ITN FACTBOOK

ITN FACTBOOK

MICHAEL O'MARA BOOKS LIMITED

First published in Great Britain in 1990 by
Michael O'Mara Books Limited
9 Lion Yard
Tremadoc Road
London SW4 7NQ

A CIP catalogue record of this book is available from the British Library.

ISBN 1-85479-065-X

Editor: Helen Armitage
Design: Mick Keates

Typeset by Florencetype Limited, Kewstoke, Avon
Printed and bound in Great Britain by The Bath Press, Bath

It is intended that the *ITN Factbook* will appear annually. While every attempt is made to incorporate correct information, errors are bound to occur. The publishers regret such errors and invite users of the *Factbook* to contribute up-to-date or additional relevant information, which should be sent to:

ITN Factbook Information
Michael O'Mara Books Limited
9 Lion Yard
Tremadoc Road
London SW4 7NQ

Dedicated to Mary Anne Sanders

CONTENTS

See also table of contents for individual factfiles.

Colour illustrations between pp. 518 and 519

ACKNOWLEDGMENTS

The publishers would like to thank the following people and organizations for their invaluable help in the preparation of the *Factbook*.

Text, graphs and maps

CIRCA Reference for the World Factfile (text and maps), compiled under the general editorship of Roger East; Thomas S. Arms for the compilation of the International Daily Review: 1989–90; Pat Brian for the compilation of the Sports Factfile; Anna Hodson for general editorship of the UK Factfile; Aporia Research; Andrew Duncan; Lyn Greenwood; Sarah Harland; Michael March; Martha Ross; First Edition; Vivitext for graphs; Richard Natkiel Associates for maps (UK Factfile).

Colour plate section

Chinese troops in Tiananmen Square (Frank Spooner Pictures)
Chinese students struggle with troops (Topham Picture Source)
Ethnic violence in Uzbekistan (Associated Press/Topham)
The funeral of Ayatollah Khomeini (Associated Press/Topham)
President Moi sets fire to ivory tusks (Frank Spooner Pictures)
John McEnroe (ITN)
Hurricane Hugo hits Puerto Rico and the Virgin Islands (Associated Press/Topham)
The wreckage of the *Marchioness* (ITN)
The B-2 stealth bomber (Associated Press/Topham)
A burning oil refinery in Lebanon (Associated Press/Topham)
Pope John Paul II in Seoul, South Korea (Associated Press/Topham)
The independence movement begins in the Baltic States (Frank Spooner Pictures)
Gerald Conlan, one of the Guildford Four (Associated Press/Topham)
The Berlin Wall (Rex Features)
The US space shuttle *Atlantis* launches the spacecraft *Galilea* on its journey to Jupiter (Frank Spooner Pictures)
Earthquake damage in the San Francisco area (Associated Press/Topham)
Alexander Dubcek and Vaclev Havel (Associated Press/Topham)
Romanian troops watch the Ceaucescus being interrogated (Rex Features)
US troops invading Panama (Associated Press/Topham)
Nicolae Ceaucescu shot dead on Christmas Day 1989 (Frank Spooner Pictures)
Manuel Noriega (Frank Spooner Pictures)
The ambulance drivers' rally in Trafalgar Squard (Gowan/Network)
Vietnamese children in Hong Kong demonstrate against repatriation (Associated Press/Topham)
Demonstrators against the 'Rebel Tour' to South Africa (© ALLSPORT/Simon Bruty)
Nelson Mandela on his release from prison (Associated Press/Topham)
Alexandra Griffiths reunited with her mother (Press Association/Topham)
Wayne Larkins at the first test in Jamaica (© ALLSPORT/Adrian Murrell)
Police officers acting as ambulance drivers (ITN)
Journalist Farzad Bazoft (ITN)
The Duke and Duchess of York with Princess Eugenie (Tim Graham)
May Day 1990 in Red Square (Associated Press/Topham)
Bette Davis (Frank Spooner Pictures)
Ava Gardner (London Features International)
Gordon Jackson (London Features International)
Lord Olivier (London Features International)
The Princess Royal and Mark Phillips (Tim Graham)
Listeria bacteria (CNRI/Science Photo Library)
Salman Rushdie (Topham Picture Source)
A soldier guarding the estate of a drug baron in Colombia (Associated Press/Topham)
The Royal Marines School of Music in Deal (Press Association/Topham)
The prison mutiny at Strangeways (Frank Spooner Pictures)
A boy carries a Kalashnikov in Ethiopia (Associated Press/Topham)
Robert Palhill arrives in the US (Associated Press/Topham)
The crew of the *Maiden* (Press Association/Topham)

Rio de Janeiro's famous statue of Christ (Associated Press/Topham)
A swimmer in the Gulf of Mexico (Sam Pierson/Science Photo Library)
Scotland defeats England in the rugby championship (Colorsport)
Mark Hughes and Nigel Martyn in the FA Cup Final (Colorsport)
Mike Tyson is knocked out in the World Heavyweight Championship (Colorsport)
The England-Republic of Ireland game in the World Cup (Colorsport)

WORLD FACTFILE

An international A–Z covering the geography, history, constitution and government, international relations, economy, communications, education and welfare of all the countries of the world

AFGHANISTAN

Dowlat-e Jumhuri-ye Dimukratik-e Afghanistan (Dari name)
Da-Afghanistan Dimukratic Jamhawriyat (Pashto name)
(Democratic Republic of Afghanistan)

GEOGRAPHY

A land-locked country in south-western Asia comprising 29 provinces, Afghanistan covers an area of 251,759 miles^2/652,225 km^2, nearly 75% of which is mountainous; average elevation about 4,265 ft/1,300 m. The largest area is occupied by the sparsely populated central highlands (154,400 miles^2/400,000 km^2), incorporating the Hindu Kush range (second highest in the world) and seismically active north-east of the country. Afghanistan's highest peak is Istoro Nal at 24,458 ft/7,455 m. South of these highlands lies the south-western plateau (including the Rigestan Desert), arid and virtually uninhabited. Densely populated regions include the Herat region and valley of Darya-ye Kunduz in the fertile north-east, although the highest concentration is found in the east between the cities of Kabul and Charikar. There are three great river basins: the Oxus, Helmand and Kabul. 3% of the total land surface area is forested while 12.4% is under permanent cultivation.

Climate

Generally semi-arid steppe, with wide regional variations, the climate varies sharply between highlands and lowlands. Subpolar in the mountainous north-east with dry, cold winters (temperature falling to –14.8°F/–26°C in the Hindu Kush) and desert in the south-west with less than 3 in/75 mm rainfall annually and summer temperatures over 95°F/35°C (120°F/49°C recorded in Jalalabad). Monsoons influence the climate of the mountains on the Pakistan border with an annual rainfall in the Sâlang pass of 51.2 in/1,300 mm. Elsewhere, summer remains hot and dry. Kabul Jan. 27°F/–2.8°C, July 76°F/24.4°C. Annual rainfall 13.3 in/338 mm.

Cities and towns

Kabul (capital)	1,036,407
Kandahar	191,345
Herat	150,497
Mazar-i-Sharif	110,367

Population

Total population (1988) is estimated at 15,090,000 excluding nomads of whom there were 2,734,000 in 1983 and approximately 4,000,000 refugees abroad in neighbouring countries. Density per miles^2 60/24.1 km^2 persons. 52.3% of the population are Pashtun; 20.3% Tadzhik; 8.7% Uzbek; 8.7% Hajara (a nomadic people inhabiting the central highlands); 2.9% Chahar Aimak; 2.0% Turkmen. 15.4% live in urban areas.

Birth rate 4.81%. **Death rate** 2.23%. **Rate of population increase** (1980–87) 2.6%. **Age distribution** under 15 = 41.8%, over 65 = 2.7%. **Life expectancy** female 37, male 36, average 37.

Religion

Islam. The majority (74%) of Afghans are Muslims of the Sunni sect. There are also approximately 3.55 m Shi'ite Muslims, a few thousand Hindus, Sikhs, and a small Jewish minority.

Language

Pashto and Dari (Persian) are the official languages. Two principal language families define the majority of the population: the Indo-European languages of the Pashtuns and Tadzhiks and the Turkic languages spoken by the Uzbeks and Turkmens. A number of Indii and Pamiri languages related to the Indo-European group are spoken in the north-east. Very small communities of Dravidian and semitic speakers survive in the far south.

HISTORY

In the 6th century BC, southern Afghanistan was part of the Persian Empire. Upon the Empire's overthrow by Alexander the Great in 331 BC, two 'Greek' kingdoms developed: to the north the Bactrian and to the south, the Indo-Greek dynasties. These were overwhelmed by nomads from central Asia in 130 BC. It was only in the 18th century that a separate and independent Afghan identity emerged.

In 1747 with the demise of Safavid rule in Persia and Mughal in India a council meeting (Jirga) of Pashtun (meaning the inhabitants of Pasht) peoples took place and laid the foundations of the first national Afghan/Pashtun state.

Durrani Ahmad Shah became paramount chieftain of the Abdali Pashtun people. However, numerous tribal groupings existed, including Tajiks and Uzbeks, which were mutually suspicious and hostile to Pashtun rule. The name 'Afghan' referred to Pashtuns, and it was the specific ethnic grouping with which a citizen identified.

The period 1838–1918 witnessed the pursuance of policies which reflected the interconnecting interests of Tsarist Russia, Afghanistan and Britain. Afghanistan was concerned with maintaining independence and territorial integrity; Russia with balancing British moves in south and central Asia and securing her own frontiers; Britain with protecting her imperial ambitions in India. In the first Anglo-Afghan war (1838–42), the British entered Kabul and attempted, without success, to install Shah Shura on the throne. Britain invaded again in Nov. 1878 and in May 1879 under the Treaty of Gandmak signed with Amir Yaqub Ali Khan, the bordering Afghan areas of Pashin, Sibi, Khyber, Kurram and Michni were annexed. It was also agreed that Britain would control the country's external relations in a bid to increase mutual trade. However, conflict again ensued between Britain and Afghanistan and after Yaqub Ali Khan was exiled to India a new treaty was signed with Amir Abdul Rahman which established the Durand Line. This treaty set up the contentious international boundary between Afghanistan and Pakistan which became known as the Northwest Frontier Province.

After World War I, on 13 Apr. 1919, Amir Amanullah Khan made a declaration of Afghanistan's independence and autonomy as a sovereign state. The Soviet Union was the first country to recognize the new Afghanistan and at the Paris Peace Conference in 1919 proposed that international guarantees be given to the effect that the Afghan government would not be overthrown by any external power. Within a month Britain declared war on Afghanistan and although an armistice was signed on 3 June 1919, Britain did not formally recognize Afghanistan as a sovereign state.

A treaty of friendship was signed with the Soviet Union on 28 Feb. 1921, although territorial disputes continued to create some tension between the two countries. However, under Muhammed Zahir Shar (r. 1933–73), Kabul's relations with the Soviet Union improved with a mutual assistance pact being concluded and a trade agreement signed in 1936.

After World War II Afghanistan's position changed. British withdrawal from India raised the old difficulty of the Northwest Frontier Province which now bordered Pakistan. A dispute soon erupted and Pakistan closed the frontier in 1950.

In 1953 Mohammed Daoud Khan was appointed prime minister and within a decade had built a close political, economic and military relationship with the Soviet Union. However, a growing chasm existed between economic and infrastructural advance and political stagnation. Daoud's proposals for democratic reforms, including the granting of a constitution and elections to a national assembly were rejected by the King and Daoud resigned from office, although not from politics. In Oct. 1964 provisions were made for the establishment of a constitutional monarchy and although two elections were held in 1965 and 1969 the provisions of the constitution were never fully implemented. On 1 Jan. 1965 the country's first Marxist party, the PDPA was formed under Nur Mohammad Taraki and Babrak Karmal. The party newspaper *Khalq* (Masses), was banned in 1966 and in 1977 the PDPA split into two factions, the Parcham (Banner) and Khalq factions. On 17 July 1973 Daoud carried out a successful coup. He abolished the monarchy and proclaimed a republic, declaring himself its Founder, President and Prime Minister; he also announced the establishment of a one-party state. Opposition mounted from the two factions of the PDPA and on 27 Apr. 1978 Daoud was killed in a coup known as the 'Saur' Revolution and a Revolutionary Council established with Taraki as leader.

Taraki's position became increasingly insecure, and in Sept. 1979 he was ousted by Hafizullah Amin. In December Amin was removed and killed in a coup that was supported by the entry into Afghanistan of some 80,000 Soviet troops. Babrak Karmal, leader of the Parcham faction of the PDPA, was installed as the new president and party general secretary. Karmal was replaced as party general secretary in May 1986 by Dr Najibullah. In Nov. 1987 Najibullah was elected President of the Republic, thereby consolidating his power. The revolution and the Soviet presence has led to civil war, with Muslim Afghan mujaheddin rebels fighting against occupation. It has also highlighted the ethnic and tribal divisions within the country and resulted in the exodus of refugees, estimated at 3.5 million, into Pakistan and Iran.

A UN-sponsored agreement under which the Soviet Union would begin withdrawing its troops from Afghanistan was signed by Afghanistan and Pakistan (the principal backer of the mujaheddin fighters) on 14 Apr. 1988 in Geneva. The Soviet Union and the United States also signed a declaration guaranteeing the agreement. The year following the final Soviet troop withdrawal on 15 Feb. 1989 was marked by the virtual collapse of the mujaheddinn as a real military threat to the Najibullah regime.

CONSTITUTION AND GOVERNMENT

Executive and legislature

The 1987 Constitution provided for an executive president (last elected 30 Nov. 1987), for a seven-year term by the Loya Jirga, a nationwide traditional gathering of tribal and other leaders. It created a bicameral National Assembly, the lower house elected for a five-year term, and the upper house partly elected and partly appointed. The president appoints the Council of Ministers, subject to the approval of the National Assembly. The constitution envisaged that the ruling People's Democratic Party of Afghanistan (PDPA) would lose its monopoly on political power. Elections to the National Assembly were held on 5–14 Apr. 1988. A 20-member Supreme Council for the Defence of the Homeland, headed by Pres. Najibullah, was established in Feb. 1989 after a state of emergency had been declared, and was described as the country's 'supreme military and political organ'.

Present government

President; C.-in-C. of the Armed Forces; Chairman of Supreme Council for Defence of the Homeland Dr Najibullah

Vice-Presidents Lt.-Gen. Mohammad Rafi, Abdol Hamid Mohat, Dr Abdol Wahed Sorabi, Abdorrahim Hatef

Chairman of Executive Committee of the Council of Ministers Sultan Ali Keshtmand

Deputy Prime Ministers Mohammad Sarwar Mangal, Sayed Amanoddin Amin, Mahbubollah Koshani, Mahmud Barialay, Mohammad Hakim

Principal Ministers Hamidollah Tarzi (Finance); Lt.-Gen. Gholam Faruq Yaqubi (State Security); Abdol Wakil (Foreign Affairs); Mohammad Bashir Baghlani (Justice)

Ruling party People's Democratic Party of Afghanistan (Jamiyat-e Demokrati Khalq-e Afghanistan)

General Secretary Dr Najibullah

Political bureau full members Dr Najibullah; Sultan Ali Keshtmand; Nur Ahmad Nur; Maj.-Gen. Mohammad Rafi; Gen. Mohammad Aslam Watanyar;

Abdol Wakil; Solayman Laeq; Lt-Gen. Gholam Faruq Yaqubi; Lt.-Gen. Sayed Mohammad Ghulabzoi; Najmoddin Kawiani; Niaz Mohammad Mohmand; Haydar Masud; Brig.-Gen. Nazas Mohammad; Mir Saheb Karwal; Farid Ahmad Mazdak

Justice

The system of law is based on a combination of constitutional provision, legislation, and the Hanafi (Islamic) jurisprudence. The highest court is the Supreme Court established in 1970, with a separate system of military courts. The death penalty is in force, but the number of executions carried out between 1985 and mid-1988 is not known.

National symbols

Flag. Three horizontal stripes in the traditional colours of black, red and green with the state coat of arms in the hoist of the black and red stripes.

Festivals. 27 Apr. (Revolution Day), 1 May (Workers' Day), 18 Aug. (Independence Day).

Vehicle registration plate. AFG.

INTERNATIONAL RELATIONS

Affiliations

NAM; Comecon (observer); ICO.

Defence

Total Armed Forces: Active: 55,000. Terms of service: Males 15–55, volunteeers 2 years, conscription 3 years.

Reserves: No formal force identified.

Army: 50,000 (mostly conscripts); 450 main battle tanks, mainly T-34, T-54/55, T-62, and light tanks PT-76.

Air Force: 5,000; 140 combat aircraft, mostly MiG-17/-19/-21F and Su-7B Fitter A and Su-22 Fitter J.

Opposition: Afghan resistance groups operate in very substantial numbers, equipped with predominantly captured tanks.

ECONOMY

Currency

The unit is the afghani, divided into 100 puls.

National finance

Budget. The fiscal 1987 (21 Mar.–20 Mar.) budget was for revenue of US$370.2 million. Main items of expenditure are defence (55%) and education (2%).

Balance of payments. The balance of payments (current account, fiscal 1987) was a deficit of US$702 million.

Inflation. 20%.

Gross Domestic Product

Estimated total GDP US$3,100 million, per capita US$220 (overall size of economy ranking 103 in the world).

Economically active population. The total number of persons active in the economy is 4,980,000.

Sector	% of workforce
industry	21
agriculture	68
services*	11

* services figure includes elements unassigned to other categories.

Energy and mineral resources

Natural gas. Production (1985) 84,754 million ft³/2,400 million m³. Most of the natural gas produced in Afghanistan is piped to the Soviet Union.

Minerals. There is only limited exploitation of the country's mineral resources. Coal and unrefined salt are mined. Other deposits include iron ore, beryllium, barite, gold, silver, lapis lazuli, asbestos, mica, sulphur, chrome and copper.

Electricity. There are at least six hydroelectric plants throughout the country. Production capacity (1988) 480,000 kW.

Bioresources

Agriculture. It is estimated that there are 34,594,000 acres/14 million ha of cultivable land in Afghanistan, of which only 19,026,700 acres/7.7 million ha were being cultivated in 1988. Agriculture is the most important sector of the economy, supporting about 80% of the population and accounting for one-third of all exports. Wheat makes up 60% of total grain production and two-thirds of the population rely on raising livestock for a major portion of their income. Substantial amounts of opium poppy and cannabis are grown for the international drug market.

The war has caused serious damage to the country's agricultural infrastructure; it was estimated in 1988 that over 30% of the land had been destroyed during the fighting.

Crop production (1988, in 1,000 tons/tonnes): wheat 2,243/2,035; maize 647/587; barley 302/274; rice 378/343.

Livestock numbers (1988): sheep 19 million; chickens 5.9 million; goats 3 million; cattle 2.7 million; horses, donkeys and mules 1.7 million.

Forestry. Forests cover over only 3% of the country and have been badly damaged as a result of the war.

Industry and commerce

Industry. Industries include cotton textiles and handwoven carpets, woollen fabrics, coalmining, small vehicle assembly plants, cement, soap, furniture, footwear manufacture, sugar manufacture and fruit canning. Most of these industries are relatively small and many are equipped with Soviet machinery.

Commerce. Afghan imports totalled US$1,404 million and exports US$552 million (1987). The main export commodities were natural gas (55%), fruits and nuts (24%), handwoven carpets, wool, cotton, hides and pelts. The main items imported were petroleum products, textiles and motor vehicles and spares. The Soviet Union and the other Comecon countries are Afghanistan's major trading partners.

Trade with UK. Afghanistan imported goods worth £11,501,000; exports to UK totalled £12,109,000 (1988).

Tourism. The tourist sector has been virtually destroyed by the war.

COMMUNICATIONS

Railways

There are only two short rail stretches, of 6 miles/10 km and 9 miles/15 km respectively, running into the USSR at Kushka and Termez.

Roads

There are 13,041 miles/21,000 km of roads, of which 1,739 miles/2,800 km hard surfaced, 1,025 miles/1,650 km gravel and improved earth, the rest unimproved earth and tracks.

Aviation
There are 34 usable airports in all, nine with permanent surface runways. Bakhtar Afghan Airlines provides international services (main airports are at Kabul and Kandahar).

Shipping
There are 745 miles/1,200 km of navigable inland waterways, chiefly on the Amu Darya, and a port at Shir Khan.

Telecommunications
There are five AM radio stations and one television channel (introduced in 1980), over 800,000 radios and 12,000 television sets. There are 31,200 telephones.

EDUCATION AND WELFARE

In principle, the state system provides free elementary and secondary education. However, the civil war has meant that large numbers of children have been unable to take advantage of the system. In August 1988 the government announced that over 1,800 schools had suffered damage estimated at US$26 million during the conflict.

School population. In 1982 there were over 1 million pupils and 35,000 teachers in primary education and 124,000 pupils and 6,000 teachers in secondary education.

Schools. Elementary schools are located throughout the country, but secondary schools exist only in Kabul and the provincial capitals.

Universities. There is a university and polytechnic in Kabul and the university of Nangarhar is situated in Jalalabad. In 1982 there were over 13,000 students in higher education, almost 4,500 in teacher-training colleges and over 1,000 in technical schools. Many students attend university or college in the Soviet Union.

Literacy. 12%.

Health
In 1982 there were some 1,200 doctors and over 6,800 hospital beds in Afghanistan.

ALBANIA

Republika Popullore Socialiste Shqipërisë)
(Albanian People's Socialist Republic)

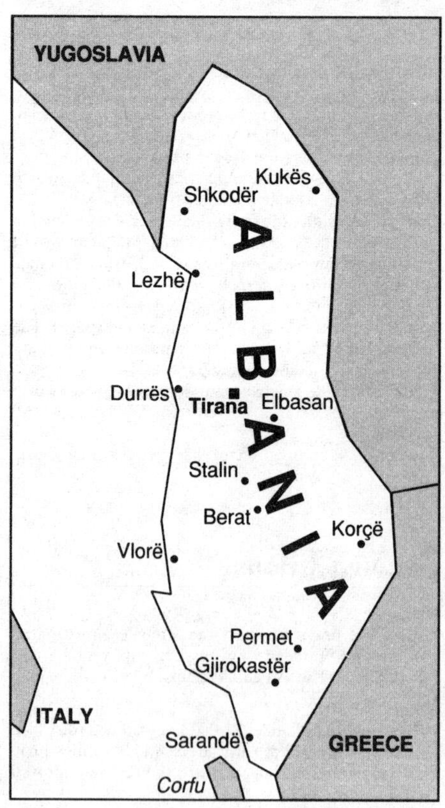

GEOGRAPHY

Located in south-eastern Europe, in the western part of the Balkan peninsula, Albania covers an area of 11,097 miles²/28,748 km², divided into 26 provinces or 'rrethet'. Approximately 50% of the population live in the cultivated and comparatively fertile lowlands on the west Adriatic coast on less than 30% of the country's total surface area. The other 70% of the country is largely mountainous and sparsely populated, composed of the northern lying Albanian Alps, the central uplands (including Albania's highest peak Mount Korab in the east, at 9,025 ft/2,751 m) and the southern highlands. Forests cover 40–47% of the territory while over 50% of the cultivated land is irrigated. The two principal river basins, the Drin and the Vijose, situated north and south respectively, characterize the country's westward-draining hydrology. The southern half of Albania lies in a geologically active zone.

Climate
Predominantly Mediterranean. Sea winds exert a moderating influence on the central regions although winter cyclones bring unstable cloudy weather with rain. In the higher northern altitudes, an altogether harsher Central European climate prevails, with severe winters and abundant snowfall. Summer weather is uniformly hot and dry (between 75°F/24°C and 84°F/29°C) particularly on the western central plains which receive less than half the average annual rainfall c. 14.7 in/375 mm. Tirana Jan. 44°F/6.8°C. July 75°F/23.9°C. Average annual rainfall 0.053 in/1,353 mm. Shkodër Jan. 39°F/3.9°C. July 77°F/25°C. Average annual rainfall 0.056 in/1,425 mm.

Cities and towns

Tirana (capital)	225,700
Durrës (Durazzo)	78,700
Elbasan	78,300
Shkodër (Scutari)	76,300
Vlorë (Vlonë or Valona)	67,600
Korçë (Koritsa)	61,500

Population

Total population is 3,134,000, of which 34% live in urban areas. Population density is 282/107 persons per miles^2/km^2. 96.7% of the population are Albanian, claiming descent from the ancient Illyrians, 2.0% Greek; 0.5% Romanian; 0.4% Macedonian; 0.2% Montenegrin; 0.2% Gypsy.

Birth rate 2.67%. **Death rate** 0.61%. **Rate of population increase** 2.1%. **Age distribution** under 15 = 34.5%; over 65 = 5.3%. **Life expectancy** female 74; male 69; average 72.

Religion

The State recognizes no religion (all religious institutions have been closed). Before 1946 Islam was the predominant faith. Today, an estimated 20.5% of the population remain Muslim, with another 5.4% Greek Orthodox and Roman Catholic.

Language

The Albanian language is Indo-European in origin and is closely related to the Balto-Slavic group. It comprises two dialects – Gheg in the north and Tosk in the south, divided geographically by the Shkumbin river. Of the two, Tosk is currently the dominant idiom. Native Albanian speakers may also be found in Yugoslavia, Southern Italy, Sicily and Greece. As well as the 2.9 million Albanian speakers, the Republic supports 58,000 Greek-speaking citizens, 10,000 Macedonians, 5,000 Montenegrins and 16,000 Romanians.

HISTORY

Inhabited from Neolithic times, the territory of present-day Albania from around 2000 BC was home to the Southern Illyrians, whose civilization was at its height from 750 to 450 BC. Rome subjugated the Southern Illyrians between 168 BC and AD 9, their lands becoming part of the province of Illyricum. Rome's decline in the late 3rd century admitted waves of invaders to the Balkans, and by the 7th century the depleted remnants of the Southern Illyrians had taken refuge in the mountains of Albania. Between the 9th and 15th centuries foreign powers (Byzantium, Bulgaria, Serbia, Epirus and the states of southern Italy) fought for control of Albania and its strategic coastline. Foreign invasions split the country into a Roman Catholic North and an Eastern Orthodox South, and allowed local power to devolve to mutually hostile native chieftains. Ottoman conquest (1385–1417) began a Turkish occupation lasting until 1912. Albanians staged a revolt in 1443–68 led by George Kastrioti or Skanderbeg, but this collapsed on Skanderbeg's death and Turkish reconquest of the country featured forced Islamization unparalleled elsewhere in the Balkans (Albanians were 70% Muslim by the early 18th century). Turkish repression and Albania's isolated backwardness prevented the emergence of a modern nationalist movement until 1878, when the Albanian League for the Defence of the Rights of the Albanian Nation (suppressed by the Turks in 1881) was established to protest against the cession of Albanian territory to Montenegro by decision of the Congress of Berlin.

Albania became independent during the Balkan Wars (1912–13), but was occupied by various foreign armies during and immediately after World War I. No proper Albanian government was established until 1921, when the country's borders were also fixed. Thereafter a brief period of democracy under the liberal Bishop Fan Noli was ended in 1924 by an invasion from Yugoslavia led by Ahmet Zogu, a conservative Albanian chieftain who proclaimed himself King Zog I in 1928. In 1926 Zogu entered into a defence pact with Mussolini's Italy giving the latter the right to intervene militarily in Albania. This it did in Apr. 1939, whereupon King Zog's regime collapsed and the crown passed to Italy's King Victor Emmanuel. In Sept. 1943 Nazi Germany occupied Albania following Italy's withdrawal from World War II hostilities, but the Nazis were expelled by partisans in the summer of 1944. By that time the Communist Party of Albania (renamed in 1948 the Albanian Party of Labour), led by Enver Hoxha since 1941, had emerged victorious from a year-long civil war against various nationalist groups. A Communist-dominated provisional government with Hoxha as prime minister on 11 Jan. 1946 formally proclaimed a republic. In the subsequent four decades Albania has remained a hardline Stalinist state: the Constitution of 27 Dec. 1976 (replacing that of Mar. 1946 and renaming the country the People's Socialist Republic of Albania) confirmed the leading role of the APL, together with bans on private property, religion (Albania was declared the world's first atheist state in 1967), foreign military alliances and acceptance of foreign economic support. Successive political purges claimed such prominent figures as Mehmet Shehu (since 1954 Hoxha's successor as prime minister) in Dec. 1981. Internationally, Hoxha's regime pursued an isolationist and extremely hard-line foreign policy, involving bitter ideological quarrels with Yugoslavia (1948), the Soviet Union (1961) and China (1977). Since Hoxha's death on 11 Apr. 1985 his successor as APL leader, Ramiz Alia, has brought about a limited rapprochement with certain Western countries.

CONSTITUTION AND GOVERNMENT

Executive and legislature

The unicameral People's Assembly, with 250 members elected every four years from a single list of candidates, elects the Presidium and the Council of Ministers. The president of the Presidium is the head of state. Effective political control, however, lies with the (communist) Albanian Party of Labour, the sole legal party.

Present government

President of the Presidium of the People's Assembly Ramiz Alia

Prime Minister (Chairman of the Council of Ministers) Adil Carcani

Principal Ministers Manush Myftiu (Prime Minister; Chairman of the State Control Commission); Pali Miska (Deputy Prime Minister; Minister of Agriculture); Simon Stefani (Deputy Prime Minister; Minister of Internal Affairs); Reis Malile (Foreign Affairs); Prokop Murra (People's Defence); Niko Gjyzari (Chairman of the State Planning Commission); Andrea Nako (Finance)

Ruling party

Albanian Party of Labour (Partia e Punës te Shqipërisë). *First secretary* Ramiz Alia. *Full members of the politburo* Ramiz Alia; Adil Carcani; Besnik

Bekteshi; Foto Cami; Hajredin Celiku; Hekuran Isai; Lenka Cuko; Manush Myftiu; Muho Asllani; Pali Miska; Prokop Murra; Rita Marko; Simon Stefani. *Central committee secretariat* Ramiz Alia; Foto Cami; Lenka Cuko; Hekuran Isai.

Justice

The system of law is based on the 1976 constitution. The highest court for the judicial review of legislation is the presidium of the People's Assembly, which elects the Supreme Court judges, while implementation of the law is the responsibility of the Office of the Procurator-General. Below the level of People's Courts, local tribunals deal with minor crimes. The death penalty is in force. The number of executions between 1985 and mid-1988 is not known.

National symbols

Flag. The flag features a black double-headed eagle, surmounted by a red five-pointed star edged with yellow.

Festivals. 11 Jan. (Proclamation of the Republic); 1 May (Workers' Day); 7 Nov. (Victory of the October Socialist Revolution); 28 Nov. (Proclamation of Independence); 29 Nov. (Liberation Day).

Vehicle registration plate. AL

INTERNATIONAL RELATIONS

Affiliations

None; member of UN; ceased participating in Comecon 1961; left Warsaw Pact 1968.

Defence

Total Armed Forces: 42,000 (22,400 conscripts). Terms of service: Army 2 years; Air Force, Navy and special units 3 years. Reserves: 155,000 (to age 56).

Army: 31,500; 190 main battle tanks (T-34/-54).

Navy: 3,300; 2 submarines (Soviet Whiskey) and 40 patrol and coastal combatants.

Air Force: 7,200; 95 combat aircraft (J-2/-4/-6/-7).

Para-Military: 12,000.

ECONOMY

Currency

The unit is the lek, divided into 100 qintars.

National finance

Budget. The 1989 budget was for expenditure of US$2,300 million and revenue of US$2,300 million.

Gross Domestic Product

Estimated total GDP US$2,800 million (1986 GNP est), per capita US$930 (overall size of economy ranking 107 in the world).

Economically active population. The total number of persons active in the economy is 1,500,000.

Energy and mineral resources

Minerals. Albania has considerable mineral resources, led by crude oil, (non-bituminous) coal and chromium ore. Output was coal 1,614 tons/1,780 tonnes; chrome ore 1,361 tons/1,500 tonnes; copper ore 152 tons/168 tonnes; phosphate 16.3 tons/18 tonnes; nickel ore 5.4 tons/6 tonnes (1984).

Oil and gas. Albania's crude oil output in 1988 was 2,721,550 tons/3 million tonnes and 148,318,800 ft^3/ 420 million m^3 of natural gas were produced in 1985.

Electricity. Production 5.25 million megawatt/hours (1988). Albania is rich in hydroelectric potential, which is the country's main source of electricity. 2 million megawatt/hours of electricity were exported in 1984 to Yugoslavia, Bulgaria, Romania and Greece.

Bioresources

Agriculture. Albania is self-sufficient in food, although much of the country is so mountainous that little can be produced from it. There were an estimated 1,753,916 acres/709,800 ha of arable land in 1983, of which 55% was irrigated. 75% of it was held by co-operatives in 1989. Much of the rest of it is in the form of state farms.

Crop production (1986 in 1000 tons/tonnes): wheat 595/ 540; maize 459/410; sugar beet 358/320; fruit 218/ 198; potatoes 150/136; barley 40/36; oats 33/30; tobacco 22/20; rice 15/14.

Livestock numbers (1987 in millions): sheep 1.2; goats 705,000; cattle 619,000; pigs 229,000.

Forestry. 40–47% of Albanian territory is forest, mainly oak, elm, pine and birch. It is almost wholly owned by the state.

Fisheries. Total fish catch in 1984 was 3,629 tons/4,000 tonnes.

Industry and commerce

Industry. All industry is nationalized. Output is small and the principal industries are agricultural product processing, textiles, oil products and cement. Chemical, engineering and metallurgical industries are being developed.

Commerce. Albania's exports were an estimated US$428 million in 1986. Main exports were mineral and agricultural products and electricity. Imports were US$363 million, mainly of machinery and industrial products. Main trading partners were Greece, Yugoslavia and the Eastern bloc countries.

Trade with UK. Albania imported UK goods worth £1.1 million and exported to the UK goods worth £2.8 million (1988).

COMMUNICATIONS

Railways

There are 316 miles/509 km of railways.

Roads

There are 10,370 miles/16,700 km of roads (4,161 miles/6,700 km of main roads).

Aviation

Albtransport provides international services (there is no regular domestic service). Main airport is Rinas (17.4 miles/28 km from Tirana). There are 10 airports in all.

Shipping

Albanian waterways include sections of Lake Shkodër, Lake Ohrid and Lake Prespa. Main ports are Durrës, Shengjih and Vlorë. The 11 merchant marine ships are of at least 1,000 GRT.

Telecommunications

There are an estimated 210,000 radios and 52,000 television sets; TV broadcasting began in 1971. Radio Tiranan broadcasts internationally in 18 languages.

EDUCATION AND WELFARE

Education

Free and compulsory primary education for 7- to 15-year-olds is provided by the state. Secondary education is available in 12-year (general), technical–professional or lower vocational schools. Periods of productive work and military service are intermingled with full-time adult education.

School population. 721,057 under 15, with 35,846 teachers, a teacher–pupil ratio of 1:20 (1984–85); 69,700 in higher stages (1979–80).

Technical–professional schools. 116 (1979–80).
Universities. The Enver Hoxha University of Tirana (founded 1957) with 820 teachers and some 12,000 students (1985–86), as well as 35 other institutes of higher education with some 25,000 students (1979–80).

Health

Free health care. There were 4,967 doctors or 1 doctor per 560 people and 17,600 hospital beds or 1 per 150 people (1983).

ALGERIA

Al-Jumhuriya al-Jazairiya ad-Dimugratiya ash-Shabiya (The Democratic and Popular Republic of Algeria)

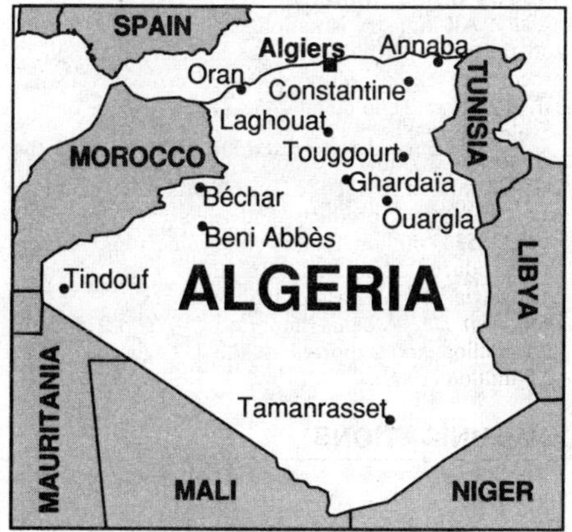

GEOGRAPHY

Situated on the north coast of Africa, Algeria has a total area of 919,352 miles²/2,381,741 km². The narrow fertile coastal strip, area about 147,066 miles²/381,000 km², supports the bulk of the population. Farther south, in comparatively fertile soil, the Atlas Mts run EW (highest point 7,578 ft/2,310 m). Further south, the sparsely populated grassland plains of the Chott plateau extend towards the Saharan Atlas (highest point 7,644 ft/2,330 m) also sparsely populated and semi-arid. The southern part of the country (Algérie Saharienne), area about 772,000 miles²/2,000,000 km², is arid and largely uninhabited, consisting of a vast sandstone plain traversed by valleys and rocky mountains including the Ahaggar (Hoggar) range in the south (highest point Mt Tahat 9,875 ft/3,010 m, Algeria's highest mountain). The desert is advancing progressively.

Climate

Mediterranean in the north, with cool rainy winters and hot dry summers (average Jan. 54°F/12°C, July 77°F/25°C); typical tropical desert climate in the south, with very low rainfalls (less than 4 in/100 mm per year) and extremes of temperature, e.g. from 95°F/35°C daytime to 41°F/5°C nighttime (average Jan. 54°F/12°C, July 95°F/35°C).

Cities and towns

Algiers (capital)	1,721,607
Oran	663,504
Constantine	448,578
Annaba	348,322
Blida	191,314
Setif	186,978
Side-Bel-Abbes	146,653
Tlemcen	146,089
Skikda	141,159
Bejaia	124,122
Batna	122,788
El-Asnam	117,886
Boufarik	112,000
Tizi-Ouzou	100,749

Population

Total population is 22.9 million, of which 96% live in the north on 17% of the land area; 49% of the population live in urban areas. Arabic speakers are 75% of the population, Berber speakers 25%; French speakers are now an insignificant minority (less than 50,000).
Birth rate 846,000. **Death rate** 137,974. **Rate of population increase** 0.8% (annual). **Age distribution** under 15 = 46.1%; over 65 = 4.3%. **Life expectancy** female 62; male 59; average 60.

Religion

Islam is overwhelmingly dominant, with some 19 million adherents. There are about 60,000 Roman Catholics and a small Jewish community (less than 1,000).

Language

Arabic is the official language, French is still widely used.

HISTORY

Inhabited from Palaeolithic times, Algeria was for long the home of nomadic Berber peoples. It became a Roman province (Numidia) in 106 BC, and was an important source of corn for Rome. St Augustine (354–430 AD) was bishop of Hippo (later Bône, now Annaba). Roman rule was destroyed by the invasion of the Vandals (429), and there was disorder until the region came under Byzantine control early in the 6th century. The Arabs arrived in the late 7th century and brought with them Islam. Apart from the Spanish capture of some of the coastal cities in the Middle Ages, Algeria remained under Arab rule until it became part of the Ottoman empire in the mid-16th century. It was notoriously a stronghold of piracy and slave-trading, and the pirates' activities became increasingly troublesome to the other countries trading round the Mediterranean. The crisis came in 1827 when the ruler of Algiers hit the French consul with a fly-whisk; French honour had to be avenged, so Algeria was first blockaded by the French fleet and then invaded (1830). Resistance by the Algerians, particularly the Berbers under Abd al-Kadir, was ferocious, and it was not until 1848 that the French (their army led by Gen. Bugeaud) had subdued the country. It became a colony with three departments.

In spite of continuing unrest, many colonists moved in from France, and by the 1880s there were 375,000 Europeans in Algeria, who had appropriated most of the fertile farmland. Many of the settlers were French ex-soldiers, others were from Spain, Italy and Malta. Government of the colony was military until 1870 when a civil administration (controlled from Paris) was set up; in 1900 this became locally autonomous under the governor-general. Muslim Algerians, although French subjects, did not have political rights, and they remained economically and socially separate from the colonists. The colony flourished, though the benefits of its prosperity went almost entirely to the European settlers.

After World War I, two political movements developed among the Muslims: one (led by Ferhat Abbas) called for full assimilation with France, with Muslims becoming full French citizens on equal terms with European colonists; the other was nationalist. The latter began in Paris as l'Etoile nord-africaine, a workers' movement led by Messali Hadj, which merged with various Muslim groups to become the Mouvement pour le triomphe des libertés démocratiques (MTLD).

During World War II the Vichy regime controlled Algeria until 1942, when it became the Allied armies' North African base. After the war nationalists hoped that their support for Gen. de Gaulle's Free French government would be rewarded with some progress towards independence. Peaceful progress became impossible after a spontaneous riot at a victory celebration in May 1945: nationalists killed 88 Europeans, and the French killed several thousand Muslims in reprisal. France granted Algeria a national assembly (Sept. 1947), but voting rights were restricted so that only a few Muslims could qualify, and control was kept in European hands. Nationalist sentiment grew, and an activist group split from the MTLD to form the Front de libération nationale (FLN). They launched attacks on police posts in 1954, and in 1955 massacred dozens of settler families. By 1956 the FLN controlled much of the country, but during 1957, a combination of massive French troop deployment combined with a ruthless use of torture drove them back into the rural areas. Still no solution was in sight, and in May 1958 the colonists began to suspect that the French government would negotiate with the guerrillas. Their riots in support of keeping Algeria French brought on the crisis in France that returned Gen. de Gaulle to power with the establishment of the Fifth Republic. In Oct. 1958 de Gaulle offered cease-fire terms to the FLN, which by that time had organized itself into a provisional government (Gouvernement provisoire de la république algérienne, GPRA) based in Tunis under Ferhat Abbas as prime minister.

The fighting continued, however, with heavy casualties (68,000 Muslims and 5,800 French killed in 12 months). De Gaulle was forced to concede (15 Sept. 1959) that the Algerians should determine their own future with a universal vote. In response, the colonists and extremists in the French army formed the terrorist group, l'Organisation de l'armée secrète (OAS) in a desperate attempt to prevent the inevitable move to independence, and in Apr. 1961 four generals attempted a coup against de Gaulle. France reopened negotiations with the GPRA and signed an agreement (18 Mar. 1962) under which Algeria would become independent; this agreement was approved by the French people in a referendum held on 8 Apr. On 20 Apr. Gen. Salan, leader of the OAS, was captured, and the army revolt collapsed; colonists flooded out of Algeria. The Algerian people voted virtually unanimously for independence, and on 3 July 1962 the French government recognized the new state.

The moderate Ben Khedda formed the first government, but was soon replaced by Ahmed Ben Bella who had more support from the FLN; his policies included confiscation of European-owned farms and nationalization of key industries. On 15 June 1965, he was deposed in a bloodless coup by his defence minister, Col. Houari Boumédienne, who suspended the constitution and ruled via a revolutionary council. Radical measures were taken to reconstruct the economy, still in ruins after the war: in Feb. 1971 the French oil and natural gas companies were nationalized (with compensation) and became the mainstay of the economy. A national health service was introduced in Dec. 1973. A National Charter, approved by a 99% majority on 27 June 1976, stipulated that socialism and Islam would be the guiding principles of government. Another referendum that year (19 Nov.) approved a new constitution establishing a one-party (FLN) state with an executive president. Col. Boumédienne died on 27 Dec. 1978, and Col. Bendjedid Chadli (sole candidate) was elected president on 7 Feb. 1979 (re-elected 13 Jan. 1983).

In Dec. 1985 a new National Charter was published which provided for a private sector in the economy; it was approved by a 98% majority in a referendum on 16 Jan. 1986. In spite of the new direction in the economy there were desperate problems, especially in the cities, and in Nov. 1986 anti-government demonstrations were staged by students at Constantine and Setif (3 dead); the subsequent trial of some of the students in Feb. 1987 gave rise to yet more rioting. Further economic reforms were approved in a referendum in Sept. 1988, but more riots followed, with over 170 people killed during disturbances in several cities in Oct. 1988, representing the most serious challenge yet faced by the government. A new prime minister, Kasdi Merbah, was appointed in November 1988, but dismissed the following September, blamed for failing to pursue Chadli's reform programme energetically enough, and for failing to prevent food shortages and price rises. Meanwhile a referendum in February 1989 effectively nullified the one-party State, and parties were legalized in July.

CONSTITUTION AND GOVERNMENT

Executive and legislature

The executive president (who is also head of the armed forces) is nominated by the congress of the ruling party (the Front de libération nationale, or National Liberation Front) and elected by universal adult suffrage for a five-year term; last election 22 Dec. 1988. The president appoints and presides over the Council of Ministers. Legislative power is shared by the president and the 281-member National Assembly, which is also elected every five years; last general election 26 Feb. 1987. Amendments to the 1976 Constitution, approved by referendum (Nov. 1988 and Feb. 1989), transferred power away from the presidency and effectively marked the end of one-party state socialism. Laws approving the formation of new political parties were passed in July 1989.

Present government

President Col. Chadli Bendjedid

Prime Minister Mouloud Hamrouche

Principal ministers: Sid-Ahmed Ghozali (Foreign Affairs); Mohammed Saleh Mohammedi (Interior); Said Chibane (Religious Affairs); Ghazi Hidouci (Economy); Ali Benflis (Justice).

Justice

The system of law is based on French and Islamic traditions and socialist principles. The highest court is the Supreme Court, which also has a constitutional role as the Council of State. The criminal justice system is based on the French model, with courts of first instance in each of 17 areas, and three appeal courts. At the local level, justices of the peace have a major role. Parallel with the criminal justice system, there is a system of commercial courts. The death penalty is in force. There were 12 executions between 1985 and mid-1988. Capital offences: murder.

National symbols

Flag. Two vertical stripes, green and white, with a red crescent and a five-pointed star in its centre, the star positioned so that two of its points touch the edge of the green stripe.

Festivals. 1 May (Labour Day); 19 June (Ben Bella's Overthrow); 5 July (Independence); 1 Nov. (Anniversary of the Revolution).

Vehicle registration plate. DZ.

INTERNATIONAL RELATIONS

Affiliations

NAM; Arab League; AMU; ICO; OPEC; OAPEC; OAU.

Defence

Total Armed Forces: 139,000 (70,000 conscripts). Reserves: some 150,000, to age 50.

Army: 120,000; 900 main battle tanks, mainly T-34, T-54/-55, T-62, T-72, and light tanks PT-76.

Navy: 7,000; 4 submarines (Soviet Kilo and Romeo), 3 frigates and 26 patrol and coastal combatants.

Air Force: 12,000; 266 combat aircraft and 48 armed helicopters.

ECONOMY

Algeria's economy is organized by a series of development plans. The 2nd 5-year Plan (1985–89) envisaged expenditure of 550 thousand million DA with priority for housing, industrial development, and agricultural and water resources.

Currency

The unit is the dinar, divided into 100 centimes.

National finance

Budget. The 1987 budget was for expenditure of $23,100 million and revenue of $20,600 million.

Balance of payments. The balance of payments (current account, 1987) was a deficit of 406 million.

Inflation. 11 %.

Gross Domestic Product

Estimated total GDP US$64,600 million, per capita US$2,645 (overall size of economy ranking 36 in the world).

Economically active population The total number of persons active in the economy is 370,000; unemployed = 19 %.

Sector	% of workforce	% of GDP
industry	40	42
agriculture	30	12
services*	27	45

* services figure includes elements unassigned to other categories.

Energy and mineral resources

Oil and gas. Production is nationalized; output is 27,215,520 million tons/30 million tonnes of crude oil (1988 – 16th in the world) and 169,507 million ft^3/ 48,000 million cubic metres of natural gas (1987 – 7th in the world).

Minerals. Output (1987 in million tons/tonnes): iron ore 3.36/3.7; lead 5.4/6.0; zinc 13.2/14.6; copper 0.09/0.1; mercury 0.272/0.3; phosphates 0.90/1.0. Algeria has small deposits of uranium.

Electricity. Production is 12.41 million megawatt/hours (1986). Three AGC nuclear reactors have 20 megawatt capacity.

Bioresources

Agriculture. There are an estimated 16.8 million acres/ 6.8 million hectares of arable land in Algeria (1978–9). The country has 70% self-sufficiency in food.

Crop production (1986 in 1,000 tons/tonnes): wheat 1,311/1,445; barley 9,980/1,100; dates 172/190; potatoes 771/850; oranges 200/220; mandarines and tangerines 95.2/105; tomatoes 249/275; olives 127/140; wine 163/180.

Livestock numbers (1987): cattle 1.6 million, sheep 1.5 million, goats 3.16 million, horses, mules and asses 755,000 million and camels 130,000 million.

Forestry. Algeria's 2.9 million acres/1.2 million hectares of Aleppo pine and cork oak trees produce some 212,100 ft^3/60,000 m^3 of timber for industrial and firewood purposes.

Fisheries. Total fish catch is 82,740 tons/91,200 tonnes (1987).

Industry and commerce

Industry. The main industries are petroleum refining (the major plant is at Skikda has a capacity of 22 million tons/20 million tonnes per year) and natural gas liquifaction (a plant at Arziew has a 423,768,000 ft^3/ 312 million m^3 capacity). Other significant industries are cement (output of 5.07 million tons/4.6 million tonnes in 1986), processed foods, steel and textiles.

Commerce. Algeria's exports totalled US$8,100 million and imports totalled US$6,100 million (1988). Imports were capital goods 35%; consumer goods 36%; food 20%. Exports were petroleum and natural gas 98%.

Trade with UK. Algeria imported goods worth £86.6 million and exported to the UK goods worth £160 million (1988).

Tourism. There were 553,000 visitors (1987).

COMMUNICATIONS

Railways

There are 2,336 miles/3,761 km of railways, 185 miles/ 298 km electrified.

Roads

(1986) 48,693 miles/78,410 km of roads including 27,988 miles/45,070 km concrete or bitumenized; in 1984 there were 505,492 passenger vehicles; 7 miles/11.2 per km of road.

Aviation

Air Algeria provides domestic and international services (5 international airports). Air traffic (1985) was 4.82 million passengers and 44,623 tons/40,482 tonnes of freight.

Shipping

(1986) 144,283,440 tons/128,790,000 tonnes of freight were handled at Algerian ports.

Telecommunications

There are (1988) 735,400 telephones, 25% are in Algiers.

Broadcasting

The state broadcasting company Radiodiffusion Télévision algérienne broadcasts 12 hrs of television per day to about (1987) 2.3 million sets, and broadcasts radio in Arabic, Kabyle and French to an estimated audience of over 10 million.

EDUCATION AND WELFARE

Education

The education system is modelled on that of France. All teaching is in Arabic for the first two years, then in French as well. There is compulsory schooling from 6 to 14 years.

School population. 5.5 million (1987), with an attendance rate of 83.3%.

Schools. There are 11,692 primary schools with 133,250 teachers and 3,625,000 pupils (a teacher/pupil ratio of 1:28) and 1,900 secondary schools with 95,000 teachers and 1,877,000 pupils (a ratio of 1:20).

Universities. There are a total of 72,200 students in higher education, including universities at Algiers, (two of them with a total of 28,500 students), Oran, Constantine, Annaba, Sétif and Boumerdes.

Literacy. Estimated literacy rate is 45%.

Health

There is a national health service providing for basic health care. There are a total of 48,280 hospital beds (1 per 460 people) and 15,361 doctors (1 per 1,500 people) (1986).

ANDORRA

Principat d'Andorra
(Principality of Andorra)

GEOGRAPHY

Andorra is a small, neutral European co-principality (formed by a treaty in 1278) situated in the Eastern Pyrenees roughly midway between Barcelona and Toulouse. It has an area of approximately 175 m/453 km^2 with a maximum length of 19 miles/30 km and breadth of 12 miles/20 km, and consists of gorges and valleys running between mountains between 6,168 ft/1,880m and 9,665 ft/2,946 m (Coma Pedrosa) in height. The River Valira, flowing south into Spain, provides over 30,000 kW of hydroelectric power, half of which is exported.

Climate

Alpine. The climate is cold for six months with much snow in winter, but mild in spring and warm in summer. Average temperature at Les Escaldes, Jan. 36°F/2.3°C, July 67°F/19.3°C. Average annual rainfall 32 in/808 mm.

Cities and towns

Andorra la Vella (capital)	18,463

Population

Total population is 51,400, of which 65% in urban areas. Ethnic composition = Spanish 55.1%; Andorran 27.5%; French 7.4%; Portuguese 4.1%; British 1.5%.

Birth rate 1.16%. **Death rate** 0.38%. **Rate of population increase** 0.78%. **Age distribution** under 15 = 19.0%, over 65 = 8.6%. **Life expectancy** female 70; male 70; average 70.

Religion

Christianity, mainly Roman Catholics (94.2%). Andorra is part of the diocese of See de Urgel. 0.4% are Jewish, 0.3% Jehovah's Witnesses and 0.2% are Protestant.

Language

The official language is Catalan, but French and Castillian Spanish are widely spoken.

HISTORY

Tradition has it that Andorra was granted a self-government charter by Charlemagne (r. 768–814) for helping the King of the Franks in his war against the Saracens in Spain. Amid the dismemberment of the Frankish Empire, Charlemagne's grandson, Charles II of what became France (r. 843–77), granted overlordship of Andorra to the Count of Foix in 843. Later, however, the Bishopric of Urgel (in Spain) claimed that Andorra was an endowment of its cathedral. The solution adopted (1278) was to make Andorra a co-principality under the joint suzerainty of the Count of Foix and the Bishop of Urgel. Three centuries later the rights of the former passed to Henry IV of France (r. 1589–1610) and thence to his successors as French head of state. In 1793 the revolutionary government in Paris renounced co-suzerainty over Andorra, but this was restored by Napoleon in 1806 on the petition of the Andorran people.

Historically protective of the right to Andorran citizenship, Andorrans reacted to a modest extension of the franchise in 1933 by staging a mild revolution, which was eventually ended by a force of French gendarmes. In the post-war era, as tourism rapidly developed into the main industry, the non-Andorran (mainly Spanish) population increased. Previously confined to male citizens of the third generation, the franchise was progressively extended to all citizens in the 1970s, although with a higher age qualification for first-generation Andorrans. Under a 1981 constitutional agreement providing for a separation of legislative and executive functions, Andorra's first executive council (government) was formed in Jan. 1982 under the leadership of a prime minister, an office initially held by Óscar Ribas Reig and since May 1984 by Josep Pintat Solens. The Dec. 1985 elections to the General Council of the Valleys produced, in the absence of formal parties, a mainly conservative new legislature, which confirmed Pintat in his post. In a general election in Dec. 1989, however, Ribas Reig was returned to office.

CONSTITUTION AND GOVERNMENT

Executive and legislature

Joint sovereignty is held as co-princes by the president of France and the bishop of See de Urgel (in Spain); they are represented in Andorra by the Veguer de França and the Veguer Episcopal respectively. Permanent delegations for Andorran affairs are headed respectively by the prefect of the département des Pyrénées-Orientales in France and a vicar general from the Urgel diocese. The executive functions of government are exercised by the Executive Council, appointed by the 28-member General Council of the Valleys, whose members are elected for a four-year term.

Present government

Co-Princes François Mitterrand, Joan Martí Alanís
Permanent French Delegate Jean Keller
Permanent Episcopal Delegate Maj. Ramón Vilardell Mitjaneta
Veguer de França Enric Benoît de Coignac
Veguer Episcopal. Francesc Badia-Batalla
Prime Minister. Óscar Ribas Reig

Justice

The system of law is based on French and Spanish civil codes. The highest courts for criminal cases are the 'Corts', made up of nominees of the co-princes and representatives elected by the General Council of the Valleys. For civil cases, a plaintiff may choose between going before the 'bayle' appointed by the French or Episcopal co-prince. The death penalty is nominally in force. No executions were carried out between 1985 and mid 1988.

National symbols

Flag. Three vertical stripes of blue, yellow and red, and in the centre there is the Andorran coat of arms with a coronet.
Festivals. 8 Sep. (National Holiday).
Vehicle registration plate. AND.

INTERNATIONAL RELATIONS

Affiliations

None.

ECONOMY

Currency

The units are the French franc/Spanish peseta, divided into 100 centimes/centimos.

Energy and mineral resources

Electricity. Production capacity is 35,000 kW. Actual production in 1988 was 140,000,000 kWh or 2,830 kWh per person.

Bioresources

Agriculture. Mainly sheep-raising. Also small quantities of tobacco, rye, barley, oats and some vegetables. Timber is also grown.

Industry and commerce

Industry. Manufacturing is small-scale and mainly of cigarettes, cigars and furniture.
Commerce. Banking and smuggling (the principality has duty-free status) are both important sources of income.
Trade with UK. Andorran exports to the UK totalled £46,000 in 1988, while imports from the UK totalled £10,780,000.
Tourism. The economy relies chiefly on tourism, especially skiing, and there are around 12,000,000 visitors a year.

COMMUNICATIONS

Railways

There are no railways in Andorra.

Roads

There are 60 miles/96 km of roads.

Aviation

None.

Shipping

None.

Telecommunications

Andorra has one AM radio station, no television broadcasting, 8,000 radios and 4,000 television sets. There are 17,700 telephones.

EDUCATION AND WELFARE

Education

There were 1,866 pupils at infant school, 3,458 at primary school, 3,271 at secondary school, 320 at technical school and 46 at special school (1986–87).

Health

There is 1 doctor per 450 inhabitants and 1 hospital bed per 440 inhabitants.

ANGOLA

República Popular de Angola
(People's Republic of Angola)

GEOGRAPHY

Angola is situated on the west coast of Africa with an area of 481,226 miles²/1,246,700 km² divided into 18 provinces. Cabinda, the northernmost district is divided from the rest of the country by the estuary of the River Congo and Zaïrean territory. The 'planalto central' (average elevation 3,609–4,593 ft/1,100–1,400 m) occupies nearly two-thirds of the country's area (south and south-east) rising northwards within the central massif of the Bie Plateau to 7,116 ft/2,619 m at Serro Môco. North and east of the mid-section massif, the land slopes gradually towards the Congo and Zambezi river basins. The southwestern coastal desert strip extends as far north as Benguela. Semi-desert conditions continue north to Luanda, Angola's capital, supporting an estimated 12% of the total population. Forests and woodlands occupy approximately 40% of Angola's surface area concentrated in the north-west and scattered elsewhere although absent in the desert south-west.

Climate

Predominantly Tropical Plateau climate. Wet season lasts from Oct. to Mar. (May, in the north) followed by a long dry season. Temperatures and rainfall averages are much reduced on the coast, influenced by the cold south-north flowing Benguela current. The extreme aridity of the south-west (average annual rainfall 2.17 in/55 mm, average maximum daily temperature between 72°–81°F/22–27°C) contrasts sharply with the 23.6 in/600 mm rainfall received in the far north and 70 in/1,750 mm in the extreme north-east. Luanda Jan. 78°F/25.6°C. July 69°F/20.6°C. Average annual rainfall: 12.7 in/323 mm. Lobito Jan. 77°F/25°C. July 68°F/20°C. Average annual rainfall 13.9 in/353 mm.

Cities and towns

Luanda (capital)	480,613
Huambo (Nova Lisboa)	61,885
Lobito	59,258
Benguela	40,996
Lubango	31,674
Malanje	31,559

Population

Total population is 9,481,000, of which 30% live in urban areas. Population density is 19.7/7.3 persons per miles²/km². Major ethnic groups include the Bakongo; the Mbundu; the Ovumbundu; the Lunda-tchokwe; the Nganguela; the Nyaneka-humbe; the Herero and the Ambo. About 40,000 Mbuti Pygmies inhabit the Ituri forest of Zaïre and approximately 8,000 nomadic Angolan San (Bushmen) survive in the south-west. The post-independence exodus of the mid-1970s has left 30,000 Europeans (mainly Portuguese) in Angola.

Birth rate 4.73%. **Death rate** 2.22%. **Rate of population increase** 2.51%. **Age distribution** under 15 = 44.6%; over 65 = 3.0%. **Life expectancy** female 43.6; male 40.4; average 42.

Religion

A considerable minority (860,000) of the population still follow traditional beliefs. Of the 65.7% of the population who are affiliated Christians, 4.7 million (55.1%) are Roman Catholic and 9.2% Protestant.

Language

The official language is Portuguese, but Bantu dialect and other African languages are also in common use, including Umbundu (38% or 3.38 million speakers); Kimbundu; Lunda; Kikongo.

HISTORY

The territory now known as Angola was probably first inhabited by Khoisan-speaking hunters-gatherers. In the first millenium AD large-scale migrations of Bantu-speaking peoples into southern Africa occurred and the occupation of what is now Angola was probably completed by about 1600. The first Portuguese explorers arrived in 1482 and established a presence along the northern coast. In 1575 the Portuguese founded Luanda. The slave trade developed as a valuable source of income for the Portuguese, with between 5,000 and 10,000 slaves a year being exported from Luanda during the early 17th century.

The frontiers of Angola were fixed by the conventions of 1891, following the 1884–5 Congress of Berlin which divided the map of Africa among the colonial powers. As a junior colonial power, Portugal was granted 'rights of occupation' over Angola, but Portuguese rule did not effectively begin until 1910–20. Following the overthrow of the Portuguese Republic in 1926 and the establishment of Dr Antonio Salazar's Estado Novo four years later, the decentralization policy of the early colonial period ended and was replaced by a system whereby the interests of the colonies were more directly subjugated to the immediate interests of Portugal.

Under Dr Salazar and, latterly, Marcello Caetano, the colonial regime imposed itself more on the Angolan people, eventually leading to a rebellion in Luanda in Feb. 1961. Severe repression followed, but armed resistance to Portuguese rule in Angola was under way. In the 13 years until Apr. 1974, when a military coup in Lisbon led directly to the ending of the Portuguese colonial wars, the nationalist guerrilla armies were able to establish military and political control over large parts of eastern Angola and to press westwards towards the country's central and western districts.

Three nationalist movements were involved in the struggle for independence. The Popular Movement for the Liberation of Angola (Movimento Popular de Libertação de Angola – MPLA) was formed in Dec. 1956 with the aim of ending colonial rule and building a new and unified society. It was led by Agostinho Neto. The National Front of Angolan Liberation (Frente Nacional de Libertação de Angola – FNLA), essentially a tribalist movement, was formed in 1962, operating in the north of the country and led by Holden Roberto. The National Union for the Total Independence of Angola (União Nacional para a Independência Total de Angola – UNITA) was formed in 1966 under Dr Jonas Savimbi, operating mainly in eastern Angola.

Following the military coup in Portugal a tripartite 'government of transition' was formed by the three nationalist movements, but armed conflict soon broke out between the MPLA and the others. The conflict intensified following superpower involvement, with the Soviet Union and allies (including a major Cuban troop presence) supporting the MPLA while South Africa, with Western support, backed UNITA. In 1975 South African troops invaded and occupied parts of southern Angola, ostensibly to protect South African workers in Angola, and subsequently to take military action against Namibian guerrilla camps. In Oct. 1975 a further South African incursion was halted 300 km south of Luanda by MPLA and Cuban troops.

The MPLA on 11 Nov. 1975 proclaimed the People's Republic of Angola, with Neto as president, and the other two nationalist movements also claimed to have established governments of the new state. However, on 24 Nov. the Nigerian Government recognized the MPLA government and prompted other states to follow suit. As 350,000 Portuguese settlers left Angola, the Cuban intervention proved decisive and on 25 Mar. 1976 South Africa announced that its troops would be withdrawn from southern Angola.

A socialist regime was established in the new republic and in Dec. 1977 the MPLA was restructured as a Marxist–Leninist party, with the state becoming an instrument of the party. Pres. Neto died on 10 Sept. 1979 and was succeeded by another MPLA veteran, José Eduardo dos Santos. Elections to the National People's Assembly, consisting of 289 deputies, were held in 1980 and 1986, but political power remained firmly in the control of the 90-member central committee and the 15-member political bureau of the MPLA.

From 1978 South Africa made periodic incursions into Angola, purportedly in pursuit of Namibian nationalist guerrillas. In 1981 these incursions occurred on a greatly increased scale and in 1983 South African forces occupied large parts of Cunene province, 450 km inside Angola. South African incursions into Angola continued on a sporadic basis until Aug. 1988, despite a formal withdrawal in Apr. 1985 following the signing of the Lusaka Accord in Feb. 1984. South Africa also continued to provide logistical backing to UNITA as the latter maintained a guerrilla campaign in support of its claim to be included in the central government. The US Congress in June 1985 voted to repeal the Clark Amendment (enacted in 1976) which prohibited US military and financial support for UNITA.

As part of the peace process designed to bring independence to Namibia, South African forces were finally withdrawn from Angola on 30 Aug. 1988 and, under a US-mediated agreement signed in New York on 22 Dec. 1988, Cuba and Angola agreed on a gradual and total withdrawal of the estimated 50,000 Cuban troops from Angola, while South Africa agreed to withdraw from Namibia to allow free elections to be held there prior to independence. In Dec. 1988 the Angolan government offered a one-year amnesty to UNITA supporters, but this was rejected by the UNITA leadership. Pres. dos Santos had declared in mid-1987 that the war against UNITA and its South African backers had cost Angola $12,000 million in terms of economic sabotage, 60,000 citizens killed and 600,000 displaced.

CONSTITUTION AND GOVERNMENT

Executive and legislature

The ruling MPLA-PT party, restructured in 1977 as a Marxist-Leninist vanguard party, exercises effective political control. It is responsible for Angola's political, economic and social leadership, and its chairman is also head of state. The National People's Assembly is composed of 289 full and 29 alternate members elected indirectly for a five-year term; last elections were in late 1986.

Present government

C.-in-C. of the Armed Forces; Chairman of the Council of Ministers; Minister of State for the Economic and Social Sector José Eduardo dos Santos

Principal ministers Kundi Paihama (Minister of State for Inspection and Control; State Security); António Henriques da Silva (Planning); Lt.-Col. Pedro de Castro Van-Dúnem 'Loy' (External Relations); Col.-Gen. Pedro Maria Tonha 'Pedalé' (Defence); Augusto Teixeira de Matos (Finance); Domingo das Chagas Simoes Rangel (Foreign and Internal Trade, Industry); Lt.-Col. Francisco Antonio Magalhaes Paiva 'Nvunda' (Interior); Fernando José França Van-Dúnem (Justice)

Ruling party Popular Movement for the Liberation of Angola, Workers' Party (Movimento Popular de Libertaçao de Angola, Partido de Trabalho)

Chairman José Eduardo dos Santos

Political bureau full members José Eduardo dos Santos; Afonso Van-Dúnem 'Mbinda'; Lt.-Col. Antonio dos Santos Franca 'Ndalu'; Lt.-Col. Francisco Antonio Magalhaes Paiva 'Nvunda'; Col. Juliao Mateus Paulo 'Dino Matross'; Kundi Paihama; Lt.-Gen. Manuel Alexandre Rodrigues 'Kito'; Pascoal Luvualu; Lt.-Col. Pedro de Castro Van-Dúnem 'Loy'; Col.-Gen. Pedro Maria Tonha 'Pedalé'; Roberto Antonio de Almeida

Justice

The system of law, originally based on Portuguese and customary law, has been modified in line with socialist principles. The highest courts are the Supreme Court and Court of Appeal in Luanda. The death penalty is in force. There were 15 executions between 1985 and mid-1988. Capital offences: crimes against the security of the state; homicide.

National symbols

Flag. Two horizontal stripes, red over black; in its centre there is a yellow emblem consisting of half a cogwheel (with nine cogs), a machete and a five-pointed star.

Festivals. 4 Feb. (Anniversary of the outbreak of the armed struggle against Portuguese colonialism); 27 Mar. (Victory Day); 1 May (Workers' Day); 1 Aug. (Armed Forces Day); 17 Sep. (National Heroes' Day, birthday of Dr. Agostinho Neto); 11 Nov. (Independence Day); 1 Dec.(Pioneers' Day); 10 Dec. (Anniversary of the Foundation of the MPLA).

INTERNATIONAL RELATIONS

Affiliations

NAM, OAU, ACP, Comecon (observer).

Defence

Total Armed Forces: 100,000 (including some 10,000 Guerrilla Forces; ODP People's Defence Organisation militia; 24,000 conscripts). Reserves: Militia 50,000.

Army: 91,500; 500 main battle tanks, mainly T-34, T-54/-55, T-62, and light tanks PT-76.

Navy: 1,500; 24 patrol and coastal combatants.

Air Force: 7,000; 133 combat aircraft, mainly MiG-23 and MiG-21 MF/bis, and 21 armed helicopters.

Opposition: UNITA; Total Armed Forces: 28,000 regulars and 37,000 militia equipped with tanks mainly T-34 and T-55.

ECONOMY

Currency

The unit is the kwanza, divided into 100 lwei.

National finance

Budget. The 1986 budget was for expenditure of US$2,700 million.

Gross Domestic Product

Estimated total GDP US$4,700 million, per capita US$600 (overall size of economy ranking 89 in the world).

Economically active population. The total number of persons active in the economy is 2,783,000.

Energy and mineral resources

Minerals. Angola has reserves of diamonds; salt; iron ore; phosphates; copper; feldspar; gold; bauxite; uranium. Only diamonds (625,000 carats in 1985) and salt (55,000 tonnes in 1983) are fully exploited.

Oil. Total production was about 24.8 tons/22.5 million tonnes (1988). Oil production is the most lucrative sector of the economy, contributing about one-third of GDP.

Electricity. Production 737 million kWh (1988); capacity 501,000 kW, mainly hydroelectricity.

Bioresources

Agriculture. Over 80 % of the population is engaged in subsistence agriculture. Some 2% of the land is arable, with virtually no permanent cultivated crops; meadows and pastures constitute 23%.

Crop production: cash crops (1986 production figures in tons/tonnes): sugar-cane 275,575/250,000; coffee 38,580/35,000; bananas 308,644/280,000; palm oil 44,092/40,000; palm kernels 13,228/12,000; seed cotton 36,376/33,000. Tobacco, citrus fruits and sisal are also cultivated. Food crops: cassava 2,171,531/1,970,000; maize 253,529/230,000; sweet potatoes 198,414/180,000; beans 44,092/40,000; and other local foodstuffs. Disruption caused by civil war and marketing deficiencies have necessitated food imports.

Livestock numbers (1987): cattle 3.39 million; sheep 260,000; goats 970,000; pigs 475,000.

Forestry. Forest and woodland cover 43% of the country, with tropical rainforest in the north, from which mahogany and other hardwoods are exported. Production 31,782,600 ft^3/9 million m^3 (1984).

Fisheries. Total catch 79,932 tons/70,700 tonnes (1984).

Industry and commerce

Industry. Some 15% of the workforce is employed in industry (1985 estimate). Principal industrial activities are mining; fish processing; brewing; tobacco; sugar; textiles; cement; food production; building construction.

Commerce. Exports US$1,278 million; imports $1,062 million (1986). Exports in 1986 included oil; coffee; diamonds; sisal; fish; fish products. Imports included capital equipment (machinery and electrical equipment); food; vehicles and spare parts; textiles and clothing; medicines; military hardware. Principal trading partners are USA; Soviet Union; Cuba; Portugal; Brazil.

Trade with UK. Angola imported goods from the UK worth £20,154,000 and exported to the UK goods worth £10,036,000 in 1988.

COMMUNICATIONS

Railways

There are 1,833 miles/2,952 km of railway. Civil war has meant closure of important sections of the Benguela railway.

Roads

There are 44,898 miles/72,300 km of roads.

Aviation

There are over 200 airfields in all, 26 with permanent surface runways. Linhas Aereas de Angola provides domestic and international services (main airport is at Luanda).

Shipping

There are 804 miles/1,295 km of navigable waterways. Main ports are Luanda, Lobito, Namibe and Cabinda. There are 12 merchant ships of 1,000 GRT or over.

Telecommunications

There are 40,300 telephones. Television is broadcast on two channels and radio on a large number, both AM and FM; there are 400,000 radios and 32,000 television sets.

EDUCATION AND WELFARE

Education

School population. 2.4 million pupils in primary schools; 153,000 in secondary schools; 4,746 students in higher education (1983).

Universities. The Universidade de Angola was founded in Luanda in 1963, and has faculties at Huambo and Lubango. There were 3,500 students in 1982.

Literacy. 20% of the adult population.

Health

Doctors 436, hospital beds 20,700 (1980).

ANGUILLA

GEOGRAPHY

An island in the eastern Caribbean, Anguilla covers an area of 35 miles^2/91 km^2; the terrain is flat, formed of limestone and coral. Its capital is The Valley.

Climate

Tropical, with north-east moderating trade winds; hurricanes are frequent particularly July to Oct.

Population

Total population (1989) estimated at 6,850, mainly of black African descent.
Birth rate 2.4%. **Death rate** 0.9%. **Rate of population increase** 0.5%. **Life expectancy** female 76; male 71.

Religions

Christianity: Anglican; Methodist; Roman Catholic.

Language

English.

HISTORY

Anguilla's earliest inhabitants were Arawak Indians who lived on the island for several centuries before the arrival of European settlers in 1650. British settlers from St Christopher (St Kitts) colonized the island and it remained a British possession. In 1816 it was joined for administrative purposes with St Kitts and Nevis. African slaves were imported to the island until the abolition of slavery in 1834.

Universal suffrage was introduced in 1951. In 1967 Anguilla became part of the Associated State of St Kitts-Nevis-Anguilla, which gave the territory greater internal self-government. The islanders, however, resented their subordination to St Kitts and in May 1967 St Kitts policemen were expelled from the island in a movement led by Ronald Webster, leader of the People's Progressive Party (PPP). Attempts to find a solution failed and in Mar. 1969 British troops landed on the island to restore British control. In 1971 Anguilla was separated from St Kitts-Nevis and in 1980 formally returned to dependent status. After losing a vote of 'no confidence' Webster was replaced as Chief Minister in 1977 by Emile Gumbs. Webster returned to power in 1980 as leader of the Anguilla United Party, but his administration collapsed in 1981, leading to early general elections which were again won by Webster, but this time at the head of another party, the Anguilla People's Party (APP). The APP was defeated in elections held on 9 Mar. 1984 by the Anguilla National Alliance (formerly the PPP), and Gumbs became chief minister. The Gumbs administration was returned to power in a general election on 27 Feb. 1989; the ANA won three seats in the seven-member parliament but maintained a working majority through the support of an independent MP.

CONSTITUTION AND GOVERNMENT

A dependent territory of the UK, Anguilla under its 1982 Constitution has a governor (Geoffrey Whittaker) who chairs the seven-member Executive Council, and a House of Assembly comprising 11 members, last elected in March 1989 for a five-year term.
Chief Minister Emile Gumbs

National symbols

Flag. Three orange dolphins in a circular design on a white ground, with a light blue horizontal band at the base.
Festivals. 30 May (Anguilla Day).

ECONOMY

Anguilla is heavily dependent on tourism, benefiting from a boom in recent years, and offshore banking. Development plans also involve light industry, a response to high unemployment.

Currency

East Caribbean dollar

COMMUNICATIONS

There are no railways; 37 miles/60 km of surfaced road; and three airports in all, only one of which (Wallblake) has a permanent-surfaced runway. There is a modern internal telephone system, three AM radio broadcasting stations and one FM station, and no television.

EDUCATION AND WELFARE

There are seven schools. Education is free and compulsory up to 14. There is one 21-bed hospital.

ANTIGUA AND BARBUDA

GEOGRAPHY

The country consists of three islands situated in the eastern Caribbean, lying along the outer rim of the Leeward Islands chain in the West Indies. The largest of the islands, Antigua (108 miles^2/280 km^2), rises to 1,328 ft/405 m in the west at Boggy Peak and is atypical of the other Leeward Islands in the absence of forests, mountains and rivers. The nation's capital, St. John's, lies in the north-west parish with approximately 36,000 inhabitants (nearly half the total population). The flat, coral island game reserve of Barbuda (62 miles^2/160 km^2) lies 28 miles/40 km to the north of Antigua and is comparatively well wooded. The one town is Codrington, located on a lagoon in the western half of the island. The uninhabited rocky islet of Redonda (39 miles^2/1.0 km^2) lies 28 miles/40 km south-west of Antigua. Total area of the islands is 170 miles^2/441.6 km^2.

Climate

Tropical, moderated by constant sea breezes and trade winds with a mean annual rainfall of 44 in/ 1,118 mm, which is slight compared with other islands of the Lesser Antilles. Temperatures range from 75°F/ 24°C in Jan. to 81°F/27°C average in Aug. but can rise to 91°F/33°C between May and Oct.

Cities and towns

St John's (capital)	36,000

Population

Total population is 84,000 of which 30.8% live in urban areas. Most are of African descent. Population density is 494 persons per mile^2/186.6 per km^2. Ethnic composition: 94.4% Black; 3.5% mulatto; 1.3% White. **Birth rate** 1.48%. **Death rate** 0.5%. **Rate of population increase** 0.98%. **Age distribution** under 15 = 38.5%; over 65 = 5.4%. **Life expectancy** female 74.2; male 70.4; average 73.

Religion

The majority of the population are Christian, 44.5% of whom belong to the Anglican Church. Other Protestants (principally Moravian, Methodist and Seventh Day Adventist) make up a further 42.2%. 10.2% are Roman Catholic and 0.7% Rastafarian.

Language

English is the official language, but the local English patois/argot is commonly used.

HISTORY

The earliest inhabitants of Antigua and Barbuda were Arawak and Carib Indians. The first European to visit Antigua was Columbus in 1493. He named the island after the church of Santa Maria de la Antigua in Seville, Spain. A permanent settlement was not established on the island until 1632 and Antigua formally became a British colony in 1667. During the 18th century the island flourished under a plantation system using African slave labour to produce sugar. Slavery was abolished in 1834. The island of Barbuda, which had formerly been owned by the Codrington family, was incorporated into the territory in 1860.

Universal adult suffrage was introduced into the colony in 1951 when the Antigua Labour Party (ALP), the political arm of the Antigua Trade and Labour Union, led by Vere Bird, won all eight elective seats on the Legislative Council. A system of ministerial government was introduced in 1956 and in 1960 Bird became chief minister. The territory became an Associate State in 1967 with full internal government. The ALP lost the 1971 general election to the opposition Progressive Labour Movement, and George Walter became premier. The ALP regained power at elections held in 1976 and after elections in 1980 opened negotiations with Britain for full independence. Opposition to independence came from the island of Barbuda which wanted greater autonomy for itself. The territory became an independent state within the Commonwealth on 1 Nov. 1981. Vere Bird became the first prime minister. The ALP retained power by winning elections in 1984 and 1989.

CONSTITUTION AND GOVERNMENT

Executive and legislature

The British sovereign as head of state is represented by a governor general, appointed on the advice of the Antiguan prime minister. The governor general formally appoints the prime minister, who is responsible to Parliament (a bicameral body), the lower chamber of which is popularly elected for a maximum term of five years (last general elections Mar. 1989). Barbuda has a considerable degree of autonomy in its own internal affairs.

Present government (1 Feb 1990)

Governor General Sir Wilfred Ebenezer Jacobs
Prime Minister; Defence; Information C. Vere Bird Sr.
Principal Cabinet Ministers Lester Bird (Deputy Prime Minister; External Affairs; Economic Development; Tourism; Energy); Christopher O'Marde (Home Affairs); John St. Luce (Finance); Keith Ford (Legal Affairs; Attorney General); Hugh Marshall (Trade and Industry).

Justice

The system of law is based on English common law. The highest court is the British Caribbean Court of Appeal. The death penalty is in force. There was 1 execution between 1985 and mid-1988. Offence: murder.

National symbols

Flag. The red flag bears a large isosceles triangle, the base of which is at the upper edge of the flag and the apex in the middle of the lower edge. The triangle is divided into three horizontal sections of black, blue and white. The black stripe bears a yellow rising sun with nine rays.

Festivals. 1 May (Labour Day); 5 June (11 June in 1990, Queen's Official Birthday); 1 Nov. (Independence Day).

INTERNATIONAL RELATIONS

Affiliations

Caricom; Commonwealth.

ECONOMY

Currency

The unit is the EC dollar, divided into 100 cents.

National finance

Budget. The 1987 budget was for expenditure of US$140 million and revenue of US$70 million.

Inflation. 1%.

Gross Domestic Product

Estimated total GDP US$215 million, per capita US$3380 (overall size of economy ranking 162 in the world).

Economically active population. The total number of persons active in the economy is 30,000; unemployed = 10%.

Sector	% of workforce
industry	7
agriculture	11
services*	82

* services figure includes elements unassigned to other categories.

Energy and mineral resources

Minerals. Antigua and Barbuda has no significant mineral resources.

Electricity. Production capacity (1987) 48,800 kW.

Bioresources

Agriculture. 18% of the total land area of Antigua and Barbuda is used for arable purposes and a further 7% consists of meadows and pastures. Cotton and fruits are the main agricultural products.

Crop production (1986 in 1000 tons/tonnes): cotton 77/70; fruit 9.92/9. Livestock numbers (1987): cattle 18,000; sheep 13,000; goats 13,000; pigs 4,000.

Forestry. Forests cover 16% of the country.

Fisheries. Total fish catch 1,117 tons/1,013 tonnes (1983).

Industry and commerce

Industry. Tourism is the country's largest industry. Other economic activities include light manufacturing (clothing; alcohol; household appliances) and construction. An oil refinery was opened in 1982.

Commerce. Antigua and Barbuda's exports totalled US$30.8 million; imports US$278.9 million (1987). Exports included petroleum products 46%; manufactures 29%; food and live animals 14% and machinery and transport equipment 11%. Imports included food and live animals; machinery and transport equipment; manufactures; chemicals; oil. Countries exported to were Trinidad and Tobago 40%; Barbados 8%. Imports came from US 27%; UK 14%; Caricom 7%; Canada 4%.

Trade with UK (1988). Antigua and Barbuda imported UK goods worth £20,755,000 and exported to the UK goods worth £10,845,000.

Tourism (1986). 149,000 tourists (excluding cruise ship visitors) entered Antigua and Barbuda.

COMMUNICATIONS

Railways

There are no railways.

Roads

There are 7,235 miles/1,165 km of roads, of which 238 miles/384 km are concrete or bituminized.

Aviation

Leeward Islands Air Transport Services (LIAT) provides services to 22 islands in the West Indies and to Caracas (main airport is Vere Bird International Airport, on Antigua).

Shipping

The port of St John's is located on Antigua. There are 58 merchant ships of 1,000 GRT or over.

Telecommunications

There is a good telephone system and 6,700 telephones; some 20,000 radio and television sets.

EDUCATION AND WELFARE

Education

Most schools are run by the state, although a minority are operated privately, usually by religious denominations.

School population. 15,657.

Schools. 48 primary schools with 436 teachers (1 per 24.2 pupils); 16 secondary schools with 304 teachers (1 per 16.8 students).

Literacy. 90%

Health

The country has a general hospital with 215 beds, a psychiatric hospital with 200 beds and a geriatric unit with 150 beds. In rural areas health care is provided by health centres and dispensaries. The government operates a Medical Benefits Scheme which provides free medical attention and hospital facilities for most illnesses, and a Social Security Scheme which provides pension, sickness and maternity benefits.

ARGENTINA
República Argentina
(Argentine Republic)

GEOGRAPHY

Argentina occupies almost the whole of the southern part of the South American continent and extends from Bolivia to Cape Horn, a total distance of nearly 2,149 miles/3,460 km; its greatest breadth is about 981 miles/1,580 km with a coastline (excluding the Rio de la Plata estuary) 1,599 miles/2,575 km in length. Argentina is divided into four main geographical regions: the Andes (west, running north-south); the forest and flood plain of the north and Entre Rios (area 224,942 miles^2/582,750 km^2); the fertile Pampa plains of the Argentinian heartland, area 250,900 miles^2/650,000 km^2, supporting some 67% of the total population including Greater Buenos Aires (east of the Andes, west of the Atlantic); and finally Patagonia, south of the Rio Colorado, with an area of 301,080 miles^2/780,000 km^2 but comprising only 2.7% of the total population. Dominating the immense western Chilean frontier, the Cordilleras range (highest point: Mount Aconcagua 22,834 ft/6,960 m) extends from the northern to the southern boundaries rising from the Southern Patagonian glaciated trough into the high and arid north-west plateaux of the Bolivian Altiplano.

The Republic consists of 22 provinces, one territory (Tierra del Fuego) and one federal district (Buenos Aires, supporting 40% of the population), comprising in all an area of 1,068,019 miles^2/2,766,889 km^2. Argentina also claims the Falkland Islands (known in Argentina as the Islas Malvinas), South Georgia, the South Sandwich Islands and part of Antarctica.

Climate

Sub-tropical in the Chaco region of the north with mild winters, rainfall decreasing east-west (average temperatures Jan. 77°F/25°C, July 57.2°F/14°C, Santiago del Estero); cold temperate in Patagonia and Tierra del Fuego with total annual rainfall not more than 8–9 in/200–250 mm, strong winds but mild average temperatures Jan. 51°F/10.5°C, July 36°F/2°C. In the Andes, temperatures for Mount Aconcagua regularly fall below –4°F/–20°C at night even in the warm summer months, winds gusting 100 mph +. Temperatures in Buenos Aires are generally between 41°F/5°C and 84°F/29°C but can rise to 95°F/35°C in Jan. and Feb.

Cities and towns

Buenos Aires	(capital) 2,922,829
Cordoba	983,969
Rosario	957,301
Mendoza	605,623
La Plata	564,750
San Miguel de Tucuman	498,579

Population

Total population is 31,960,000, of which 85% live in urban areas. Population density fluctuates from 5,655/14,651 per miles^2/km^2 in the Federal district of Buenos Aires to less than 1.4 per km^2 in Patagonia. According to Argentina's own governmental census of 1980, a total of 1.9 million foreign-born citizens made up 6.8% of the national population, 56.5% of whom were of European origin. Immigrants from neighbouring countries made up a further 2.7% of the national total. The largest indigenous Indian communities included the Andean Colla (35,100); the Chiriguan in the Gran Chaco (23,700); the Araucan Mapuches in Patagonia (21,600).

Birth rate: 2%. **Death rate** 0.9%. **Rate of population increase** 1.2%. **Age distribution** under 15 = 30.6%; over 65 = 8.5%. **Life expectancy** female 74; male 67; average 71.

Religion

Christianity. Approximately 91.6% of the population are Roman Catholic, 2.5% are Protestant. A variety of different Christian denominations including the Armenian Orthodox and Ukrainian Catholic churches make up a further 1.5%. 2% are Jewish, 75% of whom live in Buenos Aires.

Language

Spanish. Some Indian languages survive as first or secondary languages in a few areas e.g. Quechua in the north-west; Chiriguan; Charoti in the Gran Chaco; Guarán in Entre Rios; Araucano Mapuche; Tehuelche in the Pampa and in Patagonia.

In 1980, 95% spoke Spanish; 3% Italian; 1% Guarán; 1% other languages including Welsh in Patagonia.

HISTORY

Archaeological work, at sites from the north-west of Argentina to the southern tip of Tierra del Fuego, has established the presence of hunter-gatherers and fishermen as far back as 12,000 years ago. The more sedentary tribes, dating from approximately 500 BC, were distinguished by their cultivation of crops and domestication of animals, alongside their perfection of tools, weapons, pottery and belief systems (a notable example being the Diaguitas of the north-west who were not fully conquered by the Spanish until the late 17th century).

The Spanish 'conquistadores' arrived in the first half of the 16th century, founding Buenos Aires in 1536. In remote areas such as the northern Gran Chaco swamps and the vast plains of the Pampas groups like the Guaycurans and the Tehuelches, were barely affected and persisted in their nomadic life-style. However, by the 1700s many of the nomads were using horses and began cattle raids on Spanish settlements from the Chaco to Patagonia. After their subjugation and partial assimilation, many of these mounted nomads became, in the late 19th century, the celebrated 'Gauchos', the cowboys of the Pampas.

Up to 1776, what is now Argentina was part of the Spanish viceroyalty of Peru (1544–1824). In 1776, Charles III of Spain established the viceroyalty of Río de la Plata (which also comprised present-day Paraguay, Uruguay and Bolivia), with Buenos Aires as its capital. Here, immigrants from Spain gradually concentrated economic and political power and began to threaten the interests of the provincial creole Spaniards.

After 1816, when the Congress of Tucumán declared the United Provinces of the Río de la Plata to be independent from Spain, the division between the capital and the interior provinces widened, with a constant power struggle between the 'Unitarians' of Buenos Aires and the 'Federalist' leaders in the provinces (powerful local chiefs or 'caudillos' who wished to remain self-governing). The federalist dictator Juan Manuel de Rosas, who came to power in 1835, imposed a form of stability but was overthrown in 1852. An attempt made the following year to establish a federalist constitution was resisted by the province of Buenos Aires, and the antagonism developed into open civil war in 1858. In 1861 the army of Buenos Aires, led by Bartolomé Mitre, defeated the provincial forces at the battle of Pavón. An unpopular war with Paraguay (1865–70), which increased taxes, temporarily revived the dying spirit of provincial separatism. However, Mitre, who had become Argentina's first truly national president in 1862, devoted his tenure of office (as did his two successors) to pacifying the country and developing the institutions of government. The Congress, which was moved from Paraná to Buenos Aires, began to meet regularly, a national judiciary was established and the city of Buenos Aires became a federal distict with a separate existence from the province of the same name.

From 1880 to the 1920s, the attraction of foreign investment and labour became the primary concern of governments. Argentina's population, numbering barely 1,500,000 (the majority of whom lived on subsistence agriculture in the countryside) was boosted by European immigration (especially from Italy), the rate of arrivals increasing from 40,000 in 1870 to 110,000 in 1885, and 200,000 in 1890. In step with this, infrastructural development, primarily through British financing, opened up the country, the railway system alone expanding from 3,200 km in 1860 to 32,000 km in 1910. Agriculture benefited substantially, the amount of cultivated land expanding from less than 0.6 million hectares to more than 24.3 million hectares between 1860 and 1910. The introduction of barbed wire and the refrigeration of meat made possible a large increase in cattle-ranching. The country also became a major exporter of cereals and pastoral products.

The provincial legislatures and the National Congress were dominated during this period of economic growth by a small landowning elite (estancieros) and the powerful commercial and livestock interests based in the city and province of Buenos Aires. Represented by the Conservative Party, this ruling elite barred political representation to the majority of the population and, significantly, to the emerging middle class. The latter, concentrated in the bureaucracy and professions, had begun to articulate their beliefs through the founding of the Radical Civic Union (UCR) in 1890. These Radicals, convinced that the ruling class would never allow them to achieve an electoral victory, boycotted all elections prior to 1912, opting for rebellions in 1890, 1893 and 1905, all of which failed. However, the honest administration of the 1912 Electoral Law (brought in by the Conservatives in an effort to legitimize their rule and to co-opt their middle-class opponents), which insisted on universal and compulsory male suffrage, secret ballots and permanent voter registration, brought the Radicals to power in 1916 under Hipólito Yrigoyen. The Radicals, who promised 'national renovation', held the presidency for the next 14 years but never seriously threatened the power base of the ruling class. With so many newly registered voters (rising from 190,000 in 1910 to 1,460,000 in 1928), the chances of further Conservative electoral success were seriously diminished; however, in Sept. 1930, amid economic crisis, government corruption and popular disillusionment with Yrigoyen's second term as president, a coup brought Argentina's first military government to power. Far from providing stability, the coup brought harsh repression and corruption, the period 1930-43 being known as the 'Era of Patriotic Fraud', when the Conservatives, together with civilian and military political opportunists, rigged successive elections. Such abuses in turn antagonized the growing industrial middle class (who were profoundly dissatisfied with the economic policies of the landed elite) and an increasingly militant working class. The heightened tension developing between these two new forces persuaded the military to take the helm again in 1943.

The 1943 coup brought Col. Juan Domingo Perón on to the political stage. As the military's minister of labour, Perón believed that the State could play the key role in industrializing and diversifying the economy and that it could be assisted in this task by the rapidly expanding urban working class. For Perón, this meant reforms and, in the teeth of Conservative opposition, he sanctioned progressive labour legislation, encouraged trade union growth and organization, and substantially raised wages. In the presidential elections of Feb. 1946 Perón, now the candidate of the Argentine Labour Party, defeated the single candidate of the traditional parties. He, along with his second wife Eva (who as 'Evita' became a legend for her social welfare programmes), mobilized the labour movement into a single General Labour Confederation (CGT) fiercely loyal to him. Such loyalty persisted even when Perón (re-elected in 1951 as the automatic candidate of the new Peronist Party) became increasingly authoritarian as economic growth slowed. Strikes were repressed, wages driven down and opposition leaders were harassed or exiled. By 1955, Peronism had strained its appeal among the rank-and-file of the labour movement, and the Catholic Church had withdrawn its support. In September, disillusioned sections of the military overthrew Perón, forcing him into what was to be an 18-year exile.

The succeeding twenty years were characterized by accelerating inflation, strikes, high unemployment and political instability. The military, who had closed the Congress and dissolved all political parties in 1966, were unable to deal with the high level of political violence which their own repression had stoked up. Gen. Alejandro Lanusse allowed the Perónists to contest the elections of Mar. 1973, and their successful candidate, Héctor Cámpora, then resigned within 50 days, forcing fresh elections to clinch the presidency for Perón, who had returned from exile. Both Perón and his third wife 'Isabelita' (who succeeded him as president after his death on 1 July 1974), in the context of a gathering world recession, failed to deliver any significant social and economic changes, with record inflation in 1975 and 1976, and in 1975 there was the threat of the first general strike against a Perónist government. As tensions heightened, the radical youth wing of the Perónist movement (the Montoneros) initated a campaign of urban guerrilla warfare to destabilize the government. This provided a green light for the military who returned to power in a coup on 24 Mar. 1976, arresting Isabel Perón and proceeding to torture, murder and abduct thousands of perceived opponents in a campaign later known as the 'dirty war'.

Gen. Jorge Videla was succeeded by Maj.-Gen. Roberto Viola as president in Mar. 1981, but at the end of that year Viola was ousted by military hardliners, and replaced by the commander-in-chief of the army, Gen. Leopoldo Galtieri. By 1982 the military had so discredited itself that it gambled on invasion of the Falkland (Malvinas) Islands on 2 Apr. to restore its national credibility. Ignominious defeat by British forces made the resignation of Galtieri's military junta inevitable and in the presidential elections of 30 Oct. 1983 the UCR's candidate Raúl Alfonsín was the surprise victor over the Perónist Italo Luder. The Alfonsín administration promised Peace, Freedom and Progress, but instead faced military unrest and a multitude of economic problems which deepened throughout its term, notably the spiralling inflation and a foreign debt which topped US$60,000 million at the close of 1988. The more immediate political problems lay with the army as groups of officers led a series of rebellions in 1987 and 1988, protesting against government efforts to bring to trial the military personnel responsible for gross human rights violations in the 'dirty war'. The Peronists returned to power with the victory of Carlos Saúl Menem over the UCR candidate Eduardo Angeloz in May 1989. They also won control of the Congress. Menem's inauguration, scheduled for December 1989, had to be brought forward to July due to the depth of the current economic crisis.

CONSTITUTION AND GOVERNMENT

Executive and legislature

Executive power is vested in the president, as head of state. The president appoints the cabinet. The president and vice-president are elected for a six-year term by an electoral college of 600 directly elected members. Last presidential elections May 1989. Argentina's Chamber of Deputies has 254 members elected directly for four-year terms with half of the seats renewable every two years; last elections May 14, 1989. The members of the 46-member Senate nominated by the legislatures of each of the provinces for nine-year terms with one-third of the seats renewable every three years. Each province has its own elected governor and legislature, concerned with all matters not delegated to the federal government.

Present government

President Dr Carlos Saúl Menem

Vice President Eduardo Duhalde

Principal members of Cabinet Humberto Romero (Defence); Antonio Erman González (Economy); Domingo Cavallo (Foreign Relations); Gulio Mera Figueroa (Interior); Alberto Jorge Triaca (Labour and Social Security); Julio Oyhanarte (Justice)

Justice

The system of law is a mix of US and western European concepts. The highest federal court is the Supreme Court, with 5 judges at Buenos Aires. Each province has its own judicial system, with a Supreme Court and several minor chambers. Justice is administered by federal and provincial courts, with jury trials for criminal cases. The death penalty is in force only for exceptional crimes. There were no executions between 1985 and mid-1988.

National symbols

Flag. Three horizontal stripes - sky blue, white and sky blue. In the centre, as a sign of freedom, there is the yellow 'Sun of May' with a human face and thirty-two rays.

Festivals. 1 May (Labour Day); 25 May (Anniversary of the 1810 Revolution); 10 June (Occupation of the Isla Malvinas); 20 June (Flag Day); 10 July (Death of General José de San Martin); 12 Oct. (Discovery of America).

Vehicle registration plate. RA.

INTERNATIONAL RELATIONS

Affiliations

NAM; OAS; SELA.

Defence

Total Armed Forces: 95,000 (40,000 conscripts). Terms of Service: Army 6–12 months; Air Force 1 year; Navy 14 months. Reserves: 377,000.

Army: 55,000; 425 main battle tanks; mainly TAM and M-4 Sherman; light tanks AMX-13.

Navy: 25,000 inclusive naval air force and marines; 4 submarines; 13 principal surface combatants: 1 carrier (capacity 18 aircraft and helicopters); 6 destroyers; 6 frigates. 13 patrol and coastal combatants.

Naval Air Force: 2,000; 26 combat aircraft; 14 armed helicopters.

Air Force: 15,000; 137 combat aircraft (mainly Canberra B-62, Mirage IIIC and IIIE, and Dagger); 18 armed helicopters.

ECONOMY

Currency

The unit is the austral, divided into 100 centavos.

National finance

Budget. The 1987 budget was for expenditure of

US$9,500 million and revenue of US$7,100 million. Main items of expenditure are housing and welfare (33%); defence (6%); education (6%).

Balance of payments. The balance of payments (current account, 1987) was a deficit of US$4,285 million.

Inflation. 188%.

Gross Domestic Product

Estimated total GDP US$71,530 million, per capita US$2,360 (overall size of economy ranking 32 in the world).

Economically active population. The total number of persons active in the economy is 10,900,000; unemployed = 6.5%.

Sector	% of workforce	% of GDP
industry	31	43
agriculture	12	13
services*	57	44

* services figure includes elements unassigned to other categories.

Energy and mineral resources

Oil and gas. Crude oil production 25,352,901 tons/ 23,000,000 tonnes (1988); natural gas 13,500,000 million m^3 (1983) with new fields offshore also discovered.

Minerals. Argentina is rich in minerals. All of the following are extracted coal; gold; silver; copper; tin; iron ore; tungsten; beryllium; mica; uranium; lead; barytes; zinc; tin; manganese; limestone.

Electricity. Production capacity 16,058,000 kW. Actual production was 48,034m kWh or 1,520 kWh per capita (1988).

Bioresources

Agriculture. The agricultural sector is an important export earner. Cereals and oilseed account for approximately two-thirds of production with the remainder largely accounted for by livestock production.

Crop production (1986, in million tons/tonnes): wheat 9.8/8.9. Other crops include cotton; potatoes; grapes; tobacco; citrus fruits; olives; rice; soya; mate tea; sugar; sunflower; ground nuts.

Livestock numbers (1987, in millions): cattle 55.7; sheep 29; pigs 4; horses 3.

Forestry. Forestry accounts for around 1% of agricultural production. Some 214,500,000 acres/ 86,806,962 hectares or around one-third of the agricultural land is woodland.

Fisheries. The fish catch was estimated at 551,150 ton/ 500,000 tonnes in 1987.

Industry and commerce

Industry. The industrial sector accounts for around 25% of GDP and comprises primarily food processing (especially meat packing); motor vehicles; consumer durables; textiles; chemicals and petrochemicals; printing; metallurgy; steel.

Commerce. Argentina's exports totalled $6,300 million in 1987, primarily to the USA; Soviet Union; Italy; Brazil; Japan; the Netherlands. Imports were $5,800 million, primarily from the USA; Brazil; West Germany; Bolivia; Japan; Italy; the Netherlands.

Trade with UK. Argentina imported UK goods worth £12,991,000; exports to UK totalled £66,281,000 (1988).

Tourism. (1986) 1,600,000 visitors.

COMMUNICATIONS

Railways

There are 21,430 miles/34,509 km of railways; only 102 miles/164 km are electrified.

Roads

There are 131,260 miles/211,369 km of roads, of which about 37,260 miles/60,000 km are surfaced.

Aviation

Aerolineas Argentinas provides international services and Austral Lineas Aereas (ALA) and Lineas Aereas del Estado (LADE) provide domestic services (main airports are: Aeroparque Jorge Newbery; Cordoba; Corrientes; El Plumerillo; Ezeiza (35 km from Buenos Aires); Jujuy; Resistencia; Rio Gallegos; Salta; San Sarlos de Bariloche).

Shipping

11,000 km of the inland waterways are navigable. The main ports are Bahia Blanca; Buenos Aires; Necochea; Rio Gallegos; Rosario; Santa Fe. There are 138 merchant ships of 1,000 GRT or over.

Telecommunications

There is an extensive modern phone system with 2,650,000 telephones including 12,000 public telephones. With a proliferation of broadcasting channels, the capital alone has over 100 radio stations and four television channels. There are 8,000,000 radios and about 6,000,000 television sets.

EDUCATION AND WELFARE

Education

Schools. There were 4,430,500 primary school pupils with 218,520 teachers (1 per 20 students), 656,500 secondary school pupils with 86,900 teachers (1 per 7.5 students), and 905,750 vocational school pupils with 119,300 teachers (1 per 7.5 students) (1984).

Universities. There are 24 national universities and 17 private universities.

Literacy. Estimated literacy is 94%.

Health

Public hospitals provide free medical care, while trade unions also give medical and dental care to members and their dependents.

ARUBA

GEOGRAPHY

An island in the Caribbean 17.4 miles/28km north of Venezuela, Aruba covers an area of 74.5 miles²/193km²; the terrain is mainly flat, with scant vegetation. The capital is Oranjestad.

Climate

Tropical, with little seasonal temperature variation. It escapes the Caribbean hurricane belt.

Population

Total population (1989) estimated at 62,500, large majority of mixed European/Caribbean Indian descent.

Birth rate 0.3%. **Death rate** 0.6%. **Rate of population increase** 0.3%. **Life expectancy** female 80; male 72.

Religions

Christianity: Roman Catholic; Protestant. Small Hindu; Moslem; Confucian and Jewish minorities.

Language

Dutch (official); Papiamento (a Spanish, Portuguese, Dutch, English dialect); Spanish.

HISTORY

Aruba's earliest inhabitants were Arawak Indians. The Spanish visited the island in 1499, but did not colonize it. The Dutch claimed Aruba in 1634, but made no concerted attempts at settlement and the island remained undeveloped and retained much of its Indian population. The construction of an oil refinery in 1929 brought employment and prosperity to the island. In 1954 the Netherlands Antilles attained internal self-government as part of the Tripartite Kingdom of the Netherlands. However, in Aruba resentment grew at Aruba's status within the Netherlands Antilles federation, particularly compared with that of Curaçao, and over its financial support for the smaller islands. Political parties in Aruba, principally the Arubaanse Volkskpartij (AVP) and the Movimento Electoral de Pueblo (MEP) campaigned for separation from the other constituent elements of the Netherlands Antilles. In 1977 a referendum on Aruba produced an 83% vote in favour of independence. The MEP led the campaign for separation and independence for Aruba and in the early 1980s negotiations started with the Netherlands government. In Mar. 1983 it was agreed that Aruba would become a separate autonomous part of the Netherlands from 1 Jan. 1986, with full independence following in 1996. The closure of the oil refinery in 1985 provoked a severe economic crisis and led to the defeat of the MEP as the majority party in the island's council. The leader of the AVP, Henny Eman, became the island's first prime minister when separate status was achieved in 1986.

CONSTITUTION AND GOVERNMENT

A self-governing part of the Netherlands, Aruba achieved autonomy in internal affairs in 1986 upon separation from the Netherlands Antilles. Independence is planned for 1996. Under its 1986 Constitution it has a governor general (Felipe B Tromp). Government is by a coalition of three parties. The last election was held in Jan. 1989.

Prime Minister Nelson Oduber (Electoral Movement Party)

National symbols

Flag. Blue, with two narrow horizontal yellow stripes across the lower section, and with a four-pointed red star outlined in white in the upper hoist corner.

Festivals. 18 Mar. (Flag Day)

ECONOMY

The Aruban economy depends heavily on a thriving tourist industry (lack of natural resources severely limits development of agriculture and manufacturing). The Dutch Government has supported the economy with loans.

Currency

Aruban florin

COMMUNICATIONS

There are no railways. There are two ports, Oranjestad and Sint Nicolaas. There is one government-owned airport. There are telephone, television and radio installations (4 AM and 4 FM).

AUSTRALIA
Commonwealth of Australia

GEOGRAPHY

Australia, the sixth largest country on Earth, is located between the Indian and Pacific Oceans bounded by latitudes 10°41' and 43°39'S (a distance of 2,447 miles/3,940 km) and by longitudes 113°9' and 153°37'E (about 2,608 miles/4,200 km). It is divided into six states and two territories and comprises a land area of some 2,965,368 miles^2/7,682,300 km^2 including Tasmania to the south-east but excluding the external territories. The elevation of the arid Western Shield (occupying over 50% of the total surface area) averages between 1,312 ft/400 and 1,968 ft/600 m, rising to 5,000 ft/1,524 m at Mount Liebig in the central MacDonnel ranges. Much of the plateau region is desert. To the east of the shield, the Great Artesian basin (a composite of the Carpentaria, Eyre and Murray basins) extends from the Gulf of Carpentaria in the north to the mouth of the Murray River in the south. The Eastern Uplands or Great Dividing Range (93–248 miles/150–400 km in width) constitute Australia's third major physiographic region traversing the continent north-south from Queensland to Tasmania and separating the fertile, populous east-southeast coastal plains from the vast Basin and Shield regions in the west. The highest points are Mount Kosciusko (7,310 ft/2,228 m) in New South Wales and Mount Oisa (5,305 ft/1,617 m) in Tasmania. The lowest is Lake Eyre (−49 ft/–15 m). Forests cover an estimated 18% of the total surface area, primarily along the varied ranges, plateaux and basins of the Great Divide. The tropical rainforest belt skirts the north-eastern Queensland coast. Australia's longest river is the Murray, fed by the Darling, Murrumbidgee and Lachlan tributaries. Off the north-east coast, the Great Barrier Reef runs almost parallel to the Great Divide over 1,199 miles/ 1,931 km.

External Territories. Australian Antarctic Territory: 2,362,250 miles^2/6,119,818 km^2; Cocos (Keeling) Islands: located in the Indian Ocean, 1,719 miles/2,768 km north-west of Perth, 2,288 miles/3,685 km west of Darwin, comprising 27 small coral islands, total area 564 miles^2/1,462 km^2. 616 inhabitants on Home and West Islands; Christmas Island: isolated peak in Indian Ocean, 259 miles/417 km north of Cocos Islands, area 52 miles^2/135 km^2. Estimated population 2,000 (1,300 Chinese; 600 Malay; 100 Australian (European origin); Norfolk Island: 869 miles/1,400 km east of Brisbane 1,398 acres/3,455 hectares. Population 1,977 (1986). Penal colony 1788–1814; 1825–1855; Heard and McDonald Islands: 3,105 miles/5,000 km south-west of Freemantle, area 159 miles^2/412 km^2; Territory of Ashmore and Cartier Islands: 323 miles/520 km north-west of Australia, area 3 miles^2/5 km^2; Territory of Coral Sea Islands: situated north-east of Great Barrier Reef, area .386 miles^2/1 km^2 (manned meteorological station on Willis Island).

Climate

Australia's large area and latitudinal span determine a wide range of climatic conditions from the Alpine (south-east New South Wales) to the tropical (north-east Queensland). Temperate conditions with consistent rainfall averages are confined to the fertile, densely populated lowlands, valleys and highland declines in the east and south-east coastal sectors (including Australian Capital Territory) and in the south-western tip of Western Australia. Melbourne averages 43–55°F/6–13°C in July and 57–79°F/14–26°C in Jan.–Feb.; average monthly rainfall 1.9–2.6 in/48–66 mm. 50% of Australia has a mean total rainfall of less than 11.8 in/300 mm per year and less than a third receives over 19.7 in/500 mm. The effectiveness of the rainfall in the northern monsoonal belt (over 31.5 in/800 mm annually) is diminished by the strict demarcation of wet and dry seasons, soaring temperatures and high potential evaporation. Roughly two-thirds of the continent is arid or semi-arid. Alice Springs, located in the semi-arid centre of the continent has average daily temperatures of 39–66°F/4–19°C in July and 70–97°F/21–36°C in Jan. with rainfall averages of 0.31 in/8 mm (July – Sept.) and 1.7 in/43 mm (Jan.). West Tasmania has the highest rainfall averages: a mean total of 60.5 in/1,536 mm falling annually in Hobart. Extremes of cold are rare due to the absence of extensive mountain masses and because of the expanse of ocean in the south. By contrast, inland desert temperatures can reach up to 122°F/50°C.

Canberra Jan. 68°F/20°C. July 42°F/5.6°C. Annual rainfall 24.8 in/629 mm.

Cities and towns

Canberra (national capital)	273,600
Sydney	3,391,600
Melbourne	2,916,600
Brisbane	1,157,200
Perth	1,001,000
Adelaide	987,100

Population

Total population is 16,358,000 of which 86% live in urban areas. Population density is 5.5 persons per miles^2/2.1 per km^2, but ranges widely between a much higher density in Australian Capital Territory and the sparsely populated Northern Territory. Approximately 94.4% of the population are white, 2.1% Asian and 1.1% Aboriginal. In 1985 78.9% of the population were native born and 21.1% foreign born, of which United Kingdom 7.5%; Italy 1.8%; New Zealand 1.2%; Greece 1.0%; Yugoslavia 1.0%; East and West Germany 0.8%; The Netherlands 0.7%; Poland 0.4%; Malta 0.4%; Lebanon 0.3%. In 1987, 3.49 million Australians were born overseas, of whom 1.2 million came from the United Kingdom and Ireland, 1.5 million from Continental Europe, 606,604 from Asia and 230,451 from New Zealand.

In 1986, there were 227,645 Aboriginal Australian and Torres Straits Islanders. The majority live in rural communities scattered throughout the northern and central areas of the country. Queensland has the largest Aboriginal population while the Northern Territory Aboriginals make up 22.4% of the total state population.

Birth rate 1.5%. **Death rate** 0.8%. **Rate of population increase** 1.4%. **Age distribution** under 15 = 23.6%, over 65 = 10.1%. **Life expectancy** female 80; male 73; average 76.

Religion

In response to the optional question on religion in the 1986 census: 73% of the population were Christian, of which 26% Catholic; 23.9% Anglican; 7.6% Uniting; 3.6% Presbyterian; 2.7% Orthodox; 1.3% Baptist; 1.3% Lutheran; 0.6% Church of Christ. An estimated 0.5% of the population are Muslim; 0.4% Jewish; 0.2% Buddhist.

Language

The official language is English. 196,000 Australians speak other languages including native Aboriginal dialects. Australian Aboriginal languages comprise a group of 260 interrelated tongues, the vast majority of which are now extinct. Of the surviving languages, Mabinag (the language of the Western Torres Strait Islands) and Western Desert Language are the most widely spoken.

HISTORY

Archaeological evidence indicates that Aborigines were living in Australia at least 40,000 years ago. In 1973 a skeleton was found at Lake Mungo in New South Wales, dating back at least 28,000 years. In pre-European times, Aborigines were hunters, fishers and gatherers, living in groups of between 25 and 50 people, and roaming over large areas of land. By the time Europeans settled, Aborigines numbered around 300,000. They were killed in large numbers by settlers, and by diseases introduced by the Europeans. In the 17th century, European explorers sailed along the coast of Australia. The Dutch explorer Abel Tasman charted the coastline of what is now Tasmania (1642–44), and in two separate voyages (1688 and 1699) the Englishman William Dampier explored the western and northwestern coastline. No country took formal possession until 1770, when Capt. James Cook charted the east coast, and claimed it for Britain.

The first settlement was a British penal colony, established on 26 Jan. 1788, at Port Jackson (now Sydney). Australia provided Britain with an alternative penal settlement, after transportation to North America had stopped because of the War of Independence. In 1803 a penal colony was established on Tasmania (then called Van Diemen's Land). Wheat and merino sheep were introduced to Australia in the late 18th century. Free settlers also emigrated to Australia from the 1790s. Land was at first granted by the government, but in 1831 a system of land sales was introduced, the proceeds of which helped finance the passage of immigrants. Over the next decade an estimated 50,000 settlers came to Australia, paid for by land sales. As more of the country was opened up, squatters began to occupy grazing land. In 1836 the government recognized the squatters, and introduced a licence of £10 a year. Free settlers began to resent the competition for jobs from convicts, and the policy of transportation also began to lose favour in Britain. Transportation to New South Wales ended in 1840, and to Tasmania in 1853, though it was re-introduced in Western Australia for a short time (1853–67) to provide labour. In all, around 160,000 convicts were sent to Australia.

Many of the free settlers brought with them ideas of representative government, and the demand for self-government grew in the 1830s and 1840s. It was granted in 1850, when Britain passed the Australian Colonies Government Act, which gave considerable independence to the colonies, including the right to alter their own constitutions, fix the franchise, and determine tariffs. The discovery of gold in New South Wales and in Victoria in 1851 attracted thousands of people. The population of Victoria quadrupled in the next four years. The Australian economy was now based on wool and gold. Most colonies tried to break up the squatters' large holdings so that small farmers could buy land, but with limited success. Miners and shearers unions began to emerge, and in the 1880s there was intermittent industrial unrest. In 1890 wharf labourers went on strike over the issue of whether or not employers were entitled to engage non-union labour. The strike spread to miners and farm workers. Troops and special police were brought in, and the strikes were put down. There were more strikes in the 1890s, over the same issue. Labor emerged as a political organization, and the party held the balance of power in New South Wales following elections in 1891. The 1890s saw bank failures and a financial crisis, brought on by drought, labour unrest, over-expansion and over-borrowing.

The independent nature of the colonies posed problems such as different railway gauges, different postal systems, and the absence of a common defence policy. Victoria introduced a policy of trade protection (1866), followed by the other colonies, with the exception of New South Wales. It became clear to many that a measure of co-operation was necessary. The first of several inter-colonial conferences was held in 1863, aimed at creating closer ties, but it was not particularly successful. In 1891 the first Australian Federal Convention met. It was made up of members of the colonial parliaments, who worked out a draft constitution which later served as a basis for federation.

On 1 Jan. 1901, the colonies of New South Wales, Victoria, Queensland, South Australia, Western Australia, and Tasmania federated to form the Commonwealth of Australia. (The Northern Territory was transferred from South Australia to the Commonwealth in 1911.) The federal government was to have control of foreign affairs, defence, trade etc. The head of state was the governor general, appointed by the crown, and a parliament was set up, consisting of a Senate and a House of Representatives. The first Commonwealth parliament passed an Immigration Restrictions Act in 1901, which put the 'White Australia' policy into effect. It was aimed in particular at keeping out Chinese immigrants, who had arrived in large numbers to work in the gold fields. The policy also caused the repatriation of Pacific Islanders. A great deal of social legislation was enacted in the years leading up to World War I. In 1902 women's suffrage was adopted by the federal government. An industrial arbitration court was established in 1906 which laid down the principle of a basic wage. Old-age and invalid pensions were brought in, along with free and compulsory education. In 1909 the first ship of the Australian Navy was ordered. In 1911, territory was acquired from New South Wales to form the federal capital of Canberra, and parliament began meeting there in 1927. In 1911 the Commonwealth Bank was established.

During World War I Australia sent about 330,000 men to Europe to fight alongside Britain. Conscription was twice defeated in a referendum, and the issue caused a split in the ruling Labor Party. In 1920 Australia was a founder member of the League of Nations. With the passage of the Statute of Westminster in 1931 Australia became a Dominion within the British Commonwealth. During the 1920s the Australian economy expanded, benefiting from high prices for wool and meat. Tariffs were introduced to protect new manufacturing industries, and primary producers were given subsidies. The world depression in the early 1930s caused widespread unemployment and hardship in Australia, which had an economy largely dependent on that of Britain. But it recovered more quickly than many countries, due to the rising price of wool and gold. It was also helped by the Ottawa Trade Agreement of 1932, which provided a preferential trade arrangement between Britain and Australia (along with the other British dominions and colonies).

In World War II Australia once again supported Britain. Australian troops fought in the Middle East between 1940 and 1942. When Japan entered the war, Australian forces returned to the Pacific theatre, and the United States made Australia the Allied base in the Pacific. The Australian Labor Party (ALP) took office in 1941, after the United Australia Party lost ground in federal elections. At the end of the war, there was an influx of displaced persons from Europe. In 1947 the Labor prime minister John Chifley made a controversial attempt to nationalize the banks, which failed in the courts. A bitter coal strike was put down with the use of troops and emergency legislation.

The ALP was voted out of office in 1949, with the bank issue being a major factor. The Liberal and the Country Parties formed a coalition government which stayed in power for the next 23 years. The new prime minister was Robert Menzies. In 1950 the High Court prevented his government from outlawing the Communist Party. The 1950s saw the trade deficit rise, along with wages, and inflation spiralled. A secret ballot for trade union elections was introduced. The banking system was reformed, with the Reserve Bank of Australia becoming the central bank for the Commonwealth. Australia's foreign policy now concentrated on non-Communist Asian nations, and on strengthening ties with the United States. Australia took a prominent part in the Colombo Plan (1950), giving economic aid to underdeveloped countries of South and South-East Asia. Australia, New Zealand and the United States signed the ANZUS defence treaty the following year. In 1954 it was a signatory to the South East Asia Treaty Organization, whose members pledged to help each other in the event of outside aggression. In 1952 Britain began testing atomic bombs on Australian territory, and continued to do so for more than a decade. The government agreed to the establishment of an American naval communications base in Western Australia, in 1963. In 1965 Australia sent troops to support the United States in South Vietnam.

At home, Aborigines were given the vote, and access to social benefits which had previously been denied them. Australia adopted decimal currency in 1966. Robert Menzies retired as prime minister in 1966. Harold Holt took over, but died in a swimming accident the following year. John Gorton became prime minister, and then, in 1971, the Liberal leader William McMahon took over the premiership. The government was beset by problems of inflation and industrial unrest. It lost a general election for the House of Representatives, to the ALP, led by the charismatic socialist, Gough Whitlam. The Whitlam government ended Australia's military involvement in the Vietnam war in 1972. Amongst the administration's domestic achievements was the introduction of a national health scheme called Medibank, to provide free health care for all. In 1974, Whitlam dissolved both Houses of Parliament, following a conflict between the government and the Senate. Labor was returned, but still without a majority in the Senate. In 1975 the Senate blocked the government's money bills, threatening the administration with bankruptcy. On 11 Nov. the Governor General, Sir John Kerr, in an unprecedented move, dismissed Whitlam and dissolved Parliament. The Liberal Party leader, Malcolm Fraser, was declared caretaker prime minister, pending new elections in December.

A coalition of Fraser's Liberals and the National Country Party subsequently won majorities in both Houses. Fraser's policy was one of moderating government expenditure, in order to reduce inflation and the overseas debt. His majority was reduced in the general election of 1977 and again in 1980. The coalition government was beaten in the Mar. 1983 general elections, by the ALP. Bob Hawke, the new prime minister, immediately called an economic summit, and an accord on pay and prices was reached between the government, trade unions and employers, which set a centralized wage-fixing mechanism. In Dec. 1983 the government began a policy of economic deregulation, with the flotation of the Australian dollar, and the removal of most exchange controls. In 1984 a law was enacted giving greater protection to sacred Aboriginal sites. The Medicare system, providing universal health insurance, was introduced. Mr Hawke called an early general election for Dec. 1984, and was returned to power with an increased majority. At the same time the electorate rejected proposals put to it in a referendum, that the terms of the Senate and the House of Representatives be aligned, and the powers of the federal government and the state be redistributed.

In July 1984 a Royal Commission was set up to investigate the British nuclear testing on Australian territory in the 1950s and 1960s. Australia banned exports of uranium to France in 1984, in protest at French testing nuclear of weapons in the South Pacific. But in 1985 the government agreed to allow a shipment of uranium to France, and in 1986 the ban was lifted.

In Aug. 1985 draft legislation was proposed, which would give Aborigines the freehold of up to 25% of the country, including national parks, vacant crown land, and former Aboriginal reserves. Ayers Rock was transferred to the Mutijulu community (Oct. 1985) who immediately leased it back to the federal government for 99 years. The government gave up its plan to impose the Aboriginal land-rights bill on the state governments in 1986, after pressure from mining companies, and adverse public opinion. The Australia Act (1986) gave the nation full legal independence from Britain, but left the Queen's status as sovereign unaltered.

In Apr. 1987 the opposition National–Liberal coalition was annulled, after a split within the National Party. An early general election was called in July 1987, which Bob Hawke's ALP won. In August, the opposition alliance was renewed. A Royal Commission was set up (1987) into high death rates of Aborigines in police custody, officially listed as suicide. It started with a few cases in New South Wales, but many more instances were discovered and additional commissioners were appointed to cope with the workload. In September voters rejected in a referendum proposals on constitutional reform, including a plan to extend the term of the House of Representatives from three years to four. In 1988 Australians celebrated the bicentenary of European settlement. There were demonstrations and other public protests by some Aborigines. In 1989 both the Liberal and National parties elected new federal leaders in order to capitalize on the unpopularity of the Hawke government prior to the next general election, due in 1990.

CONSTITUTION AND GOVERNMENT

Executive and legislature

As an independent member of the Commonwealth the Australian head of state is the British sovereign, represented by a governor general. Legislative authority lies with a bicameral parliament consisting of an elected 76-member Senate (with 12 seats apportioned to each of the country's constituent states and two each for the Northern Territory and the Capital Territory of Canberra), and a 148-member House of Representatives elected for three years; last general election July 1987.

Present government (1 Feb 1990)

Governor General Bill Hayden

Prime Minister Bob Hawke

Members of the Cabinet Lionel Bowen (Deputy Prime Minister; Attorney General); Paul Keating (Treasurer); Robert Ray (Local Government; Immigration and Ethnic Affairs); Kim Beazley (Defence); Ralph Willis (Transport and Communications); Gareth Evans (Foreign Affairs and Trade); Peter Walsh (Finance); Stewart West (Administrative Services); John Button (Industry, Technology and Commerce); John Kerin (Primary Industry and Energy); Brian Howe (Social Security and Social Justice); John Dawkins (Training; Employment; Education); Graham Richardson (Arts; Sport; Environment; Tourism; Territories); Dr Neal Blewett (Health and Community Services); Michael Duffy (Trade Negotiations); Peter Morris (Industrial Relations).

Administration

Each state has its own legislature, government and constitution.

State Governors New South Wales – Sir James Rowland; Queensland – Sir Walter Campbell; Tasmania – Sir Phillip Bennett; Victoria – Dr Davis McCaughey; South Australia – Sir Donald Dunstan; Western Australia – Prof. Gordon Reid.

Administrator of the Northern Territory Commodore Edward Johnston.

State Premiers New South Wales – Nick Greiner; Queensland – Wayne Cross; Tasmania – Michael Field; Victoria – John Cain; South Australia – John Bannon; Western Australia – Peter Dowding.

Chief Minister of the Northern Territory Steve Hatton.

Justice

The system of law is based on English common law. The highest court is the High Court of Australia (the Federal Supreme Court), beneath which there is a structure of Federal Courts (the Federal Court of Australia and the Family Court of Australia) and State Courts. Disputes beween residents of different States come under the jurisdiction of the federal courts. The death penalty was fully abolished in 1985.

National symbols

Flag. The flag comprises the British Blue Ensign bearing in the fly, instead of a badge, four white seven-pointed stars and one smaller five-pointed star.
Festivals. 26 Jan. (Australia Day); 25 Apr. (Anzac Day); 12 June (Queen's Official Birthday).
Vehicle registration plate. AUS.

INTERNATIONAL RELATIONS

Affiliations

Anzus Pact, OECD, Commonwealth.

Defence

Total Armed Forces: 70,500. Terms of service: voluntary. Reserves: 27,580.

Army: 32,000; 103 main battle tanks (mainly Leopard 1A3).

Navy: 15,800; 6 submarines; 12 principal surface combatants (3 destroyers and 9 frigates); 22 patrol and coastal combatants.

Air Force: 22,600; 85 combat aircraft (mainly F-111C and F-18A).

ECONOMY

Currency

The unit is the Australian dollar, divided into 100 cents.

National finance

Budget. The 1988 budget was for expenditure of US$73,800 million and revenue of US$78,700 million. Main items of expenditure are housing and welfare (39%); health (9%); defence (9%); education (7%).
Balance of payments. The balance of payments (current account, 1987) was a deficit of US$8,688 million.
Inflation. 7.7%.

Gross Domestic Product

Estimated total GDP US$183,280 million, per capita US$12,580 (overall size of economy ranking 16 in the world).
Economically active population. The total number of persons active in the economy is 7,700,000; unemployed = 6.9%.

Sector	% of workforce	% of GDP
industry	16	33
agriculture	6	4
services*	78	63

* services figure includes elements unassigned to other categories.

Energy and mineral resources

Minerals. Australia is rich in mineral resources. It is one of the world's largest producers of coal and iron ore and also has significant deposits of uranium and bauxite. Output (in 1,000 metric tons/tonnes) was coal 153,219/139,000; iron ore 103,616/94,000; lignite 41,887/38,000; zinc 785/712; lead 495/448; copper 273/248; gold 83/75 (1986). In 1986 the country produced 27/24.5 million tons/tonnes of crude oil.
Electricity. Production 124,369 million kWh. The largest proportion of Australia's electricity is produced by brown-coal-fired generating stations, although power is also generated from thermal and hydroelectric stations. Tasmania, in particular, generates a considerable amount of hydroelectricity as a result of its assured rainfall and high level of water storage.

Bioresources

Agriculture. Farms and ranches cover 64% of Australia's total area, although 90% of this land is used for grazing rather than crop cultivation. The main farm products are meat; dairy produce; wool; cereals; sugar; rice.

Crop production (1987 in 1,000 tons/tonnes): sugar cane 27,576/25,000; wheat 11,023/10,000; barley 3,627/3,290; oats 2,050/1,860; rice 860/780.

Livestock numbers (1987 in millions): sheep 149.2; cattle 21.9 and pigs 2.6.
Forestry. Forests cover 14% of the country but are not evenly distributed between the states, with Queensland and Tasmania having the greatest areas of forest. In 1986–87 the quantity of timber processed in Queensland was: conifers 21,675,027 ft^3/613,780 m^3; hardwoods and cabinet woods 22,513,169 ft^3/637,514 m^3. In Tasmania the production of sawn timber was 10,569,480 ft^3/299,300 m^3, with a further 234,184 ft^3/827,000 m^3 used for milling and 140,210,000 ft^3/3,970,400 m^3 for chipping or grinding.
Fisheries. Fishing is particularly important in the Northern Territory and Western Australia where the total value of fish products landed was $A40.33 million and $A138.7 million respectively (1987).

Industry and commerce

Industry. Although Australia is essentially a producer of primary products, its metal production, especially iron and steel, provides the basis for the production of a wide range of engineering, machinery and transport products ranging from motor vehicles and machine tools to chemicals, electrical goods and telecommunications equipment.
Commerce. Australia's exports totalled A$35,782.6 million; imports totalled A$37,022 million (1987). Exports included coal; cereals; petroleum; transport equipment; meat; textile fibres. Imports included machinery and transport equipment; petroleum products; manufactured items. Countries exported to were Japan 26%; US 11%; New Zealand 6%; South Korea 4%; Singapore 4%; Soviet Union 3%. Imports came from US 22%; Japan 22%; UK 7%; West Germany 6%; New Zealand 4%.
Trade with UK. Australia imported UK goods worth £1,378 million and exported to the UK goods worth £745.6 million (1988).
Tourism. Australia derived revenue of A$3,700 million from 1.7 million visitors (1987).

COMMUNICATIONS

Railways

There are 25,341 miles/40,807 km of railways.

Roads

There are 529,704 miles/852,986 km of roads (489 miles/787 km of motorways, 24,050 miles/38,728 km other main roads and 56,934 miles/91,777 km of secondary roads).

Aviation
Four Airlines provide domestic services and Australian Airlines, East-West Airlines Ltd. and Qantas Airways Ltd. provide international services.

Shipping
Major ports are Adelaide; Brisbane; Cairns; Darwin; Devonport; Fremantle; Geelong; Hobart; Launceston; Mackay; Melbourne; Sydney; Townsville. There are 72 merchant ships of 1,000 GRT or over.

Telecommunications
There are 8,700,000 telephones and good national and international services. The Australian Broadcasting Service provides a national radio and television service, with competition on both counts from a large number of commercial channels.

EDUCATION AND WELFARE

Education
The major responsibility for the provision of education rests with the Australian states. Attendance at school is compulsory between the ages of 6 and 15 (16 in Tasmania), at either a free state school (most of which are co-educational and comprehensive) or a recognized private educational institution.

School population. 2,196,742 in state schools and 808,141 in non-state institutions.

Schools. 7,575 state schools with 148,972 teachers (1 per 14.8 students); 2,504 non-state schools with 49,543 teachers (1 per 16.3 students).

Universities. Tuition fees in post-secondary education were abolished in 1974 and student allowances are provided subject to a means test. A total of 175,476 students were enrolled at university in 1985, of whom 24,554 were engaged in post-graduate courses.

Literacy. 98.5%

Health
Australia has 1,053 general hospitals with an average of 5.4 beds per 1,000 of the population. In remote areas medical care is provided by the Royal Flying Doctor Service. Under the provisions of the Medicare universal health scheme introduced in 1984, there is automatic entitlement to a single public health fund which provides substantial assistance in the payment of medical fees.

AUSTRIA
Republik Österreich
(Republic of Austria)

GEOGRAPHY
Austria is a land-locked country in central Europe, divided into nine federal states (länder) with an area of 32,368 miles²/83,855 km². 64% of the territory is occupied by the Austrian Alps, part of the European Alpine system that connects Germany, Liechtenstein, Switzerland and Italy. Austria's highest peak is the Grossglockner in the western portion of this eastern belt, rising to 12,457 ft/3,797 m. North of the Alps, the subalpine Bohemian Massif, a forested area covering 10% of the land, forms part of a general upland region extending north into Czechoslovakia. The very fertile soils of the eastern lowlands, including the Vienna Basin, support virtually all Austria's arable farming. Approximately 40% of Austria is forested, and 90% of the terrain drains into the Danube River system (chief tributaries: the Lech, Inn, Traun, Raab and Drau rivers). The federal state of Wien supports 20% of the total population.

Climate
Climate varies considerably according to altitude, from humid continental in the north-east to Alpine in the west and south-west. Rainfall increases slightly east-west (reaching 39.4 in/1,000 mm in some areas). Winters are cold with plentiful snowfall but summers are warm. Vienna: Jan. 28°F/–2°C, July 68°F/19.8°C. Average annual rainfall 25 in/640 mm. Innsbruck: Jan. 27°F/–2.7°C, July 66°F/18.8°C. Average annual rainfall 34 in/868 mm.

Cities and towns

Vienna (capital)	1,531,346
Graz	243,166
Linz	199,910
Salzburg	139,426
Innsbruck	117,287

Population
Total population is 7,493,000, of which 55% live in urban areas. Population density is 231.5/90.1 persons per mile²/km². At the last census, 96.1% of the inhabitants were Austrian; 1.7% Yugoslavian; 0.8% Turkish; 0.5% German.

Birth rate 1.22%. **Death rate** 1.21%. **Rate of increase** 0.01%. *Age distribution* under 15 = 18.6%, over 65 = 14.1%. **Life expectancy** female 78; male 71; average 74.

Religion
Christianity. Between 85 and 90% are Roman Catholic and 5.6% Protestant. There are approximately 25,000 members of the Old Catholic Church in Austria and a Jewish population of about 7,000.

Language
97% of the population is German-speaking. Linguistic

minorities include 60,000 Turks; 32,000 Slovenes and Croats; 23,000 Slovaks; 19,000 Hungarians; 10,000 Czechs.

HISTORY

The Romans conquered what is now Austria south of the Danube by the end of the 1st century BC. Overrun by Germanic and Asiatic tribes in the 4th and 5th centuries AD, the area became the eastern frontier province (Ostmark) of the Frankish Empire in the 790s and thus part of the Holy Roman Empire established by Charlemagne in 800. In 976 Emperor Otto I created a margravate in the province, which was ruled for the next 270 years by the Babenberg dynasty, one of whom, Henry II, established Vienna as his capital in 1142. After the last of the Babenbergs had been killed in battle with the Magyars in 1246, there followed a bloody interregnum, from which Count Rudolf of Habsburg (in modern Switzerland) emerged in 1273 as King of the Germans and Holy Roman Emperor. Having defeated Ottokar of Bohemia at the Battle of Marchfeld in 1278, Rudolf (r. 1273–92) declared the Austrian ducal title hereditary in 1282.

Over the next three centuries, a combination of war, diplomacy and judicious marriages achieved a remarkable expansion of the Habsburg domains, whose only major setback was Switzerland's assertion of independence by 1453. When Charles V succeeded as Archduke and Holy Roman Emperor in 1519, he was already, through his father's marriage to a Spanish princess, King of Spain and of the Spanish dominions in the Americas, Italy and the Low Countries. Before his abdication in 1555, Silesia, Bohemia, Moravia, Hungary and Croatia had been added to the Habsburg Empire, which had also defeated the first Turkish siege of Vienna in 1529. Charles V was succeeded in Spain by his son, Philip II, and in Austria by his younger brother, Ferdinand I, to whom he had progressively handed over the Austrian provinces and who became Holy Roman Emperor in 1558.

Fierce Habsburg resistance to the Protestant Reformation in Germany led inexorably to the Thirty Years' War (1618–48), in which Catholic Austria and Spain were ranged against Protestant Germany, England, Denmark, Sweden, the Netherlands, and, latterly, Catholic France, whose intervention proved decisive. The 1648 Peace of Westphalia recognized the sovereignty of the German states, notably in religious matters, and the Holy Roman Empire, although continuing in name, disappeared as a political unit. France emerged as the dominant European power and the Habsburg empire began its long relative decline. It nevertheless remained strong enough to defeat the second Turkish siege of Vienna in 1683 and thereafter gradually to push back the frontiers of the Ottoman empire in south-eastern Europe. In the War of Spanish Succession (1702–13/14), the Austrian Habsburgs failed to prevent a French Bourbon from becoming King of Spain, but the Treaty of Utrecht (1713) confirmed their claim to the former Spanish Low Countries.

The male Habsburg line died out with Charles VI (r. 1711–40), who under the 1713 Pragmatic Sanction had conferred the succession to all Habsburg lands on his daughter, Maria Theresa. This arrangement was challenged, in the War of Austrian Succession (1740–8), by Prussia, France, Spain and Bavaria. Supported by England and the Netherlands, Austria won acceptance of the Pragmatic Sanction under the Treaty of Aix-la-Chapelle (1748) and recognition of Maria Theresa's husband as Holy Roman Emperor, but was obliged to cede Silesia to Prussia. The emergence of Prussia as the Habsburgs' principal rival for leadership of the Germans was confirmed in the Seven Years' War (1756–63), in which Austria's alliance with France, Russia, Sweden and Spain, against Prussia and England, failed to win back Silesia or ward off eventual defeat by Frederick the Great of Prussia.

Under Maria Theresa and her son, Emperor Joseph II (r. 1765–90), major reforms were instituted, transforming an agglomeration of feudal lands into a centrally administered state. Serfdom was abolished and freedom of religion guaranteed, amid a flowering of the arts and the great age of Austrian classical music. But although Habsburg dominion was further extended by the partition of Poland (from 1772), imperial Austria proved unable to resist the onslaught of the French revolutionary armies under Napoleon Bonaparte. The loss of the Austrian Low Countries to France (1797) was followed by massive defeat at the Battle of Austerlitz (1805) and the creation under Napoleon's tutelage of the Confederation of the Rhine (1806). This caused the Habsburg ruler, who in 1804 had declared himself Emperor Franz I of Austria, to give the last rites to Charlemagne's 1,000-year-old creation by renouncing the title of Holy Roman Emperor. However, the defeat of Napoleon found Austria on the winning side and, through Metternich's gifted diplomacy at the Congress of Vienna (1814–15), not only a principal territorial beneficiary (notably in northern Italy) but also acknowledged as leader of a new German Confederation.

Europe's revolutionary upsurge of 1848–9 exposed the vulnerability of the Habsburg Empire to the new forces of democracy and nationalism. Although national rebellions were eventually put down (with Russian assistance in the case of the Hungarians), Emperor Ferdinand (r. 1835–48) was obliged to abdicate in favour of his less absolutist nephew, Franz Joseph (r. 1848–1916). Moreover, Austria's leadership of the German Confederation was compromised by its insistence that all the Habsburg domains should be part of a unified Germany. Weakened by its defeat by France and its partial ejection from Italy in 1859, Austria then succumbed to Bismarck's vision of a 'smaller Germany' led by Prussia. Humiliated in the 1866 Austro-Prussian War, the Empire was forced to relinquish the German stage to Prussia. In an attempt to accommodate the Empire's largest non-German nationality, the Ausgleich (compromise) of 1867 created a 'dual monarchy', under which the emperor of Austria became king of Hungary as well and each realm had its own parliament.

The final decades of the Habsburg rule were a glorious twilight of economic, social and cultural achievement. Politically, despite the introduction of universal suffrage in the Austrian part in 1907, the Empire remained essentially an autocracy, not least for its subject Slav peoples and for the growing working-class movement represented by the Social Democratic Party (founded 1889). The threat posed by Slav nationalism, and by Russia's claim to pan-Slav leadership, cemented an alliance between Austria and the new German Empire (from 1879), which underpinned Austria's expansionist policy in the Slav-populated Balkan provinces once under Ottoman rule. But Austria's annexation of Bosnia-Herzegovina (1908) was to lead indirectly to the Empire's final downfall. When a Serbian extremist assassinated the heir to the imperial throne at Sarajevo (the provincial capital) in June 1914, Austria's resultant confrontation with independent Serbia caused Russia to mobilize and thus led to the outbreak of World War I.

The 1914–18 conflict not only ended in defeat for Germany and Austria–Hungary but also unleashed a tide of revolutionary and national aspirations which swept away the old order in central Europe. Having succeeded his great-uncle in 1916, Emperor Charles abdicated in Nov. 1918 and the first Austrian Republic was proclaimed, with Karl Renner (Social Democrat) becoming chancellor. A 'Habsburg Law' enacted in 1919 barred members of the former imperial family from Austria unless they declared allegiance to the Republic. Various post-war peace treaties dismembered the Empire on the basis of national self-determination and Austria was reduced to its present-day borders, being roughly the German-speaking area except South Tirol, which was ceded to Italy. Beset by economic problems, the new Republic experienced chronic strife between left and right, leading to the suspension of parliamentary government by Chancellor Englebert Dollfuss in 1933, Dollfuss's murder by Austrian Nazis, and the suppression of the Social Democrats in 1934. Growing internal pro-fascist agitation and pressure from Nazi Germany culminated in the unopposed entry of German forces in Mar. 1938 and the Anschluss (annexation), under which Austria was fully incorporated into Hitler's Reich.

After World War II the victorious Allies established a four-power (Soviet, US, British and French) occupation regime in Austria and recognized the newly declared Second Republic in Dec. 1945. Economic recovery was assisted by the receipt of US Marshall Aid. After lengthy negotiations, the 1955 Austrian State Treaty achieved the withdrawal of all occupation forces and accorded international recognition to Austria as a 'sovereign, independent and democratic state' within its frontiers of Jan. 1938. The treaty specifically banned any future political or economic union with Germany and reaffirmed the 1919 Habsburg Law, while an associated constitutional law provided for Austria's permanent neutrality. The resumption of full sovereignty was followed by rapid industrialization and economic advance. A founder member of EFTA from 1959, Austria signed an industrial free-trade agreement with the European Economic Community (EEC) in 1972 and applied for membership of the latter in July 1989.

Meanwhile, party politics had resumed on the basis of a determination to avoid the conflict of the inter-war period. From 1945 to 1966 the country was governed by a grand coalition of the People's Party (ÖVP), heir to the old Christian Socials, and the Socialist Party (SPÖ), successor to the pre-war Social Democrats. Four years of ÖVP rule (1966–70) were followed by 13 years of SPÖ government under the chancellorship of Bruno Kreisky, whose only major setback was the narrow rejection by referendum (1978) of nuclear power generation. The 1983 elections, after which the SPÖ was obliged to form a coalition with the small Freedom Party (FPÖ), marked a transition to less stable politics, accompanied by a series of scandals compromising establishment figures and by serious financial problems in the large state-owned economic sector, parts of which were earmarked for privatization.

In June 1986 Kreisky's successor as SPÖ chancellor, Fred Sinowatz, resigned immediately after the election to the Austrian presidency of former UN Secretary-General Kurt Waldheim, amid a major national and international controversy over the latter's wartime role as a German army officer in the Balkans. Political instability increased in Sept. 1986 when the new chancellor, Franz Vranitzky, terminated the SPÖ's coalition with the FPÖ following the latter's election of Jörg Haider, a right-wing nationalist, as its leader. General elections in Nov. 1986 resulted in a doubling of the FPÖ's vote, the entry of the Greens into the Austrian Parliament and losses for both the SPÖ and the ÖVP. The two major parties accordingly formed (Jan. 1987) a grand coalition with Vranitzky as chancellor.

CONSTITUTION AND GOVERNMENT

Executive and legislature

The ceremonial head of state is the federal president (Bundespräsident or head of state), elected for a six-year term by universal suffrage; maximum two terms of office. The head of government, nominally appointed by the president, is the federal chancellor (Bundeskanzler or head of government). The bicameral Federal Assembly (Bundesversammlung) consists of a 183-member National Council (Nationalrat or lower house) and a 63-member Federal Council (Bundesrat or upper house). Last Nationalrat elections Nov. 23, 1986.

Present government

Federal President Dr Kurt Waldheim
Federal Chancellor Dr Franz Vranitzky
Principal Cabinet members Josef Riegler (Vice-Chancellor; Federalism and Administrative Reform in the Federal Chancellery); Dr Alois Mock (Foreign Affairs); Ferdinand Lacina (Finance); Dr Franz Löschnak (Interior); Dr Wolfgang Schüssel (Economic Affairs); Dr Robert Lichal (Defence); Dr Egmont Foregger (Justice).

Justice

The system of law is Roman in origin. A constitutional court has the function of judicial review of legislation. The highest criminal court is the Supreme Court of Justice (Oberster Gerichtshof) in Vienna, with 4 higher provincial courts (Oberlandesgerichte), 21 provincial and district courts (Landesund Kreisgerichte) and 205 local courts (Bezirksgerichte). The death penalty was abolished in 1968.

National symbols

Flag. Three horizontal stripes of red, white (with a black eagle in the middle) and red.
Festivals. 1 May (Labour Day); 26 Oct. (National Holiday).
Vehicle registration plate. A.

INTERNATIONAL RELATIONS

Affiliations

Neutral; member of OECD; EFTA

Defence

Total Armed Forces: 54,700 (27,300 conscripts). Terms of service: 6 months' recruit training, 60 days' reservist refresher training during 15 years' or 8 months' training and no refresher. Reserves: 242,000 ready (72 hours); 1,200,000 have a reserve commitment.

Army: 50,000; 170 main battle tanks (chiefly M-60A3 and M-60A1).

Air Force: 4,700; 23 combat aircraft, mainly SAAB 105Oe. (J-350e Draken to replace SAAB 105: 6 on strength, 18 more to be delivered.)

ECONOMY

Currency

The unit is the Schilling, divided into 100 Groschen.

National finance

Budget. The 1987 budget was for expenditure of US$37,500 million and revenue of US$31,600 million. Main items of expenditure are housing and welfare 47%; health 12%; education 10%; defence 2.8%.

Balance of payments. The balance of payments (current account, 1988) was a deficit of US$155 million.

Inflation. 2.5% (12 months to Sept. 1989).

Gross Domestic Product

Estimated total GDP US$117,660 million, per capita US$15,573 (overall size of economy ranking 24 in the world). Growth rate (1988) 4.2%.

Economically active population. The total number of persons active in the economy is 3,200,000; unemployed = 3.6% (1988).

Sector	% of workforce	% of GDP
industry	35	37
agriculture	8	3
services*	56	60

* services figure includes elements unassigned to other categories.

Energy and mineral resources

Minerals. Austria's mineral production in 1987 was (in tons/tonnes) raw steel 4,741,174/4,301,165; rolled steel 3,783,591/3,432,451; pig iron 3,803,723/3,450,714; iron ore 3,362,015/3,050,000; lignite 3,070,579/2,785,611; raw magnesite 1,043,815/946,943; tungsten ore 359,902/326,501; lead and zinc ore 355,037/322,088.

Oil. Production of crude oil was 1,168,843/1,060,367 tonnes (1987).

Electricity. Out of a capacity of 17,042,000 kW, 47,860 million kWh of electricity (or 6,310 kWh per capita) were produced in 1988.

Bioresources

Agriculture. Agriculture contributes less than 4% of GDP and employs 8.5% of the workforce. The country is nevertheless 84% self-sufficient in agricultural products. Main products are livestock; forest products; cereals; potatoes; sugar beet.

Crop production (1987, in tons/tonnes): wheat 1,599,141/1,450,731; barley 1,299,266/1,178,686; potatoes 969,469/879,497; raw sugar 395,672/358,951; rye 340,971/309,327; oats 270,866/245,728.

Livestock numbers (1987): poultry 14,503,801; pigs 3,946,997; cattle 2,589,509; sheep 260,595; horses 45,179; goats 37,534.

Forestry. Of the agricultural land 41% is forested. 415,280,000 ft^3/11,759,643 m^3 of timber were felled in 1987.

Industry and commerce

Industry. Manufacturing is the mainstay of the Austrian economy, contributing 30% of GDP. The main industries are foods; iron and steel; machines; textiles; chemicals; electrical goods; paper and pulp; tourism and mining.

Commerce. Austria's exports totalled $27,200 million and imports totalled $32,700 million in 1987. Countries exported to were West Germany 35%; Italy 10%; Eastern Europe 8%; Switzerland 7%; the USA 4%; OPEC countries 3% (1987). Primary exports are machinery and equipment; iron and steel; lumber; textiles; paper products; chemicals. Imports are primarily petroleum; foodstuffs; machinery and equipment; vehicles; chemicals; textiles and clothing; pharmaceuticals. They come from West Germany 44%; Italy 9%; Eastern Europe 6%; Switzerland 5%; USA 3%; Soviet Union 2%.

Trade with UK. Austria imported UK goods worth £509,991,000 and exported goods to the UK worth £874,430,000 (1988).

Tourism. (1987) 15,761,399 visitors.

COMMUNICATIONS

Railways

There are about 3,602 miles/5,800 km of railways, of which all main lines are electrified.

Roads

There are 66,759 miles/107,503 km of classified roads.

Aviation

Oesterreichische Luftverkehrs AG (Austrian Airlines) provides domestic and international services (main airport is Schwechat, near Vienna).

Shipping

Vienna and Linz are river ports; there are 277 miles/446 km of navigable internal waterways, principally the Danube.

Telecommunications

There is a highly developed telephone system, and 4,014,000 telephones. There are two television channels, national and regional radio broadcasting by Osterreichische Rundfunk, 2,500,000 televisions and 2,700,000 radio licences.

EDUCATION AND WELFARE

Education

The education system provides for free compulsory education for children between 6 and 15 years of age.

Schools. There are 5,128 elementary and special schools with 650,241 pupils and 68,600 teachers (1 per 9 students); 1,509 secondary schools with 503,420 pupils.

Universities. There are 12 state-maintained universities (with 176,453 students and 8,885 teachers, a ratio of 1 per 20 students) and six art colleges (with 6,405 students and 1,632 teachers a ratio of 1 per 4 students). There are also 560 commercial, training and other colleges.

Literacy The literacy rate is 98%.

Health

The compulsory social and health insurance system is funded by contributions from employers and employees, with the government making up the difference. There are 22,889 doctors (1 per 330 people) and 334 hospitals with 83,341 hospital beds (1 per 90 people).

BAHAMAS
The Commonwealth of the Bahamas

GEOGRAPHY

The West Indian coral-limestone archipelago of the Bahamas consists of 29 islands, 661 cays and about 2,387 rocks occupying a total land surface area of 5,380 miles²/13,939 km² (about the size of Wales) dispersed over 89,938 miles²/233,000 km² of ocean. There are 17 principal islands and island groups (including Grand Bahama, Andros, Eleuthera, Great Abaco) with almost two-thirds of the population concentrated on New Providence Island and in the capital Nassau. Twenty-two of the islands are inhabited. The highest point is Mount Alverina on Cat Island, at 207 ft/63 m. Approximately 55 miles²/142 km² of the territory is cultivated; there are no rivers in the Bahamas.

Climate

Subtropical with warm summers (May-Nov.) and mild winters (Dec.-Apr.). Hurricane season: July-Nov. with frequent summer thunderstorms. Rainfall averages vary from 30 in/750 mm to 59 in/1,500 mm. Most rain falls May-June and Sept.-Oct. Temperature ranges from 68°F/20°C in winter to 86°F/30°C in summer. Nassau: Jan. 71°F/21.7°C July 81°F/27.2°C Average annual rainfall 46 in/1,179 mm.

Cities and towns

Nassau (capital)	110,000

Population

Total population is 253,000, of which 54.1% live in urban areas. Population density is 47 persons per mile²/17.2 per km² rising a hundredfold on New Providence. Ethnic composition according to the last census was: 72.3% Black; 14.2% mixed; 12.9% White. Of these 13% were of British extraction.

Birth rate 2.4%. **Death rate** 0.51%. **Rate of population increase** 1.89%. **Age distribution** under 15 = 32.9%, over 65 = 5.2%. **Life expectancy** female 74.4 years; male 68.2 years; average 71.

Religion

Christianity 94.6% (25.5% Roman Catholic; 48.4% non Anglican Protestant including 50,000 Baptists; 10,000 Seventh Day Adventists; 12,000 Methodists; and 20.7% Anglican).

Language

The official language is English. Over 200,000 inhabitants speak an English Creole and 25,000 French (Haitian) Creole.

HISTORY

The earliest inhabitants of the Bahama islands were the Lucayans, a branch of the Arawak Indian peoples, most of whom were transported to the island of Hispaniola by the Spanish not long after the arrival of Columbus in 1492. There was no systematic attempt at colonization until the mid-17th century. In 1690 the islands were granted to the proprietors of Carolina, who administered the territory until the British Crown resumed control in 1717. The Bahamas were seized by American revolutionaries in 1776 and by the Spanish in 1781, but recaptured by Britain and confirmed as British territory in 1783. After the abolition of slavery the islands experienced periods of prosperity (as during the American Civil War and the prohibition period of the 1920s and 1930s) and periods of depression. Adult male suffrage was introduced in 1959, but the vote was not extended to women until 1962, and certain property qualifications were not abolished until 1964 when internal self-government was granted. The ruling United Bahamian Party (UBP), representing the white-dominated establishment, strongly resisted the introduction of reforms that could weaken its position.

At the first elections held under universal suffrage in 1967 the UBP and the opposition Progressive Liberal Party (PLP), supported mostly by black Bahamians, each gained 18 seats. The PLP, however, was able to secure the support of the one Labour Party member and therefore form a government. Fresh elections were held in 1968 which gave the PLP a decisive victory, and broke the power of the UBP. The Bahamas received a new constitution in 1969, and the 1972 elections were dominated by the issue of independence, following a PLP victory on 10 July 1973. Lynden (later Sir Lynden) Pindling, the leader of the PLP, became the country's first prime minister. The PLP have won all the elections held since independence, in 1977, 1983 and 1987.

Allegations of widespread corruption in government involving money from illegal trafficking in drugs led to a major scandal in 1983. A Royal Commission was set up to investigate the allegations and two cabinet ministers and numerous officials were implicated and forced to resign. There was no firm evidence, however, to prove Pindling's involvement, although he did reveal that he had received substantial gifts from businessmen. Arthur Hanna, the deputy prime minister, resigned after unsuccessfully trying to persuade Pindling to resign. The allegations did not affect the PLP's electoral popularity, despite attempts by the opposition Free National Movement to use the issue against the PLP.

CONSTITUTION AND GOVERNMENT

Executive and legislature
The head of state is the British sovereign, represented by a governor general. The bicameral Parliament consists of a popularly elected 49-seat House of Assembly (last general election June 1987) and an appointed Senate.

Present government (1 Feb. 1990)
Governor General Sir Henry Taylor
Prime minister, Finance Minister Sir Lynden O. Pindling
Principal Cabinet members Clement T. Maynard (Deputy Prime Minister; Charles Cantes (Foreign Affairs); Paul L. Adderley (Education); Darrell Rolle (Works and Utilities); Alfred T. Maycock (Employment and Immigration)

Justice
The system of law is based on English common law. The highest court is the British Caribbean Court of Appeal. The death penalty is in force. There were no executions between 1985 and mid-1988.

National symbols
Flag. Three horizontal stripes of blue, golden yellow and blue, with a black equilateral triangle based on the hoist.
Festivals. 3 June (Labour Day); 10 July (Independence Day); 6 Aug. (Emancipation Day); 12 Oct. (Discovery Day, Columbus Day).
Vehicle registration plate. BS.

INTERNATIONAL RELATIONS

Affiliations
NAM, ACP, Commonwealth, OAS, Caricom.

Defence
Total Security Forces: 600. Terms of Service: voluntary.
Coastguard: 600; 9 patrol and coastal combatants.

ECONOMY

Currency
The unit is the Bahamian dollar, divided into 100 cents.

National finance
Budget. The 1987 budget was for expenditure of US$468 million and revenue of US$462 million.
Inflation. 5.8%.

Gross Domestic Product
Estimated total GDP US$2,300 million, per capita US$9,632 (overall size of economy ranking 110 in the world).
Economically active population. The total number of persons active in the economy is 132,600; unemployed = 12%.

Energy and mineral resources
Minerals. The Bahamas has no significant mineral resources other than salt and aragonite.
Electricity. Production capacity (1988) 357,000 kW, most of which is supplied by the Bahamas Electricity Corporation.

Bioresources
Agriculture. Less than 1% of the total land area of the country is under cultivation, the main farm products being eggs, meat and sugar cane.
Crop production (1986, in 1,000 tonnes) sugar cane 256/232; vegetables 31/28; fruit 14/13.
Livestock numbers (1987): poultry 1 million; sheep 40,000; pigs 20,000; goats 19,000; cattle 5,000.
Forestry. Forests and woodland cover 32% of the Bahamas.
Fisheries. Red fish, snappers, marine shrimp and spiny lobster are all caught in the waters around the Bahamas. In 1986 the country exported fish worth B$21.4 million and imported B$4.5 million.

Industry and commerce
Industry. Tourism, by far the largest of the country's industries, has spawned several light ancillary industries such as the manufacture of garments, ice, furniture, purified water, perfume and jewellery. The other major economic activity is offshore banking. Other industries include the manufacture of alcoholic drinks, pharmaceutical, aragonite mining and salt production.
Commerce. The country's exports totalled B$273 million, and included pharmaceuticals, cement, rum and crawfish; imports were B$1,000 million, and included foodstuffs, manufactured goods and fuel. Countries exported to were US 90% and UK 10%; imports came from Iran 30%; Nigeria 20%; US 10%; EC 10%; Gabon 10%.
Trade with UK. The Bahamas imported UK goods worth £20,708,000 and exported to the UK goods worth £24,781,000 (1988).
Tourism. Tourism provides some 50% of the country's GDP and directly or indirectly employs 40% of the local labour force. In 1987 there were 3,002,000 foreign arrivals in the Bahamas.

COMMUNICATIONS

Railways
There are no railways.

Roads
There are some 2,111 miles/3,400 km of roads, most of which are bituminized.

Aviation
Bahamasair provides services between Nassau, Freeport, Newark, Orlando and Miami and 20 locations within the Family Islands (main airports are at Nassau on the the island of New Providence and Freeport on Grand Bahamas).

Shipping
Ports are principally Freeport and Nassau. There are 423 ships of 1,000 GRT or over registered under the Bahamas flag, whch is used as a flag of convenience registry.

Telecommunications
The highly developed automatic telephone system serves 99,000 telephones. Bahamas Broadcasting Corporation provides one television channel as well as radio broadcasts (40,000 televisions and 120,000 radios).

EDUCATION AND WELFARE

Education
The state system provides free education from primary to higher levels in competition with private schools.
School population. 60,469.
Schools. There are 190 state and 40 independent schools. There are also 5 special schools with 280 students and 49 staff.
Universities. The College of the Bahamas, opened in

1975, is the country's only state-funded tertiary level educational institution. It has 5,866 students and a staff of 128 and, among its wide range of courses, it offers degree programmes in conjunction with the Universities of Miami and the West Indies.

Literacy. 95%.

Health

State-funded general hospitals in Nassau and Freeport offer a total of 528 beds, whilst in the more remote areas of the country medical care is provided through a system of health centres and clinics. Nassau also has a private hospital.

BAHRAIN

Dawlat al-Bahrayn
(State of Bahrain)

GEOGRAPHY

Consisting of a group of 35 low-lying islands, the independent state of Bahrain is located in the Arabian (Persian) Gulf, 15 miles/24 km from the eastern coast of Saudi Arabia and 17 miles/28 km from the western coast of the Qatar peninsula. The main island of Bahrain (capital Manama pop. 151,500) occupies 223 miles^2/578 km^2 of the total state area of 265.5 miles^2/ 687.75 km^2 and is approximately 30 miles/48 km in length and between 8–15.5 miles/13–25 km in width. Causeways link Bahrain with Muharraq, the second largest island in the archipelago (approximately 3.7 miles/6 km long), Sitra (3.4 miles/5.5 km long) and mainland Saudi Arabia. The central plateau of Bahrain rises to a maximum elevation of 443 ft/135 m at Jabal Dukhan. Poor soils, semi-aridity and high salinity render the island(s) largely barren although major drainage schemes and soil imports have considerably improved fertility between Jidhafs and Wasmiah. Only 3% of the territory is arable, most of which is located near the springs and freshwater aquifers in the north of the island.

Climate

Temperate from Dec. to end of Mar. with north and north-eastern winds, rainfall of about 2.75 in/70 mm (1.38 in/35 mm in Dec.) and temperatures between 66°F/19°C and 77°F/25°C. Summer months, particularly June to Sept., are very hot and humid, reaching a peak in Aug. although occasionally moderated in June by the cool northerly 'Bara'. Average temperatures in summer 96.8°F/36°C with 97% humidity in Sept. The period June to Nov. records virtually no rainfall at all.

Bahrain: Jan. 60°F/19°C, July 97°F/36°C. Annual rainfall 5 in/130 mm.

Cities and towns

Manama (capital)	151,000
Muharraq	75,579

Population

Total population is 481,000 of which 78.9% live in urban areas. Population density is 1,811/695.9 persons per mile^2/km^2. Ethnic composition (according to last census): 67.9% Bahrain Arab; 24% Persian; Indian and Pakistani; other Arab 4.1%; European 2.5%.

Birth rate 3.1%. **Death rate** 0.45%. **Rate of population increase** 2.65%. **Age distribution** under 15 = 33.3%, over 65 = 2.0%. **Life expectancy** female 72.5 years; male 70.4 years; average 71.

Religion

Islam is the State religion. Estimated 85% of the population are Muslim, of whom almost 60% are Shi'ite and just over 40% Sunni. 7.3% are Christian (25,600). Small Jewish, Bahai, Hindu and Parsee minorities also exist.

Language

Arabic is the official language (South Central Semitic) although English has a wide commercial currency. Farsi and Urdu are also spoken.

HISTORY

Between 4,000 and 2,000 BC what is now Bahrain was the centre of the ancient civilization of Dilmun. In 1782, the al-Khalifa family and other members of a branch of the Bani Utub tribe moved from Qatar to the nearby Bahraini islands and formed a ruling merchant oligarchy over the indigenous people, many of whom were of Persian descent. The Persians contested al-Khalifa rule but were held back when Bahrain came under British influence in 1820. A treaty signed in 1835 between Britain and the states on the south side of the Persian Gulf prohibited local conflicts during the fishing and pearling seasons (known as the Trucial period) and Bahrain became the centre of the pearling industry in the Gulf region. Upon British withdrawal, Bahrain became independent in Aug. 1971 although claims to Bahrain came again from Iran in 1968 and 1979. Coup attempts believed to be linked to Iran have occurred in recent years, the most serious of which was discovered in Dec. 1981 and led to the arrest of 73 people.

Bahrain developed a constitutional form of government administered under the amir, a member of the al-Khalifa family, which provides for separate executive, legislative and judicial functions. The first parliamentary elections were held in Dec. 1973. The National Assembly was composed of 30 elected and 14 appointed cabinet members. Although political parties are not permitted in Bahrain, the loosely organized 'Popular Bloc' of the left won ten seats in the Assembly before it was dissolved by Shaikh Khalifa in 1975 for an indeterminate period on the grounds that it interfered with the administrative affairs of government.

Since 1980, the Cabinet has been headed by the prime minister, Shaikh Khalifa bin Sulman al-Khalifa, brother of the amir, and the family wields great influence within the country's political structure. Bahrain, as one of the oldest oil producers (petroleum production began in 1932) has a sophisticated labour force, although no unions are permitted. The historic territorial dispute with Qatar over the Hawar Islands continues (see entry on Qatar). Bahrain was a founding member of the Gulf Cooperation Council (GCC) in 1981 which is of political, economic and strategic importance to the region, and attempts are being made to improve relations with Iran since the ceasefire in the Iran–Iraq war.

CONSTITUTION AND GOVERNMENT

Executive and legislature

Bahrain is an absolute monarchy. The amir, the head of state, governs with the assistance of an appointed Cabinet. A National Assembly, including 30 elected members, is provided for under the 1973 constitution, but the last National Assembly was dissolved in 1975.

Present government

Amir Shaikh Isa bin Sulman al-Khalifah;
Heir Apparent Shaikh Mohammed bin Hamed Isa al-Khalifa
Prime Minister Shaikh Khalifa bin Sulman al-Khalifah

Justice

The system of law is codified on the basis of English jurisprudence and Islamic law. The death penalty is nominally in force. No executions were carried out between 1985 and mid-1988.

National symbols

Flag. Red with a white stripe in the hoist separated from the red field by eight serrations.
Festivals. 16 Dec. (National Day).
Vehicle registration plate. BRN.

INTERNATIONAL RELATIONS

Affiliations

NAM; ICO; Arab League; GCC.

Defence

Total armed Forces: 2,850. Terms of service: voluntary.
Army: 2,300; 60 main battle tanks (M-60A3).
Navy: 350; 8 patrol and coastal combatants.
Air Force: 200; 12 combat aircraft (F-5E and F-5F).

ECONOMY

Currency

The unit is the dinar, divided into 1,000 fils.

National finance

Budget. The 1987 budget was for expenditure of US$1,210 million and revenue of US$1,136 million.
Inflation. -1%.

Gross Domestic Product

Estimated total GDP US$3,500 million, per capita US$7,550 (overall size of economy ranking 99 in the world).
Economically active population. The total number of persons active in the economy is 140,000; unemployed = 3.2%.

Energy and mineral resources

Oil and gas. The government has held a 60% stake in the Bahrain oilfield (the remainder held by US interests), receipts from which account for some 20% of GDP. Crude oil output is 2,369,945 million tons/2.15 million tonnes (1988) and natural gas production (under 100% state control) is 252,431 m^3.
Electricity. Production 2.9 million MWh (1986).

Bioresources

Agriculture. Only 2% of the land area is arable, totalling 5,559 acres/2,250 ha. Fruits and vegetables are the main crops. Desertification and rapid depletion of sub-surface water resources are major problems.
Crop production (1986): fruits 49,604 tons/45,000 tonnes; vegetables 33,069 tons/30,000 tonnes.
Livestock numbers (1987): cattle 6,000; sheep 8,000; goats 16,000; camels 1,000; poultry 1 million.
Fisheries. Total fish catch (1986) conducted largely by a government fleet of 2 large and 5 small trawlers, 8,881 tons/8,057 tonnes.

Industry and commerce

Industry. Petroleum refining and processing, aluminium smelting and petrochemicals. The Aluminium Bahrain smelting operation (with a majority state holding) represents the largest non-oil industry in the Gulf, producing 198,414 tons/180,000 tonnes of aluminium (1987). A US$400 million petrochemical complex started operations in 1985.
Commerce. Bahrain's exports totalled US$2,400 million; imports totalled US$2,500 million (1988). Exports in 1988 included petroleum 80% and aluminium 7%. Imports in 1988 were crude oil 41% and non-oil 59%.
Trade with UK. Bahrain imported UK goods worth £138 million and exported to the UK goods worth £75.8 million (1988).
Tourism. Around 165,000 tourists, mainly from the Gulf area, visited Bahrain (1985).

COMMUNICATIONS

Railways

There are no railways in Bahrain.

Roads

Most inhabited areas are linked by bitumen-surfaced roads.

Aviation

Gulf Air provides international services (main airport is Bahrain International Airport).

Shipping

Ports are at Mina Salman, Mina al Manama and Sitra. The merchant marine includes two ships of over 1,000 GRT.

Telecommunications

There is an excellent international telephone service and adequate domestic network, serving 98,000 telephones. There is a state radio and television service, with some 150,000 television and radio sets.

EDUCATION AND WELFARE

Education

Free state education is provided from primary to technical school level.
School population. Approximately 100,000 (1987).
Schools. Total of 158, of which 143 general schools with 4,967 teachers and 88,132 pupils (Teacher/pupil ratio of 1:17).
Universities. In addition to Bahrain University and the Gulf Technical College, which opened in 1978 and 1986 respectively, 1,665 Bahrainis received higher education abroad (1987).

Health

There is a free medical service for all residents of Bahrain. In 1986 there were a total of eight hospitals (four of them owned by the government) and 18 state health centres. Pensions, sickness and industrial injury benefits, unemployment, maternity and family allowances were established in 1976.

BANGLADESH

Gana Prajatantri Bangladesh (People's Republic of Bangladesh)

GEOGRAPHY

Bangladesh is located in southern Asia, between the foothills of the Himalayas and the Indian Ocean, covering an area of approximately 55,583 miles^2/ 143,998 km^2. The predominantly low-lying fertile alluvial terrain occupies territory which was formerly East Pakistan. The country's physiography is dominated by the three main navigable rivers: the Ganges (Padma), the Brahmaputra (Jamuna) and the Meghna. The delta formed at their confluence in the south is the largest in the world. The highland regions in the north and north-east, including the Sylhet Hills, average 1,968–2,952 ft/600–900 m elevation with the Keokradong peak rising to 3,934 ft/1,200 m in the south-eastern Chittagong tract. The Dhaka-Rajshahi lowlands comprise the north-western part of the country, including the Bhar Basin between the Ganges and Brahmaputra, the Madhupur monsoon forest tract, and Dhaka, the national capital (population 4.5 million). The Khulna plains lie south of the Ganges-Padma, ranging from marshland and mangrove forest in the west Sundarbans to the Mengha-Padma delta in the Bay of Bengal and north to the very densely populated agricultural regions of the lower Ganges. Frequent and extensive flooding in the lowland areas maintains soil fertility but also causes severe structural damage. Over two-thirds of Bangladesh land area is arable and one-sixth is forested.

Climate

Tropical monsoon climate. High temperatures, extreme humidity and very heavy rainfall (75% of total annual rainfall) throughout the June-Oct. monsoon season. Periodic cyclones in Apr. and May and towards the end of the monsoon season with winds gusting over 99 mph/160 km/h and coastal inundation. Rainfall varies from 39–79 in/1,000–2,000 mm in the west lowlands to nearly 157 in/4,000 mm annually in the north-eastern Sylhet hills. Dhaka: Jan. 66°F/19°C, July 84°F/28.9°C. Annual rainfall 2,025 mm; Chittagong: Jan. 66°F/19°C, July 81°F/27.2°C. Annual rainfall 111.5 in/2,831 mm.

Cities and towns

Dhaka (capital)	3,430,312
Chittagong	1,391,877
Khulna	646,359
Rajshahi	253,740
Comilla	184,132
Barisal	172,905
Sylhet	168,371
Rangpur	153,174
Jessore	148,927
Saidpur	126,608

Population

Total population is 109,579,000 of which 13% live in urban areas. Population density 1,971/731.3 persons per mile^2/km^2. Ethnic composition: 97.7% Bengali; 1.3% Bihari and 1% tribal located mostly in the Chittagong Hills including the Chakma, Murung, Tippera and the Buddhist Mru peoples.

Birth rate 4.1%. **Death rate** 1.5%. **Rate of population increase** 2.8%. **Age distribution** under 15 = 45.7%, over 65 = 3.1%. **Life expectancy** female 50; male 51; average 51.

Religion

Islam was declared to be the State religion in June 1988. Roughly 86.6% of the population are Muslim (largely Sunni); 12.1% Hindu; 0.6% Buddhist; 0.3% Christian. There may be as many as 181,000 Roman Catholics and 26,500 Baptists in Bangladesh.

Language

(Bangla) Bengali is the official language (part of the Indo-Aryan) group, spoken by approximately 103 million of the population. English is retained for legal and commercial use. Ninety-six tribal dialects include Garo, Khasi, Magh, Santal, Tippera and Chakma (nearly 0.4 million speakers), some of which have Tibeto-Burman origins.

HISTORY

Until 1947, Bangladesh formed part of the British-ruled Indian provinces of Bengal and Assam. With independence and the creation of states along religious lines, Bengal was partitioned and the eastern, predominantly Muslim, wing combined with part of Assam became the province of East Pakistan. Of the two wings of Pakistan, which were separated by 11,000 miles of Indian territory, East Pakistan had more than half the country's total population.

The main reasons for the break-up of Pakistan and the emergence of Bangladesh as a separate state in 1971 lay in the lack of Bengali participation in the country's central government and the colonial-style economic exploitation of the province, in particular its jute resources, by West Pakistan. Latent dissatisfaction with Pres. Ayub Khan's regime increased between 1966 and 1969, when demands for democratic rights in West Pakistan and for autonomy for East Pakistan led to a gradual breakdown of law and order, the proclamation of martial law and the replacement of Ayub Khan by Gen. Yahya Khan as head of state in Mar. 1969. Pres. Yahya Khan announced a series of far-reaching constitutional reforms in late 1969, giving East Pakistan over half the seats in a new National Assembly. The first elections ever held in Pakistan on a basis of 'one man, one vote' took place in Dec. 1970, and resulted in an overwhelming victory for the Awami League (AL), led by Shaikh Mujib ur-Rahman, in East Pakistan. More importantly, the AL gained an absolute majority of the 291 seats in the National Assembly.

The postponement of the first National Assembly session scheduled for March 1971 and efforts by the military-bureaucratic elite in West Pakistan to block the Awami League's demands for regional autonomy led to strikes and civil disobedience in East Pakistan. The Pakistani army responded with 'Operation Searchlight', attacking Dhaka on 25 March 1971. Full-scale civil war erupted the next day when a clandestine radio broadcast announced the proclamation by Shaikh Mujib ur-Rahman and the Awami League of the 'sovereign independent people's republic of Bangladesh'. The cost of the war in terms of lives was estimated at between one and three million plus damage to property worth US$1,000 million.

Mujib returned to Dhaka from imprisonment in West Pakistan on 8 Jan, 1972 and formed a cabinet with himself as prime minister. Abu Sayeed Chowdhury replaced Mujib as president. The new constitution provided for a unitary parliamentary system and placed emphasis on nationalism, socialism, democracy and secularism. General elections followed on 7 Mar. 1973 in which Mujib's AL were swept back to power. The new administration proceeded to introduce widescale nationalization of banks, insurance companies and private companies. In spite of foreign aid, the economy drifted into crisis. Severe floods in 1974 damaged the rice crop and caused famine and severe inflation. Law and order deteriorated with left-wing revolutionary opposition parties attempting to complete Bangladesh's 'unfinished revolution'. Constitutional amendments in Jan. 1975 replaced parliamentary democracy with one-party presidential rule. This move heightened military discontent and on 15 Aug. 1975 Mujib and members of his family were killed by a group of army majors, who installed one of Mujib's ministers, Khandokar Mushtaq Ahmad, as president. Two further coups in early Nov. 1975 led to the chief justice, A. M. Sayem, being appointed president. However, the Army Chief of Staff, Maj.-Gen. Zia ur-Rahman, emerged as the country's de facto ruler.

'Young General Zia' (he was 40 in 1975) set about unifying the armed forces through improved pay and training. He reconstituted the political structure of the country, emphasizing more strongly its Islamic connections as a counter to Indian influence. He also advocated a pragmatic economic programme seeking solutions to the pressing problems of population growth, insufficient food production and illiteracy. He took over the presidency in Apr. 1977 and his re-election in June 1978 preceded that of his party, the Bangladesh Nationalist Party (BNP), in National Assembly elections of the following February. Continuing discontent in the army was reflected in numerous coup attempts before Zia was finally assassinated in Chittagong in May 1981. The Army High Command encouraged Vice-President Abdus Sattar to become acting president and, as BNP nominee, he won the presidential elections of Nov. 1981.

The seizure and maintenance of power by Lt.-Gen. Hossain Mohammad Ershad on 24 Mar. 1982 reflected the support which he had built up in the armed forces. He reimposed martial law, appointing himself chief martial law administrator, and in June returned most of the country's major industries to private ownership. Ershad took over the presidency from S.M. Ahsanuddin Chowdhury in Dec. 1983. Parliamentary elections held in May 1986, in which the AL participated, were won by Ershad's Jatiya Party amid accusations of rigged ballots. Opposition parties proceded to boycott the National Assembly. Ershad resigned his army post in August 1986 and was elected president in Oct. Martial law was formally lifted on 10 Nov. 1986. Despite efforts to gain popularity through appeals to Islam, resentment against Ershad remained widespread. In Nov. 1987 a state of emergency was declared and in Dec. parliament dissolved. The main opposition leaders, including Shaikh Mujib's daughter Shaikh Hasina and Zia's widow, Begum Khaleda Zia, denounced elections held on 3 Mar. 1988 and called for non-participation. As a result Ershad's Jatiya Party won an easy majority and formed a government under the prime ministership of Moudad Ahmed. The worst floods on record during Aug. and Sept. 1988 left three-quarters of the country under water and 25,000,000 people homeless, inflicting extensive damage on Bangladesh's economy and infrastructure.

CONSTITUTION AND GOVERNMENT

Executive and legislature

The head of state is the president, elected by universal adult suffrage for a five-year term (maximum two terms); last election Oct. 1986. An elective post of vice-president was created in July 1989. The president appoints a council of ministers and is head of the Armed Forces. The legislature is a unicameral parliament; last general elections Mar. 3, 1988.

Present government

President; C.-in-C. of the Armed Forces; President of the Council of Ministers; Minister of Defence; Minister of Establishment and Re-organization Lt.-Gen. (retd) Hussain Mohammad Ershad

Vice-President; Minister of Industry, Islam, Law and Justice Moudud Ahmed

Prime Minister, Minister of Information Kazi Zafar Ahmed

Principal Cabinet members Dr M.A. Matin (Deputy Prime Minister); Shah Moazzam Husayn (Deputy Prime Minister; Labour and Manpower); Mohammad Rezwanul Haq Chowdhury (Social Welfare and Women's Affairs); Prof. Wahidul Huq (Finance); Anisul Islam Mahmud (Foreign Affairs); Maj.-Gen. (retd) Mahmudul Hasan (Home Affairs).

Justice

The system of law, temporarily overridden by the 1987 state of emergency, had English common law as its original basis. The highest authority is a Supreme Judicial Council set up in 1977 to establish a code of conduct for Supreme Court and High Court judges, who may be removed from office by the President on the Council's recommendation. The death penalty is in force. There were over 36 executions between 1985 and mid-1988. Capital offences: murder.

National symbols

Flag. Green with a red disc which has a radius equal to one-fifth of the flag's length.
Festivals. 21 Feb. (National Mourning Day); 26 Mar. (Independence Day); 7 Nov. (National Revolution Day); 16 Dec. (National Day).
Vehicle registration plate. BD.

INTERNATIONAL RELATIONS

Affiliations

NAM; ICO; Commonwealth; SAARC.

Defence

Total Armed Forces: 101,500. Terms of service: voluntary. Reserves: 30,000.

Army: 90,000; 50 main battle tanks (chiefly Ch Type-59 and T-54/55) and light tanks (Type-62).

Navy: 7,500; 3 frigates and 37 patrol and coastal combatants.

Air Force: 4,000; about 55 combat aircraft (J-6/JJ-6, Q-5 and MiG-21MF).

Opposition: Shanti Bahini (Peace Force), Comilla Province. Total Armed Forces: 8,000.

ECONOMY

Currency

The unit is the taka, divided into 100 paise.

National finance

Budget. The 1988 budget was for expenditure of US$3,300 million and revenue of US$1,800 million. Main items of expenditure are housing and welfare 10%; education 11%; defence 10%.
Balance of payments. The balance of payments (current account, 1987) was a deficit of US$966 million.
Inflation. 11.4%.

Gross Domestic Product

Estimated total GDP US$17,600 million, per capita US$170 (overall size of economy ranking 63 in the world).
Economically active population. The total number of persons active in the economy is 35,100,000; unemployed = 30%.

Sector	% of workforce	% of GDP
industry	11	13
agriculture	74	47
services*	15	39

* services figure includes elements unassigned to other categories.

Energy and mineral resources

Oil and gas. Oil drilling is in progress in the Bay of Bengal. Reserves of natural gas are considered sufficient for 200 years. Over 125,329,076 ft^3/3,549 million m^3 of natural gas produced (1986–87).
Minerals. Large reserves of low-grade coal in the Rajshahi and Jamalpur areas. Other minerals include salt; limestone; white clay; glass; sand; uranium.
Electricity. 1,570,000 kW capacity; 4,800 million kWh produced, 45 kWh per capita (1988).

Bioresources

Agriculture. The economy is based on the output of a narrow range of agricultural products, principally jute, which is the main cash crop and major source of export earnings. The agricultural sector is constrained by low productivity and self-sufficiency in food-grain production remains a long-term goal. The agricultural sector contributes over 50% to GDP and 75% to exports, and employs over two-thirds of the labour force. Approximately 60% of the country's land is cultivable.

Crop production (1986): foodgrains 18.55 million tons/16.55 million tonnes; tea 41,226 tons/37,400 tonnes; potatoes 1.32 million tons/1.2 million tonnes; pulses 330,690 tons/300,000 tonnes; tobacco 60,627 tons/55,000 tonnes.

Livestock numbers (1987 in millions): poultry 91; cattle 23.5; goats 10.8; sheep 1.13; buffalo 1.9.
Forestry. Over 14% of the country is forested. Most of the timber produced is used as fuel.
Fisheries. With the Ganges, Jamuna, Brahmaputra and Meghna river deltas running through Bangladesh, the country possesses great potential as a fish-producing area. In 1986, 876,329 tons/795,000 tonnes of fish were caught, the majority by inland fishermen, but some by boats operating in the Bay of Bengal.

Industry and commerce

Industry. Bangladesh is the world's largest supplier of jute. About half the crop is exported in its raw form and the rest is processed in Bangladesh for export as hessian, sacking and carpet-backing. In 1987, approximately 1,332,760 million tons/1.2 million tonnes of jute was produced, 595,242 tons/540,000 tonnes of which was converted into jute goods. Jute manufacturing is the largest component of the industrial sector, which as a whole accounts for less than 15% of the country's GDP. Other industries include textiles; paper and newsprint; fertilizer; glass; iron and steel; sugar; cement; aluminium.
Commerce. Bangladesh's exports totalled US$1,200 million (1988), the principle commodities being jute goods; hide; skins; leather; tea. The main export partners are the United States 24%; Western Europe 22%; Middle East 9%; Japan 8%; Eastern Europe 7%. Imports totalled US$2,900 million (1988), the principal commodities being food; petroleum; consumer goods; semi-processed goods; capital equipment. These goods are imported from Western Europe 18%; Japan 14%; Middle East 9%; the United States 8%.
Trade with UK. Bangladesh imported UK goods worth £50,249,000; exports to UK totalled £64,018,000 (1988).
Tourism. Almost 107,000 people visited Bangladesh, of whom 47,000 were from India (1987).

COMMUNICATIONS

Railways

There are 2,826 miles/4,551 km of railways.

Roads

There are 6,523 miles/10,504 km of roads, of which 3,527 miles/5,680 km are metalled.

Aviation

Bangladesh Biman (Bangladesh Airlines) provides domestic and international services (main airport is Zia International Airport).

Shipping

Chittagong is the principal port. The merchant marine includes 45 ships of over 1,000 GRT. Internal waterways comprise 3,105–4,968 miles/5,000–8,000 km, including some 1,863 miles/3,000 km of main cargo routes.

Telecommunications

There is an adequate international radio and landline telcommunications system, and a fair domestic service, with 182,000 telephones.

EDUCATION AND WELFARE

Education

Education is not compulsory, but the government provides free primary education for five years. Secondary schools and colleges in the private sector vastly outnumber government institutions. Schools administration is controlled by the government from Dhaka.

School population. Primary school pupils 10,790,000; secondary school pupils 2,750,000 (1988).

Schools. 42,200 primary schools; 9,360 secondary schools (1984).

Universities. There are six universities and up to 100 teacher-training colleges and vocational institutes; 43,500 higher education students (1988). In addition there are over 100 degree-awarding government colleges and over 500 non-government colleges, more than half of which award degrees.

Literacy. 29%

Health

3,092 persons per hospital bed; 5,170 persons per doctor (1988).

BARBADOS

GEOGRAPHY

Located approximately 270 miles/435 km north-west of Venezuela and 199 miles/320 km north-east of Trinidad, the very densely populated east Caribbean island of Barbados covers a total area of 165 miles^2/430 km^2, divided into 11 districts. The coral-limestone relief is predominantly low-lying, marked by a coastal fringe of coral reef and by a series of inland terraces rising in the west to reach the highest point Mount Hillaby (1,115 ft/340 m) in the north-central part of the island. About 50% of the total land area is arable with sugar cane plantations accounting for 85% of the cultivated terrain. Surface water is negligible although some gullies form natural reservoirs in periods of heavy rainfall. The majority of the population inhabit the Bridgetown, St Michael and Christchurch districts in the southern part of the island.

Climate

The island experiences a moderate tropical climate with two seasons, wet (June to Nov.) with warm temperatures and high humidity, and dry (Dec. to May). Rainfall varies from 75 in/1,900 mm annually in the higher central region to 50 in/1,270 mm on the coasts. Barbados lies within the Caribbean hurricane zone.

Cities and towns

Bridgetown (capital)	7,517

Population

Total population is 257,000, of which 42.3% live in urban areas. Population density is 1,558/591 persons per miles^2/km^2. According to the last census, 91.9% of the population are Black, 3.3% White, 2.6% mulatto, 0.5% East Indian.

Birth rate 1.78%. **Death rate** 0.87%. **Rate of population increase** 0.91%. **Age distribution** under 15 = 27.1%, over 65 = 10.7%. **Life expectancy** female 76.2; male 72.0; average 74.

Religion

Christianity. 39.7% are Anglican, 25.6% other Protestant (including sizeable Methodist, Pentecostal and Seventh Day Adventist denominations). There are approximately 24,000 Roman Catholics on the island together with small communities of Hindus, Muslims and Jews.

Language

English is the official language although the bulk of the population (approximately 230,000) speak an English Creole.

HISTORY

Barbados's earliest inhabitants were Arawak Indians, but by the time of the first European settlements on the island in the 1620s the island was uninhabited. The first Europeans to visit Barbados were Portuguese, but its first settlers were British, and the island remained a British possession. The island developed a system of plantation agriculture, producing sugar using imported African slave labour. Slavery was abolished in 1834 and the former prosperity of the island began to decline.

Economic depression and labour unrest during the 1930s led to the beginnings of modern political activity and an extension to the franchise for elections to the island's Assembly in 1944 allowed the Barbados Labour Party (BLP), led by Grantly (later Sir Grantly) Adams, to win a majority of seats. In 1946 Adams and other BLP members joined the Executive Committee. Universal adult suffrage was introduced in 1951 and a full ministerial system in 1954. Successive electoral victories maintained the BLP in power, with Adams as chief minister and then premier. Between 1958 and 1962 Barbados was part of the Federation of the West Indies and Adams served as federal prime minister. Hugh Cummins replaced him as premier of Barbados, but he lost the 1961 general election (held immediately after the granting of full internal self-government) to the Democratic Labour Party (DLP), originally formed by dissident BLP members. Errol Barrow, the leader of the DLP, led the country to independence from Britain on 30 Nov. 1966, after winning a further general election earlier that month. Barrow became the country's first prime minister.

The DLP retained power in elections held in 1971, but was defeated in 1976 by the BLP under J.M.G. 'Tom' Adams, Sir Grantly's son. Adams pursued a more conservative, pro-US policy and strongly supported the US and Caribbean intervention in Grenada in Oct. 1983. The BLP had been returned to office in 1981 on the strength of its economic achievements, but in 1985 Adams died suddenly and was replaced as prime minister by Bernard St John, a former BLP leader. Elections were held shortly afterwards in 1986 and the BLP, lacking strong leadership and accused of corruption, was heavily defeated by the DLP, retaining only three of the 27 seats in the House of Assembly. Errol Barrow became prime minister again, but died suddenly in June 1987. He was succeeded by Erskine Lloyd Sandiford.

CONSTITUTION AND GOVERNMENT

Executive and legislature

The head of state is the British sovereign, represented by a governor general who nominally is responsible for appointing the prime minister and cabinet. The prime minister as head of government is responsible to the bicameral Parliament; the 27-seat House of Assembly is popularly elected every five years (last general election May 1986), and the upper house, the Senate, consists of appointed members.

Present government (1 Feb. 1990)

Governor General Sir Hugh Springer
Prime Minister; Finance and Economic Affairs; Civil Service Erskine Sandiford
Principal Cabinet members Philip Greaves (Deputy Prime Minister; International Transport, Telecommunications and Immigration); Maurice King (Foreign Affairs; Attorney General; Legal Affairs); Evelyn Greaves (Trade, Industry and Commerce); Warwick Franklin (Agriculture, Food and Fisheries); Wesley Hall (Tourism and Sports).

Justice

The system of law is based on English common law. The highest court is the Supreme Court of Judicature consisting of a High Court and a Court of Appeal; in certain cases appeals may go ultimately to the Judicial Committee of Her Majesty's Privy Council. The Chief Justice and the Puisne Judges are appointed by the Governor-General acting on the recommendation of the Prime Minister after consultation with the leader of the Opposition. The death penalty is in force. No executions were carried out between 1985 and mid-1988.

National symbols

Flag. A vertical stripe of golden yellow in the middle between two blue ones. In the centre there is a black trident of the sea god Neptune.
Festivals. 1 May (7 May in 1990, May Day); 7 Oct. (United Nations Day); 30 Nov. (Independence Day).
Vehicle registration plate. BDS.

INTERNATIONAL RELATIONS

Affiliations

NAM; ACP; Commonwealth; OAS; Caricom.

ECONOMY

Currency

The unit is the Barbadian dollar, divided into 100 cents.

National finance

Budget. The 1986 budget was for expenditure of US$543 million and revenue of US$476 million.
Inflation. 3.3%.

Gross Domestic Product

Estimated total GDP US$1,400 million, per capita US$5,405 (overall size of economy ranking 129 in the world).

Economically active population. The total number of persons active in the economy is 112,300; unemployed = 17.3%.

Sector	% of workforce
industry	22
agriculture	8
services*	70

* services figure includes elements unassigned to other categories.

Energy and mineral resources

Oil and gas. In 1987 Barbados produced 20.9 million US gallons of crude oil and 33,054 million ft^3/936 m^3 of gas.
Minerals. Barbados has no significant mineral resources.
Electricity. Production capacity 132,000 Kw (1988).

Bioresources

Agriculture. There are an estimated 54,979 acres/22,250 ha of arable land, 77% of the total area of Barbados, which is intensely cultivated to produce sugar cane and subsistence foods.
Crop production (1987 in 1,000 tons/tonnes): refined sugar 93/85; yams 2.2/2; sweet potatoes 2.2/2.
Livestock numbers (1987): poultry 1 million; sheep 56,000; pigs 49,000; goats 33,000; cattle 17,000.
Forestry. Barbados has no significant areas of forest or woodland.
Fisheries. Total fish catch 10,802 tons/9,800 tonnes (1987). Many boats are used only in the flying fish season between Oct. and July.

Industry and commerce

Industry. Although eclipsed in recent years by the rapid growth of tourism, the traditional sugar refining industry remains an important source of employment and revenue. There has also been some diversification towards light manufacturing and component assembly for export.
Commerce. The total exports of Barbados (excluding bullion and specie) in 1987 amounted to BD$214 million, of which sugar totalled BD$56.9 million and electronic components BD$51.8 million. Imports amounted to BS$1,035.9 million, of which BD$250.2 million was machinery and transport equipment, BD$309 million manufactured goods and BD$167 million food and livestock. Countries exported to were USA 30%; Caricom; UK and Canada; imports came from US 34%; Caricom; Japan; UK; Canada.
Trade with UK. Barbados imported UK goods worth £19,487,000; exports to the UK totalled £32,061,000.
Tourism. Barbados derived revenue of BD$757.2 million from 421,859 visitors (1987). The tourist industry employs over 10,000 of the island's inhabitants.

COMMUNICATIONS

Railways

There are no railways.

Roads

There 1,448 miles/2,333 km of roads, most of which are bituminized.

Aviation

Caribbean Air Cargo Ltd (CARICARGO) provides services between Miami, New York, Houston, Puerto

Rico and the Eastern Caribbean (main airport is Grantley Adams International Airport, 11.2 miles/18 km from Bridgetown).

Shipping

The merchant marine includes two ships of over 1,000 GRT. Bridgetown is the main port.

Telecommunications

The automatic telephone system connects 89,000 telephones.

EDUCATION AND WELFARE

Education

The state provides free education from primary to university level. In addition to state educational facilities there are state-assisted private schools and wholly independent schools.

School population. Over 60,000.

Schools. 105 state primary schools with 29,392 pupils; 21 state secondary schools with 21,501 pupils; 5 vocational centres with 967 students; 15 state assisted private secondary schools with 3,547 pupils; a number of wholly private schools.

Universities. There are several colleges of the University of the West Indies in Barbados which provide places for over 1,800 students.

Literacy. 99%

Health

Barbados has 2,054 hospital beds and 243 doctors.

BELAU

GEOGRAPHY

Belau is an archipelago of six island groups in the Pacific Ocean, totalling over 200 islands in the Caroline chain. The total land area is 177 miles^2/458 km^2. The islands vary in terrain from high mountains to coral reef. The capital is Koror (a new capital is being built in eastern Babelthuap).

Climate

Hot and humid, with wet season May–Nov. Typhoons June–Dec.

Population

Total population (1989 est.) 14,208. Belauans are of mixed Polynesian, Malayan and Melanesian descent. **Birth rate** 2.5%. **Death rate** 0.6%. **Rate of population increase** 0.7%. **Life expectancy** female 74; male 68.

Religion

Christianity: Roman Catholic.

Language

Belauan (official). English is widely spoken. Dialect of Trukese spoken in isolated areas.

HISTORY

Belau is at the western end of the Caroline Islands archipelago, part of the Pacific territory of Micronesia. Migrants from South-East Asia were the first to settle the islands around 1000 BC. The Carolines were relatively unaffected by European and American activities in Micronesia until the mid-19th century when whaling and trading in the islands became intensive. Protestant missionaries also established a presence. The indigenous population was subjected to forced labour, and the introduction of alien diseases caused rapid depopulation. Spain occupied the Carolines in 1886 but, following its defeat in the 1898 Spanish–American war, it sold its remaining Micronesian possessions to Germany. The Germans exploited phosphate deposits on Belau.

At the outbreak of World War I, Japanese forces quickly captured Micronesia, and in 1921 the territory was entrusted to Japan under a League of Nations Mandate. The islands were intensively developed, but as an integral part of the Japanese empire and for the benefit of Japanese settlers. In 1935 Japan withdrew from the League of Nations and began to build military installations in the territory, in clear violation of the Mandate. During World War II Micronesia assumed great strategic importance, and Japan and the Western Allies clashed throughout the territory.

In 1947 Micronesia became the Trust Territory of the Pacific, a United Nations trusteeship under US administration. In 1969 the US entered into negotiations with the Joint Commission on Future Status of the Congress of Micronesia (the territory's legislature). These led in Apr. 1978 to the Statement of Agreed Principles for Free Association, which prescribed full internal self-government for Micronesia and US responsibility for security and defence. In a referendum in July 1978, the Belau electorate rejected the Constitution of the Federated States of Micronesia (FSM) as the basis for their political future. Dismemberment of the Trust Territory followed. On 7 Jan. 1981 Belau's own popularly approved Constitution took effect. It prohibited the introduction of nuclear weaponry into Belauan territory and severely restricted the US's right to acquire land for military purposes. On 26 Aug. 1982 the Belau and US governments signed a Compact of Free Association, which would grant the US extensive military freedoms in Belau, including the right to operate nuclear weaponry in the territory. Successive referenda between 1983 and 1987 approved the Compact, but failed to achieve the 75% approval rating to overturn the non-nuclear clauses of the Constitution. Attempts by the administrations of Pres. Haruo Remiliik (first elected in 1980 and murdered on 28 Aug. 1985) and Pres. Lazarus Salii (who was elected on 30 June 1985 and committed suicide on 20 Aug. 1988) to interpret simple majority votes as sufficient for ratification of the Compact were overruled in the Belau Supreme Court. Salii saw implementation of the Compact, which would guarantee continued US economic aid, as a way out of the country's crippling indebtedness. In general elections on 2 Nov. 1988 the strongly pro-Compact Ngiratkel Etpison was elected president. With the Compact still unratified, the UN trusteeship remained formally in force. A further referendum in February 1990 again failed to approve the Compact by a sufficient majority.

CONSTITUTION AND GOVERNMENT

Belau is a UN trusteeship administered by the Office of Territorial and International Affairs, US Department of Interior. It has a directly elected national president and vice president (elected for a four-year term), a bicameral legislature and a separate judiciary. A Compact of Free Association with the US, signed in 1986 has yet to be implemented. The last elections were held in Nov. 1988.

President Ngiratkel Etpison.

National symbols

Flag. Light blue with a large yellow disc (representing the moon) shifted slightly to the hoist side.

National holiday. 9 July, Constitution Day.

ECONOMY

Belau depends heavily on US support. The government is the major employer. Agriculture and fishing are at subsistence levels. Tourism is undeveloped due to location and shortage of facilities.

Currency

US dollar.

COMMUNICATIONS

Railways

There are no railways.

Roads

18 miles/25.7 km of surfaced road.

Aviation

There are two airports with permanent-surface runway, and a port at Koror.

Telecommunications

There is one AM and one FM radio broadcasting station, and one TV station.

BELGIUM

Koninkrijke Belgie (Flemish)
Royaume de Belgique (French)
(Kingdom of Belgium)

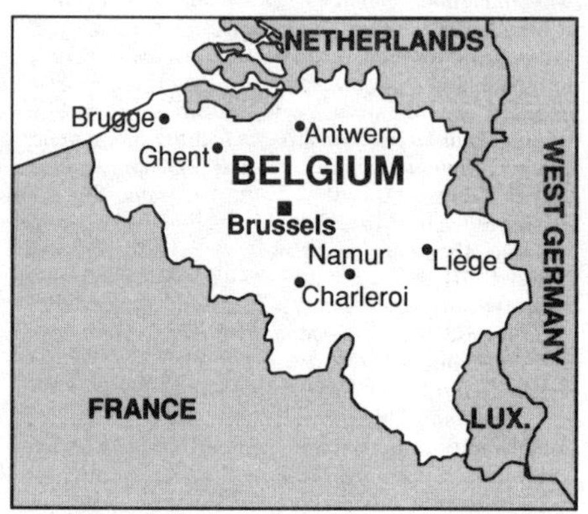

GEOGRAPHY

A small nation situated in north-western Europe and divided into nine provinces, Belgium covers an area of 11,783 miles²/30,525 km² (including the 2.7 miles²/7 km² enclave of Baarle-Hertog in the Netherlands), measuring approximately 120 miles/193 km north-south and 149 miles/240 km (maximum) east-west, with 40 miles/64 km of coastline. Upper Belgium lies to the south of the Sambre-Meuse valley, comprising the forested Ardennes region (average elevation 1,312 ft/400 m) and including Belgium's highest point, Mount Botranges (3,277 ft/694 m). North of the Sambre-Meuse, tributaries of the Scheldt traverse a fertile and intensely cultivated central region descending into Flanders in the north-west (Vlaanderen) and the marshy Campine (Kempenland) woodlands in the north-east. Lower Belgium is dissected by a number of canals and irrigation ducts with over 116 miles²/300 km² of reclaimed land in polders on the sandy North Sea coast. 52% of the total area is meadow, pasture or cultivated land and approximately 20% of Belgium is forested. 10% of the largely urban population live within the metropolitan district of the Belgian capital Bruxelles/Brussels.

Climate

Cool temperate, with maritime influences. Mild winters and cool summers (higher temperatures inland), distinguished by wet west and south-west winds. Interior temperature ranges between 32°F/0° and 73°F/23°C, dropping to 30°F/–1°C during the winter months in the Ardennes. Average rainfall between 29 in/750 mm and 39 in/1,000 mm.

Bruxelles/Brussels: Jan. 36°F/2.2°C. July 64°F/17.8°C. Annual rainfall 35 in/825 mm. Ostend: Jan. 38°F/3.3°C. July 62°F/16.7°C. Average annual rainfall 28 in/725 mm.

Cities and towns

Bruxelles/Brussels (capital)	970,346
Antwerp	476,044
Ghent	232,620
Charleroi	208,938
Liège	200,312
Brugge	117,857
Namur	103,104

Population

Total population is 9,925,000, of which 97% live in urban areas. Population density is 842/323.1 persons per mile²/km². The principal ethnic divisions within Belgium are between the Flemings (of Teutonic origin) and Walloons (French Latin) who constitute approximately 55% and 33% of the total population respectively. The Dutch-speaking majority inhabit the provinces of West and East Flanders, Antwerp, Limburg and North Brabant. Wallonia (dialectal French-speaking) comprises Hainaut, Namur, Luxembourg, Liège and South Brabant. In 1988, there were 855,650 foreigners in Belgium. Of the 878,577 citizens of foreign birth recorded in 1981, 31.8% were Italian, 11.8% French, 12.0% Moroccan and 0.72% Turkish.

Birth rate 1.2%. **Death rate** 1.2%. **Rate of population increase** 0%. **Age distribution** under 15 = 19.0%; over 65 = 13.8%. **Life expectancy** female 77.7; male 70.9; average 75.

Religion

Christianity predominates. Over 75% of the population are Roman Catholic (8,720,000) dispersed among eight dioceses and 260 deaneries. There are about 24,000 Protestants (including 2,000 members of the Belgian Evangelical Mission) and an estimated 35,000 Jewish citizens.

Language

Official languages are French, Dutch and German. Approximately 50% of the population (5,676,194) speak Flemish (Dutch) and 32% speak French. 66,445 of the inhabitants of Wallonia are German-speaking (east of Liège). Four linguistic divisions were recognized in law in 1963: the French-, Dutch- and German-speaking areas and Brussels which is bilingual.

HISTORY

Belgium takes its name from the Belgae, a fierce Celtic tribe conquered by Julius Caesar by 51 BC. Following the collapse of the Roman Empire, the area of modern Belgium was conquered by Germanic tribes, Christianized by the 7th century AD and absorbed into the Frankish Empire in the 8th century. By 1100 it was divided into four main domains: the County of Flanders in the north-west, the Duchy of Brabant in the north-east, the Bishopric of Liège in the south-east, and the County of Hainaut in the south-west. These provinces regularly fought each other, while resistance by Flanders to attempted domination by France culminated in the Battle of the Golden Spurs (1302) in which the artisans of Bruges, Ghent and other prosperous Flemish towns routed the flower of French chivalry. From 1384, however, Flanders (and later the rest of the Low Countries) passed by marriage, inheritance or purchase to the French Dukes of Burgundy, whose rule proved to be a golden age of economic and artistic achievement.

With the end of the male Burgundian line in 1477, all of the Low Countries passed by marriage to the House of Habsburg, whose greatest ruler, Emperor Charles V of Austria and Spain (r.1515–55), was himself born in Ghent. On his abdication and the separation of the Austrian and Spanish Habsburg lines, the Low Countries became a province of Spain, whereupon a great revolt, centred in the rising Protestant merchant class, began against Catholic Spanish rule (1568). During the resultant Eighty Years' War, one of the cruellest in history and later bound up with the broader Thirty Years' War (1618–48), the seven northern provinces of the Low Countries declared their independence from Spain as the Netherlands (1581), while the ten southern provinces (present-day Belgium) remained under Spanish rule. Economic factors were a key determinant of this division, which was conceded by Spain in 1609 and confirmed by the Peace of Westphalia (1648), and consolidated by migration of southern Protestants to the north. After the Spanish Habsburg line came to an end in 1700, the Spanish War of Succession (1702–13/14) resulted, under the Treaty of Utrecht (1713), in the Spanish Low Countries passing to Austrian Habsburg rule. The armies of Napoleon Bonaparte finally ended Austrian rule in the Low Countries, the southern provinces of which were incorporated into France from 1797 and, in the case of Dutch-speaking Flanders, induced to adopt French as the language of state affairs and commerce. With the eventual defeat of France, the Congress of Vienna (1814–15) created a United Kingdom of the Netherlands (including Belgium and Luxembourg) as a northern bulwark against the French. In 1830, however, the southern provinces (including over half of Luxembourg) proclaimed their independence of the Dutch, choosing an uncle of Queen Victoria, Leopold I (r.1831–65), as King of the Belgians and constitutional monarch. Under the 1839 Treaty of London, Belgium's independence and perpetual neutrality were recognized by the Netherlands and guaranteed by the Great Powers. It was this 'scrap of paper' which Germany violated by invading Belgium in 1914, thus bringing Britain into World War I. Its forces having valiantly held a strip of Belgian territory throughout the 1914–18 conflict, Belgium was rewarded under the 1919 Treaty of Versailles by the cession of a German border area.

Meanwhile, Belgium had experienced rapid industrialization and general economic advance from the mid-19th century, and had also acquired an empire in equatorial Africa. Politically, the introduction of universal suffrage in the 1890s had assisted the growth of parliamentary democracy and of the Labour Party, which after World War I became the country's second party after the Catholics, while the previously dominant Liberals declined. In 1932 the Flemish language was accorded equal official status with French. Paul-Henri Spaak became the country's first Labour prime minister in 1938, but on 10 May 1940 a further German invasion quickly overran Belgian resistance. The government went into exile to continue the struggle from London, while King Leopold III (r.1934–51), who had ordered his troops to surrender, remained as a prisoner of war. Compromised by this conduct, he finally abdicated in 1951 in favour of his son Baudouin. Belgian politics resumed after World War II with successive coalition governments being formed by combinations of the (mainly Catholic) Christian Socials, the Socialists (successors of the Labour Party) and the Liberals. Assisted by US Marshall Aid, Belgium made a speedy economic recovery, joining the Benelux economic union with the Netherlands and Luxembourg (1948) and becoming a founder member of the European Coal and Steel Community, EEC and Euratom (1951–58). It also abandoned its neutral posture by joining NATO (1949) and the WEU (1955), while in 1960 it granted independence to the Belgian Congo (now Zaïre). But whereas the main lines of external policy were agreed, internal politics came to be dominated by the 'communal question'. This centred on the competing aspirations of the numerically-dominant Dutch-speaking Flemish population in the increasingly prosperous north and the French-speaking Walloons in the south, whose heavy industries were in decline; additional complications were provided by bilingual Brussels and the small German-speaking community in eastern Belgium. Against this background, the three main political formations became split into separate Flemish and Walloon parties, while extreme nationalist parties arose in both communities.

Constitutional amendments enacted in 1970–71 sought to resolve the communal question by devolving substantial central powers to regional councils for Flanders, Wallonia and Brussels, with a cultural council also being created for German speakers. Parts of this federal solution were functioning by the early 1980s, but detailed aspects such as border delineation in Brussels and elsewhere caused numerous government crises. Typical of the complexities was the status of Les Fourons/Voeren, a group of villages in the south-east of Flanders whose French-speaking majority stubbornly resisted the authority of Flemish-speaking Limburg. Inter-party dissension over this problem caused the collapse in Oct. 1987 of the four-party centre-right Christian Social/Liberal coalition in power since 1981 and headed by Wilfried Martens (Flemish Christian Social). Under the Martens government, parliamentary approval was given in Mar. 1985 to the NATO decision that US cruise missiles should be deployed on Belgian territory, amid political controversy which only subsided with the signature of the US–Soviet INF Treaty (1987) providing for the removal of such weapons. In early elections to the 212-seat Chamber of Representatives (Dec. 1987) 11 parties secured representation, with both Christian Social parties losing ground and the Socialists gaining support. The outcome was the formation (May 1988) of a five-party centre-left coalition of the Flemish and Walloon Christian Social and Socialist parties together with the Flemish nationalist Volksunie, under the continued premiership of Martens. The new government commanded the two-thirds parliamentary majority needed to enact further constitutional reforms on inter-communal issues.

CONSTITUTION AND GOVERNMENT

Executive and legislature

The constitutional monarch, as head of state, has certain limited powers including the appointment of 'formateurs' to negotiate the formation of new governments. The legislature comprises a 212-member Chamber of Deputies elected by a system of proportional representation for a four-year term (last general election 13 Dec. 1987), and a 181-member Senate, in which 106 of the senators are directly elected.

Present government

Head of state Baudouin, King of the Belgians
Prime Minister Dr Wilfried Martens
Principal Cabinet members Philippe Moureaux (Deputy Prime Minister, Brussels Region; Institutional Reform; National Education (Francophone)); Willy Claes (Deputy Prime Minister; Economic Affairs and Planning; National Education (Flemish)); Jean-Luc Dehaene (Deputy Prime Minister; Communications; Institutional Reform); Melchior Wathelet (Deputy Prime Minister; Justice and the Middle Classes); Hugo Schiltz (Deputy Prime Minister; Budget and Scientific Policy); Mark Eyskens (Foreign Affairs); Philippe Maystadt, (Finance); Guy Göeme (National Defence); Louis Tobback (Interior, Modernization of Public Services and National Scientific and Cultural Institutions).

Justice

The system of law is heavily influenced by British constitutional theory. The highest court is the Court of Cassation, with 5 Courts of Appeal. Assize Courts try major criminal cases, while the 27 judicial districts each have courts of first instance, and each of the 222 cantons has a justice of the peace. Judges are appointed for life. The death penalty is nominally in force. No executions were carried out between 1985 and mid-1988.
Prisons. There are 6,951 prisoners.

National symbols

Flag. Three vertical stripes of black, yellow and red.
Festivals. 21 July (Independence Day).
Vehicle registration plate. B.

INTERNATIONAL RELATIONS

Affiliations

Nato; OECD; EC; Benelux; Francophonie.

Defence

Total Armed Forces: 88,300 (3,500 women, 26,500 conscripts). Terms of service: ten months in the Federal Republic of Germany or 12 months' home service. Reserves: Total reserve status 411,500.
Army: 65,100; 334 main battle tanks (Leopard 1) and 113 light tanks (Scorpion).
Navy: 4,500; four frigates (Wielingen).
Air Force: 18,700; 125 combat aircraft (mainly Mirage 5BA/BD, Mirage 5BR and F-16).

ECONOMY

Currency

The unit is the Belgian franc, divided into 100 centimes.

National finance

Budget. The 1988 budget was for expenditure of US$54,700 million and revenue of US$41,000 million. Main items of expenditure are housing and welfare 32%; education 13%; defence 5.3%.
Balance of payments. The balance of payments (current account, 1988) was a surplus of US$3,540 million for Belgium-Luxembourg.
Inflation. 3.5% (12 months to Sept. 1989).

Gross Domestic Product

Estimated total GDP US$142,300 million, per capita US$15,690 (overall size of economy ranking 20 in the world). Growth rate (1988) 4.3%.
Economically active population. The total number of persons active in the economy is 4,000,000; unemployed: 10% (1988).

Sector	% of workforce	% of GDP
industry	37	31
agriculture	5	2
services*	58	67

* services figure includes elements unassigned to other categories.

Energy and mineral resources

Gas. Gas production in 1987 was 23,802 million ft^3/674 million m^3.
Minerals. Output: (1987, in tons/tonnes) wrought steel 10,787,573/9,786,422; cast iron 9,085,560/8,242,366; finished steel 8,173,775/7,415,200; coke 5,760,920/5,226,272; coal 4,802,120/4,356,455.
Electricity. Capacity: 17,271,000 Kw; production: (1988) 60,951 million Kw; 6,160 Kwh per capita.

Bioresources

Agriculture. There are an estimated 7,541,492 acres/3,052,000 ha of agricultural land in Belgium. Livestock production predominates.

Crop production: (1987 in million tons/tonnes) sugar beet 6.11/5.43; potatoes 1.79/1.62; beet for fodder 1.3/1.15; wheat 1.15/1.05; barley 0.74/0.68.

Livestock numbers: (1987) pigs 5.9 million; cattle 3.1 million; sheep 188,000; horses 23,000; goats 9,000.

Forestry. Some 20% of the land area is forested.

Fisheries. Annual catch: (1987) 34,029 tons/30,871 tonnes.

Industry and commerce

Industry. Belgium has few natural resources and is therefore heavily dependent on imported raw materials for its diversified industrial activities. Industry is concentrated in the populous Flemish area in the north, although the government is encouraging reinvestment in Wallonia in the south, once the heart of a significant steel and heavy manufacturing industry. Main industries are engineering and metal products; processed food and beverages; chemicals; basic metals; textiles; glass; petroleum; coal.

Commerce. Belgium, Luxembourg and the Netherlands have functioned as a customs union since 1948. A full economic union of the Benelux countries came into force in 1960. Belgium's exports totalled US$99,000 million; imports totalled US$93,000 million. Countries exported to: other EC countries 74%; US 5%; socialist bloc countries 2%. Imports: from other EC countries 72%; US 5%; oil-exporting less developed countries 4%; socialist bloc countries 3%.

Trade with UK. Belgium imported UK goods worth £4,252 million; exports to UK totalled £4,956 million.

Tourism. Earnings were US$3 million (1987).

COMMUNICATIONS

Railways

There are 2,216 miles/3,568 km of railways, of which 1,366 miles/2,200 km are electrified.

Roads

There are 79,686 miles/128,319 km of roads, of which 62,100 miles/100,000 km are minor roads.

Aviation

SABENA (Societé anonyme belge d'exploitation de la navigation aérienne or Belgian World Air Lines) and Delta Air Transport (DAT) provide international services (main airport is at Brussels).

Shipping

Main ports are at Antwerp, Brugge, Ghent, Ostend and Zeebrugge. The merchant marine includes 72 ships of over 1,000 GRT.

Telecommunications

There are 4,560,000 telephones, with an excellent domestic and international service. Public broadcasting is provided as a bilingual service, RTBF in French and BRT in Flemish, each with five radio and two television channels. There are a large number of cable television services, drawing on broadcasting by neighbouring countries, and the Canal Plus Belgique subscription television service began 20 hours/day transmission in Sept. 1989. There are about 4,600,000 radio sets and 3,200,000 televisions.

EDUCATION AND WELFARE

Education

Over 50% of Belgian schools are state-controlled while the remainder are mostly Roman Catholic schools subsidized by the state. The school-leaving age is 18.

Schools. There are 8,910 infant and primary schools with 1,136,872 pupils; 2,143 middle or secondary schools with 843,255 pupils.

Universities. There are seven state universities and ten private universities with a total of 103,505 students. There are also 101 'normal' schools for teacher training.

Literacy. 98%.

Health

Health care is provided through a social security scheme to which employers, employees and the government contribute. As well as state-run hospitals there are private hospitals run by religious bodies and private health insurance funds. There are 30,942 physicians, 454 of whom are dentists (1 per 320 people) and 5,979 other dentists. With around 90,000 hospital beds there is 1 bed per 110 people.

BELIZE
Belice

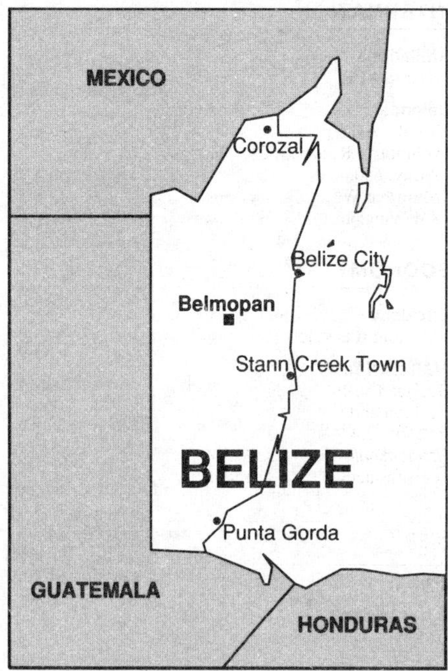

GEOGRAPHY

Situated on the Caribbean coast of Central America, the independent state of Belize occupies an area of 8,864 miles²/22,964 km² (including the mangrove 'cays' offshore), divided into six districts. Maximum lengths and breadths are 174 miles/280 km and 68 miles/109 km respectively. The Mexican frontier is marked by the Rio Hondo; the southern Guatemala Border by the Sarstun river. The Hondo, Belize and New Rivers drain the northern lowlands (average elevation less than 197 ft/60 m) and swampy coastal plain. In the south, the Maya Mountains transect the country's western border, extending north-eastward into the sparsely populated interior and towards the sea. Victoria Peak (3,648 ft/1,112 m) is Belize's highest mountain, part of the Cockscomb spur, flanked by tropical forest, grasslands and farming regions. 49% of Belize is forested and roughly 14% is cultivated. Belize's coastal waters are sheltered by the world's second largest barrier reef.

Climate

Sub-tropical, moderated by trade winds. Average annual rainfall is high (50 in/1,290 mm in the north to 175 in/4,445 mm in the south) and the range of temperature generally low, although greater in the mountainous regions; mean temperature 75°F/24°C Nov.–Jan. and 80°F/27°C May–Sept. A second dry period in Aug. (the Maugre season) succeeds the main dry season (Feb.–May). Belize lies within the hurricane zone.

Cities and towns

Belmopan (capital)	4,500
Belize City (former capital)	47,000
Corozal	10,000
Orange Walk	9,600
Dangriga	7,700

Population

Total population is 174,000, of which 51.7% live in urban areas. Population density is 19.6 persons per mile²/7.6 per km². One third of the population lives in Belize City. At the last census, 39.7% of the population were Creole (largely African descent); 33.1% Mestizo or Spanish Indian; 9.5% Mayan Indian, dominating the depopulated interior, of which 2.7% were Kekchi; 7.6% were Garifuna (Black Carib Indian); 2.1% were East Indian; and 4.2% were white.

Birth rate 4.01%. **Death rate** 0.4%. **Rate of population increase** 3.61%. **Age distribution** under 15 = 45.8%; over 65 = 4.5%. **Life expectancy** female 74.8; male 68.1; average 71.

Language

English is the official language although 90,000 inhabitants speak an English 'creole' and 31.6% of the population speak Spanish. There are 4,000 German speakers, while Mayan and Garifunan languages account for another 39,000.

Religion

Christianity. Approximately 62% of the population are Roman Catholic and 28% Protestant (including Anglican, Mennonite, Methodist, Seventh Day Adventist, Nazarene, Baptist, Jehovah's Witness and Pentecostal denominations). 1.2% are Jewish. There are also small groups of Baha'is, Hindus and Muslims.

HISTORY

The original inhabitants of Belize were the Maya Indians and the Black Carib Indians. The first foreign settlers were British adventurers, who arrived in the mid-17th century using the area as a base for attacks on Spanish shipping, and subsequently began to exploit the abundant timber resources. Later African slaves were imported and more recently foreign immigration has been encouraged to supplement the workforce.

The territory first came under British administration in 1786 and was designated a crown colony in 1862 under the name British Honduras. A new constitution was introduced in 1954 under which the country's first general elections were held, and self-government was granted in 1964. The new city of Belmopan became the capital in 1972 and the following year British Honduras was renamed Belize. Following growing domestic and international pressure Belize was declared independent on 21 Sept. 1981, retaining membership of the Commonwealth.

Although Spain recognized British sovereignty in 1802, neighbouring Guatemala has laid claim to Belize since 1821; the claim was, however, largely dormant between 1855 and 1945, and was not seriously pursued until the 1960s. Informal and inconclusive negotiations between Guatemala and the United Kingdom opened in 1972, and the first trilateral talks held in 1983 collapsed when Belize rejected a Guatemalan proposal for the annexation of the southern sector (about 25% of the total) of its territory. The first direct bilateral talks opened in Miami on 29 Apr. 1987, and although no new proposals were advanced, both sides agreed to continue negotiations.

The domestic political scene in the decades prior to independence in 1981 was dominated by the centre-left People's United Party (PUP). Under George Price, the PUP had won the country's first general election in 1954, its chief aim being the achievement of national independence. In 1982 a split developed within the party when Price was accused of allying too closely with the left-wing governments in Cuba and Nicaragua and thereby jeopardizing good relations with the United States. Price and several leading PUP members lost their seats in the House of Representatives in Dec. 1984, when the conservative United Democratic Party (UDP) won a landslide victory with 21 of the 28 seats in the House of Representatives, and UDP leader Manuel Esquivel became prime minister. Although the UDP was more right-wing in its foreign policy outlook, in the run-up to the election both parties had campaigned against the mooted replacement of the current British garrison by US troops for fear of becoming involved in the Central American conflict. In a surprise result, Price defeated Esquivel in the General Election of September 1989 and the PUP gained a narrow majority (15 out of the 28 seats) in the House of Representatives. Price promised to reverse what he termed as the UDP's previous policy of 'savage economic liberalism'.

CONSTITUTION AND GOVERNMENT

Executive and legislature

The head of state is the British sovereign, represented by a governor general appointed in consultation with the prime minister of Belize. The bicameral National Assembly consists of a 28-member House of Representatives popularly elected for five years (last general election Dec. 1984) and an appointed Senate.

Present government

Governor General Dame Minita Elvira Gordon

Prime Minister; Finance; Defence; Home Affairs George Price

Principal Cabinet members Florencio Marin (Deputy Prime Minister; Industry and Natural Resources); Said Musa (Foreign Affairs; Economic Development; Education); Glenn Godfrey (Tourism; Environment; Attorney General).

Justice

The system of law is based on English law. The highest court is the Supreme Court. Magistrates preside over district courts for civil cases, and summary jurisdiction courts for criminal cases, in the 6 judicial districts; there is a Court of Appeal, and 3 Puisne Judges. The Director of Public Prosecutions decides on bringing cases on behalf of the state. The death penalty is in force. There was 1 execution between 1985 and mid-1988. Offence: murder.

National symbols

Flag. Dark blue with a narrow red stripe at both the upper and lower edges. In the centre there is a large white circular field charged with the state coat of arms within a wreath of fifty green leaves.

Festivals. 9 Mar. (Baron Bliss Day); 1 May (Labour Day); 24 May (Commonwealth Day); 12 June (11 June in 1990, Queen's Official Birthday); 21 Sept. (Independence Day); 12 Oct. (Columbus Day; anniversary of the discovery of America); 19 Nov. (Garifuna Settlement Day).

Vehicle registration plate. BH.

INTERNATIONAL RELATIONS

Affiliations

NAM; ACP; Commonwealth; Caricom.

Defence

Total Armed Forces: 700. Terms of service: voluntary. Reserves: 350.
Army: 650.
Maritime Wing: 50; two patrol boats.
Air Wing: 15; 2 BN-2B Defender.

ECONOMY

Currency

The unit is the Belizean dollar, divided into 100 cents.

National finance

Budget. The 1988 budget was for expenditure of US$89 million and revenue of US$64 million.

Inflation. 2.4 %.

Economically active population. The total number of persons active in the economy is 51,500; unemployed: 14%.

Sector	% of workforce
industry	10
agriculture	30
services*	60

* services figure includes elements unassigned to other categories.

Energy and mineral resources

Minerals. Belize has few mineral resources. Although oil deposits were located in 1981, they have not yet been discovered in quantities sufficient for commercial exploitation.

Electricity. Production capacity: (1988) 34,000 Kw.

Bioresources

Agriculture. The economy of Belize is based primarily upon agriculture which generates over 70% of foreign exchange earnings and employs 30% of the labour force.

Crop production: (1987 in 1,000 tons/tonnes) sugar cane 870/789; citrus fruits 537/487; bananas 114/103; maize 20/18; rice 4.4/4.

Livestock numbers: (1987) poultry 1,000,000; cattle 51,000; pigs 25,000; sheep 4,000.

Forestry. Forests cover 49% of the country's total land area, and include cedar, mahogany, pine and rosewood. The export of timber generated B$4.8 million in 1987.

Fisheries. In addition to heavy domestic consumption, fish are an important export. In 1987 fish products exported to the US alone were valued at $B14 million.

Industry and commerce

Industry. The main industries are the production of sugar and molasses. Other important industries include the manufacture of cigarettes; beer; batteries; rum; fertilizer; clothing.

Commerce. Belize's exports totalled $B198.8 million and imports were $B285.9 million. Exports: sugar ($B62.5 million); molasses; citrus fruit; wood products. Imports: machinery; transportation equipment; food; manufactured goods; fuel; chemicals; pharmaceuticals. Countries exported to were US 47%; UK; Trinidad and Tobago; Canada. Imports came from US 55%; UK; Netherlands Antilles; Mexico.

Trade with UK. Belize imported UK goods worth £22,461,000 and exported to the UK goods worth £12,064,000 (1988).

Tourism. Belize derived revenue of $B41.3 million from 99,266 visitors (1987).

COMMUNICATIONS

Railways

There are no railways.

Roads

There are about 1,397 miles/2,250 km of all-weather and feeder roads, of which 186 miles/300 km are bituminized.

Aviation

Maya Airways Ltd provides international services (Philip Goldson International Airport, 14 km from Belize City).

Shipping

Belize City is the main port. There are, in addition to coastal routes, some 512 miles/825 km of seasonally navigable inland waterways.

Telecommunications

There are 8,650 telephones, connected by a system based on radio relay. Broadcasting by Belize Broadcasting Network is mainly in English, with some Spanish programmes.

EDUCATION AND WELFARE

Education

Education is compulsory for children between six and 14 years of age, with free primary education provided by the state.

School population. 48,250.

Schools. There are 226 primary schools with 40,000 pupils and 1,578 teachers (one per 25 pupils); 26 secondary schools with 7,326 pupils and 572 teachers (one per 13 pupils); eight technical schools with 932 students and 69 teachers (one per 14 students).

Universities. The University College of Belize opened in 1986. The University of the West Indies also has an extra-mural department in Belize City.

Literacy. 93%

Health

Belize has seven government hospitals with 82 doctors and 583 beds. In rural areas medical care is provided by health care centres and mobile clinics.

BENIN
République du Bénin
(Republic of Benin)

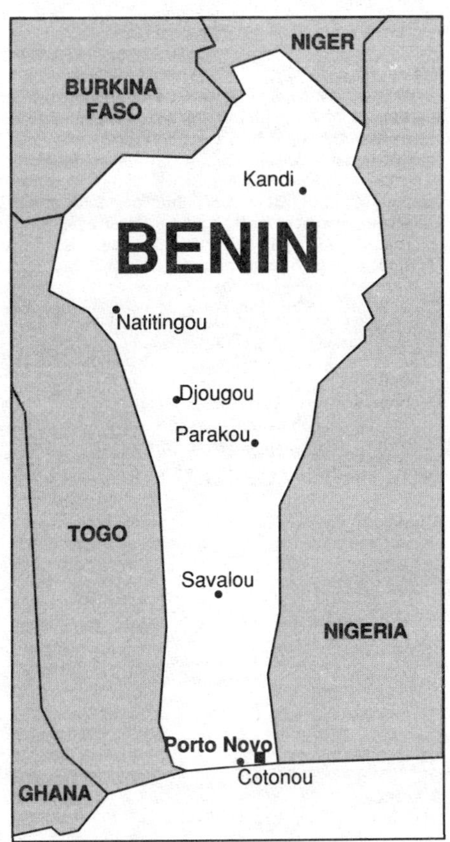

Climate

Tropical in the north with the rainy season lasting May-Sept. and temperature extremes of 115°F/46°C. Rainfall averages increase towards the south where coastal regions experience equatorial conditions with average temperatures of 68°F/20°C and rainfall of between 30 in/760 mm and 50 in/1,270 mm annually. Porto-Novo: Jan. 82°F/27.8°C. July 78°F/25.6°C. Annual rainfall 51 in/1,300 mm. Cotonou: Jan. 81°F/27.2°C. July 77°F/25°C. Annual rainfall 13 in/325 mm.

Cities and towns

Porto-Novo (capital)	144,000
Cotonou	383,250

Population

Total population is 4,448,000, of which 39% live in urban areas. Population density is 102 persons per mile^2/39.4 per km^2. Almost all (99%) of the Beninese sub-divide ethnolinguistically into 42 groups, principally the Fon (40% of the total population) in the south, the Adja, the Yoruba (10%) and Bariba (20%) in the north. The nomadic Fulani inhabit the northern semi-desert plains.

Birth rate 4.8%. **Death rate** 1.6%. **Rate of population increase** 3.2%. **Age distribution** under 15 = 46.8%; over 65 = 2.9%. **Life expectancy** female 52; male 49; average 50.

Religion

At least two thirds of the population follow traditional African animist beliefs but substantial minorities of Christians (Roman Catholic 12%, Protestant 3%) and Muslims 13%, exist.

Language

French is the official language. Almost half the population (47%) speak Fon; 12% Adja; 10% Bariba; 9% Yoruba; 6% Fulani; 5% Somba; 5% Aizo. Somba and Bariba are related to the languages of Burkina Faso and Ghana.

GEOGRAPHY

Benin is situated on the West African coast, extending 435 miles/700 km inland off the Bight of Benin and comprises six provinces totalling 43,472 miles^2/112,622 km^2 in area. It has a coastline of about 62 miles/100 km. Benin has five physiographic regions (south-north): a sandy shore-line backed by Grand-Popo and Porto-Novo, the low-lying fertile plains or 'barre' that surround the Lama Marsh, the clay savannah plateaux (rising to 755 ft/230 m) stretching west-east from Aplahové to Zagnanada, the north-western Atacora massif (highest point 2,103 ft/641 m) and the north-eastern Niger plains traversed by the Alibori river valley which joins the Niger on the border between Benin and Niger in the north-east of Borgou province. The Pendjari and Mekrou rivers flow northwards from the Atacora to the north-western border with Burkina Faso. About 15% of the land is arable, of which less than 5% is pasture; the bulk of the population (60%) is concentrated in the southern third of the country.

HISTORY

Little is known of Benin's history before the foundation of the kingdom of Abomey (later Dahomey) by the Fon people in 1625, though the Fon are thought to have been involved in the slave trade before that date. The third king of this dynasty, Ouegbajda (c.1645–85) defeated and absorbed the neighbouring kingdom of Dan, and his son Agadja (r.1708–32) conquered Allada and, further south, the coastal kingdom around Porto-Novo and Ouidah. This brought Dahomey into contact with the European trading posts established on what the Portuguese, British and French had come to call the slave coast, and gave them access to firearms. Under King Gezo (r.1818–58) Dahomey prospered from slave raids against the Yoruba. However, Gezo allowed the French to install themselves at Grand-Popo in 1857 and subsequently France hindered the slave trade. This led to hostilities, the defeat of King Behanzin (r.1889–94) and the declaration of a French protectorate in 1892. Two years later

Dahomey became a French colony; from 1904 it was governed as a division of French West Africa.

In 1960, in common with most of the French colonies in Africa, Dahomey acceded to independence (1 Aug.). Its politics rapidly proved fraught with divisions stemming from the rivalries of the historic kingdoms. Over the following 12 years there were 11 changes of government, including five military coups, a period of coalition government and two changes of constitution. In Oct. 1973, Maj. Mathieu Kerekou seized power, complaining that tribalism had rendered the existing political system anarchic; he turned politics abruptly to the left, renaming Dahomey the People's Republic of Benin (1 Dec. 1975) and launching a single party, the Parti de la révolution populaire du Bénin (PRPB). Ruling through a Conseil national révolutionnaire (CNR), Kerekou nationalized most large enterprises. Relations with France came near to breakdown following an abortive coup attempt by French mercenaries in Jan. 1977. After talks in 1978, France agreed to resume aid payments.

Constitutional reforms led to the election of a Assemblée nationale révolutionnaire (ANR) in Nov. 1979 and the unanimous election of Pres. Kerekou in Feb. 1980. The following year three former civilian presidents were released from prison, and Kerekou announced a general amnesty for political prisoners after his re-election in Aug. 1984.

Since 1980 the government has encouraged foreign investment and embarked on a programme of economic liberalization. Left-wing critics of the change of policy were removed from the government in 1982. The economic situation continued to deteriorate and the government's announcement that students could no longer be guaranteed employment led to riots in May 1985. That year Kerekou approached the International Monetary Fund, Western powers and conservative African countries for assistance. A cabinet reshuffle in Feb. 1987 continued the drift away from Marxism and served to restore the balance between ethnic groups. There were further student demonstrations in Mar. 1987. On 28 Mar. 1988 the military tried to seize power. Lt-Col. Badjo Gounmé, one of Kerekou's closest associates, was among the 150 officers arrested after the coup attempt. Marxism-Leninism was abandoned as the official ideology in late 1989.

CONSTITUTION AND GOVERNMENT

Executive and legislature

In February 1990 delegates at a national convention revoked the constitution, suspended the legislature and appointed a commission to draw up a reformed constitution, to provide for the separation of party and state. An interim Prime Minister was elected to steer the country through a transitional period to elections in 1991. The country's name was changed from People's Republic to Republic of Benin. Elections to the Assembly, whose 206 members represented socio-professional classes, all nominated on a single list system by the Benin People's Revolutionary Party, had been held in June 1989.

Present government

Head of state, President Mathieu Kerekou

Principal members of Transitional National Executive Council Nicephore Soglo (Prime Minister); Didier Dassi (Finance); Justin Gnidehou (Industry and Energy); Robert Dossou (Minister-Delegate to the Presidency in charge of Planning and Statistics); Daniel Tawena (Foreign Affairs and Co-operation); Cdr Pancras Brathier (Minister-Delegate to the Presidency in Charge of Interior, Public Security and Territorial Administration).

Ruling party (prior to March 1990) Benin People's Revolutionary Party (Parti de la révolution populaire du Bénin).

Chairman of the central committee Mathieu Kerekou.

Full members of the politburo Mathieu Kerekou; Maj. Martin Dohou Azonhiho; Joseph Degla; Girigissou Gado; Roger Imorou Garba; Justin Gnidehou; Sanni Mama Gomina; Romain Vilon Guezo; Vincent Guezodje; Idi Abdoulaye Malam; Simon Ifede Ogouma.

Justice

The system of law is based on the French civil code and customary law. The highest court is the Supreme Court at Cotonou, with magistrates' courts in seven cities, and a 'tribunal de conciliation' in each district. The death penalty is in force. There were 8 executions between 1985 and mid-1988. Capital offences: murder.

National symbols

Flag. Green; in the upper hoist there is a red five-pointed star.

Festivals. 16 Jan. (Anniversary of Mercenary Attack on Cotonou); 1 May (Labour Day); 26 Oct. (Armed Forces Day); 30 Nov. (National Day).

Vehicle registration plate. DY.

INTERNATIONAL RELATIONS

Affiliations

NAM; OAU; ACP; Francophonie.

Defence

Total Armed Forces: 4,350. Terms of service: conscription (selective), 18 months.

Army: 3,800; 20 light tanks (PT-76).

Navy: 200; seven patrol and coastal combatants.

Air Force: 350; no combat aircraft or armed helicopters.

ECONOMY

Currency

The unit is the CFA franc, divided into 100 centimes.

National finance

Budget. The 1987 budget was for expenditure of US$313 million and revenue of US$168 million.

Balance of payments. The balance of payments (current account, 1987) was a deficit of 223 million.

Inflation. 3.6%.

Gross Domestic Product

Estimated total GDP US$1,570 million, per capita US$340 (overall size of economy ranking 125 in the world).

Economically active population. The total number of persons active in the economy is 1,900,000.

Sector	% of workforce	% of GDP
industry	2	14
agriculture	60	46
services*	38	39

* services figure includes elements unassigned to other categories.

Energy and mineral resources

Minerals. There are deposits of limestone and marble.

Oil. The Seme oilfield, located ten miles offshore, began production in 1982 and produced 3.3 million barrels in 1985.

Electricity. Production capacity: (1988) 28,000 kW; 24 million kWh: hydro-electric resources on the Mono river are being developed in co-operation with Togo.

Bioresources

Agriculture. Some 15% of the land is arable; 4% is given over to permanent crops and 5% to meadows and pastures. About 90% of the population works in agriculture, which contributes 45% of GDP. Small farms produce 90% of output, with production dominated by food crops. Cotton has been introduced in the north and coffee in the south, and cocoa is also produced.

Food crop production: (1986 in tons/tonnes) cassava 800,270/726,000; yams 945,773/858,000; maize 401,237/364,000; sorghum 99,207/90,000; groundnuts 73,854/67,000; beans 48,501/44,000; also other local foodstuffs. Cash crop production: (1986 in tons/tonnes) palm kernels 19,841/18,000; palm-oil 41,887/38,000.

Livestock numbers: (1986) cattle 930,000; sheep 1,160,000; pigs 600,000; poultry 22,000,000; horses 6,000; asses 1,000.

Forestry. Forest and woodland cover 35% of land area. Roundwood production: (1985) 155 million ft^3/4.4 million m^3.

Fisheries. Total catch: (1985) 22,283 tons/20,306 tonnes, of which 80% was caught in inland waters and lagoons.

Industry and commerce

Industry. The industrial sector contributes nearly 15% of GDP; principal activities are palm-oil and palm kernel oil processing; textiles; beverages; petroleum.

Commerce. Exports totalled US$108 million (1986), comprising crude oil; cotton; palm products; cocoa. Principal partners were West Germany; France; Netherlands; Japan; Italy; UK. Imports: ($338 million in 1986) foodstuffs; beverages; tobacco; petroleum products; intermediate goods; capital goods; light consumer goods. Principal trading partners were France; Netherlands; Japan; Italy; US.

Trade with UK. Benin exported to the UK (1988) goods worth £2,450,000 and imported from the UK goods worth £8,169,000.

COMMUNICATIONS

Railways

There are 360 miles/579 km of railways (a 403 miles/650 km extension north from Parakou to Gaya, and on through Niger to Niamey, was under construction in 1988).

Roads

There are 4,623 miles/7,445 km of classified roads and 745 miles/1,200 km of tracks.

Aviation

Transports aériens du Bénin provides domestic services and Air Afrique provides international services (main airport is at Cotonou).

Shipping

Cotonou is the main port. The merchant marine has one ship of over 1,000 GRT.

Telecommunications

There are 16,200 telephones, some 70,000 radios and 20,000 television sets.

EDUCATION AND WELFARE

Education

School population. 444,232 pupils enrolled at primary level; 112,267 at secondary level; 8,315 in technical schools.

University. The University of Benin had 6,302 students in 1983. Three teacher training colleges were opened in 1987.

Literacy. 28% of the adult population (1980).

Health

In 1986 there were eight hospitals, 186 dispensaries and approximately 100 clinics. In 1979 there were 204 doctors, 13 dentists, 55 pharmacists and 1,294 midwives.

BERMUDA

GEOGRAPHY

A group of islands in the North Atlantic Ocean, Bermuda covers an area of 19.3 $miles^2$/50 km^2; the terrain consists of low hills separated by fertile depressions. There are no rivers or freshwater lakes. The capital is Hamilton.

Climate

Subtropical, gales in winter.

Population

Total population (1989 est.) 58,238: 61% Black; 31% White and other.

Birth rate 1.5%. **Death rate** 0.7%. **Rate of population increase** 0.2%. **Life expectancy** female 79; male 73.

Religion

Christianity: Anglican; Roman Catholic; African Methodist Episcopal.

Language

English.

HISTORY

The Bermudas were uninhabited when they were first discovered by Spanish explorers in the early 16th century. They remained uninhabited until 1609 when an English expedition landed and in 1612 they were colonized by the Virginia Company. The Crown assumed responsibility for the islands in 1684. African slaves were imported to serve as labour for plantations until slavery was abolished in 1834.

Universal suffrage was introduced in 1962 and internal self-government in 1968. Elections in 1968 were won by the United Bermuda Party (UBP) which favoured continued dependent status and was supported by the White establishment. The left-wing Progressive Labour Party (PLP), mainly supported by Black Bermudans and in favour of independence, became the opposition. Serious outbreaks of disorder, fuelled by racial tensions, had preceded the elections and in Mar. 1973 the governor, Sir Richard Sharples, was assassinated, six months after the murder of the Commissioner of Police. Further rioting erupted in Dec. 1977 after the execution of the Governor's murderer. A state of emergency was imposed and a Royal Commission set up to investigate the underlying problems. The Commission recommended the redrawing of constituency boundaries to allow the PLP a greater opportunity of winning seats and negotiations towards early independence. The UBP won the 1980 election and in 1985 was returned to power with an increased majority after a split in the PLP led to the formation of the National Liberal Party. John Swan, the leader of the UBP since 1982, remained premier, and won a further general election on 9 Feb. 1989.

CONSTITUTION AND GOVERNMENT

Bermuda is a dependent territory of the United Kingdom with a Constitution dating from June 1968. It has an Executive Council (cabinet) appointed by the governor (Sir Desmond Langley since Oct. 1988), which is led by a government leader. There is a bicameral legislature, with an 11-member appointed Senate and a 40-member elected House of Assembly; Supreme Court. The last general election was in Feb. 1989.

Premier John Swan.

National symbols

Flag. Red, with the flag of the United Kingdom in the upper hoist-side quadrant and the Bermudian coat of arms centred on the outer half.

National holiday. 22 May (Bermuda Day).

ECONOMY

Agriculture is severely restricted by terrain; manufacturing industry is limited. Tourism and financial services are the mainstay of the economy. Per capita income is one of the highest in the world.

Currency

Bermudian dollar.

COMMUNICATIONS

Railway

There are no railways.

Roads

130 miles/210km of public roads, 248 miles/400km of private roads.

Shipping

There are ports at Hamilton, Freeport and St George.

Aviation

There is one permanent surface runway airport.

Telecommunications

There is a modern telephone system, five AM and three FM radio broadcasting stations and two TV stations.

BHUTAN

Druk-yul

GEOGRAPHY

The Kingdom of Bhutan lies in the eastern Himalayas, comprising four regions (17 districts) and a total area of 18,142 miles²/47,000 km². The sparsely populated Greater Himalayas, bounded north by the Tibetan plateau, reach heights of over 23,950 ft/7,300 m and extend southward, losing height, to form the fertile valleys of the Lesser Himalayas divided by the Wong, Sankosh, Tongsa and Manas rivers. Monsoon influences promote dense forestation in this region and alpine growth at higher altitudes. The cultivated central uplands and Himalayan foothills support the bulk of the population. In the south, the Duars plain drops sharply away from the Himalayas into large tracts of semi-tropical forest, savannah grassland and bamboo jungle.

Climate

Varies according to altitude. The glaciated north is permanently snowcapped, but central Bhutan's climate is less severe; average monthly temperatures vary from 40°F/4.4°C (Jan.) to 63°F/17°C (July). Rainfall ranges from a modest 39–49 in/1,000–1,250 mm annually in the central interior to a torrential 197 in/ 5,000 mm in the southern Duars tropics.

Cities and towns

Thimphu (capital)	15,000

Population

Total population is 1,451,000 of which 5% live in urban areas. Population density is 79.9/28.4 persons per miles²/km². 62.5% of the population are Kuamas Bhutia or Bhote, of Tibetan extraction (northern and central Bhutan); 15.5% Gurung. In the south and south-west, the ethnic mix is dominated by the Nepalese settlers (Hindu); Bhutia, Monpa and Sherdukpen populate the east.

Birth rate 3.84%. **Death rate** 1.81%. **Rate of population increase** 2.03%. **Age distribution** under 15 = 40.0%; over 65 = 3.3%. **Life expectancy** female 47; male 49; average 48.

Religion

Mahayana (Lamaistic) Buddhism is the state religion. The majority are Buddhists of the Drukpa sect or the

Kagyupa school, which was introduced from Tibet during the twelfth century. 25% Nepalese Hindus; 5% Muslim.

Language

Official languages are Dzongkha (836,000), Lhotsan (Nepali) and English. A variety of Tibetan dialects make up Dzongkha: different dialects are for the most part mutually intelligible.

HISTORY

Migrations from Tibet into Bhutan began as early as the 9th century AD. About 1630 the Shabdrung Ngawang Namgyal, a lama of the Drukpa sect of Tibetan Buddhism, established a Buddhist theocracy centred on the Drukpa monasteries. British contact with Bhutan began when the East India Company intervened in the border dispute with Kuch Behar, a dependency of Bengal, in 1774. Bhutan was defeated in a serious border war with British India in 1865. In 1907 an hereditary monarchy was established with the selection of a local nobleman, Ugyen Dorji Wangchuk (r. 1907–26), as king.

The 1910 Treaty of Punakha between Bhutan and British India recognized Bhutan's internal autonomy in exchange for accepting Indian guidance on foreign affairs. Similar provisions were included in the 1949 Indo-Bhutan Treaty signed by independent India. In 1953 an elected assembly (the Tshogdu) was established with a narrow franchise. The king remained the sole executive authority although in 1968 the assembly acquired important powers, including the right to remove the monarch by a two-thirds vote. The Drupka monastic order, led by a high priest, the Je Khempo, still wielded formidable political power.

The present king, Jigme Singye Wangchuk, was crowned in 1972. While remaining closely allied with India, Bhutan has attempted to assert its autonomy in foreign-policy matters, conducting regular annual talks with China over border issues since 1984. Direct diplomatic contacts have been opened up with several countries and Bhutan joined the United Nations in 1971, appointing a permanent representative in 1985. Bhutan is a founder member of the South Asian Association for Regional Cooperation (SAARC) established in 1985.

CONSTITUTION AND GOVERNMENT

Executive and legislature

Bhutan is a hereditary limited monarchy. The king, as head of state, is assisted by a Royal Advisory Council, and shares power with the Council of Ministers, the National Assembly (Tshogdu) and the monastic head of the Kingdom's Buddhist priesthood. The 151-member legislature, the Tshogdu, has 105 elective seats, elected by universal suffrage, minimum voting age 17. Every three years the Tshogdu holds a vote of confidence in the king, which requires a two-thirds majority; the Tshogdu has the power to replace the monarch.

Present government

Head of state, Druk Gyalpo (Dragon King); Chairman of the Council of Ministers Jigme Singye Wangchuk

Members of Council of Ministers Princess Dechhen W. Wangchuck (Agriculture); Princess Sonam Chhoden Wangchuck (Finance); *Lyonpo* Dawa Tsering (Foreign Affairs; Secretary of the Council of Ministers); HRH Namgyel Wangchuck (Home Affairs); *Lyonpo* Dr T. Tobgyal (Social Services; Communications; Tourism).

Head (Je Khempo) of the Central Monastic Secretariat Venerable Dorji Lopon Tenzin Dhondrub.

Justice

The system of law is based on Indian law and English law. The High Court, whose 8 judges are appointed by the King, functions at the national level, with lower tiers of district and local courts. The death penalty is nominally in force. There were no executions between 1985 and mid-1988.

National symbols

Flag. Divided diagonally from the bottom of the hoist to the top of the fly, into two triangles in the traditonal Chinese colours of saffron yellow in the hoist and orange-red in the fly. Over the dividing line there is the white Bhutanese wingless dragon outlined, facing to the right and holding balls.

Festivals. 11 Nov. (birthday of HM Jigme Singye Wangchuk); 17 Dec. (National Day).

Vehicle registration plate. BHT.

INTERNATIONAL RELATIONS

Affiliations

NAM; SAARC.

Defence

Royal Bhutan Army; military age 18.

ECONOMY

Currency

The unit is the ngultrum, divided into 100 chetrum.

National finance

Budget. The 1988 budget was for expenditure of US$110 million and revenue of US$105 million.

Balance of payments. The balance of payments (current account, 1987) was a defecit of US$56 million.

Inflation. 6.8%.

Gross Domestic Product

Estimated total GDP US$250 million, per capita US$170 (overall size of economy ranking 160 in the world).

Sector	% of GDP
industry	16
agriculture	51
services*	32

* services figure includes elements unassigned to other categories.

Energy and mineral resources

Minerals. Bhutan has deposits of dolomite; limestone; marble; graphite; lead; copper; slate; talc; gypsum; beryl; mica; pyrites; tufa. Output: (1985 in tons/tonnes) dolomite 178,589/162,014; limestone 158,731/144,000; coal 33,069/30,000; gypsum 13,228/12,000.

Electricity. Bhutan possesses large hydroelectric potential from its many fast-flowing rivers. Production capacity: (1988) 353,000 kW. Over 20 towns and 90 villages have electricity.

Bioresources

Agriculture. Land under cultivation exceeds 988,400 acres/400,000 ha. The principal crops are maize; rice; oranges; wheat; barley; potatoes.

Crop production: (1986 in 1,000 tons/tonnes) maize 97/88; rice 69/63; potatoes 31/28; oranges 30/27; wheat 12/11; barley 5.5/5.
Livestock numbers: (1987) cattle 395,000; pigs 62,000; sheep and goats 55,000; yaks (1985) 31,300.
Forestry. Forests cover nearly 75% of the land area and timber is exported to neighbouring India.

Industry and commerce

Industry. The small industrial sector concentrates mainly on cement production and on wood and food processing. In 1987 there were less than 500 small-scale cottage and industrial units.
Commerce. Total exports (1988): US$60,800,000. The main exports are cement; minerals; timber; fruit products. Imports: US$105,100,000, including fuel and lubricants; grain; machinery and parts; vehicles; fabrics. India is the destination for the vast majority of Bhutan's exports and also supplies most imports.
Trade with UK. Bhutan imported from the UK (1988) goods worth £175,000 and exported to the UK goods worth £12,464,000.
Tourism. Bhutan derived revenue of US$2,040,000 from 2,524 visitors (1987). Tourism is the country's largest source of foreign exchange.

COMMUNICATIONS

Railways

There are no railways.

Roads

There are 1,344 miles/2,165 km of road, of which 1,058 miles/1,703 are concrete or bituminized.

Aviation

Druk-Air Corpn (Royal Bhutan Airlines) provides services between Paro and Calcutta and Paro and Dhaka (main airport is at Paro).

Shipping

None.

Telecommunications

The rudimentary telephone system serves some 1,900 telephones. There are 15,000 radio sets and about 100 televisions, receiving foreign broadcasts since there is no domestic television channel.

EDUCATION AND WELFARE

Education

In 1988 there were over 42,446 pupils and 1,513 teachers in primary schools; 16,350 pupils and 695 teachers in secondary schools; 1,761 pupils and 150 teachers in technical, vocational and tertiary-level schools.
Literacy. Approximately 5%.

Health

There are over 130 doctors and approximately 550 paramedics (1988); one doctor per 16,500 inhabitants. There are approximately 30 hospitals, with additional dispensaries, health units, leprosy hospitals and malaria eradication centres.

BOLIVIA
República de Bolivia
(Republic of Bolivia)

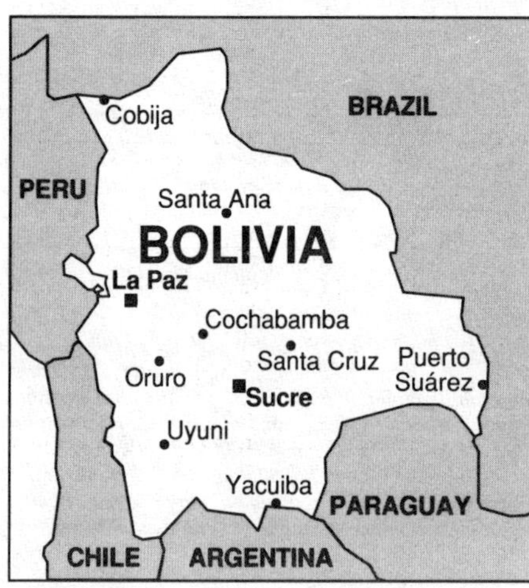

GEOGRAPHY

Bolivia is a landlocked country of west South America with an area of approximately 424,052 m²/1,098,580 km², divided into nine departments. East of the Cordillera Real range in the north-western department of La Paz, the Oriente foothills and lowlands stretch north-east into dense tropical vegetation and south-east through the humid eastern and central regions, drained by the sparsely populated Beni, Mamoré and Guaporé basins, toward the semi-arid Chaco scrublands of Santa Cruz. The south-western highlands are dominated by three principal features: the volcanic Western (Cordillera Occidental) and fluvial Eastern (Cordillera Oriental) arms of the Andes, separated by the comparatively populous Altiplano (average elevation 11,810 ft/3,600 m) running 248 miles/400 km south-north from the department of Potosí to La Paz, and covering 20% of the total land surface area. Sajama, Bolivia's highest volcanic peak, stands 21,463 ft/6,542 m above sea level in the Cordillera Occidental, north of which lies Lake Titicaca, the world's highest navigable body of water, and to the south-east Lake Poopó. Over 50% of Bolivia is forested and less than 4% is arable.

Climate

The climate varies with altitude, ranging from consistently warm (79°F/26°C) and damp conditions (71 in/1,800 mm of rainfall per year) in the north-east rain forest of the Oriente (Amazon Basin) to summer

drought conditions in the south (Chaco, Cordillera Occidental, South Cordillera Oriental and South Altiplano) for four to six months annually. Rainfall in the parched Cordillera Occidental is negligible, increasing in the North Altiplano and Lake Titicaca districts to between 22 in/570 mm and 26 in/650 mm. Above 13,123 ft/4,000 m, the temperature drops to about 45°F/7°C, and over 16,404 ft/5,000 m conditions become sub-Arctic.
La Paz: Jan. 23°F/11.7°C. July 47°F/8.3°C. Average annual rainfall 23 in/574 mm.

Cities and towns

La Paz (administrative capital)	1,013,688
Santa Cruz de la Sierra	577,803
Cochabamba	360,446
Oruro	189,278
Potosí	111,215
Sucre (legal capital)	92,917

Population

Total population is 6,918,000 of which 49% live in urban areas. 30% are Quechua Indian, 25% Aymará Indian, 25–30% mestizos (mixed Indian-Spanish extraction) and 5–10% European, principally of Spanish descent. Other Indian groupings include the Chiquitano, Chiriguano and Moxo peoples, together with a number of smaller Andean and Amazon forest groups. Approximately 4 million Indians are indigenous to the highlands and 80,000 to the lowlands.
Birth rate: 4.3%. **Death rate** 1.4%. **Rate of population increase** 2.7%. **Age distribution** under 15 = 43.8%; over 65 = 3.2%. **Life expectancy** female 53.0 years; male 48.6 years; average 51.

Religion

The State recognizes the Roman Catholic faith (95%). Traditional pantheistic beliefs survive among the Altiplano Indians. Significant protestant denominations include the Baptists and Methodists (5,000 members). 2.6% of the population are Baha'is and a small minority are Jewish.

Language

Spanish is the official language but most Indians speak Aymará (25.2%) or Quechua (34.4%). Composite dialects of Spanish-Aymará or Spanish-Quechua or all three are also very widely spoken.

HISTORY

With roots thought by archaeologists to stretch back 21,000 years, civilization in the Bolivian Andes reached twin peaks: from approximately AD 600–1200 the ceremonial centre of Tiahuanaco near Lake Titicaca held sway (the Colla empire that replaced it left, as its legacy, the current Aymará tongue) and, from the 13th century up to the 16th century, the Incas ruled an empire which encompassed most of present-day Bolivia, Ecuador, Peru, northern Chile (and a fraction of Argentina) and whose language, Quechua, is still widely spoken in the highlands.

The Spanish conquest of the Incas, initiated from Peru in 1532 by Francisco Pizarro, meant the eventual inclusion of present-day Bolivia as Upper Peru in the viceroyalty of Peru (1544–1824). Its southern Potosí mine, established 1545, became the most crucial supplier of silver to the Spanish empire.

The process of winning independence from Spain began in May 1809 but was not achieved until the decisive victory over royalist forces by Antonio José de Sucre at the battle of Ayacucho in 1824; the Republic of Bolivia being formally proclaimed on 8 Aug. 1825, at a time of profound economic crisis, with Sucre as its first president (1828–39). The temporary confederation with Peru (established 1836) failed in 1839 and decades of political turmoil and violence ensued (while, paradoxically, silver mining experienced a revival after its earlier collapse), particularly under the tyrannical rule of Mariano Melgarejo (1864–71) who launched major assaults on Indian community lands, which led to Indian uprisings in 1869, 1870, and 1871. Defeat in the War of the Pacific (1879–83), waged with Peru (in line with a mutual defence treaty of 1873) against Chile, resulted in the loss of its Pacific province of Atacama (with its nitrate fields), the port of Antofagasta and the consequent landlocking of the country.

A period of Conservative Party rule (1884–99), dominated by the silver-mining elites of the south, gave way to ascendency by the Liberal Party (assured by its victory in the civil war between the two parties in 1898), which drew its strength from the new tin magnates who allowed their political interests to be run by professional politicians (the Rosca) drawn from the rising urban professional classes of La Paz. Government policies changed little in the period of Liberal control (1899–1920) but Pres. José Manuel Pando (1899–1904) was compelled to sell off the disputed Amazonian Acre rubber region (for £2.5 million) to Brazil in 1903 although he signed a peace treaty with Chile in 1904 which included rail access to the Pacific. The construction of rail links for mineral transport greatly contributed to the growth of La Paz, which in 1898 replaced the old colonial city of Sucre as the national capital.

The Conservative–Liberal consensus began to break down with the emergence in the 1920s of the Republican Party (founded 1914), which itself split into two factions, and Pres. Bautista Saavedra (1921–25) facing the combined opposition of the Genuine Republican party of Daniel Salamanca and the Liberals. Saavedra, in classic style, brutally put down the 1920 Indian rebellion of Jesús de Machaca while, after initially courting organized labour, used troops in the bloody suppression of miners at Uncia in 1923. The unstable government of his successor Hernando Siles (1925–30) allowed Salamanca, who had galvanized cross-party opposition, to take the presidency in Mar. 1931. Economic crisis, characterized by continuing decline in world tin prices and growing labour unrest, persuaded Salamanca to waged war with Paraguay (1932–35) over control of the Chaco region, with catastrophic results. This defeat caused widespread disillusionment, opened up the country to a ferment of revolutionary ideas, and sparked off the growth of a militant labour movement which survived the six years of military rule and the re-emergence of the Conservatives in 1946. The result was the revolution of 1952 which brought to power the Nationalist Revolutionary Movement (MNR) led by Pres. Víctor Paz Estenssoro (1952–56). Although land reform and universal adult suffrage were introduced and the mining sector nationalized, the dual strategy of elevating popular consumption while simultaneously developing investment led to eventual agreement with the International Monetary Fund (IMF), in 1956, to accept an austerity programme in return for economic aid. To head off the mounting labour protest, MNR Pres. Hernán Siles Suazo (1956–60) modernized the army while Paz Estenssorro, in his second term (1960–64), and supported by the US's Alliance for Progress initiative (designed to head off Cuban-style insurrections), moved towards the creation of a mixed state–

capitalist economy. However, the MNR government, unable to break the power of the Labour left, was overthrown by the military, headed by Gen. René Barrientos, in the coup of 1964, whose tenure (1964–69) was marked by a pact to incorporate the peasantry while he systematically repressed the militant miners and put down the Nancahuazu guerrilla campaign of the Cuban Ernesto 'Che' Guevara, shot dead in Oct. 1967. The two brief 'leftist' military regimes that followed (Gen. Ovando 1969–70 and Gen. Juan José Torres 1970–71) were supplanted by that of Col. Hügo Banzer Suárez (1971–78), who ruled with an iron hand while attempting a similar policy of state-led growth. After three further military coups in 1978 and 1979, the interim Pres. Lidia Gueiler set elections for June 1980, which were contested by 73 parties but failed to produce a clear winner. Before Congress could endorse Siles Suazo as the leading candidate, power was seized in July 1982 by Gen. Luis García Meza, whose government became notorious for its violent repression and involvement in cocaine trafficking. He was overthrown by the army in 1982 and Siles Suazo was again sworn in as president, this time for the National Revolutionary Movement of the Left (MNRI). Under mounting economic and labour pressure, the next general elections were held early in July 1985 and were won by Paz Estenssoro's (1985–89) Historic Nationalist Revolutionary Movement (MNRH). Faced with dramatic declines in international tin prices, the government resorted to austerity measures (and a state of siege in 1986) to stem massive labour unrest, while increasing numbers of unemployed miners, for want of an alternative, turned to coca growing, thus adding to the government's problems in combating the burgeoning cocaine industry. The failure of any candidate to attain an outright majority in May 1989 elections meant that the Congress chose Victor Paz Zamora of the left-wing Movement of the Revolutionary Left (MIR) to be President in August. Zamora was to lead a coalition government dominated by the right-wing Democratic Action Party (ADN) led by Hugo Banzez, now a retired General who had imprisoned and exiled Zamora in 1974. The new government pledged to continue Paz Estenssoro's austerity program.

CONSTITUTION AND GOVERNMENT

Executive and legislature

The executive president is head of state and government, and appoints the Cabinet. Direct presidential elections are held every four years; if no candidate wins an overall majority, as in the last election (May 1989), the decision is made by Congress, the bicameral legislative body. The 27-member Senate and 130-member House of Representatives are both elected for four-year terms by universal adult suffrage. Last legislative elections May 1989.

Present government

President Víctor Paz Zamora
Vice-President Luis Ossio
Principal members of Cabinet Carlos Iturralde Ballivián (Foreign Affairs; Worship); Guillermo Capobianco Ribera (Interior; Justice; Migration); Gustavo Fernández Saavedra (Minister of Presidency); Héctor Hormaechea Penaranda (National Defence); David Blanco Zavala (Finance).

Administration

The country is divided for administrative purposes into nine departments, each of which is governed by a prefect appointed by the president.

Justice

The system of law is based on Spanish principles and the Code Napoleon. The highest court is the Supreme Court, which is divided into two sections, civil and criminal, and whose members are elected by the Congress. District courts and courts of local justice administer the law at lower levels. The death penalty is nominally in force. No judicial executions were carried out between 1985 and mid-1988.

National symbols

Flag. Three horizontal stripes of red, yellow and green.
Festivals. 2 May (1 May in 1990, Labour Day); 6 Aug. (Independence Day).
Vehicle registration plate. BOL.

INTERNATIONAL RELATIONS

Affiliations

NAM; OAS.

Defence

Total Armed Forces: 27,600 (some 19,000 conscripts).
Terms of service: 12 months, selective.
Army: 20,000; 36 light tanks (Steyr SK 105).
Navy: 3,600; some ten river patrol craft.
Air Force: 4,000; 35 combat aircraft (mainly 14 AT-33N and F-86F) and ten armed helicopters.

ECONOMY

Currency

The unit is the boliviano, divided into 100 centavos.

National finance

Budget. The 1987 budget was for expenditure of US$2,867 million and revenue of US$2,867 million.
Balance of payments. The balance of payments (current account, 1987) was a deficit of US$597 million.
Inflation. 21%.

Gross Domestic Product

Estimated total GDP US$4,470 million, per capita US$680 (overall size of economy ranking 91 in the world).
Economically active population. The total number of persons active in the economy is 1,700,000; unemployed: 11%.

Sector	% of workforce	% of GDP
industry	14	24
agriculture	50	24
services*	36	53

* services figure includes elements unassigned to other categories.

Energy and mineral resources

Oil and gas. Natural gas provides 25% of export income while crude oil production was around 992,070 tons/900,000 tonnes (1988).
Minerals. Mining (together with oil) employs less than 5% of the working population and contributes less than 7% of GDP but 95% of export earnings. Tin accounts for around half of all mineral production, other minerals being antimony; asbestos; bismuth salt; copper; lead; sulphur; wolfram; zinc. Gold and

silver are also mined and uranium deposits are beginning to be exploited.

Electricity. Capacity: 778,000 kW; production: 1,646 million kWh (1988) or 250 kWh per capita.

Bioresources

Agriculture. Some 50% of the working population is employed in the agricultural sector contributing about 24% of GDP, but only 2% of export earnings. Most important crops are coffee; soya beans; corn; sugar; rice; potatoes; timber; livestock. In addition Bolivia is a major coca producer for the international drug trade. The 'oriente' region east of the Andes is increasingly being developed.

Crop production: (1986 in 1,000 tons/tonnes) sugar cane 2,039/1,850; potatoes 768/697; maize 504/457; rice 147/137; wheat 89/81; coffee 21/19; cocoa 3.3/3; cotton 2.2/2. Coca is, however, easily the largest crop and production is believed to be worth around US$2,000 million annually.

Livestock numbers: (1987) sheep 9.5 million; poultry 8 million; cattle 5.38 million; goats 2.3 million; pigs 1.69 million; asses 600,000; horses 311,000.

Forestry. Tropical forests are beginning to be exploited.

Fisheries. Bolivia is a landlocked country although it shares with Peru control of Lake Titicaca.

Industry and commerce

Industry. Bolivia is the poorest country on the Latin American mainland and is heavily dependent on imports for many consumer goods. Apart from mining, smelting and petroleum, the main industries are foods and beverages; tobacco; handicrafts; clothing.

Commerce. Bolivia's exports totalled US$675 million, of which natural gas accounted for 43%, and metals for 29%. Other commodities (1988) were coffee; soya beans; sugar; cotton; timber. Imports were US$750 million, primarily food; petroleum; consumer goods; capital goods. Countries exported to were US 23%, and Argentina. Imports came from the US 15% (1988).

Trade with UK. Bolivia imported UK goods worth £6,029,000; exports to UK totalled £13,224,000 (1988).

Tourism. (1986) 133,000 visitors.

COMMUNICATIONS

Railways

There are 2,318 miles/3,733 km of railways.

Roads

There are 31,041 miles/49,987 km of roads, of which 6,710 miles/10,806 km are concrete or bituminized.

Aviation

Lloyd Aéreo Boliviano, SAM (LAB) provides domestic and international services (joint services with other national lines). International airports are at La Paz (El Alto) and Santa Cruz (Viru-Viru).

Shipping

Bolivia has a merchant marine with two ships of over 1,000 GRT, using maritime outlets in Chile and Peru.

Telecommunications

There are 144,300 telephones, the system being based on radio relay. There is a government television service and four privately owned television channels.

EDUCATION AND WELFARE

Education

There is compulsory free education for all children from six to 14 years of age.

Schools. There are 10,662 primary and elementary schools with over 1,100,000 pupils and over 50,000 teachers (one for every 22 pupils).

Universities. There are eight universities.

Literacy. 63%.

Health

There were 1,540 physicians in 1984 (1 per 4,350 people), and 2,480 nurses.

BOTSWANA

Republic of Botswana

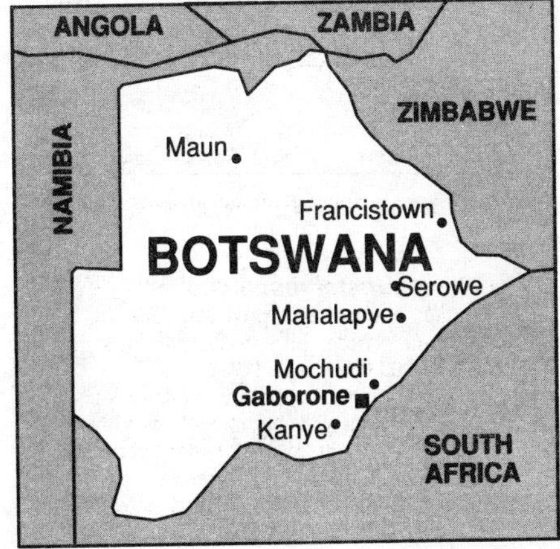

GEOGRAPHY

Botswana is a landlocked republic in southern Africa with a total area of 224,689 miles^2/582,096 km^2 divided into nine districts and six independent townships. The country's physiography is dominated by the Southern African Plateau running north-south (average height 3,281 ft/1,000 m), separating the comparatively fertile and populous eastern grasslands (veld) along the Limpopo river, from the Okavango Swamps, Kgalagadi and Kalahari desert regions in the west. About 80% of the total surface area is occupied by savannah or scrubland with actual forest confined to the banks of the Chobe River in the extreme north. Wholly barren desert conditions prevail only in the south-west.

Climate

Some latitudinal variation in climate with continental extremes, but predominantly sub-tropical with semi-arid and arid conditions in the south and south-west,

rainfall decreasing in these regions from 8 in/200 mm to 0.98 in/25 mm. Warm winter (Apr.-Sept.) days alternate with nights below 32°F/0°C, but summer (Oct.-Mar.) temperatures may reach 108°F/38°C. Mean annual rainfall is 18in/450 mm, rising in the north to 25 in/635 mm, most of which falls during the summer months.
Gaborone: Jan. 78°F/26.1°C. July 55°F/12.8°C. Average annual rainfall 21 in/538 mm.

Cities and towns

Gaborone (capital)	59,657
Francistown	31,065
Selebi-Phikwe	29,469
Serowe	23,661
Mahalapye	20,712
Molepolole	20,565
Kanye	20,215

Population

Total population is 1,198,000 of which 20.6% live in urban areas. Population density is 5.3/2.0 persons per miles^2/km^2, rising to 15 persons per km^2 in the south-east and dropping to 0.2 in the Kgalagadi south-west. The Tswana people constitute between 75 and 94% of the population, excluding the nomadic San or Bushmen of the Kalahari. The eight inter-related ethnic groups include the Batswana (of western Sotho extraction) and the Kwena and Ngwaketse, concentrated around Gabarone. The Kgatla, Malek and Tlokwa peoples inhabit the Namibian border. 2.5% of the population are Khoikhoin, 1.3% Ndebele and 1% European.
Birth rate 4.92%. **Death rate** 1.43%. **Rate of population increase** 3.49%. **Age distribution** under 15 = 48.3%; over 65 = 3.9%. **Life expectancy** female 62; male 56; average 59.

Religion

Small Muslim and Baha'i communities exist in Gabarone and Lobatse, and an estimated 30% of the population is Christian (chiefly protestant denominations) but the bulk of the population practises traditional animist faiths (over 50%).

Language

Two official languages: English and Setswana (Siswana, Tswana). 15,000 speak Ndebele, 29,000 Hottentot, 145,000 Shona and 41,000 a variety of San dialects.

HISTORY

The region of southern Africa now known as Botswana was first inhabited by hunter-gatherers known as the San. The Sotho-speaking Tswana people migrated into the area around 1600 and an early European expedition explored the region in 1801. Twelve years later a mission was established by the London Missionary Society. In 1867 gold was discovered near the Tati River, an attraction that made the Boers of neighbouring Transvaal try to annex the country. During the Conference of Berlin (1884–85), the British Bechuanaland Protectorate was established in the area. From 1900 it was administered by the High Commissioner for Basutoland, Bechuanaland and Swaziland. South Africa continued to seek annexation, but the British insisted that this should not take place without the consent of the people of Bechuanaland; after South Africa hardened its policy of apartheid in 1948 this became unthinkable.

Seretse Khama, deposed by the British as head of the main traditional Tswana ruling family and exiled for six years (1950–56) because of his marriage to a British woman, Ruth Williams, subsequently became the main figure in the transition to independent status. The first elections in the Protectorate were held in 1961, when executive and legislative councils were introduced to replace the traditional resident commission. In 1965 the Botswana Democratic Party (BDP), led by Seretse Khama, comprehensively defeated its more radical rivals and won 28 of the 31 seats in the country's first general election; in the following year Botswana was proclaimed independent (30 Sept. 1966) as a republic within the Commonwealth. Sir Seretse Khama died on 13 July 1980 and was succeeded by Vice-President Quett Masire. In Sept. 1984 the BDP won 28 of the 34 parliamentary seats, with the opposition Botswana National Front winning five. The BDP won 31 seats in October 1989 and the BNF 3.

Throughout the period since independence Botswana has attempted to maintain the delicate balance between economic dependence on South Africa, and good relations with the surrounding Black states. Sir Seretse Khama chaired the Lusaka summit meeting in Apr. 1980 at which the Southern African Development Co-ordination Conference (SADCC) was formed with the express intention of reducing southern Africa's economic dependence on South Africa. Gaborone, the Botswana capital, became the home of SADCC's permanent secretariat. Tension with South Africa has increased since 1984, with the latter alleging that Botswana was providing bases for African National Congress political and military activity. South African forces raided Gaborone in June 1985 and May 1986, killing 13 people.

CONSTITUTION AND GOVERNMENT

Executive and legislature

The executive president is elected by universal suffrage for a renewable five-year term, and appoints a vice-president from among the members of the National Assembly. The president presides over the Cabinet. Legislative elections are held every five years, most recently Oct. 1989. An advisory 15-member House of Chiefs considers draft legislation relating to alterations to the Constitution or to Chieftancy matters, and may make representation to the president on matters affecting the ethnic groups or their organizations.

Present government

President, C.-in-C. of the Armed Forces Dr Quett K.J. Masire
Vice President; Minister of Local Government and Lands Peter Mmusi
Principal members of Cabinet Dr Gaositwe K. T. Chiepe (Commerce and Industry); Ponatshego Kedikilwe (External Affairs); Patrick Balopi (Labour and Home Affairs).
Chairman of the House of Chiefs Chief Seepapitso.

Justice

The system of law is based on a combination of Roman-Dutch and customary local law. The highest court is the Botswana Court of Appeal, established in 1954, dealing with criminal and civil appeals from the High Court. The Court of Appeal has jurisdiction in all criminal and civil matters. The death penalty is in force. The number of executions between 1985 and mid-1988 is not known.

National symbols

Flag. Blue with a black horizontal stripe in the middle,

edged with two narrow white stripes.

Festivals. 15–16 July (President's Day); 30 Sept.-1 Oct. (Botswana Day).

Vehicle registration plate. RB.

INTERNATIONAL RELATIONS

Affiliations

NAM; OAU; ACP; Commonwealth; SADCC.

Defence

Total Armed Forces: 3,250. Terms of service: voluntary.

Army: 3,100.

Air Force: 150; five combat aircraft (BN-2 Defender).

ECONOMY

Currency

The unit is the pula, divided into 100 thebe.

National finance

Budget. The 1990 est. budget is for expenditure of US$1,080 million and revenue of US$1,235 million.

Balance of payments. The balance of payments (current account, 1987) was a surplus of US$458 million.

Inflation. 8.5%.

Gross Domestic Product

Estimated total GDP US$1,520 million, per capita US$1,310 (overall size of economy ranking 126 in the world).

Economically active population. The total number of persons active in the economy is 400,000; unemployed: 25%.

Sector	% of GDP
industry	57
agriculture	3
services*	40

* services figure includes elements unassigned to other categories.

Energy and mineral resources

Minerals. Diamonds are mined at Orapa and Jwaneng, and there is a nickel-copper complex at Selebi-Phikwe. There are salt and soda ash deposits at Sua Pan and an opencast coal mine at Morupule. There are also deposits of potash, iron ore, silver and natural gas. Output: (1987) diamonds 13,324,000 carats; copper-nickel 47,601 tons/43,238 tonnes; coal 638,683 tons/579,409 tonnes.

Electricity. Capacity 207,000 kW; production from coalfired power station at Morupule 631 million kWh (1988).

Bioresources

Agriculture. Botswana's economy has historically been based on cattle raising. Some 80% of the population are involved in agriculture and animal husbandry, but this provides only 50% of the country's food needs and contributes 5% of GDP. Only 2% of the land is ploughed, while pasture constitutes 75% of land use. Rainfall is erratic: successive droughts during the 1980s severely affected the livestock industry, while over-grazing and desertification have compounded the problems.

Crop production: (1987 in tons/tonnes) maize 2,204/2,000; sorghum 8,818/8,000; groundnuts 1,102/1,000; millet 1,102/1,000; wheat 1,102/1,000; roots and tubers 7,716/7,000; sunflower seeds 1,102/1,000; pulses 15,432/14,000; seed cotton 1,102/1,000; vegetables 17,636/16,000; fruit 12,125/11,000.

Livestock numbers: (1987) cattle 2.3 million; goats 1.05 million; sheep 215,000; poultry 1 million.

Wildlife. Some 17% of land area is given over to wildlife preservation, including national parks and game reserves, with controlled areas for photographic and game-viewing safaris and recreational and subsistence hunting.

Forestry. Commercial forestry is practised in the Kasana and Chobe forest reserves and in the Masame area.

Fisheries. Inland fishing in the Okavango and Kwando river systems. 80% of the land has no surface water.

Industry and commerce

Industry. The mining sector was the driving force behind the rapid economic growth of the 1970s and 1980s, with diamonds the principal factor. This sector generated over 50% of GDP in 1988. Unemployment, however, remains a problem. Considerable numbers of Batswana work in South Africa's mining industry.

Commerce. The value of exports reached US$1,300 million in 1988, of which diamonds composed 88%, copper and nickel 5%, meat 4%, and livestock and animal products the remainder. Imports reached $1,100 million (1988), comprising foodstuffs, vehicles, textiles and petroleum products. Principal trading partners were Switzerland, US, UK and EC-associated members of the Southern African Customs Union.

Trade with UK. Botswana exported goods worth £6,942,000 to the UK and imported goods worth £26,763,000 in 1988.

Tourism. There were 99,210 foreign visitors in 1986.

COMMUNICATIONS

Railways

There are about 484 miles/780 km of Botswanan railways. The main railway line from Mafikeng (South Africa) to Bulawayo (Zimbabwe), a distance of 596 miles/960 km, also passes through Botswana.

Roads

There are 8,384 miles/13,500 km of roads, of which about 994 miles/1,600 km are paved and 1,056 miles/1,700 km are gravel.

Aviation

Air Botswana (Pty) Ltd provides domestic and regional services to the neighbouring countries (main airport is Seretse Khama Airport at Gaborone).

Shipping

None.

Telecommunications

There are 17,900 telephones. Radio services are provided by Radio Botswana.

EDUCATION AND WELFARE

Education

The state system provides free primary and (since 1988) free secondary education. There is a National Literacy Programme and provision for vocational training and secondary-level correspondence courses.

School population. 239,324 pupils enrolled in primary schools, with 7,778 teachers (one per 31 pupils); 35,462 pupils in secondary schools with 1,607 teachers (one per 22 pupils); 1,332 students in teacher-training colleges with 78 teachers (one per 17 students) (1987).

There is a College of Education in Molepolole (497 students with 28 teachers in 1987).

University. The University of Botswana had 1,700 students in full-time attendance (1986–87).

Literacy. The literacy rate of those over 15 years of age is 63% (1987).

Health

Health facilities provided by central and local government are supplemented by the provisions made by medical missions, mining companies and voluntary organizations. There are 13 general hospitals, as well as health centres and local clinics. Mobile health teams also operate. There were 156 registered doctors in 1986.

BRAZIL

República Federativa do Brasil (Federative Republic of Brazil)

GEOGRAPHY

Situated in central and north-east South America, Brazil is the fifth largest country in the world and occupies a total area of 3,288,585 miles²/8,511,965 km² comprising 23 states, three territories and one federal territory (Brasília).

Two physiographic regions dominate the landscape, the Amazon Basin in the north and the Brazilian plateau in the centre (Planalto de Mato Grosso) and south. The immense highland plateau (mean elevation 1,968 ft/600 mm–2,953 ft/900 m) is bounded south by the Rio de la Plata basin, east by the thin but heavily populated coastal strip backed by the Serra do Mar and Serra do Espinhaco, and north by the Amazon basin. Most of the interior plateau (area 772,000 miles²/2 million km²) is covered by infertile savannah woodlands or 'campo cerrado', thinning northwards into semi-deciduous scrub and 'caatinga' in the north-east. The 'terra-rosa' soil in the south plateau sustains the bulk of Brazil's coffee plantations. The central highlands reach a maximum elevation of 9,482 ft/2,890 m at Pico de Bandeira in the state of Espírito Santo, although Brazil's highest peak is located in the Guiana Highlands in the north (Pico de Neblina 9,888 ft/3,014 m). The 2,231,080 miles²/5,780,000 km² Amazon River basin is the largest in the world, fed by 1,000 tributaries, and extending over 4,037 miles/6,500 km from the Peruvian Andes to the Atlantic Ocean. The majority of it is navigable and the surrounding area sparsely populated. Principal northern tributaries are the Rio Branco, Rio Negro and Japura; its southern tributaries are the Jurua, Purus, Madeira, Tapajos and Xingu systems. Beneath the dense tropical foliage (selva) of the forested basin, the condition of the heavily leached soils is extremely poor and subject to erosion where the canopy has been cleared. The Tocantin and Araguaia drain from Mato Grosso and Goias into the Gulf of Para. Other major river systems include the São Francisco (central), the Paraguay, the Uruguay and the Parana. Just over 7% of Brazil's land is arable and two-thirds is forested (one-seventh of total global forest area).

Climate

Largely tropical subject to variation according to altitude, distance from sea and prevailing winds. Amazonian conditions are consistently warm and humid with temperatures deviating very little from an average of 79°F/26°C. Rainfall averages between 79 in/2,000 and 118 in/3,000 mm in most areas of the Basin but can rise in places to 197 in/5,000 mm. The north-eastern São Francisco basin is significantly drier with frequent droughts and an average rainfall of only 24–26 in/600–650 mm annually. In the south and south-east, hot summers and warm springs contrast with cold, polar-influenced spells in winter.

Brasília: Jan. 72°F/22.2°C. July 64°F/17.8°C. Average annual rainfall 63 in/1,600 mm. Belém: Jan. 79°F/26°C. July 79°F/26°C. Average annual rainfall 96 in/2,438 mm. Rio de Janeiro: Jan. 78°F/25.6°C. July 69°F/20.6°C. Average annual rainfall 43 in/1,082 mm.

Cities and towns

Brasília (capital)	1,567,709
São Paulo	10,063,110
Rio de Janeiro	5,603,388
Belo Horizonte	2,114,429
Salvador	1,804,438
Fortaleza	1,582,414
Nova Iguaçu	1,319,491
Recife	1,287,623
Curitiba	1,279,205
Pôrto Alegre	1,272,121
Belém	1,116,578

Population

Total population is 144,427,000, of whom 75% live in urban areas; 30% live in the coastal strip. Population density 43.9/16.6 persons per miles^2/km^2. Indians are confined to the Amazon Basin; unassimilated or unmixed ethnic groups are now rare. The Indian population comprises 0.1% (240,000) of the total. Ethnic groups include Parakanãs; Txukurramae; Kreen-Akrore; Yanomani (decimated by diseases contracted through the building of the north perimeter highway); Gaviao; Arara; Nambiquara; Guayajarã; Satere Mave; Xavante; Yoruba. At the last census, 53.0% were White Brazilian (of whom 15.0% Portuguese, 11.0% Italian, 10% Spanish and 3.0% German); 22.0% were mulatto, 12.0% mestizo, 11.0% Black and 0.8% Japanese.

Birth rate: 2.8%. **Death rate** 0.8%. **Rate of population increase** 2.2%. **Age distribution** under 15 = 36.4%; over 65 = 4.3%. **Life expectancy** female 68; male 62; average 65.

Religion

Mainly Christianity; at the last census, 89% of the population were Roman Catholic; 6.6% Protestant; 2.0% Afro-American Spiritist; 1.7% Spiritist; 0.3% Buddhist; 0.2% Jewish. The Dahomeyan voodoo cult and various fetish societies remain active, together with a growing number of hybrid spiritist cults synthesized from Christian liturgy, Bantu (African) rhythms and Indian dance.

Language

The official language is Portuguese (138 million speakers). Over 120 Amerindian languages exist, spoken by 240,000 Indians. 780,000 speak German; 590,000 Italian.

HISTORY

The indigenous coastal-dwelling Tupinambá Indians initially welcomed the presence of the Portuguese, dating from the arrival of Pedro Alvares Cabral in 1500. Portugal, who named the country Brazil after the much sought-after red dyewood 'pau-brasil', established its colonial frontiers with those of Spain under the Papal Treaty of Tordesillas of 1494. In 1532 Martim Affonso de Sousa founded the settlement of São Vicente (near present-day Santos) and in 1533 the Portuguese crown divided the territory into 12 captaincies in the hope of consolidating its control (threatened by growing British, French and Spanish interest) and generating much-needed revenue. Few captaincies achieved either, and all were finally united under a captain general, Tomé de Sousa, in 1549. By 1580, Brazil was established and prosperous, drawing its principal wealth from north-eastern sugar cane plantations worked by Black African slave labour. Throughout the colonial period, whenever slaves were in short supply (due to Dutch and other pirates) southern-based Brazilian slave-hunters (the 'bandeirantes') supplied Indian replacements from unexplored interior regions, thereby extending the country's frontiers. Indian resistance was persistent but fatally handicapped by inter-tribal warfare which, along with their lack of immunity to European diseases, facilitated their defeat.

Periods of foreign rule and intervention, first the Spanish rule (1580–1640) following the annexation of Portugal's throne by Philip II of Spain in 1580, and then the Dutch occupation of the richest northern sugar-growing regions (1637–54), nurtured early movements for complete Brazilian independence. These gained momentum during the era of viceregal rule (1763–1822) when the Portuguese prime minister, the Marquis de Pombal, instituted colonial reforms to extract the maximum wealth from the colony. Four Republican conspiracies, supported by members of the colonial elite, were put down between 1788 and 1801 but it was the French invasion of Portugal in 1807 which effectively cut the tie with the Iberian peninsula. The exodus of the Portuguese court to Brazil (1807–21) created the conditions for King John VI's son, Dom Pedro, to declare himself emperor and effect a peaceful transition to Brazilian independence on 7 Sept. 1822. However, sustained resentment by the mazombos (White Americans) of the concentration of monarchical power, intensified by a costly and fruitless war with Argentina (1825–8), led to Dom Pedro's abdication in 1831. Liberal monarchists then presided over an unruly regency period (marked by the secession of the southern state of Rio Grande) until the 14-year-old Dom Pedro II became emperor in July 1840. The power of the monarchy was reaffirmed via the agency of a Conservative government and the rebels of Rio Grande were forced to negotiate peace in Feb. 1845. Decades of stability, founded on the prosperity created by international demand for Brazilian coffee, saw domestic infrastructural development and foreign success, shared with Uruguay and Argentina, in the War of the Triple Alliance (1865–70) against Paraguay. The issue of slavery, which had raised attacks on the monarchy (from Liberal leaders, intellectuals and urban middle-class groups demanding emancipation, and from plantation slave-owners demanding the opposite) gradually tipped in favour of abolition. This was made law 13 May 1888, with the support of the southern coffee interests, increasingly benefiting from European immigrant labour. In response to this perceived betrayal, the former slave-owners (especially in the declining sugar areas) joined the Republican opposition to Dom Pedro, who was overthrown in the bloodless coup of 15 Nov. 1888 and the Republic of Brazil was proclaimed.

During the first Republic (1889–1930) the federalists held sway, headed by southern coffee interests, and the 1891 constitution recognized the property rights of the landed elites and provided for their semi-feudal domination of the 20 self-governing states with complete jurisdiction over their internal affairs, while the central government had prime responsibility for national security, tariffs and the collection of import duties, cementing the massive gulf between the cities and the sertão (the interior). After 1906 the coffee states of São Paulo and Minas Gerais alternated the presidency between them; but their monopoly of power and wealth, while the weaker provinces endured endemic violence (which was spreading to the cities), stored up tensions among those denied access to one or both. The decline of coffee exports in World War I and the virtual cessation of imports, were strong stimuli to post-war urbanization and domestic industrialization. Along with this, the 1920s saw the growth of a broad movement (encompassing intellectuals, lawyers, young army officers and a nascent working class composed of European immigrants with socialist and syndicalist traditions) hostile to the rule of the corrupt rural oligarchies and demanding the regeneration and modernization of the society. Although the military revolt of young officers (tenentes) in Rio de Janeiro in July 1922 was put down, with the coffee rulers' chosen president, Artur da Silva Bernardes (1922–26) coming to power, it initiated a period of struggle for economic and social reform which, against the backcloth of the world economic crisis brought Getúlio Vargas to power, in the coup of Oct. 1930.

Vargas began with a progressive programme promoting industrialization (production doubling between 1931 and 1934), increased political participation (the July 1934 constitution extending the vote to 18-year-olds and women, but not to illiterates) and centralized authority. However, his attempt to balance ultimately irreconcilable interest groups led to his increasing political opportunism, paternalism and, finally, authoritarianism. To please the landowners, he ignored agrarian reform and artificially supported coffee prices while undermining their state autonomy; to satisfy labour he established a labour code and social legislation but unions were controlled by the Ministry of Labour and strikes brutally repressed; to please the right-wing military, the National Security Law of Mar. 1935 allowed them to suppress 'subversion', effectively depriving the left of legal of political expression (the broad popular front, the National Liberation Alliance, was banned). The latter's abortive uprising in Nov. 1935 paved the way for the ending of democracy with the establishment, on 2 Dec. 1937 of the Fascist-modelled New State (Estado Nôvo, 1937–45), with Vargas as dictator. Despite economic co-operation with Italy and Germany, Vargas's main aims remained that of economic independence and modernization, and to achieve it he used any foreign assistance available, including that of the United States. He founded national iron and steel companies and joined the allied war effort, promising a post-war era of liberty. During a period of military rule (1945–51) the rural landowners regained much of their influence, but Vargas returned to power in 1951 as the candidate of the Brazilian Labour Party (PTB), which led a broad coalition of workers, industrialists and the urban middle class. Nevertheless, his plan for further state-led industrialization (in oil and electricity) met with stiff opposition from the conservative congress (and the US government), and his labour policy, which although still paternalistic, included the doubling of the minimum wage in 1954, caused the right, backed by the military, to demand his resignation. Vargas committed suicide in Aug. 1954. The PTB-backed presidency of Juscelino Kubitschek (1956–60) offered generous incentives to attract massive foreign investment (particularly from the US) to develop modern, fast-growing sectors (chemical; metallurgy; electrical; communication; cars) at the expense of traditional ones. A new capital, Brasília (inaugurated 21 Apr. 1961), in the state of Goias, was built in three years as a symbol of a new age of national integration and growth. The cost of this development was met by foreign loans which crippled the economy. Ironically the conservative president, Jânio da Silva Quadros (1960–61), sought to break the grip of dependence on the US by diversifying trade links and by pursuing an independent policy on Cuba. This incensed the right and the powers of his successor Pres. João Goulart (1961–64) were initially curtailed by the conservative congress, until a plebiscite of Jan. 1963 restored full presidential authority. Goulart was ousted by a military coup (with full US government co-operation) on 1 Apr. 1964, when his plan for radical structural reforms raised popular expectations (in the interior and cities) so much that the bourgeoisie and urban middle classes joined the landed oligarchy in opposing him. The military, under Gen. Castello Branco (1964–67), Marshal Artur da Costa e Silva (1967–69), Gen. Emílio Garrastazú (1969–74), and Gen. Ernesto Geisel (1974–78), banned political and trade union activity (imprisoning and torturing thousands) and eliminated urban guerrilla groups, while opening up the economy to foreign investment as never before (but keeping control of the state sector to ensure cheap steel, power and raw materials to profitable foreign-owned companies). They maintained a democratic façade by establishing two 'official' parties, the National Renovating Alliance (ARENA) and an 'opposition' Brazilian Democratic Movement (PMDB). In the 1970s, however, the economic miracle began to fade as the 1973 oil crisis highlighted the country's dependence on imported oil, and as the huge foreign loans rose to become the world's largest foreign debt. The combined effect of the severe economic recession, and economic austerity measures which caused unprecedented social unrest, persuaded Gen. João Figueiredo (1979–85) to give ground to the opposition by allowing more than two parties to contest the Nov. 1982 elections, and the direct election of state governors. The opposition parties gained a majority in the Chamber of Deputies and a number of important governorships, and the 1985 indirect presidential election was won by the PMDB candidate, Tancredo Neves. On Neves' sudden death, José Sarney was sworn into office and his government promulgated a constitution in Oct. 1988 which prepared the way for a return to full democracy in 1990, but failed to cope with serious internal social and economic problems resulting firstly from an inability to service the massive foreign debt and secondly from the remaining gross inequality in rural land ownership. Fernando Collor, the candidate of the conservative National Reconstruction Party (PRN – formed in May 1989 to promote his candidacy) defeated Luiz Inacio da Silva, popularly known as 'Lula', the leader of the socialist Workers Party (PT – formed in 1980). Collor promised to renegotiate the US$110,000 million foreign debt, root out government corruption, privatise state companies and open up the highly protected domestic market to foreign competition. Collor was inaugurated on March 15 1990.

CONSTITUTION AND GOVERNMENT

Executive and legislature

Executive power is exercised by the president, elected directly by universal suffrage, who appoints and leads the Cabinet. The president's term of office, under the 1988 Constitution, is five years. There is a bicameral National Congress. The Chamber of Deputies, of variable size, is directly elected every four years, by universal and compulsory adult suffrage. The members of the 69-seat Federal Senate serve an eight-year term; two-thirds of them are elected at one time, and the other third four years later.

Present government

President. Fernando Collor de Mello
Vice-President Itamar Franco
Principal members of the Cabinet Bernardo Cabral (Justice); Francisco Rezek (External Relations); Zélia Cardoso de Mello (Economy); Ozires Silva (Infrastructure); Antonio Rogério Magri (Labour)

Administration

The federation comprises 23 States (each of which has a directly elected governor and legislature), three Territories and a Federal District (Brasília).

Justice

The system of law is based on Spanish and Portuguese codes. The highest courts at federal level, located in Brasilia, are the 11-member Supreme Federal Court of Justice (made up of 11 judges) and the 13-member Federal Court of Appeal, to which judges are appointed, for life, by the President subject to Senate approval. Under the dual system of federal and state law, each state has in effect its own judicial system and legal framework. The death penalty is in force only for exceptional crimes. No executions were carried out between 1985 and mid-1988.

National symbols

Flag. A green field bears a yellow diamond charged with a blue disc, crossed by a white band with the motto 'Ordem e Progresso'.

Festivals. 1 May (Labour Day); 7 Sept. (Independence Day); 12 Oct. (Our Lady Aparecida patroness of Brazil); 15 Nov. (Proclamation of the Republic).

Vehicle registration plate. BR.

INTERNATIONAL RELATIONS

Affiliations

OAS; SELA.

Defence

Total Armed Forces: 319,200 (145,200 conscripts). Terms of service: 12 months (can be extended by months). Reserves: Trained first line 1,115,000; 400,000 subject to immediate recall. Second-line (limited training) 225,000.

Army: 218,000 (to be 296,000); some 560 light tanks (mainly M-3 and M-41C).

Navy: 50,500; seven submarines: one Tupi (FRG T-209/1400), three Humaita (UK Oberon) and three Goias Bahia (US Gruppy III/II); 17 principal surface combatants: one carrier (UK Colossus), ten destroyers (US Gearing, Sumner and Fletcher); six frigates; 24 patrol and coastal combatants.

Naval Air Force: 700; 18 armed helicopters (mainly SH-3D and ASH-3H).

Air Force: 50,700; 215 combat aircraft (chiefly F-103E and F-103D) and some armed helicopters.

ECONOMY

Currency

The unit is the cruzado, divided into 100 centavos.

National finance

Budget. The 1986 budget was for expenditure of US$40,100 million and revenue of US$27,800 million.

Balance of payments. The balance of payments (current account, 1987) was a deficit of US$1,275 million.

Inflation. 900%.

Gross Domestic Product

Estimated total GDP US$299,230 million, per capita US$2,130 (overall size of economy ranking nine in the world).

Economically active population. The total number of persons active in the economy is 57,000,000; unemployed: 6%.

Sector	% of workforce	% of GDP
industry	25	38
agriculture	35	11
services*	40	51

* services figure includes elements unassigned to other categories.

Energy and mineral resources

Minerals. Brazil is the only source of high-grade quartz crystal in commercial quantities (1985 output 124,870 tons/113,282 tonnes raw and 9,336 tons/8,470 tonnes processed) and the largest western producer of chrome ore (reserves of 10.5 million tons/9.3 million tonnes and 1985 output of 801,292 tons/727,125 tonnes). Output of other minerals (in 1,000 tons/tonnes) was manganese ore 3,876/3,516; bauxite 1,098/9,963; tungsten ore 526/477; lead 348/316; asbestos 2,486/2,254; coal 23,553/21,367; tin ore 50/45; iron ore 185,318/168,120; gold 33/30 (processed); silver 42/38; zirconium 24/22; graphite 212/192; titanium ore 2,862/2,596 (1985).

Oil and gas. Crude oil production amounted to 29.6 million tons/26.8 million tonnes in 1988 and natural gas production was 200,795 ft^3/5,686 m^3 in 1986.

Electricity. Production 212 million MWh (1986), 193 million MWh of it hydro-electric. Brazil's potential capacity for hydoelectric power production was estimated at 106,500 MW in 1984, one of the largest in the world. One-third of this capacity comes from the Amazon basin.

Bioresources

Agriculture. 8.9% of the total land area is under cultivation (1984), 61% of the 5.16 million farms being family-operated. Coffee, cocoa and cotton are the principal agricultural commodities.

Crop production: (1986 in 1,000 tons/tonnes) coffee 2,212/2,007; cocoa 507/460; raw cotton 2,551/2,315; natural rubber 49/44; maize 22,612/20,541; sugar cane 262,890/238,493; soya beans 14,698/13,334; wheat 6,215/5,638.

Livestock numbers: (1987) cattle 132 million; pigs 32 million; sheep 19 million; goats 9.8 million.

Forestry. Timber production: (1984) 7,840 million ft^3/222 million m^3.

Fisheries. Total fish catch: (1984) 1,057,105 tons/959,000 tonnes (1984).

Industry and commerce

Industry. Iron and steel production, based substantially at Volta Redonda, produces 22.4 million tons/20.3 million tonnes of pig-iron and 23.4 million tons/21.2 million tonnes of crude steel (1986). The cement, paper, automobile and rubber tyre industries are also important.

Commerce. Brazil's exports totalled US$26,200 million; imports totalled US$16,600 million (1987). Exports in 1985 included coffee (green) US$2,369 million; soya bean bran US$1,175 million; iron ore US$1,101 million; soya beans US$763 million; cocoa beans US$361 million. Imports in 1986 were mainly of mineral and chemical products; crude oil; machinery; mechanical appliances; electrical equipment.

Trade with UK. Brazil imported UK goods worth £305 million and exported to the UK goods worth £742 million (1988).

Tourism. 1,717,659 tourists visited Brazil in 1986.

COMMUNICATIONS

Railways

There are 18,569 miles/29,901 km of railways, of which 1,300 miles/2,094 km are electrified.

Roads

There are 1,040,120 miles/1,675,040 km of roads, of which 83,216 miles/134,003 km are concrete or bituminized.

Aviation

Servicos Aéreos Cruzeiro do Sul, SA and Viação Aérea Rio Grande do Sul (VARIG) provide international services; Trans Brasil SA Linhas Aéreas and Viação Aérea São Paulo, (VASP) provide domestic services (there are 21 international airports, of which the most important are at Rio de Janeiro and two at São Paulo).

Shipping

Major ports are Belém; Fortaleza; Ilheus; Manaus; Paranagua; Pôrto Alegre; Recife; Rio de Janeiro; Rio Grande; Salvador; Santos. The merchant marine totals nearly 6 million GRT, with 289 ships of over 1,000 GRT.

Telecommunications

The telephone system is based on extensive radio relays. There are 9,860,000 telephones. Brazil has some 67 million radios and 26 million television sets, with thousands of radio stations and hundreds of television channels, most of them operating in their own local areas.

EDUCATION AND WELFARE

Education

There is compulsory elementary education to the age of 15.

School population. 24,769,736 under 15 (primary); 3,016,138 in secondary education (1985).

Schools. 187,274 primary schools with 1,040,566 teachers (one per 24 pupils); 9,260 secondary schools with 206,111 teachers (one per 29 pupils).

Universities. There are 35 federal (state) universities, the largest being that of São Paolo (44,000 students), as well as 20 private universities.

Literacy. 80% of population aged 15 or over.

Health

Total number of hospitals and clinics (1984): 27,552; total number of beds: 538,721, of which 411,184 in private institutions. There were 97,100 doctors in 1980 (one per 1,500 inhabitants).

BRITISH ANTARCTIC TERRITORY

GEOGRAPHY

The territory lies south of 60° S, stretching to the South Pole, in a segment bounded by longitudes 20° W and 80° W, with an area of about 659,828 miles^2/1,709,400 km^2. The main islands are South Orkney and South Shetland; in addition the territory includes Palmer Land and Graham Land on the Antarctic Peninsula, the Filcher and Ronne ice shelves and Coats Land.

Climate

Warmest temperatures may rise slightly above freezing in Jan. The terrain is for the most part covered with ice, although there are some ice-free coastal areas.

Population

There is no resident permanent population; the total number of personnel at research stations is generally around 300.

HISTORY

The islands and section of mainland Antarctica between 80°W and 20°W that comprise the British Antarctic Territory were uninhabited before their discovery. They were then only used as temporary bases for whalers and seal-hunters and it was not until the early 20th century that a permanent settlement was established on the South Shetland Islands, to be followed by scientific bases during the 1940s.

The South Shetland Islands were discovered by the British in 1819 and the South Orkney Islands in 1821. The coastline of Antarctica was explored in 1820 and claimed for Britain in 1832. In 1908 the territories were grouped together to be administered as the Falkland Islands and were separated from the others and the British Antarctic Territory formed.

Both Argentina and Chile have territorial claims to parts of the British Antarctic Territory. Britain established a permanent base on Deception Island in 1944 after evidence of Argentinian visits to the island. In 1952 there were clashes between British and Argentinians and in 1982 Argentinians occupied the South Shetland Islands until they were expelled by the British troops during the Falklands conflict. Argentina and Chile both maintain scientific bases in the area.

CONSTITUTION AND GOVERNMENT

Administered by a British high commissioner based on the Falkland Islands. The territory as claimed by Britain almost coincides with the Argentine claim and overlaps substantially (as to its western part) with the Chilean claim, while Brazil has also declared a zone of interest within it. Of the other 15 signatories to the Antarctic Treaty with consultative status, Australia, France, New Zealand and Norway have also made their own claims, while the other 11 (including the US and USSR) recognize none of the claims.

BRITISH INDIAN OCEAN TERRITORY

GEOGRAPHY

The British Indian Ocean Territory, a dependent territory of the United Kingdom, is an archipelago of 2,300 islands, with a total land area of 23.2 miles²/60 km². The terrain is flat and low. The largest and southernmost island is Diego Garcia, which is claimed by Mauritius. There is no capital.

Climate

Tropical marine; hot, humid, trade winds.

Population

There is no permanent civilian population. The former population was evacuated before the UK and US started defence constructions.

HISTORY

The British Indian Ocean Territory was formed in 1965 by grouping together the Chagos, Aldabra, Desroches and Farquhar Islands. The Chagos Islands were uninhabited until their discovery by the Portuguese in the 16th century. They were claimed by France in the early 18th century and settled by planters and their African slaves in the latter part of the century. The islands were administered as a dependency of Mauritius and passed into British control in 1814 when Mauritius and the Seychelles were ceded to Britain. In 1903 the Aldabra, Desroches and Farquhar Islands were included with the Seychelles when the latter was made a separate colony.

When the British Indian Ocean Territory was formed it was intended that the Chagos Islands would be developed by Britain and the United States as a joint military base. The islands were bought by the Crown in 1967 and between 1967 and 1973 the population of 1,200 working on the copra plantations was resettled in Mauritius or the Seychelles. Construction of a naval and air base was started on the atoll of Diego Garcia. On the independence of the Seychelles in 1976 the Aldabra, Desroches and Farquhar Islands were returned to the Seychelles government. Both the governments of Mauritius and the Seychelles have protested at the growing military use of Diego Garcia by the US, and Mauritius has made claims, supported by the Organization for African Unity, for the return of the Chagos Archipelago.

CONSTITUTION AND GOVERNMENT

The Territory has a commissioner, R. Edis, who is resident in the UK.
Administrator R. Crompton (since 1988).

National symbols

Flag. The UK flag is used.

ECONOMY

All economic activity is concentrated on Diego Garcia, the largest island, where joint UK-US defence facilities are located. Construction projects and various services needed to support the military installations are provided by military and contract employees from the UK and US. There is no industry or agriculture.

COMMUNICATIONS

There is a port in Diego Garcia, which also has a permanent surface runway. There is a short stretch of paved road between this port and the airfield. There is one AM, one FM and one TV station operated by the US navy.

BRUNEI

Negara Brunei Darussalam (Islamic Sultanate of Brunei)

GEOGRAPHY

Located on the north-western coast of the island of Borneo (Kalimantan), Brunei has a total area of 2,225 miles²/5,765 km² divided into four districts, the most populous of which is Brunei/Muara in the west with 114,310 inhabitants. The swampy coastal strip in the north-west is backed by foothills that rise to form a mountainous tract (average height 1,640 ft/500 m) on the Sarawak border. 75% of Brunei is covered by rainforest: the principal rivers (the Belait, Tutong and Brunei) flow northwards through the western enclave to the sea. Most agricultural activity is centred on the cleared portion of the alluvial coastal plain.

Climate

Tropical marine, high temperatures, annual humidity range of between 67 and 91%. Abundant rainfall from 100 in/2,540 mm on the coast to 200 in/5,080 mm inland. No dry season.

Bandar Seri Begawan: Jan. 80°F/26.7°C. July 82°F/27.8°C. Average annual rainfall 129 in/3,275 mm.

Cities and towns

Bandar Seri Begawan (capital) 50,500.

Population

Total population is 249,000 of which 59.4% live in urban areas. Population density is 112/41.8 persons per miles²/km². Ethnic composition: 64.6% Malay; 20% Chinese; 8.3% indigenous tribes (inhabiting the tropical interior).

Birth rate 2.98%. **Death rate** 0.35%. **Rate of population increase** 2.63%. **Age distribution** under

15 = 37.2%; over 65 = 3.0%. **Life expectancy** female 72.7; male 70.1; average 71.

Language

English and Malay are official languages. In practice, 156,000 speak Malay, 48,000 Chinese and 37,000 local dialects.

Religion

The official Islamic religion (predominantly Sunni) is practised by 63.4% of the population. 14.0% are Buddhist, 9.7% Christian (Anglican Protestant and Roman Catholic). Traditional beliefs survive in the interior.

HISTORY

Little is known of Brunei's early history but records show trade with China in the 6th century AD and evidence suggests that the country was controlled by the Hindu Javanese empire of Majapahit in the mid-14th century. By the early 16th century, due in part to its success as a port, Brunei had extended its influence over much of Borneo. The thrust of European, and particularly British, influence within South-East Asia in the 17th and 18th centuries saw a marked decline in the power and the territory of Brunei, a process which was hastened in the 19th century.

Between 1841, when Sarawak was ceded to the British adventurer James Brooke, and the mid-1880s, Brunei witnessed the gradual erosion of its territories and influence, a process which culminated in 1888 with the sultanate itself becoming a British protectorate. In 1906, a British Resident was appointed to the court to 'advise' the Sultan on all administrative matters except religion and culture.

Following Japanese occupation from 1941 to 1945, Brunei reverted to its former status as a British residency. In 1959, Brunei was provided with its first written constitution and in 1962 a partly elected Legislative Council was founded. A large-scale revolt broke out in early Dec. 1962 by elements strongly opposed to British plans to merge Brunei, Sabah, Sarawak, Malaya and Singapore into a Malaysian Federation. In late December, after the revolt had been quelled, the Sultan suspended the 1959 Constitution, dissolved the Legislative Council and announced his intention to rule by decree. In 1971 a new UK–Brunei treaty was signed under which Britain retained control of Brunei's external affairs only. A separate agreement provided for the stationing of a battalion of British Army Gurkhas in Brunei.

In the 1970s, Brunei concentrated on the economic development of its large natural gas and oil fields, a proportion of the revenue being channelled into free education and health care for its nationals. Despite the general absence of political discontent from within the country, Sultan Hassanal Bolkiah objected to the withdrawal of British troops when the idea was mooted by London in 1976, expressing concern over Malaysian and Indonesian territorial ambitions. Assurances were received from the two countries that Brunei's sovereignty would be respected, and on 1 Jan. 1984 Brunei achieved full independence from Britain, underscoring its new relationship with its neighbours by joining ASEAN in the same month. Brunei hosted the ASEAN annual ministerial meeting in July 1989.

CONSTITUTION AND GOVERNMENT

Executive and legislature

The Sultan has supreme executive authority, presiding over an advisory Council of cabinet ministers, a Religious Council and a Privy Council. The Sultan has ruled by decree and a state of emergency has been in force since Dec. 1962.

Present government

Sultan; Prime Minister; Minister of Defence Sir Hassanal Bolkiah

Principal members of Council of Cabinet Ministers *Penigran Dato* Dr *Haji* Ismail (Development); Prince Jefri Bolkiah (Finance); Prince Mohammed Bolkiah (Foreign Affairs), *Pehin Dato Hahi* Isa (Internal Affairs and Special Adviser in Prime Minister's Office); *Pehin Dato* Dr *Haji* Mohammed Zain (Religious Affairs).

Justice

The system of law is based on Islamic law, administered by Sharia Courts. In both criminal and civil cases, appeal may be made from subordinate courts to the High Court and Court of Appeal (which, together with the magistrates' courts, comprise the Supreme Court). Ultimately, final appeal is to the Judicial Committee of the Privy Council in London. The death penalty is nominally in force. No executions were carried out between 1985 and mid-1988.

National symbols

Flag. Yellow with a diagonal stripe, divided white over black. The red coat of arms of Brunei consisting of two free-standing upraised human arms with a crescent placed between them, is placed in the middle of the flag.

Festivals. 23 Feb. (National Day); May/June (Anniversary of the Royal Brunei Malay Regiment); 15 July (Sultan's birthday).

Vehicle registration plate. BRU.

INTERNATIONAL RELATIONS

Affiliations

ICO; ASEAN; Commonwealth; SAARC.

Defence

Total Armed Forces: 4,000 including 250 women. Terms of service: voluntary.
Army: 3,200; 16 light tanks (Scorpion).
Navy: 500; six patrol and coastal combatants.
Air Force: 300; six armed helicopters.

ECONOMY

Currency

The unit is the Bruneian dollar, divided into 100 cents.

National finance

Budget. The 1987 budget was for expenditure of US$1,100 million and revenue of US$1,200 million.

Balance of payments. The balance of payments (current account, 1987) was a surplus of US$2,608 million.

Inflation. 3%.

Gross Domestic Product

Estimated total GDP US$3,100 million, per capita US$13,663 (overall size of economy ranking 102 in the world).

Economically active population. The total number

of persons active in the economy is 68,000; unemployed = 3.4%.

Sector	% of workforce
industry	50
agriculture	2
services*	48

* services figure includes elements unassigned to other categories

Energy and mineral resources

Oil and gas. There are six offshore oil and gas fields (Champion; Magpie; South West Ampa; Fairley; Fairley-Baram; Gannet) and two onshore fields (Seria and Rasau). Production is carried out by Brunei Shell Petroleum in which the government has a 50% stake. Approximately 8.3 million tons/7.5 million tonnes of oil was produced in 1988. The crude oil is exported directly to Brunei's ASEAN partners, Japan, South Korea, Taiwan and the US.

Liquefied natural gas (LNG) is produced at one of the world's biggest plants at Lumut. The LNG is sold in quantities of 5.5 million tons/5 million tonnes a year to Japan to the Tokyo Electric Power Company, the Tokyo Gas Company and the Osaka Gas Company.

Electricity. Production: (1986) 470 million kWh.

Bioresources

Agriculture. Agriculture accounts for only 1% of Brunei's GDP and 80% of food is imported. Only 15% of the country is cultivated and the small farms that do exist grow mainly rice and vegetables. During the 1980s the development of agriculture became a government priority, with the ultimate aim of achieving self-sufficiency in food production.

Crop production: (1986 in tons/tonnes) bananas 1,102/1,000; other fruit 6,614/6,000; rice 3,307/3,000; roots and tubers 1,102/1,000; cassava 1,102/1,000.

Livestock numbers: (1987) chickens 2 million, pigs 14,000, buffaloes 10,000, cattle 3,000.

Forestry. Over two-thirds of Brunei is tropical forest. The government Forestry Department controls all forest reserves and activities and has recently started to encourage the timber industry to expand into higher-value activities, such as furniture production. Annual timber production averages 10,594,200 ft^3/ 300,000 m^3.

Industry and commerce

Industry. Brunei's economy is dominated by the oil and liquefied natural gas (LNG) industries. The commercial production of oil from onshore deposits at Seria began in the 1920s. Offshore oil production began in 1963 and now accounts for the vast majority of Brunei's exports. In 1972, what was then the world's largest LNG plant came on stream at Lumut. Sales of 5 million tonnes a year of LNG are sent to Japan under a 20-year contract due to expire in 1993. The petroleum sector has been adversely affected by depressed prices in the world oil market in the 1980s. Output reached a peak of about 260,000 barrels per day (bpd) in 1979, but production has steadily decreased since then. The government's fifth National Development plan (1986–90) aims to reduce Brunei's economic dependence on petroleum and natural gas by encouraging new private sector industries.

Commerce. Brunei's exports totalled US$1,995 million (1986). Crude oil accounted for 56% of the total value of the exports, liquid natural gas 40% and petroleum products 3%. Japan took almost 70% of all exports; other recipients included Thailand, South Korea, Singapore and the US. Brunei's imports totalled US$725 million (1986). The imports were mainly machinery and transport items, manufactured goods, food and chemicals from, principally, Singapore, Japan, the US and the UK.

Trade with UK. Brunei imported UK goods worth £142,461,000: exports to UK totalled £171,556,000 (1988).

Tourism. There were 500,000 visitors to Brunei in 1987.

COMMUNICATIONS

Railways

There are no public railways in Brunei.

Roads

There are about 900 miles/1,450 km of roads.

Aviation

Royal Brunei Airlines Ltd provides international services (an international airport is at Bandar Seri Begawan).

Shipping

Kuala Beleit and Muara are the main ports. The merchant marine includes seven liquefied gas carriers of over 1,000 GRT.

Telecommunications

There are 33,000 telephones, 74,000 radio receivers and 31,000 television sets, with services provided by the government Department of Radio and Television.

EDUCATION AND WELFARE

Education

Primary and secondary education is provided free by the state, although private, non-government schools exist. Children start school at the age of five and education is available for nine years (six years for primary and three for lower secondary).

School population. 42,100 primary school pupils and 22,600 secondary school pupils (1986 est.).

Schools. There are 177 primary schools and 29 secondary schools (1987).

Universities. The University of Brunei Darussalam opened in 1985. In 1988, over 900 students were studying in the university's four faculties.

Literacy. 45%.

Health

The health service is free for Brunei citizens. The service is based upon a three-tier system, with health clinics providing primary care, health centres providing secondary care and district hospitals, the tertiary and specialized care. There are four hospitals, the largest of which is the 550-bed central referral hospital in Bandar Seri Begawan.

BULGARIA

Narodna Republika Bulgaria
(People's Republic of Bulgaria)

GEOGRAPHY

Situated in south-eastern Europe, Bulgaria covers an area of 42,812 miles²/110,912 km² divided into 28 provinces (okruzi). The fertile, undulating Bulgarian lowlands (Danube plain) extend south from the Romanian frontier (marked by the Danube) across one-third of Bulgaria's total surface area. The principal Bulgarian tributaries of the Danube, the Iskur and Yantra rivers, drain northwards over this terrain from the Balkan Mountains (Stara Planina) which cross central Bulgaria west-east at an average height of 2,296 ft/700 m (highest point Botev, 7,795 ft/2,376 m). South of the Stara Planina, the Rhodope massif divides Bulgaria from Greece, rising to a maximum height of 9,596 ft/2,925 m at Musala Peak. The southern and south-western regions are drained by the Struma, Mesta, Tundzha, Maritsa and Arda rivers. Areas of high population density include the Danubian Plain, the Upper Thracian Basin and the expanding urban centres of Sofia (capital), Varna and Ruse. 35% of the territory is arable land and 35% forest and woodland.

Climate

In the south, a mediterranean climate prevails with hot, dry summers and mild winters. A transitional climatic belt extends from the central uplands to the Black Sea coast, becoming more continental further north with colder winters, lowering the average winter temperature to 30°F/-1°C. Rainfall averages between 21 in/525 mm and 28 in/700 mm, reaching 47 in/1,200 mm annually in highland areas. Sofia: Jan. 28°F/ -2.2°C. July 69°F/20.6°C. Average annual rainfall 25 in/635 mm.

Cities and towns

Sofia (capital)	1,114,759
Plovdiv	332,131
Varna	302,211
Ruse	183,746
Burgas	182,549
Stara Zagora	150,803

Population

The total population is 8,995,000, of which 64.8% live in urban areas. Population density is 210/81 persons per miles²/km². Over 85% of the population are Bulgarian, and there are significant minorities of Turks (over 800,000 or 8.5%) concentrated in the north-east and the eastern Rhodope Mountains, Gypsies (2.6%) and Macedonians (2.5%). There are also smaller communities of Armenians, Romanians, Greeks, Russians and Tatars. Since the end of World War II, internal rural-urban migration has doubled the population of the capital while Varna (Black Sea coast) and Ruse (north) have trebled in size.
Birth rate 1.21%. **Death rate** 1.14%. **Rate of population increase** 0.07%. **Age distribution** under 15 = 21.3%; over 65 = 11.3%. **Life expectancy** female 74.7; male 68.6; average 72.

Religion

No official religion exists. Despite atheistic dissuasions under the Communist regime, 80–85% of the religiously affiliated population are Eastern (Bulgarian) Orthodox and Armenian Apostolic. An estimated 60,000 Roman Catholics and 10,000 Pentecostal Protestants comprise the two next largest Christian minorities. Approximately 13% are Muslim and 0.8% are Jewish.

Language

Bulgarian, part of the South Slavonic language family, related to Serbo Croat, Slovene, Russian and Macedonian (regarded as a Bulgarian dialect by the State). The Cyrillic alphabet is used. Greek, Turkish and Albanian vocabularies have been locally assimilated. There are approximately 220,000 Romany- and 760,000 Turkish-speaking inhabitants.

HISTORY

The earliest known inhabitants of the territory of present-day Bulgaria were the Thracians, who migrated from the Eurasian steppes around 3500 BC. From the 3rd century BC the Thracians became subject first to the Macedonians and then to the Romans. The Roman provinces of Thrace and Moesia were laid waste between the 3rd and 6th centuries AD by successive waves of invaders. The Bulgars, tribes of mixed Slav and Turkic origin, arrived in the area between the 5th and 7th centuries and by the end of the 7th century a Bulgarian state had emerged. In 864 the Bulgarians converted to Christianity and in 870 an independent Bulgarian Church was established. Bulgaria was an important power in the Balkans throughout much of the medieval period.

At the end of the 14th century Bulgaria fell to Ottoman armies. Ensuing Turkish domination lasted almost 500 years and the Bulgarian church was placed under the authority of the Greek patriarch. A revival of Bulgarian culture began in the late 18th century. Nationalism was initially manifest in demands for a separate church and in 1870 an autonomous Bulgarian Church was declared. In 1876 a Bulgarian uprising against the Turks was brutally suppressed, attracting sympathy from the Great Powers. After Ottoman defeat in the Russo-Turkish war of 1877–78 the Treaty of San Stefano established a large independent Bulgarian state stretching from the Danube to the Aegean. This proved unacceptable to Great Britain and Austria, and the subsequent Treaty of Berlin (1878) left a much-reduced Bulgarian principality. Union with the province of Eastern Rumelia was achieved in 1885 and in 1908 Bulgaria gained full independence as a kingdom. There was a proliferation of political parties, which included (after 1903) the 'Narrow Socialists', the precursors of the Bulgarian Communist Party (BCP).

Bulgarian claims to Macedonia dominated foreign policy. In 1912 Bulgaria formed a coalition with Serbia and Greece and in the First Balkan War almost drove the Turks from the Balkans. The failure of a pre-emptive Bulgarian attack on Serbia and Greece in the following year, however, led to a division of Macedonia which left only the Pirin district in Bulgarian hands. Bulgaria joined World War I on the side of the Central Powers in Sept. 1915. This brought the loss of Thrace (to Greece) and Southern Dobrudja (to Romania) at the Treaty of Neuilly in Nov. 1919. Inter-war politics were turbulent. On 28 Mar. 1920 a radical Agrarian Party government was elected with Aleksandur Stamboliski as prime minister, but this was overthrown and Stamboliski was killed in a coup on 8–9 June 1923. Amid continuing political violence (including a failed Communist insurrection in Sept. 1923) a succession of coalition governments held office until a military coup on 19 May 1934. In the following year King Boris III (r.1918–43) established a personal dictatorship. At the beginning of World War II Bulgaria remained neutral, but after Nazi incursions in Mar. 1941 it joined the Axis powers and took part in the occupation of Yugoslavia. This policy was reversed in Sept. 1944 when Bulgaria declared war on Germany. The 10 Feb. 1947 peace treaty with the allies confirmed Bulgaria's pre-war borders, with the addition of Southern Dobrudja.

A left-wing Fatherland Front seized power after the Soviet army had entered Bulgaria in Sept. 1944 and the BCP gradually extended its hold over the country. A purge of pro-Axis leaders in Feb. 1945 destroyed the old centre and right-wing parties. The monarchy was abolished after a referendum on 8 Sept. 1946. Georgi Dimitrov, the veteran Comintern leader, became prime minister two months later. On 23 Sept. 1947 the Agrarian leader Petkov was executed as a traitor and his party was dissolved. By the end of 1947 the nationalization of private enterprises was completed. In the following August the Social Democrats merged with the BCP and in early 1949 the remaining opposition groups were eliminated. The five-year plan which came into effect on 1 Jan. 1949 envisaged the socialization of the economy and in the same year Bulgaria became a founder member of Comecon. Agriculture was collectivized by 1958 and a heavy industrial base was built up.

The BCP in 1949 underwent an internal power struggle, as a result of which Deputy Prime Minister Traicho Kostov was arrested and in December hanged as a Titoist. Dimitrov died in July 1949 and was succeeded as BCP first secretary by Vulko Chervenkov. By Apr. 1951 more than one in five party members and many non-Communists had been purged. Chervenkov, who had already relinquished the post of first secretary to Todor Zhivkov in 1954, was in Apr. 1956 accused of fostering a cult of personality and was replaced as prime minister by Anton Yugkov. Party in-fighting continued for the next six years. Zhivkov, who was identified with de-Stalinization, finally triumphed over his rivals, taking over from Yugov as prime minister in 1962 (this in spite of the failure of the 1959 'Zhivkov Theses' which sought to emulate China's 'great leap forward' by radically accelerating production).

An attempted army coup in Apr. 1965 failed to dislodge Zhivkov from power and thereafter frequent reshuffles ensured that no serious rival threatened his authority. Under a new constitution of 18 May 1971 Zhivkov was elected president of the State Council and relinquished the post of prime minister. Growing hopes of liberalization in the 1970s were dashed by a BCP purge in 1978 in which over 38,000 members were expelled. A slowing down of economic growth prompted the introduction of the 'New Economic Mechanism' (a limited form of market socialism) in 1979–82. Bulgaria demonstrated support for the restructuring implemented in the Soviet Union since 1985 with attacks on bureaucracy, corruption and inefficiency. A party conference in Jan. 1988 approved multiple candidacy for elections and stressed the need for socialist self-government. However, the dismissal of the reformers Chudomir Aleksandrov and Stoyan Mikhailov from the BCP politburo in July 1988 suggested a conservative backlash.

Bulgarian relations with the West were marred by accusations that the secret service had been involved in an assassination attempt on Pope John Paul II on 13 May 1981 (evidence was circumstantial). An official campaign of forced assimilation of the Turkish minority (declared to be simply 'Muslim Bulgarians') began in late 1984 with some loss of life. Its escalation in June 1989 led to a mass exodus by Aug. of over 300,000 ethnic Turks which brought renewed international criticism and domestic economic crisis. This drove Foreign Minister Petur Mladenov in Nov. to stage a 'palace coup' which ousted Zhivkov as BCP leader and head of state. Zhivkov's hardline cohorts were purged. In Dec. the new reformist BCP leadership decided to renounce the party's constitutionally-guaranteed monopoly on power, proposed free elections in 1990, and entered into dialogue with the burgeoning political opposition.

CONSTITUTION AND GOVERNMENT

Executive and legislature

Pending the formal abolition of its monopoly, power is exercised by the Bulgarian Communist Party, within an umbrella Fatherland Front also embracing the only other approved political party, the Bulgarian Agrarian People's Union. The Front draws up a single list of candidates for the elections held every five years, by universal adult suffrage, to the unicameral 400-member National Assembly, which in turn elects the State Council (a largely ceremonial body) and the Council of Ministers (government). There is no constitutional provision for a head of state, but some of the functions are performed by the president of the State Council.

Present government

President of the State Council Petur Mladenov
Prime Minister Georgi Atanasov
Principal members of the Council of Ministers Kiril Zarev (Deputy Prime Minister, Economy and Planning), Belcho Belchev (Finance), Boyko Dimitrov (Foreign Affairs), Atanas Semerdzhiev (Interior), Dobri Dzhurov (National Defence).

Justice

The system of law is based on a civil law system, influenced by Soviet law. The highest court is the Supreme Court. Below the level of the 28 provincial courts and 105 regional courts, minor offences are dealt with by 'Comrade Courts'. The Prosecutor General, elected by the National Assembly, is responsible for ensuring observance of the law, and for appointing prosecutors from national down to local level. The death penalty is in force. There were over 32 executions between 1985 and mid-1988. Capital offences: murder, terrorism, manslaughter.

National symbols

Flag. Three horizontal stripes of white, green and red with the Bulgarian state coat of arms in the hoist of the white stripe.

Festivals. 3 Mar. (National Day); 1–2 May (Labour Day); 24 May (Education Day).

INTERNATIONAL RELATIONS

Affiliations

Warsaw Pact; Comecon.

Defence

Total Armed Forces: 157,800 (94,000 conscripts). Terms of service: Army and Air Force two years, Navy three years. Reserves: 216,500.

Army: 115,000; 2,550 main battle tanks (mainly T-34, T-54 and T-72).

Navy: 8,800; four submarines (Soviet Romeo); three frigates (Soviet Riga); 25 patrol and coastal combatants.

Air Force: 34,000; 255 combat aircraft (MiG-17; MiG-23BN; MiG-23MF; MiG21PFM).

ECONOMY

Currency

The unit is the lev, divided into 100 stotinki.

National finance

Budget. The 1987 budget was for expenditure of US$23,700 million and revenue of US$23,800 million.

Inflation. 1.7%.

Gross Domestic Product

Estimated total GDP US$67,600 million (GNP), per capita US$7,540 (overall size of economy ranking 35 in the world).

Economically active population. The total number of persons active in the economy is 4,300,000.

Sector	% of workforce
industry	33
agriculture	20
services*	47

* services figure includes elements unassigned to other categories.

Energy and mineral resources

Minerals. Output: (in 1,000 tons/tonnes) coal 42,439/38,500; iron ore 660/599; manganese ore 12/10.9.

Oil and gas. Crude oil production: (1988) 308,644 tons/280,000 tonnes.

Electricity. Production: (1987) 43.5 million MWh. In the absence of significant oil, gas or high-grade coal resources, energy policy is based on the exploitation of low-grade coal and hydroelectric resources. Of the country's 135 power stations, with a combined potential of 10,700 MW, 46 (6,500 MW) were thermal, 88 (2,000 MW) were hydroelectric and one (2,260 MW) was nuclear.

Bioresources

Agriculture. There are an estimated 15,233,715 acres/6,165,000 ha of agricultural land, of which 11,490,891/4,650,300 are arable (1987). The total area of private plots (maximum 1 ha) is 1,522,877 acres/616,300 ha (1987). The remaining collective and state farms have been incorporated into 'agricultural-industrial complexes'. The main farm products are cereals, dairy products and meat.

Crop production: (1987 in 1,000 tons/tonnes) wheat 4,573/4,149; maize 2,048/1,858; barley 1,202/1,091; sugar beet 851/772; sunflower seed 452/410; tobacco 147/133. Bulgaria produces some 2,645 lb/1,200 kg of attar of roses per year, 80% of the world supply.

Livestock numbers: (1988 in millions) sheep 8.9; pigs 4; cattle 1.6; poultry 41.

Forestry. Forest area: (1987) 9,636,900 million acres/3.9 million ha (34% coniferous, 25% oak). 113,66/46,000 ha were afforested in 1987 and 236,603,800 ft^3/6.7 million m^3 of timber were cut.

Fisheries. Total catch: (1982) 127,425 tons/115,600 tonnes.

Industry and commerce

Industry. The main industries are food processing, machine and metal building, electronics and chemicals. All industry was nationalized in 1947 and a 1986 Labour Code provides for the self-management of enterprises.

Commerce. Exports: US$14,500 million; imports: US$15,300 million. Exports (1986) included machinery and equipment 53.5%; agricultural products 18.4%; fuels, mineral raw materials and metals 10%; manufactured consumer goods 9.7%. Imports (1986) included fuels and minerals 47%; machinery and equipment 33.2%; agricultural and forestry products 9.5%; manufactured consumer goods 3.8%.

Trade with UK. Bulgaria imported UK goods worth £82 million and exported to the UK goods worth £28 million (1988).

Tourism. Bulgaria received 7.59 million foreign visitors in 1987.

COMMUNICATIONS

Railways

There are 2,848 miles/4,586 km of railways, of which more than 1,273 miles/2,050 km are electrified.

Roads

There are 22,920 miles/36,908 km of roads.

Aviation

BALKAN (Bulgarian Airlines) provides domestic and international services (main airport is Sofia Airport).

Shipping

The main ports are Burgas and Varna, with river ports on the Danube, and 470 km of navigable internal waterways. The merchant marine totals 1.2 million GRT, with 108 ships over 1,000 GRT.

Telecommunications

There are 2,100,000 radio and television sets. Radio Sofia broadcasts on two radio and two television channels, and links up with Soviet television via the Intervision system.

EDUCATION AND WELFARE

Education

Free and compulsory state education is provided for children aged seven to 16. Since 1973, unified secondary polytechnical schools offering compulsory education for all children aged seven to 17 have been gradually introduced.

School population. 1,092,197 under 16; 167,845 in higher stages.

Schools. 2,891 schools with 62,054 teachers (one per 17 pupils) at ages 7–16; 554 secondary schools with 9,837 teachers (one per 19 pupils).

Universities. Bulgaria has three universities; 30 institutes of higher education; 16 post-secondary institutions; 248 technical colleges; 261 secondary vocational-technical schools.

Health

Free medical services and comprehensive social security arrangements, including retirement and disablement pensions, temporary sick pay and child allowances. There is one doctor per 330 inhabitants.

BURKINA FASO

People's Republic of Burkina

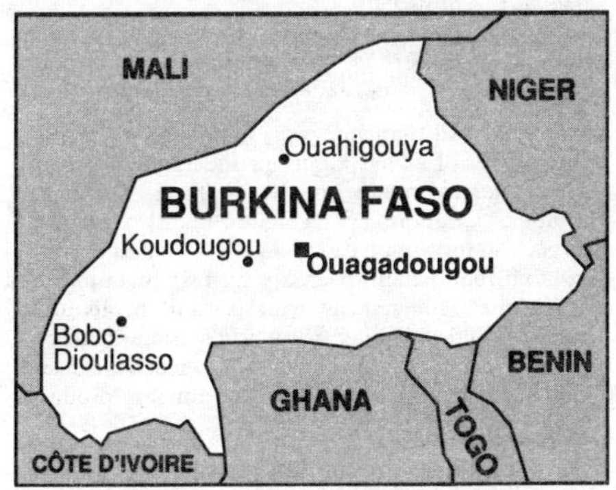

GEOGRAPHY

Burkina Faso is a landlocked republic in west Africa, lying south of the Sahara with a total area of 105,811 miles^2/274,122 km^2 divided into 30 provinces. In the western and southern regions of the country, semi-arid sandstone savannah plateaux dominate the physiography, transected by the Mouhoun, Nakambe and Nazinon rivers (all subject to reduction in the dry season). In the south-west, the Falaises de Banfora (Banfora Cliffs) reach elevations of approximately 492 ft/150 m. In the north and north-east, rocky outcrops provide residual relief. Over 90% of the population is rural-based yet only 8–10% of the Republic's land is arable. Soil conditions are generally poor with very scant irrigation. 26% of the land area is bush forested.

Climate

Sahelian in the north, sudanic (tropical savannah) in the south. Rainfall decreases south-north, falling from 39 in/1,000 mm to less than 10 in/250 mm annually. Warm, high temperatures all year with a dry season from Dec.-Apr., a wet season from June-Nov. (reaching 80% humidity in the south) and maximum temperatures from Mar.-May reaching 104°F/40°C in the shade. The dry north-east Harmattan blows throughout the dry season reducing the savannah grasslands to semi-desert. Ouagadougou: Jan. 76°F/24.4°C. July 61°F/28.3°C. Average annual rainfall 35 in/894 mm.

Cities and towns

Ouagadougou (capital)	441,514
Bobo-Dioulasso	228,668
Koudougou	51,926

Population

Total population is 8,529,000 of which 7% live in urban areas. Population density is 80.6 persons mile^2/31.1 per km^2. The population is composed of more than 50 ethnic groups of which the Mossi (48%), Fulani (10%) and Gourma (5%) nomads in the north constitute nearly two-thirds. In the south-east, the Lobi-Dagari and Mande peoples make up a further 14%. Other significant groups are the Bobo (7%) in the south-west, and Sénoufo and Gorounsi.

Birth rate 4.71%. **Death rate** 1.99%. **Rate of population increase** 2.72%. **Age distribution** under 15 = 43.8%; over 65 = 2.9%. **Life expectancy** female 49; male 46; average 47.

Religion

Almost two-thirds of the population adhere to indigenous animist beliefs. Muslims (25%) and Christians (10%) comprise the remainder. Of the Christian minority, approximately 106,467 were Protestant and 868,116 Roman Catholic.

Language

The official language is French. Ethnolinguistically, Burkina Faso is divided into two indigenous Sudanic language families, the Voltaic and the Mande. Moré, a Voltaic tongue spoken by the majority of the Mossi (nearly 4 million), predominates. Other important languages are Mande (730,000 speakers); Bobo (570,000 speakers); Fulani (690,000 speakers); Lobi (580,000 speakers).

HISTORY

Very little is known about the early history of Burkina Faso (formerly Upper Volta). Some time before the 15th century the Mossi people began to expand from their base on the Niger river, close to the modern town of Niamey. Their expansion northwards was blocked by the Songhai Empire, but from the late 16th century until colonial intervention in the late 19th century a complex of Mossi kingdoms dominated virtually all of the country. The Mossi states were very independent, practising their traditional religion and resisting the process of Islamization seen in the neighbouring states.

When European explorers began to travel through the Mossi kingdoms in the 19th century they found a relatively well developed administrative system revolving around the king or Mogho Naba. The area came under French rule at the end of the 19th century when it was incorporated into the colony of the French Soudan which itself formed part of the Federation of French West Africa. To a very large extent the traditional chiefs remained in place. In 1920 the area became a separate colony known as Upper Volta but in 1932 it was divided up between the neighbouring colonies of French Soudan, Niger and the Ivory Coast; in 1947, however, it re-emerged as a separate administrative unit in its current boundaries.

Throughout the colonial period the colony was one of the most backward of the French West African empire. There was very little investment and many of the inhabitants worked in the coffee plantations of neighbouring Ivory Coast (to which it was linked by a railway started before World War I but not completed until 1954).

After World War II the Mossi king was a pro-French conservative influence in opposition to the more radical *Rassemblement démocratique africain* (RDA) party which campaigned for independence for the whole of French West Africa as a single state.

The country became independent as Upper Volta on 5 Aug. 1960 with Maurice Yaméogo, leader of the *Union démocratique voltaïque* (UDV) party, as president. Yaméogo soon moved to a one-party state but was deposed in a coup in 1966 led by Lt-Col Sangoulé Lamizana. A new constitution, providing for a return to civilian rule, was approved in a referendum on 14 June 1970; this was followed by elections in December, contested by three parties, at which the UDV, now led by Gérard Ouedraogo, won a majority of the seats. Severe hardship caused by the Sahelian drought combined with political ineptitude led to another military intervention with Lamizana resuming full executive powers on 8 Feb. 1974. During the 1970s the trade unions became the principal mouthpiece for opposition politics and when in Feb. 1976 Lamizana formed a new, mainly civilian, cabinet he included Zoumana Traoré, a leading trade unionist. Full party politics were restored in assembly and presidential elections in Apr. and May 1978 in which the UDV again won a majority of the votes and Lamizana was confirmed as president, though only on the second round of voting.

Lamizana's regime was overthrown in a military coup in 1980 installing Col Saye Zerbo as president until he was overthrown in Nov. 1982 in a coup of junior officers led by Capt Thomas Sankara. Sankara formed a new government known as the Peoples' Salvation Council with a radical reforming programme closely modelled on policies pursued by Flt-Lt Jerry Rawlings in Ghana. On 3 Aug. 1984 Upper Volta was renamed Burkina Faso – 'the country of honest men' – a symbolic break with the past and a declaration of intent for future government. War broke out briefly with neighbouring Mali on 25–29 Dec. 1985, when Burkinabe troops crossed the disputed border but were driven back by superior Malian air power; relations were normalized the following year. Sankara's drive against corruption and his authoritarian policy of forcing city-dwellers to return to the countryside caused resentment against the urban elite and on 15 Oct. 1987 he was assassinated. His replacement had formerly been one of his closest friends, Blaise Compaoré, who was not thought to have been directly involved in the assassination, but was known to have become disaffected with Sankara's policies. With one of the lowest GNPs in the world Burkina Faso is increasingly dependent upon foreign aid for its survival.

CONSTITUTION AND GOVERNMENT

Executive and legislature

The Constitution was suspended by the 1980 military coup; since the Oct. 1987 coup executive authority has been exercised by the Popular Front, assisted by a council of ministers.

Present government

Chairman of the Popular Front; Head of Government; Minister of Popular Defence Capt. Blaise Compaoré

Principal members of Council of Ministers Thomas Sanon – Economic Promotion; Prosper Vocouma – External Relations; Pascal Zagre – Planning and Co-operation; Antoine Komy Sambo – Justice; Bintou Sanogo – Finance.

Popular Front Executive Committee

Chairman Capt. Blaise Compaoré.

Secretaries Clément Oumarou Ouedraogo (political affairs); Capt. Arsène Ye Bognessan (organization); Capt. Gilbert Diendere (defence and security).

Justice

The system of law is based on the French civil law system and customary law. The highest court is the Supreme Court in Ouagadougou and Courts of Appeal. Revolutionary People's Tribunals have replaced the former lower courts. The death penalty is in force. No judicial executions were reported between 1985 and mid-1988. A number of senior army officers were executed in September 1989 and January 1990 in connection with alleged coup plots.

National symbols

Flag. Two equal horizontal stripes, red over green with a yellow, five-pointed star in the centre.

Festivals. 3 Jan. (Anniversary of the 1966 Revolution); 1 May (May Day); 4 Aug. (National Day).

Vehicle registration plate. HV.

INTERNATIONAL RELATIONS

Affiliations

NAM; OAU; ACP; ICO; Francophonie.

Defence

Total Armed Forces: 8,700.

Army: 7,000.

Air Force: 200; some combat aircraft, no armed helicopters.

ECONOMY

Currency

The unit is the CFA franc, divided into 100 centimes.

National finance

Balance of payments. The balance of payments (current account, 1987) was a deficit of 124 million.

Inflation. –2.7%.

Gross Domestic Product

Estimated total GDP US$1,650 million, per capita US$160 (overall size of economy ranking 123 in the world).

Economically active population. The total number of persons active in the economy is 3,300,000.

Sector	% of workforce	% of GDP
industry	13	25
agriculture	82	38
services*	5	38

* services figure includes elements unassigned to other categories.

Energy and mineral resources

Minerals. Deposits of manganese, magnetite, bauxite, zinc, lead, nickel and phosphates have been found in the north near Tambao, but exploitation is currently hampered by inadeqate transport facilities. Small deposits of gold, antimony, copper and silver have also been discovered.

Electricity. Capacity: 73,000 kW; production: (1987) 141 million kWh.

Bioresources

Agriculture. Some 10% of land area is arable, with 82% of the population engaged in agriculture, mostly subsistence, forestry and fishing. Meadows and pastures constitute 37% of land area. Problems associated with drought, desertification, deforestation and overgrazing have affected agricultural production.

Crop production: food crops (1986 in tons/tonnes) sorghum 1,115,528/1,012,000; millet 757,280/687,000; maize 174,163/158,000; rice 30,864/28,000. Cash crops (1986 in tons/tonnes) groundnuts 167,550/152,000; sugar cane 380,294/345,000; seed cotton 157/142; sesame 17,637/16,000.

Livestock numbers: (1987) cattle 3.17 million; sheep 2.3 million; goats 3.43 million; horses 70,000; donkeys 200,000.

Forestry. Some 26% of land area is classified as forest and woodland, principally in the river valleys of the Mouhoun (formerly Black Volta), Nakambe (White Volta) and Nazinon (Red Volta). Timber production: (1985) 236 million ft^3/6.69 million m^3.

Fisheries. Total catch from river fishing: (1983) 7,716 tons/7,000 tonnes.

Industry and commerce

Industry. Some 13% of the population are employed in industry. The principal activities are agricultural processing; brewing; cement and brick manufacture.

Commerce. Exports in 1985 totalled US$82 million, principally livestock (on the hoof); groundnuts; shea nut products; cotton; sesame. Principal trading partners (by destination) in 1983 were Côte d'Ivoire; France; Taiwan; China; UK. Imports amounted to $324 million in 1985, comprising textiles; food and other consumer goods; transport equipment; machinery; fuels from France; Côte d'Ivoire; US.

Trade with UK. Burkina Faso exported goods worth £546,000 to the UK and imported goods worth £3,732,000 from the UK (1988).

Tourism. There were 60,000 tourists in 1986.

COMMUNICATIONS

Railways

There are 3,415 miles/5,500 km of railways (comprising 321 miles/517 km of the 729 miles/1,175 km RAN line linking Ouagadougou with Abidjan, Côte d'Ivoire.

Roads

There are 6,975 miles/11,231 km of roads (2,842 miles/4,576 km of main and 2,551 miles/4,108 of secondary roads).

Aviation

Air Afrique provides international services and Air Burkina has a monopoly of domestic flights (main airports are at Ouagadougou and Bobo-Dioulasso).

Shipping

None.

Telecommunications

There are 13,900 telephones. State television broadcasts are provided by Télévision Nationale du Burkina; there are about 20,000 television sets and over 100,000 radios.

EDUCATION AND WELFARE

Education

Schools. 1,037 primary schools with 276,732 pupils and 4,796 teachers (one per 58 pupils); 79 secondary schools with 43,001 pupils and 1,553 teachers (one per 28 pupils); 27 technical schools with 4,492 pupils and 484 teachers (one per 10 pupils) and 495 students in teacher-training establishments (1984).

University. The Université d'Ouagadougou had 3,870 students and 216 teaching staff in 1984.

Literacy. 7% of adult population.

Health

A health programme initiated in 1979 aimed to provide, within a decade, a comprehensive network of village and district health centres, backed up by larger regional and subregional medical centres, ten departmental hospitals, two national hospitals and a university centre of health sciences in Ouagadougou. By 1987 there was one doctor per 40,000 of the population.

BURMA

Myanmar Naingngan
(Union of Burma (Myanmar))

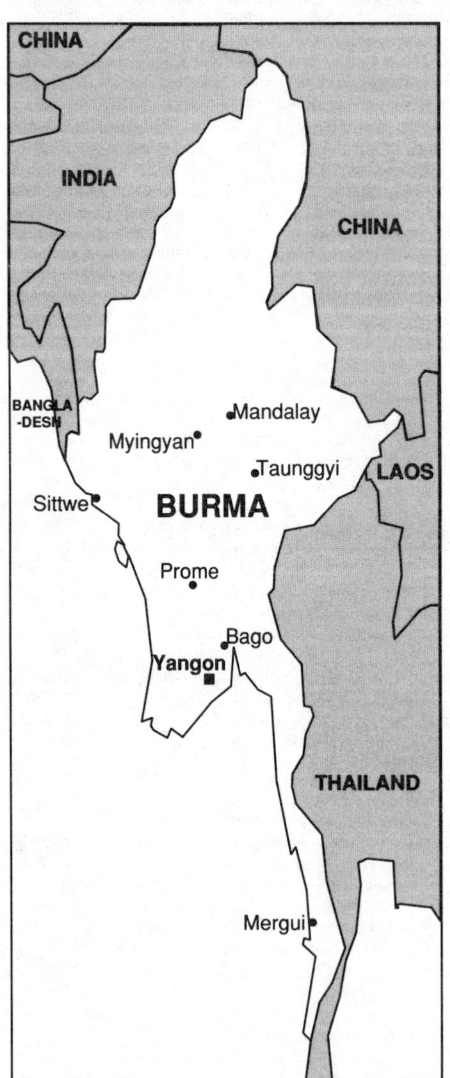

GEOGRAPHY

Situated in south-east Asia, on the eastern coasts of the Bay of Bengal and the Andaman Sea, between the Malay Peninsula and the Tibetan plateau, Burma covers an area of 261,159 miles^2/676,577 km^2 comprising 14 administrative divisions. The central lowlands, supporting the bulk (75%) of the population, are enclosed by longitudinal mountain ranges to the north and to the west and by the Shan Plateau in the east (average elevation just under 3,280 ft/1,000 m). Burma's highest peak, Hkakabo Razi (19,577 ft/5,967 m), is located in the extreme north on the Chinese frontier, forming part of the Kumon Range. In the west, the Chin Hills descend southwards into the thinly populated upland forests of the Arakan-Yoma range. The central lowlands subdivide into the north-south draining Irrawaddy, Sittang and Salween Basins and the coastal plains of Arakan and Tenasserim. Laterite soils cover most highland areas and alluvial clay deposits predominate in the intensively cultivated rice paddies of the southern-delta region. Not more than 15% of Burma's mountainous terrain is deemed arable, pasture land is negligible and nearly 49% of the total area is forested.

Climate

Predominantly tropical monsoon, equatorial on the coast and humid temperate in the extreme north. Hot, humid summers (south-west monsoon June-Sept.) followed by a cooler, drier period from Nov.-Feb. and a hotter dry spell from Mar.-May. Rainfall decreases inland from 197 in/5,000 mm on the coast to 98 in/2,500 mm in the delta region and 34 in/870 mm around Mandalay, 90% of which falls during the monsoon. Average annual temperatures range from 72°F/27°C in Rangoon to 47°F/22°C in the Shan highland plateau. Rangoon: Jan. 51°F/25°C. July 80°F/26.7°C. Average annual rainfall 103 in/2,616 mm.

Cities and towns

Rangoon (capital) (Yangon)	2,458,712
Mandalay	532,895
Moulmein	219,991
Pegu (Bago)	150,447
Bassein	144,092
Taunggyi	107,907
Sittwe	107,607
Manywa	106,873

Population

The total population is 39,966,000, of which 23.9% live in urban areas. Population density is 153 persons per mile^2/59.0 per km^2. Ethnic composition includes 68% Burman (Tibeto-Chinese extraction) and several major communities. The Chin (2%) (in the north-west) comprise several distinct groups as do the Kachin peoples of the upper Irrawaddy valley and northern hills. Similarly, the Wa and Palaung are usually identified with the Shan (9%) from the eastern plateau. In the south, the Karen (7%) populate the delta region, the Pegu Yama range and the lower basin of the Salween river. A further 3% of the population are Chinese and 2% Indian.

Birth rate 3.43%. **Death rate** 1.10%. **Rate of population increase** 2.33%. **Age distribution** under 15 = 39.2%; over 65 = 3.8%. **Life expectancy** female 62; male 58; average 60.

Religion

An estimated 85% of the population adhere to Theravada Buddhism, an ancient strain of the faith. Animist, Hindu, Muslim and Christian minorities constitute the remaining 15%.

Language

The official language is Burmese, notwithstanding the 100 indigenous languages spoken in Burma, most of which (together with Burmese) belong to the Sino-Tibetan family. The Shan language is of Tai extraction while the languages of the Mons and Wa/Palaung peoples derive from an Austro-asiatic subgroup.

HISTORY

During Burma's early history no one racial group was able to exert any significant degree of predominance until the 11th century, when the Tibeto-Burmans, by then the most numerous of the many races that populated the country, united Burma and, under its king, Anarutha the Great (r.1044–77), founded the Pagan dynasty. Anarutha's successors continued to rule Burma until the end of the 13th century – an era popularly known as Burma's Golden Age. In 1287 Kublai Khan's Mongol armies captured Pagan.

Although Mongol control ended in 1303, the second Burman kingdom was not founded until the 16th century, when the Toungoo dynasty, under King Tabinshweti (?–1551), united the country. Continuous fighting against its neighbours proved to weaken the kingdom however, and the dynasty fell into decline.

The third and final dynasty, Konbaung, rose in the 18th century and under Alaungpaya (r.1711–60) and his successors, almost all of present-day Burma, much of north-eastern India and western Thailand fell under Burman control. Inevitably, expansion in India during the late 1700s resulted in contact and conflict with the British who viewed Burma's expansionist designs as a threat to their own. This led to three Anglo-Burmese wars – 1824, 1852 and 1885 – and by 1886, Britain had succeeded in extending its control over all of Burma, incorporating it into the British Empire as a province of India.

Not surprisingly, under British rule, the fabric of Burmese society underwent an inexorable process of change. Defeat in war signalled an end both to Burma's independence and monarchy. As a province of the neighbouring subcontinent, Burma was subject to the same administrative processes but in 1937, Burma was separated from India and given its own constitution, with an elected parliament and an indigenous prime minister. Five years later, however, following a British withdrawal, the country was occupied by invading Japanese forces.

During the four-year occupation, in 1943, the Japanese installed Dr Ba Maw – a former prime minister under the British – as head of the nominally independent Burmese government. That same year, Burma declared war against Britain and the United States. Prior to the installation of the puppet regime, a group of Burmese nationalists (known as the Thirty Comrades) had been sent to Japan for military training and upon their return, collaborated with the Japanese in forming the Burma Independence Army (BIA).

The BIA, dissatisfied with the economic and political situation under the Japanese, rejected Ba Maw's government and organized an anti-Japanese resistance movement. The Anti-Fascist People's Freedom League (AFPFL) dominated the political scene in Burma up to and beyond 1945 when Britain reoccupied the country (led by Lord Mountbatten), following Japan's surrender. Under the leadership of Aung San, the AFPFL campaigned for Burmese independence which was finally granted by Britain in Jan. 1947. Aung San and six members of the executive council were assassinated at a cabinet meeting on 19 July 1947, but Burma was made independent of Britain, outside the Commonwealth, on 4 Jan. 1948.

The fledgling Union of Burma, led by U Nu, was almost immediately assailed by a widespread insurrection of communists (principally the People's Volunteer Organization – PVO) and ethnic insurgents (Karens, Shans, Kachins, Mons and others). Security problems were also posed in the north by Chinese Kuomintang forces, who entered Burma after communist victory in China in 1949. Attempts made by parliament to administer the country on a federal basis were perceived by the insurgents as largely cosmetic. Although serious, the threat to the government was mitigated in part by in-fighting amongst the insurgents and by 1951, the unrest was brought under control by government forces.

Despite two electoral successes in the early 1950s, differences within Burma's ruling party, the AFPFL, led to a intra-party split in 1958. In order to maintain law and order, the government invited the army chief, General Ne Win (one of the Thirty Comrades) to assume temporary control of the country until new elections could be organized. These were held in 1960 and U Nu's faction of the AFPFL was once again returned to power.

Increasing demands by the Shans and Kachins for wider independence, in addition to general economic mismanagement, served to frustrate Nu's attempts at forging greater racial harmony within Burma and indeed, the process of government itself. On 2 Mar. 1962, Ne Win once again regained control (as head of the Revolutionary Council – RC), this time by way of a coup. Ne Win stated that the renewed calls for ethnic independence threatened the unity of the country; he placed U Nu and other leading politicians in detention.

In 1962, a document entitled **The Burmese Way to Socialism** was published, and for ten years it served to provide the ideological framework within which the RC prosecuted its policy of government. During the early period of military rule, both the constitution and parliament were suspended. Free enterprise and private trade were abolished and privately owned companies were nationalized and placed under military control.

In July 1962, the Burma Socialist Programme Party (BSPP or Lanzin Party) was formed. Ostensibly open to the services and civilians alike, the party was, in reality, dominated by the military and the only legal political party in the country. On 2 Mar. 1974, Ne Win dissolved the RC and, under the terms of a new constitution (which was promulgated in Jan. 1974) established a one-party socialist government. The 451-member People's National Congress (Pyuthu Hluttaw) was open to legal representatives from all over Burma, including the country's various indigenous minorities.

Despite the new constitution, power continued to be held by the small military clique that had engineered the 1962 coup. Of the 29 members of the council of ministers, 11 were from the RC, with Ne Win as chairman of the council of state and first president, and San Yu as secretary of the council of ministers. San Yu eventually succeeded Ne Win as president following the latter's retirement in 1981. Ne Win, who retained charge of the BSPP, remained the real source of political power in the country. San Yu was reelected in Nov. 1985 for another four-year term from Mar. 1986.

Economic problems continued to plague the government and on various occasions – notably in 1974 – food riots and anti-government demonstrations served to illustrate the continuing popular discontent. The army's counter-insurgency campaign against the ethnic rebels continued to dominate the government's security deliberations, especially after the insurgent groups united under a common umbrella, namely the National Democratic Front.

Student-led demonstrations against the imposition of a series of demonetization measures in Sept. 1987 marked the beginning of a 12-month period of turmoil in Burma, which culminated in the assumption of power by the armed forces in mid-Sept. 1988. Massive demonstrations against Ne Win in mid-1988 compelled the ruling elite to implement a number of cosmetic political reforms before resorting to brutal raw terror in August. So, in July 1988, both Ne Win and San Yu resigned their party posts, and Sein Lwin became president, stepping down on 12 Aug. A week later, Maung Maung became president, but on 18 Sept. General San Maung, at the head of a military-dominated State Law and Order Restoration Council (SLORC), assumed power. The SLORC announced more political reforms, including the abolition of the one-party system. However, most commentators agreed that the ageing Ne Win, who held no official position in the new regime, retained supreme political power.

During 1989 the military sought to consolidate its rule through the arrest and intimidation of leading opposition figures. So, Aung San Suu Kyi, secretary general of the National League for Democracy (NCD) and Burma's main opposition leader, was placed under house arrest in July. In Dec. 1989 (five months before a general election was scheduled to be held) the NCD chairman, Gen. (retd) Tiull, was imprisoned for three years.

CONSTITUTION AND GOVERNMENT

Executive and legislature

The country's armed forces in Sept. 1988 established a military council and a cabinet, the latter also consisting almost entirely of members of the armed forces. According to an Oct. 1988 military decree the principal organs of power were (i) the State Law and Order Restoration Council, headed by a chairman; and (ii) the Government.

Present government

State Law and Order Restoration Council Chairman Gen. Saw Maung. Members Lt-Gen. Than Shwe; Rear Adml. Maung Maung Khin; Maj.-Gen. Tin Tun; Brig.-Gen. Aung Ye Kyaw; Maj.-Gen. Phone Myint; Maj.-Gen. Sein Aung; Maj.-Gen. Chit Swe; Brig.-Gen. Kyaw Ba; Col. Maung Thint; Brig.-Gen. Maung Aye; Brig.-Gen. Nyan Lin; Brig.-Gen. Myint Aung; Brig.-Gen. Mya Thinn; Brig.-Gen. Tun Kyi; Brig.-Gen. Aye Thaung; Brig.-Gen. Myo Nyunt. Secretaries Brig.-Gen. Khin Nyunt; Col Tin U.

Government (Principal members) *Prime Minister; Defence; Foreign Affairs* Gen. Saw Maung; *Home and Religious Affairs; Information and Culture* Maj.-Gen. Phone Myint.

Justice

The system of law was set up under the 1974 constitution as a People's Justice system administered by People's Courts. The highest judicial authority, the Chief Judge, is appointed by the State Law and Order Restoration Council. The death penalty is in force. The number of executions between 1985 and mid-1988 is not known.

National symbols

Flag. Red with a blue canton charged with a white cogwheel with fourteen cogs, in the centre of which are two ears of rice.

Festivals. 4 Jan. (Independence Day); 12 Feb. (Union Day); 2 Mar. (Peasant's Day, anniversary of the 1962 coup); 27 Mar. (Armed Forces Day); 1 May (Workers' Day); 19 July (Martyrs Day); 3 Dec. (National Day).

Vehicle registration plate. BUR.

INTERNATIONAL RELATIONS

Affiliations

None (member of UN).

Defence

Total Armed Forces: 186,000. Terms of service: voluntary.

Army: 170,000; 20 main battle tanks.

Navy: 7,000 inclusive 800 Marines; 39 patrol and coastal combatants.

Air Force: 9,000; perhaps 27 combat aircraft, no armed helicopters.

Opposition: Communist Party of Burma (CPB), 10,000 active; 8,000–10,000 militia. National Democratic Front (NDF), some 20,000, coalition of numerous groups. Private armies (mainly narcotics linked) with about 7,000 active.

ECONOMY

Currency

The unit is the kyat, divided into 100 pyas.

National finance

Budget. The 1988 est. budget was for expenditure of US$2,200 million and revenue of US$1,100 million. Main items of expenditure are defence (19%); education (12%).

Balance of payments. The balance of payments (current account, 1987) was a deficit of US$307 million.

Inflation. 17.8%.

Gross Domestic Product

Estimated total GDP US$9,300 million, per capita US$230 (overall size of economy ranking 69 in the world).

Economically active population. The total number of persons active in the economy is 50,800,000; unemployed (urban areas): 10.4%.

Sector	% of workforce
industry	14
agriculture	66
services*	20

* services figure includes elements unassigned to other categories.

Energy and mineral resources

Oil and gas. Production is nationalized. Output: 826,725 tons/750,000 tonnes of crude oil (1988); 38,280 million ft^3/1,084 million m^3 of petroleum (1987); 32,595 million ft^3/923 million m^3 of natural gas (1988).

Minerals. Although Burma is relatively rich in mineral deposits, production is at a low level. Small amounts of coal; tin; lead; zinc; tungsten; copper; silver; gold; marble; limestones; precious stones are mined.

Electricity. Capacity: 820,000 kW; production: 1,900 million kWh; 50 kWh per capita (1987).

Bioresources

Agriculture. Approximately 15% of Burma's total land area is cultivated. The primary crop is rice, diminishing amounts of which are exported. Other food crops include pulses; beans; maize; oilseeds; sugar cane; peanuts. Cotton, rubber and jute are also produced. Rebel organizations based in outlying areas produce large amounts of opium poppy and cannabis for the international drug trade.

Crop production: (1987–88 in tons/tonnes) rice 15.1/13.7 million; sugar cane 3.2/2.9 million; maize 305,337/277,000; wheat 265,654/241,000; butter beans 134,480/122,000; soya beans 26,455/24,000; cotton 90,389/82,000; jute 45,194/41,000; rubber 16,535/15,000.

Livestock numbers: (1987–88 in millions) poultry 39.5; cattle 9.9; pigs 3.1; buffaloes 2.2; sheep and goats 1.5.

Forestry. Teak is the most valuable timber in the forests which, despite forest loss, still cover nearly half of the country's total area. Teak has overtaken rice as the country's main export earner.

Fisheries. 1,738 tons/1,577 tonnes of sea fish and 418.9 tons/380 tonnes of freshwater fish (1987–88).

Industry and commerce

Industry. The main industries are agricultural processing; textiles and footwear; wood; wood products; petroleum refining; mining of copper, tin and tungsten; construction materials; pharmaceutical and fertilizers.

Commerce. Imports and exports are controlled by the government trading organizations. Exports in 1986–87 totalled US$353 million, of which forest products US$121.3 million; agricultural products US$113.8 million; livestock and fisheries products US$15.7 million. Imports were estimated at US$665 million, of which capital goods US$323.8 million; intermediate goods US$156.1 million; consumer goods US$50.5 million. Countries exported to included Singapore; China; UK; Japan. Imports came from Japan; Singapore; UK and other Western European countries.

Trade with UK. Burma imported UK goods worth £4,427,000; exports to UK totalled £11,685,000 (1988).

Tourism. There were 42,175 tourists in 1987.

COMMUNICATIONS

Railways

There are 1,959 miles/3,156 km of railways.

Roads

There are 14,325 miles/23,067 km of roads, of which the whole network is concrete or bituminized.

Aviation

Burma Airways Corporation (BAC) provides domestic and international services (main airport is Mingaladon Airport, near Rangoon).

Shipping

Rangoon is the main port. The merchant marine includes 34 ships of over 1,000 GRT.

Telecommunications

There are 53,000 telephones, one state television channel and seven radio stations. There are 725,000 radios and 35,000 television sets.

EDUCATION AND WELFARE

Education

The state provides free education in the primary, lower secondary and vocational schools. Upper secondary schools and universities charge fees.

School population There are 6.42 million pupils attending primary and secondary schools (1986–87).

Schools. There are over 36,000 schools (over 33,000 of which are primary schools) with a total teaching staff of 218,000.

Universities. There are Arts and Science Universities in Rangoon and Mandalay. In addition, there are numerous independent degree-giving colleges and institutions. In 1988, over 211,000 students were enrolled in universities, colleges or institutions.

Literacy. 78%.

Health

In 1986–87 there were approximately 10,500 doctors, 640 hospitals and 27,000 hospital beds.

BURUNDI

Republika y'Uburundi (Republic of Burundi)

GEOGRAPHY

Lying in east central Africa, just south of the equator across the Nile-Congo watershed, Burundi is a land-locked country with an area of 10,744 miles²/27,834 km² divided into eight provinces. Occupying a high plateau grassland (average elevation 4,922 ft/1,500 m decreasing eastwards towards Tanzania and the River Maragarazi valley) with a mountainous western belt, Burundi contains the Ruvubu River basin (south-west – north-east), the southernmost arm of the Nile drainage basin. Mount Karonje (8,809 ft/2,685 m) is Burundi's highest peak. The river Ruzizi forms part of the country's north-west frontier with Zaire and links Lake Kivu (bordering Rwanda in the north) with Lake Tanganyika in the south and east. Approximately 50% of the surface area is arable but less than 2% is forested (most of this is in mountainous areas). Over 10% of the population live in Gitega province (central east Burundi).

Climate

Equatorial, varying with altitude. Wet seasons are Mar.-May; Sept.-Dec. Average annual temperatures on the mountain slopes are generally cooler (61°F/16°C) than those along the western lakeside border and Ruzizi valley. The western frontier also receives less annual rainfall, 39 in/1,000 mm as opposed to 55 in/1,400 mm in the highlands and plateau regions. Bujumbura: Jan. 73°F/22.8°C. July 73°F/22.8°C. Average annual rainfall 33 in/825 mm.

Cities and towns

Bujumbura (capital)	172,201
Gitega	15,943

Population

Total population is 5,147,000 of whom 7% live in urban areas. Population density is 479 persons per mile^2/192.1 per km^2. At the last census, the three principal ethnic groups were Hutu (Chad/Niger origin, 83% of total), the Tutsi (Nilotic, under 15%) and the pygmoid Twa, the first Burundians (less than 1%). There are some 1,500 Asians and up to 3,500 Europeans. In 1988, there were 270,000 Rwandan refugees in Burundi.

Birth rate: 4.72%. **Death rate**: 1.9%. **Rate of population increase** 2.82%. **Age distribution** under 15 = 44.8%; over 65 = 3.3%. **Life expectancy** female 51; male 47; average 49.

Religion

Over two-thirds of the population are Christian: 62% Roman Catholic; 5% Protestant. Approximately 1% are Muslim, and almost a third of the population still follow indigenous animist beliefs.

Language

Kirundi (Bantu) and French are official languages. Kiswahili is used for commercial purposes, chiefly in the capital Bujumbura and along Lake Tanganyika.

HISTORY

Twa (Batwa) pygmies were the earliest peoples of the Burundi forests. Hutu (Bahutu) cultivators settled from the 14th century but were swept aside by Tutsi (Batutsi) herders over the next two centuries. The majority Hutu became virtual serfs. The central power of the Tutsi king or Mwami only declined towards the end of the 19th century.

Germany took control as the colonial power after 1884, merging Burundi with Rwanda (1899), and making Ruanda–Urundi part of German East Africa. Belgian troops occupied it during World War I, after which Belgium administered it under a League of Nations mandate, later (1946) a UN trusteeship. In 1959 it was split into Rwanda and Burundi.

The Parti de l'Unité et Progrés National (UPRONA) won UN-supervised elections in Sept. 1961 and Prince Louis Rwagasore became prime minister; he was assassinated less than a month later. Burundi became an independent kingdom on 1 July 1962. Two more premiers were assassinated before Oct. 1965, when an attempted coup was crushed and thousands killed.

An army coup in Nov. 1966 overthrew the monarchy and Burundi became a republic under Pres. Michel Micombero. The exiled former king, Mwami Ntare V, was killed in 1972 during an abortive attempted coup, which was blamed on the Hutu. Around 100,000 Hutu died in the subsequent Tutsi crackdown and thousands more fled. A military coup ousted Micombero in 1976 and Jean-Baptiste Bagaza became president, introducing some pro-Hutu reforms, although Tutsi dominance continued. Fellow Tutsi Pierre Buyoya deposed Bagaza in the 3 Sept. 1987 coup. Up to 20,000 Hutu were massacred by Tutsi in Aug. 1988. Ethnic fighting flared up again in Aug. 1988, resulting in many deaths and a (temporary) mass exodus of refugees, mostly Hutu, to Rwanda.

CONSTITUTION AND GOVERNMENT

Executive and legislature

The Sept. 1987 coup leaders suspended the civilian Constitution of 1981, establishing as the ruling body a 31-member Military Council for National Salvation.

Day-to-day government is run by the Council of Ministers headed by a prime minister.

Present government

President of the Republic; Chair of Military Council for National Salvation; Minister of Defence Maj. Pierre Buyoya

Members of Military Council for National Salvation Maj. Michel Mibarurwa (Chief of Staff); Lt-Col Gervais Ndikumagenge; Lt-Col Gideon Fyiroko; Lt-Col Jean-Baptiste Mbonyingingo; Lt-Col Jean-Claude Ndiyo; Lt-Col Aloys Kadoyi; Lt-Col Athanase Nziyumvira; Maj. Etienne Sindayihebura; Maj. Didace Nikuriyo; Maj. Gerard Cishahayo; Maj. Simon Rusuku; Maj. Leonidas Maregarege; Maj. Michel Nibaruta; Maj. Lucien Rufyiri; Maj. Bernard Kabwari; Maj. Jean Niyongabo; Maj. François Bizindavyi; Maj. Jean Bikomagu; Cdr Lazare Gakoryo; Cdr Evariste Niyungeko; Cdr Cyrille Bihabandi; Cdr Charles Ntancuti; Cdr Pascal Simbandumwe; Cdr Severin Nkejimana; Cdr Aloys Semujandari; Cdr Georges Mukorako; Cdr Sylvestre Nyingaba; Cdr Bernard Bijoyi; Cdr Daniel Mengeri; Cdr Gerard Ntakindi.

Prime Minister Adrien Sibomana

Principal Ministers Cyprien Mbonimpa – Foreign Relations and Co-operation; Gerard Niyibigira – Finance; Evariste Niyonkuru – Justice; Lt.-Col. Aloys Kadoyi – Interior.

Justice

The system of law is based on German and French civil codes and customary law. The highest courts are the Supreme Court and Appeal Court at Bujumbura, with provincial tribunals in each provincial capital. The death penalty is in force. No executions were carried out between 1985 and mid-1988.

National symbols

Flag. The field of the flag is divided by a white saltire into four triangles, those in the hoist and the fly being green, and the top and bottom ones red. In the centre there is a white circle with three red six-pointed stars, edged with green, forming a triangle.

Festivals. 1 May (Labour Day); 1 July (Independence Day).

Vehicle registration plate. RU.

INTERNATIONAL RELATIONS

Affiliations

NAM; OAU.

Defence

Total Armed Forces: 7,200 (inclusive Gendarmerie).
Terms of service: voluntary.
Army: 7,000.
Air Force: 200; some combat aircraft, no armed helicopters.

ECONOMY

Currency

The unit is the Burundi franc, divided into 100 centimes.

National finance

Budget. The 1986 budget was for expenditure of US$295 million and revenue of US$252 million.

Balance of payments. The balance of payments (current account, 1987) was a deficit of US$185 million.

Inflation. 7.3%.

Gross Domestic Product

Estimated total GDP US$1,150 million, per capita US$239 (overall size of economy ranking 137 in the world).

Economically active population. The total number of persons active in the economy is 1,900,000.

Sector	% of workforce	% of GDP
industry	1.5	14
agriculture	93	59
services*	5.5	27

* services figure includes elements unassigned to other categories.

Energy and mineral resources

Minerals. There are unexploited deposits of nickel, platinum and vanadium. Deposits of uranium, rare earth oxide, peat, cobalt and copper are known to exist. Gold is mined on a small scale.

Electricity. Capacity: 34,000 kW; production: (1987) 45 million kWh. Most of Burundi's electricity is supplied by Zaïre.

Bioresources

Agriculture. 85% of the population is engaged in subsistence farming. Coffee is the main cash crop, accounting for 90% of exports.

Crop production: (in tons/tonnes) cash crops are coffee 39,683/36,000 (1985); cotton 7,716/7,000; tea 3,307/3,000. Food crops: (1986) cassava 573,196/520,000; yams 7,716/7,000; bananas 1,388,898/1,260,000; dry beans 330,690/300,000; maize 176,368/160,000; sorghum 242,506/220,000; groundnuts 88,184/80,000; peas 35,274/32,000.

Livestock numbers: (1987) cattle 360,000; goats 865,000; sheep 390,000; pigs 80,000.

Forestry. Production: (1985) 127 million ft^3/3.6 million m^3.

Fisheries. Total catch: (1985) 16,424 tons/14,900 tonnes from commercial fishing industry on Lake Tanganyika.

Industry and commerce

Industry. Small-scale coffee and cotton processing in Bujumbura; light consumer goods; brewing; textiles; cement works; assembly of imports; food processing.

Commerce. Burundi's exports reached US$184.6 million (1986), principally coffee and tea. Total value of imports (comprising petrol products; food; vehicles; textiles) was $245.4 million. Principal trading partners are US; EC countries; Finland.

Trade with UK. (1988) Burundi imported goods worth £2,922,000 from the UK and exported to the UK goods worth £1,807,000.

Tourism. (1986) 66,000 visitors.

COMMUNICATIONS

Railways

There are no railways in Burundi (in 1987 plans were finalized for the construction of a line passing through Uganda, Rwanda and Burundi, to connect with the Kigoma-Dar es Salaam line in Tanzania).

Roads

There are 3,194 miles/5,144 km of roads (1,061 miles/1,710 km are national highways and 791 miles/1,274 km secondary roads).

Aviation

Air Burundi provides domestic and international services (chief airport is at Bujumbura).

Shipping

Bujumbura is a lake port on Lake Tanganyika, connecting with Tanzania and Zaïre.

Telecommunications

There are 8,000 telephones linked by a rudimentary system; 230,000 radio sets and about 4,000 televisions.

EDUCATION AND WELFARE

Education

School population. (1984) 387,710 at primary level; 13,037 at secondary level; 12,902 in technical schools; 2,783 students in higher education.

Schools. 1,023 primary; 62 secondary; 47 technical.

Literacy. 30%.

Health

(1983) 216 doctors; six dentists; 24 pharmacists; 1,126 nursing personnel; 33 hospitals with 5,709 beds.

CAMBODIA
Roat Kampuchea
(State of Cambodia)

GEOGRAPHY

Located on the south-west Indonesian peninsula in South-East Asia, Cambodia covers an area of 69,880 miles^2/181,035 km^2, divided into 18 provinces. An estimated 75% of the total land area is fertile lowland surrounding the north-west centrally situated Tonle Sap (Great Lake) which drains south-east into the north-south flowing Mekong. Highland areas border the plains to the north, north-east, east and south-west, rising to 5,948 ft/1,813 m at Phnom Aural in the sparsely populated south-western Cha¡nes des Cardamomes range (Chuor Phnum Kravanh and Chuor Phnum Damrei). 75% of the country is forested, with tropical vegetation dominating the south-west mountains and mangrove forests lining the coast. Annual monsoon flooding of the paddy-lands bordering the Mekong and Tonle Sap enriches them with alluvial deposits. The disastrous urban exodus of 1975–1978 under Pol Pot has severely depleted the populations of the major towns and cities. The vast majority of the population are rurally employed in forestry, fishing and subsistence agriculture.

Climate

Tropical conditions with high temperatures all year round, and monsoon rainfall (May-Sept.) ranging from 71 in/5,000 mm in the south-west to 51 in/1,300 mm in the interior lowlands. Average annual temperatures vary from 70°F/21°C to 95°F/35°C. Dry season Oct.-Apr. Phnom Penh: Jan. 78°F/25.6°C. July 84°F/28.9°C. Average annual rainfall 51 in/1,308 mm.

Cities and towns

Phnom Penh (capital)	700,000

Population

Accurate statistical trends and projection estimates remain difficult to establish following the mid-1970s genocide in which as many as 3 million people may have died.

Total population is variously estimated between 6,685,000 and 7,869,000 of whom 85% live in rural and 15.0% in urban areas. Population density is about 104 persons per mile^2/40 per km^2. At the last census, 93% of the total population were Khmer, 4% Vietnamese and 3% Chinese. **Birth rate** 4.55%. **Death rate** 1.97%. **Rate of population increase** 2.58%. **Age distribution** under 15 = 32.5%; over 65 = 2.6%. **Life expectancy** female 44.9; male 42; average 43.5.

Religion

The country's 1981 Constitution was amended in April 1989 elevating Buddhism to the national religion. In 1980, up to 88.4% (6 million people) practised Theravada Buddhism, 2.4% were Muslim and a small minority Roman Catholic.

Language

The official language is Khmer (Mon-Khmer derivative). French is widely understood. The written language dates from the 7th century in a script of Indian origin. Mixtures of Sanskrit, Pali, Thai, Chinese and Vietnamese vocabulary are commonplace.

HISTORY

According to Khmer myth the state of Funan was founded on the site of present-day Cambodia in the 1st century AD. The process of Indianization, which came to shape the politics and culture of subsequent Khmer states, broadened during the 4th and 5th centuries and was not halted by the subjugation of Funan in the 6th century by the rulers of the emerging state of Chenla, situated in modern north-east Cambodia.

In the early 9th century Jayavarman II, a Khmer prince, founded what is conventionally known as the Angkor Empire, based in the area north of the Tonle Sap. During the 11th century Angkor reached its peak under Suryavarman II, who consolidated Khmer rule over much of modern Cambodia, Thailand, Laos, Vietnam and Malaysia. Jayavarman VII was the last of the great Angkor god-kings and following the end of his rule sometime after 1215, the empire fell into decline. The eventual conquest of Angkor by Ayutthaya in 1444 led to the re-establishment of the Khmer kingdom at Phnom Penh, the site of the current capital. By the early 19th century competing factions of the Khmer royal house acknowledged Thai and Vietnamese suzerainty.

French rule over Cambodia evolved out of France's involvement in neighbouring Vietnam. Conquests in Cochin China during the 1850s induced the French to expand to the northwest in order to secure the Mekong against potential aggressors, principally the Thais and the British. Consequently, in 1863 King Norodom was pressured into accepting a protectorate status for his kingdom. In 1884 Norodom was forced, literally at gunpoint, into signing an agreement transforming Cambodia into a full French colony.

Japanese forces occupied Cambodia in late 1940, but left the pro-Vichy colonial administration intact. In Apr. 1941, the French authorities placed the 18-year-old Prince Norodom Sihanouk on the Cambodian throne. The French appeared to have expected that the young and inexperienced prince would be easily manipulated, a calculation that was subsequently proved imprudent. Facing impending defeat in the Pacific War, the Japanese attempted to foster genuine support within South-East Asia through the encouragement of native nationalism. In Mar. 1945 they interned the French in Indochina and offered limited independence to Cambodia, Vietnam and Laos. A few weeks later Sihanouk was pressured into proclaiming his country's independence.

After Japan's surrender in mid-1945, the French returned to Cambodia and in 1946 the absolute monarchy was abolished. A constitution was introduced in 1947 which permitted popular political activity. However, political stability was elusive and by 1950 dissident anti-French Khmer Issarak rebels controlled large areas of the countryside. Sihanouk abolished the country's National Assembly and declared martial law in early 1953 before embarking on a 'Royal Crusade for Independence'. The French, facing an increasingly stiff military test in Vietnam and Laos and concerned about the possible drift away from the conservative throne to the Viet Minh-associated wing of the Issarak, conceded Cambodia's independence on 9 Nov. 1953.

Sihanouk's royal government was accorded international recognition as the sole legitimate authority within Cambodia at the 1954 Geneva Conference. In early Mar. 1955, in order to avoid constitutional constraints on his political actions, Sihanouk abdicated from the throne. Sihanouk's newly created political party, the Sangkum, won an overwhelming victory in national elections held in September. The Sangkum repeated this in 1958, 1962 and 1966.

As head of state Sihanouk attempted to preserve Cambodia's neutrality during the Vietnam War. To this end, he approved both the establishment of Vietnamese communist sanctuaries in eastern Cambodia and America's clandestine bombing of these bases. Eventually, the overwhelming external pressures destabilized Sihanouk's government internally and in Mar. 1970 Lon Nol and Sirik Matik masterminded a successful right-wing coup and renamed the country the Khmer Republic.

In response, Sihanouk forged an alliance with his former communist enemies, the radical, rural-based Khmers Rouges. Together they formed a government-in-exile based in Beijing. Protracted conflict ensued, with the Khmers Rouges assuming an increasingly heavy burden. The overthrow of Lon Nol's regime was only narrowly averted in 1973 by US saturation bombing of Khmers Rouges forces. Eventually, in Apr. 1975, Phnom Penh fell to the Khmers Rouges.

After severing the country's links with the outside world (excepting China and North Korea), the new government embarked on a pre-planned economic and social experiment, based, to a large extent, on China's 'Great Leap Forward' of the late 1950s. The experiment failed and many hundreds of thousands of people died from brutal treatment, starvation and disease.

The Khmer Rouge leadership was deeply divided, and it was not until 1978 that an ultra-nationalist faction led by Pol Pot and Ieng Sary attained full control of the revolution. In the process, military commanders allied with this faction liquidated almost all pro-Vietnamese elements within the ruling elite. Villages and communes under the control of Pol Pot's opponents, most notably in the east of the country, were subjected to the most ferocious purges.

Border clashes between Cambodia and Vietnam broke out in May 1975 and by early 1977 Cambodian forces were carrying out deep, brutal forays into Vietnam's western border provinces. Initially, Vietnam responded to these violations with restraint, but by mid-1978 all pro-Vietnamese internal opposition to Pol Pot had been extinguished and invasion plans were formulated. After organizing anti-Pol Pot refugees from eastern Cambodia into a United Front, crack Vietnamese troops swept into Cambodia in late Dec. 1978. Pol Pot's forces put up little resistance and were quickly driven towards the Thai border. On 10 Jan. the People's Republic of Kampuchea (PRK) was proclaimed by members of the United Front and other (Hanoi-based) Khmer exiles.

Vietnam's invasion of Cambodia was criticized by China and the US, who continued to support Pol Pot from his base on the Thai border. Western pressure ensured that Pol Pot's regime retained its United Nations seat, but unease over his genocidal record led to the formation of the Coalition Government of Democratic Kampuchea (CGDK) in 1982, once again bringing together the Khmers Rouges and Sihanouk.

The CGDK guerrilla forces on the Thai border were routed by Vietnam in 1984–85. By this time, the PRK regime, with the help of Vietnam and the Soviet Union, had firmly established itself in Phnom Penh. Negotiations between the PRK and the CGDK made little headway until late 1987 when Sihanouk and the PRK premier, Hun Sen, held talks in France. During 1988 improved Sino-Soviet relations allowed even more substantive negotiations to take place.

An international conference held in Paris in July and August 1989 ended in stalemate. In late Sept. 1989 Vietnam withdrew the last of its armed forces from the country. The withdrawal heralded a period of increased fighting between the various Khmer protagonists.

CONSTITUTION AND GOVERNMENT

Executive and legislature

Political power in practice rests with the People's Revolutionary Party, the country's sole legitimate party. Under its (amended) 1981 Constitution, Cambodia is an independent sovereign state 'moving step by step toward socialism'. Executive power is held by a Council of Ministers elected by the parliament, the unicameral 117-seat National Assembly, which is elected for a five-year term by universal adult suffrage. The last elections were in May 1981; in Feb. 1986 the Assembly endorsed a resolution to postpone the next elections until 1991. The Assembly (which meets twice a year) elects a Council of State as its permanent organ from amongst its members.

The State of Cambodia government is not recognized by an overwhelming majority of UN member states on the grounds that the government was 'installed' in 1979 by Soviet-backed Vietnamese forces. Instead they recognize the tripartite Coalition Government of Democratic Kampuchea (CGDK).

Present government

State of Cambodia

President of the Council of State Heng Samrin

Chairman of Council of Ministers, and Foreign Minister Hun Sen

Vice-Chairmen Bou Thang; Say Phouthang; Chea Soth; Kong Samol; Say Chhum; Gen. Tea Banh (Minister of National Defence).

Kampuchean People's Revolutionary Party

General secretary Heng Samrin.

Coalition Government of Democratic Kampuchea
President (vacant)
Prime Minister Son Sann
Vice President, Foreign Minister Khieu Samphan.

National symbols

Flag. Red; in its centre features a yellow silhouette of five pointed towers with two steps at either side.
Festivals. 7 Jan. (Liberation Day, State of Cambodia); 17 Apr. (Independence Day, Pol Pot's former Democratic Kampuchea regime).
Vehicle registration plate. K.

INTERNATIONAL RELATIONS

Affiliations

CGDK is a member of the UN and NAM.

Defence

Total State of Cambodia Armed Forces: 60,000. Terms of service: conscription, five years; ages 18–35.
Army: some 30,000; 80 main battle tanks (mainly T-54/-55), ten light tanks (PT-76).
Navy: 1,000; 11 patrol and coastal combatants (Soviet Turya and Stenka).
Air Force: 800; 12 combat aircraft (MiG-21, reported).
Provincial Forces: some 25,000.

ECONOMY

Currency

The unit is the riel, divided into 100 sen.

Gross Domestic Product

Estimated total GDP US$570 million, per capita US$90 (overall size of economy ranking 151 in the world).
Economically active population. The total number of persons active in the economy is 3,300,000.

Sector	% of workforce
industry	7
agriculture	74
services*	19

* services figure includes elements unassigned to other categories.

Energy and mineral resources

Minerals. There are two phosphate deposits of an estimated 385,805 tons/350,000 tonnes each. One has been exploited by a jointly controlled state and private operation, and there are plans to exploit the other. There are high-grade iron-ore deposits in northern Cambodia, but difficulty of transportation prevents their exploitation. There are small-scale gold-panning and gem-mining operations.
Electricity. Capacity: 125,000 kW; production: 143 million kW; 21 kWh per capita (1988).

Bioresources

Agriculture. The vast majority of the population is involved in forestry, fishing and agriculture, the latter (except for rubber) being at subsistence level. Main crops are rice, rubber and corn. The war had a massively disruptive effect on agriculture and the country has been close to famine. In 1986 the amount of rice produced was able to meet only 80% of domestic need.
Crop production: (1985 in tons/tonnes) rubber 17,636/16,000; (1986) paddy 2.2 million/2 million. Other crops; (1986 in tons/tonnes) maize 101,412/92,000; dry beans 40,785/37,000; soya beans 2,205/2,000.
Livestock numbers: (1987 est.): cattle 1.6 million; buffaloes 700,000; sheep 1,000; pigs 1.3 million; horses 14,000; poultry 9 million.
Forestry. Over 50% of the country is forest and woodland. Some areas of woodland are over-exploited and conservation is not practised. Roundwood production: (1982) 180.1 million ft^3/5.1 million m^3.
Fisheries. Cambodia has the largest freshwater fish resources in South-East Asia. Production: (1982 est.) 92,593 tons/84,000 tonnes.

Industry and commerce

Industry. This was badly disrupted by the war. Major industries are rice milling; fishing; wood; rubber; cement. One of the biggest successes of the nation's recovery programme has been in the rubber industry. There are several thousand small family concerns in the private sector.
Commerce. Major trading partners are USSR; Vietnam. Principal imports: (1972) petroleum products; metals; machinery; food; chemicals.
Trade with UK. Cambodia imported £322,000 worth of goods from the UK and exported goods worth £55,000.

COMMUNICATIONS

Railways

There are 851 miles/1,370 km of railways.

Roads

There are some 6,831 miles/11,000 km of roads, of which about 1,242 miles/2,000 km are concrete or bituminized.

Aviation

Air Kampuchea provides domestic and limited international services (international airport is at Pochentong, near Phnom-Penh).

Shipping

Kompong Som is the maritime port; Phnom Penh operates as a port on the inland waterways which extend to 2,298 miles/3,700 km navigable all year by small craft.

Telecommunications

Telephone system is virtually non-existent except for government communications; about 7,300 telephones in all, with international links from Phnom Penh. There are two television and six radio stations, 52,000 television sets and some 200,000 radios.

EDUCATION AND WELFARE

Education

School population. In 1984 there were 1,504,840 pupils in primary schools; 147,730 in secondary schools; 7,334 in vocational establishments.
Universities. Phnom Penh University reopened in 1988.

Health

In 1984 there were 200 doctors (one per 34,190 patients); 130 pharmacists; 146 hospitals and clinics with 16,200 beds (one bed per 422 patients).

CAMEROON
République du Cameroon (Republic of Cameroon)

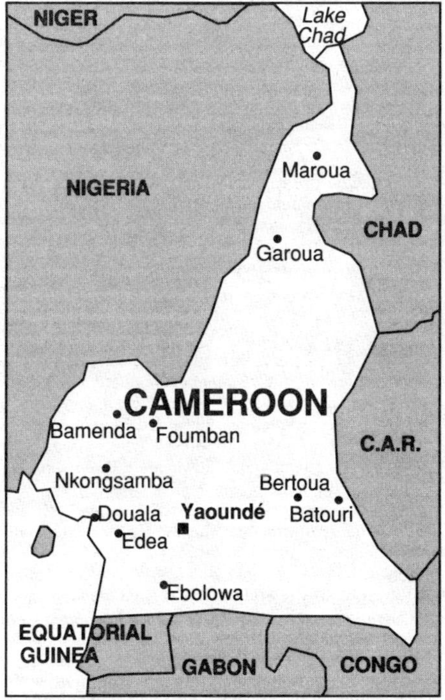

GEOGRAPHY

Situated on the west coast of central Africa, fronting the Gulf of Guinea, Cameroon comprises ten provinces covering a total area of 183,519 miles²/ 475,439 km². Topographically divisible into four regions, the southernmost area of equatorial forest, coastal plain and plateau (average elevation 984 ft/300 m) extends northwards from the southern frontier to the 326 miles/525 km-long Sanaga river traversing the country east to south-west. North of the Sanaga, deciduous and evergreen forest rises in the east towards the very sparsely populated Adamaua massif beyond which the Bénoué drains westwards into the Niger basin. The mountainous forest region north-west of the Sanaga incorporates the 13,353 ft/4,070 m-high volcano Mount Cameroon, and has pockets of very high population density. North of the Bénoué, semi-arid savannah slopes towards Lake Chad and the lower Chad border. 54% of Cameroon is forested, 13% is arable and only 2% is under permanent cultivation. The comparatively low urban population is concentrated in the southern part of the country.

Climate

Tropical climate in the south and west with high temperatures (average 79°F/26°C) and humidity, abundant rainfall Mar.-June and Sept.-Nov., decreasing south-north to semi-arid conditions north of the Bénoué. Coastal rainfall averages 150 in/3,800 mm a year, dropping to 59 in/1,500 mm in the central plateau region. The dry season lasts Oct.-Apr. in the north and in the south Dec.-Feb. and July-Sept. Yaoundé: Jan. 75°F/24.4°C. July 72°F/22.0°C. Average annual rainfall 61 in/1,555 mm. Douala: Jan. 79°F/ 26.1°C. July 75°F/23.9°C. Average annual rainfall 159 in/4,026 mm.

Cities and towns

Douala	458,426
Yaoundé (capital)	313,706
Nkongsamba	71,298
Maroua	67,187
Garoua	63,900
Bafoussam	62,239

Population

Total population is 10,674,000 of which 42.4% live in urban areas. Population density is 58.2 persons per mile²/23.2 per km². Over 200 ethnic groups constitute a diverse mix. Approximately 19.6% are Fang; 18.5% Bamileke and Bamum; 14.7% Duala, Luanda and Bassa; 9.6% Fulani; 7.4% Tikar; 5.7% Mandara; 4.9% Maka; 2.4% Chamba; 1.3% Mbum; 1.2% Hausa; 0.2% French. In 1987, over 8,500 Chadian refugees were living in Cameroon. The Pygmy Babinda people inhabit the southern forests.

Birth rate 4.43%. **Death rate** 1.73%. **Rate of population increase** 2.7%. **Age distribution** under 15 = 43.3%; over 65 = 3.9%. **Life expectancy** female 58; male 54; average 56.

Religion

Indigenous animist faiths are still practised by an estimated 39% of the population. Of the remaining 61%, roughly two-thirds are Christian (21% Catholic; 18% Protestant) and the remaining 21% are Muslim.

Language

French and English are the official languages; a number of African language groups define and divide the various peoples ethnolinguistically. The northern peoples are predominantly Sudanic-speaking (e.g. the Sao and Fulani). Elsewhere and particularly in the north-west and in the tracts of equatorial forest, Bantu speakers are prevalent (Fang, Bamilere, Duala, Luanda, Batsa and others).

HISTORY

Little is known of the earliest inhabitants of the area now known as Cameroon. The country was formed of over 150 different ethnic groups, including Bantu-speaking tribes who migrated to the south in the first millennium BC. Fulani pastoral nomads arrived in the north in the 16th century, and from 1809–48, under Mobido Adama, conquered the northern savannahs. Indigenous forest peoples may then have moved southwards after the Fulani invasions. Most groups did not settle until the late 18th and early 19th centuries.

The Portuguese arrived in 1472, and sailed up the Wouri river, naming it Rio dos Camarões (prawns), thus giving the country its name. By the early 17th century, the Dutch, Portuguese and English were competing for trade based on the export of slaves.

When Britain failed to take up the opportunity of imposing its rule in the colonial era, Germany signed a treaty with Douala chiefs on 12 July 1884, and set up the protectorate of Kamerun. During its rule, Germany developed a basic road and railway infrastructure, but ruthlessly exploited local products such as rubber, using forced local labour on the plantations. This led to uprisings in the south in 1904–10, but any resistance was brutally crushed by the military. By 1914, the country had been divided into small administrative units called residencies, headed by German advisers.

During World War I, British and French forces occupied the territory and used local people as labourers for the military. In 1922, Kamerun was made a mandate of the League of Nations with the West being controlled by the French. The status of United Nations Trust Territories was confirmed after World War II. The western part, divided into North and South Cameroons, was therefore administered by the British as part of Nigeria, while French Cameroon was treated as a French Equatorial territory. Changes in colonial policies after the war, when native Cameroonians were allowed to participate in local government, set the scene for the founding in 1948 of the Union des populations du Cameroun (UPC), which sought both reunification and independence.

In 1955, the UPC, under Ruben Um Nyobé, led an unsuccessful revolt, which was severely repressed by the French, and over 10,000 people were allegedly killed. The UPC was banned and went underground in the Bamileke region.

The French loi cadre (Framework Law) of 1956 granted a larger measure of self-government, which began with territorial assembly elections on 23 Dec. 1956. Under this system a French-Cameroonian government of 1957 had André-Marie Mbida of the Parti démocrate as prime minister, but the country was continually disturbed by a cycle of violent demonstrations and repression. Mbida was forced to resign in the political crisis, and Ahmadou Ahidjo, leader of the northern Union Camerounaise (UC), became prime minister on 19 Feb. 1958. In September, following Ruben Um Nyobé's death during a wave of repression, the legal UPC was founded, which took part in elections on 12 Apr. 1959, when France accorded the country full internal self-government.

On 1 Jan. 1960, Cameroon acceded to independence, with a presidential system of government. In the first National Assembly elections of 10 Apr. 1960, the UC won 51 out of 100 seats; Ahidjo was elected president shortly afterwards and re-elected in 1965, 1970, 1975 and 1980.

After a UN-organized plebiscite on 1 Oct. 1961, the Northern Cameroons became part of Nigeria, while the Southern Cameroons joined with the independent former French Cameroon to form a federal state, with both English- and French-speaking areas. This led to problems of merging separate educational, legal, administrative and economic systems. The federal structure lasted until 2 June 1972, when the United Republic of Cameroon was declared.

Ahidjo established an authoritarian state by merging the six legal political parties into the Union nationale camerounaise (UNC) on 1 Sept. 1966. The country became self-sufficient in food, with an economy based on the export of cocoa and coffee.

Rebellion in the West and Bamiléké regions, which had been repressed by the French, continued throughout the 1960s and 1970s, when the last remains of UPC resistance were crushed in a series of security trials. The UPC vice president, Ernest Ouandié, was arrested and sentenced to death after allegedly plotting to assassinate Ahidjo; he was publicly executed on 15 Jan. 1971.

On 7 May 1975, the post of prime minister was created with Paul Biya as incumbent. A constitutional amendment of 9 June 1979 stipulated that the prime minister would succeed to the presidency if there was a power vacancy. When Ahidjo unexpectedly resigned on 4 Nov. 1982, Biya took control; his mandate as president was renewed on 24 Apr. 1988, with a vote officially recorded as 100% in favour.

At the fourth party congress of 21–24 Mar. 1985, the UNC was renamed the Cameroon People's Democratic Movement (CPDM), as part of a programme to promote national unity by restructuring local party representation. Independent candidates were allowed to stand for the first time since 1960, but multi-partyism is not envisaged, and the ban on the UPC was confirmed in 1986.

Biya survived two coup attempts; the first of these, led on 22 Aug. 1983 by Maj. Ibrahim Oumarou and Capt. Amadou Salatou, was allegedly on Ahidjo's orders. The plotters, including Ahidjo, received the death sentence, which was later commuted to a period of detention. The following year, on 6 Apr. 1984, rebels in the presidential guard, led by Col Ibrahim Saleh, tried to seize the presidential palace. The rebellion was finally put down after three days of fighting, and with heavy civilian casualties. About fifty coup plotters were later executed. The head of state later gained control over the military by delegating the defence ministry to his office.

There have been other isolated incidents of unrest throughout Biya's rule, which have gone largely unreported in the Cameroon press. An unknown number of political prisoners are held in detention, although some were released in Sept. 1986. Biya carried out an economic restructuring programme involving strict austerity measures and a reform of the public sector in 1987.

At least 1,700 people died as they slept on 21 Aug. 1986, in a natural disaster when toxic gas (a mixture of carbon dioxide and hydrogen) from the volcanic Lake Nyos, 200 miles north of Yaoundé, engulfed lakeside villages.

CONSTITUTION AND GOVERNMENT

Executive and legislature

The executive president, head of state, head of government and C.-in-C. of the Armed Forces, is elected for a five-year term by popular vote (last held Apr. 1988). The Cameroon People's Democratic Movement is the sole and ruling party. The president rules with the assistance of a cabinet, whose ministers must not be members of the legislature, the 180-member National Assembly which meets twice a year (last elected Apr. 1988 on the basis of single party list).

Present government

Head of state, President Paul Biya

Principal members of the Cabinet Michel Meva'a M'Eboutou (Minister-Delegate at the Presidency for Defence); Ibrahim Mbombo Njoya (Territorial Administration); Sadou Hayatou (Finance); Adolphe Moudiki (Justice; Keeper of the Seals); Jacques-Roger Booh-Booh (Foreign Affairs).

Ruling party Cameroon People's Democratic Movement (Rassemblement démocratique du peuple camerounais).
National President Paul Biya.
Political Secretary François Senghat Kuo.
Members of the political bureau François Senghat Kuo; Lawrence Fonka Shang; Luc Ayang; Joseph-Charles Doumba; Ibrahim Mbombo Njoya; Basile Emah; Gabriel Mbala Bounoung; Michael Kima Tabong; Sadou Hayatou; Jean-Marcel Mengueme; Theodore Mayi; Jean Nkuete.

Justice

The system of law is based on the French civil code, influenced by English common law precepts. The highest court is the Supreme Court, based in Yaoundé, as is the High Court, while magistrates' courts operate in the provinces. The death penalty is in force. There were two executions between 1985 and mid-1988. Capital offences: murder and aggravated theft.

National symbols

Flag. Tricolour with vertical stripes in the pan-African colours of green, red and yellow and with a yellow five-pointed star in the centre of the red stripe.
Festivals. 11 Feb. (Youth Day); 1 May (Labour Day); 20 May (National Day).
Vehicle registration plate. CAM.

INTERNATIONAL RELATIONS

Affiliations

NAM; OAU; ACP; ICO; Francophonie.

Defence

Total Armed Forces: 11,600 (inclusive Gendarmerie). Terms of service: voluntary (para-military compulsory training programme in force).
Army: 6,600.
Navy: 700; six patrol and coastal combatants.
Air Force: 300; 11 combat aircraft (Alphajet and Magister) and four armed helicopters.

ECONOMY

Currency

The unit is the CFA franc, divided into 100 centimes.

National finance

Budget. The 1988 budget was for expenditure of US$2,217 million and revenue of US$2,170 million. Main items of expenditure are housing and welfare 12%; education 12.7%; defence 8.1%.
Balance of payments. The balance of payments (1987) was a deficit of US$1,112 million.
Inflation. 3.8%.

Gross Domestic Product

Estimated total GDP US$12,660 million, per capita US$1,190 (overall size of economy ranking 65 in the world).
Economically active population. The total number of persons active in the economy is 5,400,000; unemployed: 7%.

Sector	% of workforce	% of GDP
industry	11	31
agriculture	75	24
services*	14	45

* services figure includes elements unassigned to other categories.

Energy and mineral resources

Oil and gas. Production of crude petroleum from offshore fields (1987) 9.5 million tons/8.6 million tonnes.
Minerals. Production: (1985 estimated metal content of ore in tons/tonnes) tin 26,455/24,000; limestone flux and calcareous stone 87,082/79,000. Bauxite and kyanite are mined near Ngaoundere in north-central Cameroon.
Electricity. Capacity: 752,000 kW; production: 2,581 million kWh (1988).

Bioresources

Agriculture. 13% of the land is arable. The agriculture and forestry sectors contribute 25% of GDP; some 80% of the population is engaged in farming, mostly at subsistence level.
Crop production: food crops (in tons/tonnes): cassava 760,587/690,000; millet 440,920/400,000; maize 385,805/350,000; plantain 1,086,868/986,000; yam 440,920/400,000; groundnuts 144,092/140,000; bananas 73,854/67,000. Cash crops (in tons/tonnes); palm oil 93,696/85,000; palm kernels 57,650/52,300; cocoa 132,276/120,000; coffee 134,481/122,000; rubber 20,944/19,000; cotton 41,887/38,000; raw sugar 83,775/76,000.
Livestock numbers: (in millions) cattle 4.4; sheep 2.5; goats 2.45; pigs 1.2.
Forestry. 54% of the land is forest and woodland. Tropical hardwoods (mahogany, ebony and sapele) are produced in the south. Production: (1983) 350.7 million ft^3/9.9 million m^3.
Fisheries. Commercial catch: (1984–85) 11,894 tons/10,790 tonnes.

Industry and commerce

Industry. Aluminium smelting at Edea produced 85,979 tons/78,000 tonnes (1983). Other activities include cement manufacture; brewing; shoes; soap; petroleum products; rubber; food processing.
Commerce. Exports amounted to US$2,200 million (1988), of which petroleum products contributed 56%. Other principal exports were coffee; cocoa; timber. 50% of trade is with the EC. Imports were $1,700 million (1987), comprising mainly machinery; electrical equipment; transport equipment; chemical products; consumer goods. The principal trading partners are France (42% of imports); Japan; USA.
Trade with the UK. In 1988 Cameroon exported goods worth £16,180,000 to the UK, and imported goods worth £20,470,000 from the UK.
Tourism. (1986) 140,000 visitors.

COMMUNICATIONS

Railways

There are about 851 miles/1,370 km of railways.

Roads

There are 32,425 miles/52,214 km of roads (4,687 miles/7,548 km of main and 8,487 miles/13,666 km of secondary roads).

Aviation

Cameroon Airlines (Cam-Air) provides domestic and international services (international airports are at Douala and Garoua).

Shipping

The main port is Douala. The merchant marine has four cargo ships exceeding 1,000 GRT.

Telecommunications
There are 26,000 telephones. Radio is broadcast by ten stations, to 785,000 radio sets, and television was introduced in 1985.

EDUCATION AND WELFARE

Education
Education is free in state schools. Missionary and private schools also exist. Educational provisions vary according to region. Bilingual teaching was introduced at primary level (6–12) in 1972. Curricula were standardized in 1977.

School population. Enrolment at primary and secondary schools reached 67% of the school-age population (75% of boys and 59% of girls) in 1984, one of the highest rates of school attendance in Africa. In 1984–85 there were 1,638,570 pupils and 32,000 teachers at primary level (one per 51 pupils), and 238,000 pupils with 8,380 teachers at general secondary level (one per 28 pupils). There were 77,550 students at technical secondary schools and 3,880 in vocational secondary schools.

University. The State University has been decentralized to five regional campuses, each specializing in a different field of study. There were 13,750 students and 572 teaching staff in 1984–85.

Literacy. 56.2%.

Health
There were 1,003 hospitals and health centres with a total of 24,540 beds in 1981. In 1982 there were 600 doctors (one per 13,681 inhabitants); 400 midwives; 1,090 nursing personnel.

CANADA

GEOGRAPHY

Divided into ten provinces and two territories, covering 40% of the North American continent from 83°–42°N and from 52°–140°W, Canada occupies a total area of some 3,850,790 miles^2/9,976,140 km^2 with approx. 151,394 miles/243,791 km of coastline making it the second largest country in the world. The interior lowlands, surrounding Hudson Bay, constitute approximately 80% of Canada's total surface area, comprising the vast Canadian Shield (seldom more than 1,968 ft/600 m elevation), the St Lawrence-Great Lakes lowlands and the interior plains. The ancient Shield alone covers nearly 50% of Canadian territory, bounded south by the Lawrentide escarpment and west by the complex series of interwoven lakes traversing the country from the frozen north-west territories to Lake Superior (south-east). West of the Shield, the eastward sloping interior plains of Saskatchewan and Manitoba represent extensions of US prairie-land. The fertile and populous St Lawrence-Great Lakes lowlands stretch east from Lake Huron along the northern shores of Ontario and Erie and along the faulted St Lawrence River valley south of the Lawrentide Scarp, at an average height of slightly less than 1,968 ft/600 m. The rugged upland terrain of Nova Scotia and New Brunswick in the extreme south-east represents the northern spur of the Appalachians while across the Gulf of St Lawrence, the highlands of North Labrador and Baffin Island reach northwards culminating in the fragmented belt of Inuitian mountains in the Arctic Archipelago. In the west, the Canadian Cordillera dominates the topography from the Yukon/Alaskan border to the north-west United States frontier with British Columbia. Mount Logan in the north-west Yukon territory is Canada's highest peak at 19,524 ft/5,951 m.

The St Lawrence (E), Mackenzie (W), Yukon (W), Fraser (E) and Nelson rivers are among the world's 40 largest, with a combined total discharge of more than 1,149,294 ft^3/32,545 m^3 per sec. Over 35% of Canada is forested (including a coniferous belt stretching from Alaska to Newfoundland), 5% is arable and 80% of the population live within 99 miles/160 km of the US border.

Climate

Characterized by long, severe winters, Canada's climate ranges from polar and sub-polar conditions in the north to cool temperate in the south with significant variations between coastal regions and the interior. The highest winter temperatures occur on the Pacific coast near Vancouver Island with January temperatures above freezing (37°F/3°C) and warm July temperatures of 64°F/17.8°C; annual rainfall 57 in/1,458 mm. Rainfall is generally higher in coastal areas, decreasing inland, while the reverse is true of average summer temperatures. Winnipeg (south central Manitoba) receives 20 in/510 mm of rain per year and experiences mean Jan.-July temperatures of −2.7°F/−19.3°C and 67°F/19.6°C respectively. In the drier arctic latitudes, summer temperatures frequently fail to rise above freezing point and winter temperatures in the far north-west territories can drop below −33°F/−36°C.

Cities and towns

Ottawa (capital)	819,263
Toronto	3,427,168
Montreal	2,427,168
Vancouver	1,380,729
Edmonton	785,465
Calgary	671,326
Winnipeg	625,304
Quebec	603,267
Hamilton	557,029

Population

Total population is 26,093,000 of which 75.9% live in urban areas. Population density is 6.8 persons per miles^2/2.8 per km^2, falling to 0.05 persons per km^2 in the Yukon territories and markedly less than this in the virtually uninhabited north-west territories. At the last census, figures for ethnic origins were as follows; 6,332,725 of British extraction; 6,095,160 French; 709,590 Italian; 420,210 Ukranian; 896,720 German; 351,765 Dutch; 360,320 Chinese and an estimated 373,265 (approximately 1.5% of total population) aboriginal peoples, including the Metii, Dene, indigenous North American Indians and 25,000 Inuit in the north-west and Yukon territories. 6,986,345 Canadians recorded multiple origins of which 1,139,345 were Anglo/French.

Birth rate 1.52%. **Death rate** 0.71%. **Rate of population increase** (1980–87) 0.81%. **Age distribution** under 15 = 21.5%; over 15 = 10.4%. **Life expectancy** female 80; male 73; average 77.

Religion

Roman Catholic 46.5%; Protestant 41.2%; Eastern Orthodox 1.5%; Jewish 1.2%; Muslim 0.4%; Hindu 0.3%; Sikh 0.3%.

Language

English and French are both official languages. 62.7% (15,334,085) of the population speak English and 25.4% (6,159,740) speak French. In addition, native Amerindian languages claim approximately 95,000 speakers of whom 57,645 speak Cree, 16,380 Ojibway and 21,050 Eskimo (Inuktitut). Figures for other ethnolinguistic groups approximate to those stated above in Population.

HISTORY

The first human inhabitants of Canada were Indians from Asia who crossed by ice and land bridge over what is now the Bering Straits. There is also evidence that Inuit peoples regularly traversed the European, Asian and American Arctic areas. The first European settlers were Vikings who established a short-lived settlement in Newfoundland in the 11th century.

Extensive European settlement of Canada did not begin until after 1497 when the Italian navigator John Cabot, sailing on behalf of the English King Henry VII, landed at Newfoundland. In 1534, the French explorer Jacques Cartier discovered and claimed the St Lawrence River basin for France. Thus the two great European civilizations became established in Canada—English Canada in the north, northeast and western part of the country, and French Canada along the St Lawrence River, and, until the 19th century, down the Mississippi River to New Orleans.

The first European settlers engaged primarily in the fur trade. Exploration and settlement within the territory were determined by the needs of commercial concerns such as the Hudson Bay Company to find new sources of fur for the European markets. Fur and fishing remained major factors in Canadian history well into the 19th century and the Anglo-French rivalry has been a dominant force in Canadian politics until the present day.

From 1686, the French and English settlements began to clash regularly as their fur-trading operations increasingly overlapped. In 1744, the War of Austrian Succession spread to North America where it weakened but did not destroy the French position in Canada. In 1754, however, the French and Indian War broke out in North America between Britain and France (at the same time as the Seven Years' War in Europe). The result was a resounding defeat for the French in Canada and they were forced to relinquish the St Lawrence and Quebec settlements to Britain, which thereby gained control of the whole country.

The former French settlement now became known as Quebec. The British were thus faced with a large French-speaking population in control of the main transport route through Canada. Successive British governors sought to mollify French Canadian opinion by persuading the British government in London to establish a political structure which recognized Roman Catholicism, the French language and other French cultures and traditions. This was accepted and enshrined in the Quebec Act of 1774.

The next major challenge faced by Canada was the American Revolution (1775–83) which completely changed the character of Canada from a British colony dominated by Frenchmen to a British colony dominated by Englishmen intensely loyal to the British crown. Tens of thousands of British loyalists fled the American revolutionary forces in the US to seek refuge in Canada. Most of them were bitter at the expropriation of their property and Canada developed a strong anti-American element, which in turn came to be regarded by the Americans as a threat to their own independence. This led to the attempted American invasion of Canada during the war of 1812. At the end of this inconclusive war, the boundary between the US and Canada to the eastern edge of the Rocky Mountains was confirmed, except for the border between Maine and Canada, which had to wait for the Webster-Ashburton Treaty of 1842. The boundary was extended to the Pacific Coast with the Oregon Treaty of 1846.

In the first half of the 19th century Canada enjoyed an immigration boom. Its fur and fishing economy expanded to include small-scale industries based on timber and shipbuilding, and supported a growing number of ancillary professionals. With these economic changes came demands for greater political freedoms. The British government, having already lost the US, was responsive with the result that the Canadian colonies achieved effective self-government in 1848. The basic structure of the modern Canadian government is based on the British North America Act 1867, which confederated the colonies of Nova Scotia, New Brunswick, Ontario (Upper Canada) and Quebec. British Columbia joined in 1871, Prince Edward Island in 1872 and Newfoundland in 1949. Manitoba was created in 1870 from the former territory of the Hudson Bay Company and the provinces of Alberta and Saskatchewan were added in 1905. Each of the provinces retains considerable political power which results in a considerable amount of political juggling between the provincial governments and the federal government in Ottawa.

The British North America Act provided that the Constitution of the Dominion of Canada should be 'similar in principle to that of the United Kingdom'. Executive authority is vested in the British monarch who is represented by a governor general. Federal legislative authority is exercised by a parliament with two houses, the Senate and the House of Commons. In 1982 Canadians were given the right to amend their constitution without the approval of the British Parliament. The Canada Act 1982 also added to the constitution a Charter of Rights and Freedoms which recognized Canada's multicultural heritage, affirmed the existing rights of native peoples, confirmed the principle of equalization of benefits among the provinces and strengthened the provincial ownership of natural resources.

The second half of the 19th century was a period of fast growth for Canada. Immigration rose dramatically, the great wheat fields of Manitoba, Alberta and Saskatchewan were opened to settlement and the goldfields of the Klondike were exploited from 1897. Canadian control of both of these events was ensured by the completion of the transcontinental railroad in 1885 which also helped to suppress the dangerous 1885 Riel Rebellion of French Canadians and Indians.

Canada, however, remained a British colony. Although it had internal self-government, its foreign relations were determined by the government in London. This caused increasing resentment on the part of the French Canadians, who refused to fight in the Boer War. But during World War I, the English- and French-speaking communities were initially united in their support of the war effort and their battle record helped to ensure for Canada an increased voice after the war in determining its own foreign affairs and influencing Commonwealth and imperial issues. The war also helped to create a Canadian industrial base.

In the interwar years, successive Canadian governments used their wealth and increased political stature to steer a more independent course within the Commonwealth. Along with the Irish Free State and South Africa, they took a leading role in rejecting the concept of a common foreign policy for the Commonwealth and at the Commonwealth Conference of 1926 the principle of equality of status was accepted, followed shortly by a curtailment of the powers of the governor generals.

Until the 1930s, Canadian politics was dominated by two parties – the Liberals and the Conservatives. However, the failure of either party to deal with the Depression of the 1930s produced the social and political conditions for the rise of a number of special-interest and social democrat parties. These included the Cooperative Commonwealth Federation (later the New Democratic Party), the Social Credit Party and the Quebec nationalist party, the Union nationale, which provided the political roots for the Parti québécois. In an attempt to deal with the Depression, the Conservative government of R.B. Bennett introduced policies similar to Roosevelt's New Deal in the US and in 1936 laid a foundation stone for increased US-Canadian economic links with the 1936 Reciprocity Treaty. Neither one of these moves, however, resolved the economic crisis and the Depression continued until World War II, when Canadian troops again supported Britain.

World War II provided the Canadian economy with a powerful stimulus and it emerged from the conflict as a creditor nation with a powerful industrial base. World War II also marked the relative decline of Britain as a world power and the emergence of the US in this role. Canada's relations with these two countries changed to reflect these reversed roles. The US and Canada became founding members of the North Atlantic Treaty Organization (NATO) and formed military committees to coordinate policies for the defence of North America. The American Early Warning System for defence against a Soviet nuclear attack across the Arctic was based in Northern Canada. Canadian troops fought in the Korean War and were based in West Germany as part of NATO forces. Finally, in 1988, the economic links between the two countries were recognized by the signing of a free-trade agreement between the US and Canada.

US-Canadian relations, however, have not been problem-free. Canadians claim that the US takes their support too much for granted and plays too dominant a role in their national economy. There have also been differences over foreign policy. Canada had consistent doubts about the American isolation of the People's Republic of China in the 1950s and 1960s and during the Vietnam War became a refuge for thousands of young Americans evading conscription. Canada has also maintained close contacts with the Commonwealth which has become a political vehicle for friendly relations between Canada and the Third World, often at variance with both the US and Britain.

The Liberals, first under W. Mackenzie King and

then Louis St Laurent, dominated Canadian politics from the mid 1930s to the mid 1950s. A debate in 1956 over the Trans-Canada Pipeline made the long-lasting Liberal government appear complacent and arrogant and resulted in its 1957 election defeat by the Conservatives led by the impassioned and controversial orator John F. Diefenbaker. Internal dissension reduced the Diefenbaker administration to a minority government in 1962, and it was defeated in the following year by the Liberals, led by Lester Pearson, who was succeeded in 1967 by Pierre Trudeau.

Trudeau was faced with the problem of growing separatist demands, especially in his home province of French-speaking Quebec. The long-standing Anglo-French rivalry had been fuelled by changing social conditions and a politically corrupt Conservative English-speaking provincial government of premier Maurice Duplessis who remained in office until 1959. The resultant surge in French nationalism was further fuelled by an inflammatory visit by French president Charles de Gaulle in 1967, and the Parti quebécois – led by René Lévesque – was formed to demand complete separation from the federal government. The movement continued to grow through the 1970s and was accompanied by terrorist bombing campaigns, murders and the kidnapping in Oct. 1970 of British diplomat James Cross. After it had won provincial elections in 1976, it appeared as if the Parti quebécois would succeed in its aim of secession from Canada. A 1980 referendum on the issue, however, rejected Lévesque's plans for a separate government and the Parti quebécois went into rapid decline.

In the interim, the Liberal federal government of Trudeau had fallen victim to the world economic recession and, following the general election on 22 May 1979, the Conservatives formed a minority government under Joe Clark. This fell less than a year later when the government's budget proposals were defeated in Parliament. In the Feb. 1980 election, the Liberal Party and Trudeau were returned with a large majority. Trudeau resigned as prime minister in June 1984 and was replaced by the new Liberal leader John Turner who sought a popular mandate by calling elections on 4 Sept. 1984. The Liberals entered the pre-election period with revived popular support. Their following, however, receded in the face of accusations of political patronage and mismanagement by Turner. The result was a Conservative victory with the largest electoral majority in Canadian history. Although the Conservative government was soon hit by a series of damaging sex and financial scandals involving cabinet ministers, the opposition Liberal Party was unable to exploit its advantage as it was embroiled in a leadership struggle. The result was a second electoral victory for Mulroney in the general election of 21 Nov. 1988, although with a substantially reduced majority.

In 1989, Mulroney appeared to be firmly in control of the Canadian political scene. The US-Canada Free Trade Agreement, which he had negotiated and which was the central issue of the 1988 election, took effect on 1 Jan. and there were signs of a US-Canada pollution agreement to prevent American-originated acid rain which is destroying Canadian forests. The Canadian economy, in 1988, grew 4.5% compared with 3.7% the preceding year. The inflation rate, however, also increased, from 4.2% to 4.3% and this has led to curbs on public spending and unpopular higher interest rates. By the end of the year, however, the Mulroney government was recording record levels of unpopularity.

CONSTITUTION AND GOVERNMENT

Executive and legislature

The British sovereign as head of state is represented by a governor general, who appoints the prime minister. The prime minister, who is head of government and responsible to parliament, recommends the members of the Cabinet, who are formally appointed by the governor general. The Federal Parliament comprises a Senate of 104 members appointed by the governor general, and a House of Commons of 282 members elected for a maximum of five years by universal adult suffrage under a simple majority system in single-member constituencies. The last general election was on 21 Nov. 1988.

Present government (2 Feb. 1990)

Governor General Ramon John Hnatyshyn
Prime Minister Brian Mulroney
Members of the Federal Cabinet Gerald Merrithew (Veterans' Affairs); Joseph (Joe) Clark (Secretary of State for External Affairs); Marcel Masse (Communications); John Crosbie (International Trade); Donald Mazankowski (Deputy Prime Minister; Minister of Agriculture; President of the Privy Council); Elmer MacKay (Public Works); Jake Epp (Energy, Mines and Resources); John Wise (Agriculture); Doug Lewis (Justice; Attorney General; Government Leader in House); Robert De Cotret (President of the Treasury Board); Perrin Beatty (National Health and Welfare); Michael Wilson (Finance); (vacant) (Consumer and Corporate Affairs; Minister responsible for Canada post); Otto Jelinek (National Revenue); Thomas Siddon (Fisheries); Charles Mayer (Minister of State for the Canadian Wheat Board and for Grains and Oilseeds; Western Economic Diversification); William McKnight (Defence); Lucien Bouchard (Environment); Benoit Bouchard (Transport); Pierre Blais (Solicitor General; Minister of State for Agriculture); Barbara McDougall (Immigration; Minister responsible for Status of Women); Gerry Weiner (Multiculturalism and Citizenship; Secretary of State); Frank Oberle (Minister of State for Forestry and Mines); Monique Vézina (Minister of State for Employment and Immigration; Senior Citizens); John McDermid (Minister of State for Privatization and Regulatory Affairs); Lowell Murray (Government Leader in Senate; Minister of State for Federal-Provincial Relations); Paul Dick (Supply and Services); Pierre Cadieux (Indian Affairs and Northern Development); Jean Charest (Minister of State for Youth); Tom Hockin (Minister of State for Finance, Small Businesses and Tourism); Monique Landry (Minister of State for External Relations); Shirley Martin (Minister of State for Transportation); Mary Collins (Assistant Minister of Defence); Allen Redway (Minister of State for Housing, with responsibility for Central Mortgage and Housing Corporation); William Wineguard (Minister of State for Science and Technology); Kim Campbell (Minister of State for Indian Affairs and Northern Development); Jean Cordell (Minister of Labour); Giles Loiselle (Minister of State for Finance).

Administration

Canada comprises ten provinces and two territories. In each of the provinces there is a lieutenant-governor who represents the governor general, and an elected legislature and executive council, led by a premier. Considerable decentralization of federal authority to the provincial governments is provided by

Province	Total area (in miles^2/km2)	Population	Capital
Newfoundland	156,608/405,720	568,349	St John's
Prince Edward Island	2,185/5,660	126,646	Charlottetown
Nova Scotia	21,419/55,490	873,199	Halifax
New Brunswick	28,348/73,440	710,442	Fredericton
Quebec	594,702/1,540,680	6,540,276	Quebec City
Ontario	412,472/1,068,580	9,113,515	Toronto
Manitoba	250,881/649,950	1,071,232	Winnipeg
Saskatchewan	251,799/652,330	1,010,198	Regina
Alberta	255,219/661,190	2,375,278	Edmonton
British Columbia	365,851/947,800	2,889,207	Victoria
Yukon	186,612/483,450	23,504	Whitehorse
Northwest Territories	1,322,560/3,426,320	52,238	Yellowknife

a constitutional accord currently awaiting formal ratification. The two territories, in which the chief executive officer is the federally appointed commissioner, currently enjoy differing degrees of responsible government.

Provincial lieutenant-governors Alberta – Helen Hunley; British Columbia – Robert Rogers; Manitoba – Dr George Johnson; New Brunswick – George Stanley; Newfoundland and Labrador – James McGrath; Nova Scotia – Alan Abraham; Ontario – Lincoln Alexander; Prince Edward Island – Lloyd MacPhail; Quebec – Gilles de Lamontagne; Saskatchewan – Frederick Johnson.

Provincial premiers Alberta – Donald Getty; British Columbia – William Vander Zalm; Manitoba – Gary Filmon; New Brunswick – Frank McKenna; Newfoundland and Labrador – Tom Rideout; Nova Scotia – John Buchanan; Ontario – David Peterson; Prince Edward Island – Joseph Ghiz; Quebec – Robert Bourassa; Saskatchewan – Grant Devine.

Territorial commissioners Northwest Territories – John Parker; Yukon Territory – J.K. McKinnon.

Justice

The system of law is based on English common law (French civil law in Quebec). The highest court is the Supreme Court, located in Ottawa. It has general appellate jurisdiction in civil and criminal cases. The Governor-General, acting on the advice of the federal government, appoints Supreme Court judges, as well as the judges at each province's Superior Court and the county courts; provincial governments appoint the justices of the peace and magistrates operating at local level. The death penalty is in force only for exceptional crimes. No executions were carried out between 1985 and mid-1988.

National symbols

Flag. Three vertical stripes of red, white and red. In the middle of the white stripe there is a stylized red maple leaf.

Festivals. 22 May (21 May in 1990, Victoria Day); 1 July (2 July in 1990, Canada Day); 4 Sept. (3 Sept. in 1990, Labour Day); 11 Nov. (Remembrance Day).

Vehicle registration plate. CDN.

INTERNATIONAL RELATIONS

Affiliations

Nato; OECD; OAS; Commonwealth; Francophonie.

Defence

Total Armed Forces: 84,600 (planned 90,000 by 1989; 7,740 women). Terms of Service: voluntary. Reserves: 23,700.

Army: 22,500; 114 main battle tanks (Leopard C-1).

Navy: 10,000; three submarines (UK Oberon); 19 destroyers (Iroquois, Annapolis, improved Restigouche and Mackenzie); 12 patrol and coastal combatants.

Air Force: 23,100; 182 combat aircraft (CF-116/-116D, CF-18/-18D) and 32 armed helicopters (CH-124, CH-136 and CH-136).

ECONOMY

Currency

The unit is the Canadian dollar, divided into 100 cents.

National finance

Budget. The 1988 budget was for expenditure of US$89,500 million and revenue of US$75,200 million. Main items of expenditure are housing and welfare 36%; health 6.3%; defence 8.1%.

Balance of payments. The balance of payments (current account, 1988) was a deficit of US$7,498 million.

Inflation. 5.2% (year to Sept. 89).

Gross Domestic Product

Estimated total GDP US$373,690 million, per capita US$18,070 (overall size of economy ranking 8 in the world). Growth rate (1988) 5%.

Economically active population. The total number of persons active in the economy is 13,380,000; unemployed = 7.8% (1988).

Sector	% of workforce	% of GDP
industry	17	35
agriculture	4	3
services*	79	62

* services figure includes elements unassigned to other categories.

Energy and mineral resources

Minerals. Canada's principal mining regions are in the provinces of Alberta, British Columbia, Saskatchewan and Quebec. Production: (1987) copper over 83.8 tons/760 million kg; zinc 146.5 tons/1,329 million kg; lead 43 tons/390 million kg; gold 1.3 tons/117 million grammes. In addition, fuel production yielded 307,231 million ft^3/87 million m^3 of crude petroleum and 63.8 million tons/59.7 million tonnes of coal. Canada is the world's largest producer of zinc, nickel and uranium.

Electricity. Production: 482.1 million MWh. Of the net

total, hydroelectric generation accounted for over 313 million MWh with the bulk of the remainder produced by conventional steam power plants (92 million MWh). Nuclear power contributed a further 72.8 million MWh. Total national demand: 440.3 million MWh.

Bioresources

Agriculture. At the last census (1986), agricultural land made up 168 million acres/68 million ha of the total land area of 2,278 million acres/922 million ha. Over 75% of cultivable land is located in the Western Canadian prairies. Grain, dairying, fruit, fur farming and ranching are all flourishing activities.

Crop production: (1988 in 1,000 tons/tonnes) wheat 17,256.3/15,654.9; oats 3,299.6/2,993.4; barley 11,160.9/10,125.1; rye 283/257; flaxseed 456.2/413.9; canola 4,677/4,243.

Livestock numbers: (1988 in millions) cattle 12.06; sheep 0.69; pigs 10.85; chickens 22.42.

Forestry. Of the total land area, over 35% is forest, of which approximately 1.02 million miles^2/2.64 million km^2 is considered productive. Lumber output in 1985 totalled 1,839.9 million ft^3/52.1 million m^3 with sawmill shipments valued at approximately C$5,545 million for the same year. In the paper industry, 22.3 million tons/20.2 million tonnes of pulp and paper shipments of 15.7 million tons/14.2 million tonnes were valued at C$10,540.6 million (1985).

Fisheries. Total fish catch: (1986) 1.66 million tons/1.51 million tonnes, market value $2,952 million. Salmon $271 million; cod $218 million; lobster $243 million; herring $74 million.

Industry and commerce

Industry. Growth rate 5.7% (1988). Canada's economic development owes much to the continuing success of its mineral industry and to the sustained expansion of the manufacturing sector, providing the impetus over the past thirty years for a rural-urban industrial transformation. Prime industries include minerals; food; timber/paper; transportation equipment; chemicals; petroleum production.

Commerce. Exports: C$121,462 million in 1987 (US$111,500 million or 23.6% of the GNP in 1988). Imports: C$116,239 million in 1987 (US$102,100 million in 1988). Major exports in 1988 included newsprint paper; wood pulp; timber; grain; crude petroleum; natural gas; ferrous and non-ferrous ores; motor vehicles; telecommunications equipment; livestock. In 1987, food exports accounted for C$10,243 million and inedible, fabricated materials for C$41,820 million. Major imports in 1988 included processed foods; beverages; crude petroleum; chemicals; industrial machinery; motor vehicles; durable consumer goods; electronic computers. In 1987, food imports amounted to C$6,629 million and inedible end products to C$79,195 million.

Trade with UK. Canada imported UK goods worth C$4,339 million and exported to the UK goods worth C$2,850 million (1987).

Tourism. (1987) 39,595,211 visitors of whom 36,952,611 were US citizens.

COMMUNICATIONS

Railways

There are almost 120,474 miles/194,000 km of railways. The two major transcontinental systems are the government-owned Canadian National Railway and the Canadian Pacific Railway; the government operates the VIA passenger service.

Roads

There are 243,969 miles/392,864 km of roads, of which 102,466 miles/165,002 km are concrete or bituminized.

Aviation

Five airlines provide domestic and international service (chief airport is at Montreal). Air Canada is the major carrier.

Shipping

The merchant marine includes 85 ships of over 1,000 GRT. Principal ports are at Halifax, Montreal, Quebec, St John, St John's, and Vancouver on the Pacific seaboard. There are 3,000 km of inland waterways including the St Lawrence Seaway.

Telecommunications

There is a modern telephone system and 18,000,000 telephones. Broadcasting is done from 136 television and 850 radio stations, many of them local, and many of them affiliated to the national publicly owned Canadian Broadcasting Corporation (CBC) and transmitting its programmes. CBC operates in both English and French. Over 90% of Canadian households have colour television sets, and 78% subscribe to cable television services. CBC also transmits radio broadcasts, with two AM and two FM services, one each in French and English, and some services also in Indian and Inuit languages.

EDUCATION AND WELFARE

Education

Provincial legislative power over education is obliged to recognize certain minority language and denominational rights, as for example dual Roman Catholic and Protestant school board provision in Newfoundland and Quebec and the financing of Indian/Inuit education by Indian and Northern Affairs Canada.

School population. The total number of schools in 1987–88 was 15,521 including all primary, secondary, public, federal, private, blind and deaf divisions. These were attended by a total of 4,959,000 pupils and 273,190 teachers (one per 18 pupils).

Universities. A total of 474,820 full-time graduates and undergraduates were enrolled at Canadian universities for the academic year 1987–88. Of the 82,094 first degrees awarded in the same year, 36,489 were in social sciences, commerce, law, economics, political science, psychology and geography; 16,140 in education; 10,977 in humanities; 8,581 in engineering and applied sciences; 3,177 in fine arts.

Health

Canada's state-sponsored national health insurance scheme consists of a series of ten interrelated provincial hospital and healthcare programmes, drawn up in accordance with certain national stipulations, viz. provision of a wide range of hospital and medical benefits; universal population coverage; access to necessary services on uniform terms and conditions (Canada Health Act). Total health expenditure in 1988 amounted to an estimated C$50,400 million or 8.7% of the GNP. Of this figure, approximately 75% is attributable to public sector spending.

CAPE VERDE
Republica de Cabo Verde
(Republic of Cape Verde)

GEOGRAPHY

Situated approximately 385 miles/620 km west northwest of Senegal in the central Atlantic, the archipelago republic of Cape Verde comprises ten islands and five islets covering an area of 1,557 miles^2/4,033 km^2. They are divided into the Ilhas do Barlavento (windward) group in the north and the Ilhas do Sotavento (leeward) group in the south. The predominantly rugged, infertile mountainous terrain is volcanic in origin with an active volcano, Mount Cano, on Fogo Island rising to 9,281 ft/2,829 m above sea level. The semi-arid coastal plain of São Tiago (south), Santa Antão (north) and São Vicente (north) are the most densely populated regions; the bulk of the rural population inhabit a comparatively small number of fertile (irrigated) inland valleys. High aridity and a succession of prolonged droughts have repeatedly decimated the republic's agricultural yield. Less than 1% of the land area is under permanent cultivation. Poor soils and the absence of surface water outside the rainy season prohibit development.

Climate

Arid, with periodic droughts. Moderately warm, dry weather prevails Dec.–June (average Feb. temperature 42°F/22°C) with temperatures rising in the summer months to an average of 51°F/27°C (Sept.). Low, erratic annual rainfall ranges from 5 in/127 mm in the Barlavento islands to 12 in/304 mm in the Sotavento. Sea mists at higher altitude provide some compensatory moisture. Praia: Jan. 72°F/22.2°C. July 73°F/23°C. Average annual rainfall 10 in/250 mm.

Cities and towns

Cidade de Praia (capital)	57,748

Population

Total population is 358,000 of which 35.1% live in urban areas. Population density is 230 persons per mile^2/88.8 per km^2. Ethnic composition: 71% are of mixed (mulatto) origins, 28% are Black and 1% European. Well over half a million Cape Verdeans live abroad.

Birth rate 3.33%. **Death rate** 1.16%. **Rate of population increase** 2.17%. **Age distribution** under 15 = 41.7%; over 65 = 5.1%. **Life expectancy** female 61.04; male 58.95; average 60.

Religion

Well over 300,000 (perhaps as many as 97.8% of the population) are Roman Catholic and approximately 2% Protestant. Some indigenous beliefs survive.

Language

Portuguese is the official language, spoken in 19 creole (crioulo) forms throughout the islands.

HISTORY

Portuguese navigators were the first Europeans to discover the uninhabited islands in 1456, and in 1462 a settlement was established on the island of Santiago. Cape Verde became a transshipment base in the slave trade, which was only abolished there in 1876. The islands' fortunes declined in the 18th and 19th centuries with the drop in the slave traffic, recurrent two- to three-year droughts, and the migration of a significant proportion of the population to work on America's eastern seaboard as well as in Portugal and mainland Africa.

Under Portuguese colonial administration, the islands became an Overseas Province in June 1951. In 1956 Amilcar Cabral founded the Partido Africano da Independencia do Guine e Cabo Verde (PAIGC), which launched an armed struggle in 1961 for the liberation of Cape Verde and Portuguese Guinea. The party unilaterally proclaimed the independence of the latter (now Guinea-Bissau) in 1973. Following the Apr. 1974 coup by the armed forces in Portugal, a transitional government administered Cape Verde until independence on 5 July 1975. Aristides Pereira, who became the first president, had been party leader since the assassination of Amilcar Cabral in 1973.

Relations with Guinea-Bissau were soured by the Nov. 1980 coup in Bissau, and in Jan. 1981 the Cape Verde wing of the PAIGC was renamed the Partido Africano da Independencia de Cabo Verde (PAICV). Reconciliation talks were held in June 1982, relations returned to normal, and in 1988 the two countries signed a co-operation agreement.

In Jan. 1986 Pres. Pereira was re-elected for a further five-year term by the National Assembly; his leadership of the PAICV was reconfirmed at a party conference in Nov. 1988. Social tension spread in the islands in July 1987 and Jan. 1988 when laws decriminalizing abortion were passed.

In Feb. 1990 the party recommended constitutional reforms providing for a multi-party system by Dec. 1990 when elections were due.

CONSTITUTION AND GOVERNMENT

Executive and legislature

The 1980 Constitution defines Cape Verde as 'a sovereign, democratic, unitary, anti-colonialist and anti-imperialist republic'. The executive president serves a five-year term, and was last elected (unanimously) in Jan. 1986 by the National People's Assembly. The 83 Assembly members are elected by universal suffrage (most recently in Dec. 1985) from a single list of candidates put forward by the sole party, the African Party for the Independence of Cape Verde.

Present government

President Aristides Maria Pereira

Prime Minister; Finance; Planning and Co-operation Gen. Pedro Verona Rodrigues Pires

Prominent members of Council of Ministers Col. Silvino Manuel da Luz (Foreign Affairs); Maj. Osvaldo Lopes da Silva (Transport, Trade and Tourism); Maj. Julio de Carvalho (Armed Forces and Security); Maj. João Pereira Silva (Agriculture and Fisheries); Corsino Fortes (Justice).

Ruling party

African Party for the Independence of Cape Verde (Partido Africano da Independencia de Cabo Verde).

Secretary-General Aristides Maria Pereira. **Deputy Secretary-General** Gen. Pedro Verona Rodrigues Pires.

Justice

The highest court is the Supreme Court in Praia, with a network of People's Tribunals. The death penalty was abolished in 1981.

National symbols

Flag. Two horizontal stripes of yellow over green with a vertical stripe in the hoist. Just above the middle of this stripe there is an emblem dominated by a black five-pointed star.

Festivals. 20 Jan. (National Heroes' Day); 8 Mar. (Women's Day); 1 May (Labour Day); 1 June (Children's Day); 5 July (Independence Day); 12 Sept. (Day of the Nation).

INTERNATIONAL RELATIONS

Affiliations

NAM; OAU.

Defence

Total Armed Forces: 1,200. Terms of service: conscription (selective).
Army: 1,000 (Popular Militia).
Navy: 200; five patrol and coastal combatants.
Air Force: under 100.

ECONOMY

Currency

The unit is the Cape Verdean escudo, divided into 100 centavos.

National finance

Budget. The 1984 budget was for expenditure of US$27 million and revenue of US$20 million.

Inflation. 11%.

Gross Domestic Product

Estimated total GDP US$136 million, per capita US$400 (overall size of economy ranking 173 in the world).

Economically active population. The total number of persons active in the economy is 180,000; unemployed = 25%.

Sector	% of workforce
industry	14
agriculture	57
services*	29

* services figure includes elements unassigned to other categories.

Energy and mineral resources

Minerals. Salt is produced on the islands of Sal, Boa Vista and Maio. There are deposits of basalt, limestone and kaolin. Pozzolana (volcanic rock) is mined for export.

Electricity. Capacity 14,000 kW; production (1988) 18 million kWh.

Bioresources

Agriculture. 9% of the land is arable, with 6% composed of meadows and pasture. Some 57% of the population are engaged in agriculture, mostly subsistence, in the irrigated inland valleys. The volcanic islands are subject to prolonged droughts, the effects of which have been compounded by deforestation and overgrazing.

Crop production: (1986 in tons/tonnes) coconuts 11,023/10,000; sugar cane 11,023/10,000; bananas 4,409/4,000; potatoes 3,307/3,000; cassava 4,409/4,000; sweet potatoes 7,716/7,000; maize 13,228/12,000.

Livestock numbers: goats 65,000; cattle 13,000; pigs 50,000; asses 6,000.

Fisheries. Total catch: (1983) 14,330 tons/13,000 tonnes, including tuna (46%) and lobster.

Industry and commerce

Industry. The main activities are fish processing; salt mining; clothing manufacture; ship repairs.

Commerce. Exports amounted to US$5,600,000 in 1987, comprising fish, bananas and salt, principally to Portugal; Central African Republic; Guinea-Bissau; Netherlands. Imports in 1987 totalled $82,000,000 worth of petroleum; foodstuffs; consumer goods; industrial products from Portugal; West Germany; EC countries; US.

Trade with UK. Cape Verde exported goods worth £132,000 to the UK in 1988 and imported goods worth £1,812,000 from the UK.

Tourism. Approximately 2,000 visitors per year.

COMMUNICATIONS

Railways

There are no railways.

Roads

There are about 1,398 miles/2,250 km of roads, of which 410 miles/660 km are concrete or bituminized.

Aviation

Transportes Aéreos de Cabo Verde (TACV) provides international services and connects the islands.

Shipping

Mindelo and Praia are the main ports. There are four cargo ships of over 1,000 GRT.

Telecommunications

There is a radio relay telephone system between the islands, and 1,740 telephones. There are two government-owned radio stations, 47,000 radios and no television service.

EDUCATION AND WELFARE

Education

Education is compulsory between the ages of seven and 14.

Schools. There is a two-cycle system of primary education. In 1986–87 there were 347 first-level primary schools with about 50,000 pupils, and 16 second-stage primary schools with 10,300 pupils. There were four lycées providing either a three-year general course or a two-year pre-education course for the post-14 age group. There was also one industrial and commercial school and three teacher-training colleges.

Literacy. 47.4%.

Health

Health facilites are limited, but there are plans for a national health service, to include the provision of 300 local clinics. There were 21 hospitals and dispensaries in 1980, with 632 beds, 51 doctors (one per 6,550 inhabitants) and 184 nursing personnel.

CAYMAN ISLANDS

GEOGRAPHY

The Cayman Islands, (Grand Cayman, Little Cayman and Cayman Brac) cover a total area of 100 miles^2/260 km^2 in the Caribbean. They are low-lying and are within the Caribbean hurricane belt. The capital is George Town.

Climate

Tropical marine, with warm, rainy summers (May-Oct.) and cool, relatively dry winters (Nov.-Apr.).

Population

23,768.

Life expectancy female 79; male 73.

Religion

Christianity: United Church, Anglican, Baptist, Roman Catholic.

Language

English.

HISTORY

The Cayman Islands were uninhabited until their discovery by Europeans. Navigators, traders and pirates used the islands as temporary bases in the 16th and early 17th centuries, but no permanent settlements were established until the islands came under British control in 1670 and were colonized by settlers from Jamaica. The smaller islands of Cayman Brac and Little Cayman were not settled until 1833. The Cayman Islands were administered as a dependency of Jamaica until Jamaica attained independence in 1962. They then reverted to being a British dependency with an administrator, whose title was changed to governor in 1971. Offshore banking and financial services developed during the 1960s and 1970s and replaced the traditional activities of turtle fishing and farming, leading to a substantial increase in the islands' prosperity. Political parties have not developed on the islands and elections are contested by independent candidates, sometimes grouping into 'teams', although all remain in favour of continued dependent status. The last elections to the islands' Assembly were held in 1988.

CONSTITUTION AND GOVERNMENT

A dependent territory of the United Kingdom and member of the Commonwealth, with a Constitution dating from 1959, revised in 1972. There is a governor and Executive Council (three appointed official members and four elected members chosen by the Legislative Assembly from its elected members). The Legislative Assembly is unicameral, with 12 elected members and three appointed by the governor. Elections are held every five years. There are no formal political parties.

Governor A.J. Scott, who is also president of the Executive Council.

National symbols

Flag. Blue, with the flag of the UK in the upper hoist-side quadrant, and the Caymanian coat of arms on a white disc centred on the outer half of the flag. The coat of arms includes a pineapple and turtle, above a shield with three stars.

ECONOMY

The islands are heavily dependent on tourism and off-shore financial services. About 90% of the island's food and consumer goods must be imported. The standard of living is one of the highest in the region.

Currency

Caymanian dollar.

COMMUNICATIONS

There are ports in George Town and Cayman Brac, and three airports, two with permanent-surface runways. There are 99 miles/160 km of main roads. There is a telephone system and a satellite ground system linking the islands and accessing international services. There are three radio stations, but no television.

CENTRAL AFRICAN REPUBLIC

République Centrafricaine

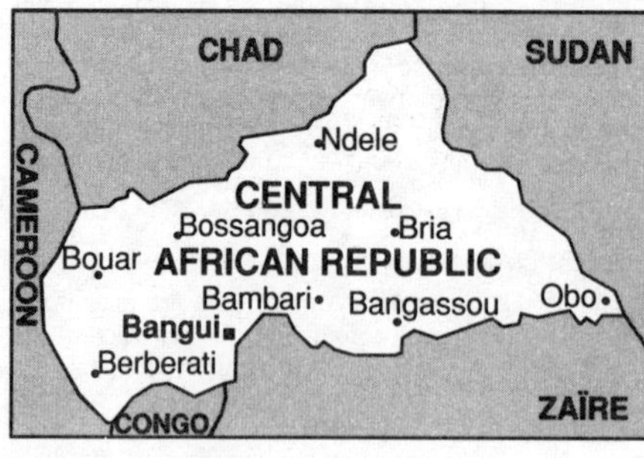

GEOGRAPHY

The Central African Republic is a landlocked country just north of the equator, occupying a low plateau area of 240,471 miles^2/622,984 km^2 divided into 15 prefectures. The CAR plateau has an average elevation of between 1,968 ft/600 m and 2,625 ft/800 m and forms the watershed that divides the Chad, Congo and Nile River basins. Highland areas include the Massif des Bongos (4,593 ft/1,400 m) in the north-east and the granite ranges of Mont Karre in the west (4,003 ft/1,220 m). The principal northern rivers drain into the Bahr Avok, a tributary of the Chari. In the south, 60% of CAR's drainage flows into the Ubangi

River on the Zaïrean border. The land surrounding the border river (north and south) also sustains the largest concentrations of CAR's predominantly rural population. Over 64% of the total surface area is forested, the greater part of which is savannah parkland. In the south and south-west regions, rainforests penetrate the interior grasslands along the river valleys. Approximately 3% of the land is arable and most agricultural activity is subsistence farming.

Climate

Tropical, with sub-Saharan conditions in the north and equatorial climate in the south. Rainfall increases south and south-west with a wider annual distribution than that of the north and north-east, 90% of which falls in a single wet season from Apr.–Sept. Average rainfall in the north is 34–39 in/875–1,000 mm, compared to 59–79 in/1,500–2,000 mm in the south. Uniformly high temperatures range between 75°F/24°C and 82°F/28°C throughout the country. Bangui: Jan. 26.5°C. July 77°F/25°C. Average annual rainfall 60 in/1,525 mm. Ndele: Jan. 83°F/28.3°C. July 77°F/25°C. Average annual rainfall 56 in/1,417 mm.

Cities and towns

Bangui (capital)	473,817
Berberati	100,000
Bouar	55,000

Population

Total population is 2,771,000 of which 37% live in urban areas. Population density is 11.5 persons per mile^2/4.5 per km^2. Of the 80 separable ethnic groups, many share common ethnolinguistic denominations. The major groups are Baya (35%); Banda (28%, centrally located); Sara (10%, north border peoples); Mandija (9%); Mbdum (9% largely in the north and north-east); M'baka (7% part of the Ubangi group). There are approximately 6,500 Europeans of whom 3,600 are French.

Birth rate 4.46%. **Death rate** 2.18%. **Rate of population increase** (1980–87) 2.28%. **Age distribution** under 15 = 42.5%; over 65 = 3.8%. **Life expectancy** female 52; male 48; average 50.

Religion

About half the total population profess Christianity, divided equally between Roman Catholicism and Protestantism. Approximately 24% follow indigenous (animist) beliefs and a further 10% are Muslim.

Language

French is the official written language, supplanted orally by Sango, the national lingua franca. In addition to the ethnolinguistic percentages listed above, approximately 290,000 persons speak Ngbandi and 270,000 Zande. Arabic, Hunsa and Swahili are also spoken.

HISTORY

Archaeologists have discovered Palaeolithic remains in the Central African Republic but there is no historical record before 1850. The region was probably part of the Gaoga empire in the 16th century and was decimated by slave raiders from the north from then until the early 19th century. A French post was established at Bangui in 1889, though it was not until 1911 that France secured complete control. In 1898 the colony, then called Oubangui-Chari and administered as one of the four territories of French Equatorial Africa, was parcelled out among commercial concessionaires who, until the 1930s, ruthlessly conscripted labour to work on plantations.

Oubangui-Chari became an overseas territory in 1946 and elected Barthélémy Boganda, a nationalist, as its representative in the French parliament. From 1 Dec. 1958, the country became the Central African Republic within the French Community, but moved to full independence on 13 Aug. 1960. Its first president was David Dacko, Boganda having died in the previous year.

In 1966 Dacko was overthrown by his cousin, Col Jean-Bedel Bokassa, who promptly abrogated the constitution and personally assumed full executive powers. Bokassa became one of Africa's most notorious and bizarre dictators, crowning himself emperor on 4 Dec. 1977 in imitation of Napoleon at a ceremony costing $20–30 million. Bokassa received substantial financial and military aid from the West, especially from France (and provoked a major political scandal there over his gifts of diamonds to President Giscard d'Estaing), but condemnation of his regime grew increasingly widespread, with Amnesty International revealing that Bokassa had participated in the massacre of 80 schoolchildren.

French paratroopers assisted in a coup to overthrow Bokassa on 20–21 Sept. 1979; the Empire was abolished and the Republic restored, with David Dacko again as president (re-elected 15 Mar. 1981 amid protests over ballot-rigging). He proved unable to reverse the country's economic decline and the military hierarchy seized power on 1 Sept. 1981 with Gen. André Kolingba becoming head of state. In Dec. 1984, opposition leaders formed a government-in-exile and in Jan. 1986 a unified opposition Front uni pledged a return to democracy. Pres. Kolingba responded by forming a new government in Sept. 1985 in which civilians held the majority of portfolios, though the military still held key posts.

A referendum on 21 Nov. 1986 backed a new constitution, granted Kolingba a six-year mandate and approved a sole party, the Rassemblement démocratique centrafricain (RDC). The first legislative elections for 20 years were held on 31 July 1987, but the turnout was disappointing, with the Front uni boycotting the poll. Kolingba secured IMF support for economic adjustment programmes and, during a visit to France in Feb. 1988, obtained increased aid from France.

Bokassa, escaping surveillance in France, returned from exile in Oct. 1986, apparently expecting an enthusiastic reception, but was arrested at Bangui airport; he was tried and sentenced to death, later commuted (Feb. 1988) to life imprisonment.

Twelve opposition figures who had fled the country after an unsuccessful coup attempt in 1982 were in Aug. 1989 extradited from Benin and placed in detention.

CONSTITUTION AND GOVERNMENT

Executive and legislature

A gradual process of returning the country to civilian rule has been undertaken. A referendum in Nov. 1986 approved establishment of a one-party state, the sole party being the Central African Democratic Assembly. A National Assembly was created as legislative organ; last elections July 1987.

Present government

President; Prime Minister, Minister of Defence; Minister of Armed Forces and Veterans' Affairs Gen. André Kolingba

Principal members of Council of Ministers Dieudonné Wazoua (Economy and Finance, Planning and International Co-operation); Michel Gbezera-Bria (Foreign Affairs); Lt-Gen. Thomas Matouka (Rural Development); Lt-Col Christophe Grelombe (Interior and Territorial Administration); Jean Willibiro-Sako (Justice; Keeper of the Seals).

Ruling party

Central African Democratic Assembly (Rassemblement démocratique centrafricain).

Founding president Gen. André Kolingba.

Executive secretary Joseph Bangui.

Justice

The system of law is based on French concepts. The highest court is the Supreme Court, which together with the Criminal Court is located in the capital, Bangui. The death penalty is in force. No executions were recorded between 1985 and mid-1988.

National symbols

Flag. Four horizontal stripes of blue, white, green and yellow, crossed by a central vertical red stripe with a yellow five-pointed star in the top left-hand corner.

Festivals. 29 Mar. (Anniversary of death of Barthelemy Boganda); 1 May (May Day); 30 June (National Day of Prayer); 13 Aug. (Independence Day); 1 Dec. (National Day).

Vehicle registration plate. RCA.

INTERNATIONAL RELATIONS

Affiliations

NAM; OAU; ACP; Francophonie.

Defence

Total Armed Forces: 6,500 inclusive Gendarmerie. Terms of service: conscription (selective), two years. Reserve obligation thereafter, term unknown.

Army: 3,500; four main battle tanks (T-55).

Air Force: 300.

ECONOMY

Currency

The unit is the CFA franc, divided into 100 centimes.

National finance

Budget. The 1986 budget was for expenditure of US$147 million and revenue of US$143 million.

Balance of payments. The balance of payments (current account, 1987) was a deficit of US$214 million.

Inflation. –7%.

Gross Domestic Product

Estimated total GDP US$1,010 million, per capita US$410 (overall size of economy ranking 141 in the world).

Economically active population. The total number of persons active in the economy is 775,000; unemployed: (in Bangui) 30%.

Sector	% of workforce	% of GDP
industry	3	13
agriculture	85	41
services*	12	46

* services figure includes elements unassigned to other categories.

Energy and mineral resources

Minerals. Gem diamonds 258,700 carats; industrial diamonds 98,700 carats (1986); gold 225 kg (1987). There are also significant deposits of uranium.

Electricity. Capacity: 35,000 kW; production: 84 million kWh (1988).

Bioresources

Agriculture. Only 3% of the land is arable, with 5% meadows and pasture. Subsistence agriculture is the mainstay of the economy, with over 80% of the population rural dwellers. The agricultural sector contributes about 40% of GDP, with agricultural products accounting for some 50% of export earnings. The northern regions are affected by desertification.

Crop production: (1986 in tons/tonnes) cassava 780,428/708,000; groundnuts 156,527/142,000; bananas 91,491/83,000; plantains 71,679/65,000; millet 44,092/40,000; maize 58,422/53,000; seed cotton 69,445/63,000; coffee 19,841/18,000; rice 17,637/16,000.

Livestock numbers: (1987) cattle 2,224,000; goats 1,135,000; sheep 116,000; pigs 371,000.

Forestry. 64% of the land is covered in forest and woodland. There are extensive hardwood forests in the south-west, producing mahogany, obeche and limba for export. Production of roundwood (1986) 111,133,000 ft^3/3,147,000 m^3.

Fisheries. Total catch: (1986) 14,329 tons/13,000 tonnes of freshwater fish.

Wildlife. Poaching has diminished the country's reputation as one of Africa's major wildlife refuges.

Industry and commerce

Industry. Principal activities are diamond mining; sawmills; brewing; textiles; footwear; assembly of bicycles and motorcycles. Mining and manufacturing contribute 14% of GDP; utilities and construction 4%. The CAR's landlocked position and underdeveloped transport infrastructure have constrained economic development.

Commerce. Exports: (1987) US$131 million, comprising diamonds; cotton; coffee; timber; tobacco. Countries exported to are France (30%); Belgium; Italy; Japan; US. Imports: (1987) $269 million, principally food; textiles; petroleum products; machinery; electrical equipment; motor vehicles; chemicals; pharmaceuticals; consumer goods; industrial products. Countries imported from are France; other EC countries; Japan; Algeria; Yugoslavia.

Trade with UK. CAR imported UK goods worth £733,000 in 1988; exports to the UK totalled £195,000.

Tourism. (1986) About 4,000 visitors.

COMMUNICATIONS

Railways

There are no railways at present but there is a long-term project to connect Bangui to the Transcameroon railway.

Roads

There are 12,593 miles/20,278 km of roads, of which only about 279 miles/450 km are concrete or bituminized.

Aviation

Air Afrique provides international services and Inter-RCA provides extensive domestic services (international airport is at Bangui-Mpoko).

Shipping

There are some 497 miles/800 km of inland waterways usable by small craft, the main link being the Oubangui river.

Telecommunications

There are about 6,000 telephones, with a rudimentary radio relay system. There are 125,000 radio sets.

EDUCATION AND WELFARE

Education

Education is compulsory between the ages of six and 14. The primary cycle begins at six years old and lasts for six years. The secondary cycle begins at the age of 12 and lasts for up to seven years.

School population. (1982) An estimated 60% of the primary age group (six to 12) attended school (79% of boys and 42% of girls). Secondary enrolment was the equivalent of 16% of the age group (24% of boys and 8% of girls). In 1985 there were 308,000 pupils at primary school and 52,780 pupils at secondary school. There were 1,300 students at technical school in 1982 and 330 at two teacher-training colleges.

University. The University of Bangui had 1,500 students in 1980.

Literacy. Adult literacy 40.2%.

Health

There were approximately 7,000 hospital beds in 1984 (one per 371 inhabitants). There were 112 physicians (one per 23,282 inhabitants). There were also 168 midwives and 710 nursing personnel.

CHAD

République du Tchad *(Republic of Chad)*

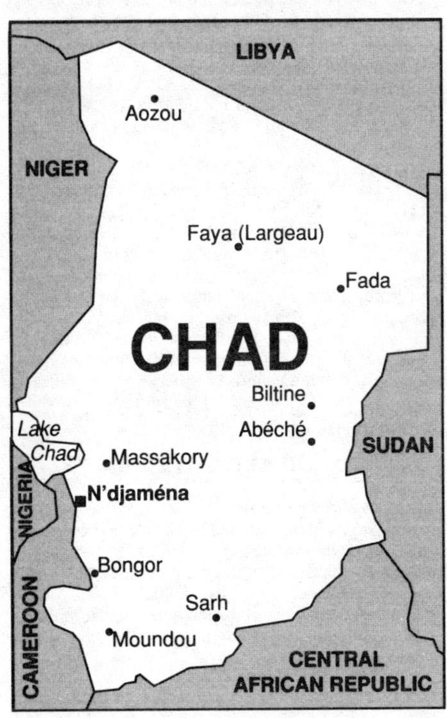

GEOGRAPHY

Located in north central Africa, Chad is a dry landlocked country extending north-east and south-east of Lake Chad on the western border, covering a total area of 495,624 miles^2/1,284,000 km^2. Chad is divided into 14 prefectures, the most densely populated of which are the Mayu-Kebbi, Chari-Baguirmi and Moyen-Chari regions in the tropical south. The northernmost Borkou-Ennedi-Tibesti prefecture stretches over 231,716 miles^2/600,300 km^2 but sustains less than 2% of the total population. Most of the terrain occupies arid semi-desert plateau scrubland (average elevation 656–1,640 ft/200–500 m) rising from the west Lake Chad basin to the volcanic Tibesti peaks in the north (11,204 ft/3,415 m at Emikoussi, Chad's highest point), the sandstone plateaux in the north-east, the Eastern Ovaddai range and the Oubangi Plateau in the south. The monotony of the north central and north-eastern desert-steppe is occasionally alleviated by palm oases. The south-east to south-west flowing Chari and Logone drain into Lake Chad. 2% of the total surface area is arable land, 11% is woodland and forest and less than 1% is irrigated.

Climate

Tropical conditions in the south, with between 32 in/800 mm and 47 in/1,200 mm of rainfall in the wet season from May-Oct. Rainfall decreases in the north, falling to 12 in/300 mm minimum in the central zone and virtually disappearing altogether in the northern half of the republic. Extreme annual temperatures vary from 54°F/12°C to 120°F/50°C, with the hot Saharan harmattan wind blowing in the north. N'djam¡bé: Jan. 75°F/23.9°C. July 82°F/27.8°C. Average annual rainfall 29 in/744 mm.

Cities and towns

N'djaména (capital)	402,000
Sarh	124,000
Moundou	87,000
Bongor	69,000
Doba	64,000
Laï	58,000

Population

Total population is 5,401,000 of which 23.9% live in urban areas. Population density is 9.2/4.1 persons per miles^2/km^2. Approximately 200 distinct ethnic groups are broadly divisible by region into northern Arabic nomads and southern Black herdsmen. Of the total, the Bagirmi, Sara and Kreish peoples constitute 30.5%; Sudanic Arab 26.1%; Tubu 7.3%; Mbum 6.5%; Masalit, Maba and Mimi 6.3%; Mubi 4.2%; Tama 6.3%. Other groups include the Fulbe, Kotoko, Hansa, Kanembou and Boulala in the north and the

Ngambaye, Mbaye, Goulaye, Moudang, Moussei and Massa in the south. An estimated 150,000 Chadians are non-native, of whom 1,000 are French.

Birth rate 4.42%. **Death rate** 2.14%. **Rate of population increase** 2.28%. **Age distribution** under 15 = 42.3%; over 65 = 3.6%. **Life expectancy** female 47; male 44; average 46.

Religion

The majority of the northern peoples are Muslim (44% of total population). Animist beliefs survive mostly in the southern districts, while the Christian minority are principally Roman Catholic.

Language

More than 100 different languages are currently spoken throughout Chad. Of these, the languages of the Sara and Bagirmi peoples belong to the Chari-Nile family, the Laka and Mbum to the Niger-Congo family, and the Buduma, Kuri and Kanemba to the Saharan group.

HISTORY

Chad has a natural division between the Sahara zone and the Sahelian belt inhabited by Arabs and Berbers in the north, and the tropical African south. The north was for many centuries dominated by the Kanem-Bornou empire founded in the 9th century, and the Baguirmi and Ouaddai kingdoms founded in the 16th and 17th centuries. The south, with its decentralized political systems, offered little resistance to raids led by the northern sultans.

In 1878, Rabah Zobeir, originally from Sudan, began the long process of conquest in Chad which over the course of the next 20 years made him dominant over the northern kingdoms and the head of the most powerful and well-organized state in the region. He was eventually overcome by the French, however, who first conquered Baguirmi (1897) and then Kanem (1899) before defeating Rabah himself at Kasseri in early 1900. French military control was effectively established by further campaigns in 1911 and 1916. Fighting in the north continued until 1930, and military administration persisted in parts of this region throughout the colonial period, whereas in the south, more amenable to French colonial control, cultivation of cotton was introduced in the 1920s, and a civilian administrative system set up through local chiefs. The colony was ruled by the French as part of French Equatorial Africa until it became an autonomous republic within the French community (28 Nov. 1958).

Chad, like most of France's former possessions in Africa, moved to full independence two years later as the French community idea crumbled. François Tombalbaye, prime minister and leader of the dominant party in the pre-independence elections of May 1959, was elected by the National Assembly as head of state on independence (11 Aug. 1960), and his Parti progressiste tchadien (PPT), purged of his rivals, became the sole party (19 Jan. 1962). Widespread discontent with Tombalbaye's dictatorship led to rebellions, notably in Fort-Lamy (later N'djaména) in 1963, and to the formation in 1966 of the first guerrilla movement, the Chad National Liberation Front (FROLINAT), which drew its strength from the northern populace. Tombalbaye appealed to France for military aid to end the rebellion.

In 1973 Libyan troops occupied the Aozou Strip in the extreme north, staking a claim to the mineral-rich region based on a Franco-Italian treaty of 1935.

Tombalbaye was assassinated in Apr. 1975 and succeeded by Gen. Malloum, who continued to accept French logistical support to counter further offensives from northern rebels. With the country seriously divided on regional and religious bases, a power struggle developed in 1979 between the prime minister, Hissène Habré (a northerner), and Malloum.

An agreement signed in Lagos (Aug. 1979) brought various factions together with the formation of the Transitional Government of National Unity (GUNT), headed by Goukouni Oueddei, with Habré as defence minister, although Habré split from GUNT a few months later. Oueddei signed a defence agreement with Libya in 1980, but Habré's forces gradually took control of Chad, seizing N'djaména in June 1982, and bringing Habré to power.

After renewed offensives from Libya and GUNT allies, French soldiers invited by Habré occupied Chad as far north as the 16th parallel. An initial reconciliation under OAU auspices failed, but Paris and Tripoli announced a simultaneous withdrawal of their troops in Sept. 1984.

In the following years, Habré rallied the south and numerous northern factions to his side. However, a fresh outbreak of fighting occurred in 1986, and French air commandos returned to help defend the north. Oueddei had meanwhile been held prisoner by Libya, and Acheikh Ibn Oumar had become the new GUNT leader. Chadian troops won a decisive victory over the Libyans at Faya (Largeau) in Mar. 1987; further successes induced cross-border raids into Libya itself. The two sides agreed to a cease-fire on 11 Sept. 1987, leading to a restoration of diplomatic relations in Oct. 1988.

A reconciliation agreement between the government and the remaining opposition factions was concluded in Nov. 1988. Many of the rebel leaders were incorporated into the government with Acheikh Ibn Oumar becoming foreign minister. In Apr. 1989, Habré survived a coup attempt by two military leaders and government minister Mahamat Itno. The country remains under threat from ethnic divisions, with insurgents operating from western Sudan. Central government authority remains patchy in many areas. Economically, the country's principal strength lies in the cotton-producing areas of the south.

CONSTITUTION AND GOVERNMENT

Executive and legislature

A one-party system in which legislative and executive power rests with the president, who governs through a Council of Ministers. A referendum on 10 Dec. 1989 approved a further 7-year presidential term for Habré and endorsed a new constitution under with a National Assembly would be elected, for a five-year term, within a single party framework.

Present government

President of Council of Ministers; Minister of National Defence, War Veterans and Victims of War Hissène Habré

Principal members of Council of Ministers Djidingar Dono Ngardoum (Minister of State); Acheikh bin Oumar (Foreign Affairs and Co-operation); Wadal Abdelkader Kamougue (Justice and Keeper of the Seals); Mbailem Bana Ngarnayal (Finance and Computers).

Ruling party

National Union for Independence and the Revolution (Union nationale pour l'indépendence et la révolution). **Chairman** Hissène Habré. **Executive Secretary** Capt. Gouara Lassou.

Justice

The system of law is based on the French civil code and on customary law. The Court of Appeal is located in N'djaména; there are criminal courts and magistrates' courts in N'djaména, Sarh and Abéché. The death penalty is in force. No judicial executions were recorded between 1985 and mid-1988.

National symbols

Flag. Tricolour with three vertical stripes of blue, yellow and red.

Festivals. 1 May (Labour Day); 25 May (Liberation of Africa, anniversary of the OAU's foundation); 11 Aug. (Independence Day); 28 Nov. (Proclamation of the Republic).

Vehicle registration plate. TCH.

INTERNATIONAL RELATIONS

Affiliations

NAM; OAU; ACP; ICO; Francophonie.

Defence

Total Armed Forces: some 17,000, excluding para-military. Terms of service: conscription, three years.

Army: 17,000.

Air Force: 200; two combat aircraft.

Para-military: perhaps 5,700.

ECONOMY

Currency

The unit is the CFA franc, divided into 100 centimes.

National finance

Budget. The 1987 est. budget was for expenditure of US$85 million and revenue of US$59 million.

Balance of payments. The balance of payments (current account, 1987) was a deficit of US$324 million.

Inflation. –3%.

Gross Domestic Product

Estimated total GDP US$980 million, per capita US$160 (overall size of economy ranking 145 in the world).

Sector	% of GDP
industry	18
agriculture	43
services*	39

* services figure includes elements unassigned to other categories.

Energy and mineral resources

Oil and gas. Exploitation of small quantities of crude petroleum in Kanem (western Chad) has been disrupted by civil war.

Minerals. Salt is mined in the Lake Chad region (about 4,409 tons/4,000 tonnes per year). Deposits of uranium, gold, bauxite, natron and kaolin have been discovered.

Electricity. Capacity: 38,000 kW; production: (1988) 69m kWh.

Bioresources

Agriculture. Four Chadians in every five are either farmers or lake fishermen, despite the fact that so much of the country is desert. Transport services and infrastructure are poor, compounding the difficulties of production and distribution of food, and making foreign aid necessary. Most farmers are involved in animal husbandry, and cotton is the only very significant cash crop.

Crop production: (1986 in 1,000 tons/tonnes) millet 661/600; sugar cane 320/290; yams 241/219; seed cotton 77/70; groundnuts 99/90; cassava 337/306; rice 28/25; dry beans 46/42; sweet potatoes 45/41; mangoes 35/32; dates 36/33; maize 58/53; cotton lint 30/27; cotton seed 44/40.

Livestock numbers: (1987 in millions) cattle 5.15; sheep 2.62; goats 2.7; chickens 4.

Fisheries. Total catch: (1985) 121,253 tons/110,000 tonnes of freshwater fish from Lake Chad and the Chari and Logone rivers.

Forestry. Roundwood production: (1986) 127.1 million ft^3/ 3.6 million m^3.

Industry and commerce

Industry. Industry is based almost entirely on the processing of agricultural products. The sector has been severely disrupted by the effects of civil war. Cotton ginning is the principal activity, with sugar refining; brewing; textiles; cigarette manufacturing; rice and flour milling.

Commerce. Exports: (1986) US$98.6 million, of which cotton 43%; cattle 35%; textiles 5%; fish. Imports: (1986) $206 million, mainly machinery and transportation equipment 39%; industrial goods 20%; petroleum products 13%; foodstuffs 9%. Principal trading partners are France and Nigeria.

Trade with UK. (1988) Chad imported goods worth £639,000 from the UK and exported goods worth £1,764,000 to the UK.

COMMUNICATIONS

Railways

There are 310 miles/500 km of railways (Trans-cameroon railway from N'gaoundéré to Sarh).

Roads

There are 19,080 miles/30,725 km of roads (2,874 miles/4,628 km of national and 2,181 miles/3,512 km of secondary roads).

Aviation

Air Afrique provides international services and Air Tchad provides domestic services and international charters (international airport is at N'djaména).

Shipping

None. There are 1,242 miles/2,000 km of inland waterways and lake transport on Lake Chad.

Telecommunications

There are 5,000 telephones, and 75,000 radio sets.

EDUCATION AND WELFARE

Education

Education is officially compulsory between the ages of eight and 14. There is a six-year primary level from age six. The secondary level lasts for seven years from the age of 12.

School population. Enrolment at primary school was equivalent to 38% of children in the primary age group (55% of boys and 21% of girls); at secondary level the attendance ratio was only 6% (11% of boys and 2% of girls). In 1984 there were approximately 288,500 pupils in primary schools, 43,000 in secondary schools and 2,560 in technical schools and teacher-training establishments.

University. The University of Chad in N'djaména had 1,643 students and 141 teaching staff in 1984.
Literacy. (1985) 25.3%.

Health

There are 32 hospitals and medical centres, and several hundred dispensaries. There were 3,373 beds in government-administered hospitals in 1978, one per 1,278 inhabitants, with 90 physicians employed in government medical services (one per 55,555 inhabitants). There were also about 1,100 midwives and nurses.

CHILE

República de Chile
(Republic of Chile)

GEOGRAPHY

Stretching 2,701 miles/4,350 km along the Pacific seaboard of South America from 17°30′ to 56°30′S, Chile covers a total area of 292,205 miles²/756,626 km² (excluding Antarctic territory) divided into 12 regions. Three parallel features running north-south dominate the country's physiography: the coastal Cordillera backed by the Intermediate Depression (Pampa Central) and the eastward-lying Chilean Andes. The Cordillera de los Andes may be further subdivided into the northern plateaux, central Andean highland (including Ojos del Salado, Chile's highest peak 22,572 ft/6,880 m) and the extensively glaciated southern Andes, dissected by fjords, lakes and sheer sea channels. The rich and fertile Pampa central, originating in the southern reaches of the desolate Atacama Desert and regularly transected by Andean spurs, includes the populous plains of Bio-Bio and Valparaiso, before submerging south of 40°S. The lower coastal cordillera dissipates at a similar latitude to become a series of islands. Of the country's comparatively short rivers, the Bio-Bio makes a substantial hydroelectric contribution discharging approximately 16,950 ft³/480 m³ per sec. 21% of the land is forested and 7% is arable (centrally located). 92% of the population live between Copiapo (27°22′S) and Puerto Montt (41°28′S).

Climate

Complex and varied across the large latitudinal span. Desert in the north with negligible rainfall and average temperature 68°F/20°C. Mediterranean-type in central Chile with winter rainfall of between 12–14 in/300–350 mm and dry summers. Cool temperate in the south with abundant rainfall and very stormy in the extreme south (Patagonia), averaging 157 in/4,000 mm of rain annually. Santiago: Jan. 67°F/19.5°C. July 46°F/8°C. Average annual rainfall 15 in/375 mm. Antofagasta: Jan. 69°F/20.6°C. July 57°F/14°C. Average annual rainfall 0.50 in/12.7 mm.

Cities and towns

Gran Santiago (capital)	4,318,305
Viña del Mar	315,947
Valparaiso	267,025
Talcahuano	220,910
Concepción	217,756

Population

Total population is 12,748,000, of which 83.6% live in urban areas. Population density is 43.6 persons per mile²/16.8 per km². An estimated 92% of the population are 'mestizo' of mixed European (Spanish) and Indian descent. The only sizeable indigenous minority left consists of the Mapuche border peoples.

Birth rate 2.42%. **Death rate** 0.63%. **Rate of population increase** 1.79%. **Age distribution** under 15 = 31.5%; over 65 = 5.8%. **Life expectancy** female 75; male 68; average 72.

Religion

No state religion but over 85% of the population are Roman Catholic, distributed among 16 dioceses. In addition, there are over 850,000 Protestants and approximately 25,000 Jewish inhabitants.

Language

The official language is Spanish. Amerindian languages have approximately 860,000 speakers (6.8%) and are primarily of Araucanian, Fuegian and Chango origin.

HISTORY

The Spanish conquest of Chile began in 1535 under the conquistador Diego de Almagro who failed either to subdue the Araucanian Indians or to establish a permanent settlement. It was Pedro de Valdivia who founded the capital, Santiago, in 1541 but large-scale colonization proceeded slowly due to fierce Araucanian resistance (which continued into the 19th century). Agriculture became the country's main staple and gave rise to a class of wealthy landowners who, failing to support initial moves for independence in 1811, allowed the reimposition of royalist control in 1814. The successful reconquest of the country (secured by royalist defeats at the battles of Chacabuco 1817 and Maipu 1818) was undertaken by the Army of the Andes led the Chilean Bernardo O'Higgins and the Argentinian José de San Martin. Named the Supreme Director of the Republic, O'Higgins ruled 1817–23, and was succeeded by a number of liberals before political anarchy erupted into civil war 1829–30 between warring powerful families and regional and ideological groups.

Under Pres. Joaquin Prieto (1831–41), a constitution was passed in 1833 which strengthened central government and the power of Diego Portales (assassinated 1837), a strong man, who really controlled affairs. It was the beginning of three decades of Conservative rule (formal political opposition narrowed to the Liberal party) which was boosted by victory in the war with Peru (1836–39). The war's hero, Gen. Manuel Bulnes (president 1841–51), supported the separation of powers between the executive, the Congress and the courts, and won general support for a successful economic policy which emphasized the export of raw materials and the import of manufactured goods. However, greatly expanding revenue collection from custom duties not only increased state power but encouraged government intervention in social and economic affairs. This antagonized both those Conservatives who wanted to retain control of rural areas, and who supported the Church's monopoly over educational, cultural and family affairs and those Liberals hostile to the centralization of political power. The two factions combined forces to replace Pres. Manuel Montt (1851–61) with Pres. José Joaquin Perez (1861–71); but the resulting diminution of presidential and congressional power (the 1871 constitution forbidding two consecutive terms, and that of 1878 granting all literate males the vote) was achieved at the price of the growing secularization of society.

Seizure of the lucrative Peruvian and Bolivian nitrate regions in the War of the Pacific (1879–83) greatly re-enhanced executive power (and revenues), especially under the controversial presidency of José Balmaceda (1886–91). Balmaceda, who launched massive public-works projects, used his personal control of state resources to guarantee political submissiveness from Liberals, Conservatives and British nitrate interests. He was deposed in the civil war of 1891 but the period of a parliamentary republic (1891–1924) saw the emergence of corrupt free-wheeling professional politicians, the fragmentation of the major parties, and increasing political chaos as the nitrate wealth dried up. The army seized power in the coup of Sept. 1924, and imposed a Labour code on the increasingly militant trade unions that placed them under strict government supervision. The non political Col. Carlos Ibañez (1927–31) was elected president but the catastrophic effects of the Great Depression on exports led to further political crisis and forced his resignation. A Socialist Republic, which was led by Col. Marmaduke Grove and lasted 13 days in June 1932, inspired the founding of the Socialist party (PSCh) in Apr. 1933 which, with the Communist Party (PCCh, founded 1912) and Radical Party (founded 1863), formed the Popular Front in 1936. This Popular Front, which outmanoeuvred the conservative Arturo Alessandri (1932–38) and took and retained power under the Radical presidents Pedro Aguirre Cerda (1938–41) and Juan Antonio Rios (1942–46), was best known for the creation, in 1939, of the State Development Corporation (CORFO) designed to stimulate domestic industrialization.

Relations with the Axis powers were broken off in 1943 and the Radical Pres. Gabriel Gonzalez Videla (1946–52), in line with cold-war US foreign policy, attacked the PCCh, having it banned in 1948, after which the Popular Front waned. An anti-Radical front, which returned (now General) Carlos Ibañez to the presidency (1952–58) quickly collapsed amid an economic recession which the government met with deeply unpopular austerity measures, adopted under the auspices of the International Monetary Fund. Pres. Jorge Alessandri (1958–64) followed a similar course with Conservative and Liberal support, cooperating with US foreign-aid policy to marginalize the left while aiming for economic stabilization.

A new Christian Democratic (PDC) government, under Pres. Eduardo Frei (1964–70) received huge grant aid (mainly from the US government) for a reform programme (especially land reform) to win popular support among potential voters of the PCCh and PSCh, but its radical measures, including the partial nationalization of the copper industry, failed to do so while alienating right-wing elements, and the 1973 elections were won by the left-wing Popular Unity party (UP) of Salvador Allende. Allende fully nationalized the copper industry (without compensation to US owners), froze prices and raised wages. However, by mid-1972, spiralling inflation, a US economic embargo, and the internal sabotage of the economy (which culminated in the Oct. 1972 strike of truck owners, merchants, industrialists, and professionals) persuaded the internally divided government to incorporate members of the military into its cabinet, but further government offers of concessions were ignored by hardline PDC members and those of right-wing parties. Congressional elections of Mar. 1973 saw an increase in the government's vote but not its ability to manoeuvre. In the coup of 11 Sept. 1973, Allende was killed, along with an estimated 15,000 in the subsequent repression, thousands more being imprisoned, tortured and exiled.

The military junta, headed by Agusto Pinochet, sought to replace party and interest group politics with techno-administrative economic and political solutions, and banned all Marxist political parties in 1973, and all other parties in 1977, and severely restricted civil and human rights. American-educated free market economists (the 'Chicago Boys') dramatically reduced state involvement in the economy, advocating the virtues of privatization and exposure to foreign competition. However the large flow of foreign funds into the country, although helping to improve the balance of payments by 1980, did not translate into higher investment and was used instead to finance speculative ventures and the massive purchase of imported consumer goods. Bankruptcies and unemployment marked the end of the Chicago experiment in 1981, the GNP falling a record 14% in 1982.

Pinochet faced constant opposition from a hostile Catholic Church, and failed to prevent the re-emergence of political parties and trade unions. The 1981 Constitution guaranteed elections in 1989 and in a referendum held on 5 Oct. 1988 the electorate rejected a clause which would have allowed Pinochet to continue as president until 1997. The government subsequently confirmed that a presidential election would take place in Dec. 1989. This resulted in victory for Patricio Aylwin, leader of the PDC and candidate of the 17 opposition party Coalition for Democracy (CPD), who defeated the non-party candidate Hernan Buchii, a former Finance Minister, who was seen by voters as the military regime's civilian representative. Aylwin was inaugurated on 11 Mar. 1990, ending 17 years of military dictatorship. However Pinochet had already confirmed that he intended to remain as Commander in Chief of the Army.

CONSTITUTION AND GOVERNMENT

Executive and legislature

Absolute power rested with the military junta under the Mar. 1981 Constitution, with Gen. Pinochet as supreme chief of state and president of the Republic. Executive and legislative authority was vested in the president and the junta, assisted by a Cabinet. A plebiscite in Oct. 1988 determined that Gen. Pinochet should not remain in office for a further eight years upon the expiry of his present term in 1990.

Present government

President Patricio Aylwin

Justice

The system of law is based on the 1857 code, deriving from Spanish law but subsequently affected by the influence of French and Austrian codes. The highest court is the Supreme Court, which may review legislation; the High Court of Justice in the capital, Santiago, is backed up by a system of tribunals of first instance in the departmental capitals with 12 Courts of Appeal distributed throughout the country. The death penalty is in force. There were 2 executions between 1985 and mid-1988. Capital offences: murder.

National symbols

Flag. Two horizontal stripes, white over red, and a blue square canton charged with a white five-pointed star in the hoist.

Festivals. 1 May (Labour Day); 21 May (Battle of Iquique); 18 Sept. (Independence Day); 12 Oct. (Day of the Race).

Vehicle registration plate. RCH.

INTERNATIONAL RELATIONS

Affiliations

OAS; SELA.

Defence

Total Armed Forces: 101,000 (33,000 conscripts). Terms of service: two years all services. Reserves: 100,000 active.

Army: 57,000; 171 main battle tanks (M-4A3, M-51, AMX-30) and 110 light tanks (M-24m M-41).

Navy: 29,000; four submarines (UK Oberon, FRG T-209/1300); 11 principal surface combatants: one cruiser (US Brooklyn); eight destroyers (UK Norfolk, ASUW, US Sumner); two frigates (modell UK Leander). Nine patrol and coastal combatants.

Naval Airforce: 500.

Marines: 5,200.

Air Force: 15,000; 96 combat aircraft (F-71, FGA-9, FR-71, F-5, F-E).

Para-military: 27,000.

Opposition: Frente Patriotico Manuel Rodriguez (FPMR) 1,000 leftist; Movement of the Revolutionary Left some 500.

ECONOMY

Currency

The unit is the peso, divided into 100 centavos.

National finance

Budget. The 1986 budget was for expenditure of US$5,100 million and revenue of US$4,900 million. Main items of expenditure are housing and welfare 43%; education 12.5%; defence 10.7%.

Balance of payments. The balance of payments (current account, 1987) was a deficit of US$871 million.

Inflation. 12.7%.

Gross Domestic Product

Estimated total GDP US$18,950 million, per capita US$1,520 (overall size of economy ranking 60 in the world).

Economically active population. The total number of persons active in the economy is 3,840,000; unemployed: 7.1%.

Sector	% of workforce
industry	44
agriculture	16
services*	40

* services figure includes elements unassigned to other categories.

Energy and mineral resources

Oil and gas. Oil production: (1988) 1.43 tons/1.3 million tonnes; gas: (1987) 157.2 million ft^3/4.45 million m^3.

Minerals. Output: (1987 in million tons/tonnes) copper 1.5/1.4; iron ore 7.3/6.6 plus 4/3.6 processed into pellet form; coal 1.9/1.7; molybdenum 18.6/16.9; zinc 19.6; manganese 35/31.8; lead 913,806/829,000. Nitrate of soda is also produced (1985) 959,001 tons/870,000 tonnes, of which iodine is a by-product (1985) 3 tons/2.7 tonnes.

Electricity. Capacity: 3.98 million kW; production: (1988) 15.57 million kWh; 1,230 kWh per capita.

Bioresources

Agriculture. There are an estimated 72 million acres/29 million ha of agricultural land in Chile. The main crops are wheat; potatoes; corn; sugar beet; onions; beans; fruits.

Crop production: (1988 in million tons/tonnes) wheat 2,066/1,874; oats 140/127; barley 53/48; maize 680/617; rice 162/147; potatoes 801/727; dry beans 89/81; lentils 28/25; green peas 26/24; sugar beet 2,921/2,650.

Livestock numbers: (1987) poultry 19 million; sheep 6.05 million; cattle 3.58 million; pigs 1.15 million; goats 600,000; horses 490,000; asses 28,000.

Forestry. Approximately 21% of the land in Chile

is forest and woodland, of which 2.84 million acres/1.15 million ha are artificial forests, mainly pine (pinus radiata, 2,298,030 acres/930,000 ha) with some eucalyptus and poplar.

Fisheries. Annual catch of fish and shellfish: 5.4 million tons/4.9 million tonnes. 1.5% of the working population are employed in the fishing industry.

Industry and commerce

Industry. The main industries are copper; other minerals; foodstuffs; fish processing; iron and steel; wood; wood products.

Commerce. Chile's exports totalled US$6,900 million including copper 48%; industrial products 33%; molybdenum; iron ore; wood pulp; fishmeal; fruits. Imports totalled US$4,800 million, including petroleum; wheat; capital goods; spare parts; raw materials

Countries exported to were EC 34%; US 22%; Japan 10%; Brazil 7%. Imports came from EC 23%; US 20%; Japan 10%; Brazil 9%.

Trade with UK. Chile imported UK goods worth £80,901,000; exports to UK totalled £179,628,000.

Tourism. (1987) 560,000 visitors.

COMMUNICATIONS

Railways

There are 5,083 miles/8,185 km of railways.

Roads

There are 49,197 miles/79,222 km of roads, of which 6,409 miles/10,320 km are concrete or bituminized.

Aviation

Linea Aérea Nacional de Chile (LAN-Chile) provides international services and Linea Aérea del Cobre SA (LADECO) provides domestic and cargo services and international services.

Shipping

Main ports are Valparaiso and also Arica; Antofagasta; Concepción; Puerto Montt; and Punto Arenas. The merchant marine includes 38 ships of over 1,000 GRT.

Telecommunications

The modern telephone system serves 768,000 telephones. There is a national television service (Canal 7, scheduled in late 1988 to be privatized), broadcasting in colour, and other channels broadcast by university-based stations; there are several hundred commercial radio stations, an estimated 30 million radios and 3.5 million television sets.

EDUCATION AND WELFARE

Education

There are three levels of education in Chile: Basic from 6–14 years; Middle from 15–18 years; University from 19–23 years.

Schools. Basic schools have 2,139,319 pupils and 66,354 teachers (one per 32 pupils). Middle schools have 392,940 pupils and 24,387 teachers (one per 16 pupils) and technical schools have 161,809 pupils and 4,176 teachers (one per 38 pupils).

Universities. There are eight universities in Chile, with a total student population of 118,978.

Health

There are 5,416 doctors (one per 2,370 people), 25,889 nursing personnel and 205 hospitals. In addition there are some 300 health centres and 900 emergency posts providing outpatient care.

CHINA

Zhonghua Renmin Gonghe Guo (People's Republic of China)

GEOGRAPHY

Covering 3,704,427 miles²/9,596,961 km² of central and east Asia, China lies between 53°–18°N and 73°–134°E, stretching about 3,105 miles/5,000 km from east-west and 3,416 miles/5,500 km north-south. The People's Republic comprises 21 provinces, five autonomous regions and three municipalities under governmental jurisdiction.

China's topography divides into three major regions: the south-western mountains (including the Tibetan Plateau, average elevation 13,320 ft/4,060 m) the north-western uplands (enclosing the vast Tarim Basin, Takla Makan Desert and the smaller Dzungarian Basin in Xinjiang province) and the eastern region, predominantly low-lying and divided by the Yangtze (Ch'ang Chiang) and Huang Ho (Yellow) Rivers. One-third of the total population inhabit China's highland regions which account for two-thirds of the total area. The highest peaks of the Tibetan plateau are found on the Nepalese border where Mount Everest, the highest mountain on earth, climbs to 29,029 ft/8,848 m. In the north-west, the Tien Shan mountains separate the Tarim and Dzungarian basins (average altitude 13,999 ft/4,267 m) while to the east, the southern reaches of the Gobi Desert form part of the Nei Mongol Plateau. In the north-east, the fertile Manchurian and North China plains constitute China's two largest low-lying areas. The Manchurian levels rise to meet the heavily forested Changpai Shai range of hills on the North Korean border while the Loess Plateau and Tsling Shan range (high point T'ai-pai Shan 12,027 ft/3,666 m) lie to the west of the North China plains. To the south, the Sichuan basin drains into the Yangtze river flowing south-east across fertile and populous lowlands to Shanghai and the East China Sea. In the south-east, the Chu Chiang Delta interrupts the south-eastern mountains which border the rocky coastline at an average height of 4,921–5,905 ft/1,500–1,800 m. 10% of all land is arable, 5% is irrigated and 14% is forested.

Climate

Mostly temperate, but wide latitudinal and altitudinal range encompasses many extremes of climate, particularly in winter. Temperatures generally increase north-south. South-east (sub-tropical) provinces experience the warmest weather with maximum average rainfall, ranging from 1.2 in/31 mm in Dec. along the coast to 16 in/394 mm in July. The typhoon season is July-Oct. Summers are hot and humid, average temperatures range 79°–88°F/26°–

31°C (Hong Kong). Average annual rainfall of over 30 in/750 mm in the south decreases north and north-east to between 9.8 in/250 mm and 30 in/750 mm on the North China plains. Manchuria experiences especially cold winters, with rivers frozen on average five months of each year. Shenyang's average daily temperature range in Jan. is 21°F/–6° to −0.4°F/–18°C, with milder July conditions reflected in daily temperatures of between 70°F/21° and 88°F/31°C. Desert conditions prevail in the north-western region of Xinjiang Uygur and western interior. Rainfall is greatest in Jan. (0.6 in/15 mm) dwindling to the minimum average of 3 mm in Feb. and Sept.–Oct. Temperature range of 12°F/–11°C to 34°F/1°C in Jan. and 68°–91°F/20°–33°C in July. The high altitudes of the Tibetan plateau (Xizang) experience harsh, frosty winters with valley temperatures varying from 14°F/–10° in Jan. to 75°F/24°C in July. Rainfall negligible Dec.–Jan., rising to 4.5 in/122 mm in July. Beijing: Jan. 24°F/–4.4°C. July 79°F/26°C. Annual rainfall 25 in/623 mm. Chongqing: Jan. 45°F/7.2°C. July 84°F/28.9°C. Average annual rainfall 43 in/1,092 mm. Shanghai: Jan. 39°F/3.9°C. July 82°F/27.8°C. Average annual rainfall 45 in/1,135 mm.

Cities and towns

Shanghai	7,180,000
Beijing (capital)	5,970,000
Tianjin	5,460,000
Shenyang	4,290,000
Wuhan	3,490,000
Guangzhou	3,360,000
Chongqing	2,830,000
Harbin	2,670,000
Chengdu	2,640,000
Xian	2,390,000
Zibo	2,330,000
Nanjing	2,290,000

Population

Total population is 1,103,983,000, of which 36.6% live in urban areas. Population density is 298 persons per mile^2/115 per km^2, ranging from a much higher figure in Shanghai to a sparsely populated Tibet. At the last census, 93.3% of the population were Han Chinese. A further 67 million people belonged to 55 distinct ethnic minorities, of which Chuang 1.33% of total population; Hui 0.72%; Uighur 0.59%; Yi 0.54%; Miao 0.50%; Manchu 0.43%; Tibetan 0.39%; Mongolian 0.34%; Tuchia 0.28%; Puyi 0.21%; Korean 0.18%; Tung 0.14%; Yao 0.14%; Pai 0.11%; Hani 0.11%; Kazakh 0.09%; Tai 0.08%; Li 0.08%. There are over 286,000 Vietnamese refugees in China.

Birth rate 1.9%. **Death rate** 0.67%. **Rate of population increase** 1.23%. **Age distribution** under 15 = 29.7%; over 65 = 5.3%. **Life expectancy** female 71; male 68; average 69.

Language

Four language families characterize the ethnolinguistic distribution of the Chinese population: Sino-Tibetan; Altaic; Indo-European; Austro-Asiatic. Within the first family, Putonghua (Mandarin Chinese) forms the basis for modern Standard Chinese with three principal regional dialectal variants: northern, western (spoken in the Sichuan Basin and Upper Yangtze) and southern (Lower Yangtze). Pinyin (Romanization of Putonghuanese characters) was introduced in Feb. 1958 as a phonetic learning-aid to transcription and pronunciation. The Altaic family (north and north-west China) includes the Turkic, Mongolian and Manchu-Tungus languages. The Tadzhiks in western Xinjiang have the same Indo-European linguistic roots as their Russian relatives, while the Kawa people in southern China derive from Mon Khmer/Austro-Asiatic origins. Tibetan was reinstated as a major language in July 1988.

Religion

Officially atheist: the Governmental Bureau of Religious Affairs was re-instated in 1979. Reliable statistics are unavailable for the predominant religious philosophies of Confucianism, Buddhism and Taoism. Ancestor worship is uniformly practised. The majority of Buddhists belong to the Chan or Pure Land sects. There are an estimated 7 million Christians in China, of whom approximately 3 million are Roman Catholic. Islam reached China in AD 651 and has an estimated 16 million adherents today, concentrated among the Wei Wuer and Hui peoples.

HISTORY

According to Chinese legend and the officially recorded imperial histories, China's first dynasty, the Xia, ruled from around the 21st century to the 16th century BC.

Recorded history begins with the founding of the Shang dynasty which lasted from the 16th to the 11th centuries. At its capital, near modern Anyang, excavations have revealed remains of palaces, temples, and government buildings.

The Shang were overthrown by the conquering Zhou people, whose capital lay near the modern-day city of Xian. Confucianism and Taoism both date from this period.

However, by about 800 BC the power of the Zhou kings had waned and they were left with only nominal authority as various kingdoms jostled for supremacy. Nevertheless the Chinese regard this period as their classical age. These last few centuries of the Zhou dynasty, known as the Warring States period (475–221 BC) came to a climax with the victory of the centralist-minded prince of Qin who founded the Qin dynasty and proclaimed himself China's first emperor, Qin Shi Huangdi. The short-lived dynasty laid the foundation of a centralized bureaucracy by abolishing feudal states, creating 36, later 41, military areas or provinces, and standardizing customs, laws, weights, and measures.

Qin Shi Huangdi's successor was assassinated in 207 BC and the victor of the ensuing power struggle, Liu Bang, established the Han dynasty (206 BC–AD 220). At its zenith the Han empire stretched from Korea in the east to present-day Xinjiang in the west while the southern border penetrated as far south as modern-day Vietnam. Through Xinjiang trade lines were established and Buddhism entered China. There was a brief interregnum during the Han (AD 8–23), sometimes known as the Xin dynasty. The subsequent period was known as the later Han, or Eastern Han as the capital was moved eastward from Chang'an to Luoyang. Imperial power over the outlying parts of the empire was reconsolidated during this period. Palace intrigues, with eunuchs and empresses' families wielding power, resulted in misgovernment and a peasant revolt occurred in 184. The uprising was put down but an ensuing palace revolution saw the fall of the emperor, by now only a puppet of the eunuchs who were also ousted. Warlords prevailed and one of China's great dynasties in terms of art and literature came to an end amidst sacking and pillage. Half a century's contention for the imperial throne followed.

Three royal houses controlled three main economically important areas, the Wei (220–65) in the north with the capital at Luoyang, the Wu (220–80) in the south, Nanking being its capital, and the Shu Han (221–64) in the west, with its capital at Chengdu. Feudalism reappeared, barter became current again and anarchy was widespread. In the succeeding centuries numerous ruling groups and states battled for dominance. Finally China was reunified under the short-lived Sui dynasty (581–618) and under the Tang (618–906). Administratively, militarily, and culturally the Tang was an era of achievement. However the 9th century saw China's borders shrink, Manchuria was lost, Tibetans continually threatened western China, the Thais attempted to invade southern China and the coast was menaced by pirates. Poor government compounded the country's problems. From 875 onwards rebellion swept China, with numerous cities laid waste. Twelve years later the uprising was crushed but the dynasty collapsed as rival military commanders squabbled amongst each other. Several secessionist movements resulted in breakaway states being founded and the period 907–60 is known as the Five dynasties and ten states.

The Sung dynasty (960–1279) restored order but invaders conquered much northern territory. By 1223 the Mongols under Genghiz Khan controlled most of China above the Huang Ho River and in 1260 Kublai Khan (grandson of Genghiz) declared himself universal sovereign. He built and extended roads and waterways, and established post stations with relays of horses. Beijing was designated as capital. In 1273 the Mongols crossed the Yangtze and the Chinese fleet bearing the remnants of the imperial household was defeated near Macao in 1279. The Yuan, or Mongol dynasty, officially dates from this year. As a result of unifying the nomadic Mongol tribes, by about AD 1300 the empire extended from Kiev to the Persian Gulf, and from Burma to Korea. Muslims, Christians and Armenians all came to China at this time. Marco Polo served under Kublai Khan. After his death in 1279 the huge empire began to fragment and traders and missionaries left China.

Chinese rule was restored in 1386 with the founding of the Ming dynasty with Nanking and then Beijing as its capital. Irrigation and defence systems were repaired, a new legal code promulgated and overseas contacts forged. Missions and expeditions were sent to Tibet, Java, Thailand, the South Pacific, India, and the Persian Gulf. However, in the early 15th century China's naval expeditions were suddenly halted, just as Europeans were testing the Chinese waters. Tibet successfully resisted Chinese suzerainty and the Mongols harassed the Chinese along their northern borders. The Portuguese ventured along China's coast in the 16th century. Expelled in 1522 they returned to found the permanent settlement of Macao on the coast south of Canton. The Spanish, who had colonized the Philippines, traded with China in the 16th century, and Chinese goods found their way to Latin America. The Dutch held Taiwan and the Pescadores or Penghu Islands throughout the Ming dynasty. Five English ships fought their way up the Pearl River to Canton in 1617 but no permanent foothold was gained. A war was fought over Korea with the Japanese towards the end of the 16th century. A tribe of farmers and herdsmen, descendants of the Jurchen, took Manchuria from the Chinese in 1636, and in 1644 established the Manchu dynasty (1644–1911) with its capital at Beijing. By 1659 the last of the Ming pretenders were expelled from China.

Under the Manchus the empire, run on Chinese lines, reached its greatest territorial extent. Over the next 150 years the Manchus gradually lost touch with their own traditions and language and were largely absorbed by the majority Han Chinese population. During this time China experienced a period of peace. Aboriginal minorities on the fringes of the empire were crushed and their lands opened to colonization. The population increased more rapidly than ever; the census of 1661 recorded a figure of 108,000,000, which in 1741 had risen to over 143,000,000. China continued to trade with the Spanish who paid for silk and porcelain with Spanish American silver. Trade increased with the Japanese, Indians, Arabs, Portuguese, and Dutch. Gradually, the pre-eminence of the Dutch in Chinese trade was lost to the English. Russian adventurers settled in the Amur Valley on the frontier with the Manchu empire and sporadic fighting occurred until a border treaty was signed in 1689. The opium poppy was introduced into China at this time, and Europeans began to import opium into China. The Chinese banned opium in 1800, but thousands of chests of the drug were being annually shipped into Canton (now Guangzhou), mainly by the British. The trade drained China of silver. In 1840 the government acted, burning a large consignment of opium. This led to the first opium war with Britain, who won the war and extracted trade concessions from China; the opium trade was finally banned by the British parliament in 1911. Meanwhile large tracts of land in China had been given over to the poppy; food shortages resulted and opium addiction was rife. The Manchu dynasty was doomed after the opium war. The imperial court, nevertheless, persisted in a policy of isolation and refused to engage in reforms to rejuvenate the country and emulate the West's Industrial Revolution. Canton was declared the single port of entry. Britain defiantly demanded and was granted a trading port at Hong Kong. Other powers demanded and obtained similar rights and territorial enclaves.

In addition to problems with foreigners, the Manchus encountered dissatisfaction among their native Chinese subjects. Corruption, maladministration and natural disasters led to frequent popular uprisings, especially towards the end of the 18th century.

In the middle of the 19th century, there were a number of more serious revolts: the Taiping rebellion (1848–64); a secret society revolt by the Nianfei (1853–68) and four Muslim uprisings in Yunnan, Shaanxi, Gansu, and central Asia between 1855 and 1878. Millions died in the suppression of the rebellions and several provinces suffered massive destruction. No reforms were effected however. Foreign powers continued to exact concessions and privileges. In 1855 China lost a war with Japan and ceded Korea, Taiwan, and the Pescadores to the Japanese empire. In 1900 the Boxer Rebellion attempted to expel all foreigners. The rebellion was suppressed by a combined foreign army led by the British, and a war indemnity was imposed on China. Legal, education, economic, and political reforms were hastily but belatedly initiated.

The opposition to Manchu rule led by Sun Yat-sen (1867–1925) and fellow revolutionaries overthrew the regime in the 1911 Chinese Revolution. Sun Yat-sen was elected president of a provisional government, and with the official abdication of the imperial government on 12 Feb. 1912 China became a republic. However, Sun Yat-sen failed to gather sufficient support and resigned on 15 Feb. 1912 in favour of the military strongman Yuan Shikai who ruled the country until his death in 1916, after which political control started to fragment.

Yuan Shikai's followers set up a government in Beijing, while Sun Yat-sen's Kuomintang (KMT) established a rival government in Canton. For the next decade much of the country was gripped by civil war conducted by contending warlords. In 1919, China's negotiations at the Versailles peace talks agreed to Japan's taking over Germany's territories in the Shandong peninsula. On 4 May Beijing's students took to the streets in protest and an intellectual revolution, known as the May 4th Movement, was born. Riding on this student agitation the Chinese Communist Party (CCP) was founded in 1921. The Russians meanwhile assisted Sun Yat-sen in reorganizing the KMT, allowing CCP members to simultaneously join its ranks. Sun Yat-sen died in 1925, and the following year the KMT, now under the leadership of Chiang Kai-shek, began a northwards drive, reaching Beijing in 1928. In 1927, Chiang had turned on the communists, attacking them in their base in Shanghai.

In 1931, Japan occupied Manchuria (which it established as the puppet state of Manchukuo the following year) and in 1933 it gained control of Jehol. The KMT government's stated priority, however, was to defeat the communists before tackling the Japanese. By 1930 the communists had won control of large tracts of territory in the south, and had established an army. In 1934, however, the KMT advance forced the communists out of the southern bases. The communists undertook the Long March 1934–5, winding through southern and western China, and finally coming to a halt in Oct. 1935 at Yanan in Shaanxi Province, where Mao Zedong emerged as the CCP leader. In Dec. 1936 Chiang Kai-shek was captured by the CCP and held near Xian until he agreed to halt his campaign against the communists and join with the CCP in fighting the Japanese. Japan launched a full-scale invasion of China in 1937 and before the year's end succeeded in occupying much of the north-east of the country. The Japanese established puppet governments in Beijing and Nanking, and the Nationalists were forced to remove the capital to Chongqing. Relations between the CCP and KMT remained poor despite their nominal pact against the common enemy.

In 1943 the Allies relinquished their privileges of extraterritoriality in China, to encourage the KMT not to make peace with the Japanese. After the Japanese surrender in 1945, the Nationalists took control of Japanese-occupied areas. The US provided transport to airlift KMT troops northwards, while at the same time attempting to mediate between the KMT and the CCP in the hope of achieving a negotiated settlement. In the south support for the KMT was weakening with Nationalist generals defecting to the communists. Beijing fell to the communists in Jan. 1949. The People's Liberation Army, as the communist forces were now known, marched south three months later. The People's Republic of China was formally established on 1 Oct. 1949 and its capital established at Beijing. The communist forces stopped at the border with Hong Kong and did not invade as many expected. In Oct. 1950 the army invaded Tibet, and in 1951 it became a so-called autonomous region of China. Taiwan, the Pescadores, Quemoy and Matsu were left in the hands of the KMT. The government moved against corruption and nepotism. Prices were stabilized, industries nationalized and the press placed under central control. On 14 Feb. China signed a thirty-year Treaty of Friendship, Alliance and Mutual Assistance with the USSR. The US imposed a trade embargo and supported the nationalist Chinese government on Taiwan under Chiang Kai-shek.

Between 1950–58 land reform was implemented in four stages. First there was redistribution of land between landlord, rich peasants, poor peasants and the landless. Production did not increase as a result and the second stage was to combine numbers of households into mutual aid teams. The third step in 1954 was to extend this system and enlarge the teams into agricultural co-operatives, pooling perhaps 500 people, their land, livestock, tools and labour. The co-operatives were headed by a management committee. The final stage carried out in 1958 was the amalgamation of cooperatives into communes of about 200,000 people. Currency reform took place in 1955. The 1953–58 first five-year plan failed due to a shortage of experts. The 1954 Constitution organized the state, in accordance with the principle of democratic centralism, into five autonomous regions, 21 provinces, about 175 municipal administrations, and 2,000 districts. A central council under the chairmanship of Mao Zedong held absolute power. Zhou Enlai was premier of the Administrative Council from 1949–76. In May 1957 the Hundred Flowers Campaign was launched with Mao's declaration, 'let a hundred flowers bloom, and a hundred schools of thought contend', ostensibly inviting constructive criticism particularly from intellectuals. The severe, perhaps unexpected criticism of the system by liberal intellectuals led to a backlash known as the Anti-Rightist Campaign against those who spoke out. The movement to root out the 'White Flags' followed. The 1958 'Great Leap Forward' that put much faith in the newly established people's communes and increasing of steel production by the use of backyard furnaces ended in economic disaster. Between 1959 and 1961 failed economic policies led to widespread famine, disease and unrest. Refugees streamed into Hong Kong. Estimates of those who died of starvation range as high as 200,000,000. As a consequence of the economic disasters that befell China as a result of the 'Great Leap Forward' there were changes in the leadership of the state with Mao remaining chairman of the party.

In 1960 Soviet technicians were withdrawn from China. Sino-Soviet relations had been deteriorating for several years, due partly to ideological conflict, and partly to nationalist pride. The Chinese resented the 'big elder brother' role the Russians assumed in the world communist movement. In 1962 CPSU-CCP relations were openly broken off, and the next year the CCP's '25-point Programme' aimed to woo other communist parties to its ideological standpoint. In 1959 the uprising in Tibet led to the flight of the Dalai Lama into India. Also in 1959 the Sino-Indian border conflict took place over the MacMahon line, with China occupying disputed territories. In 1963–64 premier Zhou Enlai and the foreign minister, Chen Yi, travelled through Asia and Africa promoting China's pro-Third World foreign policy. On 16 Oct. 1964 China detonated its first nuclear bomb.

By mid-1964 Mao Zedong had become doubtful about the fitness of his heir apparent Liu Shaoqi, and by 1966 the defence minister Lin Biao was the new putative successor. That year the 'Great Proletarian Cultural Revolution' gradually gathered steam. At its most basic level it was a means by which Mao Zedong could regain supreme power. Young people seeing themselves as revolutionary rebels banded together as Red Guards to eliminate old thought, old culture, old customs and old habits. According to the system-point charter of the 'Cultural Revolution' promulgated in August the masses were allowed to attack those in authority and those on the 'capitalist road'. In August and September, Red Guards put local authorities throughout China on trial. Chaos was total as rival Red Guards were formed. On 22 Nov. 1966 a 17-member Central Cultural Revolutionary Committee was formed with Chen Boda, Mao's secretary, as chairman and Mao's wife, Jiang Qing, as vice-chairman. This Revolutionary Committee, together with the Military Commission under Lin Biao and the State Council under Zhou Enlai, ruled China under Mao's guidance. The Red Guards ransacked property, rampaged through cities, renamed streets and humiliated foreign diplomats. In Jan. 1967 Mao ordered the army to restore order, and it consequently became an important political force. The attacks on Liu Shaoqi continued. He was put under house arrest and in Nov. 1968 the CCP Central Committee confirmed his ousting from all party and government posts. Also attacked and purged was Deng Xiaoping, the party general secretary. Throughout the 'Cultural Revolution' the premier, Zhou Enlai, seemed to exercise a moderating influence.

In Apr. 1969 the 9th Party Congress elected Mao chairman of the Party and the Central Committee. Lin Biao was elected vice-chairman and designated Mao's successor. Many China-watchers take this congress to mark the end of the 'Cultural Revolution' but the Chinese authorities take 1976 as the end of the 'ten years of chaos'. The army now accounted for about half of the posts on the Central Committee and Politburo, and the military dominated at the provincial and local levels. Because of his increasing distrust for Lin Biao, Mao Zedong decided in Mar. 1970 to abolish the position of state chairmanship coveted by Lin. In Jan. 1971 the Beijing Military Region, Lin's power base, was reorganized, and in September Lin died in a plane crash while fleeing China after the alleged discovery of an earlier plot.

On 15 Jan. 1971 the US president Richard Nixon announced that he had been invited to visit China after his foreign affairs advisor, Henry Kissinger, had concluded a secret visit to Beijing on 9–11 July. Nixon arrived in China on 21 Feb. 1972, and seven days later he signed the Sino-US Shanghai communiqué, which recognized that Taiwan was a part of China, and set the scene for increased Sino-American détente.

At the Tenth Party Congress on 24–28 Aug. 1973 the 'Cultural Revolution Group' made a bid for power and Jiang Qing was elected to the Politburo, as were her protégés Yao Wenyuan, Zhang Chunqiao, and Wang Hongwen, later to be labelled 'the Gang of Four'. In Apr. 1973 Deng Xiaoping was rehabilitated as vice-premier and was elected to the Politburo in Jan. 1974; however, the moderates still held less than half the 21 Politburo seats.

In 1974 the 'Anti-Lin, Anti-Confucius Campaign' was launched, attacking Lin Biao for his betrayal and use of Confucianism to restore capitalism. But it seemed also that Zhou Enlai was being likened to Confucius. The movement petered out in the late summer. The Fourth National People's Congress was convened in Beijing on 13–17 Jan. 1975. Mao was absent and a new constitution was approved abolishing the post of State chairman. Mao remained chairman of the CCP Central Committee and Zhou Premier of the State Council. 'Radicals' and 'moderates' uneasily and temporarily shared power. Deng Xiaoping was made first vice-premier, vice-chairman of the CCP and a member of the standing committee and chief of staff of the armed forces, while Zhang Chunqiao was made second vice-premier and chief political commissar of the armed forces.

Zhou Enlai died in Jan. 1976 and although he had wanted Deng Xiaoping as his successor, the next month the *People's Daily* launched an attack on 'capitalist roaders' which was obviously aimed at Deng. Jiang Qing was promoting Zhang Chunqiao, but on 7 Feb. the compromise figure of Hua Guo Feng, the minister of public security, was appointed acting premier. Between 29 Mar. and 4 Apr., the time of the Qing Ming Mourning Festival, people flocked to Peking's Tiananmen Square to lay wreaths in commemoration of Zhou Enlai. The security forces' removal of the wreaths enraged the people, 100,000 of whom gathered on 5 Apr. at Tiananmen Square in protest, and displayed placards praising Zhou and supporting Deng. The demonstrators were violently suppressed, and on 7 Apr. Mao recommended the Central Committee to strip Deng Xiaoping of all government and party posts. On 8 Apr. Hua was declared premier and first vice-chairman of the party.

On 9 Sept. 1976 Mao Zedong died. For years he had suffered from Parkinson's disease and had already suffered a stroke. A fierce power struggle, led by his widow, Jiang Qing, ensued. Jiang Qing controlled the media, education, and urban militia in the major cities but lacked military strength. The struggle for power continued throughout September and into October. Jiang Qing and her supporters were apparently planning a coup, but at an emergency Politburo meeting in the night of 5–6 Oct. Wang Hongwen, Zhang Chunqiao and Yao Wenyuan were arrested. Jiang Qing was arrested in her bed. The captives were placed in solitary confinement to await trial. On 7 Oct. 1976 the Politburo named Hua Guo Feng chairman of the Party Central Committee and the Central Military Commission. On the first anniversary of Zhou Enlai's death, demonstrations and wall posters in Beijing called for Deng's rehabilitation. The Third Plenum of the Tenth Central Committee in July restored Deng Xiaoping to his posts of Politburo Standing Committee member, vice-chairman of the Central Committee, first vice-premier of the State Council, vice-chairman of the Central Military Commission, and Chief of General Staff of the People's Liberation Army. Throughout 1977–78 Deng's power continued to grow. He attacked Hua's associates and all those who had risen under Mao's patronage. In May and June 1978 he announced two guiding principles to combat Maoist thought: 'Practice is the sole criterion of truth', and, 'Seek truth from facts'.

In Dec. 1978 the Third Plenum of the CCP's Eleventh Central Committee launched a decade of reform, and modernization of the economy became the priority. China welcomed foreign trade and investment; special economic zones (SEZ) were established to attract investors. Peasants were given the right to farm a piece of land on their own and were encouraged to make profits and use initiative; this was known as the responsibility system. Between Nov. 18 and Mar. 1979 the short-lived Peking Spring took place. Comprising mainly the disaffected generation of the Red Guard era, the Democracy Movement aimed to achieve greater freedom and democracy. It served Deng Xiaoping's purpose to let this anti-Maoist backlash go on for a while. On 5 Dec. 1978 a dazibao (big-character wall poster) was posted on the 'Democracy Wall' at Xidan in Beijing calling for 'The Fifth Modernization: Democracy'. Its author was Wei

Jingsheng, who was arrested in Mar. 1979 and on 16 Oct. was sentenced to 15 years' imprisonment for 'counter-revolutionary activities'. At the Fifth Plenum of the Eleventh Central Committee, 23–29 Feb. 1980, which marked Deng's emergence as China's most powerful figure. Mao's 'politics in command' seemed to have been jettisoned in favour of Deng's 'economics in command'. However, any motion of a 'Fifth Modernization' was also rejected. The 'Four Big Freedoms' (to speak out freely, to air one's views freely, to engage in mass debates, and to pen big character posters) were deleted from the constitution. Two of Deng's protégés, Zhao Ziyang and Hu Yaobang, were appointed to the Politburo standing committee. At the Third Plenum of the Fifth National People's Congress (29 Aug.–10 Sept. 1980) Hua Guo Feng resigned the premiership, to be replaced by Zhao Ziyang. Deng set about rejuvenating the entire leadership structure and attempted to retire many veteran cadres. Hua Guo Feng was replaced as premier by Zhao Ziyang, in June 1981 he was replaced as chairman of the CCP by Hu Yaobang, and as chairman of the all-important Military Affairs Commission by Deng himself. In Mar. 1982 the State Council was rationalized, and in Sept. the CCP was reorganized, the post of chairman abolished, and Hu Yaobang appointed general secretary. A Central Advisory Commission to which elderly leaders could retreat was established. China adopted a new Constitution in Dec. 1982, restoring the presidency; in June 1983 Li Xiannian was appointed head of State. The reforms of the 1980s were seen by more conservative elderly leaders as being too consumerist, too oriented towards profit. In an effort to restore socialist spiritual civilization in late 1983 and early 1984, the conservative elements of the leadership launched the abortive 'Campaign against spiritual pollution'. In Sept. 1985 at the CCP's first national delegate conference for 40 years, a number of elderly leaders stepped down from the Politburo. The new leadership was more favourably disposed to Deng Xiaoping's reforms. But elders such as Li Xiannian and Chen Yun remained, and the latter was unhappy about the pace and direction of the reforms, despite the successes of Deng's 1979–81 agricultural decollectivization experiment. Industrial reforms announced in Oct. 1984 proved far less successful than the agricultural reforms. However, most enterprises remained under the control of party cadres rather than professional managers. In Apr. 1985 policies were introduced to streamline and professionalize the army, and within a year military personnel were reduced by about 25%. Throughout the first nine months of 1986 reformers had advocated political reforms to facilitate the economic reforms. The Sixth Plenum of the Twelfth CCP Central Committee, held in Sept. 1986, attempted to assuage the fears of conservatives such as Chen Yun, but an ideological struggle nevertheless commenced. In December student street demonstrators demanded greater freedom and democracy. In January the conservative leaders condemned the students and initiated the 'Campaign against bourgeois liberalization'. The general secretary Hu Yaobang was blamed for encouraging the 'bourgeois liberalization' and on 16 Jan. resigned. Zhao Ziyang, a more careful reformer, took over with the support of Deng Xiaoping and the campaign subsided. The 13th National Congress of the CCP in Oct. and Nov. of 1987 reaffirmed support for the reforms, as did the 7th NPC held Mar.–Apr. 1988, at which the chairman of its standing committee, the conservative Peng Zhen, was replaced by the reformer Wan Li. The NPC approved Li Peng's elevation to prime minister and Yang Shankun to the presidency. Li Peng, adoptive son of Zhou Enlai, was known to be less enthusiastic about the reforms. By mid-1988 the reforms were threatened by rising double-figure inflation. In May Zhao proposed extending price reform or deregulation. But in September the conservatives obtained the deferment of price reforms for a further two years and a policy of 'rectifying the economy' was initiated. It was a major set-back for Zhao and the reforms which were already plagued by corruption and urban (and increasingly rural) dissatisfaction with falling standards of living.

Student-led pro-democracy demonstrations erupted in Beijing in April 1989 following the death of Hu Yaobang. The demonstrations intensified during May, but were halted abruptly on 4 June when troops took control of central Beijing by force, killing hundreds of unarmed civilians. Towards the end of June the dismissal of Zhao Ziyang signalled the victory of conservative elements in a two-month power struggle provoked by conflicting responses to the demonstrations. Zhao was replaced as Party General Secretary by Jiang Zemin, a former party leader in Shanghai. However, real political power rested with a clique of elderly and conservative Deng loyalists. In Nov. 1989 Deng retired as the Chairman of the Central Military Commission, his last official party post. Despite his formal retirement, most analysts agreed that Deng remained China's most influential political figure.

Tibet

Little is known of the history of Tibet before its unification in the 7th century under King Srongtsen Gampo. Despite an alliance with China's Tang Dynasty, Tibetan military conquests continued; culminating in the capture of the Tang capital in 763. In the 13th century the Mongols took control of Tibet, establishing a patron-priest relationship. Tibetan Buddhism enjoyed great cultural and religious influence over the Mongol empire until its fall. Good relations were also established with the Manchu Qing Dynasty in China in the 1640s. Extending their influence in Tibet, the Manchus attempted from 1793 to exert control over the selection of the reincarnation of the Dalai Lama, Tibet's spiritual and temporal leader.

Throughout the 19th century, Tibet was ruled by a lay and monastic hierarchy with some Manchu influence. The gradual collapse of the Qing Dynasty led Britain and Russia to seek influence in Tibet, culminating in Britain's 1904 Younghusband Expedition to Lhasa. In 1911 Tibet declared itself independent.

Reasserting Chinese suzerainty over Tibet, Communist forces 'liberated' Tibet in Oct. 1950, incorporating parts of the region into neighbouring Chinese provinces. In 1959 a short-lived revolt broke out and the 14th Dalai Lama fled to India. The Chinese instituted major political, economic, and social changes, ending the dominance of the Buddhist monks (lamas), and in 1965 formally assimilated Tibet as an Autonomous Region. Increased repression followed in the 1966–76 Cultural Revolution when monasteries were destroyed and hundreds of thousands allegedly arrested. After 1978, attempts were made to improve relations, but Tibetan independence uprisings in 1987, 1988 and 1989 prompted the imposition of martial law in Lhasa in Mar. 1989.

CONSTITUTION AND GOVERNMENT

Executive and legislature

The head of state is the president, largely a titular role. The 1982 constitution states that executive power is exercised by the State Council. The State Council is elected (most recently Apr. 1988) by the legislature, the National People's Congress (NPC), which convenes annually; when not in session the NPC is represented by a 155-member Standing Committee. The 2,978 NPC members are indirectly elected for five years. Effective political control is in the hands of the Communist Party of China (CCP) which has over 40,000,000 members. China's dominant elder statesman, Deng Xiaoping, has not held any senior formal position since Oct. 1987 (when he retired from the standing committee of the politburo) except that he retains the chairmanship of the Central Military Commission.

Present government

President of the Republic Yang Shangkun
Vice-President of the Republic Wang Zhen
Premier of the State Council; Minister in charge of the State Commission for Restructuring the Economy Li Peng
Principal members of State Council Yao Yilin (Vice Premier of State Council); Tian Jiyun (Vice Premier of State Council); Wu Xueqian (Vice Premier of State Council); Li Tieying (State Councillor; Minister in charge of the State Education Commission); Qin Jiwei (State Councillor; National Defence); Wang Bingqian (State Councillor; Finance); Song Jian (State Councillor; Minister in charge of State Scientific and Technological Commission); Wang Fang (State Councillor; Public Security); Zou Jiahua (State Councillor; Minister in charge of the State Planning Commission); Li Guixian (State Councillor; Governor of the People's Bank of China); Cheng Xitong (State Councillor); Chen Junsheng (State Councillor); Luo Gan (Secretary General); Qian Qichen (Foreign Affairs); Jia Chunwang (State Security); Cai Cheng (Justice); Hu Ping (Commerce); Zheng Tuobin (Foreign Economic Relations and Trade).
Standing Committee of National People's Congress Chairman–Wan Li.
Secretary-General Peng Chong.

Ruling party

Chinese Communist Party (Zhongguo Gongchan Dang). *General Secretary* Jiang Zemin. *Members of the Standing Committee of the politburo* Li Peng; Qiao Shi; Yao Yilan; Jiang Zemin; Song Ping; Li Ruihuan. *Other full members of politburo* Wu Xueqian; Wan Li; Tian Jiyun; Yang Shangkun; Li Tieying; Li Ximing; Qin Jiwei; Yang Rudai. *Alternate member* Deng Guangen. *Central committee secretariat* Qiao Shi; Hu Qili; Deng Guangen; Yang Baibing. *Alternate member* Wen Jiabao. *Chairman of Central Military Commission* Jiang Zemin.

Administration

The People's Republic of China is a unitary state which, according to its constitution, consists of 23 provinces or sheng (the 23rd being Taiwan), five

Government-controlled municipalities	Area (in 1,000 miles²/km²)	Population in 1986 (in 1,000s)	Density per mile²/km²	Capital
Beijing	6.8/17.8	9,750	1,434/547	–
Tianjin	1.5/4.0	8,190	5,460/2,048	–
Shanghai	2.2/5.8	12,320	5,600/2,124	–
Provinces				
Hebei	78.2/202.7	56,170	731/277	Shijiazhuang
Shanxi	60.6/157.1	26,550	438/169	Taiyuan
Liaoning	58.3/151.0	37,260	639/246	Shenyang
Jilin	72.2/187.0	23,150	321/124	Changchun
Heilongjiang	178.9/463.6	33,320	186/72	Harbin
Jiangsu	39.4/102.2	62,130	1,577/608	Nanjing
Zhejiang	39.3/101.8	40,700	1,036/400	Hangzhou
Anhui	54/139.9	52,170	966/373	Hefei
Fujian	47.5/123.1	27,490	473/223	Fuzhou
Jiangxi	63.6/164.8	35,090	552/213	Nanchang
Shandong	59.2/153.3	77,760	1,314/507	Jinan
Henan	64.5/167.0	78,080	1,211/468	Zhengzhou
Hubei	72.4/187.5	49,890	689/266	Wuhan
Hunan	81.3/210.5	56,960	701/271	Changsha
Guangdong	89.3/231.4	63,640	713/275	Guangzhou
Sichuan	219.6/569.0	103,200	470/181	Chengdu
Guizhou	67.2/174.0	30,080	447/173	Guiyang
Yunnn	168.4/436.2	34,560	205/80	Kunming
Shaanxi	75.6/195.8	30,430	403/155	Xian
Gansu	204.6/530.0	20,710	101/39	Lanzhou
Qinghai	278/721.0	4,120	14/6	Xining
Autonomous regions				
Inner Mongolia	173.7/450.0	20,290	117/45	Hohhot
Guangxi	85.1/220.4	39,460	464/179	Nanning
Tibet	471.5/1,221.6	2,030	43/2	Lhasa
Ningxia	65.6/170,0	4,240	65/25	Yinchuan
Xinjiang Uygur	635.7/1,646.8	13,840	22/8	Urumqi

autonomous regions or zizhiqu, and three municipalities or shi (Beijing, Shanghai and Tianjin). These principal units are in turn subdivided into prefectures, cities, counties and urban districts.

Justice

The system of law is an amalgam of customary and statutory (mainly criminal) law. The highest organ is the Supreme People's Court. Six new codes of law came into effect in 1980, to protect the people's courts (2,000 at basic level, 200 intermediate and some 30 higher-level courts) from intervention by other state bodies. People's courts generally comprise a president, a vice-president, judges and people's assessors. A civil code has been drawn up and has been in effect since January 1987. The death penalty is in force. There were over 500 executions between 1985 and mid-1988 for a wide range of offences: ranging from murder, rape, and robbery to printing or showing pornographic material.

National symbols

Flag. Red, with a large gold five-pointed star and four small gold stars in a crescent, all in upper quarter next to staff.

Festivals. 8 Mar. (International Women's Day); 1 May (Labour Day); 1 Aug. (Army Day); 12 Oct. (National Day).

INTERNATIONAL RELATIONS

Affiliations

Member of UN and most specialized agencies; IMF; World Bank.

Defence

Total Armed Forces: some 3,200,000 (perhaps 1,350,000 conscripts – men and women aged 18–22), being reduced. Terms of service: selective conscription; Army, marines three years; navy five years; air force four years. Technical volunteers can serve 8–12 more years to maximum age 35. Reserves: 1,200,000 inclusive military and militia service.

Strategic Forces: 90,000; one submarine.

Army: 2,300,000; 9,000 main battle tanks (T-54; Type 59; T-69); 2,000 light tanks Type-62; Type-63 amph.

Navy: 300,000 inclusive coastal defence, marines and naval air; 115 submarines (Romeo, Whiskey); 53 principal surface combatants: 19 destroyers (Type-051; Soviet Gordy); 34 frigates (Jianghu; Jiangnan). About 850 patrol and coastal combatants.

Naval Air Force: 30,000; some 900 shore-based combat aircraft (J-5/-6/-7; Q5; H-5); 12 armed helicopters.

Air Force: 470,000; some 6,000 combat aircraft (H-6; H-5; J-5; J-6/B/D/E; J7/J-7M; J-8).

Para-military: some 12,000,000.

ECONOMY

Currency

The unit is the yuan, divided into 10 jiao.

National finance

Balance of payments. The balance of payments (current account, 1987) was a deficit of US$171 million.

Inflation. (est.) 18.5%.

Gross Domestic Product

Estimated total GDP US$293,380 million, per capita US$320 (overall size of economy ranking 10 in the world).

Economically active population. The total number of persons active in the economy is 513,000,000.

Sector	% of workforce	% of GDP
industry	30	49
agriculture	61	31
services*	9	20

* services figure includes elements unassigned to other categories.

Energy and mineral resources

Minerals. There are coal deposits in most provinces, and there are 70 major production centres, of which Hebei, Shanxi, Shandon, Jilin and Anhui are the most important. Reserves are estimated at 847,867 million tons/769,180 million tonnes; production in 1987 was estimated at 1,014 million tons/920 million tonnes. There is an estimated 547,193 million tons/496,410 million tonnes of iron ore deposits, found particularly in Shanxi, Hebei and Shandong. In 1984 iron ore output was estimated at 134 million tons/122 million tonnes. The major steel producing areas are Anshan (capacity 6.6 million tons/6 million tonnes); Wuhan (capacity 3.9 million tons/3.5 million tonnes); Baotou; Maanshan; Baoshan. Tin production (1981) 16,535 tons/15,000 tonnes. China is the major world producer of tungsten ore – production in 1981 was 15,432 tons/14,000 tonnes. The most important centres are Hunan, Guangdong, and Yunnan.

Electricity. Production: (1988) 110 million kWh per capita. Over 70% of electricity is generated from coal; hydroelectric power accounts for 4%; oil 21%; gas 2%. In Shanghai and Daya Bay in Guangdong nuclear energy plants are being built.

Bioresources

Agriculture. Although only 11% of the land is cultivated, the majority of the workforce is engaged in agriculture. China is self-sufficient in grain, and is the world's largest producer of rice, millet, barley and sorghum. Peasants are now allowed to lease land from the state and to retain earnings after meeting the state's contractual obligations. In 1984 there were 2,048 state farms and 180 million peasant households. Crop production: (1986 in million tons/tonnes) rice 195/177; wheat 98/89; maize 72/65.6; soya beans 12/11.0; roots and tubers 153/138.8; tea 0.55/0.5. (1987) cotton 4.60/4.17; oilseed crops 16.81/15.25; sugar cane 51.6/46.8; fruit 17/15.5. The gross value of agricultural output (1987) was 444,700 million yuan.

Livestock numbers: (1987 in millions) horses 10.9; cattle 71.4; goats 67.5; pigs 32.6; sheep 178.3.

Forestry. Total forest area: (1985 est.) 284 million acres/115 million ha. Timber reserves: 3,623,216 ft^3/102,600 m^3. Principal forest areas are Heilongjiang, Sichuan and Yunnan. Timber production: (1985 est.) 2,228 million ft^3/63.1 million m^3.

Fisheries. Total catch: (1985) 7.77 million tons/7.05 million tonnes.

Industry and commerce

Industry. The major industries are iron; steel; coal; machine building; armaments; textiles; petroleum. Growth rate in industrial production: (1987) 14.8%. Production: (1985 est. in tons/tonnes) chemical fertilizer 14.7 million/13.3 million; pig iron 44 million/40 million; cement 156 million/142 million; steel 51 million/46.6 million; rolled steel 40.6 million/36.8 million; coke 36 million/33 million; cotton cloth 507,109 million ft^3/14,360 million m^3; motor vehicles

439,000 units; tractors 44,600 units; bicycles 32.2 million; TV sets 10 million. Gross value of 1985 industrial output: 875,960 million yuan.

Commerce. Imports: (1987) US$33.4 million; exports US$34.6 million. Main exports are textiles; oil; oil products; chemicals; light industrial goods; arms. Exports: (1985 in 1,000 tons/tonnes) crude oil 33,102/30,030; petroleum products 6,845/6,210; tea 151/137; cereals 102,845/93,300; tungsten ore 17/16; cotton cloth 590,919 million ft^3/16,733 million m^3. Major imports: machinery and transport equipment; iron and steel; chemicals. Imports: (1985 in 1,000 tons/tonnes) wheat 59,304/53,800; rolled steel 22,079/20,030; motor vehicles 353,979 units. Major trading partners: Hong Kong; USA; Federal Republic of Germany; Canada. Customs duties with Taiwan were abolished in 1980.

Trade with UK. China imported £411,563,000 worth of goods and exported £443,698,000 to the UK (1988).

Tourism. The Chinese government in Feb. 1986 relaxed to some extent the restrictions on Chinese nationals travelling abroad. Access to China for foreign tourists had also become easier and the country was becoming a popular destination for travellers from the West, at least until the Tiananmen Square massacre of mid-1989.

Earnings from tourism exceeded US$2,000 million in 1988, with over 23 million visitors in the first 9 months of the year (as compared with 3 million in the whole of 1985).

COMMUNICATIONS

Railways

There are 32,603 miles/52,500 km of railways, of which 2,732 miles/4,400 km are electrified.

Roads

There are 597,899 miles/962,800 km of roads of all types, 100,602 miles/162,000 km of paved highway.

Aviation

General Administration of Civil Aviation of China (CAAC) provides domestic and international services (international airports are at Beijing, Xiamen, Shanghai and Chengdu). There are 330 airfields in all.

Shipping

China's large merchant fleet includes a total of 1,333 ships exceeding 1,000 GRT, with a further 159 operating under Panamanian, Liberian, UK, Hong Kong and Maltese registry; the combined total approaches 25 million DWT.

Telecommunications

There is an uneven telephone system with some 7,500,000 telephones in all. There are more than 215 million radios in China, and some 16,800,000 televisions, including 6,000,000 colour sets. Broadcasting is controlled by the Ministry of Radio, Film and Television; operations are conducted by the Central People's Television Broadcasting Section and (radio) by the Central People's Broadcasting Station and Radio Beijing, the latter's foreign service being broadcast in 38 languages.

EDUCATION AND WELFARE

Education

In 1986 90% of school-age children attended school, although in 1988 there were 220 million people (of whom 70% were women) who were illiterate. An existing five-year school career is being replaced by a nine-year education, with six years of primary schooling and three years of secondary school.

School population. (1985 figures): 14.8 million children at kindergarten; 133.7 million children at primary school; 50.3 million children at secondary school; 1.7 million students in higher education.

Schools. (1985 figures): 172,262 kindergartens with 798,000 teachers, one per 18.5 pupils. 832,309 primary schools with 6.02 million teachers, one per 22 pupils.

Universities. 1,016 institutes of higher education with 0.87 million teachers, one per 1.9 pupils.

Health

Only certain groups of employees are entitled to free medical care. Costs are paid in part by the patient's employer. In 1985 there were 1,413,000 doctors (336,000 of whom practised Chinese medicine) (approximately one doctor per 758 people). In 1985 there were 59,619 hospitals (including 348 psychiatric hospitals) with 2.23 million beds (approximately one bed per 479 people).

CHRISTMAS ISLAND

GEOGRAPHY

An island in the Indian Ocean, about 186 miles/300 km south of Java, Christmas Island covers an area of 52 $miles^2$/135 km^2. With steep cliffs rising to a central plateau, it is almost completely surrounded by a reef. The capital is The Settlement.

Climate

Tropical; heat and humidity moderated by trade winds.

Population

Total population (1989 est.) 2,278, mainly of Chinese and Malay descent.

Rate of population increase 0.0.

Language

English.

HISTORY

Before 1888 Christmas Island was apparently uninhabited. It had been discovered by European explorers in the early 17th century and received its name in 1643 when an Englishman, Capt. William Mynors, sighted it on Christmas Day.

A British expedition in 1886 surveyed the island, and it was formally annexed by Great Britain in 1888. In 1891 a lease for the island was granted to John Clunies-Ross and Sir John Murray and the discovery a few years later of phosphate deposits on the island led to the transfer of the lease to the Christmas Island Phosphate Co. Ltd (of which Clunies Ross and Murray were the chief shareholders). The company exploited the deposits and imported a labour force, composed mainly of Chinese and Malays, to work on the island. In 1900 Christmas Island was included for administrative purposes as a dependency of Singapore.

In 1948 the Australian and New Zealand governments acquired the company's mining interests and on 1 Oct. 1958 the island was transferred to Australian administration. Legislation introduced in 1981 gave the inhabitants of the island the right to acquire Australian citizenship and to migrate to the mainland. In 1985 the island's first Assembly was elected. In 1987, after industrial unrest and difficulties running the mining operations, the Australian government announced that the Company would cease mining by the end of the year. Redundancy and resettlement schemes were introduced and attempts made to encourage private investment in the island, including the recommencement of mining activities.

CONSTITUTION AND GOVERNMENT

Christmas Island is a territory of Australia, with a constitution under the Christmas Island Act of 1958. The administrator is appointed by the governor general of Australia, and advised by the Advisory Council.

Administrator. The Hon. A.D. Taylor.

National symbols

Flag. The flag of Australia.

ECONOMY

The land is unsuitable for agriculture. The only significant economic activity is phosphate mining, but this is under threat of closure from the Australian government. There are plans to develop tourism.

Currency.

Australian dollar.

COMMUNICATIONS

There is a port at Flying Fish Cove. There is one airport with a permanent-surface runway. There is radio, but no television.

COCOS (KEELING) ISLANDS

GEOGRAPHY

The islands are low-lying coral atolls in the Indian Ocean (about half-way between Australia and Sri Lanka) and have a total area of 5.4 miles^2/14 km^2. They are thickly covered with coconut palms and other vegetation. The main islands are West Island, the capital, and Home Island.

Climate

Pleasant, modified by the south-east trade winds for about nine months of the year. Rainfall is moderate.

Population

Total population (1989 est.) 616. Inhabitants are mostly Europeans on West Island and Cocos Malays on Home Island.

Language

English.

HISTORY

These islands were discovered in 1609 by Capt. William Keeling of the East India Company, who found them uninhabited. In 1826 Alexander Hare from England established the first settlement, and a year later a second was set up by a Scotsman, John Clunies-Ross, who brought Malay labourers with him. The islands became a British possession in 1857 and responsibility for them passed in 1878 to the governor of Ceylon and then in 1886 to the governor of the Straits settlements. That year the British Crown granted all lands on the islands to George Clunies-Ross and his heirs in perpetuity, subject to future Crown requirements. In a naval engagement off the islands in 1914 an Australian warship destroyed a German cruiser.

After being a dependency of the Colony of Singapore from 1946, the islands became an Australian external territory in 1955. The only inhabited islands in the group are Home Island, where the Cocos Malays live, and West Island, with a small European settlement. In 1978 the Australian government purchased the bulk of John Clunies-Ross's interests in the island and the following year established an Islands Council to carry out certain functions and to advise the resident administrator, who is responsible to the minister of Home Affairs and the Environment in Canberra. In a referendum in 1984, with United Nations observers present, the Cocos Malays chose to integrate with Australia. All islanders have the full rights of Australian citizens, including voting rights in relation to the Australian Parliament.

CONSTITUTION AND GOVERNMENT

The Cocos (Keeling) Islands are an Australian territory. Under the Cocos Islands Act of 1955 there is a resident administrator, appointed by the governor general of Australia. The Cocos Malay community is represented by the Cocos Islands Council.

National symbols

Flag. The flag of Australia.

ECONOMY

Coconuts are the sole cash crop, and are grown

throughout the islands. Copra and fresh coconuts are the major export earners. Most necessities are imported from Australia.

Currency
Australian dollar.

COMMUNICATIONS

There are no ports, lagoon anchorage only. There is one airport with a permanent-surface runway. There are no roads or railways. There is one AM radio station, but no television. There are telephone, telex and fax communications via satellite with Australia.

COLOMBIA

Republica de Colombia
(Republic of Colombia)

GEOGRAPHY

Colombia is situated in the extreme north-west of South America with a Caribbean and Pacific coastline, and island territories in both: San Andrés, Providencia, San Bernado, Islas del Rosario, Isla Fuerte and Gorgona, Gorgonilla, Malpelo respectively. It has a total area of 439,621 miles^2/1,138,914 km^2 divided into 23 departments, four intendencies and five administrative territories. The Colombian Andes run north-south, separating the densely forested and very sparsely populated Llanos and Amazonian lowlands to the east from the Pacific and dry Caribbean coastal plain in the west and north-west. West-east, the Colombian Andes comprise three ranges: the Cordillera Occidental, divided from the Cordillera Central (highest point Huila 18,865 ft/5,750 m) by the Rio Cauca, and the Cordillera Oriental, also separated from the two western chains by the densely populated Magdalena River valley, draining northwards and eventually emptying into the Caribbean. Approximately 90% of the total population inhabit the temperate Andean valleys and Eastern Cordillera plateaux, and a large proportion of Colombia's arable land (5% in total) is on the fertile highland slopes of the longitudinal Cauca and Magdalena basins. 49% of Colombian territory is forested. Other major river systems are the Guarviare, Putomayo, Caqueta and Patia.

Climate
Varies according to altitude, though predominantly tropical. Where rainfall is very high (98 in/2,500 mm in the Amazonian lowlands, Magdalena Valley and west, north-west Pacific coast), rainforests (selvas) proliferate. Tropical savannah characterizes the north Magdalena Valley, becoming dry savannah on the Caribbean plains (average temperature 81°F/27°C) with rainfall no more than 24 in/600 mm annually. At comparatively low altitudes (6,561 ft/2,000 m–8,202 ft/2,500 m), rainfall is between 55 in/1,400 mm and 87 in/2,200 mm decreasing with a corresponding drop in temperature at higher elevations to become permanent snow cover above 14,737 ft/4,500 m. Bogotá: Jan. 58°F/14.4°C. July 57°F/13.9°C. Annual rainfall 41 in/1,052 mm. Cali: Jan. 75°F/23.9°C. July 75°F/23.9°C. Average annual rainfall 36 in/915 mm. Medellín: Jan. 71°F/21.7°C. July 72°F/22.2°C. Average annual rainfall 63 in/1,606 mm.

Cities and towns

Bogotá (capital)	3,982,941
Medellín	1,468,089
Cali	1,350,565
Barranquilla	899,781
Cartagena	531,426

Population
Total population is 30,566,000 of which 67.2% live in urban areas. Population density is 69.5 persons per mile^2/26.8 per km^2. Ethnic composition: 58% mestizo; 20% White; 14% mulatto; 4% Black; 3% mixed Black-Indian; 1% Indian. The Paez and Guambiano (south-west) peoples are involved in on-going territorial disputes over the expropriation of traditional Indian 'resguardos'. The Indian Council of the Cauca was formed in 1971.

Birth rate 3.1%. **Death rate** 0.77%. **Rate of population increase** 2.33%. **Age distribution** under 15 = 37.2%; over 65 = 3.8%. **Life expectancy** female 68; male 64; average 66.

Religion
95% of the population are Roman Catholic (26 bishops, 1,546 parishes and 4,020 priests). Some traditional beliefs survive among the indigenous population. A small minority of Episcopal Church

adherents, Baptists and Baha'is. The Jewish community numbers approximately 25,000.

Language

The official language is Castillian Spanish. Over 180 indigenous Indian languages and dialects survive, including Aymara; Arawak; Chibcha; Carib; Quechua; Tupi-Guarani; Yurumangi.

HISTORY

The poorly organized Chibcha-speaking Indians of the north-western mountain regions posed little resistance to the main thrust of the Spanish Conquest which proceeded from 1525 onwards. The country was incorporated into the viceroyalty of Peru in 1544 until 1739 when the current capital, Bogotá, became the centre of the new viceroyalty of New Granada (comprising present-day Colombia, Ecuador, Venezuela and Panama). Gold had been worked by the Chibchas, and New Granada was one of the world's leading gold exporters (before being eclipsed by the mid-19th-century discoveries in California and Australia) but its economy was commercially undeveloped.

National independence, finally achieved by the army of the Venezuelan liberator Simon Bolívar at the Battle of Boyaca in 1819, was followed by ten years of uneasy confederation with Venezuela and Ecuador in the shape of Gran Colombia (1821–30), until regional differences between the three finally undermined the union. In 1830 the countries went their separate ways, although Panama remained part of Colombia until 1903.

By 1850, the dominant creole elites (American-born Spanish) had split into either the Liberal or Conservative parties. These, from their founding in 1849 up to the present, succeeded in dividing almost the entire society into partisan camps, irrespective of social class and regional and economic realities. Although the division was often based on personal circumstances and family loyalties, there were ostensibly great ideological differences between the parties; the Liberals were associated with anti-clericalism, federalism and free-trade while the Conservatives were committed to a centralist state, the Church and protectionism.

During the 19th century and into the 20th, control of the government alternated between the two, the Liberals monopolizing power 1861–86 and the Conservatives 1886–1930. Political resentment and protest over unfulfilled promises of economic improvement erupted into frequent outbursts of civil war, culminating in the 'War of a Thousand Days' of 1899–1901, which occurred at a time of a slump in coffee prices (coffee having become the country's leading export at the end of the 19th century). In this political climate, third-party alternatives were absent and the newly emerging middle classes never banded together but, instead, made their way within the two traditional parties which occasionally acted in coalition.

Towards the end of the 1920s Conservative dominance waned, to be replaced by that of the Liberals, although their new president Enrique Olaya Herrera (1930–34) was elected by a coalition of Conservatives and Liberals in the country's first ever peaceful change of party in power. The situation became more complicated when a significant faction of the Liberal Party adopted a 'new liberalism' which identified the role of the state with active social reform, most forcefully expressed, if not practically realized, during the tenure of Pres. Alfonso Lopez Pumarejo (1934–38), who was also instrumental in the creation of the Confederation of Colombian Workers (CTC) in 1935. Such reform was successfully resisted by the authoritarian Conservative faction led by Laureano Gomez and the moderates from both parties who wished to maintain the status quo. Lopez was forced to resign during his second presidential term (1942–45) and in 1946 the Conservative Mariano Ospina Perez defeated two Liberal candidates for the presidency. Ten years of unprecedented violence (La Violencia, 1946–56) followed in which at least 200,000 people were killed as the Conservatives tried to consolidate a new period of power and the Liberals resisted it. The military dictatorship of Gustavo Rojas Pinilla (1953–57) which (with the support of all parties and the Church) overthrew the Conservative Pres. Laureano Gomez (1950–53), was the first of the century, but was only partially successful in stemming the spiral of violence, although it brought significant improvements to the economic infrastructure. When Pinilla himself began using repression to extend his tenure of power, he was replaced by a temporary military regime which in 1958 stepped aside for a National Front government.

The incoming National Front, the product of legal agreements guaranteeing the restriction and division of power to the Liberals and Conservatives, endured for 16 years, up to 1974, seeing two Liberal and two Conservative presidents alternate in office. As an alternative to this closed system Rojas Pinilla formed the National Popular Alliance (ANAPO) in 1961. Unable to declare itself a party in its own right, it worked as a movement within both of the traditional parties. The constitutional reforms of 1968 allowed for new parties, but they also hampered the Liberal government of Alfonso Lopez Michelsen (1974–78) by maintaining the system of parity of offices between Liberals and Conservatives. Thus, following the election of the Liberal president Julio Cesar Turbay Ayala (1978–82), Conservatives joined his executive as did Liberals that of the Conservative Pres. Belisario Betancur Cuartas (1982–86).

A number of opposition parties were created in the early 1970s but failed to shake the dominant two-party system, encouraging the emergence, in the late 1970s, of left-wing guerrilla groups, most prominently the National Liberation Army (ELN), Revolutionary Armed Forces of Colombia (FARC) and the April 19 Movement (M19). They failed to dislodge the government, but caused major national disruption. The government made several attempts at conciliation before the M19 finally declared a cease-fire in response to a peace plan, proposed by the Liberal Pres. Virgilio Barco Vargas (1986–) on 2 Sept. 1988. The other current threat existing in society was not directed at the established political system as such but set right-wing para-military death squads against any group (peasant farmers, human-rights activists, trade unionists, officials of left-wing political parties or government anti-drug squads) which attempts to oppose the powerful drug cartels in Medellín and Cali, the world's major suppliers of cocaine. These private drug armies are estimated to have murdered thousands of people each year since the early 1980s.

The assassination of the prominent Liberal Party politician Carlos Galan in Aug. 1989 provoked President Barco to declare 'war' on the drug cartels. The new strategy, which included the controversial measure to extradite drug traffickers and murderers wanted in the United States, resulted in the Drug Barons suing for peace in Jan. 1990. Their offer to cease drug shipments and surrender their weapons in return for constitutional and legal guarantees allowing them to re-integrate themselves into society were rejected by the government.

CONSTITUTION AND GOVERNMENT

Executive and legislature

There is an executive president, directly elected for a four-year term (last election 25 May 1986), who appoints the Cabinet. The legislature, the Congress, consists of a 114-member Senate and a 199-member House of Representatives, both directly elected for four-year terms (last elections 9 Mar. 1986). A 'Primer Designado' (First Delegate) is elected by Congress to act in the event of a presidential vacancy.

Present government

President Sr Virgilio Barco Vargas
Primer Designado Dr Victor Mosquera Chaux
Principal members of Cabinet Col Julio Londono Paredes (Foreign Affairs); Sr Carlos Lemos Simons (Interior); Gen. Oscar Botero (Defence); Dr Luis Fernandez Alarcon Mantilla (Finance); Dr Carlos Arturo Marulanda (Economic Development); Sr Roberto Salazar Manrique (Justice).

Justice

The system of law is based on Spanish law. The highest court is the Supreme Court at Bogotá, which can review legislation, Superior Courts are the top of the legal structure in each of the 61 judicial districts, while marriage matters are handled separately by religious courts. Communism was outlawed by government decree on 5 March 1956. The death penalty was abolished in 1910.

National symbols

Flag. Three horizontal stripes of yellow, blue and red.
Festivals. 1 May (Labour Day); 20 July (Independence Day); 7 Aug. (Battle of Boyaca); 12 Oct. (Discovery of America); 11 Nov. (Independence of Cartagena).
Vehicle registration plate. CO.

INTERNATIONAL RELATIONS

Affiliations

NAM; OAS; SELA.

Defence

Total Armed Forces: 86,300 (some 28,200 conscripts). Terms of service: 1–2 years, varies (all services). Reserves: 116,900.

Army: 69,000; 12 light tanks (M-3A1).

Navy: 10,600; two submarines (FRG T-209/1200; FRG HWT); four frigates; 19 patrol and coastal combatants.

Air Force: 6,700; 48 combat aircraft (Mirage 5); 16 armed helicopters.

Opposition: Coordinadora Nacional Guerrillera (CNG), loose coalition of guerrilla groups with together 9,300 active.

ECONOMY

Currency

The unit is the peso, divided into 100 centavos.

National finance

Budget. The 1987 budget was for expenditure of US$3,700 million and revenue of US$3,600 million.

Balance of payments. The balance of payments (current account, 1987) was a surplus of US$255 million.
Inflation. 23.3%.

Gross Domestic Product

Estimated total GDP US$31,940 million, per capita US$1,140 (overall size of economy ranking 49 in the world).
Economically active population. The total number of persons active in the economy is 11,000,000; unemployed: 11.7%.

Sector	% of workforce	% of GDP
industry	21	35
agriculture	26	19
services*	53	46

* services figure includes elements unassigned to other categories.

Energy and mineral resources

Oil. Production 19.16 million tons/17.38 million tonnes.
Minerals. Colombia has rich mineral resources. Output: (1987 in troy oz) gold 853,468; silver 167,277; platinum 22,530. Other minerals include copper; lead; mercury; manganese; emeralds. Both land salt (224,919 tons/204,045 tonnes) and sea salt (729,691 tons/661,971) are produced and coal production is 15.9 million tons/14.5 million tonnes.
Electricity. Capacity: 8.8 million kW; production: 34,700 million kWh; 1,110 kWh per capita.

Bioresources

Agriculture. Only a small percentage of the land in Colombia is cultivated despite its generally fertile soil, and there is a wide range of crops and climate. 5.36 million acres/2.17 million ha are under temporary cultivation and 2.94 million acres/1.19 million ha under permanent. Crops include coffee; rice; maize; sugar cane; plantains; bananas; cotton; tobacco. Colombia is an illegal producer of coca and cannabis for the international drug trade.

Crop production: coffee 12.9 million 132 lb/60kg sacks. Others (in 1,000 tons/tonnes) potatoes 2,584/2,344; rice 2,070/1,878; maize 978/887; sorghum 790/717.

Livestock numbers: (in millions) poultry 138.5; cattle 23.9; sheep 2.6; pigs 2.5.
Forestry. 49% of Colombia is forest and woodland.
Fisheries. Total catch: 84,750 tons/76,885 tonnes.

Industry and commerce

Industry. The main industries are textiles; food processing; oil; clothing and footwear; beverages; chemicals; metal products; cement. Mining is also important (see Minerals).
Commerce. Total exports: $4,600 million including coffee 30%; petroleum 24%; coal; bananas; fresh cut flowers. Imports: $4,300 million including industrial equipment; transportation equipment; foodstuffs; chemicals; paper products. Countries exported to were US 36%; EC 21%; Japan 5%; Netherlands 4%; Sweden 3%. Imports came from US 34%; EC 16%; Brazil 4%; Venezuela 3%; Japan 3%.
Trade with UK. Colombia imported UK goods worth £53,132,000; exports to UK totalled £61,835,000.
Tourism. (1986) 732,000 visitors.

COMMUNICATIONS

Railways

There are 1,627 miles/2,620 km of railways.

Roads
There are 65,961 miles/106,218 km of roads.

Aviation
Aérovias Nacionales de Colombia (AVIANCA) provides domestic and international services. Servicio Aéreo a Territorios Nacionales (Satena) provides internal services and Sociedad Aéronautica de Medellín Consolidada, SA (SAM) domestic and international cargo services (international airports are at Bogotá (Eldorado Airport), Medellín, Cali, Barranquilla, Bucaramanga, Cartagena, Cucuta, Leticia, Pereira, San Andrés and Santa Marta).

Shipping
Main ports are at Barranquilla; Buenaventura; Cartagena; Covenas; San Andrés; Santa Marta; Tumaco. There are 38 ships in the merchant marine exceeding 1,000 GRT. Inland waterways extend over 8,694 miles/14,000 km navigable by river boats.

Telecommunications
There are 1,890,000 telephones, connected by a national radio relay system. Television (dating from 1954) is broadcast on three channels by the state monopoly Inravision, and can now be received by some 7.8 million sets, and radio (over 500 stations) by 30 million radio sets.

EDUCATION AND WELFARE

Education
Primary education in Colombia is free (although not compulsory) but facilities are limited. There are both state-run and private schools.
Schools. There are 6,640 pre-primary schools with 291,741 pupils; 34,520 primary schools with 3,740,379 pupils; 5,181 secondary schools with 1,684,731 pupils.
Universities. There are 232 higher education establishments with 417,786 pupils.
Literacy. 88% but only 60% for Indians.

Health
There are 753 hospitals and clinics and around 860 health centres.

COMOROS
République fédérale islamique des Comores (Federal Islamic Republic of the Comoros)

GEOGRAPHY
The archipelago republic of Comoros consists of three volcanic islands (Grande Comore or Njazidja, Moheli or Mwali, Anjouan or Nzwani) situated at the north end of the Mozambique Channel between mainland Africa and Madagascar, covering a total area of 719 miles^2/1,862 km^2. The republic's highest peak is Mount Kartala (7,746 ft/2,361 m), at the southern end of the rocky and infertile though densely populated Grande Comore. The nation's capital, Moroni, is situated in the south-west. Anjouan's once fertile soils have suffered extensive erosion but the inland valleys of Moheli, smallest of the island group, are generally fertile with densely forested hillsides. Surface water is seasonal and wells can only be sunk on Anjouan and Moheli. 35% of the total area is arable and 16% is forested.

Climate
Tropical, subject to Indian monsoon (Cacassi) influences from the north. Hot, humid conditions prevail in the wet season between Nov. and Apr., with temperatures up to 82°F/28°C and maximum rainfall in Jan. (11–15 in/275–375 mm). Summer conditions also include periodic cyclones, waterspouts and tidal waves. The dry season lasts May–Oct. Moroni: Jan. 81°F/27.2°C. July 75°F/23.9°C. Average annual rainfall 111 in/2,825 mm.

Cities and towns
Moroni (capital)	17,267
Mutssamudu	13,000
Fomboni	5,400

Population
Total population is 487,000 of which 27.1% live in urban areas. Population density is 677 persons per mile^2/262 per km^2. Principal ethnic divisions are the Antalote, Cafre, Makoa, Oimatsaha and Sakalava groups of African, Arabian, Indonesian and Madagascan extraction. 0.4% are French.
Birth rate 4.64%. **Death rate** 1.59%. **Rate of population increase** 3.05%. **Age distribution** under 15 = 46.1%; over 65 = 2.8%. **Life expectancy** female 53.9; male 54.2; average 54.

Religion
Islam (official). The vast majority of the population (between 96 and 97%) are Sunni Muslims; there are about 2,000 Roman Catholics.

Language
Arabic and French are official languages. Comorian, a Bantu-Swahili-Malagasy hybrid is in common usage (96.9%). A small minority speak Makua (of Bantu origin).

HISTORY
Islamic sultanates were set up by Shirazi religious groups arriving from the north from the 10th century onwards. They ruled until the 19th century over islands inhabited by earlier immigrants of Polynesian origin, and by African and Arab elements involved in the dominant slave and spice trades. The French bought Mayotte in 1841, declared a protectorate over the other islands in 1886, and proclaimed them a colony in 1912. The strictly limited political development in the succeeding period was restricted to the French companies and the landowners who controlled the cash crop economy (principally vanilla and cocoa).

During World War II the British occupied the Comoros, at that time administered from Madagascar, which had declared for the Vichy regime in France. Returned to French control after the war, the

Comoros were separated administratively from Madagascar and remained a French Overseas Territory under France's 1958 Fifth Republic constitution. A Council of Government was set up under the Dec. 1961 autonomy law, with a Chamber of Deputies initially with a consensus in favour of retaining strong links with France.

In 1972, with both main groups in the Chamber swinging over to demand independence, its leaders resigned, precipitating elections (Dec. 1972) from which they emerged with a popular mandate to negotiate with the French on independence terms. Those terms (agreed June 1973) envisaged independence in five years, a timetable soon brought forward by two years. A referendum (22 Dec. 1974) gave overwhelming support for independence, except that a majority in Mayotte favoured continuing links with France. The French insisted that any constitutional proposals should be accepted by referendum in each of the islands, but the Chamber of Deputies voted (6 July 1975) to declare independence unilaterally. Ahmed Abdallah became president, but France kept Mayotte, making it a collectivité territoriale (Dec. 1976) after a referendum in February that year.

Meanwhile Abdallah's overthrow (3 Aug.–21 Sept. 1975) allowed coup leader Ali Soilih to become head of state (2 Jan. 1976); the Comoros joined the UN (12 Nov. 1975) but its relations with France degenerated and all French aid was cut off. Soilih's radical socialist reforms of government, administration and the economy emphasized mobilization of youth (the minimum voting age was lowered to 14), but on 13 May 1978 he was overthrown, and killed two weeks later. The French mercenary coup leader Bob Denard restored Ahmed Abdallah to power; the OAU suspended the Comoros from membership, but relations with France were re-established, links with Arab countries were developed, and a Federal Islamic Republic was declared (1 Oct. 1978).

In Feb. 1979 the OAU relented and readmitted the Comoros to membership, despite the continuing influence of Denard (his name changed to Col Said Mustapha Moidjou) and his presidential guard. Party politics were banned. Abdallah strengthened his personal grip by reshuffling the government (1980), obtaining re-election as sole candidate in presidential elections (Sept. 1984) and taking over as head of government, after modifying the constitution and abolishing the office of prime minister (Dec. 1984). He survived two coup attempts (Feb. 1983 and Mar. 1985), the second of which gave evidence of some continuing support for Soilih's left-wing ideas. France, accused by some of supporting Abdallah's regime, continued to oppose UN resolutions (1981, 1984) calling for negotiations on restoring Mayotte to the Comoros.

Abdallah was assassinated in Nov. 1989 and his presidential guard led by Denard briefly ran the country until forced to leave under French and South African pressure. A provisional national unity government was formed by various political groupings; one-party rule was abolished. Presidential elections in Feb. 1990 were abandoned in chaos, but the acting President, Said Mohammed Djohar, beat eight other candidates in the rescheduled election in March.

CONSTITUTION AND GOVERNMENT

Executive and legislature

The executive president is elected for a six-year term (last election Mar. 1990). The 42-member Federal Assembly is elected by universal adult suffrage for a five-year term, most recently in Mar. 1987.

Present government

President; Said Mohammed Djohar
Leader (vacant)

Administration

Governors of the islands, appointed by the president, have responsibility for routine economic and police administration.

Justice

The system of law has been codified to consolidate French and Muslim elements. The highest court is the Supreme Court, whose 7 members are appointed by the President, the Federal Assembly and by the island's Legislative Council. The death penalty is nominally in force. No executions were recorded between 1985 and mid-1988.

National symbols

Flag. Green with a white crescent and four white five-pointed stars between the horns of the crescent, which is placed centrally and turned towards the lower fly.

Festivals. 6 July (Independence Day).

INTERNATIONAL RELATIONS

Affiliations

NAM; OAU.

Defence

Security forces comprise the Army, the Presidential Guard and the gendarmerie.

ECONOMY

Currency

The unit is the Comoran franc, divided into 100 centimes.

National finance

Budget. The 1987 budget was for expenditure of US$70 million and revenue of US$67 million.

Inflation. 8.3%.

Gross Domestic Product

Estimated total GDP US$163 million, per capita US$390 (overall size of economy ranking 169 in the world).

Economically active population. The total number of persons active in the economy is 140,000; unemployed: over 20%.

Energy and mineral resources

Minerals. No significant mineral deposits have been located.

Electricity. Capacity: 16,000 kW; production: (1988) 24 million kWh.

Bioresources

Agriculture. Agriculture, along with fishing and forestry, is the leading sector of the economy, contributing about 40% of GDP and employing 80% of the working population. 35% of the land is arable, with 8% given over to permanent crops and 7% to meadows and pasture. The principal cash crops are vanilla; copra; cloves; essential oils (citronella; ylang-ylang; lemon grass).

Crop production: (1986 in tons/tonnes) cassava 102,514/93,000; coconuts 51,805/47,000; bananas 39,683/36,000; sweet potatoes 19,841/18,000; rice 17,637/16,000; maize 6,614/6,000.

Livestock numbers: (1987) cattle 88,000; sheep 9,000; goats 96,000; asses 4,000.

Forestry. About 16% of the land is forested. Timber is produced on the island of Njazidja.

Fisheries. Total catch: (1986 est.) 5,842 tons/5,300 tonnes.

Industry and commerce

Industry. The industrial sector contributes less than 4% of GDP. The distillation of essential oils for perfume manufacture is the principal activity.

Commerce. Exports: (1986) US$39 million, mainly vanilla (approximately 67% of total value); cloves (20%); perfume oil; copra. Countries exported to were the US 53%; France 41%; African countries 4%; West Germany 2%. Imports: $41 million, comprising rice (accounting for 90% of all imports); cement; petroleum products; consumer goods. Principal sources of imports: Europe 62% (of which France 22%); Africa 5%; Pakistan; China.

Trade with UK. (1988) The Comoros imported UK goods worth £333,000 and exported goods to the UK worth £33,000.

Tourism. (1986) approximately 5,000 visitors.

COMMUNICATIONS

Railways

There are no railways.

Roads

There are some 466 miles/750 km of roads, of which 247 miles/398 km are concrete or bituminized.

Aviation

Air Comores (Société nationale des transports aériens) provides domestic services (the international airport is at Moroni-Hahaya on Njazidja).

Shipping

Moroni and Mutsamudu are the main ports.

Telecommunications

There are 1,800 telephones, the sparse system being based on radio relay. There are about 50,000 radio sets and no television service.

EDUCATION AND WELFARE

Education

The level of education is low overall.

Schools. (1981) 236 primary schools with 59,700 pupils and 1,300 teachers (one per 46 pupils); 32 secondary schools with 13,530 pupils and 430 teachers (one per 32 pupils); two technical schools with 150 students and nine teachers (one per 17 students). There was also a teacher-training college with 120 students and eight teaching staff.

Literacy. 15%.

Health

(1978) 20 doctors (approximately one per 22,224 inhabitants); 35 midwives; 124 nursing personnel. In 1980 there were 17 hospitals and clinics with 760 beds (one bed per 585 inhabitants).

CONGO

République Populaire du Congo (People's Republic of the Congo)

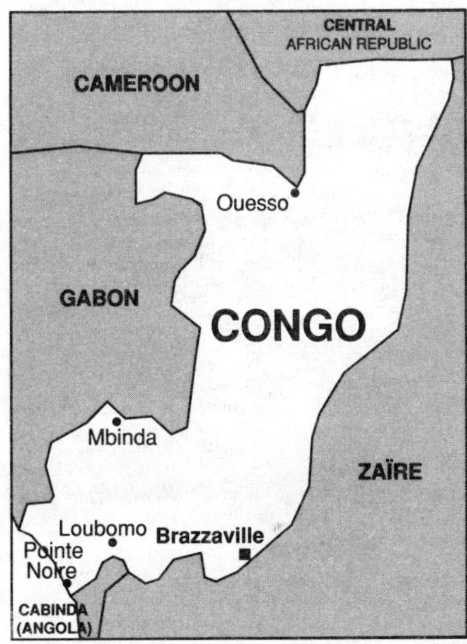

GEOGRAPHY

Located in west central Africa, the Congo republic occupies an area of 132,012 miles²/342,000 km² divided into nine provinces of which the most populous is Kouilou province in the south. The central plateaux (Bateke and Bembe) run east-west, dividing the country's hydrology into the northern Congo (Zaïre) basin, accounting for 75% of total drainage, and the smaller Niari-Konilou Basin, draining most of the south and south-east regions. The Niari basin itself rises northwards to heights of 2,133 ft/650 m in the Massif du Chaillu on the Gabon border, and 3,412 ft/1,040 m at Mont de la Leketi, while to the west of the Niari, the incised Mayombe massif (Mount Foungouti 3,051 ft/930 m) rises inland from the swampy coastal plain. The Congo Basin's relief rarely exceeds more than 984–1,148 ft/300–350 m rising to 1,476 ft/450 m on the Central African Republic and Gabon borders. Principal tributaries in the north are the Alima and Sangha, joining the Oubangi and Congo rivers as they form the country's eastern and southern frontiers. Over 60% of the Congo is covered in dense tropical rainforest. The alluvial fertility of the Niari valley is subject to erosion by wind and rain but is still the republic's most important agricultural area.

Climate

The Congo has an equatorial climate, with high humidity, small temperature range and average annual rainfall of 49–69 in/1,250–1,750 mm. Rainfall increases north-easterly with nearly 79 in/2,000 mm falling per year. The dry season in the south-western plateau uplands is May–Oct., elsewhere June–Sept. Brazzaville: Jan. 78°F/25.6°C. July 73°F/22.8°C. Average annual rainfall 58 in/1,473 mm.

Cities and towns

Brazzaville (capital)	456,383
Pool	219,329
Pointe-Noire	214,466
Bouenza	135,999
Cuvette	127,558
Niari	114,229
Plateaux	110,379

Population

Total population is 1,888,000, of which 41% live in urban areas. Population density is 14.3 persons per mile²/5.5 per km². Almost 50% of the Congo's population belong to the Kongo ethnic group, of which the major divisions are the Sundi, Kongo, Lali, Kougni, Bembe, Kamba, Dondo, Vili and Yombe, concentrated in the south. The Sangha (Gabonese Bantu) and M'bochi (Ubangi) inhabit the northern part of the country. The Teke (17%) dominate the central regions. Approximately 1.5% of the total population are Binga Pygmy; small pockets of European French, foreign African, Chinese and Portuguese make up a further 3%.

Birth rate 4.45%. **Death rate** 1.54%. **Rate of population increase** (1980–87) 2.91%. **Age distribution** under 15 = 43.6%; over 65 = 3.4%. **Life expectancy** female 61; male 57; average 59.

Religion

An estimated 42% of the population practise indigenous/animist beliefs. 50% are Christian, roughly three-quarters of whom are Roman Catholic and the remainder Protestant. Of these, the Evangelical Church of the Congo and the Church of Jesus Christ on Earth constitute the major denominations. There is also a small Muslim community.

Language

Official language is French. All indigenous speakers use a number of distinct Bantu languages (for ethno-linguistic divisions see Population). Mono Kutuba and Lingala are the chief lingua francas.

HISTORY

Scholars believe that the Congo was uninhabited before the arrival of Bantu-speaking tribes in the 15th century. By the 16th century, two kingdoms dominated the region: Loango at the mouth of the Congo River and Teke upstream. Both reached their peak in the 17th century, largely due to the lucrative slave trade with the Portuguese, who had first arrived in the region in 1483.

In 1880 and 1883, the Italian-born French explorer Pierre Savorgnan de Brazza concluded treaties with the kingdoms of Teke and Loango, leading to their incorporation as Middle Congo within French Equatorial Africa. Brazza served as commissioner until 1898 when the territory was divided among concessionary companies. These companies ruthlessly exploited the local population, causing many revolts.

Despite government reforms, the abuses persisted until 1930.

In 1958 Congo voted to become an autonomous republic within the French Community, but as the idea of this Community within Africa was discarded by the majority of emerging new states, Congo moved to full independence two years later (15 Aug. 1960) with Fulbert Youlou, a former Catholic priest, as president. Moves to create a one-party state faced growing opposition and a general strike in Aug. 1963 led to Pres. Youlou's resignation and his replacement by Alphonse Massamba-Debat. Although the new president was a moderate, the communist-inspired Mouvement national de la révolution (MNR) was established as the sole party in July 1964 and the role of the ruling party grew in strength during his rule. In Aug. 1968 he was ousted by a military coup led by Maj. Marien Ngoumbi, who became president and proclaimed on 1 Jan. 1960 the People's Republic of Congo, with the Parti congolais du travail (PCT) as the sole political party.

Opposition to single party-rule, especially in the south, culminated in Pres. Ngoumbi's assassination (for which former president Massamba-Debat was later executed) in Mar. 1977. The PCT military committee declared martial law and nominated Joachim Yhombi-Opango as head of state. However, his liberal economic policies, the expulsion of foreign workers and the deteriorating economic situation alienated him from the party. In Feb. 1979 he tendered his resignation and was replaced by his rival Col Denis Sassou-Nguesso as PCT chairman and head of state. Later that year a new constitution was approved, Marxist in tone although the government was moving towards the right.

In July 1984, Sassou-Nguesso was re-elected president and secured additional powers as head of government from the PCT congress. However, as a northerner he faced opposition from southerners and the government's decision to introduce a qualifying exam for student grants sparked off student rioting in which three died in Nov. 1985. The following month, a cabinet reshuffle reduced the predominance of northerners. In July 1987, 20 army officers from the northern Kouyou tribe were charged with undermining state security. A security court claimed that Yhombi-Opango and his former colleague, Pierre Anga, were also implicated. Yhombi-Opango surrendered to security forces; Anga, who escaped into the bush, was reported to have been killed in July 1988.

CONSTITUTION AND GOVERNMENT

Executive and legislature

A Marxist regime in which the Congolese Party of Labour (PCT) is the sole political party, and the chairman of the PCT central committee is head of state and head of government, appointing the prime minister and council of ministers (last central committee chairmanship election 30 July 1989). The legislature is a unicameral 133-seat National Assembly, with all candidates proposed by the PCT central committee. 59 of the seats are reserved for PCT delegates, 66 for mass organizations, and a further eight for individuals. The last elections were in Sept. 1989.

Present government

President; Head of Government; Minister of Defence and Security Gen. Denis Sassou-Nguesso

Prime Minister Alphonse Poati-Souchalaty

Ministers of State Pierre Moussa (Plan and Economy); Gabriel Oba-Apounou (Youth and Rural Development); Col Raymond Damas Ngollo (Forestry); Antoine Ndinga Oba (Foreign Affairs and Cooperation).

Other Principal Ministers Alphonse Nzoungou (Justice and Keeper of the Seals; Administrative Reform); Auxence Ickonga (Minister in the Presidency with responsibility for State Control); Edouard Ngakosso (Finance and Budget); Pascal Ngayama (Secretary of State for Foreign Affairs and Cooperation).

Ruling party Congolese Party of Labour (Parti congolais du travail).

Chairman Gen. Denis Sassou-Nguesso.

Secretary-General Obami Itou.

Justice

The system of law is based on the French civil law and customary law. The highest court is the Supreme Court in Brazzaville, where there is also a Court of Appeal and a criminal court; a network of tribunaux de grande instance and tribunaux d'instance covers the regions. The death penalty is in force. No executions were recorded between 1985 and mid-1988.

National symbols

Flag. Red with the state emblem in the upper hoist. The emblem consists of a crossed hammer and hoe under a yellow five-pointed star, flanked by two curved green palm branches.

Festivals. 1 May (Labour Day); 15 Aug. (Independence Day).

Vehicle registration plate. RCB.

INTERNATIONAL RELATIONS

Affiliations

NAM; OAU; ACP; Francophonie.

Defence

Total Armed Forces: 8,800. Terms of service: voluntary, two years.

Army: 8,000; 50 main battle tanks (mainly T-54/-55, Ch Type-59) and 17 light tanks (Ch Tupe-62, PT-76).

Navy: 300; nine patrol and coastal combatants.

Air Force: 500; 20 combat aircraft (MiG-17); no armed helicopters.

ECONOMY

Currency

The unit is the CFA franc, divided into 100 centimes.

National finance

Budget. The 1987 budget was for expenditure of US$743 million and revenue of US$453 million.

Balance of payments. The balance of payments (current account, 1987) was a deficit of US$298 million.

Inflation. 1.3%.

Gross Domestic Product

Estimated total GDP US$2,150 million, per capita US$1,060 (overall size of economy ranking 113 in the world).

Economically active population. The total number of persons active in the economy is 79,000.

Sector	% of GDP
industry	33
agriculture	12
services*	55

* services figure includes elements unassigned to other categories.

Energy and mineral resources

Oil and gas. There are estimated oil reserves of 551–1,102 million tons/500–1,000 million tonnes. Production: (1988) 7 million tons/6.4 million tonnes from offshore oil fields.

Minerals. Production: (1985 in tons/tonnes) lead ore 1,102/1,000; zinc ore 2,315/2,100; copper ore 3,197/2,900; gold 11 lb/5kg. There are also reserves of uranium; phosphates; bauxite; iron.

Electricity. Capacity: 133,000 kW; production: (1988) 301 kWh.

Bioresources

Agriculture. 2% of the land is arable, with 29% consisting of meadows and pasture. The agricultural sector employs 75% of the working population.

Crop production: (1986 in 1,000 tons/tonnes) cassava 683/620; sugar cane 562/510; pineapples 121/110; bananas 37/34; plantain 71/64; yam 15/14; maize 9/8; groundnuts 18/16; palm-oil 17/15.6; sweet potatoes 15.4/14; coffee 2.2/2; cocoa 2.2/2; rice 3.3/3.

Livestock numbers: (1987) cattle 71,000; pigs 45,000; sheep 64,000; goats 185,000; poultry 1,000,000.

Forestry. Over 62% (49.42 million acres/20 million ha) of land area is equatorial forest. Timber including okoume, sapele and mahogany is exported. Roundwood production: (1986) 90,898,236 ft^3/2,574,000 m^3.

Fisheries. Total catch: (1986) 33,069 tons/30,000 tonnes.

Industry and commerce

Industry. Oil is the mainstay of the economy, providing about 90% of exports and about two-thirds of government revenues. The principal activities are crude oil production; cement; sawmills; brewing; sugar refining; palm-oil production; soap and cigarette manufacturing. There is a growing manufacturing sector based in the four main towns, employing (along with other commercial activities and government service) 25% of the workforce.

Commerce. Exports: (1987) US$912 million, largely crude oil; timber; coffee; cocoa; sugar. The main recipients of exports are the US; France; other EC countries. Imports: (1987) $494.4 million, consisting mainly of foodstuffs and machinery. Principal trading partners are France; Italy; US.

Trade with UK. The Congo imported UK goods worth £8,521,000 and exported goods worth £2,016,000 in 1988.

Tourism. (1986) 39,000 visitors.

COMMUNICATIONS

Railways

There are 551 miles/887 km of railways.

Roads

There are 5,121 miles/8,246 km of roads, of which 527 miles/849 km are bituminized.

Aviation

Air Afrique and Lina Congo (Lignes nationales aériennes congolaises) provide international services. International airports are at Brazzaville (Maya-Maya) and Pointe-Noire.

Shipping

Pointe-Noire is the maritime port, while Brazzaville is a river port on the 696 miles/1,120 km of commercially navigable inland waterways on the Congo and Oubanui rivers.

Telecommunications

There are 18,100 telephones, 100,000 radios and over 4,500 televisions, with a national television and radio station.

EDUCATION AND WELFARE

Education

All schools have been run by the government since 1965. Primary education begins at six for six years. The seven-year secondary cycle begins at age 12. Officially education is compulsory between the ages of six and 16.

Schools. (1985, approximate figures) Pre-primary: 51 schools with 5,600 pupils and 540 teachers (one per 11 pupils); primary: 1,560 schools with 475,800 pupils and 7,750 teachers (one per 62 pupils); general secondary: 197,500 pupils with 4,775 teachers (one per 42 pupils); vocational secondary: 23,340 pupils with 1,360 teachers (one per 17 pupils); teacher training: 1,800 pupils with 191 teachers (one per 10 pupils).

University. The Marien Ngouabi University in Brazzaville had 9,385 students and 565 teaching staff in 1985.

Literacy. (1985 est.) 62.9% (males 71.4%; females 55.4%).

Health

The state system provides three general hospitals, a combined total of 548 medical centres, dispensaries and infirmaries and seven centres for contagious diseases, with a total of 7,048 beds (one per 272 inhabitants).

COOK ISLANDS

GEOGRAPHY

The Cook Islands, in the South Pacific Ocean, consist of low coral atolls in the north and volcanic hilly islands in the south. The capital is Avarua.

Climate

Tropical, moderated by trade winds. There are typhoons from Nov.–Mar.

Population

Total population (1989 est.) 18,092, the great majority of Polynesian descent.

Birth rate 2.2%. **Death rate** 0.5%. **Rate of population increase** 5.3% **Life expectancy** female 76; male 70.

Religion

Christianity: Cook Islands Christian Church.

Language

English.

HISTORY

The Cook Islands were first settled between 500 and 800 AD. Spanish navigators arrived in 1595. Captain James Cook explored the islands from 1773–77. British missionaries arrived in 1821 and took control of the islands, destroying the traditional culture. In 1888 Britain, seeking to check French power in the region, declared the islands a protectorate. In 1901 they were annexed to New Zealand.

In Aug. 1965 the islands became a self-governing territory in free association with New Zealand, the latter retaining responsibility for foreign relations and defence.

Sir Albert Henry, leader of the Cook Islands Party (CIP) and prime minister since 1965, fell from power in July 1978 following a judicial inquiry into vote rigging in the March parliamentary elections. Thomas Davis, leader of the Democratic Party (DP), assumed the premiership and remained in power until 1987, with only an eight-month interlude in 1983 during which Geoffrey Henry and the CIP formed a government.

In Aug. 1985 on Rarotonga the Cook Islands and seven other members of the South Pacific Forum signed the South Pacific Nuclear Free Zone Treaty. In Jan. 1986 Prime Minister Davis declared the Cook Islands a neutral country, in the belief that New Zealand could no longer fulfil its defence obligations following the virtual break-up of the ANZUS military alliance.

Amidst growing disaffection with his premiership, Davis was forced out of office in July 1987. Dr Pupuke Robati took his place. General elections in Jan. 1989 returned Geoffrey Henry and the CIP to power.

CONSTITUTION AND GOVERNMENT

Self-governing in free association with New Zealand since independence in 1965, the Cook Islands are fully responsible for internal affairs. New Zealand has responsibility for external affairs, in consultation with the Cook Islands. The New Zealand governor general appoints a representative, who represents the Queen and the New Zealand government, and who appoints the prime minister. There is an election every five years to the 24-member Parliament (last elections were in Jan. 1989)

Prime Minister Geoffrey Henry (since Feb. 1989).

National symbols

Flag. Blue, with the flag of the UK in upper hoist-side quadrant. Circle of 15 white stars (one for each island) centred in outer half of flag.

ECONOMY

Economic development is hampered by isolation from foreign markets and lack of natural resources. Agriculture is the economic base. Major exports are fruit; copra; clothing. Aid is given by New Zealand and Australia.

Currency

New Zealand dollar.

COMMUNICATIONS

Railways

There are no railways.

Roads

116 miles/187 km of road, only 22 miles/35 km paved.

Shipping

There is a port at Avatiu, and seven airports, one with a permanent-surface runway. There are two AM radio stations, but no television. There is a telephone system and one Pacific Ocean satellite station.

COSTA RICA

Republica de Costa Rica
(Republic of Costa Rica)

GEOGRAPHY

Situated in the Central American isthmus, Costa Rica covers a total surface area of approximately 19,686 miles²/51,000 km², divided into seven provinces of which the most heavily populated is San José. A series of rugged volcanic highlands form the country's north-south spine from the Cordillera de Guanacaste in the north-west to the Cordillera Central and south to the Panama border, along the Cordillera de Talamanca (including the highest peak at Chirripo Grande 12,529 ft/3,819 m). Between the Cordillera Central and the Cordillera de Talamanca, the temperate Meseta Central (average altitude 2,625–4,593 ft/800–1,400 m), Costa Rica's core coffee-producing region, supports over 50% of the population. The coastal lowlands fronting the Caribbean and south-west along the Pacific are heavily forested. In the north-west drier savannah conditions prevail. Costa Rica's main rivers are the Rio Grande, draining the Meseta Central west into the Pacific, the Rio Reventazon draining the same basin north-east into the Caribbean and the Rio General in the south-west.

Climate

Tropical, plentiful rainfall and little variation in temperature. Conditions in the central highlands are more temperate. From Dec.–May there is a dry season. Rainfall varies from 55 in/1,400 mm in the north-west to 315 in/8,000 mm in some parts of the Cordillera de Talamanca. Average rainfall: 129 in/3,300 mm. San José: Jan. 60°F/18.9°C. July 69°F/20.6°C. Average annual rainfall 71 in/1,793 mm.

Cities and towns

San José (capital)	278,561
Alajuela	147,396
Cartago	101,350
Puntarenas	86,439

Population

Total population is 2,866,000 of which 50.3% live in urban areas. Population density is 146 persons per mile^2/56.1 per km^2. Most of the population is of European (Spanish) descent (over 85%), concentrated in and around San José and the major provincial towns. On the Caribbean coast, 15,000 West Indians are centred in Limón province while the indigenous Indian population in the far south has dwindled to 1,200. In 1988 23,000 refugees entered Costa Rica, of whom 19,000 were Nicaraguan.

Birth rate 2.8%. **Death rate** 0.4%. **Rate of population increase** (1980–87) 2.3%. **Age distribution** under 15 = 36.8%; over 15 = 3.9%. **Life expectancy** female 76; male 71; average 74.

Religion

Roman Catholicism is the official state religion (one Archbishop, four bishops), accounting for 92.4% of the population. There are an estimated 40,000 Protestants, of whom a significant proportion may be found in the West Indian communities of Limón.

Language

Spanish (official). Around Limón, a Jamaican, English dialect is the basis of a creole spoken by approximately 52,000 inhabitants. In addition, a few thousand speakers of Spanish-Chibchan, Chibchan and other Indian dialects remain scattered through the Pacific South.

HISTORY

Although little is known of the Indian cultures which lay between the high civilizations of Middle America and that of the Central Andes, archaeologists date them from around 10,000 years ago and they must have had both Maya and Inca influences. By the early 16th century, when the Spanish arrived, the area was a kaleidoscope of ethnic groups which were quickly decimated by European diseases or killed outright. Spanish official interest in the area declined when it became clear that the area was not a 'rich coast' of precious metals. The country's subsequent political history has been more peaceful than that of its neighbours. Along with the rest of Central America, Costa Rica gained independence from Spain in 1821, and joined the United Provinces of Central America until 1838. It was then ruled by a succession of conservative governments with the exception of a reformist liberal period from 1870 to 1889, its economy dependent on the supply of coffee to Europe and, increasingly, bananas to the US.

In 1936 the National Republican Party (PRN) formed a government and instituted a programme of moderate social and political reforms, which became more radical in the next decade under the leadership of Rafael Calderón Guardia (president 1940–44). A disputed election in 1948 resulted in a brief civil war; the victorious Social Democratic Party (PSD – later the National Liberation Party, PLN) then formed a provisional government led by José Pepe Figueres Ferrer, who abolished the national army in Dec. 1948 and remained highly influential for nearly 30 years, serving as president 1953–58 and 1970–74. The PLN instituted social reform and followed a moderate left-wing foreign policy, the main opposition coming from the now right-wing Calderón and the conservative National Unification Party (PUN). The PLN and the PUN both split in 1976; the 1978 presidential election was won by Rodrigo Carazo Odio of the coalition Opposition Unity (which included Calderón's party), who clashed with trade unions and cooled relations with Cuba and with the Sandinistas in Nicaragua.

The PLN returned to power in 1982 under Luis Alberto Monge Alvarez, but the country's deepening economic crisis forced the government to depend much more heavily on US economic aid. Rafael Angel Calderón, son of the former president, who had personally contested the presidential elections in 1982, stood again in 1986, but was again defeated by the PLN candidate, Oscar Arias Sánchez, who asserted his commitment to developing the welfare system. In foreign policy Arias cautiously improved relations with Nicaragua and was the architect of a Central American peace plan signed in Guatemala in Aug. 1987.

CONSTITUTION AND GOVERNMENT

Executive and legislature

The executive president is directly elected for a four-year term (last election 2 Feb. 1986). The president, assisted by two vice-presidents (or, in exceptional circumstances, one vice-president) appoints and presides over the Cabinet. Legislative power is held by a unicameral Legislative Assembly similarly elected for a four-year term (last elections were in Feb. 1986).

Present government

President Sr Oscar Arias Sánchez
First Vice-President Sr Jorge Manuel Dengo Obregon
Second Vice-President Sra Victoria Garron de Doryan
Principal members of Cabinet Sr Rodrigo Arias Sánchez (Minister at the Presidency); Sr Rodrigo Madrigal Nieto (Foreign Affairs); Sr Antonio Alvarez Desanti (Interior and Police); Sr Rodrigo Bolanos (Finance); Sr Hernan Garron Salazar (Public Security); Sr Antonio Burgues (Industry, Economy and Commerce); Sr Luis Diego Escalante Vargas (Foreign Trade); Dr Luis Paulino Mora (Justice); Sr Jorge Monge Aguero (National Planning and Economy).

Justice

The system of law is based on Spanish civil law. The highest court is the Supreme Court, which may review legislation; there are 5 Appeal Courts, the Court of Cassation, the Higher and Lower Criminal Courts, and the Higher and Lower Civil Courts. The death penalty was abolished in 1877.

National symbols

Flag. Five horizontal stripes of blue, white, red, white and blue; towards the hoist of the red stripe a white oval bears the state coat of arms of 1848.

Festivals. 11 Apr. (Anniversary of the Battle of Rivas); 1 May (Labour Day); 25 July (Anniversary of the Annexation of Guanacaste Province); 15 Sept. (Independence Day); 12 Oct. (Columbus Day); 1 Dec. (Abolition of the Armed Forces).

Vehicle registration plate. CR.

INTERNATIONAL RELATIONS

Affiliations

OAS; SELA.

Defence

Total Security Forces: 9,500 inclusive 3,000 reserves.

Civil Guard: 6,000.

Rural Guard: (Ministry of Government and Police) 3,500; small arms only.

ECONOMY

Currency

The unit is the colone, divided into 100 centimos.

National finance

Budget. The 1987 budget was for expenditure of US$792 million and revenue of US$700 million. Main items of expenditure are housing and welfare 27%; health 19%; education 16%.

Balance of payments. The balance of payments (current account, 1987) was a deficit of US$377 million.

Inflation. 26%.

Gross Domestic Product

Estimated total GDP US$4,310 million, per capita US$1,529 (overall size of economy ranking 92 in the world).

Economically active population. The total number of persons active in the economy is 868,000; unemployed: 6.2%.

Sector	% of workforce	% of GDP
industry	35	29
agriculture	27	18
services*	38	53

* services figure includes elements unassigned to other categories.

Energy and mineral resources

Minerals. Output: gold 3,000 troy oz.; salt 11,023 tons/10,000 tonnes. Haematite ore reserves and sulphur deposits are found on the Nicoya peninsula and near San Carlos.

Electricity. Power is generated by hydroelectricity. Capacity: 825,000 kWh; production: 2,916 million kWh; per capita 1,010 kWh per capita (1988).

Bioresources

Agriculture. About 999,999 acres/404,694 ha of land is cultivable. 7% of the total land area is permanently cultivated and 6% is considered arable.

Crop production: (1986 in tons/tonnes) coffee 141,109/128,000; sugar cane 2.92 million/2.65 million; bananas 1.1 million/1 million; cocoa 5,511/5,000; maize 114,639/104,000; tobacco 2,205/2,000; rice 205,028/186,000; potatoes 44,092/40,000.

Livestock numbers: (1987) cattle 2.36 million; pigs 238,000.

Forestry. 34% of the total surface area is forested.

Industry and commerce

Industry. Costa Rica's principal manufacturing industries include food processing; textiles; clothing; construction materials; fertilizer production. In 1988 the economic growth rate was 4.4% (up 1.4% on the previous year's rate).

Commerce. Exports: (1987) $1,100 million or 25.6% of the GDP. Imports $1,400 million or 32% of the GDP. Principal exports included coffee $267.8 million; bananas $251 million; beef; sugar; fertilizer. Imported goods included petroleum $166.7 million; machinery $219.6 million; consumer durables; chemicals; fertilizers; foodstuffs.

Trade with UK. (1988) Imports from UK totalled £11.39 million; exports to the UK amounted to £16.9 million.

COMMUNICATIONS

Railways

There are 402 miles/647.4 km of railways, of which 174 miles/280.8 km are electrified.

Roads

There are 21,948 miles/35,343 km of roads, of which 3,128 miles/5,037 km are paved (inclusive 412 miles/663 km of the Pan-American Highway).

Aviation

Lineas Aereas Costarricenses, SA (LACSA) provides international services and Servicios Aereos Nacionales, SA (SANSA) provides domestic services (main international airport is Juan Santamaria Airport).

Shipping

Main ports are Puntarenas and Golfito on the Pacific, and Puerto Limón on the Caribbean. There are three cargo ships of over 1,000 GRT.

Telecommunications

There is a good domestic service, connecting into the Cental American system, and 292,000 telephones. There are 420,000 televisions and 470,000 radios, a government television station and six commercial stations, and some 50 radio stations.

EDUCATION AND WELFARE

Education

Both primary and secondary education are free. Elementary education is compulsory, with schools maintained by a system of local school councils.

School population. (1984) 501,990.

Schools. In 1984, 353,958 pupils attended 3,068 public primary schools with 12,223 teachers and administrative personnel (one per 29 pupils). A further 148,032 pupils attended 241 public and private secondary institutions.

University. The 13 faculties of the University of Costa Rica accommodated 2,337 professors and 38,629 students in 1980.

Literacy. 93%.

Health

(1982) 1,929 doctors, 39 hospitals and 7,706 beds. (1979) 239 dentists.

CÔTE D'IVOIRE (IVORY COAST)

République de la Côte d'Ivoire
(Republic of Côte d'Ivoire)

GEOGRAPHY

Situated on the west coast of Africa, Côte d'Ivoire covers a total area of 124,471 miles^2/322,463 km^2 divided into 26 departments. A narrow sandy coastal strip (40 miles/64 km wide) characterized by lagoon formations in the east, is backed by a (depleted) equatorial and cultivated forest region. Beyond this, the sparsely-populated interior rises in the west and north-west to an average elevation of 984–1,148 ft/300–350 m on the open savannah plateau, reaching 5,748 ft/1,752 m at Mount Nimba on the Liberian and Guinean border. Rivers include the Cavady, which marks the border with Liberia, the Sassandra, the Bandama and the Comoé. They drain north-south, emptying into the Gulf of Guinea.

Climate

Tropical, with two zones (north and south), according to relative distance from the sea. Rainfall is higher in the south, averaging 59–79 in/1,500–2,000 mm per year, with two rainy seasons (May–July; Oct.–Nov. on the coast) and one wet season in the north June–Oct. Temperatures average between 79°F/26°C and 82°F/28°C north and south. Abidjan: Jan. 81°F/27.2°C. July 75°F/23.9°C. Average annual rainfall 83 in/2,100 mm. Bouake: Jan. 81°F/27.2°C. July 77°F/25°C. Average annual rainfall 47 in/1,200 mm.

Cities and towns

Abidjan	1,423,323
Bouaké	272,640
Yamoussoukro (new capital)	120,000

Population

Total population is 11,612,000 of which 47.0% live in urban areas. Population density is 93.3 persons per mile^2/36 per km^2. Côte d'Ivoire supports over 60 distinguishable ethnic groups, the most important of which are the Baule (12%) and Anyi (11%) of the south-east; the Bete (20%) and Kru of the south-west, dispersed throughout large tracts of forest; the Senufo (14%) of the north-east savannah; the Malinke (7%) and Mande in the north-west. There are also an estimated 40,000 French and 25,000 Lebanese residents, and approximately 2 million foreign Africans.
Birth rate 5.1%. **Death rate** 1.56%. **Rate of population increase** 3.54%. **Age distribution** under 15 = 48.9%; over 65 = 2.2%. **Life expectancy** female 54; male 51; average 53.

Religion

Approximately 65% of the population follow indigenous animist beliefs while 12% are Christian (including an estimated 1,015,000 Roman Catholics) and 23% are Muslim (mostly in northern regions).

Language

The official language is French, but a diverse range of African languages is also spoken. Principal ethno-linguistic groups are the Akan-speakers of the south-east, the Voltaic peoples of the north-east (including the Lobi and Bobo) and the Mande and Malinke of the north-west.

HISTORY

The Ivory Coast was from earliest times inhabited by a large number of ethnic groups divided into local kingdoms: the Kru from Liberia had already settled in the south-west by the 16th century as had the Voltaic tribes from the Upper Volta valley in the north-east. The Mande people arrived from what is now Guinea and Mali, while the Baule people probably migrated from Ghana in the 18th to 19th centuries.

First European contacts occurred in 1637 with the arrival of French missionaries, but the Portuguese and Spanish later established trading posts in competition with the British and French, with slaves as the main commodity. From 1840 to 1900, France signed a series of treaties with local chiefs, establishing protectorates over the kingdoms in the coastal areas, and although French interest waned during the latter part of the 19th century, the trading posts remained. The territory became a colony in 1893.

From 1893 to 1898, the French pushed northwards to inland areas which they had not previously penetrated. They defeated the expanding empire of the Malinke chief, Almani Samori, from Guinea. Resistance among the Baule and other forest people was crushed by the French military in 1908, although sporadic revolts against the imposition of a poll tax continued until 1917. In 1904 the Ivory Coast became a member of the federation of French West Africa, whose capital was Dakar (Senegal).

After World War I, France imposed a uniform, centralized administrative system, and used forced labour on its road and public-works programmes. In the inter-war period, the Ivory Coast became a major producer of cocoa, coffee and tropical hardwoods; the farms were run by both European and local planters. The country was controlled by the French Vichy regime during World War II, after which France carried out a series of reforms, including the abolition of forced labour. It became possible for the inhabitants to attain French citizenship, and they gained representation in the French National Assembly, with the right to organize political parties. A French-educated elite pressed for greater African political rights rather than for independence.

In 1944, the Syndicat agricole africain (SAA) had been founded by wealthy local planter Félix Houphouët-Boigny to promote local interests against those of French planters. The SAA in 1945 set up a Parti démocratique de la Côte d'Ivoire (PDCI), which a year later joined other French West African parties in the Rassemblement démocratique africain (RDA) to oppose the colonial administration. In its aim to achieve a greater measure of self-government and higher commodity prices, the PDCI over the next two years organized mass demonstrations in Abidjan, which were put down by the French, with heavy loss of life and thousands of arrests. The PDCI, aligned with the French Communist Party, continued to face repression from France in the early 1950s, but adopted a more conciliatory position once an increase in commodity prices had been accepted. The PDCI then won a series of elections, emerging as the dominant force in the country and also holding two seats in the French parliament. Houphouët-Boigny served in the French cabinet 1956–58.

On 28 Sept. 1958, Gen. de Gaulle organized a referendum whereby French colonies in Africa were offered either immediate independence or membership within a French Community. The PDCI campaigned successfully for the latter, but opposed the creation of any West African federation which might involve the Ivory Coast in providing economic support for its poorer neighbours. As pro-independence feeling spread in the region, however, the French Community was seen to have little prospect of survival, and on 7 Aug. 1960 Houphouët-Boigny unilaterally declared independence from France.

Although multi-partyism is provided for in the republic's constitution, no formal opposition is tolerated, and the PDCI, under Pres. Houphouët-Boigny, has maintained exclusive control. Côte d'Ivoire has retained very close relations with France, relying on the former colonial power for technical assistance and investment, and for the presence of a French military garrison. In spite of an Ivorianization policy, and to the resentment of educated Ivorians, French nationals still hold many high-ranking industrial and commercial positions.

Since independence, the situation in Côte d'Ivoire has been generally calm. Political stability attracted foreign capital, so that the country enjoyed sustained economic growth through the exports of cocoa and coffee, and the discovery of large reserves of offshore oil in the late 1970s. There were sporadic regional outbreaks of unrest in 1968–70, while in June 1973 a military plot was uncovered, and seven officers were sentenced to death on 28 July.

Allegations of corruption in high places provoked a major government reshuffle in 1977, when three senior ministers were dismissed. A constitutional amendment of 1976 stated that the president of the National Assembly would succeed to the presidency if there were a vacancy. This post went first to Philippe Yacé, but he had fallen from favour by 1980, after his heavy-handedness in organizing the 1978 elections resulted in general uproar. These elections were annulled by the president. Yacé was replaced by Henri Konan Bédié, widely tipped to succeed Houphouët-Boigny on his death.

Opposition to the regime has mostly been either suppressed or absorbed into the PDCI. The clandestine Front populaire ivoirien (FPI), led by Laurent Gbagbo, has had numerous clashes with the government. Gbagbo himself returned from self-imposed exile late in 1988 to be reconciled with the president, but another FPI leader, Innocent Anaky, was arrested on 20 Nov. 1988, and later sentenced to 20 years' imprisonment for fraud. Throughout the 1980s leaders of the teachers' union SYNESCI were accused of trying to form a political opposition movement, and in 1987 some were sent to a military camp for a period of re-education.

In foreign policy, Houphouët-Boigny pursued pro-Western policies, and opposed the expansion of communist power. From 1971 onwards, he advocated dialogue between black Africa and South Africa, and held several meetings with South African leaders, notably Prime Minister John Vorster in 1979, Pres. P.W. Botha in Oct. 1988 and Pres. F.W. de Klerk in Dec. 1989. A preoccupation of the 1980s was the high level of street crime and drug trafficking. Austerity measures imposed in Feb. 1990 as part of an economic structural adjustment plea provoked nationwide unrest, with workers joining students in protests, and were hastily rescinded.

The President announced in 1986 that the country should henceforth be given its French appellation, Côte d'Ivoire.

CONSTITUTION AND GOVERNMENT

Executive and legislature

The executive president is elected by direct universal suffrage for a five-year term of office; the last election was in Oct 1985. The president of the National Assembly assumes the post of acting president on the death or incapacity of the head of state. The president appoints the Council of Ministers. Legislative power is vested in a single-chamber National Assembly of 175 members, most recently elected for five years in Nov 1985. The election for each seat is between opposing candidates all put forward by the ruling party.

Present government

President Dr Félix Houphouët-Boigny

Ministers of State Auguste Denise; Mathieu Ekra; Emile Kei Boguinard.

Other principal Ministers

Vincent Pierre Lokrou (Agriculture; Water and Forest Resources); Moïse Koumoue Koffi (Budget; Economy and Finance); Jean Konan Banny (Defence and Maritime Affairs); Siméon Ake (Foreign Affairs); Léon Konan Koffi (Interior); Gen. Issouf Kone (Internal Security; Drug Control); Noël Nemin (Justice; Attorney General).

President of the National Assembly Henri Konan Bédié.

Ruling party

Côte d'Ivoire Democratic Party (Parti démocratique de la Côte d'Ivoire).

Chairman Dr Félix Houphouët-Boigny.

Members of executive committee of the political bureau Camille Alliali; Maurice Seri Gnoleba; Jean Konan Banny; Lazeni Coulibaly; Dona Fologo; Dr Balla Keita; Gilles Laubhouet; Alphonse Djedje Madi; Bernard Ehui Koutoua; Paul Gui Dibo; Jean-Jacques Bechio; Yaya Ouattara; Nicholas Kouandi Angba.

Justice

The system of law is based on French civil law and customary law. The highest court is the Supreme Court in Abidjan, whose constitutional chamber may review legislation. There are 28 courts of first instance, 3 assize courts in Abidjan, Bouake and Daloa, and 2 courts of appeal in Abidjan and Bouake. The death penalty is nominally in force. No executions were recorded between 1985 and mid-1988.

National symbols

Flag. Three vertical stripes of orange, white and green.

Festivals. 1 May (Labour Day); 7 Dec. (Independence Day).

Vehicle registration plate. CI.

INTERNATIONAL RELATIONS

Affiliations

NAM; OAU; ACP; Francophonie.

Defence

Total Armed Forces: 7,100. Terms of service: conscription (selective), six months. Reserves: 12,000.
Army: 5,500; five light tanks (AMX-13).
Navy: 700; ten patrol and coastal combatants.
Air Force: 900; six combat aircraft (AlphaJet).
Para-military: 7,800.

ECONOMY

Currency

The unit is the CFA franc, divided into 100 centimes.

National finance

Budget. The 1988 est. budget was for expenditure of US$2,300 million.

Balance of payments. The balance of payments (current account, 1987) was a deficit of US$641 million.

Inflation. 5.3%.

Gross Domestic Product

Estimated total GDP US$7,650 million, per capita US$960 (overall size of economy ranking 73 in the world).

Economically active population. The total number of persons active in the economy is 6,000,000; unemployed: 14%.

Sector	% of GDP
industry	25
agriculture	36
services*	39

* services figure includes elements unassigned to other categories.

Energy and mineral resources

Oil and gas. Crude petroleum production from offshore oil fields: (1985) 1.5 million tons/1.4 million tonnes.

Minerals. Diamonds 700,000 carats (1985). There are iron ore deposits awaiting exploitation at Bangolo.

Electricity. Capacity: 1,081,000 kW; production: 2,438 kWh (1988).

Bioresources

Agriculture. Côte d'Ivoire is among the world's largest producers of coffee, cocoa beans and palm kernel oil, and the economy remains largely dependent on agriculture despite government attempts to diversify. The agricultural sector accounts for over one-third of GDP and about 80% of export earnings, and along with forestry and livestock raising employs over 85% of the workforce.

Crop production: (1986 in thousand tons/tonnes) cash crops; coffee 309/280; cocoa 573/520; bananas 187/170; pineapples 331/300; palm-oil 198/180; palm kernels 47/43. Food crops: yams 3,302/2,996; cassava 1,653/1,500; plantain 1,543/1,400; rice 507/460; maize 606/550; millet 36/35; groundnuts 94/86. Some sugar cane is also grown.

Livestock numbers: (1987) cattle 965,000; sheep 1.5 million; goats 1.5 million; pigs 450,000; horses 1,000; donkeys 1,000.

Forestry. 26% of the land is forested. Equatorial rainforest covers 7.4 million acres/3 million ha, producing over 30 species including teak, mahogany and ebony. Roundwood production: (1986) 416.7 million ft^3/11.8 million m^3.

Fisheries. Total catch: (1986) 107,144 tons/97,200 tonnes, including 3,748 tons/3,400 tonnes of crustaceans.

Industry and commerce

Industry. The principal activities are food processing; textiles; sawmills.

Commerce. Exports: (1987) US$3,400 million, comprising cocoa 30%; coffee 20%; tropical woods 11%; also cotton; bananas; pineapples; palm-oil. Principal trading partners: (1986) Netherlands; France; US. Value of imports: (1987), $2,700 million, chiefly composed of manufactured goods and semi-finished products 50% of imports; consumer goods 40%; raw materials and fuels 10%. Principal sources of imports: (1986) France; Nigeria; West Germany; Netherlands.

Trade with UK. Côte d'Ivoire imported goods worth £31.2 million from the UK in 1988 and exported goods worth £64 million.

Tourism. (1986) 187,000 visitors.

COMMUNICATIONS

Railways

There are 718 miles/1,156 km of railways.

Roads

There are some 34,155 miles/55,000 km of roads (96 miles/155 km are motorways).

Aviation

Air Afrique (Société aérienne africaine multinationale) provides international services and Air Ivoire domestic services (international airport is at Abidjan-Port-Bouet).

Shipping

Main ports are Abidjan and San Pedro. There are seven ships of over 1,000 GRT.

Telecommunications

There is an above-average telephone system by regional standards, with 87,700 telephones. The state television network, broadcasting in colour since 1973, reaches some 500,000 sets, and there are 1,300,000 radios.

EDUCATION AND WELFARE

Education

The state provides free education at all levels; education received the highest allocation in the 1987 budget.

School population. Enrolment at primary school was 78% of children in the 7–12 age group (92% of boys and 65% of girls). At secondary school level enrolment was the equivalent of 20% of the 13–19 age group (27% of boys and 12% of girls). Attendance at both levels was higher in urban areas. In 1984–85 there were 1,179,456 pupils enrolled in state and private primary schools, with a total of 28,561 teachers (one per 42 pupils); there were 245,342 pupils in secondary school (both general and technical).

University. The National University had 12,755 students in 1984/85.

Literacy. (1985 est.) 42.7% (males 53.1%; females 31.1%).

Health.

The state provides medical services. In 1980 there were 8,800 hospital beds (approximately one per 940 inhabitants), and 518 physicians in government medical services (one per 15,950 inhabitants).

CUBA

Republica de Cuba
(Republic of Cuba)

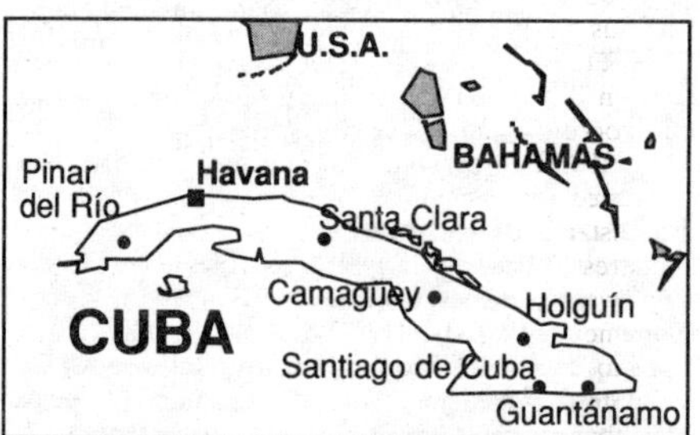

GEOGRAPHY

Lying 135 miles/217 km south of the tip of Florida, in the Caribbean Sea, Cuba comprises two main islands (Cuba 44,206 miles^2/114,524 km^2 and Isla de la Juventud 455.5 miles^2/1,180 km^2) and over 1,500 islets and keys, covering a total area of 44,662 miles^2/115,704 km^2. The country is divided into 14 provinces and the very densely populated capital city La Habana. Cuba's indented coastline is marshy in the south and south-west, and rugged and precipitous in the north. Three separate mountainous regions cover 25% of the territory east-west: the Oriental (Sierra Maestra, including Pico Turquino, Cuba's highest peak at 6,578 ft/2,005 m), Central and Occidental (Sierra de los Organos) ranges. The lowlands and basin areas occupying the remaining 75% of the surface area support sugar cane, rice and coffee plantations on fertile soil and livestock in the central savannah. The longest river is the Rio Cauto in the east, traversing the three provinces of Santiago de Cuba, Holguin and Granma. 29.5% of the total surface area is forested.

Climate

Subtropical with warm temperatures (73–81°F/23–27°C) and high humidity. Cuba lies within the hurricane zone (June–Oct.) and is influenced by the Gulf Stream and north-east trade winds. The dry season lasts from Nov.–Apr., and the wet season from May–Oct. Average annual rainfall is 54 in/1.375 mm, a large proportion of which (75%) falls during tropical storms. La Habana: Jan. 72°F/22.2°C. July 82°F/27.8°C. Average annual rainfall 48 in/1,224mm.

Cities and towns

La Habana (capital)	2,036,799
Santiago de Cuba	364,554
Camagüey	265,588
Holguín	199,861
Santa Clara	182,349
Guantánamo	179,091
Cienfuegos	112,225
Bayamo	108,716
Pinar del Río	108,109
Matanzas	106,954

Population

Total population is 10,154,000, of which 70.8% live in urban areas. Population density is 227.4 persons per miles^2/92.8 per km^2. At the last census, 66.0% of the population were White (mainly of Spanish extraction), 21.9% mulatto and 12% Black.

Birth rate 1.5%. **Death rate** 0.64%. **Rate of population increase** 0.86%. **Age distribution** under 15 = 25.7%; over 65 = 8.0%. **Life expectancy** female 76.1; male 72.7; average 74.

Religion

There is no state religion although a significant percentage (40%) of the population are Roman Catholic (over 4 million adherents but as few as 100,000 practising communicants). An estimated 3.3% of the population are Protestant (Baptist, Methodist, Presbyterian, Pentecostal and Nazarene Churches) and 1.6% are Afro-American Spiritist.

Language

Spanish is the official language, universally spoken and understood. English has some minor currency, though seldom used by the majority of the population.

HISTORY

Cuba was first inhabited by Ciboney Indians who were gradually displaced by Taino-speaking Arawak Indians coming from Haiti. The first Europeans to arrive in Cuba were those on Columbus's first expedition in 1492. Columbus claimed the territory for Spain, but it was not until 1511 that the island was settled and colonized. Spanish settlement remained underdeveloped, and centred on the coastal areas as the main impetus of Spanish colonization moved to Central and South America. Activity was confined to ports like Havana, which became a strategic link in the trade route between Spain and Mexico. The British captured Havana in 1762 and held it for ten months, before the Treaty of Paris returned it to Spain. A liberalization of trade restrictions and the import of labour, both slaves from Africa and European immigrants, bolstered the economy and favoured the cultivation of coffee and sugar cane. Easy access to the growing markets of North America dramatically increased the island's prosperity.

In the first half of the 19th century authoritarian rule by Spain increased, particularly under Miguel Tacon, captain-general 1834–38. There were a number of abortive revolts, but it was not until 1868 that a major rebellion broke out. Carlos Manuel de Céspedes, a wealthy plantation owner, declared Cuba independent, and initiated a guerrilla struggle known as the Ten Years' War. In the peace treaty signed in 1878, the Spanish government agreed to a number of concessions in return for the rebels' surrender. One of these was the abolition of slavery, which finally ended in 1886. An economic depression, caused by Cuba's over-dependence on sugar and on the US market, provoked political unrest, and led to the Second War of Independence in 1895 led by José Martí, Antonio Maceo and Mácimo Goméz. Early successes for the rebels were reversed as Spanish troops brutally reimposed order. The blowing up in Havana harbour of the USS *Maine*, which had arrived to safeguard American lives and property, heightened popular pressure in the US for military intervention in the struggle. In Apr. 1898 Pres. McKinley was authorized by Congress to declare war on Spain. Cuba was captured after a brief campaign and placed under US military government until an independent Cuban government could take over.

The US left the island in 1902 after the acceptance by the Cuban government of the Platt amendment (not repealed until 1934), which preserved American rights of intervention in Cuba, and which allowed American military bases on Cuban soil. US troops did intervene in Cuba in 1906–9 and 1919–24. Cuba prospered during World War I because of the lack of competition from the European sugar beet industry, but an economic depression soon followed and this, combined with a growing awareness of government corruption, particularly under the virtual dictatorship of Pres. Gerardo Machado after 1925, led to a revolution in 1933. The main figure to emerge from the unrest was Fulgencio Batista, an army sergeant who had led a mutiny against senior officers. Batista forced the government to resign and installed his own puppet president, then served himself as president between 1940 and 1944. The evident corruption and gangsterism of the presidents who followed provided the pretext for Batista to seize power again in a coup in Mar. 1952. Batista's final years in power were marked by increasing repression and growing support for the guerrilla campaign waged since 1954 by Fidel Castro in the mountains of the Sierra Maestra. Eventually, at the end of 1958, the regime disintegrated. Batista and his family fled the country and on 1 Jan. 1959 Castro's army captured Havana.

A civilian cabinet of ministers was appointed, with Manuel Urrutia as president and Castro as prime minister. Castro, however, gradually consolidated his position by using the Communist Party as a vehicle of government, superseding the traditional institutions as the constitution was suspended. Urrutia was removed in July 1959 and a programme of wide-ranging reform instituted, including land reform, the confiscation of illegally held assets and the nationalization of foreign-owned land and enterprises. Many of those opposed to these dramatic changes went into exile in the US. Relations with the US deteriorated rapidly and early in 1961 the American government severed diplomatic relations. A US-sponsored invasion by anti-Castro exiles was defeated at the Bay of Pigs in April. The external threat allowed Castro to strengthen his position internally and in Dec. 1961 he declared himself a Marxist–Leninist and Cuba a Communist state. Economic and political isolation within the region forced Cuba into a closer alignment with the USSR. Castro's avowed aim of bringing revolution to his neighbouring countries in Latin America was unwelcome, and he became less keen on this policy after the death in Oct. 1967 of his colleague Che Guevara, while helping guerrillas in Bolivia. The discovery in 1962 of Soviet missile bases in Cuba led to a US blockade of the island and produced the most serious superpower confrontation of the decade. The USSR became the country's principal trading partner, and in 1972 Cuba became a member of the CMEA, the socialist countries' economic grouping.

In 1965 Castro announced that his party had been renamed the Communist Party of Cuba (PCC) and was established as the sole legal party. The PCC's first congress was held in Dec. 1975, and a new constitution was approved by referendum in 1976. The party became institutionalized along Soviet lines with Castro, as first secretary of the party, becoming head of state as president of the Council of State.

Cuban troops became involved in Angola in 1976 and in Ethiopia in 1977, in support of Castro's internationalist aims. Relations with the US were further strained in 1980 by the mass exodus to the US of an estimated 125,000 Cuban refugees, including many who were criminals or mentally ill, and by the establishment in 1985 of Radio Marti, an anti-Castro propaganda station. The third congress of the PPC was held in 1986 at which a third of senior party officials lost their posts and which strengthened the influence of Gen. Raul Castro, Fidel Castro's brother and his deputy. In 1986 Castro criticized the slight moves which had been made towards economic liberalization, accusing them of causing corruption and speculation. This attitude left Cuba increasingly isolated within the Communist bloc, and somewhat distanced from the reforms of Pres. Gorbachev in the Soviet Union. Nevertheless, Cuba's relationship with the Soviet Union remained close, and Gorbachev was warmly received when he visited the island in Apr. 1989. Castro's continuing hostility to market forces, together with the collapse of communist regime in Eastern Europe, meant that by the end of 1989 Cuba's international isolation had increased considerably.

CONSTITUTION AND GOVERNMENT

Executive and legislature

Legislative authority lies with a unicameral 510-member National Assembly of People's Power, indirectly elected every four years by popularly elected local assemblies. The National Assembly elects a 31-member Council of State to represent it between its twice-yearly ordinary sessions; the president of the Council of State is the head of state. The Council of Ministers, which exercises executive and administrative authority, is appointed by the National Assembly on the recommendation of the president. In practice the major focus of power is the sole and ruling party, the Cuban Communist Party.

Present government (1 Feb. 1990)

President of the Council of State and Council of Ministers Dr Fidel Castro Ruz

First Vice President of Council of State; Minister of Revolutionary Armed Forces Gen. Raúl Castro Ruz

Vice Presidents of Council of State Dr Carlos Rafael Rodríguez Rodríguez, Sr Osmany Cienfuegos Gorriarán

Vice Presidents of Council of Ministers Dr Carlos Rafael Rodríguez Rodríguez; Sr Osmany Cienfuegos Gorriarán; Sr Antonio Esquivel Yedra; Sr Joel Domenech Benítez; Sr José Ramón Fernández Alvarez; Sr Pedro Miret Prieto; Gen. Ramiro Valdés Menéndez; Sr José López Moreno.

Other principal Ministers Sr Isidoro Octavio Malmierca Peoli (Foreign Relations); Sr Ricardo Cabrisas Ruiz (Foreign Trade); Gen. Abelardo Colomé Ibarra (Interior); Dr Juan Escalona Reguera (Justice).

Ruling party

Cuban Communist Party (Partido Comunista Cubano).

First secretary Dr Fidel Castro Ruz.

Second secretary Gen. Raúl Castro Ruz.

Full politburo members Dr Fidel Castro Ruz; Gen. Raúl Castro Ruz; Sr Juan Almeida Bosque; Sr Julio Camacho Aguilera; Sr Osmany Cienfuegos Gorriarán; Gen. Abelardo Colomé Ibarra; Sra Vilma Espín Guillois de Castro; Dr Armando Hart Dávalos; Sr Esteban Lazo Hernández; Sr José Ramón Machado Ventura; Sr Pedro Miret Prieto; Sr Jorge Risquet Valdés-Saldaña; Sr Carlos Rafael Rodríguez Rodríguez; Sr Roberto Veiga Menéndez.

Justice

The system of law is based on Spanish and US legal codes, but with modifications in line with Castro's Marxist-Leninist regime. The highest court is the Supreme Court in Havana and there are 7 regional courts of appeal. Courts for civil and criminal actions, are in the provinces, which are further divided into judicial districts. Revolutionary Summary Tribunals have wide powers. The death penalty is in force. There were 4 executions between 1985 and mid-1988. and several more for treason in 1989. Capital offences: murder, treason, 1 not known.

National symbols

Flag. Five horizontal stripes, three blue and two white, and a red equilateral triangle charged with a white five-pointed star in the hoist.

Festivals. 2 Jan. (Liberation Day); 1 May (Labour Day); 25–27 July (Anniversary of the 1953 Revolution); 9 Oct. (8 Oct. in 1990, Wars of Independence Day).

Vehicle registration plate. C.

INTERNATIONAL RELATIONS

Affiliations

NAM; Comecon; SELA.

Defence

Total Armed Forces: 180,500 (79,500 conscripts) inclusive 15,000 ready reserves. Terms of service: three years. Reserves: 130,000.

Army: 145,000; 650 main battle tanks (mainly T-54/-55, T-62, T-34); 60 light tanks (PT-76).

Navy: 13,500; three submarines (Soviet Foxtrot); three frigates (Soviet Koni); 58 patrol and coastal combatants (Soviet Osa-I/II, Turya PHI).

Air Force: 22,000; 176 combat aircraft (MiG-21F/-21PFM/-21PFMA/-21bis/-23 Flogger E), 44 armed helicopters.

ECONOMY

Currency

The unit is the peso, divided into 100 centavos.

National finance

Budget. The 1987 budget was for expenditure of US$11,800 million and revenue of US$11,300 million.

Gross Domestic Product

GDP estimates cannot be made reliably from incompatible Cuban national accounting methods. The US government records an outdated figure of GDP per capita US$2,696 (1981).

Economically active population. The total number of persons active in the economy is 3,300,000; unemployed: 7%.

Sector	% of workforce
industry	39
agriculture	13
services*	48

* services figure includes elements unassigned to other categories.

Energy and mineral resources

Oil. Crude oil production: 826,725 tons/750,000 tonnes.

Minerals. Cuba is rich in iron ore. Production: wrought iron 1,300 tons/1,180 tonnes; steel 442,573 tons/401,500 tonnes. Output of other minerals: (in tons/tonnes) copper concentrate 3,815/3,461; refractory chrome 30,092/27,300; nickel and cobalt 39,462/35,800; salt 134,811/122,300. Gold and silver are also mined,

Electricity. Capacity: 3.9 million kW; production 15,972 million kWh; 1,540 kWh per capita (1988).

Bioresources

Agriculture. In 1959 all land over 30 caballerias was nationalized and there are now approximately 1,500 co-operatives. Total land cultivated is 8.4 million acres/3.4 million ha, with 1,173,725 acres/475,000 ha privately owned. Cuba is the world's second largest producer of sugar, which represents almost 50% (by value) of the country's exports. Other crops are tobacco; rice; potatoes; tubers; citrus fruit; coffee. Rice is grown in the south of Havana province.

Crop production: sugar 7.9 million tons/7.2 million tonnes. Other crops (in 1,000 tons/tonnes): citrus fruit 866/786; potatoes 348/316; rice 63/57; tobacco 50/45; maize 40/36; coffee 25/23; kenaf 15/13; seed cotton 3.3/3.

Livestock numbers: cattle 5,007,000; pigs 2.4 million; horses 718,000; sheep 382,000; goats 110,000.

Forestry. Cuba has extensive and valuable forest resources including mahoghany (mainly for export) and cedar (mainly for cigar boxes). Other species planted include majagua; teca; eucalyptus; pine; casuarina.

Fisheries. Fishing is a major export industry. Annual catch: 269,610 tons/244,589 tonnes.

Industry and commerce

Industry. The main industries are sugar milling; petroleum refining; food and tobacco processing; textiles; chemicals; paper and wood products; metals (esp. nickel); cement; fertilizers; consumer goods; agricultural machinery.

Commerce. Exports: $5,400 million including sugar; nickel; shellfish; citrus; tobacco; coffee. Imports: $7,600 million including capital goods; industrial raw materials; food; petroleum. Countries exported to: USSR 72%; other communist countries 15%. Imports came from: USSR 72%; other communist countries 14%.

Trade with UK. Cuba imported UK goods worth £31,162,000; exports to UK totalled £28,489,000.

Tourism. (1986) 194,531 visitors.

COMMUNICATIONS

Railways

There are 7,802 miles/12,563 km of railways (of which 4,808 miles/7,743 km are used by the sugar industry) and 1,861 miles/4,820 km are public service railways (of which 94/151 are electrified).

Roads

There are 12,420 miles/20,000 km of roads, of which 5,465 miles/8,800 km are concrete or bituminized.

Aviation

Empresa Cubana de Aviacion (CUBANA) provides domestic and international services (international airports are at Havana, Santiago de Cuba, Camagüey and Varadero).

Shipping

Havana is a major port. Other principal ports are Cienfuegos; Mariel; Matanzas; Santiago de Cuba. There are 89 ships in Cuba's merchant fleet exceeding 1,000 GRT, and a further 23 under Panamanian or Maltese registry.

Telecommunications

There are 493,000 telephones, 1,530,000 television sets and 2,140,000 radios. There are five national radio networks, and Radio Habana Cuba broadcasting on short wave internationally; and two national television networks.

EDUCATION AND WELFARE

Education

Free (and compulsory) education is provided for children aged 6–14 yrs.

Schools. 1,000,971 pupils and 61,490 teachers (one per 16 pupils) in primary schools; 1,153,659 pupils and 98,105 teachers (one per 11 pupils) in intermediate schools. There are 173,295 students at adult primary schools.

Universities. 256,619 students and 21,573 teachers (one per 12 students).

Health

The state clinics provide free medical treatment although a few doctors remain in private practice. There are 21,752 doctors (one per 488 people) and 261 hospitals with 65,824 beds (one per 158 people). Cuba's budget for health and education is 2,940.2 million pesos.

CYPRUS

Kypriaki Dimokratia (Greek)
Kıbrıs Cumhuriyeti (Turkish)
(Republic of Cyprus)

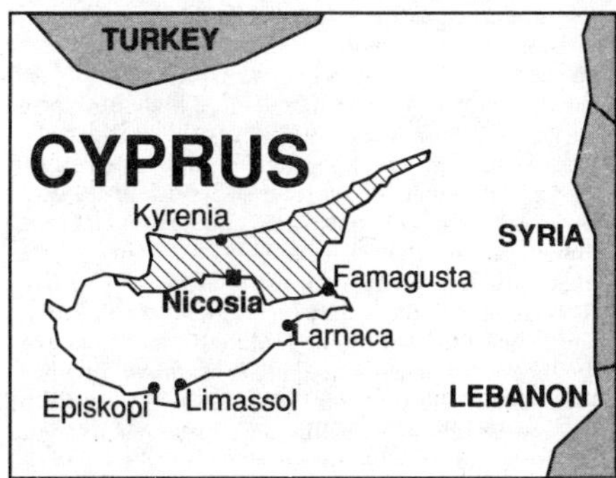

GEOGRAPHY

Located 49.7 miles/80 km south of Turkey in the north-east Mediterranean, Cyprus covers an area of 3,570 miles^2/9,251 km^2 divided into six districts. The third largest island in the Mediterranean, it subdivides into four physiographic sectors: the Kyrenian mountains along the north coast (Mount Kyparissovouno 3,360 ft/1,024 m) backed by the fertile alluvial Mesaoria Plain, the forested Troodos Massif (50% of total area, including the highest peak Mount Olympus, 6,401 ft/1,951 m) and the south-eastern plateau region sloping towards the sandy coastline. All the major rivers flow from the central massif including the Pedios, Karyota and Kouris. Nearly half the total surface area is arable (of which 20% is irrigated) and 18% of the land is forested.

Climate

Mediterranean with hot, dry summers (all water courses are dry at some point during the year) and moist, mild winters. Average annual rainfall ranges from 12–16 in/300–400 mm on the Mesaoria Plain to 47 in/1,200 mm in the Troodos Mountains. July and Jan. extremes are 112°F/44.5°C and 23°F/–5.5°C (in the mountains) respectively. The average winter temperature on the plains is 50°F/10°C. Nicosia: Jan

50°F/10°C. July 83°F/28.3°C. Average annual rainfall 15 in/371 mm.

Population

The Turkish-occupied northern sector of the island constitutes 37% of the total area. Approximately 18% of the total population are Turkish Cypriot and 77% Greek Cypriot. Armenian, Latin and Maronite minorities make up a further 5%. Total population is 687,000 of which 63.6% live in urban areas. Population density is 192.4 persons per mile^2/72 per km^2. **Births** 2.04%. **Deaths** 0.84%. **Rate of population increase** 1.2%. **Age distribution** under 15 = 25.2%; over 65 = 10.6%. **Life expectancy** female 80; male 74.

Religion

The Greek Cypriots are predominantly Orthodox Christian (estimated 544,700 members) and the Turkish minority are mostly Sunni Muslim (estimated 126,900) belonging to the Hanafi sect.

Language

Greek (81%) and Turkish (19%) are both official languages. English is also widely understood.

Cities and towns

Nicosia (capital)	
(excluding Turkish-occupied portion)	149,100
Limassol	107,200
Larnaca	48,300
Famagusta	39,500
Paphos (Turkish-occupied area)	20,800
Lefkosa (Nicosia)	
(Turkish-occupied area only)	37,400
Gazi Maguasa	19,428
Guezelyurt	10,179
Girne	6,902

HISTORY

Colonized by a succession of mainland peoples from the 15th century BC, Cyprus formed part of the empire of Alexander the Great in the 4th century BC, came under Roman rule in 58 BC and passed into the Eastern Roman, or Byzantine, Empire in AD 395. Held by Richard the Lionheart of England at the end the Third Crusade (1189–92) and then ruled by French feudal lords, it was annexed by Venice in 1489. Conquest by the Ottoman Turks in 1571 ushered in three centuries of Muslim rule, during which the island's Greek population was supplemented by a substantial admixture of Turks. Declining Ottoman power and the Russian threat to Constantinople led to the Cyprus Convention of 1878, an arrangement confirmed at the Congress of Berlin of the same year, to place Cyprus under the protection of Britain. Britain then annexed the island when Turkey joined the central powers in World War I, and a British proposal in 1915 to cede Cyprus to Greece if Greece entered the war on Britain's side was rejected by Greece and the offer was not repeated when Greece declared war on the central powers in 1917. Under the 1923 Treaty of Lausanne, Greece and Turkey recognized British sovereignty over the island, which was made a Crown Colony in 1925. Demands by Greek Cypriots for enosis (union with Greece) led to riots in 1931 in which the British governor's residence was burnt down and constitutional government suspended. Cyprus remained under British control throughout World War II.

Notwithstanding the wartime Anglo-Greek alliance, post-war British governments rejected not only the enosis option for Cyprus but also the creation of institutional links with Greece. Both of these scenarios were in any case opposed by Turkey, which joined NATO in 1952 together with Greece. The result was the emergence from 1955 of the pro-enosis EOKA terrorist organization led by Gen. George Grivas and of a powerful anti-British popular movement headed by Archbishop Makarios III, leader of the Cypriot Orthodox Church. Amid growing violence, Makarios was deported to the Seychelles in 1956, but returned to Cyprus in triumph in 1959, after Britain, Greece and Turkey had reached agreement that Cyprus would become an independent republic within the Commonwealth. Under associated treaties, Greece and Turkey became guarantors of the terms of the settlement and accorded the right to maintain a limited military presence in Cyprus, while Britain retained sovereignty over its military bases at Akrotiri and Dhekelia. In accordance with the agreement's power-sharing provisions, Makarios was elected as the country's first president (Dec. 1959) and Fazil Kutchuk, leader of the Turkish Cypriot community, as vice-president, following which Cyprus became independent in Aug. 1960.

The power-sharing arrangements quickly foundered on inter-communal conflict, which caused the withdrawal of Turkish Cypriots from the House of Representatives and Cabinet from late 1963 and the deployment of a UN peacekeeping force in Cyprus from early 1964. In 1968 the Turkish Cypriots set up an 'autonomous administration' in the north, with its own assembly and with Kutchuk as president. Among the Greek Cypriots, dissension between Makarios supporters and pro-enosis hardliners culminated in a coup by Greek-born officers of the National Guard in July 1974, the flight of Makarios and the installation of Nicos Sampson (a former EOKA leader) as president. Claiming to be acting as a guarantor of the 1959 agreement, Turkey immediately launched a large-scale military invasion of Cyprus, its forces rapidly taking control of the northern 40% of the island including the Turkish quarter of Nicosia. Sampson resigned after only a week in office, immediately after the fall of the seven-year-old military regime in Athens, which had backed his coup attempt. Glafcos Clerides (Speaker of the House of Representatives) became acting president, until Makarios returned (Dec. 1974) to resume the leadership.

Until his death in 1977, Makarios pursued UN-sponsored negotiations with the Turkish side, but the division of Cyprus hardened into an effective partition on the 'Attila' cease-fire line, as Greek Cypriots fled from the north. A Turkish Federated State of Cyprus, declared in the north in 1975 under the presidency of Rauf Denktash, was converted into the 'independent' Turkish Republic of Northern Cyprus in 1983. It secured recognition only from Turkey, which continued to maintain substantial forces in Cyprus. Makarios was succeeded as president by Spyros Kyprianou (of the centre-right Democratic Party), whose quest for a negotiated solution which preserved the country's unity made no substantive progress. Presidential elections in Feb. 1988 were won by George Vassiliou, a wealthy businessman standing as an independent with the backing of the powerful Greek Cypriot Communists. Following a thawing of relations between Athens and Istanbul, Vassiliou and Denktash met in Geneva in Aug. 1988 under UN auspices and agreed to new negotiations. However, a deadline in mid-1989 for their completion passed with the two sides still divided on major issues.

CONSTITUTION AND GOVERNMENT

Executive and legislature

Since Feb. 1975 Cyprus has been de facto divided into two states–the internationally recognized (Greek Cypriot) Republic of Cyprus, and the Turkish Cypriot part, which since 1983 has styled itself the Turkish Republic of Northern Cyprus (TRNC, not internationally recognized). The Greek-Cypriot administration continues to observe the 1960 constitution, but with the provisions for Turkish-Cypriot participation in abeyance. An executive president is directly elected by universal adult suffrage for a five-year term (last election 14 Feb. 1988). The president appoints and presides over a Council of Ministers. The unicameral House of Representatives (enlarged prior to the Dec. 1985 elections from 50 seats to 80, including a nominal allocation of 24 seats to Turkish-Cypriots) is elected by universal adult suffrage according to a system of proportional representation; last election 8 Dec. 1985.

Present government

President: Georgios Vassiliou

Principal Ministers Georgios Iacovou (Foreign Affairs); Georgios Syrimis (Finance); Christodoulos Veniamin (Interior); Andreas Aloneftis (Defence); Takis Nemitsas (Commerce and Industry); Christodoulos Chrysanthou (Justice). (Rauf Denktash (TRNC President)

Justice

The system of law has a background in common law, with modifications taken from civil codes. The highest court is the Supreme Court. Assize Courts (with unlimited criminal jurisdiction) have beneath them a District Court for every district (the courts of first instance for civil and criminal cases; there are separate Ecclesiastical Courts and Turkish Family Courts). Judges are appointed by a Supreme Council of Judicature, consisting of the Attorney-General, the President and judges of the Supreme Court. The death penalty is in force only for exceptional crimes. No executions were carried out between 1985 and mid-1988.

National symbols

Flag. The white flag bears a copper-coloured map of Cyprus above two crossed olive branches.

Festivals. 25 Mar. (Greek Independence Day); 1 Oct. (Independence Day); 28 Oct. (Greek National Day). The TRNC designates various public festivals including 23 Apr. (National Sovereignty and Children's Day); 20 July (Peace and Freedom Day, anniversary of the Turkish invasion in 1974); 1 Aug. (Communal Resistance Day); 30 Aug. (Victory Day); 29 Oct. (Turkish Republic Day)

Vehicle registration plate. CY.

INTERNATIONAL RELATIONS

Affiliations

NAM; Commonwealth.

Defence

Total Armed Forces: 13,000. Terms of service: conscription, 29 months, then reserve to age 50 (officers 65). Reserve: 60,000.

National Guard: 13,000; eight main battle tanks (T-34, AMX-30 B-2).

Para-military: 3,666.

The TRNC's defence forces (excluding Turkish forces present in strength since 1974) consist of 3,000 soldiers, with conscription for a two-year period; its army has five main battle tanks (T-34, operability questionable).

ECONOMY

Currency

The unit is the Cypriot pound, divided into 100 cents. (In the Turkish-occupied area the currency in use is the Turkish lira, divided into 100 kurus.)

National finance

Budget. The 1987 budget was for expenditure of US$911 million and revenue of US$900 million.

Inflation. 2.8%.

Gross Domestic Product

Estimated total GDP US$3,700 million, per capita US$5,670 (overall size of economy ranking 96 in the world).

Economically active population. The total number of persons active in the economy is 251,000 (Greek area); unemployed: 3.4%.

Sector	% of workforce
industry	33
agriculture	25
services*	42

* services figure includes elements unassigned to other categories.

Energy and mineral resources

Minerals. Major resources are copper; pyrites; asbestos; gypsum; timber; salt; marble; clay earth pigment. Major mineral exports: (1987 in tons/tonnes) asbestos 24,625/22,340; flotation pyrites 24,146/21,905; copper precipitates 335/304.

Electricity. Capacity 620,000 kW; production: 1,671 million kWh; 2,410 kWh per capita (1988).

Bioresources

Agriculture. Approximately 40% of Cyprus is arable land; 7% permanent crops; 10% meadow and pasture. Crop production: (1987 in 1,000 tons/tonnes) grapes 191/173; potatoes 165/150; citrus fruit 165/150. Other important crops: cereals; meat; fruit; olives.

Livestock numbers: (1987 in 1,000s) sheep 310; goats 220; poultry 266, cattle 45.

Forestry. Approximately 18% of Cyprus is forest and woodland. 34,594 acres/14,000 ha were reforested during the 1980s.

Fisheries. Total catch: (1987) 2,868 tons/2,602 tonnes.

Industry and commerce

Industry. Main activities are: mining (iron pyrites; gypsum; asbestos) and manufacture principally for local consumption of beverages; footwear; clothing; cement.

Commerce. Imports: US$1,500 million (1987). Major imports: (1987 in £C1,000s) machinery and transport material 174,000; petroleum 82,000; textiles, yarn and fabric 75,000; paper; plastics; animal feedstuffs. Exports: US$584 million (1987). Major exports: (1987 in £C1,000s) clothing 68,000; potatoes 22,000; footwear 16,000; fruit and fruit juice 8,000; cigarettes; wine; cement.

Trade with UK. In 1988 Cyprus exported £121.8 million worth of goods to the UK and imported £159.7 million.

Tourism. This is becoming increasingly important for the economy. In 1987 150,000 tourists visited the island.

COMMUNICATIONS

Railways

There are no railways in Cyprus.

Roads

There are 5,568 miles/8,966 km of roads, of which 2,749 miles/4,427 km are concrete or bituminized.

Aviation

Cyprus Airways provides international service (main airports are at Nicosia and Paphos). In the Turkish-Cypriot controlled part, Turkish Cypriot Airlines provides international services (international airports are Ercan, formerly Tymbou (Nicosia) and Gecitkale).

Shipping

The main ports are Famagusta (now under Turkish Cypriot control), Kyrenia, which is divided in two, Larnaca, Limassol and Paphos. As a major flag of convenience registry, Cyprus has a merchant fleet under its flag with 1,187 ships of over 1,000 GRT, and a total of 19 million GRT.

Telecommunications

There is a good telephone system (less good in the Turkish-Cypriot controlled part of the island) and 210,000 telephones. There are over 200,000 radios in all, 89,000 televisions (more than half of them colour) in the government-controlled sector, and contending government-controlled and Turkish Cypriot radio and television broadcasting corporations (CyBC and Bayrak Radio and TV respectively).

EDUCATION AND WELFARE

Education

School population. (1987) 20,800 pupils in primary schools; 11,100 pupils in secondary schools; 1,700 students in technical schools.

Schools. (1987) One teacher per 28 pupils in primary schools; one teacher per 16 pupils in secondary schools.

Universities. (1987) 1,640 students in higher education. One teacher per 20 students.

Health

There were 118 doctors in Cyprus in 1986; one doctor per 4,600 inhabitants.

CZECHOSLOVAKIA

Česka a Slovenská Federativní(Czech)
Česka a Slovenská Federativna(Slovak)
(Czech and Slovak Federative Republic)

GEOGRAPHY

The federal state of Czechoslovakia is a landlocked country in central Europe, comprising two Socialist Republics covering a total area of 49,362 miles^2/127,881 km^2. Two features dominate the physiography: the Bohemian Massif (Česke Masiv) in the west and the Carpathian Mountains in the east separated by the Morava river valley. In the west, the Česke Masiv (average elevation 2,953 ft/900 m) surrounds the tilted Bohemian basin, through which the Elbe-Moldau river system flows north into East Germany. Along the Polish border, the Carpathians rise to 8,737 ft/2,663 m at Gerlachovsky in the Tatra Range. The fertile Danubian levels and Eastern Slovakian lowlands are located in the south and south-east of the country, drained by the Danube-Morava river systems. 40% of the land is arable and a similar proportion is deciduous/mixed forest. There are approximately 22,000 lakes in Czechoslovakia. Internal rural-urban migration is steady but general distribution remains comparatively even.

Climate

Humid continental with cold winters and warm, rainy summers subject to thunderstorms. 20% of precipitation is in the form of snow, averaging between 20–30 in/500–750 mm annually in lowland regions, while mountainous areas receive 32 in/800 mm or more. Average temperatures range from 27°F/–3°C (Jan.) to 64°F/18°C (July). Prague: Jan. 29°F/–1.5°C. July 67°F/19.4°C. Average annual rainfall 19 in/483 mm. Brno: Jan. 31°F/–0.6°C. July 67°F/19.4°C. Average annual rainfall 21 in/525 mm.

Cities and towns

Praha (Prague, capital)	1,200,266
Bratislava	424,378
Brno	385,965
Ostrava	328,373
Košice	225,841
Plzeň (Pilsen)	174,765
Olomouc	105,969
Ústí nad Labem	104,752
Liberec	102,685

Population

Total population is 15,597,000 of which 74.1% live in urban areas. Population density is 316 persons per mile^2/121.9 per km^2. Ethnic composition: approximately Czech 31.5%; Slovak 31.5%; Hungarian 3.8%; Polish 0.5%; German 0.4%; Ukrainian 0.3%. In addition, there are an estimated 0.3 million Gypsies in Czechoslovakia.

Birth rate 1.51%. **Death rate** 1.19%. **Rate of popula-**

tion increase 0.32%. **Age distribution** under 15 = 24.5%; over 15 = 11.0%. **Life expectancy** female 74.8; male 67.3; average 71.

Religion

An estimated 20% of the population profess some religious faith. Of the many denominations, the Roman Catholic Church is the largest with approximately 3.7 million members (concentrated in Slovakia). Other denominations with significant memberships include the Hussites 475,000; the Czech Brethren 81,000; the Slovak Lutherans 40,000; the Reformed Christians 120,000; the Orthodox Church 150,000; and an estimated 6,000 Jews in Prague.

Language

Official languages are Czech and Slovak, belonging to the Slavic family and using the Roman as opposed to the Cyrillic alphabet. Hungarian is also widely spoken.

HISTORY

Traces of human settlement in the territories of present-day Czechoslovakia date back to the 4th millennium BC. The earliest known inhabitants were the Celtic Boii (from whom the name Bohemia is derived), who were supplanted at the start of the Christian era by the Germanic Marcomanni. The Slav ancestors of the Czechs and Slovaks arrived in the area between the 5th and 7th centuries. They were converted to Christianity during the 9th century. Slovakia was incorporated into the Kingdom of Hungary at the end of the 9th century (this condition lasting until 1918), but a cohesive Czech state emerged in Bohemia and Moravia between the 10th and 12th centuries; there also began an influx of German settlers. The Czech monarch Charles IV was crowned as Holy Roman Emperor in 1346. In the early 15th century the priest and scholar Jan Hus led a religious reform movement which acquired nationalist overtones, and his execution at the stake helped to precipitate almost two decades of civil and religious war. The Austrian Catholic Habsburg dynasty acceded to the thrones of the Czech lands and Hungary in 1526. A century later the predominantly protestant Czech nobility sought to throw off Habsburg rule, but a two-year revolt was put down at the Battle of the White Mountain (outside the gates of Prague) in 1620. A national revival began in the Czech lands in the late 18th century, and the 19th century was marked by bitter competition between Czech and German nationalist movements (in Slovakia economic underdevelopment and Hungarian political domination prevented the emergence of an effective national movement).

With the collapse of the Habsburg empire in 1918, an independent Czechoslovak republic was founded with Thomas Masaryk as president, Edward Beneš succeeding him in Dec. 1935. The First Republic was ruled by coalition governments comprising most or all of the main Czech and Slovak parties (apart from the Communist Party of Czecholslovakia–CPCz, which broke away from the Social Democrats in 1921). The First Republic guaranteed equal rights to all its nationalities, but with political power centred on Prague; many Slovaks and members of the German minority resented what they saw as Czech domination. The Depression after 1929 affected the German areas of Czechoslovakia (the Sudetenland) especially hard, and fomented extreme nationalist and separatist sentiment among the Germans (encouraged by the Nazis who took power in Germany in 1933). To appease the Nazis Czechoslovakia was forced (with the acquiescence of Britain and France under the Munich agreement of 29 Sept. 1938) to cede the Sudetenland to Germany. An independent Slovak state was declared on 14 Mar. 1939 under an extreme right-wing and pro-German regime. On 15 Mar. Germany occupied the Czech lands, which were turned into the Protectorate of Bohemia-Moravia.

During World War II Beneš headed a London-based Czechoslovak National Committee which was officially recognized as the country's government by the Allies in July 1941. Resistance to the Germans in the Protectorate was sporadic until late in the war, although Reinhard Heydrich, the Protector, was assassinated on 27 May 1942. Slovaks began a national uprising at the end of Aug. 1944 and resisted the German occupiers until late October.

In Mar. 1945 Beneš visited Moscow and reached agreement with CPCz General Secretary Klement Gottwald on forming a National Front government. The pre-war parties were to be reduced to six, all participating in government. On 5 Apr. the government announced its programme at Košice (east Slovakia). This included nationalization of key industries and finance, equality of Czechs and Slovaks, expulsion of the German and Hungarian minorities (later only the Germans were wholly expelled), expansion of social welfare, and a foreign policy built around the Czechoslovak–Soviet treaty of alliance signed in 1943. The government arrived in Prague on 10 May in the wake of the Soviet Red Army, the city having effectively been liberated from Nazi control by an uprising beginning on 5 May.

Following general elections in May 1946 the Communists emerged as the strongest political grouping within the National Front, and Gottwald became prime minister. In Feb. 1948 a crisis arose due to dissension within the National Front cabinet, the non-socialist ministers resigned, and a Communist-dominated government took power. Beneš resigned as president in June over provisions of a new Constitution. He died three months later and was succeeded by Gottwald, who was replaced as prime minister by Antonin Zapotocky. The Communist takeover led to full nationalization of industries and agriculture, collectivization and a purge of political opponents from all public posts. The Social Democratic Party was merged with the CPCz in Apr. 1948, while the other parties survived as subordinates to Communist policy within the National Front. Between 1950 and 1954 an extensive purge of CPCz members and officials took place, leading to the imprisonment and even execution of many leading figures (including Rudolf Slansky, Gottwald's successor as CPCz general secretary). Gottwald died in Mar. 1953, being succeeded as president by Zapotocky, while Antonin Novotny became first secretary of the CPCz later in the year and president after Zapotocky's death in 1957.

A new Constitution, modelled on that of the Soviet Union, was introduced in 1960; it changed the state's title to the Czechoslovak Socialist Republic. The Novotny regime resisted growing pressure for reforms during the 1960s, but conceded extensive economic liberalization in 1967. In Jan. 1968 Novotny was replaced as first secretary by Alexander Dubček (and as president by Ludvik Svoboda in March). There followed an eight-month period (known as the Prague Spring) of radical reform and democratization (including abolition of censorship, guarantees of basic freedoms, autonomy for Slovakia and rehabilitation of the victims of the 1950s purges). This process provoked concern amongst leaders of Czechoslovakia's communist allies, and on 20–21 Aug. troops of the Soviet Union and four other Warsaw Pact countries invaded. Dubček and his reformist colleagues were taken to Moscow and were only released after they had agreed drastically to curtail the reforms.

The only significant reform which survived was the introduction in Jan. 1969 of a federal system, with autonomous Czech and Slovak governments. Anti-Soviet protests and disturbances were followed by Dubček's replacement as first secretary (later general secretary) by Gustáv Husák on 17 Apr. The rest of the reformist leadership was removed in the succeeding months and expelled from the party. A thorough process of 'normalization' was set in motion, including expulsion from the CPCz of up to half a million members. In May 1970 a new 20-year treaty of friendship was signed with the Soviet Union. In Jan. 1977 a group of citizens issued a document entitled 'Charter 77', calling on the government to fulfil its obligations under UN covenants on human rights signed by Czechoslovakia in 1976. This spawned the Charter 77 dissident movement which persisted despite the imprisonment and harassment of its members. Economic stagnation in the early 1980s led to limited devolution of managerial powers being announced in 1987, but political restructuring on the Soviet model was rejected. Husák was replaced as general secretary of the CPCz by Miloš Jakeš on 17 Dec. 1987 (he remained president, a post he had assumed in 1975), while Lubomír Štrougal, federal prime minister since 1970 (and allegedly a supporter of more extensive restructuring) was replaced by Ladislav Adamec and removed from the CPCz presidium in Oct. 1988. Two months earlier some 10,000 people had demonstrated in Prague to mark the 20th anniversary on 21 Aug. of the Warsaw Pact invasion.

Such demonstrations grew increasingly frequent in the course of 1989, and beginning on 17 Nov. there was a dramatic upsurge in street protests in Prague. These led to the resignation of Jakes a week later. The authorities entered into a dialogue with opposition groups organized in the new Civic Forum, and at the end of Nov. they capitulated to opposition demands by abolishing the Communists' constitutionally-guaranteed monopoly on power. During Dec. a new coalition government with a non-Communist majority was sworn in, Husák resigned and was replaced as President by leading dissident Vaclav Havel, and Dubček was elected speaker of parliament.

CONSTITUTION AND GOVERNMENT

Executive and legislature

Political power was effectively in the hands of the Communist Party of Czechoslovakia (CPCz), which was organized in the Slovak SR as the Communist Party of Slovakia, and which headed a National Front including four nominally separate parties. The highest organ of state authority was the bicameral Federal Assembly, comprising a 200-seat Chamber of the People and 150-seat Chamber of Nations, both elected from approved lists of candidates by universal adult suffrage every five years. The executive is headed by the president of the Republic, who is elected by the Federal Assembly, and who in turn appoints the Federal Government.

Present government

President of the Republic Vaclav Havel
Prime Minister Marian Calfa
Principal members of the Federal Government Valtr Komarek (First Deputy Prime Minister); Jan Carnogursky (First Deputy Prime Minister); Jiri Dienstbier (Foreign Affairs); Miroslav Vacek (National Defence); Vaclav Klaus (Finance).

Administration

The Czech and Slovak Federative Republic is a federal state consisting of the Czech and Slovak Socialist Republics, each of which has its own government. The country is further subdivided into ten 'Kraj' or regions.

Justice

The system of law is based originally on the Austro-Hungarian civil code, subsequently modified in line with Communist legal precepts. The highest court is the Federal Supreme Court (with a parallel structure of military courts). Supreme Court judges are elected by the Federal Assembly; the principle of the election of judges is extended throughout the court structure, from the lay judges elected by local authorities, up through the professional judges elected by the national councils in the republics to serve on regional and district courts. The death penalty is in force. There were over five executions between 1985 and mid-1988. Capital offences: murder.

National symbols

Flag. Two horizontal stripes, white over red, with a blue triangle in the hoist, the apex of which is in the centre of the flag.
Festivals. 1 May (Labour Day); 9 May (National Day, Anniversary of the Liberation); 28 Oct. (National Day, Anniversary of Independence).
Vehicle registration plate. CS.

INTERNATIONAL RELATIONS

Affiliations

Warsaw Pact; Comecon.

Defence

Total Armed Forces: 197,000 (118,000 conscripts). Terms of service: Army and air force two years. Border troops and militia 27 months. Reserves: 280,000.

Army: 145,000; 3,400 main battle tanks (T-54/-55, T-72).

Air Force: 52,000; some 450 combat aircraft (MiG-21/-21U, MiG-23 MF, MiG23BN/Um, MiG-21SMT/U, Su-25/-22/-7BM/U), 45 armed helicopters.

ECONOMY

Currency

The unit is the koruna, divided into 100 haler.

National finance

Budget. The 1986 budget was for expenditure of US$21,900 million and revenue of US$22,400 million.
Inflation. 0.9%.

Gross Domestic Product

Estimated total GDP US$158,200 million (GNP), per capita US$10,130 (overall size of economy ranking 18 in the world).
Economically active population. The total number of persons active in the economy is 8,200,000; unemployed: 0.9%.

Sector of GDP	% of workforce
industry	37
agriculture	12
services*	51

* services figure includes elements unassigned to other categories.

Energy and mineral resources

Minerals. Czechoslovakia has both hard and soft coal reserves. Output: (in 1,000 tons/tonnes) coal 27,775/25,197; lignite and brown coal 113,248/102,738. Other minerals include uranium; glass; sand; salt; lesser amounts of iron ore; graphite; copper; lead.

Electricity. Capacity: 22.9 million kW; production: 84,900 million kWh; 5.4 million kWh per capita (1988).

Bioresources

Agriculture. Of a total of 16 million acres/6.8 million ha of agricultural land, 10.6 million acres/4.3 million ha are collective farms; 5.2 million acres/2.1 million ha are state farms; 71,000 are privately owned. There are 1,664 collective farms and 235 state farms.

Crop production: (in 1,000 tons/tonnes) sugar beet 7,865/7135; wheat 5,848/5,305; potatoes 3,871/3,512; barley 3,891/3,530; maize 1,093/992; rye 603/547.

Livestock numbers: poultry 49 million; pigs 6.8 million; cattle 5.0 million; sheep 1.1 million; horses 46,000.

Forestry. Czechoslovakia has rich forest reserves and the timber industry is an important one, 11.4 million acres/4.6 million ha are forested including spruce 50%; beech 16%; pine 7%. Timber yield: 664 million ft^3/18.8 million m^3.

Fisheries. Annual catch: 23 million tons/21 million tonnes.

Industry and commerce

Industry. Main industries: iron and steel; machinery and equipment; cement; sheet glass; motor vehicles; armaments; chemicals; ceramics; wood; paper products; footwear.

Commerce. Exports: US$23,500 million including machinery and equipment 57.4%; manufactured consumer goods 16.2%; fuels; minerals and metals 12.5%; agricultural and forestry products 6.1%; other products 7.8%. Imports: US$23,900 million including fuels; minerals and metals 39.8%; machinery and equipment 35.7%; agricultural and forestry products 11.2%; manufactured consumer goods 5.8%; other products 7.5%. Countries exported to were Soviet Union; East Germany; Poland; Hungary; West Germany; Yugoslavia; Austria; Bulgaria; Romania; US. Imports came from USSR; East Germany; Poland; Hungary; West Germany; Yugoslavia; Austria; Bulgaria; Romania; US.

Trade with UK. Czechoslovakia imported UK goods worth £130,420,000; exports to UK totalled £148,248,000.

Tourism. (1986) 10.66 million visitors, of which 770,000 from the West.

COMMUNICATIONS

Railways

There are 8,145 miles/13,116 km of railways, of which 2,192 miles/3,530 km are electrified.

Roads

There are 45,403 miles/73,112 km of roads, of which 40,862 miles/65,800 km are concrete or bituminized.

Aviation

ČSA (Československe Aerolinie) provides international services and Slov-Air domestic and charter services (there are 15 international airports, the most important being Ruzyně at Prague).

Shipping

There are 18 ships exceeding 1,000 GRT in the country's merchant marine, which uses maritime outlets in Poland, East and West Germany and Yugoslavia. There are 264 miles/425 km of navigable inland waterways.

Telecommunications

There are 4,360,000 television sets and a similar number of radios, with five national radio networks, and a national television broadcasting operation (with a separate Slovakian section).

EDUCATION AND WELFARE

Education

Free compulsory education is provided for ten years.

Schools. There are some 11,500 kindergartens for 3–6 year olds with over 50,500 teachers and 670,000 pupils; 6,300 primary schools with over 2,100,000 pupils and over 97,000 teachers; 343 secondary schools with nearly 10,000 teachers and 134,000 pupils; 561 secondary vocational schools with 258,000 pupils and 17,000 teachers.

Universities. There are five universities and 31 other higher education institutes with 136,000 students and 19,500 teachers.

Literacy. 99%.

Health

There is free medical care. There are 230 hospitals with 123,000 beds and 57,000 doctors and dentists. Pensions of 50–60% of average salary over 20 years are paid to men from age 60 and to women from 53 depending on the number of children they have raised.

DENMARK

Kongeriget Danmark
Kongarikidh Danmark (Faroese)
Danmarkip Nalagauvfia (Greenlandic)
(Kingdom of Denmark)

GEOGRAPHY

Southernmost of the Scandinavian countries, Denmark occupies the Jutland peninsula in north central Europe and the islands of Sjælland, Funen, Lolland and Falster. It has a total area of 16,629 miles²/43,080 km² including 480 other smaller islands, the island of Bornholm in the Baltic Sea but excluding the self-governing dependencies of Greenland (North Atlantic) and the Faroe Islands (Atlantic).

Denmark exhibits a low-lying, glaciated topography with an average elevation of less than 98 ft/30 m rising to 568 ft/173 m at Yding Skovhoj in east central Jutland. An undulating, marly moraine (running northwest-south) divides the sandy soils to the west from the fertile loam of East Jutland. Many of the coastal fjords penetrate the interior mainland, including Limfjorden which divides Jutland from its northernmost tip. The longest river is the Gudena (96 miles/155 km) in east central Jutland, and the most densely populated areas are the city and county of Copenhagen (København) and the borough of Frederiksberg. 61% of Denmark is arable and 12% is forest or woodland.

Climate

Temperate, modified by marine influences and Gulf Stream. Winters are cold and overcast, summer usually mild or warm and sunny. Rainfall decreases west-east with average rainfall rarely in excess of 265 in/675 mm a year. Strong winds are not uncommon.

Copenhagen: Jan. 33°F/0.5°C. July 63°F/17°C. Average annual rainfall 23 in/571 mm. Esbjerg: Jan. 33°F/0.5°C. July 59°F/15°C. Average annual rainfall 32 in/800 mm.

Cities and towns

Copenhagen (København, capital)	1,351,999
Aarhus	195,152
Odense	137,286
Aalborg	113,650
Esbjerg	71,112
Randers	55,563

Population

Total population is 5,119,000 of which 84.3% live in urban areas. Population density is 308/119 persons per miles²/km². Ethnic composition: 95.2% of the population were born in Denmark.

Greenland's total population is 54,524 (1988) of whom an estimated 42,000 are Inuit.

The Faroe Islands' total population is 46,352 (1988).

Of the 136,177 foreign nationals resident in Denmark in 1988, 23,130 were from Nordic countries; 26,875 from the EC (including a significant German contingent); 39,427 from the rest of Europe; 29,786 Asian.

Birth rate 1.03%. **Death rate** 1.11%. **Rate of population increase** (1980–87) 0.08%. **Age distribution** under 15 = 18.7%; over 65 = 14.9%. **Life expectancy** female 78; male 73; average 76.

Religion

Predominantly Christian. 90.6% of the population subscribe to the Evangelical Lutheran doctrine (National Church). Other Protestant denominations include the Methodists, German and Norwegian Lutherans, the Seventh Day Adventists and the Unitarians. There are approximately 28,188 Roman Catholic adherents in Denmark and an estimated 3,064 Jewish citizens.

Language

The Danish language derives from Old Scandinavian, like Norwegian and Swedish to which it is closely related. The Germanic influence is also a feature. (Southern Jutland supports a German-speaking minority.) Faroese and Greenlandic are also spoken in these dependencies.

HISTORY

Settled since Neolithic times, the area of present-day Denmark first made its mark on recorded European history from the 5th century AD as the source of seafaring warriors who moved by conquest into other lands, notably England, to which the conquering Angles from Jutland and Schleswig gave their name. The Angles were replaced in their original lands by the 'Dan' people from southern Sweden, who in the 10th century were unified under Gorm the Old (d.950), founder of the Danish monarchy (the oldest in Europe), and embraced Christianity under Harald Bluetooth (r.950–85). Meanwhile, since the late 8th century the Danes had been in the vanguard of a further remarkable wave of seaborne migration and conquest which took the Viking Norsemen of Scandinavia to the ends of the known world. Anglo-Saxon England bore the brunt of the Danish expansion, which by the early 11th century had united the whole of Scandinavia and England under Cnut the Great (r.1014–35).

Although Cnut's Nordic empire quickly disintegrated after his death, Valdemar the Great (r.1157–82) reasserted Denmark's Scandinavian ascendancy. Two centuries of increasing dominance culminated in the 1397 Union of Kalmar under which Queen Margrethe of Denmark (r.1387–1412) became effective ruler of both Norway and Sweden (including Finland). Protracted conflict with the Hanseatic League ensued, until in 1460 the disputed duchies of Schleswig and Holstein to the south of Jutland were united under Christian I (r.1448–81), founder of the present-day Oldenburg royal house. Sweden was lost, however, when a long rebellion against Danish rule culminated in the election of Gustavus I to the Swedish throne in 1523. The Danish Lutheran Reformation was completed under Christian III (r.1534–59). His successor, Frederick II (r.1559–88), extended Denmark's maritime domination of the Baltic and the North Sea and fought a war with the Swedes to consolidate Danish possessions in southern Sweden.

Christian IV (r.1588–1648) continued the struggle with Sweden, but overreached Danish strength in the Thirty Years' War (1618–48). Further humiliation followed at the hands of Sweden, which not only became Protestant northern Europe's champion against the Catholic Habsburgs but also drove the Danes out of southern Sweden by 1645. The 1648 Peace of Westphalia ending the Thirty Years' War confirmed the new dominance of Sweden in the Baltic region. In 1660 Frederick III (r.1648–70) established an absolute monarchy, securing the Danish burghers' support for a final breaking of aristocratic privilege. He and his successors waged further wars against the Swedes, but by the end of the Great Northern War (1700–21) it was clear that the former Danish territories across the Öresund Sound had been lost for ever (although Norway remained Danish). Through the 18th century, Denmark adopted a neutral stance towards European conflicts, while its statesmen concentrated on emancipating the peasantry and developing trade. In the Napoleonic Wars, however, Danish efforts to evade the British blockade of continental Europe caused the Royal Navy to destroy one Danish fleet at Copenhagen in 1801 and another in 1807. Denmark then allied itself with France and shared in the latter's final defeat. The price paid was the loss of her German possessions in Pomerania and of Norway, which under the 1814 Treaty of Kiel was transferred to the Swedish Crown, although Iceland, Greenland and the Faroe Islands remained under Danish sovereignty.

The long conflict left Denmark weak and impoverished, but the foundations for national recovery existed in the growth of a robust and productive class of small independent farmers. Liberal reforms, notably the introduction of compulsory universal education up to the age of 14, culminated in the granting of a democratic constitution in 1849. But while the road to political and economic progress was now open, international problems intensified over the national aspirations of the German inhabitants of Schleswig and Holstein. Ultimately, Prussia's determination to unite the German Confederation under its leadership proved irresistible. Military defeat in 1864 forced Denmark to cede both provinces, which in 1871 passed into the new German Reich. However, despite remaining neutral in World War I, Denmark gained some compensation when, as allowed under the 1919 Versailles Treaty, northern Schleswig voted in 1920 in favour of a return to Danish rule by a majority of three to one.

The introduction of universal adult suffrage in 1915 accelerated the rise of the Social Democratic Party, mainly at the expense of the Liberals. After a first experience of government 1924–26, the Social Democrats came properly to power in 1929 under Thorvald Stauning, who in the 1930s implemented advanced welfare-state legislation and other egalitarian reforms. On the outbreak of World War II in 1939 Denmark reaffirmed its neutrality, but the following year was occupied by German forces without bloodshed. A national coalition government was formed but became increasingly powerless against the Germans and their Danish collaborators. The Germans took complete control in 1943, amid mounting harassment by the Danish Resistance. In 1944 Iceland declared its independence from Denmark.

Following the defeat of Germany in 1945, Danish politics resumed with the Social Democrats maintaining their dominance in post-war coalitions. Under a major constitutional reform in 1953 a single-chamber, proportionally-elected Parliament was created and the royal succession opened to females, enabling Margrethe II to accede to the throne in 1972. The Faroes and Greenland were granted home rule in 1948 and 1979 respectively. Meanwhile, Denmark had abandoned neutrality by becoming a founder member of NATO in 1949, and had joined the Nordic Council in 1953 and EFTA in 1959. But with its rising prosperity linked increasingly to non-Nordic Europe, in 1972 Denmark voted by two to one in a fiercely-contested referendum to join the European Coal and Steel Community, EEC and Euratom as from 1 Jan. 1973, together with Britain and Ireland.

The political consequences of joining the European Communities included further fragmentation of the Danish party structure and seemingly unending minority governments. A new right-wing populist People's Party gained significant support from 1973 onwards, while on the left the Social Democrats experienced gradual electoral decline. In 1982 a minority Social Democratic administration gave way to Denmark's first Conservative-led government since 1901, headed by Poul Schlüter and also including the Venstre Liberals, the Centre Democrats, and the Christian People's Party. By late 1987 this minority 'four-leaf clover' coalition had achieved the longest tenure of any non-socialist government since the 1920s and had secured endorsement in a Feb. 1986 referendum for Danish ratification of the Single European Act, albeit by the relatively narrow margin of 56.2% for and 43.8% against. The outcome of the May 1988 elections was the formation of another non-socialist minority coalition under the leadership of Schlüter, consisting this time of the Conservatives, Venstre Liberals, and Radical Liberals.

CONSTITUTION AND GOVERNMENT

Executive and legislature

The monarch is head of state, and nominally shares legislative authority with the parliament. The prime minister is head of government, while legislative authority is exercised by the unicameral 179 member parliament (Folketing) elected for a four-year term (last elections 10 May 1988).

Present government

Queen Margrethe II
Prime Minister Poul Schlüter

Principal Ministers Uffe Ellemann-Jensen (Foreign Affairs); Henning Dyremose (Finance); Niels Helveg Petersen (Economic Affairs); Hans Engell (Justice); Anders Fogh Rasmussen (Fiscal Affairs); Knud Enggaard (Defence); Thor Pedersen (Interior; Nordic Affairs).

Justice

The system is based on civil law. The highest court is the Supreme Court in Copenhagen, which has a role in the judicial review of legislation. At the lower level the 83 tribunals (byretterne) sit with a single judge presiding; there are 34 such tribunals in Copenhagen, 13 in Arhus, 10 in Odense. More important cases are dealt with by the Landsretterne, which also function as courts of appeal for the byretterne. Appeals from the Landsretterne are to the Supreme Court. The death penalty was abolished in 1978.

Prisons. There are 3,515 prisoners.

National symbols

Flag. Red with a white cross.

Festivals. 5 June (Constitution Day).

Vehicle registration plate. DK.

INTERNATIONAL RELATIONS

Affiliations

NATO; EC; Nordic Council; OECD.

Defence

Total Armed Forces: 29,300 (8,400 conscripts, 800 women). Terms of service: 9–12 months (up to 27 months in certain ranks).

Reserves: 74,700.

Army: 17,000; 210 main battle tanks (Leopard 1, Centurion); 52 light tanks (M-41 DK-1).

Navy: 5,400; four submarines; three frigates; 49 patrol and coastal combatants.

Air Force: 6,900; 95 combat aircraft (F-16A/B, F-35, RF-35, SAAB T-17).

ECONOMY

Currency

The unit is the krone, divided into 100 ore.

National finance

Budget. The 1988 budget was for expenditure of US$34,000 million and revenue of US$34,000 million. Main items of expenditure are housing and welfare 40%; education 8.6%; defence 5.2%.

Balance of payments. The balance of payments (current account, 1988) was a deficit of US$1,810 million.

Inflation. 4.7% (12 months to Sept. 1989).

Gross Domestic Product

Estimated total GDP US$85,480 million, per capita US$19,780 (overall size of economy ranking 28 in the world by size). Growth rate (1988) −0.4%.

Economically active population. The total number of persons active in the economy is 2,860,000; unemployed: 8.6% (1988).

Sector	% of workforce	% of GDP
industry	24	29
agriculture	6	5
services*	70	66

* services figure includes elements unassigned to other categories.

Energy and mineral resources

Oil and gas. Oil production: (1988) 5.1 million tons/4.6 million tonnes.

Electricity. Capacity: 11,123,000 kW; production: (1988) 30,011 million kWh; 5,860 kWh per capita.

Bioresources

Agriculture. 61% of the country is arable land. Over the past 30 years manufacturing has progressively replaced agriculture as the most important sector. Agricultural products nevertheless provide 30% of total exports and it is still an important sector.

Crop production: (1987 in million tons/tonnes) barley 4.7/4.3; wheat 2.5/2.3; potatoes 1/0.9; rye 0.6/0.5.

Livestock numbers: (1987) poultry 15 million; pigs 9 million; cattle 2.3 million; horses 33,000.

Industry and commerce

Industry. Manufactured goods provide 60% of total exports, including food processing; machinery and equipment; textiles and clothing; furniture and other wood products; chemical products; electronics.

Commerce. Denmark's exports totalled US$25,600 million, including meat; meat products; dairy products; transport equipment; fish; chemicals; industrial machinery. Imports: (1987) US$25,500 million, including petroleum; machinery and equipment; chemicals; grain and foodstuffs; textiles; paper. Countries exported to were US 6.9%; West Germany; Norway; Sweden; UK; other EC countries; Japan. Imports came from US 5.3%; West Germany; Netherlands; Sweden; UK; other EC countries.

Trade with UK. Denmark imported UK goods worth £1,171 million; exports to UK totalled £2,028 million (1988).

Tourism. (1987) earnings 15,185 million kroner.

COMMUNICATIONS

Railways

There are 1,534 miles/2,471 km of railways, of which 90 miles/145 km are electrified (in the København area).

Roads

There are 43,773 miles/70,488 km of paved roads.

Aviation

Cimber Air A/S, Maersk Air and Conair A/S provide charter flights and Danair A/S domestic services and Sterling Airways international inclusive-tour flights (main airport is at København).

Shipping

Main ports are Aalborg, Aarhus, København (all on the Baltic) and Esbjerg on the North Sea coast. The merchant marine includes 223 ships over 1,000 GRT.

Telecommunications

The modern telephone system serves 4,237,000 telephones. There are approximately 2 million valid licences for radio receivers and a similar number for televisions. Radio Denmark transmits both radio and television programmes, while the commercial TV2 channel based in Odense began operation in Oct. 1988. There are services in both radio and television for the Faroes and Greenland.

EDUCATION AND WELFARE

Education

Free compulsory education is provided in the folkeskole (public primary and lower secondary school) for nine years with a voluntary tenth year. Children between the ages of 14 and 18 can choose alternatively to complete their compulsory education at continuation schools of which there were 188 with over 14,000 pupils in 1986–87.

Schools. There are over 2,500 folkeskole with nearly 700,000 pupils and over 64,000 teachers. Some 16% of all the schools are private schools which teach around 10% of all school children.

Universities. There are five universities plus many other tertiary colleges and schools specializing in commerce, technical and agricultural subjects.

Health

Denmark has a comprehensive health and social security system covering the entire population and providing for free medical care and full rate pensions for those resident in the country for over 40 years.

DJIBOUTI

Jumhouriyya Djibouti
(Republic of Djibouti)

GEOGRAPHY

Located on the north-eastern coast of the Horn of Africa, fronting the Strait of Bab al Mandeb. Djibouti is a small, volcanic, mostly infertile country covering a total area of 8,938 miles^2/23,310 km^2. The bulk of the population inhabit the comparatively fertile coastal strip bordering the Gulf of Tadjoura. The southern plateaux are flanked by sunken plains forming part of Ethiopia's Danakil Desert, while in the northern part of the country, the mountains rise to 6,627 ft/2,020 m at Moussa Ali. The Ambouli, a subterranean river, is an essential source of water, but 89% of the terrain is desert with some scrub vegetation, and less than 1% of the land is arable.

Climate

Semi-arid, particularly hot May–Sept. with very high temperatures on the coastal plain all year. Rainfall is sparse throughout the country, falling Nov.–Mar. on the coast and Apr.–Oct. inland. Djibouti: Jan. 78°F/25.6°C. July 96°F/35.6°C. Average annual rainfall 5 in/130 mm.

Cities and towns

Djibouti (capital)	200,000

Population

Total population is 383,000, of which 75.0% live in urban areas. Population density is 42.8 persons per mile^2/16.4 per km^2. Nearly two-thirds of the total population live in the capital. Ethnic composition: 60% Somali (Issa) concentrated in the south: 35% Afar (concentrated in the north and west); 5% French, Arab, Ethiopian, Italian.

Birth rate 4.79%. **Death rate** 1.91%. **Rate of population increase** (1980–87) 2.88%. **Age distribution** under 15 = 45.7%; over 65 = 2.2%. **Life expectancy** female and male statistics unavailable; average 47.

Religion

The vast majority of the population is Sunni Muslim (94%), the other 6% Christian (4% Roman Catholic; 1% Protestant; 1% Orthodox).

Language

Official language is Arabic. French, Somali and Afar are all widely spoken. Somali and Afar, the two principal ethnic groups, share a common Hamito-Semitic linguistic origin.

HISTORY

Despite extreme heat and aridity, Djibouti has been inhabited since Palaeolithic times. Throughout the historical period, the country's scarce pastures have been contested by Afar (sometimes called Danakil) and Somali nomadic pastoralists.

In 1861 France negotiated the cession of Obock in the north of the country from an Afar sultan but in the early 1880s the French administration moved to Djibouti, which became the capital of French Somaliland in 1892. Djibouti's port served as an important bunkering station on the Suez Canal route and a railway to Addis Ababa was completed in 1917.

In response to calls for independence from the predominant Somali community a referendum was held in Mar. 1967. Although the territory voted to retain its association with France, the Somali community contested the validity of the result. After nearly a decade of Somali agitation and pressure from the Organization for African Unity, the territory acceded to independence in June 1977. A Somali, Hassan Gouled, was elected president and an Afar, Ahmed Dini, appointed prime minister. In Dec. 1977, Ahmed Dini and four other Afar ministers resigned, alleging discrimination against Afars. As part of a policy of detribalization, the Rassemblement populaire pour le progrès (RPP) was formed in 1979 and in Nov. 1981 Djibouti became a one-party state. Pres. Gouled was re-elected in 1982 and 1987 but stood as sole candidate on both occasions. Ethnic tensions between rival Somali-speaking groups led to serious violence in March and April 1989, while in April security also moved to suppress unrest among the Afar majority.

CONSTITUTION AND GOVERNMENT

Executive and legislature

The head of state and government is the executive president, elected by direct universal suffrage (most recently in Apr. 1987); under the 1981 Constitution the president may serve for no more than two terms. The legislature is a 65-member Chamber of Deputies, elected for a term of five years from a single list put forward by the sole legal party, the Popular Rally for Progress. Last legislative elections Apr. 1987.

Present government

President; C.-in-C. of the Armed Forces Hassan Gouled Aptidon

Prime Minister; Planning and Land Development Barkat Gourad Hamadou

Principal members of Council of Ministers Mohammed Djama Elabe (Finance and National Economy); Moumin Bahdon Farah (Foreign Affairs and Co-operation); Khayreh Alaleh Hared (Interior, Posts and Telecommunications); Elaf Orbis Ali (Justice and Islamic Affairs); Hussein Barkad Siraj (National Defence)
Ruling party Popular Rally for Progress (Rassemblement populaire pour le progrès).
Chairman Hassan Gouled Aptidon
First Deputy Chairman Barkat Gourad Hamadou
Secretary-General Moumin Bahdon Farah.

Justice
The judicial system is based on a combination of French civil law, traditional practice, and Islamic law. There is a Court of First Instance and a Court of Appeal in Djibouti. The death penalty is nominally in force. There were no executions between 1985 and mid-1988.

National symbols
Flag. Two horizontal stripes, light blue over light green, with a white equilateral triangle based on the hoist; in the centre of the triangle there is a red five-pointed star.
Festivals. 1 May (Workers' Day); 27 June (Independence Day).

INTERNATIONAL RELATIONS

Affiliations
NAM; OAU; ACP; Arab League; ICO.

Defence
Total Armed Forces: 4,230 inclusive Gendarmerie.
Terms of service: voluntary.
Army: 2,780.
Navy: 60.
Air Force: 100.
Para-Military: 1,200.

ECONOMY

Currency
The unit is the Djiboutian franc, divided into 100 centimes.

National finance
Budget. The 1987 est. budget was for expenditure of US$163 million and revenue of US$117 million.
Inflation. 9.2%.

Gross Domestic Product
Estimated total GDP US$333 million (GNP), per capita US$1,070 (overall size of economy ranking 158 in the world by size).
Unemployment. Over 50%.

COMMUNICATIONS

Railways
There are 485 miles/781 km of railways.

Roads
There are 1,886 miles/3,037 km of roads, of which 400 km are bituminized.

Aviation
Air Djibouti (Red Sea Airlines) provides domestic and international services (international airport is at Ambouli, near Djibouti).

Shipping
Djibouti is an important port serving the regional hinterland.

Telecommunications
There are 7,300 telephones. The state-controlled RTD broadcasts both radio and television programmes; 30,000 radio sets and 10,000 televisions in use.

EDUCATION AND WELFARE

Education
School population. There were (1987–88) some 26,000 pupils in primary schools (aged 7–13) and over 6,000 in secondary schools.
Schools. 59 schools with some 600 teachers at primary level, and 21 secondary schools.
Literacy. 80%.

Health
Djibouti has 18 hospitals and clinics, with some 1,300 beds in all, and 90 doctors.

DOMINICA
Commonwealth of Dominica

GEOGRAPHY
Approximately 29 miles/47 km long and 16 miles/26 km wide, the volcanic island of Dominica is located in the windward group of the West Indies. It covers a total area of 290 miles^2/751 km^2 divided into ten parishes. A mountainous ridge forms the spine of the island, from which central region the Clyde, Pagua, Roseau, Rosalie and Layou rivers flow down to the indented coastline. Morne Diablotin in the northern half of the island is Dominica's highest point, rising to 4,747 ft/1,447 m above sea level. 'Boiling Lake' is situated in the south. The rich soil supports dense tropical vegetation over 41% of the total surface area, but only 9% of the land is arable.

Climate
Tropical: warm temperatures and high humidity. Small mean monthly temperature range from 78°F/25.6° to 90°F/32.2°C. Rainy season (periodic hurricanes) June–Oct. Rainfall varies from 69 in/1,750 mm average on the coast to 246 in/6,250 mm inland. Roseau: Jan. 76°F/24.2°C. July 81°F/27.2°C. Average annual rainfall 77 in/1,956 mm.

Cities and towns
Roseau (capital)	8,279
Portsmouth	2,220

Population
Total population is 79,000. At the last census, 91.2% of the population were Black; 6.0% were of mixed race; 1.5% Amerindian (including 500 Caribs); 0.5% White.
Birth rate 2.08%. **Death rate** 0.52%. **Rate of population increase** (1980–87) 1.56%. **Age distribution** under 15 = 37.6%, over 65 = 4.6%. **Life expectancy** female 76.5; male 72.8; average 74.

Religion
Predominantly Christian. An estimated 80% of the

population is Roman Catholic (approx. 65,000 members). Other Christian denominations include Anglicans; Methodists; Pentecostals; Baptists; Church of Christ; Seventh Day Adventists.

Language

Official language is English, although the local French patois is widespread.

HISTORY

Dominica was first inhabited by Arawak Indians who were displaced by Caribs moving north from South America. Attempts by Europeans to settle on the island failed owing to resistance by the Caribs and it was not until the mid-18th century that the French began to colonize the island. Dominica was seized by the British in 1759 and remained a British possession apart from brief periods of French rule. African slaves were brought to the island as labour until the abolition of the slave trade and the emancipation of the slaves in the early 19th century.

Universal suffrage was introduced in 1951 and in 1967 the island gained full internal autonomy as an Associated State. Edward LeBlanc, the leader of the ruling Dominica Labour Party (DLP), became premier. In 1974 LeBlanc retired and was succeeded by Patrick John, who led the country to full independence from Britain as a republic on 3 Nov. 1978. Controversial measures introduced by the DLP government caused a political crisis in 1979 which culminated in the resignation of John and his cabinet. An interim government was installed until elections were held in July 1980. The elections were won by the conservative Dominica Freedom Party (DFP), led by Eugenia Charles who became prime minister. There were two coup attempts in 1981, both involving John, who was eventually tried for his involvement. The DFP retained power in elections held in 1985, defeating the Labour Party of Dominica, formed from the DLP and other left-wing parties.

CONSTITUTION AND GOVERNMENT

Executive and legislature

As an independent republic within the Commonwealth, Dominica has a president who holds titular executive authority (and who is elected by the legislature, with a maximum of two five-year terms in office); in practice the president acts as a constitutional head of state, appointing the prime minister to exercise the executive role as head of the Cabinet. The unicameral 30-member House of Assembly is composed of 21 elected representatives and nine appointed senators, serving a five-year term. Last general election July 1985.

Present government (1 Feb. 1990)

President Sir Clarence Augustus Seignoret

Prime Minister; External Affairs; Finance; Defence; Economy (Mary) Eugenia Charles

Principal ministers Charles Maynard (Agriculture; Industry; Tourism; Lands and Survey; Trade); Brian Alleyne (Legal Affairs; Immigration and Labour; Attorney General).

Justice

The system of law is based on English common law. The highest court is the British Caribbean Court of Appeals; local administration of justice is through the magistrates' courts. The death penalty is in force. There was one execution between 1985 and mid-1988. Capital offences: murder.

National symbols

Flag. Dark green with a cross composed of three stripes – yellow, black and white; in the centre there is a red disc with a diameter equal to two-thirds of the flag's width.

Festivals. 6–7 Feb. (26–27 in 1990, Carnival); 1 May (7 May in 1990, Labour Day); 2 July (Caricom Day); 3–4 Nov. (Independence Day).

Vehicle registration plate. WD.

INTERNATIONAL RELATIONS

Affiliations

Commonwealth; OAS; Caricom; OECS; Francophonie.

ECONOMY

Currency

The unit is the EC dollar, divided into 100 cents.

National finance

Budget. The 1988 budget was for expenditure of US$52 million and revenue of US$60 million.

Inflation. 4.9%.

Gross Domestic Product

Estimated total GDP US$125 million (GNP), per capita US$1,320 (overall size of economy ranking 175 in the world by size).

Economically active population. The total number of persons active in the economy is 25,000; unemployed: 20%.

Sector	% of workforce
industry	32
agriculture	40
services*	28

* services figure includes elements unassigned to other categories.

Energy and mineral resources

Minerals. Pumice mining.

Electricity. Capacity: 7,000 kWh; production: 16 million kWh; 190 kWh per capita (1988).

Bioresources

Agriculture. 9% of the land is arable, 13% is under permanent cultivation and 3% is meadow or pasture. Hurricanes in 1979 and 1980 severely weakened the Dominican agricultural infrastructure.

Crop production: (1987 in tons/tonnes) bananas 71,650/65,000; coconuts 2,364/2,145. Other significant crops include citrus fruits; cocoa; yams.

Livestock numbers: (1987) cattle 4,000; pigs 9,000; sheep 4,000; goats 6,000; (1986) poultry 115,000.

Forestry. 4% of the land area is forested.

Industry and commerce

Industry. The principal industries are tourism and agricultural processing. Growth rate: (1987) 4.6%.

Commerce. Exports: (1987) US$46 million or 36.9% of the GNP. Imports: US$66 million or 53% of the GNP. Principal exports include bananas; coconuts; grapefruit; soap; galvanized sheets. Imports include foodstuffs; oil and fats; manufactured goods; machinery and equipment. Chief trading partners are UK; Jamaica; US.

Trade with UK. In 1987, the Commonwealth of Dominica imported UK goods worth £8,416,000 and exported goods to the UK worth £32,423,000.

Tourism. (1987) 41,200 visitors.

COMMUNICATIONS

Railways

There are 282 miles/454 km of railways.

Roads

There are 466 miles/750 km of roads, of which 310 miles/500 km are bituminized.

Aviation

LIAT provides domestic services (main airports are Melville Hall Airport and Canefield Airport at Roseau).

Shipping

Roseau, and Portsmouth further north, are the main ports.

Telecommunications

There are 4,600 telephones in a fully automated network. There is no television broadcasting (although some households have cable services), one government radio station and two religious ones, and some 28,000 radios in use.

EDUCATION AND WELFARE

Education

School population. 18,513.

Schools. 15,262 pupils attended 65 primary schools and a further 3,251 children received secondary education in ten schools.

Universities. There are two colleges of higher education.

Literacy. 80%.

Health

(1988) The Commonwealth of Dominica supports three hospitals with 245 beds and 31 doctors, as well as four dentists, ten pharmacists, 273 nursing staff, 44 health clinics and seven health centres.

DOMINICAN REPUBLIC

República Dominica

GEOGRAPHY

Occupying the eastern two-thirds of the West Indian island of Hispaniola in the Caribbean, the Dominican Republic covers a total area of 18,699 miles^2/48,442 km^2 including a number of small coastal islets. Running north-west–south-east, the forested Cordillera Central (average elevation 5,905 ft/1,800 m) dominates the landscape reaching a maximum elevation of 10,417 ft/3,175 m at Pico Duarte (the highest point in the Caribbean). In the north central region, the fertile Cibao valley is the focus of the republic's agricultural activity. The western part of the country is largely semi-arid desert with some savannah-type vegetation. Principal rivers are the Yaque del Norte, the Yaque del Sur and the Yuna in the east. To the southwest, the very low-lying Lake Enriquillo bisects the mountains east-west. 23% of the land is arable and 14% is forested. The republic is divided into 27 provinces, the most populous of which is the Distrito Nacional (including the nation's capital city Santo Domingo), supporting approximately 25% of the total population.

Climate

Tropical maritime, wet season May–Nov. with periodic hurricanes June–Nov. Most rain falls in the north and east regions. Average rainfall is 53 in/1,346 mm (extremes: 98 in/2,500 mm in north-east and 20 in/500 mm in west). Mean annual temperature ranges from 70°F/21°C (mountainous regions) to 77°F/25°C (plains and coast). Santo Domingo: Jan. 75°F/23.9°C. Jul. 81°F/27.2°.

Cities and towns

Santo Domingo (capital)	1,313,172
Santiago de los Caballeros	278,638
La Romana	91,571
San Pedro de Macoris	78,562
San Francisco de Macoris	64,906
Concepcion de la Vega	52,432

Population

Total population is 6,867,000 of which 55.7% live in urban areas. Population density is 367/138.5 persons per miles^2/km^2. The majority of the population are of Spanish or Spanish-Indian extraction (mulatto 73%; White 16%; Black 11%). A small Japanese colony farms the Constanza Valley.

Birth rate: 3.36%. **Death rate**: 0.75%. **Rate of increase**: 2.61%. **Age distribution** under 15 = 39.7%; over 65 = 3.2%. **Life expectancy** female 68; male 64; average 66.

Religion

Roman Catholicism is the official state religion, claiming over 90% of the population. Protestant denominations include the Baptist, Evangelist and Seventh Day Adventist Churches. There are also small (German) Jewish and Baha'i communities.

Language

Spanish is the official language, spoken by 6.57 million people; a further 130,000 speak a French (Haitian) creole.

HISTORY

The earliest inhabitants of the Dominican Republic were Taino Arawak Indians, who lived throughout the island which Columbus's expedition in 1492 named Hispaniola. The island, and its capital, Santo Domingo, became the centre of Spanish rule and activity in the region, until Spain developed its possessions in mainland Central and South America and consequently attached less importance to the island territory. A division between Spain and France in 1697 left the Spanish in control of the portion in the east and centre of the island, which remained under-developed and sparsely inhabited compared with French Haiti in the west. The territory proclaimed its independence from Spain in 1821, but was immediately invaded and subjugated by Haiti, which had become independent in 1804; this conflict was the latest of several rounds of fighting stretching back to the late 18th century.

The Haitians were ejected in 1844 and the Dominican Republic was proclaimed independent. Wars with the Haitians and the need for foreign help persuaded the Dominicans to accept the re-establishment of Spanish colonial rule in 1861. This soon proved unacceptable, and after two years of war the country again regained its independence in 1865. Political and economic instability followed, with only the dictatorship of Ulises Heureaux providing a period of strong rule between 1882 and 1899.

Inability to repay foreign debts led to growing United States involvement in the country, and in 1905 the establishment of a customs receivership by the US. The US intervened militarily between 1916 and 1924, when US troops administered the country. In 1930 the army commander, Gen. Rafael Trujillo Molina, was elected president and proceeded to establish a ruthless dictatorship, through his own presidencies and through those of puppet presidents, until his assassination in May 1961. The president at the time of Trujillo's death, Dr Joaquín Balaguer, remained in office until Jan. 1962, when a Council of State took over to prepare for presidential elections. These were held in December and were won by Dr Juan Bosch of the left-wing Partido Revolucionario Dominicano (PRD). Bosch, however, was overthrown in a military coup in Sept. 1963 and replaced by a three-man civilian junta. In Apr. 1965 the junta was in turn overthrown by a revolt of pro-Bosch supporters. Civil war broke out and US troops intervened to stop the fighting. An interim administration was set up to govern until fresh elections could be held. These were held in June 1966, and were won by Balaguer, now of the conservative Partido Reformista (PR), defeating ex-president Bosch. Balaguer was re-elected in 1970 and 1974 after the PRD had boycotted the poll in protest at Balaguer's decision to seek further terms in office. Bosch resigned from the PRD in 1973 to form his own party, and in 1978 the PRD candidate was Antonio Guzman. Guzman defeated Balaguer, but only after pressure from the US had prevented an attempt to stage a pro-Balaguer coup.

Guzman committed suicide in 1982 (after allegations of fraud were made against his family) following the election of Dr Jorge Salvador Blanco as his successor. In 1984 and 1985 there were serious disturbances in protest at price rises in essential goods, as part of an IMF austerity programme.

Violence also preceded the 1986 elections and the count was suspended after allegations of fraud by the PRD candidate, Jacabo Majluta Azar. In the event Majluta accepted defeat by Balaguer by a narrow margin. Former president Blanco was put on trial accused of corruption and, in Dec. 1988, was convicted and sentenced to 20 years' imprisonment.

CONSTITUTION AND GOVERNMENT

Executive and legislature

The head of state is an executive president, directly elected for a four-year term, who appoints and presides over the cabinet. The legislature is a bicameral National Congress consisting of a 120-member Chamber of Deputies and a 20-member Senate. The Congress is also directly elected for a four-year term. Last presidential and legislative elections 16 May 1986.

Present government (1 Feb. 1990)

President Dr Joaquín Balaguer
Vice-President Carlos Morales Troncoso
Principal members of the Cabinet Dr Rafael Bello Andino (Minister at the Presidency); Sr Guillermo Caram (Finance); Sr Joaquín Ricardo (Foreign Affairs); Sr Manuel Estrada Medina (Defence; Interior and Police).

Justice

The system of law is based on the French civil code. The highest court is the Supreme Court of Justice (which consists of eight judges chosen by the Senate, and the Procurator-General, appointed by the executive). Three tiers of courts – communal, first instance, and appeal courts – are supplemented by a system of land courts created by special legislation. The death penalty was abolished in 1966.

National symbols

Flag. The flag is divided by a white cross into four quarters, the first and fourth being blue and the second and the third red. In the centre of the cross there is the state coat of arms.
Festivals. 26 Jan. (Duarte); 27 Feb. (Independence Day); 14 Apr. (Pan American Day); 1 May (Labour Day); 16 July (Foundation of Sociedad la Trinitaria); 16 Aug. (Restoration Day); 12 Oct. (Columbus Day); 24 Oct. (United Nations Day).
Vehicle registration plate. DOM.

INTERNATIONAL RELATIONS

Affiliations

OAS; SELA.

Defence

Total Armed Forces: 20,800. Terms of service: voluntary.
Army: 13,000; 14 light tanks (AMX-13, M-41A1).
Navy: 4,000; 17 patrol and coastal combatants.
Air Force: 3,800; eight combat aircraft.

ECONOMY

Currency

The unit is the peso, divided into 100 centavos.

National finance

Budget. The 1987 budget was for expenditure of US$898 million and revenue of US$796 million.
Balance of payments. The balance of payments (current account, 1987) was a deficit of US$148 million.
Inflation. 16.7%.

Gross Domestic Product

Estimated total GDP US$4,910 million, per capita US$800 (overall size of economy ranking 84 in the world by size).
Economically active population. The total number of persons active in the economy is 2,500,000; unemployed: 25.8%.

Sector	% of workforce	% of GDP
industry	18	30
agriculture	49	17
services*	33	53

* services figure includes elements unassigned to other categories.

Energy and mineral resources

Minerals. Output: (1982) bauxite 167,825 tons/152,250 tonnes; (1983) ferronickel 57,626 tons/52,278 tonnes; gold 354,023 troy oz.; silver 1.329 million oz.

Electricity. Capacity: 1,331,000 kW; production 3,968m kWh; 560 kWh per capita (1988).

Bioresources

Agriculture. 23% of the land area is arable, 7% is under permanent cultivation and 43% is meadow or pasture. Sugar cultivation is the primary agricultural activity.

Crop production: (1986 in tons/tonnes) sugar cane 8/7.3; coffee 60,627/55,000; rice 328,485/298,000; cocoa 40,785/37,000; leaf tobacco 13,228/12,000; bananas 465,171/422,000.

Livestock numbers: (1987) cattle 2.06 million; sheep 84,000; pigs 2,64 million.

Forestry. 14% of the land area is forested.

Fisheries. Total catch: (1981) 15,983 tons/14,500 tonnes.

Industry and commerce

Industry. Industrial production growth rate 30% (1987). Key products are sugar; textiles; cement; tobacco. Other significant industrial activities include tourism and ferronickel/gold mining. Over 114,639 tons/104,000 tonnes of refined sugar were produced in 1983 and 1,058,208 tons/960,000 tonnes of cement in 1981.

Commerce. The Dominican Republic's exports totalled US$711 million or 13% of the GDP in 1987; imports amounted to US$1,800 million or 32% of the GDP. Principal exports: (1983) sugar US$263.5 million; coffee US$76.3 million; ferronickel US$83.5 million; Doré US$164.5 million. Chief imports include foodstuffs; petroleum; cotton and fabrics; chemicals; pharmaceuticals.

Trade with UK. In 1988, the Dominican Republic imported UK goods worth £17.23 million and exported goods to the UK worth £8.52 million.

Tourism. (1986) 800,000 visitors.

COMMUNICATIONS

Railways

There are 994 miles/1,600 km of railways.

Roads

There are 10,632 miles/17,120 km of roads.

Aviation

Alas del Caribe, C por A provides domestic services and Dominicana de Aviacion C por A provides international services (international airports are at Santo Domingo and Puerto Plata).

Shipping

Santo Domingo is the main Caribbean port, with Puerto Plata on the north coast the main Atlantic ocean port. The merchant marine includes eight cargo ships of over 1,000 GRT.

Telecommunications

There are 190,000 telephones in a system based on the island-wide radio relay network. There are 800,000 radios, ten government radio stations and over 100 commercial stations, 500,000 television sets, a government station broadcasting on two channels, and five commercial television stations.

EDUCATION AND WELFARE

Education

Elementary education is free and compulsory between the ages of seven and 14. All secondary, vocational or special educational institutions are either entirely state-maintained or state-aided.

School population. 1,474,179.

Schools. 1,121,851 pupils attended 5,956 primary schools with 20,607 teaching staff in the academic year 1983–84 (one teacher per 54 pupils); a further 352,328 pupils attended secondary schools.

Universities. In 1985–86, 88,000 students were registered at the University of Santo Domingo (founded 1538) and at the Republic's five other universities.

Literacy. 74%.

Health

(1980) 2,142 doctors, 8,953 hospital beds.

ECUADOR
República del Ecuador
(Republic of Ecuador)

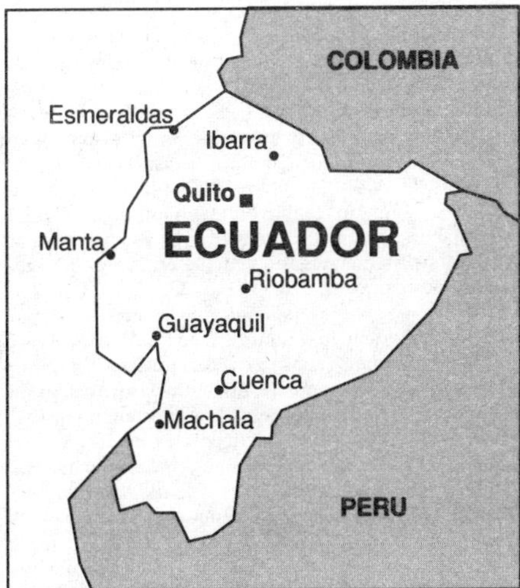

GEOGRAPHY

Located on the north-western coast of South America, astride the equator, Ecuador covers a total area of 109,455 miles²/283,561 km² including the Galápagos Islands, divided into 20 provinces. The Andean Sierras traverse the country north–south, comprising two major ranges (East and West Cordillera) divided from each other by intermontane basins, and separating the western coastal plains (Costa) from the alluvial forest plains in the east (Oriente). The Sierra highlands rise to 20,561 ft/6,267 m at Chimborazo and to 19,344 ft/5,896 m at Cotopaxi, the world's highest active volcano. Two river systems dominate the Ecuadorian hydrology: the Rio Guayas (draining west) and the Napo-Aguarico basin, draining eastwards. The south-western coastal sector experiences greatest aridity, supporting savannah-type vegetation, but over half the total surface area is forested, consisting largely of lowland rainforest, and 9% is either arable or under permanent cultivation. Approximately 49% of the population inhabit the lowland Costa, 47% live in the Sierra and 3% in the Oriente basin. Ecuador lies in a seismically active zone; volcanic activity also characterizes the basaltic Galápagos Islands, 621 miles/1,000 km west of the republic's Pacific Coast.

Climate

Varies according to altitude, though predominantly hot and humid. Rainfall decreases north-south on the coast from 79 in/2,000 mm to 8 in/200 mm; the coastal dry season is May–Dec., twice as long as the dry spell in the central sierra which only lasts June–Sept. Temperatures decrease with altitude. Hot, equatorial conditions in the Oriente, with even annual rainfall distribution. Quito: Jan. 59°F/15°C. July 58°F/14.4°C. Average annual rainfall 44 in/1,115 mm. Guayaquil: Jan. 79°F/26.1°C. July 75°F/23.9°C. Average annual rainfall 39 in/86 mm.

Cities and towns

Guayaquil	1,509,108
Quito (capital)	1,093,278
Cuenca	193,012
Machala	137,321
Portoviejo	134,393
Manta	129,578
Ambato	122,139
Esmeraldas	115,138

Population

Total population is 10,203,000 of which 52.8% live in urban areas. Population density is 93 persons per mile²/35.9 per km². Ethnic composition: Indian 25%; Mestizo 55%; Spanish 10%; African 10%. The Puruha in Chimbaraza province constitute the largest (and most impoverished) Indian community. Most of the indigenous peoples inhabit the intermontane basins in the Sierra region. The Amazonian Jivaro are scattered throughout the Oriente.

Birth rate: 3.68%. **Death rate**: 0.81%. **Rate of population increase** (1980–87) 2.87%. **Age distribution** under 15 = 41.8%; over 65 = 3.7%. **Life expectancy** female 68; male 63; average 66.

Religion

No official religion, although Roman Catholicism is the prevalent Christian doctrine (90%) with three archdioceses and ten dioceses. The Baptists, Methodists and Episcopalians are also represented as are Baha'i and Jewish minorities in Quito and Guayaquil.

Language

Spanish is the official language spoken by some 93% of the population. The principal Indian language is Quechua. The Jivaros and Colorados peoples converse in their own dialects.

HISTORY

The highlands around the present capital, Quito, had been settled by Indian tribes for thousands of years, the Incas being the latest and most sophisticated. On the execution of the Inca emperor Atahualpa by the Spanish in 1533, Chief Rumiñavi marshalled the remains of the Inca army and fought on against the twin attacks of Pedro de Alvarado and Sebastián de Benalcázar before being executed in 1534. The Spanish refounded the city of Quito on the same site in 1534.

The colonial system, which very quickly took shape, endured for 300 years, a small conservative highland Spanish elite dominating economic and social affairs. Although these aristocrats overthrew the local Spanish administration in 1809, primarily to break the Spanish trade monopoly, they were more afraid of instigating popular rebellion amongst the landless peasant populations and chumas (rabble) of the cities than of Spanish retribution from the viceroyalty of Peru (1544–1824), which duly quelled this protest and a subsequent more popular one in 1810–12.

The thrust for independence came from another source, the emerging landowning and commercial bourgeoisie, centred on the coastal city of Guayaquil, who wished for free trade and the opportunity to expand the cocoa industry. They needed outside assistance which came from the armies of the Argentinian general José de San Martín and that of the Venezuelan Simón Bolívar, and at the Battle of Pichincha in 1822 they secured independence, in which a neutral Quito was not included. This reinforced the existing antagonism between the Highlands and the coast, which has continued up to the present. From 1822 to 1830 the area administered from Quito formed part of Bolívar's visionary state of Gran Colombia (1821–30) until gaining full independence in 1830 under the presidency of Gen. Juan José Flores, a Venezuelan.

During the period 1830–95, 21 different governments and juntas occupied the presidency 34 times, with only six completing their terms. Most of these governments represented conservative highland landowners (suffrage was extended to literate adults in 1861) who remained antagonistic to the anti-clerical, market-oriented agro-exporters of the coast. The latter triumphed in the Liberal Revolution of 1895 led by Eloy Alfaro (president 1895–1901, 1906–11). Apart from curbing the power of the Church, the Liberals sought to promote civil rights, public health and education while improving the country's infrastructure and financial climate. Alfaro was killed by pro-clericals in 1912 and was succeeded by Gen. Leónidas Plaza, who managed to effect a compromise between the coastal and highland power blocs. During World War I Liberal governments borrowed heavily to stave off the economic and social crisis which resulted from plummeting world prices, particularly those for cocoa, the country's principal export crop. Despite criticism from the conservative highland landlords, the Liberals hung onto power until 1925 when rampant inflation and the spiralling cost of living released a storm of social unrest which the army felt only it could control. The 1925 July Revolution of young officers introduced a brief reformist phase, which initiated a measure of social concern that outlived the government's collapse. A series of fiscal reforms under Pres. Isidro Ayora (1925–31) served to restore the status quo but the ensuing world crisis from 1928 onwards halved the country's export revenues, and Ayora was overthrown in a coup. Twenty-one governments held temporary office between 1931 and 1948, a period of economic instability during which political life was dominated by José Maria Velasco Ibarra (who succeeded to the presidency five times, the last being 1968–72), whose rich brand of populist politics never tackled the underlying social and economic problems or threatened the power of the elites. Velasco's overthrow by the military in 1947 led, paradoxically, to 12 years of more liberal government sustained by a boom in the export of coffee and bananas. An increase in state spending, particularly during the presidency of Galo Plaza (1948–52) encouraged the growth of a modernizing capitalist class, linked to the commercial and banking sector, at the expense of those landed interests who refused to adapt.

Velasco was returned to office in 1960 with the greatest popular mandate in the country's history, but his attempt to present himself as a left-wing reformer proved alarming to the army at the time of the Cuban revolution, and he was ousted in 1962. His successor, Carlos Julio Arosemena, was overthrown in July 1963. The army then chose to remain in power until 1966, intent on delivering major reforms, but the military government collapsed because of internal dissent, and two interim presidents maintained formal control until Velasco was returned to the presidency in 1968. His tenure was a display of erratic and arbitrary leadership, with Congress dissolved in 1970. The military, with the prospect of utilizing newly tapped oil wealth for structural change, once more deposed Velasco on 15 Feb. 1972, only to divide themselves on how they should simultaneously rule and develop the country. Power was returned to the reformist coalition government of Pres. Jaime Roldós who, elected on 29 Apr. 1979, was beset by political and economic difficulties, and only succeeded in galvanizing the country around a border dispute with Peru in 1981. Roldós' death in a plane crash (1981) brought Osvaldo Hurtado (1981–84) to the presidency at a time of falling oil revenues, high inflation and a burgeoning foreign debt. His introduction of austerity programmes to meet the crisis led to large-scale social unrest. León Febres Cordero (1984–88) of the conservative National Reconstruction Front, elected president in a run-off election in May 1984, adopted ultimately unsuccessful monetarist policies towards the same end. Rodrigo Borja of the Social Democratic Left, who became president in run-off elections in May 1988, pledged to form a national consensus of government, business and labour to cope with the economic crisis. However by Aug. 1988 he was forced to announce emergency economic measures which resulted in general strikes called by trade unions in Nov. 1988 and July 1989. A new oil company Petroecuador created in Sept. 1990 took back into state ownership the trans-Amazonian pipeline and Amazonian oilfields.

CONSTITUTION AND GOVERNMENT

Executive and legislature

Under the 1979 Constitution the executive president is directly elected, together with a vice-president for a single four-year term (last election May 1988). The president appoints and presides over the Cabinet. The legislature, the 72-member unicameral National Congress, consists of 60 members elected on a provincial basis every two years and 12 members elected for a four-year term on a national basis.

Present government

President Sr Rodrigo Borja Cevallos
Vice-President Sr Luis Parodi
Principal members of the Cabinet Sr Andres Vallejo (Government and Justice (Interior)); Gen. (retd) Jorge Félix (Defence); Sr Jorge Gallardo (Finance and Public Credit); Sr Diego Cordovez (Foreign Affairs); Sr Jacinto Jouvin (Industry, Commerce and Integration).

Administration

Ecuador comprises 20 provinces, including the Galápagos Islands, each administered by an appointed governor.

Justice

The system is based on codified civil law. The highest court is the Supreme Court in Quito; each province has its superior court as well as lower and special courts. The death penalty was abolished in 1906.

National symbols

Flag. Three horizontal stripes of yellow, blue and red; in the centre of the flag there is the state coat of arms.

Festivals. 6–7 Feb. (26–27 in 1990, Carnival); 1 May (Labour Day); 24 May (Battle of Pichincha); 24 July (Birth of Simón Bolívar); 10 Aug. (Independence of Quito); 9 Oct. (Independence of Guayaquil); 12 Oct. (Discovery of America); 3 Nov. (Independence of Cuenca); 6 Dec. (Foundation of Quito).

Vehicle registration plate. EC.

INTERNATIONAL RELATIONS

Affiliations

NAM; OAS; OPEC.

Defence

Total Armed Forces: 40,000. Terms of service: conscription two years, selective; most are volunteers. Reserves: system in force, ages 18–47, numbers unknown.

Army: 33,000; about 150 light tanks (M-3, AMX-13).

Navy: 4,000 inclusive some 1,000 marines; two submarines (FRG T-209/1300); two principal surface combatants: one destroyer (US Gearing); one frigate (US Lawrence). 18 patrol and coastal combatants.

Air Force: 3,000; 52 combat aircraft (Mirage F-1JE, Jaguar S, Kfir C-2 or F21).

ECONOMY

Currency

The unit is the sucre, divided into 100 centavos.

National finance

Budget. The 1987 budget was for expenditure (current and capital) of US$2,600 million and revenue of US$1,800 million. Main items of current expenditure are education 25%; defence 11.8%; health 7.3%.

Balance of payments. The balance of payments (current account, 1987) was a deficit of $1,251 million.

Inflation. (1988) 85.7%.

Gross Domestic Product

Estimated total GDP US$10,610 million, per capita US$940 (ranking 67 in the world by size).

Economically active population. The total number of persons active in the economy was 2,800,000; unemployed: 8.5%.

Sector	% of workforce	% of GDP
industry	17	31
agriculture	52	16
services*	31	53

* services figure includes elements unassigned to other categories.

Energy and mineral resources

Oil and gas. Crude oil production (1988) 17,416,340 tons/15,800,000 tonnes, much less than in previous years because of the Mar. 1987 earthquake which destroyed 20 miles/32 km of oil pipeline and caused a loss of revenue estimated at US$950 million. Some 214,869,450 million ft^3/608,454 million m^3 of natural gas were produced (1985).

Minerals. The most important metals mined were gold 608 troy oz; silver 3,138 troy oz; zinc 14,820 kg; copper 7,960 kg (1983).

Electricity. Capacity 1,834,000 kW; production (1988) 5,777 million kWh; 565 kWh per capita.

Bioresources

Agriculture. Of the land 6% is arable; 3% is under permanent cultivation; 17% meadows and pastures. The most important crops are bananas; coffee; cocoa; sugar cane; maize; potatoes; rice; also coca for the illegal drug trade.

Crop production: (1987 in thousand tons/tonnes) sugar cane 5,732/5,200; bananas 2,631/2,387; plantains 935/848; rice 861/781; maize 414/376; potatoes 390/354; soya beans 161/146; cassava (manioc) 144/131; coffee (green) 130/118; oranges 86/78; pineapples 83/75; cocoa beans 64/58

Livestock numbers: (1987) cattle 3,884,300; sheep 1,619,800; pigs 1,293,200.

Forestry. 51% of Ecuador is forested. In 1986 307 million ft^3/8.7 million m^3 of wood was felled, almost double that felled five years earlier. Nearly 75% of the wood cut was used as fuel.

Fisheries. Total catch: (1986) 1,123,574 tons/1,019,300 tonnes.

Industry and commerce

Industry. The main industries are food processing; textiles; chemicals; fishing; timber; petroleum.

Commerce. Exports US$2,400 million, primarily petroleum (44%); coffee; bananas; cocoa products; shrimp and fish products. Imports (1988) US$1,700 million primarily transport equipment; vehicles; machinery; chemicals and petroleum. Countries exported to: US 58%; Latin America; Caribbean; EC countries. Imports came from US 28%; Latin America; Caribbean; EC countries; Japan.

Trade with UK. Ecuador imported UK goods worth £50,417,000; exports to UK totalled £13,120,000 (1988).

Tourism. (1986) 252,443 visitors.

COMMUNICATIONS

Railways

There are 599 miles/965 km of railways.

Roads

There are 22,593 miles/36,382 km of roads, of which 6,283 miles/10,118 km are concrete or bituminized.

Aviation

Empresa Ecuatoriana de Aviacion (EEA) provides international services and Transportes Aereos Nacionales Ecuatorianos (TAME) provides domestic services (international airports are at Quito and Guayaquil). In 1984 the number of passengers carried on scheduled services was 0.6 million.

Shipping

There are 932 miles/1,500 km of inland waterways. Guayaquil is the main port. Other ports are Puerto Bolívar and Esmeraldas. There are 49 merchant ships of 1,000 GRT or over. Freight loaded: (1985) 14.9 million tons/13.5 million tonnes; unloaded 2.8 million/2.5 million.

Telecommunications

There are 318,000 telephones, and the domestic facilities are generally regarded as inadequate. There are 1,900,000 radios and 600,000 televisions; several hundred radio stations and 12 television stations including the state corporation CET.

EDUCATION AND WELFARE

Education

The state provides free compulsory primary education. Private primary and secondary schools are subject to state inspection.

Schools. There were 11,480 primary schools with 1,407,898 pupils and 41,973 teachers (one per 34 pupils); 2,198 secondary schools with 955,658 pupils and 54,578 teachers (one per 18 pupils) (1983/84).

Universities. There are nine universities and three other higher education institutes with a total of 227,233 students and 8,854 teachers (one per 26 students) (1983/84).

Literacy. 85%.

Health

(1984) 11,000 doctors (one per 800 people); 337 hospitals with 15,455 beds (one per 575 people).

EGYPT

Al-Jumhuriyat Misr Al-Arabiya (Arab Republic of Egypt)

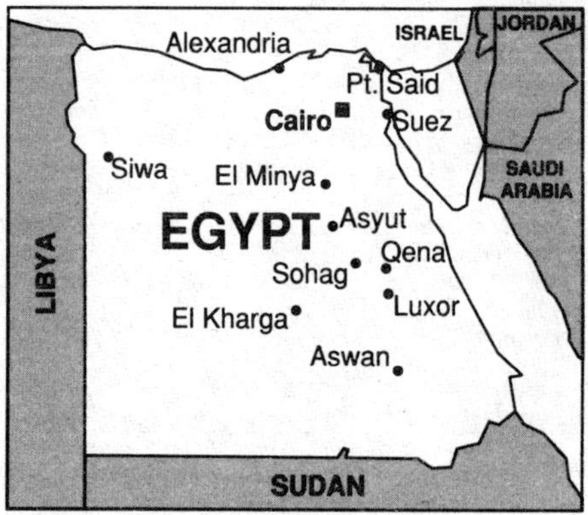

GEOGRAPHY

Situated in north-east Africa, Egypt occupies a total surface area of 386,559 miles^2/1,001,449 km^2 divided into 25 governorates. 99% of the population inhabits the fertile Nile Valley and Delta but the densely populated and intensively cultivated flood plains and oases represent only 3% (13,734 miles^2/35,580 km^2) of the country's total area: over 90% of the territory is barren desert. The Aswan High Dam (completed 1965) has regulated the flow of the Nile and relieved the threat of flooding downstream. The delta fans out north of Cairo to a width of 155 miles/250 km. South of the capital, scarp slopes mark the edge of the river valley; on either side stretch huge tracts of desert. The low-lying Western Desert (as-Sahra-al-Charbiyah) is largely arid while the sparsely populated Eastern Desert (as-Sahra-ash-Sharqiyah), dissected by wadis, supports isolated pockets of scrub vegetation and climbs south-east to 7,175 ft/2,187 m at Shayib el Banat. Egypt's highest peak rises in the south of the Sinai Peninsula (another desert region east of the Gulf of Suez) to 8,651 ft/2,637 m at Gebel Katherina. The chief islands belonging to Egypt in the Gulf of Suez and Red Sea are Shadwan, Jubal, Gafatin and Yebgerged.

Climate

Arid, rainfall low (higher on Mediterranean coast, especially during winter) and unevenly distributed. Mild winters (average day temperature 64°F/18°C) alternate with hot summers (100°F/43°C), particularly in the south. Rainfall decreases north-south from 7 in/175 mm at Alexandria to .98 in/25 mm at Cairo and .098 in/2.5 mm or just a trace near Aswan. Cairo: Jan. 56°F/13.3°C. July 83°F/28.3°C. Average annual rainfall 1.1 in/28 mm. Alexandria: Jan. 57.9°F/14.4°C. July 79°F/26.1°C. Average annual rainfall 7 in/178 mm. Ismailia: Jan. 56°F/13.3°C. July 84°F/28.9°C. Average annual rainfall 1.4 in/37 mm. Aswan: Jan. 62°F/16.7°C. July 92°F/33.3°C. Average annual rainfall trace.

Cities and towns

El-Qahira (Cairo, capital)	5,875,000
Al-Iskandariyah (Alexandria)	2,905,000
El-Gîza	1,640,000
Shoubra el-Kheima	497,000
Bur Sa'id (Port Said)	364,000
El-Mahalla el-Koubra	355,000
Tanta	344,000
El-Mansoura	323,000

Population

Total population is 51,453,000 of which 48.8% live in urban areas. Population density is 133 persons per mile^2/51.4 per km^2. The majority of the Egyptian population, along the valley and Delta, is of Hamito-Semitic origin (at least 90%). In the Western and Arabian deserts, the Bedouin nomads subdivide into the genuinely nomadic peoples and the sedentary tent-dwellers (north Sinai). The Arabdah and Bisharin (Hamiti-Beja) inhabit the southern part of the Eastern Desert; the Sa'adi and Murabatin (Arab and Berber stock) are dispersed throughout the Western Desert. The Arab-Negro Nubians inhabit the upper Nile Valley. **Birth rate** 3.97%. **Death rate** 1.19%. **Rate of population increase** 2.78%. **Age distribution** under 15 = 40.5%; over 65 = 3.9%. **Life expectancy** female 62; male 59; average 61.

Religion

An estimated 90% of the population are Muslim (predominantly Sunni) and approximately 7% (2 million) are Coptic Christians. Another 1 million Christians are divided between seven different Catholic rites and three Protestant denominations. The last census recorded 1,631 Jews in Egypt.

Language

Arabic is the official language, with several distinct dialects spoken by the Sinai/Eastern Desert Bedouin and the Western Desert nomads; also regional variants spoken in Cairo and Upper Egypt (as-Sa'id). Other ethnolinguistic minorities include To Badawi spoken by the Eastern desert Hamitic Beja, the Hamito-Sudanic language of the Nubians and the

Berber-related tongue of the Siwah tribes, located east of the Quattara depression in Egypt.

HISTORY

Egypt was the first country to develop a politically organized society: a Predynastic culture that exploited land and used domestic animals, and was able to support craftsmen, developed around 5000 BC. From about 4000 BC, two kingdoms arose in the Nile Valley and in the Delta, which were unified under one Pharaoh about 1,000 years later. In the following 3,000 years, the Egyptian state was ruled by 30 dynastic families: the agriculture-based Old Kingdom (3rd–6th dynasties) built the pyramids; the Middle Kingdom (2060–1785 BC) evolved a more complex administrative system and expanded trade with Asia; under the New Kingdom (1580–1085 BC), a great imperial era began with the realization of great architectural works. Religious cults and formal art were at their peak.

Persian kings ruled from 525–404 BC, and Alexander the Great conquered the state in 332 BC. Alexander's general, Ptolemy, and his successors continued the traditions of Pharaonic rule until the defeat of the last Ptolomaic ruler, Cleopatra, in 30 BC. As Egypt became part of the Roman Empire, new cultural traditions were imposed, including the arrival of Christianity in AD 40.

The Muslim Arab conquest of AD 632 brought little change to the traditional forms of government, but Arabic had become the official language by the 8th century. Following a second expedition by the Abbasid caliphs of Baghdad in 905, the country was thrown into turmoil until the arrival of the Fatimids, who originated in the Maghreb. Under Fatimid rule, Egypt became wealthy as the focus of East-West trade, and Cairo, founded in 969, became a centre of cultural and intellectual life.

Salah al-Din (Saladin, r.1171–1193) attempted to drive Christianity out of the eastern Mediterranean, and imposed Sunnism on Egypt. His successors, the Ayyubids, continued his policies, so that Egypt became an Islamic centre.

In the mid-13th century, the Mamelukes (originally slave-soldiers) rebelled, overran the Ayyubid Empire, set up the finest regional army, and made Egypt a Sunni Muslim stronghold, ruling until the Ottomans seized Cairo in 1517. Although the Turks ruled until 1914, their control was nominal after Napoleon's occupation (1798–1801).

In 1804, an Albanian officer in the Turkish army, Mohammad Ali, seized power and became recognized as the Viceroy of Egypt by the Sultan of Constantinople. He set up an industrial base, modernized the country's institutions, and organized the army on the European model. By 1875, his successors had won total responsibility for governing Egypt. However, in order to accelerate modernization, and to sustain his enormous personal wealth, Khedive Ismail (1863–79) borrowed so heavily that his financial difficulties opened the way to foreign intervention. The Suez Canal, opened on 17 Nov. 1869, was jointly owned by Egypt and France, but in 1875 Ismail was forced to sell his shares to Britain, and to accept British and French dual control of the budget. The British and French governments, however, were unable to bring the economic situation into any kind of balance, with Ismail resisting their increased interference until they successfully put pressure on the Ottoman sultan to order Ismail to abdicate, albeit with substantial financial compensation, on 30 June 1879.

The Ottomans installed in Ismail's place his son Tewfik, but saw a growing threat to Ottoman control in an emergent 'Egypt for the Egyptians' movement, led by Col. Arabi and focussed on the Egyptian army. In a show of strength, Britain and France sent a joint squadron to Alexandria, where serious rioting in June 1881 offered a pretext for their intervention. The French hesitated, but the British fleet bombarded Alexandria and Britain then sent a powerful expeditionary force under Sir Garnet Wolseley, who routed Arabi's forces at Tel el-Kebir and occupied Cairo (1882).

Hereafter British control was to be the dominant force in Egypt, exercised from 1883 to 1907 by Sir Evelyn Baring (Lord Cromer) as consul-general, although there was no formal British colonial authority, the Egyptian khedive remaining nominally autonomous under Ottoman suzerainty, until Britain declared Egypt a protectorate in 1914. Egypt was forced to withdraw from Sudan following the Mahdist uprising in 1881, and its role in the 1899 Anglo-Egyptian Condominium Agreement for the Sudan was nominal. Development in Egypt concentrated in particular on cotton-growing as a cash crop, and the extension and modernization of irrigation works.

Nationalism gained ground after World War I when Egypt sought independence from its protectorate status. Britain, unwilling to give up its imperial communication line and control of the Suez Canal, refused to negotiate with the nationalist leader, Saad Zaghlul. In order to quell widespread unrest, Britain unilaterally declared a limited independence for Egypt (Feb. 1922), but safeguarded its defence arrangements. In spite of nationalist resentment, Egypt became a constitutional monarchy with a bicameral parliament in 1923. An election of Jan. 1924 brought Zaghlul to power as the first democratically chosen prime minister at the head of the Wafd party. He resigned shortly afterwards, following unrest in Sudan over demands for the withdrawal of Egyptian troops from that country. Tension was eased by the 1929 Nile Waters Agreement, which allowed Egypt to use a greater share of the Nile's waters for irrigation than previously.

The 1936 Anglo-Egyptian Treaty provided for the British military occupation of the Suez Canal zone, allowing Britain to mount its North African campaign in World War II to defend Egypt and the Suez from combined German and Italian forces. These were finally repulsed at El-Alamein (Nov. 1942).

The creation of the state of Israel in 1948 destabilized the monarchy as right-wing extremists, through a series of violent demonstrations, gained control of political momentum. The political parties failed to mobilize mass support especially after Egypt's defeat in the war against Israel. There was serious rioting in Cairo, and politicians accused of colluding with the West were assassinated. On 23 July 1952, the Free Officers' Movement forced the abdication of King Farouk. The Republic was proclaimed on 18 June 1953, and under first Gen. Mohammad Neguib, then Col. Gamal Abdel Nasser (1954–70), a complete economic and constitutional reorganization was undertaken.

The government proclaimed a new constitution with the National Union as the sole party (Jan. 1956). Elections in the following year established the one-party state. In the meantime, Egypt had become a leading radical force throughout the Arab world, advancing Nasser's concept of pan-Arab socialism. Moving away from the West, Egypt expounded support for the Non-Aligned Movement and Nasser approached the USSR for military and economic aid.

In 1956, Nasser nationalized the Suez Canal Company, intending that its operation should provide the necessary revenue to finance the Aswan High Dam project (from which the US and Britain had withdrawn promises of assistance). Perceiving this both as expropriation of their property in the canal, and as a threat to a vital sea route, Britain and France prepared a military response. The pretext was set up by encouraging an Israeli invasion of Sinai (29 Oct. 1956). British and French bombing began two days later, after Egypt had rejected their ultimatum for a cease-fire and withdrawal designed ostensibly to separate the combatants. The Egyptian air force was destroyed; Egypt lost 2,000–3,000 killed or captured; Cairo was bombed and Port Said captured by the Anglo-French invasion force; but the affair ended in fiasco for Britain and France and the strengthening of Egyptian popular support for Nasser. Strong US opposition to the Anglo-French plan was combined with pressure from the UN, and a cease-fire was declared, followed by UN-supervised withdrawal of the invading forces.

In furtherance of pan-Arabist objectives, Egypt joined Syria in establishing the United Arab Republic (1958), although Syria withdrew three years later. Egypt sponsored Palestinian guerrilla attacks on Israel from the Gaza Strip, but suffered a humiliating defeat in the June 1967 war, losing Gaza and the Sinai peninsula. The Suez Canal remained blocked by sunken ships from 1967 until 1975, depriving Egypt of much-needed revenue. Egypt had to seek Western financial aid to alleviate its foreign exchange shortages, but remained dependent on the USSR for its military training and equipment.

After Nasser's death (1970), Anwar Sadat was elected president. Sadat's policy was to dismantle the socialist planning and organization established by Nasser. During the 1970s, private enterprise was encouraged alongside the public sector, press censorship was relaxed, and political parties were allowed a limited degree of freedom. US food-aid shipments became an essential economic prop for Sadat's regime. In the general elections of Oct. 1976, rival candidates campaigned freely and the multi-party system returned.

On 1 Sept. 1971 the country changed its name to the Arab Republic of Egypt. A proposed confederation with Syria and Libya was approved in a referendum, but came to nothing on the ground. In Egypt itself, Sadat was under pressure to reopen hostilities with Israel. On 6 Oct. 1973, Egyptian forces caught the Israelis by surprise in the Yom Kippur War, initially gaining ground in Sinai, although a successful Israeli counter-attack led to both sides agreeing to a cease-fire. From a position of relative strength, Egypt sought a solution to the conflict. In Nov. 1977, Sadat became the first Arab leader to visit Israel. With US mediation, the two sides agreed to a peace accord ('the Camp David agreement') in Oct. 1978, leading to the treaty of Mar. 1979. Under the terms of the treaty, Israel staged a phased withdrawal from Sinai.

The Arab League headquarters was moved from Cairo to Tunis, and there was a call for a total boycott of the Egyptian government by Arab states. Libya had already broken off diplomatic relations in 1977 over Egypt's Israel policy, and there had been a number of border clashes in that year.

Sadat was assassinated in Oct. 1981 by a group of Muslim fundamentalists, and succeeded as president by Hosni Mubarak, the leader of the ruling National Democratic Party (NDP). He was re-elected for a further six years on 5 Oct. 1987. Mubarak has sought to continue the cautious policies of the Sadat administration while successfully attempting to re-insert Egypt into the mainstream of Arab politics. For the first time in elections on 27 May 1984 voters were asked to choose a party rather than a candidate. A general election (6 Apr. 1987) again showed the NDP to be the clear winner with 338 out of 448 seats, although there were widespread allegations of electoral irregularity. Elections to the Consultative *Shura* in June 1989 again reflected the NDP's dominance of electoral politics.

Throughout Mubarak's administration, waves of unrest, in protest at economic hardship, have on occasion been exploited by Islamic fundamentalists. Frequent government crackdowns on fundamentalist activities have included widespread arrests and mass trials. The most serious threat to the regime occurred in Feb. 1986, when riots by police conscripts resulted in heavy loss of life.

An important step towards Egypt's return to the Arab fold came in 1984, when Jordan re-established diplomatic relations in a bid to revive the Middle East peace process. Since 1987, Egypt's isolation has gradually been eased, as one by one, the Arab nations have restored diplomatic ties; as of early 1990, only Libya had held back from this degree of acceptance of Egypt, which returned to the Arab League at the Casablanca summit of May 1989. After several years of negotiations, culminating in arbitration, Israel returned the disputed Taba Strip to Egypt in Mar. 1989.

CONSTITUTION AND GOVERNMENT

Executive and legislature

The executive is headed by the president, who is nominated for office by the legislature, and confirmed by popular referendum for a six-year term. The president appoints the Council of Ministers. The unicameral People's Assembly is elected by universal adult suffrage (last elections Apr. 1987). There is also a 210-member consultative council, the Shura, which has advisory powers.

Present government

President Mohammed Hosni Mubarak

Assistant Presidents Field-Marshal Mohammed Abdel-Karim, Abu Ghazalah

Prime Minister Dr Atef Sidki

Principal Ministers Youssef Sabry Abu Taleb (Deputy Prime Minister; Defence and Military Production); Dr Ahmed Esmat Abdel Meguid (Deputy Prime Minister; Foreign Affairs); Dr Kamal Ahmed Ganzouri (Deputy Prime Minister; Financial and Economic Affairs; Planning); Dr Yusuf Amin Wali (Deputy Prime Minister; Agriculture and Land Reclamation); Mohammed Abdel-Halim Moussa (Interior); Dr Mohammad Ahmed Al Razaz (Finance); Dr Youssri Mustapha (Economy and Foreign Trade); Farouk Seif al Nasr (Justice).

Justice

The system of law is a complex amalgamation of English common law, French Napoleonic code law, and Islamic law. The highest court, with the power of judicial review of legislation, is the Supreme Court. There is a Court of Cassation which is the highest court of appeal in both criminal and civil cases. At lower levels, there is a functional division between the tribunals which deal with civil, commercial and criminal matters, but all serious criminal cases go before the Assize Courts, with possible reference upwards to the Courts of Appeal. The death penalty is in force. There were over 12 executions between 1985 and mid-1988. The offences were abduction and rape.

National symbols

Flag. Three horizontal stripes of green, white and red; based on the hoist there is a light blue isosceles triangle reaching to one quarter of the flag's length; in the centre of the white stripe there is the state coat of arms.

Festivals. 18 June (Evacuation Day, Proclamation of the Republic); 23 July (Revolution Day); 6 Oct. (Armed Forces Day); 24 Oct. (Popular Resistance Day); 23 Dec. (Victory Day).

Vehicle registration plate. ET.

INTERNATIONAL RELATIONS

Affiliations

NAM; Arab League; OPEC; OAPEC; OAU; ICO; ACC.

Defence

Total Armed Forces: 445,000 (some 250,000 conscripts). Terms of service: three years (selective). Reserves: 604,000.

Army: 320,000; 2,425 main battle tanks (T-54/-55,T-62, M-60A3), 15 light tanks PT-76.

Navy: 20,000; 12 submarines (mainly Soviet Romeo and Whiskey); six principal surface combatants: one destroyer (UK 'Z'); 5 frigates (Spain Descubierta, Chinese Jianghu). 41 patrol and coastal combatants.

Air Force: 25,000; 441 combat aircraft (Mirage 5E2, Mirage 5 and 2000C, MiG21, MiG-17, Alphajet, F-4E, F-16A, CH J-6); 75 armed helicopters.

Air Defence Command: 80,000.

ECONOMY

Currency

The unit is the Egyptian pound, divided into 100 piastres.

National finance

Budget. The 1988 budget was for expenditure (current and capital) of US$23,000 million and revenue of US$15,000 million. Main items of current expenditure are defence 19.5%; housing and welfare 16%; education 12%.

Balance of payments. The balance of payments (current account, 1987) was a deficit of $3,757 million.

Inflation. (1988) 25%.

Gross Domestic Product

Estimated total GDP US$34,470 million, per capita US$490 (ranking 46 in the world by size).

Economically active population. The total number of persons active in the economy was 15,000,000; unemployed: 17%. The workforce is made up of 44% in agriculture, 36% in government and public-sector enterprises, and 20% in private enterprises, including service and manufacture.

Sector	% of GDP
industry	25
agriculture	21
services*	54

* services figure includes elements unassigned to other categories.

Energy and mineral resources

Oil and gas. Crude oil production, which is under state control, is 49 million tons/44.5 million tonnes (1988).

Minerals. Production: (1981 in tons/tonnes) phosphate rock 1.1/1 million; iron ore 2.3/2.1 million; also manganese; chrome; molybdenum; uranium.

Electricity. Capacity: 9,673,000 kW; production: 42,367 million kWh; 790 kWh per capita (1988).

Bioresources

Agriculture. Despite an extensive irrigation system (including the perennial irrigation system based on the Aswan High Dam), arable land represents only 6.5% of Egypt's total land area. The country's cultivated land area is being extended progressively by irrigation work.

Crop production: (1986 in 1,000 tons/tonnes) sugar cane 10,416/9,450; maize 4,190/3,801; tomatoes 3,131/2,840; rice 2,700/2,450; wheat 2,126/1,929; potatoes 1,405/1,275; oranges 1,280/1,170; lint cotton 478/434.

Livestock numbers: (1987) cattle 1.9 million; buffaloes 2.55 million; sheep 1.16 million; goats 1.6 million; camels 70,000.

Forestry. Total removal of roundwood: (1982) 66.7 million ft^3/1.89 million m^3, of which 63.6 million ft^3/ 1.8 million was fuel wood.

Fisheries. Total Nile and lakes fish catch: (1982) 170,857 tons/155,000 tonnes.

Industry and commerce

Industry. Two-thirds of total industrial output and almost all large-scale enterprises are in the public sector. Main industries are textiles; food processing; tourism; chemicals; petroleum; cement; construction.

Commerce. Exports: US$4,400 million; imports US$11,900 million (1987). Main exports were raw cotton; crude and refined petroleum; cotton yarn and textiles. Main imports were foods; machinery; equipment; fertilizers; durable consumer goods; capital goods.

Trade with UK. Egypt imported UK goods worth £289 million and exported to the UK goods worth £163 million (1988).

Tourism. There were 1.36 million foreign visitors (43% from Arab countries) spending £E251.3 million (1986).

COMMUNICATIONS

Railways

There are some 3,504 miles/5,643 km of railways, of which 99 miles/160 km are electrified.

Roads

There are 59,589 miles/90,000 km of roads, of which 10,055 miles/16,191 km are concrete or bituminized.

Aviation

Egypt Air and Zarkani Air Services provide domestic and international services (main airports are at Heliopolis and Alexandria, near Cairo). Passengers: (1984) 2.8 million.

Shipping

There are 2,174 miles/3,500 km of inland waterways including the Nile, Lake Nasser, the Alexandria-Cairo waterway, and the Ismailia Canal. The Suez Canal is 120 miles/193.5 km in length including the approaches, and in 1987 there were 17, 541 transits through the canal. Alexandria, situated on the north coast, on the Mediterranean, is the main port. Others include Port Said, Suez, Bur Safajah and Damietta. The merchant marine consists of 142 ships of 1,000 GRT or over.

Telecommunications

Although the telecommunications system is large it is still inadequate for the country's needs. The principal centres are Alexandria, Cairo, Al Mansurah, Ismailia and Tanta and extensive upgrading is in progress. There are an estimated 600,000 telephones. There are 12 million radios and 3.86 million televisions (1985). ERTV, the state-controlled broadcasting corporation, broadcasts radio services within Egypt (in addition to which there is a commercial Middle East Radio service), external radio broadcasts in some 30 languages, and television programmes on three channels.

EDUCATION AND WELFARE

Education

There is compulsory education in the country's six-year primary schools and free state education at primary, secondary and technical levels.

School population. Total primary, preparatory and secondary school population (1982–83): 7,766,010.

Schools. There are 5,036,608 pupils in 12,013 primary schools; 1,769,768 pupils in 3,151 preparatory schools; 517,998 pupils in 823 general secondary schools; 441,636 pupils in 639 commercial secondary schools.

Universities. There are 12 universities in Egypt with a total student population of 558,527 and 74,945 graduates. El Azhar University is the largest with 65,451 students and 5,346 graduates (1980–81). In addition, there are 33 higher commercial and industrial institutes with a total of 82,211 pupils (1982).

Health

There are an estimated 85,350 hospital beds (one per 577 people); 73,300 doctors (one per 672 people).

EL SALVADOR

República de El Salvador
(Republic of El Salvador)

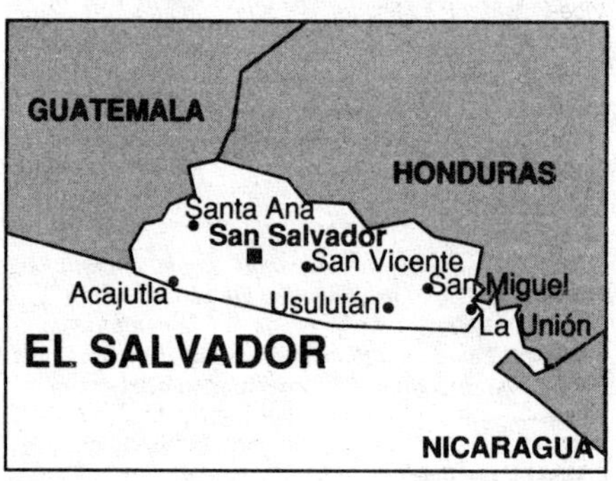

GEOGRAPHY

The smallest and most densely populated of the Central American countries, El Salvador stretches 208 miles/335 km along the Pacific coast, covering a total area of 8,259 miles^2/21,393 km^2 divided into 14 departments. Physiographically it comprises four areas: a narrow coastal strip in the south, bordering the Pacific and backed by a range of volcanic mountains (including Santa Ana, El Salvador's highest peak at 7,811 ft/2,381 m), a rich and fertile central plain (occupying 25% of the total surface area) and a range of northern mountains (the Metapan and Chalatenango uplands). The semi-navigable Lempa traverses the country east–west, bisecting the Honduras border. There are an estimated 95 miles^2/247 km^2 of inland lakes including the Lago de Ilopango and Lago de Coatepeque. The most populous departments are those of San Salvador (the capital) and Cuscatlan. 6% of the land is forested and 29% is pasture. El Salvador lies within a seismically active zone.

Climate

Varies according to altitude. Tropical, hot and humid (average temperature 73°F/23°C) in the lowlands and on the coastal belt; average rainfall between 39 in/1,000 mm and 79 in/2,000 mm, mostly falling during the single rainy season May–Sept. Rainfall increases with altitude but temperatures above 5,905 ft/1,800 m rarely exceed 44°F/18°C. San Salvador: Jan. 71°F/21.7°C. July 75°F/23.9°C. Average annual rainfall 70 in/1,775 mm. San Miguel: Jan. 77°F/25°C. July 83°F/28.3°C. Average annual rainfall 67 in/1,700 mm.

Cities and towns

San Salvador (capital)	462,652
Santa Ana	204,570
San Miguel	157,838

Population

Total population is 5,026,000 of which 42.8% live in urban areas. Population density is 609 persons per mile^2/235 per km^2. Ethnic divisions: Spainish-Indian mestizo approximately 89%; Indian 10%; White 1%. **Birth rate** 3.8%. **Death rate** 1.1%. **Rate of population increase** 2.69%. **Age distribution** under 15 = 46%; over 65 = 3.4%. **Life expectancy** female 67; male 58; average 62.

Religion

Christianity, predominantly Roman Catholic (80%). In 1982 there were approximately 200,000 Protestants. Other denominations include the Baptists; Jehovah's Witnesses; Seventh Day Adventists; Church of Jesus Christ of the Latter Day Saints (Mormons).

Languages

Spanish is the official language but Nahvatl is still spoken by some Indians.

HISTORY

The pre-Columbian inhabitants of what is now El Salvador were of the Mayan Indian language group (the Maya being the pre-eminent Middle American civilization from 1500 BC to AD 1500); the less developed Pipil tribes of the eastern and coastal regions held their lands in common until conquered and rapidly assimilated by the Spanish in the early 16th century. The Spanish came to regard the region as an outpost of their headquarters in Guatemala City. The most important factor in the political history of El Salvador, the most densely populated country in Central America, has been the ownership of land. It lacks the mountainous areas of its neighbours and has been intensively cultivated for a variety of crops, but since the late 19th century the main crops have been coffee, cotton and sugar cane for the export market.

El Salvador gained independence from Spain in 1821 as part of the United Provinces of Central America, and San Salvador became the federation's capital until the countries split in 1838. At the turn of the century the country enjoyed relative political stability, less from a respect for the political process than from the development of an economic and military oligarchy operating outside it. The new National Guard gained substantial prestige and influence, while the abolition of communal land ownership in the 1880s placed about 75% of the land in the hands of 14 families, which have held power ever since.

Following growing demand for social change the Salvadorean Labour Party (PTS) came to power in 1931, but was forced out by the army after only a few months. In 1932 the army crushed a popular insurrection led by Agustín Farabundo Martí in a campaign which saw the murder of an estimated 30,000 civilians (chiefly Indian peasants). Gen. Maximiliano Hernández Martínez became president and introduced a highly autocratic and repressive regime which lasted until 1944. The army continued in power through the Revolutionary Party of Democratic Union (PRUD) later renamed the National Reconciliation Party (PCN).

In 1972 the PCN nearly lost power to the Nationalist Democratic Union (UDN), whose presidential candidate, José Napoleón Duarte, accused the government of massive electoral fraud and attempted a coup. Disillusionment with the electoral process led to the formation of many popular organizations and guerrilla groups. There were renewed allegations of fraud after the 1977 elections, officially won by PCN candidate Gen. Carlos Humberto Romero, who was overthrown by a group of reformist officers in Oct. 1979. They formed a revolutionary junta and promised major social and political changes, including a land-reform programme, but their failure to curb the political violence of large sections of the army led to the outbreak of civil war when in Jan. 1981 the Farabundo Martí National Liberation Movement (FMLN) launched its first major military offensive.

In the new Constituent Assembly elected in 1982 Duarte's Christian Democratic Party (PDC), the largest single group, was outnumbered by right-wing members. In the presidential election of 1984 Duarte defeated the extreme right-wing Maj. Roberto d'Aubuisson of the Nationalist Republican Alliance (Arena), and in 1985 the PDC won an outright majority in the Assembly, but in 1988 Arena captured half of the 60 seats and in the presidential election of Mar. 1989 Alfredo Cristiani of Arena won 53.8% of the vote. The PDC was highly dependent on support from the United States, which has maintained a very high level of economic and military aid to El Salvador in an attempt to prevent a victory by the left-wing guerrillas, but the army has been unable to defeat the FMLN. Under Duarte attempts were made to open talks with the FMLN–FDR (Democratic Revolutionary Front), but on taking office Cristiani declared his opposition to any form of dialogue in favour of a total military solution. A major FMLN military offensive in Nov. 1989 followed the breaking down of further peace negotiations. The government declared a state of siege in the capital San Salvador, where 2,000 people were estimated to have been killed or wounded in one week of fighting. Six Jesuit priests of the University of Central America were also among the dead and five soldiers and four officers were charged with their murder in Jan. 1990.

CONSTITUTION AND GOVERNMENT

Executive and legislature

Executive power is held by the president, directly elected for a five-year term (last election 19 Mar. 1989). The president is assisted by a vice-president and a council of ministers. Legislative power is vested in the unicameral 60-member Legislative Assembly, elected for a three-year term (last elections 20 Mar. 1988).

Present government

President Sr Alfredo Cristiani Burkard

Vice-President; Minister of the Interior Sr José Francisco Merino Lopez

Principal Ministers Gen. Rafael Humberto Larios Lopez (Defence and Public Security); Sr José Manuel Pacas Castro (Foreign Affairs); Dr Oscar Alfredo Santamaría (Justice); Sr Juan Antonio Martínez Varela (Presidency); Sr Francisco Merino (Interior); Sr Rafael Alvarado Cano (Finance); Sr Arturo Zablah (Economy).

Justice

The system is based on Spanish law with some common law elements. The highest court is the Supreme Court of Justice, which has the function of judicial review of legislation; its judges, like those of the higher courts, are elected for a three-year term by the Legislative Assembly. At local level there are tribunals, and courts of first instance for more serious matters. The death penalty is in force only for exceptional crimes, and no judicial executions were recorded between 1985 and mid-1988.

National symbols

Flag. Three horizontal stripes of blue, white and blue, with the state coat of arms in its centre.

Festivals. 1 May (Labour Day); 4–6 Aug. (San Salvador Festival); 15 Sep. (Independence Day); 12 Oct. (Discovery of America); 5 Nov. (First Call of Independence).

Vehicle registration plate. ES.

INTERNATIONAL RELATIONS

Affiliations

OAS; SELA.

Defence

Total Armed Forces: 55,000 inclusive 12,000 civil defence force. Terms of service: conscription, selective, two years: all services.

Army: 39,000; 12 light tanks (AMX-13, status uncertain).

Navy: 1,000; five patrol and coastal combatants.
Air Force: 2,000; 29 combat aircraft (AC-47, A-37B, Ouragan).
Opposition: Farabundo Marti National Liberation Front (FMLN), coalition of five groups: 6,000–7,000 combatants.

ECONOMY

Currency

The unit is the colón, divided into 100 centavos.

National finance

Budget. The 1987 budget (in US$) was for expenditure (current and capital) of 642 million and revenue of 518 million. Main items of current expenditure are defence 26.8%; education 17.1%; health 7.4%.
Balance of payments. The balance of payments (current account, 1987) was a deficit of $196 million.
Inflation. (Jan. 1989) 20%.

Gross Domestic Product

Estimated total GDP US$4,750 million, per capita US$780 (ranking 87 in the world by size).
Economically active population. The total number of persons active in the economy was 1,700,000; unemployed: 30%.

Sector	% of workforce	% of GDP
industry	16	22
agriculture	40	14
services*	44	64

* services figure includes elements unassigned to other categories.

Energy and mineral resources

Electricity. Capacity: 669,000 kW; production: (1988) 1,813 million kWh; 350 kWh per capita.

Bioresources

Agriculture. Of the land 27% is arable, 8% under permanent crops, and 29% meadows and pastures. Agriculture accounts for 25% of GDP and contributes around two-thirds of exports. Coffee is the most important crop contributing 60% of export earnings. Cotton and sugar growing have declined because of the civil war.
Crop production: (1987 in tons/tonnes) maize 630,527/572,010; coffee (green) 167,532/151,984; sugar cane 165,757/150,374; millet 28,649/25,990; beans 26,468/24,012; rice 25,353/23,000.
Livestock numbers: (1987) cattle 1,024,000; pigs 398,000; goats 15,000; sheep 5,000.
Forestry. 6% of the country is forested. Some 173,003,000 ft³/4,899,000 m³ of timber was felled in 1986.
Fisheries. Total catch: (1986) 13,779 tons/12,500 tonnes.

Industry and commerce

Industry. The manufacturing sector is based on food and beverage processing. Other industries apart from food processing are textiles; clothing; petroleum products; cement.
Commerce. Exports: US$577 million, primarily coffee but also of sugar; cotton; shrimps. Imports: US$961 million, primarily petroleum products; consumer goods; foodstuffs; machinery; construction materials; fertilizer (1987). Countries exported to were US 49%; West Germany 24%; Guatemala 7%; Costa Rica 4%; Japan 4%. Imports came from US 40%; Guatemala 12%; Venezuela 7%; Mexico 7%; West Germany 5%; Japan 4%.
Trade with UK. El Salvador imported goods worth £8,186,000; exports to UK totalled £2,961,000.
Tourism. (1987) 125,000 visitors.

COMMUNICATIONS

Railways

There are about 373 miles/600 km of railways.

Roads

There are 7,554 miles/12,164 km of roads, of which 1,056 miles/1,700 km are concrete or bituminized.

Aviation

TACA International Airlines provides international services (main airport is El Salvador International Airport). Passengers: (1987) 0.4 million.

Shipping

The main ports of El Salvador are Acajutla and Cutuco. The Rio Lempa is partially navigable. Freight loaded: (1987) 0.18 million tonnes; unloaded 1.0 million tonnes.

Telecommunications

There is a nationwide trunk radio relay system. There are approximately 116,000 telephones. There are 1.2 million radios (1986) and 425,000 televisions (1987). There are 75 commercial radio stations, a state radio service and two rebel-operated stations (Radio Venceremos and Radio Farabundo Marti). There is a government TV service with two channels, and four commercial TV stations.

EDUCATION AND WELFARE

Education

Although primary education is technically compulsory there are not enough teachers or schools to provide adequate education.
Schools. There were 916 kindergartens with 62,500 pupils and 1,561 teachers (one per 40 pupils); 2,799 primary schools with 923,597 pupils and 24,295 teachers (one per 38 pupils); 285 secondary schools with 90,288 pupils and 3,880 teachers (one per 23 pupils) (1985).
Universities. Students in higher education numbered 60,994 (1985).
Literacy. 65%.

Health

There was one physician per 2,830 people and one nurse per 930 people (1984).

EQUATORIAL GUINEA
República de Guinea Ecuatorial

GEOGRAPHY

Equatorial Guinea consists of a mainland area (Río Muni) of 10,042 miles^2/26,016 km^2 on the coast of west central Africa and the islands of Bioko (formerly Acias Nguema, formerly Fernando Póo), Annobón (Paualu), Corislo, Elobey Granoe and Elobey Chico in the Gulf of Guinea, giving a total area of 10,828 miles^2/28,051 km^2. 75% of the population live on the mainland. Mangrove swamps, bordering the coastal strip are backed by the dense forests of the African plateau rising eastwards towards the Gabonese border and deeply incised by the Río Mbini (Benito) traversing the country east-west. Approximately 99 miles/160 km north-west of Rió Muni, the fertile volcanic island of Bioko rises to 9,865 ft/3,007 m at Pico de Basilé in the north, Guinea's highest point. Rugged terrain and cataracts typify the southern half of the island.

Climate

Equatorial. High temperatures and humidity. Plentiful rainfall, particularly on the coast. Bata (the capital) receives 94 in/2,388 mm annually, southern Rió Muni as much as 177 in/4,500 mm. Inland, rainfall decreases to 57 in/1,450 mm (Mikomeseng). Average yearly temperature: 93°F/26°C on the continent; 63°F/25°C on Bioko, ranging between 34°C and 17°C respectively. Monsoon deluges raise southern Bioko's rainfall total to a massive 443 in/11,250 mm per annum.

Cities and towns

Malabo (capital)	15,253
Bata	24,100

Population

Total population is 420,000 of which 27.6% live in urban areas. Population density is 42 persons per mile^2/16.1 per km^2. The majority of Rió Muni's population are Fang-Bantu (over 70%). The Mbini/Benito river divides the Ntumu Fang (to the north) from the Okak Fang in the south. Coastal-dwelling peoples include the Kombe, Mabea, Lengi and Benga. On Bioko, the indigenous peoples are the Bubi (14.7% of the total population), also of Bantu extraction.

Birth rate 4.25%. **Death rate** 2.10%. **Rate of population increase** 2.15%. **Age distribution** under 15 = 41.4%; over 65 = 4.2%. **Life expectancy** female 45; male 42; average 44.

Religion

Christianity: over 85% Roman Catholic (above 319,000 adherents). Presbyterian and Methodist missions have been established on the mainland. Local beliefs are still in evidence, particularly the Mbwiti cult.

Language

Spanish is the official language. Individual languages of different ethnic groups have been preserved e.g. Fang, Bubi, Kombe, Balemke, Bujeba (and various coastal tongues), Duala, Maka and Ibo. Pidgin English and a Portuguese-based patois are also spoken on Bioko and Annobón.

HISTORY

The island of Fernando Póo (later renamed Bioko) was discovered by the Portuguese in 1472 and ceded to Spain in 1778, together with the mainland region of Río Muni. Spain only developed the colony in earnest after the Spanish Civil War ended in 1939. Its two provinces were declared an integral part of Spain in 1959, but granted partial autonomy in 1963, when the two provinces were merged together again as Equatorial Guinea.

Independence (12 Oct. 1968) followed a constitutional referendum, and Francisco Macias Nguema, the winner of elections held in Sept. of that year, became the first president. In Feb. 1970 he outlawed all existing political parties, and in July 1972 he appointed himself president-for-life, concentrating all power in his hands and using strict security measures to suppress resistance to his increasingly brutal and arbitrary rule.

In Aug. 1979 Pres. Macias was overthrown in a coup led by his nephew, Teodoro Obiang Nguema Mbasogo; Macias was tried and later executed. The Spanish government promptly recognized and resumed financial and technical aid to the new regime of Obiang Nguema, who was reappointed president for a further seven years in Aug. 1982. A referendum in the same month approved a new constitution providing for an eventual return to civilian government. Legislative elections in Aug. 1983, and again in July 1988, returned unopposed candidates nominated by the president. In Aug. 1987 Obiang Nguema announced the formation of a 'governmental party', the Partido Democratico de Guinea Ecuatorial (PDGE). On 2 Aug. 1989 Obiang Nguema began a new presidential term after elections on 25 June in which he was the only candidate. He has survived a number of attempted coups in 1981, 1983, 1986 and Sept. 1988.

CONSTITUTION AND GOVERNMENT

Executive and legislature

The president, elected for a seven-year term (unopposed elections 25 June 1989), heads what is effectively the country's cabinet, a Supreme Military Council (composed of both military and civilians since Dec. 1981), and is also leader of its single 'party of government'. All candidates for election to the 41-member House of Representatives of the People were nominated by the president and were elected unopposed for a five-year term (election July 1988).

Present government

President of the Supreme Military Council; Minister of Defence Brig.-Gen. Teodoro Obiang Nguema
Prime Minister Capt. Cristino Seriche Bioko
Other principal members of the Supreme Military Council Isidoro Eyi Monsuy Andeme (Deputy Prime Minister; Education, Youth and Sports); Marcelino Nguema Ongueme (Minister of State, Secretary-general to the Presidency); Antonio Fernando Nve (Minister-Delegate, Economy and Financial); Santiago

Eneme Ovono (Minister-Delegate, Foreign Affairs and Co-operation); Melanio Ebendeng Nsomo (Minister-Delegate, National Defence).

Ruling party Equatorial Guinea Democratic Party (Partido Democratico de Guinea Ecuatorial).

Leader Brig.-Gen. Teodoro Obiang Nguema.

Justice

The system of law is based partly on local custom, but influenced also by Spanish law. The highest court is the Supreme Tribunal in Malabo; there are Courts of Appeal at Malabo and Bata, dealing with matters referred to them by the courts of first instance. The Constitution guarantees an independent judiciary. The death penalty is in force. There were at least 2 executions between 1985 and mid-1988. Capital offences: murder; attempting to kill or overthrow the head of state.

National symbols

Flag. Three horizontal stripes of green, white and red; based on the hoist there is a light blue isosceles triangle reaching to one-quarter of the flag's length. In the centre of the white stripe the is the state coat of arms.

Festivals. 5 Mar. (Independence Day); 1 May (Labour Day); 10 Dec. (Human Rights Day).

INTERNATIONAL RELATIONS

Affiliations

NAM; OUA; ACP; Francophonie.

Defence

Total Armed Forces: 1,400. Terms of service: voluntary.
Army: 1,100.
Navy: 200; four patrol combatants.
Air Force: 100.
Para-military: some 2,000.

ECONOMY

Currency

The unit is the CFA franc, divided into 100 centimes.

National finance

Budget. The 1987 budget (in US$) was for expenditure (current and capital) of 25 million and revenue of 23.5 million.

Inflation. (1987) -12%.

Gross Domestic Product

Estimated total GDP US$75 million (GNP), per capita US$300 (ranking 183 in the world by size).

Economically active population.

Sector	% of workforce
industry	8
agriculture	76
services*	16

* services figure includes elements unassigned to other categories.

Energy and mineral resources

Oil and gas. Exploration of crude oil deposits is taking place under concessions offered to US, French and Spanish firms.

Minerals. There are small unexploited deposits of gold; manganese; titanium; iron ore; uranium.

Electricity. Capacity: 10,000 kW; production: (1988) 17 million kWh.

Bioresources

Agriculture. Agriculture, forestry and fishing account for about 60% of GDP and almost all exports. Subsistence agriculture predominates; some 5% of the land is arable, with 4% given over to permanent crops. About 76% of the population is occupied in subsistence farming. Cocoa (185,325 acres/75,000 ha in 1986) and coffee (49,338 acres/18,000 ha) are the principal cash crops, with palm oil, palm kernels and bananas also produced for export.

Crop production: (1986 in tons/tonnes) coffee 7,716/7,000; palm-oil 7,716/7,000; palm kernels 3,197/2,900; bananas 20,944/19,000; cocoa (1984) 11,023/10,000. Food crops include cassava 60,627/55,000; sweet potatoes 38,581/35,000.

Livestock numbers: (1987) cattle 4,000; sheep 36,000; goats 8,000.

Forestry. Some 61% of the land is forested. Roundwood removals (1986 est.) 21,435,598 ft^3/607,000 m^3.

Fisheries. Total catch: (1986) 4,850 tons/4,400 tonnes.

Industry and commerce

Industry. There is little industrial activity. Timber is processed at Río Muni.

Commerce. Exports: (1986) US$39 million, comprising cocoa; coffee; timber. Chief destinations for exports were Spain 39%; Netherlands 36%; West Germany 11%; Italy 1%. Imports: (1986) $41 million, principally petroleum; food; beverages; clothing; machinery. Main trading partners: (1985) Spain 35%; Gabon 15%; Cameroon 8%; US 5%; France 4%.

Trade with UK. In 1988 Equatorial Guinea imported goods worth £1,029,000 from the UK, but made no exports to the UK.

COMMUNICATIONS

Railways

There are no railways.

Roads

There are about 730 miles/1,175 km of roads.

Aviation

Aerolineas Guinea Ecuatorial (ALGESA) and Empresa Ecuato-Guineano de Aviacion (EGA) provide international services (main airport is at Malabo).

Shipping

Malabo and Bata are the country's two main ports. The merchant marine consists of two ships of 1,000 GRT or over.

Telecommunications

There is a generally poor system although the government services are adequate. There are 2,000 telephones, 100,000 radios and 2,200 televisions (1985), and three government-operated radio stations.

EDUCATION AND WELFARE

Education

Under the Constitution education is 'the first priority of the state'. It is officially compulsory for eight years between the ages of six and 14. A major restructuring plan for primary education was planned in 1987.

School population. (1982) Enrolment at primary and secondary level was equivalent to 56% of the school-age population.

Schools. There were 550 primary schools with 65,000 pupils in 1986. There were 14 secondary schools, with 3,000 pupils and 288 teachers (one per 11 pupils). In

1986 100 Spanish teaching staff were working in the country as part of a project to assist the development of the education system.

University. There are two higher education centres, at Bata and Malabo, which are administered by the Spanish Universidad Nacional de Educación a Distancía, and had 500 students in 1986.

Literacy. 37% (1980 official estimate).

Health

Health services are limited. In 1977 there were 65 hospitals with about 3,600 beds (one per 83 inhabitants). The number of physicians had declined from 25 in 1971 to only five in 1975 (approximately one per 60,000 inhabitants).

ETHIOPIA

Hebretesebawit Ityopia
(People's Democratic Republic of Ethiopia)

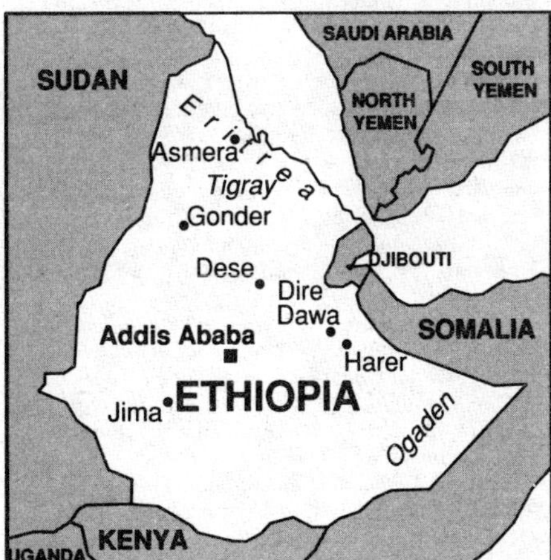

GEOGRAPHY

Ethiopia is located on the Horn of Africa, covering a total area of 471,653 miles²/1,221,900 km² divided into 15 regions. The mountainous plateau which dominates the country comprises two principal regions: the Western and Eastern highlands divided by the Great Rift Valley. The Western plateau (average height 7,874–9,842 ft/2,400–3,000 m) rises to 15,157 ft/4,620 m at Ras Deshen in the north Gonder region. Deep gorges surround the high tablelands including the Blue Nile River gorge which flows south-west from its source, Lake Tana (elevation 6,001 ft/1,829 m) encompassing the Choke Mts (high point Birhan 13,628 ft/4,154 m). In the Eastern uplands, the Bale Massif separates the mountainous courses of the South-East flowing Genale and Shebele rivers. Low-lying regions include areas of Eritrea and Tigray (north), Welo and Harerge (north-east and east). The Danikil depression descends to −380 ft/−116 m in the north-east. The fertile alluvial silts of the Blue Nile and the rich basaltic loams of the highlands are both extensively cultivated. The most densely populated regions are Shewa and Addis Ababa (capital). 12% of the total surface area is arable and about 29% is forested.

Climate

Latitudinal span and differences in elevation account for a varied climate. Plateau uplands are temperate; lowlands hot and humid. The wet season lasts Apr–Sept. (particularly June–Aug., 39 in/1,000 mm) but the north-east and eastern plains receive under 19.7 in/500 mm of rain and frequently experience severe drought. Addis Ababa: Jan. 59°F/15°C. July 59°F/15°C. Average annual rainfall 49 in/1,237 mm. Massawa: Jan. 78°F/25.6°C. July 94°F/34.4°C. Average annual rainfall 8 in/193 mm.

Cities and towns

Addis Ababa (capital)	1,412,577
Asmara	275,385
Dire Dawa	98,104
Gondar	80,886
Nazret	76,284
Dessie	68,848
Harar	62,160
Mekele	61,583
Jima	60,992

Population

Total population is 44,727,000 of which 10.6% live in urban areas. Population density is 94.8 persons per mile²/36.6 per km², concentrated in the central high plateau region, the Amhara are the dominant ethnic group. To the north, the Tigreans share the Amhara's Hamito-Semitic origins. Other people of Hamitic extraction include the Oromos (Galla) and Somalis in the south-east. The Afars inhabit a wide north-eastern belt of land stretching from Wollo to Eritrea. In 1988, there were 265,000 refugees in Ethiopia.

Birth rate 4.3%. **Death rate** 2.35%. **Rate of population increase** 1.95%. **Age distribution** under 15 = 46.2%; over 65 = 4.1%. **Life expectancy** female 49; male 45; average 47.

Religion

An estimated 40–45% of the population are Muslims and 35–40% Christians (predominantly Ethiopian Orthodox). Animist beliefs still flourish in the deep south (5–15%) and approximately 8,000 Falashas (Ethiopian Jews) remain, after the Israeli air-lifts of 1984–85.

Language

Amharic is the official language. Over 100 other provincial languages (including those of the Cushitic and Nilotic families) are still spoken but the Semitic family and its various sub-divisions remain the most important. The northern group of Semitic tongues consists primarily of Ge'Ez, Tigre and Tigrinya and the southern group of Amharic, Gurage, Hareri and Argobba. English is commercially used and understood.

HISTORY

Hominid remains dating back 1,500,000 years have been found in Ethiopia but the earliest historical civilization, known to the Egyptians as Punt, dates from the 2nd millennium BC. From the 6th century BC to the 1st century AD northern Ethiopia came under the influence of the Sabean civilization in Arabia. An independent kingdom centred on Aksum was founded in the 2nd century AD and flourished until the 9th century.

In the 4th century, Christianity was adopted as the state religion and gradually spread into the mountainous interior. As the Aksumite civilization waned in the 10th century the seat of power was transferred to central Ethiopia by the Zagwe dynasty. In 1270 they were overthrown by Amhara princes from Shoa, claiming descent from the Aksumite kingdom and Sabeans and calling themselves Solomids after King Solomon, the legendary husband of the Queen of Sheba.

Over the following four centuries the (Amhara) Solomids were almost constantly at war with Oromo invaders from the south. In 1523, Ethiopia was devastated by a Muslim invasion, only repelled with the assistance of a small Portuguese contingent in 1543. Links with Portugal led to a union of the Ethiopian Coptic Church with Rome, but the demands of Catholic missionaries forced the emperor to revoke the union in 1610 after only 15 years. When the centre of power moved east to Gondar in 1632, the empire became isolated and xenophobic, but Ethiopian civilization flourished.

By the 18th century real power had passed to Tigrayan and Oromo princes. These princes proved unable to protect Ethiopia from Egyptian attacks, and in 1855 an Amhara chief overthrew the Gondar dynasty, proclaimed himself Emperor Tewodros (or Theodore) II in 1855 and moved the capital to the mountain fortress of Magdala. There, in 1868, he committed suicide, rather than fall prisoner to a British punitive expedition sent to release British hostages. His successor, Yohannes IV, repelled Muslim incursions from Sudan but died in battle in 1889 whereupon his vassal, Menelik II, king of Shoa, assumed the throne.

Menelik pushed the borders of his empire south and eastwards, doubling its size. This brought him into contact with European colonial powers (Italians in Eritrea and Somalia, the French in Djibouti and British in north Somalia) with their own imperialist ambitions. However, an Italian invasion of Tigray was defeated at Adowa in 1896 and the colonial powers were reluctantly forced to recognise Ethiopia's independence. Following Menelik's death in 1913, his son Lij Iyasu became de facto emperor, although he was never crowned. His conversion to Islam and proposed alliance with Turkey alienated the Church and Amhara nobles who deposed him in 1916. Zauditu, Menelik's daughter, became empress with Ras Tafari as regent.

Ras Tafari secured Ethiopia's membership of the League of Nations in 1923 and embarked on a programme of modernization and reform. This accelerated after Zauditu's death and Ras Tafari's coronation in 1930 as Emperor Haile Selassie. However, in 1936 the Italians, deploying ruthlessly the weapons of modern war, conquered and occupied Ethiopia. Europe ignored Haile Selassie's appeal for protection in a moving speech at the League of Nations, but Haile Selassie was restored to power by the Allies when they drove out the Italians in 1941.

Despite his reforms of the system of government, with a constitution, a cabinet and a parliament, and the expansion of educational facilities and modernization of the armed forces, Haile Selassie retained centralized power in his own hands and never threatened the feudal system which enriched nobles at the expense of the vast majority of peasants. Popular discontent increased after an abortive coup in 1960.

Secessionist movements were also active, particularly from the late 1960s, in Eritrea. The Italian defeat in 1941 had been followed by British military administration of this former Italian colony until 15 Sept. 1952, when, according to a UN resolution, it was handed over to Ethiopia as an autonomous unit within a federal structure. Its autonomy was progressively eroded and removed, however, under the 1955 constitution and the creation of a unitary Ethiopian state on 14 Nov. 1962.

In Jan. 1974 a wave of strikes and army mutinies broke out in protest at the deteriorating economic situation, the emperor's autocratic style of government and the revelation that some 200,000 Ethiopians had died during the 1972–74 famine. To appease his critics Haile Selassie forced the entire cabinet to resign, appointed a moderate, Endalkachew Makonnen, as prime minister and promised a new constitution.

These concessions proved inadequate and Haile Selassie was deposed by the military in Sept. 1974. A Provisional Military Administrative Council (PMAC), comprising junior officers for the most part, took power. In Nov. 1974, radicals purged the PMAC, including the head of state Gen. Aman Andom, and executed 57 senior officials of the former regime. A month later, Ethiopia was declared a socialist state. Foreign investments and most industries were nationalized and the government embarked on a programme of land reform. Within the PMAC, the power struggle continued, culminating in the murder of Gen. Teferi Bante, chairman of the PMAC, in Feb. 1977 and his replacement by Col. Mengistu Haile Mariam. A radical and a staunch defender of Ethiopia's territorial integrity, Col. Mengistu stepped up the offensive against the secessionist Eritrean People's Liberation Front (EPLF) and ruthlessly eliminated rival left-wing political groups.

Taking advantage of internal disorder Somalia invaded the Ogaden in July 1977. Following initial successes, the USSR and Cuba, formerly Somalia's allies, rearmed Ethiopia and directed the Ethiopian counter-attack. By Mar. 1978, Somalia had been forced out of the Ogaden, although fighting continued intermittently until Apr. 1988 when Ethiopia and Somalia signed a non-aggression pact.

Ethiopia's alliance with the Soviet Union was sealed by a 20-year treaty of friendship and co-operation in Nov. 1978. After its victory in the Ogaden, the Ethiopian army launched an offensive in Eritrea but failed to defeat the EPLF. By the late 1970s other opponents of the regime had taken up arms: the Tigray People's Liberation Front (TPLF) in Tigray, the Oromo Liberation Front (OLF) in Wollo and Gondar, and Afars in southern Eritrea. Guerrilla warfare continued throughout the 1980s, draining Ethiopia of its financial and manpower resources. By

1988 Ethiopia's military debt to the Soviet Union amounted to $6,000 million and military expenditure absorbed half the budget.

The country suffered crippling droughts in 1980–81, 1984–85 and 1987–88; an estimated 1,000,000 people died in 1982–85 in widespread famine, which at its height attracted major Western media attention and humanitarian relief efforts (from Oct. 1984).

In 1984 the Workers' Party of Ethiopia (WPE) was established as the sole political party and a new constitution was approved by a referendum in Feb. 1987. This led to the election of a shengo (parliament) in June 1987 and the proclamation of the People's Democratic Republic of Ethiopia in Sept. 1987, with Mengistu as its first president. It also provided for the creation of five autonomous regions within Ethiopia, Pres. Mengistu's solution to the nationalities question.

The EPLF and TPLF launched a co-ordinated offensive against the government in Mar. 1988. By the end of 1988 much of Eritrea was in rebel hands and Pres. Mengistu, forced to admit that the army had suffered reverses in the north, announced a war budget under the slogan 'Everything to the War Front'. Following economic reforms in Dec. 1987, further liberalization measures were promised in Nov. 1988 in an effort to attract development aid from hitherto hostile Western countries. By the end of 1989, a string of TPLF military victories had left the rebels in effective control of most of Tigray. The prospect of renewed famine compounded the war-torn country's problem. Mengistu had made little headway in talks with EPLF leaders in 1989, but this regime did successfully survive a coup attempt by senior officers (May 1989).

CONSTITUTION AND GOVERNMENT

Executive and legislature

The president, who holds executive power as head of a 24-member State Council, is elected by the National Shengo (last Shengo elections June 1987 and May 1989). The president is also the head of the sole legal party. Government is conducted through a council of ministers headed by the prime minister.

Present government

President; President of the State Council; C.-in-C. of the Armed Forces Lt.-Col. Mengistu Haile Mariam
Vice-President; Vice-President of the State Council Lt.-Col. Fisseha Desta
Second Vice President Lt.-Col. Berhanu Bayeh
Prime Minister (acting) Ato Hailu Yimenu
Deputy Prime Ministers Ato Alemu, Ato Wole Chekol, Ato Ashagre Yigletu
Principal Ministers Ato Tesfaye Dinka (Foreign Affairs); Col. Tesfaye Wolde Selassie (Internal Affairs); Ato Tekola Dejene (Finance); Ato Wondayen Mehretu (Justice)
Ruling party Workers' Party of Ethiopia.
General secretary Lt.-Col. Mengistu Haile Mariam.
Full members of the Political Bureau Lt.-Col. Mengistu Haile Mariam; Capt. Fikre Selassie Wogderesse; Lt.-Col. Fisseha Desta; Lt.-Col. Berhanu Bayeh; Maj.-Gen. Addis Tedla; Ato Legesse Asfaw; Ato Hailu Yimenu; Ato Emanuel Amde-Mikhail; Ato Alemu Agebe; Ato Shimelis Mazengia; Ato Tesfaye Dinka.

Justice

The system of law shows influences from common law, customary law, codified civil law (it is said to be based on the Justinian Code), and Islamic law. The highest court is the Supreme Court (presided over by the Chief Justice) at Addis Ababa, and there is a circuit of high court judges visiting the provincial and district courts.

National symbols

Flag. Three horizontal stripes of green, yellow and red.
Festivals. 2 Mar. (Battle of Adowa); 6 Apr. (Victoria Day); 1 May (May Day); 12 Sep. (Popular Revolution Commemoration Day).
Vehicle registration plate. ETH.

INTERNATIONAL RELATIONS

Affiliations

NAM; OAU; ACP; Comecon (observer).

Defence

Total Armed Forces: 315,800. Terms of service: conscription, 30 months, inclusive police and border guard. Reserves: People's Militia. All citizens 18–50 do six months' training. Assigned to army, police and border guard.
Army: 313,000 (inclusive 150,000 People's Militia); 750 main battle tanks (T-54/-55, T-62).
Navy: 1,800; two frigates (Soviet Petya II); 22 patrol and coastal combatants.
Air Force: 4,000; some 150 combat aircraft (MiG-17F, MiG-21MF, MiG-23BN).

ECONOMY

Currency

The unit is the birr, divided into 100 cents.

National finance

Budget. The 1987 budget (in US$) was for expenditure (current and capital) of 1,900 million and revenue of 1,400 million.
Balance of payments. The balance of payments (current account, 1987) was a deficit of 475 million.
Inflation. (1987) -2.4%.

Gross Domestic Product

Estimated total GDP US$4,800 million, per capita US$130 (ranking 86 in the world by size).
Economically active population. Unemployed = 34% of total workforce.

Sector	% of workforce	% of GDP
industry		18
agriculture	90	42
services*		40

* services figure includes elements unassigned to other categories.

Energy and mineral resources

Minerals. There are small reserves of gold, platinum, copper and potash. Gold production: (1985/86) 923 kg; platinum 2.4 kg.
Electricity. Capacity: 330,000 kW; production: (1988) 765 million kWh.

Bioresources

Agriculture. The country's economy is based on subsistence agriculture, which accounts for over 40% of GDP and about 90% of total employment. Coffee is the most important export crop, accounting for 60% of export earnings in 1987. Drought, compounded by problems of deforestation, overgrazing, soil erosion and desertification, has led to serious famine in recent years.

Crop production: (1986 in 1,000 tons/tonnes) maize 1,653/1,500; sorghum 1,213/1,100; barley 1,102/1,000; pulses 1,041/945.

Livestock numbers: (1987 in millions) cattle 30; sheep 23.2; goats 17.3. Donkeys, horses, mules and camels are also raised.

Forestry. Roundwood removals: (1986 est.) 137,435,000 ft^3/38,918,000 m^3.

Fisheries. Total catch: (1986 est.) 4,519 tons/4,100 tonnes.

Industry and commerce

Industry. The manufacturing sector is largely composed of processing of agricultural produce. The economy is centrally-planned, with over 90% of large-scale industry being state-run.

Commerce. Exports: (1987 est.) US$390 million, mainly coffee. Principal destinations for exports: US; West Germany; Djibouti; Japan; South Yemen; France; Italy. Imports: $900 million, principally food. Main trading partners: USSR; Italy; West Germany; Japan; UK; US; France.

Trade with UK. Ethiopia exported goods worth £8,451,000 to the UK in 1988, and imported goods worth £47,661,000.

Tourism. (1986) 59,000 visitors.

COMMUNICATIONS

Railways

There are 422 miles/681 km of railways.

Roads

There are 23,518 miles/37,871 km of roads (7,973 miles/12,839 km are main roads).

Aviation

Ethiopian Airlines provides domestic and international services (there are four international airports). Passengers: (1984) 0.38 million.

Shipping

Aseb and Mitsiwa are the major ports. The merchant marine consists of 14 ships of 1,000 GRT or over. Freight loaded: (1983/4) 3.53 million tons/3.2 million tonnes; unloaded: 0.77 million tons/0.7 million tonnes.

Telecommunications

The open-wire and radio relay system is adequate for government use. There are 3 million radios and 50,000 televisions (1984); the government operates the Voice of Revolutionary Ethiopia radio service and Ethiopian Television.

EDUCATION AND WELFARE

Education

Education is free and is due to be made compulsory. Most schools are controlled by local peasants' or urban dwellers' associations. The primary cycle begins at seven years of age and lasts for six years. Secondary education begins at age 13 and lasts for a further six years.

School population. (1988) Enrolment as a proportion of male children in the relevant age group: 35% at primary level, 21% at junior level and 11% at senior level; for females the ratios were 27%, 18% and 9%. In the school year 1988/89 there were more than 2.5 million pupils in primary schools, with some 500,000 in secondary schools.

University. In 1979/80 there were 14,562 students at the National University, with faculties situated in Addis Ababa, Harar and Gondar.

Literacy. A major literacy campaign was launched in 1979, and by 1987 the adult illiteracy rate had reportedly been reduced from 93% to 29%.

Health

Health services, despite expansion since 1960, reach only a small proportion of the population, but attempts are being made to extend health services into remote rural areas. Free medical care for the needy was introduced in 1977. The number of hospital beds and doctors per head of population is the lowest among African countries. In 1987 there were about 11,400 hospital beds (one per 4,035 inhabitants), with 1,200 physicians (approximately one per 38,300 inhabitants), and 3,100 nursing personnel.

FALKLAND ISLANDS

GEOGRAPHY

The Falkland Islands, which include the two main islands of East and West Falkland and about 200 small islands, lie in the South Atlantic Ocean and cover 4,698 $miles^2$/12,170 km^2. They are rocky and hilly with some boggy undulating plains. The capital is Stanley.

Climate

Cold, with strong westerly winds. Rain on more than 180 days per year.

Population

Total population (1989) estimated at 1,943 of British origin.

Birth rate 1.08%. **Death rate** 0.7%. **Rate of population increase** 0.5%

Religion

Christianity: Anglican; Roman Catholic; United Free Church.

Language

English.

HISTORY

The first recorded landing on the islands was made in 1690 by Capt. Strong of the English ship *Welfare*, who named them the Falkland Islands. The islands were not settled until the mid-18th century; the East Falklands in 1764 by the French (who gave them the name 'Les Malouines') and the West Falklands by the British in 1765. The Spanish, basing their claim on the 1713 Treaty of Utrecht, resisted both settlements, and the French accepted financial compensation for withdrawal in 1767. The British settlement, however, survived to be recognized by Spain in 1771, but was abandoned for economic reasons in 1774, leaving behind a plaque and flag as symbolic stakes to future occupation.

In 1806 the Spanish garrison abandoned the Falklands, leaving them uninhabited. In 1820 the recently independent government of the United Provinces of the Río de la Plata (1816–28, including Argentina) proclaimed sovereignty over the islands, where US and British whaling and sealing vessels were now establishing bases. Following the seizure of US sealing boats in 1831 by Louis Vernet, a Frenchman who had gained Argentinean permission to establish a settlement on East Falkland in 1824, commanders of the USS *Lexington* intervened to declare the islands free of all government (with the support of the US government), facilitating British repossession, in the face of Argentinean opposition, and the declaration of British sovereignty in 1833.

A civilian governor was appointed in 1841 over a fledgling community which, by 1892, had been granted colonial status. Continuous years of peaceful occupation and administration (ultimately based on the disparity of power between Britain and Argentina) were undisturbed by ideas of leaseback arrangements to Argentina, raised in the 1930s, and the deliberations of the United Nations, which noted the existence of a dispute in 1965. Argentina pursued its claim more actively from 1973, but various rounds of talks proved inconclusive; and Argentine forces invaded and occupied the Islands on 2 Apr. 1982.

In response to the Argentine invasion, Britain despatched a task force which arrived in late April, established a 'total exclusion zone' around the islands, sank the Argentine battle cruiser *General Belgrano* on 2 May, effected a landing on East Falkland on May 21 and drove back the Argentinean forces (who surrendered in Port Stanley at midnight on 14–15 June). The conflict led Britain to secure the military reinforcement (and to re-emphasise the economic development) of the Islands. The British government from 1982 onwards maintained a refusal to discuss the question of sovereignty, and this policy remained unchanged despite the formal ending of hostilities between the two countries in Oct. 1989 and the restoration of full diplomatic relations in Feb. 1990.

CONSTITUTION AND GOVERNMENT

The Falkland Islands are a British Dependent Territory, with a constitution dating from Oct. 1985. The governor is assisted by a five-member Executive Council and a 10-member Legislative Council of nominated and elected members.

Governor William Fullerton, since 1988

National symbols

Flag. Blue, with the flag of the UK in the upper hoist-side quadrant, and the Falkland Islands coat of arms in a white disc centred on the outer half.

National holiday. 14 June (Liberation Day).

ECONOMY

The economy is based on sheep farming which employs most of the workforce. The major exports are high-grade wool and stamps and coins. There are plans to exploit the fish stocks. The Falkland Islands Development Corporation plans to develop tourism.

Currency

Falkland pound.

COMMUNICATIONS

There is a port at Stanley. There are 317 miles/510 km of road, 19 miles/30 km paved and 50 miles/80 km gravel. There are five airports, two with permanent-surface runways. There is a government-operated radio-telephone system and a private VHF/CB network. There are two AM and three FM radio stations, but no television.

FAROE ISLANDS

GEOGRAPHY

The Faroe Islands are an archipelago of 18 inhabited islands and a few uninhabited islands covering a total area of 540 miles^2/1,400 km^2, lying in the north Atlantic Ocean. The terrain is rugged and rocky with cliffs along most of the coast. The capital is Tórshavn.

Climate

Winters are mild and summers cool. It is usually overcast, foggy and windy.

Population

Total population (1989) estimated at 47,283.

Birth rate 1.7%. **Death rate** 0.8%. **Rate of population increase** 0.9% **Life expectancy** female 81; male 74.

Religion

Christianity: Evangelical Lutheran.

Language

Faroese (derived from Old Norse), Danish.

HISTORY

Conquered by Norwegian Vikings in the 9th century AD, the Faroe Islands were annexed to the Norwegian crown in 1035 and by tradition produced one of Norway's greatest kings, Sverre (r.1184–1202). The union of the Norwegian and Danish crowns (1380), as confirmed by the Union of Kalmar (1397), meant that the islands passed to Denmark, which administered them separately from Norway after 1709. They remained a Danish possession when Norway was transferred to Sweden in 1814 and their parliament (Lagtinget) was revived in 1852. During World War II, with Denmark under German occupation from 1940, the islands were placed under British military protection. A pro-independence movement gained some support, but the majority favoured home rule under Danish sovereignty, which was granted in 1948. When Denmark joined the European Communities in Jan. 1973, the Faroes remained outside with special associate status providing for industrial free trade. After the islands had declared a 200-mile exclusive fishing zone (1976), a Faroes–EEC agreement was reached within the framework of the EEC's common fisheries policy (1983).

Since 1948 Faroes governments have been dominated by combinations of the four main parties: the Social Democrats and Republicans on the centre-left and the People's and Union parties on the right, while the smaller Christian People's and Self-Government parties have also had periods in office. After becoming marginally the largest party in 1958, the Social Democrats headed coalitions in 1958–63, 1974–81 and 1985–88, latterly under the premiership of Atli Dam. The People's Party won the most seats in the 1988 elections and formed a centre-right coalition under Jógvan Sundstein, initially with the Republican, Christian People's and Self-Government parties and, from June 1989, with the Republican and Union parties.

CONSTITUTION AND GOVERNMENT

The Faroe Islands are part of the Danish realm. Legislative authority rests jointly with the Danish crown, acting through an appointed high commissioner, and a 32-member provincial parliament (Lagting) in matters of strictly Faroese concern. Executive power is vested in the Danish crown, acting through the high commissioner, but is exercised by a provincial cabinet responsible to the provincial parliament. Elections are held every four years (last in Nov. 1988). There is at present a ruling four-party coalition.

National symbols

Flag. White with a red cross outlined in blue; the vertical part of the cross is shifted to the hoist side, in the style of the Danish flag.

National holiday. 16 Apr. (Birthday of Danish Queen).

ECONOMY

The Faroe Islanders' standard of living is relatively high (GNP per capita, 1986, US$16,800). Because of the climate, agriculture is limited to raising sheep and growing vegetables. Fishing is the major industry. Denmark provides an annual economic subsidy.

Currency

Danish krone.

COMMUNICATIONS

There are ports at Tórshavn and Tvoroyri (plus eight smaller ports). There are 200 km of road and no railways. There is one airport with permanent-surface runways. There is a telephone system, one AM and three FM radio stations, but no television.

FIJI

Viti

(Republic of Fiji)

GEOGRAPHY

Lying in the south Pacific Ocean, approximately 1,099 miles/1,770 km north of Auckland, 1,695 miles/2,730 km north-east of Sydney, Australia and 1,198 miles/1,930 km south of the equator, the Melanesian archipelago of Fiji covers a total area of 7,077 miles^2/18,333 km^2 with 701 miles/1,129 km of coastline. Fiji consists of approximately 332 islands and 500 islets (between 15°–22°S lat. and 174°E–177°W long.). 70% of the population live on Vitu Levu (4,026 miles^2/10,429 km^2), the largest of the islands, and another 20% on Vanua Levu (2,195 miles^2/5,556 km^2). Most of the larger islands exhibit sharp, rugged relief, rising to 4,344 ft/1,324 m at Mt Victoria on Vitu Levu, with fertile river delta formations and coastal plains. Principal rivers (on Vitu Levu) are the Rewa, Sigatoka and Ba. The Great Sen Reef stretches 300 miles/483 km along the western shoreline of the archipelago. Dense tropical growth covers the windward south-east sides of the islands.

Climate

Tropical, subject to moderating oceanic influences. Cyclonic storms and hurricanes usually occur Nov.–Apr. (wet season); rainfall decreases May–Nov. under the influence of the south-east trade winds. Average temperature range 74–80°F/23.2–27.2°C (extremes 63°F//17.2°C and 92°F/33.3°C); rainfall varies from 70 in/1,780 mm per year in the north-west to 118 in/3,000 mm in the south-east. Suva: Jan. 80°F/26.7°C. July 73°F/22.8°C. Average annual rainfall 117 in/2,974 mm.

Cities and towns

Suva (capital)	69,665

Population

Total population is 727,000 of which 38.7% live in urban areas. Population density is 102.7 persons per mile^2/39.7 per km^2. At the last census, 48.7% of the population were Fijian (Melanesian-Polynesian origin), 48.7% Indian and 5.2% other races (including Europeans, Chinese settlers and other Pacific Islanders). **Birth rate** 3.11%. **Death rate** 0.54%. **Rate of population increase** 2.57%. **Age distribution** under 15 = 37.2%; over 65 3.5%. **Life expectancy** female 72.1; male 67.8; average 70.

Religion

At the last census, 378,452 people (53% of the total population) were Christians, 273,088 (38%) were Hindus, 4,674 were Sikhs, 56,002 were Muslims and 82 were Confucian.

Language

English is the official language; the indigenous Fijian

tongue is spoken in a variety of dialects including the most popular, Bavan. Hindustani is spoken by the Indo-Fijian population.

HISTORY

The archipelago has been inhabited for over 3,000 years by Melanesian peoples. In 1643 the Dutch started the era of European exploration, which resumed with the British in the last quarter of the 18th century. From the beginning of the next century until its establishment as a British Crown Colony in 1874 Fiji witnessed the settlement of traders and missionaries, and a period of intense tribal wars. British concern over the failure of European residents to establish a regular form of government and the abuses in the labour trade for the plantations in Fiji led to Britain's accepting an offer of cession by Chief Cakobau. The migrations of Indian workers for the sugar estates lasted from 1879 to 1916. European settlers secured elected political representation in the Legislative Council in 1904 and the Indians in 1929. Further major constitutional changes did not occur until the 1960s when ministerial government, universal adult franchise and political parties were established.

On 10 Oct. 1970 Fiji achieved independence as a constitutional monarchy within the Commonwealth, with the governor-general as the British monarch's representative. The Alliance Party held power from the first general election in 1972 until Apr. 1987, when it was defeated by a coalition with an Indian majority. The ensuing ethnic tensions resulted in two military coups by Maj.-Gen. Sitiveni Rabuka in May and September in order to restore indigenous Melanesian control. The declaration of a republic on 6 Oct. 1987 led to Fiji's withdrawal from the Commonwealth and former partners breaking off diplomatic relations. Though many of these were restored in 1988, Fiji has continued to attract international criticism for its discrimination against the Indian community. Although the country was to return to full civilian rule by the end of 1989, this was not in fact achieved until January 1990 when Rabuka and the other Army officers left the government. A new constitution (guaranteeing political power for Fiji's native Melanesian population) was due to be adopted during 1990, with legislative elections to follow within two years.

CONSTITUTION AND GOVERNMENT

Executive and legislature

The 1970 constitution provided that the head of state was the British sovereign, represented by a governor-general, who would appoint the prime minister and cabinet in accordance with the wishes of the bicameral Fijian Parliament. Last general election Apr. 1987. The government set up by the May 1987 coup was a military regime; civilian government was later restored, with a Council of Advisors established as an interim administration by the governor-general. The coup of 1 Oct. 1987 was followed by the revocation of the constitution and declaration of a republic. The republic's head of state, the president, was sworn in on 5 Dec. 1987.

Present government (1 Feb. 1990)

President Ratu Sir Penaia Ganilau

Prime Minister, Minister of Foreign Affairs; Home Affairs; and Public Service Ratu Sir Kamisese Mara

Principal Ministers Josefata Kamikamica (Finance and Economic Planning); Berenado Vunibobo (Trade and Commerce); Sailosi Kepa (Attorney General; Minister of Justice); Ratu William Tongiavalu (Lands and Mineral Resources).

Justice

The system of law is based on the British system. The highest court of appeal is the Supreme Court, to which appeals may be made from the Fiji Court of Appeal. The President of the Court is the Chief Justice, appointed by the President. The courts have jurisdiction to hear and determine constitutional and electoral questions including membership of the House of Representatives. Most matters at local level are dealt within the magistrates' courts. The death penalty is in force only for exceptional crimes. No executions were recorded between 1985 and mid-1988.

National symbols

Flag. Light blue ground with Union flag in top left quarter and the shield of Fiji in the fly.

Festivals. 31 July (30 July in 1990, Bank Holiday); 9 Oct. (8 Oct. in 1990, Independence Day).

Vehicle registration plate. FJI.

INTERNATIONAL RELATIONS

Affiliations

SPF; suspended from Commonwealth membership.

Defence

Total Armed Forces: 3,500. Terms of service: voluntary. Reserves: some 5,000 (to age 45).

Army: 3,200.

Navy: 300; five patrol and coastal combatants (mainly US Redwing).

ECONOMY

Currency

The unit is the Fijian dollar, divided into 100 cents.

National finance

Budget. The 1987 budget (in US$) was for expenditure (current and capital) of 340 million and revenue of 274 million.

Inflation. (1987) 5.7%.

Gross Domestic Product

Estimated total GDP US$1,120 million, per capita US$1,680 (ranking 138 in the world by size).

Economically active population. The total number of persons active in the economy was 176,000; unemployed: 15–20%. 60% are involved in agriculture.

Energy and mineral resources

Minerals. Fiji has significant gold reserves. Output: (1987) 2,647 kg.

Electricity. Capacity: 215,000 kW; production: 325 million kWh; 440 kWh per capita (1988)

Bioresources

Agriculture. Approximately 17% of the total area of Fiji is arable land and cultivated pasture, the main farm products being sugar cane; coconuts; cassava; rice; sweet potatoes; bananas.

Crop production: (1986 in 1,000 tons/tonnes) sugar cane 4,740/4,300; rice 31/28; copra 24/22; fruit 20/18; vegetables 18/16; maize 2.2/2.

Livestock numbers: (1987) poultry 2 million; cattle 159,000; goats 59,000; horses 41,000; pigs 29,000.

Forestry. Forests cover 65% of the country. In addition to supplying most of its own timber requirements, in 1987 Fiji earned F$16.5 million from timber exports.

Fisheries. Total catch: (1985) 17,527 tons/15,900 tonnes.

Industry and commerce

Industry. Fiji's industry contributes only about 10% to the total GDP. It is based primarily upon the processing of sugar, copra and gold. Fiji also has a variety of cottage industries.

Commerce. Exports: US$328 million. Imports: US$385 million (1987). Exports included sugar (49%); gold; fish; lumber; coconut oil. Imports included food (15%); petroleum products; machinery; manufactured goods. Countries exported to: UK 45%; Australia 21%; US 5%. Imports came from US 5%; New Zealand; Australia; Japan.

Trade with UK. Fiji imported UK goods worth £6,358,000 and exported to the UK goods worth £65,273,000 (1987).

Tourism. Fiji earned $F145.7 million from 389,866 visitors (1987).

COMMUNICATIONS

Railways

There are 370 miles/595 km of railways.

Roads

There are some 2,670 miles/4,300 km of road, of which 348 miles/560 km are concrete or bituminized.

Aviation

Air Coral Coast and Sunflower Airlines provide domestic services and Air Pacific Ltd. and Fiji Air Ltd provide international services (international airport is at Nadi).

Shipping

There are 126 miles/203 km of inland waterways. The ports are Lambasa, Lautoka, Savusavu, and Suva. The merchant marine consists of seven ships of 1,000 GRT or over.

Telecommunications

There are modern local, inter-island and international (wire/radio integrated) public and special-purpose telephone, telegraph and teleprinter facilities. There are an estimated 53,000 telephones and 400,000 radios (1983). The government operates Radio Fiji and controls the content of broadcasts by the 24-hour commercial radio station FM96.

EDUCATION AND WELFARE

Education

Fiji does not have a compulsory education system.

School population. 180,514 in primary and secondary schools, and over 4,000 students in vocational and technical schools.

Schools. In addition to the 647 primary and 141 secondary schools (which employ 7,082 teachers), there are 236 pre-schools and a number of vocational and technical schools.

Universities. The University of the South Pacific (USP) has facilities in Suva in which 2,344 students are enrolled; a further 4,085 students are enrolled in the USP's extension schemes elsewhere in the country.

Literacy. 80%.

Health

The country has 25 hospitals with 1,721 beds and 271 doctors (1987).

FINLAND
Suomenn Tasavalta
Republiken Finland
(Republic of Finland)

GEOGRAPHY

Situated in northern Europe and divided into 12 provinces, Finland covers a total area of 130,524 miles²/338,145 km², more than a third of which lies north of the Arctic Circle. Apart from the 'Tunturi' fells in the north-west (highest elevation Haltiatunturi, 4,357 ft/1,328 m on the Norwegian border), Finland is a predominantly low-lying country (average height 499 ft/152 m) whose lowland coastal belt in the southern and western regions rarely exceeds 66 ft/20 m elevation. Over 60,000 lakes and rivers, concentrated in the south-east, occupy 10% of the total surface area, the largest of which are Saimaa, Paijanne and Pielinen. Lake Saimaa is connected to the Russian Lake Ladoga by the Vuoksi River, the Paatsjoki drains into the Arctic Sea, while the Tornio and Kemi flow south, emptying into the Gulf of Bothnia. West of the Saaristomeri archipelago lie the Åland Islands (Ahvenanmaa), extensions of the mainland coastal plain. Fertile glacial silts and moraines are fairly evenly distributed with cultivated land comprising 8% of the total land surface area. 65% of Finland is commercially productive forest, and over 50% of the population live in the five southernmost provinces.

Climate

Extreme in regions north of the Arctic Circle, temperatures falling to −22°F/−30°C during the six-month winter and rising to 81°F/27°C from May–July, throughout the 73 days of Midnight Sun. Mean temperatures are 21°F/−6°C during winter in the south and south-west. Summers are mild and short. Moderate to light annual rainfall is evenly distributed throughout the country; over 30% falls as snow. Helsinki: Jan. 21°F/−6°C. July 62°F/16.5°C. Average annual rainfall 24 in/618 mm.

Cities and towns

Helsinki (capital)	490,034
Tampere	170,533
Espoo	164,569
Turku	160,456
Vantaa	149,063

Population

Total population is 4,951,000 of which 61.8% live in urban areas. Population density is 38/16.2 persons per miles²/km². Inhabitants are of Scandinavian-Baltic extraction. Grouped ethnolinguistically, 93.6% of the population speak Finnish and 6.2% speak Swedish. The majority of Finland's Lapp (Sami) population (between 2,000 and 4,500) inhabit the Lapland districts of Enontekio, Inari, Utsjoki and Sodankyla. An estimated 5,500 Gypsies are concentrated in the southern regions.

Birth rate 1.35%. **Death rate** 0.93%. **Rate of population increase** 0.42%. **Age distribution** under 15 = 19.4; over 65 = 12.5. **Life expectancy** female 79; male 72; average 76.

Language

The two official languages are Finnish and Swedish. Swedish is confined mainly to the Ahvenanmaa and west–south-west districts. Finnish (spoken in a variety of dialects) belongs to the Baltic-Finnic branch of the Finno-Ugric language family (which includes Hungarian) and shares common features with Estonian, Livonian, Votic, Karelian, Veps and Ingrian. Lappish constitutes a separate branch of the Finno-Ugric group with a number of markedly dissimilar dialects.

Religion

At the last census 88.9% of the population belonged to the Lutheran National Church and 1% to the Greek Orthodox Church of Finland. In addition, there are approximately 16,700 Jehovah's Witnesses; 13,192 members of the Evangelical Free Church; 1,309 Jews; 926 Muslims.

HISTORY

Inhabited from about 8000 BC, the area of modern Finland was settled by tribes from Asia, with the Lapps being pushed north (from about the 1st century AD) by the Finns, whose language took root despite the later numerical dominance of peoples of Germanic stock. Viking penetration from about AD 800 was followed by Christianization by English and Swedish missionaries in the 11th and 12th centuries, amid competition between Sweden, the republic of Novgorod, the Teutonic Knights and Denmark for control of the Gulf of Finland. Increasing Swedish dominance was confirmed by the 1323 Treaty of Pähkinäsaari with Novgorod, whereafter Finland was part of Sweden for almost 500 years. After Sweden had thrown off the Union of Kalmar with Denmark (1397–1523) and adopted Protestantism, Finland became a grand duchy (1581), with borders which Swedish military power in the 17th century steadily extended in the east and south. In the Great Northern War (1700–21), however, Sweden was defeated by Peter the Great of Russia and was forced to cede extensive territories on the Gulf of Finland as well as Finnish Karelia. Russia's further expansion westwards in the 18th century culminated, during the Napoleonic Wars, in its annexation of Finland (1809), which was confirmed by the Congress of Vienna (1815).

As a grand duchy within the Russian Empire, with Helsinki as its capital from 1819, Finland enjoyed considerable autonomy. Although its officer class served in the Russian army, a growing sense of national identity was reflected in the increasing use of Finnish, which in 1863 became an official language alongside Swedish. The introduction of universal suffrage in 1906 enabled the Social Democratic Party (founded 1899) to become dominant in a new siingle-chamber parliament, the Diet, but its social reforms were not ratified by the Tsar. World War I and the Russian Revolution presented an historic opportunity, which the Finnish Diet seized by twice declaring independence (July and Dec. 1917). A brief civil war ensued (1918) between pro-Bolshevik 'Reds' and anti-revolutionary 'Whites', from which the latter, backed by Germany, emerged victorious, although Germany's defeat forestalled plans to make a German prince King of Finland. Under the guidance of Marshal C.G.E. Mannerheim as Regent, a republic was declared (July 1919) and K.J. Staahlberg was elected president with wide powers. The 1920 Treaty of Tartu with the Soviet Union recognized Finland's independence within borders which took in Finnish Karelia and the eastern shores of the Gulf of Finland, as well as Petsamo on the Arctic coast. Under the 1921 London Convention, the Swedish-populated Åland Islands, at the entrance to the Gulf of Bothnia, were confirmed as part of Finland.

For most of the inter-war period centre-right or 'presidential' governments were in power. Weakened by the formation in 1918 of the breakaway pro-Moscow Communist Party (which remained illegal until 1944), the Social Democrats managed only one period of minority government (1926–27) before joining a centre-left coalition with the Agrarians in 1937. In between, rural hardship and fear of communism combined to impel the right-wing Lapua peasant movement into an abortive armed rebellion (1930–32). Externally, the post-1937 government sought to align Finland with neutral Sweden, but the rise of Nazi Germany resulted in increased pressure from a Soviet regime anxious to improve its strategic position. After the Hitler–Stalin non-aggression pact (Aug. 1939) had secretly given Moscow a free hand in the Gulf of Finland, unacceptable Soviet demands for territorial concessions by Finland were immediately followed by invasion (Nov. 1939). In the ensuing Winter War, stout Finnish resistance was eventually overcome by vastly superior Soviet numbers. Under the Treaty of Moscow (Mar. 1940), Finnish Karelia and the eastern shores of the Gulf of Finland (a tenth of the national territory) were ceded to the Soviet Union, which also obtained a lease on Hango peninsula, at the western end of the Gulf.

Bitterness over the 1940 defeat strengthened the pro-German faction in Finland, which the following year joined in the German assault on the Soviet Union with the aim of restoring and possibly extending the pre-war Finnish border. The outcome was a further defeat by the Red Army, causing Finland to enter peace negotiations in Aug. 1944 and to replace the discredited Pres. Ryti by Marshal Mannerheim as head of state (1944–46). As confirmed by the 1947 Treaty of Paris between Finland and the wartime allies, the Finnish-Soviet border in the south-east became that laid down by the 1940 Moscow Treaty and Petsamo was also ceded (thus depriving Finland of access to the Arctic Ocean and creating a Soviet–Norwegian border in the north). In addition, a 50-year lease was granted to Porkkala peninsula (south-west of Helsinki) for the establishment of a Soviet naval base (Soviet rights to Hango peninsula being renounced). In 1948 Finland signed a friendship treaty with the Soviet Union, in accordance with a policy of close co-operation with its superpower neighbour initiated by Pres. Juho Paasikivi (1946–56) and developed by his successor, Urho Kekkonen (1956–82). Under the treaty (which was renewed in 1955, 1970 and 1983), Finland undertook to resist any attack on the Soviet Union launched through Finnish territory by Germany or its allies. Reparations of $300 million to the Soviet Union were paid off by 1952 and Soviet forces withdrew from the Porkkala base in 1955.

In return for its accommodation of Soviet strategic interests (a process which gave the term 'Findlandization' to the international vocabulary), post-war Finland was able to develop an increasingly prosperous market economy aligned to the West and to join the Nordic Council (1955), EFTA (as an associate member from 1961 and a full member from 1986) and the OECD (1969). Finland also concluded an industrial free-trade agreement with the EEC (1973), balanced by a simultaneous co-operation agreement with Comecon, and hosted the 35-nation Conference on Security and Co-operation in Europe (1975). Internally, Finland remained a multi-party democracy, with the Social Democrats and Agrarians (renamed the Centre Party in 1965) usually forming a centre-left axis in a frequently changing pattern of coalition politics. The Finnish Communists, operating within the People's Democratic League, participated in government in 1944–48 and again on three occasions between 1966 and 1982, but in 1985–86 split into orthodox and revisionist parties. Mauno Koivisto (Social Democrat) was elected president in succession to Kekkonen (Centre Party) in 1982 and was returned for a further six-year term in 1988. Meanwhile, the (conservative) National Coalition Party, in opposition since 1966, had made strong gains in the Mar. 1987 Diet elections and had formed a four-party coalition (with the Social Democratic, Swedish People's and Rural parties) under Harri Holkeri, who in Apr. 1987 became Finland's first post-war conservative prime minister. In Oct. 1989

President Gorbachev of the USSR visited Finland, the first visit by a Soviet head of state since 1975.

CONSTITUTION AND GOVERNMENT

Executive and legislature

The president, who nominally holds supreme executive power, is elected for a six-year term, by universal adult suffrage in a direct election in the first instance, but if no candidate wins an absolute majority of votes, the president is then chosen by a college of 301 electors also elected by universal adult suffrage. Last presidential election Jan.–Feb. 1988. The president appoints a cabinet led by a prime minister, the effective head of government. The government is responsible to the legislature, the 200-member unicameral Eduskunta, which is elected for a four-year term by universal adult suffrage (last general election Mar. 1987).

Present government

President Dr Mauno Koivisto
Prime Minister Harri Holkeri
Principal Ministers Pertti Paasio (Foreign Affairs; Deputy Prime Minister); Matti Louekoski (Justice); Jarmo Rantanen (Interior); Ole Norrback (Defence); Erkki Liikanen (Finance).

Justice

The system of law is based on codified civil law using the Swedish model. The highest court is the Supreme Court in Helsinki, with a role in the judicial review of legislation. There are four superior courts, and 93 lower courts, either municipal courts (in towns) or district courts (in the country). There is an ombudsman to oversee the administration of justice, and a Chancellor of Justice who acts as public prosecutor and counsel for the state. The death penalty was abolished in 1972.

National symbols

Flag. White with a blue cross.
Festivals. 1 May (Labour Day); 24 June (Midsummer Day, Flag Day); 6 Dec. (Independence Day).
Vehicle registration plate. SF.

INTERNATIONAL RELATIONS

Affiliations

Neutral; OECD; EFTA; Nordic Council.

Defence

Total Armed Forces: 35,200 (25,000 conscripts). Terms of service: 8–11 months (11 months for officers). Reserves: some 700,000.

Army: 30,000; 150 main battle tanks (T-54/-55, t-72); 15 light tanks (PT-76).

Navy: 2,700; 23 patrol and coastal combatants (two corvettes, nine missile craft and 12 inshore patrol craft).

Air Force: 2,500; 74 combat aircraft (mainly MiG-21bis and J-35F/BS/XS Draken).

ECONOMY

Currency

The unit is the markka, divided into 100 pennia.

National finance

Budget. The 1988 budget (in US$) was for expenditure (current and capital) of 28,100 million and revenue of 26,900 million. Main items of current expenditure are housing and welfare 37%; education 13.6%; health 10.5%; defence 5.3%.
Balance of payments. The balance of payments (current account, 1988) was a deficit of $3,000 million.
Inflation. 6.7% (12 months to Sept. 1989).

Gross Domestic Product

Estimated total GDP US$77,900 million, per capita US$17,780 (ranking 30 in the world by size). Growth rate 5.2% (1988).
Economically active population. The total number of persons active in the economy was 2,570,000; unemployed: 5.1%.

Sector	% of GDP	% of workforce
industry	30	35
agriculture	10	16
services*	60	58

* services figure includes elements unassigned to other categories.

Energy and mineral resources

Minerals. Finland has significant deposits of copper; iron; nickel; zinc; lead. Output: (ir 1,000 tons/tonnes) iron concentrates and pellets 714/648; nickel concentrates 115/104.4; zin concentrates 61/55; copper concentrates 19.6/17.8; lead concentrates 2.6/2.4.
Electricity. Capacity: 13,119 MW; production 50.9 million MWh.

Bioresources

Agriculture. Just over 4,942,000 acres/2 million ha is under cultivation (around 8% of the total land area). Principal crops: cereals; hay; potatoes; sugar beet.

Crop production: (in 1,000 tons/tonnes) hay 1,474/1,337; barley 1,200/1,089; oats 797/723; potatoes 540/490; wheat 310/281; rye 82/74.

Livestock numbers: poultry 6.678 million; cattle 1.443 million; pigs 1.305 million; reindeer 364,000; horses 15,100.

Forestry. Forests cover nearly 86 million acres/31 million ha, of which 49 million acres/19.7m ha is in productive use.

Industry and commerce

Industry. Finnish industry is based principally on timber and wood processing (including pulp and paper), and metallurgy (refining, manufacturing and engineering). Other industries include shipbuilding; textiles; food processing.
Commerce. Exports: 87,564 million marks. Imports 86,696 million marks. Exports went to EC countries 37.7%; USSR 20.2%; Sweden 14.7%; US 5.4%. Imports came from EC countries 42.9%; USSR 15.2%; Sweden 13.4%; US 4.8%.
Trade with UK. Finland imported UK goods worth 6,192 million marks and exported to the UK goods worth 9,990 million marks.
Tourism. Finland derived revenue of 3,026 million marks from visitors (1986).

COMMUNICATIONS

Railways

There 3,653 miles/5,883 km of railways, of which 897 miles/1,445 km are electrified.

Roads

There are 47,334 miles/76,223 km of public roads and 32,927 miles/53,023 km of private roads.

Aviation

Finnaviation provides domestic services and Karair Oy and Finnair Oy provide international services (international airport is at Helsinki-Vantaa, 11.8 miles/19 km from Helsinki).

Shipping

Including the Saimaa Canal there are 4,145 miles/6.675 km of inland waterways. The major maritime ports are Helsinki, Oulu, Pori, Rauma and Turku. There are six secondary ports and numerous minor ones. The merchant marine has 79 ships of 1,000 GRT or over. Freight loaded: (1987) 22.4 million tonnes; unloaded 31.3 million tonnes.

Telecommunications

There are 3.14 million telephones and there is a good service from cable and radio relay network. There are 3.5 million radios and 1.84 million televisions (1987). The state YLE company broadcasts two radio channels in Finnish, one in Swedish, and local and external service programming, as well as three television channels (on which an independent TV company also makes commercial broadcasts for some 21 hours per week) and teletext news.

EDUCATION AND WELFARE

Education

The state system provides free and compulsory education in comprehensive schools for six years. Upper sections of the comprehensive schools or senior secondary schools provide further courses for up to three years.

School population. 388,465 in compulsory education; 403,115 in higher stages, including 113,117 at vocational schools.

Schools. 5,334 schools with 46,000 teachers (one per 14.8 pupils); 554 vocational schools with 16,638 teachers (one per 6.8 pupils).

Universities. There are ten universities, one of which (at Turku) caters for the Swedish-speaking minority, and ten specialist or vocational colleges. 133,933 students in 1986–87.

Literacy. 100%.

Health

Health insurance is administered by the Social Insurance Institution, with spending on the country's health service accounting for 28.8% of the total national social security expenditure (1986). There are 73,317 hospital beds, 11,452 doctors (one per 430 inhabitants) and 4,719 dentists (1986).

FRANCE

République Française
(French Republic)

GEOGRAPHY

Situated in western Europe, France is the largest central European state, with a total area of 211,150 miles^2/547,020 km^2 comprising 95 metropolitan departments including the Mediterranean island of Corsica, four overseas departments, two collectivités territoriales and four overseas territories. The major interior hill ranges, located in the north-east and west, are derived from ancient mountain masses: the Armorican massif, the Ardennes, the Vosges and the Massif Central (high point 6,188 ft/1,886 m). The country is bounded south-east by the Jura Mountains and the Alps (at 15,771 ft/4,807 m Mont Blanc is Europe's highest peak) and south by the Pyrenees (Vignemale 10,820 ft/3,298 m). A series of plains (such as the Northern plain, the plains of Saône and Alsace, the Rhône valley and the more dispersed Mediterranean coastal plains) divide the ancient massifs from each other and mark their points of intersection with the mountain chains. Common topographical features of the upland regions include plateau landscapes in the Massif Central, Brittany and the Ardennes and deeply incised river gorges such as the Gorges du Tarn. Principal rivers are the Rhône, Seine, Garonne and Loire (the longest at 633 miles/ 1,020 km). Approximately 60% of the total land area (77.8 million acres/31.5 million ha) is fertile and agriculturally useful. Another 35.6 million acres/14.4 million ha is forested. To the west of a line running north–south-west from Caen to Marseille, 35% of the total population is sparsely distributed over half the country's total area (major cities Toulouse and

Bordeaux). In the east intensive farming, a high degree of urbanization, good industrial liaisons with neighbouring countries and an economic output totalling 70% of the GNP continue to sustain the vast majority of the population. Major cities in this region are Paris, Marseille and Lyon. The Paris region (Ile de France) occupies only 2% of the total surface area but supports nearly 20% of the total population.

Climate

Mediterranean in the south with warm, moist winters and hot, dry summers. Maritime in the north-west with small annual temperature range, plentiful rainfall and winter temperatures moderated by the Atlantic influence. Continental in the east with particularly high rainfall are the Vosges (7 ft/2 m or more per year), Massif central, Alps and Jura; summer thunderstorms prevalent. In July mean temperatures fluctuate between 59–64°F/15–18°C in the south. Jan. temperatures vary from 23°F/−5°C in the east to 39°F/4°C in the west. In mountainous regions, high altitudes lower the average temperature but increase the daily range. The south has mild mediterranean winters, sporadically disturbed by cold winds from the north and north-west, known as the 'tramontane' or 'mistral'. Paris: Jan. 37°F/3°C. July 64°F/18°C. Average annual rainfall 23 in/573 mm. Bordeaux: Jan. 41°F/5°C. July 68°F/20°C. Average annual rainfall 31 in/786 mm.

Cities and towns

Paris (capital)	2,188,918
Marseille	878,689
Lyon	418,476
Toulouse	354,289
Nice	338,486
Strasbourg	252,264
Nantes	247,227
Bordeaux	211,197
Saint-Etienne	206,688
Montpellier	201,067
Le Havre	200,411
Rennes	200,390
Toulon	181,985
Reims	181,980
Lille	174,039
Brest	160,355
Grenoble	159,503
Clermont-Ferrand	151,092
Le Mans	150,331

Population

Total population is 55,840,000 (1988), of which 74% live in urban areas. Population density 264.5/102.7 persons per miles^2/km^2. The estimated population of the Paris and Nord departments are 2,127,400 and 2,501,300 respectively. At the last census (1982) there were 3,680,100 persons of foreign origin; of these 1.47% (795,920) were Algerian; 1.41% Portuguese (764,860); 0.79% Moroccan (431,120); 0.61% Italian (333,740); 0.59 % Spanish (321,440).

Birth rate 1.4% **Death rate** 1.0% **Rate of population increase** 0.5%. **Age distribution** Under 15 = 22%; over 65 = 13.3% **Life expectancy** female 80; male 74; average 77.

Religion

Christianity is the dominant religion, although there is no recognized state religion and the law of 9 Dec. 1905 codified the separation of Church and State. The Roman Catholic Church has approx 42.35 million adherents in France and there are 850,000 Protestants. Other significant groupings include 2.5 million Muslims, 0.75 million of whom live in Marseille.

Languages

French-speakers make up 93.4% of the total population. 2.9% are wholly or partially bilingual in Occitan (the old language of the south, or Langue d'oc). 2.3% speak German; 1.0% Breton; 0.4% Catalan; 2.6% Arabic.

HISTORY

(It must be remembered that the boundaries of what is now France have changed a great many times during its history, and that therefore the political units described below, eg the Frankish kingdoms or the Napoleonic Empire, are not necessarily equivalent even approximately to modern France.)

France is the site of some of the earliest prehistoric remains in Europe: there are important Neanderthal skeletons from the Dordogne valley, and the post-Ice Age cultures of the Aurignacians and Magdalenians produced brilliantly refined flint tools and the cave paintings at Lascaux. The Neolithic age reached France in the 4th millennium BC, and the spectacular achievements of the Megalithic culture (stone circles, menhirs, chambered tombs) were centred on the coastal regions, especially Brittany.

Recorded history starts with the foundation of Marseille as a Greek colony about 600 BC. By the time Caesar conquered Gaul (as France was then known) in 57–52 BC and incorporated it into the Roman Empire he found three predominant but disunited tribes: the Belgae between the Seine and the Rhine, the Celts from the Garonne to the Seine and the Marne, and the Aquitanians south of the Garonne. The region was Christianized, but from the 3rd century AD onwards it was repeatedly attacked by barbarians from the north – Visigoths, Burgundians, Franks, and Huns. In 486 Clovis I, King of the Franks, defeated the last Roman governor; he converted to Christianity and founded the Merovingian dynasty which ruled France until 751. The Frankish Empire expanded under the succeeding Carolingian dynasty into what are now Italy, Hungary, Czechoslovakia and Germany, and reached its zenith under Charlemagne (r.768–814), who was crowned Roman Emperor by the Pope in 800. However, in the subsequent Partition of Verdun (843) German-speaking Franconia was separated from what was to become France, and faction-fighting between the numerous feudal lords controlling the different regions in France led in 987 to the election of Hugh Capet as King. His dynasty lasted until 1328 – a time of prosperity and increasing civilization in France. Towns grew, universities were founded and cathedrals were built. Louis IX (St Louis) was renowned for taking a leading part in the Crusades.

When the Capetian dynasty petered out the crown passed to the house of Valois, the first king being Philip VI (r.1328–50). At that time nearly half of France belonged to the English King Edward III, and Philip began the Hundred Years' War (1337–1453) in which the Black Prince, Joan of Arc, and Henry V all fought. Despite Henry V's victory at Agincourt (1415) the English were eventually driven out of France (except for Calais which was not recaptured until 1558). At home Charles VIII of France (r.1483–98) laid the foundations of the ancien régime's centralized absolutism. Abroad he invaded Italy in 1494 provoking the first of the Habsburg-Valois Wars, which did not end until 1559 when Henry II (r.1547–59) concluded the two Treaties of Cateau-Cambrésis under which French claims to Italy were abandoned but France was given the three bishoprics of Metz,

Toul and Verdun as well as confirmed possession of Calais. Henry II, like his two predecessors, Louis XII (r.1498–1515) and Francis I (r.1515–47), continued to strengthen and centralize the Crown's powers. In the French Wars of Religion (1562–98), Roman Catholic and Protestant noble factions fought for control of the Crown following the sudden death of Henry II in 1559. The Protestant Huguenots suffered persecution, most notably at the Massacre of St Bartholomew's in 1572 when some 4,000 were murdered, before achieving permission to worship in the Edict of Nantes (1598). It was King Henry of Navarre, crowned Henry IV, the first of the Bourbon kings, in 1589, who was to bring the country out of the wars. A Protestant who judiciously converted to Catholicism in 1593, he reconstructed and centralized royal power after the wars and continued the traditional French anti-Habsburg tendency in foreign policy but was assassinated in 1610.

In the 17th century France's status as an international power increased further. First Cardinal Richelieu, chief minister of Louis XIII (r.1610–43), and later Cardinal Mazarin, chief minister of Louis XIV (r.1643–1715) during his minority, successfully extended Bourbon influence, gaining territories by diplomacy and later by fighting in the Thirty Years' War (1618–48). Under Louis XIV, the 'Sun King', French absolutism reached its peak. At home centralized power was reinforced with legal codifications, tax and governmental reforms, while literature and the arts flourished at the Versailles court. In foreign policy a series of expansionist wars culminated in the War of the Spanish Succession (1702–13/14) as a result of which Louis XIV's grandson succeeded the Spanish throne as Philip V. However, Louis XIV's successors, Louis XV (r.1715–74) and Louis XVI (r.1774–93), and the inflexibility of the ancien régime proved incompetent and inadequate to maintain the monarchy's position either at home or abroad. The Seven Years' War (1756–63), which was fought in Europe against the increasing power of Frederick II of Prussia and in the colonies and at sea against Britain, drained the treasury and led to the loss of France's colonies in India, the West Indies, and North America. Not long afterwards, France's support for the Americans in their War of Independence (1776–83) against Britain was another financial disaster and gave hope to opponents of French absolutism.

The country's economic crisis brought out discontent among the bourgeoisie who sought more political power and the land owners of all ranks who resented the hugely increased taxation. Louis XVI attempted to control the situation by calling (May 1789) a meeting at Versailles of the Estates-General, the formal representative body of France that had not met since 1614; it consisted of 300 nobility, 300 clergy and 600 commoners – the 'Third Estate'. On 17 June the Third Estate declared themselves to be the National Assembly; joined by many clergy and some nobles they drew up an agenda of reforms to rationalize the monarchy. Louis's response of vacillation and threats excited the mob in nearby Paris: they stormed the Bastille on 14 July. During August peasants in many parts of the country rose against the feudal lords, in an unorganized way. Meanwhile the National Assembly drew up the formal deeds of the Revolution: the abolition of feudalism, the Declaration of the Rights of Man (27 Aug.), and the limitation of the royal veto. The King hesitated to accept these, but matters were once again precipitated by the Paris mob; by now (October) they were nearly starving, and a band (mostly of women) marched to Versailles petitioning for bread. They did not get bread, but they captured the royal family and brought them back to Paris as hostages. On 14 July 1790 the National Assembly announced the constitution. Among its provisions was the nationalization of Church property, and sale of this to the people in 'shares' raised the money to save the country's finances. In June 1791 the royal family attempted to escape in disguise from France; they were recognized at Varennes and brought back to Paris, and the damage to the King's prestige was irreparable. On 14 Sept. he accepted the new constitution, which replaced the National Assembly with the Legislative Assembly of 745 members. There were many monarchists, but the dominant party was the Girondists who wanted a federal republic, and there was also an important group of republican extremists who belonged to the Jacobin and Cordelier clubs. Outside France, royalist emigrés were seeking help from European rulers, who feared that revolutionary ideas might spread; Prussia and Austria formed an alliance against France. The Girondists hoped that a foreign war would rally the nation to republicanism, so with both sides wanting it war was inevitable: on 20 Apr. 1792 the French Revolutionary Wars began. Rumours of treason by Louis and particularly his Austrian-born queen Marie Antoinette brought the mob into action again: on 10 Aug. they stormed the Tuileries Palace and installed a provisional government (the Commune of Paris) in place of the legally elected commune. The Paris Commune, led by Danton, seized all police power and connived at the killing of hundreds of royalist prisoners by the mob (2–7 Sept.). The National Assembly, now virtually powerless, dissolved itself in favour of the National Convention of 749 elected members. It was composed entirely of republicans, and at its first meeting (21 Sept. 1792) it abolished the monarchy, and began proceedings against Louis for treason. He was convicted on 15 Jan. 1793, and on the next day the Convention voted by 361 to 360 for the death penalty. His execution on 21 Jan. led to royalist uprisings especially in the Vendée (south-west France), and was followed by the Reign of Terror, in which Robespierre, as leader of the Committee of Public Safety, removed first the leading Girondists, then the rival factions led by J.R. Hébert and by Danton. Robespierre's excesses finally frightened the National Convention into the coup of 9 Thermidor (27 July 1794) which resulted in his execution and a period of relative moderation. Meanwhile the French Revolutionary Wars had been a success for the Republic, with French influence and territory considerably extended in the north. On 22 Aug. 1795 a new Constitution was enacted, which brought in the Directory, comprising two parliamentary chambers (the Council of the Ancients and the Council of the Five Hundred). Ruling at a time of instability and high inflation, the Directory became increasingly corrupt, inefficient and divided, and the army (conducting a particularly successful campaign in Italy under Napoleon Bonaparte) became a critical factor in political life. Returning to France unexpectedly, Napoleon toppled the Directory in the coup of 18 Brumaire (9 Nov. 1799) and installed himself initially as First Consul and in 1802 as Consul-for-life.

In a renowned ceremony in Dec. 1804 Napoleon took the crown from the Pope and crowned himself 'Emperor of the French'. His rule was in many ways similar to the former absolute monarchy but with a modern and efficient administration. At home he brought the financial crisis under control, reforming the tax systems, and introducing the legal Code

Napoléon. Napoleon continued to be successful abroad, achieving major victories against Russia and Austria at Austerlitz (Dec. 1805) and against Prussia at Jena (Oct. 1806). However, his disastrous campaign against Russia in 1812 ultimately led to the Austrians and Prussians capturing Paris (31 Mar. 1814) and the forced abdication of Napoleon on 11 Apr. He was banished to Elba, from where he made a brief reappearance in 1815 for the so-called 'Hundred Days' War' which ended at Waterloo.

A constitutional monarchy was restored in 1814 under Louis XVIII (Louis XVI's brother), who reigned until his death in 1824, when his brother Charles X introduced a much more reactionary regime. He was overthrown in the 'July revolution' of 1830 after which Louis Philippe, Duke of Orleans, was chosen by the bourgeoisie to rule as 'citizen king'. Political conditions in France as elsewhere were changing, with the sudden rise of industrialization, creating a wealthier bourgeoisie and a new class of proletariat. A year of famine and a government attempt to block any extension of the suffrage brought about Louis Philippe's fall in the Revolution of 24 Feb. 1848, which itself triggered similar uprisings throughout Europe. In the Second Empire, declared in Dec. 1848, direct male suffrage was introduced (although women were to wait until 1945 for this right) and Louis Napoleon Bonaparte (a nephew of Napoleon I) was elected 'Prince-President' nominally for a non-renewable four-year term. Lacking truly republican sentiments, he extended his presidential authority in a coup on 2 Dec. 1851 before being crowned exactly one year later as Emperor Napoleon III. The Second Empire was authoritarian and repressive at home, although it was also a time of material prosperity. In alliance with the British in the Crimean War (1854–56) Napoleon III curtailed Russian influence in the Black Sea area, and in the 1859 Franco-Piedmontese War against Austria obliged Austria to cede Lombardy despite heavy French casualties in the battles of Magenta and Solferino. However, by the 1860s his plans became more grandiose and impractical. He attempted in 1863 to establish a Catholic Empire in Mexico with Maximilian, a brother of Emperor Francis Josef of Austria, as Emperor but was forced to withdraw French troops in Mar. 1867.

In the Franco-Prussian War of 1870–71 Napoleon III was captured in September, ushering in the Third Republic on 4 Sept. 1870. The four-month siege of Paris and the eventual entry of a joint Prussian, Russian and Austrian army into the city on 28 Jan. 1871, led radical Parisians to establish the Paris Commune in March. A bloody suppression of the Commune (20,000 killed, 13,000 imprisoned and 7,500 deported to New Caledonia) was led by the wily Adolphe Thiers. He was obliged to cede Alsace and most of Lorraine to the Germans and was proclaimed president in mid 1871. Although under Marshal Patrice MacMahon (elected president in 1873 in place of Thiers) the re-establishment of the monarchy seemed a possibility, in 1875 a republican constitution was adopted and MacMahon resigned in 1879. The Third Republic's greatest political problem lay in the instability of its governments; between 1870 and 1940 there were no less than 109 ministries with an average life of seven months. However, the country continued to prosper and railways and public education were expanded, the latter reviving the age-old quarrel between Church and State. This conflict was epitomized by the Dreyfus affair concerning Capt. Alfred Dreyfus, an Alsatian Jew, convicted in 1894 of treason for supplying military secrets to Germany on what turned out to be the forged evidence of a military hierarchy riddled with anti-semitism. The affair had the effect of uniting and bringing to power the French left wing, who rallied behind Dreyfus, while monarchists, Army leaders and clericalists were discredited. Dreyfus was eventually acquitted in 1906 and the affair marked the final separation of Church and State (1905). In foreign policy the years before 1914 were marked by continued colonial expansion in Africa (Morocco, Tunisia, much of West Africa, Madagascar) and Indochina, bringing conflict with both Britain and Germany in the race to acquire territory. Morocco was partitioned with Spain in 1912 following the 'Moroccan crisis' of 1905, as agreed at the 1911 conference of Algeciras, in which Germany attempted unsuccessfully to undermine a growing alliance between Britain and France.

While the Radicals were prominent in government even before the official founding of the Radical–Socialist Party in 1901, conflict with the Socialists split the political left-wing and in 1905 the Socialist Party (PS) was founded. Georges Clemenceau, a Radical known as 'the Tiger' and perhaps the strongest politician of the Third Republic, became prime minister in 1906. His term of two years and nine months (the second longest in the Third Republic) was marked by violent attacks on the Socialists and attempts to contain a growing strike movement. It was Clemenceau who united the country in the face of war when he became prime minister again in Nov. 1917. Sparked by growing nationalism in the Balkans and the assassination at Sarajevo in 1914, the fighting in World War I was concentrated in the trenches along the Western Front, where for nearly four years neither side advanced more than a few miles along a line from Nieuport on the Belgian coast to Verdun. The Germans eventually broke through Allied defences at Verdun in early 1917 but were driven back into Belgium. The US entry into the war in Apr. 1917 shifted the military balance on the western front in favour of the Allies, while in the east (following the Bolshevik revolution in November) Lenin had withdrawn from the war. On 11 Nov. 1918 Germany was forced to sign an armistice. In the resulting Treaty of Versailles (June 1919) Alsace–Lorraine was returned to France and the Saar was placed under League of Nations administration for 15 years pending a plebiscite. Despite the harshness of the terms which were to lead to military resurgence in Germany, Clemenceau was seen at home as having been too lenient and he fell from power in a right-wing backlash in the Nov. 1919 elections.

The inter-war years, with the worldwide Depression causing severe economic problems in France, were marked by continued government instability with 44 governments headed by 20 different prime ministers. The trade union movement (legally recognized in 1884) was split when a majority of delegates at the Dec. 1920 Socialist Party congress in Tours decided to support the Moscow-based Third International and formed the Communist Party (PCF). However, faced with rising fascism throughout Europe, Radicals, Socialists and Communists forged an alliance which resulted in an overall left-wing majority in the Apr.–May 1936 elections, bringing Léon Blum to power as the country's first Socialist prime minister at the head of a broad-based 'popular front' government. This and ensuing popular front governments introduced extensive social reforms including a 40-hour working week. However, socialist and communist suspicion of Radical Prime Minister

Edouard Daladier following the gross miscalculation of the Sept. 1938 Munich Agreement, which allowed the annexation of the Sudetenland by Adolf Hitler in exchange for apparent peace in Europe, led to the break-up of the front.

In Sept. 1939, upon Hitler's invasion of Poland, France and Britain declared war on Germany. With France overrun by the Nazis in May and June 1940, Marshal Henri Philippe Pétain signed an armistice with the Germans on 22 June (only six days after becoming prime minister). French forces were disarmed and 60% of France was controlled directly by Germany, while the remaining part (Vichy France) was governed by Pétain as a German lackey. Gen. Charles de Gaulle immediately pronounced from London an alternative 'Free French' government. The Allied invasion of North Africa (Nov. 1942) gave him a base at Algiers, but was also the trigger for German occupation of the rest of France. Under repressive Nazi rule in France, thousands of civilians were taken hostage and shot in reprisal for attacks on Germans, and later in the war hundreds of thousands of French workers were taken to Germany to provide slave labour in factories. France was liberated following the Allied landings in mid-1944 and on 23 Aug. Paris was liberated when citizens rose against the Nazi occupiers as Allied troops approached the city.

After the war France became one of the five great powers in the United Nations and was one of the four powers to occupy Germany. De Gaulle was provisional president of France but resigned before a referendum on 13 Oct. 1946 approved the adoption of the Fourth Republic's constitution. Similar to the Third Republic, particularly in the instability of its governments which numbered 26 between 1946 and 1958, the Fourth Republic's constitution also provided for the colonies to be formed into a French Union, under which they gained varying degrees of autonomy. At home, economic reconstruction was the priority and the generally socialist policies introduced included the nationalization of banks and major industries. US aid under the Marshall Plan was significant, but even more so was France's role in the economic rapprochement with western Germany. Robert Schuman and Jean Monnet were chief architects in the formation of the European Coal and Steel Community at the Treaty of Paris in 1951, which was followed by the establishment of the EEC and Euratom in the twin Treaties of Rome of Mar. 1957. (The Jan. 1963 Franco-German Friendship Treaty further cemented this Franco-German rapprochement and in 1987 it was agreed to establish a joint Franco-German brigade.) France was likewise a founder member of NATO (1949).

At the same time France expended huge military effort in an attempt to defeat the communist movement in Indochina led by Ho Chi Minh. Eventually, after a humiliating defeat at Dienbienphu (7 May 1954) France was forced at the Geneva Conference that year to withdraw from Indochina. Soon afterwards the struggle for independence in Algeria threatened civil war and de Gaulle, whose prestige was still immense, was persuaded to return to politics in a newly-established Fifth Republic (5 Oct. 1958), in which the president (a post held by de Gaulle until 1969) had greatly enhanced powers. Taking a realistic view of France's relationship to the former colonies, he reorganized the French Union as the French Community, within which most of the African territories became fully independent by 1960. Algerian independence (granted 1962) was negotiated in spite of a terrorist campaign by right-wing French soldiers, without loss of either France's or de Gaulle's prestige.

Restoring France to its status as a leading world power was de Gaulle's main concern, to which end he developed France's own nuclear weapons (first test 13 Feb. 1960) and withdrew French troops from NATO's integrated command structure (29 Mar. 1966). He also gave a celebrated 'non' to Britain's entry into the Common Market (14 Jan. 1963). But there were problems at home: in May 1968 students protesting against France's obsolete education system were joined by farmers and striking workers. Riot police were deployed against students in Paris and car-workers at several plants, and three people were killed. De Gaulle dissolved the National Assembly (30 May) and, blaming the Communists for the trouble, won a landslide victory at elections in June, the Gaullists gaining the first absolute majority in French history. But de Gaulle resigned the following year (28 Apr. 1969) after his proposals for regional reform were defeated in a referendum. On 15 June 1969 (in the second presidential elections to be held by direct universal suffrage, the first having been won by de Gaulle in Dec. 1965) the Gaullist Georges Pompidou was elected president. Economic difficulties continued, and the franc was devalued in August. Pompidou supported British entry into the Common Market, which took place on 22 Jan. 1973, and he won a greatly reduced majority in the March 1973 election, in part due to the formation of a 'Union of the Left' between the PS and PCF.

Pompidou died on 2 Apr. 1974, and in a presidential election the following month his finance minister, the right-wing Valéry Giscard d'Estaing, was narrowly elected president. The oil crisis of the early 1970s hit France, as a non-oil producer, very hard; measures were taken to conserve energy and nuclear energy was developed. Under Prime Minister Jacques Chirac public expenditure increased, consequently reducing socialist agitation, but inflation soon took hold, and Chirac resigned to be replaced by Raymond Barre (Aug. 1976) with austerity measures including a planned increase in unemployment and deregulation of prices of necessities such as bread. The National Assembly elections in Mar. 1978 gave the ruling centre-right coalition a continuing comfortable majority: although relations between Chirac's Gaullist Rally for the Republic (RPR, founded in 1976 as the successor to de Gaulle's Rally of the French People formed in 1947) and the three smaller centrist formations in the coalition had deteriorated to the extent that a non-Gaullist, centrist Union for French Democracy (UDF) was formed immediately before the election, policy differences between the PS and the PCF split the left-wing vote.

In the May 1981 presidential election François Mitterrand was elected with the support of the PCF as the first Socialist president of the Fifth Republic. (Giscard's defeat was attributed at least in part to a scandal which broke in Oct. 1979 concerning his receipt in 1973 when finance minister of $250,000-worth of diamonds from Emperor Bokassa of the Central African Republic.) In National Assembly elections the following month the PS again triumphed, and Pierre Mauroy took office as the PS prime minister of a cabinet which included four PCF ministers for the first time since 1947. Mitterrand's policies included the introduction of voluntary retirement on half-pension at 60, significantly increased social security contributions for those working beyond retirement, improved job training programmes, and a decentralization of government. An ambitious programme of nationalization was stalled by a Constitutional Council ruling in Jan. 1982, which added over one-third to the cost of the compensation offered. Inflation and a rapidly increasing trade deficit was tackled with higher taxes and cuts in public spending. In addition, in July 1984 the government was forced to abandon plans to introduce a unified state-controlled education system. The education minister's resignation was followed by that of Mauroy, leading to the appointment of the brilliant Laurent Fabius (at only 37) as prime minister of a new government from which the Communists withdrew their support.

On 11 July 1985 the Rainbow Warrior, a ship of the environmentalist protest group Greenpeace, sank in a limpet-mine attack, killing one crew member. The ship was in Auckland harbour, New Zealand, to protest at French nuclear testing in the Pacific. Although at first the French government denied any involvement, two months later it admitted that the two French secret service agents arrested after the attack (Alain Mafart and Dominique Prieur) had acted under orders from the Defence Ministry. The minister concerned resigned, the head of the secret service was sacked, France had to apologize to New Zealand and compensate Greenpeace, but French public opinion continued to support France's policy of independent nuclear deterrence and was not much perturbed.

Facing disaster in the Mar. 1986 Assembly elections, Mitterrand brought in income tax cuts in July 1985 and pleased liberal opinion by imposing sanctions on South Africa. This was not enough and, although the PS remained the largest single party, a right-wing coalition led by the RPR and the UDF won an overall majority of five seats, while the neo-fascist National Front (founded 1972) entered parliament for the first time. The result was an unprecedented 'cohabitation' of a Socialist president with a right-wing Gaullist prime minister in the shape of Chirac, since both parliament (which determined the composition of the government) and the President were elected directly and for differing terms of five and seven years respectively. Initially continual rivalry between Chirac and Mitterrand hampered the passage of legislation, with Mitterrand refusing to countersign ordinances and Chirac forcing legislation through by severely curtailing debate, but an uneasy 'cohabitation' did eventually emerge. Chirac was beset by a number of strikes in the public sector, which he met with intransigence, possibly successful in financial terms but losing him political support. In August, students demonstrated against reforms which would have restricted their choice of university, and there was street fighting reminiscent of 1968. Chirac's government was also made to appear weak in its failure to control bomb attacks in the second half of 1986. The left-wing extremist Action directe (Direct Action) assassinated Renault's boss in November and attackers with Arab connections attempted in a series of bombings in Paris in September to pressurize the government on French hostages in Lebanon. By 1987 this situation was brought under greater control with the arrest of almost all the Action directe leaders and of 16 people connected with the pro-Iranian Hezbollah movement.

In elections on 24 Apr. and 8 May 1988 Mitterrand became the first president to be directly elected for a second seven-year term. The right-wing vote was split not just between Chirac (for the RPR) and Barre (for the UDF) but also for Jean-Marie Le Pen, the neo-fascist National Front leader, who gained 14% of votes in the first round (and as many as 20% in parts of the south). Upon Chirac's resignation as prime minister Mitterrand appointed the Socialist Michel Rocard in his place but he lacked a workable majority. In general elections held the following month (5 and 12 June) the PS made substantial gains as did the RPR and UDF, while PCF support continued to decline and the National Front won only one seat compared with 35 in 1986. Rocard accordingly formed a government dominated by Socialists but with members of the UDF and the Left Radical Movement (MRG, formed 1978 by Radical-Socialists not joining the UDF), and some technocrats. In a policy speech on 29 June, Rocard gave priority to the reintroduction of a wealth tax and an increase in the statutory minimum wage. As a believer in the mixed economy, he proceeded with a cautious privatization scheme (already begun under Chirac); during 1988 the bank Crédit Agricole and the defence and electronics firm Matra were sold. In August the chairman of SNCF, the French national railways, resigned after two major train crashes occurred in two months (Gare de Lyon, Paris, 27 June, 56 dead; Gare de l'Est, Paris, 6 Aug., 1 dead). A referendum throughout France on 6 Nov. 1988 approved legislation providing for the political and economic development of New Caledonia in the Pacific pending a referendum on independence in 1998.

CONSTITUTION AND GOVERNMENT

Executive and legislature

The Constitution of the Fifth Republic came into effect in 1958 and was revised in 1960, 1962, 1963, 1974 and 1976. The president, who holds executive power, is directly elected for a seven-year term by universal suffrage (minimum voting age 18) and must win an absolute majority of votes cast, so a second round run-off election between the top two candidates may be necessary. The country is governed by a council of ministers, led by a prime minister. Appointed by the president, the prime minister is responsible to the bicameral parliament, the highest legislative body. The 575-seat National Assembly (lower house) is elected for a five-year term by universal suffrage; the upper house is the 319-member Senate (upper house), in which a third of the seats are renewed every three years in indirect elections.

The four overseas departments (French Guiana, Guadeloupe, Martinique and Réunion) participate in the French electoral system in the same way as the departments of metropolitan France. There are in addition two overseas 'collectivités territoriales' (Mayotte and St Pierre and Miquelon), with a status between that of an overseas department and an overseas territory, and four overseas territories – New Caledonia, with special transitional arrangements towards greater autonomy, and French Polynesia, Wallis and Futuna Islands, and the French Southern and Antarctic Territories.

The last legislative elections were on 5 June and 12 June 1988. The last presidential election was on 24 Apr. and 8 May, 1988.

Present government

President François Mitterrand
Prime Minister Michel Rocard
Ministers of State Lionel Jospin (National Education, Youth and Sport); Pierre Bérégovoy (Economy, Finance and Budget); Roland Dumas (Foreign Affairs); Michel Durafour (Civil Service and Administrative Reforms).

Ministers Pierre Arpaillange (Keeper of the Seals; Justice); Jean-Pierre Chevènement (Defence); Pierre Joxe (Interior); Roger Fauroux (European Affairs); Michel Delebarre (Equipment and Housing; Transport; the Sea); Jean-Pierre Soisson (Labour, Employment and Vocational Training); Jacques Pelletier (Co-operation and Development); Jack Lang (Culture, Communication and Major Works); Louis Le Pensec (Overseas Departments and Territories); Henri Nallet (Agriculture and Forestry); Paul Quilès (Postal Services, Telecommunications and Space); Jean Poperen (Relations with Parliament); Claude Evin (Solidarity, Health, Social Protection and Government Spokesman); Hubert Curien (Research and Technology); Jean-Marie Rausch (Foreign Trade).

Administration

The controversial reorganization programme introduced under Mitterrand in 1981–82 created elected regional councils in 22 regions, into which the historic divisions, the departments created by Napoleon, were grouped. The departmental prefects were renamed Commissioners of the Republic. Regions are as follows:

Alsace Bas-Rhin, Haut-Rhin (Strasbourg)
Aquitaine Dordogne, Gironde, Landes, Lot-et-Garonne, Pyrénées-Orientales (Bordeaux)
Auvergne Allier, Cantal, Haute-Loire, Puy-de-Dôme (Clermont-Ferrand)
Basse-Normandie Calvados, Manche, Orne (Caen)
Bourgogne Côte-d'Or, Nièvre, Saône-et-Loire, Yonne ((Dijon)
Bretagne Côtes-du-Nord, Finistère, Ile-et-Vilaine, Morbihan (Rennes)
Centre Cher, Eure-et-Loir, Indre, Indre-et-Loire, Loir-et-Cher, Loiret (Orléans)
Champagne-Ardennes Ardennes, Aube, Marne, Haut-Marne (Reims)
Corse Corse-du-Sud, Haute-Corse (Ajaccio)
Franche-Comté Doubs, Haute-Saône, Jura, Territoire-de-Belfort (Besançon)
Haute-Normandie Eure, Seine-Maritime (Rouen)
Ile-de-France Essone, Haute-de-Seine, Seine-et-Marne, Seine-St. Denis, Val-de-Marne, Val-d'Oise, Ville de Paris, Yvelines (Paris)
Languedoc-Roussillon Aude, Gard, Hérault, Losère, Pyrénées-Orientales (Montpellier)
Limousin Corrèze, Creuse, Haute-Vienne (Limoges)
Lorraine Meurthe-et-Moselle, Meuse, Moselle, Vosges (Nancy)
Midi-Pyrénées Ariège, Aveyron, Haute-Garonne, Gers, Lot, Hautes Pyrénées, Tarn, Tarn-et-Garonne (Toulouse)
Nord Nord, Pas-de-Calais (Lille)
Pays-de-la Loire Loire-Atlantique, Maine-et-Loire, Mayenne, Sarthe, Vendée (Nantes)
Picardie Aisne, Oise, Comme (Amiens)
Poitou-Charentes Charente, Charente-Maritime, Deux-Sèvres, Vienne (Poitiers)
Provence-Alpes-Côte d'Azur Alpes-de-Haute-Provence, Alpes-Maritime, Bouches-du-Rhône, Hautes-Alpes, Var, Vaucluse (Marseille)
Rhône-Alpes Ain, Ardèche, Drôme, Isère, Loire, Rhône, Savoie, Haute-Savoie (Lyon)

Justice

The legal system is historically based on the principles of Roman law, as codified under the Code Napoléon, and the judicial process in criminal cases is inquisitorial rather than adversarial in character. The judiciary is independent of the government. Petty offences under the criminal law are dealt with by police courts, and more serious offences, with penalties of up to five years' imprisonment, are handled by non-jury correctional tribunals, usually of three judges. Civil cases go before one of the 471 tribunaux d'instance, or in more serious cases the 181 tribunaux de grande instance. Labour disputes are dealt with by the 282 Conciliation Boards (Conseils de Prud'hommes) each made up of an equal number of employers and employees, while commercial litigation goes to one of the 229 Commercial Courts. There are 35 Courts of Appeal, to which appeal may be made from any of these tribunals, and 103 Courts of Assizes, which deal with severe criminal offences involving imprisonment of over five years. Decisions of these Appeal and Assize courts may be annulled by the Court of Cassation only if the law has been interpreted incorrectly or the proper procedures not followed. The first Ombudsman (mediateur) was appointed for a six-year period on 24 Jan. 1973. The death penalty was abolished in 1981.

Prisons. There are 44,898 prisoners.

National symbols

Flag. Vertical stripes of blue, white and red. The tricolour, the flag of the French Revolution, dates in this form from 1794. It is based on colours first used in 1789, the royal white combined with the red and blue of Paris.

Festivals. 1 May (Labour Day); 8 May (Liberation Day); 14 July (National Day, Fall of the Bastille).

Vehicle registration plate. F.

INTERNATIONAL RELATIONS

Affiliations

The UN and its specialized agencies, NATO (outside military structure); WEU; OECD; European Communities; Council of Europe; Francophone Community.

Defence

Total Armed Forces: some 456,900 (13,500 women, 238,500 conscripts).
Reserves: 356,000.
Army: 280,900; 1,340 main battle tanks (AMX-30), 230 light tanks (AMX-13).
Navy: 66,500 inclusive Naval Air; 24 submarines (Rubis ASW/ASUW, Agosta, Daphne); 43 principal surface ships: two carriers (capacity 40 aircraft); two cruisers; 15 destroyers; 24 frigates. 22 patrol and coastal craft.
Naval Air Force: 9,000; 110 combat aircraft and 24 armed helicopters.
Air Force: 95,000; 580 combat aircraft, no armed helicopters.

Defence expenditure US$31,880 million plus US$37,090 million in contributions to NATO (1988). Per capita expenditure on defence was US$623 or 3.9% of GDP.

Deployment of forces French forces abroad include substantial forces in overseas possessions (Antilles-Guyana 8,000; Mayotte-La Réunion 5,100; New Caledonia 9,500; Polynesia 5,000) plus also forces in the Central African Republic 1,200; Chad 1,900; Côte d'Ivoire 500; Djibouti 3,900; Gabon 500; Senegal 1,200. 1,750 French troops serve with UNIFIL in Lebanon.

ECONOMY

The French economy, an industrialized market economy, has been planned under a series of multiyear national plans, most recently the 10th National Plan for 1989-92, adopted by the National Assembly on 28 Apr. 1989, which emphasises tackling unemployment and preparing for the single European market due to come into effect on 1 Jan. 1993.

Currency

The unit is the franc (F) divided into 100 centimes.

National finance

Budget. The 1989 budget was for expenditure of F1,083,845 million and revenue of F968,862 million, giving a deficit of F114,983 million. Main items of expenditure are housing, social security and welfare 38.5% (1987); health 20.8%; education 7.8%; defence 6.3%.

Balance of payments. The balance of payments (current account, 1988) was a deficit of US$3.58 billion, compared with 4.44 billion the previous year.

Inflation. 3.4% (12 months to Sept. 1989).

Gross National Product

Estimated total GDP US$879,900 million, per capita US$15,818 (the 28th richest country in the world in terms of per capita income). Growth rate (1988) 3.4%.

Economically active population. The total number of persons active in the economy (1988) was 24,124,000; unemployed: 10% (1988).

Sector	% of workforce	% of GDP
services*	59	63
industry	32	32.5
agriculture	7.9	3.5
mining	1	1

* services figure includes elements unassigned to other categories.

Energy and mineral resources

Oil and gas. Production in 1988 totalled 3.9 tons/3.5 million tonnes of crude oil and some 353,140 ft^3/10,000 m^3 of natural gas. The majority of oil refined in France is imported.

Minerals. Mining is relatively unimportant, amounting to less than 0.5% of GNP, mainly from coal; uranium; iron ore; sulphur; potash.

Electricity. Production: 378.3 million MWh, of which 70 % is from nuclear reactors, the highest proportion in the world, and most of the remainder from hydroelectric schemes.

Bioresources

Agriculture. There are an estimated 77.8 million acres/31.5 million ha. of agricultural land in France.

Crop production: wheat 30 million tons/27 million tonnes; maize 13/12 million; other cereals 13/12 million; sugar beet 28.3/25.7 million (white sugar 4.3/3.9 million); potatoes 7.9/7.2 million; wine 249,995 ft^3/70.8 million hectolitres; paper 11.4 million tons/10.3 million tonnes; fruits 1.8 million tons/1.6 million tonnes.

Livestock numbers: poultry 218 million; cattle 22.8 million; pigs 12 million; sheep 10.6 million; sheep 10.6 million; goats 976,000; horses 310,000.

Forestry. Forests cover 86,319 miles^2/139,000 km^2 or 25% of the total land area, and some 988,792 million ft^3/28,000 million m^3 of wood is produced annually.

Fisheries. Annual catch: fish 565,480 tons/513,000 tonnes; shellfish and crustaceans 275,575 tons/250,000 tonnes.

Industry and commerce

Industry. The main heavy industries are oil refining; steel (1986) 19.7 million tons/17.9 million tonnes; cement 24.8 million tons/22.5 million tonnes; aluminium. Also important are paper production; chemicals; textiles; food products; aircraft; motor manufacturing.

Commerce. Exports: (1987) US$147,900 million; (1988) US$ 167,500 million. Imports: (1987) US$153,200 million; (1988) US$173,000 million. Main countries exported to: (1987) West Germany 16.6%; Italy 12.1%; Belgium-Luxembourg 9.3%; UK 8.8%; US 7.3%. Imports came principally from West Germany 19.8%; Italy 11.7%; Belgium-Luxembourg 9.4%; US 7.2%; UK 7.1%.

Trade with UK. In 1988 France imported UK goods worth £9.39 million and exported to the UK goods worth £8.27 million.

Tourism. (1987) 36,974,000 visitors, mainly from West Germany; UK; Netherlands; Belgium; Switzerland. Receipts from tourism F19,927 million.

COMMUNICATIONS

Railways

There are 21,536 miles/34,680 km of railways, of which 7,260 miles/11,692 km are electrified, run by the state Société Nationale des Chemins de fer Français (SNCF). A high-speed train de grande vitesse (TGV) connects Paris and Lyon. Paris has an extensive underground network (the Métro, linked with the bus system under the RATP umbrella) and regional express railway system (RER).

Roads

There are 934,568 miles/1,504,940 km of roads in all, including 3,999 miles/6,440 km of motorways, operated as toll roads, 17,698 miles/28,500 km of national highways and 217,350 miles/350,000 km of secondary highways. 21,970,000 passenger vehicles, or one per 2.7 inhabitants.

Aviation

Air France provides international services and Air Inter domestic services. International airports are at Orly, Roissy/Charles de Gaulle and Le Bourget (the three Paris airports); Bordeaux; Lille; Lyon; Marseille; Nice; Strasbourg; Toulouse.

Shipping

101.6 million tons/92.2 million tonnes of crude and refined petroleum products, and 104.4 million tons/94.7 million tonnes of other freight, were unloaded at French ports in 1987, while outgoing seaborne traffic totalled 68.2 million tons/61.9 million tonnes. Passenger traffic amounted to 21,500,000.

Telecommunications

614 telephones per 1,000 inhabitants in 1986; relatively advanced communications through introduction of Minitel, free videotex data screens installed in millions of homes and allowing users to access electronic information sources.

Broadcasting. 394 television sets per 1,000 inhabitants (22 million in total, and 49 million radio sets). Three state radio stations, France Inter (24 hours per day), France Musique and France Culture; privately-owned radio is mostly local, except for foreign-based stations such as RTL (Luxembourg), Europe 1 (Saarbrücken) and Radio Monte Carlo. Radio France International broadcasts within France in about ten other languages for foreign workers (on France Culture network) and has 24-hour external broadcasting, mainly in French, worldwide. The state-run television channel TF1 was privatized in 1986, leaving two state-run television channels, Antenne 2 and France Régions 3, the privately-owned Canal Plus, La 5 and M6, and broadcasts which can be received in France from Télé-Luxembourg, Télé-Belge and Télé-Monte Carlo. The satellite television system TDF-1 was launched in Oct. 1988.

Newspapers. The daily press is mainly regional, with 72 provincial dailies selling an average daily total of 6.7 million copies, the largest being Ouest-France, based in Rennes (783,000); 14 dailies based in Paris have national circulation, totalling 2.5 million copies, including *France-Soir* (410,000); *Le Figaro* (434,000); the prestigious *Le Monde* (365,000); *Le Parisien Libéré* (340,000); the sports paper *L'Equipe* (240,000); *Libération* (166,000); the Communist Party paper *L'Humanité* (117,000). Of the news weeklies, *L'Express* sells 670,000; *Le Point* 330,000; and *Le Nouvel Observateur* 325,000; *Paris-Match* has a circulation of 690,000 and the satirical *Le Canard Enchaîné* 450,000.

EDUCATION AND WELFARE

Education

France has a highly centralized education system based on a national curriculum and with compulsory attendance for ages 6–16. The five years of primary school are followed by a first cycle of secondary education, for four years, at a lycée (grammar school), a collège d'enseignement secondaire (CES) or a collège d'enseignement générale (CEG); a second cycle follows, leading to the baccalauréat after three years at the lycée, or a professional qualification after one, two or three years at the CES or CEG. At tertiary level, there are 69 state universities and three national polytechnics, as well as five Catholic and various private universities and, outside the university system, over 400 schools and institutes of higher education, including the highly prestigious grandes écoles and the institutions which provide preparatory classes for students seeking admission to these elite bodies.

School and university population. 6,664,000 pupils in some 64,000 nursery and primary schools (14% in private schools); 4,482,000 pupils at 7,342 state secondary schools; 1,193,000 at 3,905 private secondary schools; 980,400 students at state universities; over 50,000 at Catholic and private universities; 200,000 in higher education outside the university system proper.

Student-teacher ratio. One teacher per 17 pupils in primary schools; one per 17.5 pupils in secondary schools.

Health

Health insurance is part of the state social security scheme for those not covered by private insurance schemes. There is one doctor for every 435 inhabitants; total number of doctors 139,000; nurses 294,000; midwives 10,000; dentists 35,000; hospitals 3,730 with 574,000 beds (one per 105 inhabitants).

Welfare

Contributions to the national social security scheme are payable by employees (deducted from earnings) and employers. Medical insurance under this scheme refunds, in large part but generally not in full, the cost of the medical treatment which is bought by the patient. The scheme also covers maternity insurance, sickness benefit and compensation for industrial injuries. Unemployment benefit is means tested, and payable at full rate for only the first three months. Family allowances and family income supplements are also covered by the scheme, which is administered by the state social security organization.

FRENCH GUIANA

GEOGRAPHY

French Guiana lies on the northern shore of South America, and has borders with Brazil and Suriname. It covers a total area of 35,126 million^2/91,000 km^2. The terrain consists of low-lying coastal plains rising to hills and small mountains. The population is mainly limited to the coastal area. The capital is Cayenne.

Climate

Tropical; hot and humid, with little seasonal variation.

Population

Total population (1989) estimated at 94,702.

Birth rate 2.7%. **Death rate** 0.6%. **Rate of population increase** 3.2%. **Life expectancy** female 75; male 68.

Religion

Christianity: Roman Catholic.

Language

French.

HISTORY

The earliest inhabitants of French Guiana were Amerindian tribes, including the Caribs, Arawaks, Palicur, Wayana and Oyampi. The first European explorers of the Guiana coast in the early 16th century included French, Spanish and Dutch adventurers. A French settlement was established at Cayenne in 1637, but the area was in dispute between the French, Dutch, Portuguese and English until the Treaty of Utrecht in 1713. African slaves were imported as labour for plantations and the colony gradually prospered. Portugal occupied the colony between 1809 and 1817. Slavery was abolished in 1848 and several groups, including Asians and Chinese, were imported to help overcome the labour shortage. In 1852 the first penal colony in the territory was created and from then until 1939 many convicts were deported from France to serve their sentences in French Guiana.

French Guiana became a department of France in 1946 and a region in 1974. Attempts to stimulate the economy and promote the development of the interior were outlined in the Green Plan of 1976. Industrial and social unrest in the department was reflected in the increase in support for political parties demanding greater autonomy, in particular the Parti socialiste guyanais (PSG). Some measure of greater autonomy was granted in the 1982 decentralization legislation, and since then the PSG, together with other left-wing parties, has increased its representation on both Regional and General Councils, securing the presidencies of both. The PSG consolidated its position by victories over right and centre parties in the General Council election and municipal elections held in Mar. 1989.

CONSTITUTION AND GOVERNMENT

French Guiana is an overseas department of France. It has a popularly-elected 16-member General Council. The last General Council election was held in Oct 1988. (Only half the General Council is elected each time.)

Leader Jean-Pierre Lacroix, Commissioner of the Republic (since Aug 1988).

National symbols

Flag. The flag of France.

National holiday. 14 July (Bastille Day).

ECONOMY

The economy is closely linked with that of France through subsidies and imports. There is a French space centre at Kourou. Main exports are fish and fish products. The sawmill industry is expanding due to the reserves of tropical hardwood. Unemployment: 15%.

Currency

French francs.

COMMUNICATIONS

There are 422 miles/680 km of road, 317 miles/510 km of which are paved. There are 285 miles/460 km of inland waterway navigable by small ocean-going vessels and 2,049 miles/3,300 km navigable by native craft. There is a port at Cayenne. There are 11 airports, five with permanent-surface runways. There is a telephone system, five AM and seven FM radio stations, and nine TV stations.

FRENCH POLYNESIA

GEOGRAPHY

French Polynesia includes five archipelagos with a total area of 1,521 miles^2/3,941 km^2. The capital is Papeete.

Climate

Tropical but moderate.

Population

Total population (1989 est.) 196,246, mainly of Polynesian descent.

Birth rate 2.7%. **Death rate** 0.4%. **Rate of population increase** 2.7% **Life expectancy** female 74; male 70.

Religion

Christianity: Protestant; Roman Catholic.

Language

French (official); Tahitian.

HISTORY

Islands in the French Polynesia group were first settled about 2,000 years ago. The first contact with Europeans came in 1767. In 1797 the London Missionary Society established a presence on Tahiti, quickly converting the islanders to Christianity. French colonization dates from 1842. The Tahitians resisted their new rulers in a three-year guerrilla war.

In 1957 the islands became a French Overseas Territory. Local autonomy, particularly in economic matters, was increased in 1977 and again in 1984. A French high commissioner remains head of the administration and the territory is represented in the French National Assembly and Senate.

In 1985 the French Government reaffirmed its strategic interests in the Pacific and its policy of testing nuclear devices on Mururoa Atoll, in defiance of the signatories of the South Pacific Nuclear Free Zone Treaty.

Following the five-yearly elections for the islands' 41-seat Territorial Assembly in Mar. 1986, Gaston Flosse of the Tahoeraa Huiraatira Party, aligned with the Réassemblement pour la Républiqve (RPR) was re-elected as president of the territory's Council of Ministers. However, Flosse resigned in Feb. 1987 after complaints against him concerning the misuse of public funds. Jacques Teuira replaced him as president. In Oct. 1987 the break-up of a dock strike led to serious rioting in the capital, Papeete. Discontent with Teuira's policies led to his resignation in Dec. 1987 and Alexandre Léontieff was elected president. The government was thrown into crisis in Mar. 1989 when half of Léontieff's ministerial appointments were declared unconstitutional by the Administrative Court.

CONSTITUTION AND GOVERNMENT

French Polynesia is an overseas territory of France. There is a popularly elected 30-member Territorial Assembly, which elects a five-member Council of Government. One senator is elected to the French Senate. Elections are held every five years.

Leadership Jean Montpezat, High Commissioner of the Republic (since Nov 1987); Alexandre Leontieff, President of the Territorial Government (since Dec 1987).

National symbols

Flag. The flag of France.

National holiday. 14 July (Bastille Day).

ECONOMY

Since France stationed military personnel in the region in 1962, the economy has changed from subsistence to one in which a high proportion of the workforce is employed by the military or supports tourism. Tourism accounts for 20% of the GDP.

Currency

Comptoirs français du Pacifique franc.

COMMUNICATIONS

There are 373 miles/600 km of road. There are ports at Papeete and Bora-bora. There are 43 airports, 25 with permanent-surface runways. There is a telephone system, five AM and two FM radio stations and six TV stations, and one satellite ground station.

FRENCH SOUTHERN AND ANTARCTIC TERRITORIES

GEOGRAPHY

The French Southern and Antarctic Territories lie in the southern Indian Ocean, covering a total area of 3,003 miles^2/7,781 km^2. This figure includes Ile Amsterdam, Ile Saint-Paul, (both extinct volcanoes) Iles Kerguelen and Iles Crozet, but excludes about 193,000 mile^2/500,000 km^2 in antarctica known as Terra Adélie. The French claim to this area is not recognized by the United States.

Climate

Antarctic

Population

Total population (1989 est.) 210 (mostly researchers).

HISTORY

The islands and section of mainland Antarctica that comprise the French Southern and Antarctic Territories were uninhabited prior to their discovery by European seafarers. Seasonal visits were made by whalers and seal hunters, but no permanent settlements were made until the establishment of scientific bases in the area, the main base being Port-aux-Français on Kerguelen Island, set up in 1950.

The Crozet Islands were discovered by the French in 1772, together with the Kerguelen Islands. The island of Nouvelle Amsterdam, discovered in 1552, was annexed by France in 1843, together with the island of Saint Paul, which had been used by fishermen from Réunion since the 18th century. Adélie Land, the part of Antarctica claimed by France, was first explored by the French in 1840 and formally claimed as the section of land between 136°E and 142°E in 1938. Between 1924 and 1955 all the southern islands and Adélie Land were administered as dependencies of the French colony of Madagascar. In 1955 the Southern Islands and French Antarctic were formed into a separate overseas territory, administered by special statute.

CONSTITUTION AND GOVERNMENT

The French Southern and Antarctic Territories are an overseas territory of France.

Leader Vice Admiral Claude Piere, High Administrator.

National symbols

Flag. The flag of France.

ECONOMY

Economic activity is limited to servicing meteorological and geophysical research stations and French and other fishing fleets.

COMMUNICATIONS

There are no ports, only offshore anchorage. There are no permanent telecommunications facilities.

GABON

Republique Gabonaise (Republic of Gabon)

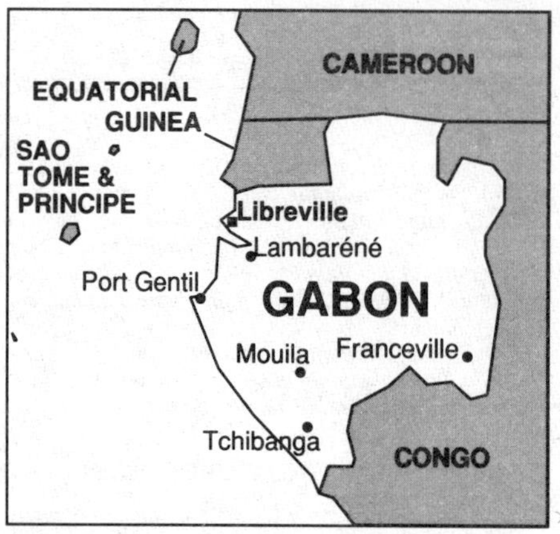

GEOGRAPHY

Gabon is an equatorial country on the west coast of Africa, covering a total area of 103,062 mile^2/ 267,000 km^2. The coastal plain is characterized by longshore bars, estuaries (including the mouth of the Ogooué river) and lagoons backed by gently rising land, climbing towards the African central plateau. The Ogooué river basin dominates Gabon's hydrology, occupying over 60% of the total surface area. The river itself flows from south-east to north-west, skirting the Massif du Chaillu which rises to 3,215 ft/980 m (Gabon's highest point) at Mont Ibounoji and draining a number of lakes west of Lambaréné. The northern Woleu-ntem basin drains into Río Muni (Equatorial Guinea) and Cameroon. Only a very small area of land is cultivated and two-thirds of the republic is covered by equatorial rainforest. Estuaire, on the north-west coast, is the most densely populated of the nine provinces.

Climate

Equatorial; hot and humid with plentiful rainfall. Inland, rainfall averages from 49/1,250–79/ 2,000 in/mm, increasing in coastal areas to 98 in/ 2,500 mm. The dry season lasts from mid-May to mid-Sept. Temperature is consistently high all year; mean annual temperature 81°F/27°C. Libreville: Jan 80°F/ 26.7°C. July 75°F/23.9°C. Average annual rainfall 99 in/2,510 mm.

Cities and towns

Libreville (capital)	251,400
Port-Gentil	77,611
Lambaréné	22,682

Population

Total population is 1.1 million, of which 43% live in urban areas. Population density is 10.7 persons per mile^2/4.1 per km^2. Over 40 distinct ethnic groups of Bantu origin make up the indigenous population, of which the largest groups are the Fang 30% (north of the Ogooué river); the Eshira 25%; the Bateke and Bapounou (south of the river). An estimated 10% of the population are expatriate Europeans and Africans. **Birth rate** 3.38%. **Death rate** 1.8%. **Rate of population increase** 1.57%. **Age distribution** under 15 = 34.3%; over 65 = 5.9%. **Life expectancy** female 54; male 51; average 52.

Religion

Approximately 60% of the population are Christian, predominantly Roman Catholic (over 560,000 adherents), although the Evangelical Church of Gabon and the Christian Missionary alliance also have significant memberships. 1% of the population are Muslims. Nearly 40% of the population follow traditional animist beliefs.

Language

French is the official language, but Fang, Myene, Bateke and other Bantu dialects are widespread.

HISTORY

Palaeolithic and Neolithic artefacts have been discovered in Gabon, but the immigration of Bantu-speaking peoples, the present inhabitants, is probably contemporary with the early Christian era. The Fang, now predominant, arrived in the late 18th century, attracted by the opportunities for trade with Europeans on the coast. Portuguese explorers discovered the Gabon estuary in 1483 and were soon followed by French, British and Dutch slave traders. France secured treaties with Mpongwe chiefs in 1838–42 and from 1843 to 1886 Gabon came under French naval administration. In 1886 Gabon became a French colony, administered as part of French Equatorial Africa. The colony was divided between concessionary companies in 1898. These companies treated conscripted native labourers ruthlessly but, despite widespread protests, the concessions were not abolished until 1930.

In 1958 Gabon became an autonomous republic within the French community; it moved to full independence on 17 Aug. 1960. Léon M'ba, a former mayor of Libreville, was elected president in Feb. 1961. In Jan. 1964 M'ba dissolved the national assembly, promising new elections the following month, but the military deposed him (18 Feb. 1964) and installed his rival Jean-Hilaire Aubame, former foreign minister, as head of state. France intervened (under the terms of a defence agreement signed in 1960) and M'ba was reinstated as president.

Mba's Bloc démocratique gabonais (BDG) won a majority at the Apr. 1964 elections and in Mar. 1967 no opposition candidates stood for election. When M'ba died (Nov. 1967) his vice-president, Albert-Bernard Bongo, acceded to the presidency. In Mar. 1968, Pres. Bongo instituted single-party government through the Parti démocratique gabonais (PDG). Although there was some opposition to single-party rule and the government's liberal economic policies, which afford foreign investors considerable benefits, the country was politically stable throughout the 1970s. Influenced by Libya, Bongo broke off relations with

Israel in Sept. 1973, became a Muslim and changed his name to Omar. Nevertheless, the government retained close ties with France and the west.

At the Jan. 1979 PDG congress several of Bongo's close allies lost their seats and delegates were critical of some government policies. In 1981 there were anti-government demonstrations at the University, organized by the Mouvement de redressement national (MORENA), a moderate opposition group. Members of MORENA were given harsh sentences at a trial in Nov. 1982 but subsequently reprieved. In May 1985 Pres. Bongo appealed to opposition leaders to return to Gabon but reaffirmed his commitment to single-party government. A MORENA candidate who stood in the Nov. 1987 presidential elections was prevented from organizing his campaign. MORENA responded by forming a government-in-exile. Political opposition or public criticism of the regime was discouraged. In early 1988, French newspapers were seized after they published allegations that Bongo had misused French aid.

Unrest in the form of strikes and protests in Jan. and Feb. 1990 provoked by IMF-sponsored economic austerity measures caused the government to postpone legislative elections scheduled for April, and to initiate meetings to discuss constitutional reform. In Feb. 1990 the PDG was dissolved and reformed as the Rassemblement social-democrate gabonaise to encourage wider popular participation.

CONSTITUTION AND GOVERNMENT

Executive and legislature

The president is head of state, and holds executive authority, appointing the prime minister (who is designated head of government) and the council of ministers. The president is elected directly, for a seven-year term (last elections Nov. 1986), as the sole candidate nominated by the ruling and sole legal party. The party's single list of approved candidates is also the basis for elections held by universal adult suffrage every five years to choose 111 members of the National Assembly; a further nine deputies are appointed by the president.

Present government

President El Hadj Omar Bongo

Prime Minister; Head of Government, Minister of Finance, Budget and State Shareholdings, Planning, Development and Economy Léon Mebiame

Other principal members of Council of Ministers

Ministers of State without portfolios: Georges Rawiri; Guy-Etienne Mouvagha-Tchioba; Emile Kassa Mapsi; Simon Essimengane

Jean Ping (Information, Posts and Telecommunications, Reform of Parastatals; Relations with Parliament, Government Spokesman); Ali Ben Bongo (Foreign Affairs and Co-operation); Julien Mpouho-Epigat (National Defence, Veterans' Affairs and Public Security; Mines and Hydro-carbons).

Ruling party The Gabonese Democratic Party (Parti démocratique gabonais) was replaced by the Gabonese Social Democrat Rally in Feb. 1990. *Founding chairman and secretary general* El Hadj Omar Bongo. *First secretary* Léon Mebiame.

Justice

The system is based on the French codified civil law system and customary law. The highest court is the Supreme Court, which may conduct judicial review of legislation, and is the highest appeal court. The superior courts are the tribunaux de grande instance at Libreville, Port-Gentil, Lambaréné, Mouila, Oyem, Masuku and Koulamoutou; in Libreville there is a central Criminal Court and Court of Appeal. The death penalty is in force. There was 1 execution between 1985 and mid-1988, for the capital offence of plotting to overthrow the government.

National symbols

Flag. Tricolour with horizontal stripes coloured green, yellow and blue.

Festivals. 12 Mar. (Anniversary of the Renovation, foundation of the Parti démocratique gabonais); 1 May (Labour Day); 17 Aug. (Anniversary of Independence).

Vehicle registration plate. G.

INTERNATIONAL RELATIONS

Affiliations

NAM; OAU; ACP; OPEC; ICO; Francophonie.

Defence

Total Armed Forces: 3,000. Terms of service: voluntary.

Army: 1,900.

Navy: 500; six patrol and coastal combatants.

Air Force: 600; ten combat aircraft (Mirage 5) and five armed helicopters.

Para-military: Coastguard 2,800; Gendarmerie 2,000.

ECONOMY

Currency

The unit is the CFA franc, divided into 100 centimes.

National finance

Budget. The 1988 budget (in US$) was for expenditure (current and capital) of 1,200 million and revenue of 927 million.

Balance of payments. The balance of payments (current account, 1987) was a deficit of $231 million.

Inflation. (1987) –1%.

Gross Domestic Product

Estimated total GDP US$3,500 million, per capita US$3,300 (ranking 100 in the world by size).

Economically active population. The total number of persons active in the economy was 120,000.

Sector	% of workforce	% of GDP
industry	30	41
agriculture	65	11
services*	5	48

* services figure includes elements unassigned to other categories.

Energy and mineral resources

Oil and gas. Crude petroleum production 8,730,216 tons/7,920,000 tonnes (1987); natural gas 8 petajoules (1985). There are two oil refineries, at Port-Gentil and Pointe Clairette.

Minerals. Uranium ore production: (1986) 1010 tons/917 tonnes; manganese ore (1985) 1.3 million tons/1.2 million tonnes; gold (1985) 68 lb/31 kg. The exploitation of an estimated 937 million tons/850 million tonnes of iron ore reserves at Mekabo in the north-east is dependent upon the completion of a branch railway line.

Electricity. Capacity: 310,000 kW; production: (1988)

976 million kWh, mainly from thermal plants, although hydroelectric schemes are being developed.

Bioresources

Agriculture. The agricultural sector is relatively underdeveloped, although a large proportion of the population is engaged in subsistence farming.

Crop production: (1986 in 1,000 tons/tonnes) sugar cane 143/130; cassava 281/255; plantain 187/170; maize 12/11; groundnuts 8.8/8; bananas 8.8/8; palm-oil 4/3.6; cocoa 2.2/2; coffee 1.1/1; rice 1.1/1.

Livestock numbers: (1987) cattle 9,000; sheep 83,000; goats 63,000; pigs 153,000.

Forestry. Nearly 80% of the land area is equatorial forest. Production of okoumé and other softwoods was 48.73 million ft^3/1.38 million m^3 (1985). Hardwoods including mahogany, ebony and walnut are also exported.

Fisheries. Total catch of freshwater and marine fishes, including shrimp: (1986 est.) 22,486,920 tons/20,400,000 tonnes

Industry and commerce

Industry. The industrial sector accounts for only 8% of GDP. Most manufacturing is based on the processing of food (including sugar refining), timber and mineral resources. The economy is dominated by the oil sector. During the period 1981–85 oil accounted for about 46% of GDP, 83% of export earnings and 65% of government revenue, on average. In 1986 however GDP declined for the first time in a decade following the fall in oil prices in 1985.

Commerce. Gabon's exports amounted to US$1,950 million (1986 est.), of which crude oil accounted for 67%; manganese 11%; wood 11%; uranium 6%. Principal destinations for exports: France 53%; US 22%; West Germany; Japan. Imports $950 million, comprising foodstuffs; chemical products; petroleum products; construction materials; manufactures; machinery. Principal trading partners France 48%; US 2.6%; West Germany; Japan; UK.

Trade with UK. Gabon exported goods worth approximately £5 million to the UK in 1988, and imported goods worth £18.8 million.

COMMUNICATIONS

Railways

There are some 559 miles/900 km of railways.

Roads

There are 4,284 miles/6,898 km of roads, of which 456 miles/735 km are concrete or bituminized.

Aviation

Air Affaires Gabon provides domestic serivices and Compagnie Nationale Air Gabon provides international services (main airports are at Libreville, Port-Gentil and Franceville). Passengers (1984) 0.4 million.

Shipping

994 miles/1,600 km of the inland waterways are navigable all year round. The maritime ports on the Gulf of Guinea are Owendo, Port-Gentil and Libreville. The merchant marine has two cargo ships of 1,000 GRT or over. Freight loaded: (1986) 6.5 million tons/5.9 million tonnes; unloaded: 1.1 million tons/1.0 million tonnes.

Telecommunications

There are 13,800 telephones and an adequate facility of open-wire and radio-relay systems. There are 102,000 radios and 20,000 televisions (1983). Broadcasting is principally by the state-owned RTG and the commercial stations Africa No. 1 (radio) and Tele-Africa.

EDUCATION AND WELFARE

Education

Education is officially compulsory for ten years between the ages of six and 16. There are state-run and mission-run schools. There is a six-year primary cycle, beginning at age six, and a seven-year secondary cycle, from age 12.

School population. An estimated 75% of children in the relevant age group attended primary and secondary schools in 1984, representing 78% of boys and 72% of girls.

Schools. (1984/85) 940 primary schools with 178,111 pupils and 3,837 teachers (one per 47 pupils); 51 secondary schools with 25,815 pupils and 1,894 teachers (one per 14 pupils); 29 technical and teacher-training establishments with 13,529 students and 720 teachers (one per 19 students).

University. The Université Omar Bongo at Libreville had 2,505 students in 1985.

Literacy. Adult literacy (1985 est.) 61.6% (males 70.2%; females 53.4%).

Health

In 1985 there were 565 physicians (approximately one per 2,170 inhabitants). There were 28 hospitals, 87 medical centres and 312 dispensaries, with a total of 5,156 beds (one per 238 inhabitants).

GAMBIA

Republic of the Gambia

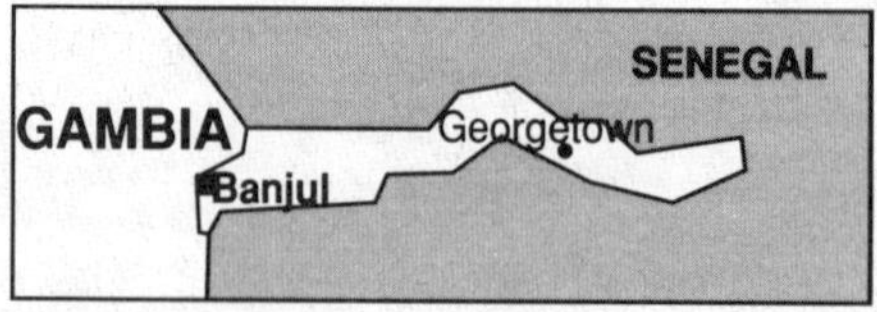

GEOGRAPHY

Gambia is a narrow 200 miles/322 km-long enclave within Senegal on the west coast of Africa. 20% of its total surface area of 4,359 miles^2/11,295 km^2 is occupied by the River Gambia, which flows east-west. The river flows over a low undulating landscape (82/25–246/75 ft/m elevation, high point 295 ft/90 m) through dry savannah and swampland and is navigable for 124 miles/200 km of its middle-lower course. Approximately 25% of the land is arable. Gambia is divided into eight local government areas, of which Banjul is the most densely populated.

Climate

Subtropical. Wet season lasts June–Oct., with the south-west monsoon bringing abundant rainfall and increased humidity. Annual rainfall averages range between 30/760 and 55/1,400 in/mm. The dry season lasts Nov.–May with light rainfall and substantially reduced humidity. Annual temperatures range from 61°F/16°C–109°F/43°C. Banjul: Jan. 73°F/22.8°C. July 80°F/26.7°C. Average annual rainfall 51 in/ 1,295 mm.

Cities and towns

Serekunda	68,433
Banjul (capital)	44,188
Birkama	19,584
Bakau	19,309
Farafenni	10,168
Sukuta	7,227
Gunjur	7,115

Population

Total population is 812,000 of which 21.2% live in urban areas. Population density is 186.3 persons per mile²/71.9 per km². Principal ethnic groups are the Madinka 37.7%; Fula 16.2%; Wolof 14%; Jola 8.5%; Sarahulis 6%. Non Gambians: 10.5%.

Birth rate 4.82%. **Death rate** 2.31%. **Rate of population increase** 2.51%. **Age distribution** under 15 = 43.4%; over 65 = 2.9%. **Life expectancy** female 44; male 40; average 42.

Religion

The majority (85%) of the population consists of Muslims. Approximately 14% are Christians, of whom 14,300 are Roman Catholic. A few isolated groups pursue animist customs and beliefs, particularly the Jola and Karonika peoples.

Language

English is the official language. Arabic is taught in some schools. The chief regional languages are Madinka, Wolof and Fula.

HISTORY

Both banks of the Gambia river had been inhabited for several centuries by black pastoralists before Muslim Arab traders arrived in the 13th century. The area came under the sway of the Mali Empire in the 14th to 16th centuries. From the time of the first contacts with Europeans along this coast in the 15th century, the history of the Gambia is scarcely distinguishable from that of Senegal until 1816, when Lt-Col. Charles MacCarthy, lieutenant-governor of the British colony of Sierra Leone, founded the town of Bathurst on St Mary's Island, at the mouth of the River Gambia. The establishment of a British colony there was largely his personal initiative, motivated by resentment of the British government's decision to return the Senegalese colonies of Dakar and Gorée to the French after they had been briefly administered by the British during the Napoleonic wars.

For much of the 19th century The Gambia, which the British governed mostly from Sierra Leone, was used as a bargaining counter in the European carve-up of Africa. In 1888 it became a formal British colony and its current boundaries were agreed with the French the following year. Like Senegal its principal source of revenue was groundnuts (peanuts), first exported from the colony in 1835. The British did little to develop the colony until the 1950s when the harbour facilities at Bathurst were improved, a road-building programme initiated and the education system (which boasted no more than six primary schools in 1940) was rapidly expanded in anticipation of independence.

The Gambia became independent on 18 Feb. 1965, having already enjoyed a considerable degree of self-government since 1960. In Apr. 1970 the country became a republic. Sir Dawda Jawara's People's Progressive Party has been in power continuously since independence. In July 1981, whilst Sir Dawda was in London for the wedding of the Prince of Wales, a coup attempt was put down by Senegalese troops. The following year plans were announced by the Senegalese and Gambian administrations for the creation of the Senegambian Confederation but despite some move towards economic union, harmonization of tariff barriers and improvement of transport links, the Confederation (formed 1 Feb. 1982) with its Confederal Parliament was mainly a symbolic gesture against the absurdity of the colonial boundaries. The Confederation was formally dissolved in Sept. 1989 after Senegal unilaterally withdrew the troops it had stationed in The Gambia since the 1981 coup attempt. Like other countries in the region, The Gambia has suffered great hardships during the droughts of the 1970s and 1980s. However, the economy is now less dependent upon groundnuts for foreign exchange, as the country has developed a flourishing tourist industry.

CONSTITUTION AND GOVERNMENT

Executive and legislature

As an independent republic within the Commonwealth since Feb. 1965, Gambia's head of state is the president, in whom executive power is vested; the president is elected by universal suffrage for a five-year term. The legislature, the unicameral House of Representatives, is also elected for a five-year term (last elections May 1987).

Present government

President; Minister of National Defence; C.-in-C. of the Armed Forces Sir Dawda Kairaba Jawara

Vice-President, Minister of Education, Youth and Sports Bakary Bunja Darbo

Principal Ministers: Omar Amadou Jallow (Agriculture and Natural Resources); Memba Jatta (Economic Planning and Industrial Development); Omar Sey (External Affairs); Saihou S. Sabally (Finance and Trade); Lamin Kiti Jabang (Interior); Hassan Jallow (Justice, Attorney General).

Justice

The system of law is based on a composite of English common law, customary law, and Islamic law. The highest court is the Supreme Court, which consists of the Chief Justice and Puisne Judges, all appointed by the President, advised by a Judicial Service Commission. There is a Court of Appeal and various subordinate Courts and Islamic courts. The death penalty is in force. No executions were recorded between 1985 and mid-1988.

National symbols

Flag. Three horizontal stripes of red, blue and green, separated by two narrow white stripes.

Festivals. 1 Feb. (Senegambia Confederation Day); 18 Feb. (Independence Day); 1 May (Labour Day).
Vehicle registration plate. WAG.

INTERNATIONAL RELATIONS

Affiliations

NAM; OAU; ACP; ICO; Commonwealth.

Defence

Total Armed Forces: 600. Terms of service: voluntary, some compulsory conditions authorized.
Para-military: 400 (Gendarmerie).

ECONOMY

Currency

The unit is the dalasi, divided into 100 bututs.

National finance

Budget. The 1987 budget (in US$) was for expenditure (current and capital) of 75 million and revenue of 66 million.
Inflation. (1988) 13.2%.

Gross Domestic Product

Estimated total GDP US$145 million, per capita US$180 (ranking 171 in the world by size).
Economically active population. The total number of persons active in the economy was 400,000. Agriculture accounts for 75% of the workforce.

Energy and mineral resources

Minerals. Reserves of heavy minerals including ilmenite, zircon and rutile have been discovered but remain to be exploited.
Electricity. Capacity: 29,000 kW; production: (1988) 64 million kWh.

Bioresources

Agriculture. Crop production and livestock raising on a subsistence basis is the activity of most of the population. Groundnuts are the only important cash crop, accounting for over 75% of total export revenue. Cotton is produced in small quantities. Fish and rice are the principal foods. About one-third of all food needs is imported.
Crop production: (1987 in tons/tonnes) groundnuts 132,276/120,000; rice 35,274/32,000.
Livestock numbers: (1987) cattle 300,000; goats 200,000; sheep 195,000; pigs 13,000; poultry (1982) 300,000.
Fisheries. Total catch: (1986) 11,100 tons/ 10,077 tonnes.
Forestry. Roundwood removals: (1986 est.) 30,228,784 ft^3/856,000 m^3.

Industry and commerce

Industry. Small-scale industrial activity includes processing of groundnuts, fish and hides.
Commerce. Exports: (1987 financial year) US$70 million, comprising groundnuts; groundnut products; fish; cotton lint; palm kernels. Principal destination for exports: Ghana 49%; Europe 27%; Japan 12%; US 1%. Imports: $117.5 million, chiefly foodstuffs; manufactures; raw materials; fuel; machinery; transport equipment. Principal trading partners: (1986) EC countries 39%; other European countries 16%; Asia 20%; US 11%; Senegal 4%.
Trade with UK. The Gambia exported goods worth £2.9 million to the UK in 1988 and imported goods worth £19.2 million from the UK.
Tourism. (1985/86) 78,268 visitors.

COMMUNICATIONS

Railways

There are no railways.

Roads

There are some 1,490 miles/2,400 km of roads, of which 312 miles/504 km are concrete or bituminized.

Aviation

Gambia Air Shuttle provides international services (main airport is at Yundum, 16.8 miles/27 km from Banjul).

Shipping

There are 248 miles/400 km of inland waterways. The maritime port is Banjul.

Telecommunications

There are 3,500 telephones and an adequate network of radio relay and wire systems. There are 110,000 radios (1986), with services from the government Radio Gambia and commercial Radio Syd. Television transmissions from Senegal can be received.

EDUCATION AND WELFARE

Education

Free primary education is provided but is not compulsory. The six-year primary-level cycle begins at age eight. A common entrance examination offers access to secondary school, where pupils choose either a four-year course at a technical secondary school or five years at a secondary high school.
School population. (1985 est.) 68% of children in the relevant age group were enrolled at primary school (representing 84% of boys and 53% of girls). At secondary level enrolment was equivalent to only 17% of children aged between 14 and 19 (23% of boys and 10% of girls).
Schools. (1984/85) 189 primary schools with 66,257 pupils and 2,640 teachers (one per 25 pupils); 16 secondary technical schools, with 10,102 pupils and 502 teachers (one per 20 pupils); eight secondary high schools, with 4,348 pupils and 235 teachers (one per 19 pupils); eight post-secondary schools, with 1,489 students and 179 teachers (one per 8 students).
University. Students must travel abroad for university-level education.
Literacy. (1985 est.) 25.1% (males 35.6%; females 15.1%).

Health

(1980) 43 government doctors (one per 18,329 inhabitants), four hospitals, 12 health centres, 17 dispensaries and 68 maternity and child welfare clinics.

GERMANY, EAST

Deutsche Demokratische Republik – DDR (German Democratic Republic – GDR)

GEOGRAPHY

East Germany is located in north central Europe and covers a total area of 41,817 miles²/108,333 km² excluding West Berlin (185 miles²/480 km²). Extending south from the 155 miles/250 km Baltic coastline, the fertile north German plain (average elevation 328 ft/100 m) exhibits a typical glaciated lowland physiography with rolling morainic hills and lakes (incl. Lake Müritz 45 miles²/117 km²). A belt of rich loess spanning the country from Magdeburger Borde to the Nieder/Oberlausitz marks the southernmost extremity of the lowlands and the beginning of the Mittelgebirge (Middle German Highlands) which range from the Harz Mountains and Thüringer Wald in the west to the Erzgebirge (Ore Mts) on the Czech border (including Fichtelberg, the highest peak at 8,983 ft/1,214 m) and on to the Polish/Czechoslovak Sudeten range. The River Elbe traverses the country south-east to north-west draining approx. 75% of the land surface area along with its tributaries the Spree, Saale and Havel. The River Oder, flowing south-north along the Polish frontier, is connected to the Elbe by the Hohenzollern canal and the Elbe to the Ruhr by the Mittelland canal. The most densely populated of East Germany's 15 counties are East Berlin, Karl Marx Stadt and Leipzig. Almost 50% of the land is arable and 30% is forested.

Climate

Temperate continental, giving warm summers and clear, generally mild winters interspersed with freezing spells and considerable snowfall. Lowland winter temperatures average between 30°F/−1°C and 34°F/1°C rising to between 59°F/15°C and 70°F/21°C in July. Interior highland temperatures can drop to a mean 19°F/−7°C during the winter months, climbing to between 50°F/10°C and 59°F/15°C in summer. Rainfall is rarely above 31 in/780 mm in low-lying areas but commonly exceeds 39 in/1,000 mm at higher altitudes. Berlin: Jan. 30°F/−0.5°C. July 66°F/19°C. Average annual rainfall 22 in/563 mm. Dresden: Jan. 30°F/−1°C. July 65°F/18.5°C. Average annual rainfall 27 in/680 mm.

Cities and towns

East Berlin (capital)	1,246,872
Leipzig	549,229
Dresden	519,524
Karl Marx Stadt	313,347
Magdeburg	289,627
Rostock	250,727
Halle an der Saale	235,730
Erfurt	217,961

Population

Total population is 16,645,000 of which 76.6% live in urban areas. Population density is 398/153.2 persons per mile²/km². 99.7% of the population are German, but there are an estimated 110,000 Sorbs (Slav minority) concentrated in the south-eastern counties of Cottbus and Dresden.

Birth rate 1.41%. **Death rate** 1.36%. **Rate of population increase** 0.5%. **Age distribution** under 15 = 19.3%; over 65 = 13.6%. **Life expectancy** female 76; male 70; average 73.

Religion

An estimated 58% of the population are Christian (50% Protestant; 8% Roman Catholic). 25% of the population belong to one of the affiliated churches of the Bekdor (Synod of Lutheran Churches). There are an estimated 5,000 Jewish citizens in the Democratic Republic.

Language

German. Regional dialects, eg Plattdeutsch (north Mecklenburg) and Saxon (south Saxony) are still in common use. The Sorbian minority retain their own language. (See West Germany for further information on German language variants).

HISTORY

Recorded German history traditionally begins in AD 9, when a Germanic tribe called the Cherusci defeated three Roman legions in the Teutoburg Forest, thus preventing Roman penetration beyond the Rhineland. West Germanic tribes overran Roman Gaul and adjoining regions in the 4th and 5th centuries AD and established the Frankish Empire, which was Christianized from the late 7th century and reached its zenith under Charlemagne (r.768–814), who was crowned Roman Emperor by the Pope in 800. After the Partition of Verdun (843) had separated German-speaking Franconia from what was to become France,

Duke Conrad was elected the first German king in 911. The monarchy was strengthened and its realms expanded by Otto I of the Saxon dynasty (r.936–73), for whom the title Emperor was revived in 962. After a great age under Henry III (r.1039–56), the Empire was weakened by the investiture dispute with Pope Gregory VII, to whom Henry IV (r.1056–1106) was forced to do penance at Canossa (1077). Frederick I Barbarossa (r.1152–90) revived imperial power, but his successors were unable to halt the fragmentation of Germany into a myriad of semi-sovereign states. German expansion eastward among the Slav peoples was continued by the Teutonic Knights, a Christian military order founded in 1190, while the Hanseatic League of the north German and allied cities established a virtual monopoly of Baltic and North Sea trade by the 13th century.

Following the fall of the Hohenstaufen dynasty (1254), Count Rudolf of Habsburg emerged as King of the Germans and Holy Roman Emperor (1273). For the next 600 years the history of Germany was inextricably bound up with that of the Austrian Habsburg dynasty. Although Emperor Charles IV's Golden Bull of 1356 vested the election of the German king in the seven leading German princes (electors), from 1438 the Habsburg emperors held a virtual monopoly of the German and imperial titles. About 1448 Germany made one of its greatest contributions to civilization when Johann Gutenberg of Mainz invented the process of printing with movable type. In the 16th century, the Catholic imperial system was challenged in Germany by the Protestant doctrines of Martin Luther (1483–1546), which inspired a bloody peasants' revolt (1524–25) and provoked a century of religious wars. The Peace of Augsburg (1555) accorded Protestants equal rights with Catholics and empowered German princes to opt for Protestantism if they wished. The Habsburg-led Counter-Reformation caused renewed Catholic–Protestant conflict, culminating in the Thirty Years' War (1618–48) and the wholesale devastation of Germany. The Peace of Westphalia (1648) confirmed the political and religious sovereignty of the German states within a weakened Empire, while German territories in the east and north were ceded to France and Sweden.

From the late 17th century the age of absolutism enabled the leading German states, notably Prussia/Brandenburg, Bavaria, Saxony and Hanover, to become considerable powers in their own right. In the War of Austrian Succession (1740–48), Frederick the Great of Prussia (r.1740–86) acquired Silesia from Austria, thus emerging as the Habsburgs' principal rival for leadership of the Germans. In the Seven Years' War (1756–63), Frederick led Prussia to the brink of defeat against heavy odds, but finally triumphed over the Austrians. Both Austria and Prussia gained territory from the first partition of Poland (from 1772), but both were overwhelmingly defeated by the French revolutionary armies of Napoleon Bonaparte (1796–97, 1805–06). Under Napoleon's tutelage, the political map of western Germany was redrawn by the enforced merger of the host of mini-principalities into 16 larger states, which were themselves bound together in the French-dominated Rhenish League (1806). Austria's Emperor then renounced the imperial title, bringing a final end to the Holy Roman Empire. On Napoleon's defeat, the Congress of Vienna (1814–15) created a new German Confederation (largely maintaining the Napoleonic restructuring) under the nominal leadership of Austria. Prussia and Austria were major territorial beneficiaries under the settlement, the former in Germany and the latter in northern Italy.

Post-1815 aspirations to German unification were apparent in the creation of the Zollverein customs union embracing 18 states including Prussia (Jan. 1834), but the pro-unification forces of democracy and nationalism were blocked by autocratic regimes. Austria's powerful Chancellor Metternich (1809–48) reached agreement with Frederick Wiliam III of Prussia on the need for strict censorship and surveillance of revolutionaries, implemented also in nine other German states under the Carlsbad Decrees (Sept. 1819), and Germany was little affected by the European unrest of 1830. When the upsurge of revolutionary movements throughout Europe encouraged liberals in the Confederation's directly elected but powerless parliament at Frankfurt to demand a united, constitutional Germany, the Austrian Emperor rejected a Germany excluding the non-German Habsburg domains; Frederick William IV of Prussia (r. 1840–61) was offered the post of Emperor under a constitution approved by the Frankfurt parliament in Mar. 1849, but declined the throne of a 'smaller Germany' (ie without Austria). The Confederation was re-established under Austrian leadership (1850), until in the 1860s Otto von Bismarck brought about 'smaller' German unification from above. Appointed Prussian chancellor in 1862, Bismarck showed great diplomatic skill in warding off wider European intervention as the Prussian army under von Moltke firstly, with Austria, dispossessed Denmark of the mainly German provinces of Schleswig and Holstein (1864), next turned south to crush Austria (June–July 1866, the decisive battle being at Sadowa on 3 July) and thus forced the Habsburgs to vacate the German stage, and finally routed the French armies of Louis Napoleon (Aug. 1870 to Jan. 1871, the French capitulating as Paris came under Prussian artillery bombardment). The southern German states then opted to join a new German Empire, declared at Versailles on 1 Jan. 1871 with William I of Prussia (r.1861–88) as Emperor and Berlin as its capital. Under the Treaty of Frankfurt (1871), France ceded Alsace and Lorraine to Germany and agreed to pay war reparations.

Rapid industrialization made the new Germany a major economic as well as military power, although politically it was dominated by the Junkers, the Prussian officer class. In the Kulturkampf, known in English as the 'conflict of beliefs' (1871–87), Bismarck waged an unproductive campaign against Catholic opposition to his system. The May Laws in Prussia (1873) and their extensions over the next two years in particular established civil authority over church appointments and over marriage and other ceremonies, and dissolved religious orders. Bismarck also moved to outlaw (1878–90) the Social Democratic Party (SPD, founded 1875), while enacting progressive social legislation in an attempt to placate the expanding working class, but failed thereby to prevent the development by the end of the century of a disciplined and well-organized socialist movement.

Externally, Bismarck constructed a system of alliances to isolate France, notably the Alliance with Austria-Hungary (1879), expanded into the Triple Alliance including Italy (1882), and the Reinsurance Treaty with Russia (1887). The accession of William II (r.1888–1918) led to Bismarck's resignation (1890) amid policy differences with the new Emperor, who replaced him initially with the more conciliatory Caprivi (1890–94). The new Kaiser aspired to a world role for Germany and allowed the Russian treaty to lapse. Germany had acquired colonies in Africa and the Pacific in 1884–85 (when the Partition of Africa was mapped out by the European powers at the Conference of Berlin), became Britain's main commercial competitor, and from 1898 constructed a battle fleet to rival Britain's, with the support of a popular campaign mobilized by Tirpitz's Navy League (founded 1898) to push through the celebrated Navy Bill passed in Mar. 1898. France and Britain reacted by forming an Entente (1904), which was extended to Russia in 1907. Tension between the two blocs strengthened the German military at the expense of the Emperor's ministers and the Reichstag (parliament), in which the SPD became the largest party in 1912, although it played no part in government.

A series of incidents on the international stage illustrated the growing dangers of Franco–German, and increasingly Anglo–German, rivalry which might precipitate war. When in southern Africa the British-backed Jameson Raid failed to overthrow the Transvaal Boer republic (Dec. 1895) the Kaiser stung British feeling by sending the congratulatory Kruger telegram to the Boer leader; in Oct. 1904 he offered Russia his support if war between Britain and Russia were to follow from the Dogger Bank incident (when Russian ships fired on British fishing boats); in Mar. 1905 he landed at Tangier to speak out for Moroccan independence despite French ambitions there, but had to back down the following year at the Algeciras conference (Jan. 1906). Another Moroccan crisis erupted when the German gunboat Panther was sent to Agadir, bringing Britain to the support of France and Europe to the brink of war before the Germans backed down, grudgingly allowing a French protectorate over Morocco in return for territorial concessions in the Congo. However, it was not on the imperial stage but in the Balkans, where Germany underwrote Austria–Hungary's expansionism in the Slav-populated former Ottoman provinces, that the spark ignited European war. After a Serbian nationalist had assassinated Archduke Ferdinand at Sarajevo in June 1914, Austria–Hungary's declaration of war on Serbia caused Russia to mobilize, whereupon Germany declared war on Russia and France, and then brought in Britain by violating Belgian neutrality.

German expectations of speedy victory in World War I were disappointed, as the western front against France and Britain became bogged down in attritional trench warfare. The Central Powers (Germany, Austria–Hungary, Bulgaria and Turkey) fared better in the east, where Russia's heavy defeats precipitated revolution and acceptance by the new Bolshevik regime of the humiliating Brest-Litovsk Treaty (Mar. 1918). By then, the United States had entered the war (Apr. 1917) on the side of Britain and France, whose allies included Japan and Italy. After a push for victory in the west had turned into general retreat, Germany signed an armistice (Nov. 1918) tantamount to accepting defeat. Emperor William immediately abdicated (9 Nov.) and fled to the Netherlands, whereupon a Republic was declared. Friedrich Ebert (SPD) formed a government, put down the Communist uprising of the Spartakists led by Karl Liebknecht and Rosa Luxemburg (Jan. 1919) with the help of the Free Corps irregular volunteers, and in Bavaria crushed an attempt to create a soviet republic (Apr. 1919). A right-wing coup attempt, the Kapp Putsch, was put down the following year, but with notable leniency towards the army officers involved.

Meanwhile constituent assembly elections (19 Jan. 1919) saw Ebert's Majority Socialists emerge with enough support to ensure his election (10 Feb.) as first president of the Weimar Republic. The Versailles Peace Treaty (June 1919) imposed harsh terms on Germany, including surrender of all colonies, demilitarization of the Rhineland, return of Alsace–Lorraine to France, curbs on military capacity, payment of huge reparations, and acceptance of 'war guilt'. The treaty was signed under protest by the Weimar Republic, which in 1922–23 weathered Bolshevik insurgency, financial collapse, French occupation of the Ruhr and a putsch attempt (1923) by an obscure Austrian fascist called Adolf Hitler. A period of stability followed, under the presidency of Field Marshal von Hindenburg from 1925, accompanied by a cultural renaissance in Berlin. Guided by Gustav Stresemann, first briefly as chancellor in 1923 and then until 1929 as foreign minister, Germany signed the Locarno Pact (Dec. 1925) regulating relations in Europe and was admitted to the League of Nations (1926).

The post–1929 world recession, bringing mass unemployment to Germany, exposed the fragility of the Weimar Republic, which came under attack from the powerful Communist Party (formed by SPD leftists in 1918) and also from Hitler's National Socialist German Workers' Party (NSDAP or Nazis). Propagating a potent mix of mystical nationalism, rejection of the Versailles terms and anti-semitism, the Nazis advanced electorally from 18.3% in 1930 to 37.4% in July 1932, replacing the SPD as the largest party. Heinrich Brüning, appointed chancellor by Pres. Hindenburg (28 Mar. 1930) when the ruling coalition of middle-class and socialist parties fell apart, had been trying for two years to govern, amid economic and political turmoil, by the exercise of the presidential emergency powers, but in May 1932 he gave way to the Papen government. Nazi street violence reached a peak that summer as Hitler's supporters sought to show that the country was ungovernable without him. Although in elections in Nov. 1932 the Nazis fell back to 33.2% (less than the combined SPD and Communist share), Hindenburg reluctantly appointed Hitler as Chancellor on 30 Jan. 1933 at the head of a coalition whose non-Nazi ministers were supposed to curb Nazi extremism. The burning of the Reichstag building (27 Feb. 1933) gave Hitler an excuse to assume emergency powers and to call new elections (Mar. 1933), in which the Nazis took 43.9% and 288 of the 647 seats. An immediate Enabling Act, approved by the centre-right parties, then gave Hitler absolute power to eliminate his opponents and to establish centralized one-party rule.

German industrialists, fearful of communism, welcomed the suppression of the labour movement. Many Catholics were impressed by his Concordat with the Vatican (July 1933) assuring the Church full religious freedom, in return for its loyalty to the state, to be sworn by its bishops under oath, and the abstention of the clergy from political involvement. The military establishment applauded Hitler's withdrawal from the League of Nations (1933) and his 'night of the long knives' against the leadership of his own party's paramilitary Sturmabteilungen or SA (June 1934). On Hindenburg's death (Aug. 1934), Hitler was proclaimed Führer (leader) of the German Empire (known as the Third Reich), combining the roles of head of state and commander-in-chief.

Assisted by improved international conditions, Hitler quickly brought about economic recovery by reflationary expenditure on state projects such as rearmament and motorway construction. From 1934 German Jews were gradually deprived of civic and human rights; the notorious Nuremberg Laws, depriving Jews of citizenship, and outlawing extramarital sexual relations between Jew and non-Jew, were promulgated at the Nazi party congress in 1935, as the skilful Nazi propaganda techniques of Joseph Goebbels whipped popular support for Hitler into near-idolatry. On Kristallnacht (9–10 Nov. 1938) over 100 Jews died as mobs attacked their synagogues, shops and homes, and 30,000 were arrested, the beginning of the full-scale state pogrom.

The return of the Saar to full German sovereignty and Germany's abrogation of the Versailles armament restrictions (1935) were followed by the entry of German forces into the Rhineland (Mar. 1936). The Axis alliance with fascist Italy and the Anti-Comintern Pact with militarist Japan were concluded in 1936, while crucial German assistance was given to Franco's fascist revolt in Spain (the Spanish Civil War). In Mar. 1938 German forces marched unopposed into Austria, which under the Anschluss (annexation) was incorporated into the Reich. In the Munich agreement (Sept. 1938), Britain and France acceded to Germany's annexation of the German-populated Sudetenland in Czechoslavakia, the whole of which came under German control by Mar. 1939, as did the Memel territories of Lithuania. But these proved to be the last of Hitler's 'bloodless' victories. Following the signature of the Nazi–Soviet non-aggression pact in Aug. 1939, also known as the Molotov-Ribbentrop pact, which secretly partitioned eastern Europe, German forces invaded Poland, causing Britain and France on 3 Sept. to declare what became World War II.

Having quickly defeated Poland, German forces occupied Denmark and Norway (Apr.–May 1940) and overran the Low Countries and France (by June 1940), at which point Italy joined the war on Germany's side. Only Britain and its dominions then stood between Hitler and complete victory, although the anticipated German invasion of Britain did not occur. Instead, Hitler turned to the east, invading Yugoslavia and Greece (Apr. 1941) and then, in alliance with Finland, Hungary and Romania, he launched a massive invasion of the Soviet Union (June 1941). This took his forces to the outskirts of Leningrad and Moscow by mid-1942 and was not repelled until 1944 by which time some 20 million Soviet citizens had died in the struggle. In the German-controlled areas, Jewish communities and gypsies were rounded up and deported to extermination camps. Auschwitz-Birkenau in Poland was the most notorious, and by far the largest, of these death camps; out of 6 million Jews killed under Hitler, 2.5 million went to the gas chambers in that camp, from 1941 onwards, and another 500,000 died of disease and starvation there.

Germany and Italy had declared war on the US after the Japanese attack on Pearl Harbor (Dec. 1941). The tide turned against the Axis powers in late 1942, when Allied victory in North Africa led to invasion of Italy (which surrendered in Sept. 1943) while the Red Army began to advance from the east. In June 1944 Allied forces landed in Normandy, pushed the Germans back across France and the Low Countries and crossed the German border in Feb. 1945, as Allied bombing was reducing German cities to rubble. Having survived an assassination attempt by German officers in July 1944, Hitler committed suicide on 30 Apr. 1945. Germany's unconditional surrender was signed at Rheims (France) on 7 May 1945.

In accordance with decisions taken by the victorious Allies at Yalta and Potsdam, defeated Germany was placed under a four-power occupation regime consisting of Soviet, US, British and French zones. In a 'partition within a partition', Berlin was divided into a Soviet sector and three Western sectors under joint four-power control. Under post-war border changes, which were accompanied by the enforced migration of millions of ethnic Germans from eastern Europe to Germany, German territory to the east of the Oder–Neisse line was given to Poland and the Soviet Union took northern East Prussia (as well as pre-war eastern Poland and part of Czechoslovakia). Regarded as final by the Soviet Union, these changes were viewed by the Western Allies as provisional pending a formal peace treaty with Germany, whose borders under international law were deemed to be those in force at the end of 1937 (ie before Hitler's annexations). The onset of the Cold War (1947) created special strains in Germany, where the Soviet Union vigorously opposed Western plans for economic integration and self-government. When the Western powers included West Berlin in a West German currency reform (1948), the Soviet authorities imposed a blockade on road and rail access to Berlin from the West, forcing the Allies to mount a massive airlift to keep West Berlin supplied (1948–49). This episode hastened the political division of Germany into two states, one a free-market democracy aligned with the West and the other a Communist-ruled state within the Soviet bloc.

For history after 1949, please see separate entries for **Federal Republic of Germany** and **German Democratic Republic** below.

The German Democratic Republic (GDR) was proclaimed on 7 Oct. 1949 in the Soviet-occupied zone of Germany, some four months after the creation of the Federal Republic of Germany (FRG) in the three Western zones. By the time of the proclamation, effective political power resided in the Soviet-backed Socialist Unity Party (SED), created in Apr. 1946 by a merger of the Communist Party of Germany and the Social Democrats (SPD) in the Soviet zone (in GDR elections since 1949, all candidates have been nominated by the SED-dominated National Front, embracing four other parties as well as mass organizations). The GDR was immediately recognized by the Soviet Union (whereas the Western powers and the FRG maintained that it had no legal basis) and was admitted to membership of the Council for Mutual Economic Assistance (Comecon) in Oct. 1950. Walter Ulbricht (1893–1973), a Weimar Republic Communist who had fled to Moscow in 1933, became SED general secretary in 1951 and over the next two decades (from 1960 as head of state as well as party leader) imposed rigid Stalinism. Anti-government uprisings by workers in East Berlin and other cities in 1953 were ruthlessly suppressed with assistance from the Soviet occupation forces.

Following the FRG's accession to NATO (May 1955), the GDR the same month became a founder member of the Warsaw Pact. From 1958 Soviet moves to integrate the whole of Berlin into the GDR created tensions with the three Western powers leading, by decision of the Warsaw Pact, to the construction of the Berlin Wall (Aug. 1961). Later extended along the whole GDR–FRG border (officially to prevent Western subversion of the GDR), the barrier was seen in the West as an attempt to staunch the exodus of East Germans to the FRG. Assisted by the absence of tariff barriers on trade with the FRG, the GDR became the most successful of the Comecon economies, but lagged far behind the FRG in living standards. GDR forces participated in the Soviet-led crushing of the 'Prague Spring' in Czechoslovakia (1968). In the same year, a new constitution declared the GDR to be 'a socialist state of the German nation' seeking unification 'on the basis of democracy and socialism'. However, in amendments approved in 1974, the words 'of the German nation' and the whole of the article about eventual unification were deleted, the GDR being now described as 'an inseparable part of the socialist community' linked 'irrevocably and for ever' to the Soviet Union.

Ulbricht resigned in May 1971 and was replaced by Erich Honecker, under whose leadership the GDR signed a treaty with the FRG guaranteeing the inviolability of the intra-German border (Dec. 1972); this enabled both states to become members of the UN (Sept. 1973). Meanwhile, tensions in Berlin had been eased by a new Quadripartite Agreement (Sept. 1971) specifying that the status quo could not be changed unilaterally. In 1975 both the GDR and the FRG signed the Final Act of the Conference on Security and Co-operation in Europe, in which the existing borders of all European states were declared to be inviolable. Honecker thereafter remained cool to further rapprochement with the FRG, and relations continued to be marred by disclosures about each side's espionage activities against the other. Moreover, Honecker repeatedly maintained that the reform measures instituted in the Soviet Union following Mikhail Gorbachev's accession to power (Mar. 1985) had little relevance to GDR conditions. Nevertheless, in Sept. 1987 Honecker became the first GDR leader to pay an official visit to Bonn (the FRG capital), during which various co-operation agreements were signed.

Despite the reform being introduced in the Soviet Union and elsewhere in Eastern Europe, Honecker refused to concede that such measures might be appropriate in East Germany. In May 1989 the opposition protested at the rigging of communal elections. As 1989 progressed tens of thousands of East Germans fled to the West most notably across the now open Austro-Hungarian border. Protests broke out immediately after East Germany's 40th anniversary on 7 Oct., most notably in Leipzig where weekly Monday demonstrations were regularly attended by 100,000 or more citizens, forcing Honecker to resign on 18 Oct. His successor Egon Krenz was unable, despite opening the Berlin Wall on 9 Nov., to quell growing demands for reform or to stem the exodus to the West (which totalled 344,000 by the end of 1989). On 17 Nov. Krenz was replaced as head of government by Hans Modrow, the reformist SED party leader in Dresden. Demonstrations continued especially in protest at corruption among former SED bosses and against the hated 'Stasi' secret police. Calls for German reunification, fuelled by West German politicians and media, grew increasingly vociferous, obliging Modrow to bring the planned general election forward from 6 May to 18 Mar. 1990.

CONSTITUTION AND GOVERNMENT

Executive and legislature

The head of state is the chairman of the 25-member Council of State, elected by the legislature, the 500-member unicameral Volkskammer (People's Chamber). The Volkskammer, which is designated as the highest state authority, also elects the Council of Minister. . It is itself elected by universal suffrage from a single list of candidates for a term of five years. Political power has in practice been monopolised by the (communist) Socialist Unity Party of Germany, which is the dominant partner in the National Front, an umbrella organization to which the four other legal political parties belong.

Present government

(The government given below was correct as of 1 Mar. 1990, but the whole nature and status of this government was provisional in that elections were scheduled and there was overwhelming support for unification with West Germany.)

Chairman of the Council of State Manfred Gerlach

Members of the Council of Ministers Hans Modrow (Chairman); Christa Luft (Deputy Chair; Economy); Peter Moreth (Deputy Chair; Local State Bodies); Lothar de Maiziere (Deputy Chair; Church Questions); Karl Grünheid (Chair of the Economic Committee); Oscar Fischer (Foreign Affairs); Adml Theodore Hoffmann (National Defence); Kurt Wuñsche (Justice); Lothar Ahrendt (Internal Affairs).

Justice

The system of law was based on codified civil law modified according to Communist legal practices. The highest court, the Supreme Court, was responsible to the People's Chamber. The administration of justice was overseen by the Prosecutor General and a network of public prosecutors' offices. Judges were elected by the people's representative organs at the appropriate level, from local and district level upwards. The death penalty was abolished in 1987.

National symbols

Flag. A tricolour with horizontal stripes of black, red and deep yellow (officially gold) to which the state coat of arms of the GDR was added in 1959.

Festivals. 1 May (May Day); 7 Oct. (National Day).

Vehicle registration plate. DDR.

INTERNATIONAL RELATIONS

Affiliations

Warsaw Pact; Comecon.

Defence

Total Armed Forces: 172,000 (94,500 conscripts). Terms of service: Army, Air Force 18 months; Navy (sea-going) 36 months. Reserves: 390.000.

Army: 120,000; 2,850 main battle tanks (mainly T-54/-55, T-72, T-34).

Navy: 15,000; 19 frigates and 37 patrol and coastal combatants.

Air Force: 37,000; 330 combat aircraft (MiG-23BN, Su-22, MiG-21RF, MiG-21F/MF/PF/U), 100 armed helicopters.

ECONOMY

Currency

The unit is the GDR mark (Ostmark), divided into 100 pfennigs.

National finance

Budget. The 1986 budget (in US$) was for expenditure (current and capital) of 123,200 million and revenue of 123,500 million.

Inflation. (1987) 0.9%.

Gross Domestic Product

Estimated total GDP US$207,200 million (GNP), per capita US$12,500 (ranking 15 in the world by size).

Economically active population. The total number of persons active in the economy was 8,960,000.

Sector	% of workforce
industry	44
agriculture	10.8
services*	45

* services figure includes elements unassigned to other categories.

Energy and mineral resources

Minerals. Lignite is the GDR's only major mineral resource, 343 million tons/311 million tonnes being produced in 1986. Small deposits of uranium, cobalt, bismuth, arsenic and antimony are also expoited.

Electricity. Capacity: (1988) 24,144 MW (more than 80% in lignite-fired power stations). Production: (1988) 120 million MWh.

Bioresources

Agriculture. The land area in agricultural use is 15 million acres/6.2 million ha, of which 11. 6 million/ 4.7 million ha is sown to crops and 3.08 million acres/ 1.25 million ha is meadows and pasture. The main products are potatoes; sugar beet; cereals.

Crop production: (1986 in 1,000 tons/tonnes) potatoes 11,120/9,997; sugar beet 8,540/7,747; barley 4,732/ 4,293; wheat 4,624/4,195; rye 2,652/2,406.

Livestock numbers: poultry 50 million; pigs 12.84 million; cattle 5.8 million; sheep 2.65 million.

Forestry. The forested area in 1985 was 7,357,649 acres/ 2,977,600 ha. Timber production in 1986 was 357,720,100,000 ft^3/10,115,000 m^3.

Fisheries. Total catch: (1986) 300,377 tons/ 272,500 tonnes, of which inland catch was 27,360 tons/ 24,821 tonnes.

Industry and commerce

Industry. The GDR is the most industrialized country in Eastern Europe. Extensive iron and steel production provides the basis for machine building and metal fabrication (especially motor cars). Other major industries are cement; chemicals (especially artificial fertilizers); petrochemicals; textiles; food processing; electronics.

Commerce. Exports: 91,505 million Valuta-Marks. Imports: (1986) 90,465 million Valuta-Marks. Principal trading partners: USSR (39%); Czechoslovakia; Poland; West Germany.

Trade with UK. The GDR imported UK goods worth £113.24 million, and exported to the UK goods worth £152.98 million (1988).

COMMUNICATIONS

Railways

There are 8,699 miles/14,008 km of railways, of which 1,920 miles/3,092 km are electrified.

Roads

There are 76,197 miles/122,700 km of roads.

Aviation

Interflug, Gesellschaft fuer internationalen Flugverkehr mbH provides international flights (international airports are at Berlin-Schoenefeld, Dresden, Erfurt und Leipzig). Passengers: (1987) 1.5 million.

Shipping

There are 1,440 miles/2,319 km of inland waterways. The maritime ports on the Baltic Sea are Rostok, Wismar, Stralsund, and Sassnitz. The river ports of East Berlin, Riesa, Magdeburg and Eisenhuttenstadt are on the Elbe or Oder Rivers and connecting canals. 145 ships of the merchant marine are over 1,000 GRT. Goods loaded and unloaded: (1987) 27.3 million tons/ 24.8 million tonnes.

Telecommunications

There are 6.6 million radios and 6.0 million televisions (1985). Radio broadcasting is conducted by Berliner Rundfunk, Radio DDR and Stimme der DDR, with external services by Radio Berlin International in 11 languages, and broadcasts on Radio Volga in Russian for Soviet forces. The state television service Fernsehen der DDR operates on two channels, while 80% of the population can also receive West German TV broadcasts.

EDUCATION AND WELFARE

Education

The state provides free and compulsory education for ten years. This may be followed by two years in a secondary school or in an apprenticeship; in either case pupils receive a state stipend.

School population. (1986) 779,700 in pre-school institutions; 2,041,013 in general education schools; 369,100 in vocational schools; 160,379 in technical schools.

Schools (1986) 13,265 pre-school institutions; 5,895 general education schools with 170,277 teachers (one per 12.0 pupils); 959 vocational schools with 16,244 teachers (one per 22.7 pupils); 239 technical schools.

Universities There are nine universities and 45 other higher-education institutions, with 131,560 full-time students (1986).

Health

Medical care is provided free and funded by compulsory social insurance. In 1986 there were 538 hospitals and 162 sanatoria with 169,179 beds (one per 98.3 inhabitants), and 598 health centres. There were 39,157 doctors (one per 425 inhabitants), and 12,182 dentists.

GERMANY, WEST

Bundesrepublik Deutschland – BRD
(Federal Republic of Germany – FRG)

GEOGRAPHY

West Germany is located in north central Europe, covering an area of 96,001 miles²/248,706 km². West Berlin is a separate enclave within the territory of East Germany. Physiographically the country divides into four principal regions, the North German Plain, the Mid-German Highlands, the South German Uplands and the Bavarian Alps and plateau. The northern lowland plains (rarely more than 328 ft/100 m above sea level) extend south towards the Harz Mountains in the east and to the Ruhr valley and lower Rhineland in the west. The central uplands, including Hessen, Rheinland Pfalz, Saarland and the remote Odenwald, are frequently densely forested at higher altitudes, the forests giving way to arable farmland and vineyards in the valleys. Prosperous industrial locations (Ruhr-Main, southern Hessen) alternate with sparsely populated forested regions. To the west of Frankfurt, the deeply incised Rhine gorge cuts through the lowland mountains that link Eifel and Hünsruck with Siebengorge and Taunus. Flowing west from Mainz, the Main river forms a natural border between the Central Uplands and the high plateau region of the south. Rising out of Switzerland, the western arm of the Jura mountains forms the Schwarzwald (Black Forest). To the south-east the Bavarian forest borders the slopes of the Danube valley. In the far south the Bavarian Alps (high point Zugspitze 9,717 ft/2,962 m, West Germany's highest mountain) represent the northern tip of the continental Alpine chain. 30% of West Germany's land is forested and a similar proportion is arable. Soils vary in composition and quality. The Borde region is particularly fertile, comprised of fine silt or 'Loess' deposits. The industrial region of the Ruhr valley sustains 10% of the total population.

Climate

Primarily temperate, continental-type climate with prevailing west winds. Oceanic influence in the north-west with milder, though frequently stormy, winters. Eastern and southern winter temperatures are lower with clear weather, frost and considerable snowfall. Summer (July) temperatures average between 63°F/17°C and 66°F/19°C, and winter (Jan.) temperatures between 28°F/−2°C and 36°F/2°C throughout the country, excluding the high Alps. Average temperatures: Frankfurt: Jan. 33°F/0.6°C. July 66°F/18.9°C. Average annual rainfall 24 in/601 mm. Cologne: Jan. 36°F/2.2°C. July 66°F/18.9°C. Average annual rainfall 27 in/676 mm. Munich: Jan. 36°F/2.2°C. July 63°F/17.2°C. Average annual rainfall 34 in/855 mm.

Cities and towns

West Berlin	1,879,200
Hamburg	1,571,300
München (Munich)	1,274,700
Köln (Cologne)	914,300
Essen	615,400
Frankfurt am Main	592,400
Dortmund	568,200
Stuttgart	556,500
Düsseldorf	560,600
Bremen	522,000
Duisburg	514,600
Hannover	505,700
Nürnberg (Nuremberg)	467,400
Bochum	381,200
Wuppertal	374,200
Bielefeld	299,400
Mannheim	296,400
Bonn (capital)	291,400

Population

Total population is 61,200,000, of which 86% live in urban areas. There is a high average population density, which rises steeply in West Berlin (total population for West Berlin 1,879,200). Of the 4,630,200 foreigners resident in West Germany 1,481,400 are Turks; 597,600 Yugoslavs; 544,400 Italians; 279,900 Greeks. 0.3% are Spanish and 0.2% Dutch. In 1988 there were 9,705 defectors from the German Democratic Republic.

Birth rate 1.0% **Death rate** 1.2% **Rate of population increase** 0.1% **Age distribution** Under 15 = 15.0%; over 65 = 14.8% **Life expectancy** female 78; male 72; average 75.

Religions

Predominantly Christian (92.8%). 47.3% (28.82 million) are Protestant, including 23.5% Lutheran Reformed; 21.7% Lutheran; 0.7% reformed. The Baptists, Methodists, Nemonites and Lutheran Free Church make up a further 400,000 of the Protestant total. 26.7 million are Roman Catholic. Other significant religious groups include 1,400,000 Muslims and a Jewish community of 32,000 (0.1%).

Language

In addition to the 58 million native German-speakers, there are 1,040,000 Turkish-; 610,000 Italian-; 370,000 Greek-; 300,000 Dutch-; 180,000 Spanish; 120,000 English-speaking citizens. Apart from the standard hybrid German tongue, three major regional dialectal categories exist. These are Upper German (Allemanic); Central German (Franconian); Low German (Plattdeutsch). Frisian, the dialect most closely related to English in structure and composition, is still spoken in some small northern communities.

HISTORY

For history before 1949 please see **East Germany** entry above.

The Federal Republic of Germany (FRG) achieved partial sovereignty on 23 May 1949 with Bonn as its capital, following the adoption of a Grundgesetz (Basic Law) by an assembly representing the three Western occupation zones. Purposely not called a constitution to signify its interim nature pending an overall German settlement, the Basic Law proclaimed the FRG to be a 'democratic and social federal state' consisting of constituent Länder linked in a federal parliamentary structure, with West Berlin participating indirectly. It also stated that its authors were acting on behalf of 'those Germans to whom participation was denied', ie those in the Soviet zone, which in Oct. 1949 became the German Democratic Republic (GDR).

The war-devastated economy in the three Western occupation zones had faced an enormous extra burden in the immediate aftermath of war because of the inflow of Germans from the east, from the Soviet-occupied zone and from what is now Poland. This influx continued (totalling over 3 million people from the GDR and 9 million from further east) up to 1961, when the East Germans built the Berlin Wall (13 Aug. 1961, later extended along the whole FRG–GDR border). It had quickly become evident that this mainly youthful addition to the population was contributing towards the promotion and sustenance of the 'economic miracle' of growth in the FRG in the 1950s and 1960s, and correspondingly depriving the GDR of much-needed skills.

In the first elections to the Bundestag (federal lower

house) in Aug. 1949, the Christian Democrats won the most seats led by Konrad Adenauer who became federal chancellor at the head of a centre-right coalition with the liberal Free Democrats (FDP) and the small German Party (DP). At the same time (Sept. 1949), Theodor Heuss (FDP) was elected as the FRG's first president with Christian Democratic support (and was re-elected for a second term in 1954). In Oct. 1950 Adenauer's followers, then an amalgam of Land parties descended from pre-war Catholic and Protestant formations, launched the Christian Democratic Union (CDU), with the associated Christian Social Union (CSU) maintaining a separate role in Bavaria. In the 1953 elections, the CDU/CSU greatly increased its strength, as several smaller parties (including the Communists) failed to surmount a new 5% national threshold (parties gaining less than 5% of the vote did not get seats in the Bundestag).

Under Adenauer's leadership, the FRG achieved full sovereignty on 5 May 1955 when it acceded to the Western European Union and NATO under the Paris Agreements of Oct. 1954. These forbade the FRG to manufacture nuclear, biological and chemical weapons and placed restrictions on its possession of conventional weapons which were not entirely lifted until 1986. Simultaneously, the Western powers (which had rejected a 1952 Soviet proposal for a neutral Germany) reasserted their goal of a 'fully free and unified Germany' within borders to be decided in a peace settlement. On 1 Jan. 1957 the coal-rich Saarland (which had been under French control since 1945) became a Land of the FRG, after its voters had rejected (Oct. 1956) a Franco-German 'Europeanization' plan.

In the 1950s and 1960s the FRG made a rapid economic recovery from post-war hardships and shortages, assisted by US Marshall Aid and its membership of the three European Communities, the European Coal and Steel Community, the EEC and Euratom (1951–58). In 1957 the CDU/CSU obtained the first (and so far only) overall majority in German parliamentary history, but maintained a coalition with the DP. In the Godesberg Programme (1959), the opposition Social Democrats (SPD) formally abandoned Marxism in favour of the social market economy and accepted the FRG's participation in NATO and European integration (until then opposed as harmful to the goal of reunification). Heinrich Lübke (CDU) became FRG president in 1959 (being re-elected in 1964); his successors were Gustav Heinemann (SPD), 1969–74, Walter Scheel (FDP), 1974–79, Prof. Karl Carstens (CDU), 1979–84, and Richard von Weizsäcker (CDU), from 1984.

The ageing Adenauer sustained the tension in relations with the East German regime, refusing to consider recognition of the GDR, and opposing Soviet-backed pressure for an agreement on Berlin. Moving towards the integration of the whole of Berlin into the GDR, the Soviet leader Nikita Kruschchev set a Dec. 1961 deadline for a Berlin treaty; the new US president John Kennedy, and West Berlin mayor Willy Brandt, led a robust Western stance in response, as the Berlin Wall went up (13 Aug.), but both sides backed away from confrontation and the crisis was defused with inconclusive negotiations. Adenauer, however, lost prestige, appearing less dynamic by comparison with younger men like Kennedy and Brandt. The CDU/CSU lost its overall majority at the 1961 elections, and the SPD made gains, giving the balance of power to the FDP (the only other party to win seats) and obliging Adenauer to form a CDU/CSU/FDP coalition. His government was then hit by the *Spiegel* affair (Oct. 1962), in which CSU defence minister Franz Josef Strauss ordered police action against the news magazine *Der Spiegel* for treason over an article critical of the army's performance on manoeuvres. Strauss was forced to resign amid protests over his strong-arm repressive tactics.

Having consummated Franco-German reconciliation by signing a friendship treaty with Gen. de Gaulle (Jan. 1963), Adenauer finally retired (Oct. 1963) and was succeeded by Ludwig Erhard, the architect of the 'economic miracle' but, as chancellor, less successful. Although returned to power in 1965, the CDU/CSU/FDP coalition collapsed in Oct. 1966. It was replaced by a 'grand coalition' or 'black–red' coalition between the two main parties, the CDU/CSU and the SPD, which Adenauer had always denigrated as a stalking-horse for Communism, but which now entered government for the first time, under Kurt Kiesinger (CDU), and with Brandt, the SPD leader, as foreign minister. The CDU/CSU left office after the 1969 elections, when SPD gains produced an SPD/FDP coalition under Willy Brandt.

The revolutionary leftist Baader–Meinhof Group (founded 1968), and the Red Army Faction which grew out of it, first emerged in the 'grand coalition' period as an extremist minority phenomenon within a broader climate of extra-parliamentary opposition. The German Socialist Students' Union (SDS) articulated the values and aspirations of a new younger generation, less inclined than their parents to esteem good order and material well-being; the SDS decried the grand coalition as revealing the absence of opposition voices within the parliamentary system. A wave of mass protests in the late 1960s and early 1970s encompassed opposition to Western complicity in the Vietnam war, criticism of the Shah of Iran's visit (June 1967), attacks on the domination of the newspaper industry by Axel Springer's companies (Apr. 1968), demands for reform of the university system and protests at housing shortages in West Berlin and other large cities. The Baader–Meinhof Group saw itself as the spark which would ignite a revolution to create a true communist society; its bomb and arson attacks and bank robberies met an energetic police response, backed by security legislation which was greatly strengthened for this purpose (1972). Arrested and brought to trial, Baader–Meinhof members would typically present their actions as political, not criminal, and demand prisoner-of-war status in captivity. Ulrike Meinhof was found hanged in her cell during her trial in Stuttgart (9 May 1976); Andreas Baader, like many of his followers, was sentenced to life imprisonment (28 Apr. 1977); attacks, arrests and trials involving the Red Army Faction continued into the late 1980s.

To combat the perceived threat of subversion and the spread of subversive ideas throughout society, the Berufsverbot (literally 'profession-ban') provisions (27 Jan. 1972) allowed the Land governments to screen the political background of all applicants for public-service jobs, including the teaching profession. (In 1985 it was estimated by anti-Berufsverbot campaigners that 6.5 million job applicants had been screened, and 7,000 debarred from employment. After 13 years of its operation, two courts ruled in June 1985 that Berufsverbot did not apply to members of the German Communist Party, which was not illegal.) The most dramatic event of 1972 was not German but Middle Eastern in origin. Eight Arab 'Black September' guerrillas attacked the Israeli building at the Munich Olympics, killing two and taking nine hostages, and demanding the release of Palestinian prisoners in Israel. All nine hostages and four of the kidnappers died in a failed rescue attempt when German police tried to prevent the guerrillas boarding the aircraft they had demanded.

Both as foreign minister (1966–69) and as chancellor (1969–74), Brandt sought, in his policy towards the east, or Ostpolitik, a reconciliation with eastern Europe, signing treaties with the Soviet Union (Aug. 1970), Poland (Nov. 1970) and the GDR (Dec. 1972) in which the inviolability of existing borders 'now and in the future' was affirmed. These agreements were ratified by the FRG parliament (1972–73) despite CDU/CSU reservations, as a result of which a resolution was adopted (May 1972) asserting that they 'do not create any legal basis for the frontiers existing today'. In Sept. 1973 both the FRG and the GDR were admitted to full UN membership. Meanwhile, tensions in Berlin had been eased by a new Quadripartite Agreement (Sept. 1971) specifying that the status quo could not be changed unilaterally.

Although the SPD/FDP coalition had increased its majority in the 1972 elections (when the SPD had outpolled the CDU/CSU for the first time), Brandt resigned as chancellor in May 1974 after one of his aides was found to be a GDR spy. He was succeeded by Helmut Schmidt, who led the coalition to further election victories in 1976 and 1980 and steered the country's economy through the shocks of sharp world oil-price rises and the associated international recession.

The Schmidt government's participation in NATO's 'twin-track' decision (Dec. 1979), providing for the deployment of US intermediate-range nuclear (INF) missiles in the FRG, provoked controversy, not least within the SPD. As the debate raged, vast numbers of demonstrators marched against the weapons (Pershing IIs and Cruise missiles), the peace movement reaching its peak in 1982–83 and in many cases fusing with growing environmentalist opposition to nuclear power. The FDP withdrew from its coalition with the SPD (Sept. 1982) and formed one with the CDU/CSU under Helmut Kohl (CDU). This coalition was returned to power at the next elections (Mar. 1983), in which the environmentalist Greens (formed 1980) entered the Bundestag for the first time and the SPD lost ground. Final parliamentary approval was given to deployment of the INF missiles in Nov. 1983, with the SPD and the Greens voting against. Kohl's CDU/CSU/FDP coalition retained a majority in Jan. 1987, as the SPD registered its lowest vote share since 1961 and the Greens gained seats.

Led by Hans-Jochen Vogel from Mar. 1987, the SPD made a partial recovery in subsequent Land elections (and entered a coalition with the Greens in West Berlin in Mar. 1989), whereas the CDU lost ground to the extreme right-wing Republicans (founded 1983; an earlier neo-fascist group, the National Democratic Party, founded 1964, had attracted appreciable electoral support at Land level in the late 1960s). The Hitler period and its significance, uncomfortably evoked by the re-emergence of a neo-fascist right, proved exceptionally problematic for Germans to evaluate as an integral part of their history. A misjudged attempt by Bundestag speaker Philipp Jenninger to air his reflections on Hitler's rule and the complicity of the German people, delivered during commemorations of the 50th anniversary of the Kristallnacht pogrom, provoked a storm of protest and Jenninger's immediate resignation (11 Nov. 1988).

The US–Soviet treaty on the dismantling of INF missiles in Europe (Dec. 1987) ended one debate in the FRG but started another on the desirability of modernizing short-range nuclear (SNF) missiles on FRG soil. Opponents of SNF missiles deployed the telling slogan 'the shorter the range, the deader the German' to dramatize their fears over Germany, East and West, becoming the 'theatre of war' in East–West strategic thinking.

Problems in the economy, post-'miracle', emerged with unemployment the most notable symptom in the 1980s, as jobless figures rose from 4% in 1979 to 10% by 1988. One effect was to increase pressure on the country's 4.7 million foreign workers, the Gastarbeiter. Drawn in from Turkey, Yugoslavia and elsewhere to fill menial jobs when labour was scarce, the Gastarbeiter had formed a social and economic under-class, while attracting the hostility of the far right on racial grounds. A policy of assisting Gastarbeiter to return to their countries of origin, with financial incentives, was introduced from 1988.

The fall of Honecker in East Germany in October 1989 and the opening of the Berlin Wall in November led Kohl on 28 Nov. to propse the formation of a German confederation uniting the two states. As the prospect of German reunification became increasingly imminent, Kohl championed the introduction of the West German Mark in East Germany and argued for a united Germany within NATO.

CONSTITUTION AND GOVERNMENT

Executive and legislature

The 1949 Basic Law (constitution) defines the Federal Republic of Germany as a 'democratic and social federal state'. The federal president (Bundespräsident) is elected for a five-year term by the Federal Assembly (Bundesversammlung), which is constituted for this purpose and consists of the members of the Bundestag and an equal number of delegates nominated by the Länder parliaments. The Federal Government (Bundesregierung) is headed by the federal chancellor (Bundeskanzler). Elected by the Bundestag, nominally on the proposal of the federal president, the chancellor is responsible to parliament. On the proposal of the chancellor, the federal president appoints, and dismisses, the government ministers. The Federal Diet (Bundestag), the lower house of parliament, is elected for a four-year term in direct elections by universal adult suffrage (minimum voting age 18). Last general election Jan 1987. The indirectly-elected Federal Council (Bundesrat), the upper house of parliament, is made up of 45 members, 41 of them drawn from the governments of the Republic's eight Länder (states) and the city governments of Hamburg and Bremen, and four from West Berlin.

West Berlin is not a constituent part of the Federal Republic but sends delegates to both the Bundestag and Bundesrat; these do not, however, have full voting rights in either body.

Present government

President Dr Richard von Weizsäcker
Chancellor Dr Helmut Kohl
Ministers: Hans-Dietrich Genscher (Vice-Chancellor; Foreign Affairs); Wolfgang Schäuble (Interior); Hans A. Engelhard (Justice); Theo Waigel (Finance); Helmut Haussmann (Economics); Ignaz Kiechle (Food, Agriculture and Forestry); Norbert Blüm (Labour and Social Affairs); Gerhard Stoltenberg (Defence); Ursula M. Lehr (Women, Youth, Family Affairs, and Health); Friedrich Zimmermann

(Transport); Klaus Töpfer (Environment, Nature Conservation and Nuclear Reactor Safety); Christian Schwarz-Schilling (Post and Telecommunications); Gerda Hasselfeldt (Building); Dorothee Wilms (Inter-German Relations); Heinz Riesenhuber (Research and Technology); Jürgen Möllemann (Education and Science); Jürgen Warnke (Economic Co-operation); Rudolf Seiters (Minister at the Chancellery); Hans Klein (Government Spokesman)

Minister Presidents of the Länder Baden-Württemberg – Lothar Späth (CDU); Bavaria – Max Streibl; Hesse – Walter Wallmannn (CDU); Lower Saxony – Ernst Albrecht (CDU); North Rhine-Westphalia – Johannes Rau (SPD); Rhineland-Palatinate – Hans Otto Wilhelm (CDU); Saarland – Oskar Lafontaine (SPD); Schleswig-Holstein – Björn Engholm (SPD); Mayor of Bremen – Klaus Wedemeier (SPD); Mayor of Hamburg – Henning Voscherau (SPD); Governing Mayor of West Berlin – Eberhard Diepgen (CDU).

Administration

The Federal Republic comprises eight Länder (states) and two free Hanseatic towns (Bremen and Hamburg), plus West Berlin which has a separate status under the 1972 Four Power Agreement. Each Land has its own constitution, government and parliament with the right to enact laws on such matters as education, culture, environmental protection, and the police. Federal responsibilities include foreign affairs, defence, federal citizenship, immigration and emigration, extradition, currency, customs, commercial and navigational agreements, federal railways and air traffic, post and telecommunications, and co-operation between the federal republic and the Länder on criminal police matters, protection of the constitution and international crime.

Land	Capital	Area (km^2)
Baden-Württemberg	Stuttgart	35,751
Bavaria (Bayern)	Munich	70,553
Bremen	Bremen	404
Hamburg	Hamburg	755
Hessen	Wiesbaden	21,115
Lower Saxony (Niedersachsen)	Hanover	47,438
North Rhine-Westphalia (Nordrhein-Westfalen)	Düsseldorf	34,068
Rhineland-Palatinate (Rheinland-Pfalz)	Mainz	19,848
Saarland	Saarbrücken	2,569
Schleswig-Holstein	Kiel	15,727
West Berlin	West Berlin	480

Justice

The system is based on codified civil law. The highest court, for consideration of constitutional matters and the acceptability of legislation at federal level, is the Federal Constitutional Court (Bundesverfassungsgericht) elected by the Federal Assembly and Federal Council. The Länder have their own Constitutional Courts. At federal level, different aspects of the law are handled by the Federal Labour Court (Bundesarbeitsgericht), the Federal Social Court (Bundessozialgericht), the Federal Finance Court (Bundesfinanzhof) which deals with tax matters, and the Federal Administrative Court (Bundesverwaltungsgericht) for administrative matters. Most cases, however, are dealt with within the Länder, at the appropriate level in a system of local courts (Amtsgerichte), regional courts (Landgerichte) and courts of appeal (Oberlandesgericht). The death penalty was abolished in 1949.

Prisons. There are 53,039 prisoners.

National symbols

Flag. Tricolour with horizontal stripes of black, red and gold. First adopted in 1848 and again in 1918, the German tricolour was abolished by Hitler in 1933 and later adopted by both German republics in 1949.

Festivals. 1 May (Labour Day); 17 June (Day of German Unity, anniversary of 1953 uprising in East Germany).

Vehicle registration plate. D.

INTERNATIONAL RELATIONS

Affiliations

West Germany is a member of the UN and its main specialized agencies; NATO; WEU; OECD; European Communities; and the Council of Europe.

Defence

Defence expenditure is US$30,310 million plus US$36,850 million in contributions to NATO (1988). Per capita expenditure on defence was US$561 or 3.2% of GDP (1987). Compulsory military service for males aged 18–45 (and for officers to 60) was increased in 1989 from 15 to 18 months, while the alternative community service for conscientious objectors was increased from 20 to 24 months.

Total Armed Forces: 488,700 (222,600 conscripts). Reserves: 850,000 (men to age 45, officers to 60).

Army: Strength 332,100; 4,937 main battle tanks (mainly Leopard 1A1 and Leopard 2).

Navy: Strength 36,400; 24 submarines (chiefly Type 206 SSC, Type 205 SSC, 16 principal surface combatants (seven destroyers, nine frigates) and 45 patrol and coastal combatants.

Air Force: Strength 108,700; 459 combat aircraft (mainly Tornado, F-4 and AlphaJet).

ECONOMY

West Germany has an industrialized market economy. The principal instrument of economic planning is the annual budget.

Currency

The unit is the Deutsche Mark (DM) divided into 100 Pfennigs.

National finance

Budget. The 1989 federal budget provided for expenditure of DM290,300 million (an increase of 5.4%) and revenue of DM318.200 million, giving a federal surplus of DM27,900 million. The balance of payments on the current account (1988) was a surplus of US$48,510 million (excluding transactions with East Germany) compared with a surplus of US$45,170 million the previous year. The total external debt was US$262,926 million (1988).

Inflation. 3.1% (12 months to Sept. 1989).

Gross National Product

Estimated total GNP US$1,205,397 million. Per capita GNP US$21,311 (in terms of per capita income the 23rd richest country in the world). Growth rate (1988) 3.6%.

Economically active population. The total number of persons active in the economy (1988) was 28,402,000; unemployed 2,242,000: 7.9%. As a percentage of the workforce 40.1% worked in industry; 18.6% in commerce and communications; 4.9% in agriculture, forestry or fishing.

Energy and mineral resources

Oil and gas. Production: (1987) petroleum 19.8 million tons/17.98 million tonnes; diesel oil 12.05 million tons/10.93 million tonnes; gas 560,468.5 million ft^3/15,871 million m^3. The main oilfields are in Emsland (Lower Saxony).

Minerals. Output: (1987 in thousand tons/tonnes) lignite 119,929/108,799; coal 84,105/76,300; potash 28,434/25,795; crude oil 4,189/3,800.

Electricity. Production: 418.3 million MWh. Nuclear energy provided 31.3% of electricity production from five stations.

Bioresources

Agriculture. There is an estimated 45,780 miles^2/118,600 km^2 of agricultural land in West Germany.

Crop production: (1987 in 1,000 tons/tonnes) sugar beet 20,998/19,049; wheat 10,948/9,932; barley 9,448/8,571; potatoes 7,535/6,836; oats 2,213/2,008; rye 1,763/1,599.

Livestock numbers: (1987) cattle 14,886,900; sheep 1,413,700; pigs 23,669,600.

Forestry. Quantity of timber felled: (1986) 1,024,106 million ft^3/29 million m^3. 42% of the country's forested area of 11.1 million acres/5.3 million ha was owned by the state (1987).

Fisheries. Total sea catch: (1987) 175,945 tons/159,616 tonnes live weight caught by 14 trawlers and 635 cutters.

Industry and commerce

Industry. The manufacturing industry forms the backbone of the West German economy, accounting for 32.4% of the country's GDP.

Commerce. Exports: DM567,750 million, of which DM272,860 million was machinery and transport equipment; DM102,560 million was manufactured goods; DM78,950 million was chemicals; DM62,370 million was miscellaneous manufactured articles; DM23,650 million was food and live animals. Countries exported to: France 12.6%; US 8.1%; Belgium-Luxembourg 7.4%; Switzerland 6.1%; Austria 5.6%; centrally planned economies 4.4%.

Trade with UK. West Germany imported UK goods worth DM30,461 million; exports to UK totalled DM52,873 million.

Tourism. (1987) 8,470,000 overnight visitors.

COMMUNICATIONS

Railways

There are 17,068 miles/27,484 km of state-owned railways, of which 7,100 miles/11,433 km are electrified.

Roads

There are 305,829 miles/492,478 km of roads, most of which are concrete or bitumenized. There are 27,908,200 passenger cars.

Aviation

Deutsche Lufthansa provides domestic and international services (main airports are at Berlin (West), Cologne-Bonn, Düsseldorf, Frankfurt, Hamburg, Hanover, Munich and Stuttgart). Air traffic: (1987) 48.74 million passengers and 928,137 tons/842,000 tonnes of freight.

Shipping

Sea-going ships carried 150.1 million tons/136.1 million tonnes of freight (1987) and inland waterways 253 million tons/229.5 million tonnes (1986). The principal sea ports for freight are Bremen, Hamburg, and Wilhelmshaven.

Telecommunications

There were 40.29 million telephones (1987).

Broadcasting

The Artbeitsgemeinschaft der öffentlich-rechtlichen Rundfunkanstalten der Bundesrepublik Deutschland (Association of public law broadcasting organizations or ARD) is the co-ordinating body of the various regional radio and television organizations, including also Deutsche Welle and Deutschlandfunk which broadcast radio programmes in Europe and overseas. RIAS Berlin is represented as an observer. As well as these three radio stations each regional organization broadcasts 2–3 channels. Of the three television channels the first is produced by ARD and the second (Zweites Deutsches Fernsehen or ZDF) is separately controlled by a public corporation of all the Länder and is partly financed by advertising. The third channel of educational and cultural programmes is contributed to by several regional bodies. There were 26.39 million radio and 23.39 million television licences (1987).

Newspapers

There are 375 daily newspapers with a total circulation of 20.6 million copies plus also five Sunday papers (total circulation 3.8 million), and 44 weeklies (total circulation 1.8 million). Major national dailies include *Bild Zeitung* (circulation 5.1 million), *Frankfurter Allgemeine Zeitung*, *Süddeutsche Zeitung* (Munich), and *Die Welt* (Hamburg). Weekly newspapers include, most importantly, *Die Zeit*, *Bild am Sonntag*, *Welt am Sonntag*. In 1987 6,908 periodicals were published (total circulation 275.49 million) and included the illustrated news weeklies *Der Spiegel*, *Stern*, and *Quick*. 63,679 books were also published. The chief West German news agency is Deutsche Presse-Agentur (dpa).

EDUCATION AND WELFARE

Education

Under the Basic Law or constitution education in West Germany is controlled by the regional Land governments. There is compulsory schooling from 6 to 18 years, nine years of which must be full-time. After 4–6 years at primary school (Grundschule), children go on to three main types of school: the general school (Hauptschule) attended by approximately half of all pupils, the secondary modern (Realschule) or the grammar school (Gymnasium). There are also experimental comprehensives (Gesamtschulen), while the handicapped are educated at special schools (Sonderschulen). Education at the Hauptschule or Realschule is for five or six years after which pupils receive vocational training on either a part- or full-time basis. To go on to higher education pupils must pass the Abitur (grammar school leaving certificate).

School population. There were 9,179,000 pupils enrolled in primary and secondary education, including vocational education (1987).

Schools. There were 21,072 primary and 15,516 secondary schools (1987). There were 3,721,800 pupils and 212,100 teachers (one per 18 pupils) in primary schools and in secondary schools, including those for vocational training, there were 5,732,100 pupils and 326,600 teachers (one per 18 pupils).

Universities. There were 61 institutes with university status including 39 universities proper (1986–87) with a total of 1,410,800 students (1987). Of the relevant age group 30% were in tertiary education.

Health

There is no national health service as such, although there is compulsory health and accident insurance. In 1987 there were 165,015 doctors, including 79,216 in hospitals, (one per 371 patients), plus 38,055 dentists. In 1987 3,071 hospitals, including 941 private hospitals, had 674,384 beds (one per 91 patients).

Welfare

Insurance for disability, retirement and unemployment is compulsory for all employees and covers some 80% of the population. Pensions are among the highest in Europe. They are based on contributions paid and linked to average national earnings which are regularly adjusted. There is also accident and sickness insurance, the latter paying for all medical attention and providing a benefit of 85–90% of the normal wage.

GHANA

Republic of Ghana

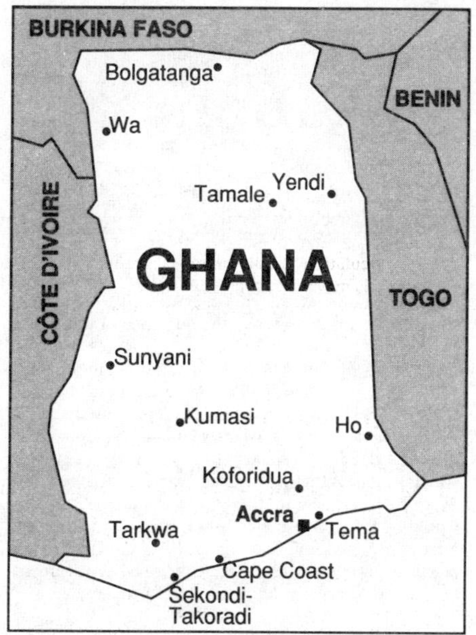

GEOGRAPHY

Situated on the west African (Gold) Coast, Ghana covers an area of 92,133 miles^2/238,686 km^2 divided into nine regions. Inland from the lagoons and sandbars of the coastal plain, the land rises either side of the Volta river basin (60% of the total surface area) to form the Ashanti plateau in the west and the Akwapin Toto Mts, east of Lake Volta (highest point Mt Afadjado 2,904 ft/885 m). The dissected northern savannah, bordered on the western frontiers by the Black Volta river, is less fertile than the laterite soils of the forest zone in the south or the Akuse clays of the populous south-eastern coastal savannah. Approx. 11% of the country is cultivated and one-third covered by evergreen and semi-deciduous tropical forest.

Climate

Equatorial on the coast with high temperatures and increased humidity in the south-west and dry heat in the south-east; hot savannah in the north. The southern and central regions (around Kumasi) receive up to 79 in/2,000 mm rainfall annually and experience two distinct wet seasons (May-June and Oct.); further north, a single rainy season (July–Sept.) yields less than 49 in/1,250 mm rainfall. In the north, the Harmattan blows throughout the dry season. Accra: Jan. 80°F/26.7°C. July 77°F/25°C. Average annual rainfall 29 in/724 mm. Kumasi: Jan. 77°F/25°C. July 76°F/24.4°C. Average annual rainfall 55 in/1,402 mm. Tamale: Jan. 82°F/27.8°C. July 78°F/25.6°C. Average annual rainfall 40 in/1,026 mm.

Cities and towns

Accra (capital)	964,879
Kumasi	348,880
Tamale	136,828
Tema	99,608
Sekondi-Takoradi	61,527
Cape Coast	57,700

Population

Total population is 14,130,000 of which 31.3% live in urban areas. Population density is 153.4 persons per mile^2/59.2 per km^2. Divided ethnolinguistically, the population falls into 75 ethnic groups, the most numerous being the Akan (44%) in the south and west; the Mole-Dagbani (11%) in the north; the Ewe (13%); the Ga (8%) centred around Accra; the Fante on the coast.

Birth rate 4.52%. **Death rate** 1.42%. **Rate of increase** 3.1%. **Age distribution** under 15 = 45.3%; over 65 = 2.3%. **Life expectancy** female 56; male 52; average 54.

Religion

Christianity (52%), of whom 37% are Protestant and 15% Roman Catholic. Muslims represent 13% of the total and 30% pursue traditional animist customs and beliefs.

Language

English is the official language. The Ashanti and Fante of the southern and central regions speak Akan, of the Kwa language family. The two other major African languages are Mole-Dagbani (belonging to the Gur family) and Ewe.

HISTORY

The modern state of Ghana is named after the Ghana empire which ruled in the western Sudan, with its centre some 500 miles north-west of modern Ghana, from the 8th to the 12th centuries. Around the 13th century Akan settlers founded states in the coastal and forest region. Mande traders arrived in the north of the country in the 14th century and Hausa merchants, in search of kola nuts, in the 16th century. During the 15th century the Mande founded the states of Dagomba and Mamprussi. In the 17th century other Mande-speaking tribes founded the kingdom of Gonja.

A Twi-speaking Akan people, the Ashanti, established a centralized empire in the forest belt in the 17th century. They traded slaves first with the Portuguese who founded a trading post at Elimina, and later with British, Dutch and Danish traders. When Britain abolished the slave trade in 1807 fighting broke out, with the Ashanti defeating Britain in 1824. However, fifty years later, a British expedition captured the Ashanti capital in 1874 which led to the foundation of the Gold Coast Colony in the southern provinces of the Ashanti empire. It was not until 1901 that the remainder of the empire was absorbed into the colony and the northern territories became a protectorate.

In 1947 moderate nationalists founded the United Gold Coast Convention (UGCC). Radicals, led by Dr Kwame Nkrumah, broke off to form the Convention People's Party (CPP) in 1949. Campaigning for immediate independence the CPP won elections in 1951, 1954 and 1956. On 6 Mar. 1957 the Gold Coast became independent when it merged with the former British Togoland to form Ghana.

Nkrumah's autocratic style of government and inability to solve Ghana's economic problems led to mounting discontent. In 1960 Ghana became a republic with Nkrumah as executive president, and in 1964 it became a 'socialist single-party state'. During a state visit to China in Feb. 1966 Nkrumah was overthrown by the military, and a National Liberation Council (NLC), comprising four military and four police officers chaired by Gen. Joseph Ankrah, took power.

A transitional government, the NLC prepared the way for return to civilian rule, lifting the ban on political parties in May 1969 and holding elections for the national assembly that August. Dr Kofi Busia's Progress Party (PP) won decisively and Busia became prime minister on 1 Oct. The Busia administration was unable to control inflation, aggravated by the devaluation of the cedi in 1971, and its unpopularity was increased by rumours of corruption. In Jan. 1972 the army, under Lt.-Col. Ignatius Acheampong, seized power. Acheampong banned political parties and established a National Redemption Council (NRC) of army and police officers.

The NRC's policies of self-reliance and austerity were initially successful, allowing the government to reschedule its debts, but the government was unpopular, facing five coup attempts in as many years. In 1975 Acheampong dismissed three of his colleagues, disbanded the NRC and founded a seven-member Supreme Military Council (SMC). Over the following two years food prices rose by between 300 and 600% and the parallel black market flourished. Acheampong advocated 'union government' (UNIGOV) as a means of overcoming fundamental economic and political problems but civilians feared this was a means of prolonging military rule. In June 1977 the Bar and Medical Associations went on strike and Acheampong was forced to give a timetable for general elections. Even so, Acheampong went ahead with UNIGOV, which was approved by a referendum in Mar. 1978, though the result was discredited by government intimidation at the polls.

In July 1978 Acheampong was replaced by Lt-Gen. Fredrick Akuffo as head of the SMC. Akuffo legalized political parties in Jan. 1979 and planned to hold elections in June. However, in May, preparations were interrupted by a coup led by Flight-Lt. Jerry Rawlings. The coup leaders were initially unsuccessful, and Rawlings and others were imprisoned, but an army mutiny spread, and Rawlings was freed on 4 June to become leader of an Armed Forces Revolutionary Council (AFRC). The AFRC executed leaders of the former regime, including Acheampong and Akuffo, but went ahead with the elections as scheduled on 18 June 1979. Dr Hilla Limann's People's National Party (PNP) won a majority, and Limann formed a civilian government. Weakened by accusations of corruption, and by personal rivalries, the Limann government was overthrown on 31 Dec. 1981, when Rawlings seized power for the second time, abrogating the constitution, abolishing political parties and dissolving parliament. A Provisional National Defence Council (PNDC), comprising four officers and three civilians with Rawlings as chairman, was set up to administer a radical programme of 'democratization', which included the transfer of some judicial powers to People's Defence Committees (PDC) and an economic policy emphasizing national self-sufficiency. The deteriorating economic situation and the leftward drift of the PNDC prompted attempted army coups in Mar. and Nov. 1982, and on 19 June 1983 military exiles from Ghana tried to topple the government. After this coup attempt, the most serious the government had faced, the PNDC renamed the PDCs Committees for the Defence of the Revolution (CDR) and sought to increase popular participation. World Bank funding was negotiated in Nov. 1983 and a three-year structural adjustment programme initiated. However, as the economic situation began to improve, the demands of the Trade Union Congress (TUC) for higher wages became more strident. In Mar. 1985 there were student protests at government plans to make them pay for their education. Preparations for a raid on Ghana by American mercenaries, paid by Ghanaian exiles, were discovered in Mar. 1986 and five officers, suspected of plotting against the government, were arrested in July 1986. In Dec. 1986 the PNDC announced that there would be local council elections in mid-1987 but these were postponed until the end of 1988 and the ban on political parties remained in force. The government also initiated a Programme of Action to Mitigate the Social Costs of Adjustment (PAMSCAD) in early 1988, targeting aid at the underprivileged groups worst affected by the government's IMF-backed economic reforms.

CONSTITUTION AND GOVERNMENT

Executive and legislature

The de facto head of state is the chairman of the Provisional National Defence Council (PNDC); executive power is vested in the PNDC which rules by decree. The Committee of Secretaries functions as a cabinet. Elections to district assemblies with executive powers were held in Dec. 1988 and Jan. and Feb. 1989.

Present government

Chairman of Provisional National Defence Council; Chief of Defence Staff Flt-Lt. Jerry Rawlings

Members of the Provisional National Defence Council Flt-Lt. Jerry Rawlings; Capt. (retd) Kojo Tsikata; Justice D.F. Annan; Alhaji Mahamad Idrisu; Maj.-Gen. Winston Mensah-Woode; Lt.-Gen. Arnold

Quainoo; Ebo Tawiah; Zachariah Ali; P.V. Obeng; Mary Grant.

Chairman of the Committee of Secretaries (Cabinet) P.V. Obeng

Principal secretaries (ministers) Dr Kwesi Botchwey (Finance and Economic Planning); Alhaji Mahamad Idrisu (Defence); Dr Obed Y. Asamoah (Foreign Affairs); G.E.K. Aikins (Justice; Attorney-General); Yaw Akrasi-Sarpong (National Defence Committee); Nii Okaidjah Adamafio (Interior).

Administration

Each region is governed through a regional PNDC secretary, as follows: Greater Accra – Lt.-Col. (retd.) W.A. Thompson; Eastern – F. Ohene-Kena; Volta – Dr Francis Agbleh (acting); Brong Ahafo – J.H. Owusu-Acheampong; Ashanti – Col. (retd) Osei Owusu; Western – J.R.E. Amenlemah; Central – Ato Austin; Northern – John Bawa; Upper East – Kandab Molbila; Upper West – Yelibora Antumini.

Justice

The system of law is based on English common law and customary law. The highest court is the Supreme Court, with a function of constitutional review of legislation, as well as the role of final court of appeal. The Chief Justice is president of the Supreme Court and of the Court of Appeal. The High Court handles civil, criminal, industrial and labour law matters at the level of major importance. At lower levels, there are public tribunals and traditional courts. The death penalty is in force. There were over 37 executions between 1985 and mid-1988. Capital offences: armed robbery, murder, embezzlement, economic sabotage.

National symbols

Flag. Tricolour with horizontal stripes of green, yellow and blue.

Festivals. 6 Mar. (Independence Day); 1 May (Labour Day); 5 June (Anniversary of the 1979 coup); 1 July (Republic Day); 31 Dec. (Revolution Day).

Vehicle registration plate. GH.

INTERNATIONAL RELATIONS

Affiliations

NAM; OAU; ACP; Commonwealth.

Defence

Total Armed Forces: 10,600. Terms of service: voluntary.

Army: 9,000.

Navy: 800; eight patrol and coastal combatants.

Air Force: 800; nine combat aircraft (B-326).

Para-military: 5,000 (People's Militia).

ECONOMY

Currency

The unit is the cedi, divided into 100 pesewas.

National finance

Budget. The 1986 budget (in US$) was for expenditure (current and capital) of 604 million and revenue of 611 million. Main items of current expenditure are education 23.9%; health 8.3%; defence 6.5%.

Balance of payments. The balance of payments (current account, 1987) was a deficit of $275 million.

Inflation. (1987) 39%.

Gross Domestic Product

Estimated total GDP US$5,080 million, per capita US$410 (ranking 83 in the world by size).

Economically active population. The total number of persons active in the economy was 3,700,000; unemployed: 26%.

Sector	% of workforce	% of GDP
industry	18.7	16
agriculture	54.7	51
services*	26.6	33

* services figure includes elements unassigned to other categories.

Energy and mineral resources

Oil and gas. Known reserves of petroleum amount to about 7 million bbls but are not yet exploited.

Minerals. Production: (1987) gold ore 1,124 ton/10,200kg; diamonds 44,000 carats; manganese ore 279,984 tons/254,000 tonnes; bauxite 214,949 tons/195,000 tonnes.

Electricity. Capacity: 1,172,000 kW; production: (1988) 4,106 million kWh.

Bioresources

Agriculture. Agriculture, including forestry and fishing, is the backbone of the economy. Food production remains low however, because of insufficient incentives and support services. In addition, the north is prone to drought, and production is severely affected by deforestation, overgrazing and soil erosion. Cocoa is the chief cash crop, contributing 60% of export revenues in 1986. Production was in decline between 1970 and 1982, when a rehabilitation programme was implemented. Other cash crops include tobacco; coffee; some rubber; pepper; ginger; pineapple. Avocado and citrus fruits are also grown for export.

Crop production: (1987 in 1,000 tons/tonnes) maize 610/553; rice 89/81; millet (1986) 143/130; sorghum 331/300; cassava 3,244/2,943; cocoyam 1,102/1,000; yam 1,103/1,001; plantain 1,108/1,005; cocoa 241/218.8.

Livestock numbers: (1987) cattle 1.1 million; sheep 1.9 million; goats 1.9 million; pigs 398,000; poultry 8.2 million.

Forestry. Some 37% of the land is forested. In 1988 a closed forest zone covered 20.5 million acres/8.3 million ha, of which 6.2 million acres/2.5 million ha were reserves and 115,149/46,600 ha were unreserved forest land. Roundwood removals: (1986 est.) 339 million ft^3/9.6 million m^3.

Fisheries. Total catch: (1986) 340,276 tons/309,200 tonnes.

Industry and commerce

Industry. The principal industrial activity is aluminium smelting at Tema, which produced 132,276 tons/120,000 tonnes in 1986.

Commerce. Exports: (1986) US$863 million, comprising cocoa (60%); timber; gold; tuna; bauxite; aluminium. Principal destinations US 23%; UK; other EC countries. Imports: (1986) $783 million, comprising petroleum 16%; consumer goods; foods; intermediate goods; capital equipment. Principal trading partners: US 10%; UK; West Germany; France; Japan; South Korea; East Germany.

Trade with UK. Ghana in 1988 exported goods worth £106.3 million to the UK, and imported goods worth £126.1 million from the UK.

Tourism. (1986) 92,550 tourists.

COMMUNICATIONS

Railways

There are 588 miles/947 km of railways.

Roads

There are some 17,574 miles/28,300 km of roads, of which 2,344 miles/3,775 km are bituminized.

Aviation

Ghana Airways Corporation provides domestic and international services (main airport is at Kotoka (Accra). Passengers: (1984) 261,000.

Shipping

104 miles/168 km of the Volta, Ankobra and Tano rivers are navigable all year round. Lake Volta provides 696 miles/1,125 km of arterial and feeder waterways. The main maritime ports are Tema and Sekondi-Takoradi. The merchant marine consists of four cargo ships of 1,000 GRT or over. Goods loaded: (1985) 1.1 million tons/1.0 million tonnes; unloaded: 2.8 million tons/2.5 million tonnes.

Telecommunications

There are 38,000 telephones and a poor to fair system of open-wire and cable radio relay links. There are 2.9 million radios and 175,000 televisions (1988). The Ghana Broadcasting Corporation operates radio and TV services (the latter including some colour services since 1987), and broadcasts external radio in English and French.

EDUCATION AND WELFARE

Education

Primary and secondary level schooling is free and officially compulsory. Under a new system introduced experimentally in 1974, primary education begins at age six for six years, and is followed by three years of junior secondary school. Pupils then choose between technical and vocational secondary school, or senior secondary leading to General Certificate of Education 'Ordinary' examinations. The old system is still in operation, however, consisting of six years' primary education followed by four years at a middle school.

School population. (1984) Enrolment at primary level was equivalent to 67% of children in the relevant age group (75% of boys and 59% of girls). At secondary level enrolment was 36% (45% of boys; 27% of girls).

Schools. In 1985/86 there were 9,000 primary schools with 1,491,162 pupils; 5,310 middle schools with 617,613 pupils; 110 junior secondary schools with 18,372 pupils; 233 secondary schools with 133,435 pupils. There were 45 training colleges with 15,210 students, and 26 vocational-technical schools with 19,547 students.

Universities. There are three universities, all offering free education.

Literacy. (1985) 53.2% (males 64.1%; females 42.8%)

Health

There are 46 government hospitals; 40 private hospitals; 35 mission hospitals; three university hospitals; three psychiatric hospitals; 34 mission clinics; 252 health centres. According to World Bank estimates, the number of physicians working in Ghana declined from 1,665 in 1981 to 817 in 1984 (approximately one per 15,000 inhabitants). The 1986–88 Economic Recovery Programme aims to expand health services and to make them accessible to all Ghanaians by the year 2000.

GIBRALTAR

GEOGRAPHY

The Rock of Gibraltar has a strategic location on the Strait of Gibraltar which links the North Atlantic Ocean and the Mediterranean. It has a total area of 2.5 miles^2/6.5 km^2, and has a .74 mile/1.2 km border with Spain. A narrow coastal lowland borders the Rock. There are very few fresh water sources and no land suitable for cultivation.

Climate

Mediterranean with mild winters and warm summers.

Population

Total population (1989 est.) 29,528, of mostly Italian, English, Maltese, Portuguese and Spanish origin.
Birth rate 1.8%. **Death rate** 0.8%. **Rate of population increase** 0.2%. **Life expectancy** female 78; male 72.

Religion

Christianity: majority Roman Catholic.

Language

English (official) and Spanish.

HISTORY

After more than 700 years of Moorish rule, Gibraltar was captured by the Spanish in 1462 and annexed to Spain in 1502. In the War of Spanish Succession, a combined British and Dutch force took the Rock (1704), which was ceded to Britain under the Treaty of Utrecht (1713). Most of the Spanish inhabitants fled during the fighting and were later replaced by a mixed non-Spanish population. British proposals to exchange Gibraltar for other territory came to nothing, and Spanish military efforts to recover the Rock (1727, 1739, 1779–83) were unsuccessful. Confirmed as British territory under the 1783 Treaty of Versailles, Gibraltar became a Crown Colony in 1830, as well as a major Royal Navy dockyard and base. As such, it played an important military role in both World Wars, although in the post–1945 era its strategic importance declined.

Spain's claim to Gibraltar was revived in 1939 by the fascist regime of Gen. Franco on the expectation of Britain being defeated in World War II. The Spanish claim was maintained after the war, and pressed when Gibraltar attained a measure of self-government in 1964. UK-Spanish negotiations were initiated at the request of the UN General Assembly (1965), although with talks in progress Franco unilaterally closed the Spain-Gibraltar border to all but pedestrian traffic (1966). A referendum in Gibraltar (1967), showing almost unanimous support for British status, led to the granting of full self-government under British sovereignty (1969). Spain reacted by closing the border completely, thus preventing thousands of Spaniards from getting to their jobs in Gibraltar.

Franco's death in 1975 and the new democratic Spain's application to join Britain within the European Communities (EC) and NATO created a scenario for resumed UK–Spanish negotiations, which produced the Lisbon agreement (1980) envisaging the reopening of the border. After a delay caused by the UK–Argentinian war over the Falklands/Malvinas (1982), the border was reopened in Feb. 1985 on the basis of an agreement reached in Brussels (Nov. 1984) specifying, for the first time, that Britain would discuss the sovereignty of Gibraltar. Although Spain had joined NATO in 1982 and became a full EC member in Jan. 1986, subsequent UK–Spanish negotiating rounds failed to resolve the basic dispute, not least because of the Gibraltarians' unyielding opposition to Spanish rule. An Anglo-Spanish agreement in Dec. 1987 providing for joint use of Gibraltar's airport was rejected by Gibraltarians.

Internally, the Rock's politics were dominated by the (conservative and pro-British) Gibraltar Labour Party (GLP) before and after the attainment of full self-government in 1969. The GLP leader, Sir Joshua Hassan, was chief minister from 1972 until his retirement in 1987, but came under increasing criticism for appearing to contemplate concessions to Spain. In the Mar. 1988 elections, the (left-wing and pro-British) Gibraltar Socialist Labour Party won the maximum permissible eight seats out of 15 in the House of Assembly and formed a government under Joe Bossano. Shortly before the election three unarmed IRA members who had been planning a car-bomb attack were shot dead on the Rock by members of the British security forces. The incident fuelled controversy about the 'summary execution' of terrorist suspects, while a television programme on the killings broadcast in the UK in the following month was described by Margaret Thatcher, the UK prime minister, as 'trial by television'.

CONSTITUTION AND GOVERNMENT

Under the Constitution dating from May 1969, there is a parliamentary system comprising the Gibraltar House of Assembly (15 elected members and three ex officio members), the Council of Ministers headed by the chief minister, and the Gibraltar Council.

Leader The Governor, Admiral Derek Rafell since Dec. 1989, is appointed by the UK crown. The chief minister is Joe Bassano (since Mar. 1988).

National symbols

Flag. Two horizontal bands of white and red, with a three-towered red castle in the centre of the white band.

National holiday. Second Monday of March, Commonwealth Day.

ECONOMY

The economy depends heavily on British defence expenditure. Nearly 50% of the work force is employed by the UK base and civil government. Other important industries are tourism; shipping; banking; finance.

Currency

Gibraltar pound.

COMMUNICATIONS

Gibraltar is an important port. There is a railway system in the dockyard area only. There are 31 miles/50 km of surfaced road. There is a telephone system, one AM and six FM radio stations and four TV stations, and one satellite station.

GREECE
Elliniki Dimokratia
(Hellenic Republic)

GEOGRAPHY

The maritime state of Greece occupies the southernmost sector of the Balkan peninsula in south-east Europe. Over 1,400 Ionian and Aegean islands compose 20% of its territory, 80% of the terrain is rugged, mountainous relief and the eroded mainland coastline, including the Peloponnese, is some 2,484 miles/4,000 km in length. Apart from the narrow fragmented coastal strips surrounding the mainland and most of the islands, the lowland areas are concentrated along the north Aegean from Thraki to Makhedonia, recurring only in the fertile intermontane valleys and riverine plains of the interior. The Pindhos Mts (an extension of the Dinaric Alps, rising to 8,638 ft/2,633 m at Kónitsa) dominate the physiography, traversing the mainland north to south-east from Albania to Peloponnese, resurfacing in Crete (Kríti), the largest of the Greek Islands (3,218 miles^2/8,336 km^2) and Rhodes (Ródhos). Mt Olympus, Greek's highest peak at 9,570 ft/2,917 m, is part of the eastern coastal mountain chain. In the north-east, the Rodopi Planina (Rhodope Mts) divides Greece from southern Bulgaria. The principal rivers include the Néstos, Strimón, Arakhthos, Akhelóos, Aliákmon and Piníos systems. The majority of the population live on the mainland and nearly a third live in Greater Athens. About 30% of the land is either arable or under permanent cultivation and a further 20% is forested. Greece has a total area of 509,930 miles^2/131,944 km^2.

Climate

Mediterranean with mild moist winters and hot, bright, dry summers. The island of Corfu in the north-west receives maximum rainfall (52 in/1,320 mm); rainfall decreases east and south-eastwards, reaching 16 in/414 mm minimum at Athínai (Athens). Winter temperatures can be severe in the mountains, but elsewhere range between 43°F/6°C and 54°F/12°C, summer temperatures from 79–82°F/26–28°C. Athens: Jan. 47°F/8.6°C. July 83°F/28.2°C Average annual rainfall 16 in/414.3 mm.

Cities and towns

Athens (Athinai, capital)	3,027,331
Thessaloniki	406,413
Piraeus	196,389
Patras	142,163
Larissa	102,426
Iraklion	102,398

Population

Total population is 10,013,000 of which 61% live in urban areas. Population density is 196.6/75.9 persons per mile^2/km^2. The vast majority of the population are Greek (97.7% of which 1.5% Macedonian); 1.3% Turkish; 1% Albanian, Slav or Vlach.
Birth rate 1.2%. **Death rate** 1.0%. **Rate of population increase** 0.5%. **Age distribution** under 15 = 21.3%; over 65 = 13.3%. **Life expectancy** female 79; male 74; average 76.

Religion

The Greek Orthodox Church is the dominant religious faith to which 97% of the population adhere. There are also an estimated 47,759 Roman Catholics (divided between the Latin, Byzantine and Armenian rites) and 5,000 Jews. 1.3% of the population are Muslims (concentrated in western Thrace). The self-governing religious community of Mount Athos, easternmost of the three projections that form the Chalcidice peninsula, is made up of 20 monasteries. The Greek government recognized the community's autonomy on 10 Sept. 1926.

Language

Greek is the official language, comprising two branches: Katharevousa (classical Greek) and Demotiki (the spoken and written language). English and French are also widely understood.

HISTORY

The Minoan civilization, Europe's earliest advanced civilization, flourished in Crete from 2300 BC to around 1400 BC. Named after King Minos of Knossos, it spread to Mycenae on the mainland, where magnificent tombs attest to the wealth and power of the ancestors of King Agamemnon of Mycenae, who with his brother King Menelaus of Sparta was to lead the Greeks in the attack on Troy. The ten-year siege was ended through the subterfuge of the wooden horse in around 1184 BC but was only formally chronicled much later by the poet Homer in the Iliad (Homer's *Odyssey* told of Odysseus's adventures on his way home from Troy). After this an invasion of tribes from Asia Minor ushered in the Greek Dark Ages, when hundreds of little states, each known as a polis, had their own separate governments, the largest to emerge being Athens. A first invasion by King Darius of Persia was defeated by the Athenians at Marathon in 491 BC. A second by the Persian King Xerxes was also beaten back (with Spartan help) in

480–479 BC, ushering in the golden age of classical Greece when the philosophers, writers and artists of Athens laid down the intellectual foundations of Western civilization. The Spartans eventually forced the Athenians to surrender in 404 BC at the end of the Peloponnesian Wars but were themselves beaten by Philip of Macedon in 338 BC. Philip's son Alexander the Great (356–23 BC) in turn conquered the Persian empire, founding Alexandria in 331 BC and spreading Greek civilization throughout his vast but shortlived empire.

Conquered by the Romans in the 2nd century BC, Greece formed part of the heartland of the Eastern Roman, or Byzantine, Empire (founded AD 395), which from its capital at Constantinople preserved versions of the Greek language and heritage while assimilating many races. Doctrinal disputes between Constantinople and the Church of Rome led to the Great Schism (1054), after which the Greek Orthodox Church regarded itself as the sole spiritual embodiment of the universal Empire. Weakened by the depredations of Latin crusaders in the 13th century, the Byzantine Empire gradually succumbed to the Ottoman Turks, to whom Constantinople fell in 1453 (and became Istanbul) followed by mainland Greece in 1456. The larger Greek-populated islands of the Aegean held out much longer under the powerful Italian city-states, of which Venice occupied the Morea peninsula in 1686–1715. Nevertheless, for several centuries most, and eventually all, of the eastern Mediterranean Greek world was under Muslim Turkish rule.

Cultural revival in the late 18th century led to the Greek war of independence (1821–29), in which the Greeks were championed by many eminent British and French (including the English poet Byron, who died at the siege of Missolonghi in 1824), and by a Russian regime seeking advantage from the Ottoman Empire's decline. Greek independence was declared at Epidauros in Jan. 1822, but not until a British-French-Russian squadron had destroyed the Turkish–Egyptian fleet at Navarino (1827) were the great powers able to force Turkish recognition of an independent Greece (1829), albeit confined to the Peloponnese and the western Aegean islands. Prince Otto of Bavaria, created King of the Hellenes (1832), accepted constitutional rule in 1843, but his despotic tendencies led to his deposition in 1862 and replacement by Prince George of Denmark. Britain's cession in 1863 of the Ionian Islands (a British protectorate since 1815) was followed by the acquisition from Turkey of Thessaly (1881) and of Macedonia, southern Epirus, Crete and the eastern Aegean islands in the Balkan Wars (1912–13). George I was assassinated in the newly acquired northern port of Salonika in Mar. 1913, and was succeeded by Constantine I.

The outbreak of World War I divided Greeks between the pro-German King and the Liberal Prime Minister, Eleftherios Venizelos (1864–1936), who in 1917 secured Constantine's abdication and Greece's entry into the war on the Allies' side and against Turkey. But Venizelos's 'greater Greece' aims, as partially envisaged under the Versailles and Sèvres treaties (1919, 1920), foundered when King Alexander (r.1917–20) died from a monkey bite and Constantine I was restored (Dec. 1920). Without Allied support, Greece sought to impose the Sèvres terms on the reinvigorated Turkey of Kemal Ataturk, who proceeded to eject the Greek army and population from Smyrna in Anatolia (1921–22), whereupon Constantine again abdicated and was succeeded by George II (Sept. 1922). Under the Treaty of Lausanne (1923), 'greater Greece' aspirations were abandoned and Greece accepted British rule in Cyprus, the Turkish presence in Anatolia, and Italy's acquisition of the Dodecanese Islands. A turbulent decade followed, in which George II gave way to a republic (May 1924) until being restored to the throne by plebiscite in Nov. 1935. In 1936, with the rising Communist Party (founded 1918) holding the parliamentary balance between Monarchists and Liberals, he gave the premiership to Gen. Joannis Metaxas, who set up a fascist-style dictatorship called the 'Third Civilization'.

In World War II, Greece repelled an attempted invasion by Italy (1940) but was then overrun by German forces (1941). Occupation by the Axis powers was resisted by the military wing of the Communist-led National Liberation Front (EAM) and, less effectively, by the Free Democratic Greek Army (EDES), which adopted a royalist stance as hostility between the two movements erupted into civil war on the liberation of Greece in late 1944. Against EAM opposition, a plebiscite restored George II to the throne (Oct. 1946), although he died in Apr. 1947 and was succeeded by his brother Paul (ruled 1947–64). Under the 1947 Paris peace treaty between the Allies and Italy, the Dodecanese Islands were ceded to Greece. Supported by British and (from 1947) US troops and aid, royalist forces led by Marshal Alexander Papagos eventually defeated the EAM 'republic' in northern Greece (Aug. 1949), after Yugoslavia had ceased to support the insurgents. The brutality of the conflict, in which 27,000 soldiers and civilians perished, created lasting divisions in Greek society, not least because the EAM remained outlawed and thousands of Communists went into exile. Greece (with Turkey) joined NATO in 1952, as the right gained electoral ascendancy under the premierships of Papagos (1952–55), who signed a Balkan Pact with Turkey and Yugoslavia (1954), and Constantine Karamanlis (1955–63), who reached agreement with Britain and Turkey on independence for Cyprus (1959–60) and took Greece into associate membership of the European Communities (EC) in 1962. During this era, the electoral system was repeatedly adjusted in the quest for greater stability, but never to universal satisfaction.

The 1963 elections brought to power a minority Centre Union government led by George Papandreou who won a landslide parliamentary majority in 1964. In July 1965, however, Papandreou resigned over a clash with the new king, Constantine II (r.1964–73), arising from an alleged plot by left-wing army officers (the Aspida group) to install a dictatorship under Andreas Papandreou (son of George). Chronic government instability and popular pressure forced the calling of elections, which were pre-empted by a military coup on 21 Apr. 1967. Led by Colonels George Papadopoulos and Stylianos Pattakos, the new regime suspended parliamentary government, banned left-wing organizations and drove democratic leaders into exile. Use of torture and other human-rights violations intensified international ostracism of the regime, although the US government (accused by the Greek left of having instigated the 1967 coup through the CIA) maintained close relations for strategic reasons. An abortive counter-coup by Constantine in Dec. 1967 forced the King into exile in Rome, where his continued plotting impelled the Athens regime to proclaim a republic (June 1973) with Papadopoulos as president. Subsequent democratization moves provoked a further military coup (Nov. 1973) led by Gen. Demetrios Ioannides, and the installation of Gen. Phaidon Ghizikis as president. Events in Cyprus caused the final downfall of the Athens regime, whose support for a right-wing coup attempt in Nicosia precipitated a Turkish invasion of the island (July 1974), whereupon the Greek military relinquished power on 23 July 1974.

Returning from exile in Paris, Karamanlis became premier of a government of national salvation, which suspended Greek military participation in NATO in protest against the Turkish action in Cyprus. His newly founded New Democracy (ND) party won a large majority in general elections (Nov. 1974), with a centrist alliance and Andreas Papandreou's Pan-Hellenic Socialist Movement (Pasok) forming the main opposition. After a 2:1 referendum verdict (Dec. 1974) against restoration of the monarchy, a new constitution (June 1975) declared a democratic republic, and the unicameral parliament elected Constantine Tsatsos (ND) as president. Of 20 leaders of the former military regime brought to trial in Aug. 1975, Papadopoulos and Pattakos were first sentenced to death and later to life imprisonment. Returned to power with a reduced majority in the Nov. 1977 elections, when Pasok became the main opposition party, Karamanlis was elected president in May 1980 and replaced as prime minister by George Rallis. In Oct. 1980 Greece rejoined NATO's military wing, although relations with Turkey remained strained over Cyprus and conflicting continental shelf claims in the Aegean. Greece acceded to full EC membership on 1 Jan. 1981, a step which was expected to benefit Greek agriculture and to accelerate development of an economy heavily dependent on the rapidly expanding tourist industry.

Voters' doubts about EC membership contributed to the ND's defeat in the Oct. 1981 elections and the installation of the country's first socialist administration, committed to withdrawal from the EC, the removal of US bases from Greece, and radical economic reforms. Under Papandreou's leadership, however, the Pasok government switched to a pro-EC stance after securing changes in the Greek entry terms (Apr. 1983). It also signed (Sept. 1983) a new defence agreement with the US, allowing its four military bases to remain at least until the end of 1988 (although a resumed boycott of NATO military exercises was maintained). Also in 1983, Greece signed a ten-year economic co-operation agreement with the Soviet Union. When Papandreou announced that Pasok would not renominate him, Karamanlis resigned the presidency shortly before the end of his five-year term (Mar. 1985); later the same month Christos Sartzetakis, the Pasok nominee, was elected president in controversial circumstances, the post becoming largely ceremonial under constitutional changes passed in Mar. 1986. Amid worsening economic conditions, Pasok retained power in the June 1985 elections with a reduced majority. In Aug. 1986 Greece formally ended the state of war which had technically existed with Albania since 1940, while a further crisis in relations with Turkey (1986–87) was eased in June 1988 by the first visit to Greece of a Turkish prime minister since 1952. The closure of the US air base at Hellenikon (near Athens) was announced in Aug. 1988.

In late 1988 a major financial scandal, known as the Koskotas affair, broke centring on the alleged involvement of Pasok ministers and officials in massive fraud and embezzlement at the Bank of Crete. Also controversial was Papandreou's announcement (Sept. 1988), shortly after undergoing heart surgery in London at the age of 69, that he intended to divorce his wife and marry his much younger mistress.

During 1989 the Koskotas affair and its ramifications dominated Greek politics. Papandreou stepped down after an inconclusive general election on 18 June and a broad-based coalition of the ND and the communist-led Coalition took office – their first collaboration since the bitter clashes of the post-war years. Under ND Prime Minister Tzannis Tzannetakis the new government sought to investigate the Koskotas affair and other scandals of recent years in advance of further elections on 5 Nov. On 26–27 Sept. parliament voted that Papandreou and four other former ministers should be tried in connection with the Koskotas affair. The November election did not significantly change the balance of power and an all-party government was formed. Led by Zenofon Zolotas the new government was intended to combat the country's increasingly serious economic problems in advance of yet another general election on 8 April 1990.

CONSTITUTION AND GOVERNMENT

Executive and legislature

The president, the head of state, is elected by Parliament for a five-year term, to what is now a largely ceremonial office. The president appoints the prime minister, who is head of government. The legislature is a unicameral 300-member parliament, elected for a four-year term by universal adult suffrage under a system of reinforced proportional representation (last general election Nov. 1989).

Present government

President Khristos Sartzetakis

Prime Minister Xenofon Zolotas

Principal Ministers Niko Themelis (Minister to the Prime Minister); Tzannis Tzannetakis (Defence; Tourism); Antonis Samaras (Foreign Affairs); Theodoros Katrivanos (Interior); Georgios Gennimatos (Economy); Georgios Souflias (Finance); Konstantinos Stamatis (Justice); Dimitris Manikas (Public Order)

Justice

There is a Special Supreme Court with which the final jurisdiction lies. There are three divisions of the Greek legal system – administrative, civil and criminal. The Supreme Court has final jurisdiction. Judges are appointed for life by the President. The death penalty is nominally in force. No executions were carried out between 1985 and mid-1988.

Prisons. There are 4,178 prisoners.

National symbols

Flag. Nine horizontal stripes of five blue alternating with four white ones and a white cross in a blue square canton.

Festivals. 25 Mar. (Independence Day); 1 May (Labour Day); 28 Oct. (Ochi Day, anniversary of Greek defiance of Italy's 1940 ultimatum).

Vehicle registration plate. GR.

INTERNATIONAL RELATIONS

Affiliations

NATO; OECD; EC.

Defence

Total Armed Forces: 214,000 (112,500 conscripts, 1,400 women). Terms of service: Army 21, Navy 25,

Air Force 23 months. Reserves: some 404,000 (to age 50).

Army: 170,500; 1,893 main battle tanks (mainly M-48, M-47, AMX-30, Leopard 1A3), 267 light tanks (M-24, M-41A3).

Navy: 19,500; ten submarines (mainly FRG T-209/1100), 21 principal surface combatants: 14 destroyers (US Gearing, US Sumner and US Fletcher), seven frigates (chiefly US Cannon). 37 patrol and coastal combatants.

Air Force: 24,000; 329 combat aircraft, plus 55 in store (mainly F-104, F104G, F-5 and F-5A).

ECONOMY

Currency

The unit is the drachma, divided into 100 lepta.

National finance

Budget. The 1987 budget (in US$) was for expenditure (current and capital) of 20,200 million and revenue of 15,300 million.

Balance of payments. The balance of payments (current account, 1988) was a deficit of $1,000 million (1988).

Inflation. 14.3% (12 months to Sept. 1989).

Gross Domestic Product

Estimated total GDP US$40,900 million, per capita US$4,670 (ranking 43 in the world by size). Growth rate 4% (1988).

Economically active population. The total number of persons active in the economy was 3,860,000; unemployed: 7.7% (1988).

Sector	% of workforce	% of GDP
industry	27	29
agriculture	27	16
services*	46	56

* services figure includes elements unassigned to other categories.

Energy and mineral resources

Minerals. Greece mines asbestos; bauxite; chrome; some coal; emery; iron ore; iron pyrites; lead; manganese; magnesite; marble; nickel; zinc. Aluminium, nickel, and iron and steel products are now processed in Greek factories.

Electricity. Capacity: 10,531,000 kW; production: (1988) 33,110 million kWh; 3,310 kWh per capita.

Bioresources

Agriculture. The relatively large and inefficient agricultural sector contributes 14% to GDP. Of the land 23% is arable; 8% is under permanent crops; 40% is meadows and pastures. Greece is nearly self-sufficient in food; the most important crops are wheat; olives; tobacco; cotton; raisins; citrus fruit; other fruit.

Crop production: (1987 in thousand tons/tonnes) wheat 2,439/2,213; maize 2,377/2,156; sugar beet 2,232/2,025; tomatoes 1,835/1,665; grapes 1,653/1,500; olives 1,213/1,100; potatoes 1,045/948; watermelons 691/627; cotton 649/589; oranges 638/579; peaches and nectarines 634/575; barley 632/573; apples 334/303; tobacco leaves 171/155.

Livestock numbers: (1987) poultry 31,000,000; sheep 11,412,000; goats 5,000,000; pigs 1,226,000; cattle 743,000; asses 185,000; mules 91,000; horses 65,000; buffaloes 1,000.

Forestry. Some 20% of the land is forested. Around 1,021,630,000 ft^3/2,893,000 m^3 of wood was felled (1986).

Fisheries. Total catch: (1986) 135,583 tons/123,000 tonnes plus an estimated 27,006 tons/24,500 tonnes from small vessels of less than 19 HP.

Industry and commerce

Industry. The industrial sector provides 50% of exports. The chief industries are food and tobacco processing; textiles; chemicals; metal products; tourism; mining; petroleum.

Commerce. Exports: US$5,600 million, most importantly manufactured goods; food and live animals; fuels and lubricants; raw materials. Imports: US$12,500 million, most importantly machinery and transport equipment; light manufactures; fuels and lubricants; foodstuffs; chemicals. Countries exported to: West Germany 24%; Italy 14%; non-oil-producing developing countries 11.8%; France 9.5%; US 7.1%; UK 6.8%. Imports came from West Germany 22%; non-oil-producing developing countries 13%; Italy 12%; France 8%; US 3.2%.

Trade with UK. Greece imported UK goods worth £468 million; exports to UK totalled £357 million (1988).

Tourism. (1986) 7,025,000 visitors.

COMMUNICATIONS

Railways

There are 1,600 miles/2,577 km of railways.

Roads

There are 21,420 miles/34,492 km of roads.

Aviation

Olympic Airways SA provides domestic and international services (main airports are Athens; Thessaloniki; Alexandroupolis; Corfu).

Shipping

The major ports are Eleusis, Piraeus, Thessaloniki and Volos. There are 20 secondary and 35 minor ports. 1,026 of the merchant marine ships are of 1,000 GRT or over. It should be noted that Greeks also own large numbers of ships under the registry of Liberia, Panama, Cyprus and Lebanon. International goods loaded: (1987 est.) 24.3 million tonnes. International goods unloaded: (1987 est.) 30.7 million tonnes.

Telecommunications

There are 4.1 million telephones and the adequate, modern networks reach all areas. There are 4 million radios and 1.71 million televisions (1985). Hellenic National Radio-Television (ERT) is the main state-controlled broadcasting service; ERA-4 provides a fourth radio channel and ET2 a second television channel.

EDUCATION AND WELFARE

Education

The state provides compulsory free education from 6 to 15.

Schools. There were 5,203 nursery schools with 160,079 pupils and 7,617 teachers (one per 21 pupils); 8,675 primary schools with 887,735 pupils and 37,994 teachers (one per 23 pupils); 2,654 high schools and lyceums with 704,119 pupils and 41,782 teachers (one per 17 pupils); 480 technical and vocational schools with 107,422 pupils and 7,992 teachers (one per 13 pupils).

Universities. There are 13 universities with 94,574 students and 7,638 lecturers (one per 12 students), plus also teacher-training, technical education, vocational and ecclesiastical schools.

Literacy. 99%.

Health

There were 30,481 doctors (one per 330 people) and 488 hospitals with 52,864 beds (one per 190 people) (1986).

GREENLAND

GEOGRAPHY

Greenland is an island in the Arctic Ocean covering 839,782 miles^2/2,175,600 km^2, of which 131,896 miles^2/341,700 km^2 is ice-free. There is continuous permafrost over the northern two-thirds of the island, and settlement is confined to the narrow, rocky coastal area. The capital is Nuuk.

Climate

Arctic to subarctic.

Population

Total population (1989 est.) 55,415.

Birth rate 2.1%. **Death rate** 0.8%. **Rate of population increase** 1.2%. **Life expectancy** female 68; male 62.

Religion

Christianity: Evangelical Lutherans.

Language

Eskimo dialects; Danish.

HISTORY

Settlement of Greenland by Norwegian Vikings began in the late 10th century and Norwegian sovereignty was confirmed in 1262. The union of the Norwegian and Danish crowns (1380), as confirmed by the Union of Kalmar (1397), placed Greenland under Danish rule, but by the late 15th century contact with the original European settlements had been lost. From 1721 Danish missionaries and settlers re-established the colony, which remained Danish when Norway was transferred to Sweden in 1814. In the 20th century, conflicting Danish and Norwegian claims to Greenland were resolved in Denmark's favour by the International Court of Justice (1933). US bases established in Greenland during World War II were retained within the framework of Denmark's accession to NATO (1949). Declared an integral part of Denmark under the 1953 constitution, Greenland joined the EEC, European Coal and Steel Community, and EFTA on Denmark's accession (Jan. 1973), although Greenlanders had voted heavily against membership in the Oct. 1972 Danish referendum.

Dissatisfaction with the European Communities (EC), combined with concern to safeguard Greenland's fisheries and mineral resources, fuelled pressure for internal autonomy, which was achieved in May 1979 after securing 70% approval in a referendum (Jan. 1979). The first home rule-government was formed by the socialist Forward party (Siumut) led by Jonathan Motzfeldt, which had won a narrow election victory over the moderate Community (Atassut) party (Apr. 1979). A further referendum in Feb. 1982 showed a 52% majority in favour of withdrawal from the EC, which took place on 1 Feb. 1985, although the acquisition of the EC's overseas countries and territories (OCT) status meant little practical change. A coalition formed in 1984 between Forward and the small left-wing Eskimo Community party collapsed in 1987, amid differences over the status of the US base at Thule. It was re-formed by Motzfeldt after early elections (May 1987) had again produced stalemate between the two major parties.

CONSTITUTION AND GOVERNMENT

Greenland is a self-governing overseas administrative division of the Danish realm. Legislative authority rests jointly with the elected 27-seat Landsting and Danish parliament, where Greenland is represented by two MPs; executive power is vested in a home rule chairman and four-person council or Landsstyre. Elections are held every four years, most recently in May 1987.

Leaders Queen Margrethe II of Denmark (since Jan 1972); Jonathan Motzfeldt, Home Rule Chairman (since May 1979).

National symbols

Flag. The flag of Denmark is used.

National holiday. 16 Apr. (Birthday of Queen Margrethe).

ECONOMY

Greenland is heavily dependent on an annual subsidy from Denmark. Fishing is the most important industry, accounting for over 60% of exports. Exploitation of mineral resources is limited to lead and zinc. The public sector is a major employer. There is a social welfare system similar to Denmark's.

Currency

Danish krone.

COMMUNICATIONS

There are seven major ports and at least ten minor ports. There are eleven airports, five with permanent-surface runways. There is a domestic cable and radio relay system, five AM and seven FM radio stations, 11 TV stations and one satellite station.

GRENADA
State of Grenada

GEOGRAPHY

Grenada is the most southerly of the Windward Isles in the eastern Caribbean, 90 miles/145 km north-west of Trinidad. Divided into six parishes, the total land area of 132.8 miles/344 km^2 includes the dependent Southern Grenadines to the north-north-west, a crescent of small islands stretching from Grenada to St Vincent. The main island is volcanic in origin with fertile soils, a forested mountainous ridge running north-south (highest point Mt St Catherine 2,756 ft/840 m) dissected by springs and rivers, a number of lakes including the Grand Etang (elevation 1,739 ft/ 530 m), a precipitous western coastline and a gentler southern coastal landscape of beaches and some natural harbours. The population is predominantly rural. 15% of the land is arable and 9% is forested.

Climate

Subtropical. The dry season lasts Jan.–May with some differentiation between daytime and cooler night-time temperatures. Mean annual temperature is 74°F/23°C (range 70–90°F/21–32°C). Rainfall varies from 148–197 in/3,750–5,000 mm inland to 59 in/ 1,500 mm on the coast. The wet season lasts June–Dec. Grenada lies within the Caribbean hurricane zone.

Cities and towns

St George's (capital) 7,500

Population

Total population is 100,000 of which 25% live in urban areas. Population density is 753 persons per miles^2/301.4 persons per km^2. 84% of the population are of Black African extraction; 12% of mixed (mulatto) origin; 3% East Indian and 1% White. **Birth rate** 2.51%. **Death rate** 0.7%. **Rate of population increase** 2.0%. **Age distribution** under 15 = 39.1%; over 65 = 7.3%. **Life expectancy** female 69; male 65; average 67.

Religion

Christianity: at the last census an estimated 64.4% were Roman Catholic. Other denominations include Anglicans; Methodists; Presbyterians; Baptists.

Language

English is the official national language. A French-African patois is also spoken.

HISTORY

Grenada's earliest inhabitants were Arawak Indians who were displaced by Caribs moving up from South America. French settlers eliminated the Caribs in the 1650s, and the island remained a French possession until it was captured by the British in 1762. African slaves were imported as labour until the abolition of slavery in 1834.

Universal suffrage was introduced in 1951, and full internal self-government in 1967 when Grenada became an Associated State. Elections in 1967 were won by the Grenada United Labour Party (GULP), which defeated the Grenada National Party (GNP), led by Herbert Blaize. Eric (later Sir Eric) Gairy became premier. Grenada attained full independence from Britain on 7 Feb. 1974. Gairy's rule became increasingly corrupt and erratic during the 1970s, and on 13 Mar. 1979 he was replaced in a virtually bloodless coup by members of the left-wing New Jewel Movement (NJM). The constitution was suspended and a People's Revolutionary Government (PRG) set up. The NJM's leader, Maurice Bishop, became prime minister.

Under the PRG the country came under growing external pressure over its failure to draft a new constitution or hold elections as promised. The United States, in particular, feared the growth of Cuban influence in the country, and viewed the construction of an airport at Point Salines with Cuban assistance as a threat. In Oct. 1983 a faction within the PRG, led by Bishop's deputy, Bernard Coard, and the army commander, Gen. Hudson Austin, seized power in a coup. In the confusion that followed Bishop and nine of his associates were murdered. The Governor General and the Organization of East Caribbean States both appealed for outside intervention, and on 25 Oct. US troops, together with contingents from Caribbean countries, invaded and overran the island.

The Governor General appointed a non-partisan interim council to administer the country until parliamentary elections could be held. Political prisoners were released, and the 1974 constitution reinstated. Traditional political parties and a number of new groupings emerged to contest the elections. Fear of a return to power by Gairy prompted several centre and centre-right parties to join forces to keep Gairy out of office. A united front was eventually achieved by the creation of the New National Party (NNP), formed from the GNP, the National Democratic Party (NDP) and the Grenada Democratic Movement (GDM). The NNP won an overwhelming majority in the election held in Dec. 1984, and Herbert Blaize became prime minister.

Dissatisfaction among many NNP members over Blaize's style of leadership, ill-health and alleged favouritism of former GNP members rapidly developed into factional discord between the different component groups of the party. Several members resigned, but it was not until Apr. 1987 that three cabinet ministers, including the former leaders of the NDP and GDM, resigned and proceeded to form a new political party, the National Democratic Congress (NDC), combining all opposition members within the House of Representatives. At the NNP convention in Jan. 1989 Blaize lost the post of party leader to his main rival within the party, Dr Keith Mitchell. Blaize remained as prime minister. Nicholas Brathwaite, the head of the 1983–84 interim council, was elected unopposed as leader of the NDC. Factional fighting within the NNP intensified, and in mid–1989 the coalition disintegrated when Blaize dismissed Mitchell from the Cabinet, a move which led to the resignation of several other members of the government and the loss of the Prime Minister's legislative majority. Despite increasing ill-health, Blaize clung on to power by advising the Governor General to prorogue parliament in August, and by launching a new political party called National Party (TNP). Blaize died on 19 Dec. and was succeeded by Ben Jones, the TNP's Vice President. A general election was constitutionally due by Mar. 1990 and it was not expected that the TNP would retain power.

In Dec. 1986 17 people were convicted of the murder of Bishop and his associates and 14 of them were sentenced to death. The appeals against the convictions were still in progress at the end of 1989.

CONSTITUTION AND GOVERNMENT

Executive and legislature

The head of state of Grenada is the British sovereign represented by a governor general. Legislative power is vested in a bicameral parliament, an elected House of Representatives and a 13-member appointed Senate. Last election Dec. 1984.

Present government (1 Feb. 1990)

Governor General Sir Paul Scoon

Prime Minister Ben Jones (also Minister of Finance; Trade; Industry and Economic Planning; Energy; Information; National Security; Home Affairs; External Affairs; Carriacou and Petit Martinique Affairs)

Other principal Ministers George McGuire (Education; Culture; Sports; Youth Affairs; Labour; Local Government; Fisheries; Social Security); Felix Alexander (Health; Housing; Physical Planning; Legal Affairs; Attorney General).

Justice

The system of law is based on English common law. The highest court is the Grenada Supreme Court, which consists of the High Court of Justice and the two-tier Court of Appeals – the Court of Magisterial Appeal, and the Itinerant Court of Appeal which hears appeals from the High Court itself. At lower levels most cases are dealt with in the Magistrates' Courts. The death penalty is in force. No executions were carried out between 1985 and mid-1988.

National symbols

Flag. A broad red border bearing three yellow five-pointed stars at the upper and lower edges. The inner rectangular field is divided diagonally into four triangles, the left and right ones being green and the upper and lower ones being yellow. In the centre of the flag there is a red disc charged with another yellow star.

Festivals. 7 Feb. (Independence Day); 1 May (Labour Day); 7–8 Aug. (6–7 Aug. in 1990, Emancipation Holidays).

Vehicle registration plate. WG.

INTERNATIONAL RELATIONS

Affiliations

NAM; ACP; Commonwealth; OAS; Caricom.

Defence

Royal Grenada Police Force; no army as such.

ECONOMY

Currency

The unit is the EC dollar, divided into 100 cents.

National finance

Budget. The 1986 budget (in US$) was for expenditure (current and capital) of 66 million and revenue of 35 million.

Inflation. (1987) -0.9%.

Gross Domestic Product

Estimated total GDP US$119 million, per capita US$1,400 (ranking 176 in the world by size).

Economically active population. The total number of persons active in the economy was 36,000; unemployed: 20%.

Sector	% of workforce
industry	13
agriculture	24
services*	63

* services figure includes elements unassigned to other categories.

Energy and mineral resources

Minerals. None.

Electricity. Capacity: 1,400 kW; production 24 million kWh; 280 kWh per capita (1988).

Bioresources

Agriculture. Over 40% of the country's total land area is used for crop production. Agriculture accounts for 90% of exports.

Crop production: (1986 in 1,000 tons/tonnes) bananas 8.8/8; nutmegs 3.3/3; cocoa 3.3/3.

Livestock numbers: (1987) poultry 260,000; sheep 17,000; pigs 11,000; goats 11,000; cattle 4,000.

Forestry. Forests and woodland cover 9% of the country.

Fisheries. Total catch: (1983) 1,985 tons/1,801 tonnes.

Industry and commerce

Industry. Grenada remains primarily an agrarian economy. Its small manufacturing sector is based on agricultural processing, making products such as chocolate; sugar; alcoholic beverages; jam. Small quantities of garments and furniture are produced, principally for export to Trinidad and Tobago.

Commerce. Exports: (1987) US$31.6 million. Imports US$88 million. Exports included nutmeg 35%; cocoa beans 15%; bananas 13%; mace 7%. Imports included food 22%; machinery 24%; manufactured goods 19%; petroleum 8%. Countries exported to: US 4%; UK; West Germany; Netherlands; Trinidad and Tobago. Imports received from: US 32%; UK; Trinidad and Tobago; Japan; Canada.

Trade with UK. Grenada imported UK goods worth £7,162,000 and exported to the UK goods worth £6,115,000 (1988).

Tourism. After agriculture, tourism is the second most important sector of the economy. Grenada received 171,000 visitors, including 114,000 cruise ship passengers (1986).

COMMUNICATIONS

Railways

There are no railways.

Roads

There are about 621 miles/1,000 km of roads, of which some 410 miles/660 km are concrete or bituminized.

Aviation

LIAT provides international services (main airport is at Point Salines, 6.2 miles/10 km from St. George's).

Shipping

The Caribbean port of Grenada is St George's. Estimated freight traffic 1985: goods loaded 29,762 tons/27,000 tonnes; unloaded 57,320 tons/52,000 tonnes.

Telecommunications

There is an automatic, island-wide system with 5,650 telephones. There are 50,000 radios (1986), broadcasts by Radio Grenada, and a small television station; TV broadcasts can also be received from Trinidad and Barbados.

EDUCATION AND WELFARE

Education

Education is free and compulsory between the ages of six and 14.

School population. 22,093 primary and 6,249 secondary.
Schools. 16 secondary, four junior and 20 primary, in addition to 46 schools which cover the entire age range.
Universities. The Extra-Mural Department of the University of the West Indies is located in Grenada.
Literacy. 85%

Health

There are 11 medical districts, each in charge of a medical officer. In addition to the country's three hospitals (providing 330 beds), there are five health centres and 28 medical stations.

GUADELOUPE

GEOGRAPHY

Guadeloupe, a group of islands in the Caribbean, is an overseas department of France. Basse-Terre is volcanic in origin, Grand-Terre is low limestone formation. La Soufrière is an active volcano. The capital is Basse-Terre.

Climate

Subtropical, tempered by trade winds. Relatively high humidity. Subject to hurricanes (June–Oct).

Population

Total population (1989 est.) 341,430.
Birth rate 2.1%. **Death rate** 0.7%. **Rate of population increase** 0.8%. **Life expectancy** female 77; male 70.

Religion

Christianity: Roman Catholic; Hindu minority.

Language

French, Creole patois.

HISTORY

The first inhabitants of Guadeloupe were Arawak and Carib Indians. The first European inhabitants were French settlers who arrived in 1635. The French colonized the islands and imported African slaves to work on sugar plantations. Guadeloupe was occupied by the British several times in the 18th and early 19th centuries, but confirmed as French territory in 1815. Guadeloupe's dependency of Saint Barthélemy was first occupied by the French in 1648, but granted to Sweden in 1784 before being returned to France in 1877. The French half of the island of Saint Martin was obtained when the island was divided between the Dutch and French in 1648. Slavery in all French territories was abolished in 1848.

In 1946 Guadeloupe was granted departmental status. A plebiscite in 1962 reflected any changes in that status, but during the 1960s and 1970s demands for greater autonomy grew, chiefly expressed by the principal left-wing parties, the Parti socialiste (PS) and the Parti communiste guadeloupéen (PCG). In 1974 the islands became a region of France and in 1982 were granted a measure of greater autonomy under the French government's decentralization legislation. Centre and right-wing parties have traditionally been in control of the local administration, but this pattern was broken in 1985 when the left-wing parties gained a majority on the General Council. In 1986 they also secured a majority on the Regional Council, thereby gaining the presidencies of both councils. This trend was continued in elections to the General Council in 1988, although in February the PCG announced that it would be pursuing independence for Guadeloupe rather than greater autonomy. In July 1985 there was a general strike and rioting over the detention of a member of one of the small pro-independence parties.

CONSTITUTION AND GOVERNMENT

There is a prefect appointed by the French government and a popularly elected General Council of 36 members (elections held every three years), and a Regional Council composed of members of the local General Council and the locally elected deputies and senators to the French parliament.
Leader Bernard Sarazin, Commissioner of the Republic (since 1987).

National symbols

Flag. The flag of France is used.
National holiday. 14 July (Bastille Day).

ECONOMY

Guadeloupe is dependent on France for subsidy and for imported food. The economy depends on agriculture, tourism, light industry and services. The traditionally important sugar-cane crop is being replaced by bananas, aubergines and flowers. Most manufactured goods and fuel are imported. There is much unemployment among the young.

Currency

French franc.

COMMUNICATIONS

There are 1,025 miles/1,940 km of road. There are ports at Pointe-a-Pitre and Basse-Terre, and nine airports, eight with permanent-surface runways. There is an inter-island radio relay to Antigua and Barbuda, Dominica and Martinique. There are two AM and eight FM radio stations and nine TV stations.

GUAM

GEOGRAPHY

Guam, largest and southernmost island in the Mariana Islands archipelago, is an island covering 209 miles^2/ 542 km^2 in the North Pacific Ocean. It is of volcanic origin, surrounded by coral reefs. It has a relatively flat coralline limestone plateau (source of most fresh water), with steep coastal cliffs and narrow coastal plains in the north, low-rising hills in the centre and mountains in the south. The capital is Agana.

Climate

Tropical marine, generally warm and humid, moderated by north-east trade winds. The dry season is Jan.–June; the rainy season July–Dec., during which there are frequent squalls. Occasional typhoons. Little seasonal variation in temperature.

Population

Total population (1989 est.) 138,093. (Approx 80% residents and 20% US military personnel/ dependents).

Birth rate 2.5%. **Death rate** 0.4%. **Rate of population increase** 2.8%. **Life expectancy** female 75; male 70.

Religion

Christianity: Roman Catholic.

Language

English and Chamorro, most residents bilingual; Japanese is also widely spoken.

HISTORY

Guam was settled in the second millennium BC by Malay-Filipino peoples. In 1521 Ferdinand Magellan became the first European to reach the island. After formally claiming Guam in 1565, the Spanish did not settle there for another century. The arrival of Jesuit missionaries, protected by a garrison, threatened the way of life of the indigenous Chamorro people and led to a protracted rebellion (1670–95). Guam served until 1815 as a port of call for the annual galleon trade between Mexico and the Philippines. During the 19th century foreign vessels called more frequently and in 1855 the United States established a consulate there. Following her defeat in the Spanish–American war of 1898, Spain ceded Guam to the US. From 1899 to 1950 the island was administered by the US Navy, except during the Japanese occupation (1941–44) in World War II. The Organic Act of 1950 made Guam an unincorporated territory of the US, granting US citizenship to its people, but without the right to vote in US national elections. This Act returned Guam to civilian administration under the US Department of the Interior and provided for local self-government. The first popular elections for governor and a non-voting delegate to the US House of Representatives took place in 1970 and 1972 respectively. During the Vietnam War Guam was used as a base for bombing Indochina. Referenda in 1982 and 1987 have indicated the Guamanians' wish to redefine their status and relationship with the US.

CONSTITUTION AND GOVERNMENT

Guam is a territory of the United States. Relations between Guam and the US are under the jurisdiction of the Office of Territorial and International Affairs, US Department of the Interior; Guamanians are US citizens, and elect a non-voting delegate to the US House of Representatives. They may not vote in US presidential elections. Guam's Constitution dates from the Organic Act of Aug. 1950. There is a governor, elected for a four-year term, and a senate with 21 members elected for a two-year term.

Leader Joseph Ada, Governor since 1986.

National symbols

Flag. Dark blue with a narrow red border on all four sides. Centred is a vertical ellipse, containing a beach scene, outrigger canoe with sail, and a palm tree with the word GUAM superimposed in red.

National holiday. First Monday in March (Guam Discovery Day).

ECONOMY

The economy is based on US military spending and tourism. There is a small manufacturing sector. Most food and industrial goods are imported, mainly from the US.

Currency

US dollar.

COMMUNICATIONS

There are 419 miles/674 km of all-weather roads; a port at Apra Harbor; five airports, three with permanent-surface runways. There is a telephone system, three AM and three FM radio stations and three TV stations.

GUATEMALA

Republica de Guatemala
(Republic of Guatemala)

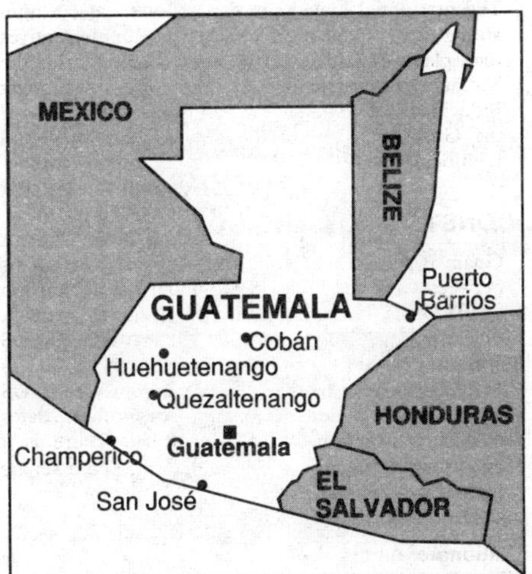

GEOGRAPHY

Located in the north-west corner of the Central American isthmus, Guatemala covers a total area of 42,031 miles^2/108,889 km^2 divided into 22 departments, the most populous of which are Guatemala City and the south-west coastal districts. Lowland areas include the well-watered and fertile Pacific coastal plain in the south, the tropically vegetated Petén tableland in the north (over 13,510 miles^2/ 35,000 km^2) and the Atlantic littoral containing Lake Izabal, part of the Río Polochic river valley which drains north into the Caribbean. The Guatemalan highlands extend south-east to north-west across the country (50% of the total surface area) comprising two principal ranges, the northern Altos Cuchumatanes and the southern Sierra Madres, including 33 volcanic peaks climbing to 13,844 ft/ 4,220 m at Tajumulco. The 248 miles/400-km-long Río Motagua drains north-east into the Golfo de Honduras. 12% of the land is arable and 40% forested.

Climate

Tropical with minimal seasonal variations in temperature. Humidity increases in the north and north-east on the Petén tableland and along the Caribbean coast. The rainy season lasts May-Oct., with the most rain falling on the warm Atlantic coast (up to 197 in/ 5,000 mm). Inland, rainfall decreases from 79–32 in/ 2,000–1,000 mm or less in the east central highlands. Above 6,562 ft/2,000 m temperatures can drop to 55°F/13°C. Guatemala City: Jan. 63°F/17.2°C. July 69°F/20.6°C. Average annual rainfall 52 in/1,316 mm.

Cities and towns

Guatemala City (capital)	754,243
Escuintla	75,442
Quezaltenango	72,922
Puerto Barrios	46,882
Retalhuleu	46,652
Chiquimula	42,571

Population

Total population is 8,680,000 of which 32.8% live in urban areas. Population density is 206/77.5 persons per miles^2/km^2. 56% of the population are Ladino (mixed Hispanic-Indian, mestizo origin). The remaining 44% are Indian (of Maya descent), divided into 21 separate groups. There are White and Black minority populations.

Birth rate 4.1%. **Death rate** 0.9%. **Rate of population increase** 2.9%. **Age distribution** under 15 = 45.9%; over 65 = 2.9%. **Life expectancy** female 64; male 60; average 62.

Religion

Roman Catholicism is the dominant faith to which approximately 75% of the population adhere. An estimated 25% are Protestants, chiefly Lutherans and Presbyterians. Some Indians continue to practise Mayan religious customs and beliefs.

Language

Spanish is the official language, although 40% of the population speak one of 20 different indigenous Indian dialects, including Quiche, Cakchiquel and Kekchi.

HISTORY

Contemporary Indians in Guatemala are the remnants of the Maya-Quiché nation (1500 BC to AD 1500) whose civilization was one of the richest ever known, but which had largely disappeared by the time of the arrival of the Spanish in the 1520s. Guatemala became the political heart of Spanish rule in Central America, although its mineral reserves were the poorest in the region. Its population has always been the largest and contained by far the greatest proportion of pure-blooded Indians (54%).

The region, known since 1549 as the Kingdom of Guatemala, declared its independence from Spain in 1821, and Guatemala City was the federation's first capital until 1834, when a liberal and largely European government was established in San Salvador. In 1837 the Guatemalan Rafael Carrera led a (mainly Indian) peasants' revolt which split the federation, and he became the country's first president in 1838 until his death in 1865. There was a period of liberal rule from 1871 to 1885, and in 1920 an elected government under the Central American Unionist Party replaced a 22-year dictatorship, but was overthrown by a military coup in 1921. The right-wing Gen. Jorge Ubico, who took power in 1931, allied with the coffee and banana plantation owners, disbanded trade unions and cracked down on all left-wing parties, until his forced resignation in 1944.

The new elected progressive government of Juan Jose Arevalo Bermejo restored trade union rights and introduced many social, political and economic reforms. These policies were continued under the government of Col. Jacobo Arbenz Guzman, elected in 1950, which launched a controversial land reform programme in 1952, providing for the confiscation of 387,000 acres owned by the United States Fruit Company (UFCO), offering $1,185,115 in compensation. As a result the Arbenz government was denounced by the US administration as communist, and in 1954 a US-backed coup replaced Arbenz by the right-wing Col. Castillo Armas. Most of the reforms were rescinded and all UFCO's lands were restored.

Since 1955 three separate constitutions have been promulgated (1956, 1965 and 1986), there have been four military coups (1957, 1963, 1982 and 1983), and all the governments except those of Julio Cesar Mendez Montenegro (1966–70) and of Vinicio Cerezo Arevalo (installed in Jan. 1986), were headed by military officers. In the early 1960s many left-wing politicians began to form guerrilla groups, which were very active until the army's intensive insurgency campaign of 1966–68, when thousands died, disappeared or were tortured. Guerrilla activity on a major scale resumed in 1978, and the army again became more repressive towards left-wing activists, trade unionists, university staff and human-rights workers. In the early 1980s the military counter-offensive against the guerrillas involved intimidation and even massacre of sections of the rural population (largely Indians) deemed to be guerrilla supporters.

The acclaimed winner in the Mar. 1982 presidential elections, Gen. Angel Anibal Guevara, was prevented from taking office by a group of young officers, headed by Gen. Efrain Rios Montt and promising to restore authentic democracy. Rios Montt became increasingly authoritarian and was overthrown in Aug. 1983 by Brig.-Gen. Oscar Mejia Victores, who organized constituent elections in July 1984 and fresh presidential and legislative elections in Nov. 1985, which were won by Vinicio Cerezo and his Guatemalan Christian Democratic Party (DCG). In Oct. 1987, two months after the signing of the Central American peace plan, very informal talks were held between delegations from the government and the guerrillas (now grouped in the Guatemalan National Revolutionary Unity, URNG).

Military coups against the government failed in May and Dec. 1988. According to a June 1989 report by Amnesty International, human-rights violations carried out by members of the police and security forces also acting in the guise of death squads had increased markedly over the previous 18 months.

CONSTITUTION AND GOVERNMENT

Executive and legislature

Executive power is held by the president, directly elected for a five-year term, and assisted by a vice-president. Last presidential election Nov.–Dec. 1985. The president appoints the cabinet. Legislative authority is vested in a unicameral National Congress, with 100 members elected for five years by universal adult suffrage. Of the total seats, 75 are filled by direct election and 25 on the basis of proportional representation. Last election 3 Nov. 1985.

Present government

President Sr Mario Vinicio Cerezo Arévalo
Vice-President Sr Roberto Carpio Nicolle
Principal Ministers: Sr Ariel Rivera Irias (Foreign Affairs); Sr René Armando de León Schlotter (Development); Sr Francisco Pinto Casarola (Public Finance); Sr Oscar Humberto Pineda Robles (Economy); Gen. Carlos Morales Villatoro (Interior); Gen. Héctor Alejandro Gramajo Morales (Defence); Sr Alfonso Cabrera Hildago (Special Affairs).

Justice

The system is based on civil law. The highest court is the Constitutional Court, for the review of legislation. The judges of the seven-member Supreme Court, and of the six appeal courts, are elected by Congress. At lower level there are 28 courts of first instance, with judges appointed by the Supreme Court. The death penalty is in force. No judicial executions were recorded between 1985 and mid-1988.

National symbols

Flag. Three vertical stripes of blue, white and blue; in the centre there is the state coat of arms of 1871.
Festivals. 1 May (Labour Day); 15 Sep. (Independence Day); 12 Oct. (Columbus Day); 20 Oct. (Revolution Day).
Vehicle registration plate. GCA.

INTERNATIONAL RELATIONS

Affiliations

OAS; SELA.

Defence

Total Armed Forces: 42,000. Terms of service: conscription; selective 30 months. Reserves: 5,200.
Army: 40,000; ten light tanks (M-41A3).
Navy: 1,200 inclusive of 650 marines; eight patrol craft (inshore).
Air Force: 850; 19 combat aircraft (serviceability of aircraft is perhaps less than 50%), six armed helicopters.

ECONOMY

Currency

The unit is the quetzal, divided into 100 centavos.

National finance

Budget. The 1987 budget (in US$) was for expenditure (current and capital) of 1,000 million and revenue of 821 million.
Balance of payments. The balance of payments (current account, 1987) was a deficit of $555 million.
Inflation. (1988) 12%.

Gross Domestic Product

Estimated total GDP US$7,040 million, per capita US$1,110 (ranking 74 in the world by size).
Economically active population. The total number of persons active in the economy was 2,500,000; unemployed: 12%.

Sector	% of workforce
industry	18.4
agriculture	57
services*	24.6

* services figure includes elements unassigned to other categories.

Energy and mineral resources

Minerals. Zinc; lead; copper; antimony; tungsten; small quantities of cadmium and silver.
Electricity. Capacity: 803,000 kW; production: 2,543 million kWh; 290 kWh per capita (1988).

Bioresources

Agriculture. The economy is based on agriculture

which supplies two-thirds of exports. The main crop is coffee; there are about 12,000 coffee plantations and 1,500 large coffee farms. Other crops are cotton; bananas; maize; beans; sugarcane.

Crop production: (in tons/tonnes) coffee (1988) 171,959/156,000; (1987) bananas 781,531/709,000; cotton 33,069/30,000.

Livestock numbers: (1987) cattle 2.3 million; pigs 865,000; sheep 690,000; horses 100,000; poultry 15 million.

Forestry. 40% of Guatemala is forest and woodland including considerable mahogany reserves in the department of Petén. Production: (1980) 396.58 ft^3/ 11.23 m^3.

Fisheries. (1980) Exports valued at 11.8 million quetzales.

Industry and commerce

Industry. Main industries are sugar; textiles and clothing; furniture; chemicals; petroleum; metals; rubber and tourism.

Commerce. (1988) Exports US$1,100 million or 11% of GDP, including coffee 40%; cotton 7%; cardamom 5%; bananas 4%. Imports: US$1,500 million and including fuel and petroleum products; machinery; grain; fertilizers; motor vehicles. Countries exported to: US 41%; El Salvador; West Germany; Costa Rica; Italy. Imports came from US 39%; Mexico; Japan; West Germany; El Salvador.

Trade with UK. Guatemala imported UK goods worth £15,387,000; exports to UK totalled £10,678,000.

Tourism. (1986) 287,000 visitors.

COMMUNICATIONS

Railways

There are 592 miles/953 km of railways.

Roads

There are 10,757 miles/17,315 km of roads, of which 1,793 miles/2,887 km are bituminized and 4,084 miles/ 6,576 km gravel.

Aviation

AVIATECA – Empresa Guatemalteca de Aviacion provides international services (main airport is at Santa Elena Peten). Passengers: (1984) 124,000.

Shipping

161 miles/260 km of the inland waterways are navigable all year round. A further 453 miles/730 km becomes navigable during the high-water season. The maritime ports Puerto Barrios, Puerto Quetzal and Santo Tomas de Castilla are situated on the Caribbean coast. The merchant marine consists of one cargo ship of 1,000 GRT or over. Freight loaded: (1987) 1.5 million tons/1.4 million tonnes; unloaded: 2.5 million tons/2.3 million tonnes.

Telecommunications

There are 97,670 telephones and a fairly modern network centred on Guatemala City. There are 350,000 radios and 207,000 television sets; radio stations include five government, six educational and nearly 100 commercial operations; and there are five television stations, four of them commercial and one a government-owned educational channel.

EDUCATION AND WELFARE

Education

Schools. Education is theoretically free but there is a serious shortage of state schools and private schools flourish as a result. In 1984 there were 11,587 schools (public and private) with 1,331,294 pupils and 45,611 teachers. There are 1,237 secondary schools with 194,484 pupils and 13,891 teachers (one per 14 pupils).

Universities. (1984) There are five universities with an estimated total of 45,550 students.

Literacy. 50%.

Health

There are approximately 60 public hospitals and 100 dispensaries with 1,250 doctors (one per 7,293 people).

GUINEA
République de Guinée (Republic of Guinea)

GEOGRAPHY

Located on the west coast of Africa, Guinea covers an area of 94,901 miles^2/245,857 km^2, divided into the four regions of Guinée-Maritime, Moyenne-Guinée, Haute-Guinée and Guinée-Forestière. The mangrove swamps and lagoons of the coast and cultivated coastal plains are backed by the Fonta Djallon highlands in the east, rising to 4,970 ft/1,515 m and 5,043 ft/1,537 m (Mt Tangue) in the north. The Niger, Sénégal and Gambia rivers all rise in the Fonta massif. The north-eastern savannah is incised by river valleys that flow towards the River Niger's upper basin. South and south-west, the forested massif rises to 5,748 ft/1,752 m at Mt Nimbu on the Liberian border. The predominantly rural population is comparatively evenly distributed. 6% of the land is arable (in the south-east) and 42% forested.

Climate

Tropical, with high coastal rainfall, the wet season lasting from May-Nov. (May-Oct. inland). Average dry season temperatures increase towards the coast, reaching 90°F/32°C. Mean annual highland temperature 77°F/25°C.

Cities and towns

Conakry (capital)	525,671
Kankan	60,000

Population

Total population is 6,540,000 of which 26.0% live in urban areas. Population density is 69/25.9 persons per miles^2/km^2. The principal ethnic groups are Fulani (40.3%, concentrated in the Fouta Djallon or in Moyenne-Guinée); Malinké (25.8%, Haute-Guinée); Susu (10%, Guinée-Maritime); Kissi (6.5%); Kpelle (4.8%, Guinée-Forestière) and several others including Dialonka; Loma (4.6%).

Birth rate 4.6%. **Death rate** 2.3%. **Rate of population increase** 2.4%. **Age distribution** under 15 = 43.1; over 15 = 2.9. **Life expectancy** female 44; male 41; average 42.

Religion

85% of the population are Muslim; 10% are Christian (including over 44,300 Roman Catholics); 5% follow traditional tribal/animist beliefs.

Language

The official language is French, but the eight principal indigenous languages of Fulani, Malinké, Kissi, Susu, Kpelle, Loma, Basari and Koniagi are all spoken and taught in Guinean schools.

HISTORY

The southward migration of Susa tribes, related to the Malinke, from the desert in the 9th century AD forced the original inhabitants, the Baga, south to the coast. By the 13th century the Susa kingdoms had extended their authority over the coastal region. During the 16th century the Fulani conquered the Fouta Djallon plateau and from 1725 prosecuted a holy war to convert its inhabitants to Islam.

The Portuguese arrived at the coast in the mid-15th century and the slave trade soon developed. In the early 19th century French traders established a settlement on the Nunez River and proclaimed the coastal region a French Protectorate in 1849. Initially administered from Senegal, the region became the colony of French Guinea in 1890. Opposition to colonial rule was particularly fierce in Fouta Djallon.

In 1958 Guinea chose full independence from France when most other French colonies became autonomous members of the French community. France immediately withdrew its financial support. Ahmed Sekou Touré, the newly elected president, established the Parti démocratique de Guinée (PDG) as the sole party, eliminated all opposition and embarked on a programme of political and economic centralization. Guinean exiles founded the Front pour la libération nationale de Guinée (FLNG) in 1965. In Nov. 1970 Guinean exiles led by Portuguese officers from neighbouring Portuguese Guinea attacked Conakry. They failed to unseat Pres. Touré and at least 90 suspected conspirators were executed in the following months. A demonstration by market women in Conakry in Aug. 1977, which spread nationwide, forced the government to relax controls on small-scale private trading. The following year, France restored diplomatic relations and the government agreed to allow some foreign investment.

Shortly after the death of Touré (26 Mar. 1984), the military seized power (3 Apr), forming a Comité militaire de redressement national (CMRN). Col. Lansana Conté became president and Col. Diara Traoré prime minister. By releasing political prisoners, promising to return property confiscated by the previous regime, and liberalizing the economy, the CMRN persuaded some of the two million Guinean exiles to return. However, following his demotion to minister of education, Col. Traoré led a coup attempt (5 July 1985). Troops loyal to Pres. Conté regained control and Traoré was arrested, together with 200 suspected conspirators. In Dec. 1987 the government admitted that Traoré had been executed immediately after the coup and that another 60 people had been sentenced to death in May 1987. However, 67 political prisoners were granted amnesties in Jan. 1988. After the coup, Pres. Conté pressed ahead with economic reforms and austerity measures, including reduction in the size of the civil service. This, together with rampant inflation, prompted demonstrations in Jan. 1988. In Oct. 1989 Pres. Conté promised a return to a two-party system with an elected President and National Assembly after a five-year transitional period. A new Constitution would be proposed in the course of 1990, after which a new ruling body, the National Recovery Council, composed of military and civilians would oversee the transition to democracy.

CONSTITUTION AND GOVERNMENT

Executive and legislature

Power rests with the Military Committee for National Recovery, headed by the president who is head of state and government, and presides over the Council of Ministers.

Present government

President; Head of Government; Minister of Defence, Security, Planning and Co-operation, Information Brig.-Gen. Lansana Conté

Members of the Military Committee for National Recovery Brig.-Gen. Lansana Conté (chairman); Maj. Babacar N'Diaye (permanent secretary with ministerial rank, in charge of relations with non-governmental organizations); Maj. Kerfalla Camara; Lt.-Col. Sory Doumbouya; Maj. Sekou Mantong Camara; Maj. Alhousśeny Fofana; Maj. Jean Traoré; Capt. Mamadou Baldet; Capt. Abdourahmane Diallo; Maj. Facine Touré; Capt. Joseph Gbago Zoumanigui (executive committee members); Maj. Kekoura Camara; Maj. Alfa Oumar Diallo; Maj. Jean Kolipe Lama; Maj. Babacar N'Diaye; Maj. Ousmane Sow; Capt. Mohamed Traoré (ordinary members).

Principal Ministers: Maj. Henri Tofani (National Defence); Maj. Henri Foula (Economic and Financial Control); René Alseny Gomez (Secretary-General to the Presidency); Ibrahim Sylla (Planning and International Co-operation); Bassirou Barry (Justice; Keeper of the Seals); Maj. Jean Traoré (Foreign Affairs); Edouard Benjamin (Economy and Finance); Capt. Mamadou Baldt (Interior and Decentralization).

Administration

With government based in the capital Conakry, provincial authority is exercised by resident ministers (all of them members of the Council of Ministers) in Maritime Guinea (Kindia), Middle Guinea (Labé), Upper Guinea (Kankan), and Forest Region (N'Zerékoré).

Justice

The system of law is based on French civil law, customary law, and decree; legal codes are undergoing revision. There is a High Court, a Court of Appeal and a Superior Tribunal of Cassation at Conakry, and two main courts of first instance, at Conakry and Kankan. The death penalty is in force. There were at least two executions between 1985 and mid-1988.

National symbols

Flag. Tricolour with vertical stripes of red, yellow and green.

Festivals. 1 May (Labour Day); 27 Aug. (Anniversary of Women's Revolt); 28 Sep. (Referendum Day); 2 Oct. (Republic Day and Mouloud, birth of Mohammed); 22 Nov. (Day of 1970 Invasion).

Vehicle registration plate. RG.

INTERNATIONAL RELATIONS

Affiliations

NAM; OAU; ACP; ICO; Francophonie.

Defence

Total Armed Forces: 9,900 (perhaps 7,500 conscripts).
Terms of service: conscription, two years.
Army: 8,500; 30 main battle tanks (T-34, T-54), 20 light tanks (PT-76).
Navy: 600; 22 patrol and coastal combatants.
Air Force: 800; perhaps six combat aircraft (MiG-17F).

ECONOMY

Currency

The unit is the Guinean franc, divided into 100 centimes.

National finance

Budget. The 1987 budget (in US$) was for expenditure (current and capital) of 443 million and revenue of 358 million.

Balance of payments. The balance of payments (current account, 1987) was a deficit of $114 million.

Inflation. (1987) 34%.

Gross Domestic Product

Estimated total GDP US$1,700 million, per capita US$270 (ranking 121 in the world by size).

Economically active population. The total number of persons active in the economy was 2,400,000. Agriculture accounts for 82% of the workforce.

Energy and mineral resources

Minerals. Production: (1985) bauxite 14.4 million tons/ 13.1 million tonnes; alumina 639,334 tons/580,000 tonnes; gem diamonds 105,000 carats; industrial diamonds 7,000 carats. Iron ore production commenced in 1981.

Electricity. Capacity: 108,000 kW; production: 243 million kWh; 35 kWh per capita (1988).

Bioresources

Agriculture. 6% of Guinea's land area is arable, with little or no irrigation. Cash crop production is dominant.

Crop production: (1986 in 1,000 tons/tonnes) cassava 551/500; rice 529/480; plantains 386/350; sugar cane 220/200; bananas 116/105; groundnuts 83/75; sweet potatoes 77/70; yams 67/61; maize 55/50; palm-oil 44/ 40; palm kernels 51/46; pineapples 22/20; pulses 55/50; coffee 17/15; coconuts 17/15.

Livestock numbers; (1987) cattle 1.8 million; sheep 460,000; goats 460,000; pigs 50,000.

Forestry. 42% of the country is under forest and woodland. Roundwood production: (1985) 130.3 million ft^3/3.69 million m^3.

Fisheries. Total catch: (1985 est.) 33,069 tons/ 30,000 tonnes.

Industry and commerce

Industry. Main industries are bauxite and diamond mining and alumina production, as well as light manufacturing and agricultural processing.

Commerce. Exports: (1987) US$571 million; imports: US$560 million. Main exports: alumina; bauxite; diamonds; coffee; pineapples; bananas; palm kernels. Main imports: petroleum products; metals; machinery; foodstuffs; textiles.

Trade with UK. Guinea imported from the UK goods worth £10.1 million and exported to the UK goods worth £7.6 million (1988).

COMMUNICATIONS

Railways

There are some 621 miles/1,000 km of railways.

Roads

There are 18,076 miles/29,108 km of roads, of which 2,674 miles/4,306 km are concrete or bituminized.

Aviation

Air Guinée provides domestic and international services (main airport is at Conakry-Gbessia). Passengers: (1982) 131,000.

Shipping.

804 miles/1,295 km of the inland waterways are navigable by shallow-draught native craft. The maritime ports are Conakry and Kamsar. Freight loaded: (1985) 11.1 million tons/10.1 million tonnes; unloaded: 539,025 tins/489,000 tonnes.

Telecommunications

There are 10,000 telephones and a fair system of open-wire lines, small radiocommunication stations and new radio-relay systems. There are 200,000 radios and 10,000 television sets, with broadcasting (including colour television) by the state radio and TV network RTG.

EDUCATION AND WELFARE

Education

School population. There were a total of 347,447 pupils in primary and secondary education (1980–81).

Schools. There were 257,547 pupils and 7,165 teachers in primary education (one per 36 pupils) and 89,900 pupils and 3,520 teachers in secondary education (one per 26 pupils) (1980–81). There were also 18,720 students in higher education.

Health

Guinea had a total of 7,650 hospital beds (one per 850 people) and 277 doctors (one per 23,000 people) in 1976.

GUINEA BISSAU

Republica da Guiné-Bissau
(Republic of Guinea-Bissau)

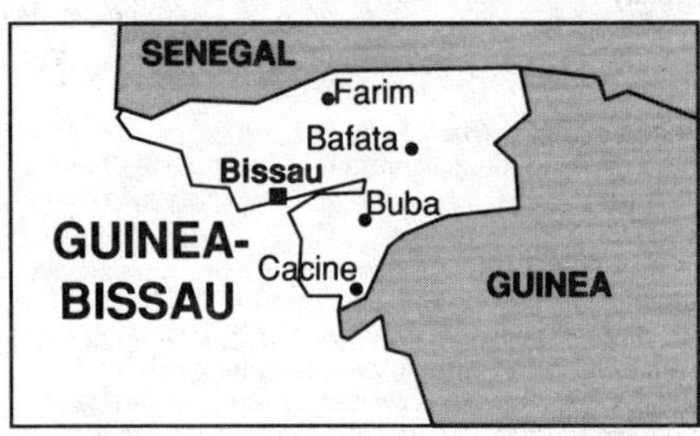

GEOGRAPHY

Situated on the west coast of Africa, Guinea-Bissau covers a total area of 13,942 miles^2/36,120 km^2 including the densely forested Bissagos Archipelago off the Atlantic coast to the south-west. The coastal lowlands consist of extensive mangrove swamps on the coast itself, backed by a system of cultivated Rias, reaching north-east to the savannah plateau-highlands of Guinea's Fouta Djallon (high point 1,017 ft/310 m on the border), the Planalto de Bafatá and the Planalto de Gabu. The interior plain is crossed and defined by the Cacheu, Geba and Corubal rivers. 9% of the total surface area is arable land and 38% forest woodland. The predominantly rural population is fairly evenly distributed throughout Guinea-Bissau's eight regions.

Climate

Tropical. Wet season June-Oct./Nov., with abundant rainfall particularly along the coast (98 in/2,500 mm). The dusty Harmattan blows Dec.-May, raising temperatures and reducing humidity. Bissau: Jan. 76°F/24.4°C. July 80°F/26.7°C. Average annual rainfall 76.8 in/1,950 mm.

Cities and towns

Bissau (capital)	109,214
Bolama/Bijagós	25,743
Monsoa	5,390
Catio	5,170

Population

Total population is 945,000 of which 27.0% live in urban areas. Population density is 67/25.2 persons per miles^2/km^2. Ethnic composition: estimated 99% African of which 30% Balanta; 20% Fula; 14% Manjaca; 13% Mandinga; 7% Papel. European and mulatto minorities make up the remaining 2%.

Birth rate 4.07%. **Death rate** 2.1%. **Rate of population increase** 1.9%. **Age distribution** under 15 = 40.7%; over 65 = 4.3%. **Life expectancy** female 44; male 41; average 42.

Religion

Approximately one-third of the population are Muslims, 5% are Christians (predominantly Roman Catholic), the rest practise traditional animist faiths.

Language

The official language is Portuguese, locally rendered in its Creole (Crioulo) form. The indigenous peoples all speak African dialects derived from the Niger-Congo family. The population statistics above are grouped ethnolinguistically.

HISTORY

From the 12th to 14th centuries the area was part of the Mali empire. Although Portuguese slave traders and merchants were active along the coast from the 1440s, followed by the French and British who set up trading stations in the 17th and 18th centuries, it was not until 1879 that Portugal proclaimed the territory of Portuguese Guinea as a colony. Britain and France recognized Portugal's rights in the area through the Treaty of Berlin (1884) and the Luso-Franco Convention of 1886. Portuguese military campaigns to subjugate all the inhabitants of the territory continued until 1915, with some parts resisting until 1936.

In the mid-1950s small nationalist groups developed, and the Partido Africano da Independencia da Guiné e Cabo Verde (PAIGC) was formed in 1956. Its leading theoretician and founder, Amilcar Cabral, was assassinated in 1973; another co-founder, Aristides Pereira, is now the president of Cape Verde. The PAIGC launched an armed struggle for independence in 1962, and by 1973 it had liberated 75% of the country and was able to organize elections in the areas under its control to a National People's Assembly, which unilaterally proclaimed the country's independence on 23 Sept. 1973, with Luiz Cabral as first president. After the armed forces coup in Portugal in Apr. 1974, Portugal recognized Guinea-Bissau's independence on 10 Sept. 1974. On 14 Nov. 1980 João Bernardo Vieira, prime minister since 1978, seized power in a military coup, only four days after the adoption of a new constitution aimed at achieving unification with Cape Verde. The Cape Verde government condemned the coup and the arrest of Luiz Cabral, although the two countries held reconciliation talks in June 1982 and subsequently normalized their relations. In March 1984 Prime Minister Victor Saude Maria was dismissed and two months later constitutional changes came into effect, abolishing the post of prime minister and strengthening the president's position. In the government reshuffle which followed, the number of ministers was reduced and several younger technocrats with expertise in economics were appointed. In Nov. 1985 First Vice-President and Justice Minister Paulo Correia and several military officers were accused of plotting against Vieira. They were motivated in part by the President's campaign against corruption in the ruling elite. Six of the alleged plotters died in mysterious circumstances, and six others (including Correia) were executed after a trial in July 1986. At the fourth PAIGC congress in Nov. 1986, Vieira continued the policy of economic liberalization initiated three years earlier and proposed further reductions in state controls over trade and the economy. The congress re-elected him as party secretary-general for a further four years. A boundary dispute with Guinea over offshore waters was resolved in Bissau's favour by the International Court of Justice in Jan. 1985. However, in July 1989 an arbitration tribunal ruled against Guinea-Bissau in a similar dispute over maritime boundaries with Senegal. Guinea-Bissau rejected the ruling and began legal proceedings against Senegal at the ICJ, with the legal and diplomatic support of Portugal.

CONSTITUTION AND GOVERNMENT

Executive and legislature

Effective power is exercised through the sole party, which according to the 1984 constitution defines policy in all fields. The National Assembly consists of 150 members elected from the eight directly elected regional councils; the party provides the sole list of candidates for these councils. Last Assembly elections June 1989. The Assembly elects a 15-member Council of State, to which its powers are delegated between sessions of the Assembly. The president of the Council is automatically Head of Government and C.-in-C. of the Armed Forces.

Present government

President of the Council of State; C.-in-C. of the Armed Forces; Head of Government; Minister of Defence and the Interior Brig.-Gen. João Bernardo Vieira

Members of the Council of State Brig.-Gen. João Bernardo Vieira; Col. Ifai Camara; Dr Vasco Cabral; Carlos Correia; Maj. José Pereira; Filinto de Barros; Tiago Aleluia Lopes; Buato Na Batcha; Bengate Na Beate; Júlio Semedo; Francisca Pereira; Mário Mendes; Teoboldo Barboza; Bana Match.

Principal Ministers: Col. Iafai Camara (First Vice-President; Minister of State for the Armed Forces); Dr Vasco Cabral (Second Vice-President); Dr Fidelis Cabral D'Almada (Minister of State at the Presidency in charge of Social Affairs); Nicandro Pereira Barreto (Justice); Maj. José Pereira (National Security and Public Order); Júlio Semedo (Foreign Affairs); Vítor Freire Monteiro (Finance).

Ruling party

African Party for the Independence of Guinea and Cape Verde (Partido Africano da Independência da Guiné e Cabo Verde).

Secretary-General Brig.-Gen. João Bernardo Vieira.

Permanent Secretary to the Central Committee Dr Vasco Cabral.

Administration

There are resident ministers heading provincial administrations in the Northern, Southern and Eastern provinces.

Justice

The death penalty is in force. There were at least seven executions between 1985 and mid-1988. Capital offences: murder and crimes against the security of the state.

National symbols

Flag. A red vertical stripe in the hoist which occupies one-third of the flag's length and is charged with a black five-pointed star; the remaining part of the flag is divided into two horizontal stripes of yellow and green.

Festivals. 20 Jan. (Death of Amilcar); 1 May (Labour Day); 3 Aug. (Anniversary of the Killing of Pidjiguiti); 24 Sep. (National Day); 14 Nov. (Anniversary of the Movement of Readjustment).

INTERNATIONAL RELATIONS

Affiliations

NAM; OAU.

Defence

Total Armed Forces: 9,200 (all services inclusive gendarmerie are part of the army). Terms of service: conscription (selective).

Army: 6,800; ten main battle tanks (T-34) and 20 light tanks (PT-76).

Navy: 300; 14 patrol and coastal combatants.

Air Force: 100; no combat aircraft.

ECONOMY

Currency

The unit is the peso, divided into 100 centavos.

National finance

Budget. The 1986 budget (in US$) was for expenditure (current and capital) of 93 million and revenue of 60 million.

Inflation. (1988) 17%.

Gross Domestic Product

Estimated total GDP US$168 million, per capita US$170 (ranking 166 in the world by size).

Economically active population. Agriculture accounts for some 90% of the workforce.

Energy and mineral resources

Minerals. Bauxite deposits amounting to an estimated 220 million tons/200 million tonnes have been located but there has been very little development.

Electricity. Capacity: 22,000 kW; production: 28 million kWh; 30 kWh per capita.

Bioresources

Agriculture. 9% of Guinea-Bissau's land area is arable. Crop production: (1986 in 1,000 tons/tonnes) groundnuts 32/29; sugar cane 5.5/5; plantains 28/25; coconuts 28/25; rice 138/125; rubber 25/23 (1981); palm kernels 15/14; millet 20/18; palm-oil 3/2.8; sorghum 36/33; maize 32/29; cashew nuts 11/10.

Livestock numbers: (1987) cattle 340,000; sheep 205,000; goats 210,000; pigs 290,000; poultry 1 million.

Forestry. 38% of the country is forest and woodland. Wood production: (1985) 19,740,526 ft^3/559,000 m^3.

Fisheries. Total catch: (1985) 3,968 tons/3,600 tonnes.

Industry and commerce

Industry. Main industries are agricultural processing and beer and soft drinks production.

Commerce. Exports: US$16.5 million; imports US$48.8 million (1987). Main exports: cashews; fish; peanuts; palm kernels. Main imports: capital equipment; consumer goods; semi-processed goods; foods; petroleum.

Trade with UK. Guinea-Bissau imported from the UK goods worth £925,000 and exported to the UK goods worth £22,000 (1988).

COMMUNICATIONS

Railways

There are no railways.

Roads

There are 1,552 miles/2,500 km of roads, of which 248 miles/400 km are bituminized.

Aviation

Transportes Aéreos da Guiné-Bissau (TAGB) provides domestic and international services (major airport is at Bissalanca).

Shipping

There are scattered stretches of inland waterways which are important to coastal commerce. The maritime port is Bissau.

Telecommunications

There are 3,000 telephones and an adequate system of open-wire lines, radio-relay links and radiocommunication stations. There are 31,000 radios, with state broadcasting on AM and FM wavelengths, and an experiment under way to set up a state television station.

EDUCATION AND WELFARE

Education

School population. Total primary and secondary school population is 93,154 (1984).

Schools. There are 658 primary schools with 3,153 teachers and 81,444 pupils (one per 26 pupils) and 12 secondary schools with 718 teachers and 11,710 pupils (one per 16 pupils) (1984). There are also four technical schools and teacher-training establishments with 1,027 students and 107 teachers.

Health

17 hospitals and clinics with 1,570 beds (one per 592 people); 108 doctors (one per 8,611 people) (1981).

GUYANA
Co-operative Republic of Guyana

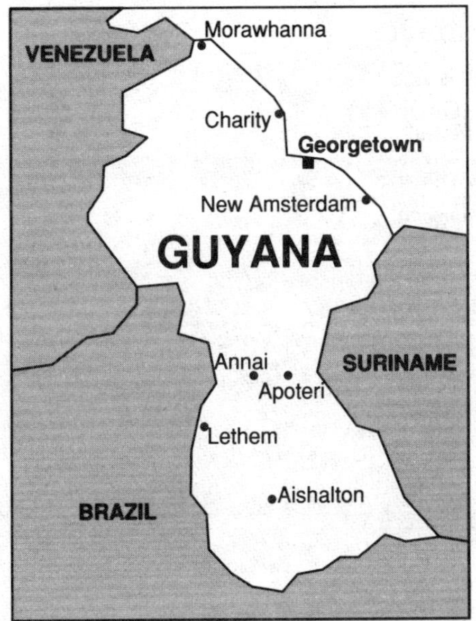

GEOGRAPHY

Occupying a total land surface area of 82,978 miles^2/ 214,969 km^2, Guyana lies on the north-east coast of South America, 1° north of the equator. The terrain is dominated by dense upland rainforest covering 85% of the total area, and rising in the west to 9,432 ft/ 2,875 m at Mt Roraima in the Pakaraima Mountains. The Essequibo, Demerara and Berbice rivers all flow north towards the Atlantic from their spectacular precipitous upper courses in the southern highlands (eg Kaietew Falls, on the Potaro river). The Rupununi grassland savannah in the south-west covers 10% of Guyana's territory marking the hinterland to the low-lying coastal plain (10–40 miles/ 16–65 km wide, 199 miles/320 km long) which supports 94% of the population. The reclaimed eastern reaches of the coastal plain are fertile and intensively cultivated.

Climate

Tropical conditions, high humidity and temperatures modified by maritime breeze. There are two wet seasons, Apr.-July and Nov.-Jan. (inland only one wet season, Apr.-Sept.). Coastal temperatures vary from 73–94°F/23–34°C, decreasing on the interior plateau from 88°F/31°C to 60°F/16°C minimum. Rainfall averages range from 90 in/2,280 mm on the coast to over 138 in/3,500 mm in the forest zone. Georgetown: Jan. 79°F/26.1°C. July 81°F/27.2°C. Average annual rainfall 86 in/2,175 mm.

Cities and towns

Georgetown (capital)	72,049
	(metropolitan area 187,056)
Linden	29,000
New Amsterdam	23,000
Corriverton	17,000

Population

Total population is 1,006,000 of which 32.1% live in urban areas. Population density is 12/3.7 persons per mile^2/km^2. Ethnic composition: 51% of the total population is East Indian; 43% Black and mixed Afro-Indian; 4% Amerindian (of which Carib 2.8%; Arawak 1.1%); 2% European and Chinese.
Birth rate 2.85%. **Death rate** 0.59%. **Rate of population increase** 2.26%. **Age distribution** under 15 = 37.0%; over 65 = 3.9%. **Life expectancy** female 71; male 65; average 68.

Religion

Christianity 57% (of whom at least 34% are Protestant and 18% Roman Catholic); Hindu 33%; Muslim 9%. The remainder follow traditional beliefs.

HISTORY

The earliest inhabitants of Guyana were Amerindians, including the Arawaks, Caribs, Warraus, and Akawaios. During the 17th and 18th centuries the Dutch founded three colonies in the region: Essequibo, Demerara, and Berbice. African slaves were imported as labour for plantations producing sugar, coffee and cotton. The territories were finally ceded to Britain in 1814, and in 1831 they were combined to form the colony of British Guiana.

The abolition of slavery in 1834 led to the importation of labourers, in particular from India, many of whom settled in the country after serving their indentures. In 1879 gold was discovered in the Orinoco region, and a long-running dispute between Britain and Venezuela flared up. The United States supported Venezuela and came close to declaring war on Britain. Political reforms were introduced after World War II, and in 1953 the first elections held under universal suffrage were won by the left-wing People's Progressive Party (PPP), led by Dr Cheddi Jagan. The British authorities, claiming that the PPP planned a communist take-over, suspended the constitution and installed an appointed legislature. In 1957 a founder-member of the PPP, Forbes Burnham, founded his own party, the People's National Congress (PNC). The PPP won elections in 1957 and 1961. Gradually, however, the two parties became more racially distinct: the PPP drew much of its support from the Asian 'East' Indian community, while the PNC appealed to those of African descent. Elections in 1964 were held under a system of proportional representation and the PPP, although winning most seats, was replaced as the government by a coalition of the PNC and United Force. Burnham became premier and, after the country's attainment of independence as Guyana on 26 May 1966, the country's first prime minister. On 23 Feb. 1970 Guyana was declared a Co-operative Republic, with a non-executive president. The PNC was re-elected in 1968 and again in 1973, after which the PPP boycotted the National Assembly, accusing the PNC of electoral fraud. The PPP returned to the Assembly in 1976 to give Burnham support for his programme of nationalizing the country's major foreign-owned enterprises. A referendum held in July 1978 gave the Assembly the power to amend the constitution. A new constitution was duly drafted with an executive presidency, to which Burnham was nominated in Oct. 1980. Elections in December gave the PNC an overwhelming majority, and Burnham declared himself elected president, despite the opinion of an international team of observers who pronounced the election fraudulent.

Jonestown, a village in the Guyana jungle, was the scene on 18 Nov. 1978 of the largest mass suicide of modern times. Over 900 people, mostly Americans, poisoned themselves at the instigation of Jim Jones and his People's Temple sect.

The country's economic situation worsened considerably during the early 1980s as the production and price of bauxite, sugar and rice declined. The government responded to growing unrest by strengthening its control of the media and harassment of opposition leaders, and by seeking aid from socialist countries to replace loans from Western countries and the International Monetary Fund.

Burnham died suddenly on 6 Aug. 1985, and was succeeded by the first vice-president and prime minister, Desmond Hoyte. At elections in December the PNC won another majority and Hoyte was elected president, although both the PPP and the Working People's Alliance alleged electoral malpractice, and increased their criticisms of government policies. They later joined with other opposition parties to form a joint Patriotic Coalition for Democracy (PCD) which boycotted municipal elections in Dec. 1986. During 1987 and 1988 Hoyte began a process of reversing some of his predecessor's policies, reacting to opposition criticism, liberalizing the economy and seeking Western aid and investment. However the three-year austerity programme, launched by the government in Dec. 1988, plunged the country into a serious social and economic crisis in 1989 and led to the suspension of foreign aid and widespread calls for free and fair elections.

CONSTITUTION AND GOVERNMENT

Executive and legislature

The president, directly elected for a five-year term, is head of state and holds executive power. Legislative authority is vested in the single-chamber National Assembly, with 65 members (53 elected for five years by universal adult suffrage, on the basis of proportional representation, and 12 regional representatives). The president appoints a first vice-president and prime minister who must be an elected member of the National Assembly, and a cabinet which may include non-elected members and is collectively responsible to the legislature. Last general election 9 Dec. 1985.

Present government

President (with responsibility for Home Affairs) Desmond Hoyte

Principal members of Cabinet: Hamilton Green (First Vice-President and Prime Minister (Youth and Sports, Housing, Health)); Viola Burnham (Vice-President (Culture and Social Development); Deputy Prime Minister); Keith Massiah (Attorney General; Justice); William Haslyn Parris (Deputy Prime Minister (Planning and Development)); Carl Greenidge (Senior Minister of Finance); Rashleigh Jackson (Senior Minister of Foreign Affairs); Winston Murray (Senior Minister of Trade and Tourism).

Justice

The system is based on English common law, with some elements of Roman-Dutch law. The highest court is the Supreme Court of Judicature, consisting of a Court of Appeal and a High Court. There are courts of summary jurisdiction at lower levels. The death penalty is in force. There were nine executions between 1985 and mid-1988. Capital offences: murder.

National symbols

Flag. Red triangle with a black border, pointing from hoist to fly, on a yellow triangle with white border, all on a green field.

Festivals. 23 Feb. (Republic Day); 1 May (Labour Day); 5 May (Indian Heritage Day); 3 July (2 July in 1990, Caribbean Day); 7 Aug. (6 Aug. in 1990, Freedom Day).

Vehicle registration plate. GUY.

INTERNATIONAL RELATIONS

Affiliations

NAM; ACP; Commonwealth; Caricom.

Defence

Total Armed Forces: 5,450. Terms of service: voluntary. Reserves: some 2,000 People's Militia.
Army: 5,000.
Navy: 150; six patrol craft.
Air Force: 300.
Para-Military: Guyana People's Militia: some 2,000; Guyana National Service: 1,500.

ECONOMY

Currency

The unit is the Guyanese dollar, divided into 100 cents.

National finance

Budget. The 1987 budget (in US$) was for expenditure (current and capital) of 293 million and revenue of 110 million.

Inflation. (1987) 29%.

Gross Domestic Product

Estimated total GDP US$344 million, per capita US$450 (ranking 157 in the world by size).

Economically active population. The total number of persons active in the economy was 268,000; unemployed: 13%. 34% work in agriculture.

Energy and mineral resources

Minerals. Bauxite is a mainstay of Guyana's economy, total output of four grades (calcined, chemical, metallurgical and abrasive) being 1.7 million tons/ 1.5 million tonnes (1986). Other resources include gold; diamonds; manganese; uranium; oil; copper; molybdenum.

Electricity. Capacity: 200 MW; production 500,000 MWh (1986).

Bioresources

Agriculture. Only 3% of Guyana's land area is arable, and a further 6% is meadow and pasture. Sugar is the main crop, followed by rice; fruits; beans; tobacco.
Crop production: (in 1,000 tons/tonnes) sugar 3,638/ 3,300; rice 386/350; coconuts 44/40; oranges 12/11.
Livestock numbers: poultry 15 million; cattle 210,000; pigs 185,000; sheep 120,000; goats 77,000.

Forestry. Forests and woodland cover 83% of Guyana's total land area. Timber production: (1986) 4,647,322 ft^3/131,600 m^3.

Fisheries. Fish production: (1986) 43,651 tons/39,600 tonnes; shrimp production 3,913 tons/3,550 tonnes.

Industry and commerce

Industry. Bauxite production and sugar refining are the mainstays of Guyana's industry. Other significant industries are rice milling; timber; textiles; also gold, diamond and manganese mining.

Commerce. Exports: G$1,092; imports: G$1,618 million (1986). Countries exported to were UK 26%; CARICOM territories 17%; Canada 5%. Imports came from CARICOM 35%; US 25%; UK 16%; Canada 4%.

Trade with UK. Guyana imported UK goods worth £10,590,000 and exported to the UK goods worth £43,518,000 (1988).

COMMUNICATIONS

Railways

There are two railways, used for transport of bauxite and minerals.

Roads

There are 3,540 miles/5,700 km of roads.

Aviation

Guyana Airways Corporation provides domestic and international services (main airport is Timehri International, 26 miles/42 km from Georgetown).

Shipping

There are 3,726 miles/6,000 km of navigable waterways. The Berbice, Demerara and Essequibo Rivers are navigable by ocean-going vessels for 93 miles/150 km, 62 miles/100 km, and 50 miles/80 km, respectively. The maritime port is Georgetown.

Telecommunications

There are over 27,000 telephones and a fair system with a radio-relay network. There are 350,000 radios, served by the state-owned Guyana Broadcasting Corporation, but no televison service.

EDUCATION AND WELFARE

Education

The government in 1976 assumed responsiblity for the entire education system, abolishing private education.

School population. 223,723 (1983).

Schools. 368 nursery schools, 418 primary schools, 34 community high schools and 56 general secondary schools (1984).

Universities. The University of Guyana was founded in 1963. Higher education is also provided in seven technical, vocational and craft schools, the Kuru-Kuru Co-operative College, two agricultural colleges and a school of art. There are 2,250 students (1987).

Health

There are 271 hospitals and clinics, with 142 doctors (one per 5,400 inhabitants).

HAITI
République d'Haïti
(Republic of Haiti)

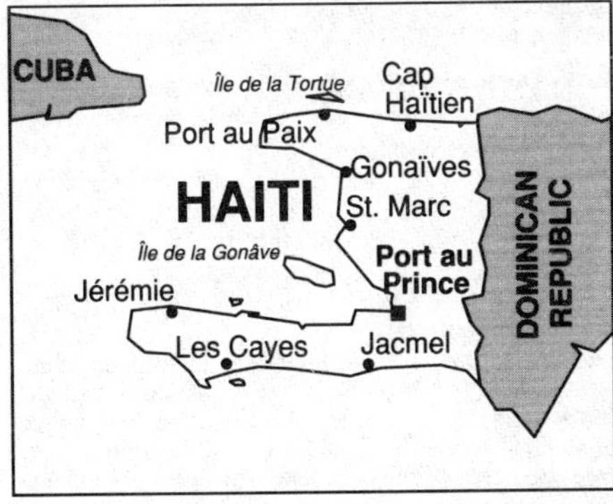

GEOGRAPHY

Haiti occupies the western third of the seismically active island of Hispaniola in the Caribbean and a number of smaller West Indian islets, about 621 miles/1,000 km south-east of Florida, USA. It covers a total area of 10,712 $miles^2$/27,750 km^2 divided into nine departments, the most populous of which is the 'Ouest'. 75% of the terrain is mountainous, concentrated in the two peninsulas (north and south) comprising the Massif du Nord (4,921 ft/1,500 m) extending east into the Dominican Republic, the Massif de la Hotte (south-west) and the Massif de la Selle (highest point La Selle 7,480 ft/2,280 m). The largest of the very densely populated fertile lowland area is the Plaine du Nord. Other low-lying regions include the Plaine du Cul-de-Sac (extending east from Port-au-Prince to the border) and the Artibonite river plain which connects the southern and north-western peninsulas. Haiti's largest lake is the Etang Saumâtre in the south-east. About one third of the land is arable and 4% is forested.

Climate

Tropical maritime with variable rainfall and high temperatures mitigated by altitude and sea breezes. Mean monthly temperatures vary from 75°F/24°C – 84°F/29°C. Over much of the country, the annual rainfall averages 58.1 in/1,475 mm to 76.8 in/1,950 mm, dropping dramatically to 19.7 in/500 mm on the leeward side. The two rainy seasons are Apr.-June and Aug.-Nov. Haiti lies within the tropical hurricane belt. Port au Prince: Jan. 77°F/25°C. July 84°F/28.9°C. Average annual rainfall 52 in/1,321 mm.

Cities and towns

Port-au-Prince (capital)	738,342
Cap Haïtien	54,691
Gonaïves	36,736

Population

Total population is 6,263,000 of which 28.9% live in urban areas. Population density is 584.7 persons per $mile^2$/201.9 persons per km^2. 95% of all Haitians are Black, descended from the African slave population granted independence in 1804; 5% are mulatto or European.

Birth rate 3.54%. **Death rate** 1.39%. **Rate of population increase**,(1980–87) 2.15%. **Age distribution** under 15 = 40.2%; over 65 = 3.5%. **Life expectancy** female 56; male 53; average 55.

Religion

Predominantly Christian: Roman Catholic 75–80%. However, orthodox Christian tenets and practices are commonly syncretized with the folk religion Voodoo (Vaudou). 10% of the religious population is Protestant.

Languages

The official language (French) is spoken by only 10% of the population, but the Haitian French-African Creole is universally understood (90% French in origin, 10% African) and intelligible to other French-creole speaking inhabitants of the Caribbean (e.g. Louisiana creole, Antilles creole, Tobago, Trinidad and Martinique creole).

HISTORY

The earliest known inhabitants of Haiti were Taino Arawak Indians. The first European settlers arrived in the years following the discovery of the island by Columbus in 1492, who named it Hispaniola and claimed it for Spain. In 1697 the presence of French settlers in the western third of the island was recognized by Spain in the Treaty of Ryswick, and the area was ceded to France. Known as Saint-Domingue, the territory developed a highly profitable plantation system of agriculture based on the use of imported African slave labour.

Political events surrounding the French Revolution and the outbreak of a slave rebellion in 1791 started 13 years of war, only resolved in 1804 with the declaration of the world's first independent Black republic. Jean-Jacques Dessalines, who had succeeded Toussaint L'Ouverture, the original leader of the insurrection, became the first president. He soon proclaimed himself emperor, but was assassinated in 1806. A succession of presidents (as well as one king and one emperor) followed as army generals and politicians vied for power. France recognized Haiti's independence in 1825, but only after payment of a huge indemnity. Haiti occupied the eastern part of the island (now the Dominican Republic) between 1822 and 1844.

Growing instability during the early 20th century, caused by political rivalries, financial insolvency, peasant uprisings and fear of foreign influence, prompted the United States to intervene after the murder of Pres. Guilliame Sam in 1915. US marines administered the country until 1934. In 1946 the then president, Elie Lescot, attempted unconstitutionally to prolong his term of office and was deposed in a military coup. Elections were held and won by Dusmarsais Estimé, who was replaced in 1950 by Gen. Paul Magloire after another coup. Magloire also tried to extend his term of office, and was overthrown in 1956. A succession of provisional presidents followed until elections in Sept. 1957, which were won by Dr François Duvalier. Duvalier gradually strengthened his position, establishing a one-party state, removing political opponents particularly among the mulatto elites and creating a militia, the National Security Volunteers (popularly known as the Tontons Macoutes) to enforce his power and counterbalance that of the army. In 1964 Duvalier declared himself president-for-life. On his death in Apr. 1971 'Papa Doc' was succeeded by his 19-year-old son, Jean-Claude Duvalier, who also became president-for-life.

Jean-Claude Duvalier continued his father's policies, although there were periods of political and economic amelioration, mainly to attract foreign aid. These were usually followed by renewed repression and harassment of political opponents. In Dec. 1985 food riots in the town of Gonaïves spread rapidly to the capital, Port-au-Prince. Demonstrations against Duvalierism grew, and eventually on 7 Feb. 1986 Duvalier was persuaded to leave the country. He was replaced by an interim council, headed by the army chief of staff, Gen. Henri Namphy. Exiles returned and numerous political parties were established to prepare for presidential elections after a new constitution had been drafted and approved by a referendum in Mar. 1987. The elections, held on 29 Nov. 1987 were abandoned after serious violence and intimidation disrupted voting. Fresh elections, controlled by the army, were held on 17 Jan. 1988. Most political parties boycotted the poll and the turnout was very low. The army's preferred candidate, Leslie Manigat of the Rassemblement de démocrates nationaux progressistes, was elected president. On 20 June, however, Manigat was overthrown in a coup led by Gen. Namphy who proclaimed himself president. In a coup three months later Namphy was himself deposed by NCOs and junior soldiers, who installed Lt-Gen. Prosper Avril as president. In Apr. 1989 Avril survived two attempts to overthrow him by sections of the army. Faced with increasing popular unrest, Avril stepped down in March 1990 and was replaced by Ertha Pascal-Trouillot, a Supreme Court Justice. Elections were expected to be held later in the year.

CONSTITUTION AND GOVERNMENT

Executive and legislature

The head of state and government is the president, installed by the most recent military coup and governing with the assistance of a Council of Ministers.

Present government

President Ertha Pascal-Trouillot

Justice

The legal system is based on French law. All judges are appointed by the president. The death penalty was abolished in 1987.

National symbols

Flag. Two vertical stripes of black and red; in the centre there is a white rectangle featuring the 1806 state coat of arms of Haiti.

Festivals. 1 Jan. (Independence Day); 2 Jan. (Heroes of Independence); 14 Apr. (Pan-American Day); 1 May (Labour Day); 18 May (Flag Day); 22 May (National Sovereignty); 24 Oct. (United Nation Day);

18 Nov. (Army Day and Commemoration of the Battle of Vertieres); 5 Dec. (Discovery Day).
Vehicle registration plate. RH.

INTERNATIONAL RELATIONS

Affiliations
OAS; SELA.

Defence
Total Armed Forces: 7,600. Terms of service: voluntary.
Army: 7,000 (has police/gendarmerie, fire-fight, immigration, etc, roles).
Six light tanks (M-5A1).
Navy: 300 (Coastguard); four patrol craft.
Air Force: 300; ten combat aircraft.

ECONOMY

Currency
The unit is the gourde, divided into 100 centimes.

National finance
Budget. The 1987 budget (in US$) was for expenditure (current and capital) of 402 million and revenue of 237 million.
Inflation. (1987) -11.5%.

Gross Domestic Product
Estimated total GDP US$2,250 million, per capita US$360 (ranking 111 in the world by size).
Economically active population. The total number of persons active in the economy was 2,300,000; unemployed: 50–70%.

Sector	% of workforce
industry	9
agriculture	66
services*	25

* services figure includes elements unassigned to other categories.

Energy and mineral resources
Minerals. None.
Electricity. Capacity: 230,000 kW; production: 447 million kWh; 70 kWh per capita (1988).

Bioresources
Agriculture. 33% of Haiti is arable land, much of which is divided amongst over 500,000 small farms and used for subsistence farming.
Crop production: (1986 in 1,000 tons/tonnes) sugar cane 3,472/3,150; mangoes 386/350; plantains 303/275; sweet potatoes 397/360; cassava 298/270; bananas 259/235; rice 198/180; maize 176/160; sorghum 121/110; sisal 11/10; cotton 7/6; cocoa 6/5.
Livestock numbers: (1987) poultry 8 million; cattle 1.5 million; goats 1.1 million; horses 425,000; sheep 93,000.
Forestry. Haiti has been subjected to radical deforestation; forests and woodlands cover only 4% of the country.
Fisheries. Production: (1984) 5,512 tons/5,000 tonnes.

Industry and commerce
Industry. The majority of Haiti's population is involved in subsistence farming. In addition to sugar refining, flour milling and cement manufacturing, the country also has some light manufacturing industries producing shoes, textiles and cooking utensils.
Commerce. Exports: US$201 million; imports US$315 million (1987). Exports included light manufactures 65%; coffee 17%; other agricultural products 8%. Imports included machinery and manufactured goods 36%; food 21%; chemicals 12%; petroleum products 11%. Countries exported to were US 77%; France 5%; Italy 4%; FRG 3%. Imports came from US 65%; Netherlands Antilles 6%; Japan 5%; France 4%; Canada 2%; Japan 2%.
Trade with UK. Haiti imported UK goods worth £6,760,000 and exported to the UK goods worth £844,000 (1988).
Tourism. Widespread lawlessness within Haiti has blighted the tourist industry; the country received 112,000 visitors in 1986.

COMMUNICATIONS

Railways
The only railway (50 miles/80 km) is used to transport sugar cane.

Roads
There are 1,987 miles/3,200 km of roads, of which 373 miles/600 km are bituminized.

Aviation
Air Haiti scheduled cargo and mail services (main airport is at Port-au-Prince).

Shipping
There are less than 62 miles/100 km of navigable waterways. The maritime ports are Port-au-Prince, situated in the Golfe de la Gonave, and Cap-Haîtien on the North Atlantic coast. Freight loaded: (1985) 186,289 tons/169,000 tonnes; unloaded: 750 tons/680 tonnes.

Telecommunications
There are 36,000 telephones, but domestic facilities are barely adequate. International facilities are slightly better. There are about 200,000 radios, with 25 radio stations, and 25,000 television sets served by the Télévision nationale d'Haiti.

EDUCATION AND WELFARE

Education
The education system, modelled on that of France, is provided by the state and by the Roman Catholic and missionary churches, and, in theory, is compulsory up to the age of 12.
School population. 756,664 pupils.
Schools. Haiti has 360 primary schools (221 state and 139 religious), 21 public lycées, 123 private secondary schools, 18 vocational training centres and 42 domestic science centres.
Universities. The state-controlled University of Haiti was established in 1944, and has 4,100 enrolled students (1980).
Literacy. 15–20%.

Health
In 1972 Haiti had 44 hospitals and 196 health centre and rural clinics, employing 332 doctors and providing 3,329 beds, of which 776 were in private institutions.

HONDURAS

Republica de Honduras
(Republic of Honduras)

GEOGRAPHY

Honduras is the second largest country of the Central American isthmus. It covers an area of 43,266 miles^2/112,088 km^2, containing the Caribbean Bay Islands and a further 288 islands in the Golfo de Fonseca of the Pacific coast. At least 75% of the surface area is mountainous terrain, traversing the country north-east to south-west. In the south, Honduras' highest peak, Cerro de las Minas, rises out of the surrounding volcanic plateau to a height of 9,347 ft/2,849 m. The soils are generally of poor quality with the exception of the coastal plains drained in the south by the Rio Choluteca and in the north by the Ulúa, Agúa and Patuca rivers. Over 50% of the population live in scattered rural settlements. 14% of the land is arable and 34% is forested, attaining tropical density on the Nicaraguan border.

Climate

Tropical, with high temperatures and plentiful rainfall. Rainfall reaches a maximum in the northern lowlands and on the Caribbean coast (70–10 in/1,780–2,790 mm). Average annual temperatures are 66–79°F/19–26°C. In highland areas, two wet seasons last May-July and Sept.-Oct. Tegucigalpa: Jan. 66°F/19°C. July 74°F/23°C. Average annual rainfall 63.8 in/1.621 mm.

Cities and towns

Tegucigalpa (capital)	640,900
San Pedro Sula	429,300
La Ceiba	66,000
Choluteca	64,500
El Progreso	61,100

Population

Total population is 4,830,000 of which 40.7% live in urban areas. Population density is 111.6 persons per mile^2/41.5 persons per km^2. Ethnic divisions: Mestizo (mixed Indian and European) 90%; Indian 7% (including Black Carib); Black 2%; White 1%. The principal aboriginal peoples are the Miskito, Payas and Xicaques.

Birth rate 4.23%. **Death rate** 0.9%. **Rate of population increase** 3.33%. **Age distribution** under 15 = 46.4%; over 65 = 3.2%. **Life expectancy** female 66; male 62; average 64.

Religion

Roman Catholicism is the dominant faith, accounting for 97% of the population. A very small protestant minority includes Episcopal and Baptist denominations.

Language

Official language is Spanish. A number of Indian dialects are spoken by the aboriginal population, the most important of which are Black Carib or Garifuna (95,000) and Miskito (14,000). An English creole is also spoken in the Islas de la Bahía.

HISTORY

Indian sites date back to 1700–1600 BC. A section of the Mayan people, whose civilization reached its height between AD 250–900, flourished around such centres as Copán in what is now Honduras, but was in demise by the time of the Spanish invasion in the early 16th century. Although Honduras possessed silver and some gold mineral reserves, since the late 19th century its economy has depended on the export of bananas, and by the 1980s the country had one of the lowest per-capita incomes in Latin America. Political life has been unstable, with a tendency to seek a solution in rewriting the constitution; new documents have been promulgated ten times (1848, 1865, 1880, 1894, 1906, 1925, 1936, 1957, 1965 and 1982).

Honduras gained independence from Spain in 1821 along with the other four Central American countries, and left the United Provinces of Central America (1823–38) as a separate country in 1838. The rest of the 19th century saw swings between relatively weak conservative and liberal governments, and from the 1890s the greatest political influence came to rest with foreign (mostly American) fruit companies. The election in 1923 of Gen. Tiburcio Carías Andino of the National Party (PNH) marked the political ascendancy of the army, as after a disputed result Andino used military force to assure the installation of his own candidate. Andino won the 1932 election and amended the constitution in order to continue in office until 1948. The PNH stayed in power until 1954.

The army held power for most of the period between 1954 and 1975, taking control by means of military coups staged in 1956, 1963 and 1972. A series of moderate social and economic reforms were introduced by the Liberal Party (PLH) in 1957–63, including a programme of land reform and the establishment of the state social security system, but were seen as a threat to the traditional ruling class.

Throughout the 1970s the principal concern in Honduras was the so-called Football War with El Salvador, which broke out in 1969. Ostensibly a war over the result of a football match, the conflict reflected mounting economic tensions between the two countries (Honduras being the least industrialized country in the region and El Salvador the most) and Honduran resentment of Salvadorean migration in search of work. Hostilities lasted only two weeks (the war being finally resolved by treaty in 1980), but placed an enormous strain on the Honduran economy, further hit by a serious hurricane in 1974 which destroyed 75% of the banana crop.

Criticized for the army's incompetence in the war and for its slowness in dealing with the effects of the hurricane, the military government of Gen. Oswaldo Lopez Arellano was overthrown in 1975 by a group of young officers led by Col. Juan Alberto Melgar Castro. The new administration renewed the earlier land-reform programme, but was removed by a right-wing military coup in 1978. Under strong pressure from the United States Gen. Policarpo Paz García prepared for a return to democratic government, and a new PLH administration under Roberto Suazo Cordova was inaugurated in Jan. 1982, although considerable power remained with the army commander-in-chief Gen. Gustavo Adolfo Alvarez Martinez, until his removal in 1984. Despite rumours of further military intervention in 1985, an elected government was peacefully succeeded by another for the first time since 1929 when on 27 Jan. 1986 the newly elected José Azcona del Hoyo of the PLH took office. Hoyo was succeeded by Rafael Leonardo Callejas of the right-wing opposition National Party (PN) in Jan. 1990, following his victory over the PLH candidate Carlos Flores Facussé in the presidential election of Nov. 1989.

CONSTITUTION AND GOVERNMENT

Executive and legislature

The president holds executive authority, and is elected directly for a four-year term, in theory requiring only a simple majority of votes. Last presidential and general elections 24 Nov. 1985. There are 134 seats in the legislative body, the unicameral National Assembly.

Present government

President Rafael Leonardo Callejas

Principal members of the Cabinet Mario Carias Zapata (Foreign Affairs); Ramón Medina Luna (Economy); Benjamin Villanueva (Finance); Manlio Martínez (Planning); Col. Francisco Zepeda Andino (Defence).

Justice

The system of law is rooted in Spanish and Roman civil law, with English common law influences. The highest court is the Supreme Court, whose judges are appointed by Congress, and who in turn appoint the judges of the courts of appeal, labour tribunals and the district attorneys. The death penalty was abolished in 1956.

National symbols

Flag. Three horizontal stripes of blue, white and blue. Five blue five-pointed stars are borne in the centre of the white stripe.

Festivals. 14 Apr. (Pan-American Day, Bastilla's Day); 1 May (Labour Day); 15 Sep. (Independence Day); 12 Oct. (Discovery Day); 21 Oct. (Army Day).

INTERNATIONAL RELATIONS

Affiliations

OAS; SELA.

Defence

Total Armed Forces: 18,700 (12,700 conscripts). Terms of service: conscription, 24 months. Reserves: 50,000.

Army: 15,400; 12 light tanks (mainly Scorpion).

Navy: 1,200 inclusive 600 marines; 13 patrol craft.

Air Force: some 2,200; 27 combat aircraft (A-37B, 2F-F5, F-5/F).

ECONOMY

Currency

The unit is the lempira, divided into 100 centavos.

National finance

Budget. The 1989 est. budget (in US$) was for expenditure (current and capital) of 1,100 million and revenue of 750 million.

Balance of payments. The balance of payments (current account, 1987) was a deficit of $330 million.

Inflation. (1989) 20%.

Gross Domestic Product

Estimated total GDP US$3,530 million, per capita US$840 (ranking 98 in the world by size).

Economically active population. The total number of persons active in the economy was 1,300,000; unemployed: 13–20%.

Sector	% of workforce	% of GDP
industry	12	24
agriculture	62	22
services*	26	55

* services figure includes elements unassigned to other categories.

Energy and mineral resources

Minerals. Minerals mined and exported include gold; silver; lead; copper; zinc; iron ore.

Electricity. Capacity: 655,000 kW; production: 1,983 million kWh; 400 kWh per capita (1988).

Bioresources

Agriculture. Agriculture is the most important sector of the economy, and produces up to two-thirds of exports. However, less than 25% of the total land area is cultivated and only a fraction of this is irrigated. The main agricultural crops are: bananas; coffee; corn; beans; sugar cane; rice; tobacco.

Livestock numbers: (1987) poultry 6 million; cattle 2,859,000; pigs 567,000; horses 170,000; goats 29,000; sheep 7,000.

Forestry. Forest and woodland cover over one third of the total land area. Hard- and soft-wood exports: (1986) 74 million lempiras.

Fisheries. Shrimp and lobster are significant exports. Value: (1986) 88 million lempiras.

Industry and commerce

Industry. Industry is still in its early stages, but nevertheless generates 20% of the country's exports. The main industries are agricultural processing (particularly sugar and coffee); textiles; clothing; wood products.

Commerce. Exports (1987) US$863 million, including bananas; shrimp; lobster; coffee; timber; meat; metals; sugar; soap; cotton. Main export partners: United States 50%; Japan; Italy; West Germany; Belgium; UK. Imports: (1987) US$969 million, including petroleum; chemicals; basic manufactures; machinery; transport equipment; foodstuffs. Main import partners: United States 42%; Central American Common Market (CACM) countries 15%; Venezuela 11%; Mexico; West Germany.

Trade with UK. Honduras imported UK goods worth £8,295,000; exports to UK totalled ££7,891,000.

Tourism. (1986) 204,000 visitors.

COMMUNICATIONS

Railways

There are 593 miles/955 km of railways.

Roads

There are 8,798 miles/14,167 km of roads (1,376 miles/2,216 km of main and national roads).

Aviation

Servicio Aereo de Honduras, SA (SAHSA) and Transportes Aereos Nacionales, SA (TAN) provide domestic and international services, Aerovias Nacionales de Honduras, SA (ANHSA) and Lineas Aereas Nacionales, SA (LANSA) provide domestic service (there are three international airports). Passengers: (1985 est.) 313,000.

Shipping

289 miles/465 km of inland waterways are navigable by small craft. The maritime ports are Puerto Castilla, and Puerto Cortes, both situated on the Caribbean Sea, and San Lorenzo on the North Pacific Ocean. The merchant marine has 141 ships of 1,000 GRT or over. Freight loaded: (1985 est. in million tons/ tonnes) 1.5/1.4; freight unloaded: (1985 est. in million tons/ tonnes) 1.2/1.1.

Telecommunications

There 35,100 telephones and although the telecommunications system has improved it is still inadequate. There are some 1.6 million radios and 280,000 television sets; the government-owned official Radio Nacional de Honduras and several hundred commercial stations broadcast radio programmes and there are three main television stations and one additional subscriber channel.

EDUCATION AND WELFARE

Education

There is free and compulsory education for children between seven and 15 years of age.

School population. Over 700,000 primary school pupils and approximately 130,000 secondary and technical school pupils (1983).

Schools. Approximately 6,500 primary schools (19,300 teachers) and 350 secondary and technical schools (6,000 teachers) (1983).

Universities. Three universities; over 30,000 students (1985).

Literacy. 56%

Health

71 hospitals (25 private) and over 600 health centres (1987).

HONG KONG

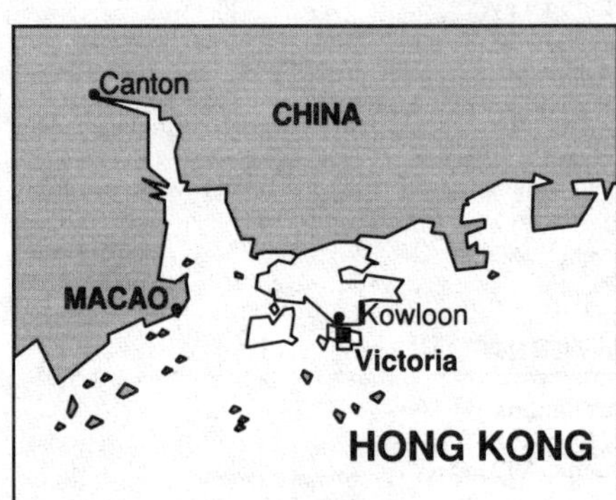

GEOGRAPHY

The island of Hong Kong itself lies off the south-east coast of China adjoining Guangdong province. The nearest point of the mainland, a peninsula with Kowloon at its southern tip, faces Victoria, the capital, on Hong Kong island, across a superb natural harbour. The territory of Hong Kong (414 miles^2/ 1,072 km^2) comprises the original Hong Kong island and adjacent islands (just under 31 miles^2/80 km^2), Kowloon (4 miles^2/10.6 km^2), and the New Territories on the mainland north of Kowloon, with adjacent islands (about 378 miles^2/980 km^2). The terrain is mostly too hilly to be cultivable, with a sharply indented coastline, and much of the most built-up area, surrounding the harbour itself, consists of land which has been artificially levelled or reclaimed. The highest point is Tai Mo Shan (3,140 ft/957 m) in the mountain range between Kowloon and the New Territories.

Climate

Sub-tropical, wet and humid in the monsoon season (May-Sept.), cool and dry in winter. Average annual rainfall 88 in/2,225 mm, mean temperatures Jan. 61°F/ 16°C. July 84°F/29°C.

Population

Total population was 5,431,234 at the March 1986 census, currently estimated at 5,730,000, and growing at 1% per annum. Population density was 13,119 per mile^2/5,355 per km^2 in all. 98% are ethnic Chinese, 2% other including Europeans; 59% were born in Hong Kong and 37% in China.

Birth rate 1.3%. **Death rate** 0.5%. **Age distribution** under 15 = 22.6%. **Life expectancy** female 81; male 75.

Religion

The majority are Buddhist, with a large Taoist and Confucianist element (the three sometimes mixed together); 10% are Christians, including Catholics and several Protestant denominations; and there are Muslim, Hindu, Sikh and Jewish communities.

Language

English and Chinese (official languages); most Chinese speak Cantonese, while Mandarin is widely understood.

HISTORY

Hong Kong was inhabited in prehistoric times, probably by peoples from northern China, and settled from the 2nd century BC by Cantonese. By the end of the 18th century Britain had become the principal European trading partner with China and in the 1820s Hong Kong became a shelter for opium-carrying vessels. Chinese efforts to ban the import of opium and the British desire to improve conditions for foreign traders led to war between them 1839–42. The British requirement for a free port was met by the Treaty of Nanjing in 1842, whereby Hong Kong island was ceded in perpetuity to the British crown. Britain needed to protect a harbour of such commercial and strategic significance from uncertain conditions on the mainland and growing international rivalries in east Asia. This was achieved through the Conventions of Peking in 1860 and 1898, by which Britain secured a perpetual lease on Kowloon peninsula and a 99-year lease on the New Territories (consisting of a mainland area adjoining Kowloon and 235 adjacent islands). A recurring feature of Hong Kong's history in the 20th century has been its importance as a centre for refugees. Large numbers of refugees entered Hong Kong after the revolutions in China of 1911 and 1949, and also after the Sino-Japanese War in 1937. Hong Kong was affected by trade boycotts and strikes 1925–27 as a result of anti-foreign sentiment in China. The Japanese invasion and occupation of Hong Kong during World War II lasted 1941–45. Post-war development under resumed British rule saw the industrialization and commercial diversification required to support an expanding population. During 1967 the influence of the Cultural Revolution in China caused civil disturbances and temporary economic paralysis in Hong Kong. The 1970s saw increases in illegal immigration from China and further problems have arisen in the 1980s with growing numbers of Vietnamese 'boat people' arriving in the territory.

Plans for increased self-government for Hong Kong after World War II were abandoned following the communist revolution in China in 1949, and the territory continued to be administered by a governor under its 1917 constitution. Talks between Britain and China on the future of Hong Kong started in 1982, leading to the ratification in May 1985 of a Sino-British Joint Declaration. Under the terms of this, on 1 July 1997 China will regain sovereignty over Hong Kong, which will become a Special Administrative Region (SAR) with its present economic and social systems remaining unchanged for 50 years afterwards. A draft Basic Law or constitution for the future Hong Kong SAR was produced by a joint Anglo-Chinese committee in Apr. 1988, for public consultation. A final version was produced by the basic law drafting committee in Feb. 1990 for promulgation by the Chinese National People's Congress in March. In the intervening period, confidence in a future under Chinese rule had been badly shaken by the bloody suppression of China's pro-democracy movement in the Tiananmen Square massacre of June 1989. The draft basic law was therefore given an especially guarded reception in Hong Kong, where there was concern that democratic representation was to extend only to a 30% directly elected Legislative Council from 1997, rising to 50% by 2003. Meanwhile Britain had been criticized for not allowing right of abode to 3,000,000 people born in Hong Kong and thus entitled to British passports in the 'British National (Overseas)' category specially established in 1981. The year 1989 also witnessed, in December, the first 'involuntary repatriation' of 'boat people' from Hong Kong to Vietnam, the British authorities having pressed for this drastic measure to deter further arrivals, with 55,000 'boat people' currently in camps in Hong Kong.

CONSTITUTION AND GOVERNMENT

Currently, under British administration, an appointed governor (Sir David Wilson) presides over an executive council, four of whose members hold their seats ex officio while the remaining ten are nominated. A legislative council (Legco), again with the governor presiding, has limited powers to advise on and approve legislation and expenditure; its 56 members are a combination of ex officio members of the executive council, appointees, and 26 elected indirectly or in 'functional constituencies'. Elections are held every three years, and are restricted to voters over 21 who meet the criteria for one of the functional constituencies.

The draft basic law on the form of Chinese rule from 1 July 1997 provides that China will have direct control over foreign affairs and defence; the chief executive of the special autonomous region shall be elected indirectly by an electoral college (with a referendum in 2011 to decide whether to go over to direct election); and the region's legislature shall be in part directly elected, in part indirectly elected by 'functional constituencies'.

Justice

There are magistrates' courts, four district courts and a High Court, from which appeals may be made to the Court of Appeal. There are nine Appeal Court justices and the Appeal Court is presided over by the Chief Justice.

National symbols

Flag. Hong Kong's coat of arms on a white disc superimposed on the blue body of the British 'Blue Ensign' flag, which has the Union Jack in the upper quadrant at the hoist.

Festivals. Several Christian and Chinese festivals, with public holidays also marking the Queen's official birthday (16–18 June in 1990) and Liberation Day (29 Aug.).

INTERNATIONAL RELATIONS

Affiliations

Hong Kong is a member in its own right of the ADB and GATT, IMO and WMO.

Defence

Currently a UK responsibility, with 7,540 Army personnel (4,500 Gurkhas) stationed there and some 1,000 navy, marine and air force personnel. From 1997 the Chinese National People's Army may station troops in Hong Kong.

ECONOMY

Currency

The currency is the Hong Kong dollar, divided into 100 cents.

National finance

Budget. The 1988/89 budget provided for an overall surplus of HK$14,200 million.

Balance of payments. The balance of payments (current account, 1987) was a surplus of US$2,480 million.

Inflation. 9.9% (Aug. 1989).

Gross Domestic Product

Estimated total GDP US$55,000 million, per capita $9,600, growth rate 14%.

Bioresources

Natural resources are very limited, and food and raw materials have to be imported. Farming and fishing account for 2% of the workforce; the output of vegetables, pigs, poultry and fish goes for local consumption. There are some 350,000 pigs and 10,000,000 poultry. There is very little crop cultivation, confined to narrow valleys and alluvial lowlands. There is some mining of feldspar (output 25,353 tons/23,000 tonnes in 1987).

Industry and commerce

Industry. Of the total workforce of 2.7 million, 30% work in manufacturing; 19% in wholesale, retail, export and import service industries; 9% in finance and business services; 7% in hotels and restaurants. Principal manufactures include clothing, textiles and footwear (41% of domestically produced exports by value in 1987); electrical and electronic appliances 28%; toys, watches and clocks.

Commerce. Exports: (1988) US$63,200 million, including $35,300 million re-exports. Imports: (1988) $63,950 million. Principal customers for domestic exports were US 37% (1987); China 14%; West Germany 7.6%; UK 6.6%; while re-exports went principally to China (33%) and the USA (18%). Imports were mainly from China 31%; Japan 19%; Taiwan 9%; US 8.5%.

Trade with UK. In 1988 Hong Kong imported goods worth £1,030 million from the UK and exported goods worth £1,789 million to the UK.

Tourism. 4.5 million visitors per year, with earnings from tourism (1987) US$3,261 million.

COMMUNICATIONS

Railways

A line 21 miles/34 km long connects Kowloon with the Chinese border and is heavily used by commuters. The various parts of the territory are linked together by a three-line Mass Transit Railway system, carrying 593 million passengers in 1987, and now complemented by a light rail transit system on the mainland.

Roads

Road tunnels connect Hong Kong island with Kowloon and pass from Kowloon to the New Territories and from the northern to the southern parts of Hong Kong island (which is also connected by bridge to Ap Lei Chau island). Total 720 miles/1,160 km of highway, of which 493 miles/794 km is paved; 322,000 registered motor vehicles of which over 50% are private cars.

Aviation

Hong Kong International Airport (Kai Tak) handled over 12 million passengers in 1987, one of the busiest in Southeast Asia.

Shipping

Hong Kong is the busiest container port in the world. Total freight handled: (1987) 67 million tons/61 million tonnes of cargo; 15,241 ocean-going ships. Also 14 million passengers landing or embarking (mostly Macao traffic by hydrofoil).

Telecommunications

There were 2,650,000 telephones and a modern service both within Hong Kong and internationally; an estimated 3 million radios and 1.4 million television sets were in use, with the government Radio Television Hong Kong providing public service and educational programmes, but not having its own television transmitters. Its programmes, in English and Chinese, are broadcast by the commercial stations. There are three commercial television stations and two radio stations.

EDUCATION AND WELFARE

Education

School is free and compulsory for nine years, to junior secondary level. Total school enrolment 1,206,000 including (private) kindergartens.

Higher education. There were (1987) about 16,000 full-time and part-time university students and over 100,000 attending full- or part-time at other higher education institutions. Besides the University of Hong Kong, the Chinese University of Hong Kong and the University of Science and Technology, there are eight technical colleges, four teacher-training colleges, two post-secondary colleges, two polytechnics and a Baptist college.

Literacy. 75%.

Health

There are 25,000 beds in government-run, government-assisted and private hospitals (4.4 per 1,000 people).

HUNGARY
Magyar Koztársaság
(Hungarian Republic)

GEOGRAPHY

Located in the Danube basin in east central Europe, Hungary is a landlocked country covering a total area of 35,910 miles²/93,030 km² divided into 19 counties. Occupying over 50% of the total surface area, the Great Hungarian Plain (Nagy Magyar Alfold – Little Plain) is separated by a low transdanubian alpine spur (elevation 1,312–2,297 ft/400–700 m), which runs south-west to north-east to meet the northern Carpathian mountains and includes Lake Balatón (143 miles²/370 km²). On the Czechoslovakian border, Hungary's highest peak, Mt Kékesteto, rises to 3,327 ft/1,014 m. The Danube and Tisza rivers drain Hungary north to south, flowing into Yugoslavia. Flooding is commonplace (spring and summer) particularly on the fertile Alfold plains east of the Danube. 54% of all land is arable and 18% is forested. An estimated 25% of the total population lives within the confines of metropolitan Budapest.

Climate

Humid continental with warm summers and cold (occasionally severe) winters. Maximum and minimum temperatures for summer and winter are 106°F/41°C and -29°F/-34°C respectively but mean temperatures vary less dramatically from 32°F–39°F/0°C–4°C in Jan. to 64°F–73°F/18°C-23°C in July. The bulk of Hungary's annual rainfall (23.6 in/600 mm average) falls during springtime. Budapest: Jan. 32°F/0°C. July 70°F/21.5°C. Average annual rainfall 24.6 in/625 mm. Pécs: Jan. 30.7°F/–0.7°C. July 70.7°F/21.5°C. Average annual rainfall 26 in/661 mm.

Cities and towns

Budapest (capital)	2,104,700
Debrecen	217,364
Miskolc	209,807
Szeged	187,800
Pécs	181,356
Györ	130,703
Nyiregyháza	119,040
Székesfehérvár	113,442
Kecskemét	105,107

Population

Total population is 10,450,000 of which 56.8% live in urban areas. Population density is 291 persons per mile²/112 per km². 96.6% of the population are Hungarian (Magyar); 1.6% German; 1.1% Slovak; 0.2% Romanian; 0.3% Yugoslav. In 1985 there were an estimated 320,000 Gypsies in Hungary.

Birth rate 1.25%. **Death rate** 1.37%. **Rate of population increase** –0.12%. **Age distribution** under 15 = 21.5%; over 65 = 12.4%. **Life expectancy** female 74; male 67; average 70.

Religion

An estimated 67.5% of the population professing a religious faith are Catholic (6,366,000 adherents) following Latin and Byzantine rites, 20% are Calvinist, 5% Lutheran. A variety of orthodox denominations are also represented including Hungarian, Serbian, Bulgarian, Russian and Romanian Orthodoxies. There are an estimated 3,000 Hungarian Muslims and a Jewish community of 88,000.

Language

98.2% of the population speak Hungarian Magyar, a member of the Finno-Ugric branch of the Uralic language family. Its European relatives are Finnish and Estonian. The Ugric group also comprises the Ob-Ugric sub-family, including two Western Siberian languages, Mansi and Khanty. A significant proportion of the Gypsy population speak Romany.

HISTORY

The central area of the Carpathian Basin irrigated by the Danube lay on the frontiers of the Roman provinces of Pannonia and Dacia. After invasions by the Huns and Avars between the 4th and 6th centuries AD the area was settled between the 8th and 10th centuries by the Finno-Ugrian Magyars moving west from the middle Volga. In AD 904 Prince Arpád founded a dynasty which lasted until 1301. His descendant St Stephen completed Hungary's conversion to Christianity and became the first king of Hungary in AD 1000.

During its first two centuries, the Hungarian Kingdom asserted itself over its neighbours, incorporating present-day Slovakia, Trans-Carpathian Ukraine, Transylvania and most of northern Yugoslavia, and successfully resisting Byzantine, German and Turkish encroachments. The 14th and 15th centuries saw recurrent internal strife between native feudal lords and a succession of short-lived dynasties from all over Europe. Despite this, the reign of King Matthias Corvinus (r.1458–90) produced a flowering of Renaissance thinking and artistic creativity.

In 1514 Gyorgy Dózsa led a resistance movement against Turkish invaders which turned into a peasant insurrection; its brutal suppression by the feudal lords left the way open for the Turks to seize central Hungary. Western Hungary submitted to the Austrian Habsburgs. By the 1699 Treaty of Carlowitz the Austrian Habsburgs finally expelled the Turks from all of Hungary, reuniting it under their own absolutist rule. The revolt of Prince Ferenc II Rákóczi soon afterwards secured a degree of autonomy, but the Magyar people found themselves a minority in the kingdom. The reforming Emperor Jozef II (r.1780–90) declined the Crown of St Stephen to avoid being bound by Hungarian custom, but his attempts to end serfdom, to re-introduce religious tolerance and to Germanize the administration were blocked by the Magyar aristocracy.

Magyar national culture revived in the early 19th century. On 15 Mar. 1848, on receiving news of revolution in Paris, the young radical poet Sandor Petofi launched a democratic revolution. The Habsburg Emperor-King accepted democratic reforms and appointed a government responsible to the Hungarian Diet (parliament), but peasant unrest and nationalist grievances triggered a civil war. Hungarian radicals deposed the new Austrian Emperor Franz-Jozef as King of Hungary and declared Lajos Kossuth Regent. Austrian control was only re-established by a Russian army which defeated the Hungarians at Villágos in 1849. There followed a period of repression and direct rule from Vienna.

In 1861 the Hungarian Diet demanded equality between Hungary and Austria. After Austria's humiliation in war against Prussia in 1866, the Compromise of 1867 created the dual monarchy of Austria-Hungary, in which only defence and foreign affairs came under joint ministries. Count Gyula Andrassy became the first Hungarian prime minister and Franz-Jozef was crowned king. Hungarian governments of the later 19th century made some cultural concessions to the non-Magyar peoples and supervised a modest industrialization and the modernization of communications. The new capital Budapest became a major centre of European culture. The conservative governments of Kálmán Tisza and his son István Tisza refused to countenance a democratic franchise, however, and supported the expansionist foreign policy of Austria-Hungary's ally, Germany, with the result that Hungary shared in the defeat of the Central Powers in World War I.

On 30 Oct. 1918 the last Habsburg Emperor-King Karl IV appointed the liberal Count Mihály Károlyi as Hungary's prime minister. On 16 Nov. Károlyi became president of a Hungarian Republic beset by Allied hostility, secessionist movements and class tension. Czech, Serb and Romanian forces occupied all but the purely Magyar heartland. Independent Hungary was reduced to a mere 35,910 miles^2/93,030 km^2, with a population of eight million. On 21 Mar. 1919 a Soviet Republic was established under the Communist Béla Kún, but it was overthrown when Romanian troops entered Budapest on 4 Aug. The Romanians handed over power to Adml. Miklós Horthy of Nagybanya.

On 1 Mar. 1920 Horthy became regent, but despite protestations of loyalty Horthy twice refused to allow King Karl to return to Hungary. Horthy's authoritarian and clerical regime failed to overcome Hungary's internal social problems or to establish positive relations with its neighbours. Under Prime Minister Gyula Gombos (1932–36) Hungary moved into the orbit of Nazi Germany. It was rewarded in 1938 and 1940, and again after joining the Axis war against Russia in 1941, with Czechoslovak, Yugoslav and Romanian territories which had once belonged to Hungary. Concerned at the possible defection of Horthy from the Axis, the Germans occupied Hungary on 19 Mar. 1944, arresting the underground opposition and exterminating Hungary's Jews and Gypsies. When Horthy tried to leave the war in Oct. 1944 he was forced to abdicate, leaving the country under the brutal administration of the Hungarian fascist Ferenc Szálasi.

On 21 Dec. 1944 Stalin authorized the formation in Debrecen of a provisional government comprising all the non-fascist parties. The last German forces left Hungary on 4 Apr. 1945. In the free elections of Nov. 1945 the Smallholders gained 57% of the vote while the Communists trailed with 17%, but the provisional government coalition was continued. Elections in 1947 saw the Communists emerge as the majority party, and in June 1948 the Social Democrats were forcibly merged with the Communists to form the Hungarian Workers' Party (HWP). Leading non-Communists such as Smallholder Prime Minister Ferenc Nagy were intimidated into emigration, opposition political parties were eliminated by 1949, and all the junior government coalition partners by 1954. In Jan. 1949 the Roman Catholic Primate Cardinal Jószef Mindszenty was sentenced to life imprisonment. The HWP split into a 'Muscovite' and a 'native' faction: in 1949 the (Muscovite) party general secretary Mátyás Rákosi purged Lászlo Rajk from the top leadership as a Titoist, while Rajk's successor as interior minister, János Kádár, was purged in 1951. Rákosi's dictatorship supervised the collectivization of agriculture and the rapid creation of a heavy industrial base.

Following Stalin's death in 1953 Rákosi was instructed by the new Soviet leadership to yield the premiership to Imre Nagy. Nagy's first premiership (July 1953–Apr. 1955) heralded a 'New Course' involving a reduction of political terror and the release of political prisoners, permission for peasants to leave collective farms, and an improvement in workers' conditions. In 1955 Rákosi condemned Nagy as a 'right deviationist' and deposed him. However, following Khrushchev's denunciation of Stalin in Feb. 1956 Rajk was rehabilitated and on 18 July 1956 Rákosi surrendered the party leadership to Erno Gero.

Between 18–21 Oct. 1956 the Polish Communist leadership successfully defied Khrushchev in insisting on their right to run their own affairs. The news electrified Hungary and triggered a demonstration on 23 Oct. demanding the reinstatement of Imre Nagy and the withdrawal of Russian forces. Clashes between demonstrators and Hungarian militia led to Soviet military intervention. On 24–25 Oct. Nagy became prime minister and Kádár first secretary of the HWP (renamed the Hungarian Socialist Workers' Party – HSWP – on 1 Nov). As the revolution gained strength, Nagy went with the tide, authorizing the restoration of multi-party democracy and announcing Hungary's neutrality. On 2 Nov. the Soviet Army launched a massive offensive, deposed Nagy and installed a puppet government under Kádár. An estimated 25,000 were killed in Budapest alone. Nagy was arrested and executed for treason on 16 June 1958.

After three years of repression and consolidation Kádár moved towards policies of national reconciliation: he inverted Lenin's slogan to declare that 'whoever is not against us is with us.' Economic experimentation included the market socialist 'New Economic Mechanism' launched in 1968 (but restricted in 1972–77). Tolerance of freedom of expression slowly increased, although Hungarian forces participated in the suppression of Czechoslovakia's 'Prague Spring' in 1968. By the mid-1980s the authorities had been forced by declining living standards and heavy foreign debt to recognize the need for further economic reforms. In 1988–89 they were propelled towards political reforms by popular disaffection expressed in pro-democracy demonstrations and the emergence of independent political groups and trade unions. At a special conference in May 1988, Kádár was replaced as HSWP general secretary by Karoly Grósz. In Jan. 1989 a law was introduced to permit formation of new political parties, while the HSWP ws thrown into crisis when a leading reformist member, Imre Pózsgay, repudiated the 'counter-revolution' label applied to the 1956 uprising. Rehabilitation of Imre Nagy followed, his remains being disinterred from their unmarked grave and reburied after a state funeral on the 31st anniversary of his execution. Also in June leadership of the HSWP effectively passed from Grósz to Reszö Nyers, and in early Oct. reformists including Nyers and Pózsgay secured the party's reconstitution as the Hungarian Socialist Party. The National Assembly on 17–20 Oct. approved a new transitional constitution and electoral law introducing a full multi-party democratic system. On 23 Oct., the anniversary of the start of the 1956 uprising, a Republic was proclaimed instead of the People's Republic declared in 1949.

CONSTITUTION AND GOVERNMENT

Executive and legislature

The transitional constitution introduced in Oct. 1989 created the post of State President, currently filled by the National Assembly speaker pending an election. The legislature is the unicameral National Assembly (*Országgyüles*), currently made up of 352 deputies directly elected from a list allowing choice between candidates, and 35 elected unopposed from a list of prominent public figures; a new electoral law passed in Oct. 1989 increased the number of deputies to 386 from the next general election (176 to be directly elected from local constituencies, 152 to be elected by proportional representation from county and metropolitan lists, and 58 to be indirectly elected from national 'compensation' lists nominated by political parties). The Assembly elects the Council of Ministers (government), whose Chairman is effectively the Prime Minister.

Present government

President of the Presidential Council (acting) Mátyás Szürös Prof. Bruno Ferenc Straub

Principal members of the Council of Ministers Miklós Németh (Chairman); Péter Medgyessy (Deputy Chairman; Chairman of Planning and Economic Committee); Imre Pózsgay (Minister of State); Rezso Nyers (Minister of State); Lt.-Gen. Ferenc Kárpáti (Defence); Dr Lászlo Bekesi (Finance); Gyula Horn (Foreign Affairs); Ferenc Horváth (Industry); Zoltan Pál (Interior – acting); Prof. Kálmán Kulcsár (Justice).

Justice

The legislature elects a procurator-general, who is in charge of the administration of justice. Civil and criminal cases fall under the jurisdiction of the district courts (which act only as courts of first instance), county courts (which are either courts of first instance or appeal) and the Supreme Court in Budapest (which functions as an appeal court). Judges of district or county courts are elected by the district or county councils. Parliament elects members of the Supreme court. The death penalty is in force. There were at least two executions between 1985 and mid-1988. The offences were murder.

National symbols

Flag. Three horizontal stripes of red, white and green.

Festivals. 15 Mar. (Anniversary of 1848 uprising against Austrian rule); 4 Apr. (Liberation day); 1 May (Labour Day); 20 Aug. (Constitution Day).

Vehicle registration plate. H.

INTERNATIONAL RELATIONS

Affiliations

Warsaw Pact; Comecon.

Defence

Total Armed Forces: 99,000 (64,000 conscripts). Terms of service: Army (inclusive Border Guard) 18 months; Air Force 24 months.

Army: 77,000; some 1,300 main battle tanks (mainly T-54/-55, T-72), 100 light tanks (PT-76).

Air Force: 22,000; 135 combat aircraft (MiG-23M, MiG-21/F/PF/bis/U), 40 armed helicopters.

ECONOMY

Currency

The unit is the forint, divided into 100 filler.

National finance

Budget. The 1987 budget (in US$) was for expenditure (current and capital) of 13,100 million and revenue of 12,600 million. Main items of current expenditure are housing and welfare 26.2%; defence 4%; health 3.6%.

Balance of payments. The balance of payments (current account, 1987) was a deficit of US$676 million.

Gross Domestic Product

Estimated total GDP US$91,800 millions (GNP), per capita US$8,670 (ranking 26 in the world by size).

Economically active population. The total number of persons active in the economy was 4,860,000.

Sector	% of workforce	% of GDP
industry	38.5	40
agriculture	18.3	15
services*	43.2	44

* services figure includes elements unassigned to other categories.

Energy and mineral resources

Oil and gas. Oil and natural gas resources are exploited in the Szeged basin and in Zala county. Output: gas 251,365 million ft³/7,118 million m³; oil (1988) 2.1 million tons/1.9 million tonnes.

Minerals. Output: (in 1,000 tons/tonnes) brown coal 14,618/13,261; lignite 7,962/7,223; bauxite 3,418/3,101; coal 2,601/2,360.

Electricity. Capacity: 7,253 MW; production: 29.735 million MWh (10,985 MWh from the 880 MW nuclear power station at Paks). Imports: 12.61 million MWh.

Bioresources

Agriculture. The land area in agricultural use is 16.1 million acres/6.5 million ha, of which 11.6 million acres/4.7 million ha is sown to crops, 3 million acres/1.2 million ha is meadow and pasture, and 595,511 acres/241,000 ha is orchards and vineyards. The main products are cereals; sugar beet; potatoes; sunflowers. Crop production: (in 1,000 tons/tonnes) maize 7,702/6,987; wheat 6,255/5,674; sugar beet 4,656/4,224;

sunflower seed 867/787; barley 861/781; potatoes 765/694.

Livestock numbers: poultry 36.2 million; pigs 8.2 million; sheep 2.3 million; cattle 1.6 million; horses 88,000.

Forestry. The forested area is 4.13 million acres/1.67 million ha. Production of cut timber: (1987) 289.6 million ft^3/8.2 million m^3.

Fisheries. Commercial catch from fisheries in the Danube and Tisza rivers and Lake Balaton, and from 64,246 acres/26,000 ha of commercial fishponds (1984) 42,963 tons/38,976 tonnes.

Industry and commerce

Industry. Mining, metallurgy and engineering are the dominant industries, followed by cement; chemicals (especially artificial fertilizers and pharmaceuticals); textiles; food processing.

Commerce. The Hungarian economy is heavily dependent on foreign trade. Exports: 450,100 million forints; imports 463,100 million forints. Exports went principally to: USSR 32.7%; West Germany 9.8%; East Germany 5.6%. Imports came from: USSR 28.5%; West Germany 13.9%; East Germany 6.4%.

Trade with UK. Hungary imported UK goods worth £131.212 million and exported to the UK goods worth £96.288 million (1988).

Tourism. 11.83 million tourists (1987) of whom 2.68 million came from the West.

COMMUNICATIONS

Railways

There are 5,279 miles/8,500 km of railways, of which 1,192 miles/1,920 km are electrified.

Roads

There are 56,322 miles/90,696 km of roads.

Aviation

Magyar Legikoezlekedesi Vallalat – MALEV (Hungarian Airlines) provides international services (main airport is at Budapest). Passengers: (1987) 1.3 million.

Shipping

There are 1,007 miles/1,622 km of inland waterways. Budapest and Dunaujvaros are river ports on the Danube. The maritime outlets are Rostock (GDR); Gdansk (Poland); Szczecin (Poland); Galati (Romania); Braila (Romania). The merchant marine consists of 14 cargo ships of 1,000 GRT or over. Freight carried: (1987) 4.2 million tons/3.8 million tonnes.

Telecommunications

There are an estimated 1.6 million telephones; over 2.6 million radio licences before their abolition in 1980; and nearly 3 million television licences. The state Magyar Radio runs three channels as well as external broadcasting in Hungarian, English and four other languages; the state televison station broadcasts on two channels, in colour, but not on Mondays, while cable and satellite television are spreading, with the capability to receive television broadcasts by satellite from several sources in Western Europe.

EDUCATION AND WELFARE

Education

The state provides free and compulsory education at primary schools for ages six to 14. Thereafter education may be continued in a secondary, secondary technical or secondary vocational school, leading to a diploma entitling a student to apply for higher education, or at a vocational training school leading to a trade diploma.

School population. 398,325 in kindergarten; 1,227,300 in primary schools; 239,800 in secondary schools; 177,200 in vocational training schools.

Schools. 4,786 kindergartens with 33,896 teachers (one per 10.9 pupils); 3,540 primary schools with 90,925 teachers (one per 14 pupils); 608 secondary schools with 19,184 teachers (one per 12.5 pupils); 284 vocational training schools with 11,651 teachers (one per 15.2 pupils).

Universities. There are four universities offering a full range of courses (at Budapest, Pécs, Szeged and Debrecen); 14 specialized universities (six technical; four medical; three arts; one economics), and 36 other higher education institutions. 66,700 students and 15,302 teachers in 1987.

Health

Medical treatment is provided free of charge, although patients must pay 15% of the cost of prescription medicines. The state provides sickness benefit at 75% of wages. 35,423 doctors and dentists. 104,581 hospital beds (one per 101 inhabitants).

ICELAND
Lýdhveldidh Ísland
(Republic of Iceland)

GEOGRAPHY

Situated in the north Atlantic Ocean, approximately 186 miles/300 km south-east of Greenland, 559 miles/900 km west of Norway and 497 miles/800 km north of Scotland, the volcanic island of Iceland covers an area of 39,758 miles^2/103,000 km^2 divided into eight regions. With an average elevation of 1,640 ft/500 m, the Icelandic terrain is largely basaltic plateau, interspersed with highland spurs, icefields and grassy lowlands (in the north central region) enclosed by a heavily indented coastline whose fjord sides climb inland to form ridges which reach a height of 6,952 ft/2,119 m at Hvannadalshnjúkur in the south-east. Glaciers cover 10% of the total surface area. Large icefields include Vatnajokull, Hofsjokull and Langjokull. Hot springs and solfataras discharge at over 250 different locations on the island. There are about 200 volcanoes and seismic disturbances are frequent although seldom of serious intensity. The River Thjorsá drains an area of 1,727 miles^2/4,474 km^2 rising between the Vatnajokull and Hofsjokull glaciers. Only 1% of the land is forested, and less than 1% is arable, but nearly 25% of the total surface area is suitable for grazing. The majority of the population is concentrated in coastal urban settlements.

Climate

Variable, but largely cool temperate oceanic, moderated by the Gulf Stream and prevailing south-westerly winds. Precipitation (mostly snow) increases in upland areas and decreases south-east to north central from 120.1 in/3,050 mm to less than 29.5 in/750 mm. Reykjavik: Jan. 33.8°F/1°C. July 51.8°F/11°C. Average annual rainfall 33.9 in/860 mm.

Cities and towns

Reykjavik (capital)	93,270

Population

Total population is 249,999 of which 89.7% live in urban areas. Population density is 6.3 persons per mile^2/2.4 per km^2. 96.9% of the population are native Icelandic. In 1987, out of the 3,874 foreign nationals resident in Iceland, 1,042 were Danish, 736 American, 380 British, 296 Norwegian and 264 German citizens.

Birth rate 1.82%. **Death rate** 0.69%. **Rate of population increase** 1.13%. **Age distribution** under 15 = 26.5%; over 65 = 10.1%. **Life expectancy** female 79; male 75; average 77.

Religion

95% of the population belong to the Evangelical Lutheran Church. Other Protestant denominations include the Free Lutherans and Seventh Day Adventists. There are about 2,000 Roman Catholics.

Language

Icelandic (Islensk) is part of the West Scandinavian branch of North Germanic languages related to Norwegian and Faeroese.

HISTORY

Settled in the late 9th century AD by Vikings mainly of Norwegian origin, although with a Celtic admixture, Iceland established its own parliament (Althing) in 930, was Christianized c.1000 and enjoyed a golden literary age in the 12th and 13th centuries, when the great Icelandic sagas were written. Hitherto an independent commonwealth, Iceland declared allegiance to Norway in 1262. On the union of the Norwegian and Danish crowns (1380), as confirmed by the Union of Kalmar (1397), Iceland came under Danish sovereignty. It adopted Lutheranism in the 16th century but fell into political and economic decline as a result of the royal absolutism and mercantilism practised from Denmark. In 1707–9 about a third of the 50,000-strong population died in a smallpox epidemic and in 1783–84 Iceland was devastated by a volcanic eruption. Having remained Danish when Norway was transferred to Sweden at the end of the Napoleonic Wars (1814), Iceland experienced national awakening under the leadership of Jón Sigurosson (d.1879). The revival of the Althing (1843) led to limited home rule (1874) and the introduction of universal suffrage (1915). Full sovereignty was established in 1918, although still under the Danish crown.

During World War II, with Denmark under German control, Iceland was occupied by British and American troops and declared itself an independent republic (1944) under the presidency of Sveinn Bjornsson. Post-war Iceland underwent rapid economic modernization and, despite considerable domestic opposition, became a founder member of NATO (1949); it also joined the Nordic Council (1953) and EFTA (1970), and signed a trade agreement with the European Economic Community (1972). With its economy heavily dependent on fishing, Iceland came into conflict with Britain (and to a lesser extent West Germany) over extensions of its exclusive fishing limits from four to 12 miles (1958), to 50 miles (1972) and then to 200 miles (1975). The second 'cod war' with Britain (1972–76) involved serious incidents at sea, before a compromise settlement gave British trawlers limited access to the zone claimed by Iceland. Opposition to the US/NATO base at Keflavík continued in the 1980s, without procuring its removal, although in 1985 the

Althing unanimously declared Iceland a nuclear-free zone.

Successive post-independence governments were formed by combinations of two or more of the four main parties, namely the conservative Independence Party (IP), the centrist Progressive Party (PP), the Communist-dominated People's Alliance (PA) and the Social Democratic Party (SDP). Amid deepening economic problems, some erosion of the dominance of the four traditional parties occurred in the 1983 Althing elections, when a new Women's Alliance (WA) secured representation, assisted by the fact that Vigdís Finnbogadóttir (independent) had been elected as Iceland's first woman president in 1980. This process continued in the Apr. 1987 elections, when the WA doubled its representation and a new Citizens' Party, formed by IP dissidents, also won seats, while the SDP for the first time outpolled the PA. A coalition of the IP, PP and SDP, led by Thorsteinn Pálsson (IP) was formed in July but collapsed in Sept. 1988, whereupon a centre-left combination of the PP, SDP and PA took office (Sept. 1988) under Steingrímur Hermannsson (PP). Vigdís Finnbogadóttir was re-elected for a third presidential term in June 1988. A year later Hermannsson's government again foundered and in Sept. 1989 the right-wing citizen's Party (CP) joined the coalition assuming the two portfolios of Economic Planning and Justice and Ecclesiastical Affairs.

CONSTITUTION AND GOVERNMENT

Executive and legislature

The head of state, with largely ceremonial duties, is the president who is elected every four years by universal adult suffrage (last election 25 June 1988). The president appoints a prime minister and cabinet who exercise effective executive authority. The legislature, the 63-member Althing (parliament), is a bicameral body, the members for both houses being elected by universal adult suffrage for four years (last elections 25 Apr. 1987); these members then meet and elect one-third of their number to serve as the upper house, while the lower house comprises the remaining two-thirds.

Present government

President Vigdís Finnbogadóttir

Prime Minister Steingrímur Hermannsson

Principal Ministers Jón Baldvin Hannibalsson (Foreign Affairs and Foreign Trade); Ólafur Ragnar Grímsson (Finance); Halldór Asgrímsson (Fisheries); Jón Sigurthsson (Commerce, Industry, Nordic Co-operation); Júlíus Sólnes (Economic Planning); Óli Gudbartsson (Justice and Ecclesiastical Affairs).

Justice

There is a Supreme Court in Reykjavik, with eight judges, which hears appeals from the lower courts of justice, the provincial magistrates and town judges. The death penalty was abolished in 1928.

Prisons. There are 102 prisoners.

National symbols

Flag. The flag is blue with a red Scandinavian cross edged with white.

Festivals. 17 June (18 June in 1990, National Day); 7 Aug. (6 Aug. in 1990, Bank holiday).

Vehicle registration plate. IS.

INTERNATIONAL RELATIONS

Affiliations

NATO; OECD; EFTA; Council of Europe; Nordic Council.

Defence

Police and coastguard only; there is a US military presence at the Keflavík base near the capital.

ECONOMY

Currency

The unit is the krone, divided into 100 aurar.

National finance

Budget. The 1987 budget (in US$) was for expenditure (current and capital) of 1,200 million and revenue of 1,040 million.

Balance of payments. The current account balance for 1988 was a deficit of $230 million.

Inflation. 19.2% (12 months Sept. 1989).

Gross Domestic Product

Estimated total GDP US$5,300 million, per capita US$21,660 (ranking 81 in the world by size). Growth rate (1988) – 1.3%.

Economically active population. The total number of persons active in the economy was 122,800; unemployed: 0.9% (1988).

Energy and mineral resources

Electricity. Capacity in publicly owned plants: 921.9 MW, of which hydroelectric plants comprised 81.5%; production: 4.2 million MWh (publicly owned plants); 5,000 MWh (private plants).

Bioresources

Agriculture. Only around 321,230 acres/130,000 ha (1.3% of the total area) is under cultivation. Around 5.7 million acres/2.3 million ha (23% of the total land area) is meadow and pasture. Main products are: dairy produce; meat; hay; potatoes; turnips.

Crop production: hay 128,652,000 ft^3/3,643,101 m^3; potatoes 19,952 tons/18,100 tonnes; turnips 1,213 tons/ 1,100 tonnes.

Livestock numbers: (1987) sheep 624,262; poultry 274,210; cattle 69,029; horses 59,218; pigs 3,351.

Forestry. Negligible. Forests cover only about 1% of Iceland's total land area.

Fisheries. The total annual fish catch is 181,880 tons/ 65,000 tonnes. The fishing industry is the dominant economic activity and provides nearly 75% of export earnings.

Industry and commerce

Industry. The main industry is fish processing. Other significant industries are aluminium smelting and ferro-silicon production.

Commerce. Exports: 55,053 million kronur (of which marine products 40,322m kronur); imports: 61,231 million kronur. EC countries accounted for more than 50% of both exports and imports.

Trade with UK. Iceland imported UK goods worth 5,033 million kronur and exported to the UK goods worth 10,321 million kronur.

Tourism. (1987) 129,315 visitors.

COMMUNICATIONS

Railways

There are no railways.

Roads

There are 7,063 miles/11,373 km of roads (2,366 miles/3,805 km of main roads).

Aviation

Eagle Air (Arnarflug) and Icelandair (Flugleidir hf) provide domestic and international services (international airport is at Keflavík, 29 miles/47 km from Reykjavik).

Shipping

The major ports on the North Atlantic coast are Reykjavik, Hafnarfjordhur, Keflavík and Vestmannaeyjar. Akureyri, Seydhisfjordhur, Siglufjordur, and Vestmannaeyjar are situated on the north coast on the Greenland Sea. The merchant marine consists of 24 ships of 1,000 GRT or over.

Telecommunications

There are 135,000 telephones and an adequate domestic service and wire and radio communications system. There are 83,000 licensed radio sets and 75,000 televisions, with the Icelandic National Broadcasting Service broadcasting two radio channels and one television channel. Reykjavik also has a commercial radio station and a commercial TV channel, while the US forces provide a radio and TV service for the Keflavík military base.

EDUCATION AND WELFARE

Education

The state system provides free and compulsory education from ages seven to 15. Upper secondary schools then provide further four-year courses.

School population. 41,800 under 16 (attendance rate 94%); 13,900 in higher stages.

Universities. There is a university in Reykjavik (founded 1911), together with a teacher-training college and a technical high school. In 1987 there were 4,700 university and college students, of whom around 25% were studying abroad.

Literacy. 100%

Health

Health insurance, including sickness benefits, is provided under social security legislation. In general hospitals are both municipally and state-run, and all offer free medical care. The cost of medical treatment outside hospitals, including most prescribed medication, is partly paid by the patient.

INDIA

Bharatavarsha
(Republic of India)

GEOGRAPHY

Located in Southern Asia, India is the seventh largest country in the world, with an area of 1,222,396 miles²/ 3,166,829 km² divided into 25 states and seven union territories. North of Delhi, the rugged, heavily glaciated terrain of the Himalayas covers 15% of the total surface area, rising to elevations over 22,966 ft/ 7,000 m in the Ladakh and Karakoram ranges and soaring to 28,215 ft/8,600 m at K2 (Godwin Austen) on the Tibetan border. The Plains region (45% of the land area) stretches south from the Thar Desert in the north-west and the Ganges basin in the north-east to the fertile western and south-east coastal lowlands which enclose the wide hills and valleys of the Deccan plateau (40% of the total surface area). The Vindhya Range separates the plateau region from the Indo-Gangetic plain. This east central part of the country constitutes the republic's agricultural and populous urban heartland, irrigated and drained by the great Ganges, Yamuna, Ghagari and Brahmaputra rivers and lying, for the most part, below 558 ft/170 m elevation. In the far north, the Indus flows south-west from its Himalayan source into Pakistan while the Godavari and Krishna rivers in the south traverse the peninsula west-east. On the very tip of the Indian peninsula, the cultivated Western and Eastern Ghats (coastal lowlands) merge in the Karnataka and Tamil Nadu uplands. 55% of the land is arable and 23% is forested, mostly on the lower slopes of the Himalayas and in those coastal areas that have not been cleared for rice cultivation.

Climate

Four separately defined seasons characterize India's Asiatic monsoonal climatic profile. Cold weather with chill northerly winds predominates Dec.-Mar., succeeded by two months of hotter weather and subsequently by four months of monsoonal rains from the south-west. The monsoon retreats during Oct. and Nov. Rainfall varies greatly from a colossal 450 in/ 11,430 mm per year at Cherrapunji in Assam to below 3.9 in/100 mm in the Thar desert, averaging between 39 and 78.7 in/1,000 and 2,000 mm in the central river plains region. Annual temperatures are affected primarily by relief, ranging from between 54–59°F/ 12–15°C in the Himalayan tracts to 79–84°F/ 26–29°C over the rest of the land mass. New Delhi: Jan. 57°F/13.9°C. July. 88°F/31.1°C. Average annual rainfall 25.2 in/640 mm. Bombay: Jan. 75°F/23.9°C. July. 81°F/27.2°C. Average annual rainfall 71.2 in/ 1,809 mm. Darjeeling: Jan. 41°F/5°C. July. 62°F/ 16.7°C. Average annual rainfall 119.5 in/3,035 mm. Cherrapunji: Jan. 53°F/11.7°C. July. 68°F/20°C. Average annual rainfall 425.1 in/10,798 mm.

Cities and towns

Greater Bombay	8,243,405
Delhi (capital)	4,884,234
Calcutta	3,305,006
Madras	3,276,622
Bangalore	2,628,593
Hyderabad	2,187,262
Ahmedabad	2,159,127
Kanpur	1,486,522
Nagpur	1,219,461
Poona	1,203,351

Population

Total population is 822,421,982 of which 25.5% live in urban areas. Population density is 672.8 persons per mile^2/247.3 per km^2. The principal strains that make up India's heterogenous ethnic mix are Australoid, Caucasoid, Mongoloid and Negroid. 72% of the population are Indo-Aryan, 25% Dravidian and 3% Mongoloid or other.

Birth rate 3.17%. **Death rate** 1.23%. **Rate of population increase** 1.94%. **Age distribution** under 15 = 37.7%; over 65 = 4.3%. **Life expectancy** female 58; male 57.

Religion

At the last census, 82.63% of the population were Hindus (549.7 million); 11.36% were Muslims (75.6 million); 2.43% were Christians (16.2 million); 1.96% were Sikhs (13.1 million); 0.7% were Buddhists (4.7 million); 0.48% were Jains (3.2 million).

Language

There are two official languages: Hindi and English. The diverse cultural identities of the Indian peoples are better represented by ethnolinguistic than by racial distinctions. Indo-European languages (Indo-Iranian and Indo-Aryan branches) include Hindi; Urdu; Bengali; Panjabi; Marathi; Oriya; Sanskrit; Gujarati; Assamese; Kashmiri. Dravidian languages, concentrated more in southern India, are Telugu; Malayalam; Tamil. Within these two broad categories, the main languages are Hindi (spoken by 30% of the population); Bengali; Marathi; Telugu; Urdu (speakers of these four languages comprising in total another 30% of the population). Other languages include Manipuri (Assam), Newari (Nepal) and the Austro-Asiatic Munda languages Santali and Khasi.

HISTORY

There are numerous sites of human settlement in India dating from the Upper Paleolithic Age (c.40,000 BC). The urban Indus Valley civilization (c.2500–1700 BC) had its centre in modern Pakistan but extended into contemporary India. During the second millenium BC tribal people of the Aryan language group from central Asia began to settle in the Ganges valley. Their language, religious beliefs and social institutions fused with those of the local inhabitants, laying the foundations for many key elements of Indian culture, in particular Sanskrit, Hinduism and the caste system. By the third century BC the Mauryan empire under Asoka (c.272–232 BC) encompassed all of modern India except the far south.

Over subsequent centuries the dominance of relatively centralized empires – like that of the Guptas in the north (AD 320–540) or the Cholas in the south (AD 850–1278) – alternated with periods of dispersed political authority. In 1206 Turkish invaders from Afghanistan established a sultanate in Delhi, initiating a long period of Muslim political dominance. In 1526 the Mongol chief Babur defeated the last of the Delhi sultans at the battle of Panipat, thereby beginning the Mughal (Mongol) era. The Mughal empire was consolidated and extended under the emperors Akbar (1556–1605), Jahangir (1605–27), Shah Jahan (1628–57), and Aurangzeb (1658–1707) until it incorporated all of the sub-continent except the far south.

The Portuguese explorer Vasco da Gama landed at Calicut in 1498 and in 1510 the Portuguese annexed Goa. In 1600 the English East India Company was formed and in 1701 it received a grant of land from the Mughal emperor, just outside contemporary Calcutta. In southern India the East India Company, based at Madras, became embroiled in a vigorous commercial and military rivalry with the French. Victory over the French coincided with a challenge from the Mughal Nawab (viceroy) of Bengal, who was defeated by Company forces at the Battle of Plassy in 1757. The East India Company took charge of the revenue management of Bengal in 1765 and steadily extended its territorial power both through negotiating treaties with Indian princely states and by direct annexation. In 1857–58 the Company's authority was threatened by the 'Indian Mutiny', as grievances in the ranks of the Company's army fused with discontent among Muslim noblemen and peasant unrest over high taxation.

The Mughal emperor supported the rebels' cause, and their defeat led to the end of the Mughal dynasty. But the mutiny also provoked the British government into assuming direct responsibility for the adminis-tration of India in 1858. Under British rule ultimate power lay with the secretary of state for India, acting through and on the advice of the governor-general. The country was divided into 'British India', administered directly, and the Princely States, which retained a measure of local autonomy. Indians soon began to press for greater political influence. Associations for social and political reform were formed by members of the western-educated middle class from the 1830s onwards, and in 1884 the Indian National Congress was created to press for greater participation in public affairs. Indian nationalism identified its goals as swadeshi (economic self-sufficiency) and swaraj (home rule). In 1906 the Muslim League was formed to defend Muslim interests.

The British decision to partition Bengal province between Hindu and Muslim regions in 1905 provoked a major nationalist reaction and increased the influence of more militant nationalist currents. In 1909 the Morley-Minto reforms provided for a limited extension of Indian participation in government and introduced the principle of separate electorates for the country's different religious communities. Further reforms in 1919 allowed elected Indian ministers to take charge of some areas of administration at the provincial level.

After World War I the nationalist movement took a new direction under the influence of Mohandas Gandhi, who had returned to India from South Africa in 1915. Gandhi supported the demand for immediate swaraj and directed Congress towards becoming a mass movement committed to extra-constitutional but non-violent methods of struggle. In 1920 he launched his first civil disobedience campaign, abruptly terminating it in 1922 when violence erupted.

Gandhi dominated the nationalist movement for the next 30 years, drawing around him a diverse array of talented lieutenants ranging from the conservative Vallabhai Patel to the radical Jawaharlal Nehru. Further civil disobedience campaigns were undertaken throughout the early 1930s and Gandhi represented Congress at the Round Table Conference on constitutional reform held in London in 1931.

In 1935 the British government introduced further constitutional changes which provided for elected responsible government at the provincial level, albeit with a narrow franchise. Congress agreed to participate in the ensuing elections, and succeeded in capturing eight out of 11 provincial governments. The Muslim League, led by Mohammed Ali Jinnah, did poorly and political rivalry led to a deterioration in relations between the League and Congress.

In 1939 Congress withdrew from the provincial administrations in protest at the British decision to declare India a party to World War II without consultation. The Muslim League cooperated with the British administration during the war and at its 1940 Congress in Lahore called for 'independent states' in Muslim majority areas. In Mar. 1942 a mission led by Sir Stafford Cripps offered Indian political leaders Dominion status after the war in exchange for support of the war effort. However a mutually agreeable formula could not be reached. In Aug. 1942 Gandhi launched the Quit India movement to force the British to leave. Mass civil disobedience was widely supported but effectively contained by the administration, who imprisoned thousands of Congress supporters including Gandhi and Nehru.

The end of the war saw a major upsurge in nationalist sentiment, expressed in events like the mutiny of Indian naval ratings in Feb. 1946. The British Labour Government began to prepare in earnest for Indian independence. However attempts to resolve differences between Congress and the Muslim League failed. In February 1947 the British government announced that it would withdraw from India by June 1948 and appointed Lord Louis Mountbatten governor-general to oversee the process. Mountbatten decided that partition was the only solution and secured the reluctant acquiescence of Congress to a formula that provided for the creation of two states – India and Pakistan – with Punjab and Bengal provinces partitioned between Muslim- and Hindu-majority areas. On 15 Aug. 1947 India became an independent state with Jawaharlal Nehru as prime minister.

Partition proved to be a traumatic experience. In the divided provinces inter-communal conflict produced half a million deaths and over ten million refugees. Gandhi's attempts to calm the situation culminated in his assassination at the hands of a Hindu extremist on 20 Jan. 1948. In 1948 war broke out with Pakistan over the Muslim-majority state of Kashmir, whose Hindu ruler had decided to accede to India. The conflict ended indecisively in 1949 when the UN negotiated a cease-fire that effectively divided Kashmir between the two countries but left the issue unresolved.

In 1950 a new Indian constitution came into effect declaring the country a republic and a federal union with a parliamentary system of government. The first post-independence elections, in 1951–52, gave Congress some 364 of 489 seats but only 45% of the popular vote. Under Nehru, who dominated the political leadership after the death of home minister Vallabhai Patel in 1951, the government pursued moderate left policies, centred around state-directed industrial development at home and non-alignment in foreign affairs. Elections in 1957 and 1962 confirmed Congress's political influence and Nehru's great personal popularity. In the autumn of 1962 a disastrous border conflict broke out with China, which culminated in a Chinese invasion of the north-eastern border area and the humiliating defeat of the Indian army.

Nehru died in May 1964 and was succeeded by Lal Bahadur Shastri. In Aug. 1965 war broke out again with Pakistan over Kashmir. The Indian army repelled Pakistan's forces and successfully counter-attacked across the border. Both countries accepted a Soviet offer of mediation and peace was concluded at Tashkent in Jan. 1966. However Prime Minister Shastri died at the conclusion of the peace conference. Nehru's daughter Indira Gandhi now became prime minister.

Internal economic difficulties and foreign policy problems combined to produce a serious reversal for Congress in the 1967 election, in which it lost 80 parliamentary seats. Mrs Gandhi moved to form an alliance with the radical wing of the party, but she met with determined opposition from the party's right-wing, headed by deputy Prime Minister Morarji Desai, who eventually led a split in 1969. Mrs Gandhi won the Mar. 1971 election, in which she campaigned around the slogan of 'abolish poverty'.

In Dec. 1971 war again broke out with Pakistan as India intervened in support of the secessionist forces in East Pakistan, underwriting the emergence of independent Bangladesh. In 1974 opposition to Congress began to take the form of mass civil disobedience and in 1975 Mrs Gandhi responded by imposing a state of emergency that suspended established civil liberties and postponed elections due for 1976. When elections were finally held in Mar. 1977 Mrs Gandhi's Congress (I) was pitted against a united opposition grouped into the Janata Party. Janata won a resounding victory, stripping Congress of more than half its seats.

Under Morarji Desai Janata formed the first non-

Congress government since independence. However it failed to develop a coherent set of policies and became riddled with factionalism. In July 1979 Desai resigned as prime minister to be briefly succeeded by his fellow Janata member and rival, Charan Singh. Singh, however, was unable to form a viable government, and resigned in August.

In Jan. 1980 fresh elections saw Congress fortunes almost fully restored and Mrs Gandhi again became prime minister. Throughout her period in office she followed cautious policies, chastened by her defeat in 1977. However her personalist and autocratic style of leadership weakened Congress and distorted the conduct of public affairs.

Beginning in 1983 serious unrest developed in the state of Punjab over Sikh demands for regional autonomy. While Mrs Gandhi opened negotiations with Sikh political leaders she refused to offer any substantial concessions. Political influence in the Punjab shifted towards the militants, typified by Jarnail Singh Bhindranwale, a figure who had earlier benefited from Congress patronage. Operating from the holiest of Sikh shrines, the Golden Temple of Amritsar, Bhindranwale's supporters organized the murder of political opponents and attacks on the security forces. In June 1984 the army launched an assault on the Golden Temple – 'Operation Bluestar'. The militants were routed and Bhindranwale killed in the attack, but Sikh religious sentiments were deeply offended.

On 31 October Mrs Gandhi was assassinated by two of her Sikh bodyguards acting in revenge. There followed a terrible outbreak of communal violence, especially in Delhi, as some 2,500 Sikhs were massacred by mobs often led by local Congress politicians. The Congress leadership chose Mrs Gandhi's son, Rajiv, as her successor only hours after her death. He called elections for Dec. 1984 in which Congress won the largest popular vote and strongest parliamentary representation in its history.

In July 1985 Rajiv Gandhi signed an accord with the leader of the Sikh Akali Dal party, Longowal, granting several Sikh demands. Elections were scheduled for Punjab, but before they could be held Longowal was killed by an extremist assassin. Under his lieutenant, Surjit Singh Barnala, the Akali Dal went on to win the elections in Sept. 1985. However, the central government failed to deliver many of the promised concessions and Barnala proved incapable of containing the militants. In May 1987 the Barnala government was dismissed and the state again placed under central control. In the absence of a political solution the influence of the militants continued unabated and the level of violence increased.

Rajiv Gandhi began his period of office promising to cleanse Indian politics of its pervasive corruption and bring the country 'into the twenty-first century'.

However, Congress proved difficult to reform and he gradually began to adopt an autocratic style reminiscent of his mother. This produced growing unrest within the Party. In 1987 the popular finance minister, V.P. Singh, was moved to the defence ministry after organizing raids on businesses suspected of tax avoidance. In the defence ministry he came into conflict with the party leadership by launching an investigation into corruption in the award of defence contracts, and was forced to resign. Singh joined with other dissident Congress figures to launch the Jan Morcha, later fused into the Janata Dal, and formed a broad National Front of opposition parties. Elections to the Lok Sabha held in late Nov. 1989 resulted in a defeat for the Congress (I) and victory for the Janata Dal-led National Front coalition. Following the election President Venkataraman received assurances of 'outside' support for a minority National Front government from the right-wing, Hindu-revivalist Bharatiya Janata Party and from the Left Front parties and in early December V.P. Singh was sworn in as the Prime Minister in place of Rajiv Gandhi. In an address to a joint session of parliament on 20 Dec., President Venkataraman announced that the primary objective of the new Singh government would be to 'restore the dignity of the nation and of the individual'.

From 1983 onwards India has been concerned with the situation in the north of Sri Lanka, where a separatist insurgency has developed among the Tamil minority. In July 1987 an agreement was reached with the Sri Lankan government that allowed Indian forces to occupy the north of the island to disarm the separatists and preside over the implementation of a package of political concessions. The operation proved to be a difficult one, with the key insurgent group putting up bitter resistance, and the southern Sinhalese majority becoming increasingly hostile to the Indian presence. The final withdrawal from Sri Lanka was completed in Mar. 1990.

CONSTITUTION AND GOVERNMENT

Executive and legislature

India is defined as 'a sovereign socialist secular democratic republic'. The head of state is the president, elected for a five-year term by an electoral college consisting of the elected members of the upper and lower Houses of Parliament (the Rajya Sabha and the Lok Sabha respectively) and of the Legislative Assemblies of the States. The president appoints a prime minister, who is the head of government. On the prime minister's advice, the president appoints a council of ministers, which is responsible to Parliament. The members of the 544-member Lok Sabha are elected directly by universal suffrage on a constituency basis and serve a five-year term; last elections Nov. 1989. Most of the 244 members of the Rajya Sabha are indirectly elected by the State Assemblies, and one-third are replaced every two years.

Present government

President Ramaswamy Venkataraman

Vice-President Dr Shankar Dayal Sharma

Prime Minister, Minister of Defence V.P. Singh

Principal Ministers Devi Lal (Deputy Prime Minister and Agriculture); Madhu Dandavate (Finance); Ajit Singh (Industry); Mohammad Sayeed (Home Affairs); I.K. Gujaral (External Affairs); Arun Kumar Nehru (Commerce and Tourism); George Fernandes (Railways); Sharad Yadav (Textiles and Food Processing Industries); Arif Mohammas Khan (Energy and Civil Aviation); Ram Vilas Paswan (Labour and Welfare); Nilamani Routray (Health and Family Welfare); M.S. Gurupadasamy (Petroleum and Chemicals); P. Upendra (Information and Broadcasting, Parliamentary Affairs); K.P. Unnikrishnan (Surface Transport and Communication); Dinesh Goswani (Law and Justice, Steel and Mines); Murasoli Maran (Urban Development); Nathu Ram Mirdha (Food and Civil Supplies).

Administration

The Union of India comprises 25 self-governing states and seven union territories. The legislative field is divided between the Union and the states, the former

Name	Area in miles²/km²	Population (1981)	Seats in Lok Sabha	Seats in Rajya Sabha
Andhra Pradesh	106,850/276,814	53,403,619	42	18
Arunachal Pradesh	32,261/83,578	628,050	2	1
Assam	30,277/78,438	19,902,826	14	7
Bihar	67,116/173,876	69,823,154	54	22
Goa	1,429/3,701	1,003,136	1	–
Gujarat	75,650/195,984	33,960,905	26	11
Haryana	17,070/44,222	12,850,902	10	5
Himachal Pradesh	21,490/55,673	4,237,569	4	3
Jammu and Kashmir	39,095/101,283	5,981,600	6	4
Karnataka	74,024/191,773	37,043,451	28	12
Kerala	15,002/38,864	25,403,217	20	9
Madhya Pradesh	170,937/442,841	52,131,717	40	16
Maharashtra	118,796/307,762	62,693,898	48	19
Manipur	8,629/22,356	1,433,691	2	1
Meghalaya	8,681/22,489	1,327,824	2	1
Mizoram	8,140/21,087	487,774	1	1
Nagaland	6,379/16,527	773,281	1	1
Orissa	60,132/155,782	26,272,054	21	10
Punjab	19,440/50,362	16,669,755	13	7
Rajasthan	132,095/342,214	34,102,912	25	10
Sikkim	2,817/7,299	315,682	1	1
Tamil Nadu	50,207/130,069	48,297,456	39	18
Tripura	4,044/10,477	2,060,189	2	1
Uttar Pradesh	113,643/294,413	110,858,019	85	34
West Bengal	33,911/87,853	54,485,560	42	16
Union Territories				
Andaman and Nicobar Islands	3,201/8,293	188,254	1	–
Chandigarh	44/114	450,061	1	–
Dadra and Nagar Haveli	190/491	103,677	1	–
Daman and Diu	42/110	78,981	1	–
Delhi	573/1,485	6,196,414	7	3
Lakshadweep	12/32	40,237	1	–
Pondicherry	185/480	604,136	1	1

Name	Capital	Ruling Party	Chief Minister
Andhra Pradesh	Hyderabad	Congress (I)	Marri Chenna Reddi
Arunachal Pradesh	Itanagar	Congress (I)	Gagong Apang
Assam	Dispur	Asom Gana Parishad	Prafulla Kumar Mahanta
Bihar	Patna	Janata Dal	Lallu Prasad Yadav
Goa	Panaji	Congress (I)	Pratap Singh Rane
Gujarat	Gandhinagar	Janata Dal	Chimanbhai Patel
Haryana	Chandigarh	Janata Dal	Om Prakash Chauthala
Himachal Pradesh	Simla	Bharatiya Janata Party	Shanta Kumar
Jammu and Kashmir	Srinagar (s) Jammu (w)	Under Governor's Rule	Veerendra Patil
		Congress (I)	
Karnataka	Bangalore	CPI – M (in coalition)	E.K.Nayanar
Kerala	Trivandrum	Bharatiya Janata Party	Sunderlal Patna
Madhya Pradesh	Bhopal	Congress (I)	Sharad Pawar
Maharashtra	Bombay	Manipur People's Party/	Raj Kumar Ranbir Singh
		Janata Dal (in coalition)	
Manipur	Imphal	Congress (I)	P.A. Sangma
Meghalaya	Shillong	Congress (I)	Lalthanhawla
Mizoram	Aizawl	Congress (I)	S.C. Jamir
Nagaland	Kohima	Janata Dal	Biju Patnaik
Orissa	Bhubaneswar	Under President's Rule	
Punjab	Chandigarh	Bharatiya Janata Party/	Bhairon Singh Shekhawat
		Janata Dal (in coalition)	
Rajasthan	Jaipur	Sikkim Samgram Parishad	Nar Bahadur Bhandari
Sikkim	Gangtok	Dravida Munnetra	
Tamil Nadu	Madras	Kazhagam	M. Karunanidhi
Tripura	Agartala	Congress (I)	Sudhir Ranjan Majumber
		(in coalition)	
Uttar Pradesh	Lucknow	Janata Dal	Mulayem Singh Yadav
West Bengal	Calcutta	CPI – M	Jyoti Basu
		(in coalition)	

(s) = summer (w) = winter

possessing exclusive powers to make laws with respect to matters grouped under 97 headings in the Constitution including foreign affairs, defence, citizenship and trade with other countries.

Justice

There is a Supreme Court (the highest court of appeal) of not more than fourteen judges (including the Chief Justice) appointed by the president and only removeable by his order following an address passed by each House of Parliament. The Court has sole jurisdiction in all disputes between State and Union or between State and State. Immediately below it are the High Courts and subordinate courts of each state. The death penalty is in force.

National symbols

Flag. Three horizontal stripes of saffron, white and green; in the centre of the white stripe there is the image in blue of Emperor Asoka's 'dharma chakra' ('wheel of life').

Festivals. 26 Jan. (Republic Day); 15 Aug. (Independence Day); 2 Oct. (Mahatma Gandhi's Birthday).

Vehicle registration plate. IND.

INTERNATIONAL RELATIONS

Affiliations

NAM; Commonwealth; SAARC.

Defence

Total Armed Forces: 1,362,000. Terms of Service: voluntary. Reserves: 240,000 (obligation to age 60).

Army: 1,200,000; 3,150 main battle tanks (mainly Vijayanta, T-55, T-72), 100 light tanks (PT-76).

Navy: 52,000; 14 submarines (Soviet Charlie-I, Soviet Kilo and Foxtrott, FRG T-209/1500), 31 principal surface combatants: two carriers (UK light fleet), five destroyers (Soviet Kashin), and 24 frigates (UK Leander, Whitby, and Leopard and Soviet Petya. 32 patrol and coastal combatants.

Naval Air Force: 2,000; 28 combat aircraft.

Air Force: 115,000; 714 combat aircraft (MiG-23 BN/UM, MiG-21 MF/U, Jaguar IS, MiG-27, MiG-29, MiG-21/FL/bis/U), 12 armed helicopters.

ECONOMY

Currency

The unit is the rupee, divided into 100 paise.

National finance

Budget. The 1987 budget (in US$) was for expenditure (current and capital) of 50,800 million and revenue of 46,200 million. Main items of current expenditure are defence 21.5%; housing and welfare 5.7%.

Balance of payments. The balance of payments (current account, 1987) was a deficit of $4,068 million (est.).

Inflation. (1987) 8.8%.

Gross Domestic Product

Estimated total GDP US$220,830 million, per capita US$290 (ranking 13 in the world by size).

Economically active population. The total number of persons active in the economy was 284,400,000; unemployed: 10%.

Sector	% of workforce	% of GDP
industry	n/a	30
agriculture	67	30
services*	n/a	40

* services figure includes elements unassigned to other categories.

Energy and mineral resources

Oil and gas. India's main oilfields are in Assam and offshore in the Gulf of Cambay. Crude oil production: (1988) 34.7 million tons/31.5 million tonnes; natural gas production: (1985) 233,072 million ft^3/6,600 million m^3.

Minerals. India has the fourth largest coal reserves in the world (171,959 million tons/156,000 million tonnes est.). The coal industry is nationalized and is based in the states of Bihar, West Bengal and Madhya Pradesh. Other minerals mined include iron ore; bauxite; chromite; copper ore; manganese ore; gold. There are also deposits of lead; zinc; limestone; apatite; phosphorite; dolomite; magnetite; silver.

Electricity. Capacity: 55,000,000 kW; production: 205,000 million kWh; 250 kWh per capita (1988).

Bioresources

Agriculture. Agriculture is the principal industry; 70% of India's vast population are dependent on the land for a living. Agricultural output has expanded during the 1980s, reflecting the greater use of modern farming techniques and improved seed. India is currently self-sufficient in food grains and a net agricultural exporter. Crops grown include rice; wheat; pulses; oilseed; cotton; jute; sugar cane; tobacco; tea; coffee. India is a legal producer of opium poppy for the pharmaceutical trade, but also an illegal producer of opium poppy and cannabis for the international drug trade.

Crop production: (1987–88 in 1,000 tons/tonnes) foodgrains 152,574/138,414 (of which rice 62,207/56,434; wheat 49,709/45,096); sugar cane 216,848/196,723; oilseeds 13,644/12,378; pulses 12,169/11,040; tea 685/621. Also cotton 1,093,100 tons/6.43 million bales (of 170 kg); jute 1,150,801 tons/5.8 million bales (of 180 kg).

Livestock numbers: (1987) cattle 199.3 million; goats 105 million; buffaloes 74.3 million; sheep 55.4 million; pigs 8.8 million; asses 1.3 million; horses 950,000.

Forestry. The total forest area is 185 million acres/75 million ha (1985). Lands under state government control are classified as 'reserved forests' (to be maintained for timber supplies or the protection of water supplies), 'protected forests' or 'unclassed' forest land.

Fisheries. Total catch (1986–87) 3.22 million tons/2.92 million tonnes, of which 1.90 million tons/1.72 million tonnes are sea fish.

Industry and commerce

Industry. Despite the prominence of the agricultural sector, India ranks among the ten leading industrial nations in the world. The emphasis of the seventh five-year plan (1985–90) is on improving the energy sector, the incompetent performance of which has contributed towards industrial production shortfalls. The government of Rajiv Gandhi pursued a policy of economic liberalization aimed at modernizing existing industries, introducing new electronic and computer-based industries and curbing the 'black economy'. The central government retains a high-level of control over the industrial sector. The main industries are textiles; food processing; steel; machinery; transportation equipment; cement; jute manufactures; mining; petroleum. Production: (1986–87) cloth 10,859 million yd/12,988 million m^2; finished steel 10.7 million tons/9.7 million tonnes; cement 38.3 million tons/34.8 million tonnes; nitrogenous fertilizers 6 million tons/5.4 million tonnes; automobiles 237,600.

Commerce. Exports US$11,400 million; imports US$16,700 million (1987). Exports in 1986–87 included gems and jewellery US$1,457 million; garments US$858 million; engineering goods US$616 million; cotton yarn and fabrics US$396 million; tea and mate US$387 million. Imports included petroleum and lubricants US$1,887 million; non-electrical machinery, apparatus and appliances US$2,615 million; iron and steel US$1,020 million; pearls and precious stones US$1,053 million; chemical elements and compounds US$729 million; fertilizers US$545 million. Main trading partners: exports – EC countries 22%; Soviet Union and Eastern Europe 19%; US 19%; Japan 11%; imports – EC 32%; Middle East 19%; Japan 13%; US 10%; Soviet Union and Eastern Europe 8%.

Trade with UK. India imported UK goods worth £560 million and exported to the UK goods worth £1,112 million (1988).

Tourism. Arrivals (excluding visitors from Pakistan and Bangladesh) 1,163,744 (1987); total visitor expenditure US$1,254 million.

COMMUNICATIONS

Railways

There are 38,386 miles/61,813 km of railways (the largest railway system in Asia).

Roads

There are 965,161 miles/1,554,204 km of roads (19,721 miles/31,756 km of national highways).

Aviation

Air India provides international services; Indian Airlines and Vayudoot Private Ltd provide domestic services.

Shipping

Of 10,048 miles/16,180 km of inland waterways, 2,255 miles/3631 km are navigable by large vessels. The ports on the coast of the Arabian Sea are Bombay, Cochin, Kandla, and New Mangalore. Calcutta and Madras are both ports on the Bay of Bengal. Port Blair is situated in the Andaman Islands. The merchant marine consists of 300 ships of 1,000 GRT or over. Freight loaded: (1983/4 in million tons/tonnes) 29.8/27; unloaded: 40.5/36.7.

Telecommunications

There are over 4 million telephones and although international radio communications are adequate there is a poor domestic telephone service. It is estimated that there are over 60 million radio sets in use, and some 12.5 million televisions, many of them installed by the government in community centres. The broadcasting network is run by the government-financed All India Radio and the government television service Doordarshan India, which reaches 70% of the population through its network of stations and relay centres, broadcasting 280 hours of programmes in total per week, some of the programmes having been in colour since 1981.

EDUCATION AND WELFARE

Education

Education is primarily the responsibility of individual state governments, although the union government has a number of direct responsibilities relating mainly to higher education. Free primary education in the age group 6–11 is available to all children and some state governments have passed legislation making primary education compulsory. Education at the senior basic and higher secondary levels is also provided free in some states.

School population. Junior basic schools: 86,465,189 pupils; senior basic schools: 28,124,756; higher secondary schools 15,105,934 (1985–86).

Schools. 528,079 junior basic schools with 1,509,910 teachers; 134,074 senior basic schools with 967,988 teachers; 61,314 higher secondary schools with 1,158,745 teachers.

Universities. There are 132 universities with 3.57 students (1985–86). In addition there are over 600 institutions awarding degrees and diplomas in engineering and technology and over 100 community polytechnics.

Literacy. 36%.

Health

Medical relief and service is primarily the responsibility of individual state governments, although family planning is centrally sponsored and the centre has also supported schemes for disease prevention. There are 2,350 persons per doctor and 1,096 persons per hospital bed (1987).

INDONESIA
Republik Indonesia
(Republic of Indonesia)

GEOGRAPHY

Located between the South-East Asian and Australian mainland, the Indonesian archipelago consists of some 13,667 islands covering a total area of 735,164 miles²/1,904,569 km² from the Malay Peninsula in the west to New Guinea in the east. The principal islands of Sumatra, Java, Kalimantan (approx. 60% of Borneo), Sulawesi and Irian Jaya are all characterized by their mountainous volcanic terrain covered by dense equatorial rainforest.

Volcanic activity on the fertile and densely populated island of Java is particularly pronounced Between the two ocean shelves of Sunda (Malaysian and Indo-Chinese extension) and Sahul (emanating from northern Australia) the Lesser Sundas, the Maluku and Sulawesi form the island summits of subaquatic mountain ranges flanked by sea trenches 14,763 ft/4,500 m in depth. The Kapuas and Barito rivers dominate the Indonesian hydrological profile, draining Kalimantan to the west and to the south. Lake Toba is situated on Sumatra at an altitude of 2,953 ft/900 m. Of the total surface area, 8% is arable land and over two-thirds is forest or woodland, including mangrove swamps along the Sumatran and Kalimantan coastlines.

Climate

Predominantly tropical monsoon, with variations attributable to latitudinal span and island structure. Temperatures reach a maximum 87.8°F/31°C in coastal areas, decreasing inland. The dry season lasts June-Sept. (eastern monsoon) and the wet season Dec.-Mar. (except in the Moluccan islands which receive the bulk of their rainfall June-Sept). Rainfall amounts vary according to leeward/windward situation. Jakarta: Jan. 78°F/25.6°C. July 78°F/25.6°C. Average annual rainfall 69.9 in/1,775 mm. Padang: Jan. 80°F/26.7°C. July 80°F/26.7°C. Average annual rainfall 174.3 in/4,427 mm. Surabaya: Jan. 81°F/27.2°C. July 78°F/25.6°C. Average annual rainfall 50.6 in/1285 mm.

Cities and towns

Jakarta (capital)	7,347,800
Surabaya	2,223,600
Bandung	1,566,700
Medan	1,378,955
Semarang	1,205,800
Palembang	873,900
Ujung Pandang (Makassar)	840,500
Padang	656,800
Malang	547,100

Population

Total population is 174,951,000 of which 25.3% live in urban areas. Population density is 238 persons per mile²/89.7 per km². At the last census, 40.1% of the total population were Javanese; 15.3% Sudanese; 12.0% Bahasa Indonesian; 48% Madurese. Principal ethnic divisions are: (by island group) the Minangkabaus, Aceh and Bataks in Sumatra; the Javanese and Sundanese in Java; the Madurese in Madura; the Balinese (Bali); the Sasaks in Lombok; the Torajas, Minakas, Menadonese and Buginese in Sulawesi; the Kalimantan Dayaks; the Irianese in Irian Jaya; the Timorese in Timor Timw; the Moluccan Ambonese. **Birth rate** 3.22%. **Death rate** 1.27%. **Rate of population increase** 1.95%. **Age distribution** under 15 = 38.6%; over 65 = 3.69%. **Life expectancy** female 62; male 58; average 60.

Religion

An estimated 87% of the population are Muslims and 9% Christians (of which 6% Roman Catholic and 3% Protestant). The 3.5 million Hindus (2%) are concentrated on Bali. In addition, there are about 1.6 million Buddhists, primarily Chinese.

Language

Bahasa Indonesia (based on Malay, Bahasa

Melayu) is the official language although Dutch has considerable unofficial currency. Of the other Indonesian/western Austronesian languages (25 languages, 250 dialects), Javanese is spoken by 69 million inhabitants, Sundanese by 26 million and Balinese, Banjarese, Batak, Bugi, Madurese and Minang by a further 25.5 million.

HISTORY

Situated on the sea-route between China and India, and possessing abundant natural resources, the islands of the Indonesian archipelago have long attracted the attention of outside influences. From 3000 BC onwards Malay peoples from western China began to settle in the archipelago. Beginning in the 1st century AD, Indonesia came into contact with the Hindu-Buddhist culture of India. The Buddhist, Sumatra-based Sri-Vijaya empire ruled the archipelago between the 7th and 13th centuries. It was succeeded in 1293 by the Hindu-Buddhist, Java-centred Majapahit empire, which controlled much of the archipelago until the mid-15th century. Majapahit's decline coincided with the growth in Indonesia of Islam, introduced by traders.

The first European intrusion came in the early 16th century, when the Portuguese gained control of the Moluccan clove trade. In 1602 the Dutch United East India Company (VOC) was formed under a charter issued by the Dutch parliament. Operating from Batavia (now Jakarta), it established a monopoly over regional trade, took control of parts of Java and the other islands, and forced local rulers into vassalage. By 1780, however, the company was bankrupt and in 1799 the charter was allowed to expire. The archipelago reverted to official Dutch rule and from 1808–11 Governor-General Daendels introduced a number of laissez-faire reforms. During the French occupation of the Netherlands in the early 19th century, Britain took temporary control of the East Indies, in the process liberalizing many of the harsher policies introduced by the Dutch. In the post-Napoleonic era the Dutch returned to the East Indies, only to be confronted by a major Java-based rebellion during 1825–30.

The end of the Java War marked the start of a period during which the Dutch intensified their exploitation of the archipelago's vast resources. In 1830 the Dutch introduced the Culture System, entailing forced cultivation of commercial crops for export. One-third of Holland's domestic budget was thus provided, but the indigenous Javanese economy was seriously distorted. Criticism of the Culture System on humanitarian grounds led to its abandonment in 1870, but this, along with the Dutch government's fear of British imperialistic designs, encouraged the 'Forward Movement' and Dutch expansion to the Outer Islands; by 1910 all of present-day Indonesia was under Dutch control. In 1901 the Dutch introduced a new Ethical Policy which aimed at providing limited educational and administrative opportunities for the indigenous population. A by-product of the Ethical Policy was the emergence in the early 20th century of a class of western-educated, urban Indonesian intellectuals, whose nationalist aspirations were given impetus by events outside the archipelago, most notably Japan's defeat of the Soviet Union in 1905.

In 1912 the Sarekat Islam was formed, its membership growing to around 500,000 in 1919. The Partai Komunis Indonesia (PKI) was first established in 1920. It led revolts in 1926 (in West Java) and 1927 (in Sumatra). In 1927 the Partai Nasional Indonesia (PNI) was formed under the leadership of Sukarno and Hatta. Dutch repression and nationalist divisiveness led to a hiatus in political activity throughout the 1930s.

In 1942 the Japanese overran the archipelago. Indonesia was to be granted 'independence' within Japan's 'Greater East Asia Co-Prosperity Sphere'. Preparations were made for this, and Sukarno worked with the Japanese, though all the time promoting his own vision of Indonesian independence. On 17 Aug. 1945, three days after the Japanese surrender, independence was declared, with Sukarno as president and Mohammad Hatta as vice-president. The Dutch returned to Indonesia but faced a Republican guerrilla war. Negotiations were entered into, and on 27 Dec. 1949 the Republic of the United States of Indonesia came into being. This federal arrangement was short-lived, however, and on 17 Aug. 1950 the unitary Republic of Indonesia was proclaimed. West New Guinea remained in Dutch hands.

A period of western-style constitutional democracy was now initiated. However, the country lacked the prerequisites necessary for the system to work, and between 1950 and 1957 six governments were formed, none of which possessed the necessary authority to address the country's mounting political and economic problems. In the mid-1950s attempts by Sukarno and the army chief of staff, Gen. Nasution, to curb the powers of military officers stationed in the Outer Islands precipitated a crisis that threatened the existence of the nation. The unrest convinced Sukarno that Indonesia was not ready for full-blown parliamentary democracy, and in late 1956 he initiated a more authoritarian, anti-parliamentary system of government, described by him as 'Guided Democracy'. Martial law was proclaimed in Mar. 1957 and in July 1959 Sukarno issued a presidential decree reinstating the 1945 Constitution, with its emphasis on broad presidential authority, and dissolving the legislature. The next year a new, fully-appointed, military-dominated legislature was created.

During the Guided Democracy period Indonesia pressed the Netherlands over its claim to West Irian (West New Guinea), and the territory was finally handed over in 1963. Also in 1963, Sukarno launched 'Confrontation' (Konfrontasi) against the new Malaysian Federation, because of a perceived threat to Indonesia. In the first half of the 1960s Indonesia established close relations with China, and on 1 Jan. 1965 left the United Nations. Sukarno's exceptional political adeptness during the period of 'Guided Democracy' was demonstrated through his ability to balance the two great contending power factions, the PKI and the Armed Forces (ABRI). Sukarno's increasing support for the PKI, and the party's growing influence within sections of the army, meant that by 1965 the ABRI-PKI equilibrium was moving inexorably towards disintegration. Konfrontasi and chronic economic mismanagement all added to the atmosphere of dangerous instability and the impression that Sukarno had lost control. On 30 Sept. 1965 the precarious balance of hostile forces broke down when junior army officers attempted a coup. Six top right-wing generals were murdered, with the participation of PKI elements. Gen. Suharto (commander of the army's Strategic Reserve) took control of the situation whilst Sukarno attempted to regain power. ABRI used the confusion as an excuse to take action against the PKI, which was quickly proscribed, and by late 1965 as many as 500,000 communists, leftists and supporters of the 'old order' had been killed during violent protests in Java, Bali and Sumatra. In Mar. 1967 Sukarno was stripped of all his governmental powers, and in Mar 1968 Suharto became president. His New Order government reversed Sukarno's anti-western foreign policies. The army used the Golkar (Functional Groups) organization to take control of the bureaucracy and to win parliamentary elections for the government in 1971, 1977, 1982, and 1987. The opposition parties were reduced to ineffective 'partners' of the government.

In 1969 a disputed Act of Free Choice was held in West Irian (renamed Irian Jaya in 1973). The Organisasi Papua Merdeka (OPM) subsequently began fighting a guerrilla war against Indonesia.

On 12 Sept. 1984 Muslim protestors clashed with troops in the Tanjung Priok area of Jakarta. At least 30 were killed. This incident marked a resurgence of Islamic protest in Indonesia in the 1980s. The government was seen as being anti-Muslim because of the 1985 Societies Law, which required all organizations to adopt the state ideology Pancasila as their sole ideological foundation, and as having too close links with Chinese business interests.

In Mar. 1988 Suharto was sworn in as president for another five-year term.

East Timor

East Timor came under Portuguese colonial administration in 1702. Moves towards decolonization began in 1974. A civil war in the territory in Aug. 1975 and the breakdown of Portuguese authority led to a declaration of independence by the Frente Revolucionaria de Timor Leste (Fretilin) on 27 Nov. 1985. Indonesian forces invaded on 7 Dec. 1975, and the territory was incorporated as Indonesia's 27th province in July 1976. By early-1989 several hundred Fretilin guerrillas continued to fight. Indonesia's claim to East Timor remained unrecognized by the United Nations.

CONSTITUTION AND GOVERNMENT

Executive and legislature

Indonesia is a a unitary state, headed by an executive president who is elected for a five-year term, together with a vice-president, by a 1,000-member People's Consultative Assembly. The last presidential elections were 10–11 Mar. 1988. The president rules with the assistance of an appointed cabinet. The legislature is the 500-member House of Representatives, with 400 members elected for a five-year term by direct universal adult suffrage (last legislative elections were in April 1987) and 100 appointed by the president. To form the People's Consultative Assembly, which is described in the Constitution as the embodiment of the whole Indonesian people, the 500 Representatives are joined by 500 government appointees, delegates of the regional assemblies and appointed representatives of parties and groups.

Present government

President Gen. (retd) Suharto

Vice-President Lt.-Gen. (retd) Sudharmono

Principal members of Cabinet Adml. (retd) Sudomo (Political Affairs and Security); Dr Radius Prawiro (Economy, Finance, Industry and Development Supervision); Gen. (retd) Supardjo Rustam (Public Welfare); Gen. Rudini (Internal Affairs); Ali Alatas (Foreign Affairs); Gen. L.B. (Benny) Murdani (Defence and Security); Lt.-Gen (retd) Ismail Saleh (Justice).

Leading members of the armed forces Gen. Try Sutrisno (Commander in Chief of the Indonesian Armed Forces and head of the Co-ordinating Agency for the Reinforcement of National Stability (Bakorstranas)); Lt.-Gen. Edi Sudrajat (Army Chief of Staff).

Justice

The system of civil and commercial law is based on Roman-Dutch and French codes, modified by indigenous concepts. Three different law systems are applicable to the three subdivisions of the country's population, Indonesians, Europeans and foreign Orientals, although all three groups are subject to the same code of criminal law and procedure. The highest court is the Supreme Court. The death penalty is in force. There were 19 executions between 1985 and mid-1988. The offences were murder, subversion, rebellion.

National symbols

Flag. A red-and-white flag.

Festivals. 17 Aug. (Indonesian National Day).

Vehicle registration plate. RI.

INTERNATIONAL RELATIONS

Affiliations

NAM; ASEAN; ICO; OPEC.

Defence

Total Armed Forces: 284,000. Terms of service: voluntary conscription, two years selective authorized. Reserves: 800,000.

Army: 215,000; some 100 light tanks (AMX-13, PT-76).

Navy: 43,000 inclusive 1,000 naval air and 12,000 marines; two submarines (FRG T-209/1300, FRG HWT, 15 frigates (Netherland Van Speijk, UK Ashanti, US Claud Jones) and 29 patrol and coastal combatants.

Naval Air: 1,000; 15 combat aircraft, nine armed helicopters.

Marines: 12,000; 30 light tanks (PT-76).

Air Force: 27,000; 70 combat aircraft (A-4, F-5, F-5E).

Para-military: some 115,000 inclusive Perintis ('special police' riot squads) and Police 'Mobile brigade'.

ECONOMY

Currency

The unit is the rupiah, divided into 100 sen.

National finance

Budget. The 1988 budget (in US$) was for expenditure (current and capital) of 13,900 million and revenue of 10,500 million. Main items of current expenditure are education 8.8%; defence 8.6%.

Balance of payments. The balance of payments (current account, 1987) was a deficit of $2098 million.

Inflation. (1987) 9.3%.

Gross Domestic Product

Estimated total GDP US$69,670 million, per capita US$880 (ranking 34 in the world by size).

Economically active population. The total number of persons active in the economy was 67,000,000; unemployed: 3%.

Sector	% of workforce	% of GDP
industry	14	33
agriculture	55	26
services*	31	41

* services figure includes elements unassigned to other categories.

Energy and mineral resources

Oil and gas. Indonesia is a major world producer of crude petroleum and a member of OPEC. Pertamina (the state oil company) produces only a fraction of total output; most petroleum is produced under work contracts with foreign oil companies or under production-sharing agreements with foreign joint ventures. Oil remains vital to the Indonesian economy, despite the government's successful pursuance of policies during the 1980s to increase non-petroleum revenue. In addition, natural gas reserves are well utilized; large amounts of gas are pumped to liquefaction plants and exported (as liquified natural gas–LNG) to Japan and South Korea. The output of crude oil is 68 million tons/ 62 million tonnes and natural gas (1988) 1,666,821 ft^3/ 47,200 million m^3.

Minerals. Other minerals mined in significant quantities include coal; tin; nickel; bauxite; iron ore; silver; gold.

Electricity. Capacity: 11,000,000 kW; production; 36,500 million kWh; 200 kWh per capita (1988).

Bioresources

Agriculture. Agriculture, including forestry and fishing, is the most important sector of the Indonesian economy, accounting for 25% of GDP and over 50% of the labour force. The staple crop is rice. Once the world's largest rice importer, Indonesia is now nearly self-sufficient.

Crop production: (1987 in million tons/tonnes) rice 30.26/27.45; copra and coconuts 2.2/2; rubber 1.26/ 1.13; palm-oil 1.55/1.41; cassava 15.96/14.48; cane sugar 2.35/2.13; coffee 0.394/0.357.

Livestock numbers: (1987) poultry 428 million; goats 12.9 million; cattle 6.5 million; pigs 6.2 million; sheep 5.3 million; buffaloes 2.9 million; horses 715,000.

Forestry. Indonesia has the largest forest resources in Asia, covering approximately 279 million acres/ 113 million ha. Production: sawn timber 261.3 million ft^3/7.4 million m^3; plywood 187.2 million ft^3/ 5.3 million m^3 (1986–7).

Fisheries. Large commercial enterprises (often foreign-owned) dominate the sea-fishing industry, which is primarily export-orientated. Inland fishing is largely for internal consumption. Annual catch of sea fish: 2.1 million tons/1.9 million tonnes; inland fish: 661,380 tons/600,000 tonnes (1986).

Industry and commerce

Industry. Production: (1987–88) textiles 3,504 yds^2/ 2,930 million m^2; steel 1.47 million tons/1.33 million tonnes; vehicle assembly 160,000; cement 13.6 million tons/12.3 million tonnes; cigarettes 133,000 million; plywood 229.5 million ft^3/6.5 million m^3. In addition there are four shipyards, paper, match, tyre and glass factories.

Commerce. Exports: (1988) US$16,500 million, mainly comprising gas and oil; timber; handicrafts; coffee; rubber; shrimps; tin; copper; pepper; palm-oil. Main export partners are: Japan 45%; US 20%; Singapore 8%; EC countries 13%. Imports: (1988) US$11,200 million, comprising machinery; chemical products; base metals; transport equipment; food; beverages; tobacco; textiles; paper; printed matter. Indonesia's main import partners are Japan 29%; US 14%; EC countries 13%; Singapore 9%; Saudi Arabia 6%.

Trade with UK. Indonesia imported UK goods worth £233,807,000; exports to UK totalled £203,275,000 (1988).

Tourism. 1,050,000 visitors (1987).

COMMUNICATIONS

Railways

There are 4,050 miles/6,521 km of railways, of which 68.3 miles/110 km are electrified.

Roads

There are 136,005 miles/219,009 km of roads (8,037 miles/12,942 km of main or national roads).

Aviation

PT Bouraq Indonesia and PT Merpati Nusantara provide domestic services; PT Garuda Indonesia provides international services (international airports are at Cengkareng (near Jakarta), Medan (North Sumatra), Denpasar (Bali), Surabaya (East Java), Manado (North Sulawesi), and Ujung Pandang (South Sulawesi). Passengers: (1985) 6.3 million.

Shipping

There are 13,401 miles/21,579 km of inland waterways. Sumatra has 3,398 miles/5,471 km, Java and Madura 509 miles/820 km. Kalimantan has 6,496 miles/10,460 km, Celebes 150 miles/241 km, and Irian Jaya 2,849 miles/4,587 km. Cilacap, Cirebon, Jakarta, Semarang and Surabaya are maritime ports on Java. Kupang is a martime port on Timor. Ujungpandang is a martime port on Celebes. Palembang is an inland port on Sumatra. The merchant marine consists of 323 ships of 1,000 GRT or over. Freight loaded: (1985) 101.2 million tons/ 91.8 million tonnes; unloaded: 69.9 million tons/63.4 million tonnes.

Telecommunications

There are 763,000 telephones. The domestic service with an inter-island microwave system is fair. The international service is good. There are about 33 million radios and 5 million television sets; the state-controlled radio RRI operates a network of some 50 stations, while external broadcasts are made in English and ten other languages by Voice of Indonesia. There is a state-run television service (TVRI) and one private TV channel (RCTI).

EDUCATION AND WELFARE

Education

In theory, education is compulsory up to the age of 12, but the implementation of this regulation faces numerous obstacles.

School population. 30,960,000 primary school pupils and 10,340,000 secondary school pupils (1988).

Universities. 1,440,000 students attending the country's 700 universities and technical institutes (1988). Approximately 640 universities and institutes are private.

Literacy. 62%.

Health

1,560 persons per hospital bed and 7,400 persons per doctor (1988).

IRAN

Jomhori-e-Islami-e-Iran
(Islamic Republic of Iran)

GEOGRAPHY

Located in south-west Asia, Iran covers an area of 646,128 miles²/1,648,000 km² divided into 24 provinces. Iran's physiography is dominated by the arid central plateau (average elevation 3,937 ft/ 1,200 m) most of which is barren salt desert, containing the Dasht-e-Lut (Great Sand Desert) and largely unexplored Dasht-e-Kavir (Great Salt Desert). The plateau is surrounded by mountain ranges: north by the volcanic Elburz range, climbing to 18,602 ft/5,670 m at Qolleh-Ye Damavand, east and south-east by the Khorasan and Baluchestan ranges and north-west–south-east along the Persian Gulf by the Zagros Mt chain. Lowland areas include the comparatively fertile Mesopotamia Plains on the Iraqi border, forming part of the Karun River basin, the narrow coastal strip fronting the Persian Gulf and Gulf of Oman and the low-lying marshes (–98 ft/ –30 m) of the Caspian shoreline. 8% of the land is arable and 11% is forested, most of which is concentrated in the Gilan and Mazandaran provinces bordering the Caspian Sea. Tehran is by far the most densely populated province supporting an estimated 18.2% of the total population.

Climate

Predominantly desert climate, becoming temperate in the north on the Caspian coast. Marked seasonal variation between hot summers and very cold winters. Most of the light annual rainfall (average below 11.8 in/300 mm, rising to 39.4 in/1,000 mm along the Caspian Sea) falls during the winter or spring months. Tehran: Jan. 36°F/2.2°C. July 85°F/29.4°C. Average annual rainfall 9.7 in/246 mm. Abadan: Jan. 54°F/ 12.2°C. July 97°F/36.1°C. Average annual rainfall 8 in/ 204 mm.

Cities and towns

Tehran (Teheran, capital)	6,022,029
Mashhad	1,500,000
Esfahan	1,000,000
Tabriz	852,296
Shiraz	800,416
Bakhtaran	531,350
Karaj	526,272

Population

Total population is 53,126,999 of which 51.4% live in urban areas. Population density is 82.2 persons per mile²/30.4 per km². Ethnic divisions: 63% ethnic Persian; 18% Turkic; 13% other Iranian; 3% Kurdish; 3% Arab and other Semitic. The indigenous Lurs inhabiting the Western mountains are related to the Bakhtyari tribes of the Zagros Mts and the Baluchs of Baluchestan.

Birth rate 4.19%. **Death rate** 0.97%. **Rate of population increase** (1980–87) 3.22%. **Age distribution** under 15 = 43.2%; over 65 = 3.3%. **Life expectancy** female 64; male 62; average 63.

Religion

Shi'a Islam is the official religion, also known as Ithna-shariyya, recognizing 12 Imams (spiritual successors of Mohammed). Of the total population, 93% are Shi'a Muslim, 5% Sunni Muslim, 2% Zoroastrian, Jewish, Christian or Baha'i.

Language

Iranian languages belong to the Indo-Iranian subgroup of the Indo-European language family. Farsi Persian is the official national language spoken by 45% of the population. 23% speak related languages such as Kurdish, Luri and Baluchi. 26% speak Turkic languages, including Afshari, Azerbaijani, Qashqa'i, Shahsavani and Turkish, and a further 2 million speak Semitic languages.

HISTORY

The history of Iran (known as Persia until 1935) dates from the 6th century BC. The Medes and the Persians were united in 533 BC by Cyrus the Great, leading to the founding of the first Persian empire. Cyrus and successive rulers of the Achaemenid dynasty ushered in a golden age of Persian civilization which extended to present-day Turkey, the eastern Mediterranean and Egypt. The Empire was overthrown in 331 BC by Alexander the Great and upon his death was divided among his generals. The Seleucid dynasty was in power until 247 BC, followed by the Parthian Empire of the Arsacids who ruled for 500 years. The last Empire of the Sassanids (AD 22–637), weakened by numerous conflicts with the Byzantine Empire, was defeated by Muslim Arabs in AD 637, dismembered and ruled from Damascus and later Baghdad by various Arab and Persian governors.

By the 16th century, with the rise of the Safavids under Ismail Safavi (r.1502–24), Persia re-emerged with the same general boundaries which exist today and Shi'ism was declared the state religion. The Safavids ruled until 1750 and after a short interregnum under Karim Khan Zand (r.1750–79), the

Qajar dynasty assumed and remained in power until 1926, when it was replaced by the recent Shah's father. The Qajar period was characterized by international power rivalry for commercial and strategic advantage, with the imperial ambitions of Britain and Russia met through favourable territorial and economic concessions which profoundly compromised the Qajar dynasty. The trading agreements with regard to the exploitation of mineral resources occasioned domestic demands for reform and these were met with the introduction of a Constituent National Assembly (Majlis) in 1906. This move was repudiated in 1907 as a result of an Anglo-Russian agreement which effectively divided the country into three zones of influence: Russian in the north, British in the south and a neutral buffer zone. A coup ensued, part of an unsuccessful effort to limit foreign interference. This was followed by a period of political turbulence which was cast against the background of Britain acquiring a controlling interest in the Anglo-Persian Oil Co. (APOC) in 1914. World War I witnessed the interference of Britain, Russia and Germany in Persian internal affairs to the effect that by 1918 the country was in chaos. In 1920 a short-lived autonomous Soviet Republic of Gilan was established in the north. This situation was brought to an end by Col. Reza Khan, Commander of the Cossack Brigade, in a coup on 20 Feb. 1921. In 1923 he became prime minister and in 1926 was crowned Reza Shah Pahlavi.

His rule was significant in that he attempted to modernize the country through the secularization of the legal system, educational reforms, the expansion of the army and the institution of a national civil service. However, he alienated the clergy and during the 1930s became more reliant on Germany as a source of machinery and advice for his modernization programme. He even changed the Hellenistic name of Persia to Iran (meaning Aryan) in 1935 in an effort to curry favour with the Nazis. It was this suspected affinity with Germany, coupled with his hesitation in expelling German expatriates which led to Britain and Russia invading in 1941 and his abdication in favour of his son, Mohammed Reza. In the early post-war years the young Shah encountered difficulties particularly with regard to the nationalization of the Anglo-Iranian Oil Co. (AIOC) which had been approved by the Majlis with the enthusiastic support of Prime Minister Mohammed Mossadeq, leader of the National Front. With the British instituting a boycott of Iranian oil and the consequent loss of oil revenues, a schism developed between the Shah and Mossadeq and a power struggle ensued. Aided by Britain and the US the Shah replaced Mossadeq in 1953 with Gen. Fazlollah Zahedi. In 1954 an agreement was devised in Washington and London for Iran to pay compensation to AIOC (renamed British Petroleum) and a consortium of seven oil companies was created to run former AIOC operations. As a consequence, Iran remained closely tied to the US and the West.

With Iran receiving a 50% share in the oil consortium the economy improved and the Shah, in 1963, launched a programme of land reform and social and economic modernization known as the 'White Revolution'. The period was marked with some success as party politics functioned and elections were held in 1967, 1971 and 1975. Amir Abbas Hovieda, a supporter of the Shah's reform plan, was elected prime minister in 1965 and remained in office for ten years. Opposition to the increasing Westernization and secularization of Iranian society was articulated by Islamic clergy, notably Ayatollah Khomeini, exiled to Turkey and then Iraq after 1964. The Shah became reliant on SAVAK, a secret police force established in 1957, to exert control over the opposition, who included the Marxist-Leninist Tudeh Party and the National Front. The death of Khomeini's son in Oct. 1977 and the consequent mourning processions led to demonstrations against the Shah and the death of a number of people. Riots and strikes ensued throughout 1978 and Khomeini's expulsion from Iraq to France in Oct. 1978 highlighted his role as opposition leader and ensured ample media coverage. The rising wave of popular discontent with the Shah ultimately led to his flight from Iran on 16 Jan. 1979. The remaining government headed by Dr Shapour Bakhtiar, a member of the main secular organization, the National Front, and critic of the Shah, aimed for a compromise with Khomeini. But following the tumultuous reception given to Khomeini on his return to Iran, the Bakhtiar government fell on 11 Feb. 1979, after which the alliance between the secular and religious movements split.

Khomeini further consolidated his power by launching an 'Islamic Cultural Revolution'. When Revolutionary Guards stormed the American embassy, taking the staff as hostages (4 Nov. 1979), Khomeini ordered that women and black staff be released (17 Nov.), but ultimately backed the militants in his regime's growing confrontation with the United States. The fiasco of a US military attempt to rescue the remaining 53 hostages (25 Apr. 1980) further humiliated the US administration, and the eventual release (21 Jan. 1981) came too late to save the Carter presidency. Abolhassan Bani Sadr was elected as the Islamic Republic's first president on 25 Jan. 1980, following a referendum on 2–3 Dec. 1979 which provided for a nationally-elected president and a unicameral parliament. A Council of Guardians composed of clerics and judges would ensure the maintenance of Islamic law. Between March and June 1980, the government nationalized two leading newspapers, *Kayhan* and *Ettelaat*; banks; insurance companies and most medium/large scale industrial enterprises. On 22 Sept. 1980 Iraq invaded Iran. This provided a pretext for the demise of Bani Sadr who, as commander-in-chief, was in an invidious position. He had repeatedly clashed with the growing radicalism of the clerical leadership. In June 1981 impeachment proceedings on the grounds of incompetence were instituted against him in the Majlis and Khomeini formally ordered his dismissal.

The Iran/Iraq war was caused by a long-standing dispute over the Shatt al-Arab waterway, but quickly escalated into a contention over territorial rights with Iraq claiming the Iranian province of Khuzistan (which it referred to as 'Arabistan'), in the south-west of the country. Iraqi forces made rapid gains in the first months of the war, but failed to achieve outright victory. After a period of stalemate, Iran launched the first of a series of counter-attacks in Mar. 1982, recapturing the city of Khorramshahr. Over the next six years, Iraq was on the defensive, resorting at times to chemical weapons in an effort to stem successive Iranian attacks, which on occasion succeeded in overwhelming Iraqi positions through the use of massed 'human-wave' infantry assaults. Iran rejected all peace initiatives, demanding the overthrow of the Iraqi president, Saddam Hussein, as the first condition for a truce. Its forces failed to achieve a decisive breakthrough, however, and by early 1988 Iran was suffering from a severe shortage of arms and ammunition, largely due to its status as an international pariah, with both the US and Soviet Union seeking to cut it off from war supplies. (Meanwhile, however, US covert attempts were mounted to win Iranian support for the release of hostages kidnapped by radical Shiites in Lebanon, by the expedient of offering secret arms deals, from mid-1985; what became known as the Iran-contra affair was not uncovered until Nov. 1986.) A flurry of Iraqi victories left Iran with no alternative but to sue for peace in July 1988 on the basis of a UN resolution passed the previous year.

Internally, Bani-Sadr was succeeded (July 1981) by Mohammed Ali Radjai, a long-time supporter of Khomeini and key figure in the ruling Islamic Republic Party. The following month, however, Radjai and his prime minister, Bahonar, were the victims of the most spectacular of a wave of bomb attacks mounted by the Mujaheddin-e Khalq, an opposition group which had initially supported Khomeini, but had fallen out with him over the extent of fundamentalist control of the government. The Mujaheddin's challenge was eventually beaten off in 1982, while the remaining focus of opposition, the Communist Tudeh Party, was banned in 1983.

Political control remained in the hands of the radicals under Pres. Seyed Ali Khamenei and Prime Minister Hossein Moussavi. From the mid-1980s onwards, however, the leadership was marked by divisions, with more 'moderate' figures, notably Hashemi Rafsanjani, coming to the fore. After Khomeini's death in June 1989, Rafsanjani emerged as the pre-eminent leader. He was elected president in July, and as head of a 20-member Expediency Council in October, while Khomeini's title of wilayat-e faqih or wali faqih (spiritual leader) passed to the former president, Ali Khamenei.

CONSTITUTION AND GOVERNMENT

Executive and legislature

Overall authority is exercised by the wali faqih, the country's spiritual leader. The president is elected by universal adult suffrage for a four-year term; last election 28 July 1989. The President appoints the ministers, subject to the role of the legislature, which approves or rejects ministerial appointments. The legislature, the 270-seat Majlis (Islamic Consultative Assembly), is elected by universal adult suffrage every four years; last elections Apr.-May 1988. A 12-member Council of Guardians ensures that all legislation conforms with the Islamic constitution and has the power to veto candidates to high elected office on the same grounds. A 20-member Expediency Council, appointed by the country's spiritual leader, adjudicates on points of contention between the Majlis and the Council of Guardians.

Present government

Spiritual leader (wali faqih); C.-in-C. of the Armed Forces Ayatollah Seyed Ali Khamenei

President Hojatolislam Hashemi Ali Akbar Rafsanjani

Presidential Advisor on Domestic and Foreign Policy Hossain Moussavi

Vice-Presidents Hassan Ebrahim Habibi; Seyed Ataollah Mohajerani (in charge of Legal and Parliamentary Affairs); Massoud Roghani Zanjani (Head of Plan and Budget Organization); Reza Amrollahi (Head of Atomic Energy Organization of Iran); Mansour Razavi (Head of Organization for State Employment and Administrative Affairs); Mehdi Manafi (Head of Environment Protection Organization); Hassan Ghafurifard (Head of Physical Education Organization).

Speaker of the Majlis Ayatollah Mehdi Karrubi

Principal members of Council of Ministers Dr Ali Akbar Vellayati (Foreign Affairs); Gholamreza Agazadeh (Oil); Abdollah Nouri (Interior; Chairman of State Security Council); Mohsen Nourbakhsh (Economic Affairs and Finance); Gholamreza Foruzesh (Jihad ['crusade'] for Reconstruction); Hojatolislam Ismail Shostari (Justice); Akbar Torkan (Defence and Armed Forces Logistics); Hojatolislam Ali Fallahiyan (Intelligence and Security).

Justice

The system of law is Islamic in origin and structured according to the 1979 constitution, which places at its head the spiritual leader or wali faqih, in turn responsible for appointing the President of the Supreme Court and the public Prosecutor-General. The Supreme Court has 16 branches and 109 offences carry the death penalty. The death penalty is in force. There were over 743 executions between 1985 and mid-1988, for offences ranging from murder, political violence, and adultery, to being at enmity with God.

National symbols

Flag. Three horizontal stripes of green, white and red. The Iranian coat of arms in red is carried in the centre of the white stripe.

Festivals. 11 Feb. (National Day/Fall of the Shah); 20 Mar. (Oil Nationalization Day); 1 Apr. (Islamic Republic Day); 2 Apr. (Revolution Day).

Vehicle registration plate. IR.

INTERNATIONAL RELATIONS

Affiliations

NAM; OPEC; ICO.

Defence

Total Armed Forces: 604,500. Terms of service: 24–30 months. Reserves: 350,000.

Army: 305,000; perhaps 1,000 main battle tanks (T-54/-55, CH T-59, T-62, M-60A1), 40 light tanks (Scorpion).

Revolutionary Guard Corps (Pasdaran Inqilab): 250,000.

Navy: 14,500; eight principal surface combatants: three destroyers (UK Battle, US Sumner), five frigates (UK Vosper Mk5 and two US PF-103) and 34 patrol and coastal combatants.

Air Force: 35,000; some 50 serviceable combat aircraft (F-4D/E, F-5E/F, F-14).

ECONOMY

Currency

The unit is the rial, divided into 100 dinars: 10 rials = 1 toman.

National finance

Budget. The 1988 budget (in US$) was for expenditure (current and capital) of 55,100 million. Main items of current expenditure are education 19.6%; housing and welfare 17.4%; defence 14.2%.

Inflation. (1988) 30%.

Gross Domestic Product

Estimated total GNP US$93,500 million, per capita US$1,800 (ranking 25 in the world).

Economically active population. The total number of persons active in the economy was 15,400,000; unemployed: 30%. One third of the population works in agriculture.

Energy and mineral resources

Oil and gas. All operating companies were nationalized in 1979 and operations are now run by the National Petrochemical Company. Production was seriously disrupted by the 1979 revolution and important refineries and terminals were put out of action during the Gulf war with Iraq. Crude oil output: (1988) 125 million tons/113 million tonnes. Iran has the second largest reserves of natural gas in the world, production: (1983) 987,409 million ft^3/27,944 m^3.

Minerals. Iran has substantial but relatively undeveloped mineral deposits. Output: (1985 in 1,000 tons/tonnes) iron ore 2,314/2,099; coal 743/674; zinc and lead 62/56; manganese 51/46; chromite 62/56.

Electricity. Capacity: 14,151,000 kW; production: 43,383 million kWh; 840 kWh per capita (1988).

Bioresources

Agriculture. Cultivable land area totals 36.8 million acres/14.9 million ha, of which 14.1 million acres/5.7 million ha are irrigated (1982).

Crop production: (1986 in 1,000 tons/tonnes) wheat 7,857/7,128; barley 2,756/2,500; rice 1,730/1,569; sugar beet 5,181/4,700; sugar cane 1,213/1,100; tobacco 24/22.

Livestock numbers: (1987) sheep 34.5 million; goats 13.6 million; cattle 8.35 million; horses 316,000; camels 27,000; buffaloes 230,000. Wool production: (1972) 22,046 tons/20,000 tonnes.

Forestry. Iran has a forest area of 31.4 million acres/12.7 million ha (1982).

Fisheries. The Caspian Fisheries Company (Shilát) is a government monopoly. Fish catch in the north: (Caspian, in tons/tonnes) non-caviar fish 4,834/4,385; caviar 272/247; clupeonella deliculata 1,830/1,660 (1984–5). In the south: (in tons/tonnes) output of canned fish 6,830/6,196; non-canned fish 18,135/16,452; shrimp 1,073/973.

Industry and commerce

Industry. Main industries are petroleum refining; petrochemicals; textiles; cement; food processing (particularly sugar refining and vegetable oil production); automobile manufacture.

Commerce. Exports: US$9,400 million, of which 90% was petroleum and most of remainder carpets; hides; fruits; nuts. Imports: US$11,000 million (1988), mainly machinery; military supplies; foodstuffs; pharmaceuticals.

Trade with UK. Iran imported UK goods worth £248 million and exported to the UK goods worth £140 million (1988).

COMMUNICATIONS

Railways

There are 2,836 miles/4,567 km of railways.

Roads

There are 84,687 miles/136,372 km of roads, of which 24,881 miles/40,066 km are concrete or bituminized.

Aviation

Iran Air (Airline of the Islamic Republic of Iran) provides international services and Iran Asseman Airlines provides domestic services (main airports are at Tehran and Abadan). Passengers((1984) 4.1 million.

Shipping

There are 561 miles/904 km of inland waterways. Approximately 81 miles/130 km of the Shatt al Arab is usually navigable by maritime traffic, but it has been closed since Sept. 1980 because of the Iran-Iraq war. The inland ports of Abadan and Khorramshahr were largely destroyed in fighting during the 1980–88 war. The ports on the Persian Gulf are Bandar-e Abbas, Bandar-e Khomeyni and Bushehr. Chah Bahar is further along the coast in the Gulf of Oman. The port of Bandar-e Shahid Raja'i is on the Caspian Sea. The merchant marine has 133 ships of 1,000 GRT or over. Freight loaded: (1985) 86.8 million tons/78.7 million tonnes; unloaded: 13.4 million tons/12.2 million tonnes.

Telecommunications

The radio relay system centred in Tehran extends throughout the country. There are 2.14 million telephones, over 10 million radios and 2 million television sets. Of the three state-run national radio stations, one is devoted to readings from the Koran and other religious material; the state television system provides two national channels (including colour programming) and also caters for local TV channels.

EDUCATION AND WELFARE

Education

The great majority of primary and secondary schools are state schools.

School population. Total number of pupils in elementary, orientation and general secondary schools is 3,556,776 (1984).

Universities. Universities and other institutes of higher education had 145,809 students in 1984.

Literacy. 48% (1988). A literacy movement was established in 1981 and by 1985 3 million citizens had participated.

Health

There were 589 hospitals with 70,152 beds in 1984 (one per 770 people) and 15,945 doctors in 1982 (one per 3,125 people).

IRAQ

Al-Jumhouriya al'Iraqia (Republic of Iraq)

GEOGRAPHY

Located north-west of the Persian/Arabian Gulf in south-west Asia, Iraq covers a total area of 167,881 miles²/434,924 km² divided into 18 governorates. The predominantly low-lying terrain (average elevation 984 ft/300 m) is interrupted in the north-east by a mountainous ridge on the Turkish/Iranian border rising to 11,811 ft/3,600 m at Rawanoiz (Kuhe Haji Ebrahim). Much of the rest of the country falls into two broad physiographic categories: the lowland desert (highest point 328 ft/100 m) sloping towards the head of the Arabian Gulf (37–40% of the total surface area) and the Tigris-Euphrates Basin (north-west–south-east), formerly known as Mesopotamia. North of Baghdad the courses of the two rivers are divided by the plain of Al Jazirah; south and south-east the gentle incline of the two channels promotes dense swampland vegetation. 118 miles/190 km before emptying into the Arabian Gulf, the two rivers merge to form the navigable Shatt Al'Arab. The bulk of Iraqi agricultural activity (much of it irrigated) takes place in the alluvial Tigris-Euphrates plain, although high soil salinity reduces the cultivable potential of much of the land. Over 25% of the population live within the Governorate of Baghdad. 12% of the land is arable and 3% is forested.

Climate

Mostly arid with light to negligible rainfall, wide annual temperature range, hot summers and cold winters. The humid Tigris-Euphrates basin receives approx. 15.7 in/400 mm of rainfall annually compared with 39.4 in/1,000 mm in the north-eastern highlands and less than 3.94 in/100 mm over the south-western desert region. Basra: Jan. 55°F/12.8°C. July 92°F/33.3°C. Average annual rainfall 6.9 in/175 mm. Baghdad: Jan. 50°F/10°C. July 95°F/35°C. Average annual rainfall 5.5 in/140 mm. Mosul: Jan. 44°F/6.7°C. July 90°F/32.2°C. Average annual rainfall 15.1 in/384 mm.

Cities and towns

Baghdad (capital)	3,236,000
Basra	1,540,000
Mosul	1,220,000
Kirkuk	535,000

Population

Total population is 17,656,000 of which 70.6% live in urban areas. Population density is 105.2 persons per mile²/37.7 per km². Ethnic groupings comprise 79% Arabs; 16% Kurd (in the north-east); 3% Persian; 2% Turkish.

Birth rate 4.44%. **Death rate** 0.87%. **Rate of population increase** (1980–87) 3.57%. **Age distribution** under 15 = 46.9%; over 65 = 2.7%. **Life expectancy** female 65; male 63; average 64.

Religion

Islam is the official religion. 60–65% of the population are Shi'a; 32–37% Sunni Muslim. About 3% are Christians, of which a substantial proportion are Catholic (Latin, Armenian, Chaldean and Syrian rites) and 35,000 Syrian or Armenian orthodox. There are an estimated 2,500 Jews, 30,000 Yazidis and 20,000 Sabeans in Iraq.

Language

Arabic is the official language spoken by up to 80% of the population. Kurdish predominates in Kurdish regions. About 140,000 inhabitants speak Assyrian; 140,000 Persian; 60,000 Turkish; 220,000 Turkmen. English is also widely spoken.

HISTORY

The Sumerians of the 1st millennium BC are the first well understood peoples of what is modern Iraq. Many dynasties followed. In the 7th century BC the Persians seized Babylon, and Iraq became part of Persia's Achaemenid empire until it was conquered by Alexander the Great in 334–327 BC. In the two centuries before and after Christ, Partha and Rome fought over Iraq until, in the 2nd century AD, it was absorbed by the Persian Sassanian Empire.

In AD 637 Muslim armies from Arabia defeated the Sassanians and Iraq became Muslim. In 750 the Umayyad dynasty centred on Damascus was broken up by the Abbasids who promptly moved their capital to Baghdad, the modern Iraqi capital. The early Abbasids were Shias, followers of Ali, the fourth Caliph and the son-in-law of the Prophet Muhammad. The Abbasids were themselves all but destroyed by the Mongol hordes in the 13th century. After periods of Turcoman, then Persian Safavid rule, Iraq was absorbed by the Ottoman Sultan Sulayman (1534). It was to remain part of the Ottoman Empire until the end of World War I.

The 19th century saw the region come increasingly under European influence. The British, who had maintained a consulate at Baghdad since 1802, wielded considerable influence. Reforms were also initiated by the Ottomans; newspapers appeared and hospitals and factories were built. In World War I the Ottoman Sultan sided with the Germans and the British quickly occupied the Shatt al-Arab waterway and turned Basra into a modern port. In Mar. 1917 the British took Baghdad. Under British control and encouraged by British promises of independence, a nationalist movement blossomed but was to be bitterly disappointed when the San Remo Conference of Apr. 1920 made Iraq a British Mandate with virtual colonial status. However, the creation of an Arab Council of State at the end of the year helped soothe nationalist passions. On 23 Aug. 1921 the Amir Faisal ibn Husayn (the son the of the Sharif Hussain of Mecca) formally acceded to the Iraqi throne.

Despite nationalist opposition, an Anglo-Iraqi Treaty was signed on 10 Oct. 1922. In 1930 a new treaty was signed, involving an Anglo-Iraqi alliance for 25 years and granting the British the use of two Iraqi air bases. On 3 Oct. 1932 the mandate was terminated and Iraq entered the League of Nations as a nominally independent state.

Oil was discovered in 1923 near the Iranian border although Iraq's main oilfields are in the area of Kirkuk, where the first major discoveries were made in 1927. Concessions were granted to the Iraq, Mosul and Basra Petroleum Companies and by 1934 the Iraq Petroleum Company was exporting oil via Tripoli in Lebanon and Haifa in Palestine. Other small fields were discovered in the 1950s.

Relations with Britain deteriorated in the years leading up to World War II because of what the Iraqis saw as Britain's pro-Zionist policies in Palestine. German influence increased and was to be represented by an Iraqi officer group called the Golden Square. Although Iraq broke relations with the Axis powers on the outbreak of war, an officer coup in 1941 led to overt pro-German sentiments. Threatened by these, Britain occupied Basra and Baghdad (May 1941). From then on Iraq cooperated with the Allies and declared war on the Axis powers in 1943. Iraq was effectively occupied by Britain until the end of the war.

By 1958 an educated elite existed that made Iraq ripe for revolution. The corrupt group that ruled from 1945, headed by the pro-British Prime Minister Nuri as-Said, was to be swept away with the monarchy in July. The royal family and Nuri were killed. The new government was headed by the Free Officers under Brig. Abd al-Karim al-Qasim. However, major political differences emerged, with the nationalists supporting union with Nasser's United Arab Republic (comprising Egypt and Syria), and the Communists opposing this. Qasim himself differed ideologically from the Communists, but did not wish to defer to Nasser. Increasing violence led to a coup in Feb. 1963 in which nationalists and Baathists (representing an ideology committed to Arab unity) seized power and unleashed a reign of terror against the Left. The next, confused five years saw a bitter war with the Kurds of the north.

On 17 July 1968 Baathist officers led by Ahmed Hasan al-Bakr carried out another successful coup. Embittered by the humiliation of the Arabs' 1967 defeat and by American support for the victorious Israelis, the new regime turned to the Soviet Union. In Mar. 1970 the Kurds were offered an element of autonomy. In 1971 the new regime issued its National Action Charter with a socialist programme and in June the following year it nationalized the Iraq Petroleum Company. By the end of 1974 a major conflict broke out with the Kurds, now united under Mustafa Barzani. However at the 1975 Algiers agreement the Shah of Iran agreed to withdraw his support for the Kurds and Kurdish resistance declined.

From the 1970s, opposition also arose among sections of the Shia community, who form 60% of the population but enjoy little power. This increased as the moment of the Iranian revolution approached. Until 1978 the Ayatollah Khomeini had lived in exile in the Iraqi holy city of Najaf. However, the government responded ruthlessly to all dissent and the war with Shia Iran which followed the revolution immediately associated Shia dissent in Iraq with treason. On 16 July 1979 Bakr had resigned and was succeeded as president by Saddam Hussain Takriti. A coup attempted against Saddam ten days later was ruthlessly crushed and its leaders executed.

Saddam was tempted to attack Iran at a time when the recently purged Iranian army was at its weakest. Moreover, he claimed to be responding to Iran's avowed goal of exporting its Islamic revolution. However, what was intended as a quick victory became a devastating eight-year war in which about one million were killed or wounded on both sides. For much of the war Iraq was on the defensive but by 1988 it had regained the offensive and the previously heroic Iranian morale had sagged. On 18 July 1988, Iran, with bitter reluctance, accepted UN resolution 598 and on 20 Aug. a cease-fire came into effect. Negotiations leading to a permanent peace commenced, but were making only tortuous headway by early 1990.

CONSTITUTION AND GOVERNMENT

Executive and legislature

The president is head of state with executive power, and appoints the council of ministers. The Revolutionary Command Council (RCC) elects the president by a two-thirds majority from among its own members. Legislative authority is shared between the RCC and the 250-member National Assembly, which is elected every four years by universal adult suffrage under a system of proportional representation; last elections Apr. 1989. Real political power is exercised through the 17-member Regional Command of the ruling party, the Arab Baath Socialist Party, which together with the state-sponsored National Progressive Patriotic Front controls all the Assembly seats.

Present government

President; Prime Minister; Chairman of the Revolutionary Command Council Saddam Hussein

Vice-President Taha Mohieddin Maarouf

Members of the Revolutionary Command Council Izzat Ibrahim (Vice-Chairman); Khaled Abdel-Moneim Rasheed (Secretary-General); Taha Yasin Ramadhan; Sa'adoun Shaker; Tariq Aziz; Hassan Ali-Nassar al-Amiri; Sa'adoun Hammadi; Taha Mohieddin Maarouf.

Principal members of Council of Ministers Taha Yasin Ramadhan (First Deputy Prime Minister); Tariq Aziz (Deputy Prime Minister; Foreign Affairs); Sa'adoun Hammadi (Deputy Prime Minister); Gen. Abdel-Jabbar Khalil Shanshal (Defence); Samir Muhammad Abdul Wahhab (Interior); Akram Abdel-Qader Ali (Justice); Issam Abdel Rahim al Chalabi (Oil); Mohammad Mehdi Saleh (Trade; Finance [acting]).

Ruling party

Arab Baath Socialist Party. *Secretary-General of Regional Command* Saddam Hussein. *Deputy Secretary-General of Regional Command* Izzat Ibrahim.

Justice

The court of cassation at Baghdad, the courts of appeal and first instance (18 with unlimited and 150 with limited powers) deal with civil and criminal matters while the Shara' courts deal with religious matters. The death penalty is in force. Hundreds of executions reported every year between 1985 and mid-1988. Offences were burglary, theft, murder, desertion from the army and forgery of official documents.

National symbols

Flag. Three horizontal stripes coloured red, white and black; the white stripe contains three green five-pointed stars.

Festivals. 6 Jan. (Army Day); 8 Feb. (Ramadan Revolution, anniversary of the 1963 coup); 14 July (Republic Day, anniversary of the 1968 coup).

Vehicle registration plate. SRQ.

INTERNATIONAL RELATIONS

Affiliations

NAM; Arab League; OPEC; ICO; ACC.

Defence

Total Armed Forces: 1,000,000. Terms of service: basic 21–24 months, extended for war. Reserves: 650,000 (People's Army).

Army: 955,000; some 4,500 main battle tanks (T-54/-55/-62/-72, T-59/-69, Chieftain Mk3/5, M-60/-47/-77), 100 light tanks (PT-76).

Navy: 5,000; five frigates (It Lupo), 38 patrol and coastal combatants.

Air Force: 40,000; some 500 combat aircraft (MiG-23BN/-25/-21/-29, Mirage F-1EQ5/EQ5–200, Mirage F-1BQ).

ECONOMY

Currency

The unit is the dinar, divided into 1,000 fils.

National finance

Budget. The 1987 budget (in US$) was for expenditure (current and capital) of 18,600 million and revenue of 20,000 million.

Inflation. (1988) 25–30%.

Gross Domestic Product

Estimated total GNP US$34,000 million, per capita US$1,950 (ranking 48 in the world by size).

Economically active population. The total number of persons active in the economy was 3,500,000; unemployed: 5%.

Sector	% of workforce
industry	28
agriculture	33
services*	39

* services figure includes elements unassigned to other categories.

COMMUNICATIONS

Railways

There are 1,260 miles/2,029 km of railways.

Roads

There are 20,640 miles/33,238 km of roads, of which 14,825 miles/23,872 km are concrete or bituminized.

Aviation

Iraqi Airways Co. provides international services (international airports are at Baghdad, Bamerni and Basra). Passengers: (1984) 435,000.

Shipping

There are 630 miles/1,015 km of inland waterways. The Shatt al Basrah, Tigris and Euphrates are navigable only by shallow-draft vessels. The Shatt al Arab was navigable by maritime traffic for about 81 miles/130 km, but was closed in 1980 because of the Iran-Iraq war. The port of Al Faw on the Persian Gulf was largely destroyed during the 1980–88 war. Other inland ports are Al Basrah, Umm Qasr, and Khawr az Zubayr. The merchant marine has 43 ships of 1,000 GRT or over.

Telecommunications

There are 632,000 telephones and a good telecommunications network. There are estimated to be at least 2.2 million radios and 600,000 television sets There are two state-run TV channels, a state-run national radio broadcasting system, with an external service in seven languages, and also local channels.

Energy and mineral resources

Oil and gas. Iraq's economy is dominated by the oil sector, which provides about 95% of foreign exchange earnings. The Gulf War caused considerable damage to Iraqi oil facilities; at the time of the July 1988 cease-fire, Iraq was totally reliant on the pipeline from Kirkuk to the Mediterranean through Turkey. The oil sector is nationalized and is administered by the Iraqi National Oil Company (INOC). Production: (1988) crude petroleum 141 million tons/128 million tonnes; natural gas 1,766 million ft^3/50 million m^3.

Minerals. There are deposits of iron ore; chromite; copper; lead; zinc; limestone; gypsum; salt; dolomite; phosphates; sulphur.

Electricity. Capacity: 8,692,000 kW; production: 22,839 million kWh; 1,300 kWh per capita (1988).

Bioresources

Agriculture. Although the agricultural sector was privatized in 1987, development remains hampered by labour shortages, salinization, and dislocation caused by previous land-reform and collectivization programmes. Iraq's annual date crop (1,102 tons/100,000 tonnes) provides approximately 80% of the world demand for dates. Other crops include wheat and barley (winter) and rice (summer).

Livestock numbers: (1987) chickens 75 million; sheep 8.7 million; cattle 1.5 million; goats 1.4 million; buffaloes 140,000; camels 55,000; horses 55,000.

Industry and commerce

Industry. Iraq's industrial sector is under-developed, despite being accorded high priority by the government. New investment funds are generally allocated to projects which rely heavily on local raw materials and result either in import substitution or foreign exchange earnings. The main industries, apart from petroleum, are textiles; construction materials; food processing.

Commerce. Exports: (1988) US$12,400 million, principally crude oil and refined products. Countries exported to were Brazil; Italy; Turkey; France; Japan; Spain; USSR; Yugoslavia; USA. Imports: (1988) US$13,000 million, including food; manufactures; consumer goods. Main import partners are Turkey; USA; West Germany; UK; France; Japan; USSR; Italy.

Trade with UK. In 1988 Iraq imported UK goods worth £43,406,000; exports to UK totalled $412,091,000.

Tourism. Over 1 million tourists visited Iraq (1986).

EDUCATION AND WELFARE

Education

Education is compulsory for children aged 6–12 and free between the ages of six and 18.

School population. 2.6 million primary school pupils; 1 million secondary school pupils; 82,000 vocational school students (1981).

Schools. 10,800 primary schools; 1,600 secondary schools; 160 vocational schools (1981).

Universities. There are six universities; 15 other higher-education establishments; over 60 teacher-training colleges.

Literacy. 55% (est.).

Health

Iraq has over 220 hospital establishments; an estimated 32,000 hospital beds; over 6,000 doctors (1986).

IRELAND
Eire
(Republic of Ireland)

GEOGRAPHY

Located in the Atlantic Ocean, 50 miles/80 km west of Great Britain, the Republic of Ireland occupies the south, central and north-west regions of the island, covering a total surface area of 27,129 miles^2/70,282 km^2 divided into 20 counties. The predominantly low-lying (197–394 ft/60–120 m) limestone landscape is punctuated by lakes, undulating hills, valleys, peat bogs and enclosed by a mountainous coastal belt. On the west coast, the highland spurs of Donegal, Mayo, Connaught and Kerry jut out into the Atlantic, giving a deeply incised coastal profile. Errigal in County Donegal rises to 2,467 ft/752 m, Croagh Patrick in Mayo to 2,510 ft/765 m, Mureelrea to 2,687 ft/819 m and in the south-west, Carrauntoohil to 3,415 ft/1041 m, Ireland's highest peak. The River Shannon drains the central plain from Sligo Bay to Limerick, feeding a number of lakes from Lough Ailen to Lough Derg. Under 15% of the total surface area is arable land (though very fertile) and 5% or less is forested. Rural-urban migration, particularly from the poorer west coast regions inland east of the Shannon, is a continuing demographic trend.

Climate

Uniformly mild and equable, due to the Gulf Stream influence. Rainfall is highest along the west coast, reaching 118 in/3,000 mm in Mayo, Kerry and Donegal, decreasing to approximately 30.7 in/780 mm in Dublin. Mean annual temperature range is a moderate 54°F/12°C, the coldest months of the year (Jan.-Feb.) averaging 39–45°F/4–7°C and the warmest (July-Aug.) 57–61°F/14–16°C. Dublin: Jan. 41°F/5°C, July 59°F/15°C. Average annual rainfall 29.5 in/750 mm. Cork: Jan. 43°F/6.1°C, July 60°F/15.6°C. Average annual rainfall 40.4 in/1,025 mm.

Cities and towns

Dublin (capital)	920,956
Cork	173,694
Limerick	76,557
Galway	47,104
Waterford	41,054

Population

Total population is 3,650,000 of which 57% live in urban areas. Population density is 134.5 persons per mile^2/51.7 persons per km^2. The population is predominantly Celtic in origin (94%) with a small English minority.

Birth rate 1.97%. **Death rate** 0.94%. **Rate of population increase** 1.03%. **Age distribution** under 15 = 29.7%; over 65 = 10.6%. **Life expectancy** female 76; male 71; average 74.

Religion

The majority of the population (an estimated 94–95%) are Roman Catholic. At the last census, 2.8% belonged to the Anglican Church of Ireland and 0.4% were Presbyterian. There were also small Methodist, Lutheran, Baptist, Baha'i and Jewish minorities.

Language

Erse, Gaelic, Gaeille. Constitutionally, Irish is the first official language, English the second. Irish Gaelic, spoken primarily in the Gaeltacht (the Gaelic-speaking Western districts of Ireland), is related to Scots Gaelic. The Latin alphabet was introduced some time after the 5th century AD.

HISTORY

Gaelic-speaking Celts conquered Ireland in about 300 BC and developed a culture which flowered into artistic and literary brilliance after the introduction of Christianity, traditionally by St Patrick in 432. According to Celtic tradition, five main kingdoms (Ulster, Leinster, Meath, Connaught and Munster) owed allegiance to a high king at Tara, until the collapse of the central monarchy in 563. From the late 8th century Viking raiders encroached on the disunited Irish kingdoms, settling the coastal areas, reputedly founding Dublin (840) and developing trade. In c.1000 Brian Boru united most of the Irish and effectively ended Norse power at Clontarf (1014), but his death after the battle led to renewed disunity. After Adrian IV (the only Englishman ever to become Pope) had authorized Henry II of England to subjugate Ireland for the Church of Rome, from 1167 Anglo-Norman adventurers rapidly extended their feudal rule westward from Dublin. Their descendants embraced Irish ways to such an extent that the Statutes of Kilkenny (1366) forbade intermarriage between English and Irish and also outlawed the Irish language. Thereafter, purely English overlordship was secure only within the 'Pale', an area reaching inland from Dublin for about 50 miles, beyond which assimilated Anglo-Irish barons (including most notably the Earl of Kildare who served as Lord Deputy of Ireland under Henry VII) and hostile Irish tribes held sway.

After Poynings' Law (1494) had decreed that no Irish parliament could initiate legislation without the King of England's consent and that English laws would also apply in Ireland, Henry VIII broke the power of the Irish feudal lords and adopted the title King of Ireland (1541). Efforts to impose Protestantism under Elizabeth I were resisted by the Irish, who staged several unsuccessful rebellions and gave support to England's Catholic enemies abroad. Under James I's policy of granting confiscated Irish lands to Protestant settlers, over 100,000 Scottish Presbyterians established the Ulster 'plantation' in the north-east (from 1607). The English Civil War provoked another revolt by the Irish, which was ruthlessly suppressed after Oliver Cromwell's victory at Drogheda (1649). When the Catholic James II was deposed in England by William of Orange (1688), Catholic Irishmen flocked to his colours but were defeated at the Battle of the Boyne (1690), which has been celebrated ever since by the Protestant 'Orangemen' of Ulster. A new penal code deprived Catholics of citizenship and the right to own property, and the government of Ireland resided exclusively in the Protestant 'Ascendancy'.

The cautionary experience of the American Revolution led Britain to grant the Irish parliament a measure of independence (1782) and to repeal Poynings' Law and the more oppressive penal laws. Nevertheless, the French Revolution inspired the United Irishmen led by Wolfe Tone (a Protestant) to launch a rebellion, which was crushed in 1798. Under the Act of Union (1800), the Dublin parliament was abolished and the Irish obtained representation at Westminster, although not until 1829, after a campaign by Daniel O'Connell, were Catholics allowed to sit in the UK parliament. A devastating famine in the late 1840s, caused by the failure of the potato crop, killed 1 million Irish people and forced many more to emigrate, (2 million crossing the Atlantic between 1847 and 1861). The limited nature of land reform measures stimulated Irish nationalism, as represented by the Young Ireland movement until its suppression in 1848 and later by the Fenians (founded 1858), who perpetrated acts of violence in Britain and assassinated Thomas Burke, the permanent under-secretary for Ireland, and Lord Frederick Cavendish, the newly appointed chief secretary, in Dublin's Phoenix Park (1882). From the mid-19th century industrialization came to the Protestant north, especially Belfast, whereas the agricultural south remained economically backward.

Demands for constitutional change were pressed at Westminster by Charles Stewart Parnell (a Protestant), whose Irish nationalist contingent forced Gladstone's Liberal government to introduce a home-rule bill. This was defeated (1886) by Conservatives and pro-union Liberals, as was another in 1893. Not until 1914 did a Liberal home-rule bill finally obtain the royal assent. By then the northern Protestants, led by Sir Edward Carson, were determined to defend the union by force, although the immediate crisis was averted by the outbreak of World War I and the deferral of home rule for the duration.

While moderate Irish nationalists supported the war effort, militant and left-wing elements, including Sinn Féin (founded 1905), launched the abortive Easter Rising in Dublin (1916) under the leadership of Patrick Pearse and James Connolly. In the 1918 elections Sinn Féin won 72 of the 105 Irish seats in the House of Commons on an all-Ireland Republican platform and convened the first modern Daíl Eireann (Irish parliament) in Dublin (1919). Guerrilla war followed, causing Britain to reinforce the Irish constabulary with the hated 'Black and Tans' and to accept partition as the only viable solution.

Under the Government of Ireland Act (Dec. 1920), the six Protestant-dominated counties of Ulster were given their own home rule parliament at Stormont. An Anglo-Irish Treaty (Dec. 1921) then created the Irish Free State as a self-governing dominion within the Commonwealth. Northern Ireland opted at once to remain within the UK, so that the new state consisted of 26 of the 32 Irish counties, including the three Catholic-majority counties of Ulster. Civil war followed in the Free State (1922–23) between those accepting the Treaty and a majority of Sinn Féin, led by Éamonn de Valera and supported by the Irish Republican Army (IRA), who opposed partition. The pro-Treaty side prevailed, and in 1927 de Valera took his Dáil seat as leader of the new Fianna Fáil party (founded 1926), in opposition to a government led by the forerunner of the Fine Gael party (founded 1933). Following Fianna Fáil's election victory in 1932, de Valera became prime minister (Taoiseach) and brought in a new constitution (1937), still largely in force, which described the national territory as 'the whole island of Ireland' and enshrined Roman Catholic moral and social precepts.

The Dublin government remained neutral during World War II and maintained Irish neutrality in the post-war era. The 1948 elections brought to power a four-party coalition led by Fine Gael and the Labour Party (founded 1912), following which the country adopted the name Republic of Ireland and left the Commonwealth (1949). In the same year, British legislation guaranteed that Northern Ireland would not cease to be part of the UK without the consent of the Stormont parliament. De Valera was again prime minister 1951–54 and 1957–59, then became president of the Republic until his death in 1973. Fianna Fáil remained the ruling party until 1973, first under Seán Lemass (1959–66), whose government achieved significant economic progress and established free trade with the UK, and then under Jack Lynch (1966–73), who took the Republic into full membership of the European Communities (Jan. 1973) to the considerable financial benefit of Irish agriculture. A 1972 referendum approved the deletion of the 'special position' accorded to the Catholic Church under the 1937 constitution. Lynch resigned following the general election of Feb. 1973 in which Fianna Fáil was defeated and was replaced by a Fine Gael/Labour coalition under Liam Cosgrave (1973–77).

Successive Dublin governments sought a UK-Irish cooperative framework within which to address the conflict of aspirations between Protestants and Catholics in Northern Ireland, where escalating violence from the late 1960s had impelled the UK government to impose direct rule 1972–73 and again from May 1974. The murder in July 1976 of Christopher Ewart-Biggs, the British ambassador to Ireland, led to the declaration of a state of emergency in Ireland in August and the passage of new anti-terrorist legislation. Criticism of Pres. Carroll O Dailaigh's referral to the Supreme Court of the legislation led to his resignation and Patrick Hillery, a former Fianna Fáil Cabinet minister, was elected unopposed as president in 1976 (and re-elected in 1983).

In August 1979 Admiral of the Fleet Earl Mountbatten of Burma, a prominent British figure, was assassinated by the IRA at Mullaghmore (County Sligo), and 18 British soldiers at Warrenpoint (County Down, Northern Ireland) were killed on the same day. As a result Lynch (who had succeeded Cosgrave as prime minister following the election of June 1977) agreed to strengthen border security. In 1979 Charles Haughey (whose career had survived allegations of gun-running for the IRA in 1970) became Fianna Fáil leader and prime minister but elections two years later brought another Fine Gael/Labour coalition to power under Garret FitzGerald, who gave way briefly to Haughey in 1982 but then resumed the premiership until 1987.

Talks initiated at prime ministerial level in 1980 resulted in the creation of the Anglo-Irish Inter-Governmental Council (AIIC) in June 1981, but renewed efforts to set up a power-sharing system in Northern Ireland (1982) were rebuffed by both sides of the religious divide. In Nov. 1985 FitzGerald and his UK counterpart, Margaret Thatcher, signed the Anglo-Irish Agreement (also known as the Hillsborough Accord), under which the Dublin government obtained a consultative role in Northern affairs in return for accepting that reunification could be achieved only with the consent of a Northern majority. Having in opposition condemned the agreement for its alleged abandonment of the principle of reunification, Haughey undertook, on regaining power in 1987, to abide by its provisions. Nevertheless, UK-Irish strains over extradition and other matters, combined with unyielding Unionist opposition to any Dublin involvement in the affairs of Northern Ireland, presented major obstacles to progress. Efforts to make the Republic's social regime more acceptable to Protestants had meanwhile encountered setbacks when referendums showed 2:1 majorities in favour of enshrining the legal ban on abortion in the constitution (1983) and against lifting the constitutional ban on divorce (1986).

Haughey and Fianna Fáil returned to power as a minority government after both Fine Gael and Labour, blamed for serious economic problems, had lost ground sharply in the Feb. 1987 Dáil elections, while the new Progressive Democrats (PDs), formed in 1985 by Fianna Fáil dissidents, emerged as the third strongest party. The Haughey government intensified its predecessor's economic austerity programme, seeking in particular to reduce a huge budget deficit. Calling a premature general election in June 1989, Haughey failed to win the absolute majority he had hoped for and was obliged to form a coalition government with Desmond O'Malley of the Progressive Democrats.

CONSTITUTION AND GOVERNMENT

Executive and legislature

The head of state is the president (Uachtarán na hÉireann) elected directly for a seven-year term by universal adult suffrage. The president is advised by a Council of State and holds specific constitutional powers, but executive authority is exercised by the head of government, the prime minister (Taoiseach), who is responsible to the Dáil Éireann or House of Representatives, the lower house of parliament. The National Parliament (Oireachtas) consists of the president, the 166-member Dáil (elected for a five-year term by universal adult suffrage on the basis of proportional representation by means of a single transferable vote – last election June 1989) and a 60-member Senate (Seanad Éireann).

Present government

President Dr Patrick Hillery

Prime Minister (Taoiseach), Minister for Irish-Speaking Affairs (Gaeltacht) Charles Haughey

Principal members of Cabinet Brian Lenihan (Deputy Prime Minister [Tanaiste], Defence); Gerard Collins (Foreign Affairs); Albert Reynolds (Finance); John Patrick Wilson (The Marine); Michael O'Kennedy (Agriculture and Food); Desmond J. O'Malley (Industry and Commerce); Ray Burke (Justice and Communications).

Justice

The judicial system comprises Courts of First Instance and a Court of Final Appeal, called the Supreme Court. The Courts of First Instance include a High Court and Courts of local and limited jurisdiction, with a right of appeal as determined by law. The High Court alone has original jurisdiction to consider the question of the validity of any law having regard to the provisions of the Constitution. The Supreme Court has appellate jurisdiction from all decisions of the High Court, with such exceptions and subject to such regulations as may be prescribed by law. Judges are appointed by the president on the advice of the government. The death penalty is nominally in force. No executions between 1985 and mid-1988.

Prisons. There are 1,973 prisoners.

National symbols

Flag. Tricolour with vertical stripes of green, white and orange.

Festivals. 5 June (4 June in 1990, Bank Holiday); 7 Aug. (6 Aug. in 1990, Bank Holiday); 30 Oct. (29 Oct. in 1990, Bank Holiday).

Vehicle registration plate. IRL.

INTERNATIONAL RELATIONS

Affiliations

Neutral; OECD; EC; Council of Europe.

Defence

Total Armed Forces: 13,200. Terms of service: voluntary, three-year terms to age 60, officers 56–65. Reserves: 15,800.

Army: 11,600; 14 light tanks (Scorpion).

Navy: 800; five patrol and coastal combatants.

Air Force: 800; 14 combat aircraft (CM-170–2 Super Magister).

ECONOMY

Currency

The unit is the Irish pound (punt), divided into 100 pence.

National finance

Budget. The 1988 budget (in US$) was for expenditure (current and capital) of 14,100 million and revenue of 12,300 million. Main items of current expenditure are housing and welfare 30.3%; health 13%; education 11.4%; defence 3.1%.

Balance of payments. The balance of payments (current account, 1988) was a deficit of $670 million.

Inflation. 4.5% (12 months to Sept. 1989).

Gross Domestic Product

Estimated total GDP US$21,910 million, per capita US$8,640 (ranking 56 in the world by size). Growth rate (1988) 1.2%.

Economically active population. The total number of persons active in the economy was 1,300,000; unemployed: 16.7% (1988).

Sector	% of workforce	% of GDP
industry	21.4	37
agriculture	12.9	10
services*	65.7	53

* services figure includes elements unassigned to other categories.

Energy and mineral resources

Minerals. Lead, zinc, and some coal is mined. Peat is an important source of energy.

Electricity. Capacity: 4,647,000 kW; production: 13,794 million kWh; 3,890 kWh per capita.

Bioresources

Agriculture. Some 14% of the land is arable and 71% meadow and pasture. Most important are livestock and dairy products. Main crops are turnips; barley; potatoes; sugar beet; wheat. Ireland is 85% self-sufficient in food.

Crop production: (1987 in 1,000 tons/tonnes) sugar beet 1,789/1,623; barley 1,763/1,599; potatoes 768/697; wheat 443/402; oats 117/106.

Livestock numbers: (1987 in thousands) cattle 6,647; sheep 4,575; pigs 999.

Forestry. About 5% of the land is forested. 51,064,044 ft^3/1,446,000 m^3 of timber was felled in 1987.

Fisheries. Total sea fish catch: (1986) 186,536 tons/169,224 tonnes.

Industry and commerce

Industry. Industry has now overtaken agriculture as the most important sector of the economy. Main products are food products; brewing; textiles; clothing; chemicals; pharmaceuticals; machinery; transportation equipment; glass and crystal.

Commerce. Exports: US$17,700 million, including primarily live animals; animal products; chemicals; data processing equipment; industrial machinery. Imports: US$14,600 million, comprising primarily food; animal feed; chemicals; petroleum and petroleum products; machinery textiles and clothing (1988). Countries exported to: EC countries 74% (of which UK 34%; West Germany 11%; France 9%); US 8%. Imports came from EC countries 66% (of which UK 42%; West Germany 8%; France 4%); US 17%.

Trade with UK. Ireland imported UK goods worth £4,057 million; exports to UK totalled £3,876 million (1988).

Tourism. 2,096,000 visitors (1987).

COMMUNICATIONS

Railways

There are 1,165 miles/1,876 km of railways, of which 23 miles/37 km are electrified.

Roads

There are 57,320 miles/92,303 km of roads, of which some 53,881 miles/86,765 km are bituminized.

Aviation

The national airline Aer Lingus Plc provides international services (main airports are at Shannon (used for transatlantic flights), Dublin, Cork and Knock). Passengers: (1987) 2.7 million.

Shipping

The inland waterways are of limited use for commercial traffic. The major ports are Dublin and Cork on the coast of the Irish Sea. There are ten secondary and numerous minor ports. The merchant marine has 49 ships of 1,000 GRT or over.

Telecommunications

There are 900,000 telephones and a small, but modern system using cable and radio relay circuits. There are almost 1 million radio sets and nearly as many televisions, over 80% of them colour. Radio Telefis Eireann (RTE) controls and operates the radio and television system, with two national radio and two TV channels, as well as financing the Gaelic radio broadcasting service. Commercial TV and radio broadcasting was made possible under legislation passed in 1989.

EDUCATION AND WELFARE

Education

Primary education is free. Voluntary secondary schools (mostly run by religious orders) all receive state grants, vocational schools are run by vocational education committees (VECs) and are mainly state-financed, comprehensive schools are fully financed by the state. An increasing number of community schools are being set up by merging voluntary secondary and vocational schools where feasible to provide both secondary-level and adult education.

Schools. There are 3,383 state primary schools (including over 100 special schools) with 565,000 pupils together with about 60 private primary schools with some 8,500 pupils. There are 500 recognized voluntary secondary schools with some 215,000 pupils; 253 vocational education committee schools with nearly 85,000 pupils, 16 comprehensive schools with 8,900 pupils, and 45 community schools with over 32,000 students.

Universities. There are five university colleges with some 27,500 students as well as technical, agricultural and horticultural colleges. In total there are around 59,500 full-time tertiary level students.

Literacy. 99%.

Health

There are three categories of people entitled to health care: those on low incomes who receive all health services free, while those on two higher income bands receive progressively fewer free services. In 1984 there was one physician for every 680 people and one nurse for every 140 people.

ISRAEL

Medinat Yisrael (Arabic: *Dawlat Isra'tl*) *(State of Israel)*

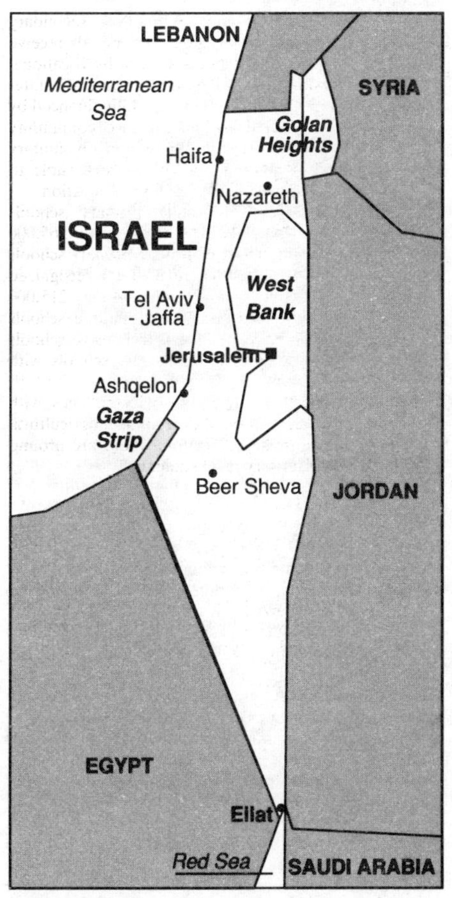

GEOGRAPHY

Located in the Middle East (western Asia) on the extreme south-eastern Mediterranean seaboard, Israel covers an area of approximately 8,017 miles/20,770 km^2 within limits defined by the 1949 Arab-Israeli armistice, ie excluding occupied territories in the Gaza Strip (south-west), the West Bank (east) and Syria's Golan Heights (north). Inland from the fertile Mediterranean coastal plain of Sharon (irrigated by the Qishon, Soreq and Sarida rivers), the terrain rises to form an upland ridge (average height 2,789 ft/850 m) stretching from the northern border (3,963 ft/1,208 m at Mt Meron near the Sea of Galilee) through the occupied West Bank (1,640–3,281 ft/500–1,000 m) to the Jordan-Red Sea rift valley. The River Jordan drains through this valley flowing 689 ft/210 m below sea level as it enters the freshwater Lake Tiberias (Sea of Galilee) and 1,345 ft/410 m below sea level as it empties into the Dead Sea. To the south the Negev Desert (60% of the total surface area) extends from the Beersheb (north) to Elat (south) at the northernmost extremity of the Gulf of Aqaba. Of the six administrative districts, Tel Aviv is by far the most densely populated. Of the total land area 17% is arable, 6% is forested and 11% is under irrigation (mostly in the Negev Desert). Relative Areas: West Bank (Judea and Samaria) 2,269 miles^2/5,879 km^2. Gaza Strip 140 miles^2/363 km^2.

Climate

Mediterranean in north and central Israel. Humid, warm winters and hot, dry summers. Northern uplands receive rainfall in excess of 15.7 in/400 mm annually, increasing to 39.4 in/1,000 mm in the extreme north, most of which falls Oct.-Apr. 50% of Israeli territory averages less than 7.9 in/200 mm rainfall annually, the Negev Desert receives only 3.9 in/100 mm. Temperatures range from 50°F/10°C in the north during winter to 63°F/17°C in the south, and from 73–93°F/23 to 34°C during the summer months. Jerusalem: Jan. 48°F/9°C. July 73°F/23°C. Average annual rainfall 21 in/528 mm. Tel Aviv: Jan. 57°F/14°C. July 81°F/27°C. Average annual rainfall 21.7 in/550 mm.

Cities and towns

*Jerusalem	428,668
*Tel-Aviv-Jaffa	327,625
Haifa	235,775
Holon	133,460
Petach-Tikva	123,868
Ramat Gan	117,072
Beersheba	110,813

* The controversial Israeli intention to establish Jerusalem as its capital is not recognized by many countries which maintain their embassies in Tel Aviv.

Population

Total population is 4,442,000 of which 89.4% live in urban areas. Population density is 554 persons per mile^2/214.9 per km^2. 83% of the population is Jewish and 16.8% Arab. The occupied West Bank has a population of some 866,000 (97% Palestinian Arabs), and the Gaza Strip a population of 564,000 (98% Arabic-speaking Muslims).

Birth rate Jewish 2.05%; Muslim 3.44%; Christian 2.23%; Druze and others 3.07%. **Death rate** Jewish 0.74%; Muslim 0.36%; Christian 0.52%; Druze and others 0.34%. **Rate of population increase** 1.70%. **Age distribution** under 15 = 32.6%; over 65 = 8.8%. **Life expectancy** female 77; male 74; average 75.

Religion

Judaism is the faith of 82% of the population. The two dominant Jewish communities are the Ashkenazim (deriving from northern, central and eastern Europe) and the Sephardim (Balkan States, North Africa and Middle East). There are an estimated 10,000 Falashas (Ethiopian Jews airlifted to Israel over the past 16 years). The Karaites recognize only the written law; the Samaritans recognize only the Torah. In addition, there are 614,000 Muslims (mostly Sunni), 76,000 Druzes and 103,000 Christians in Israel. Of the Christian faiths, Catholicism is practised according to six rites (Armenian, Chaldean, Latin, Maronite,

Melkite and Syrian). A number of orthodox Christian churches have significant representations in Israel (including Greek, Armenian, Coptic and Russian). A very small minority of Israeli Christians belong to the Church of Scotland.

Language

Hebrew (official) is spoken by 66% of the population. 15% speak Arabic (also an official language) and a diverse range of European languages make up the bulk of the remaining 19%, including English, French, German, Hungarian, Romanian, Russian, Spanish. A total of 95,000 Israelis speak Yiddish.

HISTORY

The modern state of Israel covers land that is holy to the three great sister religions, Judaism, Christianity and Islam – a fact which has led to it being a focus of conflict down the ages.

The land of Israel includes some of the earliest evidence of human life outside Africa, including a population of Neanderthal humans. Its present Jewish population claim descent from ancient Israelites, Semitic nomads who entered the land some 4,000 years ago. They adopted the first ethical monotheistic religion of Judaism, and their history is recorded in the Bible. After slavery in Egypt, the 12 tribes of Israel returned to the 'Promised Land' under Moses. They conquered and occasionally absorbed local peoples, including Canaanites, Philistines and Phoenicians. But sandwiched between the civilizations of Egypt and Mesopotamia, they were never paramount rulers of the area.

In 721 BC Assyrians sacked the capital ,Jerusalem, and destroyed ten of the tribes; in 586 BC Babylonians took the rest into exile. The Israelites (whom we may now call Jews) returned and rebuilt their temple, to be reconquered by other empires, notably the Persians, Greeks and ultimately Romans, who set up the semi-autonomous province of Palestrina in 63 BC. Christianity arose out of Judaism in Palestine in the 1st century AD. An abortive revolt against Rome in AD 138 cost the Jews their statehood. Most fled into exile, where they joined fellow-Jews in what became known as the Diaspora ('the scattering'); only a minority remained.

Later a Christian Eastern Roman Empire ruled Palestine from Byzantium until Muslim Arabs conquered Jerusalem (636). In time most of the population became Muslim and adopted the Arabic language. Christian rule over Palestine resumed in 1099 after the Crusades, but the Crusaders were defeated by the Muslim leader Salah al-Din (Saladin) in 1187. In 1517 the Muslim Ottoman Turks conquered Arab Palestine, and ruled it till 1918 as a province of Syria, largely neglecting its economic and political potential.

Over the years, Diaspora Jewry dreamt of returning to Palestine, but it was only in the 19th century that these desires were channelled into political Zionism by the Austrian Jew, Theodore Herzl, who saw a return to Palestine as a way of 'normalizing' the Jewish condition. In 1897 he convened the first Zionist conference.

The Zionist immigrants farmed land bought mainly from absentee Arab landlords living in Lebanon. They revived the ancient Hebrew language and in 1909 founded the first modern all-Jewish city, Tel-Aviv. Increased immigration brought Arab resentment; in 1914 anti-Zionist groups were founded in major cities and some Arabs raided Jewish sites, although a few welcomed the economic advances brought by Jewish immigrants. By the outbreak of World War I more than 60,000 Jews had come to Palestine, compared with the estimated 450,000 Arab residents.

Turkey sided with Germany, and Britain recruited Palestinian Arab and Jewish legions to help expel them from Palestine. This they did in 1917, and the Ottoman Empire subsequently collapsed. A vacuum now existed in Palestine. Conflicting British promises were made to Arabs and Jews but Zionist leader Chaim Weizmann won the clearest statement with the British Balfour Declaration (Nov. 1917). It called for a Jewish national home in Palestine as long as this did not prejudice the civil and religious rights of other communities. Encouraged by the declaration, Zionist immigration was stepped up. Britain was given a League of Nations mandate over Palestine in 1922. The new immigrants set up a Jewish Agency to co-ordinate the settlement activity, and founded schools, kibbutzim (communal farms), the Histadrut union and Hagana defence force. Rivalry between the indigenous Palestinian Arabs and the increasingly assertive and numerous incomers grew, and in Aug. 1929 serious riots broke out in Jerusalem, Hebron and Safed, killing 133 Jews and 116 Arabs. A British commission suggested restricting Jewish immigration and land purchases.

Though dropped, these plans were revived in 1933, when Hitler's Nazis took power in Germany and threatened European Jewry. Zionist anger at a perceived British bias towards the Arabs boiled over in new riots (Dec. 1933). Intercommunal clashes escalated, with the Hagana and Irgun guerrillas fighting Arab fedayeen (guerrillas). An Arab Higher Committee was formed to oppose Jewish settlement (1936) and start a national strike, which soon developed into the Arab Revolt. British troops were caught in the middle as London vacillated. By 1939 517 Jews, more than 3,000 Arabs and 150 British police had died. The 1937 Peel Commission recommended partition of the land into Arab and Jewish states. Zionists under David Ben Gurion accepted the plan, though it granted them only 15% of the total land; but the Higher Committee rejected it in favour of an end to mandate and a single state of Palestine ruled by the Arab majority.

Britain shelved the partition proposals in 1939. A new White Paper that year cut back immigration to 75,000 over five years. Since 1933 some 225,000 Jews had entered Palestine, raising them to 30% of the population. The advent of World War II doused inter-communal violence and some Jewish units joined Britain in its war with Germany; though other Hagana members smuggled in 'illegal' immigrants, refugees from Nazi Europe. In May 1942 Zionists in New York committed their movement to achieving an independent state, by military means if needed. Members of the Zionist Stern Gang, led by Itzhak Shamir, killed Lord Moyne, British High Commissioner to Egypt.

After the war, Palestinian Arabs and the new Arab League of independent states rejected new British partition plans. As details emerged of the Nazi Holocaust which had killed six million Jews, Zionists impatient with the mandate turned to violence. The King David Hotel (Jerusalem) bombing of 1946 killed 91. Arab nationalists countered with atrocities of their own. In Feb. 1947 Britain referred the problem to the newly formed United Nations. It came up with a new partition plan, with a Jewish state in eastern Galilee, the coastal plain and the Negev Desert; an Arab state in western Galilee, Jaffa, central Palestine and a southern strip bordering Egypt; international zones in Jerusalem and Bethlehem; and economic union between all regions. Again, Zionists accepted it but Arabs rejected it. In December Britain announced that it would leave Palestine.

Civil war erupted. Among the worst incidents were an Arab bombing in Jerusalem which killed 55, and Irgun's raid on the Arab village of Deir Yassin, which killed 254. On 14 May 1948 the State of Israel was proclaimed in Tel-Aviv. The Arab League – Egypt, Transjordan, Syria, Iraq and Lebanon – invaded it. By early 1949 Israel had survived the war and added linking territory to land granted by the UN. Jordan absorbed East Jerusalem and the West Bank; Egypt took over the Gaza Strip to the south. Most significantly, some 780,000 Palestinian Arabs were displaced from their homes, leaving 760,000 Jews as a majority.

Israel became a mixed-economy democratic state, with a proportionately elected Knesset, or parliament, controlled from 1948 till 1977 by Mapai Socialists in coalition with smaller religious parties. Menachem Begin led the right-wing Herut opposition. A Ministry of Absorption was set up to cope with new immigrants; the Law of Return allows any Jew to settle in Israel. Today 20% of world Jewry are Israeli, speaking Hebrew as the official language. At first most immigrants came from Europe, but some 640,000 Sephardim (Oriental Jews) entered by 1979, making their descendants the majority in Israel today.

In 1948 Israel was ruled by President Weizmann and Prime Minister Ben Gurion. Armistice agreements were signed with the defeated Arab states, but UN-sponsored peace talks broke down over the Palestinian refugee question, and Arab opposition to Israel grew. Egypt restricted Israeli seaborne trade and backed fedayeen raids from Gaza. Backed by Britain and France in the Suez War (1956), Israel attacked Egyptian positions in Gaza and soon overran the Sinai peninsula which it sought as a buffer zone. It withdrew following UN condemnation. Afterwards the USSR, which had previously favoured Israel, supported the pan-Arabism of Egypt's Col. Nasser; the United States drew closer to Israel.

During the 1950s the economy revived and grew at an average of 10% annually till 1967. Education was emphasized; five new universities were built after 1948. Nonetheless, Israel was and remains dependent on funds from Diaspora Jews via the Jewish Agency and World Zionist Organization. In 1965 Ben Gurion led the breakaway Rafi and Levi Eshkol succeeded him as prime minister; the opposition was too fragmented to take power.

The Arab League gave its blessing to the Palestine National Council (PNC) in Jan. 1964 and its charter, which called for an 'armed struggle to liberate Palestine'. To this end the PNC founded the PLO (June 1964), which on New Year's Day, 1965, launched the first of several raids into Israel. In early 1967 Israel clashed with Syria. Nasser called for war with Israel, and on 19 May forced UN peacekeeping forces to leave the Sinai. Begin joined a government of National Unity. As Arab states mobilized their armies, Israel launched a pre-emptive strike on 5 June.

Thus began the Six Day War, in which Israel soundly defeated all its enemies. By capturing the Sinai peninsula and Gaza from Egypt, the West Bank from Jordan and the Golan Heights from Syria, Israel almost tripled the land under its control. It now ruled over almost a million Palestinians, but did not annex the territories as it did not wish to enfranchise Palestinians. It called on Arab leaders to recognize Israel and discuss a 'permanent peace', but the offer was rejected. The UN Security Council passed Resolution 242 (22 Nov.), calling for Israeli withdrawal from captured territory and 'mutual respect for the sovereignty of all states within secure boundaries'. Israel accepted UN 242 as a basis for future negotiations, as did all other parties involved apart from Syria and the PLO.

Two months after the war the Land of Israel Movement was founded to pressurize the Israeli government never to surrender any territory. To the original security argument they added the emotional claim that the land was an integral part of Biblical 'Greater Israel'. In time settlements were built in the territories administered by the Israeli military, technically contravening the law. In 1969 Prime Minister Eshkol died and was replaced by Golda Meir (17 Mar.). The national unity government was dissolved in 1970. Meanwhile a war of attrition had broken out, consisting of cross-border raids by PLO fedayeen and Israeli-Egyptian clashes. When it ended in 1972, more Israelis had died than in the 1967 war, and so had thousands of Egyptians and PLO fighters. By this stage King Hussein of Jordan had expelled the PLO, now led by Yasser Arafat. Most guerrillas regrouped in Lebanon, from where they raided Israeli settlements. In counter-attacking Israel often killed non-combatants, thus offending international opinion. For its part the PLO gained notoriety from a spate of hijackings and other terrorist acts.

On 6 Oct. 1973 Egypt and Syria launched an attack on Israel during the holiest Jewish festival, Yom Kippur. Caught unawares, Israel lost ground at first but fought back to regain equity by the cease-fire of 24 Oct. Arab states imposed an oil embargo on Israel's western allies. After Israel's brush with defeat, the ruling Mapai party (now called the Labour Alignment) lost seats in the December election, but kept power. Meir and Defence Minister Dayan resigned four months later. Itzhak Rabin took over the premiership.

Terrorist attacks escalated – there were 144 casualties in Jerusalem alone in 1975. Israel was angered by UN decisions to allow Arafat to address them (13 Nov. 1974), and to equate Zionism with racism in 1976. That year municipal elections on the West Bank returned a majority of pro-PLO candidates, another shock for Israel. Palestinians protested against nearby Jewish settlements, and an alleged plan to expropriate Arab land in Galilee. In Apr. 1977 Rabin resigned as premier after a financial scandal and on 13 May 1977 Labour was swept from office for the first time since independence. Begin's Likud became the biggest single party with 45 seats, six more than in 1974, and with religious parties formed a 62-strong coalition in a Knesset of 120. Begin won with the backing of poorer Sephardi voters who resented their exclusion from power. Labour feared Likud's right-wing ethos, but it was Begin who made the first full peace treaty with an Arab state.

Begin committed Israel to encouraging Jewish settlement in the occupied territories, which the US opposed. His first task was to revive the economy; he eased financial restrictions, although this also exacerbated inflation. In April US Pres. Carter met Egyptian ruler Anwar Sadat, who had just broken ties with the USSR. Begin accepted Sadat's peace offer and on 9 Nov. 1977 Sadat became the first Arab leader to visit Israel and address the Knesset. Thus began the long Camp David peace process which culminated in the signing of an Israeli-Egyptian peace treaty on 26 Mar. 1979. Israel withdrew from Sinai in Mar. 1982, Egypt opened the Suez Canal to Israeli ships and both nations restored relations. Less successful was the plan for Palestinian autonomy. The PLO accused Sadat of usurping their role as sole voice of the Palestinians (accepted by the Arab League in 1974), and of abandoning the struggle for a separate peace with Israel. Israel refused to talk to the PLO, considering it to be a 'terrorist organization'.

Throughout 1978 Palestinian protests and bombings grew in Israel and the territories. Israel backed anti-PLO 'village leagues' and detained protesters to quell violence, but to little avail. In January Israel attacked PLO bases in Lebanon, in retaliation for PLO raids on Israeli border settlements. Some 1,000 civilians and 250 troops died in the conflict, adding to the civil war which had raged since 1975. On 14 Dec. Israel annexed the Golan Heights, an action condemned by the UN and US. As Palestinians protested, orthodox Jewish settlers in Yamit, Sinai, fought Israeli troops sent in to evict them.

Besieged from right and left, Begin authorized Israel's biggest invasion of Lebanon on 6 June 1982 after an attempt to assassinate the Israeli ambassador in London. Soon Israelis encircled the capital Beirut, and by September forced 5,000 PLO fighters to leave the city. On 16 Sept. Christian Phalangists entered the Palestinian refugee camps of Sabra and Chatila and killed about 700. Some 350,000 Israelis demonstrated in Tel-Aviv on 25 Sept. against alleged Israeli collusion in the massacre. In Feb. 1983 a judicial inquiry held top military and political figures responsible, and Defence Minister Ariel Sharon resigned. Faced with dissent at home and among troops, Israel agreed to withdraw from Lebanon by 1986.

The war achieved little – the PLO returned to Lebanon, Israel's economy suffered, and many felt shamed at the conduct of the war. In late 1982 new peace moves came from the US and Saudi Arabia, the latter calling for a West Bank Palestinian state, but Israel rejected any deviation from the Camp David agreement. Between 1967 and 1982, 109 settlements were built or planned in the territories; on 10 Apr. 1983 Israel announced a further 57. After new protests, West Bank mayors were dismissed. The PLO was handicapped by deep divisions between pro- and anti-Arafat factions over the latter's increasing reliance on diplomacy.

With inflation at 400%, Israel devalued twice in late 1983. Begin resigned and was replaced by Itzhak Shamir. In elections (July 1984) Labour won 44 seats and Likud 41; on 31 Aug. they formed a coalition government to last for four years. As prime minister, Peres slowed settlement building, but violence continued on the West Bank, with about 20 bombings a month by Mar. 1986. In May 1985 the Knesset banned racist parties and arrested Jewish extremists, but also forbade MPs to talk to the PLO. Peres favoured giving up land for peace, but Shamir opposed this. On 1 Oct. Israel bombed PLO headquarters in Tunis. In 1986 Shamir resumed the premiership with Peres as foreign minister. Israel rebuilt ties with Egypt, while the PLO split with Jordan and Syria routed pro-Arafat factions in Lebanon.

On 9 Dec. 1987 the intifada (Palestinian uprising) began, claiming over 795 Arab and 44 Jewish lives by Dec. 1989. Again Israel was condemned, even by the United States, for excessive violence in quelling the unrest, but the government said there was no alternative to deal with stone-throwing Palestinians. On 31 July 1988 Jordan dropped its claim to the West Bank. A meeting of the Palestine National Council (PNC – the Palestinian 'parliament in exile') in Algeria on 12–15 Nov. culminated in the proclamation of an independent Palestinian state with Jerusalem as its capital. A PNC also approved a new moderate political programme endorsing, for the first time, UN Security Council resolution 242 as the basis for a Middle East peace settlement. To date, Israel has publicly refused to talk with the PLO, despite the US's first official talks with PLO leaders in December.

On 1 Nov. 1988 Israeli polls returned another split verdict, 40 seats to Labour and 41 to Likud. Shamir formed a new coalition government, which collapsed in March 1990 as a result of internal divisions over the direction of policy on the Palestinian question. Talks with the ultimate aim of arranging elections among Palestinians in the occupied territories had started in May 1989, but by early 1990 they had become complex and meandering. The lack of progress generated a growing sense of disillusionment with the peace process.

CONSTITUTION AND GOVERNMENT

Executive and legislature

The head of state (largely a ceremonial role) is a president elected every five years; the president appoints a prime minister on the basis of the distribution of power between parties in the legislature. The prime minister is head of government, and is responsible, as is the Cabinet, to the legislature, the unicameral Knesset (parliament), which is itself elected for a maximum of four years; last elections 1 Nov 1988.

Present government

President Chaim Herzog

Prime Minister, Minister of Labour Itzhak Shamir

Principal Ministers Shimon Peres (Vice Prime Minister; Minister of Finance); David Levi (Second Vice Prime Minister; Minister of Housing and Construction); Itzhak Navon (Deputy Prime Minister; Minister of Education and Culture); Moshe Arens (Foreign Affairs); Itzhak Rabin (Defence); Chaim Bar-Lev (Police); Moshe Shahal (Energy and Infrastructure); Itzhak Moda'i (Economy and Planning); Ezer Weizmann (Science and Technology); Moshe Nissim (Trade and Industry); Dan Meridor (Justice); Zevulun Hammer (Religious Affairs); Arie Der'i (Interior).

Justice

The system of law was based originally on Ottoman law, English law and the law enacted under the British mandate for Palestine prior to 1948, with subsequent codification in many areas of commercial law. The highest court is the Supreme Court, the highest appellate court in a pyramid structure with municipal and magistrates' courts at the base and appeals through District Courts, which also act as courts of first instance on more serious matters. The rabbinical courts, for the Jewish community, have exclusive jurisdiction in personal/legal matters of marriage and divorce. The death penalty is in force only for exceptional crimes. There were no executions between 1985 and mid-1988.

National symbols

Flag. Two blue horizontal stripes near the upper and

lower edges of the flag, and there is a blue six-pointed Shield of David in the centre.
Festivals. 10 May (29 Apr. in 1990, Independence Day); 9 Oct. (29 Sept. in 1990, Yom Kippur).
Vehicle registration plate. IL.

INTERNATIONAL RELATIONS

Affiliations

Special relations with US.

Defence

Total Armed Forces: 141,000 (110,000 male and female conscripts). Terms of service: officers 48 months, men 36 months, women 24 months (Jews and Druze only; Christians, Circassians and Muslims may volunteer). Reserves: 504,000.
Army: 104,000; 3,850 main battle tanks (Centurion, M-48Ar, M-60/A1/A3, T-54/-55/-62, Merkava I/II).
Navy: 9,000; three submarines (UK Vickers) and 59 patrol and coastal combatants.
Air Force: 28,000; 577 combat aircraft (F-15, F-4E, Kfir C2/C7, F-16, A-4H/N Skyhawk), 80 armed helicopters.

ECONOMY

Currency

The unit is the new Israeli shekel, divided into 100 new agorot.

National finance

Budget. The 1987 budget (in US$) was for expenditure (current and capital) of 23,300 million and revenue of 23,500 million. Main items of current expenditure are defence 30.1%; housing and welfare 17%; education 7.6%; health 3.2%.
Balance of payments. The balance of payments (current account, 1987) was a deficit of $4,495 million.
Inflation. (1988) 16%.

Gross Domestic Product

Estimated total GDP US$35,000 million, per capita US$8,400 (ranking 44 in the world by size).
Economically active population. The total number of persons active in the economy was 1,400,000; unemployed: 8%.

Sector	% of workforce
industry	29.3
agriculture	5.5
services*	65

* services figure includes elements unassigned to other categories.

Energy and mineral resources

Minerals. The potash and bromine deposits of the Dead Sea are Israel's most valuable natural resources. Other minerals include copper; clay; sand; asphalt; manganese; small amounts of natural gas and crude oil.
Electricity. Capacity: 4,192,000 kW; production: 17,317 million kWh; 4,030 kWh per capita (1988).

Bioresources

Agriculture. Israel has developed its agriculture sector on an intensive scale over the past 20 years and is currently a world leader in irrigation techniques. Land is farmed privately or collectively; the most popular types of collective rural settlement are the Moshav (workers' co-operative smallholders' settlement) and the Kibbutz and Kvutza (communal collective settlement). Citrus fruit is the main export crop; total agricultural exports totalled US$613 million (1987).
Crop production: (1987 in 1,000 tons/tonnes) citrus fruit 1,662/1,508; vegetables 1,033/937; wheat 328/298; avocados 149/135; pomegranates 138/125; melons and pumpkins 171/155; grapes 98/89; bananas 89/81; olives 28/25; stone fruit 64/58.
Livestock numbers: (1987) poultry 23 million; cattle 319,000; sheep 281,000; pigs 130,000; goats 128,000.

Industry and commerce

Industry. As with agriculture, Israel has developed its industrial sector on an intensive scale over the past 20 years. This policy has transformed the economy into that of a modern industrial and service-orientated state. The main industries are food processing; diamond cutting and polishing; textiles; clothing; chemicals; metal products; military equipment; transport equipment; electrical equipment; miscellaneous machinery; potash mining; high-technology electronics.
Commerce. Exports: US$9,400 million; imports US$12,900 million (1988). Exports include polished diamonds; citrus and other fruits; textiles and clothing; processed foods; fertilizer and chemical products; military hardware; electronics. Imports include military equipment; rough diamonds; oil; chemicals; machinery; iron and steel; cereals; textiles; vehicles; ships; aircraft. Main trading partners are: US; UK; West Germany; France; Belgium; Switzerland; Luxembourg.
Trade with UK. Israel imported goods worth £460,289,000 and exported to the UK goods worth £487,255,000.
Tourism. Approximately 1.5 million tourists visited Israel (1987).

COMMUNICATIONS

Railways

There are 537 miles/865 km of railways.

Roads

There are 7,963 miles/12,823 km of roads, all of which are bituminized.

Aviation

El Al Israel Airlines Ltd provides international services and Arkia Israeli Airlines Ltd provides domestic services (main airport is Ben Gurion Airport at Tel-Aviv).

Shipping

The main ports are Ashod and Haifa on the Mediterranean Sea and Elat on the Gulf of Aqaba in the Red Sea. There are 39 ships in the merchant marine of 1,000 GRT or over. Freight loaded: (1987) 8.9 million tons/8.1 million tonnes; unloaded: 12.5 million tons/11.3 million tonnes.

Telecommunications

Israel's telecommunications system, although not the largest, is the most highly developed in the Middle East. There are 1.8 million telephones, 3 million radios and nearly 1 million television sets; the Israeli Broadcasting Authority operates six radio channels (in addition to which there are services by the defence forces station Galei Zahal), and a colour TV channel, in Hebrew and Arabic, as well as a highly developed educational television system. Authorization has been given for commercial radio and television services.

EDUCATION AND WELFARE

Education

The state provides free and compulsory education from age five to 16; a further two years of free education is available. Legislation passed in 1953 established a unified state-controlled elementary school system. Most schools are maintained by municipalities, although there are a number of private schools maintained by religious foundations and private societies.

School population. Hebrew education: primary schools 480,616; intermediate division 109,365; secondary schools 191,519; vocational schools 96,403 (1986–87). Arab education: primary schools 140,777; intermediate division 23,393; secondary schools 35,805; vocational schools 6,336 (1986–87).

Schools. Hebrew education: 1,310 primary schools (37,799 teachers); 291 intermediate division schools (12,952 teachers); 850 secondary and vocational schools (22,865 teachers) (1986–87). Arab education: 308 primary schools (6,610 teachers); 55 intermediate division schools (1,578 teachers); 122 secondary and vocational schools (2,208 teachers) (1986–87).

Universities. There are five universities with over 57,000 students (1986–87).

Literacy. 88% Jews; 70% Arabs.

Health

Israel has 150 hospitals with over 27,000 beds and 9,500 doctors (1986).

ITALY

Repubblica Italiana (Italian Republic)

GEOGRAPHY

Italy lies in the south of central Europe, occupying a total area of 116,273 miles²/301,225 km² divided into 20 regions including the islands of Sicily (Sicilia) (south-west), Sardegna (Sardinia) (west), Elba and approx. 70 other smaller islands. From the fertile and populous Lombardo plains in the north, the boot-shaped Italian peninsula extends about 497 miles/800 km south-east into the Mediterranean. Along the northern frontier, the Alps arch east-west, rising to 15,203 ft/4,634 m at Monte Rosa on the Swiss border, converging with the Appenine Mountains on the Ligurian Coastal Front. The Appenine Chain stretches north-south over approximately 758 miles/1,220 km, climbing to elevations above 6,562 ft/2,000 m east of Rome and continuing south-south-west into the Sicilian Massifs of Monti Nebrodi and the volcanic summit of Mt Etna (10,902 ft/3,323 m). The eastward facing basin of the River Po, enclosed north and south by the Alps and Appenines drains and irrigates approximately two-thirds of the total lowland area. The northern tributaries of the Po expand to form a chain of Alpine Lakes, including Lago Maggiore, Lugano, Lago Como and Lago di Garda. Other major rivers include the Adige (north), the Arno (north-west) and the Tiber (west central). In Sardinia, the crystalline relief reaches a maximum height of 6,020 ft/1,835 m at Monti del Gennargentu. The most densely populated regions are Lombardia in the north and Campania in the south-west. Of the total surface area over half is cultivated or pastureland and 22% is forested. Southern Italy and Sicily periodically experience serious geo-seismic instability and disturbance. South of Naples, Mt Vesuvius rises to 4,190 ft/1,277 m.

Climate

Warm temperate and Mediterranean in the south, with mild winters and hot dry summers becoming cool temperate in the north, especially on the drier Adriatic coast subject to cold north-east winds such as the 'bara'. Temperatures on Sicily and Sardegna are generally warmer than on the mainland, averaging 48–50°F/9–10°C in winter and 79°F/26°C in summer. Rainfall increases with altitude, reaching 40 in/1,010 mm in the highlands, decreasing to 30 in/750 mm in the River Po lowlands. Florence: Jan. 42°F/5.6°C. July 77°F/25°C. Average annual rainfall 35.5 in/901 mm. Rome: Jan. 45°F/7°C. July 77°F/25°C. Average annual rainfall 26 in/657 mm. Venice: Jan. 38°F/3.3°C. July 75°F/23.9°C. Average annual rainfall 28.5 in/725 mm.

Cities and towns

Rome (capital)	2,817,227
Milan	1,478,505
Naples	1,200,958
Turin	1,025,390
Palermo	728,843
Genoa	722,026

Population

Total population is 57,265,000 of which 67.4% live in urban areas. Population density is 492.5 persons per mile^2/190 per km^2. At the last census, an estimated 4,907,000 of the total population were Sicilian and 1,594,000 Sardinian. The population is predominantly (and homogenously) Italian in ethnic origin with German-Italian, French-Italian and Slovene-Italian minorities scattered throughout the northern borderlands and a few Albanian-Italians resident in the south.

Birth rate 1.07%. **Death rate** 0.95%. **Rate of population increase** (1980–87) 0.12%. **Age distribution** under 15 = 19.6%; over 65 = 12.7%. **Life expectancy** female 80; male 74; average 77.

Religion

Almost all of the 85% of the population who profess a religious faith are Roman Catholic. The total membership of the Federation of Protestant Churches is an estimated 50,000 while the Union of Italian Jewish Communities represents approximately 21 separate Jewish Communities within the republic.

Language

Italian. A significant German-speaking minority and a number of neo-Latin Ladinese speakers inhabit the province of Bolzano in the upper reaches of the Adige River. French and Slovene speaking minorities are found in the Valle d'Aosta and the Trieste-Gorizia areas. Smaller Greek, Albanian and Catalan communities populate the northern provinces.

HISTORY

Pre-Roman Italy contained various peoples and civilizations, including the Etruscans in Tuscany, Latins and Sabines in central Italy, Greek colonies in the south, and Gauls in the north. From c.400 BC the Latins developed a powerful state centred on Rome (founded by Romulus in 753 BC). Rome became a republic around 510 BC when the cruel King Tarquin the Proud was driven out, and the city gradually absorbed the surrounding peoples until after the conquest of Taranto (272 BC), Rome united the whole of Italy under its rule. Meanwhile in the three Punic Wars Rome first won Sicily from the Carthaginians and took control of Sardinia and Corsica (264–241 BC), then in the second war (218–201 BC) eventually defeated Hannibal (who had marched his army from Spain through Gaul and across the Alps to challenge the Romans) and decisively defeated the Carthaginians at Zama (on the north coast of Africa) in 202 BC. The third war which began in 149 BC resulted in the razing of Carthage after which Rome progressively won control over most of the known world along the north coast of Africa, from the Iberian peninsula in the west, England (to Hadrian's Wall) in the north, to Armenia, Mesopotamia, Judea and Egypt in the east. The Roman Empire officially adopted Christianity in AD 313 and Rome became the seat of the Papacy.

Rome's long hegemony finally ended in the 5th century AD, when barbarian Visigoth invaders penetrated to the heart of the Empire and sacked Rome itself (410). The Ostrogoth kingdom of Theodoric the Great (489–526) was followed by the reconquest of Italy by the Eastern Roman (Byzantine) Empire under Justinian (6th century), but under his successors Italy fell to assorted new invaders. Amid the power struggles and fragmentation of the post-imperial era, the Papacy (supported by Pepin the Short, King of the Franks, who recognized the 'patrimony of St Peter') emerged as a territorial power in the 8th century.

Charlemagne, who annexed the Lombard kingdom in the north of Italy to his vast Frankish realms, was crowned in Rome as Roman Emperor by Pope Leo III (800). This title was revived in 961 when Otto I of Germany was crowned in Rome by Pope John XII, marking the beginning of the Holy Roman Empire. Thereafter, Italy's history until the 13th century was in part determined by the long struggle for supremacy between Papacy and Emperors.

In the south, the Norman conquest of Sicily (11th century) led to the creation of the Kingdom of Naples, but in central and northern Italy there was no overall dominion, and instead there emerged several powerful city-state republics, notably Venice, Florence, Milan and Genoa. From c.1300 these cities were in the vanguard of the great European cultural revival, the Renaissance (literally 'rebirth'), which fostered the work of such artists as Botticelli, Piera della Francesca and later of Michelangelo, Leonardo da Vinci and Raphael. Moreover, Venice, Genoa, Pisa and Amalfi built great commercial empires on the basis of trade with the East. By the end of the 15th century, however, the Italian cities were exhausted by constant wars, and economic conditions were changing adversely. In the Mediterranean, Ottoman conquests had the effect of cutting traditional Italian trade routes. In any case, these were being supplanted by the new Atlantic and Cape routes (many of them discovered by Italian mariners, but in the service of Spain or Portugal). As a result, Italy became a battleground for the rising powers of France and Spain, the latter gaining ascendancy in the 16th and 17th centuries, when the Spanish Hapsburgs ruled Milan and Naples and controlled the Papacy. When the War of Spanish Succession (1701–14) ended Spain's domination, the successor power in northern Italy was Hapsburg Austria, although the dukes of Savoy assumed the crown of Sardinia (Piedmont) in 1720.

In the French revolutionary wars, most of divided Italy succumbed to a brilliant military campaign (1796–97) by Napoleon Bonaparte who became King of Italy (1805) as well as Emperor of France. The Congress of Vienna (1815) restored the old order in Italy. The main territorial units were Piedmont and Austrian-ruled Lombardy and Venetia in the north; the duchies of Parma, Modena and Tuscany, and the Papal States, in the centre; and the Bourbon-ruled Kingdom of the Two Sicilies (Sicily and Naples) in the south. However, the impact of French revolutionary ideas was apparent in the formation of the anti-Bourbon Carbonari in the south (1815) and in the creation (1831) of the Young Italy movement by Giuseppe Mazzini (1805–72), intellectual father of the Risorgimento (literally 'resurrection').

The democratic upsurge of 1848 began well for the nationalists but ended in disaster when Piedmontese forces, moving to assist rebelling Lombardy and Venetia, were defeated by the Austrians at Novara (1849). French troops called in by Pope Pius IX (who some nationalists hoped upon his election would prove a liberal and progressive Pope but who emerged as a reactionary) overthrew a Roman republic declared by Mazzini, whose republican wing of the national movement lost momentum thereafter. The initiative passed to the new king of Piedmont, Victor Emmanuel II (r.1849–78), and to his able chief minister, Count Camillo Cavour (1810–61). After Piedmontese troops had fought on the Anglo-French side in the Crimean War (1854–56), allied French and Piedmontese forces were sufficiently victorious in the 1859 Franco-Austrian war for Austria to cede Lombardy to France, which handed it to Piedmont in exchange for Savoy and Nice. Parma, Modena, Tuscany, and most of the Papal States, then united with Piedmont (1859–60), while in 1860–61 the Redshirt soldiers of Giuseppe Garibaldi (1807–82) overran Sicily and Naples on Piedmont's behalf, with friendly British warships waiting offshore. With most of Italy now united, Victor Emmanuel assumed the title King of Italy (Mar. 1861). Of the remaining areas, Venetia was secured through an alliance with Prussia in its 1866 war with Austria, while Rome was occupied by Italian troops in 1870 (after the French garrison had been withdrawn) and declared the capital of Italy.

Liberties enshrined in the 1848 Piedmontese constitution were extended throughout Italy and representative government developed under Umberto I (r.1878–1900). Founded by Cavour, the monarchist Liberal Party (PLI) provided the two major premiers of this period (Francesco Crispi and Giovanni Giolitti), although the Republican Party (PRI, founded 1894) became influential and the Socialist Party (PSI, founded 1892) represented the growing working-class and syndicalist movement. Umberto I was assassinated by an anarchist in 1900 and succeeded by his son, Victor Emmanuel III (r.1900–46). Rivalry with France over Tunisia led Italy to join the Triple Alliance with Germany and Austria-Hungary (1882), but their support for Italian colonial expansion did not ensure success. Although Eritrea and part of Somalia were acquired by 1895, an attempt to seize neighbouring Abyssinia (Ethiopia) ended in humiliating defeat at Adowa (1896). War with Ottoman Turkey (1911–12) resulted in Italy securing Libya and the Dodecanese Islands.

On the outbreak of World War I, Italy reneged on the Triple Alliance with Germany and Austria-Hungary, and eventually (in May 1915) joined the conflict on the side of the Entente powers, after securing promises concerning its irredentist claims against Austria-Hungary. Italy's armies suffered colossal defeat at Caporetto (1917) but recovered just before the end of the war. Under the Paris peace treaty (1919), Italy was awarded South Tirol, Trento and Trieste, but at American insistence its other claims on the Adriatic coast (including Istria and Dalmatia) went to the new state of Yugoslavia.

Dissatisfaction with the Versailles terms was a major reason for the rapid rise of the Fascist Party (founded 1919) led by Benito Mussolini, a former PSI agitator who had espoused right-wing views during the war. Mussolini backed the seizure of the disputed Adriatic city of Fiume by Gabriel D'Annunzio (1919) and condemned the government when it ended the adventure (1921) in compliance with pledges to Yugoslavia. Economic depression and the perceived revolutionary threat posed by the Communist Party (PCI), formed by PSI left-wingers (1921), also aided the Fascists, whose Blackshirt militia adopted terror tactics against opponents. Amid growing unrest, and the threat of a Fascist 'march on Rome', Victor Emmanuel asked Mussolini to form a government (Oct. 1922).

Using the title Duce ('leader'), Mussolini governed in alliance with nationalist groups until 1924, when the murder of PSI leader Giacomo Matteoti caused such protest that the parliamentary system was suspended. In the same year, Fiume came under Italian rule. Fascist one-party rule and corporatism were imposed in 1928–29, accompanied by job-creating public works such as the draining of the Pontine Marshes. The Lateran Treaties with the Vatican (Feb. 1929) which recognized the sovereignty of the Holy See in the Vatican and declared Roman Catholicism to be Italy's state religion, resolved disputes outstanding since 1870. Italy avenged its 1896 defeat by conquering Abyssinia (1935–36), in the face of international censure which led to its withdrawal from the League of Nations (1937). It also aided Gen. Franco in the Spanish Civil War.

Despite earlier doubts about Hitler's aims, Mussolini formed an Axis (his term) with Nazi Germany (1936) and also joined the German-Japanese Anti-Comintern Pact (1937). The German alliance was formalized by the 'pact of steel' (May 1939), shortly after Italy's annexation of Albania (Apr. 1939), whose crown was assumed by Victor Emmanuel. In the event, Italy did not join World War II until June 1940, after the fall of France, whereas its subsequent declarations of war on the Soviet Union (June 1941) and the United States (Dec. 1941) coincided with those of Germany. The Italian forces fared badly in the war, being defeated by Greece (1940) and in East and North Africa. When Italy itself was invaded by the Allies (July 1943), Victor Emmanuel responded by dismissing Mussolini and having him imprisoned. The new prime minister, Marshal Pietro Badoglio (1871–1956), concluded an armistice with the Allies (Sept. 1943), after which Italy declared war on Germany (Oct. 1943). Meanwhile, Mussolini had been released by German paratroopers and had set up a puppet regime in northern Italy, where he was later captured and executed by Italian partisans (Apr. 1945). Following the liberation of Rome (Apr. 1944), an interim government of anti-Fascist parties took office. From Dec. 1945 it was headed by Alcide De Gasperi

(1881–1954) of the Christian Democratic Party (DC), which had been formed (1944) as an alliance of six pre-Mussolini Catholic parties. Post-war legislation made any reconstitution of the Fascist Party illegal.

In May 1946 Victor Emmanuel formally abdicated in favour of his son, Humberto II. The following month a national referendum showed a narrow majority in favour of republican government, whereupon Humberto II, with some reluctance, also abdicated, being replaced as head of state by Enrico De Nicola (non-party). In simultaneous constituent assembly elections, a PCI/PSI popular front outpolled the DC, but the centre-right secured an aggregate majority, which increased when the PSI right broke away (Jan. 1947) to form what became the Democratic Socialist Party (PSDI). Six months later, with the onset of Cold War accentuating left-right divisions, the PCI and PSI were excluded from the government (July 1947). Meanwhile, Italy had signed a peace treaty with the Allies (Feb. 1947), obliging it to cede border areas to France and Yugoslavia, and the Dodecanese to Greece, and to waive all rights to its former colonies. (Of these, Eritrea went to Ethiopia in 1950, Libya became independent in 1951, and Italian Somalia, after reverting to Italian administration under UN auspices in 1950, became part of Somalia in 1960.)

Following the promulgation of a new constitution (Dec. 1947), the Italian Republic came into being on 1 Jan. 1948. The first elections proper (Apr. 1948) showed sharply increased support for De Gasperi and the DC, which formed a centrist coalition with the PSDI, PLI and PRI (the last two much reduced from their pre–1922 strength). The new Parliament elected Luigi Einaudi (PLI) as president of Italy. His successors in the post were Giovanni Gronchi (DC), 1955–62, Antonio Segni (DC), 1962–64, Giuseppe Saragat (PSDI), 1965–71, Giovani Leone (DC), 1971–78, Sandro Pertini (PSI), 1978–85, and Francesco Cossiga (DC), from 1985.

Italy became a founder member of NATO in 1949 and of the WEU in 1955, in which year it was also admitted to the UN. Under a defence agreement with the United States (1950), US military bases were established in Italy within the NATO framework. Under De Gasperi's leadership (until 1953), Italy was an enthusiastic participant in the creation of the European Coal and Steel Community (1951–52) and later, under his successors, of the other two European Communities (EC). Assisted by US Marshall Aid, and later by EC membership, Italy made a steady recovery from post-war economic privations and in the 1960s entered a phase of rapid industrial growth. Serious economic problems remained, however, one of the most intractable being the poverty and under-development of the south (Mezzogiorno). Although successive governments allocated substantial resources to projects in the south, the gap between it and the prosperous north continued to widen. In addition, various initiatives by the state authorities appeared to make little impact on the pervasive power of the Mafia in southern Italy.

The PCI and PSI, led respectively by Palmiro Togliatti and Pietro Nenni, both remained in opposition to successive DC-led centrist coalitions in the 1950s. After the Hungarian uprising (1956), however, Nenni gradually distanced his party from the pro-Soviet PCI. This facilitated the 'opening to the left' (1962–63) by which DC-led centre-left governments either included PSI members or accepted the party's external support. The first such coalition with actual PSI participation was that formed by Aldo Moro (DC) in Dec. 1964. One effect was a decline in DC electoral support to under 40% in the 1960s and 1970s, compared with its high of 49% in 1948, and the rise of the extreme right-wing Italian Social Movement (founded 1946) to a peak of 9% in the 1972 elections. At the same time, the PCI steadily increased its electoral support as Italy's second-strongest party, reaching over 34% in 1976; under the leadership of Enrico Berlinguer (from 1972), the PCI had by then moved to a moderate 'Euro-communist' line (including support for NATO and EC membership).

A particular challenge faced by centre-left administrations in the 1970s was that of escalating urban terrorism by groups of the extreme left and right. The leftist Red Brigades (founded 1969), in 1978, abducted and murdered Moro (by then DC president), while neo-fascist extremists planted a bomb at Bologna which exploded on 2 Aug. 1980 killing 84 and wounding nearly 200 others. The 1980s saw a gradual reduction in such violence, however.

The DC's post-war monopoly of the premiership finally ended in June 1981, when it agreed to serve in a five-party coalition headed by Giovanni Spadolini of the PRI. Although the DC resumed the premiership the following year, it suffered a major setback in the 1983 Chamber elections (falling to 33%), while the PSI, PSDI, PRI and PLI gained ground, and the PCI fell back to under 30%. The result was DC participation in Italy's first PSI-led government, under Bettino Craxi, whose centre-left coalition created a post-war record by surviving for nearly four years.

In the 1987 elections, the Greens entered the Chamber for the first time and PSI continued its advance (to 14.3%), partly at the expense of the post-Berlinguer PCI (whose 26.6% was its lowest share since 1963). But the DC recovered to 34.3% (and the smaller centre parties lost ground), enabling it to head further five-party centre-left coalitions, under Giovanni Goria until Apr. 1988, when Ciriaco De Mita took power. However, increasing criticism of De Mita's government programme by the PSI led him to resign in May 1989. Protracted negotiations interrupted by elections to the European Parliament in June eventually led to the formation of Italy's 49th government since the War. The coalition comprised the same five parties as before (DC, PSI, PRI, PLI, PSDI) and was headed by the Christian Democrat Giulio Andreotti, who had been Prime Minister five times previously.

CONSTITUTION AND GOVERNMENT

Executive and legislature

The head of state is the president of the Republic, whose duties are largely ceremonial, and who is elected for a seven-year term by an electoral college made up of both Houses of Parliament and 58 regional representatives. The president of the republic appoints the president of the council (prime minister), who is the head of government. The legislature is a bicameral Parliament elected by universal adult suffrage using proportional representation; the upper house, the Senate, is made up of 315 senators elected for five years on a regional basis, and seven life senators. The lower house, the 630-member Chamber of Deputies, is also elected for a maximum term of five years: last elections were in June 1987.

Present government

President of the Republic Francesco Cossiga

Prime Minister Giulio Andreotti
Principal Ministers Claudio Martelli (Deputy Prime Minister); Gianni De Michelis (Foreign Affairs); Mino Martinazzoli (Defence); Antonio Gava (Interior); Giuliano Vassalli (Justice); Guido Carli (Treasury); Cirino Pomicino (Budget); Salvatore (Rino) Formica (Finance).

Justice

Italy is divided for judicial purposes into 23 appeal court districts, subdivided into 159 tribunal districts. These are in turn divided into 899 'mandamenti' each with its own magistracy. There is a Court of Cassation in Rome and 90 first degree assize courts and 26 assize courts of appeal. The death penalty is in force only for exceptional crimes. There were no executions between 1985 and mid-1988.
Prisons. There are 35,589 prisoners.

National symbols

Flag. Tricolour with vertical stripes of green, white and red.
Festivals. 25 Apr. (Liberation Day); 1 May (Labour Day); 12 May (Festival of the Tricolour); 5 Nov (National Unity Day).
Vehicle registration plate. I.

INTERNATIONAL RELATIONS

Affiliations

NATO; OECD; EC; Council of Europe.

Defence

Total Armed Forces: 386,000 (270,500 conscripts). Terms of service: All services 12 months. Reserves: 769,000 (obligation to age 45).
Army: 265,000; 1,720 main battle tanks (mainly M-47/-60A1 and Leopard).
Navy: 48,000 inclusive 1,500 air arm, 600 special forces; ten submarines (mainly 184 HWT, US Tang), 30 principal surface combatants: one carrier (with 16 SH-3 Sea King helicopters), three cruisers, four destroyers and 22 frigates. 15 patrol and coastal combatants.
Navy Air Arm: 1,500; 98 armed helicopters.
Air Force: 73,000; 399 combat aircrafts (mainly Tornada, F-104, F-104S).

ECONOMY

Currency

The unit is the lira, divided into 100 centesimi.

National finance

Budget. The 1987 budget (in US$) was for expenditure (current and capital) of 311,000 million and revenue of 218,000 million. Main items of current expenditure are housing and welfare 36.3%; health 9.6%; education 7.4%; defence 3.2%.
Balance of payments. The balance of payments (current account, 1988) was a deficit of $5,570 million.
Inflation. 6.6% (12 months to Sept. 1989).

Gross Domestic Product

Estimated total GDP US$748,620 million, per capita US$14,200 (ranking 6 in the world by size). Growth rate (1988) 3.9%.
Economically active population. The total number of persons active in the economy was 23,670,000; unemployed: 12.2% (1988).

Sector	% of workforce	% of GDP
industry	37.9	34
agriculture	5.4	4
services*	56.7	61

* services figure includes elements unassigned to other categories.

Energy and mineral resources

Oil and gas. Oil production was 4,304,481.5 tons/3,905,000 tonnes (1987), around 25% of which came from Sicily. Gas production was 573,600 million ft^3/16,243 m^3.
Minerals. Italy is poor in mineral resources with only mercury (accounting for over 25% of world production) and sulphur being produced in sufficient quantities for export. Production: (1987 in tons/tonnes) raw steel 25,197,476/22,859,000; rolled iron 22,979,648/20,847,000; cast-iron ingots 12,494,571/11,335,000; iron pyrites 865,306/785,000; aluminium 284,393/258,000; zinc 74,956/68,000; lead 65,636/59,000; bauxite 16,535/15,000; manganese 4,409/4,000.
Electricity. Capacity: 54,000,000 kW; production: 197,450 kWh; 3,440 kWh per capita (1988).

Bioresources

Agriculture. Some 32% of the land is arable, 10% is used for permanent crops and 17% is meadows and pastures. Main products are fruits; wine; vegetables; cereals; potatoes; olives, which together account for 4% of GDP. The country is 95% self-sufficient in foodstuffs.
Crop production: (1987 in 1,000,000 tons/tonnes) sugar beet 17.1/15.5; grapes 12.7/11.5; wheat 10.4/9.4; maize 6.4/5.8; tomatoes 5.3/4.8; olives 3.9/3.5; potatoes 2.8/2.5; citrus fruit 2.5/2.3; apples 2.4/2.2; barley 1.9/1.7; peaches 1.7/1.5; rice 1.1/1.0.
Livestock numbers: (1987 in millions); sheep 11.5; pigs 9.4; cattle 8.8; goats 1.2; horses 0.25.
Forestry. About 22% of the land is forested. Some 339,826,622 ft^3/9,623,000 m^3 of timber was felled in 1986.
Fisheries. Annual catch: (1986) 383,600 tons/348,000 tonnes plus 604,060 ons/548,000 tonnes of shrimps; other crustaceans; mussels; squid; octopus; other molluscs etc.

Industry and commerce

Industry. The main industries are machinery and transportation equipment; iron and steel; chemicals; food processing; textiles; motor vehicles. The country is still divided between the developed industrialized north dominated by large private companies and state enterprises, and the underdeveloped south.
Commerce. Exports: US$128,600 million, including textiles; clothes; metals; transportation equipment; chemicals. Imports: (1988) US$138,500 million, including petroleum; industrial machinery; chemicals; metals; food; agricultural products. Countries exported to: EC countries 56%; US 10%; OPEC 5%. Imports came from: EC countries 56%; OPEC 8%; US 5%.
Trade with UK. Italy imported UK goods worth £4,057 million; exports to UK totalled £3,879 million (1988).
Tourism. (1987) 52,700,000 visitors.

COMMUNICATIONS

Railways

There are 9,932 miles/15,983 km of railways, of which 5,661 miles/9,110 km are electrified.

Roads

There are 187,229 miles/301,307 km of roads.

Aviation

Alitalia provides international services; Aero Trasporti Italiani SpA (ATI) and Alisarda SpA provide domestic services. Passengers: (1986) 13.8 million.

Shipping

There are 994 miles/1,600 km of inland waterways used for commercial traffic, but they have limited overall value. The major coastal ports are Genoa, La Spezia and Livorno (on the Ligurian Sea); Naples and Piombino (on the Tyrrhenian Sea); Ancona, Trieste and Venice (on the Adriatic coast) and Taranto (on the Ionian Sea). Palermo and Augusta are maritime ports of Sicily. Cagliari and Porto Foxi are maritime ports of Sardinia. The merchant marine has 545 ships of 1,000 GRT or over. Freight loaded: (1986) 105 million tons/95.3 million tonnes; unloaded: 282.5 million tons/256.3 million tonnes.

Telecommunications

There are 28 million telephones and the Italian system is well engineered, constructed and operated. There are some 15 million radio sets and a similar number of televisions. RAI-TV, a public company with a parliamentary commission to supervise its operations, claimed a monopoly of broadcasting until 1976, but its three national radio and three TV channels now face competition from seven private nationwide TV networks, some 500 local TV and 1,000 local radio stations. Radio Roma runs external broadcasts in 27 languages.

EDUCATION AND WELFARE

Education

The state provides free, compulsory education between the ages of six and 14. The first five years of compulsory education are spent at primary school and the remaining three at junior secondary school (scuola media). After this pupils may go on to attend a senior secondary school (secondaria superiore), such as a lyceum, technology institute, commercial or industry school or teacher-training college. University education is not free although students with higher entrance qualifications pay less.

Schools. There are 1,587,000 pupils in 28,400 kindergartens (for 3–5 year olds); 3,107,000 pupils in 24,300 public primary schools; 2,619,000 pupils in 10,000 junior secondary schools; 2,719,000 pupils in 7700 various different senior secondary schools.

Universities. There are over a million students at the 35 state and 14 private universities, six of which (Bologna, Genoa, Macerata, Naples, Padua, and Perugia) are among the world's oldest and were founded in the 13th century.

Literacy. 93%.

Health

In 1978 a national health service providing comprehensive free health care was introduced in place of a national insurance system. There were 237,578 doctors (one per 240 people) and 470,579 hospital beds (one per 120 people) (1985). The social security system run by the Instituto Nazionale della Previdenza Sociale gives comprehensive pension cover. An earnings-related scheme is financed by employee, employer and government contributions with special schemes for public employees, certain professional groups and the self-employed. There is a government-funded, means-tested pension scheme for those not eligible for the earnings-related scheme. There is also a family allowance scheme.

JAMAICA

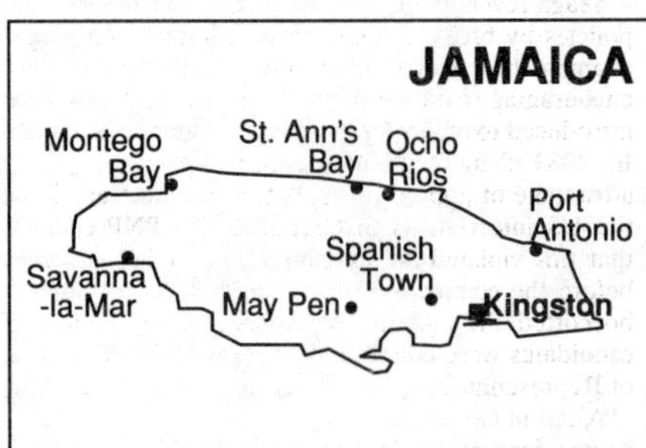

GEOGRAPHY

Located in the Caribbean Sea, 89 miles/144 km south of Cuba and 99 miles/160 km south-west of Haiti, Jamaica covers an area of 6,830 miles^2/10,991 km^2 divided into three counties. An incised limestone plateau (average elevation 1,509 ft/460 m) occupying an estimated 50% of the total surface area east-west and pitted with sinkholes in its upper reaches, encompasses the densely forested Blue Mountains in the east (rising to 7,402 ft/2,256 m at Blue Mountain Peak). In the west and south-west, the River Black is navigable for about 19 miles/30 km of its lava course. The densely populated lowland coastal fringe is extensively cultivated, dominated by sugar cane plantations. Of the land, 19% is arable and 28% is forest or woodland.

Climate

Tropical, becoming temperate at highest elevations. High coastal humidity encompasses temperatures ranging from 75–88°F/24–31°C, moderated by sea breezes. Abundant rainfall in the north (up to 199 in/ 5,060 mm) particularly during May and Aug.-Nov. (78 in/1,980 mm mean total). Rainfall decreases dramatically in the south and south-west. Jamaica lies within the tropical hurricane zone. Kingston: Jan.

76°F/24.4°C. July 81°F/27.2°C. Average annual rainfall 31.5 in/800 mm.

Cities and towns

Kingston (capital)	104,000
Montego Bay	42,800
Spanish Town	41,600

Population

Total population is 2,446,000 of which 49.1% live in urban areas. Population density is 358 persons per mile^2/215.2 per km^2. Ethnic divisions: 76.3% African; 15.1% Afro-European; 3.4% East Indian and Afro-East Indian; 3.2% White; 1.2% Chinese and Afro-Chinese; 0.8% other.

Birth rate 2.81%. **Death rate** 0.56%. **Rate of population increase** (1980–87) 2.25%. **Age distribution** under 15 = 36.7%; over 65 = 6.1%. **Life expectancy** female 77; male 71; average 74.

Religion

Christianity: largely Protestant (70.7% est.) the majority of whom are Anglican, Presbyterian or Baptist. About 7–8% of the population are Roman Catholic (archdiocese of Kingston, Jamaica includes Cayman Islands and diocese of Montego Bay). Some spiritualist cults have strong representations including Pocomania, an Afro-Christian rite. Rastafarianism (belief in the divinity of the late Emperor Haile Selassie) continues to flourish. There are an estimated 250 Jews.

Language

English is the official language, although the local Jamaican creole-patois has wide currency with morphological and syntactical borrowings from English, Spanish, French and African languages.

HISTORY

The earliest inhabitants of Jamaica were Arawak Indians, probably migrating from South America about AD 700. In 1494 Columbus claimed the island for Spain. The Spanish colonized the island in 1510, exterminating the Arawak population through war, disease and forced labour. The island remained sparsely inhabited and was easily seized by an English expeditionary force in 1655. Although initially established as a base for English privateering ventures in the Caribbean, Jamaica soon developed into a plantation society, using the labour of imported African slaves to produce sugar and coffee. The colony prospered during the 18th century, but the abolition of the slave trade in the early 19th century, the fear of slave uprisings, and the eventual emancipation of the slaves in 1838 ruined the plantation economy. A revolt by disaffected ex-slaves at Morant Bay was put down by the Governor with excessive force, leading to his dismissal and the establishment of Crown Colony government over the island in 1866.

Political unrest and discontent in many sectors of society was fuelled during the 1930s by economic depression. Labour unrest and rioting erupted in 1938, leading to the formation of a trade union, the Bustamente Industrial Trade Union, led by Alexander (later Sir Alexander) Bustamente. In 1939 the left-of-centre People's National Party (PNP) was founded by Norman Manley, Bustamente's cousin. Political reforms were introduced in the wake of the unrest, and in 1944 the first elections under universal suffrage were held and won by the Jamaica Labour Party (JLP), formed by Bustamente. The JLP won the elections held in 1949, but lost to the PNP in 1954, after Manley had purged his party of its more left-wing supporters. A ministerial system had been established in 1953, and full internal self-government was introduced in 1959. Jamaica joined the Federation of the West Indies in 1958, but when it became clear that the British government would allow Jamaica to become independent outside of the Federation, Manley held a referendum in which the majority supported secession. The JLP won the general election held shortly before Jamaica left the Federation and achieved independence on 6 Aug. 1962, with Bustamente as the country's first prime minister.

Bustamente retired in 1967 and was succeeded by Donald (later Sir Donald) Sangster, and after his sudden death Hugh Shearer became prime minister. The JLP had won elections in 1967, but growing disenchantment with the JLP administration, including alleged corruption and the events surrounding the 'Rodney riots' in 1968, allowed the PNP under Norman Manley's son, Michael, to win the 1972 election. Michael Manley then embarked on a radical left-wing programme of policies, including land reform, social programmes, and a foreign policy of non-alignment and support for other Third World states, with closer ties to Cuba. Support for these policies from the urban and rural poor helped secure another term in office for the PNP at elections in 1976.

However, the worsening economic situation, caused by the price of petroleum and world depression, placed an increasing strain on the PNP's management of the economy at a time when the party was moving politically further to the left. The Marxist rhetoric used by the PNP and its close ties with the communist Workers' Party of Jamaica (WPJ) persuaded many Jamaicans to emigrate.

Growing economic difficulties led to further dependence on the International Monetary Fund (IMF), but in 1979 Manley decided to break with the IMF by refusing to accept conditions imposed for further loans to the country, and called a general election to secure a mandate for his negotiating position. The 1980 election campaign was held in an atmosphere of violence and bitterness between the two main parties. Over 700 people were killed in politically-related violence, as armed gangs of supporters fought with each other. In the election, held in Oct. 1980, the PNP was heavily defeated by the JLP under Edward Seaga.

Seaga reversed many of the previous government's policies by breaking diplomatic relations with Cuba, aligning the country more closely with the US, and encouraging free enterprise. Austerity measures were introduced to deal with the severe economic situation. In 1983 Seaga called a general election, taking advantage of popular support for his endorsement of the US intervention in Grenada. The PNP claimed that this violated an agreement not to call elections before the completion of a new electoral roll, and it boycotted the election in protest. As a result JLP candidates were elected to all the seats in the House of Representatives.

A fall in earnings from bauxite (the country's main export earner) worsened the economic situation and forced the government to introduce further austerity measures. In Jan. 1985 a rise in the price of petrol led to several days of unrest, with seven people killed. In Sept. 1988 the country was devastated by hurricane Gilbert, which caused widespread damage to homes, communications, and crops. 20% of the population was rendered homeless, and Prime Minister Seaga appealed for international aid and assistance. A general election, delayed until 9 Feb. 1989, was won by the PNP, projecting the more centrist image it had developed since its defeat in 1980. Michael Manley returned to power as prime minister.

CONSTITUTION AND GOVERNMENT

Executive and legislature

The head of state is the British sovereign, represented by a governor general. The prime minister, who is head of government, is nominally appointed by the governor general but is responsible to parliament. The bicameral parliament consists of a 60-member House of Representatives, elected directly by universal adult suffrage for a maximum term of five years (last elections 9 Feb. 1989), and a 21-member appointed senate.

Present government

Governor General Sir Florizel Glasspole
Prime Minister, Minister of Defence Michael Manley
Deputy Prime Minister; Production, Development and Planning Percival Patterson
Principal Ministers David Coore (Foreign Affairs); Seymour Mullings (Finance); Carl Rattray (Justice and Attorney General); K.D. Knight (National Security); Claude Clark (Industry and Commerce).

Justice

There is a Supreme Court and Court of Appeal. The president of the Court of Appeal and the chief justice of the Supreme Court are appointed by the governor general on the advice of the prime minister after consultation with the leader of the opposition. The death penalty is in force. There were 30 executions between 1985 and mid-1988. The offences were murder.

National symbols

Flag. Divided by a golden yellow saltire into four triangles, the upper and lower ones being green and those in the hoist and fly being black.
Festivals. 23 May (Labour Day); 7 Aug. (6 Aug. in 1990, Independence Day); 16. Oct. (15. Oct. in 1990, National Heroes' Day).
Vehicle registration plate. JA.

INTERNATIONAL RELATIONS

Affiliations

NAM; ACP; Commonwealth; OAS; Caricom.

Defence

Total Armed Forces: 2,500. Terms of service: voluntary. Reserves: some 750.
Army: 2,200.
Coastguard: 150; five inshore patrol craft.
Air Force: 150; no combat aircraft, no armed helicopters.

ECONOMY

Currency

The unit is the Jamaican dollar, divided into 100 cents.

National finance

Budget. The 1987 budget (in US$) was for expenditure (current and capital) of 973 million and revenue of 914 million.
Balance of payments. The balance of payments (current account, 1987) was a deficit of $160 million.
Inflation. (1987) 6.7%.

Gross Domestic Product

Estimated total GDP US$2,860 million, per capita US$1,160 (ranking 106 in the world by size).
Economically active population. The total number of persons active in the economy was 728,700; unemployed: 21%.

Sector	% of workforce	% of GDP
industry		41
agriculture	32	6
services*		53

* services figure includes elements unassigned to other categories.

Energy and mineral resources

Minerals. Jamaica is the world's third largest producer of bauxite, and also has deposits of marble; gypsum; silica sand; limestone. Output: (in 1,000 tons/tonnes) bauxite ore 8,598/7,800; gypsum 194.3/176.3; marble 0.6/0.5; industrial lime 7,592.6 ft^3/2.15 m^3 (1987).
Electricity. Capacity: 1,437,000 kW; production: 2,400 million kWh; 980 kWh per capita.

Bioresources

Agriculture. There are an estimated 380,534 acres/ 154,000 ha of cultivated land, 14% of the country's total area. The main crops are sugar; bananas; citrus fruits; spices; cocoa; coffee; coconuts; tobacco.
Crop production: (1987 in 1,000 tons/tonnes) sugar cane 2,164/1,963; sugar 205/186; molasses 78.9/71.6; bananas 37.5/34; citrus fruit 33.7/30.6; cocoa 2.9/2.6; spices 2.6/2.4.
Livestock numbers: (1987) poultry 5 million; goats 440,000; cattle 290,000; pigs 246,000.
Forestry. Forests cover 28% of the country.

Industry and commerce

Industry. Jamaica's main industries are related to bauxite production (in 1987 1.8 million tons/1.6 million tonnes of alumina was produced through processing bauxite), and the processing of agricultural products to produce sugar, rum, condensed milk, cigars and cigarettes. Jamaica also has a variety of other industries manufacturing clothing and shoes; textiles; paint; cement; agricultural machinery.
Commerce. Exports: US$650 million; imports US$1,210 million (1987). Exports in 1988 included bauxite; alumina; sugar; bananas. Imports included petroleum; machinery; food; consumer goods; construction goods. Countries exported to: US 40%; UK; Canada; Trinidad and Tobago; Norway. Imports were received from: US 46%; UK; Venezuela; Canada; Japan; Trinidad and Tobago.
Trade with UK. Jamaica imported UK goods worth £48,855,000 and exported to the UK goods worth £89,693 (1988).
Tourism. Jamaica derived revenue of US$595 million from 1,037,634 visitors (1987).

COMMUNICATIONS

Railways

There are 229 miles/369 km of railways.

Roads

There are 9,317 miles/14,994 km of roads, of which 2,270 miles/3,653 km are concrete or bituminized.

Aviation

Air Jamaica provides international services and Trans-Jamaican provides domestic services (main airports are the Norman Manley International Airport, 14 miles/22 km outside Kingston, and the Donald Sangster International Airport, 3 miles/5 km from Montego Bay). Passengers: (1984) 747,000.

Shipping

Kingston, on the south coast of the island and Montego Bay on the north are the major ports. The merchant marine consists of four ships of 1,000 GRT or over. Freight loaded: (1985) 6.1 million tons/ 5.5 million tonnes; unloaded: 4.7 million tons/ 3.7 million tonnes.

Telecommunications

There are 127,000 telephones and a fully automatic domestic network. There are about 1.5 million radios and 460,000 television sets; the publicly owned Jamaica Broadcasting Corporation (JBC) provides both television and radio services, and there is in addition the RJR commercial and public service radio station and an educational broadcasting service.

EDUCATION AND WELFARE

Education

Primary education is compulsory and is free in most districts; children wishing to enter secondary school are obliged to take a common entrance examination at the age of 11.

School population. 622,224 (of whom 122,380 were in pre-primary schools).

Schools. 1,585 pre-primary schools; 293 primary schools; 141 secondary and vocational schools; 492 schools catering for all ages.

Universities. Six of the eight faculties of the University of the West Indies are based in Jamaica.

Literacy. 85%.

Health

Jamaica's health service has 23 general hospitals and seven public specialist hospitals, providing a total of 5,472 public beds and 305 private. Health care is also provided through 361 primary health centres.

JAPAN
Nippon (Nihon)

GEOGRAPHY

Located off the east Asian coast in the north Pacific, Japan comprises four principal islands and more than 3,000 small islands (islets containing a total area of 145,795 miles^2/377,708 km^2. Volcanic mountainous terrain typifies the physiography of the Japanese islands. Hokkaido (north), area 32,238 miles^2/83,519 km^2, is traversed north-south by a range of mountains (often above 6,562 ft/2,000 m high) surrounded by fertile coastal plains. A low-lying coastal belt also encloses the Hioa Alps, Mt Fuji-San (Japan's highest peak at 12,388 ft/3,776 m) and the Chugoku Mts on the densely populated island of Honshu (89,194 miles^2/231,073 km^2). To the east, the Kanto plain (which includes Tokyo) is the most populous and heavily industrialized of the southern Honshu regions. A complex of lava peaks and undulating uplands stretches from south-western Honshu across Shikoku (7,257 miles^2/18,800 km^2) and Kyushu (16,270 miles^2/42,150 km^2) islands to the volcanic Ryukyu archipelago which sweeps south towards Taiwan. Drainage basins tend to be small: the five largest rivers are the Tone, the Ishikari, the Kitikami, the Kiso and the Shinano. Offshore submarine earthquakes triggering tsunami waves can cause extensive structural damage along the Pacific coast. 11% of the land is arable and over two-thirds (68%) is forest or woodland.

Climate

Lying north-east of the Southeast Asian monsoonal belt, the islands of Japan experience a generally temperate oceanic climate with warm (humid) summers and mild winters, although winter precipitation (snow) in NW Honshu and W Hokkaido can be heavy and temperatures severe. The month-long wet season June-July brings the heaviest rainfall to most parts of Japan: weather conditions are most equable during spring and autumn though typhoons are not uncommon throughout Sept. Tokyo: Jan. 40°F/4.7°C. July 77°F/25.2°C. Average annual rainfall 575 in/1,460 mm. Hiroshima: Jan. 40°F/4.3°C. July 78°F/25.6°C. Average annual rainfall 63 in/1,603 mm. Sapporo: Jan. 23°F/–4.9°C. July 68°F/20.2°C. Average annual rainfall 46 in/1,158 mm.

Cities and towns

Tokyo (capital)	8,155,781
Yokohama	3,121,601
Osaka	2,543,520
Nagoya	2,099,546
Sapporo	1,582,073
Kobe	1,426,838
Kyoto	1,419,390
Fukuoka	1,157,111
Kawasaki	1,114,173
Hiroshima	1,042,629
Kitakyushu	1,035,053

Population

Total population is 122,424,000 of which 76.2% live in urban areas. Population density is 840 persons per mile^2/323.2 persons per km^2. Ethnic divisions by nationality: 99.4% Japanese (including the indigenous Ainu peoples on Hokkaido island); 0.67% other (mostly Korean).

Birth rate 1.27%. **Death rate** 0.62%. **Rate of population increase** (1980–87) 0.65%. **Age distribution** under 15 = 21.5%; over 65 = 10.3%. **Life expectancy** female 81; male 75; average 78.

Religion

The majority of the Japanese observe both Shinto and Buddhist rites (107,576,000 Shinto adherents and 92,947,000 Buddhists). There are an estimated 1,081,387 Christians, nearly 446,000 of whom are Roman Catholic. Other minority religious groups include a small community of Muslims in Tokyo and a number of new religions of predominantly Buddhist doctrinal foundation, e.g. Rissito Kosei-Kai and Soka Gakkai.

Language

Japanese is the national language (part of the Ural-Altaic language family), composed of two chief dialects, Hondo and Nanto, and a range of sub-idioms (eastern and western Hondo, Kyuishu, Kinki, Izumo and Nansei). It is also spoken in Korea and Taiwan as a second language.

HISTORY

The origins of Japanese society are obscured by uncertain archaeological evidence and a veil of political and religious myth, which strove to legitimize the Yamato dynasty by linking it with the creation of the world itself, through the person of the Sun Goddess, Amaterasu Omikami, alleged ancestor of the Japanese imperial line. Japanese tradition, still taught in schools as historical fact as recently as 1945, regarded the accession of a reputed first emperor, Jimmu, in 660 BC as marking the beginning of the Japanese state and inaugurating an unbroken line of 125 emperors. This dynastic continuity, coupled with a language only tenuously related to any other, and combined with an absence of ethnic or religious minorities has imparted a strong sense of distinctiveness and homogeneity to Japanese society.

Palaeolithic tool finds suggest human settlement stretching back at least 30,000 years, and there are pottery remains from 10,000 BC. By the 5th century AD a strong rice-growing kingdom under the rule of the Yamato family controlled south-central Honshu; and its people, a mixture of Micronesian, Malay and Mongol ethnic groups, were driving the Ainu, the aboriginal inhabitants of the archipelago, into the cold north and ultimately to the island of Hokkaido, which was not formally made part of Japan until 1868. From the 6th century onwards came cultural influences from mainland Asia, often via Korea. The Japanese court, led by the reforming Regent, Prince Shotoku Taishi, eagerly adopted Buddhism but saw no need to discard the native cult of Shinto, which expressed a profound reverence for nature. The Chinese calendar, writing system and craft skills in lacquer, silk and ceramics were likewise adapted. Following China's example a fixed capital was established for the first time in 710 at Nara and in 794 the capital was moved to nearby Kyoto, which retained this status, in theory at least, until 1868. Japan's first written literature, consisting of collections of ancient chronicles (Kojiki) and poetry (Manyoshu) date from this period. Significantly they authenticate and celebrate the distinctiveness of Japanese culture. By the 9th century mainland influences had begun to diminish as the cultural imports of the previous two centuries became Japanized.

Real political power slipped gradually from the hands of the emperors into those of court officials and after a period of turmoil known as the Heike wars, there arose a new breed of ruler, the shogun or military dictator, who monopolized effective power while maintaining the fiction of obedience to the emperor. This system of shogunal rule lasted from 1192 to 1867 and helped to foster the samurai code of bushido (the path of the warrior) which stressed loyalty, frugality and unflinching courage. The Zen form of Buddhism, which cultivated self-awareness through disciplined self-control, represented the spiritual embodiment of this ideology. The power of the shogunate based on the coastal stronghold of Kamkura (1192–1333) was broken by the effort of fending off massive Mongol invasion fleets in 1274 and 1281, when the timely intervention of destructive typhoons (Kamikaze – 'Divine Wind') confirmed Japanese confidence in heavenly protection for the 'Land of the Gods'. After a brief interval, during which the emperor Go-Daigo vainly attempted to seize direct power, a new shogun line was established by the Ashikaga family (1338–1573). They succumbed to internal challenges which degenerated into a century of civil wars. Despite this turmoil the period also saw the emergence of such new cultural forms as tea-ceremony (cha-no-yu) and flower-arranging (ikebana) and the creation of such national treasures as the Kinkakuji (Golden Pavilion) and the stone and gravel garden at Tyoanji monastery in Kyoto.

The reunification of the country was begun by the warlord Oda Nobunaga, who vowed to put 'all the country under one sword' and made very effective use of guns in doing just that. The process was virtually completed by one of his lieutenants, Hideyoshi Toyotomi, who disarmed the peasantry and then launched a savage invasion of Korea, with a view to the conquest of China. This project was aborted at his death and the work of domestic pacification resumed by Tokugawa Ieyasu, who brought his rivals to decisive defeat at Sekigahara in 1600 and assumed the vacant title of shogun in 1603. He created a framework of semi-centralized feudalism whereby the authority of the Tokugawa family and its vassals was balanced against the power of some 250 daimyo (literally 'great name') who ran their own vast estates under the surveillance of inspectors and spies and subject to an elaborate system of hostage-taking and costly ritual court attendances (sankin-koai). Ruling from their gigantic fortress at Edo (now Tokyo) the Tokugawa shoguns brought peace and stability at the price of excluding contact with the outside world, a policy of 'closed country' (sakoku). From 1543 onwards Western traders and missionaries had introduced the Japanese to guns, clocks, carpets and Christianity. Ieyasu's successors banned Christianity as potentially subversive, fearing the involvement of foreign troops in the event of renewed disorders. From 1639 onwards Japanese were forbidden to travel abroad and trading contacts were limited to a single Dutch settlement in Nagasaki harbour. From 1720 onwards the importation of Western books was permitted and a group of 'rangaku' (Dutch learning) scholars maintained an interest in such practical matters as astronomy, anatomy and cartography, in which 'barbarian' expertise was conceded to exist. Sheltered from alien influences and bolstered by the prosperity of the great commercial city of Osaka and the towns which grew up around daimyo castles, Japanese culture developed further distinctive art-forms.

Japan's long seclusion was forcefully ended in 1853 when a squadron of American warships, commanded by Commodore Matthew Perry, coerced the shogunal government into conceding trading rights to the Western powers. After a period of political hesitancy the humiliated Tokugawa regime was overthrown following a brief civil war in 1868. Edo was taken over in the name of Emperor Meiji ('Enlightened Rule') and re-named Tokyo ('Eastern Capital'). Proclaiming their intention to 'restore' power to the young emperor, a clique of dissident samurai from south-western Honshu initially attempted to eliminate Western influences. The Iwakura mission of 1871–72, however, though it failed in its diplomatic objective of re-negotiating the 'unequal treaties', convinced the leaders of the new government of the industrial and military superiority of the West. A far-reaching programme of modernization along western lines was initiated under the slogan 'Fukoku kyohei' (Rich country, strong army). The privileges of samurai rank were abolished, commerce fostered rather than despised, universal elementary education introduced and a constitution, modelled on that of Bismarck's Germany, promulgated in 1889. Aided by foreign experts, the Japanese rapidly learned how to build railways, make steel and train doctors in Western medicine. Great care was taken, however, to rely ultimately neither on foreign expertise nor on foreign capital for development. The Japanese found what they needed for investment by squeezing it out of the long-suffering peasantry through taxes on agriculture rather than on rapidly growing industry, and by promoting silk as a major export crop. In half a lifetime the Japanese modernizers created a state sufficiently powerful to defeat first of all China (1894–95) and then Russia (1904–5) annexing Formosa (Taiwan) and Korea as a result.

Japan made further territorial gains in the Pacific at the Paris Peace Conference of 1919 but was frustrated by the failure to insert a racial equality clause in the charter of the new League of Nations. American limits on Japanese immigration caused further resentment. In 1923 a catastrophic earthquake wiped out the port of Yokohama and half of Tokyo, at the cost of some 140,000 lives. The disaster was worsened by widespread attacks on the Korean minority, accused of looting the ruins. The social and economic strains which accompanied breakneck modernization were aggravated by the collapse of world trade after 1929. The fumbling of venial politicians contrasted sharply with the eager decisiveness of a seemingly selfless military, and served to discredit methods and an internationalist stance. The army had a record of more than 50 years of victories, unblemished by defeat. Recruiting its soldiers and junior officers from the hard-pressed peasantry it could plausibly claim to have a sympathetic understanding of the plight of the nation's most distressed class. Radical nationalism and expansion at the expense of weaker neighbours seemed to offer the best path forward for over-crowded and beleaguered Japan. Having seized resource-rich Manchuria in 1931 and created the puppet-state of Manchukuo, Japan launched a full-scale invasion of China in 1937. Meanwhile Japan itself experienced increasing restrictions on civil liberties, though an attempt by young officers to seize power in the name of the emperor in Feb. 1936 was discountenanced by Emperor Hirohito himself. Determined to create its own autarkic trading-bloc, Japan posed as the redeemer of Asian peoples from white colonial rule and proclaimed the establishment of a 'Greater East Asia Co-Prosperity Sphere'. Extremists avowed the aspiration of 'Hakko ichiu' – 'all the eight corners of the world under one roof' – ie Japanese imperial rule. The domestic expression of this aim was the dissolution of all political parties to form the Imperial Rule Assistance Association, which provided a veneer of popular legitimacy for the military regime henceforth effectively in power.

Under increasing US pressure to withdraw from China, Japan launched full-scale war in the Pacific with a surprise attack on the main US naval base at Pearl Harbour on 7 Dec. 1941. Japan's whirlwind conquest of the region's European colonies was halted at the border of India and her sea-power broken in the battles of Midway Island and the Coral Sea in mid-1942. The Japanese military exploited the native populations of the conquered territories, as well as conscripting Allied prisoners-of-war, many of whom died as a result of forced labour on construction projects. Most notorious of these among British POWs was the Burma railway, which the Japanese sought to build between their conquest of Burma (Feb. 1942) and its eventual reconquest in the British offensive of May 1945. The dropping of atomic bombs on Hiroshima and Nagasaki and the declaration of war by the Soviet Union eventually forced Japan to surrender in Aug. 1945. Defeat cost Japan more than two million dead and the destruction of 100 cities. Industrial production was reduced to 10% of its pre-war level and the ocean-going fleet limited to 17 surviving ships. The immediate post-war years were, therefore, clouded by near-starvation, inflation and a crime wave as seven million were repatriated from the armed forces and Japan's lost overseas empire.

The Occupation of 1945–52, Allied in theory and American in practice, saw the firm establishment of a democratic constitution and far-reaching reforms affecting civil liberties, education and land-reform. Gen. Douglas MacArthur, the supreme commander of the Allied Powers, epitomized American self-confidence in the possibilities of reform and Emperor Hirohito provided a valued element of continuity while co-operating enthusiastically with the task of reconstruction. The trial and execution of war-time leaders, including Gen. Tojo Hideki, was accepted by the Japanese as an inevitable instance of victor's justice. Under the terms of its new constitution Japan renounced the right of belligerency but the rise of Communist power in China prompted American pressure for rearmament leading to the eventual creation of a Self-Defence Force and the conclusion of a security treaty between the United States and its former enemy.

The Korean war of 1950–53 boosted Japan's recovery by means of procurement orders and by 1955 industrial output was back at its pre-war peak level. Despite its lack of natural resources Japan set its sights on building an advanced industrial sector. In 1960 Prime Minister Ikeda announced his plan to double real incomes in ten years. Large-scale riots that year accompanied the renewal of the US security treaty which remained the basis of Japan's international policy. The alliance was affirmed but the scale of popular discontent was symptomatic of ambivalent attitudes towards American patronage. The 1964 Tokyo Olympics saw the inauguration of the famous 'bullet train' service, a foreshadowing of Japan's emerging technological capability. In the same year Japan was admitted to the Organization for Economic Co-Operation and Development, the 'club' of advanced industrial nations. Ikeda's income-doubling target was achieved by 1967 but swiftly gave way to a concern about the environmental costs of uncontrolled industrial growth. New 'citizens' groups' forced action on pollution problems and showed that democracy was more than a formality.

EXPO'70, held outside Osaka, was the first world exposition ever to be held in Asia and confirmed Japan's right to claim a place among the world's industrial powers. But the 'oil shock' of 1973 revealed how far Japan had become dependent on the benign expansion of world trade and cruelly exposed her lack of domestic energy supplies, hastening an unpopular commitment to growing reliance on nuclear power. Growth faltered badly for the first time for more than a decade but the crisis prompted a fundamental revaluation of economic strategy and set Japan on a new path, down-grading energy-intensive, polluting industries, like steel and chemicals, in favour of high value-added hi-tech manufactures such as videos, robots and computers. The second oil crisis of 1979 saw Japan, now a world leader in energy-saving technology, scarcely pause in its seemingly inexorable rise to economic eminence. Japan's industrial prowess, however, was unmatched by cultural prestige or diplomatic influence. No Japanese statesman could command world headlines, though ex-prime minister Sato was awarded the Nobel Prize for Peace in 1974 in recognition of his efforts for nuclear disarmament.

Apart from the ebullient Tanaka Kakuei, whose premiership ended abruptly in financial scandal, Japanese politicians seemed to outsiders either faceless time-servers or colourless technocrats. The Liberal Democratic Party (LDP), having achieved parliamentary dominance in 1955, appeared eternally capable of weathering such electoral damage as it caused itself by its own factional in-fighting.

Japan's relentless export success, fuelled domestically by anxieties about her long-term future prosperity, created major frictions with her western trading-partners, which were only partly mollified by the voluntary restraints accepted by Japanese exporters and their willingness to invest in production facilities overseas, a process further hastened by the advent of the single European market in 1992, which raised fears of protectionist barriers against Japanese products. The 1986 Plaza Accords obliged Japan to accept a 40% upward revaluation of the yen but even this seemed to have little effect in denting Japan's export performance, though the Maekawa Report did lead to market-opening measures which boosted Japan's imports of manufactures, chiefly to the benefit of the newly industrializing economies of eastern Asia.

By 1988 Japan had become the world's largest donor of foreign aid and supplier of capital, as well as the world's largest producer of motor-cars, washing-machines and watches and a technological leader in such fields as biotechnology, automated manufacturing processes and computerized translation. Japan did not, however, appear to have acquired the diplomatic capability to cope with its enhanced global role, despite the prevailing passion for 'kokusaika' (internationalization). During 1989 international hesitancy was compounded by major domestic political distractions. The death of Emperor Hirohito after a lengthy illness ended the longest imperial reign in Japanese history and removed a powerful symbol of continuity in a period of dizzying change. Revelations of corrupt political contributions by the Recruit employment agency forced the resignation of Prime Minister Takeshita and allegations of sexual misconduct brought down his successor, Uno, after only two months. Prime Minister Kaifu, representing a younger generation of politicians, was left with the uphill task of restoring public confidence in the LDP, whose long hold on power had been successfully challenged at the polls by the Socialist-led opposition for the first time in 34 years. In elections to the House of Representatives in February 1990, however, the LDP retained the overall majority.

CONSTITUTION AND GOVERNMENT

Executive and legislature

A constitutional monarchy, Japan has an emperor as its head of state, while the prime minister is head of government and is responsible to the parliament. The bicameral legislature, the Diet, is elected by universal adult suffrage; the lower house, the 512-member House of Representatives, has a maximum term of four years (last elected 1990), while members of the upper house, the 252-member House of Councillors, serve a six-year term, with half of the membership coming up for election every three years.

Present government

Emperor Tsegu no Miya Akihito
Prime Minister Toshiki Kaifu
Principal Ministers Shin Hasegawa (Justice Minister); Taro Nakayama (Foreign Minister); Ryutaro Hashimoto (Finance Minister); Kabun Muto (International Trade and Industry); Keiwa Okuda (Home Affairs); Misoji Sakanoto (Chief Cabinet Secretary); Yozo Ishikawa (Director-General of Defence Agency); Hideyaki Aizawa (Director-General of Economic Planning Agency).

Justice

The civil law system has influences from both English and American law. The highest court is the Supreme Court, which is independent of the legislative and executive branches, and which has a role in the judicial review of legislation. The Chief Justice is appointed by the Emperor, and the other 14 supreme court judges are appointed by the Cabinet. There are 8 regional courts, a network of district courts in each prefecture, and local courts. The death penalty is in force. There were nine executions between 1985 and mid-1988. The offences were murder.

National symbols

Flag. White with a red disc ('Hi-no-maru' or the sun disc).

Festivals. 11 Feb. (National Foundation Day); 29 April (Emperor's Birthday); 3 May (Constitution Memorial Day); 5 May (Children's Day); 15. Sept. (Respect for the Aged Day); 10 Oct. (Sports Day); 3 Nov. (Culture Day).

Vehicle registration plate. J.

INTERNATIONAL RELATIONS

Affiliations

OECD.

Defence

Total Armed Forces: 245,000. Terms of service: voluntary. Reserves: 46,400.

Army: 156,000; 1,170 main battle tanks (Type 61, Type 74).

Navy: 44,000; 14 submarines (US Mk 37, GRX-2 HWT) and 61 principal surface combatants: 36 destroyers (mainly DDH) and 25 frigates. 14 patrol and coastal combatants.

MSDF Air Arm: 12,000; 83 combat aircraft (P-3C/-2J) and 70 armed helicopters.

Air Force: 45,000; 340 combat aircraft (F-1, F-15J/DJ, F-4/EJ).

ECONOMY

Currency

The unit is the yen, divided into 100 sen.

National finance

Budget. The 1988 budget (in US$) was for expenditure (current and capital) of 433,000 million and revenue of 349,000 million.

Balance of payments. The balance of payments (current account, 1988) was a surplus of $79,630 million.

Inflation. 2.6% (12 months to Sept. 1989).

Gross Domestic Product

Estimated total GDP US$2,376,420 million, per capita US$15,030 (ranking 3 in the world). Growth rate (1988) 5.7%.

Economically active population. The total number of persons active in the economy was 60,290,000; unemployed: 2.5% (1988).

Sector	% of workforce	% of GDP
industry	33	41
agriculture	8	3
services*	59	57

* services figure includes elements unassigned to other categories.

Energy and mineral resources

Minerals. Japan has negligible mineral deposits. 1987 output: (in 1,000 tons/tonnes) coal 17,650/16,012; iron ore 320.3/290.6; zinc 275/222; lead 44/40; copper 39/35. In 1988 the country produced 716,495 tons/650,000 tonnes of crude oil and 74,337 million ft^3/2,105 million m^3 of natural gas, almost all of which came from oilfields on the island of Honshu.

Electricity. Capacity: 188,000,000 kW; production: 696,000 million kWh; 5,680 kWh per capita is produced by nuclear energy (46.9% in 1988).

Bioresources

Agriculture. There are an estimated 13,194,959 acres/5,340,000 ha of cultivated land producing rice; meat; cereals; root crops.

Crop production: (1987 in 1,000 tons/tonnes) rice 12,838/11,647; sugar 10,025/9,095; fruit 4,912/4,456; sweet potatoes 1,661/1,507; wheat 952/864; barley 389/353; soya beans 270/245.

Livestock numbers: (1987) poultry 343 million; pigs 11.4 million; cattle 4.7 million; goats 48,000; sheep 27,000; horses 22,000.

Forestry. Forests cover some 61.7 million acres/25 million ha, 68% of the country. In 1986 1,483 million ft^3/42 million m^3 of timber were felled, and 13.6 million tons/12.3 million tonnes of paper and 9.7 million tons/8.8 million tonnes of paperboard were produced.

Fisheries. Total fish catch: (1988) 7,496 million tons/6,800 million tonnes.

Industry and commerce

Industry. Japan's metal industry provides the basis for the production of a wide range of engineering, machinery and transport products, particularly motor vehicles (12.3 million produced in 1988) and machine tools. Although declining, shipbuilding remains an important sector of the economy; in 1986 7,646,000 gross tons were launched. Japan also has important chemical and textile industries. Output in the latter was cotton yarn 490,524 tons/445,000 tonnes; cotton cloth 2,361 million yards^2/1,974 million m^2; woollen yarn 123,458 tons/112,000 tonnes; woollen fabrics 374 million yards^2/313 million m^2; rayon woven fabrics 765 million yards^2/640 million m^2; synthetic woven fabrics 3,419 million yards^2/2,859 million m^2; silk fabrics 129 million yards^2/108 million m^2 (1988). In recent years Japan has been extremely successful in the innovation and manufacture of high technology products such as computers, telecommunications equipment and electrical goods, producing 44.8 million colour television sets and VCRs in 1988.

Commerce. Exports: US$231,200 million; imports US$150,800 million (1987). Exports in 1988 included machinery 33%; motor vehicles 26%; consumer electronics 8%. Imports included manufactures 34%; fossil fuels 31%; foodstuffs 18%; raw materials 16%. Countries exported to were US 38%; Southeast Asia 20%; Western Europe 18%; Eastern Europe 7%; Middle East 5%. Imports were received from Southeast Asia 23%; US 23%; Middle East 15%; Western Europe 14%; Eastern Europe 7%.

Trade with UK. Japan imported UK goods worth £1,743 million and exported to the UK goods worth £6,509 million (1988).

Tourism. Japan derived US$2,097 million from 2.15 million visitors (1987).

COMMUNICATIONS

Railways

There are 13,177 miles/21,206 km of railways, of which 7,239 miles/11,649 km are electrified.

Roads

682,863 miles/1,098,931 km of roads.

Aviation

All Nippon Airways-ANA and Japan Air Lines-JAL provide domestic and international services, Japan Asia Airways Co provides international services; Nihon Kinkyori Airways Co, Nippon Airlines System and Southwest Air Lines Co Ltd provide domestic services (international airports are at Tokyo, Osaka and Narita). Passengers: (1986) 53,640.

Shipping

There are 1,100 miles/1,770 km of inland waterways. All coastal inland seas are accessible to sea vessels. Chiba, Kobe, Nagoya, Osaka, Yokkaichi, Tokyo, and Yokohama are the maritime ports of the main island of Honshu. The maritime ports of the north island, Hokkaido, are Hakodate and Kushiro. Kitakyushu is the martime port of the south island of Kyushu. The merchant marine totals 1,197 ships of 1,000 GRT or over. Freight loaded: (1986) 97.1 million tons/88.1 million tonnes; unloaded 660 million tons/599 million tonnes.

Telecommunications

There are 64 million telephones and an excellent domestic and international service. There are about 95 million radio sets in use, and 32 million licensed television sets. The Japan Broadcasting Corporation (Nippon Hoso Kyokai–NHK) is a public corporation running two television and three radio networks and operating a satellite broadcasting serice. Grouped within the National Association of Commercial Broadcasters (MINPOREN) there are over 100 television companies and 70 companies broadcasting radio programmes, and almost 100 more TV companies operate without being part of the MINPOREN framework.

EDUCATION AND WELFARE

Education

The state system provides free and compulsory education from age six to 15.

School population. 9.87 million in primary; 5.9 million in secondary; 1.99 million in higher education.

Schools. Japan has 15,060 kindergartens with 98,905 teachers (one per 20.3 pupils); 24,024 elementary schools with 448,977 teachers (one per 22.8 pupils); 11,132 junior high schools with 292,057 teachers (one per 20.8 pupils); and 5,322 senior high schools with 274,931 teachers (one per 19.6 pupils).

Universities. Japan has seven long-standing state universities. In addition to these there are 467 state, municipal and private universities and colleges, employing 115,863 teaching staff.

Health

Japan has 9,699 hospitals. It has one bed per 67 inhabitants, and one doctor per 640 inhabitants.

JORDAN

Al-Urdun Al-Mamlakah Al Urdunniyah Al-Hashimiyah (Hashemite Kingdom of Jordan)

GEOGRAPHY

Located in south-west Asia, the middle eastern kingdom of Jordan covers an area of 37,129 miles²/ 96,188 km² (2,565 miles²/6,644 km² of which comprises the Israeli occupied West Bank). The Red Sea-Jordan rift valley, containing the Jordan river valley, the Dead Sea (–1,293 ft/–394 m), the Sea of Galilee (–695 ft/–212 m) and Wadi'Araba divides the country into West and East banks. The Eastern Desert (80% of the total surface area) is basaltic plateau in the north and sandy plateau in the south. The El Ghor highlands immediately to the east of the rift valley are irrigated but the bulk of Jordan's useful arable land lies in the West Bank. In the far south-west, near the Gulf of Aqaba, Jabal Ramm rises to 5,754 ft/1,754 m. Less than 0.5% of the land surface is forested, mainly near the Syrian border in the east. Of the eight governorates (Muhafazas) of Amman, Irbid, Al Balqa, Al Karak, Ma'an, Jerusalem, Hebron and Nablus, the last three constitute the occupied West Bank territory.

Climate

Mediterranean, with cool, moist winters and hot, dry summers. Temperatures decrease in the highlands and increase in the rift valley regions below sea level. Desert conditions prevail in the east. In the comparatively fertile north-west, rainfall averages 31.5 in/800 mm per annum. Amman: Jan. 46°F/7.5°C. July 77°F/24.9°C. Average annual rainfall 11 in/ 290 mm. Aqaba: Jan. 61°F/16°C. July 89°F/31.5°C. Average annual rainfall 1.4 in/35 mm.

Cities and towns

Amman (capital)	972,000
Zarqa	392,220

Irbid	271,000
Salt	134,100

Population

Total population is 2,850,482 or 3,943,000 including West Bank populace (see entry on Israel) of which 66% live in urban areas. Population density is 106 persons per mile^2/38.9 per km^2. Ethnic composition: 98% of the population are Arab; 1% Circassian; 1% American.

Birth rate 4.42% **Death rate** 0.79% **Rate of population increase** 3.63%. **Age distribution** under 15 = 48.1%; over 65 = 2.7% **Life expectancy** female 68; male 64; average 66.

Religion

Over 80% of the population are Sunni Muslims. The predominantly urban Christian minority of 5% includes Roman Catholic, Anglican, Coptic, Greek Orthodox and Evangelical Lutheran denominations. There are some small Shi'a Muslim communities.

Language

Arabic is the official language spoken by an ethnically homogenous population descended from the Arabian Qaysi and Yemeni tribes.

HISTORY

According to Biblical tradition the descendants of Esau, Isaac's elder son, were the Edomites of Transjordan, in a line stretching down through King Herod the Great. In the 2nd century BC the beautiful city built at the oasis of Petra, a hidden valley within the south Jordan mountains, was the centre of the Nabataean kingdom. Conquered by Muslim Arabs in the 7th century, the area of modern Jordan experienced Christian Crusader rule from Jerusalem (12th century) and later (1517) became part of the Ottoman Empire.

During World War I Arab nationalism joined forces with British imperialism in the Arab Revolt against Turkish dominion. Turkish rule was, however, effectively only replaced by British rule, the area of what is now Jordan being included within the League of Nations mandate for Palestine (1920), but administered under the proviso that it could be closed to Jewish immigration. Transjordan (the mandated area east of the Jordan river) was granted autonomy in 1923 under Emir Abdullah (1882–1951) of the Hashemite dynasty, semi-independence (apart from finance and foreign affairs) in 1928 and full independence in May 1946. The British Gen. J.B. Glubb, known as Glubb Pasha, was instrumental during this time in training the Bedouin desert patrol in the Transjordanian army, the Arab Legion, a force which he commanded until the mid-1950s.

In the 1948–49 Arab-Israeli war, the Arab Legion took central Palestine west of the Jordan (part of the Arab-designated area under the 1947 UN partition plan) and expelled Jewish forces from East Jerusalem (the Old City). Renamed Jordan (1949), the country annexed the West Bank and East Jerusalem (1950), becoming 60% Palestinian in population content. On Abdullah's assassination by a Palestinian extremist (1951), his unstable son Tallal became king, until being deposed (1952) in favour of his 16-year-old son Hussein.

Hussein proved adept at surviving coup attempts by radical Nasserist elements, after one of which he banned political parties (1957). Having terminated Jordan's defence treaty with Britain (1957), Hussein formed a federation with Iraq (1958) which lasted until the overthrow of the Iraqi monarchy a few months later. Efforts to incorporate Palestinians into the Jordanian polity were resisted by the Palestine Liberation Organization (PLO, founded 1964), which insisted on separate statehood.

In the 1967 Arab-Israeli war, Jordan was ejected from the West Bank and East Jerusalem, and received a further influx of Palestinian refugees. Tensions between the Jordanian authorities and PLO guerrillas culminated in the expulsion of the latter from Jordan (1970–71). In the 1973 Arab-Israeli war, Jordan confined its participation to sending an armoured brigade to help Syria. The Arab League's Rabat summit decision (1974) that the PLO was the sole legitimate representative of the Palestinians was accepted by Hussein; he accordingly dissolved Jordan's National Assembly, which under the 1952 constitution included West Bank representatives (and had last been elected in 1967). A free-trade agreement with the European Community was signed in Jan. 1977.

Jordan joined other Arab states in condemning Egypt for signing a peace treaty with Israel (1979), but restored full relations with Cairo in 1984 to form a moderate Arab bloc against the radicals led by Syria and Libya. Reconciled with PLO leader Yasser Arafat in 1983, Hussein strove to unblock Middle East negotiations, holding secret talks with Israel's prime minister, Shimon Peres, in Paris (Oct. 1985) and urging recognition of the PLO; but his interest in a Palestinian-Jordan federation, favoured by the United States and some Israelis, caused a further breach with the PLO (Feb. 1986). Jordan then reasserted its responsibility for the West Bank by approving increased Palestinian seats in an enlarged National Assembly (which had been reconvened and brought up to strength in partial elections in 1984). However, in a reversion to the 'Rabat line', occasioned by the Palestinian uprising (intifada), Hussein announced plans to sever ties with the West Bank to enable the PLO to assume full responsibility (July 1988). He dissolved the lower house of the National Assembly indefinitely (Oct. 1988). The PLO's implicit recognition of Israel and renunciation of terrorism, and the resultant opening of US-PLO talks (Dec. 1988), were welcomed by Jordan. From the mid-1980s onwards Jordan has been facing increasing economic difficulties, with food riots breaking out in several towns. The most serious such riots, in April 1989, in response to the announcement of IMF-backed austerity measures, brought about the replacement of the Prime Minister. Elections were held in November, in which opposition groups and particularly the Moslem Brotherhood won more support than the pro-government candidates. The second new Prime Minister of the year, Mudar Badran, announced the freezing (29 Nov.) of martial law regulations in force since 1967.

CONSTITUTION AND GOVERNMENT

Executive and legislature

Jordan is a constitutional monarchy in which the king, as head of state, plays a major role in government. The king appoints the prime minister, who exercises executive authority in his name and chooses the members of a council of ministers which is responsible to the bicameral National Assembly. The lower house, the House of Representatives, has 80 seats (last elections 8 Nov. 1989, the first for 22 years), no longer including representation for the Israeli-occupied West Bank.

Present government

King of Jordan Hussein Ibn Talal

Prime Minister, Defence Minister Mudar Badran

Principal members of Council of Ministers Salim Masaidah (Deputy Prime Minister; Interior); Marwan al Qasem (Deputy Prime Minister; Foreign Affairs); Basil Jardana (Finance and Customs); Yusuf al-Mubayydin (Justice).

Justice

The death penalty is in force. There were at least 14 executions between 1985 and mid-1988. The offences were murder.

National symbols

Flag. Three horizontal stripes of black, white and green with a red triangle in the hoist reaching to almost one-half of the flag's length, charged with a white seven-pointed star.

Festivals. 22 Mar. (Arab League Day); 25 May (Independence Day); 11 Aug. (King Hussein's Accession); 14 Nov. (King Hussein's Birthday).

Vehicle registration plate. HKJ.

INTERNATIONAL RELATIONS

Affiliations

NAM; Arab League; ICO; ACC.

Defence

Total Armed Forces: 82,250. Terms of service: voluntary; conscription, two years authorized. Reserves: 35,000.

Army: 74,000; some 979 main battle tanks (M-47/-48A5, M-60A1/A3, Khalid, Tariq).

Navy: 250; boats only.

Air Force: 11,000; 114 combat aircraft (F-5, F-7F, Mirage F-1).

ECONOMY

Currency

The unit is the dinar, divided into 1,000 fils.

National finance

Budget. The 1989 budget (in US$) was for expenditure (current and capital) of 2,300 million and revenue of 1,200 million. Main items of current expenditure are defence 30.3%; education 13.8%.

Balance of payments. The balance of payments (current account, 1987) was a deficit of US$350 million.

Inflation. (1987) –0.3%.

Gross Domestic Product

Estimated total GDP US$4,270 million, per capita US$1,780 (ranking 94 in the world by size).

Economically active population. The total number of persons active in the economy was 550,000; unemployed: 10%.

Sector	% of workforce	% of GDP
industry	20	28
agriculture	20	9
services*	60	64

* services figure includes elements unassigned to other categories.

Energy and mineral resources

Minerals. Output: phosphates 6.89 million tons/6.25 million tonnes (1986); potash 1.3 million tons/1.2 million tonnes (1987).

Oil and gas. Oil was discovered in 1982. Deposits of oil shale are estimated at 11,023 million tons/10,000 million tonnes

Electricity. Capacity: 979,000 kW; production: 3,310 million kWh; 1,160 kW per capita (1988).

Bioresources

Agriculture. Eastern Jordan is largely desert and the south is semi-arid.

Crop production: (1987 in tons/tonnes) tomatoes 220,460/200,000; olives 16,535/15,000; citrus fruit 83,775/76,000; wheat 126,765/115,000.

Livestock numbers: (1987) sheep 1 million; goats 450,000; cattle 33,000; camels 14,000.

Industry and commerce

Industry. Phosphate mining; petroleum refining; cement and potash production; light manufacturing.

Commerce. Exports: US$723 million; imports US$2,500 million (1987). Main exports: fruits and vegetables; phosphates and fertilizers. Main imports: crude oil; textiles; capital goods.

Trade with UK. Jordan imported UK goods worth £183.5 million and exported to the UK goods worth £21.3 million in 1988.

Tourism. There were 1.9 million foreign visitors in 1987.

COMMUNICATIONS

Railways

There are some 717 miles/1,154 km of railways.

Roads

There are 3,495 miles/5,625 km of roads.

Aviation

Royal Jordanian Airline provides international services (international airports are at Amman and Aqaba). Passengers: (1986) 1.13 million.

Shipping

The major port is Aqabah in the Gulf of Aqaba in the Red Sea. The merchant marine consists of three ships of 1,000 GRT or over. Freight loaded: (1987) 12.5 million tons/11.3 million tonnes; unloaded: 9.8 million tons/8.7 million tonnes.

Telecommunications

There are 81,500 telephones and an adequate telecommunications system. There are 1,100,000 radio sets and 250,000 televisions, more than half of them colour; the government-owned Jordan Radio and Television Corporation broadcasts in both Arabic and English.

EDUCATION AND WELFARE

Education

School population. There were a total of 856,048 pupils in elementary, preparatory and secondary education (1987).

Schools. There were 1,294 elementary schools with 18,448 teachers and 542,519 pupils (one per 29 pupils); 1,124 preparatory schools with 10,495 teachers and 214,743 pupils (one per 20 pupils); 510 secondary schools with 7,028 teachers and 98,786 pupils (one per 14 pupils).

Literacy. 71% (1988 est.).

Health

There were 56 hospitals with 5,672 beds (one per 524 people) and 4,500 doctors (one per 660 people).

KENYA
Jamhuri ya Kenya
(Republic of Kenya)

GEOGRAPHY

Situated on the east coast of Africa, bisected east-west by the equator, Kenya contains an area of 150,943 miles^2/582,640 km^2 (divided into eight provinces) of which 5,172 miles^2/13,400 km^2 is water. Semi-arid or arid conditions prevail in the sparsely populated northern desert regions and in the south around Lake Magadi. In the north-west, Lake Turkana (elevation 1,230 ft/375 m) lies at the northern extremity of the Rift Valley which divides the north-south highland plateau into two regions: to the west, the Mau escarpment and south-west Lake Victoria basin; to the east, the Aberdare range (13,104 ft/3,994 m Mt Lesatima) and Mt Kenya (the highest peak at 17,060 ft/5,200 m). The River Tana, draining an estimated 15% of the total surface area, rises in the eastern highlands and flows south-east over the gently sloping Nyika plain towards the increasingly populous and fertile coastal belt, fringed by coral reefs, small island clusters and mangrove swamps. South of the River Tana, the River Athi also drains south-east into the Indian Ocean. 3% of the land surface is arable and 4% is forested.

Climate

Tropical on the coast with rainy seasons Apr.-May and Oct.-Nov. Mean annual rainfall of approximately 39 in/1,000 mm increasing south-north; average daily temperature range 81–88°F/27–31°C. The plateau interior experiences cooler conditions with rainfall from 20 in/500 mm (south) to 10 in/250 mm (north). West central Kenya has two wet seasons (totalling 38 in/960 mm per annum) and an average daily temperature range of 70–79°F/21–26°C. Nairobi: Jan 65°F/18.3°C. July 60°F/15.6°C. Average annual rainfall 38 in/958 mm. Mombasa: Jan 81°F/27.2°C. July 76°F/24.4°C. Average annual rainfall 47 in/1,201 mm.

Cities and towns

Nairobi (capital)	509,286
Mombasa	274,073
Nakuru	47,151
Kisumu	32,431
Thika	18,387
Eldoret	18,196

Population

Total population is 23,100,000 of which 19.7% live in urban areas. Population density is 153 persons per mile^2/38.5 persons per km^2. There are an estimated 70 ethnolinguistically distinguishable groups in Kenya. As a percentage of the total population: 21% are Kikuya; 14% Luhya; 13% Luo; 11% Kalenjin; 11% Kamba; 6% Kisii; 6% Meru; 1% Asian, European and Arab.

Birth rate 5.39%. **Death rate** 1.37%. **Rate of population increase** 4.02% **Age distribution** under 15 = 51.2%; over 65 = 3.1%. **Life expectancy** female 60; male 56; average 58.

Religion

An estimated 28% of the population are Roman Catholic; 38% Protestant (more than 1 million belong to the Anglican Communion); 6% Muslim. The remaining 26% follow traditional animist/indigenous beliefs.

Language

English and Swahili are the official languages. There are three principal language families: the west central Bantu group (Kikuya, Embu, Kamba, Meru, Gusii, Luhya and Nyika), the west/north-west Nilotic peoples (Luo, Masai, Kalenjin and Twkana) and the Cushitic-speaking tribes of the north-east.

HISTORY

The earliest known ancestors of modern man lived in Kenya, where Stone and Iron Age cultures thrived. Migrant cattle-herders and cultivators formed small-scale communities, very different to the kingdoms of neighbouring Uganda. Arabs settled the coastal area (from the 10th century) and intermingled with local peoples to form the Swahili language and culture. The Portuguese established forts and trading posts in the 16th century, but the Arabs regained control in the 17th century; they also made inroads into the interior but did not take over the Kamba-run slave trade until the 19th century. Epidemics and civil war destroyed much of the power of the Masai pastoralists of the highlands in the late 19th century.

European missionary–explorers aroused British and German interest in the region. The British East Africa Company traded here until the British East Africa Protectorate was established (1895), largely to secure a route to landlocked Uganda. By the turn of the century white settlement was being encouraged in the highlands and large areas of African land were taken by Europeans, South Africans and other white immigrants, sowing the seeds of resistance among impoverished squatters. When Africans refused to build the Uganda railway, Indian labourers were brought in, staying on as traders.

White settlers strengthened their hold on government during World War I, but by the 1920s African political organization was stirring. In 1920 the country became a British colony, Kenya. The Kikuyu Central Association was formed (1928), headed by Jomo Kenyatta (then Johnstone Kamau Ngengi). He went to London (1930) to voice Kikuyu grievances to the government, but did not return for 15 years. Growing urbanization, unemployment and pressure on the land led to the formation of the pan-ethnic Kenyan African Union (KAU) in 1944; Kenyatta returned from his studies to lead it. African rebellion reached a peak with the birth in 1952 of so-called Mau Mau (the Land and Freedom Army, as its adherents called it) a largely Kikuyu-led campaign to restore land to Africans. Some Europeans were attacked in the so-called White Highlands; many more Africans were attacked as colonial collaborators. (The final death toll, including those killed by the British, was 32 Europeans, around 13,000 Africans.) A state of emergency was declared (1952) and lasted nearly eight years. Kenyatta and other KAU leaders were arrested, charged with organizing Mau Mau (which Kenyatta always denied) and jailed. On his release, Kenyatta was confined to a remote district. Guerrilla leader Dedan Kimathi was caught and hanged (1957). By 1960, 80,000 Kikuyu were being held in concentration camps.

Tom Mboya and Oginga Odinga formed the Kenya African National Union (KANU) and elected Kenyatta president in his absence (1960). KANU was largely supported by Kikuyu and Luo, while the Kenyan African Democratic Union (KADU) was formed to represent the smaller ethnic groups. Kenyatta, freed in Aug. 1961, led a delegation to London to demand independence. KANU won elections (1963) and Kenya became independent on 12 Dec. 1963 and a republic a year later, with Kenyatta as president and Oginga Odinga as vice-president. KADU was dissolved (1964). Kenyatta launched land reforms (the million-acre scheme) which were later abandoned.

The more radical Odinga defected in 1966 to form the opposition Kenya People's Union (KPU); he was detained in Oct. 1969 and the KPU banned. Meanwhile Tom Mboya had been assassinated in July 1969. Former minister and government critic J.M. Kariuki was murdered (1975) sparking riots. Unrest within KANU caused the postponement of national elections (1977).

Relations with Uganda deteriorated through the years of Idi Amin's rule there (1971–79) and the nine-year-old East African Community (of Uganda, Kenya, Tanzania) broke up in June 1977; Tanzania closed its border with Kenya (re-opened 1983). When Kenyatta died (1978) vice-president Daniel arap Moi temporarily assumed the presidency, and was the sole presidential candidate at elections in Nov. 1979, proclaiming his Nyayo (footsteps) philosophy to keep Kenyatta's ideas alive. He launched drives against corruption and tribalism. A Kalenjin, he has tried to maintain a tribal balance in government, preventing Kikuyu dominance.

Moi has formed close ties with Western powers, especially the United States. Opposition to him has grown since 1980. Air force officers attempted a coup (Aug. 1982); Odinga was placed under house arrest. Cabinet minister Charles Njonjo was dropped (1983) amid accusations of plotting against Moi. Students rioted (1985, 1987) and Nairobi University was closed. Hundreds of people have been detained on suspicion of belonging to the rebel movement Mwakenya, sparking international accusations of human-rights abuses. Muslims rioted in Mombasa (1987). Moi was returned unopposed in presidential elections in Mar. 1988 and the law was amended in August, allowing Moi to dismiss judges at will and widening police powers to detain suspects without charge. Legislative elections in September were marred by widespread allegations of fraud. The 25th anniversary of independence was celebrated in Dec. 1988. The murder of Foreign Affairs minister R. Ouko in Feb. 1990 provoked anti-government riots in Kisumu and Nairobi, after which the government banned all demonstrations.

CONSTITUTION AND GOVERNMENT

Executive and legislature

The head of state is the executive president, who appoints the cabinet; the president is elected by direct universal adult suffrage, but was last confirmed in office for a further five-year term in Feb. 1988 without a vote, there being no other candidate. The concentration of effective political power is in the hands of the sole legal political organization, the Kenya African National Union (KANU), which nominates the sole presidential candidate and draws up the list of nominees from which the members of parliament are elected. The parliament is the unicameral National Assembly, comprising 188 elected members and 12 members nominated by the president; last general election Mar. 1988.

Present government

President; C.-in-C. of the Armed Forces Daniel T. arap Moi

Vice-President; Minister of Finance Prof. George Saitoti

Principal Ministers Davidson Ngibuini Kuguru (Home Affairs and Natural Heritage); Wilson Ndelo Ayah (Foreign Affairs and International Co-operation); Maina Wanjigi (Agriculture); D. Otieno (Industry); Arthur J. Magugu (Commerce).

Ruling party

Kenya African National Union. *President* Daniel T. arap Moi. *Vice-President* Prof. George Saitoti. *Secretary-general* John Joseph Kamotho.

Justice

The system of law is based on English common law, indigenous concepts and Islamic law. The highest court is the High Court, which has a role in the judicial review of legislation, and is headed by the Chief Justice. It has full jurisdiction in both civil and criminal matters. Subordinate Courts in the districts are presided over by Senior Resident, Resident or District Magistrates. Moslem Subordinate Courts operate in predominantly Moslem areas. There were 32 executions between 1985 and mid-1988. Offences were murder, robbery with violence, treason.

National symbols

Flag. Three horizontal stripes of black, red, and green.

Festivals. 1 May (Labour Day); 1 June (Madaraka Day, anniversary of self-government); 20 Oct. (Kenyatta Day); 12 Dec. (Independence Day).

Vehicle registration plate. EAK.

INTERNATIONAL RELATIONS

Affiliations

NAM; OAU; ACP; Commonwealth.

Defence

Total Armed Forces: 23,000. Terms of service: voluntary.
Army: 19,000; 76 main battle tanks (Vickers Mk3).
Navy: 1,000; 11 patrol and coastal combatants.
Air Force: 3,000; 24 combat aircraft (mainly F-5, F-5E, F-5F), 38 armed helicopters.

ECONOMY

Currency

The unit is the shilling, divided into 100 cents.

National finance

Budget. The 1987 budget (in US$) was for expenditure (current and capital) of 2,600 million and revenue of 2,300 million. Main items of current expenditure are education 23.1%; defence 9.1%.
Balance of payments. The balance of payments (current account, 1987) was a deficit of $639 million.
Inflation. (1987) 5.2%.

Gross Domestic Product

Estimated total GDP US$6,930 million, per capita US$370 (ranking 75 in the world by size).
Economically active population. The total number of persons active in the economy was 7,400,000.

Sector	% of workforce	% of GDP
industry		19
agriculture	15	31
services*		50

* services figure includes elements unassigned to other categories.

Energy and mineral resources

Minerals. Output: (1985 in K£1,000) soda ash 13,002; fluorspar ore 3,550; salt 1,029; gold 61.1. Other minerals include limestone; diotomite; magnesite; sapphires; garnets.
Electricity. Capacity: 587,000 kW; production: 2,147 million kWh; 90 kWh per capita (1988).

Bioresources

Agriculture. Tropical, sub-tropical and temperate crops can be grown and mixed farming is practised. At high altitudes (up to 9,842 ft/3,000m) coffee; tea; sisal; pyrethrum; maize; wheat are the main crops while at lower altitudes tobacco; coconuts; cashew nuts; cotton; sugar; sisal; maize are mainly grown. Kenya is an illegal producer of cannabis and there is some international drug trade trafficking.
Crop production: (1987 in 1,000 tons/tonnes) tobacco 5,512/5,000; sugar cane 4,079/3,700; maize 2,381/2,160; fruit 810/735; potatoes 805/730; cassava 595/540; vegetables 515/467; sweet potatoes 418/380; wheat 177/161; tea 172/156; sorghum 143/130; coffee 116/105; pyrethrum 103/93; millet 55/50; sisal 41/37; flowers 41/37; rice 33/30; cotton 26/24; barley 20/18.
Livestock numbers: (1986) poultry 21 million; cattle 9 million; goats 8.5 million; sheep 7.1 million; pigs 98,000.
Forestry. Kenya's forested areas amount to 6,484 miles^2/16,800 km^2, mostly in areas over 5,905 ft/1,800 metres above sea level. Bamboo grows mainly on higher ground and coniferous and broadleaved trees at lower altitudes. Production: (1985 in ft^3/m^3) softwood 14,372,798/407,000; hardwood 19,140,188/542,000.
Fisheries. Catch: (1987 in tons/tonnes) freshwater fish 130,130/118,216; marine fish 6,720/6,096; crustaceans 330/299. Total catch value K£18,84 million.

Industry and commerce

Industry. The main industries are small-scale consumer goods (plastic; furniture; batteries; textiles; soap; cigarettes; flour); agricultural processing; oil refining; cement; tourism.
Commerce. Exports: (1987) US$1,200 million or 14.8% of GDP, including coffee 20%; tea 18%; manufactures 15%; petroleum products 10%. Imports: $1,800 million, including machinery and transportation equipment 36%; raw materials 33%; fuels and lubricants 20%; food and consumer goods 11%. Countries exported to: Western Europe 45%; Africa 22%; Far East 10%; US 4%; Middle East 3%. Imports came from: Western Europe 49%; Far East 20%; Middle East 19%; US 7%.
Trade with UK. In 1988 Kenya imported UK goods worth £202,094,000; exports to UK totalled £142,455,000.
Tourism. (1987) 662,100 visitors.

COMMUNICATIONS

Railways

There are 1,698 miles/2,733 km of railways.

Roads

There are 32,346 miles/52,055 km of roads, of which 4,099 miles/6,598 km are bituminized.

Aviation

Kenya Airways Ltd. provides domestic and international services (main airport is Jomo Kenyatta international airport at Nairobi and at Mombasa). Passengers: (1985) 589,000.

Shipping

Part of the Lake Victoria system of inland waterways is within the boundaries of Kenya. The principal inland port is at Kisumu. Mombasa and Lamu are the major maritime ports on the Indian Ocean.

Telecommunications

There are 260,000 telephones and one of the best telecommunications systems in Africa. There are 3.4 million radios and about 250,000 televisions, with services provided by the state-owned Kenya Broadcasting Corporation (successor to the Voice of Kenya) which runs four TV channels and three national radio services.

EDUCATION AND WELFARE

Education

Schools. (1987) 13,849 primary schools with 5.03 million pupils and 149,151 teachers (one per 33 pupils); 2,952 secondary schools with 522,261 pupils and 24,251 teachers (one per 21 pupils); 18 technical colleges with 9,258 pupils and 368 teachers (one per 25 pupils).
Universities. (1987–88) Four public universities with a total enrolment of 18,881 students.
Literacy. 47%.

Health

There is free medical service for children and adult out-patients. There are 2,071 hospitals and health centres with 31,356 hospital beds (one per 776 people).

KIRIBATI

Republic of Kiribati (formerly Gilbert Islands)

GEOGRAPHY

Comprising three coral island groups and one volcanic island (Banaba, area 1.9 miles²/5 km². high point 285 ft/87 m), the independent republic of Kiribati covers a total land area of 276.8 miles²/717.1 km², scattered over 772,000 miles²/two million km² of central Pacific Ocean. Of the 33 constituent atolls, the 16 Gilbert Islands cover 114 miles²/295 km², the eight Phoenix Islands cover 21 miles²/55 km² and eight of the 11 Line Islands contain a total area of 127 miles²/329 km². Enclosed by coral reefs, the majority of the islands never rise above 13 ft/4 m elevation. Arable land is non-existent although coconuts, babais, bananas, pandanus, papayas and breadfruit are grown. 3% of the land is forest or woodland and 33.2% of the population live on Tarawa, the capital.

Climate

Maritime equatorial on Banaba, Line and Phoenix Islands; tropical at northern and southern extremities. Temperatures are modified by eastern trade winds, averaging 81°F/27°C. Rainfall varies from an equatorial average of 49 in/1,250 mm to over 118 in/3,000 mm in the north, and occasionally, as little as 7.8 in/200 mm in the southern Gilbert Islands. Wet season Nov.-Apr. Subject to typhoons. Tarawa: Jan. 83°F/28.3°C. July. 82°F/27.8°C. Average annual rainfall 78 in/1,977 mm.

Cities and towns

Tarawa (capital) 24,400

Population

Total population is 66,000 of which 33.4% live in urban areas. Population density is 238 persons per mile²/90.7 per km². The indigenous inhabitants are Micronesian. There are small Polynesian and non-Pacific minorities.

Birth rate 3.49%. **Death rate** 1.39%. **Rate of population increase** 2.10%. **Age distribution** under 15 = 38.9%; over 60 = 5.8%. **Life expectancy** female 56; male 51; average 54.

Religion

48% of the population are Roman Catholic and 45% Protestant (predominantly Congregational). Small Seventh Day Adventist and Baha'i communities.

Language

English is the official language but I-Kiribati (Gilbertese) is recognized as the unitary Micronesian dialect.

HISTORY

The islands were invaded early in the 14th century by Fijians and Tongans, who subsequently mixed with the Micronesian population, whose origins can be traced back nearly 2,000 years. After probable sightings by Spanish ships in the 16th century, further European discovery did not occur for over 200 years. The remaining islands were discovered by the 1820s when the group was named the Gilbert Islands. Missionary and commercial activity increased from the middle of the century, but the abuses of the trade in plantation workers for other Pacific regions led in 1892 to Britain's declaring the Gilbert and Ellice Islands a protectorate. These became a Crown Colony in 1916. During World War II the Japanese occupied the Gilbert group, but were driven out by American forces. Constitutional advances to internal self-government and eventual independence date from 1963. The Polynesian Ellice Islanders voted in a referendum in 1974 to separate from the Gilbertese, with the official separation taking effect a year later. The Gilbertese became self-governing in 1977 and the independent Republic of Kiribati came into being on 12 July 1979 as a member of the Commonwealth. The United States ratified a treaty of friendship with Kiribati in 1983, whereby the US recognized Kiribati's sovereignty over the Line and Phoenix Islands. After the general election in Mar. 1987 Ieremia Tabai was re-elected president.

CONSTITUTION AND GOVERNMENT

Executive and legislature

As an independent republic within the Commonwealth, Kiribati has a president as its head of state, exercising executive power (with the assistance of appointed ministers). The president is elected from amongst members of the legislature, the unicameral 37-member House of Assembly (Maneaba). This parliament has one appointed member, representing the Banaban community; the other 36 are popularly elected for up to four years.

Present government

President; Minister of Foreign Affairs Ieremia Tabai
Vice President; Minister of Finance Teatao Teannaki
Minister of Home Affairs and Decentralization Babera Kirata
Attorney General Michael Takabwebwe.

Justice

The Commissioner of Police, head of the 232-strong police force, is also in charge of prisons, immigration, fire service and firearms licensing. The death penalty was abolished before independence.

National symbols

Flag. The flag is based on the state coat of arms. The upper part is red, while the lower part is divided into six wavy stripes, alternately white and blue.
Festivals. 12 July (Independence Day); 4 Aug. (Youth Day).

INTERNATIONAL RELATIONS

Affiliations

Commonwealth; South Pacific Forum.

ECONOMY

Currency

The unit is the Australian dollar, divided into 100 cents.

National finance

Budget. The 1987 budget (in US$) was for expenditure

(current and capital) of 20 million and revenue of 21 million.

Inflation. (1987) 5%.

Gross Domestic Product

Estimated total GDP US$25 million, per capita US$370 (ranking 191 in the world by size).

Economically active population. The total number of persons active in the economy was 8,000.

Energy and mineral resources

Minerals. Phosphate was mined until 1979.

Electricity. Capacity: 2,750 kW; production: 8 million kWh; 120 kWh per capita (1988).

Bioresources

Agriculture. Of the total land area, approximately 50% is under permanent cultivation. The land consists chiefly of coral reefs with a layer of coral sand. The main tree is the coconut, other food-bearing trees being the pandanus palm and the breadfruit.

Crop production: (1987 in tons/tonnes) copra 13,228/12,000; coconuts 99,207/90,000.

Livestock numbers: (1987) poultry 163,000; pigs 10,000.

Forestry. Approximately 3% of the land is forested.

Fisheries. Mainly tuna fishing.

Industry and commerce

Industry. Fishing; handicrafts; tourism.

Commerce. Exports: (1987) $2.3 million or 9.3% of GDP, including fish 55% and copra 42%. Imports: $17.5 million, including foodstuffs; fuel; transportation equipment. Countries exported to: EC 20%; Marshall Islands 12%; US 8%; American Samoa 4%. Imports came from Australia 39%; Japan 21%; NZ 6%; UK 6%; US 3%.

Trade with UK. Kiribati imported UK goods worth £522,000; exports to UK totalled £128,000.

Tourism. Total income: (1984) US$1.4 million.

COMMUNICATIONS

Railways

There are no railways.

Roads

There are 397 miles/640 km of roads (suitable for motor vehicles).

Aviation

Air Tungaru Corporation provides domestic service (there are 18 airfields in Kiribati).

Shipping

There is a small network of canals, totaling 3 miles/5 km, in the Line Islands. The port of Betio is in the Tarawa district of the Gilbert Islands. The island of Banaba acts as another port.

Telecommunications

There are 1,400 telephones and about 10,000 radios, with broadcasting by Radio Kiribati.

EDUCATION AND WELFARE

Education

Schools. There are 112 primary schools with 13,192 pupils, six secondary schools with 1,649 pupils and one community high school with 232 pupils. There is also a state-run boarding school with 470 pupils.

Further education. There is a government-run teacher-training college, a marine training college and a technical institute.

Literacy. 90%.

Health

Medical services are free. There are 16 doctors (1986), with beds in the hospital on Tarawa and clinics on other islands totalling 283 (one per 243 people).

KOREA, NORTH

Choson minjujuui in'min konghwaguk
(Democratic People's Republic of Korea)

GEOGRAPHY

Situated in the northern half of the Korean peninsula in east Asia, North Korea occupies a surface area of 46,528 miles²/120,540 km² divided into nine provinces. Approx 80% of the country is mountainous. In the north-east, the volcanic peak of Mount Paek-tu rises to 9,003 ft/2,744 m surrounded by the upland expanse of the Kaema Plateau (average elevation 3,280 ft/1,000 m). Other major mountain chains include the north-south Nangnim-sanmaek range and the Hamyong-sanmaek along the east coast. In the north-west, the Yalu river valley marks the Korean-Chinese border, while to the south-west, the fertile Chaeryong and Pyongyang plains provide the focus for all agricultural activity. The narrow eastern coastal plains are the most densely populated regions. 18% of the total surface area is arable and 74% of the terrain is forested. North Korea is divided from South Korea by a 487 miles²/1,262 km² demilitarized zone.

Climate

Warm temperate but with severe winters and prolonged exposure to icy winds from Siberia and Manchuria. Rivers and coastal waters generally freeze for up to four months. In the north-west, winter temperatures range from 8.6°F/–13°C to 27°F/-3°C compared with slightly warmer conditions on the east coast (18°F/–8°C to 34°F/1°C). Summer temperatures in the same location vary from 68–84°F/20–29°C (west) to 66–81°F/19–27°C (east). The wettest season lasts July-Sept. with appreciably more rain falling on the east coast. Pyongyang: Jan: 18°F/–7.8°C. July: 75°F/23.9°C. Average annual rainfall: 36 in/916 mm.

Cities and towns

Pyongyang (capital)	1,500,000
Chongjin	300,000
Hungnam	260,000
Kaesong	240,000

Population

Total population is 21.9m of which 62% live in urban areas. Population density is 471 persons per mile^2/174.8 per km^2. The population is ethnically homogenous with over 99.8% Korean and less than 0.2% Chinese.

Birth rate: 3.05%. **Death rate**: 0.6%. **Rate of population increase**: 2.45%. **Age distribution** under 15 = 38.1%; over 60 = 6%. **Life expectancy** female 71; male 64.6; average 68.

Religion

Buddhism, Confucianism, Shamanism and Ch'ondogyo are the traditional religious philosophies formally discouraged by the state and now practised by a relatively small minority of the population (3 million Chondoists, 0.4 million Buddhists).

Language

Korean is the official language, related to Japanese and influenced by Chinese vocabulary.

HISTORY

For history of Korean peninsula prior to 1953 see under South Korea.

After the signing of the armistice on 27 July, 1953, which brought to an end the Korean War, the communist Korean Worker's Party (KWP) concentrated on post-war economic reconstruction and the consolidation of its own position of political primacy.

Although there had been several well-defined factions within the KWP, these were gradually liquidated until, by 1958, the leadership of Kim Il Sung was absolute. The growth of Kim's extraordinary personality cult was inextricably linked to the development of his highly personal interpretation of Marxism–Leninism, an all-embracing ideology known as Juche. Since its initial formulation in Dec. 1955, Juchism has come to embody the principles of primacy of the party, self-sufficiency, self-defence and the extension of respect to all parties within the international communist movement regardless of their overall size.

In accordance with the Juche principle of self-sufficiency, the country's early state economic plans concentrated on the collectivization of agriculture and the rapid development of heavy industry. The six-year plan, implemented in 1971, involved the import of advanced technology from Japan and the West which, whilst having a beneficial effect on the country's industrial development, left it with foreign debts in excess of $2,000 million by the end of 1976. A seven-year plan, involving more realistic targets for annual growth, was adopted in 1978, although the regime's obsessive secrecy and unreliable statistics made it impossible to divine the plan's success with any degree of precision. A third seven-year plan, covering the period 1987–93, was adopted in Apr. 1987.

Kim's long period of rule has been characterized by skilful diplomacy with the Soviet Union and China. Despite the Sino-Soviet rift of the late 1950s, Kim managed to remain on good terms with both of his giant communist neighbours without allowing North Korea to become the satellite of either.

The ageing Kim Il Sung has groomed his son, Kim Chong Il, as his successor. Despite the construction of a personality cult almost as extravagant as that of his father, there have been persistent rumours that the younger Kim lacks sufficient support within the KWP and the army to continue his father's rule.

CONSTITUTION AND GOVERNMENT

Executive and legislature

An effective monopoly of political power lies with the (communist) Korean Workers' Party. Nominally, political authority is held by a unicameral 615-member Supreme People's Assembly (SPA), represented by a standing committee when it is not in session. The president, elected by the SPA, is an executive head of state, exercising this role in conjunction with a central people's committee and an appointed administrative council (Cabinet). The assembly is elected by universal adult suffrage, from the party's sole list of candidates, for a four-year term.

Present government

President Kim Il Sung
Premier Yon Hyong Muk
Head of People's Armed Forces Vice-Marshal Oh Jin Wu
Principal Ministers Lt.-Gen. Paek Hak Nom (Public Security); Ms Yun Ki Chong (Finance).

Ruling party

Korean Workers' Party. *General Secretary* Kim Il Sung. *Members of Presidium* Kim Il Sung; Kim Chong Il; Vice-Marshal Oh Jin Wu. *Full members of the politburo* Kim Il Sung; Kim Chong Il; Vice-Marshal Oh Jin Wu; Yi Kun Mo; Hong Song Nam; Pak Son Chol; Yi Chong Ok; So Chol; Yon Hyong Muk; Kang Song San; O Kuk Yol; So Yun Sok; Ho Dam; Kim Yong Nam; Kim Hwan; Kye Ung Tae.

Justice

There is a Supreme Court, whose judges are elected by the National Assembly for three years, and there are provincial and city or county people's courts. While the Supreme Court controls the judicial administration, the Procurator-General, appointed by the Assembly, has supervisory powers over the judiciary and the administration. The death penalty is in force. The number of executions between 1985 and mid-1988 is not known.

National symbols

Flag. Three stripes of blue, red, blue, separated from each other by two narrow white lines. The hoist of the red stripe is charged with a white disc containing a red five-pointed star.
Festivals. 15 Apr. (Kim Il Sung's Birthday); 1 May (Labour Day); 15 Aug. (Anniversary of Liberation); 9 Sep. (Independence Day); 10 Oct. (Anniversary of the Foundation of the Korean Worker's Party); 27 Dec. (Anniversary of the Constitution).
Vehicle registration plate. K.

INTERNATIONAL RELATIONS

Affiliations

Observer status at UN and member of several UN specialized agencies; NAM; Comecon (observer).

Defence

Total Armed Forces: 842,000. Terms of service: Army 5–8 years, Navy 5–10 years and Air Force 3–4 years. Reserves: 540,000.
Army: 700,000; some 3,000 main battle tanks (T-34/-54/-55/-62, Type 59), 300 light tanks (Type-63, Type-62, M-1985).
Navy: 39,000; 21 submarines (Soviet Romeo and Whiskey), two frigates and 365 patrol and coastal combatants.

Air Force: 53,000; some 800 combat aircraft (Su-7/-25, Ch J-2/-4/-6/Q-5, MiG-21/-23).
Para-military: 38,000 (Security Troops).

ECONOMY

Currency

The unit is the North Korean won, divided into 100 chon.

National finance

Budget. The 1988 budget (in US$) was for expenditure (current and capital) of 15,200 million and revenue of 15,200 million.

Gross Domestic Product

Estimated total GDP US$20,000 million (GNP), per capita US$910 (ranking 57 in the world by size).

Economically active population. The total number of persons active in the economy was 6,100,000. Agriculture accounts for 48% of the workforce.

Energy and mineral resources

Oil. Crude oil production: (1986) 70,000 barrels.

Minerals. North Korea is rich in mineral resources. Estimated reserves: (in million tons/tonnes) coal 13,228/12,000; iron ore 3,638/3,300; manganese 7,165/6,500; uranium 29/26; zinc 13/12; lead 7/6; copper 2.3/2.1. In 1984 coal production was 41 million tons/37 million tonnes and iron ore 18 million tons/16 million tonnes.

Electricity. Capacity: 6,440 milion kW; production: 40,250 million kWh; 1,830 kWh per capita (1988). Three thermal power and four hydro-electric power plants.

Bioresources

Agriculture. 5.2 million acres/2.1 million ha of arable land of which 33% are paddy fields. Approximately 90% of the cultivated land is farmed by co-operatives.

Crop production: (1986 in million tons/tonnes) rice 2.2/2; other grains 5.3/4.83; potatoes 2.0/1.8.

Livestock numbers: (1987 in millions) poultry 19; pigs 3; cattle 1.2.

Forestry. 1,976,773 acres/800,000 ha are forested

Fisheries. Total catch: (1983) 1.8 million tons/1.6 million tonnes.

Industry and commerce

Industry. The main industries are machine building; military products; hydro-electric power; cotton spinning and weaving; chemical fertilizers; mining; metallurgy; textiles; food processing.

Commerce. Exports: (1988) $2,400 million or 12% of GDP, including minerals; metallurgical products; agricultural products; manufactures. Imports: $3,100 million, including petroleum; machinery and equipment; coking coal; grain. Countries exported to: USSR; China; Japan; FRG; Hong Kong; Singapore. Imports came from: USSR; Japan; China; West Germany; Hong Kong; Singapore.

Trade with UK. (1988) North Korea imported UK goods worth £3,125,000; exports to UK totalled £824,000.

Tourism. Non-communist tourists have only been able to enter North Korea since 1986.

COMMUNICATIONS

Railways

There are 2,796 miles/4,500 km of railways, of which 1,678 miles/2,700 km are electrified.

Aviation

Chosonminhang/Civil Aviation Administration of the DPRK provides domestic and international services.

Shipping

The 1,400 miles/2,253 km of inland waterways are navigable by small craft only. The east-coast marine ports are Ch'ongjin, Hungnam, Songnim, and Wonsan,and face on to the Sea of Japan. The west-coast marine ports of Haeju and Namp'o face the Yellow Sea. There are 68 merchant marine ships of 1,000 GRT or over.

Telecommunications

There are about 4 million radios in use, with the government programmes reaching a wider audience as they are relayed through loudspeakers in factories and in the parks and squares in all the main towns. External radio services are broadcast in eight languages. Television is broadcast by the state Mansudae Television Station.

EDUCATION AND WELFARE

Education

There is 11 years of free (compulsory) primary and secondary education in North Korea.

Schools. 47,600 kindergartens (1988) and approximately 10,000 11-year schools (1980). 5.2 million pupils and 110,000 teachers (one per 47 pupils) (1982–83).

Universities. There are 216 institutes of higher education including three universities and an Academy of Sciences. In 1982–83 there were approximately 1 million students in higher education.

Literacy. 95%.

Health

There is free medical treatment in North Korea. In 1982 there were approximately 7,900 hospitals and clinics and in 1983 there was a ratio of one doctor per 416 people and one hospital bed per 76 people.

KOREA, SOUTH
Taehan min'guk
(Republic of Korea)

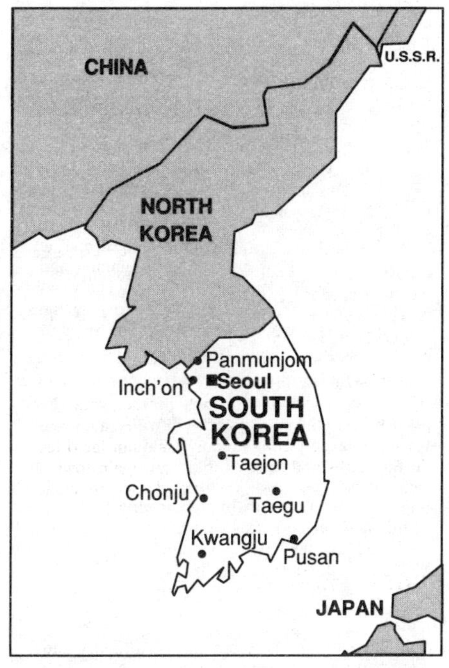

GEOGRAPHY

Occupying the southern half of the Korean peninsula in eastern Asia, the densely populated Korean republic contains an area of 38,015 miles^2/98,484 km^2 divided into nine provinces. Over 80% of the terrain is mountainous. The eastern coastal Taebaek-sanmaek mountains descend north to south-west from altitudes of 2,953 ft/900 m to the low-lying, populous and extensively cultivated western plains which occupy 15% of the total surface area. About 3,000 small islands lie off the west and south coasts, including Cheju do from which Korea's highest peak, Halla-san, rises to 6,398 ft/1,950 m. The Han-gang river basin in the north-west and the Naktong-gang basin in the south-east dominate South Korea's hydrography. 21% of the land is arable and over two-thirds is forested (subtropical vegetation on the south coast).

Climate

Continental temperate over most of the country with hot summers and cold winters; warm temperate in the extreme south. Winter and summer alternate with only a very short transitional period. Most rain falls Apr.-Sept., ranging from 40–60 in/1,020 to 1,520 mm (annual average). Periodic typhoons from June to Sept. Average temperatures decrease south-north. Pusan: Jan. 36°F/2.2°C. July 76°F/24.4°C. Average annual rainfall 55 in/1,407 mm. Seoul: Jan. 23°F/–5°C. July 77°F/25°C. Average annual rainfall 49 in/1,250 mm.

Cities and towns

Soul (Seoul, capital)	9,639,110
Pusan	3,514,798
Taegu	2,029,853
Inchon	1,386,911
Kwangju	905,896
Taejon	866,148
Ulsan	551,014

Population

Total population is 42,621,000 of which 65.4% live in urban areas. Population density is very high: 1,121 persons per mile^2/424.7 per km^2. The population is ethnically homogenous: 99.9% are Korean, 0.1% Chinese.

Birth rate 2.13%. **Death rate** 0.63%. **Rate of population increase** 1.5%. **Age distribution** under 15 = 30%; over 65 = 4.3%. **Life expectancy** female 73; male 66; average 69.

Religion

Confucianism, Mahayana Buddhism, ancestor worship, Shamanism and Ch'ondogyo are practised by two-thirds of the population. A sizeable Christian minority (28%) comprises an estimated 9,723,596 Protestants and 2,148,607 Roman Catholics.

Language

Korean is the official language (Han'gul writing system), possibly related to Japanese although probably of Altaic origin. English is widely taught in many schools.

HISTORY

Evidence of human habitation within the Korean peninsula dates back at least to 3000 BC, when nomads entered the territory whilst migrating south from the Asian mainland. The establishment of competing kingdoms within the peninsula, together with frequent Chinese intervention from the north, produced a protracted period of instability. In AD 668 the kingdom of Shilla finally established mastery of the peninsula, and was succeeded in 935 by the kingdom of Koryo, from which the Western term Korea is derived. The Yi dynasty was founded in 1392 and ruled Koryo from Seoul for the next 518 years. Weakened by wars against invading Mongols, Chinese and Japanese, however, the territory became a vassal state of China in 1644.

Japan conquered Korea in 1904 and formally annexed it as a colony in 1910. Following Japan's defeat in the Pacific War in 1945, as had been agreed by the Allies, Korean territory north of the 38th parallel was occupied by Soviet troops whilst that to the south was occupied by American forces. Faced with widespread Korean nationalism, the two superpowers each sponsored Korean leaders and embryonic administrations within their separate halves of the territory with a view to ensuring that the government of a reunified and independent Korea was ideologically sympathetic. Prospects for reunification dwindled with the growth of the Cold War, however, and in 1948 the peninsula's division was formalized by the proclamation of the Republic of Korea in the south and the Democratic People's Republic of Korea in the north. Both governments of these new states claimed sovereignty over the entire Korean peninsula.

Armed clashes between the two states increased following the withdrawal of US and Soviet troops in 1948–49. This hostility escalated into full-scale war when, on 25 July, 1950, North Korean forces crossed the 38th parallel in strength. Despite immediate US support, by late July only the south-eastern tip of the peninsula and the port of Pusan remained in South Korean hands. At this point United Nations' forces – the bulk of which were US units – halted the North Korean advance and, in mid-September, dramatically outflanked the invaders with an amphibious landing at Inchon near Seoul. Capitalizing on the success of this counter attack, UN forces captured the North Korean capital of Pyongyang in October and, by November, they had reached the Chinese border. At this point huge numbers of Chinese volunteers entered the war and the UN forces were once again driven south. The frontline eventually stabilized in the vicinity of the 38th parallel in mid-1951 and remained there until the war was ended by an armistice signed on 27 July 1953.

Between 1948 and 1960 South Korea was ruled by the aged and increasingly authoritarian and corrupt Pres. Syngman Rhee. The regime's clumsy manipulation of the 1960 presidential election, compounded by long-term discontent over economic failure and administrative incompetence, led to its overthrow in Apr. 1960 by popular revolt. The coercive apparatus of Rhee's regime was torn down and replaced with constitutional liberalism in the form of the Second Republic. The instability associated with this experiment in democracy was the pretext for a military coup on 16 May 1961.

Gen. Park Chung Hee emerged to dominate the military junta which followed the coup. After a process of political purification designed to eliminate the forces of the liberal-left and the corrupt associates of the Rhee regime, military rule was terminated at the end of 1962 with Park becoming the civilian president of the newly constituted Third Republic. Park was re-elected in 1967 and 1971 but, in the face of growing popular unrest, suspended the constitution and dissolved the National Assembly in Oct. 1972. He produced a new constitution with greatly expanded presidential powers and, at the end of 1972, he was indirectly elected president of the newly created Fourth Republic. Over the next seven years Park faced widespread protests by those demanding greater liberalism and the destruction of the authoritarian 1972 constitution. His response varied between attempts at conciliation and the use of the draconian powers at his disposal to intimidate and coerce opponents. Park was re-elected in Dec. 1978 but was assassinated on 26 Oct. 1979, by the head of his secret police force in what appeared to be a poorly organized coup attempt.

The basis for the economic success of the modern South Korean state was laid under the 18-year rule of Park who combined state planning with capitalist incentives. His regime's abrogation of labour rights and denial of general political liberties produced a largely stable, disciplined and low-wage environment which attracted foreign capital and investment.

The process of liberation for the hitherto suppressed forces of opposition, which had been unleashed by Park's death, was abruptly curtailed by a military coup on 12 Dec. 1979. Widespread unrest by workers and students led to a tightening of military rule and, in May 1980, there was a popular uprising in the southern city of Kwangju. The insurrection was suppressed with the utmost brutality and there followed a nationwide purification campaign to destroy anti-social and politically subversive elements. With the opposition crushed, the presidency was assumed in Aug. 1980 by Chun Doo Hwan, who had been a key figure in the 1979 coup and had exercised increasing control over the government during the first half of 1980.

Chun drew up a new constitution which ushered in the Fifth Republic in Oct. 1980. Controlled political activity was gradually introduced and martial law, in force since Park's assassination, was lifted in Jan. 1981. In February an electoral college chose Chun as president for a single seven-year term. Under an electoral system heavily weighted in its favour, Chun's newly established right-wing Democratic Justice Party (DJP) won an overall majority in National Assembly elections in Mar. 1981.

Although the Chun regime remained essentially repressive and continued to face outbreaks of popular unrest, it became sufficiently self-confident to release from prison key opponents and to permit many of them to re-engage in controlled political activity. US pressure on Chun to improve the country's human-rights image was also instrumental in this respect. At the beginning of 1985 the anti-Chun opposition established the New Korea Democratic Party (NKDP). It was constructed around the veteran dissidents Kim Dae Jung and Kim Young Sam and, following the legislative elections of Feb. 1985, it became the dominant opposition force.

In the face of escalating constitutional and extra-constitutional opposition, Chun agreed to consider undertaking constitutional reforms to provide for the direct election of his successor. He later reneged on the promise and chose as his successor Roh Tae Woo, a former general who had played a key role in the 1979 coup. By mid-1987, however, popular unrest had reached such a pitch that there was a real possibility that the Olympic Games – due to be held in Seoul in 1988 – would be removed to an alternative venue. On 29 June Roh announced his acceptance of the opposition's demands for reform. A new democratic constitution, including the provision for a popularly elected president, was drawn up and overwhelmingly approved by a referendum in Oct. 1987.

Notwithstanding their repeated commitments to avoid splitting the opposition vote, neither of the two Kims would stand down in favour of the other, and each eventually contested the elections at the helm of his own party. Profiting from this division, Roh was elected president on 16 Dec. with less than 36% of the total vote.

Roh was formally inaugurated as president of the Sixth Republic on 25 Feb. 1988. Elections for a new National Assembly were held on 26 Apr., with the DJP winning 125 of the 299 seats. Despite this minority position, the Roh government has remained largely stable and true to its commitment to ensuring the full restoration of democracy and the rule of law within South Korea. Although it has continued to face outbreaks of popular unrest they have been small in comparison to those which destabilized the Chun regime, and have been contained without recourse to excessive authoritarianism. The protesters have also lacked the support of the mainstream opposition which has used its majority in the legislature to work constructively with Pres. Roh.

Roh has also attempted to build upon the success of the Olympics by fostering economic and diplomatic contacts with communist countries which had previously refused to recognize the South Korean state. Relations with North Korea have also improved, although contacts between the two states remain limited in scope and shrouded in mutual suspicion. In early 1990, Roh reached an agreement to merge the DJP with two of the country's three opposition parties. The resulting grouping, the Democrat Liberal Party, controlled more than two-thirds of the seats in the legislature.

CONSTITUTION AND GOVERNMENT

Executive and legislature

The head of state is an executive president, elected by direct popular vote for a five-year term; last election 16 Dec. 1987. The president appoints the prime minister and state council (cabinet). The legislature, the 299-member National Assembly, is elected for a four-year term by universal adult suffrage; last elections 26 Apr. 1988.

Present government

President Roh Tae Woo

Prime Minister Kang Young Hoon

Principal members of State Council Cho Soon (Deputy Prime Minister; Economic Planning Board); Choi Ho Joong (Foreign Affairs); Kim Tae Ho (Home Affairs); Lee Kyu Sung (Finance); Huh Hyung Koo (Justice); Lee Sang Hoon (Defence).

Justice

The death penalty is in force. There were 23 executions between 1985 and mid-1988. Offences were murder, rape.

National symbols

Flag. White field charged with a circular red-and-blue pictograph, the yin and yang symbol.

Festivals. 1 Mar. (Sam Il Chul, Independence Movement Day); 5 May (Children's Day); 6 June (Memorial Day); 17 July (Constitution Day); 15 Aug. (Liberation Day); 1 Oct. (Armed Forces Day); 3 Oct. (National Foundation Day); 9 Oct. (Hangul Nal, Anniversary of Proclamation of Korean Alphabet).

Vehicle registration plate. ROK.

INTERNATIONAL RELATIONS

Affiliations

Observer status at UN, member of World Bank, IMF and many UN specialized agencies.

Defence

Total Armed Forces: 629,000. Terms of service: 30–36 months. Reserves: 4,500,000.

Army: 542,000; 1,500 main battle tanks (mainly M-47/-48A5, Type 88).

Navy: 54,000 inclusive 25,000 marines; three submarines and 29 principal surface combatants: 11 destroyers (US Gearing, Sumner and Fletcher), 18 frigates. 105 patrol and coastal combatants.

Naval Air: 17 combat aircraft and 21 armed helicopters.

Marines: 25,000; 40 main battle tanks (M-47).

Air Force: 33,000; 473 combat aircraft (F-16/-C/-D, F-5B/E/F, F-4).

Para-Military: Civilian Defence Corps (to age 50): 3,500,000.

ECONOMY

Currency

The unit is the South Korean won, divided into 100 chon.

National finance

Budget. The 1989 budget (in US$) was for expenditure (current and capital) of 28,700 million and revenue of 28,700 million. Main items of current expenditure are defence 27.3%; education 18.3%.

Balance of payments. The balance of payments (current account, 1987) was a surplus of $9,835 million.

Inflation. (1988) 7%.

Gross Domestic Product

Estimated total GDP US$121,310 million, per capita US$4,045 (ranking 23 in the world by size).

Economically active population. The total number of persons active in the economy was 16,900,000; unemployed: 3%.

Sector	% of workforce	% of GDP
industry	27	43
agriculture	21	11
services*	52	46

* services figure includes elements unassigned to other categories.

Energy and mineral resources

Minerals. The Sangdong mine has one of the world's largest deposits of tungsten, output: (1985) 5,126 tons/4,650 tonnes. Other minerals (in tons/tonnes) include anthracite coal 24.7 million/22.4 million; iron ore 738,541/670,000; kaolin 698,858/634,000; silver 138,890/126,000; zinc ore 105,270/92,500; lead ore 20,944/19,000; gold 25,904/23,500.

Electricity. Capacity: 7,687 million kW; production: 19,539 million kWh; 10,080 kWh per capita (1988).

Bioresources

Agriculture. 21% of the land is arable with 1% given over to permanent crops and 1% meadows and pastures.

Crop production: (1986 in 1,000 tons/tonnes) rice 6,181/5,607; total crops from dry fields 1,504/1,364; vegetables 8,520/7,729; fruits 1,626/1,475.

Livestock numbers: (1987 in millions) poultry 57; pigs 3.3; cattle 2.8.

Forestry. 67% of the land is forest and woodland.

Fisheries. Total catch: (1986) 4.03 million tons/3.66 million tonnes.

Industry and commerce

Industry. South Korea has experienced huge economic growth recently, mainly the result of the export-oriented economy. The main industries are textiles; clothing; footwear; food processing; chemicals; steel; electronics; automobile production; ship building.

Commerce. Exports: $60,700 million, or 35% of GDP, including textiles; clothing; electrical machinery; footwear; steel; automobiles; ships; fish. Imports: $51,800 million, including machinery; oil; steel; transport equipment; textiles; organic chemicals; grains. Countries exported to: US 35%; Japan 20%. Imports came from: Japan 31%; US 25%.

Trade with UK. South Korea imported UK goods worth £1,742,747,000; exports to UK totalled £1,135,107,000.

Tourism. (1986) 1,471,811 visitors.

COMMUNICATIONS

Railways
There are 3,929 miles/6,323 km of railways.

Roads
There are 31,692 miles/51,003 km of roads, of which 14,672 miles/23,613 km are concrete or bituminized.

Aviation
Korean Air provides domestic and international services and Seoul Air Lines provides domestic service, to undertake international flights by 1991 (main airports are at Kimpo (Seoul), Pusan and Cheju). Passengers: (1987) 10.55 million.

Shipping
The 1,000 miles/1,609 km of inland waterways are restricted to use by small native craft. The marine ports of Inchon, Kunsan and Mokpo face the Yellow Sea on the west coast. The ports of Ulsan and Pusan are on the south-east coast. The merchant marine consists of 425 ships of 1,000 GRT or over.

Telecommunications
There are 4.8 million telephones and adequate domestic and international services. There are some 42 million radios and 8,600,000 televison sets; the KBS and MBC corporations, broadcasting both radio and television, compete with religious radio stations and with the US Forces Korea network.

EDUCATION AND WELFARE

Education
Schools. In 1986 South Korea had 6,535 elementary schools with 4,798,323 pupils; 2,412 middle schools with 2,765,629 pupils; 1,627 high schools with 2,262,397 pupils.
Universities. There are 256 universities and colleges with 1,262,493 students (1986). There are a further 203 graduate schools with 70,000 students, and also four Open Universities.
Literacy. Over 90%.

Health
There are 31,616 doctors and 4,041 oriental medical doctors. In 1986 there were 19,600 hospitals and clinics with a total of 107,907 beds (one per 401 people).

KUWAIT
Dowlat al Kuwait
(State of Kuwait)

GEOGRAPHY
Situated at the north-west head of the Persian/Arabian Gulf, the state of Kuwait covers an area of 6,879 miles^2/17,820 km^2 divided into four governorates. The capital governorate also includes nine Gulf islands, the largest of which is Bubiyan. The bulk of Kuwait's surface area comprises a low-lying plateau, rising westward to a maximum elevation of 951 ft/290 m at Ash Shaqaya on the Iraqi-Saudi Arabian border. Along the western border, the plateau is incised to a depth of 148 ft/45 m by the Wadi al Batin. In the north-west, the Jal az-Zawr escarpment stretches 37 miles/60 km along the coast. Over 90% of the population reside within 6 miles/10 km of the Gulf and approximately 92% of the terrain is stony desert.

Climate
Dry desert conditions with regular dust storms and scant rainfall (average 4.4 in/111 mm). Very hot and humid during the summer months (above 113°F/45°C and 90% humidity). Cooler during winter with some frost at night. Kuwait: Jan. 56°F/13.5°C. July 98°F/36.6°C. Average annual rainfall 49 in/125 mm.

Cities and towns

Kuwait City (capital)	44,335
as-Salimiya	153,369
Hawalli	145,126
Faranawiya	68,701
Abraq Kheetan	45,120

Population
Total population is 1,938,000 of which 93.7% live in urban areas. Population density is 281 persons per mile ^{2}/105.1 per km^2. Ethnic composition: 39% Kuwaiti; 39% other Arab; 9% South Asian; 4% Iranian. Foreign nationals constitute approx 60% of the total population.
Birth rate 3.56%. **Death rate** 0.32%. **Rate of population increase** 3.24% **Age distribution** under 15 = 40%; over 65 = 1.3%. **Life expectancy** female 75; male 71; average 73.

Religion
85% of the population are Muslims (of which 30% Shi'a; 45% Sunni; 10% other); 15% are Christians, Hindus, Parsis and other. Of the 15% Christian minority, about 54,700 are Roman Catholic.

Language
Arabic is the official language, but Persian and English are also widely spoken.

HISTORY

In 1716 an offshoot of the Unayzah tribal confederation of Central Arabia, named Bani Utub ('the people who wandered') founded present-day Kuwait. Subsequently, several leading clans of the original settlers combined to create an oligarchical merchant principality presided over by the Al Sabah clan. In 1899 Mubarak Al Sabah, referred to as Mubarak the Great (r.1896–1915) who had expanded Kuwaiti influence along with Al Sabah preeminence, allowed the country to enter into a protected-state relationship with Britain, in order to prevent the Ottoman Empire, which claimed nominal suzerainty, from attempting to exert political control.

Under Mubarak, Kuwaiti rule expanded until 1922 when Britain, under the Treaty of Ugayr, oversaw the return of half of the country's enlarged territory to Iraqi and Saudi control. The Treaty also created the Saudi-Kuwaiti Neutral Zone, which was split equally between the two countries in 1970. Britain's indirect rule in Kuwait was transformed as a result of the discovery of oil in 1938; the Kuwait Oil Company was jointly owned by British Petroleum Company (formerly the Anglo-Iranian Oil Company) and the Gulf Oil Company. In 1961 Kuwait regained full independence from the British but was troubled by renewed claims to sovereignty from Iraq on the historic grounds that it was part of the Basra province in Ottoman times. Britain, operating under treaty provisions, sent troops to Kuwait and the crisis was subdued. In 1963 Kuwait became a member of the United Nations and although later that year Iraq recognized its independence, the country still pursued territorial claims to the Kuwaiti islands of Warbah and Bubiyan, which command the approaches to the Iraqi naval base at Umm Qasr. In May 1973, Iraq occupied the Kuwaiti border post of Samitah on the mainland and a military clash ensued. Iraq withdrew in 1974.

The constitution, inaugurated in 1962 under Amir Abdullah al Salim Al Sabah, provides for the establishment of a legislature, an executive and an independent judicial system. The National Assembly was granted the right of petition to the Amir concerning cabinet appointees. The electoral base has remained limited to citizens who are male, literate and over 21 years of age, and political parties are illegal. The National Assembly's criticism of the government led to its dissolution in Aug. 1976 and again in July 1986. The Amir now rules by decree. Kuwait's monarchical rulers have traditionally been chosen from descendants of the Al Sabah family, sons of Mubarak the Great: the Salims and the Jabirs. Two factors have had an impact on Kuwaiti stability in the 1980s: the Iran–Iraq war and terrorism. The proximity of Kuwait to the war was highlighted in 1981 when Iran bombed two Kuwaiti border areas, and in 1982 when Iranian aircraft attacked a Kuwaiti oil facility. Terrorist attacks within Kuwait have been perpetrated by Shia groups with suspected, but unproven, links with Iran.

Kuwait was one of the five founder members of the Organization of Petroleum Exporting Countries (OPEC) in 1960 and the country stressed economic and political co-operation when it co-founded the Gulf Co-operation Council in 1981. The oil glut in the 1980s and declining oil reserves have resulted in government attempts to diversify the economy into the fields of petrochemicals and fertilizer production. Thus far, most industrial enterprise is carried on by state-owned corporations with the private sector active mainly in retail marketing and investment banking.

CONSTITUTION AND GOVERNMENT

Executive and legislature
The Amir, who is chosen by and from among the royal family, is head of state and appoints the prime minister and council of ministers; he dissolved the National Assembly in July 1986 and now promulgates legislation by Amiri decree.

Present government
Amir Shaikh Jabir al Ahmad al Jabir as Sabah
Prime Minister Crown Prince Shaikh Saad al Abdullah as Salim
Principal Ministers Shaikh Sabah al Ahmad al Jabir as Sabah (Deputy Prime Minister; Foreign Affairs); Jassim Mohammed al Kharafi (Finance and Economy); Shaikh Salim as Sabah as Salim as Sabah (Interior); Dari Abdullah al Uthman (Justice, Legal and Administrative Affairs); Shaikh Ali al Khalifa al Adhibi as Sabah (Oil); Shaikh Nawaf al Ahmad al Jabir as Sabah (Defence).

Justice
The system of law is based on civil law with Islamic Sharia law of importance in the personal area. The highest courts are the Supreme Court of Appeal, Court of Cassation, Constitutional Court and State Security Court. Cases of lesser importance may be brought before the Courts of Summary Justice, or go before courts of First Instance. The death penalty is in force. There were at least six executions between 1985 and mid-1988. Offences were premeditated murder.

National symbols
Flag. Three horizontal stripes of green, white and red, and in the hoist there is a black trapezium.
Festivals. 25 Feb. (Kuwaiti National Day).
Vehicle registration plate. KWT.

INTERNATIONAL RELATIONS

Affiliations
NAM; Arab League; OPEC; OAPEC; GCC.

Defence
Total Armed Forces: 20,300. Terms of service: conscription, two years (university students one year).
Army: 16,000; 275 main battle tanks (Vickers Mk 1, Centurion, Chieftain).
Navy: 2,100; 23 patrol and coastal combatants.
Air Force: 2,200; 70 combat aircraft (mainly A-4KU, TA-4KU, Mirage F-1CK).

ECONOMY

Currency
The unit is the dinar, divided into 1,000 fils.

National finance
Budget. The 1988 budget (in US$) was for expenditure (current and capital) of 10,500 million and revenue of 7,100 million. Main items of current expenditure are housing and welfare 22%; education 14.2%; defence 14%.

Balance of payments. The balance of payments (current account, 1987) was a surplus of US$4,572 million.
Inflation. (1988) 0.8%.

Gross Domestic Product
Estimated total GDP US$17,940 million, per capita US$10,410 (ranking 62 in the world by size).
Economically active population. The total number of persons active in the economy was 566,000; unemployed: 0%.

Sector	% of workforce	of GDP
industry	32	51
agriculture	2	1
services*	66	48

* services figure includes elements unassigned to other categories.

Energy and mineral resources
Oil. The oil sector dominates the economy. Crude oil production: (1988) 80 million tons/73 million tonnes; production of petroleum products: (1984) 26.74 million tons/24.26 million tonnes.
Electricity. Capacity: 7.68 million kW; production: 19,539 million kWh; 10,080 kWh per capita (1988).

Bioresources
Agriculture. The majority of the land is unsuitable for cultivation. 8% is meadow and pasture and 27 dairy farms produce a total of 33,069 tons/30,000 tonnes of fresh milk.
Crop production: (1986 in 1,000 tons/tonnes) tomatoes 16.5/15; melons 2.2/2; onions 2.2/2; dates 2.2/2.
Livestock numbers: (1987) cattle 25,000; sheep 265,000; goats 320,000; poultry 23 million.
Fisheries. Shrimp fishing is being developed.

Industry and commerce
Industry. The main industries are petroleum; petrochemicals; desalination; food processing; salt; construction. The economy is heavily dependent on foreign labour and Kuwaitis account for less than 20% of the workforce.
Commerce. Exports: US$8,700 million or 45% of GDP, oil comprising 90%. Imports: US$4,900 million, including food; construction materials; vehicles and parts; clothing. Countries exported to: Japan; Italy; FRG; US. Imports came from: Japan; US; FRG; UK.
Trade with UK. Kuwait imported UK goods worth £237,515,000; exports to UK totalled £72,318,000.
Tourism. (1985) 116,000 visitors.

COMMUNICATIONS

Railways
There are no railways.

Roads
There are 2,231 miles/3,590 km of roads.

Aviation
Kuwait Airways Corporation (KAC) provides international services (main airport is Kuwait International Airport). Passengers: (1984) 1.49 million.

Shipping
The major marine ports are Shuwaykh, Shuaibah, and Mina al-Ahmadi. The merchant marine consists of 38 ships of 1,000 GRT or over.

Telecommunications
There are 285,000 telephones and although international facilities are excellent, domestic facilities are only adequate. There are 500,000 radios and a similar number of television sets, with the state controlling broadcasting; there are two channels on Kuwait Television.

EDUCATION AND WELFARE

Education
Schools. In 1984–5 there were 562 government schools with a total of 350,604 pupils: 24,150 in kindergartens; 126,441 in primary schools; 119,037 in intermediate schools; 77,626 in secondary schools. There were also 42 Arab and 30 foreign schools with a total of 60,000 pupils.
Universities. The University of Kuwait has 15,990 students and 877 teachers (one per 18 students) (1988).
Literacy. 71%.

Health
There is free medical treatment in Kuwait. 25 hospitals and sanitoria with 2,692 beds (one per 341 people); 2,692 doctors (one per 745 people) and 8,557 nursing personnel.

LAOS
Lao People's Democratic Republic

GEOGRAPHY

Located in the middle of the south-east Asian Indochinese peninsula, Laos is a landlocked country covering a total area of 91,405 miles²/236,800 km². The northern peaks of this predominantly mountainous country (90% of the terrain is above 591 ft/180 m elevation) reach altitudes of 9,026 ft/2,751 m on the densely forested Vietnamese frontier and 9,252 ft/2,820 m at Phou Bia on the Plateau de Xianghoang. A number of rivers traverse the country east-west from the Chaine Anamatique to the River Mekong on the western border, including the Banghiang, the Noi, the Wa and the Theun. The fertile Mekong floodplains in the west represent the only extensively cultivable Laotian lowland and support over 50% of the total population. 4% of the land is arable and 58% forest or woodland.

Climate

Sub-equatorial, tropical monsoonal. Temperatures are consistently high all year round, averaging between 61–70°F/16–21°C Dec.-Feb. and above 98°F/32°C Mar.-Apr. The wet season lasts from May-Oct. followed by a dry spell Nov.-Apr. Average annual rainfall increases from 59–66.9 in/ 1,500–1,700 mm on the western levels to 118 in/ 3,000 mm in the mountains. Vientiane: Jan. 70°F/ 21.1°C. July 81°F/27.2°C. Average annual rainfall 67.5 in/1,715mm.

Cities and towns

Vientiane (capital)	176,637
Savannakhet	50,690
Pakse	44,860
Luang Prabang	44,244

Population

Total population is 3,874,000 of which 17% live in urban areas. Population density is 42 persons per mile^2/15.9 persons per km^2 with the eastern border population severely depleted by war. The population is divisible into four principal categories: the Lao-Lu (50%) inhabiting the lowlands and valleys; the Lao-Tai (20%) including the Black Tai, Red Tai, Tai Phuan and Phon-Tai peoples; the Lao-Theung (15%) also known as the Mon-Khmer peoples; the Lao-Seung, including the Miao and Yao (15%) mountain-dwellers.

Birth rate 4.47%. **Death rate** 1.87%. **Rate of population increase** 2.6% **Age distribution** under 15 = 42.6%; over 65 = 2.9%. **Life expectancy** female 50; male 47; average 48.

Religion

The bulk of the population adhere to Theravada Buddhism (approx 85%). Small Chinese and Vietnamese minorities practise Mahayana Buddhism and Confucianism. An estimated 15% of the population pursue traditional animist faiths (largely the Lao-Theung) and a very small proportion observe Christian tenets.

Language

Laotian. The four ethnic categories also denote linguistic/dialectal difference. The Lao-Lu, Lao-Tai, Lao-Theung and Lao-Seung all speak dialects of Laotian-Tai, most of which are mutually intelligible. Laotian vocabulary is enriched by some loanwords from Pali, the scriptural language of Theravada Buddhism. French, English and Vietnamese are also spoken in the major urban centres.

HISTORY

The Lao trace their ancestry back to the great southward migration of Tai people from southern China to lands on the periphery of the great Khmer empire of Angkor, between the 6th and the 13th centuries. In 1353, Fa Ngum, a Lao prince raised at Angkor, brought together a number of scattered Lao principalities into the powerful Kingdom of Lan Xang (a million elephants), with its capital at Luang Prabang. The kingdom was weakened by warfare among rival princes in the 18th century, and both Vietnam and Siam (Thailand) made large-scale territorial acquisitions.

By 1885 France had colonized all of Vietnam, including some Lao territories. In 1893, Siam ceded to the French all Lao territory to the east of the Mekong and by 1907, French control had been extended to include Sayaboury and parts of Champasssak to the west of the river. Once in control, the French took little interest in Laos; it was enough that the country acted as a buffer between Siam and France's valuable holdings in Vietnam.

Japan occupied Laos 1940–45, ruling through the Vichy French administration. In 1945 the Japanese pressured King Sisavang Vong into declaring Laotian independence. The King reaffirmed France's protectorate role after Japan's capitulation in Aug. 1945, provoking nationalist elements to proclaim a Lao Issara (Free Laos) government. However, by early 1946, France had regained control of Laos, which was designated a free state within the French Union.

Disparate anti-French forces eventually came together in 1950 to form the Land of the Lao (Pathet Lao – PL). Led by 'Red' Prince Souphanouvong, the Pathet Lao developed close links with the forces of the Democratic Republic of Vietnam (North Vietnam). Meanwhile, Souphanouvong's elder half-brother, Souvanna Phouma, formed a Royal Lao Government (RLG) in 1951, and two years later Laos was granted full independence.

Laos emerged intact from the 1954 Geneva Conference on Indochina, although the PL was granted 'regroupment areas' in the north-east. The PL boycotted elections in 1955, but subsequent negotiations between Souvanna and Souphanouvong resulted in the formation, in late 1957, of a broad-based coalition government. The coalition soon collapsed in favour of a staunchly anti-Communist regime after the United States withdrew all aid to Laos. By Dec. 1960 the country was divided, with a 'neutralist' regime led by Souvanna based in the Plain of Jars and a 'rightist' regime in Vientiane under the control of 'strongman' Phoumi Nosavan. The PL, often fighting alongside North Vietnamese troops, took advantage of the confusion to extend the areas under its control. In 1962, another attempt to establish a coalition regime collapsed within months and the fighting intensified. The US started to carry out clandestine bombing missions into Laos in 1964 in an attempt to smash North Vietnamese sanctuaries. The bombing reached saturation level in the late 1960s. On the ground, the PL and the RLG fought a war of attrition, with neither side relinquishing much territory.

A cease-fire was signed in Feb. 1973 and 14 months later the third, and last, coalition government was established. In the wake of the Communist victories in Vietnam and Cambodia in early 1975, the Pathet Lao gradually, and peacefully, gained total control of the administration.

On 2 Dec. 1975, the People's Democratic Republic of Laos was declared, with Souphanouvong as president and Kaysone Phomvihane (general secretary of the Lao People's Revolutionary Party) as chairman of the council of ministers. A Supreme People's Assembly was appointed to draft a constitution, as yet unfinished. Souphanouvong suffered a stroke in Sept. 1986 and was replaced, on an acting basis, by Phoumi Vongvichit in Oct. 1986.

CONSTITUTION AND GOVERNMENT

Executive and legislature

An acting president and a council of ministers, whose chairman operates as head of government, were installed after the end of the war in 1975 by a National Congress of People's Representatives. An appointed 45-member Supreme People's Assembly, chaired by the president, was charged with drafting a constitution; elections to a 79-member Supreme People's Assembly were held on 26 Mar. 1989. Effective political power is exercised by the ruling Lao People's Revolutionary Party.

Present government

Acting President Phoumi Vongvichit
Chairman of Council of Ministers Kaysone Phomvihane
Principal members of Council of Ministers Sisomphone Lovansay (Vice-Chairman); Gen. Khamtay Siphandon (Vice-Chairman; Defence); Gen. Phoune Sipaseuth (Vice-Chairman; Foreign Affairs); Saly Vongkhamsao (Vice-Chairman; Economics, Planning and Finance); Kou Souvannamethi (Justice).

Ruling party

Lao People's Revolutionary Party (Phak Pasason Pativat Lao). *General Secretary* Kaysone Phomvihane. *Full members of the political bureau* Kaysone Phomvihane; Nouhak Phoumsavan; Souphanouvong; Phoumi Vongvichit; Gen. Khamtay Siphandon; Gen. Phoune Sipaseuth; Sisomphone Lovansay; Gen. Sisavat Keobounphanh; Saly Vongkhamsao; Maychantane Sengmany; Lt.-Gen. Saman Vignaket. *Members of the secretariat* Kaysone Phomvihane; Gen. Khamtay Siphandon; Gen. Sisavat Keobounphanh; Saly Vongkhamsao; Maychantane Sengmany; Lt.-Gen. Saman Vignaket; Oudom Khatthi-gna; Brig.-Gen. Choummali Saignakong; Somlak Chanthamat.

Justice

The death penalty is in force (according to available information). The number of executions between 1985 and mid-1988 is not known.

National symbols

Flag. Three horizontal stripes of red, dark blue and red. In the centre of the blue stripe there is a white disc.
Festivals. 2 Dec. (National Day).
Vehicle registration plate. LAO.

INTERNATIONAL RELATIONS

Affiliations

NAM; Comecon (observer).

Defence

Total Armed Forces: 55,500. Terms of service: conscription, 18 months minimum.
Army: 52,500; 30 main battle tanks (T-34/-55), 25 light tanks (PT-76).
Navy: some 650; about 40 patrol craft (river).
Air Force: 2,000; 30 combat aircraft (MiG-21).
Foreign Forces: Vietnam: Army: 50,000.

ECONOMY

Currency

The unit is the new kip, divided into 100 at.

National finance

Budget. The 1987 budget (in US$) was for expenditure (current and capital) of 156 million and revenue of 111 million.
Inflation. (1988) 19%.

Gross Domestic Product

Estimated total GDP US$551 million, per capita US$140 (ranking 152 in the world by size).
Economically active population. The total number of persons active in the economy was 1,500,000; unemployed: 17%. Between 85% and 90% of the population work in agriculture.

Energy and mineral resources

Minerals. Resources include gypsum; tin; gold; gemstones; iron; potash. There are two tin mines. In 1986 617 tons/560 tonnes of tin concentrates were produced. Most mineral resources are under-exploited.
Electricity. Capacity: 175,000 kW; production: 900 kWh; 230 kWh per capita. Electricity is available to only a limited area.

Bioresources

Agriculture. The majority of the population is engaged in subsistence agriculture.
Crop production: rice is by far the largest crop (1.64 million tons/1.49 million tonnes in 1986). Other crops include maize; vegetables; tobacco; coffee; cotton. There are food shortages (including rice). The opium poppy and cannabis are produced illegally for the international trade.
Livestock numbers: (1987) buffaloes 1.05 million; cattle 593,000; goats 1.5 million; poultry 8 million.
Forestry. There has been deforestation and soil erosion, but forests still cover over 50% of the country.

Industry and commerce

Industry. Tin mining; timber; beer; cigarettes; matches; soft drinks; bricks. Industrial growth is hampered by poor infrastructure and limited internal and external telecommunications.
Commerce. Exports: US$48.7 million (f.o.b. 1987) which accounted for 9% of the GDP. Major trading partners are Thailand; Malaysia; Vietnam; USSR; US. Major exports are coffee; tin; wood; wood products. Imports: US$218.8 million (c.i.f 1987). Major trading partners are Thailand; Japan; France; Vietnam. Major imports are food; fuel; consumer goods.
Trade with UK. Laos imported £1.3 million worth of goods from the UK and exported £2,000 worth of goods.

COMMUNICATIONS

Railways

There are no railways.

Roads

There are 8,067 miles/12,983 km of roads, of which 2,524 miles/4,062 km are bituminized.

Aviation

Lao Aviation provides domestic and international services (main airport is Wattai airport, Vientiane). Passengers: (1986) 25,000.

Shipping

The Mekong and its tributaries account for most of the 2,850 miles/4,587 km of inland waterways. There are no ports.

Telecommunications

There are 7,390 telephones (1986). The service to the general public is poor and the radio network service to government users is erratic. There are about 420,000 radios and 32,000 television sets in use; both radio and TV are state-owned, the domestically produced television service being supplemented by Soviet television relayed by satellite.

EDUCATION AND WELFARE

Education

School population. In the year 1982–83 there were

400,000 elementary school pupils; 65,000 secondary school pupils; 17,000 senior high school students; 13,000 students at vocational schools.

Schools. In the year 1982–83 there were 6,525 elementary schools; 420 secondary schools; 60 senior high schools; 55 vocational schools.

Universities. There is one-teacher training college; one college of education; one school of medicine; one agricultural college. Sisavangvong University in Vientiane was founded in 1958 and in 1984 had 1,600 students.

Literacy Officially literacy improved from 40% to 60% between 1978 and 1981.

Health

In 1985 there were 430 doctors and 11,650 hospital beds (approximately one per 310 patients).

LEBANON

Al-ibnan or *Al-Jumhouriya al-Lubnaniya* *(Republic of Lebanon)*

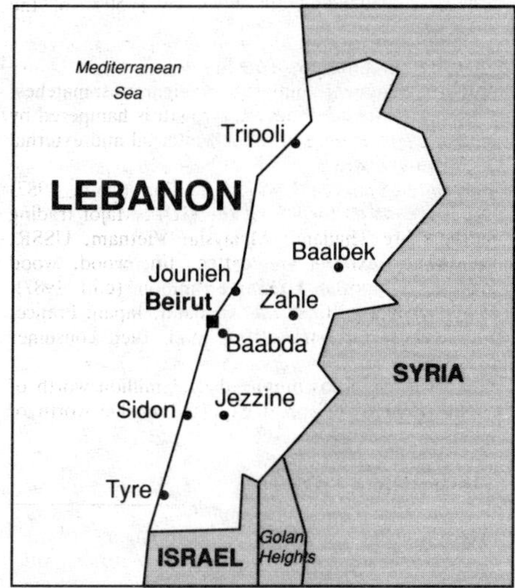

GEOGRAPHY

Located on the east coast of the Mediterranean in south-west Asia, the republic of Lebanon has an area of 4,014 miles²/10,400 km² divided into five regional governments or moafazats. From the narrow Mediterranean littoral, the land rises eastward to form the Lebanon Mountains (Jabal Lubnan) stretching north-south over approximately 30% of the entire surface area and climbing to 10,128 ft/3,087 m at Qornet es Saouda, Lebanon's highest peak. Between the harsh eastern slopes of this principal range and the Anti-Lebanon chain (Jebel esh Sharqi) bordering Syria, the fertile El Beqa'a plateau (average elevation 3,281 ft/1,000 m) is traversed by the River Litani flowing southwards before emptying into the Mediterranean north of Sour. 21% of the land is arable and 8% is forested. The majority of the urban population live in Beirut and Tripoli.

Climate

Mediterranean with long, hot, dry summers and significantly shorter, warm winters. Summer humidity reaches a maximum in coastal areas. Most rain falls during the winter months, varying with altitude and west-east location, from about 35–36 in/900–920 mm at Beirut to 15 in/380 mm per annum on the El Beqa'a plateau. Winter precipitation in the Lebanon mountains may often turn to snow. Beirut: Jan. 55°F/13°C. July 81°F/27°C. Average annual rainfall 35 in/893 mm.

Cities and towns

Beirut (capital)	1,500,000
Tripoli	160,000
Zahleh	45,000

Population

Note: Reliable estimates are difficult to establish.

Total population is 3,300,802 of which 83.7% live in urban areas. Population density is 822 persons per mile²/270 per km². Ethnic divisions: 93% Arab; 7% Armenian; Kurdish; Assyrian; Turkish; Greek.

Birth rate 2.93%. **Death rate** 0.88%. **Rate of population increase** 2.05% **Age distribution** under 15 = 37.5%; over 65 = 5.1%. **Life expectancy** female 70; male 65; average 67.5.

Religion

Note: Reliable estimates are difficult to establish.

An estimated 75% are Muslim and 25% Christian. The overwhelming majority of the Jewish population left Lebanon after the 1975–76 civil war. The 17 legally recognized religious sects are as follows: Armenian, Greek, Nestorean and Syriac Orthodox Christian; seven Uniate Christian (Armenian Catholic, Chaldean, Greek Catholic, Maronite, Protestant, Roman Catholic, Syrian Catholic); Alawite, Nusayri, Druze, Isma'ilite, Shi'a and Sunni Muslim – and Jewish.

Language

Arabic (93%) and French are both official languages. English and Armenian (6%) are also spoken. English is used increasingly as the international language of trade and commerce.

HISTORY

Part of the Phoenician empire from c.500 BC and later of the Hellenistic world, Lebanon came under Roman rule in the 1st century AD and was Christianized by the 4th century. Conquest by the Arabs (635) entailed Islamicization, although the Maronite Christians (named after the founder of their sect) retained their Catholic faith, secure in their central mountain strongholds. The 11th-century Druze heresy of Islam gained many adherents in Lebanon, who became an enclosed community.

Criss-crossed by the Crusades for two centuries of Christian–Muslim confrontation (late 11th to late 13th centuries), the Levant provided opportunities for colonies of merchants, who remained after the Crusaders themselves had been driven out, as did the chain of Crusader fortresses epitomized by Krak des Chevaliers near the Lebanon–Syria border. Conquest by the Ottoman Turks in 1516 brought greater religious toleration and encouragement for a Christian entrepreneurial class, which maintained close ties with Europe. Ottoman decline strengthened the interest of the great powers, who intervened in Lebanon in 1832 to prevent an Egyptian/Maronite takeover. Intercommunal fighting in 1859–60, in which over 10,000 Christians were killed, led to the establishment of a French protectorate (1860), under which Maronite interests prospered.

Conquest of the Ottoman Middle East by British and French forces during World War I led to the area being mandated to Britain and France by the League of Nations (1920). The French mandate for Syria encompassed Lebanon, which was separated from Syria and established as a semi-autonomous Republic (1926) with a French-drafted constitution. A 1932 census found that about 55% of the population were Christians, headed by the Maronites but including numerous other denominations. During World War II Lebanese leaders, Christian and Muslim, declared independence (Nov. 1941) and in 1943 reached an understanding (the unwritten National Covenant) that the distribution of institutional power in the new state should reflect its religious composition. Endorsed by the Free French authorities (Dec. 1943) under American and British pressure, Lebanon's independence took effect on 1 Jan. 1944.

Under the presidency of Bechara al-Khoury, Lebanon participated in the Arab League's 1948–49 war against Israel and accommodated a first wave of refugee Palestinians. It was not to join in any of the later Arab-Israeli wars. Forced to resign by Muslim and Christian opposition to official corruption (1952), al-Khoury gave way to Camille Chamoun, who achieved some stability until a revolt by Nasserist Muslim leftists persuaded him to call in United States Marines to restore state authority (1958). Under a negotiated settlement, Chamoun was replaced as president by Fuad Chehab, whose alliance of moderate Christian and Muslim parties secured a measure of reconciliation (1958–64). The same 'Chehabist' alliance maintained stability under the presidency of Charles Helou (1964–70), during which Lebanon achieved rapid economic progress as a financial and trading centre.

Under Helou, however, a new Palestinian influx from the 1967 Arab-Israeli war increased the presence of the Palestine Liberation Organization (PLO) in Lebanon, with resultant internal strains. An agreement concluded in Cairo (1969) regulated PLO activities but did little to ease Christian fears of the Palestinians becoming 'a state within a state'. Under Pres. Suleiman Franjié (1970–76), tensions increased when PLO guerrillas, expelled from Jordan (1970–71), moved to Lebanon and became a regular target for Israeli reprisal actions. Following the 1973 Arab-Israeli war, PLO moves to build an alliance with Lebanese Muslim leftists caused further alarm among Christians anxious to preserve their political and economic dominance. A series of clashes between the PLO and the Maronites' armed militia, the Phalange, culminated in the massacre by Phalangists of a busload of Palestinians in Beirut (Apr. 1975) and descent into full-scale civil war.

In the first phase of the conflict (1975–76), leftist Lebanese Muslims (including Druzes) allied with PLO groups, took the offensive on a platform of constitutional and economic reforms in favour of the Muslim community, by now generally regarded as outnumbering Christians. Under various names, and with shifting composition, this movement and its aims remained core elements in the subsequent struggle. When the mainly Christian Lebanese Front seemed on the verge of defeat, Syrian forces entered Lebanon at Pres. Franjié's request (Apr. 1976) and halted further Muslim advances. In Oct. 1976 an Arab League summit approved the Syrian intervention and created an Arab Deterrent Force (ADF), nominally of mixed composition but in reality almost wholly Syrian. Meanwhile, the convention that the presidency should be held by a Maronite had been maintained with the election of Elias Sarkis (May 1976), whose government concluded a free-trade agreement with the European Community (1977).

Despite the ADF presence, hostilities were regularly resumed in 1977–78, as efforts to find a political solution failed and the contending factions built up their armed militias. Kamal Jumblatt, the veteran Druze leader, was assassinated in Mar. 1977 and succeeded by his son, Walid Jumblatt, who became a key figure in Syrian-backed fronts seeking constitutional change.

In Mar. 1978 Israeli forces responded to PLO attacks by occupying southern Lebanon and establishing a surrogate militia of Christian Lebanese to police the border. Israel's withdrawal (June 1978) was accompanied by the deployment of a UN peacekeeping force (UNIFIL) in southern Lebanon. Over the next four years the Syrian ADF forces maintained the status quo on the 'green line' between Christian east and Muslim west Beirut, although fighting frequently erupted there and elsewhere, as various negotiated settlements proved to be stillborn.

In June 1982 Israeli forces launched a further invasion with the aim of eradicating the PLO from Lebanon. After heavy Israeli bombardment of Beirut, PLO forces withdrew to other Arab countries (Aug. 1982) under the supervision of a Multinational Force (MNF) of US and other Western troops. The murder of President-elect Bashir Gemayel (Phalangist) on 14 Sept. 1982 was followed two days later by a massacre of Palestinian civilians in the Chatila and Sabra camps in west Beirut by Israeli-backed Phalangists. Amin Gemayel (brother of Bashir) was elected president and concluded a US-mediated agreement with Israel (May 1983) for the removal of foreign troops from Lebanon. Syria, whose forces remained in control of northern and eastern Lebanon, rejected this agreement, which was also opposed by pro-Syrian leftists and Christians in Lebanon. Israel's withdrawal to southern Lebanon led to fierce fighting in mid-1983 between Jumblatt's Druze militia and Christian forces, and the creation of a virtual Druze mini-state in the central Chouf mountains. Having suffered heavy casualties from suicide bombers, the MNF was withdrawn in early 1984.

In Mar. 1984 Gemayel bowed to Syrian pressure by withdrawing from the May 1983 agreement and appointing (May 1984) a government of national unity under Rashid Karami (a Sunni Muslim) committed to fundamental reforms. Like other such initiatives before and since, this one foundered on factional intransigence (and Karami himself was assassinated in June 1987). Although Israeli forces finally completed their withdrawal in mid-1985, they remained in effective control of the border area and watchful of both the Syrian ADF forces and the resumed presence in Lebanon of the PLO. Thereafter, the fundamental Christian–Muslim divide became overlaid by more immediate, and often more ferocious, conflicts between rival factions within the two broad camps. On the Christian side, a Syrian-sponsored peace plan was backed by one Phalangist faction (Dec. 1985) but opposed by Pres. Gemayel and his followers. On the Muslim side, the pro-Syrian Amal movement and the Iranian-backed Hezbollah vied for support within the Shia community, and both came into conflict with the Druzes, Sunni militias and the PLO (1986–88).

Moreover, militant Muslim groups resorted to the kidnapping of Western nationals, amid a total breakdown of government authority and inexorable destruction of the economic infrastructure. In Jan. 1987, when 18 Westerners were known to be held hostage (some for nearly two years already), Terry Waite arrived in Beirut as a special envoy of the Archbishop of Canterbury, apparently seeking to build on some earlier successes in obtaining the release of hostages; instead he himself disappeared, presumed kidnapped, on 20 Jan., becoming perhaps the most famous, but not the last, of the Western hostages in Lebanon.

On the expiry of Gemayel's six-year term (Sept. 1988), it proved impossible to elect a successor, with the result that his final presidential act was to appoint a transitional military government headed by Gen. Michel Aoun, the Maronite army commander. However, the Muslim nominees refused to serve under Gen. Aoun and declared their support for the government of Selim al-Hoss (appointed in June 1987), from which Christian support had been withdrawn earlier. Aoun launched a 'war of liberation' against Syria in March 1989, thereby initiating a new round in Lebanon's bloody conflict. Intervention by the Arab League to halt the ensuing fighting resulted in the drawing up of an 'accord for national reconciliation', which was approved on 22 Oct. by a majority of Lebanese MPs meeting in Taif, Saudi Arabia. Aoun vehemently rejected the accord on the grounds that it failed to provide for an immediate Syrian withdrawal. Under the terms of the Taif accord, MPs elected a new president, René Mouawad, on 5 Nov. Mouawad was brutally assassinated 17 days later and was replaced on 24 Nov. by Elias Hrawi. On the following day Selim al-Hoss formed a new government. As of early 1990, an increasingly isolated Gen. Aoun continued to occupy the Presidential palace in East Beirut, from where he voiced his condemnation of the 'illegal' Hrawi regime.

CONSTITUTION AND GOVERNMENT

Executive and legislature

According to a 'National Covenant' agreed in 1943, institutional power was allocated between religious groups; the president to be a Maronite Christian, the prime minister a Sunni Moslem, the speaker of the (unicameral) National Assembly a Shia Moslem and the chief of staff of the Armed Forces a Druze. The president was elected by the National Assembly. Effective political power rests with the rival militias organized along religious lines, and with occupying Syrian forces. Lebanon was without a President between Sept. 1988 and Nov. 1989, with executive power being contested by Gen. Michel Aoun (the Maronite Christian Army Commander) and Selim al-Hoss (the Prime Minister since mid-1987). Aoun claimed still to head the country's (transitional) constitutional government despite the election of Elias Hrawi as President in late Nov. 1989.

Present government

President Elias Hrawi

Members of the Hoss Cabinet Selim al Hoss (Prime Minister; Foreign Affairs); Michel Sassin (Deputy Prime Minister; Labour); Nazih al Bizri (Economy and Trade); Ali al-Khalil (Finance); Edmond Rizq (Justice; Information); Souren Khanamirian (Industry and Oil); Abdullah al-Rassi (Health; Tourism); Nabbi Berri (Hydroelectric Resources; Housing and Co-operatives); Walid Jumblatt (Public Works); Albert Mansur (Defence); Ilyas al-Khazin (Interior); Umar Karami (Education); Muhsin Dallul (Agriculture).

Members of the Aoun Government Gen. Michel Aoun (Prime Minister; Defence; Information); Col. Islam Abu Jamrah (Deputy Prime Minister; Posts and Communications; Housing and Co-operatives; Economy and Trade); Brig.-Gen. Adgar Ma'luf (Finance; Health; Social Affairs; Industry and Oil).

Militia leaders Amal (Shia) Nabi Berri; Progressive Socialist Party (Druze) Walid Jumblatt; South Lebanon Army – Maj.-Gen. Antoine Lahad; Phalangist Party (Christian) George Sa'adah; Lebanese Forces (Christian) Samir Geagea.

Justice

The death penalty is in force. The number of judicial executions between 1985 and mid-1988 is not known.

National symbols

Flag. Three horizontal stripes of red, white and red.

Festivals. 22 Mar. (Arab League Anniversary); 22 Nov. (Independence Day); 31 Dec. (Evacuation Day).

Vehicle registration plate. RL.

INTERNATIONAL RELATIONS

Affiliations

NAM; Arab League; ICO.

Defence

Army: some 15,000; some 90 main battle tanks (M-48 A1/A5), 50 light tanks (AMX-13).

Navy: some 500 (Christian controlled); four inshore patrol craft.

Air Force: some 800 (chiefly Christian controlled); some combat aircraft (operational status doubtful).

Christian Militias:

Lebanese Forces Militia: 5,000 active, 35,000 all told; some 100 main battle tanks (T-54/-55, M-48/-4A/E-4), 20 light tanks (AMX-13).

Phalange: 800–1,000 active, 6,000 all told.

Muslim Militias:

Amal (Shi'a, pro-Syria) some 5,000 active, some 15,000 all told; about 50 main battle tanks (mainly T-54/-55).

Hezbollah (The Party of God; Shi'a, fundamentalist, pro-Iranian) some 3,500 active; perhaps 15,000 all told.

Progressive Socialist Party (Druze) 5,000 active; perhaps 12,000 all told; 70 main battle tanks (T-34/-54/-55).

South Lebanese Army (SLA, mainly Christian, some Shi'a and Druze, supported by Israel) 70 main battle tanks (M-4, T-54/-55).

Foreign Forces:
United Nations Interim Force in Lebanon (UNIFIL); some 5,500.
Syria; 30,000.
Iran; some 2,000.
Palestine Liberation Organization (PLO); all significant factions together some 7,100 active.

ECONOMY

Currency
The unit is the Lebanese pound, divided into 100 piastres.

Gross Domestic Product
Estimated total GDP US$1,800 million, per capita US$690 (ranking 120 in the world by size).
Economically active population. The total number of persons active in the economy was 650,000; unemployed: 33%. 11% work in agriculture.

Energy and mineral resources
Minerals. Limestone; iron ore; salt; iron pyrites; copper; asphalt; phosphates.
Electricity. Capacity: 1,380 million kW; production: 4,839 million kWh; 1,480 kWh per capita (1988).

Bioresources
Agriculture. Since the major disruption caused to industry by the war, agriculture has played an increasingly important part in Lebanon's economy. The country is not self-sufficient in food. Approximately 20% of the land is suitable for arable farming and 10% for permanent crops.
Crop production: fruit; wheat; barley; potatoes; tobacco; olives; onions; illegal production of opium poppy and cannabis for the international drug trade.
Production of citrus fruit: (1986) 403,442 tons/366,000 tonnes.
Livestock numbers: (1987 est.) goats 465,000; sheep 140,000; cattle 50,000; pigs 21,000.
Forestry. 8% of land is forested. Forest has been greatly reduced by overexploitation.

Industry and commerce
Industry. Industry has been badly affected by the war and has not recovered. Production figures are not available. Traditional areas of activity were banking; food processing; textiles; cement; oil refining; chemicals. Main trading partners were Saudi Arabia 16%; Switzerland 8%; Jordan 6%; Kuwait 6%; US 5%.
Commerce. Exports: (f.o.b.1987) US$1,000 million or 55% of GDP. Most important were agricultural products; chemicals; textiles; precious and semi-precious metals. Imports: (c.i.f.1987) US$1,500 million. Main trading partners were Italy 14%; France 12%; US 6%; Turkey 5%.
Trade with UK. Exports to the UK: (1988) £14.2 million; imports from the UK totalled £55.6 million.

COMMUNICATIONS

Railways
There are some 256 miles/412 km of railways.

Roads
There are 4,412 miles/7,100 km of roads (1,237 miles/1,990 km of main roads).

Aviation
Middle East Airlines (MEA) provides international services (principal airport is at Beirut). Passengers: (1984) 411,000.

Shipping
The major ports of Beirut, Tripoli and Ra's Sil'ata, Jounieh, Sidon, Az Zahrant and Tyre are not under the direct control of the Lebanese Government. The northern ports are occupied by Syrian forces and the southern ports are occupied or partially quarantined by Israeli forces. There are illegal ports along the central coast owned and operated by various Christian, Druze and Shi'a militias. The merchant marine consists of 76 ships of 1,000 GRT or over.

Telecommunications
There are 325,000 telephones. The rebuilding programme has been disrupted. There are over 2 million radios and 800,000 televisions. The state-owned Lebanese Broadcasting Station has both domestic and external radio services. Télé-Liban is a multi-channel commercial service, and there are two TV channels (Arabic and French) run by the Lebanese Broadcasting Commission which is controlled by the Christian Lebanese Forces militia.

EDUCATION AND WELFARE

Education
There are government and private primary and secondary schools.
Universities. Five universities: Lebanese (State) University; American University of Beirut; French University of St Joseph; The Arab University; Beirut University College. The French Government runs the Ecole Supérieure de Lettres and the Centre d'Etudes Mathématiques. Maronite monks run the University of the Holy Spirit at Kaslik.
Literacy. 75%.

Health
There are government-run and private hospitals.

LESOTHO
Muso oa Lesotho
(Kingdom of Lesotho)

GEOGRAPHY

Lesotho is a landlocked enclave within the Republic of South Africa, covering an area of 11,715 miles^2/ 30,350 km^2 divided into ten districts. Approximately two-thirds of the terrain is mountainous, rising to 11,424 ft/3,482 m at Thabana-Ntleayana in the north-east to east Drakensberg range and 10,157 ft/3,096 m at Thaba Putsoa, the southernmost tip of the north-east to south-west Mulati mountain chain. The highlands are dissected by a number of river valleys and gorges including the westward-flowing River Orange which rises in the central Mulatis. To the west, an 18–40 mile/30–65 km-wide belt of fertile land flanks the Caledon River, supporting the majority of the population and providing the bulk of Lesotho's agriculturally useful land. 10% of all land is arable and vegetation is limited to scattered willow, brushwood and olive growth.

Climate

Temperate and sub-tropical with mean annual rainfall (mainly Oct.-Apr.) of 285 in/725 mm in most regions. In the west lowland frosts and snowfall at higher altitudes occur frequently throughout the winter. Lowland temperatures range from a Jan. minimum of 20°F/–6.7°C to a July maximum of 90°F/32.2°C. Average summer and winter temperatures are 77°F/ 25°C and 59°F/15°C respectively.

Cities and towns

Maseru (capital) 288,951

Population

Total population is 1,676,000 of which 19% live in urban areas. Population density is 143 persons per mile^2/53.6 persons per km^2. 99.7% of the population are Sotho (subgroup: Kwena, including Molibeli, Monaheng, Hlakawana, Kxwakxwa and Fokeng ethnic groups); Zulu, Tembu and Fingo tribes comprise the remainder along with 1,600 Europeans and 800 Asians.

Birth rate 4.16%. **Death rate** 1.39%. **Rate of population increase** 2.77% **Age distribution** under 15 = 42.6%; over 65 = 3.6% **Life expectancy** female 57; male 54; average 56.

Religion

80% Christian (mostly Roman Catholic). Strongly represented Protestant denominations include the Lesotho Evangelical Church, the Anglican Communion, Providence Baptists and the United Methodists. The remaining 20% observe traditional/ indigenous beliefs.

Language

Sesotho or Southern Sotho (Bantu) and English are both official languages. Other languages spoken include Zulu; Afrikaans; French; Xhosa.

HISTORY

The area was first inhabited by the San people (bushman hunter-gatherers), who were largely displaced by the Zulu-speaking Nguniin the 18th century. Later that century the Sotho-speaking tribes settled harmoniously in the region until attacked by the Zulu King Shaka in the early 19th century.

King Moshoeshoe I united the people and repulsed the Zulu before negotiating British protection in 1843 as tension rose between the Basotho and the Boers. In 1868 the country (then known as Basutoland) became a British territory, in 1871 it was annexed to Cape Colony without the consent of the Basotho, and in 1884 became a British Crown Colony. From 1906 it was administered by the High Commissioner for Basutoland, Bechuanaland and Swaziland. The Basotho remained steadfastly opposed to incorporation into South Africa, although this was provided for under the 1910 Act of Union that founded South Africa. Britain granted Basutoland a new constitution in 1960, and Lesotho became an independent kingdom within the Commonwealth on 4 Oct. 1966, with Moshoeshoe II as king and Chief Lebua Jonathan as prime minister. Tensions between the King and his prime minister resulted in constitutional crisis in Dec. 1966; in Jan. 1970 a state of emergency was declared after the opposition Basotholand Congress Party claimed to have defeated Jonathan's Basotho National Party in the general election. The King went into exile but returned before the end of the year.

Chief Jonathan survived an attempted coup in Jan. 1974 and, despite the increasing unpopularity of his rule, was not finally overthrown until 20 Jan. 1986 when Maj.-Gen. Justin Lekhanya, the head of the Paramilitary Force, led a successful military coup. South Africa had applied increasing political and military pressure against Chief Jonathan's regime, allegedly supporting the opposition Lesotho Liberation Army and launching raids against African National Congress houses in Maseru in Dec. 1982 and Dec. 1985, during which some 50 people were killed. After the 1986 coup executive and legislative powers were invested in Moshoeshoe II, assisted by the Military Council, chaired by Maj.-Gen. Lekhanya, and a Council of Ministers. The King's powers were greatly reduced in Feb. 1990 after he objected to a purge of the Military Council carried out by Maj.-Gen. Lekhanya, and soon afterwards he left the country for what was described as a 'brief sabbatical'.

CONSTITUTION AND GOVERNMENT

Executive and legislature

Executive and legislative powers rest with the king, but government is effectively conducted by the Military Council, which appoints the Council of Ministers.

Present government

Head of state King Moshoeshoe II

Members of the Military Council Maj.-Gen. Justin Metsing Lekhanya (Chairman); Col. Elias Tutsoane Ramaema; Col. Michael Mkhahle Tsotetsi.

Principal Ministers Maj.-Gen. Justin Metsing Lekhanya (Defence and Internal Security; Public Services;

Youth and Women's Affairs; Agriculture; Cabinet Office); Chief Evaristus Retselisitsoe Sekhonyana (Finance); Tom Thabane (Foreign Affairs, Information and Broadcasting); Chief Patrick Molapo (Interior, Chieftancy Affairs and Rural Development); A.K. Maope (Justice and Prisons).

Justice

The Lesotho Courts of Law consist of the Court of Appeal, the High Court, Magistrates' Courts, Judicial Commissioners' Court and Central and Local Courts. Magistrates' and Higher courts administer the laws of Lesotho. They also adjudicate appeals from the Judicial Commissioner's and Subordinate Courts. The death penalty is in force. There were no executions between 1985 and mid-1988.

National symbols

Flag. Diagonally white over blue over green with the white of double width, and an assegai and knobkerrie on a Basotho shield in brown in the upper hoist.
Festivals. 28 Jan. (Anniversary of overthrow of Chief Jonathan's Government); 2 May (King's Birthday); 1 July (Family Day); 4 Oct. (National Independence Day); 7 Oct. (National Sports Day).
Vehicle registration plate. LS.

INTERNATIONAL RELATIONS

Affiliations

NAM; OAU; ACP; Commonwealth; SADCC.

Defence

Army, Army Air Wing and Police Department.

ECONOMY

Currency

The unit is the loti (plural maloti), divided into 100 lisente.

National finance

Budget. The 1988 budget (in US$) was for expenditure (current and capital) of 219 million and revenue of 145 million. Main items of current expenditure are education 15.5%; defence 9.6%.
Balance of payments. The balance of payments (current account, 1987) was a deficit of $16 million.
Inflation. (1988) 9.2%.

Gross Domestic Product

Estimated total GDP US$270 million, per capita US$245 (ranking 159 in the world by size).
Economically active population. The total number of persons active in the economy was 689,000; unemployed: 23%.

Sector	% of workforce	of GDP
industry	n/a	28
agriculture	86	21
services*	n/a	51

* services figure includes elements unassigned to other categories.

Energy and mineral resources

Minerals. Diamonds.
Electricity. Power supplied by South Africa.

Bioresources

Agriculture. Mostly at subsistence level, employing about 86% of the workforce and accounting for about 20% of GDP.
Crop production: principal crops (with 1986 production figures) are maize 94,798 tons/86,000 tonnes; wheat 12,125 tons/11,000 tonnes; pulses; sorghum; barley; oats; beans; peas.
Livestock numbers: (1987) sheep 1.4 million; goats 1 million; cattle 520,000; donkeys 125,000; horses 118,000.

Industry and commerce

Industry. Diamond mining ceased in 1982. Tourism.
Commerce. Lesotho is a member of the South African customs union by an agreement dated 29 June 1910. Exports: (f.o.b. 1986) US$25 million, 6% of GDP. Main exports are wool; mohair; wheat; cattle; peas; beans; hides; baskets. Main trading partners are South Africa 87%; EC 10% (1985).
Trade with UK. In 1988 Lesotho exported £977,000 worth of goods to the UK and imported £1,260,000 worth of goods from the UK.
Tourism. In 1986 there were 213,000 visitors.

COMMUNICATIONS

Railways

The territory is linked with the railway system of the Republic of South Africa by a short line of 1.2 miles/2 km in length from Maseru to Marseilles.

Roads

There are 1,917 miles/3,085 km of roads, of which 295 miles/475 km are bituminized.

Aviation

Lesotho Airways Corporation provides domestic and international services (main airport is at Thota-Moli, about 12.4 miles/20 km from Maseru). Passengers: (1983) 57,340.

Telecommunications

There are 5,290 telephones and a modest telecommunications system of a few land lines. There are about 400,000 radio sets in use, with domestic programmes broadcast by Radio and Television Lesotho. South African broadcasts can be received.

EDUCATION AND WELFARE

Education

Three main missions, Paris Evangelical, Roman Catholic and English Church, under the direction of the Ministry of Education, are largely responsible for education.
School population. 314,000 primary school pupils; 35,400 secondary school pupils; 2,000 students in teacher-training and Technical schools.
Schools. 1,141 primary schools; 143 secondary schools; eight technical schools; one teacher-training college.
Universities. The National University of Lesotho was founded in 1975 at Roma. In 1985 it had 1,100 students and 146 teaching staff.
Literacy. 65%

Health

There are approximately 100 doctors and 11 government hospitals, with approximately 2,000 beds, (one per 800 patients).

LIBERIA
Republic of Liberia

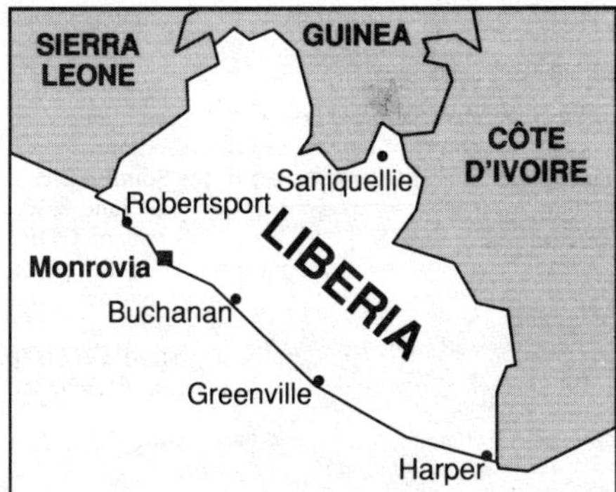

GEOGRAPHY

Situated on the west African coast, Liberia contains an area of 42,988 miles²/111,369 km² divided into 13 counties. There are three major physiographic regions. The low Atlantic coastal strip (348 miles/560 km long, 50 miles/80 km wide) is characterized by lagoon formations and mangrove swamps backed by an undulating plateau region (1,969–2,625 ft/600–800 m) rising inland to form a mountainous belt that reaches 5,801 ft/1,768 m altitude on the Guinean border (Mt Nimba). Most of the plateau region is grassland or forest. Important upland ranges include the Bomi hills in the west and the Niete mountains in the south-east. Rivers traversing the plateau include the Mano, Moro, the St Paul, St John, the Douobe and the semi-navigable Cavalla. Between 20–25% of the population live in the county of Montserrado on the Atlantic Coast. Only 1% of the land is arable and 39% is forest or woodland.

Climate

Equatorial with uniformly high temperatures all year and abundant rainfall (mostly during the May-Oct. wet season). Mean annual temperature range is between 64–84°F/18–29°C. Rainfall decreases inland from 200 in/5,080 mm on the coast to an interior low of 69 in/1,750 mm. The Saharan Harmattan wind affects coastal areas during Dec. Monrovia: Jan 79°F/26.1°C. July 76°F/24.4°C. Average annual rainfall 202 in/5,138 mm.

Cities and towns

Monrovia (capital)	425,000

Population

Total population is 2,396,000 of which 38.8% live in urban areas. Population density is 55.7 persons per mile²/23.8 per km². 95% of the population are indigenous African tribes including Kpelle, Bassa, Gio, Kru, Grebo, Mano, Krahn, Gola, Gbandi, Loma, Kissi, Vai and Bella peoples. 5% are Americo-Liberian, descendants of repatriated slaves.

Birth rate 4.5%. **Death rate** 1.45%. **Rate of population increase** 3.05% **Age distribution** under 15 = 45%; over 65 = 3.2%. **Life expectancy** female 56; male 53; average 54.

Religion

70–75% of the population follow traditional animist beliefs, 20% are Muslim and 10% Christian including Roman Catholic, Methodist, Baptist, Episcopalian, Pentecostal and African Methodist denominations.

Language

English is the official language but 20 languages/dialects of the Niger-Congo are also spoken, comprising three main linguistic groups: Mande; West Atlantic; Kwa.

HISTORY

In 1816, with the support of a US congressional grant, the American Colonization Society began to transport to Africa those freed slaves who wished to return to the continent of their ancestors. Between 1822 and 1892 some 22,000 freed slaves were resettled along the 'Grain Coast', 75% of them from America. On 26 July 1847 the Republic of Liberia was declared, formed by these settlers with their slogan 'the love of liberty brought us here', but until the 1890s the government, based in Monrovia, only controlled isolated coastal settlements. The peoples of the interior, particularly the Kru, put up a staunch resistance but were finally subdued in the 1930s.

Liberia's government was dominated from 1870 by the True Whig Party and the '300 Families' who formed the settler social elite, with their Christian faith and American colonial lifestyle. Firestone Rubber Co. began to operate in 1926 and, under the terms of a loan to the Liberian government, brought the budget under US supervision. Pres. William Tubman, inaugurated in 1944, adopted an 'open door' policy to promote foreign investment and, unlike his predecessors, encouraged some local participation in government. He died in 1971 and was succeeded by William R. Tolbert, who continued the free-enterprise policies but sought a less conservative image and strengthened ties with West African nations. An attempt to promote domestic rice production through higher prices led to demonstrations in Apr. 1979, and students and recently formed opposition political groups called for a general strike. Riots were bloodily suppressed and emergency powers were used to restore order in time for the July 1979 summit of the Organization for African Unity, lavishly hosted by Tolbert in Monrovia.

On 12 Apr. 1980 a small group of soldiers led by Master Sgt. Samuel K. Doe assassinated Tolbert and overthrew the government. As chairman of the People's Redemption Council (PRC), comprising NCOs for the most part, Doe abrogated the constitution and ruled in conjunction with a council of ministers drawn from former opposition groups. The Doe regime doubled army pay and publicly executed 13 leading officials of the former regime, in a backlash against the power and prestige of the Americo-Liberian settler elite. Despite international protests over these executions (notably from West African states), the US recognized the regime and increased the level of assistance.

In Aug. 1981 five members of the PRC were

executed, including Thomas Weh Syen, PRC vice-chairman, after a coup attempt, and in Nov. 1983 another coup attempt was uncovered, blamed on the army commander, Thomas Quiwonkpa, who fled abroad.

A new constitution was approved by referendum in July 1984, and took effect on 6 Jan. 1986, introducing universal adult suffrage without property qualifications for the first time. The PRC was dissolved in favour of an interim national assembly and the ban on political parties was lifted. Doe won the presidential elections held on 15 Oct. 1985 and his National Democratic Party of Liberia (NDPL) secured a majority in the national assembly, amid accusations of electoral malpractice. Jackson Doe, leader of the Liberian Unification Party (LUP), and William Kpolleh, leader of the Liberian Action Party (LAP), refused to accept the results. Few members of the opposition parties agreed to join the government, which nevertheless survived another coup attempt in November, when Quiwonkpa and many others died. In Mar. 1986 the LAP, the LUP and the Unity Party formed a united front as the Liberia Grand Coalition (LGC) led by Kpolleh; in succeeding months most of its leaders were arrested but later released. Talks between government and opposition ended inconclusively in June 1987, and in Mar. 1988 Kpolleh was once again arrested, with other opposition politicians. On 10 Oct. Kpolleh and nine others received ten-year prison sentences for plotting to overthrow the government. There were also reports of armed rebels active in the north of the country, led by a former Doe associate and one-time vice-president, Nicholas Podier, who reportedly crossed back into Liberia from neighbouring Côte d'Ivoire and was killed in July 1988 in yet another coup attempt. In early 1990 an armed rebellion in the north-east, led by a group calling itself the National Patriotic Forces of Liberia, was suppressed by the army with US military assistance. Hundreds of people reportedly died in the fighting, which also provoked a mass movement of refugees into Guinea and Côte d'Ivoire.

CONSTITUTION AND GOVERNMENT

Executive and legislature

The head of state is the executive president, directly elected (together with a vice-president) by universal adult suffrage (18+); last elections Oct. 1985. The legislature is a bicameral National Assembly, made up of a 26-member Senate and a 64-member House of Representatives; last elections Oct. 1985.

Present government

President; C.-in-C. of Armed Forces Gen. Samuel K. Doe

Vice-President Dr Harry Moniba

Principal Ministers Brig.-Gen. Boimah Barclay (National Defence); Emmanuel Shaw II (Finance); Jenkins Scott (Justice); Ansumana Kromah (Internal Affairs); Dr Elijah Taylor (Planning and Economic Affairs); Scott Gblorzuo Toweh (Agriculture); J. Rudolph Johnson (Foreign Affairs); Sylvester Moses (National Security).

Justice

The highest court is the People's Supreme Court, whose 5 judges have full judicial powers; there is a network of 14 circuit courts and lower courts. There was at least one execution between 1985 and mid-1988. The offence was murder.

National symbols

Flag. Eleven horizontal stripes (six red and five white), with a five-pointed white star on blue field in the upper corner, next to flagstaff.

Festivals. 11 Feb. (Armed Forces Day); 12 Mar. (Decoration Day); 15 Mar. (J.J. Robert's Birthday); 12 Apr. (National Redemption Day, Anniversary of the 1980 Coup); 14 May (National Unification Day); 26 July (Independence Day); 24 Aug. (Flag Day); 12 Nov. (National Memorial Day); 29. Nov. (Pres. Tubman's Birthday).

Vehicle registration plate. LB.

INTERNATIONAL RELATIONS

Affiliations

NAM; OAU; ACP.

Defence

Total Armed Forces: 5,800. Terms of service: voluntary. Reserves: 50,000.

Army: 5,300.

Navy: 500 (Coast Guard); five patrol craft.

Para-military: 2,000 (National Police).

ECONOMY

Currency

The unit is the Liberian dollar, divided into 100 cents.

National finance

Budget. The 1988 budget (in US$) was for expenditure (current and capital) of 248 million and revenue of 217.5 million. Main items of current expenditure are education 16.2%; defence 8.9%.

Balance of payments. The balance of payments (current account, 1987) was a deficit of $163 million.

Inflation. (1987) 3.6%.

Gross Domestic Product

Estimated total GDP US$990 million, per capita US$410 (ranking 144 in the world by size).

Economically active population. The total number of persons active in the economy was 510,000.

Sector	% of workforce	of GDP
industry	4.5	28
agriculture	70.5	37
services*	25	35

* services figure includes elements unassigned to other categories.

Energy and mineral resources

Minerals. Iron ore production: (1982) US$241 million; gold (1986) US$7.3 million; diamonds (1982) US$20.8 million.

Electricity. Capacity: 400,000 kW; production: 728 million kWh; 300 kWh per capita (1988).

Bioresources

Agriculture. 1% of the land is used for arable farming, 3% for permanent crops, 2% for meadows and pasture.

Crop production: main crops are rubber; rice; oil palm; cassava; coffee.

Livestock numbers (1987): 42,000 cattle, 140,000 pigs, 240,000 sheep, 235,000 goats.

Forestry. 39% of the land is forest and woodland. Liberia has west Africa'a largest tropical rainforest, which is however subject to deforestation. There are large rubber plantations. The Firestone Plantation

Co has about 1,000,741 acres/405,000 ha of rubber plantation and employs over 40,000 people. The company's concession expires in 2025.

Fisheries. Total catch: (1982) 14,991 tons/13,600 tonnes.

Industry and commerce

Industry. Rubber and mining of iron ore and diamonds are the most important industries. Also food processing; furniture; palm-oil processing. Small factories make bricks; soap; nails; paint; plastics.

Commerce. Exports: (f.o.b.1987) US$458, represented 25% of GDP. Major exports were iron ore; rubber; timber; coffee; cocoa; palm kernal oil. Main trading partners were: US; EC; Netherlands. Imports (c.i.f.1986) US$259 million. Major imports were rice; mineral fuels; chemicals; machinery; transport equipment; foodstuffs. Main trading partners were: US; EC; Japan; China; Netherlands; ECOWAS.

Trade with UK. Exports to UK (1988) totalled £9.6 million. Imports from the UK totalled £11.7 million.

COMMUNICATIONS

Railways

There are 304 miles/490 km of railways (used for transport of iron ore concentrates).

Roads

There are 3,363 miles/5,412 km of roads, of which some 186 miles/300 km are bituminized.

Aviation

Air Liberia provides domestic and international services (main airports are Roberts Field International Airport, 35 miles/56 km from Monrovia, and James Spriggs Payne Airport). Passengers: (1985) 108,495.

Shipping

The marine ports are Monrovia, Buchanan, Greenville and Harper (on Cape Palmas). The merchant marine consists of 1,412 ships of 1,000 GRT or over, Liberia being one of the main 'flag of convenience' registries.

Telecommunications

There are 8,500 telephones. Monrovia is the main centre for telecommunications. There are 566,000 radios and 43,000 televisions (one-third of them colour) in use; ELTV is a government-supported commercial TV station, and ELBC its radio equivalent; there is a government-operated rural radio communications network, the religious Radio ELWA, and broadcasts from Monrovia by Voice of America.

EDUCATION AND WELFARE

Education

Mission schools, supported by foreign missions and subsidized by the government, are staffed by qualified missionaries and local teachers. Also private schools.

School population. 440,000 (1986 est.)

Schools. 1,830 schools with some 8,700 teachers, (one per 50 pupils).

Literacy. 20%.

Health

(1981) 236 doctors; 3,000 hospital beds (one per 730 people).

LIBYA

Al-Jamahiriya al-Arabiya Al-Libya Al-Shabiya Al-Ishtirakiya Al-Uzma (Socialist People's Libyan Arab Jamahiriya)

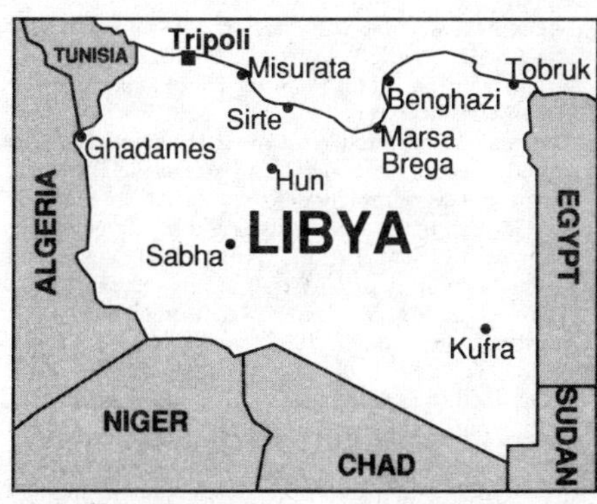

GEOGRAPHY

Situated on the north African Mediterranean coast, Libya covers a total surface area of 679,182 miles^2/ 1,759,540 km^2. Approx 93% of the country is contained by the arid Saharan plateau. To the north-west, coastal cultivation and comparatively fertile conditions in the Gefara plain and Jabal Nafusah plateau (average elevation 1,969–2,953 ft/ 600–900 m) make Tripolitania the most populous and agriculturally significant region. To the north-east, the Green Mountain district of Al-Jabal-al-Akhdar separates the coastal belt (north) from the encroaching desert and semi-desert to the south. The predominantly low-lying terrain (656–1,969 ft/ 200–600 m) rises southwards to a high point of 7,500 ft/2,286 m at Pic Belle on the Chadian border in the Tibesti range and south-east to just under 6,234 ft/

1,900 m on the Sudanese and Egyptian frontiers. Apart from a few scattered oases, Libya's surface water and perennial river hydrography is non-existent, but artesian wells and subterranean reserves supply nearly two-thirds of the country. 1% of the land surface is arable and less than 1% is forested.

Climate

The harsh climate of the Saharan interior is modified along the coast by Mediterranean maritime influences. Rain falls Oct.-Mar., concentrated in the north-west and north-east upland regions (from 15.7–23.6 in/400–600 mm), with average coastal temperatures of 52°F/11°C in winter and 82°F/28°C during the summer months. Further south, temperatures reach a mean 63°F/17°C in winter and 100°F/38°C in July with annual rainfall of less than 3.9 in/100 mm. Tripoli: Jan. 52°F/11.1°C. July 81°F/27.2°C. Average annual rainfall 15.7 in/400 mm. Benghazi: Jan. 56°F/13.3°C. July 77°F/25°C. Average annual rainfall 10.5 in/267 mm.

Cities and towns

Tripoli (capital)	481,295
Benghazi	219,317
Misurata	42,815
Az-Zawia	39,796
Ajdabiya	31,047
Derna	30,241

Population

Total population is 4,232,000 of which 64.5% live in urban areas. Population density is 6.2 persons per mile^2/2.3 per km^2. 97% of the population are of Berber and Arab origin. Minority populations of Greeks, Maltese, Italians, Egyptians, Pakistanis, Turks, Indians and Tunisians comprise the remaining 3%, together with a few scattered groups of Tebou and Touareg nomads in the south.

Birth rate 4.56%. **Death rate** 1.09%. **Rate of population increase** 3.47%. **Age distribution** under 15 = 46.4%; over 65 = 2.3%. **Life expectancy** female 63; male 59; average 61.

Religion

Islam. 97% of the population are Sunni Muslims. An estimated 2.5% are Christians, including approximately 38,000–40,000 Roman Catholics and some smaller Anglican Communion and Coptic Orthodox contingents. There are up to 6,000 Jews.

Language

Arabic is the official language, although some Berbers still converse in their own Hamitic tongue. English and Italian are widely spoken and understood in the metropolitan areas of Tripoli and Benghazi.

HISTORY

Phoenician traders arrived in Tripolitania (in the north-west of present-day Libya) around 700 BC, and founded three ports, while Cyrenaica (in the north-east) was first settled by Dorian Greeks, and became part of Alexander the Great's empire. Both provinces were later occupied by Rome for 500 years, but administered separately, together with Fezzan in the south, where an impressive Roman infrastructure was developed.

In AD 429, the Romans allied with the Vandals when they conquered Tripolitania. The Byzantines took over in the 6th century, and remained until Arab conquest in 642. The second wave of Arab invaders reduced the area to chaos in the 11th century, and almost all settled life there ceased. The Almohads arrived in Tripolitania from Morocco in 1158 and ruled for 350 years, while Cyrenaica was under the control of the Egyptian Fatimids.

As part of the Ottoman Empire, Libya enjoyed a degree of autonomy under hereditary rulers. Ahmad Caramanli founded a hereditary dynasty in Tripoli in the early 18th century, one of several which profited from the vulnerability of merchant shipping to attacks by corsairs. European powers generally had sufficient naval strength to protect their interests, or at least to punish the perceived offenders. The United States, however, when newly independent, needed to negotiate treaties with the Barbary states to buy protection, and fought a war with Yusuf Caramanli's forces in Tripoli (1801–5) to resist demands for higher payments; William Eaton led an unsuccessful US attempt to depose Yusuf in a march on Tripoli from Alexandria. The Ottoman Turks intervened in 1835, removing the over-powerful Caramanli ruler in an unpopular move which caused unrest in Cyrenaica.

In 1843, the Sanusi sect, which called for a return to the purity of Islam, was founded, drawing much of its strength from Fezzan and the south. Sayyid Mohamed Ali el Sanusi set up a network of zawiya (colleges and fortresses) which resecured the area after centuries of chaos. Over the next 75 years, there were 33 Turkish governors in Libya, many of whom enriched themselves at the country's expense.

On 3 Oct. 1911, Italy, seeking an outlet for colonial expansion and frustrated when the French secured the position they might have coveted themselves in Tunisia, launched an attack on Tripoli and other Libyan ports. They sought to appeal to the Arabs as liberators from the Ottoman yoke, and encountered little opposition. The Ottoman Sultan sued for peace, accepting the Oct. 1912 Treaty of Lausanne, by which he gave up his rights in Libya. By the spring of 1914, Italy had completed its military occupation, but faced persistent Sanusi attacks on its outposts in Fezzan. Italy's position was weakened in World War I as it came into direct conflict with Turkey. The Sanusi, fortified with Turkish and German arms, attacked the British in Egypt, while the Tripolitanians turned on Italy.

In 1917, with Italy holding only a few towns and Cyrenaican ports, Libyan leaders sought self-government. Italy countered by appointing the hard-line Giuseppe Volpi as governor of Tripolitania (1921), which he subdued by force of arms. Fighting continued for six years and spread to Cyrenaica, which was finally brought under control by the end of 1932. Volpi's ruthless methods involved herding the civilian population into concentration camps and taking all possible steps to deprive the enemy of supplies.

The next step was colonization. Mussolini's Fascist government settled over 30,000 Italian peasant farmers on the Jefara Plain of Tripolitania, and the Green Hills of Cyrenaica, during 1938–39.

When Italy entered World War II in June 1940, its large forces in Libya moved to attack the British in Egypt, but were rapidly defeated. After driving back the German forces, the British captured Tripoli (Jan. 1945) with the support of Sayyid Idris el Sanusi, and set up a military administration. In the immediate post-war period, a Four-Power Commission (US, France, USSR and the UK) met to decide Libya's future. In 1948, all claims to trusteeship were abandoned, and Cyrenaica, Tripolitania and Fezzan were granted full freedom to form an independent and united Libya. With the approval of a special constituent assembly of Libyan notables, the United

Kingdom of Libya was proclaimed in Dec. 1951 under its first hereditary ruler, King Idris. National Assembly elections were held in Mar. 1952, but were not contested on party lines, although conservatives won a majority. In return for aid, the new state allowed Britain and the US to maintain military bases.

After the discovery of oil in the 1960s, increased revenue allowed for the expansion of irrigated agriculture. It also led to an increase in private wealth and mass rural migration to the cities. Idris was slow to respond to the changes this brought. Social tension grew, and young radicals were angered by the King's failure to enter the Six Day War against Israel (1967).

Against this background, a coup by young army officers, led by Col. Moamar al Gaddafi, took place on 1 Sept. 1969. King Idris was deposed and went to live in Egypt (where he died in May 1983), while in Libya a Revolutionary Command Council of army officers took control. The new regime immediately closed the Western military bases, and promoted an Arab nationalist ideology. Gaddafi developed a political philosophy based on Islam, Arabism and popular socialism. On 11 June 1971, the Arab Socialist Union (ASU) was created as part of an effort to involve all the people in government. Two years later, Gaddafi set up People's Committees as the basic level of local democracy. The ASU was transformed into the General People's Congress, representing People's Committees and other associations in 1976, while in 1977 a new constitution was brought in with a major government reorganization signifying the 'installation of people's power'. Thus was established the 'Socialist People's Libyan Arab Jamahiriyah ('Society of the masses')'.

Gaddafi survived a coup attempt in Aug. 1975, and from 1980 waged a widely condemned assassination campaign against Libyan exiles in Europe as part of a purge of his opponents. Underground opposition groups have surfaced periodically, notably in 1984, when Tripoli witnessed a major gun battle on 8 May.

In foreign policy, Gaddafi proposed several abortive declarations of union with neighbouring countries: Egypt and Syria (1969, 1971); Egypt (1972); Tunisia (1974); Syria (1980); Chad (1981); and Morocco (1984). Relations with these and other Arab and African states have been strained on occasion, with Libya being accused of destabilizing other governments. It was involved in a lengthy, ultimately unsuccessful war in Chad until 1987.

Libya's relations with the West have regularly had a cold-war flavour, with the US and European governments frequently denouncing Gaddafi for supporting terrorism. Britain severed relations in Apr. 1984 after a policewoman died when a Libyan diplomat opened fire on demonstrators outside Libya's London embassy. Libya has played a war of nerves with the US, and there have been several incidents, notably air battles in Aug. 1981 and Jan. 1989, while in Jan. 1986 the US accused Libya of being involved in Palestinian terrorist attacks on Rome and Vienna airports on 27 Dec. 1985. The culmination of months of tension was the US bombing of Tripoli and Benghazi (15 Apr. 1986). Demanding a Libyan promise to cease supporting terrorism, and further accusing Libya of involvement in bombing a West Berlin nightclub where a US soldier and a Turkish woman died on 5 April, the US mounted this attack with eight F-111 aircraft from bases in southern England (one of which was shot down in the Mediterranean) and 15 A-6 bombers as well as A-7s and F-18s from aircraft carriers in the Mediterranean. Casualties were estimated at 30 killed in Benghazi and 100 in Tripoli, among them Gaddafi's adopted baby daughter killed at the El Azziziya barracks.

Declining oil revenue in the mid-1980s led to growing economic problems. Tunisian and Egyptian nationals working in Libya were expelled in Aug. 1985, provoking Tunisia to sever diplomatic relations. In an effort to improve the situation, Gaddafi announced a series of economic reforms in Sept. 1988, including allowing a greater role for private enterprise. Earlier the same year, a series of political liberalizations included the release of most political prisoners. In mid-1989 the first stage of the massive Great Man-Made River irrigation project came into operation.

CONSTITUTION AND GOVERNMENT

Executive and legislature

Gaddafi is 'the leader of the revolution' but neither he nor Maj. Abdel Salem Jalloud, 'the Libyan number two', holds an official post. In theory the head of state is the secretary of the General People's Congress. This body, effectively the parliament, is indirectly elected through a structure of local 'basic people's congresses'. A General People's Committee, broadly equivalent to a Council of Ministers, has a secretary-general who operates as prime minister.

Present government

Col. Moamar al Gaddafi – Leader of the revolution
Maj. Abdel Salem Jalloud – Senior adviser

General People's Congress Dr Muftah al-Usta Umar (Secretary-General); Ibrahim Bukhizam (Assistant Secretary-General); Ms Salmin Ali al-Uraybi (Assistant Secretary-General); Umar Ishkal (Secretary for People's Congress Affairs); Soleiman Sasi al-Shuhumi (Secretary for People's Committees Affairs); Bashir Huwayj Huwaydi (Secretary for the Affairs of Vocational Congresses).

Principal members of General People's Committee Umar Mustafa al-Muntasir (Secretary-General [Prime Minister]); Jadallah Azouz al-Talhi (Secretary for Foreign Liaison); Fawzi al-Shakshuki (Secretary for Petroleum); Dr Farhat Sharnanah (Secretary for Economy and Foreign Trade); Dr Mohammed Lutfi Farhat (Secretary for Planning); Mohammed Madani al-Bukhari (Secretary for the Treasury); Izz al-Din al-Hinshiri (Secretary for Justice).

Justice

The system of law is based on Italian and Islamic law, with Civil, Commercial and Criminal codes substantially following Egyptian models. There are civil and penal (assize and appeal) courts in Tripoli and Benghazi, with subsidiary courts at Misurata and Derna. Separate religious courts deal with matters of personal status of family or succession matters affecting Moslems according to the Islamic law. The death penalty is in force. There were at least nine executions between 1985 and mid-1988. Offences were murder and other offences apparently politically motivated.

National symbols

Flag. Plain emerald green flag.
Festivals. 28 Mar; 11 June; 7 Oct. (Evacuation Day); 1 Sep. (Revolution Day).
Vehicle registration plate. LT.

INTERNATIONAL RELATIONS

Affiliations

NAM; Arab League; OPEC; OAU; ICO; AMU.

Defence

Total Armed Forces: 71,500. Terms of service: selective conscription, term varies: 2–4 years. Reserves: People's Militia, some 40,000.

Army: 55,000; 1,800 main battle tanks (T-54/-55/-62/-72).

Navy: 6,500; six submarines (Soviet Foxtrot), three frigates (UK Vosper and Soviet Koni) and 55 patrol and coastal combatants.

Air Force: 10,000; 509 combat aircraft (mainly Tu-22, Mirage F-1ED, F-1BD, MiG-21/-23/-25) and 16 armed helicopters.

ECONOMY

Currency

The unit is the dinar, divided into 1,000 dirhams.

National finance

Budget. The 1986 budget (in US$) was for expenditure (current and capital) of 11,300 million and revenue of 6,400 million.

Balance of payments. The balance of payments (current account, 1987) was a deficit of US$13 million.

Inflation. (1988) 20%.

Gross Domestic Product

Estimated total GNP US$20,000 million, per capita US$5,410 (ranking 58 in the world by size).

Economically active population. The total number of persons active in the economy was 1,000,000; unemployed: 2%.

Sector	% of workforce
industry	31
agriculture	18
services*	51

* services figure includes elements unassigned to other categories.

Energy and mineral resources

Oil and gas. Production: (1988) 53.5 million tons/48.5 million tonnes, with reserves estimated at 23,000m bbls. The Libyan National Oil Corporation, a state organization founded 1970, has a majority share in all but two oil-producing companies.

A 1987 agreement with Algeria and Tunisia allowed for the construction of a gas pipeline to supply western Libya with Algerian gas.

Water. The Great Manmade River Project (costing approximately US$3,300 million), the largest water development scheme in the world, is being built to bring water from large aquifers under the Sahara to coastal cities. Completion is planned for 1990.

Minerals. Gypsum.

Electricity. Capacity: (1988) 4.6 million kW; production: 13.4 million kWh; 3,380 kWh per capita.

Bioresources

Agriculture. As only 1% of land is suitable for arable use and only 8% is meadow/pasture, 75% of food is imported. Major crops grown in the Mediterranean area of Libya: date palm; olives; oranges; peanuts; potatoes. Grown in coastal oases: cereals; olives; almonds; oranges; mulberries. Grown in steppe district: poplars; pines; acacias. Grown in dunes which are gradually being afforested: olives; figs; vines. Fruit trees are grown in Jebel (mountain district). There are some fertile oases in the desert: Ghat; Ghadames; Socna; Sebha.

Crop production: (1987 in tons/tonnes) wheat 209,437/190,000; barley 110,230/100,000; milk 146,606/133,000; meat 184,504/167,000.

Livestock numbers: sheep 5.7 million; goats 960,000; cattle 212,000; poultry 26 million (1987).

Fisheries. Catch: (1982) 8,185 tons/7,425 tonnes.

Industry and commerce

Industry. Petroleum; food processing; textiles; cement. The post-revolution development of the building material, foodstuffs and textiles industries has been hampered by the fall in oil revenues dating from 1980.

Commerce. Exports: (f.o.b. 1988 est.) US$6,100 million, or 30% of GDP. Major exports were petroleum; peanuts; hides. Main trading partners: Italy; USSR; West Germany; Spain; Belgium/Luxembourg. Imports (c.i.f 1988) US$5,000 million. Major imports were machinery; transport equipment; food. Main trading partners: Italy; USSR; West Germany; UK; Japan.

Trade with UK. 1988 exports to UK totalled £111 million, imports totalled £236 million.

Tourism. 100,000 people visited Libya in 1984.

COMMUNICATIONS

Railways

There are no railways at present in Libya.

Roads

There are 15,954 miles/25,675 km of paved roads.

Aviation

Libyan Arab Airlines provides domestic and international services and Jamahiriya Air Transport provides domestic services (main airports are Tripoli International Airport, 21 miles/34 km from Tripoli; Benina Airport at Benghazi; Sebha Airport). Passengers: (1984) 1.58 million.

Shipping

The main ports are Tobruk; Tripoli; Benghazi; Misratah; Marsa el Brega. The merchant marine consists of 30 ships of 1,000 GRT or over.

Telecommunications

There are 370,000 telephones and a modern telecommunications system. There are about 500,000 radios and half that number of televisions. Government radio channels broadcast in English and in Arabic, including external services; and there is a national TV service, mainly in Arabic with additional English, Italian and French channels.

EDUCATION AND WELFARE

Education

School population. (1981–82) 718,000 pupils attended primary school; 286,400 preparatory and secondary schools; 44,800 technical schools; 25,700 higher education.

Universities. Al Fatah (Tripoli); Garyounes (Benghazi).

Literacy. 50–60%.

Health

(1981) 74 hospitals with 15,400 beds (one per 230 people); some 5,000 doctors, 314 dentists, 5,300 nurses.

LIECHTENSTEIN
Fürstentum Liechtenstein
(Principality of Liechtenstein)

GEOGRAPHY

Liechtenstein is an alpine principality in central Europe, occupying a total area of only 61.8 miles^2/160 km^2 making it the fourth smallest country in the world. In the western third of the country, the reclaimed floodplains of the River Rhine provide fertile agricultural land at an average elevation of 1,476 ft/450 m. To the east, the forested Rhätikon alpine massif climbs to 9,809 ft/2,599 m at Grauspitz in the south, drained by the northward-flowing Samina River. 25% of the land is arable and 18% is forested.

Climate

Despite high relief, Liechtenstein experiences a mild and equable climate with average annual precipitation varying from 41–47 in/1,050–1,200 mm in the west to 70.9 in/1,800 mm in the Alpine east. Modified by the warm southerly wind (known as the Foehn), temperatures range from a minimum 5°F/–15°C in winter to temperatures of 68–82°F/20–28°C throughout the summer.

Cities and towns

Vaduz (capital)	4,920
Schaan	4,757
Balzers	3,477
Triesen	3,180

Population

Total population is 28,000 of whom 5,000 live in Vaduz. Population density is 453 persons per mile^2/171.8 per km^2. 95% of the population are Liechtensteiners of Alemannic origin. The remainder (5%) is made up of Italian and various other European minorities.

Birth rate 1.28%. **Death rate** 0.67%. **Rate of population increase** 0.61%. **Age distribution** under 15 = 21.5%; over 65 = 9%. **Life expectancy** female 83; male 78; average 81.

Religion

Approximately 87% of the population are Roman Catholic and 8.6% Protestant, belonging to the parish of Vaduz.

Language

German (official), spoken in the regional Alemannic idiom.

HISTORY

Created in the 14th century, the fiefs of Vaduz and Schellenberg were acquired by the Austrian Liechtenstein family in 1699 and 1713 respectively and became an independent principality within the Holy Roman Empire in 1719 bearing the family name. It came under French domination in the Napoleonic era but regained independence in 1815 within the new German Confederation. Following the dissolution of the Confederation (1866), the principality disbanded its army and declared its permanent neutrality (1868), which was respected in both world wars of the 20th century. In 1919 Liechtenstein entrusted its external relations (previously handled by Austria) to neutral Switzerland, with which it established currency, customs and postal unions in 1921–24. Prince Franz Josef II succeeded his grand-uncle as ruler in 1938, since when the principality has been governed by a coalition of the two main parties, the Patriotic Union (VU) and the Progressive Citizens' Party (FBP). Early in 1939 there was a 95% vote for continued independence and the Swiss link, after some citizens had demanded union with Germany.

In the post-war era Liechtenstein became increasingly prosperous as a financial centre, achieving one of the world's highest per capita incomes. The FBP was the senior coalition partner from 1938 to 1970 and again in 1974–78, with the VU heading the government in 1970–74 and again since 1978, latterly in the person of Hans Brunhart. In Aug. 1984 Prince Franz Josef (then 78) transferred his executive powers to Crown Prince Hans Adam, while remaining titular head of state. Narrowly approved by referendum in July 1984, female suffrage at national level was introduced for the Feb. 1986 elections, in which an environmentalist Free Voters' List (FW) just failed to win the 8% vote share required for representation. In a premature general election in March 1989 the balance of power remained largely unchanged and in May Brunhart of the FBP reached agreement with the VU to continue in government with an unchanged cabinet. Prince Franz Josef died in Nov. 1989 and was succeeded by his son Hans Adam.

CONSTITUTION AND GOVERNMENT

Executive and legislature

Under the constitutional and hereditary monarchy, the prince appoints the government on the proposal of the Landtag (parliament), which currently comprises 25 seats; last elections Mar. 1989.

Present government

Prince Hans Adam von und zu Liechtenstein

Cabinet Hans Brunhart (Head of Government; Foreign Relations; Education; Construction); Herbert Wille (Deputy Head of Government; Interior; Justice; Agriculture; Environmental Protection; Culture and Sport); René Ritter (Economy); Peter Wolff (Health; Welfare); Wilfried Büchel (Transportation).

Justice

The lowest court in the principality is the county court (Landgericht), which decides minor civil cases and summary criminal offences. The criminal court (Kriminalgericht) is for major crimes. The superior courts (Obergericht) and Supreme Court (Oberster Gerichtshof) are courts of appeal for civil and criminal cases. The death penalty was abolished in June 1987.

National symbols

Flag. Equal horizontal bands of blue over red; gold crown on blue band near staff.

Festivals. 1 May (Labour Day).

Vehicle registration plate. FL.

INTERNATIONAL RELATIONS

Affiliations

EFTA; Council of Europe.

Defence

Defence is the responsibility of Switzerland.

ECONOMY

Currency

The unit is the Swiss franc, divided into 100 centimes/ rappen/centesimi.

National finance

Budget. The 1986 budget (in US$) was for expenditure (current and capital) of 189 million and revenue of 171 million.

Inflation. (1987) 1.5%.

Gross Domestic Product

Estimated total GDP US$405 million (GNP), per capita US$15,000 (ranking 155 in the world by size).

Economically active population. The total number of persons active in the economy was 12,000; unemployed: 0%.

Energy and mineral resources

Electricity. Capacity: (1988) 23,000 kW; production: 150 million kWh; 5,390 kwh per capita.

Bioresources

Agriculture. The main element of agriculture is livestock production. 25% of the land is put to arable use, 38% is meadow and pasture.

Crop production: vegetables; maize; wheat; potatoes; grapes.

Livestock numbers: (1988) cattle 6,000 (2,800 milk cows); sheep 2,300; pigs 3,200.

Forestry. 18% of the land is covered in forest/ woodland.

Industry and commerce

Industry. Liechtenstein is a highly industrialized country. There are a variety of light industries, including textiles; ceramics; precision instruments. The sale of postage stamps totals an estimated US$10 million per annum and accounts for 10% of revenue. Low business taxes (maximum rate 20%) and easy incorporation rules have encouraged approximately 25,000 holding companies to establish nominal offices in Liechtenstein. These companies, incorporated for tax purposes, provide 30% of state revenue.

Commerce. Exports: (1986 est.) US$807 million. Exports include small machinery; dental products; stamps. Major trading partners are: EC 40%; EFTA 26%. Main imports include machinery; textiles; foodstuffs; motor vehicles.

Trade with UK. Since 1968 trade figures have been tied to those of Switzerland.

Tourism. Some 76,000 in 1987.

COMMUNICATIONS

Railways

There are 11.5 miles/18.5 km of railways, of which the whole line is electrified.

Roads

A road tunnel connects the Rhine and Samina valleys, and there are good roads between all the towns and villages. In 1988 an experiment was introduced with free public transport in an attempt to reduce pollution from cars; there are 15,900 cars (one per 1.75 people).

Aviation

There is no national airline and no airport.

Shipping

None.

Telecommunications

The telephone system is automatic and there are about 14,000 telephones; there are some 9,000 radios and a similar number of television sets, but no national broadcasting operation.

EDUCATION AND WELFARE

Education

School population. 3,500.

Schools. 14 primary schools; three upper schools; five secondary schools; one grammar school; 250 teachers, (one per 14 pupils).

Literacy. 100%.

Health

One hospital. Under an agreement with the Swiss cantons of St Gallen and Graubünden, and with the Austrian state of Vorarlberg, certain Swiss and Austrian hospitals may be used by Liechtensteiners.

LUXEMBOURG
Grand-Duché de Luxembourg
Gross-Herzogtum Luxemburg (German)
Grousherzogdem Lëtzebuerg (Letzeburgish)
(Grand Duchy of Luxembourg)

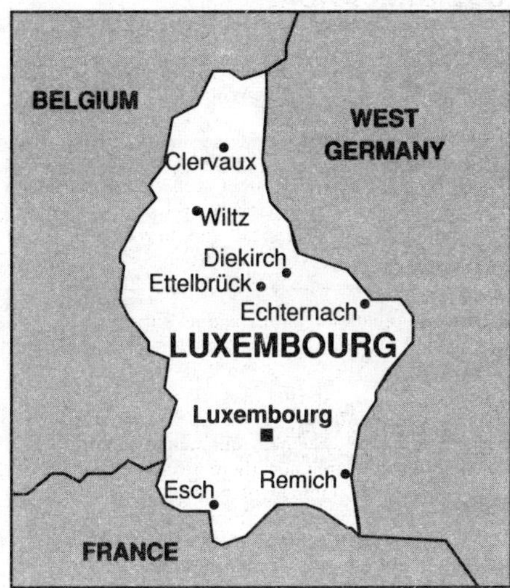

GEOGRAPHY

Located in the north-west corner of the European continent, Luxembourg is a landlocked country covering an area of 998 miles^2/2,586 km^2 divided into three districts and 12 cantons. Luxembourg's physiography comprises two distinct regions, the relatively fertile Osling in the north and the Gutland or Bon Pays in the south. The northern region occupies an estimated 32% of the territory (average elevation 1,476 ft/450 m) consisting largely of an extension of the densely forested Ardennes massif and rising to a maximum elevation of 1,834 ft/559 m in the far north at Buurgplaatz. The fertile, undulating Gutland (average elevation 820 ft/250 m) in the south covers the remaining 68% of the total surface area with rich iron ore deposits in the south-west and flourishing viticulture in the south-east. Principal rivers are the Sûre, the Our and the Moselle. 24% of the land is arable and 21% is forested. Over two-thirds of the population are concentrated in the major urban centres.

Climate

Continental with moderating maritime influences blocked by the Ardennes. High humidity, drier in the south. Winters can be harsh with 28 days' snow cover on high ground. Mean annual temperature is 46°F/8°C and average annual precipitation 32 in/810 mm. Luxembourg: Jan. 33°F/0.7°C. July 64°F/17.5°C. Average annual rainfall 30 in/764 mm.

Cities and towns

Luxembourg-Ville (capital)	77,500
Esch-sur-Alzette	25,100
Differdange	16,700
Dudelange	14,100
Petange	12,100

Population

Total population is 367,000 of which 77.6% live in urban areas. Population density is 367 persons per mile ^{2}/141.9 per km^2. Ethnic composition: Celtic, Ligurian, Roman and Frankish origin. The two dominant ethnic groups are the French and the Germans with a foreign population of 99,400, a significant proportion of whom are Italian.

Birth rate 1.16%. **Death rate** 1.12%. **Rate of population increase** 0.02%. **Age distribution** under 15 = 17.3%; over 65 = 13.2%. **Life expectancy** female 77; male 71; average 74.

Religion

95–97% are Roman Catholic. The remaining 3% are either Protestant (the Evangelical Church in the Grand Duchy of Luxembourg) or Jewish.

Language

Letzeburgish is the official spoken tongue (Moselle-Frankish origin). French and German are used for civil administrative and commercial purposes respectively. English is also widely understood.

HISTORY

Settled by the Franks in the mid-5th century AD, Luxembourg became an autonomous county within the Holy Roman Empire in 963 and rose to prominence when its ruler was elected Emperor Henry VII in 1308. Created a duchy in 1354, it passed under French Burgundian rule in 1443 before becoming part of the Habsburg Empire in 1482. On the abdication of Emperor Charles V in 1555, it became part of the Spanish-ruled Low Countries, which it remained, except for a period of French rule in 1684–97, until the end of the War of Spanish Succession (1702–13/14), when it passed to the Austrian Habsburgs. In 1795 Luxembourg was annexed to revolutionary France, but at the 1815 Congress of Vienna it became a grand duchy within the new United Kingdom of the Netherlands (which also included Belgium) and was obliged to accept a Prussian garrison as a check against France. On Belgium's secession from the Netherlands (1830), the greater part of Luxembourg went with it (and today forms the Belgian province of that name). The remainder won autonomy in 1848 and Prussian troops were withdrawn in 1867.

The link with the Netherlands was finally severed in 1890, when the accession of a female to the Dutch throne impelled Luxembourg, where Salic Law applied, to choose a male sovereign from the House of Nassau. Salic Law was eventually revoked in 1912 to allow the accession of Grand Duchess Marie-Adelaide, whose sympathies for Luxembourg's

German occupiers during World War I attracted much criticism nationally and abroad. Following an abortive republican coup attempt in early 1919, French pressure obliged Marie-Adelaide to abdicate in favour of her sister Charlotte. Under the 1919 Versailles Treaty Luxembourg was declared perpetually free of all ties with Germany, and in 1922 the Belgium–Luxembourg economic union was formed. Successive inter-war governments were dominated by the Christian Social Party (CSV), although in 1937 the Social Democrats joined a coalition which enacted modern social legislation. During World War II Luxembourg was again overrun by the Germans (1940) and annexed to the Third Reich (1942). Grand Duchess Charlotte and her ministers escaped to London. Her son, Prince Jean, was one of the first allied soldiers to enter liberated Luxembourg in 1944.

In the post-war era Luxembourg joined the Western alliance system by becoming a founder member of NATO (1949) and of the WEU (1955). It also joined the Benelux economic union with Belgium and the Netherlands (1948) and the European Coal and Steel Community, EEC, and Euratom (1951–58), rapidly achieving renewed prosperity on the basis of its large iron and steel industry. A national unity government including the Communists was in power in 1945–47, after which the CSV headed successive coalitions with the (liberal) Democratic Party (PD) in 1947–51, with the Socialist Workers' Party (LSAP), successor to the pre-war Social Democrats, in 1951–59, and with the PD again in 1959–64. In 1964 Grand Duchess Charlotte abdicated in favour of Prince Jean. The CSV continued in government with the LSAP in 1964–68 and with the PD in 1968–74, but then went into opposition to an LSAP/PD combination (1974–79). Returning to power in 1979, the CSV governed with the PD in 1979–84 and then, following Socialist and Green gains in the 1984 general elections, formed a centre-left coalition with the LSAP under the premiership of Jacques Santer (CSV). He was re-elected in a general election in June 1989.

CONSTITUTION AND GOVERNMENT

Executive and legislature

As a constitutional monarchy the grand duke exercises executive power through a council of ministers, whose president (i.e. the prime minister) is head of government. Primary legislative authority is exercised through the unicameral Chamber of Deputies, elected every five years; last election June 1989. The 21-member Council of State, nominated by the Grand Duke, is the supreme administrative tribunal and has some legislative functions.

Present government

Grand Duke Jean

Prime Minister; Treasury and Culture Minister Jacques Santer

Principal Cabinet members Jacques Poos (Deputy Prime Minister; Foreign Affairs; Security Services; Foreign Trade; Aid and Development); Jean Spautz (Interior; Public Housing; Urbanism); Fernand Boden (Family; Middle Classes; Tourism); Jean-Claude Juncker (Finance; Labour; Budget); Marc Fischbach (Education; Justice; Civil Service).

Justice

The death penalty was abolished in 1979.

Prisons. There are 382 prisoners.

National symbols

Flag. Three horizontal stripes of red, white and light blue.

Festivals. 1 May (Labour Day); 23 June (National Day).

Vehicle registration plate. L.

INTERNATIONAL RELATIONS

Affiliations

Nato; OECD; EC; Council of Europe; Benelux; Francophonie.

Defence

Total Armed Forces: 800. Terms of service: voluntary, minimum three years.

Army: 800.

Air Force: Luxembourg has no air force of its own, but for legal purposes NATO's E-3A AEW aircraft have Luxembourg registration.

ECONOMY

Currency

The unit is the Luxembourg franc, divided into 100 centimes.

National finance

Budget. The 1986 budget (in US$) was for expenditure (current and capital) of 1,800 million and revenue of 1,800 million.

Inflation. 0.3% (12 months to Sept. 1989).

Gross Domestic Product

Estimated total GNP US$4,900 million per capita US$13,380 (ranking 85 in the world by size). Growth rate (1988) 5.2%.

Economically active population. The total number of persons active in the economy was 161,000; unemployed: 1.5% (1988).

Sector	% of workforce
industry	33.5
agriculture	4.4
services*	62

* services figure includes elements unassigned to other categories.

Energy and mineral resources

Minerals. Output: (1987 in tonnes) steel 3,301,860; pig iron 2,305,100.

Electricity. Capacity: 1,497,000 kW; production: 1,108m kWh; 3,030 kWh per capita (1988).

Bioresources

Agriculture. 24% of the land area is arable (approximately 6,500 people are employed in agriculture), 1% is under permanent cultivation and 20% is meadow or pasture. In 1987, an estimated 312,722 acres/126,557 ha were cultivated.

Crop production: (1987 in 1,000 tons/tonnes) barley 66.4/60.2; wheat 34.9/31.7; potatoes 24.8/22.5; wine grapes 15.8/14.3; oats 23.9/21.7; rye 3.4/3.1.

Livestock numbers: (1987) cattle 217,254; poultry 97,468; pigs 74,944; sheep 6,164; horses 1,669.

Forestry. 21% of the land area is forested.

Industry and commerce

Industry. Growth rate 0% (1987). Industrial activity includes banking; iron and steel; food processing;

chemicals; metal products; engineering; tyres; glass and aluminium production.

Commerce. Exports: US$2,810 million (1985) or 57% of GDP. Imports amounted to $3,100 million for the same year or 63% of GDP. Principal exports (1986) included base metals and manufactures 47%; plastics and rubber products 13.5%; machinery/electrical goods 9%. Imported goods included minerals; metals; foodstuffs; quality consumer goods. 75% of all export trade was with the EC; 6% with the US. Import trading partners included FRG 40%; Belgium 35%; France 15%; US 3%.

Trade with UK. Luxembourg imported £7.04 million worth of UK goods in 1987 and exported over £134 million worth of goods to the UK in the same year.

Tourism. (1987) 476,000 tourists.

COMMUNICATIONS

Railways

There are 168 miles/270 km of railways, of which 101 miles/162 km are electrified.

Roads

There are 3,244 miles/5,220 km of roads.

Aviation

Luxair provides international services (international airport is near Luxembourg-Ville).

Shipping

The major inland waterway is the Moselle River which flows through the country's only river port, Mertert.

Telecommunications

There are 230,000 telephones and the system is adequate and efficient. There are about 230,000 radios and 90,000 television sets. The Luxembourg-based SES company has launched a European satellite television broadcasting operation, and the private company RTL operates both TV and radio stations with a wide audience outside as well as within the country.

EDUCATION AND WELFARE

Education

Elementary and secondary education is obligatory for all children aged 6–15.

School population. Total: 56,092.

Schools. Of the total school population, 8,315 attend nursery schools; 24,381 at primary schools; 23,251 at technical and secondary schools.

Universities. 3,034 students (1984/5).

Literacy. 100%.

Health

(1987) 666 doctors, 4,661 hospital beds (one per 78 people).

MACAO

GEOGRAPHY

Macao consists of a peninsula with a 0.21 miles/0.34 km border with China, and two islands; the southernmost island, Liha de Coloâne, is connected to Liha da Taipa by a causeway, and Liha da Taipa is connected to the mainland of Macao by a bridge. The terrain is flat and essentially urban. There is no land suitable for cultivation.

Climate

Subtropical: cool winters, warm summers.

Population

Total population (1989 est.) 436,480, 95% of Chinese descent.

Birth rate 1.7%. **Death rate** 0.5%. **Rate of population increase** 1.3%. **Life expectancy** female 79; male 75.

Religion

Christian: Roman Catholic.

Language

Portuguese official; Cantonese is the language of commerce.

HISTORY

The Portuguese colonized Macao in 1557 and for the next 200 years the territory flourished as one of the world's major East–West trading posts for silks, gold, spices and opium. Britain's occupation of Hong Kong in the mid-19th century undermined Macao's position as a trading centre. In 1849 the Portuguese declared Macao independent from China, an assertion not recognized by the Chinese until 1887. In 1951, Portugal proclaimed Macao as an Overseas Province. Macao suffered widespread rioting at the height of the Cultural Revolution in China during the mid-1960s. The protests unnerved the Portuguese and served to increase Beijing's influence in the territory.

Shortly after the 1974 Portuguese revolution, the new Portuguese government offered to return Macao to Chinese rule. China turned the offer down, but indicated that it had a comprehensive plan to resume sovereignty over both Macao and Hong Kong. In early 1976 Portugal promulgated an 'organic statute' granting Macao greater autonomy and providing for a directly elected minority on the 17-member Legislative Assembly.

In Feb. 1979 Portugal and China established diplomatic relations, Macao being defined as 'Chinese territory under Portuguese administration'. Sino-Portuguese talks opened in Beijing in June 1986 and ended ten months later in the formal signing of an agreement on the reversion of Macao to China in 1999. The agreement was based upon the 'one country, two systems' principle which had formed the basis of China's negotiated settlement with the UK in 1984 concerning the future of Hong Kong.

In elections in Oct. 1988, three of the six directly elected seats on the Legislative Assembly were won by a pro-liberal grouping; the remaining seats were retained by the conservative Electoral Union group, which had gained four seats in 1984 elections.

CONSTITUTION AND GOVERNMENT

Macao is a Chinese territory under Portuguese administration, and, under an agreement signed in

1987, is scheduled to become a Special Administrative Region of China in 1999. Administratively it is divided into two districts, Macao and Ilhas. There is a governor assisted by five secretaries-adjunct (all appointed by the president of Portugal), and a 17-member Legislative Assembly, five of whom are appointed by the governor, six elected by direct suffrage, and six elected indirectly.

Leader Carlos Melancia, governor since July 1987.

National symbols

Flag. The flag of Portugal is used.

National holiday. 10 June (Day of Portugal).

ECONOMY

The economy depends largely on tourism (including gambling), and textile and fireworks manufacture. There have been efforts to diversify (into toys, artificial flowers, electronics). Macao depends on China for most of its food, energy and fresh water. Japan and Hong Kong are the main suppliers of raw materials.

Currency

The pataca.

COMMUNICATIONS

There is a port in Macao. There are no airports or railways. There are 26 miles/42 km of paved roads. There is a telephone system, four AM and three FM radio stations, but no television. Access to international communications carriers is provided via Hong Kong and China.

MADAGASCAR

Republika Demokratika n'i Madagaskar (Democratic Republic of Madagascar)

GEOGRAPHY

Situated approximately 248 miles/400 km off the south-east African coast in the Indian Ocean, Madagascar (comprising the world's fourth largest island and a number of very much smaller islets) covers an area of 226,597 miles^2/587,040 km^2 divided into six provinces. Of the three longitudinal physiographic regions, the central mountainous plateau is the largest, occupying approximately 60% of the total surface area (north-south) and rising to 8,720 ft/2,658 m in the Andringitra massif (south), 8,671 f/2,643 m in the Ankaratra highlands (central) and 9,406 ft/2,876 m at Maromokotra (Madagascar's highest peak) in the North Tsaratananan range. To the east, the plateau drops precipitously down to the littoral through a densely forested cliff region, dissected by several torrential streams. A gentler descent on the west side, irrigated by the Onilahy and Mangoky rivers, leads down to broad and fertile plains and a heavily indented north-west coastline. Madagascar's predominantly rural population is concentrated in the central plateau regions. Only 4% of the land is arable and 26% is forested.

Climate

Tropical, with extremely variable rainfall. Temperate conditions in the highlands with a warm, wet season Nov.-Apr. (rainfall 39–59 in/1,000–1,500 mm) and lower temperatures the rest of the year. Rainfall averages and temperatures increase in coastal areas (Toamasina) but rainfall decreases markedly to the west and south-west from 83 in/2,100 mm (north-west) to 14 in/350 mm (south-west). Periodic cyclones from the east can cause extensive flooding. Antananarivo: Jan. 70°F/21.1°C. July 59°F/15°C. Average annual rainfall 53 in/1,350 mm. Toamasina: Jan. 80°F/26.7°C. July 70°F/21.1°C. Average annual rainfall 128 in/3,256 mm.

Cities and towns

Antananarivo (capital)	406,366
Antsirabe	78,941
Toamasina	77,395
Fianarantsoa	68,054
Mahajanga	65,864

Population

Total population is 11,238,000 of which 21.8% live in urban areas. Population density is 49 persons per mile^2/18.1 per km^2. The native population is of Malayo-Indonesian origin, comprising 18 separate ethnic groups, of which the most significant are the Merina (26%, central plateau); the Betsileo (12%, southern plateau); the east coastal Betsimisaraka (15%). Other Cötier (coastal) peoples include the Tsimihety; the Antaisaka; the Sakalava. Principal foreign nationals are the European French; Indians of French nationality; Chinese; Comorians; Arabs.

Birth rate 4.58%. **Death rate** 1.54%. **Rate of population increase** 3.04% **Age distribution** under 15 = 44.5%; over 65 = 3%. **Life expectancy** female 55; male 52; average 54.

Religion

52% of the population pursue traditional animist beliefs. An estimated 41% are Christian, of which the majority is Roman Catholic. Most of the Protestant remainder adhere to the Fiangonan'i Jesosy Kristy eto Madagascar. 7% are Muslim.

Language

Official languages are French and Malagasy. Malagasy is spoken by all ethnic divisions in a variety of dialects including the official Merina idiom. Malagasy belongs to the Austronesian language family with loanwords from Bantu; Swahili; Arabic; French; English.

HISTORY

Madagascar's first settlers are believed to have arrived in the 5th century AD. Within the island, coastal and inland populations, variously of African and Polynesian origin, were not brought together as a single political unit until they felt the pressures of French influence in the 19th century. The French were not the first European visitors; the Portuguese explorers da Cunha and d'Albuquerque arrived in 1506, but took no steps to occupy the island, or adjacent smaller islands, judging them to be without sufficient strategic importance or commercial value. The gradual growth of European (especially French) contacts, the taking of quantities of slaves, and the influence of Christian missionaries, was paralleled by the growing internal dominance of the Polynesian-speaking highland Merina kingdom based in Tananarive (from the late 18th century). The Merina conquest of effectively all of the island, by late 19th century, proved shortlived as the French invaded (1895), deposed the Queen, made Madagascar a French colony (1896) and suppressed the ensuing anti-French revolt (1898–1904).

Acquisition of land by French settlers, building up plantations for coffee and other cash crops, created a dispossessed peasantry, while French-educated members of a small local elite could seek advancement only in the image of Black Frenchmen within the colonial, political and social structure. Resistance continued throughout this period, culminating in the uprising of 1947–48 which was put down by French troops at the cost of thousands of Malagasy dead. During World War II, when the French authorities in Madagascar declared for the Vichy regime, the British invaded (1942) to prevent the possibility of the island falling into Japanese hands.

In the postwar period the gradual development of French structures for self-government, as elsewhere in Africa, led to the creation of an autonomous Malagasy Republic within the French community (Oct. 1958) and a subsequent decision to move to full independence (26 June 1960). The president of the First Republic (1960–72), Philibert Tsirinana, led a Parti social démocrate (PSD) which the French had encouraged and which drew its support primarily from coastal tribes as opposed to the traditional Merina highland ruling elites. Tsirinana's regime maintained close relations with France. The former colonial power kept military bases in Antananarivo and on Diego Suarez, while French companies dominated trade in coffee and other cash crops developed in the colonial period.

Economic difficulties, growing unrest, and the brutality of government forces suppressing a revolt in the south (1971) undermined support for the regime. Amid a wave of protests by students and workers in the main towns, Tsirinana resigned, and a military regime dissolved parliament, launching a drive to 'Malagasize' education, industry and government. Village assemblies were revived and elections arranged (Oct. 1973) to a People's National Development Council. As foreign minister, Didier Ratsiraka ordered the closure of foreign military bases, established relations with the USSR and China, and broke off contact with South Africa. A developing economic and political crisis, the resignation of the head of government (Jan. 1975) and the assassination of his successor (11 Feb. 1975), ended with Ratsiraka coming to power in June 1975. A Second Republic (the Democratic Republic of Madagascar) was declared and approved in a referendum (Dec. 1975) with Ratsiraka as president.

The Ratsiraka regime stated as its goal the creation of a socialist society by the year 2000. It governed through a Supreme Revolutionary Council (CSR), with the Avant-garde de la révolution malgache (AREMA) as the nucleus for what was intended to become one national political party (the Front national pour la défense de la révolution–FNDR). AREMA won elections (1977), but regional rivalries and economic difficulties kept unrest high, and Ratsiraka's security forces were used to put down demonstrations, strikes and two alleged coup attempts, while opposition leader Monja Jaona was arrested (1980). Jaona was subsequently released and rejoined the CSR, but then opposed Ratsiraka in presidential elections (Nov. 1982), winning almost half of the vote in the capital. AREMA confirmed its dominance at National Assembly elections the following year.

Meanwhile, the emphasis on socialist development had been tempered by the need for support from the International Monetary Fund (IMF), in view of high external debts and trade deficits; structural adjustment programmes accompanied a series of IMF credit agreements (from 1980). In foreign relations, Madagascar sought African support for a territorial claim to several small French-administered islands off the coast, notably Juan de Nova where France had built airport facilities.

Urban and youth unrest was reflected in the so-called kung fu riots which erupted when the government moved to suppress the alleged 'state within a state' created by the cult of this martial art (50 dead Dec. 1984, 20 more killed July-Aug. 1985). In early 1987 many families of Indian and Pakistani origin fled the country after attacks on their retail businesses in which 14 died. Ratsiraka won a further presidential term (Mar. 1989) and AREMA again dominated the Assembly (elected May 1989), despite the emergence of a Democratic Alliance which mustered the support of an unprecedented number of voters (over one-third) prepared to show their opposition to the regime's monopoly of political power. In Mar. 1990 the CSR approved a decree permitting political parties to operate outside the FNDR. Prior to this all parties had been required to belong to the FNDR.

CONSTITUTION AND GOVERNMENT

Executive and legislature

The executive president is elected for a term of seven years by universal adult suffrage (last elections 12 Mar. 1989). The president is also chairman of the Supreme Revolutionary Council, which is defined in the Constitution as 'the guardian of the Malagasy Socialist Revolution'. Two-thirds of the members are nominated by the president, who also selects the rest from a list nominated by the parliament. The prime minister is appointed by the president; the government is responsible to parliament, the 137-member National People's Assembly, directly elected by universal adult suffrage (last elections 28 May 1989).

Present government

President; Chairman of the Supreme Revolutionary Council; Head of Government Didier Ratsiraka

Members of the Supreme Revolutionary Council Lt.-Col. Victor Ramahatra; Richard Andriamanjato; Dr Jérôme Marojama Razanabahiny; Solo Norbert Andriamorasata; Justin Rakotoniaina; Manandafy Rakotonirina; Col. Jean Ferlin Fiakara; Col. Ferdinand Jaotombo; Lt.-Col. Max Valirien Marson; Jean-Baptiste Ramanantsalama; Lt.-Col. Jean de Dieu Randriantanany; Arsène Ratsifehera; M. Rakotovao-Razakaboana; Célestin Radio; Georges Thomas Indrianjafy; Maharanga Tsihozony; Michel Mahatsanga; Théophile Andrianoelisoa; André Sosohany; Victor Henri Boanoro; Rémy Tiandraza; Bruno Rakotomavo.

Prime Minister Lt.-Col. Victor Ramahatra

Principal Ministers Jean Robiarivuny (Economy); Leon Rajaobelina (Finance); Gen. Christopher Raveloson-Mahasampo (National Defence); Jean Bemananjara (Foreign Affairs); Augustin Ampy Portos (Interior); Joseph Bedo (Justice; Keeper of the Seals).

Justice

There are a Supreme Court and a Court of Appeal in Antananarivo. Most towns have ordinary criminal courts for criminal cases and Courts of First Instance for civil and commercial cases. The death penalty is nominally in force. There were no executions between 1985 and mid-1988.

National symbols

Flag. A white vertical stripe in the hoist and two horizontal ones coloured red over green.

Festivals. 29 Mar. (Commemoration of 1947 Rebellion); 1 May (Labour Day); 26 June (Independence Day); 30 Dec. (Anniversary of the Democratic Republic of Madagascar).

Vehicle registration plate. RM.

INTERNATIONAL RELATIONS

Affiliations

NAM; OAU; ACP.

Defence

Total Armed Forces: 21,000. Terms of service: conscription (inclusive for civil purposes), 18 months.
Army: some 20,000; 12 light tanks (PT-76).
Navy: 500; one patrol craft.
Air Force: 500; 12 combat aircraft (MiG-17F/-21FL).
Para-military: 7,500 (Gendarmerie).

ECONOMY

Currency

The unit is the Malagasy franc, divided into 100 centimes.

National finance

Budget. The 1986 budget (in US$) was for expenditure (current and capital) of 255 million and revenue of 276 million.

Balance of payments. The balance of payments (current account, 1987) was a deficit of $241 million (est.).

Inflation. (1987) 15.5%.

Gross Domestic Product

Estimated total GDP US$2,070 million, per capita US$195 (ranking 115 in the world by size).

Economically active population. The total number of persons active in the economy was 4,900,000.

Sector	% of GDP
industry	16
agriculture	43
services*	42

* services figure includes elements unassigned to other categories.

Energy and mineral resources

Oil. The Toamasina oil refinery has a daily production capacity of 12,000 bbls.

Minerals. Output: (1987 in tons/tonnes) graphite 14,957/13,569; chromite 117,696/106,773; mica 444/403; unrefined salt 46,670/42,339. 285,511 lb/129,507 kg of industrial beryl was produced in 1985 along with 115 lb/52.2 kg of industrial garnet.

Electricity. Capacity: 119,000 kW; production: 431 million kWh; 40 kWh per capita.

Bioresources

Agriculture. Approximately 85% of the labour force are employed in agricultural activities including fishing and forestry, accounting for 43% of the GDP and 80% of all export revenue. 4% of the land is arable and 1% is under permanent cultivation. 58% of the surface area is meadow or pasture.

Crop production: (1987 in 1,000 tons/tonnes) cassava 2,701/2,450; rice 2,458/2,230; sugar cane 1,984/1,800; sweet potatoes 518/470; potatoes 291/264; bananas 275/250; mangos 209/190; maize 167/153; coffee 92/83; oranges 90/82; pineapples 56/51; cotton 45/41; groundnuts 36/33; sisal 23/21; tobacco 4.4/4.

Livestock numbers: (1987 in millions) cattle 10.56; poultry 29; pigs 1.36; goats 1.24; sheep 0.6.

Forestry. 26% of the land is forested. Madagascar's forests contain a wide variety of commercially valuable woods. Total production: (1986) 249.32 million ft^3/7.06 million m^3.

Fisheries. (1985) Total catch 70,106 tons/63,600 tonnes.

Industry and commerce

Industry. Industrial activity is limited to the processing of agricultural produce and textile manufacturing, accounting (1985) for 16% of the GDP and utilizing 4% of the labour force. Growth rate 1.3% (1986).

Commerce. Exports: (1987) $310 million or 14.7% of GDP. Imports amounted to $315 million for the same year or 15% of GDP. Principal exports include coffee 45%; vanilla 15%; cloves 11%; sugar; petroleum products. Imports include intermediate manufactures 30%; capital goods 28%; petroleum 15%; consumer goods 14%; foods 13%. Trading partners are

(exports) France; Japan; Italy; FRG; US and (imports) UK and other EC countries.
Trade with UK. Madagascar imported UK goods worth £4.75 million in 1988 and exported £7.15 million worth of goods to the UK.
Tourism. (1986) 27,000 visitors.

COMMUNICATIONS

Railways

There are some 579 miles/933 km of railways.

Roads

There are 36,086 miles/58,110 km of roads, of which 3,363 miles/5,415 km are bituminized.

Aviation

Air Madagascar provides domestic and international services (international airport is at Antananarivo). Passengers: (1987) 343,000.

Shipping

The inland waterways are only of local importance. The major marine ports are Toamasina (on the east coast), Antsiranana (at the northern tip of the island), Mahajanga and Toliara (on the west coast). The merchant marine consists of 14 ships or 1,000 GRT or over. Freight loaded: (1987) 1.1 million tons/1 million tonnes; unloaded: 1.8 million tons/1.6 million tonnes.

Telecommunications

There are 96,000 telephones and an above average telecommunications system. There are 2 million radios and 55,000 televisions (1986). The state-controlled RTM broadcasts radio and (since 1968) television programmes in French and Malagasy, with some English radio programmes as well. Radio Madagasikara is also state-controlled.

EDUCATION AND WELFARE

Education

Elementary education is obligatory between the ages of six and 14.
School population. 1,894,763.
Schools. (1984) Over 35,370 primary school staff teach an estimated 1,608,722 pupils in 13,973 elementary schools (one teacher per 45 pupils). 275,000 secondary school pupils are given instruction by 10,383 teachers (one per 26 pupils). 11,041 pupils attend technical schools and four agricultural colleges have been established at Nanisana, Ambatondrazaka, Maraovoay and Ivoloina.
Universities. In 1986, 37,475 students attended the University of Madagascar.
Literacy. 53%.

Health

901 doctors, 770 nursing staff, 839 midwives, 87 pharmacists and 52 dentists work in over 740 hospitals and dispensaries with 20,625 beds, (one per 554 people).

MALAWI
Republic of Malaêi

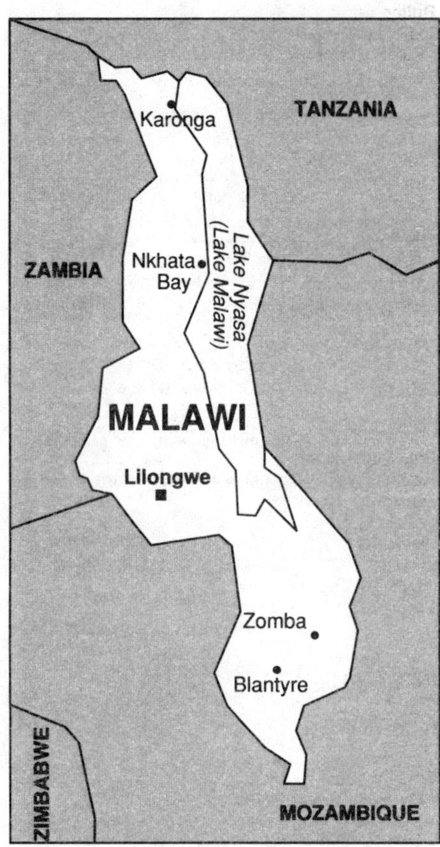

GEOGRAPHY

Located in south-east Africa, Malawi is a narrow landlocked country covering an area of 45,735 miles²/ 118,484 km² divided into three regions. Traversing the country north-south, the Great Rift Valley contains both Lake Nyasa, Africa's third largest lake (20% of Malawi's total surface area) and the Shire River valley, draining south-eastward from the lake. The largely infertile western central plateau (2,625–4,593 ft/800–1,400 m elevation) rises in the north to 8,530 ft/2,600 m in the Nyika uplands. To the south, the widely cultivated Shire highlands (average altitude 1,968–5,249 ft/600–1,600 m) reach maximum altitudes of 6,988 ft/2,130 m (Mt Zomba) and 9,842 ft/ 3,000 m in the Mulanje massif. The bulk of the population is concentrated in the southern regions, thinning northwards. 25% of the land is arable and 50% is forested.

Climate

Equatorial monsoonal. The dry season lasts May-Oct. and the wet season Nov.-Apr. High temperatures in Nov. vary from 72°F/22°C in the uplands to 81°F/27°C in the lowlands. Maximum temperatures range from 75–90°F/24–32°C, with corresponding minima of 58–67°F/14.4–19.4°C. Rainfall averages reach a maximum of 98 in/2,500 mm per annum in the northern highlands in contrast with lowland totals of 30 in/750 mm or less. Lilongwe: Jan. 73°F/22.8°C. July 60°F/15.6°C. Average annual rainfall 35 in/900 mm. Blantyre: Jan. 75°F/23.9°C. July 63°F/17.2°C. Average annual rainfall 44 in/1,125 mm.

Cities and towns

Blantyre	289,000
Lilongwe (capital)	175,000

Population

Total population is 7,884,000 of which 12.3% live in urban areas. Population density is 172 persons per mile²/79 per km². Ethnic composition: Black African of which nearly 60% is Maravi (comprising the Chewa, Nyanja, Tonga and Tumbuka ethnic groups); 18.4% Lomwe; 13.2% Yao; 6.7% Ngoni. Some small Asian and European minorities.

Birth rate 5.31%. **Death rate** 2.14%. **Rate of population increase** 3.17%. **Age distribution** under 15 = 46%; over 65 = 2.6%. **Life expectancy** female 48; male 44; average 46.

Religion

The majority of the population are Christian. 55% are Protestant (including Baptist, Presbyterian, Evangelist and Lutheran denominations) and 20% Roman Catholic. Another 20% are Muslim. Traditional animist beliefs are also widespread.

Language

English and Chichewa (spoken by 50% of the population) are official languages. Chilomwe, Chiyao and Chitumbuka are also commonly spoken (Bantu derivatives).

HISTORY

The prehistoric forebears of the early Twa and Fula inhabitants of Malawi date back to 8000–2000 BC. Bantu-speaking peoples first entered the area in the 1st to 4th centuries AD. Early political states were established by Bantu-speakers and in 1480 the Maravi Confederacy was founded in what is currently central and southern Malawi. In northern Malawi the Ngonde founded a kingdom in 1600 and in the 18th century immigrants from the eastern shore of Lake Nyasa established the Chikulamayembe state. During the 18th and 19th centuries the slave trade flourished in the region. Swahili-speaking peoples entered the area in 1830–60 and, along with the Yao people, established spheres of influence. European exploration, by Livingstone in particular, was followed in the latter half of the 19th century by a strong Scottish missionary effort.

The British established colonial authority over the region in 1891, forming the Nyasaland Districts Protectorate, which in 1893 became the British Central African Protectorate before becoming Nyasaland in 1907. A Central African Federation formed in 1953, comprising Nyasaland, Northern and Southern Rhodesia, was dissolved in 1963 under pressure from the nationalist movements. The Malawi Congress Party (MCP), formed in 1959 under the leadership of Dr Hastings Kamuzu Banda, led Malawi to independence on 6 July 1964 as a republic within the Commonwealth. Dr Banda was elected president in July 1966, as Malawi became a one-party state, and life president in 1971.

Dr Banda's regime was recognized as one of the most conservative in Africa. He opened diplomatic ties with South Africa, and maintained close ties with the Portuguese colonial authorities in neighbouring Mozambique until 1975. Nevertheless, Malawi recognized the Marxist government in Angola in 1976 and has refused to recognize the 'independent' South African homelands. In 1980 Malawi became a member of the Southern African Development Co-ordination Conference, which has the expressed aim of reducing the region's economic dependence on South Africa.

Pres. Banda has a reputation for ruthlessness in dealing with opposition and his regime was believed to be responsible in 1983 for the assassination, in Zimbabwe, of Dr Attati Mpakati, leader of the opposition Socialist League of Malawi (LESOMA). A power struggle in 1983 over the succession to Dr Banda, involving Dick Matenje (minister without portfolio) and John Tembo (governor of the Reserve Bank of Malawi) ended when Matenje and three other senior politicians died on 19 May in what was officially described as a road accident. Tembo, for his part, has not been promoted in Banda's frequent Cabinet reshuffles, the main apparent purpose of which has been to maintain his own dominance of Malawian politics. The government denied it was responsible for a fire bomb attack on the home of an officer of the exiled opposition Malawi Freedom Movement (MAFREMO) in Zambia in Oct. 1989, when nine people were killed. Parliamentary elections were most recently held in May 1987, when the 112 elective seats in the National Assembly were contested by 213 MCP members.

During the mid-1980s, relations with neighbouring Mozambique were severely strained as a result of the Mozambique government's belief that the Malawian authorities were assisting the rebel Resistencia Nacional Mocambicana (MNR or Renamo). However, during 1988 agreement was reached whereby Malawi would not permit its territory to be used as a sanctuary by the MNR; Malawi also committed troops in Mozambique to protect the railway line linking the two countries. By mid-1988 the UN High Commissioner for Refugees estimated that some 570,000 Mozambicans had taken refuge in Malawi as a consequence of the continuing conflict in Mozambique.

CONSTITUTION AND GOVERNMENT

Executive and legislature

Malawi, a republic within the Commonwealth, is a one-party state with an executive president; Banda was proclaimed life president in July 1971. The president appoints cabinet ministers, the chief justice, senior civil servants, and senior officers of the armed forces. Legislative power is vested in the unicameral 112-member National Assembly, with constituency members elected by universal direct adult suffrage for a five-year term (last election May 1987); the president is empowered to appoint an unlimited number of additional deputies to the Assembly.

Present government

Life President; Head of Government; Minister of External Affairs, Agriculture, Justice, Works and Supplies Dr Hastings Kamuzu Banda

Other principal Cabinet ministers Maxwell Pashane (Without portfolio); Louis Chimango (Finance); Robson W. Chirwa (Trade and Industry; Tourism).

Ruling party

Malawi Congress Party. *Life President* Dr Hastings Kamuzu Banda. *Members of National Executive Committee* Maxwell Pashane (administrative secretary); Katola Phiri (deputy administrative secretary); Robson W. Chirwa; John Tembo (Treasurer-general); Wadson Bini Deleza; Bester Bisani; Edward C.I. Bwanali; Kapichira Banda; Malani Lungu; Stanford Demba; Mfungo Mwaki-kunga.

Justice

The system of law is based on English common law and customary law. The highest court is the Supreme Court of Appeal, with a role in the review of legislation. There is a High Court, 23 magistrates' courts and a network of traditional courts, with procedures for judgments to be appealed from each level to the superior level up to the Supreme Court of Appeal. The death penalty is in force. Number of executions between 1985 and mid-1988 not known.

National symbols

Flag. Tricolour with horizontal stripes of black, red and green.

Festivals. 3 Mar. (Martyrs' Day); 14 May (Kamuzu Day, Birthday of Pres. Banda); 6 July (Republic Day); 17 Oct. (Mothers' Day); 21 Dec. (National Tree Planting Day).

Vehicle registration plate. MW.

INTERNATIONAL RELATIONS

Affiliations

NAM; OUA; ACP; Commonwealth.

Defence

Total Armed Forces: 5,250 (all services form part of the Army). Terms of service: voluntary, seven years.
Reserves: some 1,000.
Army: 5,000.
Navy: 100; one patrol craft, some boats.
Air Force: 150; two armed helicopters.
Para-military: 1,000.

ECONOMY

Currency

The unit is the kwacha, divided into 100 tambala.

National finance

Budget. The 1988 budget (in US$) was for expenditure (current and capital) of 390 million and revenue of 246 million. Main items of current expenditure are education 10.8%; health 7.1%; defence 6.6%.

Balance of payments. The balance of payments (current account, 1987) was a deficit of $53 million.

Inflation. (1986) 20%.

Gross Domestic Product

Estimated total GDP US$1,110 million, per capita US$170 (ranking 139 in the world by size).

Economically active population. The total number of persons active in the economy was 428,000.

Sector	% of workforce	% of GDP
industry	23	18
agriculture	43	37
services*	34	45

* services figure includes elements unassigned to other categories.

Energy and mineral resources

Minerals. 164,523 tons/149,254 tonnes of marble were extracted in 1976. Coal output: (1987) 25,938 tons/23,531 tonnes.

Electricity. Capacity: 172,000 kW; 535 million kWh; 70 kWh per capita (1988). Hydro-electric power stations at Tedzani and Nkula Falls contribute 124 MW (1984) and thermal power plants are located at Blantyre, Mtunthama, Mzuzu and Lilongwe.

Bioresources

Agriculture. Agriculture forms the mainstay of the economy, accounting for 37% of the GDP and 90% of all export earnings. 25% of the land is arable and 20% is meadow or pasture.

Crop production: (1986 in tons/tonnes) maize 1.51 million/1.37 million; tea 46,297/42,000; tobacco 78,263/71,000; sugar cane 1.8 million/1.6 million.

Livestock numbers: (1986) cattle 930,000; sheep 180,000; pigs 240,000; goats 690,000.

Forestry. 50% of the land area is forested; sawn timber production: (1983/4) 39,267,910 ft^3/11,108 m^3.

Fisheries. Catch: (1984) 71,730 tons/65,073 tonnes.

Industry and commerce

Industry. Growth rate 1.7% (1986). Principal industries are agricultural processing (tea, tobacco, sugar); sawmilling; cement; consumer goods.

Commerce. Exports: US$277 million (1987) or 23% of GDP; imports amounted to $296 million in the same year or 25% of GDP. Chief exports include: (1985) tobacco; tea; sugar; groundnuts; pulses; rice. Imported products include foodstuffs; petroleum; semimanufactures; consumer goods; transportation equipment. Trading partners are: (imports and exports) US; UK; Zambia; South Africa; FRG. (Imports only) Japan; Zimbabwe.

Trade with UK. Malawi imported £27.6 million worth of UK goods in 1988; exports amounted to £30.18 million.

Tourism. (1985) 41,145 visitors.

COMMUNICATIONS

Railways

There are some 491 miles/790 km of railways.

Roads

There are 7,586 miles/12,215 km of roads, of which 1,653 miles/2,662 km are bituminized.

Aviation

Air Malawi Ltd provides domestic and international services (main airport is Kamuzu International Airport at Lilongwe). Passengers: (1986) 324,983.

Shipping

The inland waterways consist of Lake Nyasa (Lake Malawi) and the Shire River. Chipoka, Monkey Bay, Nkhata Bay, and Nkotakota are all inland ports on Lake Nyasa (Lake Malawi).

Telecommunications

There are 36,800 telephones and a fair telecommunications system. There are 1.06 million radios (1983). Malawi Broadcasting Corporation is partly state and partly commercially financed, with programmes in English and Chichewa. There is no television.

EDUCATION AND WELFARE

Education

Eight years of primary school instruction are followed by four years at secondary school.

Schools. 1,022,765 pupils in primary schools are taught by 25,013 members of staff (one per 41 pupils); a further 25,681 secondary schools students receive instruction from 1,229 teachers (one per 21 pupils). In addition 777 pupils attend technical colleges and 1,802 students are enrolled at teacher-training establishments.

Universities. 2,323 students are registered on degree courses at the University of Malawi.

Literacy. 25%.

Health

Of Malawi's 51 hospitals, 21 are government district hospitals. The figure also includes one mental institution and two leprosaria. There are 7,081 hospital beds in all, one per 1,234 people.

MALAYSIA

Federation of Malaysia

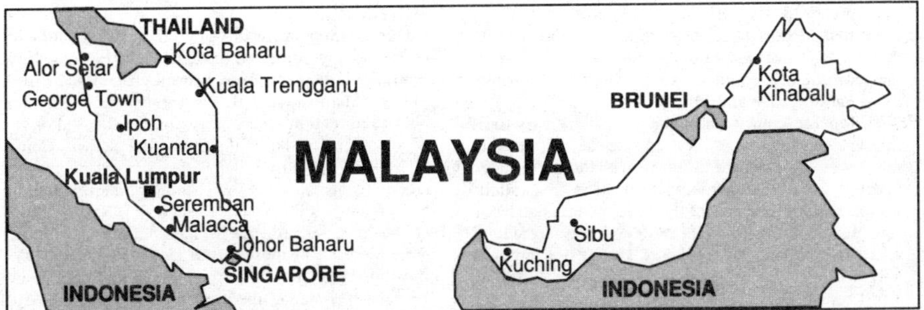

GEOGRAPHY

Malaysia consists of two separate parts (West and East Malaysia) in Southeast Asia, covering a total area of 127,225 miles²/329,750 km². West Malaysia comprises the southern half of the Malay or Kra peninsula (50,797 miles²/131,598 km²). Climbing to 7,181 ft/2,189 m at Gunong Tahan, the central chain of mountains (running north-south) divides the narrow eastern coastal belt from the fertile and populous alluvial plains in the west. East Malaysia consists of the states of Sarawak in the north-west (48,037 miles²/124,449 km²) and Sabah in the north-east (28,452 miles²/73,710 km²) on the island of Borneo. From the swampy coastal plain, the land rises through a foothill region in the north-west to a mountainous interior on the Indonesian border and a maximum elevation of 13,432 ft/4,094 m at Gunong Kinabalu in the north-east. West Malaysia is drained by the Pahang river and East Malaysia by the Rajang and Kinabatangan rivers. 3% of the land is arable and 63% covered by tropical rain forest supporting one of the world's most diverse bird populations.

Climate

North-east and south-west monsoons last Nov.-Mar. and June-Oct. respectively. Temperatures are consistent all year, averaging 77–86°F/25–30° C in low-lying areas and 72–82°F/22–28°C in the upland districts. High humidity (85%) accompanies plentiful rainfall, ranging from 124 in/3,150 mm in Sabah to 89 in/2,250 mm in Sarawak and 98 in/2,500 mm in peninsular Malaysia. Kuala Lumpur: Jan. 81°F/27.2°C. July 81°F/27.2°C. Average annual rainfall 96 in/2,441 mm. Penang: Jan. 82°F/27.8°C. July 82°F/27.8°C. Average annual rainfall 108 in/2,736 mm.

Cities and towns

Kuala Lumpur (capital)	1,103,200
Ipoh	293,849
George Town	248,241
Johor Baharu	246,395
Petaling Jaya	207,805
Kelang	180,296
Kota Baharu	167,872

Population

Total population is 16,573,000 of which 38.2% live in urban areas. Population density is 130 persons per mile²/48.9 per km² (higher in West Malaysia). Ethnic composition: 59% Malay and indigenous inhabitants, including the Orang Asli of West Malaysia and the Iban, Land Dayak, Bajan and Kadazan peoples of East Malaysia; 32% Chinese; 9% Indian, Pakistani or Sri Lankan Tamil.

Birth rate 2.95%. **Death rate** 0.6%. **Rate of population increase** 2.35%. **Age distribution** under 15 = 37.8%; over 65 = 3.8%. **Life expectancy** female 72; male 68; average 70.

Religion

The vast majority of the Malay population in the peninsular region are Muslim. Most of the Chinese are practising Buddhists. The Indian population is predominantly Hindu. East Malaysia. Sabah: 38% Muslim; 17% Christian; 45% other including tribal animist. Sarawak: 35% tribal animist; 24% Buddhist or Confucian; 20% Muslim; 16% Christian (Church of England, Roman Catholic, Methodist and Seventh Day Adventist).

Language

Bahasa Malaysia is the official language, belonging to the Indonesian branch of the Austronesian language family and related to other Malayan dialects including Iban (Sea Dayak) spoken in Borneo; Brunei Malay; Sambai Malay; Kutai Malay; Banjarese. Mandarin and Hakka dialects are spoken by the Chinese population. The Tamils speak a mixture of Dravidian and Indo-European languages. Numerous local languages.

HISTORY

Archaeological evidence indicates that areas of modern Malaysia were inhabited as long ago as 50,000 BC. Between the 3rd and 14th centuries, the peninsula was subject to various external cultures, chiefly Indian and Hindu. Chinese sources in the 3rd century AD record that the Malay peninsula was an amalgam of small states, the most important of which, Lankasuka, extended its control over northern parts of the peninsula and where temple ruins still remain. By the 1300s, the peninsula was dominated by the Javanese Majapahit Empire, which extended its control as far south as present-day Singapore. Following an invasion of Singapore by the Thai Ayuthia empire in 1400, its ruler, Paramesvara, escaped to the peninsula and established a base in Malacca.

Thus the Malacca Sultanate was founded, marking 100 years of Malay economic cultural expansion. The centralized authority wielded by the sultan formed the basis of the political state that was to characterize Malaya's future political structure. Islam was propagated from east Bengal via trading links with Arab merchants and, although introduced 200 years previously, the conversion of the Sultan encouraged the spread of the religion as Malacca's territory expanded. Prior to 1511, when Malacca fell to Portuguese forces led by Alberquerque, its influence and control had extended to the states of Pahang, Trengganu, Kedah and Johor.

Portuguese control of Malacca lasted up to 1641, during which time it exerted varying degrees of influence. For Portugal, Malacca was found to be too isolated from its other trading outposts in Goa and the Moluccas and, for much of the time, it was engaged in the defence of the port against deposed Malay sultans and the Sumatra Achehanese. Portugal eventually succumbed when the Dutch joined with Acheh to wrest control of Malacca in 1640.

By the mid-17th century, Malacca had lost much of its economic vitality and despite efforts by the Dutch to revive the port, it slipped into decay through neglect. The power vacuum was exploited by the Buginese from the Celebes, who during the 18th century used Malacca to penetrate the peninsula. By 1745, they had managed to secure the position of one of their own number as sultan of Selangor.

The decline in both Dutch and Buginese influence was directly linked to the rise in British interest in the region. By the late 18th century, merchant houses in London were becoming aware of the need for trading commodities with China. Tin and spices from the Malay peninsula were identified as being viable products. In 1786, Francis Light of the East India Company set up a trading post in Penang, and in 1795 and 1819 Malacca and Singapore respectively, were acquired by the Company. Britain's position was clarified in 1824 by the Anglo–Dutch Treaty which effectively demarcated the respective spheres of their influence. In 1826, Singapore, Malacca and Penang were incorporated into an administrative unit known as the Straits Settlements (SS), which, in 1867, came under the direct control of the British Colonial Office.

Following the formation of the Straits Settlements, the UK had attempted to distance itself from the other peninsula territories. Economic developments in the residual states, and particularly the discovery of tin deposits, made this impossible. Disputes over commercial interests, notably in Perak and Selangor, began to have an adverse effect on trading in the region. The lack of administrative control outside of the Settlements led European and Chinese merchants to petition Britain to restore order. Eventually, the British government accepted the need for intervention, possibly in an attempt to pre-empt what were perceived as German ambitions to exploit the disorder. In 1874 Britain accepted administrative responsibility for Perak and by 1888 this had been extended to include Selangor, Negri Semilan and Pahang. These four states were brought together in 1896 as the Federated Malay States, with the federal capital at Kuala Lumpur. In 1914, British authority was extended to the whole peninsular when the five remaining Malay states, Kedah, Perlis, Trenganu, Kelantan and Johor, were united as the Unfederated Malay States.

British control was maintained by providing the Malay elite (and especially the aristocracy) with an English education at Kuala Kangsar College which opened in 1905, its graduates then being employed in the Malay Administrative Service. By the early 20th century, Malaya was a leading producer of tin and rubber but with increasing immigration of Chinese – mainly to the tin mines on the east coast – and Indians – mainly to rubber plantations, the demographic composition shifted radically. By 1931, Chinese accounted for 39% of the population, and the Malays, 45%.

During the inter-war years, the plural nature of Malay society became more entrenched and political aspirations and concerns became communal-based. Malay Indians looked to the sub-continent for their political direction and radical Chinese focused on the development of the communist movement in China. A Malay Communist Party (MCP) and its parallel labour organization, the Malay General Labour Movement (MGLU) were formed in 1930.

The invasion of the Malay peninsula and the surrender of Singapore to the Japanese in Feb. 1942, was the culmination of both strategic imperatives and military mis-management by the British. In Sept. 1940, Whitehall publicly acknowledged the primacy of Europe over the Far East. Preference of military supplies and advisers were therefore given over to Europe and, consequently, armed forces in Malaya remained ill-equipped, under-supplied and under-trained. The long standing belief that in Singapore, Britain wielded a deterrent sufficient to deter any aggression in Southeast Asia was spectacularly undermined when in Dec. 1941 Japanese forces swept down through Malaya to Singapore in little over two months.

Upon its return to Malaya in early 1946, Britain announced plans to remodel its administration of the peninsular. It was proposed that sovereignty be transferred from the Malay rulers to the British crown, that all the Malay states (with the exception of Singapore) be unified into a Malayan Union, and that all Chinese and Indian immigrants be awarded citizenship and equal rights. The Malayan Union was formally introduced in Apr. 1946, but it met with such resistance from the Malay community (brought together in a new political grouping, the United Malays National Organization–UMNO) that its provisions were never brought into full effect. Following negotiations between Britain, UMNO and the Malay rulers it was agreed to form a Federation of Malaya (eventually inaugurated in Feb. 1948), which formalized the policy of unification, but allowed the sultans to maintain sovereign control and introduced restrictive citizenship provisions for members of the Chinese and Indian communities. The MCP, which had formed the principal opposition to the Japanese during World War II, began to incite labour unrest throughout the colony and, following a series of murders, the government declared a state of emergency in June 1948.

Britain's counter-insurgency effort, for the first three years, was an ad hoc affair without proper coordination. However, by 1952, with a unified military command under Gen. Templer and by shelving the Union and re-endorsing Malay status, Britain demonstrated that it was prepared to cede independence to Malaya and support for the communists dissipated. By 1954, the insurgency had been reduced to minor proportions and was declared over in 1960. It was not until Dec. 1989 that the MCP signed a formal peace treaty with Kuala Lumpur.

In federal elections held in 1955, UMNO, the Malay Chinese Association (MCA) and the Malay Indian Association (MIA) formed an alliance under the leadership of Tunku Abdul Rahman, and won 51 of the 52 seats contested. Following the preparation of a constitution, Malaya secured its independence (merdeka) from Britain on 31 Aug. 1957 (the alliance was later expanded to include other parties under a national coalition).

Malaysia was established in Sept. 1963, through the Union of the Independent Federation of Malay, the internally self-governing state of Singapore, and the former British colonies of Sarawak and North Borneo (Sabah). The incorporation of Singapore into the new Federation had been proposed by Tunku Abdul Rahman, who was apparently reluctant to allow the emergence of a (predominantly Chinese) rival power on Malaya's southern coastline. Sabah and Sarawak, neither of which had been prepared by the British for independence, were included in the Federation partly in order to secure the numerical superiority of the Malay community. Tensions arose in 1963, when Indonesia pursued a policy of confrontation towards Malaysia over the formation of the Federation but this was reduced by Malaysian and Commonwealth forces and a reconciliation was secured following the rise to power of Pres. Suharto of Indonesia in 1966. Problems also arose in Singapore, where Lee Kuan Yew's People's Action Party was threatening the Alliance by openly competing against the MCA for Chinese support. Against Lee's wishes, Singapore was removed from the Federation in Aug. 1965, reducing the number of Malaysia's component states from 14 to 13.

On 13 May 1969, serious racial clashes between the Chinese and Malay communities precipitated the declaration of another state of emergency. Many hundreds were killed and the government cited the underlying causes of the disturbances as being economic disparity between the Chinese and Malays. In order to redress the balance, it embarked on a New Economic Policy (NEP) designed to eradicate poverty and create a bumiputra (indigenous Malay) commercial and industrial community that would hold at least 30% of the equity in every Malaysian company by 1990.

Malaysia's development during the 1980s was guided by UMNO – still the dominant party in the governing federal National Front coalition – under the leadership of Datuk Seri Dr. Mahathir Mohamad (who succeeded Dato Hussein bin Onn as prime minister in 1981 and was most recently re-elected in Aug. 1986). Despite economic successes, concern over political freedoms, human rights and more recently, the independence of the judiciary have been expressed by opposition groups. Such concerns, in part, resulted in a close-run but unsuccessful challenge for the leadership of UMNO, which culminated in the de-registration of the old UMNO configuration and the registration of UMNO Baru (new) in 1988.

CONSTITUTION AND GOVERNMENT

Executive and legislature

Malaysia is a parliamentary monarchy whose (largely ceremonial) monarch, the Yang di-Pertuan Agong, is elected every five years by the nine hereditary Malay rulers of Peninsular Malaysia from among their own number. The Yang di-Pertuan Agong appoints a Cabinet headed by a prime minister, who is head of government. Parliament (Parlimen) consists of: (i) a 69-member Senate (Dewan Negara), serving a six-year term, two members of which are elected by the Legislative Assemblies of each of the states, the remaining 43 members being nominated by the Yang di-Pertuan Agong; and (ii) a 177-member House of Representatives (Dewan Rakyat) elected by universal adult suffrage for a five-year term and by simple majority in single-member constituencies. Last elections Aug. 1986.

Present government

Head of State (King, or Yang di-Pertuan Agong). Sultan Azlan Muhibbuddin Shah

Prime Minister; Minister of Home Affairs and Justice. Datuk Seri Dr Mahathir Mohamed

Other Principal Ministers Encik Abdul Ghafar Baba (Deputy Prime Minister; National and Rural Development); Tengku Ahmad Rithauddeen (Defence); Datuk Haji Abu Hassan Omar (Foreign Affairs); Encik Daim Zainuddin (Finance).

Administration

Malaysia has a federal form of government, with some legislative powers resting with the states. The ruling party at federal level, the multi-racial National Front coalition (Barisan Nasional), retained an absolute majority in simultaneous elections in all 11 Peninsular Malaysian state assemblies held concurrently with the federal general elections in Aug. 1986. The Federation of Malaysia consists of the 11 states of Peninsular Malaysia and the two states of Sarawak and Sabah situated on the northern coast of the island of Kalimantan (Borneo).

Chief Ministers of state governments Johor – Datuk Abdul Ajib Ahmad; Kedah Datuk Osman Aroff; Kelantan – Datuk Haji Mohamed bin Yaacob; Malacca – Datuk Rahim Thamby Chik; Negri Sembilan – Datuk Abdul Samad; Pahang – Datuk Najib Tun Razak; Penang – Dr Lim Chong Eu; Perak – Datuk Seri Ramli Ngah Talib; Perlis – Datuk Haji Ali Ahmad; Sabah – Datuk Joseph Pairin Kitingan; Sarawak – Datuk Patinggi Abdul Taib Mahmud; Selangor – Datuk Ahmad Razali Ali; Trengganu – Datuk Wan Mokhtar Ahmed.

Justice

The Judicial System consists of a Supreme Court and two High Courts, one in Peninsular Malaysia and one for Sabah and Sarawak (sitting alternately in Kota Kinabalu and Kuching).

The Supreme Court comprises a president, the two chief justices of the High Courts and other judges. It possesses appellate, original and advisory jurisdiction. Each of the High Courts consists of a chief justice and not less than four other judges. In Peninsular Malaysia the Subordinate Courts consist of the Sessions Courts and the Magistrates' Courts. In Sabah/Sarawak the Magistrates' Courts constitute the Subordinate Courts.

Judges are appointed by the Yang di Pertuan Agong on the advice of the Prime Minister after consulting the Conference of Rulers, but before tendering his advice, the Prime Minister is required to consult the Lord President of the Federal Court, and, in certain cases, the Chief Justices of the High Courts and the chief ministers of Sabah and Sarawak.

The death penalty is in force. There were over 50 executions between 1985 and mid-1988. Offences were drug-trafficking; murder; kidnapping.

National symbols

Flag. Fourteen horizontal stripes (seven red and seven white). There are also 14 rays of the yellow star which, together with a yellow crescent, appears in the blue canton.

Festivals. 1 May (Labour Day); 7 June (Official

Birthday of HM the Yang di-Pertuan Agong); 31 Aug. (National Day).
Vehicle registration plate. MAL.

INTERNATIONAL RELATIONS

Affiliations

NAM; Asean; ICO; Commonwealth; SAARC.

Defence

Total Armed Forces: 113,000. Terms of service: voluntary. Reserves: 47,600.
Army: 90,000; 26 light tanks (Scorpion).
Navy: 12,500; four frigates (FS-1500, UK Mermaid) and 37 patrol and coastal combatants.
Air Force: 12,000; 58 combat aircraft (mainly F-5, F-5E, A-4, A-4PTM).
Para-military: 18,000 (Police Field Force).

ECONOMY

Currency

The unit is the ringgit, divided into 100 sen.

National finance

Budget. The 1988 budget (in US$) was for expenditure (current and capital) of 10,000 million and revenue of 8,000 million.
Balance of payments. The balance of payments (current account, 1987) was a surplus of $2,170 million.
Inflation. (1988) 2.7%.

Gross Domestic Product

Estimated total GDP US$31,230 million, per capita US$2,092 (ranking 52 in the world by size).
Economically active population. The total number of persons active in the economy was 6,000,000; unemployed: 8%.

Sector	% of workforce
industry	21
agriculture	34
services*	45

* services figure includes elements unassigned to other categories.

Energy and mineral resources

Oil and gas. Oil output: (1988) 30 million tons/27 million tonnes. Malaysia has natural gas reserves estimated at 49.4 million ft^3/1.4 million m^3. In 1986 Japan imported most of Malaysia's total LNG output of 5.8 million tons/5.3 million tonnes.
Minerals. Output: (1986 in 1,000 tons/tonnes) iron ore 229/208; bauxite 624/566; copper 127/115; tin 32/29.
Electricity. Capacity: 5,551,000 kW; production: 15,835 million kWh; 970 kWh per capita (1988).

Bioresources

Agriculture. 3% of the land area is arable and 10% is under permanent cultivation. Manufacturing has supplanted agriculture in recent years as the largest sector of the economy. Malaysia remains the world's most important producer of natural rubber and palm-oil. Subsistence farming has consistently failed to meet the demands for national self-sufficiency in food. Rice production in particular, is insufficient in all areas.
Crop production: (1987 in 1,000 tons/tonnes) rubber 1,743/1,581; pineapples 165/149.7; cocoa 143/130; tobacco leaves 13/12; pepper 17/15.
Livestock numbers: (1987) buffaloes 245,000; cattle 620,000; goats 347,000; pigs 2.2 million; sheep 75,000.
Forestry. 63% of the land surface area is forested. Most of the country's rubber and palm-oil plantations are located in peninsular Malaysia. The World Bank's US$9 million financial incentive to check the rate of deforestation resulted in a 6.9% fall in timber exports in 1988. Over 7.4 million acres/3 million ha of forest were cleared during the period 1974–84.
Fisheries. Total catch: (1986) 679,347 tons/616,300 tonnes.

Industry and commerce

Industry. Growth rate 8.3% (1987). The main industries on the peninsular are rubber and palm-oil processing and manufacturing; light manufacturing industry; electronics; tin mining; smelting; logging and processing timber. Principal activities on Sabah and Sarawak include logging; petroleum production; agriculture processing.
Commerce. Exports: (1988) US$20,000 million; imports: $14,900 million in the same year. Exports for 1987 included M$18,147 million of manufactured goods; M$3,784 million of natural rubber; M$3,038 million of palm-oil; crude petroleum; sawn logs; tin. Imports were chiefly foodstuffs; crude oil; consumer goods; machinery/transportation equipment. Malaysia's export partners included Singapore; Japan; USSR; EC; Australia; US. Goods were imported mainly from Japan; Singapore; West Germany; UK; Thailand; China; Australia; US.
Trade with UK. Malaysia imported UK goods worth £310.5 million in 1988; exports to the UK totalled £525 million.
Tourism. (1986) 3.1 million visitors (peninsular Malaysia).

COMMUNICATIONS

Railways

There are 1,321 miles/2,127 km of railways.

Roads

There are 19,132 miles/30,809 km of roads, of which 15,301 miles/24,640 km are concrete or bituminized.

Aviation

Malaysian Airline System (MAS) provides domestic and international services (international airports are at Kuala Lumpur, Kota Kinabalu, Penang, Johore Bahru and Kuching). Passengers: (1987) 10.87 million.

Shipping

Peninsular Malaysia has 1,993 miles/3,209 km of inland waterways; Sabah 974 miles/1,569 km and Sarawak 1,564 miles/2,518 km. The marine ports on Peninsular Malaysia are Penang, and Port Kelan. The marine ports in Sarawak are Kidurong and Kuching. Kota Kinabalu, Sandakan and Tawau are the marine ports of Sabah. The merchant marine consists of 155 ships of 1,000 GRT or over.

Telecommunications

There are 994,860 telephones. There is a good intercity system to peninsular Malaysia and an adequate intercity system between Sabah and Sarawak via Brunei. There are 6.85 million radios and 1.8 million televisions (1986). Radio Television Malaysia (RTM) controls as well as operates broadcasting services. Suara Malaysia (Voice of Malaysia) broadcasts external radio services in English and seven regional languages. There are three state-owned television networks run by Television

Malaysia, as well as the TV3 station run by the ruling UMNO party, and the commercial TVB network.

EDUCATION AND WELFARE

Education

Schools. There are an estimated 2,325,462 pupils and 103,983 teachers at state-aided primary schools (one per 22 pupils); 5,130 pupils at private elementary institutions taught by 224 members of staff (one per 22 pupils). 60,863 secondary-school teachers work at over 1,220 establishments with 1,329,299 pupils (one per 22 pupils). Approximately 28,251 students attend teacher-training colleges.

Universities. Malaysia's 12 higher educational institutions (excluding teacher-training colleges) include seven universities; five polytechnics; the MARA Institute of Technology; the Tunku Ab Rahman College of Kuala Lumpur. The International Islamic University was founded in 1983.

Literacy. 65%.

Health

Peninsular Malaysia: 163 hospitals, private and special medical institutions (of which only 60 are state-maintained) contain a total of 32,685 beds (one per 512 people).

Sabah: 16 hospitals; 2,799 beds.

Sarawak: 17 government hospitals; 272 dispensaries (including 118 mobile clinics); 302 doctors; 55 dentists.

MALDIVES

Divehi Jumhuriyya

(Republic of Maldives)

GEOGRAPHY

The Maldive archipelago comprises some 1,190 islands (202 of which are inhabited) in a chain of 20 coral atolls, located in the Indian Ocean 416 miles/670 km south-west of Sri Lanka, covering an area of 116 miles^2/300 km^2. Protected from monsoon devastation by barrier reefs (faros), none of the islands rises above 5 ft/1.8 m elevation. Tropical crops include breadfruit, mango, banana, cassava, and screwpine. 10% of the total surface area is arable and 3% is forested.

Climate

Hot and humid. The wet season (south-west monsoon) lasts May-Aug.; the dry season (north-east monsoon) Dec.-Mar. Average annual rainfall is 84 in/2,130 mm. Temperatures constant. Malé: Average temperature 81°F/27°C.ıAverage annual rainfall 59 in/1,500 mm.

Cities and towns

Malé (capital) 46,334

Population

Total population is 202,000 of which 25.5% live in urban areas. Population density is 1,741 persons per mile^2/637.6% per km^2. Ethnic composition is a combination of Sinhalese, Dravidian, Arab and Black races.

Birth rate 4.7%. **Death rate** 1.0% **Rate of population increase** 3.7%. **Age distribution** under 15 = 44.6%; over 60 = 4.6%. **Life expectancy** female 58; male 57; average 57.5.

Religion

State religion is Islam (Sunni). The Republic supports a total of 689 mosques.

Language

Divehi, a Sinhalese dialect of Arabic extraction is the official language (Indo-European). Arabic, English and Hindi are also spoken.

HISTORY

The Maldive islands, settled by its original Dravidian inhabitants from southern India perhaps as early as the 4th century BC, came under the domination of Indo-Aryans mainly from Ceylon who arrived some 400 years later. The king converted in AD 1153 from Buddhism to Islam, ordering the population to do likewise. The islands were ruled as a Muslim sultanate, with a brief interlude under Portuguese control from Goa (1558–73).

The British established a protectorate in Dec. 1887. The powers of the sultans were circumscribed by provisions of a 1932 constitution, and a short-lived modernizing regime set up a republic (1953–54) before a coup restored the sultanate. Ibrahim Nasir, prime minister to the last of the sultans (from 1957) and effective leader of the country at the time of independence (26 July 1965), became president when a referendum approved a republican constitution (11 Nov. 1968); he strengthened the powers of the presidency (March 1975) but then stood down and left the country (1978), and Maumoon Abdul Gayoom was elected to succeed him.

Re-elected for successive presidential terms (Sept. 1983, Sept. 1988), Gayoom survived three attempted coups (1980, 1981 and Nov. 1988), in each of which he saw the hand of his predecessor Nasir. The 1988 coup was suppressed only when Indian troops were dispatched to defeat the mercenaries, who apparently came from Sri Lanka. Meanwhile Gayoom had confirmed a non-aligned foreign policy. His predecessor had rejected in 1977 a Soviet bid to lease the island of Gan, where the British no longer needed the air-force staging post which they had secured and built after complex negotiations in the latter part of the 1950s. The Maldives joined the Commonwealth as a special status member (July 1982) and became a full member on 20 June 1985.

CONSTITUTION AND GOVERNMENT

Executive and legislature

The executive president is elected for a five-year term by universal adult suffrage (last re-elected by referendum 23 Sept. 1988), and appoints and presides over the Cabinet. The legislature is a 48-member Citizens' Assembly (Majilis), 40 of whose members are elected for five years and the remaining eight appointed by the president.

Present government

President; Minister of Defence; Minister of Finance Maumoun Abdul Gayoom

Principal members of Cabinet Fathhulla Jameel (Foreign Affairs); Umar Zahir (Home Affairs; Sports); Mohamed Rashid (Justice).

Justice

The legal system is based on the Islamic Shari'a. The death penalty is nominally in force. No executions between 1985 and mid-1988.

National symbols

Flag. Green with a broad red border and a white crescent in the middle.

Festivals. 7 Jan. (National Day); 26 July (Independence Day); 11 Nov. (Republic Day).

INTERNATIONAL RELATIONS

Affiliations

Commonwealth; NAM; SAARC.

Defence

No military forces as such.

ECONOMY

Currency

The unit is the rufiyaa, divided into 100 laris.

National finance

Budget. The 1988 budget (in US$) was for expenditure (current and capital) of 50 million and revenue of 51 million.

Inflation. (1988) 14%.

Gross Domestic Product

Estimated total GDP US$70 million, per capita US$440 (ranking 184 in the world by size).

Economically active population. The total number of persons active in the economy was 66,000.

Energy and mineral resources

Electricity. Capacity: 5,000 kW; production: 10 million kWh; 50 kWh per capita (1988).

Bioresources

Agriculture. The coconut palm grows prolifically and is the main crop. Others include millet; yams; cassava; pumpkins; melons; other tropical fruit.

Crop production: (1987 in 1,000 tons/tonnes) coconuts 14.3/13; copra.

Forestry. 3% of the Maldives is forest and woodland.

Fisheries. Annual catch: (largely tuna) 62,831 tons/57,000 tonnes.

Industry and commerce

Industry. The main industries are fishing; fish processing; tourism; shipping; boat building; coconut processing; garments; woven mats; coir (rope); handicrafts.

Commerce. Exports: US$31.2 million, including fish 57%; clothing 39%. Imports were US$73.9, including intermediate and capital goods 47%; consumer goods 42%; petroleum products 11%. Countries exported to were Thailand; Western Europe; Sri Lanka. Imports came from Japan; Western Europe; Thailand.

Trade with UK. The Maldives imported UK goods worth £1,689,000; exports to UK totalled £1,859,000.

Tourism. (1987) 131,399 visitors.

COMMUNICATIONS

Railway

There are no railways.

Roads

Only 6 miles/9.6 km of highway, constructed from coral, in the capital.

Aviation

Air Maldives provides domestic and international services (international airport is on Hulule island).

Shipping

The ports of the Maldives are Malé and Gran. The merchant marine consists of 16 ships or 1,000 GRT or over.

Telecommunications

There are 2,325 telephones and minimal domestic and international facilities. There are 22,044 radios and 4,136 televisions (1988). Broadcasting is by Voice of Maldives (radio) and Television Maldives (since 1978).

EDUCATION AND WELFARE

Education

Schools. (1987) 300 primary schools with 53,412 pupils and 1,134 teachers (one per 47 pupils); six secondary schools with 1,313 pupils and 116 teachers (one per 11 pupils).

Literacy. 36%

Health

There is one hospital in Malé with 84 beds, and a further three regional hospitals. In 1987 there were seven doctors (one per 30,000 people).

MALI
République du Mali
(Republic of Mali)

GEOGRAPHY

Situated in west Africa, Mali is a landlocked country with an area of 478,640 miles²/1,240,000 km² divided into six administrative regions. The low-lying, featureless terrain is dominated in the north by the virtually uninhabited Saharan plains of Tanezrouft and Taoudenni (984–1,640 ft/300–500 m elevation) rising north-east to meet the Ahaggar massif (high point Ad Ouzzeine range 3,280–4,921 ft/1,000–1,500 m) as it transects the Mali-Algerian frontier. The River Niger flows north-east from the Guinean border in the south-west, irrigating the semi-arid savannah and forming a fertile inland delta in the central regions as it turns east to south-east at Tombouctou. 2% of the land is arable and 7% forest or woodland (mostly scrub vegetation in the south-west).

Climate

Sub-tropical in the south and south-west with rainfall totals reaching 39 in/1,000 mm throughout June-Oct. (maximum rainfall in Aug.). North of the Sudanese zone, the Sahelian savannah receives 7.9–19.7 in/200–500 mm of rain with average temperatures 73–97°F/23–36°C. In the saharan north, rain is almost non-existent and temperatures fluctuate between 117°F/47°C during the day and 39°F/4°C at night. Bamoko: Jan. 76°F/24.4°C. July 80°F/26.7°C. Average annual rainfall 44 in/1,120mm. Tombouctou: Jan. 71°F/21.7°C. July 90°F/32.2°C. Average annual rainfall 9 in/230mm.

Cities and towns

Bamako (capital)	600,000
Segou	65,000
Mopti	54,000
Sikasso	47,000
Kayes	45,000

Population

Total population is 8,824,000 of which 20.8% live in urban areas. Population density is 18 persons per mile²/6.8 per km². Ethnic groups: 50% Mande (Bambara, Malinke, Sarakole); 17% Peul (Fulani nomads of the Sahel regions); 12% Voltaic including the Bwa, Senoufo and Minianka; 6% Songhai; 5% Tuareg and Moor.

Birth rate 5.06%. **Death rate** 2.25%. **Rate of population increase** 2.81%. **Age distribution** under 15 = 46.3%; over 65 = 2.7%. **Life expectancy** female 49; male 46; average 47.

Religion

90% of the population are Muslim. 9% pursue traditional animist beliefs and 1% are Christian (of whom approximately 50% [94,000] are Roman Catholic and a similar proportion Protestant).

Language

French is the official language but the indigenous Mande language of Bambara is spoken by an estimated 60% of the population. Other Mande dialects include Soninke, Malinke and Dogou. Other native (non-Mande) languages include Fulani; Songhai; Senoufo; Mininanka.

HISTORY

Mali is named after the Malinka Empire of Mali, founded in the 8th century AD, expanded in the 13th century, and reaching its height in the 14th century as the region's medieval Muslim empire under Mansa Moussa (1307–32). Rival power grew in the Songhai empire based on Timbuktu and Gao in the 15th century. With Moroccan support, Tuareg peoples from the north conquered much of the area within Mali's present national boundaries (1737), after which the central-southern Bambara kingdom achieved a dominance which lasted until the French conquered the area of present-day Mali between 1881 and 1895. In 1892 the districts along the upper and middle Niger and Senegal rivers were united to form the colony of French Soudan, which in 1895 became part of the federation of French West Africa. After 1899 the French Soudan was divided between neighbouring French colonies. From 1920 it was again a separate colony, directly administered through a governor, 16 district commanders and French civil servants backed by selected traditional chiefs.

The country's most prominent political leader in the period up to independence, Modibo Keita, was a founder member in 1946 of the Rassemblement démocratique africain (RDA), which became the umbrella for the affiliated parties that were to come to power in many of the erstwhile French colonies. On 24 Nov. 1958, French Soudan was renamed the Soudanese Republic, as an autonomous state within the French Community. On 4 Apr. 1959, the Soudanese Republic and the neighbouring Republic of Senegal united to form the Federation of Mali, having given up hopes of a wider West African federation. On 20 June 1960 the Federation of Mali became independent, but Senegal seceded on 22 Aug. of the same year, and the independent Republic of

Mali was then declared on 22 Sept. 1960 with Modibo Keita as its first president and his Union soudanaise as its sole legal party. Having embarked on a path of struggle against French domination, Keita dissolved the National Assembly on 17 Jan. 1968, taking over full powers himself, but on 19 Nov. 1968 he was overthrown in a bloodless army coup (and he died in detention nine years later).

The new military regime set up a Military Committee for National Liberation (CMLN), which assumed all state power; the CMLN Chairman, Moussa Traoré's Union démocratique du peuple malien (UDPM) remaining as the sole political party. His regime retained a firm grip on power (with a purge following an alleged coup attempt in Feb. 1978) despite Mali's slow economic growth. Elections to the National Assembly in 1979, 1982, 1985 and 1988 each gave the UDPM an almost unanimous vote; recurring protests by school pupils, students and teachers, however, were suppressed and many schools and colleges were closed for long periods. War broke out briefly with neighbouring Burkina Faso on 25–29 Dec. 1985, when Burkinabe troops crossed the disputed border but were driven back by superior Malian air power; relations were normalized the following year.

CONSTITUTION AND GOVERNMENT

Executive and legislature

A republic with an executive president, Mali is a one-party state ruled by a Military Committee for National Liberation. The 82-member National Assembly is elected by universal adult suffrage for a three-year term from a list of candidates drawn up by the party, based on local branch committee nominations; last elections June 1988.

Present government

President; C.-in-C. of Armed Forces; Head of government; Minister of National Defence Gen. Moussa Traoré

Principal members of Council of Ministers Django Cissoko (Secretary-General to the Presidency); Ngolo Traoré (Foreign Affairs and International Co-operation); Souleymane Dembele (Planning); Mamadou Sissoko (Justice); Tienan Coulibaly (Finance and Trade); Brig.-Gen. Mamadou Coulibaly (Minister-Delegate for National Defence).

Ruling party

Mali People's Democratic Union (Union démocratique du peuple malien). *Secretary-general* Gen. Moussa Traoré. *Political secretary* Djibril Diallo.

Justice

The Supreme Court (established in Bamako in 1969) has both judicial and administrative powers. There is a system of regional tribunals and local juges de paix, and a Court of Appeal. The death penalty is in force. There were no executions between 1985 and mid-1988.

National symbols

Flag. Tricolour with vertical stripes of green, yellow and red.

Festivals. 20 Jan. (Armed Forces Day); 1 May (Labour Day); 25 May (Africa Day, anniversary of the OAU's foundation); 22 Sep. (Independence Day); 19 Nov. (Anniversary of the 1968 coup).

Vehicle registration plate. RMM.

INTERNATIONAL RELATIONS

Affiliations

NAM; OAU; ACP; ICO; Francophonie.

Defence

Total Armed Forces: 7,300 (all services form part of the army). Terms of service: conscription (inclusive for civil purposes), two years (selective).
Army: 6,900; 21 main battle tanks (T-34), 18 light tanks (Type 62).
Navy: under 100.
Air Force: 400; 27 combat aircraft (Mig-17F/-19/-21).
Para-military: 1,800 (Gendarmerie).

ECONOMY

Currency

The unit is the CFA franc, divided into 100 centimes.

National finance

Balance of payments. The balance of payments (current account, 1987) was a deficit of $313 million.

Gross Domestic Product

Estimated total GDP US$1,960 million, per capita US$180 (ranking 118 in the world by size).

Economically active population. The total number of persons active in the economy was 3,100,000.

Sector	% of workforce	% of GDP
industry	1	12
agriculture	80	54
services*	19	35

* services figure includes elements unassigned to other categories.

Energy and mineral resources

Minerals. Gold; marble (at Bafoulabé); phosphates; kaolin; salt; limestone (at Diamou); uranium. Bauxite; iron ore; manganese; tin and copper deposits are known but not exploited.

Electricity. Capacity: 92,000 kW; production: 165 million kWh; 20 kWh per capita (1988).

Bioresources

Agriculture. 80% of Mali's land area is desert or semi-desert and most activity is confined to the riverine area irrigated by the Niger. The main crops are millet; sorghum; rice; maize; peanuts. Main cash crops are peanuts; cotton; livestock.
Crop production: (1986 in 1,000 tons/tonnes) millet 1,415/1,284; sugar cane 231/210; groundnuts 132/120; rice 274/249; maize 220/200; seed cotton 215/195; cotton lint 77/70; cassava 84/76; sweet potatoes 63/57.
Livestock numbers: (1987) cattle 4.47 million; horses 62,000; asses 550,000; sheep 5.7 million; goats 5.5 million; camels 241,000; chickens 15 million.

Forestry. 7% of the land in Mali is forested. Production: (1985) was 173 million ft^3/4.9 million m^3.

Fisheries. Total river catch: (1986) 66,138 tons/60,000 tonnes.

Industry and commerce

Industry. The main industries are small local consumer goods and processing; construction; phosphate; gold; fishing.

Commerce. Exports: US$260 million, including livestock; peanuts; dried fish; cotton; skins. Imports: US$493 million, including textiles; vehicles; petroleum products; machinery; sugar; cereals. Countries exported to were mostly franc zone and

Western Europe; imports came from mostly franc zone and Western Europe.

Trade with UK. Mali imported UK goods worth £12,732,000; exports to UK totalled £2,240,000.

Tourism. (1986) 54,000 visitors.

COMMUNICATIONS

Railways

There are 399 miles/642 km of railways.

Roads

There are 8,075 miles/13,004 km of roads, of which 1,021 miles/1,644 km are bituminized.

Aviation

Air Mali provides domestic services (main airport is at Bamako-Senou). Passengers: (1982) 79,000.

Shipping

1,127 miles/1,815 km of the inland waterways are navigable.

Telecommunications

There are 9,500 telephones. The domestic system is poor but improving through expansion of radio relay systems. There are 300,000 radios and 1,000 televisions (1986). The state controls the radio broadcasting system and also transmits a small number of television programmes (since 1983).

EDUCATION AND WELFARE

Education

Schools. In 1982 there were 1,558 primary and intermediate schools with 364,382 pupils and 10,912 teachers (one per 33 pupils); 20 senior schools with 13,227 pupils and 890 teachers (one per 15 pupils). There were also 11 technical schools with 12,612 students.

Higher education. In 1979 there were seven higher education establishments with a total of 5,792 students and 491 teachers (one per 11 students).

Literacy. 10%.

Health

There are 12 hospitals and 772 health centres and dispensaries with a total of 3,200 beds (one per 2,769 people). There are 319 doctors (one per 27,957 people) and 1,312 nursing staff.

MALTA

Repubblika ta' Malta

(Republic of Malta)

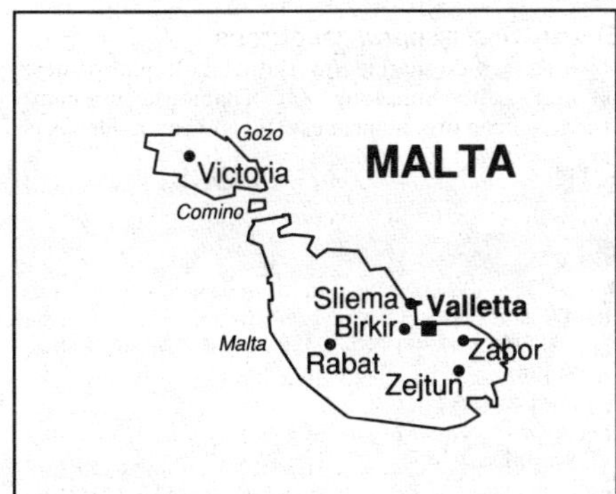

GEOGRAPHY

The 122 miles²/316 km² Maltese archipelago in the central Mediterranean Sea consists of the islands of Malta (95 miles²/246 km²), Gozo (26 miles²/67 km²) and Comino (1 mile²/2.7 km²) together with the uninhabited islets of Cominotto, Filfla and St Paul. The low-lying topography of these islands reaches a high point of 801 ft/244 m on the island of Malta. Natural harbours and rocky coves indent the coastlines of the inhabited islands. Soil conditions are poor, mostly shallow and suffer from the combined effects of high temperatures and the absence of regular drainage. 38% of the land is arable but there is no woodland growth.

Climate

Mediterranean with hot, dry summers and cool, rainy winters. Rainfall is concentrated in the period Oct-Mar., averaging approximately 19.7 in/500 mm a year. Valletta: Jan. 55°F/12.8°C. July 78°F/25.6°C. Average annual rainfall 22.7 in/578 mm.

Cities and towns

Sliema	20,071
Birkirkara	18,041
Qormi	17,130
Valletta (capital)	14,013

Population

Total population is 347,000 of which 85.4% live in urban areas. Population density is 2,844 persons per mile²/1,099 per km². Ethnic composition: approximately 94% are native islanders, of mixed Arabic, Sicilian, Norman, Spanish, English and Italian racial origin.

Birth rate 1.7%. **Death rate** 0.93%. **Rate of population increase** 0.77%. **Age distribution** under 15 = 24.1%; over 65 = 9.9%. **Life expectancy** female 76; male 72; average 74.

Religion

98% of the population are Roman Catholic. Most of the remaining 2% belong to the Anglican Communion.

Language

English and Maltese are the official languages. Maltese is a semitic tongue of the Southern Central branch related to Arabic dialects spoken in Algeria and Tunisia. Maltese is the only Arabic idiom to use the Latin alphabet.

HISTORY

Successively under Phoenician, Carthaginian, Greek and Roman rule, Malta later fell to the Arabs (AD 870), was conquered by Norman Sicily (1090) and then by Spain (1282), before being granted by the Habsburg Emperor Charles V to the Knights Hospitallers (1530). Surrendered to Bonapartist France (1798), the island was quickly taken by the British (1800), who reneged on a pledge to return it to the Knights and were confirmed in possession by the Congress of Vienna (1815). Of enhanced strategic importance following the opening of the Suez Canal (1869), Malta became a major British base. It received its first constitution in 1887 and a representative assembly in 1921. From 1929 the British authorities became embroiled in conflict with the Catholic Church and in local constitutional disputes, as Mussolini's Italy laid claim to the island. During World War II Malta withstood heavy bombing by the Axis powers and was awarded the George Cross (1942).

Granted self-government in 1947, Malta suffered from British naval cutbacks and in Feb. 1956 voted by 3:1 for full integration with Britain, as proposed by the then ruling Malta Labour Party (MLP) led by Dom Mintoff. UK reservations later caused both the MLP and the Nationalist Party (NP) to opt for full independence, which was achieved in Sept. 1964 under an NP government (1962–71), as a 10-year defence and financial agreement with Britain came into force. An association agreement with the European Communities (EC), operative from Apr. 1971, aided the island's development, especially as a tourist centre. Assisted by the lifting of a Catholic Church proscription on the MLP, Mintoff returned to power in 1971 (and was re-elected in 1976). In Mar. 1972 the 1964 agreement with Britain was replaced by a seven-year arrangement giving both Britain and NATO use of Malta's facilities in return for higher rent and aid. Malta became a Republic within the Commonwealth in 1974 and under Mintoff's leadership developed relations with Communist and Arab states, notably Libya. On the final withdrawal of British/NATO forces (Mar. 1979), Malta declared its neutrality and non-alignment. Following tensions with Libya over offshore rights, Malta secured an Italian guarantee of its neutrality (Sept. 1980), to which other countries, including the Soviet Union, later subscribed.

Mintoff and the MLP retained a parliamentary majority in the 1981 elections, but with fewer popular votes than the NP. In protest, the latter boycotted the House of Representatives for 15 months, until agreement was reached on constitutional amendments to the effect that a party winning a majority of votes would if necessary be allocated additional seats to enable it to govern. Having concluded a controversial pact providing for Libyan training of Malta's armed forces, Mintoff retired in Dec. 1984 and was succeeded as MLP leader and prime minister by Carmelo Mifsud Bonnici. In the May 1987 elections the MLP retained 34 seats and the NP 31, but with 48.9% and 50.9% of the vote respectively. Accordingly, the NP was awarded four bonus seats, enabling it to form a government under Edward Fenech Adami, committed to economic liberalization and full EC membership. In April 1989, Vincent Tabone was elected president.

CONSTITUTION AND GOVERNMENT

Executive and legislature

The (largely ceremonial) head of state is the president, elected for a five-year term, most recently in Apr. 1989, by the legislature, the 65-member House of Representatives. The president appoints the prime minister and, on the latter's advice, the other members of the government. The House is elected for a five-year term (subject to dissolution) by direct universal adult suffrage under a system of proportional representation (last elections 9 May 1987).

Present government

President Vincent Tabone

Prime Minister, Minister of Foreign Affairs Dr Edward Fenech Adami

Other Principal Ministers Dr Guido De Marco (Deputy Prime Minister; Interior; Justice); Dr George Bonello Dupuis (Finance).

Justice

The Constitution provides for Superior Courts, one of which is known as the Constitutional Court and which has the jurisdiction to hear and determine disputes over membership of the House of Representatives and appeals from other courts on constitutional, electoral and certain other matters. The Chief Justice, Judges and the Attorney General are appointed by the president on the advice of the prime minister. The death penalty is in force only for exceptional crimes. There were no executions between 1985 and mid-1988.

Prisons. There are 68 prisoners.

National symbols

Flag. Two vertical stripes of white and red with a grey George Cross edged with red in the upper hoist.

Festivals. 31 Mar. (National Day); 1 May (May Day); 13 Sep. (Republic Day).

Vehicle registration plate. M.

INTERNATIONAL RELATIONS

Affiliations

Commonwealth; NAM; Council of Europe.

Defence

Total Armed Forces: 1,216. Terms of service: voluntary.

Task Force: 751.

Armed Forces of Malta: 465.

Para-military: 700.

ECONOMY

Currency

The unit is the Maltese lira, divided into 100 cents.

National finance

Budget. The 1987 budget (in US$) was for expenditure (current and capital) of 762 million and revenue of 639 million.

Inflation. (1987) 0.4%.

Gross Domestic Product

Estimated total GDP US$1,600 million, per capita US$4,310 (ranking 124 in the world by size).

Economically active population. The total number of persons active in the economy was 125,000; unemployed: 4.4%.

Sector	% of workforce
industry	32
agriculture	4
services*	64

* services figure includes elements unassigned to other categories.

Energy and mineral resources

Oil and gas. An offshore oil exploration programme was begun in 1988.
Minerals. Limestone; salt.
Electricity. Capacity: 328,000 kW; production: 1,010 million kWh; 2,740 kWh per capita (1988)

Bioresources

Agriculture. The main products are potatoes; cauliflowers; grapes; wheat; barley; tomatoes; citrus fruits; cut flowers; green peppers; pigs; poultry.
Crop production: (1987 value in Lm) potatoes 589,589; seeds, cut flowers and plants 518,774; wine 21,458; hides and skins 23,281.
Livestock numbers: (1987) cattle 14,000; pigs 95,000; sheep 5,000; goats 5,000; poultry 1 million.
Fisheries. Annual catch: (1986) 1,176 tons/1,067 tonnes.

Industry and commerce

Industry. The main industries are tourism; ship repair; clothing; construction; food manufacturing; textiles; footwear; beverages; tobacco.
Commerce. Exports: (1987) US$600 million, including clothing; textiles; footwear; ships. Imports: US$1,130 million, including food; petroleum; non-food raw materials. Countries exported to were West Germany 31%; UK 14%; Italy 14%. Imports came from West Germany 19%; UK 17%; Italy 17%; US 11%.
Trade with UK. In 1988 Malta imported UK goods worth £121,696,000; exports to UK totalled £40,189,000.
Tourism. (1987) 745,943 visitors.

COMMUNICATIONS

Railways
There are no railways.

Roads
There are 801 miles/1,290 km of roads, of which 686 miles/1,104 km are concrete or bituminized.

Aviation
Air Malta Co Ltd provides international services (international airport is at Luqa, 5 miles/8 km from Valletta). Passengers: (1984) 364,000.

Shipping
The marine ports of Malta are Valletta and Marsaxlokk. There are 261 merchant marine ships of 1,000 GRT or over. Freight loaded: (1987) 216,000 tons/196,000 tonnes; unloaded: 1.8 million tons/1.6 million tonnes.

Telecommunications
There are 153,000 telephones and a modern automatic system centred in Valletta. There are 26,973 radios and 136,302 televisions (1988). Radio Malta and Televison Malta broadcasts, in Maltese and English, are supplemented by Radio Mediterranean and the Valletta-based Voice of the Mediterranean broadcasting operation which is owned jointly by the Maltese and Libyan governments.

EDUCATION AND WELFARE

Education
Schools. Compulsory from age five to 16 and free in government schools (25,337 pupils in 80 schools). There are 6,253 pupils in eight Junior Lyceums and 31 other government secondary schools with a total of 7,358 pupils. Three techncial institutes have 1,094 students with 5,698 in the 12 trade schools for boys and six for girls. There are also 80 private schools with a total population of 21,100 pupils.
Universities. 2,500 students at the University of Malta.
Literacy. 83%

Health
There are 710 doctors (one per 523 people) and seven hospitals with 3,217 beds (one per 115 people).

MARIANA ISLANDS, NORTHERN

Commonwealth of the Northern Mariana Islands

GEOGRAPHY

The Northern Mariana Islands lie in the North Pacific Ocean, covering an area of 184 miles^2/477 km^2. The southern islands are limestone with fringing coral reefs; the northern islands are volcanic. The capital is Saipan.

Climate
Tropical marine, moderated by north-east trade winds; little seasonal temperature variation. The dry season is Dec.-July; the rainy season is July-Oct.

Population
Total population (1989 est.) 21,312.
Birth rate 4.2%. **Death rate** 0.6%. **Rate of population increase** 2.3%
Life expectancy female 70; male 65.

Religion
Christianity (Roman Catholic), also traditional beliefs.

Language
English, Chamorro and Carolinian.

HISTORY

Habitation of the Mariana Islands dates back to 1500 BC. Spanish explorers arrived in the 16th century, but Spanish colonial rule did not begin until 1668. Resistance by the indigenous Chamorro people was finally crushed in 1681. After the 1898 Spanish-American War, Spain ceded Guam to the United States and sold the rest of the Marianas to Germany. With the outbreak of World War I Japan took possession of the islands.

In 1920 the League of Nations mandated control of Micronesia to Japan. In Aug. 1944 Japanese forces in the Marianas were defeated by the US and in 1945 the US Navy assumed control of Micronesia.

In 1947 the UN established the Trust Territory of the Pacific Islands, a 'strategic trust' under US administration. The Northern Marianas remained under US naval control until 1962. In a plebiscite in June 1975 the people of the Northern Marianas voted to become a self-governing US 'commonwealth' territory separate from the rest of the Micronesian territories. The new status came into force in Jan. 1978, elections for the territory's governorship and bicameral legislature having been held in Dec. 1977. In 1984 the US government entered into negotiations with landowners on Tinian Island over the use of their land for military purposes. In Nov. 1986 the Northern Mariana islanders were granted US citizenship. However the UN Security Council had yet to officially terminate the UN trusteeship due to uncertainty over the future status of another Micronesian territory, Palau.

CONSTITUTION AND GOVERNMENT

The Commonwealth of the Northern Mariana Islands is a commonwealth associated with the US. It has a governor elected by popular vote, and a bicameral legislature consisting of a nine-member Senate elected for a four-year term and a fifteen-member House of Representatives elected for a two-year term.

Leader Pedro P. Tenorio, Governor since 1978.

National symbols

Flag. Blue with a white five-pointed star superimposed on the grey silhouette of a latte stone (a traditional foundation stone used in building) in the centre.

National holiday. 8 Jan (Commonwealth Day).

ECONOMY

The economy is dependent on tourism, which employs about 10% of the workforce, and on support from the US. The agricultural sector is made up of cattle ranches and small farms producing coconuts, breadfruit, tomatoes and melons. Industry is small-scale – mostly handicrafts and fish processing.

Currency

The US dollar.

COMMUNICATIONS

There are ports at Saipan, Rota and Tinian; six airports, three with permanent surface runways, and 186 miles/300 km of road. There are two AM radio stations, but no FM or television stations.

MARSHALL ISLANDS

GEOGRAPHY

The Marshall Islands consist of two archipelagic island chains of 30 atolls and 1,152 islands, which include Bikini and Eniwetak, former US nuclear test sites. The total land area is 70 miles^2/181.3 km^2. The capital is Majuro.

Climate

Hot and humid, with wet season May-Nov. The islands border the typhoon belt.

Population

Total population (1989 est.) 42,018, almost entirely Micronesian.

Birth rate 3.9%. **Death rate** 0.5%. **Rate of population increase** 3.4%. **Life expectancy** female 75; male 70.

Religion

Christian: Protestant.

Language

English (official) universally spoken; two major Marshallese dialects; Japanese.

HISTORY

Human settlement in the Marshall Islands dates back about 1000 BC. Spanish seafarers reached the islands in 1529. An influx of American and European whalers, traders, and missionaries in the 19th century caused major social upheaval. The Marshalls were formally annexed by Spain in 1874, but in 1885 they became a German protectorate. With the onset of World War I Japan took possession of the islands. In 1920 the League of Nations gave Japan a mandate to administer Micronesia. At the end of the Pacific War in 1945 the US Navy took control.

In 1947 the UN established the Trust Territory of the Pacific Islands, under US control. From 1946–58 the US used Bikini and other atolls in the Marshalls to test nuclear weapons.

Preparations for Micronesian self-government led to a referendum in July 1978 on a common constitution for the whole territory. The Marshallese voted against, and in 1979 the Republic of the Marshall Islands' separate constitution took effect. In 1982 over 1,000 dispossessed landowners from Kwajalein Atoll launched Operation Home-coming, a four-month protest against the US military's use of the atoll as a missile testing range.

In Oct. 1986 a Compact of Free Association between the Marshall Islands and US governments came into effect. Under the Compact the Marshalls would be internally self-governing whilst the US would retain responsibility for foreign relations and defence. The Compact also ensured that the US would maintain its military bases in the islands for at least 15 years and annually provide $30 million in economic aid. US administration of Micronesia formally ended in Nov. 1986 but the UN Security

Council had yet to formally terminate the trusteeship owing to uncertainty over the future status of the Micronesian territory of Palau.

CONSTITUTION AND GOVERNMENT

The Marshall Islands form a constitutional government in free association with the US; the Compact of Free Association came into force in Oct 1986. The Constitution dates from May 1979. There is parliamentary government, with legislative authority vested in the 33-member Nitijela (parliament) and a Council of Iroij (chiefs), a consultative body.

Leader Amata Kabua (president since 1979).

National symbols

Flag. Blue with two stripes radiating from the lower hoist-side corner – one orange, one white. There is a white star with four large rays and 20 small rays on the hoist side above the two stripes.

National holiday. 1 May (Proclamation of the Republic of the Marshall Islands).

ECONOMY

The economy is heavily dependent on agriculture and tourism, and on grants from the US government. The islands have few natural resources, and the tourist industry is the major source of foreign exchange. The most important commercial crops are coconuts; tomatoes; melons; breadfruit.

Currency

The US dollar.

COMMUNICATIONS

There are no railways or airports. The major islands (Majuro, Kwajalein) have tarmac or concrete roads, otherwise roads are surfaced in stone, coral or laterite. Majuro and Ebeye have telephone systems, and the islands are interconnected by short-wave radio. There is one AM and two FM radio stations and one TV station, and a US government satellite communications system on Kwajalein.

MARTINIQUE

GEOGRAPHY

Martinique is a Caribbean islands with a total area of 425 miles^2/1,100 km^2. The terrain is mountainous with an indented coastline. There is a dormant volcano. Martinique is subject to hurricanes and flooding. The capital is Fort-de-France.

Climate

Tropical, moderated by trade winds. Rainy season June-Oct.

Population

Total population (1989 est.) 331,511.

Birth rate 1.8%. **Death rate** 0.7%. **Rate of population increase** 0.4%

Life expectancy female 77; male 71.

Religion

Christianity. Mainly Roman Catholic, with a small Hindu minority.

Language

French, creole patois.

HISTORY

The earliest inhabitants of Martinique were Arawak Indians who were succeeded by Caribs moving from the south. The island was first discovered by Europeans during Columbus's voyages, but no attempts were made to settle on Martinique until the French colonized the island in 1635. African slaves were imported as labour for large plantations producing sugar and coffee. Martinique was occupied by the British in 1762–63 and again during the Revolutionary and Napoleonic wars, and was finally confirmed as French territory in 1816. Slavery was abolished in 1848. In 1902 the island's capital, St Pierre, was completely destroyed during the volcanic eruption of Mt Pelée.

In 1947 Martinique became a department of France. Demands for greater autonomy were expressed during the 1950s by the Parti progressiste martiniquais (PPM), founded and led by Aimé Césaire. Rioting in 1959 led to the French government devolving some powers in 1960, but a plebiscite in 1962 produced a majority in favour of retaining departmental status. In 1974 Martinique also became a region of France and in 1982 was granted a measure of greater autonomy. The left-wing parties, led by the PPM, succeeded in gaining a small majority on the new Regional Council, but the General Council remained controlled by the right-wing and centre parties. In 1986 the left-wing parties maintained their control of the Regional Council, but in elections to the General Council in 1988, although they secured a majority of the seats for the first time, they failed to gain the presidency of the council.

CONSTITUTION AND GOVERNMENT

Martinique is an overseas department of France, and as such shares the French constitution dating from 28 Sept. 1958. It has a prefect appointed by Paris; a popularly elected General Council of 36 members, and a Regional Council, which includes all members of the Council and the locally elected deputies and senators to the French parliament.

Leader Jean Jouandet, Commissioner of the Republic since 1987.

National symbols

Flag. The flag of France is used.

National holiday. 14 July (Bastille Day).

ECONOMY

The economy is based on sugar cane, bananas, tourism and light industry. Most sugar cane is now used for the production of rum. Most basic foodstuffs are imported from France, leading to a chronic trade deficit. France gives annual aid. Tourism has become more important than agriculture as a source of foreign exchange. Unemployment is a problem.

Currency

The French franc.

COMMUNICATIONS

There is a port at Fort-de-France; three airports, one with a permanent surface runway; there are no railways. There are 1,043 miles/1,680 km of road, 807 miles/1,300 km of which are paved. There is a telephone system, inter-island radio relay links to Guadeloupe, Dominica and St Lucia; two Atlantic Ocean satellite antennae, one AM and six FM radio stations and ten TV stations.

MAURITANIA

Al-Jumhuriyah al-Islamiyah al-Muritaniyah (Islamic Republic of Mauritania)

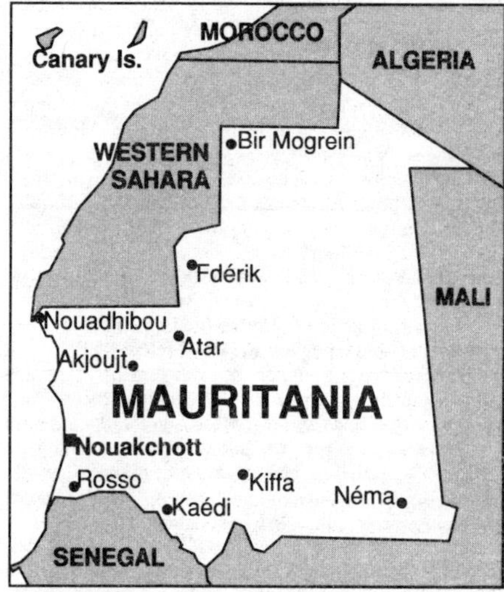

GEOGRAPHY

Located in north-west Africa, Mauritania covers an area of 397,850 miles^2/1,030,700 km^2 divided into 12 regions and the densely populated capital district of Nouakchott. To the north, the Saharan desert (47% of the total surface area) rises to 3,002 ft/915 m at Kiediet Ijill, an isolated peak surrounded by desolate low-lying plains and sand dunes. The coastal plains lie less than 148 ft/45 m above sea level; inland, the grassland plateaux are dissected by a number of (seasonal) wadis. The south to south-west-draining Sénégal river provides Mauritania with its most fertile agricultural land. 1% of the land is arable, 5% is forested.

Climate

Arid tropical conditions with minimal and unreliable rainfall averages. Tornadoes may accompany the rainy season in the south from May-Sept. Rainfall decreases north and west from 12.6 in/320 mm in the Sahelian region to below 0.98 in/25 mm on the coast. Saharan temperatures range from 32°F/0°C to above 120°F/49°C. Nouakchott: Jan. 71°F/21.7°C. July 82°F/27.8°C. Average annual rainfall 6.2 in/158 mm.

Cities and towns

Nouakchott (capital)	134,986
Nouadhibou	21,961
Kaedi	20,848
Zouerate	17,474
Rosso	16,466
Atar	16,326

Population

Total population is 1,916,000 of which 34% live in urban areas. Population density is 4.8 persons per mile^2/1.8 persons per km^2. Ethnic divisions: 40% mixed Maur-Black; 30% Maur; 30% Black.
Birth rate 4.65%. **Death rate** 2.05%. **Rate of population increase** 2.6%. **Age distribution** under 15 = 44.2%; over 65 = 3.1%. **Life expectancy** female 48; male 44; average 46.

Religion

The overwhelming majority of Mauritanians are Sunni Muslims (99%) of the Quadiriyah sect. There are approximately 6,150 Roman Catholics.

Language

French is the official language and Hassaniya Arabic is the national language spoken by over 80% of the total population. The Tukulor and Fulani peoples of the south speak Fulfulde. Other ethnolinguistic groups include the Soninke (Sarakole) and Wolof tribes of the South Sénégal river valley.

HISTORY

There is archaeological evidence of neolithic settled agriculture in the (then more fertile) Saharan areas of what is now Mauritania. From the 7th to the 11th century, southern Mauritania was part of the medieval West African states of Ghana and Takrur, while Sanhadja Berbers, who arrived in the 3rd century, formed states in the north. In the mid-11th century, Mauritania formed part of the Islamic religious Almoravid state, which subjugated Ghana, Morocco and western Algeria. The northern Almoravid empire, which by 1091 also dominated Muslim Spain, had collapsed by 1150. The strength of Islam in Mauritania has its origins in this period, while in the 13th and 14th centuries the south of Mauritania was influenced by the medieval state of Mali. In the 13th, 14th and 15th centuries Mauritania was invaded by bedouin Arab Maquil tribes, whose growing rivalry late in the 17th century with the Sanhadja Berbers led ultimately to a 30-year war, the Char Bouba, which culminated in the defeat of the Berbers in 1674. The

Hassaniya language of the principal Maquil tribe spread through the upper (Maquil bedouin and Sanhadja berber) castes of a highly stratified Moorish society, with Berber-Negroid commoners and an abid (slave) class. The Chinguetti oasis was the chief religious and political centre of Mauritania in this period, essentially operating as a loose confederation of pastoral nomadic sheikdoms.

From the 15th century the Portuguese and Spanish established trading settlements on the coast. They were followed by the French, who at first set up posts principally along the Sénégal river, but gradually (notably by the Treaty of Paris in 1814) gained formal control of the coastal region. France established a protectorate in 1903, incorporating the 'civil territory of Mauritania' within French West Africa in 1904, and crushing the remaining Moorish emirs by 1910 (in parallel with the extension of French control of Morocco). In 1920, Mauritania became a French colony, but was administered from St Louis (in Senegal) and governed by a system of indirect rule which allowed traditional rulers to retain their privileges (and the caste system).

On 28 Nov. 1958, Mauritania became an autonomous state, electing to remain within the French Community. Full independence outside the Community, as the Islamic Republic of Mauritania, was declared at Nouakchott on 28 Nov. 1960. The Mauritanian constitution came into force in May 1961, and the leader of the Mauritanian Regroupment Party (PRM), Mokhtar Ould Daddah, became president in Aug. 1961. In Dec. 1961 the PRM merged with other parties to form the Mauritanian People's Party (PPM), which subsequently became the only legal party by an amendment to the constitution. Morocco recognized the independence of Mauritania only in 1969, having harboured its own 'Greater Morocco' aspirations. In 1973 Mauritania left the franc zone, and also joined the Arab League; the country's Arab identity has been resisted and resented within the black African population, with riots notably over making Arabic an official language (in 1966), and over a resolution of Arab-Islamic identity (1979). After Spain's withdrawal from Spanish (Western) Sahara on 28 Feb. 1976, Mauritania and Morocco occupied the area; and under an agreement reached between them in Apr. 1976, Mauritania incorporated the southern part of the territory under the name of Tiris el Gharbia. Mauritania, however, renounced its claims and withdrew three years later, signing a peace treaty on 5 Aug. 1979 with the Polisario movement, whose Saharan Arab Democratic Republic (SADR) was recognized by Mauritania in Feb. 1984. Mauritania has consistently adopted a neutral attitude to the continuing conflict between Morocco and Polisario, but cannot effectively police the country's long borders, and Polisario use of Mauritanian territory has often led to tension between Morocco and Mauritania.

A military coup on 10 July 1978, provoked by hostility to the war then continuing with Polisario, deposed Ould Daddah, suspended the constitution and dissolved the National Assembly; the regime of Col. Moustapha Ould Saleck was in turn overthrown in a coup on 6 April 1979. Under a Military Committee for national Salvation (CMSN), the government was headed by Prime Minister Lt. Col Ahmed Ould Bouceif, whose death in an aircraft on 27 May brought Lt. Col Ould Heydalla into office. In a coup on 4 Jan. 1980, Heydalla took over the presidency, with a new constitution making the president the executive head of government. He survived a series of attempted coups until 12 Dec. 1984, when a successful and bloodless coup was led by the Army Chief of Staff (and former prime minister) Col Moaouia Ould Sidi Mohamed Taya. Promising democratization, the Taya regime arranged municipal elections in principal towns in Dec. 1986 where, for the first time, voters could choose between rival (albeit non-party) candidates; in the period 1960–78, ie prior to the military takeover, all polls had involved the unopposed return of PPM lists. Taya also restored relations with Morocco and with Libya, both countries having been previously accused of involvement in attempts to destabilize the Heydalla regime. Relations with Senegal were seriously strained in 1989, and diplomatic relations were broken off in Aug. The immediate cause of the dispute was the death of two people in April over competing claims to farming rights on the common border. The dispute quickly assumed an ethnic dimension, with violent attacks on nationals of each country resident in the other costing the lives of many hundreds of people. The Mauritanian authorities were subsequently accused of forcibly expelling up to 40,000 black Mauritanians into Senegal (this group was a minority in Mauritania where the Moorish population dominated society). Arillery fire was exchanged across the Senegal River boundary in Jan. 1990. The powerful interior minister, Col. Djibril Ould Abdullah, who was seen as an impediment to any resoluion of the problem, was removed from the Council of Ministers and the CMSN in Feb. 1990.

CONSTITUTION AND GOVERNMENT

Executive and legislature

The chairman of the Military Council of National Salvation is president of the Republic and holds executive power under the 1978 Constitutional Charter, which suspended the National Assembly. The president appoints the council of ministers.

Present government

President of the Republic; Chairman of the Military Council of National Salvation; Prime Minister; Minister of Defence Col. Moaouia Ould Sidi Mohamed Taya

Members of the Military Committee for National Salvation Lt.-Col. N'Diaye Kane (permanent secretary); Col Cheikh Ould Boyda; Col Ahmedou Ould Abdallah; Maj. Cheikh Sidi Ahmed Ould Babamine; Maj. Ahmed Ould Minnih; Lt.-Col. Ann Amadou Babaly; Lt.-Col Gabriel Cimper; Lt.-Col Moulaye Ould Boukhreiss; Lt.-Col Brahim Ould Alioune N'Diaye; Lt.-Col Sidina Ouir; Lt.-Col Diallo Mohammed; Lt.-Col Sidi Ould Mohamed Lemine; Maj. Sidiya Ould Mohamed Yehya; Maj. Ahmedou Haida; Maj. Mohamed Ould Lekhal; Maj. Sidi Ahmed Ould Boylil; Maj. Sidibi Toumani; Capt. Jiddou Ould Haki; Capt. Diop Djibril; Capt. Niang Arouna; Capt. Ely Ould Mohamed Fall.

Principal members of the Council of Ministers Maj. Cheikh Ahmed Ould Bada (Foreign Affairs and Co-operation); Col. Mohammed Sidina Ould Sidya (Interior); Hamdi Samba Diop (Justice); Mohamed Ould Nany (Economy and Finance); Ahmedou Ould Sidi (Secretary of State in charge of Maghreb affairs).

Justice

The juridicial system is based on Islamic jurisprudence. There are tribunaux de première instance, an Appeal Court and a Supreme Court in

Nouakchott. The death penalty is in force. There were three executions between 1985 and mid-1988. The offences were murder.

National symbols

Flag. Green, bearing a yellow crescent with its horns pointing upwards and a yellow five-pointed star above it.

Festivals. 1 May (Labour Day); 25 May (African Liberation Day, anniversary of the OAU's foundation); 28 Nov. (National Day).

Vehicle registration plate. RIM.

INTERNATIONAL RELATIONS

Affiliations

NAM; Arab League; ICO; OAU; AMU; ACP; Francophonie.

Defence

Total Armed Forces: 11,000. Terms of service: voluntary; conscription (two years) authorized.
Army: 10,400.
Navy: 350; eight inshore patrol craft.
Air Force: 250; five combat aircraft (BN-2 Defender).
Para-military: 6,400.

ECONOMY

Currency

The unit is the ouguiya, divided into five khoums.

National finance

Budget. The 1986 budget (in US$) was for expenditure (current and capital) of 273 million and revenue of 265 million.

Balance of payments. The balance of payments (current account, 1987) was a deficit of $164 million (est.).

Inflation. (1987) 8.8%.

Gross Domestic Product

Estimated total GDP US$840 million, per capita US$440 (ranking 149 in the world by size).

Economically active population. The total number of persons active in the economy was 465,000; unemployed: 50%.

Sector	% of GDP
industry	22
agriculture	37
services*	41

* services figure includes elements unassigned to other categories.

Energy and mineral resources

Minerals. 10.5 million tons/9.5 million tonnes of iron ore were extracted in 1984 from the substantial deposits around Zouérate. SOMIMA, a nationalized mining company, reopened the Akjoujit copper mine in 1983. Gypsum mining is also a feature.

Electricity. Capacity: 189,000 kW; production: 135 million kWh; 70 kWh per capita (1988).

Bioresources

Agriculture. Cultivated land is centred around the Sénégal river valley in the southern part of the country. 1% of the land is arable and 38% is meadow or pasture.

Crop production: (1986 in 1,000 tons/tonnes) millet 104/94; rice 18/16; dates 13/12; groundnuts 2.2/2; sweet potatoes 2.2/2; potatoes 1.1/1; maize 1.1/1.

Livestock numbers: (1987) sheep 3.95 million; goats 3.06 million; cattle 1 million; camels 800,000; asses 149,000; horses 17,000.

Forestry. 5% of the land area is forested, with gum arabic, the main cash crop, derived from wild acacias.

Fisheries. Total catch in Mauritanian coastal waters approximately 385,805 tons/350,000 tonnes per annum, of which 55,115 tons/50,000 tonnes (1985) is landed. Inland waters yield a further 11,023 tons/10,000 tonnes.

Industry and commerce

Industry. Growth rate 5%. Ore production, fishing and agriculture constitute the main industries. The rich Mauritanian fishing grounds are subject to heavy and potentially threatening over-exploitation by foreigners.

Commerce. Exports: (1986) US$428 million or 51% of GDP; imports: $329 million for the same year or 39% of the GDP. Principal exports include iron ore 40%; processed fish; small quantities of gum arabic and gypsum; some cattle trading with Senegal. Imports include foodstuffs; consumer goods; petroleum products; capital goods.

Trade with UK. £7.26 million worth of goods were exported to the UK in 1988; £3.05 million worth of UK goods were imported.

Tourism. (1975) 20,700 tourists.

COMMUNICATIONS

Railways

There are 416 miles/670 km of railways (primarily for transporting iron ore).

Roads

There are about 4,555 miles/7,335 km of roads, of which about 956 miles/1,540 km are concrete or bituminized.

Aviation

Air Afrique provides international services and Air Mauritanie provides domestic services (international airports are at Nouadhibou and Nouakchott). Passengers: (1984) 158,000.

Shipping

The marine ports are Nouadhibou and Nouakchott. Goods loaded: (1985) 11 million tons/10 million tonnes; unloaded: 535,718 tons/486,000 tonnes.

Telecommunications

There are 5,200 telephones and a poor system of telecommunications. There are 260,000 radios, served by broadcasting in five languages by the stateowned ORTM, and 1,000 televisions (1986), in Nouakchott, for which there are a limited number of transmissions.

EDUCATION AND WELFARE

Education

School population. 150,833 excluding 4,340 students in higher education.

Schools. Of the total school population, 119,337 pupils attended primary schools; 27,924 were at secondary schools; 3,572 at vocational or teacher-training institutions.

Universities. In 1984 a total of 984 students were registered at the University of Nouakchott.

Literacy. 17%.

Health

(1984) 170 doctors, 129 midwives, 16 pharmacists, eight dentists and 582 nursing staff worked in 13 hospitals and clinics with 1,325 beds.

MAURITIUS

Mauritius

GEOGRAPHY

Situated approximately 497 miles/800 km east of Madagascar, the island state of Mauritius comprises the main island, 20 adjacent islets and the dependencies of the Agalega and Rodrigues Islands and the Cargados Carajos shoals (St Brandon). It has an area of 718 miles^2/1,860 km^2. The island of Mauritius itself is volcanic in origin, fringed by coral reefs and rising to elevations of 1,804–2,395 ft/550–730 m in the heavily dissected central upland plateau. To the west and south-west, Little Black River Mt. climbs to 2,710 ft/826 m in the Black River-Savanne range. Savannah woodland predominates along the dry coastal plain. The two principal rivers are the Grand River South East and the Grand River North West, both major sources of hydroelectric power. Over 40% of the population inhabit the western urban strip from Curepipe to Port Louis. 54% of the land is arable and 31% is forested.

Climate

Humid, sub-tropical. Considerable variation between winter and summer. Most rain falls during the summer months ranging from 33.5 in/850 mm (annual total) in the north-west to 197 in/5,000 mm on the interior plateau. Temperatures decrease with increasing altitude, varying from 72–79°F/22–26°C on the coast to an annual average of 66°F/19°C at 1,968 ft/600 m. Mauritius lies within the Indian Cyclone belt. Port Louis: Jan. 73°F/22.8°C. July 81°F/27.2°C. Average annual rainfall 39 in/1,000mm.

Cities and towns

Port-Louis (capital)	136,323
Beau Bassin/Rose Hill	91,786
Quatre Bornes	64,506
Curepipe	63,181
Vacoas-Phoenix	54,430

Population

Total population is 1,077,000 of which 41.1% live in urban areas. Population density is 1,500 persons per mile^2/509.6 per km^2. Ethnic divisions: 68% Indo-Mauritian; 27% Creole; 3% Sino-Mauritian; 2% Franco-Mauritian.

Birth rate 2.25%. **Death rate** 0.59%. **Rate of population increase** 1.66%. **Age distribution** under 15 = 30.6%; over 65 = 3.5% **Life expectancy** female 71; male 64; average 67.

Religion

At the last census in 1983, 52.5% of the population were Hindu (506,270); 25.7% were Roman Catholic (247,743); 12.9% were Muslim (160,190); 4.4% were Protestant (6,049 Church of England and Church of Scotland).

Language

The official language is English but creole-English (the Mauritian lingua franca), French, Hindi, Urdu, Bojpoori and Hakka are also spoken.

HISTORY

Visited by Arab, Malay, Portuguese and then Dutch sailors (15th–17th centuries) and briefly and unsuccessfully settled by the Dutch who imported slaves for ebony logging, Mauritius was settled by the French and their slaves from 1715 (under Compagnie des Indes administration to 1767, then under direct French government control). British conquest (1810) and the abolition of slavery (1835) were followed by the massive importation of indentured labour for the sugar plantations, mostly from India, while the Franco–Mauritian plantation owners struggled to maintain their privileges.

Indian workers formed the basis of the Labour Party (founded 1936) and a wave of strikes was bloodily suppressed, but from 1953 onwards the party was increasingly dominated by intellectuals and merchants. Among these new leaders Seewoosagur Ramgoolam emerged as Labour leader and successfully led demands for the introduction of ministerial government (1957) and universal suffrage (1959). As independence became the main political issue, the Parti mauricien social démocrate (PMSD) rallied Creole opposition, fearing Hindu domination. Ramgoolam brought together a coalition as the Independence Party, broadening his support by attracting Muslim and some Creole support, and won a decisive 39 seats in general elections (1967). The Assembly, which under the London constitutional conference agreement of Sept. 1965 was to vote on the country's future status, opted for independence, which duly followed (12 Mar. 1968).

After independence, Duval was brought into the governing coalition (1969–73) with broad support across all ethnic groups. From the early 1970s, a left-wing youth-based Mouvement militant mauricien (MMM) led by Paul Bérenger built up influence in the unions. The government postponed elections until 1976, declared a state of emergency (1971) and cracked down with arrests of MMM leaders and unionists to break a dock strike (Aug. 71) and to prevent disruption of a visit by Queen Elizabeth II (Mar. 1972).

Duval's PSMD left the coalition (Dec. 1973) over foreign policy differences, having tried to promote a pro-French stance and a conciliatory attitude towards South Africa. Ramgoolam, with the island enjoying an economic boom based on high sugar prices, lifted a number of the repressive security regulations and lowered the voting age to 18 in the run-up to elections (Dec. 1978). The MMM, calling for a republic, won 34 of the 70 seats, but was kept out of government by the reconstitution of the Labour-PSMD coalition (1976–82). Clampdowns on the MMM followed in July 1978 and again over strikes in the key sugar industry (Aug. 1979), as unemployment, inflation and unrest grew.

For the June 1982 elections, the MMM worked in alliance with a Labour splinter group, Harish Boodhoo's Parti socialiste mauricien (PSM). Together they swept the board (MMM 42, PSM 18), but the resulting government broke down when the MMM split; Bérenger's supporters, now favouring acceptance of an IMF austerity plan, expelled the party president and current prime minister, Anerood Jugnauth (Mar. 1983). The Prime Minister then formed his own party, the Mouvement socialiste militant (MSM), winning fresh elections (Aug. 1983) in alliance with Labour, the PMSD and the PSM, and subsequently forming an umbrella Alliance Party.

Jugnauth's government retained demands for the return of Diego Garcia atoll, ceded to the UK in 1965 and then given over for use as a US naval base. It also advocated the creation of an Indian Ocean zone of peace, but failed to get enough support in the Assembly for legislation to create a republic within the Commonwealth (Dec. 83).

Rocked by a drugs scandal when four Alliance MPs were arrested at Amsterdam airport carrying heroin (Dec. 85), the government was further weakened by resignations and a Labour Party split (Feb. 1986). With a series of IMF credit agreements supporting structural adjustment programmes, good sugar harvests in 1985–87, the growth of tourism and manufacturing and the creation of a regional financial services sector, Jugnauth was able to fight and win fresh elections primarily on his economic record (Aug. 1987). He became prime minister again, with Duval as his deputy and Alliance supporters holding 46 out of 70 Assembly seats. The MMM remained the main opposition to the left. Duval resigned over economic policy disagreements (Aug. 1988), taking the PMSD out of the government; he was arrested in June 1989 in connexion with his alleged involvement in a political assassination in 1970. Two attempts have been made on Jugnauth's life, in Nov. 1988 and Mar. 1989, both of which he blamed on the 'drugs mafia'.

CONSTITUTION AND GOVERNMENT

Executive and legislature

The head of state is the British monarch, represented by a governor general. The governor general appoints the prime minister and the council of ministers, who are responsible to the Assembly. The unicameral Legislative Assembly has 70 seats, 62 of them elected by universal adult suffrage for five years (last elections Aug. 1987).

Present government

Governor General Sir Veerasamy Ringadoo
Prime Minister; Minister of Defence, Internal Security, Information, Reform Institutions and External Relations Aneerood Jugnauth
Other principal Ministers Sir Satcam Boolell (Deputy Prime Minister and Constitutional Assistant; Foreign Affairs; Emigration; Justice and Attorney General); Seetanah Lutchmeenaraidoo (Finance); Dr Beergoonath Ghurburrun (Planning and Economic Development).

Justice

The death penalty is in force. There was one execution between 1985 and mid-1988. The offence was murder.

National symbols

Flag. The flag consists of four horizontal stripes of red, blue, yellow and green.
Festivals. 17 Feb. (Chinese Spring Festival); 12 Mar. (National Day); 1 May (Labour Day).
Vehicle registration plate. MS.

INTERNATIONAL RELATIONS

Affiliations

NAM; OAU; ACP; Commonwealth; Francophonie.

Defence

Para-military Special Mobile Force and Special Support Units.

ECONOMY

Currency

The unit is the rupee, divided into 100 cents.

National finance

Budget. The 1987 budget (in US$) was for expenditure (current and capital) of 414 million and revenue of 351 million.
Balance of payments. The balance of payments (current account, 1987) was a surplus of $47 million.
Inflation. (1987) 1%.

Gross Domestic Product

Estimated total GDP US$1,480 million, per capita US$1,280 (ranking 128 in the world by size).
Economically active population The total number of persons active in the economy was 335,000; unemployed: 10%.

Sector	% of workforce	% of GDP
industry	22	32
agriculture	27	15
services*	51	53

* services figure includes elements unassigned to other categories.

Energy and mineral resources

Electricity. Capacity: 233,000 kW; production: 423 million kWh; 380 kWh per capita (1988).

Bioresources

Agriculture. 54% of the total land area is considered arable, 4% is under permanent cultivation and 4% is meadow or pasture. Sugar production remains the dominant agricultural and industrial activity. Sugar cane occupies approximately 90% (204,480 acres/82,752 ha in 1987) of the cultivated land area and accounts for 40% of all export revenue.

Crop production: (1987 in tons/tonnes) sugar 761,837/691,134; molasses 208,897/189,510; potatoes 17,124/15,535; maize 4,260/3,865; tea 0.79 tons/7.15 million kg; tobacco 0.99 tons/0.9 million kg.

Livestock numbers: (1987) cattle 38,000; goats 95,000; poultry 2 million.

Forestry. 31% of the land area is forested (52,288 acres/21,161 ha total, of which plantations constitute about 28,910 acres/11,700 ha). Timber production: (1987) 987,180 ft^3/27,954 m^3.
Fisheries. Total catch (1987): 18,121 tons/16,439 tonnes.

Industry and commerce

Industry. Main industries include food (sugar) processing; textiles; clothing; chemical products; metal products; transport equipment; non-electrical machinery; tourism.
Commerce. Exports: (1986) US$676 million or 52% of GDP; imports: $684m in the same year or 53% of GDP. Principal exports include textiles 44%; sugar 40%; light manufactures 10%. Imports include manufactured goods 50%; capital equipment 17%; foodstuffs 13%; petroleum products 8%; chemicals 7%. Trading partners are (imports and exports) EC countries; US; (imports only) South Africa; Japan.
Trade with UK. Mauritius imported UK goods worth £38.5 million; exports to UK totalled £186.2 million.
Tourism. (1987) 207,560 visitors.

COMMUNICATIONS

Railways

There are no railways.

Roads

There are 1,115 miles/1,795 km of roads, of which 1,004 miles/1,615 km are bituminized.

Aviation

Air Mauritius provides international services (main airport is Sir Seewoosagur Ramgoolam International Airport at Plaisance). Passengers: (1986) 232,000.

Shipping

Port Louis is Mauritius' port. There are seven merchant marine ships of 1,000 GRT or over. Freight loaded: (1987) 965,615 tons/876,000 tonnes; unloaded: 1.32 million tons/1.2 million tonnes.

Telecommunications

There are 48,000 telephones and a small but good system with good service. There are 250,000 radios (1985) and 200,000 televisions (1987), served by the national radio and television operation MBC.

EDUCATION AND WELFARE

Education

Schools. Elementary education is free with 137,935 pupils attending 267 primary schools (95% attendance) and 69,825 pupils attending 125 secondary schools. In addition, there are 962 students in technical and vocational institutions, eight special schools and 631 students at teacher-training establishments.

Universities. The University of Mauritius has a total enrolment of 618 students.

Literacy. 79%.

Health

Of the 800 doctors practising in Mauritius, 136 are specialists. There are 2,814 hospital beds (one per 398 people).

MAYOTTE

GEOGRAPHY

Mayotte is an island in the Mozambique Channel between Mozambique and Madagascar, forming part of the Comoro Archipelago and covering a total area of 145 miles^2/375 km^2. The terrain is generally undulating with ancient volcanic peaks and deep ravines. The capital is Dzaoudzi.

Climate

Tropical, with a hot, humid rainy season during the north-eastern monsoon (Nov.-May) and a cooler dry season (May-Nov.). The island is subject to cyclones during the rainy season.

Population

Total population (1989 est.) 69,481.
Birth rate 5.1%. **Death rate** 1.2%. **Rate of population increase** 3.8%. **Life expectancy** female 58; male 54.

Religion

Mainly Islam (99%), with a small Christian minority.

Language

Mahorian (a Swahili dialect): French.

HISTORY

The earliest inhabitants of Mayotte were a Melano-Polynesian people who had migrated from the Far East in the 6th century AD. Arab and African settlers followed as the islands became an important stage in the trade between Arabia and the east African coast. Islamic sultanates were established on all the Comoro Islands. European traders began to visit the islands in the 17th century but it was not until 1841 that colonization took place when the Sultan of Mayotte was persuaded to hand his island over to the French. In 1912 Mayotte was combined with the other Comoro Islands to form a dependency of Madagascar. In 1946 they became a separate French overseas territory.

Internal autonomy was granted in 1961. Elections to the Chamber of Deputies in Dec. 1972 produced a strong majority for the coalition of parties in favour of independence. In Mayotte, however, the local Mouvement populaire mahorais (MPM), which supports continued links with France, won most of the vote. A referendum on 22 Dec. 1974 resulted in a 96% majority throughout the Comoros for independence, but a 64% vote against in Mayotte. In July 1987 the Comoran Chamber of Deputies unilaterally declared the islands independent, despite the protests of Mayotte. France remained in control of Mayotte and proposed a referendum on the island's future while accepting the Comoros' independence. This referendum, held on 8 Feb. 1976, produced a 99% vote in favour of retaining links with France. Another referendum on the status of the island was held in April, but manipulated by the MPM so that the ballot slips supported the MPM's aim for departmental status. The French government refused to consider making the island a department, but granted the status of a territorial collective, a status in between that of a department and an overseas territory.

The Comoros government continued to claim Mayotte as a part of its territory and following a coup in 1978 the new government offered to include Mayotte in a new federal system. Mayotte, however, refused. In 1979 the French National Assembly voted to extend Mayotte's special status for a further five years, but the referendum after this period was postponed indefinitely in Dec. 1984. Negotiations between France and the Comoros resumed in 1984 but the French reiterated the view that Mayotte could not be handed back without the consent of the population. In Mar. 1987 there were outbreaks of rioting between the local population and illegal immigrants from the Comoros.

CONSTITUTION AND GOVERNMENT

Although claimed by Comoros, Mayotte is administered as a territorial collectivity of France, and shares the French Constitution (dating from 28 Sept. 1958). It has an elected 17-member General Council.

Leader Akli Khider, Representative of the Government (since 1983) and Younoussa Bamana, President of the General Council (since 1976).

National symbols

Flag. The French flag is used.

National holiday. 14 July (Bastille Day).

ECONOMY

Economic activity is based on agriculture and fishing although much of the island's food is imported from France; the economy is dependent on French aid.

Currency

The French franc.

COMMUNICATIONS

There is a port at Dzaoudzi, one airport with a permanent surface runway, and 53 miles/85 km of tarred road. There is a telephone system and one AM radio station. There is no television.

MEXICO

Estados Unidos de México

(United Mexican States)

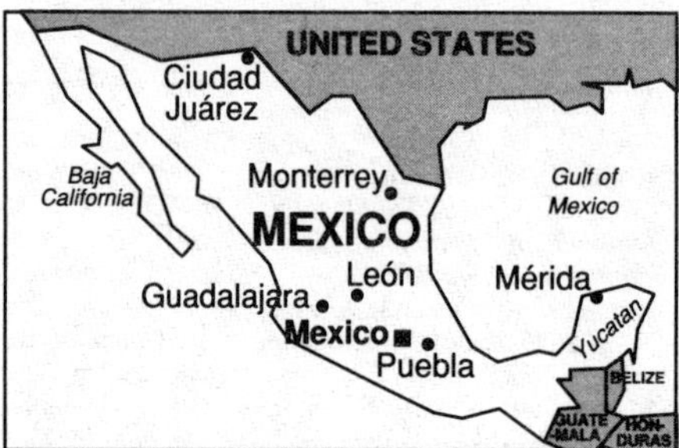

GEOGRAPHY

Containing the southern portion of the North American continent, Mexico is the largest country in Central America, covering a total area of 761,404 miles^2/1,972,550 km^2 divided into 31 states and the Federal district of Mexico City (supporting nearly 15% of the total population). Situated at the southern extremity of the North American Western Cordillera, Mexico's physiography is dominated by the central plateau rising from the northern desert and western/eastern alluvial coastal plains to an altitude of 7,874 ft/2,400 m around Mexico City. The plateau is flanked by the Sierra Madre Occidental to the west and the Sierra Madre Oriental to the east, and is enclosed to the south and north-west by the Isthmus of Tehuantepec and the arid Baja California peninsula. To the south, the peaks of the Sierra Volcánica Transversal reach maximum elevations of 18,697 ft/5,699 m (Citlaltépetl), 17,887 ft/5,452 m (Popcatépetl) and 17,342 ft/5,286 m (Ixtaccihuatl). The Sierra Madre del Sur converges with the Sierra Soconusco and Chiapas uplands on the isthmus of Tehuantepec whose fertile soils, drained by the Papaloapan and Grijalua-Usamacinta river systems are cultivated by a number of mestizo and indigenous Indian communities. Nearly 25% of Mexico's total surface area is occupied by tropical rain forest, including the south-east Yucatán peninsula. From Ciudad Juarez to Matamoros in the north-east, the Rio Bravo del Norte (R. Grande) marks the Mexican/Texan border. 12% of the land is arable, nearly 50% of the territory experiences arid/semi-arid conditions and over 25% of the population live in the three major metropolitan districts of Mexico City, Guadalajara and Monterrey.

Climate

Varies according to altitude. Elevation determines classification. Lowland zones are known as 'tierra caliente' (hot land) with mean temperatures of 79°F/26°C. Above 1,968 ft/600 m, the 'tierra templada' (temperate land) registers a mean temperature of 70°F/21°C and above 5,905 ft/1,800 m on the central plateau average annual temperatures fall to 63°F/17°C (tierra frío). 'Tierra helada' (frozen land) above 13,976 ft/4,260 m seldom records temperatures in excess of 50°F/10°C. The northern and western parts of the country are arid and subject to severe conditions. To the south, the tropical climate raises temperatures and humidity. Rainfall averages range from 3.9–7.8 in/100–200 mm in the north and north-west to 39–113 in/1,000–2,875 mm in coastal areas to 197 in/5,000 mm in the extreme southern highlands. Mexico City: Jan. 55°F/12.6°C. July 61°F/16.1°C. Average annual rainfall 29.4 in/747 mm. Guadalajara: Jan. 59°F/15.2°C. July 69°F/20.6°C. Average annual rainfall 36 in/902 mm. La Paz: Jan. 64°F/17.8°C. July 85°F/29.4°C. Average annual rainfall 5.7 in/145 mm. Monterrey: Jan. 58°F/14.4°C. July 81°F/27.2°C. Average annual rainfall 23 in/588 mm.

Cities and towns

Mexico City (capital)	9,191,295
Netzahualcóyotl	2,331,351
Guadalajara	1,906,145
Monterrey	1,064,629
Heroica Puebla de Zaragoza	710,833
Ciudad Juárez	625,040
León	624,816
Tijuana	566,344

Population

Total population is 84,884,000 of which 69.7% live in urban areas. Population density is 111 persons per mile^2/41.5 per km^2. Ethnic divisions: 60% mestizo (Indian-Spanish); 30% Amerindian or predominantly Amerindian; 9% White or predominantly White.

Birth rate 3.17%. **Death rate** 0.63%. **Rate of population increase** 2.54%. **Age distribution** under 15

= 42.2%; over 65 = 3.5% **Life expectancy** female 72; male 65; average 69.

Religion

Approximately 96–97% of the population are Roman Catholic and a further 3.3% Protestant (chief denominations: Episcopalian, Evangelical Lutheran and Methodist). The Baha'i spiritual assembly also has members in over 900 localities.

Language

Over 92% of the population speak Spanish, the official language. However, some 59 distinct native dialects belong to five major indigenous language families: the Náhuatl, Maya, Zapotec, Otomi and Mixtec groups. Other indigenous languages include Chol, Huastec, Huichol, Mazahua, Mixe, Tarahumara, Tarasco, Tlapanec, Totonac, Tzeltal and Tzotzil.

HISTORY

Mexico had the most highly developed pre-Columbian civilization in Latin America under first the Toltecs from the beginning of the 10th century, and then the Aztecs from the mid 12th century. The Aztecs built their empire through military conquest and it is estimated that there may have been up to 15,000,000 native inhabitants when Hernando Cortés and his party of 600 conquistadores landed in 1519, yet within two years the Spanish had defeated the forces of Moctezuma (Montezuma) II and captured the city of Tenochtitlan.

The chief attraction for the Spaniards was the area's mineral wealth, and the major silver strikes at Zacatecas in 1546–48 and Guanajuato ten years later made Mexico, or New Spain as it was designated, an important centre of the Spanish colonial empire, with considerable influence wielded by the Roman Catholic Church and a tight control over the population through the labour system of the encomienda (a form of semi-slavery under which Indians paid tribute or labour to a landowner or tribute to the Spanish crown in return for conversion and 'civilization'; it was abolished in 1829).

Moves for independence were triggered off by conservative reaction to events on the Iberian peninsula. In 1810, two years after Napoleon invaded Spain, Fr Miguel Hidalgo led an abortive rising from his small village of Dolores. Hidalgo was executed in 1811, and José María Morelos took on the leadership of the independence movement. In 1821 (a year after liberal revolution in Spain) Agustin de Iturbide forced the Spanish viceroy to leave. Iturbide proclaimed himself emperor in 1822, but was forced to abdicate in 1823, and the following year a federal republic was established under Guadalupe Victoria. The Spanish government attempted to regain control by a military expedition in 1829, but formally recognized Mexican independence in 1836.

The early decades of Mexican independence were characterized by political instability and strained relations with the United States. Mexico's northern neighbour had been the first country to recognize its independence and from 1823 Texas (then part of Mexico) was opened to US colonization, but in 1836 the state declared its independence from Mexico, and war broke out between the two countries in 1846. Under the Treaty of Guadalupe Hidalgo, concluded ih 1848, Mexico ceded about half of its territory (modern California, New Mexico, Arizona, Nevada, Utah and part of Colorado) to the US in return for a payment of $15,000,000 and the cancellation of its debts of $3,250,000. During this period the dominant personality of Mexican politics was Antonio López de Santa Anna, and after his fall in 1855 there was a period of feuding between the centralist conservatives and the federalist and anti-clerical liberals, culmination in the 'War of the Reform' 1858–61.

The leader of the ultimately victorious liberals was Benito Juárez, president from 1855 to 1872. Political turbulence and war had taken a heavy toll of the national economy, however, and in 1861 Mexico suspended payment on the foreign debt, provoking a swift reaction from France, Britain and Spain. An initial European military expedition launched in 1862 was unsuccessful, but the next year Napoleon III took Mexico City and established the Habsburg Archduke Ferdinand Maximilian of Austria as emperor. When the French troops were withdrawn in 1867 Maximilian was defeated by Juárez' forces, court martialled and shot.

A new era opened with the seizure of power in 1876 by Porfirio Díaz, who was president continuously until 1911 except for the period 1880–84. He strengthened the central government, drastically reduced the size of the armed forces, formed an alliance with the landed interests and built a solid economic base; in addition to gold and silver, copper, zinc and lead reserves were exploited, cash crops encouraged, railways extended, considerable foreign investment was attracted, and by the beginning of the 20th century Mexico had regained its international credit-worthiness and become one of the world's leading petroleum exporters. Díaz' rule ended the anarchy of earlier years, but his erosion of the land reform attempts made by Juárez, the influence gained by foreign interests in the economy and the easing of restrictions on the Roman Catholic Church provoked a nationalist and reformist reaction in the 'epic revolution' (1910–20). The overthrow of Díaz by Francisco Madero in 1911 sparked off a guerrilla war in the north led by, among others, Pancho Villa, and a southern peasant revolt led by Emiliano Zapata, calling for social change and, above all, land reform. Madero was deposed and murdered in 1913 and an estimated 250,000 people died in the ensuing civil war. (Zapata was ambushed and killed in 1919; Villa was murdered in 1923.) A new constitution was promulgated in 1917 severely curtailing the power of the Church, establishing state education, declaring mineral and subsoil rights the inalienable property of the nation, and introducing a number of social reforms including the protection of labour rights.

The revolution was not immediate and reforms were introduced only gradually, with xenophobia and anti-clericalism being the dominant themes. Church-state relations reached their nadir with the Cristero rebellion by militant Catholic priests of 1926–29, and the year 1929 also saw the last serious military revolt of the period and the formation of the National Revolutionary Party (PNR, renamed the Mexican Revolutionary Party – PRM – in 1938 and the Institutional Revolutionary Party – PRI – in 1946), which has held power ever since. The most significant phase in the implementation of the revolution occurred during the presidency of Gen. Lázaro Cárdenas in 1934–40, when organized labour was encouraged, land reform accelerated, co-operative farms established, the major part of the railway system nationalized, and the US and British oil companies expelled and their property expropriated.

Cárdenas' successors were less concerned with social reform than with pursuing industrial and infrastructural development through a mixed economy relying on substantial public investment. There was a considerable boost to the economy through collaboration with the US war effort in World War II, and the 'economic miracle' of the 1940s helped to ensure political stability under the PRI, with gross domestic product increasing by a factor of five between 1940–65 against only a doubling of the population. In the 1970s, however, the country began to face economic reverses as the rapidly rising population (growing at a rate of over 3% annually) and its increasing drift towards the cities ended agricultural self-sufficiency and international petroleum prices slumped.

Mexico reached a crisis in Aug. 1982 when the government was forced to declare that it no longer had the means to cover payments on its foreign debt, which at around $80,000 million was second only to that of Brazil. Banks had been eager to lend to Mexico in the 1970s at negligible rates of interest, but the rapid rise in US interest rates converted the debt from $21,400 million in 1978 to $106,700 million by 1987. In 1983 and 1984 Mexico met with other Latin American debtors, but discounted talk of a 'debt cartel' favoured by some of the other countries. The government was forced to amend its economic policy in order to reach agreements with the International Monetary Fund in 1982 and 1986, and after rescheduling negotiations with foreign banks in 1984 it relaxed the laws on direct foreign investment in contravention of the constitution. Since 1982 the currency has been repeatedly devalued, and there was a further economic blow in Sept. 1985 when Mexico City was hit by a severe earthquake, causing $3,700 million worth of damage and an estimated $425,000,000 in economic disruption; the death toll was set officially at 7,000 and unofficially at up to 30,000.

The 1982 crisis coincided with a change of government and brought to the surface a certain amount of discontent with the status quo and the PRI in particular. The incoming president, Miguel de la Madrid Hurtado, received only 74% of the vote compared with 95% for José López Portillo in 1976, and the PRI faced further losses in mid-term elections (although without any real threat to its dominance). De la Madrid undertook to combat corruption in public life, and opened investigations into officials working for the state petroleum concern Pemex, resulting in the sentencing in May 1987 of former Pemex chief Jorge Díaz Serrano to ten years' imprisonment and a fine of $54,000,000 after being found guilty of embezzlement. Meanwhile the government was criticized for its inefficient response to the earthquake and for its economic austerity measures which in de la Madrid's term of office saw record inflation figures and helped to halve real incomes. Consequently the PRI presidential candidate in the 1988 elections, Carlos Salinas de Gotari, who as minister of planning and federal budget since 1982 was strongly identified with these economic policies, gained only 50.3% of the vote. The selection of Salinas, who in accordance with usual practice was de la Madrid's personal nominee, was opposed within the PRI by a dissident faction headed by Cuauhtémoc Cárdenas (son of the former president), who gained 31.1% of the vote as the candidate of the Authentic Party of the Mexican Revolution (PARM). In July 1989, the PRI suffered its first defeat in sixty years when it conceded victory to the centre-right National Action Party (PAN) following the election for the state governorship of Baja California. However, PRI victories in the elections held simultaneously for six state legislators and mayorships were strongly disputed by opposition parties.

Within Central America and the Caribbean, Mexico has been generally friendly towards Cuba and Nicaragua, and in 1983 it launched a peace process as part of the Contadora Group. Outstanding problems with the US have been the illegal passage of drugs and immigrants across the border.

CONSTITUTION AND GOVERNMENT

Executive and legislature

Executive power is held by a president who is elected for a six-year term, in elections held concurrently with the legislative elections; last election 6 July 1988. The president appoints the cabinet. Legislative power is vested in a bicameral National Congress consisting of a 400-member Federal Chamber of Deputies elected every three years (300 by majority vote in single-member constituencies and the remaining 100 by proportional representation from minority parties' lists) and a 64-member Senate (comprising two senators from each state and two from the Federal District) elected at the same time as the president. All elections are by universal adult suffrage.

Present government

President Sr Carlos Salinas de Gortari

Principal members of the Cabinet Sr Fernando Gutiérrez Barrios (Government); Sr Fernando Solana Morales (Foreign Relations); Gen. Antonio Riviello Bazán (Defence); Dr Pedro Aspe Armella (Finance and Public Credit); Dr Ernesto Cedillo Ponce de León (Planning and Federal Budget).

Administration

Mexico is a federal republic comprising 31 states and a Federal District around the capital. Each state has its own constitution and is administered by a governor. With the exception of the governor of the Federal District (who is appointed by the president and holds a seat in the federal Cabinet), the state governors are elected for a six-year term, and the state Chambers of Deputies are elected for a three-year term.

Justice

The structure of Mexican justice mixes US constitutional theory with a civil-law system. The highest court is the Supreme Court with a role in the judicial review of legislation, and with independence from the executive and legislative branches. Supreme Court justices are appointed by the president, subject to Senate confirmation; within the period of their six-year term, they can be removed only by impeachment. There are 12 collegiate circuit courts (with 3 judges each), as well as single-judge circuit courts and district courts. The death penalty is in force only for exceptional crimes. There were no executions between 1985 and mid-1988.

National symbols

Flag. Tricolour with vertical stripes of green, white and red, bearing in the centre the state coat of arms.

Festivals. 5 Feb. (Constitution Day); 21 Mar. (Birthday of Benito Juárez); 1 May (Labour Day); 5 May (Anniversary of the Battle of Puebla); 1 Sep. (president's Annual Message); 16 Sep. (Independence Day); 12 Oct. (Discovery of America); 20 Nov. (Anniversary of the Revolution).

Vehicle registration plate. MEX.

INTERNATIONAL RELATIONS

Affiliations
OAS.

Defence
Total Armed Forces: 254,500. Active: 138,000. Terms of service: voluntary. Reserves: 300,000.
Army: 105,500; 45 light tanks ((M-3).
Navy: 26,000 inclusive 3,000 marines and 500 naval air force; three destroyers (US Gearing and Fletcher) and 103 patrol and coastal combatants.
Naval Air Force: 500; 11 combat aircraft.
Air Force: 7,000; 103 combat aircraft (F-5E, F-5F, AT-33, PC-7).

ECONOMY

Currency
The unit is the Mexican peso, divided into 100 centavos.

National finance
Budget. The 1987 budget (in US$) was for expenditure (current and capital) of 62,700 million and revenue of 41,100 million. Main items of current expenditure are education 8.7%; housing and welfare 8.5%; defence 1.4%.
Balance of payments. The balance of payments (current account, 1987) was a surplus of $3,509 million.
Inflation. (1988) 52%.

Gross Domestic Product
Estimated total GDP US$141,940 million, per capita US$1,640 (ranking 21 in the world by size).
Economically active population. The total number of persons active in the economy was 26,100,000; unemployed: 19%.

Sector	% of workforce	% of GDP
industry	25	34
agriculture	26	9
services*	49	57

* services figure includes elements unassigned to other categories.

Energy and mineral resources
Oil and gas. 158 million tons/143 million tonnes of crude petroleum were produced in 1988 and 1,312,268 ft^3/37,160 million m^3 of natural gas in 1985.
Minerals. Mexico has sizeable coal and uranium reserves estimated at 6,005 million tons/5,448 million tonnes and 165,345 tons/150,000 tonnes respectively. Uranium is mined in the states of Chihuahua, Durango, Sonora, Queretaro and Nuevo León. Output: (1987 in 1,000 tons/tonnes) coal 4,687/4,252; coke 2,579/2,340; gypsum 2,709/2,458; pig iron 5,473/4,965; sulphur 2,540/2,304; fluorite 798/724; phosphorous 698/633; barite 442/401; dolomite 399/362; zinc 299/271; copper 255/231; lead 195/177. 2,662 tons/2,415 tonnes of silver were extracted in 1987 and 2,662 tons/8,000 kg of gold.
Electricity. 34% of all power is hydroelectrically generated. Capacity: 24,962,000 kW; production: 91,250 million kWh; 1,090 kWh per capita (1988).

Bioresources
Agriculture. 12% of the land area is arable (54.1 million acres/21.9 million ha) and 1% is under permanent cultivation (3.9 million acres/1.6 million ha) with 39% used as meadow or pasture (183.8 million acres/74.4 million ha). Cultivated land is dominated by maize 43%; sorghum 10%; wheat 5%. Mexico is also an illegal producer of opium poppies and cannabis for the international drug trade.
Crop production: (1987 in million tons/tonnes) sugar cane 47/42.6; maize 12.11/10.99; sorghum 5.3/4.8; wheat 4.9/4.4; oranges 2.4/2.2; tomatoes 1.9/1.73; bananas 1.7/1.5; dry beans 1.1/1.03. Other crops grown include potatoes; lemons; barley; rice; chickpeas; cotton; soya beans; coconuts; coffee; pineapples; apples; grapes; mangoes.
Livestock numbers: (1987 in millions) cattle 31.3; pigs 18.7; sheep 5.8; horses 6.14; goats 10; donkeys 3.18; mules 3.13; poultry 229.
Forestry. 24% of the land is forested. A variety of valuable hardwoods are grown including pine; spruce; cedar; mahogany; logwood; rosewood. The total forested area contains 1,976,773 acres/800,000 ha of forest reserves and 1,853,225 acres/750,000 ha of national park land. Roundwood output: (1984) 333,717,000 ft^3/9,450,000 m^3.
Fisheries. Total catch: (1984) 1.25 million tons/1.13 million tonnes (shrimps; prawns; oysters; tunny; shark; perch; bass).

Industry and commerce
Industry. Mexico's main industries are food and beverages; tobacco; chemicals; iron and steel; petroleum; mining; textiles; clothing; transportation equipment; tourism.
Commerce. Exports: US$22,900 million (1988) or 17% of GDP; imports: $18,600 million in the same year or 13.7% of GDP. Chief exported commodities were crude oil; oil products; coffee; shrimp; engines; cotton. Imports included grain; metal manufactures; agricultural machinery; electrical equipment. Main trading partners are (imports and exports) US; EC countries: Japan.
Trade with UK. Mexico imported UK goods worth £190 million in 1988; exports to the UK totalled £144.9 million.
Tourism. (1987) 5,407,000 visitors.

COMMUNICATIONS

Railways
There are 12,369 miles/19,906 km of railways.

Roads
There are 140,237 miles/225,684 km of roads, of which 63,387 miles/102,009 km are concrete or bituminized.

Aviation
Aeromexico and Mexicana provide domestic and international services (main airport is at Mexico City). Passengers: (1984) 14.56 million.

Shipping
There are 1,802 miles/2,900 km of navigable rivers and coastal canals. The marine ports on the west, north Pacific coast are Acapulco, Ensenada, Manzanillo, Mazatlen, and Salina Cruz. Those on the east, Gulf of Mexico coast are Coatzacoalcos, Tampico, and Veracruz. Guayamas is in the Gulf of California. The merchant marine consists of 76 ships or 1,000 GRT or over. Freight loaded: (1987) 95.8 million tons/89.6 million tonnes; unloaded: 12.3 million tons/11.2 million tonnes.

Telecommunications
There are 6.41 million telephones and a highly developed system. There are 21.4 million radios (1986) and 9.5 million televisions (1988), literally

hundreds of commercial radio stations and over 100 commercial TV stations.

EDUCATION AND WELFARE

Education

Elementary and secondary education is obligatory and state-maintained.

Schools. Over 31,000 nursery schools employ 72,325 teachers with 2.15 million pupils (one per 30 pupils). 15.2 million children attend 76,183 primary schools with 437,000 members of staff (one per 35 pupils). 4,396,087 secondary school pupils receive instruction from 230,656 teachers (one per 19 pupils). A further 1.84 million students attend vocational or teacher-training establishments.

Universities. There are approximately 1.12 million students in higher education. The three most important universities in Mexico City are the Universidad Nacional Autónoma de México, the Instituto Politécnico Nacional and the Universidad Autónoma Metropolitana. Other major universities outside Mexico City are Veracruzana, Nueva León, Puebla, Sinaloa and Michoacana.

Literacy. 88%.

Health

66,373 doctors serve 6,315 hospitals with 82,717 beds (one per 1,044 people).

MICRONESIA, FEDERATED STATES OF

GEOGRAPHY

The Federated States of Micronesia consist of four major island groups in the North Pacific Ocean with a total area of 271 miles²/702 km². The 607 islands vary geologically from high mountainous terrain to low coral atolls. The capital is Kolonia on the island of Pohnpei. (A new capital is being built in the Palikir valley).

Climate

Tropical. There is heavy year-round rainfall and occasional typhoon damage.

Population

Total population (1989 est.) 102,134.
Birth rate 3.4%. **Death rate** 0.5%. **Rate of population increase** 2.8%. **Life expectancy** female 73; male 68.

Religion

Christianity, mainly Roman Catholic and Protestant.

Language

English (official) plus several indigenous languages.

HISTORY

The Caroline Islands, in which the Federated States of Micronesia (FSM) are situated, were first settled around 1000 BC. Spanish seafarers arrived in 1565. In the mid-1800s the Carolines suffered severe depopulation as American and European whalers, traders, and missionaries brought with them alien diseases and subjected the islanders to forced labour. In 1874 Spain formally annexed the Carolines, but sold them to Germany in 1899. At the outbreak of World War I Japan took possession of the German Pacific colonies. In 1920 the League of Nations mandated control of Micronesia to Japan. Truk Lagoon in the Carolines was one of Japan's most important bases during World War II. The American Navy took command of Micronesia following Japan's defeat in 1945.

In 1947 the UN established the Trust Territory of the Pacific Islands, under United States control. Moves towards preparing Micronesia for self-government began in the 1960s. In a referendum in July 1978, of the six Trust Territory districts only Ponape, Kosrae, Truk, and Yap voted in favour of a common constitution. They became the FSM. In Oct. 1982 the FSM and US governments signed a Compact of Free Association, under which the FSM would be internally self-governing while the USA maintained responsibility for defence. The US's primary strategic interest in the FSM was denial of access to other powers rather than the establishment of bases. US administration of Micronesia formally ended in Nov. 1986 but the UN Security Council has yet to officially terminate the trusteeship owing to uncertainty over the future status of the Micronesian territory of Palau.

CONSTITUTION AND GOVERNMENT

The Federated States of Micronesia have a constitutional government in free association with the United States, under the Compact of Free Association which came into force on 3 Nov. 1986. The constitution dates from May 1979. There is a national president and vice president, elected for four-year terms from the ranks of popularly elected senators. There is a unicameral National Congress.

Leader John Haglelgam (president since 1986).

National symbols

Flag. Light blue with four white stars centred, arranged in a diamond pattern.

National holiday. 10 May (Proclamation of the Federated States of Micronesia).

ECONOMY

Fishing and farming are at subsistence level. The main source of revenue is financial aid from the US. There are few mineral resources, except for highgrade phosphate.

Currency

The US dollar.

COMMUNICATIONS

There are ports at Kolonia, Truk and Okat; 11 airports, seven with permanent surface runways, and 24 miles/39 km of paved and concrete roads on the major islands. Minor islands have coral or laterite roads. There is a telephone network, five AM and one FM radio stations and six TV stations, also four satellite communications system terminals.

MONACO

Principauté de Monaco (Principality of Monaco)

GEOGRAPHY

The tiny, coastal principality of Monaco (0.73 miles²/1.9 km²), an enclave of south-eastern France, is situated in western Europe in the hills fronting the Côte d'Azur. It is the second smallest independent state in the world, divided into four administrative districts: Monaco-ville (the capital), la Condamine, Monte-Carlo and Fontvieille.

Climate

Mediterranean: hot, dry summers and cool, rainy winters. Jan. 50°F/10°C. July 74°F/23.3°C. Average annual rainfall 30 in/758 mm.

Population

Total population is 28,000. Density is 38,356 persons per mile²/18,121 per km². Ethnic composition: 47% French; 16% Monegasque; 16% Italian; 21% other. **Birth rate** 1.96%. **Death rate** 1.66%. **Rate of population increase** 0.3% **Age distribution** under 15 = 11.9%; over 65 = 22.5% **Life expectancy** female 80; male 72.

Religion

95% Roman Catholic (single archdiocese). The Church of England is also represented in Monaco and there is a synagogue within the principality.

Language

French is the official language but Italian, English and Monegasque (a French Provençal–Italian Ligurian hybrid) are also spoken.

HISTORY

Phoenicians, Greeks, Romans, Visigoths, and Saracens featured in turn in the early history of Monaco, which took its name from the Ligurian 'Monoikos' tribe of the 6th century BC. Construction of a fortress by the Genoese (AD 1215) was followed by the imposition of lordship by the house of Grimaldi (1297), whose association with the papal Guelph faction had caused its expulsion from Genoa by the imperial Ghibellines. Grimaldi service for France led to French recognition of Monaco's independence (1489), but Spanish protection was accepted in 1542 and Honoré II adopted the title of Prince in 1616. Having reverted to French protection (1641), Monaco united with revolutionary France (1793) but regained independence in 1815 as a Sardinian protectorate. After the 1859 Franco–Austrian war in Italy, Monaco again came under French protection (1861), minus Menton and Roquebrune, which opted for full French sovereignty. Princely absolutism gave way to constitutional rule in 1911. France recognized Monaco's sovereignty under agreements in 1918 and 1919, subject to its acting 'in complete conformity' with French interests.

Occupied by the Italians (1940) and then by the Germans (1943), post-war Monaco re-established itself as a major tourist centre and, by virtue of economic union with France, became an integral part of the European Communities in the 1950s. Prince Rainier III succeeded to the throne in 1949 and on 19 Apr. 1956 married US film star Grace Kelly, who died on 14 Sept. 1982 after the car she was driving plunged off a mountain road probably as a result of brake failure.

In the face of growing pressure for increased powers from the elected National Council (in particular following the collapse in 1955 of Monaco's leading bank, the Société Monégasque de Banque) Prince Rainier asserted his sovereign powers in 1959 by suspending the Council. However, a revised constitution promulgated in 1962 guaranteed representative government and renounced royal divine right. Tensions with France over the principality's role as a tax haven were eased in 1963 by a convention placing certain Monaco-based companies under French fiscal law. Since 1963 the pro-Rainier National and Democratic Union group has dominated the National Council, and won all 18 seats in the National Council in elections in 1978, 1983 and 1988.

CONSTITUTION AND GOVERNMENT

Executive and legislature

The monarch, as head of state, nominates the Minister of State (who heads the Council of Government) from a list of three French diplomats submitted by the French government. The legislature, the National Council, is elected for a five-year term by universal adult suffrage.

Present government

Head of state Prince Rainier III

Members of the Council of Government Jean Ausseil (Minister of State); Raoul Biancheri (Finance and Economics); Louis Caravel (Public Works and Social Affairs); Jean-Charles Rey (President of the National Council).

Justice

There are a 'Juge de Paix', a Tribunal of the First Instance, a Court of Appeal, Criminal Tribunal, 'Cour de Révision Judiciaire' and a Supreme Tribunal. The death penalty was abolished in 1962.

National symbols

Flag. Two horizontal stripes, red over white.

Festivals. 1 May (Labour Day); 19 Nov. (National Day).

Vehicle registration plate. MC.

INTERNATIONAL RELATIONS

Affiliations

Observer status at UN and member of some UN specialized agencies.

Defence

Defence is the responsibility of France.

ECONOMY

Currency

The unit is the French franc, divided into 100 centimes.

Energy and mineral resources

Electricity. Standby capacity (1988) 8,000 kW; power supplied by France.

Industry and commerce

Industry. Industries are pharmaceuticals; food processing; precision instruments; glassmaking; printing; tourism.

Commerce. Full customs integration with France, which collects and rebates Monacan trade duties. Monaco also participates in the EC market system through a customs union with France.

Tourism. (1987) 214,149 overnight visitors.

COMMUNICATIONS

Railways

There are 1.06 miles/1,7 km of railways.

Roads

There are 29 miles/47 km of roads.

Aviation

There is a helicopter shuttle service between the international airport at Nice, France, and Monaco's heliport at Fontvieille.

Telecommunications

Monaco is served by the French communication system. There are 38,200 telephones and an automatic system. There are 27,000 radios and 20,000 televisions (1986). Radio Monte Carlo has audiences stretching well into France and Italy for its commercially sponsored programmes, as well as running the official programme on long wave.

EDUCATION AND WELFARE

Education

Schools. Approximately 5,160 pupils receive instruction from over 420 teachers (one per 12 pupils).

Literacy. 99%.

Health

There are 53 doctors and 432 hospital beds (one per 68 people).

MONGOLIA

Bügd Nayramdakh/Mongol Ard Uls (Mongolian People's Republic)

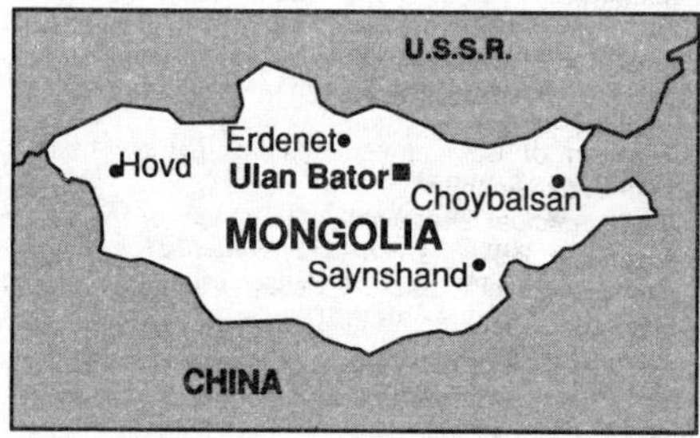

GEOGRAPHY

A sparsely populated country in north-central Asia, Mongolia covers an area of 604,090 miles²/1,565,000 km² divided into 18 counties or 'aimag' of which Töv is by far the most populous containing the capital city of Ulan Bator (500,000 inhabitants). With a mean elevation of 5,184 ft/1,580 m, Mongolia's physiographic formation is dominated by the Mongolian Altai mountain chain, running north-west to south-east and massing in the west to form the Nayramdal ridge (14,347 ft/4,373 m at Tavan-Bogdo-Uli, Mongolia's highest peak). To the east, the Khenti mountains descend south-eastwards into the semi-arid Gobi desert (33% of the total surface area). In the north-west, the great lakes include Uvs Nuur, Hösgol Nuur and Hyargas Nuur. The north-central regions are drained by the River Selenga and the north-west by the River Hovd. High aridity in the lowland plains is to some extent compensated for by the pasture land of the mountain steppe, occupying 79% of the total surface area. 1% of the land is arable and 10% is forested.

Climate

Extreme continental. Little winter precipitation but prolonged sub-zero temperatures, although summer temperatures can reach 75°F/24°C at Ulan Bator. Rainfall diminishes north to south-east from 9.8–1.8 in/250–375 mm in the mountainous uplands to below 4.7 in/120 mm in the Gobi. Rainfall is usually limited to the months May-Sept. Ulan Bator: Jan. – 14°F/–25.6°C. July 61°F/16.1°C. Average annual rainfall 8.2 in/208 mm.

Cities and towns

Ulan Bator (capital)	480,000

Population

Total population is 2,092,000 of which 51.8% live in urban areas. Population density is 3.5 people per mile²/1.3 per km². Ethnic divisions: 90% Mongol (Khalka, Dörbed, Buryat, Dariganga); 4% Kazakh; 2% Russian; 2% other.

Birth rate 3.95% **Death rate** 0.85%. **Rate of population increase** 3.10% **Age distribution** under 15 = 41.6%; over 65 = 3.2% **Life expectancy** female 65.2; male 61.1; average 63.

Religion

Formerly Tibetan Buddhist Lamaism (formally suppressed during the 1930s). Today a single monastery remains in Ulan Bator with 100 lamas. An estimated 4% of the population are Muslim.

Language

Over 90% of the population speak Khalka Mongol. The Mongolian languages form an Altaic subset related to other Altaic sub-families such as the Turkic (also spoken) and Manchu-Tungu languages. West Mongolian languages include Kalmyk, Oyrat and Mongol; East Mongolian languages comprise Mongol, Buryat, Daghur, Monguour and Santa. Russian and Chinese are also spoken by their respective minority populations.

HISTORY

The Central Asiatic Plateau has been home since at least the 2nd millennium BC to pastoral nomads. From the 3rd century BC a succession of tribal empires were formed there as various of the region's peoples became pre-eminent. Mongol tribes were consolidated into the first Mongol state in 1206 by Chingis (Genghis) Khan, and in the next 60 years Mongol armies conquered territories from Eastern Europe to the Pacific.

From the 14th century the Mongol empire disintegrated because of internal feuding and foreign attacks. It collapsed in the 17th century, overwhelmed by the Manchus (who were expanding out of Manchuria and conquered China in 1644–62): the last Mongol emperor died in 1636 and the Mongol princes became tributaries to the Manchus before finally accepting Manchu Chinese overlordship in 1691.

Chinese control lasted until 1911. In that year the aristocracy and church hierarchy in the province of Outer Mongolia (supported by Tsarist Russia) seized upon the collapse of China's imperial regime to declare an independent monarchy. The Living Buddha of Urga (the head of the lamaist church) became Bogdo Gegen (head of state). Inconclusive war with China ended in agreement in 1915 that Mongolia should become autonomous under Chinese suzerainty, although it enjoyed the de facto status of a Russian protectorate. The fall of the Russian Tsarist regime in 1917 and Russia's ensuing turmoil enabled the Chinese to abrogate Mongolia's autonomy and to occupy it in 1919–20. White Russian forces expelled the Chinese at the beginning of 1921, and they were in turn expelled in July 1921 by Mongolian partisans organized by the Mongolian People's Party (later the Mongolian People's Revolutionary Party–MPRP), with Soviet military support. Mongolia's independence was proclaimed and the Bogdo Gegen was nominally restored to power; in fact the country was firmly under Soviet direction. When the Bogdo Gegen died in 1924 the MPRP took power, and a constitution on the Soviet model established the People's Republic.

In 1925 the MPRP declared that Mongolia would be transformed into a socialist country without passing through a capitalist stage. In 1928 campaigns began to collectivize the economy and to dispossess the nobility and the Buddhist priesthood. However, resistance was so strong that collectivization of agriculture was partially reversed in 1932 (it was encouraged again after 1947 and completed during the 1950s). Political purges between 1922 and 1939 liquidated not only the nobility and clergy but most of the revolutionary old guard. Horloogiyn Choybalsan (the only member of the original MPRP leadership to survive the purges) became prime minister in 1936 and thereafter power was concentrated in his hands. In mid-1939 a Japanese invasion was repulsed with Soviet help. China formally recognized Mongolia's independence in 1946 (although relations became strained after Mongolia sided with the Soviet Union in the Sino–Soviet split of the early 1960s). Industrialization began in 1948.

Choybalsan died in 1952 and was succeeded as prime minister by Yumjaagiyn Tsedenbal, the MPRP first secretary (Tsedenbal relinquished the latter post in 1954 to Dashiyn Damba, but resumed it in 1958). Tsedenbal was elected president in 1974 and Jambyn Batmönh took over as prime minister. In 1984 Tsedenbal was unexpectedly removed from office, and Batmönh succeeded him both as president and MPRP leader. Since then Mongolia has begun to emulate (albeit cautiously) Soviet reform policies: Tsedenbal has been blamed for 'stagnation' in Mongolia's socio-economic development, and a campaign against 'negative phenomena', including official corruption, was stepped up in 1986. Peaceful demonstrations (in support of the introduction of a multi-party system and the acceleration of the process of reconstruction and renewal) during late 1989 and early 1990 constituted the first ever significant challenge to the MPRP. The demonstrations were arranged by the Mongolian Democratic Union, an organisation formed by students and intellectuals in Dec. 1989.

CONSTITUTION AND GOVERNMENT

Executive and legislature

The sole and ruling party, dominating political life, is the (communist) Mongolian People's Revolutionary Party. The head of state is the chairman of the Presidium of the People's Great Hural, the 370-member unicameral legislature, whose members are elected every five years by universal suffrage from a single list of officially nominated candidates. The Council of Ministers is also, nominally, elected by the legislature.

Present government

Chairman of the Presidium of the People's Great Hural Jambyn Batmönh

Chairman of Council of Ministers (Prime Minister) Dumaagiyn Sodnom

Other principal members of Council of Ministers Myatavyn Peljee (Deputy Chairman; Chairman of Commission for Comecon Affairs); Puntsagiyn Jasray (Deputy Chairman; Chairman of Planning and Economy Commission); Dashiyn Byambasuren (Deputy Chairman); Lt.-Gen. Luvsangombyn Molomjamts (Defence); Demchigjavyn Molomjamts (Finance); Tserenpilyn Gombosuren (Foreign Affairs); Origiyn Jambaldorj (Justice).

Ruling party

Mongolian People's Revolutionary Party (Mongol Ardyn Khuv'sgat Nam). *General secretary* Jambyn Batmönh. *Full politburo members* Jambyn Batmönh; Bat-ochiryn Altangerel; Bugyn Dejid; Banzragchiin Lamzav; Demchigjavyn Molomjamts; Tserendashiyn Namsray; Dumaagiyn Sodnom; Paavangiyn Damdin.

Justice

There is a Supreme Court, whose judges are elected by the National Assembly while the Procurator-General is appointed. In addition there are provincial, town and district courts. Cases are judged by lay assessors who work alongside professional judges. The death penalty is in force. The number of executions between 1985 and mid-1988 is not known.

National symbols

Flag. Three vertical stripes of red, light blue and red.

The red stripe in the hoist is charged with a yellow ideogram with a yellow five-pointed star.

Festivals. 8 Mar. (International Women's Day); 1 May (Labour Day); 11 July (National Day); 7 Nov. (USSR's October Revolution).

INTERNATIONAL RELATIONS

Affiliations

Comecon.

Defence

Total Armed Forces: 24,500 (perhaps 17,000 conscripts). Terms of service: conscription: males 18–28, three years authorized, actual service may only be two. Reserves: 200,000.

Army: 21,000; 650 main battle tanks (T-54/-55/-62).

Air Force: 3,500 (100 pilots); about 30 combat aircraft (MiG-21).

ECONOMY

Currency

The unit is the tughrik, divided into 100 möngös.

National finance

Budget. The 1987 budget (in US$) was for expenditure (current and capital) of 2,190 million and revenue of 2,200 million.

Gross Domestic Product

Estimated total GDP US$1,700 million, per capita US$880 (ranking 122 in the world by size).

Energy and mineral resources

Minerals. In addition to the 18,739 million tons/17,000 million tonnes of coal reserves, there are substantial deposits of copper; zinc; nickel; molybdenum; tin; phosphorites; wolfram; fluorspar. Output: (1984 in tons/tonnes) coal 5.9 million/5.4 million; fluorspar 823,418/747,000.

Electricity. Capacity: 657,000 kW: production: 2,950 million kWh; 1,430 kWh per capita (1988) from six thermal power plants.

Bioresources

Agriculture. Mongolia's agricultural sector is dominated by livestock breeding, with the highest number of livestock per capita in the world. Cattle raising accounts for over two-thirds of all production. The total cultivated area (308.83 million acres/124.98 million ha in 1983) is divided into collective or state farms. 1% of the land area is arable and 79% is meadow or pasture. Over 80% of the arable sector was cereal producing in 1985, 17% fodder and 2% vegetables.

Crop production: (1986 in 1000 tons/tonnes) wheat 732/664; barley 161/146; oats 55/50; potatoes 147/133.

Livestock numbers: (1987) cattle 2.48 million; horses 2.02 million; sheep 13.2 million; goats 4.4 million; camels 550,000.

Forestry. 10% of the land is forested. Output: (1983) timber 24,123,318 ft^3/683,100 m^3.

Industry and commerce

Industry. Developing industry has recently supplanted agriculture in the size of its percentage contribution to the GNP. The main industries are animal product processing; construction materials; food and beverages (20% of all production); coal mining.

Commerce. Exports: (1985) US$388 million or 23% of GDP; imports: $1,000 for the same year or 59% of GDP. Principal exports include livestock; animal products; wool; hides; fluorspar; non-ferrous metals; minerals. Minerals and fuels account for 40% of all export revenue. Imports include machinery and equipment; fuels; foodstuffs; industrial consumer goods; chemicals; building materials; sugar; tea. Virtually all trade is conducted with communist countries (80% with USSR).

Trade with UK. Mongolia imported UK goods worth £1.4 million in 1988; exports to UK totalled £1.86 million.

COMMUNICATIONS

Railways

There are 1,103 miles/1,775 km of railways.

Roads

There are 5,344 miles/8,600 km of roads, of which 621 miles/1,000 km are bituminized.

Aviation

Mongolian Civil Air Transport (MIAT) provides domestic and international services (main airport at Ulan Bator).

Shipping

There are 247 miles/397 km of inland waterways.

Telecommunications

There are 210,000 radios and 120,000 televisions (1987). Ulan Bator Radio is state-run, while much of the TV service involves Soviet programmes transmitted via satellite, supplemented by the locally originated Mongoltelevidz programmes.

EDUCATION AND WELFARE

Education

Children attend school from the age of seven.

Schools. In addition to the 680 nurseries accommodating 62,500 children, 444,000 pupils attend 911 general education institutions with 15,900 teachers (one per 28 pupils) and 48,000 students attend 68 secondary or vocational technical schools.

Universities. The Ulan Bator state university employs 40 professors and 240 lecturers with, an enrolment of 10,000 students. There are seven other higher educational establishments with 1,400 teachers supervising 26,000 students (one per 19 students). Approximately 6,000 students study abroad each year.

Literacy. 80% (est.); 100% claimed (1985).

Health

There are an estimated 240 doctors and 1,100 hospital beds per 100,000 of the population.

MONTSERRAT

GEOGRAPHY

Montserrat is a Caribbean island with a total land area of 39 miles^2/100 km^2. The terrain is volcanic, mostly mountainous with small coastal lowland. The capital is Plymouth.

Climate

Tropical, with little daily or seasonal temperature variation. The island is subject to severe hurricanes June-Nov.

Population

Total population (1989 est.) 12,428.
Birth rate 1.4%. **Death rate** 1.0%. **Rate of population increase** 0.3%. **Life expectancy** female 80; male 74.

Religion

Christianity.

Language

English.

HISTORY

The earliest inhabitants of Montserrat were Arawak and Carib Indians. The first Europeans to settle on the island were British colonists from St Christopher (St Kitts), who arrived in 1632. Slaves were imported from Africa to provide labour for plantations. Slavery was abolished in 1834 and the island's economy declined, although the cultivation of limes revived the agricultural sector. Between 1871 and 1956 Montserrat was administered as part of the Federal Colony of the Leeward Islands and between 1958 and 1962 participated in the Federation of the West Indies. In 1960 a new constitution was granted providing greater autonomy for the island.

In 1978 the ruling Progressive Democratic Party (PDP) was defeated in elections by the opposition People's Liberation Movement (PLM) which won all seven seats in the Legislative Council. John Osborne, the leader of the PLM, became chief minister. The PLM won elections in 1983 and Osborne stated that he would be in favour of eventual independence for the territory. In June 1984 a state of emergency was declared after a strike by public service employees disrupted services. An early general election was held in Aug. 1987 and again won by the PLM, which defeated the PDP and the more recent National Development Party.

CONSTITUTION AND GOVERNMENT

Montserrat is a UK dependent territory with a Constitution dating from June 1960. It has an Executive Council (presided over by the governor, which consists of two ex officio members, and four unofficial members) and a Legislative Council. Elections are held at least every five years, most recently in Aug. 1987.

Leader Christopher Turner, governor since 1987. John Osborne, chief minister since 1978.

National symbols

Flag. Blue, with the flag of the UK in the upper hoist-side quadrant, and the Montserratian coat of arms (featuring a woman standing beside a yellow harp with her arm round a black cross) centred in the outer half.

National holiday. 10 June (Birthday of Queen Elizabeth II).

ECONOMY

The economy is based on tourism and construction. It is heavily dependent on imports.

Currency

Eastern Caribbean dollar.

COMMUNICATIONS

There is a port at Plymouth, and one airport with a permanent surface runway. There are 174 miles/ 280 km of road. There is a telephone system, eight AM and four FM radio stations, and one television station.

MOROCCO

Al-Mamlaka al-Maghrebia (Kingdom of Morocco)

GEOGRAPHY

Situated in the north-west corner of Africa, Morocco covers an area of 172,368 miles²/446,550 km² divided into seven provinces. 80% of Morocco's terrain is upland plateau or mountain range. 50% of the total surface area is semi-arid plateau comprising the east Moroccan, Rabat coastal and Saharan high plains. The Atlas mountain system dominates the high relief from the Er Rif range along the Mediterranean coast in the north through the Middle Atlas to the Haut Atlas in the south climbing to 13,665 ft/4,165 m at Jbel Toubkal, Morocco's highest point. The fertile Moulouyan (north-east), Rharb (north-west), Sous (south-west) and High Atlas (south-central) plains provide virtually all of Morocco's cultivable land. Principal rivers include the Dra'ar (south and south-west) and the Moulouya (north) which drains into the Mediterranean. The bulk of the population lives on the urbanized west Atlantic coast. 18% of the land is arable and 12% is forested.

Climate

Semi-arid in the south (virtually rainless in the Saharan regions) with very hot daytime summer temperatures and equally severe winter nights. Cooler temperatures in high mountainous regions becoming warm temperate along the Mediterranean coast with rainfall averages in the north of between 15.7–31.5 in/400–800 mm per year. Rabat: Jan. 55.2°F/12.9°C. July 72°F/22.2°C. Average annual rainfall 22.2 in/564 mm. Agadir: Jan. 57°F/13.9°C. July 72°F/22.2°C. Average annual rainfall 88 in/224 mm. Casablanca: Jan. 54°F/12.2°C. July 72°F/22.2°C. Average annual rainfall 15.9 in/404 mm. Marrakesh: Jan. 52°F/11.1°C. July 84°F/28.9°C. Average annual rainfall 9.4 in/239 mm.

Cities and towns

Casablanca	2,408,600
Rabat (capital)	841,800
Fez	562,000
Marrakesh	548,700
Meknès	486,600
Oujda	470,500
Kénitra	449,700

Population

Total population is 23,910,000 of which 43.9% live in urban areas. Population density is 138.7 persons per mile²/50.4 per km². Ethnic divisions: 99.1% Arab Berber; 0.7% non-Moroccan; 0.2% Jewish.

Birth rate 3.82%, **Death rate** 1.15%. **Rate of population increase** 2.67% **Age distribution** under 15 = 42.2%; over 65 = 3.9% **Life expectancy** female 63; male 59; average 61

Religion

The state religion is Islam. 98.7% of the population are Sunni Muslims (of the Maliki order). 1.1% are Christians (predominantly Roman Catholic) and 0.2% Jews.

Language

Arabic is the official language with a number of Berber dialects (including Rif, Tamazight and Shluh groupings). French is widely used as the language of commerce, education and governmental administration.

HISTORY

The first inhabitants of Morocco were Berbers: the Masmoudas in the Rif region and the Sanhajas. For many centuries, clan loyalties divided the country, and it was not until the 10th century that nationalism gained ground. In AD 429 the Vandals occupied the area from Tangier to Carthage, and remained until the Idrissid kingdom gained control in the 8th century. Idris was reputedly a descendant of the prophet Mohammed, and he brought Islam to the kingdom. After the fall of the Idrissid dynasty in 920, there was a power vacuum for 140 years, until the Almoravid sultan Youssef ben Tachfin conquered Morocco and western Algeria in 1062. This empire was in turn overrun by the Almohads in 1147, whose rule lasted about 100 years. The Zenatas from the Sahara conquered Morocco in the 13th century, and were themselves ousted by the Saadians 300 years later. At around this time, several coastal areas came under Spanish control.

The first Alaouit ruler, Moulay Rashid, whose dynasty rules today, captured Morocco from the Saadians in the mid-17th century. His successor, Moulay Ismail, brought peace to the country and reduced Spanish influence to the enclaves of Ceuta and Melilla.

Throughout the 19th century, there was fighting with France and Spain, both of whom coveted the territory, which lay sandwiched between their existing African possessions. Sultan Moulay Hassan (r.1873–94) gained some success in curtailing European interference by playing off the colonial powers against one another, but France secured important diplomatic advantages among the

European powers with regard to its sphere of influence in Morocco by complex diplomatic manoeuverings in the early years of the 20th century. Britain, as part of its 1904 Entente Cordiale with France, agreed to give the latter a free hand in Morocco if France did not interfere with British domination of Egypt. In the same year France and Spain concluded a secret agreement to partition Morocco; Spain received acknowledgement of a smaller sphere of influence in the north, in return for allowing France to dominate the south of the country. German claims to equal economic influence were staved off by the 1906 Algeçiras conference, ostensibly guaranteeing Moroccan integrity while mandating France and Spain to maintain order there. German ambitions flared up again in 1911, when the German chancellor sent the gunboat Panther to Agadir, but that crisis ended with German acceptance of French rights to 'pacify' Morocco.

France, whose troops had entered eastern Morocco when civil war broke out after the death of Moulay Hassan, had by now occupied first Oujda, then Casablanca, and in 1911 a French army entered Fez to relieve Sultan Abd al-Hafiz, who was under siege from rivals. He duly signed the treaty (Mar. 1912) setting up the French Protectorate, thus becoming the last of Morocco's independent sultans. Spain, which had meanwhile led expeditions to the north to strengthen its positions, signed an agreement with France (1912) defining the limits of the Spanish zone of influence.

The first French resident-general, Marshal Lyautey, saw his efforts to pacify the country interrupted by World War I. After 1918, however, the French started a vast public works programme to rebuild and extend towns, although bitter fighting against the Berbers lasted until 1920. The following year, Abd el-Krim from the Rif mountains in the north defeated Spanish forces, and advanced on the capital. It took France and Spain six years to conquer his vastly outnumbered forces. Seven years later, France finally penetrated the Anti-Atlas region, entering Tindouf, in present-day Western Algeria, in 1934. It was from the Spanish protectorate in northern Morocco that Gen. Franco launched the military rebellion which began the Spanish Civil War in 1936.

The period between the World Wars was a time of sustained economic growth for Morocco. Sidi Mohammed ben-Yusuf had come to the throne in Rabat in 1927, and declared for the Free French in World War II. The Allies landed in 1942, and shortly afterwards Gen. de Gaulle was appointed governor-general of French North Africa.

After the war, the Sultan headed the independence movement by promoting national unity, within the framework of the Istiqlal (Independence) party's 1947 manifesto. In 1953, he was exiled by the French to Madagascar, but the popular support for him was such that France was forced to give way before a full-scale revolt occurred. He returned to Rabat in Nov. 1955, and concluded an independence agreement with France, whereby the French protectorate became the independent Sultanate of Morocco the following year (2 Mar. 1956). The Spanish protectorate was joined to the independent sultanate the following month, and the status of Tangier as an international zone (since 1923) was terminated in October.

The following year, the Sultan changed his title to that of King. A National Consultative Assembly was appointed with the King taking on the premiership pending the promulgation of a Constitution, which was eventually adopted by referendum in 1962. Sidi ben-Yusuf died in Feb. 1961, and was succeeded by his son, Prince Moulay Hassan, as King Hassan II. Radical groups opposing the monarchy were active in the late 1960s and early 1970s, and attempts were made on the King's life in 1971 and 1972. Against this background, the independence constitution was suspended, its replacement (approved by referendum in Mar. 1972) abolished the single party, and stipulated that only two-thirds of the deputies would be elected by direct vote: the remainder by provincial councils and professional associations. The Chamber of Representatives was eventually elected in June 1977, and again in Sept.-Oct. 1984. There are now 14 political parties covering every tendency from conservatives to the progressive left, but they are all monarchists. In spite of relative freedom, there are still political prisoners. Student strikes and labour unrest have periodically beset the regime, with occasional political trials of opponents. At one such trial, in Casablanca in Feb. 1986, 27 left-wing activists received long sentences for 'subversion'.

Since the mid-1970s, Morocco has been embroiled in conflict over its attempts to annex the Western (formerly Spanish) Sahara. After a guerrilla war with the pro-independence Polisario organization, the Spanish withdrew in 1975. Morocco immediately laid claim to the territory, and on 6 Nov. 1975, the King led the 'Green March', when some 350,000 unarmed Moroccans entered the Western Sahara in a gesture of peaceful occupation. The southern third of the territory was occupied by Mauritania, which withdrew in 1979. This left Morocco fighting the Polisario for the whole of the Western Sahara. The war has been long and costly for Morocco. An estimated 100,000 troops maintain the 1,400 miles of defensive walls built with United States aid to defend the economically valuable areas. Polisario, which has been supported by Algeria and Libya, seeks independence for the territory as the 'Saharan Arab Democratic Republic'.

Throughout the 1980s, Morocco suffered increasing isolation over its Western Sahara policy; in Nov. 1984, it left the Organization of African Unity temporarily in protest at the SADR's admission as a full member. UN mediation eventually led to both sides accepting a peace formula in Aug. 1988, and direct talks opened in Jan. 1989, the aim being to decide the future of the territory through a referendum of its inhabitants. Polisario launched a fresh offensive in Oct. 1989, frustrated by the lack of progress in negotiations.

In an effort to halt Libyan support for the Polisario, Morocco agreed in 1984 to Col Gaddafi's proposal for a treaty of union between them. This was abrogated by Morocco in Aug. 1986, following ferocious Libyan criticism of King Hassan's controversial meeting with the Israeli prime minister the previous month. Morocco and Algeria restored relations after a 12-year break (caused by the latter's support for Polisario) in May 1988, opening the way to the creation of the Arab Maghreb Union, an economic federation grouping Algeria, Libya, Mauritania, Morocco and Tunisia, in Marrakesh in Feb. 1989.

Despite a series of amnesties announced by King Hassan in 1988–89, the existence and treatment of political prisoners became a focus of criticism of the regime.

CONSTITUTION AND GOVERNMENT

Executive and legislature

Under Morocco's constitutional monarchy, the prime minister as head of government is appointed by the king. Legislative authority rests with a 306-member Chamber of Representatives, elected for a six-year term, 206 of the seats being directly elected by universal adult suffrage (last election 1984) and the remainder by an electoral college composed of local councillors and representatives of professional bodies.

Present government

Head of state King Hassan II

Prime Minister Dr Azzedine Laraki

Principal Ministers Moulay Ahmed Alaoui (Minister of State); Haj Mohamed Bahnini (Minister of State); Mohamed Berrada (Finance); Abdel Latif Filali (Foreign Affairs and Co-operation); Driss Basri (Interior and Information); Abdelkebir Alaoui M'Daghri (Religious Endowments and Islamic Affairs); Moulay Mustapha Ben Larbi Alaiou (Justice).

Justice

The legal system is based on Islamic law and on French and Spanish civil law codes. The highest court is the Supreme Court, with a special Constitutional Chamber responsible for the judicial review of legislation. The judiciary is constitutionally independent of the executive and legislative branches. At lower levels, justice is administered through magistrates' courts, with regional tribunals and courts of appeal. The death penalty is in force. There were no executions between 1985 and mid-1988.

National symbols

Flag. A red field with green interlaced five-pointed star in the centre.

Festivals. 3 Mar. (Festival of the Throne, anniversary of King Hassan's accession); 1 May (Labour Day); 6 Nov. (Anniversary of the Green March); 18 Nov. (Independence Day).

Vehicle registration plate. MA.

INTERNATIONAL RELATIONS

Affiliations

NAM; Arab League; ICO; AMU.

Defence

Total Armed Forces: 203,500 (inclusive Gendarmerie). Terms of service: conscription 18 months authorized, most enlisted personnel are volunteers. Reserves: obligation, details unknown.

Army: 170,000; 173 main battle tanks (M-48A5), 50 light tanks (AMX-13).

Navy: 6,500 inclusive 1,500 naval infantry; one frigate (Spain Descubierta) and 19 patrol and coastal combatants.

Air Force: 15,000; 109 combat aircraft (mainly Mirage F-1EH and F-1CH, F5A/-5B/-5E/-5F, AlphaJet) and 24 armed helicopters.

ECONOMY

Currency

The unit is the dirham, divided into 100 centimes.

National finance

Budget. The 1987 budget (in US$) was for expenditure (current and capital) of 5,000 million and revenue of 4,000 million. Main items of current expenditure are education 16.9%; defence 14.5%.

Balance of payments. The balance of payments (current account, 1987) was a surplus of US$164 million.

Inflation. (1988) 4.5%.

Gross Domestic Product

Estimated total GDP US$16,750 million, per capita US$740 (ranking 64 in the world by size).

Economically active population. The total number of persons active in the economy was 7,400,000; unemployed: 15%.

Sector	% of workforce	% of GDP
industry	15	31
agriculture	50	19
services*	35	50

* services figure includes elements unassigned to other categories.

Energy and mineral resources

Oil and gas. Morocco produced 19,290 tons/17,500 tonnes of crude oil in 1981 and a further 5 million tons/4.5 million tonnes of refined oil in 1983.

Minerals. Phosphate extraction constitutes the principal mining activity with 23,589,220 tons/21,400,000 tonnes produced in 1986. Output: (1985 in 1000 tons/tonnes) anthracite 798.6/724.5; lead 169.3/153.6; iron ore 209.8/190.3; copper 65/59; zinc 30/27; manganese 48.2/43.7; baryt 510.7/463.3; fluorine 82/74; salt 130/118.

Electricity. Capacity: 2,064,000 kW; production: 7,757 million kWh; 310 kwh per capita (1988).

Bioresources

Agriculture. The agricultural sector, including fishing, provides 30% of all export earnings. Of the 19 million acres/7.7 million ha of cultivable land in 1984, 11.1 million acres/4.5 million ha were used for cereal crops; 988,386 acres/400,000 ha for leguminous vegetables; 370,645/150,000 for market gardening; 271,806/110,000 sown to fodder and 988,386/400,000 covered by extensive fruit plantations. Some illegal cannabis is also grown.

Crop production: (1986 in 1000 tons/tonnes) wheat 4,199/3,809; barley 3,927/3,563; sugar beet 2,756/2,500; fruit 1,901/1,725; maize 338/307; pulses 433/393; sugar cane 871/790; olives 364/330; tomatoes 440/400; onions 287/260; potatoes 62/56; sunflower seeds 23/21; groundnuts 40/36.

Livestock numbers: (1987 in millions) cattle 2.85; sheep 15; goats 5.3.

Forestry. An estimated 12.4 million acres/5m ha of land is covered by forest.

Fisheries. Total catch: (1986) 651,459 tons/591,000 tonnes.

Industry and commerce

Industry. Main industries are phosphate rock mining and processing; food processing; leather goods; textiles; construction; tourism.

Commerce. Exports: (1988) US$3,300 million or 18.3% of GDP; Imports: $4,200m in the same year or 23.3% of GDP. Principal exports include food and beverages 30%; semi-processed goods 23%; consumer goods 21%; phosphates 17%. Imported commodities include capital goods 24%; semi-processed goods 22%; raw materials 16%; fuel and lubricants 16%; foods and beverages 13%; consumer goods 10%. Chief trading partners are (imports and exports) EC countries; USSR; US; Japan and (imports only) Canada and Iraq.

Trade with UK. Morocco imported UK goods worth £79 million in 1988; exports to UK totalled £78.9 million.

Tourism. (1986) 1.47 million visitors.

COMMUNICATIONS

Railways

There are 1,176 miles/1,893 km of railways, of which 605 miles/974 km are electrified.

Roads

There are 35,824 miles/57,651 km of roads, of which 16,479 miles/26,519 km are paved.

Aviation

Royal Air Maroc provides domestic and international services (international airports are at Casablanca, Rabat, Tangier, Marrakesh, Agadir, Oujda, Al-Hocima and Fez). Passengers: (1984) 1.04 million.

Shipping

Agadir, Casablanca, El Jorf Lasfar, Kénitra, Mohammedia, Safi and Tangier are all ports onto the Atlantic Ocean. Ceuta and Melilla (both Spanish-controlled) and Nador are on the Mediterranean coast of Morocco. The merchant marine consists of 53 ships of 1,000 GRT or over. Freight loaded: (1986) 22.2 million tons/20.1 million tonnes; unloaded: 14.2 million tons/12.9 million tonnes.

Telecommunications

A good communications system whose principal centres are Casablanca and Rabat. There are 280,000 telephones. There are 4.3 million radios and 1.2 million televisions (1988). The government RTM operation broadcasts domestic radio services in French, Arabic, Berber, Spanish and English, a foreign service radio network, and television programmes in French and Arabic (since 1962). There is competition from the private television company 2M International. Voice of America has a radio station in Tangier.

EDUCATION AND WELFARE

Education

Education is obligatory between the ages of seven and 13. Since 1959, efforts have been made to streamline the French, Spanish, Muslim and Israeli systems of education. Primary and secondary education is conducted in Arabic.

Schools. A total of 75,094 primary school teachers serve 3,144 schools and 2,550,000 pupils (one per 34 pupils). A further 1,050,000 pupils receive instruction from 51,711 secondary school teachers (one per 20 pupils). In addition 36,110 students attend technical schools, teacher-training colleges or vocational establishments.

Universities. Six universities employ 3,146 members of staff (lecturers and tutors) with 99,637 registered students.

Literacy. 28%.

Health

Private medical healthcare provides about 2,000 doctors, and about 700 nurses. In the state sector, over 5,000 doctors and about 4,500 registered nurses serve approximately 1,000 medical centres and dispensaries. The total number of qualified nurses is around 15,000.

MOZAMBIQUE

República Popular de Moçambique
(People's Republic of Mozambique)

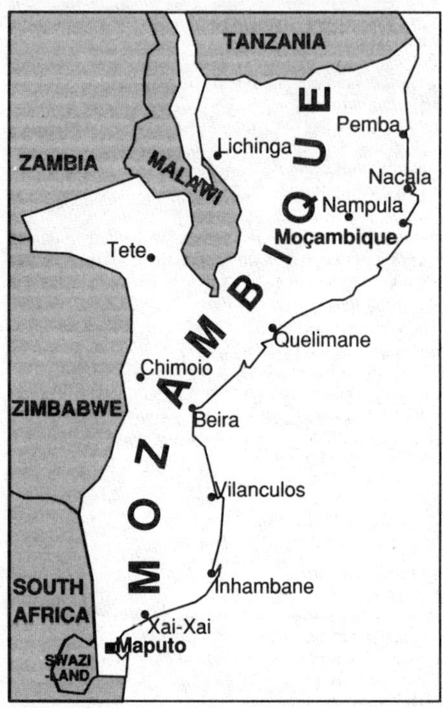

GEOGRAPHY

Situated on the south-east African coast, Mozambique covers a total area of 308,568 miles^2/799,400 km^2 divided into ten provinces of which the most populous are north-central Zambezia and Nampula. The River Zambezi bisects the country, flowing south-east from the Zimbabwean and Zambian frontiers and passing through the Carona Bassa dam before emptying into the Mozambique Channel south of Chinde. South of the Zambezi, the terrain is predominantly semi-arid lowland savannah (average elevation 656 ft/200 m) with a coastal belt characterized by mangrove swamps and sandy beaches. North of the comparatively fertile Zambezi delta, the coastal plain is narrower, backed by a rugged interior savannah plateau (2,625–3,281 ft/800–1,000 m) abutting the tropical vegetation of the north-west highlands. The highest peak, Mt Binga (7,992 ft/2,436 m) is located south-west of the Zambezi in the Serra de Gorongosa. Other principal rivers include the Limpopo (south) and the Lurio (north). 4% of the land area is arable and 20% is forested.

Climate

Tropical, with high humidity. The wet season lasts Dec.–Mar. Rainfall decreases north-south, ranging from 56 in/1,420 mm in the north-west to 20–30 in/500–750 mm in the south-east. Average Jan./July temperatures in the lowlands are 79–86°F/26–30°C and 59–68°F/15–20°C respectively, with corresponding highland temperature ranges of 72–77°F/22–25°C and 52–59°F/11–15°C. Drought conditions affect many southern regions. Maputo: Jan. 78°F/25.6°C. July 65°F/18.3°C. Average annual rainfall 30 in/760 mm. Beira: Jan. 82°F/27.8°C. July 69°F/20.6°C. Average annual rainfall 60 in/1,522 mm.

Cities and towns

Maputo (capital) 1,006,765

Population

Total population is 14,845,000 of which 23% live in urban areas. Population density is 48 persons per mile^2/18.5 persons per km^2. The bulk of the population is made up of indigenous ethnic groups of which the Makua/Lomwe peoples comprise 52%, living in the far northernmost provinces. Other significant groupings include the Shona 6%, Malawi 12%, and Yao 3% in Manica, Sofala and Tete provinces and the Thonga (24%) in the south.

Birth rate 4.57%. **Death rate** 2.01%. **Rate of population increase** 2.56%. **Age distribution** under 15 = 43.7%; over 65 = 3.2% **Life expectancy** female 50; male 47; average 48.

Religion

60% of the population practise indigenous animist beliefs; 30% are Christian (of whom 1.7 million are Roman Catholic) and 10% are Muslim.

Language

Portuguese is the official language, although its influence beyond the major urban centres is limited. A variety of indigenous Bantu dialects (see ethnic groupings) and Swahili are widely spoken throughout Mozambique.

HISTORY

The early inhabitants of present-day Mozambique were probably related to the San (Bushman) peoples, before Bantu-speaking peoples settled in the area in the 1st to 4th centuries AD. Arab traders established settlements in the 8th century, which subsequently developed into independent city-states. The Maravi kingdom of Mwene Matapa controlled most of the Zambezi basin when the Portuguese explorer Vasco de Gama landed in 1498.

The Portuguese had established two inland trading settlements by 1531 and a century later, in 1629, the Mwene Matapa kingdom recognized Portuguese sovereignty. In this period Portugal exercised little effective control, treating its imperial status primarily as a claim to exclusive rights in exploiting the local trade in slaves, gold and ivory. In the late 17th century, the Changamire of the Rozwi kingdom conquered the Mwene Matapa and pushed the Portuguese south of the River Zambezi. Portuguese control was slowly re-established north of the Zambezi and in 1752 the first colonial governor was appointed. From the late 17th century the slave trade became a major factor in the Mozambique economy, continuing for some years after it became illegal in the 19th century.

By the late 19th century Mozambique was administered partly by the Portuguese authorities in Lisbon and partly by private companies. Private Portuguese landowners had conquered, or been granted, large estates or prazos in the Zambezi valley and elsewhere in Mozambique from the 17th century onwards, deriving revenue from a feudal-type imposition on peasant farmers; in addition, in the late 19th century, territorial concessions were granted to three charter companies over wide areas in the northern part of the colony. In 1929 and 1940 the Portuguese government took control of the company lands. In 1951 Mozambique became an overseas province of Portugal.

The Front for the Liberation of Mozambique (FRELIMO – Frente de Libertação de Moçambique) was formed in 1962, with Eduardo Mondlane as its leader, following the merger of three nationalist movements. An armed struggle against Portuguese rule was launched in 1964, and continued until a cease-fire was called in Sept. 1974 (the situation having been changed dramatically by Portugal's Apr. 1974 revolution). Mozambique became independent on 25 June 1975, under the presidency of Samora Machel, the leader of FRELIMO since the assassination of Mondlane by the Portuguese in 1969.

FRELIMO's efforts towards economic growth and political stability were hampered from the outset by the rapid departure of some 250,000 Portuguese settlers, who left a trail of destruction behind them. The country also faced destabilization first by Rhodesia and latterly by South Africa. In Mar. 1976 the Mozambican government closed its border with Rhodesia, and continued to provide bases and support for the guerrillas fighting the minority settler regime there. Considerable devastation was caused by Rhodesian cross-border raids. The Rhodesian intelligence service helped to found and foster the Mozambique National Resistance (MNR – Resistência Nacional Moçambicana, or RENAMO); the South African military took over as backers of the MNR following Zimbabwean independence in 1980. The MNR waged a terror campaign against the local population and also disrupted road, rail and oil pipeline links from Mozambican ports. Zimbabwean troops have been deployed since 1982 to help protect the Beira-Mutare pipeline.

As the MNR's activities grew more widespread, severe food shortages and increasing numbers of refugees became evident. A joint UNICEF/ Mozambican report, published in Mar. 1989, estimated that 600,000 people had been killed as a result of the civil war and that 494,000 children had died 'from causes directly attributed to malnutrition associated with war'. Under the Nkomati accord, signed on 16 Mar. 1984, South Africa agreed to stop supporting the MNR as the Mozambican government committed itself to ending facilities previously made available to South African nationalist guerrillas. The South Africans appeared not to honour this commitment, although a further series of meetings between the two sides in 1988–89 seemed to herald improved relations.

FRELIMO's third party congress in Feb. 1977 provided for the reconstitution of FRELIMO as a Marxist-Leninist vanguard party with a restricted membership. The fourth party congress in Apr. 1983, however, introduced significant changes in economic policies and the expansion of the membership of the party's central committee. After maintaining close ties with eastern Europe and China, Mozambique began to develop closer links with the West during the 1980s, and in Oct. 1987 Mozambique was granted observer status at the meeting of Commonwealth heads of government.

Pres. Machel died on 19 Oct. 1986 in mysterious circumstances in a plane crash inside South Africa, close to the Mozambique–Swaziland border. He was succeeded by Foreign Minister Joaquim Chissano. Elections were last held in Dec. 1986; 299 candidates were nominated by the sole party, FRELIMO, for membership of the 250-seat People's Assembly. At the fourth FRELIMO congress, in July 1989, the party adopted reforms intended to make it a broader-based party of national unity. Congress also approved a 12-point plan put forward by Chissano for a negotiated settlement to the civil war; this envisaged initially indirect negotiations with RENAMO, but ruled out any form of power sharing with the rebels.

CONSTITUTION AND GOVERNMENT

Executive and legislature

The ruling Front for the Liberation of Mozambique is the sole legal political organization; the president of Frelimo is head of state and commander-in-chief of the armed forces. Legislative power is vested in the People's Assembly, to which representatives are elected from the armed forces and each of the ten provinces (last elections 1986); the Assembly also has as ex officio members the Frelimo Central Committee, Executive Committee, and Permanent Commission, the members of the Council of Ministers, and the provincial governors.

Present government

Head of state, President of Frelimo; C.-in-C. of the Armed Forces Joaquim Alberto Chissano

Principal members of the Council of Ministers Mario da Graça Machungo (Prime Minister; Planning); Lt.-Gen. Alberto Joaquim Chipande (Defence); Lt.-Gen. Antonio Hama Thai (Chief of General Staff of the Armed Forces, Deputy Minister of Defence); Pascoal Mocumbi (Foreign Affairs); Maj.-Gen. Jacinto Soares Veloso (International Co-operation); Mariano Matsinhe (Security); Manuel António (Interior); Abdul Magid Osman (Finance); Ossmane Ali Dauto (Justice).

Ruling party

Front for the Liberation of Mozambique (Frente da Libertação de Moçambique – FRELIMO). *President* Joaquim Alberto Chissano. *Members of the Political Bureau* Joaquim Alberto Chissano; Marcelino dos Santos; Lt.-Gen. Alberto Joaquim Chipande; Lt.-Gen. Armando Emílio Guebuza; Jorge Rebelo; Mariano de Araújo Matsinhe; Maj.-Gen. Jacinto Soares Veloso; Mario da Graça Machungo; Pascoal Mocumbi; Eduardo da Silva Nihia; Feliciano Gundana; Rafael Maguni.

Administration

The country is divided into ten provinces.

Provinces and provincial governors Cabo Delgado – António Simbine; Gaza – Francisco Pateguana; Inhambane – José Pascoal Zandamela; Manica – Rafael Maguni; Maputo – Raimondo Manuel Vila; Nampula – Jacob Jeremias Nyambir; Niassa – Julio Ntchola; Sofala – Francisco Masquil; Tete – Cadmiel Muthemba; Zambezia – Carlos Agostinho do Rosario. Maputo City Council Chairman – João Baptista Cosme.

Justice
The system of law is based on Portuguese civil codes and indigenous practice, substantially modified by the Marxist principles applied locally during the anti-colonial struggle, and nationally since independence. A system of People's Courts exists at all levels. The death penalty is in force. There were at least four executions between 1985 and mid-1988. Offences were treason, armed rebellion.

National symbols
Flag. Three horizontal stripes of green, black and yellow, with a narrow white stripe above and below the black stripe. Based on the hoist is a red triangle.

Festivals. 3 Feb. (Heroes' Day, anniversary of the assassination of Eduardo Mondlane); 7 Apr. (Day of the Mozambican Woman); 1 May (Workers' Day); 25 June (Independence Day); 7 Sep. (Victory Day, anniversary of the end of the Armed Struggle); 25 Sept. (Anniversary of the launching of the Armed Struggle for National Liberation, and Day of the Armed Forces of Mozambique); 25 Dec. (National Family Day).

INTERNATIONAL RELATIONS

Affiliations
NAM; OAU; SADCC; ACP; Comecon (observer).

Defence
Total Armed Forces: 36,700 (some 10,500 conscripts). Terms of service: conscription (selective), two years (inclusive women).

Army: some 35,000; 250 main battle tanks (T-34/-54/-55).

Navy: 700; 23 patrol and coastal combatants.

Air Force: 1,000; some 70 combat aircraft (MiG-17/-21), 12 armed helicopters.

Opposition: Mozambique National Resistance (MNR or RENAMO), supported by South Africa: 20,000 reported, some 10,000 trained.

Foreign Forces: Zimbabwe: 6,000–12,000 (varies); Tanzania: some 3,000; Malawi: 600 (varies).

ECONOMY

Currency
The unit is the metical, divided into 100 centavos.

National finance
Budget. The 1987 budget (in US$) was for expenditure (current and capital) of 321 million and revenue of 122 million.

Balance of payments. The balance of payments (current account, 1987) was a deficit of $676 million (est.).

Inflation. (1987) 15%.

Gross Domestic Product
Estimated total GDP US$1,490 million, per capita under US$100 (ranking 127 in the world by size).

Sector	% of GDP
industry	12
agriculture	50
services*	38

* services figure includes elements unassigned to other categories.

Energy and mineral resources
Minerals. Coal, titanium.

Electricity. Capacity: 2.26 million kW; production: 1,741 million kWh; 120 kWh per capita (1988).

Bioresources
Agriculture. Main cash crops are cotton; cashew nuts; sugar; tea; copra; sisal; rice. Other crops: maize; wheat; peanuts; potatoes; beans; sorghum; cassava.

Crop production: (1986 in 1,000 tons/tonnes) cereals 672/610; tea 16.5/15; maize 386/350; bananas 83/75; sisal 3.3/3; rice 66/60; groundnuts 72/65; copra 74/67; vegetables 211/191; citrus fruits 46/42; potatoes 72/65; cashews 33/30; sunflower seeds 22/20; cotton 19/17; sugar 29/26.

Livestock numbers: (1987) cattle 1.35 million; goats 370,000; sheep 117,000; pigs 155,000; asses 20,000.

Forestry. 20% of land area is forested. Production: (1985) 1,236,006 ft^3/35,000 m^3 of cut timber.

Fisheries. Total prawn catch: (1984) 6,393 tons/5,800 tonnes; other fish 12,897 tons/11,700 tonnes.

Industry and commerce
Industry. The main industries are food; beverages; chemicals; petroleum products; textiles; non-metallic mineral products (cement, glass, asbestos); tobacco.

Commerce. Exports: (1987) US$85.9 million, including shrimps 48%; cashews 21%; sugar 10%; copra 3%; citrus fruits 3%. Imports: US$642 million, including food; clothing; farm equipment; petroleum. Countries exported to were US; western Europe; East Germany; Japan. Imports came from US; western Europe; USSR.

Trade with UK. Mozambique imported UK goods worth £24,218,000; exports to UK totalled £5,574,000.

COMMUNICATIONS

Railways
There are 2,388 miles/3,843 km of railways.

Roads
There are 24,326 miles/39,173 km of roads (7,398 miles/11,905 km are classified as first-class roads).

Aviation
Linhas Aéreas de Moçambique provides domestic and international services (main airport is at Maputo). Passengers: (1986) 267,300.

Shipping
There are about 2,330 miles/3,750 km of navigable inland waterways. The marine ports are Maputo, Beira and Nacala. There are five merchant marine cargo ships of 1,000 GRT or over. Freight loaded: (1985) 2.3 million tons/2.1 million tonnes; unloaded: 2.6 million tons/2.4 million tonnes.

Telecommunications
There are 57,400 telephones and a fair communications system. There are 500,000 radios and 10,000 televisions (1986). The government-controlled broadcasting services include a limited television experiment.

EDUCATION AND WELFARE

Education
Schools. (1985) 4,382 primary schools with 1,251,391 pupils; 208 secondary schools with 144,012 pupils.

Universities. (1985) 2,500 students enrolled in the Universidade Eduardo Mondlane.

Literacy. 14%.

Health
In 1985 there were 258 hospitals and health centres with 12,472 beds (one per 1,152 people) and 317 doctors (one per 45,032 people).

NAMIBIA

Namibie (Afrikaans: formerly known as *Suidwes-Afrika)*
Namibia (German: formerly known as *Südwestafrika)*
Namibia (English: formerly known as *South West Africa)*

GEOGRAPHY

Located on the south-west coast of Africa and bisected by the Tropic of Capricorn, Namibia covers a total area of 318,176 miles²/824,290 km², including the enclave of Walvis Bay (some 347 miles²/900 km²) over which South Africa maintains control, but which Namibia's 1990 independence constitution declares to be part of Namibian territory.

From north to south, the arid and infertile Namib desert forms a rocky coastal belt averaging 62 miles/100 km in width. North of Walvis Bay, Brandberg rises to 8,550 ft/2,606 m, Namibia's highest peak. Inland, the central plateau (mean elevation 4,921 ft/1,500 m) includes the Tsaris (south-west), Anas (central) and Erongo (west) massifs, sloping in the south and east to meet the grassland of the Kalahari desert. The Okavango (north), Orange (south), Kunene and Zambezi rivers are the chief perennial water-bodies. The northern (administrative) districts are the most densely populated (inhabited by the Ovambo). 1% of the land is arable and 22% is (scrub) forest or woodland.

Climate

Arid, continental tropical. Temperatures vary from a mean annual range of 66–72°F/19–22°C on the central plateau to a summer (Nov.–Apr.) high of 120°F/49°C in the coastal desert (Namib). Sparse rainfall along the coast is frequently less than 1 in/25 mm per year (Walvis Bay). Inland, rainfall averages increase to 14 in/360 mm per year at Windhoek. Daytime temperatures average 68–86°F/20–30°C.

Cities and towns

Windhoek (capital)	120,000
Swakopmund	15,500
Rehoboth	15,000
Rundu	15,000

Population

Total population is variously estimated at between 1,300,000 (internal government estimate pre-independence) and 1,700,000 (UN estimate) and is predominantly rural. Population density is 4–5.3 persons per mile²/1.6–2 per km². Ethnic divisions (based on total population est. 1.27 million): 86% Black; 6.5% White; 7.5% mixed (45% of the population belong to the Ovambo ethnic group).

Birth rate 4.44%. **Death rate** 1.37%. **Rate of population increase** over 3%. **Age distribution** under 15 = 45.1%; over 65 = 3.3%. **Life expectancy** female 49.9; males 46.6; average 48 (Whites 68–72).

Religion

Approximately 90% of the population are Lutheran, Roman Catholic, Dutch Reformed and Anglican Christians. Of the remaining 10% a significant proportion follow traditional animist beliefs.

Language

Afrikaans is spoken by 60% of the White population, the rest having German or English as their mother tongue. Afrikaans and English are official languages. Bantu-speaking groups in the northern regions include the Ovambo, the largest single group, and the Okavango, East Caprivian and Kaokolander ethnic groups. To the south, the major ethnolinguistic divisions are the Bantu-speaking Herero and Tswana and the Khoisan-speaking Bergdama, Nama and San peoples. The Rehoboth Basters represent a racial mix of Afrikaners and Nama.

HISTORY

Prior to European contact, South West Africa was occupied by the Khoikhoi, the San (or Bushmen) and the Bantu-speaking Herero. In the late 1480s Portuguese navigators first explored the coastal regions at Cape Cross, Walvis Bay and Dias Point, and they were followed in the 17th to early 19th centuries by Dutch and British explorers. The German connection began in the 1840s with the arrival of the Rhenish Missionary Society. In 1878 Britain annexed Walvis Bay; an Anglo-German agreement of 1890 acknowledged German control of South West Africa, with Britain retaining Walvis Bay (which it administered as part of Cape Colony). German colonization was characterized by the progressive alienation of land and cattle from the indigenous population and the creation of a dispossessed African wage-labour force. The Herero rose against the colonizers in 1904 but were ruthlessly suppressed, their population being reduced from 80,000 to 16,000 starving refugees.

During World War I South African troops defeated the Germans and occupied South West Africa. The territory was mandated to South Africa by the League of Nations in 1920, to be administered on behalf of Britain, with the duty of preparing it for eventual self-determination; the mandate required the administering power to 'promote to the utmost the material and moral well-being and the social progress of the inhabitants'. In 1946 the United Nations rejected South Africa's request to incorporate South West Africa and in 1950 the International Court of Justice ruled that the territory remained under an international mandate.

The UN General Assembly on 27 Oct. 1966 revoked the South African mandate and from 1968 referred to the territory as Namibia. South Africa, however, having contested the conversion from League of Nations mandate to UN trusteeship status in 1946, did not accept the UN's right to terminate its administration. In 1949 the territory's European voters had been given representation in the South African parliament and in 1966 South Africa had extended its apartheid laws to Namibia, with retrospective effect from 1950. In so doing, implementing the 1964 Odendaal Commission report, it had divided the territory between ethnically based 'homelands', a reserved area for Whites (43% of the total area) and an area directly administered by South Africa, including the diamond zone which was the major economic resource (together with the Rössing uranium mine, increasingly important from its inception in 1970, and majority-owned by the multinational RTZ).

The South West African People's Organization (SWAPO) was founded in 1958, under the leadership of Sam Nujoma, and in Oct. 1966 it launched the armed struggle, having failed to persuade the South African regime to negotiate independence for Namibia. The UN in 1973 recognized SWAPO as the 'authentic representative of the Namibian people' and the UN's first Commissioner for Namibia was appointed. South Africa pursued its own plans for an 'internal settlement', setting up a political structure under the 1975 Turnhalle Conference proposals. Negotiations involving SWAPO, South Africa and internal Namibian leaders supported by South Africa, were held at various stages through the 1970s and 1980s, including the unsuccessful Geneva conference in 1981, with a Western 'contact group' seeking to broker a solution.

UN Security Council Resolution 435, which was passed in 1978, embodied terms for an internationally recognized settlement and provided for UN-supervised elections prior to independence. The terms of Resolution 435 were finally set in motion as part of the tripartite agreement formally signed at the UN in New York on 22 Dec. 1988 by Angola, Cuba (which was to withdraw troops from Angola) and South Africa.

Implementation of the settlement began officially on 1 Apr. 1989, marred initially by large-scale violence as SWAPO guerrillas sought to cross into Namibia and clashed with South African forces (casualties amounted to 259 SWAPO guerrillas and 26 South African troops in the first week of April). A cease-fire was worked out to allow the transition process to proceed, and elections were held effectively on schedule (7–11 Nov. 1989) under the supervision of a UN Transition Assistance Group. The poll gave SWAPO 41 seats in a 72-member Constituent Assembly; the constitution was formally adopted on 9 Feb. 1990, to take effect at independence on 21 Mar. 1990, when Nujoma became the country's first president, his government consisting primarily but not exclusively of SWAPO members.

CONSTITUTION AND GOVERNMENT

Executive and legislature

Under the 1990 Constitution, Namibia is a multi-party republic. The head of state is the executive president, elected directly for a maximum term of five years and limited to a maximum of two such terms. The first holder of the post, Sam Nujoma, was elected prior to independence by a unanimous vote of the Constituent Assembly (16 Feb. 1990). The president exercises the functions of government with the assistance of a cabinet headed by a prime minister. The president may declare a state of emergency, but only subject to National Assembly approval within 30 days. Legislative authority lies with the parliament: the former Constituent Assembly was converted upon independence into the lower house of a bicameral parliamentary structure, known as the National Assembly and with 72 members serving a five-year term. A proportional representation system was to apply to future elections. An upper house representing regional leaders was to be created two years after independence.

Present government

President Sam Nujoma

Principal Cabinet members Hage Geingob (Prime Minister); Theo Ben Gurirab (Foreign Affairs); Peter Mueshihange (Defence); Andimba Toivo ja Toivo (Mines and Energy); Hifikepunje Pohamba (Home Affairs); Ngarikutuke Tjiriange (Justice); Otto Herrigel (Finance).

Justice

Prior to independence, under South African administration, the system of justice was based on Roman-Dutch and customary law. The independence constitution provides for an independent judiciary, with a Supreme Court as its highest body, and a bill of rights (including rights to fair trial and cultural and religious freedoms) entrenched against amendment. The constitution makes apartheid a criminal offence, outlaws torture and forced labour, and formally bans the death penalty.

National symbols

Flag. Diagonal stripes of blue, red and green separated by white lines, with a golden sun at the top near the hoist.

Festivals. 21 Mar. (Independence Day).

INTERNATIONAL RELATIONS

Affiliations

Already recognized prior to independence as a member of the FAO, ILO, UNESCO and WHO, an independent Namibia was to become a full member of the UN, NAM, Commonwealth, OAU and SADCC, and to seek World Bank membership while remaining for at least two years a part of the Southern African Customs Union.

Defence

Namibia's post-independence armed forces were to be based on the integration of locally recruited units with former SWAPO guerrillas. The first integrated units, comprising 500 men, began training in Feb. 1990 under supervision by Kenyan members of the UN Transition Assistance Group. Britain sent military instructors to assist with the formation of a national force.

ECONOMY

Currency

The South African rand, divided into 100 cents, is to continue in use after independence for a transitional period probably of at least two years.

National finance

Budget. The budget deficit in the first year of independence was expected to be about US$200 million, or double that of 1989/90, with priority going to increased spending on social infrastructure and amenities.

Balance of payments. The balance of payments (current account, 1988) was a deficit of US$37 million.

Gross Domestic Product

Estimated total GDP (1989) US$1,800 million, per capita US$1,060–1,300.

Energy and mineral resources

Minerals. Mining accounts for over 30% of total GDP. Export earnings from mining: (1988) $682 million, the principal current activities being diamond mining (dominated by CDM, a company wholly owned prior to independence by De Beers of South Africa), and the Rössing uranium mine, in which the government has 50% voting rights and RTZ Corporation is the major foreign partner. Other mineral resources (industrial minerals including coal, base metals including lead, zinc and tin, and gold and silver) are underdeveloped. Production from the Navachab gold mine came on stream in Dec. 1989.

Bioresources

Agriculture. Some 5,000 White ranchers owned, at independence, about 80% of cultivable land and produced 95% of agricultural output (primarily cattle and sheep for export, and karakul sheep pelts).

Crop production is principally wheat, maize and sunflower seeds. Subsistence farming provides the livelihood of about 20% of the total population. A declared objective of the independence government was to implement land reform in co-operation with White landowners.

Livestock numbers: (1987 in millions) cattle 1.8; sheep 2.8; goats 1.6.

Fisheries. Total catches in offshore deep-sea fishing have averaged over 1,102,300 tons/1,000,000 tonnes annually, while some 440,920 tons/400,000 tonnes of pilchards, anchovies and mackerel are caught inshore. However, these activities have been based entirely on South African operations from Walvis Bay, the principal fishing activity elsewhere being lobster-catching.

Industry and commerce

Industry. Manufacturing, accounting for only some 5% of total GDP, is based on processing of primary products, including meat packing and fish processing. A development priority will be greater value-added processing particularly of mining production, for example diamond-cutting.

Commerce. Exports: (1988) US$850 million, of which 72% minerals. Imports: (1988) $780 million. Principal trading partner is South Africa.

Trade with UK. In (1988) Namibia imported goods worth £3,259,000 from the UK and exported goods worth £10,729,000 to the UK.

COMMUNICATIONS

Railways

There are 1,453 miles/2,340 km of railways, the main line running from the border with South Africa in the south-east, to Windhoek, on north-west to Swakopmund and south again to Walvis Bay.

Roads

There are 33,845 miles/54,500 km of roads (2,484 miles/4,000 km paved, 1,553/2,500 gravel, remainder unsurfaced).

Aviation

The international airport is at Windhoek. Nearly 200,000 passengers flew in or out on international flights in 1987/8. There are some 150 other airports or airstrips in the country, of which 20 have permanent-surfaced runways.

Shipping

Walvis Bay has handled the great majority of shipping hitherto, the only other port being Lüderitz.

Telecommunications

There are 63,000 telephones. The two AM radio stations prior to independence were the mutually hostile South West Africa Broadcasting Corporation operating from Windhoek (and also broadcasting television programmes in three languages) and the exile-based SWAPO Broadcasts transmitting its Voice of Namibia programmes. There were over 60,000 licensed radio sets and nearly 30,000 televisions in 1988.

EDUCATION AND WELFARE

Education

In 1985–86 there were 1,150 schools in all, and 12,000 teachers, with a total enrolment of some 375,000 pupils. Higher education facilities comprised three technical institutes, three agricultural colleges, four teacher-training colleges and one academy. The new government has announced its intention to make education free and compulsory for all up to 16 years of age.

Literacy. 100% among Whites; 16% among Blacks.

Health

The UN in 1983 estimated per capita expenditure on health services as 5.4 rand for Blacks and 270 rand for Whites. By 1988 there were in all some 300 doctors, nearly 70 hospitals and 170 clinics, with 5.5 beds per 1,000 population. Infant mortality is estimated at 72 per 1,000 live births.

NAURU

Republic of Nauru

GEOGRAPHY

The island Republic of Nauru lies approximately 2,486 miles/4,000 km north-east of Sydney, Australia, 186 miles/300 km west of Kiribati, 2,423 miles/3,900 km south-west of Hawaii and 25 miles/40 km south of the equator. It encloses an area of 8.1 miles^2/21 km^2 rising to 197 ft/60 m elevation in the central plateau and encircled by a fertile belt of semi-cultivated land supporting the bulk of the population. The island is fringed by reefs and is very sparsely vegetated. 15% of the land is farmed.

Climate
Tropical, hot and humid (70–80%), Modified by sea breezes, daytime temperatures nevertheless register a mean 86°F/30°C. Annual rainfall average: 78.7 in/ 2,000 mm, with periodic droughts. The westerly monsoon lasts Nov.-Feb. Jan. 81°F/27.2°C. July 82°F/ 27.8°C. Average annual rainfall 73.3 in/1,862 mm.

Cities and towns
Nauru has no official capital.

Population
Total population is 8,000 of which 100% live in urban areas. Population density is 987.7 persons per mile^2/ 382.1 per km^2. Ethnic composition: 61.7% Nauruan; 26.5% Pacific Islanders; 8.5% Asian; 3.3% Caucasian.

Religion
Christianity is the dominant faith with strong Nauruan Protestant (Independent and Congregational Churches) and Roman Catholic representations.

Language
The Nauruan language is a Polynesian, Melanesian and Micronesian hybrid spoken by the entire population. English is also widely understood.

HISTORY

Little is known of the Polynesian inhabitants of this island before the arrival from Britain in 1798 of Capt. John Fearn, who named it Pleasant Island. From the 1830s Western traders and beachcombers established themselves there, but by the 1870s increasing concern over the scale of clan warfare among the ethnic population led German traders to request the island's incorporation within the German Marshall Islands. From 1888, when the island assumed the name of Nauru, until 1914 it was administered by Germany. In 1899 a British company discovered that the island contained the world's richest phosphate deposits and mining started a few years later. The Germans surrendered Nauru in 1914 to an Australian force and in 1920 it became a British-mandated territory under the League of Nations, administered by Australia. The Japanese occupied Nauru from 1942 to 1945, and after World War II it continued under Australian administration as a United Nations trust territory. Political advancement for the Nauruans began in 1951 with the creation of the Local Government Council, and by 1966 a large measure of self-government had been granted. Independence was achieved on 31 Jan. 1968 and Nauru was accorded special member status of the Commonwealth later that year. Australia, New Zealand and Great Britain handed over in 1970 their joint control of the phosphate industry. Nauru has yet to apply to join the UN. After political uncertainties in 1986, when Kennan Adeang briefly held power, Hammer DeRoburt became president again following the general election in Jan. 1987. He was forced to resign in Aug. 1989 after a vote of no confidence, and was succeeded by Kenas Aroi. Following a general election on 9 Dec. 1989, the legislature elected Bernard Dowiyogo as president.

CONSTITUTION AND GOVERNMENT

Executive and legislature
The head of state is an executive president, who appoints the cabinet. The president is selected by the 18-member unicameral Parliament from among its members; the Parliament is elected for a three-year term.

Present government
President; Minister of Internal Affairs, External Affairs, Island Development and Industry, Public Service; Civil Aviation Bernard Dowiyogo
Other Ministers Vincent Detundamo (Works and Community Services; Minister assisting the President); Kinza Clodumar (Finance); Vinci Clodumar (Health; and Education); Kenna Adeung (Justice).

Justice
A Supreme Court of Nauru is presided over by the chief justice. The District Court, which is subordinate to the Supreme Court, is presided over by a resident magistrate. Both the Supreme Court and the District Court are Courts of Record. The Supreme Court exercises both original and appellate jurisdiction. A large number of British statutes and the common law have been adopted for Nauru. The death penalty is nominally in force. There were no executions between 1985 and mid-1988.

National symbols
Flag. Dark blue with a narrow yellow horizontal stripe in the middle and a white twelve-pointed star in the bottom left.
Festivals. 31 Jan. (Independence Day).

INTERNATIONAL RELATIONS

Affiliations
Commonwealth (associate member); SPF.

Defence
No armed forces as such.

ECONOMY

Currency
The unit is the Australian dollar, divided into 100 cents.

National finance
Budget. The 1986 budget (in US$) was for expenditure (current and capital) of 52 million and revenue of 70 million.

Gross Domestic Product
Estimated total GNP US$160 million, per capita US$20,000 (overall size of economy ranking 170 in the world).

Energy and mineral resources
Minerals. Phosphates, reserves of which are expected to be exhausted by 1995. Sales of phosphates: (1984) $A100 million.
Electricity. Capacity: 13,250 kW; production: 48 million kWh; 5,390 kWh per capita (1988).

Bioresources
Agriculture. Neglibible. Nauru is almost completely dependent on imports for food and water.

Industry and commerce
Industry. Phosphate mining; financial services; coconuts.
Commerce. Exports: (1984) US$93 million, consisting almost entirely of phosphates. Imports were US$73 million, consisting of food; fuel; manufactures; machinery. Countries exported to were Australia; New Zealand. Imports came from Australia; New Zealand; UK; Japan.
Trade with UK. Nauru imported UK goods, worth £759,000; exports to UK totalled £642,000.

COMMUNICATIONS

Railways
There are 3.2 miles/5.2 km of railways (serving the phoshate workings).

Roads
There are 12 miles/19 km of roads.

Aviation
Air Nauru provides international services.

Telecommunications
There are 1,600 telephones and 5,500 radio receivers. An adequate intra-island and international radio communications system is provided by Australian facilities. There is a government radio station.

EDUCATION AND WELFARE

Education
Schools. Schooling is compulsory for children aged six to 16 in Nauru. In 1983 there were eight infant and primary schools and two secondary schools. In infant, primary and secondary schools combined there were 2,164 pupils and 44 teachers. There was also a trade school with four teachers and 74 students. Scholarships are awarded for secondary and higher education and vocational training in Australia and New Zealand.

Literacy. 99%.

NEPAL

Nepal Adhirajya (Kingdom of Nepal)

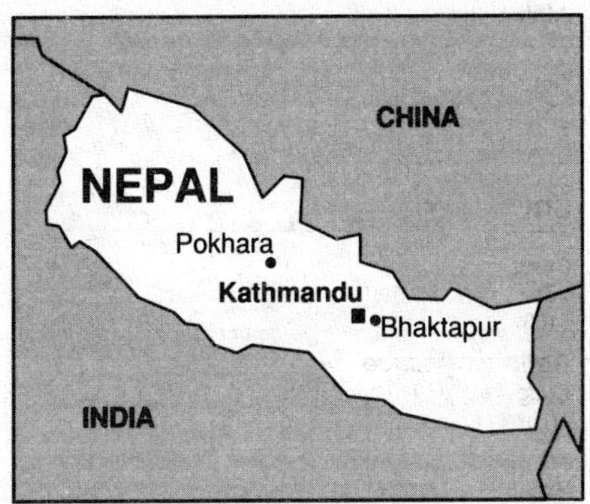

GEOGRAPHY

Nepal occupies a landlocked area of 54,349 miles^2/140,800 km^2, along the southern slopes of the Himalayas in south-central Asia. To the south, the Terai/Ganges river plain covers 17% of the total surface area. On the Indian border its fertile soils are well cultivated, but further north at the intersection of the Tarai plain and thinly populated Churia foothills, marshland and forest predominate. The fertile and densely populated central uplands enclose the Kathmandu and Pokhara Valley (4,386 ft/1,337 m above sea level, drained by the Baghmati and Seti rivers), while to the north the sparsely inhabited, glaciated Himalayan peaks soar to 29,029 ft/8,848 m at Mt Everest, the world's highest mountain. The Himalayas are cut by three principal river systems, the Karnali, Kosi and Gandak. 17% of the land is arable and one third is covered by forests.

Climate
Subtropical monsoon in the Tarai regions (monsoon lasts July-Oct.) with average winter and summer temperatures of 59°F/15°C and 86°F/30°C respectively. Conditions in the Himalayas are Alpine/Artic, with most land above 10,827 ft/3,300 m elevation permanently frozen. Rainfall reaches a maximum of 70 in/1,778 mm in the east, diminishing westward to 35 in/889 mm or less. Kathmandu: Jan 32°F/0°C. July 76°F/24.4°C. Average annual rainfall 56 in/1,428 mm.

Cities and towns

Kathmandu (capital)	235,160
Biratnagar	94,000
Lalitpur	81,000
Bhaktapur	50,500
Pokhara	48,500

Population
Total population is 18,234,000 of which 8% live in urban areas. Population density is 335 persons per mile^2/119.4 per km^2. At the last census, 58.4% were Nepalese (native Mongolian); 18.7% Bihari (including Maithiri and Bhojpuri); 3.3% Tharu; 3.5% Tamang; 3% Newar.

Birth rate 4.29% **Death rate** 1.7% **Rate of population increase** 2.6% **Age distribution** under 15 = 42.3%; over 65 = 3.0% **Life expectancy** female 50; male 52; average 51.

Religion
Nepal is the only official Hindu state in the world. 88–90% of the population are Hindu, 5% Buddhist and 3% Muslim. There are an estimated 35,000 Christians of whom 1,600 are Roman Catholic.

Language
Nepali is the official language, spoken by approximately 58% of the population. Another 20 languages subdivide into numerous dialects. Chief ethnolinguistic divisions are Bhojpuri; Bhutia (Sherpa); Gurung; Hindi; Limbu; Magar; Maithili; Newari; Rai; Kirati; Tamang; Tharu.

HISTORY

There is evidence of links between Nepal and India's

Gangetic plain from about 1500 BC onwards. The Buddha was born in southern Nepal about 568 BC and the Buddhist Newar culture flourished from about the 4th century BC onwards. There are several columns bearing Buddhist inscriptions erected by the Indian emperor Asoka in about 250 BC. The Lichchavi dynasty of Hindu kings was established in the 4th–5th centuries AD. Between AD 500–700 strong cultural and trading ties were established with Tibet.

By the 16th century a number of hill principalities had been created by Rajput nobles fleeing the Muslim invasions of India. The foundations of the modern state of Nepal and its current ruling family were laid in 1769 when the king of Gurkha, Prithvi Narayan Shah (1743–75), conquered the valley and moved his capital to Kathmandu. After a period of expansion Nepal's boundaries were set in a series of wars with her neighbours.

The 1814–16 border war with the East India Company led to acceptance of a British resident and the beginning of British influence over Nepal. Power in Nepal passed from the king to a succession of influential families, first the Thapas (1806–37) and then the Ranas (1846–1951), who became hereditary prime ministers. British influence grew under the Ranas, who secured support for their authority in domestic matters in exchange for accepting British 'guidance' in foreign affairs.

In the 1930s a nationalist political opposition, influenced by the Indian national movement, began to emerge and an attempt was mounted in 1940 to overthrow the Rana government. In 1946 the Nepali Congress was formed. In 1950 King Tribhuvan (1911–55), implicated in a plot to overthrow Rana rule, fled to India and an armed revolt broke out under Nepali Congress leadership. Order was restored through Indian mediation which produced an effective end to Rana domination and a division of power between the monarchy and the political parties. In 1951 the Congress leader, Bisweswore Prasad Koirala, became the first non-Rana prime minister of Nepal for more than a century. It proved difficult to establish stable governments, however, and under King Mahendra (1955–72) a struggle for power developed between the monarchy and the Nepali Congress. In 1959 Nepal's first constitution was promulgated and the country's first elections, held in Feb. 1959, gave the Nepali Congress 74 of 109 seats.

In Dec. 1960 King Mahendra suspended the constitution and banned all political parties. A new constitution was introduced in 1962 which established a non-party panchayat (council) system, with legislative power in the hands of the indirectly elected Rashtriya Panchayat. King Mahendra died in 1972 and was succeeded by his son Birendra. In May 1980 Birendra responded to popular protests against the panchayat system by holding a referendum which gave voters a choice between a party-based system and a reformed version of the existing order. The result was close, with 54.8% of electors opting for the King's reformed panchayat system. After the referendum direct elections for the Rashtriya Panchayat were restored on a non-party basis. Elections took place in 1981 and 1986. Despite a boycott by the Nepali Congress, both elections returned a large number of independents opposed to the panchayat system. In June 1985 violence erupted in the country as an opposition group launched a bombing campaign in which eight people died, including an MP. The government responded by arresting some 4,000 opposition supporters.

The Rana government signed a treaty with India in 1950 that established a 'special relationship' with India. But under the monarchy Nepal has tried, with limited success, to reduce its dependent status. Nepal is a founding member of the South Asian Association for Regional Cooperation (SAARC) established in 1985. SAARC's secretariat is based in Kathmandu. Nepal's relations with India deteriorated sharply during 1989 after New Delhi imposed in March what amounted to an economic blockade of its land-locked neighbour. The new Indian National Front government, which came to power in late 1989, adopted a more conciliatory approach to the dispute (which centred on Nepal's alleged abuse of transit rights, but also reflected India's concern over a Nepalese weapons purchase from China); nevertheless, the crisis had not been resolved as of early 1990.

CONSTITUTION AND GOVERNMENT

Executive and legislature

The king of Nepal is a constitutional monarch, with significant executive powers. The panchayat (council) democracy system as reformed in 1980 provides for direct, but non-party, elections (last held in May 1986) by universal adult suffrage for 112 seats in the 140-member unicameral legislature, the Rashtriya Panchayat. The king appoints the other 28 members and presides over the legislature, which elects the prime minister.

Present government

Head of state King Birendra Bir Bikram Shah Deva

Prime Minister; Minister of Defence and Royal Palace Affairs Marich Man Singh Shrestha

Other Principal Ministers Shailendra Kumar Upadhya (Foreign Affairs); Bharat Bahadur Pradhan (Finance); Badri Prasad Mandal (Law and Justice).

Administration

There are elected panchayats or councils at village level which in turn elect members to district councils and thence to zonal councils.

Justice

The system of law is based on Hindu legal concepts and English common law. The highest court is the Supreme Court, consisting of a Chief Justice and up to 6 other justices. The death penalty is in force. No executions between 1985 and mid-1988.

National symbols

Flag. Exceptional shape, composed of two crimson blue-edged triangles of unequal height placed one above the other. The upper triangle bears a stylized white moon in outline and the lower one bears the sun.

Festivals. 18 Feb. (National Day); Oct. over a week (Dasain-Durga Puja Festival); Nov. two days (Tihar – Festival of Lights); 16 Dec. (Mahendra Jayanti and Constitution Day); 28 Dec. (King Birendra's birthday).

Vehicle registration plate. NEP.

INTERNATIONAL RELATIONS

Affiliations

NAM; SAARC.

Defence

Total Armed Forces: 35,000 (to be 40,000). Terms of service: voluntary. Reserves: none.

Army: 35,000.
Para-military: 28,000 (Police Force).

ECONOMY

Currency

The unit is the Nepalese rupee, divided into 100 paisa.

National finance

Budget. The 1989 budget (in US$) was for expenditure (current and capital) of 813 million and revenue of 388 million.

Balance of payments. The balance of payments (current account, 1987) was a deficit of $194 million.

Inflation. (1988) 10.9%.

Gross Domestic Product

Estimated total GDP US$2,560 million, per capita US$170 (overall size of economy ranking 108 in the world).

Economically active population. The total number of persons active in the economy was 4,100,000; unemployed: 5%.

Sector	% of workforce	% of GDP
industry	2	14
agriculture	93	57
services*	5	29

* services figure includes elements unassigned to other categories.

Energy and mineral resources

Minerals. Quartz; also small deposits of lignite; copper; cobalt; iron ore.

Electricity. Capacity: 203,000 kW; production: 530 million kWh; 30 kWh per capita (1988).

Bioresources

Agriculture. The main crops are rice; maize; wheat; sugar cane; oilseeds. Nepal is an illegal producer of cannabis for the international drug trade.

Crop production: (1986 in 1,000 tons/tonnes) rice 2,590/2,350; maize 970/880; wheat 659/598; sugar cane 615/558; potatoes 394/357; millet 152/138.

Livestock numbers: (1987) cattle 6.37 million; buffaloes 2.89 million; sheep 821,000; goats 5.07 million; pigs 467,000; poultry 10 million.

Forestry. 33% forest and woodland, with valuable forest in the south of the country.

Fisheries. Annual catch: (1983) 2,315 tons/2,100 tonnes.

Industry and commerce

Industry. The main industries are rice, jute, sugar and oilseed production; cigarettes; textiles; cement; bricks; tourism. Production: (1982 in 1,000 tons/tonnes) jute goods 17.3/15.7; sugar 23.2/21.1; cement 33/30; iron goods 8.2/7.4.

Commerce. Exports: (1987) US$139 million (not including unrecorded border trade with India) including clothing; carpets; leather goods; grain;. Imports: US$507 million, including petroleum products 20%; fertilizer 11%; machinery 10%. Countries exported to were India 43%; US 26%; UK 10%; other European countries 17%. Imports came from India 40%; Europe 13%; Japan 13%; US 2%.

Trade with UK. Nepal imported UK goods worth £4,968,000; exports to UK totalled £9,384,000.

Tourism. (1986) 223,000 visitors.

COMMUNICATIONS

Railways

There are 63 miles/101 km of railways.

Roads

There are 3,738 miles/6,015 km of roads, of which 1,243 miles/2,000 km are metalled.

Aviation

Royal Nepal Airlines Corporation provides domestic and international services (main airport is at Kathmandu). Passengers: (1987/88) 596,192.

Telecommunications

There is a poor telephone and telegraph service but a fair radio communication and broadcast service although international radio communication service is poor. There are 30,000 telephones, 2 million radios and 27,000 televisions (1986). The government owns Radio Nepal. A TV service around Kathmandu began in 1986.

EDUCATION AND WELFARE

Education

Schools. (1984) 1,748,000 primary school pupils; 454,000 secondary school pupils.

Universities. Tribhuvan University.

Literacy. 20%.

Health

In 1979 Nepal had approximately 420 doctors and 2,590 hospital beds.

NETHERLANDS

Koninkrijk der Nederlander (Kingdom of the Netherlands)

GEOGRAPHY

The maritime kingdom of the Netherlands, the largest of the Low Countries, lies in north-western Europe, covering a total area of 16,159 miles^2/41,863 km^2 of which 13,101 miles^2/33,940 km^2 is land. The highest point in the country is Mt Vaalserberg in the south-east, but the bulk of the terrain is extensively cultivated lowland, formed by the common delta of the Rhine, Maas, Waal, Ijssel and Schelde rivers. 27% of the total area is below sea level, reaching a low point of –19.7 ft/–6.7 m north of Rotterdam, inhabited by nearly two-thirds of the population. A series of dykes and coastal sand dunes protects the reclaimed coastal territory from tidal flooding. Over 3,940 miles/6,340 km of navigable waterways connect the Netherlands to the rivers and canals of Belgium and Germany. 25% of the land is arable, 34% is occupied by meadows or pasture and 9% is forested. Reclaimed areas include the Noordholland-Wieringen Barrage (1.6 miles/2.5 km), the Wieringermeer Polder (81 miles^2/210 km^2), the Wieringen-Friesland Barrage (19 miles/30 km), the Noordoost Polder (194 miles^2/502 km^2), the Oost Flevoland (233 miles^2/604 km^2) and the Zvidelijk Flevoland (193 miles^2/499 km^2).

Netherlands Antilles Caribbean island group: autonomous region of the Netherlands. Population: 170,000. Area: 309 miles^2/800 km^2.

Aruba South Caribbean island, 15 miles/24 km north of Venezuela. Population: 62,500. Area: 74 miles^2/193 km^2.

Climate

Temperate maritime with periodic continental influences, bringing cold winter winds. Generally mild winter and summer conditions, (cooler inland during winter, warmer throughout the summer months) averaging 35°F/1.7°C in Jan. and 63°F/17°C in July. The rainfall average of 28 in/700 mm is fairly evenly distributed with a July/Aug. maximum. The Hague: Jan. 37°F/2.7°C. July 61°F/16.3°C. Average annual rainfall 32 in/820 mm. Amsterdam: Jan. 36°F/2.3°C. July 62°F/16.5°C. Average annual rainfall 33 in/850 mm. Rotterdam: Jan. 37°F/2.6°C. July 62°F/16.6°C. Average annual rainfall 32 in/800 mm.

Cities and towns

Amsterdam (capital)	682,702
Rotterdam	572,642
The Hague	445,127
Utrecht	229,326
Eindhoven	190,962
Groningen	168,019
Tilburg	153,625
Haarlem	149,099
Nijmegen	146,639
Apeldoorn	145,696
Enschede	144,227

Population

Total population is 14,648,000 of which 88.4% live in urban areas. Population density is 906 persons per mile^2/430.6 per km^2, rising to 1,080 persons per km^2 in the province of Zuid Holland. 99% of the population are Dutch (Germanic/Gallo-Celtic stock) and 1% Indonesian/Surinamese (from the Netherland Antilles and former colony of Suriname).

Birth rate 2.2%. **Death rate** 0.8%. **Rate of population increase** 0.4%. **Age distribution** under 15 = 19.5%; over 65 = 12.17%. **Life expectancy** female 80; male 74; average 77.

Religion

Christianity. 40% of the population are Roman Catholics, 31% are Protestants, of which the chief denominations are the Netherlands Reformed Church (2.7 million members); the Reformed Churches in the Netherlands (0.83 million members) and the Christian Reformed Churches in the Netherlands (75,000 members). 24% of the population are unaffiliated and 5% atheist/agnostic.

Language

The official language is Dutch (Netherlands), a West Germanic language descended from Low Franconian. Netherlandic is also spoken in northern Belgium and in one or two very small French communities. It occurs in standard form (Algemeen Beschaafd Nederlands) and in a wide variety of dialectal idioms. It is also the parent tongue of Afrikaans, one of two official South African languages.

HISTORY

The Romans colonized the southern part of what is now the Netherlands, which later, together with the rest of the Low Countries, was penetrated by Germanic tribes (5th century AD) and became fully Christianized as part of the Frankish Empire (7th–8th century AD). Viking incursions in the 9th and 10th centuries helped to fragment the area into feudal fiefdoms owing loose allegiance to the Holy Roman Emperor, with the County of Holland becoming dominant by the 12th century. But wealth and power resided increasingly in the new trading and manufacturing towns on the river estuaries, while the steady reclamation of North Sea marshes created an independent peasantry free of feudal bonds. The resultant eclipse of the local nobility left the way open for the French Dukes of Burgundy to establish dominion over the Low Countries, beginning with the acquisition of Flanders by marriage in 1384 and continuing, by inheritance, purchase and other marriages, until they ruled the whole of the present-day Benelux region. There followed the Pax Burgundica of economic progress and artistic achievement.

The death in battle of Charles the Bold (1477) left the House of Burgundy without male issue, whereupon the Low Countries passed by marriage to the Habsburg dynasty, becoming part of an empire which, with the joining of the Spanish and Austrian successions in Charles V (r.1515–55), extended over half the known world. The imperial connection brought growing prosperity to the Low Countries, where the new doctrines of Calvinist Protestantism took firm root despite fierce opposition from the staunchly Catholic Habsburgs. Following the abdication of Charles V and the separation of the Austrian and Spanish Habsburg lines (1555), the Low Countries became a province of Spain under Charles's son, Philip II, who determined to fight heresy with fire and sword. The result in the Low Countries was a great revolt led by William (the Silent) of Orange and the merciless Eighty Years' War (1568–1648), during which the seven northern provinces declared their independence from Spain as the United Provinces of the Netherlands (1581). Dictated in large part by economic factors, this division was conceded by Spain in 1609 and confirmed by the Treaty of Münster, signed in Jan. 1648, ten months before the Peace of Westphalia, which ended the broader Thirty Years' War (1618–48), and was consolidated by the northward migration of Protestants from the mainly Catholic south, which remained under Spanish rule.

For the new Republic the 17th century was a golden age of commercial prosperity, religious tolerance and artistic achievement. Power was vested in the provincial Estates (assemblies) dominated by an oligarchic 'regent' class, although in times of crisis the office of Stadholder (head of state), first held by William the Silent until his assassination in 1584, was revived. The Netherlands played a key role in European power politics, successfully resisting French designs on the Low Countries and obliging Louis XIV in the Treaties of Nijmegen (1678–79) to return the Dutch provinces he had invaded in 1672. Meanwhile the powerful United East India and West India companies began to build a Dutch empire in the Americas, Africa and Asia. This led to mercantile competition with England, however, and a series of Anglo-Dutch naval wars in the mid-17th century. Despite some Dutch victories, English maritime supremacy was eventually confirmed, and in 1666 the Dutch surrendered their North American colony of New Amsterdam, later New York, to England. Only when William III of Orange accepted the invitation of the English parliament to depose the Catholic James II and became Protestant King of England (1688) did Anglo-Dutch relations improve.

In the War of Spanish Succession (1702–13/14) the Netherlands formed part of the alliance which failed to prevent a French Bourbon ascending the throne of Spain, although the transfer of the Spanish Low Countries to the Austrian Habsburgs provided some check against French northward expansion. Thereafter, the Dutch retreated from direct involvement in the European power struggle, while compensating for their declining role in world trade by making Amsterdam a major financial centre. The War of Austrian Succession (1740–48) and a renewed French threat resulted in William IV of Orange-Nassau being made hereditary Stadholder (1747), although he and his successor were unable to curb the power of the oligarchies. Mounting pressure for reform was resisted by William V, who called in Prussian troops to maintain his authority in 1787, but the French Revolution (1789) reignited popular disaffection. In 1794–95 a French revolutionary army, supported by local dissidents, overran the whole of the Low Countries and forced William V to flee to England. The Austrian provinces were immediately annexed to France, while the Dutch provinces first became the Batavian Republic (1795–1806), then a kingdom ruled by Napoleon Bonaparte's brother Louis (1806–10) and latterly a province of the French Empire.

Amid the death throes of the Napoleonic Empire, Dutch leaders reasserted the country's independence (1813) and opted to replace the old federal system by a centralized constitutional monarchy with a revived Estates-General (which had last met in 1632). William V's son accepted the crown and, as determined at the Congress of Vienna (1814–15), became William I (r.1815–40) of the United Kingdom of the Netherlands, including Belgium and Luxembourg, which was intended to form a northern bulwark against France. Although Ceylon, Cape Colony (South Africa) and half of Dutch Guyana were ceded to Britain, the rest of the colonial empire in the East Indies and Americas was restored to the Netherlands. William I began to modernize the economy, but his authoritarian tendencies alienated the mainly Catholic southern provinces, where French revolutionary ideas had taken deeper root than in the north. In 1830 these provinces (including the greater part of Luxembourg) declared their independence as Belgium, which was recognized by the Netherlands in 1839. A year later William I abdicated in favour of his son, William II (r.1840–49), who in 1848 granted a new constitution providing for ministerial accountability to the Estates-General.

Largely the work of J.R. Thorbecke (the father of Dutch liberalism), the new constitution ushered in an era of economic progress, based in part on an increasing flow of wealth from the colonies. Within a loose party structure, the Liberals enjoyed broad hegemony, although in the 1880s the Calvinists and Catholics formed a powerful confessional coalition. On the death of William III (r.1849–90), his wife Emma became regent until their daughter Wilhelmina came of age in 1898, one effect of this female succession being the final end of the union with Luxembourg (where Salic Law then applied). Extensions of the franchise in 1887 and 1894 benefited first the religious parties and later the Social Democratic Workers' Party (founded 1894) at the expense of the older political currents. Externally, the Netherlands pursued a policy of neutrality, hosting two international peace conferences (1898 and 1907) which resulted in the creation of what later became the International Court of Justice at The Hague. Dutch neutrality was observed by the belligerents in World War I, during which adult male franchise became universal in 1917 (women had to wait until 1922) and the great Zuyder Zee reclamation project was launched.

In the inter-war period the Netherlands shared in the traumas experienced by other European economies, while a proportional electoral system created a multiplicity of political parties and consequential government instability. With the Social Democrats refusing to join coalitions with 'bourgeois' parties, the confessional formations took the dominant role, sometimes in alliance with the Liberals. The post–1929 slump assisted the emergence of a Dutch fascist movement on the German model and also stimulated increased Communist agitation, although neither extreme obtained substantial popular support. From 1936 reflationary measures by the confessional government of H. Colijn were supported by the Social Democrats, who on the eve of World War II accepted ministerial office. But the government's efforts to maintain Dutch neutrality proved abortive: German forces launched a surprise attack in May 1940 and quickly overran the country. The Queen and her government fled to London to continue the struggle, which broadened when Japan conquered the Dutch East Indies in 1942. The German occupation regime, despite appeals to common Nordic origins, met with stubborn resistance from the Dutch, who suffered great privations culminating in the 1944–45 'winter of starvation'.

Following the German surrender, Dutch politics resumed with the Catholic People's Party (CVP) and a new moderate Labour Party (PvdA) formed in 1946 by the pre-war Social Democrats and other progressive elements becoming the dominant formations, although post-war aspirations to a two-party system on the British model were to founder on the continued use of proportional representation. From 1948 to 1958 Willem Drees of the PvdA led successive centre-left coalitions with the CVP which, backed by US Marshall Aid, laid the foundations for future economic prosperity, despite devastating North Sea floods in 1953, when 2,000 people died. Queen Wilhelmina abdicated in 1948 in favour of her daughter Juliana, whose reign (1948–80) proved to be controversial, firstly because of the marriage (in 1965) of her daughter Beatrix to a German diplomat who had been a member of the Hitler Youth, and latterly because of the involvement of her consort, Prince Bernhard, in an international financial scandal. Queen Juliana abdicated in 1980 and was succeeded by Beatrix, amid fierce anti-royalist rioting in Amsterdam.

Externally, the Netherlands participated fully in post-war European construction, joining the Benelux economic union with Belgium and Luxembourg (1948) and becoming a founder member of the ECSC, EEC and Euratom (1951–58). It also abandoned its neutral posture by joining NATO in 1949 and the WEU in 1955. The Dutch failed to re-establish colonial authority in the East Indies, most of which attained virtual independence as Indonesia (1949). The remaining links between Indonesia and the Netherlands were severed in 1956, whereas Western New Guinea (West Irian/Irian Jaya) remained under Dutch rule until being placed under UN administration in 1962 and ceded to Indonesia the following year. Dutch Guyana (Suriname) and the Netherlands Antilles were granted internal autonomy as 'equal partners' with the Netherlands in 1954. In 1975, however, Suriname became a fully independent republic, while in 1986 the Caribbean island of Aruba attained separate status from the other Netherlands Antilles (Curaçao, Bonaire, St Eustatius, Saba and St Maarten) and was scheduled to achieve full independence in 1996. Social and economic problems created by large-scale immigration from the former colonies and dependencies to the Netherlands were compounded in the mid-1970s by terrorist actions by South Moluccan exiles who blamed the Dutch government for the integration of their homeland into Indonesia in the early 1950s.

Having been in opposition to centre-right coalitions for most of the previous 15 years, the PvdA returned to power in 1973 under the leadership of Joop den Uyl. His centre-left coalition contained, for the first time in Dutch history, a majority of left-wing ministers, although such was the fragmentation of the left that these came from three different parties. In a move to reduce divisions on the centre-right, the CVP and the two main Protestant parties (the Anti-Revolutionary Party and the Christian Historic Union) federated in 1975 as the Christian Democratic Appeal (CDA), prior to a full merger in 1980. Both the CDA and the right-wing Liberals (VVD) gained ground in the 1977 general elections and formed a centre-right coalition, which lasted until 1981. After a brief centre-left interregnum (1981–82), another CDA/VVD coalition emerged in Nov. 1982 under the premiership of Ruud Lubbers (CDA) and continued in power after the 1986 elections, in which nine parties gained representation in the Second Chamber. Under the Lubbers government, the Netherlands was the last of the five designated European NATO members to give final parliamentary approval (Feb. 1986) to the deployment of US cruise missiles on its territory, amid fierce controversy which only subsided with the signature of the US–Soviet INF Treaty (1987) providing for the dismantling of such weapons. When in May 1989 the VVD withdrew from the coalition in disagreement over the financing of a national environmental policy a premature general election was held on 6 Sept. The VVD lost support, however, and in November Lubbers formed a new centre-left coalition of his CDA and the labour PvdA.

CONSTITUTION AND GOVERNMENT

Executive and legislature

The powers of the constituional monarch are largely formal. Executive authority is exercised through a prime minister as head of government, who presides over the council of ministers. Legislation may be proposed by the crown (advised by a council of state) or put forward in the main legislative house, the 150-member Second Chamber (Tweede Kamer) of the bicameral parliament (Staten-Generaal). Elections, which are on a proportional representation system with a minimum voting age of 18, were last held on 6 Sept. 1989. The upper house, the First Chamber (Eerste Kamer), whose 75 members are elected by the 12 provincial councils, has the power to approve or reject, but not amend, such bills. Both houses have a maximum term of four years.

Present government

Head of state Beatrix, Queen of the Netherlands
Prime Minister Ruud Lubbers
Other Principal Ministers Wim Kok (Deputy Prime Minister and Minister of Finance); Ien Dales (Home Affairs); Hans van den Broek (Foreign Affairs); Jan Pronk (Development Co-operation); Relus ter Beek (Defence); Koos Andriessen (Economic Affairs); Hirsch Ballin (Justice).

Justice

The judiciary consists of the High Court of the Netherlands (Court of Cassation), five courts of justice (Courts of Appeal), 19 district courts, which deal with more serious crimes, and 62 cantonal courts, which deal with minor offences. All judges are appointed for life by the Sovereign. They can be removed only by a decision of the High Court. The death penalty was abolished in 1982.

Prisons. There are 5,291 prisoners.

National symbols

Flag. Three horizontal stripes coloured red, white and blue.

Festivals. 30 Apr. (Queen's Day); 5 May (National Liberation Day).

Vehicle registration plate. NL.

INTERNATIONAL RELATIONS

Affiliations

NATO; OECD; EC; Benelux.

Defence

Total Armed Forces: 106,100 (inclusive 3,900 Royal Military Constabulary); 12,600 women; 50,000 conscripts. Terms of service: Army 14–16 months, Navy and Air Force 14–17 months. Reserves: 175,000 (men to age 35, officers to 45).

Army: 66,000; 913 main battle tanks (Leopard 1A4 and Leopard 2).

Navy: 17,100 inclusive naval air and marines; five submarines and 16 principal surface combatants: four destroyers, 12 frigates.

Naval Air Arm: 1,378; 13 combat aircraft, 17 armed helicopters.

Marines: 2,800.

Air Force: 18,100; 227 combat aircraft (mainly F-16A/B, NF-5A).

ECONOMY

Currency

The unit is the guilder, divided into 100 cents.

National finance

Budget. The 1988 budget (in US$) was for expenditure (current and capital) of 91,400 million and revenue of 78,600 million. Main items of current expenditure are housing and welfare 13.8%; education 11.9%; health 11%; defence 5%.

Balance of payments. The balance of payments (current account, 1988) was a surplus of $5,090 million.

Inflation. (1988) 1.3% (12 months to Sept. 1989).

Gross Domestic Product

Estimated total GDP US$214,420 million, per capita US$15,170 (overall size of economy ranking 14 in the world). Growth rate (1988) 2.9%.

Economically active population. The total number of persons active in the economy was 5,300,000; unemployed: 8.3% (1988).

Sector	% of workforce	% of GDP
industry	28.2	30
agriculture	5.8	4
services*	66	66

* services figure includes elements unassigned to other categories.

Energy and mineral resources

Oil and gas. Natural gas production: (1987) 74,247,000 million kJ. Crude oil is also produced.

Minerals. Salt mines at Hengelo and Delfzijl, production: (1987) 4,386,052 tons/3,979,000 tonnes.

Electricity. Capacity: 21,931 million kW; production: 63,409 million kWh; 4,310 kWh per capita (1988).

Bioresources

Agriculture. Mainly animal husbandry, also horticultural crops; grains; potatoes; sugar beet. Annual production of cheese is 627,414 tons/569,186 tonnes.

Crop production: (1988 in tons/tonnes) wheat 898,926/815,500; rye 29,762/27,000; barley 343,036/311,200; oats 69,114/62,700; peas 114,125/113,800; colza 25,243/22,900; flax 34,502/31,300; potatoes 5 million/4.6 million.

Livestock numbers: (1988) cattle 4.71 million; pigs 13.93; horses 64,800; sheep 1.16 million; poultry 95.15 million.

Forestry. 9% of the total land area is forest and woodland.

Fisheries. Total catch from sea and inshore fisheries: (1981) 440,301 tons/399,438 tonnes.

Industry and commerce

Industry. The main industries are agroindustries; metal and engineering products; electrical machinery and equipment; chemicals; petroleum; fishing; construction; microelectronics.

Commerce. Exports: (1987) US$92,400 million, including agricultural products; processed foods and tobacco; natural gas; chemicals; metal products; textiles and clothing. Imports: US$91,300 million, including raw materials and semi-finished products; consumer goods; transportation equipment; crude oil; food products. Countries exported to were EC countries 74.9%; US 4.7%. Imports came from EC countries 63.8%; US 7.9%.

Trade with UK. In 1988 The Netherlands imported UK goods worth £5,583,280,000; exports to UK totalled £8,279,747,000.

Tourism. (1987) 3,114,000 visitors.

COMMUNICATIONS

Railways

There are 1,782 miles/2,867 km of railways, most of which are electrified.

Roads

There are 69,528 miles/111,891 km of roads.

Aviation

NLM Dutch Airlines provides domestic services; Air Holland provides domestic and international services; KLM (Koninklijke Luchtvarrt Maatschappij NV) and Martinair Holland provide international services (main airport is at Schiphol, near Amsterdam).

Shipping

Of the 3,940 miles/6,340 km of inland waterways 35% are navigable by craft of 900 metric ton capacity or larger. The marine ports are Den Helder, Delfzijl, Eemshaven, Ijmuiden, Scheveningen, and Terneuzen. The inland ports are Amsterdam, Dordrecht, and Rotterdam. The merchant marine consists of 344 ships of 1,000 GRT or over. Freight loaded: (1987) 91.2 million tons/82.7 million tonnes; unloaded: 275.1 million tons/249.6 million tonnes.

Telecommunications

There is a highly developed, well maintained and extensive telecommunications system. There are 9.4 million telephones; 4.8 million radios; 4.7 million televisions (1988). Radio and television broadcasting is regulated to allow scope to the various broadcasting associations, which may be political or religious in character, in line with the size of their membership. Radio Nederland Wereldomroep (Radio Netherlands International), broadcasting from Hilversum, transmits external services in ten languages. A feature of Dutch television is the high level of access to cable and satellite TV, in addition to the three nationally broadcast channels.

EDUCATION AND WELFARE

Education

Schools. There are 8,465 basic schools with 1,447,776 pupils, 1,000 special schools with 103,047 pupils and 1,354 secondary schools with 775,826 pupils. There are also a number of junior and senior secondary vocational schools.

Universities. There are 21 universities with a total of 160,947 students.

Literacy. 99%.

Health

There are 34,573 doctors (one per 427 people) and approximately 67,500 hospital beds (one per 219 people).

NETHERLANDS ANTILLES

GEOGRAPHY

The Netherlands Antilles consist of two island groups – Curaçao and Bonaire, located off the coast of Venezuela, and St Maarten, Saba and St Eustatius, 497 miles/800 km to the north. The total land area is 371 miles^2/960 km^2. The terrain is generally hilly, with volcanic interiors. The capital is Willemstad.

Climate

Tropical, modified by north-eastern trade winds. The St Maarten, Saba and St Eustatius group are subject to hurricanes July-Oct.

Population

Total population (1989 est.) 183,076.

Birth rate 1.8%. **Death rate** 0.5%. **Rate of population increase** 0.2%. **Life expectancy** female 79; male 74.

Religion

Christianity, mainly Roman Catholic.

Language

Dutch (official). Papiamento (Spanish–Portuguese–Dutch–English dialect) predominates. English and Spanish are also spoken.

HISTORY

The earliest inhabitants of the three 'Leeward' islands of the Netherlands Antilles (Curaçao, Aruba and Bonaire) were Arawak Indians, while the three 'Windward' islands (St Maarten, St Eustatius and Saba) were inhabited by small groups of Arawaks and Caribs. The first Europeans to visit the islands were Spanish, who settled in Curaçao in 1511, though colonization remained small-scale. In 1634 Curaçao was seized by the Dutch, who were also involved in settlements in the Lesser Antilles at about the same time. Curaçao rapidly developed as a centre for trade in the Caribbean region, in particular the slave trade from Africa. Slavery was abolished in the Dutch West Indies in 1863.

In 1954 the Netherlands Antilles attained internal self-government as part of the 'Tripartite Kingdom' of the Netherlands. The system of proportional representation used in elections to the islands' legislature led to a series of coalitions between different political parties, usually based on different islands. The parties from Curaçao predominated, principally the Democratische Partij (DP) and the Nationale Volkspartij (NVP). The centrist coalition led by Silvio Rozendal of the DP collapsed in 1979 and was replaced after elections by a centre-left coalition led by Don Martina, the leader of the Movementu Antiyas Nobo (MAN). In Sept. 1981 the Aruban Movimento Electoral di Pueblo withdrew from the coalition after disagreements over the terms of Aruba's progress to separate status, but Martina's government survived to form another administration which lasted until mid-1984. It was then replaced by a centre-right coalition led by the leader of the NVP, Maria Liberia Peters. After elections in Nov. 1985 caused by the withdrawal of Aruba from the federation, Martina was again able to form a coalition government which lasted until 17 May 1988 when he was again replaced as prime minister by Liberia Peters after the withdrawal of members representing St Maarten led to the collapse of his administration.

CONSTITUTION AND GOVERNMENT

Netherlands Antilles is part of the Dutch realm. Full autonomy in internal affairs was granted in 1954. Federal executive power rests nominally with the governor, appointed by the Dutch crown. Actual power is exercised by a council of ministers, presided over by a minister-president. Legislative power rests with a 22-member Legislative Council. Each island has an island council headed by a lieutenant governor. Elections are held every four years, most recently in Nov. 1989.

Leader Maria Liberia Peters, prime minister since May 1988; Dr Rene Römer, Governor General (since 1983)

National symbols

Flag. White, with a horizontal blue stripe in the centre, superimposed on a vertical red band also centred; five white stars (representing the five main islands) arranged in an oval in the centre of the blue band.

National holiday. 30 April (Queen's Day).

ECONOMY

The economy is dependent on tourism, petroleum refining and offshore banking. The islands have a relatively high per capita income and well developed infrastructure compared with others in the region. Almost all consumer and capital goods are imported, mainly from the US. The government also seeks support from the Netherlands.

Currency

Netherlands Antilles guilder.

COMMUNICATIONS

There are ports at Willemstad, Philipsburg, and Kralendijk; seven airports with permanent surface runways, and 590 miles/950 km of road. There are extensive inter-island radio relay links, one TV station, nine AM and four FM radio stations; two Atlantic Ocean satellite antennae.

NEW CALEDONIA

Nouvelle Calédonie et Dépendances (New Caledonia and Dependencies)

GEOGRAPHY

The territory administered by France as New Caledonia and Dependencies comprises a group of islands in the South Pacific Ocean, 1,087 miles/1,750 km east of Australia, with a total area of some 7,334 miles^2/19,000 km^2. The terrain of the principal island, Grande Terre (6,320 miles^2/16,372 km^2), consists of coastal plains with mountains in the interior. To the east are the Loyalty Islands or Îles Loyauté, to the south-west the Île des Pins, and to the north-west the Bélep archipelago. Other islands are small and uninhabited. The capital is Nouméa, on the coast in the south of the main island.

Climate

Tropical, modified by south-east trade winds. Mean temperatures in Nouméa are 77°F/25°C in January and 66°F/19°C in July. Average annual rainfall 43 in/1,083 mm.

Population

Total population (1989 est.) 152,386, of whom some 43% are Melanesian Kanaks, the next largest group (37%) being the settler population of European descent; over 10% are Polynesian. The main island has some 90% of the total population.

Birth rate 2.4%. **Death rate** 0.6%. **Rate of population increase** 1.0%. **Life expectancy** female 73; male 66.

Religion

Over 70% Roman Catholic, 16% Protestant; others include some 4% Muslim.

Language

French; Melanesian-Polynesian dialects.

HISTORY

New Caledonia was first settled by the indigenous Kanak people as long ago as 4000 BC. Spanish and other navigators arrived in the 16th and 17th centuries AD. The islands were named by Capt. James Cook in 1774. In 1853 the territory was annexed by France. By the end of the 19th century settlers owned 90% of all land, with the Kanaks confined to reservations. Colonization caused the decimation of the Kanak population.

During World War II the US forces made New Caledonia their South Pacific headquarters. In 1946 the islands became a French Overseas Territory. Increasing political tensions and violence in the 1980s led to various French attempts to reform the New Caledonian political structure. Elections in Nov. 1984 for a new Territorial Assembly with greater powers of self-government were boycotted by most of the pro-independence parties, and in December the newly formed Front de libération nationale kanake socialiste (FLNKS) formed a 'provisional government' led by Jean-Marie Tjibaou. In 1985 a plan drawn up by French Prime Minister Laurent Fabius met with some success. However, the accession of the Gaullist Jacques Chirac to the French premiership in Mar. 1986 heralded a harder French line on the issue of New Caledonian independence. His government's political initiatives failed to win the co-operation of the FLNKS. Tensions increased, and in April and May 1988 serious armed clashes occurred between Kanaks and security forces.

In June 1988 the new socialist French prime minister, Michel Rocard, FLNKS leader Tjibaou, and the president of the settlers' anti-independence party the Rassemblement pour la Calédonie dans la République (RPCR), Jacques Lafleur, signed the Matignon Accord. This ten-year plan provided for the division of the territory into three administrative regions and for elections to regional assemblies (two of which would come under Kanak rule), which duly took place in June 1989. A referendum on self-determination would be held in 1998, with only those resident in the territory for ten years or more, and their direct descendants, eligible to vote. The issue of eligibility was crucial to the Kanaks, who made up only 43% of the population, the rest consisting of Caldoches (French settlers) and people of other origin. On 4 May 1989 the FLNKS president, Tjibaou, and vice-president, Yeiwéné Yeiwéné, were assassinated by Djubelly Wéa, a Kanak extremist. Wéa and others believed that in signing the Matignon Accord the FLNKS leaders had betrayed the Kanak people.

CONSTITUTION AND GOVERNMENT

New Caledonia is an overseas territory (territoire d'outre-mer) of France. As such it is administered by a government-appointed high commissioner, and participates in the election of the French parliament (sending two deputies to the National Assembly and having one senate member). Its principal elected local leaders are the presidents of the three provinces, namely Jacques Lafleur (South), Léopold Jorédié (North) and Richard Kaloi (Loyalty Islands), each elected (most recently in June 1989) by the provincial assemblies. These assemblies exercise local power and their combined membership forms a 54-member congress through which the territory as a whole exercises a measure of self-government.

National Symbols

Flag. The flag of France is used (three equal vertical bands of blue, white and red).
Festivals. 14 July (Bastille Day).

ECONOMY

New Caledonia has more than 40% of the world's known nickel resources; chrome ore is also exported, and other metals (including gold and silver) have been mined. In recent years the economy has suffered due to decreased international demand for nickel, the principal source (over 60%) of export earnings. 33% of the working population work in agriculture but very little land is suitable for cultivation and food accounts for 25% of imports. There were over 60,000 tourists in 1987, mainly French and Japanese.
Gross national product. Estimated at $860 million in 1985, or $5,810 per capita.
Currency. Comptoirs Français du Pacifique (CFP) franc.

COMMUNICATIONS

There are 3,383 miles/5,448 km of road of which 347 miles/558 km are paved and 1,398 miles/2,251 km improved earth. Nouméa is the main port. There are 27 usable airports (29 in total) including four with permanent-surface runways. There are 32,578 telephones, five AM and three FM radio stations and two TV stations.

NEW ZEALAND

GEOGRAPHY

The independent state of New Zealand is located in the South Pacific Ocean, 994 miles/1,600 km south-east of Australia, comprising two main islands (North and South, divided by the Cook Strait), Stewart Island and a number of much smaller islands. The combined area is 103,856 miles^2/269,057 km^2 comprising 13 statistical divisions. The principal islands measure 1,100 miles/1,770 km from their northernmost extremity to the southernmost. New Zealand lies in a geo-seismically and geo-thermally active zone exemplified in its physiography by the hot springs and geysers of North Island, central mountainous region (high points 9,177 ft/2,797 m at Mt Ruapehu and 8,261 ft/2,518 m at Mt Egmont). Lake Tampo, the largest natural lake in New Zealand, occupies an ancient volcanic crater, and the River Waikato measures some 264 miles/425 km in length. South Island is dominated by the Southern Alps climbing to 12,349 ft/3,764 m at Mt Cook, New Zealand's highest point. 75% of the terrain is above 656 ft/200 m elevation. Major lakes include Te Anau (133 miles^2/344 km^2), and Wakatipu (113 miles^2/293 km^2). The bulk of the population lives on North Island, with over 30% of the total concentrated around Central Auckland and the Bay of Plenty. Most of the clay-based soils are relatively infertile, but meadow and pasture constitute 63.9% of the total land area and a further 5.1% is forested.

Climate

Cool temperate becoming almost subtropical in the extreme north. Plentiful rainfall all year, decreasing north-south from 60 in/1,525 mm to 25 in/635 mm. Mean sea level temperatures range from 59°F/15°C (north) to 48°F/9°C (south). Only the extreme south region experiences a cold winter. The highest peaks are permanently snow-capped. New Zealand is subject to periodic sub-tropical cyclones (eg Bola in 1988 caused NZ$1,000 million-worth of damage). Auckland: Jan. 65°F/18.6°C. July 50°F/10.2°C. Average annual rainfall 41 in/1,053 mm. Christchurch: Jan. 61°F/16.3°C. July 42°F/5.8°C. Average annual rainfall 29 in/737 mm. Dunedin: Jan. 57°F/14.1°C. July 43°F/6.2°C. Average annual rainfall 38 in/968 mm. Hokitika: Jan. 56°F/13.4°C. July 43°F/6.4°C. Average annual rainfall 132 in/3,357 mm.

Cities and towns

Auckland	889,225
Wellington (capital)	352,035
Christchurch	333,191
Hamilton	167,711
Dunedin	113,592

Population

Total population is 3,327,000 of which 83.7% live in

urban areas. Population density is 32 persons per mile²/12.5 per km². At the last census, 84.5% of the population were native residents. Of the foreign-born population 196,872 were from the UK. 46,839 from Australia; 24,159 from the Netherlands; 33,864 from Samoa; 15,540 from the Cook Islands. In 1986 the Maori population totalled 294,201 (9%).

Birth rate 1.6%. **Death rate** 0.81%. **Rate of population increase** (1980–87) 0.79%. **Age distribution** under 15 = 24.4%; over 65 = 10.5%. **Life expectancy** female 78; male 72; average 75.

Associated territories comprise the autonomous Cook Islands and Niue, and the Ross/Tokelau dependencies. Their populations are as follows:

	Area	Population
Cook Islands:	91.5 miles²/237 km²	17,185
Niue:	100 miles²/259 km²	3281
Ross Dependency:	154,400 miles²/400,000 km²	uninhabited
Tokelau:	3.9 miles²/10 km²	1690

Religion

81% of the population are Christian with a total of nearly 0.5 million Roman Catholics and 0.9 million Anglicans. Other denominations include the Baptist, Methodist and Presbyterian Churches. Maori churches have a combined membership of approximately 30,000, dispersed throughout the Rataria, Ringatu, Te Kooti Rikirangi, and Absolute Maori and Unified Maori denominations.

Language

English is the official language, but the indigenous Maoris have their own language spoken by 9% of the total population.

HISTORY

The discoverers and first colonists of New Zealand, in around AD 800, came from eastern Polynesia, (the region which includes the present-day Society, Marquesas and Cook Islands). Thereafter there were few influences from anywhere in the Pacific. The basis of the early Maori economy was horticulture, fishing and hunting.

Abel Tasman, leading a Dutch East India Company expedition, was probably the first European to sight New Zealand. He reached South Island in 1642, naming it Staten Landt. It was soon renamed Nieew Zeeland. In 1769 James Cook became the first European to land. In 1772 Marion du Fresne, the leader of a French expedition, was killed, and 250 Maoris were massacred in retaliation. From the 1790s onwards European sealers, whalers and traders landed in New Zealand. Missionaries came from 1814, and the first permanent settlers in the 1830s. Deep-sea whaling peaked in the 1830s, and flax and timber were also important. In 1827 the Maori language was first recorded in print, when the Bible was translated.

In 1814 the Maori people were declared to be 'under the protection of His Majesty'. New Zealand became British Territory by the Proclamation of May 1840. William Hobson was appointed the first lieutenant-governor. The legal code of New South Wales was extended to cover New Zealand in 1840.

Under the Treaty of Waitingi, signed in Feb. 1840 by Hobson and 46 Maori chiefs, all rights and powers of sovereignty were ceded to Queen Victoria. The chiefs held possession of all land, which the crown alone had the right to buy. The English and Maori versions did not exactly tally, and were later the subject of much violent dispute. (The Treaty of Waitingi is still cited in Maori protest movements today). In 1841 New Zealand was proclaimed a separate Crown Colony. Auckland became the capital.

In 1852 the British Constitution Act was passed by Parliament in London. A General Assembly with two chambers was created, and the colony was divided into six provinces, each of which had an elected Provincial Council. All non-Maori males aged 21 and over were granted the vote, subject to a property qualification. (Most Maoris were disenfranchised). Power over foreign policy was retained by the British Government, and laws passed by the General Assembly needed the Royal Assent. In 1867 four Maori seats were created in the General Assembly. In 1879 the property qualification was abolished, and any male over 21 could vote. Women were given the vote in 1893.

Large tracts of land were purchased from the Maoris. There was fighting in Taranaki in 1860 over land which the crown had allegedly bought, but which its inhabitants declined to sell. The 'Maori Wars' continued until 1872.

In 1855 there were 750,000 sheep – in 1870 there were 10 million. Starting in 1861 there was a series of gold rushes. Wool and gold became the largest overseas earners.

The capital moved to Wellington in 1865. In the 1870s groups of Scandinavians, Irish and English came under special settlement schemes. In 1882 the first shipment of refrigerated meat took place, marking the start of a trade which is still vital to New Zealand's prosperity.

At the end of the 19th century less than 20% of land was in Maori ownership, and Maoris formed only 7% of the population.

In 1907 New Zealand became a dominion under the British Crown. New Zealanders fought alongside the British in the Boer War. In World War I 103,000 New Zealanders served abroad and 18,000 died, out of a population of just over one million.

New Zealand was hit by the Depression of the 1930s, during which up to 12% of the workforce were unemployed. In 1935 the Labour party (founded 1916) won its first election and introduced guaranteed prices for dairy farmers, compulsory trade-union membership, a 40-hour week, and undertook large-scale public spending. The Social Security Act of 1938 provided free medical treatment, family allowance and increased old age pensions, and New Zealand became the first welfare state. In 1936 the conservative New Zealand National Party was formed by the merger of the Reform and Liberal parties. Labour and National remain the two major parties, and have dominated New Zealand politics since World War II.

In Nov. 1926 New Zealand, along with Canada, Australia, South Africa and Newfoundland, became self-governing dominions with status equal to that of Britain, as members of the British Commonwealth. Full independence was achieved by the Statute of Westminster, adopted by the British parliament in 1931 and accepted by New Zealand in 1947.

During World War II 12,000 New Zealanders died fighting with the Allies. The war forced New Zealand to become more self-sufficient and less reliant upon the UK. In 1951 New Zealand, Australia and the United States signed the ANZUS defence treaty. In 1953 New Zealand became a member of the South-East Asia Treaty Organisation and in 1961 joined the

International Monetary Fund. Western Samoa, (which had been administered by New Zealand under a League of Nations mandate of 1920) achieved independence in 1962.

Labour won the general election in 1984. The ANZUS treaty and relations with Australia and the US were strained when all vessels were banned from New Zealand ports if they were believed to be carrying nuclear weapons or powered by nuclear energy. New Zealand was excluded from ANZUS council meetings, but did not formally withdraw. In 1985 the Greenpeace vessel Rainbow Warrior (which was to have led a protest against testing of nuclear weapons in French Polynesia) was blown up in Auckland harbour. A Portuguese photographer was killed in the blast. Two French secret service agents were arrested and convicted of manslaughter. The French Government, having at first applied trade sanctions, formally apologized and paid compensation.

The Labour government of Prime Minister David Lange was returned with an increased majority in 1987, but was subject to a growing rift between supporters and opponents of the finance minister, Roger Douglas. The free-market economic policies which Douglas had pursued since 1984, which were seen by some as the foundation of the country's economic stability, were criticized by others as a fundamental betrayal of social democracy. In Dec. 1988 Douglas was dismissed from the Cabinet and unsuccessfully challenged Lange for the leadership of the Labour Party. Douglas was re-elected to Cabinet in August 1989, whereupon Lange resigned as Labour leader and prime minister. He was succeeded by Geoffrey Palmer.

CONSTITUTION AND GOVERNMENT

Executive and legislature

The head of state is the British sovereign, represented by a governor general. The head of government is the prime minister, who is responsible to the legislature and appointed by the governor general acting upon its advice. Legislative authority is vested in a unicameral 95-member House of Representatives elected on a constituency basis by universal adult suffrage (minimum voting age 18) for a term of up to three years. Elections were last held on 15 Aug. 1987.

Present government

Governor General Sir Paul Reeves

Prime Minister and minister of the Environment Geoffrey Palmer

Other Principal Ministers Helen Clark (Deputy Prime Minister; Health; Labour); Michael Moore (External Relations and Trade: Foreign Affairs, Overseas Trade and Marketing); Koro Wetere (Maori Affairs); David Caygill (Finance); Michael Cullen (Social Welfare); Phil Goff (Education); Margaret Shields (Consumer Affairs; Statistics; Women's Affairs); Bill Jeffries (Justice; Transport; Civil Aviation).

Justice

The judiciary consists of the Court of Appeal, the High Court and District Courts, all of which deal with both civil and criminal cases. There is also an Office of Ombudsman created in 1962 (there are currently two). The death penalty is in force only for exceptional crimes. There were no executions between 1985 and mid-1988.

National symbols

Flag. The flag is blue and comprises the British Blue Ensign, bearing in the fly four red five-pointed stars edged in white and arranged in the form of the constellation of the Southern Cross.

Festivals. 6 Feb. (Waitangi Day, anniversary of 1840 treaty); 25 Apr. (ANZAC Day, anniversary of 1915 landing at Gallipoli); 5 June (Queen's Official birthday); 23 Oct. (Labour Day).

Vehicle registration plate. NZ.

INTERNATIONAL RELATIONS

Affiliations

OECD; Commonwealth; Anzus Pact (suspended).

Defence

Total Armed Forces: 12,800. Terms of service: voluntary, supplemented by Territorial Army service: seven weeks basic, 20 days per year. Reserves: 9,700.

Army: 6,000; 26 light tanks (Scorpion).

Navy: 2,600; four frigates (UK Leander); eight patrol and coastal combatants.

Air Force: 4,200; 43 combat aircraft (mainly A-4); seven armed helicopters.

ECONOMY

Currency

The unit is the NZ dollar, divided into 100 cents.

National finance

Budget. The 1988 budget (in US$) was for expenditure (current and capital) of 15,300 million and revenue of 15,400 million. Main items of current expenditure are housing and welfare 29.7%; health 12.4%; education 11.1%; defence 4.7%.

Balance of payments. The balance of payments (current account, 1988) was a deficit of US$350 million.

Inflation. 7.2% (12 months to Sept. 1989).

Gross Domestic Product

Estimated total GDP US$31,850 million, per capita US$8,390 (overall size of economy ranking 50 in the world). Growth rate (1988) –1%.

Economically active population. The total number of persons active in the economy was 1,592,000; unemployed: 6.2% (1988).

Sector	% of workforce	% of GDP
industry	19.8	31
agriculture	9.3	8
services*	70.9	61

* services figure includes elements unassigned to other categories.

Energy and mineral resources

Oil and gas. There are six gasfields in production: Kapuni, Maui, McKee, Kaimiro, Tariki, Ahuroa. 30% of primary energy consumption is supplied by natural gas.

Minerals. Iron ore; gold (production: (1987) 2,531 lbs/ 1,148 kg); limestone. (1987) bentonite 3,462 tons/ 3,140 tonnes; clay for bricks and tiles 70,547 tons/ 64,000 tonnes; potters' clays 27,558 tons/25,500; iron sand 2.5 million tons/2.3 million tonnes; limestone for agriculture 903,886 tons/820,000 tonnes; limestone for industry 229,278 tons/208,000 tonnes.

Electricity. Capacity: 7.7 million kW; production: 27,400 million kWh; 8,200 kWh per capita (1988).

Bioresources

Agriculture. Approximately two-thirds of the land is used for agriculture and grazing. New Zealand produces a food surplus. Agricultural exports have been suffering from a drop in world commodity prices and shrinking quotas in the key EC market.

Crop production: (1987) grassland, lucerne, tussock 34 million acres/13.8 million ha; horticulture 217,445 acres/88,000 ha; grain or fodder crops 887,077 acres/359,000 ha; plantations 2.9 million acres/1.2 million ha. Total meat production 1.33 million tons/1.21 million tonnes; total liquid milk production 1,849 million gallons/7,000 million litres. Wool production 385,805 tons/350,000 tonnes.

Livestock numbers: (1987) sheep 64.2 million; cattle 8 million; goats 1.1 million; deer, 500,000.

Forestry. 15.3 million acres/6.2 million ha of indigenous forest, most protected in National Parks or State Forests. 2.5 million acres/1 million ha of productive exotic forest. 1987 total timber produced, 74.2 million ft^3/2.1 million m^3; 450 sawmills; five plywood and veneer plants; eight pulp and paper mills.

Fisheries. Total exports: 345.7 million lb/156.8 million kg.

Industry and commerce

Industry. Food processing; wood and paper products; textiles; machinery, dairy products; oil refining; petrochemicals; iron and steel; aluminium.

Commerce. Exports: (f.o.b. 1988) US$7,900 million or 28% of GDP. Major exports are wool; lamb; mutton; beef; fruit; fish; cheese. Main trading partners are the US 16%; Japan 15%; Australia 15%; UK 9%. Imports: (c.i.f.1988) US$6,900 million, mainly petroleum; consumer goods; motor vehicles; industrial equipment. Main trading partners are Japan 21%; Australia 18%; US 16%; UK 10%; West Germany 6%.

Trade with UK. Exports (1988) to UK totalled £443 million; imports from UK totalled £300 million.

Tourism. The tourist industry is expanding; (1988) 856,000 visitors.

COMMUNICATIONS

Railways

There are 2,655 miles/4,273 km of railways.

Roads

There are 57,771 miles/92,971 km of roads.

Aviation

Air New Zealand Ltd provides international services and Ansett New Zealand and Mount Cook Airlines provide domestic services (international airports are at Auckland, Christchurch and Wellington). Passengers: (1985) 3.3 million.

Shipping

There are 999 miles/1,609 km of inland waterways. The marine ports of Auckland, Tauranga and Wellington are located on the North Island. Christchurch and Dunedin are on the South Island. The merchant marine consists of 23 ships of 1,000 GRT or over. Freight loaded: (1987) 10.6 million tons/9.6 million tonnes; unloaded 8.2 million tons/7.4 million tonnes.

Telecommunications

There is an excellent international and domestic system with 2.1 million telephones. There is a state radio company, transmitting on three non-commercial networks, and a state-owned television broadcasting company which operates two commercially-backed TV channels, as well as 19 privately owned commercial radio stations. There are 949,810 televisions (1988).

EDUCATION AND WELFARE

Education

Compulsory between six and 15, and free up to 19. Between the ages of three and four, children may attend one of 560 free kindergartens.

School population. 407,000 primary school pupils; 215,700 in state secondary schools; 11,900 in private schools.

Schools. 2,370 state primary schools with 18,400 teachers; 314 state secondary schools with 14,500 teachers. Teacher/pupil ratio approximately 1:14.

Universities. Six universities, with a total of approximately 66,500 students; six teacher-training colleges with approximately 4,000 students.

Health

(1987) 8,300 doctors; 24,500 hospital beds (one per 134 people).

NICARAGUA
República de Nicaragua (Republic of Nicaragua)

GEOGRAPHY

Nicaragua is the largest and most densely populated of the Central American republics, covering a total area of 49,985 miles²/129,494 km² including Lago de Nicaragua and Lago de Managua situated in the mountainous western half of the country, behind the volcanic Pacific coastal range. Along the northwestern border with Honduras, the Cordillera Entre Rios climbs to 6,913 ft/2,107 m at Pico Moyoton, Nicaragua's highest summit. Other western ranges include the forested peaks of the Cordilleras Isabella and Darien, divided by fertile basins and river valleys. To the east, the terrain slopes towards the Caribbean marshes of the Mosquito Coast. Main rivers include the Coco (forming the Nicaragua/Honduras frontier) and the San Juan (forming part of the south Nicaraguan/Costa Rican border). 9% of the land is arable and 35% forested. Nicaragua is divided into 16 departments of which Managua (in the west) is by far the most populous. The Nicaraguan republic lies in a seismically active zone.

Climate

Tropical. The wet season lasts May-Jan. Rainfall increases west-east from approximately 74.8 in/1,900 mm on the Pacific Seaboard to 148 in/3,750 mm (decreasing inland) on the Caribbean coast. Mean annual temperatures vary west to east from 81°F/27°C to 79°F/26°C. Managua: Jan. 79°F/26°C. July 86°F/30°C. Average annual rainfall 45 in/1,140 mm.

Cities and towns

Managua (capital)	615,000
León	158,577
Chinandega	144,291
Masaya	78,308
Granada	72,640

Population

Total population is 3,622,000 of which 58% live in urban areas. Population density is 72 persons per mile²/29.5 per km². Ethnic divisions: 69% mestizo; 17% White; 9% Black; 5% Indian including the Sumo, Mikito and Ramaguie peoples of the northeast.

Birth rate 4.42%. **Death rate** 0.97%. **Rate of population increase** (1980–87) 3.45%. **Age distribution** under 15 = 46.7%; over 65 = 2.5%. **Life expectancy** female 65; male 62; average 63.

Religion

95% of the population are Roman Catholic, 5% are Protestant (of which the major denominations are the Episcopalian and Baptist Churches).

Language

Spanish is the official language spoken by the majority of the population. Indigenous Indian languages are spoken along the Atlantic Coast and English has a fairly widespread currency, especially in its creole form.

HISTORY

Little is known of indigenous pre-Columbian tribes occupying what is now Nicaragua, but by the early 16th century the Lenca Indians (influenced by the higher civilizations of the Maya to the north and the Incas to the south) were typical of the complex intermixing of languages and cultures in the tribes of the region. They proved no match for the Spanish invasion in the early 16th century.

Nicaragua's political history has been one of great instability, with frequent foreign interventions. In the early 19th century there were clashes with British troops in the east of the country where the British protectorate of the Mosquito Coast lasted from 1816–60. Nicaragua was the focus of Anglo-American rivalry in the region, as early plans for a trans-isthmian canal envisaged it running through Nicaraguan territory.

Like its neighbours, Nicaragua gained independence from Spain in 1821 and separated from the Central American federation (founded 1823) in 1838. Conservative rule was punctuated in 1855–57 by William Walker, a US citizen, who invaded the country with mercenaries to support the Liberals, declared himself president in 1856 and was later removed by a joint Central American force with British support. Liberal rule returned in 1893 under Jose Santos Zelaya, but he was overthrown in 1909 by a conservative, Juan Estrada, backed by foreign financial interests and by the United States. As political chaos increased the government turned to the US, and in 1911 under the Knox–Castillo Treaty Nicaragua became a US protectorate. The US supervized elections and US troops were present from 1912 until 1933, during which time the National Guard was formed under the leadership of Gen. Anastasio Somoza Garcia. A number of opponents of the US presence took to the hills and launched a guerrilla war; the most famous of these, Lt. Augusto Cesar Sandino, was murdered by members of the

National Guard in 1934 (while attending peace negotiations in good faith).

For the next 45 years the Somoza family used the National Guard and the new National Liberal Party (PLN) to maintain its dictatorship, and also dominated much of the country's economic activity. Elections were held during that period, but winning candidates were always members of the Somoza family or their nominees, and the Conservative party took the role of a loyal opposition. The US continued its support of the Somozas and also maintained its financial interests in the country; when Gen. Somoza was shot and fatally wounded in 1956 he was attended by US military medical personnel on the orders of US Pres. Eisenhower. Gen. Somoza's elder son, Col Luis Somoza Debayle, succeeded him as president and his second son, Anastasio, became head of the National Guard. In 1967 Luis died and Gen. Anastasio Somoza was elected president in succession to a civilian PLN incumbent.

In Dec. 1972 a violent earthquake virtually destroyed the capital, Managua, and extended Somoza's control over national life still further through his chairmanship of the newly-created National Emergency Committee, which became notorious for its apparent corrupt diversion of the international aid received. In the years which followed the regime alienated most sectors of the population by its ban on all forms of political opposition and its growing abuse of human rights, and the possibility of any form of political settlement disappeared with the assassination in Jan. 1978 of the moderate politician Pedro Joaquín Chamorro.

The Sandinista National Liberation Front (FSLN), formed in 1961, staged its first main guerrilla action in 1974, occupied the National Palace in Aug. 1978, launched an insurrection one month later, and finally succeeded in entering Managua and overthrowing Somoza in July 1979. A 'provisional junta of national reconstruction' was formed, which later named Daniel Ortega Saavedra as co-ordinator, and in Apr. 1980 legislative power was vested in a new council of state incorporating seven political parties along with mass organizations, trade unions and professional bodies. By 1981, however, there had been a number of divisions within the ranks of those who had supported the 1979 revolution. In the Catholic Church many senior clergy, led by the Archbishop of Managua (now Cardinal) Miguel Obando y Bravo, became strongly antagonistic to the Sandinistas, especially when some priests were appointed to government office. Most junior clergy, however, continued to support the considerable social reforms and the substantial improvement in the country's human-rights record. Some leading politicians, including former junta members, joined opposition party groupings such as the Democratic Co-ordinating Board (CD), while others fled north to Honduras or south to Costa Rica to establish guerrilla groups, which the government dubbed 'counter-revolutionaries' or 'contras'.

Contra attacks began in 1982 and have concentrated chiefly on projects of economic sabotage, although by the mid-1980s there were also reports of contra campaigns of intimidation against civilians. Official US financial support for the contras was first passed through the US Congress in Dec. 1982, and the US Central Intelligence Agency (CIA) was reported to have been actively promoting anti-Sandinista activities since 1981.

In keeping with an undertaking given in 1981, general elections were held on 4 Nov. 1984 for the posts of president and vice-president and for 96 seats in a new National Assembly, to replace the junta and the Council of State. Ortega was elected president as the candidate of the FSLN, and the party won 61 seats; six other parties gained representation, but the elections were boycotted by the CD. The new government took office on 10 Jan. 1985, but was criticized by some sectors, in particular the Church hierarchy, for its economic austerity measures, for its curtailment of press freedom and for the reintroduction in Oct. 1985 of the state of emergency (first declared in Mar. 1982 and lifted except in war zones in Oct. 1984). A new constitution was promulgated on 9 Jan. 1987 incorporating a commitment to democracy and political pluralism, but some of its articles were suspended immediately by a renewal of the state of emergency.

Despite pressure from the US the Sandinista government refused to enter into negotiations with the contras, although it fell into line with the regional peace plan drawn up by Pres. Arias of Costa Rica, which was signed in Guatemala City on 7 Aug. 1987. Under the terms of the treaty each of the Central American governments promised the opening of negotiations with non-combatant groups, the declaration of a cease-fire, the holding of free elections, the restoration of full civil rights and a ban on the use of their territories for activities aimed to destabilize their neighbours. The Nicaraguan government made it clear that its compliance with these terms depended on the cessation of US aid to the contras. Although this US aid continued the government proceeded with elections which were held on 25 Feb. 1990. Ortega, the FSLN presidential candidate and pre-poll favourite, was heavily defeated by Violetta Chamorro, the candidate of the 14 party National Opposition Union (UNO) which also gained a clear majority in the National Assembly. The president-elect, who was to take office in April, immediately called for national unity, the demobilization and reduction in size of the Sandanistas Peoples' Army and the disbanding of the contras.

CONSTITUTION AND GOVERNMENT

Executive and legislature

Executive power is vested in the president, who is the head of state and commander-in-chief of the Defence and Security Forces and who governs with the assistance of a vice-president and an appointed cabinet. In practice the ruling Sandinista party plays a dominant role in government. Both the president and the vice-president are directly elected for a six-year term; last elections 4 Nov. 1984. Legislative power under the new constitution is to be exercised by a unicameral national assembly. The composition of the Assembly includes 90 representatives (each with an alternate) directly elected in Feb. 1990 for a six-year term by a system of proportional representation and, in addition, those unelected presidential and vice-presidential candidates (as representatives and alternates respectively) whose support exceeds a specified threshold.

Present government

President Cdr. Daniel Ortega Saavedra

Vice-President Dr Sergio Ramírez Mercado

Principal members of the Cabinet Fr Miguel d'Escoto Brockman (Foreign Affairs); Cdr. Humberto Ortega Saavedra (Defence); Cdr. Tomas Borge Martínez (Interior); Sr William Hupper Argüello (Finance).

Justice

The highest judicial authority is the Supreme Court of Justice at Managua. At local level there are over 150 tribunals, and there are 5 chambers of second instance. The death penalty was abolished in 1979.

National symbols

Flag. Three horizontal stripes of blue, white and blue, bearing the 1908 state coat of arms in the centre.

Festivals. 1 May (Labour Day); 19 July (Liberation Day); 10 Aug. (Managua local holiday); 14 Sept. (Battle of San Jacinto); 15 Sep. (Independence Day).

Vehicle registration plate. NIC.

INTERNATIONAL RELATIONS

Affiliations

NAM; OAS; Comecon (observer).

Defence

Total Armed Forces: 77,000 inclusive active duty reserves and militia (some 20,500 conscripts). Terms of service: conscription, males 17–50, two years' service plus commitment to age 45. Reserves: 120,500.

Army: 70,000; 35,000 active, 35,000 recalled reserves and militia; some 130 main battle tanks (T-54/-55) and 22 light tanks (PT-76).

Navy: 4,000; 20 patrol and coastal combatants.

Air Force: 3,000; nine combat aircraft (mainly Cessna 337, SF-260), ten armed helicopters.

Opposition: The main 'contra' guerrilla forces were the Nicaragua Democratic Force (FDN) based mainly in Honduras, with some 12,000 active fighters, US-backed, and the Southern Opposition Bloc (BOS) and Misurasata (Miskito, Sumo, Rama and Sandinista Unity) with up to 3,000, not all active.

ECONOMY

Currency

The unit is the cordoba, divided into 100 centavos.

National finance

Budget. The 1987 budget (in US$) was for expenditure (current and capital) of 1,400 million and revenue of 900 million.

Balance of payments. The balance of payments (current account, 1987) was a deficit of $799 million.

Gross Domestic Product

Estimated total GDP US$3,200 million, per capita US$610 (overall size of economy ranking 101 in the world).

Economically active population. The total number of persons active in the economy was 1,086,000; unemployed: 22%.

Sector	% of workforce	% of GDP
industry	13	34
agriculture	44	21
services*	43	46

* services figure includes elements unassigned to other categories.

Energy and mineral resources

Minerals. Production: (1980) gold 67,000 troy oz; silver 167,000 troy oz; copper 3,307 tons/3,000 tonnes; tungsten; lead; zinc.

Electricity. Capacity: 379,000 kW; production: 1,258 million kWh; 370 kWh per capita (1988).

Bioresources

Agriculture. Export of agricultural products, especially coffee and cotton, is the foundation of the economy. Farm production fell 5.4% in 1986, the third successive year of decline. 9% of land is arable; 1% permanent crops; 43% meadows/woodlands. Over 50% of agricultural and industrial firms are state-owned.

Crop production: (1986) cotton 50,706 tons/46,000 tonnes; coffee 48,501 tons/44,000 tonnes; sugar cane 3 million tons/2.8 million tonnes; rice; maize.

Livestock numbers: cattle 2.1 million; pigs 750,000.

Forestry. Mahogany; cedar; rosewood; dyewood. Timber production has fallen.

Fisheries. Catch: (1984) 4,740 tons/4,300 tonnes.

Industry and commerce

Industry. Cane sugar; cooking oil; cigarettes; beer; leather; metal products; petroleum refining; cement.

Commerce. There are severe shortages of basic consumer goods. Exports: (1988 est. f.o.b.) US$240 million, or 11% of GDP. Mainly coffee; cotton; sugar; bananas; seafood; chemicals. Main trading partners; Comecon 40%; OECD 39%. Imports: (c.i.f. 1988 est.) petroleum; food; chemicals; clothing. Main trading partners; Comecon 52%; EC countries 12%; Mexico 10%.

Trade with UK. In 1988 Nicaragua imported UK goods worth £6,856 million and exported to the UK goods worth £725,000.

COMMUNICATIONS

Railways

There are 199 miles/321 km of railways.

Roads

There are 15,378 miles/24,748 km of roads, of which 2,737 miles/4,408 km are paved.

Aviation

Aérolineas Nicaraguenses (AERONICA) provides domestic and international services (main airport is Contiguo Aeropuerto Internacional Augusto C. Sandino, near Managua). Passengers: (1982) 100,000.

Shipping

There are 1,379 miles/2,220 km of inland waterways including the two lakes Lago de Manague and Lago de Nicaragua. The marine port of Corinto on the west coast faces the North Pacific Ocean. Rama, accessible from the Caribbean Sea, is the main inland port. Other marine ports on the east coast are Puerto Cabezas and El Bluff (damaged by Hurricane Joan in Oct. 1988). There are seven secondary and ten minor ports. The merchant marine consists of two cargo ships of 1,000 GRT or over. Freight loaded: (1985) 367,066 tons/333,000 tonnes; unloaded: 1.5 million tons/1.4 million tonnes.

Telecommunications

There is a low capacity radio relay and wire system being expanded. There are 60,000 telephones, 870,000 radios and 200,000 televisions (1986). Among the 50-odd radio stations are the government-run La Voz de Nicaragua, the ruling party's Radio Sandino, and the Church-run Radio Catolica which has at times been banned for anti-government broadcasts. Television programmes are broadcast on Sistema Sandinista de Television.

EDUCATION AND WELFARE

Education

School population. 535,000 primary school pupils; 151,000 secondary school pupils.
Schools. 5,000 primary schools with 14,000 teachers; 323 secondary schools.
Literacy. 88%. (est.)

Health

2,200 doctors, 200 dentists, 49 hospitals with 5,000 beds (approximately one bed per 650 people).

NIGER

République du Niger
(Republic of Niger)

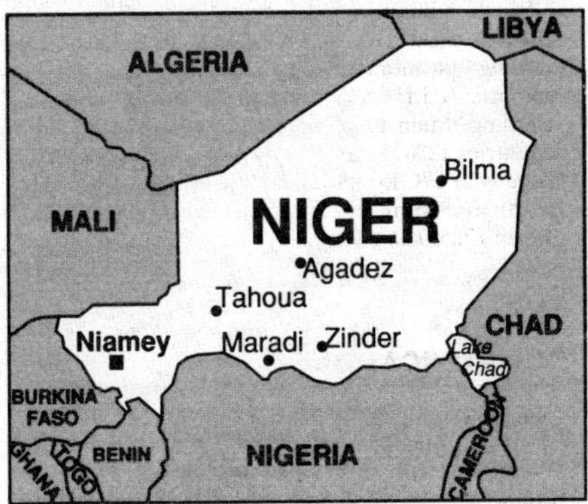

GEOGRAPHY

Located in West Africa, the landlocked Republic of Niger contains a total area of 489,062 miles²/ 1,267,000 km² divided into seven departments. Niger's predominantly arid physiography is dominated by the Hamada Manguene highlands in the north-east (dividing the Chadian Tibesti mountains from the Algerian Hoggar range), and the Massif de l'Air in the centre. Flanking the central massif east and west are the Saharan desert plains of Tenere du Tafassasset and the Western Talk. Sand or thin, sandy soil covers much of west, north and central Niger, but to the south-west around the Niger river basin (40% of the total surface area) and in the south-east around Lake Chad, soils are rich and fertile. Niger's highest peak is Mt Gréboun at 6,562 ft/2,000 m in the extreme north-west. The majority of the population is concentrated in the fertile southern regions; northern Niger is virtually uninhabited with the exception of a few scattered oases. Between 2 and 3% of the terrain is considered arable and 2% is (scrub) forest. Over two-thirds of Niger's territory is barren inhospitable desert.

Climate

Niger can be divided into three broad climatic zones. In the southern third of the country, a June-Oct. wet season provides 22in/560 mm of rainfall annually. During the rainy season, temperatures decrease to between 28.4°F/–2°C (nightime) and 61°F/16°C (daytime), increasing from Feb. to May to reach a maximum of 106°F/41°C. Rainfall decreases in the central zone, diminishing in the north to 0.8 in/20 mm per year or less in the desert area, scoured by the dry Saharan Harmattan wind.

Cities and towns

Niamey (capital)	225,314
Zinder	58,436
Maradi	45,852
Tahoua	31,265
Agadèz	20,475
Birni N'Konni	15,227

Population

Total population is 6,688,000 of which 19.8% live in urban areas. Population density is 13.7 persons per mile²/5.9 per km². Ethnic divisions: 50% Hausa; 22% Djerma and Songhai; 8.5% Fulani; 8% Tuareg; 4.3% Beriberi (Kanouri); 1.2% Arab; Toubou; Gourmantche; about 4,000 French expatriates.
Birth rate 4.42%. **Death rate** 0.97%. **Rate of population increase** (1980–87) 3.45%. **Age distribution** under 15 = 46.7%; over 65 = 2.5%. **Life expectancy** female 65; male 62; average 63.

Religion

Approximately 80% of the population are Muslims (predominantly Tijaniyya, Senoussi and Hamallist). Most of the remaining 20% practise independent beliefs although a significant minority are Christians (including 15,000 Roman Catholics).

Language

French is the official language although five major independent languages are also commonly spoken: Hausa, Songhai, Fulfulde (the Fulani dialect), Tamashek (the Tuareg language) and Arabic.

HISTORY

Archaeological remains and cave drawings show settlements in present-day Niger dating from Neolithic times. In the medieval period some parts of the area belonged to Sudanese states, and the western and south-western regions belonged to the Songhai empire of Gao (in present-day Mali). In the mid-18th century regions along the Niger river came under the power of nomadic Tuareg peoples; and in the early 19th century the southern regions were part of the Fulani Empire.

The first European explorer of the area, Mungo Park, disappeared on the river Niger in 1806. The French established their first military posts in Niger in the 1890s, and extended this conquest, marked by violent incidents such as the 1898 Zinder massacre, until in 1901 Niger was constituted as a French territory. In 1904, the territory was incorporated in the colony of Upper Sénégal-Niger, which was part of French West Africa. Niger became a separate administrative unit of French West Africa in 1922.

On 18 Dec. 1958 Niger became an autonomous republic, electing to remain within the French Community, despite a strong campaign by radical proponents of immediate independence. In the Dec. 1958 elections to the National assembly, Hamani Diori's Niger Progressive Party (PPN), an affiliate of the Rassemblement démocratique africain (RDA), won a majority of seats and formed a one-party government. On 3 Aug. 1960, full independence was proclaimed with Hamani Diori as president; the Republic of Niger was admitted to the UN in Sept. 1960, and on 8 Nov. 1960 a new constitution was adopted, confirming a system of government with an executive presidency.

Diori's regime survived the hostility of exiled Sawaba forces in the early and mid-1960s, but not the great drought of 1973; it was overthrown on 15 Apr. 1974 in a military coup led by Lt.-Col (later Maj.-Gen.) Seyni Kountché. Kountché suspended the constitution, dissolved the National Assembly, outlawed all political organizations and established a Supreme Military Council, with himself as president. Unsuccessful coup attempts against Pres. Kountché took place in 1976 and 1983. The President's constitutional initiatives led up to a referendum on 14 July 1987 which approved a National Charter designed to provide for an eventual return to civilian rule.

Kountché died on 10 Nov. 1987 and was succeeded as president by Army Chief of Staff Col Ali Saibou, who like Kountché was a member of the Djerma Songhai ethnic group. In February 1990 police opened fire on students protesting against austerity measures imposed as part of an economic restructuring programme; three people were killed according to the authorities, and at least ten according to student sources. The Interior Minister and the political secretary of the party's National Executive Bureau, whom the students had held responsible for the incident, were removed from their posts in Mar. 1990, and the post of Prime Minister was reinstated.

CONSTITUTION AND GOVERNMENT

Executive and legislature

After the 1974 coup Niger was ruled by a Supreme Military Council, with an executive president appointing the council of ministers. A single party, the country's sole legal political grouping, known as the National Movement for the Development Society (Mouvement National pour la Société de Développe-ent–MNSD), was formed in Aug. 1988 as part of a process of returning to civilian rule. A new supreme ruling body, a half-military and half-civilian Conseil Supérieure d'Orientation National, was set up under the president's chairmanship in May 1989, and a new Constitution was adopted by referendum in Sept. 1989. Saibou – the sole candidate – was confirmed as head of state in elections in Dec. 1989. At the same time a list of 93 deputies, all nominated by the party, the National Movement for a Development Society, was approved by the electorate. The deputies had been chosen by a process of elimination at meetings at local and regional levels.

Present government

President of the Higher Council for National Orientation; C.-in-C. of the Armed Forces; Minister of Defence Brig. Ali Saibou
Prime Minister Aliou Mahamidou
Other Principal Ministers Wassalke Boukary (Finance); Sani Bako (Foreign Affairs and Co-operation); Lt. Col. Tanja Mamadou (Interior); Ali Bandiere (Justice and Security).

Ruling party

National Movement of the Development Society (Mouvement National de la Société de Développement). *Chairman* Brig. Ali Saibou.

Justice

The system of law is based on both the French civil code and customary law. At local level justice is administered by justices of the peace in most towns, with regional magistrates', assize and appeal courts in the main towns (Niamey, Zinder and Maradi). The death penalty is nominally in force. There were no executions between 1985 and mid-1988.

National symbols

Flag. Three horizontal stripes of orange, white and green with an orange disc in the centre of the white stripe.
Festivals. 15 Apr. (Anniversary of the 1974 coup); 1 May (Labour Day); 3 Aug. (Independence Day); 18 Dec. (Republic Day).
Vehicle registration plate. NIG.

INTERNATIONAL RELATIONS

Affiliations

NAM; OAU; ACP; ICO; Francophonie.

Defence

Total Armed Forces: 3,300. Terms of service: selective conscription (two years).
Army: 3,200.
Air Force: 100.
Para-military: 4,500 (Gendarmerie, Presidential and Republican Guard and National Police).

ECONOMY

Currency

The unit is the CFA franc, divided into 100 centimes.

National finance

Budget. The 1988 budget (in US$) was for expenditure (current and capital) of 452 million and revenue of 226 million.
Balance of payments. The balance of payments (current account, 1987) was a deficit of $201 million.
Inflation. (1987) –6.7%.

Gross Domestic Product

Estimated total GDP US$2,160 million, per capita US$310 (overall size of economy ranking 112 in the world).
Economically active population. The total number of persons active in the economy was 2,500,000.

Sector	% of workforce	% of GDP
industry	6	24
agriculture	90	34
services*	4	42

* services figure includes elements unassigned to other categories.

Energy and mineral resources

Oil and gas. In 1978 oil was found in the Lake Chad area, but this has yet to be exploited.

Minerals. Large uranium deposits at Arlit and Akouta; phosphates found in Niger valley. There is opencast coal mining. Other minerals include iron ore and tin.

Electricity. Capacity: 102,000 kW; production: 227 million kWh; 30 kWh per capita.

Bioresources

Agriculture. 3% of the land is put to arable use, 7% is pasture or meadow. Niger suffers from recurrent drought and desertification caused by overgrazing and soil erosion.

Crop production: Food crops: millet 1.1 million tons/1 million tonnes; rice 66,138 tons/60,000 tonnes; sorghum 407,851 tons/370,000 tonnes; sugar cane 121,530 tons/110,000 tonnes. Cash crops: groundnuts 45,194 tons/41,000 tonnes; cotton.

Livestock numbers: (1987) cattle 3.4 million; sheep 3.6 million; camels 416,000; asses 500,000; goats 7.6 million.

Forestry. 2% of the country is forest and woodland. Production: (1985) 138.43 million ft^3/3.92 million m^3.

Fisheries. Catch: (1983) 7,540 tons/6,840 tonnes.

Industry and commerce

Industry. Some small manufacturing industries, mainly in Niamey, produce textiles; food products; furniture; chemicals.

Commerce. Exports: (f.o.b. 1988 est.) US$371 million or 16% of GDP. Over 75% of export revenue came from uranium. Other exports include livestock; cowpeas; onions; hides. Main trading partners are France; Japan; Nigeria. Imports: (c.i.f.1988) US$441 million, mainly petroleum products; primary materials; vehicles and parts; electronics equipment; pharmaceuticals; foodstuffs. Main trading partners are France; Nigeria.

Trade with UK. In 1988 Niger exported £1.4 million worth of goods to the UK and imported £7.5 million.

COMMUNICATIONS

Railways

There are as yet no railways.

Roads

There are 11,806 miles/19,000 km of roads, of which about 2,007 miles/3,230 km are concrete or bituminized.

Aviation

Air Afrique provides international flights and Air Niger provides domestic services (major airports are at Arlit, Diffa, Tahoua and Zinder). Passengers: (1984) 118,000.

Shipping

The Niger River is navigable for 186 miles/300 km from Niamey to Gaya on the Benin frontier from mid-Dec.–Mar.

Telecommunications

There is a small system of wire, radiocommunications and radio relay links in the south-western area, and 11,900 telephones. There are 350,000 radios and 15,000 televisions (1986). The government runs Télé Sahel, with programmes four days a week, and broadcasts a radio service in nine languages.

EDUCATION AND WELFARE

Education

Schools. 230,000 pupils, 5,500 teachers in 1,700 primary schools. 46,000 pupils, 1,400 teachers in secondary schools. Teacher-pupil ratio approximately 1:40.

Universities. The University of Niamey has about 2,000 students and 300 teachers.

Literacy. 8%.

Health

Two hospitals, 26 medical centres 116 dispensaries (1982). In 1980 there were 136 doctors.

NIGERIA

Federal Republic of Nigeria

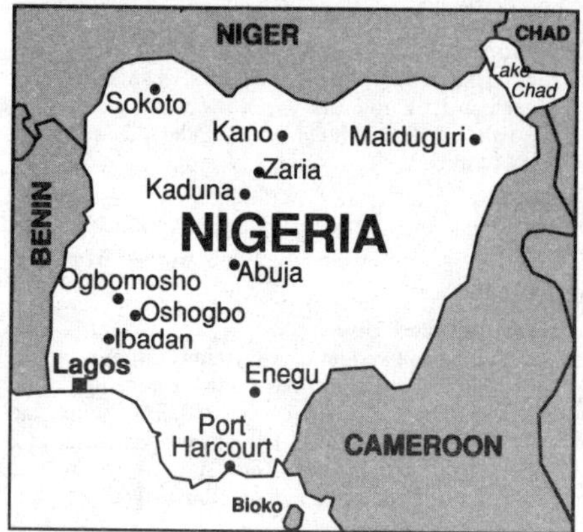

GEOGRAPHY

Nigeria lies on the south coast of West Africa, containing a total area of 356,575 miles²/923,770 km², divided into 19 states and a Federal Capital Territory. It comprises four main physiographic regions. The narrow sandy coastal strip fronting the Bight of Benin and Gulf of Guinea is characterized by mangrove swamps, lagoons and waterways dominated by the Niger Delta. Inland, a tropical rainforest belt rises northwards, opening out onto the semi-arid central Savannah plateaux (and Jos Plateau, climbing to 5,840 ft/1,780 m at Share Hill). Northern Nigeria lies on the edge of the Sahara desert, typified by tall, gently undulating grasslands. Nigeria's highest peak is situated in the Gotel Mountains on the border (south-east) with Cameroon (Mount Vogel 6,640 ft/2,024 m). The Niger-Benue basin dominates the country's hydrology, draining some 60% of the total surface area. In the extreme north-east lies the south-western tip of Lake Chad. Nigeria is the most populous country in the African continent, with particularly large demographic densities in the forest region, west of the River Cross and in the coastal lowland zone. 31% of the land is considered arable and 15% is forested.

Climate

Tropical, with uniformly high temperatures. Temperatures average 90°F/32°C on the coast with high humidity and rainfall total of 70–167 in/1,780–4,250 mm. Inland the rainy season lasts Apr.-Oct with July temps often above 100°F/38°C. Northern Nigeria is subject to the influence of the Saharan Harmattan, a dry, dusty, desert wind. Rainfall decreases markedly to an average of 20 in/500 mm or less. Lagos: Jan. 81°F/27.2°C. July 78°F/25.6°C. Average annual rainfall 72 in/1,836 mm. Kano: Jan 70°F/21.1°C. July 79°F/26.1°C. Average annual rainfall 34 in/869 mm. Port Harcourt: Jan. 80°F/26.1°C. July 77°F/25°C. Average annual rainfall 98 in/2,497 mm.

Cities and towns

Lagos (federal capital)	1,060,848
Ibadan	847,000
Ogbomosho	432,000
Kano	399,000
Oshogbo	282,000
Ilorin	282,000
Abeokuta	253,000
Port Harcourt	242,000
Zaria	224,000
Onitsha	224,000
Iwo	214,000
Ado-Ekiti	213,000
Kaduna	202,000

Population

Total population is 105,471,000, of which 16.1% live in urban areas. Population density is 296 persons per mile²/108.9 per km². Out of the 250 (or more) ethnic groups, the Hausa and Fulani of the north, Yoruba of the south-west and Ibo of the south-east constitute 65% of the total population. The Kanuri, Tiv, Edo, Nupe and Ibidio make up another 25%.

Birth rate 5.04%. **Death rate** 1.71 %. **Rate of population increase** (1980–87) 3.33%. **Age distribution** under 15 = 48.3%; over 65 = 2.4%. **Life expectancy** female 53; male 49; average 51.

Religion

An estimated 50% of the population are Muslim and 40% Christian including an estimated 7.8 million Roman Catholics; 0.8 million Anglicans; 0.5 million Baptists; 0.48 million Methodists. 10% of the population practise indigenous animist faiths.

Language

English is the official language, although Hausa is the most widely spoken (African) language, followed by Yoruba and Ibo. Other Niger–Congo dialects include Bura; Edo; Ibibio; Ijaw; Kanuri; Nupe; Tiv.

HISTORY

There is evidence of a variety of late stone-age cultures in most of the regions of Nigeria. Between 500 BC and AD 200 there was a flourishing civilisation, known as 'Nok', covering a large area of central Nigeria. The Nok culture was probably based on trade in iron and tin but is best known for the terracotta figurines which it produced. The historical development of the country from these early times varies from region to region.

In the northern half of the country the Hausa people evolved a series of city-states of which Kano, Katsina and Zaria were the most powerful. With their distinctive fortified walls these towns not only became important commercial centres in the trans-Saharan trade in gold, slaves and cotton but also centres of Islam as by the 16th century most of the Hausa rulers were Muslim. In the early 19th century the political structure of the Hausa states was transformed by a series of jihads (holy wars) inspired by the Islamic reformer, Uthman dan Fodio in Sokoto which brought almost all of Hausaland under the control of the Sokoto caliphate.

In the south-west of the country the history is dominated by the emergence of the Yoruba states of Ife, Oyo, Ijebu and Benin. In the course of the 17th century the Oyo kingdom in the north of Yorubaland started to expand, conquering other Yoruba states on its borders so that by the end of the 18th century it was the dominant power in Yorubaland.

In the south-east of the country on the Niger delta, there were no states equivalent in size to the Hausa and Yoruba kingdoms. The Niger Delta states were based on relatively self-contained fishing communities but with the development of the Atlantic trade they came to occupy a strategic commercial position controlling trading networks which extended far into the interior.

European contact with Nigeria dates back to the Portuguese traders of the 15th century. The Gulf of Guinea became one of the biggest centres of the slave trade and during the 18th century it is estimated that over 15,000 slaves were exported annually from the Bight of Benin on the southern edge of Yorubaland and a further 15,000 from the Bight of Biafra. In the 19th century, following the abolition of the slave trade and the growing interest in produce such as palm-oil kernels, British merchants established a more permanent presence in southern Yorubaland, around Lagos, along the Niger Delta and in Calabar on the Cross River but it was not until the annexation of Lagos in 1861 that the process of formal colonization began.

Much of the impetus for colonization came from commercial interests, led by George Goldie's Royal Niger Company (RNC), who feared that the French would be allowed to dominate trade. In 1885 the company was given responsibility for government along the Niger and Benue rivers which the British claimed as their sphere of influence. Around the same time the British sent military expeditions into Yorubaland and the Niger Delta where local rulers were either coerced or persuaded into accepting British rule. In 1897 the West African Frontier Force (WAFF) under the leadership of Sir Frederick Lugard was formed and the following year the RNC's charter to govern on behalf of the British government was revoked. The WAFF embarked on a campaign to bring the north under British rule and in 1900 the British Protectorate of Northern Nigeria was established with Lugard as high commissioner. The caliph of Sokoto, Attihuru, continued to resist British conquest until he was killed in 1903. In 1906 the colony of Lagos was incorporated into a newly formed Protectorate of Southern Nigeria, and in 1914 the Northern and Southern Protectorates were joined together to form the colony of Nigeria.

The British made extensive use of local leaders; particularly in the north where the precolonial emirate system was left largely intact. This policy, associated in particular with Lugard, came to be known as indirect rule. Until after World War II Africans had very limited political rights; political activity was confined to a number of ethnic associations and independent African churches and was dominated by the urban, mission-educated intelligentsia of the coast.

After the war the two leading Nigerian nationalists, Dr Nnamdi Azikiwe and Chief Obafemi Awolowo, led cautious demands for greater independence, enthusiastically backed by the African press and by the trade union movement. However, ethnic divisions were already evident in the 1951 elections in which the National Convention of Nigeria and Cameroon (NCNC) led by Azikiwe won in the Ibo-dominated Eastern Region, Awolowo's Action Group (AG) won in the Yoruba Western Region and the Northern Peoples' Congress (NPC) won in the Hausa-Fulani Northern Region. The constitution of 1954 established a federal system of government, and a timetable for independence was agreed following a series of constitutional conferences in 1957 and 1958.

Nigeria became independent as a federal republic on 1 Oct. 1960. The northern part of the British-administered UN trust territory of the Cameroons was incorporated within Nigeria as part of the northern region in June 1961. Within two years of independence regional and ethnic tensions were already putting the constitution under strain. In Jan. 1966 the army staged a coup, killing many leading politicians including the federal prime minister, Sir Abubakar Tafawa Balewa and the Northern Regional premier, Ahmadu Bello, the Sardauna (caliph) of Sokoto. The coup, led by Maj.-Gen. Ironsi, was seen as having been carried out in the selfish interests of the east (where huge oil reserves had recently been discovered). Ironsi and many of his officers were killed in a counter-coup on 29 July which was followed in September and October by a spate of massacres of Ibo living in the north.

Gen. Gowon, a Christian from the middle belt of Nigeria, succeeded in establishing his authority in the north and west but was rejected in the east which followed the lead of Lt.-Col Odemegwu Ojukwu in calling for greater autonomy. Attempts at reconciliation between the two sides failed and in May 1967 Ojukwu announced the formal secession of the east, under the new name 'Biafra'. From May 1967 until Jan. 1970 Nigeria was plunged into civil war in which thousands perished before the federal forces defeated the Biafran army. Gen. Gowon revived constitutional plans for the creation of 12 states out of the three regions and initiated a policy of national reconciliation. At the same time Nigerian society was being transformed by the wealth of its oil reserves and by 1975 oil revenue accounted for more than 90% of all export earnings.

Gen. Gowon was toppled in a bloodless coup in July 1975 and replaced by Brig. Murtala Mohammed who was murdered in an abortive coup in Feb 1976. The new head of the Federal Military government, Gen. Obasanjo, continued Mohammed's plan for a return to civilian rule and established a further seven states, bringing the total to 19. Political parties became legal in Sept. 1978 providing that they could show that they were truly national parties. The Federal Electoral Commission (FEDECO) recognized five parties which contested elections in July and Aug. 1979. These were narrowly won by the National Party of Nigeria (NPN) under the leadership of Alhaji Shehu Shagari who became president of Nigeria's Second Republic. Despite winning a further election in 1983 Shagari and his administration were unable to offer any solution to the country's pressing social and economic problems of squandering foreign exchange, rampant inflation and corruption.

On 31 Dec. 1983 the army staged a coup, and on 3 Jan. 1984 Maj.-Gen. Mohammed Buhari became head of a 19-member Supreme Military Council. Buhari's 'War Against Indiscipline' programme failed to cure the country's ills and the military regime's restrictions on freedom of expression were politically unpopular. Buhari was replaced by Maj.-Gen. Ibrahim Babangida in an internal military coup on 27 Aug. 1985. Babangida promised a return to civilian rule by 1992; the difficult task of framing a civilian constitution to satisfy the various ethnic, regional and religious demands was made more difficult still by the unpopularity of his package of economic reforms designed to reduce public-sector spending and encourage foreign investment. A ban on political party activity was lifted in May 1989 and a number of parties applied for registration. Babangida, however, rejected all the applications and instead announced the creation of two entirely new parties, the Social Democratic Party and the National Republican Convention, situated respectively on the left and on the right of the political spectrum. These were to be the only parties allowed to contest elections in the transition to civilian rule.

CONSTITUTION AND GOVERNMENT

Executive and legislature

The principal decision-making body under the post-1985 military regime, the Armed Forces Ruling Council (AFRC), is composed of 18 senior officers and members of the police force, plus the president as chairman. A 22-member Council of States consists of the president and the 21 state governors. There is a national council of ministers appointed by the AFRC, which is responsible for federal administration. A timetable providing for a return to civilian rule by 1992 was announced in July 1987.

Present government

President; C.-in-C. of the Armed Forces; Minister of Defence Gen. Ibrahim Babangida

Principal Ministers Rilwann Lukman (Defence); Maj.-Gen. Ike Nwachukwu (External Affairs); Cdr. Lamba Dung Gworn (Internal Affairs); Prince Bola Ajibola (Justice; Attorney General); Jabril Laminu (Petroleum Resources).

Administration

Nigeria is a federal republic, with military governors appointed by the President to head the administrations of all the 21 states.

States and their military governors Akwa Ibom – Col Gordon Abbey; Anambra – Col Bob Akonobi; Bauchi – Col Joshua Madaki; Bendel – Col Tunde Ogbeha; Benue – Lt.-Col Fidelis Maka; Borno – Col. M. I. Minan Mohammed; Cross River – Lt.Col-E.K. Attah; Gongola – Grp Capt. Salihu; Imo – Lt.-Cdr Amadi Ikwechegh; Kaduna – Col Abdullahi Muktar; Kano – Col Idris Garba; Katsina – Lt.-Col. J.Y. Madaki; Kwara – Col. A.J. Kazir; Lagos – Col Raji Rasaki; Niger – Lt.-Col Lawan Gwadabe; Ogun – Navy Capt. M.A. Lawal; Ondo – Navy Capt. Olabode Ibiyinka George; Oyo – Col S. Ore Sawyer; Plateau – Lt. Col A. Kama; Rivers – Group Capt. E.O. Adeleye; Sokoto – Col Ahmed Daku.

Justice

The system of law is based on English and indigenous common law and Islamic law. All judges are appointed under the current regime by the Armed Forces Ruling Council. The highest court is the Federal Supreme Court headed by the Chief Justice of the Republic, together with up to 15 Justices. The Federal Supreme Court has jurisdiction in disputes between states, or between the federal republic and any state. Each state has its own High Court and Chief Justice, while the northern states also have an Islamic Sharia Court of Appeal and Court of Resolution, and Alkali courts applying Moslem Law codified in a Penal Code. The death penalty is in force. There were at least 439 executions between 1985 and mid-1988. Offences included armed robbery.

National symbols

Flag. Three vertical stripes of green, white and green.
Festivals. 1 Oct. (National Day).
Vehicle registration plate. WAN.

INTERNATIONAL RELATIONS

Affiliations

NAM; OAU; OPEC; ICO; ACP; Commonwealth.

Defence

Total Armed Forces: 94,500. Terms of service: voluntary. Reserves: planned; none organized.
Army: 80,000; 132 main battle tanks (T-55, Vickers Mk 3), 100 light tanks (Scorpion).
Navy: 5,000; two frigates and 51 patrol and coastal combatants.
Air Force: 9,500; 84 combat aircraft (AlphaJet, MiG 21/-21U/-21MF, Jaguar).

ECONOMY

Currency

The unit is the naira, divided into 100 kobos.

National finance

Budget. The 1989 budget (in US$) was for expenditure (current and capital) of 5,675 million.
Balance of payments. The balance of payments (current account, 1987) was a deficit of $380 million.
Inflation. (1988) 25%.

Gross Domestic Product

Estimated total GDP US$24,390 million, per capita US$720 (overall size of economy ranking 53 in the world).
Economically active population. The total number of persons active in the economy was 45–50,000,000; unemployed: 7.5%.

Sector	% of GDP
industry	43
agriculture	30
services*	27

* services figure includes elements unassigned to other categories.

Energy and mineral resources

Oil and gas. There are oil refineries at Port Harcourt, Warri and Kaduna. Oil constitutes 95% of Nigeria's total exports. Natural gas reserves are estimated at 141 million ft^3/4 million m^3; gas is used at two electric power stations.
Minerals. Tin; columbite; coal (126,627 tons/114,875 tonnes 1981); iron ore (reserves estimated at 270 million tons/245 million tonnes); lead; zinc.
Electricity. Capacity: 4.7 million kW; production: 11.2 million kWh; 100 kWh per capita (1988).

Bioresources

Agriculture. Nearly half the total workforce is engaged in agriculture. Recent droughts in the north have severely affected marginal agricultural activities. In 1987 agricultural production fell 10%. Nigeria suffers from desertification and soil degradation.
Crop production: main food crops are (in million tons/tonnes) yams 21/19; cassava 15/14; rice 1.7/1.5; millet 3.3/3; sorghum 5/4.5; plantains; oil palms; rubber.

Cannabis is illegally produced for the international trade.

Livestock numbers (1987): 12.2 million cattle, 13.2 million sheep, 26 million goats.

Forestry. 15% of the country is forest or woodland, products include mahogany; iroko; ebony.

Fisheries. Total catch: (1984) 412,260 tons/374,000 tonnes.

Industry and commerce

Industry. The mining industry includes crude oil; natural gas; coal; tin; columbite. There are primary processing industries producing palm oil; peanuts; cotton; rubber; petroleum; wood; hides. Manufacturing industries include building materials; food products; footwear; chemicals.

Commerce. Exports: (f.o.b. 1987) US$6,700 million. Major products are oil; cocoa; palm kernels; rubber. Main trading partners are EC countries 51%; US 32%. Imports: (c.i.f. 1987) US$5,800 million. Major products are consumer goods; capital equipment; chemicals; raw materials. Main trading partners are EC countries; US.

Trade with UK. In 1988 Nigeria exported £128,000 worth of goods to the UK and imported £330,500 worth of goods from the UK.

Tourism. There were 340,000 visitors to Nigeria in 1985.

COMMUNICATIONS

Railways

There are about 2,180 miles/3,505 km of railways.

Roads

There are 67,104/107,990 km of roads, of which 18,773 miles/30,212 km are concrete or bituminized.

Aviation

Central Airlines and Kabo Air provide domestic services; Nigeria Airways and Intercontinental Airlines provide domestic and international services (main airports are at Lagos ((Murtala Muhammad Airport) and Kano). Passengers: (1984) 2.3 million.

Shipping

There are 5,328 miles/8,575 km of inland waterways including the Niger and Benue Rivers. Calabar is an inland port. Port Harcourt, Warri and Sapele are located on the Niger delta. Lagos is the major maritime port. The merchant marine consists of 35 ships of 1,000 GRT or over. Freight loaded: (1985) 69.2 million tons/62.8 million tonnes; unloaded: 12.7 million tons/11.49 million tonnes.

Telecommunications

There is an above average telecommunications system limited by poor maintenance, and major expansion is in progress. There are 155,000 telephones, 9.5 million radios and 5.6 million televisions (1988). The federal government controls radio broadcasting through the Federal Radio Corporation of Nigeria and the Nigerian Television Authority.

EDUCATION AND WELFARE

Education

Primary education is free.

School population. Approximately 15 million primary school pupils; 2.5 million secondary school pupils.

Schools. Some 200 teacher-training schools.

Universities. 23 federal and nine state universities.

Literacy. 25–30%.

Health

(1980) 8,000 doctors and 75,000 hospital beds (approximately one bed per 1,300 people).

NIUE

GEOGRAPHY

Niue, one of the world's largest coral islands, lies in the South Pacific Ocean covering a total area of 100 miles^2/260 km^2. It has steep limestone cliffs along the coast, with a central plateau. Most land is put to arable use. The capital is Alofi.

Climate

Tropical, modified by south-easterly trade winds. The island is subject to typhoons.

Population

Total population (1989 est.) 2,112; falling by some 6.6% per year.

Religion

Christianity, mainly Ekalesia Nieue (Niuean Church), a Christian Protestant Church. Also other Christian minorities.

Language

Polynesian language closely related to Tongan and Samoan. English.

HISTORY

Niue was settled by AD 900 by Polynesian people, probably from Samoa, and migrations from Tonga probably occurred in the 16th and 17th centuries. The first European to visit Niue, Capt. James Cook in 1774, named it Savage Island. After previous unsuccessful attempts the London Missionary Society established a mission in 1846 and within a decade virtually the entire population had become Christians. In the 1860s the islanders were subjected to kidnapping raids from Peruvian slaving vessels and in the following decade European settlers helped to develop the trade in cotton. After rejecting earlier offers of cession by the Niuean king, Britain proclaimed its sovereignty over the island in 1900 and a year later Niue was annexed to New Zealand as part of the Cook Islands. In 1904 Niue was made a separate administrative territory with its own resident commissioner and island council. Further constitutional change did not take place until 1960, when an elected assembly was established. In Oct. 1974 Niue became a self-governing territory in free association with New Zealand, with its population possessing New Zealand citizenship. The New

Zealand Government appoints a resident representative and remains responsible for the island's defence and external affairs. Sir Robert Rex, who has been the island's political leader since the 1950s, retained the premiership after the 1987 general election. By the mid-1980s the scale of the migration of Niueans to New Zealand and the subsequent decrease in the island's population had become a cause for concern to the New Zealand Government.

CONSTITUTION AND GOVERNMENT

Niue is a self-governing territory in free association with New Zealand. It has no formal written constitution. The executive consists of a cabinet of four members (the premier, elected by the Assembly, and three ministers, chosen by the premier from among Assembly members). The Legislative Assembly consists of 20 members (14 village representatives and six elected on a common roll). New Zealand will legislate for the island if requested to do so. Elections are held every three years, most recently in Mar. 1987.

Leader Sir Robert Rex Premier since early 1950s.

National symbols

Flag. Yellow, with the flag of the UK in the upper hoist-side quadrant. The UK flag has five yellow stars.

National holiday. 6 Feb. (Waitingi Day, commemorating Treaty of Waitingi, establishing British sovereignty in New Zealand).

ECONOMY

The economy is heavily dependent on New Zealand aid. Agriculture is mainly at subsistence level. Industry consists of small factories processing passion fruit, lime oil, honey and coconut cream. The sale of postage stamps to foreign collectors is an important source of revenue.

Currency

The New Zealand dollar.

COMMUNICATIONS

There is offshore anchorage only; one airport with permanent surface runways; 76 miles/123 km of all-weather roads. A single-line telephone system connects all villages on the island. There is one AM and one FM radio station. No television.

NORFOLK ISLAND

GEOGRAPHY

Norfolk Island is a volcanic island in the South Pacific Ocean with a total land area of 13.3 miles^2/34.6 km^2. The administrative centre is Kingston; the commercial centre is Burnt Pine.

Climate

Subtropical, little seasonal temperature variation.

Population

Total population (1989 est.) 2,490.
Rate of population increase 1.7%.

Religion

Christianity.

Language

English (official); Norfolk (mixture of 18th-century English and ancient Tahitian.

HISTORY

Norfolk Island is the oldest of Australia's external territories and was uninhabited when discovered in 1774 by Capt. James Cook. The island served as a penal colony from 1788 to 1814, when it was abandoned, and again from 1825 to 1856. During the second penal settlement Norfolk Island earned considerable notoriety. Owing to overcrowding on Pitcairn Island the entire population, who were descendants of the Bounty mutineers, were resettled on Norfolk Island in 1856 and allowed to establish their own social systems. Increasing concern in Sydney over the islanders' attitude to authority and their inability to develop commercial trade led in 1897 to Norfolk Island becoming a dependency of New South Wales. It became a Territory of Australia in 1914. Between then and 1979 various forms of locally elected advisory bodies were established to help run the island, but relations between the islanders and the Australian Government were often strained. The Nimmo Report in 1976 recommended Norfolk Island's integration into the Australian political and legal system, but the islanders' opposition to this was instrumental in the Australian Government's decision to develop a form of self-government for the territory. The 1979 Norfolk Island Act established a Legislative Assembly with executive and legislative responsibility in certain municipal matters and its powers were increased in 1985 when the Norfolk Island government assumed responsibility for public works and services and civil defence. The Australian Government continues to have overall responsibility for Norfolk Island and is represented there by a resident administrator.

CONSTITUTION AND GOVERNMENT

Norfolk Island is a territory of Australia. Its constitution dates from the Norfolk Island Act of 1957. There is a nine-member elected legislative assembly. The chief executive is an Australian administrator named by the governor general. Everyone born on the island is an Australian citizen.

Leader David Buffet, chief minister (since 1983).

National symbols

Flag. Three vertical bands of green, white and green, with a large green Norfolk Island pine tree centred in the white band.

National holiday. 8 June (Pitcairners Arrival Day).

ECONOMY

The major economic activity is tourism, which has given the island a favourable balance of trade. The agricultural sector is self-sufficient in production of beef, poultry and eggs.

Currency

The Australian dollar.

COMMUNICATIONS

There are no ports; one airport with permanent surface runway; 50 miles/80 km of road. One AM radio station, no FM radio or television.

NORWAY

Kongeriket Norge
(Kingdom of Norway)

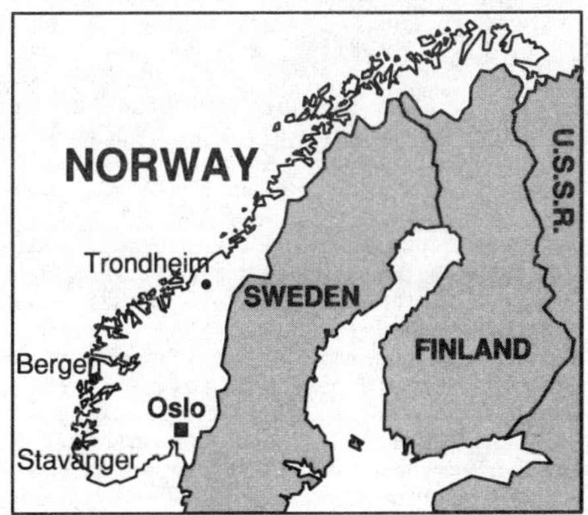

GEOGRAPHY

Norway ('The Northern Way') occupies the western part of the Scandinavian peninsula, containing an area of 125,149 miles^2/324,220 km^2 divided into 19 counties or 'fylker'. The deeply indented and glaciated coastline measures some 13,624 miles/21,925 km in length including 10,000 miles/16,093 kms of fjords and a major island circumference of 1,499 miles/2,413 km (including Lofoten and Vesteralen off the northwestern coast). The three principal fjords are Sogne fjorden (north of Bergen), Hardanger fjorden (south of Bergen) and Oslo fjorden (south east). Much of Norway's interior is dominated by mountainous or high plateau terrain ('fjell' or 'vidde') including Hardangervidda and Darrefjell in the central southwest. To the south, the centrally located Jotunheimen range rises to 8,100 ft/2,469 m at Galdhopiggen and 8,104 ft/2,470 m at Glittertind (Norway's highest peak). To the north, the Kjolen Mountains mark the Swedish border. The largest of Norway's 160,000 lakes is Lake Mjosa (142 miles^2/368 km^2) in the southeast, and principal rivers include the Dramselv, Glama and Lagen. Only about 1,976,773 acres/800,000 ha of land is considered arable, mostly in the fertile fjord/lakeside valleys, and 27% of the total surface area is forested. The most densely populated counties are those of Oslo, Østfold and Vestfold (all in the south-east) and the most depopulated are those of Finnmark and Troms in the far north. Norwegian dependencies comprise Bouvet Island, Jan Mayen Island, the Svalbard achipelago (population 3,942 in 1986) and Queen Maud Land in Antarctica.

Climate

Arctic in the northern highlands throughout the winter months, with heavy snowfall and strong winds. Conditions are considerably ameliorated on the coast by the Gulf Stream. Precipitation decreases west-east from 79 in/2,000 mm to 29.5 in/750 mm. Mean temperatures in the north and inland range from 50°F/10°C in July to 14°F/–10°C in Jan., and in the south from 63°F/17°C to 28°F/-2°C. Oslo: Jan. 25°F/–3.9°C. July 63°F/17°C. Average annual rainfall 27 in/683 mm. Bergen: Jan. 35°F/1.5°C. July 61°F/16.1°C. Average annual rainfall 77 in/1,958 mm. Trondheim: Jan 26°F/-3.5°C. July 57°F/14°C. Average annual rainfall 34 in/870 mm.

Cities and towns

Oslo (capital)	451,099
Bergen	208,809
Trondheim	134,496
Stavanger	95,437
Kristiansand	63,293
Drammen	51,324

Population

Total population is 4,188,000, of which 74% live in urban areas. Population density is 33 persons per mile^2/12.9 per km^2. 97% of the population are of Germanic (Nordic, Alpine, Baltic) origin, with a Sami/Lapp minority of 20,000 in the extreme north. **Birth rate** 1.23%. **Death rate** 1.02%. **Rate of population increase** (1980–87) 0.21%. **Age distribution** under 15 = 20.4%; over 65 = 15.5%. **Life expectancy** female 80; male 74; average 77.

Religion

Christianity. 94% of the population belong to the Evangelical Lutheran Norwegian State church. Of the remaining 6%, two-thirds are Baptists, Pentecostalists, Methodists or Roman Catholics (21,500 adherents).

Language

Norwegian (North Germanic language). Two forms of the official Norwegian language are recognized: Bokmål, the more urban Dano-Norwegian language, and Nynorsk (or New Norwegian), taught in 16–20% of the schools and instated by Ivor Aasen (language scholar) in the mid-19th century. Small Lappish and Finnish-speaking minorities inhabit the far northern regions.

HISTORY

The area of present-day Norway, where settlement dates back over 10,000 years, was penetrated in the early centuries AD by Germanic tribes, who established numerous petty kingdoms. First unified under Harald I Fairhair (c.900), Norway was Christianized under St Olaf II (r.1015–30). Norwegians participated in the great northern wave of Viking expansion and conquest (800–1100), conquering Normandy, Iceland and Greenland and parts of the British Isles, and reaching as far as North America. Dynastic conflict involving Denmark and Sweden was followed by the consolidation of royal power under King Sverre (r.1184–1202) and an era of peace and prosperity under Haakon IV (r.1217–63) and Magnus VI (r.1263–80). The accession of Magnus VII (1319) unified the Norwegian and Swedish crowns until his son became Haakon VI of Norway in 1343. The Black Death (1349–50) killed up to two-thirds of Norway's population, creating institutional weakness. Under the 1397 Union of Kalmar, secured by Queen Margrethe of Denmark and preceded by a union of the Norwegian and Danish crowns in 1380, Norway and Sweden passed to Denmark. Sweden reasserted its independence in 1523, but Norway remained a Danish province for over four centuries.

The Lutheran Reformation, not fully embraced in Norway until c.1600, strengthened Danish control, as symbolized by the foundation of Christiania as the capital after medieval Oslo had been destroyed by fire in 1624. Denmark's adoption of absolute monarchy in 1660 strengthened Danish influence, although some Norwegian institutions survived. In the 17th and early 18th centuries Norway featured in wars between Denmark and Sweden, notably in the Great Northern War (1700–21), in which the Norwegian naval hero Peder Wessel Tordenskiold destroyed the Swedish fleet at Dynekilen (1716). Swedish ambitions against Norway were thus thwarted until the end of the Napoleonic Wars, when Denmark's alliance with France resulted, on the defeat of Napoleon, in Norway being transferred to the Swedish crown under the Treaty of Kiel (1814), although Iceland, Greenland and the Faroe Islands remained Danish. The Norwegians immediately rebelled, causing a Swedish invasion, whereupon a compromise enabled Norway to retain its own parliament (Storting) and some autonomy under Swedish sovereignty.

Under the union with Sweden some economic and social progress was made, although Norway remained a relatively poor rural country. Nationalism became the dominant force and the 19th century brought a remarkable literary renaissance, although the competing claims of Dano–Norwegian and the rural vernacular raised still unresolved controversies. Political life centred on competition between the Venstre Liberals and the Conservatives (both organized as parties from 1884), while the Labour Party (DNA) was formed in 1887 to represent the growing industrial labour force. Increasing strains with Sweden came to a head in 1905 over moves by the government of Christian Michelsen (Liberal) to create separate overseas representation for Norway. When Sweden resisted, the Storting assumed the royal powers and secured overwhelming support for independence in a plebiscite. Sweden then formally concurred in the separation and Prince Carl of Denmark ascended the Norwegian throne as Haakon VII. The 1814 constitution was reaffirmed and universal male suffrage introduced. Women obtained the vote in 1913, almost a century later.

Norway remained neutral during World War I, enjoying an economic boom by virtue of the belligerents' demand for its raw materials and fish. After the immediate post-war slump, the 1920s saw rapid industrialization and exploitation of natural resources such as hydroelectricity, minerals and timber. Christiania reverted to its old name of Oslo in 1925. Although weakened by the formation of a pro-Moscow Communist Party (1923), the DNA had its first experience of government in 1927 after becoming the largest parliamentary party. Amid economic recession, the DNA returned to office in 1935 under Johan Nygaardsvold and remained in power for the next 30 years (except for the war years). Like other Scandinavian countries, Norway declared its neutrality in World War II but was invaded by Nazi Germany in 1940 and was quickly overrun. With the King and government in London, the Norwegian people mounted determined resistance to a repressive occupation regime, in which the Germans were assisted by Norwegian fascists such as Vidkun Quisling.

After the liberation in 1945, the Labour leadership passed to Einar Gerhardsen, who headed an all-party coalition (including the Communists) until the DNA won an absolute majority in elections to the Storting in Dec. 1945. The next three elections (1949, 1953 and 1957) also produced absolute DNA majorities, under the successive premierships of Gerhardsen until 1951, Oscar Torp (1951–55), and Gerhardsen again from 1955. During its long hegemony the DNA government implemented a major programme of reconstruction and built a comprehensive welfare state on foundations laid in the pre-war period. Having acquired, as a result of World War II territorial changes, a northern frontier with the Soviet Union, Norway abandoned neutrality by joining NATO in 1949; it also joined the Nordic Council in 1953 and EFTA in 1959. King Haakon died in 1957 and was succeeded by his son, who became Olav V. The 1961 elections marked a political watershed in that the DNA lost its absolute majority and has not succeeded in regaining it since. Although it continued as a minority government supported by the left-wing Socialist People's Party (SPP), it lost power briefly in mid-1963 and finally went into opposition after being defeated in the 1965 elections.

The post–1965 non-socialist coalition, headed by Per Borten of the Centre (formerly Agrarian) Party, included the Conservatives, Liberals and Christian People's Party (CPP). It continued after the 1969 elections but resigned in 1971 amid differences over whether Norway should join the European Communities (EEC, European Coal and Steel Community and Euratom). The succeeding DNA minority government under Trygve Bratteli signed an EC accession treaty, but in a fiercely-contested referendum (Sept. 1972) Norwegian voters rejected membership by 53.5% to 46.5%. Bratteli immediately resigned and was replaced by Lars Korvald at the head of a minority coalition (of his own CPP, the Centre Party and the anti-EEC Liberals), which concluded an industrial free trade agreement with the EEC (1973). Defections to the SPP-led Socialist Electoral Alliance (SEA) sharply reduced DNA representation in the 1973 elections, but equivalent disarray on the centre-right enabled Bratteli to form another minority government with the external support of the SEA (which became the Socialist Left Party in 1975). In 1976 Bratteli was succeeded by

Odvar Nordli, who in Feb. 1981 gave way to Gro Harlem Brundtland, Norway's first woman prime minister. Although the economy had been greatly strengthened by North Sea oil and gas production, international recession contributed to the DNA's defeat in Sept. 1981. The Conservatives, by now the dominant non-socialist party, formed a one-party minority government under Kaare Willoch, who in June 1983 brought in the Centre Party and CPP. This coalition continued after the 1985 elections but collapsed in May 1986 over an economic austerity package, whereupon Brundtland formed a minority DNA government. The country was shaken in mid-1987 by revelations that the state-owned engineering and defence equipment company Kongsberg Vaapenfabrikk (KV) had violated NATO restrictions on the sale to Eastern bloc countries of sensitive material when it had in cooperation with a Japanese company exported computer systems to the Soviet Union. Later in the year serious mismanagement of the state-owned Statoil company, which controlled the country's oil industry, led to another political row and the restructuring of Statoil during 1988. In a general election on 11 Sept. 1989 both the two largest parties, the Labour Party and the Conservatives, lost ground and a month later Jan Syse took office at the head of a minority liberal-conservative coalition of the Conservatives, the CPP and the Centre Party. The new government depended on the right-wing populist Progress Party, which had performed well in the elections, for support.

CONSTITUTION AND GOVERNMENT

Executive and legislature

The monarch, a largely ceremonial head of state, nominally exercises authority through a council of state (cabinet) headed by a prime minister. In practice the prime minister, as head of government, is responsible to the legislature, the bicameral 157-member parliament (Storting). The Storting is elected for a fixed term of four years by universal adult suffrage (minimum voting age 18), using a complex system of proportional representation within 19 districts. Last elections were on 11 Sept. 1989. The Storting divides itself into an Upper House (Lagting) of 25% of its members, and a Lower House (Odelsting) of 75%.

Present government

Head of state Olav V, King of Norway

Prime Minister Jan P. Syse

Other Principal Ministers Kjell Magne Bondevik (Foreign Affairs); Arne Skauge (Finance); Per Ditliv-Simonsen (Defence); Else Bugge Fougner (Justice).

Justice

The system of law is a mixture of customary law, civil law and common law. The highest court is the Supreme Court, which may be called upon for an advisory judicial opinion on legislation. There are in all over 100 lower courts, as well as the Court of Impeachment and a Conciliation Council. Serious offences are prosecuted through a public prosecution authority, headed by the Attorney General and operated by the district attorneys and legally qualified officers of the ordinary police force. The death penalty was abolished in 1979.

Prisons. There are 1,951 prisoners.

National symbols

Flag. Red with a blue Scandinavian cross edged with white.

Festivals. 17 May (National Independence Day).

Vehicle registration plate. N.

INTERNATIONAL RELATIONS

Affiliations

Nato; OECD; EFTA; Nordic Council; Council of Europe.

Defence

Total Armed Forces: some 35,800 (23,000 conscripts). Terms of service: Army, 12 months plus four to five refresher training periods, Navy and Air Force 15 months. Home Guard 12 months. Reserves: 285,000; obligation to 45 (officers: reserves: 55, regulars: 60).

Army: 19,000; 80 main battle tanks (Leopard); 70 light tanks (NM-116).

Navy: 7,000, inclusive 2,000 coast artillery; 12 submarines (Kobben SSC), five frigates (Oslo); 40 patrol and coastal combatants.

Air Force: 9,100; 88 combat aircraft (mainly F-5A/B, F-16, F-16A).

ECONOMY

Currency

The unit is the krone, divided into 100 ore.

National finance

Budget. The 1989 budget (in US$) was for expenditure (current and capital) of 43,850 million and revenue of 41,440 million. Main items of current expenditure are housing and welfare 26%; health 10.5%; education 8.7%; defence 8.3%.

Balance of payments. The balance of payments (current account, 1988) was a deficit of $3,660 million.

Inflation. 4.2% (12 months to Sept. 1989)

Gross Domestic Product

Estimated total GDP US$83,080 million, per capita US$19,768 (overall size of economy ranking 29 in the world). Growth rate (1988) 2.3%.

Economically active population. The total number of persons active in the economy was 2,128,000; unemployed: 3.2% (1988).

Sector	% of workforce	% of GDP
industry	24.6	35
agriculture	7.2	4
services*	68.2	62

* services figure includes elements unassigned to other categories.

Energy and mineral resources

Oil and gas. Oil production: (1988) 62 million tons/ 56 million tonnes. Gas production: (1987) 1,038,246 ft^3/29,400 million m^3.

Minerals. Production: (1986 in tons/tonnes) copper 128,906/116,943; pyrites 418,801/379,934; nickel 42,110/38,202; iron ore; zinc; lead.

Electricity. Capacity: 26.18 million kW; production: 118,141 million kWh; 28,190 kWh per capita (1988). Some 99% of Norway's total production comes from hydroelectric plants. Most is used for industrial purposes, especially the chemical and metal industries and the paper and pulp industries.

Bioresources

Agriculture. Approximately 80% of land area is unproductive and only 2% under cultivation, mainly around the fjords and lakes. Animal husbandry and fish farming (salmon) predominate. Main crops are feed grains; potatoes; fruits; vegetables.

Crop production: (1987 in 1,000 tons/tonnes) wheat 273/248; rye 3/3; barley 625/567; oats 515/467; potatoes 409/371; hay 3,182/2,887.

Livestock numbers: (1987) cattle 945,500; sheep 2.24 million; horses 16,500; goats 91,900; pigs 778,900; hens 3.98 million.

Forestry. 27% of the land is forest and woodland, of which 80% is conifer and broadleaf forest. An average of 303.7 million ft^3/8.6 million m^3 of timber is produced, of which 293.1 million ft^3/8.3 million m^3 is used by industry.

Fisheries. Total catch: (1987) 2.12 million tons/ 1.93 million tonnes.

Industry and commerce

Industry. The main industries are petroleum and gas; food processing; shipbuilding; pulp and paper products; metals; chemicals; timber; mining, textiles; fishing.

Commerce. Exports: (1987) US$21,500 million, including petroleum and petroleum products 28%; natural gas 12%; ships 7%; fish 6%; aluminium 6%; pulp and paper. Imports: US$22,600 million, including machinery; fuels and lubricants; transportation equipment; chemicals; foodstuffs; clothing; ships. Countries exported to were UK 28%; West Germany 20%; less developed countries 14%; Sweden 10%; Netherlands 6%; US 5%; Denmark 4%. Imports came from Sweden 18%; West Germany 17%; UK 9%; less developed countries 8%; US 7%; Japan 7%; Denmark 7%.

Trade with UK. Norway imported UK goods worth £1,053,613,000; exports to UK totalled £3,074,000,000.

COMMUNICATIONS

Railways

There are 2,622 miles/4,219 km of railways, of which 1,523 miles/2,451 km are electrified.

Roads

There are 53,528 miles/86,143 km of roads (15,978 miles/25,713 km of national roads).

Aviation

Wideroe's Flyveselskap A/S, Braathens South American and Far East Airtransport A/S and Partnair A/S provide domestic services; Det Norske Luftfarselskap A/S (DNL) and Scandinavian Airways (SAS) provide international services (main airport is at Oslo). Passengers: (1986) 7.4 million.

Shipping

There are 980 miles/1,577 km of inland waterways along the west coast. The major ports: Oslo, Bergen, Drammen, Fredrikstad, Stavanger, Trondheim are all located in the lower half of the country. The merchant marine consists of 429 ships of 1,000 GRT or over. Freight loaded: (1987) 67.7 million tons/61.4 million tonnes; unloaded: 22.7 million tons/20.6 million tonnes.

Telecommunications

There is a good domestic and international telecommunications system with 3.1 million telephones. There are 3 million radios and 1.4 million televisions (1988). The government operates a monopoly over radio and television through NRK, with two radio channels and some 40 hours of television per week.

EDUCATION AND WELFARE

Education

Schools. School attendance is compulsory between seven and 16 years. There are 3,500 primary schools with 505,942 pupils and 87 special schools with 2,620 pupils. Total number of pupils attending secondary and vocational secondary schools is 206,068.

Universities. There are four universities and 11 other equivalent institutions with a total of 44,303 students.

Health

(1985) 10,324 doctors (one per 407 people) and (1987) 66,373 beds (one per 63 people).

OMAN
Saltanat Uman
(Sultanate of Oman)

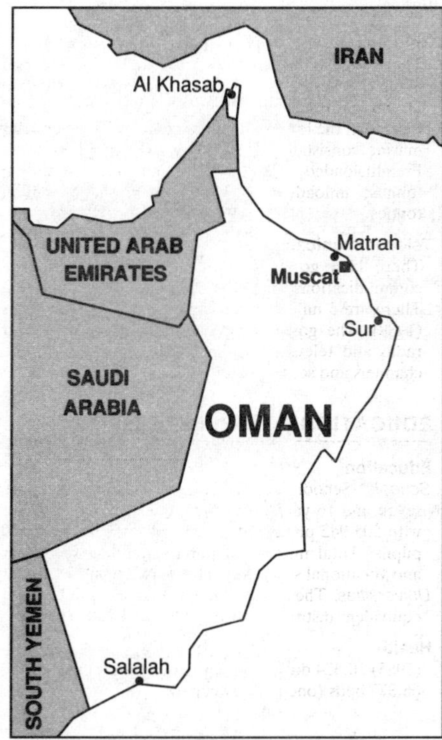

GEOGRAPHY

Located on the south-eastern coast of the Arabian peninsula, Oman covers an area of 82,008 miles^2/212,457 km^2. including the tip of the Musandam peninsula and the islands of Masirah, Kuria Maria and Daymaruyat. To the north, the fertile coastal plain of al-Batinah is separated from the arid plateau desert dominating 75% of the territory, by the Hajjar mountain range (north-west – south-east) rising to 10,194 ft/3,107 m in the Jabal Akhdar ridge. Soil conditions in the upland region are poor but seasonal wadis dissecting the Akhdar spur, underground canals (falajs) and wells provide some irrigation. North of the Dhofar uplands in the south-west, the desert interior meets the sandy wastes of the Saudi Arabian Rubal Khali (empty quarter). Subsistence agriculture occupies approximately 158 miles^2/410 km^2 of arable land. The bulk of the population lives along the alluvial al-Batinah strip in the north, where date gardens stretch over 155 miles/250 km.

Climate

Desert, hot and arid, with very high temperatures and humidity along the coastal areas Apr.-Oct. (maximum temperature 117°F/47°C). Conditions become less extreme Dec.-Mar. Rainfall varies from 2 in/50 mm to 4 in/100 mm; light rainfall waters the south June-Sept. Muscat: Jan. 72°F/22.2°C. July 92°F/33.3°C. Average annual rainfall 3.9 in/99.1 mm.

Cities and towns

Muscat (capital)	400,000

Population

Total population is 1,304,882 of which 8.8% live in urban areas. Population density is 15.9 persons per mile^2/4.4 per km^2. Ethnic composition: predominantly Arab with small Baluchi, Zanzibari Iranian, Indian, Pakistani and West European minorities.

Birth rate 4.3%. **Death rate** 1.2%. **Rate of population increase** (1980–87) 3.1%. **Age distribution** under 15 = 44.3%; over 65 = 2.5%. **Life expectancy** female 57; male 54; average 55.

Religion

Islam. 75% of the population are Ibadhi Muslim (a sub-branch of the Kharijites). A mixture of Sunni Muslims, Shi'a Muslims and Hindus comprise the remaining 25%.

Language

Arabic is the official language, but English, Baluchi (and other Mahri languages), Urdu and a variety of Indian dialects are also spoken.

HISTORY

In the first millenium the Magan civilization arose in Oman and farming communities existed in the Hajar Mountains. A Persian occupation in the mid-18th century was ended under the leadership of Ahmad bin Sa'id Al bu Sa'id who was subsequently elected imam (ruler). The imamate was a combination of religious and political leadership uniquely developed by the Ibadi Muslims of Oman who were part of the Kharijite schism dating from AD 650.

However, there was a marked division between the coastal plain in the Muscat-Matrah region, an area traditionally involved in maritime trade, responsive to new cultural influences and the home of a relatively cosmopolitan, predominantly Hindu population, and the interior, centred on the fertile plateau and the oasis of Nizwa, the stronghold of the Ibadi Muslims. This geographical division was reflected in a division of power, whereby the legitimacy and authority of the Muscat-based Al bu Sa'id Sultans were not fully accepted in the interior where a politically autonomous, theocratic Ibadi imamate ruled. Periodically, an imam would challenge the power of the sultan and after one such display of strength the sultan was compelled to agree, in 1920, not to interfere in the affairs of the interior. This resulted in a 35-year peace between the two areas, although the continuing division was expressed in the country's official name: the Sultanate of Muscat and Oman, the agreement failed to resolve the issue.

A Saudi-backed insurrection broke out in the interior in the mid-1950s when the imam proclaimed an independent state and sought membership of the

Arab League. Sultan bin Taymur (ruler since 1932) was assisted by the British, whose treaties dating from 1798 gave Oman protectorate status, and the imam suffered military defeat. However, the Sultanate was more seriously threatened by the rebellion in the western province of Dhofar, which had been annexed in the late 19th century after years of quasi-autonomous existence. By 1968 the Marxist oriented Popular Front for the Liberation of the Occupied Arabian Gulf (latterly known as the Popular Front for the Liberation of Oman), supported by the neighbouring People's Republic of Yemen, were active in large tracts of the region. The revolt in Dhofar was only finally overcome in late 1975 with the support of Britain and Iran.

In a palace coup in 1970, the Sultan was replaced by his son, Sultan Qabus, who in a symbolic gesture of unification changed the name of the country to the Sultanate of Oman. Under Sultan Qabus, Oman entered a new era, with oil revenues (exports began in 1967) facilitating a programme of socio-economic development in an effort to modernize the country. In 1976, the Sultan reorganized regional and local government by establishing 37 divisions (wilayats) within the country. These are administered by governors appointed by the Sultan, who collect taxes, provide local security, settle disputes and advise the Sultan. Dhofar, governed as a separate province, still has more local autonomy than other regions, while Muscat municipality has special status. In 1981, Oman established an advisory council to advise the Sultan on matters of social, educational and economic policy. The members, drawn from the ethnic, merchant and government communities, are appointed by the sultan and the total rose to 51 in 1985. Nevertheless, modern political institutions are relatively embryonic. There is no constitution or modern judicial system and there are no political parties or elections. Final legal and administrative power is vested in the sultan and as head of state all authority emanates from him. Since 1970, Sultan Qabus has created a formal council of ministers headed by an appointed prime minister. Oman was a founder member of the Gulf Cooperation Council in 1981 and has sought to improve relations with its member states, particularly with Saudi Arabia, from whom it had been estranged since 1955.

CONSTITUTION AND GOVERNMENT

Executive and legislature

The sultan is head of state with absolute powers. He rules by decree. He is advised by a cabinet, which he appoints, and by a 55-member consultative assembly. There are no political parties.

Present government

Sultan of Oman; Prime Minister; Minister of Foreign Affairs, Defence, Finance Sultan Qabus bin Said

Principal Members of the Cabinet Sayyid Fahr bin Taimour al-Said (Deputy Prime Minister for Security and Defence); Sayyid Fahad bin Mahmoud al-Said (Deputy Prime Minister for Legal Affairs); Qais Abdel-Moneim al-Zawawi (Deputy Prime Minister for Financial and Economic Affairs); Sayyid Thuwaini bin Shihab (Special Representative of the Sultan and governor of Muscat); Sayyid Hilal bin Saud bin Hareb al-Busaidi (Justice, Waqfs (Religious Endowments) and Islamic Affairs); Said Ahmed al-Shanfari (Petroleum and Minerals); Sayyid Badr bin Saud bin Hareb (Interior).

Administration

In 1976, the Sultan reorganized regional and local government by establishing 37 divisions within the country. These are administered by governors appointed by the sultan, who collect taxes, provide local security, settle disputes and advise the sultan. Dhofar is governed as a separate province and has more local autonomy than other regions. Muscat municipality has special status.

Justice

The death penalty is in force. The number of executions between 1985 and mid-1988 is not known.

National symbols

Flag. Three horizontal stripes of white, red and green with a red vertical stripe in the hoist.

Festivals. 18 Nov. (National Day); 19 Nov. (birthday of the Sultan).

INTERNATIONAL RELATIONS

Affiliations

NAM; Arab League; GCC.

Defence

Total Armed Forces: 25,500 inclusive of some 3,700 foreign personnel. Terms of service: voluntary.

Army: 20,000; 39 main battle tanks (M-60A1, Chieftain).

Navy: 2,500; 11 patrol and coastal combatants.

Air Force: 3,000; 51 combat aircraft (chiefly Jaguar, Mk 1, Hunter FGA-73).

ECONOMY

Currency

The unit is the rial, divided into 1,000 baiza.

National finance

Budget. The 1989 budget (in US$) was for expenditure (current and capital) of 4,200 million and revenue of 3,100 million. Main items of current expenditure are defence 43.9%; education 11.3%.

Balance of payments. The balance of payments (current account, 1987) was a deficit of US$966 million.

Inflation. (1987) 10%.

Gross Domestic Product

Estimated total GDP US$8,150 million, per capita US$6,110 (overall size of economy ranking 72 in the world).

Economically active population. The total number of persons active in the economy was 430,000.

Sector	% of workforce	% of GDP
industry	n/a	43
agriculture	60	3
services*	n/a	54

* services figure includes elements unassigned to other categories.

Energy and mineral resources

Oil and gas. Oman's economy is dominated by the oil industry. Production: (1988) 32.5 million tons/ 29.5 million tonnes. Gas production: (1986) 7,995,197 ft^3/226,400 m^3.

Minerals. Copper; asbestos; some marble; limestone; chromium; gypsum.

Electricity. Capacity: 1.13 million kW; production: 3,591 million kWh; 2,840 kWh per capita (1988).

Bioresources

Agriculture. Based on subsistence farming (fruits; dates; cereals; cattle; camels). Main crops are dates; limes; bananas; coconuts; mangoes; alfalfa.

Crop production: (1987) dates 84,877 tons/77,000 tonnes.

Livestock numbers: (1987) camels 80,000.

Fisheries. Catch: (1985) 125,662 tons/114,000 tonnes.

Industry and commerce

Industry. Main industries are crude oil production and refining; natural gas production; construction; cement; copper.

Commerce. Exports: US$3,600 million, including petroleum; re-exports; processed copper; dates; nuts; fish. Imports: US$1,900 million, including machinery; transportation equipment; manufactured goods; food; livestock, lubricants. Countries exported to were Japan; Korea; Thailand. Imports came from Japan; United Arab Emirates; UK; West Germany; US.

Trade with UK. In 1988 Oman imported UK goods worth £344,875,000; exports to UK totalled £146,751,000.

COMMUNICATIONS

Railways

There are no railways.

Roads

There are some 11,676 miles/18,790 km of roads, of which some 2,486 miles/4,000 km are bituminized.

Aviation

Oman Aviation Services Co (SAO) provides domestic services and Gulf Aviation Ltd (Gulf Air) provides international services (main airports are Seeb International Airport at Muscat and Salalah Airport). Passengers: (1984) 674,000.

Shipping

The marine ports are Mina' Qabus on the north coast facing the Gulf of Oman and Mina' Raysut facing the Arabian Sea. Freight loaded: (1985) 24.6 million tons/ 22.2 million tonnes; unloaded: 4.4 million tons/ 4 million tonnes.

Telecommunications.

There are 50,000 telephones and a fair telecommunications system. There are 850,000 radios (1986) and 45,000 televisions (1983), with TV services in both Muscat and Dhofar.

EDUCATION AND WELFARE

Education

Schools. 531 schools with 195,847 pupils and 9,236 teachers (one per 21 pupils). Technical and vocational training schools are being developed at intermediate and secondary level.

Universities. Sultan Qaboos University.

Literacy. 20%.

Health

In 1984 there were 15 hospitals with 2,142 beds (one per 609 people) and 572 doctors (one per 2,281 people). There were also 95 health clinics and dispensaries and Save The Children Welfare Clinics at Sohar and Sur.

PAKISTAN

Islami Jamhuriya-e Pakistan (Urdu)
(Islamic Republic of Pakistan)

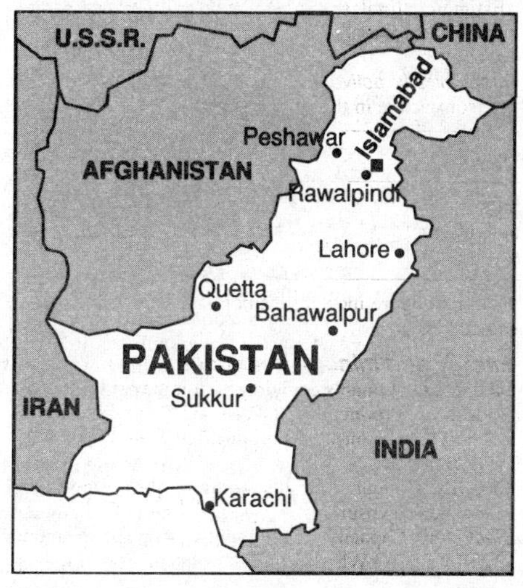

GEOGRAPHY

Located in the western reaches of the Indo-Gangetic Plain, north-west of the Indian sub-continent, Pakistan covers a total area of 310,321 miles^2/ 803,940 km^2, divided into four provinces, a federal capital territory and 10,507 miles^2/27,220 km^2 of Tribal Areas. To the north, the Karakoram and Pamir Himalayas form the Great Highlands, climbing to 28,251 ft/8,611 m at K2 and 26,660 ft/8,126 m at Nangu Parbat. To the south-west, another fragmented highland region, the Baluchistan Plateau averages approximately 984ft/300 m in elevation, transected by a number of mountainous ridges. The River Indus flows south from the Himalayas to Karachi on the Arabian sea coast, forming a vast, fertile and densely populated flood plain in the east. Other major rivers include the Jhelum, Chenab, Ravi and Sutlej. To the south-east, the terrain is largely barren desert. 26% of the land is arable and 4% is forest or woodland. Pakistan has the largest irrigation system in the world: total area irrigated is over 32 million acres/13 million ha.

Climate

Continental, with many temperature variations, and severe winters in mountainous areas. Rainfall ranges from 5.9–7.9 in/150–200 mm per annum in coastal areas to 18.7 in/475 mm on the alluvial plain to 59 in/1,500 mm in the mountainous north. The mean seasonal temperature range is –4°F/–20°C (north) to 57°F/14°C (Indus Plain) in Jan. and 32°F/0°C (mountains) to 95°F/35°C (desert regions) in July. Islamabad: Jan. 50°F/10°C. July 90°F/32.2°C. Average annual rainfall 35 in/900 mm. Karachi: Jan. 61°F/16.1°C. July 86°F/30°C. Average annual rainfall 77 in/196 mm. Lahore: Jan. 53°F/11.7°C. July 89°F/31.7°C. Average annual rainfall 18 in/452 mm.

Cities and towns

Karachi	5,180,562
Lahore	2,952,689
Faisalabad	1,104,209
Rawalpindi	794,843
Hyderabad	751,529
Multan	722,070
Gujranwala	658,753
Peshawar	566,248
Sialkot	302,500
Sargodha	291,000
Quetta	286,000
Islamabad (capital)	204,000

Population

Total population is 110,407,376, of which 29.8% live in urban areas. Population density is 355.8 persons per mile^2/133.4 per km^2. Pakistan's ethnic composition is a complex and heterogeneous combination of indigenous elements. Nearly two-thirds of the population are Punjabi. Other major ethnic groups include the Sindhi, Pashtan (Pathan), Baluch and Muhajir. There are over 3 million Afghan refugees in Pakistan.

Birth rate 4.3%. **Death rate** 1.4%. **Rate of population increase** (1980–87) 2.7%. **Age distribution** under 15 = 44.6%; over 65 = 2.8%. **Life expectancy** female 54; male 55; average 55.

Religion

97% of the population are Muslim (77% Sunni, 20% Shi'a). The remaining 3% is composed of Christian, Hindu, Parsee and Buddhist minorities, including 0.6 million Roman Catholics.

Language

Urdu and English are the official languages, although in practice, 64% of the population speak Punjabi; 12% Sindhi; 8% Pashto; 7% Urdu; 1% Baluchi and Brahvi.

HISTORY

The region now comprising Pakistan has been inhabited from Lower Palaeolithic times. From around 3500 BC, an expansion of agricultural settlements began to take place, culminating in the Indus (or Harappan) civilization c.2500 BC. The arrival from the west of semi-nomadic pastoral tribes known as Indo-Aryans represented a sharp contrast to the urban culture of the Harappans. Gradually tribal identities made way for territorial ones and independent kingdoms of varying sizes. In 710–716 AD, Sind and southern Punjab were conquered by the Umayyad Arab general, Muhammad bin Qasim, who introduced Islamic law. Between 1000 and 1026, Mahmud of Ghazni extended his empire eastwards to include Punjab, the northwest frontier areas and Sind. Ghaznavid rule was followed by that of Muhammad of Ghur, under whom Muslim power spread to all parts of north-west India as well as to Bihar and Bengal in the east. The Delhi Sultanate (1206–1526) and the Mughals (1526–1858) exercised control over much of the region although later Mughal rulers faced repeated challenges along their borders.

British expansion in the shape of the East India Company resulted in the annexation of Sind (1843) and Punjab (1849). After the great rebellion or mutiny in India in 1857, the company ceded government to the British crown. Under the British raj, a growing number of Indian Muslims came to see themselves as forming a distinct political minority, encouraged by the introduction of separate electoral representation along religious lines. The 1930s and early 1940s witnessed increased demands for the establishment of a separate Muslim state in the areas in which Muslims were in a numerical majority, spearheaded by the Muslim League (founded 1906) and its leader, Muhammad Ali Jinnah. With the rejection of the federal compromise offered by the Cabinet Mission Plan of May 1946, partition of India and Pakistan took place on 14 Aug. 1947, accompanied by much bloodshed and large-scale transfers of population. The Indian Empire came to an end with the formal transfer of power by Britain to the two new Dominions of India and Pakistan. Jinnah was immediately appointed as the first governor-general of Pakistan.

Following Jinnah's death in 1948, the prime minister, Liaqat Ali Khan, found it difficult to establish his own authority. He was still overseeing the discussions on the formulation by the Constituent Assembly when he was assassinated in Oct. 1951. He was succeeded by Khwaja Nazimuddin, whose government was widely accused of indecision and of failure to take the firm action necessary to cope with the economic situation and to maintain public order. In Apr. 1953 Pakistan's ambassador to the United States, Mohammad Ali, was appointed as the new prime minister. Elections to the East Pakistan provincial assembly in 1954 resulted in the defeat of the Bengal Muslim League by the opposition United Front and signalled a growing challenge by new parties to the ascendancy of the Muslim League.

The 1956 Constitution declared Pakistan to be an Islamic republic with a national assembly composed of an equal number of members representing East and West Pakistan (the four provinces of West Pakistan – Punjab, Sind, North West Frontier Province (NWFP) and Baluchistan – having been amalgamated into 'One Unit' in 1955). Politics soon began to dissolve into factionalism, and Prime Minister Mohammad Ali faced a revolt by dissident Muslim League assembly members and resigned in Aug. 1956. Pres. Iskander Mirza was forced to accept a predominantly East Pakistani Awami League (AL) government headed by H.S. Suhrawardy. But a dispute over the basis of constituencies for general elections due to be held in 1958 led to Suhrawardy's resignation and a number of short-lived administrations. On 7 Oct. 1958, a presidential proclamation announced the imposition of martial law. Chief martial law administrator, Gen. Ayub Khan was sworn in as prime minister but shortly afterwards Pres. Mirza was himself exiled and Gen. Ayub assumed the presidency.

Gen. Ayub's 1962 constitution differed quite radically from its predecessor by introducing a more centralized system of government with the executive branch under the full control of an indirectly-elected president, chosen by an electoral college of 80,000 Basic Democrats or union councillors. The principle of parity between East and West Pakistan was preserved but Pakistan was no longer described as an Islamic republic. In the Jan. 1965 presidential elections, Ayub shook off a challenge from the Combined Opposition Party (COP) candidate, Fatima Jinnah, but the narrowness of the victory shook his confidence as did public reactions to the war with India over Kashmir in the same year. Growing political opposition culminated in Ayub's resignation in Mar. 1970 and Pakistan was placed under martial law by Gen. Yahya Khan, the commander-in-chief of the Armed Forces. Preparations went ahead for the country's first direct national elections, which eventually took place in Dec. 1970. They resulted in an overwhelming victory for Sheikh Mujibur Rahman's East Pakistan-Sajal Awami League (AL). The AL's success and the reluctance of West Pakistan to accept an East Pakistani-led national government precipitated war with India, civil war and the creation of Bangladesh in 1971 (see entry on Bangladesh for further details of the war and Bangladesh's subsequent history).

The war ended in Dec. 1971 following the intervention, on the side of Bangladesh, of Indian forces. That month, Yahya Khan handed over the presidency to Zulfikar Ali Bhutto, leader of the Pakistan People's Party (PPP), which had won a majority in the West in the 1970 elections. Following the lifting of martial law and the introduction of the 1973 Constitution, Bhutto became prime minister of what remained of Pakistan. The new constitution set up a parliamentary system with powers divided between the central government and provinces. One of Bhutto's first moves was to normalize relations with India and in July 1972 Pakistan and India signed the Simla accord. The same year, Bhutto pulled Pakistan out of the Commonwealth. Pakistan's relations with the United States improved as did its relations with the Muslim world, encouraged by economic aid and employment opportunities for Pakistani workers in Saudi Arabia and other Gulf states. Committed to 'Islamic socialism', Bhutto nationalized private banks, insurance companies, heavy industries and educational institutions. Salaries for government employees were increased but high rates of inflation considerably eroded Bhutto's popularity in the cities. In Mar. 1977 the PPP won a decisive victory over the Pakistan National Alliance (PNA) in general elections. But allegations of vote rigging combined with other dissatisfactions led to rioting and in July Gen. Zia ul Haq deposed Bhutto and once more imposed martial law.

After the 1977 coup, the office of prime minister, together with the federal and provincial assemblies were suspended. Legislative authority rested with Zia who assumed the presidency in 1978. The objectives of the armed forces' Operation Fair Play, which led to Bhutto's imprisonment and later execution in 1979, were to restore democracy and hold elections within 90 days. The elections, however, were repeatedly postponed as Zia made moves towards establishing 'a truly Islamic order' in Pakistan. Zia was helped in maintaining power by the Soviet Union's invasion of neighbouring Afghanistan in 1979 which resulted in US support for his regime. In 1981, his Provisional Constitutional Order established a consultative Federal Council known as the Majlis i Shura to advise the presidency. Encouraged by a national referendum on his Islamization programme in which more than 60% of the electorate were said to have voted in favour of his changes, Zia held general elections on a non-party basis in early 1985 which were boycotted by the PPP-led opposition. A civilian government under the premiership of Muhammad Khan Junejo was sworn in but earlier sweeping changes to the 1973 constitution meant that power was still concentrated in the hands of the president. On 30 Dec. 1985, martial law was lifted and the Pakistan Muslim League revived under Junejo's leadership. Public response to the return to Pakistan of Benazir Bhutto, daughter of Zulfikar Ali Bhutto and co-chairperson of the PPP, in Apr. 1986, illustrated the large amount of support which existed for the opposition. However, her return from exile did not seriously damage the government's authority. Ethnic riots in Karachi in Dec. 1986, which claimed hundreds of lives and inflicted damage to property worth millions of dollars, shook Junejo's confidence and allowed Zia to consolidate his position. In May 1988 he dismissed Junejo, dissolving the country's assemblies, and announced elections within 90 days: these too were subsequently postponed.

On 17 Aug. 1988 Zia was killed in a plane crash. Acting-President Ghulam Ishaq Khan confirmed that elections would take place as scheduled in November and the military stood aside from the constitutional process. The PPP, under Benazir Bhutto's leadership, emerged as the largest party in the National Assembly and so in Dec. 1988 she became the first woman premier of a modern Islamic state. She faced pressing problems, including a vast budget deficit, severe ethnic conflict and the repercussions of the Afghan war, which had forced 3,000,000 Afghans to seek refuge in Western Pakistan. Bhutto's government faced a growing domestic and political crisis during the latter half of 1989, culminating in an opposition vote of no confidence held on 1 Nov., which the government narrowly survived.

CONSTITUTION AND GOVERNMENT

Executive and legislature

The head of state is the president, elected for a five-year term by an electoral college comprising the national assembly, the senate and the four provincial assemblies; last election 12 Dec. 1988. The head of government, responsible to parliament, is the prime minister. The lower house of the federal legislature, the 237-member National Assembly, has 217 members elected directly by universal adult suffrage for a five-year term (last elections Nov. 1988) and 20 women members nominated by the provincial assemblies. The upper house, the senate, has 87 members elected by the provincial assemblies and tribal areas for a six-year term, one-third of the seats coming up for election every two years.

Present government

President Ghulam Ishaq Khan

Prime Minister; Minister of Defence and Finance Benazir Bhutto

Other Principal Ministers Begum Nusrat Bhutto (Senior Minister Without Portfolio); Aitzaz Ahsan (Interior); Syed Iftikhar Hussein Gilani (Law and Justice); Sahibzada Yaqub Khan (Foreign Affairs).

Administration

Pakistan is divided into four provinces, each with their own governments and provincial legislatures. There are also designated tribal areas and a federal capital territory.

Provincial Chief Ministers. Baluchistan – Akbar Bugti; North-West Frontier Province – Afteb Ahmad Khan Sherpao; Punjab – Mian Mohammad Nawaz Sharif; Sind – Aftab Shahban Mirani.

Justice

The system of law had its origins in English common law, but was transformed under the Zia regime to incorporate the tenets of Islamic Sharia law, with an Islamic court structure existing alongside the Supreme Court and provincial high courts. The death penalty is in force. There were over 115 executions between 1985 and mid-1988. The offences were murder.

National symbols

Flag. The green field bears the symbols of Islam, a white crescent and a white five-pointed star. A white vertical stripe occupies one-quarter of the flag's length.

Festivals. 23 Mar. (Pakistan Day, proclamation of republic in 1956); 1 May (Labour Day); 14 Aug. (Independence Day); 6 Sept. (Defence of Pakistan); 11 Sept. (Anniversary of Death of Quaid-i-Azam); 25 Dec. (Birthday of Quaid-i-Azam).

Vehicle registration plate. PAK.

INTERNATIONAL RELATIONS

Affiliations

Commonwealth (under Benazir Bhutto, Pakistan applied to rejoin the Commonwealth and formally reacceded on 1 Oct. 1989); NAM; ICO; SAARC.

Defence

Total Armed Forces: 480,600. Terms of service: voluntary. Reserves: 513,000.

Army: 450,000; 1,600 main battle tanks (Type-59, M-47/-48, T-54/-55), light tanks (Type-63).

Navy: 16,000 inclusive Naval Air; six submarines (Fr Agosta and Daphne), eight destroyers (UK Devonshire, US Gearing and Battle) and 29 patrol and coastal combatants.

Naval Air: three combat aircraft; nine armed helicopters.

Air Force: 17,600; 338 combat aircraft (Mirage IIIEP, Mirage 5, J-6/JJ-6, F-16, Q-5).

Para-military: National Guard: 75,000; Frontier Corps: 65,000; Pakistan Rangers: 15,000.

ECONOMY

Currency

The unit is the rupee, divided into 100 paisa.

National finance

Budget. The 1987 budget (in US$) was for expenditure (current and capital) of 9,100 million and revenue of 5,800 million. Main items of current expenditure are defence 29.5%; housing and welfare 8.7%.

Balance of payments. The balance of payments (current account, 1987) was a deficit of $719 million.

Inflation. (1988) 6.3%.

Gross Domestic Product

Estimated total GDP US$31,650 million, per capita US$370 (overall size of economy ranking 51 in the world).

Economically active population. The total number of persons active in the economy was 28,900,000; unemployed: 3.6%.

Sector	% of workforce	% of GDP
industry	13	28
agriculture	54	23
services*	33	49

* services figure includes elements unassigned to other categories.

Energy and mineral resources

Oil and gas. Oil is produced from fields in the Potowar Plain production: (1988) 2.6 million tons/2.4 million tonnes and at Dhodak. There are extensive natural gas reserves; production: (1987) 390,048 ft^3/ 11,045 m^3.

Minerals. Coal; iron ore; copper; salt; limestone.

Electricity. Capacity: 6.9 million kW; production: 29,000 million kWh; 270 kWh per capita (1988).

Bioresources

Agriculture. Agriculture is almost entirely dependent on the irrigation provided by five large rivers and their tributaries. The main crops are cotton; rice; wheat; sugar cane; fruits; vegetables. Pakistan is an illegal producer of opium poppy and cannabis for the international drug trade.

Crop production: (1987 in 1,000 tons/tonnes) rice 3,843/3,486; wheat 13,244/12,015; sugar cane 32,986/ 29,925; cotton 1,454/1,319; cotton seed 2,909/2,639; maize 1,225/1,111; potatoes 655/594.

Livestock numbers: (1987 in millions) cattle 16.9; buffaloes 13.7; sheep 26.6; goats 31.9; poultry 121.7.

Forestry. 4% of the land area is forest and woodland of which 3.19 million acres/1.29 million ha are productive forest. Production: (1987) 25,885,162 ft^3/ 733,000 m^3.

Fisheries. Catch: (1987) Approximately 369,271 tons/ 335,000 tonnes of marine fish and 92,593 tons/ 84,000 tonnes of inland fish.

Industry and commerce

Industry. The main industries are textiles; food processing; beverages; petroleum products; construction materials; clothing; paper products; international finance; shrimps.

Commerce. Exports: US$4,300 million, including rice; cotton; textiles; clothing. Imports: US$6,900 million, including petroleum; petroleum products; machinery; transportation equipment; vegetable oils; animal fats; chemicals. Countries exported to were EC countries 31%; US 11%; Japan 11%. Imports came from EC countries 26%; Japan 15%; US 11%.

Trade with UK. Pakistan imported UK goods worth £263,300,000; exports to UK totalled £175,337,000.

Tourism. (1986) 432,395 visitors.

COMMUNICATIONS

Railways

There are 7,868 miles/12,660 km of railways.

Roads

There are 64,269 miles/103,428 km of roads (27,008 miles/43,464 km of main roads).

Aviation

Pakistan International Airlines Corpn (PIA) provides domestic and international services (main airport is at Karachi).

Shipping

The marine ports are Gwadar and Karachi. The merchant marine consists of 29 ships of 1,000 GRT or over. Freight loaded: (1987/88) 3.7 million tons/ 3.4 million tonnes; unloaded: 15.8 million tons/ 14.3 million tonnes.

Telecommunications

There is a good international but poor domestic service by radio telephone. There are 564,500 telephones, 9.8 million radios and 1.5 million televisions (1988). Pakistan Broadcasting Corporation operates a home service radio in 21 languages, and external services in 15 languages, while TV services are provided daily by the Pakistan Television Corporation Ltd.

EDUCATION AND WELFARE

Education

Schools. Free and compulsory primary education, 49% of children enrolled. There is an emphasis on technical and vocational education. There are 7,368 pupils in primary schools, 2,004 pupils in middle schools and 690 pupils in high schools.
Universities. There are 64,443 students enrolled in universities and 65,376 in other colleges.
Literacy. 26%.

Health

679 hospitals and 3,501 dispensaries with a total of 59,987 beds (one per 1,840 people) and 51,020 doctors (one per 2,163 people).

PALESTINE

The phrase 'Palestinian' is as much a political definition as a cultural or ethnic one; it stands for the Arabs who dwelt in the biblical land of Palestine, or are descendants of people whose origins lie there, and who consider themselves dispossessed of that land by the creation of the State of Israel in 1948. In recent years it has been extended to include Arabs who stayed in Israel after 1948 and are full citizens of that state, but who still call themselves Palestinian; and, more contentiously, to Israeli Jews whose families lived in Palestine prior to Zionist colonization, or who consciously eschew Zionism. The recent history of the Palestinians is bound up with that of Israel.

Today there is no Palestinian state, though Palestinians form approximately 50% of the population of Israel's eastern neighbour, Jordan. Apart from the 700,000 Israeli Arabs, living within Israel itself, some 1.6 million Palestinians today live under Israeli rule in the occupied territories of Gaza and the West Bank. In all there are an estimated 4 million Palestinians living in historical Palestine, or dotted throughout the Middle East and elsewhere. The name Palestinian derives from the Philistines, a coastal tribe who were eventually subdued by the Jews under King David (according to the Bible), in land which was to become the Roman province of Palestrina, which included Jerusalem, Acre, Jaffa and the Biblical Holy Land generally. After an abortive revolt against Rome in AD 135, Jewish rule of Palestine ended, and the area came under direct rule from Rome.

Today's Palestinians carry the ethnic fingerprints of both Philistine and Jew, as well as later invaders of this land – Persian, Crusader, Turk – but most importantly Arab, for it was the latter who gave them their language (Arabic) and religion (Islam). A minority (perhaps 10%) are Christian. Ottoman Turks ruled Palestine 1517–1918, and afforded the Palestinians only very limited autonomy. Following Ottoman defeat in World War I, Palestine became a British Mandate. By this stage Zionist Jews from Europe had entered in great numbers, encouraged by Britain's Balfour Declaration of 1917 which promised them a 'national home' in Palestine. Feeling that their own rights had been overlooked, Arabs waged a violent struggle against the new settlers and the British, and rejected repeated plans for partitioning the land into Arab and Jewish zones, up to and including the partition plan of 1947 accepted by the UN General Assembly (29 Nov.) which created a Jewish state of Israel.

The seminal event in recent Palestinian history was the departure of a majority of them (about 780,000) from the land in the Israeli War of Independence, 1948–49, whereby Israeli forces repulsed an Arab attempt to deny their newborn state its existence, and then went on to conquer most of the territory which the partition had allocated to the Palestinian Arabs. The displacement of Palestinians gave the new State of Israel a Jewish majority, and efforts to solve the refugee problem failed after Israel and the Arab states proved unable to reach a general peace settlement. That position persists today, exacerbated by Arab-Israeli wars in 1956, 1967, 1973 and 1982, despite Egypt's bilateral peace deal with Israel in 1979. Hundreds of thousands of Palestinians have thus lived for over 40 years, or been born and raised, in refugee camps.

The Palestine Liberation Organization (PLO) was founded in 1964 on the initiative of Iraq and Egypt to co-ordinate resistance with a view to liberating all Palestine. In 1967 Israel conquered the West Bank from Jordan and the Gaza Strip from Egypt but chose not to annex them. Though the Israelis built universities, offered employment (40% of Palestinians now work in Israel itself) and kept an 'open doors' policy in these areas, they also restricted Palestinian economic and political activity and refused to talk to the PLO. The PLO in turn encouraged acts of terrorism and raids on Israel from their bases in Lebanon. Despite periodic divisions in PLO ranks (including bitter in-fighting in Lebanon in the early 80s) no other group has managed to rival their claim to be the 'voice of the Palestinian people', a claim backed by the Arab League summit of 1974, West Bank municipal elections in 1976 and increasing international recognition. Since 1977 more Jewish settlements have been built on the West Bank, which Palestinians see as provocation.

Israel's attempt to flush out PLO guerrillas from Lebanon in 1982 ultimately failed, and Israel has also not managed to stifle the 'intifada' (uprising) in the territories which broke out in Dec. 1987 and which, by its second anniversary on 10 Dec. 1989, had claimed 795 Arab and 44 Israeli lives. In Nov. 1988 the Palestine National Council (the PLO's 'parliament-in-exile') apparently changed tack by supporting UN Resolution 242 of 1967 which implicitly meant recognizing the existence of Israel, by rejecting terrorism, and by calling for a two-state solution based on Israeli withdrawal from the West Bank and Gaza. It declared also the existence of the 'independent state of Palestine'. Although Israel's US ally opened talks with the PLO for the first time, Israel itself still refuses to recognize it as a negotiating partner. Meanwhile, PLO leader Yasser Arafat's willingness to compromise (in May 1989 in Paris he declared as 'a thing of the past' the PLO's 1964 National Charter whereby the state of Israel had been categorized as totally illegal) puts him in danger of a backlash from more hard-line colleagues. Through it all, Palestine remains the one issue which unifies an otherwise fragmented Arab world.

PALESTINIAN POLITICAL STRUCTURE

The 'independent state of Palestine', as declared in Nov. 1988 in Algiers by the Palestine National Council (PNC), has been recognized by Arab states, other members of the non-aligned movement and China. The declaration confirms Jerusalem to be the capital of an independent Palestinian state, and provides for a provisional government; Yasser Arafat, the PLO leader, was nominated by the PLO executive committee in Mar. 1989 as president, with Farouk Qaddumi as foreign minister. Within the PLO structure, the PNC is the 'parliament-in-exile' and decides on general PLO strategy, while tactical matters are decided by the PLO executive committee, and the 60-member PLO central council acts as an advisory body. The PLO had already, prior to the Nov. 1988 Algiers Declaration, been accepted by the majority of states as the 'sole legitimate representative of the Palestinian people'.

The PLO is itself an alliance of Palestinian factions, the largest of which is Arafat's Al-Fatah. Other factions accepting the decisions of the (19th) PNC meeting in 1988 include the more radical Popular Front for the Liberation of Palestine led by Georges Habash and Democratic Front for the Liberation of Palestine led by Naif Hawatmeh; the Palestine Liberation Front; and the Palestine Popular Struggle Front. By the late 1980s the Abu Nidal Group, previously notorious for attacks on PLO moderates as well as for dramatic acts of terrorism like the 1985 Rome and Vienna airport attacks, had apparently come more into line with PLO strategy. Underground organizations co-ordinating the 'intifada' within the occupied territories also express loyalty to the PLO.

Anti-Arafat and pro-Syrian 'rejectionist' Palestinian factions are principally:

the Popular Front for the Liberation of Palestine – General Command, led by Ahmed Jibril;

a group led by Saed Abu Musa which split from Fatah in 1983 to form the Fatah Revolutionary Council;

Al-Saiqa, originally formed in 1968 with Syrian government backing.

PANAMA
República de Panamá
(Republic of Panama)

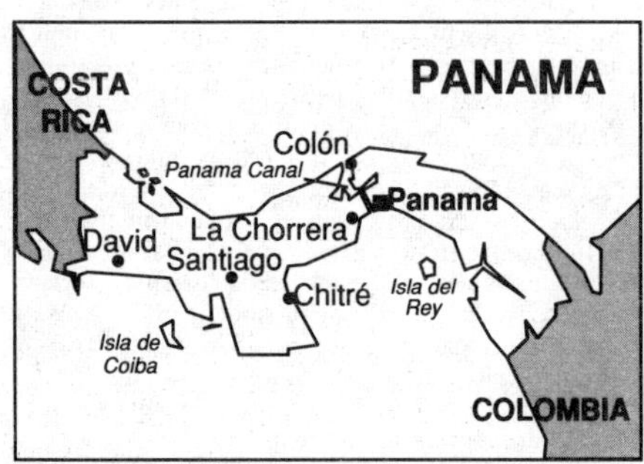

GEOGRAPHY

Occupying the southernmost portion of the isthmus that links North and South America, Panama covers a total area of 30,185 miles²/78,200 km², divided into nine provinces and one Indian territory. 85% of the terrain lies below 2,297 ft/700 m elevation. Principal lowland regions include the Caribbean littoral, the Bayano and Chucunaque river basins and the province of Chiriqui Panamá. In the west central regions, the Serranía de Tabasará range rises to 11,401 ft/3,475 m at Volcán Barú. Major rivers draining into the Caribbean include the Sixaola, Changuinola and Indio, while the Bayano, Chucunaque, Chiriquíviejo and Santa María flow south into the Pacific. 6% of the moderately fertile land surface area is arable and nearly 54% is covered by rainforest. The central province of Panama is the most populous region, bisected by the 51 miles/82 km-long Panama Canal connecting the Pacific and Atlantic Oceans.

Climate

Tropical with uniformly high temperatures and dry weather Jan.-Apr. only. Rainfall increases markedly to the north. Panama City: Jan. 80°F/26.1°C. July 81°F/27.2°C. Average annual rainfall 69.7 in/1,770 mm. Colón: Jan. 80°F/26.7°C. July 80°F/26.7°C. Average annual rainfall 125 in/3,175 mm.

Cities and towns

Panama City (capital)	608,890
Colón	59,840
David	50,016

Population

Total population is 2,373,053 of which 52.2% live in urban areas. Population density is 78.6 persons per mile²/29.5 per km². Ethnic composition: 70% mestizo (Indian/European ancestry); 14% West Indian; 10% White; 6% Indian. The three largest indigenous Indian peoples are the Guaymí (west), the Cuna and the Chocoe (south-east).

Birth rate 2.6%. **Death rate** 0.5%. **Rate of population increase** (1980–87) 2.1%. **Age distribution** under 15 = 37.5%; over 65 = 4.5%. **Life expectancy** female 74; male 70; average 72.

Religion

Christianity. Over 93% of the population are Roman Catholic, and 6% Protestant. Small Jewish, Muslim and Baha'i minorities comprise the remainder.

Language

Spanish is the official language although up to 14% of the population are English-speaking. Major indigenous languages include 'movere' or the 'language of the plains'; Cuna; Chibchan; Choco.

HISTORY

Indian tribes such as the Guaymís and Cunas in what is now Panama never reached the sophistication of the Maya or the Inca, although they were probably influenced by both. Under the Spanish colonial system Panama was the seat of government for an area stretching as far south as Peru. Consequently, when it gained independence from Spain in 1821 it did not join the Central American federation but was incorporated into Gran Colombia (1821–30). A dominant feature of its history has been the construction of a trans-isthmian canal, first suggested in the 16th century to ship Peruvian mineral wealth to Spain, raised again in the 19th century by the United States, and eventually completed in 1914. US troops intervened in Panama to restore order several times in the second half of the 19th century, chiefly to protect US trading interests, and it was with US assistance that Panama gained independence from Colombia in 1903.

The US retained considerable influence in Panama, supervising all elections held between 1908 and 1928 (usually at the prompting of at least one of the candidates), but by the 1930s there was growing internal opposition to US influence. The 1903 Canal Treaty, which had accorded the US 'sovereign rights' in the Canal Zone (for $10 million), was revised in 1936, increasing the rent paid to Panama for the canal and revoking the US right of intervention to preserve order in Panama. The Canal Treaty was revised again in 1955, further increasing the rent (although to a sum still far below half that proposed by Panama), but anti-US feeling continued to grow, and in 1959 there were riots in Panama City in protest that the US and not the Panamanian flag was flown in the Zone.

Panama has not had the same degree of violence in its political history as many of its Central American neighbours, but it has experienced similar volatility. Elected governments were overthrown in 1941, 1949, 1951 and 1968 (usually after disputed elections), and there were serious constitutional crises in 1918, 1948 and 1968, while in 1955 Pres. José Ramón Guizado was impeached after being implicated in the assassination of his predecessor, Lt.-Col. José Antonio Remón. In 1968 the National Guard (responsible for national security as the formation of an army was banned under the 1904 constitution) intervened under the command of Col. Omar Torrijos Herrera, to depose the recently-inaugurated right-wing Arnulfo Arias Madrid (president 1940–41 and 1949–51). Torrijos (1968–81), who was named 'the Supreme leader of the Panamanian Revolution', dissolved political parties, introduced a number of social reforms including a wide-ranging agrarian reform programme and adopted a more left-wing foreign policy. His principal achievement was the negotiation of two new Canal treaties with the United States, which abolished the Zone and prepared for a transition of jurisdiction over the Canal to Panama by the year 2000.

Preparations began in 1978 for a return to elected government and new parties were allowed to form. Presidential elections held on 6 May 1984 were won by Nicolás Ardito Barletta of the Democratic Revolutionary Party (PRD – formed by Torrijos in 1978) by a narrow margin over Arias Madrid, and the PRD, in coalition with five other parties, gained 47 of the 60 seats in the new Legislative Assembly. Ardito resigned in Sept. 1985, and his successor, Eric Arturo Delvalle, was replaced by Manuel Solis Palma on 26 Feb. 1988, after an abortive attempt to dismiss the commander of the National Guard, Gen. Manuel Antonio Noriega Morena; Delvalle went into hiding but maintained his claim to the presidency. Meanwhile demands continued both in Panama and the United States for the removal of Gen. Noriega, who had been implicated in drug smuggling, electoral fraud and even political assassination. Guillermo Endara, the representative of the Democratic Opposition Alliance (ADOC) generally considered to have been denied victory in the May 1989 presidential election whose result was annulled by Noriega, was installed as 'constitutional President' following the Dec. 1989 military invasion by US troops. Noriega, who had taken refuge in the papal nunciature in the capital, Panama City, finally gave himself up to the US authorities on 3 Jan. 1990 and was flown to Miami, Florida to stand trial on drug-trafficking charges.

CONSTITUTION AND GOVERNMENT

Executive and legislature

A major political role is played by the commander of the Defence Forces, Gen. Manuel Antonio Noriega Moreno. Executive power is, however, nominally vested in the president, who is directly elected for a five-year term, assisted by two elected vice-presidents and an appointed cabinet. The last presidential elections, on 7 May 1989, had their results annulled by Gen. Noriega, whose preferred choice was sworn in as provisional president on 4 Sept. The unicameral Legislative Assembly consists of 67 members elected for five-year terms by universal and compulsory adult suffrage; the May 1989 elections, like the concurrent presidential elections, were annulled.

Present government

President Sr Guillermo Endara

Principal Ministers Sr Ricardo Arias (First Vice-President; Minister of Government; Justice); Sr Mario Galindo (Second Vice-President; Treasury and Finance); Sr Guillermo Ford (Planning; Economic Policy); Sr Julio Linares (Foreign Affairs).

Justice

The system of law is based on civil law; the highest court is the Supreme Court whose justices are appointed for 10-year terms by the President, subject to confirmation by the legislature. The Supreme Court has a role in the judicial review of legislation. The Penal Code of 1922 stipulated that the death penalty was abolished for all offences.

National symbols

Flag. Four quarters; the first is white with a blue five-pointed star, the second red, the third blue, and the fourth white with a red five-pointed star.

Festivals. 9 Jan. (National Martyrs' Day); 1 May (Labour Day); 15 Aug. (Foundation of Panama City; Panama City only); 11 Oct. (Revolution Day); 1 Nov. (National Anthem Day); 3 Nov. (Independence from Colombia); 4 Nov. (Flag Day); 10 Nov. (First Call of Independence); 28 Nov. (Independence from Spain).

Vehicle registration plate. PA.

INTERNATIONAL RELATIONS

Affiliations

NAM; OAS; SELA.

Defence

Total Armed Forces: 7,300; Terms of service: voluntary.
Army: 6,000.
Navy: 900; six inshore patrol craft.
Air Force: 400.
Para-military: Police and National Guard: 12,300.
Foreign Forces: US: some 12,900.

ECONOMY

Currency

The unit is the balboa, divided into 100 centesimos.

National finance

Budget. The 1988 budget (in US$) was for expenditure (current and capital) of 800 million and revenue of 600 million. Main items of current expenditure are education 15.9%; health 15.5%.

Balance of payments. The balance of payments (current account, 1987) was a surplus of $229 million.

Inflation. (1988) 2%.

Gross Domestic Product

Estimated total GDP US$5,490 million, per capita US$1,850 (overall size of economy ranking 79 in the world).

Economically active population. The total number of persons active in the economy was 770,000; unemployed: 23%.

Sector	% of workforce	% of GDP
industry	16	18
agriculture	26	9
services*	58	73

* services figure includes elements unassigned to other categories.

Energy and mineral resources

Minerals. There are known copper reserves, especially at Cerro Colorado (Chiriqui province) where reserves are estimated at 1,433 million tons/1,300 million tonnes.

Electricity. Capacity: 1.1 million kW; production: 3,374 million kWh; 1,450 kWh per capita (1988).

Bioresources

Agriculture. Main cash crops are bananas; sugar cane; coffee. Other crops are rice; maize; beans.

Crop production: (1987 in 1,000 tons/tonnes) bananas 999/907; sugar 136/123; oranges 40/36; mangoes 31/28; rice 183/166; maize 99/90; cocoa 2.2/2; coffee 17/15; coconuts 24/22.

Livestock numbers: (1987) cattle 1.49 million; pigs 205,000; poultry 8 million.

Forestry. Production: (1984) 72.4 million ft^3/ 2.05 million m^3.

Fisheries. Catch: (1982) 371,475 tons/337,000 tonnes.

Industry and commerce

Industry. Main industries are manufacturing and construction activities; petroleum refining; brewing; cement and other construction materials; sugar mills; paper products.

Commerce. Exports: (1988) US$298 million, including bananas 28%; shrimps 17%; coffee 5%; sugar; clothing. Imports: US$700.5 million, including capital goods; petroleum products; consumer goods; foodstuffs; chemicals. Countries exported to were US 66%; Central America and Caribbean; EC countries. Imports came from US 43%; Central America and Caribbean; Mexico; Japan; EC countries; Venezuela.

Trade with UK. Panama imported UK goods worth £32,497,000; exports to the UK totalled £12,230,000.

Tourism. (1986) 467,000 visitors.

COMMUNICATIONS

Railways

There are 359 miles/578 km of railways.

Roads

There are 6,024 miles/9,694 km of roads.

Aviation

Air Panama International and Compañia Panameña de Aviación, SA (COPA) provide international services (main airport is Omar Torrijos). Passengers: (1986 provisional) 1.3 million.

Shipping

There are 497 miles/800 km of inland waterways navigable by shallow draught vessels. The Panama Canal is 51 miles/82 km in length. The two major ports are Cristóbal on the Caribbean Sea at the north exit of the Panama Canal and Balboa, on the Pacific Ocean, at the south exit. The merchant marine consists of 3,159 ships 1,000 GRT or over. All are foreign-owned and operated.

Telecommunications

There are 220,000 telephones and a well-developed domestic and international system. There are 900,000 radios (1986) and 475,990 televisions (1987), about 100 radio stations and six TV stations (mainly commercial apart from the educational Canal 11).

EDUCATION AND WELFARE

Education

Schools. Schooling is compulsory for children between seven and 15 years and there are an estimated 552,200 pupils enrolled in schools.

Universities. The University of Panama, Panama City has a total of 55,000 students while the Catholic University Sta Maria La Antigua has an estimated 2,000.

Literacy. 90%.

Health

There are approximately 2,200 doctors (one per 1,078 people) and 50 hospitals with 7,500 beds (one per 318 people).

PAPUA NEW GUINEA

GEOGRAPHY

Located east of Indonesia and north of the north-eastern tip of Australia, the island state of Papua New Guinea (PNG) has a total area of 178,213 miles^2/461,691 km^2, divided into 19 provinces and a National Capital District. Of the total area, 152,379 miles^2/394,765 km^2 forms the eastern half of the island of New Guinea. Approximately 600 smaller islands constitute the remaining 25,833 miles^2/66,926 km^2, including the northern reaches of the Solomon Islands (Bougainville and Buka) and the Bismarck Archipelago (New Britain, New Ireland and Manus). On the New Guinean mainland, the River Daru forms a vast swampy delta plain in the south-west rising towards the central east-west mountains, reaching 14,793 ft/4,509 m elevation at Mount Wilhelm. Principal rivers include the Fly, Sepik and Ramu, draining south, north and east respectively. The Fly and Sepik basins are the most depopulated regions. The major islands (Bougainville, New Ireland and New Britain) are mostly volcanic in origin with rugged relief, enclosed by coral formations. Nearly three-quarters of Papua New Guinea is covered by dense tropical rainforests. Soils are largely of indifferent quality, heavily leached and fertile only in lowland areas and on the peripheral isles.

Climate

Typical Monsoon, with consistently high temperatures and humidity, growing more temperate at higher altitudes. Rainfall averages between 78.7 and 98.4 in/2,000 and 2,500 mm, most of which falls Dec.-Mar. Mean maximum and minimum temperatures are 91°F/33°C and 72°F/22°C respectively. Papua New Guinea: Jan. 82°F/27.8°C. July 78°F/25.6°C. Average annual rainfall 39.9 in/1,011 mm.

Cities and towns

Port Moresby (capital) 139,300

Population

Total population is 3,804,000, of which 14.3% live in urban areas. Population density is 21 persons per mile^2/7.6 per km^2 (average). Papua New Guinea's complex ethnic composition comprises two principal groups: Papuan (over 80%) and Melanesian (less than 15%). The Papuan peoples predominate in the mainland interior and on the south coast, while the ethnic Melanesians populate the northern and eastern regions and occupy many of the peripheral islands. Polynesian, Chinese and European minorities comprise the remainder.

Birth rate 3.88%. **Death rate**: 1.31%. **Rate of population increase** (1980–87) 2.57%. **Age distribution** under 15 = 41.6%; over 65 = 2.4%. **Life expectancy** female 55; male 53; average 54.

Religion

At the last census (1980) 64% of the population were Protestant and 33% were Roman Catholic. However, indigenous pantheistic beliefs are nevertheless widespread and traditional rituals are integral to Papuan culture.

Language

Of the 750 indigenous languages spoken in Papua New Guinea, between 350–450 are inter-related, constituting the Central New Guinea Macrophylum. English (spoken by 2% of the population) and Motu are the official parliamentary languages, although the majority speaks a Melanesian pidgin known as Tok Pisin. 150,000 people speak Hiri and 130,000 speak Enga.

HISTORY

The island of New Guinea was first inhabited at least 50,000 years ago by settlers from Asia. In 1828 the Dutch, seeking to protect their East Indies empire, formalized their long-standing claim to sovereignty over the western half of the island. In 1884 Britain claimed the south-eastern quarter of the island, and Germany the north-eastern quarter. In 1906 British New Guinea became the Territory of Papua, as control was transferred to newly-independent Australia. With the outbreak of World War I, Australia also took control of German New Guinea, and in 1920 this became a League of Nations Mandated Trust Territory under Australian trusteeship. Following Japanese occupation during World War II, the eastern half of New Guinea reverted to Australian control as a single colony, the Territory of Papua and New Guinea. In 1963 Indonesia took control of Dutch New Guinea, and incorporated it into the Indonesian state as the territory of Irian Jaya.

PNG achieved self-government in 1973 and full independence on 16 Sept. 1975, with a parliamentary system of government. The country has been ruled by a series of unstable coalitions composed of political parties based on patronage rather than ideology. In 1980 Michael Somare, leader of the Pangu Party and prime minister since 1972, was ousted from power after a parliamentary vote of no confidence led by Julius Chan and his People's Progress Party. Chan, who had previously been Somare's deputy, became prime minister. In the 1982 general election Somare was returned to power. In Mar. 1985 deputy premier Pias Wingti defected to the opposition along with about 15 other Pangu MPs. Following a vote of no-confidence in Nov. 1985, Wingti replaced Somare as prime minister, Chan becoming his deputy. After general elections in 1987, Wingti assumed the premiership once again. On 4 July 1988 the Wingti coalition, which had been subject to corruption inquiries and was highly unstable, was toppled by a no-confidence motion in parliament. Rabbie Namaliu, who had replaced Somare as the Pangu Party leader in May, became prime minister.

At independence PNG faced serious secessionist threats, which were quelled by the introduction in 1976 of an extensive system of decentralized provincial government. However, unrest resurfaced on Bougainville island in late 1988, when local landowners demanded compensation for damage done to their land by the island's giant copper mine, and gave vent to ethnic grievances.

Problems of law and order led to the declaration of states of emergency in Port Moresby in 1979 and 1985, and in the Highlands (where there was severe ethnic unrest) in 1979.

Although a Treaty of Mutual Respect, Friendship and Co-operation was signed with Indonesia in Oct. 1986, relations between the two countries remained delicate. The principal cause of friction was the use of PNG territory by the Organisasi Papua Merdeka (OPM) – a guerrilla movement composed of native Melanesians committed to ending Indonesian control of Irian Jaya. In Aug. 1980 PNG armed forces assisted newly independent Vanuatu in putting down a secessionist movement on Espiritu Santo. A more assertive role in regional affairs was also indicated by the formation (with Vanuatu and the Solomon Islands) of the Melanesian Spearhead Group, which signed a set of Agreed Principles on 14 Mar. 1988.

CONSTITUTION AND GOVERNMENT

Executive and legislature

The head of state is the British sovereign, represented by a governor general. The head of government is the prime minister, who is assisted by the National Executive Council (Cabinet). The government is responsible to the National Parliament, a unicameral 109-member body elected for up to five years by universal adult suffrage (last election June 1987). Government has been based on coalition arrangements which have on several occasions broken down, leading to changes of government following votes of no confidence by the parliament.

Present government

Governor General Sir Kingsford Dibela
Prime Minister Rabbie Namaliu
Other Principal Ministers Arnold Marsipal (Defence); Michael Somare (Foreign Affairs); Bernard Narakobi (Justice); Timothy Bonga (Home Affairs); Paul Pora (Finance and Planning); Akoka Doi (Deputy Prime Minister and Minister for Public Services); Ted Diro (Special Minister of State).

Justice

The judiciary consists of the National Court and district and local courts. The death penalty is in force only for exceptional crimes. There were no executions between 1985 and mid-1988.

National symbols

Flag. Divided into two triangular fields: black (in the hoist) and red (in the fly). The black field is charged with five white five-pointed stars. The red field bears a stylized design of a yellow bird of paradise.
Festivals. 5 June (Queen's Official birthday); 23 July (Remembrance Day); 16 Sept. (Independence Day and Constitution Day).
Vehicle registration plate. PNG.

INTERNATIONAL RELATIONS

Affiliations

Commonwealth; ACP; SPF.

Defence

Total Armed Forces: 3,200. Terms of service: voluntary.
Army: 2,900.
Navy: 200; five patrol and coastal combatants.
Air Force: 100.
Para-military: Border Patrol Police: 4,600.

ECONOMY

Currency

The unit is the kina, divided into 100 toea.

National finance

Budget. The 1988 budget (in US$) was for expenditure (current and capital) of 998 million and revenue of 962 million. Main items of current expenditure are education 16.4%; health 9.7%.
Balance of payments. The balance of payments (current account, 1987) was a deficit of $530 million.
Inflation. (1988) 5%.

Gross Domestic Product

Estimated total GDP US$3,030 million, per capita US$745 (overall size of economy ranking 105 in the world).
Economically active population. The total number of persons active in the economy was 1,660,000; unemployed: 5%.

Sector	% of GDP
industry	26
agriculture	34
services*	40

* services figure includes elements unassigned to other categories.

Energy and mineral resources

Minerals. Production: (1986) 646,557 tons/586,553 tonnes of copper concentrate; 1,804 tons/16,367 kg of gold; 5,554 tons/50,385 kg of silver.
Electricity. Capacity: 364,000 kW; production: 1,300 million kWh; 360 kWh per capita (1988).

Bioresources

Agriculture. Main crops are copra; cocoa; coffee; rubber; oil palm; tea.
Crop production: (1986 in 1,000 tons/tonnes) coffee 60/54; copra 160/145; cocoa beans 33/30; palm-oil 138/125.
Livestock numbers: (1987) cattle 123,000; pigs 1.5 million; goats 17,000; poultry 3 million.
Forestry. 71% of the land area is forest and woodland and timber production is increasingly important. Sawn timber production: (1986) 2,966,416 ft^3/84,000 m^3, of which 262,670 ft^3/7,438 m^3 was exported.
Fisheries. Catch: (1980) 36,376 tons/33,000 tonnes, mainly tuna. Exports of crustacea: (1986) 1,736 tons/1,575 tonnes.

Industry and commerce

Industry. Copra crushing; oil palm processing; plywood processing; wood chip production; gold; silver; copper; construction; tourism.
Commerce. Exports (1987) US$1,170 million,

including gold; copper ore; coffee; copra; palm-oil; timber; lobster. Imports: $US1,100 million, including machinery and transport equipment; fuels; food; chemicals; consumer goods. Countries exported to were West Germany; Japan; Australia; UK; Spain; US. Imports came from Australia; Singapore; Japan; US; New Zealand; UK.

Trade with UK. Papua New Guinea imported UK goods worth £20,521,000; exports to UK totalled £44,291,000.

Tourism. (1986) 32,000 visitors including 8,500 tourists.

COMMUNICATIONS

Railways

There are no railways.

Roads

There are 12,256 miles/19,736 km of roads (3,023 miles/4,865 km are classified as highways or trunk roads).

Aviation

Air Niugini provides international services; Douglas Airways Pty Ltd and Talair Pty Ltd provide domestic services (main airport is at Port Moresby). Passengers: (1984) 711,000.

Shipping

There are 6,798 miles/10,940 km of inland waterways. The marine ports of Lae, Madang, and Port Moresby are on the main island. Rabaul is situated on the smaller New Britain Island. The merchant marine consists of 11 ships of 1,000 GRT or over. Freight loaded: (1986) 2.3 million tons/2.1 million tonnes; unloaded: 2.0 million tons/1.8 million tonnes.

Telecommunications

There are 51,700 telephones and the telecommunications system is adequate and being improved; facilities provide radiobroadcast, radiotelephone and telegraph, coastal radio, aeronautical radio and international radiocommunication services. There are 229,500 radios and 5,000 televisions (1988).

EDUCATION AND WELFARE

Education

Schools. There are 2,461 primary schools with an estimated 375,000 pupils and 234 secondary, technical and vocational schools with 60,100 students.

Universities. An estimated 3,200 students are enrolled in the University of Papua New Guinea and the Papua New Guinea University of Technology.

Literacy. 32%.

Health

283 doctors (one per 13,202 people); 19 hospitals; 460 health centres; 2,230 aid posts.

PARAGUAY

República del Paraguay
(Republic of Paraguay)

GEOGRAPHY

Paraguay is a landlocked state in central South America, containing an area of 157,006 miles^2/406,752 km^2, divided into 19 departments and one capital district. The Paraguay River bisects the country north-south, dividing it into the Región Occidental (Western Region) and the Región Oriental (Eastern Region). The sparsely populated Western Region covers approximately 60% of the total surface area and forms part of the semi-arid Chaco plains that stretch north-west and south-west into Bolivia and Argentina. To the east, the Paraná Plateau averages 984–1,969 ft/300–600 m elevation, reaching 2,297 ft/700 m in the Cordillera de Caaguazu[a], falling to 164 ft/50 m in the fertile plains that divide the River Paraguay and River Paraná in the south-east. 80% of Paraguay's frontiers are river-navigable, the Paraguay in the north, the Alto Paraná to the south and to the east, and the Pilcomayó in the west, draining the Chaco flatlands. Approximately 35% of the total surface area is forested and 20% is considered arable.

Climate

Subtropical with a summer temperature range of 77–112°F/25–40°C and a winter range of 50–68°F/10–20°C. A maximum of 67 in/1,702 mm rain falls in the south-east, decreasing westwards to 54 in/1,375 mm along the Paraguay river valley and 22 in/570 mm further west. Intermittent flooding and drought can cause severe agricultural disruption. Asunción: Jan. 81°F/27.2°C. July 64°F/17.8°C. Average annual rainfall 52 in/1,316 mm.

Cities and towns

Asunción (capital)	455,517
San Lorenzo	74,359
Fernando de la Mora	66,810
Lambare	65,145

Population

Total population is 4,040,000, of which 43.9% live in urban areas. Population density is 25.7 persons per mile^2/9.6 per km^2. 95% of the population are mestizo (mixed Spanish/Guaraní Indian ancestry). Amerindian, Black, European and Asian minorities comprise the bulk of the remainder. Also resident in the Chaco region are some 13,000 Germano-Canadian Mennonites, together with approximately 7,000 Japanese in the Región Oriental.

Birth rate 3.58%. **Death rate** 0.67%. **Rate of population increase** (1980–87) 2.91%. **Age distribution** under 15 = 41%; over 65 = 3.5%. **Life expectancy** female 69; male 65; average 67.

Religion

97% of the population are Roman Catholic but small Mennonite minorities and Baptist/Anglican denominations are also present.

Language

Spanish is the official language, but over 40% of the population speak Guariní and 48.2% are proficient in both Spanish and Guaraní.

HISTORY

Long before the arrival of Europeans, the area between the Paraguay and Paraná rivers was occupied by Guaraní Indians, semi-nomadic people who, in the process of subduing their enemies in the Gran Chaco region, extended their influence to the fringes of the Inca empire. The first Spanish colonists arrived in 1536 in search of El Dorado. They founded the capital Asunción in 1537 but instead of discovering gold, learnt how to coexist with the indigenous tribes, producing the distinctive racial mixture of habits and customs still present in the rural population. There was a particularly strong Jesuit presence in Paraguay, but the Spanish crown saw this as a threat to its own authority and expelled the Jesuits in 1767, thus destroying their Indian communities in the south-east of the country. Although extremely paternalistic, the Jesuits had provided protection for some 100,000 Indians who now became prey to colonial landlords and Brazilian slave runners.

Independence from Spain was declared on 14 May 1811 but full statehood came only after a struggle with the government of Buenos Aires on 12 Oct. 1813. For the next 27 years, the country prospered under the paternalistic rule of Dr José Gaspar Rodríguez de Francia who outlawed political parties, stripped the church and creole nobility of power and wealth and severely limited external commerce. On his death in 1840, he was succeeded by Carlos Antonio López (president 1844–62) whose all-embracing power was legitimized by the country's first constitution, passed by the Congress in 1844. López's rule was significant for the opening up of the country and for its militarization in an attempt to deter the growing territorial designs of Brazil and Argentina. His son, Francisco Solano López (president 1862–70), who succeeded him on his death, lacked the father's diplomatic skills. In a gross overestimation of Paraguay's military capability, he pursued a bellicose foreign policy which ended in the ruinous war against the triple alliance of Uruguay, Brazil and Argentina (1865–70) which, in war dead, reduced the population from an estimated 525,000 to about 220,000. Allied armies occupied Asunción, installing a provisional government which promulgated an ineffectual liberal constitution (with limited male suffrage), alien to the Paraguayan authoritarian tradition, in 1870.

The occupying forces withdrew in 1876 and those vying for power coalesced into the Colorado and Liberal parties which shared a preference for personality politics, violence, electoral manipulation and opportunism. The Colorados with the support of Brazil held power from 1887 to 1904, and the Liberals with the backing of Argentina from 1904 until 1936. The whole period 1870–1936 was one of economic collapse and financial fraud. The nation was united briefly by the Chaco war with Bolivia (1932–35), in which a Paraguayan army successfully resisted the attempt of the landlocked Bolivians to force access to the upper Paraguay river, a right subsequently granted in the truce terms of 1935, while Paraguay gained about 75% of the disputed territory.

A group of reformist officers, supported by disgruntled war veterans, overthrew Pres. Eusebio Ayala in Feb. 1936 but in the elections of 1939 the Liberals were returned, with the war hero, Marshal José Félix Estigarribia as president. Estigarribia's attempt to build a state-dominated society, reflected in a constitution of Feb. 1940, was abruptly ended by his death in an air crash in September. The provisional president, Gen. Higinio Moríngo quickly antagonized the Liberals by favouring Colorado interests, provoking Liberal-inspired revolts in 1947, which left thousands dead. Moríngo was replaced by the Colorados in 1948 and in the following six years, six presidents enjoyed the briefest of tenures until the Army took control, in 1954, under Gen. Alfredo Stroessner.

The Stroessner dictatorship maintained its grip on power for 35 years, bringing economic and political stability, modernization of the country's infrastructure and such huge developments as the Itaipú Dam project on the Paraná river. Although elections were held every five years in compliance with the constitution, political activity was severely curtailed and the government was heavily criticized for its flagrant abuses of human rights. Presidential and congressional elections held in May 1989, which were considered to have been relatively free and open by international observers, resulted in a sweeping victory for the Colorado candidate Gen. Andres Rodriguez, who had led the military coup of Feb. 1989 which overthrew the Stroessner dictatorship.

CONSTITUTION AND GOVERNMENT

Executive and legislature

The executive president is directly elected (and re-eligible) for a five-year term (last elections 1 May 1989), and governs with the assistance of an appointed council of minsters. Legislative power is vested in a bicameral national congress consisting of a senate of at least 30 members and a chamber of deputies of at least 60 members, both directly elected for five-year terms (subject to dissolution) at the same time as the president. The party receiving the largest number of votes (since 1947 the Partido Colorado) is allotted two-thirds of the seats in both houses of congress.

Present government

President Gen. Andres Rodriguez

Principal Members of Council of Ministers Gen. Orlando Machuca Vargas (Interior); Sr Luis Maria Argaña (Foreign Affairs); Sr Enzo Debernardi (Finance); Sr Alexis Frutos Vaesken (Justice and Labour); Gen. Adolfo Samaniego (Defence).

Justice

The system of law is based on Argentine and French codes, and Roman law. The highest court is the Supreme Court, which has a role in the judicial review of legislation. The judicial interests of the state are represented by the Attorney General. At local level, judges of first instance deal with civil, commercial and criminal cases, while for each of these categories there is a Chamber of Appeal. The death penalty is nominally in force. There were no executions between 1985 and mid-1988.

National symbols

Flag. Three horizontal stripes of red, white and blue. In the centre of the white stripe there is the state coat of arms.

Festivals. 1 Mar. (Heroes' Day); 1 May (Labour Day); 14–15 May (Independence Day Celebrations); 12 June (Peace of Chaco); 15 Aug. (Founding of Asunción); 25 Aug. (Constitution Day); 29 Sep. (Battle of Boqueron); 12 Oct. (Day of the Race, anniversary of the discovery of America).

Vehicle registration plate. PY.

INTERNATIONAL RELATIONS

Affiliations

OAS; SELA.

Defence

Total Armed Forces: 16,000 (9,800 conscipts). Terms of service: 18 months; Navy two years.

Army: 12,500; six main battle tanks (M-4A3), 34 light tanks (M-3A1).

Navy: 2,500; eight patrol and riverine combatants.

Marines: 500.

Air Force: 1,000; 16 combat aircraft (EMB-326, AT-6).

Para-military: Special Police Service: 7,500.

ECONOMY

Currency

The unit is the guarani, divided into 100 centimos.

National finance

Budget. The 1987 budget (in US$) was for expenditure (current and capital) of 1,098 million and revenue of 1,084 million. Main items of current expenditure are housing and welfare 32.3%; education 12.2%; defence 12.1%.

Balance of payments. The balance of payments (current account, 1987) was a deficit of $422 million (est.).

Inflation. (1987) 33.3%.

Gross Domestic Product

Estimated total GDP US$4,570 million, per capita US$1,740 (overall size of economy ranking 90 in the world).

Economically active population. The total number of persons active in the economy was 1,300,000; unemployed: 11%.

Sector	% of workforce	% of GDP
Industry	n/a	26
agriculture	44	27
services*	n/a	47

* services figure includes elements unassigned to other categories.

Energy and mineral resources

Minerals. Large deposits of limestone; salt; kaolin; apatite. Known reserves of iron ore and manganese but these are not considered commercially exploitable.

Electricity. Capacity: 2.36 million kW; production: 1,200 million kWh; 275 kWh per capita (1988).

Bioresources

Agriculture. Main crops are oilseed; soya beans; cotton; wheat; manioc; sweet potatoes; tobacco; maize; rice; sugar cane. Paraguay is an illegal producer of cannabis for the international drug trade.

Crop production: (1986 in 1,000 tons/tonnes) manioc 3,169/2,875; soya beans 730/662; maize 517/469; seed cotton 413/375; wheat 279/253; rice 85/77; tobacco 20/18; sugar cane 1,429/1,296; coffee 19.8/18.

Livestock numbers: (1987) cattle 7.33 million; horses 317,000; pigs 1.69 million; sheep 398,000.

Forestry. 35% of the land area is forest and woodland. In 1986 203,105 tons/184,256 tonnes of timber were exported.

Industry and commerce

Industry. Main industries are meat packing; oilseed crushing; milling; brewing; textiles; other light consumer goods; cement; construction.

Commerce. Exports (1987) US$380 million, including cotton; soya beans; timber; vegetable oils; coffee; meat products. Imports: US$620 million, including capital goods 35%; consumer goods 20%; fuels and lubricants 19%; raw materials 16%; foodstuffs, beverages and tobacco 10%. Countries exported to were EC countries 37%; Brazil 25%; Argentina 10%; Chile 6%; US 6%. Imports came from Brazil 30%; EC countries 20%; US 18%; Argentina 8%; Japan 7%.

Trade with UK. In 1988 Paraguay imported UK goods worth £22,024,000; exports to UK totalled £1,950,000.

Tourism. (1986) 200,000 visitors.

COMMUNICATIONS

Railways

There are some 1,243 miles/2,000 km of railways.

Roads

There are 7,034 miles/11,320 km of roads, of which 1,301 miles/2,094 km are concrete or bituminized.

Aviation

Lineas Aereas Paraguayas (LAP) provides international services (main airport is Aeropuerto Presidente Stroessner at Asunción). Passengers: (1983) 282,520.

Shipping

There are 1,926 miles/3,100 km of inland waterways. The inland port of Asunción is on the Paraguay River. The merchant marine consists of 17 ships of 1,000 GRT or over.

Telecommunications

There are 78,300 telephones and a fair intercity network centred in Asunción. There are 624,000 radios and 88,000 televisions (1986), a government Radio Nacional del Paraguay, a dozen main commercial radio stations and three commercial TV stations.

EDUCATION AND WELFARE

Education

Schools. Education is free and compulsory. There are 4,101 primary schools with 579,687 pupils and 21,136 teachers (one per 27 pupils) and 740 secondary schools with 148,516 students and 2,448 teachers (one per 60 pupils).

Universities. The National University of Asunción has 18,700 students and 2,694 teachers (one per 6 students) and the Catholic University has 10,500 students and 900 teachers (one per 11 students).

Literacy. 81%

Health

There are an estimated 2,200 doctors (one per 2,055 people) and 3,380 hospital beds (one per 1,370 people).

PERU

República del Perú
(Republic of Peru)

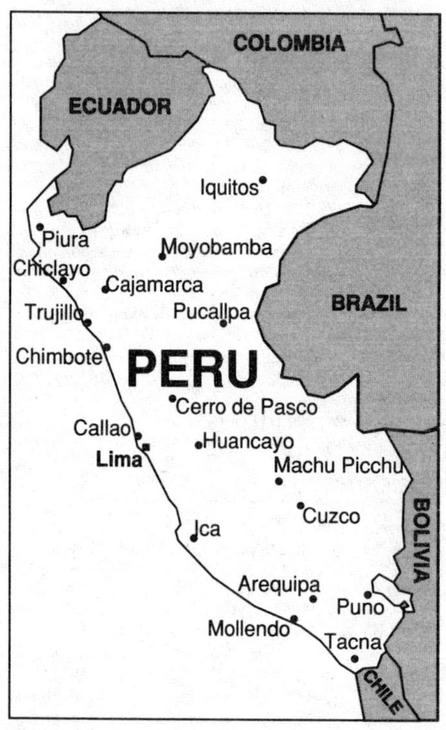

GEOGRAPHY

Located on the western coast of South America, Peru covers an area of 496,095 miles^2/1,285,220 km^2, divided into 24 departments and the constitutional province of Lima. West-east, Peru's physiography can be divided into three distinct regions. To the west, the coastal plains contain 11% of the total surface area, supporting a little over 40% of the population on predominantly infertile terrain. Further inland, the Andean Sierra (average elevation 9,842 ft/3,000 m) comprises two principal ranges (Cordillera Occidental and Oriental) deeply cut by a number of rivers to form steep-sided fertile valleys and basins. Mount Huascaran (to the west) is Peru's highest peak at 22,204 ft/6,768 m. The mountains occupy an estimated 26% of the total area and support approximately 50% of the entire population. To the east, the sparsely populated forest or selva descends from the Andean high ground to tropical lowland, forming part of the Amazon basin, drained by the Maranón and Ucayali rivers. The selva covers 62% of the land surface. In the south, on the Bolivian frontier, Lake Titicaca lies 12,507 ft/3,812 m above sea level, making it the highest navigable waterbody in the world. 3% of the land area is arable and 55% is forested.

Climate

Peru exhibits a diverse range of climatic conditions, from the equatorial tracts of rainforest in the east to the semi-arid desert in the southern Costa. Annual temperature ranges are as follows: 54–90°F/12–32°C on the western coastal plains, with increased humidity May-Sept.; 34–57°F/1–14°C in the Sierra, with a wet season Nov.-Mar., and 75–95°F/24–35°C in the tropical Selva or Montana. Rainfall decreases east-west from 125–75 in/3,175–1,900 mm in the forests to 3.9 in/100 mm or less on the west coast. Lima: Jan. 74°F/23.3°C. July 62°F/16.7°C. Average annual rainfall 1.9 in/48 mm. Cuzco: Jan. 56°F/13.3°C. July 50°F/10°C. Average annual rainfall 31.7 in/804 mm.

Cities and towns

Lima (capital)	5,008,400
Arequipa	531,829
Callao	515,200
Trujillo	438,709
Chiclayo	347,702
Piura	256,150
Chimbote	253,289
Cuzco	225,683
Iquitos	215,275

Population

Total population is 21,448,501 of which 70.2% live in urban areas. Population density is 43 persons per mile^2/16.1 per km^2. South American Indians comprise 45% of the total population; 37% are mestizo (mixed European and Indian descent); 15% White; 3% Black, Japanese or Chinese.

Birth rate 2.9%. **Death rate** 0.8%. **Rate of population increase** 2.1%. **Age distribution** under 15 = 40.5%; over 65 = 3.6%. **Life expectancy** female 63; male 60; average 61.

Religion

An estimated 90% of the population are Roman

Catholic. Peru is divided ecclesiastically into seven archdioceses, 14 dioceses, 12 territorial prelatures and eight Apostolic Vicariates. In addition, there are considerable Anglican and Methodist representations and a minority of Peruvian Baha'is.

Language

Spanish and Quechua are both official languages, spoken by 68% and 27% of the population respectively; 3% speak Aymará.

HISTORY

Human occupation of Peru dates from at least 8000 BC, with advanced cultures (the Charin, Chima, Nazca, Tiahuanaco) starting from approximately 1250 BC. The Incas came much later, their thirteen emperors dating from the reign of Manco Capac (c. AD 1200) up to that of Atahualpa (1532–33), the latter being captured, ransomed and executed in 1533 by the Spanish conquistador Francisco Pizarro, who founded the coastal capital of Lima, in 1535. The rebellion of the last Inca leader, Túpac Amaru, ended with his beheading in 1572, marking the effective end of a dynasty which at its height had ruled over an area extending from present-day Colombia, down to central Chile.

The Spanish crown, eager to limit the power of the conquistadores, passed the New Laws of the Indies in 1546, which restricted their Indian tributes, freed Indian slaves and forbade forced labour. In retaliation, the conquistadores assassinated the Spanish Viceroy in 1544. It was not until the viceregal rule of Francisco de Toledo (1569–81) that civil war was ended and Spanish authority fully restored. In the ensuing period of stability Peru emerged as the most powerful of the viceroyalties, with massive mineral wealth in the Potosí silver mines of Upper Peru (Bolivia), and Lima establishing itself as a sophisticated cultural and commercial centre and the seat of Church and judicial power. However 18th century colonial reforms of the Spanish Bourbon kings seriously weakened this power, Peru losing its northern territories to the viceroyalty of New Granada (1739–1819 Ecuador, Venezuela, Colombia) and most crucially Upper Peru, along with its mineral wealth, to the Viceroyalty of Río de la Plata (1777–1810). This humiliation came in a period of renewed internal strife, most notably the rebellion of Túpac Amaru II (the 'mestizo' José Gabriel Condorcanqui) of 1780–83. Paradoxically, this fall from grace did not produce a widespread movement for independence from Spain. Peru remained loyal to the crown while neighbouring countries proclaimed their independence, its final liberation, in 1824, being secured by 'outsiders', the Argentinian general José de San Martín and the Venezuelan Simón Bolívar.

The post-independence era witnessed, despite the passing of a liberal constitution in 1828, the battles of rival chieftains (caudillos) for the presidency, with coups and counter-coups being a feature of the period up to the early 1840s. During this period there were also sporadic outbreaks of fighting with Bolivia and Ecuador over territorial disputes.

The strongest leader of the time was Gen. Ramón Castilla (1845–51, 1855–62) who abolished the Indian tribute system and prepared for the emancipation of Black slaves in 1854 (although allowing the importation of some 100,000 Chinese as cheap labour) while presiding over a period of economic growth based on the discovery that coastal 'guano' (preserved bird droppings rich in nitrogen and known to the Incas as a first-class fertilizer), was in great demand in Europe. The 'Guano Age' provided the government with an economic bonanza but one wasted in political favours by such presidents as José Rufino Echenique (1851–54). Nicolás de Piérola, a young treasury minister, prevented financial collapse by trading the foreign debt with the French firm Adolph Dreyfus in exchange for the latter's monopoly over the purchase and sale of guano. The country's first civilian president, Manuel Prado (1872–76), whose Civilista Party represented powerful landlords and merchants, increased the foreign debt through such projects as the construction of a Trans-Andean railway.

This indebtedness, coupled with crippling defeat by Chile in the War of the Pacific (1879–83), which resulted in the loss of lucrative nitrate fields in the southern Atacama desert region, brought Peru to the brink of bankruptcy. This was staved off only by Pres. Andrés Cáceres (1885–90) signing the Grace Contract which ceded control of its railways (for sixty-six years) and guano deposits to British creditors.

Piérola, who became president in 1895, restored sound economic management and introduced direct suffrage while strengthening municipal government. Economic recovery (but not political development) took place over the next 30 years but became heavily dependent on United States investment in public works, particularly under the second autocratic presidency of Augusto Leguía (1919–30) who, in return, gave US companies extensive rights to exploit Peru's mineral and oil deposits. Although Leguía approved a new constitution in 1920, he failed to implement the key clause which guaranteed the protection of Indian communal land. This betrayal encouraged the growth of 'Indianism' among intellectuals (based on fanciful interpretations of past Inca collectivism), one such, Víctor Rául Haya de la Torre, founding the American Revolutionary Popular Alliance (APRA) in 1924. Haya argued for the unity of all American Indians and the elimination of US imperialism and nationalization of their assets.

A military junta, headed by Col Luis Sánchez Cerro (president 1931–33) overthrew Leguía in 1930 and in the following year, defeated Haya in presidential elections. APRA accused the government of fraud and refused to accept the result. Its supporters staged a rebellion in the northern city of Trujillo in 1932, executing ten military officers and assassinating Sánchez Cerro himself in 1933. The military shot 1,000 suspected 'Apristas' and determined that the party should never come to power.

Gen. Oscar R. Benavides, the 'interim' president (1933–39), attempted to reduce polarization of the country through state-led economic growth. He succeeded in blunting the appeal of APRA by the wider provision of social benefits. Pres. Manuel Prado (1939–45) a moderate civilian, received widespread support for his pro-allied stance in World War II, as did Pres. José Luis Bustamente y Rivero (1945–48) until his overthrow, in a coup of 1948 led by Gen. Manuel Odría (president 1948–56), for his alleged failure to clamp down on APRA, but more accurately because his agricultural diversification plans threatened powerful sugar barons.

Odría, although encouraging foreign investment and ensuring that Peru benefited from US demands for raw materials during the Korean War, left the country in a financial crisis. Manuel Prado returned to office in 1956, and used austerity policies and the record receipts from the sale of Peruvian fishmeal to restore economic equilibrium, but at the expense of heightened political tension. The elections of 1962 produced no clear winner, the military allowing Fernando Belaúnde Terry (president 1963–68), of the National Democratic Front, to take the presidency in 1963. Belaúnde's optimistic social and economic reconstruction programme foundered and a self-styled progressive military junta, led by Gen. Juan Velasco Alvarado (1968–75), seized power in 1968.

Initially popular for nationalizing US assets and sweeping land reforms, the increasing bureaucratization of society alienated almost everyone and this, coupled with the collapse of the fishmeal industry and declining copper and sugar prices, led to Velasco's replacement by Gen. Francisco Morales Bermúdez (1975–80), who reversed the policies and opted for austerity measures to deal with inflation and the swollen foreign debt.

Pres. Belaúnde Terry (president 1980–85), who returned to power as the Popular Action candidate in 1980, stuck to the same economic recipe in the hope of qualifying for International Monetary Fund (IMF) support. In response, nationwide strikes, along with the initiation of violent insurgency in the Andes by the Maoist Shining Path (Sendero Luminoso) guerrilla group, bred great political instability.

In this climate, much was expected from Alán García (president 1985–), the 36-year-old APRA presidential candidate elected to office with a large majority in Apr. 1985. He quickly improved general living standards hoping that greater demand would encourage economic growth. He also promised to devote no more than 10% of export earnings to service the foreign debt. However, his pledge to curtail military power crumbled as he increasingly relied upon the army to combat left-wing insurrection. By the end of 1988 and throughout 1989 García faced three-figure inflation, which had decimated wages and salaries, and the threat of a full-scale civil war as military offensives of Sendero Luminoso and the Tupac Amaro Revolutionary Movement (MRTA) gained in strength and audacity. In response the government extended the existing States of Emergency in the central and southern Andes region to cover most of the country. This was intended to guarantee the holding of municipal elections in Nov. 1989, which were subsequently won by the right-wing Broad Democratic Alliance (FREDEMO), and Presidential and congressional elections in April 1990.

CONSTITUTION AND GOVERNMENT

Executive and legislature

The executive president is directly elected in a nationwide ballot for a five-year term (last election 14 Apr. 1985), and governs with the assistance of two elected vice-presidents and an appointed council of ministers. Legislative authority is vested in a bicameral national congress. The lower house, the 180-seat Chamber of Deputies, is directly elected by proportional representation within constituencies, for a five-year term (last elections Apr. 1985, simultaneously with the presidential poll). The Senate has 60 members elected for a five-year term, together with past Peruvian presidents who have the status of life senators.

Present government

President Sr Alan García Pérez
First Vice-President vacant
Second Vice-President Sr Luis Alva Castro
Prime Minister; President of the Council of Ministers and Minister of the Presidency Dr Luis Alberto Sánchez Sánchez
Other Principal Ministers Sr Augustín Mantilla (Interior); Sr Julio Velasquez Giacarini (Defence); Sr Cesar Vasquez Bazan (Economy and Finance); Sr Guillermo Larco Cox (Foreign Affairs); Sr César Delgado Barreto (Justice).

Justice

The system of law is based on civil codes. The highest court is the Supreme Court with a President and 12 members. At local level, justices of peace deal with minor criminal cases and civil cases, above which there is a structure of courts of first instance, for more significant cases, and superior courts. The death penalty is in force only for exceptional crimes. No executions between 1985 and mid-1988.

National symbols

Flag. Three vertical stripes of red, white and red; in the centre there is the shield from the coat of arms of 1825.
Festivals. 1 May (Labour Day); 24 June (Day of the Peasant, half-day only); 28–29 July (Independence); 9 Oct. (for Battle of Angamos).
Vehicle registration plate. PE.

INTERNATIONAL RELATIONS

Affiliations

NAM; OAS.

Defence

Total Armed Forces: 118,000 (74,000 conscripts). Terms of service: two years, selective. Reserves: 188,000 (Army only).
Army: 80,000; 300 main battle tanks (T-54/-55); 110 light tanks (AMX-13).
Navy: 23,000; 12 submarines (FRG T-209/1200, US Guppy and Mackerel) and 14 principal surface combatants: two cruisers (NL De Ruyter and De 7 Provincien); eight destroyers (US Daring, NL Friesland); four frigates (It Lupo). Six patrol and coastal combatants.
Naval Air Force: seven combat aircraft and ten armed helicopters.
Marines: 2,500.
Air Force: 15,000; 117 combat aircraft (Mirage 2000, Mirage 5, Su-22, Cessna A-37B, Canberra B-2/-8).
Opposition: Sendero Luminoso (Shining Path): some 2,000–5,000.
Movimiento Revolucionario Túpac Amaru (MRTA): 500.

ECONOMY

Currency

The unit is the inti, divided into 1,000 soles.

National finance

Budget. The 1986 budget (in US$) was for expenditure (current and capital) of 3,700 million and revenue of 3,200 million.
Balance of payments. The balance of payments (current account, 1987) was a deficit of $1,419 million.
Inflation. (1988) 1,700%.

Gross Domestic Product

Estimated total GDP US$45,150 million, per capita US$920 (overall size of economy ranking 42 in the world).

Economically active population. The total number of persons active in the economy was 6,800,000; unemployed: 9.5%.

Sector	% of workforce	% of GDP
industry	19	33
agriculture	37	11
services*	44	56

* services figure includes elements unassigned to other categories.

Energy and mineral resources

Oil and gas. 1988 production from the jungle oilfields was 7.7 million tons/7 million tonnes.

Minerals. Copper; silver; gold; iron ore; coal; phosphate.

Electricity. Capacity: 4.63 million kW; production: 14,800 million kWh; 700 kWh per capita (1988).

Bioresources

Agriculture. Main crops are wheat; potatoes; beans; rice; barley; coffee; cotton; sugar cane. Peru is the world's leading producer of coca and an illegal supplier for the international drug market.

Crop production: (1987 in 1,000 tons/tonnes) sugar cane 6,723/6,099; potatoes 1,884/1,709; cotton 223/202; coffee 108/98; rice 1,289/1,169; maize 1,008/914.

Livestock numbers: (1987) alpacas 2.48 million; vicuña 25,000; cattle 3.96 million; sheep 13.3 million; pigs 2.3 million; poultry 50 million.

Forestry. 55% of the land area is forest and woodland, including valuable hardwoods (oak and cedar 40%).

Fisheries. Catch: (1987) 4.7 million tons/4.27 million tonnes, mainly anchovies and sardines.

Industry and commerce

Industry. Main industries are mining; petroleum; fishing; textiles; clothing; food processing; cement; auto assembly; steel; shipbuilding; metal fabrication.

Commerce. Exports: (1988) US$2,600 million or 13% of GDP, including fishmeal; cotton; sugar; coffee; copper; iron ore; refined silver; lead; zinc; crude petroleum and byproducts. Imports: US$2,600 million, including foodstuffs; machinery; transport equipment; iron and steel semimanufactures; chemicals; pharmaceuticals. Countries exported to were US 28%; EC countries 22%; Japan 11%; Latin America 8%; USSR 4%. Imports came from US 20%; Latin America 16%; EC countries 12%; Japan 7%; Switzerland 3%.

Trade with UK. Peru imported UK goods worth £31,384,000; exports to UK totalled £90,844,000.

Tourism. (1986) 305,000 visitors.

COMMUNICATIONS

Railways

There are 1,491 miles/2,399 km of railways.

Roads

There are 43,461 miles/69,942 km of roads, of which some 12,428 miles/20,000 km are concrete or bituminized.

Aviation

Aeronaves del Peru, SA and Compania de Aviacion Faucett provide domestic services, and Aeroperu provides international services (main airport is Jorge Chavez Airport, near Lima). Passengers: (1986) 2.8 million.

Shipping

There are 5,344 miles/8,600 km of navigable tributaries of the Amazon system and 129 miles/208 km of Lago Titicaca. The inland port of Iquitos on the Amazon river creates more direct access for the North Atlantic Ocean. The west coast marine ports are Callao, Ilo, Matarani, and Talara. The merchant marine consists of 34 ships of 1,000 GRT or over. Freight loaded: (1987) 8.6 million tons/7.8 million tonnes; unloaded: 5.4 million tons/4.9 million tonnes.

Telecommunications

There are 544,000 telephones and an adequate telecommunications system including a nationwide radio relay network. There are 5.2 million radios (1987) and 1.6 million televisions (1988). The government runs Radio Nacional del Peru, two other radio stations and a cultural TV station, while there are also commercial radio operations and five main commercial TV stations.

EDUCATION AND WELFARE

Education

Schools. Both primary (compulsory) and secondary education are free for children from seven to 16 years. There are 3,763,730 pupils in primary schools and 1,732,466 in secondary schools.

Universities. There are 35 universities with a total number of 409,654 students.

Literacy. 80%.

Health

There are 353 hospitals and 920 health centres.

PHILIPPINES

Republika ng Pilipinas
(Republic of the Philippines)

GEOGRAPHY

Lying in the west Pacific Ocean, some 497 miles/ 800 km off the South-East Asian coast, the Philippine Archipelago (7,100 islands) occupies a total land area of approximately 115,800 miles^2/300,000 km^2. Luzon to the north (40,410 miles^2/104,688 km^2) and Mindanao (36,527 miles^2/94,630 km^2) to the south are the two largest islands containing two-thirds of the total area. The other nine main islands are Samar, Negros, Palawan, Panay, Leyte, Mindore, Bohol, Cebu and Masbate. The Philippines exhibit a predominantly mountainous, volcanic topography with narrow coastal belts, north-south upland ridges, and north-draining river systems. On Luzon, the Sierra Madre (east) and Cordillera Central (west) are divided by the fertile Cagayan River Valley, converging north of the populous central plain which extends south to Manila Bay. Mount Apo, the Philippines' highest peak, rises to 9,692 ft/2,954 m on the island of Mindanao. South-east of Manila, the country's largest lake, Lagunalde Bay, covers an area of over 347 miles^2/900 km^2. 40% of the total surface area is forested and 20% is considered arable.

Climate

Maritime tropical with variations according to altitude. Predominantly warm and humid in low-lying areas with consistently high temperatures, deviating little from 81°F/27°C. Rainfall varies from 35 in/ 890 mm to 216 in/5,490 mm on Luzon with a rainy season June-Nov., brought on by the south-westerly monsoon. Lying across the typhoon zone, up to 15 storms strike the archipelago every year. Other natural hazards include tsunamis (tidal waves) and seismic disturbance. Manila: Jan 77°F/25°C. July 82°F/ 27.8°C. Average annual rainfall 82 in/2,083 mm.

Cities and towns

Manila (capital)	1,630,485
Quezon City	1,165,865
Davao	610,375
Cebu	490,281
Caloocan	467,816
Zamboanga	343,722

Population

Total population is 64,906,990 of which 41.0% live in urban areas. Population density is 561 persons per mile^2/191.2 per km^2 with severe overcrowding resulting from rural-urban migration. The Filipinos are of Malay origin with some Chinese, US and Spanish admixtures. See Language for ethnolinguistic composition.

Birth rate 3.4%. **Death rate** 0.7%. **Rate of population increase** (1980–87) 2.7%. **Age distribution** under 15 = 41.1%; over 65 = 3.4%. **Life expectancy** female 65; male 62; average 63.

Religion

83% of the population are Roman Catholic; 9% Protestant; 5% Muslim; 3% Buddhist. Animists and unaffiliated persons number 400,000. The majority of the Muslims live in or around the capital, Manila.

Language

Pilipino (from Tagalog, a Malay dialect) is the national language. English is the other official language. Over 87 languages are endemic to the Philippines. Only 23.8% of the population at the last census spoke Pilipino, whereas 24.2% spoke Cebuano; 10.3% Ilocano; 9.2% Hiligaynon Ilongo; 5.6% Bicol; 4.0% Samar-Leyte; 2.8% Pampango; 1.8% Pangasinan.

HISTORY

Prior to Spanish colonization in the 16th century, the 7,000 or so islands which today comprise the Republic of the Philippines had no central government and little cultural homogeneity. The common unit of social and economic organization within the territory was the barangay, a small settlement based on subsistence agriculture.

In the century after Ferdinand Magellan's voyage to Cebu in 1521, Spain increased its control over the Philippines, as the islands became an important transhipment point on the important trade route between the Far East and the Spanish colonies in Latin America. Catholicism was successfully implanted within the territory, although in the southern islands of Mindanao and the Sulu archipelago Islam, which had been established for a century before the arrival of the Spanish, remained the dominant religion. In the 18th century an increasing number of plantations, or haciendas, were established which, together with the application of steam power in the 19th century, transformed the Philippines into a huge sugar producer. The territory's economic development in conjunction with the decline of Spain, stimulated native nationalism and by the end of the 19th century the colonial authorities were struggling to contain a flourishing independence movement.

In 1898 the colony was occupied by US forces during the Spanish–American war and, under the terms of the Treaty of Paris, was formally ceded to the US. Although the US colonial administration was more enlightened than its predecessor, and granted significant concessions towards self-government, the nationalist movement continued to press for full independence. On 15 Nov. 1935, the Commonwealth of the Philippines was established under Pres. Manuel Quezon as a transitional stage prior to full independence which was to follow in ten years.

Following the outbreak of the Pacific War in Dec. 1941, Japanese forces invaded and conquered the Philippines. There followed a period of harsh occupation during which the country was exploited to fulfil Japan's military needs and the autarchic aims of its Greater East Asia Co-Prosperity Sphere. In the latter half of 1942, as the military struggle began to run in favour of the Allies, Japan sought to harness its faltering war effort to the engine of native nationalism and thereby build a genuine basis for popular support within the occupied territories. A greater emphasis was placed upon Filipino values and culture, and on 14 Oct. 1943, the territory was declared independent. Nevertheless, the continuing brutalities of the occupation (particularly the conscription of labour), combined with Japanese attitudes of racial superiority, served to foster pro-American sentiments amongst much of the population.

US forces invaded the Philippines in Oct. 1944. In Feb. 1945 Manila was liberated and the Filipino government-in-exile under Sergio Osmena (who had become president following the death of Quezon in 1944) was reinstated. At a presidential election in Apr. 1946 Osmena was defeated by the Liberal Party candidate Manuel Roxas. On 4 July 1946 the Republic of the Philippines was proclaimed as an independent sovereign state with Roxas as its first president.

During the next 20 years the country's political process featured a series of one-term presidents drawn either from the Liberal or Nationalist Parties. There was little ideological distinction between these two groupings, however, as each tended to be based around a leader who could dispense patronage. In Nov. 1965 the incumbent president was defeated by Ferdinand Marcos, the candidate of the Nationalist Party. Marcos was re-elected in 1969 amid charges that his victory had been secured by ballot rigging and intimidation.

Economic stagnation, together with rising inflation and endemic corruption, fuelled popular opposition to the Marcos administration. The government was also challenged by insurgency campaigns waged by communist and Muslim secessionist guerrillas. By the early 1970s, the New People's Army (NPA), the military wing of the banned Maoist Communist Party of the Philippines, had succeeded in harnessing peasant grievances to the extent that it constituted the de facto government in many of the more remote areas of the country, including parts of Luzon. In Mindanao and the southern islands the government was challenged by the Moro National Liberation Front (MNLF), which demanded greater autonomy or independence for the country's 2,100,000 Muslims.

Marcos attempted to crush his opponents and extend his period in office by imposing martial law in Sept. 1972. Although a new constitution was created in 1973, Marcos ruled as a virtual dictator until 1981 when martial law was lifted in all but the southernmost provinces. In June 1981 he was elected to a new six-year term as president in an election which was largely boycotted by the opposition and tarnished by charges of fraud.

The relaxation of the autocratic grip of Marcos allowed the opposition to achieve a greater degree of unity, and in mid-1983 its most prominent figure, Benigno Aquino, decided to return from exile in the US. Aquino, a former senator who had been sentenced to death after the imposition of martial law but reprieved following US pressure, arrived at Manila airport on 21 Aug. and was shot dead on the tarmac as he disembarked from the airliner. Although Marcos attempted to conceal his involvement in the murder, Aquino's death provided a focus for the opposition to extend its campaign against the regime.

In an attempt to bolster his position Marcos bowed to US pressure and called a presidential election for 7 Feb. 1986. The opposition united around the candidacy of Corazón Aquino, widow of Benigno. Although Marcos claimed victory, most neutral observers dismissed his clumsy attempts to alter the figures and accepted that Aquino had polled more votes. She launched a mass campaign of peaceful resistance which, backed by a revolt within the army, succeeded in ousting Marcos. Aquino was sworn in as president on 25 Feb. 1986. A year later a new, liberal constitution was overwhelmingly approved in a referendum, and in May 1987 Aquino's supporters won a majority in both houses of the new Congress.

Since her election victory Aquino has survived defections from her government and several attempted military coups by right-wing elements and supporters of Marcos. Although her survival has returned a degree of constitutionality to the country's political process, she has been unable to resolve the most pressing problems of the Philippines. Despite negotiations and the establishment of a temporary cease-fire, the insurgency campaigns have continued. Limited military victories have been achieved against the NPA but only at the cost of sponsoring right-wing vigilante squads which have added a further element of lawlessness to Filipino society. After some delay, a land reform programme was drawn up, but it has been widely criticized as inadequate in both its scope and application. In Dec. 1989 the Aquino government was shaken by the most serious coup attempt to date. The rebellion lasted for 10 days and resulted in over 100 deaths.

CONSTITUTION AND GOVERNMENT

Executive and legislature

The directly elected president has executive power, governing with the assistance of an appointed cabinet. The overwhelming popular approval of the constitution was accepted as a de facto election of Corazón Aquino as president. Legislative authority is vested in a bicameral popularly-elected congress consisting of a 250-member house of representatives (last election 11 May 1987) and a 24-member senate.

Present government

President Corazón Aquino

Vice-President Salvador Laurel

Principal Members of Cabinet Gen. Fidel Ramos (Defence); Franklin Drilon (Justice); Jesus Estanislao (Finance); Catalino Macaraig (Executive Secretary); Raul Manglapus (Foreign Affairs).

Justice

The judiciary consists of a Supreme Court, which can declare a law or treaty unconstitutional, an intermediate appellate court, regional trial courts (one for each judicial region) and metropolitan trial courts in each metropolitan area. The death penalty was abolished in 1987.

National symbols

Flag. Two horizontal stripes, blue over red, with a white triangle inserted in the hoist. In the centre of the triangle there is a yellow sun with eight triple rays and in each corner of the triangle there is a yellow five-pointed star.

Festivals. 25 Feb. (Freedom Day, anniversary of the People's Revolution); 1 May (Labour Day); 12 June (Independence Day, anniversary of 1898 declaration); 28 Aug. (National Heroes' Day); 21 Sep. (National Thanksgiving Day).

Vehicle registration plate. PI.

INTERNATIONAL RELATIONS

Affiliations

ASEAN.

Defence

Total Armed Forces: 147,500 inclusive Philippine Constabulary. Terms of service: voluntary. Reserves: 48,000.

Army: 65,000; 28 light tanks (Scorpion).

Philippine Constabulary: 43,500.

Navy: 23,000 inclusive 9,500 marines; three frigates (US Savage and Cannon), 51 patrol and coastal combatants.

Air Force: 16,000; some 50 combat aircraft (mainly F-5, SF-260 WP).

Opposition: Bangsa Moro Army (armed wing of Moro National Liberation Front (MNLF), Muslim): some 15,000.

Moro Islamic Liberation Front (breakaway from MNLF; Muslim): 2,900.

New People's Army (NPA; Communist): 25,500 (perhaps 16,000 armed).

ECONOMY

Currency

The unit is the peso, divided into 100 centavos.

National finance

Budget. The 1988 budget (in US$) was for expenditure (current and capital) of 7,040 million and revenue of 5,720 million. Main items of current expenditure are education 18%; defence 9.2%.

Balance of payments. The balance of payments (current account, 1987) was a deficit of $736 million.

Inflation. (1987) 3.8%.

Gross Domestic Product

Estimated total GDP US$34,580 million, per capita US$546 (overall size of economy ranking 45 in the world).

Economically active population. The total number of persons active in the economy was 23,000,000; unemployed: 11.3%.

Sector	% of workforce	ofGDP
industry	n/a	33
agriculture	47	24
services*	n/a	43

* services figure includes elements unassigned to other categories.

Energy and mineral resources

Minerals. Production: (1987 in tons/tonnes) nickel 9,381/8,510; zinc 1,243/1,128; copper 236,006/214,103; cobalt 99/90; salt 514,142/466,427; silica sand 235,239/213,407. Other minerals include chromite; cement; rock asphalt. In 1987 mining of precious metals amounted to 1.05 million troy ounces/32.7 million grams of gold and 1.6 million troy ounces/49.8 million grams of silver.

Electricity. Capacity: 6.6 million kW; production: 25,000 million kWh; 400 kWh per capita (1988).

Bioresources

Agriculture. Of the total area of 74 million acres/30 million ha, 36.3 million acres/14.7 million ha are under cultivation. Main crops are rice; maize; coconuts; sugar cane; bananas; abaca; tobacco. The Philippines is an illegal producer of cannabis for the international drug trade.

Crop production: (1987 in 1,000 tons/tonnes) rough rice 9,874/8,958; copra 2,677/2,429; coconuts 3,597/3,263; sugar 2,051/1,861; shelled corn 4,426/4,015; bananas 4,139/3,755; tobacco 64/58; abaca fibre 93/84.

Livestock numbers: (1987 in millions) buffaloes 2.86; cattle 1.74; pigs 7.03; goats 2.01; poultry 58.

Forestry. Some 40% of the land area is forest and woodland. Log production: (1987) 145.85 million ft^3/4.13 million m^3.

Fisheries. Production: (1987) 233.8 tons/2,213 million kg.

Industry and commerce

Industry. Main industries are textiles; pharmaceuticals; chemicals; wood products; food processing; electronics assembly; petroleum refining; fishing.

Commerce. Exports: (1987) US$5,600 million or 16% of GDP, including electrical equipment 19%; textiles 16%; minerals and ores 11%; farm products 10%; coconuts 10%; chemicals 5%; fish 5%; forest products 4%. Imports were US$7,100 million, including raw materials 53%; capital goods 17%; petroleum products 17%. Countries exported to were US 36%; EC countries 19%; Japan 18%; other ASEAN countries 7%. Imports came from US 25%; Japan 17%; EC countries 11%; other ASEAN countries 10%; Middle East 10%.

Trade with UK. In 1988 the Philippines imported UK goods worth £123,974,000; exports to UK totalled £223,571,000.

Tourism. (1987) 794,700 visitors.

COMMUNICATIONS

Railways

There are about 1,553 miles/2,500 km of railways (mainly confined to the islands of Luzon and Panay).

Roads

There are 100,484 miles/161,709 km of roads, of which 44,211 miles/71,148 km are concrete or bituminized.

Aviation

Aero Filipinas provides international services and Philippine Airlines Inc (Pal), provides domestic and international services (main airports are at Manila and Mactan on Cebu). Passengers: (1985) 4.6 million.

Shipping

There are 2,000 miles/3,219 km of inland waterways, but these are only accessible to shallow-draught vessels. The marine ports are Manila and Legaspir (both on the main island of Luzon); Davao and Cagayan de Oro (both on Mindanao Island, further south); Guimaras, and Iloilo (on Panay Island), and Cebu, on the island of Cebu. The merchant marine consists of 34 ships of 1,000 GRT or over. Freight loaded: (1987) 14.3 million tons/13 million tonnes; unloaded 27.2 million tons/24.7 million tonnes.

Telecommunications

There are 872,900 telephones; good international radio and submarine cable services; and adequate domestic and inter-island services. There are 7.5 million radios and 2 million televisions (1986), five main TV networks, and at least ten main radio broadcasting networks, including the Far East Broadcasting Co. Inc. based in Valenzuela, Metro Manila, with a region-wide external service.

EDUCATION AND WELFARE

Education

Schools. Public elementary education (six years) is free, whilst the majority of secondary education (four years) is private. There are also adult literacy classes, agricultural training programmes and various community programmes. There are 9,230,378 pupils in primary schools, 3,420,921 in secondary schools and 1,704,618 in further education.

Universities. In 1984 The University of the Philippines had 15,316 students.

Literacy. 88%.

Health

(1985) 51,461 doctors and (1987) 87,697 hospital beds (one per 640 people).

POLAND

Polska Rzeczpospolita
(Polish Republic)

GEOGRAPHY

Located in north-eastern central Europe, Poland covers a total area of 120,694 miles²/312,680 km², divided into 49 provinces (voivodships). Apart from the Carpathian and Sudetes mountains in the south, marking the Czechoslovakian border and rising to a maximum elevation of 8,199 ft/2,499 m at Mount Rysy, the Polish landscape is mostly low-lying (part of the North European plain) with an average elevation of less than 656 ft/200 m. North of the Carpathians, the plateau regions of Little Poland and the Middle Polish heartland are traversed by the San, Bug and Vistula Rivers. The fluvioglacial lowland terrain of the north is studded with lakes, surrounded in the north-east by harder moraine deposits to form the undulating topography of the Mazurian Lake District. The swamps and sand-dunes of the Baltic coastal plain form suitable harbours only at the mouths of the Odra and Vistula Rivers as they empty into the Baltic. The population is fairly evenly distributed reaching a maximum density in the voivodship of Warsaw and nearly 50% of the total surface area is arable. 29% of the land is covered by forests.

Climate

Continental with some oceanic influences. Severe winters alternate with hot summers. Rainfall is never excessive, falling mostly during the summer months. Average annual total: 26 in/650 mm. Warsaw: Jan. 25°F/–3.9°C. July 66°F/18.9°C. Average annual rainfall 22 in/550 mm. Gdansk: Jan. 29°F/–1.7°C. July 63°F/17.2°C. Average annual rainfall 22 in/559 mm. Szezecin: Jan. 30°F/–1.1°C. July 65°F/18.3°C. Average annual rainfall 22 in/550 mm. Wroclaw: Jan. 30°F/–1.1°C. July 66°F/18.9°C. Average annual rainfall 23 in/574 mm.

Cities and towns

Warszawa (Warsaw, capital)	1,664,700
Łódź	847,400
Kraków	744,000
Wroclaw	640,000
Poznań	578,100
Gdańsk	468,400
Szczecin	395,000
Bydgoszcz	369,500
Katowice	367,300
Lublin	329,700

Population

Total population is 38,169,841 of which 60.2% live in urban areas. Population density is 316 persons per mile²/120.8 per km². Ethnic divisions: 98.7% Polish,

0.6% Ukrainian, 0.5% Byelorussian and less than 0.05% Jewish.

Birth rate 1.6%. **Death rate** 1.0%. **Rate of population increase** (1980–87) 0.5%. **Age distribution** under 15 = 25.5%; over 65 = 9.4%. **Life expectancy** female 76; male 68; average 72.

Religion

Religious broadcasting was resumed in 1980. Church-state links are ordered and regulated in accordance with agreements of 1950, 1956 and 1972. The radical priest Jerzy Popieluszko was murdered in Oct. 1984 by secret policemen (subsequently tried, convicted and imprisoned). 95% of the population are Roman Catholic (about 75% are regular communicants); full diplomatic relations between Poland and the Holy See were re-established in July 1989 after a break of 44 years. Other Christian denominations include the Polish Autocephalous Orthodox Church, the Lutheran, Uniate, Old-Catholic Mariavite, Methodist, Baptist, United Evangelical and Seventh Day Adventist Churches. There are an estimated 12,000 Jews and 2,500 Muslims.

Language

Polish (Jezyk Polski) is a West Slavic tongue related to Czech, Slovak and East German 'Sorbian'. It belongs to the Lekhitic Slavic sub-family and has a number of district dialectal variants: Great Polish, Pomeranian, Silesian, Little Polish, Mazovian and Kashubian.

HISTORY

Neolithic cultures developed in the territory of present-day Poland from the 4th millennium BC. Celtic tribes arrived around 400 BC and Germanic tribes in the 1st century AD; in the 5th and 6th centuries the area was overrun by the Huns and the Avars. Slavs moved north from the Carpathians to settle between the Oder and Vistula rivers in the 7th and 8th centuries, designating themselves as the Polanie ('people of the open fields'). In AD 966 Prince Mieszko I of the Piast dynasty was converted to Roman Catholicism; his immediate successor Boleslaw I (r.992–1025) was the first to be crowned king. After 1138 Poland fragmented as rival branches of the Piasts fought for supremacy, but was reunified in 1320–70 under King Wladyslaw I and King Kazimierz III.

In 1386 the 11-year-old Polish Queen Jadwiga married Jagiello, Grand Prince of Lithuania. After Jadwiga's death in 1399 Jagiello and his descendants (from a later marriage) continued as rulers of the dual Polish–Lithuanian realm, although constitutional union creating the Polish–Lithuanian Rzeczpospolita ('Commonwealth' or 'Republic') was not effected until 1569 (prompted by the impending extinction of the Jagiellonian dynasty). Poland-Lithuania at its height was the largest nation in Europe, with lands as far as the Black Sea and military power enough to challenge the Teutonic Knights for control of the south-eastern Baltic coast.

Following the death in 1572 of Zygmunt II August, the last Jagiellonian king, Poland–Lithuania was progressively weakened by the constitutional arrangement whereby an elective monarchy shared power with the Sejm (parliament), by the election of foreign nobles to the throne, and by intermittent wars with neighbouring powers. The election of Duke Frederick Augustus of Saxony as king of Poland–Lithuania in 1697 made the country a principal battleground of the Great Northern War (1700–21) which pitted Saxony's ally Russia against Sweden. In 1717 Poland–Lithuania effectively became a Russian protectorate by a treaty forced on the Sejm which wholly emasculated the state apparatus.

In 1772, 1793, and 1795 Russia, Prussia, and Austria partitioned Poland-Lithuania amongst themselves, ultimately wiping it from the political map. In 1807–13 Poland was partially reincarnated during the Napoleonic wars as the Duchy of Warsaw, but after Napoleon's defeat most of the Duchy was annexed by Russia. Here in 1815 the Congress Kingdom of Poland was established within the Russian Empire, with the Tsar as king but with an autonomous government system. Unsuccessful Polish revolts occurred in 1830–31 and 1863–64, the latter prompting the dissolution of the Congress Kingdom and Russia's adoption of policies to suppress Polish culture. From the 1870s similar cultural policies were instituted in the Prussian (German) partition; only in the Austrian partition did Poles continue to enjoy political autonomy and cultural freedom.

An independent Poland re-emerged in Oct.–Nov. 1918 upon the military collapse of Austria and Germany which ended World War I (by the time of Russia's Nov. 1917 Bolshevik revolution German and Austrian forces had already overrun Russia's Polish provinces, and these had been detached from Russia by the Mar. 1918 Treaty of Brest–Litovsk whereby the Bolsheviks withdrew from the war). Provisional governments which sprang up in several Polish regions placed themselves by 14 Nov. 1918 under the command of Marshal Jozef Pilsudski, who was proclaimed chief-of-state of the Second Polish Republic. The Treaty of Versailles (28 June 1919) fixed the frontiers with Germany, but to the east Polish military encroachments led to the outbreak of war with the Bolsheviks in Feb. 1920: between 16–23 Aug. 1920 the Poles inflicted a decisive defeat on the Bolshevik Red Army outside Warsaw, and went on to seize central Lithuania and the western areas of Byelorussia and the Ukraine, Polish possession of these territories being confirmed by the 18 Mar. 1921 Treaty of Riga.

A Constitution of 17 Mar. 1921 established a parliamentary democracy and guaranteed racial and religious tolerance (Ukrainians, Jews and other minorities made up over 30% of Poland's population). The weakness of successive coalition governments, however, prompted Pilsudski to stage a military coup on 12–15 May 1926, and thereafter he ruled Poland until his death on 12 May 1935 (first as head of government, but after 1930 without formal office); the façades of parliamentary democracy nevertheless were maintained, while stability was threatened by Ukrainian separatism, growing anti-semitism and economic crisis. Authoritarian rule was continued after Pilsudski's death by a council of generals.

Nazi Germany invaded Poland on 1 Sept. 1939, followed 17 days later by the Soviet Union (a Nazi–Soviet non-aggression pact signed on 23 Aug. had included secret protocols on the partition of Poland and the rest of Eastern Europe; Polish–Soviet and Polish–German non-aggression pacts of 1932 and 1934 were summarily abrogated). Great Britain and France stood by guarantees of support to Poland, on 3 Sept. declaring war on Germany. Much of western Poland was incorporated into the German Reich, the population being either deported to Germany as forced labour or despatched to the unincorporated Nazi-occupied area, known as the General Gouvernement. Here repression was extreme, with arbitrary mass executions, starvation rations for the population, and the extermination in concentration camps of over 90% of Poland's Jewish community (some 3.5 million people). The Soviet Union annexed eastern Poland, and in the nearly two years until the Nazis invaded in June 1941 over one million Poles were deported eastward (including over 14,000 Polish officers, of whom the remains of 4,321 were discovered in Apr. 1943 in mass graves at Katyn near Smolensk). 20% of Poland's population, some six million people, perished during World War II.

The Polish government under Gen. Wladyslaw Sikorski moved to London (Sikorski died in an air crash at Gibraltar on 4 July 1943, being succeeded as premier by Stanislaw Mikolajczyk). At the end of 1943 Stalin ordered the formation of a rival communist Polish government-in-exile: on 21 July 1944 this set up a Polish Committee of National Liberation, which on 31 Dec. was reorganized as a provisional government at Lublin. The Soviet Red Army liberated Warsaw on 17 Jan. 1945 (although close to the city since July 1944 the Red Army had refrained from coming to its aid during the 63-day Warsaw uprising of Aug.–Oct. 1944, ordered by the London-based Polish government-in-exile, in which some 200,000 inhabitants died). In early July 1945 a Polish Government of National Unity dominated by the communist Polish Workers' Party (PPR) was established in Warsaw with Boleslaw Bierut as acting president, and recognized by Great Britain and the US.

At the Teheran Conference in Nov.–Dec. 1943, Churchill and Roosevelt had agreed, without consulting the Poles, to Stalin's territorial claims to eastern Poland (an area of 178,220 km^2); at the postwar Potsdam conference on 2 Aug. 1945 Poland received in compensation former German lands to the west and north-east (an area of 101,200 km^2). In effect Poland was moved 250 km westward, keeping barely half of its prewar territory. Poland's right to the German territories was recognized by the German Democratic Republic in June 1950, but by the Federal Republic of Germany only in Dec. 1970.

In the immediate postwar period opposition to the communists was ruthlessly suppressed. In elections on 19 Jan. 1947 the PPR and its allies (the Socialists, the Democratic Party and the Peasant Party) won an overwhelming parliamentary majority as a result of vote rigging and coercion, and the new Sejm elected Bierut as president. Shortly afterwards opposition parties were dissolved (opposition leaders, including Mikolajczyk, fled the country). In 1949 the PPR and the Socialists merged to become the Polish United Workers' Party (PZPR). A period of Stalinism ensued: a purge of elements considered hostile to Soviet control extended in 1948 to the PPR general secretary Wladyslaw Gomulka, who was replaced by Bierut, stripped of party membership and imprisoned. Nationalization of industry and collectivization of agriculture began in the late 1940s.

In June 1956 workers in Poznan staged strikes and demonstrations to demand better living standards and political freedoms. Although the protest was crushed by troops it led to major changes in the political leadership, despite a threatened Soviet military intervention, Gomulka being elected PZPR first secretary on 21 Oct. (Bierut had died in March). Subsequently there was limited economic and political liberalization (compulsory collectivization of agriculture was abandoned and greater religious and intellectual freedom was tolerated); relations with the Soviet Union were 'normalized' by the withdrawal of Soviet 'advisers' from the army and government apparatus. In the following year, however, the leadership under Gomulka reverted to conservatism. In Aug. 1968 Gomulka ordered Polish participation in the Warsaw Pact invasion of Czechoslovakia. Gomulka was ousted on 20 Dec. 1970 in the wake of the violent suppression of riots a week earlier in the Baltic ports over price rises. His successor, Edward Gierek, embarked on ambitious industrial development financed by heavy foreign borrowing, but by the mid-1970s worldwide economic recession had undermined Gierek's plans for export-led growth. Price rises again led to strikes in June 1976.

National euphoria surrounded the election of the Polish Cardinal Karol Wojtyla as Pope John Paul II on 16 Oct. 1978. He made a triumphant return to his homeland in June 1979.

A two-month strike wave in the Baltic ports and Silesian coalfields in the summer of 1980 forced the government on 31 Aug. to concede the 'Gdańsk accords' allowing workers to form free trade unions and to strike. On 22 Sept. 1980 the independent Solidarity trade union was formed under Lech Walesa (a Gdańsk shipyard electrician and a chief negotiator of the 'Gdańsk accords'); it claimed a membership of up to 10 million. The PZPR and government were in chaos: on 6 Sept. Gierek was replaced as PZPR leader by Stanislaw Kania, who was in turn replaced on 19 Oct. 1981 by Gen. Wojciech Jaruzelski (premier since Feb. 1981). There was persistent industrial unrest during 1981, and radicals came to dominate the Solidarity leadership. On 12 Dec. 1981 Solidarity's national commission voted to call a national referendum on establishing an interim government and holding free elections. This prompted Jaruzelski on 13 Dec. to declare martial law, ban strikes, suspend all trade unions and arrest Solidarity's leaders, including Walesa (he was detained for 11 months). Western countries imposed sanctions which compounded Poland's economic problems.

Solidarity was outlawed on 8 Oct. 1982, but continued underground. Martial law was suspended on 30 Dec. 1982 and lifted formally on 22 July 1983. Subsequent government efforts to dispel public apathy and mistrust (including the release of all political prisoners in 1986, and a referendum on reforms on 29 Nov. 1987) were largely unsuccessful. Economic austerity measures introduced in 1988 caused strike waves in April-May and August, the latter prompting negotiations between Interior Minister Czeslaw Kiszczak and Walesa in August-September resulting in the promise of round-table talks on resolving Poland's economic and social crises. These convened in Feb. 1989. The resulting package of agreements unveiled in April included Solidarity's relegalization, a market economy, and changes to the constitution and legal system which created a bicameral parliamentary system with more democratic elections, an executive presidency, freedom of association, media access for the opposition, and a more independent judiciary. The new National Assembly was elected in June: contests for the seats in the Senate (upper house) were completely free, and all but one were won by Solidarity candidates; in the Sejm (lower house) elections contests for 65% of the seats were restricted to candidates from the PZPR and from its traditional coalition partners the United Peasants' Party (ZSL) and the Democratic Party (SD), or from three lay Roman Catholic groups, while the remainder were contested by opposition or independent candidates and were all won by Solidarity. In July the new National Assembly elected Jaruzelski to the new presidency: he was unopposed, but won by the narrowest of margins. Efforts to constitute a new PZPR-led coalition government collapsed when the ZSL and SD unexpectedly entered rival negotiations with Solidarity. In late Aug. Solidarity's Tadeusz Mazowiecki was elected Prime Minister, and three weeks later he formed a coalition government dominated by Solidarity but including members not just of the ZSL and SD but also the PZPR.

At the end of 1989 the National Assembly changed the country's name from the Polish People's Republic (in use since 1947) to the Polish Republic.

CONSTITUTION AND GOVERNMENT

Executive and legislature

The constitutional amendments of Apr. 1989 created the office of executive state president, elected (for the first time on 19 July 1989) for a six-year term by the National Assembly, a new bicameral legislature in which both houses sit for simultaneous four-year terms. The 460-seat Sejm (the former unicameral legislature) became the lower house, with a new 100-seat Senate as the upper house. Direct elections for the two houses took place in June 1989. 65% of the Sejm seats were restricted to candidates from the ruling Polish United Workers' Party and its traditional coalition partners the United Peasants' Party and the Democratic Party, or from three lay Roman Catholic organizations; the remaining 35% were open to be contested by candidates from opposition or independent groups (and were all won by the Solidarity Citizens' Committee). The Senate seats, all openly contested, were won (with only one exception) by Solidarity candidates. The Sejm elects the prime minister, who must secure its endorsement for the composition of the Council of Ministers.

Present government

President Gen. Wojciech Jaruzelski

Chairman of the Council of Ministers (Prime Minister) Tadeusz Mazowiecki

Other Principal Members of Council of Ministers Leszek Balcerowicz (Deputy Chairman; Finance); Prof. Czeslaw Janicki (Deputy Chairman; Agriculture, Forestry and Food Economy); Prof. Jan Stanislaw Janowski (Deputy Chairman; Minister-Head of the Office for Advancement and Applications of Science and Technology); Lt.-Gen. Czeslaw Kiszczak (Deputy Chairman; Internal Affairs); Jacek Ambroziak (Minister-Head of the Office of the Council of Ministers); Aleksander Bentkowski (Justice); Gen. Florian Siwicki (National Defence); Prof. Krzystof Skubiszewski (Foreign Affairs); Marcin Swiecicki (Foreign Economic Co-operation); Tadeusz Syryjczyk (Industry).

Justice

There is a Supreme Court, whose judges are elected for a term of five years by the president in consultation with a National Judicial Council. There are district and special courts. The office of the prosecutor general, appointed by the president, is separate from the judiciary. An ombudsman's office was established in 1987. The death penalty is in force. There were at least 11 executions between 1985 and mid-1988. Offences were murder.

National symbols

Flag. Two horizontal stripes, white over red.

Festivals. 1 May (Labour Day); 9 May (Victory Day); 22 July (Polish National Day).

Vehicle registration plate. PL.

INTERNATIONAL RELATIONS

Affiliations

Warsaw Pact; Comecon.

Defence

Total Armed Forces: 406,000 (231,000 conscripts). Terms of service: Army, international security forces, Air Force two years; Navy, special service, afloat three years, ashore two years.

Army: 230,000; 3,950 main battle tanks (T-34/-54/-55/-72); 100 light tanks (PT-76).

Navy: 19,000; four submarines (Soviet Kilo and Whiskey) and two principal surface combatants: one destroyer (Soviet Kashin); one frigate. 24 patrol and coastal combatants.

Naval Aviation: 2,300; 45 combat aircraft (MiG-17); 15 armed helicopters.

Air Force: 92,000; 625 combat aircraft (chiefly MiG-21/U, MiG-23MF, Su-7B/7U, Su-20/-22).

ECONOMY

Currency

The unit is the zloty, divided into 100 groszy.

National finance

Budget. The 1988 budget (in US$) was for expenditure (current and capital) of 24,000 million and revenue of 23,000 million.

Balance of payments. The balance of payments (current account, 1987) was a deficit of $578 million.

Inflation. (Jan 1989) 74%.

Gross Domestic Product

Estimated total GDP US$276,300 million (GNP), per capita US$7,280 (overall size of economy ranking 12 in the world).

Economically active population. The total number of persons active in the economy was 18,630,000. Some 30% work in agriculture.

Energy and mineral resources

Oil and gas. Crude oil production: (1988) 154,322 tons/140,000 tonnes. Natural gas production: (1987) 202,879 ft^3/5,745 m^3.

Minerals. Large coal (approximately 132,276 million tons/120,000 million tonnes) and sulphur reserves; also reserves of copper; silver; lead; salt. Production: (1987 in million tons/tonnes) coal 213/193; brown coal 81/73.2; copper ore (1985) 32/29.4; silver 916/831.

Electricity. Capacity: 31.38 million kW; production: 129,400 million kWh; 3,410 kWh per capita (1988).

Bioresources

Agriculture. There are 35.8 million acres/14.5 million ha of arable land. About 75% of agricultural production comes from the private sector and the rest from state farms. Main crops are grain; sugar beet; oilseed; potatoes. Poland is an exporter of livestock products and sugar.

Crop production: (1987 in 1,000 tons/tonnes) wheat 8,754/7,942; rye 7,513/6,816; barley 4,778/4,335; oats 2,676/2,428; potatoes 39,961/36,252; sugar beet 15,418/13,987.

Livestock numbers: (1987 in millions) cattle 10.52; pigs 18.54; sheep 4.73; horses 1.14; poultry 65.

Forestry. 29% of land area is forest and woodland. Timber production: (1987) 865.2million ft^3/24.5 million m^3.

Fisheries. Catch: (1985) 717,156 tons/650,600 tonnes.

Industry and commerce

Industry. Main industries are machine building; iron and steel; extractive industries; chemicals; shipbuilding; food processing; glass; beverages; textiles.

Commerce. Exports: (1987) US$26,000 million or 9% of GDP, including machinery and equipment 49%; fuels, minerals and metals 23%; manufactured consumer goods 13%; agricultural and forestry products 10%. Imports were US$24,300 million, including machinery and equipment 33%; fuels, minerals and metals 38%; manufactured consumer goods 9%; agricultural and forestry products 13%. Countries exported to were USSR 25%; West Germany 11%; Czechoslovakia 6%. Imports came from USSR 27%; West Germany 12%; Czechoslovakia 6%.

Trade with UK. Poland imported UK goods worth £175,685,000; exports to UK totalled £328,013,000.

Tourism. (1987) 4,776 million visitors.

COMMUNICATIONS

Railways

There are 16,683 miles/26,848 km of railways, of which 5,873 miles/9,452 km are electrified.

Roads

There are 95,694 miles/154,000 km of roads, most of which are concrete or bituminized.

Aviation

Polskie Linie Lotnicze-LOT provides domestic and international services (main airport is at Warsaw). Passengers: (1987) 1.9 million.

Shipping

There are 2,479 miles/3,989 km of navigable rivers and canals. The principal inland ports are Gliwice on Kanal Gliwice, Wroclaw on the Oder and Warsaw on the Vistula. The main marine ports are Szczecin, Swinoujscie, Gdańsk and Gdynia. The merchant marine consists of 240 ships of 1,000 GRT or over. Freight loaded: (1987) 34.8 million tons/31.6 million tonnes; unloaded: 19.2 million tons/17.4 million tonnes.

Telecommunications

There are some 4.6 million telephones in use, 10.8 million radios and 9.9 million televisions (1987). Polish Radio and Television runs four programmes on home service radio, external services in 12 languages, and two TV channels.

EDUCATION AND WELFARE

Education

Schools. Education is free and compulsory for children between seven and 15 years with free secondary education in either general or vocational schools. There are 26,289 kindergartens with 1.4 million pupils and 88,000 teachers (one per 15 pupils); 18,129 primary schools with 5.13 million pupils and 277,000 teachers (one per 18 pupils); 1,138 secondary schools with 422,000 pupils and 22,000 teachers (one per 19 pupils); 9,421 vocational schools with 1.66 million pupils and 82,000 teachers (one per 20 pupils).

Universities. There are 11 universities, 18 polytechnics and 11 medical schools.

Literacy. 98%.

Health

There are 710 hospitals with 249,000 beds (one per 153 people) and 77,300 doctors (one per 493 people). There are also some 10,000 health centres and dispensaries.

PORTUGAL
República Portuguesa
(Portuguese Republic)

GEOGRAPHY

Located in south-western Europe on the Atlantic coast of the Iberian peninsula, mainland Portugal covers an area of 34,308 miles^2/88,880 km^2. In addition, the republic includes two semi-autonomous archipelagos in the Atlantic, the Azores (921 miles^2/ 2,387 km^2) and the Madeira Islands (314 miles^2/ 813 km^2). Most of Portugal's highland lies to the north of the Rio Tejo which bisects the country east – south-west. In the far north, the Spanish Galician mountains traverse the Portuguese border rising to 5,906 ft/1,800 m, while to the south, the Serra da Estrela climbs to a maximum elevation of 6,539 ft/ 1,993 m. The northern (Spanish) meseta slopes towards the coastal lowlands drained by the River Douro, and to the south of the Rio Tejo, the gently undulating terrain seldom exceeds 984 ft/300 m above sea level. In general, the northern part of the country is more populous than the southern half, although both north-west (Minho) and south (Algarve) regions experience serious overcrowding. The Azores lie in a seismically active zone. 32% of the land surface is arable and 40% is forested.

Climate

Cool, Atlantic maritime in the north; warmer Mediterranean type in the south. From June to August, rainfall dwindles to less than 5% of the annual total. The northern regions receive the bulk of the winter precipitation and are subject to continental influences that produce considerable temperature variation. Lisbon: Jan 52° F/11°C. July 72°F/22°C. Average annual rainfall 27 in/686 mm. Porto: Jan 48°F/8.9°C. July 67°F/19.4°C. Average annual rainfall 45 in/1,151 mm.

Cities and Towns

Lisbon (capital)	808,000
Oporto	327,000
Amadora	96,000
Setúbal	78,000
Coímbra	75,000

Population

Total population is 10,459,701 of which 29.6% live in urban areas. Population density is 305 persons per mile^2/111.6 per km^2. Homogeneous Mediterranean ethnic identity. Black African immigrants, repatriating in the wake of decolonization, number less than 100,000.

Birth rate 1.5%. **Death rate**: 0.9%. **Rate of population increase** (1980–87) 0.7%. **Age distribution** under 15 = 23.5%; over 65 = 12.0%. **Life expectancy** female 77; male 70; average 73.

The Azores Nine islands; 1,200–1,600 km west of Lisbon. Population: (1986 est.) 253,500 (243,410 at last census, 1981). Half the total population lives on São Miguel.

Madeira Islands Two main islands and two uninhabited clusters of islets. Population: (1986 est.) 269,500 (252,844 at last census, 1981).

Macao Portuguese overseas territory. A peninsula enclave (6.05 km^2) on the southern China mainland linked to the islands of Taipa (3.78 km^2) and Coloane (7.09 km^2). Population: 261,680 at last census (1981); 426,400 (1986 est.).

Religion

Christianity. 97% Roman Catholic, 1% Protestant. There are an estimated 15,000 Muslims in Portugal.

Language

Portuguese (Portugues), a Romance language. Dialectal variations comprise Northern Portuguese (Galician), Central Portuguese, Southern Portuguese and Insular Portuguese (Brazilian and Madeiran idioms).

HISTORY

Conquered by the Carthaginians (3rd century BC), the ancient Lusitanians of Portugal came under Roman rule in the 2nd century BC. Invasion by Germanic tribes led to the creation of a Swabian kingdom (AD 410), which was later absorbed by Visigoth Spain (585) and Christianized. Conquest by the Muslim Moors (712–16) resulted in rule by the Ommayad caliphs, although Viking raids from the mid-9th century weakened Moorish authority and opened the way for Christian reconquest.

After Henry of Burgundy had become the first Count of Portugal (1095) under the king of León, Count Alfonso established Portugal's independence (1128) and was declared king after defeating the Moors at Ovrique (1139). The capture of Lisbon (1147) led to papal recognition of the Portuguese monarchy (1179) and the final defeat of the Moors by Alfonso III (1249). Wars with Castile caused Ferdinand I (r.1367–83) to conclude an alliance with England (1373), which survived through the centuries. The end of the Burgundian line (1383) provoked a Spanish claim to the crown, but Ferdinand's half-brother John of Aviz (r.1385–1433), founded a new dynasty which presided over a golden age of exploration and expansion. From c.1450 and in particular under the reign of Manoel I (r.1495–1521), Portugal built an empire in Africa, India, the Far East, and the Americas so that by the early 16th century Portugal had become a major maritime power. Bartolomeu Dias discovered the sea route to India when he rounded the Cape of Good Hope in 1487–88, Vasco da Gama opened up this route to trade in two voyages starting in 1498 and 1502, and Pedro lvares Cabral claimed Brazil for Portugal in 1500. A series of papal decrees dividing the New World territories between the Spanish and Portuguese was consolidated in the Treaty of Tordesillas (1494) while the Treaty of Zaragoza (1529) confirmed the Moluccas in the Pacific as Portuguese.

With the end of the Aviz line (1580), Portugal was seized by Philip II of Spain and went into decline. Many of its Indian and Far East possessions fell to England or the Netherlands in their wars with Spain, a process which continued after Portugal had reasserted its independence (1640) under John IV (r.1640–56) of the house of Braganza. Spain's formal recognition of a separate Portugal in the Treaty of Lisbon (1668) was followed by the imposition of absolute monarchy by John V (r.1706–50). Portugal remained a backwater in the 18th century, although the great Lisbon earthquake (1755) was much discussed by philosophers as evidence of the non-existence of God. Allied with Britain in the Napoleonic wars, Portugal was invaded by French forces (1807) and the royal family fled to Brazil. In the ensuing Peninsular War (1809–14) British troops led by Sir Arthur Wellesley (later Duke of Wellington) eventually expelled the French from Portugal in 1811 and from Spain in 1814. John VI (r.1816–26) remained in Brazil, however, until he was forced out (1821) and succeeded there by his son Pedro, who declared Brazil independent (1822). Back in Portugal, John first accepted, then changed, a liberal constitution (1822–23), initiating a century of struggle between liberals and conservatives. The abolition of slavery in the colonies (1869) did nothing to alleviate acute poverty in Portugal, where republicanism became a powerful force and a Socialist Party (PS) was formed (1875).

The assassination of King Carlos (r.1889–1908) increased instability, which escalated into insurrection in Lisbon in 1910. Manuel II was forced to flee and a Republic was declared (5 Oct. 1910), Manuel de Arriagas being elected as its first president (1911). Portuguese support for Britain in World War I caused Germany to declare war on Portugal (1916), whose losses on the western front were heavy. From 1917 Portugal experienced renewed turmoil, as disappointed hopes of reform under the Republic gave rise to revolutionary coups, military counter-coups and abortive royalist uprisings. Stability returned with the election to the presidency of Gen. António Carmona (1928), who named António de Oliveira Salazar (1889–1970) as finance minister. Such was Salazar's firm impact that in 1932 he became prime minister with dictatorial powers to implement his fascist Estado Novo (New State) programme. Social reforms and public works were implemented, and opposition to his National Union (founded 1930) was suppressed. Salazar kept Portugal out of World War II, but the Anglo-Portuguese alliance ensured that the Royal Air Force had use of bases in the Azores (from 1943). Limited post-war liberalization allowed the formation of opposition parties, although severe restrictions, enforced by the PIDE secret police, prevented them from making an electoral challenge to the regime. Portugal became a founder member of NATO (1949) and was admitted to the UN (1955). Although Portuguese Goa was seized by Indian troops (1961), the Salazar regime insisted that the African colonies were 'inalienable' and engaged in increasingly costly wars against emerging nationalist movements.

Salazar finally vacated the premiership in 1968 (after suffering a stroke) and was succeeded by Marcello Caetano. He sought to broaden the regime's appeal by reorganizing the ruling party as the Popular National Action (1970) and relaxing curbs on opposition parties. However, his continuation of essentially authoritarian government and of the African wars attracted growing criticism within the military, culminating in a bloodless coup on 25 Apr. 1974 by leftist officers, who installed a military-dominated government committed to building socialism. Radical left-wing officers gained the ascendant in 1975, but an attempted Communist takeover was foiled by moderates in co-operation with the PS leader, Mário Soares. In Assembly elections (Apr. 1976), held under a new constitution enshrining socialist goals and institutionalizing the role of the armed forces, the PS was confirmed as the strongest party. It then supported the successful presidential candidature of Gen. António Ramalho Eanes (June 1976), who appointed Soares prime minister of a minority PS government. Meanwhile, the new regime had recognized the independence of Guinea-Bissau, Mozambique, Cape Verde, São Tomé and Príncipe, and Angola (1974–75) and had been powerless to prevent Indonesia's seizure of East Timor (1975–76). Following Soares's resignation (1978), the PS was outvoted in the 1979 and 1980 elections by the centre-right, which provided four of the five prime ministers appointed in 1978–80, one of whom, Francisco Sá Carneiro of the (conservative) Social Democratic Party (PSD), died in an air crash (1980).

Re-elected in Dec. 1980, Pres. Eanes appointed a coalition headed by Francisco Pinto Balsemão (PSD), who secured the enactment of constitutional amendments restoring full civilian government (1982). The 1983 elections restored the PS as the largest Assembly party, enabling Soares to form a coalition with the PSD. Beset by economic and internal security problems, it resigned in June 1985, one day after the signature of Portugal's treaty of accession to the European Communities from 1 Jan. 1986 (together with Spain). On becoming the largest party in the Oct. 1985 elections, the PSD formed a minority government under Aníbal Cavaço Silva; but in the 1986 presidential election Soares secured a narrow second-round victory, thus becoming Portugal's first civilian head of state for 60 years. Having contracted with China (Mar. 1987) that Portuguese Macao would revert to Chinese rule in 1999, in further elections (July 1987) Cavaco Silva led the PSD to an overall Assembly majority, the first since the 1974 revolution. Amendments to the constitution agreed between the PSD and PS (Oct. 1988) and approved by parliament in June 1989 included deletion of its reference to socialism being a state goal. In Nov. 1988 Portugal signed, with Spain, an accession protocol to become a member of the WEU. A poor showing by the PSD in municipal elections in December 1989 led Cavaço Silva to undertake a major reorganization of his cabinet in Jan. 1990.

CONSTITUTION AND GOVERNMENT

Executive and legislature

The head of state is the president, elected by universal adult suffrage for a five-year term. The prime minister is head of government, appointed by the president but responsible to the legislature. The unicameral 250-member assembly of the republic is elected by universal adult suffrage for up to four years under a system of proportional representation; last elections 19 July 1987.

Present government

President Dr Mário Soares

Prime Minister Prof. Aníbal Cavaço Silva

Other Principal Ministers Carlos Brito (Defence); Fernando Nogueira (Minister of State; Justice); Antonio Capucho (Parliamentary Affairs); Miguel Beleza (Finance); Prof. Luis Valente de Oliveira (Planning and Territorial Administration); Manuel Periera (Interior); João de Deus Pinheiro (Foreign Affairs).

Justice

The Republic of Portugal is divided for civil (including commercial) and penal cases (including labour, military, administrative and fiscal) into 217 comarcas; in every comarca there is at least one court or tribunal. The death penalty was abolished in 1976.

Prisons. There are 8,222 prisoners.

National symbols

Flag. Two vertical stripes, green in the hoist and red in the fly. The shield and armillary sphere from the state coat of arms are placed on the dividing line.

Festivals. 7 Feb. (Carnival); 25 Apr. (Liberty Day); 1 May (Labour Day); 10 June (Portugal Day); 5 Oct. (Proclamation of the Republic); 1 Dec. (Restoration of Independence).

Vehicle registration plate. P.

INTERNATIONAL RELATIONS

Affiliations

Nato; WEU; OECD; EC; Council of Europe.

Defence

Total Armed Forces: 73,000 (44,800 conscripts). Terms of service: Army 16 months; Navy 24 months; Air Force 21–24 months. Reserves: 190,000 (obligation: men to 45, officers to 70).

Army: 44,000; 66 main battle tanks (M-48A5).

Navy: 16,300; three submarines (Fr Daphne); 15 frigates; 20 patrol and coastal combatants.

Marines: 2,800.

Air Force: 13,600; 89 combat aircraft (mainly A-7, A-7P, G-91, G-91R4/T3).

Para-military: National Republican Guard: 17,000.

ECONOMY

Currency

The unit is the escudo, divided into 100 centavos.

National finance

Budget. The 1987 budget (in US$) was for expenditure (current and capital) of 11,100 million and revenue of 8,000 million.

Balance of payments. The balance of payments (current account, 1988) was a deficit of $580 million.

Inflation. 12.7% (12 months to Sept. 1989).

Gross Domestic Product

Estimated total GDP US$34,290 million, per capita US$3,250 (overall size of economy ranking 47 in the world). Growth rate (1988) 4.1%.

Economically active population. The total number of persons active in the economy was 4,580,000; unemployed: 5.8% (1988).

Sector	% of workforce	% of GDP
industry	34	40
agriculture	22	9
services*	44	51

* services figure includes elements unassigned to other categories.

Energy and mineral resources

Minerals. Considerable mineral reserves. Production: (1985 in tons/tonnes) coal 257,292/233,414; cupriferous pyrites 391,889/355,519; kaolin 114,700/104,055; gold (refined) 0.252/0.229; uranium 143/130; wolframite 3,282/2,977. Other minerals are tungsten; iron ore; marble.

Electricity. Capacity: 6.59 million kW; production: 15,555 million kWh; 1,500 kWh per capita (1988).

Bioresources

Agriculture. Generally underdeveloped. Main crops are grains; potatoes; olives; grapes for wine (1986 wine production: 4,317 million pints/7.6 million hectolitres. Crop production: (1986 1,000 tons/tonnes) wheat 551/500; maize 681/618; oats 169/153; barley 99/90; rye 110/100; rice 164/149; dried beans 49/44; potatoes 1,176/1,067.

Livestock numbers: (1987) cattle 1.08 million; sheep 5.15 million; pigs 2.92 million; goats 745,000; asses 175,000; mules 90,000; horses 29,000.

Forestry. 7.4 million acres/3 million ha of forest, mainly pine; cork oak; other oak; eucalyptus; chestnut. Portugal is the world's leading producer of cork oak, production: (1985) 116,340 tons/105,543 tonnes.

Fisheries. The fishing industry is important, especially sardines. Sardine catch: (1986) 113,958 tons/103,382 tonnes.

Industry and commerce

Industry. Main industries are textiles and footwear; wood pulp; paper and cork; metalworking; oil refining; chemicals; fish canning; wine; tourism.

Commerce. Exports: (1987) US$9,200 million or 27% of GDP, including cotton textiles; cork and cork products; canned fish; wine; timber and timber products; resin; machinery; appliances. Imports were US$13,400 million, including petroleum; cotton; foodgrains; industrial machinery; iron and steel; chemicals. Countries exported to were EC countries 71%; other developed countries 14%; US 7%. Imports came from EC countries 64%; other developed countries 14%; less developed countries 17%; US 5%.

Trade with UK. In 1988 Portugal imported UK goods worth £810,537,000; exports to UK totalled £928,015,000.

Tourism. (1986) 13,056,871 visitors.

COMMUNICATIONS

Railways

There are 2,229 miles/3,588 km of railways, of which 270 miles/434 km are electrified.

Roads

There are about 32,312 miles/52,000 km of roads (11,731 miles/18,878 km of national roads).

Aviation

TAP – Air Portugal provides international services and LAR – Ligacoes Aéreas Regionais, SA provides domestic services (main airports are at Lisbon, Porto and Faro).

Shipping

There are 509 miles/820 km of navigable inland waterways, but these are relatively unimportant to the economy. The marine ports are Leixoes, Lisbon, Oporto, Puerto das Vellas, Setubal, Sines and Ponta Delgada (in the Azores). There are 34 minor ports. The merchant marine consists of 53 ships of 1,000 GRT or over. Freight loaded: (1985) over 13.2 million tons/12 million tonnes; unloaded: over 26.5 million tons/24 million tonnes.

Telecommunications

There are 2.2 million telephones and the telecommunications system is adequate. There are 2.1 million radios and 1.6 million televisions (1988). Nationalized radio stations were merged together in 1975 to form RDP, with four home service programmes and an international service, in addition to which there are a number of private radio stations including the Catholic RR. The state RTP operates two TV channels, TV being a government monopoly.

EDUCATION AND WELFARE

Education

Schools. Compulsory education. In 1985 there were 10,448 state primary schools with 837,760 pupils and 40,773 teachers (one per 20 pupils); 668 private elementary schools with 61,611 pupils and 2,882 teachers (one per 21 pupils); 1,918 basic preparatory schools with 375,516 pupils and 31,248 teachers (one per 12 pupils); 499 secondary schools with 604,727 pupils and 45,559 teachers (one per 13 pupils).

Universities. There are 13 universities of which eight are in Lisbon.

Literacy. 83%.

Health

(1986) 227 hospitals, 363 health centres and 25,696 doctors (one per 407 people).

PUERTO RICO

GEOGRAPHY

The Commonwealth of Puerto Rico is an island covering 3,514 miles^2/9,104 km^2 in the Caribbean Sea. The terrain is mostly mountainous, with a coastal plain belt in the north. The capital is San Juan.

Climate

Tropical marine, with little seasonal variation.

Population

Total population (1989 est.) 3,300,707.
Birth rate 1.9%. **Death rate** 0.7%. **Rate of population increase** 0.2%. **Life expectancy** female 77; male 69.

Religion

Christianity, mostly Roman Catholic.

Language

Spanish (official); English is widely spoken.

HISTORY

The earliest inhabitants of Puerto Rico were Arawak Indians who reached the island about AD 800. The first European discoverers of the island were with Columbus's expedition of 1493. The Spanish settled on the island in 1508, but raids from Caribs, European adventurers and pirates prevented the colony from growing quickly. African slaves were imported as labour for sugar and coffee plantations and for cattle ranches. The island prospered during the 18th century as its population was swelled by the arrival of refugees from neighbouring territories. During the 19th century there were demands for greater integration with Spain and also for independence, leading to failed insurrection in 1863. Slavery was abolished in 1872 and during the latter part of the 19th century many Puerto Ricans favoured greater autonomy from Spain. A new autonomous government structure was granted in 1897 but the outbreak of the Spanish–American war in 1898 prevented its implementation.

American troops invaded the island in May 1898 and in December the island was ceded to the US. It became an unincorporated territory of the US and US citizenship was granted to Puerto Ricans in 1917. Many islanders, however, wanted greater internal self-government and economic and social reforms, a policy advocated by the Partido Popular Democratico (PPD). The PPD gained a majority in the Senate in elections in 1940 and the first elections to the post of Governor in 1947 were won by the PPD's leader, Luis Muñoz Marín. Puerto Rico was granted a new constitution in 1952 when it became a 'Commonwealth' in association with the US. Under the PPD administration a programme of investment and industrialization developed the island's economy and improved social conditions. In 1967 a plebiscite produced a majority in favour of commonwealth status, rather than statehood, with only a very small minority in favour of independence. The PPD remained in power until 1968 when it was defeated by the Partido Nuevo Progressista (PNP), which favours statehood. Luis A. Ferré became governor. In 1972 the PPD was returned to power with Rafael Hernández Colón elected governor. The PNP's candidate for governor, Carlos Romero Barceló, won in the 1976 elections, but in 1980 the PNP lost its majority in both houses of the Legislative Assembly, although Romero Barceló retained the governorship. Internal factionalism within the PNP led to divisions in the party over Romero Barceló's leadership. In 1984 Romero Barceló was defeated by Hernández Colón for the governorship and the PPD maintained its majority in the Assembly. Hernández Colón retained the governorship in the election held in Nov. 1988, defeating Baltasar Corrada del Rio of the PNP by a narrow margin.

CONSTITUTION AND GOVERNMENT

Puerto Rico is a commonwealth associated with the United States. It has a Constitution dating from 1952. The governor is elected by direct vote for a four-year term. There is a bicameral legislature (a senate with 27 members and a house of representatives with 51 members, all popularly elected for four-year terms).

Leader Governor Rafael Hernández Colón.

National symbols

Flag. Five equal horizontal bands of red alternating with white. A blue triangle based on the hoist side has a large white star in the centre.

National holiday. 25 July (Constitution Day).

ECONOMY

Industry has outstripped agriculture as the major sector of economic activity. US firms have invested heavily encouraged by tax incentives. Tourism is an important source of income. Pharmaceuticals, electronics, textiles and petrochemicals are important industries.

Currency

The US dollar.

COMMUNICATIONS

There is 621 miles/100 km of rural narrow gauge railway for sugar cane only; ports at San Juan, Ponce, Mayaguez and Arecibo; 33 airports, 19 with permanent surface runways; 8,552 miles/13,762 km of road. Telephone system; 69 AM, 42 FM radio stations; 24 television stations.

QATAR

Dawlat al-Qatar
(State of Qatar)

GEOGRAPHY

Situated on the eastern coast of the Arabian peninsula, the State of Qatar comprises the Qatar peninsula and several offshore islands. Bahrain lies to the north-west. The predominantly low-lying, arid and monotonous terrain rises in the west to form the Dukhan Heights, reaching 292 ft/98 m elevation. Sand desert, salt flats and barren plains, dissected by shallow wadis, occupy 95% of the 4,400 miles^2/11,400 km^2 area. 5% of the total surface area is used as pasture, and two-thirds of the population live in the capital city of Doha on the east coast.

Climate

Hot, humid (90% during the summer) desert type. Mean winter/summer temperatures of 73 and 95°F/23 and 35°C respectively. Total rainfall of no more than 3 in/75 mm, most of which falls in winter storms. Doha: Jan. 62°F/16.7°C. July 98°F/36.7°C. Average annual rainfall 2.4 in/62 mm.

Cities and towns

Doha (capital) 217,294

Population

Total population is 468,632, of which 88.0% live in urban areas. Population density is 107 persons per mile^2/36.3 per km^2. Ethnic divisions: 40% Arab (including 20–25% indigenous Qatari); 18% Pakistani; 18% Indian; 10% Iranian.

Birth rate 2.6%. **Death rate** 0.4%. **Rate of population increase** (1980–88) 5.4%. **Age distribution** under 15 = 33.9%; over 65 = 1.6%. **Life expectancy** female 72; male 68; average 70.

Religion

95% of the population are Muslim, adhering to the Wahhabi reading of Sunni Islam.

Language

Arabic is the official language spoken by the majority of the population. English is a commonly used second language.

HISTORY

In the mid-18th century a branch of the Bani Utub tribe moved from Kuwait to Qatar and established a fishing and pearling mini-state at Subarah. Qatar came under British influence in 1869 and under a treaty signed in 1916 Britain gained effective control over Qatar's foreign relations together with responsibility for security and commercial privileges. This protectorate status continued until Qatar gained independence in 1971. In 1972 a palace coup occurred when Shaikh Khalifa ibn Hamad al-Thani ousted his cousin, Shaikh Ahmad. A year before independence, Qatar promulgated a written constitution which provided for a council of ministers and an advisory council. It stipulated that the former was to be appointed by the ruler and that a majority of the advisory council be elected by the general population. To date no elections have been held and the council has become little more than a recommendatory authority being unempowered, by itself, to initiate legislation.

The al-Thanis constitute the largest ruling family in the region and members hold ten of the 15 cabinet portfolios, including defence, finance, and foreign affairs. There are no political parties. Prior to the production of oil in 1949, the population, who are largely Sunni Muslims, were one of the poorest in the region, with most livelihoods dependent upon fishing and pearling. Petroleum production and export together with the nationalization of both major oil producers, Qatar Petroleum Company and Shell Oil of Qatar, have led to the government providing considerable investment for infrastructural development. Qatar has been a member of the Gulf Cooperation Council since its inception in 1981 and is a member of the Organization of Arab Petroleum Exporting Countries and the Organization of Petroleum Exporting Countries. The historic territorial dispute with Bahrain continues over the Hawar islands, which flared up in 1986 when Qatari troops briefly occupied Fasht al-Dibal, a coral reef which was being reclaimed from the sea by Bahrain. It was later destroyed by agreement of both parties.

CONSTITUTION AND GOVERNMENT

Executive and legislature

Qatar is an absolute monarchy. The Amir is head of state, appoints the cabinet, and occupies the office of prime minister. There is also a 30-member advisory council. Qatar has no legislature or political parties.

Present government

Amir; Prime Minister Shaikh Khalifa Bin Hamad al-Thani

Heir Apparent; Minister of Defence; C.-in-C. of the Armed Forces Shaikh Hamad Bin Khalifa al-Thani

Principal Other Ministers Shaikh Abdul Aziz Bin Khalifa al-Thani (Finance and Petroleum); Shaikh Hamad Bin Jasim Bin Hamadi al-Thani (Economy and Commerce); Shaikh Abdullah Bin Khalifah al-Thani (Interior); Sayed Abdullah Bin Khalifah al-Attiya (Foreign Affairs).

Justice

The system of law is based on Islamic law and decided through Sharia courts in personal matters, but the Amir controls a legal structure allowing him substantial discretion, limited only to some extent by the development of civil codes. There is a Court of Appeal, a Labour Court, a Lower and a Higher Criminal Court, and a Civil Court. The death penalty is nominally in force. There were two executions in Oct. 1988 – the first known executions for over ten years.

National symbols

Flag. Maroon with a white stripe in the hoist separated from the brown field by nine serrations.

Vehicle registration plate. Q.

INTERNATIONAL RELATIONS

Affiliations

NAM; Arab League; ICO; OPEC; OAPEC; GCC.

Defence

Total Armed Forces: 7,000. Terms of service: voluntary.

Army: 6,000; 24 main battle tanks (AMX-30).

Navy: 700 inclusive Marine Police; 11 patrol and coastal combatants.

Air Force: 300; 23 combat aircraft (mainly Mirage F-1 and AlphaJet), some 18 armed helicopters.

ECONOMY

Currency

The unit is the riyal, divided into 100 dirhams.

National finance

Budget. The 1988 budget (in US$) was for expenditure (current and capital) of 3,400 million and revenue of 1,700 million.

Inflation. (1987) 1.6%.

Gross Domestic Product

Estimated total GDP US$5,400 million, per capita US$17,070 (overall size of economy ranking 80 in the world).

Economically active population. The total number of persons active in the economy was 104,000.

Energy and mineral resources

Oil and gas. Oil is the backbone of the economy and accounts for 90% of export earnings and more than 80% of government revenues. Oil reserves are estimated at 3,300 million barrels, and output should continue at current levels for another 25 years. Oil is responsible for Qatar having one of the world's highest GDPs per capita. Production: (1988) 16.8 million tons/15.2 million tonnes.

12% of the world's known natural gas reserves are contained in the North West Dome oilfield.

Electricity. Capacity: 1.3 million kW; production: 4.2 million kWh; 9,500 kWh per capita.

Bioresources

Agriculture. There is little land suitable for arable purposes or for permanent crops, and only 5% used as meadow or pasture.

Crop production: tomatoes; melons; aubergines; dates.

Livestock numbers: horses 1 million; camels 22,500; sheep 121,300; goats 86,500.

Forestry. There is no forest or woodland.

Fisheries. Commercial fishing is increasing in importance. The Qatar National Fishing Company has a refrigeration unit which processes some 3,307 tons/3,000 tonnes of shrimps annually.

Industry and commerce

Industry. Crude oil production and refining is the most important industry. Others include fertilizers; petrochemicals; steel; cement.

Commerce. Exports: (f.o.b. 1988 est.) US$2,200 million; oil (90%); steel; fertilizer. Major trading partners are France; West Germany; Italy; Japan; Spain. Imports: US$1,000 million (excluding military equipment) consisting mainly of foodstuffs; beverages; chemicals; machinery. Major trading partners are EC countries; Japan; Arab countries; Australia.

Trade with UK. In 1988 Qatar imported £88.9 million worth of goods from the UK and exported £3.9 million to the UK.

COMMUNICATIONS

Railways

There are no railways in Qatar.

Roads

Nearly 62.1 miles/100 km total length, of which half is hard surfaced.

Aviation

One international airport, at Doha, with permanent runway suitable for jumbo jets. Airport passengers: (1987) 962,000.

Shipping

Freight loaded (1985) 14.9 million tons/13.5 million tonnes, unloaded 2.3 million tons/2.1 million tonnes.

Telecommunications

There is a modern system centred in Doha and 110,000 telephones. There are 158,888 radios, with broadcasts in four languages by the government's Qatar Broadcasting Service, and 128,000 televisions (1988) with eight TV channels transmitted throughout the Gulf by Qatar Television.

EDUCATION AND WELFARE

Education

School population. 33,300 primary school pupils; 12,400 intermediate school pupils; 7,700 secondary school pupils.
Universities. University of Qatar has approximately 5,500 students.
Literacy. 40%.

Health

There are three hospitals with a total of approximately 1,000 beds (one per 500 people), some 600 doctors, 60 dentists and 1,500 nurses.

REUNION
Réunion

GEOGRAPHY

Réunion is an island in the Indian Ocean covering 969 miles^2/2,510 km^2. The terrain is mostly rugged and mountainous, with fertile lowlands along the coast. The capital is Saint-Denis.

Climate

Tropical. Cool and dry May-Nov., hot and rainy Nov.-Apr. Subject to periodic devastating cyclones.

Population

Total population (1989 est.) 565,548.
Birth rate 2.5%. **Death rate** 0.5%. **Rate of population increase** 1.5%.
Life expectancy female 75; male 69.

Religion

Christianity (Roman Catholic).

Language

French (official); Creole is widely used.

HISTORY

Ownership of the unpopulated 'Ile Bourbon' (Réunion) was granted by the French king to the Compagnie des Indes in 1664, ostensibly in perpetuity, although in fact the French government resumed control 100 years later. French settlers, encouraged under the Compagnie's aegis, moved over after 1715 from self-sufficient farming to cash crop production, growing coffee and food for neighbouring Mauritius. For their plantations they brought in quantities of slaves, particularly from Madagascar, and in the late 18th century the plantation owners backed an independence movement to resist the French revolutionary regime's attempt to enforce abolition of slavery.

Briefly occupied by the British from 1810 but restored to French control in 1814, Réunion's economy was switched over primarily to sugar-growing, with indentured labourers brought over in their thousands from India after 1861 to replace Black slave labour. A French colony until 1946, it then became a French overseas department, but it was not in practice integrated with metropolitan France, and from 1959 onwards the influential local communist party has campaigned for a change of status to autonomy. Communists dominate the Anti-Colonialist Front for the Self-Determination of Réunion (FRACPAR, or FRA), formed in 1978. A Regional Council was elected for the first time in Feb. 1983.

CONSTITUTION AND GOVERNMENT

Réunion is an overseas department of France, and as such has the French Constitution dating from Sept. 1958. It is administered by a prefect appointed by the French minister of the interior, assisted by a secretary general and an elected 36-member general council. In 1974 France created an elected 45-member regional assembly to coordinate economic and social development policies.
Leader Jean Anciaux, Commissioner of the Republic.

National symbols

Flag. The flag of France.
National holiday. 14 July (Bastille Day).

ECONOMY

Traditionally based on agriculture, especially sugar cane (the major export). The tourist industry is being developed in response to high unemployment. The economy is heavily dependent on financial aid from France.

Currency

The French franc.

COMMUNICATIONS

There is a port at Pointe des Galets; two airports, both with permanent surface runways; 1,740 miles/2,800 km of road. There is a telephone system; three AM and 13 FM radio stations; two TV stations; one Indian Ocean satellite station.

ROMANIA
România

GEOGRAPHY

Located in south-east Europe, Romania covers a total area of 91,675 miles²/237,500 km² divided into 41 counties. Approximately 30% of the land area is occupied by the Carpathian Mountains (Carpatii Orientali, Carpatii Occidentali and Carpatii Meridionali) which divide the central Transylvanian tablelands from Old Romania (Moldavia and Walachia in the east and south). The highest peak rises in the Meridionali (Southern Carpathians) to 8,360 ft/2,548 m at Mount Negoiul. On the periphery of the sickle-shaped Carpathian range, the fertile sub-Carpathians provide the focus for Romanian viticulture. Further south, the rich, well cultivated Baragan and Oltenian Plains are dissected by many rivers including the Jiu, Olf and Teleorman, all tributaries of the Danube, forming the southern (Bulgarian) frontier. The most densely populated rural areas are to be found in North Moldavia. An estimated 3,500 glaciated lakes or lagoons are concentrated to the south-east in the Danube delta region. 43% of the land is arable and 28% is forested (including the wooded passes of the Eastern Carpathians).

Climate

Continental, with cool, wet Carpathian summers and warmer, drier weather elsewhere at the same time with periodic drought conditions on the Northern and Eastern Plains. Winter weather can be severe (milder on the Black Sea Coast) with low temperatures and abundant snowfall. Average annual temperatures range from 45°F/7°C in the north to 52°F/11°C further south and rainfall increases south-east – north-west from 16 in/400 mm to 54 in/1,375 mm in the Carpathians. Bucharest: Jan 27°F/–2.7°C. July 74°F/23.5°C. Average annual rainfall 22.8 in/579 mm. Constanta: Jan 31°F/–0.6°C. July 71°F/21.7°C. Average annual rainfall 15 in/371 mm.

Cities and towns

Bucharest (capital)	1,989,823
Braşov	351,493
Constanţa	327,676
Timişoara	325,272
Iaşi	313,060
Cluj-Napoca	310,017
Galaţi	295,372
Craiova	281,044
Brăila	235,620
Ploieşti	234,886
Oradea	213,846

Population

Total population is 23,153,475 of which 50.8% live in urban areas. Population density is 253 persons per mile²/96.5 per km². Ethnic divisions: 89.1% Romanian; 7.8% Hungarian; 1.5% German; 1.6% Ukrainian, Serb, Croat, Russian, Turk and Gypsy (approximately 1 million Gypsies).
Birth rate 1.6%. **Death rate** 1.1%. **Rate of population increase** (1980–87) 0.5%. **Age distribution** under 15 = 24.7%; over 65 = 9.5%. **Life expectancy** female 73; male 68; average 70.

Religion

Of the religiously affiliated population, 80% are Romanian Orthodox Christian, 6% Roman Catholic, 4% Calvinist, Lutheran and Baptist. There are an estimated 30,000 Jewish and 40,000 Muslim inhabitants.

Language

Romanian, a Romance language, is the official language, composed of four major dialects: Daco-Romanian; Aromanian or Macedo-Romanian (spoken in isolated Greek, Yugoslavian, Bulgarian and Albanian communities); Megleno-Romanian; Istro-Romanian. Hungarian and German are also spoken by their respective minorities.

HISTORY

The area now forming Romania was home in classical times to Thracian tribes known as the Dacians. It was part of the Roman Empire from AD 106 to about AD 273 (Roman influence survives in the country's name and in the Latin-derived Romanian language). Invasions of Slavic peoples took place in the 7th and 8th centuries and of Magyars between the 9th and 11th centuries, the latter forming a colony in Transylvania whose descendants remain as a distinct community in the region. The Daco–Roman population was converted to Orthodox Christianity around the 9th century. Transylvania was conquered in the 11th century by Hungary. Separate principalities under Romanian rulers emerged in Wallachia and Moldavia in the 13th and 14th centuries. Ottoman suzerainty was first established over Wallachia at the end of the 14th century and over Moldavia a century later. Transylvania came under Turkish domination as a tributary state in 1526; in 1699 the Habsburgs (then holders of the Hungarian crown) gained the region.

In the 19th century ideas of Romanian national unity and liberation spread. The Congress of Paris in 1856 (following the Crimean War) recognized the independence of Wallachia and Moldavia within the Ottoman Empire. On 17 Jan. 1859 both principalities elected the same ruler, Alexandru Cuza, who promoted their legal union in 1861. Following Cuza's overthrow in Feb. 1866, Prince Karl of Hohenzollern-Sigmaringen was elected to the throne of the United Principalities. In May 1877 the Romanians took advantage of the Russo–Turkish War to declare full independence, which was recognized internationally by the Treaty of Berlin (13 July 1878). On 22 May 1881 Karl was crowned as King Carol I of Romania (he reigned until 1914). At the outset of World War I Romania remained neutral, but in Aug. 1916 joined the Allies. Under the postwar peace settlement (1920) Romania gained Transylvania (from Hungary), Bessarabia (from Russia) and southern Dobrudja (from Bulgaria), more than doubling the country's size.

Inter-war politics were corrupt and were marked in the 1930s by the emergence of a powerful fascist movement, the 'Iron Guard'. At the beginning of World War II Romania remained neutral, but in June 1940 it was obliged to cede Bessarabia to the Soviet Union and in July–August to restore Southern Dobrudja to Bulgaria and much of Transylvania to Hungary. Faced with this national humiliation King Carol II (who took the throne in 1930) abdicated on 6 Sept. 1940 in favour of his son Michael. Shortly afterwards Romania formally became an ally of the Axis powers. On 23 Aug. 1944, with Soviet troops already at the frontier, King Michael renounced this alliance. War was declared on Germany and a coalition government was formed which included the Romanian Communist Party (RCP – formed in 1921 by a breakaway faction of the Social Democrats, but banned in 1924). The following March Michael had to accept a more radical left-wing government under Petru Groza. On 15 Sept. 1947 the peace treaty with the Allies confirmed the loss of Bessarabia and Southern Dobrudja, although Romania recovered all of Transylvania. A purge of democratic parties began, the Peasant and Liberal parties being dissolved in Aug. 1947. In December that year Michael was forced to abdicate and a People's Republic was declared.

The Social Democratic Party merged with the RCP in Feb. 1948 to form the Romanian Workers' Party, which became the sole legal party. An internal power struggle followed and 192,000 members were expelled in a purge during 1948–50. Industries and services were nationalized, while collectivization of agriculture was implemented. Gheorghe Gheorghiu-Dej became prime minister in June 1952, and leading figures who had fled to the Soviet Union after 1924 were removed from the leadership. In Oct. 1955 Gheorghiu-Dej resumed the post of party first secretary (which he had briefly relinquished); he was elected president in Mar. 1961. Under his leadership Romania increasingly asserted its independence of the Soviet Union (the withdrawal of Soviet troops was negotiated in 1958). Romania strongly resisted attempts in 1963–64 to foster specialization within Comecon, and adopted a neutral stance in the Sino–Soviet dispute. Gheoghiu-Dej died in Mar. 1965 and was succeeded as first secretary by Nicolae Ceausescu; Chivu Stoica became president. At its congress in July the party reverted to calling itself the Romanian Communist Party and Ceausescu was elected general secretary. He became president in Dec. 1967. He continued the policy of promoting Romanian independence, maintaining links (unlike his allies) with Israel after the Six-Day War of June 1967, and in Aug. 1968 condemning the invasion of Czechoslovakia by the Soviet Union and other Warsaw Pact countries. In July-Aug. 1984 Romania was the only Warsaw Pact country to compete in the Los Angeles Olympic Games.

Ceausescu reinforced his control by frequent changes within the RCP and government leadership and extensive nepotism. During the 1970s Romania borrowed extensively from the West in order to develop its industrial base, but after 1981 a concerted effort was made to maximize exports and hold down imports to pay off the country's foreign debt. This caused extreme privations for the Romanian population and led to outbreaks of workers' protests (notably in Brasov on 15 Nov. 1987). During the 1980s the authorities also pursued an increasingly assimilatory policy towards the Magyar and German national minorities, straining relations with Hungary. Furthermore, rural culture was threatened when in Mar. 1988 Ceausescu announced a policy of systematization, under which some 7,000 villages were to be demolished and their inhabitants resettled in agro-industrial centres. On 17 Dec. 1989 demonstrations began in the western city of Timoşoara against the Ceausescu regime. The authorities tried to suppress them using armed force, but they spread on 21 Dec. to Bucharest. On 22 Dec, the army joined the revolutionaries after Defence Minister Vasile Milea committed suicide rather than obey Ceausescu's order to open fire on demonstrators. Revolutionaries stormed the RCP headquarters, and Ceausescu and his wife Elena fled by helicopter from the roof. They were captured shortly afterwards, and were executed by firing squad on 25 Dec. after a military tribunal found them guilty of genocide, corruption and destruction of the economy. A National Salvation Front (NSF) took power on 22 Dec., and by the end of Dec. all resistance to the revolutionaries by the Securitate secret police had been put down by the army. The NSF abolished the RCP's monopoly on power and promised free elections for 1990, and began to repeal the most hated decrees of the Ceausescu regime including the rural systemization programme and a prohibition on abortion.

CONSTITUTION AND GOVERNMENT

Executive and legislature

The 145-member Council of the National Salvation Front, represented by an 11-member Executive Bureau, assumed legislative power after the Dec. 1989 revolution, pending a free multi-party election. A provisional Council of Ministers was given executive responsibility.

Present government

President of the National Salvation Front Council Executive Bureau Ion Iliescu
Prime Minister Petre Roman
Principal Other Ministers Mihai Draganescu (Deputy Prime Minister); Gelu Voican-Voiculescu (Deputy Prime Minister); Gen. Nicolae Militaru (Defence); Sergiu Celac (Foreign Affairs); Col.-Gen. Mihai Ghitac (Interior); Col.-Gen. Victor Stanculescu (National Economy).

Justice

Justice is administered by the Supreme Court, the 40 district courts, and lower courts. Elected lay assessors participate in most court trials. The Procurator-General, appointed by the National Salvation Front Council, is independent of any organs of justice or administration, and exercises 'supreme supervisory power to ensure the observance of the law' by all authorities and citizens. Military tribunals were given responsibility by the National Salvation Front Council for trying cases connected with the

Dec. 1989 revolution and with abuse of power under the Ceausescu regime. The death penalty was abolished on 1 Jan. 1990.

National symbols

Flag. Three vertical stripes of dark blue, yellow and red.
Festivals. 1–2 May (International Labour Day); 23–24 Aug. (National Day).
Vehicle registration plate. R.

INTERNATIONAL RELATIONS

Affiliations

Warsaw Pact; Comecon.

Defence

Total Armed Forces: 179,500 (107,500 conscripts). Terms of service: Army, Air Force 16 months, Navy 24 months. Reserves: 556,000.
Army: 140,000; some 1,860 main battle tanks (T-34/-54/-55/-72, M-77).
Navy: 7,500; one submarine (Soviet Kilo); five principal surface combatants: one destroyer; four frigates (Soviet Koni). 105 patrol and coastal combatants.
Air Force: 32,000; 350 combat aircraft (mainly MiG-17/-23/-21F/PF/U).

ECONOMY

Currency

The unit is the leu (plural lei), divided into 100 bani.

National finance

Budget. The 1987 budget (in US$) was for expenditure (current and capital) of 21,600 million and revenue of 26,000 million.
Inflation. (1987) 0%.

Gross Domestic Product

Estimated total GDP US$151,300 million (GNP), per capita US$6,570 (overall size of economy ranking 19 in the world).
Economically active population. The total number of persons active in the economy was 10,690,000.

Sector	% of workforce
industry	34
agriculture	28
services*	38

* services figure includes elements unassigned to other categories.

Energy and mineral resources

Oil and gas. Oil production: (1988) 11 million tons/10 million tonnes; methane gas production: (1986) 945,109 ft^3/26,763 m^3.
Minerals. Brown coal and lignite production: (1986) 42 million tons/38 million tonnes; iron ore 2.4 million tons/2.2 million tonnes; copper ore; bauxite; chromium; manganese; uranium. Salt is also mined in the Carpathians and Transylvania. Production: (1985) 5.5 million tons/5 million tonnes.
Electricity. Capacity: 22.43 million kW; production: 78,500 million kWh; 3,410 kWh per capita (1988).

Bioresources

Agriculture. In 1986 there were 37 million acres/15 million ha of agricultural land of which 10 million were arable, and 3 million people worked in agriculture.
Crop production: (1986 in 1,000 tons/tonnes) wheat and rye 8,760/7,947; barley 2,425/2,200; maize 22,046/20,000; potatoes 9,384/8,513; sunflower seeds 1,107/1,004; sugar beet 7,716/7,000.
Livestock numbers: (1987 in millions) cattle 7; pigs 14.7; sheep 18.7; poultry 137.
Forestry. 28% of the land area is forest and woodland. Total forest area: 15.67 million acres/6.34 million ha.

Industry and commerce

Industry. Main industries are mining; timber; construction materials; metallurgy; chemicals; machine building; food processing; petroleum. Production: (1986 in tons/tonnes) pig-iron 10,283/9,329; steel 15,736/14,276; steel tubes 1,722/1,565; blast furnace coke 5,609/5,088; rolled steel 11,251/10,207; chemical fertilizers 3,613/3,278; caustic soda 933/846; cement 15,670/14,216; sugar 539/489; cotton 806/731; man-made fibres 333,645/302,681.
Commerce. Exports: (1986) US$12,500 million or 8% of GNP, including machinery and equipment 34.7%; fuels, minerals and metals 24.7%; manufactured consumer goods 16.9%; agricultural materials and forestry products 11.9%. Imports: US$10,600 million, including fuels, minerals and metals 51%; machinery and equipment 26.7%; agricultural and forestry products 11%; manufactured consumer goods 4.2%. Countries exported to (1987) were USSR 27%; Eastern Europe 23%; EC countries 15%; China 4%. Imports (1987) came from Communist countries 60%; non-Communist countries 40%.
Trade with UK. In 1988 Romania imported UK goods worth £50,111,000; exports to UK totalled £100,906,000.

COMMUNICATIONS

Railways

There are 6,968 miles/11,221 km of railways, of which 2,067 miles/3,328 km are electrified.

Roads

There are 45,208 miles/72,799 km of roads, of which 22,337 miles/35,970 km are concrete or bituminized.

Aviation

Transporturile Aeriene Române – TAROM provides domestic and international services (main airports are at Bucharest-Otopeni, M. Kogalniceanu-Constanţa, Timişoara and Arad).

Shipping

There are 1,071 miles/1,724 km of inland waterways. The inland ports are Braila, Galaţi, Giurgiu, Drobeta-Turnu Severin and Orsova. The marine ports are Constanţa and Mangalia. The merchant marine consists of 282 ships of 1,000 GRT or over.

Telecommunications

There were nearly 2,000,000 telephone subscribers in 1986. There are 3.2 million radios and 3.8 million televisions (1988). The state controls both radio and TV broadcasting, and also operates an external service radio station with programmes in 13 languages.

EDUCATION AND WELFARE

Education

Schools. Education is free and compulsory from 6–16 years. There are 12,548 kindergartens with 836,225 pupils and 32,789 teachers (one per 25 pupils);

14,046 primary and secondary schools with 3,017,339 pupils and 144,878 teachers (one per 20 pupils); 981 lycées with 1,196,949 pupils and 46,124 teachers (one per 25 pupils); 747 professional schools with 257,196 pupils and 2,420 teachers (one per 106 pupils). There are also 44 institutes of higher education.

Universities. There are six universities located at Iaşi, Bucharest, Cluj, Timişoara, Craiova and Brasov.
Literacy. 98%.

Health

(1986) 213,560 hospital beds (one per 117 people) and 40,706 doctors (one per 568 people).

RWANDA
Republika y'u Rwanda
(Republic of Rwanda)

GEOGRAPHY

Rwanda is a landlocked country, situated just south of the equator in east-central Africa, containing a total area of 10,167 miles²/26,340 km² divided into ten prefectures. Lying a mean 4,921 ft/1,500 m above sea level, Rwanda rises to 14,787 ft/4,507 m at Mount Karisimbi in the north-westerly Virunga range. On the western border, Lake Kivu (4,790 ft/1,460 m above sea level) drains into the southerly-flowing Ruzizi River. Further east, the River Kagera marshlands encircle a number of lakes including Lake Rwanye, Lake Ihema and Lake Mugesera. Rwanda is the most densely populated country in Africa. 29% of the land is arable and 10% is forested.

Climate

Tropical, modified by high altitude. Average annual temperature of 68°F/20°C. The two wet seasons last Oct.-Dec. and Mar.-May respectively with the months June-August receiving less than 6% of the annual rainfall total. Precipitation increases to the west, from 30 in/760 mm to 70 in/1,770 mm maximum. Kigali: Jan. 67°F/19.4°C. July 70°F/21.1°C. Average annual rainfall 39 in/1,000 mm.

Cities and towns

Kigali (capital)	117,749
Butare	21,691
Ruhengeri	16,025
Gisenyi	12,436

Population

Total population is 7,322,039 of which only 5.1% live in urban areas. Population density is 720 persons per mile²/246.3 per km². Ethnic divisions: 90% Hutu; 9% Tutsi; 1% Pygmoid Twa.

Birth rate 5.3%. **Death rate** 1.6%. **Rate of population increase** (1980–87) 3.8%. **Age distribution** under 15 = 49.0%; over 65 = 2.4%. **Life expectancy** female 50; male 47; average 49.

Religion

65% Roman Catholic; 17% indigenous beliefs; 9% Protestant; 9% Muslim.

Language

French and Kinyarwanda (an indigenous Bantu tongue) are the official languages. More people speak Kinyarwanda than any other Bantu language. A dialectal variant of Kiswahili is also commonly used.

HISTORY

The original inhabitants, Twa (Batwa) pygmies, were displaced by Hutu (Bahutu) farmers who began arriving in the 14th century. Tutsi (Batutsi) pastoralists migrated from the north in the 15th and 16th centuries and imposed their rule under powerful monarchs. Rwanda, together with Burundi, came under the colonial rule of Germany and the two were merged in 1899 and renamed Ruanda-Urundi. Belgian troops occupied the colony during World War I (1916). After the war Belgium was given a League of Nations mandate to rule Ruanda-Urundi, later a UN trusteeship (1946).

A Hutu revolution in 1959 demolished the monarchy and Tutsi power. Hundreds of people were killed and many Tutsi fled Rwanda, which became a republic in 1961 and fully independent on 1 July 1962, when the Hutu-led Parti du Mouvement de l'Emancipation Hutu (PARMEHUTU) came to power under Pres. Grégoire Kayibanda.

Up to 20,000 Tutsi were reportedly killed by Hutu following border raids by Tutsi refugees in Dec. 1963. Kayibanda was overthrown in a bloodless military coup (5 July 1973) and former defence minister Gen. Juvénal Habyarimana became president. In 1975 Habyarimana formed a new ruling party of civilian and military members, the Mouvement Révolutionnaire National pour le Développement (MRND). Rwanda returned to constitutional government in 1978. Habyarimana was re-elected in 1983 and again in Jan. 1989. Tensions have simmered between central and northern Hutu; northern elements took the upper hand in government, which remains civilian-military. Ethnic tensions in Burundi (Aug. 1988) brought around 38,000 Hutu refugees fleeing to Rwanda; most have now returned.

CONSTITUTION AND GOVERNMENT

Executive and legislature

The executive president is elected for a five-year term by universal adult suffrage (last elections Dec. 1988), and governs with the assistance of a council of ministers. Legislative power is exercised jointly by the president and the 70-member National Development Council, whose members are also directly elected for five years from a list of candidates put forward by the sole legal party; last elections Dec. 1988.

Present government

President; President of the Council of Ministers; Minister of Defence Maj.-Gen. Juvénal Habyarimana
Principal Ministers Juvénal Uwilingiyimana (Economy and Consumption); Benoît Ntigulirwa (Finance); Dr Casimir Bizimungu (Foreign Affairs and Co-

operation); Jean Marie Vianney Mugemana (Interior and Community Development); Theoneste Muryanama (Justice).

Ruling party

National Revolutionary Movement for Development (Mouvement Révolutionnaire National pour le Développement).

President Maj.-Gen. Juvénal Habyarimana. **Secretary-general** Bonaventure Habimana.

Justice

The judiciary consists of Courts of First Instance and provincial courts which refer appeals to Courts of Appeal and a Court of Cassation at Kigali. The death penalty is in force. There were no executions between 1985 and mid-1988.

National symbols

Flag. Tricolour with vertical stripes of red, yellow and green.

Festivals. 28 Jan. (Democracy Day); 1 May (Labour Day); 1 July (National Holiday, anniversary of independence); 5 July (National Peace and Unity Day, anniversary of 1973 coup); 25 Sept. (Kamarampaka Day, anniversary of 1961 referendum); 26 Oct. (Armed Forces Day).

Vehicle registration plate. RWA.

INTERNATIONAL RELATIONS

Affiliations

NAM; OAU.

Defence

Total Armed Forces: 5,200. Terms of service: voluntary.

Army: 5,000;

Air Force: 200; two combat aircraft.

Para-military: 1,200 (Gendarmerie).

ECONOMY

Currency

The unit is the Rwandese franc, divided into 100 centimes.

National finance

Budget. The 1987 budget (in US$) was for expenditure (current and capital) of 330 million and revenue of 270 million.

Balance of payments. The balance of payments (current account, 1987) was a deficit of $250 million.

Inflation. (1987) 4.1%.

Gross Domestic Product

Estimated total GDP US$2,100 million, per capita US$340 (overall size of economy ranking 114 in the world).

Economically active population. The total number of persons active in the economy was 3,600,000.

Sector	% of workforce	% of GDP
industry	2	23
agriculture	93	37
services*	5	40

* services figure includes elements unassigned to other categories.

Energy and mineral resources

Minerals. Gold; cassiterite (tin ore); wolframite (tungsten ore); natural gas; hydropower.

Electricity. Capacity: 26,000 kW; production: 112 million kWh; 15 kWh per capita (1988).

Bioresources

Agriculture. 30% of the land is put to arable use, 10% to permanent crops and 20% to meadows and pastures.

Crop production: cash crops are coffee 33,069 tons/30,000 tonnes; tea 8,818 tons/8,000 tonnes; pyrethrum (insecticide made from chrysanthemums); main food crops are bananas; cassava; sweet potatoes; livestock farming.

Livestock numbers: goats 1 million; cattle 673,000; sheep 350,000.

Forestry. Approximately 10% of the country is forest or woodland.

Industry and commerce

Industry. Main industries are mining of cassiterite and wolframite; food manufacturing; cement; soap; furniture; shoes; textiles; plastic goods; cigarettes.

Commerce. Exports: (f.o.b. 1987) US$113 million. Major exports are coffee 85%; tea; tin; cassiterite; wolframite; pyrethrum; main trading partners are West Germany; Belgium; Italy; Uganda; UK; France; US. Imports: (c.i.f.1987). US$352 million. Major imports are textiles; foodstuffs; machinery; capital goods; steel; petroleum products; cement and construction material; main trading partners are US; Belgium; West Germany; Kenya; Japan.

Trade with UK. In 1988 Rwanda imported £1.6 million worth of goods from the UK and exported £8.4 million worth of goods to the UK.

COMMUNICATIONS

Railways

There are no railways in Rwanda at present.

Roads

There are 7,495 miles/12,070 km of roads.

Aviation

Air Rwanda provides domestic passenger services and international cargo services (main airport is Grégoire Kayibanda Airport at Kigali). Passengers: (1984) 107,000.

Shipping

Lac Kivu, a border of Rwanda, is only navigable by shallow-draught barges and native craft.

Telecommunications

There is a fair system with low-capacity radio relay centred on Kigali. There are 6,600 telephones and 411,735 radios (1988). There is no television service in Rwanda.

EDUCATION AND WELFARE

Education

School population. 706,000 pupils (1981).

Schools. 1,600 primary schools with 12,000 teachers; 118 secondary schools.

Universities. National University at Butare has approximately 1,600 students.

Literacy. About 35%.

Health

Some 200 hospitals and health centres with approximately 9,000 beds (approximately one per 600 people) some 200 doctors and 550 nurses.

SAINT CHRISTOPHER AND NEVIS

Federation of Saint Christopher and Nevis

GEOGRAPHY

Located at the northern end of the Leeward Islands chain of the West Indies, the Federation comprises the islands of St Christopher, more commonly known as St Kitts (65 miles^2/168.4 km^2) and Nevis (36 miles^2/93.2 km^2) divided by a 2 mile/3 km-wide sea strait known as The Narrows. Both islands are volcanic in origin and are dominated by mountains that rise to 3,793 ft/1,156 m at Mount Misery on St Kitts and 3,232 ft/985 m on Nevis. Over 75% of the population live on St Kitts. 22% of the land is arable and 17% is forest-covered. Both islands are satisfactorily drained by rivers.

Climate

Tropical. Temperatures vary between 63 °F/17°C and 91°F/33°C with an average annual temperature of 79°F/26°C. Average annual rainfall is approximately 54 in/1,375 mm (48 in/1,220 mm on Nevis). Sea winds modify the high temperatures and hurricanes may occur July-Oct.

Cities and towns

Basseterre (capital)	14,161

Population

Total population is 40,068 of which 35.8% live in urban areas. Population density is 396.7 persons per mile^2/153.2 per km^2. Ethnic composition: the population is primarily of Black African descent. At the last census 94.3% were Black; 3.3% mulatto; 0.9% White.

Birth rate 2.4%. **Death rate** 1.0%. **Rate of population increase** (1980–87) 0.2%. **Age distribution** under 15 = 32.4%; over 65 = 6.0%. **Life expectancy** female 70; male 64; average 67.

Religion

Christianity. 36.2% Anglican; 32.3% Methodist; 7.9% other Protestant; 10.7% Roman Catholic.

Language

English is the official language, widely spoken in its creole form.

HISTORY

The earliest inhabitants of the islands of St Christopher and Nevis were Arawak and Carib Indians. The British were the first European settlers, arriving in 1623. Disputes with the French over the possession of the islands were not finally resolved until 1783. The island of Anguilla was joined administratively to the other two islands in 1816. African slaves were imported as labour for sugar and cotton plantations until the abolition of slavery in 1834.

Universal suffrage was granted in 1951 and in 1967 the territory attained full internal self-government. Robert Bradshaw, the leader of the ruling Labour Party, became premier. In May 1967 Anguilla declared itself independent of control from St Kitts. British troops intervened in Mar. 1969 and in 1971 the island reverted to being a British dependent territory, formally separated from St Kitts-Nevis in 1980.

Bradshaw died in May 1978 and was succeeded by Paul Southwell, who also died a year later. The new premier, Lee Moore, called elections for Feb. 1980, but the Labour Party lost and was replaced as the government by a coalition of the People's Action Movement (PAM) and the Nevis Reformation Party (NRP), which sought greater autonomy for Nevis. Dr Kennedy Simmonds of the PAM became premier and then prime minister on the attainment of full independence from Britain on 19 Sept. 1983. The PAM/NRP coalition remained in power after winning general elections in 1984 and 1989, in spite of the PAM achieving a clear majority of seats in the National Assembly.

CONSTITUTION AND GOVERNMENT

Executive and legislature

The head of state is the British sovereign, represented in the islands by a governor general, who holds the formal authority to appoint the prime minister. The prime minister, as head of government, is responsible to the unicameral national assembly. This legislature comprises a speaker, three senators (appointed by the governor general in accordance with the wishes of the prime minister and leader of the oppositon) and 11 representatives elected directly by universal adult suffrage; last election Mar. 1989. The island of Nevis has its own legislature (consisting of five elected and three nominated members) and executive which has exclusive responsiblility for the island's internal administration and through which its population may exercise its constitutional rights to secede from the union with St. Christopher.

Present government

Governor General Clement Athelston Arrindell

Prime Minister; External Affairs; Home Affairs; Finance Kennedy Alphonse Simmonds

Principal Members of Cabinet Michael Oliver Powell (Deputy Prime Minister; Labour; Tourism); Hugh Heyliger (Agriculture, Lands, Housing and Development); Sydney Earl Morris (Education, Health and Community Affairs, Communications, Works and Public Utilities); Fitzroy Jones (Trade and Industry);

Justice

The system of law is based on English common law. The highest court is the Court of Appeal of the Leeward and Windward Islands. Justice, in both civil and criminal matters, is administered by the Supreme Court and by Magistrates' Courts. The death penalty is in force. There was one execution between 1985 and mid-1988.

National symbols

Flag. Divided diagonally by a black band edged in yellow and bearing two white stars whose upper points are directed towards the top left-hand side. The triangle based on the hoist is green and the other is red.

Festivals. 1 May (Labour Day); 10 June (Queen's Official birthday); 19 Sep. (Independence Day); 14 Nov. (Prince of Wales Day); 31 Dec. (Carnival).

INTERNATIONAL RELATIONS

Affiliations
Commonwealth; OAS; Caricom; OECS.

Defence
Police force only.

ECONOMY

Currency
The unit is the East Caribbean dollar, divided into 100 cents.

National finance
Budget. The 1986 budget, in US$, was for expenditure of 24.4 million and revenue of 20.7 million.
Inflation. 0.9%.

Gross Domestic Product
Estimated total GDP US$83 million, per capita US$2,210 (overall size of economy ranking 182 in the world).
Economically active population. The total number of persons active in the economy was 20,000; unemployed = 20–25%.

Energy and mineral resources
Electricity. Capacity: 11,400 kW; production: 32 million kWh; 800 kWh per capita (1988).

Bioresources
Agriculture. Main crops are sugar on St Christopher and cotton on Nevis. Other crops are coconuts and copra. Crop production: sugar (1987) 31,405 tons/28,490 tonnes; cotton (1986) 33.6/30.5; copra 260,383 lb/118,109 kg.
Livestock numbers: (1987) cattle 7,000; pigs 10,000; sheep 15,000; goats 10,000; donkeys (1984) 1,365; poultry 67,030.
Forestry. 17% of the land area is forest and woodland.
Fisheries. Total catch: (1983) 1,213 tons/1,100 tonnes.

Industry and commerce
Industry. Main industries are sugar processing; tourism; cotton; salt; copra; clothing; footwear; beverages.
Commerce. Exports (1987) US$27.2 million or 32% of GDP, including sugar; manufactures; postage stamps. Imports: US$79.5 million, including foodstuffs; intermediate manufactures; machinery; fuels. Countries exported to were US 44%; UK 30%; Trinidad and Tobago 12%. Imports came from US 35%; UK 18%; Trinidad and Tobago 10%; Canada 6%; Japan 4%.
Trade with UK. In 1988 St Christopher and Nevis imported UK goods worth £8,025,000; exports to UK totalled £4,271,000.
Tourism. (1987) 91,383 visitors.

COMMUNICATIONS

Railways
There are 36 miles/58 km of railways, serving the sugar plantations.

Roads
There are 186 miles/300 km of roads, of which 78 miles/125 km are concrete or bituminized.

Aviation
Main airport is Golden Rock Airport, 2½ miles/4 km from Basseterre.

Shipping
There are two ports: Basseterre on St Christopher and Charlestown on Nevis. Freight loaded: (1985) 36,376 tons/33,000 tonnes; unloaded: 40,785 tons/37,000 tonnes.

Telecommunications
There are 2,400 telephones, good inter-island radio connections and an international link via Antigua and Barbuda and St Martin. There are 22,850 radios and 7,000 televisions (1988). The government owns the commercial ZIZ Radio and Television station and there are three other radio stations including the religious Radio Paradise.

EDUCATION AND WELFARE

Education
Schools. Primary education is compulsory between five and 14 years and pupils may stay up to 16 years if they wish.
Higher Education. There is an Extra-Mural Department of the University of the West Indies, a Technical College and a teacher-training college.
Literacy. 80%.

Health
(1987) 22 doctors; four hospitals with 258 beds (one per 155 people); 17 clinics.

SAINT HELENA AND DEPENDENCIES

GEOGRAPHY

The group of islands which includes St Helena, Ascension, Gough Island, Inaccessible Island, Nightingale Island and Tristan da Cunha, lies in the South Atlantic Ocean, and covers a total land area of 158 miles^2/410 km^2. The terrain is rugged and volcanic, with small scattered plateaux and plains. There are few streams. The capital is Jamestown on St Helena.

Climate
Tropical marine; mild, tempered by trade winds.

Population
Total population (1989 est.) 7,200.
Birth rate 1.3%. **Death rate** 0.7%.
Rate of population increase 0.6%.
Life expectancy female 75; male 70.

Religion
Christianity; mostly Anglican.

Language
English

HISTORY

St Helena was uninhabited when it was first discovered by the Portuguese in 1502. The island was visited by other European navigators but was not settled until 1659 when it was occupied by the British East India Company. Slaves were imported from mainland Africa until freed between 1826 and 1836. Napoleon Bonaparte, after his defeat at Waterloo (1815), spent the last six years of his life in exile on St Helena. Responsibility for the island was transferred to the British crown in 1834.

Ascension Island was discovered by the Portuguese but uninhabited until 1815 when a British naval garrison was established. It became a dependency of St Helena in 1922. Tristan da Cunha was discovered in 1506, but first settled by the British in 1816. The island and its dependencies became a dependency of St Helena in 1938. The island was evacuated between 1961 and 1963 after a volcanic eruption.

Greater autonomy was granted to St Helena in 1966, providing for an elected legislative council. However, political activity remained slight and in 1981 a Constitutional Commission was set up to investigate further amendments that could be made to the Constitution. The Commission reported that there were no changes that could command the support of a majority of the islanders. The last elections to the Legislative Council were held in Oct. 1984.

CONSTITUTION AND GOVERNMENT

St Helena is a dependent territory of the United Kingdom, with a constitution dating from Jan. 1967. There is an executive council and 12-member elected legislative council. The last general election was held in Oct. 1984.

Leader Francis Baker, Governor and Commander in Chief (since 1984)

National symbols

Flag. Blue, with the flag of the UK in the upper hoist-side quadrant and the St Helena shield centred on the outer half of the flag – the shield features a rocky coastline and three-masted ship.

National holiday. 10 June (birthday of Queen Elizabeth II).

ECONOMY

The economy is heavily dependent on aid from the UK. Economic activity is centred on fishing and agriculture. Because of unemployment, many people have left to seek work overseas.

Currency

The St Helenian pound.

COMMUNICATIONS

There are ports at Jamestown (St Helena) and Georgetown (Ascension); one airport with a permanent surface runway on Ascension; 54 miles/87 km of surfaced road on St Helena, 50 miles/80 km of surfaced road on Ascension, 1.7 miles/2.7 km of surfaced road on Tristan da Cunha. There is one AM radio station, no FM or television. There are HF radio links to Ascension, then into worldwide submarine cable and satellite networks; major coaxial cable relay point between South Africa, Portugal and UK at Ascension.

SAINT LUCIA

GEOGRAPHY

Saint Lucia, the second largest island in the Windward group of the West Indies, is situated in the East Caribbean 24 miles/39 km south of Martinique and 20 miles/32 km north of Saint Vincent. The major physiographic features on this tropical volcanic island are forested mountains stretching north to south, cut by a number of fertile river valleys, rising to 3,146 ft/959 m at Mount Gimie, the sulphurous springs of Qualibou in the south-west and the twin peaks of the Gros and Petit Pitons (2,618 ft/798 m, 2,461 ft/750 m). 8% of the land is arable and 13% is forested. St Lucia contains a total area of 238 miles^2/616 km^2.

Climate

Tropical, average annual temperature of 79°F/26°C, with little variation. The wet season lasts May-Aug., and the dry season Jan.-Apr. Annual rainfall totals vary according to altitude from 59 in/1,500 mm in the lowlands to 138 in/3,500 mm in the mountainous zones.

Cities and towns

Castries (capital)	52,868

Population

Total population is 149,577 of which 52.1% live in urban areas. Population density is 628 persons per mile^2/ 243 per km^2. Ethnic divisions: 90.3% of African origin; 5.5% mixed; 3.2% East Indian; 0.8% Caucasian.

Birth rate 3.4%. **Death rate** 0.5%. **Rate of population increase** (1980–87) 2.5%. **Age distribution** under 15 = 44.4%; over 65 = 5.7%. **Life expectancy** female 74; male 67; average 70.

Religion

Christianity. 90% Roman Catholic; 7% Protestant; 3% Anglican.

Language

English is the official language, although a large proportion of the population speak a local French/English creole.

HISTORY

The earliest inhabitants of St Lucia were Arawak Indians who were followed by Caribs migrating from the South American continent. During the 17th century both England and France made attempts to colonize the island, and ownership alternated between Britain and France many times before it was finally ceded to Britain in 1814. African slaves were imported as labour until slavery was abolished in 1834.

Universal suffrage was introduced in 1951 and full internal autonomy in 1967. Elections in 1974 were won by the ruling United Workers' Party (UWP), led by John Compton, campaigning for full independence, which was attained on 22 Feb. 1979. The UWP, however, was defeated in elections held shortly afterwards by the St Lucia Labour Party (SLP), led by Allan Louisy. Defections by left-wing SLP members, principally George Odlum, the deputy prime minister, in May 1981 forced Louisy to resign and led eventually to the collapse of the SLP government in Jan. 1982 amid strikes and demonstrations. An all-party interim administration was installed prior to fresh elections. These were won overwhelmingly by the UWP and Compton returned as prime minister. In elections held in Apr. 1987 the UWP was returned to power, but with a majority of only one seat over the SLP. Compton called a fresh election for later the same month hoping to obtain a more decisive mandate, but the distribution of seats remained the same.

CONSTITUTION AND GOVERNMENT

Executive and legislature

The head of state is the British sovereign represented by a governor general, who has the nominal power to appoint the prime minister. As head of government, the prime minister is responsible to the legislature, the bicameral parliament which consists of an appointed senate and a 17-member house of assembly. The assembly is elected directly for a five-year term by universal adult suffrage; last election 30 Apr. 1987.

Present government

Governor-General Sir Vincent Floissac

Prime Minister; Minister of Finance, Home Affairs, Planning and Development John Compton

Other Principal Members of the Cabinet George Mallet (Deputy Prime Minister; Trade, Industry and Tourism); Neville Cenac (Foreign Affairs); Parry Husbands (Attorney General; Legal Affairs).

Justice

The Eastern Caribbean Supreme Court (formerly known as the West Indies Associated States Supreme Court) operates from St Lucia. There is an itinerant Court of Appeal consisting of a Chief Justice and three Justices of Appeal; a High Court with a resident judge, a senior magistrate and four other resident magistrates. The other Eastern Carbbean states which share the Supreme court are Antigua, British Virgin Islands, Dominica, Montserrat, St Kitts and St Vincent. There is a High Court with one resident judge in each of the states. The death penalty is in force. There was one execution between 1985 and mid-1988. The offence was murder.

National symbols

Flag. Blue with an upright black isosceles triangle which has a white stripe along the upper two sides.

Festivals. 6–7 Feb. (Carnival); 22 Feb. (Independence Day); 1 May (Labour Day); 10 June (Queen's Official birthday); 7 Aug. (Bank Holiday).

Vehicle registration plate. WL.

INTERNATIONAL RELATIONS

Affiliations

NAM; Commonwealth; OAS; Caricom; OECS.

Defence

Police force only.

ECONOMY

Currency

The unit is the East Caribbean dollar, divided into 100 cents.

National finance

Budget. The 1987 budget, in US$, was for expenditure of 79.3 million and revenue of 71.7 million.

Inflation. 7.0%.

Gross Domestic Product

Estimated total GDP US$166 million, per capita US$1,250 (overall size of economy ranking 167 in the world).

Economically active population. The total number of persons active in the economy was 43,800; unemployed = 18.6%.

Sector	% of workforce
industry	18
agriculture	43
services*	39

* services figure includes elements unassigned to other categories.

Energy and mineral resources

Minerals. There are some reserves of pumice.

Electricity. Capacity: 20,000 kW; production: 80 million kWh; 590 kWh per capita (1988).

Bioresources

Agriculture. Main crops are bananas; copra; coconut oil; sugar; cocoa; spices.

Livestock numbers: (1987) cattle 12,000; pigs 12,000; sheep 15,000; goats 12,000.

Forestry. 13% of the land area is forest and woodland.

Industry and commerce

Industry. Main industries are clothing; assembly of electronic components; beverages; corrugated boxes; tourism; lime processing; coconut processing.

Commerce. Exports: (1987) US$76.8 million or 46% of GDP, including bananas 67%; cocoa; vegetables; fruits; coconut oil; clothing. Imports: US$178.1, including manufactured goods 22%; machinery and transportation equipment 21%; food and live animals 20%; mineral fuels; foodstuffs; machinery and equipment; fertilizers; petroleum products. Countries exported to were UK 55%; Caricom 21%; US 18%; other 6%. Imports came from US 33%; UK 16%; Caricom 14.8%; Japan 6.5%; other 29.7%.

Trade with UK. In 1988 St Lucia imported UK goods worth £19,750,000; exports to UK totalled £58,385,000.

Tourism. (1986) 171,000 visitors.

COMMUNICATIONS

Railways

There are no railways.

Roads

There are some 602 miles/970 km of roads.

Aviation

Main airports are Hewanorra International (40 miles/64 km from Castries) and Vigie (in Castries).

Shipping

The port of St Lucia is Castries. Freight loaded: (1986) 214,949 tons/195,000 tonnes; unloaded: 309,746 tons/281,000 tonnes.

Telecommunications

There are 9,500 telephones, a fully automatic telephone system and a direct radio link with Martinique and St Vincent and the Grenadines. There are 99,120 radios (1988) and 2,200 televisions (1985). Television is broadcast commercially by Saint Lucia Television Services Ltd, and the three radio stations include the government-owned RSL.

EDUCATION AND WELFARE

Education

Schools. Primary education is free and compulsory. There are 79 primary schools with 32,273 pupils and 12 secondary schools with 5,665 pupils (1986).

Higher education. (1986) one technical college with 223 students and one teacher-training college with 123 students.

Literacy. 78%.

Health

There is one hospital in Castries with 213 beds, four other hospitals including one mental hospital, and 209 health centres. In 1984 there were 58 doctors (one per 2,578 people).

SAINT PIERRE AND MIQUELON

GEOGRAPHY

St Pierre and Miquelon are islands in the North Atlantic Ocean covering a total area of 93 miles^2/242 km^2. The terrain is mostly barren rock. The capital is St Pierre.

Climate

Cold, wet, misty, foggy. Spring and autumn are windy.

Population

Total population (1989 est.) 6,303.
Birth rate 1.7%. **Death rate** 0.7%. **Rate of population increase** 0.4%. **Life expectancy** female 79; male 72.

Religion

Christianity (Roman Catholic).

Language

French

HISTORY

The islands of the archipelago of Saint Pierre and Miquelon were uninhabited prior to their discovery by the Portuguese in 1520. The islands were soon claimed by France and the first permanent settlement was established in 1604. The islands served as a base for fishermen and were populated by settlers from Normandy, Brittany and the Basque region, added to later by refugees from areas of French Canada occupied by the British. The British administered the islands 1713–63 and 1794–1816, when they were finally restored to French control.

The importance of France's last possession in North America was that it allowed the French to exploit the rich fishing grounds of Newfoundland. Fishing for cod allowed the islands to prosper until the introduction of factory ships and frozen fish facilities reduced the importance of the islands' harbours. Saint Pierre and Miquelon became an overseas territory of France in 1946 and in 1976 was made a department, against the wishes of many of the islanders. General strikes and unrest over departmental status intensified during the late 1970s and early 1980s. In 1976 Canada declared a 200-mile economic interest zone around its shores, prompting the French to declare a similar zone around Saint Pierre, although the Canadians only recognized a 12-mile limit. In 1987 it was agreed to take the dispute to the International Court of Justice. However, in October negotiations over future fishing quotas broke down and French vessels were banned from Canadian waters. In Apr. 1988 several fishermen and island politicians were arrested by the Canadian authorities for fishing in Canadian waters, while in May a Canadian vessel was arrested by the French.

CONSTITUTION AND GOVERNMENT

The Territorial Collectivity of Saint Pierre and Miquelon is a territorial collectivity of France, and shares the French Constitution dating from Sept. 1958. There is a government commissioner appointed by Paris, and a popularly elected 14-member general council.

Leader Bernard Leurquin, Commissioner of the Republic; Marc Plante-Genest, President of the General Council.

National symbols

Flag. The flag of France.

National holiday. 14 July (National Day).

ECONOMY

The economy has traditionally been dominated by fishing and the servicing of fishing fleets operating off the coast of Newfoundland. However, recently the number of ships stopping at St Pierre has fallen. There has also been a dispute between France and Canada since Oct. 1987 over cod quotas, and St Pierre's trawlers have been confined within the islands' 200-mile/300-km zone where cod catches are declining. Most imports come from Canada. The economy is dependent on French subsidies.

Currency

The French franc.

COMMUNICATIONS

There is a port at St Pierre; two airports, both with permanent surface runways; 75 miles/120 km of roads. There is a telephone system, one AM and three FM radio stations, no television.

SAINT VINCENT AND THE GRENADINES

GEOGRAPHY

The Windward Islands nation of St Vincent and the Grenadines lies in the East Caribbean, 93 miles/160 km west of Barbados, occupying a total area of 150 miles^2/388 km^2 of which the chief island, St Vincent, comprises 93 miles^2/240 km^2. Among the larger coralline Grenadines spanning the 37 miles/60 km between Grenada and St Vincent are Bequia, Canouan, Mayreau, Mustique, Union Island, Petit St Vincent and Prune Island. The densely populated volcanic island of St Vincent is dominated by a northern-southern spur of densely forested mountains, dissected east-west by many short, torrential water courses. To the north, Mt Soufrière rises to 4,049 ft/1,234 m. The majority of the population live on the coastal perimeter. 38% of the land is arable and 41% is forested.

Climate

Tropical, temperatures range from 64 to 90°F/18 to 32°C, with an annual average temperature of 80.1°F/26.7°C. Rainfall increases with altitude from 59 in/1,500 mm in the southern coastal regions to 148 in/3,750 mm in the mountainous interior of St Vincent. St Vincent and the Grenadines are less prone to hurricanes than many of the other Caribbean islands.

Cities and towns

Kingstown (capital) 30,000

Population

Total population is 104,891 of which 25.7% live in urban areas. Population density is 699 persons per mile^2/287.7 per km^2. Ethnic divisions: 82% Black (African origin); 13.9% mixed racial origin; the remainder comprises a number of White, Asian and Amerindian minorities.

Birth rate 2.7%. **Death rate** 0.6%. **Rate of population increase** (1980–87) 0.6%. **Age distribution** under 15 = 37.8%; over 65 = 4.4%. **Life expectancy** female 74; male 69; average 71.

Religion

At the last census in 1981, 42% were Anglican; 21% Methodist; 12% Roman Catholic.

Language

English is the official language, although the regional French patois is also commonly used.

HISTORY

St Vincent was first inhabited by Arawak Indians who were displaced by Caribs migrating from South America. No major attempts by Europeans at colonization occurred until the mid-18th century. African slaves were imported to provide labour for plantations. The majority of the Carib population was deported by the British to the Bay of Honduras after the suppression of a revolt in 1795. Serious eruptions of the island's volcano, La Soufrière, in 1812 and 1902 caused widespread damage.

Universal suffrage was introduced in 1951 and full internal self-government in 1969. Elections in 1972 resulted in the People's Political Party (PPP) and the St Vincent Labour Party (SVLP) each winning six seats in the House of Assembly. The balance of power was held by an independent, James Mitchell, who joined the PPP to form a government with himself as premier. Mitchell's government collapsed in 1974 and was replaced after elections by a coalition of the PPP and SVLP, whose leader, Milton Cato, led the country to full independence from Britain on 27 Oct. 1979. The SVLP retained power at elections in 1979, but discontent at the government's record and failure to improve the economy led to its defeat in 1984 by the New Democratic Party (NDP), founded by Mitchell. Mitchell became prime minister and strengthened the NDP's position by polling 71% of the vote and winning all 15 seats in the House of Assembly in elections in May 1989.

CONSTITUTION AND GOVERNMENT

Executive and legislature

The head of state is the British sovereign, represented within the islands by a governor general, who has the nominal authority to appoint the prime minister. As head of government, the prime minister is responsible to parliament, the unicameral national assembly which sits for five years and consists of six appointed senators and 15 popularly elected representatives. Last elections May 1989.

Present government

Governor General Sir Joseph Lambert Eustace
Prime Minister; Minister of Foreign Affairs and Finance James F. Mitchell
Other Principal Members of the Cabinet Allan Cruickshank (Agriculture; Industry and Labour); Parnell Campbell (Information; Legal Affairs; Attorney General).

Justice

St Vincent retains its connection with the West Indies Associated States Supreme Court, which is known in St Vincent as the Eastern Caribbean Supreme Court. It consists of a Court of Appeal and a High Court. There are at present two puisne judges of the Eastern Caribbean Supreme Court resident in St Vincent. The Judicial Committee of the Privy Council remains the final Court of Appeal. The death penalty is in force. There were two executions between 1985 and mid-1988. The offences were murder.

National symbols

Flag. Three vertical stripes of blue, yellow and green. In the middle of the yellow stripe there is a green breadfruit leaf surmounted by the coat of arms of St. Vincent.
Festivals. 22 Jan. (Saint Vincent and the Grenadines Day); 1 May (7 May in 1990, Labour Day); 3 July (Caricom Day); 4 July (Carnival Tuesday); 7 Aug. (Emancipation Day); 27 Oct. (Independence Day).
Vehicle registration plate. WV.

INTERNATIONAL RELATIONS

Affiliations
Commonwealth; OAS; Caricom; OECS.

Defence
Police force only.

ECONOMY

Currency
The unit is the East Caribbean dollar, divided into 100 cents.

National finance
Budget. The 1988 FY budget, in US$, was for expenditure of 67.5 million and revenue of 42.7 million.
Inflation. 0.5%.

Gross Domestic Product
Estimated total GDP US$95 million, per capita US$900 (overall size of economy ranking 179 in the world).
Economically active population. The total number of persons active in the economy was 67,000; unemployed: 40%.

Energy and mineral resources
Electricity. Capacity: 16,600 kW; production: 63.7 million kWh; 610 kWh per capita (1988).

Bioresources
Agriculture. 38% of land area is arable and 12% under permanent crops. Main crops are coconuts and bananas, others are cocoa; citrus fruits; mangoes, avocados; guavas.
Crop production: (1987 in tons/tonnes) coconuts 22/20; bananas 52/47.
Livestock numbers: (1987) cattle 8,000; pigs 7,000; sheep 14,000; goats 4,000.
Forestry. 41% of the land area is under forest and woodland.

Industry and commerce
Industry. Main industries are food processing (sugar, flour); cement; furniture; rum; starch; sheet metal; beverages.
Commerce. Exports: US$63.8 million or 67% of GDP, including bananas; eddoes and dasheen; arrowroot starch; copra. Imports: US$87.3 million, including foodstuffs; machinery and equipment; chemicals and fertilizers; minerals and fuels. Countries exported to were Caricom 60%; UK 27%; US 10%. Imports came from US 37%; Caricom 18%; UK 13%.
Trade with UK. St Vincent imported UK goods worth £8,011,000; exports to UK totalled £29,709,000.
Tourism. (1987) 127,776 visitors.

COMMUNICATIONS

Railways
There are no railways.

Roads
There are 633 miles/1,019 km of roads, of which 270 miles/435 km are concrete or bituminized.

Aviation
Main airport is at Arnos Vale, 1.9 miles/3 km from Kingstown.

Shipping
The port is Kingstown on the island of St Vincent. The merchant marine consists of 128 ships of 1,000 GRT or over. Freight loaded: (1987) 94,798 tons/86,000 tonnes; unloaded: 232,585 tons/211,000 tonnes.

Telecommunications
There are 6,500 telephones and an island-wide fully automatic telephone system. There are 58,190 radios and 10,000 televisions (1988). The National Broadcasting Corporation competes with a commercial radio station and a cable TV service.

EDUCATION AND WELFARE

Education
Schools. There are 61 primary schools with 25,152 pupils; 21 state secondary schools; one private secondary school.
Literacy. 82%.

Health
There is a general hospital in Kingstown with 204 beds; five rural hospitals; one psychiatric hospital; one geriatric hospital; one private hospital; 35 clinics. There are 39 doctors (one per 2,689 people).

SAMOA, AMERICAN

GEOGRAPHY

American Samoa is a group of five volcanic islands and two coral atolls in the South Pacific Ocean, covering a total of 77 miles^2/199 km^2. The capital is Pago Pago.

Climate
Tropical marine, moderated by south-east trade winds. Rainy season Nov.-Apr.; dry season May-Oct. Little seasonal temperature variation.

Population
Total population (1989 est.) 40,625.
Birth rate 4.2%. **Death rate** 0.4%. **Rate of population increase** 2.7%. **Life expectancy** female 74; male 69.

Religion
Christianity (Christian Congregationalist, Roman Catholic, Protestant).

Language
Samoan; English (most people are bilingual).

HISTORY

The islands have been settled since 800 BC by Polynesian peoples. The Dutch made the first European contact in 1722, and though deserters and escaped convicts settled there from the beginning of the 19th century, the arrival of British missionaries in 1830 marked the start of continuous western involvement in Samoa. The Americans, in their search for a strategic harbour for their navy, gained exclusive rights from the High Chief in 1872 to use the harbour of Pago Pago on Tutuila, the main island in the eastern group. Rivalries between Germany, Britain and the US in the Samoan Islands eventually led to a convention between them, whereby the US acquired Eastern Samoa. The territory, which became known as American Samoa in 1911, was administered by the US Navy from 1900 to 1951, after which the US Department of the Interior took over responsibility. American Samoa remains an unincorporated territory of the United States, whose people are US nationals, but not citizens. The 1960 constitution, combining traditional practices with the needs of a modern state, gives American Samoans self-government with certain powers reserved to the US secretary of the interior. A non-voting delegate is elected to the US House of Representatives. In 1978 Peter Tali Coleman became the first popularly elected American Samoan governor. He was succeeded in 1984 by A.P. Lutali. A revised constitution was drawn up in 1986, which still excludes commoners and women from voting, but this has yet to be ratified by the US Congress.

CONSTITUTION AND GOVERNMENT

The Territory of American Samoa is an unincorporated and unorganized territory of the United States. The governor is popularly elected to a four-year term, and exercises authority under the direction of the US secretary of the interior. There is a bicameral legislature (known as the Fono), with a senate of 18 members chosen by county councils to serve four-year terms; the House of Representatives has 20 popularly elected members serving two-year terms. American Samoa sends one non-voting delegate to the US House of Representatives.

Leader Peter Coleman, governor since Nov. 1988.

National symbols

Flag. Blue, with a white triangle edged in red. A brown and white American bald eagle flies toward the hoist side, carrying a staff and a war club, traditional Samoan symbols of authority.

National holiday. 17 April (Flag Day).

ECONOMY

90% of foreign trade is conducted with the US. The government and the tuna processing industry are the major employers. Primary export is tinned tuna. There is a developing tourist industry.

Currency

The US dollar.

COMMUNICATIONS

There are ports at Pago Pago and Ta'u; a small railway in Pago Pago harbour; three airports, one with permanent surface runways; 217 miles/350 km of road, 93 miles/150 km of which are paved. There is a telephone system and one AM radio station, but no FM or television.

SAN MARINO

Repubblica di San Marino
(Republic of San Marino)

GEOGRAPHY

San Marino is a landlocked republic situated on the slopes of Monte Titano in east-central Italy, 12 miles/20 km west of the Adriatic Sea. The world's smallest republic, it covers a total area of 24 miles^2/61 km^2. divided into nine castles or districts. The terrain is dominated by the limestone mass of Mt. Titano (2,425 ft/739 m) and the Ausa river valley, draining eastwards into the Adriatic. 17% of the land is arable and approximately one-third of the entire population lives in the northern town of Serravalle.

Climate

Temperate, with cool, mild winters (temperatures seldom below 21°F/–6°C) and warm summers (maximum temperature 79°F/26°C). Annual rainfall totals range from 22 in/560 mm to 31 in/800 mm.

Cities and towns

San Marino (capital)	4,179

Population

Total population is 22,980, of which 90.1% live in urban areas. Population density is 958 persons per mile^2/361.2 per km^2. Ethnic composition: 87.1% are Sanmarinesi (citizens of San Marino); 12.4% Italian. An estimated 11,000 Sanmarinese live abroad.

Birth rate 0.8%. **Death rate** 0.7%. **Rate of population increase** (1980–87) 0.6%. **Age distribution** under 15 = 19.3%; over 65 = 11.5%. **Life expectancy** female 79; male 74; average 77.

Religion

Roman Catholic (at least 95%).

Language

Italian is the official language. The prevailing regional dialect is identifiably Celto-Gallic, related to Piedmont, Lombardy and Romagna dialects.

HISTORY

Claiming to be the world's oldest republic, San Marino was by tradition established in the 4th century AD by St Marinus, a Christian stonemason who fled from Dalmatia to the Apennines. The community he reputedly founded became one of Italy's many ministates and secured papal recognition in 1631. In the Risorgimento (literally 'resurrection'), Garibaldi marched through San Marino in 1849 but the Republic declined to join the unified Italian state created in 1861, preferring to conclude a friendship treaty with it (1862). San Marino volunteers fought for Italy in World War I and from 1923 the Republic came under the domination of Mussolini's fascist regime. In World War II, San Marino followed Italy in declaring war on Britain (1940) but abolished the fascist system and declared its neutrality shortly before Italy's surrender (Sept. 1943). A year later San Marino declared war on Germany after German forces had entered its territory and captured its 300-strong army.

The post-war party structure reflected Italy's. A Communist/Socialist (PCS/PSS) coalition (1945–57) was followed (1957–73) by one between the Christian Democrats (PDCS) and the Independent Social Democrats (PSDIS), a PSS breakaway party. By virtue of its economic union with Italy, San Marino became an integral part of the European Communities in the 1950s. Women obtained the vote in 1960 and became eligible for election in 1973. A PDCS/PSS coalition governed in 1973–77, followed from 1978 by a left-wing coalition of the PCS and PSS plus the Unitarian Socialists (PSU), formed in 1975 when the PSDIS split into left and right factions. In June 1986, however, the PDCS and the PCS, as the two largest parties, formed a grand coalition, which was returned to power in the May 1988 elections.

CONSTITUTION AND GOVERNMENT

Executive and legislature

Every six months, the parliament elects two of its members to act as captains-regent, with the functions of head of state. They exercise executive authority with the assistance of a cabinet, the congress of state. The parliament, the 60-member Grand and General Council, is elected every five years by universal adult suffrage according to proportional representation; last elections 29 May 1988.

Present government

Captains-Regent Leo Achilli, Gloriana Ranocchini II

Principal Members of the Congress of State Gabriele Gatti (Secretary of State for Foreign and Political Affairs); Clara Boscaglia (Secretary of State for Finance and Budget); Alvaro Selva (Secretary of State for Internal Affairs, Civil Protection and Justice).

Justice

The system of law is based on civil law influenced also by Italian practice. The highest court is the Council of Twelve (Consiglio dei XII). There are commissioners respectively for civil and criminal cases, whose rulings may be the subject of appeals to a civil- or criminal-appeals judge. The death penalty was abolished in 1848 (last known execution was carried out in 1468).

National symbols

Flag. Two horizontal stripes of white and blue and the state coat of arms in the centre.

Festivals. 5 Feb. (Liberation Day); 25 Mar. (Anniversary of the Arengo); 1 Apr. and 1 Oct. (Investiture of the new captains-regent); 1 May (Labour Day); 28 July (Fall of Fascism); 3 Sept. (San Marino and Republic Day).

Vehicle registration plate. RSM.

INTERNATIONAL RELATIONS

Affiliations

Observer status in NAM; Council of Europe; member of some UN specialized agencies.

Defence

Small police force only.

ECONOMY

Currency

The unit is the Italian lira, divided into 100 centesimi.

Inflation. 6.4%.

Economically active population. The total number of persons active in the economy was 4,300; unemployed: 6.5%.

Energy and mineral resources

Electricity. Supplied by Italy.

Bioresources

Agriculture. Approximately 17% of the land is put to arable use.

Crop production: wheat; grapes; fruit; vegetables; animal feedstuff; dairy produce; olives.

Industry and commerce

Industry. Wine; olive oil; cement; leather; textiles; tourism. The sale of postage stamps to foreign collectors is an important source of income. Payments are made by the Italian Government in exchange for a monopoly in retailing tobacco, petrol and a few other goods.

Commerce. Trade data are included with statistics for Italy; commodity trade consists primarily of exchanging building stone; lime; wood; chestnuts; wheat; wine; hides; ceramics for a variety of consumer goods.

Tourism. The country relies heavily on the tourist industry as a source of revenue. There are more than 2 million tourists each year, who contribute about 60% to the GDP.

COMMUNICATIONS

Railways

The capital is connected by funicular railway with the Italian town of Borgo Maggiore.

Telecommunications

There are 11,700 telephones, an automatic telephone system and radio relay and cable links into Italian networks; there are no communications satellite facilities and, under an agreement with Italy, no local radio or television station.

EDUCATION AND WELFARE

Education

School population. 1,500 elementary school pupils; 1,400 secondary school pupils.

Schools. 13 elementary schools; four secondary schools, also schools for foreign languages, trade, handicraft and technical skills. (Teacher/pupil ratio 1:12)

Health

150 hospital beds; 60 doctors (approximately one bed per 153 people).

SAO TOME AND PRINCIPE

República Democrática de São Tomé e Príncipe (Democratic Republic of São Tomé and Príncipe)

GEOGRAPHY

Comprising two main islands, São Tomé and Príncipe and the rocky islets of Caroco, Pedras, Tinhosas and Rolas, this democratic republic covers a total area of 372 miles²/964 km², situated in the Bight of Biafra, off the West African coast. São Tomé (326 miles²/845 km²) lies 273 miles/440 km off the north Gabonese coast and rises to a maximum elevation of 6,640 ft/2,024 m at the Pico de São Tomé in the central volcanic uplands. Lowlands to the north-east and south-west characterize the physiography of the two principal islands. Streams drain to the sea from the forested mountainous interiors. Well over 80% of the total population live on the island of São Tomé. 1% of the land is arable and 75% is forested.

Climate

Tropical, temperatures varying slightly according to altitude and the moderating influence of the cool Benguela current. Average annual temperature 77°F/25°C. The rainy season lasts Oct.-May, but rainfall totals increase southwards from 39 in/1,000 mm in the humid north-eastern lowlands to 150-197 in/3,800–5,000 mm on the highland plateau. São Tomé: Jan. 79°F/26.1°C. July 75°F/23.9°C. Average annual rainfall 37 in/951 mm.

Cities and towns

São Tomé (capital)	25,000

Population

Total population is 120,993 of which 33.5% live in urban areas. Population density is 325 persons per mile²/112.4 per km². Ethnic divisions – racially mixed: Mestico; angolares (descendants of Angolan slaves); forros (descendants of emancipated slaves); servicais (contract labouring foreign nationals); tongas (children of servicais); European (mostly Portuguese).

Birth rate 3.8%. **Death rate** 0.7%. **Rate of population increase** (1980–87) 3.0%. **Age distribution** under 15 = 46.4%; over 65 = 4.8%. **Life expectancy** female 70; male 66; average 68.

Religion

Approximately 80% of the population are Roman Catholic. Of the remaining 20%, a substantial proportion are either Seventh Day Adventist or Evangelical Protestant.

Language

The official language is Portuguese. A number of creoles (including a Portuguese crioulo) are also spoken.

HISTORY

After São Tomé's discovery in the 1470s, the Portuguese established sugar plantations in the late 15th century, using slave labour from the mainland. Cocoa was introduced in the 19th century, but production declined after 1905, when an international boycott was imposed over the conditions of virtual slavery suffered by plantation labourers.

In 1960 a nationalist liberation group was set up, which reorganized itself in 1972 as the Movimento de Libertação de São Tomé e Príncipe (MLSTP) under the leadership of Dr Manuel Pinto da Costa. After the armed forces' coup in Portugal in Apr. 1974 the MLSTP was recognized as the sole representative group, and when independence was achieved on 12 July 1975 Dr da Costa became the first president. In Mar. 1978 a coup attempt by foreign mercenaries organized from Gabon was suppressed, and in Mar. 1979 the alleged conspirators were sentenced to imprisonment. In late 1984 Pres. da Costa proclaimed the islands to be non-aligned, and in 1985 the ministers of foreign affairs and planning, both supporters of co-operation with the Soviet Union, were dismissed. Major constitutional changes were announced in Oct. 1987, providing for the election by universal suffrage of the president and the national people's assembly. In Mar. 1988 an invading force of 46 armed men landed and attempted to seize police headquarters near the capital on São Tomé island. Two were killed and the rest captured, including their leader, Afonso dos Santos, head of a dissident faction of the exiled São Tomé National Resistance Front. During their trial which began in July 1989 the would-be invaders, among them Cape Verdeans and Angolans, admitted that they had been trained in South Africa.

CONSTITUTION AND GOVERNMENT

Executive and legislature

The head of state is the president, who under 1987 constitutional amendments is elected directly by universal adult suffrage with a secret ballot. The legislature, the unicameral 40-member National People's Assembly designated as 'the supreme organ of the state', is also to be elected directly, for a five-year term. Last elections were in Aug. 1985, when all candidates were nominees of the ruling and sole legal party, which has held an effective monopoly of political power since independence, although the recent constitutional changes provide for the election to public office of independents and candidates put forward by 'organizations with recognized representation'.

Present government

President; C.-in-C. of the Armed Forces Dr Manuel Pinto da Costa

Prime Minister Celestino Rocha da Costa

Other Principal Members of the Cabinet Raul Bragança Neto (Defence and Internal Security); Agapito Mendes Dias (Economy and Finance); Carlos da Graça (Foreign Affairs); Francisco Fortunado Pires (Justice and Public Affairs).

Ruling party

Movement for the Liberation of São Tomé and Príncipe (Movimento de Libertação de São Tomé e Príncipe). **General Secretary** Dr Manuel Pinto da Costa.

Justice

There is a Supreme Court, whose judges are appointed by the People's Assembly. The death penalty is in force only for exceptional crimes. There were no executions between 1985 and mid-1988.

National symbols

Flag. Three horizontal stripes of green, yellow and green and a red triangle in the hoist, reaching one-quarter of the flag's length.
Festivals. 12 July (independence Day).

INTERNATIONAL RELATIONS

Affiliations

NAM; OAU; ACP.

Defence

Army and Navy.

ECONOMY

Currency

The unit is the dobra, divided into 100 centivos.

National finance

Budget. The 1987 budget, in US$, was for expenditure of 25.1 million and revenue of 19.2 million.
Inflation. 4.2%.

Gross Domestic Product

Estimated total GDP US$38 million, per capita US$340 (overall size of economy ranking 188 in the world).
Economically active population. The total number of persons active in the economy was 21,100.

Energy and mineral resources

Electricity. Capacity: 6,000 kW; production: 7 million kWh; 60 kWh per capita.

Bioresources

Agriculture. The land is subject to deforestation and soil erosion and drought. Most is state-owned. 1% is arable, 20% permanent crops. The economy is dependent on cocoa, but production is in decline, leading to balance-of-payment problems. The vast majority of food has to be imported.
Crop production: cocoa; copra; coconuts; coffee; palm-oil; bananas. Food crops are sweet potato; yams; cassava.
Livestock numbers: goats 4,000; cattle 3,000; pigs 3,000; sheep 2,000.
Forestry. 75% of the land is forest and woodland.
Fisheries. Total catch: (1985) 4,960 tons/4,500 tonnes. Tuna and shrimps are important.

Industry and commerce

Industry. Light construction; fisheries; shrimp processing; shirts; soap; beer.
Commerce. Exports: (f.o.b. 1987 est.) US$9.8 million or 26% of GDP, including cocoa 90%; copra; coffee; palm-oil. Imports: (c.i.f. 1987 est.) US$26 million, including machinery and electrical equipment 60%; food products 30%; fuels 10%. Main trading partners Portugal; US; West Germany; East Germany.
Trade with UK. São Tomé imported £416,000 worth of goods from the UK and exported £20,000 worth to the UK.
Tourism. Considerable potential exists for expansion of the tourist industry, and the government has started to develop facilities.

COMMUNICATIONS

Railways

There are no railways in São Tomé and Príncipe.

Roads

There are 178 miles/287 km of roads, of which 124 miles/199 km are bituminized.

Aviation

Equatorial Airlines of São Tomé and Príncipe provides domestic services between the islands and to Libreville (chief airport is at São Tomé).

Shipping

There are two ports: São Tomé (on São Tomé) and Santo Antonio (on Príncipe).

Telecommunications

There are 2,200 telephones and a minimal telecommunications system. There are 28,000 radios, with a state-controlled service in Portuguese, and no television service (1986).

EDUCATION AND WELFARE

Education

School population. Some 20,000 primary school pupils; some 7,000 secondary school pupils; some 400 technical school students.
Schools. 65 primary schools with 550 teachers; 11 secondary schools with 300 teachers; two technical schools with 35 teachers. (Pupil/teacher ratio 31:1)

Health

Some 40 doctors.

SAUDI ARABIA

Al-Mamlaka al-'Arabiya as-Sa'udiya (Kingdom of Saudi Arabia)

GEOGRAPHY

Occupying approximately 80% of the Arabian peninsula in south-western Asia, the Kingdom of Saudi Arabia covers an area of 829,780 miles^2/ 2,149,690 km^2 divided into 14 provinces. Backing the Red Sea coastal plain (Tihamah), a broad range of mountain extends north-west to south-west climbing to 4,921 ft/1,500 m in the north and 10,278 ft/3,133 m at Jebel Abha in the south-west, Arabia's highest peak. The south-western Asir highlands constitute the only region with reliable rainfall. The high central desert (Nejd) plateau declines to the north and east, merging with two of the world's largest desert regions, the Great Nafūd in the north, and the Rub'al-Khali to the south. Salt flats abound to the east, and the north-eastern regions are dissected by a number of wadis. Over 95% of the terrain is arid or semi-arid desert. Approximately one-third of the population lives in the cities of Riyadh, Jiddah and Mecca (Makkah) and the surrounding urban areas. 0.5% of the land is considered arable (irrigated) and less than 2% is forested.

Climate

Hot, dry, predominantly desert conditions. Average temperatures range from 79°F/26°C in the south to 70°F/21°C in the north. Summer temperatures for the same regions vary from 120°F/49°C to 100°F/38°C, reaching as much as 129°F/54°C in the interior. Maximum humidity occurs May-Sept.; winter temperatures are mild. In the south-west, the Asir highlands receive up to 15 in/370 mm of rainfall annually, but the national average is less than 2 in/ 50 mm a year with many sectors remaining rainless for years. Riyadh: Jan. 57.9°F/14.4°C. July 91.9°F/33.3°C. Average annual rainfall 4 in/100 mm. Jiddah: Jan. 73°F/22.8°C. July 87.1°F/30.6°C. Average annual rainfall 3 in/81 mm.

Cities and towns

Riyadh (royal capital)	666,840
Jiddah (administrative capital)	561,104
Mecca (Makkah)	366,801
Ta'if	204,857
Medina	198,186
Dammam	127,844
Hufuf	101,271

Population

Total population is 16,108,539 of which 73.0% live in urban areas. Population density (average) is 19 persons per mile^2/7.4 per km^2. Ethnic divisions: 90% Arab; 10% Afro-Asian. The nomadic population at the last census was 1,883,987.
Birth rate 3.8%. **Death rate** 0.7%. **Rate of population increase** (1980–88) 3.7%. **Age distribution** under 15 = 44.9%; over 65 = 2.6%. **Life expectancy** female 65; male 62; average 63.

Religion

Almost 100% of the population are Sunni Muslims. Mecca, birthplace of the prophet Muhammad, is visited by over 1.5 million Muslims every year. Most native Saudis adhere to the orthodox Wahhabi rites. A small Christian minority is represented by the Roman Catholic, Anglican and Greek Orthodox faiths.

Language

Arabic is the official language, some English is taught in secondary schools.

HISTORY

The new religion of Islam was the force which unified Arabia in the 7th century AD. Prior to its emergence, the peninsula was divided between a number of Arab tribes, many nomadic or semi-nomadic, with major trading centres at Medina and Mecca, the latter also being the site of a pagan religious sanctuary. The majority of the peninsula's peoples were animist, but there were also small Jewish and Christian communities. The Prophet Muhammad was born in AD 570 in Mecca where he received revelations from God and founded Islam. Within a few years most of what is today Saudi Arabia had become Muslim. However, following the Prophet's death the political focus of Islam moved out of Arabia, first to Damascus and then to Baghdad. The unity of Muslim Arabia collapsed and gave away to tribal rivalries although some order was restored by the Seldjuk Turks who invaded the peninsula in 1174. In the early 16th century the Egyptian Mamelukes invaded but were soon swept aside by the Ottomans who established their authority over much of the peninsula.

In 1744 a pledge was made near Riyadh between a Muslim preacher, Mohammad ibn abd al-Wahhab, and the ancestor of the kingdom's present rulers, Mohammad ibn Saud. The alliance was to spearhead a politico-religious campaign to reform the Arabian peninsula. 'Wahhabism' (correctly 'Unitarianism') sought a return to Islamic purity.

Mohammad ibn Saud was succeeded by his son, Abd al-Aziz, who captured Riyadh in 1765. In 1792 al-Wahhab died and in 1803 the Saudis marched on the Hejaz defeating the Sharif Husayn of Mecca. Saudi authority now extended from Hasa in the east to the Hejaz in the west and as far south as Najran. Alarmed by this new power, the Ottoman Sultan Mahmoud II called on his viceroy in Egypt, Mohammad Ali, to reconquer the Hejaz. The Egyptians took the Hejaz and the Najd and in 1819 destroyed the Saudi capital, Dir'iyya. The ruler, Abdullah ibn Saud, was sent to Istanbul and executed. In 1838 Muhammad Ali's armies returned to Najd, defeated Faisal, the Saudi ruler of the time, and sent him captive to Cairo. In 1843 he escaped and began a second 20-year reign by the end of which he had reconquered most of Najd and Hasa. His death caused internal family squabbles and the rise of the Rashid family in Hail. By 1884 the Rashid had conquered Riyadh and by 1890 most of the Saudi clan had found refuge in Kuwait.

The creation of today's kingdom dates from 1902 when the 21-year-old Abd al-Aziz (commonly known as Ibn Saud) took Riyadh by night with a small group of followers. In 1906 he defeated the Rashid and over the next seven years conquered the eastern territory of Hasa, the home of Shia tribes. After World War I, Abdul Aziz continued to expand his domain, taking in Hail and Najd. Eager to gain control of the lucrative pilgrimage trade at Mecca and Medina, Abdul Aziz took advantage of the fact that Sharif Hussain, Mecca's current ruler, had proclaimed himself Caliph. Abdul Aziz succeeded in having him condemned for such presumption by a conference of Islamic clergy. With British support, Abdul Aziz's followers captured Mecca in 1924, and Medina the following year. In 1926 he took the title of King of Hijaz, and on 18 Sept. 1932 he announced the creation of the Kingdom of Saudi Arabia. In 1937 Socal (Standard Oil Company of California), under its new name Aramco (the Arabian American Oil Company), struck oil near Riyadh. Production started in Hasa in May 1939 and during the following decade Aramco began work on the Trans-Arabian Pipeline (Tapline).

On 9 Nov. 1953 Abd al-Aziz died in Taif and was succeeded by his son, Crown Prince Saud. Saud did not have the makings of a ruler and after severe financial problems he stepped down in 1964 in favour of his astute brother Faisal. Despite financial chaos, Saudi Arabia was producing 33.5% of the total oil output of Middle East countries by Faisal's death in 1975. Aware of the impact of such wealth on his country he prepared two five-year development plans which aimed to absorb the best of Western technology without, if possible, compromising the kingdom's spiritual values.

By the 1950s, Faisal was playing a key role in Middle Eastern politics at a time when Egypt's Pres. Nasser was the dominant influence in the region. From 1962 until 1967 Saudi Arabia supported the monarchists against the Egypt-backed republicans in the civil war in North Yemen. The war came to an end with the withdrawal of support from both sides and attention moved to Israel which was to heavily defeat Egypt in the 1967 war.

After the 1973 war with Israel, Saudi Arabia put pressure on the United States to encourage Israel to withdraw from the occupied territories of Palestine by cutting oil production and placing an embargo on all exports to the US. The Israeli occupation of Jerusalem, the holiest city in Islam after Mecca and Medina, shocked the Saudis. At home Faisal inaugurated a programme of social and economic reforms which included the abolition of slavery and the creation of a free health service for all Saudis and, despite conservative opposition, opportunities for women in education and in employment.

On 25 Mar. 1975 King Faisal was assassinated by his nephew. The succession passed to his brother Khaled although effective authority was to be in the hands of another brother, Fahd.

Throughout this period, the Saudi rulers presented themselves as guardians of Islam. However, in Nov. 1979, they faced a serious fundamentalist challenge when the Great Mosque at Mecca was occupied by some 250 fanatical followers of Juhaiman ibn Saif al-Otaibi, a militant Wahhab leader, who was to reveal the Mahdi (messiah) within the mosque on that day, the first day of the Muslim year 1400. The siege ended after two weeks of bloody fighting in which 102 rebels and 27 Saudi soldiers were killed. On 9 Jan. 1980, 63 of the rebels were led into the squares of various towns and publicly beheaded.

In December of that year riots exploded in the towns of the Qatif Oasis, the heartlands of the kingdom's 300,000 Shias, who were inspired by the success of Khomeini's Shia revolution in Iran. The government responded by putting down the riots with severity but also promising reforms for the Shias, who felt with justice that although they occupied the territory of the kingdom's wealth, they were not reaping the benefits of that wealth.

In the face of Iranian threats to 'export' its Islamic revolution, Saudi Arabia lent moral and material support to Iraq in the Gulf War. In May 1981, it joined with the UAE, Bahrain, Oman, Qatar and Kuwait to form the Gulf Co-operation Council with its secretariat in Riyadh. In March, the US agreed to sell Saudi Arabia five airborne warning and control systems (AWACS) aircraft.

King Khaled died on 14 June 1982, aged 69, and was succeeded by Fahd, the eldest of seven full brothers (the Sudeiri Seven) whose mother comes from the Sudeiri clan. Fahd had for the previous eight years been the main formulator of Saudi policy so that there was little change in policy. Saudi diplomats played an active part in mediation efforts in Lebanon and between Iraq and Iran during the mid-1980s, although its increasing support for Iraq brought it to the brink of war with Iran. The 1987 haj to Mecca was the occasion of bloody clashes between Iranian pilgrims and Saudi security forces. Since the end of the Gulf War in 1988, relations with Iran have begun to improve. Economically, the kingdom invests considerable manpower and finance in efforts to develop a substantial agricultural base.

CONSTITUTION AND GOVERNMENT

Executive and legislature

The king holds supreme executive and legislative power, and is assisted by an appointed cabinet. His official title is Custodian of the Two Holy Mosques (ie Mecca and Medina). There is no parliament.

Present government

Custodian of the Two Holy Mosques; Prime Minister King Fahd ibn Abdul Aziz

Crown Prince; First Deputy Prime Minister; Commander of National Guard Prince Abdullah ibn Abdul Aziz

Second Deputy Prime Minister; Minister of Defence and Civil Aviation Prince Sultan ibn Abdul Aziz

Other Principal Ministers Prince Nayef ibn Abdul Aziz (Interior); Prince Saud al Faisal (Foreign Affairs); Muhammad Ali Abdul Khail (Finance and National Economy); Muhammad ibn Ibrahim ibn Jubair (Justice); Shaikh Hisham Nazer (Petroleum and Mineral Resources; Planning (acting)); Shaikh Abdul Wahhab Ahmad Abdul Wasi (Haj (Pilgrimage) Affairs and Waqfs (Religious Endowments)).

Justice

The legal system is based on Islamic law, which is the common law of the country. The judiciary consists of religious courts, at the head of which is a chief judge, who is responsible for the Department of Sharia (legal) Affairs. Sharia courts are concerned primarily with family inheritance and property matters. The death penalty is in force. There were over 140 executions between 1985 and mid-1988. Offences were murder, robbery with violence, adultery and drug offences.

National symbols

Flag. Green with a white Arabic inscription and a sword with a straight blade.
Festivals. 23 Sept. (Unification of the Kingdom); Islamic holidays.
Vehicle registration plate. SA.

INTERNATIONAL RELATIONS

Affiliations

NAM; Arab League; OPEC; OAPEC; ICO; GCC.

Defence

Total Armed Forces: 72,300 inclusive 10,000 National Guard. Terms of service: voluntary; conscription, males 18–35, authorized.
Army: 38,000; 550 main battle tanks (AMX-30, M-60A1, M-60A39).
Navy: 7,800 inclusive 1,200 marines; eight frigates (Fr Type F.2000, US Tacoma) and 13 patrol and coastal combatants.
Air Force: 16,500; 182 combat aircraft (F-5FE, F-15C, Tornados IDS).
Para-military (National Guard): 56,000.

ECONOMY

Currency

The unit is the riyal, divided into 100 halalas.

National finance

Budget. The 1988 budget, in US$, was for expenditure of 37,900 million and revenue of 24,000 million.
Balance of payments. The balance of payments, in US$ (current account, 1987) was a deficit of 6,270 million.
Inflation. 1.0%.

Gross Domestic Product

Estimated total GDP US$71,470 million, per capita US$5,840 (overall size of economy ranking 33 in the world).
Economically active population. The total number of persons active in the economy was 4,200,000; unemployed: 0%.

Sector	% of workforce	% of GDP
industry	28	50
agriculture	16	4
services*	56	46

* services figure includes elements unassigned to other categories.

Energy and mineral resources

Oil and gas. Crude oil, proven reserves 169,000 million bbls (1988). Crude oil production: (1988) 277 million tons/251 million tonnes, 97% produced by Aramco which is a state-owned company. There are 14 major oilfields, Ghawar, Abqaiq, Safaniyah being the most important. There are five domestic refineries. Gas production equivalent to 355,000 bbls per day (1984).
Minerals. Iron ore; gold (produced at Mahd Al-Dahab); copper; phosphate; bauxite; uranium.
Electricity. Capacity: 24.4 million kW; production: 53.5 million kWh; 3,460 kWh per capita.

Bioresources

Agriculture. 1% of the land is put to arable use. There are no perennial rivers or permanent water bodies. Extensive coastal seawater desalination plants are being developed. Not self-sufficient in food, except wheat. There are large government schemes for desert reclamation and irrigation.
Crop production: (1987) dates 551,150 tons/500,000 tonnes; wheat 2.2 million tons/2 million tonnes; water melons 468,478 tons/425,000 tonnes; poultry 3,307 tons/3,000 tonnes; red meat 148,811 tons/135,000 tonnes.
Livestock numbers: sheep 3.8 million; goats 2.4 million; cattle 530,000; camels 165,000.
Fisheries. Annual catch 17,637–22,046 tons/16–20,000 tonnes.

Industry and commerce

Industry. By far the most important economic activity is the production of petroleum and petroleum products. The petroleum sector accounts for about 85% of budget revenue, 80% of GDP and almost all export earnings. Saudi Arabia has the largest reserves of petroleum in the world, and is the largest exporter of petroleum. Industries include crude oil production; petroleum refining; basic petrochemicals; cement; small steel-rolling mill; construction; fertilizer; plastic. Two important industrial centres are Jubail and Yanbu.
Commerce. Exports: (f.o.b.1988) US$24,000 million (approximately 32% of GNP), including petroleum and petroleum products 89%. Main trading partners Japan; US; France; Bahrain. Imports: US$18,500 million, mainly manufactured goods; transportation equipment; construction materials; processed food products. Major trading partners US; Japan; UK; Italy.
Trade with UK. In 1988 Saudi Arabia exported £614,144 worth of goods to the UK, and imported £1.7 million worth of goods from the UK.
Tourism. The principal reason for 'tourist' units to Saudi Arabia is the annual pilgrimage to Mecca (Makkah), which attracts over 2 million of the faithful from throughout the Islamic world.

COMMUNICATIONS

Railways

There are some 621 miles/1,000 km of railways.

Roads

There are 56,728 miles/91,350 km of roads, of which 21,020 miles/33,848 km are bituminized.

Aviation

Saudia (Saudi Arabian Airlines) provides domestic and international services (main airports are the King Abd al-Aziz International Airport in Jiddah, the King

Khalid International Airport at Riyadh and the New Eastern Province Airport). Passengers: (1984) 11.4 million.

Shipping

Jiddah, Jizzan, and Yanbu al Bahr are all ports on the Red Sea. Ad Dammam, Al Jubayl, and Ras Tannura are located on the east coast of Saudi Arabia in the Persian Gulf. The merchant marine consists of 99 ships of 1,000 GRT or over. Freight loaded: (1985 est.) 181 million tons/163.8 million tonnes; unloaded: 41 million tons/37.5 million tonnes.

Telecommunications

There are 1.6 million telephones and a good telecommunications system with an extensive microwave and coaxial cable network. There are 3.8 million radios and 3.2 million televisions (1986). The government operates a television service in Arabic and English, while the private non-commercial Channel 3 provides a film service in English; the Aramco Radio station provides music and programmes in English in addition to the government radio stations, which broadcast in Arabic and English with overseas services in six other languages.

EDUCATION AND WELFARE

Education

Education is free at primary, intermediate and secondary levels; boys and girls are educated separately.

School population. Some 1.3 million primary school pupils; some 530,000 intermediate and secondary school pupils.

Schools. Some 7,600 primary schools with 79,000 teachers; 3,300 intermediate and secondary schools with some 40,300 teachers. Pupil/teacher ratio approximately 15:1.

Universities. King Abdul Aziz University, Jiddah; King Saud University, Riyadh; King Faisal University, University of Petroleum and Minerals.

Literacy. 52%.

Health

Some 140 hospitals with 24,000 beds (approximately one per 670 people); 8,500 doctors; 16,500 nurses and midwives.

SENEGAL

République du Sénégal
(Republic of Senegal)

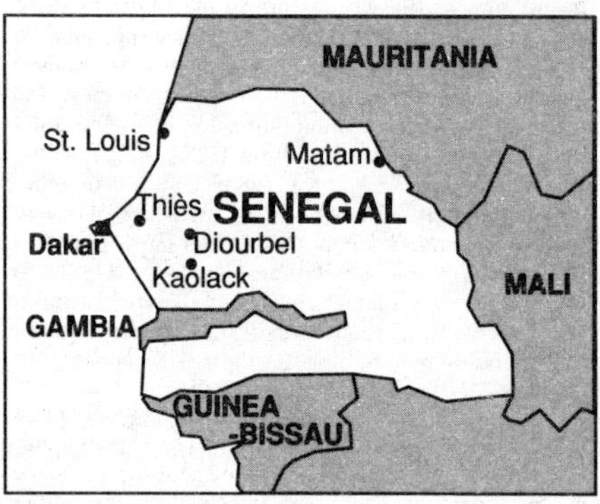

GEOGRAPHY

Located on the west coast of Africa, Senegal contains an area of 75,729 miles^2/196,190 km^2, divided into ten regions. North of Cape Verde, the westernmost extremity of the African continent, the Senegalese coastline is typified by sand dunes and to the south by rias (drowned valleys), dunes and mangrove forests. The lowland savannah and semi-desert regions of the north drain into the River Sénégal, forming the north and north-eastern boundary with Mauritania. To the south, the land inclines gradually towards the Guinean frontier, reaching a maximum elevation of 1,640 ft/500 m. The bulk of the population inhabits the northern Sahel and Savannah regions. 27% of the land is arable and 31% is forested.

Climate

Tropical, with well-demarcated wet and dry seasons: most rain falling in the hot and humid period June-Oct. Rainfall increases north-south from 12–14 in/300–350 mm to 39–59 in/1,000–1,500 mm per annum. The dusty Saharan Harmattan blows in from the north-east during the dry season. Dakar: Jan. 72°F/22.2°C. July 82°F/27.8°C. Average annual rainfall 21 in/541 mm.

Cities and towns

Dakar (capital)	800,000
Thiès	117,000
Kaolack	106,000
Saint-Louis	88,000
Ziguinchor	73,000
Diourbel	51,000

Population

Total population is 7,506,197 of which 35.0% live in urban areas. Population density is 99.1 persons per mile^2/38.3 per km^2. Ethnic composition: 36% Wolof; 17% Fulani; 17% Serer; 9% Toucouleur; 9% Diola; 9% Mandingo; 1% European and Lebanese.

Birth rate 4.6%. **Death rate** 1.5%. **Rate of population increase** (1980–87) 3.1%. **Age distribution** under 15 = 44.4%; over 65 = 3.0%. **Life expectancy** female 49; male 46; average 48.

Religion

At the last census 91% of the population were Sunni Muslims; 6% Christian (predominantly Roman Catholic); 3% followed traditional animist beliefs.

Language

French is the official language. The principal ethnic groups each speak a separate language eg Wolof, Pulaar, Diola and Mandingo.

HISTORY

The earliest inhabitants of Senegal were Black pastoralists, ancestors of the Wolof and Serer ethnic groups. Little is known about the early history of the region until North African traders began to record their impressions of the Bilad al-Sudan, the Land of the Blacks. By the 11th century AD Muslim Arabs had become a major influence in the politics of the Senegal valley. The king of Takrur, an important gold-rich kingdom in the upper valley of the River Sénégal, was reported to have converted to Islam in the mid-11th century and to have introduced Islamic law. By the 14th century the whole of Senegal was incorporated into the vast Mali empire which from its base in the bend of the River Niger extended westwards to the Atlantic. By the end of the 16th century the Mali empire had disintegrated and from then until the 19th century the history of Senegal was dominated by the smaller pagan kingdoms of Walo, Cayor, Baol and Sine-Saloum which occupied the region between the Senegal and Gambia valleys.

European contact with Senegal dates back to the late 15th century when Portuguese merchants began to buy gold and slaves at coastal entrepots. By the mid-17th century the French had replaced Portuguese, Dutch and English merchants as the principal trading partners. The French established a trading post in St Louis on the mouth of the River Sénégal in 1637 and in 1677 took over the fortified island of Gorée which had originally been settled by the Dutch in 1627. The traffic in slaves came to dominate what had originally been a varied commerce in gold, ivory, hides and furs. During the height of the slave trade Gorée was a major slave depot through which up to 5,000 slaves were exported annually. By the early 19th century the French decided to expand their influence inland, establishing a sequence of river forts along the Sénégal valley where the trade in gum arabic was now the main source of wealth.

The decisive period of French expansion started in the mid-1860s under the governorship of Louis Faidherbe. French military imperialism coincided with a period of intense change further east as a result of the foundation of a militant reformist Islamic state under the leadership of al-hajj Umar Tall in the Futa Toro region of the upper valley of the Sénégal. Al-hajj Umar had imperialist ambitions of his own as he attempted to extend his empire westwards but although he succeeded in holding up the French occupation of the interior neither he nor his successors could match the firepower of the French. By the end of the century the French army (composed largely of African soldiers) had overcome the last African resistance.

Around the turn of the century the French organized their various West African colonies into the federation of French West Africa (Afrique occidentale Française, AOF) with its administrative centre in Dakar, the capital of Senegal. During the colonial period Senegal, and especially Dakar, prospered from being the administrative capital of this federation. Senegal's economy was based on the cultivation of groundnuts which became a virtual monoculture.

Political life in the colony was very active. Since 1848 the 'Four Communes' of St Louis, Dakar, Gorée and Rufisque, had enjoyed the same status as a metropolitan department and citizens regardless of race or creed were allowed to vote and elect a deputy to the French parliament. In 1914 Blaise Diagne was elected as the first ever Black deputy and by the late 1930s there was a relatively well developed party system. During the period of France's wartime collaborationist Vichy regime (1940–43) Africans were denied political rights but as part of the post-war settlement there was a big increase in the franchise and elections were fiercely contested. After the war the two leading politicians were both socialists: Lamine Guèye and Léopold Senghor, the poet and philosopher of negritude. In 1948 Senghor split from Gùye to found his own party. Although both Guèye and Senghor pressed for a greater degree of autonomy neither envisaged independence. Senghor's originality lay in his recognition of the importance of rural voters; despite being a Catholic his power-base came increasingly to lie in the Muslim countryside where the conservative Muslim leaders became key actors in Senegalese politics.

By the late 1950s political attitudes were changing and a new party, Parti africain de l'indépendance (PAI) with its roots in the urban educated elite, campaigned for independence. Throughout French West Africa many African politicians were anxious to preserve the unity of the federation but French policy was to allow colonies to become independent as individual sovereign states. Senegal became independent on 20 June 1960 as part of the Mali Federation incorporating Senegal, Mali, Upper Volta and Dahomey as they were then called. The Federation did not survive long and within two months Senegal seceded, becoming the independent Republic of Senegal on 20 Aug. 1960.

Léopold Senghor became president of the Republic with Mamadou Dia as prime minister. Senghor ousted Dia in 1962 following allegations of an attempted coup and approved a new constitution (promulgated 7 Mar. 1963) to strengthen the position of the president. Legislative elections the following year consolidated the position of Senghor and his ruling Union Progressiste Sénégalais (UPS) over opposition parties led by Cheikh Anta Diop's populist Bloc des masses sénégalais. Party politics went into decline and by 1966 there were no legally recognized opposition parties.

In 1968 Senghor had to ask for French assistance in overcoming internal student and trade union unrest as the economic situation worsened. In 1970 Senghor appointed Abdou Diouf, a technocrat, to the newly revived position of prime minister. Senghor continued to rule with an astute combination of firmness and flexibility, allowing the foundation of a new opposition party, Parti démocratique sénégalais (PDS) led by Abdoulaye Wade in 1974. In 1976 a new constitution was introduced, enshrining the principle of multi-party politics but limiting the permitted number to three, whose ideologies were also prescribed in the constitution. The PDS became the legal liberal democratic party and the old PAI was allowed back into existence as the marxist democratic party. At the same time the UPS was renamed the Parti socialiste (PS).

In Jan. 1981 Senghor announced his retirement, naming Abdou Diouf as his successor. Diouf won a comfortable majority in the 1983 elections in which the opposition parties were given a high level of access to state media. Despite winning another big majority in elections in 1988 against a hopelessly divided opposition (which now consisted of 13 legally recognized parties) Diouf has faced increasing problems as a result of poor harvests, worsening social and economic conditions, and unpopular IMF-backed economic structural adjustment policies dating from 1980. During the 1980s secessionist demands from the southern province of Casamance, the most fertile and prosperous region of the country, have posed a major threat to Senegal's stability.

CONSTITUTION AND GOVERNMENT

Executive and legislature

The president, the head of state and head of government, is elected directly by universal adult suffrage for a five-year term, at the same time as elections to the national assembly; last general election Feb. 1988. The unicameral Assembly has 120 seats, half elected on a constituency basis and half by proportional representation.

Present government

President; Head of Government; Commander of the Armed Forces Abdou Diouf

Principal Members of the Council of Ministers Jean Collin (Minister of State, Secretary-General to the President's Office); Medoune Fall (Defence); Seydou Madani Sy (Justice; Keeper of the Seals); Ibrahima Fall (Foreign Affairs); André Sonko (Interior); Serigne Lamine Diop (Finance and Economic Affairs; Djibo Kâ (Planning and Co-operation).

President of the National Assembly Abdoul Azizi Ndaw.

Justice

The system of law is based on French civil law. The highest court is the Supreme Court, which has a role in the judicial review of legislation. At local level, justice is administered by the *juges de paix* in each *departement*, with a court of first instance in each region. There are assize courts in Dakar, Kaolack, Saint-Louis and Ziguinchor, and a court of appeal in Dakar. The death penalty is nominally in force. There were no executions between 1985 and mid-1988.

National symbols

Flag. Tricolour with vertical stripes of green, yellow and red. In the yellow stripe there is a green five-pointed star.

Festivals. 1 Feb. (Confederal Agreement Day); 4 Apr. (National Day); 1 May (Labour Day); 14 July (Day of Association).

Vehicle registration plate. SN.

INTERNATIONAL RELATIONS

Affiliations

NAM; OAU; ACP; ICO; Francophonie.

Defence

Total Armed Forces: 9,700. Terms of service: conscription, two years selective. Reserve: exists, no details known.

Army: 8,500.

Navy: 700; eight patrol and coastal combatants.

Air Force: 500; 11 combat aircraft (CM-170, R-235 Guerrier).

ECONOMY

Currency

The unit is the CFA franc, divided into 100 centimes.

National finance

Budget. The 1988/89 FY budget, in US$, was for expenditure of 1,573 million and revenue of 1,573 million.

Balance of payments. The balance of payments, in US$ (current account, 1987) was a deficit of 608 million.

Inflation. 4.3%.

Gross Domestic Product

Estimated total GDP US$4,720 million, per capita US$290 (overall size of economy ranking 88 in the world).

Economically active population The total number of persons active in the economy was 2,509,000; unemployed: 3.5%.

Sector	% of GDP
industry	27
agriculture	22
services*	52

* services figure includes elements unassigned to other categories.

Energy and mineral resources

Minerals. Phosphate extraction constitutes Senegal's principal mining activity. An estimated 2 million tons/1.8 million tonnes of calcium phosphate and 0.41 million tons/0.37 million tonnes of aluminium phosphate were produced in 1985. Other significant mineral reserves include titanium ores and zirconium found along the coast and approximately 1,080 million tons/980 million tonnes of iron ore deposits.

Electricity. Capacity: 210,000 kW; production: 758 million kWh; 100 kWh per capita (1988).

Bioresources

Agriculture. 27% of the land is arable, 30% is meadow or pastureland. About 40% (5.29 million acres/2.14 million ha) of the total cultivated land area (13.22 million acres/5.35 million ha) is used to grow peanuts, an important export crop.

Crop production: (1986 in 1,000 tons/tonnes) sugar cane 882/800; groundnuts 794/720; millet 775/703; rice 141/128; maize 141/128; seed cotton 55/50; mangoes 37/34; onions 35/32; tomatoes 28/25.

Livestock numbers: (1987) cattle 2.2 million; sheep 2.2 million; goats 1.1 million; asses 210,000; pigs 210,000; horses 208,000; camels 6,000.

Forestry. 31% of the land area is forested. Timber production: (1985) 144.8 million ft^3/4.1 million m^3.

Fisheries. Total catch: (1985) 268,961 tons/244,000 tonnes. Fishing accounted for 25% of all foreign exchange earnings in 1987.

Industry and commerce

Industry. Senegal's main industries are fishing; agricultural processing; phosphate mining; petroleum refining; building materials. The slump in phosphate production over recent years is attributable to the decline in global demands for fertilizer. Tourism is currently a growth industry. Dakar is a major industrial centre with extensive shipbuilding and repair facilities for vessels of up to 28,000 tonnes. Production: (1983 in 1,000 tonnes) cement 395; petroleum products 336; peanut oil 217.

Commerce. Exports: (1987) US$749 million or 37% of GDP; imports $983 million or 49% of GDP. Chief exports included manufactures 30%; fish products 27%; peanuts 11%; petroleum products 11%; phosphates 10%. Imports were semi-manufactures 33%; food 26%; durable consumer goods 17%; petroleum 14%; capital goods 14%. Export trading partners were US; France; other EC countries; Côte d'Ivoire; India. Import trading partners included US; France; other EC countries; Nigeria; Algeria; China; Japan.

Trade with UK. Senegal imported UK goods worth

£14.8 million in 1988; exports to the UK amounted to £11.3 million.
Tourism. (1986) 235,000 visitors.

COMMUNICATIONS

Railways

There are 642 miles/1,034 km of railways.

Roads

There are 9,315 miles/15,000 km of roads, of which 2,795 miles/4,500 km are concrete or bituminized.

Aviation

Air Afrique provides international service and Air Sénégal - Société Nationale des Transports Aériens (SONATRA) provides domestic services (main airports are at Dakar-Yoff, Saint-Louis, Ziguinchor and Tambacounda). Passengers: (1984) 126,000.

Shipping

There are 602 miles/970 km of inland waterways. The main ports are Kaolack (inland) and Dakar (marine). The merchant marine consists of three ships of 1,000 GRT or over. Freight loaded: (1987) 2.1 million tons/ 1.9 million tonnes; unloaded: 2.3 million tons/ 2.1 million tonnes.

Telecommunications

There are 40,200 telephones and an above-average urban system using radio relay and cable. There are 440,000 radios and 6,000 televisions (1983). The state ORTS controls radio and TV broadcasting, and in addition an agreement in 1989 provided for direct television transmissions from France.

EDUCATION AND WELFARE

Education

Schools. An estimated 583,500 pupils attend 2,170 primary schools served by 11,500 members of staff (one per 51 pupils). 113,653 secondary school pupils receive instruction from 2,346 teachers (one per 48 pupils) in 162 schools modelled on the French educational system.
Universities. 11,470 students are registered at the University of Dakar. The University of St. Louis is still under construction.
Literacy. 10%.

Health

A total of 1,766 state nursing staff and 450 doctors serve 44 hospitals with 7,092 beds (one per 1,058 members of the population). In addition there are some 70 dentists, 326 midwives and about 140 pharmacists.

SEYCHELLES

Republic of Seychelles

GEOGRAPHY

Located in the Indian Ocean, approximately 994 miles/1,600 km east of Kenya, the Republic of Seychelles comprises 115 islands and islets dispersed over 250,900 miles^2/650,000 km^2 of ocean, covering a total land area of 175 miles^2/453 km^2. The principal island groups are the Mahé or Granitic group, consisting of 40 central, rugged islands with narrow coastal borders and dense tropical vegetation (92 miles^2/239 km^2) and the Outer Coralline islands, flat, waterless and for the most part uninhabited (total population 400). 90% of the population live on Mahé island (59 miles^2/153 km^2), which rises to a maximum elevation of 2,972 ft/906 m. Other islands in the Granitic group include Praslin, La Digue, Silhouette, Fregate and North. 4% of the total land area is arable and 18% is forested.

Climate

Tropical with uniformly high temperatures all year round and a wet, humid season Dec.-May. Cooler conditions prevail June-Nov. Victoria: Jan. 80°F/ 26.7°C. July 78°F/25.6°C. Average annual rainfall 93.5 in/2,375 mm.

Cities and towns

Victoria (capital)	23,334

Population

Total population is 69,719 of which 37.2% live in urban areas. Population density is 398 persons per mile^2/145.6 persons per km^2. The population is predominantly Seychellois (Asian, African and European admixtures); 3.1% are Malagasy; 1.6% Chinese; 1.5% English.
Birth rate 2.8%. **Death rate** 0.7%. **Rate of population increase** (1980–87) 1.6%. **Age distribution** under 15 = 36.8%; over 65 = 6.4%. **Life expectancy** female 76; male 67; average 72.

Religion

90% Roman Catholic; 8% Anglican; 2% other.

Language

English and French are the official languages; the bulk of the population speaks the Coral French-English creole patois (95%).

HISTORY

The islands, uninhabited when the French occupied them in 1742, were first settled by the French in the late 18th century, but ceded to Britain in 1810. The British administered them from neighbouring Mauritius until 1888, when an administrator was appointed to govern from Victoria on Mahé island. The Seychelles became a crown colony in 1903.

The political influence of plantation owners was unchallenged until the emergence of nationalist parties in the 1960s. James Mancham's Seychelles Democratic Party, initially advocating association with Britain rather than full independence, had by 1974 gone over to seeking independence. He formed a coalition government in 1975 (after a constitutional conference in March) with his more radical rival France-Albert René of the Seychelles People's United Party, leading the country to independence (28 June

1976) with Mancham as executive president and René as prime minister.

René, increasingly critical of Mancham's 'international jet-set' image, overthrew him in June 1977 (while Mancham was at the Commonwealth conference in London). He launched a social reform programme and sought to diversify away from excessive dependence on tourism. René's party, retitled the Seychelles People's Progressive Front, became sole party under the June 1979 constitution. Mancham, accusing the regime of communistic policies and pro-Soviet leanings, was in turn accused by René of backing unsuccessful coup attempts involving mercenaries (Apr. 1978, Nov. 1979, Nov. 1981). The last of these, launched from South Africa, led to the trial and imprisonment there of its organizer, Col 'Mad Mike' Hoare. Tanzanian troops supported the René regime and suppressed a mutiny (Aug. 1982). Exiled opponents formed (Nov. 1984) a Seychelles National Movement, whose president, Gérard Horeau, was assassinated at his London home (30 Nov. 1985).

CONSTITUTION AND GOVERNMENT

Executive and legislature

A one-party state, Seychelles has an executive president, who is elected for a five-year term by direct suffrage (last election 9–11 June 1989), and appoints the council of ministers, as well as members of the judiciary and the holders of certain public offices. The unicameral 25-member National Assembly is elected by direct popular vote, from the party list, apart from two members appointed by the president. The Assembly, like the president, has a term of five years; last elections Dec. 1987.

Present government

President; Head of Government; C.-in-C. of the Armed Forces; Minister of Defence, Administration, Finance, Legal Affairs France-Albert René

Principal Members of the Council of Ministers Maj. James Michel (Finance); Danielle de St Jorre (Planning and External Affairs).

Ruling party

Seychelles People's Progressive Front. **Secretary-General** France Albert René. **Deputy Secretary-General** Maj. James Michel.

Justice

The death penalty is in force only for exceptional crimes. There were no executions between 1985 and mid-1988.

National symbols

Flag. The upper part of the flag is red, the lower one green, separated by a wavy white stripe.

Festivals. 1 May (Labour Day); 5 June (Liberation Day, anniversary of 1977 coup); 29 June (Independence Day).

Vehicle registration plate. SY.

INTERNATIONAL RELATIONS

Affiliations

NAM; OAU; ACP; Commonwealth; Francophonie.

Defence

Total Armed Forces: 1,300. Terms of service: conscription: two years.
Army: 1,000.
Marines: 200; six patrol and coastal combatants.
Air: 100.
Para-military (People's Militia): 5,000 reported.

ECONOMY

Currency

The unit is the rupee, divided into 100 cents.

National finance

Budget. The 1987 budget, in US$, was for expenditure of 130 million and revenue of 106 million.

Inflation. 2.6%.

Gross Domestic Product

Estimated total GDP US$192 million, per capita US$2,924 (overall size of economy ranking 164 in the world).

Economically active population. The total number of persons active in the economy was 27,700; unemployed: 15%.

Sector	% of workforce
industry	31
agriculture	12
services*	57

* services figure includes elements unassigned to other categories.

Energy and mineral resources

Electricity. Capacity: 25,000 kW; production: 67 million kWh; 980 kWh per capita (1988).

Bioresources

Agriculture. 4% of the land is arable; 18% is permanently cultivated. Crops grown for domestic consumption include sweet potatoes; cassava; yams; sugar cane; bananas. The bulk of the islands' food supply including the staple food, rice, must be imported.

Crop production: (chief cash crops 1987 in tons/tonnes) coconuts 23,148/21,000; copra 1,440/1,307; cinnamon bark 42/38; tea 120/109.

Livestock numbers: (1987) pigs 15,000; cattle 2,000; goats 4,000.

Forestry. 18% of the land is forested.

Fisheries. Total catch: (1987) 4,347 tons/3,944 tonnes.

Industry and commerce

Industry. The main industry is tourism. Other activities include coconut and vanilla processing; fishing; coir rope manufacture; boat building; printing; furniture; beverages. Brewery production: (1987) 17.6 million US gallons/4.65 million litres (16.7 million US gallons/4.4 million litres of soft drinks); 67.8 million cigarettes were also produced.

Commerce. Exports: (1986) US$19 million or 10% of GDP; imports: $106 million or 55% of GDP. Principal exports are fish; copra; cinnamon bark; petroleum products (re-exports). Main imports include manufactured goods; food; tobacco; beverages; machinery and transportation equipment; petroleum products. Export trading partners are Pakistan; France; Réunion; UK; Mauritius. Imported goods come from Bahrain; UK; South Africa; Singapore; Japan; France.

Trade with UK. The Seychelles imported UK goods worth £10.5 million in 1988; exports amounted to £1.3 million.

Tourism. (1987) 71,626 visitors.

COMMUNICATIONS

Railways

There are no railways in the Seychelles.

Roads

There are 161 miles/259 km of roads, of which 97 miles/157 km are bituminized.

Aviation

Air Seychelles provides domestic and international services. Passengers: (1985) 152,000.

Shipping

Freight loaded: (1985) 4,960 tons/4,500 tonnes; unloaded: 25,041 tons/235,000 tonnes.

Telecommunications

There are 13,000 telephones and direct radio communications with adjacent islands and African coastal countries. There are 27,255 radios and 5,500 televisions (1988). Television services began in 1983, controlled by the state RTS which also provides radio programmes in French, creole and English. The Far East Broadcasting Association is a Christian missionary operation with a station in Mahé.

EDUCATION AND WELFARE

Education

Schools. 14,663 primary school pupils receive elementary instruction from 681 teachers (one per 22 pupils). A further 112 secondary school staff teach 2,433 pupils (one per 22 pupils). Some 240 students receive some form of higher education or vocational training overseas, largely in the UK.

Universities. 152 Seychelles students are at university abroad; a total of 1,541 students attend the Polytechnic at home.

Health

373 hospital beds (one per 187 members of the population); 57 doctors; 275 nursing staff; nine dentists.

SIERRA LEONE

Republic of Sierra Leone

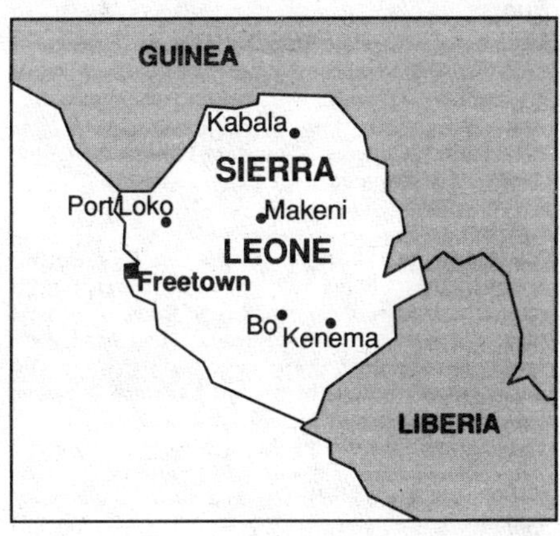

GEOGRAPHY

Located on the West African coast, the Republic of Sierra Leone covers a total area of 27,692 miles^2/71,740 km^2 divided into four provinces. The swampy coastal plain, dominated by mangrove forests, is interrupted by the Freetown or Sierra Leone (Lion's Range) peninsula, and backed by a wooded upland region rising to 2,913 ft/888 m at Picket Hill. The interior plateau exhibits a diverse topography, from savannah grassland to undulating forest. In the east (south-east of the Loma Mountains) the Tingi hills climb to 6,079 ft/1,853 m. The highest peak in Sierra Leone is Loma Marisa (6,391 ft/1,948 m) near the Guinean border. Principal rivers are the Great Scarcies, Little Scarcies, Rokal, Gbangbaia, Jong, Sewa, Moa, Mano and Wanje. Soils are mainly iron-rich, heavily leached and weathered. 23% of the total surface area is arable, and 29% forested. Approximately 40% of the population live in the northern province.

Climate

Tropical, high temperatures all year round with distinct wet and dry seasons, Apr.-Nov. and Dec.-Mar. respectively. Most rain falls in July and August. Additional relief rainfall in the peninsular zone augments Freetown's annual total. Freetown: Jan. 80°F/26.7°C. July 78°F/25.6°C. Average annual rainfall 135 in/3,434 mm.

Cities and towns

Freetown (capital)	469,776
Koidu	80,000
Bo	26,000
Kenema	13,000
Makeni	12,000

Population

Total population is 4,063,519 of which 28.3% live in urban areas. Population density is 146.7 persons per mile^2/53.0 per km^2. Ethnic composition: 99% of the population are of native African origin. The chief groups are the Temnes (30%), Limbas, Korankos and Lokos in the northern part of the country; the centrally situated Temnes; the Mendis in the south (30%); the Kissis and Konos people of the eastern regions. **Birth rate:** 4.6%. **Death rate:** 2.1%. **Rate of population increase** (1980–87) 2.5%. **Age distribution** under 15 = 43.9%; over 65 = 3.1%. **Life expectancy** female 42; male 40; average 41.

Religion

Over two-thirds of the population follow traditional customs and beliefs. An estimated 25% are Sunni Muslims and 5–10% are Christian (6% Protestant, 2% Catholic). The Temne peoples are predominantly Muslim.

Language

English is the official language. Mende and Temne are

indigenous to the south and to the north. Krio (an Anglo-African hybrid) is the Sierra Leonean lingua franca.

HISTORY

The Bulom, probably the earliest inhabitants, were joined by Krim and Gola peoples by the 14th century and by the Mende and Temne in the 15th century. In the mid-15th century Portuguese traders first visited the coast and a fort was established at Freetown in 1495. There were British trading posts on Bund and York islands in the 17th century when the country was an important source of ivory and slaves.

Abolitionists founded Freetown in 1787 as a refuge for freed slaves but after Britain abolished the slave trade in 1807 the British government took over the settlement as a naval base; the colony, formerly run by the Sierra Leone Company, became a Crown Colony. The hinterland became a British protectorate in 1896. Many settlers were killed in a war with indigenous peoples in 1898, precipitated by the introduction of a hut tax.

With the preparation after World War II for progression to self-government, elections were held to a new assembly in 1951, and won by Milton Margai's Sierra Leone People's Party (SLPP). An emerging alliance between the SLPP's supporters, mainly Mende southerners, and the minority Creole elite which dominated the professions and civil service, kept Margai in office, as prime minister from 1958 and as the first leader of independent Sierra Leone following independence (27 Apr. 1961). The SLPP won the May 1962 elections but Milton Margai died in Apr. 1964 and his successor, his half-brother Albert, alienated the Creoles by his Africanization policies. The opposition All-People's Congress (APC), led by Siaka Stevens and supported mainly by Temne northerners, won the Mar. 1967 elections, but the army seized power before Stevens could take office. The National Reformation Council (NRC) was itself overthrown by NCOs in Apr. 1968 and civilian rule was subsequently restored with Siaka Stevens as prime minister.

Following a period of instability, Brig. John Bangura tried to overthrow Stevens' leftist government in Mar. 1971 but the mutiny was put down with assistance from Guinea. Sierra Leone became a republic in Apr. 1971, with Stevens as executive president. Discontent increased as the economic situation deteriorated. In Feb. 1977 there was widespread rioting. The government declared a state of emergency and called a general election, which returned the APC with a reduced majority. Subsequently, Pres. Stevens put forward a new constitution providing for a one-party state, arguing that this was the only means of preventing ethnic factionalism. It was approved by a referendum in June 1978. However, as the economic situation continued to deteriorate and evidence of corruption was revealed, the government declared a state of emergency in Aug. 1981 to prevent a general strike. Elections in May 1982 were again marred by violence and there was another wave of demonstrations and strikes in 1984–85.

Stevens retired in Aug. 1985 (died 29 May 1988) and the APC convention appointed Gen. Joseph Momoh as his replacement – an appointment endorsed at the polls in Oct. 1985. After further demonstrations in Jan. 1987, Gabriel Kai Kai, head of the anti-smuggling unit, and Francis Minah, first vice-president, tried to seize power on 23 Mar. They were arrested, and sentenced to death in Oct. 1987; both were executed along with four other conspirators in Oct. 1989. Meanwhile, Pres. Momoh initiated a drive against corruption; he also imposed a state of economic emergency following strikes by public employees in Nov. 1987, giving the government new powers. This was extended for 12 months in Mar. 1988.

CONSTITUTION AND GOVERNMENT

Executive and legislature

A one-party state and a republic within the Commonwealth, the head of state is an executive president, elected by popular vote for a seven-year term, after endorsement as party leader; last election Oct. 1985. The unicameral House of Representatives comprises 105 members elected on a constituency basis, ten elected paramount chiefs and ten presidential nominees; last elections May 1986. Parliamentary candidates must obtain party approval, but there may be several candidates for any one seat.

Present government

President; Minister of Defence and Public Services Maj.-Gen. Joseph Saidu Momoh
First Vice-President Abu Bakar Kamara
Second Vice-President Salia Jusu-Sheriff
Principal Members of the Cabinet Tommy Taylor Morgan (Finance); Dr Sheka Kanu (Economic Planning and National Development); Alhaji Abdul Karim Koroma (Foreign Affairs); Ahmed Sesay (Internal Affairs); Abdulai Conteh (Attorney-General; Justice).

Ruling party

All-People's Congress. **Secretary-General** Maj-Gen. Joseph Saidu Momoh.

Justice

The system of law is based on a blend of English common-law traditions with indigenous concepts. The highest courts are the Sierra Leone Court of Appeal and Supreme Court; at local level, justice is administered by magistrates in the various districts, and by native courts, headed by a court chairman. Appeals from the decisions of magistrates' courts go to the High Court, and from there ultimately to the Court of Appeal and Supreme Court. The death penalty is in force. The number of executions between 1985 and mid-1988 is not known.

National symbols

Flag. Three horizontal stripes of green, white and cobalt blue.
Festivals. 27 Apr. (Independence Day).
Vehicle registration plate. WAL.

INTERNATIONAL RELATIONS

Affiliations

NAM; OAU; ACP; ICO; Commonwealth.

Defence

Total Armed Forces: 3,100. Terms of service: voluntary.
Army: 3,000.
Navy: 150; three patrol and coastal combatants.
Para-military: 800.

ECONOMY

Currency

The unit is the leone, divided into 100 cents.

National finance

Budget. The 1987 FY budget, in US$, was for expenditure of 181.6 million and revenue of 98.5 million.

Balance of payments. The balance of payments, in US$ (current account, 1987) was a deficit of 9 million.

Inflation. 167.1%.

Gross Domestic Product

Estimated total GDP US$900 million, per capita US$250 (overall size of economy ranking 146 in the world).

Economically active population. The total number of persons active in the economy was 1,500,000; unemployed: 12%.

Sector	% of workforce	% of GDP
industry	19	19
agriculture	65	45
services*	16	36

* services figure includes elements unassigned to other categories.

Energy and mineral resources

Minerals. The principal minerals mined are diamonds 243,500 carats; gold 11,168 oz/347,372 g; bauxite 1.1 million tons/1 million tonnes; rutile 84,767 tons/76,900 tonnes; others are titanium ore; iron ore; chromite.

Electricity. Capacity: 65,000 kW; production: 116 million kWh; 30 kWh per capita (1988).

Bioresources

Agriculture. Main crops are palm kernels; coffee; cocoa; rice; yams; millet; ginger; cassava. Much of the cultivated land is devoted to subsistence farming.

Crop production: (1986 in 1,000 tons/tonnes) rice 579/525; cassava 125/113; palm-oil 49/44; palm kernels 33/30; coffee 12/11; cocoa 10/9.

Livestock numbers: (1987) cattle 330,000; goats 180,000; sheep 330,000; chickens 6 million.

Forestry. 29% of the land area is forest and woodland.

Fisheries. Total catch: (1983) 138,998 tons/126,098 tonnes. This does not meet the country's needs and approximately 276 tons/250 tonnes of fish are imported.

Industry and commerce

Industry. Main industries are mining (diamonds, bauxite, rutile); small-scale manufacturing (beverages, textiles, cigarettes, footwear); petroleum refinery.

Commerce. Exports: (1987) US$129 or 13% of GDP, including diamonds 20%; cocoa 20%; rutile 21%; bauxite 17%; coffee. Imports: US$137 million, including capital goods 40%; food 32%; petroleum 15%; consumer goods 7%; light industrial goods. Countries exported to were US; UK; Netherlands; West Germany; West Europe. Imports came from US; EC; Japan; China.

Trade with UK. In 1988 Sierra Leone imported UK goods worth £14,256,000; exports to UK totalled £14,462,000.

Tourism. (1986) 194,000 visitors.

COMMUNICATIONS

Railways

There are 52 miles/84 km of railways, linking iron ore mines.

Roads

There are 4,592 miles/7,395 km of roads, of which 689 miles/1,110 km are concrete or bituminized.

Aviation

Sierra Leone Airlines provides domestic and international services (main airport is at Lungi). Passengers: (1984) 80,000.

Shipping

Freight loaded: (1985) 1.3 million tons/1.2 million tonnes; unloaded: 669,096 tons/607,000 tonnes.

Telecommunications

There are 23,650 telephones and a fair telephone and telegraph service; the national microwave radio relay system is unserviceable at present. There are 700,000 radios and 25,000 televisions (1986). The government SLBS broadcasts radio programmes and a television service (since 1963, and in colour since 1978).

EDUCATION AND WELFARE

Education

Schools. Primary education is partially free but not compulsory and in 1984 there were 1,267 primary schools with a total of 276,911 pupils. There were 184 secondary schools with 66,464 pupils, approximately 40% of which are government-funded, and also four technical institutes and a rural institute.

Universities. The University of Sierra Leone has two constituent colleges, Fourah Bay College (1,400 students) and Njala University College.

Literacy. 15%.

Health

There are 13 government hospitals and six government health centres in the Western Area; three private hospitals in Freetown; 14 government hospitals, six associated with the mining companies and seven mission hospitals in the provinces. There are also 156 government dispensaries and health centres and two military hospitals.

SINGAPORE

Republik Singapura (Malay)
Hsin-Chia-P'o Kung-Ho-Kuo (Chinese)
Singapore Kudiyarasu (Tamil)
(Republic of Singapore)

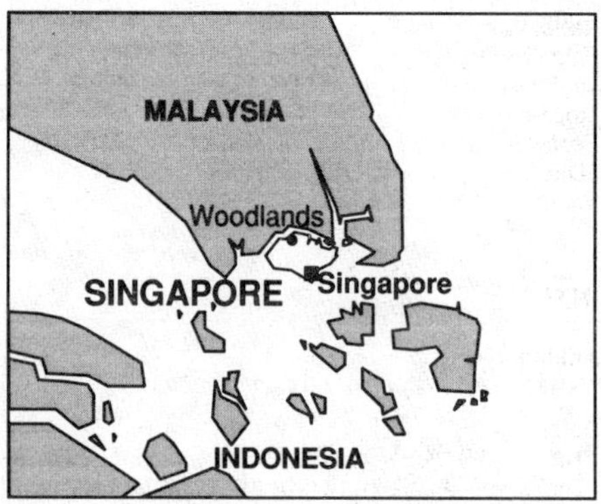

GEOGRAPHY

The island city-state of Singapore is located off the southernmost extremity of the Malay Peninsula (approximately 77 miles/124 km north of the equator) to which it is linked by a causeway. The republic comprises the main island of Singapore and 57 smaller islands, covering a total area of 239 miles^2/620 km^2. For the most part low-lying, Singapore rises to 581 ft/177 m at Bukit Timah. Urban development has accelerated deforestation and swamp reclamation. The Selatar River drains the island north-eastwards. 4% of the land is arable and 5% forested.

Climate

Equatorial, with high temperatures and high humidity. Abundant rainfall all year. No clearly defined wet or dry seasons. Average temperatures 75–80.6°F/24–27°C. Jan.: 78°F/25.6°C. July 80.8°F/27.1°C. Average annual rainfall 93 in/2,367 mm.

Cities and towns

Singapore City (capital)

Population

Total population is 2,674,362 of which 100% live in urban areas. Population density is 11,130 persons per mile^2/4,205.8 per km^2. Ethnic divisions: 76.4% Chinese; 14.9% Malay; 6.4% Indian; 2.3% other. **Birth rate** 1.6%. **Death rate** 0.5%. **Rate of population increase** (1980–87) 1.1%. **Age distribution** under 15 = 24.5%; over 65 = 5.2%. **Life expectancy** female 77; male 71; average 73.

Religion

Buddhism, Taoism, Islam, Christianity and Hinduism. The Chinese population is predominantly Buddhist and virtually all the Malays are Muslim. At the last census, 56% of the population were either Buddhist or Taoist. Small Sikh and Confucian minorities also exist.

Language

English is the official language, and Malay is the national tongue. Mandarin (Chinese) and Tamil are also widely spoken.

HISTORY

The island of Singapore is first mentioned historically in the Malay Annals, where it is called Temasek and is referred to as a busy 14th-century trading centre. At about this time it became known as Singapura (Sanskrit for Lion City) and was claimed by the rival expanding empires of Javanese Majapahit and Thai Ayuthia. Attacked by armies from both empires, and further divided by internal dissension, Singapura was laid to waste at the end of the 14th century.

The island remained almost deserted for 400 years, with European interest centred primarily on Java and the Moluccas. However, the opening of trade routes meant that Singapore, situated at the southernmost tip of the Malay Peninsular and the Straits of Malacca, assumed a fresh commercial and strategic value as a base from which to protect the new trade routes and challenge the Dutch monopoly in the region. Therefore in 1819, an employee of the East India Company, Sir Stamford Raffles, established on Singapore a new trading settlement. Its position was clarified in 1824 by the Anglo-Dutch Treaty which effectively demarcated the respective spheres of European influence. In 1826, Singapore, Malacca and Penang were incorporated into an administrative unit known as the Straits Settlements. In 1867, it came under the direct control of the British Colonial Office which exercised authority through a British governor, and legislative and executive councils, which were comprised almost exclusively of Europeans.

Singapore's success as a port was underpinned by the principle of laissez-faire. Free of customs tariffs and restrictions, the port attracted a large number of (mainly Chinese) immigrants and, following the opening of the Suez Canal in 1869, a burgeoning trade in rubber and tin from the Malayan hinterland. The island soon became the leading trading centre of the region and following World War I, in a bid to secure its commercial and strategic position, construction began on a large naval base designed to protect both Singapore and the Malay Peninsula. The defences of Singapore were therefore designed for defence against sea-attack, and in Feb. 1942 the island fell to a Japanese land attack down the Malay Peninsula.

With the re-establishment of British control in 1945 came a desire to re-administer the Peninsula as a single unit. However, the Malay Union and later the Federation of Malaya, excluded Singapore from the new structure, mainly because Malays feared Singapore's predominantly Chinese population would upset the racial composition of the new federation. In Apr. 1945, with the restoration of civil rule, the Straits

Settlements were dissolved and Singapore became a Crown Colony. A new Constitution came into force in early 1955, allowing Singapore a large measure of self-government. A fresh Constitution was promulgated in 1959, with the establishment of a self-governing State of Singapore.

Elections held in 1959 saw the People's Action Party (PAP) led by Lee Kuan Yew sweep to power, winning 43 out of 51 seats. Under Lee's leadership the PAP has remained in power ever since. The Federation of Malaysia came into being in 1963, with Singapore as a constituent state. The association was strained from the start, and in 1965 the central government of Kuala Lumpur forced Lee Kuan Yew to agree to a separation. On 9 Aug. 1965 the Malaysian parliament approved legislation providing for Singapore to become an independent state within the Commonwealth. By legislation passed in Dec. 1965, with retrospective effect of 9 Aug., Singapore became a republic. In Jan. 1968, the British government announced its intent to withdraw its troops from Singapore by 1971, a threat to Singapore's economy since the bases accounted for 20% of the country's GNP. The PAP called a snap election and contested seats on the basis of wide economic reforms designed to develop its economy and attract investment.

Since the mid-1960s, government has focused the bulk of its attention on the economy and engineered the 'economic miracle' of Singapore's industrialization. However, opposition groups within Singapore including the Workers' Party, stated that economic success had been achieved at the expense of political freedom, especially after a number of individuals were charged in 1988 with being involved in a Marxist plot to overthrow the government and were held without trial under the Internal Security Act (ISA). Despite criticism from international human-rights groups, elections in Sept. 1988 returned the PAP to power though with a slight erosion in the popular vote from 62.9% in 1984 to 61.6% in 1988. In October 1989, Lee Kuan Yew confirmed that he would retire from his post as prime minister by the end of 1990.

CONSTITUTION AND GOVERNMENT

Executive and legislature

The head of state is the (largely ceremonial) president elected by parliament for a five-year term, most recently in Aug. 1989. The president appoints a cabinet headed by a prime minister, who is the executive head of government and is responsible to parliament. The unicameral 81-member parliament is elected by adult suffrage for five years; last elections 3 Sept. 1988.

Present government

President Wee Kim Wee

Prime Minister Lee Kuan Yew

Other Principal Members of the Cabinet Goh Chok Tong (First Deputy Prime Minister; Defence); Ong Teng Cheong (Second Deputy Prime Minister); Suppiah Dhanabalan (National Development); Dr Tony Tan Keng Yam (Education); Prof. Shanmugam Jayakumar (Home Affairs; Law); Dr Richard Hu (Finance); Wong Kan Seng (Community Development; Foreign Affairs); Brig.-Gen. (reserve) Lee Hsien Loong (Trade and Industry; Second Minister for Defence (Services)).

Justice

The system of law is based on English common law. The highest court, the Supreme Court, is composed of a Chief Justice and 6 Judges. There is a High Court with civil and criminal jurisdiction, and separate courts of appeal for civil and criminal cases. At the lower level, there are 12 district courts and 14 magistrates' courts, with certain matters being dealt with by bodies with specific responsibilities – the juvenile court, the coroner's court and the small claims tribunal. The death penalty is in force. There were at least two executions between 1985 and mid-1988. Offences were drug-trafficking.

National symbols

Flag. Two horizontal stripes of red and white. In the hoist of the red stripe there is a white crescent together with five small white five-pointed stars.

Festivals. 1 May (Labour Day); 9 Aug. (National Day).

Vehicle registration plate. SGP.

INTERNATIONAL RELATIONS

Affiliations

NAM; Asean; Commonwealth; SAARC.

Defence

Total Armed Forces: 55,500 (34,800 conscripts). Terms of service: conscription; 24–30 months. Reserves: some 180,000.

Army: 45,000; some 350 light tanks (AMX-13).

Navy: 4,500; 26 patrol and coastal combatants.

Air Force: 6,000; 151 combat aircraft (mainly F-5E, F-5F, F-74, A-4S/S1), some armed helicopters.

ECONOMY

Currency

The unit is the Singapore dollar, divided into 100 cents.

National finance

Budget. The 1988 FY budget, in US$, was for expenditure of 6,200 million and revenue of 5,800 million. Main items of expenditure are defence 19%; education 18.2 %; housing and welfare 15.9%.

Balance of payments. The balance of payments, in US$ (current account, 1987) was a surplus of 561 million.

Inflation. 1.5%.

Gross Domestic Product

Estimated total GDP US$19,900 million, per capita US$8,870 (overall size of economy ranking 59 in the world).

Economically active population. The total number of persons active in the economy was 205,000; unemployed: 3.3%.

Sector	% of GDP
industry	38
agriculture	1
services*	62

* services figure includes elements unassigned to other categories.

Energy and mineral resources

Electricity. Capacity: 3.9 million kW; production: 11,500 million kWh; 4,350 kWh per capita (1988).

Bioresources

Agriculture. Only 1% of the labour force is employed in agriculture and most food is imported, although Singapore is self-sufficient in pork and eggs. Orchids are an important export.

Forestry. Only 5% of the land area is forest and woodland.

Fisheries. Various projects have been introduced in recent years to help make Singapore self-sufficient in fish and a major fishing base. The ornamental fish industry is important and exports of aquarium fish (1987) are valued at S$53.9 million.

Total fresh fish: (1987) 123,545 tons/112,079 tonnes.

Industry and commerce

Industry. Main industries are petroleum refining; electronics; oil drilling equipment; rubber processing and rubber products; processed food and beverages; ship repair; financial services; biotechnology.

Commerce. Exports: (1988) US$39,000 million, including petroleum products; rubber; electronics; manufactured goods. Imports: US$42,500 million, including capital equipment; petroleum; chemicals; manufactured goods; foodstuffs. Countries exported to were US 24%; Malaysia 13%; Japan 9%; Hong Kong 6%; Thailand 6%; Australia 3%; West Germany 3%. Imports came from Japan 22%; US 16%; Malaysia 14%; EC countries 12%; Kuwait 1%.

Trade with UK. In 1988 Singapore imported UK goods worth £632,452,000; exports to UK totalled £579,368,000.

Tourism. (1987) 3,678,809 visitors.

COMMUNICATIONS

Railways

There are 16 miles/26 km of railways and a new Mass Rapid Transit with a total length of 42 miles/67 km.

Roads

There are 16 miles/26 km of railways and a new Mass Rapid Transit with a total length of 42 miles/67 km.

Aviation

Singapore Airlines Ltd (SIA) provide international services (main airport is at Changi). Passengers: (1987) over 10 million.

Shipping

Freight loaded: (1987) 52 million tons/47 million tonnes; unloaded: 79 million tons/71.3 million tonnes.

Telecommunications

There are 1.1 million telephones, good domestic facilities, good international service and good radio and television broadcast coverage. There are 745,907 radios and 538,196 televisions (1988). The state SBC runs radio services in five languages, and three TV channels.

EDUCATION AND WELFARE

Education

Schools. At the primary level, there are 169 government schools with 199,174 pupils and 8,062 teachers (one per 24 pupils); 60 government-aided schools with 62,225 pupils and 2,371 teachers (one per 26 pupils); one private school with 204 pupils and nine teachers (one per 22 pupils). At the secondary level, there are 113 government schools with 148,240 pupils and 6,960 teachers (one per 21 pupils); 44 government-aided schools with 52,885 pupils and 2,341 teachers (one per 22 pupils); four private schools with 1,732 pupils and 68 teachers (one per 25 pupils).

Universities. The Nanyang Technological Institute (3,940 students and scheduled to be a University of Technology by 1992); Singapore Polytechnic (13,750 students); Ngee Ann Polytechnic (10,860 students). The Institute of Education is responsible for teacher training and the Vocational and Industrial Training Board offers vocational training in 16 centres.

Literacy. 87%.

Health

There are nine government hospitals with 7,717 beds (one per 346 people) and 2,941 doctors (one per 909 people).

SOLOMON ISLANDS

GEOGRAPHY

Located in the south-western Pacific Ocean and scattered over 249,000 square nautical miles between Papua New Guinea to the north-west and Vanuatu to the south-east, the Solomon Islands archipelago consists of several hundred islands with a total land area of 10,980 miles^2/28,446 km^2. The six main islands are Guadalcanal, Malaita, New Georgia, San Cristobal (now Makira), Santa Isabel and Choiseul. The larger islands are typified by densely forested mountain ranges with deeply incised river valleys, ringed by narrow coastal plains supporting the bulk of the population and coral reefs. Mount Makarakomburu reaches an elevation of 8,028 ft/2,477 m on Guadalcanal. Most of the outer islands are small, evolving coral atolls with the exception of the Santa Cruz and eastern Anuta, Fataka and Tikopia islands, which are volcanic. 1% of the land is considered arable and 93% is forested.

Climate

Equatorial and tropical monsoon with minor seasonal variations. A mean temperature of 81°F/27°C accompanies a humidity range of 60–90%. Maximum rainfall occurs Nov.-Apr. when the north-westerly trade winds affect the windward shores. Periodic cyclones. Annual rainfall totals range from 79 in/2,000 mm to 118 in/3,000 mm.

Cities and towns

Honiara (capital)	30,499

Population

Total population is 323,545 of which 15.7% live in

urban areas. Population density is 29 persons per mile^2/11.3 persons per km^2. Ethnic divisions: 93% Melanesian; 4.0% Polynesian; 1.5% Micronesian; 0.8% European; 0.3% Chinese.
Birth rate 4.1%. **Death rate** 0.5%. **Rate of population increase** (1980–87) 3.6%. **Age distribution** under 15 = 49.1%; over 60 = 5.5%. **Life expectancy** female 71; male 66; average 69.

Religion
At the last census, 33.9% of the population were Anglican and 41.1% other Protestant (including 17.6% South Sea Evangelical). 19.2% were Roman Catholic.

Language
English is the official language, cultivated in its pidgin form as the nation's lingua franca and spoken in the majority of urban settlements. In addition, at least 90 indigenous Melanesian, Papuan and Polynesian languages are spoken.

HISTORY

This double chain of islands has been settled since at least 1000 BC by Melanesian peoples. Spanish explorers reached them in AD 1568 and a colony was founded on the island of Santa Cruz at the end of that century. But its existence was brief and Western contact with the islands remained spasmodic until the establishment of missions and trading posts in the latter part of the 19th century. The need for workers on the sugar plantations of Queensland and Fiji attracted labour recruiters to the islands, but the abuses of this trade led Britain in 1893 to establish a protectorate over the southern Solomons. In 1900 Britain acquired by treaty the northern Solomons from Germany. Commercial development began early in the 20th century with the development of the copra industry on a large scale until a fall in prices in the 1920s. During World War II the Japanese occupied the main islands from 1942–43 before Allied forces drove them out after fierce fighting. Anti-government movements, notably Marching Rule, emerged for a time in the post-war period. But after their decline and a lessening of the political tension that had hampered development and administration, there was a gradual increase in the establishment of local government councils. Constitutional development accelerated quite rapidly at the beginning of the 1970s in preparation for independence. In 1976 self-government was introduced and the name Solomon Islands was officially adopted in place of the British Solomon Islands Protectorate.

The country became independent on 7 July 1978 as a constitutional monarchy within the Commonwealth, with the governor-general as the British monarch's representative. A cyclone caused widespread destruction in 1986 and it could take ten years to rebuild the economy. In a scandal which developed over the allocation of cyclone-damage aid, Prime Minister Sir Peter Kenilorea resigned in late 1986 and was succeeded by Ezekiel Alebua, a colleague from the ruling Solomon Islands United Party. The Alebua government was decisively defeated at a general election in Feb. 1989 and was replaced by a government led by Solomon Mamaloni, the leader of the People's Alliance Party.

CONSTITUTION AND GOVERNMENT

Executive and legislature
The head of state is the British sovereign represented by a governor general. The head of government is the prime minister, elected by and responsible to the legislature, the unicameral 38-member national parliament, itself elected by universal suffrage for up to four years. The last election was in Feb. 1989.

Present government
Governor General Sir George Lepping
Prime Minister Solomon Mamaloni
Other Principal Ministers Sir Baddeley Devesi (Foreign Affairs and Trade); Christopher Abe (Finance and Planning); Allen Kemakeza (Police and Justice); Danny Philips (Home Affairs).

Justice
The system of law is based on the principles of English common law. The highest court is the High Court of Solomon Islands, dealing with both civil and criminal matters at the highest level, and consisting of a Chief Justice and two or three Puisne Judges. A system of native courts remains in place throughout the islands, together with magistrates' courts. The death penalty was abolished in 1966.

National symbols
Flag. The flag is divided by a yellow diagonal into two fields, the upper one being blue and the lower one dark green. In the hoist of the blue field there are five white five-pointed stars.
Festivals. 9 June (Queen's Official birthday); 7 July (Independence Day).

INTERNATIONAL RELATIONS

Affiliations
Commonwealth; ACP; SPF.

ECONOMY

Currency
The unit is the Solomon Islands dollar, divided into 100 cents.

National finance
Budget. The 1987 budget, in US$, was for expenditure of 154.4 million and revenue of 139 million.
Inflation. 11.0%.

Gross Domestic Product
Estimated total GDP US$141 million, per capita US$469 (overall size of economy ranking 172 in the world).
Economically active population. The total number of persons active in the economy was 23,400.

Energy and mineral resources
Minerals. The islands are rich in undeveloped mineral resources such as lead; zinc; nickel; gold; bauxite; phosphate. There is a small amount of gold (65,807 g in 1986) and silver production by panning.
Electricity. Capacity: 15,000 kW; production: 30 million kWh; 100 kWh per capita (1988).

Bioresources
Agriculture. About 90% of the population depend on subsistence agriculture and fishing for their livelihood. Main crops are copra; cocoa; palm-oil; rice; fruits; vegetables; spices; tobacco.
Crop production: (1987 in tons/tonnes) copra 30,255/27,447; palm-oil 13,225/11,998; cocoa 3,267/2,964;

palm kernels 2,680/2,432; (1983) milled rice 5,079/4,608.

Livestock numbers: (1987) cattle 23,000; pigs 51,000.

Forestry. 93% of the land area is forest and woodland, and forest covers 5.9 million acres/2.4 million ha with approximately 367.3 ft^3/10.4 million m^3 of commercial timber. Production of logs: (1987) 10,654,234 ft^3/301,700 m^3; sawn timber 621,526 ft^3/17,600 m^3.

Fisheries. Catch of tuna: (1987) 35,505 tons/32,210 tonnes.

Industry and commerce

Industry. Palm-oil milling; rice milling; fish canning; saw milling; food, tobacco; soft drinks.

Commerce. Exports: (1987) US$64.5 million or 45% of GDP, including fish 46%; timber 31%; copra 5%; palm-oil 5%. Imports: US$67.4 million, including plant and machinery 30%; fuel 19%; food 16%. Countries exported to were Japan 51%; UK 12%; Thailand 9%; Netherlands 8%; Australia 2%; US 2%. Imports came from Japan 36%; US 23%; Singapore 9%; UK 9%; New Zealand 9%; Australia 4%; Hong Kong 4%; China 3%.

Trade with UK. Solomon Islands imported UK goods worth £2,576,000; exports to UK totalled £5,153,000.

Tourism. (1987) 12,555 visitors.

COMMUNICATIONS

Railways

There are no railways.

Roads

There are 807 miles/1,300 km of roads.

Aviation

Solomon Islands Airways Ltd (Solair) provide domestic and international services.

Shipping

The major ports are Honiara on the island of Guadalcanal and Ringi Cove. Freight loaded: (1987) 43,866 tons/39,795 tonnes; unloaded: 155,250 tons/140,842 tonnes.

Telecommunications

There are 3,000 telephones; 40,500 radios (1987) receiving Solomon Islands Broadcasting Corporation programmes mainly in pidgin; no television service.

EDUCATION AND WELFARE

Education

Schools. There are 462 primary schools with 42,374 pupils and 2,124 teachers (one per 19 pupils); 12 provincial and eight national secondary schools with 5,604 pupils and 300 teachers (one per 18 pupils).

Higher education. Teacher and vocational training is carried out at the College of Higher Education.

Literacy. 60%.

Health

There are eight hospitals and 31 doctors (one per 10,436 people).

SOMALIA

Jamhuriyadda Dimugradiga Somaliya
(Somali Democratic Republic)

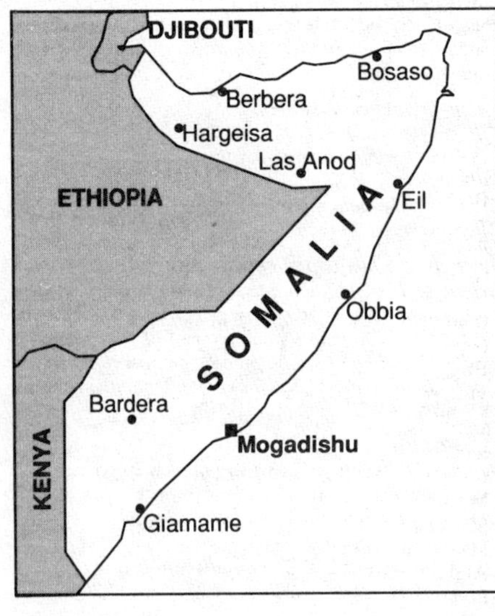

GEOGRAPHY

Situated on the north-east coastal Horn of Africa, Somalia covers a total area of 246,136 $miles^2$/637,657 km^2 divided into 16 regions. To the north, the semi-arid Guban coastal plain along the Gulf of Aden is backed by a mountainous belt stretching from the easternmost tip of the horn to the north-western Ethiopian border and rising to 7,926 ft/2,416 m at Shimbiris in the Woqooyi Galbeed region. To the south, the arid coastal plain rises inland to the Haud Plateau (3,281 ft/1,000 m average elevation) and the flat land of the deep south. Between the Jubba and Wadi Shebelle rivers which traverse the country west-east from Ethiopia to the Indian Ocean, the soils are rich and fertile with a considerable area given over to meadowland and pasture. 70% of the population is nomadic; the greatest sendentary concentrations are found in the Jubba and Wadi Shebelle river valleys. 2% of the land is arable and 14% is forested.

Climate

Predominantly arid, with rainfall increasing north to south-east from 2.4 in/61 mm to 19.3 in/490 mm annually. Maximum temperatures occur Apr.-Sept.

although cooler maritime influences modify high temperatures on the east coast. Drought represents a constant threat. Mogadishu: Jan. 79°F/26.1°C. July 78°F/25.6°C. Average annual rainfall 16.9 in/429 mm. Berbera: Jan. 76°F/24.4°C. July 97°F/36.1°C. Average annual rainfall 2 in/51 mm.

Cities and towns

Mogadishu (capital)	1,000,000
Hargeisa	150,000
Kismayu	70,000
Berbera	65,000
Merca	60,000

Population

Total population is 8,248,133 of which 33% live in urban areas. Population density is 33.5 persons per mile^2/9.7 per km^2. Ethnic divisions: 85% Somali; the remaining 15% are primarily Bantu, with Arab (30,000), European (3,000) and Asian (less than 1,000) minorities.

Birth rate 4.7%. **Death rate** 1.5%. **Rate of population increase** (1980–87) 3.2%. **Age distribution** under 15 = 45.9%; over 65 = 2.7%. **Life expectancy** female 49; male 45; average 47.

Religion

Islam; the population is almost exclusively Sunni Muslim (at least 99.8%). There is a tiny Christian minority.

Language

The official Somali language is almost universally spoken, with the exception of the very small Arabic-speaking communities.

HISTORY

The Somali people, who probably originated in the highlands of Ethiopia, spread south and east from the northern steppes of present-day Somalia following their conversion to Islam in the 14th century. Today there are Somali communities in Djibouti, Kenya, and the Ogaden region of Ethiopia. Arab trading communities established towns on the coast during the Middle Ages, which came under Omani rule in the 16th century, but they did not impose their authority over the pastoral nomads of the interior.

In 1875 Egypt took control of Northern Somalia but was forced to withdraw in 1884, at which point the British stepped in, declaring a Protectorate in 1885. Meanwhile, Italy asserted its claim on the Benadir (eastern) coast which became a Protectorate in 1889. Whereas Italy strove to develop Somalia as a colony, encouraging Italians to found cotton, sugar and banana plantations, Britain made no attempt to colonize its Protectorate. Even so, opposition to European rule was strongest in northern Somalia where Muhammad Abdallah Hassan maintained control of the interior from 1899 until his death in 1920.

After Italy's defeat in 1941, southern Somalia was returned to Italy as a UN trusteeship in 1950 on condition that it became independent by 1960. Elections followed in southern Somalia in 1956 and were won by the nationalist Somali Youth League (SYL). Then, in Feb. 1960, the Somali National League (SNL) secured a majority in elections in northern Somalia and declared its intention to reunify the north and south at independence. This was achieved on 1 July 1960.

Re-unification proved difficult since the new Republic lacked a national infrastructure and rivalries soon developed between ethnic groups. Moreover, the coalition government's irredentist policies led to war with Ethiopia over the Ogaden in 1964. A period of democratic rule, characterized by a proliferation of parties, corruption and electoral malpractice, followed the first national elections in Mar. 1964. This ended with the assassination of Pres. Shermakhe and a week later, on 21 Oct. 1969, a military coup which brought Maj.-Gen. Mohammed Siyad Barre to power.

Governing through a 25-strong Revolutionary Council, Gen. Barre adopted a policy of 'scientific socialism'. One lasting achievement was the creation and dissemination of a written Somali language. In 1977 Somalia launched an attack on Ethiopia in order to enforce its claims to the Ogaden. The rout of the Somali army in Mar. 1978 marked a turning point. Gen. Barre abandoned his Soviet allies in favour of the United States. The economic situation deteriorated sharply. Despite the formation of a Somali Revolutionary Socialist party in 1976 and single-party elections in Aug. 1979 discontent at the autocratic style of government grew. There was an attempted military coup in Apr. 1978 and the surviving leaders founded the opposition Somalia Salvation Democratic Front (SSDF) in 1979. Another Issaq-dominated opposition group, the Somali National Movement (SNM), was founded in 1981. From bases in Ethiopia they carried out a guerrilla war in Somalia until reconciliation between Ethiopia and Somalia in Apr. 1987 led the SNM to occupy northern Somalia. The civil war continued throughout 1988 and 1989; the SNM on two occasions, in Nov. 1988 and Dec. 1989 took effective control of the second largest city, Hargeisa.

CONSTITUTION AND GOVERNMENT

Executive and legislature

A one-party state in which 'political leadership of party and state are indivisible', Somalia has an executive president, proposed by the party and elected by direct universal suffrage for a seven-year term. Last election Dec. 1986. The People's Assembly, the unicameral legislative body, is elected for a five-year term by direct popular vote; last elections Dec. 1984. The constitution was under review as of late 1989, with the president promising in November that 1990 would see free elections in which 'all political currents will be able to express themselves and share power.'

Present government

President; C.-in-C. of the Armed Forces; Chairman of the Council of Ministers Maj.-Gen. Mohammed Siyad Barre

Prime Minister Lt.-Gen. Mohammed Ali Samater

Other Principal Members of the Council of Ministers Col. Ahmed Mahmoud Farah (Deputy Prime Minister); Maj.-Gen. Hussein Kulmiye Afrah (Economic Planning); Abdulkadir Haji Mohammad (Interior); Hussein Abdurahman Matan (Defence); Brig.-Gen. Mohammed Ghelle Yusuf (Finance and Treasury); Ahmed Jaba Abdulle (Foreign Affairs).

Ruling party

Somali Revolutionary Socialist Party. **Secretary-General** Maj.-Gen. Mohammed Siyad Barre. **Members of the politburo** Maj.-Gen. Mohammed Siyad Barre; Lt.-Gen. Mohammed Ali Samater; Maj.-Gen. Hussein Kulmiye Afrah; Brig.-Gen. Ahmed Suleiman Abdullah; Col Ahmed Mahmoud Farah.

Justice

There is a Supreme Court at Mogadishu, two Courts of Appeal, eight regional courts and 84 district courts, each with a civil and criminal section. The death penalty is in force. There were over 150 executions between 1985 and mid-1988. Offences were murder; embezzlement; organizing a subversive organization.

National symbols

Flag. A blue field bearing a large white five-pointed star.

Festivals. 1 May (Labour Day); 26 June (Independence Day); 1 July (Foundation of the Republic); 21–22 Oct. (Anniversary of military coup in 1969).

Vehicle registration plate. SP.

INTERNATIONAL RELATIONS

Affiliations

NAM; OAU; ACP; Arab League; ICO.

Defence

Total Armed Forces: 65,000. Terms of service: conscription (males 18–40), 18 months selective.
Army: 61,300; 293 main battle tanks (Centurion, M-47, T-34, T-54/-55), ten light tanks (M-41).
Navy: 1,200; 12 patrol and coastal combatants.
Air Force: 2,500; 66 combat aircraft (mainly MiG-17/-21MF, J-6, SF-260W).
Para-military: 29,500.

ECONOMY

Currency

The unit is the shilling, divided into 100 centesimi.

National finance

Budget. The 1987 budget, in US$, was for expenditure of 477.6 million and revenue of 74.7 million.

Balance of payments. The balance of payments, in US$ (current account, 1987) was a deficit of 59 million.

Inflation. 28.1%.

Gross Domestic Product

Estimated total GDP US$1,890 million, per capita US$190 (overall size of economy ranking 119 in the world).

Economically active population. The total number of persons active in the economy was 2,200,000.

Sector	% of GDP
industry	9
agriculture	65
services*	26

* services figure includes elements unassigned to other categories.

Energy and mineral resources

Minerals. Uranium and largely unexploited reserves of iron ore; tin; gypsum; bauxite; copper; salt.

Electricity. Capacity: 71,000 kW; production: 86 million kWh; 10 kWh per capita (1988).

Bioresources

Agriculture. Somalia is predominantly a pastoral country and approximately 80% of the population depend on livestock-rearing (cattle, sheep, goats and camels). Bananas, cotton, sugar cane and cereals are also grown.
Crop production: (1986 in 1,000 tons/tonnes) sugar cane 606/550; bananas 77/70; maize 421/382; sorghum 277/251; grapefruit 10/9; seed cotton 3.3/3.
Livestock numbers: (1987) goats 18.5 million; sheep 11.5 million; camels 6.35 million; cattle 5.5 million; horses 1000; asses 25,000; mules 23,000.

Forestry. 14% of the land area is forest and woodland. Timber production: (1984) 183.6 million ft^3/ 5.2 million m^3.

Fisheries. Catch: (1984) 16,865 tons/15,300 tonnes.

Industry and commerce

Industry. Main industries are sugar refining; food processing; textiles; petroleum refining.

Commerce. Exports: (1987) US$95 million or 6% of GDP, including livestock; hides; skins; bananas; fish. Imports: US$418 million, including textiles; petroleum products; foodstuffs; construction materials. Countries exported to were US 0.5%; Saudi Arabia; Italy; West Germany. Imports came from US 13%; Italy; West Germany; Kenya; UK; Saudi Arabia.

Trade with UK. In 1988 Somalia imported UK goods worth £10,379,000; exports to UK totalled £1,151,000.

COMMUNICATIONS

Railways

There are no railways in Somalia.

Roads

There are 13,225 miles/21,297 km of roads, of which 3,647 miles/5,873 km are concrete or bituminized.

Aviation

Somali Airlines provide domestic and international services (main airport is at Mogadishu). Passengers: (1984) 130,000.

Shipping

The ports of Mogadishu and Chisimayu are on the Indian Ocean, Berbera is located on the Gulf of Aden. The merchant marine consists of two cargo ships of 1,000 GRT or over. Freight loaded: (1985) 256,836 tons/233,000 tonnes; unloaded: 1.1 million tons/1 million tonnes.

Telecommunications

There are 6,000 telephones and a minimal telephone and telegraph service. There are 363,292 radios, some installed in public places and tuned to the Somali Broadcasting Service as the main government service. Reception of the television service, broadcast for 2–3 hours daily, is limited to a 30 km radius of Mogadishu.

EDUCATION AND WELFARE

Education

Schools. A large percentage of the population lead a nomadic life. In 1982 there were 220,680 pupils and 9,460 teachers (one per 23 pupils) in primary schools and 53,391 pupils and 2,201 teachers (one per 24 pupils) in secondary schools.

Universities. The National University of Somalia in Mogadishu (2,332 students in 1980).

Literacy. 60%.

Health

(1986) There are 450 doctors (one per 18,329 people).

SOUTH AFRICA
Republiek van Suid-Afrika
(Republic of South Africa)

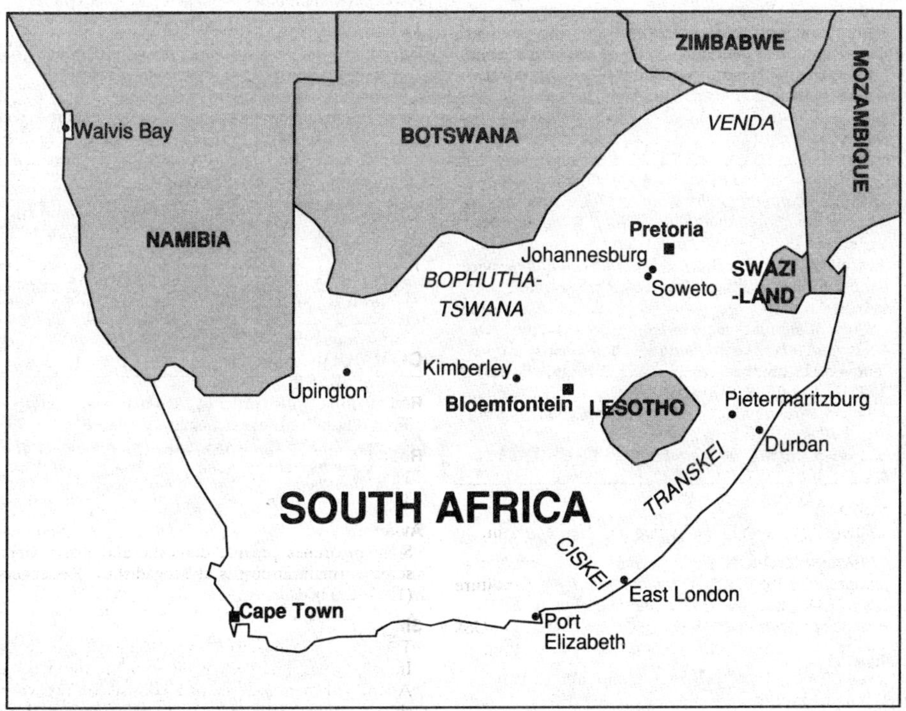

GEOGRAPHY

South Africa occupies the southernmost territory of the African continent, covering a total area of 476,094 miles²/1,233,404 km² including the homelands of Bophuthatswana, Ciskei, Transkei and Venda whose 'independent' status is recognized by South Africa alone. The independent state of Lesotho also lies within South Africa's main frontiers. The country divides physiographically into three major zones: the interior African plateau extending northwards to form part of the semi-arid and sparsely populated Kalahari Basin and rising eastwards to 6,562 ft/2,000 m elevation; the rugged, semi-circular Great Escarpment encompassing the plateau and rising north-eastwards to a maximum altitude of 11,424 ft/3,482 m (Thabana Ntleyana) in the Drakensberg range; the peripheral coastal plains forming narrow, fertile lowland strips in the west, south and east. Other highland ranges to the south and west of the Drakensbergs include the Roggeveldberg, Sneeuberge and Noweveldberge systems. South Africa's principal river is the River Orange (tributaries Vaal and Caledon) traversing Orange Free State east to west before emptying into the Atlantic at Alexander Bay. 10% of the land is arable and 3% is forested. Of the four provinces (Cape, Natal, Orange Free State and Transvaal) Orange Free State is the most densely populated.

Climate

Temperate, sub-tropical with plentiful sunshine and average annual rainfall of 19 in/485 mm. The warm Mozambique current promotes rich vegetation and high temperatures along the Natal coast with average annual rainfall above 39 in/1,000 mm. To the south, the cooler Benguela current moving north from the Antarctic meets the Mozambique stream and continues north along the west coast of the republic where dry conditions prevail with a minimum annual average rainfall of less than 1 in/30 mm in the north-western coastal desert zone. Generally, summer temperatures range between 70 and 75°F/21 and 24°C with a corresponding winter range of 46–52°F/8–11°C. Pretoria: Jan. 70°F/21°C. July 52°F/11.1°C. Average annual rainfall 31 in/785 mm. Bloemfontein: Jan. 73°F/22.8°C. July 47°F/8.3°C. Average annual rainfall 22.2 in/564 mm. Durban: Jan. 75°F/23.9°C. July 62°F/16.7°C. Average annual rainfall 39.7 in/1,008 mm.

Cities and towns

Cape Town (legislative capital)	1,911,521
Johannesburg	1,609,408
Durban	982,075
Pretoria (administrative capital)	822,925

Port Elizabeth	651,993
Vereeniging	540,142
Bloemfontein (judicial capital)	232,984
East London	193,819
Pietermaritzburg	192,417
Kimberley	149,667

Population

South Africa's official population census, last carried out in 1985, excludes 'citizens' of the four nominally 'independent' homelands. Their total number of residents, rather than 'citizens' (many of whom may be resident elsewhere in South Africa) has been estimated (1989) at 8.11 million out of a total population of some 38.51 million. In view of the apartheid restrictions on where non-whites may be legally resident, there is widespread resistance to registration of population data, and official census figures must be considered in this light. The 1985 census recorded a total population, excluding 'citizens' of Bophuthatswana, Ciskei, Transkei and Venda, of 23.39 million, breakdown by colour classification 15.2 million Black (65%), 4.57 million White (19.5%), 2.8 million Coloured (12%) amd 0.82 million Asian (3.5 %).

Current population estimates for the four 'independent' and six Black National homelands are as follows: Bophuthatswana 2,287,701 growth rate 2.77%; Ciskei 996,457 growth rate 2.89%; Transkei 4,187,559 growth rate 4.23%; Venda 639,947 growth rate 3.88%; Gazankulu 713,244 (4.01%); Ka Ngwane 536,093 (3.65%); Kwa Ndebele 337,227 (3.32%); Kwa Zulu 5,158,425 (3.64%); Lebowa 2,600,481 (3.93%); Qwaqwa 768,641 (2.5%).

In 1986 13,711 emigrants left South Africa of whom 6,741 went to Europe (5,407 to the UK) and nearly 4,000 to Australia. In the same year, there were 6,994 immigrants over 3,800 of whom came from Europe, 1,860 from Zimbabwe, 360 from the Americas and an estimated 232 from Asia.

Religion

60% of the Black population and almost all the White and Coloured peoples are Christian. Major denominations include: Anglican communion 2 million; Dutch Reformed Church 2.38 million: Evangelical Lutherans 0.83 million; Roman Catholic Church 2.3 million. An estimated 60% of the Asian population are Hindus and another 20% are Muslims. There are an estimated 120,000 South African Jews.

Language

The official languages are Afrikaans and English. A wide variety of African languages are also spoken, including Nguni dialects (Zulu, Xhosa, Swazi, Ndebele) with approximately 10 million speakers (excluding nominally 'independent' homelands); Sotho 5.5 million speakers; Tsonga 0.9 million speakers; Venda 0.17 million speakers. Indian languages spoken include Hindi; Gujarati; Urdu; Tamil.

HISTORY

In the late Stone Age, around 8000 BC, the San (or Bushmen) and the Khoikhoi lived as hunters and gatherers in what is now South Africa. The Khoikhoi had developed a pastoral culture by the time of European contact. In the Iron Age and until the 15th century AD Bantu-speaking peoples migrated southwards, developing more complex community structures, sophisticated gold- and copper-mining industries and an active East African trade.

The Portuguese navigator, Bartolomeu Dias sailed round the southern tip of South Africa in 1488. More than 150 years later, in 1652 Jan van Riebeeck established a colony at the Cape of Good Hope to serve as a shipping port for the Dutch East India Company. The colonists were initially known as Boers and latterly as Afrikaners (after their language – Afrikaans). Inter-breeding occurred between the San, Khoikhoi and Afrikaners which led to the formation of a new ethnic group known as the Cape Coloureds.

The Afrikaners ventured inland from the Cape, becoming semi-nomadic pastoral farmers. They encountered the populous and settled agricultural (Bantu-speaking) Xhosa people in the area of Fish River. In the late 18th century minor cattle raids developed into frontier wars between the Afrikaners and the Xhosa, which lasted intermittently for a century. Within the Cape colony, meanwhile, the Khoikhoi were displaced to labour as serfs on the Afrikaner farms and the San were driven out into arid or mountainous areas; thousands were killed in retaliation for livestock raids.

In 1795 the British captured the Cape. They relinquished control in 1802 but recaptured the colony four years later. The British continued to subdue the Bantu-speaking peoples along the frontier. The 'Great Trek' began in the 1830s when the Afrikaners, resisting British domination and resenting in particular the British order of 1834 that slaves in Cape Colony should be emancipated, gathered up their property (and their slaves) and migrated north. In large numbers they crossed the Orange and Vaal Rivers, establishing the South African Republic, later Transvaal, in 1838, Natal, which was proclaimed a British colony in 1843, and the Orange Free State in 1854. The Transvaal and Orange Free State gained independence from British colonial rule in the 1850s. In 1877 they briefly became British protectorates after seeking protection against the Zulus, but regained independence by defeating the British in the First Boer War (1881). The discovery of diamonds in 1868 and gold in 1886 led to an economic boom in the late 19th century, and the pattern of reliance on black migrant labour began to emerge as the indigenous Africans, dispossessed in a series of land wars, congregated around the labour-hungry mines. Importation of labour from the Indian subcontinent created the basis for what is now treated as another separate ethnic group, the Indians among whom Mohandas Gandhi was to gain his early political experience as a lawyer and organizer of passive resistance (1907–14).

The Boer Republics resisted British attempts to reabsorb them into the South African confederation. Cecil Rhodes, epitomizing the thrusting expansionism of British mining companies allied to imperial ambitions, founded the British South Africa Company (1887) for the development of Rhodesia in the hope that this area to the north would prove equally attractive. Disappointed in this, he turned his attention (as premier of Cape Colony 1890–96) to efforts to gain control over the Transvaal, encouraging anti-Boer sentiments among European 'Uitlander' mineworkers there and becoming involved in the adventurism of the Jameson Raid (Dec. 1895–Jan. 1896). Jameson's mounted troops from Bechuanaland were quickly captured by the Boers loyal to Paul Kruger's government, the Uitlanders having proved unwilling to rise in revolt against him. Rhodes resigned; Kruger, strongly anti-British and believing in the prospect of German backing, later launched the Second Boer War (1899–1902) with attacks on Natal and Cape Colony. Initially successful, the Boers laid siege to Ladysmith, Mafikeng and Kimberley, but British counter-offensives led by Lord Roberts turned the tide of the war, the Boer capital Pretoria fell (June 1900), and the British, now under Kitchener, broke down the Boer guerrilla resistance, controversially rounding up civilian sympathizers in concentration camps. Under the Treaty of Vereeniging (May 1902) the Transvaal and Orange Free State were again incorporated within the British Empire, but granted self-government some four years later. The South African Act, which was passed on 31 May 1910, established the Union of South Africa, a dominion under the British Crown.

South Africa supported the British during World War I and by July 1915 its troops had forced the Germans to capitulate in South West Africa (now known as Namibia). The League of Nations in 1919 mandated this former German colony to be administered by South Africa.

The South African Party, under the leadership of Louis Botha and Gen. Jan Smuts, ruled the country until 1924. The government wished to keep the Africans in reserves both to prevent the white population from being 'swamped' and to act as a labour pool. In 1924 the South African Party was heavily defeated at the polls and J.B.M. Hertzog became prime minister at the head of a National-Labour coalition. Herzog's main objectives were to win complete emancipation from imperial control, and to provide greater protection for the Whites from the Africans and for the Afrikaners from the British. The Balfour Report (1926) and the Statute of Westminster (1931) gave statutory definition to the established convention that the British government could not exercise authority over a dominion. White supremacy was bolstered during this period by (i) the provision of sheltered employment for 'poor whites' in the state enterprises; (ii) the Mines and Works Amendment Act of 1926 which made existing legislation more effective in shutting Africans out of skilled mining trades; (iii) the Native Administration Act of 1927 and the Riotous Assembly Act of 1930 which gave the executive wide powers over individuals; and (iv) the Franchise Acts of 1930–31 which extended the suffrage to all white men and women. In 1933 Hertzog and Gen. Smuts formed a coalition government and their two parties merged the following year to form the United Party. However, a small group of irreconciled Afrikaners split off to form the Purified Nationalist Party under the leadership of D.F. Malan.

Tensions between Hertzog and Smuts grew during the build-up to World War II, since Hertzog appeared sympathetic to Nazi Germany and moved in the House of Assembly on 4 Sept. 1939 that South Africa should adopt a neutral position in the war. Gen. Smuts argued that South Africa should support Britain and won the debate with an 80:67 vote. The following day Gen. Smuts formed a new government with the support of the Labour Party, the Dominion Party and the majority of the United Party, and war was declared on Germany. In the 1943 general election Gen. Smuts' coalition won a majority of 67 seats but Malan's Nationalists won all 43 opposition seats.

The National Party, with the support of H.C. Havenga's small Afrikaner Party, secured an overall majority of five in the House of Assembly after the 1948 election, with a policy of reducing South Africa's links with Britain, the Commonwealth and the United Nations, to advance the power of the Afrikaner people and, above all, to preserve White supremacy. The National Party expressed horror at the 'liberalism' of the United Party and proclaimed the policy of apartheid by which each race would be able to 'develop along its own lines in its own area'. The National Party has consolidated its power in the years since 1948 under the leadership of Malan (1948–54), J.G. Strijdom (1954–58) and Dr Hendrik Verwoerd (1958–66), while enacting a mass of racial legislation to preserve White supremacy. Under Verwoerd South Africa left the Commonwealth and became a republic (31 May 1961).

The principal opposition to government policy initially took the form in the 1950s of a civil disobedience campaign organized by the multi-racial African National Congress (ANC). In 1955 the ANC and other organizations signed the 'Freedom Charter' which called for equal political rights for all racial groups. Four years later a split in the ANC led to the formation of the exclusively African Pan-Africanist Congress (PAC). The ANC and the PAC in 1960 conducted a campaign against the notorious pass laws, which regulated the movement of Blacks within the country.

State violence against pass law demonstrations led to 67 Africans being shot dead at a demonstration in Sharpeville in March 1960. The ANC and the PAC were declared illegal organizations by the government and both subsequently formed military wings outside South Africa to conduct sabotage campaigns. The ANC's leader Nelson Mandela was gaoled for life after the Rivonia trial in 1963, when he was convicted of sabotage. In prison for over a quarter of a century, he nevertheless remained in touch with the development of nationalist opposition to the apartheid regime, a figure of genuine authority rather than a mere figurehead.

B.J. Vorster, the former minister of justice, became prime minister in Sept. 1966 when Verwoerd was assassinated in Sept. 1966. Vorster continued to implement the policy of apartheid. He resigned in Sept. 1978 and was succeeded by P.W. Botha, the former minister of defence. In Mar. 1982, 17 right-wing members broke away from the Nationalist Party in protest at what they perceived to be P.W. Botha's liberalizing of apartheid. They formed the Conservative Party under the leadership of Dr Andries Treurnicht.

Under Verwoerd's 'Grand Apartheid' policy, the government had established ten homelands (or bantustans) comprising 13% of all land, for African ethnic groups. Transkei was the first to be given self-governing status (1963). Four homelands were later granted 'independence': Transkei in Oct. 1976; Bophuthatswana in Dec. 1977; Venda in Sept. 1979; Ciskei in Dec. 1981. None have been recognized outside South Africa. South Africa's mines and industry depended on Black workers, many millions of whom were drawn in from neighbouring Black states and had no citizenship rights; the creation of 'independent' homelands was designed to extend this pattern, giving South African Blacks their 'own' national identity, excluding them from the political development of White South Africa, and exploiting the flexibility of a non-citizen workforce with an influx control system to match the labour requirements of the White-run economy.

Numerous discriminatory laws and stringent security legislation has led to the detention without trial of many of the government's opponents, the banning of African political organizations outside the homelands, a large prison population and the forced removal of hundreds of thousands of Africans under the provisions of the Group Areas Act and the homelands policy. The African response to these measures in 1976 took the form of uprisings in the Soweto township of Johannesburg. Several hundred Africans, including many schoolchildren, were killed by the security forces after initial protests against a new regulation which made Afrikaans the compulsory language of instruction in African schools. South African methods of repression caused further international outrage in Sept. 1977 over the death in detention of Black Consciousness leader Steven Biko. Further serious rioting broke out in the townships in Sept. 1984, which was met by violent repression and in July 1985 the declaration of a state of emergency. By Mar. 1986, when the state of emergency was ended, some 8,000 people had been arrested and 757 killed. In June 1986 a new state of emergency was declared as censorship was tightened and the ANC guerrilla campaign continued. South African Church leaders, notably Anglican Archbishop Desmond Tutu and Rev. Allan Boesak, emerged as a major focus of mass opposition to apartheid, the regime having banned not only the PAC and ANC but also the United Democratic Front (UDF, established Aug. 1983, progressively restricted and finally prohibited Feb. 1988) and a wide range of other political, union, community and detainee support groups.

Under the premiership of P.W. Botha a number of reforms of the apartheid system were introduced which failed to satisfy Black aspirations whilst also antagonizing the right-wing of the National Party. African trade unions were legalized in 1979 and some petty apartheid restrictions were also lifted. Constitutional reforms introduced in 1983 provided for separate chambers for the Coloured and Indian communities, but not for Blacks. These separate chambers, which were effectively subordinate to the White chambers, were implemented in 1984 when P.W. Botha was unanimously elected as state president, with wider executive powers under the new constitution. The government also introduced in 1983 the Black Authorities Act which provided for Black community councils to be replaced by town councils giving Blacks, in theory, greater powers in local government. The UDF, formed in Aug. 1983 to mobilize resistance on a national scale to Coloured and Indian participation in the constitutional reforms, led a boycott campaign which resulted in a 20% turnout in the Black council elections in Nov. and Dec. 1983, and less than 11% in Soweto. In Apr. 1985 the government repealed the 1927 Immorality Act and the 1949 Prohibition of Mixed Marriages Act (which forbade sexual relations and marriage between members of different races). However, the government began to adopt a more cautious approach to reform in the light of fierce right-wing opposition to the relaxation of apartheid laws. P.W. Botha, who suffered a stroke in Jan. 1989, resigned as leader of the NP in Feb., but remained State President. F.W. de Klerk, then the NP leader in the Transvaal, leader of the House of Assembly and Minister of National Education became leader of the NP. Botha announced in April that he would not seek a futher term as president in elections called for Sept. 1989; he resigned as state president in Aug., following a row between de Klerk and himself, in which de Klerk had the support of the cabinet.

In the election, held on 6 Sept. 1989, the NP again won an overall majority, with 93 out of the 166 elective seats, although for the first time since 1948 it won less than half of all votes; the CP won 39 seats with nearly one-third of the vote; 33 seats (20%) went to the Democratic Party – formed by an amalgamation of liberal groups earlier in the year. In the previous general election, in May 1987, the right-wing CP, winning 22 seats and nearly 27% of the vote, had replaced the Progressive Federal Party as the official opposition in the House of Assembly. De Klerk was chosen as President by an electoral college on 14 Sept. 1989. De Klerk acknowledged the urgent need for the government to open negotiations with legitimate black leaders, prompted by a wish to end South Africa's international islolation; however he was known to favour the retention of 'group rights', ie entrenched privilege for the white majority.

In Oct., seven veteran ANC activists, the most prominent of whom was Walter Sisulu, were released from gaol after serving long sentences, and soon afterwards the ANC, in spite of the state of emergency restrictions, held a huge rally of its supporters. In Feb. 1990 de Klerk stepped up the pace of change and confounded right-wingers by announcing the unbanning of the ANC, the South African Communist Party (SACP) and the PAC, and the lifting of restrictions on various other anti-apartheid organizations, including the UDF, although the state of emergency remained in force. On 11 Feb. 1990, to scenes of worldwide jubilation, Nelson Mandela was released after 27 years in gaol and immediately set about consolidating the ANC's position as the principal liberation movement. After being reunited with the exiled leadership in Zambia, and with its President Oliver Tambo, convalescing from an illness in Sweden, Mandela was elected deputy President of the Congress in Mar. The ANC announced that it would transfer its headquarters back to South Africa and preparations began for a series of high-level negotiations with the government on constitutional reform.

South Africa had grown increasingly isolated politically within southern Africa following the independence of the Portuguese colonies in 1975 and Zimbabwe in 1980. The South African policy of regional destabilization during the 1980s involved a military presence in Angola, support for anti-government movements in Angola and Mozambique and military raids and acts of sabotage in other neighbouring states. The lengthy international wrangle over the future of Namibia appeared likely to resolve itself following the withdrawal of South African forces from Angola and the reduction of the South African military presence in Namibia, together with the phased withdrawal of Cuban troops from Angola. Namibia achieved independence in Mar. 1990. Facing economic recession, South Africa began feeling in the late 1980s a significant impact of Western disapproval of apartheid; the withdrawal of multinationals, difficulties in obtaining new investment and loans, and the imposition of some trade sanctions. A group of seven Commonwealth heads of government (excluding Britain's) supported in Aug. 1986 a wide-ranging sanctions package; more limited measures were adopted by the European Communities (Sept. 1986) and the United States (Oct. 1986, reinforced Dec. 1987).

CONSTITUTION AND GOVERNMENT

Executive and legislature

South Africa's social and political structure is based on the policy of racial segregation. The tricameral

Parliament has a separate House of Assembly (178 members) representing Whites, a House of Representatives (85 members) representing people of mixed race ('Coloureds'), and a House of Delegates (45 members) representing Indians, but no representation for the majority Black population. Last elections to all three houses were on 6 Sept. 1989. In each of the three houses of Parliament there is a ministers' council, each chamber having separate responsibility for the affairs of the population group it represents (including housing, social welfare, health, education), while joint parliamentary responsibility is taken for 'general' or national affairs (including foreign policy, defence, finance, law and order), each of these functions at national level being reflected in a portfolio in the cabinet itself. The executive state president is head of government, nominating the cabinet, and is chosen by an electoral college composed of 50 members of the House of Assembly, 25 members of the House of Representatives, and 13 from the House of Delegates; last election 14 Sept. 1989. A 60-member president's council acts as an advisory body, to which are referred, among other things, disagreements on general affairs among the three chambers of parliament.

Present government

State President; C.-in-C. of the South African Defence Force F. W. de Klerk

Principal Members of the Cabinet Roelof F. Botha (Foreign Affairs); Dr Gerrit van N. Viljoen (Constitutional Development); Gen. Magnus A. Malan (Defence); Dr D.W. de Villiers (Minerals and Energy, Public Enterprises and Privatization); Kobie (H.J.) Coetsee (Justice, Chair of the Ministers' Council of the House of Assembly); Barend J. du Plessis (Finance); Adriaan J. Vlok (Law and Order); W. Louw (Home Affairs; National Education); Dr W.J. de Villiers (Administration and Economic Co-ordination).

Administration

The main administrative division is into the four provinces:

Cape Province population: 4.9 million (1986); area including the Walvis Bay enclave on the coast of Namibia 247,572 miles^2/641,379 km^2; provincial capital Cape Town.

Natal population: 2.15 million (1985); area excluding Kwa Zulu 21,505 miles^2/55,712 km^2; provincial capital Pietermaritzburg.

Orange Free State population: 1.86 million (1987); area including Qwaqwa 49,405 miles^2/127,993 km^2; provincial capital Bloemfontein.

Transvaal population: 7.5 million (1985); area including Gazankulu, Lebowa, Ka Ngwane and Kwa Ndebele 101,325 miles^2/262,499 km^2; administrative capital Pretoria.

Ten parts of South Africa (not necessarily contiguous geographical entities but based on ethnic groupings) have been designated by the government as 'homelands' for Africans; four of these (Bophuthatswana, Ciskei, Transkei, Venda) have been declared independent sovereign states but are recognized only by South Africa and by each other; the remainder (Gazankulu, Ka Ngwane, Kwa Ndebele, Kwa Zulu, Lebowa and Qwaqwa) are at various stages of 'self-government'. The administration of apartheid regulations is highly complex, particularly such measures as the Group Areas Act controlling which population groups may live within designated areas.

Justice

The system of law is based on Roman-Dutch law, but with English law followed in the Cape Province and influencing civil and criminal procedure elsewhere. The highest court is the Supreme Court with its Appellate Division in the judicial capital, Bloemfontein, and provincial divisions in each of the four provinces. Local courts deal with all but the more serious cases in the first instance. For what are defined as specifically Black judicial affairs, there are separate Black Appeal Courts, Black Divorce Courts and Courts of Black Affairs Commissioners. The judiciary has sought to preserve its reputation for acting independently from political control. The death penalty is in force. There were over 537 executions between 1985 and mid-1988. Offences were murder; rape; aggravated robbery and house-breaking; treason.

National symbols

Flag. Three horizontal stripes of orange, white and blue.

Festivals. 31 May (Republic Day); 5 Sept. (Settlers' Day); 10 Oct. (Kruger Day); 16 Dec. (Day of the Covenant).

Vehicle registration plate. ZA.

INTERNATIONAL RELATIONS

Affiliations

Member of the UN (although not participating in General Assembly meetings since 1974); GATT; the World Bank and IMF; and several UN agencies, but membership in others is suspended.

Defence

Total Armed Forces: 103,500 (67,900 White conscripts; 3,200 women). Terms of service: 24 months' National Service, followed by 12 years' part-time service in Citizen Force. Races other than Whites may volunteer for Full Time Force, National Service, and Commando service but are not conscripted. Reserves: 455,000.

Army: 75,000. Full-time Force 19,900 (12,000 White; 5,400 Black and Coloured; some 2,500 women); some 250 main battle tanks (Centurion/Olifant 2B).

Navy: 7,500 inclusive 900 marines; three submarines (Fr Daphne) and nine patrol and coastal combatants.

Air Force: 13,000; 324 combat aircraft inclusive 93 with Citizen Force (mainly Canberra B(I) 12, Buccaneer S-50, Mirage F-1AZ, MB-326M/K, Impala I/II), 14 armed helicopters.

Para-military (South African Police): 55,000.

Opposition: African National Congress (ANC): combat wing Umkhonto we Sizwe: perhaps 10,000 trained; up to 1,000 based in Angola.

Pan Africanist Congress: (PAC): Azanian People's Liberation Army.

ECONOMY

Currency

The unit is the rand, divided into 100 cents.

National finance

Budget. The 1989 FY budget, in US$, was for expenditure of 23,300 million and revenue of 18,900 million.

Balance of payments. The balance of payments, in US$ (current account, 1987) was a surplus of 2,911 million.

Inflation. 12.3%.

Gross Domestic Product
Estimated total GDP US$74,260 million, per capita US$2,360 (overall size of economy ranking 31 in the world).

Economically active population. The total number of persons active in the economy was 11,000,000; unemployed: 19%.

Sector	% of workforce	% of GDP
industry	36	44
agriculture	30	6
services*	34	50

* services figure includes elements unassigned to other categories.

Energy and mineral resources
Minerals. Production: (1986) gold in troy weight, 1,701,943 lbs/635,233 kg; silver in troy weight 580,321 lbs/216,599 kg; chromium; antimony; coal 187 million tons/170 million tonnes; iron ore 27 million tons/24.5 million tonnes; manganese ore 4 million tons/3.7 million tonnes; nickel; phosphates 3.1 million tons/2.9 million tonnes; tin; uranium; diamonds 10.1 million carats; platinum; copper 216,051 tons/196,000 tonnes; vanadium; salt; natural gas.

Electricity. Capacity: 34.2 million kW; production: 155,000 million kWh; 4,025 kWh per capita (1988). 20 coal powered stations; three hydroelectric; two gas-turbine.

Bioresources
Agriculture. South Africa is self-sufficient in food. 10% of the land is put to arable use, 65% is meadow and pasture. Lack of important arterial rivers or lakes necessitates extensive water conservation and control measures.

Crop production: (1987) maize 8.1 million tons/7.3 million tonnes; wheat 2.9 million tons/2.6 million tonnes; sugar cane 22 million tons/20 million tonnes; tobacco; citrus fruit; cattle and dairy products; sheep; wool 100,309 million tons/91,000 tonnes; cotton; viticulture.

Livestock numbers: sheep 29.7 million; cattle 11.8 million; 5.8 million goats; 1.5 million pigs.

Forestry. About 4 million acres/1.6 million ha of forest are commercially exploited.

Fisheries. Total catch (1986) 680,009 tons/616,900 tonnes (anchovy and Cape hake form the largest proportion of the catch).

Industry and commerce
Industry. The economy is based on mining and manufacturing; almost 65% of exports come from mining, with gold contributing 40%. Manufacturing contributes approximately 20% to GDP. Other important industries are finance; insurance; food processing; beverages; tobacco; wood pulp and paper; chemicals; rubber; fertilizers. There is high unemployment (15–20%) especially among Black workers.

Commerce. Exports: (f.o.b. 1987) US$18,500 million or 22% of GDP: gold 40%; minerals and metals 23%; food 6%; chemicals 3%. Main trading partners US; UK; West Germany; Japan; other EC countries; Hong Kong.

Trade with UK. In 1988 South Africa exported £807 million worth of goods to the UK and imported £1,074.8 million worth of goods from the UK.

Tourism. Some 600,000 tourists visited South Africa in 1986.

COMMUNICATIONS

Railways
There are 14,660 miles/23,607 km of railways (of which 1,453 miles/2,340 km in Namibia, 174 miles/280 km in Transkei, 165 miles/265 km in Bophuthatswana, 60 miles/96 km in Ciskei and 1.2 miles/2 km in Lesotho are controlled by the South African Transport Services Board).

Roads
There are 115,413 miles/185,851 km of roads, of which 31,854 miles/51,295 km are concrete or bituminized.

Aviation
Air Cape (Pty) Ltd, COMAIR (Commercial Airways (Pty) Ltd) and United Air (Pty) Ltd provide domestic service; South African Airways (SAA) provide domestic and international services (main airports are S.A. Airways Centre at Johannesburg and Malan Airport at Cape Town). Passengers: (1985) 3.9 million.

Shipping
The ports of Cape Town and Saldanha face onto the South Atlantic Ocean, Mosselbaai, Port Elizabeth, Richard's Bay and Durban are on the coast of the Indian Ocean. Walvis Bay, situated in an exclave of South Africa in Namibia, is also a port facing onto the South Atlantic.

Telecommunications
There are 4.5 million telephones and the system is the best developed, most modern and has the highest capacity in Africa, with key centres in Bloemfontein, Cape Town, Durban, Johannesburg, Port Elizabeth and Pretoria. There are 10.3 million radios and 3.1 million televisions (1986). The government's SABC operates radio services in 19 languages, external broadcasts (Radio RSA) in 12 languages, and a television service (since 1976 only) with one channel for English and Afrikaans programmes, another two for Sotho, Tswana, Xhosa and Zulu language broadcasts, and sports and entertainment on Channel 4.

EDUCATION AND WELFARE

Education
School attendance is compulsory for Whites, Coloureds and Indians between seven and 16, and for Blacks between seven and 11. Primary and secondary public education are the responsibility of the Provincial Administration. Education policy is determined according to the National Education Policy Act 1967. The Department of Black Education and Training has responsibility for Blacks, and the Department of Internal Affairs has responsibility for Coloureds and Indians.

School population. Some 952,000 White primary school pupils; 823,000 Coloured pupils; 236,000 Indian pupils; 4.7 million Black pupils (1987).

Schools. Pupil/teacher ratios: White 13:1; Coloured 19:1; Indian 18:1; Black 34:1.

Universities. Students at tertiary level: Whites 247,000; Coloureds 31,500; Indians 25,000; Blacks 95,000. There are 17 universities in the Republic of South Africa, ten of which are for whites (although admission restrictions have been relaxed and numbers of other races are now enrolled); three are for Blacks only (plus one Medical University); one for Coloureds; one for Indians; one offering correspondence tuition for all races. There is one university in each of the four 'independent' homelands.

Literacy. Whites 93%; Asians 71%; Coloureds 62%; Blacks 32%.

Health

Some 23,000 medical practitioners; 4,000 dentists; 650 hospitals. There is considerable disparity between health care for Whites and non-Whites (for example five times more hospital beds are available for Whites than for Blacks and eight times more beds for Whites than for Asians).

SPAIN
España
(Spanish State)

GEOGRAPHY

Situated on the Iberian Peninsula in south-western Europe, Spain, the third largest country in Europe, has an area of 194,846 miles^2/504,782 km^2 including the Canary and Balearic Islands and the municipalities of Ceuta and Melilla on the northern Moroccan coast. Continental Spain's physiography is dominated by the central Meseta (average elevation 2,297 ft/700 m), an elevated tableland surrounded by mountain ranges to the north (Cordillera Cantábrica), to the south (Sierra Morena), to the south-west (Sistema Ibérico) and north-west. In the south-east, the Andalucian Sierra Nevada mountains rise to a maximum elevation of 11,411 ft/3,478 m at Mulhacén, while the north-eastern Pyrenees reach 11,168 ft/3,404 m at Pico a'Aneto. Also in the north-east, the Ebro river valley flows south-east from the Basque Country through Rioja and Aragón before emptying into the Mediterranean at Cabo de Tortosa. The central plateau is drained by three major rivers, divided by mountain ranges: the Douro and Tajo in the north and the Guadiana in the south. Flowing east to south-west, the Río Guadalquivir traverses Andalucía from the Sierra de Segura to Cádiz. Arable land is concentrated in the northern regions; viticulture predominates on the southern Meseta and in the eastern provinces. Irrigation in the south-east province of Almería has helped promote agricultural activity in an otherwise semi-arid and infertile district. The combined populations of Madrid and Barcelona account for nearly 25% of the total population. 31% of the land area is considered arable and a similar proportion is forested.

Climate

Although the influence of the Mediterranean is paramount, Spain nevertheless experiences a broad range of climatic conditions from the continental climates of the Ebro Basin and the central Meseta to the African 'calina' (haze) of Murcia in the south-east. Three principal climatic zones are distinguishable. On the northern and eastern seaboards, coastal conditions prevail with Jan. and July temperatures of 48°F/9°C and 64°F/18°C respectively and annual rainfall of 38 in/965 mm. The continental plateau varies in temperature according to altitude. Below 9,000 ft/2,743 m, average Jan. and July temperatures are 39°F/4°C and 75°F/24°C with rainfall of 15 in/375 mm. Rainfall increases markedly in mountainous regions, to as much as 44 in/1,125 mm, but average temperatures are 32°F/0°C in Jan. and 52°F/11°C in July. Madrid: Jan. 41°F/5°C. July 77°F/25°C. Average annual rainfall 16.5 in/419 mm. Barcelona: Jan. 46°F/8°C. July 74°F/23.5°C. Average annual rainfall 21.5 in/525 mm. La Coruña: Jan. 50.9°F/10.5°C. July 66.2°F/19°C. Average annual rainfall 31.5 in/800 mm. Balearic Islands: Jan. 51.8°F/11°C. July 77°F/25°C. Average annual rainfall 14 in/347 mm. Canary Islands: Jan. 64.2°F/17.9°C. July 75.9°F/24.4°C. Average annual rainfall 8 in/196 mm.

Cities and towns

Madrid (capital)	3,188,297
Barcelona	1,754,900
Valencia	751,734
Sevilla	653,833
Zaragoza	590,750
Málaga	503,251
Bilbao	433,030
Las Palmas de Gran Canaria	366,454
Palma de Mallorca	304,422
L'Hospitalet de Llobregat	294,033
Murcia	288,631
Córdoba	284,737
Granada	262,182
Vigo	258,724
Gijón	255,969
Alicante	251,387

Population

Total population is 39,417,220 of which 75.8% live in urban areas. Population density is 202.3 persons per mile^2/76.9 per km^2. Ethnic divisions: basically homogeneous, ethnic groups (eg Basque) are separable only by language. Accurate statistics for the considerable Gypsy population are unavailable, but this semi-nomadic minority is estimated to be several hundred thousand strong.

Birth rate 1.3%. **Death rate** 0.8%. **Rate of population increase** 0.5%. **Age distribution** under 15 = 22.9%; over 65 = 12.1%. **Life expectancy** female 80; male 74; average 77.

The mid-decennial census in 1986 gave the following figures:

Balearic Islands population: 754,777 (population density 390 per mile^2/151 per km^2).

Canary Islands population: 1,614,882 (population density 575 per mile^2/221 per km^2).

Ceuta population: 71,403.

Melilla population: 55,613.

Religion

There is no official state religion, as of 29 Dec. 1978. 99% of the population is nominally Roman Catholic. Of the 250,000 other Christians (including Anglican, Baptist and Evangelical denominations), a significant proportion are Mormons or Jehovah's Witnesses. The Muslim community is estimated at between 0.2 and 0.3 million. There are approximately 13,000 Spanish Jews.

Language

Constitutionally, the official language is Castilian Spanish (a Romance language). The majority of Catalonians, Balearic Islanders and Valencians speak Catalan (16.4%), influenced by and related to the Occitan/Provençal tongues of southern France. In the north-west, Galician (Gallego) bears strong resemblances to modern Portuguese. Basque, perhaps the most important of the ethnolinguistic divisions, is widely spoken in the Basque country and the provinces of Guipúzcoa, Vizcaya, Alava and north-western Navarra. The origins of Basque are obscure, it is unrelated to any extant Romance or Indo-European patterns. It was designated a local official language in 1978.

HISTORY

Flourishing Iberian Stone and Bronze Age cultures preceded Phoenician trading settlements in Spain (from c.1100 BC) and Celtic penetration across the Pyrenees (from c.1000 BC). Greek coastal colonization from the 7th century BC was followed by conquest by the Carthaginians (3rd century BC), who were ousted by the Romans in the second Punic war (218–201 BC). Finally pacified by the Romans in 27 BC, Spain was a Roman province until it was overrun in the late 4th century AD by Germanic tribes, one of which, the Visigoths, established a powerful kingdom in 419. The conversion of King Recared I to Christianity (587) helped to integrate the Visigoths with the Christian Romano-Spanish, whose vernacular language was adopted by the invaders (7th century). Muslim rule began when Moors from North Africa ended Visigoth power at the Battle of Guadalete (711), which led to their conquest of the whole peninsula except the far north. The Ommayad Caliphate of Córdoba (755–1031) attained the zenith of Moorish power and artistic achievement under Abdurrahman III (r.912–61), but was eventually destroyed by internal conflict, as vigorous Christian feudal kingdoms (Castile, Aragón, Navarre, León and Asturias, and Catalonia) emerged in the north.

The long Christian reconquest began in earnest in 962 and culminated in decisive victory at the Battle of Navas de Tolosa (1212), after which the Moors were confined to Granada. By the mid-13th century the smaller Spanish kingdoms had been absorbed by either Castile or Aragón, which were themselves united by the marriage (1469) and subsequent accession of King Ferdinand of Aragón (d.1516) and Queen Isabella of Castile (d.1504). Granada was captured from the Moors in 1492, in which year Columbus reached America on behalf of Spain and Jews were given the option of Christian baptism or expulsion, those choosing the former being tested for sincerity by the Spanish Inquisition (founded 1478). Under Ferdinand and Isabella, Spain's administration was centralized, southern Italy came under Spanish rule (1501–4) and Spanish Navarre was conquered (1512) and annexed to Castile (1515). Abroad, four voyages by Christopher Columbus (c.1451–1506), who sought to reach Asia by sailing westwards, led to the discovery of the Americas. The Treaty of Tordesillas (1494) consolidated a series of papal rulings and divided the world into two spheres for respective Spanish and Portuguese exploration. Meanwhile Ferdinand Magellan (c.1470–1521), a Portuguese, led a Spanish expedition on the first ever circumnavigation of the world.

On Ferdinand's death (1516), the Spanish crown passed to his distaff grandson, Charles of Habsburg, who had already inherited the Low Countries from his father (1504) and subsequently succeeded his paternal grandfather as Archduke of Austria and Holy Roman Emperor (1519). Spanish colonization of the New World continued with Hernando Cortés's conquest of the Aztecs in Mexico and Francisco Pizarro's ruthless overthrow and destruction of the Inca empire in Peru. When the greatest of the Habsburg emperors abdicated (1555) and divided the Spanish and imperial successions between his son and brother, the Spain inherited by the former, Philip II (r.1556–98), was the dominant world power.

Philip II further expanded Spain's overseas empire in the Americas and the Far East (where the Philippines was named after him) and brought Portugal under Spanish rule (1580). But his later years marked the start of decline, as his absolutism and fierce Catholicism led to corruption and persecution, while unearned colonial bullion undermined the economy. A Protestant revolt in the Low Countries opposed Philip's centralizing absolutist tendencies and his ruthless attempts to root out heresy, and resulted in the northern half (the later Netherlands) led by William of Orange, winning independence in 1581. Anglo-Spanish relations, which had begun to deteriorate following Philip's barren marriage with the Catholic Queen Mary (d.1558), worsened further with Francis Drake's piratical expeditions to the Spanish West Indies and Queen Elizabeth I's support for the Dutch and for the Huguenots in France. However, Philip's invasion of Protestant England, in which an armada of 130 ships with 22,000 men set sail in May 1588, ended in decisive defeat. In the Thirty Years' War (1618–48), Portugal regained independence (1640) and the Catholic forces of Habsburg Spain and Austria failed to impose the Counter-Reformation on Protestant northern Europe. Under the Peace of Westphalia (1648), France became the leading European power, while England and the Netherlands supplanted Spain at sea. The death of the childless Charles II (ruled 1665–1700) ended the Habsburg dynasty in Spain and gave rise to the War of Spanish Succession (1702–13), in which France secured the accession of the Bourbon Duke of Anjou as Philip V. Under the post-war treaties (1713–14), Spain lost its Italian possessions and the southern Low Countries (to Austria) as well as Gibraltar (to Britain).

Spain recovered southern Italy in 1735 but experienced continued relative decline in the 18th century despite the 'enlightened despotism' of Charles III (r.1759–88), who introduced social and economic reforms and expelled the Jesuits. Drawn into the Napoleonic wars against France, the Spanish house of Bourbon was overthrown by Emperor Napoleon, who made his brother Joseph King of Spain (1808). Rebellion by the Spanish people, who convened the first national Cortes (parliament) in 1810, was assisted in the Peninsular War (1809–14) by British troops led by Sir Arthur Wellesley (later the Duke of Wellington), which ejected the French and restored Ferdinand VII (r.1814–33), although southern Italy passed to another Bourbon branch. By 1830 Spain's American colonies, in revolt since 1810, had won independence, except for Cuba and Puerto Rico. Bequeathed the crown in abrogation of Salic Law, Ferdinand's daughter, Isabella II (r.1833–68), abolished the Inquisition (1834) and promised modernization of Spain's ossified social and economic structures. However, her right to the crown was challenged by Ferdinand's brother, whose Carlist revolt, although unsuccessful, weakened Spain and led to Isabella's deposition by army generals (1868). Duke Amadeo of Savoy, elected king in 1870, abdicated in 1873, whereupon the Cortes declared a Republic. It lasted until a further military revolt (1874) restored the Bourbon Alfonso XII (r.1875–85), who finally defeated the Carlists (1878). Under Alfonso XIII (r.1886–1931), rebellion in Cuba (1895) led to war with the United States (1898), whose victory resulted in Cuba, Puerto Rico and the Philippines becoming possessions of the new US empire.

Spain remained neutral during World War I, which strengthened the republicanism of the Socialist Workers' Party (PSOE, founded 1879) and Communist Party (PCE, founded 1920), as anarchist and regional autonomist movements also gained in support. Military disaster in Spanish Morocco (1921) led to the imposition of military dictatorship by Gen. Primo de Rivera (1923), who essayed a form of fascism and remained prime minister until 1930. Local elections in 1931 produced a republican majority, whereupon King Alfonso abdicated in favour of the Second Republic, which immediately introduced universal adult suffrage. A centre-right administration (1933–36) survived revolt in Asturias and Catalonia (1934), being succeeded, in the 1936 elections, by a Popular Front government under the presidency of Manuel Azaña (1881–1940) and including the PSOE and PCE. This provoked military rebellion in North Africa led by Gen. Francisco Franco (1892–1975), whose Nationalist forces invaded metropolitan Spain and, with the support of the right-wing Spanish Falangists (founded 1933), fascist Italy and Germany, eventually defeated the Republican government in the Spanish Civil War (1936–39). Some 750,000 people died in the war before government forces, increasingly beset by internal intrigues and starved of Soviet aid, were forced to surrender Barcelona to the nationalists in Jan. 1939 and Madrid in Mar. 1939. Earlier German planes had bombed Guernica on 27 Apr. 1937, devastating the town and killing hundreds of civilians. The attack marked the first large-scale aerial bombardment of civilians for military ends and was commemorated by the artist Pablo Picasso in one of his most famous paintings. The war served as an ideological battleground for fascists and socialists from all countries. Over 50,000 Italians fought for the nationalists, while many prominent left-wing writers and thinkers such as George Orwell and Ernest Hemingway supported the anarchist and communist side or fought in the government's 'international brigade'.

As 'chief of the Spanish state' (Caudillo), Gen. Franco established a personal dictatorship based on corporatism, banned opposition to the Falangist Party (later called the National Movement) and restored Catholic Church privileges. He also withdrew from the League of Nations (1939) and revived Spain's claim to Gibraltar in expectation of a British defeat in World War II, in which Spain combined neutrality with pro-Axis sympathies. Notwithstanding the defeat of German and Italian fascism, Franco maintained his authoritarian regime in the post-war era, while declaring (1947) that on his death or retirement the monarchy would be restored. Although the Cortes was revived (from 1942), its members were either elected on a corporatist basis or appointed, within the framework of a one-party system. Excluded from West European integration, Spain remained economically backward in many respects, with a large rural population, although from the mid-1950s the tourist industry developed rapidly, producing capital for industrial development. While remaining outside NATO, Spain signed (1953), and later renewed, a defence treaty with the United States providing for US bases on Spanish soil. Admitted to the UN in 1955, Spain the following year began the transfer of its Moroccan possessions to newly-independent Morocco, culminating in the cession of Ifni (1969), although Morocco's claim to the enclaves of Ceuta and Melilla was rejected by Spain. Similarly, Britain continued to reject Spain's claim to Gibraltar, whose achievement of self-government under British sovereignty caused Franco to close the Spain-Gibraltar border (June 1969). Having granted independence to Equatorial Guinea in 1968, Spain effectively closed its colonial history in Nov. 1975 by withdrawing from Western Sahara.

Following the investiture of Juan Carlos (grandson of Alfonso XIII) as crown prince and Franco's designated successor as head of state (1969), the Caudillo's last years saw a measure of liberalization, although Catalan and Basque separatism continued to elicit a stern response. In its most spectacular action to date, the militant Basque separatist Euskadi ta Askatasuna (ETA) assassinated Prime Minister Admiral Luis Carrero Blanco in a Madrid bomb explosion (20 Dec. 1973). New laws were introduced in 1975 to combat such extremist attacks but in a serious miscalculation by the ageing Franco as to the strength of international outrage he allowed the execution on 27 Sep. 1975 of five of 11 extremists sentenced to death for murders committed in 1974 and 1975 with the result that many European and Scandinavian governments recalled their ambassadors from Madrid in protest.

On Franco's death (20 Nov. 1975), Juan Carlos duly ascended the throne and began the gradual restoration of democracy, which accelerated with the appointment of moderate conservative Adolfo Suárez González as prime minister (July 1976). The disbandment of the National Movement and the legalization of political parties and trade unions (1976) was followed by general elections (June 1977), the first since 1936, in which Suárez's Democratic Centre Union (UCD) became the largest party, with the PSOE as the main opposition. A new constitution, overwhelmingly approved by referendum (Dec. 1978), declared Spain to be a democratic, parliamentary monarchy, while the granting of autonomy to the regions reduced separatist militancy (except in the Basque country). Further elections in Mar. 1979 confirmed the dominance of Suárez and the UCD, although Francoist elements in the military and elsewhere remained unreconciled to the new Spain. When Suárez resigned the premiership (Jan. 1981), amid dissension within the UCD, his successor, Leopoldo Calvo Sotelo, faced an attempted military coup on 23 Feb. 1981 when armed civil guards led by Lt.-Col. Antonio Tejero stormed the Congress of Deputies taking Calvo Sotelo, other members of the government and all the MPs hostage. The attempt was only foiled by King Juan Carlos, who took firm preventive action and won pledges of loyalty from the military commanders behind the coup.

Admitted to the Council of Europe (1977), democratic Spain applied the same year, with Portugal, for membership of the European Communities (EC) and NATO. It also resumed negotiations with Britain on the Gibraltar question, but implementation of the resultant Lisbon agreement (1980), envisaging the reopening of the border, was deferred because of the UK-Argentinian war over the Falklands (Malvinas) (1982). In May 1982 Spain became the 16th member of NATO, although negotiations on its military integration were suspended when the PSOE, which had opposed entry, won a large majority in the Oct. 1982 general elections and the right-wing Popular Alliance (AP) became the main opposition. Headed by Felipe González Márquez (who became at 40 Europe's youngest contemporary prime minister), the PSOE government then opted for remaining in NATO, subject to the verdict of a popular referendum, and launched a major programme of economic and social reform, including the partial legalization of abortion (enacted in 1983). Resumed talks with Britain on Gibraltar produced the Brussels agreement (1984), specifying for the first time that sovereignty could be discussed; accordingly, Gibraltar's border with Spain was reopened (Feb. 1985), although the basic dispute remained unresolved. On 1 Jan. 1986 Spain and Portugal became full members of the EC, on terms expected to benefit their agricultural sector. Eventually held in Mar. 1986, the NATO referendum endorsed the government's pro-membership line, on the basis that Spain would remain outside the NATO command structure, would not allow nuclear weapons on its soil, and would reduce US forces in Spain.

Despite increasing economic difficulties, González and the PSOE were returned to power, with a reduced majority, in early general elections in June 1986, when the AP-led Popular Coalition took second place and Suárez's new Democratic and Social Centre third place, while Basque and Catalan regional parties also polled strongly. Thereafter, dissension and splits among the centre-right formations highlighted the political dominance of the PSOE, although the government continued to face a major security threat from ETA, which continued its attacks in particular on civil guards but also in its most dramatic recent attack placed a car bomb in a Barcelona department store's underground car park which killed 19 people. González also came under increasing pressure from trade unions opposed to its economic austerity programme. A Spain–UK agreement signed in Dec. 1987 envisaged joint use of Gibraltar's airport (but was roundly condemned by the Gibraltarians). In accordance with the government's 1986 NATO referendum pledge, the US–Spain defence treaty was replaced (1988) by a new agreement under which combat planes would be withdrawn from one of the three US air bases in Spain. In Nov. 1988 Spain and Portugal both signed an accession protocol to join the Western European Union. González was returned to power for a third term in elections held on 29 Oct. 1989. However, continuing controversy over the results in several constituencies was not resolved until March 1990 when a repoll in the Spanish north African enclave of Melilla deprived him of his overall majority.

CONSTITUTION AND GOVERNMENT

Executive and legislature

The monarch is head of state. The head of government, appointed by the monarch but responsible to parliament, is the president of the government (prime minister). The bicameral parliament, the Cortes

Name	Area (mile²/km²)	Population	Capital
Andalusia	33,685/87,268	6,875,628	Sevilla
Aragon	18,400/47,669	1,214,729	Zaragoza
Asturias	4,078/10,565	1,114,115	Oviedo
Baleares	1,935/5,014	754,777	Palma de Mallorca
Basque Country	2,803/7,261	2,133,002	Vitoria
Canary Islands	2,807/7,273	1,614,882	*Las Palmas/Santa Cruz de Tenerife
Cantabria	2,047/5,289	524,670	Santander
Castilla-La Mancha	30,581/79,226	1,665,029	+Toledo
Castilla-León	36,341/94,147	2,600,330	Valladolid
Catalonia	12,325/31,930	5,977,008	Barcelona
Extremadura	16,058/41,602	1,088,543	Mérida
Galicia	11,362/29,434	2,785,394	Santiago de Compostela
Madrid	3,086/7,995	4,854,616	Madrid
Murcia	4,368/11,317	1,014,285	**Murcia
Navarra	4,023/10,421	512,676	Pamplona
Rioja, La	1,943/5,034	262,611	Logroño
Valencian Community	8,996/23,305	3,772,002	Valencia

*Dual and alternative capitals
+As of 1988 Castilla-La Mancha had not chosen a capital town; the seat of its legislature and executive is at Toledo.
**Regional parliament at Cartagena
NB: Spain's population also includes the two enclaves on the Moroccan coast, Ceuta (population 71,403) and Melilla (population 55,613).

Generales, comprises the 350-member Congress of Deputies, elected by proportional representation, and the 280-member directly elected Senate. Both houses are elected by universal adult suffrage and for terms of no longer than four years; last elections 29 Oct. 1989.

Present government

King of Spain; C.-in-C. of the Armed Forces; Head of the Supreme Council of Defence. Juan Carlos

President of the Government (Prime Minister). Sr Felipe González Márquez

Principal Members of Council of Ministers. Sr Alfonso Guerra (Deputy Prime Minister); Sr Narcís Serra Serra (Defence); Sr José Luis Corcuero (Interior); Sr Francisco Fernández Ordóñez (Foreign Affairs); Sr Carlos Solchaga (Economy and Finance); Sr Enrique Múgica Herzog (Justice); Sr José Claudio Aranzadi Martínez (Industry and Energy).

Administration

Spain is divided into autonomous regions, each with its own elected legislative assembly, a governing council with executive and administrative functions, and a president of the government (prime minister) elected by the assembly from its members. Many of the autonomous regions are in turn subdivided into provinces.

Presidents of the Governments of the autonomous regions. Andalucía – Sr José Rodríguez de la Barbolla; Aragón – Sr Hipólito Gómez de las Roces; Asturias – Sr Pedro de Silva Cienfuegos Jovellanos; Baleares (Balearic Islands) – Sr Gabriel Cañellas Fons; Basque Country – Sr José Antonio Ardanza; Canary Islands – Sr Lorenzo Olarte Cullen; Cantabria – Sr Juan Hormaechea Cazón; Castilla y León Sr José María Aznar; Castilla-La Mancha – Sr Josí Bono Martínez; Catalonia – Sr Jordi Pujol i Soley; Extremadura – Sr Juan Carlos Rodríguez Ibarra; Galicia – Sr Fernando González Laxe; Madrid – Sr Joaquín Leguina Herrán; Murcia – Sr Carlos Collado Mena; Navarra – Sr Gabriel Urralburu Tainta; La Rioja – Sr Joaquín Espert Pérez-Caballero; Valencia – Sr Joan Lerma.

Justice

A Tribunal Constitucional (Constitutional Court) has specific responsibilities in adjudging whether legislation is in accordance with the constitution and in resolving conflicts between the State and Autonomous communities; it is also the court of last resort in matters relating to individual liberties as defined in the constitution. The judicial function at the local level is exercised by some 7,500 justices of the peace; there are about 750 Juzgados de Distrito (District Courts) and over 500 Juzgados de Primera Instancia (Courts of First Instance), with the higher courts organized as 50 Audiencias Provinciales (Provincial High Courts), 16 Audiencias Territoriales (Division High Courts) and the Tribunal Supremo (Supreme High Court). The death penalty is in force only for exceptional crimes. There were no executions between 1985 and mid-1988.

Prisons. There are 27,793 prisoners.

National symbols

Flag. Three horizontal stripes of red, yellow and red with the state coat of arms in the centre of the yellow stripe.

Festivals. 1 May (St Joseph the Workman); 24 June (King Juan Carlos's Saint's Day); 12 Oct. (National Day, anniversary of the discovery of America).

Vehicle registration plate. E.

INTERNATIONAL RELATIONS

Affiliations

Nato; OECD; EC; Council of Europe.

Defence

Total Armed Forces: 309,500 (to be reduced); 206,000 conscripts. Terms of service: volunteers 16, 18, 24 or 36 months, conscripts 12 months. Reserves: 2,400,000 (all services to age 38).

Army: 232,000; 838 main battle tanks (AMX-30,

M-47E1, M-47E2, M-48A5E), 127 light tanks (M-41).
Navy: 45,000 inclusive marines; eight submarines (Fr Agosta and Daphne) and 23 principal surface combatants: two carriers (about 20 and 18 aircraft); seven destroyers; 14 frigates. 63 patrol and coastal combatants.
Naval Air: 13 combat aircraft; 33 armed helicopters.
Marines: 8,500; 18 main battle tanks (M-48E).
Air Force: 32,500 (to be reduced); 209 combat aircraft (Mirage, F-5, EF-18 A/B).
Para-military (Guardia Civil): 72,700.

ECONOMY

Currency

The unit is the peseta, divided into 100 centivos.

National finance

Budget. The 1987 budget, in US$, was for expenditure of 66,700 million and revenue of 57,800 million. Main items of expenditure are housing and welfare 40.4%; health 12.7%; defence 5.6%; education 5.5%.
Balance of payments. The balance of payments, in US$ (current account, 1988) was a deficit of 3,690 million.
Inflation. 6.8% (12 months to Sept. 1989).

Gross Domestic Product

Estimated total GDP US$287,970 million, per capita US$7,390 (overall size of economy ranking 11 in the world). Growth rate (1988) 5%.
Economically active population. The total number of persons active in the economy was 14,200,000; unemployed: 19.5% (1988).

Sector	% of workforce	% of GDP
industry	32	37
agriculture	16	6
services*	52	57

* services figure includes elements unassigned to other categories.

Energy and mineral resources

Oil and gas. Crude oil production: (1988) 1.7 million tons/1.5 million tonnes; natural gas production: (1986) 248,018 tons/225,000 tonnes.
Minerals. Spain has a wide range of mineral reserves but none in large quantities. Production: (1987 in 1,000 tons/tonnes) coal 9,814/8,903; lignite 24,208/21,961; uranium 419/380; iron 2,251/2,042; pyrites 1,093/992; copper 12/11; lead 86/78; zinc 248/225; tin 78/71; wolfram 71/64; fluorspar 216/196; potassium salts 1,777/1,612.
Electricity. Capacity: 45.1 million kW; production: 149,565 million kWh; 3,810 kWh per capita (1988).

Bioresources

Agriculture. Main crops are grains; citrus and other fruits; vegetables; wine grapes. There are approximately 3.7 million acres/1.5 million ha under vine production and the preparation of wines and fruits is an important activity.
Crop production: (1987 in 1,000 tons/tonnes) wheat 6,365/5,774; barley 10,530/9,533; oats 553/502; rye 354/321; rice 531/482; maize 3,679/3,338; onions 1,173/1,064; potatoes 6,118/5,550; sugar beet 8,419/7,638; oranges and mandarins 3,969/3,601; lemons 685/621; sunflowers 1,021/926; cotton 277/251; olive oil 646/586; tobacco 46/42.
Livestock numbers: (1987) cattle 4.9 million; pigs 16.9 million; horses 248,000; asses 10,000; mules 117,000; (1986) sheep 17.1 million; goats 2.9 million; poultry 53 million.
Forestry. 31% of the land area is forest and woodland and the total forest area is 28.9 million acres/11.7 million ha. Production (1986) 550.9 million ft^3/15.6 million m^3 of wood; resins, cork and esparto are also produced.
Fisheries. Total catch (1987) 1.1 million tons/1 million tonnes, including molluscs 179,675 tons/163,000 tonnes; crustaceans 37,478 tons/34,000 tonnes.

Industry and commerce

Industry. Main industries are textiles and apparel (including wool and cotton cloth and yarn); footwear; food and beverages; metals and metal manufactures; cement; chemicals; shipbuilding; automobiles; machine tools. Production: (1987 in 1,000 tons/tonnes) steel 13,021/11,813; cement 25,366/23,012; 1.4 million cars and 302,000 commercial vehicles were also built.
Commerce. Exports: (1987) US$34,200 million or 11% of GNP, including foodstuffs; live animals; wood; footwear; machinery; chemicals. Imports: US$49,100 million, including petroleum; footwear; machinery; chemicals; grain; soya beans; coffee; tobacco; iron and steel; timber; cotton; transport equipment. Countries exported to were EC countries 64%; Switzerland 11%; US 8%; Middle East; Japan; Portugal. Imports came from EC countries 55%; Mexico 10%; US 8%; Middle East; USSR.
Trade with UK. In 1988 Spain imported UK goods worth £2,691,662,000; exports to UK totalled £2,482,360,000.
Tourism. (1987) 50.5 million visitors.

COMMUNICATIONS

Railways

There are 9,811 miles/15,798 km of railways, of which 3,855 miles/6,207 km are electrified.

Roads

There are 198,093 miles/318,991 km of roads.

Aviation

IBERIA, Lineas Aereas de España, SA provides domestic and international services; Aviacion y Comercio, SA (AVIACO) provides domestic services; Spantax Transportes Aereos, Hispania Lineas Aereas and Air España/Air Europa provide international charter services (there are 20 international airports). Passengers: (1987 provisional) 33.7 million.

Shipping

The 649 miles/1,045 km of inland waterways have little economic importance. The ports of Alicante, Almería, Barcelona, Cartagena, Málaga, Sagunto, Tarragona and Valencia face on to the Mediterranean Sea. Algeciras is situated on the strait of Gibraltar. Cádiz and Rota, on the south coast, face onto the North Atlantic Ocean. La Coruña and El Ferrol, both situated on the north-west tip of Spain, and Vigo, further west along the coast, face onto the North Atlantic coast. Bilbao is on the north coast on the Bay of Biscay. Las Palmas is the major port of the Canary Islands, Mahon is the port of Menorca, and the port of Tenerife is Santa Cruz de Tenerife. The ports of Ceuta and Melilla, situated on the Moroccan coast, face onto the Mediterranean. There are some 175 minor ports. The merchant marine totals 363 ships of 1,000 GRT or over. Freight loaded: (1983 provisional) 81 million tons/80 million tonnes; unloaded: 150 million tons/136 million tonnes.

Telecommunications

There are 15.3 million telephones and a generally adequate system with modern facilities. There are 11.5 million radios and 12.5 million televisions (1986). The state RTVE is the controlling body for broadcasting, and TVE was a monopoly TV service until 1988, broadcasting two national channels. There are also Basque, Galician and Catalan channels, and new commercial TV stations such as Television Madrid. Radio is broadcast domestically on five RNE channels, as well as by Basque, Catalan and Galician government stations and several hundred private radio stations. The state REE provides external service radio broadcasting in Spanish worldwide, as well as services in English, French and Arabic.

EDUCATION AND WELFARE

Education

Schools. Primary education is free and compulsory for children between six and 14 years. There are 39,190 pre-primary schools with 1,326,917 pupils and 39,105 teachers (one per 33 pupils); 185,658 primary schools with 6,649,521 pupils and 192,217 teachers (one per 34 pupils). Secondary schooling (14–17 years) is divided into 2,638 middle schools with 1,263,841 pupils and 77,163 teachers (one per 16 pupils) and 2,199 vocational schools with 727,212 pupils and 50,480 teachers (one per 14 pupils). There are also 602 adult education centres and 4,817 schools for physically or mentally handicapped pupils.

Universities. There are 34 universities: 23 state universities; two autonomous universities; four polytechnic universities; four private universities and the Universidad Nacional de Educación a Distancia which teaches through correspondence, radio and TV.

Literacy. 97%.

Health

There are 131,000 doctors (one per 300 people) and 935 hospitals with a total of 179,192 beds (one per 219 people).

SRI LANKA

Sri Lanka Prajathanthrika Samajavadi – Jan Arajya (Sinhala)
(Democratic Socialist Republic of Sri Lanka)

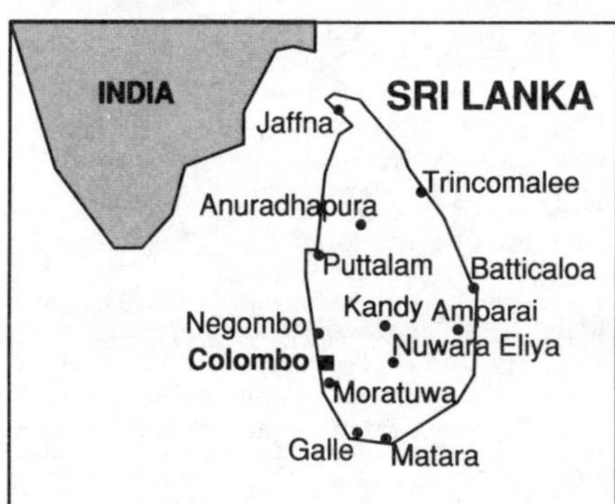

GEOGRAPHY

Lying south-east of the Indian sub-continent, from which it is divided by the Palk Strait, the island state of Sri Lanka covers a total area of 25,325 miles²/ 65,610 km², including one large island and several smaller coral islets to the north-west known collectively as Adam's Bridge. 273 miles/440 km long and 137 miles/220 km wide, the island's physiography is dominated by the rugged terrain of the central uplands, typified by high mountains, intermontane plateaux and river gorges. To the south-west of the highest point, Mount Pidurutalagala (8,281 ft/ 2,524 m), a series of undulating declines extend towards the sandy coastal lowlands. The fertile northern plains are dissected by a number of rivers and bordered to the south-east by the Mahaweli Ganga river as it drains north-eastwards out of the highlands. Deforestation has severely reduced the extent of Sri Lanka's jungle, but tropical vegetation and open woodland still cover 37% of the total surface area. 16% of the land is arable. Of the nine provinces, the western province (including the districts of Colombo, Gampaha and Kalutara) is the most densely populated.

Climate

Equatorial, with slight temperature variation and high humidity modified in the interior according to altitude. The south-western coastal and mountainous zones receive most rainfall, especially Apr.-June and Oct.-Nov. under south-western monsoonal influences. Rainfall decreases to the north-east, where the monsoon season lasts Dec.-Feb. and conditions are dry (becoming semi-arid) for the rest of the year. Colombo: Jan. 79.7°F/26.5°C. July 81.1°F/ 27.3°C. Average annual rainfall 99.5 in/2,527 mm. Trincomalee: Jan. 78.6°F/25.9°C. July 86.1°F/30.1°C. Average annual rainfall 63.6 in/1,615 mm. Nuwara Eliya: Jan. 58.5°F/14.7°C. July 60.3°F/15.7°C. Average annual rainfall 80.5 in/2,044 mm.

Cities and towns

Colombo (capital)	683,000
Dehiwala-Mount Lavinia	191,000
Jaffna	143,000
Moratuwa	138,000
Kandy	130,000
Galle	109,000
Kotte	104,000

Population

Total population is 16,881,130 of which 21.1% live in urban areas. Population density is 666.6 persons per mile²/249.2 per km². Ethnic composition 74% Sinhalese; 18% Tamil; 7% Moor; 1% Burgher, Malay and Veddha.

Birth rate 2.1%. **Death rate** 0.6%. **Rate of population increase** 1.5%. **Age distribution** under 15 = 34.1%; over 65 = 4.7%. **Life expectancy** female 73; male 68; average 70.

Religion

69% Buddhist; 15% Hindu; at least 8% Christian (including an estimated 1.4 million Roman Catholics); 8% Muslim.

Language

Sinhala is the official language (spoken by an estimated 74% of the population). Tamil and Sinhala are both national languages. English is commonly used for governmental administrative purposes and is spoken or understood by approximately 10% of Sri Lankans.

HISTORY

There are extensive traces of Stone Age settlements dating from c.10,000 BC throughout Sri Lanka. A complex, irrigation-based civilization flourished on the island from the 1st century BC to the 13th century AD, after which date the centre of power shifted towards the central Kandyan highlands. The island has long been peopled by two cultural groups, the Hindu Tamils of the north and the Buddhist Sinhalese of the south. The 6th-century Sinhalese chronicle, the Mahavamsa, traces the origin of the Sinhalese to the migration of a north Indian prince, Vijaya, to the island in about 500 BC. But it is more likely that the two communities evolved gradually in response to diverse cultural influences from the mainland.

The coastal regions came under the influence of successive European powers: Portugal from 1600 to 1658; Holland until 1795; and then Britain. With the conquest of the Kandyan kingdom in 1815 the entire island came under British rule.

Ceylon's constitutional development took place with very little conflict. The Ceylon National Congress was formed in 1919 and the Tamil Congress in 1921 but they remained moderate, elite organizations. The first elections were held to a Legislative Council, on a restricted franchise, in 1924. The colonial office introduced the principle of universal suffrage into the political system in the Donoughmore constitution of 1931. In 1947 Britain introduced a new constitution in anticipation of independence and the ensuing elections were won by the United National Party (UNP) of D.S. Senanayake, an offshoot of the Ceylon National Congress. Ceylon became an independent state on 4 Feb. 1948.

One of the first acts of the new state was to strip 800,000 Tamil plantation workers of Indian origin of their citizenship and suffrage rights. In 1951 the UNP minister of health and local government, Solomon Bandaranaike, left the party to form the Sri Lanka Freedom Party (SLFP). The UNP retained power in the 1952 election, called after the sudden death of D.S. Senanayake and the succession of his son Dudley Senanayake. A massive general strike in Aug. 1953 in protest at the imposition of economic austerity measures led to Senanayake's resignation and his replacement by his cousin, Sir John Kotelanala.

In 1954 the SLFP took up the demand that Sinhala be made the country's sole official language. By the 1956 election this had become the dominant national political issue and the SLFP's united front organization – the People's United Front (Mahajana Eksath Peramuna–MEP) – won a sweeping majority, reducing the UNP to only eight seats. The proclamation of Sinhala as the official language was met with a wave of Tamil civil disobedience.

In response supporters of the new legislation launched violent anti-Tamil pogroms. Bandaranaike tried to work out a compromise formula, but was blocked by his own supporters. In Sept. 1959 he was assassinated by a militant Buddhist monk who felt he had betrayed the Sinhalese cause.

An indecisive election in Apr. 1960 was followed by a further poll in July. In the interim, leadership of the SLFP was assumed by Bandaranaike's widow, Sirimavo, who negotiated an electoral pact with the left parties, enabling the SLFP to win a clear majority. In 1964 the SLFP brought the former Trotskyist party, the Lanka Sama Samaja Party (LSSP) into the government. The coalition fell the following year when 13 MPs from the right wing of the SLFP defected to the opposition.

The UNP won a majority in the 1965 election and formed a 'National Government' of six parties under Dudley Senanayake. Concessions on the 'reasonable use of Tamil' in administrative affairs were introduced, easing the language crisis. Over the next five years inflation and unemployment began to rise and social and economic issues dominated the 1970 election. The SLFP, in a United Front with the LSSP and the Communist Party, cut the UNP's parliamentary representation to 17.

Shortly after taking office, the United Front government ordered the mass arrest of supporters of the Sinhalese Maoist Janata Vimukthi Peramuna (JVP, People's Liberation Front). In consequence, the JVP launched a revolt in April, which was quickly crushed by the army and police. A new constitution was proclaimed by the United Front government in 1972. It left the parliamentary system intact but declared the country a Republic and changed its name from Ceylon to Sri Lanka. Much of the United Front's programme was implemented, but it did not bring the economic gains that had been promised. In 1975 the right wing of the SLFP forced the LSSP out of the United Front government and the Communist Party was similarly removed in 1977.

General elections held in July 1977 resulted in a heavy defeat for the SLFP and the victory of the UNP, led by J.R. Jayawardene. The scale of the SLFP's defeat was unprecedented, with the UNP winning 139 out of 168 seats. The LSSP and the Communist Party both failed to return a single member. The moderate Tamil United Liberation Front (TULF), which had been formed in 1976, won 17 seats from the northern and eastern provinces. The worst communal riots since the late 1950s occurred in Aug. 1977, when 125 people were killed in attacks on the Tamil minority by the Sinhalese community.

The National Assembly approved the adoption of a presidential system of government, based broadly on the French model, in Oct. 1977. The following February, Jayawardene was sworn in as president; he was replaced as prime minister by Ranasinghe Premadasa. The new presidential system was enshrined in a new Consititution promulgated in Sept. 1978. In Oct. 1982, Jayawardene won Sri Lanka's first presidential election and two months later the current term of the National assembly, due to expire in Aug. 1983, was extended for another six years under a constitutional amendment approved by parliament, the government and a national referendum.

From 1983 onwards the conflict between the Sinhalese majority of the south and the northern

Tamil minority came to dominate Sri Lankan politics. A state of emergency declared in May 1983 after serious communal unrest has been routinely extended in an attempt to contend with a mounting security threat posed by Tamil guerrillas fighting for a separate Tamil state – Eelam – in the north and east of the island.

By 1987 the militant Tamil groups, the most important of which was the Liberation Tigers of Tamil Eelam (LTTE or 'Tamil Tigers'), had fought the Sri Lankan armed forces to a standstill. India had long been concerned at the potential repercussions of the unrest in northern Sri Lanka among Tamils in southern India, and in July 1987 the Sri Lankan government was persuaded to sign an agreement which allowed Indian forces to enter the north and disarm the rebels in exchange for substantial political reforms for the Tamil areas, (including the temporary merger of the northern and eastern provinces ahead of a referendum on the merger issue). The LTTE rejected the deal and put up vigorous resistance to the Indian forces, although other groups, notably the Eelam People's Revolutionary Liberation Front (ERRLF), collaborated with the Indian army. By 1988 violent opposition to the accord emerged in the south, led by a resurgent JVP and fuelled by differences in the UNP. In Dec. 1988 Prime Minister Ranasinghe Premadasa defeated two opponents to become Sri Lanka's new President. In general elections in Feb. 1989 the ruling UNP won a 25-seat majority; a new Cabinet was subsequently sworn in headed by D.B. Wijetunge.

A protracted dispute between Sri Lanka and India over a formula for the withdrawal of the Indian troops policing the island's northern and eastern provinces was resolved in Sept. 1989 with the establishment of a withdrawal deadline of 31 Dec. 1989. The change of government in India in Dec. 1989 rendered the deadline infeasible and the last Indian troops were not withdrawn until March 1990. Meanwhile, the JVP's southern-based insurgency, which had become increasingly violent during 1989, was dealt a devastating blow by the government in November when almost all JVP leaders were either killed or arrested.

CONSTITUTION AND GOVERNMENT

Executive and legislature

The executive president is directly elected for a six-year term (last election 19 Dec. 1988) and has powers to appoint or dismiss members of the cabinet, including the prime minister, and to dissolve parliament. The unicameral parliament is normally elected for a six-year term; the first general elections, for 225 seats under a new system of proportional representation, were held on 15 Feb. 1989.

Present government

President; Minister of Defence; Buddha Sasana; Policy Planning and Implementation Ranasinghe Premadasa
Prime Minister, Minister of Finance D.B. Wijetunge
Other Principal Members of the Cabinet M. Vincent Perrera (Justice; Parliamentary Affairs); U.B. Wijekoon (Home Affairs; Public Administration; Provincial Councils); Ranjan Wijeratne (Foreign Affairs).

Justice

The system of law is a complex amalgam of Roman-dutch law, English law (in particular in the commercial sphere), Muslim law, and the indigenous legal systems, namely Kandyan law and the Tesawalamai (applied to Tamils). The highest court is the Supreme Court, with a role in maintaining the constitution; there is a Court of Appeal, a High Court (for major crimes), and District Courts with jurisdiction in civil matters. At lower levels, minor matters are dealt with by Magistrates' Courts and Primary Courts. The death penalty is nominally in force. No judicial executions between 1985 and mid-1988.

National symbols

Flag. A yellow-edged, dark red field with a yellow lion holding a sword. In the hoist there are vertical stripes of green and orange, with a yellow border around them.
Festivals. 4 Feb. (Independence Commemoration Day); 1 May (May Day).
Vehicle registration plate. CL.

INTERNATIONAL RELATIONS

Affiliations

NAM; Commonwealth; SAARC.

Defence

Total Armed Forces: some 48,000 inclusive active Reservists. Active: 22,000. Terms of service: voluntary. Reserves: some 25,000; obligation: seven years' post-Regular service.
Army: 40,000, inclusive recalled Reservists.
Navy: 5,000; 36 patrol and coastal combatants.
Air Force: 3,700 inclusive active Reservists; six combat aircraft (SF-260PT); 15 armed helicopters.
Para-military (Police Force): 21,000 (increase to 28,000 planned).

ECONOMY

Currency

The unit is the rupee, divided into 100 cents.

National finance

Budget. The 1987 budget, in US$, was for expenditure of 2,200 million and revenue of 1,500 million. Main items of expenditure are housing and welfare 11.7%; defence 9.6%; education 7.8%.
Balance of payments. The balance of payments, in US$ (current account, 1987) was a deficit of 572 million.
Inflation. 7.7%.

Gross Domestic Product

Estimated total GDP US$6,040 million, per capita US$370 (overall size of economy ranking 77 in the world).
Economically active population. The total number of persons active in the economy was 6,600,000; unemployed: 19%.

Sector	% of workforce	% of GDP
industry	13	27
agriculture	46	27
services*	41	46

* services figure includes elements unassigned to other categories.

Energy and mineral resources

Minerals. Precious and semi-precious stones include sapphire; ruby; chrysoberyl; beryl; topaz; spinel; garnet; ziran; tourmaline. Also graphite, production: (1986) 8,497 tons/7,708 tonnes; mineral sands (including ilmenite and rutile); phosphates. Salt is also produced, by solar evaporation of sea water, production: (1986) 114,947 tons/104,279 tonnes.

Electricity. Capacity: 1.2 million kW; production: 4,200 million kWh; 250 kWh per capita (1988).

Bioresources

Agriculture. Approximately 4.9 million acres/2 million ha are under cultivation and 45% of the population are engaged in agriculture. Main crops are paddy rice; coconuts; tea; rubber; sugar cane.

Crop production: (1986 in tons/tonnes) paddy rice 2.9 million/2.6 million; rubber 151,015/137,000; tea 232,585/211,000; coconuts 3,350/3,039; nuts.

Livestock numbers: (1987) cattle 1.8 million; buffaloes 1 million; pigs 97,000; goats and sheep 530,000; poultry 9 million.

Forestry. 37% of the land area is forest and woodland.

Fisheries. Production: (1986) 205,010 million tons/ 185,984 million tonnes.

Industry and commerce

Industry. Main industries are processing of rubber; tea; coconuts; cement; petroleum refining; textiles; tobacco; clothing.

Commerce. Exports (1987) US$1,400 million or 23% of GDP, including tea; textiles and garments; petroleum products; coconuts; rubber; agricultural products; gems and jewellery; marine products. Imports: US$2,060 million, including petroleum; machinery and equipment; textiles and textile materials; wheat; transportation equipment; electrical machinery; sugar; rice. Countries exported to were US 22%; Egypt; Iraq; UK; West Germany; Singapore; Japan. Imports came from Japan; Saudi Arabia; US; India; Singapore; West Germany; UK; Iran.

Trade with UK. Sri Lanka imported UK goods worth £92,528,000; exports to UK totalled £56,661,000.

Tourism. (1986) 230,000 visitors.

COMMUNICATIONS

Railways

There are 1,207 miles/1,944 km of railways.

Roads

There are 94,655 miles/152,423 km of roads.

Aviation

Air Lanka provides domestic and international services (main airports are at Batticaloa, Colombo, Gal Oya, Jaffna and Trincomalee). Passengers: (1987) 588,000.

Shipping

The 267 miles/430 km of inland waterways are only navigable by shallow-draught vessels. The major ports are Colombo on the west coast on the Gulf of Mannar and Trincomalee on the east coast on the Bay of Bengal. The merchant marine consists of 51 ships of 1,000 GRT or over. Freight loaded: (1987 provisional) 3.6 million tons/3.3 million tonnes; unloaded: 6 million tons/5.4 million tonnes.

Telecommunications

There are 109,900 telephones (1982) and a good international service. There are 2.8 million radios and 460,000 televisions (1986). All broadcasting is controlled by the Sri Lanka Broadcasting Corporation, with home service programmes in English, Sinhalese and Tamil, as well as external services in these and seven other languages. Trans World Radio is a religious station in Colombo. There are six hours' of television programmes broadcast each day.

EDUCATION AND WELFARE

Education

Schools. Education is free from kindergarten age to university. There are 10,099 schools of which 9,656 are government-run. The government schools have 3.7 million pupils and 142,630 teachers (one per 25 pupils).

Universities. There are eight universities including one Open University at Ruhuna.

Literacy. 87%.

Health

(1986) 497 hospitals with 46,005 beds (one per 366 people); 341 dispensaries. There are 2,222 doctors (one per 7,597 people).

SUDAN

Jamhuryat es-Sudan, Ad-Dimuqratiyah (Republic of the Sudan)

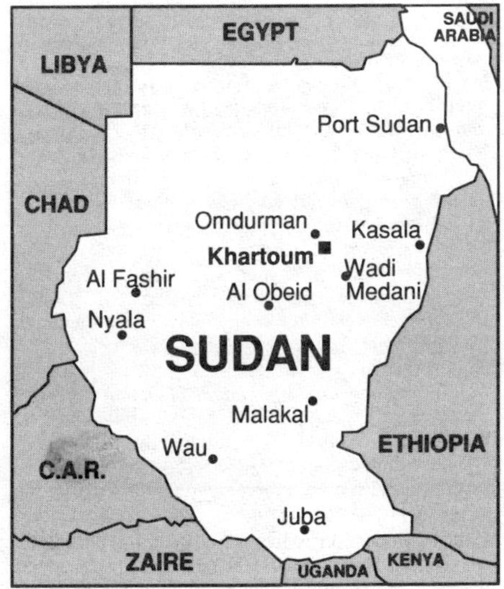

GEOGRAPHY

Sudan, in north-eastern Africa, is the largest country on the continent, occupying 967,243 miles^2/ 2,505,810 km^2 divided into seven regions. The bulk of the population is concentrated along the banks of the River Nile and in the fertile central provinces of El Gezira, Khartoum and al-Abyad (White Nile). The northern part of the country consists of the barren, rocky Saharan desert plain stretching westwards to an area of sand-dunes and rising further south to 10,075 ft/3,071 m elevation at Jebel Marra in the Darfur massif. Other highland areas include the Red Sea Coastal region (average elevation 6,562 ft/ 2,000 m) and the Imatong mountains in the extreme south, bordering Kenya and Uganda, and climbing to a maximum elevation of 10,456 ft/3,187 m at Mount Kinyeti. The River Nile traverses Sudan south-north; the capital city of Khartoum lies at the confluence of the White and Blue Niles. 5% of the land is arable and 20% is wooded, from the soils and swamplands of the central regions to the tropical vegetation of the southern highlands.

Climate

Tropical continental with maritime influences on the Red Sea Coast. Desert conditions prevail in the north with rainfall of 6.3 in/160 mm or less. Rainfall increases north-south, most rain falling Apr.-Oct. Temperatures in the north seldom fall below 75.2°F/ 24°C during the two hottest months of July and August and brief sandstorms (haboobs) are a common occurrence. Khartoum: Jan. 73.9°F/23.3°C. July 89.1°F/31.7°C. Average annual rainfall 6.2 in/157 mm. Juba: Jan. 82.9°F/28.3°C. July 78.1°F/25.6°C. Average annual rainfall 38.1 in/968 mm. Port Sudan: Jan. 73.9°F/23.3°C. July 93.9°F/34.4°C. Average annual rainfall 3.7 in/94 mm. Wadi Halfa: Jan. 60.1°F/15.6°C. July 90°F/32.2°C. Average annual rainfall 0.1 in/ 2.5 mm.

Cities and towns

Omdurman	526,287
Khartoum (capital)	476,218
Khartoum North	341,146
Port Sudan	206,727
Wadi Medani	141,065
Al-Obeid	140,024
Atbara	73,009

Population

Total population is 24,476,290 of which 30.6% live in urban areas. Population density is 25.3 persons per mile^2/10.2 per km^2. Ethnic divisions: 52% Black; 39% Arab; 6% Beja; 2% foreign nationals. Of the 975,000 refugees in Sudan in 1987, 337,544 were from Ethiopia. The Arab and Nubian peoples predominate in the north, while the Nilotic and Sudanic peoples inhabit the south.

Birth rate 4.4%. **Death rate** 1.4%. **Rate of population increase** (1980–87) 2.7%. **Age distribution** under 15 = 45%; over 65 = 2.8%. **Life expectancy** female 51; male 49; average 50.

Religion

The twelve northern provinces are populated almost exclusively by Sunni Muslims. 70% of the total population are Muslim, and 5% Christian (largely in the south). Approximately 20% of the population follow traditional animist beliefs.

Language

Arabic is the official language, spoken by just over 50% of the population. Northern languages (including Darfurian) account for 18% of the population. A further 23% speak Nilotic (Dinka and Nver) or Nilo-Hamitic languages, while the remaining 8% speak a variety of Sudanic dialects.

HISTORY

Sudan's history has always been closely linked with that of Egypt. The first recorded inhabitants were Hamites, ancestors of the present-day Azande, Shilluk and Dinka tribes. In AD 641, Muslim Arabs took over from the Byzantines, and ruled for five centuries. In 1276, Nubia (present-day northern Sudan) was conquered by Egypt's Bahri Mameluk. By the 17th century, the caravan trade across the Sahara had created wealth for the Fung and Fur sultanates of central and western Sudan. Arab nomads had migrated to Darfur and intermarried, promoting the spread of the Arabic language.

The Viceroy of Egypt, Mohammed Ali, conquered the north (1821) and opened trade routes across the Sudd swamps to the south. The southern population was decimated by the slave trade.

Britain, seeking a foothold in Central Africa, financed Egyptian expeditions to the south. Gen. Gordon, in the service of Khedive Ismail of Egypt, administered the Sudan (1874–80) and energetically set about tackling the slave trade, as Western influences and Western missionary endeavours began to make their presence increasingly felt. This contributed to the religious dimension of the Mahdist uprising (1881), a holy war in defence of Islam, based around the Ansar religious brotherhood and led by Muhammad Ahmed, the Mahdi (saviour), but fuelled also by resentment at the burden of rule from Egypt and the heavy taxation which this entailed. Britain, seeking to promote a policy which would separate Sudan from Egypt and perhaps build a link with British East Africa, brought Gordon back from South Africa and despatched him with a force (1884) to secure the evacuation of isolated Egyptian garrisons, but Gordon and his troops became trapped in Khartoum, besieged by the Mahdists for ten months and ultimately massacred there two days before a relief column arrived (Jan. 1885).

In 1898, Anglo-Egyptian troops under Kitchener finally defeated the Mahdists at Omdurman, establishing British control of the Upper Nile. Egypt and Britain signed a Condominium Agreement, allowing British domination of Sudan and excluding the possibility of a rival French claim.

By the 1920s, an economy based on gum arabic and cotton exports had been created. Faced with the rise of nationalism in the early 1920s, Britain avoided nationwide rebellion by isolating the south. When the Anglo-Egyptian Treaty of 1936 ratified Britain's occupation, the nationalist movement gained added impetus with the formation of the Ashiqpa party, the forerunner of the National Union Party (NUP, founded 1943) and the Umma (People's) Party (founded 1945).

After World War II, Sudan remained dependent on foreign capital for the development of vast irrigation schemes along the Nile. The independence movement became more organized, and Britain agreed to self-determination for Sudan. Meanwhile discontent was rising in the mainly Christian and animist south, which was economically undeveloped and dominated by the Muslim north. This culminated in 1955 in the Equatoria Corps mutiny, led by anti-Muslim officers, who in 1963 formed the nucleus of the Anya-nya ('snake poison') secessionist movement. When the south's demands for secession were rejected, civil war ensued. At independence on 1 Jan. 1956, the country was in chaos.

The new democratic government had to face internal conflicts and economic ruin, and on 17 Nov. 1958, Gen. Ibrahim Abboud's junta took control. The military regime lasted until 1964, but foundered over its inability to end the expensive southern war, which had led to popular revolt and a general strike.

In the 1965 elections, an Umma-NUP coalition was formed, with Sayyid Sadiq el-Mahdi, the Umma leader, coming to power on 25 July 1966. From 1966–69, the economic situation worsened as cotton prices fell and foreign aid was curtailed after the Arab–Israeli War. The south was in complete turmoil, and military takeover was inevitable. On 25 May 1969, Col Jaafar el Nemery seized power in a bloodless coup. El-Mahdi was sent into exile, but returned in 1977. The Communist Party which had brought Nemery to power was transformed into the Sudan Socialist Union (SSU), the sole legal party.

Unsuccessful coup attempts were made in 1971 and 1976. In 1972, the debilitating civil war was brought to a temporary end by the Addis Ababa agreement, which granted limited regional autonomy.

In Aug. 1979 there were demonstrations against rising prices and chronic food shortages. In the ensuing political crisis, Nemery cracked down heavily on the opposition. He was re-elected for a third six-year term in Apr. 1983, and in September he introduced Islamic (Sharia) Law. Meanwhile, a southern rebellion, led by the Sudan People's Liberation Army (SPLA) of Col John Garang, re-emerged.

Nemery was overthrown on 16 Apr. 1985 by Gen. Abdul Rahman Swaredahab, after Khartoum had been immobilized by food riots and a general strike. Elections for a return to civilian rule were held in Apr. 1986, but were cancelled in the rebel-controlled south. On 6 May, Sadiq el-Mahdi returned as prime minister at the head of the coalition between Umma and the Democratic Unionist Party (DUP – formerly NUP) to face challenges of a ruined economy and continuing civil war. Fighting in the south escalated in 1986–87, and several attempts at peace failed. On 26 July 1987, a state of emergency was declared in an effort to salvage the economy and curb social unrest. The fragile coalition lurched from crisis to crisis, with Islamic fundamentalists continuing to play a major role. In Dec. 1988, following reports of an attempted coup, a new state of emergency was declared as demonstrations and strikes were held in protest at food price increases. El Mahdi's failure to deal with the country's problems led to an army takeover on 30 June 1989, in a coup led by Brig. Omar Hassan Ahmad al-Bashir. Hopes for an early peace settlement with the southerners were dashed after the breakdown of negotiations in July, and a further round of talks, mediated by former US president, Jimmy Carter, also foundered over the regime's determination to apply Islamic Sharia law with its full rigours and punishments. There was speculation that the Khartoum government, facing the intractable civil war, was seeking to provoke the SPLA to back secession by the non-Moslem south.

CONSTITUTION AND GOVERNMENT

Executive and legislature

Since the June 1989 coup, power has been held by a 15-member Revolutionary Command Council for National Salvation, whose chairman is both head of state and prime minister.

Present government

Chairman of the Revolutionary Command Council; Prime Minister; Minister of Defence Lt.-Gen. Omar Hassan Ahmad al-Bashir

Principal Ministers Brig.-Gen Zubir Mohammed Saleh (Deputy Prime Minister); Lt.-Col. Tayib Ibrahim Mohammed Khayr (Minister of Presidential Affairs); Ali Sahlul (Foreign Affairs); Brig.-Gen. Faisal Ali Abu Salih (Interior); Hassan Ismail al-Billi (Justice, Attorney-General); Sayed Ali Zaki (Finance and National Economic Planning).

Justice

The system of law was based substantially on the English common law, with the judiciary functioning as a separate and independent department of state, responsible to the President. In the 1980s successive regimes, beginning with that of Nemery, have grappled with pressures to apply the Islamic Sharia law in a country where the non-Muslim south has been in a state of open rebellion. The introduction of Islamic justice in personal matters (inheritance, marriage, divorce, family relationship and charitable trusts) for the Muslim population has not satisfied the demand for a fully Islamic state as increasingly espoused by the Bashir regime. The death penalty is in force. There were nine executions between 1985 and mid-1988. Offences were murder, subversion and apostasy.

National symbols

Flag. Three horizontal stripes of red, white and black. In the hoist there is a green isosceles triangle reaching to one-third of the flag's length.

Festivals. 1 Jan. (Independence Day); 3 Mar. (Unity Day); 6 Apr. (Uprising Day, anniversary of 1985 coup); 1 July (Decentralization Day).

Vehicle registration plate. SUD.

INTERNATIONAL RELATIONS

Affiliations

NAM; OAU; ICO; ACP; Arab League.

Defence

Total Armed Forces: 57,000. Terms of service: voluntary; (conscription is legislated, but not implemented).

Army: 54,000; 155 main battle tanks (T-54/-55, M-60A3); 60 light tanks (Ch Type-62).

Navy: 700; six patrol craft.

Air Force: 3,000; 52 combat aircraft (MiG-21/-23, F-5E, J-5, J-6).

Opposition: Sudanese People's Liberation Army (SPLA): some 20,000.

ECONOMY

Currency

The unit is the Sudanese pound, divided into 100 piasters.

National finance

Budget. The 1988 FY budget, in US$, was for expenditure of 1,500 million and revenue of 867 million.

Balance of payments. The balance of payments, in US$ (current account, 1987) was a deficit of 702 million.

Inflation. 55%.

Gross Domestic Product

Estimated total GDP US$8,210 million, per capita US$340 (overall size of economy ranking 71 in the world).

Economically active population. The total number of persons active in the economy was 6,500,000.

Sector	% of workforce	% of GDP
industry	10	15
agriculture	80	37
services*	10	48

* services figure includes elements unassigned to other categories.

Energy and mineral resources

Oil and gas. 15,000 bbls per day of good quality oil are produced by two oil wells in the south-west, production (1982) 165,345 tons/150,000 tonnes.

Minerals. Gold; graphite; iron ore; copper; chromium ore; zinc; tungsten; mica; silver; limestone; dolomite; pumice.

Electricity. Capacity: 606,000 kW; production: 1,259 million kWh; 50 kWh per capita (1988).

Bioresources

Agriculture. Sudan is a predominantly agricultural country and cotton is the most important cash crop. One of the largest sugar-processing plants in the world, with a capacity of 330,000 tonnes per year, is located at Kenana. Main crops are cotton; sorghum; sugar cane; millet; wheat; sesame; peanuts; beans; barley; gum arabic.

Crop production: (1986 in 1,000 tons/tonnes) sorghum 3,974/3,605; sugar cane 5,732/5,200; groundnuts 500/454; seed cotton 485/440; millet 600/544; wheat 219/199; sesame 332/301; cotton seed 303/275.

Livestock numbers: (1987) cattle 20.4 million; sheep 19 million; goats 14 million; poultry 32 million.

Forestry. 20% of the land area is forest and woodland, and gum arabic is the only major forest product. Production: (1986) 742 million ft^3/21 million m^3.

Industry and commerce

Industry. Main industries are cotton ginning; textiles; cement; edible oils; sugar; soap distilling; shoes; petroleum refining.

Commerce. Exports: (1988) US$502 million or 5% of GNP, including cotton 44%; sesame; gum arabic; peanuts. Imports were US$1,300 million, including petroleum products; manufactured goods; machinery and equipment; medicines and chemicals.

Trade with UK. In 1988 Sudan imported UK goods worth £86,480,000; exports to UK totalled £9,910,000.

Tourism. (1986) 42,000 visitors.

COMMUNICATIONS

Railways

There are 3,416 miles/5,500 km of railways.

Roads

There are some 33,031 miles/53,190 km of roads.

Aviation

Sudan Airways Co. Ltd provides domestic and international services (main airport is at Khartoum). Passengers: (1984) 485,000.

Shipping

There are 3,298 miles/5,310 km of navigable inland waterways. Port Sudan and nearby Suakin on the Red Sea are the major ports. There are ten ships of 1,000 GRT or over in the merchant marine. Freight loaded: (1985) 730,825 tons/663,000 tonnes; unloaded: 2.5 million tons/2.3 million tonnes.

Telecommunications

There are 68,800 telephones and a large, well-equipped system by African standards but scarcely adequate and poorly maintained. There are 5.4 million radios and 1.1 million televisions (1985). Government corporations provide radio services in six languages and 35 hours of TV programmes per week.

EDUCATION AND WELFARE

Education

Schools. (1985) 6,707 primary schools with 1.7 million pupils; 2,167 secondary schools with 490,583 pupils.

Universities. There are four universities: Khartoum University (9,000 students); a branch of Cairo University at Khartoum (5,000 students); the Islamic University of Omdurman (1,500 students); Juba University (500 students).

Literacy. 31%.

Health

In 1981 there were 158 hospitals with 17,205 beds (one per 1,422 people); 887 dispensaries; 1,619 dressing stations; 220 health centres. There were 2,122 doctors (one per 11,534 people).

SURINAME

Republiek Suriname (Dutch)

(Republic of Suriname – formerly Dutch Guiana)

GEOGRAPHY

Situated on the north-central coast of South America, Suriname contains an area of 63,022 miles²/163,270 km², divided into nine districts of which the most densely populated is Paramaribo, the nation's capital. Suriname exhibits a diverse physiographic profile from the swampy coastal lowlands in the north, through undulating grassland to the forest-clad highland interior, deeply dissected by mountain streams. Suriname's highest peak, Juliana Top (4,035 ft/1,230 m) rises in the southern central region, part of the Wilhelmina Gebergte massif projecting north from the Brazilian border. The seven principal rivers traversing the country south-north are the Marowijne (east), Correntyne (west), Suriname, Commewijne, Koppename, Saramacca and Nickerie. Only a few minor coastal and fluvial areas are considered suitable for agricultural activity. 97% of the territory is forested.

Climate

Equatorial, uniformly high temperatures all year round and abundant rainfall. Most rainfall occurs Apr.-Aug. and Nov.-Feb. There is no clearly defined dry season. Paramaribo: Jan. 80.1°F/26.7°C. July 81°F/27.2°C. Average annual rainfall 87.6 in/2,225 mm.

Cities and towns

Paramaribo (capital)	67,718

Population

Total population is 401,497 of which 45.2% live in urban areas. Population density is 6.4 persons per mile²/2.5 per km². Ethnic composition: 37% Hindustani (East Indian); 31% Creole (Black and mixed); 15.3% Javanese; 10.3% Bush Black; 2.6% Amerindian; 1.7% Chinese; 1% European.

Birth rate 2.7%. **Death rate** 0.6%. **Rate of population increase** (1980–87) 1.6%. **Age distribution** under 15 = 37.2%; over 65 = 4.3%. **Life expectancy** female 71; male 66; average 69.

Religion

27.4% Hindu; 19.6% Muslim; 22.8% Roman Catholic; 25.2% Protestant (largely Moravian, although Reformed Church, Lutheran, Jehovah's Witnesses and Seventh Day Adventist denominations are also represented); 5% indigenous customs and beliefs.

Language

Dutch is the official language. English is widely understood. A broad spectrum of languages denotes the heterogeneous ethnic mix: Hindustani, Javanese, Chinese and Spanish are all spoken, along with the Creole lingua franca Sranan Tongo (also known as Taki-Taki or Surinamese).

HISTORY

Suriname's earliest inhabitants were Amerindian peoples; European settlers did not arrive until the 17th century, when several countries sought to establish trading posts and settlements. In 1677 the colony was ceded by England to the Dutch. It remained a Dutch possession, apart from two brief periods of British rule. African slaves were imported as labour for large plantations producing sugar, coffee and cotton. The abolition of slavery in 1863 caused a labour shortage in the plantations, alleviated by the immigration of Portuguese and Chinese labourers, and after 1873 by indentured labourers from India, followed by Javanese from the Dutch East Indies after 1894. Many of these indentured labourers settled in the country, giving it a diverse racial character.

Universal suffrage was granted in 1948, internal self-government in 1950 and in 1954 Suriname became an equal partner in the 'Tripartite Kingdom' of the Netherlands. Legislative elections in 1949 were won by the mainly creole (Black) Nationale Partij Suriname (NPS). Other political parties tended to be formed on racial lines also, most notably the Verenigde Hindostaanse Partij (VHP), supported by the Hindustani (or Indian-descended) population. Between 1958 and 1969 Suriname was governed by an alliance between the NPS and the VHP and its two leaders, Johan Pengel and Jaggernath Lachmon, who used their personal friendship to overcome shifting majorities and coalitions in the country's legislature. At elections in 1969 the VHP won most seats, but allowed Jules Sedney of the creole Progressieve Nationale Partij (PNP) to become prime minister. Elections in 1973 were won by an alliance of four parties, led by the NPS and its new leader, Henck Arron, campaigning for full independence. The country duly achieved independence on 25 Nov. 1975. Elections in 1977 confirmed the ruling coalition in power, although without the support of the left-wing Partij Nationalische Republiek (PNR).

On 25 Feb. 1980 a group of soldiers staged a coup with support from the PNR, and Dr Henk Chin A Sen was appointed prime minister. In August the army chief-of-staff, Sgt.-Maj. (later Lt.-Col) Desi Bouterse, led another coup dismissing the president, dissolving the legislature and declaring a state of emergency. The struggle between competing political and military groups led to the dismissal of Chin A Sen in Feb. 1982 and a failed counter-coup. A civilian cabinet was appointed, although the army remained in effective control. In December, faced by strikes and demonstrations, the armed forces killed 15 leading citizens during the unrest. In response, the Netherlands suspended its large aid programme. In Feb. 1983 a new civilian cabinet was appointed, but strikes and opposition to Bouterse's rule continued. In Jan. 1984 a new cabinet was appointed after consultations with the trade unions and private business sector to prepare for a transition to constitutional rule. A nominated National Assembly was established in Jan. 1985, and in November the ban on traditional political parties was lifted, with Arron, Lachmon and Willy Soemita of the Indonesian party (KPTI) joining the ruling military-dominated council. A new constitution was approved by referendum in Sept. 1987.

In 1986 anti-government guerrillas, led by Ronny Brunswijk, began attacking miliary outposts and disrupting the country's bauxite production. The cabinet resigned in Mar. 1987 over the conduct of the war, and was replaced by a government led by Jules Wijdensbosch, a Bouterse supporter. In November elections to a new National Assembly were held. The three main traditional parties, the NPS, VHP, and KPTI joined together to form an electoral alliance known as the Front for Democracy and Development (FDD), and won 40 of the 51 seats in the Assembly. The party led by Wijdensbosch gained only three seats. In Jan. 1988 Ramsewak Shankar was elected president with Henck Arron as vice-president and prime minister. Bouterse remained as leader of the military council formed to oversee the transition to democracy.

CONSTITUTION AND GOVERNMENT

Executive and legislature

Under the 1987 constitution ultimate authority rests in theory with a 51-member national assembly, elected for a five-year term on 25 Nov. 1987. The executive president is elected by the national assembly (most recently on 12 Jan. 1988) as head of state, head of government, head of the armed forces, chair of the council of state and chair of the security council (which is charged with assuming all government functions in the event of 'war, state of siege or exceptional circumstances to be determined by law'). The army remains the 'vanguard of the people'.

Present government

President Ramsewak Shankar

Vice-President, Prime Minister Henck Arron

Members of the Council of State Lt.-Col Désiré 'Desi' Bouterse; Cdr. Ivan Granoogst (Army Chief-of-Staff); Capt. Chas Mijnals; Maj. Badressein Sital; Lt. Lieuw Yen Tai.

Principal Members of the Council of Ministers A. Sedoc (Foreign Affairs); Subhes Chandra Mungra (Finance and Planning); Evelyn Alexander-Vanenburg (Home Affairs, District Administration and People's Mobilization); J. Adjodhia (Justice and Police); Maj. A. Sheikkariem (Army).

Justice

There is a court of justice, whose members are nominated by the president, and there are three cantonal courts. The death penalty is in force. There were no executions between 1985 and mid-1988.

National symbols

Flag. Five horizontal stripes of green, white, red, white and green. In the middle of the red stripe there is a yellow five-pointed star with a diameter.

Festivals. 25 Feb. (Revolution Day); 1 May (Labour Day); 1 July (National Union Day); 25 Nov. (Independence Day).

Vehicle registration plate. SME.

INTERNATIONAL RELATIONS

Affiliations

NAM; ACP; OAS.

Defence

Total Armed Forces: 3,000. Terms of service: voluntary.
Army: 2,700.
Navy: 200; six inshore patrol craft.
Air Force: about 100.
Para-military (National Militia): 900.
Opposition: Surinamese Liberation Army or 'Jungle Commando': 200–300.

ECONOMY

Currency

The unit is the guilder, divided into 100 cents.

National finance

Budget. The 1988 budget, in US$, was for expenditure of 650 million and revenue of 346 million.

Inflation. 53.4%.

Gross Domestic Product

Estimated total GDP US$1,190 million, per capita US$2,800 (overall size of economy ranking 136 in the world).

Economically active population. The total number of persons active in the economy was 104,000; unemployed: 32%.

Energy and mineral resources

Minerals. Bauxite is the most important mineral, production: (1985) 4,120,397 tons/3,738,000 tonnes. Most is exported but some is processed locally into alumina and aluminium. There are also modest amounts of nickel; copper; platinum; gold.

Electricity. Capacity: 439,000 kW; production: 1,922 million kWh; 4,870 kWh per capita (1988).

Bioresources

Agriculture. Suriname has very little arable land (about 216,213 acres/87,500 ha) and this is restricted to the alluvial coastal zone. Main crops are rice; bananas; palm-oil.

Crop production: (1986 in 1,000 tons/tonnes) sugar cane 132/120; rice 331/300; oranges 11/10; grapefruit 1.1/1; coconuts 7.7/7; palm-oil 7.9/7.2; cassava 3.3/3.

Livestock numbers: (1987) cattle 66,000; sheep 3,000; goats 5,000; pigs 23,000; poultry 6 million.

Forestry. 97% of the land area is forest and woodland and Suriname has extensive timber resources. Production: (1983) 7,212,920 ft^3/204,251 m^3 of logs; 640,384 ft^3/18,134 m^3 of plywood; 111,416 ft^3/3,155 m^3 of particle board.

Fisheries. Catch: (1980 in tons/tonnes) Fish 2,315/2,100; shrimp 3,417/3,100.

Industry and commerce

Industry. Main industries are bauxite mining; alumina and aluminium production; lumber; food processing; fishing. There is a shortage of skilled personnel.

Commerce. Exports: (1987) US$338.8 million or 28% of GDP, including alumina; bauxite; aluminium; rice; wood and wood products; shrimp and fish; bananas. Imports: US$274.3 million, including capital equipment; petroleum; foodstuffs; cotton; consumer goods. Countries exported to were Netherlands 25%; Norway 22%; US 20%; Japan 13%; Brazil 7%; UK 4%. Imports came from US 31%; Netherlands 20%; Trinidad and Tobago 10%; Brazil 9%; UK 2%.

Trade with UK. Suriname imported UK goods worth £6,107,000; exports to UK totalled £11,256,000.

COMMUNICATIONS

Railways
There are 97.5 miles/157 km of railways.

Roads
There are 5,520 miles/8,889 km of roads.

Aviation
Surinaams Luchtvaart Maatschappij NV (SLM) and Gonini Air Service Ltd provide domestic and international services (main airport is Zanderij International Airport, 28 miles/45 km from Paramaribo). Passengers: (1987) 1.3 million.

Shipping
The 745 miles/1,200 km of inland waterways are the most important means of travel. Ocean-going vessels can navigate many of the principal waterways. The major port is Paramaribo, on the North Atlantic Ocean. Moengo, a smaller port, is situated inland. The merchant marine consists of three merchant ships of 1,000 GRT or over. Freight loaded: (1987) 2 million tons/1.8 million tonnes; unloaded: 1.9 million tons/1.7 million tonnes.

Telecommunications
There are 27,500 telephones, good international facilities and a domestic radio relay system. There are 245,000 radios and 35,000 televisions (1987). The government owns a commercial and a non-commercial TV station, and also operates one commercial radio station (with four competing companies) and Radio Suriname International, broadcasting news and other material including international services in three languages.

EDUCATION AND WELFARE

Education
Schools. (1985) 321 primary schools with 89,624 pupils and 3,880 teachers (one per 23 pupils); 63 secondary schools with 22,814 pupils and 839 teachers (one per 27 pupils).
Universities. There is one university with 2,353 students and 155 teachers (one per 15 students).
Literacy. 65%.

Health
(1985) 1,964 hospital beds (one per 204 people); 219 doctors (one per 1,833 people).

SWAZILAND
Umbuso Weswatini (Siswati)
(Kingdom of Swaziland)

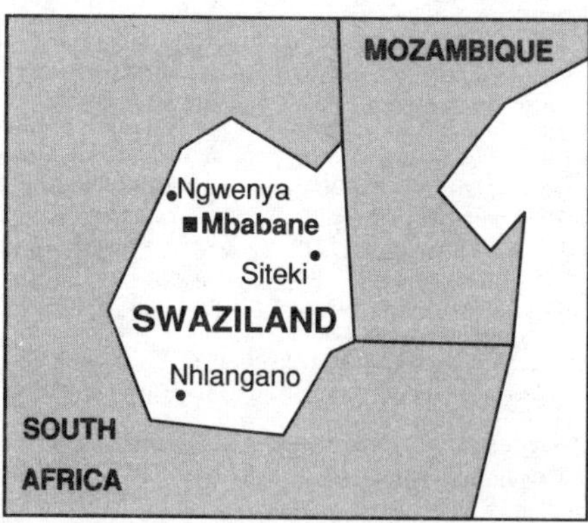

GEOGRAPHY
The landlocked kingdom of Swaziland in southern Africa covers a total area of 6,702 miles²/17,363 km² divided into the districts of Shiselweni, Lubombo, Manzini and Hhohho. Four topographical regions are identifiable from west to east. In the western part of the country, the Highveld (average elevation 3,609–4,593 ft/1,100–1,400 m) rises to 6,102 ft/1,860 m at Emblembe peak, the highest point in Swaziland. The Highveld contains an estimated 30% of the total surface area and is backed to the east by the more populous Middleveld, sloping eastwards again to the bush-covered Lowveld (average elevation 492–984 ft/150–300 m). Finally, the Lubombo escarpment ascends to plateau elevations of between 1,312–2,707 ft/400–825 m, covering 9% of the territory. The four principal rivers (Komati, Usutu, Mbuluzi and Ngwavuma) all flow west-east. 8% of the land is arable and 6% is forested. Most of the country's agricultural activity is focused on the mixed farming areas of the Middleveld.

Climate
Temperate. The rainy season lasts Nov.-Mar. with high temperatures and thunderstorms. A cooler, drier season prevails May-Sept. Rainfall totals vary from 19.7 in/500 mm in the east to 88.6 in/2,250 mm in the west. Mbabane: Jan 68°F/20°C. July 54°F/12.2°C. Average annual rainfall 55.2 in/1,402 mm.

Cities and towns

Mbabane (capital)	38,636
Manzini	13,893

Population
Total population is 756,195 of which 26.3% live in urban areas. Population density is 112.8 persons per mile²/41.2 per km². Ethnic composition: 97% African; 3% European.
Birth rate 4.6%. **Death rate** 1.5%. **Rate of population increase** (1980–87) 2.8%. **Age distribution** under 15 = 46.8%; over 65 = 3.0%. **Life expectancy** female 54; male 47; average 51.

Religion

60% of the population are Christian (including an estimated 40,000 Roman Catholics and Anglican, Mennonite, Methodist and Evangelical Lutheran denominations). 40% follow traditional animist customs and beliefs.

Language

English and Siswati (Swazi) are the official languages. Ethnolinguistically, Swaziland divides into 70 groups, 90% of whom are Swazi-speaking. Swazi is part of the Benue-Congo sub-family of Niger-Congo languages.

HISTORY

Bantu-speaking peoples migrated southwards along the Mozambican coast in the 16th century. A group of Swazi settled in the region between the Pangola and the Great Usutu rivers but, under pressure from the Zulus, then moved north to the Little Usutu river. In the mid-19th century the Swazi under King Mswati (1839–68) sought British support against Zulu expansion, and also faced pressure from the Transvaal Boers. White settlers obtained concessions over much Swaziland in the 1880s. In 1888 the Swazi consented to the establishment of a provisional government of British, South African and Swazi representatives. Britain assumed sovereignty in 1894, and in 1903 the governor of Transvaal was empowered to administer Swaziland. In 1906 these powers were transferred to a high commissioner for Basutoland, Bechuanaland and Swaziland. Limited self-government was granted in 1963; the British resisted South African pressure for incorporation of the High Commission Territories within South Africa, and the Imbokodvo (Grindstone) National Movement formed by King Sobhuza II won all 24 seats in the House of Assembly in 1967 as a kingdom was proclaimed under British protection. Full independence was achieved on 6 Sept. 1968.

Swaziland maintained close links with South Africa in the 1970s and joined the South African Customs Union. The Swazi government signed a secret non-aggression pact with South Africa in Feb. 1982, and expelled several ANC members. Nevertheless, the South Africans launched a raid in June 1986 in the Swazi capital Mbabane, killing three ANC members. In 1973 and 1977 King Sobhuza II dismissed parliament and abolished the constitution, only to replace it with a new one two years later. Sobhuza II died in Aug. 1982 and was succeeded by his teenage son, Prince Makhosetive. A power struggle ensued between the traditionalists and the modernists, which continued through the 1980s. Makhosetive was crowned as Mswati III on 25 Apr. 1986.

CONSTITUTION AND GOVERNMENT

Executive and legislature

Under the terms of the 1978 Constitution, executive power is vested in the paramount chief or king, and exercised by a cabinet appointed by him. The bicameral legislative body, the Libandla, has limited powers. The senate has ten members appointed by the king and ten indirectly elected; the house of assembly has ten appointed and 40 indirectly elected members. The normal full parliamentary term is five years. Last elections took place on 5 Nov. 1987, by means of the election of an 80-member electoral college, with two representatives from each of the 40 traditional chieftancies (Tinkhundla).

Present government

Head of state King Mswati III
Prime Minister (acting) Obed Dlamini
Other Principal Members of the Cabinet Sibusiso Barnabas Dlamini (Finance); Sir George M. Mamba (Foreign Affairs); Senzenjani Enoch Tshabalala (Interior and Immigration); Reginald Dladla (Justice).

Justice

The system of law combines the Roman-Dutch system (on the South African model) in statutory courts, and a traditional Swazi structure with 16 Swazi courts of first instance, 2 Swazi courts of appeal and a Higher Swazi Court of Appeal; the highest law officer is the Chief Justice, and the judiciary is constitutionally independent of the executive arm of government, although administered as part of the Ministry of Justice. The death penalty is in force. No executions between 1985 and mid-1988.

National symbols

Flag. Five horizontal stripes coloured blue, yellow, crimson, yellow and blue.
Festivals. 13 Mar. (Commonwealth Day); 25 Apr. (National Flag Day); 22 July (birthday of the late King Sobhuza); 24 Aug. (Umhlanga-Reed Dance-Day); 6 Sept. (Somhlolo-Independence-Day); 24 Oct. (United Nations Day).
Vehicle registration plate. SD.

INTERNATIONAL RELATIONS

Affiliations

NAM; OAU; ACP; Commonwealth; SADCC.

Defence

Umbutfo Swaziland Defence Forces; police force.

ECONOMY

Currency

The unit is the lilangeni (plural emalangeni, divided into 100 cents.

National finance

Budget. The 1989 FY budget, in US$, was for expenditure of 163 million and revenue of 149 million.
Inflation. 13%.

Gross Domestic Product

Estimated total GDP US$539 million (GNP), per capita US$750 (overall size of economy ranking 153 in the world).
Economically active population. The total number of persons active in the economy was 195,000.

Energy and mineral resources

Minerals. Production: (1987) asbestos 28,577 tons/25,925 tonnes; coal 182,289 tons/165,371 tonnes; quarry stone 3,394,170 ft^3/96,114 m^3. Also tin; haematite; small gold and diamond deposits.
Electricity. Capacity: 50,000 kW; production: 130 million kWh; 180 kWh per capita (1988).

Bioresources

Agriculture. The cultivated area is some 405,244 acres/164,000 ha and the main crops are maize; cotton; rice; sugar; citrus fruits; tobacco.

Crop production: (1987 in 1,000 tons/tonnes) sugar cane 4,502/4,084; citrus fruits 64/58; rice 5.5/5; seed cotton 16.5/15; maize 166/151; sorghum 3.3/3; pineapples 45/41; tomatoes 4.4/4; potatoes 7.7/7.

Livestock numbers: (1987) cattle 641,000; goats 309,000; sheep 22,000; poultry 1 million.

Forestry. 6% of the land area is forest and woodland and the commercial forest area amounts to some 262,667 acres/106,300 ha. Wood pulp is a major export.

Industry and commerce

Industry. Mining (coal and asbestos); wood pulp; sugar.

Commerce. Exports: (1987 US$300 million or 55% of GNP, including sugar; asbestos; wood pulp; citrus fruits; canned fruit. Imports: US$381 million, including motor vehicles; chemicals; petroleum products; foodstuffs. Countries exported to were South Africa; UK; US. Imports came from South Africa; US; UK.

Trade with UK. In 1988 Swaziland imported UK goods worth £1,564,000; exports to UK totalled £27,973,000.

Tourism. (1986) 256,000 visitors.

COMMUNICATIONS

Railways

There are 230 miles/370 km of railways.

Roads

There are 1,689 miles/2,719 km of roads, of which 422 miles/680 km are bituminized.

Aviation

Royal Swazi National Airways Corporation provides international services (main airport is at Matsapa, near Manzini, about 25 miles/40 km from Mbabane). Passengers: (1983) 35,800.

Shipping

None.

Telecommunications

There are 15,400 telephones and a system with carrier-equipped open-wire lines and low-capacity radio relay links. There are 105,000 radios and 8,000 televisions (1986). The government runs radio and TV services, in addition to which there is a private Swaziland Commercial Radio company, based in South Africa and broadcasting throughout the region. South African SABC broadcast services can be received.

EDUCATION AND WELFARE

Education

Schools. There are 590 schools with 147,743 primary class pupils and 32,942 secondary class pupils. Technical and vocational classes are run at the government Swaziland College of Technology (498 students) and four other vocational centres. There is also a police college, an Institute of Health Sciences, a college of nursing and three teacher-training colleges.

University. University of Swaziland (1,270 students).

Literacy. 68%.

Health

(1984) 80 doctors (one per 9,452 people); 1,608 hospital beds (one per 470 people).

SWEDEN

Konungariket Sverige (Kingdom of Sweden)

GEOGRAPHY

Sweden is situated in north-west Europe, occupying about 60% of the Scandinavian peninsula. It covers an area of 172,786 miles²/449,964 km² with a heavily indented coastline 4,732 miles/7,620 km in length. 15% of the country lies north of the Arctic Circle. Some 96,000 lakes account for 8.6% of the total area, including Lake Väneru (2,156 miles²/5,585 km²), the third largest lake in Europe. Another 57% of the total land surface is forested. The least populous northern part of the country (Norrland) stretches across an area of 90,324 miles²/234,000 km² incorporating the Kjolën mountain range in the west (highest peaks Kebnekajse 6,926 ft/2,111 m and Sarektjåkkå 6,854 ft/2,089 m located in north-west Lapland) and the intermittently cultivated lowland coastal strip in the east. Central Sweden (Swealand) is mostly low-lying and 50% forest-covered with farming regions concentrated on fertile clay soils surrounding the four major lakes (Väneru, Vattern, Hjälmaren and Mälaren). Apart from the predominantly infertile Småland uplands (886 ft/270 m above sea level) southern Sweden (Gotland) is extensively cultivated with large fertile areas in Vastergotland, Ostergotland, Skåne and the Island of Gotland. Swealand and Gotland have areas of 30,880 and 33,582 miles²/80,000 and 87,000 km² respectively. Sweden is divided into 24 counties (Län), the most populous of which are Stockholm in the east and Malmöhus in the south.

Climate

Generally continental, with cold winters and mild summers, although colder in winter and substantially drier than Norway. Continuous daylight in the north during the Arctic summer produces a mean July temperature of 59°F/15°C, but the January mean temperature is 14°F/-10°C and the freeze can last up to 250 days of the year. Further south, the mean July temperature is 63°F/17°C in Stockholm and Göteborg although winter temperatures average 26.6°F/–3°C in January. Ice begins to accumulate in the Gulf of Bothnia by November, and near Stockholm by early January. The Northern Baltic surface waters may remain frozen for up to six months. Precipitation is lowest in north-east Sweden, particularly during winter. Karesuando on the Finnish border records a mean annual total of only 12.6 in/320 mm. By contrast Göteborg, in the south-west, records 28 in/710 mm while the mountains on the Norwegian frontier may receive between 74.8 and 80 in/1,900 and 2,030 mm annually.

Cities and towns

Stockholm (capital)	666,810
Göteborg	431,521
Malmö	230,838
Uppsala	159,962
Orebro	119,066
Norrköping	119,001
Vaesteras	118,602
Linköping	108,962
Helsingborg	106,982
Boras	100,395

Population

Total population (mid-1987) is 8,414,083 of whom 84% live in urban areas. Population density of 48.7 persons per mile²/18.6 per km² over 70% of the total area. Approximately 401,000 of the above total are foreign citizens. By far the largest proportion of these are Finns (130,000 in 1987). Other significant nation-specific minorities in 1987 included citizens of Yugoslavia 39,000; Poland 15,000; Turkey 23,000; Iran 20,000; West Germany 12,000; Chile 12,000. Ethnic minorities with Swedish citizenship include approximately 15,000-17,000 Lapps, 2,000 gypsies and 16,000 Jewish inhabitants (5,000 of them in Stockholm).

Birth rate 1.2%. **Death rate** 1.3%. **Rate of population increase** (1980–87) 0.1%. **Age distribution** under 15 = 17.8%; over 65 = 17.7%. **Life expectancy** female 80; male 73; average 77.

Religion

Predominantly Christian. 93% are adherents of the Evangelical Lutheran Church. The Roman Catholic Diocese of Stockholm claims in excess of 120,000 members – 1.4% of the population. Of the non-conformist churches, both the Pentecostal movement (100,442) and the Salvation Army (28,691) have significant memberships. Sweden also has the largest Scandinavian Jewish population at around 16,000.

Language

Swedish is derived from Old Norse and related to German and English; it shares a number of common features with Norwegian and Danish. Finnish and Lapp are still spoken in the far north where 30,000–50,000 Finnish speakers are located in the Torne Valley. The Statute for Nomad Schools permits Lapp children to receive instruction in Lapp although the variety of dialects means that Lapps from different regions often cannot understand one another.

HISTORY

Inhabited from about 8000 BC, Sweden takes its name from the Germanic 'Svear' people, whose early kingdom in the area of present-day Stockholm extended to much of central Sweden by the 7th century AD. Swedish warriors and traders participated in the great Viking expansion (800–1100), penetrating deep into what is now Russia, founding Novgorod and reaching Constantinople and the Black Sea. Introduced by English and German missionaries, Christianity was fully established under St Eric IX (r.1150–60), whose dynasty brought the more southerly Goths into the Swedish kingdom. Under Magnus II (r.1319–65), Swedish rule over what is now Finland was confirmed by treaty with Novgorod (1323) and trade in Swedish metals developed with the Hanseatic League. Denmark's assertions of Scandinavian supremacy culminated in the Union of Kalmar (1397), under which Sweden and Norway passed to the Danish crown. Rebellion by the Swedes, launched with the convening of the first Riksdag (parliament) in 1435, was reignited by a massacre of over 80 Swedish nobles in Stockholm (8 Nov. 1520). This event led directly to the election of Gustav I Vasa (r.1523–60) as king of independent Sweden, although Norway and southern Sweden remained under Danish rule.

The first Vasa ruler improved royal finances by establishing Lutheranism as the state religion (1527) and confiscating the property of the Roman Catholic Church; he also established a centralized hereditary monarchy (1544). Growing Swedish power in the Baltic facilitated the acquisition of Estonia and Ingria under his sons, Eric XIV (r.1560–68) and Johan III (r.1568–92), while the latter's marriage to the Queen of Poland resulted in their son Sigismund becoming king of both Sweden and Poland from 1592. Sigismund's Catholicism and prolonged absences provoked his deposition in Sweden (1599) by Gustav Vasa's third son, who later took the throne as Karl IX (r.1604–11). He was succeeded by Gustav II Adolf (r.1611–32), Sweden's greatest monarch. An able administrator and brilliant general, he quickly vanquished the threatening armies of Poland and Russia, annexing Polish Livonia and the eastern littoral of the Gulf of Finland, thus depriving Russia of access to the Baltic. He then turned the tide of the Thirty Years' War (1618–48) in favour of the Protestant cause by invading Germany and defeating the Habsburg-led forces of the Counter-Reformation at Breitenfeld (1631). Although he was killed at the Battle of Lützen the following year, further Swedish military successes, combined with the intervention of France from 1635, ensured the eventual defeat of Habsburg ambitions in northern Europe and also drove the Danes out of southern Sweden by 1645. The Peace of Westphalia (1648) confirmed Sweden's ascendancy in the Baltic region and its new status as one of the great powers of Europe.

Queen Christina's successful reign (1632–54) began as a regency and ended, on her conversion to Catholicism, in abdication in favour of her cousin, Carl X Gustav (r.1654–60). In further wars he and his successor, Carl XI Gustav (r.1660–97), successfully resisted Denmark's efforts to recover southern Sweden (and with it sole control over the strategic Öresund Sound between the North Sea and the Baltic), although Norway remained under the Danish crown. Under the 'Reduction' of 1679, Carl XI created an absolute monarchy, obtaining the support of the Riksdag for the appropriation of estates from the nobility and the reversal of aristocratic encroachment on royal prerogatives. Carl XII Gustav (r.1697–1718), the austere 'warrior-king', led Sweden into the Great Northern War (1700–21), but spectacular early victories against the Danes, Russians and Poles turned into disaster when he invaded the Russian heartland. Crushing defeat by Peter the Great at the Battle of Poltava (1709) forced him to flee to Turkey, while advancing enemies, which by then included Prussia and England/Hanover, threatened Sweden's very survival. Carl XII eventually returned to his homeland (1715), but his death in battle in Norway (1718) forced Sweden to conclude peace treaties ceding most of its southern and eastern Baltic possessions. The main beneficiary was Russia, which obtained Estonia, Livonia, Ingria and Finnish Karelia and became the dominant power on the Gulf of Finland, although most of Finland remained Swedish.

Internally, the collapse of Sweden's Baltic empire led directly to the adoption of a parliamentary constitution (1723) under which the Riksdag came to exercise greater authority than the crown. Two factions, the mercantilist and aristocratic 'Hats' and the liberal 'Caps', alternated in power, respectively pursuing alliance with France and rapprochement with Russia and England, although without beneficial result in either case. Considerable economic and social progress was made in this era, but the parliamentary system's bureaucracy and partisan animosities enabled Gustav III (r.1771–92), a nephew of Frederick the Great of Prussia, to re-establish a measure of absolutism and to preside over a flowering of the arts and literature until his assassination by opposition noblemen (1792). In the Napoleonic Wars Sweden's alliance with Britain led to disaster when the Treaty of Tilsit (1807) between France and Russia enabled the latter to conquer Finland (1809). Blamed for this defeat, Gustav IV Adolf (r.1792–1809) was deposed in a bloodless revolution and replaced by his uncle, Karl XIII (r.1809–18), who accepted a parliamentary constitution. The new monarch being elderly and childless, the Riksdag elected as his heir one of Napoleon's marshals, Jean-Baptiste Bernadotte, who as crown prince (1810) took his adopted country into the anti-Napoleon alliance. Sweden's reward at the Congress of Vienna (1814–15) was the transfer of Norway from Denmark to the Swedish crown, although Finland remained part of the Russian Empire and Sweden lost its remaining possessions in northern Germany.

Bernadotte eventually ascended the Swedish throne in 1818 as Carl XIV Johan (r.1818–44), a reign which eventually led in 1840 to the so-called 'departmental reform' and a measure of ministerial accountability. The introduction of compulsory school education (1842) was followed, under Oscar I (r.1844–59), by other social reforms and moves to a free trading and enterprise system, although the principle of a public economic role was established with the decision that railways should be built and operated by the state (1854). Oscar I abandoned alignment with Russia to support Britain and France in the Crimean War (1854–56), although Swedish hopes of recovering Finland were disappointed. Under Carl XV (r.1859–72) pan-Scandinavian sentiment flourished, but Sweden failed to honour its pledge to assist Denmark in the defence of Schleswig-Holstein against Prussia (1864) and thereafter was increasingly influenced by German political and economic methods. In 1865–66 Justice Minister Louis De Geer masterminded the replacement of the old four-chamber Riksdag (of nobility, clergy, burghers and peasants) by a parliament of two houses with equal rights, although with franchise qualifications which ensured that the first chamber was dominated by wealthy landowners and industrialists and the second by better-off farmers. In the late 19th century Sweden remained a predominantly agricultural country, where endemic rural poverty fuelled large-scale emigration to North America. As industrialization gathered pace, however, an organized labour movement emerged, represented by the Social Democratic Labour Party (founded 1889), which made common cause with the Liberal Party (founded 1900) for full democracy, while the Conservative Party (founded 1904) defended the status quo and the maintenance of crown prerogative.

Under Oscar II (r.1872–1907) severe strains in the union of Sweden and Norway culminated in the latter's becoming fully independent in 1905. Two years later adult male franchise and proportional representation were introduced for second chamber elections, with the result that the Liberals won a landslide majority in 1911 and Gustav V (r.1907–50) was obliged to appoint a Liberal, Karl Staaff, as prime minister. However, royal resistance to full parliamentary government led to the installation of a Conservative administration (1914), even though a general election had made the Social Democrats the strongest second chamber party. The internal political struggle was then overtaken by the outbreak of World War I, in which Sweden remained neutral and enjoyed an economic boom as a result of heavy demand for its industrial products by the German war machine. Retaliatory action by Britain contributed to the fall of the Hammarskjöld government in 1917, when elections gave the Social Democrats and Liberals an increased majority in the second chamber and brought them to power under Nils Edén (Liberal). The new government reached an accommodation with the western powers by agreeing to limit Swedish exports to Germany, but displeasure over Sweden's wartime role was apparent in the decision of the League of Nations (1921) to confirm the sovereignty of newly-independent Finland over the Swedish-populated Aaland Islands.

The Edén government quickly introduced universal adult suffrage (1919), after which the coalition partners parted company on economic policy issues. Affected by the formation of a breakaway Communist party (1917), the Social Democrats embraced nationalization and other radical policies, while the Liberals shared the preference of the Conservatives and a new Farmers' Party for the free enterprise system. The pattern of the present-day division of the parties into socialist and non-socialist blocs was thus set, although differences within the latter and the effects of proportional representation produced much political fluidity during the economically prosperous 1920s.

The Social Democrats formed their first government in 1920 under Hjalmar Branting, who was again prime minister 1921–23 and 1924–25. Economic depression in the early 1930s facilitated, in the 1932 elections, a major advance by the Social Democrats, who formed a government under Per Albin Hansson which was to remain in power, under succeeding leaders and with different coalition partners, for 44 years, except for a short interval of Farmers' Party rule in 1936. In addition to beginning the creation of a welfare state, the Hansson government also inaugurated a new era of industrial relations harmony under the 1938 Saltsjöbaden collective bargaining agreement. Sweden remained neutral during World War II, during which a national unity coalition was in office, and again came under Allied criticism, in particular for continuing to trade with Nazi Germany and for granting transit rights to German forces (until 1943).

In the post-war era the Social Democrats continued to dominate Swedish politics, under Tage Erlander from 1946 and as a minority government until forming a coalition with the Farmers' Party in 1951–57, after which they again governed alone until 1976. During this period legislation was enacted establishing Sweden as the world's most advanced welfare state, while economic progress made it one of the world's most affluent countries. Eschewing outright nationalization, the Social Democrats pursued a strategy of 'functional socialism' under which the economy was left largely in private hands but made subject to measures designed to eliminate anti-social aspects, to give workers a voice at their workplace and to promote equality. In the external sphere, Swedish neutrality, non-alignment and active participation in the UN secured all-party support, as did the allocation of substantial resources to national defence and overseas aid. Sweden was a founder member of the Nordic Council (1953) and EFTA (1959), and in 1972 signed an industrial free trade agreement with the European Economic Community. Having from 1957 relied in part on the external support of the Communists (renamed the Left Communists in 1967), in 1968 the Social Democrats obtained their first absolute majority since 1940. Erlander was succeeded as party leader and prime minister by Olof Palme in 1969, when a major constitutional reform (fully implemented in 1975) created a unicameral Riksdag with a three-year term and reduced the monarch to purely ceremonial functions. In 1973 Carl XVI Gustav succeeded his grandfather, Gustav VI Adolf (r.1950–73), and in 1980 the succession was opened to females, enabling Princess Victoria to become heir to the throne.

Having lost ground in the 1970 and 1973 elections, the Social Democrats finally went out of office in 1976, when a non-socialist coalition came to power under Thorbjörn Fälldin of the Centre Party (successor to the Farmers' Party) and also including the Moderates (successor to the Conservatives) and the Liberals. The coalition collapsed in 1978 over differences on the nuclear energy issue (being replaced by a Liberal minority government under Ola Ullsten) but was re-established after the 1979 elections, again under Fälldin. A national referendum in 1980 showed a majority in favour of a limited expansion of nuclear power generation prior to its being phased out by the early 21st century. The Moderates left the coalition in 1981 after disagreements on taxation policy, whereupon the Centre and Liberal parties formed a two-party cabinet until 1982. In the elections of that year the Social Democrats gained seats and returned to power as a minority government supported by the Left Communists, a situation which continued after the 1985 elections despite Social Democratic losses. The post–1982 Palme government maintained its immediate predecessor's closer alignment with the West, as Swedish relations with the Soviet Union continued to be strained by repeated Soviet violations of Swedish territorial waters and air space.

In Feb. 1986 Palme was shot dead in a Stockholm street. He was succeeded as prime minister by Ingvar Carlsson, whose government was troubled not only by the lack of progress in the Palme murder investigation but also by a series of political scandals and by continuing economic problems. In the 1988 elections the Social Democrats and the three centre-right parties all lost ground, while the Left Communists gained seats and the Swedish Greens entered the Riksdag for the first time. The outcome was a further minority Social Democratic government under the continued premiership of Carlsson.

CONSTITUTION AND GOVERNMENT

Executive and legislature

Sweden is a parliamentary democracy; the functions of King Carl XVI Gustav as head of state are purely ceremonial. A cabinet led by a prime minister is responsible to a unicameral parliament (Riksdag) which is elected directly every three years by universal suffrage (minimum voting age 18) using proportional representation. The last general election was on Sept. 18, 1988.

Present government

Prime Minister Ingvar Carlsson

Principal ministers: Odd Engström (Deputy Prime Minister); Sten Andersson (Foreign Affairs); Roine Carlsson (Defence); Allan Larsson (Finance); Laila Freivalds (Justice); Rune Molin (Industry, including energy affairs); Birgitta Dahl (Environment).

Justice

The system of law is based on civil law influenced by customary law. The highest court is the Supreme Court of Judicature, with 6 Courts of Appeal and 97 district courts, which deal in the first instance with both civil and criminal law. Senior law officers are the Attorney-General and the Parliamentary Commissioners (Justitieombudsmannen) for the Judiciary and Civil Administration. The death penalty was abolished in 1973.

Prisons. There are 5,150 prisoners.

National symbols

Flag. Blue with a yellow Scandinavian cross. The colours are derived from the national arms of the three gold crowns on a blue background. The flag dates from the 16th century with the Scandinavian form being used since 1665.

Festivals. 1 May (May Day); 24 June (Midsummer Day).

Vehicle registration plate. S.

INTERNATIONAL RELATIONS

Affiliations

Neutral; UN and its main subsidiary organizations; OECD; EFTA; Council of Europe; Nordic Council.

Defence

As a neutral country, Sweden has not participated in any military alliance since the early 19th century. Its defence budget is US$4,430 million (1987/88). There is compulsory military service in the Army and Navy of 7½–15 months, and in the Air Force of 8–12 months. Abroad it provides 770 soldiers for the UNIFIL force in Lebanon.

Total Armed Forces: 67,000 (48,950 conscripts). Reserves: 709,000 (obligation to age 47).

Army: 47,000; some 800 main battle tanks (Strv-101/-102/-104, Strv-103B), 200 light tanks (Ikv-91).

Navy: 12,000; 14 submarines and 51 patrol and coastal combatants.

Air Force: 8,000; 446 combat aircraft (mainly SK-50, AJ-37 Viggen, SK-37, JA-37 Viggen).

ECONOMY

Sweden has an industrialized and prosperous market economy in which the chief government instrument of control is the annual budget.

Currency

The unit is the krona (pl. kronor), which is divided into 100 öre.

National finance

Budget. The 1988/89 budget (in US$) provided for expenditure of $57,700 million and revenue of $56,600 million, giving a deficit of $1,100 million. The balance of payments on the current account (1988) was a deficit of US$2,500 million as compared with one of US$1,000 million the previous year.

Inflation. (1988) 6.6%, up from 5.3% the year before.

Gross national product

Total GNP was US$160,000 million, representing a GNP per capita of US$19,000 (1987). Growth rate (1988) 2.5%.

Economically active population. The total number of persons active in the economy (1988) was 4,517,000; unemployed: 1.6% (1988).

Energy and mineral resources

Minerals. Sweden has rich mineral resources including some 15% of the world's known reserves of uranium. There are also significant iron ore deposits which mean the country accounts for around 10% of global iron ore production. Output: (in 1,000 tons/tonnes) iron ore 21,723/19,707; pyrites 472/428.6; zinc ore 355.5/322.5; silver and lead ore 146.7/133.1 (1987).

Electricity. Production: 147,200 million kWh. The largest proportion of Sweden's electricity is produced by nuclear energy (46.9% in 1988). However, the country's 12 nuclear power stations are due as a result of a 1980 referendum, to be phased out completely by 2010. Currently the country's remaining energy requirements are almost entirely met by hydro-electricity with imports of natural gas expected to be a likely alternative to nuclear power in the future.

Bioresources

Agriculture. There are an estimated 7,142,077 acres/2,890,359 ha of arable land (on holdings of over 4.9 acres/2 ha) and 832,060 acres/336,730 ha of cultivated pastures, the main farm products being dairy produce, meat, cereals, and potatoes.

Crop production: (1987 in 1,000 tons/tonnes from holdings of over 4.9 acres/2 ha) tame hay 4,947/4,488; barley 2,102/1,907; sugar beet 1,873/1,699; wheat 1,717/1,558; oats 1,587/1,440; potatoes 1,055/957; rapeseed 326/296; rye 151/137.

Livestock numbers: (1987) poultry 10.8 million; pigs 2.2 million; cattle 1.7 million; sheep 397,000.

Forestry. Forests cover over 50% of the country and broadly are 25% publicly-owned, 25% by companies with the remainder privately-owned. Timber felled in

1987/88 amounted to 1,861 million ft^3/52.7 million m^3. Timber and the related sawmill, wood-pulp and paper industries account for some 18% of exports. Paper industry output in 1988 was 9 million tons/8.2 million tonnes of which 7.1 million tons/6.4 million tonnes were exported (22% to the UK), while of the 11.5 million tons/10.4 million tonnes of pulp produced, 4.4 million tons/4 million tonnes were exported.

Fisheries. Total catch (1988) 252,427 tons/229,000 tonnes.

Industry and commerce

Industry. Sweden has a successful and sophisticated manufacturing industry based on metal production, especially of steel but also of iron, copper, aluminium and lead. This metalworking industry provides the basis for the production of a wide range of engineering, machinery and transport products ranging from cars, aeroplanes and machine tools to chemicals, electrical goods and telecommunications equipment. The shipping industry and the merchant marine are, however, in decline.

Commerce. Exports: (1987) US$44,388 million or 27.9% of GDP; imports US$40,596 million or 25.5% of GDP. Exports: (1988) machinery and transport equipment 42.8%; basic manufactures 26.7%; other manufactured articles 9.4%; crude materials including forestry products 9.2%; chemicals and related products 7.2%; food and live animals 1.6%. Imports: (1988) machinery and transport equipment 39.6%; basic manufactures 16.8%; various manufactured articles 15.1%; chemicals and related products 10%; mineral fuels and lubricants 6.8%; food and live animals 5.5%.

Trade with UK. Sweden imported UK goods worth 24,000 million kronor and exported to the UK goods worth 34,200 million kronor (1988).

Tourism. Sweden derived revenue of 12,881 million kronor from visitors (1987).

COMMUNICATIONS

Railways

There are 6,978 miles/11,236 km of railways, of which 4,344 miles/6,995 km are electrified.

Roads

There are 81,248 miles/130,834 km of roads and 3,366,570 passenger cars (one per 2.6 inhabitants).

Aviation

Scandinavian Airlines (the national carrier of Denmark, Norway and Sweden) provide international services and Linjeflyg AB provides domestic services; main airports are at Arlanda (26 miles/42 km from Stockholm), Landvetter (15.5 miles/25 km from Göteborg) and at Sturup (17 miles/28 km from Malmö).

Shipping

The merchant fleet has a gross registered tonnage of 2,028,000. Total freight unloaded at Swedish ports: 62 million tons/56 million tonnes; loaded: 47.8 million tons/43.4 million tonnes.

Telecommunications

5,480,000 main telephone lines (one per 1.54 inhabitants).

Broadcasting

Sveriges radio broadcasts three home-service channels as well as short-wave overseas broadcasts. There is a network of 24 independent radio stations. Sveriges Radio also controls two non-commercial television channels. There are 3,293,000 television licence holders and 7,271,556 radios (1988).

Newspapers

178 dailies, total circulation 4.9 million; a strong provincial press (*Göteborgs-Posten*, circulation 283,000) and four major Stockholm-based dailies: *Dagens Nyheter* (407,000) and its evening paper *Expressen* (571,000), the conservative *Svenska Dagbladet* (227,000) and the union-owned Social Democrat paper *Aftonbladet* (387,500).

EDUCATION AND WELFARE

Education

The state system provides free and compulsory education in comprehensive schools from age seven to 16. Upper secondary schools then provide further courses for 2–4 years.

School population. 928,000 under 16, 285,000 in higher stages.

Schools. 4,674 schools with 99,030 teachers (one per 9.4 pupils) at age 7–16; 484 upper secondary schools with 29,080 teachers (one per 9.8 students).

Universities. New integrated higher education institutions, högskola, created under 1977 legislation, bring together the professional and vocational training colleges and the universities in the six higher education regions. 163,200 students in 1987.

Health

Comprehensive health care and social security arrangements (32% of GDP on social expenditure in 1986), including compulsory sickness insurance and employment injury insurance. One doctor per 400 inhabitants.

SWITZERLAND
Confédération Suisse (French)
Schweizerische Eidgenossenschaft (German)
Confederazione Suizzera (Romansch)
(Swiss Confederation)

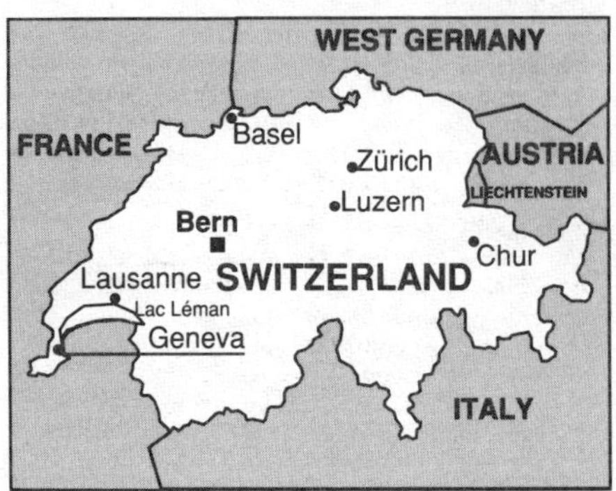

GEOGRAPHY

Switzerland is a landlocked country in central Europe, with an area of 15,939 miles^2/41,293 km^2 divided into 23 cantons. 60% of the land surface is covered by the Alps, stretching east-west across the southern regions (mean elevation 5,577 ft/1,700 m). The Mittelland or Central Plateau, supporting the bulk of the nation's urban economic and agricultural activity, occupies a further 30% of the territory, drained by the River Aare and bordered by the Brienz, Biel, Thun and Neuchâtel lakes. Further north, the sparsely forested Jura Mountains comprise the remaining 10% of the surface area with an average altitude of 2,297 ft/700 m. The entire transcontinental Alpine range arcs through France, Italy, Switzerland, Bavaria, Austria and Yugoslavia over 3,281 ft/1,000 km (160,839 miles^2/259,000 km^2), rising to a maximum Swiss elevation of 15,203 ft/4,634 m at Dufourspitze in the Valais Alps. The Alpine region is drained longitudinally by the Rhône and Upper Rhine, and latitudinally by the Reuss and Ticino river systems. 10% of the land is arable and 26% is forested.

Climate

Transitional. Variable according to relief: subject to Atlantic, Mediterranean, east and central European continental influences. Average annual temperatures decrease as elevation increases, from 45°F/7°C (central plateau) to 36°F/2°C at higher altitudes. Rainfall increases south-west to north-east from 21 in/533 mm (Rhône Valley) to 112 in/2,850 mm. Perennial snow cover above 9,842 ft/3,000 m. Bern: Jan. 32°F/0°C. July 65°F/18.5°C. Average annual rainfall 39 in/986 mm.

Cities and towns

Zürich	840,000
Genève	382,000
Basel	363,600
Bern (capital)	301,100
Lausanne	260,200
Luzern	160,000
St. Gallen	125,400
Winterthur	107,400

Population

Total population is 6,611,019 of which 58.2% live in urban areas. Population density is 415 persons per mile^2/159.5 per km^2. Ethnic composition: (of Swiss Nationals) 74% German; 20% French; 4% Italian; 1% Romansch; 1% other. (See Languages for ethnolinguistic divisions.

Birth rate 1.2%. **Death rate** 1.0%. **Rate of population increase** (1980–87) 0.3%. **Age distribution** under 15 = 16.9%; over 65 = 14.6%. **Life expectancy** female 80; male 74; average 77.

Religion

Christianity. 49% of the population are Roman Catholic; 48% belong to a variety of Protestant denominations collected under the Federation of Swiss Protestant Churches. The Jewish minority comprises 0.3% of the total population.

Language

At the last census, 65.0% of the population were German-speaking; 18.4% spoke French; 9.8% Italian; 1.6% Spanish; 0.8% Romansch (Rhaeto-Roman, spoken mostly in the Graubünden canton, officially designated the fourth national language on 8 July 1937); 0.6% Turkish.

HISTORY

Under Roman rule from 58 BC, the area of modern Switzerland was penetrated by Germanic tribes in the 5th century AD, becoming part of the Swabian lands (c.600). It later passed to Burgundian rule (9th century), although the Swiss cantons which emerged from the Dark Ages enjoyed autonomy in their Alpine fastnesses.

Defined as a province of the Holy Roman Empire from 1033, Switzerland came under the overlordship of the house of Habsburg (named after its domains in north-west Switzerland), whose accession to the imperial title as dukes of Austria (1273) intensified revolt by the Swiss. The Perpetual League set up (1291) by the Waldstätte ('forest cantons') of Schwyz, Unterwalden and Uri (home of legendary resistance hero William Tell) to oppose Austrian encroachments on Swiss liberties was later joined by other cantons. A long struggle finally resulted in the achievement of virtual independence within the Empire (late 15th century).

The Protestant Reformation of the early 16th century caused religious wars in Switzerland, as some cantons embraced Calvinism and the more rural areas remained loyal to Rome. In Zürich the Reformation owed most to Huldreich Zwingli, who made the city a stronghold of Protestantism in the early 1520s and strongly affected similar revolutions in the religious and political life of Bern (1528) and Basel (1529). He led military campaigns against rural Catholic cantons in 1529 and 1531, and was killed in battle at Kappel (11 Oct. 1531). Jean Calvin, based from 1536 in Geneva, saw the city adopt religious reform in May of that year, at the same time as siding with Bern and Fribourg for independence from the House of Savoy. He was forced to leave the city in 1538, however, as the mildly reformist Libertines gained ascendancy, but was invited back in 1541 and devoted the remaining 23 years of his life to the (ultimately successful) effort to secure the ascendancy of his more radical views both in theological teaching and in political organization of the city under strict Church control.

None of the Swiss cantons joined in the Thirty Years' War (1618–48), which began as a conflict between Protestant Europe and the Habsburg-led Counter-Reformation and became a struggle for supremacy between France and Austria. Benefiting from the victory of France, the Swiss Confederation achieved full independence under the Peace of Westphalia (1648), outside a Holy Roman Empire reduced to a purely nominal existence.

Allied to Louis XVI's France from 1777, Switzerland was invaded by French revolutionary armies in 1798 and converted into a centralized Helvetic Republic, although later mediation by Napoleon (1803) restored the power of the cantons. The Congress of Vienna (1815) reaffirmed the Confederation, which was joined by Geneva (hitherto a separate republic) and Valais, and declared to be perpetually neutral. Pressure by liberals for a more unitary and democratic Switzerland led to an almost bloodless civil war (1847), in which the conservative Catholic cantons of the Sonderbund (Lucerne, Zug, Fribourg and Valais) were defeated by Confederation forces. Modelled on that of the United States, a new constitution (1848) gave the central government and parliament substantial powers, while also guaranteeing cantonal rights in important areas. In 1857 the Confederation was joined by Neuchâtel, hitherto a principality under Prussian sovereignty (1707–1806 and again from 1815). The horrors of the Franco-Austrian war in Italy (1859) impelled Henri Dumant of Geneva to found the International Red Cross (1864), enhancing Switzerland's neutral and non-belligerent vocation.

Revisions to the constitution (1874) increased federal powers in the defence and educational spheres and established the referendum as a means of national decision-making. These changes generated renewed opposition in conservative cantons anxious to maintain their cultural autonomy and were not fully accepted until 1884. Industrialization in the late 19th century led to the growth of organized trade unions (from 1880) and the formation (1888) of the Swiss Socialist Party (SPS); however, Switzerland remained largely immune from the revolutionary upsurge experienced elsewhere in Europe (and a Communist Party formed by SPS leftists in 1918–20 obtained little support). The other main elements of the modern party structure came into being when liberal groups derived from the anti-Sonderbund movement of the 1840s formed the Radical Democratic Party (FDP) in 1894 and Catholic groups established a Conservative Party (1912), forerunner of the inter-denominational Christian Democratic People's Party (CVS). An Agrarian Party, formed in 1917 from 19th-century farmers' and burghers' movements, became the main component of the present-day People's Party (SVP). The introduction of proportional representation (1919) ensured that subsequent federal governments were dominated by combinations of these four parties.

Swiss neutrality was observed by the belligerents in both World Wars, during both of which Switzerland played a major humanitarian role. In what was seen as a gesture of appeasement to Nazi Germany, the Swiss government banned the Communist Party (1940), whose activists joined with dissident Socialists in 1944 to form the Party of Labour (PdA).

Although it had been a member of the inter-war League of Nations (from 1920), Switzerland decided on neutralist grounds to remain outside the post-1945 UN, which it saw as originating in the wartime alliance against the Axis powers. It nevertheless accepted UN observer status and became an active member of the UN agencies (except the World Bank and International Monetary Fund), several of which established their headquarters in Geneva. Switzerland also became a founder member of EFTA (1959). In the 1970s support for membership of the UN developed in government circles and secured parliamentary approval in 1984. However, a national referendum held in Mar. 1986 resulted in a 3:1 majority against membership. Post-war relations with other states have been largely untroubled, although the secrecy laws surrounding Switzerland's international banking role have attracted criticism for their alleged protection of illegal activities.

Increasing economic prosperity (Swiss citizens enjoy one of the highest per capita incomes in the world) produced a large measure of stability in post-war Swiss politics, with successive elections showing minimal changes. The FDP's leading role in the federal government gave way, in 1959, to a four-party coalition in which the FDP, SPS and CVP each took two posts and the SVP one, an arrangement which has been maintained ever since. The 1967 and 1971 elections saw the emergence of radical right-wing movements urging curbs on the number of foreign workers and other aliens in Switzerland. Although such propositions were twice defeated in referendums (1970, 1974), the government felt constrained to impose certain restrictions on foreign workers and was defeated in a further referendum when it sought to relax them (1982). The 1971 elections were the first in which women were able to vote and be elected at federal level, this having been approved by a 2:1 majority of male voters in a referendum in Feb. 1971. (By Apr. 1989 only the half-canton of Appenzell Innerhoden still denied this right to women at cantonal level.) Elisabeth Kopp of the FDP became Switzerland's first woman minister in 1984 (but was forced to resign in Dec. 1988 over claims that she had abused her position as justice minister).

The SPS, usually returned as the largest parliamentary party in the 1960s and 1970s, was overtaken by the FDP in 1983 and by the CVP in 1987. The smaller SVP maintained its position as fourth party. Of the 13 formations that won representation in 1987, two Green lists took 13 seats between them, benefiting from the growing importance attached to environmentalist issues in Switzerland.

CONSTITUTION AND GOVERNMENT

Executive and legislature

The president and vice-president are elected each December by the parliament, the bicameral Federal Assembly (Bundesversammlung), from among the members of the Federal Council (Bundesrat). This seven-member body, also elected by the Federal Assembly, exercises executive power. The Federal Assembly comprises the 46-member Upper House or Council of States (Ständerat) of representatives from the cantons, and the 200-member Lower House (Nationalrat or National Council) which is directly elected by universal adult suffrage (minimum voting age 20) for a four-year term using a proportional representation system. The last general election was on 18 Oct. 1987.

Present government

President in 1990 Arnold Koller

Vice-President in 1989 Flavio Cotti

Members of Federal Council René Felber (Political (Foreign) Affairs); Otto Stich (Finance and Customs); Jean-Pascal Delamuraz (Public Economy); Adolf Ogi (Transport, Communications and Energy); Flavio Cotti (Interior); Arnold Koller (Justice and Police); Kaspar Villiger (Military (Defence)).

Chancellor of the Swiss Confederation Walter Buser.

Administration

The Swiss Confederation has a republican, federal constitution in which the 20 cantons and six half-cantons retain considerable power.

Justice

The system of law is decentralised to a large extent to the cantons which make up the confederation; justice is based on civil law influenced by customary law. The highest court, with responsibility for the review of legislation, is the Federal Tribunal (Bundesgericht) in Lausanne whose members are appointed by the Federal Assembly for 6 years. The Tribunal also operates as a court of appeal in respect of decisions by other federal authorities, and in respect of cantonal authorities applying federal laws. The death penalty is in force only for exceptional crimes. No executions between 1985 and mid-1988.

Prisons. There are 4,968 prisoners.

National symbols

Flag. Red with a white couped cross.

Festivals. 1 Aug (anniversary of founding of Swiss Confederation in 1291).

Vehicle registration plate. CH.

INTERNATIONAL RELATIONS

Affiliations

Neutral; OECD; EFTA; Council of Europe.

Defence

Total Armed Forces: about 3,500 regular and recruits (two intakes of 18,000 each for 17 weeks only). Mobilizable to some 1,100,000 inclusive 460,000 Civil Defence, in 48 hours. Terms of service: 17 weeks' recruit training at age 20, followed by reservist refresher training of three weeks over an eight-year period between ages 21–32 for 'Auszug' (call out). Reserves: 625,000.

Army: 560,000 on mobilization; some 850 main battle tanks (Leopard 2, Centurion, Pz-61/-68).

Air Corps: 45,000 on mobilization; 272 combat aircraft (Hunter F-58, F-5E, Mirage IIIS).

Para-military (Civil Defence): 480,000 (300,000 fully trained).

ECONOMY

Currency

The unit is the Swiss franc, divided into 100 centimes/rappen/centesimi.

National finance

Budget. The 1987 budget, in US$, was for expenditure of 16,100 million and revenue of 16,200 million.

Balance of payments. The balance of payments, in US$ (current account, 1988) was a surplus of 8,560 million.

Inflation. 3.4% (12 months to Sept. 1989).

Gross Domestic Product

Estimated total GDP US$170,880 million, per capita US$16,900 (overall size of economy ranking 17 in the world) Growth rate (1988) 3%.

Economically active population. The total number of persons active in the economy was 3,050,000; unemployed: 0.7%.

Sector	% of workforce
industry	39
agriculture	7
services*	54

* services figure includes elements unassigned to other categories.

Energy and mineral resources

Minerals. There are few natural resources. Salt is mined.

Electricity. Capacity: 17.7 kW; production: 58.4 million kWh; 8,870 kWh per capita (1988). Hydroelectric power provides more than 50% of electricity output; nuclear power provides about 37%.

Bioresources

Agriculture. About 10% of land is put to arable use, and 40% is meadow and pasture. Switzerland is less than 50% self-sufficient in food. Dairy farming predominates. Fish, refined sugar, fats and oils other than butter, grains, eggs, fruit, vegetables, meat have to be imported.

Crop production: wheat 584,219 tons/530,000 tonnes; potatoes 870,817 tons/790,000 tonnes; sugar beet 870,817 tons/790,000 tonnes; maize 173,061 tons/157,000 tonnes; fruit; grapes; milk 4.2 million tons/3.8 million tonnes.

Livestock numbers: cattle 1.8 million; pigs 1.9 million; sheep 355,000; poultry 6 million.

Forestry. About 25% of the country is forest and woodland. Timber production: softwood 161,385 ft^3/4,570 m^3; hardwood 40,894 ft^3/1,158 m^3.

Industry and commerce

Industry. Industrial production is expanding and there are few industrial disputes. Major industries are precision engineering (especially clocks and watches); heavy engineering; pharmaceuticals; chemicals; chocolate. Machine building provides approximately 30% of export earnings; the chemical industry provides 20%.

Commerce. Switzerland is an international financial centre. Total exports: (f.o.b.1987) US$45,500 million or 40% of GDP. Major commodities are machinery and equipment; precision instruments; metal products; foodstuffs; textiles and clothing. Main trading partners are EC countries 56%; US 9%; Japan 4%. Imports: (c.i.f.1987) US$50,700 million, mainly agricultural products; machinery; chemicals; textiles. Main trading partners are EC countries 72%; US 5%.

Trade with UK. 1988 Switzerland exported £3,841 million worth of goods to the UK and imported £1,855 million from the UK.

Tourism. Tourism in both summer and winter is important to the economy, and is equivalent to some 15% of merchandise exports.

COMMUNICATIONS

Railways
There are 3,133 miles/5,045 km of railways, of which 1,788 miles/2,879 km are electrified.

Roads
There are 43,829 miles/70,578 km of roads.

Aviation
Crossair and Swissair provide international services (main airports are at Geneva and Basel-Mulhouse).

Shipping
There are 40 miles/65 km of inland waterways, ie the Rhine, from Basel, the major inland port, to Rheinfeden and from Schaffhausen to Bodensee. The merchant marine has 23 ships of 1,000 GRT or over. Freight loaded: (1987) 342,595 tons/310,800 tonnes; unloaded: 8.7 million tons/7.9 million tonnes.

Telecommunications
There are 5.8 million telephones and excellent domestic, international and broadcast services. There are 2.5 million radios and 2.3 million televisions (1989). The privately-owned Swiss Broadcasting Corporation fulfils certain public broadcasting functions on behalf of the government, and has separate operations to provide radio and TV broadcasts in French (RTSR), German and Romansch (DRS) and Italian (RTSI). Swiss Radio International broadcasts on short-wave worldwide in nine languages.

EDUCATION AND WELFARE

Education
Compulsory and free at primary level. It is administered by the cantons, with costs met either by communes, or by cantons and communes.
School population. 133,000 pupils in nursery schools; 375,000 in primary schools; 314,000 pupils in secondary schools.
Universities. There are seven universities.
Literacy. 99%.

Health
18,400 doctors; 37,500 nurses; 4,700 dentists; 432 hospitals.

SYRIA
al-Jumhuriya al-Arabya as-Suriya
(Syrian Arab Republic)

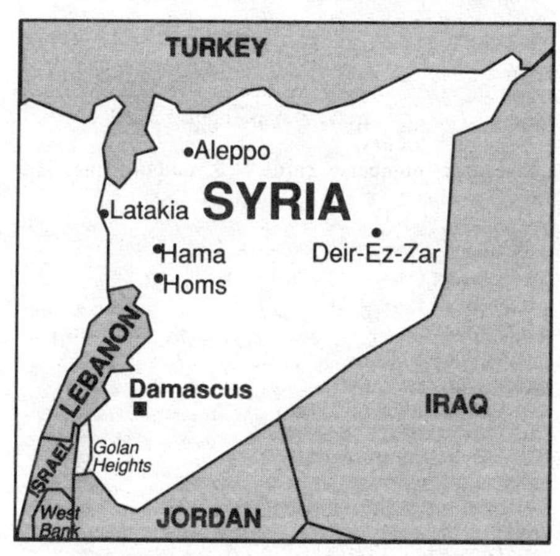

GEOGRAPHY

Situated in the Middle East, on the far east coast of the Mediterranean, the Syrian Arab Republic covers a total area of 71,480 miles^2/185,180 km^2 divided into 14 governorates or mohofazats. Syria's tripartite physiographic profile consists of the western coastal strip (well watered from subterranean sources, intensely cultivated and densely populated), the interior mountain ranges (Jabal Alawite and al-Jabal ash-Sharqi, divided by the River Orontes) and the eastern reaches of the Syrian Desert, traversed north-west to south-east by the Euphrates River. Irrigation projects such as the Euphrates Dam (in the north-east) have rendered hitherto barren terrain cultivable and agriculturally useful. Jesh Sheikh (Mount Hermon) on the Lebanese border is Syria's highest peak at 9,232 ft/2,814 m elevation. 28% of the land is arable and 3% is forested.

Climate
Mediterranean on the coast with hot, dry summers and mild, moist winters. Rainfall increases in the mountainous interior but decreases again in the eastern semi-desert where annual rainfall is frequently below 8 in/200 mm. Summer temperatures may rise to between 109–120°F/43–49°C in the desert zones, augmented by the hot khamsin wind, blowing from the east. Damascus: Jan. 45°F/7°C. July 81°F/27°C. Average annual rainfall 8.9 in/225 mm. Aleppo: Jan. 43°F/6.1°C. July 83°F/28.3°C. Average annual rainfall 15.8 in/401 mm.

Cities and towns

Damascus (capital)	1,112,214
Aleppo	985,413
Homs	346,871
Latakia	196,791
Hama	177,208

Population
Total population is 12,010,564, plus 10,500 Jewish settlers in the Golan Heights. 49.1% of the population live in urban areas. Population density is 168.1 persons per mile^2/64.9 per km^2. Ethnic divisions: 90.3% Arab; 9.7% Kurds, Armenians, Turks, Circassians and Assyrians.
Birth rate 4.4%. **Death rate** 0.6%. **Rate of population**

increase (1980–87) 3.6%. **Age distribution** under 15 = 48.1%; over 65 = 2.8%. **Life expectancy** female 67; male 63; average 65.

Religion
74% Sunni Muslim; 16% Alawite; Druse and other Muslim sects. 10% of the population are Christians, including Greek, Syrian and Armenian Catholics, adherents of the Greek, Syrian and Armenian Orthodox Doctrines and a number of other Protestant denominations. There are also small Jewish and Yezide communities.

Language
Arabic is the official language (spoken by 89% of the total population). Kurdish, Armenian, Aramaic, Circassian, French and English are also spoken.

HISTORY

Although the area which now comprises modern Syria has been incorporated into the Assyrian, Babylonian, Persian and Greek empires, its heritage as an independent state can be traced to the 7th-century Umayyad caliphate. In 634 AD Syria was captured from the Byzantine Empire by followers of the Prophet Mohammad, and in the 660s AD, Muawiyah, the governor of Damascus, became the fifth Caliph, or leader, of the Muslim community. Damascus became the capital and Syria the hub of an empire which expanded to Spain and India. The Christian majority at that time were largely unaffected by their Muslim rulers. With the overthrow of the Umayyad dynasty in 750 AD by the Abbasids and the removal of the capital to Baghdad, Syria became vulnerable to attack. The rule of the Shi'ite Fatimid dynasty of Egypt in the 10th century did however produce tensions between Syrian Muslim and Christian communities. Christian states established by western European crusaders in Syria and neighbouring Palestine in the 11th century proved short-lived as Salah al-din (Saladin) won military supremacy (1187–1193) and established stronger government in Syria as well as in Egypt.

Under the control of the Ottoman Empire (1516–1918) autonomy was given to local governors and various religious groups. Syria was not however governed as one province, but included Aleppo and Damascus as competing regional centres. The concept of Arab nationalism developed under Ottoman rule and upon the Empire's demise after World War I, Amir Faisal called for a sovereign and free Syria with himself as the constitutional monarch. The victorious European powers however placed the country under French mandatory authority at the San Remo Conference in Apr. 1920. The French divided Syria into several zones: Alexandretta for the Turks, Jabal Druze for the Druse with the majority Sunni Muslims separated between Aleppo and Damascus.

Resistance to French rule in the form of riots and strikes occurred until full independence was achieved in 1946 under an elected nationalist government led by Pres. Shukri al-Kuwatly. After coming under military rule in Dec. 1949, Syria's first indigenous constitution was drafted which protected the rights of all citizens, although the president was required to be a Muslim, and Islamic law was established as the foundation of state law. The transition was not easy and the numerous coups of the 1950s and 1960s undermined constitutional political structures. An important development in 1953 was the establishment of the Arab Socialist Renaissance Party (Ba'ath) which resulted from the merger of Akram Hourani's Arab Socialist party and the Arab Renaissance (Ba'ath) party led by Michel Aflaq and Salah Bitar. The Ba'ath party's political stance emphasized social and economic reform, greater Arab unity through a form of pan-Arabism and the recognition of the relationship between Islam and Arabism whilst promoting religious tolerance. After a period in government in 1956 and the abortive formation of the United Arab Republic with Egypt in 1958, a Ba'athist-supported junta seized control in 1963 and the Ba'ath party has dominated Syrian politics ever since. The military wing of the party, led by Hafez al-Assad, seized power in Nov. 1970. The domination of the majority Sunni populace by Assad's own Alawite community has remained a focus of tension.

Within the legislature, (People's Council), the state-approved National Front embraces shades of opinion including Arab socialists, Communists and trade unionists, all of whom are appointed by the president. Under the provisions of the 1973 constitution, the president also selects the prime minister and cabinet and may dismiss the Peoples' Council at any time.

One of the most serious challenges to Ba'athist political dominance in recent years has come from Sunni Islamic fundamentalists Between 1976 and 1982, attacks by the Muslim Brotherhood were common in major urban centres. In Feb. 1982, the Brotherhood staged an ambitious but ultimately unsuccessful uprising in the city of Hanna. From the mid-1970s, Syria has been increasingly involved in Lebanon. Several factors underline this, most notably the widespread view that Lebanon as a whole, especially the non-Christian territories included by the French in 1920 were essentially part of Syria; and also Syria's dependence on Lebanese ports and its antipathy towards Israel. Syria intervened militarily in 1976 at the time of the Lebanese civil war (officially as the 'Arab Deterrent Force'). Syria's fear of Israeli aggrandizement and its opposition to the Israeli presence from Lebanon has led to tension with the United States. Its relations with the Palestine Liberation Organization have also been strained, in part due to its sponsorship of Damascus-based radical factions opposed to the 'moderate' approach of Yasser Arafat. In Feb. 1987 a large-scale military operation consisting of some 7,000 Syrian troops, supported by tanks and artillery, was launched in an effort to end the fighting in Beirut. This intervention brought some respite but has raised questions as to the long-term directions of Syrian policy in Lebanon. Syria's presence in the country came under direct attack in 1989 when the Christian leader, Gen. Michel Aoun, launched a 'war of liberation' in an effort to drive them out.

CONSTITUTION AND GOVERNMENT

Executive and legislature
The executive president is elected directly every seven years, and appoints the vice-presidents and the council of ministers. The legislature, the 195-member People's Assembly, is elected for a four-year term on a constituency basis; there is universal adult suffrage and voting is compulsory. Elections were last held in Feb. 1986. In practice, political power is to a great extent in the hands of the Ba'ath Party's regional command.

Present government
President Lt.-Gen. Hafez al-Assad

Vice-Presidents Abdel Halim Khaddam, Zuheir Masharqa
Prime Minister Mahmoud Zubi
Other Principal Members of the Cabinet Gen. Mustafa Tlass (Deputy Prime Minister; Defence); Dr Salim Yassin (Deputy Prime Minister for Economic Affairs); Mahmud Qaddur (Deputy Prime Minister for Public Affairs); Dr Mohammad Harbah (Interior); Dr Mohammad al-Imadi (Economy and Foreign Trade); Farooq ash-Shar' (Foreign Affairs); Khaled al-Mahayni (Finance); Khalid Ansari (Justice).

Ruling Party
Arab Socialist Renaissance (Ba'ath) Party. **Secretary-general** Lt.-Gen. Hafez al-Assad. **Assistant secretary-general** Abdullah al-Ahmar. **Assistant regional secretary-general** Zuheir Masharqa.

Justice
The system of law is based on a combination of Islamic law and the French civil code. The highest appeal court is the Court of Cassation in Damascus, and there are appeal courts also in each of the 14 provinces. At local level, justices of the peace operate in summary courts in each sub-district, and there are separate district courts for civil and for criminal cases. The death penalty is in force. There were 31 executions between 1985 and mid-1988. Offences: espionage, rape of minors, murder, incitement to commit murder, drug-trafficking.

National symbols
Flag. Three horizontal stripes of red, white and black with two five-pointed stars in the white stripe.
Festivals. 8 Mar. (Revolution Day); 23 July (Egypt's Revolution Day); 1 Sept. (Union of Syria, Egypt and Libya); 6 Oct. (Beginning of October War); 16 Nov. (National Day).
Vehicle registration plate. SYR.

INTERNATIONAL RELATIONS

Affiliations
NAM; OPEC; OAPEC; ICO; Arab League.

Defence
Total Armed Forces: 404,000. Terms of service: conscription, 30 months. Reserves: 272,500 (to age 45).
Army: 300,000; 4,050 main battle tanks (T-54/-55, T-62M/K, T-72/-72M).
Navy: 4,000; three submarines (Soviet Romeo); two frigates (Soviet Petya); 18 patrol and coastal combatants.
Air Force: 40,000; 448 combat aircraft (mainly Su-7/-22, MiG-17/-25/-25U, MiG-21PF/PFMA/bis, MiG-23MF); 148 armed helicopters.
Air Defence Command: 60,000.

ECONOMY

Currency
The unit is the Syrian pound, divided into 100 piasters.

National finance
Budget. The 1988 budget, in US$, was for expenditure of 4,600 million. Main items of expenditure are defence 38.9%; education 9.4%.
Balance of payments. The balance of payments, in US$ (current account, 1987) was a deficit of 1,365 million.
Inflation. About 70%.

Gross Domestic Product
Estimated total GDP US$23,990 million, per capita US$1,962 (overall size of economy ranking 54 in the world).
Economically active population. The total number of persons active in the economy was 2,400,000; unemployed: 5.0%.

Sector	% of workforce	% of GDP
industry	32	19
agriculture	32	27
services*	36	54

* services figure includes elements unassigned to other categories.

Energy and mineral resources
Oil and gas. 14.9 million tons/13.5 million tonnes of crude oil were produced in 1988. Gas production: (1983) 2,676.8 million ft^3/75.8 million m^3.
Minerals. Phosphates; chrome; manganese ore; asphalt; iron ore; rock salt; marble; gypsum.
Electricity. Capacity: 2.6 million kW: production: 9,173 kWh; 790 kWh per capita.

Bioresources
Agriculture. Although land is subject to deforestation, overgrazing, soil erosion and desertification, agricultural output increased in 1988. 28% of the land is put to arable use.
Crop production: (1987) cotton 386,907 tons/351,000 tonnes; wheat 1.8 million tons/1.6 million tonnes; barley 634,925 tons/576,000 tonnes; tobacco; olives; sugar beet.
Livestock numbers: sheep 12.7 million; goats 1.6 million; cattle 710,000; asses 184,000.
Fisheries. Total catch: (1986) 5,291 tons/4,800 tonnes.

Industry and commerce
Industry. The industrial sector is largely government-controlled. Major industries are textiles; food processing; beverages; tobacco; phosphate rock; mining; petroleum; cement.
Commerce. Exports: (f.o.b. 1987 est.) US$1,300 million or 6.4% of GDP, including petroleum; textiles; fruit; phosphates. Major trading partners are Italy; Romania; USSR; US; Iran; France. Imports: (f.o.b. 1987) US$2,700 million, mainly machinery; foodstuffs; beverages; crude oil. Major trading partners are Iran; West Germany; USSR; France; East Germany; Libya; US.
Trade with UK. 1988 exports to the UK totalled £36.1 million; imports from the UK totalled £24.6 million.
Tourism. 1.1 million visitors (1986).

COMMUNICATIONS

Railways
There are 2,716 miles/4,374 km of railways.

Roads
There are some 18,009 miles/29,000 km of roads, of which 13,225 miles/21,296 km are bituminized.

Aviation
Syrian Arab Airlines (Syrianair) provides domestic and international services (main airport is at Damascus). Passengers: (1986) 458,600.

Shipping
The 417 miles/672 km of inland waterways have little economic importance. The major ports are Tartous,

Latakia and Baniyas on the Mediterranean coast. The merchant marine consists of 14 ships of 1,000 GRT or over. Freight loaded: (1986) 8.5 million tons/7.7 million tonnes; unloaded: 10.9 million tons/9.9 million tonnes.

Telecommunications

There are 512,600 telephones and a fair telecommunications system which is currently undergoing significant improvement. There are 2.5 million radios and 600,000 televisions (1985). Radio and television broadcasting are both state-controlled; external service radio broadcasts include programmes in about a dozen languages.

EDUCATION AND WELFARE

Education

Primary education (from 6–12 years) is officially compulsory.

School population. 2.02 million primary school children; 84,000 secondary school children (1986).

Schools. 9,000 primary schools, with some 78,000 teachers.

Universities. Four universities, with some 135,000 students.

Health

There are about 200 hospitals, with some 12,300 beds (one bed per 850 people). There are some 6,800 doctors; 2,000 dentists; 10,300 nurses and midwives.

TAIWAN

Chung-hua Min-kuo

(Republic of China – formerly Formosa*)*

GEOGRAPHY

Located approximately 81 miles/130 km off the southeast coast of mainland China, the island republic of Taiwan (comprising Taiwan island, the P'eng-hu Lien-tao Islands to the west, Lau Hsu and Lu Tao to the east, Quemoy, Matzu and a few smaller islands to the north) covers a total area of 13,965 miles^2/36,179 km^2, divided into 16 counties (hsien). Taiwan island itself is dominated by a north-south mountainous region occupying two-thirds of the total surface area, rising in the east to 13,113 ft/3,997 m (Taiwan's highest point) at Hsin-kao Shan in the Yu Shan range. The fertile, cultivated and densely populated lowlands lie on the western side of the island, irrigated by several rivers including the Cho-Shui. Forests cover 55% of the territory.

Climate

Tropical monsoon type, similar to southern China. Hot and humid, with abundant rainfall May-Sept. Rainfall above 79 in/2,000 mm on low-lying land, increasing with altitude. Midsummer typhoons bring additional heavy rain. Rainfall decreases during the cooler winter months. Taipei: Jan. 59.5°F/15.3°C. July 84.6°F/29.2°C. Average annual rainfall 98 in/2,500 mm.

Cities and towns

Taipei (capital)	2,367,100
Kaohsiung	1,342,797
Taichung	715,107
Tainan	656,927
Panchiao	506,220

Population

Total population is 19,700,000 of which 72.1% live in urban areas. High population density: 1,410 persons per mile^2/545.3 per km^2, reaching a higher density in the western basins. Approximately 84% of the population are Taiwanese (Han Chinese extraction) and 2 million mainland Chinese. In addition there are an estimated 332,169 aboriginals.

Birth rate 1.59%. **Death rate** 0.49%. **Rate of population increase** 1.1%. **Age distribution** under 15 = 29.6%; over 60 = 8.2%. **Life expectancy** female 75.8; male 70.8; average 73.

Religion

2.05 million Taoists (including 23,430 priests); 3.56 million Buddhists (5,860 priests); 477,650 Protestants; 291,592 Catholics.

Language

Mandarin (northern Chinese) is the official language. South Fukien Chinese and Taiwanese dialects are commonly spoken. Hakka dialects, a form of 'Hokkien', and various aboriginal tongues are also used.

HISTORY

Taiwan, also identified as Formosa, was originally inhabited by Malayo-Polynesian aborigines. Europeans exploited its strategic value during the 15th century, but towards the end of the 17th century the island was brought under the political control of mainland China. Large numbers of Chinese immigrants from Fujian and Guangdong provinces were encouraged to settle on the island.

China's defeat in the 1894–95 Sino–Japanese War meant that Taiwan was ceded to Japan. The Chinese inhabitants objected and declared Taiwan a republic, which the Japanese subdued by force. As well as establishing Taiwan as an important military base, the Japanese also promoted educational and economic development, thereby establishing the foundations for Taiwan's recent economic success.

Following Japan's defeat in World War II in 1945, the island reverted back to China. The Taiwanese, however, revolted against Chinese Nationalist rule in Feb. 1947. Claiming that the revolt was Communist-initiated, the Chinese brutally suppressed the rebellion and introduced a series of repressive security measures.

As the Chinese Communists occupied the mainland, the Nationalist Kuomintang (KMT) forces under Generalissimo Chiang Kai-shek fled en masse to Taiwan in late 1949, establishing the Republic of China (ROC). Chiang maintained that the Communists had usurped the Nationalists' rightful authority over the whole of China. The ROC occupied the China seat in the United Nations.

Chiang imposed martial law in 1949 to guard against the threat of internal communist subversion. Opposition parties were banned and the mainland Chinese-dominated KMT assumed control of all governmental organs. At the same time, the Nationalists concentrated on the economic development of the island economy which, with the support of heavy economic and military aid from the United States, rapidly expanded.

The US announced in Jan. 1951 that it recognized the Nationalist Chinese government in Taiwan as the only legal representative of China, and until 1960 the US succeeded in having discussion of the Chinese UN membership question deferred. From 1961 onwards the question of the admission of the People's Republic of China (PRC, communist China) was, at the insistence of the US, judged to be an 'important' one to be decided upon only by a two-thirds majority in accordance with the UN Charter. However, in Oct. 1971 the General Assembly adopted by 76 votes to 35 (with 17 abstentions) an Albanian resolution appointing the PRC to the Chinese seat in all its functions and to exclude the Taiwan government, as having usurped these rights, from the organization.

Following the improvement in relations between the US and the PRC in 1972, the US reduced its forces on and around the island. Eventually, on 1 Jan. 1979, the US formally recognized the PRC, announcing at the same time that it would give Taiwan a year's notice that their two countries' mutual defence agreement was being terminated. That April the US Congress passed as law the Taiwan Relations Act which, in the absence of diplomatic relations and a defence treaty, provided for Taiwan's security.

Chiang Kai-shek died in 1975 and was replaced as KMT leader by his son the prime minister Gen. Chiang Ching-kuo and as president by Dr Yen Chia-kan. In 1978, Dr Yen retired and Gen. Chiang became president, a post to which he was re-elected for a second six-year term in Mar. 1984. In Sept. 1986 the opposition Democratic Progress Party (DPP) was formed. The formation of the DPP contravened Taiwan's martial law regulations, but although technically illegal it was allowed to contest elections to the Legislative Yuan and the National Assembly in Dec. 1986. Pres. Chiang announced in July 1987 the lifting of martial law and its replacement by a new National Security Law. During 1987–88 the government started to encourage the opening of informal relations with the PRC.

Pres. Chiang Ching-kuo died in Jan. 1988, and, in accordance with the constitution, was immediately succeeded by Lee Teng-hui, hitherto vice-president. Pres. Lee was the first native Taiwanese to be appointed head of state. Yu Kuo-hwa, the last remaining political leader with direct ties to Chiang Kai-shek, resigned as prime minister in May 1989; he was replaced by Lee Huan, the secretary-general of the KMT. Lee Huan was replaced in his KMT position in June by James Soong. The results of national elections held in Dec. 1989 constituted a serious setback for the KMT which lost control in central and local seats to the opposition democratic Progressive Party.

CONSTITUTION AND GOVERNMENT

Executive and legislature

Executive power is exercised by a president, elected indirectly (for a six-year term) by the 940-delegate National Assembly. The president appoints the cabinet or Executive Yuan (council), which is headed by the premier. Legislative authority is nominally vested in the National Assembly, but in fact exercised principally by the highest legislative body, the 312-member Legislative Yuan (last election 6 Dec. 1986, but most members hold lifetime seats as nominal representatives of mainland China constituencies). The three other councils in the five-council structure of government are the Judicial Yuan, Examination Yuan and Control Yuan. Martial law, imposed in 1949, was revoked in July 1987. The one-party regime was relaxed in 1989 to allow the formation of opposition parties.

Present government

President of the Republic Lee Teng-hui
Premier Lee Huan
Vice-Premier Shih Chi-yang
Secretary-General of Executive Yuan Robert C. Chien
Other principal ministers Hsu Shui-teh (Interior); Lien Chan (Foreign Affairs); Cheng Wei-yuan (National Defence); Ms Shirley Kuo (Finance); Chen Li-an (Economic Affairs).

Ruling party

Kuomintang. **Chairman** Lee Teng-hui. **Secretary-General** James Soong.

Administration

The government of Taiwan is derived from that which ruled the Chinese mainland before 1949. It maintains its claim to legal jurisdiction of this lost territory. Within this framework, Taiwan is considered a province, with a provincial assembly and provincial governor.

Justice

The death penalty is in force. There were over 17 executions between 1985 and mid-1988. Offences were murder; robbery; rape; narcotics- and firearms-trafficking.

National symbols

Flag. Red, with blue quarter at top next to staff, bearing a twelve-pointed white sun.
Festivals. 1 Jan. (Founding of the Republic); 29 Mar. (Youth Day); 8 June (28 May in 1990, Dragon Boat Festival); 28 Sept. (Teacher's Day – birthday of

Confucius); 10 Oct. (Double Tenth Day, anniversary of 1911 revolution); 25 Oct. (Retrocession Day, anniversary of end of Japanese occupation); 31 Oct. (birthday of Chiang Kai-shek); 12 Nov. (birthday of Sun Yat-sen); 25 Dec. (Constitution Day).
Vehicle registration plate. RC.

INTERNATIONAL RELATIONS

Affiliations

None: UN membership ceased 1971.

Defence

Total Armed Forces: 405,500. Terms of service: two years. Reserves: 1,657,000.
Army: 270,000; 309 main battle tanks (M-48A5); 275 light tanks (M-24).
Navy: 35,500; four submarines (NI model Zwaardvis, US Guppy II); 36 principal surface combatants: 26 destroyers (US *Gearing*, US *Sumner*, US *Fletcher*), 10 frigates (US *Lawrence/Crosley*, US *Rudderow*). 69 patrol and coastal combatants.
Naval Air: 12 armed helicopters.
Marines: 30,000.
Air Force: 70,000; some 500 combat aircraft (F-5E, F-5F, F-104G); no armed helicopters.

ECONOMY

Currency

The unit is the New Taiwan dollar, divided into 100 cents.

National finance

Budget. The 1988 FY budget, in US$, was for expenditure of 17,200 million and revenue of 17,200 million.
Balance of payments. The balance of payments, in US$ (current account, 1987) was a surplus of 17,917 million.
Inflation. 4.0%.

Gross Domestic Product

Estimated total GDP US$91,700 million (GNP), per capita US$4,325 (overall size of economy ranking 27 in the world).
Economically active population The total number of persons active in the economy was 7,880,000; unemployed: 2.0%.

Sector	% of workforce
industry	41
agriculture	20
services*	39

* services figure includes elements unassigned to other categories.

Energy and mineral resources

Minerals. There are small deposits of coal; natural gas; limestone; marble; asbestos. Coal output: (1987) 1.7 million tons/1.5 million tonnes; natural gas 37,327 million ft^3/1,057 million m^3.
Electricity. Capacity: (1988) 16.7 million kW; production: 65,000 million kWh; 3,250 kWh per capita. There are three nuclear power stations, and a fourth is planned.

Bioresources

Agriculture. The importance of agriculture to the economy is steadily declining as the industrial sector continues to thrive. 24% of the land is put to arable use; 5% is meadow and pasture.
Crop production: (1987) rice 2.1 million tons/ 1.9 million tonnes; sweet potatoes 380,294 tons/ 345,000 tonnes; sugar cane 5.7 million tons/5.2 million tonnes; bananas 224,869 tons/204,000 tonnes; pineapples; citrus fruit; peanuts.
Livestock numbers: (1987) pigs 7.1 million; goats 207,000; cattle 171,000.
Forestry. Some 55% of the island is forest and woodland. Timber production (1987) 14,450,489 ft^3/ 409,200 m^3.
Fisheries. Catch: (1987) 1,362,630 tons/1,236,170 tonnes.

Industry and commerce

Industry. Main industries are textiles; clothing; chemicals; electronics; food processing; plywood; sugar milling; cement; shipbuilding; petroleum.
Commerce. Exports: (f.o.b. 1988) US$59,000 million, or 64% of GNP; textiles 20.5%; electrical machinery 19%; general machinery and equipment 9%; basic metals and metal products 7%; foodstuffs 5.4%. Main trading partners US 39%; Japan 14%.
Trade with UK. Taiwan imported UK goods worth £355,786,000 in 1988; exports to the UK totalled £1,150 million.
Tourism. 1.7 million tourists visited Taiwan in 1987.

COMMUNICATIONS

Railways

There are 1,661 miles/2,675 km of railways.

Roads

There are 12,386 miles/19,946 km of roads, most of which are asphalt-paved.

Aviation

China Air Lines Ltd provides domestic and international services and Far Eastern Air Transport Corpn provides domestic services and charter flights (two international airports are at Taoyuan and Kaohsiung). Passengers: (1987) 12.4 million.

Shipping

The marine ports are Kao-hsiung, Chi-lung, Hua-lien, Su-ao and T'ai-tung. The merchant marine has 216 ships of 1,000 GRT or over. Freight loaded: (1987) 20 million tons/18.1 million tonnes; unloaded: 88 million tons/80 million tonnes.

Telecommunications

Taiwan has 6 million telephones and the best developed system in Asia apart from Japan's, with extensive microwave transmission links on east and west coasts. There are 8 million radios and 6 million television sets. There are three TV companies and over 30 radio companies, including three main national operations; the Broadcasting Corporation of China (BCC), based in Taipei, runs seven domestic radio networks, as well as external services in 15 languages.

EDUCATION AND WELFARE

Education

Education is free and compulsory between the ages of six and 15.
School population. (1988) 2,472 primary schools with some 76,000 teachers and 2.4 million pupils. Pupil-teacher ratio 31:1. 1,059 secondary schools with some 78,700 teachers and 1.7 million students.

Universities. 39 universities and colleges, with 465,000 students.
Literacy. 94%.

Health

88 public hospitals, with 31,500 beds (one per 642 people); 817 private hospitals with 46,500 beds. 78,600 medical personnel.

TANZANIA

Jamhuri ya Muungano wa Tanzania
(United Republic of Tanzania)

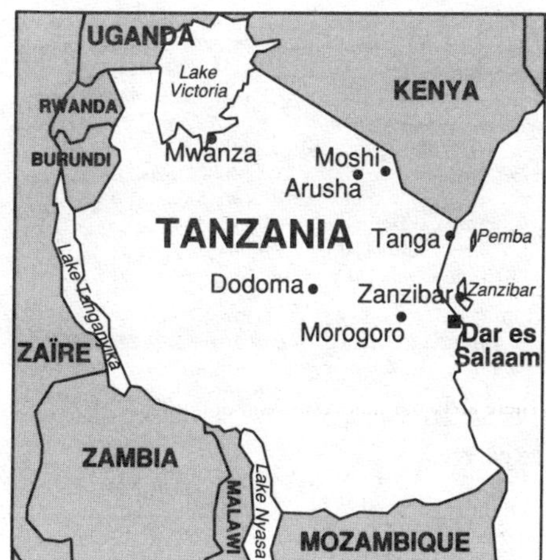

Climate

Equatorial, subject to variation according to altitude. There are three principal climatic zones in Tanzania. High temperatures in coastal regions (average 79.9°F/26.6°C) accompany high humidity levels which lessen considerably on the semi-arid central plateau. Coastal rainfall (39.4 in/1,000 mm) decreases inland to 9.8 in/250 mm, the greater part of which falls Dec.-May. Above 4,921 ft/1,500 m, semi-temperate conditions prevail with perennial snowcover on the higher peaks and even distribution of precipitation. Dodoma: Jan. 75°F/23.9°C. July 66.9°F/19.4°C. Average annual rainfall 22.5 in/572 mm. Dar es Salaam: Jan. 59.8°F/27.8°C. July 73.9°F/23.3°C. Average annual rainfall 41.9 in/1,064 mm.

Cities and towns

Dar es Salaam (capital)	757,346
Zanzibar	110,669
Mwanza	110,611
Tanga	103,409

GEOGRAPHY

Situated just south of the equator on the east African coast, Tanzania covers a total area of 364,805 miles²/945,090 km² of which c.20,458 miles²/c.53,000 km² is inland water and 1,100 miles²/2,850 km² island territory (Zanzibar, Pemba and Matia). The long coastal sandbars and reefs are interspersed with mangrove swamps where the Pangini, Mandera, Mbemkuku and Rufiji rivers empty into the Indian Ocean. Inland, the narrow coastal lowland climbs to a mean elevation of 3,280 ft/1,000 m on the central plateau which forms part of the upland complex stretching north-south from Mount Kilimanjaro (19,340 ft/5,895 m), the highest mountain in Africa, to the Ulugura mountains west of Dar es Salaam and the southern-lying Kipengere and Livingstone ranges. The Rift system divides into two branches at a point just north of Lake Nyasa on the Malawi/Mozambique border. To the east of Lake Victoria in the north, the eastern arm of the Rift Valley traverses the length of the country containing Lakes Natron, Manyara and Eyasi, and the Serengeti National Park, while the western branch skirts the Zaïrean border containing Lakes Tanganyika and Rukwa. Population distribution is affected by the semi-arid conditions in some northern regions and by the predominance of the tsetse fly in western central areas. Rural concentrations are found on the fertile shores of Lake Victoria, along river valleys and in the highlands. Only 5% of the land is arable and 47% is forested.

Population

Total population is 25,206,263 of which 17.9% live in urban areas. Population density is 69 persons per mile²/26.2 per km². 99% of the population is of indigenous Bantu extraction (including an estimated 21.1% Nyamwezi and Sukuma, 8.8% Swahili, 6.9% Hehet and Bena, 5.9% Makonde and 5.9% Haya). The remaining 1% consists of Asian, European and Arab minorities.
Birth rate 5.0%. **Death rate** 1.6%. **Rate of population increase** (1980–87) 3.3%. **Age distribution** under 15 = 48.6%; over 65 = 2.3%. **Life expectancy** female 55; male 51; average 53.

Religion

Approximately 33% of the mainland population are Christian (Roman Catholic, Anglican and Lutheran) and a similar proportion pursue traditional animist beliefs. A further 33% are Muslim. The religiously affiliated population of Zanzibar is almost exclusively Muslim with a 4% Hindu minority.

Language

Kiswahili and English are the official languages. English is used primarily for commercial, administrative and educative purposes. Swahili facilitates inter-tribal communication, bonding the main Bantu-, Nilotic- and Cushitic-speaking peoples.

HISTORY

In the 1st millenium BC Caucasoid peoples, probably southern Cushites from Ethiopia, inhabited northern Tanganyika and subsequently spread to southern regions. In the period up to 500 AD, small groups of iron-using and Bantu-speaking peoples from west Africa settled there. By the end of the lst century AD, trading contacts existed between Arabia, the East African coasts and possibly India.

Until the arrival of the Portuguese in the late 15th century, the coastal trading centres were mainly Arab settlements. The Portuguese gradually undermined the position of the Arabs along the coast, but made little effort to explore the interior, where Arab traders extended their search for slaves, particularly in the south-east towards Lake Nyasa. In the 1840s the Portuguese did venture towards Lake Tanganyika and established trading centres. At the same time German colonizers began to show an interest and Tanganyika was declared a German colony in 1884.

During World War I the German colonial possessions were occupied by the British and at the end of the war a League of Nations mandate gave Tanganyika over to British administration. The British retained control, after World War II, in what was now designated a UN Trust Territory. In pre-independence elections in Sept. 1960, the Tanganyika African National Union (TANU) won 70 of the 71 parliamentary seats. Tanganyika gained its independence on 9 Dec. 1961 under the leadership of Dr Julius Nyerere, who in the first year of independence concentrated on the party leadership, but who was then elected (Dec. 1962) by an overwhelming majority to be the first president of the Republic of Tanganyika.

Zanzibar, an island off the coast of the mainland, which had been a British protectorate since 1890, became an independent sultanate in Dec. 1963. Following an armed uprising by the Afro-Shirazi party in Jan. 1964, the Sultan was deposed and a republic proclaimed. In Apr. 1964, the new government signed the Act of Union with Tanganyika, which gave rise to the formal creation of Tanzania in Oct. 1964.

Tanzania effectively became a one-party state in July 1965, although TANU and the Afro-Shirazi Party did not formally amalgamate to form Chama Cha Mapinduzi (CCM – the Revolutionary Party of Tanzania) until Feb. 1977.

Pres. Nyerere, who was re-elected in 1965, 1970, 1975 and 1980, finally stepped down in Nov. 1985, but remained as CCM chairman. The Vice-President and President of Zanzibar, Ali Hassan Mwinyi, was elected in Oct. 1986 to succeed Nyerere as president of Tanzania. Nyerere was re-elected as CCM chairman in Oct. 1987 with a large majority and it was reported that he was continuing in office to pursue the cause of the traditional socialists against the pragmatist supporters of the new president.

Under Dr Nyerere Tanzania maintained support for the African liberation movements fighting surviving colonial regimes elsewhere in southern Africa. Tanzania also offered military support to the Mozambican government in its war against anti-government guerrillas. When Pres. Amin's forces from neighbouring Uganda invaded Tanzania in 1978, the Tanzanian army repulsed the attack and invaded Uganda in retaliation, only withdrawing in 1981 after the Amin regime had been overthrown. Relations remained strained with neighbouring Kenya, particularly after the dissolution of the East Africa Federation in 1977, and the border between the two countries was not reopened for six years.

CONSTITUTION AND GOVERNMENT

Executive and legislature

The executive president is nominated by the ruling party and elected by direct popular vote for a five-year term, renewable once only; last presidential election Oct. 1985. The president appoints two vice-presidents, one of whom is the president of Zanzibar and the other the prime minister of the Union government. The president, in consultation with the prime minister, appoints the cabinet. The unicameral National Assembly, serving a normal five-year term, has 243 members (118 directly elected from the mainland, 50 from Zanzibar, 25 ex-officio, 15 nominated and 35 indirectly elected). All candidates must be approved by the party. Last legislative elections Oct. 1985.

Present government

President; Minister of Defence and National Service Ali Hassan Mwinyi

First Vice-President; Prime Minister Joseph Warioba

Second Vice-President; President of Zanzibar Idris Abdul-Wakil

Principal Members of the Cabinet Rashidi Mfaume Kawawa (Without Portfolio); Steven A. Kiboua (Finance); Benjamin Mkapa (Foreign Affairs); Nalaila Kiula (Home Affairs); Damian Lubuva (Attorney-General).

Ruling party

Revolutionary Party of Tanzania (Chama Cha Mapinduzi). **Chairman** Dr Julius Nyerere. **Vice-Chairman** Ali Hassan Mwinyi. **Secretary-general** Rashidi Kawawa.

Justice

The system of law is based on English common law. The highest legal officer is the Chief Justice, who is head of the Court of Appeal and of the judiciary department. The judicial review of legislation is limited to matters of interpretation. At local level there are Primary Courts, District and Resident Magistrates' Courts; more serious matters are dealt with in the High Court. The death penalty is in force. There were no executions between 1985 and mid-1988.

National symbols

Flag. The flag is divided into two triangles by a broad black stripe running diagonally from the lower hoist to the upper fly, bordered by two narrow yellow stripes. The triangle in the hoist is green and the other is blue.

Festivals. 12 Jan. (Zanzibar Revolution Day); 26 Apr. (Union Day); 1 May (International Labour Day); 9 Dec. (Independence Day).

Vehicle registration plate. EAT or EAZ.

INTERNATIONAL RELATIONS

Affiliations

NAM; OAU; ACP; Commonwealth; SADCC.

Defence

Total Armed Forces: 40,050 (perhaps 20,000 conscripts). Terms of service: national service inclusive civil duties, two years. Reserve: 10,000: armed element of Citizen's Militia.

Army: 38,350; 30 main battle tanks (Ch Type-59); 66 light tanks (Ch Type-62, Scorpion).

Navy: 700; 18 patrol and coastal combatants.

Air Force: 1,000 22 combat aircraft (Ch J-7, Shenyang=J-6/-4).

ECONOMY

Currency

The unit is the shilling, divided into 100 cents.

National finance

Budget. The 1988/89 budget, in US$, was for expenditure of 902 million and revenue of 902 million.
Balance of payments. The balance of payments, in US$ (current account, 1987) was a deficit of 605 million.
Inflation. 29.9%.

Gross Domestic Product

Estimated total GDP US$3,080 million, per capita US$258 (overall size of economy ranking 104 in the world).
Economically active population. The total number of persons active in the economy was 732,200.

Sector	% of workforce	% of GDP
industry	n/a	8
agriculture	90	61
services*	n/a	31

* services figure includes elements unassigned to other categories.

Energy and mineral resources

Oil and gas. There are offshore gas reserves near Songo Songo island and at Kimbiji, and crude petroleum has been discovered off Pemba island. Natural gas is beginning to be exploited. The petroleum refinery at Dar es Salaam has a capacity of 826,725 tons/750,000 tonnes per annum.
Minerals. Phosphates; iron ore; diamonds (reserves estimated at 3.87 million carats 1988); gold; nickel; salt. Coal and tin deposits are large but not exploited to any great extent.
Electricity. Capacity: 401,000 kW; production: 895 million kWh; 35 kWh per capita (1988). More than 70% of electricity is produced by hydroelectric power.

Bioresources

Agriculture. The economy is heavily dependent on agriculture, but activity is limited by lack of water and the tsetse fly. The strength of the Tanzanian economy is linked to international market prices, especially for coffee. 5% of the land is put to arable use, 1% is permanent crops, 40% is meadow and pasture.
Crop production: (1987) maize 2.5 million tons/ 2.3 million tonnes; coffee 56,217 tons/51,000 tonnes; sisal 24,251 tons/22,000 tonnes; tobacco 19,841 tons/ 18,000 tonnes; vegetables; fruit. Most of the world's cloves are grown in Zanzibar (some 9,370 tons/ 8,500 tonnes in 1985). The coconut industry is also important.
Livestock numbers: cattle 14.5 million; goats 6.5 million; sheep 4.5 million; poultry 32 million.
Forestry. Some 40% of the country is woodland and forest. Timber production: (1986) 78.1 million ft^3/ 23.8 million m^3.
Fisheries. Total catch: (1986 est.) 440,920 tons/ 400,000 tonnes.

Industry and commerce

Industry. The industrial sector is limited and consists primarily of agricultural processing (sugar, beer, cigarettes, sisal twine); diamond mining; oil refining; shoes; cement; textiles; fertilizer.
Commerce. Exports: US$411 million (f.o.b 1987) or 8% of GDP. Major exports are coffee; cloves; cotton; sisal; cashew nuts; tobacco; tea; diamonds; coconuts and coconut products; pyrethrum (an insecticide made from chrysanthemums). Main trading partners are West Germany; UK; US; Netherlands; Japan. Imports: (c.i.f. 1987) US$1,500, mainly manufactured goods; machinery; transport equipment; crude oil; foodstuffs. Main trading partners are West Germany; UK; US; Iran; Japan; Italy.
Trade with UK. In 1988 total exports to UK were £26.3 million, total imports from UK were £88.6 million.
Tourism. The tourist industry is expanding. Earnings: (1987) US$15.3 million.

COMMUNICATIONS

Railways

There are some 2,770 miles/4,460 km of railways.

Roads

There are 50,857 miles/81,895 km of roads, of which some 1,987 miles/3,200 km are concrete or bituminized.

Aviation

Air Tanzania Corporation provides domestic and international services (main airport is at Dar es Salaam, 8 miles/13 km from the city centre). Passengers: (1984) 498,000.

Shipping

The major inland waterways are Lake Tanganyika, Lake Victoria and Lake Nyasa. Dar es Salaam, Mtwara, Tanga and Zanzibar are the marine ports. The inland ports are Mwanza on Lake Victoria and Kigoma on Lake Tanganyika. The merchant marine has seven ships of 1,000 GRT or over. Freight loaded: (1985) 699,961 million tons/635,000 million tonnes; unloaded: 2.9 million tons/2.6 million tonnes.

Telecommunications

There are 103,800 telephones and a fair system of open wire, radio relay and troposcatter. There are 2 million radios in Tanzania and 13,000 televisions in Zanzibar; there is no television service on the mainland, although Television Zanzibar has been operative since 1973 and broadcasts in colour. Radio Tanzania, government-run, broadcasts in Swahili as well as its English programme for schools and its external service in English, Afrikaans and various southern African languages.

EDUCATION AND WELFARE

Education

Primary education between the ages of seven and 14 is free and compulsory. There is a government-determined fee for secondary education.
School population. In 1987 there were some 10,300 primary schools, with 3.2 million pupils. Enrolment in primary schools is just over 50% of those eligible; secondary school enrolment is less than 10%.
Universities. The University of Dar es Salaam and the Sokoine University of Agriculture have some 3,500 students between them.
Literacy. 80%.

Health

Medical care is provided by the state and by Christian missions. 152 hospitals, with 22,800 beds (one per 1,100 patients); about 1,065 doctors.

THAILAND

Prathes Thai or *Muang-Thai* (formerly Siam) *(Kingdom of Thailand)*

GEOGRAPHY

Located in the west of the Southeast Asian Indochinese peninsula, Thailand contains a total area of 198,404 miles²/514,000 km² divided into 73 provinces or Changwat. Geographically, the country divides into four sections. To the north, a complex system of forested mountain ranges divided by the precipitous but fertile Ping, Yom, Wang and Nan river valleys, rises to a maximum elevation of 8,510 ft/2,594 m at Doi Inthanon. To the north-east, the Khorat plateau (average 984 ft/300 m elevation) is only sparsely vegetated and largely infertile. Occupying the heartland, the central plains support the bulk of the population and sustain the greater part of the country's agricultural and industrial growth. This fertile terrain consists largely of the Chao Phraya delta flood plain. The mountainous southern provinces, situated on the northern half of the Malay Peninsula, are dominated by dense tropical rainforest and bordered by mangrove-forested islands off the coast. In the north and north-eastern provinces, the River Mekong forms the border with Laos. 34% of the land is arable and 30% is forested.

Climate

Tropical, high temperatures and humidity. Three seasons may be distinguished. The wet season lasts June-Oct., succeeded by a cool season Nov.-Feb. and, subsequently, a hot season Mar.-May. Rainfall varies according to region and increases east to west with altitude from 39.4 in/1,000 mm in the Chao Phraya delta to 118 in/3,000 mm in mountainous areas. Average annual temperatures range from 75 to 86°F/24 to 30°C. Bangkok: Jan. 78°F/25.6°C. July 83°F/28.3°C. Average annual rainfall 55 in/1,400 mm.

Cities and towns

Bangkok (capital)	5,468,915
Songkhla	172,604
Chon Buri	115,350
Nakhon Si Thammarat	102,123
Chiang Mai	101,594

Population

Total population is 55,524,352 of which 19.8% live in urban areas. Population density is 280 persons per mile²/104.7 per km². Ethnic divisions: 75% Thai; 14% Chinese; 11% other, including Khmer and Mon minorities.

Birth rate 2.4%. **Death rate** 0.7%. **Rate of population increase** (1980–87) 1.7%. **Age distribution** under 15 = 36.5%; over 65 = 3.6%. **Life expectancy** female 66; male 63; average 64. Indigenous groups include the Karen (hill people), Semang, Lana and Chao Nam (coastal nomads).

Religion

95.5% of the population adhere to the national religion of Theravada Buddhism. Muslims, Hindus, Sikhs and Christians account for the remaining 4.5%. Confucianism is also prevalent among the Chinese population.

Language

Thai is the official national language, also known as Siamese, belonging to the Tai language family of South East Asia. A number of Chinese dialects, Malay and some English as well as several regional tongues are also spoken.

HISTORY

Between the 7th and the 11th centuries Thai people from northern parts of Burma and from the Yunnan province of China migrated to the fertile Chao Phraya river basin, the heart of modern Thailand.

The establishment of the kingdom of Sukhothai, in AD 1238, in what is today north-central Thailand, signalled a 200-year period of expansion during which Thai identity and culture developed as the influence and power of the neighbouring Khmer empire of Angkor receded. Under the rule of King Ramkamheng, Thai influence expanded southwards in the late 13th and early 14th century. In the mid-14th century a new Thai state, Ayuthia, emerged at a point on the Chao Phraya river, hitherto the locus of a Mon civilization, easily attainable by sea-going ships. Ayuthia not only subsumed Sukhothai, but pursued a successful policy of expansion, conquering Angkor and taking Burmese land to the west, Thai principalities in the north and Malay territories to the south.

In the mid-15th century King Trailok introduced radical changes to the system and nature of government. Previously, the king had been a paternalistic provider, dispensing benefaction and justice to his subjects. During Trailok's reign, the monarch began to be viewed more as a god-king and a concomitant system of hierarchy developed with duties, obligations and loyalties at each level. Through the promulgation of a code of law and the high degree of centralization in the bureaucratic structure of government, administration of the country – and collection of taxes – was greatly increased.

During the 16th century, contact with Europe began to develop via trading links. In 1511, following Portugal's conquest of Malacca, Portuguese missionaries, adventurers and commercial missions began arriving in Siam and, with the emergence of the Dutch as a trading competitor to the Portuguese, Ayuthia soon became entangled in European intrigues and rivalries. During the reign of King Narai (1657–88) a French mission was accepted as a means to counterbalance Portuguese and Dutch expansionist designs. However, fears that the French meant to convert the King and court to Catholicism lead to an anti-Western coup in 1688 which signalled the beginning of a 150-year period during which contact with Europeans was kept to a minimum.

In 1767, following a Burmese invasion, Ayuthia was sacked and a new Thai state was founded at Thonburi by a Chinese noble, Phraya Taskin. Although he succeeded in ousting the Burmese, he was overthrown in 1781 and Chao Phraya Chakri assumed control. Amongst the first of his decisions was to relocate the capital to the nearby settlement of Bangkok. The rule of the first Chakri kings in the 18th and early 19th centuries was marked by attempts to reimpose Siamese (Thailand was then known as Siam) authority over southern Laos, western Cambodia and northern Malaysia.

Under the rule of King Chulalongkorn (Rama V, 1868–1910), a major restructuring of the state was undertaken. The restructuring was motivated partly by economic necessity, especially in an attempt to counter the effects of the Bowring Treaty imposed by Britain in 1855 to break the King's export monopoly. However, the reforms also arose out of the ruling elite's interest in western ideas and technology. It is possible to identify two distinct phases of political re-organization; (i) the Chakri Reformation of 1872–92, when reforms were introduced in finance, communications, transport, education and personnel administration; and (ii) the Radical Reorganization of 1892 when a western-style council of minutes was established. By establishing a modern, bureaucratic monarchy and by yielding Lao and Cambodian territory to France and Malay territory to Britain, King Chulalongkorn managed to maintain Siam as the sole Southeast Asian country to avoid colonial control.

The collapse of the international rice market during the Great Depression of the late 1920s-early 1930s created severe budgetary problems for King Prajadhipok (Rama VII), who responded by making deep cuts in civil service and military spending. In 1932, a European educated civilian-military group carried out a successful and bloodless coup (commonly referred to as a 'revolution'), aimed at removing Siam's absolute monarchical system in favour of a system modelled on the European constitutional monarchies. The ideological leader of the coup was Dr Pridi Phanomyong, and he was accompanied by Col Phahon Phomphayuhasena (representing the older generation of officers) and Maj. (later Field Marshal) Phibun Songkhran (representing the younger generation).

Following the setting up of a constitutional regime, Pridi and Phahon split over the political direction Thailand was to take. This divergence between the civilian radicals and the military came to a head when, soon after the coup, the King dissolved the Assembly, when it appeared that an economic plan emphasizing the nationalization of land would be accepted by the radicals. Aware that the royalists might regain power, however, the military established a conservative constitutionalist regime, headed, ostensibly, by Phahon, despite an abortive royalist counter-coup in 1933.

Phahon introduced into his Cabinet a younger circle of military officers led by Phibun, and they quickly emerged as the country's ruling power bloc. In 1939, Phahon was retired and Phibun was appointed prime minister. He immediately embarked on a militantly anti-Chinese and anti-Western campaign. An admirer of the fascist Führerprinzip, he stressed his position as the powerful leader of a modern society and, in 1939, Siam adopted the more nationalist name of Thailand. The Phibun regime collaborated with the Japanese invasion of Thailand in 1941, declaring war on the Allies early the next year. However, when it became evident that the Axis powers were going to be defeated, Phibun's power base diminished. He was formally overthrown in mid-1944 by a vote of the National Assembly and was replaced by Khuang Apaiwong, a civilian who enjoyed the support of Dr Pridi (who, during the war, had led the Free Thai Movement which had clandestinely co-operated with the Allies). After the Japanese surrender, Seni Pramoj (Thai ambassador to the US at the outbreak of war) replaced Khuang as prime minister.

Post-war economic and political turmoil did much to undermine the ability of the new liberal government to administer the country. Following the mysterious death of King Ananda (Rama VIII) in 1946 and the identification of communism by Western powers as the major threat to regional security, the army seized control in 1947. The next year Phibun again assumed control of the government.

During the 1950s and up to the early 1970s, political power rested predominantly with the military. For nine years, Phibun remained a major influence in the government, balancing the interests of Thai bureaucrats and militarists against the economically powerful Chinese. Following what was seen as only a cosmetic attempt at liberalizing the country, he announced elections in 1957 but so blatantly were they rigged that his government lost credibility and Marshal Sarit Thanarat gained control of the government and became premier in 1958. Sarit called for a restoration of 'old values', including (for the first time since the 1932 Revolution) an appeal for loyalty to the king.

Sarit abandoned Phibun's ostensive policy of liberality and imposed on Thailand an authoritarian regime – abolishing the constitution and elections. US involvement in Vietnam provided an opportunity for economic expansion and Sarit created the environment in which foreign investment and manufacture became attractive. Sarit died in 1963, and his successors, Thanom Kittikachorn and Praphat Charusathien attempted to revive the democratic process by inaugurating a new constitution. In 1969, a partly elected National Assembly was formed.

However, both the constitution and assembly were suspended in 1971.

Discontent over military rule, acute social and regional divides and the withdrawal of the US from Southeast Asia combined to undermine Thanom and Praphat and following student protests and the withdrawal of support by King Bhumibol Adulyadej (Rama IX, 1946–) and the army commander-in-chief, Gen. Krit Siwara, the government collapsed and a democratic government was formed.

During its three-year existence, the democratic interregnum gave free rein to liberal form but little in the way of democratic substance was achieved. Such was the polarization between right and left, that a national consensus was difficult to accomplish and consecutive governments failed to rule with any tangible degree of authority. Following the return from exile of Thanom and the consequent student protests in 1976, the military once again took control of the government and in 1977, Gen. Kriangsak Chamanand became premier.

In 1979, Thai politics and foreign policy initiatives became dominated by Vietnam's invasion and occupation of Kampuchea and the concomitant refugee problem along the Thai–Kampuchea border. Kriangsak remained in power until Mar. 1980 when he was replaced by Gen. Prem Tinsulanond. Prem restored elements of democracy to the governmental structure and, although the military wielded ultimate power, a right-of-centre coalition contributed to the running of the state. Prem defeated two coup attempts, in 1981 and 1985, by a group of young officers nicknamed the 'Young Turks' (after the secret society of officers responsible for the Turkish revolution of 1908). All were aged about 40, and had graduated together from the Chulachomklo Military Academy, in Bangkok. Following a general election in July 1988, Prem stepped down from the premiership when the Chart Thai party secured a majority of seats. In Aug. 1988, Maj.-Gen. Chatichai Choonhaven (the Chart Thai leader) became prime minister and formed his new cabinet on 9 Aug. 1988.

CONSTITUTION AND GOVERNMENT

Executive and legislature

A constitutional monarchy, the head of government is the prime minister, appointed by the king on the advice of the National Assembly. The prime minister governs with the assistance of a Council of Ministers. The bicameral parliament consists of (i) a 261-member Senate appointed by the king on the recommendation of the prime minister and (ii) a 347-member House of Representatives elected for a four year term by adult suffrage of persons 21 or more years old. Martial law remains in force although some powers have been relaxed. Last general election 24 July 1987.

Present government

Head of state, King of Thailand; Head of the Armed Forces Bhumibol Adulyadej (Rama IX)

Prime Minister Maj.-Gen. Chatichai Choonhaven

Deputy Prime Ministers Pong Sarasin; Chuan Leekpai; Gen. Tienchai Sirisamphan; Gen. Cheovalit Yongchaiyut (Defence)

Ministers attached to Prime Minister's Office Boon-eua Prasertsuwan; Korn Dapparungsi; Anuwat Wattanapongsiri; Chaisiri Ruangkanchanaset; Supatra Masdit; Col Phol Rerngprasertvit; Police Capt. Chalerm Yubamrung.

Other Principal Ministers Pramual Sabhavasu (Finance); Air Chief Marshal Siddhi Savetsila (Foreign Affairs); Banham Silpa-Archa (Interior); Police Lt.-Gen. Chamras Mangkalarat (Justice).

Army Commander in Chief Gen. Suchinda Kraprayooz

Justice

The system of law is a civil law system influenced by customary law. The highest court is the Supreme Court, exercising judicial authority in the name of the King and with judges appointed by him. At local level there are magistrates' courts for civil and minor criminal matters, and 85 provincial courts, with appeals as appropriate going to the Court of Appeal. The death penalty is in force. There were at least 34 executions between 1985 and mid-1988. Offences were drug-trafficking; murder; aggravated rape; homicide.

National symbols

Flag. Five horizontal bands of red, white, dark blue, white and red (the blue band twice the width of the others).

Festivals. 1 May (Labour Day); 5 May (Coronation Day); 12 Aug. (Queen's birthday); 5 Dec. (King's birthday); 10 Dec. (Constitution Day).

Vehicle registration plate. T.

INTERNATIONAL RELATIONS

Affiliations

ASEAN.

Defence

Total Armed Forces: 256,000. Terms of service: two years. Reserves: 500,000.

Army: 166,000; 95 main battle tanks (CH type-69, M-48A5), some 480 light tanks (Scorpion, M-41/-24).

Navy: 42,000; five frigates (US PF-103 and Tacoma); 53 patrol and coastal combatants.

Naval Air: 900; 22 combat aircraft; eight armed helicopters.

Air Force: 48,000; 143 combat aircraft (mainly F-5E, F-5A/B, RF-5A).

Opposition: Communist Party of Malaysia (CPMAL): some 650, surrendered in June 1987. Communist Party of Thailand (CPT): some 600. Thai People's Revolutionary Movement (TPRM), also known as Pak (or Phak) Mai (New Party); New Communist Party/Sayam Mai (New Siam): 1,500 claimed; active guerrillas about 100. Vietnam/Laos-backed Communist Party.

Islamic: Patani United Liberation Organisation; Barisan Revolusi Nasional (BRN) (National Revolution Party): together 400.

ECONOMY

Currency

The unit is the baht, divided into 100 satang.

National finance

Budget. The 1989 FY budget, in US$, was for expenditure of 11,300 million and revenue of 10,400 million. Main items of expenditure are education 19.3%; defence 18.7%.

Balance of payments. The balance of payments, in US$ (current account, 1987) was a deficit of 723 million.

Inflation. 4.5%.

Gross Domestic Product

Estimated total GDP US$48,200 million, per capita US$965 (overall size of economy ranking 40 in the world).

Economically active population. The total number of persons active in the economy was 26,000,000; unemployed: 6.4%.

Sector	% of workforce	% of GDP
industry	11	35
agriculture	73	16
services*	16	49

* services figure includes elements unassigned to other categories.

Energy and mineral resources

Oil and gas. 160 million bbls proven oil reserves. The main oilfield is at Sirikit and further exploration is being conducted in the Gulf of Thailand. Crude oil production: (1988) 2.1 million tons/1.9 million tonnes; gas production: (1987) 178,548 ft^3/5,056 m^3.

Minerals. Tin ore; tungsten; tantalum; lead; gypsum; lignite; fluorite; gemstones. Output: (1986 in tons/tonnes) iron 41,149/37,330; manganese 5,388/4,888; tin 25,682/23,299; lead 68,216/61,885; zinc 412,076/373,833; gypsum 1,835,944/1,665,557; fluorite 209,120/189,712.

Electricity. Capacity: 7,044,000 kW; production: 27,500 million kWh; 500 kWh per capita (1988).

Bioresources

Agriculture. Of the total land area, 34% is arable, 4% under permanent crops, 1% meadow and pasture, 30% forest and woodland. The importance of agriculture to the economy has declined in the last ten years although it is still the major employer. Rice is the dominant crop and an important export (21.4 million tons/19.46 million tonnes of paddy in 1988). Other crops are sugar; maize; rubber; manioc; pineapples; seafood. Thailand is an illegal producer of opium poppy and cannabis for the international drug trade.

Crop production: (1988 in tons/tonnes) maize 5.4 million/4.9 million; sugar cane 30.3 million/27.5 million; coconut 859/780; mung beans 342/310; tapioca root 24.4 million/22.1 million.

Livestock numbers: (1987 in 1,000s) cattle 4,931; buffaloes 6,350; horses 19; pigs 4,200; sheep 73; goats 80; poultry 99,000.

Forestry. 30% of the land area is forest and woodland consisting of mixed deciduous and tropical evergreen forests, including teak. Production: (1987) teak 1,345,463 ft^3/38,100 m^3; yang and other woods 74.2 million ft^3/2.1 million m^3. Rubber production: (1988) 1,069,231 tons/970,000 tonnes. Charcoal, bamboo and yang oil are other forest products.

Fisheries. Sea catch: (1986) 2,588,862 tons/2,348,600 tonnes; freshwater catch 155,645 tons/141,200 tonnes.

Industry and Commerce

Industry. Tourism is the largest source of foreign exchange. Other industries are textiles; agricultural processing; beverages; tobacco; furniture; plastics. Thailand is the world's second largest tungsten producer and the third largest tin producer.

Commerce. Exports: (1988) US$16,000 million or 30% of GNP, including textiles 12%; rice 8%; tapioca 8%; jewellery 6.6%; maize; tin. Imports: US$19,700 million, including machinery and parts 23%; petroleum products 13%; chemicals 11%; iron and steel; electrical appliances. Countries exported to were US 18%; Japan 14%; Singapore 9%; Netherlands; Malaysia; Hong Kong. Imports came from Japan 26%; US 14%; Singapore 7%; West Germany; Malaysia; UK.

Trade with UK. In 1988 Thailand exported to UK goods worth £321,241,000; imports from UK were £279,717,000.

Tourism. The tourist industry is expanding. 3.5 million visitors (1987).

COMMUNICATIONS

Railways

There are 2,732 miles/4,400 km of railways.

Roads

There are 47,392 miles/76,315 km of roads.

Aviation

Thai Airways International Ltd (TAI) provides international services (main airports are Don Muang (near Bangkok), Chiang Mai, Haadyai and Phuket). Passengers: (1987) 5.3 million.

Shipping

There are approximately 2,484 miles/4,000 km of inland waterways of which 2,298 miles/3,700 km are navigable throughout the year, having a depth of 2.95 ft/0.9m or more. The marine ports of Bangkok, Pattani and Sattahip are situated around the Gulf of Thailand. Phuket, on the west coast, faces the Andaman Sea. The merchant marine has 119 ships of 1,000 GRT or over. Freight loaded: (1987) 20.9 million tons/19 million tonnes; unloaded: 26.5 million tons/24 million tonnes.

Telecommunications

There are 739,500 telephones and an adequate service to the general public whilst the bulk of service to government activities is provided by a multichannel cable and radio-relay network. There are 7.7 million radios and 3.3 million televisions (1986). Radio Thailand (RTH) operates a series of stations and three national radio channels as well as external services in ten languages; there is also a Voice of Free Asia station broadcasting in five languages from Bangkok. TVT is the government-run television service, in addition to which there are several commercial stations.

EDUCATION AND WELFARE

Education

Schools. Education is compulsory between the ages of seven and 14 years and free in local municipal schools. Total enrolment at primary and secondary schools was 64% of all school-age children in 1985.

Universities. There are 16 universities and technical institutes.

Literacy. 91%.

Health

408 hospitals, more than 8,000 doctors. Ministry of Social Welfare and Labour created 1989.

TOGO
République Togolaise
(Republic of Togo)

GEOGRAPHY

Located in west Africa, the narrow Togolese republic covers an area of 21,921 miles^2/56,790 km^2 divided into five regions of which the most densely populated is the maritime sector, backed by a series of low-lying plains. Further inland, the Chaîne du Togo Mountains traverse the northern region south-west to north-east, climbing to 3,235 ft/986 m at Pic Baumann, Togo's highest peak. Granite tableland typifies the far north-western areas. Togo's two principal rivers are the Oti, flowing south-westerly into Ghana in the northern part of the republic, and the Mono which drains southwards (forming part of the Benin–Togo frontier) into the Gulf of Guinea. 25% of the land is arable, but the most fertile soils occur in the forested regions which cover 28% of the total surface area.

Climate

Tropical conditions with a wet season Mar.-July and again Oct.-Nov. Further north, a single rainy season lasts Apr.-July. The west, south-west and central highlands receive the bulk of the rainfall. In the north, the dry Saharan Harmattan blows from the north-east Oct.-Apr. Temperatures and humidity levels are high. Lomé: Jan. 81°F/27.2°C. July 75.9°F/24.4°C. Average annual rainfall 34.4 in/875 mm.

Cities and towns

Lomé (capital)	229,400
Sokodé	33,500
Kpalimé	25,500
Atakpamé	21,800
Bassar	17,500
Tsévié	15,900

Population

Total population is 3,448,939 of which 15.2% live in urban areas. Population density is 157 persons per mile^2/55.6 per km^2. Ethnic divisions: there are approximately 37 separate ethnic groups of which the most important are the Ewe, Mina and Kabyè groups. European and Syrian–Lebanese minorities comprise less than 1% of the total population.

Birth rate 4.7%. **Death rate** 1.3%. **Rate of population increase** (1980–87) 3.3%. **Age distribution** under 15 = 44.8%; over 65 = 3.2%. **Life expectancy** female 55; male 51; average 53.

Religion

About 70% of the population follow traditional (animist) beliefs. 20% are Christian (predominantly Roman Catholic) and 10% are Muslim.

Language

The official language is French. Ewe-speaking tribes predominate in the south, while the Hamitic peoples of the north are mostly Voltaic-speaking (Kabyè, Gurma, Tem, Basari, Moba, Mossi and Konkomba). 47% of the population speak Ewe.

HISTORY

The original inhabitants, Voltaic peoples in the north and Kwa in the south-west, were joined by Ewe tribes from Nigeria before the 16th century and the Ane from Ghana in the 18th century. Danes occupied the coastal region in the 18th century but, following the arrival of German missionaries (1847), many of the coastal chiefs accepted German protection (1884), and Togoland became a German colony (1894). In World War I the Germans were driven out by British and French forces (1914) and after the war the League of Nations divided the former German colony into two mandated territories (1922), entrusted to British and French administration. These mandated territories, British and French Togoland, became UN trust territories in 1946.

British Togoland was incorporated into present-day Ghana following a UN plebiscite (1956–57) whereas French Togoland voted (Oct. 1956) for autonomous republic status within the French community (1958) and then moved to full independence (27 Apr. 1960).

The first president was Sylvanus Olympio, leader of the Unité togolaise (UT) party which had dominated the pre-independence election in Apr. 1958. He banned the opposition parties from the Apr. 1961 elections, driving his brother-in-law and rival Nicolas Grunitzky into exile. Olympio was assassinated in a coup led by Sgt Etienne Gnassingbe Eyadéma in Jan. 1963. Eyadéma recalled Grunitzky to become president (1963–67) and arranged a referendum to approve a new constitution, and fresh elections in which all the main parties were represented in the single list of candidates. In Jan. 1967 Gen. Eyadéma seized power for himself in a bloodless coup. He abrogated the constitution and abolished existing political parties, forming the Rassemblement du peuple togolais (RPT) in 1969. His rule was legitimized by a referendum (Jan. 1972), and the armed forces were gradually moved to a back seat in political life.

In 1977 there were demonstrations and strikes, followed by reports of a coup plot (Jan. 1978). A new Third Republic constitution was approved by referendum, a list of RTP candidates elected to the new national assembly and Pres. Eyadéma re-elected in Dec. 1979. Tight security prevented political opposition, although candidates did not have to be proposed by the RTP in the Mar. 1985 election. In Aug. 1985 there was a wave of bomb attacks in Lomé and another terrorist attack was reported in Sept. 1986, giving rise to tension as Eyadéma alleged the involvement of neighbouring countries, particularly Ghana. French and Zaïrean troops were brought in to support the Togolese regime. The evidence of internal discontent, and international protests at the treatment of political prisoners, prompted Pres. Eyadéma to hold talks (June 1987) with the leaders of the political parties banned since 1967. Direct elections were also allowed for local government bodies (June 1987). Pres. Eyadéma pardoned 230 detainees (Oct. 1987) and subsequently freed another 296 prisoners (Jan. 1988) as well as commuting death sentences imposed in connection with the 1987 coup attempt; meanwhile he had had himself re-elected unopposed (Dec. 1986) for a further seven-year presidential term.

CONSTITUTION AND GOVERNMENT

Executive and legislature

The sole ruling party has effectively monopolized poitical power since its establishment in Nov. 1969, and the party's political bureau, appointed by the president, is the country's chief policy-making body. The executive president is elected by universal adult suffrage for a seven-year term; last elections Dec. 1986. The National Assembly is elected directly for a five-year term; last legislative elections Mar. 1990. In practice the Assembly has limited powers.

Present government

President; C.-in-C. of the Armed Forces; Minister of National Defence Gen. Gnassingbe Eyadéma

Principal Members of Council of Ministers Yaovi Adodo (Foreign Affairs and Co-operation); Gen. Mawulikplimi Amegi (Interior); Komlan Alipui (Economy and Finance).

Ruling party

Rally of the Togolese People (Rassemblement du peuple togolais). **Chairman** Gen. Gnassingbe Eyadéma. **Members of the political bureau** Gnassingbe Eyadéma; Kpotivi Tevi-Djidjogbe Laclé; Moussa Barry Barque; Samon Kortho; Gbegnon Amegboh; Mawupe Vovor; Komla Agbetiafa; Palli Tchalla; Koffi Edoh; Bitokotipou Yagninim; Kunale Eklo; Nangbog Barnabo; Dr Tchaa-Kozah Tchalim.

Justice

The system of law is based on the French model. The highest court is the Supreme Court, and there are separate Courts of Appeal for criminal and for civil and commercial cases. Tribunals administer justice at the local level. The death penalty is nominally in force. There were no executions between 1985 and mid-1988.

National symbols

Flag. Three green horizontal stripes alternating with two yellow stripes and a red square canton charged with a white five-pointed star.

Festivals. 13 Jan. (Liberation Day, anniversary of the 1967 coup); 24 Jan. (Day of Victory, anniversary of the failed attack at Sarakawa); 24 Apr. (Day of Victory); 1 May (Labour Day); 24 Sept. (Anniversary of the failed attack on Lomé).

Vehicle registration plate. TG.

INTERNATIONAL RELATIONS

Affiliations

NAM; OUA; ACP; Francophonie.

Defence

Total Armed Forces: 5,900 (all services, inclusive Gendarmerie, form part of the Army). Terms of service: conscription, two years (selective).

Army: 4,000; two main battle tanks (T-54/-55); nine light tanks (Scorpion).

Navy: 100; two patrol and coastal combatants.

Air Force: 250; 13 combat aircraft (mainly AlphaJet, EMB-326GC).

ECONOMY

Currency

The unit is the CFA franc, divided into 100 centimes.

National finance

Budget. The 1987 budget, in US$, was for expenditure of 391 million and revenue of 363 million. Main items of expenditure are education 13.1%; housing and welfare 9.9%; defence 7.6%.

Balance of payments. The balance of payments, in US$ (current account, 1987) was a deficit of 147 million.

Inflation. 2.5%.

Gross Domestic Product

Estimated total GDP US$1,230 million, per capita US$390 (overall size of economy ranking 134 in the world).

Economically active population. In formal sector, unemployed: 2.0%.

Sector	% of workforce	% of GDP
industry	n/a	18
agriculture	78	29
services*	n/a	54

* services figure includes elements unassigned to other categories.

Energy and mineral resources

Minerals. There are rich reserves of phosphate (1984 production of phosphate rock 2.8 million tonnes) and bauxite. Other deposits include limestone; iron ore; marble.

Electricity. Capacity: 116,000 kW; production: 155 million kWh; 45 kWh per capita (1988).

Bioresources

Agriculture. The main cash crops are coffee, cocoa and cotton, which together account for 30% of export earnings. Food crops are yams; cassava; corn; beans; rice; millet; sorghum. Some 80% of the population depend on subsistence agriculture.

Crop production: (1986 in 1,000 tons/tonnes) cassava 487/442; yams 370/336; maize 147/133; sorghum 99/90; millet 77/70; seed cotton 77/70; rice 17/15; groundnuts 24/22; coffee 11/10; tomatoes 7/6.

Livestock numbers: (1987) cattle 290,000; sheep 950,000; goats 740,000; pigs 300,000; horses 1,000; asses 3,000.

Forestry. 28% of the land area is forest and woodland. Roundwood production: (1983) 2,411 ft^3/735 m^3.

Fisheries. Catch: (1984) 16,035 tons/14,547 tonnes.

Industry and commerce

Industry. Main industries are phosphate mining; agricultural processing; cement; handicrafts; textiles; beverages.

Commerce. Exports: (1987) US$296.1 million or 22% of GDP, including phosphates; cocoa; coffee; cotton; manufactures; palm kernels. Imports: were US$358 million, including food; fuels; durable consumer goods; other intermediate goods; capital goods. Countries exported to were EC countries 70%; Africa 9%; US 2%; other 19%. Imports came from EC countries 69%; Africa 10%; Japan 7%; US 4%; other 10%.

Trade with UK. Togo imported UK goods worth £22,231,000; exports to UK totalled £690,000.

Tourism. (1986) 100,000 visitors.

COMMUNICATIONS

Railways

There are 326 miles/525 km of railways.

Roads

There are 3,347 miles/7,000 km of roads.

Aviation
Air Afrique provides international services and Air Togo domestic services (main airports are at Tokoin, near Lomé, and at Niamtougou). Passengers: (1984) 72,000.

Shipping
There are 31 miles/50 km of coastal lagoons and tidal creeks and the inland waterways also include a section of the Mono River. There are two main ports, Lomé, on the coast, and Kpeme, a phosphate port. The merchant marine has six ships of 1,000 GRT or over. Freight loaded: (1987) 214,949 million tons/195,000 million tonnes; unloaded: 1.3 million tons/1.2 million tonnes.

Telecommunications
There are 12,000 telephones and a fair system based on open-wire lines suppplemented by radio-relay routes. There are 680,000 radios and 16,000 televisions (1986). The state controls the radio and television broadcasting stations.

EDUCATION AND WELFARE

Education
Schools. (1986) 2,345 primary schools with 475,000 pupils and 10,209 teachers (one per 46 pupils); 86,327 pupils in secondary schools; 5,050 pupils and 198 teachers (one per 25 pupils) in technical schools.
Universities. The University of Benin at Lomé (4,500 students in 1986).
Literacy. 18%.

Health
In 1979 there were 69 hospitals with (1982) 3,655 beds (one per 943 people) and (1985) 168 doctors (one per 20,529 people).

TONGA
Pule'anga Tonga
(Kingdom of Tonga)

GEOGRAPHY
The Kingdom of Tonga consists of an archipelago of some 172 islands (36 of which are permanently inhabited) located in the south-west Pacific, 404 miles/650 km east of Fiji and 1,863 miles/3,000 km north-east of Sydney, Australia, covering a total area of 289 miles^2/748 km^2. The archipelago is divided physically into two parallel belts: low fertile coralline-limestone formations in the east, higher volcanic terrain in the west. The three principal island groups are Vava'u, Ha'apai and Tongatapu-Eua. The highest Tongan peak is Mount Kao, rising to 3,379 ft/1,030 m. 66% of the total population inhabit the main island of Tongatapu (99.8 miles^2/258.6 km^2). Surface water on the non-volcanic isles is negligible. 25% of the land area is arable and 12% is forested.

Climate
Warm, semi-tropical. Mean annual temperatures vary from 81°F/27°C in the north to 73°F/23°C in the south. Rainfall totals range from 68.9/1,750 on the main island to 108 in/2,750 mm on Vava'u. Maximum temperatures are recorded between the humid months of January and March. Tonga suffers periodic hurricanes throughout the summer months. Nuku'alofa: Jan. 78.1°F/25.6°C. July 70°F/21.1°C. Average annual rainfall 62 in/1,576 mm. Vava'u: Jan. 80.1°F/26.7°C. July 73°F/22.8°C. Average annual rainfall 108 in/2,750 mm.

Cities and towns
Tongatapu	63,614
Nuku'alofa (capital)	28,899
Vava'u	15,170

Population
Total population is 100,465 of which 31.8% lives in urban areas. Population density is 348 persons per mile^2/126.4 per km^2. Over 98% of the population are Polynesian Tongan. There is a small European community of about 300.

Birth rate 2.7%. **Death rate** 0.5%. **Rate of population increase** (1980–87) 0.8%. **Age distribution** under 15 = 39.6%; over 60 = 5.7%. **Life expectancy** female 74; male 69; average 72.

Religion
The dominant faith is Christianity, made up of over 30,000 Free Wesleyan Methodists, and sizeable Roman Catholic, Mormon and Anglican minorities.

Language
The official languages are Tongan (a member of the Austronesian family) and English.

HISTORY
The islands have been inhabited by Polynesian peoples for 3,000 years and the line of ruling dynasties can be traced back to AD 950. European contact began with the Dutch in the 17th century and resumed with the British in the 18th century when Capt. Cook named them the Friendly Islands. A period of civil wars ended during the reign of King George Tupou I (1845–93), who created a unified and independent nation with a modern constitution. Wesleyan missionaries arrived in 1822 and within a generation most of the population had become Christians. Germany, Britain and the United States recognized the kingdom's independence in separate treaties, but in 1900 Tonga signed a Treaty of Friendship and Protection with Britain in order to ward off German advances. Under this treaty Tongan foreign policy was conducted through a British consul. King George Tupou II died in 1918 and was succeeded by his daughter as Queen Salote Tupou III. During World War II she placed Tonga's resources at the disposal of the Allies. On the Queen's death in 1965 her son, Prince Tungi, became King Taufa'ahau Tupou IV. Tonga and Britain signed a new Treaty of Friendship in 1958 and complete independence from Britain came in 1970, when Tonga also joined the Common-

wealth. Although the 1987 general election indicated areas of discontent, and resulted in several new representatives being elected to the Commoners' seats in the Legislative Assembly, overall political power has remained with the King's appointees and the nobility, who together constitute a permanent majority within the legislature. The King's 70th birthday in July 1988 was marked by official celebrations. Elections in February 1990, resulted in several prominent pro-democracy commoners entering the legislature.

CONSTITUTION AND GOVERNMENT

Executive and legislature

The Tongan sovereign is the executive head of state. He governs with the assistance of an appointed ten-member privy council (cabinet). The 29-member unicameral Legislative Assembly consists of the king, privy council, nine hereditary nobles (elected by their peers) and nine popularly elected representatives. Elected representatives hold office for three years; the most recent elections were held in Feb. 1987.

Present government

King Taufa'ahau Tupou IV

Principal Members of the Privy Council Prince Fatafehi Tu'ipelehake (Prime Minister; Agriculture; Forestry and Fisheries; Marine Affairs); Baron Tuita (Deputy Prime Minister; Lands, Survey and Natural Resources); Crown Prince Tupouto'a (Foreign Affairs; Defence); Cecil Cocker (Finance).

Justice

The death penalty is in force. There were no executions between 1985 and mid-1988.

National symbols

Flag. Red with a white canton which contains a red couped cross taken from the state coat of arms of 1862.

Festivals. 25 Apr. (ANZAC Day); 4 May (HRH the Crown Prince's birthday); 4 June (Independence Day); 4 July (HM the King's birthday); 4 Nov. (Constitution Day); 4 Dec. (Tupou Day).

INTERNATIONAL RELATIONS

Affiliations

Commonwealth; SPF.

Defence

Land Force and Maritime Force.

ECONOMY

Currency

The unit is the pa'anga, divided into 100 seniti.

National finance

Budget. The 1988 FY budget, in US$, was for expenditure of 36 million and revenue of 35.5 million.

Inflation. 8.2%.

Gross Domestic Product

Estimated total GDP US$66 million, per capita US$670 (overall size of economy ranking 185 in the world).

Energy and mineral resources

Electricity. Capacity: 5,000 kW; production: 8 million kWh; 80 kWh per capita (1988).

Bioresources

Agriculture. Some 70% of the population are employed in agriculture, and coconuts, bananas and vanilla beans are the main crops, making up two-thirds of exports. Other crops are cocoa; coffee; ginger; black pepper.

Crop production: (1986 in 1,000 tons/tonnes) coconuts 57/52; fruit and vegetables 21/19; copra 6.6/6; cassava 19/17.

Livestock numbers: (1987) cattle 8,000; pigs 65,000; goats 11,000; horses 9,000; poultry (1982) 175,000.

Forestry. 12% of the land area is forest and woodland.

Fisheries. Catch (1982) 2,756 tons/2,500 tonnes.

Industry and commerce

Industry. Main industries are tourism and fishing.

Commerce. Exports: (1987) US$5.9 million or 8% of GDP, including coconut oil; desiccated coconut; copra; bananas; taro; vanilla beans; fruits; vegetables; fish. Imports: US$46.2 million, including food products; beverages and tobacco; fuels; machinery and transport equipment; chemicals; building materials. Countries exported to were New Zealand 54%; Australia 30%; US 8%; Fiji 5%. Imports came from New Zealand 39%; Australia 25%; Japan 9%; US 6%; EC 5%.

Trade with UK. In 1988 Tonga imported UK goods worth £856,000; exports to UK totalled £145,000.

Tourism. (1987) 44,677 visitors.

COMMUNICATIONS

Railways

There are no railways.

Roads

There are 119 miles/192 km of all-weather metalled roads.

Aviation

Friendly Island Airways Ltd/Tavake Ome provides domestic services (main airport is Fua'amotu Airport, 14 miles/22 km from Nuku'alofa).

Shipping

The chief ports are Nuku'alofa in the Tongatapu Group of Islands, Neiafu in the Vava'u Group and Pangai in the Ha'apai Group. The merchant marine has four ships of 1,000 GRT or over.

Telecommunications

There are 3,529 telephones and 81,000 radios (1986), with programmes broadcast in Tongan and English by the commercially operated Tonga Broadcasting Commission. There is no television service.

EDUCATION AND WELFARE

Education

Schools. (1986) 101 government and ten denominational primary schools with a total of 16,912 pupils. Covering secondary education, there are five government, 45 mission and one private school with a total of 14,321 pupils.

Higher education. There is one government teacher-training college, three government and eight non-government technical and vocational colleges.

Literacy. 90–95%

Health

(1987) 47 doctors (one per 2,137 people); four hospitals with 307 beds (one per 327 people).

TRINIDAD AND TOBAGO

Republic of Trinidad and Tobago

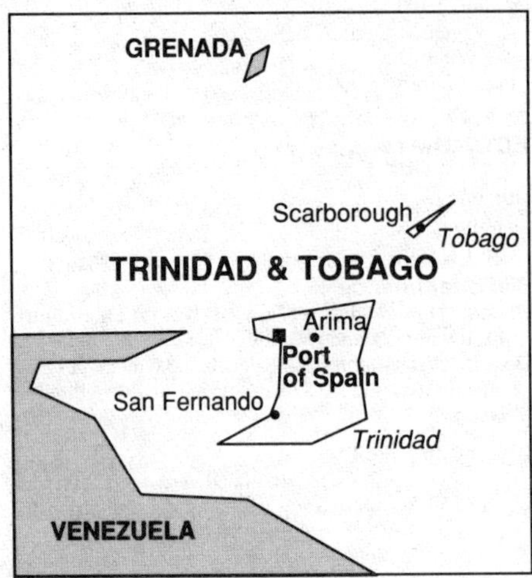

GEOGRAPHY

Trinidad, southernmost of the Caribbean islands, lies approximately 7 miles/11 km north of the Venezuelan mainland, with an area of 1,863 miles^2/4,828 km^2. 20 miles/32 km to the north-east lies the island of Tobago (116 miles^2/300 km^2). 96.3% of the population live on Trinidad Island which is traversed by three mountain ranges (northern, central and southern) rising to 3,084 ft/940 m elevation at El Cerro del Aripo and drained by the Caroni, Ortoire and Oropuche rivers. Apart from these highland ridges, the Trinidadian terrain is mostly low-lying, fringed by mangrove swamps. Tobago Island is dominated by the Main Ridge, a volcanic upland range rising to a maximum of 1,890 ft/576 m. 14% of the land is arable and 44% of the republic is covered by tropical rainforest.

Climate

Tropical. The wet season lasts June-Dec., interrupted by a short dry spell (Petit Carême) Sept.-Oct. The main dry season lasts Jan.-May. Average annual temperature 84°F/29°C. Rainfall varies from 50 in/1,270 mm to 120 in/3,048 mm (north-east). Port-of-Spain: Jan. 78.1°F/25.6°C. July 79°F/26.1°C. Average annual rainfall 64 in/1,631 mm.

Cities and towns

Port-of-Spain (capital)	59,649
San Fernando	34,200
Arima	24,600

Population

Total population is 1,244,160 of which 49.1% live in urban areas. Population density is 668 persons per mile^2/238.3 per km^2. Ethnic divisions: 43% Black; 40% East Indian; 14% mixed; 1% White; 1% Chinese; 1% other.

Birth rate 2.6%. **Death rate** 0.6%. **Rate of population increase** 2.0%. **Age distribution** under 15 = 32.9%; over 65 = 5.4%. **Life expectancy** female 73; male 67; average 70.

Religion

36.2% of the population are Roman Catholic; 23.0% Hindu; 13.1% Protestant (Anglican, Presbyterian, Pentecostal and Seventh Day Adventist); 6.0% Muslim; 21.7% unknown or unaffiliated.

Language

English is the official language, although Hindi, Spanish and French are also spoken.

HISTORY

Trinidad and Tobago's earliest inhabitants were Arawak and Carib Indians. The islands were first visited by Europeans in 1488. Trinidad was colonized by Spain, but it remained under-developed during the 17th and 18th centuries. The island was seized by the British in 1797, and remained a British possession. African slaves had been brought over as labour for sugar and cocoa plantations, but the abolition of slavery in 1834 led to a severe shortage of labour. This was alleviated by the immigration of Chinese, Madeiran and, in particular, Indian labourers. Many of the indentured labourers settled in the country, giving it a sizeable Asian-descended 'East Indian' population. Tobago was settled by Europeans in the mid-17th century, but ownership passed through many hands, and it was not until 1814 that it was confirmed as a British possession. It remained a separate colony until 1888, when it was linked to Trinidad.

Demands for greater self-government increased after World War I. Universal suffrage was introduced in 1945, and elections in 1956 were won by the newly formed People's National Movement (PNM), led by Dr Eric Williams. Ministerial government was introduced in 1959, and full internal self-government in 1961. Trinidad and Tobago joined the Federation of the West Indies in 1958, but after the secession of Jamaica the PNM decided to secede also in order to seek full independence. Williams led the country to independence from Britain on 31 Aug. 1962 and became the first prime minister.

In Apr. 1970 a political crisis was caused by 'Black Power' demonstrations and a mutiny in the army, but the PNM retained control and won all the seats in the 1971 elections after the opposition boycotted the poll. The discovery and exploitation of petroleum reserves made the country prosperous during the 1970s and financed major government expenditure. On 1 Aug. 1976 Trinidad and Tobago became a republic within the Commonwealth. The PNM won elections the following month, with the trade union-led United National Front (ULF) and the Tobago-based Democratic Action Congress (DAC) winning seats as opposition parties.

Williams died in Mar. 1981, and was succeeded by George Chambers, who led the party to victory in elections in Nov. 1981. The ULF, DAC and Tapia House Movement had joined together to form the Trinidad and Tobago National Alliance, while a new party, the Organization for National Reconstruction, failed to win any seats, in spite of securing over 20% of the vote. During 1983 and 1984 the opposition parties moved closer together to form a united coalition to oppose the PNM. In Feb. 1986 the four parties merged to form one party, the National Alliance for Reconstruction (NAR), with A.N.R. Robinson, the leader of the DAC and a former deputy prime minister under the PNM, as leader. Elections were held in Dec. 1986, and the NAR won convincingly, taking advantage of the discontent caused by the PNM's austerity measures and its long tenure in office. Robinson became prime minister, but the NAR soon began to suffer internal divisions and public unpopularity from its own measures introduced to deal with the deteriorating economic situation. In Nov. 1987 three cabinet ministers were dismissed, including Basdeo Panday, the former leader of the ULF, for criticizing Robinson's leadership. They were then suspended and expelled from the party. In Apr. 1989 they proceeded to form a new opposition party, the United National Congress.

CONSTITUTION AND GOVERNMENT

Executive and legislature

The president is elected by a parliamentary electoral college; the head of government is the prime minister, responsible to parliament. The 36-member House of Representatives is elected for a five-year term by universal adult suffrage (last elections Dec. 1986) and the upper house, the Senate, is appointed by the president on the advice of the prime minister and leader of the opposition.

Present government

President Noor Mohammed Hassanali

Prime Minister; Minister of Finance and the Economy Arthur Napoleon Raymond Robinson

Other Principal Ministers Selby Wilson (Finance); Selwyn Richardson (Justice and National Security); Dr Sahadeo Basdeo (External Affairs and International Trade); Kenneth Gordon (Industry and Enterprise and Tourism); Anthony Smart (Attorney General).

Administration

Tobago, the smaller of the country's two main constituent islands, achieved full internal self-government in early 1987.

Justice

There is a Supreme Court of Judicature, consisting of a High Court, Court of Appeal and 12 Magistrates' Courts. The chief justice is appointed by the president acting on the advice of the prime minister. Puisne judges are appointed by the president acting in accordance with the advice of the Judicial and Legal Service Commissions. The death penalty is in force. There were no executions between 1985 and mid-1988.

National symbols

Flag. Red with a black diagonal stripe bordered by two narrow white stripes.

Festivals. 6–7 Feb. (Carnival); 19 June (Labour Day); 1 Aug. (Emancipation Day); 7 Aug. (Discovery Day); 31 Aug. (Independence Day); 24 Sept. (Republic Day).

Vehicle registration plate. TT.

INTERNATIONAL RELATIONS

Affiliations

NAM; ACP; Commonwealth; OAS; Caricom.

Defence

Total Armed Forces: 2,750. Terms of service: voluntary.
Army: 2,100.
Coastguard: 600; ten inshore patrol craft.
Air Wing: 50.
Para-military: 4,000 (Police).

ECONOMY

Currency

The unit is the Trinidad and Tobago dollar, divided into 100 cents.

National finance

Budget. The 1988 budget, in US$, was for expenditure of 2,100 million and revenue of 1,400 million.

Balance of payments. The balance of payments, in US$ (current account, 1987) was a deficit of 184 million.

Inflation. 10.7%.

Gross Domestic Product

Estimated total GDP US$4,260 million, per capita US$3,550 (overall size of economy ranking 95 in the world).

Economically active population. The total number of persons active in the economy was 464,000; unemployed: 21.6%.

Sector	% of workforce	% of GDP
industry	33	39
agriculture	11	4
services*	56	57

* services figure includes elements unassigned to other categories.

Energy and mineral resources

Oil and gas. Although currently in decline because of the sharp fall in the price of oil, Trinidad's oil production and refining industry remains the most important source of all export revenue (71.6% of total in 1986). Output: crude oil (1988) 8.6 million tons/7.8 million tonnes; distilled oil 305,000 bbls per annum. Gas production: (1985) 7,409 million ft^3/209.8 million m^3.

Minerals. Asphalt production: (1986) 189 million ft^3/5.36 million m^3 from Pitch Lake.

Electricity. Capacity: 1,176,000 kW; production: 3,312 million kWh; 2,720 kWh per capita (1988).

Bioresources

Agriculture. 14% of the land is arable, 17% is under permanent cultivation and 2% is meadow or pasture. Cocoa and sugar plantations covered 96,369 acres/39,000 ha in 1984. Irrigation and conservation projects have been implemented to help promote rice cultivation and improve forest management. 101,742/92,300 tonnes of sugar were produced in 1986. Other crops include coffee; rice; citrus fruits; bananas, but the republic is still heavily dependent on imported foodstuffs.

Livestock numbers: (1987) cattle 77,000; pigs 83,000; goats 50,000; sheep 12,000; poultry 8 million.

Forestry. Forests cover 44% of the territory.

Industry and commerce

Industry. Trinidad and Tobago's main industries are

petroleum production; chemicals; tourism; food processing; cement; beverage and cotton textiles manufacturing. Output: (1985) iron and steel 0.52 million tons/0.47 million tonnes; ammonia 1.46 million tons/1.32 million tonnes; (1986) fertilizers 2.08 million tons/1.89 million tonnes; cement 0.37 million tons/0.34 million tonnes; rum 2.3 million gallons/10.5 million litres; beer 4,557 gallons/20,716 litres; cigarettes 2.03 lb/0.92 kg.

Commerce. Exports: (1987) US$1,400 million or 33% of GDP; imports: $1,200 million in the same year or 29% of GDP. Chief exported commodities include petroleum and petroleum products 70%; fertilizers, chemicals 15%; steel products; sugar; coffee; cocoa; citrus. Imports include raw materials 41%; capital goods 30%; consumer goods 29%. Trading partners are (imports and exports) US; EC countries; Caricom; Latin America; Canada; (imports only) Japan.

Trade with UK. Trinidad and Tobago imported UK goods worth £39.9 million in 1988; exports to the UK amounted to £35.7 million.

Tourism. (1986) 182,640 visitors.

COMMUNICATIONS

Railways

There are no railways.

Roads

There are 4,906 miles/7,900 km of roads, of which 2,236 miles/3,600 km are concrete or bituminized.

Aviation

BWIA International provides domestic services (linking the Eastern Caribbean islands with each other) and international services (main airport is Piarco International, 16 miles/25.7 km from Port-of-Spain). Passengers: (1985 UN est.) 1.4 million.

Shipping

The ports of Port-of-Spain, Point Lisas, and Pointe-a-Pierre are situated in the Gulf of Paria on the island of Trinidad. Freight loaded: (1985 UN est.) 9.1 million tons/8.3 million tonnes; unloaded: 4.7 million tons/4.3 million tonnes.

Telecommunications

There are 109,000 telephones with good local service and excellent international service via tropospheric scatter links to Barbados and Guyana. There are 552,000 radios and 345,000 televisions (1986). The government NBS and commercial Radio Trinidad stations provide radio services, and the state owns the commercial TV station Trinidad and Tobago Television.

EDUCATION AND WELFARE

Education

Schools. An estimated 172,424 pupils attend primary schools. A further 39,188 are enrolled in junior secondary schools with over 12,600 pupils at state schools, 17,570 in state-assisted institutions, 21,600 in senior comprehensive schools and over 4,400 in vocational or technical colleges.

Universities. Approximately 2,700 students are registered at the University of the West Indies site in St Augustine.

Literacy. 98%.

Health

1,103 physicians; 496 pharmacists; 129 dentists; 3,344 nurses and midwives; 980 auxiliary nursing staff serve 31 hospitals and nursing homes with a total of 4,087 beds (one per 304 members of the population).

TUNISIA
Al-Jamhuriya at-Tunisiya
(Republic of Tunisia)

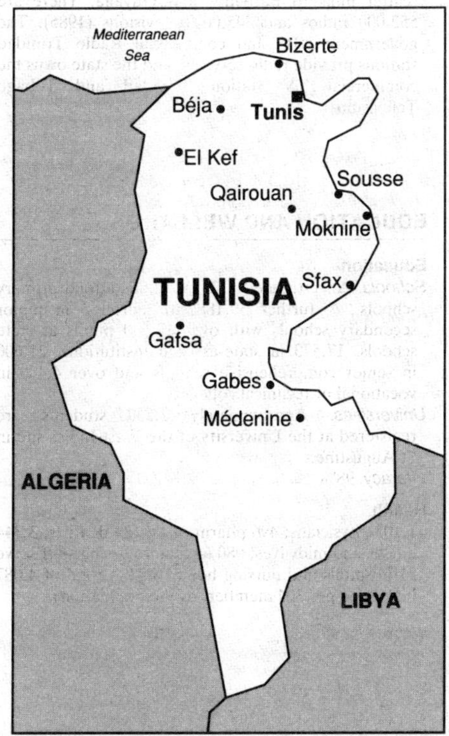

GEOGRAPHY

Located in north Africa, on the Mediterranean coast, Tunisia covers an area of 63,153 miles²/163,610 km² divided into 18 governorates. In the populous northern part of the country, the Northern Tell and High (Southern) Tell Atlas mountains occupy an estimated 30% of the total surface area, climbing to 5,066 ft/1,544 m maximum at Jabal Ash-Sha'nabi. To the south, the dry expanse of plateau-steppe gives way to a series of saline lakes or shawati including the Shatt al-Jarid (49 ft/15 m below sea level), bending west-eastwards. Further south, this semi-arid depression merges into the barren and very sparsely populated terrain of the Sahara desert, interspersed with cultivated artesian oases. The Majardah river valley provides Tunisia with its most fertile soil and its chief source of hydroelectrical power generation. 20% of the land is considered arable and 4% is forested.

Climate

Warm temperate (Mediterranean) in the north with hot, dry summers and mild, rainy winters. Extreme desert-continental type in the far south, with large annual temperature range and negligible rainfall. Tunis: Jan. 48°F/8.9°C. July 78.1°F/25.6°C. Average annual rainfall 15.7 in/400 mm. Bizerta: Jan. 52°F/11.1°C. July 77°F/25°C. Average annual rainfall 24 in/622 mm. Sfax: Jan. 52°F/11.1°C. July 78.1°F/25.6°C. Average annual rainfall 8 in/196 mm.

Cities and towns

Tunis (capital)	596,654
Sfax	231,911
Ariana	98,655
Bizerte	94,509
Djerba	92,269
Gabès	92,258
Sousse	83,509
Kairouan	72,254
Bardo	65,669
La Goulette	61,609

Population

Total population is 7,916,104 of which 52.8% live in urban areas. Population density is 125 persons per mile²/49.4 per km² (average), rising considerably higher in the Tunis region. Ethnic composition: 98% Arab; 1% European; less than 1% Jewish. **Birth rate** 2.9%. **Death rate** 0.6%. **Rate of population increase** (1980–87) 2.3%. **Age distribution** under 15 = 39.6%; over 65 = 3.8%. **Life expectancy** female 66; male 65; average 65.

Religion

98% of the population are Sunni Muslims (Islam is recognized as the state religion). 1% of the population are Christian (including approximately 20,000 Roman Catholics). There are an estimated 9,000 Tunisian Jews.

Language

Arabic is the official language. French and Berber are also widely used.

HISTORY

The area of North Africa now known as Tunisia was since earliest times inhabited by the Zenata Berbers, who were nomadic horsemen. In 1101 BC Phoenician sailors founded Utica and other trading posts, while in 814 BC the Phoenician Queen Elyssa (Dido) founded Carthage, which soon became a vast trading centre for gold and precious metals, and extended its rule all along the Mediterranean coast. The Nomadic shepherds (Numidians) remained in the mountains.

Carthage's power lasted until 264 BC, when the Romans started their campaigns in the Punic Wars, although it was not until 146 BC that the city was completely destroyed, and Caesar incorporated it with Numidia into the province of Africa Nova.

The Vandals overran the area in AD 439, but they were conquered by the Byzantine Empire in 534. In spite of frequent Berber rebellions, this rule lasted for over 100 years until the Arab conquest brought Islam to North Africa. The Aghlabid kingdom ruled Tunisia until conquering tribes from Egypt devastated the country in the 11th century. In 1148 the Sicilian king Roger II arrived in Djerba, to become 'King of Africa'. The Governor of Ifriqiya (roughly equivalent to Tunisia) in 1230 proclaimed himself Emir, founded the Hafsid dynasty and renamed the country after the new capital: Tunisia.

The country became an Ottoman province in 1574, but in the following centuries the Italians, French and English fought for control. By the Convention of La Marsa in 1883, Tunisia became a French Protectorate. Nationalism gained ground 1920–34 with the Constitutional Party (Destour) demanding internal autonomy. The party split and was supplanted by the Neo-Destour Party, led by Habib Bourguiba.

During World War II, Tunisia was occupied by the Axis powers, who were driven out by British forces in 1943. The war over, Bourguiba's influence increased and armed resistance to France grew. Bourguiba returned from exile (1955) to negotiate the country's independence of 20 Mar. 1956, becoming the first president of the Republic in 1957, at the head of the Parti Socialiste Destourien (PSD).

Diplomatic relations with France were broken off in 1961, when Tunisia called for the evacuation of the Bizerte naval base. In 1967, land collectivization was attempted, but output fell dramatically; the minister in charge was imprisoned, and private ownership was restored. Bourguiba was re-elected president-for-life on 15 Sept. 1974. He survived occasional student and labour unrest in 1968 and 1978, and an attempted coup in 1980. The most serious rioting occurred on 2 Jan. 1984 in the wake of a sharp government-imposed rise in the price of bread.

In the 1980s, Bourguiba attempted to halt the rise of Islamic fundamentalism by imposing severe penalties and death sentences. In foreign policy, a fraternity treaty was signed with Algeria on 19 Mar. 1983, ending a 20-year dispute, while relations with Libya were broken off in Sept. 1985, after the expulsion of Tunisian nationals working in Libya. They were eventually restored in Dec. 1987.

On 8 Nov. 1987, Bourguiba, suffering advanced senility, was deposed in a bloodless palace coup by his recently appointed prime minister, Zine el-Abidine Ben Ali. Following constitutional reforms, the government party, renamed the Rassemblement Constitutionnel Démocratique (RCD), won a resounding victory in general elections on 2 Apr. 1989, in which newly legalized opposition parties also competed.

President Ben Ali dismissed Prime Minister Hedi Baccouche in Sept. 1989 after a reported disagreement over economic policy; the Justice Minister, Hamed Karoui, became the new prime minister.

CONSTITUTION AND GOVERNMENT

Executive and legislature

The executive president is elected directly every five years (but is now limited to a maximum of three terms), and appoints the prime minister and the council of ministers. The unicameral 141-seat National Assembly is elected for a maximum five-year term by universal adult suffrage, most recently on 2 Apr. 1989, at the same time as presidential elections. The ruling Destour Socialist Party (PSD) ceased to be the sole legal party in 1981, and was renamed the Constitutional Democratic Rally (Rassemblement constitutionnel démocratique – RCD) in Feb. 1988.

Present government

President Gen. Zine el-Abidine Ben Ali
Prime Minister Dr Hamed Karoui
Principal Other Members of Cabinet Habib Ammar (Special Adviser to the President); Chedli Neffati (Interior); Abdelhamid Escheikh (Foreign Affairs); Mohamed Jeri (Secretary General for the Presidency); Abdallah Kallal (Secretary General for National Defence); Mohamed Ghanouchi (Planning and Finance); Moncef Belaid (National Economy).

Justice

The judiciary consists of 51 magistrates' courts, 13 courts of first instance, three courts of appeal and the High Court in Tunis. The death penalty is in force. There were 30 executions between 1985 and mid-1988. Offences were murder; rape; aggravated robbery.

National symbols

Flag. Red with white disc in the middle, containing a red Osmanli Turkish crescent and a five-pointed star.
Festivals. 20 Mar. (Independence Day); 21 Mar. (Youth Day); 9 Apr. (Martyrs' Day); 1 May (Labour Day); 25 July (Republic Day); 13 Aug. (Women's Day); 15 Oct. (Evacuation of Bizerta).
Vehicle registration plate. TN.

INTERNATIONAL RELATIONS

Affiliations

NAM; OPEC; OAPEC; OAU; ICO; Arab League; AMU.

Defence

Total Armed Forces: 38,000 (26,400 conscripts). Terms of service: 12 months' selective.
Army: 30,000; 68 main battle tanks (M-48A3, M-60A3), 104 light tanks (AMX-13, M-41, Steyr SK-105 Kuerassier).
Navy: 4,500; one frigate (US *Savage*) and 23 patrol and coastal combatants.
Air Force: 3,500; 31 combat aircraft (F-5E, F-5F, MB-326K, MB-326L).

ECONOMY

Currency

The unit is the dinar, divided into 1,000 millimes.

National finance

Budget. The 1987 budget, in US$, was for expenditure of 3,420 million and revenue of 3,080 million.
Balance of payments. The balance of payments, in US$ (current account, 1987) was a deficit of 99 million.
Inflation. 7.2%.

Gross Domestic Product

Estimated total GDP US$8,450 million, per capita US$1,270 (overall size of economy ranking 70 in the world).
Economically active population. The total number of persons active in the economy was 2,250,000; unemployed: 18%.

Sector	% of workforce	% of GDP
industry	n/a	32
agriculture	32	18
services*	n/a	50

* services figure includes elements unassigned to other categories.

Energy and mineral resources

Oil and gas. Output: crude oil (1988) 5.3 million tons/ 4.8 million tonnes; natural gas (1984) 15,185 million ft^3/430 million m^3.
Minerals. Tunisia has significant reserves of iron ore;

phosphates; lead, zinc; salt. Output: (1984) iron ore 340,611 tons/309,000 tonnes; phosphates 5,936 million tons/5.385 million tonnes; lead ore 7,165 tons/ 6,500 tonnes; zinc ore 13,338 tons/12,100 tonnes; pig iron 106,923 tons/97,000 tonnes; crude steel 115,742 tons/105,000 tonnes.

Electricity. Capacity: 1,493,000 kW; production: 4,209 kWh; 540 kwh per capita (1988).

Bioresources

Agriculture. 20% of the land area is arable; 10% is under permanent cultivation; 19% is meadow or pasture. Agriculture constitutes one of Tunisia's primary industries. An estimated 22.2 million acres/ 9m ha of land are cultivable.

Crop production: (1987 in 1000 tons/tonnes) wheat 1,499/1,360; barley 592/537; citrus fruits 316/287; olive oil 125/113; dates 82/74; wine 77,161 tons/70,000 tonnes. Other crops grown include apricots; pears; apples; peaches; figs; pomegranates; henna; cork; shaddocks; almonds; pistachios; esparto grass.

Livestock numbers: (1987 in 1,000s) cattle 610; asses 218; horses 55; mules 75; sheep 5,800; goats 1,127; camels 182; pigs 4.

Forestry. 4% of the land is forested.

Fisheries. Total catch: (1987) 105,821 tons/96,000 tonnes.

Industry and commerce

Industry. Tunisia's main industries are petroleum; mining; agriculture; textiles; footwear; food and beverages. Important industrial plants include sugar and petroleum refineries in Béja and Bizerte, cellulose production in Kassérine, steel works in Menzel Bourguiba and marble works at Mégrine. Output: (1984 in 1,000 tons/tonnes) crude steel 183/ 166; lime 534/484; cement 3,023/2,742, phosphoric acid 606/550; petrol 237/215.

Commerce. Exports: (1987) US$2,100 million or 22% of GDP; imports:$3,000 million or 31% of GDP. Principal exports include hydrocarbons 40%; agricultural products 18%; phosphates and chemicals 18%. Imported commodities were chiefly industrial goods and equipment 57%; hydrocarbons 13%; food 12%; consumer goods. Export trading partners are EC countries; Middle East; US; Turkey; USSR. Imports are received from EC countries; US; Canada; Japan; USSR; China; Saudi Arabia; Algeria.

Trade with UK. Tunisia imported UK goods worth £30.8 million in 1988; exports to the UK amounted to £36 million.

Tourism. (1986) 1.54 million visitors.

COMMUNICATIONS

Railways

There are 1,351 miles/2,175 km of railways.

Roads

There are 16,574 miles/26,689 km of roads.

Aviation

Tunis Air (Société Tunisienne de l'Air) provides international services and Tunisavia (Société de Transports, Services et Travaux Aériens) provides domestic services (main airports are at Tunis-Carthage, Tunis-el Aouina, Djerba, Monastir and Tozeur). Passengers: (1984) 1.3 million.

Shipping

The ports of Tunisia are Bizerte, Gabès, Sfax, Sousse, Tunis and La Goulette. Freight loaded: (1985) 5 million tons/4.5 million tonnes; unloaded: 8.3 million tons/7.5 million tonnes.

Telecommunications

There are 233,000 telephones and the system is better than most in Africa, consisting of open-wire lines, multiconductor cable and radio relay. There are 1.2 million radios and 500,000 televisions (1986). There are two TV channels, and radio programmes in Arabic, French and Italian, broadcast by the government RTT service.

EDUCATION AND WELFARE

Education

Free, nationally aligned state education is available from primary school to university. All distinctions between religious and public schools have been abrogated and the 208 independent Koranic schools nationalized.

Schools. An estimated 1,338,900 pupils are enrolled in 3,605 primary schools with 43,190 teachers (one per 31 pupils). A further 437,600 pupils attend 436 secondary schools and are taught by 22,373 members of staff (one per 20 pupils). An additional 60,137 students receive instruction at vocational or technical schools; 4,101 students are in teacher-training institutions.

Universities. 38,830 students are registered at the University of Tunis, taught by 5,019 tutors and lecturers. There are two other universities at Sousse and Sfax.

Health

Medical staff include 1,800 doctors, 176 dentists and 313 pharmacists serving 98 hospitals with 13,571 beds (one per 583 members of the population).

TURKEY

Türkiye Cumhuriyeti (Republic of Turkey)

GEOGRAPHY

Located partly in south-eastern Europe and partly in western Asia, the Republic of Turkey contains a total area of 300,868 miles²/779,452 km² divided into 67 provinces. The relatively small European sector known as Eastern Thrace covers only 9,173 miles²/ 23,764 km², separated from the Asian continent by the Turkish Straits. The Asian provinces, known as Anatolia, cover 291,696 miles²/755,688 km². The semi-arid Central Anatolian plateau (altitude 3,280–6,562 ft/1,000–2,000 m) is enclosed to the north and to the south by the Pontic and Taurus mountains, stretching east-westerly across the Anatolian peninsula, bordered by narrow coastal plains. In the east, the Mount Agri Dagi (Ararat) rises to a maximum elevation of 16,945 ft/5,165 m. In the west, narrow mountainous spurs extend towards the Aegean, with the Yildiz uplands dominating the European provinces. The Gokso, Seyan and Orontes drain into the Mediterranean; the Tigris and Euphrates rise in the east and drain southwards. The bulk of the urban, settled population inhabits the western half of the country. 30% of the land is arable and 26% is forested, particularly along the Black Sea Coast.

Climate

Mediterranean on the coast with hot, dry summers and mild, wet winters. Mean July temperature on the southern and western Mediterranean coasts is 84°F/ 29°C; average precipitation on the Black Sea Littoral is 96 in/2,438 mm. Winter temperatures fall sharply in the north-eastern plateau regions to an average low of 10°F/–12°C. Rainfall decreases west-east, with negligible precipitation during the summer months in eastern plateau provinces. Ankara: Jan. 32.5°F/0.3°C. July 73°F/23°C. Average annual rainfall 14 in/367 mm. Istanbul: Jan. 41°F/5°C. July 73°F/23°C. Average annual rainfall 28.5 in/723 mm. Izmir: Jan 46°F/8°C. July 81°F/27°C. Average annual rainfall 27.6 in/ 700 mm.

Cities and towns

Istanbul	5,475,982
Ankara (capital)	2,235,035
Izmir	1,489,772
Adana	777,554
Bursa	612,510
Gaziantep	478,635
Konya	439,181
Kayseri	373,937
Eskişehir	366,765
Mersin	314,350
Diyarbakir	305,940

Population

Total population is 55,355,831 of which 53.0% live in urban areas. Population density is 184 persons per mile²/67.8 per km². Ethnic divisions: 85% Turkish; 12% Kurd (most inhabiting the depopulated eastern and south-eastern reaches of Anatolia); 3% other. **Birth rate** 3.0%. **Death rate** 0.8%. **Rate of population increase** (1980–87) 2.1%. **Age distribution** under 15 = 36.4%; over 65 = 4.2%. **Life expectancy** female 66; male 63; average 64.

Language

Turkish is the official language (Türkce), related to Azerbaijani, Turkmen and Gagauz and forming with them the Oguz sub-division of the Turkic-Altaic language family. Turkish is spoken by approximately 90% of the population. Kurdish and Arabic are also spoken, with smaller Greek, Armenian and Yiddish ethnolinguistic minorities in the major cities.

Religion

Over 98% are Muslim, although Islam is not the official state religion, Turkey being a secular state. The head of the Orthodox Church in Turkey, the Oecumenical Patriarch, has his seat at Istanbul.

HISTORY

Turkey traces its pre-Anatolian history in the changing fortunes of the 16 main Turkish tribes which became powerful in Asia and Europe between c. 2000 BC and AD 1500 (all of them symbolized in the present-day presidential coat of arms). Asia Minor was won from the Persians by Alexander the Great of Macedonia in the 4th century BC as he expanded his empire eastwards as far as India. Eventually incorporated into the Roman Empire it was Constantine, Rome's first Christian Emperor, who in the early 4th century AD established an eastern capital (Constantinople in Byzantium at the entrance to the Black Sea), which became the centre of the Byzantine empire. Later the Seldjuk Turks (one of the 16 Turkish tribes) embraced Islam in the 7th century and penetrated the area of modern Turkey in the 11th century, when it formed part of the Byzantine Empire and the Greek Christian world. The Seldjuks' victory over the Byzantines at Manzikert in 1071 enabled them to settle in Anatolia and to form a sultanate (1098), which repulsed Christian Crusader raids (12th century) but disintegrated before the Mongol hordes (13th century). The Ottoman Turks of north-western Anatolia began their rise under Osman I (r.1288–1326) and became dominant in Anatolia under Murad I (r.1359–89), who also conquered Thrace, Macedonia, Bulgaria and Serbia in Europe. Having routed a Christian counter-attack, Bayezid I

Chinese troops at student demonstration in Tiananmen Square in June 1989

Students struggling hopelessly against troops as their occupation of the square is ended

Ethnic violence in Uzbekistan resulted in many deaths as problems mounted in the Soviet Union

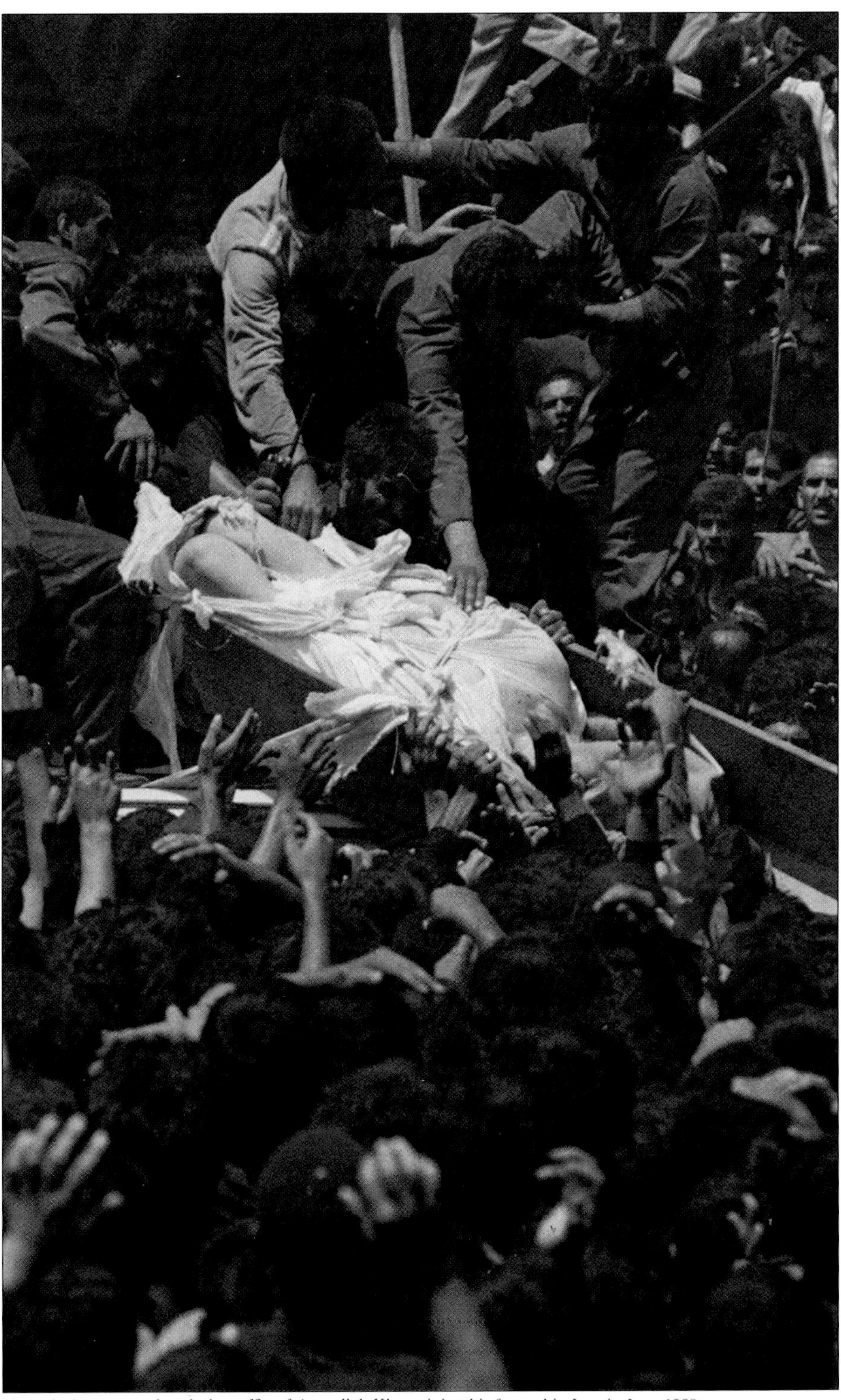

Hysterical mourners break the coffin of Ayatollah Khomeini at his funeral in Iran in June 1989

President Moi of Kenya sets fire to a mountain of tusks at the start of a new campaign to end world trade in ivory

John McEnroe contemplates his early exit from Wimbledon 1989

Hurricane Hugo hits Puerto Rico and the Virgin Islands with winds of 140 miles per hour. Thousands of homes are destroyed and 25 people killed

The wreckage of the *Marchioness* at low tide in the Thames, the day after 56 people died when the craft sank after being struck by the *Bowbelle*

The B-2 stealth bomber on a test flight. The hugely expensive project was cancelled due to increasing costs

A burning oil refinery blackens the Beirut sky as fighting continues in strife-torn Lebanon

Pope John Paul II is greeted by a crowd of 700,000 in Seoul, South Korea

1989 saw the beginning of the independence movement in the Baltic States

Gerald Conlan, one of the 'Guildford Four', who were released from prison after serving 14 years. A Court of Appeal found that the police had faked evidence

When East Germany opened its borders the Berlin Wall, once the symbol of the Cold War, became a place of celebration

The US space shuttle *Atlantis* launches the spacecraft *Galilea* on its six-year journey to the planet Jupiter

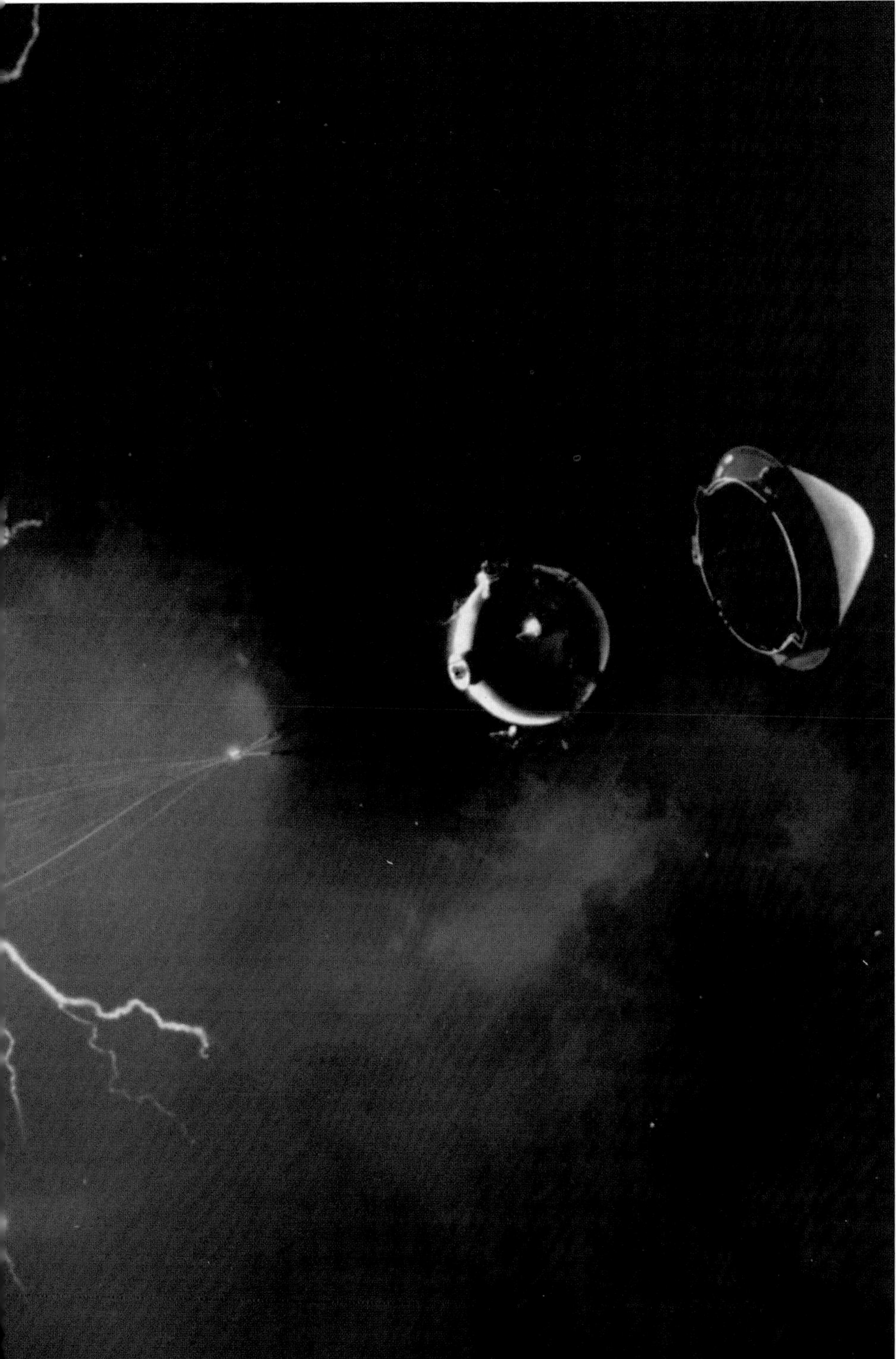

Seventy people died and 3,000 were injured when an earthquake rocked the San Francisco area

Former Czech leader Alexander Dubcek and leading dissident Vaclev Havel about to address a crowd in Prague. Within months, Havel would be elected the nation's leader

Romanian troops watch a television broadcast of Nicolae and Elena Ceaucescu being interrogated

In December 1989 US troops invaded Panama in order to topple the regime of Manuel Noriega

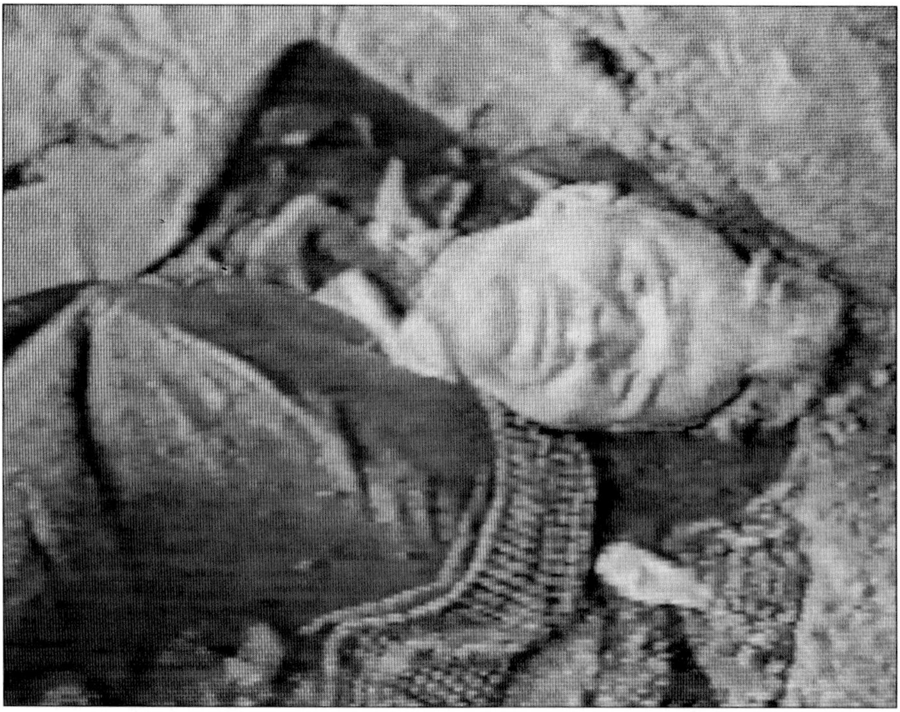

Ceaucescu and his wife were shot by a firing squad, after a two-hour 'trial', on Christmas Day, 1989

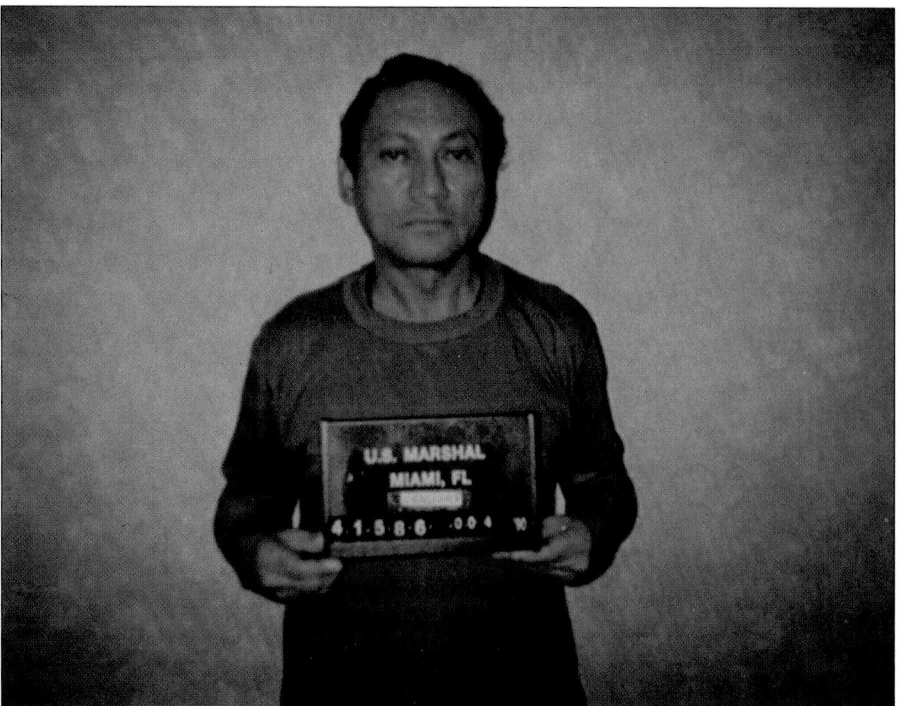

A 'mug shot' of Manuel Noriega taken in the US where he was flown after giving himself up to US troops in Panama

A January 1990 rally in Trafalgar Square highlighted the long-term dispute between the government and ambulance drivers

In January 1990, Vietnamese children demonstrated in a Hong Kong detention centre against plans to repatriate them

Demonstrators outside the cricket ground voice their feelings about the 'Rebel Tour' to South Africa. Their presence caused an early return to Britain by Mike Gatting and his team

Nelson Mandela, with his wife Winnie, greets the jubilant crowd on his release from prison on 11 February 1990

Alexandra Griffiths who had been kidnapped from a London hospital is reunited with her mother, Dawn

Wayne Larkins celebrates after scoring the winning run against the West Indies in the first test in Jamaica

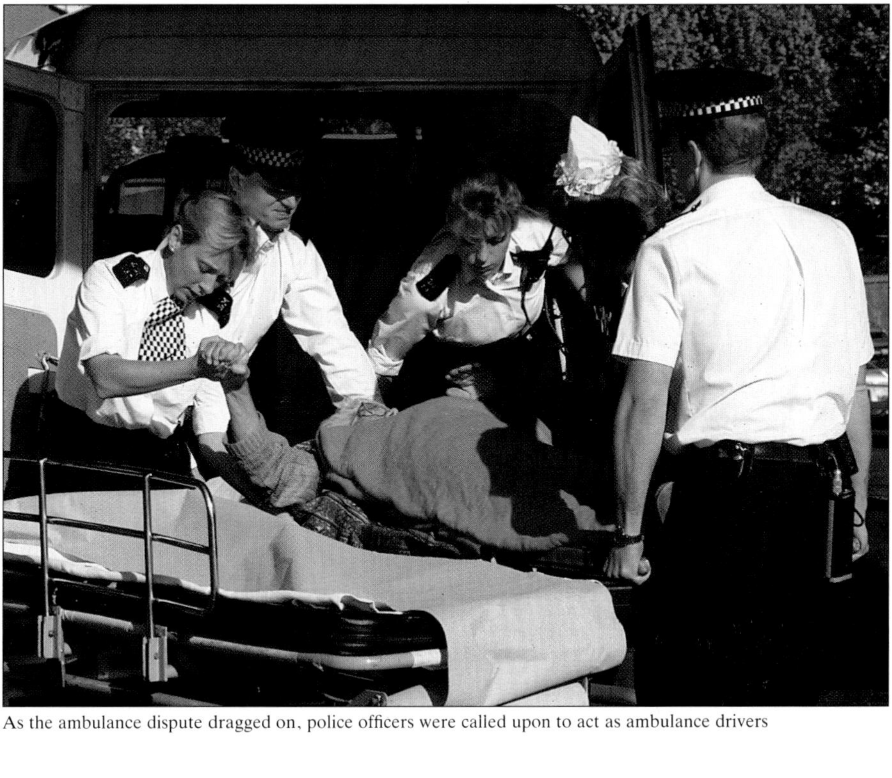

As the ambulance dispute dragged on, police officers were called upon to act as ambulance drivers

Journalist Farzad Bazoft as he appeared on Iraqi television 'confessing' to spying on Iraq. Despite international appeals he was hanged on 15 March 1990

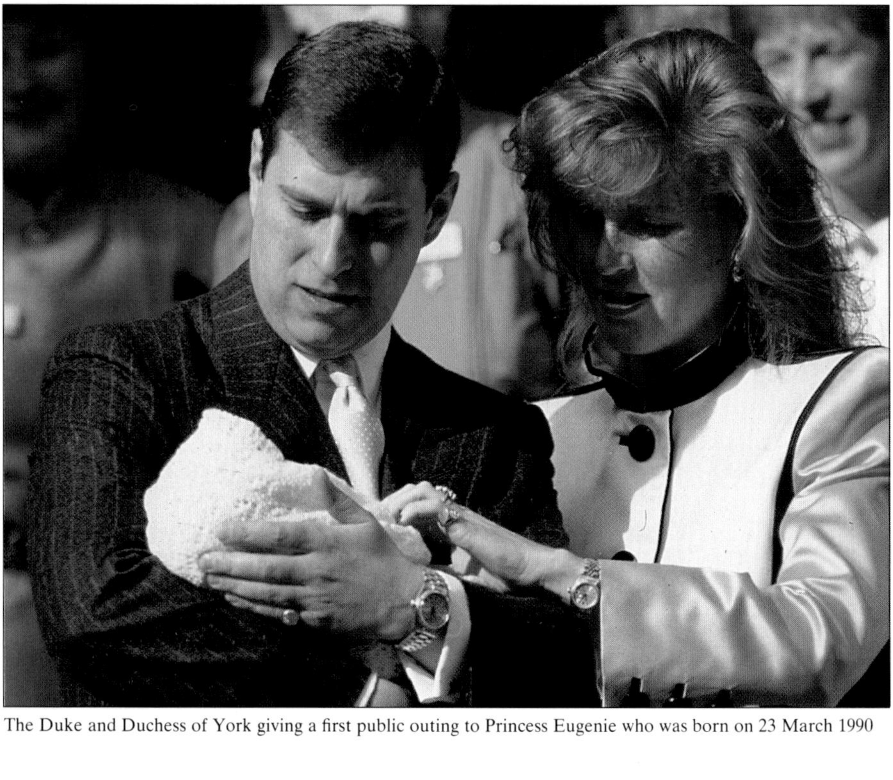

The Duke and Duchess of York giving a first public outing to Princess Eugenie who was born on 23 March 1990

May Day, 1990, in Red Square, but this year the marchers are anti-government protesters

Bette Davis, Ava Gardner, Gordon Jackson and Lord Olivier – four stars who died in the past year

The Princess Royal and Mark Phillips decided to go their separate ways in 1990, although divorce has not been discussed

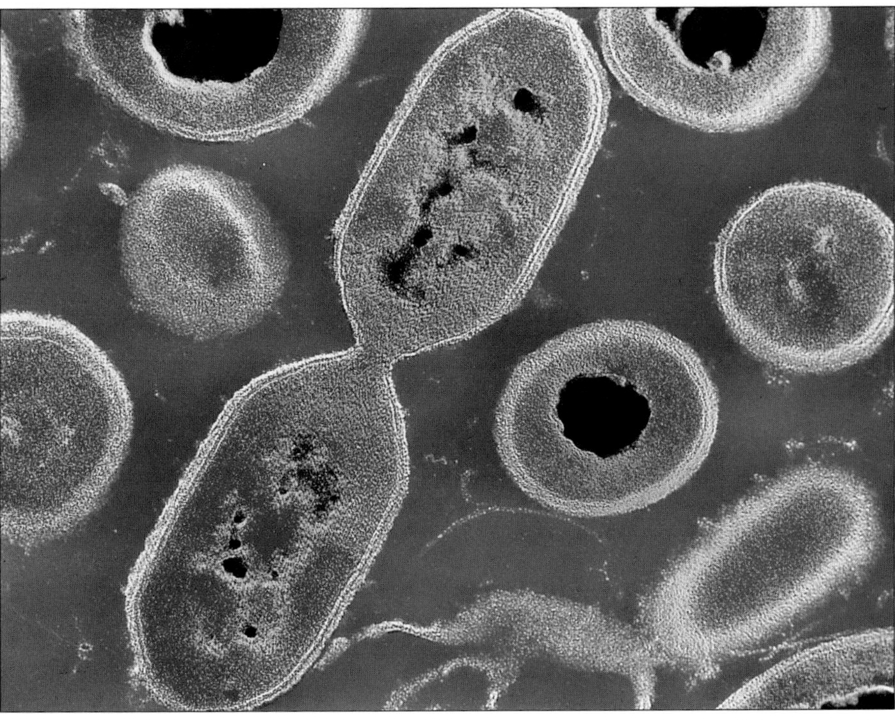

A colony of listeria bacteria, found in prepared foods in supermarkets where foods were not being kept at sufficiently low temperatures

The controversy over Salman Rushdie's book *The Satanic Verses* persisted as Muslim fundamentalists continued to call for his death. Rushdie has remained in hiding

The drug war in Colombia raged on. The picture shows a soldier guarding the estate of drug baron Vasquez

A soldier and a policeman stand guard at the Royal Marines School of Music in Deal, Kent where an IRA bomb killed ten bandsmen

The prison mutiny at Strangeways was the longest in British history. A handful of prisoners kept police and warders at bay for several weeks by barricading themselves on the roof

19

A small boy carries a Kalashnikov rifle in Ethiopia as the civil war continues

A very happy Robert Palhill arrives in the US after being released by his Beirut kidnappers

The crew of the *Maiden* celebrate the completion of their long journey in the Whitbread Round the World Yacht Race

In May 1990 restoration work began on Rio de Janiero's famous statue of Christ

America suffered several severe oil spills in the past year. The photo shows a swimmer emerging from the Gulf of Mexico in Texas covered in oil from a recent spill

Scotland's Gary Armstrong gets the ball away under pressure from England's Brian Moore in Scotland's 13–7 defeat of England which gave them the rugby championship

Mark Hughes beats Nigel Martyn to level the score at 3–3 during extra time in the FA Cup Final. Manchester United beat Crystal Palace 1–0 in the replay

James 'Buster' Douglas did the seemingly impossible when he knocked out Mike Tyson for the undisputed World Heavyweight Championship

England's Gary Lineker beats Mick McCarthy and Chris Morris of the Republic of Ireland to score England's goal in their 1–1 draw during the World Cup

(r.1389–1403) was recognized as Sultan (1396) but was defeated and captured by the Mongols under Tamerlane (1402). Murad II (r.1421–51) restored Ottoman power, enabling Mohammed II 'the Conqueror' (r.1451–81) to overthrow what was left of the Byzantine Empire by storming Constantinople (1453), which became, as Istanbul, the Ottoman capital.

Mohammed II later overran Greece, Montenegro, Serbia, Bosnia–Hercegovina, Wallachia and Bukovina in Europe and extended Ottoman borders in the south, east and north, capturing Christian Trebizond (the last Byzantine remnant) and the Crimea. Under Bayezid II (r.1481–1512), Moldavia and Bessarabia were conquered. Kurdistan and the Arab lands of Mesopotamia, Palestine, Syria, Hejaz and Egypt were added by Selim I (r.1512–20), to whom the Abbasid version of the Islamic Caliphate passed with the capture of Cairo. His successor, Suleiman 'the Magnificent' (r.1520–66), conquered the eastern Black Sea littoral, Baghdad, the Greek islands of Rhodes, Samos and Chios, Belgrade and Hungary, and unsuccessfully besieged Vienna (1529). His navy under Khaireddin Barbarossa imposed Ottoman suzerainty on North Africa, becoming the scourge of Christian ships in the Mediterranean. The millions of Christians passing under Ottoman rule were granted religious tolerance as a 'people of the Book' (the Koran); but failure to pay Ottoman taxes, or other signs of rebellion, called down ruthless repression.

The Empire's long decline set in under Suleiman's much inferior immediate successors, as the Ottoman system lost its earlier dynamism. Fratricidal succession struggles strengthened the authority of the Grand Viziers, some competent but drawn from family dynasties which became endemically corrupt. Later, power to make or unmake Sultans fell to the elite Janissaries, the semi-hereditary corps of palace guards descended from Christian captives. Islamic social rigidities contributed to economic inertia and cultural stagnation, in contrast to the new post-Reformation vibrancy of Christian Europe, whose military techniques also became superior to the unchanging methods of the Ottomans. In the first great Christian victory over the Turks, the Holy League led by Habsburg Spain and Austria destroyed the Ottoman fleet at Lepanto (1571), a disaster only partly offset by the Ottoman capture of Cyprus the same year. The able Grand Viziers of the Kiuprili family (1648–1703) extended Ottoman domains in Europe, taking Crete (1669) and Podolia in the Ukraine (1672). But the abortive second siege of Vienna (1683), the fall of Buda (1686), and of Belgrade (1688) marked the beginning of the Empire's territorial decline.

Under the Treaty of Carlowitz (1699), most of Hungary, Transylvania and Croatia were ceded to Austria, Podolia to Poland, and Dalmatia and the Morea to Venice. Further cessions to Austria, notably Belgrade and surrounding provinces and the rest of Hungary, were made under the Treaty of Passarowitz (1718), whereas the Ottomans recovered the Morea. In the east, Ottoman suzerainty over the Caucasus and Luristan came under severe challenge from Russia and Persia from the 1720s. Internally, the reign of Ahmed III (r.1703–30) was ended by the Janissaries amid popular uprising, but the ruling caste resisted real reform. War with Catherine the Great's Russia (1768–74) resulted, under the Treaty of Kutchuk-Kainardji (1774), in the loss of the Crimea and Azov, and Ottoman recognition of Russia's right to protect Christian Moldavia and Wallachia (later Romania). The cession of Bukovina to Austria (1775) preceded more Russian wars (1787–92, 1806–12), in which Bessarabia and western Georgia were ceded. An attempt by Napoleonic France to capture Ottoman Egypt (1798–1802) was defeated by British naval forces. By the early 19th century, the Ottoman Empire was seen as the 'sick man of Europe' and the focus of the Eastern Question, arising from the desire of the subject peoples for freedom and the great powers' competing designs on Ottoman territory.

The granting of autonomy to Serbia (1817) was followed by an uprising by the Greeks (1821), who with British, French and Russian assistance achieved a small independent state (1830), as France established a protectorate over Algiers and Egypt became self-governing. Internally, Mahmud II (r.1808–39) began the process of reform by eliminating the Janissaries (1824), but modernization attempts by Abdul Mejid I (r.1839–61) made little headway. Ottoman reverses in another conflict with Russia (1853) led to Anglo-French intervention in the Crimean War (1854–56). Appalling organization on both sides was only mitigated by the dedicated nursing of Florence Nightingale and 30 other nurses, although Russian designs on the Dardanelles and Bosphorus straits were thwarted. Ottoman atrocities against Bulgarian insurgents (1875–76) provoked the next war with pan-Slavist Russia (1877–78), whose draconian terms in victory were softened by the powers at the Congress of Berlin (1878). Nevertheless, the Empire was forced to recognize the independence of Romania, Serbia and Montenegro, the autonomy of Bulgaria, Austrian protectorates over Bosnia–Hercegovina, a British protectorate in Cyprus and Russia's acquisition of the Caucasus. The cession of Thessaly to Greece and the establishment of a French protectorate over Tunisia (1881) were followed by Britain's occupation of Egypt (1882) and Bulgaria's assertion of independence (1885).

A parliamentary constitution granted by Abdul Hamid II (r.1876–1909) on his accession was revoked during the 1877–78 war. Pressure for its restitution by reformers known as the Young Turks intensified when the Sultan was obliged to place his bankrupt finances in the hands of the European powers (1881). Ruling through reactionary clerics, Abdul Hamid used Kurdish irregulars to put down an Armenian nationalist revolt with much slaughter (1894–96). Rebellion by military elements of the Young Turks forced the Sultan to restore constitutional rule and convene a parliament in 1908; the following year he was deposed after attempting a counter-coup and succeeded by Mohammed V (r.1909–20). Further military defeats followed in wars with Italy (1911–12), which seized Libya and the Dodecanese, and with the Balkan states (1912–13). Most of the remaining Ottoman territories in Europe were lost, mainly to Greece and Serbia, although an independent state of Albania was formed while Bulgaria, which had also fought against Turkey, was obliged to drop its claims to territory in Macedonia and Thrace and even to cede territory to Romania. These setbacks, and the perceived designs of the Entente powers on Ottoman dominions, strengthened the pro-German inclinations of the nationalist Young Turks who dominated the government. Accordingly, Turkey fought on the side of the central powers in World War I and shared in their eventual defeat.

Under the Treaty of Sèvres (1920), Turkey accepted the loss of its Arab territories in the Middle East (which were mandated to their British and

French conquerors by the League of Nations); Greece was awarded eastern Thrace just short of Istanbul as well as the city of Izmir/Smyrna and its Anatolian hinterland; and an independent Armenian Republic was created in eastern Anatolia. Signed by the Sultan's government, the treaty was, however, repudiated by a provisional government set up in Apr. 1920 by Mustapha Kemal (1881–1938), hero of Turkey's 1915 victory at Gallipoli and later surnamed Atatürk ('father of the Turks'). His nationalist forces proceeded to quash the Armenian Republic and to eject the Greeks from Izmir (1922), assisted by the reluctance of Britain and France to intervene and the support of the new Soviet government. The last Sultan, Mohammed VI, was deposed in Oct. 1922 and the Sultanate abolished. By the Treaty of Lausanne (July 1923), Turkey regained Eastern Thrace and Izmir and was confirmed within the Anatolian borders which, with some later adjustments, exist today, in return for renouncing all other former Ottoman territories (including Cyprus). An accompanying exchange of their Greek and Turkish minorities by Turkey and Greece caused great dislocation and hardship.

On 29 Oct. 1923 a Turkish Republic was declared, with Atatürk as president and Ankara as its capital. A new constitution (1924) abolished the Caliphate and secularized the state. In succeeding years, state institutions and laws were Westernized, Arabic script gave way to the Latin alphabet, monogamy and Western dress became obligatory, and Western-style surnames were introduced. A Muslim business class emerged, with beneficial economic results which state investment in industrial projects assisted. The forms of parliamentary democracy were observed, but Atatürk's Republican People's Party (RPP) exercised effective one-party rule. On Atatürk's death in 1938, Gen. Ismet Inönü (1884–1974) succeeded to the presidency committed to maintaining the 'Kemalist' system. Turkey signed a non-aggression pact with the Soviet Union (1925), joined the League of Nations (1932) and signed the Montreux Convention (1936) restoring Turkish sovereignty over the Bosphorus and Dardanelles. Alignment with France and Britain resulted in the Sanjak of Alexandretta (in French-mandated Syria) becoming part of Turkey as Hatay (1939). Turkey remained neutral in World War II until Feb. 1945, when it declared war on Germany and Japan as a member of the UN.

In Turkey's first multi-party elections (1946), Inönü and the RPP won a large majority over the new opposition Democratic Party (DP), formed by RPP dissidents. The Soviet Union having abrogated the 1925 pact (1945), the RPP government accepted US Marshall Aid and signed a defence agreement with the United States (1947). In the 1950 elections, the DP came to power under Adnam Menderes, who took Turkey into NATO (1952), with Greece, and helped to conclude an independence agreement for Cyprus (1959). Mounting economic and internal security problems, and criticism of his alleged abandonment of 'Kemalism', impelled Menderes to curtail political liberties, whereupon his government was overthrown by the military (May 1960). Menderes was later hanged (Sept. 1961). Under a new constitution, providing for a bicameral rather than unicameral parliament, elections in Oct. 1961 restored civilian government under the premiership of Inönü (but with a military president), who concluded an association agreement with the EEC in 1963. The 1965 elections were won by the DP's successor, the Justice Party (JP) led by Süleyman Demirel, under whose premiership violence by the extreme right and left increased sharply, with the result that army leaders forced his resignation and imposed martial law (Mar. 1971).

After an interregnum of rule by military nominees, elections in Oct. 1973 brought to power (Jan. 1974) a short-lived coalition dominated by the RPP under the new left-wing leadership of Bülent Eçevit. His government authorized Turkey's invasion and occupation of Turkish-populated northern Cyprus (July 1974), precipitating a major (and unresolved) crisis with Greece which was exacerbated by a continuing dispute over the delimitation of the Aegean Sea continental shelf. Between 1975 and 1980 Demirel and Eçevit alternated in office at the head of a precarious coalition of minority governments, as economic conditions worsened and political violence intensified. After some 2,000 people had been killed in the ten months from Nov. 1979 (when a DP minority government took office under Demirel), the armed forces seized power on 12 Sept. 1980, suspended parliamentary government and imposed martial law. Under the leadership of Gen. Kenan Evren, a National Security Council (NSC) then held effective power for three years, during which existing political parties were dissolved (Oct. 1981) and internal stability was restored by harsh methods.

A new constitution approved by referendum in Nov. 1982 reaffirmed Turkey's democratic, secular and parliamentary identity, although certain temporary articles specified inter alia that Gen. Evren would remain head of state until 1989. A restrictive political parties law was also introduced (Apr. 1983). Elections to a new unicameral parliament held in Nov. 1983 under close military supervision were contested by only three authorized parties. The conservative Motherland Party (MP) won an overall majority and its leader, Turgut Özal, formed a civilian government, after which the NSC was dissolved (Dec. 1983). By Mar. 1987 martial law had been lifted in all provinces except the four with Kurdish majorities. Turkey submitted a formal application for full EC membership in Apr. 1987, but the reaction of existing members indicated that entry would not be achieved speedily, if at all. A referendum held in Sept. 1987 showed a narrow majority in favour of lifting a ten-year ban on over 100 political figures prominent before the 1980 coup (although a ban on Marxist and religious fundamentalist parties remained in force). In further elections held in Nov. 1987 the MP again secured an overall majority, although with only 36.3% of the vote, and the Social Democratic Populist Party (SHP) became the main opposition. Subsequent partial and local elections showed a major erosion of electoral support for Özal and the MP in favour of the SHP. A further crisis in relations with Greece (1986–87) was eased in June 1988, when Özal became the first Turkish prime minister to visit Athens since 1952. Özal, who narrowly escaped an assassination attempt in June 1988, was elected by parliament in Oct. 1989 to succeed Evren as president, taking office in the following month.

CONSTITUTION AND GOVERNMENT

Executive and legislature

The president, as head of state, is elected by the legislature; last election 31 Oct. 1989. The prime minister is head of government. The 450-seat legislature, the Grand National Assembly, is elected under a proportional representation system, by universal adult suffrage; last elections 29 Nov. 1987.

Present government

President Turgut Özal
Prime Minister Yildirim Akbulut
Principal Members of Cabinet Prof. Ali Bozer (Deputy Prime Minister; Minister of State); Safa Giray (National Defence); Abdulkadir Aksu (Interior); Mesut Yilmaz (Foreign Affairs); Ekdem Pakdermirli (Finance and Customs).

Justice

The system of law is based on a mixture of models taken from different European traditions, primarily Swiss (Neuchatel) for civil law, German for the commercial law code, and Italian for the Penal Code. At the local level, justices of peace have limited criminal and civil jurisdiction; more serious matters may go before courts of first instance, while the central criminal courts deal with crimes for which terms of imprisonment of more than 5 years may be imposed. Special state security courts try offences against the integrity of the state. The judiciary is defined constitutionally as independent of the executive and legislative branches. The death penalty is in force. There were no executions between 1985 and mid-1988.
Prisons. There are 50,160 prisoners.

National symbols

Flag. Red with a white crescent and a white five-pointed star.
Festivals. 23 Apr. (National Sovereignty and Children's Day); 1 May (Spring Day); 19 May (Youth and Sports Day); 30 Aug. (Victory Day); 29 Oct. (Republic Day).
Vehicle registration plate. TR.

INTERNATIONAL RELATIONS

Affiliations

NATO; OECD; ICO.

Defence

Total Armed Forces: 635,000 (575,800 conscripts). Terms of service: 18 months. Reserves: 951,000 (to age 46).
Army: 522,900; some 3,600 main battle tanks (M-47, M-48A1/A2, M-48A5, Leopard 1A3); 108 light tanks (M-41).
Navy: 55,000; 17 submarines (FRG Type 209/1200, US *Guppy* and *Tang*) and 19 principal surface combatants: 12 destroyers (US *Gearing*, *Carpenter* and *Sumner*) and seven frigates (FRG MEKO 200 and Koeln). 46 patrol and coastal combatants.
Naval Aviation: 22 combat aircraft, 9 armed helicopters.
Marines: 4,000.
Air Force: 57,400; 409 combat aircraft (F-5A/B, F-100D/F Super Sabre, F-4E, F-104S/TF 104G).
Forces Abroad: 27,000 on Cyprus.

ECONOMY

Currency

The unit is the Turkish lira, divided into 100 kurus.

National finance

Budget. The 1989 budget, in US$, was for expenditure of 16,225 million and revenue of 18,435 million. Main items of expenditure are education 12.6%; defence 11.4%.
Balance of payments. The balance of payments, in US$ (current account, 1987) was a deficit of 1,335 million.
Inflation. 78%.

Gross Domestic Product

Estimated total GDP US$60,820 million, per capita US$1,180 (overall size of economy ranking 37 in the world).
Economically active population. The total number of persons active in the economy was 18,800,000; unemployed: 15.3%.

Sector	% of workforce	% of GDP
industry	14	36
agriculture	56	17
services*	30	46

* services figure includes elements unassigned to other categories.

Energy and mineral resources

Oil and gas. Crude oil production: (1988) 2.8 million tons/2.5 million tonnes. The four oil refineries have a total refining capacity of 26.8 million tons/24.3 million tonnes.
Minerals. Turkey has rich mineral reserves and is a major producer of chrome. Production: (1987 in 1,000 tons/tonnes) coal 7,809/7,084; lignite 51,236/46,481; chrome 1,156/1,049; iron 5,915/5,366; boron 1,796/1,629.
Electricity. Capacity: 13.4 million kW; production: 49,951 million kWh; 870 kWh per capita (1988).

Bioresources

Agriculture. The soil is generally very fertile and main crops are cotton; tobacco; cereals (especially wheat); sugar beet; figs; olives and olive oil; dried fruits; nuts; silk; livestock products. Turkey is a legal producer of opium poppy for the pharmaceutical trade.
Crop production: (1987 in 1,000 tons/tonnes) wheat 20,833/18,900; barley 7,606/6,900; maize 2,646/2,400; rye 419/380; tobacco 201/182; oats 358/325; sugar (refined) 1,575/1,429; olive oil 471/427, grapes 3,307/3,000; oranges 772/700; lemons 375/340; hazelnuts 309/280; apples 1,852/1,680; potatoes 4,409/4,000; tea 728/660; rice 182/165.
Livestock numbers: (1987) sheep 40.4 million; goats 13.1 million; cattle 12 million; asses 1.2 million; horses 620,000; buffaloes 540,000.
Forestry. Total forest area is 49.7 million acres/20.1 million ha. Timber production: (1987 in 1,000 ft^3/m^3) logs 139,490/3,950; pit props 23,025/652; industrial wood 17,657/500; poles 6,568/186; firewood 175,016/4,956.
Fisheries. Catch: (1987 in tons/tonnes) sea fish 620,261/562,697; crustaceans and molluscs 22,218/20,156; freshwater fish 46,032/41,760.

Industry and commerce

Industry. Main industries are textiles; food processing; mining (coal, chromite, copper, boron minerals); steel; petroleum; construction; lumber, paper. Production: (1987 in tons/tonnes) fuel oil 8.9 million/8.1 million; motor oil 7.2 million/6.5 million; crude oil 4.5 million/4.1 million; pig iron 372,577/338,000; steel ingots 7.7 million/7 million; super phosphate 4 million/3.6 million; coke 3.3 million/3 million; cement 24.1 million/21.9 million; paper 586,878/532,412.
Commerce. Exports: (1987) US$10,200 million or 16% of GDP, including industrial products 70%; crops and livestock products 25%. Imports: £13,300 million, including crude oil; machinery; transport equipment; metals; pharmaceuticals; dyes; plastics; rubber; mineral fuels; fertilizers; chemicals. Countries exported to were West Germany 19.4%; US 10.6%;

Italy 7.8%; Iran 7.6%; Iraq 7.4%; Japan. Imports came from West Germany 15.9%; US 10.6%; Italy 7.8%; Iraq 6.9%; Japan 6.2%.

Trade with UK. In 1988 Turkey imported UK goods worth £477,539,000; exports to UK totalled £509,636,000.

Tourism. (1987) 2.89 million visitors.

COMMUNICATIONS

Railways

There are 6,410 miles/10,328 km of railways, of which 352 miles/567 km are electrified.

Roads

There are 199,155 miles/320,700 km of roads (36,723 miles/59,136 km of which are highways).

Aviation

Türk Hava Yollari AO (THY) provides domestic and international services (main airports are at Atatürk (Istanbul), Esenboga (Ankara), Adana and Dalaman). Passengers: (1988) 3.9 million.

Shipping

There are about 745 miles/1,200 km of inland waterways. There are 13 secondary and 18 minor ports, but the main ones are Iskenderun, Istanbul and Mersin. The merchant marine consists of 338 ships of 1,000 GRT or over. Freight loaded: (1985) 60.3 million tons/54.7 million tonnes; unloaded: 41 million tons/37 million tonnes.

Telecommunications

There are 3.1 million telephones and a fair domestic and international system with a trunk radio-relay network. There are 8.2 million radios and 8.3 million televisions (1986). There are two national TV channels and four radio networks, as well as the Voice of Turkey external radio service in 17 languages, run by the state-owned TRT corporation.

EDUCATION AND WELFARE

Education

Schools. Primary education is free, compulsory and co-educational. There are secondary schools, lycées and vocational schools.

Universities. There are 28 universities and over 100 other institutes of further education.

Literacy. 70%.

Health

(1986) 38,829 doctors (one per 1,425 people) and 111,135 beds (one per 498 people) in 661 hospitals and 95 health centres (1987).

TURKS AND CAICOS ISLANDS

GEOGRAPHY

The Turks and Caicos Islands are a group of 30 islands (eight of which are inhabited) in the North Atlantic Ocean. The terrain is low, flat limestone with extensive marshes and mangrove swamps. The land is not suitable for cultivation. The capital is Grand Turk.

Climate

Tropical marine, moderated by trade winds; sunny and relatively dry.

Population

Total population (1989 est.) 9,531.

Birth rate 2.5%. **Death rate** 0.5%. **Rate of population increase** 2.4%

Religion

Christianity. Anglicans; Roman Catholics; Baptists; Methodists; Church of God; Seventh Day Adventists.

Language

English.

HISTORY

The Turks and Caicos Islands were apparently uninhabited at the time of the arrival of Europeans in the early 16th century, although Lucayan and Arawak Indians had lived on the islands. No attempts were made by Europeans at settlement for many years and it was not until the late 17th century that British settlers from Bermuda began to visit the islands regularly in order to obtain salt. Permanent settlement followed gradually, augmented in the late 18th century by the arrival on the Caicos Islands of planters from the United States after the War of Independence who settled on the islands with their African slaves. Slavery was abolished in 1834.

The islands were at first placed under the control of the Bahamas but, at the request of the inhabitants, they became a separate colony in 1848. In 1873 the islands became a dependency of Jamaica and remained so until 1959 when they received their own governor. On Jamaica's independence from Britain in Aug. 1962 the islands again became a British Crown Colony. The Turks and Caicos received their own governor again in 1972 and greater internal autonomy in 1976. In 1980 the ruling pro-independence People's Democratic Movement (PDM) agreed with the British government that independence would be achieved if the PDM won the 1980 general election. The PDM, however, lost the election to the Progressive National Party (PNP), which supported continued dependent status. The leader of the PNP, Norman Saunders, became chief minister. The PNP retained power in elections in 1984 but in 1985 Saunders and two of his associates were arrested and convicted in the US on drugs charges. The PNP maintained itself in power by winning the by-elections held as a result, but on 24 July 1986 the Governor dissolved the government and replaced it with an advisory council after a report on allegations of arson and fraud found that the chief minister, Nathaniel Francis, two other ministers and two PDM members of the Legislative Council were unfit to hold office. A Constitutional Commission was created to suggest possible revisions to the constitution and electoral process. A general election under the provisions of the new constitution with voting in multi-member constituencies was held on 3 Mar. 1988. It was won convincingly by the PDM whose leader, Oswald Skippings, became prime minister.

CONSTITUTION AND GOVERNMENT

Turks and Caicos Islands are a dependent territory of the United Kingdom. The constitution was introduced on 30 Aug. 1976, suspended in 1986, and at present is being reviewed by a Constitutional Commission. There is an executive council and a 14-member legislative council.

Leader Michael Bradley, Governor since 1987; Oswald Skippings, Chief Minister since 1988.

National symbols

Flag. Blue, with the flag of the UK in the upper hoist-side quadrant, and with a shield (yellow, and containing a conch shell, lobster and cactus) centred on the outer half.

National holiday. 30 Aug. (Constitution Day).

ECONOMY

The economy is based on fishing, tourism and offshore banking. Subsistence farming exists only on the Caicos Islands. Most food has to be imported.

Currency

US dollar.

COMMUNICATIONS

There are ports at Grand Turk, Salt Cay, Providenciales, Cockburn Harbour. There are seven airports, four with permanent surface runways; 75 miles/121 km of road. There is a telephone system, three AM radio stations, but no FM; several TV stations; one satellite ground station.

TUVALU

Tuvalu (formerly Ellice Islands)

GEOGRAPHY

Covering a total land area of 9.2 miles²/23.96 km², the nine atolls comprising the constitutional monarchy of Tuvalu lie in the west central Pacific 652 miles/1,050 km north of Fiji and 2,496 miles/4,020 km north-east of Sydney, Australia. The coral chain is 360 miles/579 km long, consisting of the islands of Funafuti, Nukufetau, Nukulailai, Nanumea, Niutao, Nanumanga, Nui, Vaitupu and Niulakita, all low-lying with a maximum elevation of 15 ft/4.6 m on Niulakita. Poor soils restrict vegetation to coconut palms and salt-resistant bush.

Climate

Warm and pleasant with slight temperature variation (annual temperature range 79–90°F/26–32°C) and some moderating, cooling trade-wind influences. Average annual rainfall totals vary from 102 in/2,600 mm in the northern atolls, increasing southwards to 144 in/3,650 mm or more. Funafuti: Jan. 84°F/28.9°C. July 81°F/27.2°C. Average annual rainfall 158 in/4,003 mm.

Cities and towns

Funafuti (capital)	2,856
Vaitupu	1,231
Niutao	904
Nanumea	879

Population

Total population is 8,624 of which 34.2% live in urban areas. Population density is 937 persons per mile²/342.2 per km². Ethnic divisions: 96% Polynesian (Samoan and Tokelavan related).

Birth rate 2.7%. **Death rate** 1.0%. **Rate of increase** 1.7%. **Age distribution** under 15 = 33.8%; over 60 = 7.7% (1979). **Life expectancy** female 63; male 60; average 62.

Religion

Christianity. 97% of the population belong to the Protestant Church of Tuvalu but there are a few groups of Roman Catholics, Seventh Day Adventists and Baha'is, and a very small Muslim community.

Language

Tuvaluan is a Polynesian-Samoan dialect. English is also widely spoken and a Kiribati dialect is in use on the island of Nui.

HISTORY

The language and traditions of these Polynesian islands indicate that they were invaded by Tongans and Samoans in the early 14th century. After probable sightings by Spanish ships in the 16th century, further European contact did not take place until later in the 18th century and it took until 1826 to discover the whole group, which became known as the Ellice Islands. Missionaries and recruiters for labour on the plantations of Queensland and Fiji became active on the atolls from the 1860s, but the abuses of the labour trade led to the British decision in 1892 to annex the islands and form the Gilbert and Ellice Islands Protectorate. In 1916 these became a Crown Colony. In 1942, during World War II, American forces occupied the Ellice Islands to counter the advance of the Japanese, who had invaded the Gilberts. The period 1963–77 saw the steady constitutional development towards the present system of government in Tuvalu. In 1974 the Ellice Islanders voted in a referendum to separate from the Micronesian Gilbertese, with the official separation taking effect a year later. Tuvalu achieved independence on 1 Oct. 1978 as a constitutional monarchy within the Commonwealth, with the governor general as the Queen's representative. In Mar. 1984 Tuvalu established diplomatic relations with Kiribati and in 1987 the Tuvalu Trust Fund was set up by Britain, New Zealand, Australia and South Korea to provide development aid. Dr Tomasi Puapua, who became prime minister following the general election of 1981, was re-elected prime minister by a ballot of MPs after the general election in 1985.

CONSTITUTION AND GOVERNMENT

Executive and legislature

The head of state is the British sovereign, represented by a governor general. The head of government is the prime minister (who is elected by MPs from amongst their number), who determines the composition of the Cabinet, ministers then being appointed by the governor general. The unicameral 12-member Parliament is popularly elected for up to four years.

Present government

Governor General Sir Tupua Leupena
Prime Minister; Minister of Local Government and Foreign Affairs Dr Tomasi Puapua
Deputy Prime Minister; Finance Henry Faati Naisali.

Justice

There are eight island courts and a High Court in the capital, but without its own senior law officers, the Chief Justice of Fiji being its president. Appeals must similarly be dealt with in the Fiji Court of Appeal. The death penalty was abolished before independence.

National symbols

Flag. Blue ground with Union Jack in top-left quarter and nine five-pointed stars in the fly.
Festivals. 13 Mar. (Commonwealth Day); 19 June (Queen's Official Birthday); 7 Aug. (National Children's Day); 1–2 Oct. (Tuvalu Day, Anniversary of Independence); 14 Nov. (Prince of Wales's birthday).

INTERNATIONAL RELATIONS

Affiliations

Commonwealth (with special status); ACP; SPF.

Defence

No armed forces as such.

ECONOMY

Currency

The unit is the Australian or Tuvaluan dollar, divided into 100 cents.
Inflation. 3.9%.

Gross Domestic Product

Estimated total GDP US$4 million (GNP), per capita US$450 (overall size of economy ranking 195 in the world).

Energy and mineral resources

Electricity. Capacity: 2,600 kW; production: 3 million kWh; 350 kWh per capita (1988).

Bioresources

Agriculture. The soil is of poor quality and farming is at subsistence level. Main crops are coconuts; coconut palms; copra.
Crop production: (1984) copra 948 tons/860 tonnes.
Fisheries. Sea fishing is excellent but largely unexploited by local people.

Industry and commerce

Industry. Main industries are fishing; tourism; copra. A large source of income is from Tuvaluans working abroad, especially those employed in the phosphate industry on Nauru.
Commerce. Exports: (1983) US$1 million, including copra. Imports were US$2.8 million, including food; animals; mineral fuels; machinery; manufactured goods. Trading partners: (imports and exports) Fiji; Australia; New Zealand.
Trade with UK. In 1988 Tuvalu imported UK goods worth £105,000; exports to UK totalled £1,000.
Tourism. (1987) 474 visitors.

COMMUNICATIONS

Aviation

Air Marshall (Kiribati) operates a weekly service between Tarawa (Kiribati) and Funafuti, and Air Fiji flies between Suya and Funafuti three times a week.

Shipping

The ports are the atolls of Funafuti and Nukufetau. There is one merchant marine ship of 1,000 GRT or over.

Telecommunications

There are 108 telephones, 300 radio telephones and one AM station (no FM). There are 2,500 radios and no television service (1986). Radio Tuvalu broadcasts in Tuvaluan and English.

EDUCATION AND WELFARE

Education

Schools. In 1984 there were nine primary schools with a total of 924 pupils and one secondary school with 250 pupils.
Literacy. Under 50%.

Health

In 1984 there were four doctors (one per 2,156 people); one hospital with 36 beds (one per 239 people).

UGANDA

Republic of Uganda (English)
Jamhuri ya Uganda (Swahili)

GEOGRAPHY

Located on the equator, the landlocked country of Uganda in east Africa covers a total area of 91,111 miles^2/236,040 km^2 divided into ten provinces. The bulk of Ugandan territory forms part of the Central African plateau, scored by mountains and depressions. In the populous west, the volcanic Virunga range rises to 13,540 ft/4,127 m at Mount Muhavura while Mount Margherita attains a maximum elevation of 16,765 ft/5,110 m in the Ruwenzori chain on the Zaïrean border between Lake Albert and Lake Edward. Lake Albert lies within the western portion of the Great Rift Valley system which also contains the Albert Nile River valley. The Victoria Nile drains north-east of Lake Albert. The Kenyan frontier is marked by the volcanic Mount Elgon massif and in the extreme north-east by the Karasuk and Turkana hills. In the south, Lake Victoria, Africa's largest lake, dominates the country's hydrological profile. Other major lakes include Kyoga, Kqania, George and Bisina. The eastern and south-western regions are generally speaking the areas of highest population density. 23% of the land area is arable (ferralite soil) and 30% is forested. Savannah vegetation predominates in the central regions and to the north; 15,054 miles^2/39,000 km^2 of the total surface area is swamp. Kabalega is the largest of Uganda's four national parks.

Climate

Tropical, mitigated by altitude and by the influences of Lake Victoria. Rainfall decreases south-west to north-east. Lakeside rainfall totals of 59 in/1,500 mm and above dwindle to less than 39 in/1,000 mm in the central and north-eastern plateau. Most rain falls Mar.-June. Temperatures range between 59°F/15°C and 86°F/30°C. Kampala: Jan. 74°F/23.3°C. July 70°F/21.1°C. Average annual rainfall 45 in/1,150 mm. Entebbe: Jan. 72°F/22.2°C. July 69°F/20.6°C. Average annual rainfall 59 in/1,506 mm.

Cities and towns

Kampala (capital)	330,700
Jinja and Njeru	52,509
Bugembe planning area	46,884
Mbale	23,544
Entebbe	21,096

Population

Total population is 17,007,530 of which 14.4% live in urban areas. Population density is 187 persons per mile^2/78.7 per km^2. Ethnic divisions: 99% African; 1% European, Asian and Arab. Principal ethnic groups are the Ganda, Teso, Nkole, Nyoro and Soga peoples.

Birth rate 4.9%. **Death rate** 1.5%. **Rate of population increase** 1980–87 3.4%. **Age distribution** under 15 = 48.1%; over 65 = 2.5%. **Life expectancy** female 50; male 47; average 48.

Religion

33% Roman Catholic; 33% Protestant; 18% animist; 16% Muslim.

Language

English is the official language. The 40 separate ethnic groups that constitute Uganda's heterogeneous African mix fall into three linguistic groups. 70% of the population are Bantu-speaking (Ganda, Soga, Nyoro and Nkole); 16% are Nilotic in linguistic origin (Lango and Aholi); the remaining 14% are predominantly Nilo-Hamitic. English and Swahili are both commonly used, but Luganda (Ganda) is the most widely acknowledged tongue.

HISTORY

Palaeolithic hand axes dating from 50,000 BC have been found along the Kagera River in Uganda, although it was not until the first millennium AD that agriculture developed in the region. By the 14th century the Chwezi people had founded a centralized kingdom with its capital at Bigo. This was superseded by the rise of the Ganda in the 17th century

During the reign of Kabaka (King) Mutesa I (1856–84) European explorers first entered the country of Buganda, followed by Anglican and Catholic missionaries. At about this time, traders from Sudan brought Islam to the country. Following the Anglo–German Agreement of 1886, the territory of present-day Uganda, incorporating Buganda and 28 other ethnic groups, came under the British sphere of influence. It was administered by a trading company until 1893 when it was formally incorporated into the empire as a Protectorate. In 1900 an agreement was signed with the Kabaka that privileged Buganda with a degree of autonomy. The Ganda, together with other Bantu peoples from the south, subsequently played an important role in the administration of Uganda while the armed forces were recruited among the Acholi and Langi from the north of the country.

In 1955, the Namirembe Agreement, giving Ugandans a majority in the Protectorate's executive and administrative councils, signalled that independence was on its way. Rival political parties were formed, divided along ethnic and religious rather than ideological lines. In order to prevent the country splitting up, the British imposed a federal constitution at independence in 1962 which gave considerable autonomy to the four kingdoms, including Buganda, and ten administrative districts. The first government, formed by an alliance of Ganda and northern groups, was led by the Kabaka as president and Milton Obote, a Langi, as prime minister.

In 1966 Obote suspended the constitution, declared himself executive president and moved government policy abruptly to the left. Resistance in Buganda had to be put down by the army, under Idi Amin, who, in turn, seized power in 1971.

During the eight years of Amin's rule, an estimated 300,000 Ugandans were killed, the Langi and their neighbours the Acholi being particularly victimized. Meanwhile, the economy collapsed. As part of his 'economic war' against foreign domination, Amin ordered the expulsion in 1972 of Asians living in Uganda who did not hold Ugandan citizenship. Many of them held British nationality, and 27,200 went to Britain, several thousand British Asians also being resettled in Canada and others in India, Pakistan and elsewhere.

An Air France Airbus, carrying 12 crew and 247 passengers from Tel Aviv via Athens to Paris, was hijacked on 27 June 1976 by two West Germans and two Palestinians and flown via Benghazi to Entebbe in Uganda. The non-Israeli passengers were released there, where six more men joined the hijackers. Accusing Uganda of collusion with the terrorists, an Israeli commando force flew into Entebbe on 3 July, killed 20 Ugandan soldiers and seven terrorists, and rescued all the hostages except three who were killed and one (Mrs Dora Bloch) who had been taken to Kampala hospital before the commando raid and was believed to have been murdered afterwards by Ugandan security forces.

Idi Amin was overthrown by Ugandan exiles supported by the Tanzanian army in 1979. After a year of political chaos, in which two leaders were deposed by the northern-dominated Uganda National Liberation Army (UNLA), elections were held in Dec. 1980. These returned Milton Obote as president. Accusing the provisional government of electoral malpractice, opposition leader Yoweri Museveni formed the National Resistance Army (NRA) and started a guerrilla war against Pres. Obote. Civilian casualties from the government's anti-guerrilla operations exceeded those of Idi Amin's rule: the populous Luwero region was devastated. Pres. Obote alienated the Acholi faction in the army by appointing a Langi as commander-in-chief in 1983, over the heads of Acholi candidates. In July 1985, Acholi units mounted a coup bringing Gen. Tito Okello to power at the head of a Military Council. Okello was, however, unable to defeat the NRA which occupied Kampala in Jan. 1986 and was in effective control of most of the country by mid-1986.

Yoweri Museveni, sworn in as president on 29 Jan. 1986, set up a National Resistance Council (NRC) as the government. Although rival political parties were banned, the government included a wide range of political allegiances in a fragile coalition, with a cabinet numbering 68 ministers in Feb. 1988. This assured the Museveni administration of considerable support. Nevertheless, resistance continued in the north and east, where guerrillas and a messianic cult, the Holy Spirit Army, led by Alice Lakwena, operated. In Dec. 1987, Alice Lakwena was captured in Kenya and her army disbanded. Six months later, in June 1988, the government signed a peace agreement with one of the main opposition groups, the Uganda People's Democratic Party (UPDA).

A mutiny in the NRA was suppressed in April 1988, and in Oct. a coup plot was discovered and foiled. In Nov. 1989 Museveni replaced the Army Commander, the Chief of Staff and the Minister of State for Defence in what was seen as part of the armed forces' process of transition from guerilla force to regular army.

CONSTITUTION AND GOVERNMENT

Executive and legislature

The executive president is head of government, assisted by a prime minister and cabinet composed of representatives of a number of political parties; although the parties continue to exist, political activity is prohibited. The 278-member National Resistance Council (NRC) functions as a legislature pending the arrangement of a transition to full democratic rule; NRC elections (in Feb. 1989) were conducted on a non-party indirect election basis through a system of local and provincial councils, with in addition 68 presidentially appointed members.

Present government

President; Minister of Defence Yoweri Museveni
Prime Minister Dr Samson Kisekka
Other Principal Members of the Cabinet Eriya Kategaya (First Deputy Prime Minister); Paul Semogerere (Second Deputy Prime Minister, Minister of Foreign Affairs and Regional Co-operation); Abubakar Mayanja (Third Deputy Prime Minister); Sam Njuba (Constitutional Affairs); Dr Crispus Kiyonga (Finance); Ibrahim Mukiibi (Internal Affairs); George Kanyeihamba (Justice; Attorney General).

Justice

The system of law as reinstated under the Museveni regime is based on a combination of English common law and customary law. The highest court is the Court of Appeal of Uganda which hears appeals from the High Court. At local level, justice is administered by magistrates of the first, second and third grades; Chief Magistrates preside over the subordinate courts, from which appeal is to the High Court. The death penalty is in force. There were over 11 executions between 1985 and mid-1988. Offences: armed robbery, murder.

National symbols

Flag. Six horizontal stripes of black, yellow, red, black, yellow and red. In the centre of the flag is an old badge of Uganda, the crested crane on a white disc.
Festivals. 25 Mar. (Anniversary of the Formation of the UNLF); 1 May (Labour Day); 3 June (Martyrs' Day); 9 Oct. (Independence Day).
Vehicle registration plate. EAU.

INTERNATIONAL RELATIONS

Affiliations

NAM; OAU; ACP; Commonwealth.

Defence

Total Armed Forces: 35,000. Terms of service: voluntary.
National Resistance Army (NRA).
Aviation: six combat aircraft (SF-260W, AS-202).
Opposition: Holy Spirit Movement: numbers not known, small arms only.

ECONOMY

Currency

The unit is the shilling, divided into 100 cents.

National finance

Budget. The 1988 FY budget, in US$, was for expenditure of 790 million and revenue of 470 million. Main items of expenditure are defence 26.3%; education 15%.

Balance of payments. The balance of payments, in US$ (current account, 1987) was a deficit of 200 million.

Inflation. 155%.

Gross Domestic Product

Estimated total GDP US$3,560 million, per capita US$220 (overall size of economy ranking 97 in the world).

Economically active population. The total number of persons active in the economy was 4,500,000.

Sector	% of workforce	% of GDP
industry	n/a	5
agriculture	over 80	76
services*	n/a	19

* services figure includes elements unassigned to other categories.

Energy and mineral resources

Minerals. Substantial deposits of copper and cobalt. Copper ore production: (1984) 1,213 tons/1,100 tonnes.

Electricity. Capacity: 173,000 kW; production: 312 million kWh; 18 kWh per capita (1988).

Bioresources

Agriculture. Approximately 80% of the work force are employed in agriculture. Coffee accounts for 93% of exports; other crops are cotton; tobacco; tea.

Crop production: (1986 in 1,000 tons/tonnes) tobacco 4.4/4; coffee 215/195; cotton lint 8.8/8; tea 3.3/3; sugar cane 606/550.

Livestock numbers: (1987) cattle 5.2 million; sheep 1.72 million; goats 3.32 million; pigs 260,000; poultry 19 million.

Forestry. 30% of the land area is forest and woodland and almost all the exploitable forest consists of hardwoods.

Fisheries. Uganda has 8.6 million acres/3.5 million ha of lakes and a large number of rivers. Fish production: (1983) 189,596 tons/172,000 tonnes. Fish farming (mainly tilapia and carp) is being developed.

Industry and commerce

Industry. Main industries are sugar; brewing; tobacco; cotton textiles; cement.

Commerce. Exports: (1987) US$414 million or 11% of GDP, including coffee 93%; cotton; tea. Imports were US$492 million, including petroleum products; machinery; cotton piece goods; metals; transportation equipment. Countries exported to were US 27%; UK 14%; France; Spain. Imports came from Kenya 39%; UK 17%; Japan 7%.

Trade with UK. In 1988 Uganda imported UK goods worth £35,340,000; exports to UK totalled £30,487,000.

Tourism. (1986) 35,000 visitors.

COMMUNICATIONS

Railways

There are 787 miles/1,268 km of railways.

Roads

There are 17,594 miles/28,332 km of roads, of which 3,871 miles/6,233 km are concrete or bituminized.

Aviation

Uganda Airlines Corporation provides international services (main airport is at Entebbe, on Lake Victoria, some 25 miles/40 km from Kampala). Passengers: (1984) 50,000.

Shipping

The inland waterways consist of the Victoria, Albert, Kyoga, George and Edward lakes, and the Victoria Nile, and Albert Nile rivers. Jinja and Port Bell, the major inland ports, are both on Lake Victoria. The merchant marine consists of one roll-on/roll-off cargo ship of approximately 1,000 GRT.

Telecommunications

There are 61,600 telephones and a fair system with radio-relay and radio-communications stations. There are 340,000 radios (1985) and 100,000 televisions (1986). Radio Uganda, and the Uganda TV Service, are both government-controlled.

EDUCATION AND WELFARE

Education

Schools. There are 7,905 primary schools with 2.2 million pupils. There are 50 technical schools and institutes with 6,556 students, five technical colleges, five colleges of commerce and ten teacher-trainng colleges.

Universities. Uganda Polytechnic (504 students); Uganda College of Business Studies (333 students); Makerere University (1,318 students); Mbale Islamic University (163).

Literacy. 52%.

Health

In 1983 there were 76 hospitals with a total of 20,343 beds (one per 836 people).

UNION OF SOVIET SOCIALIST REPUBLICS

Soyuz Sovietskikh Sotsialisticheskikh Respublik

GEOGRAPHY

The Union of Soviet Socialist Republics (USSR) is the largest country in the world: it covers a total area of 8,647,172 miles^2/22,402,000 km^2, nearly 1/6th of the total global land surface, and extends east-west across northern Eurasia for nearly 6,210 miles/10,000 km from the Pacific Ocean to the Baltic Sea, and for nearly 3,105 miles/5,000 km north-south at its widest point. The USSR consists of 15 Union (constituent) Republics: the Russian Soviet Federative Socialist Republic (RSFSR or Russian Federation), the largest and most populous with 77% of the total territory and 53% of the total population, covers the larger portion of the territory in both the European and Asian parts of the country; the Ukraine, the second largest in population, lies in the south-west of the European part of the USSR; Byelorussia lies immediately north of the Ukraine; Lithuania, Latvia and Estonia border the Baltic Sea; Moldavia is sandwiched between the Ukraine and the Romanian border in the extreme south-west; Georgia, Armenia and Azerbaijan form Transcaucasia, stretching south-west from the Black to the Caspian Seas; Kazakhstan, the second largest republic in area, stretches from the Caspian Sea to the Chinese border, and together with Turkmenia, Uzbekistan, Tadjikistan and Kirghizia to the south, forms Soviet Central Asia.

The USSR is divided geographically by the Ural Mountain chain (high point Narodnaya, 6,214 ft/ 1,894 m in the sub-polar north) traversing the country over 1,490 miles/2,400 km from the Arctic Ocean in the north, to Kazakhstan. To the west of the Urals (Ural'skiy Khrebet), the East European plain (average elevation 558 ft/170 m above sea level) provides broad areas of fertile land interspersed with a number of low-lying glaciated features, boulder clays, sands, lakes and hills. In this region, the major north-flowing rivers are the Pechora, Severnaya Dvina, and Mezen systems, while the Dnestr, Dnepr, Don and Volga all drain southwards. The Caucasus mountains in the south, between the Black and Caspian Seas, include Mt Elbrus, Europe's highest peak (18,510 ft/5,642 m). To the east of the Urals, the low-lying West Siberian steppelands stretch eastwards to the Yenisey river and climb southwards towards the Kazakh Uplands and Turgay Plateau. Beyond the Yenisey lies the central Siberian plateau (elevation 1,476–2,953 ft/450–900 m) bounded to the east by the central Yakut plain and north by the North Siberian lowland (Khatanga). The North Siberian plain is bounded south and east by a series of complex fold-mountain chains marking the Soviet-Chinese and Soviet-Mongolian frontiers and the Pacific seaboard. Principal mountain ranges (other than the Urals) in the USSR are the Pamir, Tien Shan and Altay ranges (in Central Asia rising to heights in excess of 16,404 ft/

Union Republics

	Area (miles²/km²)	Capital	Pop. (millions)	Ethnic composition (1979 census)
Armenia	11,580/30,000	Yerevan	3.4	Armenian 89.7%; Azerbaijani 5.3%; Russian 2.3%; Kurd 1.7%
Azerbaijan	33,582/87,000	Baku	6.8	Azerbaijani 78.1%; Armenian 7.9%; Russian 7.9%; Daghestani 3.4%
Byelorussia	80,288/208,000	Minsk	10.1	Byelorussian 79.4%; Russian 11.9%; Polish 4.2%; Ukrainian 2.4%; Jewish 1.4%
Estonia	17,370/45,000	Tallinn	1.6	Estonian 64.7%; Russian 27.9%; Ukrainian 2.5%; Byelorussian 1.6%; Finnish 1.2%
Georgia	27,020/70,000	Tbilisi	5.3	Georgian 68.8%; Armenian 9.0%; Russian 7.4%; Azerbaijani 5.1%; Ossetian 3.2% Abkhazian 1.7%
Kazakhstan	1,048,762/2,717,000	Alma-Ata	16.2	Russian 40.8%; Kazakh 36.0%; Ukrainian 6.1%; Tatar 2.1%
Kirghizia	76,814/199,000	Frunze	4.1	Kirghiz 47.9%; Russian 25.9%; Uzbek 12.1%; Ukrainian 3.1%; Tatar 2.0%
Latvia	24,704/64,000	Riga	2.6	Latvian 53.7%; Russian 32.8%; Byelorussian 4.5%; Ukrainian 2.7%; Polish 2.5%
Lithuania	25,090/65,000	Vilnius	3.6	Lithuanian 80.1%; Russian 8.6%; Polish 7.7%; Byelorussian 1.5%
Moldavia	13,124/34,000	Kishinev	4.2	Moldavian 63.9%; Ukrainian 14.2%; Russian 12.8%; Gagauz 3.5%; Jewish 2.0%; Bulgarian 2.0%
Russian Federation	6,590,950/17,075,000	Moscow	145.3	Russian 82.6%; Tatar 3.6%; Ukrainian 2.7%; Chuvash 1.2%
Tadjikistan	55,198/143,000	Dushanbe	4.8	Tadjik 58.8%; Uzbek 22.9%; Russian 10.4%; Tatar 2.1%
Turkmenia	188,368/488,000	Ashkhabad	3.4	Turkmen 68.4%; Russian 12.6%; Uzbek 8.5%; Kazakh 2.9%
Ukraine	233,144/604,000	Kiev	51.2	Ukrainian 73.6%; Russian 21.1%; Jewish 1.3%
Uzbekistan	172,542/447,000	Tashkent	19.0	Uzbek 68.7%; Russian 10.8%; Tatar 4.2%; Kazakh 4.0%; Tadjik 3.9%; Karakalpak 1.9%

5,000 m), the mountains of Uzbekistan, Tadjikistan, Kirgizia and Kazakhstan, the volcanic Kamchatka Peninsula including Siberia's highest peak, Mt Klyuchev (15,584 ft/4,750 m), and the maritime ranges in the far east and the Pacific. The Soviet Union's highest peak is Pik Kommunizma in the Pamirs at 24,590 ft/7,495 m.

Only 25% of the USSR's total land area is put to agricultural use, with less than half of that being sown with crops. Over 33% of the land is covered by swampy coniferous forest or taiga. Major vegetation zones extend almost uniformly east-west, with tundra covering the extreme north beside the Arctic Ocean, and giving way to taiga and then to the fertile steppes of the Ukraine, southern European Russia and northern Kazakhstan. Most of Central Asia is desert or semi-desert.

Climate

Climatic conditions vary dramatically, ranging from northerly polar conditions (–90°F/–68°C has been recorded near Verkhoyansk in north-east Siberia) through sub-arctic and humid continental, to subtropical and semi-arid conditions in the south. In summer temperatures may reach 122°F/50°C in central Asia. Permafrost covers almost the whole of Siberia, and ranges in depth from one metre in the south to over 1,181 ft/360 m in the far north. Precipitation decreases from 98 in/2,500 mm in the south-west to less than 2 in/50 mm in eastern Siberia. Areas of greatest precipitation are those regions bordering the Baltic, Black, and Caspian Seas and at the southern end of the USSR's Pacific coast, where summer monsoon conditions prevail. Moscow: Jan. 15°F/–9.4°C. July 65°F/18.3°C. Average annual rainfall 24 in/630 mm. Kiev: Jan. 21°F/–6.1°C. July 68°F/20°C. Average annual rainfall 22 in/554 mm. Vladivostok: Jan. 6°F/–14.4°C. July 65°F/18.3°C. Average annual rainfall 23.6 in/599 mm.

Cities and towns

Moskva (Moscow, capital)	8,703,000
Leningrad	4,901,000
Kiyev (Kiev)	2,495,000
Tashkent	2,073,000
Baku	1,722,000
Kharkov	1,567,000
Minsk	1,510,000
Gorky	1,409,000
Novosibirsk	1,405,000
Sverdlovsk	1,316,000
Kuybyshev	1,267,000
Tbilisi	1,174,000
Dnepropetrovsk	1,166,000
Yerevan	1,148,000
Odessa	1,132,000
Omsk	1,124,000
Chelyabinsk	1,107,000
Alma-Ata	1,088,000
Donetsk	1,081,000
Ufa	1,077,000
Perm	1,066,000
Kazan	1,057,000
Rostov-na-Donu (Rostov-on-Don)	1,004,000
Volgograd	988,000
Saratov	918,000
Riga	900,000
Krasnoyarsk	899,000
Voronezh	872,000
Zaporozhye	865,000
Lvov	767,000
Krivoi Rog	698,000
Kishinev	663,000
Yaroslavl	634,000
Karaganda	633,000
Frunze	632,000
Izhevsk	631,000
Togliatti	627,000
Krasnodar	623,000
Vladivostock	615,000
Irkutsk	609,000
Barnaul	596,000
Khabarovsk	591,000
Ulyanovsk	589,000
Novokuznetsk	589,000
Dushanbe	582,000
Vilnius	566,000
Penza	540,000
Tula	538,000
Orenburg	537,000
Mariupol	529,000
Kemerovo	520,000
Lugansk	509,000
Astrakhan	509,000
Ryazan	508,000
Nikolayev	501,000
Tomsk	489,000
Gomel	488,000
Naberezhnye Chelny	480,000
Ivanovo	479,000
Tallinn	478,000
Lipetsk	465,000
Tyumen	456,000
Makeyevka	455,000
Kalinin	447,000
Bryansk	445,000
Kursk	434,000
Murmansk	432,000
Magnitogorsk	430,000
Nizhnii Tagil	427,000
Kirov	421,000
Kaunas	417,000
Arkhangelsk	416,000
Cheboksary	414,000
Grozny	404,000
Kaliningrad	394,000
Chimkent	389,000
Samarkand	388,000
Vinnitsa	383,000
Ashkhabad	382,000
Mogilev	359,000
Kherson	358,000
Kurgan	354,000
Ulan-Ude	351,000
Sevastopol	350,000
Chita	349,000
Vitebsk	347,000
Gorlovka	345,000
Vladimir	343,000
Smolensk	338,000
Simferopol	338,000
Orel	335,000
Pavlodar	331,000
Semipalatinsk	330,000
Saransk	323,000
Ust-Kamenogorsk	321,000
Makhachkala	320,000
Sochi	317,000
Komsomolsk-na-Amure (Komsomolsk-on-Amur)	316,000
Djambul	315,000
Cherepovets	315,000
Ordzhonikidze	313,000
Poltava	309,000

Kaluga	307,000
Stavropol	306,000
Tambov	305,000
Taganrog	295,000
Belgorod	293,000
Namangan	291,000
Chernigov	291,000
Andizhan	288,000
Zhitomir	287,000
Cherkassy	287,000
Dneprodzerzhinsk	279,000
Vologda	278,000
Prokopyevsk	278,000
Tselinograd	276,000
Kostroma	276,000
Orsk	273,000
Gendzhe	270,000
Kirovograd	269,000
Sumy	268,000
Petrozavodsk	264,000
Grodno	263,000
Angarsk	262,000
Volzhsky	257,000
Rybinsk	254,000
Chernovtzy	254,000
Petropavlovsk-Kamchatskii	252,000
Sterlitamak	251,000
Bratsk	249,000
Aktyubinsk	248,000
Yoshkar-Ola	243,000
Severodvinsk	239,000
Brest	238,000
Nalchik	236,000
Sumgait	234,000
Rovno	233,000
Petropavlovsk (North Kazakhstan)	233,000
Bobruisk	232,000
Biisk	231,000
Kremenchug	230,000
Temirtau	228,000
Novgorod	228,000
Leninakan	228,000
Shakhty	225,000
Ivano-Frankovsk	225,000
Syktyvkar	224,000
Kutaisi	220,000
Bukhara	220,000
Kustanai	212,000
Podolsk	209,000
Osh	209,000
Zlatoust	206,000
Kamensk-Uralskii	204,000
Fergana	203,000
Pskov	202,000
Blagoveshchensk	202,000
Uralsk	201,000
Klaipeda	201,000
Berezniki	200,000

Population

Total population is 283,555,000, of which around 70% live in the European part of the country. 65.6% live in urban areas. Average population density is 33 persons per mile^2/12.7 per km^2. 99.9% of population is native-born. Total population expected to reach 318,909,000 by year 2000. Principal nationalities recorded at the last (1979) census were: Russians 137.4 million; Ukrainians 42.3 million; Uzbeks 12.5 million; Byelorussians 9.5 million; Kazakhs 6.6 million; Tatars 6.3 million; Azerbaijanis 5.5 million; Armenians 4.1 million; Georgians 3.6 million; Moldavians 3.0 million; Tadjiks 2.9 million; Lithuanians 2.9 million; Turkmenians 2.0 million; Germans 1.9 million; Kirghiz 1.9 million; Jews 1.8 million; Chuvashes 1.8 million; Latvians 1.4 million; Bashkirs 1.4 million; Mordovians 1.2 million; Poles 1.2 million; Estonians 1.0 million. Out of a total of 104 nationalities recognized officially in the USSR a further 27 number over 100,000 people, and a further 28 over 10,000.

Birth rate 1.96%. **Death rate** 0.97%. **Rate of population increase** (1980–87) 1.0%. **Age distribution** under 15 = 24.8%; over 60 = 13.1%. **Life expectancy** female 75.4; male 66.5.

Religion

The USSR Constitution enshrines the separation of Church and State, and recognizes the right to conduct both religious worship and atheistic propaganda. The Russian Orthodox Church constitutes the largest single religious denomination, with an estimated 35–40 million believers dispersed throughout 76 dioceses and attending some 6,500 churches. The next most numerous Christian communities are the Armenian and Georgian Orthodox Churches. Up to 5 million Roman Catholics (principally in Lithuania, Byelorussia and the Ukraine) attend 1,035 churches. Uniate (Eastern Rite) Catholicism, common in the west Ukraine, was officially proscribed and practised clandestinely until Dec. 1989, when its more than 3 million adherents were allowed legally to register congregations. There are over 500,000 Evangelical Christian Baptists, and nearly 1 million Lutherans, mostly in the Baltic states. An estimated 18% of the population (40–45 million) are Muslims, predominantly Sunnis. In 1987, 365 mosques were officially registered in the USSR, with as many as 1,800 operating unofficially. Soviet Jews attend 109 synagogues throughout the Union. The Buryat, Tuvan and Kalmyk peoples practise Buddhism. Shamanism survives among some of the peoples of Siberia.

Language

The USSR officially has 112 languages. The Slavic language group predominates (58% of the total population are native Russian speakers and a further 17% speak Ukrainian, Byelorussian, Polish, Czech, Slovak or Bulgarian, all Slavic languages). Other Indo-European languages spoken in the USSR include Lithuanian; Latvian; Moldavian; Armenian; Albanian; German; Greek; Gypsy; Yiddish; Tajik; Kurdish; Ossetian.

The ancient languages of the Caucasus include Abkhazian; Adzhar; Chechen; Cherkess; Georgian; Ingush; Kabardin. Around 12.5% of the population speak Turkic languages, including Altay; Azerbaijani; Balkar; Bashkir; Chuvash; Dolgan; Gagauz; Karachay; Karakalpak; Kazakh; Khakass; Kirghiz; Meskhetian; Turkish; Tatar; Turkmen; Tuvan; Uzbek; Yakut. Other language groups represented are Finno-Ugric (including Estonian; Finnish; Hungarian; Karelian; Khanty; Komi; Komi-Permyak; Mansi; Mari; Mordvin; Udmurt); Samoyed (including Nenets); Mongolian (Buryat and Kalmyk); Tungus-Manchu (including Evenk); and Paleo-Siberian (including Chukchi and Koryak). Other languages used by communities in the USSR include Eskimo, Aleut, Ainu, Arabic, Assyrian and Korean.

HISTORY

Nomads settled the vast plain of northern Eurasia from at least the 2nd millennium BC. The most renowned of these peoples were the Scythians, fierce warriors mentioned in the annals of classical Greece. Apart from Greek settlements on the northern Black Sea coast from the 2nd century BC and the ancient civilizations of Transcaucasia, the nomads were the only inhabitants of almost the whole territory now forming the Soviet Union until the 6th century AD. At that time Slavic peoples began migrating eastward from central Europe to settle the forested zone between the Carpathian mountains and the upper Volga river. The Slavs subjugated or assimilated the indigenous (mostly Finno-Ugrian) peoples, but they in turn became subjects of a ruling class of Norse warriors and merchants who spread through the region along river trade routes from the Baltic to the Black and Caspian Seas. Towards the end of the 9th century the first unified Russian state emerged when the Slav principalities which had grown up along the trade routes were gathered into a confederation centred on Kiev and known as Kievan Rus. Strong Byzantine influences led to the conversion of Kievan Rus to Orthodox Christianity in 988, and to the development of rich spiritual and cultural traditions. In the 12th century Kievan Rus went into decline as a result of internal power struggles and external pressures. Finally in 1237–40 the Russian principalities were overrun by the Tatars (warrior nomads from Mongolia), and they were made subject to Tatar overlordship as part of the vast Mongol-Tatar empire stretching from eastern Europe to the Pacific.

A struggle to reassert Russian independence began in 1380 when Russian princes took up arms against the Tatars at the battle of Kulikovo Polye, and within a century Tatar overlordship was wholly thrown off. By this time Muscovy had emerged as paramount among the Russian principalities, and under Grand Prince Ivan III (r.1462–1505) Muscovy's annexation of the other independent principalities and republics began the process of territorial expansion which created the modern Russian state. Ivan III's grandson Ivan IV ('The Terrible') was the first to be proclaimed 'Tsar of all the Russias'. Although his long reign (1533–84) is remembered mostly for his degeneration into extreme despotism, it saw the achievement of Muscovy's expansion eastward across the Volga into the Urals and Siberia (Russians reached the Pacific coast in 1639). The Rurik dynasty (the royal house since the earliest Norse rulers) died out in 1598 with Ivan IV's idiot son Fyodor. For the next 15 years Muscovy was rocked by the so-called 'time of troubles', the throne passing first to Fyodor's brother-in-law, Boris Godunov (d.1605), and then (amid nationwide political turmoil, economic collapse and foreign intervention) successively to a Polish-backed pretender, to a Boyar nobleman, and to the Polish King Sigismund III (whose forces occupied Moscow in 1609). After an uprising ousted the Poles in 1612, the dynastic void was filled in the following year with the election of Mikhail Romanov as Tsar by an assembly of Boyars, clergy, officials and merchants.

The first Tsars of the Romanov dynasty oversaw Muscovy's recovery and began westward territorial expansion and the absorption of western ideas. Tsar Peter I ('The Great', r.1696–1725) made the greatest contribution to this westward orientation. During his reign Muscovy was formally renamed Russia, territories along the Baltic (including modern Estonia and Latvia) were annexed from Sweden, a new capital city (St Petersburg, Russia's 'window on the West') was founded at the head of the Gulf of Finland, and European customs and dress were adopted. Peter also originated the state administrative structure, including the system of ranked nobility, which survived until 1917. Peter's reign saw Russia supplant Sweden as the great military power of north-east Europe. By the end of the reign of Catherine II ('The Great', r.1763–96) the partitions of Poland and war with Turkey had added the territories of present-day Lithuania, Byelorussia, the Ukraine, Crimea and North Caucasus to Russia's domains, giving access to the Black Sea and rich agricultural lands which boosted Russia's economic might. Catherine's immediate successors began the conquest of the Caucasus in 1801 when Georgia was annexed upon the abdication of its last native king. Finland was seized from Sweden in 1809, and Bessarabia (present-day Soviet Moldavia) from Turkey in 1812. Around this time Russian incursions began against the Muslim khanates of Central Asia, although conquest of that region took most of the next century.

Napoleon's abortive invasion of Russia in 1812 culminated in the pursuit of his armies across Europe by a Russian army led by Tsar Alexander I (r.1801–25), who entered Paris in Mar. 1814 at the head of Russian, Austrian and Prussian forces. This triumph allowed Alexander to claim a leading role in the post-Napoleonic settlement of Europe, and to extend Russia's territory (by acquisition of the Duchy of Warsaw) to frontiers which remained virtually unchanged in Europe for the next century. Another consequence of the Russian march into Western Europe was contact with European notions of government by younger members of Russia's nobility, prompting unfavourable comparisons with Russia's own system and the first stirrings of a revolutionary movement. In Dec. 1825 a group of young noblemen attempted a coup during the interregnum between Alexander's death and the installation as Tsar of his brother Nicholas. This failed, and the execution of the leading 'Decembrists' marked the start of 30 years of reactionary and oppressive autocracy under Nicholas I. Russia's humiliating defeat in the Crimean War (1853–56) against Turkey, France and Great Britain came a year after Nicholas's death, and prompted a crisis of confidence in the existing order. Tsar Alexander II (r.1855–81) introduced major political and social reforms, notably the 1861 emancipation of the serfs (peasants bonded to a private landlord). At the same time revolutionary movements such as the Populists emerged, their adoption of increasingly anarchist and terrorist positions culminating in the assassination of Alexander II on 1 Mar. 1881. The assassination brought a return to repressive autocracy under Tsar Alexander III (r.1881–94). It also discredited the Populist cause, leaving the way open for the emergence of Russian Marxist organizations. In 1895 Vladimir Ilich Lenin founded the League of the Struggle for the Emancipation of the Working Class, which in 1898 joined other Marxist groups to form the Russian Social Democratic Labour Party, but in 1903 this split over Lenin's conception of the party as a vanguard of professional revolutionaries: its supporters became known as Bolsheviks ('majoritarians') and its opponents as Mensheviks ('minoritarians'). In 1904–5 Russia went to war with Japan over spheres of influence in Manchuria and Korea. In late 1904 workers' unrest broke out in St Petersburg, and on 22 Jan. 1905 troops fired on a 150,000-strong crowd demonstrating outside the Winter Palace (the Tsar's residence) to voice demands including greater workers' rights and an end to the war. The killing of up to 200 demonstrators sparked off a nationwide revolt which lasted for most of the year and witnessed the first appearance of revolutionary soviets (councils) of people's deputies. The 1905 revolution forced Tsar Nicholas II (who had ascended the throne in 1894) at the end of October to grant a constitutional manifesto proclaiming certain fundamental civil liberties and promising the creation of an elected parliament, the Duma (which met for the first time in May 1906).

Russia entered World War I against the Central Powers in Aug. 1914, and almost immediately was on the retreat. By early 1917 army morale was collapsing, and when in March spontaneous demonstrations and strikes broke out in the capital (now renamed Petrograd), troops mutinied in their tens of thousands. On 15 Mar. Tsar Nicholas II abdicated in favour of his brother, Grand Duke Michael, but the latter refused the throne and a provisional government took power (the royal family was imprisoned and on 18 July 1918 was executed by Bolshevik guards). The provisional government forfeited popular support by opting to stay in the war, and it suffered both from internal dissensions and the challenge to its authority by the burgeoning soviets in which the Bolsheviks increasingly held sway. On 7 Nov. 1917 the Bolsheviks overthrew the provisional government in a bloodless coup and established a Council of People's Commissars with Lenin as chairman (prime minister), but elections held on 25 Nov. for a Constituent Assembly gave the Bolsheviks only a quarter of the seats, and an absolute majority for the Socialist Revolutionaries. When the Assembly convened on 18 Jan. 1918 the majority of deputies rejected Bolshevik demands that it should be subordinate to the Congress of Soviets, whereupon the Assembly was broken up by Bolshevik Red Guards. For the next three years the Bolshevik regime fought for survival. The war against the Central Powers ended in Mar. 1918 with the Treaty of Brest-Litovsk (its draconian terms forced the Bolsheviks to surrender Estonia, Latvia, Lithuania and the Russian part of Poland to Germany and Austria, and to recognize the independence of the Ukraine, Georgia and Finland), but by this time Russia was sliding into civil war, with the Bolsheviks challenged by the White armies led by former Tsarist officers and actively supported by Great Britain, France, the United States and Japan. It took the Bolsheviks until the beginning of 1920 to gain the upper hand against the Whites, whereupon they became embroiled in a year-long war with Poland. During 1921 the Bolsheviks seized power in Georgia, Armenia and Azerbaijan (independent states since early 1918), and in Central Asia. The civil war period closed with the withdrawal of Japanese forces from Russia's Pacific coast provinces at the end of 1922.

The Bolsheviks renamed Russia the Russian Soviet Federated Socialist Republic in 1918 (with Moscow reinstated as the capital), and in Dec. 1922 this became part of the Union of Soviet Socialist Republics following the consolidation of Soviet power in the Ukraine, Transcaucasia and Central Asia. The Bolshevik party became the Russian Communist Party (Bolsheviks) in 1918, the All-Union Communist Party (Bolsheviks) in 1925, and the Communist Party of the Soviet Union (CPSU) in 1952.

During the civil war the Bolsheviks pursued a policy of 'war communism', involving highly centralized economic administration, conscription of all private and public wealth and manpower, a ban on private trade, and forcible requisitioning of grain and other foodstuffs from the peasantry. A response to the exigencies of the military threat, 'war communism' gradually alienated the regime from the workers and peasants and prompted manifestations of discontent culminating in a mutiny in Mar. 1921 at the Kronstadt naval garrison near Petrograd. Shortly afterwards, recognizing the need to recoup popular support for the regime as well as to restore the war-ravaged industrial base, Lenin announced the New Economic Policy (NEP). Originally limited to replacing forcible requisitioning of peasants' produce with a tax-in-kind on surpluses, the NEP became a general retreat from principles of a socially owned economy towards what Lenin termed 'state capitalism', combining state ownership of the 'commanding heights' of the economy (heavy industry, public utilities and the financial system) with a free market and private ownership of small-scale industry and agriculture.

Lenin died in Jan. 1924. By then the party leadership was split into four factions led by Leon Trotsky; Yosef Stalin; Grigory Zinoviev and Lev Kamenev; and Nikolai Bukharin, Alexei Rykov and Mikhail Tomsky. Zinoviev and Kamenev allied with Stalin to ensure that Trotsky did not succeed Lenin as leader, and were instrumental in convincing the party central committee to ignore Lenin's recommendation (made shortly before his death) that Stalin should be ousted as party general secretary (an office he had assumed in 1922) because he was accumulating unlimited authority. However, fear of Stalin's growing power prompted Zinoviev and Kamenev to break with him in 1925, and in the following year they allied with Trotsky, while Stalin allied with Bukharin's group. Stalin's opponents were expelled from the party in 1927; Zinoviev and Kamenev were subsequently readmitted, but Trotsky was forced into exile in 1929. Economic policy was a key issue in the factional struggle: Trotsky advocated accelerated industrialization, financed at the peasants' expense, whereas Bukharin favoured conciliation of the peasantry. In this he was supported initially by Stalin, but once the 'left opposition' was defeated in 1927 Stalin turned against the 'right deviation' and in 1929 secured the expulsion of Bukharin, Rykov and Tomsky from the politburo. At the beginning of 1928 Stalin launched a policy of rapid industrialization under the first five-year plan, signalling the end of the NEP. Meanwhile, in the countryside a growing crisis over the withholding of grain supplies by the kulaks (the richest peasant farmers who were generally hostile to government agricultural policy) prompted a government terror campaign in 1929–30 during which the kulaks were 'liquidated' as a class (they were either executed or banished to desolate areas) and a programme was begun of forcing the rest of the peasantry into collective farms. These measures met with fierce resistance and caused massive disruption to agriculture, leading to widespread famine in 1932–33. During the 17th party congress in Jan. 1934 there were suggestions that Stalin should be replaced by Sergei Kirov (the party leader in Leningrad). In Dec. 1934 Kirov was assassinated (probably on Stalin's orders) and his death was made the pretext for a reign of terror which reached its height in 1936–38. An estimated half a million people were executed and millions more were imprisoned (mostly without trial) in forced labour camps, while at show trials Stalin's former opponents in the party leadership (including Zinoviev, Kamenev, Bukharin and Rykov) were condemned to death after making obviously false confessions of treason and terrorism. Trotsky was also sentenced to death in absentia, and was murdered by a Soviet agent in Mexico in 1940. Severe political repressions lasted until Stalin's death in Mar. 1953.

Unsuccessful Soviet attempts to form an alliance with Great Britain and France were followed by the signing in Aug. 1939 of a non-aggression pact with Nazi Germany. In accordance with the pact's secret protocols dividing Eastern Europe into German and Soviet spheres of influence the Soviet Union annexed eastern Poland in Sept. 1939, and Estonia, Latvia, Lithuania (independent republics since 1918) and territories in northern and eastern Romania in June 1940. On 22 June 1941 Germany abrogated the non-aggression pact and invaded the Soviet Union, capturing vast territories and inflicting massive human and material damage in the European part of the country. The German armies were finally expelled in 1944 after a struggle in which about 20 million Soviet citizens lost their lives. Soviet troops went on to liberate the nations of Eastern Europe, Soviet-backed communist regimes took power there, and in 1955 the Warsaw Pact created a formal military alliance of the Soviet Union and these nations (except Yugoslavia, which had broken with the Soviet Union in 1948). Meanwhile, the wartime alliance with Great Britain, France and the US was supplanted in the post-war period by the 'cold war' of mutual suspicion, hostility and a contest to achieve military supremacy.

Stalin was succeeded by a triumvirate comprising Georgy Malenkov (Stalin's successor as prime minister and party leader), Vyacheslav Molotov (the foreign minister) and Lavrenti Beria (the notorious head of the secret police). However, after little more than a week Malenkov was forced to relinquish the party leadership to Nikita Khrushchev, while Beria was expelled from the party in July 1953 and was later executed for treason. At the 20th party congress in Feb. 1956 Khrushchev launched a bitter attack on Stalin's dictatorship and cult of personality. In the following year Malenkov, Molotov and Lazar Kaganovich attempted to depose Khrushchev, whereupon they were expelled from the party central committee. By the early 1960s Khrushchev's erratic domestic policies (including unworkable overhauls of regional administration and economic planning) and his conduct of international relations were arousing strong opposition. In Oct. 1964 his critics in the leadership engineered his replacement as party first secretary (later general secretary) by Leonid Brezhnev, under whom Khrushchev's comparatively liberal policies were largely reversed and there was a limited rehabilitation of Stalin; furthermore, after the invasion of Czechoslovakia in 1968 the so-called Brezhnev Doctrine enunciated the right of the Soviet Union to intervene in socialist countries where socialism was under threat of being overturned (later this was put into practice when Soviet troops entered Afghanistan in 1979). Brezhnev died in Nov. 1982 (aged 75) whereupon Yury Andropov succeeded him both as party general secretary and president of the presidium of the Supreme Soviet (ceremonial head of state – a post Brezhnev had acquired in 1977). Andropov introduced cautious economic reforms and a major anti-corruption campaign, and began to remove leading officials associated with Brezhnev, but he fell seriously ill after less than a year in office and died in Feb. 1984 (aged 69). He was succeeded in both posts by Konstantin Chernenko (a conservative former Brezhnev protégé). In the 13 months until Chernenko's death on 10 Mar. 1985 (aged 73) Andropov's limited reforms were continued, albeit at a more cautious pace and without any major new initiatives.

Mikhail Gorbachev (at 54 the youngest member of the party politburo) was elected by the party central committee as Chernenko's successor on 11 Mar. 1985. Formerly an Andropov protégé, he immediately resumed the campaign to remove 'Brezhnevite' officials and to root out corruption, leading to a massive turnover in the government and party leadership. Complaining that the economy had been stagnating since the 1970s he announced a policy of complete 'restructuring' (perestroika), to involve technical innovation, more efficient use of labour and materials, and managerial autonomy; subsequent initiatives introduced limited private enterprise, including private farming, and a reduction in central planning. However, by the end of 1989 this had failed significantly to improve economic performance. Perestroika in the economy was accompanied in the political and cultural spheres by the policy of glasnost ('openness'). A watershed in ending obsessive official secrecy came on 26 Apr. 1986 when a reactor at the Chernobyl nuclear power station in the north Ukraine exploded during an unauthorized experiment by operators, sending a trail of radioactive fallout across northern Europe. Subsequent disasters were handled with equal candour by the Soviet authorities and media, notably the devastating Armenian earthquake of 7 Dec. 1988 which killed some 25,000 people. Glasnost led to a freer press, official willingness to acknowledge unwelcome developments, a frequently damning reappraisal of Soviet history, and greater tolerance of individual expression; by the end of 1988 virtually all political prisoners had been freed. However, loosening the fetters on Soviet political life had the unwelcome effect of unleashing pent-up ethnic tensions. In Feb. 1988 a dispute flared between Armenians and Azerbaijanis over the status of Nagorny Karabakh (an enclave with a majority Armenian population, but part of Azerbaijan); massive demonstrations and strikes gripped Armenia and Azerbaijan intermittently throughout 1988–89, and sporadic intercommunal violence left nearly 100 people dead and forced thousands to flee their homes. During 1989 intercommunal violence and nationalist unrest erupted in other southern republics, notably Uzbekistan and Georgia. Also in 1988–89 Estonia, Latvia and Lithuania witnessed a coalescence of the goals of unofficial nationalist agitation with official initiatives for greater autonomy: in all three republics the authorities permitted the establishment in Oct. 1988 of independent movements which combined support for Gorbachev's reforms with radical autonomy programmes and proposals for political pluralism, while the official initiatives featured unilateral declarations of the republics' 'sovereignty' and open condemnation of their 1940 annexation by the Soviet Union. They culminated at the end of 1989 in the Lithuanian Communist Party's splitting from the CPSU. In the foreign policy sphere a global diplomatic offensive began. Four summit meetings between Gorbachev and US president Ronald Reagan culminated in May 1988 in the Treaty on Intermediate Nuclear Forces, providing for the elimination over a three-year period of all intermediate-range land-based nuclear weapons held by the Soviet Union and the United States. Soviet troops were withdrawn in full from Afghanistan by Feb. 1989.

Gorbachev became ceremonial head of state on 1 Oct. 1988, succeeding Andrei Gromyko (who had assumed the post in July 1985 after nearly 30 years as foreign minister). In accordance with constitutional amendments passed on 1 Dec. 1988 elections were held in early 1989 for a new supreme representative body, the 2,250-member Congress of People's

Deputies. These produced striking victories for Communist Party reformists, members of unofficial political groups and Baltic nationalists, and a rout of conservative party figures. When the Congress convened on 25 May 1989 it overwhelmingly elected Gorbachev to a new executive presidency. For the rest of 1989 the work of the Congress and of a restyled Supreme Soviet, notably the freedom and contentiousness of debate, demonstrated a radical change in the conduct of Soviet politics.

(N.B. Russia used the Julian calendar until Feb. 1918, when the Gregorian calendar (13 days ahead) was adopted to conform with the West. Therefore, what are commonly known as the February and October 1917 revolutions occurred in March and November according to the modern calendar.)

CONSTITUTION AND GOVERNMENT

The USSR, which was formally established in 1922, is a federation of the 15 Union (Soviet Socialist) Republics, which according to the 1976 Constitution are of equal status, are linked voluntarily, and each have in theory the right to secede.

Constitutional amendments passed in Dec. 1988 created a new supreme representative body, the 2,250-member Congress of People's Deputies, which partly supersedes the former USSR Supreme Soviet. It serves a five-year term during which it meets once or twice a year to decide on major constitutional, political and socio-economic questions. The new Congress was constituted at the end of May 1989 as a result of elections in March and April, when two-thirds of the seats were filled by direct popular vote from 750 single-member constituencies organized to include roughly equal numbers of voters and another 750 constituencies designed to give representation to the majority of the Soviet Union's recognized ethnic groups; the remaining 750 seats were reserved for members of approved political and social organizations (in future elections there will be no reserved seats). The Congress elects from among its own members a restyled bicameral 542-member Supreme Soviet which serves as a standing legislature, meeting twice a year for three- or four-month sessions and having responsibility for all legislative and administrative matters.

The Congress also elects an executive president, known as the Chairman of the Supreme Soviet, who is the country's head of state. The president's extensive powers include the appointment, subject to approval by the Congress, of the First Deputy Chairman of the Supreme Soviet (the first vice-president) and of the Chairman and members of the Council of Ministers.

The Communist Party of the Soviet Union (CPSU) is the only legal political grouping and is the dominant force in government. It is led by a central committee, which elects as its executive a general secretary, a politburo and a secretariat.

Each Union Republic has its own constitution and a state administrative structure modelled on the central USSR administration. This includes a unicameral Supreme Soviet for each Union Republic, elected for a five-year term, which in turn elects a Presidium and a Council of Ministers to deal with internal affairs. Each republic except the Russian Federation has its own Communist Party subordinate to the CPSU; they are statutorily subordinate to the CPSU, but in Dec. 1989 the Lithuanian Communist Party unilaterally declared itself independent.

Present government and CPSU leadership

The government

Chair of the USSR Supreme Soviet (head of state) Mikhail Gorbachev

First Deputy Chair of the USSR Supreme Soviet Anatoly Lukyanov

Presidents of the Presidiums of the Supreme Soviets of the Union Republics (ex officio Deputy Chairs of the Presidium of the USSR Supreme Soviet): Armenia – Grant Voskanyan; Azerbaijan – Elmira Kafarova; Byelorussia – Nikolai Dementei; Estonia – Arnold Rüütel; Georgia – Givi Gumbaridze; Kazakhstan – Makhtay Sagdiyev; Kirghizia – Tashtambek Akhmatov; Latvia – Anatoly Gorbunov; Lithuania – Algirdas Brazanskas; Moldavia – Mircha Snegur; Russian Federation – Vitaly Vorotnikov; Tadjikistan – Gaibnazar Pallayev; Turkmenia – Saparmurad Niyazov; Ukraine – Dr Valentina Shevchenko; Uzbekistan – Mirzaolim Ibragimov.

Chairs of USSR Supreme Soviet Chambers: Yevgeny Primakov (Chair of the Soviet of the Union); Rafik Nishanov (Chair of the Soviet of Nationalities).

Chair and Vice-Chairs of the Council of Ministers: Nikolai Ryzhkov (Chair); Yury Maslyukov (First Deputy Chair; Chair of USSR State Planning Committee (Gosplan)); Vladilen Nikitin (First Deputy Chair); Lev Voronin (First Deputy Chair, responsible for general questions); Dr Leonid Abalkin (Deputy Chair; Chair of State Commission for Economic Reform); Igor Belousov (Deputy Chair; Chair of Bureau for the Military Industrial Complex); Aleksandra Biryukova (Deputy Chair; Chair of Bureau for Social Development); Vitaly Doguzhiyev (Deputy Chair; Chair of State Commission for Emergency Situations); Vladimir Gusev (Deputy Chair; Chair of Bureau for Chemical and Timber Complex); Nikolai Laverov (Deputy Chair; Chair of State Committee for Science and Technology); Pavel Mostovoi (Deputy Chair; Chair of State Committee for Material and Technical Supply); Lev Ryabev (Deputy Chair; Chair of Bureau for the Fuel and Energy Complex); Ivan Silayev (Deputy Chair; Chair of Bureau for Machine Building); Stepan Sitaryan (Deputy Chair; Chair of State Foreign Economic Commission).

Ministers of USSR All-Union Ministries: Nikolai Pugin (Automobile and Agricultural Machine Building); Apollon Systsov (Aviation Industry); Nikolai Lemayev (Chemical and Oil Refining Industry); Col-Gen. Aleksandr Volkov (Civil Aviation); Mikhail Shchadov (Coal Industry); Vladimir Chirskov (Construction of Oil and Gas Industry Enterprises); Gen. Dmitry Yazov (Defence); Boris Belousov (Defence Industry); Oleg Anfimov (Electrical Equipment Industry and Instrument Making); Vladislav Kolesnikov (Electronics Industry); Nikolai Kotlyar (Fisheries Industry); Konstantin Katushev (Foreign Economic Relations); Oleg Shishkin (General Machine Building); Grigory Gabrielyants (Geology); Vladimir Velichko (Heavy Machine Building); Nikolai Panichev (Machine Tool and Tool Making Industry); Valery Bykov (Medical Industry); Yury Volmer (Merchant Marine); Serafim Kolpakov (Metallurgy); Vitaly Konovalov (Nuclear Power Generation and the Nuclear Industry); Leonid Filimonov (Oil and Gas Industry); Vladimir Shimko (Radio Industry); Nikolai Konarev (Railways); Igor Koksanov (Shipbuilding Industry); Vladimir Brezhnev (Transport Construction); (vacant) (Water Resources Construction).

Ministers of USSR Union Republican Ministries Erlen

Pervyshin (Communications); Nikolai Gubenko (Culture); Valentin Pavlov (Finance); Eduard Shevardnadze (Foreign Affairs); Vladimir Melnikov (Forestry Industry); Dr Yevgeny Chazov (Health); Aleksandr Mikhalchenko (Installation and Special Construction Work); Vadim Bakatin (Internal Affairs); Veniamin Yakovlev (Justice); Yury Semenov (Power and Electrification); Kondrat Terekh (Trade).

Chairs of USSR All-Union State Committees: Boris Tolstykh (Computer Technology and Information Science); Yury Izrael (Hydrometeorology); Valery Sychev (Output Quality Control and Standards).

Chairs of USSR Union Republican State Committees: Aleksandr Kamshalov (Cinematography (Goskino)); Valery Serov (Construction (Gosstroy)); Aleksandr Isayev (Forests); Vladimir Shcherbakov (Labour and Social Affairs); Nikolai Rusak (Physical Culture and Sports); Nikolai Yefimov (Press); Vyacheslav Senchagov (Prices); Prof. Nikolai Vorontsov (Protection of the Environment); Prof. Gennady Yagodin (Public Education); Gen. Vladimir Kryuchkov (State Security (KGB)); Vadim Kirichenko (Statistics); Vadim Malyshev (Supervision of Work Safety in Industry and the Nuclear Power Industry); Mikhail Nenashev (Television and Radio (Gosteleradio).

Other Chairs Viktor Gerashchenko (Chair of the Board of USSR State Bank (Gosbank)); Mikhail Shkabardnya (Chief Administrator of the USSR Council of Ministers);

Chairs of the Councils of Ministers of Union Republics (ex officio members of USSR Council of Ministers) Armenia - Vladimir Margaryants; Azerbaijan - Gasan Azizogly Gasanov; Byelorussia - Mikhail Kovalev; Estonia - Indrek Toome; Georgia - Nodar Chitanava; Kazakhstan - Uzabakay Karamanov; Kirghizia - Apas Dzhumagulov; Latvia - Vilnis Bresis; Lithuania - Vytautas Sakalauskas; Moldavia - Pyotr Paskar; Russian Federation - Aleksandr Vlasov; Tadjikistan - Izatullo Khayeyev; Turkmenia - Khan Akhmedov; Ukraine - Vitaly Masol; Uzbekistan - Irakhmat Mirkasymov.

The leadership of the Communist Party of the Soviet Union

(Kommunisticheskaya Partiya Sovietskogo Soyuza)

General secretary Mikhail Gorbachev.

Full politburo members Mikhail Gorbachev; Vladimir Ivashko; Gen. Vladimir Kryuchkov; Yegor Ligachev; Yury Maslyukov; Vadim Medvedev; Nikolai Ryzhkov; Eduard Shevardnadze; Nikolai Slyunkov; Vitaly Vorotnikov; Aleksandr Yakovlev; Lev Zaikov.

Candidate members Aleksandra Biryukova; Anatoly Lukyanov; Yevgeny Primakov; Boris Pugo; Georgy Razumovsky; Aleksandr Vlasov; Gen. Dmitry Yazov.

Central committee secretariat Mikhail Gorbachev; Oleg Bakhlanov; Ivan Frolov; Andrei Girenko; Yegor Ligachev; Yury Manayenkov; Vadim Medvedev; Georgy Razumovsky; Nikolai Slyunkov; Yegor Stroyev; Gumer Usmanov; Aleksandr Yakolev; Lev Zaikov.

Republican party leaders Armenian CP - Suren Arutyunyan; Azerbaijan CP - Ayaz Niyaz ogly Mutalibov; Byelorussian CP - Yefrem Sokolov; Estonian CP - Vaino Vaelaes; Georgian CP - Givi Gumbaridze; Kazakh CP - Nursultan Nazarbayev; Kirghiz CP - Absamat Masaliyev; Latvian CP - Janis Vagris; Moldavian CP - Pyotr Luchinsky; Tadjik CP - Kakhar Makhkamov; Turkmen CP - Saparmurad Niyazov; Ukrainian CP - Vladimir Ivashko; Uzbek CP - Islam Karimov.

Administration

The eight larger Union Republics (Byelorussia, Kazakhstan, Kirghizia, Russian Federation, Tadjikistan, Turkmenia, Ukraine and Uzbekistan) are subdivided for purely administrative purposes into oblasts (regions) or krays (territories). Additionally, in order to give administrative-territorial autonomy to the majority of the USSR's recognized ethnic groups, five Union Republics contain within them Autonomous Soviet Socialist Republics (ASSRs), Autonomous Oblasts, or National Okrugs (districts), as follows:

Republic	ASSR	AO	NO
Azerbaijan	Nakhichevan	Nagorny Karabakh	
Georgia	Abkhazia	South Ossetia	
	Adzharia		
Russian Federation	Bashkiria	Adygei AO	Agin Buryatia
	Buryatia	Gorny Altai	Chukotka
	Checheno-Ingushetia	Jewish AO	Evenk NO
	Chuvashia	Karachayevo-Cherkessia	Khanty-Mansi NO
	Daghestan	Khakassia	Komi-Permyak NO
	Kabardino-Balkaria		Koryakia
	Kalmykia		Nenetia
	Karelia		Taymyr (Dolgano-Nenetia)
	Komi ASSR		Ust-Ordyn Buryatia
	Mari ASSR		Yamalo-Nenetia
	Mordovia		
	North Ossetia		
	Tartaria		
	Tuvinia		
	Udmurtia		
	Yakutia		
Tadjikistan		Gorny Badakhshan	
Uzbekistan	Karakalpakia		

The 20 ASSRs each have their own unicameral Supreme Soviet, elected for a five-year term, which in turn elects a presidium and council of ministers responsible for local government. The oblasts, autonomous oblasts, krays and national okrugs are each administered by a soviet (council) elected for a 2½-year term. Elected soviets extend down to the level of local districts and municipalities. Each ASSR, oblast or kray also has an autonomous Communist Party committee, led by a first secretary.

Justice

The system of law is a civil code system modified by the application of communist legal theories. The highest court is the Supreme Court of the USSR, elected by the Supreme Soviet of the USSR; there are equivalent structures at the level of the republics, which each have their Supreme Courts elected by their Supreme Soviets, and within the administrative subdivisions, with Territorial, Regional and Area Courts each with members elected by the appropriate Soviet. At the local level, the judge and two assessors for each People's Court are chosen by direct popular election. The USSR's senior law officer is the Procurator-General, appointed for 5 years by the Supreme Soviet, and responsible in turn for appointing the procurator of each republic. The death penalty is in force. There were more than 60 executions between 1985 and mid-1988, for offences including theft of social property, aggravated bribe-taking, aggravated rape and murder, war crimes and espionage.

National symbols

Flag. Adopted as the national flag in Nov. 1923, the design superimposes upon the basic red revolutionary flag the symbols of soldiers, workers and peasants, ie the red star of the Red Army (also used by the Bolshevik party), the hammer representing industrial workers, and the sickle for the peasants. The hammer and sickle are crossed, in yellow, with the red star outlined in yellow above them, in the upper hoist. Each of the 15 Union Republics also has its own flag; these tend to be similar to the USSR flag with additions, for example a dark blue vertical strip at the hoist (RSFSR); a light blue horizontal strip (Ukraine SSR); a green horizontal strip at the base and white pattern on red at the hoist (Byelorussian SSR). However, during 1988–89 the Supreme Soviets of Estonia and Lithuania restored to official use the flags of the pre-1940 independent Estonian and Lithuanian republics (respectively three horizontal bands of blue, black and white, and three horizontal bands of yellow, red and green); in most instances these flags supplanted official Estonian and Lithuanian flags modelled on that of the USSR.

Festivals. 23 Feb. (Soviet Army and Navy Day); 8 Mar. (International Women's Day); 1–2 May (May Day Celebrations); 9 May (Victory Day); 7 Oct. (Constitution Day); 7–8 Nov. (October Revolution); 19 Nov. (Agricultural and Agro-Industrial Workers' Day).

Vehicle registration plate. SU.

INTERNATIONAL RELATIONS

Affiliations

Member of the UN (permanent member of Security Council) and of many of its specialized agencies but not the IMF/World Bank/IDA/IFC, nor the FAO/IFAD; member of IAEA; member of Warsaw Treaty Organization (Warsaw Pact); CMEA (Comecon) and its International Bank for Economic Co-operation and International Investment Bank.

As well as USSR membership of the UN, Byelorussia and the Ukraine also have separate membership of the UN and of many of its specialized agencies. This arrangement dates from the foundation of the UN, and represents a partial accommodation of the demand voiced at that time by the USSR that each of its Union Republics should have membership on the grounds that the USSR was constitutionally a 'voluntary union' of nations.

Defence

Total Armed Forces: 5,096,000 inclusive of some 1,476,000 railroad, construction, labour, civil defence and Kommandatura troops; perhaps 3,000,000 are conscripts.

Terms of service: two years, then discharged into Reserves. Women with medical and other special skills may volunteer. Reserves: total 6,217,000.

Strategic Nuclear Forces: 298,000.

Navy: 15,500; 63 nuclear-fuelled ballistic-missile submarines; 12 ballistic-missile submarines.

Strategic Rocket Forces: 298,000; 1,386 intercontinental ballistic missiles (ICBM).

Strategic Aviation: 95,000; about 1,400 combat aircraft: 1,195 bombers (175 long-range, 570 medium-range, 450 short-range).

Ground Forces: 1,900,000; 53,300 main battle tanks (T-54/-55/-62/-64-A/-B, T-72-L/-M and T-80); 1,200 light tanks (PT-76).

Air Defence Troops: 520,000; some 2,300 fighters (mainly MiG-23 Flogger/MiG-25 Foxhound A, Su-15 Flagon, Su-27).

Navy: 458,000; 372 submarines (75 strategic, 263 tactical); 268 principal surface combatants: four carriers (37,000-tonnes); 36 cruisers; 62 destroyers; 166 frigates. 410 patrol and coastal combatants.

Naval Aviation: 70,000; 400 bombers (mainly Tu-26 Backfire B/C, Tu-16 Badger C/G/G-mod); about 220 combat aircraft (mainly Yak-38 Forger, Su-17 Fitter C).

Naval Infantry (Marines): some 17,000; 230 main battle tanks (T-54/-55, T-72).

Air Force: 440,000 inclusive Strategic Aviation; some 4,400 combat aircraft (mainly MiG-21, MiG-27 Flogger D/J, Su-17 Fitter, Su-24, MiG-23 Flogger B/G).

Defence expenditure Official defence expenditure is equivalent to US$32,080 million (1988), although this does not cover spending on research and development.

Deployment of forces The Western, Southern (or Near Eastern) and Far Eastern strategic theatres (HQs respectively Kiev, Tashkent and Irkutsk) are defended by centrally controlled force deployments in five Theatres of Military Operations (north-west; west; south-west; south; far-eastern), four oceanic theatres (Atlantic, Arctic, Indian and Pacific) and three sea theatres (Baltic, Black Sea and Mediterranean). Strategic forces, wherever deployed, come under central Supreme High Command. The Central Reserve HQ is in Moscow.

Soviet troops stationed outside the Soviet Union, as estimated by the London-based International Institute for Strategic Studies, comprise:

Western strategic theatre: the Group of Soviet Forces Germany in East Germany (HQ Zossen-Wünsdorf, strength 380,000); the Central Group of Forces in Czechoslovakia (Milovice, 80,000); the Northern Group Forces in Poland (Legnica, 40,000); the southern group of forces in Hungary (Budapest,

65,000). The northern Arctic fleet is headquartered at Severomorsk, the Baltic fleet at Kaliningrad and the Black Sea fleet at Sevastopol, with bases on the Black Sea to be complemented by a base under development at Tartus, Syria.

Southern strategic theatre: Soviet troops which were stationed in Afghanistan were withdrawn by Feb. 1989. A naval flotilla on the Caspian is headquartered at Baku.

Far Eastern theatre: between 50,000 and 55,000 Soviet troops are stationed in Mongolia but the withdrawal of around 75% of these troops began in May 1989. The Pacific/Indian Ocean fleet headquartered at Vladivostock uses Soviet naval bases abroad at Cam Ranh Bay (Vietnam) and Aden (South Yemen).

There are in addition an estimated 8,000 Soviet military personnel stationed in Cuba including advisers and technicians, and smaller numbers also in Syria 4,000; Vietnam 2,500; Libya 2,000; Ethiopia 1,700; and various other countries.

ECONOMY

The Soviet economy is a centrally planned economy currently undergoing a process of restructuring (perestroika), involving decentralization of much of the planning of production and distribution to the republics, and the encouragement of elements of a market economy (notably, in agriculture, the introduction of supply contracts between state-purchasing organizations and farmers). The fundamental instruments of economic policy remain the five-year plans (guidelines for 12th 5-year Plan covering 1986–90 presented Mar. 1986 to party congress, and plan endorsed by Supreme Soviet June 1986, including targets to year 2000). An annual plan is formulated within this framework; state plan and budget for 1989 approved Nov. 88 by Supreme Soviet. The crucial emphasis is on raising living standards.

Currency

The unit is the rouble, divided into 100 kopeks.

National finance

Budget. The 1989 budget was for expenditure of 495,000 million roubles (up by 11%), income of 459,000 million roubles (up by 3%) and a deficit of 36,000 million roubles, the first time that a budget deficit had been acknowledged. The deficit would have been greater, except that a total of 63,400 million roubles borrowed from the state banking system had been included in the figure for total income. Expenditure was predominantly (56%) on running the national economy, but also included 4.1% on defence and 33% on social and cultural services.

Balance of payments. The balance of payments (current account, 1988) was a surplus of 4,000 million roubles, down from 7,400 million roubles in 1987 primarily because of lower prices for fuel and energy exports.

Inflation. Unofficially estimated at 6–8% in early 1989; the government had insisted in early 1989 that prices were rising no faster than 2% per annum on average.

Gross National Product

Official figures were given in Jan. 1989 not only for 1988 GNP (866,000 million roubles, up 5%) but also for national income, the usual Soviet measure (625,000 million roubles, up 4.4%). By the official exchange rate, this GNP figure converts to $1,368,000 million and per capita GNP of $4,800. Figures some 10% lower are commonly quoted.

Economically active population. The total number of persons active in the economy, as last recorded in the 1979 census, was 135,423,642; employment in the 'socialized' sector, plus employment on collective farms, totalled 130,000,000, divided as follows: industry 29%; agriculture on state farms etc. (including forestry) 9.7%; collective farms 9.6%; transport and communications 9.7%; construction 8.8%; distribution, supplies and catering 7.7%; other services and administration 25%.

Energy and mineral resources

Oil and gas. Production (1988) 688 million tons/624 million tonnes of crude oil and 27,262,408 million ft^3/772,000 million m^3 of natural gas. More than 50% of gas is produced in the Tyumen (West Siberian) complex.

Minerals. The Soviet Union claims 88% of the world's manganese deposits; 58.7% of its oil; 58% of its coal; 54% of its potassium salts; 41% of its iron ore. Production: (1988) coal 851 million tons/772 million tonnes; iron ore 277 million tons/251 million tonnes; steel 851 million tons/772 million tonnes.

Electricity. Production: (1987) 1,665 million MWh. There is an integrated power grid, covering over 900 power stations, controlled centrally from Moscow. Nuclear power accounts for 12.6% of total electricity produced; over 80% is produced by burning fossil fuels, while hydroelectric power is being expanded.

Bioresources

Agriculture. Total area under cultivation was 519.7 million acres/210.3 million ha in 1986. Crop production: (1987 in million tons/tonnes) wheat 91.8/83.3; barley 64.4/58.4; maize 16.3/14.8; (1988) milk 117.3/106.4; sugar beet 96.8/87.8; potatoes 69.1/62.7. Livestock numbers: (1987 in millions) cattle 122.1; pigs 79.5; sheep 142.2; horses 5.9; poultry 1,174.2.

Forestry. Forests cover 2,003.7 million acres/810.9 million ha, of which 1,957.3 million acres/792.1 million ha is state-owned, the rest common land. Timber production: (1986) 16,845 million ft^3/477 million m^3.

Fisheries. Annual catch: fish 11.7 million tons/10.6 million tonnes; shellfish and crustaceans 12.3 million tons/11.2 million tonnes. Commercial whaling ceased in 1987.

Industry and Commerce

Industry Soviet investment in heavy industry over a long period has made it a major producer and exporter within the Comecon area, although it is now energy production which dominates Soviet export trade. Major industries besides electricity generation are steel; coal (see above for figures); cement 151 million tons/137 million tonnes; tractors (1987) 52.1 million; mineral fertilizer 1.8 million tons/1.6 million tonnes; automobiles (1988) 1.3 million. Also important are textiles; chemicals; paper; food products.

Commerce. Exports: 68,142 million roubles. Imports: 60,741 million roubles (1987). Main trading partners are Bulgaria; Czechoslovakia; East Germany; Hungary; Cuba.

Trade with UK. Imports from UK £491,615,000; exports to UK £875,431,000 in 1987.

Tourism. Tourism is controlled by the State Committee on Tourism, part of the USSR Council of Ministers. Numbers of hotels more than quadrupled between 1960 and 1987. In 1988 there were 6 million foreign visitors to the USSR, and 4.2 million Soviet citizens visited foreign countries. Most visitors came from Poland; Finland; East Germany,

COMMUNICATIONS

Railways

There are 90,728 miles/146,100 km of railways, of which 32,106 miles/51,700 km are electrified; almost all non-electric locomotives are now diesel-powered. The network continues to expand; the large-scale ten-year BAM project to build a new link over 1,863 miles/3,000 km to the east-coast ports, using a line north of the existing Trans-Siberian Railway, completed construction in 1985 and became fully operational in 1989, with additional branches already under construction. Soviet railways carried 4,483 million tons/4,067 million tonnes of freight and 4,360 million passengers in 1987. The 16 largest Soviet cities, excepting only Odessa, all have, or are building, underground urban rail systems.

Roads

(1984) 941,871 miles/1,516,700 km of roads, of which 681,299 miles/1,097,100 km are concrete or bitumenized.

Aviation

Aeroflot, the world's largest airline, provides domestic and international services (main airports are at Moscow and Leningrad). It is the sole operator of all air services. There were 124 million passenger journeys in 1988 (119 million in 1987), and air freight amounted to 3.5 million tons/3.2 million tonnes.

Shipping

The merchant fleet in 1988 amounted to 1,960 ships and 15.8 million gross registered tonnage.

Telecommunications

35.3 million telephones or approximately 12 per 1,000 population.

Broadcasting

83 million radio sets and 87 million televisions, or approximately 31 per 1,000 population. Three programmes are broadcast throughout the USSR, originating in Moscow, and additional programmes are broadcast at republic and sometimes also local level. Moscow radio foreign service broadcasts to over 60 foreign countries. Moscow has four television programmes; over 100 other TV centres broadcast one or more programmes, and distant regions are served through satellite links.

Newspapers.

Total circulation of daily newspapers is 207.9 million; there are 640 dailies, and newspapers in over 50 languages. The Communist Party daily *Pravda* ('*Truth*'), circulation 9,664,000, and the USSR Supreme Soviet's newspaper *Izvestiya* ('*News'),* circulation 10,500,000, are the most influential, while the largest circulations are those of the trade union daily *Trud* ('*Labour*') at 20,200,000 and *Komsomolskaya Pravda*, published by the Komsomol or Leninist Young Communist League.

EDUCATION AND WELFARE

Education

Education in the USSR is free, and almost all schools and higher education establishments are state-run (a small number of colleges are run by public organizations or co-operatives). Teaching is based on a national curriculum. School attendance is compulsory for ages seven to 17. After three years in primary school pupils at age seven enter a general secondary school with either an eight-year or a ten-year curriculum. A pupil completing an eight-year curriculum must transfer either to a ten-year school or to a vocational or specialized technical secondary school for the last two years of compulsory education, while pupils in a ten-year school may also transfer to a vocational or specialized technical secondary school after the eighth year. Graduates from vocational or specialized technical secondary schools are automatically offered work in the profession for which they have trained. There are also special secondary schools providing intensive tuition in foreign languages, and for exceptionally gifted children. Almost half of the USSR's 112 recognized languages are used for school tuition.

At tertiary level, entrance to university or technical college is by competitive examination (the number of new places available each year is set out in the annual national economic plan). In addition to free tuition students receive stipends and other benefits from the state.

School and university population. 16,600,000 children at 142,700 pre-school nurseries and kindergartens; 53,600,000 pupils in 135,000 primary and secondary schools (including 9,800,000 in vocational and specialized technical secondary schools); 4,500,000 students at 4,508 technical colleges; 5,000,000 students (including 1,800,000 taking correspondence or evening courses) at 898 universities, institutes or other higher education establishments

Student-teacher ratio. One teacher per 13 pupils in primary and general education secondary schools.

Health

Health services are provided free of charge, although patients must pay for prescription medication. Holiday sanatoria (2,414 in 1986, with accommodation for 605,000 patients) are also provided at a nominal charge either by the state or the trade unions, and sanatoria are provided free for sick children and tuberculosis sufferers. Private medical practice exists, although currently only on a small scale. Total number of doctors (including dentists) 1,232,000; 23,600 hospitals with 3,700,000 beds (one per 76 inhabitants).

Welfare

Workplace trade-union organizations administer the payment of social insurance and security (using funds provided by the state), including disability and maternity benefits and pensions to compensate for the loss of a wage earner. The social insurance budget for 1988 was planned at 58,708 million roubles. Men may retire on pension at age 60 and women at age 55, their pensions averaging 60–70% of salary prior to retirement. Workers certified by a doctor as temporarily unable to work through illness receive sick-leave benefit. No system of unemployment benefit exists since USSR economic policy is committed to maintaining full employment.

UNITED ARAB EMIRATES

Ittihad Al-Imarat Al-Arabiyah

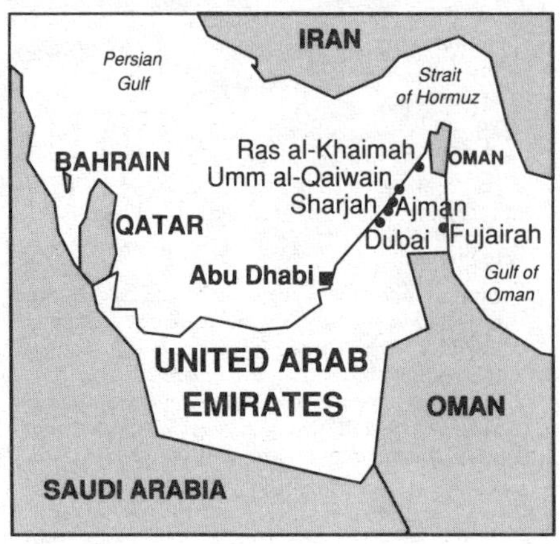

GEOGRAPHY

The federation of seven emirates comprising the UAE is located along the east-central coast of the Arabian Peninsula, occupying a total surface area of 32,270 miles^2/83,600 km^2. The Emirates of Abu Dhabi, Dubai and Sharjah support over 90% of the total population. The Arabian Gulf coast is marked by salt marshland merging inland with barren and infertile desert plain with very scant scrub vegetation. The Emirate of Al-Fujairah fronts the Gulf of Oman, and contains the only highland expanse with the al-Hajar mountains rising to 3,700 ft/1128 m in the east. Less than 0.2% of the total surface area is considered arable. Virtually all agricultural activity is based in the northern emirates of Sharjah, Ras al-Khaimah, Ajman and Fujairah.

Climate

Predominantly desert-type with very irregular and scant rainfall and extreme temperatures during the summer months, exceeding 104°F/40°C. Rainfall averages approximately 3.1 in/80 mm annually. Winter temperatures are milder. Shamal dust storms blow periodically from the north and north-west. Dubai: Jan. 74.1°F/23.4°C. July 108°F/42.3°C. Average annual rainfall 2.4 in/60 mm. Sharjah: Jan. 64°F/17.8°C. July 89.6°F/32°C. Average annual rainfall 4.1 in/105 mm.

Cities and towns

Abu Dhabi (capital)	670,125
Dubai	419,104
Sharjah	268,722
Ras al-Khaimah	116,470
Ajman	65,318
Fujairah	54,425

Population

Total population is 2,115,109 of which 77.8% live in urban areas. Population density is 65 persons per mile^2/23.9 per km^2. Ethnic divisions: 19% Emirian; 23% other Arab; 50% South Asian; 8% other expatriates. In 1982, under 20% of the population were UAE citizens. Approximately 10% of the population are nomadic.

Birth rate 3.2%. **Death rate** 0.4%. **Rate of population increase** (1980–88) 4.9%. **Age distribution** under 15 = 31.0%; over 65 = 1.5%. **Life expectancy** female 73; male 69; average 71.

Religion

96% Muslim (16% belonging to the Shi'a sect); 4% Christian (the UAE forms part of the Roman Catholic Apostolic Vicariate of Arabia), Hindu and other.

Language

Arabic is the official language. English and Farii are commonly spoken in the major urban centres. Urdu and Hindi are also spoken.

HISTORY

The maritime Emirates of the Gulf prospered as a result of seaborne trade which reached its zenith during the reign of the Abbasid caliphs in Baghdad (AD 750–1258). It was this trading capacity which later attracted the colonial powers of Portugal, Holland and Britain. In 1820 Britain, in a bid to protect trading routes from pirates operating from ports along the lower Gulf, devised and imposed on the littoral emirates the first of what became a series of truces designed to quell naval warfare. As a result, the area, formerly known as the Pirate Coast, came to be called the Trucial Coast and the seven small principalities which dotted its shores, the Trucial States. These principalities remained under British protectorate status until 1971. Britain had since 1968 favoured, on independence, the creation of a federation which would include the seven Trucial States, plus Qatar and Bahrain. Qatar and Bahrain withdrew and on 1 Dec. 1971 Abu Dhabi, Dubai, Sharjah, Ajman, Umm al-Qaiwain and Fujairah formed the new United Arab Emirates. Ras al-Khaimah joined in early 1972.

From its inception, the UAE faced numerous difficulties. Abu Dhabi had an unresolved dispute with Saudi Arabia and Oman over the Buraymi Oasis which lay in the eastern region of the Emirate and Iran resurrected a claim against Ras al-Khaimah for the Greater and Lesser Tunbs islands. It also had a claim against Sharjah for the Abu Musa island. Iran occupied all three islands and this led to a conflict between Ral al-Khaimah with loss of life on both sides. By 1974, however, an agreement was settled over the Buraymi Oasis.

Territorially, Abu Dhabi is the largest of the shaikhdoms. It also contains more than half the total population of the UAE. Before the discovery of oil in Abu Dhabi in 1958, only Dubai and Sharjah had developed an extensive entrepot trade. This led to rivalry when Dubai began to eclipse Sharjah commercially when the latter's harbour began to silt up in the 1940s. Since the discovery of petroleum

Abu Dhabi Town has grown into a major city with developed administrative and social welfare services. Dubai and Sharjah, though smaller oil producers, have also undertaken extensive development projects. The contrast between the three affluent shaikhdoms and the other four remains significant although the gap has been lessened in recent years. Federal government money, largely from Abu Dhabi, has financed numerous development projects in the poorer states. The federal legislative, executive and judicial bodies are provided for under the UAE constitution of 1971. The legislature, the Federal National Council, is essentially a consultative assembly. Its 40 members are nominated by the president and approved by the rulers of the seven states, who constitute the Federal Supreme Council (FSC). In the absence of political parties overall authority is vested in the FSC. Abu Dhabi and Dubai have the power of veto, which is an expression of their political predominance, though this has occasioned contention among the other emirates. Since independence, Shaikh Zaid of Abu Dhabi has been president of UAE, on a five-year termly basis, with Shaikh Rashid of Dubai as vice-president, and since 1979 as prime minister as well. Within the shaikhdoms politics has traditionally been tribally based and autocratic, so the emergence of a federal system has presented many challenges. UAE is an active member of the Gulf Cooperation Council and increasingly uses the forum as a medium for Gulf regional issues. In the recent Iran/Iraq war UAE contributed $5 billion to Iraq.

CONSTITUTION AND GOVERNMENT

Executive and legislature

Overall authority is vested in the Supreme Council of the seven emirate rulers (each of whom is an absolute monarch in his own state), and the Council's decisions require the approval of at least five rulers; the rulers of Abu Dhabi and Dubai each have a veto. The Supreme Council elects the head of state and government, ie the president of the UAE, together with the vice-president: the president then appoints a prime minister and council of ministers. An appointed Federal National Council considers legislative proposals submitted by the Council of Ministers.

Present government

Supreme Council of Rulers Shaikh Zaid bin Sultan al-Nahayan; President (head of state), Ruler of Abu Dhabi.

Shaikh Rashid bin Said al-Maktoum; Vice-President; Prime Minister; Ruler of Dubai.

Other Members Shaikh Sultan bin Muhammed al-Qassimi (Ruler of Sharjah); Shaikh Saqr bin Muhammed al-Qassimi (Ruler of Ras al-Khaimah); Shaikh Hamad bin Mohammed al-Sharqu (Ruler of Fujairah); Shaikh Rashid bin Ahmed al-Mualla (Ruler of Umm al-Qaiwain); Shaikh Humaid bin Rashid an-Nu'aymi (Ruler of Ajman).

Principal Ministers Shaikh Maktoum bin Rashid al-Maktoum (Deputy Prime Minister); Shaikh Hamdan bin Mohammed al-Nahayan (Deputy Prime Minister); Shaikh Hamdan bin Rashid al-Maktoum (Finance and Industry); Shaikh Mubarak bin Mohammed al-Nahayan (Interior); Shaikh Mohammed bin Rashid al-Maktoum (Defence); Dr Sayed Manah Said al Oteiba (Petroleum and Mineral Resources).

Administration

The UAE is composed of the emirates of Abu Dhabi, Dubai, Sharjah, Ras al-Khaimah (which acceded in 1972), Fujairah, Umm al-Qaiwain and Ajman.

Justice

Systems of law are based throughout the UAE originally on Islamic legal principles, with a trend towards the introduction of secular codes, but their operation is dealt with differently by the local courts in the various emirates; Abu Dhabi has a Ruler's Court presided over by a professional (Jordanian) judge, and Dubai's court is run by a qadi (Islamic legal expert), whereas the ruling families in other emirates deal directly with legal issues themselves. The death penalty is in force. There were seven executions between 1985 and mid-1988. Offences were murder, rape, armed robbery.

National symbols

Flag. Three horizontal stripes of green, white and black, with a red vertical stripe in the hoist, the width of the red stripe being a quarter of the length of the flag.

Festivals. 6 Aug. (Accession of the Ruler of Abu Dhabi); 2 Dec. (National Day).

Vehicle registration plate. UAE.

INTERNATIONAL RELATIONS

Affiliations

NAM; ICO; Arab League; OPEC; OAPEC; GCC.

Defence

Total Armed Forces: 43,000 (perhaps 30% expatriates). Terms of service: voluntary.

Army: 40,000; 136 main battle tanks (AMX-30, OF-40 MK); 80 light tanks (Scorpion).

Navy: 1,500; 15 patrol and coastal combatants.

Air Force: 1,500 (inclusive Police Air Wing); 44 combat aircraft (Mirage 5AD, Hawk Mk 63, MB-339A, MB-326KD/LD); 25 armed helicopters.

ECONOMY

Currency

The unit is the Emirian dirham, divided into 100 fils.

National finance

Budget. The 1987 budget, in US$, was for expenditure of 3,900 million and revenue of 3,000 million.

Balance of payments. The balance of payments, in US$ (current account, 1987) was a surplus of 6,486 million.

Inflation. 5–6%.

Gross Domestic Product

Estimated total GDP US$23,720 million, per capita US$11,900 (overall size of economy ranking 55 in the world).

Economically active population. The total number of persons active in the economy was 580,000; unemployed: negligible.

Sector	% of workforce	% of GDP
industry	85	57
agriculture	5	2
services*	10	41

* services figure includes elements unassigned to other categories.

Energy and mineral resources

Oil and gas. The UAE's high per capita income is founded on its oil and gas. Crude oil production: (1985) 442.3 million bbls; reserves estimated in 1988 are 32,850 million bbls, which at present levels of production are expected to last for approximately 100 years. Most petroleum is produced by Abu Dhabi and Dubai. Abu Dhabi has most of the natural gas reserves, estimated at 184 million ft^3/5.2 million m^3 in 1988.

Water. There is a solar-powered station at Umm al Nar producing some 18,014 US gallons/15,000 gallons per day. The largest solar-powered water-production plant in the Gulf region is under construction at Taweela, with an intended output of 48 million US gallons/40 million gallons per day.

Electricity. Capacity: 5.5 million kW; production: 14.5 million kWh; 7,320 kWh per capita (1988).

Bioresources

Agriculture. Although hampered by lack of natural fresh water, frequent dust and sand storms and by locusts, the number of farmers has increased four-fold in the last ten years as a result of government incentives. The Ministry of Agriculture and Fisheries plans investing Dh1,172 million in agricultural development 1983–93, and it is hoped that self-sufficiency in wheat will be achieved by 2000. Much food still has to be imported.

Crop production: dates (1987) 70,547 tons/64,000 tonnes; alfalfa; vegetables; fruit; tobacco.

Livestock numbers: goats 825,000; sheep 400,000; camels 121,000; cattle 48,000.

Fisheries. It is hoped that with the help of investment, near self-sufficiency in fish will by achieved by 2000. Catch: (1986 est.) 79,807 tons/72,400 tonnes.

Industry and commerce

Industry. Petroleum; fishing; petrochemicals; fertilizers; construction materials; some boatbuilding; handicrafts; pearling.

Commerce. Exports: (f.o.b 1988 est.) US$11,600 million or 52% of GNP, mainly crude oil 75%; natural gas; dried fish; dates. Major trading partners are US; EC countries; Japan. Imports: (f.o.b. 1988 est.) US$6,400 million, mainly food; consumer and capital goods. Major trading partners are EC countries; Japan; US.

Trade with UK. Total exported to the UK 1988 £58,651,000; imported goods from the UK totalled £128,838,000.

COMMUNICATIONS

Railways

There are no railways.

Aviation

Abu Dhabi Airline provides domestic and international services; Emirates (EK) Dubai and Gulf Air Dubai provide international services (international airports are at Dubai, Abu Dhabi and Ras al-Khaimah). Passengers: (1984) 674,000.

Shipping

The major marine ports are Port Rashid and Jebel Ali in Dubai, and Port Zayed in Abu Dhabi. Other smaller ports are Fujairah and Umm al-Qaiwain, Port Khalid in Sharjah, and Port Saqr in Ras al-Khaimah. The merchant marine consists of 46 ships of 1,000 GRT or over. Freight loaded: (1984) 64.5 million tons/58.5 million tonnes; unloaded: 8.3 million tons/ 7.5 million tonnes.

Telecommunications

There are 386,600 telephones and an adequate system of radio-relay and coaxial cable. There are 350,000 radios and 130,000 televisions (1985). Abu Dhabi and Dubai have their own radio and TV stations, and several of the smaller emirates have radio broadcasting operations.

EDUCATION AND WELFARE

Education

Primary education is compulsory between six and 12 years.

School population. 1986–87 some 123,000 primary school pupils; 36,800 preparatory school pupils; 21,000 secondary school pupils.

Schools. Pupil:teacher ratio approximately 32:1.

Universities. One university at al-Ain in Abu Dhabi. Many students study abroad.

Literacy. 54%.

Health

Medical care is free for nationals of the UAE, and if specialist treatment is required abroad grants are available. There are 28 hospitals and 119 clinics, and approximately 2,000 doctors. The Ministry of Health aims to reduce the ratio of beds per head of population to 1:100.

UNITED STATES OF AMERICA

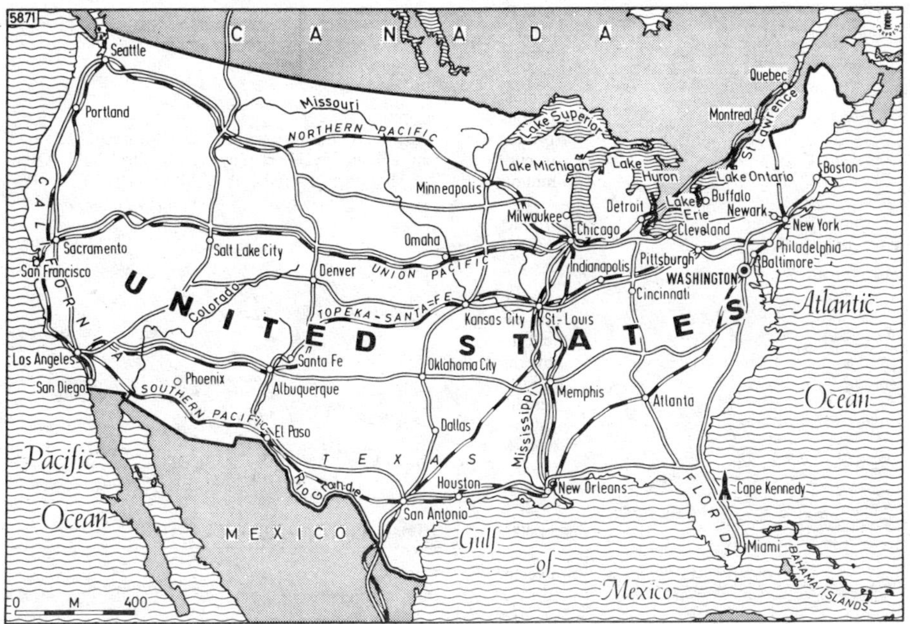

GEOGRAPHY

The United States proper covers a total area of 3,617,829 miles²/9,372,614 km². It comprises 48 contiguous states in mainland North America (bounded by Canada to the north and Mexico to the south), and the separate states of Alaska, to the north-west of Canada, and Hawaii, in the central Pacific. The continental US can be divided into five major physical areas. There are (east to west) the Atlantic coastal plain (including the Florida peninsula and the Gulf Coast in the south), the Appalachian Mountains, the Interior Plain, the North American Cordillera and the Western Intermontane Plateau. The widely forested Appalachian Mountains run south-southwest to north-northeast from northern Alabama to the Great Lakes, and consist of a number of parallel chains: the Allegheny, the Blue Ridge and the Catskill Mountains (high point Mount Mitchell 6,683 ft/2,037 m). West of the Appalachians, the Interior Plain consists of two principal subsections: the eastern central lowlands, combining both the (north) Corn and (south) Cotton Belts, and the Great Plains rising east to west to meet the Rocky Mountains. The US Rockies (highest point Mount Elbert 14,432 ft/4,399 m, in Colorado) are the eastern arm of the North American Cordillera. The western arm of the Cordillera includes, in the south, the Sierra Nevada (highest point Mount Whitney 14,495 ft/4,418 m, in California), and the Cascade Mountains (Oregon and Washington, highest point Mount Rainier 14,409 ft/4,392 m); the Cordillera then runs north through western Canada to Alaska, where the highest peak is Mount McKinley (20,318 ft/6,193 m, highest in the US). Between the two arms of the Cordillera lies the high tableland of the Intermontane Plateau, dominated by the Great Interior Basin which includes the Great Salt Lake (in Utah).

Dominating the US river networks, the Red Mississipi-Missouri system traverses the country north-south over 5,970 km to its mouth in the Gulf of Mexico. Of its many tributaries, the Yellowstone, Platte, Arkansas and Ohio rivers are the largest. Further west, the Colorado of Texas and the Rio Grande, a long river forming part of the boundary with Mexico, also both drain south into the Gulf of Mexico. The rivers flowing east into the Atlantic Ocean (Hudson, Delaware, Susquehanna, Potomac, James, Roanoke and Savannah) are comparatively smaller. The principal rivers flowing west into the Pacific are the Columbia-Snake which forms the border between Washington and Oregon, the Sacramento which flows into San Francisco Bay, and the Colorado which rises in the Rockies and flows through the Grand Canyon and thence west and south to the Golfo de California.

The Eastern States, forming the most densely populated portion of the country, are extensively forested. Deserts cover much of Texas, New Mexico, Arizona, Nevada and Utah. The lowest point of dry land in the US is in Death Valley (Inyo, California), 282 ft/86 m below sea level.

Climate

On the Pacific Coast, polar conditions in North Alaska give way to cool and warm temperate zones further south, with moderate rainfall, and temperate desert in southern California. The Mountain States (Arizona, Colorado, Idaho, Montana, Nevada, New Mexico, Utah, Wyoming) exhibit very varied climatic

States

State	Capital	Date/ Order	Area (mile^2/km^2*)	Population	Governor
Alabama	Montgomery	1819/22nd	51,595/ 133,665	3,893,888 (73.8% White 25.6% Black)	Guy Hunt (1990) R
Alaska	Juneau	1959/49th	586,156/ 1,518,539	401,851 (77.1% White 3.4% Black)	Stephen Cowper (1990) D
Arizona	Phoenix	1912/48th	113,879/ 295,023	2,718,215 (83.2% White 2.7% Black)	Rose Mofford (1990) D
Arkansas	Little Rock	1836/25th	53,088/ 137,533	2,286,435 (82.7% White 16.3% Black)	William Clinton (1990) D
California	Sacramento	1850/31st	158,651/ 411,013	23,667,901 (76.2% White 7.7% Black)	George Deukmejian (1990) R
Colorado	Denver	1876/38th	104,313/ 270,240	2,889,964 (89.0% White 3.5% Black)	Roy Romer (1990) D
Connecticut	Hartford	1788/5th+	5,008/ 12,973	3,107,576 (90.1% White 7% Black)	William A. O'Neill (1990) D
Delaware	Dover	1787/1st+	2,057/ 5,328	594,338 (82.1% White 16.2% Black)	Michael N. Castle (1992) R
District of Columbia		1791	69/179	638,333 (26.9% White 70.3% Black)	Seat of federal government
Florida	Miami	1845/27th	58,556/ 151,700	8,746,324 (85.4% White 13.8% Black)	Robert Martinez (1990) R
Georgia	Atlanta	1788/4th+	58,865/ 152,500	5,464,265 (72.3% White 26.8% Black)	Joe Frank Harris (1990) D
Hawaii	Honolulu	1959/50th	6,448/ 16,705	964,691 (34.4% White 24.9% Japanese 13.7% Filipino 12.3% Hawaiian 5.8% Chinese)	John D. Waihee (1990) D
Idaho	Boise	1890/43rd	83,535/ 216,412	943,935 (95.5% White 0.3% Black)	Cecil D. Andrus (1990) D
Illinois	Springfield	1818/21st	56,385/ 146,075	11,426,518 (80.8% White 14.7% Black)	James R. Thompson (1990) R
Indiana	Indianapolis	1816/19th	36,262/ 93,994	5,490,224 (91.2% White 7.6% Black)	B. Evan Bayh (1992) D
Iowa	Des Moines	1846/29th	56,275/ 145,790	2,913,387 (97.4% White 1.4% Black)	Terry Brandstad (1990) R
Kansas	Topeka	1861/34th	82,242/ 213,063	2,364,236 (91.7% White 5.3 Black)	Mike Hayden (1990) R
Kentucky	Frankfort	1792/15th	40,384/ 104,623	3,660,777 (92.3% White 7.1% Black)	Wallace G. Wilkinson (1991) D
Louisiana	Baton Rouge	1812/18th	48,511/ 125,675	4,203,972 (69.2% White 29.4% Black)	Charles 'Buddy' Roemer (1991) D
Maine	Augusta	1820/23rd	33,206/ 86,027	1,125,027 (98.7% White 0.3% Black)	John R. McKernan (1990) R
Maryland	Annapolis	1788/7th+	10,574/ 27,394	4,216,975 (74.9% White 22.7% Black)	Willian D. Schaefer (1990) D
Massachusetts	Boston	1788/6th+	8,235/ 21,385	5,737,037 (93.5% White 3.9% Black)	Michael S. Dukakis (1990) D

States – cont.

State	Capital	Date/ Order	Area (mile²/km²*)	Population	Governor
Michigan	Lansing	1837/26th	58,200/ 150,777	9,262,078 (85% White 12.9% Black)	James J. Blanchard (1990) D
Minnesota	St Paul	1858/32nd	84,045/ 217,735	4,075,970 (96.6% White 1.3% Black)	Rudy Perpich (1990) DFL
Mississippi	Jackson	1817/20th	47,703/ 123,584	2,520,638 (64.1% White 35.2% Black)	Ray Mabus (1991) D
Missouri	Jefferson City	1821/24th	69,656/ 180,455	4,916,686 (88.4% White 10.5% Black)	John D. Ashcroft (1992) R
Montana	Helena	1889/41st	147,099/ 381,085	786,690 (94.1% White 4.7% Indian 0.3% Asiatic 0.2% Black)	Stan Stephens (1992) R
Nebraska	Lincoln	1867/37th	77,214/ 200,036	1,569,825 (94.9% White 3.1% Black)	Kay A. Orr (1990) R
Nevada	Carson City	1864/36th	110,512/ 286,300	799,184 (87.5% White 6.4% Black)	Bob Miller (1990) D
New Hampshire	Concord	1788/9th+	9,303/ 24,100	920,610 (98.9% White 0.4% Black)	Judd Gregg (1990) R
New Jersey	Trenton	1787/3rd+	7,834/ 20,295	7,364,823 (83.2% White 12.6% Black 1.4% Asiatic)	James A. Florio (1993) D
New Mexico	Santa Fé	1912/47th	121,641/ 315,133	1,302,894 (89.3% White 8.1% Indian 1.9% Black)	Garrey E. Carruthers (1990) R
New York State	Albany	1788/11th+	49,562/ 128,400	17,557,288 (79.5% White 13.7% Black)	Mario M. Cuomo (1990) D
North Carolina	Raleigh	1789/12th+	52,698/ 136,523	5,874,429 (75.8% White 22.4% Black)	James G. Martin (1992) R
North Dakota	Bismarck	1889/39th	70,646/ 183,020	562,717 (95.8% White 0.4% Black)	George A. Sinner (1992) D
Ohio	Columbus	1803/17th	41,192/ 106,714	10,797,630 (88.9% White 10% Black)	Richard F. Celeste (1990) D
Oklahoma	Oklahoma City	1907/46th	69,900/ 181,088	3,025,290 (85.9% White 6.8% Black 5.6% Indian)	Henry Bellmon (1990) R
Oregon	Salem	1859/33rd	83,059/ 215,180	2,633,105 (94.6% White 1.4% Black 1.3% Asiatic 1% Indian)	Neil Goldschmidt (1990) D
Pennsylvania	Harrisburg	1787/2nd+	45,321/ 117,412	11,863,895 (89.8% White 8.8% Black)	Robert P. Casey (1990) D
Rhode Island	Providence	1790/13th+	1,202/ 3,114	947,154 (94.7% White 2.9% Black)	Edward D. DiPrete (1990) R
South Carolina	Columbia	1788/8th+	31,047/ 80,432	3,121,833 (68.9% White 30.4% Black)	Carrol A. Campbell (1990) R
South Dakota	Pierre	1889/40th	77,026/ 199,550	690,178 (92.6% White 0.3% Black)	George S. Mickelson Jr (1990) R

States – cont.

State	Capital	Date/ Order	Area (mile²/km²*)	Population	Governor
Tennessee	Nashville	1796/16th	42,233/ 109,412	4,591,120 (83.5% White 15.8% Black)	Ned R. McWherter (1990) D
Texas	Austin	1845/28th	267,269/ 692,407	12,228,383 (78.7% White 12% Black)	William P. Clements (1990) R
Utah	Salt Lake City	1896/45th	84,893/ 219,931	1,461,037 (94.6% White 1.3% Indian 1% Asiatic 0.6% Black)	Norman H. Bangerter (1992) R
Vermont	Montpelier	1791/14th	9,606/ 24,887	511,456 (99.1% White 0.3% Asiatic 0.2% Black)	Madeleine M. Kunin (1990) D
Virginia	Richmond	1788/10th+	40,804/ 105,711	5,346,818 (79.1% White 18.9% Black)	L. Douglas Wilder (1993) D
Washington	Olympia	1889/42nd	68,173/ 176,615	4,132,156 (91.5% White 2.6% Black 1.5% Indian)	Booth Gardner (1992) D
West Virginia	Charleston	1863/35th	24,175/ 62,629	1,949,644 (96.2% White 3.3% Black)	Gaston Caperton (1992) D
Wisconsin	Madison	1848/30th	56,139/ 145,438	4,705,642 (94.4% White 3.9% Black)	Tommy G. Thompson (1990) R
Wyoming	Cheyenne	1890/44th	97,888/ 253,595	469,557 (95.1% White 0.7% Black)	Mike Sullivan (1990) D

* Area includes inland water.
** All of the governors serve four-year terms except for those of New Hampshire, Rhode Island and Vermont.
\+ One of the 13 original states.
D = Democratic Party. DFL = Democrat-Farmer-Labour. R = Republican Party.

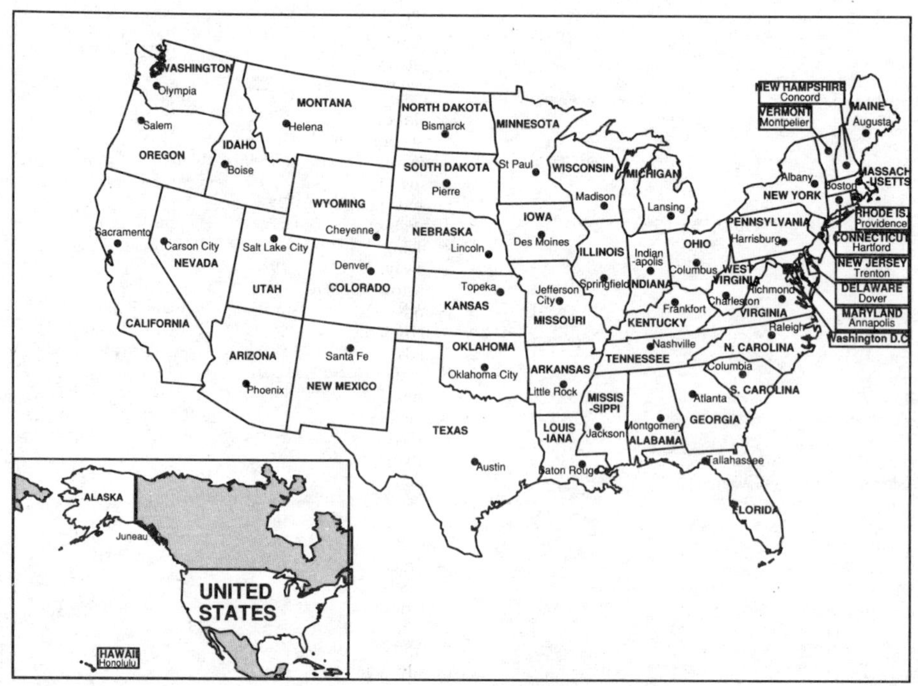

conditions, usually determined principally by local mountain features. Very cold in the north in winter with considerable snowfall. Aridity and high temperatures in the south produce desert conditions. The High Plains (Intermontane Plateau) have a continental climate and suffer summer dust storms and winter blizzards. The Central Plains are temperate continental, the Mid West is continental, as are the Great Lakes, but with especially cold winters while the lakes are frozen. The Appalachians are cool temperate in the north, warm temperate in the south, with abundant precipitation, particularly further south. On the Gulf Coast conditions fluctuate from warm temperate to sub-tropical with plentiful rainfall. The Atlantic Coast is temperate maritime with temperature varying considerably according to latitude; heavy winter snowfall in the north is not unusual. New England is cool temperate, with severe winters and warm summers.

Mean annual temperatures range from 84°F/29°C in Florida to 8°F/–13.3°C in Alaska. Temperature ranges are at their most extreme in the north-central plain. Chicago averages 27°F/–3°C in Jan. and 75°F/24°C in July while temperatures in Phoenix, Arizona vary from 52°F/11.1°C in Jan. to 90°F/32.2°C in July. Annual rainfall averages 29 in/735 mm, ranging from 65 in/1,640 mm in Alabama to 7 in/180 mm in Arizona. Both Alaska and Hawaii are very humid, with annual rainfall 60–200 in/1,524–5,080 mm.

Cities and towns

	State	Population*
Akron	Ohio	237,177(1980)
Albuquerque	New Mexico	366,750
Anaheim	California	219,311(1980)
Anchorage	Alaska	231,422(1987)
Atlanta	Georgia	421,910
Aurora	Colorado	220,066(1986)
Austin	Texas	466,550
Baltimore	Maryland	745,900(1987)
Baton Rouge	Louisiana	242,184(1987)
Birmingham	Alabama	284,413(1980)
Boston	Massachusetts	573,600
Buffalo	New York	324,820
Charlotte	North Carolina	352,070
Chicago	Illinois	3,009,530
Cincinnati	Ohio	369,750
Cleveland	Ohio	535,830
Colorado Springs	Colorado	215,150(1980)
Columbus	Ohio	566,030
Corpus Christi	Texas	231,999(1980)
Dallas	Texas	1,003,520
Dayton	Ohio	203,371(1980)
Denver	Colorado	505,000
Detroit	Michigan	1,086,220
El Paso	Texas	491,800
Fort Worth	Texas	429,550
Fresno	California	218,202(1980)
Honolulu	Hawaii	372,330
Houston	Texas	1,728,910
Indianapolis	Indiana	719,820
Jackson	Mississippi	202,895(1980)
Jacksonville	Florida	638,212(1987)
Jersey City	New Jersey	223,532(1980)
Kansas City	Missouri	441,170
Las Vegas	Nevada	217,360(1987)
Lexington-Fayette	Kentucky	204,165(1980)
Los Angeles	California	3,259,340
Long Beach	California	361,334(1980)
Louisville	Kentucky	298,451(1980)
Memphis	Tennessee	652,640
Miami	Florida	417,714(1987)
Milwaukee	Wisconsin	605,090
Minneapolis	Minnesota	356,840
Mobile	Alabama	200,452(1980)
Nashville-Davidson	Tennessee	473,670
Newark	New Jersey	316,240
New Orleans	Louisiana	555,641(1987)
New York	New York State	7,262,700
Norfolk	Virginia	266,979(1980)
Oklahoma City	Oklahoma	446,120
Oakland	California	356,960
Omaha	Nebraska	349,270
Philadelphia	Pennsylvania	1,642,900
Phoenix	Arizona	894,070
Pittsburgh	Pennsylvania	387,490
Portland	Oregon	419,810(1987)
Richmond	Virginia	219,214(1980)
Rochester	New York	241,741(1980)
Sacramento	California	323,550
St Louis	Missouri	426,300
St Paul	Minnesota	270,230(1980)
St Petersburg	Florida	263,352(1987)
San Antonio	Texas	914,350
San Diego	California	1,015,190
San Francisco	California	749,000
San José	California	712,080
Santa Ana	California	203,713(1980)
Seattle	Washington	419,300(1987)
Shreveport	Louisiana	217,718(1987)
Tampa	Florida	291,617(1987)
Toledo	Ohio	340,680
Tucson	Arizona	358,850
Tulsa	Oklahoma	373,750
Virginia Beach	Virginia	333,400
Washington DC	(capital)	626,000
Wichita	Kansas	279,272(1980)

* Population figures refer to estimated mid-1986 population unless indicated otherwise. The last official census was in Apr. 1980.

Population

Total population (1 Jan. 1989 est.) 246,900,000, compared with 243,600,000 one year earlier. The last census (1980) records the following statistical data: United States (50 states and Federal District of Columbia) 226,545,805; Puerto Rico 3,196,520; Outlying Areas 368,856; Territories including Medway, Wake, Canton and Eudebuy Island and Johnston Atoll 235,927; Guam 105,979; Virgin Islands 95,569; American Samoa 32,297; Pacific Islands Trust Territory 116,144; Northern Mariana Islands 16,780. Figures exclude armed service personnel abroad and US citizens living abroad.

The 1980 census recorded 188,372,000 people as White (83.15%), 26,495,000 as Black (11.7%) and 11,679,158 as 'other races', of whom 1,364,033 were (Native) Indian; 700,974 Japanese; 806,040 Chinese; 774,652 Filipino. 1986 figures: 84.8% White, 12.2% Black. Population projections for the country as a whole estimate 268,266,000 inhabitants by the year 2000. Hispanic population ('of Spanish origin', any race) estimated 1980 at 14,609,000 and 1989 at 19,358,000 rising to 25,223,000 by the year 2000. American Indian populations are concentrated in Oklahoma, Arizona, New Mexico, California and North Carolina. More than 50% live on reservations, mostly below the poverty line. The median Indian

family income falls far below the national average. The Bureau of Indian Affairs recognizes 266 ethnic groups in the US and 216 Eskimo and Indian communities in Alaska. Navajo reserves cover 17,000,233 acres/6,879,900 ha and support 150,000 people.
Population density 68 per mile^2/27 per km^2 (but only 1.5 per mile^2/0.27 per km^2 in Alaska). 74% live in urban areas.
Birth rate (1987) 3,829,000 (15.7 per 1,000 population); (1988 est.) 3,900,000. **Death rate** (1987) 2,127,000 (8.7 per 1,000); (1988 est.) 2,200,000. **Rate of population increase** 1.35%. **Age distribution** Under 15 = 21,9%; over 65 = 11.7%. **Life expectancy** female 78.1; male 70.6; average 74.3.
Immigration In 1986, 601,708 immigrants entered the US of whom 104,383 were admitted as permanent residents. In the year ending 30 Sept. 1987 there were 601,516 immigrants, of whom 68,000 were from Europe (15,889 from the UK); 248,000 from Asia (58,317 from the Philippines, 35,397 from South Korea, 32,669 from China including Taiwan, 26,394 from India, 16,489 from Thailand, 13,073 from Vietnam and 10,323 from Iran); 265,026 from the Americas and Caribbean (72,511 from Mexico, 27,363 from Cuba, 24,947 from Dominican Republic and 22,430 from Jamaica); 15,700 from African countries. The 1988 immigration total was 606,000.

Religion

An estimated 60% of the population are members of a religious body. Christianity is the predominant religion; the 52,655,000 Roman Catholics form the largest single denomination, although Protestants outnumber Catholics by 3:2, the largest Protestant groups being the 25.8 million adherents of Baptist churches (including 14.6 million in the Southern Baptist Convention and 5.5 million in the National Baptist Convention); 12.8 million Methodists; 8.5 million Lutherans; 3.4 million Presbyterians; 3.1 million Pentecostalists; 2.5 million Episcopalians. There are 3.9 million Mormons; 4.3 million members of Orthodox Christian churches; an estimated 2 million Muslims; and 5.9 million Jews (2% of the total population), 1.5 million of whom are affiliated to the United Synagogue of America, 1.3 million to the (reform) Union of American Hebrew Congregations and 1 million to the Union of Orthodox Jewish Congregations of America. There are 250,000 Buddhists, 110,000 Bahá'is and an estimated 9,500 Sikhs.

Languages

Approximately 216,180,000 persons speak English as their first language. 13.6 million speak Spanish; 1.84 million German; 1.83 million French; 1.84 million Italian; 0.75 million Chinese; 417,000 speak American Indian or Native American Dialects. There are approximately 358,000 Yiddish-speakers.

HISTORY

The earliest American settlers were Amerindian tribes which are believed to have crossed the Bering Straits from Asia to North and South America. In North America, they established cultures ranging from the nomadic dwellers of the Plains to elaborate civilizations such as that of the Aztecs in Mexico.

European civilization first made its impact on America at the end of the 15th century with the voyages of Christopher Columbus, who had set out to discover a route to the Orient and instead opened the mineral-rich regions of South and Central America to Spanish exploitation. Explorers, however, continued to search for a route to the Orient. Blocked at the south, they turned to the north where French and English adventurers established early fur-trading settlements in Canada. The area between Canada and Mexico, which was later to become the original 13 states and later still the Eastern Seaboard of the United States, was largely shunned as a mosquito-infested region devoid of worthwhile natural resources.

It was not until 1587 that the British navigator Sir Walter Raleigh made an unsuccessful attempt to establish a colony on the island of Roanoke off the coast of Virginia. Although this colony mysteriously disappeared, it fired the imagination of the British public and in the following 50 years a number of British settlers embarked for the New World and established colonies stretching from Maine to Georgia.

The Spanish and Portuguese empires established in the previous century were distinguished by their heavy reliance on the imperial armies, the close relationship with the Roman Catholic Church and exploitation of the colonies and their mineral resources. By contrast, the British colonies from the start had little or no connection with the government in London. They were, in the main, private business ventures financed by wealthy British individuals seeking to establish a long-term return on their capital by employing settlers to farm land granted to them by royal charter. They also functioned as havens for non-conformist Protestants seeking to escape persecution.

For a variety of reasons, the British government eventually moved to establish its authority in the colonies by appointing royal governors for each of the 13 colonies. But the commercial and religious foundations of the colonies engendered an independent streak among the settlers. This was generally either encouraged or ignored by the government in London as it meant that the colonies were less of a political and economic burden on the government of the day. But the Seven Years' War (1757–63) brought a reversal of this policy of benign neglect.

The war was largely fought for the benefit of the American settlers against the French Canadians and their Indian allies. It resulted in the defeat of the French, marked notably by the fall of Quebec in 1759. At the Treaty of Fontainbleu (1762), the French ceded to Britain their remaining possessions in Canada and all American land west of the Missisipi. In 1763, the French also ceded Lousiana to Spain, which in turn ceded Florida to Britain. The war cost the British exchequer the then staggering sum of £101,500,000 and the government in London decided to try to recoup some of the expense by imposing taxes on the colonies such as the Stamp Act (1765 – repealed the following year), the Townshend Duties (1769) and the Tea Act, which together provoked the American settlers to rally round the flag of 'no taxation without representation'. The British also negotiated an unpopular treaty with the Indian Chief Pontiac which restricted colonial settlement to the area east of the Appalachian Mountains.

The new taxes coincided with an economic recession in the colonies and together they provided fertile ground for the radical politicians of the day, such as Patrick Henry and Samuel Adams, who advocated independence from Britain. Frequent clashes between American demonstrators and British troops culminated in the 'Boston Massacre' (1770), in which a number of civilians were shot dead. After a widespread campaign against the Tea Act, marked by protests such as the famous 'Boston Tea Party' (1773), when settlers threw crates of British tea into the harbour, the British Parliament overreacted with the 1774 'Intolerable Acts' which attempted to strangle the economic life of Boston, regarded as the hotbed of revolutionary activities. Instead of suppressing rebellion, the Intolerable Acts united the formerly divided 13 colonies against the British. Common cause between the colonies was made at the first Continental Congress (1774), and open fighting broke out the following year with the battles of Lexington, Concord and Bunker Hill. With no compromise in sight, representatives of the 13 colonies signed a 'Declaration of Independence' from Britain on 4 July 1776. Initially, Britain had the upper hand, forcing American commander George Washington to take refuge in Valley Forge (1777). British success was short-lived, however, and their defeat at Yorktown (1781) marked the effective end of the war, leading to a peace agreement (1783) in which Britain recognized American independence.

Following the defeat of Britain, the 13 colonies, which had united against the common foe, quickly divided again. This was not surprising. Although the colonies shared a common British heritage and a common enemy, they differed widely in their political beliefs and social and economic structures. The colonies remained loosely tied together under the Articles of Confederation (drawn up 1777), but the central authority created by this wartime agreement was too weak to deal with the crippling wartime debts or fend off increasing British antipathy and Spanish and French encroachments. At a constitutional convention in Philadelphia (1786–87), it was agreed to construct a strengthened federal government, but with significant rights and responsibilities reserved for the individual states. The result was the American Constitution (1788), the world's first written constitution, and the establishment of the present United States of America, with a directly elected executive president, presidentially appointed cabinet ministers, an elected bicameral legislature and a presidentially appointed independent judiciary with the power to overturn legislation on constitutional grounds. The first elections were held in 1788, with Washington elected unopposed as president. The first ten amendments to the constitution, which together became known as the Bill of Rights, were passed by Congress in 1791.

Washington was succeeded by John Adams (1797–1801) and Thomas Jefferson (1801–09). Washington himself died in 1799 at the age of 67. The following year, Philadelphia was replaced as US capital by the newly created city of Washington (DC).

One of the first acts of the new government was to reject Britain's 1763 treaty with Chief Pontiac which restricted European settlement to east of the Appalachians. This immediately opened up all the lands between the Appalachians and the Mississippi and started the great drive west. In 1803, Pres. Thomas Jefferson purchased the French-held territory of Louisiana from the financially hard-pressed Napoleon. This astute real-estate deal effectively doubled the size of the US and secured the vital Mississippi waterway. An unsuccessful second war with Britain (1812) increased American determination to remain aloof from European affairs. This stance was epitomized by the so-called 'Monroe Doctrine', named after the incumbent president (1823). The Oregon Territory was ceded to the US by Britain in 1818. Texas joined the Union in 1845 after a brief period as an independent state and New Mexico, Arizona, California, Utah and Colorado were acquired in 1850, following the defeat of Mexico. This westward expansion received a further boost by the discovery of gold in California in 1849.

Unfettered expansion demanded the dispossession of the Indian nations who were already in occupation, albeit sparsely, of much of the West. This was achieved by a mixture of treaty, deception and war. The 'Five Civilized Nations' group of Indians were compelled to take the so-called Trail of Tears, from their eastern lands to Oklahoma (1838), while the western Indians were subdued in a series of conflicts: most notably the Cheyenne–Arapaho wars (1861–64); the Sioux wars (1862–67; 1875–76 – which included the last significant American military defeat on its soil, when Custer was crushed at Little Big Horn); and the Apache Wars (1881–87). Armed Indian defiance collapsed completely after the Ghost Dance Uprising (1890).

The first half of the 19th century also witnessed an unprecedented growth in the American economy, the start of the industrial revolution in the north-east and the strengthening of the institution of slavery. Slave-produced cotton from the southern states was demanded by the textile mills of the north as well as providing the United States' principal export to the textile mills of Britain.

Slavery, however, had become anathema to many Northerners by the mid-19th century. The Southerners, at the same time, regarded the institution as an essential element of their economic and social life. After the 1860 election victory of apparently pro-abolitionist Abraham Lincoln, the Southern states seceded from the Union (1861) and formed the Confederate States of America. Lincoln and the North rejected the secession, and the result was the American Civil War. The conflict was unequal from the start. The Northern states had a population of 21 million compared with 9 million in the South. The North had 70% of the railway lines and 93% of the factories, including all of the iron, cannon and gun-manufacturing businesses. The only reason that the war lasted for four years was that the South possessed the country's finest military leaders and was fighting a defensive war in its own territory. Broken by Sherman's capture of Atlanta (1864) and march across the confederacy, the southern states surrendered in 1865. Following the victory, slavery was formally abolished throughout the US by the 13th amendment (1866). Tragically, Lincoln was assassinated while attending a theatre performance later the same year. The next 40 years were to see two further presidential assassinations – that of Garfield (1881) and McKinley (1901). It took the south nearly 100 years to recover fully from their defeat and the subsequent Reconstruction period, and American politics and business were dominated by the north-eastern establishment until after the 1950s.

Following the Northern victory, the country was again able to return to its 'Manifest Destiny' of westward expansion. A large area of territory was added with the purchase of Alaska from Russia in 1867. A rapid increase in industrialization and railway building reached its ceremonial peak with the completion of the transcontinental railway in May 1869. This and subsequent east-west railways opened the eastern markets to western products of beef, grain and timber as well as providing a means for transporting settlers and manufactured eastern goods to the west.

The years before and after the Civil War also saw a major change in the demographic structure of the US. At the time of independence, the population of the US was drawn almost entirely from British stock with a few Germans and Dutch from the early settlements in New York. But from about 1850, the lure of gold in California and jobs in factories in the north, attracted an increasing number of workers from Central Europe. These were further swelled by thousands of Chinese who constructed the transcontinental railroads. By 1870, the country was beginning to develop its English-dominated polyglot character.

The virgin western territories meant that from 1781 to the end of the 19th century, the US was occupied entirely with the establishment of its own continental base and the resolution of basic political and economic problems. But by the end of the 19th century, the US had become a leading economic power, although its relatively small-standing defence forces and isolationist political establishment meant that internationally the country was a minor force.

The Spanish-American War of 1898 catapulted the US out of its isolationism and into European-dominated international affairs. The war left it a major power in the Caribbean and in the Pacific with the acquisition of Puerto Rico, Guam and the Philippines and effective control of the island of Cuba. America's expansion outside the continental US continued with the acquisition of the Hawaiian Islands in 1898, the opening of the Panama Canal (1914) and the acquisition of the Danish Virgin Islands (1916). During the same period, the US formulated its 'Open Door' policy towards China which was designed to force Europeans to accept American businessmen on an equal footing. The Open Door policy had the corollary effect of pledging the US to the support of Chinese political integrity, a pledge which later led to the extended American involvement in the political development of Asia.

But despite these developments, the vast bulk of the American hinterland and the slow development of internal trade meant that the US remained a basically isolationist country. When World War I broke out in Europe, the vast majority of Americans were in favour of staying neutral. Pres. Woodrow Wilson reflected these sentiments and spent the first three years of the war trying to mediate between Britain and Germany and keep America out of the war. But the German decision in Jan. 1917 to launch an all-out submarine attack against neutral shipping quickly led to the US entering the war on the Allied side. The infusion of 1,250,000 American soldiers was an important factor in defeating the German Western Offensive (Mar. 1918), after which Germany was forced to accept an armistice.

At the subsequent Paris Peace Conference, Wilson dominated the negotiations with his 14-point proposal for freedom of the seas, open diplomacy, free trade, general disarmament and a League of Nations to oversee a new world order based on peace and social justice. The idealism of Wilson's position was undermined, however, by the Allies' desire to exact vengeance upon their defeated enemies. The success of the League of Nations, the arbiter of Wilson's new world order, was also heavily dependent on American participation. Although Wilson campaigned enthusiastically for the treaty's ratification by the Senate, Republican isolationists succeeded in securing its rejection, with the result that the US remained outside the League and returned to its isolationist roots.

The immediate post-war years saw a short depression as the economy wound down from its war footing and encountered inevitable difficulties in absorbing the demobilized servicemen. But by 1925, the economy was booming once more, and throughout the 1920s industrial production increased by 50%. The rapid growth in the American economy was partly fuelled by the repayment of two billion dollars in wartime loans which shifted the world's capital base from London to New York. The growth was stimulated by the laissez-faire economic policies of the administrations of presidents Warren Harding (1921–23) and Calvin Coolidge (1923–29). But this unbridled growth also encouraged rampant speculation and in Oct. 1929 the New York stock-market collapsed. The crash came to symbolize the onset of a severe economic depression which lasted throughout the 1930s.

Republican president Herbert Hoover (elected Nov. 1928) attempted some remedial action but was hampered by his commitment to the concept of laissez-faire economics. In 1932, Hoover was defeated by Democrat Franklin D. Roosevelt, who promised a 'New Deal' of unprecedented government intervention to bring the US out of the Depression. In his first 100 days in office, Roosevelt sent Congress bills that created the Tennessee Valley Authority, unemployment relief, an agricultural recovery programme, federal supervision of investment securities and prevented the foreclosure of mortgages on private homes. This legislation was later followed by other basic social and economic foundation stones such as the Social Security Act and the Fair Labour Standards Act which established a minimum wage. By 1938, government spending had become the primary device for stimulating the American economy.

The New Deal did much to alleviate the personal hardships of the Depression, but failed to correct the structural weaknesses which had created it and which were eventually eliminated by the outbreak of World War II in Europe. Renewed hostilities between Britain and Germany forced Britain to turn again to the US for capital and defence material, which was made available on generous terms under the Lend-Lease Act (1941). The US entered the war on 7 Dec. 1941, after the Japanese bombed the US Pacific fleet at Pearl Harbor.

The US played a much larger role in World War II than it had in World War I. An estimated 16 million men and women went into uniform. They fought in North Africa, Western Europe, Asia and the Pacific. Factory output doubled with the result that the US produced 196,400 aeroplanes, 6,500 naval vessels and 86,300 tanks. World War II also saw the American development of the atomic bomb which would come to dominate international relations in the postwar period. The war in Europe ended in May 1945 and in Asia on 14 Aug. (formally on 2 Sept.), after the dropping of the atomic bomb on Hiroshima and Nagasaki.

Roosevelt died on 12 Apr. 1945 and was succeeded by his inexperienced vice-president, Harry S. Truman. Immediately prior to Roosevelt's death the relationship between the Western Allies and the Soviet Union had been deteriorating as the common threat posed by Nazi Germany receded. Efforts to find common ground, such as the Yalta Conference (1945), were only partially suceessful. Disputes broke out in eastern Europe and Korea over the political complexion of governments which were to be installed in the liberated territories. This antipathy developed into the Cold War as the US and the Soviet Union each sought to prevent the other from extending its influence. The position of the US was epitomized by the Truman Doctrine of Mar. 1947 which committed it to 'support free peoples who are resisting attempted subjugation by armed minorities or by outside pressures'.

Logical extensions of the Truman Doctrine were the Marshall Plan (also known as the European Economic Recovery Programme), which sought to undermine Communist influence by revitalizing Western European economies with American aid, and the 1949 formation of the North Atlantic Treaty Organization (NATO) which committed the US to the defence of Western Europe and eventually led to over 300,000 American troops being permanently based in Europe.

In Asia, US policies initially centred on China and an attempt to mediate between the recognized government of Chiang Kai-shek and the Chinese Communists led by Mao Zedong. The mediation attempt failed and in the subsequent civil war the Chinese Communists drove Chiang off the mainland of China to the island of Taiwan where he established a government-in-exile. During the war years, Chiang had developed strong connections in the American political establishment but alienated professional American diplomats by his failure to stamp out corruption or establish a popular political base. On the advice of his diplomats, Pres. Truman refused to throw full American military support behind Chiang. This later led to accusations that Truman and various American diplomats had 'lost' China.

In the charged anti-Communist atmosphere of the late 1940s and early 1950s, Americans were prepared to believe that the success of the Chinese Communists was part of a global strategy orchestrated by the Soviet Union with the aid of disloyal Americans. The loss of China also encouraged Truman and successive presidents to take an increasingly interventionist line in Asian affairs. This led to the Korean War (1950–53), support for the French in their Indochina War (1946–54), the Quemoy and Matsu crises of 1956 and 1958, and finally the Vietnam War (1964–75). In Europe, some of the major Cold War crises were the Berlin Blockade of 1948 and the Berlin Crises of 1959 and 1961, the year of the completion of the Berlin Wall. Fear of the Soviet Union spilled over into domestic politics with the rise of the demagogic senator Joseph McCarthy, whose Communist witch hunt of innuendo destroyed the lives of thousands of innocent American public employees.

In the early Cold War years, the US enjoyed a monopoly of atomic weapons. Then, in Sept. 1949, the Soviet Union exploded its first atomic bomb. The US responded with the development of the hydrogen bomb, which the USSR quickly matched. The two countries then competed in developing the quantity and quality of nuclear weapons and delivery systems as well as increasingly expensive conventional forces.

In the late 1940s and early 1950s, the US was able to absorb this heavy defence expenditure without any damage to the economy. The US emerged from the war with its production base intact and considerably improved and the world's main creditor nation. In 1950 its gross national product was $381 billion, more than the combined gross national products of Britain, the Soviet Union, France, West Germany, Italy and Japan. There was sufficient money for Pres. Truman to propose an extension of Roosevelt's pre-war New Deal which was renamed the Fair Deal. Congress, however, was dominated by the opposition Republican Party which rejected all but the pension provisions of the 1950 Social Security Act.

Truman was succeeded by Republican president Dwight Eisenhower (1953–61) who adopted a laissez-faire policy towards the economy. Government intervention increased under the successive Democratic administrations of John F. Kennedy (1961–63) and Lyndon Baines Johnson (1963–69). By the time of the Johnson administration, the economy was beginning to feel the strain of heavy defence expenditures and increased social spending. These strains continued through the Nixon, Carter and Reagan administrations and the US federal deficit and the trade deficit became a source of increasing concern.

Another source of concern was the lack of civil rights for American Blacks. Although they had been freed from slavery during the Civil War, they continued to be subjected in many states to a policy of racial discrimination and segregation. In 1954, the US Supreme Court ruled that racial segregation in public schools was unconstitutional. The Black community, under the leadership of Martin Luther King Jr., embarked on a campaign of civil disobedience to secure its constitutional rights. The civil disobedience erupted into race riots in the 1960s and eventually led to the passage of the Civil Rights Act (1964). But the deep-seated prejudices of some White Americans were underscored by the assassination of Martin Luther King in Apr. 1968.

Throughout the first 20 years of the post-war period, the US based its claim to world leadership on a superior New World morality. This belief reached its zenith during the administration of Pres. John Kennedy whose combination of youth and charisma appeared to personify the vibrant new America and offer hope and opportunity to billions around the world. Kennedy's assassination in Nov. 1963 shocked the world and to some extent marked the end of these illusions.

The death of Kennedy was quickly followed by the Vietnam War – a conflict which for many people closely resembled the oppressive imperialist wars of the 19th century which the US had ostensibly disdained. The Vietnam War seriously split American society and culminated in America's first major military defeat. The US had become involved in a limited capacity supporting the French colonial government in the 1950s; their involvement escalated in 1961, and dramatically three years later when Congress passed the 'Tonkin Gulf' resolution (1964) authorizing the president to take whatever steps were necessary to prosecute the war. Over 541,000 US troops saw combat (including 32,000 in Cambodia in 1970). Under Pres. Richard Nixon, the troops were gradually withdrawn, but by the fall of Saigon (1975), official casualty figures revealed that 46,079 Americans had been killed, and 303,640 wounded.

Public opposition to the war was fuelled by reports of atrocities such as the My Lai massacre of Vietnamese civilians (1969). Four students protesting against the incursion into Cambodia were shot dead by National Guard troops at Kent State University in 1970.

Towards the end of the Vietnam period, American political society was rocked by the revelation that the Democratic Party's Washington DC campaign headquarters had been burgled by a team hired by the campaign committee of Pres. Nixon. The subsequent investigation led to the Watergate Scandal and Nixon's resignation in Aug. 1974.

While Nixon's handling of the Watergate Scandal was deemed reprehensible, his foreign policy marked America's coming of age as a Super Power. Under the direction of Henry Kissinger, the US discarded the naivety that had characterized the foreign policy of other administrations and adopted a realpolitik approach to foreign affairs that more closely resembled the balance-of-power diplomacy of Kissinger's hero, the 19th-century diplomat Count Metternich. Nixon paid a historic visit to China (1972) and developed a working relationship with the Soviet Union which became known as détente. Diplomatic relations with China were eventually established in 1979. At the same time, suspicion grew of US covert involvement in attempts to destabilize or overthrow left-wing regimes, notably in the case of the Allende government bloodily deposed in Gen. Pinochet's coup in Chile (Sept. 1973), and the civil war in Angola (from 1975). The CIA, embroiled with anti-Castro Cubans since their abortive Bay of Pigs invasion in Apr. 1961 and apparently even prepared to consider schemes to kill Castro with exploding cigars, gained a reputation for 'dirty tricks' to the extent that conspiracy theorists would see its hand in the Kennedy assassination, and almost everything else.

Part of the reason for improved relations with the Communist Bloc was the change in the structure of international relations from the bipolar world of the early postwar years to a more complex multipolar system of conflicting national aspirations. US dominance of the world's economy was challenged by the growing power of the European Economic Community and Japan, and the emerging nations of Asia and Africa were establishing governments and pursuing policies which failed to fit into the capitalist-versus-Communist formula.

Nixon was succeeded by his vice-president Gerald Ford (1974–77) who retained Kissinger as secretary of state and maintained his predecessor's foreign and domestic policies. In 1976 the relatively unknown Democrat Jimmy Carter was elected president. Carter offered a fresh face and unblemished past to an American electorate seeking a politician untainted by Vietnam or the discredited Washington power circles. Carter, however, failed to live up to the public expectation of a man capable of restoring American prestige, and, although he scored a notable foreign-policy success with the conclusion of the US-sponsored Egyptian-Israeli 'Camp David' agreement (1978), he was humiliated by the seizure of American hostages in Tehran (1979).

In 1980, Carter was defeated by Ronald Reagan, the former film actor who promised to restore the US to its position as 'a shining city on the hill'. For many Americans, Reagan and his policies typified basic national values which predated the Roosevelt years. On domestic issues, he stressed the importance of family, thrift and industriousness. In foreign affairs, he took a tough anti-Soviet position and backed this up with increased defence spending. Reagan secured public support for these policies with a relaxed manner and a series of televised homespun homilies which struck a basic chord with the American public. Towards the end of his term, the administration underwent a volte-face in its attitude towards the Soviet Union, marked by summit meetings between Reagan and Mikhail Gorbachev at Geneva (1985), Reykjavik (1986) and Washington (1987).

Relations with several third-world countries with whose regimes the Reagan regime was at odds, whether fundamentalist Islamic (Iran), third-world maverick radical (Libya) or socialist-too-close-to-home (Nicaragua, Cuba), showed his administration far from surefooted on unpredictable terrain. While Iran reviled the US in public as the 'Great Satan', covert attempts were mounted to win Iranian support for the release of hostages kidnapped by radical Shi'ites in Lebanon, by the expedient of offering secret arms deals (from mid-1985). The intended by-product was cash to go in back-door military aid to the contras in Nicaragua, where Congress had become unwilling to fund Reagan's proxy crusade against the left-wing Sandinista government. The upshot, however, was the uncovering of what became known as the Iran-contra affair (Nov. 1986), implicating former national security adviser Robert Macfarlane, his successor Adml. Poindexter, Marine Lt.-Col Oliver North and others, and leading to protracted inquiries as to whether George Bush as vice-president, or Reagan as president, had ignored, known of, or authorized, illegal actions. Less convoluted was US hostility towards Libya, whose leader Col Gaddafi the administration held responsible for supporting acts of terrorism in the Middle East. Punitive retaliatory US air strikes against Libyan cities (15 Apr. 1986), launched from aircraft carriers and from USAF bases in southern England, caused numerous civilian casualties (estimates suggested 100 dead in Tripoli and 30 in Benghazi).

Reagan left office in 1989, one of the few genuinely popular American presidents. He was succeeded by his vice-president, George Bush, who defeated Democratic contender Michael Dukakis in the Nov. 1988 elections. Bush was faced with two major problems, the continuing American trade deficit and international financial instability, and the lack of a clear response to the wave of liberalization within Communist regimes.

By the mid-1980s the Soviet economy was clearly unable to cope with the country's overextended foreign and defence commitments. Following the accession to power of Mikhail Gorbachev in 1985, the Soviet Union began to cut back on defence spending and foreign aid. At the same time, in order to secure public support for difficult economic measures, Gorbachev sought to widen his political base by introducing a measure of representative government. This in turn led to Soviet-dominated governments in Eastern Europe introducing their own democratization programmes and Soviet-supported guerrilla movements seeking diplomatic solutions as the Soviet Union became unwilling and unable to continue its financial aid.

With many American policy makers still locked into the political concepts of the Cold War years, the Reagan and Bush administrations have been slow to react to the changes within the Communist Bloc countries. This has meant that other, more directly affected, countries such as Japan and the West European countries have been forced to act more and more independently of the US.

CONSTITUTION AND GOVERNMENT

Executive, legislature and judiciary

The federal government embodies the separation of powers which is a cornerstone of the Constitution. The distribution of powers, as between the separate branches of government, however, is in continuous evolution, and shifts in the balance are frequently at issue in Supreme Court deliberations on constitutional issues. The executive branch is headed by a president (who is head of state and head of government) and vice-president, elected for four years, and a government nominated by the president, subject to confirmation by the Senate; these appointees may have cabinet rank, but the cabinet is not a formal collegiate body, nor does it have the same degree of collective decision-making responsibility as cabinets have in some other Western government systems. The legislative branch (Congress) comprises a Senate of 100 members and a House of Representatives of 435 members. Legislation passed by Congress (ie in both houses) may be vetoed by the president, but this veto may be overridden by a two-thirds majority in both houses. The Senate has a particularly pronounced role in foreign affairs, since the ratification of treaties requires a two-thirds Senate majority; the declaration of war rests with Congress. The judicial branch is headed by the Supreme Court, to which recourse may be had in disputes over the constitutionality of legislative and executive actions; its decisions may then only be counteracted by constitutional amendments, for which approval must be obtained from two-thirds majorities in the House and the Senate, and from three-quarters of the states. In addition to this basic tripartite division, federal regulatory agencies have grown up, in the 20th century, with a semi-independent status, run by commissions named by the president with the Senate's approval. Such bodies include the Federal Reserve System (the Fed, the country's central bank), the General Accounting Office, the Federal Trade Commission, the Security and Exchange Commission, the Federal Communications Commission and the Nuclear Regulatory Commission.

The states

The sovereign powers of the 50 individual states of the Union, while in theory protected under the constitution, have in practice declined as the sphere of federal goverment involvement has extended, a process more or less continuous since the Civil War. In the states the executive branch is headed by a governor, there is a bicameral state congress, usually an assembly or house of representatives and a senate (except in Nebraska where there is a single chamber), elected for terms which vary from state to state. (The terms of office for state governors are four years except New Hampshire, Rhode Island and Vermont, where two-year terms apply.)

Federal electoral system

Presidential elections are held every four years, on the Tuesday following the first Monday in November. A 538-member electoral college is constituted by elections on the basis of universal adult suffrage (minimum age 18) in each state and the District of Columbia, the number of electoral college members per state being determined by population (but with a minimum of three). The formal process is that this electoral college meets in mid-December and chooses a president, whose name is announced on Jan. 6; in practice the result of the November election is known shortly after polling ends. The political process at this level is dominated by the rival organizations of the two main parties, the Republicans and the Democrats, whose candidate selection process involves a protracted round of party caucuses and primary contests in different states (the first primary elections being in New Hampshire, in mid-February), culminating in party conventions in July-August to choose the party candidate.

Legislative elections At the same time as the presidential election, and at presidential mid-term (ie two years later), elections take place for the federal Congress; state-wide for senators (one-third of the Senate seats being up for election at each of these occasions, for a six-year term) and in single-member constituencies for the House of Representatives (all seats up for election every two years). Elections at state and local level may also be held at the same time.

The most recent presidential election was held on 8 Nov. 1988. The Republican candidate and incumbent vice-president, George Bush, defeated his Democratic rival, Michael Dukakis, and duly took office as president on 20 Jan. 1989. The Democrats, however, retained control over Congress, winning 262 out of 435 seats in the House of Representatives and controlling 55 seats in the Senate.

Present government

President (head of state); Commander-in-Chief; Head of Executive Branch George Bush

Members of the Cabinet J. Danforth Quayle (Vice-President); James Baker (Secretary of State); Nicholas Brady (Secretary of the Treasury); Richard (Dick) Cheney (Secretary of Defence); Munuel Lujan (Secretary of the Interior); Clayton Yeutter (Secretary of Agriculture); Robert Mosbacher (Secretary of Commerce); Jack Kemp (Secretary of Housing and Urban Development); Sam Skinner (Secretary of Transportation); Louis Sullivan (Secretary of Health and Human Services); Richard Thornburgh (Attorney General); Elizabeth Dole (Secretary of Labour); James Watkins (Secretary of Energy); Lauro Cavazos (Secretary of Education); Ed Derwinsky (Secretary of Veterans' Affairs).

Other leading executive branch officials John Sununu (White House Chief of Staff); Richard Darman (Director of Office of Management and Budget (OMB)); Gen. Brent Scowcroft (Assistant to the President for National Security Affairs); Carla Hills (Representative for Trade Negotiations); William H. Webster (Director, Central Intelligence Agency (CIA)); Michael Boskin (Chairman, President's Council of Economic Advisers); William Bennett (Director, Office of National Drug Control Policy).

Legislative branch

Senate J. Danforth Quayle (the vice-president) is president of the Senate. Leading Democrats in the Senate are George Mitchell – Senate majority leader and Alan Cranston – majority whip; Robert Dole is Senate minority (Republican) leader and Alan K. Simpson is minority whip. The principal committees are all chaired by Democrats, as follows: Claiborne Pell – foreign relations; Sam Nunn – armed services; Jim Sasser – budget; Lloyd Bentsen – finance; Joseph R. Biden – judiciary.

House Thomas S. Foley (Democrat) is speaker of the house; other leading Democrat officials are Richard Gephardt – majority leader and William Gray – majority whip, while the leading Republicans are Robert H. Michel – minority leader and Newt Gingrich – minority whip. The principal committees are all chaired by Democrats, as follows: Dante B. Fascell – foreign affairs; Les Aspin – armed services; Leon Panetta – budget; Dan Rostenkowski – ways and means; Jack Brooks – judiciary.

Supreme Court

Chief Justice – William H. Rehnquist. Associate Justices – William J. Brennan; Byron R. White; Thurgood Marshall; Harry A. Blackmun; John Paul Stevens; Sandra Day O'Connor; Antonin Scalia; Anthony Kennedy.

Administration

The states, under the federal structure, retain responsibility for the majority of government functions. Save only for topics pre-empted by federal legislation, and the requirement that they should not contravene the constitution, they pass their own laws, raise their own income from taxation (although income tax is also levied federally, and federal grants accounted for one-third of the income of the states by 1980), and administer the provision of services – law enforcement, prisons, schools, highways and public works etc. States are in turn subdivided (except for a few cases such as Alaska and Rhode Island) into counties, with a sheriff in charge of maintaining law and order, and in some cases responsible for local roads, tax collection and perhaps even school management. Cities, operating under charters or laws passed by the relevant state, have administrations typically headed by a mayor, who in the case of major cities such as New York will be a figure of major political significance, but whose city government nevertheless is subordinate to the state government.

Justice

The highest court is the Supreme Court, which reviews cases from the lower federal courts, and is final arbiter of all questions involving federal statutes and the Constitution.

The federal court system has 13 Courts of Appeal and 94 District Courts (one or more in each of the 50 states, and one each in the District of Columbia, Puerto Rico, Guam, the Northern Marianas and the US Virgin Islands). These are the trial courts for federal offences and for civil cases involving the government, or bankruptcy; they may also hear civil cases involving parties from different states, or federal statutes such as labour, tax, anti-trust and civil-rights laws. The federal system also includes special federal courts of limited jurisdiction – the US Claims Court, for claims against the federal government, and the Court of International Trade. The judges of all these courts are appointed by the president with the approval of the Senate.

State court systems are usually arranged like the federal court system, with trial and appeal courts and a state supreme court, having as their lowest tier the justices of the peace and municipal and police courts, which can deal with misdemeanours and minor civil actions, and commit for trial in criminal matters. The state courts try criminal and civil cases arising under state laws.

Prisons Total prison population at end June 1989 was 673,575. Crime statistics for 1987 covered 13.5 million offences in all, including 20,096 cases of murder and non-negligent manslaughter, and 91,111 cases of rape. The death penalty was effectively in abeyance under an unofficial moratorium for ten years to 1977, while various states awaited, and then revised their laws in line with, key decisions of the Supreme Court (notably Furman v. Georgia, 1972 and Gregg v. Georgia, 1976). The death penalty is currently authorized, for aggravated murder, in 36 states – Alabama, Arizona, Arkansas, California, Colorado, Connecticut, Delaware, Florida, Georgia, Idaho, Illinois, Indiana, Kentucky, Louisiana, Maryland, Mississippi, Missouri, Montana, Nebraska, Nevada, New Hampshire, New Jersey, New Mexico, North Carolina, Ohio, Oklahoma, Oregon, Pennsylvania, South Carolina, South Dakota, Tennessee, Texas, Utah, Virginia, Washington and Wyoming. There were six executions between 1977 and 1982; five in 1983; 21 in 1984; 18 in 1985; 18 in 1986; 25 in 1987. As of 1 May 1988 there were 2,048 prisoners under sentence of death in 35 states.

National symbols

Flag. The Stars and Stripes. The 13 stripes are horizontal, alternately red and white, and there are 50 white stars on a blue canton (rectangle) which forms the upper quarter of the flag nearest the hoist. The 13 stripes represent the 13 original colonies; in the flag raised by George Washington in 1775, a Union Jack was in the canton, signifying the British connection, but this was replaced in 1777 by a star for each of the colonies. The number of stars and stripes was accordingly increased to 15 in 1795, but the stripes were put back to 13 in 1818, and only the stars kept pace with the increasing number of states, reaching 50 in 1960 following the admission of Hawaii.

National anthem. The Star-spangled Banner.

Festivals. 20 Jan. (Martin Luther King Day); 20 Feb. (Washington-Lincoln Day); 29 May (Memorial Day); 4 July (Independence Day); 4 Sept. (Labour Day); 9 Oct. (Columbus Day); 13 Nov. (for Veterans' Day).

Vehicle registration plate. USA.

INTERNATIONAL RELATIONS

Affiliations

The UN and its specialized agencies (except for UNESCO); GATT; the OECD; the OAS; NATO; Anzus.

Defence

Total Armed Forces: 2,163,200 (203,000 women).

Terms of service: voluntary.

Reserves: Ready Reserves: 1,637,900 (National Guard 576,700 and Reserve 1,061,200). Standby Reserve: 37,900. Retired Reserve: 176,600.

Strategic Nuclear Forces: Navy: 640 submarine-launched ballistic missiles in 36 ballistic-missile submarines (*Ohio*, *Franklin*, *Madison*, *Lafayette*).

Strategic Air Command: 1,000 intercontinental ballistic missiles, 432 combat aircraft (337 long-range and 56 medium-range bombers).

Army: 776,400 (76,000 women); some 15,600 main battle tanks (M-48A5, M-60/M-60A1/-60A2/-60A3, M-1/M-1A1 Abrams).

Navy: 585,000; 137 (36 strategic and 99 tactical) submarines (mainly *Los Angeles*, *Sturgeon* and *Permit*) and 239 principal surface combatants: five nuclear-fuelled aircraft carriers (*Nimitz* and *Enterprise*); nine carriers (average 86 aircraft, dependent on ship); three battleships (*Iowa*); 38 cruisers (surface-to-air missile cruisers; nine nuclear-fuelled); 69 destroyers (mainly *Spruance* and *Adams*); 115 frigates (mainly *Oliver*, *Hazard*, *Perry* and *Knox*); 30 patrol and coastal combatants.

Naval Aviation: some 1,601 combat aircraft (F-14, F/A-18, F-5E/F/T-38); some 314 armed helicopters.

Marine Corps: 198,200 (10,500 women); 716 main battle tanks (M-60A1). Aviation: 528 combat aircraft; 92 armed helicopters.

Air Force: 603,600; strategic: 393 combat aircraft (B-52/-G/-H, B-1B, FB-111A); tactical: 3,583 (mainly F-4/-15/-16).

Defence expenditure Defence expenditure was US$283,500 million (1987) and US$289,000 million (1988) plus US$288,433 million in contributions to NATO (1987). Per capita expenditure on defence was US$1,209 or 6% of GDP (1987).

Deployment of forces Forces deployed abroad are under Unified Commands. The European Command (EUCOM) of 317,000 men is headquartered at Stuttgart-Vaihingen, West Germany, and includes an army of 204,700 in West Germany, and air force bases in West Germany (41,000); Greece (2,700); Italy (5,800); Spain (7,200); UK (27,500); naval fleets of 20,100 in the Mediterranean; 4,500 at Rota, Spain; 2,300 based at Holy Loch, UK. The Pacific Command

(USPACOM) includes the US Pacific Fleet and US Third Fleet, headquartered at Pearl Harbor, Hawaii, and the Seventh Fleet, headquartered at Yokosuka, Japan; army forces stationed in the region include Hawaii (18,900 men); S. Korea (29,100); air force personnel include Philippines (9,300); Japan (16,200); South Korea (11,200). Central Command (USCENTCOM) takes command of forces deployed in the Middle East area and includes a joint task force at sea and an army of 1,200 in Sinai, Egypt. Southern Command (USSOCOM), headquartered in Panama comprises armies in Honduras (1,000); Panama (10,200); naval forces of 450 men in Panama; an air force of 2,250 also in Panama. The Atlantic Command (USLANTCOM), headquartered in Norfolk, Virginia, US, includes naval forces in Guantánamo, Cuba (2,000); Keflavik, Iceland (1,800); the Azores, Portugal (400); an air force of 1,800 also in the Azores.

ECONOMY

The US has a developed market economy; the main instrument of government economic policy is the annual budget, proposed by the president and debated in Congress, and the main focus of controversy over the budget in recent years has been the size of the budget deficit. Under the Gramm-Rudman legislation the Congress now requires the president to meet targets for reducing the budget deficit year by yearm to zero by fiscal year 1993, the fiscal 1990 target being a deficit under $100,000 million.

Currency

The unit is the dollar (US$) divided into 100 cents.

National finance

Budget. The budget for the 1989 fiscal year (beginning 1 Oct. 1988) was for expenditure of $1,149,500 million and revenue of $979,300 million, with a deficit of $170,200 million. The fiscal 1990 budget, as presented on 9 Feb. 1989, envisaged increasing spending only slightly, to $1,160,400 million, with revenue to rise to 1,065,600 million, mainly as a result of expected economic growth and with no need to increase taxation; the deficit was budgeted at 94,800 million. Main expenditure items would be social security and Medicare 29.4%; defence 25.9%; federal pensions, unemployment and other income security 11.9%; health and education 7.8%; veterans' benefits 2.5%; transportation 2.5%; energy, environment and natural resources 1.5%; foreign aid and other international programmes 1.5%; agriculture 1.3%; science, space and technology 1.3%.

Balance of payments. The balance of payments (current account, 1988) was a deficit of US$135.3 billion, compared with US$154 billion the previous year.

Inflation. (1988) 4.1%, slightly up from 3.7% the year before.

Gross Domestic Product

Estimated total GDP $4,805,500 million, per capita $18,338.

Economically active population. The total number of persons active in the economy (1988) was 121,666,000; unemployed 6,695,000 = 5.5%.

Sector	% of workforce
Services	69.9
Industry	27.1
Agriculture: forestry & fishing	3.0

Energy and mineral resources

Oil, gas and coal. Oil output: (1986) 15,960,412 million ft^3/451,951 million m^3; crude petroleum output: 503 million bbls. The US nevertheless remains a significant net importer of petroleum and petroleum products. Coal output 837 million tons/760 million tonnes of hard coal plus 77 million tons/70 million tonnes of brown coal.

Minerals. Output: (1987 in million tones) phosphate rock 45.1/40.9; sulphur 4.0/3.6; copper 1.3/1.2; lead 0.33/0.3; zinc 0.22/0.2. Mining of precious metals includes output of 4,966,000 troy oz of gold and 39,800,000 troy oz of silver.

Electricity. Total generation (1987) 2,732 gigawatt hours of which nuclear 482.6 (17.7%); coal 1,566 (57%).

Bioresources

Agriculture. There are an estimated 1,665,204 miles^2/ 4,314,000 km^2 of agricultural land in the US, of which 44% is arable. The country is a major food exporter (net surplus on agricultural trade $6,717 million).

Crop production (1987): maize 7,000 million bushels/ 178 million tonnes; wheat 2,100 million bushels/ 57 million tonnes; rice 12,773 million lb/5.8 million tonnes; soybeans 1,900 million bushels/51.5 million tonnes; potatoes 38,600 million lb/17.5 million tonnes; sugar beet 28 million short tons/25.4 million tonnes; apples 9,950 million lb/4.5 million tonnes; peaches 2,430 million lb/1.1 million tonnes; grapes 5.2 million tons/5.3 million tonnes; tobacco 1,225 million lb/ 450,000 tonnes; peanuts 3,585 million lb/1.63 million tonnes.

Livestock numbers: (1988) cattle 99 million; pigs 53.8 million; sheep 10.8 million; chickens 377.5 million.

Industry and commerce

Industry. Principal industries are the manufacture of machinery; electrical machinery; transport equipment (particularly motor vehicles and aircraft); fabricated metal products; food and beverages; chemicals; paper manufacturing; printing and publishing.

Commerce. Exports: (1987) $252,866 million, including machinery and transport equipment 43%; chemicals 10.4%; food; live animals; beverages and tobacco 9%. Imports: $405,901 million, including machinery and transport equipment 44%; basic manufactures such as paper, textiles, iron and steel 13%; oil and gas 10.9% Main countries exported to were Canada 24%; Japan 11.2%; Mexico 5.8%; UK 5.7%; West Germany 4.6%. Imports came from Japan 20.8%; Canada 17.5%; West Germany 6.7%; Taiwan 6.1%; Mexico 5%; UK 4.3%; South Korea 4.2%. The US had a net deficit in its merchandise trade with all of these main trading partners.

Trade with UK. In 1988 the US imported UK goods worth £10,768 million; exports to UK totalled £10,544 million.

Tourism. 29,657,000 tourist arrivals in 1987; receipts from tourism $14,778 million (3.5% of export earnings).

COMMUNICATIONS

Railways

There are 210,396 miles/338,590 km of railways. Million passenger miles/km travelled: (1987) 12,112/ 19,504; revenue from freight traffic: $25,637 million.

Roads

There are 3,955,502 miles/6,365,590 km of roads, of which 3,238,926 miles/5,212,404 km are concrete or bituminized. A total of 137.3 million passenger cars and taxis were registered in use in 1987 (563 per 1,000 population) and there were 602,000 buses and coaches, 41.1 million goods vehicles and 4,886,000 motor cycles. There were 2.6 million road accidents in 1986; 46,090 deaths.

Aviation

Eastern Air Lines Inc., United Airlines and Western Airlines provide domestic services; American Airlines provides domestic and international services; Continental Airlines Inc., Delta Air Lines Inc., Northwest Airlines Inc., Pan American World Airways, Trans World Airlines Inc. (TWA) and United Airlines provide international services. Scheduled carriers carried 416 million passengers for a total of 324,481 million passenger miles.

Shipping

A total of 792.1 million tons/718.6 million tonnes of freight was handled at US ports (1987). The US merchant fleet as at mid-1988 included 686 vessels of over 1,000 gross tons.

Telecommunications

There are 760 telephones per 10,000 population.

Broadcasting

There are over 500 million radios in use, and 90 million households own one or more television sets (total 800 television sets per 1,000 population). There are some 4,000 FM radio stations (and another 1,270 educational FM stations), and 5,000 AM stations. In addition to commercial radio networks there is a National Public Radio system, and government-controlled external broadcasting by the Voice of America (in 42 languages worldwide), and by Radio Free Europe/Radio Liberty broadcasting from Munich, West Germany, to Eastern Europe and the USSR, in 23 languages. The principal commercial television networks are CBS, NBC, Capital Cities/ABC and the cable television operation Turner Broadcasting; there is also a non-commercial Public Broadcasting Service (PBS) financed by the federal government and by private subscription.

Newspapers

1,645 English-language dailies had a total end-1987 circulation of almost 63 million copies per day, and of these 39 had circulations in excess of 250,000. Total circulation of Sunday newspapers was similar to that for dailies. The primary characteristic of the US press is its strongly regional and local character; the main newspapers with national readerships are the *New York Times* (circulation 1,057,000 but 1,645,000 on Sundays); the *Washington Post* (797,000/1,113,000); the *Los Angeles Times* (1,118,000/1,397,000); the *Wall Street Journal* (2,026,000); *USA Today* (1,467,000). The influential news weekly *Time* sells 4,720,000 copies and *Newsweek* 3,181,000.

EDUCATION AND WELFARE

Education

The provision of primary and secondary education is largely the responsibility of individual states (approximately 50% of funding) and local government (44% of funding) with some federal input (6%) to cover special needs. In every state public education is free at both elementary and secondary (high school) level. There are also private fee-paying schools, attended by some 12% of pupils, most of these being controlled by a religious organization. The three main educational structures followed are (i) the K8–4 plan (kindergarten, eight elementary grades, and four high-school grades); (ii) the K6–3-3 plan (kindergarten, six elementary grades, three years at junior high school, and three years at senior high school); (iii) the K6–6 plan (kindergarten, six elementary grades, and six years' high school). All systems finish with high school graduation generally at 17 or 18 years. In most states school is compulsory between seven and 16 years; some states start earlier, a few states (Hawaii, Ohio, Utah) have compulsory schooling as late as 18, while pupils can leave at 15 in Kentucky, Louisiana and Washington, and in New Hampshire school is not compulsory after age 14 in areas without a local high school.

School population. 27,900,000 enrolled in public primary schools; 12,100,000 in public secondary schools; 4,300,000 in private primary schools; 1,300,000 at private secondary schools. Total 45,600,000 (1987/88 academic year). In 1987 2,428,000 students graduated from public high schools; 265,000 from private high schools; around 25,000 from adult education and evening courses. 74.5% of the relevant age group gain secondary qualifications.

Schools. In 1987/88 there were 60,784 public elementary schools; 23,389 public secondary schools. There were 1,267,000 primary public school teachers and 24,201,000 pupils (one per 19 pupils); 977,000 public school teachers and 15,636,000 pupils at secondary level (one per 16 pupils). In 1985/86 private elementary schools numbered 20,252, with 250,000 teachers and 4,300,000 pupils (one per 17 pupils) and there were 7,387 private secondary schools with an estimated 98,000 teachers and 1,300,000 pupils (one per 13 pupils).

Universities. There are around 3,600 degree-awarding universities and colleges (1987/88), at which over 12,500,000 students are enrolled. 1,385,200 degrees were awarded in 1986/87. 63.6% of the relevant age group enter higher education.

Literacy. Among those over 25 years old 2.4% of the population (and 5.1% of non-whites) were 'functionally illiterate' (having received less than five years' elementary schooling) as estimated in Mar. 1987.

Health

Basic health care is provided through the two-part federal insurance programme (Medicare). Part A provides for basic hospital care for those over 65 (and certain younger disabled people). It is non-contributory since the programme is funded by payroll taxes but beneficiaries pay part of the costs and their length of stay in hospital for each illness is limited. Voluntary medical insurance is administered through Part B in which beneficiaries must pay monthly contributions. In addition a federal and state programme administered by the states (Medicaid) assists those in need, particularly the aged and families with dependent children, through payments made direct to the health services.

There are 6,091 hospitals (1985) with 1,087,750 beds (one per 219 people). In 1986 there were 544,800 practising doctors (one per 442 people) although distribution between the different states and between town and country varied. There were 143,000 dentists (one per 1,697 people). Total health expenditure amounted to 10.9% of GDP (1986).

Welfare

A federal system of social welfare was first introduced with the Social Security Act of 1935. As progressively amended this now provides for a federal Old Age, Survivors and Disability Insurance scheme or OASDI (an earnings-related scheme covering about 90% of employees and self-employed people and providing for a pension automatically adjusted in line with inflation); supplemental security income or SSI (a means-tested allowance for the old, blind and disabled); Medicare and Medicaid (see under Health above); federal assistance to maternal and child-health services; federal state unemployment insurance.

URUGUAY

República Oriental del Uruguay (Eastern Republic of Uruguay)

GEOGRAPHY

Located in eastern South America, Uruguay covers a total area of 68,021 miles²/176,220 km² divided into 19 departments. Uruguay's physiography marks the transition from Argentinian pampas to Brazilian highland. The low savannah plains in the south rise gradually towards a sandy central plateau traversed south-east and north-west by two highland chains (the Cuchilla Grande and Cuchilla de Haedo rising to 1,644 ft/501 m at Cerro Mirador) separated by the Rio Negro basin. Flowing south-westerly, the Rio Negro drains into the Rio Uruguay on the Argentinian frontier. Nearly half the total population live in Montevideo. 8% of the land is arable and 4% is forested.

Climate

Warm temperate, with warm summers and mild equable winters. Average summer temperatures of 72°F/22°C and winter temperatures of 50°F/10°C vary little by region. The large proportion of Uruguay's 35 in/890 mm annual precipitation falls during the autumn months of April and May. Montevideo: Jan. 72°F/22.2°C. July 50°F/10°C. Average annual rainfall 37.4 in/950 mm.

Cities and towns

Montevideo (capital)	1,246,500
Salto	77,400
Paysandú	75,200
Las Piedras	61,300
Rivera	55,400

Population

Total population is 2,988,813 of which 86.2% live in urban areas. Population density is 44 persons per mile²/17.5 per km². Ethnic divisions: 88% White (Iberian and Italian origin); 8% mestizo; 4% Black. **Birth rate** 1.7%. **Death rate** 1.0%. **Rate of population increase** (1980–87) 0.4%. **Age distribution** under 15 = 26.9%; over 65 = 10.7%. **Life expectancy** female 74; male 68; average 71.

Religion

Mainly Christianity. 66% nominally Roman Catholic; 2% Protestant (Anglican, Baptist, Methodist); 2% Jewish; 30% unaffiliated.

Language

The official language is Spanish spoken by all but 3% of the population.

HISTORY

Unable to find gold or silver, and with few indigenous Indians to exploit, the Spanish took little interest in the area east of the Uruguay river (the Banda Oriental) until the Portuguese founded Colonia do Sacramento in 1680 to further their smuggling operations into Argentina. To counter this threat, the Spanish founded the city of Montevideo in 1726 which encouraged settlement of the territory and the development of cattle ranching on its vast plains.

The struggle for independence lasted nearly 30 years, José Artigas, a rancher and regional chieftain (caudillo) establishing the shortlived Autonomous Government of the Eastern Province in 1811 before defeat by the Portuguese and its annexation to Brazil. Independence finally came in 1828 through the mediation of Great Britain who saw geo-political and trade benefits for itself in a buffer state between Brazil and Argentina.

Despite the passing of the 1830 national constitution, 40 years of civil war divided the country into warring bands distinguished by the colours they sported: Blancos (Whites) and Colorados (Reds). Their chief aim was to gain territory from each other and they each courted the support of either Argentina or Brazil, and European economic interests, to achieve it.

The internecine strife continued throughout the 19th century, as the two groups evolved into political parties (the Blanco Party was conservative and the Colorado Party liberal), and a formal territorial agreement was concluded in 1896. Despite the political instability, the economy developed rapidly. The 1830s and 1840s saw successive waves of European immigration (representing an estimated 40% of the population by 1880), and the growing demand for meat and wool, from industrializing countries, offered unprecedented opportunities to the landowning elite. They backed the 1876 military coup in the belief that a strong centralized government would complement their economic power.

By the 1880s European investment was pouring in, providing the railways and telecommunications and the barbed wire that transformed the productivity of ranching. However, this economic expansion stimulated the growth of groups competing for a greater share in it. The immigrant community (some of whom were small manufacturers, while the majority filled the front ranks of industrial workers) had settled in Montevideo and, drawing on European syndicalist and anarchist traditions, developed their own trade and trade-union organizations to press their claims. These were strenuously resisted by elites and bitter strikes occurred throughout the 1890s.

The Colorado leader José Batlle y Ordóñez now played a crucial role in using this reservoir of immigrant resentment to achieve power in 1903. In balancing the economic growth with increasing state intervention (in welfare provision and public sector enterprises), 'Batllismo' succeeded in creating a mixed economy which promoted class harmony, social mobility and middle-class values; the rural landowners trading their acquiesence to such reforms in return for social peace and respect for their economic primacy. Batlle (president 1903–07, 1911–15), in an attempt to encourage political co-operation, also managed to restrict the power of the presidential office in favour of a Council of National Administration upon which the two traditional parties would always enjoy either two-thirds or one-third representation in accordance with election results On Batlle's death in 1929, the Colorado president Gabriel Terra (1931–34, joint dictator with Luís Alberto de Herrera 1934–36) with the support of a right-wing Blanco faction, immediately redirected the State away from the role of public provider to that of bestower of personal patronage and, by the coup of 1933, had excluded opposition groups (within the Colorados and the Blancos) from involvement in political dialogue. It was Pres. Alfredo Baldomir (1938–42), who, by dismissing his government in Feb. 1942, attempted to re-introduce the principles of state independence and political integration but it was not until 1947 that a version of 'Batllismo' re-emerged under Luis Batlle Berres (Pres. 1947–51, and president of the National Council of Government 1955–56). This was assisted by a period of prosperity when Uruguay enjoyed the highest per capita income (US$937) in Latin America.

This was not to last. In the late 1950s tumbling world prices for the country's agricultural products exposed the underlying weakness of this sector and the government's attempt to maintain its spending, while riding out the storm on its gold and foreign exchange reserves, failed to stem the flight of capital abroad. Political consensus gave way to the class polarization that brought the Blancos to power for the first time in 1959. The resulting formation, in 1964, of the National Confederation of Workers (CNT), which united all the major unions, was not just insurance against spiralling inflation (100% in 1965), but an effective recognition that workers could no longer expect a favourable response from the state. In 1966, the collegiate system of government, which had operated since 1951, was ended and the Colorados were re-elected. On the death of the successful Colorado candidate, Jórge Pacheco Areco was sworn in as president (1967–71) but, because he lacked a policy for economic or social reform, used press censorship in an attempt to stem the protest produced by an austerity programme and wage freezes. The start of an urban guerrilla campaign by the Tupamaros, founded in 1967, dramatically heightened political tension and led to the introduction, in Sept. 1971, of special security laws which, in their broadened interpretation by the military, severely curtailed general civil rights. The military, who brutally suppressed the Tupamaros in 1971–72, expanded on this success to seize power (ousting Pres. Juan María Bordaberry) in June 1973, the first such military takeover of the century. However, the military's plan to open up the economy to private domestic and international investment, while simultaneously denying even the traditional parties political expression (and brutally repressing trade unionists and the left) led not only to the mass emigration of an estimated 400,000 people (mostly to Argentina) but to the short-term growth provided by increased banking (attracted by easy terms) and speculation. Amidst a continuing social and economic crisis, the military regime eventually agreed terms, in Aug. 1984, for a return to democracy. The Colorado candidate Julio María Sanguinetti, who was elected president in Nov. 1984, pledged national reconstruction and signed an amnesty law in Dec. 1986 which granted immunity to military and police officers accused of gross human-rights abuses between 1973 and 1985. When the Broad Left campaign to annul this law secured the requisite number of signatures in Mar. 1988 to force a national referendum on the issue, Sanguinetti appealed to the 'silent majority' to oppose it for the sake of future democracy and peace. In the first free presidential and congressional elections to be held in 18 years, Luis Alberto Lacalle Herrera defeated the Colorado candidate Jorge Battle to become only the third Blanco ever to be elected President. However, the lack of an overall parliamentary majority persuaded Lacalle, who was inaugurated on 1 March, to announce a coalition government, with the Colorados receiving four ministerial seats in the new Cabinet.

CONSTITUTION AND GOVERNMENT

Executive and legislature

An executive president and a vice-president are elected directly for a five-year term; last elections 26 Nov. 1989. The legislature, the National Congress, comprises a 99-member chamber of deputies and a 30-member senate, also elected directly (at the same time as the president) for a five-year term. The president appoints the council of ministers.

Present government

President Luis Alberto Lacalle Herrara
Vice-President Gonzala Aguirre Ramirez
Principal Members of the Council of Ministers Sr Juan Andres Ramirez (Interior); Dr Hector Gros Espiell (Foreign Relations); Sr Enrique Braga (Economy and Finance); Sr Mariano Brito (Defence).

Justice

The system of law is based on Spanish law. The highest court is the Court of Justice, whose members are appointed by the Council of the Nation for a term of five years. There are four Courts of Appeal. At the local level, justice is administered by justices of the peace, and each department has its departmental court.

National symbols

Flag. Four blue horizontal stripes on a white field, ie nine horizontal stripes of equal width, alternately white and blue.
Festivals. 19 Apr. (Landing of the 33 Patriots); 1 May (Labour Day); 18 May (Battle of Las Piedras); 19 June (birth of Gen. Artigas); 18 July (Constitution

Day); 25 Aug. (National Independence Day); 12 Oct. (Discovery of America).
Vehicle registration plate. U.

INTERNATIONAL RELATIONS

Affiliations
OAS.

Defence
Total Armed Forces: 24,400. Terms of service: voluntary; 1–2 years, extendable.
Army: 17,200; 67 light tanks (M-24, M-3A1, M-41A1).
Navy: 4,200 (inclusive naval air, naval infantry); one frigate (US *Dealey*) and seven patrol and coastal combatants.
Naval Air Force: 400; six combat aircraft.
Naval Infantry: 400.
Air Force: 3,000; 12 combat aircraft (A-37B, IA-58B).

ECONOMY

Currency
The unit is the New Uruguayan peso, divided into 100 centisimos.

National finance
Budget. The 1987 budget, in US$, was for expenditure of 1,300 million and revenue of 1,200 million. Main items of expenditure are housing and welfare 49.5%; defence 10.2%; education 7.1 %.
Balance of payments. The balance of payments, in US$ (current account, 1987) was a deficit of 132 million.
Inflation. 69%.

Gross Domestic Product
Estimated total GDP US$6,420 million, per capita US$2,530 (overall size of economy ranking 76 in the world).
Economically active population. The total number of persons active in the economy was 1,300,000; unemployed: 9.0%.

Sector	% of workforce	% of GDP
industry	19	32
agriculture	11	13
services*	70	55

* services figure includes elements unassigned to other categories.

Energy and mineral resources
Oil and gas. Petroleum output: (1981) 203,926 tons/185,000 tonnes.
Electricity. Capacity: 1,889,000 kW; production: 4,204 million kWh; 1,410 kWh per capita (1988).

Bioresources
Agriculture. 8% of the land area is arable and 78% is meadow or pasture. 90% of the 16.6 million ha of farmland is used to raise livestock. Uruguay is self-sufficient in most basic foodstuffs, including rice. Viticulture thrives in the departments of Canelones, Colonia and Montevideo. Output: (1987) 74,000 tonnes.
Crop production: (1987 in 1,000 tons/tonnes) wheat 350; barley 99/90; linseed 8.8/8; maize 115/104; oats 33/30; rice 390/354. Fruit crops include oranges; tangerines; pears; peaches.
Livestock numbers: (1987 in 1,000s) cattle 10,323; horses 500; sheep 25,560; pigs 190; goats 12; poultry 6,000.
Forestry. 4% of the land area is forested. Roundwood removals: (1985) 105 million ft^3/2.98 million m^3.
Fisheries. Catch: (1985) 153,306 tons/139,078 tonnes.

Industry and commerce
Industry. Uruguay's main industries are meat processing; wool and hides; sugar; textiles; footwear; leather apparel; tyres; cement; fishing; petroleum refining; wine.
Commerce. Exports: (1988) US$1,300 million or 17.3% of GDP. Imports amounted to $1100 in the same year or 14.7% of the GDP. Main exports were hides and leather goods 17%; beef 10%; wool 9%; fish 7%; rice 4%. Imports included fuels and lubricants 15%; metals; machinery; transportation equipment; industrial chemicals. Principal trading partners are (imports and exports) Brazil; US; West Germany; Argentina.
Trade with UK. Uruguay imported UK goods worth £34.99 million in 1988; exports to the UK totalled £35.4 million.
Tourism. (1986) 1.17 million tourists.

COMMUNICATIONS

Railways
There are 1,857 miles/2,991 km of railways.

Roads
There are 32,292 miles/52,000 km of roads.

Aviation
TAMU provides domestic services and Primeras Lineas Uruguayas de Navegacion Aerea (PLUNA) provides international services (main airport is Carrasco, 13 miles/21 km from Montevideo). Passengers: (1984) 343,000.

Shipping
There are 994 miles/1,600 km of inland waterways. The marine ports are Montevideo and Punta del Este. The merchant marine has six ships of 1,000 GRT or over. Freight loaded: (1985) 656,971 tons/596,000 tonnes; unloaded: 1.7 million tons/1.5 million tonnes.

Telecommunications
There are 337,000 telephones with the most modern facilities being concentrated in Montevideo, and a new nationwide radio-relay network. There are 1.8 million radios and 520,000 televisions (1986). About 100 radio and 20 TV stations, many locally based, provide a variety of programmes, with a government service run by SODRE.

EDUCATION AND WELFARE

Education
Both compulsory primary education and secondary instruction are free.
Schools. There are an estimated 356,000 primary and 188,175 secondary school pupils in Uruguay. Special educational establishments include a number of religious seminaries, schools for the blind, deaf and dumb and a college of Arts and Trades with an enrolment of approximately 33,000 students.
Universities. An estimated 18,000 students attend the University of the Republic at Montevideo, divided into ten faculties. Tuition is free.
Literacy. 94%.

Health
5,736 physicians serve an estimated 23,400 hospital beds (one per 128 members of the population).

VANUATU
Republic of Vanuatu

GEOGRAPHY

Located in the South Pacific Ocean, 621 miles/1,000 km west of Fiji and 249 miles/400 km north-east of New Caledonia, Vanuatu covers a total area of 5,697 miles^2/14,760 km^2. The archipelago consists of 13 large islands and 70 islets, the majority of which are mountainous and volcanic in origin with coral beaches, reefs, thick forest cover, and some coastal cultivation. The principal islands are Vanua, Lava, Espiritu Santo, Maewo, Pentecost, Aoba, Malekula, Ambrym, Epi, Efate, Erromango, Tanna and Aneityum. The highest summit, on Espiritu Santo, climbs to 6,194 ft/1,888 m. 1% of the land is arable and nearly two-thirds of the total population inhabit the four main islands of Efate, Espiritu Santó, Malekula and Tanna.

Climate

Tropical, with high temperatures and abundant rainfall Nov.-Apr. Oceanic influences, and trade winds May-Oct. Cyclones may occur during the wet season (rainfall totals vary from 89–153 in/2,250–3,875 mm south-north). Vila: Jan. 80°F/26.7°C. July 72°F/22.2°C. Average annual rainfall 83 in/2,103 mm.

Cities and towns

Port Vila (capital)	14,184
Luganville	5,621

Population

Total population is 159,830 of which 14.5% live in urban areas. Population density is 28 persons per mile^2/11.9 per km^2. Ethnic divisions: 94% indigenous Melanesian, 4% French, the remaining 2% is composed of Vietnamese, Chinese and other Pacific Islander minorities.

Birth rate 3.8%. **Death rate** 0.5%. **Rate of population increase** (1980–87) 3.2%. **Life expectancy** female 71; male 67; average 69.

Religion

80% are Christian (Presbyterian, Anglican and Roman Catholic). Traditional animist beliefs account for the bulk of the remainder. The Jon Frum cargo cult is pre-eminent on the island of Tanna.

Language

Bislama, English and French are the official languages. The majority of the Melanesian dialects in use derive from languages indigenous to Fiji and New Caledonia. Bislama (or pidgin) is the national and parliamentary lingua franca.

HISTORY

The chain of islands has been inhabited since about 5000 BC by Melanesian peoples. The first European visitors were the Portuguese in 1606. Capt. Cook systematically explored the islands in 1774 and named them the New Hebrides. Britain and France both developed trading posts and missions in the 19th century and set up in 1887 a joint naval commission to govern the islands. This was formalized into a condominium in 1906, under which British and French citizens had political dominance over the indigenous peoples. On 30 July 1980 the islands achieved independence as the Republic of Vanuatu, which became a member of the Commonwealth. In September the same year a secession movement in Espiritu Santo, the largest island, was put down with help from Papua New Guinea.

In Mar. 1983 Vanuatu became a member of the Non-Aligned Movement, and later in the year the ruling left-wing Vanuaaku Party, under the leadership of Prime Minister Walter Lini, was returned to government. The party won a further election in Nov. 1987 but was subject to increasing internal dissension as Barak Sope attempted to wrest the leadership from Lini, who had suffered a cerebral haemorrhage in early 1987. Following Sope's expulsion from the Vanuaaku Party his uncle, George Sokomanu – the country's president – tried to dismiss Lini's agreement and swear in Sope as prime minister. This constitutional coup was defeated and both Sope and Sokomanu were imprisoned for mutiny, although the latter was later released on appeal. In Mar. 1989 Fred Timakata, a former member of Lini's cabinet, was elected president of Vanuatu.

CONSTITUTION AND GOVERNMENT

Executive and legislature

The (largely ceremonial) post of president is filled by an election every five years by an electoral college which is composed of the parliament and the presidents of the regional councils (local government bodies to which a considerable degree of power is constitutionally devolved). The head of government is the prime minister, elected by parliament from among its members, who appoints the council of ministers. The legislature, the unicameral 46-member Parliament, is elected for a four-year term on the basis of universal adult franchise. Last general elections Nov. 1987.

Present government

President Fred Timakata
Prime Minister; Minister of Public Services; Planning and Information Fr Walter Lini
Other Principal Members of the Council of Ministers
Iolu Abbil (Home Affairs); Sela Molisa (Finance); Donald Kalpokas (Foreign Affairs; Judicial Services).

Justice

The death penalty was abolished before independence.

National symbols

Flag. Two horizontal stripes, red over green, with a black triangle based on the hoist.
Festivals. 1 May (Labour Day); 30 July (Independence Day); 5 Oct. (Constitution Day); 29 Nov. (Unity Day).

INTERNATIONAL RELATIONS

Affiliations

NAM; Commonwealth; SPF.

Defence
A para-military internal and external security force; no military forces as such.

ECONOMY

Currency
The unit is the vatu, divided into 100 centimes.

National finance
Budget. The 1986 budget, in US$, was for expenditure of 58 million and revenue of 53 million.
Inflation. 3.6%.

Gross Domestic Product
Estimated total GDP US$84 million, per capita US$580 (overall size of economy ranking 181 in the world).

Energy and mineral resources
Minerals. Reserves are negligible. Manganese and pozzolana extraction ceased in 1978 and 1985 respectively.
Electricity. Capacity: 10,000 kW; production: 20 million kWh; 130 kWh per capita (1988).

Bioresources
Agriculture. 1% of the land area is arable, 5% is under permanent cultivation and 2% is meadow or pasture. The principal cash and export crops are copra; cocoa; coffee; fish. Subsistence farming supports about 80% of the population.

Crop production: (1987) copra 44,092 tons/40,000 tonnes; cocoa 1,102/1,000; coffee 72/65. Subsistence crops include yams; taro; sweet potatoes; manioc; bananas.

Livestock numbers: (1987) cattle 103,000; pigs 73,000; goats 12,000.
Forestry. 1% of the land is covered by forest. Sawn timber output:(1985) 1,338,419 ft^3/37,900 m^3.
Fisheries. Tuna catch: (1985) 4,070 tons/3,962 tonnes.

Industry and commerce
Industry. Vanuatu's main industries are food and fish freezing; forestry processing; meat canning. Other industrial activities comprise a cement plant; a print works; construction materials; soft drinks production.
Commerce. Exports: (1987) US$17 million or 20% of GDP. Imports amounted to $68 million or 81% of GDP. The chief exported commodities were copra 37%; cocoa 11%; meat 9%; fish 8%; timber 4%. Imported goods included machines and vehicles 25%; food and beverages 23%; basic manufactures 18%; raw materials and fuels 11%; chemicals 6%. Countries exported to included Netherlands; France; Japan; Belgium; New Caledonia; Singapore. Imports came from Australia; Japan; NZ; France; Fiji.
Trade with UK. Vanuatu imported UK goods worth £856,000 in 1988; exports to the UK amounted to £5,000 in the same year.
Tourism. (1986) 18,000 visitors.

COMMUNICATIONS

Railways
There are no railways in Vanuatu.

Roads
There are some 621 miles/1,000 km of roads, of which 22 miles/35 km are sealed.

Aviation
Air Melanesiae provides services to 24 destinations within the archipelago and Air Vanuaku provides services between Port Vila and Sydney (main airports are at Bauerfield (Efate) and Pekoa (Santo).

Shipping
The major ports are Port Vila on the island of Efate. Luganville on Espiritu Santo, Palikoulo and Santu. The merchant marine has 63 ships of 1,000 GRT or over. Freight loaded: (1985) 65,036 tons/59,000 tonnes; unloaded: 67,240 tons/61,000 tonnes.

Telecommunications
There are 3,000 telephones and two AM stations (no FM). There are 18,000 radios and no television service (1986). Radio Vanuatu is government-owned and broadcasts in English, French and Bislama.

EDUCATION AND WELFARE

Schools. About 13,000 pupils attend 224 English primary schools and 10,000 pupils attend 105 French primary schools. An additional 2,000 secondary school pupils are divided between 11 State and Denominational establishments and Matevalu college. The Teachers' College and Vanuatu Technical Institute are the islands' tertiary education and vocational training institutions.
Literacy. 10–20% (est.)

Health
19 doctors; two dentists; three pharmacists; five midwives; 266 nursing staff serve ten state-run hospitals.

VATICAN
Stato della Cittá del Vaticano
(Vatican City)

GEOGRAPHY

The ecclesiastical State of the Vatican City, seat of the Holy See, lies within the city of Rome, Italy, on the western bank of the River Tiber, containing a total area of 0.17 $mile^2$/0.44 km^2 making it the world's smallest state. The three public entrances to the city are 'The Bronze Doors', 'The Arch of the Bells', and the 'Via di Porta Angelica'.

Climate
Mediterranean.

Population
Total population 755 (July 1989). **Growth rate** 0.3%.

Religion
Roman Catholicism.

Language
Italian, Latin.

HISTORY

The Papacy's temporal authority, dating from the 8th century when it was recognized by Pepin the Short, King of the Franks, and exercised from 1377 from a palace built on Rome's Vatican hill, extended by the 16th century to much of central Italy. In the 19th-century Risorgimento ('resurrection'), the so-called Papal States were, from 1859, incorporated into the emerging Italian state, culminating (1870) in the entry of Italian troops into Rome, which became Italy's capital. In protest, successive Popes refused to leave the Vatican until, in Feb. 1929, Pope Pius XI and Mussolini concluded the Lateran Treaties recognizing the Holy See's sovereignty in the Vatican City State and incorporating a concordat by which Catholicism became Italy's state religion. During World War II Pope Pius XII incurred much international criticism by adhering to strict neutrality.

In the post-war era, the Vatican combined its spiritual role with active diplomacy as a neutral sovereign state, signing the Final Act of the Conference on Security and Co-operation in Europe (1975) and establishing diplomatic relations with over 100 countries, including Britain (1982) and the United States (1984). In 1978 Cardinal Karol Wojtyla of Poland became, as Pope John Paul II, the first non-Italian pontiff since the 16th century. He undertook an unprecedented number of papal visits abroad and survived two assassination attempts, one in Rome in 1981 (in which Bulgarian agents were later implicated) and another in Portugal a year later.

The privileged status of the Catholic Church in Italy was ended under a revised concordat signed in Feb. 1984. In a major reorganization of Vatican administration (Apr. 1984), the Pope delegated most of his temporal duties to the Secretary of State, Cardinal Agostino Casaroli, amid concern over the alleged involvement of the Vatican Bank in the fraudulent bankruptcy in 1982 of the Banco Ambrosiano in Milan. Ambrosiano's collapse was precipitated by the death of Roberto Calvi, the bank's chairman, who was found hanging beneath Blackfriars Bridge in London on 18 June 1982. Calvi's death was first found to be suicide, then at a second inquest in June 1983 an open verdict was returned, while in Feb. 1989 a Milan court ruled that his death had been murder. Under a financial settlement agreed in May 1984 the Vatican Bank agreed to pay 109 creditor banks $250 million of the $406 million it owed following the liquidation of Banco Ambrosiano.

CONSTITUTION AND GOVERNMENT

Executive and legislature The Pope, as head of state and head of the Roman Catholic Church, is elected for life by a conclave comprising members of the Sacred College of Cardinals. Routine administration of the Vatican is delegated to the Secretary of State, and the adminstrative affairs of the Vatican City are conducted by a pontifical commission, appointed by the Pope.

Present government
Head of state His Holiness Pope John Paul II
Secretary of State Cardinal Agostino Casaroli

National symbols
Flag. Two vertical stripes, yellow and white. In the middle of the white field are crossed keys, turned outwards.
Vehicle registration plate. V.

ECONOMY

Currency
The unit is the Vatican lira, divided into 100 centesimi.
Budget. The 1986 budget, in US$, was for expenditure of 113.7 million and revenue of 57 million.
Economically active population. The total number of persons active in the economy was 1,500.
Electricity. 3,000 kW standby capacity (1988), power supplied by Italy.
Industry. Global banking and financial activities.
Trade with UK. Imports from the UK totalled £447,000 in 1988; exports to the UK amounted to £111,000.

COMMUNICATIONS

Railways
There is a small railway, 2,828 ft/862 m, which runs from the Vatican into Italy.

Telecommunications
There is a 2,000-line automatic telephone exchange. Radio Vatican broadcasts information and Papal teaching and forms a link with Catholics throughout the world while Vatican Television Centre produces and distributes religious programmes.

VENEZUELA

República de Venezuela
(Republic of Venezuela)

GEOGRAPHY

Located on the north coast of South America, Venezuela covers a total area of 352,051 miles^2/ 912,050 km^2 divided into 20 states, two territories and one federal district. 40% of the total surface area is dominated by the sparsely populated Guiana Highlands (Macizo de Guayana) in the south-east. A further 30% of the area is covered by the central Llanos, a grassland plain drained by the Orinoco River. In the north-western part of the country, Lake Maracaibo is surrounded by marshy but fertile lowlands. South of Lake Maracaibo, the Cordillera de Mérida stretches from the Colombian border as far north as Barquisimeto, rising to 16,427 ft/5,007 m at Pico Bolívar. The Coastal Cordillera continues eastwards from Valencia, climbing to 9,072 ft/2,765 m. The River Orinoco rises in the southern highlands and traverses the whole country, draining 75% of the terrain before emptying into the Atlantic through the Delta Amacuro. 3% of the land is arable and 39% is forested. Approximately 15% of the total population lives in Caracas.

Climate

Predominantly tropical, becoming warm temperate on the coast. Climatic zones are defined by differences in precipitation rather than by temperature range. Coastal rainfall varies considerably from the arid northern coastal lowlands to 343 in/1,000 mm in the east. Rainfall increases in the Llanos (39.3–59 in/ 1,000–1,500 mm) and Guiana highlands (59in/1,500 mm). The dry season lasts Dec.-Apr. Caracas: Jan. 65°F/18.3°C. July 69°F/20.6°C. Average annual rainfall 32.8 in/833 mm. Ciudad Bolívar: Jan. 79°F/26.1°C. July 81°F/27.2°C. Average annual rainfall 40 in/1,016 mm. Maracaibo: Jan. 81°F/27.2°C. July 86°F/29.4°C. Average annual rainfall 22.7 in/577 mm.

Cities and towns

Caracas (capital)	3,247,698
Maracaibo	1,295,421
Valencia	1,134,623
Maracay	857,982
Barquisimeto	718,197
Ciudad Guayana	466,418
Barcelona/Puerto La Cruz	417,501
San Cristobál	338,188
Departamento Vargas	320,576

Population

Total population is 19,263,376 of which 85.7% live in urban areas. Population density is 54.7 persons per mile^2/20.0 per km^2, dwindling to much less in the south-eastern highlands. Ethnic divisions: 67% mestizo; 21% White; 10% Black; 2% Indian (200,000 Amerindians). Land boundary disputes are ongoing between Guajibo and Yaruro Indians and local cattle ranchers.

Birth rate 3.0%. **Death rate** 0.6%. **Rate of population increase** (1980–87) 2.5%. **Age distribution** under 15 = 39.5%; over 65 = 3.4%. **Life expectancy** female 73; male 67; average 70.

Religion

Christianity, mainly Roman Catholicism, which accounts, nominally, for at least 96% of the population. Approximately 2% are Protestant.

Language

Spanish is the official language, but over 30 separate languages are spoken by the Amerindian minority in the interior, most of which belong to the Arawak, Cariban and Chibcha ethnolinguistic categories.

HISTORY

Although the area was visited by Columbus on his third voyage to the New World in 1498, it was Alonso de Ojeda, on his Caribbean expedition in 1499, who named the country Venezuela or 'little Venice' when he encountered huts of the indigenous Jirajara Indians built on stilts on the swampy shore of Lake Maracaibo (archaeological remains point to their ancestors' presence in the area at least 3,750 years ago).

The first Spanish settlement was established about 1500 but due to subsequent fierce Caracas Indian resistance to conquest, and lack of gold, the Spanish crown, in 1528, allowed the German Banking House of Welser to settle and develop the country. The Spanish resumed control in 1556, transferring responsibility for the country's supervision from Santo Domingo to the Viceroyalty of New Granada (1739–1819), the future capital, Caracas, being founded in 1567.

Colonial neglect during the 16th and 17th centuries encouraged illicit trading with the French, English and Dutch, which the Spanish attempted to eradicate by the granting of a trade monopoly to the Guipuzcoana Company of Basque merchants in 1728. The resulting local resentment fuelled an abortive revolt in 1749 but it was not until 5 July 1811 that the creole elites (American-born Spaniards) declared independence from Spain, one of the first Latin-American countries to do so. However, ten years of civil war between the creole patriots and royalist forces passed before independence was secured at the Battle of Carabobo in 1821. The hero of the campaign, Simón Bolívar, went on to assist in the liberation of Colombia, Ecuador, Peru and Bolivia but his ideal of a Gran Colombian confederation (of Venezuela, Colombia and Ecuador) did not survive his death in 1830, when a new constitution guaranteed Venezuela true independence.

Gen. José Antonio Páez, a popular conservative mestizo (mixed race) war hero from the great plains (Llanos), dominated political life, as president and president-maker, for the next 18 years, bringing a degree of stability and development to the country. After his defeat in 1848, there followed a period of strife in which the liberals emerged victorious, and stability was restored under Antonio Guzmán Blanco (1873–88), but he was succeeded by a string of corrupt strong men (caudillos), the last and most notorious of whom was Juan Vicente Gómez (1908–35).

Gómez ran the country as a personal fiefdom and silenced all opposition, but, by creating a national army, ensured the centralization of power. The discovery of oil in the 1920s accelerated the country's transformation from being agriculturally dependent and backward into an emerging modern nation. Oil also changed the pattern of life, stimulating peasant migration to the cities, replacing the landed aristocracy by local and foreign industrialists and creating a new opposition, especially among students and intellectuals, openly critical of nepotism, corruption and repression who called for the end of the dictatorship. Gen. Eleazar López Contreras, who became president on Gómez's death in 1935, initiated the process of political and economic liberalization which his chosen successor Gen. Isaís Medina Angarita extended. In the run-up to the 1945 presidential elections the first real political opening appeared when young army officers invited the Democratic Action party (AD) of Rómulo Betancourt to join them in overthrowing Angarita. For the next three years Betancourt, a skilled politician, headed the governing junta and sought to mobilize the support of workers and peasants through the passing of legislation beneficial to the under-privileged and through the creation of a new constitution which respected human and social rights. Although the AD's presidential candidate, the novelist Rómulgo Gallegos, was elected in 1948, he was ousted by the military ten months later for threatening to cut their budget. The military government of Marcos Pérez, who enjoyed US support, by its corruption and approval of large-scale development projects funded by foreign capital, alienated not only the Church and the now better-organized students, workers and peasants, but significant sections of the military who were denied access to the spoils. Following a general strike, the military deposed Pérez in Jan. 1958 and Betancourt returned as president in free elections held at the end of the year. The AD administration, whose ideology blended the needs of development with those of social justice, was successful in creating a mass cross-class party which also cemented ties with labour unions, the armed forces, industrialists and the Church. At the same time, Betancourt was successful in isolating and discrediting the left, especially the guerrillas who failed to receive the support of the peasantry in their attempt to repeat the success of the recent Cuban Revolution. The AD president Raúl Leoni, who took power in 1963, carried on the process and it was only differences in the AD leadership that allowed Rafael Caldera of the Social Christian party (COPEI) to win the presidency in 1968. Although the COPEI government carried out a programme almost identical to that of its predecessor, it faced an obstructionist AD-dominated Congress which facilitated the victory of Carlos Andréz Pérez in 1973. Pérez's government nationalized the iron and petroleum industries but came to be seen as both dishonest and lacking in technical competence. This allowed Luís Herrera Campíns to regain the presidency for the COPEI in 1978, but his ruinous economic policy, especially the failure of the huge Workers' Bank, and general lacklustre political performance led to a landslide victory for the AD's Jaime Lusinchi in 1983. Lusinchi's measures to reactivate the economy, coupled with a serious decline in international oil prices, meant the introduction of austerity programmes, wage freezes and the removal of fuel subsidies. As unemployment and inflation spiralled upwards, the government's tri-partite social pact (of the State, business and Labour), to deal with the current debt crisis, broke down. Amid increasing student and union unrest (200,000 workers demonstrating in the capital on 1 May 1988) and despite a bitter faction fight within the AD for the presidential nomination, Carlos Andréz Pérez, running a populist campaign, managed to clinch victory for the AD in the Dec. 1988 elections. However, in a climate of deepening economic recession, the AD, although winning the highest overall total of seats in local and provincial government, suffered a setback in regional and municipal elections held in Dec. 1989, when opposition parties won control of the most important and populous of the provinces.

CONSTITUTION AND GOVERNMENT

Executive and legislature

The executive president appoints and presides over a council of ministers. The legislature, a bicameral National Congress, comprises a senate of 44 elected members (with additionally, as life members, the country's former presidents) and a 196-member chamber of deputies. The president and national congress are directly elected by universal adult suffrage for concurrent five-year terms; last elections 4 Dec. 1988.

Present government

President Sr Carlos Andrés Pérez

Principal Members of the Council of Ministers Sr Alejandro Izaguirre Angeli (Interior); Sr Reinaldo Figueredo Planchart (Foreign Affairs); Sr Eclée Iturbe de Blanco (Finance); Gen. Filmo Lopéz Uzcategui (Defence); Sr Luis Beltran Guerra (Justice).

Administration

The country comprises 20 States, two Federal Territories, a Federal District around the capital and 72 Federal Dependencies. The states are autonomous, each with their own executive governor, appointed by the president, and an elected legislature, but must comply with the laws and Constitution of the Republic.

Justice

The judiciary consists of the Supreme Court with five members elected by Congress for five years, a supreme court with three members in each state, superior courts or superior tribunals, courts of first instance, district courts (the country is divided into 20 legal districts) and muncipal courts. The procurator-general is appointed for five years. The death penalty was abolished in 1863.

National symbols

Flag. Three equal horizontal stripes coloured yellow, blue and red.

Festivals. 6–7 Feb. (Carnival); 19 Apr. (Declaration of Independence); 2 May (for Labour Day); 24 June (Battle of Carabobo); 5 July (Independence Day); 24 July (Birth of Simón Bolívar and Battle of Lago de Maracaibo); 4 Sept. (Civil Servants' Day); 12 Oct. (Discovery of America).

Vehicle registration plate. YV.

INTERNATIONAL RELATIONS

Affiliations

OAS.

Defence

Total Armed Forces: 69,000 inclusive National Guard; (18,000 conscripts). Terms of service: two years; Navy 2½ years; selective, varies by region for all services.

Army: 34,000; 81 main battle tanks (AMX-30); 71 light tanks (M-18, AMX-13).

Navy: 10,000; three submarines (FRG T-209/1300, US *Guppy III*); 6 frigates (It Lupo); 13 patrol and coastal combatants.

Naval Air Force: 2,000; four combat aircraft; six armed helicopters.

Marines: 5,200.

Air Force: 5,000; 104 combat aircraft (Bombers: B-82, B(I)-82, PR-83, T-84; Fighter: F-5, T-2D, Mirage, F-16).

National Guard: 20,000.

ECONOMY

Currency

The unit is the bolívar, divided into 100 centivos.

National finance

Budget. The 1987 budget, in US$, was for expenditure of 13,700 million and revenue of 12,900 million. Main items of expenditure are education 19.6%; housing and welfare 11.7%; health 10%; defence 5.8%.

Balance of payments. The balance of payments, in US$ (current account, 1987) was a deficit of 1,103 million.

Inflation. 35.5%.

Gross Domestic Product

Estimated total GDP US$49,610 million, per capita US$2,520 (overall size of economy ranking 39 in the world).

Economically active population. The total number of persons active in the economy was 5,800,000; unemployed: 7.0%.

Sector	% of workforce	% of GDP
industry	28	38
agriculture	16	6
services*	56	56

* services figure includes elements unassigned to other categories.

Energy and mineral resources

Oil and gas. Petroleum dominates the economy and in 1987 accounted for 87% of export earnings. 1986 proven crude oil reserves were approximately 55,521 bbls, with other new fields estimated at up to 40,000 bbls; crude oil production: (1988) 103 million tons/93 million tonnes. Gas production: (1985) 1,165,378 ft^3/33,000 m^3.

Minerals. Gold (1982) 1,989 lb/902 kg; diamonds (1977) 687,000 carats; iron ore (1985) 16.4 million tons/14.9 million tonnes. There are known reserves of manganese; phosphate rock 16.5 million tons/15 million tonnes; coal 176 million tons/160 million tonnes; bauxite is being mined in the Guayana region.

Electricity. Capacity: 18.2 million kW; production: 51.9 million kWh; 2,760 kWh per capita (1988)

Bioresources

Agriculture. Main crops are cereals; fruits; sugar; coffee; rice. Venezuela is an illegal producer of small quantities of coca and cannabis for the international drug trade.

Crop production: (1987 in 1,000tons/ tonnes) rice 331/300; maize 1,323/1,200; cassava 347/315; sugar cane 7,716/7,000; bananas 1,102/1,000; oranges 432/392; potatoes 215/195; tomatoes 138/125; coffee 73/66; sesame seed 88/80; tobacco 17/15; cocoa 15/14.

Livestock numbers: (1987) cattle 12.6 million; pigs 3.3 million; goats 1.34 million; sheep 422,000; poultry 54 million.

Forestry. 39% of the land area is forest and woodland and the resources are largely unexploited. There are 600 known species of wood.

Fisheries. Catch: (1985) 290,831 tons/263,840 tonnes.

Industry and commerce

Industry. Main industries are petroleum; iron-ore mining; construction materials; food processing; textiles; steel; aluminium; motor vehicle assembly. Production: (1985) 3.0 million tons/2.7 million tonnes of steel; 448,636 million tons/407,000 tonnes of aluminium; 540,127 tons/490,000 tonnes of ammonia; 716,495 tons/650,000 tonnes of fertilizers; 5.6 million tons/5.1 million tonnes of cement; 606,625 tons/550,000 tonnes of paper.

Commerce. Exports: (1988) US$10,400 million or 21% of GDP, including petroleum 81%; bauxite and aluminium; iron ore; agricultural products; basic manufactures. Imports: US$10,900 million, including foodstuffs; chemicals, manufactures; machinery; transport equipment. Countries exported to were (1987) US 50%; West Germany 4.7%; Japan 3.1%; Netherlands 2.6%. Imports came from US 44%; West Germany 8.5%; Japan 6%; Italy 5%; Brazil 4.4%.

Trade with UK. In 1988 Venezuela imported UK goods worth £177,787,000; exports to UK totalled £76,563,000.

Tourism. (1986) 317,300 visitors.

COMMUNICATIONS

Railways

There are some 373 miles/600 km of railways (there are plans to construct a 1,243-mile/2,000-km rail network by the year 2000).

Roads

There are 62,494 miles/100,571 km of roads, of which 20,685 miles/33,289 km are bituminized.

Aviation

Aerovias Venezolanas, SA (AVENSA), Aeronaves del Centro and Aerotuy, CA provide domestic services; Linea Aeropostal Venezolana (LV) and Venezolana Internacional de Aviacion, SA (VIASA) provide international services (main airports are Maiquetia (domestic) and Simón Bolívar (international), both 8 miles/13 km from Caracas). Passengers: (1984) 4.5 million.

Shipping

There are 4,412 miles/7,100 km of inland waterways. The Rio Orinoco and Lago de Maracaibo can accommodate ocean-going vessels. The marine ports are Amuay Bay, Bajo Grande, El Tablazo, La Guaira, Puerto Cabello, Puerto Ordaz. The merchant marine has 72 ships of 1,000 GRT or over. Freight loaded: (1985) 79.7 million tons/72.3 million tonnes; unloaded: 16.4 million tons/14.9 million tonnes.

Telecommunications

There are 1.4 million telephones and a modern and expanding system. There are 7.5 million radios and 2.5 million televisions (1986). There are three government and three private TV companies providing numerous channels nationally and locally, the state Radio Nacional and nearly 200 commercial radio stations.

EDUCATION AND WELFARE

Education

Schools. In 1985 there were 14,277 primary schools with 3,256,554 pupils and 125,140 teachers (one per 26 pupils).

Universities. There are 11 universities and over 100 higher education institutes.

Literacy. 86%.

Health

In 1983 there were 21,502 doctors (one per 895 people) and a total of 43,650 beds (one per 441 people) in hospitals and clinics.

VIETNAM

Công Hòa Xã Hôi Chu Nghĩa Viêt Nam
(The Socialist Republic of Vietnam)

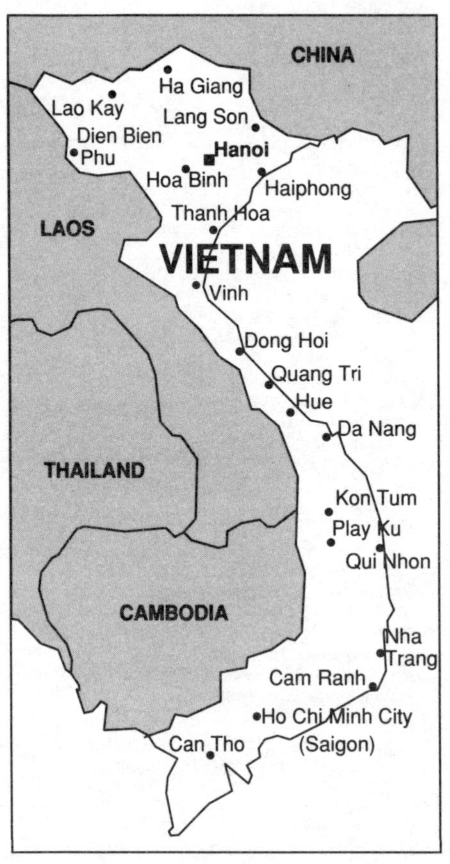

GEOGRAPHY

Located on the eastern coast of the Southeast Asian Indochinese peninsula, Vietnam covers a total area of 127,210 miles^2/329,560 km^2 divided into 40 provinces. An estimated 66% of the total area is dominated by the rugged, heavily forested terrain of the Chaîne Annamitique stretching north-south between the intensively cultivated and densely populated Red River (north) and Mekong River (south) deltas. The highest peak in Vietnam is Fan-si-Pan (10,312 ft/3,143 m) in North Vietnam, south of the Chinese border. A long, narrow coastal plain links the two major river deltas. 22% of the land is arable and 40% is forested.

Climate

Tropical monsoon (sub-tropical in the north). Summer temperatures vary little by region, commonly exceeding 100°F/38°C. Winter temperatures drop in the north to 59°F/15°C or less, affected by cold polar air masses moving over southern Asia. Most rain falls May-Oct., giving a mean annual precipitation of 59–79 in/1,500–2,000 mm (rising to more than 157 in/4,000 mm in the west-central highlands). Typhoons affect north and south-western regions. Hanoi: Jan. 62°F/16.7°C. July 84°F/28.9°C. Average annual rainfall 72 in/1,830 mm.

Cities and towns

Ho Chi Minh City (formerly Saigon)	3,419,978
Hanoi (capital)	2,674,400
Haiphong	1,279,067
Da Nang	492,194
Nha Trang	216,227
Qui Nhon	213,757
Hue	209,043

Population

Total population is 66,820,544 of which 19.0% live in urban areas. Population density is 525 persons per mile^2/188.4 per km^2. Ethnic divisions: 85–90% Vietnamese (Kinh); 3% Chinese. Ethnic minorities include Muong; Thai; Meo, Khmer; Man; Cham; various mountain-dwellers.

Birth rate 3.3%. **Death rate** 0.8%. **Rate of population increase** (1980–87) 2.5%. **Age distribution** under 15 = 40.6%; over 65 = 4.5%. **Life expectancy** female 68; male 64; average 66.

Religion

Buddhism is the principal religion. In addition, there are sizeable Taoist, Confucian, Hoa Hao, Caodaist, Muslim and Christian minorities, including an estimated 180,000 Protestants.

Language

The official language is Vietnamese, part of the Viet-Muong sub-branch of the Mon-Khmer (Austro-Asiatic) language family. Other languages spoken include French, Chinese, English, Khmer and a variety of Mon-Khmer and Malayo-Polynesian local dialects.

HISTORY

The Han Chinese established a military garrison in northern Vietnam in 214 BC, and a century later most of the area of present-day northern Vietnam was annexed as the Chinese province of Giao Chi. After 1,000 years of Chinese domination the Empire of Vietnam attained its independence in 939, although it nominally remained a tributary state of China. Originally confined to the Red River delta area, the Empire gradually expanded southward, reaching the Gulf of Siam in the 18th century. Christian missionary activity, carried on particularly by French priests, began in the 17th century, and despite recurrent outbursts of persecution resulted in the establishment of a sizeable Vietnamese Catholic community.

The persecution of French missionaries provided France with the pretext for armed intervention against Vietnam, and in 1859 French troops captured Saigon. Eight years later they had completely conquered the whole of southern Vietnam, which became the French colony of Cochin China. After a new war in 1883 France secured Hanoi and the following year they took over Annam (central Vietnam) and Tonkin (northern Vietnam) as protectorates. Limited guerrilla resistance to French domination continued until 1916 under the leadership of members of the imperial family and the mandarin class. Many underground nationalist organizations were founded in the 1920s, and in 1930 the Indochinese Communist Party was founded by Ho Chi Minh. A nationalist uprising in Tonkin in 1930 was followed by a peasant revolt under Communist leadership, both rebellions being brutally repressed by the French.

Japanese forces occupied Vietnam in 1940, and in Mar. 1945 ousted the French authorities and established a puppet regime headed by Emperor Bao Dai. Ho had meanwhile established the Viet Minh in China in 1941 as an alliance of Communist and nationalist organizations, and Viet Minh bands carried on a guerrilla resistance to the Japanese, with some assistance from the US military authorities. After the surrender of Japan in Aug. 1945 the Viet Minh took over Hanoi and Saigon; Bao Dai abdicated, and the Democratic Republic of Vietnam (DRV) was established on 2 Sept. with Ho as president and Hanoi as its capital.

Under the Potsdam Agreement concluded by the United States, Britain and the Soviet Union at the end of World War II in 1945, Vietnam was temporarily divided into two zones, the North being occupied by Chinese and the South by British troops. Whereas the Chinese recognized the Hanoi government, the British military authorities refused to do so and rearmed the French troops interned by the Japanese, who seized control of Saigon.

A compromise agreement between the French and Vietnamese governments was signed in Mar. 1946, with the DRV being recognized as a 'free state' within the French Union. Repeated clashes occurred between French and Vietnamese forces, however, and in late November the French navy bombarded Haiphong, killing 6,000 people. Ho Chi Minh's government left Hanoi, and war began.

In June 1948 France established a satellite 'State of Vietnam' government in Saigon with former emperor Bao Dai as chief of state. Whilst the new state was granted diplomatic recognition by the Western Powers, the Communist countries officially recognized the DRV in 1950. The Viet Minh took the offensive in late 1950, and by the beginning of 1954 partly or wholly controlled almost all the rural areas of Tonkin and Annam, as well as large areas of Cochin China. The decisive battle of the war was fought at Dien Bien Phu, in north-west Tonkin, where after a seige lasting 55 days 10,000 French troops were forced to surrender on 7 May 1954. Peace negotiations opened in Geneva on the following day.

The Geneva Agreements of July temporarily divided Vietnam into two zones, the North being controlled by Ho Chi Minh's government and the South by the Bao Dai regime, but provided that the country should be reunited following general elections in July 1956. All North Vietnamese proposals for the holding of elections, however, were rejected by Pres. Ngo Dinh Diem who had deposed Bao Dai in 1955 and declared South Vietnam a republic, and the country remained divided into a Communist North and a US-supported South.

Diem soon alienated important sections of the South Vietnamese community through the introduction of unduly oppressive security measures. The intensification of Diem's repression in 1959 resulted in a commensurate reaction from the rural population, and there was a marked increase in communist-led guerrilla warfare. In Dec. 1960 the various southern-based guerrilla groups united to form the National Liberation Front (NLF or Viet Cong). The intensification of NLF activity caused increasing anxiety to the US, and in June 1961 the Kennedy administration increased its economic and military assistance to Diem. Over the next few years the number of American military 'advisors' in South Vietnam rose from 2,000 in 1961 to 23,000 in 1964.

Conflict between Diem's government and the savagely persecuted Buddhist community led to a major political crisis in South Vietnam during late 1963, culminating in the overthrow of the regime by a military coup in November. A prolonged period of political instability followed with 12 changes of government occurring before the establishment of a military regime in Feb. 1965 under Gen. Nguyen Van Thieu and Air Vice-Marshal Nguyen Cao Ky.

In Aug. 1964 North Vietnamese patrol boats allegedly attacked US vessels patrolling in the Gulf of Tonkin. The US launched retaliatory airstrikes over the North and the US Congress passed the Tonkin Gulf resolution sanctioning the use of US armed forces in Southeast Asia. Sustained US bombing of the North started early the next year and in March the first US combat troops landed in Danang. By the year end, 185,000 US troops were stationed in Vietnam.

During the Tet (lunar new year) holiday early in 1968 the NLF launched a massive offensive in the South. Saigon, Hue and many other towns and military installations were attacked. Although the NLF suffered high casualties and were expelled from all the towns they had penetrated by late February, the attack highlighted the overall weakness of the South Vietnamese government and at the same time served to shift US public opinion against the war.

Peace talks involving all the warring factions opened in early 1969 and US Pres. Nixon began to withdraw US troops under the pretext of 'Vietnamizing' the war. Nevertheless, while the diplomats talked, the war intensified with saturation bombing of North Vietnam and secret air and ground attacks into Laos and Cambodia being carried out during 1970.

Protracted negotiations involving ceasefire and peace proposals by both sides led to the 1973 Paris Peace Agreements, but in fact the war ended only with the fall of the Saigon regime and the de facto reunification of the country on 30 Apr. 1975. It had been the longest conflict of the 20th century. In the years 1965–72 alone, according to estimates by the US Senate and Department of Defence, between 195,000 and 415,000 civilians were killed in South Vietnam, and 'enemy' dead totalled at least 850,000, many of them civilians. A UN report on war damage in June 1976 stated that 183 dams and 884 irrigation works had been bombed and over 350 km of railways destroyed, and that in the South 1,000,000 ha of arable land had been destroyed. There were 3,000,000 people unemployed, 1,000,000 with venereal disease and 1,000,000 drug addicts.

Vietnam's reunification, under the name of the Socialist Republic of Vietnam, was officially proclaimed in July 1976. Pham Van Dong, the North Vietnamese premier, formed a government on the following day which included South Vietnamese representatives.

In late 1978, after two years of attacks across the Vietnamese border, Hanoi invaded neighbouring Cambodia, overthrowing the hostile Khmer Rouge regime and establishing a friendly government. China responded by launching a brief punitive attack into northern Vietnam in Feb. 1979. Vietnam withdrew the last of its troops from Cambodia in Sept. 1989.

Le Duan, the leader of the Communist Party of Vietnam (CPV) since Ho Chi Minh's death in 1969, died in mid-1986. He was replaced at the party's sixth congress held in December by the southern reformist, Nguyen Van Linh. During 1987–88 Van Linh achieved only minor success in his efforts to reconstruct Vietnam's war-shattered economy and increase the general efficiency of governmental control.

CONSTITUTION AND GOVERNMENT

Executive and legislature

Vietnam has a collective presidency, the Council of State, elected by the legislature, and a government, the Council of Ministers, also elected by the legislature and headed by a chairman (prime minister). The legislature is a 496-member national assembly; last elections 19 Apr. 1987. The ruling Communist Party is described in the 1980 Constitution as 'the only force leading the state and society'.

Present government

President of the Council of State Vo Chi Cong
Chairman of the Council of Ministers Do Muoi
Other Principal Members of Council of Ministers Senior Gen. Vo Van Kiet (First Vice-Chairman); Nguyen Co Thach (Vice-Chairman; Foreign Affairs); Senior Gen. Vo Nguyen Giap (Vice-Chairman); Senior Gen. Dong Sy Nguyen (Vice-Chairman); Nguyen Khanh (Vice-Chairman; General Secretary of Council of Ministers); Tran Duc Luong (Vice-Chairman); Maj.-Gen. Mai Chi Tho (Interior); Senior Gen. Le Duc Anh (National Defence).

Ruling party

Communist Party of Vietnam (Dang Cong San Viet Nam).
Secretary general Nguyen Van Linh
Full members of the political bureau Nguyen Van Linh; Vo Chi Cong; Do Muoi; Senior Gen. Vo Van Kiet; Senior Gen. Le Duc Anh; Nguyen Duc Tam; Nguyen Co Thach; Senior Gen. Dong Sy Nguyen; Tran Xuan Bach; Nguyen Thanh Binh; Lt.-Gen. Doan Khue; Maj.-Gen. Mai Chi Tho.
Members of the secretariat Nguyen Van Linh; Nguyen Duc Tam; Tran Xuan Bach; Dao Duy Tung; Tran Kien; Le Phuoc Tho; Lt.-Gen. Nguyen Quyet; Lt.-Gen. Dam Quang Trung; Vu Oanh; Nguyen Khanh; Lt.-Gen. Tran Quyet; Pham The Duyet.

Justice

The system of law originates with the French civil code, modified by Communist legal theory. The highest court is the Supreme People's Court, whose president is responsible to the National Assembly. The Assembly also elects the Procurator-General, the senior law officer, who heads the Supreme People's Office of Supervision and Control. At the local level, justice is administered through a network of local people' courts and military courts. The death penalty is in force. There were at least three executions between 1985 and mid-1988. Offences were treason and espionage.

National symbols

Flag. A red field bearing a yellow five-pointed star.
Festivals. 30 Apr. (Liberation of Saigon); 1 May (May Day); 2–3 Sept. (National Day).
Vehicle registration plate. VN.

INTERNATIONAL RELATIONS

Affiliations

NAM; Comecon.

Defence

Total Armed Forces: 1,252,000. Terms of service: three years; specialists four years; some ethnic minorities two years. Reserves: 3,000,000.
Army: 1,100,000; some 1,800 main battle tanks (T-34/-54/-55, Type-59); 450 light tanks (PT-76, Type 62/63).
Navy: 6,000 plus some 27,000 Naval Infantry; seven frigates (US *Barnegat* and *Savage*); 62 patrol and coastal combatants.
Air Force: 12,000; some 250 combat aircraft (mainly MiG-21bis/PF); 30 armed helicopters.
Air Defence Force: 120,000.
Forces Abroad: Laos: 50,000; Kampuchea: 100,000 as at 1 June 1988, withdrawn in 1989.
Opposition: 25,000 inclusive; United Front for the Liberation of the Oppressed Races (FULRO) some 2,500. National Salvation Movement; Army of the Republic of Vietnam.

ECONOMY

Currency

The unit is the new dong, divided into 100 xu.

National finance

Budget. The 1987 budget, in US$, was for expenditure of 4,300 million and revenue of 3,200 million.

Inflation. 301%.

Gross Domestic Product Estimated total GDP US$12,600 million (GNP), per capita US$198 (overall size of economy ranking 66 in the world).

Economically active population. The total number of persons active in the economy was 32,900,000; unemployed: 10%.

Energy and mineral resources

Minerals. Most mineral resources are located in the north, including coal, anthracite and lignite. Coal is the major export item and provides the vast majority of energy produced. Phosphates; manganese; bauxite; chromate; offshore oil deposits (discovered by Soviet-Vietnam joint enterprise 1984). Petroleum exports are unofficially estimated as the third largest source of foreign exchange. There is a nuclear research reactor at Da Lat.

Electricity. Capacity: 2.02 million kW; production: 5,525 million kWh; 85 kWh per capita (1988). There is a hydroelectric dam at Tri An, produced with Soviet aid, and with an anticipated annual output of 1.7 million kWh.

Bioresources

Agriculture. The balance between the state-controlled economy and market incentives in agriculture is a major focus of the current debate on economic reform; the current arrangements include a state-farm system, agricultural co-operatives and production collectives. Agriculture is the basis of the economy, with rice as the staple crop. Some 20% of the land is put to arable use, with 3% permanent crops, meadow and pasture.

Crop production: (1987) rice 16.9 million tons/15.3 million tonnes; soya beans 99,207 tons/90,000 tonnes; rubber 62,831 tons/57,000 tonnes; sweet potatoes 2.3 million tons/2.1 million tonnes; fruit and vegetables; maize; cassava; sugar cane. Major food imports are wheat; maize; dairy products.

Livestock numbers: (1987) pigs 11.7 million; cattle 2.7 million; goats 432,000; poultry 100 million.

Forestry. 19.5 million acres/7.9 million ha of the country is forest and woodland.

Fisheries. Total catch: (1986 est.) 881,840 tons/800,000 tonnes.

Industry and commerce

Industry. Vietnam has received aid from communist and non-communist countries and from international organizations. Industry is state-owned and centrally controlled. It suffered severe damage during the war, and has since suffered from shortages of raw materials and spare parts for machines. The government has reported increases in gross industrial output since 1983. Main industries are food processing; cement; metallurgy; chemicals; paper; engineering; textiles.

Commerce. Exports: (f.o.b. 1987) US$880 million or 7% of GNP, mainly agricultural and handicraft products; coal; minerals. Main trading partners USSR; Eastern Europe; Japan; Singapore. Imports: (c.i.f. 1987) US$2,900 million, mainly petroleum; steel products; railway equipment; chemicals; medicines; raw cotton; fertilizer; grain. Main trading partners USSR; Eastern Europe; Japan; Singapore.

Trade with UK. In 1988 Vietnam exported £492,000 worth of goods to the UK, and imported £2.2 million worth of goods from the UK.

COMMUNICATIONS

Railways

There are 1,616 miles/2,600 km of railways.

Roads

There are 232,550 miles/374,243 km of roads (37,283 miles/60,000 km of main roads).

Aviation

Hang Khong Viet-nam provides domestic and international services (main airports are Tan Son Nhat, Ho Chi Minh City and Thu Do, near Hanoi). Passengers: (1983) 12,000.

Shipping

There are about 11,000 miles/17,702 km of navigable inland waterways of which more than 3,107 miles/5,000 km is navigable all the time by craft with up to 5.9 ft/1.8 m draught. The marine ports are Da Nang, Haiphong and Ho Chi Minh City, which all face onto the South China Sea. The merchant marine has 72 ships of 1,000 GRT or over. Freight loaded: (1985) 335,099 tons/304,000 tonnes; unloaded: 1.5 million tons/1.4 million tonnes.

Telecommunications

There are 35,000 telephones in Ho Chi Minh City. There are 6 million radios and 2.3 million televisions. Broadcasting is government-run, through Central TV and the Voice of Vietnam which also operates foreign-service radio in ten languages.

EDUCATION AND WELFARE

Education

There is compulsory free education for children aged between six and 16. Primary school enrolment in 1985 was 86% of the relevant age group, and 43% for secondary schools.

School population. Some 12 million pupils.

Universities. 93 universities and colleges of higher education with 115,00 students and some 19,000 teachers (1985).

Health

There is a state system of social security.

VIRGIN ISLANDS, BRITISH

GEOGRAPHY

The British Virgin Islands are a group of islands in the Caribbean covering a total of 58 miles²/150 km². The coral islands are relatively flat while the volcanic islands are hilly. The capital is Road Town.

Climate

The climate is subtropical and humid. Temperatures are moderated by trade winds. The islands are subject to hurricanes and tropical storms July-Oct.

Population

Total population (1989 est.) 12,124.
Birth rate 2.0%. **Death rate** 0.5%. **Rate of population increase** 1.1%. **Life expectancy** female 77; male 71.

Religion

Christianity.

Language

English.

HISTORY

The earliest inhabitants of the Virgin Islands were Arawak Indians who were succeeded by Caribs migrating from the south. The first European to visit the islands was Christopher Columbus in 1493. The islands were used as bases by English and Dutch privateers and adventurers in the mid-16th century and it was not until 1672 that the main island, Tortola, was formally annexed by the British. The colony grew gradually as African slaves were imported to work on the plantations. In 1773 the islands were granted their own government and House of Assembly. Slavery was abolished in 1834 and the economy of the islands declined. An appointed Council replaced the elected Assembly in 1867 and between 1872 and 1956 the British Islands were administered as part of the Federal Colony of the Leeward Islands.

A new constitution granting greater internal self-government was introduced in 1977. Elections in 1975 had resulted in the Virgin Islands Party (VIP) and the United Party (UP) each winning three seats. An independent member, Willard Wheatley, a former chief minister, held the balance of power. He formed a government with the VIP with himself as chief minister. In 1979 Wheatley's deputy H. Lavitty Stoutt was able to secure enough support after elections in that year to become chief minister. Another tied election result in 1983 allowed the one independent member, Cyril Romney, to form a government with the UP with Romney as chief minister. In 1986 Romney faced allegations over illegal conduct and he called an early general election rather than face a vote of 'no confidence'. In the elections, held on 30 Sept., the VIP won a majority of the seats and Stoutt returned to power as chief minister.

CONSTITUTION AND GOVERNMENT

The British Virgin Islands are a dependent territory of the United Kingdom, and have a constitution dating from June 1977. The cabinet consists of the governor, four members of the legislature and an ex officio member. The legislative council consists of the speaker, nine elected members and an ex officio member. In both chambers the ex officio member is the attorney general. Elections are held at least every five years (most recently in Sept. 1986).

Governor and Chairman of the Executive Council Mark Herdman

National symbols

Flag. Blue with the flag of the UK in the upper hoist-side quadrant and the Virgin Islands coat of arms centred in the outer half. The coat of arms depicts a woman flanked by six oil lamps and a scroll with the word 'Vigilate' (Be watchful).

National holiday. 1 July (Territory Day).

ECONOMY

The economy is highly dependent on the tourist industry. Since 1985 the islands have become an offshore financial centre. The soil is too poor for all food requirements to be met. Major trading partners are the US Virgin Islands, Puerto Rico and the US.

Currency

The US dollar.

COMMUNICATIONS

There is a port at Road Town; three airports, two with permanent surface runways; 66 miles/106 km of road. There is a telephone system, submarine cable communication links to Bermuda; one AM radio station, but no FM or TV stations.

VIRGIN ISLANDS, UNITED STATES

GEOGRAPHY

The US Virgin Islands are a group of islands in the Caribbean covering a total of 136 miles²/352 km². The terrain is mostly hilly or rugged and mountainous. There is a lack of fresh water, and the area is subject to frequent severe droughts, floods and earthquakes. The capital is Charlotte Amalie.

Climate

Subtropical, tempered by easterly trade winds. Rainy season May-Nov.

Population

Total population (1989 est.) 109,105.
Birth rate 2.0%. **Death rate** 0.5%. **Rate of population increase** 1.4%. **Life expectancy** female 76; male 70.

Religion
Christianity.

Language
English (official); Spanish and creole are widely spoken.

HISTORY

The earliest inhabitants of the Virgin Islands were Ciboney Indians who were gradually displaced by Arawak Indians. The Arawaks in turn suffered from raids and settlement by Caribs migrating north-westwards. Although Columbus found the islands in 1493, settlement by Europeans did not take place until the 17th century, when the islands were used by privateers and traders from many nations. St Thomas was first settled by the Danes in 1665 for use as a base for Denmark's trading activities in the region. The Danish West India Company enlarged its possessions by colonizing St John in 1718 and buying St Croix from France in 1733. The Danish Crown assumed responsibility for the islands in 1746. African slaves were imported as labour for large sugar plantations. Slavery was abolished in the Danish West Indies in 1848. During the 19th century the island's agricultural economy went into decline and the growing financial burden of the islands prompted Denmark to open negotiations in 1867 for their sale to the United States. The US Senate, however, refused to ratify the treaty. Further attempts to sell the islands took place in the 1890s and in 1902 a treaty drawn up by the US was rejected by the upper house of the Danish parliament. The islands were eventually sold to the US in 1916 for US$25,000,000 and transferred to US military administration in 1917.

US citizenship was granted in 1927 and in 1931 a civil administration replaced control by the Navy Department and the islands came under the control of the Department of the Interior. Revisions to the Organic Act in 1954, which created an elected senate, prompted the development of political parties, the principal parties being affiliates of the US Republican and Democratic parties. The Virgin Islands were given the right to elect their own governor in 1968 and the first election in 1970 was won by Melvin Evans of the Republicans. In 1974 Cyril King, the leader of a breakaway faction of the Democratic Party known as the Independent Citizen's Movement, was elected governor. King died in 1978 and was succeeded by his deputy, Juan Luis, who was re-elected in 1982. The elections in 1986 were won convincingly by the Democrats and Alexander Farrelly became governor. The last referendum on a constitution giving greater autonomy to the islands failed to achieve a sufficient majority in favour when it was held in Nov. 1981.

CONSTITUTION AND GOVERNMENT

The Virgin Islands of the United States are an organized, unincorporated territory of the US. The Revised Organic Act of July 1954 serves as the constitution. There is a governor elected to a four-year term, and a unicameral legislature – a senate with 15 members elected to two-year terms.

Leader Alexander Farrelly

National symbols
Flag. White with a modified US coat of arms (showing an eagle holding an olive branch in one talon and three arrows in the other with a superimposed shield of red and white stripes) in the centre, between large blue initials 'V' and 'I'.

National holiday. 31 March (Transfer Day – from Denmark to US).

ECONOMY

The main economic activity is tourism (70% of GDP and 70% of employment). Small agricultural sector, most food is imported. Manufacturing sector includes textiles; electronics; pharmaceuticals. Main trading partners are the US and Puerto Rico.

Currency
The US dollar.

COMMUNICATIONS

There are ports at Christiansted and Frederiksted on St Croix; Long Bay, Crown Bay and Red Hook on St Thomas; Cruz Bay on St John. There are three airports with permanent surface runways; 538 miles/865 km of road. There is a telephone system; four AM and six FM radio stations; three TV stations.

WALLIS AND FUTUNA ISLANDS

GEOGRAPHY

The Wallis and Futuna Islands are volcanic islands in the South Pacific Ocean covering a total area of 106 miles^2/274 km^2. The capital is Mata-Utu.

Climate
Tropical; the hot rainy season lasts Nov.-Apr.; the cool dry season lasts May-Oct.

Population
Total population (1989 est.) 14,575.

Birth rate 2.9%. **Death rate** 0.6%. **Rate of population increase** 2.3%. **Life expectancy** female 70; male 69.

Religion
Christianity (Roman Catholic)

Language
French; Wallisian (indigenous Polynesian language).

HISTORY

The Wallis and Futuna Islands were first settled over 2,000 years ago. Dutch navigators arrived at Futuna in 1616 and Wallis takes its name from the English sea captain who was the first European to land there in 1767. In 1886 Wallis became a French protectorate, Futuna following in 1887. The islands assumed the official status of a colony of France in 1924. During World War II Wallis was an important American military base and the runway at Hihifo remains a strategic prize for the French.

In a referendum in Dec. 1959 the islanders voted in favour of becoming a French Overseas Territory. Under this arrangement a chief administrator runs the territory on behalf of the French government and the islands have one seat in the French National Assembly and one in the French Senate.

In Nov. 1983 the two traditional kings of Futuna Island sought a division of the Wallis and Futuna island groups into two separate overseas territories of France. They claimed that Wallis was dominating to an excessive degree the affairs of the territory.

In Apr. 1985 a new political party was formed by the president of the Territorial Assembly, Falakiko Gata. The Union populaire local (UPL) was committed to giving more emphasis to local issues as opposed to metropolitan concerns, but did not seek independence. Following quinquennial general elections for the 20-seat Territorial Assembly in Mar. 1987, Gata was re-elected president by an alliance of Rassemblement pour la République (RPR) and UPL members.

CONSTITUTION AND GOVERNMENT

The Territory of the Wallis and Futuna Islands is an overseas territory of France, and shares the French constitution (dating from Sept. 1958). There is a territorial assembly of 20 members. Elections are held every five years. There are popular elections of one deputy to the French National Assembly and of one representative to the French Senate.

Leader Jacques Le Henaff, High Administrator.

National symbols

Flag. The flag of France.

National holiday. 14 July (Bastille Day).

ECONOMY

The economy is limited to subsistence agriculture, the major employer. Exports are negligible. Fuel and construction materials have to be imported. Support from France is essential to the economy.

Currency

Comptoirs Français du Pacifique francs.

COMMUNICATIONS

There are ports at Mata-Utu and Leava; two airports, one with a permanent surface runway; 62 miles/100 km of road on Wallis Island and 12 miles/20 km of earth-surface road on Futuna Island. There is a telephone system; one AM radio station but no FM radio or TV.

WESTERN SAHARA

GEOGRAPHY

Western Sahara lies on the north-west coast of Africa and covers an area of 102,676 miles^2/266,000 km^2. The terrain is mostly low, flat desert with large areas of rocky or sandy surfaces rising to small mountains in the south and north-east.

Climate

Hot, dry desert; rain is rare. Cold offshore currents produce fog and heavy dew. Hot, dry sirocco wind during winter and spring. Widespread harmattan haze often severely restricts visibility.

Population

Total population (1989 est.) 186,488, mainly of Arab and Berber descent.

Birth rate 4.8%. **Death rate** 2.3%. **Rate of population increase** 2.8%. **Life expectancy** female 41; male 39.

Religion

Muslim.

Language

Hassaniya Arabic; Moroccan Arabic.

HISTORY

The indigenous inhabitants of the Western Sahara were Sanhadja Berbers who moved into the area in the 3rd century AD. They were nomadic camel herders who continued to live in largely independent groups even after the Arab conquests of the 7th and 12th centuries, and this prevented the rise of a unified nation. Islam became established in the region in the middle of the 11th century.

The 19th century was a period of Spanish expansion in North Africa. After a war with Morocco in 1859, Spain sent a commercial mission in 1884 and two years later signed a protectorate treaty, establishing the Spanish Sahara. The desert interior was left to the nomads. Spain negotiated with France over Morocco in 1886–91; there were further hostilities between the Spanish and Morocco in 1893. Subsequent Franco-Spanish treaties in the early 20th century restricted Spanish claims. Spain maintained a tenuous presence in Morocco and the Spanish Sahara, but on 21 July 1921 suffered a terrible defeat at Anual against Moroccan forces. Spanish armies were heavily occupied in the Rif region until 1926 when Moroccan forces were finally defeated. There was little economic development in the territory. Scientific exploration planned by Spain did not start until 1945, and phosphate exploitation began in the 1970s.

Indigenous resistance to Spain's rule culminated in open revolt in 1957, which was put down by a joint Franco-Spanish military expedition in Feb. 1958. The United Nations in 1966 proposed a referendum on self-determination, but this was rejected by Spain. At this time, Morocco made a claim for the Spanish Sahara based on historical allegiance; Mauritania also staked its claim. Against this background, the Sahara desert peoples sought independence. A Sahrawi liberation movement, formed in 1967, was crushed by the colonial authorities in 1970. In 1973 a new nationalist organization, the Frente Polisario (Polisario Front), led by Mustapha El Ouali Sayed, initiated a campaign of guerrilla warfare, which encouraged a Spanish decision to withdraw from the colony.

The UN favoured self-determination but on 6 Nov. 1975 the northern, phosphate-rich section was claimed by Morocco when 300,000 'volunteers' staged the 'Green March' into the territory. On 14 Nov. Spain agreed to a partition of the territory between Morocco and Mauritania. Spanish control formally ended on 28 Feb. 1976, whereupon Moroccan and Mauritanian troops entered. They met continued resistance from Polisario. Mauritania's fragile economy and ill-equipped army could not sustain this unpopular war over a largely unproductive area. On 5 Aug. 1979, Mauritania withdrew its claim and Morocco occupied this southern part of the region also.

Meanwhile, Polisario on 27 Feb. 1976 had proclaimed the Saharan Arab Democratic Republic (SADR). Its secretary-general, Mohammed Abdelaziz, became SADR president in Oct. 1982. Polisario, from its beginnings, had enjoyed Algerian support; and in Feb. 1982 the SADR was admitted to the Organization of African Unity (OAU), against Moroccan opposition. The SADR was subsequently recognized by more than 70 countries worldwide.

The war with Morocco continued into the 1980s with heavy losses on both sides. From 1980 the advantage had turned to Morocco, thanks to its use of a defensive wall of sand, equipped with sophisticated US-supplied electronic detection devices which enabled it to anticipate Polisario attacks. The wall protected most of the population centres and industry and severely limited the extent of Polisario's operations. Polisario said that a self-determination referendum would only be held if Moroccan troops first left the Western Sahara, while Morocco refused direct negotiation with the organization.

The UN called for direct negotiations between Morocco and Polisario (Dec. 1985). Indirect talks in 1986 failed, but on 30 Aug. 1988 both sides accepted a new UN peace initiative calling for a cease-fire and a referendum of the territory's indigenous people. The first meeting between King Hassan and Sahrawi leaders took place on 4 Jan. 1989. Polisario declared a unilateral truce at the end of February and at its congress in May reaffirmed its commitment to peace through negotiation. Lured by generous financial incentives many Moroccans settled in coastal areas, notably the town of El Aaiún. However, in Oct. 1989, heavy fighting erupted between Polisario and the Moroccan Army reflecting, in part, the growing impatience of the rebel forces with the slow pace of the UN-sponsored peace efforts.

ECONOMY

Poor in natural resources and with a very low rainfall, Western Sahara has a per capita GDP of under $500. Fishing and phosphate mining are the main sources of income and most food has to be imported. All trade and economic activities are controlled by the Moroccan government.

Currency

The Moroccan dirham.

COMMUNICATIONS

There are 3,790 miles/6,100 km of roads, of which 839 miles/1,350 km are surfaced, and 16 airports (14 usable) including three with permanent-surface runways. There is a limited telecommunications network with 2,000 telephones, two AM radio stations and two TV stations (no FM station) linked to Morocco's system.

WESTERN SAMOA

Malotutu' Atasi O Samoa I Sisifo

(Independent State of Western Samoa)

GEOGRAPHY

Located in the south-western Pacific Ocean, approximately 1,600 miles/2,575 km north-east of New Zealand (Auckland), Western Samoa comprises two main islands (Upolu and Savai'i) and a number of smaller islands of which two are inhabited (Apolima and Manono). On Savai'i, the rugged, volcanic interior rises to a maximum elevation of 6,000 ft/1,829 m. Upolu's highest peak attains an altitude of 3,599 ft/1,097 m. Both islands exhibit similar geographical features: a mountainous central region, covered by dense tropical forest and cut by swift, torrential rivers, encompassed by narrow coastal plains and coral reefs. Major streams include the Sili and Faleata on Savai'i and Vaisingano on Upolu. 19% of the land is arable and 47% is forested. The total area of the island state is 1,093 miles^2/2,831 km^2.

Climate

Tropical marine, distinguished by two seasons. The wet season lasts Dec.-Apr. with temperatures as high as 97°F/36°C, followed by a cooler, drier season May-Nov., average temperature 72°F/22°C. Periodic typhoons Jan.-Mar. Rainfall is plentiful but unevenly distributed, averaging 98–118 in/2,500–3,000 mm but reaching as much as 271 in/6,875 mm on the windward shores. Apia: Jan. 80°F/26.7°C. July 78°F/25.6°C. Average annual rainfall 110 in/2,800 mm.

Cities and towns

Apia (capital) 33,170

Population

Total population is 181,984 of which 21.2% live in urban areas. Population density is 166 persons per mile^2/57.0 per km^2. Ethnic divisions: Western Samoans constitute the second largest Polynesian group after the New Zealand Maoris. Approximately 7% are Euronesian (mixed European and Polynesian); 0.4% European.

Birth rate 3.4%. **Death rate** 0.7%. **Rate of population increase** (1980–87) 2.2%. **Age distribution** under 15 = 44.3%; over 60 = 5.4%. **Life expectancy** female 69; male 64; average 67.

Religion

99.7% Christian, of which 5% affiliated to the London Missionary Society. Congregational, Roman Catholic, Methodist, Mormon and Seventh Day Adventist denominations are all represented.

Language
The two official languages are English and Samoan, a Polynesian dialect.

HISTORY

These Polynesian islands were invaded by Fijians in the early 13th century, but they may have been settled as far back as 1000 BC. The Dutch made the first European contact in 1722, but it was the arrival of a British missionary in 1830 that marked the continuous involvement of the Western powers in Samoa. Britain, Germany and the United States appointed representatives there and began to obtain commercial and legal privileges for themselves and their nationals on the islands. International rivalries eventually led in 1899 to a convention in which Germany and the US acquired Western and Eastern Samoa respectively, while Britain renounced all claims. New Zealand annexed Western Samoa in 1914 and administered it 1920–62 on behalf of the League of Nations and the United Nations. The inter-war period was marked by nationalist disturbances and the activities of the Mau movement. Constitutional advances towards self-government and independence began in 1947 and a constitution combining British and Polynesian practices was drawn up in 1962. In the following year Western Samoans voted for independence on the basis of this in a UN-supervised plebiscite. On 1 Jan. 1962 Western Samoa became independent and later that year signed a treaty of friendship authorizing New Zealand to act as its agent in foreign relations when requested. Western Samoa became a full member of the Commonwealth in 1970 and joined the UN in 1976. The general election in Feb. 1988 resulted, after a period of uncertainty, in the defeat of the incumbent coalition government of Va'ai Kolone and his replacement as prime minister by Tofilau Eti.

CONSTITUTION AND GOVERNMENT

Executive and legislature
The head of state, the O le Ao O le Malo, acts as a constitutional monarch, appoints the head of government (the prime minister) on the recommendation of parliament, and may dissolve the unicameral 47-member Fono (the legislative assembly). The Fono is elected for up to three years, with two of its members elected by universal suffrage and the remainder chosen by Mati (elected clan leaders). Last elections 26 Feb. 1988.

Present government
Head of state, the O le Ao O le Malo Susuga Malietoa Tanumafili II

Prime Minister; Minister of Foreign Affairs; Labour; Broadcasting; Justice; Police and Prisons; Attorney General Tofilau Eti Alesana

Other Principal Ministers Tuilaepa Sailele Malielegaoi (Finance); Tanuvasa Livi (Economic Affairs).

Justice
The death penalty is nominally in force. There were no executions between 1985 and mid-1988.

National symbols
Flag. Red field with a blue canton containing five white five-pointed stars of unequal size.

Festival. 1 June (National Day).

Vehicle registration plate. WS.

INTERNATIONAL RELATIONS

Affiliations
Commonwealth; SPF.

Defence
No military forces as such.

ECONOMY

Currency
The unit is the tala, divided into 100 sene.

National finance
Budget. The 1988 budget, in US$, was for expenditure of 54 million and revenue of 54 million.

Inflation. 2.9 %.

Gross Domestic Product
Estimated total GDP US$100 million, per capita US$570 (overall size of economy ranking 178 in the world).

Economically active population. The total number of persons active in the economy was 37,000. Some 59% work in agriculture.

Energy and mineral resources
Electricity. Capacity: 19,000 kW; production: 30 million kWh; 170 kWh per capita (1988).

Bioresources
Agriculture. This employs two-thirds of the labour force and is the source of 90% of exports. The main crops are coconuts; bananas; taro; yams.

Crop production: (1987 in 1,000 tons/tonnes) coconuts 220/220/200; taro 43/39; copra 29/26; bananas 25/23; papayas 13/12; mangos 7/6; pineapples 7/6; cocoa beans 2.2/2.

Livestock numbers: (1987) cattle 27,000; pigs 65,000; horses 3,000; poultry 1 million.

Forestry. 47% of the land area is forest and woodland.

Fisheries. Total catch (1983) 3,472 tons/3,150 tonnes.

Industry and commerce
Industry. Main industries are timber; tourism; food processing; fishing. Tourism has become the most important growth industry.

Commerce. Exports: (1987) US$8.4 million or 8% of GDP, including coconut oil and cream 42%; taro 19%; cocoa 14%; copra; timber. Imports: US$47.3 million, including intermediate goods 58%; food 17%; capital goods 12%. Countries exported to were New Zealand 30%; EC countries 24%; Australia 21%; American Samoa 7%; US 9%. Imports came from New Zealand 31%; Australia 20%; Japan 15%; Fiji 15%; US 5%; EC countries 4%.

Trade with UK. In 1988 Western Samoa imported UK goods worth £757,000; exports to UK totalled £1,323,000.

Tourism. (1986) 49,710 visitors.

COMMUNICATIONS

Railways
There are no railways in Western Samoa.

Roads
There are 1,295 miles/2,085 km of roads, of which some 248 miles/400 km are bituminized (733 miles/1,180 km are plantation roads).

Aviation
Polynesian Airlines Ltd provides international

services (international airport at Faleolo, 25 miles/40 km from Apia).

Shipping

The port of Apia is coastally situated on the island of Upolu. The merchant marine has three ships of 1,000 GRT or over. Freight loaded: (1985) 47,399 tons/ 43,000 tonnes; unloaded: 95,900 tons/87,000.

Telecommunications

There are 7,500 telephones, 70,000 radios and 2,500 televisions (there is no TV station but the American Samoan television channel is widely received, linking in with US television networks).

EDUCATION AND WELFARE

Education

Schools. (1986) The total number of pupils in primary, junior and secondary schools is 51,940.

Universities. There are two universities, the University of the South Pacific School of Agriculture, and the National University.

Literacy. 90%.

Health

There is one national hospital; seven district hospitals; 23 health centres and subcentres. There are 44 doctors (one per 4,136 people).

YEMEN, NORTH

Al Jamhuriya Al Arabiya Al Yamaniya
(Yemen Arab Republic)

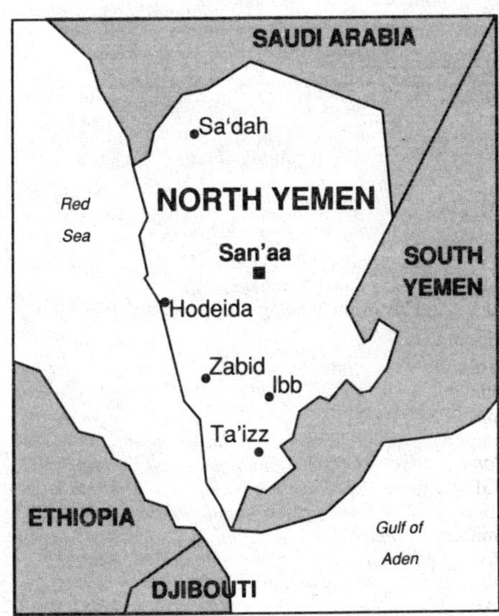

GEOGRAPHY

Located on the seismically active south-western tip of the Arabian peninsula, North Yemen (San'aa) covers a total area of 75,270 miles²/95,000 km² divided into ten provinces. Backing the narrow, barren Red Sea Coastal plain of Tihamat in the west, the comparatively fertile and well cultivated mountainous interior rises to a maximum elevation of 12,336 ft/3,760 m at Hadur Shu'ayb, the highest point on the Arabian peninsula. A number of rivers drain eastwards as the land slopes towards the perimeter of the arid Rub-al-Khali (Empty Quarter), covering 60% of the total surface area. The bulk of the population inhabits the Tihamat coastal strip and the rugged hinterland. 14% of the land is arable and 8% is forested.

Climate

Predominantly desert, mitigated by relief. Hot and humid on the Tihamat coastal belt (mean temperature 84°F/29°C) becoming mild and temperate in the interior highlands with cool winters. Rainfall decreases easterly from the annual average of 15–20 in/ 380–500 mm to below 4.7 in/120 mm. San'a: Jan. 57°F/13.9°C. July 71°F/21.7°C. Average annual rainfall 20 in/508 mm.

Cities and towns

San'aa (capital)	277,818
Hodeida	126,386
Ta'iz	119,573
Ibb	48,806
Dhamar	47,733

Population

Total population is 6,942,202 of which 14.4% (1984) live in urban areas. Population density is 92 persons per mile²/62.0 per km². Ethnic divisions: 90% Arab; 10% Afro-Arab.

Birth rate 5.2%. **Death rate** 1.6%. **Rate of population increase** (1980–87) 3.1%. **Age distribution** under 15 = 48.0%; over 65 = 3.2%. **Life expectancy** female 52; male 50; average 51.

Religion

Islam. 39–40% of the population are Sunni Muslims, 59–60% are Shi'a (Sunni in the south, Shi'a in the north). There is also a very small community of Yemeni Jews.

Language

Arabic is the official language, but English is also commonly understood.

HISTORY

The first historical civilization in Yemen was the kingdom of Ma'in which flourished on the trade in frankincense and spices with Egypt from the 14th century BC. To the south-east was the kingdom of Saba' (biblical Sheba). By the 1st century BC maritime trade had taken over from the overland routes and the highly sophisticated irrigation system at Marib had fallen into disrepair. As Sabean influence waned, the Himyaris, originally subject to Qataban in present-day South Yemen, moved their capital to San'aa and extended their control over southern Arabia. During their rule Jews and Christians settled in Yemen. In

AD 525 the last Himyarite king, a Jew, was defeated by the Christian Ethiopian kingdom. Persian Sassanids took control in 575 and were converted to Islam in the late 7th century. At the end of the 9th century the Shia Imam al-Hadi founded the 'Alid Zayid dynasty, which was to have a hand in government until 1962. In 1517 Yemen was conquered by the Ottomans, but they were expelled by the Zaydi Imams in 1636. The Ottomans recaptured Sana'a in 1872 but Yemen secured its independence in 1918.

Under the Zaydi Imams, who ruled as absolute monarchs, Yemen was politically and economically isolated. Muhammad al-Badr succeeded after the death of his father, Imam Ahmad, in Sept. 1962, but, after a week, he was overthrown by the military under Col Adbullah as-Sallal and a republic proclaimed. A civil war ensued: Britain and Saudi Arabia supporting the royalists while the Egyptians fought alongside the republicans. The withdrawal of Egyptian troops in 1968 led to swift royalist victories but the tide turned in 1969, following the deposition of the Imam by his followers and the withdrawal of Saudi finance. By 1970 the republicans had emerged victorious and diplomatic relations with Saudi Arabia and Britain were restored. A new constitution was promulgated in Dec. 1970 providing for a consultative council with elections in 1971. Fighting broke out with the People's Democratic Republic of Yemen (South Yemen) in Sept. 1972, but a peace agreement providing for the eventual unification of the two countries was agreed in October. In 1974 a coup led by Lt.-Col Ibrahim Hamadi toppled the civilian government of Hassan Makki and abrogated the constitution. Civilian administrations were appointed, first under Moshin al-Aini then, in Jan. 1975, under Abdelaziz al-Ghani, and a return to constitutional rule was promised. In Oct. 1977 Hamadi was assassinated. His successor, Lt.-Col Ahmad al-Ghashimi, appointed a constituent assembly of 99 members in Feb. 1978 to chart the course towards civilian rule. Following Pres. al-Ghashimi's assassination in June 1978, Lt.-Col. Ali Abdullah Saleh was elected president. Fighting with PDR Yemen, suspected of complicity in Pres. al-Ghashimi's murder, broke out in Feb. 1979, with the PDR supporting the opposition National Democratic Front. Peace was restored with another agreement on unification in March. Pres. Saleh has gradually introduced democratic procedures, culminating in a general election for a newly created 159-member Consultative Council on 5 July 1988, which replaced the appointed Constituent Assembly. 25% of the seats were won by supporters of the Muslim Brotherhood. The council re-elected Pres. Saleh for a third five-year term on 17 July 1988 and Prime Minister al-Ghani, who had held the post since Nov. 1983, was reappointed.

Progress towards Yemen's unification increased dramatically in late 1989, culminating in the publication of a draft joint constitution for a unified nation on 1 Dec. and a summit meeting of the two leaders on 23–26 Dec. The border was finally opened in Feb. 1990 and unification was expected imminently.

CONSTITUTION AND GOVERNMENT

Executive and legislature

The executive president appoints a council of ministers headed by a prime minister; the president is elected by a constituent people's assembly, whose 159 members are themselves selected by presidential decree. There is also a general people's congress, consisting of 700 elected and 300 appointed members, which meets every two years and is elected every four years.

Present government (Feb. 1990)

President; Secretary-General of the General People's Congress; C.-in-C. of the Armed Forces Col. Ali Abdullah Saleh

Vice-President Abdel-Karim al-Arashi

Prime Minister Abdel Aziz Abdel Ghani

Other Principal Ministers Abdel Karim al-Iryani (Deputy Prime Minister; Foreign Affairs); Muhammad Said al-Attar (Deputy Prime Minister; Development; Head of Central Planning Organization); Lt.-Col Mujahid Abu Shawrib (Deputy Prime Minister for Internal Affairs); Dr Hassan Muhammad Makki (Deputy Prime Minister); Dr Abd at-Wahhab Mahmud Abd al-Hamid (Economy, Supply and Trade); Alawi Salih al-Salami (Finance); Abdullah Hussain Barakat (Interior); Lt.-Col Muhsin Muhammad al-Ulufi (Justice).

Justice

The death penalty is in force. There were over 34 executions between 1985 and mid-1988. Offences were murder, aggravated robbery.

National symbols

Flag. Three horizontal stripes of red, white and black with a green five-pointed star in the centre.

Festivals. 13 June (Corrective Movement Anniversary); 26 Sept. (Revolution Day); 14 Oct. (PDRY National Day).

Vehicle registration plate. YMN.

INTERNATIONAL RELATIONS

Affiliations

NAM; ICO; Arab League; ACC.

Defence

Total Armed Forces: 36,600 (perhaps 25,000 conscripts). Terms of service: conscription, three years. Reserves: perhaps 40,000.

Army: 35,000; 680 main battle tanks (mainly T-34/-54/-55/-62/-60A1).

Navy: 600; eight inshore patrol craft.

Air Force: 1,000; 73 combat aircraft (mainly MiG-21, Su-22, F-5E).

ECONOMY

Currency

The unit is the riyal, divided into 100 fils.

National finance

Budget. The 1986 budget, in US$, was for expenditure of 1,680 million and revenue of 1,180 million. Main items of expenditure are defence 22.2%; education 16.5%.

Balance of payments. The balance of payments, in US$ (current account, 1987) was a deficit of 607 million.

Inflation. 21.7%.

Gross Domestic Product

Estimated total GDP US$4,270 million, per capita US$690 (overall size of economy ranking 93 in the world).

Sector	% of workforce	% of GDP
industry	n/a	17
agriculture	70	28
services*	n/a	55

* services figure includes elements unassigned to other categories.

Energy and mineral resources

Oil and gas. Export earnings from the oil reserves located in 1984 began to accrue in 1987 with the opening of North Yemen's first major oilfield and pipeline.

Minerals. Salt deposits amount to an estimated 25 million tonnes. Output: (1984) 169,000 tonnes.

Electricity. Capacity: 415,000 kW; production: 499 million kWh; 75 kWh per capita (1988).

Bioresources

Agriculture. 14% of the land (1.3 million ha) is arable, 30% is meadow or pasture. Cotton growing predominates along the coastal belt (Tihama) near Zabid and Bait al Faqih, assorted fruit crops and vine-growing flourish in the San'a district. Qati, a mildly narcotic shrub, is grown for domestic consumption.

Crop production: (1987 in 1,000 tons/tonnes) sorghum 526/477; wheat 110/100; grapes 142/129; potatoes 121/110; barley 44/40; maize 53/48; dates 17/15.

Livestock numbers: (1987 in 1,000s) cattle 1,023; sheep 2,604; goats 1,594; camels 61; poultry 18,000.

Forestry. 8% of the land area is covered by forest or woodland.

Fisheries. Catch: (1984) 93,696 tons/18,300 tonnes.

Industry and commerce

Industry. North Yemen's main industries are crude oil production; small-scale production of cotton textiles and leather goods; food processing; handicrafts; fishing; a small aluminium products factory; cement manufacture, output (1982) 93,696 tons/85,000 tonnes.

Commerce. Exports: (1987) US$51.1 million or 1.13% of GDP. Imports: $1,400 million or 31% of GDP. Exported goods included crude oil; cotton; coffee; hides; vegetables. Imported commodities were largely textiles and other manufactured consumer goods; petroleum products; sugar; grain; flour; other foodstuffs; cement. Main trading partners were US; South Yemen; Japan. Imports were received from Italy; Saudi Arabia; US; Japan; UK.

Trade with UK. North Yemen imported UK goods worth £42.6 million in 1988; exports to the UK totalled £1.53 million.

Tourism. (1986) 44,000 visitors.

COMMUNICATIONS

Railways

There are no railways in the Yemen Arab Republic.

Roads

There are23,136 miles/ roads.

Aviation

Yemen Airways (Yemenia) provides domestic and international services (main airports are San'aa International (8 miles/13 km from the city), al-Ganad (at Taiz) and Hodeida Airport). Passengers: (1984) 456,000.

Shipping

The major ports of North Yemen are Al Hudaydah, Al Mukha, Salif and Ra's Kathib situated on the coast of the Red Sea. Freight loaded: (1983 est.) 110,230 tons/100,000 tonnes; unloaded: 3.0 million tons/2.7 million tonnes.

Telecommunications

There are 50,000 telephones and a poor but gradually improving system, with new radio-relay and cable networks. There are 200,000 radios and 50,000 televisions (1986). The government controls all three radio stations, which broadcast in Arabic, and the television service which began nationwide broadcasting in 1980.

EDUCATION AND WELFARE

Education

Schools. An estimated 904,490 pupils are enrolled at primary schools with a further 112,920 pupils in secondary education. Over 11,600 students attend teacher-training institutions.

Universities. Approximately 6,720 students are registered at the University of San'aa (founded 1974).

Literacy. 15%.

Health

1,234 physicians serve 60 hospitals and health clinics with a total of 5,986 beds (one per 1,160 members of the population).

YEMEN, SOUTH

Jumhuriyah Al-Yemen Al-Dimuqratiyah Al Sha'abiyah (People's Democratic Republic of Yemen)

GEOGRAPHY

Situated on the southern coast of the Arabian Peninsula, South Yemen covers a total area of 128,526 miles²/332,970 km² divided into six governorates, including the islands of Socotra, Perim and Kamaran. The sandy, fragmented coastal plain rises inland to form the steep and rugged Yemen Plateau (10,587 ft/3,227 m at Jabal Al-Hasha), dissected by the Wadi Mayfa'ah and Wadi Hadramawt. To the north, the plateau descends to meet the uninhabited gravel wastes of the Rub al-Khali (Empty Quarter). 1% of the land is considered arable and 7% is (sparsely) vegetated. The predominantly rural population includes 10% nomadic peoples.

Climate

Desert climate. Coastal areas and north-eastern desert regions receive less than 3.9 in/100 mm of rainfall annually. Most rainfall is relief-influenced; reaching 27.5 in/700 mm on occasions near the North Yemen border. Extremely hot and humid in the summer months, temperatures soaring to 129°F/54°C; winter conditions in the highlands can be very cold. Aden: 75°F/Jan. 24°C. July 90°F/32°C. Average annual rainfall 1.8 in/46 mm.

Cities and towns

Aden (capital)	270,000

Population

Total population is 2,503,641 of which 33.2% live in urban areas. Population density is 19 persons per mile²/6.8 per km². Ethnic composition: predominantly Arab, with Indo-Pakistani, Somali, Amhara and Swahili, Jewish, Persian and European minorities making up an estimated 4.3% of the total population. **Birth rate** 4.8%. **Death rate** 1.5%. **Rate of population increase** (1980–87) 3.2%. **Age distribution** under 15 = 45.1%; over 65 = 2.8%. **Life expectancy** female 52; male 49; average 51.

Religion

Sunni Muslim (Shafi'i) about 99.5%, with very small Christian, Hindu and Jewish communities.

Language

Arabic is spoken by the vast majority of the population, many of whom also understand English.

HISTORY

During the 1st millennium BC present-day PDR Yemen was divided between the Qataban and Hadramawt kingdoms. Qataban was conquered by the neighbouring Sabeans during the 5th century BC. By 100 BC they had given way in their turn to the Himyarite kingdom. Following the defeat of the last Himyarite king in AD 525 by Ethiopians, Southern Arabia was occupied by the Persian Sassanids. During the 7th century the region was converted to Islam. From 1174 to 1451 the Egyptian Ayyubids and the Rasulids, descendants of Ayyubid governors, ruled, but by 1517 the region had become part of the Ottoman empire. In 1635 the Ottomans were expelled by the Zaydis, although they only managed to keep control of Aden until 1735. The region then came under the rule of tribal sheikhs. Britain occupied the port of Aden in 1839, to provide a guaranteed chandling station on the route to India. The town was administered by British India until 1937, when it became a Crown Colony and the interior a Protectorate, where tribal leaders retained nominal authority.

Aden was amalgamated with the Protectorate in 1963 to form the Federation of South Arabia. This was opposed by many Aden citizens and rioting followed. In June 1964, a constitutional conference agreed that the Federation would accede to independence in 1968, but the violence continued. The British government tried to secure an orderly transfer of power by establishing a broad-based provisional administration in July 1967, including the Front for the Liberation of Occupied South Yemen (FLOSY), the National Liberation Front (NLF) and the sultans. However, the nationalists refused to co-operate with the federal authorities and in Sept. 1967 the British government entered negotiations with them alone. The last British troops were pulled out of Aden in Nov. 1967 and the People's Republic of Yemen was proclaimed by the NLF, the dominant nationalist group, with Qahtan ash-Sha'abi as its first president. He resigned in June 1969 and was replaced by Rubayi Ali. The following November, Yemen became a People's Democratic Republic. Fighting broke out with the Yemen Arab Republic (North Yemen) in Sept. 1972, but a peace agreement providing for eventual unification was signed the following month. Pres. Rubayi was deposed in June 1978 by his radical rival Abdalfattah Ismail, who reorganized the National Front (NF), established in 1975, into the Yemen Socialist Party (YSP) and signed a 20-year friendship treaty with the Soviet Union in Oct. 1979. Renewed fighting with North Yemen broke out in 1979 but ended with another agreement on unification.

In Apr. 1980, Pres. Ismail was replaced by Ali Nasser Muhammad who pursued a more moderate policy, restoring diplomatic relations with Oman and Saudi Arabia in 1983. Following a cabinet reshuffle in Feb. 1985, former president Ismail returned from exile in Moscow and was reappointed to the YSP Central committee along with many of Pres. Muhammad's critics. On 13 Jan. 1986 Pres. Muhammad tried to purge his opponents in the political bureau, killing Abdalfattah Ismail and other leaders. Heavy fighting between rival factions continued until 28 Jan. when Pres. Muhammad fled to Ethiopia. Haider Abu Bakr al Attas, the former prime minister, became president on 8 Feb. Subsequently, Pres. Muhammad's supporters within the administration were purged and, in Dec. 1987, death sentences were passed on 35 conspirators, 19 of them in absentia. A joint oil exploration company was established with North Yemen in May 1988 and in October Pres. Attas visited Oman, the first visit by a PDR Yemen head of state.

Progress towards Yemen's unification dramatically increased in late 1989, culminating in the publication of a draft joint constitution for a unified nation on 1 Dec. and a summit meeting of the two leaders on 23–26 Dec. The border was finally opened in Feb. 1990 and unification expected imminently.

CONSTITUTION AND GOVERNMENT

Executive and legislature

Overall authority is in the hands of the ruling party. The president is elected for a five-year term (most recently in Nov. 1986) by a presidium which is itself elected by the 111-member Supreme People's Council (SPC).

Present government (Feb. 1990)

Head of state, Chairman of the Presidium of the Supreme People's Council Haider Abu Bakr al Attas

Chairman of Council of Ministers (Prime Minister) Dr Yasin Said Numan

Other Principal Members of the Council of Ministers Salih Munassar as-Siyayli (Deputy Chairman; Internal Affairs); Saleh Abu Bakr Bin Hussain (Deputy Chairman; Energy and Minerals); Dr Abdel Aziz ad-Dali (Foreign Affairs); Said Salih Salim (National Security); Salih Ubayd Ahmed (Defence); Said Ahmed Bakr al-Dinawi (Finance).

Ruling party

Yemen Socialist Party.

Secretary-general Ali Salim al-Bid.

Assistant secretary-general Salim Salih Muhammad.

Full politburo members Ali Salim al-Bid; Haider Abu Bakr al Attas; Salih Munassar as-Siyayli; Salim Salih Muhammad; Dr Abdel Aziz ad-Dali; Dr Yasin Said Numan; Muhammad Said Abdullah Mohsin; Said Salih Salim; Fadl Mohsin Abdullah.

Members of the secretariat Salim Salih Muhammad; Fadl Mohsin Abdullah; Muhammad Said Abdullah Muhsin; Dr Salim Umar Bukayr; Shafal Umar Ali.

Justice

The system of law is based on Islamic law, particularly in personal matters, and influenced by English common law principles in the commercial law area. The highest court is the Federal High Court, with a role in the interpretation of the constitution. At the local level, justice is administered through the magistrates' courts. The death penalty is in force. There were more than five executions between 1985 and mid-1988. Offences: treason.

National symbols

Flag. Three horizontal stripes of red, white and black with a light blue isosceles triangle charged with a red five-pointed star based on the hoist.

Festival. 14 Oct. (National Day).

Vehicle registration plate. ADN.

INTERNATIONAL RELATIONS

Affiliations

NAM; ICO; Arab League; Comecon (observer).

Defence

Total Armed Forces: 27,500 (perhaps 18,000 conscripts). Terms of service: two years. Reserves: Army 45,000.

Army: 24,000; 470 main battle tanks (T-34/-54/-55/-62).

Navy: 1,000; ten patrol and coastal combatants.

Air Force: 2,500 (may be some Soviet and Cuban aircrew); 117 combat aircraft (bombers: I1–28; fighters: MiG-17/-21/-27, Su-20/-22); 12 armed helicopters.

ECONOMY

Currency

The unit is the dinar, divided into 1,000 fils.

National finance

Budget. The 1987 budget, in US$, was for expenditure of 848 million and revenue of 474 million.

Balance of payments. The balance of payments, in US$ (current account, 1987) was a deficit of 178 million.

Inflation. 0.8%.

Gross Domestic Product

Estimated total GDP US$840 million, per capita US$480 (overall size of economy ranking 148 in the world).

Economically active population. The total number of persons active in the economy was 477,000.

Sector	% of workforce	% of GDP
industry	24	23
agriculture	45	16
services*	31	61

* services figure includes elements unassigned to other categories.

Energy and mineral resources

Oil and gas. Oil reserves were located in 1987 in the Shabwa district by Soviet prospectors. A pipeline from Shabwa to Bir Ali is currently under construction. Exploratory drilling is carried out in other regions by a number of Western companies. Crude oil output: (1988) 687 million tons/624 million tonnes.

Electricity. Capacity: 245,000 kW; production: 601 million kWh; 250 kWh per capita (1988).

Bioresources

Agriculture. 1% of the land is arable. Abyan cotton is the chief cash crop. Subsistence crops include sorghum; sesame; millet; wheat; barley; dates; qat. The modernization and expansion of South Yemen's irrigation systems continues.

Crop production: (1987 in 1,000 tons/tonnes) millet 94/85; wheat 19/17; cotton seed 11/10; cotton lint 5.5/5; sesame 3.3/3; barley 2.2/2.

Livestock numbers: (1987) cattle 96,000; goats 1.4 million; sheep 0.93 million; poultry 2 million.

Forestry. 7% of the land is covered by forest or woodland.

Fisheries. Catch: (1985) 88,184 tons/80,000 tonnes.

Industry and commerce

Industry. South Yemen's main industries are petroleum refining (operates on imported crude oil); fishing. A number of paint and textile factories constitute the country's chief light industrial activities.

Commerce. Exports: (1987) US$54 million or 5.3% of GNP. Imports: $497 million or 49.2% of GNP. Exported goods included cotton; hides; skins; dried and processed fish. Imported commodities were largely grain; consumer goods; crude oil; machinery; chemicals. Partners in export trade were Japan; YAR (North Yemen); Singapore. Imports were received in quantity from USSR; Australia; UK.

Trade with UK. South Yemen imported UK goods worth £20.86 million in 1988; exports to the UK totalled £1.83 million.

COMMUNICATIONS

Railways

There are no railways in the People's Democratic Republic of Yemen.

Roads

There are 6,521 miles/10,495 km of roads, of which 843 miles/1,356 km are bituminized.

Aviation

Alyemda (Democratic Yemen Airlines) provides domestic and international services (main airport is Aden Civil Airport, 6.8 miles/11 km from Khormaksar). Passengers: (1982) 190,000.

Shipping

The major ports are Aden, Al Khalf and Nishtun on the Gulf of Aden. The merchant marine has four ships of 1,000 GRT or over.

Telecommunications

There are 15,000 telephones and a small system of open-wire, radio-relay, multiconductor cable and radio communications stations. There are 300,000 radios and 40,000 televisions (1986). The Democratic Yemen Broadcasting Service operates both the radio and TV services.

EDUCATION AND WELFARE

Education

Schools. An estimated 310,840 pupils attend 989 primary schools with an additional 31,530 pupils in secondary education at 62 schools. The total school population is above 400,000.

Universities. There is one state university in Aden, with 4,386 students. There are nine teacher-training colleges.

Literacy. 25%.

Health

652 doctors serve 54 hospitals with a total of 4,499 beds (one per 556 members of the population).

YUGOSLAVIA

Socijalistička Federativna Republika Jugoslavija
(Socialist Federal Republic of Yugoslavia)

GEOGRAPHY

Located in south-eastern central Europe, Yugoslavia covers an area of 98,739 miles²/255,800 km² divided into six federal republics (Serbia, Croatia, Slovenia, Montenegro, Bosnia-Hercegovina and Macedonia). Mountains dominate nearly 75% of the total area in the central, north-western, eastern and south-eastern regions. The Slovenian Alps, situated in the north-west, rise to a high point of 9,393 ft/2,863 m at Triglav in the Julian range (Julijske Alpe). Along the Adriatic coast, the limestone topography of the Dinaric Alps merges to the south with a complex of transverse mountain ranges dissected by steep river valleys including the northward-flowing Morava and the southward-flowing Vardar. In the north, the Drava, Sava and Danube rivers irrigate the most fertile agricultural regions. Rural-urban migration constitutes the chief demographic trend, approximately 10% of the population live in the cities of Belgrade and Zagreb. 28% of the land is arable and 36% is forested.

Climate

Largely moderate (European) continental with cold winters (temperatures decreasing from 30°F/–1°C on the Danube plain to 18°F/–8°C above 7,218 ft/ 2,200 m) and hot summers (70°F/21°C on the plains). Coastal areas experience a Mediterranean-type climate with milder, moist winters and hot, dry summers. Rainfall varies from 30 in/760 mm along the coast to 98 in/2,500 mm in the Alpine regions. Belgrade: Jan. 32°F/0.°C. July 72°F/22°C. Average annual rainfall 24 in/610 mm. Sarajevo: Jan. 31°F/ –0.5°C. July 67°F/19.6°C. Average annual rainfall 34 in/856 mm. Split: Jan. 47°F/8.5°C. July 78°F/25.6°C. Average annual rainfall 34 in/870 mm.

Cities and towns

Belgrade (capital)	1,470,073
Osijek	867,646
Zagreb	768,700
Niš	643,470
Skopje	505,547
Sarajevo	448,519
Ljubljana	305,211
Novi Sad	257,685
Split	235,922
Priština	210,040

Population

Total population is 23,724,919 of which 46.5% live in urban areas. Population density is 240 persons per mile^2/91.6 per km^2. Ethnic composition: (at the last census, 1981), 36.3% Serb; 19.7% Croat; 8.9% Bosnian Muslim; 7.8% Slovene; 7.7% Albanian; 5.9% Macedonian; 5.4% unspecified Yugoslav; 2.5% Montenegrin; 1.9% Hungarian.

Birth rate 1.5%. **Death rate** 0.9%. **Rate of population increase** (1980–87) 0.6%. **Age distribution** under 15 = 24.1%; over 65 = 8.5%. **Life expectancy** female 75; male 68; average 71.

Religion

Predominantly Christian. 50% Eastern Orthodox (Serbian and Macedonian Orthodox); 30% Roman Catholic; 1% Protestant; 9% Muslim. The Yugoslavian Jewish community is approximately 6,000-strong.

Language

Serbo-Croatian, Macedonian and Slovene are all official languages (South Slav). The two strands that combine to form Serbo-Croat ie Serbian and Croatian, have been claimed as separate languages in the past. Serbian may be written using the Cyrillic alphabet.

HISTORY

Intermittently inhabited from Lower Palaeolithic times, the territory of present-day Yugoslavia after around 2000 BC was home to the Illyrians. These were subjugated by Rome between 168 BC and AD 9, their lands becoming the Roman provinces of Illyricum and Moesia; Roman cities included Sirmium (modern Sremska Mitrovica), an imperial capital in the late 3rd century. With the decline of Rome in the 4th century Illyricum and Moesia came under the nominal control of the Eastern Empire at Constantinople, but they were laid waste by the invading Huns and Bulgars in the 5th century and the Avars in the late 6th century. As vassals of the Avars, Slavs arrived in the region in the late 6th and early 7th centuries, becoming vassals of the Byzantine Empire after a Byzantine victory over the Avars in AD 626.

During the 7th century two Slavic tribes, the Croats and the Serbs, came to prominence. In the north and west the Croats broke away from the influence of Byzantium in 879 and oriented themselves politically and spiritually towards Rome, but this led to the end of Croat independence in 1089 when the Pope invited the Hungarians to invade Croatia, resulting in the election of the Hungarian King to the Croatian throne. To the south and east, the Eastern Orthodox Christian Serbs were absorbed into the Bulgarian Empire at the turn of the 10th century but later enjoyed a period of autonomy under Byzantine suzerainty. In 1036 Stephen Vojislav, prince of Zeta, broke away from the influence of Byzantium, and began to annex neighbouring Serbian principalities. His successor, King Constantin Bodin, continued this expansionist policy, but upon his death in 1101 the nascent Serbian state collapsed into civil war. From 1165 a Serbian Empire was created under the Nemanjids dynasty, reaching its height under King Stefan Dušan (r.1331–55). However, the Empire did not long outlast Dušan's death, falling prey to the empire of the Ottoman Turks to the east: in 1371 Macedonia became a Turkish vassal, and on 15 June 1389 the Ottoman sultan Murad I decisively defeated the Serbian forces of Prince Lazar at the Battle of Kosovo.

In 1463 Bosnia, the last major Serbian outpost in the Balkans, fell to the Ottoman Turks, leaving only tiny Montenegro independent in the high mountains along the Adriatic coast. During the reign of Suleiman I ('the Magnificent', r.1520–66) the Ottoman Empire in the Balkans reached its height: the Turks sacked Belgrade in 1521, and in 1526 they defeated the Hungarians at Mohács, but in 1529 they failed to take Vienna, setting the limit to their westward expansion. Only after 1683 when the Turks again failed to take Vienna did Ottoman power in the Balkans begin to wane, and under the Treaty of Carlowitz (1699) the Turks ceded to the Austrian Habsburgs Hungary, Transylvania, Croatia and large parts of northern Serbia (although the Serbian territories were regained by the Turks in 1739). In 1809, during the Napoleonic Wars, Austria was forced to cede its Balkan territories to France, which organized them into the Illyrian Provinces (they were regained by Austria following France's defeat in 1815). With a population of Serbs, Croats and Slovenes, and a constitutional government, the Illyrian Provinces have been described as the first Yugoslav state. In Serbia there was an anti-Turkish uprising in 1804–13, while as a result of the Russo-Turkish war of 1828–29 the Russians obliged the Turks (under the 1829 Treaty of Adrianople) to respect Serbian autonomy.

Serbia achieved full independence as a principality in 1878 under the Treaty of San Stefano (which followed Ottoman defeat in the Russo-Turkish war of 1877–78). Shortly afterwards amendments to the Treaty of San Stefano, made by the Congress of Berlin, recognized Serbian and Montenegrin independence, but mandated Austria to occupy Bosnia-Hercegovina and left Macedonia under Ottoman control. The period 1878–1914 in the Balkans witnessed increasing international conflict, as local nationalist aspirations and rivalries clashed with the regional interests of the Great Powers. In 1909 the Austro-Hungarian Empire annexed Bosnia-Hercegovina, and only pressure from Germany averted war with Serbia and its ally, Russia. In the First Balkan War of 1912 a Serbian-Bulgarian-Greek military alliance pushed the Turks virtually out of Europe, but in the following year the victorious allies fell out amongst themselves, and the Second Balkan War resulted in a joint Serbian-Greek defeat of Bulgaria. On 28 June 1914, World War I began when a Serb revolutionary, Gavrilo Princip, assassinated the Austrian archduke Franz Ferdinand in the Bosnian capital, Sarajevo. The resultant conflagration saw Austria-Hungary, Germany and the Ottoman Turks allied against Serbia, Russia, France and Great Britain.

Upon the collapse of the Central Powers in Nov. 1918 the Serbian King Alexander united Serbia and Montenegro with the former Austro-Hungarian territories of Slovenia, Croatia and Bosnia-Hercegovina, and on 1 Dec. 1918 the Kingdom of Serbs, Croats and Slovenes was proclaimed. It was renamed Yugoslavia in 1929. A new unitary Constitution was promulgated in 1921 and there followed a period of democratic government, albeit marred by worsening Croat-Serb rivalry. In 1929 King Alexander imposed his own dictatorship. This exacerbated Croat hostility to centralization and Serbian dominance, and on 9 Oct. 1934 the King was assassinated in France by Croat separatist terrorists. A regency under Prince Paul ruled the country thereafter in the name of the child-king Peter II. Internationally, Yugoslavia was threatened by the growing power of Nazi Germany after 1933, and the hostility of the Soviet Union, which encouraged the Communist Party of Yugoslavia (CPY – formed in the Soviet Union in 1919 and outlawed in Yugoslavia in 1921) to work towards the break-up of the country. Yugoslavia was overrun by German armies in Apr. 1941; a puppet state of Croatia was created (incorporating much of Bosnia-Hercegovina) and the rest of the country was partitioned between Germany, Italy, Hungary and Bulgaria. Two rival Yugoslav guerrilla groups developed, the Serbian royalist Chetniks led by Draža Mihailović and the Communist Partisans led by Josip Broz Tito (head of the CPY since 1937). Attempts at co-operation failed early in the war, and thereafter the Chetniks frequently collaborated with the occupiers against the Partisans, prompting the Allies in 1943 to transfer their support from Mihailović to Tito. In 1943 a provisional government known as the Anti-Fascist National Liberation Council (AVNOJ) was formed with Tito as prime minister, and in 1945 it took power after the Partisans and the Soviet Red Army had expelled the Nazis.

The provisional government on 29 Nov. 1945 abolished the monarchy and established the Federative People's Republic of Yugoslavia, and in Jan. 1946 a Constitution was adopted which was modelled on the Soviet Constitution of 1936. Industry, transport and banking were nationalized, and collectivization of agriculture began. Tito broke with the Soviet Union in June 1948, unwilling to allow Yugoslavia to be merely a Soviet satellite. Thereafter a self-managed and progressively decentralized Yugoslav version of socialism was implemented in new Constitutions of 1953, 1963 (when the country was renamed the Socialist Federal Republic of Yugoslavia) and 1974. Tito died on 4 May 1980, and was replaced both as head of state and of the party (renamed the League of Communists of Yugoslavia in 1952) by collective leaderships.

Steady economic progress took place in the 1950s and 1960s, but by the 1980s the economy was in crisis, burdened with heavy foreign debt and rampant inflation. In the 1970s Croatian nationalism re-surfaced, involving mass demonstrations within Yugoslavia and a terrorist campaign by Croat emigrés against Yugoslav targets abroad. Between March and May 1981 the majority Albanian population in Serbia's Kosovo province staged an uprising against their treatment by the Serbian administration. Ethnic unrest centred on Kosovo flared up again from mid-1988 because of Serbian moves drastically to curtail provincial autonomy. The hardline position of the Serbian political leadership, which favoured a centralized state with a strong authoritarian ruling party, brought it into conflict during 1988–89 with the more liberal leaderships in Slovenia and Croatia, which favoured still greater decentralization and political pluralism.

Internationally, Yugoslavia adopted a non-aligned foreign policy after the split with the Soviet Union (in 1961 it became a founder member of the Non-Aligned Movement). In Mar. 1988 a Soviet-Yugoslav rapprochement took place when Soviet leader Mikhail Gorbachev visited Yugoslavia and reaffirmed declarations negotiated between Tito and Nikita Khrushchev in 1955 and 1956 concerning the sovereignty and independence of the Soviet and Yugoslav social systems.

CONSTITUTION AND GOVERNMENT

Executive and legislature

The ruling party exercises an effective monopoly of real power. The collective state presidency has eight members (one from each republic and province) elected for five years (most recently in May 1989) by the bicameral Federal Assembly (parliament). Within the collective state presidency there are annual rotations of the offices of president and vice-president of the presidency. Deputies to the Federal Assembly, which is made up of the Federal Chamber (220 seats) and the Chamber of Republics and Provinces (88 seats), are elected by a multi-tiered system of communal assemblies, and serve for four years. Each new Federal Assembly elects the Federal Executive Council (cabinet).

Present government

President of the Collective State Presidency Dr Janez Drnovsek

Vice-President Borisav Jović

Members of the Presidency Stipe Suvar; Riza Sapunziju; Nenad Bucin; Dr Dragutin Zelenović; Bogic Bogicević; Dr Vasil Tupurkovski.

President of the Federal Executive Council (Federal Prime Minister) Ante Marković

Other Principal Members of the Federal Executive Council Aleksandar Mitrović (Vice-President); Zivko Pregl (Vice-President); Budimir Loncar (Federal Secretary for Foreign Affairs); Col-Gen. Veljko Kadijevic (Federal Secretary for National Defence); Col-Gen. Petar Gracanin (Federal Secretary for Internal Affairs); Branko Zekan (Federal Secretary for Finance); Franc Horvat (Federal Secretary for Foreign Economic Relations).

Ruling party

League of Communists of Yugoslavia (Savez Komunista Jugoslavije).

President of the central committee presidium Milan Pancevski.

Secretary to the Presidium Stefan Korosec.

Elected members of the presidium Ivan Brigić and Ugljesa Uzelac (Bosnia-Hercegovina); Marko Lolić (Croatia); Milan Pancevski and Ljubomir Varoslija (Macedonia); Miomir Grbovic and Perko Vukotic (Montenegro); Dušan Ckrebic and Petar Skudric

(Serbia); Stefan Korosec and Boris Muzevic (Slovenia). There are vacancies for Croatia, Kosovo and Vojvodina.

Ex-officio members of the presidium Dr Nijaz Durakovic (Bosnia-Hercegovina); Ivica Racan (Croatia); Rahman Morina (Kosovo); Petar Gosev (Macedonia); Milica Pejanović (Montenegro); Bogdan Trifunovic (Serbia); Cyril Ribicić (Slovenia); Nadeljko Sipovac (Vojvodina); Col-Gen. Petar Simic (People's Army).

Executive secretaries Marko Lolic; Vukasin Loncar; Boris Muzevic; Stanislav Stojanovic; Ljubomir Varoslija.

Administration

Yugoslavia is a federation of six constituent republics: Bosnia-Hercegovina, Croatia, Macedonia, Montenegro, Serbia and Slovenia. Within the republic of Serbia there are two autonomous provinces, Kosovo and Vojvodina, whose status has been the focus of much nationalist unrest.

INTERNATIONAL RELATIONS

Affiliations

NAM; OECD (observer); Comecon (associate); joint committee with EFTA.

Defence

Total Armed Forces: 188,000 (103,500 conscripts). Terms of service: 12 months. Reserves: 510,000.
Army: 144,000; 1,570 main battle tanks (T-34/54/-55/-72, M-84/-47/-4); 13 light tanks (PT-76).
Navy: 11,000 inclusive 900 marines, 2,300 coastal defence; five submarines; three frigates (Soviet Koni); 71 patrol and coastal combatants.
Air Force: 33,000; 431 combat aircraft (MiG-21F/PF/M/bis,MiG-21U/-29, P-2 Kraguj, Jastreb, Super Galeb, Orao); some 150 armed helicopters.

ECONOMY

Currency

The unit is the dinar, divided into 100 paras.

Name	Area (miles^2/km^2)	Population	Capital
Bosnia & Hercegovina	19,736/ 51,129	4,124,256	Sarajevo
Croatia	27,824/ 56,538	4,601,469	Zagreb
Macedonia	9,925/ 25,713	1,909,136	Skopje
Montenegro	5,331/ 13,812	584,310	Titograd
Serbia	21,604/ 55,968	9,313,676	Belgrade
Kosovo	4,202/ 10,887	1,584,441	Pristina
Vojvodina	8,301/ 21,506	2,034,772	Novi Sad
Slovenia	7,817/ 20,251	1,891,864	Ljubljana

*Figures for Serbia excluded the autonomous provinces of Kosovo and Vojvodina.

Republican and Provincial Presidents Bosnia-Hercegovina – Dr Obrad Piljak; Croatia – Ivo Latin; Kosovo – Hisan Kajdomcaj; Macedonia – Jezdimir Bogdanski; Montenegro – Branko Kostic; Serbia – Slobodan Milosevic; Slovenia – Janez Stanovnik; Vojvodina – Jugoslav Kostic.

Republican and Provincial Prime Ministers Bosnia-Hercegovina – Marko Ceranic; Croatia – Antun Milovic; Kosovo – Jusuf Zejnulaju; Macedonia – Gligorije Gogovski; Montenegro – Dr Radoje Kontic; Serbia – Stanko Radmilović; Slovenia – Dušan Sinigoj; Vojvodina – Rademan Bozović.

Justice

The system of law is based on codified civil law modified by communist theories; the highest court is the Supreme Court at federal level, with Supreme Courts also in each constituent republic (which enact their own criminal legislation). At the local level, the District Courts and County Tribunals are presided over by judges assisted by lay assessors, both being popularly elected. The death penalty is in force. There were four executions between 1985 and mid-1988. Offences were murder.

National symbols

Flag. Three horizontal stripes of blue, white and red; in the centre there is a red five-pointed star edged with yellow.

Festivals. 1–2 May (Labour Days); 4 July (Fighters' Day); 29–30 Nov. (Republic Day).

Vehicle registration plate. YU.

National finance

Budget. The 1989 budget, in US$, was for expenditure of 4,500 million and revenue of 4,500 million. Main items of expenditure are defence (55% of federal spending); housing and welfare 11.2%.

Balance of payments. The balance of payments, in US$ (current account, 1987) was a surplus of 817 million.

Inflation. 230%.

Gross Domestic Product

Estimated total GDP US$59,960 million, per capita US$6,540 (overall size of economy ranking 38 in the world).

Economically active population. The total number of persons active in the economy was 9,600,000; unemployed: 15%.

Sector	% of workforce	% of GDP
industry	27	43
agriculture	22	11
services*	51	45

* services figure includes elements unassigned to other categories.

Energy and mineral resources

Oil and gas. Crude oil output: (1988) 4.1 million tons/3.7 million tonnes.

Minerals. Yugoslavia's varied mineral deposits include iron ore mines of considerable importance at Vares and Ljubija. Siderite and limonite ores are extracted around Sanski Most, Prijedor and Topusko. Other minerals mined include copper; lead; chrome; gold; antimony. Output (1985 1,000 tons/tonnes) coal 440/400; lignite 62,429/56,635; bauxite 3,582/3,250; manganese ore 35/32; salt 452/410; iron ore 6,038/5,478; copper ore 28,843/26,166; lead and zinc ore 5,060/4,590; antimony ore 78/71; pyrite 559/507; magnesite 460/417; gold (1983) 9,343 lb/4,238 kg; silver 343,915 lb/156,000 kg.

Electricity. Capacity: 20,000,000 kW; production: 83,500 million kWh; 3,540 kWh per capita. Approximately 35% of the total output is hydroelectrically generated. The nuclear plant at Krsko has a 664 mW production capacity.

Bioresources

Agriculture. 28% of the land is arable. 3% is under permanent cultivation and 25% is meadow or pasture. 20.1 million acres/8.14 million ha of the total cultivated area (24.3 million acres/9.85 million ha) is privately farmed with the remaining 4.25 million/1.72 million belonging to an estimated 3,474 agricultural combines. Main crops are corn; wheat; tobacco; sugar beet; sunflowers.

Crop production: (1986 in 1,000 tons/tonnes) maize 13,807/12,526; sugar beet 6,172/5,599; wheat 5,232/4,746; potatoes 2,922/2,651; sunflowers 495/449; tobacco 106/96; rye 82/74; grapes 1,707/1,549; plums 772/700; apples 702/637; wine 4,317 million pints/7.6 million hectolitres.

Livestock numbers: (1987 in millions) cattle 5.03; sheep 7.82; pigs 8.46; poultry 79.7.

Forestry. 23,192,806 acres/9,396,000 ha or 26% of the land area is forested. Beech, oak and fir are the predominant species. Timber cut: (1986) 804.8 million ft^3/22.79 million m^3.

Fisheries. Saltwater catch: (1986) 56,749 tons/51,482 tonnes; freshwater catch 28,750 tons/26,082 tonnes.

Industry and commerce

Industry. Industrial activity is concentrated in the north-west. The main industries with their respective outputs given in 1,000 tonnes for 1986 are steel 4,519; cement 9,128; pig-iron 3,063; sulphuric acid 1,595; fertilizers 2,700; plastics 774,240 million yd^2/647,358 million m^2 of cotton and 132 million yd^2/110 million m^2 of woollen fabrics were produced in the same year. A total of 228,000 motor vehicles were manufactured.

Commerce. Exports: (1987) US$11,400 million or 7.4% of GNP. Imports: $12,600 million or 8.2% of GNP. Principal exports were in raw materials and semi-manufactures 50%; consumer goods 31%; capital goods and equipment 19%. Imported commodities were chiefly raw materials and semi-manufactures 79%; capital goods and equipment 15%; consumer goods 6%. Export and import trading partners included EC countries 30%; CEMA 45%; less developed countries 14%; US 5%; other 6%.

Trade with UK. Yugoslavia imported UK goods worth £203.1 million in 1988; exports to UK totalled £197.3 million.

Tourism. (1987) 8.91 million visitors.

COMMUNICATIONS

Railways

There are 5,837 miles/9,393 km of railways, of which 2,063 miles/3,320 km are electrified.

Roads

There are 73,165 miles/117,744 km of roads.

Aviation

Jugoslovenski Aerotransport (JAT) and Air Yugoslavia provide international services; Adria Airways provides domestic and international services (main airports are at Belgrade, Dubrovnik, Ljubljana, Sarajevo, Skopje, Titograd and Zagreb). Passengers: (1987) 6.9 million.

Shipping

There are 1,616 miles/2,600 km of inland waterways. Belgrade is the major inland port. Rijeka, Split, Koper, Bar, Ploče are the marine ports. The merchant marine has 269 ships of 1,000 GRT or over. Freight loaded: (1987) 6.7 million tons/6.1 million tonnes; unloaded 21.5 million tons/19.5 million tonnes.

Telecommunications

There are 3.5 million telephones, 4.7 million radios and 4.5 million televisions. Each republic has its own radio and television service, in most cases offering at least two TV channels, and Radio Yugoslavia foreign services are broadcast in ten languages.

EDUCATION AND WELFARE

Education

Eight years of general education is obligatory, followed by 3–4 years of secondary education.

Schools. 140,357 teachers serve 11,978 primary schools with 2,843,253 pupils (one per 20 pupils). Approximately 945,590 pupils attend 1,246 secondary schools and receive instruction from 57,788 teaching staff (one per 16 pupils). There are about 10,600 adult primary school and 38,736 secondary school pupils at 330 institutions. Yugoslavia also supports 1,370 Albanian, 220 Hungarian, 43 Bulgarian, 12 Czech, 33 Slovak, 39 Italian, 38 Romanian, 77 Turkish and two Ukrainian schools for ethnic minorities. 349,654 students are enrolled at 326 higher educational establishments with 17,601 members of staff.

Literacy. 91.5%.

Universities. There are 18 Yugoslavian universities.

Health

51,775 doctors and dentists. There are 142,579 hospital beds available, (one per 166 members of the population) of which 10,107 are in psychiatric departments.

ZAÏRE

République du Zaïre
(Republic of Zaïre)

GEOGRAPHY

Located in central equatorial Africa, Zaïre is the third largest country on the continent occupying a total area of 905,328 miles^2/2,345,410 km^2 divided into nine regions. Approximately 60% of the Congo/Zaïre river basin lies within Zaïre. The densely vegetated central river basin is situated in the north-western part of the country, surrounded by forested plateau formations rising eastwards to meet the Mitumba Mts on the western perimeter of the Great Rift Valley and the Massif du Ruwenzori straddling the Ugandan frontier. Margherita Peak rises 16,765 ft/5,110 m above sea level in the Mount Stanley massif while Karisimbe reaches an elevation of 14,787 ft/4,507 m on the Zaïre-Rwanda border. The River Zaïre/Congo is one of the world's largest rivers, and the second largest (after the Nile) in Africa. Rising in southern Zaïre as the River Lualaba it traverses the continent north, north- westerly, west and south-westerly, fed by innumerable tributaries including the Kasai and Oubangui before emptying into the Atlantic south of Cabinda. 3% of the land area is arable, but nearly 78% is covered by dense tropical rainforest. Over 10% of the population live in Bas-Zaïre and Kinshasa City on less than 24,704 miles^2/64,000 km^2 of the total surface area. Lake Albert, Lake Edward, Lake Kiuu and Lake Tanganyika lie along the eastern frontier.

Climate

Equatorial; hot and humid in the central basin with relatively uniform temperatures all year (75–79°F/24–26°C) and rainfall frequently exceeding 78,7 in/2,000 mm in mountainous areas. South of the equator, wet and dry seasons are well differentiated, lasting Dec.-Mar. and May-Sept. respectively, temperature range 79–91°F/26–33°C. North of the equator the dry season lasts Dec.-Feb. Kinshasa: Jan. 79°F/26.1°C. July 73°F/22.8°C. Average annual rainfall 44.3 in/1,125 mm. Kananga: Jan. 76°F/24.4°C. July 74°F/23.3°C. Average annual rainfall 62.4 in/1,584 mm. Lubumbashi: Jan. 72°F/22.2°C. July 61°F/16.1°C. Average annual rainfall 49 in/1,237 mm.

Cities and towns

Kinshasa (capital)	2,443,876
Kananga	704,211
Lubumbashi	451,332
Mbuji-Mayi	382,632
Kisangani	339,210
Bukavu	209,051
Kikwit	172,450
Matadi	162,396
Mbandaka	149,118
Likasi	146,394

Population

Total population is 34,279,472 of which 44.2% live in urban areas. Population density is 37.9 persons per mile^2/14.6 per km^2. Ethnic composition: the majority of Zaïre's 200 ethnic groups are of Bantu origin. The Mongo, Kongo, Luba (Bantu) and Mangbetu-Azande (Hamitic) peoples constitute 45% of the total population. Other major groups include the Sudanese Azande, Banda and Abarambo in the north, the Nilotic tribes of the north-east and the riverine-forest Pygmies.

Birth rate 4.5%. **Death rate** 1.4%. **Rate of population increase** (1980–87) 2.9%. **Age distribution** under 15 = 46.1%; over 65 = 2.5%. **Life expectancy** female 54; male 51; average 52.

Religion

Nearly 50% Roman Catholic (15.7 million adherents in 1988); 20% Protestant, 10% Kimbanguist (Church of Simon Kimbangu); 10% other Christian/animist sects and traditional beliefs.

Language

French is the official language. Kiswahili is prevalent in the east and is recognized as a national language along with Tshiluba (south), Kikongo (spoken in and around Kinshasa and Bas-Zaïre) and Lingala, the lingua franca. The other 190 or so languages belong to the Bantu, Nilo-Saharan and Pygmy language families.

HISTORY

Early pygmies were joined by migrants of Bantu, Sudanic and Nilotic origin. From the Middle Ages, many great kingdoms were established, including those of Kongo, Kuba, Luba and Lunda. The Kongo was particularly powerful, conquering other coastal states to control much of what is today Angola. The Portuguese arrived in 1482 and relations between the Kongo and Portugal were initially friendly, but by the 17th century the pressures of the European slave trade had begun to destroy the Kongo. Portuguese demands for slaves to work plantations in Brazil became insatiable; warring broke out and the Kongo went into decline. The kingdoms of Kuba, Luba, Lunda and Zande thrived, much of their wealth built on trading in copper, ivory and slaves, with new avenues opened up by Arab slavers who had pushed inland from the East African coast during the 19th century.

The slave trade was challenged by European explorers such as David Livingstone, but as travellers took news of the riches of the African interior home to Europe, so the 'scramble' for control of these regions began. King Leopold II of Belgium staked a claim, cloaking his empire-building designs in humanitarian and scientific objectives. The Berlin Conference (1885) settled various European claims to the region in favour of King Leopold's International Association of the Congo (IAC). The Congo Free State was declared (July 1885), ruled from Brussels by King Leopold without any Belgian government control. The next 23 years was a period of brutal colonization by extortion, forced labour and frequent massacre of Africans who failed to comply. Africans were forced to gather rubber for the state. Those who failed to deliver were often killed. Famine set in as crops were neglected. Protests were voiced in Europe and African resistance spread in a series of rebellions (from 1895). King Leopold, who had accrued enormous personal wealth from rubber, was eventually forced in 1908 (after an international outcry) to hand the Congo Free State to Belgium, which renamed it the Belgian Congo. Belgian rule remained harsh, though the system of forced rubber-gathering was phased out. Copper, gold and diamond mining flourished.

African political associations formed in the 1950s began calling for independence, the most powerful being the Alliance des Ba-Kongo (ABAKO) led by Joseph Kasavubu and Patrice Lumbumba's Mouvement National Congolais (MNC). Riots in Leopoldville (now Kinshasa) in 1959 precipitated the Belgian decision to move hastily and without proper preparation to independence the following year. The MNC won elections (May 1960) and Lumumba became the first prime minister of the Republic of the Congo (30 June) and Kasavubu president. Within days, however, the army mutinied and Katanga province broke away (11 July) under its governor Moise Tshombe, who appealed for (and got) Belgian support. The Lumumbae government appealed for United Nations help, and UN troops were sent in to restore order. Belgians fled the country in panic. A second secessionist state formed in Kasai proved shortlived, but the secession of Katanga, supported by Belgium, was more durable and more significant.

The crisis deepened in Sept. 1960 when Kasavubu broke with Lumumba, and army chief of staff Joseph Mobutu (with the acquiescence of Kasavubu) dismissed Lumumba, later handing him over to his enemies in Katanga (Jan. 1961), where he was murdered. His killing prompted widespread anger at home and abroad. Lumumba supporters formed a rebel government in Stanleyville (now Kisangani) which was not put down until early 1962. Mobutu dominated Leopoldville until a new central government was formed in Feb. 1961; this was replaced in August by the government of Cyrille Adoula.

UN forces, seeking to end the Katanga secession principally by reaching an agreement with Tshombe, became controversially involved in fighting in Elisabethville in Aug. 1961; not until 24 Nov. did the UN Security Council formally empower them to use force to expel foreign mercenaries. By this time UN Secretary General Dag Hammarskjold had been killed in a plane crash on 17 Sept. en route for a meeting with Tshombe.

Tshombe in Dec. 1961 renounced the Katanga secession which ended in Jan. 1983, and he went into exile. When fresh revolts broke out in the centre and east in 1964, based on Kwilu, Tshombe was invited back from exile to become prime minister. Belgian troops helped his government to crush the revolts, recapturing Stanleyville in Nov. 1964. Tshombe scored a success in elections held in April 1965, but was suddenly ousted by Pres. Kasavubu (Oct. 1965) and in the confusion that followed, Gen. Mobutu took control, ousting Kasavubu.

Mobutu has ruled ever since (Nov. 1965). He Africanized all place names the following year, changed the name of the country to Zaïre (1971) and, styling himself Mobutu Sese Seko, he ordered all personal names Africanized (1972), which led to conflicts with the powerful Catholic Church. The sole and ruling party, the Mouvement Populaire de la Révolution (MPR) was formed in 1967. Former Kwilu rebel leader Pierre Mulele, exiled in Brazzaville, was invited home amid promises of amnesty, then executed (1968). Tshombe died in exile in Algeria.

A copper boom in the early 1970s was followed by a disastrous slump as world prices plummeted, generating more unrest. After Angolan independence, exiled soldiers from the Katanga secession invaded Zaïre from Angola (Mar. 1977), sweeping through Shaba province (formerly Katanga). Western and African allies sent troops to help quell the rebellion. In a second invasion of Shaba (May 1978) rebels captured a major mining centre killing over 100 Europeans, and Western governments sent troops to assist Mobutu.

Human-rights organizations have made numerous allegations of atrocities by Zaïrean troops; while largely rejecting the charges, Mobutu agreed to a major military retraining programme, condemned widespread corruption and offered amnesties to political exiles. An attempt to form a second political party was crushed (1982) and insurgencies put down (1984). Repeated student protests (since 1968) against economic strife reached a head with a peaceful march on the presidential palace (Oct. 1988) and riots (Feb. 1989) in which up to 27 students were killed by troops. Relations with Belgium hit crisis point in late 1988, over debt repayments and criticism of Mobutu's regime in the Belgian press.

CONSTITUTION AND GOVERNMENT

Executive and legislature

The leader of the sole legal political party is ex officio head of state, with executive powers, and appoints the members of the National Executive Council (Cabinet) as well as determining the composition of the party's political bureau. The unicameral National Legislative Council (CNL) is elected for a five-year term by compulsory, direct and universal adult suffrage, on the basis of a list of candidates nominated by the ruling party, whose central committee has the power to overrule the legislature's decisions. Last elections Sept. 1987.

Present government

President; Armed Forces C.-in-C.; President of the National Executive Council and of the National Legislative Council; Minister of Defence and Veterans' Affairs Marshal Mobutu Sese Seko

Principal Members of the Executive Council (State Commissioners) Kengo wa Dondo (First State Commissioner); Nimy Mayidika Ngimbi (Deputy First State Commissioner for Social and Cultural Affairs; State Commissioner for Citizens' Rights and

Liberties); Mwando Nsimba (Deputy First State Commissioner for Economic, Financial and Monetary Affairs; State Commissioner for Rural Development); Mozagba Ngbuka (Deputy First State Commissioner for Political and Administrative Affairs; State Commissioner for Territorial Administration and Decentralization); Gen. Singa Boyenge Mosambay (Territorial Security); Nguza Karl I. Bond (Foreign Affairs); Nyiwa Mobutu (International Co-operation); Katanga Mukumadi ya Mutumba (Finance); Mananga wa Pholo (Budget).

Ruling party

Popular Movement of the Revolution (Mouvement Populaire de la Révolution).

Chairman Marshal Mobutu Sese Seko.

Members of the political bureau Bapa-Banze Mudiangombe; Derikoye Tita Avungara; Engulu Baanga Mpopgo Bakokele-Lokanga; Epee Ganbwa; Ileo Songo Amba; Kakule Mbahingana; Kankolongo Ndaye; Kishiba Kasangula; Kithima Bin Ramazani; Kptitvboumansi Benga Ntupdu; Mosagba Ngbuka; Ndolela Siki Konde; Nsona Kukabusu; Nyembo Mwana Ngongo; Takizal Luyan Muis Mbingin; Wembi Kakesi.

Justice

The system of law is based on Belgian civil codes and indigenous legal traditions. The highest court is the Supreme Court at Kinshasa. Courts of first instance deal with important cases within their area of jurisdiction, the country being divided for this purpose into 32 areas; in each province, and in Kinshasa, there is a court of appeal. The death penalty is in force. There were at least four executions between 1985 and mid-1988. Offences: armed robbery with murder; armed rebellion.

National symbols

Flag. Light green field with a yellow disc in its centre on which a human arm holding a brown torch with red flames is depicted.

Festivals. 4 Jan. (Commemoration of the Martyrs of Independence); 1 May (Labour Day); 20 May (Anniversary of the Mouvement Populaire de la Révolution); 24 June (Anniversary of Zaïre currency, Promulgation of the 1967 Constitution and Day of the Fishermen); 30 June (Independence Day); 1 Aug. (Parents' Day); 14 Oct. (Youth Day, birthday of Pres. Mobutu); 27 Oct. (Anniversary of the country's change of name to Zaïre); 17 Nov. (Army Day); 24 Nov (Anniversary of the Second Republic).

Vehicle registration plate. ZRE.

INTERNATIONAL RELATIONS

Affiliations

NAM; OAU; ACP; Francophonie.

Defence

Total Armed Forces: 51,000 inclusive Gendarmerie. Terms of service: voluntary.

Army: 22,000; some 50 tanks (Ch Type-62).

Navy: 1,500 inclusive 600 marines; four patrol and coastal combatants.

Air Force: 2,500; 28 combat aircraft (Mirage-5M/-5DM, MB-326K, AT-6G).

Para-military: 25,000 (Gendarmerie); 25,000 (Civil Guard).

ECONOMY

Currency

The unit is the zaïre, divided into 100 makuta.

National finance

Budget. The 1988 budget, in US$, was for expenditure of 1,600 million and revenue of 878 million.

Balance of payments. The balance of payments, in US$ (current account, 1987) was a deficit of 851 million.

Inflation. 90.4%.

Gross Domestic Product

Estimated total GDP US$5,770 million, per capita US$170 (overall size of economy ranking 78 in the world).

Economically active population. The total number of persons active in the economy was 15,000,000.

Sector	% of workforce	% of GDP
industry	13	33
agriculture	75	32
services*	12	35

* services figure includes elements unassigned to other categories.

Energy and mineral resources

Oil and gas. Zaïre's large potential energy and mineral resources have not been able to prevent the country's recent economic difficulties. Zaïre has large offshore petroleum reserves, estimated at 140 million bbls. Petroleum revenue represents about 20% of government income. Crude oil production in 1988 was 1.5 million tons/1.4 million tonnes.

Minerals. The major source of Zaïre's wealth is its copper mines. Other minerals include cobalt (65% of world's reserves); cadmium; gold; silver; manganese; tin; germanium; zinc; uranium; radium; bauxite; iron ore; coal; hydropower potential. Zaïre is the world's largest producer of industrial and gem diamonds.

Electricity. Zaïre has great hydroelectric potential, and hydroelectric power stations produce over 90% of electricity. Capacity: 2.5 million kW; production: 5,547 million kWh; 170 kWh per capita (1988).

Bioresources

Agriculture. 3% of land is put to arable use, 4% is meadow and pasture. Agricultural exports are hampered by the lack of infrastructure.

Crop production: (1987) cash crops are coffee; palm-oil; rubber; quinine. Food crops are cassava 17 million tons/16 million tonnes; plantains 1.6 million tons/1.5 million tonnes; sugar cane 1.19 million tons/1.08 million tonnes; maize; bananas. Zaïre is an illegal producer of cannabis for the international trade.

Livestock numbers: cattle 1.4 million; sheep 777,000; goats 2.9 million; pigs 792,000; poultry 19 million.

Forestry. Nearly 80% is forest and woodland. The potential for exploitation of timber reserves is not developed.

Fisheries. Total catch: (1985) 112,435 tons/102,000 tonnes. There is very little sea fishing, most fish is caught inland.

Industry and commerce

Industry. Copper is a key export earner, and the country's economy is very dependent on international copper prices. Mining and mineral processing account for one-third of GDP and two-thirds of total export earnings. Other industries include foodstuffs; tobacco; cement; textiles; footwear; cigarettes.

Commerce. Exports: (f.o.b. 1987) US$1,800 million, including copper 37%; coffee 24%; diamonds 12%; cobalt; crude oil. Main trading partners US; Belgium; France; West Germany; Italy; UK; Japan. Imports: (f.o.b. 1987) US$1,600 million, mainly consumer goods; foodstuffs; mining and other machinery; transport equipment. Main trading partners US; Belgium; France; West Germany; Italy; Japan.

Trade with UK. In 1988 Zaïre exported goods worth £7.7 million to the UK, and imported goods worth £26.1 million from the UK.

Tourism. 1986 51,000 visitors.

COMMUNICATIONS

Railways

There are 2,952 miles/4,750 km of railways, of which 533 miles/858 km are electrified.

Roads

There are 90,101 miles/145,000 km of roads.

Aviation

Air Zaïre, SARL, Scibe Airlift Cargo Zaïre (SBZ Cargo) and Zaïre Aero Service, SARL provide domestic and international services (international airports are Ndjili (for Kinshasa), Luano (for Lubumbashi), Bukavu, Goma and Kisangani).

Shipping

There are 15,000 km of inland waterways including various lakes and the Congo and its tributaries. The ports of Zaïre are Matadi, Boma and Banana which are located on the estuary of the Congo where it meets the South Atlantic Ocean. The merchant marine consists of four ships of 1,000 GRT or over. Freight loaded: (1985) 2.3 million tons/2.1 million tonnes; unloaded: 858,692 tons/779,000 tonnes.

Telecommunications

There are 31,200 telephones and a barely adequate wire and radio-relay service. There are 3.4 million radios and 16,000 televisions (1987). Zaïre television is a government commercial station, and La Voix du Zaïre broadcasts domestic radio services in five languages.

EDUCATION AND WELFARE

Education

Between the ages of six and 12 primary education is officially compulsory.

School population. In 1983 some 75% of school-age children were enrolled in primary school and some 49% were enrolled in secondary school. That year there were 4.65 million primary school pupils in 10,065 schools (pupil/teacher ratio 40:1), and 1.6 million secondary school pupils.

Universities. Three universities: Kinshasa, Kisangani and Lubumbashi.

Literacy. 61%.

Health

Up-to-date figures are not available. In 1979 there were some 950 hospitals with 1,900 doctors and 79,000 beds.

ZAMBIA

Republic of Zambia

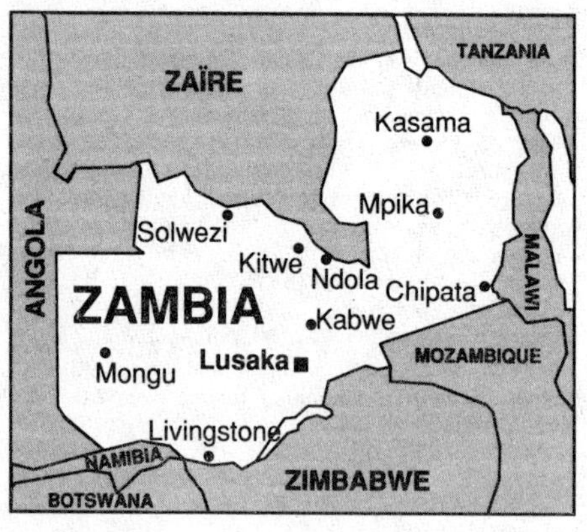

GEOGRAPHY

Zambia is a landlocked country in southern Africa covering a total area of 290,507 miles^2/752,610 km^2 divided into eight provinces, of which the most populous is the north-west central copper belt. Most of Zambian territory comprises an elevated plateau (3,281–4,593 ft/1,000–1,400 m above sea level) with isolated peaks and hill ranges such as the Muchinga mountains rising in the north to 5,866 ft/1,788 m at Chimbwingombi and 6,781 ft/2,067 m (highest point) south-east of Lake Tanganyika. In the northern part of the country, a number of rivers drain southwards to join the River Zambezi, including the River Luangwa which occupies a 350 miles/563 km-long rift valley. The Zambezi River defines part of the Zambia–Zimbabwe border; navigation is impeded by its torrential rapids and falls including Victoria Falls to the south-west. The River Chambeshi drains the north-eastern sector, flowing southwards to one of the major global inland swamps around Lake Bangweulu. 7% of the land is arable and 27% is forested.

Climate

Tropical, with three separate seasons. Two dry seasons, one cool, one hot, lasting May-Aug. and Sept.-Nov. respectively, followed by a rainy season with high temperatures and humidity. Lusaka: Jan. 70°F/21.1°C. July 61°F/16.1°C. Average annual rainfall 33 in/836 mm. Livingstone: Jan. 75°F/23.9°C. July 61°F/16.1°C. Average annual rainfall 26 in/673 mm. Ndola: Jan. 70°F/21.1°C. July 59°F/15°C. Average annual rainfall 51 in/1,293 mm.

Cities and towns

Lusaka (capital)	818,994
Kitwe	449,442
Ndola	418,142
Mufulira	192,323
Kabwe	190,752
Chingola	187,310
Luanshya	160,667
Livingstone	94,637

Kalulushi	89,065
Chililabombwe	79,010

Population

Total population is 7,875,448 of which 49.5% live in urban areas. Population density is 27 persons per mile^2/9.5 per km^2. Ethnic divisions: 98.7% African; 1.1% European; 0.2% other. Principal ethnic groups include the Bantu-speaking Bemba, Nyanja, Barotse, Mambwe, Tumbuka and Swahili peoples and a minority of San-Bushmen.

Birth rate 5.0%. **Death rate** 1.27%. **Rate of population increase** (1980–87) 3%. **Age distribution** under 15 = 48.7%; over 65 = 2.3%. **Life expectancy** female 55; male 51; average 53.

Religion

Between 50–75% of the population are Christians (equal proportions Catholic/Protestant). Christianity has largely displaced traditional animist worship. An estimated 1% of the population is either Muslim or Hindu.

Language

English is the official language, although an estimated 70 indigenous languages are also spoken of which Bemba, Tonga, Nyanja, Lozi, Lunda, Kaonde and Luvale are the most important.

HISTORY

Early humans are believed to have inhabited Zambia some one to two million years ago. Stone-Age sites have been discovered, as well as the Iron-Age remains of Bantu-speaking peoples who probably began arriving in about the 8th century AD. These were the ancestors of the Tonga peoples of southern Zambia. In the modern era, the penetration of what is now Zambia from Zaïre and Angola did not begin until the 17th and 18th centuries.

A Portuguese trading mission was established on Lake Mweru in 1798 and 37 years later a group of Bantu-speaking Ngoni settled in the Lake Nyasa-Luangwa watershed. Dr David Livingstone, the Scottish explorer, reached the upper Zambezi River in 1851 and four years later became the first White man to see the Victoria Falls.

Emissaries from Cecil Rhodes and the British South Africa Company signed treaties with Zambian chiefs during the 1890s which resulted in the Company administering the country until 1924. Northern Rhodesia (the entity formed in 1911 by the merger of two protectorates) passed from the administration of the Company to that of the British government in 1924. The country's mining industry began to develop in the early 20th century; lead and zinc mining at Broken Hill (Kabwe) began in 1906, and railway connections were soon established through to Katanga in the Belgian Congo. The discovery of the mineral wealth of the copper belt along the border with Katanga fuelled rapid development in the 1920s–40s.

In 1935 the country's capital was moved from Livingstone to Lusaka. Northern Rhodesia became part of the Central African Federation in 1953, despite strong internal opposition. African nationalists, with a power base in the mining unions, formed the African National Congress (founded 1951) to resist the prospect of White settler domination of the Federation. The more radical United National Independence Party (UNIP) emerged following the 1958 split in the ANC. UNIP won 55 out of 65 seats in the first elections under universal suffrage, in 1963, and pressed for the dissolution of the Federation (dissolved in Dec. 1963). Northern Rhodesia became the independent Republic of Zambia on 24 Oct. 1964, with UNIP leader Kenneth Kaunda (prime minister since Jan. 1964) as its first president.

Pres. Kaunda embarked upon a policy of industrial and commercial nationalization in 1969, established a one-party state under the hegemony of UNIP in Dec. 1982 and introduced a new constitution the following August in which the Cabinet was subordinate to the UNIP Central Committee. Pres. Kaunda was re-elected for a sixth term of office in 1988.

The Zambian economy was dominated by the mining of copper (which accounted for 86.8% of the country's total export earnings in 1986) and other minerals, including lead, zinc and cobalt. In 1973 the government took control of the country's two largest copper-mining groups, merged in 1982 to form Zambia Consolidated Copper Mines. Being so dependent on a single export, Zambia was vulnerable to fluctuations in the world market price for copper. A deepening economic crisis in 1985–87 led to the imposition of unpopular austerity measures and to civil unrest. In Nov. 1989 the former Army Commander and three other officers went on trial, charged with conspiring to overthrow the government in mid-1988.

The Zambian government has played a major foreign policy role in southern Africa since independence, with its support for the guerrilla movements fighting for the independence of neighbouring Angola, Mozambique and Zimbabwe. The Zambian economy suffered significantly as a consequence of this policy, and most directly as a result of the imposition of sanctions against Rhodesia from 1965 and the closure of the Rhodesian border in 1973. More recently Pres. Kaunda has taken a leading part in attempts to resolve the issue of Namibian independence and to seek a peaceful resolution to the South African conflict.

CONSTITUTION AND GOVERNMENT

Executive and legislature

The executive president, who is also leader of the sole legal party and appoints the Cabinet, is elected directly by popular vote for a five-year term, concurrently with elections to the unicameral National Assembly. The Cabinet is subordinate to the party's Central Committee. The Assembly has ten presidential appointees and 125 elective seats, for which the party conducts a primary selection procedure in each locality to draw up a list with two or more candidates for each constituency; last elections Oct. 1988.

Present government

President; C.-in-C. of the Armed Forces Dr Kenneth Kaunda

Principal Members of the Cabinet Gen. Malimba Masheke (Prime Minister); Alex Shapi (Secretary of State for Defence and Security); Frederick S. Hapunda (Defence); Gen. Kingsley Chinkuli (Home Affairs); Luke Mwananshiku (Foreign Affairs); Gibson Chigaga (Finance and National Commission for Development Planning); Frederick Chomba (Legal Affairs; Attorney General).

Ruling party

United National Independence Party.

President Dr Kenneth Kaunda.

Secretary General (with Cabinet rank) Alexander Grey Zulu.

Justice

There is a Supreme Court, a High Court, a Court of Appeal and four classes of magistrates' courts. A Judicial Service Commission deals with the appointment, discipline and removal from office of the magistracy and advises the president on the appointment of puisne judges. The death penalty is in force. There were 11 executions between 1985 and mid-1988. Offences were murder; aggravated robbery.

National symbols

Flag. Green, the bottom of the fly bears a tricolour of vertical stripes of red, black and orange, above which is an orange eagle from the state coat of arms, with spread wings.

Festivals. 11 Mar. (Youth Day); 1 May (Labour Day); 24 May (African Freedom Day, anniversary of OAU's foundation); 5 July (Heroes' Day); 8 July (Unity Day); 5 Aug. (Farmers' Day); 24 Oct. (Independence Day).

Vehicle registration plate. Z.

INTERNATIONAL RELATIONS

Affiliations

NAM; OAU; ACP; Commonwealth; SADCC.

Defence

Total Armed Forces: 16,200. Terms of service: voluntary.

Army: 15,000; 30 main battle tanks (T-54/-55, Ch Type-59), 30 light tanks (PT-76).

Air Force: 1,200; perhaps 53 combat aircraft (MiG-21MF, Ch J-6, MB-326GB).

ECONOMY

Currency

The unit is the kwacha, divided into 100 ngwee.

National finance

Budget. The 1987 budget, in US$, was for expenditure of 787 million and revenue of 540 million. Main items of expenditure are education 8.3%; health 4.7%.

Balance of payments. The balance of payments, in US$ (current account, 1987) was a deficit of 12 million.

Inflation. 58.0%.

Gross Domestic Product

Estimated total GDP US$2,030 million, per capita US$240 (overall size of economy ranking 116 in the world).

Economically active population. The total number of persons active in the economy was 2,455,000.

Sector	% of workforce	% of GDP
industry	6	36
agriculture	85	12
services*	9	52

* services figure includes elements unassigned to other categories.

Energy and mineral resources

Minerals. Production: (1985) copper is the largest export earner, 598,549 tons/543,000 tonnes; cobalt; zinc is the second largest export earner, 35,274 tons/32,000 tonnes; lead 16,535 tons/15,000 tonnes; coal; emeralds; gold 223,965 gm/7,900 oz; silver; uranium.

Electricity. The country is self-sufficient in hydro-electricity. Capacity: 1.9 million kW; production: 8,244 kWh; 1,090 kWh per capita 1988.

Bioresources

Agriculture. The government plans to reduce the economy's dependence on copper by expanding the agricultural industry are hampered by the land being subject to drought, deforestation and soil erosion. Basic foodstuffs have to be imported.

Crop production: (1987 in tons/tonnes) sugar cane 1.38 million/1.25 million; maize 1,051,594/954,000; seed cotton 62,831/57,000; groundnuts 15,432/14,000; tobacco 4,409/4,000.

Livestock numbers: cattle 2.85 million; goats 420,000; pigs 221,000; sheep 80,000; poultry 14 million.

Forestry. Approximately 25% of the land is forest and woodland.

Fisheries. Total catch: (1984) 71,650 tons/65,000 tonnes.

Industry and commerce

Industry. The mining and processing of copper are the foundation of the economy, providing more than 80% of export earnings. Zambia Consolidated Copper Mines, which is government-controlled, is the world's second largest copper concern. The industry, and hence the Zambian economy, is affected by variations in the world market, by deficiencies in transportation and equipment, and by unrest in the labour force. Copper reserves are not expected to last into the 21st century. Other industries include transport; foodstuffs; beverages; chemicals; fertilizers.

Commerce. Exports: (f.o.b. 1987) US$866 million or 43% of GDP. Mainly copper; zinc; cobalt; lead; tobacco. Main trading partners EC countries; Japan; South Africa; US. Imports: (c.i.f. 1987) US$765 million, including machinery; transportation equipment; foodstuffs. Main trading partners EC countries; Japan; South Africa; US.

Trade with UK. Exports to the UK in 1988 totalled £24.8 million and imports from the UK totalled £85.7 million.

Tourism. (1985) 100,000 visitors.

COMMUNICATIONS

Railways

There are 1,340 miles/2,157 km of railways.

Roads

There are 23,136 miles/37,232 km of roads, of which 3,826 miles/6,157 km are bituminized.

Aviation

Zambia Airways Corporation provides domestic and international services (main airport is at Lusaka). Passengers: (1987) 600,000.

Shipping

There are 1,398 miles/2,250 km of inland waterways including the Zambezi and Luapula rivers, and Lake Tanganyika where the main inland port of Mpulungu is situated. Freight loaded: (1987 in 100 lb/kg) 54,071/24,527; unloaded (1987 in 100 lb/kg) 168,457/76,412.

Telecommunications

There are 71,700 telephones and facilities are among the best in sub-Saharan Africa; high-capacity radio relay connects most larger towns and cities. 528,000 radios and 100,000 televisions (1986). The national broadcasting corporation offers television in English and radio broadcasts also in seven Zambian languages.

EDUCATION AND WELFARE

Education

Between the ages of seven and 14 primary education is compulsory.

School population. Primary school attendance is approximately 80%. About 1.1 million pupils attend some 3,000 primary schools, and some 105,000 secondary school pupils attend 150 schools (1984).

Universities. University of Zambia at Lusaka, Copperbelt University at Kitwe.

Literacy. 76%.

Health

(1981) 636 hospitals with 20,600 beds; 821 doctors.

ZIMBABWE

Republic of Zimbabwe

(formerly: 1911–64 Southern Rhodesia; 1964–79 Rhodesia; 1979–80 Zimbabwe Rhodesia)

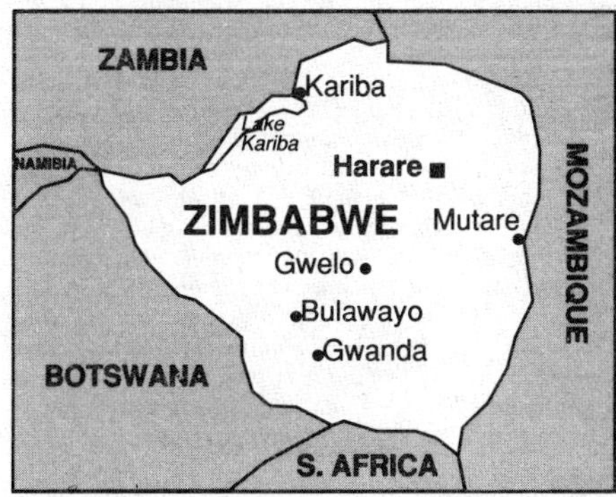

GEOGRAPHY

Located in southern Africa, the landlocked republic of Zimbabwe covers a total area of 150,764 miles²/ 390,580 km² divided into eight provinces. 25% of the area is occupied by the Highveld ridge which traverses the country south-west to north-east to join the Inyanga mountains on the north-eastern Mozambique border where Inyangani, the highest peak, climbs to an elevation of 8,507 ft/2,592 m. The Highveld is flanked by the 'Middleveld' (2,953–3,937 ft/900–1,200 m elevation) declining north-west and south-eastwards into the riverine 'Lowveld' regions which contain roughly 30% of the total surface area. The Zambezi in the north-west, the Limpopo and Sabi in the south-east are the three principal rivers draining eastwards into the Indian Ocean. 7% of the land is arable and 62% is forested. Nearly 75% of the population is rural-based.

Climate

Subtropical, modified by altitude. Humidity levels checked by inland situation. Rainfall varies from 16–24 in/400–600 mm in the warm, temperate climes of the Lowveld to between 47–59 in/1,200–1,500 mm in the mountainous east. Most rain falls in the main wet season Nov.-Mar. Cooler temperatures prevail mid-May-mid Aug. Harare: Jan. 69°F/20.6°C. July 57°F/13.9°C. Average annual rainfall 33 in/828 mm. Bulawayo: Jan. 71°F/21.7°C. July 57°F/13.9°C. Average annual rainfall 23 in/594 mm. Victoria Falls: Jan. 78°F/25.6°C. July 61°F/16.1°C. Average annual rainfall 28 in/710 mm.

Cities and towns

Harare (capital)	656,000
Bulawayo	413,800
Chitungwiza	172,600
Gweru	78,900
Mutare	69,600
Kwekwe	47,600
Kadoma	44,600

Population

Total population is 10,119,037 of which 25.7% live in urban areas. Population density is 67 persons per mile²/22.1 per km². Ethnic divisions: 98% African (of which 71% Shona, 16% Ndebele); 1% White; 1% Asian or mixed. In 1988, there were an estimated 135,000 refugees in Zimbabwe, mainly from Mozambique.

Birth rate 4.2%. **Death rate** 0.9%. **Rate of population increase** (1980–87) 3.4%. **Age distribution** under 15 = 46.2%; over 65 = 2.7%. **Life expectancy** female 60; male 56; average 58.

Religion

Approximately 50% of the population pursue syncretic Christian/local beliefs. 25% profess Christianity alone, 24% follow indigenous animist beliefs and there is a small Muslim minority.

Language

English is the official language; Shona and Ndebele are the most widely spoken.

HISTORY

The remains of Stone Age cultures dating from 500,000 years ago have been found in Zimbabwe, but the first Bantu-speaking peoples did not reach the region until the second half of the 1st millenium AD, driving the San (or Bushmen) into the desert. Antonio Fernandes in the 16th century was probably the first European to reach Zimbabwe and in 1569 an abortive Portuguese military expedition entered the region in search of gold. A second migration of Bantu-speakers, fleeing from the Zulu chief Shaka, arrived in Zimbabwe around 1830. The Ndebele people carved out a kingdom in the Zulu pastoral tradition, subduing the indigenous Shona tribes. During the 19th century British and Afrikaner hunters, traders and prospectors moved north from South Africa with the missionaries.

Southern Rhodesia (as the country was then

known) was founded by Cecil Rhodes' British South Africa Company in 1890 after the Ndebele leader Lobengula had been duped into signing away African land rights. Uprisings by the Ndebele in 1893 and the Shona and Ndebele together in 1896–97 were put down by the better armed settlers and the country continued to be administered by the Company until 1923. In a referendum held in 1922 some 34,000 European settlers chose to become a self-governing colony rather than joining the Union of South Africa and a year later responsible self-government was granted to the settlers as the territory was annexed by the British crown. A number of discriminatory legislative measures were introduced to ensure continued White supremacy in Southern Rhodesia, including the 1931 Land Apportionment Act and the 1957 Land Husbandry Act.

The Central African Federation was formed in 1953, comprising Northern and Southern Rhodesia (now Zambia and Zimbabwe) and Nyasaland (now Malawi) under the premiership of Sir Godfrey Huggins (1953–56) and Sir Roy Welensky (1956–63). The Federation was bitterly opposed by the nationalist movements in all three countries and the Federation broke up in 1963 as both Malawi and Zambia made rapid progress towards independence the following year. Within Southern Rhodesia, however, with its more powerful White settler community fearing the loss of its privileged position under majority rule, Garfield Todd, the prime minister, was replaced as leader of the United Federal Party (UFP) in 1958 because of his liberal statements on racial issues and in 1962 the right-wing Rhodesian Front, led by Winston Field, defeated Sir Edgar Whitehead's UFP in a general election. As the Federation broke up, Southern Rhodesia submitted a formal application for independence to the British government but this was rejected. Ian Smith, who had succeeded Field as prime minister in 1964, on 11 Nov. 1965 unilaterally declared independence (UDI) for Rhodesia.

The first African nationalist movement in Rhodesia, the African National Congress, formed in 1934, was revived in 1957, under the leadership of Joshua Nkomo, as the country's main nationalist movement. Renamed as the National Democratic Party and then the Zimbabwe African People's Union (ZAPU), the party was banned in 1962. In Aug. 1963 the nationalist movement split; a new party, the Zimbabwe African National Union (ZANU), was formed with Rev. Ndabaningi Sithole as its leader. Both ZANU and the People's Caretaker Council (as ZAPU was then briefly known) were banned and many of their leaders detained by the Smith regime. The nationalist movement then went underground; the first shots in the guerrilla war were fired in 1964, and both ZANU and ZAPU mounted guerrilla operations in the 1960s, but the armed struggle did not get under way in earnest until Dec. 1972.

The British government invoked selective international sanctions against Rhodesia following UDI and continued to make efforts to restore Rhodesia to 'legality', although it was not prepared to use force. Harold Wilson, the British Labour prime minister, met Smith twice on board HMS *Tiger* in 1966 and HMS *Fearless* in 1968 in an unsuccessful bid to negotiate a settlement. However, the Conservative foreign minister Sir Alec Douglas-Home finally reached an agreement for a proposed settlement with Smith in 1971. A British commission under the chairmanship of Lord Pearce toured the country in 1972 to ascertain if the Home-Smith proposals were acceptable to the people of Rhodesia as a whole. Country-wide opposition to the proposals, organized by the newly formed African National Council (ANC) under the leadership of Bishop Abel Muzorewa, ensured that the proposals were rejected.

Beginning in Dec. 1972 ZANU, operating from bases in Mozambique, infiltrated north-eastern Rhodesia, while ZAPU, operating from bases in Zambia, began more slowly to establish a guerrilla presence in western Rhodesia. The guerrilla campaign forced the Smith regime to negotiate at intervals during the 1970s notably during the 'detente' period of 1974–75 which resulted in the release of many detainees including Robert Mugabe (ZANU's secretary-general), Nkomo and Rev. Sithole. Mugabe replaced Sithole as leader of ZANU in the same year after Sithole had lost the confidence of the guerrillas in the field. ZANU and ZAPU formed a loose alliance, known as the Patriotic Front, which represented both organizations in international negotiations from 1976 to 1980. Seven years of guerrilla war cost at least 27,000 lives, before talks eventually culminated in the British-organized Lancaster House Conference (Sept.-Dec. 1979), at which an agreement was hammered out on a transition to independence based on majority rule.

Lord Soames was appointed governor of Southern Rhodesia in late 1979 to oversee the cease-fire and election processes agreed at Lancaster House. He played a significant role in defusing the tension of this transitional period. ZANU secured an overall majority in pre-independence elections (Feb. 1980), winning 57 of the 80 common-roll seats, while ZAPU won 20 and Bishop Muzorewa's United African National Council only three seats; 20 seats were reserved for Whites under 'entrenched' provisions of the constitution agreed at Lancaster House.

Zimbabwe became an independent Republic within the Commonwealth on 18 Apr. 1980, with a non-executive president (Canaan Banana) and Mugabe as the new country's first prime minister at the head of a coalition government. This coalition broke up in Feb. 1982 when Nkomo and two of his ZAPU colleagues were dismissed from the Cabinet following the discovery of arms caches on farms owned by ZAPU. A wave of unrest in Matabeleland resulted, and several hundred people were killed in 1983 as the government cracked down on dissident activities.

Mugabe convincingly defeated Edgar Tekere, his sole rival in March 1990 presidential elections, winning 78% of the vote. Tekere, a former leading member of ZANU, had formed the breakaway Zimbabwe Unity Movement (ZUM) in April 1989 after being expelled from the ruling party in Oct. 1988 for persistently criticizing Mugabe's leadership. In legislative elections held at the same time, marked by a relatively low turnout of 54%, ZANU won 116 of the 120 elective seats in the enlarged House of Assembly. ZUM won two seats and Sitole's party retained its single seat; polling was postponed in one constituency. Tekere challenged the election results in court, alleging irregularities. Mugabe claimed before the elections that a win for ZANU would provide him with a mandate to establish a one-party system.

In elections held in 1985 ZANU won 64 of the 80 Black seats, ZAPU 15 and Sithole's ZANU only one. The 20 White seats were abolished in Sept. 1987 under the terms of the constitution agreed at Lancaster House and all were replaced by ZANU nominees (including 11 Whites). Following further constitutional reforms agreed in Oct. 1987, Mugabe was elected as Zimbabwe's first executive president

(30 Dec. 1987). In the same month Mugabe and Nkomo signed a unity agreement, which was ratified by both parties in Apr. 1988 and which provided for a merger of the two parties. Nkomo and two other former ZAPU members were appointed to the Cabinet on 31 Dec. 1987, with Nkomo assuming one of the senior posts in the office of the president.

Since 1980 Zimbabwe has been an important member of the Southern Africa Development Co-ordination Conference, which aimed to reduce the region's economic dependence on South Africa. Zimbabwe has also played an important role in international efforts to stabilize the region and to end apartheid in South Africa. The South African Defence Force in May 1986 launched a raid against an alleged African National Congress (ANC) base in Harare, and in May and Oct. 1987 and Jan. 1988 further bomb attacks were launched against ANC targets in Harare and Bulawayo. Zimbabwe has continued to maintain close relations with Mozambique, which originally arose from the latter's support for ZANU during the guerrilla war. Some 12,000 Zimbabwean troops were deployed in Mozambique in the late 1980s to guard the Beira-Mutare rail and oil pipeline against anti-government sabotage; in retaliation the rebel Mozambique National Resistance has launched raids into Zimbabwe since 1987.

CONSTITUTION AND GOVERNMENT

Executive and legislature

The executive president combines the posts of head of state and head of government, and is elected by parliament for a six-year term; last presidential election Mar. 1990. The post-independence bicameral parliament comprised a 40-member indirectly elected Senate and a 100-seat House of Assembly. The provision to reserve 20 seats for Whites in the House of Assembly and ten in the Senate was abolished in 1987. A new unicameral legislature was elected in Mar. 1990, comprising 120 elective seats, 20 presidential nominees and 10 traditional chiefs. The provisions of the Lancaster House agreements expired in April 1990, the tenth anniversary of independence, after which only a two-thirds majority in the legislature was required in order to alter the Bill of Rights which provided for a multi-party system.

Present government

President, C.-in-C. of the Defence Forces Robert Gabriel Mugabe

Vice-President, Minister for Political Affairs Simon Vengesai Muzenda

Principal Members of the Cabinet Joshua Nkomo (Senior Minister in the President's Office; Local Government, Community Co-operative Development and Women's Affairs, National Housing); Dr Bernard Chidzero (Senior Minister in the President's Office, Finance, Economic Planning and Development, Industry and Technology); Dr Nathan Shamuyarira (Foreign Affairs); Moven Mahachi (Home Affairs); Emmerson Munangagwa (Justice, Legal and Parliamentary Affairs).

Justice

The system of law is based on a mixture of Roman-Dutch law, English common law traditions, and African customary law. The highest court is the Supreme Court, which is headed by the Chief Justice (who also presides over the High Court) and which is Zimbabwe's final court of appeal. The High Court handles both civil and criminal cases. At the local level, there are over 1,000 village courts, with locally elected presidents assisted by lay assessors, handling minor civil matters. Appeals from village courts may go to one of the 50 community courts, which also deal with minor criminal matters. At the higher level are some 20 Magistrates' Courts, handling both civil and criminal cases, and (for criminal cases) two Regional Courts based in Harare and Bulawayo. The death penalty is in force. There were 24 executions between 1985 and mid-1988. Offences: murder.

National symbols

Flag. Seven horizontal stripes of green, yellow, red, black, red, yellow and green; a white isosceles triangle, based on the hoist, reaches to one-third of the flag's length.

Festivals. 18 Apr. (Independence Day); 1 May (Workers' Day); 25 May (Africa Day, anniversary of OAU's foundation); 11–12 Aug. (Heroes' Day).

Vehicle registration plate. ZW.

INTERNATIONAL RELATIONS

Affiliations

NAM; OAU; ACP; Commonwealth; SADCC.

Defence

Total Armed Forces: 47,000. Terms of service: conscription; term unknown.

Army: 46,000; 43 main battle tanks (T-54, Ch Type-59).

Air Force: 1,000; 53 (estimated 30 operational) combat aircraft (bombers: Canberra B-2, T-4; fighters: Hunter FGA-90/T-81, Ch J-6/J-7, Hawk Mk 60).

Forces abroad: Mozambique: some 6,000–12,000 (varies).

ECONOMY

Currency

The unit is the Zimbabwean dollar, divided into 100 cents.

National finance

Budget. The 1988 FY budget, in US$, was for expenditure of 2,800 million and revenue of 2,200 million. Main items of expenditure are education 20.3%; defence 14.2%.

Balance of payments. The balance of payments, in US$ (current account, 1987) was a deficit of 22 million.

Inflation. 12.5%.

Gross Domestic Product

Estimated total GDP US$5,240 million, per capita US$540 (overall size of economy ranking 82 in the world).

Economically active population. The total number of persons active in the economy was 3,100,000; unemployed: 20%.

Sector	% of workforce	% of GDP
industry	10	43
agriculture	74	11
services*	16	46

* services figure includes elements unassigned to other categories

Energy and mineral resources

Minerals. Output: (1987 in 1,000 tons/tonnes) coal 5,306/4,814; chromium ore 620/562; asbestos 213/193.3; nickel 12,028/10,912; copper 21.6/19.6; iron ore 1,464/1,328; tin 1,143/1,037; cobalt 118/107; vanadium; lithium. Also gold 29,874 lb/13,551 kg.

Electricity. Capacity: 2 million kW; prooduction: 5,457 million kWh; 560 kWh per capita (1988).

Bioresources

Agriculture. Main crops are tobacco; maize (the staple food crop of much of the population); tea; sugar; cotton. Tobacco is the most important single product, production: (1985) 141,094 tons/128,000 tonnes. Coffee and sugar production are becoming increasingly important.

Crop production: (1987 in 1,000 tons/tonnes) maize 1,206/1,094; wheat 237/215; coffee 14/13; tea 19/17; sorghum 58/53; barley 33/30; millet 89/81; soya beans 115/104; seed cotton 331/300; fruit 146/132.

Livestock numbers: (1987) cattle 5.5 million; pigs 180,000; sheep 570,000; goats 1.6 million.

Forestry. 62% of the land area is forest and woodland.

Fisheries. Trout, prawn and bream are farmed to supplement the quantity of fish caught in lakes and dams. 200,000 trout were caught in 1986 and bream production is expected to be approximately 551 tons/500 tonnes per year.

Industry and commerc

Industry. Main industries are mining; steel; clothing and footwear; chemicals; foodstuffs; fertilizers; beverages; transportation equipment; wood products.

Commerce. Exports: (1988) US$1,600 million or 29% of GDP, including agricultural products 34% (tobacco 21%, other 13%); manufactures 19%; gold 11%; ferrochrome 11%; cotton 6%. Imports: US$1,100 million, including machinery and transportation equipment 37%; other manufactures 22%; chemicals 16%; fuels 15%. Countries exported to were Europe 55% (EC 41%, Netherlands 6%, other 8%); Africa 22% (South Africa 12%, other 10%); US 6%. Imports came from EC countries 31%; Africa 29% (South Africa 21%, other 8%); US 8%; Japan 4%.

Trade with UK. In 1988 Zimbabwe imported UK goods worth £58,077,000; exports to UK totalled £86,268,000.

Tourism. (1987) 454,779 visitors.

COMMUNICATIONS

Railways

There are 1,706 miles/2,745 km of railways.

Roads

There are 53,305 miles/85,784 km of roads.

Aviation

Air Zimbabwe Corporation (AirZim) provides domestic and international services (main airport is at Harare). Passengers: (1986) 451,600.

Shipping

The inland waterway of Lake Kariba is a potential line for communication.

Telecommunications

There are 247,000 telephones and the system was once one of the best in Africa but now suffers from poor maintenance. There are 480,000 radios and 130,000 televisions (1986). The Zimbabwe Broadcasting Corporation provides two TV and four radio channels.

EDUCATION AND WELFARE

Education

Schools. Education is compulsory, and free at primary level. All teaching is in English. There are also some 3,800 private primary schools and 950 private secondary schools. There are 2.2 million pupils in primary schools and 653,350 pupils in secondary schools. Zimbabwe has ten teacher-training colleges.

Universities. The University of Zimbabwe at Harare has nine faculties and 7,699 students.

Literacy. 45–55%.

Health

In 1985 there were 162 hospitals, 1,062 rural clinics and health centres and 32 mobile rural clinics.

INTERNATIONAL ORGANIZATIONS

UNITED NATIONS

The United Nations (UN) is an organization of states formed in 1945 as the successor to the League of Nations. Its main aims are to maintain international peace and security and to co-operate in finding solutions for political, economic, social, cultural and humanitarian problems on an international level.

The UN Charter, which is the governing treaty of the organization, has its roots in a Conference of Foreign Ministers held in Moscow in 1943. Further discussions involving the UK, USA, USSR and China at Dumbarton Oaks (Washington DC) from 21 Aug. to 7 Oct. 1944 resulted in a series of proposals being submitted to the UN Conference on International Organization at San Francisco from 25 Apr. to 26 June 1945. After much discussion, criticism and amendment to the proposals, they were finally accepted as the Charter of the UN and signed on 26 June 1945 by delegates representing 50 countries. The formal existence of the UN began on 24 Oct. 1945, after the US Department of State had received the necessary number of ratifications of the Charter. The permanent headquarters of the UN are in Manhattan, New York. It has six official languages which are Arabic, Chinese, English, French, Russian and Spanish. The flag of the UN is light blue with a white UN emblem in the centre, and its official day is 24 October.

Membership of the UN is open to all states following a policy of peaceful co-existence. The General Assembly effects their admission after receiving the recommendation of the Security Council.

The six main organs of the UN are: (1) the General Assembly; (2) the Security Council; (3) the Economic and Social Council; (4) the Trusteeship Council; (5) the International Court of Justice; (6) the Secretariat.

THE GENERAL ASSEMBLY

All the members of the UN make up the General Assembly. Each Member has one vote but may have five representatives at the annual meeting of the Assembly, which begins on the third Tuesday in September and usually lasts for about three months. At the beginning of every annual session a new President is elected by the Assembly. Apart from the annual sessions, special sessions are also allowed and have been held on areas ranging from Palestine to Namibia.

As the chief deliberative body of the UN, the General Assembly may discuss and make recommendations on any matter within the sphere of the Charter, with the exception of issues under Security Council consideration. A majority of Members present and voting is usually acceptable for making decisions, but if the matter is important a two-thirds majority is required. If the Security Council fails to fulfil its main role of maintaining international peace and security because of an impasse between permanent members and there appears to be a threat to peace, the General Assembly immediately considers the matter. It then makes the necessary recommendations to Members for collective methods of maintaining or restoring international peace.

The General Assembly's work is divided among the following seven Main Committees: (1) Disarmament and related international security questions (an additional Special Political Committee exists to assist with this work); (2) Economic and Financial Affairs; (3) Social, Humanitarian and Cultural affairs; (4) Decolonization (including Non-Self-Governing Territories); (5) Administrative and Budgetary affairs; (6) Legal Affairs. Every Member has the right to be represented on each of the Main Committees.

The two procedural committees of the Assembly are the General Committee, which co-ordinates the proceedings of the Assembly and its Committees, and the Credentials Committee, which checks the credentials of delegates. The two standing committees are the Advisory Committee on Administrative and Budgetary Questions and a Committee on Contributions. The General Assembly occasionally appoints ad hoc committees for specific purposes, such as the Commission on Human Rights. Subsidiary bodies, including the Board of Auditors, the Committee on Conferences and the International Law Commission, assist the Assembly with its work.

The General Assembly passes the UN budget and sets assessments. It also receives reports from the Security Council and the other bodies of the UN for its consideration. The Secretary-General submits an annual report on the work of the UN.

THE SECURITY COUNCIL

The Security Council consists of 15 members. Each member has one representative and one vote. Five of the members are permanent, with the ten non-permanent members being elected for a two-year term by the General Assembly. Members of the UN are occasionally invited to contribute to discussions concerning questions of specific interest to them, but are not allowed a vote. Each member state is President for one month, in a rotation system based on the English alphabetical order of the names of the states.

The Security Council operates on a continuous basis. Its main responsibility is to maintain peace and security. An affirmative vote of nine members is needed to make decisions on procedural questions, but on other matters the unanimous agreement of the permanent members plus four affirmative votes is needed. Any permanent member may exercise the right of 'veto' by voting negatively on a non-procedural proposal, which results in the dropping of the proposal even if it has received nine affirmative votes. An abstention by a permanent member is not considered a veto in practice.

If the Security Council is considering ways of settling a dispute peacefully, parties to the dispute are obliged to abstain from voting.

Members of the UN, the General Assembly or the Secretary-General can alert the attention of the Council to matters which may pose threats to international peace and security. The Council can either make recommendations on how to deal with these threats or take action, which may be either economic sanctions or military action. A non-Member state can bring a dispute before the Council only if it first accepts the UN Charter obligations for peaceful settlement. The Council is exempt from the ban on domestic intervention stated in the Charter.

The Security Council has the power to set up ad hoc committees and commissions for particular purposes.

Permanent members: China, France, UK, USA, USSR.

Non-permanent members: Algeria, Brazil, Canada, Colombia, Ethiopia, Finland, Malaysia, Nepal, Senegal, Yugoslavia.

THE ECONOMIC AND SOCIAL COUNCIL

The Economic and Social Council consists of 54 members elected by the General Assembly for three-year terms. Eighteen members are elected each year. Each member has one vote and on retirement is eligible for immediate re-election. Decisions are taken by a majority vote of members present. The President holds office for one year but may be re-elected immediately. The Council meets twice a year but is able to hold special sessions if they are needed.

The Economic and Social Council has the responsibility, under the auspices of the General Assembly, for carrying out the operations of the UN in international cultural, educational, health, economic, social and related areas. By the end of 1977 a relationship had been formed with 15 'specialized' intergovernmental agencies working in this sphere. Consultations with international non-governmental organizations were arranged by the Council, which also approached national organizations after consulting the member state concerned. By 1983, 600 non-governmental organizations had been given consultative status.

The Council is also involved in making recommendations for the co-ordination and streamlining of the policies and activities of other organizations and agencies in the UN system. It supplies the General Assembly and other UN bodies with reports of its work and general progress.

Much of the Council's work is done by Functional and Regional Commissions. The Regional Commissions, such as the Economic Commission for Africa (ECA), have been formed to help countries in major world regions to co-operate on solving mutual problems and supply economic information. Functional Commissions include the Commission on Human Rights, the Commission on Narcotic Drugs and the Population Commission.

The Council's 54 members for 1989 are: Bahamas, Belize, Bolivia, Brazil, Bulgaria, Cameroon, Canada, China, Colombia, Cuba, Czechoslovakia, Denmark, France, Federal Republic of Germany, Ghana, Greece, Guinea, India, Indonesia, Iran, Iraq, Ireland, Italy, Japan, Jordan, Kenya, Lesotho, Liberia, Libya, Netherlands, New Zealand, Nicaragua, Niger, Norway, Oman, Poland, Portugal, Rwanda, Saudi Arabia, Somalia, Sri Lanka, Sudan, Thailand, Trinidad and Tobago, Tunisia, Ukraine, USSR, United Kingdom, United States, Uruguay, Venezuela, Yugoslavia, Zaire and Zambia.

President Kjeld Mortensen (Denmark)
Vice Presidents Chandrashekhar Dasgupta (India), Hassen Elghouayel (Tunisia), Guennadi Oudovenko (Ukraine), Felipe Hector Paolillo (Uruguay)

THE TRUSTEESHIP COUNCIL

The Trusteeship Council consists of China, France, USSR, UK and the US. It administers the only remaining trust territory, the Pacific Islands (Micronesia). Each member has one vote and decisions are taken by a majority of members present and voting. The Council meets annually and is able to hold special sessions if necessary.

The role of the Council is to ensure that the interests of the inhabitants of territories that are not yet self-governing are protected. It examines reports from the administering authority and makes routine inspection visits to Micronesia. Conditions in the territory are checked by means of an annual questionnaire on the political, economic, social and educational advancement of the inhabitants. Petitions are examined in consultation with the US.

INTERNATIONAL COURT OF JUSTICE

The International Court of Justice, the successor to the World Court, is the main judicial organ of the UN. It was created by the Statute of Court, an international treaty, which is an essential part of the UN Charter. The Court consists of 15 judges, each from a different Member state, chosen by the General Assembly and Security Council for nine-year terms. Judges are eligible for immediate re-election. They are chosen from a list of nominees supplied by national groups in the Permanent Court of Arbitration. Nations that are not represented in the Permanent Court of Arbitration appoint special national groups to nominate their candidates. The President and Vice-President are elected by the Court for a three-year term.

The Court sits at The Hague, and is permanently in session with the exception of judicial vacations. A quorum of nine judges is necessary for the Court to sit. Decisions are reached by a majority vote of judges present, with the President having a casting vote. English and French are the official languages of the Court.

The Court hears disputes between Member states and issues advisory opinions on matters presented by UN bodies and other international organizations. It has limited jurisdiction in questions of international law, breaches of international obligations and reparations for breachments. In reaching its decision the Court may make use of international conventions; international custom; the general principles of law recognized by civilized nations; and judicial decisions and the teachings of authorities on international law. The judgments of the Court are not appealable, and are binding only for the particular case and parties. There is no system of precedent. Although parties are unable to appeal they may apply for a revision of the judgment within a ten-year period of the date of judgment if new decisive factors should arise. In the event of a party to a case failing to abide by the judgment of the Court, the other party may consult the Security Council.

President J.M. Ruda (Argentina, 1991)
Vice-President K. Mbaye (Senegal, 1991)
Judges M. Lachs (Poland, 1994), R.S. Pathak (India, 1991), T.O. Elias (Nigeria, 1994), S. Oda (Japan, 1994), R. Ago (Italy, 1997), M. Shahabuddeen (Guyana, 1997), S. Schwebel (US, 1997), Sir R. Jennings (UK, 1991), M. Bedjaoui (Algeria, 1997), Ni Zhengyu (China, 1994), J. Evensen (Norway, 1994), N.K. Tarasov (USSR, 1997), G. Guillaume (France, 1991).

The judges are listed in order of precedence, with dates of expiry of office.

THE SECRETARIAT

The Secretariat consists of the Secretary-General and a large international staff. The Secretary-General is the chief administrative officer and usually serves for a five-year term. The Secretary-General appoints the staff under regulations laid down by the General Assembly, which is responsible for appointing the Secretary-General and the High Commissioner for Refugees.

The Secretariat performs all the UN administrative functions. The Secretary-General acts as chief administrative officer in all meetings of the principal organs of the UN, with the exception of the International Court of Justice. The Secretariat acts as an impartial party when effecting conciliation. It is responsible for bringing situations to the attention of appropriate UN organs, and has the power to perform functions which are entrusted to it by other UN bodies.

The financial year is arranged in accordance with the calendar year, and the accountancy is in US$.

Secretary-General Javier Perez de Cuellar (Peru) until 1 Jan. 1991

The United Nations Information Office for the UK is at Ship House, 20 Buckingham Gate, London SW1E 9LB, tel. 071 630 1981.

SPECIALIZED AGENCIES OF THE UNITED NATIONS

Agency	Date affiliated with UN;[1] headquarters	Number of members[2]	Purpose and function	Budget
Food & Agriculture Organization (FAO)	1945; Rome	158	Improves rural conditions, agricultural production, and distribution by investing in agriculture. Raises nutritional levels and standard of living of rural populations. Promotes conservation and rational use of fertilizer. Transfers technology and develops research. Collects, analyses and disseminates information on natural resources and agricultural production.	US$492,000,000 (1988–89)
General Agreement on Tariffs and Trade (GATT)	1958; Geneva	96	Lays down common code of conduct in international trade and trade relations. Acts as forum for negotiation and consultation to overcome trade problems and reduce trade barriers and tariffs. Lays down principles to assist trade of developing countries.	Sw.F.61,122,300 (1987)
International Atomic Energy Agency (IAEA)	1957; Vienna	113	Accelerates and enlarges contribution of atomic energy to worldwide peace, health and prosperity. Ensures that atomic energy used for peaceful aims, not for military purposes. Buys and sells fuels and materials; assists in peaceful applications.	US$137,337,000 (1988)
International Bank for Reconstruction and Development (IBRD)	1945; Washington	151	Provides funds and technical assistance to help economic development in poorer member countries. Helps member countries identify and prepare development projects by drawing on expertise of FAO, WHO, UNIDO and UNESCO. Trains Member state officials. IBRD and the IDA make up the World Bank. Affiliated to IFC.	US$77,526,969,000 (Subscribed capital)

SPECIALIZED AGENCIES OF THE UNITED NATIONS ***continued***

Agency	Date affiliated with UN;[1] headquarters	Number of members[2]	Purpose and function	Budget
International Civil Aviation Organization (ICAO)	1947; Montreal	158	Establishes technical standards for safe, efficient air navigation, airworthiness, pilot licensing. Develops regional plans for ground facilities and services needed for international flying. Encourages orderly aviation growth. Disseminates air transport statistics.	US$30,816,000 (1987)
International Development Association (IDA)	1960; Washington	135	Extends credit to poorer developing countries that do not qualify for IBRD loans. Loans are to governments only. It is part of the World Bank.	US$43,308,000,000
International Finance Corporation (IFC)	1957; Washington	133	Encourages growth of productive private enterprises in less developed member countries. Provides risk capital. Assists established enterprises to expand, improve or diversify operations.	US$1,300,000,000 (Subscribed share capital)
International Fund for Agricultural Development (IFAD)	1977; Rome	130	Mobilizes additional funds for agricultural and rural development in developing countries. Promotes projects directly benefiting the poorest rural populations: improved food production, raised nutritional levels.	(not available)
International Labour Organization (ILO)	1946; Geneva	150	Improves labour conditions and living standards of workers. Promotes social justice and protects foreign workers. Encourages human resources development and training. Does research into unemployment problem in developing countries.	US$324,000,000 (1988–89)
International Maritime Organization (IMO)	1948; London	131	Promotes co-operation on technical matters, maritime safety and navigation. Encourages anti-pollution measures. Facilitates international maritime traffic. Provides technical assistance for countries wishing to develop maritime activities. Drafts international maritime conventions.	US$21,627,200 (1988–89)
International Monetary Fund (IMF)	1945; Washington	151	Promotes international monetary co-operation, currency stabilization, trade expansion. Assists in the removal of exchange restrictions and the establishment of a multilateral system of payments. Meets balance-of-payments difficulties.	(not available)

SPECIALIZED AGENCIES OF THE UNITED NATIONS ***continued***

Agency	Date affiliated with UN;[1] headquarters	Number of members[2]	Purpose and function	Budget
International Telecommunication Union (ITU)	1947 (founded 1865); Geneva	154	Regulates, standardizes, plans, co-ordinates and maintains international telecommunications. Allots radio frequencies. Promotes the development of technical facilities and their efficient operation. Offers technical assistance to developing countries.	Sw.F.125,967,000 (1988)
United Nations Educational, Scientific and Cultural Organization (UNESCO)	1946; Paris	158[3]	Reduces social tensions by encouraging interchange of ideas and cultural achievements. Improves quality of education. Seeks to further universal respect for justice, the rule of law, human rights and fundamental freedoms through promotion of education, science and culture.	US$350,386,000 (1988–89)
Universal Postal Union (UPU)	1947 (1875); Bern	159	Unites countries for reciprocal exchange of correspondence. Aids and advises on improvements to postal services.	Sw.F.22,487,630 (1987–88)
World Bank *see*	International Bank for Reconstruction and Development and International Development Association.			
World Health Organizaton (WHO)	1948; Geneva	166	Promotes highest health standards. Sets drugs and vaccine standards, health and research guidelines. Collaborates with governments, specialized agencies, etc. regarding strengthening of health services. Encourages improved standards of teaching and training and promotes environmental health.	US$633,980,000 (1988–89)
World Intellectual Property Organization (WIPO)	1974 (1883); Geneva	121	Promotes protection of intellectual property, inventions, copyrights, access to patented technology. Administers various international treaties. Encourages creative intellectual activity. Facilitates the transfer of technology, especially to developing countries.	(not available)
World Meteorological Organization (WMO)	1950 (1878); Geneva	155	Encourages co-operation between world meteorological stations. Standardizes observations. Promotes research and encourages training in meteorology. Furthers application of meteorology to aviation, shipping, water problems, etc. Improves co-operation between meteorologcal and hydrological services.	Sw.F.170,000,000 (1988–91)

Notes:

[1] Date in parentheses is the date that predecessor organizations began operation.

[2] In almost all cases, agencies have member states that are not Members of the UN General Assembly.

[3] The UK withdrew from UNESCO on 31 Dec. 1985, but was later granted observer facilities by the Executive Board at the 124th session.

SELECTED OTHER UNITED NATIONS AGENCIES

Name	Purpose and function
United Nations International Children's Emergency Fund (UNICEF)	Provides post-war relief for children. Assists development activities improving quality of life for mothers and children in developing countries. Concentrates on supplying basic services for children such as nutrition, water supply, sanitation and education. Promotes oral rehydration therapy; expanded immunization; child growth monitoring; and breast feeding. Provides training, equipment and services of healthcare professionals. Received the Nobel Peace Prize, 1965.
United Nations Conference on Trade and Development (UNCTAD)	Accelerates economic growth in developing countries. Reviews policies of developing and industrial countries influencing trade and development.
United Nations High Commissioner for Refugees (UNHCR)	Provides international protection for refugees. Seeks permanent solutions to their problems through voluntary repatriation, local integration or resettlement. Provides emergency relief and material assistance to most-needy groups. Co-ordinates voluntary agency efforts. Received the Nobel Peace Prize, 1954, 1981.
United Nations Industrial Development Organization (UNIDO)	Assists developing countries with financial, design, technological, market, research advice. Helps formulate industrial development policies.
United Nations Relief and Works Agency for Palestinian Refugees in the Near East (UNRWA)	Provides food, health services, education and vocational training for approximately 2 million refugees displaced by Arab–Israeli wars. Carries out emergency relief programmes for Palestinian refugees. Is financed by voluntary contributions from governments.

MEMBER COUNTRIES OF THE UN IN ALPHABETICAL ORDER

Country	% contribution to UN budget	Date of joining	Country	% contribution to UN budget	Date of joining
Afghanistan	0.01	1946	Chad	0.01	1960
Albania	0.01	1955	*Chile*	0.08	1945
Algeria	0.15	1962	*China*	0.79	1945
Angola	0.01	1976	*Colombia*	0.14	1945
Antigua and Barbuda	0.01	1981	Comoros	0.01	1975
Argentina	0.66	1945	Congo	0.01	1960
Australia	1.57	1945	*Costa Rica*	0.02	1945
Austria	0.74	1955	Côte d'Ivoire	0.02	1960
Bahamas	0.02	1973	*Cuba*	0.09	1945
Bahrain	0.02	1971	Cyprus	0.02	1960
Bangladesh	0.01	1974	*Czechoslovakia*	0.66	1945
Barbados	0.01	1966	*Denmark*	0.69	1945
Belgium	1.17	1945	Djibouti	0.01	1977
Belize	0.01	1981	Dominica	0.01	1978
Benin	0.01	1960	*Dominican Republic*	0.03	1945
Bhutan	0.01	1971	*Ecuador*	0.03	1945
Bolivia	0.01	1945	*Egypt*	0.07	1945
Botswana	0.01	1966	*El Salvador*	0.01	1945
Brazil	1.45	1945	Equatorial Guinea	0.01	1968
Brunei	0.04	1984	*Ethiopia*	0.01	1945
Bulgaria	0.15	1955	Fiji	0.01	1970
Burkina Faso	0.01	1960	Finland	0.51	1955
Burma	0.01	1948	*France*	6.25	1945
Burundi	0.01	1962	Gabon	0.03	1960
Byelorussian SSR	0.33	1945	Gambia	0.01	1965
Cambodia	0.01	1955	German Democratic Rep.	1.28	1973
Cameroon	0.01	1960	Germany, Federal Rep. of	8.08	1973
Canada	3.09	1945	Ghana	0.01	1957
Cape Verde	0.01	1975	*Greece*	0.40	1945
Central African Republic	0.01	1960	Grenada	0.01	1974

MEMBER COUNTRIES OF THE UN IN ALPHABETICAL ORDER ***continued***

Country	% contribution to UN budget	Date of joining	Country	% contribution to UN budget	Date of joining
Guatemala	0.02	1945	*Peru*	0.06	1945
Guinea	0.01	1958	*Philippines*	0.09	1945
Guinea-Bissau	0.01	1974	*Poland*	0.56	1945
Guyana	0.01	1966	Portugal	0.18	1955
Haiti	0.01	1945	Qatar	0.05	1971
Honduras	0.01	1945	Romania	0.19	1955
Hungary	0.21	1955	Rwanda	0.01	1962
Iceland	0.03	1946	St Christopher and Nevis	0.01	1983
India	0.37	1945	St Lucia	0.01	1979
Indonesia	0.15	1950	St Vincent and the Grenadines	0.01	1980
Iran	0.67	1945	São Tomé and Príncipe	0.01	1975
Iraq	0.12	1945	*Saudi Arabia*	1.02	1945
Ireland	0.18	1955	Senegal	0.01	1960
Israel	0.21	1949	Seychelles	0.01	1976
Italy	3.99	1955	Sierra Leone	0.01	1961
Jamaica	0.01	1962	Singapore	0.11	1965
Japan	11.38	1956	Solomon Islands	0.01	1978
Jordan	0.01	1955	Somalia	0.01	1960
Kenya	0.01	1963	*South Africa*	0.45	1945
Kuwait	0.29	1963	Spain	1.95	1955
Laos	0.01	1955	Sri Lanka	0.01	1955
Lebanon	0.01	1945	Sudan	0.01	1956
Lesotho	0.01	1966	Suriname	0.01	1975
Liberia	0.01	1945	Swaziland	0.01	1968
Libya	0.28	1955	Sweden	1.21	1946
Luxembourg	0.06	1945	*Syria*	0.04	1945
Madagascar	0.01	1960	Tanzania	0.01	1961
Malawi	0.01	1964	Thailand	0.10	1946
Malaysia	0.11	1957	Togo	0.01	1960
Maldives	0.01	1965	Trinidad and Tobago	0.05	1962
Mali	0.01	1960	Tunisia	0.03	1956
Malta	0.01	1964	*Turkey*	0.32	1945
Mauritania	0.01	1961	Uganda	0.01	1962
Mauritius	0.01	1968	*Ukrainian SSR*	1.25	1945
Mexico	0.94	1945	*USSR*	9.99	1945
Mongolia	0.01	1961	United Arab Emirates	0.19	1971
Morocco	0.04	1956	*UK*	4.86	1945
Mozambique	0.01	1975	*US*	25.00	1945
Nepal	0.01	1955	*Uruguay*	0.04	1945
Netherlands	1.65	1945	Vanuatu	0.01	1981
New Zealand	0.24	1945	*Venezuela*	0.57	1945
Nicaragua	0.01	1945	Vietnam	0.01	1977
Niger	0.01	1960	Western Samoa	0.01	1976
Nigeria	0.20	1960	Yemen Arab Republic	0.01	1947
Norway	0.55	1945	Yemen, P.D.R.	0.01	1967
Oman	0.02	1971	*Yugoslavia*	0.46	1945
Pakistan	0.06	1947	Zaïre	0.01	1960
Panama	0.02	1945	Zambia	0.01	1964
Papua New Guinea	0.01	1975	Zimbabwe	0.02	1980
Paraguay	*0.03*	*1945*			

Note:
Founder members are in italic.

EUROPEAN COMMUNITY

Member states: Belgium, Denmark, France, Federal Republic of Germany, Greece, Republic of Ireland, Italy, Luxembourg, the Netherlands, Portugal, Spain, United Kingdom.

HISTORY

At the end of World War II there was a strong desire amongst European countries to create a united Europe in which member countries would have such strong bonds that war would cease to be a recurring threat. Thus after the war, instead of demanding reparations, European countries concentrated on rebuilding the whole of Europe, including Germany. The European Community evolved from France's proposal (1950) that the coal and steel industries of France and Germany should be combined under an independent European authority. Membership of this community was open to any European country, and, under the Treaty of Paris of 1951, six nations – Belgium, France, West Germany, Italy, Luxembourg and the Netherlands – joined together to form the European Coal and Steel Community.

In 1957 the Treaty of Rome was signed, bringing into existence the European Economic Community (EEC) and the European Atomic Energy Community (EURATOM). The formation of these two communities was intended to advance economic integration within Europe. Britain was invited to join but wanted to continue to give preferential trading terms to her former colonies, which would not have been allowed under EEC rules.

Under the terms of the treaty, member states were to attempt to improve and harmonize living standards. Customs duties and quotas in trade between member states were to be abolished (by a process of reduction in fixed steps) and a common trade policy towards third countries set up. Co-ordination and co-operation in economic matters were necessary to ensure an overall balance of payments. There was to be free movement of persons, services and capital between member states. Common policies for agriculture and transport were inaugurated, and the European Investment Bank was established. An association of overseas countries and territories was created to increase trade.

The success of the early years in increasing trade between the member nations ('the Six') was remarkable. In Dec. 1969, a meeting was held at The Hague between the heads of state or government of the Six to discuss the completion, strengthening and possible enlargement of the Community (if other European countries were prepared to accept the Treaties of Paris and Rome). The Commission was instructed to prepare a plan for economic and monetary union, while the foreign ministers were required to investigate possible steps towards political unification and report back at the end of July. It was also decided to concentrate on the co-ordination of research and development programmes.

Britain, the Irish Republic, Denmark and Norway were invited to begin negotiations concerning their applications to join the Community, in June 1970. These negotiations continued during 1971 and were finally completed with the UK Conservative government at the end of June, whereupon a White Paper detailing the results was issued. The Treaty of Accession was signed by the four applicant countries on 22 Jan. 1972 in Brussels. Norway, however, was obliged to withdraw its application following a negative response to a domestic referendum. The enlarged Community of the Nine came into being on 1 Jan. 1973.

In 1974, a Labour government gained power in the UK, and promptly began to renegotiate the terms of Britain's entry into the Community. A referendum was held on 5 June 1975 to determine whether Britain should remain a member. Two-thirds of the voters were in favour of Britain remaining in the Community and thus the British Labour Party representatives, after a period of boycotting the European Parliament, finally took up their 18 allotted seats.

The community was enlarged again when Greece joined in 1981, followed by Portugal and Spain in 1986. Turkey has applied (1987) for membership.

CONSTITUTION

The European Community is governed by a dialogue between the Commission, which represents the interests of the Community itself, and the Council of Ministers, representing the member states. The European Parliament has the role of exercising democratic control. The final arbiter in all matters concerned with the Community Treaties is the Court of Justice.

The Commission

The Commission has the role of an independent executive within the Community. Each Commissioner is appointed by his or her country, but must work independently of government or national interests.

The Commission's main responsibility is implementing and safeguarding the various Treaties. It initiates Community action and also mediates between member governments in Community affairs. It may submit proposals to the Council of Ministers for action and after the Council's decision may be responsible for carrying them out. If any of the member states or other institutions within the Community renege on their obligations under any Treaty, the Commission has power to take them before the Court of Justice.

The Commission was reduced from 14 members to nine on 1 July 1970. West Germany, France and Italy each had two members while Belgium, the Netherlands and Luxembourg each had one member. After the enlargement of the Community in 1973, the number of members rose to 13, with Britain receiving two seats and Ireland and Denmark each receiving one seat. Greece received one seat on her admission in 1981. In 1986 when Spain and Portugal joined the Community, the former received two seats and the latter one seat, thus bringing the total number of Commissioners to 17.

The 12 member governments appoint the members of the Commission by agreement, for a four-year renewable term. The president and vice-presidents of the Commission are chosen from among the members for a two-year term, which is also renewable. The decisions of the Commission are taken by a majority vote, with all members accepting joint responsibility for decisions taken. It usually meets every Wednesday in Brussels.

Members of the Commission and their areas of responsibility

President

Jacques Delors (France) Secretariat General, juridical service, monetary affairs, office of security, interpretation at conferences, common service, etc.

Vice-presidents

Frans Andriessen (Netherlands) Agriculture, forestry

Henning Christophersen (Denmark) Budget, financial control, personnel and administration

Sir Leon Brittan (UK) Financial institutions, fiscal matters, department of customs, internal markets

Manuel Marin (Spain) Social affairs and employment, education, planning

Martin Bangemann (Germany) Industrial affairs, research and science, information technology

Filipo Pandolfi (Italy) Co-operation and development

Members

Carlo Ripa di Meana (Italy) Institutional questions, problems concerning European citizens, office of information and communication, cultural action, tourism

Antonio Cardoso e Cunha (Portugal) Fishing

Abel Matutes (Spain) Credit, investments, etc., strategy for small and medium enterprises

Peter Schmidhuber (Germany) Economic affairs, regional politics, office statistics

Christiane Scrivener (France) Mediterranean politics, north–south relations

Bruce Millan (UK) Environment, nuclear security, transport

Jean Dondelinger (Luxembourg) Energy, Euratom, office of publications, office of provisions

Ray McSharry (Ireland) Parliamentary relations, competition

Karel van Miert (Belgium) External relations and commercial strategy

Vasso Papandreou (Greece) Co-ordination of structural instruments, protection of consumers

Secretary General

D. Williamson (UK)

The Commission for the European Community has an information office at 8 Storey's Gate, London SW1P 3AT, tel. 071 222 8122.

THE COUNCIL OF MINISTERS

The Council is composed of the foreign ministers from the governments of each of the member states, and represents national rather than Community interests. The Council is the main decision-taking body within the Community legislative process. According to the Treaty of Rome, decisions should be taken by a majority vote, but since 1966 the Council has tended to seek unanimity wherever possible.

The Council generally operates on the basis of proposals presented by the Commission, which attends Council sessions in order to participate in the shaping of measures taken. The views of the European Parliament and the Economic and Social Committee on the Commission proposals are usually obtained before the Council examines them. The Council acts by issuing Regulations, Directives, Decisions, Recommendations and Opinions. 'Regulations' are completely binding on all member states, whereas 'Directives' allow national governments a certain amount of choice in the methods used to achieve the end result. 'Decisions' are binding only on the members named in them, and 'Recommendations' and 'Opinions' are not binding.

'European Council' meetings, attended by heads of state and government, have been held three times a year since the first such 'summit' in Dec. 1974. Specialist Councils such as the Agriculture Council have meetings to discuss matters concerning individual policies.

The presidency of the Council is held in rotation for a six-month term. A Committee of Permanent Representatives of member states is responsible for preparing the session of the Council. A general secretariat services the Council and its committees.

European Parliament

The European Parliament is designed to increase the democratic control that the people of Europe can exert over Community affairs. Parliament is consulted on all important issues, and on a wide range of legislative proposals. Apart from having powers of supervision and consultation, it also questions the Council of Ministers and the Commission, which it has the power to dismiss by vote of censure.

The Budgetary Authority which proposes the Community's budget is composed of the Council and the Parliament acting jointly. This gives the Parliament considerable control over the budget, as it can either reject the budget as a whole or amend items of non-obligatory expenditure, which can amount to 27% of the total budget.

The Parliament usually meets in Strasbourg, while its committees meet in Brussels. The Parliamentary Secretariat is in Luxembourg. Sessions last for a week and are held 12 times a year: monthly except for August, which is a holiday month, and October, when two sessions are held.

Number of seats

The number of seats allocated to each country is in theory related to the size of the population. Each country can choose what electoral system to use for elections. Direct elections were first held in 1979, then in 1984 and 1989.

Country	No. of seats	Population per seat
Belgium	24	410,833
Denmark	16	320,000
France	81	686,667
Germany, Federal Republic of	81	753,086
Greece	24	415,416
Ireland	15	236,000
Italy	81	707,407
Luxembourg	6	61,583
Netherlands	25	584,800
Portugal	24	428,750
Spain	60	648,333
United Kingdom	81	688,642
TOTAL	518	

Political groupings

Members of the European Parliament sit in political not national groupings, even though there is no one-to-one correspondence between political parties in different countries.

Socialists – 180

European People's Party (Christian Democratic Union) – 123

European Democratic Group (formerly European Conservatives) – 34

Communists and Allies – 41

Liberal, Democratic and Reform Group – 44

European Democratic Alliance – 20

'Rainbow' group – 39

Independents – 16

European Right – 21

European Members of Parliament for the United Kingdom

Constituency	Member	Party	% of vote gained
Bedfordshire South	Peter Beazley	Con.	38.6
Birmingham East	Christine Crawley	Lab.	53.7
Birmingham West	John Tomlinson	Lab.	50.5
Bristol	Ian White	Lab.	39.5
Cambridge & Beds North	Sir Fred Catherwood	Con.	44.5
Cheshire East	Brian Simpson	Lab.	41.2
Cheshire West	Lyndon Harrison	Lab.	47.2
Cleveland & Yorkshire North	David Bowe	Lab.	50.1
Cornwall & Plymouth	Christopher Beazley	Con.	38.9
Cotswolds	Lord Plumb	Con.	45.1
Cumbria & Lancashire North	Richard Vane	Con.	41.2
Derbyshire	Geoffrey Hoon	Lab.	42.5
Devon	Lord O'Hagan	Con.	46.4
Dorset East & Hampshire West	Bryan Cassidy	Con.	55.4
Durham	Stephen Hughes	Lab.	65.8
Essex North East	Anne McIntosh	Con.	44.5
Essex South West	Patricia Rawlings	Con.	41.1
Glasgow	Janey Buchan	Lab.	55.4
Greater Manchester Central	Eddy Newman	Lab.	51.7
Greater Manchester East	Glyn Ford	Lab.	49.7
Greater Manchester West	Gary Titley	Lab.	71.6
Hampshire Central	Edward Kellett-Bowman	Con.	48.6
Hereford & Worcester	Sir James Scott-Hopkins	Con.	41.3
Hertfordshire	Derek Prag	Con.	46.7
Highlands & Islands	Winifred Ewing	SNP	51.6
Humberside	Peter Crampton	Lab.	45.4
Kent East	Christopher Jackson	Con.	43.9
Kent West	Ben Patterson	Con.	43.4
Lancashire Central	Michael Welsh	Con.	42.1
Lancashire East	Michael Hindley	Lab.	51.5
Leeds	Michael McGowan	Lab.	52.2
Leicester	Mel Read	Lab.	42.6
Lincolnshire	Bill Newton Dunn	Con.	45.4
London Central	Stan Newens	Lab.	42.2
London East	Carole Tongue	Lab.	49.5
London North	Pauline Green	Lab.	41.1
London North East	Alf Lomas	Lab.	53.9
London North West	Lord Bethell	Con.	41.3
London South & Surrey East	James Moorhouse	Con.	45.4
London South East	Peter Price	Con.	38.2
London South Inner	Richard Balfe	Lab.	51.9
London South West	Anita Pollack	Lab.	38.3
London West	Michael Elliot	Lab.	43.0
Lothians	David Martin	Lab.	41.3
Merseyside East	Terence Wynn	Lab.	65.7
Merseyside West	Kenneth Stewart	Lab.	49.8
Midlands Central	Christine Oddy	Lab.	38.5
Midlands West	John Bird	Lab.	53.4
Norfolk	Paul Howell	Con.	42.3
Northamptonshire	Anthony Simpson	Con.	41.7
Northumbria	Gordon Adam	Lab.	56.1
Nottingham	Ken Coates	Lab.	43.8
Oxford & Buckinghamshire	James Elles	Con.	46.8
Scotland Mid & Fife	Alex Falconer	Lab.	46.1
Scotland North East	Henry McGubban	Lab.	30.6
Scotland South	Alex Smith	Lab.	39.8
Sheffield	Roger Barton	Lab.	58.2
Shropshire & Stafford	Christopher Prout	Con.	41.0
Somerset & Dorset West	Margaret Daly	Con.	45.0
Staffordshire East	George Stevenson	Lab.	50.3
Strathclyde East	Ken Collins	Lab.	56.2
Strathcylde West	Hugh McMahon	Lab.	42.7
Suffolk	Amédée Turner	Con.	43.6
Surrey West	Tom Spencer	Con.	49.8
Sussex East	Sir Jack Stewart-Clark	Con.	48.2
Sussex West	Madron Seligman	Con.	47.4
Thames Valley	John Stevens	Con.	42.7

European Members of Parliament for the United Kingdom ***continued***

Constituency	Member	Party	% of vote gained
Tyne & Wear	Alan Donnelly	Lab.	69.3
Wales Mid & West	Dave Morris	Lab.	46.9
Wales North	Anthony Wilson	Lab.	33.1
Wales South	David Wayne	Lab.	54.7
Wales South East	Llewellyn Smith	Lab.	64.3
Wight & Hampshire East	Richard Simmonds	Con.	44.8
Wiltshire	Caroline Jackson	Con.	44.4
York	Edward McMillan-Scott	Con.	43.3
Yorkshire South	Norman West	Lab.	69.4
Yorkshire South West	Tom Megahy	Lab.	57.9
Yorkshire West	Barry Seal	Lab.	49.9

Northern Ireland

Three candidates were elected by single transferable vote:

Member	Party	% of first-preference votes
Ian Paisley	Democratic Unionist	29.9
John Hume	Social Democratic & Labour	25.4
Jim Nicholson	Official Unionist	22.2

Seven other candidates shared the remaining 22.5% of the Northern Ireland vote.

THE EUROPEAN COURT OF JUSTICE

The European Court of Justice has as its main responsibility to act as adjudicator of disputes that have arisen from the application of the Treaties. The findings of the Court are enforceable in all member countries. Apart from acting as a judge in cases involving member states and the Community, it also has to safeguard the law in the interpretation and application of Community Treaties. It is responsible for deciding whether decisions made by the Council of Ministers of the Commission are legal, and for determining whether or not the Treaties have been violated in particular instances. Member states, community institutions, firms or individuals may bring cases to the court.

The Court has 13 judges and six advocates-general who are appointed for renewable six-year terms by the member governments in mutual agreement. The Court sits on Tuesdays, Wednesdays and Thursdays, apart from when it has its summer break (mid July – mid September). In 1988 the Court had 372 new cases and 238 judgments were reached. There were 193 new cases in 1989, plus a further 599 brought over from 1988.

COMMUNITY FINANCES

The annual budget is created by the Council of Ministers and the Parliament, who act together as the Budgetary Authority. The member states pay levies, duties and a VAT charge under the terms of the Treaty of Rome.

The European Community had a budget requirement of nearly 45,000 million ECU (European Currency Unit) for 1989, in order to meet the Community expenditure. The largest part of this budget (almost 30,000 million ECU) was devoted to agricultural market sectors, although for the first time agricultural spending was reduced and some of the savings were channelled into increased food aid for developing countries. The other main areas of expenditure were on (1) regional policy and transport, (2) social policy, and (3) research, energy and industry. Over 1,000 million ECU were devoted to assisting developing and other non-member countries. The administration of the Commission and other EC institutions claimed over 2,000 million ECUs.

This expenditure is financed by money raised from the 12 member states. The greatest part of the finance for the budget is derived from VAT payments, which totalled over 26,000 million ECU. Customs duties brought in almost 10,000 million ECU, whereas agricultural and sugar levies accounted for just under 2,500 million ECU. Britain's contribution for 1989 was set at 637,333,981 ECU, or about £431 million.

The European Community Annual Budget

(a) Receipts: where the money comes from

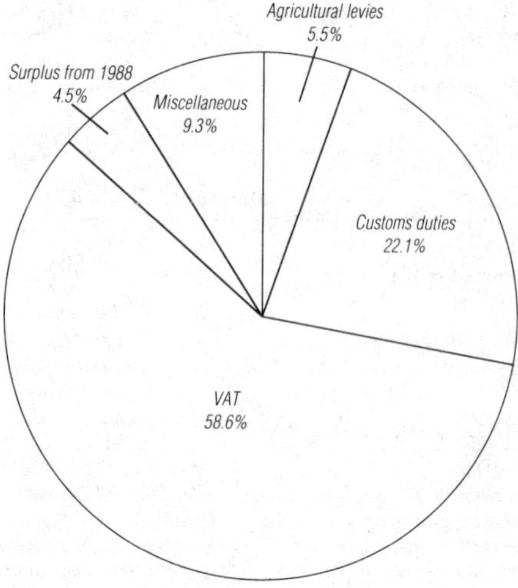

(b) Expenditure: how it is spent

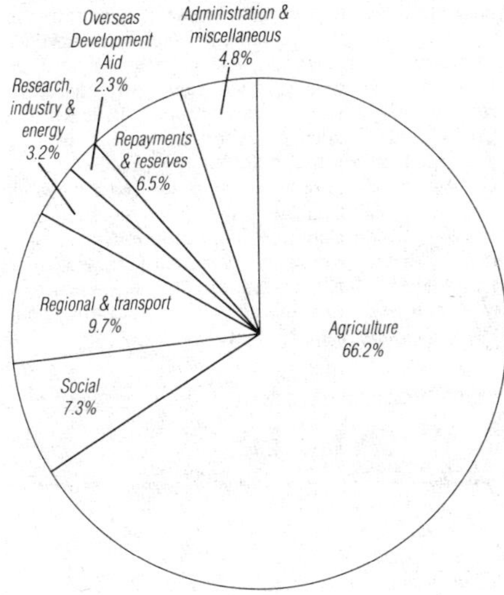

COMMON AGRICULTURAL POLICY (CAP)

Begun in 1962, the CAP aims to ensure reasonable standards of living for Europe's farmers, the great majority of whom (especially on the continent) farm on a small scale. The policy works in two ways: first by giving grants for farm improvements (this accounts for about one-third of the CAP budget), and secondly by supporting prices. The target price for each commodity is set annually, and if the market price falls below this the EC itself buys up the product at the guaranteed price and stores it. This has led over the years to immense surpluses (notably of beef and butter), which themselves cost money to maintain and are a further charge on the CAP. In response to this the EC has imposed upon farmers fixed quotas for the production of certain items, particularly milk. The CAP is resented by British farmers, who feel that they are made to subsidize the less efficient methods of continental farmers. The annual cost of Britain's contribution to the CAP is 175 million ECU (£120 million) in agricultural levies and 72.5 million ECU (£50 million) in sugar levies (1989 figures).

Storage

The costs for 1989 of storage of surplus agricultural products bought in by CAP intervention were:

	Million ECU	£ million
Beef/veal	794	537
Skimmed-milk powder	5	3
Butter and cream	439	297
Wine and alcohol	1,170	791
TOTAL	2,408	1,628

EUROPEAN MONETARY SYSTEM (EMS)

The European Monetary System was begun in 1979, to assist trading relations between member countries by preventing unduly wide variations in exchange rates. All members of the Community are in the EMS except Greece, Spain, Portugal and the UK. Currencies within the EMS have their value limited to a fixed range within their value calculated in terms of the European Currency Unit (ECU).

The ECU is the monetary unit used in all EC accounting. It is recalculated annually in relation to the value of the member states' currencies. At present, the ECU is composed of the following amounts of the currencies of 10 of the member states as follows:

Currency Amount	
0.71900	German marks
0.08780	Pounds sterling
1.31000	French francs
140.00000	Italian lire
0.25600	Dutch guilders
3.71000	Belgian francs
0.14000	Luxembourg francs
0.21900	Danish kroner
0.00871	Irish pounds
1.15000	Greek drachmas

The value of 1 ECU in sterling is 0.677p, and £1 = 1.476 ECU (as at 1 Sept. 1989).

THE EUROPEAN INVESTMENT BANK (EIB)

The European Investment Bank was created in 1958, to finance capital investment projects that would assist in the steady development of the European Community. The 12 member states of the Community are the members of the EIB. Each of the member countries nominates one minister (usually the finance minister) to the Board of Governors of the EIB.

The Bank's capital of 28,000 million ECU is made up of members' subscriptions, and the Bank also borrows the major part of its current funds from the capital markets of the Community and non-member countries, and on the international market. The EIB operates on a non-profit-making basis.

The EIB grants long-term loans to private enterprises, public authorities and financial institutions for projects that advance the economic development of less developed regions and protect the environment. Other projects that it is prepared to finance include the improvement of communication networks between states, the modernization of enterprises and the promotion of schemes involving co-operation between member states. In 1988 the EIB provided finance totalling over 10,200 million ECU for investments within the Community (including over £790 million in the UK). It has also signed contracts for about 700 million ECU for projects in countries outside the EEC.

EUROPEAN COAL AND STEEL COMMUNITY (ECSC)

Since starting operations in 1952, the ECSC has abolished customs duties and quantitative restrictions on coal, iron ore and scrap, as well as revoking the dual pricing system whereby different prices were charged on exported coal and steel from those charged to home consumers. It has also abolished currency restrictions, discrimination in transport rates and special frontier charges, all of which made the transport of its goods so much more expensive within the Community than within national boundaries. The ECSC has also applied for rules for fair competition and is attempting to set a harmonized external tariff for the whole Community. It has powers to set quotas and minimum prices.

All members of the European Economic Community are also members of the ECSC.

EUROPEAN ATOMIC ENERGY COMMUNITY (EURATOM)

Euratom was set up on 25 Mar. 1957, following discussions between members of the ECSC on further means of co-operation. Euratom's main task is to create the technical and industrial conditions necessary to utilize nuclear discoveries and produce nuclear energy on a large scale, in as short a period as possible. It is not involved in any way with the military uses of nuclear power.

Euratom has one substantial research institute of its own at Ispra in Italy, but the majority of its work is done in co-operation with research institutes in member states, or in international undertakings. In recent years, Euratom has gone into a decline. Quarrels over finance have repeatedly disrupted research programmes. Some states have been worried by the rising number of Green groups and growing public concern regarding the safety of nuclear power. Despite the increased awareness of the dangers of nuclear power after Chernobyl, member states have still not been able to agree on procedures for licensing or on standards of safety and quality control. The supply agency has been made redundant because of the ample supply of uranium ore, despite the Commission's attempts to revive it.

THE COMMONWEALTH

The Commonwealth is an informal association of sovereign states, without charter or constitution but co-ordinated by the Commonwealth Secretariat in London. It was inaugurated by the Imperial Conference in 1926 and originally was based on countries being members of the British Empire, i.e. owing allegiance to the Crown. In 1949 India led the way to a new concept of the Commonwealth, declaring her intention of remaining a member of the Commonwealth after becoming a republic. Many other former Empire countries or mandated territories have become republics on gaining independence, and most have opted to remain within the Commonwealth (those that did not were Aden, British Somaliland, Burma, Egypt, Iraq, Palestine, South Cameroons, Sudan, Transjordan). Republics (27) and local monarchies (5) now easily outnumber the Queen's realms (17) in the Commonwealth.

The heads of government of the Commonwealth countries hold a conference every two years, meeting in a different city each time. There are also annual meetings of finance ministers, and of other ministers (e.g. health, education) as appropriate.

Many Commonwealth countries have a formal link with Britain in that their highest court of appeal is the Privy Council. Most of these are countries which are still the Queen's realms (Antigua and Barbuda, the Bahamas, Barbados, Belize, Jamaica, Mauritius, New Zealand, St Christopher and Nevis, St Lucia, St Vincent and the Grenadines, Tuvalu), but some are republics (Dominica, the Gambia, Kiribati, Singapore, Trinidad and Tobago), and one is a local monarchy (Brunei).

Commonwealth Day is celebrated round the world on the second Monday in March.

Secretary General Sir Shridath S. Ramphal CMG QC
Headquarters Marlborough House, Pall Mall, London SW1Y 5HX, tel. 071 839 3411

Members of the Commonwealth

Antigua and Barbuda (1981)
Australia (1931)
Bahamas (1973)
Bangladesh (1972)
Barbados (1966)
Belize (1981)
Botswana (1966)
Britain
Brunei (1984)
Canada 1931)
Cyprus (1961)
Dominica (1978)
Gambia, the (1965)
Ghana (1957)
Grenada (1974)
Guyana (1966)
India (1947)
Jamaica (1962)
Kenya (1963)
Kiribati (1979)
Lesotho (1966)
Malawi (1964)
Malaysia (1957)
Maldives (1982)
Malta (1964)
Mauritius (1968)
Nauru (1968)
New Zealand (1931)
Nigeria (1960)
Pakistan (left 1972; rejoined 1989)
Papua New Guinea (1975)
St Christopher and Nevis (1983)
St Lucia (1979)
St Vincent and the Grenadines (1979)
Seychelles (1976)
Sierra Leone (1961)
Singapore (1965)
Solomon Islands (1978)
Sri Lanka (1948)
Swaziland (1968)
Tanzania (1961)
Tonga (1970)
Trinidad and Tobago (1962)
Tuvalu (1978)
Uganda (1962)
Vanuatu (1980)
Western Samoa (1970)
Zambia (1964)
Zimbabwe (1980)

Dates in brackets indicate the date that countries joined the Commonwealth.

Countries that have left the Commonwealth

Fiji (lapsed 1987)
Ireland (left 1949)
South Africa (left 1961)

NORTH ATLANTIC TREATY ORGANIZATION

The North Atlantic Treaty Organization (NATO) was founded shortly after World War II with the aim of increasing the ability of the Western powers to resist the perceived threat from the Communist bloc. The Treaty was signed on 4 Apr. 1949 by the foreign ministers of 12 countries: Belgium, Canada, Denmark, France, Iceland, Italy, Luxembourg, the Netherlands, Norway, Portugal, the United Kingdom and the United States. The Treaty came into force on 24 Aug. 1949. The terms of the Treaty included a commitment to keep to the United Nations principle of peaceful settlement of international disputes, but also stated (Article 5) that 'the parties agree that an armed attack against any one or more of them in Europe or North America shall be considered an attack against them all'. Later, four more countries were admitted: Greece and Turkey in 1952, the Federal Republic of Germany in 1955, and Spain in 1982. France withdrew her forces from military participation in 1966 but continues to take part in NATO's political activities.

Affairs of the Organization are controlled by the North Atlantic Council in which all member countries have equal status. Regular meetings are held twice a year attended by foreign ministers, and there are also occasional meetings at heads of government level. Matters specifically relating to defence are handled by the subsidiary Defence Planning Committee, at which defence ministers (of all member countries except France) meet twice a year. Both these bodies are also in permanent session to handle day-to-day affairs, with meetings attended by each country's Ambassador to NATO. There is also a Nuclear Planning Group, which meets twice yearly and consists of the defence ministers of all countries except France.

MILITARY COMMITTEE

This controls the military operations and the activities of the Allied Commanders, under the direction of the Defence Planning Committee. It consists of the Chiefs-of-Staff of all member countries (except France, and Iceland which has no military forces). Spain does not participate in military operations; Greece does sometimes but is held back by difficult relations with her neighbour Turkey. There is also the Canada–US Regional Planning Group, meeting alternately in Washington and Ottawa and dealing with the defence of North America.

Apart from the above, NATO's forces consist in theory of all the armed forces of all the member states. Since in practice no country could commit more than a proportion of its forces to NATO duties even in an emergency, the actual strength of NATO is hard to estimate. See p. 610, table following entry for Warsaw Treaty Organization (Warsaw Pact) for estimates of the relative strengths of NATO and the Warsaw Pact.

Secretary General Lord Carrington (UK)
Headquarters 1110 Brussels, Belgium

Command	Commander	Headquarters	Permanent force
Allied Command Europe (ACE)	Supreme Allied Commander Europe (SACEUR)	Supreme Headquarters Allied Powers in Europe (SHAPE), at Mons	ACE Mobile Force (land and air units)
Atlantic Command	Supreme Allied Commander Atlantic (SACLANT)	Norfolk, US	Standing Naval Force Atlantic (STANAVFORLANT)
Channel Command	Allied Commander-in-Chief Channel (CHINCHAN)	Northwood, UK	Standing Naval Force Channel (STANAVFORCHAN)

WARSAW TREATY ORGANIZATION (WARSAW PACT)

The Warsaw Treaty Organization (Warsaw Pact) was formed in response to the establishment and growth of the North Atlantic Treaty Organization (NATO) (formed 1949). At the instigation of the USSR, eight countries met in Warsaw and on 14 May 1955 signed a 20-year treaty of co-operation. They were: Albania, Bulgaria, Czechoslovakia, the German Democratic Republic, Hungary, Poland, Romania and the USSR. (Albania formally withdrew from the Pact in 1968, having not participated since the split away from the USSR in 1961.) The Treaty contains a clause similar to the one in NATO's treaty stating that 'in case of armed aggression in Europe against one or several States . . ., each State member of the pact will afford to the State or States which are the object of such aggression immediate assistance . . . including the use of armed force'. It also includes, unlike NATO, a clause (Article 11) that commits the Warsaw Pact to dissolving itself immediately 'in the event of a system of collective security being set up in Europe and a pact to this effect being signed – to which each party to this treaty will direct its efforts'. Another clause states that the contracting parties will set up a joint command of their armed forces.

The Warsaw Pact's forces, with command headquarters at Moscow, are believed to consist of two divisions in Poland, twenty in the German Democratic Republic, four in Hungary and five in Czechoslovakia.

NATO AND WARSAW PACT FORCES

In preparation for the conventional Stability Talks held in March 1989, ministers from the Defence Committees of NATO and the Warsaw Pact drew up the following estimates of their own and the opposite side's strengths.

NATO's forces	Own estimate	Warsaw Pact's estimate
Personnel (ground forces only)	2,213,593	2,493,200
Tanks	16,424	30,690
Combat helicopters	2,419	5,270
Combat aircraft	3,977	7,130

Warsaw Pact's forces	Own estimate	NATO's estimate
Personnel (ground forces only)	2,809,900	3,090,000
Tanks	59,430	51,500
Combat helicopters	2,785	3,700
Combat aircraft	7,876	8,250

Other types of forces were listed by both sides, but not in the same categories, so no direct comparisons can be made.

INTERNATIONAL DAILY REVIEW: 1989-90

1 JUNE

● Two IRA men, Harry Maguire and Alexander Murphy, are found guilty of the murder of two British soldiers who blundered into an IRA funeral procession in Mar. 1988. Both are sentenced to life imprisonment.

● Chancellor Nigel Lawson denies that there is a sterling crisis as the pound falls against the dollar in what the Chancellor calls a 'dollar phenomenon'.

● US President George Bush starts a two-day visit to Britain to reaffirm the Anglo-American special relationship. He holds talks with Mrs Thatcher and lunches with the Queen at Buckingham Palace.

● Soviet leader Mikhail Gorbachev agrees to establish a commission to determine whether or not the Baltic states of Estonia, Latvia and Lithuania were forcibly annexed in 1940. At the same time he blames the massacre of nationalist demonstrators in Georgia on the disgraced local Communist Party leader.

● The Portuguese parliament approves a package of constitutional reforms that dispenses with the vestiges of socialist ideology embedded in the 1976 constitution.

● Sri Lankan President Ranasinghe Premadasa demands the withdrawal of the Indian peace-keeping forces in Sri Lanka.

2 JUNE

● An estimated 5000 unarmed Chinese troops attempt to march on Tiananmen Square and are forced to retreat when they are blocked by Chinese students and Beijing residents.

● US President George Bush returns from a tour of Western Europe to tell a cheering crowd that 'we have a great and historic opportunity to shape the changes that are transforming Europe'.

● 6-month-old Andrew Little is savaged in his cot by a Rottweiler dog.

● Soviet dissident Andrei Sakharov is howled down in the Soviet Congress of People's Deputies after he accuses Soviet troops of atrocities in Afghanistan.

● IRA bomber Gerard Kelly is released for 'good behaviour' after serving only half of a five-year sentence. His early release raises a storm of protest from Conservative backbenchers.

● The Soviet newspaper *Pravda* reveals that in 1962 Soviet soldiers fired on a crowd of unarmed striking factory workers, killing up to 24 people.

● In Japan, Sosuke Uno is formally elected as Prime Minister.

3 JUNE

● The pro-democracy demonstrations in Beijing's Tiananmen Square are ruthlessly suppressed as tens of thousands of Chinese troops open fire on student demonstrators. Casualty figures among the students range between 5000 and 10,000.

● Hundreds are killed in the Soviet Union when a gas pipeline explodes and engulfs two passing railway trains in flames near the town of Ufa in the Ural Mountains. The accident is the worst rail disaster in Soviet history and raises questions about the safety of the Soviet gas pipeline from Siberia to Western Europe.

● Leonid Zamyatin, the Soviet Ambassador in London, accuses British intelligence of planting listening devices in the walls of the Russian trade delegation and in the London homes of Soviet diplomats.

● Foreign Secretary Sir Geoffrey Howe attacks Labour leader Neil Kinnock whom he claims lacks Mrs Thatcher's qualities of 'character, conviction and competence' and is 'a man who regards words as a substitute for thought and confuses ranting with resolution'.

● Irish poet Seamus Heaney is elected Oxford University's Professor of Poetry.

4 JUNE

● Mrs Thatcher says that Britain is 'deeply shocked and appalled' at the massacre in Tiananmen Square. Labour leader Neil Kinnock brands the killings as 'a crime against humanity'.

● Clashes between civilians and the army continue in China. There are reports of a mutiny within the Chinese Army. There are also reports of a power struggle within the Chinese leadership.

● Demonstrations in support of Chinese students break out in Hong Kong where the residents become increasingly concerned about Britain handing the colony over to China in 1997.

● The death of Iranian leader Ayatollah Khomeini is announced in the early hours. He had died shortly before midnight.

● President Ali Khameini succeeds Ayatollah Khomeini as Iran's supreme religious leader but Hojatoleslam Ali Akbar Hashemi Rafsanjani, Speaker of the House, is poised to take political power.

● The Polish Communist Party suffers a humiliating defeat as Solidarity candidates win 92 out of 100 open seats in parliamentary elections. The Communists and their coalition partners, however, have been guaranteed 65% of the seats in the Polish Sejm (parliament)

● Newly installed Japanese Prime Minister Sosuke Uno is implicated in a sex scandal.

5 JUNE

● Britons in China flee to the safety of the British embassy compound as troop movements and shootings continue.

● US President George Bush announces a package of sanctions against the Chinese government in response to the crackdown in Beijing. But he stresses that he does not want to break off relations.

● Eight people are crushed to death as hundreds of thousands of Iranians press around the body of Ayatollah Khomeini for a final viewing.

● More than 1000 North Sea oil-industry construction workers stage a one-day strike in support of higher pay and improved safety conditions.

● Torrential rains in Sri Lanka leave 100,000 homeless and 310 dead.

● Pakistan Prime Minister Benazir Bhutto starts a six-day visit to the United States. She and President George Bush discuss the war in Afghanistan, Pakistan's nuclear capability and US aid for Pakistan.

6 JUNE

● Iranian leader Ayatollah Khomeini is buried among chaotic scenes which involve rescuing his body by helicopter after a grief-stricken crowd surges forward.

● Mrs Thatcher says Britain will stand by its agreement to hand Hong Kong over to China in 1997. The Foreign Office announces a ban on arms sales to China and France announces a freeze on diplomatic relations with China.

● The first official Chinese government accounts of the Tiananmen Square massacre are issued. They claim that only 300 were killed after students attacked soldiers.

● US Congressman Thomas S. Foley is elected Speaker of the House of Representatives in succession to the disgraced Jim Wright.

● Polish leader Gen. Wojciech Jaruzelski calls on Solidarity to join the Communist Party in a broad coalition government. The proposal is rejected by Solidarity.

● The West German government, under pressure from environmentalists, formally scraps plans to build a controversial nuclear reprocessing plant at Wackersdorf in Bavaria.

7 JUNE

● Mrs Thatcher says that Britain cannot provide a home to all 3.25 million British passport holders in Hong Kong but may be able to offer an eventual refuge to key business leaders and civil servants.

● Chinese leaders say they will expel all Party members who played a role in the 'counter-revolution' and warn other countries not to interfere in China's internal affairs.

● Hong Kong Governor Sir David Wilson leaves for London for talks with Mrs Thatcher on the crisis in China and its implications for the Crown Colony.

● Oil ministers from the Organization of Petroleum Exporting Countries (OPEC) agree to a higher production ceiling in an effort to hold oil prices at $18 a barrel.

● Govan Mbeki, the highest ranking African National Congress leader at liberty in South Africa, visits ANC leader Nelson Mandela in prison.

● A Surinam Airways DC-8 jet airliner crashes near the capital of Surinam, Parmaribo, killing 169 of the 182 passengers aboard.

8 JUNE

● Thousands of dockers take unofficial strike action at five British ports.

● The Commons Select Committee on Transport is told that London Underground management plans to raise fares in order to discourage people from using the service during peak periods.

● Soviet Prime Minister Nikolai Ryzhkov promises to cut Soviet defence spending by between one-third and a half by 1995.

● A Soviet MiG 29 jet crashes at the Paris Air Show. The test pilot, Anatoly Kvochur, ejected from the plane just before the crash and survives with multiple injuries.

● The Royal Australian Air Force is forced to take over air traffic control at Sydney International Airport after civilian air traffic controllers start industrial action in support of a 42% pay rise.

9 JUNE

● The Chinese authorities start arresting hundreds of pro-democracy activists. Reformist-minded Party leader Zhao Ziyang is dropped from photographs of the Chinese leadership.

● The British government imposes a ban on the importation of ivory in an effort to save elephant herds from extinction. The United States, Japan and other EC countries join the ban.

● El Salvadorean cabinet minister José Antonio Rodriguez Porth is assassinated by leftist guerrillas. He was minister for the presidency.

● EC environment ministers formally adopt anti-pollution standards for small cars.

● 31 people are killed in the Soviet Union when an express train crashes into a stalled bus.

● South Africa's three-year-old state of emergency is extended for a further 12 months.

10 JUNE

● Chinese authorities expel ITN journalist Peter Newport after he videotaped a student demonstration in Shanghai. Newport is the first foreign correspondent to be expelled for covering the unrest.

● Polish leader Gen. Wojciech Jaruzelski visits Britain for talks with Mrs Thatcher, who promises £25 million in British aid to boost Polish economic reforms.

● US Secretary of State James Baker meets Chinese Ambassador Han Xu to discuss the fate of Chinese dissident Fang Lizhi who took refuge in the US Embassy in Beijing following the Tiananmen Square massacre.

● Admiral William Crowe, Chairman of the US Joint Chiefs of Staff, starts a 10-day tour of the Soviet Union. He is the first US Joint Chiefs Chairman to visit the Soviet Union.

● A McDonald's restaurant in Milton Keynes is fire-bombed by animal-rights activists after a vegetarian pop star criticizes the fast-food chain.

11 JUNE

● Former US President Ronald Reagan arrives in London for a four-day private visit during which he will dine at Buckingham Palace and Downing Street and deliver the Churchill Memorial Lecture on 'The

Problems, Perils, Challenges and Opportunities Confronting the English-Speaking Peoples of Today'.

● Two Chinese diplomats at the Chinese consulate in San Francisco announce that they are seeking political asylum in the United States; in China, a warrant is issued for the arrest of dissident Fang Lizhi in spite of a US appeal yesterday.

● Venezuelan troops storm police stations throughout Caracas to crush a strike by the capital's police force.

● Alfredo Cesar, a leading Contra rebel, returns to Nicaragua to join forces with opposition parties hoping to defeat the Sandinista government in elections in February.

● The Hungarian Communists and opposition groups reach an agreement to start political negotiations on the country's future. The agreement includes a commitment to multi-party elections.

12 JUNE

● The Civil Aviation Authority grounds all 12 Boeing 737–400 airliners flown by British operators after two engine failures identical to the one that led to the M1 plane crash.

● Britain suffers its most serious outbreak of the deadly disease botulism. The outbreak is traced to a hazelnut yogurt.

● Soviet leader Mikhail Gorbachev starts a four-day visit to West Germany; he is warmly welcomed.

● 90 die when ethnic violence erupts in the Soviet Union's Central Asian republic of Uzbekistan. The deaths stem from clashes between majority Uzbecks and minority Meskhetians.

● US President George Bush presents proposals for a clean-air programme. The aim is to reduce smog in 78 US cities, cut acid rain by 50% and cut industrial toxic emissions by 75%.

● Argentine President Raul Alfonsin announces that he will resign five months early as it becomes increasingly apparent that he cannot control the economy following the election of Peronist candidate Carlos Saul Menem as President to succeed him.

13 JUNE

● Mrs Thatcher tells the House of Commons that Chancellor Nigel Lawson has her 'full and unequivocal and generous backing'. The statement is Mrs Thatcher's reply to reports that she and Mr. Lawson are split over British membership of the European Monetary System.

● Home Secretary Douglas Hurd says that Britain's independent broadcasting licences will be put up for sale to the highest bidder from Jan. 1993.

● Disgraced Canadian sprinter Ben Johnson admits to a Toronto federal inquiry that he is a long-time user of anabolic steroids and had lied about not using the substances.

● The Hungarian Communist Party and leaders of opposition factions start formal talks in Budapest on a transition to a multi-party political system.

● José Antonio Zorrilla Perez, the former head of Mexico's federal police agency, is arrested for the 1984 murder of well-known Mexican journalist Manuel Buenida.

● Soviet leader Mikhail Gorbachev and West German Chancellor Helmut Kohl sign a declaration pledging that 'every state has the right to freely choose its own political and social system'.

14 JUNE

● A 60-nation Geneva conference on the Vietnamese boat people agrees proposals to stem the tide of Vietnamese refugees. Britain and Vietnam agree to further talks on the forcible repatriation of boat people in Hong Kong.

● Foreign Secretary Sir Geoffrey Howe says that Britain has 'inescapable' obligations to the people of Hong Kong in the event of of an 'overwhelming cataclysmic series of events' but rejects calls to grant British passport holders automatic right of abode in the United Kingdom.

● Gen. Arnaldo Ochoa Sanchez, a senior Cuban Army officer, is arrested in Havana on charges of drug smuggling.

● French President François Mitterrand starts a three-day visit to Poland. On his arrival he announces that France will restructure $1200 million of Poland's debt with France and offers the Polish government a further $100 million in fresh loans.

● Former US President Ronald Reagan is made an honorary Knight of the Order of the Bath.

● Two suspected IRA men, Terence McGeough and Gerard Hanratty, are indicted in West Germany on charges related to bomb attacks in 1987 and 1988 against British military bases in West Germany. A total of 46 people were injured in the attacks.

15 JUNE

● The Conservatives suffer a major setback in the European Parliamentary elections. Labour polls 40% of the votes and gains 14 seats compared with only 35% for the Conservatives. The election also sees the emergence of the British Green Party as a political force.

● The Labour Party increases its majority in two parliamentary by-elections, in Glasgow Central and the London constituency of Vauxhall.

● Irish Prime Minister Charles Haughey fails to win an absolute majority in the general election. The result leads to a political crisis in Ireland.

● Soviet leader Mikhail Gorbachev tells a press conference in Bonn that the Berlin Wall need not stand for 'an eternity'.

● Three young workers in Shanghai are sentenced to death for helping to set fire to a train at the height of the anti-government protests.

● Dr Jan Cools, a Belgian doctor held captive in Lebanon for 13 months, is released by the Fatah Revolutionary Council, the Palestinian splinter group led by Abu Nidal.

● The US House of Representatives approves a $157,000 million bail-out of the American savings and loan industry.

16 JUNE

● Among those knighted in the Birthday Honours List

are the actor Rex Harrison and the Queen's couturier, Hardy Amies.

● A ballot of workers at British passport offices approves a nationwide ban on overtime. The Civil and Public Servants Association has called for a three-fold increase in staffing levels. The overtime ban seriously affects the issuing of passports and disrupts many holidays.

● Chinese leader Deng Xiaoping is reported to have told senior army commanders that the Communist Party leadership was forced to crush the pro-democracy movement to prevent its own downfall.

● ITN journalists Vernon Mann and John Elphinstone are expelled from China for violating the terms of their tourist visas.

● Gen. Dan Shomron, Chief of Staff of the Israeli armed forces, rejects calls for a purely military solution to the Palestinian uprising on the West Bank and Gaza Strip.

● Hungarians rebury the remains of Premier Imre Nagy who had been executed and buried in an unmarked grave after he led the 1956 Hungarian Revolution. The reburial service is accompanied by a nine-hour memorial service in Budapest.

● Six more Cuban Army officers are arrested on charges of drug smuggling.

17 JUNE

● Hundreds of young Muslims clash with mounted police in Bradford during a demonstration against Salman Rushdie and his novel *The Satanic Verses*.

● More than 300 people are arrested at a rock festival at Pilton, near Shepton Mallet, Somerset. Most of the arrests were for drug offences.

● Turkish Prime Minister Turgut Ozal opens his country's borders with Bulgaria to allow tens of thousands of persecuted ethnic Turks to flee Bulgaria.

● The Iranian authorities publicly hang 15 people convicted of drug trafficking. The hangings bring to 676 the number of people executed for drug trafficking since the start of 1989.

● 17 people die when an East German airliner en route to Moscow bursts into flames during takeoff from East Berlin's Schönefeld Airport.

18 JUNE

● The Conservative Party starts a major inquest into its poor showing in the European Parliamentary elections. The elections saw big gains for left-wing and environmentalist parties throughout Europe.

● Greece's New Democracy Party wins the most seats in the general election but fails to secure an absolute majority and the Communists hold the balance of power. The Socialist government of Andreas Papandreou was badly damaged by the Bank of Crete scandal.

● Poland holds run-off elections to fill the 303 parliamentary seats left vacant in the first round of voting on 4 June. The final result leaves Solidarity in control of 99 of the 100 seats in the Senate (the upper house) and 161 seats in the Sejm (lower house of the parliament).

● The Spanish peseta formally enters the European Monetary System, a year earlier than scheduled.

● Romania starts construction of a wall along its border with Yugoslavia and Hungary.

19 JUNE

● The High Court in London refuses British Rail's request for an injunction to stop a threatened rail strike because 200 of the union's 71,000 workers had not had a chance to vote on strike action.

● Labour leader Neil Kinnock says that the Labour result in the European Parliamentary elections left him 'very confident of a strong majority at the next general election'. Mrs Thatcher admits that the result was 'disappointing' and blames it on inflation, but other senior Conservatives attribute the defeat to the Prime Minister's EC-bashing tactics.

● Spanish Prime Minister Felipe Gonzalez visits Mrs Thatcher at Downing Street to urge her to drop her outright opposition to monetary union and an EC social pact.

● US–Soviet Strategic Arms Reduction Talks (START) resume in Geneva after a seven-month recess. Parallel bilateral negotiations on space weapons resume in Geneva on the same day.

● Transport Secretary Paul Channon gives his approval to plans to extend the London Underground to the Docklands.

● EC finance ministers agree measures to create an open internal market in banking and financial services.

20 JUNE

● Britain has the hottest June day since 1976 as temperatures in London soar to 30°C (86°F). The temperature rise is accompanied by drought warnings.

● Soviet dissident Andrei Sakharov tells the Royal Institute for International Affairs that the Soviet Union faces an upheaval so huge that even civil war could not be excluded.

● The United States suspends all high-level contacts between US and Chinese government officials and urges international financial institutions to 'postpone consideration' of Chinese loan applications.

● Angry West Bank Jewish settlers hold a demonstration march outside the Israeli Knesset (parliament) after a fellow settler is stabbed to death on the West Bank.

● A Soviet cruise ship, the *Maxim Gorky*, hits an iceberg in the Greenland Sea. Nearly 1000 people, mainly West German tourists, are rescued by the Norwegian Coast Guard.

● Ali Akbar Hashemi Rafsanjani, Speaker of the Iranian parliament, starts a visit to the Soviet Union. He signs economic agreements worth $6000 million and signs a joint declaration with Soviet leader Mikhail Gorbachev stating that 'relations between the two countries have entered a new stage'.

21 JUNE

● Today saw the first of a series of one-day official strikes by the National Union of Railwaymen. The strike is compounded by identical action on London's buses and the London Underground. Railway workers are demanding a higher pay offer and protesting against a change in working practices.

● The government announces voluntary measures to curb malpractices by estate agents. The measures mean that estate agents can be banned from practising for activities such as bidding up prices, unfair or misleading contract terms or forcing purchasers to arrange finance through them.

● Mrs Thatcher denies that her policies were responsible for the Conservatives' defeat in the European Parliamentary elections and blames the loss on Conservative Central Office's handling of the campaign.

● More than 250 people are arrested during the hippies' traditional attempt to visit Stonehenge at the summer solstice. An 800-strong cordon of police prevented this year's attempt.

● The US Supreme Court rules that burning the American flag is protected by the First Amendment's guarantee of free speech. The ruling provokes an outcry and President George Bush announces that he will seek a constitutional amendment prohibiting the burning of the flag.

● Australian Prime Minister Bob Hawke starts a three-day visit to Britain during which he will hold talks with Mrs Thatcher on Australian and British sanctions against China and South Africa. Mr Hawke will go on to visit West Germany, Hungary, France and the United States.

22 JUNE

● Manslaughter charges are brought against three former directors of P&O European Ferries for the deaths of 188 people drowned when the *Herald of Free Enterprise* capsized off Zeebrugge in Mar. 1987. Also charged for manslaughter were the captain, the first officer, a crewman, the assistant boatswain and the ship's senior master.

● The Hanson Trust bids £3100 million for the British mining house Consolidated Gold Fields.

● Emergency water tenders and standpipes are sent to southeast London after a broken water main leaves 150,000 people without water.

● The London Underground unveils plans to spend more than £500 million on upgrading the Northern Line.

● The Socialist International meeting in Stockholm embraces the market economy and rejects widescale nationalization of industry as a 'remedy for social ills'. The new policy line is seen as a major revision of basic principles.

● Angola's Marxist government and the UNITA rebels led by Jonas Savimbi announce a formal truce in their 14-year-old civil war following a one-day summit in Gbadolite, Zaire.

23 JUNE

● Nine prisoners being transferred from Plymouth to Exeter gaol hijack their van. Four of the prisoners escape.

● Two British merchant naval officers die when two ships collide in the Atlantic off the coast of Spain.

● F. W. de Klerk, leader of South Africa's National Party, visits Britain for talks with Mrs Thatcher who urged de Klerk to release gaoled ANC leader Nelson Mandela. De Klerk will also visit West Germany and Portugal during his seven-day European tour.

● The Greek oil-tanker *World Prodigy* runs aground off Newport, Rhode Island, US, spilling 420,000 gallons of fuel oil. On the same day, a Panamanian-registered freighter *Rilhand B* collides with an oil-tanker barge in Galveston Bay, Texas, causing the spillage of a further 250,000 gallons.

● Polish leader Gen. Wojciech Jaruzelski says that the Communist Party's poor showing in the elections underscored the need for the Party to change.

● Greek caretaker Prime Minister Andreas Papandreou is rushed to hospital suffering from pneumonia in the middle of his unsuccessful efforts to form a minority government.

24 JUNE

● Protestant Ulster Freedom Fighters murder Catholic barman Liam McKee in Lisburn, Northern Ireland. McKee's family says he had no Sinn Fein or paramilitary connections.

● Dr John Vincent, the head of the British Methodist Church, attacks Mrs Thatcher's policies as a 'perversion' of the Christian tradition.

● Hang-glider Charles Collins dies when his hang-glider crashes near Shaftesbury, Dorset.

● Zhao Ziyang, the reform-minded general secretary of the Chinese Communist Party, is formally ousted in a leadership reshuffle. Zhao, who was denounced for fostering a 'counter-revolutionary rebellion', is replaced by hard-liner Jiang Zemin.

● A 100,000-strong rally in Ankara calls on the Turkish government to invade neighbouring Bulgaria to protect persecuted ethnic Turks.

● Israeli troops kill six pro-Iranian guerrillas during battles in Lebanon's Bekaa Valley. An Israeli soldier is slightly wounded.

● A Uruguayan oil-tanker *Presidente Rivera* hits a rock in the Delaware River and dumps 310,000 gallons of heating oil; this is the third US oil spillage in two days.

25 JUNE

● A Grenadier guardsman who accidentally shot dead a Sinn Fein election worker at a Northern Ireland border crossing returns to duty in West Germany. Guardsman David Holden had initially been charged with manslaughter, but the charge was later dropped.

● TUC General Secretary Norman Willis attacks government proposals to give bonuses to workers who refuse to join closed shops.

● The Chinese Communist Party leadership calls for a purge of all Party officials who supported the pro-democracy movement.

● Japan's ruling Liberal Democratic Party loses a major parliamentary by-election to the Japan Socialist Party, underscoring the political impact of financial and sex scandals involving the Party leadership.

● An estimated 40,000 Moldavians rally to protest against the 1940 creation of the republic which was ceded to the Soviet Union by Romania.

● In Hungary, Reformist Imre Pozsgay is named as the Communist Party's nominee for state President. At the same time, the Party issues a statement saying that 'The goal is democratic socialism, based on a multi-party system and a market economy based on the decisive role of communal property.'

26 JUNE

● Alan Bond, the Australian businessmen who controls 28% of British Satellite Broadcasting, is ruled unfit to hold a broadcasting licence by the Australian Broadcasting Tribunal.

● Defence Secretary George Younger says the crisis in China may force the government to delay the withdrawal of the Gurkha regiment from Hong Kong.

● A Soviet nuclear submarine off the coast of Norway is forced to shut down its reactors after an onboard accident. The submarine manages to limp back to Murmansk using diesel engines.

● At least 24 people are killed when a bomb explodes on a Chinese train. The explosion is linked to the pro-democracy movement.

● The World Bank announces that it is indefinitely suspending $708 million in loans to China.

● US Secretary of State James Baker proposes the establishment of a 'pan-Pacific entity' to facilitate the free flow of goods, services, capital, technology and ideas among the countries bordering the Pacific.

27 JUNE

● Mrs Thatcher, attending an EC heads of government summit in Madrid, agrees to a compromise communiqué affirming the EC's 'determination progressively to achieve economic and monetary union'.

● The Transport and General Workers' Union votes in favour of the Labour Party retaining the policy of unilateral nuclear disarmament.

● The EC announces a series of sanctions against China in protest against the 'brutal repression' of the pro-democracy movement. The sanctions include the suspension of high-level diplomatic contacts and of military cooperation and sales between EC countries and China.

● Three Chinese diplomats in London apply for political asylum in Britain.

● The Supreme Soviet (the Soviet parliament) rejects six nominated cabinet ministers proposed by Premier Nikolai Ryzhkov. It is the first time in Soviet history that the parliament has not automatically approved cabinet nominees.

● The West German government starts an inquiry into American reports that a West German company has helped Iran to manufacture mustard gas.

● An estimated 80% of New Delhi's businesses are closed by a general strike in protest against the Indian government's failure to check terrorism in the Punjab.

28 JUNE

● The second in a series of one-day strikes again stops Britain's rail and underground services.

● Prince Charles launches an attack on the standard of the teaching of English.

● The Sri Lankan government and the Tamil Tigers sign a cease-fire.

● Hundreds of thousands of Serbs from across the globe gather at Kosovo to mark the 600th anniversary of the Battle of Kosovo. The gathering underscores the continuing threat of Serbian nationalism to Yugoslavia.

● The European Commission warns that rising inflation and diverging budgetary and trade imbalances could jeopardize sustained economic growth among the 12 member states.

● American film stuntman Clinton Carpenter is killed and five other people are injured when a helicopter being used in the film *Freedom or Death* crashes in Corfu, Greece.

29 JUNE

● Mrs Thatcher asks the Treasury to draw up an alternative plan to the European Monetary System.

● The Commons Select Committee on Social Services publishes a report attacking the government for a delayed and confused response to the sharp increase in cases of listeria.

● A 12-year-old schoolgirl and a teacher die when a coach carrying schoolchildren overturns and hits a car in
West Sussex. More than 30 other children from Calthorpe Comprehensive School are injured.

● Labour leader Neil Kinnock is heckled by left-wingers at the Transport and General Workers' Union when he reaffirms the new Labour Party policy of multilateral nuclear disarmament.

● Five members of the French left-wing terrorist group Action Directe are sentenced to heavy prison terms at the end of a month-long trial. They were charged with kidnapping and murder.

● Zairean President Mobutu Sese Seko is welcomed at the White House where he is praised by US President George Bush for helping to open negotiations between the MPLA government of Angola and the UNITA rebels led by Jonas Savimbi.

30 JUNE

● The Commons Foreign Affairs Committee supports the government's refusal to grant the right of residence in Britain to all British passport holders in Hong Kong.

● Home Secretary Douglas Hurd says that specialist units are being set up throughout London to deal with the growing problem of domestic violence.

● A Greenpeace activist boards a Soviet nuclear-powered submarine in the Baltic and fixes a nuclear warning flag on top of it.

● European Commissioner Sir Leon Brittan urges Mrs Thatcher not to delay British entry into the Exchange Rate Mechanism of the European Monetary System.

● A military coup in Sudan ousts the civilian government of Prime Minister Sadiq el-Mahdi. The new leadership pledges itself to ending the country's long-running North–South civil war.

● Hundreds of Jewish settlers stage a protest march through West Jerusalem to assert their right to live and move freely in the Occupied Territories.

1 JULY

● The Labour Party takes a 10-point lead in an opinion poll. The MORI poll published in the *Sunday Times* gives Labour 47% of the vote, the Conservatives 37%, the Greens 7%, the Democrats 4% and the SDP 3%.

● More than 20,000 people attend an anti-poll-tax rally in Manchester where Labour politicians said the tax would cost the Conservatives the next general election.

● One of Britain's last remaining Spitfires crashes into a hillside, killing its millionaire pilot–owner Charles Church.

● Opinion poll in the *Observer* reports that 79% of the public are opposed to the government's plans to privatize the water industry.

● Tzannis Tzannetakis, leader of Greece's conservative New Democracy Party, is sworn in as Prime Minister at the head of a conservative–Communist coalition pledged to bringing to justice former socialist ministers guilty of corruption.

● Soviet leader Mikhail Gorbachev warns that ethnic unrest poses 'an enormous danger' to the Soviet Union and says the 'most decisive measures' will be taken against those who promote separatism.

2 JULY

● Foreign Secretary Sir Geoffrey Howe starts a three-day visit to Hong Kong. He is greeted by angry crowds who denounce Britain's refusal to grant refuge to Hong Kong residents with valid British passports.

● A British Army corporal is killed and his wife and children injured when an IRA car bomb explodes outside his home in Hanover, West Germany. A second bomb found under a nearby car belonging to another British serviceman is defused.

● The flotation of Abbey National shares is oversubscribed 2.7 times.

● Andrei Gromyko, the long-serving Soviet Foreign Minister and President of the USSR, dies in Moscow. He was Foreign Minister from 1957 to 1985.

● Japan's ruling Liberal Democratic Party suffers a major setback in the Tokyo municipal elections, the result of sex and financial scandals involving the LDP leadership.

● The Mexican conservative opposition party National Action Party (PAN) wins the election for governor in the state of Baja. It is the first time in 60 years that the ruling Institutional Revolutionary Party (PRI) has conceded defeat.

● A group of liberal White South Africans fly to the Zambian capital of Lusaka for a meeting with ANC President Oliver Tambo.

3 JULY

● The Post Office announces that it will reintroduce some Sunday postal collections from October and that second and first class stamps will rise by 1p.

● The Labour Party attacks senior British executives for awarding themselves the largest pay rises of the century while calling on workers to moderate their pay claims.

● A High Court judge lifts the injunction halting building work on the site of Shakespeare's Rose Theatre in Southwark.

● Poland's Solidarity offers to help form the first non-Communist government in Eastern Europe for 40 years.

● Panos Koupparis, a businessman who tried to blackmail the government of Cyprus for £9 million by threatening to release a poisonous gas cloud over the island, is gaoled for five years by Old Bailey judge Justice MacPherson.

● Anti-abortionists in the United States suffer a major blow when the US Supreme Court strengthens the individual states' rights to legislate on laws related to abortion.

● The West German police start an investigation into electoral and financial fraud in West Germany's far-right Republican Party.

4 JULY

● The British Society of Motor Manufacturers reports a surge in British car exports. Car production for export in May leapt by 60% compared to May 1988.

● Soviet leader Mikhail Gorbachev starts a three-day visit to France.

● A Soviet MiG 23 jet fighter crashes into a Belgian house killing a 19-year-old man. The plane was placed on autopilot when the pilot bailed out over Poland.

● The Hanson Trust buys the mining company Consolidated Gold Fields for £3500 million.

● The European Commission decides to take Britain to the European Court of Justice for overfishing waters stretching from Scotland to the Bay of Biscay.

● A US delegation of scientists, politicians and journalists starts an inspection tour of a Soviet Cruise-missile site and two secret military facilities.

● Former US President Ronald Reagan is injured in a riding accident in Mexico.

5 JULY

● Holiday campers Peter and Gwenda Dixon are murdered by a shotgun blast while walking along the Pembrokeshire coastline. Police warn ramblers to keep off the coastal footpaths.

● Former White House aide Lt-Col. Oliver North is spared a prison sentence for his part in the Iran–Contra scandal, but he is given a three-year suspended sentence and fined $150,000 after being found guilty on three of the nine charges brought against him.

● Christopher Patten, Minister for Overseas Development, signs a British aid package aimed at protecting the Brazilian rain forest.

● The third one-day strike by Britain's train drivers paralyses the nation's transport system.

● David Evans, the farmworker who strangled schoolgirl Anna Humphries and then fled to France, is gaoled for life with a recommendation that he serve a minimum of 30 years.

● South African Prime Minister P. W. Botha and gaoled ANC leader Nelson Mandela meet secretly at Botha's Cape Town office.

● Israeli Prime Minister Itzhak Shamir hardens proposals for a Middle East peace initiative in order to win the support of his right-wing Likud Party. The changes discourage the United States, EC and Arab countries.

6 JULY

● Mrs Thatcher warns that the rail strikes are threatening rail workers' jobs.

● A Palestinian extremist grabs the wheel of an Israeli bus forcing it off the road. The action causes the deaths of 14 people and seriously injures 46 others after the bus bursts into flames. The Palestinian survived.

● Pakistan Prime Minister Benazir Bhutto visits London for talks with Mrs Thatcher on Pakistan rejoining the Commonwealth, the drug trade, increased British aid and the Afghan civil war.

● Collet's bookshop in Charing Cross Road, London, is fire-bombed by Islamic fundamentalists protesting against the shop's sale of Salman Rushdie's novel *The Satanic Verses*.

● Nine survivors are found clinging to an upturned bathtub in the North Sea after a fishing boat sinks.

● Former Hungarian Premier Imre Nagy, who led the 1956 Hungarian Uprising, is posthumously rehabilitated by the Hungarian Supreme Court. On the same day, former Hungarian Communist Party leader Janos Kadar dies.

● Soviet leader Mikhail Gorbachev addresses the Council of Europe and speaks of his belief in 'a common European home'.

7 JULY

● At a Warsaw Pact summit meeting in Bucharest, Soviet leader Mikhail Gorbachev calls for a 'new atmosphere' of tolerance among Pact members that accepts 'independent solutions of national problems'. The statement is interpreted as a renunciation of the Brezhnev Doctrine which justified the 1968 Soviet-led invasion of Czechoslovakia.

● The High Court upholds Environment Secretary Nicholas Ridley's decision to allow military training on grazing land in the North Pennines. The decision has been strongly opposed by environmentalists. The same day, Ridley also gives provisional approval for the building of Foxley Wood, a new town of 4800 homes at Bramshill, Hampshire.

● The Chinese government invites Hong Kong leaders to Beijing for talks with top officials in a bid to restore confidence in the colony's future.

● Three RUC policemen are wounded when their car is blown off the road by an IRA bomb planted in a lay-by on the Antrim coast in Northern Ireland.

● Convicted Cuban drug smuggler, Arnald Ochoa Sanchez, is executed by a Cuban firing squad. Ochoa was a former army Major General and war hero. Three other drug smugglers were executed at the same time.

● John McEnroe is knocked out of Wimbledon in the semi-finals.

8 JULY

● Sheila McCarthy, mother of kidnapped Worldwide Television News journalist John McCarthy, dies of cancer. Her son's Beirut kidnappers had ignored Mrs McCarthy's appeals to let her see her son before she died.

● A woman's body is found in the River Brent in west London. Police say she had been sexually attacked, beaten and thrown into the river while still alive.

● 27 people are arrested in the latest of a series of police raids on acid parties.

● The City of London celebrates its 800th anniversary.

● East German leader Erich Honecker goes into hospital suffering from a gall-bladder complaint.

● Carlos Menem is inaugurated as President of Argentina. The inauguration marks Argentina's first transfer of power from one democratically elected civilian government to another for 61 years.

● News of the secret meeting on 5 July between South African Prime Minister P. W. Botha and gaoled ANC leader Nelson Mandela is leaked to the press.

9 JULY

● US President George Bush arrives in Poland and says the changes in that country are an inspiration to the world. During his visit, Bush meets President Wojciech Jaruzelski and Solidarity leader Lech Walesa.

● The Afghan Army breaks a four-month rebel siege of Jalalabad. The government victory is a major setback for the US- and Pakistan-backed guerrilla forces.

● Argentine President Carlos Menem announces an emergency austerity package which includes a 600% increase in public-sector prices and the privatization of nationalized industries.

● The Archbishop of Canterbury, the Rt Rev. Dr Robert Runcie, warns that religious fundamentalism leads to dangerous intolerance equivalent to an 'ecclesiastical apartheid'.

● West German tennis players sweep the board at Wimbledon as Boris Becker wins the men's singles trophy and Steffi Graf the women's title.

● Former Irish Prime Minister Dr Garret FitzGerald announces that he will retire from politics at the end of the present parliament.

10 JULY

● British dockers begin their strike in 60 ports in protest against the abolition of the National Dock Labour Scheme.

● Trade and Industry Secretary Lord Young tones down the Monopolies and Mergers Commission's proposals for ownership of British pubs. Under Lord Young's plan, brewers that own more than 2000 pubs will have to rent at least half the number of pubs over 2000 to tenants allowed to operate free houses.

● Environment Secretary Nicholas Ridley hits out at what he terms the 'constant barrage of misinformation' from the Green Party and other environmentalist organizations. He also says that the Green Party's 'wish list' is made up of 'unscientific rubbish based on myths, prejudices and ignorance'.

● A series of nationwide strikes by coalminers starts in the Soviet Union. Grievances include low wages, lack of compensation for night shifts, unsafe working conditions, inadequate housing and medical care and shortages of food and consumer goods.

● Soviet negotiator Viktor Karpov gives qualified approval to an American plan for trial monitoring of long-range nuclear weapons before the signing of a formal treaty to reduce strategic nuclear weapons.

● The Israeli Labour Party considers pulling out of the coalition government because of Prime Minister Itzhak Shamir's hard-line proposals for for the West Bank and Gaza Strip.

11 JULY

● Lord Olivier, Britain's foremost actor, dies.

● Financier Sir James Goldsmith announces a £13,000 million 'leveraged buyout' offer for BAT Industries. The takeover bid is the largest ever made in Europe and sends shares soaring on the London Stock Exchange.

● 500,000 local government workers start a two-day strike in support of their claim for a 12% pay rise plus the guaranteed right to national pay bargaining.

● The President of the Royal Institute of British Architects, Max Hutchinson, criticizes Prince Charles for wanting architects to 'mimic' 18th-century architecture rather than create new styles.

● US President George Bush ends his visit to Poland with an appeal to Poles to support a movement of 'national reconciliation'. He flies to Hungary where he promises that the United States will work with Hungary to continue its economic and political reforms.

● The Chinese government hints that ousted Communist Party Secretary Zhao Ziyang may be put on trial for his handling of the pro-democracy demonstrations in May and June.

● 47 Ugandan youths suffocate after being locked in a railway carriage. The youths were among 200 arrested by the Ugandan Army as suspected rebel guerrillas.

12 JULY

● British Rail and the London Underground again grind to a halt in the fourth one-day strike in support of higher wages.

● Ireland's Fianna Fail leader, Charles Haughey, succeeds in forming a coalition government with the Progressive Democrats.

● Argentine President Carlos Menem says he is willing to declare a formal end to hostilities with Britain if Britain opens its 150-mile exclusion zone around the Falkland Islands.

● 15 people are killed and another 10 injured when a gunman goes berserk in the tiny French village of Luxiol in eastern France. Christian Dornier killed his mother and sister and then went on a shooting spree which ended when police sharpshooters wounded him.

● Mrs Thatcher, on the eve of the bicentenary of the French Revolution, creates a stir when she says that human rights did not begin with the French Revolution and had been proclaimed by Magna Carta.

● Environment Secretary Nicholas Ridley reorganizes government environmental agencies because the existing arrangements were 'inefficient, insensitive and mean that conservation issues in both Scotland and Wales are determined with too little regard for the particular requirements in these countries'.

● American FBI agents arrest three suspected IRA terrorists who are alleged to have assembling an anti-aircraft system for use in Northern Ireland.

13 JULY

● Honda announces that it is to invest £300 million in building its first European car-assembly plant in Britain. The Japanese car manufacturer will also take a 20% stake in the Rover Group. The projects will create 8250 jobs, but mean the loss of 3000 jobs at the Rover plant in Cowley.

● Foreign Secretary Sir Geoffrey Howe upgrades Britain's contacts with the PLO by meeting Bassam Abu Sharif, a close advisor of Yasser Arafat.

● Former Conservative Prime Minister Edward Heath attacks government plans to give only top Hong Kong Chinese the right of abode in Britain. He says it would lead to accusations of discrimination.

● NATO negotiators at the Conventional Forces in Europe negotiations formally present an American plan for a reduction in NATO and Warsaw Pact conventional forces. The proposals include a 15% reduction in the number of NATO combat aircraft and a 40% reduction in the number of Warsaw Pact combat aircraft.

● Former Greek Prime Minister Andreas Papandreou, aged 70, marries his mistress, 34-year-old former airline hostess Dimitra Liani.

● The Polisario Front drops its insistence on an unconditional withdrawal of Moroccan troops from the disputed Western Sahara. The move opens the way for UN-sponsored talks between the Polisario Front and Morocco's King Hassan II.

14 JULY

● Celebrations to mark the bicentenary of the French Revolution reach their climax with an elaborate parade and spontaneous street parties in Paris. The festivities cost $75 million.

● The leaders of the seven leading industrialized western countries (Britain, the United States, Canada, Japan, France, West Germany and Italy) start a summit meeting in Paris.

● Chancellor Nigel Lawson says that inflation has peaked at 8.3% and is likely to be much lower by the end of the year.

● French air traffic controllers stage industrial action, creating chaos and long delays for British holidaymakers bound for the continent.

● Andrew Collins, QC, counsel to the inquiry into the Hillsborough disaster, which claimed 95 lives, says the disaster was 'avoidable' and caused by 'ignorance, complacency, lack of foresight' but 'not deliberate callousness'.

● Somali police open fire on anti-government rioters

in the capital of Mogadishu. The government later reports that 10 people were killed and 32 wounded.

15 JULY

● British Rail's white-collar workers in the Transport Salaried Staffs Association accept the management's pay offer of 8.8%.

● A research team from Leeds finds that 10% of the paté samples tested from the shelves of British supermarkets were contaminated with listeria bacteria.

● The waters off Italy's northern Adriatic coast are plagued by a pollution-created glutinous mass of algae which causes hotel bookings to fall by up to 40%.

● The Chinese government bans foreign publications as part of a fight against 'Western bourgeois ideas'.

● A car bomb explodes in the centre of Kabul, the capital of Afghanistan, killing 12 people and wounding 50.

● Two Indian soldiers in the peace-keeping force in Sri Lanka are killed when Sri Lankan troops open fire on their battalion. It is the first time that Indian and Sri Lankan troops have clashed and occurs when tensions between the two countries are rising.

16 JULY

● On the last day of the industrialized countries' summit in Paris, Soviet leader Mikhail Gorbachev writes to the leaders proposing East–West cooperation in economic matters, but the seven leaders give him a gentle but firm rebuff. In their final communiqué they endorse western support for changes in Hungary and Poland and support the Brady Plan for relieving the international debt problem.

● The Israeli government confirms reports that Foreign Minister Moshe Arens held meetings with prominent Palestinians to discuss government plans for elections on the West Bank and Gaza Strip.

● Herbert von Karajan, one of the world's most brilliant conductors, dies in Vienna at the age of 81.

● Ethnic unrest in the Abkhazia region of Georgia between Abkhazians and Georgians leads to riots, and 11 die and 130 are injured.

● French driver Alain Prost wins the British Grand Prix at Silverstone. Britain's Nigel Mansell comes second.

● Pakistan Prime Minister Benazir Bhutto offers to hold arms control talks with Indian Prime Minister Rajiv Gandhi. She says that 'Pakistan is ready to join any arrangmeent which can guarantee non-proliferation of nuclear weapons in South Asia.'

17 JULY

● The strike by Soviet coalminers spreads to take in the entire Kuznetsky Basin in Siberia and the Donetsk Basin in the Ukraine.

● Austria formally applies for membership of the European Community. It faces a stumbling block in the Austrian aim to remain militarily neutral.

● The US government offers to pay compensation of between $100,000 and $250,000 for each of the 290 victims who died when the USS *Vincennes* accidentally shot down an Iranian airliner over the Persian Gulf on 3 July 1988.

● West Germany's Social Democratic Party puts forward a proposal to ban low-flying military training over Germany by German, American and British pilots. Defence planners say such exercises are an essential part of NATO strategy.

● Poland and the Vatican restore diplomatic relations after a break of 44 years.

● America's controversial B2 Stealth bomber takes off on its first test flight. US Defense Secretary Richard Cheney is reported to be delighted with the performance of the $22,500 million plane capable of avoiding Soviet radar.

● The Commons Select Committee on Energy calls on the British government and its EC partners to set aside a specific sum for research into the greenhouse effect. The all-party committee says: 'Global warming may be an assault on the security of the world, and every country should be able to contribute to environmental defence.'

18 JULY

● The Executive Committee of the National Union of Railwaymen rejects British Rail's 8.8% pay rise offer and the advice of General Secretary Jimmy Knapp. The rejection leads to a drop in support. The fifth one-day strike again paralyses the rail system.

● Five suspected IRA terrorists appear at separate court hearings in Paris and Dublin. Their arrests are hailed as a major breakthrough in the search for IRA men responsible for attacks on British servicemen on the European continent.

● Christopher Tugenhadt, Chairman of the Civil Aviation Authority, proposes easing restrictions on night flights at Gatwick and allowing charter flights to use Heathrow to ease the growing air traffic chaos and long delays for travellers.

● US and Soviet negotiators reach agreement on some key issues in a proposed international treaty to ban chemical weapons. Agreements include the reduction of their stockpiles to an equal size and then a gradual elimination of chemical weapons over a ten-year period.

● Kenyan President Daniel arap Moi sets fire to a £2 million pile of ivory elephant tusks as part of his campaign for a worldwide ban on the trade in ivory in an effort to halt the illegal poaching of elephants.

● The Soviet government imposes a state of emergency and curfew on towns in the Abkhazia region of Georgia. The new regulations are described by Moscow Radio as 'a special regime of civil behaviour'.

19 JULY

● Environment Secretary Nicholas Ridley encounters an angry Commons response when he unveils his 'safety net' proposals for the poll tax.

● The government publishes its White Paper on the reform of the legal profession, officially accepting many of the proposals of Lord Mackay, the Lord Chancellor.

● The Polish parliament elects Gen. Wojciech Jaruzelski President with the minimum number of necessary votes.

● The strike by the Soviet Union's Siberian coalminers ends, but miners in the Ukraine continue their industrial action. Soviet President Mikhail Gorbachev declares that the labour unrest has precipitated a 'very acute' crisis.

● A United Airlines DC-10 jumbo jet crash-lands at Sioux City, Iowa after the jet suffers a complete hydraulic failure. A total of 111 of the 296 people on board are killed and 60 are injured.

● The European Commission proposes regulations that would prevent any EC government from vetoing cut-price air fares proposed by airlines.

20 JULY

● By a vote of three-to-one, Britain's general practitioners reject new performance-related contracts agreed in May after talks between the government and the British Medical Association. Health Secretary Kenneth Clarke says he will impose the contracts from 1990 regardless of the vote.

● The Department of Trade and Industry accuses National Westminster Bank of disregarding its own standards of integrity and propriety over the issue of Blue Arrow Shares in 1987.

● US President George Bush proposes the establishment of a permanent orbiting space station, a permanent base on the moon and a manned mission to Mars.

● The US Senate defeats an amendment that would have put severe limits on the dialogue between the Bush Administration and the Palestine Liberation Organization.

● More than 6000 holidaymakers and residents are evacuated from the Landes region of southwest France as forest fires spread through the area.

● Comedian Harry Worth, aged 71, dies at his home in Berkhamsted, Hertfordshire.

21 JULY

● Comedian Ken Dodd is cleared of charges of tax fraud and false accounting after a 23-day trial and five-year investigation by the Inland Revenue. But he still faces an £825,000 tax bill and large legal fees.

● The Anglo-French Eurotunnel Consortium announces that it will need to raise more money to finish the Channel Tunnel. The estimates for the cost of the tunnel are believed to have risen from £4800 million to £6000 million pounds.

● US President George Bush submits his clean-air bill to Congress. The bill proposes to tighten controls against pollution by manufacturers and cars.

● The US State Department announces that Felix Bloch, a senior diplomat, is under investigation for 'illegal activities' involving a foreign intelligence service.

● Marshal Sergei Akhromeyev, senior military adviser to Soviet leader Mikhail Gorbachev, appears before the Armed Services Committee of the US House of Representatives.

● Mexico reaches an historic agreement to reduce its $54,000 million commercial bank debt, becoming the first country to do so under the new debt strategy plan launched by US Treasury Secretary Nicholas Brady.

22 JULY

● The Thames Water Authority advises 100,000 residents of Kent and southeast London to boil their water after reports that some supplies had been contaminated.

● Temperatures in London reach a near-record 34°C (93°F) and hosepipe bans are enforced on residents throughout southern England and Wales.

● Mrs Thatcher attacks top executives for taking exorbitant pay rises after it is revealed that Lord King, Chairman of British Airways, had his salary increased from £178,000 to £386,000.

● Soviet leader Mikhail Gorbachev appeals to striking miners in the Ukraine to return to work and says that he is 'inspired' by the fact that the miners are 'taking matters into their own hands' although strikes are 'not the way to take'.

● Giulio Andreotti is sworn in as Prime Minister of Italy's 49th post-war government in succession to Ciriaco de Mita.

● The Welsh extremist group Meibion Glyndwr (Sons of Glendower) fire-bomb a Mercedes parked outside a holiday cottage in the village of Abersoch.

23 JULY

● In Senate elections in Japan, the ruling Liberal Democratic Party loses its majority in the upper house of the Diet (parliament) for the first time since coming to power in 1955.

● The board of directors of National Westminster Bank holds a crisis meeting after the Department of Trade and Industry's damning report on the bank's handling of the 1987 Blue Arrow flotation.

● A Harris opinion poll in the *Observer* puts the Labour Party seven points ahead of the Conservatives with 44% of the voters' support compared with 37% for the Conservatives, 7% for the Greens, 6% for the Democrats and 3% for the SDP.

● More than 18,000 people are evacuated when forest fires sweep through several million acres of the northern part of the Canadian province of Manitoba.

● Israel's coalition government averts a possible coalition split when Labour Party members join other members of the government in voting to reaffirm support for Prime Minister Itzhak Shamir's election plans for the West Bank and Gaza Strip.

● Gabor Roszik, a 35-year-old Lutheran clergyman, becomes the first opposition candidate in more than 40 years to be elected to the Hungarian parliament.

24 JULY

● Mrs Thatcher reshuffles her cabinet. Changes include Sir Geoffrey Howe being replaced by John Major and Nicholas Ridley being moved from Environment to the Department of Trade and Industry. Chris Patten takes over the Department of Environment, George Younger resigns as Defence Secretary and is replaced by Tom King and Education Secretary Kenneth Baker is promoted to post of Conservative Party Chairman.

● Japanese Prime Minister Sosuke Uno resigns in the wake of the ruling Liberal Democratic Party's defeat in Senate elections. 'All the responsibility of this election defeat is on me, and so I have decided to step down,' he says at a Tokyo press conference.

● A government inquiry into Nazi war criminals in Britain says that action should be taken against the criminals or Britain will be tainted with 'the slur of being a haven for war criminals'.

● Cambodian Prime Minister Hun Sen and rebel leader Prince Norodom Sihanouk meet outside Paris to prepare for an international conference on Cambodia.

● Foreign Office Minister William Waldegrave meets Israeli Deputy Foreign Minister Benjamin Netanyahu who tells him that Britain's decision to upgrade relations with the PLO is 'an historic mistake'.

● A woman is killed in South Africa when a limpet mine explodes outside a court building in Athlone, near Cape Town.

25 JULY

● It is reported that an angry Sir Geoffrey Howe nearly resigned after being moved from the Foreign Office and that he had to be mollified with the post of Deputy Prime Minister as well as Leader of the Commons.

● Lord Boardman, chairman of National Westminster Bank, and three of his fellow directors, resign over the Blue Arrow share-rigging scandal. The other directors are Charles Green, Terry Green and John Plastow, all of whom had been accused by the Department of Trade and Industry of failing to supervise the 'lawful conduct of business'.

● 16 shop stewards at Tilbury docks are sacked by employers determined to break the dockworkers' strike.

● The Confederation of British Industry reports that confidence in British business prospects has fallen to its lowest level for nearly seven years as manufacturers report drops in exports and investment.

● The US Congress cuts President George Bush's budget for Strategic Defense Initiative (Star Wars) research by $2000 million to $2900 million.

● Jamil Tarifi, a pro-PLO lawyer and former Deputy Mayor of the West Bank town of El Bireh, admits to participating in talks with the Israeli government on elections in the West Bank and Gaza Strip.

26 JULY

● British railwaymen start to cross picket lines as support for the national rail strike wanes.

● Strikes by the Soviet Union's Ukrainian coalminers start to end after the government gives in to most of the miners' demands.

● Donald Kell, aged 66, is shot dead trying to stop a raid on a security van delivery to a Lloyds Bank branch in Finchley Road, North London.

● The government announces that it will write off £1000 million of British Coal's debts in preparation for privatization planned in 1993. The same day, British Coal reports an operating profit of £498 million.

● Polish Solidarity's parliamentary caucus initially rejects proposals to form a grand coalition with the Communist Party.

● Soviet Defence Minister Gen. Dimitri Yazov visits Britain and makes the first tour of British military bases by a Soviet defence minister.

27 JULY

● A government White Paper proposes to register all food premises – from hot-dog stands to hypermarkets – under a new Food Bill. The proposal, however, is criticized by Labour and environmental health officers as not going far enough.

● Backbench Conservative MPs cheer Sir Geoffrey Howe on his first day as Leader of the House of Commons. The warm reception is seen as an attack on Mrs Thatcher by her own backbenchers.

● French President François Mitterrand warns that Britain could be left out of a new EC treaty on economic and monetary union unless concessions are made by Mrs Thatcher.

● The Israeli press reports that the Palestine Liberation Organization has offered specific conditions under which it might approve of the Israeli government's plans for elections on the West Bank and Gaza Strip.

● Carl Gustav Christer Pettersson, aged 42, is convicted of the 1986 murder of Swedish Prime Minister Olof Palme.

● A Korean Airlines DC-10 jet with 199 people aboard crashes in heavy fog while trying to land at Tripoli airport in Libya.

28 JULY

● The National Union of Railwaymen becomes the third and last union to accept British Rail's improved offer of an 8.8% basic pay increase. Workers in London and the southeast will also get increases of between 10% and 15% and the company's plan to dispense with national bargaining is scaled back.

● Israeli commandos in Lebanon kidnap pro-Iranian Shiite cleric Sheikh Abdul Karim Obeid as a hostage for the release of captured Israeli soldiers. The pro-Iranian Hezbollah responds by threatening to hang American hostage Lt-Col. William Higgins.

● Shares on the London Stock Exchange close at their highest level since the Oct. 1987 crash when the share index breaks through the 2300 points barrier to 2306.

● Hojatoleslam Ali Akbar Hashemi Rafsanjani wins a landslide victory in Iran's presidential elections. According to final returns, he received 94.5% of the votes.

● The Soviet newspaper *Pravda* attacks Mikhail Gorbachev in a front-page editorial in which it says 'one must not...destroy a mechanism without knowing what the new one will be'.

● Polish Communist Party members, at a meeting of the Central Committee, attack their own leadership for failing to achieve serious economic reform.

29 JULY

● The flights of thousands of British holidaymakers are delayed for up to seven hours after technical hitches and industrial action by French air-traffic controllers. The worst affected were Manchester and Gatwick airports.

● Two men die when two London Underground trains collide at West Brompton station.

● A police guard is provided for England cricketer Ian Botham after he receives death threats.

● Gen. Wojciech Jaruzelski, the newly elected President of Poland, resigns as leader of the Polish Communist Party. He also resigns from the Party Politburo and Central Committee. Jaruzelski is succeeded as Party leader by Miecyzyslaw Rakowski.

● More than 140 people die in Sri Lanka after a fresh outbreak of communal fighting between Sinhalese and Tamils.

● The first tentative opposition political group, the Inter-Regional Group, is formed in the Soviet Union. The group comprises about 250 members of the Congress of People's Deputies and is led by Boris Yeltsin, former Communist Party leader in Moscow.

30 JULY

● The Royal Institute of British Architects says that few British football grounds are capable of staging important matches in safety.

● US Secretary of State James Baker warns Britain against the forcible repatriation of Vietnamese boat people in Hong Kong.

● A 19-nation peace conference on Cambodia opens in Paris. The conference includes representatives from the Vietnamese and Cambodian governments and the three rebel groups fighting government and Vietnamese troops.

● Chileans overwhelmingly approve a package of constitutional reforms negotiated between military ruler Gen. Augusto Pinochet and the civilian opposition.

● More than 20,000 protesters march through Kishinev, the capital of Moldavia in the Soviet Union, demanding that Moldavian become the main language and that the local Party leadership be purged.

● Mexican police reveal that convicted Mexican drug dealers are living in luxury prisons with saunas, a discotheque, colour television and hand-carved furniture and are being regularly supplied with drugs.

31 JULY

● The pro-Iranian Hezbollah releases a videotape showing that it hanged American Marine Lt-Col. William Higgins in retaliation for the kidnapping of Sheikh Abdul Karim Obeid. American experts, however, believe Higgins died before the Israeli kidnapping of the Shiite cleric.

● More than 9000 key staff at 140 local authorities go on strike after the National Association of Local Government Officers (NALGO) rejects an improved pay offer of 8.15%.

● A group of nine young British holidaymakers on the Spanish holiday island of Ibiza drag a 19-year-old Spanish waiter from his moped and beat him to death.

● A 1000-lb IRA car bomb explodes in front of the Northern Ireland High Court. A half-hour warning was given before the explosion which broke windows up to half a mile away.

● East Germans start entering Hungary in the hope that they can reach the West through the recently opened Austro-Hungarian border. They are initially captured by Hungarian border guards and returned to East Germany.

● Cuba's former Minister of the Interior, Gen. José Abrantes Fernandez, and four other senior officials are arrested as part of a government crackdown on 'corruption and cronyism'.

1 AUGUST

● The national dock strike ends with the Transport and General Workers' Union failing to save or replace the National Dock Labour Scheme.

● Baroness Susan de Stempel is cleared at Worcester Crown Court of battering her husband to death.

● Work starts on dismantling the Cruise missile base at Greenham Common as part of the Dec. 1987 US–Soviet INF Treaty.

● The Israeli government is reported to be engaged in secret negotiations to secure the release of western hostages held by terrorists in the Lebanon.

● The Polish Peasant Party, nominal allies of the Communist Party, refuses to back Communist Czeslaw Kiszczak for the premiership.

● The Polish government lifts controls on nearly all food prices and cushions the blow with modest wage increases.

2 AUGUST

● US President George Bush orders American warships to steam towards the Lebanese coast as the terrorist Hezbollah movement threatens to execute American hostage Joseph Cicippio.

● Argentine President Carlos Menem ends restrictions on trade with Britain. The restrictions had been in place since the Falklands War. He also promises to tone down the United Nations debate on the Falklands.

● Scotland Yard announces that it has smashed an international organized crime network involving Indian and Pakistani gangs connected with drugs, extortion, illegal immigration, fraud and armed robberies.

● Forest fires in southeast France and Corsica reach 'catastrophic proportions' with 50,000 acres destroyed in Corsica and 25,000 acres in France.

● South African anti-apartheid activists stage a protest against South Africa's segregated hospitals by bringing Blacks in need of medical care to Whites-only casualty departments. The hospital authorities, under orders from the government, admit the Blacks.

● The Chairman of the UK Atomic Energy Authority, John Collier, condemns the government plans to privatize the electricity industry as 'terribly messy'.

3 AUGUST

● The American hostage in the Lebanon, Joseph Cicippio, is temporarily reprieved after US President Bush tells Iranian leaders that he holds them responsible for the safety of US hostages in the Lebanon.

● A Middle East terrorist bomber dies in an explosion that rips apart two floors of a London hotel. The bomber is believed to be linked to the groups opposing the publication of *The Satanic Verses*.

● The Midland Bank reports a pre-tax loss of £531 million after setting aside £846 million to cover bad debts to Third World countries.

● PLO leader Yasser Arafat opens a meeting of Al-Fatah with a pledge to continue his policy of peace through diplomacy and the Intifada (the Palestinian uprising).

● An Olympus Airways Short-330 aircraft crashes on the Greek island of Samos, killing all 34 Greek passengers and crew.

● The New Zealand parliamentary Labour Party snubs Prime Minister David Lange by re-electing former Finance Minister Roger Douglas whom Lange had sacked from his cabinet.

● Ali Akbar Hashemi Rafsanjani is sworn in as President of Iran and promises to 'improve and expand' Iran's foreign relations.

4 AUGUST

● Most of the blame for the Hillsborough football disaster is placed on the shoulders of the South Yorkshire Police in a report by Lord Justice Taylor. The publication of the report is followed by the suspension on full pay of Chief Supt David Duckenfield, the officer in command of the Hillsborough operation.

● Suffolk businessman John Ward leaves for Kenya to try to prove that his daughter Julie was murdered and that the murder had been covered up by Kenyan police.

● Iranian President Ali Akbar Hashemi Rafsanjani says that there is a solution to the hostage problem and urges the Bush administration to secure the release of Israeli-held Sheikh Abdul Karim Obeid.

● Hundreds of political prisoners in Turkey start a hunger strike after two Kurdish activists die when police attempt to end their month-long hunger strike.

● An American cruiser, the USS *Thomas S. Gates*, visits the Soviet port of Sevastopol. It is the first visit by a US warship to the Soviet Union since 1975.

● Two passenger trains crash head-on outside Havana, Cuba, killing 18 people and injuring 87.

5 AUGUST

● Presidents from five Central American countries meet in Honduras to discuss ways of ending the civil war in Nicaragua.

● Hungary's opposition Hungarian Democratic Forum (HDF) wins two parliamentary by-elections with large majorities.

● Toshiki Kaifu, Japanese Prime Minister-designate, admits he had received £67,000 in political donations from the Recruit Company but denies that he had done any favours in return.

● London's Savoy Hotel celebrates its 100th birthday.

● 50 people are arrested in North London after skirmishes break out between rival demonstrations organized by the Irish Freedom Movement and the British National Party.

● A British Rail train from Oxford to Paddington is derailed after vandals place masonry and a railway sleeper on the tracks. No one is seriously injured.

6 AUGUST

● The Lebanese kidnappers of American Joseph Cicippio demand the release of Sheikh Abdul Karim Obeid and 450 other Arab prisoners held by Israel as their price for the release of Cicippio.

● Soviet Foreign Minister Eduard Shevardnadze flies unexpectedly into the Afghan capital of Kabul in the middle of a rocket attack. His trip is to brief President Najibullah on Soviet–Iranian talks and to review the military situation.

● Water authorities in Wales announce that thousands of fish died when farm slurry escaped into a tributary of the River Dee in North Wales.

● Six Sri Lankan Tamils are sentenced to death by the High Court of the Maldives after being found guilty of attempting to overthrow President Maumoon Abdul Gayoom. Eight other Sri Lankan Tamils are banned to a desert island for life.

● The award-winning film *The Killing Fields* about the Khmer Rouge reign of terror in Cambodia is shown in the Cambodian capital of Phnom Penh for the first time.

● Former Greek Prime Minister Andreas Papandreou announces that he will continue to lead the Greek Socialist Party despite his ill health and the possibility of criminal charges being brought against him.

7 AUGUST

● Lloyds Bank, the registrars responsible for the Abbey National flotation, admit that between 300,000 and 400,000 share certificates worth about £50 million were deliberately burnt.

● The Argentine Foreign Ministry issues a statement looking forward to Anglo-Argentine talks on the renewal of diplomatic relations as 'the ideal way of resolving the differences' between the two countries.

● New Zealand Prime Minister David Lange resigns after the Labour Party turns against him in his dispute with former Finance Minister Roger Douglas.

● Mozambique peace talks open in Nairobi in an effort to end the 14-year-old Mozambican civil war between the Frelimo government and right-wing Renamo guerrillas.

● Central American leaders agree to start disbanding Nicaragua's Contra rebels within 30 days.

● Labour Energy spokesman Tony Blair demands that the government disclose whether electricity privatization will lead to the closure of up to 20 British Coal pits.

● The Hanson Trust claims victory in the battle for control of one of the world's biggest mining companies, Consolidated Gold Fields. The company was bought for £3500 million after the South African-controlled Minorco company failed in its bid.

8 AUGUST

● US President George Bush rejects an Iranian offer

to help free American hostages in Lebanon in return for assurances that $12,000 million in frozen Iranian assets will be released from the United States.

● Assistant Chief Constable Walter Jackson, the most senior police officer at the Hillsborough disaster, is moved to a desk job from his post of operational control with South Yorkshire Police.

● Liverpool dockworkers return to work, finally ending the unsuccessful national dock strike in protest against the cancellation of the National Dock Labour Scheme.

● A United Nations team flies into Phnom Penh to start a study on ways to end the 20-year conflict in Cambodia.

● Geoffrey Palmer is chosen to succeed David Lange as New Zealand's new Prime Minister and leader of the New Zealand Labour Party.

● Commonwealth foreign ministers split on the issue of trade with South Africa. African countries called for a complete cessation of trade while the Canadian and Australian foreign ministers reserved their judgement. Britain was not represented because of its anti-sanctions stand.

9 AUGUST

● London Underground management accepts an ACAS (Advisory Conciliation and Arbitration Service) formula to end the long-running dispute over drivers' pay. The formula boosts drivers' pay to an average of £17,300 from £15,000.

● A 15-year-old Catholic boy in North Belfast is killed by a plastic bullet on the 18th anniversary of internment in Northern Ireland.

● An estimated 20,000 Russians go on strike in Estonia in protest at an Estonian law curbing the electoral rights of recent immigrants to the Baltic state.

● Toshiki Kaifu is chosen as the new Prime Minister of Japan.

● A Lebanese Hezbollah militant dies in a suicide bomb attack on an Israeli military convoy in southern Lebanon. He injured five soldiers in the attack.

● A Soviet ship loaded with Canadian toxic waste is turned away from Tilbury Docks after British dock-workers refused to unload it.

10 AUGUST

● The Conservative-controlled Commons Select Committee on Health and Social Services calls on the government to slow down its plans for reforming the National Health Service, warning that patient care could be put at risk by 'premature' change.

● Education Secretary John McGregor tells his history advisers that he wants schools to place more emphasis on British history and the teaching of names and dates.

● The dispute over local government pay ends when 700,000 members of NALGO (National Association of Local Government Officers) agrees to an average 8.6% pay rise.

● The leadership of Poland's Solidarity meets the Communist-allied United Peasants' Party to discuss the possibility of creating a non-Communist coalition government.

● The Soviet government announces that it will pay farmers in hard currency in an effort to boost food production.

● US President George Bush names General Colin Powell as Chairman of the Joint Chiefs of Staff. He will be the first Black and, at 52, the youngest man to hold the top US military job.

● French air traffic-control technicians start a seven-day strike.

11 AUGUST

● A fire in a chemical factory in Aughton, near Ormskirk, Lancashire, releases a toxic gas over the area. A total of 60 homes are evacuated and ten firemen are rushed to hospital.

● The Soviet Union warns Poland that attempts to exclude the Communist Party from the government were 'not conducive to good Soviet–Polish relations'.

● Sheikh Mohammed Hussein Fadlallah, the spiritual leader of the Lebanon Hezbollah movement, offers to work for an end to the hostages crisis.

● 20 people are killed and 15 seriously injured when a bus runs off a road in the North Indian state of Himachal Pradesh.

● Kurdish guerrillas raid hamlets in southeastern Turkey, killing 14 people and kidnapping 22 others.

● Bus services in the East Midlands are disrupted by a pay strike involving 600 drivers. The drivers want an 8.3% pay rise. The Derby- based Trent Bus Company offered 7%.

12 AUGUST

● Nevill Grant, the alleged 'godfather' of the West Indian mafia, is extradited from Britain to Jamaica on drug charges.

● A middle-aged couple from Hilperton, near Trow-bridge, Wiltshire, are found stabbed to death. Police believe that Brian and Ursula Randall disturbed a burglar. Their 20-year-old daughter Sarah is seriously wounded.

● The Soviet Union reports crime figures which reveal that it is suffering its worst crime wave in 20 years, with overall crime up 32% over the previous year and serious crime up 40%.

● Venice International Airport grinds to a halt when hundreds of thousands of swallows swarmed onto the runways.

● A curfew is imposed on the northeast Indian state of Assam after four days of violence in which more than 160 die.

● US and Panamanian troops confront each other after Panama seizes four American vehicles. American helicopters and troops are moved into the area to recover the vehicles.

13 AUGUST

● Republicans in Northern Ireland mark the 20th anniversary of the arrival of British troops in Northern Ireland with a peaceful march through West Belfast.

● Syrian tank and infantry forces launch a major

offensive against Christian strongholds near Beirut but are repulsed.

● West Germany shuts its embassy in Budapest to prevent any more asylum-seeking East Germans from joining the estimated 200 refugees already inside.

● The bodies of US Congressman Mickey Leland and 15 others are found in plane wreckage in Ethiopia. Congressman Leland was visiting a refugee camp.

● An estimated 50,000 Serbs defy the Yugoslav authorities to hold an anti-government rally in Bosnia.

● 13 people are killed when a hot-air balloon crashes near Alice Springs, Australia.

14 AUGUST

● South African President P. W. Botha resigns after a bitter showdown with National Party leader F. W. de Klerk who succeeds Botha as President.

● Polish Prime Minister Czeslaw Kiszczak resigns after only two weeks in office because of his failure to form a government.

● 50 West Midlands CID police officers are transferred or suspended from duty after allegations that the police force's Serious Crimes Squad had fabricated confessions.

● The South Yorkshire Police Authority rejects the proffered resignation of Chief Constable Peter Wright over the Hillsborough disaster.

● London Underground drivers vote to work normally, accepting an average 8.5% pay rise.

● West German and Hungarian foreign ministers meet to discuss what action to take over the increasing number of East Germans using Hungary as a springboard to West Germany.

● Peru's 70,000 miners start an indefinite strike in support of their claim for higher wages.

15 AUGUST

● The crisis deepens in Lebanon as Syrian and Iranian-backed forces step up attacks on Christian positions and France orders a missile-bearing destroyer to the eastern Mediterranean.

● Noraid publicity director, Martin Galvin, is arrested in Northern Ireland and flown to London for deportation back to the United States. He had been banned from entering Northern Ireland for five years on the grounds that his presence would not be conducive to the public good.

● US President George Bush urges Iran to send 'a clear and good signal' of its desire to improve relations with the United States by securing the release of American hostages held in Lebanon.

● Indian Prime Minister Rajiv Gandhi uses independence-day celebrations to attack the opposition parties as 'traitors' trying to weaken and divide the country and impede its economic and social progress.

● Pakistan Foreign Minister Sahabzada Yakub Khan visits Iran in an effort to mediate in the hostage crisis with the United States.

● Filipino soldiers end a prison riot in the southern city of Davao by storming the prison. All 15 rioting prisoners and five hostages, including 36-year-old Australian missionary Jacqueline Hamill, a 16-year-old girl and a nine-year-old boy, are killed.

16 AUGUST

● Britain and Argentina hold their first formal talks since 1985. The talks about talks are between Sir Crispin Tickell, British Ambassador to the United Nations, and Argentine Special Envoy Lucio Garcia del Solar. They meet at the UN headquarters in New York.

● Thieves escape with £1 million after robbing a security van delivering cash to a Midland Bank branch in Cheam, Surrey.

● West Midlands Police announce that the Hillsborough disaster will be the subject of a criminal inquiry by West Midlands Chief Constable Geoffrey Dear.

● Poland moves closer to having a non-Communist Prime Minister as Solidarity leader Lech Walesa is nominated for the post. Walesa, however, says: 'There are better candidates than me.'

● A fragile cease-fire takes effect in Lebanon after an appeal by the UN Security Council.

● The Israeli government announces that Israeli Trade and Industry Minister Ariel Sharon will visit the Soviet Union, the first Israeli minister to do so since 1967.

17 AUGUST

● Poland's Democratic and Peasants' parties agree to support Solidarity in a coalition government, thus giving the key opposition movement a majority in the Polish parliament.

● The Commons Defence Committee criticizes the Ministry of Defence for poor management which resulted in increased costs of £50 million.

● The US Pentagon admits to fundamental miscalculations in the design of the new Trident D-5 ballistic missile which is being developed for the American and British nuclear defence forces.

● Up to 700 people are killed in an explosion at a secret Iraqi defence establishment near Baghdad. The incident was not fully reported until September.

● British Rail's fleet of 30 new electric locomotives is removed from service after a fault is discovered in the brake system.

● 121 Vietnamese boat people voluntarily return to Vietnam from Hong Kong.

● Colombian judge Carlos Ernesto Valencia is shot dead in Bogota, only hours after upholding an arrest warrant for an alleged Medellin drugs cartel leader.

18 AUGUST

● Victor Cracknell, the 32-year-old son of a British millionaire businessmen, is freed after being kidnapped and held for ransom for £1 million. Three men and three women were arrested in connection with the kidnapping.

● British and Argentine foreign ministers agree to meet in Madrid in October to continue talks on the restoration of full diplomatic relations.

● The Court of Appeal rules that a 17-month-old baby of mixed race is to be taken from its White foster parents and moved to a Black family because of its colour.

● Colombian presidential candidate Senator Luis Carlos Galan is assassinated by drugs cartel gunmen. Immediately afterwards, President Virgilio Barco announces measures permitting the extradition of drug traffickers and the confiscation of their assets.

● The African National Congress is expelled from Zambia.

● British Airways services are disrupted by a 24-hour cabin-crew strike in protest against the sacking of a stewardess.

● Former Liberian Defence Minister Gray Allison is found guilty of the ritual murder of a police private. Gen. Allison ordered the killing to obtain blood for use in rites to gain power to overthrow President Samuel Doe. Allison was sentenced to death by firing squad.

19 AUGUST

● 56 people die when the Thames pleasure-boat cruiser *Marchioness* sinks after colliding with the dredger *Bowbelle* near Southwark Bridge.

● Solidarity activist Tadeusz Mazowiecki is formally asked by President Wojciech Jaruzelski to become Poland's first post-war non-Communist Prime Minister.

● Eight people are killed and 27 injured when a car loaded with fireworks explodes in a car park in the Spanish resort town of Alicante.

● Irish Republicans stage a march through Dublin to mark the 20th anniversary of the arrival of troops in Northern Ireland. Among those leading the march are British Labour MP George Galloway, Sinn Fein leader Gerry Adams and wanted Catholic priest Father Patrick Ryan.

● 150 tonnes of crude oil leak into the Mersey from a Shell pipeline linking a terminal at Tranmere to a refinery at Stanlow, Ellesmere Port. The oil spill endangers Merseyside wildlife.

● Hundreds of East Germans rush across the border between Hungary and Austria at a celebration to mark the removal of Hungary's barbed-wire fence.

● Millionaire publisher Malcolm Forbes celebrates his 70th birthday with an elaborate million-pound birthday party in Tangier, Morocco.

20 AUGUST

● Thames River Police arrest the captain and the second mate of the dredger *Bowbelle* in connection with the sinking of the pleasure-boat cruiser *Marchioness*.

● Egyptian police arrest 41 Shiite Muslims suspected of attempting to overthrow President Hosni Mubarak.

● Maj.-Gen. Mohammad Farouk Zaif, a senior military adviser to Afghanistan's President Najibullah, defects to the Mujaheddin guerrillas.

● A low-pay report says that British women earn 75% of men's hourly pay.

● An estimated 30,000 Serbs gather in Niksic, Montenegro to rally in support of Serbian leader Slobodan Milosevic and protest against inflation and poverty.

● Police in Czechoslovakia arrest 370 dissidents in preparation for the 21st anniversary of the Warsaw Pact invasion of Czechoslovakia.

21 AUGUST

● Transport Secretary Cecil Parkinson announces measures to tighten passenger safety on the Thames in the wake of the *Marchioness* disaster. The measures include the mandatory compilation of a record of passengers before sailing, with the record to be kept ashore, and emergency instructions to be given to passengers.

● Senior foreign ministry officials from the EC countries meet in Paris to discuss emergency aid for Lebanon.

● George Adamson, the British conservationist who devoted his life to lions in Africa, is murdered by bandits in Kenya after trying to save a friend from an ambush.

● The Organization of African Unity (OAU) issues a statement saying that circumstances now exist 'which could create the possibility to end apartheid through negotiations'.

● More than 12,000 people are arrested and 134 aircraft seized as the Colombian government starts a major crackdown on drug traffickers.

● The Bangladesh government calls in police to crush a general strike. In the following riots, 100 people are injured and 55 arrested.

22 AUGUST

● A Monopolies and Mergers Commission report criticizes the five big banks for making excessive profits on their credit-card business. The commission says this is 'against the public interest' and recommends that cash-paying customers be given discounts.

● Polish Communists agree to join a grand coalition government with Solidarity after a 40-minute telephone conversation between Soviet leader Mikhail Gorbachev and Polish Communist Party leader Mieczyslaw Rakowski.

● An East German refugee trying to flee from Hungary to West Germany via Austria is shot dead by Hungarian border guards. The incident is later described as an accident.

● The captain and crew of the *Bowbelle* are cleared of any apparent wrongdoing in the sinking of the Thames pleasure cruiser, *Marchioness*.

● The Commons Select Committee on Transport calls on the government to increase spending on overcrowded roads and railways.

● The Central Electricity Generating Board reveals plans to dig a tunnel from Clapham Common to St John's Wood to carry two 1200 MW cables.

23 AUGUST

● Hundreds of thousands of Estonians, Lithuanians and Latvians form a human chain linking the Baltic states to mark the 50th anniversary of the Molotov–Ribbentrop Pact which set the diplomatic framework for the Soviet annexation of the three states.

● South African police fire tear gas on demonstrators outside a Cape Town church. Anglican Archbishop Desmond Tutu is among the demonstrators.

● The government reports a near-record trade deficit of £2060 million, up £500 million over the previous month.

● America's *Voyager Two* satellite beams back pictures of Neptune's moon Triton as it approaches the planet itself.

● The Australian Air Force is ordered to help maintain an air service after domestic airlines start working-to-rule in a pay dispute.

● The Greek parliament impeaches former Socialist minister Nikos Anatasopoulos on corruption charges related to the forging of state documents linked with a £6.4 million EC grain sales scandal.

24 AUGUST

● Solidarity member Tadeusz Mazowiecki is confirmed as Prime Minister of Poland.

● Chancellor Nigel Lawson says that interest rates will have to remain high until inflation is under control.

● American satellite *Voyager Two* sends back startling pictures of Neptune and discovers two new moons circling the planet.

● The New York Stock Exchange closes on an all-time high.

● Bass Breweries becomes the world's biggest hotelier after buying the American hotel chain Holiday Inns for £2000 million.

● More than 100 East German refugees sheltering inside the West German embassy in Budapest are given free passage to the West through an agreement between the Hungarian and West German governments.

● Colombian drug barons launch bomb attacks on the offices of the country's two main political parties in the drug capital, Medellin. The drug barons announce that they declared 'total war' on the government.

25 AUGUST

● The United States announces that it will provide the Colombian government with $65 million in aid, including combat helicopters and jets, to help fight the country's drug barons.

● Media magnate Rupert Murdoch attacks British television for its obsession with the past and its anatagonism to money-making businessmen.

● It is revealed that the 10 regional water authorities are spending nearly £22 million in public relations and advertising in the run-up to privatization.

● Acting South African President F. W. de Klerk and Zairean President Mobutu Sese Seko meet in Goma, Zaire, and agree to try to salvage a faltering peace plan for Angola.

● A supermarket assistant is stabbed to death after he tackles an armed raider who tried to snatch £300 from a Europa Foods branch in Fulham Road, West London.

● The outlawed Loyalist Ulster Freedom Fighters murder 28-year-old Catholic John Maginn, a father of four, in his home in Co. Down.

26 AUGUST

● A MORI opinion poll shows Labour Party support at 45% of the electorate and the Conservatives at 40%. The Green Party is in third position with 6% and the Social and Liberal Democrats have slipped to 4% and the Social Democratic Party to 3%.

● The Central Committee of the Soviet Communist Party attacks the Baltic states of Estonia, Latvia and Lithuania for whipping up 'nationalist hysteria' and accuses the nationalists of driving the Baltic people 'towards an abyss'.

● The Foreign Office orders an investigation into the activities of British mercenaries allegedly helping Colombian drug barons in their war against the Colombian government.

● Another 100 East Germans escape across the open border between Austria and Hungary.

● An 11-car pile-up on the M23 motorway near Gatwick results in the death of a woman and in a man being seriously injured.

● Japan's Prince Aya, second in line to the Japanese throne, announces his engagement to fellow student Kiko Kawashima, the daughter of an economics professor.

27 AUGUST

● American drug officials break up a major drug-laundering operation which was channelling £32 million a year back to the drug barons in Colombia.

● An estimated 300,000 Moldavians gather in the capital, Kishinev, to demonstrate in favour of proposed laws making Moldavian the official language of the southwestern Soviet republic.

● Solidarity leader Lech Walesa says that new Prime Minister Tadeusz Mazowieceki has a year at most to produce tangible results. If he fails, Walesa warns that Solidarity will lose public confidence.

● Israel bombs a Hezbollah base in southern Lebanon and exiles five Palestinians accused of leading the Intifada (the Palestinian uprising) in the Occupied Territories.

● The World Health Organization reports that some 170,000 people around the world are suffering from AIDS. Britain ranks fifth in Europe with 2400 cases. The United States has a total of 98,255 cases of AIDS.

● Sikh militants kill 20 people and wound another 30 during a machine-gun attack on a passenger train in the northwestern Indian state of Punjab.

28 AUGUST

● The Notting Hill Carnival in London ends in violence as riot police are called in after fighting breaks out in Portobello Road and nearby streets.

● Acting South African President F. W. de Klerk and Zambian President Kenneth Kaunda hold an historic meeting at Victoria Falls on the Zambezi River. Kaunda says he is impressed by de Klerk's commitment to a negotiated solution to South Africa's problems.

● Irish police intercept a 1500-lb package of explosives near the border with Northern Ireland.

● A British Army staff sergeant foils a bomb attack in Hanover, West Germany, when he notices a bomb under his Rover car.

● Mozambique makes an urgent appeal for pledges of 184,000 tonnes of food aid to relieve shortages that are expected to become critical within four months.

● Nigerian President Ibrahim Babangida announces the creation of a new riot police force to patrol the country's borders and handle civil disorder.

29 AUGUST

● An estimated 120,000 ethnic Russians in Moldavia go on strike in protest against a draft law that would make Moldavian the official language of the region.

● Nine seamen die when a Maltese-registered tanker tries to run a Syrian-imposed blockade of South Lebanon's Christian enclave.

● Cambodian peace talks in Paris break down. The talks involved 19 foreign ministers.

● The Colombian government asks for a further $19 million in US aid to protect judges from the gun squads of the drug barons. 50 judges have been killed in 10 years.

● Soviet Interior Minister Vadim Bakatin reveals that extra detachments of special troops have been despatched to Armenia and Azerbaijan to quell ethnic violence.

● Home Secretary Douglas Hurd calls for a report on the disturbances at the Notting Hill Carnival as the police are criticized for provoking the violence by overmanning and Conservative backbench MPs call for a Carnival ban.

30 AUGUST

● On the third day of her trial, bank clerk Alison Anders pleads guilty to conspiring to defraud Britoil of £23 million.

● Leah Tutu, wife of South Africa's Archbishop Desmond Tutu, is among 174 women arrested during a Cape Town protest over capital punishment and child detentions.

● British ornithologist and broadcaster Sir Peter Scott dies at the age of 79.

● Mrs Leona Helmsley, one of the richest women in America, is found guilty on 39 counts of tax evasion and other charges. During her trial, her housekeeper testified that Helmsley told her: 'We don't pay taxes. The little people pay taxes.'

● Cholera breaks out among Vietnamese boat people packed into refugee camps in Hong Kong. The diagnosis comes two weeks after the United Nations warned about sanitary conditions in the camps.

● Thomson Holidays, Britain's biggest tour operator, responds to a crisis in the package holiday industry by cutting half a million holidays from its 1990 summer programme and increasing prices by up to 15%.

31 AUGUST

● Buckingham Palace announces the separation of Princess Anne and Capt. Mark Phillips after a marriage of 15 years.

● Hungary and West Germany reach an agreement to allow 20,000 East Germans on 'holiday' in Hungary to leave Hungary for Austria and then West Germany.

● The nationalist movements of Latvia, Estonia and Lithuania accuse the Soviet Communist Party of trying to halt the 'peaceful democratization process' under way in the three Soviet Baltic states.

● Uppark House in West Sussex, one of the most important 17th-century mansions in Britain, is badly damaged by fire at the end of a major restoration.

● The government announces that boats on the Thames will be required to maintain a bow lookout in the aftermath of the *Marchioness* disaster.

● The Department of Transport announces that British Rail will spend £257 million on 400 new carriages for the chronically congested southeast region.

● The European Community announces a £5.8 million emergency food and medical-aid package for Lebanon.

1 SEPTEMBER

● More than 1000 dockworkers are made redundant at Devonport Dockyard in Plymouth, Europe's largest ship-repair complex.

● South Africa's Anglican Archbishop Desmond Tutu is arrested by South African police during a Cape Town protest march against the government response to the campaign against the general election. Tutu was released after three hours.

● Nationalists in Estonia, Latvia and Lithuania write to
the United Nations appealing for protection against a possible Soviet intervention.

● Today is the 50th anniversary of the German invasion of Poland and the start of World War II.

● French President François Mitterrand meets Mrs Thatcher at Chequers where the two leaders discussed monetary union and the proposed EC Social Charter.

● The US government severs diplomatic relations with Panama in protest against the installation of a government subservient to Gen. Manuel Noriega.

2 SEPTEMBER

● Yegor Ligachev, the Soviet Communist Party's leading hard-liner, appears on television to call for measures to stop the 'erosion of socialism'. He said that the Kremlin had a 'constitutional duty' to tighten the reins on nationalist unrest.

● Gurkha troops are sent into refugee camps in Hong Kong to stop riots in which one man died and 15 were injured.

● Plain-clothes soldiers chase and shoot dead an Ulster Volunteer Force gunman after he murdered a Roman Catholic grocer in the Ardoyne district of Belfast.

● The brother of Argentine President Carlos Menem, Senator Eduardo Menem, arrives in London. The official purpose of his visit is the centenary conference of the Inter-Parliamentary Union, but he also plans unofficial talks on the Falkland Islands.

● West Germany charges a former US Army sergeant,

Clyde Lee Conrad, with selling nuclear and military secrets to Hungary and Czechoslovakia.

● The body of Antonio de Vasconcellos, the host of the ill-fated party aboard the Thames pleasure cruiser the *Marchioness*, is recovered from the Thames.

3 SEPTEMBER

● Labour leader Neil Kinnock and his wife Glenys survive a multiple car crash in Dublin in which their chauffeur, 52-year-old Tom Conlon, dies after suffering a heart attack.

● Three people are injured in a bomb explosion on the ground floor of the London department store Liberty's in Great Marlborough Street.

● Two Royal Naval vessels help the US Coast Guard to chase and seize an American trawler carrying 12 tons of marijuana off the coast of Mexico.

● Ethiopia releases 907 political prisoners, including three relatives of the late Emperor Haile Selassie, on the eve of peace talks with Eritrean rebels.

● Thousands of Black South Africans invade 'Whites Only' beaches in Durban in protest against the segregation laws.

● A 115-vehicle multiple crash on a West German autobahn near Munich leaves 26 people injured.

● A Cuban airliner carrying Italian tourists crashes into a village at the end of the runway of Havana International Airport, killing at least 129 people. The crash is Cuba's worst air disaster.

4 SEPTEMBER

● British football fans riot on a North Sea ferry. One fan, 24-year-old Patrick Ayling, falls overboard and drowns after coming under the influence of LSD. The ferry is forced to turn back to Harwich where 20 men were taken in for questioning.

● The Fatah Revolutionary Council, the Palestinian terrorist organization led by Abu Nidal, announces that it has executed a 24-year-old Palestinian for betraying information about the Provisional IRA to British intelligence.

● Cpl Cameron Hastie of the Royal Scots returns to duty after being convicted of leaking documents that found their way into a Loyalist terrorist group in Northern Ireland. His reinstatement sparks off protests from the Dublin government.

● Workers in the Azerbaijani capital of Baku begin a week-long strike to demonstrate opposition to Moscow's direct rule of the disputed territory of Nagorno-Karabakh.

● The Trades Union Congress doubles the number of seats reserved for women on the TUC's general council.

● The Latvian Popular Front outlines proposals for independence from the Soviet Union, claiming that 'only in an independent, democratic Latvia can the economic, social and political crisis be overcome'.

5 SEPTEMBER

● The Trades Union Congress passes a resolution effectively demanding complete immunity from civil legal action. The resolution clashes with Labour Party policy.

● US President George Bush unveils a $7800 million anti-drugs campaign, saying that 'drugs are sapping our strength as a nation'.

● Hundreds of children are sent home from London schools on the first day of the school term because of a shortage of teachers.

● A two-day general strike by more than 1 million South African Black workers starts in protest against the exclusion of the country's Black majority from the general election.

● In Belize, the left-of-centre People's United Party, led by Mr George Price, wins the general elections.

● Indian Prime Minister Rajiv Gandhi proposes the establishment of an $18,000 million a year international environment fund to develop environment-friendly technologies which would be available to fund members.

● A Boeing 737 missing in the Amazon jungle for three days with 54 people on board is found with 43 survivors.

6 SEPTEMBER

● The general election in South Africa results in the re-election of the ruling National Party but with a reduced majority as the liberal anti-apartheid Democratic Party increased its representation; the rigidly pro-apartheid Conservative Party also lost support.

● Four small children missing for over 24 hours from their homes in the Scottish village of Stonehouse are found alive and well in a coal cellar.

● Ruud Lubbers, leader of the Dutch Christian Democrats, emerges as the winner of the Dutch general election, ensuring himself a third term as Prime Minister.

● Swedish police arrest over 200 British football fans after outbreaks of rioting and looting in Stockholm before and after the World Cup match between England and Sweden.

● Mrs Thatcher writes to the leaders of West Germany, France and the United States calling on them to provide more aid for the governments of Poland and Hungary.

● Belgian author Georges Simenon, creator of the famous character Inspector Maigret, dies at the age of 86.

7 SEPTEMBER

● The TUC General Congress abandons its unilateral nuclear-disarmament policy in line with the changed Labour Party line.

● The wife of a British soldier based in Dortmund, West Germany, is shot dead in her car parked outside married quarters. The IRA claims responsibility for her death.

● Sports Minister Colin Moynihan instructs the Football Association to withdraw from a friendly international between Holland and Britain because the match carried a 'totally unacceptable risk' of violence.

● Polish Prime Minister Tadeusz Mazowiecki names his cabinet: it is dominated by Solidarity which receives six full ministries and four cabinet-level posts. Four ministries go to the Communist Party.

● New Zealand Labour MPs vote to participate in a controversial ANZAC project to build naval frigates.

● The Non-Aligned Movement's summit meeting in Belgrade ends with a declaration praising US–Soviet efforts to reduce world tension.

● The Philippines government starts the trial *in absentia* of former President Ferdinand Marcos and his wife Imelda for allegedly plundering the nation of $100,000 million of its wealth.

8 SEPTEMBER

● Management and workers of the Belfast shipyard Harland and Wolff conclude a £15 million management buyout of the Northern Ireland company, saving 2300 jobs in the company and over 1000 jobs in other firms.

● The President of the Scottish Conservative Party, 54-year-old Professor Ross Harper, resigns after newspaper reports that he consorted with a prostitute.

● The Ukrainian nationalist organization Popular Front opens its founding congress in Kiev.

● 116 East Germans inside the West German mission in East Berlin are allowed to leave for West Germany.

● A total of 55 people aboard a Norwegian charter plane are killed when it plunges into the sea off northwest Denmark.

● Former US President Ronald Reagan enters hospital to remove fluid on his brain after a riding accident.

9 SEPTEMBER

● Soviet leader Mikhail Gorbachev attacks critics of his *perestroika* campaign, claiming that they were spreading alarm with predictions of a coup or civil war. The remarks are believed to be aimed at Party hardliner Yegor Ligachev.

● The Labour Party's annual report reveals debts of £1.2 million despite a £600,000 package of job cuts.

● Four men are charged with drug smuggling after customs officers seize £7 million worth of cannabis resin during a routine check at Ipswich.

● Juan Archibaldo Lanus, the Argentinian Foreign Affairs Secretary and assistant to Foreign Minister Domingo Cavallo, resigns in protest against the government's policy of improving relations with Britain.

● Algerian President Chadli Benjedid names Mouloud Hamrouche as Prime Minister, but his predecessor Kasdi Merbah leaves under protest on the grounds that the President has no power to dismiss the government unless parliament has passed a motion of no confidence.

● Gen. Florian Siwicki, Polish Defence Minister, says his country should not have participated in the 1968 Warsaw Pact invasion of Czechoslovakia.

10 SEPTEMBER

● Social and Liberal Democrats leader Paddy Ashdown rejects a proposal from Social Democratic Party leader Dr David Owen that the two parties should join a broad anti-Thatcher alliance. The statement is made at the start of the SLD conference in Brighton.

● The British Army confirms that a list of suspected IRA members has disappeared from Ballykinlar Army Camp in Co. Down, Northern Ireland. It is feared that the list has fallen into the hands of Loyalist terrorists.

● Over 150 people drown when a Romanian pleasure cruiser sinks on the Danube after colliding with a Bulgarian tugboat.

● More than 200 British scientists living in the United States sign an open letter to Mrs Thatcher calling on her to invest more government money in British scientific research.

● Boris Yeltsin, former Moscow Communist Party leader, says on American television that the Soviet Union faces a continuing economic and social crisis.

● A United Nations panel calls for tougher economic sanctions against South Africa after a three-day public hearing in Geneva.

11 SEPTEMBER

● Thousands of East Germans start flooding out of Hungary into Austria and West Germany as the Hungarian government decides to lift restrictions on the Austro-Hungarian border.

● Mrs Thatcher warns of a period of sustained high interest rates in order to win the fight against 'the cancer of inflation'.

● The IRA launches a mortar attack on RAF Bishopscourt, a radar-tracking station in Co. Down, Northern Ireland. There are no injuries.

● The London Stock Exchange suspends dealing in shares of British defence contractor Ferranti International after reports of financial irregularities.

● A committee of Greek MPs recommends that former Prime Minister Andreas Papandreou should stand trial on charges of instigating widespread illegal telephone tapping.

● Soviet politician Boris Yeltsin, during a tour of the United States, predicts that Soviet leader Mikhail Gorbachev has a year to achieve domestic progress or face revolution.

● The general election in Norway results in a setback for Labour Prime Minister Gro Harlem Brundtland and the start of a period of political uncertainty as no party emerges with an absolute majority.

12 SEPTEMBER

● The East German government officially protests to the Hungarian government over its decision to allow East German citizens to cross into the West without East German exit visas and demands that the Hungarians stop the flood of refugees.

● Lindsay MacFairlaine, the chief press officer for South Yorkshire Police, is reinstated in her job. She had been sacked after allegations that she passed confidential information to journalists after the Hillsborough disaster.

● The Social and Liberal Democrat Party conference votes overwhelmingly to adopt a nuclear defence policy of multilateralism, including the retention of the Trident missile system.

● Simon Hayward, former Life Guards captain, is

freed from prison in Sweden after serving half of his five-year sentence for smuggling cannabis.

● The Polish parliament overwhelmingly approves the cabinet nominations of Prime Minister Tadeusz Mazowiecki, giving Poland its first government not dominated by Communists in more than 40 years.

● Anton Lubowski, a senior White official of the South West Africa People's Organization (SWAPO) is assassinated outside his home in Windhoek. His murder is seen to endanger the fragile peace accord for Namibia.

13 SEPTEMBER

● David Howell, Chairman of the Commons Foreign Affairs Committee, says that the reform process in Poland risks collapse within a year unless western countries rapidly coordinate their aid programmes.

● British ambulancemen start an overtime ban after rejecting a 6.5% pay offer.

● A peaceful protest march by 100,000 anti-apartheid demonstrators is allowed to take place by the South African authorities.

● 79 beagles die of suffocation on a ferry shipping them from kennels in Worcestershire to a pharmaceuticals company in Sweden.

● New York Mayor Ed Koch loses in the Democratic Party's mayoral primaries to Black candidate David Dinkins. Rudolph Guiliani wins the Republican nomination.

● Australian Prime Minister Bob Hawke vows not to concede to the demands of Australian airline pilots, on strike in support of a 29% pay claim.

● The Islamic Party of Britain is launched to contest local government and parliamentary elections. The Party's manifesto says it intends to put into practice Islamic principles laid out in the Koran.

● The ruling on 26 June by the Australian Broadcasting Tribunal that Alan Bond was unfit to hold a broadcasting licence is reversed.

14 SEPTEMBER

● A reorganization of BP operations worldwide results in the loss of 1700 jobs, mainly in Scotland.

● Gunman Anthony Hughes shoots himself after ruthlessly murdering 49-year-old Manchester Police Inspector Raymond Codling. After the murder, Hughes fled to Barnsley and shot himself after being cornered by South Yorkshire Police.

● The Royal Ulster Constabulary admits that a list of 12 suspected IRA members and photographs have been stolen from a Belfast police station.

● Sam Nujoma, President of the South West Africa People's Organization (SWAPO) returns to Namibia after 30 years in exile.

● The Social and Liberal Democrat Party conference approves a resolution to reduce the voting age to 16.

● A Greek parliamentary committee recommends that former Prime Minister Andreas Papandreou be charged with embezzlement from the Bank of Crete in addition to earlier charges of illegal wiretapping.

15 SEPTEMBER

● Independent accountants are called in to investigate 'significant irregularities' in Ferranti International Signal's major overseas contracts.

● Peter Brooke, Northern Ireland Secretary, and Irish Foreign Minister Gerry Collins hold an Anglo-Irish intergovernmental conference in Dublin to discuss security leaks from the Ulster Defence Regiment and the Royal Ulster Constabulary.

● South West Water Authority closes three reservoirs to the public because they are polluted by poisonous algae.

● Hong Kong's main political groups reach an outline agreement to demand that Britain increase the pace of democratic reform in the colony.

● The East German Socialist Unity (Communist) Party cancels a visit to East Berlin by a delegation from the West German Social Democratic Party (SPD). The move is in protest against increasing SPD criticisms of East Germany and the flood of East German refugees to the West.

● Sir Shridath Ramphal, Secretary General of the Commonwealth, announces that Pakistan will rejoin the Commonwealth on 1 October.

16 SEPTEMBER

● The Polish Communist Party newspaper *Trybuna Ludu* accuses Soviet troops of 'massive crimes' during the Soviet invasion of Poland in 1939. Solidarity marks the 50th anniversary of the Soviet invasion with a wreath-laying ceremony in Warsaw.

● Viscount Althorp, brother of the Princess of Wales, marries Victoria Lockwood.

● Lord Trafford, a Minister of State for Health, dies at the age of 57 from lung cancer.

● Ten Welsh soccer fans convicted of football hooliganism are gaoled for 16 months by a Greek court.

● Hungary's largest opposition group, the Hungarian Democratic Front, wins its fourth consecutive by-election victory against the ruling Communist Party.

● The Azerbaijan parliament calls for an end to Moscow's direct rule of the disputed region of Nagorno-Karabakh.

17 SEPTEMBER

● The Liberian-registered oil-tanker *Phillips Oklahoma* and the Maltese-registered *Fiona* collide in the mouth of the Humber, causing a 20-mile oil slick.

● The *Sunday Correspondent* is launched with a print run of 680,000 copies.

● Indian troops kill 40 Tamil guerrillas when they destroy a base on the eastern coast of Sri Lanka. 350 people died during one of the country's most violent weeks.

● Nearly 100,000 Ukrainians march through the city of Lvov to demand the reinstatement of the banned Ukrainian Catholic Church.

● Former US President Jimmy Carter visits Nicaragua

to assess the validity of the political structures established for elections in February.

● Foreign Secretary Francis Maude starts a three-day fact-finding mission to Hong Kong.

18 SEPTEMBER

● Hurricane Hugo hits Puerto Rico and the Virgin Islands with winds of 140 miles per hour. Thousands of homes are destroyed and 25 killed.

● The Hungarian Communist Party and the main opposition groups agree a legislative package which paves the way for free elections. The package includes a new electoral law and modified constitution.

● The National Union of Railwaymen claims that safety on the London Underground remains jeopardized by cost-cutting operations despite new Home Office regulations.

● India agrees to suspend military operations against the Tamil Tigers and to withdraw its troops from Sri Lanka by the end of the year.

● Israeli Defence Minister Yitzhak Rabin flies to Cairo for talks with Egyptian President Hosni Mubarak to discuss Egypt's plans for continuing the Middle East peace process.

● Argentine President Carlos Menem says he will pardon military officers facing trial for human-rights abuses as a first step towards healing divisions over the 1976–83 'dirty war' in which nearly 10,000 Argentines died.

19 SEPTEMBER

● Soviet leader Mikhail Gorbachev promises rebellious republics expanded economic and political rights enshrined in a new Soviet constitution. But he refuses to countenance secession.

● US Secretary of State James Baker drops the US demand for a ban on mobile missiles, removing an obstacle to a US–Soviet agreement on nuclear weapons.

● Hurricane Hugo brushes past the Dominican Republic and heads for the Bahamas.

● The Ford Motor Company announces plans to become a 'major shareholder' in Jaguar, the British luxury car manufacturer.

● The Rt Rev. Dr Robert Runcie, the Archbishop of Canterbury, says in an interview with an Italian magazine that he personally would accept some kind of papal authority 'linked to a renewed ecumenical and universal primacy'.

● A French DC-10 airliner belonging to UTA explodes after taking off from Ndjamena Airport in Chad. All 154 people on board, including a Chadian cabinet minister and the wife of the American Ambassador, are killed.

20 SEPTEMBER

● Soviet leader Mikhail Gorbachev drops five Communist Party hard-liners from the ruling Politburo and promotes four reformist figures. However, the leader of the hard-liners, Yegor Ligachev, remained in place.

● EC Commissioner for the Environment, Carlo Ripa di Meana, announces that the EC will take the British government to court for failing to meet EC drinking water standards.

● US President George Bush orders troops into the US Virgin Islands to prevent looting and violence in the aftermath of Hurricane Hugo.

● During a visit to Japan, Mrs Thatcher warns that unless it eliminates trade barriers it could trigger protectionism in which 'we shall all be losers'.

● F. W. de Klerk is sworn in as South Africa's President. He promises to develop a new constitution which will allow all races to participate in government within five years.

● The US Federal Aviation Authority announces that Pan American, the American airline whose aircraft was blown up over Lockerbie, was guilty of security lapses at Heathrow and Frankfurt airports and faces fines of £409,000.

21 SEPTEMBER

● NATO negotiators present a new conventional arms control package at East–West talks in Vienna. The proposals include East–West exchange of detailed military information on air, artillery, ground-support units, air defences, combat units, bombers and other units as well as weapons limits, limits on military exercises and advance notification of major military changes.

● Mrs Thatcher says that the West must not be lured into destroying its defences simply because Communism appears to be in 'terminal decline'.

● Saudi Arabia publicly beheads 16 Kuwaitis convicted of involvement in two bomb blasts which killed a pilgrim and wounded 16 during the Islamic Haj (pilgrimage) to Mecca.

● Inland Revenue Inspector Michael Cormode is gaoled for three years for stealing £136,000 from the Inland Revenue because he felt that his salary of £16,000 was not enough.

● The Green Party conference opens with a warning from Party activist Sara Parkin that members be on their guard against 'parasites' trying to infiltrate the Party and derail it from within.

● The Institute for Public Policy Research proposes that motorists should pay a daily charge of £3–4 to drive in central London in an effort to relieve traffic congestion.

● The Polish government says it will not force the repatriation of East Germans trying to escape to the West through its territory.

22 SEPTEMBER

● Ten Royal Marine Guards bandsmen are killed in a bomb explosion at the Royal Marines School of Music in Deal, Kent. The IRA admits responsibility.

● The Green Party's conference votes to delete its specific target of reducing Britain's population to 30 million. Party activists believe that the policy laid the Greens open to charges of advocating mandatory birth control.

● US Secretary of State James Baker and Soviet

Foreign Minister Eduard Shevardnadze meet in Wyoming to discuss a Gorbachev–Bush summit and reductions in US–Soviet strategic nuclear weapons.

● Hurricane Hugo hits the historic South Carolina city of Charleston, destroying many important buildings with its 135 mph winds.

● The Scottish National Party conference singles out the Labour Party as its main opponent at the next general election.

● 12 schoolchildren are killed and 20 injured in Yugoslavia when a train hits a schoolbus.

23 SEPTEMBER

● Mrs Thatcher meets Soviet leader Mikhail Gorbachev in Moscow, and in an interview on Soviet television appeals to the Soviet people to stick by the Soviet leader.

● Soviet Foreign Minister Eduard Shevardnadze says the controversial Krasnoyarsk radar station in Siberia will be pulled down. He makes the promise after his meeting with US Secretary of State James Baker.

● Talks between the ambulance drivers' union and employers break down, leaving half of the ambulance crews off the road as the national overtime ban takes effect.

● Finance ministers and central bankers from the seven leading industrialized western countries – Britain, France, the United States, Japan, Canada, West Germany and Italy – agree to take measures to stop the rise in the value of the dollar.

● The Lithuanian parliament declares invalid the 1940 vote which resulted in the republic joining the Soviet Union.

● Lebanese peace hopes rise when Gen. Michel Aoun, leader of Lebanon's Christian forces, accepts Arab League proposals for ending the country's civil war.

24 SEPTEMBER

● The number of East Germans crossing the Austro-Hungarian border passes the 20,000 mark.

● Chancellor Nigel Lawson, speaking at the IMF (International Monetary Fund) and World Bank annual meeting in Washington, says British interest rates will remain high and adds that there is little danger of recession.

● Beirut International Airport reopens as the Lebanese cease-fire takes effect. It had been closed since 11 March.

● 50 people are injured in Ireland when a train carrying pilgrims to the Knock shrine is derailed in a collision with a herd of cattle.

● 60 football fans are charged with public order offences when pub fights break out after a second-division match between Stoke City and Port Vale.

● Responsibility for the bombing of the French airliner over Chad is claimed by an organization calling itself the Clandestine Chadian Resistance.

25 SEPTEMBER

● US President George Bush, in an address before the United Nations General Assembly, proposes that the United States and Soviet Union agree a mutual 80% reduction in chemical weapons' stockpiles.

● Two passengers die after a fire breaks out on board the Danish ferry *Tor Scandinavia* bound for Harwich from Gothenburg.

● Conservative Party Chairman Kenneth Baker says that 'quality of life' issues such as improving public services and environment protection will dominate the political agenda in the 1990s.

● Former Irish embassy official Kevin McDonald is gaoled for 21 months after pleading guilty to obtaining false passports for Middle Eastern clients.

● Soviet Finance Minister Valentin Pavlov proposes an austerity budget to deal with the Soviet Union's economic crisis. He says he plans to cut the Soviet budget deficit from £119,000 million to £60,000 million in a year.

● The South Korean Prosecutor's office announces that it is investigating 21 South Korean MPs for either corruption or pro-Communist activities.

26 SEPTEMBER

● Soviet Foreign Minister Eduard Shevardnadze counters US President George Bush's proposal for an 80% cut in chemical weapons' stocks with a proposal that the superpowers completely destroy their chemical weapons.

● British nursing unions launch a claim for a 12% pay rise.

● Education Secretary John McGregor announces that the government is allocating £600 million for 1990 pay increases to 400,000 teachers in England and Wales.

● Left-wing guerrillas in Athens shoot dead Greek MP Paul Bakyoannis, son-in-law of Greek conservative leader Constantine Mitsotakis.

● The Italian government refuses to accept a European Commission ruling that it close a steel plant in Bagnoli as part of a restructuring plan for the European steel industry.

● A general election in Quebec returns Liberal Premier Robert Bourassa to office with a substantially increased majority.

27 SEPTEMBER

● The pound slides sharply on foreign-exchange markets, leading to fears of another rise in interest rates.

● The Royal Navy frigate HMS *Alacrity* and SAS instructors are sent to Colombia as part of a British 'package of assistance' for the Colombian government's war against the drug barons.

● A bomb threat forces Dr David Owen to give his keynote address at the Social Democratic Party conference on the steps of the town's promenade. Dr Owen warns that Britain faces another decade of Conservative government if opposition parties fail to unite against Mrs Thatcher.

● The European Commission publishes proposals for a Social Charter which include proposals for workers' rights to information and the right to participation in company management. Many of the proposals are opposed by the British government.

● Khmer Rouge guerrillas launch an attack on Pailin in western Cambodia as Vietnamese troops complete their withdrawal from the country.

● The Soviet Communist Party delivers a stern public reprimand to six senior government officials for failing to ensure a decent supply of basic goods in shops. The most prominent scapegoat is Vladimir Gusev, a Deputy Prime Minister and Minister of the Chemical Industry.

28 SEPTEMBER

● Britain's university Vice-Chancellors agree to investigate funding an expansion in universities by asking students to pay for tuition.

● Former Philippines President Ferdinand Marcos dies in exile in Hawaii at the age of 72. Filipino President Corazon Aquino refuses to allow his body to be buried in the Philippines.

● The Conservatives hold a one-seat majority in the key London Borough of Wandsworth after a council by-election shows a 2.2% swing to the Conservatives.

● Foreign Secretary John Major says Britain would not stand in the way if Colombia sought the extradition of British mercenaries alleged to have trained gunmen employed by Colombian drug barons.

● Anti-Slovene demonstrations are staged in many Yugoslav towns after Slovenia claims it has the right to secede from Yugoslavia.

● Vladimir Shcherbitsky is ousted as the Communist Party chief of the Ukraine. He is the last important political survivor from the Brezhnev years.

29 SEPTEMBER

● The government is forced to delay its timetable for the privatization of the electricity industry by six months. The delay is caused by disputes over the supply contracts under which the new privatized companies will operate.

● About 400 police launch a major drugs raid on the Broadwater Farm Estate in north London. 24 suspected drug dealers are arrested.

● The government pulls out of an £8,000 million NATO project to build a common frigate because of a failure to agree on design features and a production timetable. The frigate was meant to replace the Type 42 destroyer.

● Thousands line the streets of Deal when the band of the Royal Marines School of Music parades through the town in tribute to the 10 comrades who died in the IRA bomb blast.

● British and Chinese negotiators meet in London to discuss the future of Hong Kong. It is the first Sino-British meeting since the Tiananmen Square massacre. The meeting ends on a sour note when the Chinese insist on the right to station troops in Hong Kong after 1997.

● A Harris opinion poll for ITN shows that Labour has overtaken the Conservatives in 50 Conservative-held marginal parliamentary seats.

30 SEPTEMBER

● 4000 East Germans who sought refuge in West German embassies in Prague and Warsaw are allowed to leave for West Germany on trains travelling through East Germany.

● The Rt Rev. Dr Robert Runcie, the Archbishop of Canterbury, finishes two days of talks in Rome with Pope John Paul II. The talks lead to protests from many Protestants, including the Rev. Ian Paisley.

● 60 football fans are arrested after drunken Birmingham City fans rampage through Blackpool before a third-division match in the town's football stadium.

● Shaun Cunliffe, a 20-year-old member of the Royal Artillery based in West Germany, is charged in Belfast with leaking confidential photographs, names and addresses of suspected members of the IRA.

● The Lebanese parliament meets in Taif, Saudi Arabia, in an attempt to reach an agreement on political reforms, the election of a new President, the formation of a new national unity government and a phased withdrawal of Syrian troops from Lebanon.

● Khmer Rouge guerrillas capture the important town of Sisophon on the Thai–Cambodian border.

1 OCTOBER

● A trainload of East German refugees arrives in West Germany from Czechoslovakia and Poland. The success of the refugees spurs thousands more East Germans to seek sanctuary in the West German embassies in Prague and Warsaw.

● Labour Shadow Chancellor John Smith says a future Labour government would maintain a tight rein on public spending. Mr Smith also supported early British entry into the European Monetary System.

● West Germany's ruling Christian Democratic Union suffers a major setback in local elections in North Rhine–Westphalia. The CDU dropped its share of the vote from 42.2% to 37.5% while the opposition Social Democratic Party, Green Party and Free Democratic Party all increased their share of the vote.

● Pakistan re-enters the Commonwealth.

● China celebrates the 40th anniversary of Communist Party rule with parades and fireworks in Beijing's Tiananmen Square. Only invited guests and performers were allowed in the square.

● Japan's ruling Liberal Democratic Party receives a boost when it wins a by-election for a seat in the upper house of the Diet (parliament). The victory came in the wake of a series of sex and financial scandals and the loss of the LDP majority in the upper house in the July elections.

2 OCTOBER

● The Labour Party Conference at Brighton accepts the end of its policy of unilateral nuclear disarmament but also votes in favour of heavy cuts in defence spending.

● The number of East Germans seeking sanctuary in the West German embassy in Prague exceeds 5000.

● A large pro-democracy demonstration is held in the East German industrial city of Leipzig. The demonstrations were largely organized by New Forum, a new East German umbrella opposition group which demanded the establishment of a multi-party political system.

● Channel Tunnel cost estimates rise by at least £2000 million, threatening the financing of the scheme. Joint Chairman Alastair Morton blamed the higher estimate on cost overruns by the contractors.

● Egyptian President Hosni Mubarak meets US President George Bush in Washington to discuss his new 10-point Middle East peace plan. The plan included Israeli–Palestinian talks in Cairo to discuss proposed elections in the Occupied Territories.

● Cambodian rebels launch a new offensive from Thailand a week after the last Vietnamese troops withdraw. An estimated 5000 rebels participated in the 'general offensive' and three towns and 10 Cambodian outposts were overrun on the first day.

3 OCTOBER

● Labour leader Neil Kinnock's keynote address to the Party conference at Brighton claims that the Party's radical shift in policies means it is now 'fit to serve'.

● East Germany suspends unrestricted travel to Czechoslovakia in an attempt to stem the flow of refugees.

● An attempted military coup in Panama fails to overthrow Gen. Manuel Antonio Noriega.

● The European Community agrees a plan to regulate television transmissions from October 1991. The plan allows any transmission company to show its programmes throughout the EC.

● A curfew is imposed in the Indian town of Badaun in Uttar Pradesh after 30 people are killed in communal violence.

● PLO leader Yasser Arafat visits Japan and meets Prime Minister Toshiki Kaifu. This was the PLO leader's first visit to Japan and was at the invitation of the Japanese government.

4 OCTOBER

● The East German government allows a second trainload of East German refugees to travel from Prague to West Germany through East Germany. An estimated 11,000 refugees were on board and some East Germans attempted to halt the train in order to climb aboard.

● The Labour Party conference in Brighton rejects a proposal from miners' leader Arthur Scargill that would allow a return to mass picketing and industrial action with or without ballots. But the conference also voted in favour of extending the right of workers to take industrial action.

● Lebanese parliamentarians end five days of talks in the Saudi Arabian mountain resort of Taif by accepting an Arab League plan to end the fighting in the latest round of Lebanese civil war. But Palestinian, Druze and Christian factions vowed to continue the fighting.

● Environment Secretary Chris Patten reverses the plans of his predecessor Nicholas Ridley and stops the construction of a new town at Foxley Wood, Hampshire.

● The Canadian government announces that the nationalized rail passenger network will be axed by half as an economy measure.

● Soviet Foreign Minister Eduard Shevardnadze visits Nicaragua and unveils a proposal for the United States and the Soviet Union jointly to guarantee peace and security in Central America.

5 OCTOBER

● British interest rates jump another percentage point to 15%.

● The Labour Party conference in Brighton votes by a three-to-one margin against the introduction of proportional representation in Britain.

● A regular session of the Anglo-Irish conference in London is dominated by Irish protests about the leaks of sensitive documents to Protestant paramilitary groups. The Irish government demanded tighter vetting of members of the Protestant-dominated Ulster Defence Regiment.

● Tibet's exiled Dalai Lama is awarded the Nobel Peace Prize for his efforts to free his homeland from Chinese rule using non-violent means.

● Dissident South Korean clergyman Rev. Moon Ik Hwan is sentenced to 10 years' imprisonment for visiting North Korea. The visit was a violation of South Korea's national security law which prohibits private individuals from contacting North Korea.

● American television evangelist Jim Bakker is found guilty of swindling his followers of more than $150 million.

6 OCTOBER

● Soviet leader Mikhail Gorbachev arrives in East Berlin and urges the hard-line East German leadership to discuss economic and political reforms with 'all groups in society'.

● Israel's inner cabinet rejects Egyptian President Hosni Mubarak's Middle East peace plan. The vote was six Labour ministers in favour of the plan and six Likud ministers against it. Under Israeli cabinet rules a tie vote is a rejection.

● Two Burmese students hijack a Burmese airliner in protest against human-rights abuses by the Burmese military government.

● Lindy Chamberlain, the Australian mother in the Dingo baby case, announces she is seeking $4.3 million in damages for wrongful imprisonment.

● Soviet Defence Minister Dimitri Yazov ends a six-day visit to the United States. Yazov was the highest ranking Soviet defence official ever to visit the United States.

● Film actress Bette Davis dies.

7 OCTOBER

● The Royal Ulster Constabulary thwarts a major bomb attack on Belfast's Crumlin Road prison when the police discover an industrial digger equipped with 500 lbs of explosives outside the prison wall.

● East German police use water cannons to dispel rioters in the industrial city of Leipzig.

● The Hungarian Socialist Workers' Party (Communist) votes to transform itself into a social democratic party.

● Weekend opinion polls put the Labour Party lead over the Conservatives at between 8% and 11%.

● Pope John Paul II starts a 10-day tour of Asia. It is the 44th world trip of his papacy and his fourth visit to Asia.

● Composer Andrew Lloyd Webber announces that he is quitting musicals to produce films.

● The Burmese student hijackers surrender in Thailand.

8 OCTOBER

● 28 members of the Ulster Defence Regiment are arrested during a dawn sweep by police in Northern Ireland. The arrests were related to leaks of sensitive documents to Protestant paramilitaries. 18 of those arrested were released without being charged.

● Environment Secretary Chris Patten continues to reverse the policies of his predecessor Nicholas Ridley when he announces that he will end plans to force the Nature Conservancy Council to sell land.

● 70 people are evacuated from a North Sea gas rig 40 miles from Great Yarmouth because of a gas leak on a nearby platform.

● A Congress of the Latvian Popular Front demands independence from the Soviet Union, a multi-party political system, free market economic systems and a programme of human rights.

● Nigerian President Ibrahim Babangida blocks the creation of 13 new political parties. He said the military government would organize and finance two parties under a new 'grass roots democratic two-party system'.

● Seven people are killed and eight seriously injured when a bomb explodes on a bus in Colombia. Drug traffickers were blamed for the explosion.

9 OCTOBER

● Thousands of East German students take to the streets in spontaneous anti-government demonstrations after leader Erich Honecker warns that any attempt to topple his government will fail and threatens to use the army to quell the riots.

● The pound plummets against all major currencies. The fall was the steepest for three years and led to fears of a fresh increase in interest rates.

● A MORI opinion poll places Michael Heseltine second behind Margaret Thatcher as the choice of leader of the Conservative Party. The poll was conducted among Conservatives and the general public.

● The Supreme Soviet (the Soviet parliament) approves a bill giving workers the legal right to strike, but severely restricts the conditions under which strikes can be called.

● Former Greek Premier Andreas Papandreou abandons his efforts to form a coalition government.

● Journalists on the *Daily Telegraph* launch a 36-hour strike after the management announces plans for 33 redundancies and a seven-day working week.

● American scientists J.Michael Bishop and Harold Varmus win the Nobel Prize for medicine for work which helps to show how normal human cells become cancerous.

10 OCTOBER

● Conservative Party Chairman Kenneth Baker opens the Party conference in Blackpool by defending interest rate rises, the poll tax and privatization programmes and by attacking Neil Kinnock as 'a character in which arrogance, conceit and stupidity are each struggling to get the upper hand'.

● The pound drops to a new low against the West German Deutschmark of 2.95 DM to the pound.

● Alfred Morris, the Shadow Minister for the Disabled, says that a Labour government will make an 'immediate and substantial' increase in the basic pension.

● The South African government announces that it will release eight leading Black Nationalist leaders including leading ANC figure Walter Sisulu.

● A rebel rocket attack on the Afghanistan capital of Kabul leaves 23 people dead.

● 37 people die in Colombia in a series of bomb-and-gun attacks by drug traffickers.

11 OCTOBER

● David Hunt, Minister of State for Local Government, reveals the 'safety net' arrangement for the poll tax. The safety net pledged an additional £300 million to ease the costs to pensioners and the disabled and contained new incentives for local governments not to increase spending. Labour attacked the changes as 'an electoral bribe'.

● East German leader Erich Honecker says he is prepared to discuss ways of improving life in the country but refuses to talk about relinquishing the Communist Party's stranglehold on power.

● A Syrian airforce pilot defects to Israel with his Soviet-made MiG 23 fighter-bomber. The pilot, Maj. Mohammed Bassem Adel, was the first Arab airman to defect to Israel in 23 years.

● The Hong Kong government announces a $16,000 million plan to build a major new international airport and harbour for container shipping. The plan is meant to be a vote of confidence in the future of Hong Kong as the work is due to be completed in 1997, the date of transfer to Chinese rule.

● Japanese newspapers report that the country's powerful pinball gambling industry contributed at least $1.1 million to Japanese politicians in both the ruling Liberal Democratic Party and the opposition Japan Socialist Party.

● The PLO agrees to defer its bid to become a member of UNESCO. The United States had warned that it would never rejoin the organization if UNESCO admitted the PLO as the state of Palestine.

12 OCTOBER

● Ireland's Director of Public Prosecutions says there is insufficient evidence to bring charges against Patrick Ryan, the former Irish priest sought in Britain on terrorism charges.

● Transport Secretary Cecil Parkinson says that plans to privatize British Rail are 'not at the top of my list of priorities at the moment'.

● Chancellor Nigel Lawson, speaking at the Conservative Party conference, admits that using high interest rates to curb inflation is unpopular. But he added that 'there is no alternative and the policy will work'.

● A Swedish Court of Appeal overturns the conviction of Carl Gustav Christer Pettersson who was found guilty of the murder of the Swedish Prime Minister Olof Palme. Court President Birgitta Blom said: 'Our present judgment is that the investigation into the case is insufficient for a conviction.'

● Poland's Solidarity-led government unveils a detailed programme to fight 400%-plus inflation and create a free-market economy. Specific provisions included an end to restrictions on private property, privatization of state enterprises, introduction of monetarist policies, devaluation, creation of a stock market and the introduction of value-added tax.

● Australia's opposition Liberal–National coalition proposes to reduce the top rate of personal income tax from 47% to 39%.

13 OCTOBER

● Mrs Thatcher, speaking at the Conservative Party conference, gives full backing to Nigel Lawson's economic polices. She also attacks Labour's scrapping of unilateral nuclear disarmament as a 'confidence trick'.

● US stock markets suffer their steepest fall since the crash of 1987. The Dow Jones Industrial Average fell 190.58 points in a day of hectic trading.

● Treasury figures show inflation at 7.6% a year.

● Foreign Secretary Douglas Hurd meets the leader of the Angolan rebel force UNITA, Dr Jonas Savimbi, at Blackpool, and urges him to end the fighting with the MPLA government.

● The exact site of Shakespeare's Globe Theatre is unearthed by archaeolgists working in Southwark. The site's owners, Hanson plc, said they would ask the British government to ban construction on the site without governmental approval.

● French President François Mitterrand ends a tour of Latin America with a promise to support Colombia's war against the drug barons.

14 OCTOBER

● The Rt Rev. Dr Robert Runcie, the Archbishop of Canterbury, reports that he has been told by Iranian officials that Anglican envoy Terry Waite is alive.

● The Colombian governnment sends three suspected cocaine traffickers to the United States to stand trial. Bernard Palez Roldan was taken to Detroit where he had already been convicted *in absentia*. Peter Carolini Arrico was taken to Orlando, Florida, and Ana Rodriguez de Tamayo was flown to Miami.

● 15 people are killed and 100 injured after clashes between Hindus and Muslims in the Indian city of Indore.

● Former Japanese Premier Kakuei Tanaka, aged 71, announces his retirement from politics. Tanaka was embroiled in the Lockheed bribery scandal and was forced to resign in 1974.

● Three men posing as detectives steal rare coins valued at £50,000 from an American dealer visiting London.

● 20 people are killed in Sri Lanka and their bodies placed on a funeral pyre of burning tyres as the death toll continues to rise in the intercommunal violence.

15 OCTOBER

● Consultation among the world's leading banks and finance ministers successfully stems a potential crash in world stock markets after an anxious week on the stock exchanges and money markets.

● The South African government frees leading African National Congress member Walter Sisulu and seven other prominent ANC figures. The same evening, Sisulu held a news conference and rally in Soweto.

● Irish Prime Minister Charles Haughey makes a public call for the reform of the Ulster Defence Regiment. He said that confidence in British justice in Northern Ireland 'cannot prevail if there is a perception that individual members of the security forces are colluding with sectarian assassins'.

● Shadow Trade and Industry spokesman Bryan Gould says a future Labour government would impose credit controls by tightening limits on mortgages for homeowners 'trading up'.

● Former Philippines President Ferdinand Marcos is buried in Honolulu, Hawaii after the government refuses to allow the body to be returned to the Philippines.

● The Beijing branch of the Chinese Communist Party votes to purge itself of 'hostile and anti-party elements' and wealthy private businessmen. The move was seen as further evidence of the hard-liners' tightening grip in China.

16 OCTOBER

● The 103-nation Convention on International Trade in Endangered Species votes to ban all trade in ivory in an attempt to save Africa's dwindling elephant herds from extinction at the hands of poachers. The meeting also placed the elephant on its most-endangered species list.

● An estimated 100,000 people stage a pro-democracy demonstration in the East German city of Leipzig.

● The Social and Liberal Democrats vote to change their name to the Liberal Democrats.

● North and South Korea agree to allow a limited number of family reunification visits.

● Egyptian President Hosni Mubarak and Libyan leader Moamar al-Gaddafi meet in Egypt as part of Gaddafi's efforts to end Libya's international isolation.

● Jan Syse, leader of Norway's Conservative Party, is sworn in as Norway's Prime Minister. He heads a three-party centre–right minority coalition and succeeded Socialist Premier Gro Harlem Brundtland.

17 OCTOBER

● A major earthquake rocks the area around San

Francisco, California. Approximately 70 died and 3000 were injured. Most of the dead were crushed when a mile-long section of a double-decker motorway collapsed. 14,000 people were displaced from their homes. More than 100,000 homes were damaged and the estimates of the economic damage were $7000 million.

● Foreign Office Minister of State Francis Maude visits Hong Kong to discuss the issue of repatriation of the Vietnamese boat people in detention centres in the colony.

● Anglo-Argentine talks on the normalization of relations between the two countries are held in Madrid.

● Indian Prime Minister Rajiv Gandhi calls early elections on 22 and 24 November.

● South Korean President Roh Tae Woo holds talks with US President George Bush at the White House. The two men reaffirmed Korean–American defence ties.

● Colombian federal judge Hector Jimenez Rodriguez is assassinated. Responsibility was claimed by the Extraditables, a group set up by drug traffickers to fight against extradition.

18 OCTOBER

● Hard-line East German leader Erich Honecker is ousted from power and replaced by former internal security chief Egon Krenz.

● The Commonwealth heads of government summit opens in Malaysia. Mrs Thatcher came under continuing strong criticism for her opposition to sanctions against South Africa. Nigerian Chief Emeka Anyaoku is elected Secretary General of the Commonwealth in succession to Sir Shridath Ramphal.

● The Hungarian parliament amends the country's constitution to end the Communist Party's monopoly on power and to allow multi-party elections. The parliament also renamed the country the Republic of Hungary, codified civil liberties and human rights and separated the governmental functions of the executive, legislative and judicial branches.

● The US space shuttle *Atlantis* launches the spacecraft *Galileo* on its six-year journey to the planet Jupiter.

● Peace talks end between the El Salvador government and the rebel Farabundo Marti National Liberation Front (FMLN). The three days of talks in Costa Rica ended with a joint communiqué listing their differences, but both sides said the meeting was a small step in the right direction.

● Cuba is elected a non-permanent member of the United Nations Security Council for the first time since the 1959 revolution which brought Fidel Castro to power.

19 OCTOBER

● The Court of Appeal voids the convictions of the four 'Guildford pub bombers'. Patrick Armstrong, Gerald Conlon, Carole Richardson and Paul Hill were in 1975 sentenced to life imprisonment for the 1974 bombings of pubs in Guildford and Woolwich. They were released after an investigation revealed that police faked evidence.

● Unemployment continues to drop as the jobless rate falls to 6%, the lowest since 1980.

● Chancellor Nigel Lawson defends his economic policies in his annual Mansion House speech in the City of London. This was his last major speech before resigning.

● The Court of Appeal rules that an original libel award of £630,000 to Sonia Sutcliffe, wife of the Yorkshire Ripper, against the magazine *Private Eye* was excessive. Mrs Sutcliffe later accepted damages of £60,000 from the magazine, which also had to pay her legal costs and another £100,000 relating to two other libel charges.

● The Hungarian parliament passes a law formally legalizing Hungary's opposition parties. The parliament also rescinded a law allowing the Communist Party to base Party cells at places of work, established the shape of a future parliament and disbanded a 60,000 strong paramilitary organization controlled by the Communist Party.

● The US House of Representatives approves an $837.5 million aid package for Poland and Hungary. Other western aid for Eastern Europe included $1900 million for Poland from West Germany, $400 million for Poland in Italian export credits, $36 million from Canada for Poland and $642 million in aid for Poland from France.

20 OCTOBER

● A French headmaster bans three Muslim schoolgirls for insisting on wearing headscarves in school. The move sparks off a major political row over the issue of religious symbols in schools.

● US Congressman Robert Garcia and his wife Jane Lee Garcia are convicted of extortion and conspiracy charges related to a corruption scandal involving the defence contractor Wedtech Corporation.

● The Polish government reports that industrial production dropped 1.6% in the first nine months of 1989.

● Former US President Ronald Reagan starts an eight-day lecture tour of Japan for which he receives a $2 million fee.

● 22 people are killed, including six members of one British family, when a passenger bus collides with a truck near the town of Grafton in New South Wales, Australia.

● Rebel forces from the Somali National Movement are reported to be threatening the government of President Siad Barre. On the same day, President Barre marked the 20th anniversary of his rule by freeing 1178 political prisoners and calling on opposition figures to help him introduce political reforms.

● Actor Anthony Quayle dies of cancer.

21 OCTOBER

● US President George Bush vetoes a bill that would have allowed the use of Medicaid funds to pay for abortions for poor women who were the victims of rape or incest.

● Reports of renewed famine in Eritrea start pouring into the West. The famine is a result of the continuing war and another severe drought.

● A Honduran jet airliner crashes into the side of a Honduran mountain killing 131 of the 146 passengers.

The crash was the worst in Central American aviation history.

● The experimental drug AZT – used in fighting AIDS – is approved for distribution in the United States by the Food and Drug Administration. The drug was developed by the British pharmaceutical company Burroughs Wellcome.

● A group of Soviet military officers calls for the establishment of an independent trade union for military personnel.

● Child prodigy Ruth Lawrence becomes Oxford University's youngest Doctor of Philosophy at the age of 18.

22 OCTOBER

● Commonwealth heads of government agree to a compromise declaration on the environment that encourages increased international spending on environmental protection.

● Three fire-bombs are defused in London. Responsibility is claimed by the Welsh extremist group Meibion Glyndwr (Sons of Glendower).

● A Russian nationalist group, the Popular Front of the Russian Federation, is formed and demands a multi-party system.

● A Greek airforce warrant officer is killed while planting a bomb in a theatre where the conservative Constantine Mitsotakis was due to speak.

● West Germany's far-right Republican Party makes significant advances in communal elections in Baden-Württemberg.

● Environmental pollution officers force the closure of three out of 12 of the cooling towers at Drax power station in Yorkshire, the largest coal-fired station in Western Europe.

23 OCTOBER

● Police vans in London are used to take 999 calls for ambulance crews as the ambulance pay dispute worsens.

● The government freezes child benefit at £7.25 a week for the following year. It was the third year in succession that the government had frozen the benefit, which prompted protests from Conservative backbenchers as well as the Labour opposition.

● Soviet Foreign Minister Eduard Shevardnadze says that his country's 1979 invasion of Afghanistan was an illegal act. He also conceded that the Soviet radar complex at Krasnoyarsk violated the 1972 ABM missile treaty.

● 250,000 East German pro-democracy demonstrators march through the centre of Leipzig. The demonstrators shouted: 'Free elections,' 'We are the people,' and 'Freedom for detainees.' Police did not interfere.

● The Commonwealth heads of government summit in Malaysia ends with Britain refusing to agree to the joint communiqué calling for tightened credit and arms sanctions against South Africa. Zimbabwe Prime Minister Robert Mugabe described the British move as 'despicable' and Australian Prime Minister Bob Hawke said it was 'astounding'.

● Hungary marks the 23rd anniversary of the 1956 uprising with an official 'day of national reconciliation'. It was the first time that the anniversary was officially and openly commemorated in Hungary.

● The Khmer Rouge guerrillas announce that they have captured the key Cambodian town of Pailin.

24 OCTOBER

● Chancellor Nigel Lawson publicly rebukes Sir Alan Walters, the Prime Minister's personal economic adviser, and demands that he refrain from making any further statements on the government's economic policy. Sir Alan, unlike Mr Lawson, publicly opposed British membership of the European Monetary System.

● Mrs Thatcher criticizes the United States for its opposition to the forced repatriation of Vietnamese boat people from Hong Kong.

● Lebanese Christian and Muslim parliamentarians approve a national charter designed to end the long-running civil war. Christian and Muslim militiamen, however, remain sceptical.

● US President George Bush says that he does not 'share the concern that some European countries have about a reunified Germany'.

● The Polish Red Cross opens soup kitchens in Warsaw and in the depressed Katowice region.

● Actress Zsa Zsa Gabor is sentenced to a three-day prison term for slapping a policeman. Ms Gabor was also ordered to pay a $2350 fine and perform 120 hours of community service.

25 OCTOBER

● Foreign Secretary John Major announces that Britain will forcibly repatriate 40,000 Vietnamese boat people in Hong Kong. The refugees will each receive £380 when they are returned.

● The House of Lords votes against the government to curb sales of rural homes intended for the low-paid and to limit tenants' rights to buy council homes suitable for the elderly and disabled.

● The Post Office uncovers a £10 million fraud involving recycled used stamps donated to charities.

● NATO defence ministers say the Alliance will maintain nuclear weapons even if the Warsaw Pact's conventional forces are substantially reduced.

● Soviet leader Mikhail Gorbachev makes his first visit to Finland. Gorbachev hailed Finland as 'a model of relations between a big country and a small country, a model of relations between states with different social systems, a model of relations between neighbours'.

● The Soviet government devalues the rouble by 90% against the US dollar to bring its value into line with western market rates.

26 OCTOBER

● Chancellor Nigel Lawson resigns from the Cabinet over differences with Mrs Thatcher, and her personal economic adviser Sir Alan Walters, over Britain's membership of the European Monetary System. John Major is moved from the Foreign Office to the Treasury to fill the vacancy. Douglas Hurd is moved from the Home Office to the Foreign Office and David Waddington is brought into the cabinet as Home Secretary.

● A Royal Air Force corporal and his six-month-old daughter are killed in a gun attack on their car in Wildenrath, West Germany. The IRA claimed responsibility.

● Soviet Foreign Minister Eduard Shevardnadze pledges non-interference in the internal affairs of East European countries. Shevardnadze made the pledge at a meeting of Warsaw Pact foreign ministers in Warsaw.

● East German government officials open a formal dialogue with opposition leaders in East Berlin and Dresden.

● A China Airlines jetliner crashes after taking off from the eastern Taiwanese city of Hualien. All 54 people on board were killed.

● The Booker Prize is awarded to Japanese-born author Kazuo Ishiguro for his novel *The Remains of the Day*.

27 OCTOBER

● The new Chancellor of the Exchequer, John Major, pledges that interest rates will remain high. Mrs Thatcher denies that she is shaken by Nigel Lawson's resignation and says it is 'business as usual'.

● Transport Secretary Cecil Parkinson rules out government subsidies for a high-speed rail link between London and the Channel Tunnel. Two private companies had expressed an interest in the scheme, but both said their involvement was contingent on a billion-pound government subsidy.

● Australia and Indonesia sign an agreement on the economic development of a stretch of the Timor Sea between the Indonesian island of Timor and the north Australian coast.

● Jean-Pierre Hocke, United Nations High Commissioner for Refugees, resigns after allegations that he had mismanaged the UN agency and made personal use of agency funds.

● At least four policemen were killed and 40 injured when a bomb exploded on a police bus in the Colombian drug capital of Medellin.

● US newspapers and television produce reports claiming that Israel secretly aided South Africa to develop an intermediate-range ballistic missile capable of carrying a nuclear warhead. The missile was tested on 5 July.

28 OCTOBER

● Deputy Prime Minister Sir Geoffrey Howe delivers a strongly worded speech calling on Mrs Thatcher to reaffirm the government's commitment to the European Exchange Rate Mechanism.

● Foreign Secretary Douglas Hurd says that his relationship with Mrs Thatcher will continue being 'loyal and cooperative, but clearly not subservient'.

● An opinion poll in the *Sunday Correspondent* shows the Labour Party 15 points ahead of the Conservatives in the opinion polls.

● Six men are charged with attempting to smuggle £37 million worth of cannabis into Britain. The four Dutchmen and two Lebanese were arrested at Dover.

● Riot police in Czechoslovakia use clubs to break up a pro-democracy demonstration by 10,000 people in central Prague.

● Nicaraguan President Daniel Ortega announces an end to a 19-month unilateral cease-fire against the Contra rebels. He said this was necessary because increased attacks endangered the Nicaraguan electoral process.

● Former US President Richard Nixon starts a six-day visit to China. He apparently went with the approval of President George Bush.

29 OCTOBER

● Mrs Thatcher says that a number of major barriers would need to be dismantled before Britain could join the European Monetary System.

● An opinion poll in the *Independent* gives Mrs Thatcher the lowest popularity rating of any Prime Minister for 50 years. 62% of those polled were dissatisfied with her leadership and only 24% said they were satisfied with her record.

● Spanish Prime Minister Felipe Gonzalez is re-elected to a third term with a one-seat majority. The Socialists, however, lost 800,000 votes compared with elections in 1986.

● Michael Heseltine says he will not challenge Margaret Thatcher for the party leadership 'under any circumstances I can foresee'.

● Nearly 70,000 people attend an African National Congress rally in a soccer stadium halfway between Soweto and Johannesburg. The rally was permitted by President F. W. de Klerk.

● Former Japanese Prime Minister Zenko Suzuki, aged 78, announces that he is retiring from politics.

30 OCTOBER

● The executive committee of the 1922 Committee, the committee which represents Conservative backbenchers, warns Mrs Thatcher that she must change her style of leadership and take a more collective approach to decision-making.

● Moscow riot police charge and club demonstrators after a candlelight vigil outside KGB headquarters in memory of Stalin's victims.

● St Helens South MP Gerry Birmingham becomes the first Labour MP to be de-selected under the Labour Party's new rules.

● An Israeli court gives a Palestinian 16 life sentences for killing 16 Jews by forcing their bus off a road into a ravine.

● Talks are held between Turkey and Bulgaria on the issue of Bulgaria's ethnic Turks. Some 300,000 ethnic Turks had fled persecution in Bulgaria.

● A man left mute and paralysed after a car accident is awarded £860,000 by a High Court in London. Adam Davidson, aged 20, was struck by a van when aged 16.

31 OCTOBER

● In his first Commons speech since his resignation, former Chancellor Nigel Lawson launches a full-scale attack on the style and substance of Mrs Thatcher's leadership. He also said that Britain should enter the European Monetary System as soon as possible.

● The Turkish parliament elects former Prime Minister Turgut Ozal the country's President.

● The Hungarian parliament votes to cancel Hungary's participation in a controversial joint hydroelectric project with Czechoslovakia to dam the Danube River. The project was strongly opposed by environmentalists.

● *Observer* journalist Farzad Bazoft appears on Iraqi television to confess to being an Israeli spy. The confession was derided by both the *Observer* and the Foreign Office, who linked Bazoft's arrest and confession to his coverage of a mid-August explosion at a secret Iraqi arms factory.

● Trade and Industry Secretary Nicholas Ridley announces that the government will not use its 'golden share' to block the Ford Motor Company's proposed hostile takeover of Jaguar Cars.

● Ten people are killed in El Salvador by a bomb blast at the country's anti-government labour federation headquarters. The dead included prominent trade unionists.

1 NOVEMBER

● Elections to Labour's Shadow Cabinet return all existing members. New faces included Paul Boateng, the first Black to win a seat. He was appointed to the Treasury and Economic Affairs section. Four women were elected to the 18 shadow cabinet posts.

● The High Court rules that money market transactions by Hammersmith and Fulham councils were illegal.

● Pakistan Prime Minister Benazir Bhutto wins a vital no-confidence vote in the National Assembly.

● East Germany reopens its border with Czechoslovakia, spurring an immediate movement of 50,000 East German refugees to West Germany through Czechoslovakia and Hungary.

● The new East German leader Egon Krenz visits Moscow and after meeting Soviet leader Mikhail Gorbachev promises to introduce Gorbachev-type reforms.

● An anti-drug parliamentarian in Colombia and a federal judge are assassinated by the country's drug traffickers.

2 NOVEMBER

● The British government publishes its own plan for economic and monetary union. The plan called for a fuller development of the European Monetary System and opposed the creation of a common currency, a European central bank and the irrevocable fixing of European exchange rates.

● The Ford Motor Company announces that it will buy Jaguar plc for £1600 million.

● British Rail announces fare increases of up to 15%. The biggest increases are borne by long-distance commuters into London. The average price rise was 9%.

● The El Salvador rebel group Farabundo Marti National Liberation Front (FMLN) withdraws from peace talks with the government.

● Colombia's judges start a series of strikes in support of demands for tighter protection from assassination following the deaths of judges at the hands of the country's drug traffickers.

● US President George Bush dismisses speculation that he would drop Vice-President Dan Quayle as his running mate in the 1992 presidential election. He said: 'I think he has been an oustanding Vice-President, doing exactly what I want him to do.'

3 NOVEMBER

● The East German leader Egon Krenz promises sweeping economic and political reforms in a nationally televised address.

● More than 500,000 people participate in a pro-democracy demonstration in East Berlin. This was believed to be the largest protest in East German history.

● Northern Ireland Secretary Peter Brooke creates a political stir when he appears to suggest that the British government might negotiate with Sinn Fein if the IRA renounced violence.

● An estimated 10,000 people demonstrate in Sofia, the capital of Bulgaria, in favour of free elections and democratic reform. It was the first such demonstration in Bulgaria since World War II.

● The Lithuanian parliament approves legislation that would allow Lithuanians to decide by a referendum whether or not they wanted to secede from the Soviet Union.

● An important hoard of Bronze and Iron Age swords and jewellery is discovered near Peterborough, Cambridgeshire, by archaeologists.

4 NOVEMBER

● Lebanese Christian militia leader Gen. Michel Aoun issues a declaration dissolving parliament. He accused the parliamentarians of 'violating the constitution by approving...an agreement that damages the independence' of Lebanon.

● Soviet KGB Chief Vladimir A. Kryuchkov admits in a nationally televised interview that the KGB had been a 'mechanism of repression' and pledged that the Stalinist abuses 'would never happen again'. Kryuchkov's comments were part of a KGB public relations effort to improve its image.

● The Princess of Wales is praised for shaking hands with lepers in a leper colony in Jakarta, Indonesia.

● Iranian fundamentalists celebrate the 10th anniversary of the takeover of the US embassy in Teheran with rallies around the country. But the event was played down by President Ali Akbar Hashemi Rafsanjani.

● A Soviet poll shows that 90% of those questioned considered the Soviet economic situation to be bad or critical. Only 17% thought that the country's leadership had a well-thought out economic reform plan.

5 NOVEMBER

● In an interview with the *Sunday Correspondent*, Mrs Thatcher says she will step down as leader of the Conservative Party after the next election.

● Former Chancellor Nigel Lawson denies Mrs Thatcher's claims that she did everything possible to stop him from resigning.

● The Greek general election ends with the second

inconclusive result in five months. The conservative New Democracy Party led in the voting, but fell three short of an overall majority.

● Syrian-backed Christian, René Moawad, is elected President of Lebanon by the Lebanese parliament. His election is opposed by supporters of Christian militia leader Gen. Michel Aoun, who riot for two days through the streets of East Beirut.

● The Iranian government hangs four men charged with spying for the CIA.

● About 250 people die when Typhoon Gay sweeps across the Gulf of Thailand. 93 of the dead were from a capsized US gas-drilling ship.

6 NOVEMBER

● Environment Secretary Chris Patten estimates that the average poll tax will be £278.

● A survey of building societies shows that house prices fell 2% in the previous two months.

● A pro-democracy crowd of 300,000 people marches through the East German industrial city of Leipzig.

● The United States unfreezes $567 million in Iranian assets frozen since the hostage crisis of 1979. The State Department insisted that the move was unconnected with the holding of western hostages in Beirut.

● Kitty Dukakis, the wife of former US presidential candidate Michael Dukakis, is hospitalized after drinking rubbing alcohol.

● The Chinese leadership agrees to a series of economic austerity measures including major reductions in the importation of consumer goods and raw materials.

7 NOVEMBER

● Troops are called in to man ambulances in London and to take over 999 calls for ambulance crews as the ambulance dispute worsens.

● The Church of England Synod votes in favour of women priests by a margin of 64.1%.

● An international environmental meeting in Noordwijk, the Netherlands, adopts a compromise resolution aimed at stabilizing carbon-dioxide emissions which play a major part in the 'greenhouse effect'.

● Democrats make major gains in state gubernatorial and mayoral elections in the United States. The elections also see two Blacks elected to leading posts: David Dinkins as Mayor of New York and Douglas Wilder as Governor of Virginia.

● Israeli Defence Minister Yitzhak Rabin says that Palestinians had gained 'a certain self-respect' from the Intifada (the Palestinian uprising) in the Occupied Territories.

● The Chinese leadership announces that it has closed 2.2 million private businesses in the previous year.

8 NOVEMBER

● Half the remaining members of the Politburo of East Germany's ruling Socialist Unity Party are removed from office by the Central Committee.

● West German Chancellor Helmut Kohl promises a 'new dimension' of economic aid for East Germany if the East German Communist Party relinquishes its monopoly of power. Speaking in the West German Bundestag, Kohl also pledged that West Germany would remain in NATO.

● Mrs Thatcher, addressing the United Nations General Assembly, says: 'The most pressing task which faces us at the international level is to negotiate a framework convention on climate change – a sort of good-conduct guide for all nations.' She promised that Britain would establish a Centre for the Prediction of Climate Change.

● Edward Browning is convicted at Shrewsbury Crown Court of the June 1988 murder of Marie Wilks on the M50 motorway near Tewkesbury, Gloucestershire. He was sentenced to life imprisonment.

● Three people die when a car ferry heading for Britain collides with a freighter in the North Sea off Hamburg.

● Former US Air Force Maj.-Gen. Richard V. Secord pleads guilty to making a false statement to congressional investigators probing the Iran–Contra arms scandal.

9 NOVEMBER

● The East German government opens its border with the West. Within hours of the announcement, tens of thousands of East and West Berliners gathered at the Wall for an emotional impromptu celebration that lasted well into the next day. West Berlin Mayor Walter Momper said: 'The long-awaited day has arrived. The Berlin Wall no longer divides Berliners.'

● Energy Secretary John Wakeham announces that none of the government's nuclear reactors would be sold off in the privatization of the electricity industry. He also indicated that plans to build three new reactors would be scrapped.

● 11 City of London financial figures are charged with fraud and conspiracy in connection with a 1987 stock issue for Blue Arrow plc. Also involved in the charges were National Westminster Bank plc, County NatWest and stockbrokers Phillips and Drew. The individuals charged were Charles Villiers and Jonathan Cohen, the former number one and number two, respectively, at both NatWest Investment Bank and County NatWest.

● Chinese paramount leader Deng Xiaoping resigns his last official post as Chairman of the Central Military Commission. Jiang Zemin, the Chinese Communist Party's general secretary, is named Chairman of the Military Commission in succession to Deng.

● The US House of Representatives passes anti-oil-spill legislation which demands double hulls on all tankers operating in US waters. The legislation also tightened laws relating to liability and clean-up operations.

● Yildirim Akbulut is named Prime Minister of Turkey by Turgut Ozal who is sworn in as President on the same day.

10 NOVEMBER

● East German bulldozers start punching holes in the Berlin Wall as Berliners literally dance in the streets.

● Hundreds of thousands of East Berliners pour into West Berlin by foot, car and special shuttle bus.

● West German Chancellor Helmut Kohl breaks a trip to Poland to visit Berlin and call for a reunited Germany.

● Bulgaria's long-serving hard-line Communist leader Todor Zhivkov unexpectedly resigns and is replaced by Foreign Minister Petur Mladenov.

● Islamic fundamentalists make major gains in Jordan's first general election in 22 years. The Muslim Brotherhood won 20 of the 26 seats it contested and other fundamentalist candidates 12 seats, to give the fundamentalists a total of 32 seats out of 80 and make them the largest voting bloc in the new parliament.

● EMI and Capitol records reach an agreement with the Beatles to end a 10-year-long legal battle during which the Beatles alleged underpayment of royalties.

11 NOVEMBER

● Four days of elections are completed in Namibia. The South West Africa People's Organization (SWAPO) failed to win the two-thirds majority needed to dictate the terms of the constitution, although it did win 57.3% of the vote.

● The government of El Salvador declares a state of siege and a curfew after 80 people are killed in attacks by the rebel Farabundo Marti National Liberation Front.

● British crewman Anthony Phillips dies after being swept overboard in the South Atlantic in the Whitbread round-the-world yacht race.

● Spanish Civil War heroine Dolores Ibarrui, popularly known as La Passionaria, dies in Madrid at the age of 93. A former Communist parliamentarian, she spent 38 years in exile in the Soviet Union to escape the Franco regime.

12 NOVEMBER

● The El Salvador rebel group Farabundo Marti National Liberation Front launches a major military offensive which takes their forces into the capital San Salvador.

● A Fabian Society report says that the Labour Party fails to offer a clear alternative to the Conservative government's pro-market economic policies.

● EC President Jacques Delors says that the Community could absorb East Germany and still complete its plans for political and economic unity.

● American pro-abortionists stage a series of rallies across the United States. The biggest was held in Washington DC where 150,000 people gathered.

● The centre–right Democratic Front coalition makes impressive gains in municipal elections in Peru. There was a heavy turnout at the polls despite threats by the left-wing guerrilla group Shining Path to kill or cripple anyone who voted.

● 2000 Soviet troops are airlifted to Moldavia to maintain order after police clashes with nationalist demonstrators.

13 NOVEMBER

● Mrs Thatcher calls on the West to support changes in Eastern Europe but warns that the speed of events could put the goal of democracy at risk.

● Hans Modrow, East Germany's reform-minded Dresden Communist Party leader, is elected Premier in a secret ballot. He replaced Willi Stoph who accepted responsibility for 'all the failures of the former government'.

● Lord Marshall resigns as Chairman of the Central Electricity Generating Board. He had been a major proponent of nuclear power.

● EC health ministers agree that cigarette packaging should carry health warnings and that the maximum allowable levels of tar in cigarettes should be reduced. The regulation is opposed by Britain which said that such rules should be left to member states.

● West Germany's opposition Social Democratic Party (SPD) calls for a conference of the four victorious World War II powers – the United States, France, Britain and the Soviet Union – to consider the future of the two Germanies. The proposal was rejected by West German Chancellor Helmut Kohl.

● Rohana Wijeweera, the leader of Sri Lanka's radical Sinhalese group the People's Liberation Front, is shot dead in Colombo. The murder was a major blow to the island's Sinhalese community.

14 NOVEMBER

● Lt-Gen. Sir David Ramsbotham, commander of Britain's Field Army, escapes death when a bomb is discovered under a car outside his Kensington home.

● Soviet leader Mikhail Gorbachev issues a stern warning to the West not to exploit the political turmoil in Eastern Europe. The warning was made during a visit by French Foreign Minister Roland Dumas and reported by the Soviet news agency Tass.

● West German Chancellor Helmut Kohl ends a visit to Poland with a pledge of $1900 million in German aid for Poland, a promise to respect the current German-Polish border and a joint Polish–German declaration outlining future bilateral economic and political co-operation.

● Czechoslovak Prime Minister Ladislav Adamec announces the easing of restrictions on travel by Czechoslovaks to Yugoslavia and the West. The new legislation included the abolition of exit visas.

● Auditors of Bond Corporation Holdings Ltd warn that there is 'some doubt' that the company can 'continue as a going concern' in the face of mounting debts.

15 NOVEMBER

● Chancellor John Major, in the annual autumn Economic Statement, predicts a slowdown for the British economy in 1990. He also announced plans to boost spending on transport, the National Health Service and the plight of the homeless.

● 1400 top Soviet managers and economists end an unprecedented three-day debate on the future course of Gorbachev's economic reform programme. The meeting was chaired by Deputy Premier Leonid Abalkin who said he was surprised by the level of conservative resistance.

● Three serving detectives on the West Midlands Serious Crime Squad are suspended from duty and told that they face charges of perjury and intent to pervert the course of justice following an inquiry into allegations of a falsified confession.

● Palestinians on the West Bank and Gaza Strip celebrate the first anniversary of the declaration of a Palestinian state. By this date, 94 countries had recognized the PLO as the representative of the Palestinian state.

● Polish Solidarity leader Lech Walesa addresses a joint session of the US Congress. He called for a new Marshall Plan to rebuild Eastern Europe.

● Pope John Paul II calls for a 'global plan to combat AIDS and drug addiction'. His comments came at the end of a three-day Vatican conference on AIDS.

16 NOVEMBER

● Ramon Canale is freed after the Court of Appeal quashes his conviction for conspiracy to rob and transporting a firearm. The conviction was quashed because of what Lord Lane, the Lord Chief Justice, called 'flagrant, deliberate and cynical' breaches of interview rules by West Midlands detectives.

● Transport Secretary Cecil Parkinson announces that the Underground's Jubilee Line will be extended from Charing Cross through Docklands to Stratford in East London. He said that private developers would pay 40% of the costs.

● Six Jesuit priests and two female employees are killed in El Salvador by a right-wing death squad.

● The Supreme Court of Canada rules that a father of an unborn child does not have a legal basis for seeking a civil injunction to prevent a woman from obtaining an abortion.

● A federal district judge in Washington DC approves a *sub poena* requiring former President Ronald Reagan to produce notes and provide testimony for the Iran–Contra trial of former national security adviser John Poindexter.

● Israeli Prime Minister Itzhak Shamir visits the United States. While he was there, US Jewish leaders said they opposed his hardline policies on the principle of exchanging 'land for peace with secure borders'.

17 NOVEMBER

● Czechoslovak students are attacked and beaten by security forces during an anti-government protest by 20,000 in Prague. The police used dogs, tear gas and truncheons.

● Home Secretary David Waddington warns the public to be extra vigilant after a series of IRA bomb attacks and discoveries by British police.

● A White South African ex-police captain admits that he was a member of an official assassination squad which targeted apartheid opponents.

● Romania closes its border with Hungary.

● East Germany's new Premier Hans Modrow announces a new 27-member cabinet which includes 11 non-Communists.

18 NOVEMBER

● The European Community holds a special summit in Paris to discuss events in Eastern Europe. The meeting ended with a promise of economic aid to East European countries which embraced democracy.

● A military policeman and his wife are seriously injured in an IRA car-bomb attack in Colchester, Essex. On the same day three British soldiers are killed and one seriously injured in an IRA bomb attack near Newry, Co. Down.

● Michael Heseltine warns that Britain risks being left behind in a 'two-speed Europe' and EC Commissioner Leon Brittan calls on Mrs Thatcher to commit Britain to early membership of the European Monetary System.

● Eight Coldstream Guards are killed and 13 injured when an Army truck plunges over a precipice in Cyprus.

● El Salvador Attorney General Mauricio Eduard Colorado urges Pope John Paul II to withdraw the nine Roman Catholic bishops from his country on the grounds that he has 'tremendous concern' for their 'fate and fortune'.

19 NOVEMBER

● The Czechoslovak opposition group Civic Forum is founded. In the following weeks the group, headed by dissident playwright Vaclav Havel, organized anti-government demonstrations and demanded political reforms and talks with the Communist government.

● The Georgian Supreme Court rules that the Soviet republic has the right to secede from the Soviet Union and override Soviet laws that affect Georgia.

● Terry Clarke, a leading Irish Republican, is gaoled for nine years because he failed to stop the violence at the IRA funeral at which two Army corporals were beaten, stripped and shot dead. Clarke was the chief steward at the IRA funeral.

● The pound slides against the dollar and the West German Deutschmark after worse than expected monthly trade figures.

20 NOVEMBER

● A crowd of 200,000 marches peacefully through Prague in support of pro-democracy demands. Smaller demonstrations take place in other Czechoslovak cities and towns.

● Former Labour deputy leader Denis Healey announces that he is quitting the House of Commons at the next general election.

● The editor of the *Sunday People*, Wendy Henry, is sacked. Publisher Robert Maxwell said she was dismissed for publishing 'deeply offensive' photographs of the royal children.

● The British Film Institute calls on the government to establish a National Television Archive to hold and preserve taped records of programmes for future generations.

● France announces the sale of fighter aircraft engines to Israel. These were the first French military sales to Israel since the 1967 war.

● The United Nations General Assembly adopts a Convention on the Rights of the Child. The pact outlined international standards on education, adoption, protection from sexual abuse and other issues.

21 NOVEMBER

● The House of Commons is televised for the first time

following the Queen's Speech. The first MP to be televised live was Labour MP Bob Cryer. The first formal speech was given by Conservative Ian Gow.

● The Queen's Speech lists 15 pieces of legislation. These included the restructuring of the National Health Service, the Broadcast Bill, reform of the legal profession, a freeze on student grants, a ban on wildcat strikes and tighter controls on waste disposal and emissions.

● The El Salvador rebel group Farabundo Marti National Liberation Front seizes the Hotel El Salvador in San Salvador. Trapped inside were 17 civilians and 12 members of the US Green Berets.

● Czechoslovak Premier Ladislav Adamec begins talks in Prague with the new opposition group Civic Forum.

● Greece's three major political parties agree to form a coalition government headed by the 85-year-old former head of the Bank of Greece, Xenophon Zolotas. The coalition was a stopgap measure designed to last until a general election was held after presidential elections in March 1990.

● Talks between the Sandinista government in Nicaragua and the Contra rebels break down when the Sandinistas proposed that 2300 rebels withdraw to their camps in Honduras.

22 NOVEMBER

● Lebanese President René Moawad is assassinated by a car bomb only 17 days after becoming President.

● The ambulance dispute worsens as crews outside London refuse to answer non-emergency calls.

● Health Secretary Kenneth Clarke unveils new legislation for the National Health Service. The proposals include the creation of an internal market in health care which would allow health authorities to buy services from NHS and private hospitals.

● Lord Justice Stuart-Smith is named the first independent watchdog over MI5.

● US President George Bush, in a Thanksgiving Day broadcast, says that 'America believes that liberty is an idea whose time has come in Eastern Europe'.

● An oil-tanker and a tug collide in Milford Haven Harbour, Wales, causing 50 tonnes of oil to spill from the *Texaco Westminster*.

23 NOVEMBER

● Alexander Dubcek, leader of Czechoslovakia's 1968 Prague Spring, re-emerges to address a crowd of pro-democracy demonstrators in Bratislava.

● The Rover Car Company announces that it is investing £130 million in its Cowley car plan for a new range of executive cars.

● The government establishes a £19,000 million fund for haemophiliacs who have contracted AIDS from tainted blood provided by the National Health Service.

● The Italian Communist Party votes to change its name and abandon its hammer-and-sickle emblem. It was decided to choose a new name at a party congress in 1990.

● A five-year-old boy, Richard Cooney, dies and four other children are injured when a wall collapses on top of them in the playground of Sir James Barrie School in Clapham, London.

● Several thousand gallons of acid solution leak into the River Ebbw in Gwent.

24 NOVEMBER

● Czechoslovakia's Communist Party General Secretary Milos Jakes and the other 12 members of the ruling Politburo resign en masse. Jakes admitted failing to understand the liberalization process sweeping Eastern Europe.

● Mrs Thatcher visits US President George Bush at Camp David, Maryland. The two leaders discussed events in Eastern Europe and Hong Kong. Bush expressed his 'profound disagreement' with Britain's plans for the forcible repatriation of Vietnamese boat people from Hong Kong.

● In an interview with *The Times*, Mrs Thatcher says she is willing to lead the Conservative Party into the next two elections. This appeared to contradict her interview in the *Sunday Correspondent* on 5 Nov.

● The government announces that anonymous AIDS testing will start in 1990.

● Romanian Communist leader Nicolae Ceaucescu is unanimously re-elected President at the 14th Congress of the Romanian Communist Party. In his keynote address, Ceaucescu ruled out economic and political reforms.

● The South African government opens four 'free settlement areas' to all races for integrated residential living. They were the first areas in South Africa where the Group Areas Act, a key pillar of apartheid, would officially no longer apply.

25 NOVEMBER

● Pro-democracy demonstrators hold a major demonstration in Prague, the ninth consecutive demonstration in as many days. The crowd was estimated at 800,000.

● Fines for breaking food safety laws are raised from £2000 to £20,000 under the proposed Food Safety Bill.

● The European Court rules that British laws governing Sunday trading do not breach EC regulations. But the ambiguous wording of the ruling enabled both sides to claim victory.

● Canadian Prime Minister Brian Mulroney ends a five-day visit to the Soviet Union during which he told Soviet leader Mikhail Gorbachev: 'It is my deep conviction that it is very clearly in everyone's interest that your reforms succeed.'

● The European Commission pledges to introduce measures to reduce barriers to corporate takeovers across European borders.

26 NOVEMBER

● Hungarians approve a constitutional amendment which calls for a strong executive president to be chosen by a parliament to be directly elected in 1990.

● The EC and Soviet Union reach preliminary agreement on a 10-year trade and economic cooperation treaty. The treaty would phase out EC quotas on industrial imports from the Soviet Union in return for freer access to the Soviet market.

● Luis Alberto Lacalle is elected President of Uruguay.

His closest opponent was Senator Jorge Batlle.

● President Ahmed Abdallah Abbderemane of the Comoros archipelago is assassinated during an attempted coup. The coup was quelled by loyalist troops and power was temporarily assumed by Said Mohammed Djohar, head of the Supreme Court.

● Opposition presidential candidate Rafael Leonardo Callejas wins elections in Honduras.

● Swiss voters vote two to one in favour of retaining their national army. But the surprisingly high 'no vote' of 35.6% was expected to lead to defence changes.

27 NOVEMBER

● Deutsche Bank AG, the largest West German commercial bank, announces that it will purchase the London merchant bank Morgan Grenfell for £950 million.

● A national two-hour general strike takes place in Czechoslovakia as part of demands for democratic reform.

● Chancellor John Major says he is prepared to raise interest rates further if the pound continues to come under pressure from foreign exchanges and in order to fight inflation.

● The Lome IV Convention between the EC and the African–Caribbean–Pacific (ACP) countries agrees a $12,100 million EC trade and aid package to 66 of the world's poorest countries.

● All 107 passengers on board an Avianca Airlines Boeing 727 die when the jet exploded in mid air a few minutes after takeoff from Bogota, Colombia. Drug traffickers claimed responsibility for the bomb explosion.

● El Salvador's rebel Farabundo Marti National Liberation Front launches a fresh offensive in the capital San Salvador which leads to their temporarily occupying the homes of conservative politicians and American diplomats.

● Israeli Premier Itzhak Shamir says he is prepared 'to speak with Satan for the sake of peace' but he is not ready to talk to the PLO 'because talks with the PLO mean the establishment of a Palestinian state, and that jeopardizes the survival of Israel'.

28 NOVEMBER

● The National Audit Office issues a report claiming that the government-set sale price of British car manufacturer the Rover Group 'fell significantly short of the real value' of the company which was sold to British Aerospace in 1988 for £150 million. The National Audit Office said the real value was estimated to be at least £206.5 million.

● Czechoslovak Premier Ladislav Adamec opens formal power-sharing negotiations with the opposition group Civic Forum.

● West German Chancellor Helmut Kohl outlines plans for a confederation of East and West Germany. He stressed that the development of intra-German relations would take place within a framework of 'pan-European development'.

● The Organization of Petroleum Exporting Countries (OPEC) reaches an agreement on new oil-production quotas. The agreement increased the cartel's total production ceiling to 22 million barrels a day from 20.5 million barrels.

● EC environment ministers agree to establish a European Environmental Agency to provide environmental information to the European Commission.

● South African President F.W. de Klerk announces that he is scrapping the controversial security organization, the National Security Management System.

29 NOVEMBER

● Indian Premier Rajiv Gandhi's Congress (I) Party loses a general election. He is replaced by Vishwanath Pratap Singh, leader of the opposition coalition.

● The Czechoslovak parliament approves a constitutional amendment removing the Communist Party's 'leading role' in society.

● Soviet Foreign Minister Eduard Shevardnadze says he is concerned about West German 'revanchism' and expresses opposition towards German reunification.

● The US government threatens to cut off all funds to the United Nations if it introduces a resolution to upgrade the PLO's diplomatic status at the UN from observer level to that of a non-member state.

● A group of 29 right-wing French parliamentarians flies to Lebanon to meet Christian militia leader Gen. Michel Aoun as an expression of their support for his cause.

30 NOVEMBER

● Ferranti International Signal plc charges the company's former deputy chairman, James Guerin, and three other former executives with siphoning off £126.4 million from the company.

● The *Guardian* reports leaked documents showing that the government gave British Aerospace secret concessions worth £38,000 million to encourage it to buy the Rover Group. Labour leader Neil Kinnock accused the government of seeking 'to deceive Parliament', 'selling short' taxpayers and perpetrating a 'rip-off'.

● A High Court jury awards libel damages of £1.5 million to Lord Aldington who claimed he had been libelled by Count Nikolai Tolstoy who accused him of being a war criminal who ordered the forced repatriation of 70,000 Cossacks to the Soviet Union in 1945.

● Soviet leader Mikhail Gorbachev, during a visit to Italy, proposes a Europe of 'sovereign democratic states with a high level of equitable interdependence and easily accessible borders, open to the exchange of products, technologies and ideas and wide-ranging contacts among people'.

● The French government orders a naval vessel and hospital ship to sail to Lebanon in case French citizens need to be evacuated. The move is also interpreted as a measure of military support for the Christian militia led by Gen. Michel Aoun.

● A terrorist bomb kills Alfred Herrhausen, the head of Deutsche Bank AG, West Germany's largest bank. Responsibility was claimed by the Red Army Fraction.

● Arab League foreign ministers call on US President George Bush and Soviet leader Mikhail Gorbachev to focus their attentions on the Middle East and support a direct PLO role in the peace process.

1 DECEMBER

● Soviet leader Mikhail Gorbachev visits Pope John Paul II at the Vatican. It was the first ever meeting between a Pope and the leader of the Soviet Union.

● US President George Bush arrives in Malta for talks with Soviet leader Mikhail Gorbachev.

● A military coup attempt starts in the Philippines with a series of air attacks, including one on the presidential palace. President Corazon Aquino was forced to call on the US for American planes to protect her and her government.

● The East German parliament revokes a constitutional clause guaranteeing the Socialist Unity Party (Communist) its 'leading role' in society.

● New Indian Premier Vishwanath Pratap Singh promises a thorough investigation of the Gandhi government's role in the Bofors arms scandal. He also promised to devote more government funds to rural areas.

2 DECEMBER

● Soviet leader Mikahil Gorbachev arrives in Malta for talks with US President George Bush. The talks were originally scheduled to be held on a US ship offshore, but stormy weather forced the discussions onto the Soviet cruise ship *Maxim Gorky* in Valetta Harbour.

● On the second day of a military coup attempt in the Philippines, the rebel forces seize the financial district. An estimated 2000 foreigners were reported to be trapped.

● Polish Solidarity leader Lech Walesa meets Mrs Thatcher at Downing Street. Walesa was invited by the Trades Union Congress and during his visit he also met Labour leader Neil Kinnock and Foreign Secretary Douglas Hurd who told him that Britain was increasing its emergency aid to Poland to £50 million.

● A general election in Taiwan results in the opposition Democratic Progressive Party securing more than 30% of the popular vote. They also secured enough seats to enable the party to introduce legislation in parliament.

● Audrey Mclauglin is elected leader of Canada's New Democratic Party, becoming the first woman to head a major Canadian political party.

● The Azerbaijan Popular Front, the republic's nationalist movement, imposes a renewed rail blockade on landlocked Armenia.

3 DECEMBER

● US President George Bush and Soviet leader Mikhail Gorbachev end two days of talks in Malta. At a joint press conference, Bush said that the world was on the 'threshold of a brand new era of US–Soviet relations'. Gorbachev said that he and Bush agreed that 'the characteristics of the Cold War should be abandoned'.

● The entire leadership of East Germany's Socialist Unity Party (Communist) resign from their Party posts. This included General Secretary Egon Krenz, Premier Hans Modrow, the entire Politburo and all 163 members of the Central Committee. Before stepping down, the Central Committee expelled former leader Erich Honecker from the party.

● Shadow Environment Secretary Bryan Gould says the privatization of the British water industry will cost the taxpayers £3300 million. The figure included a government debt write-off, the cost of incentives to buy shares and promotion costs.

● Three leading British doctors are accused of being involved in the kidneys-for-sale affair in which Turks were paid to donate their kidneys for transplant operations. Dr Raymond Crockett, Michael Bewick and Michael Joyce were charged with serious professional misconduct.

● Filipino Vice-President Salvador H. Laurel expresses support for the continuing coup attempt and calls on President Corazon Aquino to resign.

● The Czechoslovak opposition group Civic Forum rejects the government's proposals for a coalition government. They said the proposals left the Communists in complete control.

● The Greek government introduces an austerity budget which involved price increases on public utilities, petrol, taxes, public transport, cigarettes and alcohol.

4 DECEMBER

● A Warsaw Pact heads of government meeting in Moscow condemns the 1968 invasion of Czechoslovakia.

● US President George Bush meets other NATO heads of government to brief them on his Malta talks.

● East German Premier Hans Modrow promises to form a special commission, including opposition figures, to conduct a full-scale investigation of Party and government corruption.

● The US Navy successfully test launches the Trident II missile from an underwater-based submarine. Three previous tests had failed. The environmentalist ship *Greenpeace* tried to disrupt the test and was rammed by a US Navy ship.

● Labour peer and former Lord Chancellor Lord Elwyn-Jones dies of cancer at his Brighton home at the age of 80.

5 DECEMBER

● Mrs Thatcher easily wins the first contested election for the leadership of the Conservative Party since she secured the post in 1975. Her challenger was moderate Conservative MP Sir Anthony Meyer who hoped to win enough votes to force a change of policy.

● EC Commissioner for Competition, Sir Leon Brittan, announces that he will investigate the details of the sale of the Rover Group to British Aerospace.

● Seven regional commanders of the East German security police are dismissed after allegations of corruption.

● Leading Soviet dissident Andrei Sakharov calls for a two-hour general strike as part of a campaign to withdraw the constitutional clause guaranteeing the Communist Party's monopoly of power.

● Thousands of East German demonstrators storm and ransack the offices of the security police in Dresden.

● EC transport ministers reach agreements that allow air carriers more freedom to set air fares and open new routes from the start of 1993.

6 DECEMBER

● Gunman Marc Lepine goes on a shooting spree at the Ecole Polytechnique in Montreal, killing 14 young women before turning his gun on himself. A suicide note indicated a deep hatred for women.

● Bob Reid, Chairman of Shell UK, is appointed Chairman of British Rail in succession to Sir Robert Reid. He will receive a salary of £200,000 a year.

● French President François Mitterrand and Soviet leader Mikhail Gorbachev meet in Kiev to discuss German reunification. Mitterrand said he was 'not afraid of reunification' but added: 'We must avoid at all costs anything that could poison what is already a very complex situation.'

● The EC announces a $1100 million loan to Hungary over five years to help Hungary's balance of payments' problems.

● The Lithuanian and Estonian parliaments repeal the constitutional clause guaranteeing the Communist Party its monopoly of political power.

● 52 people are killed and 600 injured when a truck bomb explodes outside the offices of Colombia's security and intelligence agency in Bogota. The authorities blamed drug traffickers.

● The French government announces plans to tighten immigration. The move followed a landslide by-election victory by the right-wing National Front.

7 DECEMBER

● The government's Broadcast Bill is published. It calls
for ITV licences to go to the highest bidders, a new Channel 5 to be auctioned off, Channel 4 to become a separate non-profit corporation and a new Independent Television Commission to replace the Independent Broadcasting Authority.

● 21 people are injured when an IRA car bomb explodes in Belfast's shopping district. On the same day two British soldiers are killed and one wounded in an IRA attack on a border security post.

● Czechoslovak Premier Ladislav Adamec resigns over his continuing failure to reach an agreement with the opposition Civic Forum on a coalition government. Dissident playwright Vaclav Havel, on the same day, announces that he is a candidate for the Czechoslovak presidency.

● The military coup attempt in the Philippines effectively ends as rebel troops either surrender to loyalist forces or return to their barracks.

● The East German government and opposition groups agree to free elections on 6 May 1990 and to the establishment of 'confederative structures' with West Germany and the disbandment of party-controlled paramilitary groups. The election date was later moved forward to 25 March 1990.

● Nine independent Bulgarian political groups form an opposition coalition known as the Union of Democratic Forces.

● US Secretary of State James Baker and Soviet Foreign Minister Eduard Shevardnadze hold an hour-long telephone conversation on the issue of the shipment of Soviet arms to Central America.

8 DECEMBER

● EC heads of government meeting in Strasbourg agree to a December 1990 intergovernmental conference aimed at establishing European Monetary Union.

● Former East German leader Erich Honecker, and five other former high-ranking officials, are charged with corruption and abuse of power.

● Four supporters of former Bulgarian leader Todor Zhivkov are forced out of the Politburo of the Bulgarian Communist Party.

● Iraq announces that it has launched a rocket capable of putting a satellite in space, making it the first Arab nation with such a capacity.

● Benin President Mathieu Kerekou announces that his government is abandoning Marxism in favour of political reform and private enterprise.

● Indian housemaid Laxmi Swami wins £300,000 in damages for being kept prisoner and horsewhipped by two Arab princesses in their London home.

9 DECEMBER

● EC heads of government end a two-day summit in Strasbourg with support for German 'unity through free elections'. But they also added that unification should be in the context of 'relevant agreements and treaties...and East–West cooperation'. Mrs Thatcher dissented from an EC heads of government agreement in support of a European Social Charter backing basic rights for workers.

● Soviet leader Mikhail Gorbachev threatens to resign the leadership of the Communist Party in the face of conservative opposition to his reform programme.

● Hundreds of exotic birds are found dead on arrival at Heathrow Airport. The birds were part of a cargo of 15,000 birds en route from Dar es Salaam, Tanzania to Miami.

● East Germany's Socialist Unity Party (Communist) votes to restructure the party and support free elections and elects liberal lawyer Gregor Gysi as its chairman in succession to Egon Krenz.

● Seven Chinese students stage an anti-government protest outside the Ministry of Radio and Television. It was the first protest since the suppression of the student demonstrations in June.

● 4500 delegates from anti-apartheid organizations across South Africa meet in Johannesburg for the Conference for a Democratic Future. It was the largest gathering of its kind since 1955. ANC official Walter Sisulu told the conference that the ANC was ready for negotiations with the government.

10 DECEMBER

● A non-Communist coalition government comes to power in Czechoslovakia. Communist hard-line President Gustav Husak immediately resigns. A crowd of about 200,000 celebrated the event in Prague's Wenceslas Square.

● 50,000 Bulgarians stage a pro-democracy march in the capital Sofia. It was believed to be the largest unsanctioned demonstration in Bulgaria in 43 years.

● Two top American officials, National Security Adviser Brent Scowcroft and Deputy Secretary of State Lawrence Eagleburger, visit Beijing to brief Chinese leaders on the US–Soviet Malta talks. The visit was criticized by those who opposed contacts with China after the Tiananmen Square massacre.

● United Nations observers arrive in Central America in an attempt to prevent countries in the region from being used as bases for guerrilla attack against neighbours.

● The total number of East Germans fleeing to West Germany reaches 650,000. West German Social Democrat Oskar Lafontaine proposed that no more East Germans be allowed in without first having a job and place to live.

● Nationalists in Estonia and Latvia win up to 70% of the vote in local elections.

11 DECEMBER

● The government increases pensions for pre-1973 war widows by £40 a week.

● A new government Employment Bill proposes to make closed shops illegal and allow employers to dismiss workers taking unofficial industrial action.

● Most of London's major hospitals close their doors to non-emergency cases as a flu epidemic provokes a red alert in 32 health districts.

● An estimated 200,000 East Germans march through Leipzig demanding the reunification of the two German states. A similar rally was held in Karl Marx Stadt involving 40,000 demonstrators.

● West German Chancellor Helmut Kohl denies that it is his intention to create an 'all-powerful Germany in the middle of Europe'.

● Bulgarian leader Petur Mladenov supports free elections and an end to the Communist Party's constitutional monopoly of power.

12 DECEMBER

● The British water industry is floated on the London Stock Exchange as 10 separate companies. The flotation netted the government £5240 million as the issue was over-subscribed by nearly 600%.

● Britain starts the forcible repatriation of Vietnamese boat people from Hong Kong. The first contingent of 51 boat people was flown back on a chartered Cathay Pacific passenger plane. The US administration declared that 'involuntary repatriation is unacceptable until conditions improve in Vietnam'.

● US Secretary of State James Baker becomes the first high-ranking American official to visit East Germany. In a speech in West Berlin, he proposed that NATO's emphasis shift from a military to a political role.

● Five Central American presidents end two days of talks in San José, Costa Rica. The presidents reached a new peace accord which supported the government of El Salvador President Alfredo Cristiani and called for an increaserd UN role in Nicaragua.

● Soviet leader Mikhail Gorbachev blocks an attempt by dissident Andrei Sakharov to stage a parliamentary debate on the Communist Party's constitutional position as holding the leading role in Soviet society.

● Bulgarian leader Petur Mladenov reveals that Bulgaria's foreign debt stands at $10,000 million and annual interest payments alone were $4500 million.

13 DECEMBER

● South African President F. W. de Klerk and ANC leader Nelson Mandela meet in de Klerk's Cape Town office to discuss the political future of South Africa.

● Thousands of Vietnamese boat people stage demonstrations in their Hong Kong detention centres against the British government's policy of forcible repatriation. The repatriation scheme is temporarily suspended in the face of international condemnation.

● Health Secretary Kenneth Clarke rules out any further concessions to ambulance workers involved in the 13-week-old dispute.

● The Bulgarian Communist Party votes to renounce its constitutionally guaranteed monopoly of political power and expels former leader Todor Zhivkov from the Party.

● US President George Bush authorizes $240 million in aid to fight cocaine production in Colombia and Peru.

● Financial representatives from the world's wealthiest 24 countries meet in Brussels to agree a $1000 million emergency-aid package for Poland and plans to help the other economies of Eastern Europe.

14 DECEMBER

● London ambulance crews refuse to take calls from controllers at the London Ambulance Service Headquarters. All 999 calls were passed to army, police and volunteers. Army ambulances were called on to provide emergency cover in Birmingham and North Bedfordshire.

● Soviet dissident scientist and human-rights campaigner Andrei Sakharov dies in Moscow of a heart attack at the age of 68. His funeral was attended by 80,000 mourners. Soviet leader Mikhail Gorbachev and several other members of the Politburo paid their respects.

● The European Parliament passes a resolution saying it is 'appalled' at Britain's decision forcibly to repatriate Vietnamese boat people from Hong Kong.

● Christian Democratic opposition leader Patricio Aylwin wins a landslide victory in Chile's presidential elections.

● 20,000 Bulgarian students demonstrate in the capital Sofia for an immediate end to Communist Party rule.

● The West German government postpones signing an agreement on ending border checks with France, the Netherlands, Luxembourg and Belgium because of complications arising from the flood of refugees from East Germany.

15 DECEMBER

● Panamanian 'strong man' Gen. Manuel Noriega is

named head of government and 'maximum leader of the struggle for national liberation' by Panama's parliament. The parliament also declared the country to be in a state of war with the United States.

● Romanian secret police attempt to arrest dissident Romanian pastor Laszlo Tokes in the Transylvanian town of Timisoara but are prevented from doing so by a large crowd of his supporters.

● Gales hit Britain. Six fishermen died after their boat sank in the Firth of Clyde, Channel ferry services were disrupted, two youths were swept out to sea at Folkestone and the Isle of Man, and the captain of an Irish vessel is swept overboard in the Bay of Biscay.

● Chief Constable George Esson, one of those leading the investigation into the Lockerbie air disaster, says that the investigators have achieved 'remarkable progress' and obtained 'hard evidence' implicating several individuals in the bombing. But he said that the evidence was insufficient to seek arrrests or extraditions.

● South Africa's Supreme Court reverses the controversial 1988 convictions of 11 Black activists on charges of treason and terrorism.

● Gonzalo Rodriguez Gacha, the number two man in Colombia's Medellin drug cartel, is killed in a gun battle with Colombian commandos. Killed with him was his 17-year-old son Alfredo.

● The leaning Tower of Pisa is closed for repairs after experts warn that the landmark is in danger of falling over.

16 DECEMBER

● US Marine Lt Robert Paz is killed by Panamanian soldiers after his car is stopped at a roadblock. US President George Bush described the incident as an 'enormous outrage'.

● Anti-government demonstrations break out in the Romanian city of Timisoara following the government's attempt to arrest dissident pastor Laszlo Tokes. The Internal Security and army send in troops and thousands are killed when they open fire.

● Soviet leader Mikhail Gorbachev expresses his support for political changes in East Germany.

● US President George Bush and French President François Mitterrand meet on the Dutch–French Caribbean island of St Martin. The meeting was seen as part of Bush's attempts to improve relations with France and West Germany.

● Egypt's hard-line Interior Minister General Zaki Badr survives an assassination attempt when a car bomb explodes near his Cairo motorcade.

● A French water-supply company, Lyonnaise des Eaux, acquires a 10% stake in the newly privatized Anglian Water.

17 DECEMBER

● Labour Employment spokesman Tony Blair announces that the Party is abandoning its support for the pre-entry closed shop.

● In Brazil, Conservative presidential candidate Francisco Collor de Mello narrowly defeats left-winger Luis Inacio da Silva (Lulu) to win the presidential election.

● The Confederation of British Industry reports a recovery in export demand for British manufactured products from a drop earlier in the year.

● Transport Secretary Cecil Parkinson says airport security does not need further tightening in spite of an American warning of a possible terrorist attack.

● The Sudanese military government of Gen. Omar Hassan starts a crackdown on civilian dissidents which involves executions for offences ranging from the illegal possession of foreign currency to fomenting a strike.

● Chinese President Yang Shangkun leaves Beijing for a tour of the Middle East which takes him to Egypt, the United Arab Emirates, Kuwait and Oman. China is eager to increase economic links with the region.

18 DECEMBER

● The EC rejects Turkey's application to join the European Community.

● Romania closes its borders with Hungary as violence continues to mount in the city of Timisoara and other towns and cities.

● Polish inflation hits 557%.

● Five people are killed at Biggin Hill Aerodrome when a helicopter crashes in bad weather.

● Yugoslavia adopts an austerity economic plan which includes a six-month wage freeze and a devaluation of the dinar. The plan is opposed by Serbia, the largest of the Yugoslav republics.

● A survey of Hong Kong's civil service and professional staff reveals that fewer than a third of these key personnel intend to stay in Hong Kong after it reverts to Chinese rule in 1997.

● El Salvador's rebel Farabundo Marti National Liberation Front admits that more than 400 of its guerrillas died during the FMLN's offensive against the capital San Salvador.

19 DECEMBER

● West German Chancellor Helmut Kohl visits Dresden for talks with East German Premier Hans Modrow. The two men agreed to an opening in the Berlin Wall at the historic Brandenburg Gate, immediate West German economic aid of $2000 million, collaboration on transport, environmental, cultural and social issues and greater economic cooperation.

● The government provides £150 million compensation to investors in the crashed Barlow Clowes investment group.

● Soviet Foreign Minister Eduard Shevardnadze visits NATO headquarters in Brussels. He was the first Warsaw Pact envoy to make such a visit. Shevardnadze said: 'The Warsaw Pact and NATO at this critical stage in European development are able to play a very important stabilizing role in Europe.'

● Anti-government protests in Romania spread from Timisoara to other towns and cities.

● The EC and European Free Trade Association agree to start talks on the free flow of goods, services, capital and labour between the EC countries and the seven EFTA countries.

20 DECEMBER

● US troops invade Panama in the largest US military operation since the Vietnam War. President Bush said the invasion was launched to safeguard American lives, defend Panamanian democracy and bring Panamanian 'strong man' Gen. Manuel Noriega back to America to stand trial on drugs charges. Noriega, however, initially escaped the American invaders. The invasion was welcomed in America and by Mrs Thatcher but universally condemned elsewhere.

● Foreign Secretary Douglas Hurd announces that Britain will grant full citizenship to up to 225,000 Hong Kong residents before the colony reverts to Chinese rule in 1997. The Labour Party called the plan elitist and discriminatory. Right-wing Conservatives opposed the potential massive influx of immigrants.

● The government publishes its Environment Protection Bill which appears substantially to tighten environmental regulations on emissions, hazardous wastes and the storing of radioactive materials.

● The Lithuanian Communist Party declares itself independent of the Communist Party of the Soviet Union. The Party then declared that it wanted an 'independent democratic Lithuanian state'.

● A demonstration by 50,000 anti-government protestors is staged in the Romanian city of Timisoara where thousands have already been killed by security police.

● Czechoslovak Premier Marian Calfa meets Soviet leader Mikhail Gorbachev in Moscow where the two men agree to discuss the withdrawal of Soviet troops from Czechoslovakia.

21 DECEMBER

● Anti-government riots break out in the Romanian capital of Bucharest while President Nicolae Ceaucescu is giving a speech from the balcony of the presidential palace.

● Education Secretary John McGregor says the government will start its student loan scheme in September 1990 despite the refusal of the major banks to participate in the plan.

● Trade and Industry Secretary Nicholas Ridley backs a proposal for shopowners to give discounts for cash payments over credit-card purchases.

● US-backed Guillermo Endara is sworn in as President of Panama.

● Former US President Ronald Reagan is ordered to submit his diaries for scrutiny in case they are relevant to the defence of former National Security Adviser Admiral John Poindexter on charges related to the Iran–Contra scandal.

● A Congress of the Czechoslovak Communist Party suspends former leader Gustav Husak from membership of the Party.

22 DECEMBER

● Romanian Communist leader Nicolae Ceaucescu is overthrown in a popular uprising. His demise was welcomed by both the United States and Soviet Union.

● US President George Bush sends an additional 2500 troops to Panama to join the 22,500 already in the country. US commanders are forced to admit that they have encountered stronger opposition than anticipated.

● Berlin's famous Brandenburg Gate is reopened in a ceremony attended by West German Chancellor Helmut Kohl and East German Premier Hans Modrow.

● 40 people die when two buses collide in the town of Frederickton, New South Wales, Australia.

● The Khmer Rouge claim to have captured the important Cambodian town of Anlong Ven.

● Irish-born playwright Samuel Beckett dies in Paris at the age of 83.

23 DECEMBER

● Czechoslovakia opens its border with West Germany in a ceremony attended by West German Foreign Minister Hans-Dietrich Genscher.

● Poland signs a letter of intent with the International Monetary Fund. The move committed the government to inflation cuts and spending cuts. In return, the IMF provided $725 million in standby credits and agreed to act as a conduit for more aid from western banks and governments.

● M-19 guerrillas in Colombia suspend a peace agreement with the government because of Congress's failure to implement key points in the agreement. The same day, 10 government soldiers died in an ambush.

● An Iranian student, Mehrdad Kokabi, is charged with involvement in an arson attack on Dillons bookshop. He was questioned, along with three other Iranian students, about a planned attempt on the life of British author Salman Rushdie.

● Essex police launch a murder hunt after the bodies of a man and a woman are found shot dead in a car parked in a secluded lane in Epping Forest.

24 DECEMBER

● Panamanian 'strong man' Gen. Manuel Noriega seeks sanctuary in the Vatican's diplomatic mission in Panama City.

● South African President F.W. de Klerk appeals to South African churches to join and help facilitate 'broad-based and in-depth talks' on South Africa's political future.

● The Israeli Supreme Court orders the army to court-martial Col. Yehuda Meir for ordering his men to break the limbs of Palestinian prisoners.

● Two British climbers die in an avalanche in the French Alps.

● Three sisters die in a fire in southeast London. A fourth sister survived the flames.

● Tory MP Patrick Cormack launches a campaign to win state aid to preserve the nation's cathedrals.

25 DECEMBER

● Romanian Communist leader Nicolae Ceaucescu and his wife Elena are executed by firing squad after a two-hour trial by an 'extraordinary military tribunal'.

● The Queen's annual Christmas Day broadcast deals with the problem of protecting the environment.

● Iran releases 50 Iraqi prisoners of war as a 'gesture of goodwill'.

● The number of drink–driving cases drops dramatically compared with the 1988 Christmas period. Avon and Somerset Police reported that out of 1200 drivers breathalysed only 97 failed the test and Wiltshire Police reported a 36% drop in positive tests.

● The number of homeless people rises dramatically. One temporary shelter in southeast London served 1200 Christmas dinners.

26 DECEMBER

● Ion Iliescu is named interim President of Romania. The new government quickly announced limits on the amount of food Romanians could buy, the legalization of birth control and abortion and freedom to travel abroad.

● Soviet leader Mikhail Gorbachev attacks the decision of the Lithuanian Communist Party to break with the national party. Gorbachev said the move was 'illegitimate'.

● A woman dies and four people are injured when a car collides with a taxi during a high-speed police car chase through Walsall, West Midlands. Police launched an official inquiry.

● The Central Committee of the Yugoslav Communist Party proposes that the Party consider relinquishing its constitutionally protected monopoly of power.

● South African Anglican Archbishop Desmond Tutu visits the occupied West Bank of Israel and compares the plight of the Palestinians to that of the Blacks in South Africa.

● Israeli forces mount air and ground attacks against bases of the Lebanese Communist Party in the area north of Sidon.

27 DECEMBER

● The death toll in the US invasion of Panama reaches 23 Americans and 700 Panamanians. An estimated 2000 Panamanians were reported injured and 5000 were homeless.

● The United Nations Food and Agriculture Organization reports that Ethiopia needs more than 1 million tons of food aid in order to avoid a repetition of the 1984–5 famine disaster.

● Egypt and Syria restore full diplomatic relations – the first time since the 1979 Camp David Agreement.

● The Bulgarian Communist Party agrees to start talks on sharing political power with opposition groups led by the Union of Democratic Forces.

● Afghan rebels fire 55 rockets at the centre of the capital, Kabul.

● Sir Walter Bromley-Davenport, Conservative MP for Knutsford for 25 years, dies at the age of 86.

28 DECEMBER

● The pound falls to a record low against the West German Deutschmark as it hits 2.7204 DM to the pound.

● The government estimates that up to 1000 people will die in the severe influenza epidemic.

● The Lithuanian government formally registers the 2000-member Party of Democrats. This was the first non-communist party to be legally sanctioned anywhere in the Soviet Union.

● The Latvian parliament abolishes the Communist Party's constitutional monopoly of political power.

● Northwest Airlines warns passengers that it has received a bomb threat to its 30 Dec. Paris to Detroit flight. The flight went ahead without incident with only 17 passengers on board.

● The Japanese Department of Trade and Industry unveils a series of proposals designed to increase imports over the next 10 years.

29 DECEMBER

● US troops in Panama raid the residence of the Nicaraguan Ambassador where they find a weapons cache which includes grenade launchers, AK-47 assault rifles and an anti-tank weapon. The Nicaraguan government retaliated by ordering 20 US diplomats to leave the country.

● A United Nations General Assembly resolution is passed deploring America's 'flagrant violation of international law' in its invasion of Panama.

● Dissident playwright Vaclav Havel is elected President of Czechoslovakia and former Czech leader Alexander Dubcek is elected Speaker of Parliament.

● 11 people are killed and 120 injured in an earthquake in Newcastle, New South Wales, Australia.

● One person dies and 40 are injured as fighting breaks out between police and the Vietnamese boat people held in Hong Kong detention centres. Aid workers warn of the danger of more violence and suicides because of the government's policy of forcible repatriation.

● The Victoria Supreme Court in Australia forces the brewing assets of Bond Corporation Holdings Ltd into receivership.

30 DECEMBER

● The Polish parliament approves an economic reform programme which will transform Poland into the most market-oriented economy in Eastern Europe.

● Angolan President Eduardo dos Santos offers new peace proposals in an effort to end the civil war between the ruling MPLA and the UNITA forces led by Dr Jonas Savimbi. The proposals allowed UNITA to participate in national elections, but ruled out a multi-party system.

● A crowd of 30,000 Jews, Palestinians and Europeans form a human chain around the walls of Jerusalem's old city in protest against the Israeli government's refusal to hold negotiations with the PLO.

● The Soviet newspaper *Pravda* publishes its first ever criticism of Lenin, written by dissident writer Alexander Solzenitsyn.

● Soviet leader Mikhail Gorbachev is voted 'Man of the Year' by the listeners to Radio Four's 'Today' programme. *Time Magazine* named him 'Man of the Decade'.

● Five people are arrested after four police officers are injured when they are attacked by a mob of 200 youths outside a nightclub in Bletchley.

31 DECEMBER

● Israeli Prime Minister Itzhak Shamir dismisses leading cabinet dove and Science Minister Ezer Weizman for allegedly meeting PLO officials.

● A MORI opinion poll shows the Labour Party leading the Conservatives by 46% to 39% of the vote.

● The Meteorological Office reports that 1989 was the hottest year on record in Britain.

● Former South Korean President Chun Doo Hwan testifies before the National Assembly about alleged corruption and abuses of power during his eight-year government. Chun denied any personal wrongdoing but accepted 'moral responsibility' for abuses that occurred during his government.

● Philippines President Corazon Aquino announces a cabinet shakeup in the wake of the attempted military coup earlier in the month.

1 JANUARY 1990

● A Panamanian, Fernando Manfredo, takes over as administrator of the Panama Canal.

● A New Year's message from US President George Bush is broadcast on Soviet television and a message from Soviet leader Mikhail Gorbachev is broadcast on American television.

● The provisional Romanian government of the National Salvation Front announces the disbandment of the feared secret police, the Securitate. The government is headed by President Ion Iliescu.

● The conservative National Peasants Party is revived in Romania. The party had been banned by the Communists.

● An attempted coup in Liberia fails to overthrow President Samuel Doe.

● Argentina's armed forces warn that the nation is descending into a state of political and economic chaos and call on the citizens to rally round the democratically elected leaders.

2 JANUARY

● 30 members of the Romanian Communist Party's Politburo are placed under arrest by the provisional government.

● London-based Amnesty International accuses Israel of encouraging its defence forces to kill Palestinian civilians to help quell the Intifada on the West Bank and Gaza Strip. The Israeli Ministry of Foreign Affairs said the Amnesty Report was 'total nonsense and absolutely baseless'.

● Czechoslovak President Vaclav Havel visits both East and West Germany.

● Israeli Science Minister Ezer Weizmann is brought back into the cabinet, but with a reduced role.

● Portugese Prime Minister Anibal Cavaco Silva reshuffles his cabinet. Among those ousted were Finance Minister Miguel Cadilhe and Deputy Premier Enrico de Melo.

● Andrew Knight is appointed chief executive of Rupert Murdoch's News International.

3 JANUARY

● Panamanian 'strongman' General Manuel Antonio Noriega surrenders to US troops and is immediately flown to Miami to stand trial for drug trafficking.

● Employment Secretary Norman Fowler resigns from the cabinet and is honoured with a knighthood. Michael Howard is named as his successor.

● South African Foreign Minister Pik Botha visits Hungary and the two countries agree to establish diplomatic relations.

● Thousands of Azerbaijanis demonstrate for an open border with Iran and increased contacts with Azerbaijanis living in Iran.

● A group of Afghanistan generals are arrested and charged with plotting to overthrow President Najibullah.

● The Secretary General of the Vietnamese Communist Party, 74-year-old Nguyen Van Linh, announces his intention to resign.

4 JANUARY

● A baby boy who had an historic heart operation while still in the womb is born at Guy's Hospital in London.

● Human Rights Watch attacks the Bush administration for 'widespread disregard for human rights'. The organization was especially critical of President Bush's policy towards China in the aftermath of the Tiananmen Square massacre.

● The Soviet authorities ban foreign journalists from Azerbaijan. Government spokesman Gennadi Gerasimov said their presence would 'fuel conflict'.

● Six East German opposition groups form a united front called the Electoral Alliance to contest the March elections.

● The rebel Sudan People's Liberation Army reports that a pro-government Arab militia massacred 2000 Black residents of the town of el-Jebelein in the White Nile region.

● Brush fires destroy 125,000 acres of farmland in New South Wales. Tens of thousands of ship and cattle were killed and dozens of homes were destroyed.

5 JANUARY

● Health Secretary Kenneth Clarke says he is willing to release more money to ambulance workers if they drop their demand for a long-term link to other public-sector workers.

● Hundreds of thousands of Bulgarians strike and march in protest against the government's proposals to allow Turkish Muslims religious freedom.

● The Swiss government agrees to hand over to the Filipino government £160 million held in bank accounts in the name of former Filipino President Ferdinand Marcos.

● Geidar Isayev, the local Communist Party leader in the riot-torn Azeri town of Nakhichevan, resigns after protesters demanded the opening of the Iranian–Azeri border and attacked border control posts.

● Colombia's Medellin drug cartel kidnaps 20 people as part of its battle against the government's anti-drug campaign.

● Maj.-Gen. Sitiveni Rabuka, who led two military coups in Fiji in 1987, quits his post of Home Affairs Minister and withdraws from the interim government to return to his post as Commander of the Army.

6 JANUARY

● Soviet Foreign Minister Eduard Shevardnadze visits Romania and promises Soviet support for any future government. 'What political parties will lead Romania is the business of Romanians themselves,' he said.

● Angry Muslim mobs in Azerbaijan attack and destroy Soviet border stations between Iran and Azerbaijan.

● The Sri Lankan and Indian governments reach agreement on the withdrawal of 25,000 Indian peacekeeping troops in Sri Lanka.

● Polish Communist Party leaders approve plans to dissolve the party and replace it with a social democratic alternative.

● EC President Jacques Delors says a democratic East Germany would be entitled to membership of the European Community.

● East German Communist Party leader Gregor Gysir calls on East and West Germany to halve their armed forces by 1991 and force the removal of all foreign troops by 1999.

7 JANUARY

● Thousands of Romanians demonstrate against the presence of former high-ranking Communist Party members in the new National Salvation Front government.

● Soviet troops are sent to Georgia to quell riots between rival ethnic groups and to prevent nationalist demonstrations.

● Japanese Prime Minister Toshiki Kaifu starts a European tour aimed at reassuring western Europeans about trade and offering East Europeans Japanese aid.

● Roman Catholic taxi driver Martin Byerne, aged 28, is murdered in Co. Armagh.

● Khmer Rouge guerrillas launch a major offensive against Battambang, Cambodia's second largest city.

● Actor Ian Charleson, who played the Scottish missionary Eric Liddell in the film *Chariots of Fire*, dies of AIDS at the age of 40.

8 JANUARY

● US President George Bush abandons a plan for US naval ships to to monitor airborne drug traffic off the coast of Colombia.

● The East German opposition parties threaten to quit round-table talks with the government and call a general strike unless the government gives a full account of Stasi (secret police) personnel and disarms all agents with weapons.

● The Home Office orders the sudden end of a pilot scheme in Nottingham of electronic tagging of bailed defendants.

● National Westminster Bank reports that Britain's North Sea oil production fell by 25.7% in 1989.

● Five children drown when a fishing boat capsizes and sinks in Nelson Bay, New South Wales. 43 other people aboard the boat were rescued by marine police. Overcrowding was blamed for the disaster.

● Actor Terry-Thomas dies at the age of 78 of Parkinson's Disease.

9 JANUARY

● An international bank syndicate providing finance for the Channel Tunnel agrees to release new funds after the contractors agreed to bear 30% of the cost of overruns.

● Labour MP Ron Brown is found guilty of causing damage to his ex-mistress's flat, but is acquitted of stealing from Nonna Longden. Brown was fined £1000 and ordered to pay costs and compensation.

● Northern Ireland Secretary Peter Brooke tells a meeting of businessmen that there is now a 'common ground' for the start of negotiations aimed at ending Westminster rule in Northern Ireland.

● The Armenian parliament passes a bill incorporating the disputed region of Nagorno-Karabakh into an overall 1990 socio-economic plan for Armenia. The legislation is immediately denounced by the Kremlin and the Azerbaijan government.

● Japanese Premier Toshiki Kaifu offers a total of $1000 million in aid to Poland and Hungary while on a tour of Germany and Eastern Europe.

● The provisional Romanian government lifts restrictions on Romanians travelling abroad.

10 JANUARY

● Martial law is lifted in Beijing. Premier Li Peng warned, however, that 'hostile forces' within China and abroad still threatened 'to subvert the social system' of the country.

● Danny Morrison, a senior official in Sinn Fein, is charged with conspiracy to commit murder and two other terrorist offences. The charges stemmed from the alleged abduction of Alexander Joseph Lynch.

● Former East German leader Erich Honecker undergoes surgery to remove a cancerous tumour from his kidney.

● The Governor of Hong Kong, Sir David Wilson, visits Beijing for the first talks with Chinese officials since the Tiananmen Square massacre.

● British Customs and Excise report that they seized £259 million worth of drugs in 1989.

● Iraq and Iran both accept Soviet mediation in an effort to settle the unresolved Gulf War.

● A meeting of Comecon finance ministers and prime ministers agrees to the gradual adoption of free market principles in their trading policies.

11 JANUARY

- Soviet leader Mikhail Gorbachev starts a three-day trip to Lithuania in an attempt to dissuade the local Communist Party from splitting with Moscow.
- Three-day-old baby girl Alexandra Griffiths is kidnapped from St Thomas's Hospital in London by a bogus health worker.
- China's Tiananmen Square is reopened to the public for the first time since the massacres in June.
- Tommy Lyttle, the West Belfast leader of the Protestant paramilitary Ulster Defence Association, is arrested by officials investigating links between Protestant paramilitary organizations and British security forces.
- The Armenian parliament adopts a resolution asserting Armenia's right to override Soviet laws that affect the Republic of Armenia.
- Hard-line Deputy Foreign Minister Zhou Nan is named as head of the New China News Agency in Hong Kong, and therefore the de facto Chinese Ambassador to the colony.
- The Spanish government launches a campaign to encourage men to do more domestic chores. The television advertisement featured Prime Minister Felipe Gonzalez.

12 JANUARY

- The ruling National Salvation Front in Romania outlaws the Communist Party.
- The Royal Ulster Constabulary foils an attempt to murder Ken Maginnis, Ulster Unionist MP for Fermanagh and Tyrone.
- A left-wing El Salvadoran politician, Hector Oqueli Colindres, and a Guatemalan human rights lawyer, Gilda Flores, are murdered in Guatemala City.
- The Albanian authorities declare a state of emergency in an attempt to head off anti-Communist demonstrations.
- The British Communist daily newspaper the *Morning Star* announces plans to cut staff following the Soviet government's decision to halve its subsidizing subscription order for the paper.
- The Meteorological Office reports that the 1980s were the warmest decade since records began.

13 JANUARY

- British undercover security forces in Ulster shoot and kill three men robbing a betting shop in West Belfast. The men carried replica weapons and had no links with the IRA.
- Soviet leader Mikhail Gorbachev ends a three-day visit to Lithuania after failing to stop the Lithuanian Communist Party from breaking away from the Moscow-based national party.
- Azeris riot against Armenians in Baku, forcing thousands of Armenians to flee Azerbaijan.
- Turkish President Turgut Ozal opens the Ataturk Dam on the Euphrates River. The dam brought protests from the Iraqi and Syrian governments which claimed that the dam increased the threat of drought to their countries.

14 JANUARY

- Israeli Prime Minister Itzhak Shamir says Israel needs more settlements on the West Bank to accommodate the 1000-a-day Soviet Jewish immigrants. 'Big immigration requires Israel to be big as well. We need the space to house the people,' he told a meeting of the Likud Party.
- Former Conservative Party chairman Norman Tebbit says he will 'fight his corner' against plans to give 225,000 Hong Kong Chinese the right to settle in Britain.
- Four men appear in a Florida court accused of trying to buy US-made ground-to-air Stinger missiles for the IRA. The men were Joseph McColgan, Kevin McKinley, Seamus Maley and Sean McCann.
- Corsican separatists blow up about 60 cabins and summer houses belonging to tourists. Residents in the area were detained by about 60 armed men from the Corsican National Liberation Front while the buildings were destroyed.
- A total of 43 people die in a discotheque fire in Zaragosa, Spain. The fire was caused by an electrical fault.
- Scottish actor Gordon Jackson of 'Upstairs Downstairs' fame dies in a London hospital.

15 JANUARY

- 24,000 Soviet troops are sent to Azerbaijan to quell the ethnic civil war in the southern republic.
- Thousands of East German protesters break into the East Berlin headquarters of the secret police and destroy files, wreck furniture and steal documents.
- Amnesty International claims that thousands of Vietnamese boat people face persecution back in Vietnam because of 'critical shortcomings' in the Hong Kong authorities' screening process.
- The Bulgarian parliament votes to end the Communist Party's constitutionally protected monopoly of power.
- The Soviet Union and Czechoslovakia start negotiations on the withdrawal of Soviet troops from Czechoslovakia.
- Heavy air pollution in Ankara forces the closure of a number of schools and some factories.

16 JANUARY

- The five permanent members of the United Nations Security Council call for a greater UN role in resolving the Cambodian civil war. The statement came at the end of a two-day meeting in Paris.
- US Senate minority leader Robert Dole proposes that the US reduce aid to Israel and Pakistan in order to free funds for Eastern Europe, Panama and the anti-drug campaign in South America.
- Top military officials from East and West attend an unprecedented seminar on East–West military doctrine in Vienna. The participants included the US Chairman

of the Joint Chiefs of Staff, the Chief of the Soviet General Staff and the Vice-Chief of the British Defence Staff.

● The Bulgarian government starts round-table talks with opposition groups aimed at establishing a coalition government.

● Foreign Secretary Douglas Hurd asserts at the end of a trip to Hong Kong that, if Britain and China fail to reach an agreement on the governmental structure of Hong Kong, then Britain will have to make its 'own decisions' about the implementation of democratic reforms before 1997.

● More than 6000 Polish coalminers go on strike for higher wages following a series of steep price increases as a result of the Polish government's abandonment of subsidies.

17 JANUARY

● The Soviet government orders the troops in Azerbaijan to shoot radicals in order to protect civilians and in self-defence.

● It is revealed that senior Scottish judges have been questioned by the legal authorities over allegations of homosexual behaviour. One of the judges, Lord Dervaird, resigned.

● Former world light welterweight boxing champion Terry Marsh is arrested in connection with the shooting of his ex-manager Frank Warren.

● The French government reports that the annual inflation rate for 1989 was 3.6% and that the target figure for 1990 is 2.5%.

● The British budget surplus for the first quarter of the fiscal year 1989–90 is reported at £3700 million, down £8700 million on the corresponding period in the previous year.

● Colombia's Medellin drug cartel offers to halt its bombing and assassination campaign and all other illegal activities in exchange for an amnesty and government pledges to stop extraditions to the US. The proposal was rejected by President Virgilio Barco.

● Hong Kong and China say they will not comply with a global ban on the trading of ivory.

18 JANUARY

● 31 Tory rebel MPs vote against the poll tax in the House of Commons when it comes up for its final reading.

● Fraud charges against Manchester property developer Kevin Taylor are dismissed after the prosecution admits that the police lied to obtain bank records. Taylor claimed that the case was part of an attempt to discredit the work of his friend John Stalker.

● Mayor Marion Barry, the Mayor of Washington DC, is arrested on drugs charges after he was allegedly filmed purchasing and smoking cocaine.

● Former Bulgarian leader Todor Zhivkov is placed under house arrest on charges of inciting ethnic hostility, misusing government property and money and malfeasance in office.

● The Mayor of Nagasaki, Hitoshi Motoshima, is shot and wounded by a right-wing nationalist after criticizing the late Emperor Hirohito for his role in World War II.

● Britain's unemployment rate falls to its lowest in nine years with 1.6 million claiming unemployment benefits.

● Ecuador's Supreme Court orders the arrest of former President Leon Febres Cordero on embezzlement charges.

19 JANUARY

● Israeli police arrest Faisal al Husseini, one of the most prominent Palestinian nationalists in the Israeli-occupied West Bank.

● South African police use batons and tear gas to break up a demonstration against the tour of 16 English professional cricketers. The demonstration was timed to coincide with the cricketers' arrival at Johannesburg airport.

● The annual inflation rate for 1989 was revealed to be 7.7%, the highest since 1982. The Treasury said inflation was expected to remain above 7% throughout 1990.

● Sir Anthony Meyer, the MP who stood against Mrs Thatcher for the Conservative Party leadership, is dropped as parliamentary candidate by his Welsh constituency Conservative Association.

● Liverpool police break a child sex racket. The children turned to prostitution to finance their addiction to video games.

● Reformist Soviet politician Boris Yeltsin says Mikhail Gorbachev's economic reforms have failed and that he faces revolution unless he quickly introduces even more radical measures.

20 JANUARY

● According to Soviet figures 143 people die when Soviet troops enter the Azerbaijani capital of Baku to stop a week of anti-Armenian massacres and riots.

● The Haitian government of General Prosper Avril orders a state of siege and arrests opposition politicians following the murder of an Army colonel.

● Mrs Thatcher and French President François Mitterrand meet in Paris to discuss German reunification and changes in Eastern Europe.

● Portuguese air traffic controllers strike for higher pay and disrupt air services across southern Europe.

● East Germany reveals that half of the country's trees are severely damaged by industrial emissions and that Leipzig is exposed to 13 times more air pollution than the national average.

● American film actress Barbara Stanwyck dies in California at the age of 82.

21 JANUARY

● The African National Congress reaffirms its readiness to start constitutional negotiations with the South African government.

● Commercial air services between Argentina and Britain are restored for the first time since the Falklands War.

● Irish Prime Minister Charles Haughey indicates that he is ready to review the Anglo-Irish Agreement and possibly negotiate a new agreement in its place.

● More than 2500 pro-democracy protesters defy a government ban to stage a peaceful demonstration in the centre of Ulan Bator, the capital of Mongolia.

● Indian and Pakistan foreign ministers meet in New Delhi to discuss the crisis in Kashmir.

● Three men are charged with drugs smuggling offences after £3 million worth of cannabis is seized in East London. The men were Stephen Howe, Alastair Williams and Ioannis Karakantas.

22 JANUARY

● The Azerbaijani Supreme Soviet (parliament) condemns as 'unconstitutional' the Soviet military occupation of Baku and threatens secession from the Soviet Union unless the troops are withdrawn.

● South Korean President Roh Tae Woo announces that his Democratic Justice Party is merging with the Reunification Democratic Party and the New Democratic Republican Party to form a new majority coalition in the South Korean parliament.

● The Indian government files preliminary criminal charges against 14 people suspected of complicity in the Bofors arms scandal.

● The Kuwaiti authorities crush a peaceful pro-democracy rally with tear gas, water cannons and stun grenades. The march was one of several demanding the reinstatement of the Kuwaiti parliament and an end to press censorship.

● The Yugoslav Communist Party votes to abolish the party's monopoly of power.

● British defence contractor Ferranti wins a £1600 million contract to supply the radar system for the new European fighter aircraft.

23 JANUARY

● Ford workers vote to accept a two-year contract and avoid an indefinite strike. The pay pact offered a 10.2% pay rise the first year and an additional increase of 8% or, alternatively, 2.5% above the rate of inflation, in the second year.

● Chancellor of the Exchequer John Major says 'interest rates will stay high for some time to come'.

● Immediately after winning a major defence contract, the troubled electronics company Ferranti International agrees to sell its radar division to GEC for £310 million. The sale was necessary for Ferranti to recover financially from an alleged £215 million fraud involving the American-based Ferranti subsidiary International Signal Corp.

● Turkish Foreign Minister Mesut Milmaz accuses the Soviet Union of 'massive violation of human rights' in Azerbaijan.

● An extraordinary congress of Yugoslavia's League of Communists breaks down after only one day when the Slovene delegation walks out after the Serbian delegation voted down political and economic reforms proposed by the Slovenians.

● Former Canadian cabinet minister Jean Chretien announces that he is a candidate for the leadership of Canada's Liberal Party.

24 JANUARY

● Japan launches a satellite toward the moon, making Japan the third nation after the US and Soviet Union to send a satellite into lunar orbit.

● Retired US Air Force General Richard Secord is sentenced to two years' probation for making a false statement to congressional investigators probing the Iran–Contra arms scandal. After his sentencing, Secord attacked former President Reagan for failing to 'take the heat' for the arms scandal.

● Soviet naval ships in the Caspian Sea fire on ships blockading the Azeri port of Baku. At the same time, Soviet officials called for more negotiations with Azeri and Armenian nationalist organizations.

● A police traffic helicopter crashes into a block of old people's flats in Glasgow, killing one policeman and injuring three others on board. The flats were only slightly damaged.

● 20-year-old Carol Evans is jailed for 14 days after she refused to give evidence against her boyfriend, Richard Edie, who was charged with having kidnapped, imprisoned and beaten her.

● Journalist Richard Holmes wins the £22,000 Whitbread Book of the Year Prize for his biography of the poet Coleridge.

25 JANUARY

● 46 people die as hurricane-force winds sweep across the UK. The victims included two young schoolchildren killed when a school roof was blown off in Swindon. Many of the victims died when trees crashed onto their cars.

● Edinburgh Leith constituency Labour Party passes a vote of no confidence in MP Ron Brown and asks him to resign immediately.

● Soviet statistics reveal that 13 million people out of a workforce of 164 million are unemployed.

● Belgian Defence Minister Guy Coeme says Belgium is likely to withdraw its 25,000 troops in West Germany. The statement draws an immediate protest from NATO Secretary-General Manfred Woerner who says national troop withdrawals should be made after multilateral negotiations.

● Czechoslovak President Vaclav Havel visits Warsaw and tells the Polish parliament that the emerging democracies of Eastern Europe must launch a new era of cooperation and friendship.

● Ethnic Azeris in Turkey demonstrate against the actions of the Soviet army in Azerbaijan and against the Armenians.

● Indian troops are sent into Kashmir after a radical Muslim gunman kills four airforce men and wounds 10 others. The shootings resulted in riots in which 70 more died.

● American actress Ava Gardner dies in London.

26 JANUARY

● Britain's trade deficit narrows to £1120 million. The figure is better than the one expected by financial markets and the pound rises. The total figure for 1989, however, showed a record £20,300 million trade deficit.

● Strike action by dancers at the Royal Ballet is averted when the dancers accept a last-minute pay offer of 15%.

● The Vice-President of Romania, Dumitru Vazilu, resigns in protest against the ruling National Salvation Front's decision to contest elections in May.

● South Africa's bloodiest strike since 1922 comes to an end. At least 35 people died during the strike for higher wages and recognition for South Africa's Railways and Harbour Workers Union.

● France suspends aid to Haiti in protest against human rights violations by the regime of General Prosper Avril.

● The African National Congress's ruling executive backs Nelson Mandela's policy of talks with the South African government.

27 JANUARY

● Kidnapped baby Alexandra Griffiths is discovered in the Cotswold town of Burford and returned to her parents in London. A former nurse is taken into custody.

● Mieczyslaw Rakowski, First Secretary of the Polish Communist Party, refuses to start a new left-wing party. Rakowski said: 'It is time for a new generation.'

● A Harris poll in the *Observer* puts the Labour Party 13 points ahead of the Conservatives. A MORI opinion poll in the *Sunday Times* says Labour is 12 points ahead.

● Mexican President Carlos Salinas de Gortari visits Mrs Thatcher in London to argue that economic aid should not be extended to Eastern Europe at the expense of Latin America.

● Rafael Leonardo Callejas is inaugurated as President of Honduras.

28 JANUARY

● A crowd of 40,000 demonstrators attempt to storm the government building in Bucharest as protests mount against Romania's ruling National Salvation Front.

● A 17-year-old boy is killed when an IRA bomb explodes during a Republican parade in Londonderry to mark the anniversary of 'Bloody Sunday'. Four policemen and one soldier were also injured in the explosion.

● Foreign Secretary Douglas Hurd says there is no question of Britain 'rushing into' defence cuts while Eastern Europe is going through a period of instability.

● The East German government and opposition leaders agree to move the date of the election forward from 6 May to 18 March.

● South African police use tear gas and rubber bullets to disperse crowds demonstrating against the tour by the rebel England cricket team.

● A crowd of 20,000 demonstrators gather outside a Soviet army base in Czechoslovakia to demand the immediate withdrawal of Soviet troops from their country.

● The *Independent on Sunday* is published.

29 JANUARY

● Recommendations in Lord Justice Taylor's report on the Hillsborough disaster include: all-seater stadiums by 1999, electronic tagging for football hooligans, the shelving of the government's ID card scheme and the annual review of ground safety certificates. The government accepted the recommendations. The football clubs estimated that it would cost £130 million to implement the report.

● The United States announces that it will close 12 overseas bases. Among those scheduled for closure are Greenham Common in Berkshire and Fairford in Gloucestershire. The closures mean a withdrawal of 2750 US servicemen from Britain.

● Thousands of pro-government demonstrators besiege the headquarters of Romania's opposition parties. One party leader was forced to jump out of a window to escape the angry mob. Another escaped in an armoured car.

● East German Premier Hans Modrow says early elections and a 'grand coalition' with the opposition parties is the only way to halt the slide into political and economic chaos.

● The Polish Communist Party changes its name to the Social Democracy Party of the Republic of Poland and elects Alexander Kwasniewski as its leader.

● Yugoslav police kill two more Albanians on the sixth consecutive day of rioting in the province of Kosovo.

30 JANUARY

● Tens of thousands of people join across-the-nation rallies in support of the ambulance drivers' pay claim. Rallies in Liverpool and Glasgow attracted 20,000 each and in Birmingham the city's symphony orchestra played for demonstrators.

● Soviet leader Mikhail Gorbachev acknowledges the inevitability of German unification. He said: 'Basically no one can cast any doubt on the idea of a single German state.'

● Andrew Neil, editor of the *Sunday Times*, is awarded £1000 in libel damages against the *Sunday Telegraph* and its former editor Peregrine Worsthorne. Neil claimed that the *Sunday Telegraph* implied that an affair he had with Pamella Bordes made him unfit to edit a quality newspaper.

● The Ministry of Defence announces that Britain's nuclear submarine fleet is to be thoroughly checked after faults are discovered on HMS *Warspite* during a refit.

● 19 crew members aboard the Greek-registered freighter *Flag Theofano* are drowned when their ship sinks in gale-force winds in the English Channel.

● The US Senate votes 98–0 in favour of trade sanctions against China, but leaves the final say to President Bush.

31 JANUARY

● US President George Bush proposes that the US and Soviet Union reduce their conventional forces in

Central Europe to 195,000 on each side. Bush made the proposal in his first State of the Union message in which he talked of a 'new era' in world affairs.

● Mrs Thatcher admits that she was misled about a British security forces' disinformation campaign to discredit the IRA.

● Opposition groups in Bulgaria turn down 'for the time being' an offer to form a coalition with the ruling Communist Party.

● Six people die and 130 are injured when a car bomb explodes in the centre of Kabul, the capital of Afghanistan.

● The French secret service, the DGSE, advertises for 500 additional agents for its overseas operations.

● New Zealand Labour Prime Minister Geoffrey Palmer reshuffles his cabinet, moving it to the right in preparation for elections later in the year.

1 FEBRUARY

● Defence Secretary Tom King says that new information has come to light about the disinformation campaign against the IRA and says there will be an internal investigation into whether or not a senior civil servant (Colin Wallace) linked to the case had been unfairly dismissed.

● Mrs Thatcher imposes an 8% pay norm on National Health Service workers, teachers, members of the armed forces, senior civil servants and judges.

● Home Secretary David Waddington orders the deportation of nine Iranians accused of having associations with 'pro-Iranian regime organizations and individuals'. The deportees included the head of the London bureau of Iranian state television.

● East German Premier Hans Modrow proposes a reunified but neutral Germany. West German Chancellor Helmut Kohl refused to accept Modrow's condition of neutrality.

● Hungary and the Soviet Union start negotiations on the withdrawal of 65,000 Soviet troops in Hungary.

● Additional Yugoslav troops are sent to the troubled province of Kosovo after a renewed outbreak of ethnic violence. Serbian President Solobodan Milosevic threatened to arm Serbian civilians and send them to Kosovo to protect the Serbian minority.

2 FEBRUARY

● South African President F. W. de Klerk legalizes the ANC and announces that Nelson Mandela will soon be freed. He also announces the lifting of restrictions on 33 other opposition groups, the release of non-violent political prisoners, an end to most news censorship and a suspension of executions.

● The Department of Health revises downwards the estimated number of AIDS cases in Britain. The Department estimated that there were between 12,000 and 26,000 infected people in England and Wales. The previous estimate was 20,000–50,000 people.

● The Bulgarian Communist Party elects Alexander Lilov as its new leader. Former leader Petur Mladenov remained as head of state.

● Soviet Foreign Minister Eduard Shevardnadze suggests that the issue of German reunification be discussed as part of an international realignment. The proposal was quickly rejected by West German Chancellor Helmut Kohl.

● Four top aides of former Romanian dictator Nicolae Ceaucescu are found guilty of complicity to commit genocide and sentenced to life imprisonment. The aides were Emil Bobu, the number three man in the hierarchy; former Vice-President Manea Manescu; former Deputy Premier Ion Dinca; and former Interior Minister Tudor Postelnicu.

3 FEBRUARY

● Peace talks between Armenian and Azerbaijani negotiators are held in the Latvian capital of Riga.

● Heavy rains and winds sweep the UK and northern France. At least eight people died in British car accidents related to the weather conditions. Another 18 died in France.

● British Rail's intercity fares go up 15% and fares on the suburban services rise 9%.

● A 16-year-old girl is fitted with an artificial lung. The operation, performed in Salt Lake City, was the first of its kind in the world.

● Liberal Politburo member Andrei Lukanov is named Bulgaria's Prime Minister. Lukanov promised to form a government with the 'participation of all political forces in the country'.

4 FEBRUARY

● Tens of thousands of Muscovites take part in a pro-democracy rally in the centre of Moscow. The rally was reportedly the biggest demonstration since the Bolshevik Revolution.

● A Labour Party survey reveals that an estimated 400,000 mortgage payers are two or more months in arrears.

● 15 people die and eight are injured when terrorists open fire on an Egyptian bus carrying Israeli tourists.

● Suspected right-wing extremists fire on the British embassy in Pretoria, smashing embassy windows. The right-wingers are suspected because of the objections they raised to British pressure for the release of ANC Deputy President Nelson Mandela.

● The Slovene branch of the Yugoslav Communist Party votes to break away from the federal branch of the Party.

● Rafael Angel Calderon Fournier is elected President of Costa Rica.

5 FEBRUARY

● A US Federal Court judge in Washington DC orders former President Reagan to give videotaped testimony for use in the Iran–Contra arms scandal trial of former National Security adviser John Poindexter.

● Britain's Inspector of Schools says that 30% of the work in state schools is poor or very poor because of inadequate teaching and poor facilities. The report said: 'A large number of pupils and students are getting a raw deal.'

● The East German Communist Party loses its majority

in the cabinet when eight opposition figures are added to the government. Prime Minister Hans Modrow said that a 'coalition of national responsibility' was needed to prevent anarchy.

● Rolls-Royce workers receive a 10.3% pay rise and a 2-hour reduction in their working week.

● An American F-111 bomber crashes into the North Sea after an explosion on board the aircraft. The plane came from the US Air Force base at Upper Heyford in Oxfordshire.

● American political leader the Rev. Jesse Jackson meets Mrs Thatcher at Downing Street and unsuccessfully tries to persuade her to reverse her policy on sanctions towards South Africa.

6 FEBRUARY

● The West German government outlines its plan for monetary union between the two Germanies.

● Home Secretary David Waddington unveils a package of criminal justice reforms, which includes a sharper distinction between violent and non-violent crimes; a greater role for the probation service; a reduction of maximum sentences for theft; a stipulation that time served in prison should be closer to the court's sentence; and that parents should be held more responsible for crimes committed by their children.

● The government announces plans to divert National Health Service spending away from building new hospitals to refurbishing Victorian buildings. Roger Freeman, Parliamentary Under-Secretary of State for Health, said: 'Our Victorian forefathers were excellent builders. They built hospitals to last....'

● Foreign Secretary Douglas Hurd visits Germany and warns 'it would not be in the interests of the German people to achieve unification in a way which arouses anxieties throughout Europe'.

● US Secretary of State James Baker visits Czechoslovakia and outlines a four-point programme of US support for Eastern Europe. The programme included: help for free elections; economic aid; political and economic cooperation; and a redefinition of defence policies.

● A poll of British teachers reveals that one-third want to leave their jobs and nearly two-thirds are dissatisfied with their jobs.

7 FEBRUARY

● The Chinese Communist Party explicitly rejects the Soviet and East European example of abandoning the Communist Party's monopoly of political power.

● A petition signed by 1600 British scientists overseas urges Mrs Thatcher to halt the 'brain drain' by providing more government money for British science.

● Strathclyde Regional Council reveals that one-third of the adult population has fallen behind in its poll tax payments.

● The US Congress approves $10 million in aid to 'support the democratic transition in Eastern Europe'. It was promised that more money would come later.

● Sudanese military ruler Omar Hassan el Bashir says he plans to introduce one-party rule.

8 FEBRUARY

● The Vietnamese government suspends its participation in the British programme of forcible repatriation of boat people from Hong Kong.

● The 80-year-old Earl of Roden is tied up and left overnight when four masked men stole £1 million worth of silverware and furniture from his stately home in Co. Down.

● Soviet negotiators make a major concession in arms negotiations when they drop their previous link between a future START (Strategic Arms Reduction Talks) Treaty and the 1972 ABM (anti-ballistic missile) Treaty.

● East Germany for the first time accepts responsibility for the mass slaughter of Jews during World War II. Prime Minister Hans Modrow added that the East German government 'recognizes its humanitarian duties towards the survivors of the Jewish people who suffered from Nazi oppression'.

● Relatives of 58 trapped Turkish coalminers are told that there is no hope of their survival. The men were trapped 1000 feet underground after a methane gas explosion in their mine in Turkey's Amasaya province.

● The Boy Scouts announce that they will admit girls to their ranks.

9 FEBRUARY

● The US and Soviet Union agree to destroy a 'significant' portion of their chemical weapons' stock.

● The Sandinista government in Nicaragua releases all remaining political prisoners as a gesture of goodwill before the general election on 25 February.

● The Supreme Leader of Iran, Ayatollah Ali Khomeini, reaffirms the death sentence on *Satanic Verses* author Salman Rushdie.

● The Soviet Union says it will withdraw its forces from the strategic Cam Ranh Bay air and naval base in Vietnam. The base was built by the Americans during the Vietnam War.

● Labour says it would replace the poll tax with a property tax based on ability to pay. But Environment spokesman Bryan Gould admitted that the details still had to be worked out.

● Fiat announces that it is launching an electric version of its Panda car. The £12,000 car has a top speed of 50 mph and can travel 60 miles without recharging.

10 FEBRUARY

● South African President F. W. de Klerk announces that Black nationalist leader Nelson Mandela will be freed from Pollsmoor Prison the following day.

● West German Chancellor Helmut Kohl and Soviet President Mikhail Gorbachev meet in Moscow. Afterwards, Kohl said that Gorbachev agreed on 'the right of the German people alone to decide whether to live together in one state'.

● US Secretary of State James Baker completes three days of talks in Moscow with his Soviet counterpart Eduard Shevardnadze and Soviet leader Mikhail

Gorbachev. The two sides discussed Afghanistan, nuclear weapons' reductions, German reunification and the size of conventional forces in Europe.

● Michele Vermilio, the first baby to undergo heart surgery in his mother's womb, dies in his parents' arms at the age of five weeks.

● 500 people are evacuated from their Liverpool homes after an unexploded 2200 lb German wartime bomb is uncovered. The bomb was defused by bomb specialists.

● Guerrillas belonging to the rebel Eritrean People's Liberation Front capture the strategic Red Sea port of Massawa.

11 FEBRUARY

● South African Black nationalist leader Nelson Mandela is freed after more than 27 years in prison.

● The 'Open Skies' Conference begins in Ottawa. It involves the first-ever meeting of foreign ministers from the 16 NATO countries and the seven Warsaw Pact countries.

● Three British soldiers are injured when their Gazelle helicopter is shot down in Co. Tyrone by IRA machine-gun fire.

● Former French Premier Jacques Chirac narrowly wins a vote of confidence in his leadership at a convention of his party, the Rally for the Republic (RPR).

● At least 50,000 Moldavians hold a rally to demand greater autonomy from Moscow. The rally in Kishinev's Victory Square was addressed by Communist and opposition speakers.

● American billionaire Donald Trump and his wife Ivana announce that they are divorcing.

● Heavyweight boxing champion Mike Tyson is knocked out by James 'Buster' Douglas in the 10th round.

12 FEBRUARY

● South African Black nationalist leader Nelson Mandela gives his first news conference since his release and says that the ANC wants a solution to South Africa's problems that 'will suit both the Blacks and Whites of this country'.

● The Guinness share fraud trial starts at Southwark Crown Court in London. The four defendants – Ernest Saunders, Roger Seelig, Lord Patrick Spens and David Mayhew – faced 24 charges including conspiracy, false accounting, theft and destruction of documents.

● A state of emergency is declared in the Soviet Central Asian republic of Tadzhikistan after ethnic rioting broke out in the capital Dushanbe.

● Israeli Trade and Industry Minister Ariel Sharon announces his resignation from the cabinet, undermining the Israeli coalition government.

● A Metropolitan Police survey shows that 84% of Londoners are either 'fairly satisfied' or 'very satisfied' with the London police service.

● Carmen Lawrence becomes the first woman Premier of Western Australia. She was unanimously elected by the Labour Party MPs of the Western Australian parliament.

13 FEBRUARY

● The 'Open Skies' Conference in Ottawa reaches agreement on a format for high-level talks on German reunification. The format agreed is for representatives from the four Allied powers – the UK, France, the United States and the Soviet Union – to meet representatives from East and West Germany. The format is dubbed the 'four plus two' talks.

● The Soviet Union and US agree to limit their conventional forces in Central Europe to 195,000 each. The Us would be allowed to have a further 30,000 troops based in Europe outside the central zone.

● Nelson Mandela returns to his home town of Soweto and a tumulutous welcome by a crowd of more than 100,000.

● The Soviet Communist Party publishes its radical policy platform in the party newspaper *Pravda*. The proposals outlined the Party's plan to surrender its monopoly of power; allow republics to secede; reform of the economy; and transfer power from the Communist Party to the presidency and parliament.

● French President François Mitterrand calls on the EC to speed up monetary union in the light of moves towards German monetary union.

● Soviet-born cellist Mstislav Rostropovich, who defected to the US in 1974, plays his first concert in the Soviet Union in 16 years.

14 FEBRUARY

● The Abbey National Building Society raises its mortgage interest rate to 15.4%.

● East German Premier Hans Modrow says the currency talks with West German Chancellor Helmut Kohl resulted in the 'bitterest defeat' for socialism.

● Bottles of Perrier mineral water are recalled from supermarket shelves around the world after it is discovered that the water is contaminated with traces of the cancer-causing chemical benzene.

● Adrian Noble, artistic director of the Royal Shakespeare Company, says that the RSC is considering leaving its London base at the Barbican unless conditions are improved.

● Three Rottweiler dogs savage four children in a North London school playground. The children were treated in hospital and released.

● 95 people are killed when an Indian Airlines Airbus 320 crashed while preparing to land in the southern Indian city of Bangalore. It was the first crash of an Airbus in regular service.

15 FEBRUARY

● The UK and Argentina agree to restore diplomatic relations after two days of talks in Madrid. Relations were severed at the time of the Falklands War.

● US President George Bush and the leaders of Colombia, Peru and Bolivia sign an agreement to cooperate in the fight against drug smuggling.

● US Defense Secretary Dick Cheney visits South Korea and says that the US will withdraw 5000 of its 43,000 troops based in South Korea.

● Communist Party and Soviet government officials resign in the Central Asian republic of Tadzhikistan after ethnic violence claims the lives of at least 37 people.

● The Lord Chancellor, Lord Mackay, announces proposals aimed at reducing excessive jury-awarded libel damages.

● Norman Parkinson, photographer of the Royal family, dies from a brain haemorrhage while in Singapore at the age of 76.

16 FEBRUARY

● A study published by the *British Medical Journal* shows an increased risk of leukaemia in children whose fathers worked at the Sellafield nuclear power plant in Cumbria.

● Former President Reagan says he did not order any illegal acts in the Iran–Contra affair. The statement came during eight hours of videotaped testimony recorded for the trial of his former National Security adviser John Poindexter.

● Education Secretary John MacGregor calls on schools to encourage 'active citizenship' by providing more classes on the value of democracy, respect for the law and tolerance towards minority groups.

● British Satellite Broadcasting announces its launch date as 29 April.

● The burnt body of Kenyan Foreign Minister Robert Ouko is found three days after he was reported missing. Police said he was shot in the head by his own revolver.

● Australian Prime Minister Bob Hawke calls a general election for 24 March.

17 FEBRUARY

● A temporary cease-fire is announced in Beirut, ending 18 days of fierce fighting during which more than 600 people were killed and 2000 injured.

● A report on the international telephone industry reveals that British Telecom's charges are the highest in the West.

● Lecturers at polytechnics end their five-month exam boycott and accept a 7.5% pay rise.

● Czechoslovakia's Communist Party expels former leader Gustav Husak and 20 other hard-line members.

● Cuban leader Fidel Castro says he will reform the Communist Party but rules out a multi-party system. He said: 'What we are talking about is the perfecting of a single Leninist party.'

18 FEBRUARY

● Japan's ruling Liberal Democratic Party bounces back from financial and sex scandals to win the general election to the lower house of the Diet (parliament). The LDP won 275 of the 512 seats.

● Prime Minister Margaret Thatcher urges caution on the issue of German reunification. She said that NATO troops should remain in West Germany after reunification and that 'it would be quite reasonable for some Soviet troops' to remain in East German territory 'at least for a transitional period'.

● Irish Foreign Minister Gerry Collins accuses the UK of breaking its word over assurances about the conduct of the Ulster Defence Regiment and adds that this constitutes a breach of faith in an important part of the Anglo-Irish Agreement.

● A crowd of 1000 anti-Communist Romanian demonstrators storm the ruling National Salvation Front's main offices, vandalize the building and take Interim Deputy Premier Gelu Voican-Voiculescu hostage before being persuaded to leave the building.

● Foreign Office Minister Francis Maude says Britain would supply aid to Vietnam if the Hanoi government agreed to the resumption of the forcible repatriation of refugees from Hong Kong.

● The Association of Metropolitan Authorities warns that any government attempt to 'cap' local government expenditure would lead to 'poll tax chaos'.

19 FEBRUARY

● Interim Romanian President Ion Iliescu accuses 'irresponsible elements' of attempting to 'undermine stability, create havoc and make Romania ungovernable'.

● The House of Commons Select Committee rules that Conservative MP John Browne breached Commons rules when he failed to declare Arab business dealings.

● British Rail warns that it faces a loss due to a drop in passengers and pay increases. The warning was a major blow to the government's plans to privatize BR.

● ITN newsreader Sir Alastair Burnet resigns from the ITN board of directors in a dispute over the ownership of the company after the Broadcasting Bill becomes law. Sir Alastair supported the government proposal to reduce by half the shareholding of ITV companies in ITN.

● American coalminers from three states end a 10-month strike.

● Five people are killed in Katmandu when police fire on stone-throwing demonstrators calling for a multi-party democracy.

20 FEBRUARY

● The UK announces that it is unilaterally lifting its ban on new investments in South Africa. The move provoked protests from EC partners and the Commonwealth.

● Health Secretary Kenneth Clarke and Ambulance Union official Roger Poole announce that they have achieved a breakthrough in talks aimed at ending the six-month-old ambulance drivers' dispute.

● Czechoslovak President Vaclav Havel meets US President George Bush and tells him that both NATO and the Warsaw Pact are obsolete and should be abolished.

● The IRA blows up a military van in Leicester and two soldiers are injured. Damage was less than it could have been because the bomb dropped from the undercarriage of the van just before it exploded.

● US Secretary of State, Jim Baker, calls on the United Nations General Assembly to adopt a global anti-drugs campaign. Third World countries at the assembly called on the developed world to curb the demand for drugs in their countries.

● The House of Commons votes in favour of the ordination of divorced men.

21 FEBRUARY

● Hungarian Foreign Minister Gyula Horn says Hungary may become a member of NATO. 'We must strengthen our links with NATO,' he said, and added: 'I do not think it is inconceivable that Hungary might become a member of its political organizations.'

● Naval training officer Lt. Gordon Smith is found guilty on two charges of ill-treatment of a subordinate at a court martial at HMS *Nelson* in Portsmouth. The cadet he ill-treated, Lt. Simon Rowland, suffered brain damage after being in a coma for 15 days.

● Lloyds Bank raises its mortgage interest rate to 15.7%.

● A curfew is imposed in the troubled Yugoslav province of Kosovo after a fresh outbreak of violence between anti-government ethnic Albanians and the local Serbian minority.

● A report by the US State Department's Human Rights Bureau strongly criticizes the human rights record of the Israeli government. The report claimed that Israeli forces beat 10 Palestinians so badly that they later died; they were also open to criticism for illegal searches, the deportation of Arab residents and the demolition of Arab homes.

● Police arrest 20 people after a South London raid in which a large quantity of the drug 'crack' was found.

● Former Prime Minister Edward Heath celebrates 40 years in the House of Commons.

22 FEBRUARY

● The Iranian newspaper *Tehran Times* calls for the release of Western hostages in Lebanon. The paper is known to be close to President Hashemi Rafsanjani.

● The Polish Ministry of Health says that by the year 2000 a quarter of the Polish population will be suffering from cancer as a result of pollution and lack of public-health facilities.

● Police close 10 miles of beaches in the Brighton area while they search for containers of potassium cyanide believed to have been washed off the deck of a passing ship during recent gales.

● Home Secretary David Waddington announces a charter of rights for crime victims and provides an additional £17 million to the Criminal Injuries Compensation Board.

● The Malaysian government protests about an allegation by Prince Charles that 'collective genocide' is being waged against a tribe on the island of Borneo.

23 FEBRUARY

● Ambulance workers and the government reach an agreement to end the ambulance pay dispute. Pay rises (with allowances) varied between 17.6% and 23.4% over two years. But many ambulancemen remained unhappy because the deal did not include a long-term pay mechanism.

● Hassan Khan is freed after serving 14 months of a 15-year sentence for armed robbery. The Court of Appeal said that his conviction was 'unsafe and unsatisfactory' because detectives from the West Midlands Serious Crime Squad beat him and then fabricated his confession.

● High Court judge Mr Justice Hutchinson blocks plans for a Bath comprehensive school to opt out of the state system and become private. The ruling was seen as a major blow to government policy.

● Sheikh Mohammed Hussein Fadlallah, a religious leader of the Lebanese-based Hezbollah, calls on the organization to release its western hostages and 'proceed with new methods and a new mentality'.

● The Polish parliament approves an austerity budget which cuts by half the state spending of £12,100 million in 1989.

● An Ariane rocket carrying two Japanese telecommunications satellites explodes shortly after leaving its launch pad in French Guiana.

24 FEBRUARY

● The Lithuanian nationalist party, Sajudis, wins an overwhelming majority in the Soviet Baltic state's general election. Sajudis campaigned on a pledge to seek complete independence from Moscow.

● West German Chancellor Helmut Kohl and US President George Bush meet at Camp David, Maryland to discuss the issue of German reunification. Both men agreed that a united Germany should be a full member of NATO.

● One person is killed and 18 injured when a Syrian gunboat fires on a Beirut-bound Cypriot passenger ferry. RAF helicopters from Cyprus flew the injured from the ferry to hospital in Cyprus.

● A Soviet opinion poll reveals that the late Soviet dissident Andrei Sakharov is more revered than the founder of the USSR, Vladimir Lenin.

● 6 Vietnamese boat people in Hong Kong are granted permission to challenge in the colony's High Court the screening process which determines whether a person is a political or an economic refugee.

● The US, the Soviet Union and China announce that they are sending a 30-man team to sweep Mount Everest clean of the rubbish left by nearly four decades of climbers.

25 FEBRUARY

● The Nicaraguan Sandinista regime is defeated in free elections by the National Opposition Union led by Violeta Barrios de Chamorro.

● An estimated 150,000 people attend a pro-democracy march in Moscow. Other demonstrations were held throughout the Soviet Union.

● ANC Deputy President Nelson Mandela appeals for an end to inter-tribal violence. The Xhosa tribal leader was addressing a rally of 100,000 Zulus when he said: 'We come together today to renew the ties that make us one people and to reaffirm a single united stand against the oppression of apartheid.'

● Conservative Party Chairman Kenneth Baker admits that the Party is facing 'a very serious moment' as Labour continued to gain in the opinion polls.

● Soviet KGB defector Oleg Gordievsky says that there was no high-ranking mole in British intelligence after Kim Philby and adds that the allegations against former MI5 Director Sir Roger Hollis were 'malicious speculation'.

● Malcolm Forbes, the billionaire American publisher, dies at the age of 70.

26 FEBRUARY

● 2000 people are evacuated from the North Wales town of Towyn as flood waters break through the sea wall.

● 14 people die as gale-force winds gust up to 100 mph across most of the UK.

● The Rover Group agrees to a 37-hour week for its engineering workers. Bill Jordan, President of the Amalgamated Engineering Union, said: 'If anyone in manufacturing doubted that the shorter working week had arrived, they must now take notice.'

● 90 Palestinians are injured when Israeli troops fire on protesters in the Israeli-occupied Gaza Strip. The riots started after the Israeli authorities tried to prevent the wake for a Palestinian youth shot dead two days earlier.

● US President George Bush welcomes the electoral defeat of the Sandinistas and and starts negotiations aimed at lifting US economic sanctions against Nicaragua.

● Soviet troops begin a phased withdrawal from Czechoslovakia.

27 FEBRUARY

● Soviet leader Mikhail Gorbachev wins parliamentary approval for an executive-style presidency which will give him vastly extended powers.

● Gale-force winds batter Britain's coast. The sea wall at the North Wales town of Towyn is breached again and the town is flooded.

● A Royal Marine commando who was found guilty of killing his wife and baby son is freed by Judge Lord Dunpark who told Graham Sherman: 'You have punished yourself enough.'

● Irish Prime Minister Charles Haughey visits Washington and agrees with President George Bush that there should be twice-yearly meetings between presidents and foreign ministers of the US and the holder of the presidency of the EC.

● ANC leader Nelson Mandela visits Zambia, his first trip outside South Africa after 27 years in prison.

● 60 people are killed in widespread violence during state assembly elections in the north Indian state of Bihar.

28 FEBRUARY

● The Treasury announces that the UK's current account trade deficit for January jumped £1000 million to £1880 million.

● Israeli officials report that they are expecting 230,000 Soviet Jews to emigrate to Israel in 1990.

● 16 Conservative councillors on West Oxfordshire District Council resign the Tory whip in protest against the poll tax.

● Two sister ships of the *Marchioness* and the *Bowbelle*, the vessels involved in the collision disaster on the Thames, are arrested after a legal action brought on behalf of the injured and bereaved.

● The Soviet newspaper *Izvestia* admits that there was a mutiny on a Soviet anti-submarine ship in 1975. The mutineers tried to defect to Sweden, but were captured and shot.

● Former British spy Greville Wynne, who tried to help Colonel Oleg Penkovsky to escape from the Soviet Union, dies at the age of 71.

1 MARCH

● House-to-house fighting between rival Christian factions in east Beirut led to the deaths of 70 people in a single day.

● East German Premier Hans Modrow proposes that foreign companies and banks be allowed to set up branches in East Germany.

● The Prince and Princess of Wales fly over the flooded North Wales town of Towyn and visit a castle providing shelter for 150 people. Workers trying to repair the sea wall were forced to abandon their task because of high tides and heavy winds.

● Three people are killed and more than 30 injured when a passenger train and two cars collided at a level crossing in Co. Antrim.

● 16 people die and another 70 are injured in a hotel fire in Cairo. Among the dead were two Britons.

● An Indian Air Force jet kills 50 people when it crashes into a road in Uttar Pradesh.

● The England cricket team beat the West Indies by nine wickets in Jamaica. It was their first victory over the West Indies since 1974.

2 MARCH

● The first councils to set a poll tax in England announce their rates. The lowest is Conservative-controlled Wandsworth Council with a tax of £148. In contrast, Labour-controlled Haringey set its poll tax at £572.89.

● An estimated 1 million people in Baku, Azerbaijan, attended a memorial service for the 143 people who died when Soviet troops entered the city in January to stop ethnic riots.

● The African National Congress elects Nelson Mandela Deputy President, moves its headquarters from Lusaka to Johannesburg and announces that it is seeking immediate talks with the South African government.

● Peace talks between Greek and Turkish Cypriot leaders Georgios Vassilou and Rauf Denktash break down without any progress towards a settlement.

● A general strike takes place in Nepal as pressure grows on King Birendra to lift the ban on political parties.

● Kenyan President Daniel Arap Moi bans all demonstrations after anti-government riots sparked off by the death of Foreign Minister Robert Ouko.

3 MARCH

● Prime Minister Margaret Thatcher defends the poll tax at the annual conference of London Conservative councillors. She told the councillors: 'We can give it and we can take it.'

● NATO Secretary General Manfred Woerner says he favours calling a special meeting of NATO foreign ministers to discuss German reunification.

● Peruvian peasants capture 13 Maoist guerrillas, kill them and deliver their heads to the Peruvian army.

● The South Korean government claims it has discovered a tunnel built by the North Koreans for a surprise attack on the southern half of the peninsula.

● Defecting KGB Major Viktor Ivanovich Sheymov claims that the KGB plotted to assassinate Pope John Paul II and was responsible for the death of Pakistan President Zia ul-Haq.

4 MARCH

● Peter Walker, the government's longest-surviving 'Wet', resigns as Secretary of State for Wales. Mr Walker insisted that his departure was for family and business reasons and was not prompted by any disagreements with Prime Minister Margaret Thatcher.

● It is reported that the National Union of Mineworkers received funds from the Soviet Union and Libya during the 1984–5 miners' strike and that some of the funds went to union officials.

● Reform candidates and nationalists fare well in local elections in the Russian Federation, Byelorussia and the Ukraine. The three republics encompass nearly 70% of the population of the Soviet Union.

● A military coup in the South African 'homeland' of Ciskei overthrows President-for-life Lennox Sebe.

● Defence Secretary Tom King, at the end of a four-day visit to the Falkland Islands, urges the islanders to become actively involved in their own defence.

● The Romanian government removes a 30-foot statue of Lenin from the centre of Bucharest. The government planned either to sell the bronze effigy or to melt it down to provide metal for another statue commemorating the overthrow of the Communist regime.

5 MARCH

● South African troops are sent into the 'independent homeland' of Ciskei to prevent looting following the military coup.

● West German Chancellor Helmut Kohl toughens his demand for Poland to relinquish any claims to further war damages and to guarantee the rights of Germans living in Poland. The chancellor's tough stand was opposed by Foreign Minister Hans-Dietrich Genscher and strained the coalition government.

● US Secretary of State James Baker urges the Israeli government not to settle emigrating Soviet Jews on the West Bank. His appeal was refused by Prime Minister Itzhak Shamir.

● Sterling drops an entire point against a basket of international currencies.

● Sugar manufacturers Tate & Lyle are fined £250,000 for breaches of health and safety rules that led to Neil Sinclair being smothered by an avalanche of sugar inside a silo at the company's Greenock refinery.

● Environment Secretary Christopher Patten announces that Britain will stop dumping raw sewage in the North Sea by 1998.

6 MARCH

● Dozens of protesters are arrested at anti-poll tax demonstrations across Britain. The demonstrations were held outside council meetings called to set the poll tax. Police used batons to stop protesters from entering the Bristol City council chambers.

● Labour leader Neil Kinnock calls for an inquiry into allegations that the National Union of Mineworkers received money from Libya and the Soviet Union and that some of that money was misused by union officials.

● West German Chancellor Helmut Kohl backs down from his insistence that formal recognition of the existing border with Poland be linked to Poland's renunciation of war reparations against Germany.

● Energy Secretary John Wakeham announces that Nuclear Electric, the government-owned company which was due to inherit responsibility for the nuclear power industry, will receive £2500 million in state aid.

● Afghan Defence Minister Shanawaz Tanai attempts to overthrow President Najibullah.

● A study published by the Office of Population Censuses and Surveys indicates that middle-class people are less likely to suffer from cancer than those from the working class.

7 MARCH

● The Department of Trade and Industry reports that the al-Fayed brothers lied to the Office of Fair Trading when they bought the House of Fraser Store Group which includes the department store Harrods. But Trade and Industry Secretary Nicholas Ridley said it would not be in the public interest to deny the Egyptian brothers their British directorships.

● The UK is attacked for polluting the North Sea at a European environmental conference in The Hague.

● 27 demonstrators are arrested after riots break out at a meeting of Southampton Council called to set the local poll tax. Conservative Party Chairman Kenneth Baker linked the nationwide violence to the Militant Tendency.

● Conservative MP John Browne is suspended from the House of Commons for a month after admitting that he failed to declare British and Middle Eastern business dealings. His constituency party in Winchester voted to start proceedings to select a prospective candidate.

● Veteran Turkish newspaper editor Cetin Emic is shot to death in Istanbul as political violence escalates.

● Army and air force officers loyal to Afghan Defence Minister Shanawaz Tanai gain control of Bagram airbase, Afghanistan's largest airport. Kabul is placed under a strict curfew as fighting between troops loyal to President Najibullah and the dissidents spreads.

● South Africa threatens to send troops into the 'independent homeland' of Bophuthatswana after 14 people are killed in riots with police.

8 MARCH

● 40 people are arrested at riots outside Hackney District Council offices when councillors meet to set the poll tax. Police baton-charged the crowd of 800 demonstrators.

● Environment ministers from nine countries bordering the North Sea agree to a wide range of measures to protect the North Sea.

● Israeli police fire rubber bullets and tear gas into a crowd of Palestinian women demonstrating in Jerusalem to mark International Women's Day.

● The West German parliament endorses a government resolution guaranteeing the inviolability of the German–Polish border.

● Arsonists are blamed for a fire in a restaurant in Frankfurt, West Germany, which killed 11 people, including a Briton and his French wife and four Americans.

● Armed men steal £250,000 from a Securicor van after holding 15 factory workers hostage for two hours in Rainham, Essex.

9 MARCH

● The national executive of the National Union of Mineworkers orders an independent inquiry into financial irregularities by Arthur Scargill and other senior union officials.

● Labour leader Neil Kinnock denounces 'toytown revolutionaries' leading town-hall riots against the poll tax and attacks Labour MPs who are refusing to pay the tax. He said: 'Not even the poll tax . . . can excuse hooliganism.'

● The parliament of the Soviet Republic of Georgia declares illegal the treaties under which Georgia joined the Soviet Union and demands immediate negotiations with the Kremlin aimed at recognition of its claim to total independence.

● Officials from East and West Germany start formal talks on the reunification of Germany.

● The owners of one of the last two tin mines in Cornwall, Wheal Jane, near Truro, announce that they are closing it. Brian Calver, managing director of Carnon Consolidated, blamed the slump in international tin prices.

● Heroin worth £4 million is seized by Dover customs officers from a lorry driven by Turkish driver Ihsan Uskuplugoglu who was charged with illegally importing drugs.

10 MARCH

● Plans for a European Bank for Reconstruction and Development encounter difficulties when West European finance ministers fail to agree technical details. The bank was proposed by France to provide finance for free-market initiatives in Eastern Europe.

● British Coal says it is prepared to import coal in order to meet the increased demand for low-sulphur fuel.

● The Roman Catholic Archbishop of Westminster, Cardinal Basil Hume, calls for the release of the Birmingham Six because he believes that their convictions are based on flawed evidence. The Birmingham Six were each sentenced to 21 terms of life imprisonment for an IRA bomb attack on two Birmingham pubs in 1974 in which 21 people died.

● 10 people are killed and 100 injured in Haiti as General Avril Prosper hands over power to General Gerard Abraham. It was the fifth change of government since the overthrow of the Duvalier regime in February 1986.

● Hungary and the Soviet Union sign an agreement for the withdrawal of all Soviet forces from Hungary.

● The overthrown King of Lesotho, Moshoeshoe II, is sent into exile in Britain by Maj.-Gen. Justin Lekhanya, who says the king needs a 'brief sabbatical . . . for reflection'.

● Former Labour Foreign Secretary Lord Stewart dies in Charing Cross Hospital at the age of 83. Lord Stewart was Foreign Secretary from 1968 to 1970.

11 MARCH

● The Soviet republic of Lithuania declares its independence from the Soviet Union and calls on the West to recognize the new Republic of Lithuania. White House spokesman Marlin Fitzwater urged Moscow to 'respect the will of the citizens of Lithuania'.

● The British government and other EC governments appeal to Iraqi President Saddam Hussein to grant clemency to British-based journalist Farzad Bazoft who was sentenced to death for allegedly spying for Israel. Mrs Thatcher also met Jordan's King Hussein and asked him to intervene with Saddam.

● The Scottish Labour Party conference votes in favour of retaining the policy of unilateral nuclear disarmament. The vote, however, is not seen as a threat to the national party's policy to scrap unilateral nuclear disarmament.

● Patricio Aylwen is sworn in as President of Chile in succession to General Augusto Pinochet. Among those witnessing the handover to civilian rule were Deputy British leader Sir Geoffrey Howe.

● Iran hangs 39 convicted drug traffickers, bringing the total executions for drugs-related crimes to 100 for the first two and a half months of 1990.

● More than 30,000 homes in the Hamilton and East Kilbride area are cut off from their water supply after a landslide cuts two main water pipes.

12 MARCH

● 15 people are arrested after a violent anti-poll tax demonstration outside Islington Town Hall.

● The National Society for the Prevention of Cruelty to Children claims that an increasing number of children are being abused in 'bizarre sex rituals'.

● The Soviet Union starts to withdraw its 50,000 troops in Hungary.

● West German Chancellor Helmut Kohl predicts that all-German elections will be held in 1991.

● The Central Transport Consultative Committee, the transport watchdog, says that rail travellers face cuts in services and higher fares to cover safety improvements.

● Animal rights activists free 153,000 edible snails

from a factory farm in Hebburn, Tyne and Wear.

● The East German government announces that it is closing down its foreign intelligence service and calling its overseas agents home.

13 MARCH

● The High Court in Dublin blocks the extradition of two IRA Maze Prison escapees because of 'a probable risk' of beatings by prison staff. Mrs Thatcher quickly denounced the decision as 'deeply offensive and unjustified'.

● The Soviet parliament ends the Communist Party's monopoly of political power and endorses Mikhail Gorbachev's plans for a strong executive presidency.

● The Israeli coalition government collapses over the Likud members' refusal to agree to American proposals for peace talks with Palestinians.

● The government is defeated over its refusal to increase social security payments to residential homes for the elderly. A total of 32 Conservative backbenchers voted with the Labour opposition.

● Ambulance workers vote four to one in favour of a deal to end their six-month dispute with the government.

● Britain's invisible trade balance for the fourth quarter of 1989 shows a deficit of £713 million. It was the first time in over 150 years that the invisible trade balance was in deficit.

14 MARCH

● Wolfgang Schnur, one of the leaders of East Germany's Christian Democratic Party, is forced to resign when it is revealed that he had been an informer for Stasi, the former infamous East German secret police.

● David Hunt, the minister responsible for delivering the English poll tax, is named as the Secretary of State of Wales in succession to Peter Walker.

● Fire destroys a German-built alleged chemical weapons' plant in Libya. The Libyan authorities said it was arson and closed their borders.

● The Lord Chancellor, Lord Mackay, says that parents considering divorce should first think about the children of the marriage.

● Labour leader Neil Kinnock meets ANC leader Nelson Mandela in Stockholm.

● Soviet Premier Nikolai Ryzhkov threatens to resign over allegations that he was involved in the illegal export of Soviet tanks.

15 MARCH

● Iraq ignores international appeals for clemency and hangs *Observer* journalist Farzad Bazoft for spying. The British Ambassador in Baghdad was recalled but the government refused to sever diplomatic relations. Mrs Thatcher described the hanging as 'an act of barbarism which is deeply repugnant to all civilized people'.

● The government of Israeli Prime Minister Itzhak Shamir falls over the issue of peace talks with the Palestinians after Shamir loses a vital confidence vote in the Israeli Knesset (parliament). Shamir had refused to participate in American-sponsored negotiations.

● Dr Thomas Lodwig is cleared at the Old Bailey of the mercy killing of terminally ill cancer patient Roy Spratley.

● The Court of Appeal backs the government's policy of allowing immigration officers to make deportation decisions.

● Domestic electricity prices rise 9.5% in the London area – nearly 2% above the rate of inflation.

● Two game-park rangers are arrested in Nairobi by Scotland Yard detectives investigating the murder of Julie Ward in a Kenyan game reserve. The Kenyan authorities for a year claimed that 28-year-old Miss Ward had been killed by wild animals, but her father forced the Kenyans to change their position.

16 MARCH

● Dr Jonathan Mann, director of the World Health Organization's AIDs programme, resigns after a dispute about how to handle the AIDs problem in Eastern Europe.

● Carol Perry-Lewis, the widow of a Clapham Rail disaster victim, claims that 'British Rail have treated the bereaved families and the many badly injured people very, very shabbily,' after she was forced to take BR to court to receive £106,881 in compensation.

● The Hong Kong government publishes a draft bill of rights which is immediately dismissed by critics as meaningless as they fear it will be repealed as soon as Beijing takes power in 1997.

● United Nations High Commissioner for Refugees, Thorvald Stoltenberg, proposes that the problem of the Vietnamese boat people be resolved by improving the economic conditions of the Vietnamese people. He also proposed improved conditions in the detention camps in Hong Kong and better screening procedures.

● West Germany warns Libya that it will use all legal means to prevent the production of chemical weapons at the German-built plant in Rabta, Libya.

17 MARCH

● Soviet hard-liner Yegor Ligachev warns that the erosion of the Communist Party's power could lead to 'political and economic chaos'. His comments were seen as part of a continuing Kremlin power struggle between the hard-liners and Soviet leader Mikhail Gorbachev.

● Lithuania appeals for international recognition and chooses a woman, Kazimira Prunscene, as Prime Minister.

● A police station in Coalisland, Co. Tyrone, is attacked by about 100 youths hurling 60 petrol bombs. They also rammed the security fencing with fork-lift trucks.

● A 75-year-old woman is beaten and then drowned in her home in north London.

● The Queen Mother visits Berlin to present shamrock to the Irish Guards on St Patrick's Day and is in turn presented with a piece of the Berlin Wall.

● Romanian radio announces that the brother and

namesake of the late dictator Nicolae Ceaucescu will be tried for murder. The younger Nicolae Ceaucescu was head of the officer training school of Romania's dreaded secret police, the Securitate.

18 MARCH

● East Germany's conservative alliance wins the country's first – and probably last – free elections. The vote was seen as a resounding victory for West German Chancellor Helmut Kohl and his policy towards German reunification.

● Soviet troops and tanks gather on the southern border of Lithuania and Soviet aircraft fly over the capital Vilnius.

● A 20-year-old Glasgow student is killed and seven people are injured after a 24-year-old man starts shooting people emerging from a city night club. The gunman then turned his weapon on himself.

● A French Socialist Party conference ends in confusion when its members fail to agree on a common policy or a successor to President François Mitterrand.

● The human rights group Africa Watch claims that half a million Sudanese died of slaughter and deliberate starvation over the preceding four years.

● John Thaw wins the BAFTA award for Best TV Actor for his portrayal of Inspector Morse. Best TV Actress was Diana Rigg for her performance in *Mother Love*.

19 MARCH

● A report on the Thames river collision between the pleasure boat the *Marchioness* and the dredger *Bowbelle* reveals that the Department of Transport had been warned about the need for increased safety standards six years previously. But the report by the Marine Accident Investigation Bureau said that the main cause of the accident was the failure of the *Marchioness* and *Bowbelle* to see and avoid each other.

● Thieves posing as policemen break into a private Boston gallery and steal £200 million worth of art treasures – the biggest art theft in history. Among the stolen masterpieces were Rembrandt's *Storm on the Sea of Galilee* and the Manet painting *Chez Tortoni*.

● David Lashley is jailed for life for the murder of Australian heiress Janie Shepherd in 1977. He was brought to trial after he confessed to other prisoners while serving a sentence for another crime. Mr Justice Alliott told Lashley: 'In my view you are such an appalling, dangerous man that the real issue is whether the authorities can ever allow you your liberty in your natural lifetime.'

● Home Secretary David Waddington announces that a special police unit is being set up to investigate suspected Nazi war criminals living in Britain.

● Foreign Secretary Douglas Hurd arrives in South Africa and describes the government's political reform programme as 'impressive'. He added: 'It is not complete, but it's impressive.'

● Thousands of students in Taiwan demonstrate in the capital Taipei for faster moves towards democratic reform.

20 MARCH

● Chancellor of the Exchequer John Major unveils his first Budget. It was hailed as a broadly neutral Budget and its provisions included: new five-year tax-free savings accounts for small savers from 1991; raising of income-tax allowances; increases in duty on beer, wine, spirits and tobacco; a rise in duty on petrol; raising of the VAT threshold for businesses; and doubling of the savings limit from £8000 to £16,000 for those entitled to claim poll-tax benefit. The Budget was broadly welcomed by Labour leader Neil Kinnock who said: 'We may have just a tiny corner of a listening government beginning. Unfortunately, it's just too late to save them.'

● Two IRA bombs explode inside the Belfast-based Shorts guided-missile plant, injuring five workers.

● Czechoslovak President Vaclav Havel says his country's arms industry would no longer sell weapons to dictatorial regimes. 'We are studying the reconversion of our military industry,' he said.

● Westminster City Council approves plans for a £175 million redevelopment scheme proposed for the Royal Opera House in Covent Garden. The plan was strongly opposed by residents because it would destroy a number of Victorian and Georgian buildings.

● Marks and Spencer award their shop assistants a 26% pay rise over three years. But the company's warehouse staff had their pay frozen.

● The trial starts in New York of former Philippines first lady Imelda Marcos and Saudi Arabian arms dealer Adnan Khashoggi. They were charged with a 'pattern of racketeering, embezzlement, bribery and extortion' involving £213 million.

21 MARCH

● The Home Office announces a new, but limited, inquiry into the Birmingham Six by Devon and Cornwall Police. The police will examine new evidence submitted by the men's lawyer, Gareth Peirce.

● Independence day in Namibia marks the end of South African rule. Among those attending the celebrations were US Secretary of State James Baker, Soviet Foreign Minister Eduard Shevardnadze, British Foreign Secretary Douglas Hurd and South African President F. W. de Klerk.

● Soviet leader Mikhail Gorbachev orders the confiscation of guns in Lithuania and tightens border and immigration controls into the rebel republic.

● The Henley Centre of Forecasting predicts that crime and poor transport facilities will lead to a decline in London's population in the 1990s.

● Israeli Labour leader Shimon Peres starts complex negotiations aimed at forming a coalition government that can conduct peace negotiations with the Palestinians.

● Lord Rothschild, the former MI5 officer and first head of the Downing Street think tank, dies at the age of 79.

22 MARCH

● Labour has a landslide victory in the Mid-Staffordshire

by-election. Labour candidate Sylvia Heal overturned a Tory majority of 14,654 to win 27,649, votes compared with 18,200 votes for the Conservative candidate Charles Prior. Mrs Heal said: 'They voted against the poll tax. Labour is now seen as the alternative government.' Mrs Thatcher said the Conservatives were not for 'trimming or turning' but added that the voters had 'taken their chance' to send a message about mortgage rates and the high level of the poll tax.

● The Treasury announces that Britain's trade gap narrowed to £1400 million in February. The news helped to steady the pound on foreign exchange markets.

● Czech President Vaclav Havel reveals that the former Communist government in Czechoslovakia sold 1000 tons of Semtex explosives to Libya.

● Prime Minister Margaret Thatcher tells a dinner at the Royal Society that there is a danger of politicians responding too quickly to pressure from environmentalists.

● Joseph Hazelwood, captain of the *Exxon Valdez* oil-tanker, was acquitted of the major charges connected with America's worst-ever oil spill off the coast of Alaska. Hazelwood was convicted of one misdemeanour – negligent discharge of oil. He denied that he was drunk and reckless when the tanker ran aground and spilled 11 million gallons of oil into Prince William Sound.

● A Japanese porcelain figure worth an estimated £100,000 is stolen from the British Museum.

23 MARCH

● The Soviet Union sends additional troops into Lithuania and bars foreign correspondents from visiting the dissident republic. The Lithuanian government calls for support from the international community.

● West German Chancellor Helmut Kohl calls for stepped-up progress to complete political union in the EC and warns Mrs Thatcher that she will 'be swept away' if she tries to stand in the way.

● 46 Kurdish nationalists occupy the London offices of Turkish Airways for seven hours in protest against the recent killings in the Kurdish city of Cizri.

● West German Foreign Minister Hans-Dietrich Genscher tells the Western European Union that 'we must come to terms with the idea that the concept of East and West is outdated'.

● More than 400 Albanian schoolchildren in the troubled Yugoslav province of Kosovo are taken to hospital suffering from severe gastric upset. Albanian nationalists claimed that the children were poisoned by Serbs.

● The Duchess of York gives birth to a daughter at Portland Hospital in London. The new princess weighed 7 lbs 1½ oz and was delivered by Caesarean section.

24 MARCH

● Soviet tanks and paratroopers move into the Lithuanian capital of Vilnius.

● A father and son die when their light aircraft crashes on Salisbury Plain.

● Anti-porn campaigner Mary Whitehouse calls on the government to tighten obscenity laws to protect children from pornography.

● Indian soldiers complete their withdrawal from Sri Lanka. More than 50,000 troops had spent two and a half years helping to put down a Tamil revolt.

● 27 passengers are injured in an emergency evacuation from a Cathay Pacific airliner at Tokyo Airport. The evacuation was ordered after it was discovered that fuel was leaking from the plane.

25 MARCH

● Australian Labour Prime Minister Bob Hawke wins an unprecedented fourth term in Australia's general election.

● The Rt Reverend Robert Runcie, the Archbishop of Canterbury, announces his retirement.

● Labour's opinion poll lead over the Conservatives widens to 23 points in a MORI poll published in the *Sunday Times*. A *Sunday Correspondent* opinion poll gives Labour an identical lead. The *Independent on Sunday* puts Labour 19 points ahead and the *Observer* 28 points.

26 MARCH

● The first round of Hungary's first post-war free elections votes the Communist Party out of power and sets the scene for a conservative coalition government.

● Former Chancellor Nigel Lawson warns that the government's battle against inflation was at risk because of the refusal to enter Europe's Exchange Rate Mechanism (EMS).

● Eight people are injured and 100 buildings damaged by an IRA bomb attack on a police station at Castlederg, Co. Tyrone.

● French Prime Minister Michel Rocard visits London for talks with Mrs Thatcher on German reunification and the changing situation in Eastern Europe.

● Spain's ruling Socialist Party loses its absolute parliamentary majority after a by-election in Melilla. But the government of Prime Minister Felipe Gonzalez stays in office.

● Ibrahim Bohme, the leader of East Germany's Social Democratic Party, temporarily steps down while officials investigate claims that he was an informer for the East German secret police, the Stasi.

27 MARCH

● Soviet troops occupy the headquarters of the Lithuanian Communist Party and start rounding up Lithuanian deserters from the Soviet Army.

● Actress Glenda Jackson is named prospective parliamentary Labour candidate for Hampstead and Highgate.

● Transport Secretary Cecil Parkinson scraps a £2000 million roads project for London. He instead promised new emphasis on public transport, especially cross-London rail links.

● Ford announces that it is cutting 3000 jobs from its Halewood plant over the next five years.

● Ten people die and several hundred are injured in

inter-tribal riots in the South African township of Sebokeng.

● A French government commission reports that racism is spreading in France. Prime Minister Michel Rocard calls for an all-party conference to combat 'this threat to our national heritage'.

28 MARCH

● US and British customs officials foil an Iraqi attempt to smuggle 40 nuclear-bomb trigger devices. The incident raises questions about Iraq's nuclear weapons' programme.

● Defence Secretary Tom King says he wants 'smaller but better' armed forces as a consequence of the changes in Eastern Europe.

● The Governor of the Bank of England, Robin Leigh-Pemberton, says that high inflation was the only obstacle to Britain joining Europe's Exchange Rate Mechanism.

● Labour's National Executive Committee backs the local party in Haringey after it barred three councillors standing as Labour candidates after they said they would campaign against a poll tax being set.

● Mrs Thatcher makes a 50-minute telephone call to Mikhail Gorbachev to urge the Soviet leader not to use force in Lithuania.

● Foreign Secretary Douglas Hurd says France should resume full NATO membership in order to participate fully in any Alliance rethink.

29 MARCH

● Viscount Linley, the Queen's nephew, is awarded £30,000 libel damages against the *Today* newspaper. The newspaper alleged that he had been banned from a Chelsea pub for throwing beer.

● East German demonstrators march through East Berlin to demand that newly elected deputies' links to the former Stasi security police be investigated.

● The European Commission says it will be altering its job entrance requirements to give a better chance to British graduates.

● Andrew Peacock resigns as Leader of Australia's opposition conservative Liberal Party after conceding defeat in the general election.

● Political and economic reform in Vietnam suffers a setback when Vietnamese Communist hard-liners remove the reform-minded Tran Xuan Bach from all top party posts.

● The Soviet Union appoints its first Ambassador to the Vatican – career diplomat Yuri Karlov.

30 MARCH

● Former Conservative Party Chairman Norman Tebbit says he will stand against Michael Heseltine for the Tory leadership if Margaret Thatcher retires before the next general election.

● West German Chancellor Helmut Kohl meets Mrs Thatcher at Downing Street and says his goal is 'the political unification of Europe'. But Margaret Thatcher says that Europe 'is best as it is at the moment'.

● Soviet troops occupy government buildings in the Lithuanian capital of Vilnius.

● Alban Turner, who was jailed for life in 1987 after being convicted of murdering a street trader during the Notting Hill Carnival, is set free after judges decide that the chief prosecution witness was an unprincipled liar.

● Three men are jailed for life at Belfast Crown Court for aiding and abetting the 1988 murder of the two Army corporals who drove into an IRA funeral. The convicted men were Patrick Kane, Michael Timmons and Sean Kelly.

● The Duke and Duchess of York name their daughter Princess Eugenie Victoria Helena.

31 MARCH

● An anti-poll tax march turns into a riot in Trafalgar Square and the West End of London. A total of 341 rioters were arrested and 132 people were injured as shops were looted and mounted police charged demonstrators.

● Mrs Thatcher tells the Conservative Party's annual central council conference that she is not resigning.

● The Polish government offers to fly Soviet Jews to Israel after the Hungarian airlines stopped flights to Israel because of threats by radical Palestinian guerrilla organizations.

● More than a quarter of Britain's opticians claim they are in danger of going out of business as a result of eye-test charges introduced in 1989.

● Oxford wins the boat race by two and a quarter lengths.

● Texaco, Mobil and Jet raise the price of petrol above £2 a gallon.

1 APRIL

● Inmates at Strangeways Prison in Manchester riot, occupy major sections of the prison and mount a rooftop protest against their living conditions. By the end of the day, some 700 inmates are unaccounted for and many are hospitalized.

● Paddy Ashdown, leader of the Liberal Democrats, says that Mrs. Thatcher's stand on the poll tax could 'create a climate of civic disaffection which those of violence will continue to exploit for their own evil ends'.

● Hundreds of thousands of Ukrainians stage demonstrations in dozens of towns in support of Lithuanian independence and their own demands for greater autonomy or independence from Moscow. More than 100,000 demonstrated in Lvov, the capital of western Ukraine.

● Solidarity leader Lech Walesa warns the Polish government that the pace of change in Poland is not fast enough.

● Several thousand Spaniards march to an airbase used by American forces to demand the complete withdrawal of American troops and Spanish withdrawal from NATO.

● Robert Mugabe's ruling ZANU-PF wins an overwhelming victory in the Zimbabwean general election, thus paving the way for one-party rule.

2 APRIL

- The British Defence White Paper hints at cuts in the £21,100 million defence budget. Defence Secretary Tom King said defence cuts would save the taxpayers some money, but the White Paper also underscored the need for caution in a changing world.
- Iraqi President Saddam Hussein denies that he is building a nuclear bomb, but threatens to attack Israel with chemical weapons if it launches a pre-emptive strike against Iraq.
- Strangeways Prison is condemned by the Howard League for Penal Reform as one of several 'hell-hole cesspits that would not be tolerated by any other country in Europe'.
- Conservative and Labour MPs clash over the Trafalgar Square anti-poll-tax riot and Home Secretary David Waddington's assertion that the trouble was linked to 30 Labour MPs' refusal to pay the tax. Labour MP George Galloway warned of a 'long hot summer' if the poll tax was not reversed.
- An earthquake damages buildings in England, Wales and Ireland. The quake was centred on North Wales and measured 5.2 on the Richter Scale.
- Lithuanian President Vytautas Landsbergis refuses to rescind his country's 11 March proclamation of independence, but at the same time asks for negotiations with Moscow.

3 APRIL

- Strangeways prisoner Derek White, on remand for sex offences, dies in hospital from chest and head injuries received during riots at the prison.
- Environment Secretary, Chris Patten, announces that 20 Labour-controlled local authorities are to be charge-capped because of their high community budget.
- Alexander Yakovlev, one of Soviet leader Mikhail Gorbachev's closest advisers, meets a delegation from Lithuania. But, at the same time, the Soviet parliament passed laws making secession more difficult.
- London Buses bans all staff from drinking during working hours, including lunch breaks. The ban had already applied to bus crews, but was extended to cover 5,300 clerical and managerial staff.
- Petur Mladenov, a reformist Communist, is elected President by the Bulgarian parliament. Multi-party elections are set for 10 and 17 June.

4 APRIL

- Soviet leader Mikhail Gorbachev telephones Estonian President Arnold Ruutel, demanding that he declare Estonia's independence resolution 'null and void' and threatening to impose economic sanctions against Estonia.
- The General Medical Council orders that Dr Raymond Crockett be struck off the medical register for his part in the kidneys-for-cash scandal. Dr Crockett said afterwards: 'If these actions in saving the lives of my patients represent misconduct then the moon really is made of cheese.'
- Rioting prisoners at Strangeways say their actions were sparked off by poor food, mental and physical brutality, overcrowding and the use of drugs in controlling prisoners.
- US Secretary of State James Baker and Soviet Foreign Secretary Eduard Shevardnadze meet in Washington. The talks focus on arms reductions, German reunification, Lithuania and plans for the Bush–Gorbachev Summit.
- Health Secretary Kenneth Clarke seeks to allay doctors' fears about NHS standards by agreeing to establish the Clinical Standards Advisory Group to monitor clinical standards.
- Belgium's King Badouin I abdicates for 24 hours to allow the passage of a law legalizing abortion. The king, a childless Roman Catholic, did not feel he could personally agree to the bill which was signed by parliament in the absence of the monarch.

5 APRIL

- Soviet Foreign Secretary Eduard Shevardnadze, in talks with US Secretary of State James Baker, drops the Soviet demand for a neutral unified Germany.
- The Irish Supreme Court refuses to allow the extradition of Owen Carron, a former MP and member of Sinn Fein, who is wanted in Northern Ireland on firearms charges. The ruling followed a similar ruling in two other cases and was based on the view that Mr Carron's alleged offence was political.
- Mujaheddin guerrillas in Afghanistan attack a government rally attended by about 10,000 people. Two Afghan generals and several government officials were killed.

6 APRIL

- Hundreds are killed or wounded when Nepalese security forces again open fire on pro-democracy demonstrators outside the palace of King Birendra.
- The Chinese government attacks the British government's proposals for issuing 225,000 Hong Kong Chinese with British passports. The Chinese said such a move would harm Hong Kong's stability and prosperity after 1997.
- British woman Adrianne Smith, aged 21, is jailed for six years by a Spanish court after she is found guilty of throwing her baby into a rubbish bin and leaving it to die. Smith was on holiday in Majorca at the time of her baby's birth.
- PLO leader Yasser Arafat admits that he has had contacts with Israeli leaders over the issues of the Middle East peace process and the Israeli-occupied territories.
- 10,000 Mexican troops break an occupation of 19 towns by supporters of the opposition Democratic Revolution Party. The PRD claimed that the action was necessary because they were denied legitimate power by government-authorized vote-rigging.

7 APRIL

- More than 150 people die when the Norwegian ferry *Scandinavian Star* is set alight by arsonists. The ferry was travelling from Oslo to Frederikshaven in Denmark.

● Rioting breaks out in Dartmoor Prison. A total of 103 inmates take control of a prison wing and part of the prison rooftop.

● Former US National Security Adviser Admiral John Poindexter is found guilty of lying to Congress over the Iran–Contra scandal.

● Deputy Prime Minister Sir Geoffrey Howe admits that the government has made mistakes and that the British revival is 'far from accomplished'.

● The Bishop of London, the Rt Rev Graham Leonard, announces that he will retire on his 70th birthday. Dr Leonard was a leading opponent of the ordination of women.

● Four men and two women are arrested after a petrol bomb is discovered under the floorboards of a saddlery shop in the village of Warmwell, near Dorchester, Dorset.

8 APRIL

● A riot at Dartmoor Prison ends after 24 hours. One prisoner's body is found in a burnt-out cell.

● Hungary's conservative Hungarian Democratic Forum is swept to power in the country's first free elections for 45 years.

● Ireland's ruling Fianna Fail Party approves a motion opposing the extradition of Irish citizens to the UK. But Irish Premier Charles Haughey said that his government remained 'committed to using extradition as a weapon against international terrorism',

● Turkish troops kill at least 25 Kurdish guerrillas in gun battles in southeast Turkey.

● King Birendra of Nepal lifts a 30-year ban on political parties and promises to introduce multi-party elections.

● More than 100,000 Israelis sign an electoral reform petition calling for a change in the Israeli proportional representation system which gives the country's small and extremist political parties a disproportionate share of power.

9 APRIL

● A 'grand coalition' government is agreed in East Germany between the Christian Democrats, Free Democrats and Social Democrats. The coalition is led by Christian Democrat leader Lothar de Maiziere.

● Three High Court judges refuse an application by the British Muslim Action to have author Salman Rushdie and his publishers Penguin Books prosecuted under the blasphemy laws.

● South Africa's ruling National Party loses control of Johannesburg City Council to the anti-apartheid Democratic Party. The elections followed a scandal over a council-run espionage system.

● Constantin Mitsotakis, leader of Greece's New Democracy Party, forms a government after months of political crisis.

● Six men are arrested in Dublin after a raid on a suspected IRA bomb factory.

● Fires on board the Irish Sea ferry *Noronna* and the English Channel ferry *Reine Mathilde* kill two people. The fires were believed to be copycat arson attacks modelled on the Norwegian ferry blaze in which 150 people died.

10 APRIL

● Three French hostages – Jacqueline Valente, Fernand Houtekins and their 2-year-old daughter Sophie – are released by Palestinian kidnappers after two years in captivity. The French Ministry of Foreign Affairs thanked Libyan leader Moamar al-Gaddafi for his intervention in securing the French family's release.

● Polish Solidarity leader Lech Walesa announces that he is a candidate for the presidential elections scheduled for 1993.

● Prisoners riot at Shotts Prison in Lanarkshire, injuring two prison officers and taking another one hostage.

● The Treasury announces that it will issue a new £5 note, with George Stephenson, the builder of the first commercially successful steam railway engine, replacing the Duke of Wellington.

● The National Audit Office attacks the Department of Social Security for failing to do more to make former husbands provide proper maintenance for their children and divorced wives.

● British journalist William Goodwin of the magazine *The Engineer* is fined £5,000 for contempt of court after his refusal to reveal his sources for a story about a company's finances.

11 APRIL

● British customs officers impound a consignment of Iraqi-bound cylinders which they believe were designed as the barrel of a 'super gun'. The cylinders were made by the British company Sheffield Forgemasters which claimed that they were part of an oil pipeline.

● The Confederation of British Industry calls on the government to cut business taxes or face an economic crisis sparked off by a dramatic drop in investment.

● Israeli Labour Party leader Shimon Peres fails in his bid to form a peace coalition when two religious parties withdraw their support.

● An international banking task force estimates that £49,000 million a year in drug-related profits is being laundered through the Western banking system.

● The Polish parliament votes 266 to nil to abolish censorship.

● Mother Teresa, the founder of the Calcutta-based Missionaries of Charity, is forced by ill-health to resign at the age of 79.

12 APRIL

● The Ministry of Defence supports customs claims that the British steel pipes bound for Iraq were part of a supergun. Phillip Wright, chief executive of Sheffield Forgemasters, said: 'If this thing is part of a gun, then we, the DTI and many other people, have been part of the biggest con job in the history of arms manufacture.'

● Christian Democrat Lothar de Maziere is named Premier of East Germany.

● The Romanian government bans ex-King Michael from making an Easter visit to the country he once ruled. The ruling National Salvation Front said his visit would cause 'instability.'

● Mrs Thatcher declares that the dispute over sanctions against South Africa is 'yesterday's debate' and calls on the world community to acknowledge the progress made in South Africa since the release of Nelson Mandela.

● A report by the Schools Inspectorate finds that a third of primary-school work in English, mathematics and science is unsatisfactory.

● The Office of Population Censuses and Surveys reports that US residents have a 20% better chance of surviving cancer than those in the United Kingdom.

13 APRIL

● The Soviet government announces that it will impose an economic blockade against Lithuania unless the Lithuanian government rescinds its declaration of independence.

● The Soviet Union finally admits that it was responsible for the massacre of 15,000 Polish officers in Katyn Forest in 1940. The admission came during a visit to the Soviet Union by Polish President Wojciech Jaruzelski.

● Mrs Thatcher and US President George Bush meet in Bermuda. The talks are dominated by the reunification of Germany and the future role of NATO. Mrs Thatcher relaxed her insistence on the modernization of tactical nuclear weapons in Germany.

● More than 1,000 people are evacuated and 22 are treated after a fire broke at the GEC-Marconi research centre in Great Baddow, Essex. The fire created a cloud which contained chemicals including cyanide.

● Nepal's King Birendra agrees to allow an opposition alliance to form an interim government until multi-party elections can be held.

● Czech secret-police files on former dissidents such as playwright–president Vaclav Havel are handed over to the human-rights organization Charter 77.

● Indian and Pakistani troops exchange sporadic fire over the Kashmir border. Indian Prime Minister V. P. Singh accused Pakistan of 'evil designs'.

14 APRIL

● Pakistan puts its armed forces on a war footing as Indo-Pakistan tensions continue to mount over Kashmir.

● Lithuanian President Vytautas Landsbergis says that his country will defy a Soviet economic blockade. He told American television: 'We will survive in difficult conditions, but we will survive.'

● ANC Deputy President Nelson Mandela admits that the ANC tortured dissident members. He added that those responsible had been either disciplined or dismissed from the ANC.

● Muslim unrest in the northwest Chinese province of Xinjiang leaves at least 50 people dead.

● Mongolia's Communist Party leadership promises fair multi-party elections in July.

● Jill Morrell, organizer of the campaign to free British kidnap hostage John McCarthy, says that after four years of McCarthy being held captive in Lebanon she no longer wants to be referred to as his girlfriend.

15 APRIL

● A memorial service for the 95 Liverpool supporters who died in the Hillsborough Stadium disaster is held at Anfield. About 15,000 people attended.

● The Archbishop of Canterbury, the Rt Rev. Dr Robert Runcie, uses his Easter sermon to assert that 'the world's public life has been charged with powerful images of resurrection' by the changes in Eastern Europe during 1989.

● Labour Health spokesman Robin Cook says that more than 25,000 acute-care beds were lost from the National Health Service between 1979 and 1989.

● Thousands of demonstrators stone the car of the Nepalese Prime Minister and demand the immediate dissolution of the 'rubber-stamp' parliament and the establishment of an interim opposition government in preparation for the multi-party elections promised by King Birendra.

● Almost 25% of all American children under the age of 6 are living in poverty according to a report issued by Columbia University.

● More than 30 people die in Iran during clashes between the Revolutionary Guards and the regular armed forces. The clashes were mainly in the troubled province of Baluchistan.

● Leading Soviet economic reformer Leonid Abalkin visits Cuba in an attempt to persuade Fidel Castro to introduce *perestroika*.

16 APRIL

● 75,000 people attend a Wembley rock concert in honour of ANC Deputy President Nelson Mandela. Mandela used the concert to warn Mrs Thatcher that because of her stand on sanctions she would not be welcome in South Africa until the ANC had completed a peace agreement with the South African government.

● Members of the National Union of Teachers vote against the recommendation of union officials and in favour of national industrial action in protest against compulsory redundancies.

● The Scottish National Party promises to repeal the poll tax and replace it with a local income tax based on ability to pay.

● Shadow Chancellor John Smith, speaking before an audience of New York businessmen, dismisses as a 'myth' claims that Labour is hostile to the market economy. He said: 'We welcome and endorse the dynamism, efficiency and realism that markets can provide.'

● Saudi Arabia's King Fahd backs Pakistan in its dispute over Kashmir.

17 APRIL

● The Soviet Union cuts off oil and gas supplies to Lithuania in retaliation for the Lithuanian government's refusal to rescind its independence decree.

● Leaders of the National Union of Teachers refuse to implement their members' vote for national industrial action because it would breach the Industrial Relations Act.

● South African President F. W. de Klerk promises Whites that any post-apartheid constitution would entrench their political rights. He said the National Party would reject the creation of a new political system in which simplistic majority rule on the basis of one man one vote threatened the domination or suppression of 'smaller groups'.

● The anti-Communist opposition parties win parliamentary elections in the Yugoslav republic of Slovenia.

● US President George Bush says that international anti-pollution methods must be balanced against the need for continued world economic growth.

● American civil rights campaigner the Rev. Ralph Abernathy dies at the age of 64.

18 APRIL

● Trade and Industry Secretary, Nicholas Ridley, tells the House of Commons that pipes being sent to Iraq were definitely part of a 'large calibre weapon' and admits that his department had granted export licences for the pipes, as 'on the information available at that time ... it had no knowledge that the goods were designed to form part of a gun'.

● US President George Bush and French President François Mitterrand meet in Washington. They discussed German reunification and the possibility of France returning to an altered NATO.

● Published figures show that British manufacturing industry wage costs rose by 6.8% between December and February, fuelling inflation fears. On the same day, power workers vote to strike over an 8.5% pay offer.

● The Royal Opera House faces a £5 million deficit, announces general director Jeremy Isaacs.

● Opinion polls in Poland show that popular support for Solidarity has dropped by over 30% as the government's economic reforms send prices and unemployment soaring.

● 11 Beirut schoolchildren burn to death when their bus is hit by an incendiary grenade.

● Egyptian Foreign Minister Esmat Abdel Meguid calls for a ban on the spread of high-technology weapons in the Middle East. He said: 'All weapons of mass destruction – nuclear, chemical and biological – should be prohibited in the Middle East; all nations of the region should meet equal and reciprocal commitments in this regard; and verification measures should be established to ascertain full compliance of all states.'

19 APRIL

● Government legislation to give British passports to 225,000 Hong Kong residents passes its second reading in the Commons despite a revolt by Conservative backbenchers led by former Conservative minister Norman Tebbit.

● Indo-Pakistan tensions increase after former Kashmir state minister Abdul Sjabar Sheikh is assassinated by Muslim secessionists

● The government outlines measures to control unscrupulous estate agents. The measures are designed to eradicate actions such as giving misleading information, pressuring homebuyers to use their financial services, failing to disclose personal interests and 'bidding up' house prices.

● British Coal announces that 600 more South Wales miners will be made redundant after the closure of Blaenant colliery near Neath.

● Baron Michael de Stempel is found guilty of conspiring to steal more than £500,000 from Lady Margaret Illingworth, widow of a former Conservative cabinet minister.

● Czechoslovak Interior Minister Richard Sacher is accused by his deputy ministers of authorizing a private search of MPs' secret police files.

● Omar Bongo, President of Gabon, says his country's constitution will be amended to allow multi-party politics.

20 APRIL

● Greek and Turkish customs officials seize British lorries carrying parts for Iraq's 'supergun'. Lorry driver Paul Ashwell was arrested and gaoled by Greek authorities.

● The Soviet blockade of Lithuania tightens as some food supplies from Cuba and other parts of the Soviet Union are diverted from the rebel republic.

● The Albanian leader Ramiz Aliz says he is ready for improved relations with the United States and the Soviet Union and the Albanian press appeals for a 'deepening of democracy'.

● Tens of thousands of Islamic fundamentalists march on the presidential palace in Algiers to demand parliamentary elections within three months.

● The World Wide Fund for Nature calls for an international reduction in motorway speed limits to 50 miles an hour to cut 'greenhouse gas' emissions from cars.

● Circus entrepreneur Jimmy Chipperfield dies at the age of 78.

21 APRIL

● Pope John Paul II starts his first visit to Czechoslovakia by referring to communism as a 'tragic utopia'. He called for a united Christian Europe and went on to condemn communism as an ideology built on fear and said that it had collapsed because it denied God.

● EC foreign ministers warn the Soviet Union that its economic blockade of Lithuania could damage East–West relations.

● Marcus and Sophia Wilberforce and their mother Baroness Susan de Stempel are found guilty of robbing their great-aunt and aunt, Lady Mary Illingworth of more than £500,000. The family are the direct descendants of the famous anti-slavery campaigner William Wilberforce.

● Poland's Lech Walesa is re-elected chairman of Solidarity with an overwhelming 77.5% of the vote.

● Israeli troops kill six Islamic fundamentalist guerrillas during a raid into South Lebanon.

● Police arrest 19 people as anti-Fascist demonstrators attempt to stop 140 supporters of the British National Party from holding a local election rally at Bethnal Green in London.

22 APRIL

● Islamic fundamentalists in Beirut free American hostage Robert Polhill after 39 months in captivity. The US State Department praised Syria's President Assad for his help in organizing the release.

● An attempted military coup fails in Nigeria. President Ibrahim Babangida said the majority of the rebels were captured and would be tried 'very rapidly'.

● Home Secretary David Waddington visits Strangeways Prison to inspect damage to the prison as the prison siege enters its fourth week.

● The Russian Communist Party is founded in Moscow and at its first congress calls for the 'rebirth' of the largest republic of the Soviet Union, the Russian Federated State.

● The 20th anniversary of 'Earth Day' is celebrated around the world. Organizers said that more than 100 million people from 140 countries joined in environmentally focused events.

● The London Marathon is won by Scotsman Allister Hutton with the time of 2 h, 10 min and 10 sec. Wanda Panfil, a Pole, won the women's race with a time of 2 h, 26 min and 31 sec. The event was marred by the death of a 39-year-old man.

23 APRIL

● West German Chancellor Helmut Kohl brushes aside warnings from the Bundesbank and offers to exchange East German Marks for West German Marks at a generous one-to-one exchange rate as part of the plan for the economic and monetary union of the two Germanies.

● The Rover Car Group reaches an agreement with union leaders which includes a 31-hour week and the creation of 1,200 jobs. In return, the workers agreed to keep the company's Longbridge Plant in Birmingham operating seven days a week and 24 hours a day.

● Lithuania is forced to shut down its only oil refinery because of the Soviet blockade.

● Right-wing nationalists win parliamentary elections in the Yugoslav republic of Croatia. The Croatian Democratic Union campaigned on a platform for expanded borders, thus threatening Croatia's relations with other segments of Yugoslavia.

● Six people die and at least 20 are injured during violent demonstrations in the Nepalese capital of Katmandu. The demonstrations are believed to have stemmed from clashes between supporters of the pro-democracy movement and right-wing supporters of King Birendra.

● An attempted military coup in the Sudan fails to topple the 15-man military junta led by General Omar Hassan el Beshir. 28 officers are executed. The coup attempt was the tenth in 20 years.

24 APRIL

● Billionaire American financier Michael Milken pleads guilty to securities and tax-fraud charges. He is ordered to pay penalties totalling $600 million.

● The US space shuttle *Discovery* is launched with the giant Hubble space telescope on board.

● US President George Bush announces that he is holding back on imposing sanctions against the Soviet Union over its blockade of Lithuania. He said he was 'concerned we do not inadvertently do something that compels the Soviet Union to take action that would set back the whole cause of freedom around the world'.

● MPs vote by 409 votes to 152 to cut the maximum abortion time limit from 28 weeks to 24 weeks.

● Mrs Thatcher signals her intention to slow down EC talks towards political union when she tells the Commons that political union needs closer definition because it means 'very different things to different countries'.

● Oskar Lafontaine, the prospective leader of West Germany's Social Democratic Party, is stabbed in the neck by a woman with a history of mental instability. Lafontaine survived the attack.

● One of the great train robbers, Charles Wilson, is shot dead at his home in Marbella, Spain. Police said the murder was probably linked to drug dealing.

25 APRIL

● The Strangeways Prison siege ends when the five remaining prisoners surrender after 100 prison officers in riot gear storm the jail. The siege lasted 24 days.

● Liverpool customs officers discover 300 kg of cocaine worth £40 million on board the Liberian-registered ship *Sun Tempest*. A Filipino engineer was charged with drug offences.

● Chinese Premier Li Peng ends a three-day visit to Moscow. It was the first trip to Moscow by a Chinese Premier since the early 1960s.

● The European Court of Human Rights rules that the British government breached Council of Europe conventions on freedom of expression in ordering covert M15 surveillance of British civil-liberties campaigners.

● The Taiwanese government announces that it will allow mainland China to establish private liaison offices on the nationalist-ruled island if Beijing agrees to a reciprocal arrangement.

● Mrs Thatcher, Australian Premier Bob Hawke, Turkish President Turgut Ozal and New Zealand Governor General Sir Paul Reeves meet at the Turkish battlefield of Gallipoli to mark the 75th anniversary of one of the bloodiest and most futile campaigns of World War I.

● Chilean President Patricio Aylwin establishes a national commission to investigate human-rights violations committed under the 16 years of military rule.

26 APRIL

● Mrs Thatcher and Home Secretary David Waddington unite to defend the handling of the Strangeways Prison siege against backbench Tories' claims that tougher tactics should have been used. Mrs Thatcher said that it would have been wrong to 'second-guess' decisions made by those in charge.

● Indian Foreign Minister Inder Gujral and his Pakistan counterpart Sahabzada Yaqub-Khan meet in New York and agree to reduce tensions over Kashmir.

● A Lithuanian, Slanislovas Zhamaitis, burns himself to death in central Moscow in protest against the Soviet blockade of Lithuania.

● America's Pentagon scales back plans to buy 132 B-2 Stealth bombers as part of an economy drive.

● Polish Foreign Minister Krzysztof Skubiszewski tells parliament that his government wants to negotiate the withdrawal of all Soviet troops from Poland.

● Thousands of Kuwaitis demonstrate for multi-party elections to a new parliament. The crowds were dispersed by special forces using tear-gas grenades.

27 APRIL

● The Court of Appeal releases three Irish people after it rules that comments by former Northern Ireland Secretary Tom King about terrorism and the right to silence had prevented them from having a fair trial. Martina Shanahan, Finbar Cullen and John McCann had been serving 25-year sentences for conspiracy to murder Mr King.

● British author Salman Rushdie, speaking on BBC Radio 4, says that the inability to lead an ordinary life has been the greatest deprivation he has suffered as a result of Iran's death threat against him.

● Agriculture Minister John Gummer negotiates an EC package which gives British farmers 11% more for their produce.

● Prominent Northern Ireland businessman Kenneth Graham dies after an IRA bomb explodes under his BMW. The IRA said he was killed because his firm supplied building materials to the security forces.

● Greek Prime Minister Constantin Mitsotakis introduces an austerity economic package which includes a 12% rise in electricity charges, a 15% rise in postal charges, a 25% rise in the cost of public transport and a 20% rise in petrol prices.

● Soviet government figures show that in the first quarter of 1990 the national income fell by 2% while official inflation rose to a record 8%.

28 APRIL

● Labour's opinion-poll lead over the Conservative Party widens to 23%.

● A 1931 Bugatti is sold for £9 million – making it the most expensive car in the world. The car was bought by a group of Japanese businessmen.

● Northern Ireland police arrest a woman pretending to be pregnant with a bomb under her coat. She was on a bus bound for Belfast's Aldergrove Airport.

● Mrs Thatcher tells the EC Summit in Dublin that the British people need to be reassured that political union will not jeopardize the constitutional position of the Queen.

● 100 inmates riot at a prison in Lille, France. They wrecked part of the building and climbed on the roof to throw tiles on the prison guards.

● Syrian President Hafez al-Assad flies to Moscow for talks with Soviet leader Mikhail Gorbachev. A joint communiqué accused the United States of being a big obstacle to a Middle East peace settlement.

29 APRIL

● Foreign Secretary Douglas Hurd indicates that Britain is ready to concede powers to the EC on policies covering drug trafficking and the environment.

● East German Premier Lothar de Maiziere visits Moscow and is told by Soviet leader Mikhail Gorbachev that there is no question of a unified Germany being a member of NATO.

● Tens of thousands of Romanian demonstrators in Timisoara demand the resignation of acting President Ion Iliescu.

● British Airways lays on a special flight to evacuate 234 people from civil war-torn Liberia.

● About 150 neo-Nazi skinheads are arrested in East Germany after weekend riots.

● Workers and police clash in the South Korean city of Ulsan after 10,000 riot police raided the Hyundai Heavy Industries shipyard to end a three-day strike there.

30 APRIL

● Another American hostage, Frank Reed, is freed by his Islamic fundamentalist kidnappers in Beirut. The 57-year-old college administrator had been missing since 9 September 1986 and was kept blindfolded throughout his captivity.

● The 10-man crew of an RAF Shackleton airborne early-warning aircraft die after it crashes into a hill on the island of Harris in the Outer Hebrides.

● The Chinese government lifts martial law in Tibet 14 months after sending in troops to quell riots.

● Jonas Savimbi, leader of the rebel UNITA forces in Angola, says he wants to sign a ceasefire agreement with the government to end the 15-year-old civil war.

● Four people die and 25 are seriously injured when a bomb explodes on a crowded bus in New Delhi.

● The Meteorological office reports that April 1990 was the sunniest since records began more than 60 years before.

1 MAY

● Soviet leader Mikhail Gorbachev walks out in the middle of the traditional Soviet May Day Parade as demonstrators denounce the Communist Party and cheer the rebellious Baltic republic of Lithuania.

● Mrs Thatcher indicates that Britain will join the European Exchange Rate Mechanism, but adds that she wants to join within a broad band and remain outside a 'locked currency' system.

● Customs officials question executives from the companies Walter Somers and Sheffield Forgemasters about the possible illegal export of the Iraqi 'supergun'.

● Former Swindon Town Football Club manager Lou Macar is arrested by Regional Crime Squad officers in connection with alleged tax offences. Arrested with him were the club's accountant, captain and former chairman.

● The Bank of Israel reports that the wave of

immigration from the Soviet Union will require increased government spending of £2,200 million over three years.

● Ethiopian President Mengistu Haile Mariam admits in a May Day speech that his army has suffered military setbacks in the war against Eritrean and Tigrean secessionists and that his government is losing popular support.

2 MAY

● South African President F. W. de Klerk and ANC Deputy President Nelson Mandela start constitutional talks in Cape Town. The stated goal of both negotiating teams is a democratic constitution free of racial discrimination.

● Freed American hostage Frank Reed confirms that British hostages John McCarthy and Brian Keenan were alive when he was released by his Islamic fundamentalist captors in Beirut.

● The independent Police Complaints Authority issues a warning to police to adhere to guidelines governing the care of suspects as it is revealed that serious complaints against the service rose by 14% in 1989.

● The House of Commons Public Accounts Committee reports that the government may have sold the Royal Ordnance too cheaply because of its failure to use up-to-date valuations or to consider 'clawing back' windfall profits from property deals.

● IRA terrorist Sean O'Callaghan is sentenced to two life prison sentences for the murders of a woman soldier and a police inspector. O'Callaghan had given himself up to police and pleaded guilty before Belfast Crown Court.

● Peter Mitchell, the managing director of Walter Somers, one of the companies involved in the Iraqi 'supergun' affair, is charged with illegally exporting equipment.

● Egyptian President Hosni Mubarak visits Damascus for talks with Syrian President Hafez al-Assad. It was the first visit to Syria by an Egyptian leader since the Camp David Agreements of 1978. President Mubarak said that Arab reconciliation was 'a vital and necessary step' to deal with threats to the Arab world.

3 MAY

● Labour records sweeping gains in local council elections across the country, but the Conservatives achieve a landslide victory in their flagship London borough of Wandsworth – the council with the country's lowest poll-tax rate. Mrs Thatcher said that the results showed that the community charge was beginning to work and Labour leader Neil Kinnock said that Labour was now 'on course' to win the next general election with a healthy majority.

● The US government announces that it is abandoning plans to update tactical nuclear weapons in Germany. President George Bush accompanied the announcement with a proposal for a July NATO summit to prepare for US–Soviet talks to remove all short-range nuclear weapons from European soil.

● Afghan President Najibullah lifts a year-long state of emergency and promises to convene a traditional tribal council which would include the Mujaheddin guerrillas.

● West German President Richard von Weizsaecker visits Poland and lays a wreath at the monument commemorating the Warsaw ghetto uprising in which the city's Jews fought to the death rather than submit to the Nazi extermination machine.

● US President George Bush says he is worried that Soviet leader Mikhail Gorbachev could be overthrown and that this would set back the process of detente.

● Sir Terence Conran resigns as chairman of Storehouse after more than 20 years to concentrate on his expertise as a designer.

● Investigative journalist Duncan Campbell wins £50,000 libel damages from the BBC after it libelled him in the BBC2 television play *Here is the News*. Mr Campbell said he would use the money to set up an independent television production company.

4 MAY

● The African National Congress agrees to consider suspending its armed struggle against the South African government following talks between ANC Deputy President Nelson Mandela and South African President F. W. de Klerk.

● An attempted bomb attack on British military barracks at Langenhagen base in Hanover, West Germany, is foiled after three men are disturbed by a guard.

● Mrs Thatcher and French President François Mitterrand agree to increase cooperation in the defence and security fields, including nuclear weapons, in the light of changes in Eastern Europe.

● The Baltic republic of Latvia becomes the third Baltic state after Lithuania and Estonia to vote in favour of independence from the Soviet Union.

● The Metropolitan Police report that violent crime rose by 8% in London in 1989. Sexual offences rose by 28% and domestic burglaries rose by 11% after two years of staying level.

● Veteran Greek statesman Constantine Karamanlis, aged 83, is elected President of Greece.

5 MAY

● 2,000 football fans riot at a match between Bournemouth and Leeds United at Bournemouth. Police later revealed that they had advised the Football League not to go ahead with the match because it fell on a Bank Holiday weekend.

● The foreign ministers of Britain, France, the US, the Soviet Union and East and West Germany hold their first meeting on German reunification. The meetings were dubbed the 'two-plus-four' talks in reference to the four World War II allies and the two halves of Germany.

● British Coal announces that a further 500 miners' jobs will be lost in Yorkshire owing to pit closures.

● Nicaragua's Contra rebels sign an agreement with the new government of President Violeta Chamorro to hand over their weapons to United Nations forces.

● Romanian President Ion Iliescu agrees to talks with anti-Communist protesters and apologizes for calling them 'unlawful vagabonds'.

● The tenth anniversary of the murder of John Lennon is marked with a pop concert in his home town of Liverpool.

● Australian actor Paul Hogan marries Linda Kozlowski, his American co-star in the film *Crocodile Dundee*.

6 MAY

● West German Chancellor Helmut Kohl declares that all obstacles to German reunification had been removed by the meeting between the foreign ministers of Britain, the US, France, the Soviet Union and East and West Germany (the two-plus-four talks).

● Tens of thousands of Romanians swarm into Soviet Moldavia for the first time in 50 years to meet long-lost friends and relatives. Before World War II, Moldavia was part of Romania.

● Soviet leader Mikhail Gorbachev warns the Latvian government that it risks a Lithuanian-type economic blockade unless it rescinds its independence declaration.

● Former South African President P. W. Botha resigns from the ruling National Party in protest against the inclusion of South African Communist Joe Slovo in the ANC delegation holding talks with the South African government.

● Italy's Mafia is blamed for the deaths of 10 politicians in local elections in southern Italy.

● 10 prisoners at Dublin's Mountjoy Prison stage a rooftop demonstration to demand full segregation of HIV-positive inmates.

● Colombian Army troops seize 12 tons of cocaine in a raid on jungle laboratories.

7 MAY

● Britain and France agree to site a new international bank in London. The European Bank for Reconstruction and Development will provide finance for the reconstruction of Eastern Europe and will be capitalized at £7.400 million.

● Chancellor of the Exchequer John Major predicts a fall in the rate of inflation from the start of 1991. In a speech before the interim committee of the International Monetary Fund, Mr Major added that a drop in inflation would increase the opportunity for lower interest rates.

● The Latvian parliament elects outspoken nationalist Ivars Godmanis as premier, thus ensuring that the Baltic republic remains on a collision course with the Soviet leadership in Moscow.

● An aircraft of the Queen's flight is forced to make an emergency landing at Gatwick Airport after developing an electrical fault. The aircraft was flying the Princess of Wales to Italy.

● Pan American Airlines reveals that the Lockerbie air disaster cost it $250 million and that the airline had been forced into considering scaling back its European services.

● In the wake of student and workers' riots, South Korean President Roh Tae Wood admits that his government faces a loss of confidence and promises that he would now 'lead the affairs of state with an extraordinary determination'.

8 MAY

● Home Secretary David Waddington criticizes Football League authorities for their 'quite unacceptable' decision to allow the Bournemouth fixture against the advice of the police.

● Soviet leader Mikhail Gorbachev demands immediate reforms in the Soviet armed forces and criticizes the war record of former Soviet leader Joseph Stalin.

● Prince Charles make an outspoken attack on Communism while visiting Hungary. During the first Royal visit to a Warsaw Pact country, the Prince of Wales said that '70 years of horrendous totalitarianism' had turned first Russia, then the rest of Eastern Europe, 'into a form of massive Marxist prison camp'.

● West German Chancellor Helmut Kohl rejects Soviet proposals to delay a decision on the military status of a united Germany. The Chancellor's statement indicated deep disagreements over the issue with Foreign Minister Hans-Dietrich Genscher.

● The International Monetary Fund raises its financial resources by 50%, increasing the total annual membership fees to $108,000 million.

● Cardinal Thomas O'Fiach, leader of the Roman Catholic Church in Ireland and the Archbishop of Armagh, dies while on a pilgrimage to Lourdes. He was 66.

9 MAY

● Lithuanian Prime Minister Kazimiera Prunskiene meets Mrs Thatcher in an attempt to win British support for the beleaguered Baltic state. Mrs Thatcher was sympathetic but refused to take any action that damaged the 'gains made in East–West relations'.

● Employment Secretary Michael Howard calls a meeting with Channel Tunnel contractors over work safety after a series of work-related deaths leads to a ban on British sections of the project by health and safety inspectors.

● An estimated 45,000 South Korean students stage a nationwide protest against the ruling Democratic Liberal Party. Students in the capital of Seoul rioted and clashed with police.

● Former Tory cabinet minister Michael Heseltine says the poll tax needs 'urgent and considerable' changes if the Conservative Party is to win the next general election. The statement was interpreted as part of Heseltine's campaign for the Conservative leadership.

● More than 12,500 Soviet troops march through Red Square to commemorate the 45th anniversary of the surrender of Nazi Germany.

● The Albanian government relaxes the country's penal code and gives Albanians the right to a passport for foreign travel. 11 capital offences remained on the books, however, including 'economic crime'.

10 MAY

● Former Conservative cabinet minister Michael Heseltine rules out a challenge to the leadership of Mrs

Thatcher. He said: 'We fight loyally as a party for our leader, for the policies of our party'.

● The Lord Chancellor, Lord Mackay, proposes a new divorce law which would deny couples a divorce until they resolve differences over money and children. He added: 'I am very anxious at the present rate of divorce and I would like to see it very considerably reduced.'

● Gerrit Viljoen, the South African minister responsible for constitutional talks with Black leaders, said the government was determined to renounce apartheid and replace it with a qualified system of majority rule.

● The Ministry of Agriculture reports that a cat in Bristol had died from 'mad cow' disease. It was later discovered that the disease was contracted by eating contaminated cat food.

● The families in Lockerbie agree a £10 million out-of-court settlement with Pan American Airlines as a result of the 1988 air disaster which killed 259 passengers and crew and 11 residents of Lockerbie.

● The United States and Israel clash over a United Nations resolution condemning the settlement of Soviet Jews on the West Bank.

● The Pan-European weekly newspaper *The European* is launched by publisher Robert Maxwell. The paper's first front-page lead story reported that a 'Euro poll' showed that Mikhail Gorbachev was the most popular choice for a President of Europe.

11 MAY

● British inflation hits an eight-year high as the Treasury reports that figures for April reached 9.4%. Chancellor of the Exchequer John Major said: 'I cannot be precisely certain when inflation will peak.'

● Mrs Thatcher writes to Soviet leader Mikhail Gorbachev urging him to abandon his insistence that Lithuania revoke its declaration of independence before talks about the future of the Baltic state can begin.

● Security tags for new-born babies are introduced at St Thomas's Hospital in London after a series of attempted kidnappings by women posing as social workers and health visitors.

● US President George Bush calls for a manned landing on Mars within 30 years.

● United Nations Secretary General Perez de Cuellar makes his first-ever visit to Albania.

● Antiguan Prime Minister Vere Bird dismisses his son from the cabinet post of Minister of Communications and Works after he is linked with an arms shipment scandal involving Colombian drug traffickers.

12 MAY

● Leading food scientist Professor Richard Lacey calls for the slaughter of 6 million cows to prevent humans from contracting 'mad cow' disease.

● The leaders of the Latvian, Estonian and Lithuanian governments meet to coordinate strategy in their dispute with the Soviet Union. At the end of the meeting they announced the revival of the pre-war Council of Baltic States, demanded seats at the United Nations and representation at the Conference on Security and Cooperation in Europe.

● Romanian President Ion Iliescu threatens to use force to clear demonstrators away from Bucharest's central University Square. Some 70 people were staging an anti-Iliescu hunger strike in a tent city in the centre of the square in front of the Intercontinental Hotel.

● Italian customs officials in Naples impound steel tubing thought to be part of the Iraqi 'supergun'.

● Welsh Guardsman, Simon Weston, who was badly burned during the Falklands War, marries 22-year-old student Lucy Titherington. Mr Weston had become a major campaigner for the disabled.

● An oil slick heads for the North Devon coast after the 250,000-ton Liberian-registered tanker *Rose Bay* collided with a fishing trawler.

● 13 Britons are arrested after wrecking holiday flats in the Spanish resort of Magaluf.

13 MAY

● Norman Lamont, Chief Secretary to the Treasury, says there is little chance that taxes will be cut before the next general election.

● Two American servicemen are shot outside an airbase in the Philippines the day before US–Filipino negotiations on the future of American bases on the islands.

● British Defence Secretary Tom King opposes the removal of nuclear weapons from West Germany. He said: 'The de-nuclearization, the removal of the deterrent from Central Europe, would be extremely damaging and extremely dangerous.'

● West Germany's Christian Democratic Union loses state elections in the *Länder* of Lower Saxony and North Rhine–Westphalia. The results meant that the CDU lost its one-seat majority in the upper house in Bonn, the Bundesrat, which is drawn from the *Länder* governments.

● Nicaragua's Contra rebels start surrendering their weapons to the government of President Violeta Chamorro.

● Two Czechoslovak ministers – Vladmir Prikazsky and Oldrich Bursky – resign because of past links with the former Communist government's secret police.

14 MAY

● Seven people are injured when a 10lb semtex bomb explodes outside an Army education office in south-east London. The explosion was the latest in a series of IRA attacks on low-security military targets in mainland Britain.

● Foreign Secretary Douglas Hurd said that the West would be bound to apply sanctions against the Soviet Union if the Soviet Union took military action against Lithuania.

● Former cabinet minister Norman Tebbit warns that European union could 'explode' into German nationalism.

● French President François Mitterrand leads a Paris march by thousands of Frenchmen protesting against anti-Semitism. The march follows a series of attacks on Jewish cemeteries.

● British Steel and GKN announce the closure of the

Brymbo steelworks at Wrexham, North Wales, with the loss of 1,100 jobs. The closure was blamed on a slump in demand in the car industry.

● Jordanian troops use tear gas to turn back thousands of Palestinian demonstrators attempting to cross the King Hussein (Allenby) Bridge which links Jordan and the Israeli-occupied West Bank.

15 MAY

● An American presidential commission into the Lockerbie air disaster calls for retaliatory strikes against countries such as Libya. The commission also severely criticized Pan American Airlines security operations and said that security was still 'totally unsatisfactory'. The report added, however, that even with improvements civil aviation security could not be guaranteed.

● Beef is removed from the menus of 2,000 British schools in response to the 'mad cow' disease scare.

● A special meeting of the Labour Party's home policy committee passes proposals including a pledge to keep down taxes for the majority, to retain tough controls over secondary picketing and secondary strike action and to enter the European Exchange Rate mechanism 'at the earliest opportunity'.

● More than 500 ethnic Russians break into the courtyard of Estonia's parliament building in protest against the Estonian government's independence moves.

● Soviet leader Mikhail Gorbachev and Egyptian President Hosni Mubarak sign a declaration condemning the settlement of Soviet Jews on the Israeli-occupied West Bank and Gaza Strip. The two leaders also called for a UN-organized international peace conference to discuss the Israeli-occupied territories.

● The Irish Family Planning Association is fined Ir£400 for selling a condom from its stall in the Virgin Records store in Dublin. The decision by the Dublin District Court leads to calls for the reform of Irish laws restricting the sale of contraceptives.

16 MAY

● A soldier is killed and another seriously injured when an IRA bomb blows up a minibus outside an Army careers information office in Wembley, north London.

● British Steel announces the closure of the hot strip mill at its Ravenscraig steel plant in Scotland, jeopardizing the future of the entire plant and 3,500 jobs. The closure was attacked by Secretary of State for Scotland Malcolm Rifkind.

● The Commons Select Committee on Agriculture launches an investigation into 'mad cow' disease.

● West German Chancellor Helmut Kohl tells the European Parliament in Strasbourg that German unification and EC integration should be pursued in parallel and completed 'as fast as possible'.

● The Save the Children Fund claims that 'indiscriminate violence' by the Israeli Army against Palestinians had resulted in the deaths of 159 children and serious injury to 50,000–63,000 children.

● Jim Henson, creator of the Muppets, dies in New York at the age of 53.

● American actor/singer Sammy Davis Jr dies in his California home at the age of 64.

17 MAY

● Lithuanian Prime Minister Kazimiera Prunskiene and Soviet leader Mikhail Gorbachev meet in Moscow to prepare the ground for formal negotiations on the future of the Baltic state.

● US President George Bush says that the four-power authority in West Germany should end the moment the country is reunited. Mr Bush's comments came after a Washington meeting with West German Chancellor Helmut Kohl.

● Home Office Minister David Mellor says that the rebuilding of Strangeways Prison will cost £60 million. Mr Mellor said the government would 'seize the opportunity' to improve conditions in the prison.

● Soviet leader Mikhail Gorbachev blames the limited progress of his reform movement on the Soviet people's innate conservatism. In an impromptu press conference he said: 'In politics, the public does not accept pluralism and has complexes about ideological concepts and cliches. In economics, it's a case of "you mustn't touch this, you mustn't touch that". Everywhere we are hindered by complexes.'

● European Commission Vice-President Leon Brittan calls on the European Community to develop a defence policy which could include managing a European nuclear deterrent.

● The Renoir painting *A Moulin de la Galette* is sold by Sotheby's for £48 million. The painting was bought by Japanese paper manufacturer Ryouei Saito.

18 MAY

● The US and Soviet Union move closer to a nuclear arms control agreement after three days of Moscow talks between Secretary of State James Baker and Soviet Foreign Minister Eduard Shevardnadze.

● The East and West German governments sign a formal treaty committing them to economic union from 2 July and paving the way for political union. The West German Chancellor said: 'What we are experiencing is the moment in which the free and united Germany is born.'

● The Italian budget cuts government spending by £5,800 million in an attempt to bring down the budget deficit.

● Police and students clash in the South Korean city of Kwangju after 100,000 people hold a peaceful rally to mark the tenth anniversary of the bloody suppression of pro-democracy civil unrest in which more than 200 people died.

● France's high-speed TGV train breaks a world rail-speed record when it reaches speeds of 320.2 miles an hour.

● A report by the Samaritans reveals that suicides among young people have more than doubled in the last 30 years.

19 MAY

● South African President F. W. de Klerk meets Mrs

Thatcher in London and tells a press conference that racism is wrong and that he is 'in a hurry' to dismantle apartheid. He added that his country stood 'on the verge of another very exciting change and plans radical constitutional reform. We are inexorably moving on the birth of a new South Africa.'

● Four people die when two light aircraft collide in mid-air and crash near the M25 motorway.

● A Gallup survey reveals that a quarter of British households have dropped the traditional roast beef Sunday lunch because of fears about 'mad cow' disease.

● 22 people die and 90 are injured when a Soviet freight train ploughs into the rear of a stationary passenger train in the Soviet state of Georgia. One carriage was derailed and hurtled into the Black Sea.

● American customs officials in Arizona discover a 200-foot-long tunnel across the US–Mexican border. The tunnel was used by drugs smugglers to carry cocaine into the United States and linked a luxury Mexican house to a warehouse in the American town of Douglas.

● 20-year-old English student Joanna Parrish is murdered and her body dumped in a river 80 miles outside Paris.

20 MAY

● Romania's ruling National Salvation Front and acting President Ion Iliescu win the country's general election.

● Seven Palestinians are killed and hundreds injured when protest riots erupt on the West Bank and Gaza Strip after an Israeli gunman shot dead a group of eight Arab labourers.

● The Egyptian Supreme Court rules that the parliament was elected unconstitutionally in 1987 because independent candidates were discriminated against. The ruling created a political and constitutional crisis in Egypt.

● Mrs Thatcher puts Energy Secretary John Wakeham in charge of coordinating pre-election publicity for the Conservative Party.

● Vandals in Edmonton, north London, desecrate Jewish graves in the local cemetery, duplicating a wave of anti-Semitic attacks in France.

● Lee Teng Hui is inaugurated as President of Taiwan and pledges to end the 'state of war' that has existed between the Nationalist government on Taiwan and the Communist government on the mainland since 1949.

21 MAY

● Independent counsel's investigation into the case of the Maguire Seven finds that their 14-year-old conviction for possession of explosives is unsafe.

● The Malaysian government cancels a £400 million order for 12 Tornado aircraft.

● Czechoslovak politician Alexander Dubcek, who was overthrown by Soviet tanks in 1968, meets Soviet leader Mikhail Gorbachev in the Kremlin and declares that the new Soviet leader has 'a lot of humanity in him'.

● Tensions rise in Kashmir after the state's most influential Muslim leader, Moulvi Mohammed Farooq, is assassinated. After his death, police killed 30 people out of a crowd of 100,000 who gathered outside the hospital.

● Gunmen shoot dead Colombian Senator Federico Estrada Velez and his two bodyguards. Senator Estrada was an outspoken opponent of his country's drug barons.

22 MAY

● Conservative Party Chairman Kenneth Baker says that Labour's economic policies would result in millions of people paying more taxes and would 'jeopardize all the successes of this government'.

● Irishman Kevin Barry O'Donnell is arrested in a car with two loaded Kalashnikov rifles.

● Egyptian President Hosni Mubarak warns that the Middle East is in danger of plunging into war over Jewish immigration and the Israeli government's obstruction of peace efforts. He said: 'The immigration issue threatens to blow up the peace march and put the whole region on the verge of a new bloody confrontation.'

● NATO defence ministers declare that there is no longer a military threat to Western Europe from the Warsaw Pact and agree to a thorough review of the Alliance's strategies in response to the changed circumstances.

● British Coal confirms that it plans to cut at least 7,500 jobs over three years. National Union of Mineworkers president Arthur Scargill threatened industrial action and called for a 'sensible energy policy based on coal'.

● Pro-Western North Yemen and pro-Soviet South Yemen merge into a single republic. The unification had been the stated aim of Yemeni leaders for decades, but had been blocked by tribal and ideological conflicts.

23 MAY

● Trade and Industry Secretaries Nicholas Ridley and Lord Young are criticized by the Commons Trade and Industry Select Committee for their handling of the controversial takeover of the House of Fraser by the Fayed brothers in 1985.

● Police officers give Home Secretary David Waddington a silent reception at their annual conference in protest at his decision to veto a rent-allowance award.

● Jean-Marie Le Pen, the extreme right-wing French politician, is ordered to pay a token 1 franc damages to survivors of the Nazi concentration camps for calling the gas chambers a 'detail' of history.

● Soviet leader Mikhail Gorbachev accuses his rival Boris Yeltsin of trying to break up the Soviet Union.

● Western countries agree to end restrictions on high-technology exports to East Germany.

● Anti-government riots break out in Gabon after opposition leader Joseph Rendjambe is poisoned.

24 MAY

● The Labour Party publishes its pre-election manifesto which includes pledges of gradual tax increases; an environmental protection executive; increased emphasis on education; early entry into the EC Exchange Rate Mechanism; limited secondary strike action and pickets; private-sector investment in rail, road and communications; and an elected second chamber to replace the House of Lords. The manifesto also abandoned Labour's traditional policy of full employment.

● England's football manager Bobby Robson announces that he is resigning after the World Cup.

● The 50th anniversary of Dunkirk is marked by a re-enactment of the 'little ships' flotilla across the English Channel.

● Labour Environment spokesman Bryan Gould demands that Mrs Thatcher abandon her attachment to the car because of the environmental damage of car emissions.

● Veteran North Korean leader Kim Il Sung is elected for another four-year term as President at the age of 78.

● France sends 200 troops to its former West African colony of Gabon to protect French nationals after anti-government riots break out in the major cities. The number of French troops rises to 1,000 as French planes start evacuating the 20,000-strong French expatriate community.

25 MAY

● Mrs Thatcher, speaking at an international conference on global warming, issues a stark warning about the threat of environmental disaster, but says Britain will cut its carbon dioxide emissions only if other nations promise similar restraint.

● Panic buying sweeps the Soviet Union after Premier Nikolai Ryzhkov announces forthcoming price rises as part of an economic-reform package.

● Soviet leader Mikhail Gorbachev warns that if a united Germany becomes a member of NATO then the chance of building a new Europe would be 'wrecked' and the Soviet Union would be forced to rethink its foreign policy.

● PLO leader Yasser Arafat, speaking before a special session of the United Nations in Geneva, calls for a UN-sponsored force to protect Palestinians in the Israeli-occupied territories.

● 39 people are killed in Colombia by left-wing guerrillas and drug gunmen on the eve of the country's presidential elections.

● A rail strike cuts off Poland's key Baltic port of Gdansk. Prime Minister Tadeusz Mazoweicki warned that the strikes could 'destabilize the government'.

26 MAY

● Flights from Heathrow are disrupted after 7,000 British Airways engineers start an unofficial strike after an attempt by the company to impose new work patterns.

● Jailed Spanish terrorist José Manuel Sevillano dies after a 180-day hunger strike. He had been a member of the extreme-left Grapo revolutionary group. Spanish doctors stopped force feeding Sevillano after one of the medical team was assassinated.

● Joaquin Balaguer narrowly defeats Juan Bosch in presidential elections in the Dominican Republic.

● Colombian police discover 4 tons of explosives on the eve of the country's presidential elections.

● Jerry Richardson, the 'coach' of the Winnie Mandela 'football club', is found guilty of the murder of 14-year-old Stompie Moeketsi Seipei. In his summation, Justice O'Donovan implicitly found Mrs Mandela to have been an accomplice in the assaults on four boys.

● An estimated 300 Ethiopian students are arrested after anti-government demonstrations following the execution of 12 generals involved in a failed coup against President Mengistu Haile Mariam.

27 MAY

● Two Australian lawyers working in London are shot dead in the Dutch town of Roermond by IRA gunmen. The IRA later said they mistook the Australians for British servicemen. Acting Australian Foreign Affairs Minister Neal Blewett condemned the shootings as 'an outrageous and cowardly act of violence'.

● The opposition National League for Democracy wins a landslide victory in Burma's first multi-party elections in 30 years.

● Birlik, the main opposition group in the Soviet republic of Uzbekistan, calls for a gradual campaign for independence from the Soviet Union.

● Solidarity wins the majority of the seats in local authority elections in Poland. In Warsaw it won 303 out of 344 council seats.

● Swedish extremists opposed to immigration petrol bomb a refugee centre outside Stockholm. The centre housed refugees from Somalia, Ethiopia, Lebanon and Iran. No one was hurt in the attack.

● Liberian rebels fighting against the government of President Samuel Doe attack the town of Kakata, only 40 miles from the capital of Monrovia.

● The Pakistani government sends troops into Hyderabad and Karachi after clashes between police and demonstrators during which police opened fire and killed at least 80 people and wounded another 270.

28 MAY

● Northern Ireland Secretary Peter Brooke meets Irish Prime Minister Charles Haughey in Dublin and proposes a fresh framework for Anglo-Irish talks on Northern Ireland.

● 32 workers are evacuated by helicopter from the North Sea oil rig *Henry Goodrich* after inflammable liquid gas seeped into the drilling equipment.

● The all-woman crew of the racing yacht *Maiden*, skippered by Tracy Edwards, returns to a triumphant welcome at the end of the Whitbread Round the World Yacht Race. They were the first all-woman crew to sail around the world.

● 80,000 Armenians hold a demonstration to mark the anniversary of the independent Armenian Republic, which was in existence between 1918 and 1921. The demonstration followed a series of clashes between troops and Armenian nationalists in which at least 20 people died.

● Solidarity leader Lech Walesa persuades striking Polish railwaymen to suspend their indefinite freight stoppage.

● Yugoslav President Borisav Jovic warns that his country is on the brink of 'civil war' and 'foreign intervention' unless a new and tougher federal constitution is adopted.

29 MAY

● Boris Yeltsin is elected President of the giant Soviet republic of Russia, thus giving Mikhail Gorbachev's major opponent a powerful political base. Gorbachev, who was visiting Canada, said: 'We may be in for difficult times.'

● British inventor James Ashbey unveils the world's first three-dimensional television, which he named 'Deep Vision'.

● The British government warns the EC that it will reject any proposed Social Charter that includes restrictive legislation.

● The United States and Bolivia sign an agreement to use the Bolivian Army for the first time in Bolivia's fight against drugs. In return, the Bolivian government will receive US military aid worth $330.2 million.

● Liberia's anti-government rebel forces attack the country's main airport at Robertsfield outside the capital of Monrovia.

● Dominica's conservative Prime Minister Eugenia Charles is narrowly re-elected for a third consecutive term.

30 MAY

● France suspends all imports of British beef in response to the 'mad cow' disease scare.

● Alexander Yakovlev, one of Mikhail Gorbachev's closest advisers, publicly proposes that the Soviet Union be reorganized into a loose federation based on a new constitution.

● Boris Yeltsin says that the laws of the republic of Russia should have priority over Soviet laws. Yeltsin insisted, however, that he would not take the Russian republic out of the USSR.

● Arab leaders finish a summit in Baghdad with an attack on Israel's 'aggressive' policies and America's encouragement of Israeli 'expansionism'.

● Greece and the US initial a new eight-year agreement for the continued operation of two American military bases in Greece. Two other bases were closed as a result of Pentagon cutbacks.

● Veteran African statesman Julius Nyerere, aged 68, announces that he is retiring as head of Tanzania's ruling party. He resigned as President in 1985.

31 MAY

● The French government defies an EC ruling to 'immediately' revoke its ban on British beef imports. Government officials said the ban would remain in place until the commission could provide reassurances that 'lessen public anxiety' about the 'mad cow' disease.

● Soviet leader Mikhail Gorbachev and US President George Bush meet in Washington for three days of talks. A US government spokesman described the first day of talks as 'friendly and at times animated'.

● A United Nations report on global warming predicts that the homes of 30 million people will be engulfed by rising sea levels by the end of the 21st century unless controls are imposed to curb greenhouse gases.

● The Monopolies and Mergers Commission blocks the proposed purchase of the Bristol Evening Post Company by porn publisher David Sullivan. The commission said he was likely to damage 'the accurate presentation of news'.

● An American university professor, Gerard Michael Hoy, pleads guilty in a Boston court to charges of helping to develop high-technology laser weapons and rockets for the IRA.

● More than 115 people die in a Peruvian earthquake. The earthquake was Peru's worst for 20 years and buried four villages.

ARTS FACTFILE

LITERARY AWARDS

J.R. Ackerley Prize for Autobiography
(est. 1982)
PEN, 7 Dilke Street, Chelsea, London SW3 4JE, UK
Awarded to a literary biography.
1st Prize £500
1990 **Germaine Greer** *Daddy, We Hardly Knew You* (Hamish Hamilton)

Alexander Prize
The Literary Director, Royal Historical Society, University College London, Gower Street, London WC1E 6BT, UK
£100 and silver medal for an essay
1989 **Dr J.S.A. Adamson** *The Baronial Context of the English Civil War* (Transactions of the Royal Historical Society 5th series Vol. 40)

The Hans Christian Andersen Medals
(est. 1956)
British Section, Book Trust, Book House, 45 East Hill, London SW18 2QZ, UK
Biennial Award for children's fiction writer and an illustrator.
1990 winners:
Fiction: **Tormod Haugen**
Illustration: **Lisbeth Zwerger**

Angel Literary Awards
Caroline Gough, Angel Hotel, Angel Hill, Bury St Edmunds, Suffolk IP33 1LT, UK
Awarded to East Anglian writers.
1989 1st prize £1000 Fiction: **Rose Tremain** *Restoration* (Hamish Hamilton)
1st prize £500 Non-Fiction (Autobiography): **Margaret Bufford** *Celebration*

The Rosemary Arthur Annual National Award
(est. 1989)
National Poetry Foundation, 27 Mill Road, Fareham, Hampshire PO16 OTH, UK
The award, open to unpublished poets, consists of the complete funding of a book of the poet's work, a suitably inscribed brass and glass carriage clock and £100.
1990 **Robert Roberts** *Amphibious Landings*

Arts Council of Great Britain (Writers' Bursaries)
The Literature Department, Arts Council of Great Britain, 14 Gt Peter Street, London SW1 3NQ, UK
Ten bursaries for published writers who need finance for a period of concentrated work on their next book.
1989–90 **Carey Harrison, Moy McCrory, Nigel Watts, Helena Whitbread**

The Arts Council/An Chomhairle Ealaion, Ireland
The Arts Council (An Chomhairle Ealaion), 70 Merrion Square, Dublin 2, Ireland
1990 awards totalling IR£40,000
Bursaries for creative writers:

Roz Cowman (poet)	£4,000
Michael Davitt (poet in Irish)	£3,000
Anthony Glavin (poet)	£5,000
Mary Leland (fiction writer)	£3,000
Paula Meehan (poet)	£2,000
Joe O'Byrne (dramatist)	£3,000
Conor O'Callaghan (poet)	£2,000
Julie O'Callaghan (children's writer)	£2,500
Ronan Sheehan (fiction writer)	£5,000
Pádraig Standún (bilingual fiction writer and dramatist)	£5,000
Dolores Walshe (dramatist)	£2,000

Denis Devlin Memorial Award for Poetry:
Triennial award to an Irish citizen.
1st prize IR£1300

Macaulay Fellowship:
(Literature 1990, Visual Arts 1991, Music 1992)
Triennial award to a person under 30 years old (in exceptional circumstances under 35).
1st prize IR£4000
1990 **Eoin McNamee** (fiiction writer and dramatist)

Marten Toonder Award;
(Visual Arts 1990, Music 1991, Literature 1992)
Awarded to an Irish citizen.
1st prize IR£3000
1989 **John Banville**

An Duais don bhFiliocht i nGaelige (Prize for Poetry in Irish):
Triennial award.
1st prize IR£1300

Arvon Foundation International Poetry Competition
(est. 1980)
Arvon Foundation Poetry Competition, Kilnhurst, Kilnhurst Road, Todmorden, Lancashire OL14 6AX, UK
Biennial award for previously unpublished poems.
1st prize £5000
1989 **Sheldon Flory**

Authors' Club First Novel Award
(est. 1954)
Mrs Ridgeway, The Secretary, The Authors' Club, 40 Dover Street, London W1X 3RB, UK
£200 plus silver inscribed quill
1989 **Lindsey Davis** *The Silver Pigs* (Sidgwick)

Authors' Club Sir Banister Fletcher Award
(SEE ABOVE)
Most deserving book on architecture or the arts.
1st prize £200
1989 **John O'Nians** *Bearers of Meaning: The Classical Orders in Antiquity, The Middle Ages and the Renaissance* (CUP)

Authors' Club Nelson Hurst & Marsh Biography Award
(SEE ABOVE)
Biennial award for the most significant biography.
1st prize £3000 plus trophy
1989 **David Gilmore** *The Last Leopard* (Quartet)

Verity Bargate Award
(est. 1983)
Soho Poly Theatre, 16 Riding House Street, London W1P 7PD, UK
Annual award to a new play.
1st prize £1000
1989 **David Spencer** *Killing the Cat*

The Alice Hunt Bartlett Prize
Poetry Society, 21 Earls Court Square, London SW5 9DE, UK
For a volume of poetry consisting of 20 or more poems, or 400 lines.
1st prize £500
1988 **Ciaran Carson** *The Irish for No* (Bloodaxe)

H.E. Bates Short Story Competition
Tourist Information Centre, 21 St Giles Street, Northampton, Northamptonshire NN1 1JA, UK
1st prize £100
1989 **Patricia Tyrrell**

The Samuel Beckett Award
(est. 1983)
Frank Pike, Faber & Faber, 3 Queen Square, London WC1N 3AU, UK
Two 1st prizes of £1500
1988 Stage play: **Clare MacIntyre** *Low Level Panic*
Television play: **Peter Flannery** *The One about the Irishman* (a programme in the series Blind Justice)

David Berry Prize
Council of the Royal Historical Society, University College London, Gower Street, London WC1E 6BT, UK
Awarded to the author of an unpublished essay on Scottish History between James I and James VI.
1st prize £100
1988 **J. Goodare** *Parliamentary Taxation in Scotland, 1560–1603*

James Tait Black Memorial Prize
(est. 1918)
Prof. W.W. Robson, Department of English Literature, Edinburgh University, David Hume Tower, George Street, Edinburgh EH8 9JX, UK
Awards made to the best biography and to the best novel.
1989 £1500 Biography: **Ian Gibson** *Federico Garcia Lorca: A Life* (Faber)
£1500 Best Novel: **James Kelman** *A Disaffection* (Secker)

The Kathleen Blundell Trust
(est. 1987)
The Kathleen Blundell Trust, The Society of Authors, 84 Drayton Gardens, London SW10 9SB, UK
Grants for writers, under 40 years old, whose work has contributed to 'the greater understanding of existing social and economic organisation'.

Boardman Tasker Award for Mountain Literature
56 St Michael's Avenue, Bramhall, Stockport, Cheshire SK7 2PL
Awarded to a work of fiction, non-fiction or poetry concerning the mountain environment.
1989 **Joe Simpson** *Touching the Void*

Booker Prize for Fiction
(est. 26 Oct. 1968)
The Publicity Office, Book Trust, Book House, 45 East Hill, London SW18 2QZ, UK

1989 1st prize £20,000
Kazuo Ishiguro *The Remains of the Day* (Faber)
Margaret Atwood *Cat's Eye* (Bloomsbury)
John Banville *The Book of Evidence* (Secker)
Sybille Bedford *Jigsaw* (Hamish Hamilton)
James Kelman *A Disaffection* (Secker)
Rose Tremain *Restoration* (Hamish Hamilton)

Bridport Arts Centre Creative Writing Competition
The Arts Centre, South Street, Bridport, Dorset DT6 3NR, UK
Awards for unpublished poetry and short stories and, occasionally, plays.
1989
Poetry 1st prize £1000: **Judy Gahagan** *4 Apokalypsen*
Short story 1st prize £1000: **Ted Burford** *Downstairs*

Katharine Briggs Folklore Award
The Folklore Society, University College London, Gower Street, London WC1E 6BT, UK
1st prize £50 plus engraved goblet
1989 **Dr J.P. Mallory** *In Search of the Indo-Europeans* (Thames and Hudson)

Bristol Old Vic & HTV West Playwriting Competition
(est. 1987)
Playwriting Award, PO Box 60, Bristol BS99 7NS, UK
Awarded to a playwright over 18 years old.
1st prize £2000 plus trophy and production possibilities
1989 **Andrew Rattenbury** *Soundings*

The British Film Institute Book Award
(est. 1984)
Wayne Drew, Press Officer, British Film Institute, 21 Stephen Street, London W1P 1PL, UK
1989 **J. Finler** *The Hollywood Story* (Pyramid Books)
British Book: **James Robertson** *Hidden Cinema* (Routledge)

British (Granada) Press Awards
(est. 1962)
British Press Awards, Mirror Group Newspapers, Holborn Circus, London EC1P 1DQ, UK
Awarded to the journalists of the year.
1989
Journalist of the Year: **Philip Knightley** (The Sunday Times)
Reporter of the Year: **Ian Jack** (Observer)
International Reporter: **Jon Swain** (The Sunday Times)
Columnist of the Year: **Lord (Bill) Deedes** (Daily Telegraph)
David Holden Award: **David Marsh** (Bonn Correspondent, Financial Times)
Specialist Writer Award: **Roger Highfield** (Science Correspondent, Daily Telegraph)
Feature Writer: **Brian James** (The Times)
Colour Magazine Writer: **Malcom Macalister-Hall** (Telegraph Weekend Magazine)
Arthur Sandles Award (travel writing): **Michael Watkins** (The Times)
News Photographer: **David Cairns** (Today)
Critic: **Brian Sewell** (Art Critic, Evening Standard)
Sports Journalist: **Frank Keating** (Guardian)
Young Journalist Award: **Christina Lamb** (Financial Times)
Graphic Artist: **Alan Gilliland** (Daily Telegraph)
Campaigning Journalist of the Year: **Peter Trollope & Andrew Byrne** (Liverpool Echo)
Provincial Journalist of the Year: **Tony Harney & Angela Barnes** (Yorkshire Evening Post)

John W. Campbell Memorial Award
Prof. T.A. Shippey, Secretary of the JWC Award, School of English, Leeds University, Leeds LS2 9JT, UK
A stone/bronze sculpture is awarded to the best science-fiction book of the year.
1988 **Bruce Sterling** *Islands in the Net*

The Cheltenham Prize
Cheltenham Festival of Literature, c/o Town Hall, Cheltenham, Gloucestershire GL50 1QA, UK
1st prize of £250 awarded a month before the festival for a recently published work which 'has not received its due acclaim'.
1989 **Medbh McGuckian** *On Ballycastle Beach*

Children's Book Award
(est. 1980)
(Federation of Children's Book Groups)
Jenny Blanch, 30 Senneleys Park Road, Northfield, Birmingham B31 1AL, UK
Awarded for the best work of fiction for children under 14 years old.
1st prize certificate
1989 **Roald Dahl** *Matilda* (ill. Q. Blake) (Cape)

Cholmondeley Awards
(est. 1965)
The Society of Authors, 84 Drayton Gardens, London SW10 9SB, UK
An open non-competitive poetry award totalling £6000.
1989 **Peter Didsbury**
Douglas Dunn
E.J. Scovell

Arthur C. Clarke Award
c/o Science Fiction Foundation, NE London Polytechnic, Longbridge Road, Dagenham, Essex RM8 2AS, UK
Awarded for the best science-fiction book of the year.
1st prize £1000
1989 **Jeff Ryman** *The Child Garden* (Unwin Hyman)

Collins Biennial Religious Book Award
(est. 1969)
Leslie Walmsley, William Collins plc, 8 Grafton Street, London W1X 3LA, UK
Awarded for a book which has contributed most to the relevance of Christianity in the modern world.
1st prize £2000
1989 **Archbishop Warlock** *Better Together* (Hodder)

Commonwealth Poetry Prize
Prize Administrator, Commonwealth Institute, Kensington High Street, London W8 6NQ, UK
Regional winners:
1989 **Bronwen Wallace** (Canada) *The Stubborn Particulars of Grace*
Kofi Awoonor (Ghana) *Until the Morning After: Collected Poems 1963–85*
Sujata Bhatt (India) *Bruniziem*
Allen Curnow (New Zealand) *Continuum: New and Later Poems 1972–88*
John Heath-Stubbs (UK) *Collected Poems 1943–87*

Commonwealth Writers' Prize
(est. 1987)
Commonwealth Foundation, Marlborough House, Pall Mall, London SW1Y 5HY, UK
Awards for the best work of fiction and for the best first published book written by a citizen of the Commonwealth.
Fiction: 1st prize £10,000
First Book: 1st prize £1000
1989 Fiction: **Janet Frame** *The Carpathians* (Century Hutchinson)
First Book: **Bonnie Bernard** *Women of Influence* (Coteau Books, Canada)

The Constable Trophy
Book Trust, Book House, 5 East Hill, London SW18 2QZ, UK
Biennial for an unpublished novel by a writer living in the North of England.
1989 **Petronella Pulsford** *Lee's Ghost*

Thomas Cook Book Awards
(est. 1980)
Book Trust, Book House, 45 East Hill, London SW18 2QZ, UK
Narrative travel book 1st prize £7500
Guide book 1st prize £2500
Illustrated travel book £1000 (est. 1988)
1989 Travel Book: **Paul Theroux** *Riding the Iron Rooster* (Hamish Hamilton)
Guide Book: **John & Pat Underwood** *Landscapes of Madeira* (Sunflower)
Illustrated Travel: **Dr Richard B. Fisher** *The Marco Polo Expedition* (Hodder)

The Duff Cooper Memorial Prize
(est. 1954)
Viscount Norwich, 24 Blomfield Road, London W9 1AD, UK
Annual award for a book in the genre of biography, history, politics or poetry.
1st prize approx. £250
1989 **Ian Gibson** *Federico Garcia Lorca: A Life*

The Rose Mary Crawshay Prizes
(est. 1888)
The British Academy, 20–21 Cornwall Terrace, London NW1 4QP, UK
Awarded for a historical or critical work by a woman of any nationality on English Literature (preference shown to a work on Keats, Byron or Shelley).
1st prize £600, or two prizes of £300
1989 **Mrs Margaret Smith** *Charlotte Bronte's The Professor* (OUP)
Mrs Valerie Eliot *The Letters of T.S. Eliot 1888–1922* (Faber)

CWA Cartier Diamond Dagger Award
(est. 1986)
Crime Writers' Association, PO Box 172, Tring, Hertfordshire HP23 5LP, UK
Awarded for excellence in the genre of crime fiction.
1989 **Dick Francis**

CWA John Creasey Memorial Award
(est. 1973)
(SEE ABOVE)
Awarded for the best first crime novel.
1989 **Annette Roome** *A Real Shot in the Arm* (Hodder)

CWA Gold Dagger Award and Silver Dagger Award
(est. 1955)
(SEE ABOVE)
Awarded for the best piece of crime fiction.
1989 Gold: **Colin Dexter** *The Wench is Dead* (Macmillan)
Silver: **Desmond Lowden** *The Shadow Run* (Deutsch)

CWA Gold Dagger Award for Non-Fiction
(est. 1977)
(SEE ABOVE)
Awarded for the best non-fiction crime book.
1989 **Robert Lindsay** *A Gathering of Saints*

CWA Last Laugh Award
(est. 1989)
(SEE ABOVE)

In 1988 *Punch* sponsored a prize for the funniest crime book of the year. In 1989 this was superseded by the Last Laugh Award.
1989 (Last Laugh) **Mike Ripley** *Angel Touch*

Deloitte–Bookseller Award
(est. 1987)
Victoria Pugh, The Media Group, Deloitte Haskins & Sells, PO Box 207, 128 Queen Victoria Street, London EC4P 4JX, UK
Awarded for the book with the best cover design.
1st prize £1000
1989 **Jeff Fisher & Chris Jones** *Soho Square* (Bloomsbury)

The Isaac Deutscher Memorial Prize
(est. 1968)
Isaac Deutscher Memorial Prize, c/o Gerhard Wilke, 75 St Gabriel's Road, London NW2 4DU, UK
Awarded to the author of a work in the Marxist tradition of Isaac Deutscher.
1st prize £100
1989 **Terry Eagleton** *The Ideology of the Aesthetic* (Blackwell)

The Earthworm Award
The Arts for the Earth, Friends of the Earth, 26–28 Underwood Street, London N1 7JQ, UK
Awarded for environmentally conscious children's literature.
1st prize £1000
1989 **Judy Allen** *Awaiting Developments* (J. MacRae)

Mary Elgin Award
Dilly Kay, Hodder & Stoughton, 47 Bedford Square, London WC18 3DP, UK
Awarded to talented new writers on Hodder & Stoughton's list.
1st prize £50
1989 No award

Emil Award
(SEE MASCHLER, KURT)

The European Poetry Translation Prize
(est. 1983)
The Poetry Society, 21 Earls Court Road, London SW5 9DE, UK
Biennial award for the best poetry translation into English from a European language.
1st prize £500
1989 **David Luke** *Goethe's Faust* (OUP)

The Geoffrey Faber Memorial Prize
(est. 1963)
Faber & Faber Ltd., 3 Queen Square, London WC1N 3AU, UK
Awarded alternately for a volume of verse or prose judged to be of the greatest literary merit, by a writer under 40.
1st prize £1000
1989 **David Profumo** *Sea Music* (Secker)

The Eleanor Farjeon Award
(est. 1965)
Jill Coleman, Secretary (Children's Book Circle), A.& C. Black, 35 Bedford Row, London WC1R 4JH, UK
Awarded for distinguished services in the field of children's books.
1st prize £750 (minimum)
1990 **Jill Bennett**

Prudence Farmer Poetry Prize
(est. 1974)
New Statesman, Foundation House, Perseverance Works, 38 Kingsland Road, London E2 8DQ, UK
Awarded annually for the best poem published in the previous year (July to July) by *New Statesman and Society*.
1st prize £100
1989 **Jo Shapcott** *Love Song with a Flock of Sheep*

The Fawcett Book Prize
(est. 1982)
Joint General Secretary, The Fawcett Society, 46 Harleyford Road, London SE11 5AY, UK
Awarded for the book 'which does most to illuminate women's position in society today'. Awarded for fiction and non-fiction in alternate years.
1st prize £500
1989 **Stevie Davis** *Boy Blue* (Women's Press)

The Kathleen Fidler Award
Dr Anne Smith, Book Trust Scotland, 15a Lynedoch Street, Glasgow G3 6EF, UK
Awarded for a first unpublished novel for the 8–12 year olds.
1st prize £1,000
1989 **Clare Bevan** *Mightier than the Sword* (Blackie)

The John Florio Prize
K. Pool, The Translators' Association, 84 Drayton Gardens, London SW10 9SB, UK
Biennial award for the best translation into English of a twentieth-century Italian literary work.
1st prize £700.
1988 **J.G. Nichols** trans. *The Colloquies by Guido Gozzano (Carcanet)*

E.M. Forster Award
American Academy and Institute of Arts and Letters, 633 West 155th Street, New York NY 10032, USA
Awarded to enable an English writer to stay in the United States.
1989 **A.N. Wilson**

Glenfiddich Awards
11a West Halkin Street, London SW1X 8JL, UK
Awarded to the writer of the best book on food and drink. Each category winner receives £100, a gold medal and a case of Glenfiddich malt whisky. The overall winner receives a cheque for £750 and the Glenfiddich trophy.
1989 Food: **Richard Stein** *English Seafood Cookery* (Penguin)
Wine: **Charles Metcalfe & Kathryn McWhirter** *The Wines of Spain & Portugal* (Salamander Books)

Golden Pen of Freedom
International Federation of Newspaper Publishers (FIEJ), 6 rue du Faubourg, Poissonière, 75010 Paris, France
Awarded to a group or individual whose writings have contributed most to press freedoms.
1990 **Luis Gabriel Cano** (Publisher of the Colombian daily newspaper *El Espectador*)

Prix Goncourt
(est. 1903)
M. Francois Nourissier, Secretaire, Academie Goncourt, Le Figaro, 25 Avenue Matignon, 75081 Paris Cedex 02, France
One of the most prestigious of all literary prizes.

The winner still receives only 50 francs for the best French prose work.
1989 **Jean Vautrin** *Un grand pas vers le Bon Dieu*

Eric Gregory Trust Fund
(est. 1960)
The Society of Authors, 84 Drayton Gardens, London SW10 9SB, UK
Awarded for the encouragement of poets under 30.
Prizes worth over £20,000 in total
1989 **Gerard Woodward**
David Morley
Katrina Porteous
Paul Henry

Guardian Award for Children's Fiction
(est. 1967)
Stephanie Nettell, 24 Weymouth Street, London W1N 3FA, UK
Awarded for an outstanding work of children's fiction.
1st prize £500
1989 **Geraldine McCaughrean** *A Pack of Lies* (Oxford)

Guardian Fiction Prize
119 Farringdon Road, London EC1R 3ER, UK
Awarded for a novel of 'originality and promise'.
1st prize £1000
1989 **Carol Lake** *Portraits from a Midland City* (Bloomsbury)

Guinness Peat Aviation Irish Book of the Year Award
GPA House, Shannon, County Clare, Eire
1989 IR£50,000 (£47,000): **John Banville** *The Book of Evidence*
First Novel Award IR£20,000: **Vincent McDonnell** *The Broken Commandment*
IR£1000 (each): **Seamus Heaney, Shane Connaughton, Aidan Matthews, Roy Foster**

Thomas Hardy Society Book Prize
Dr James Gibson, 4 Gore Mews, Canterbury, Kent CT1 1JB, UK
Biennial award to the writer or editor of a book which contributes most to our appreciation of Hardy's writings and/or life.
1st prize £200
1988 **Professors Richard Purdy & Michael Millgate** *The Collected Letters of Thomas Hardy* (OUP)

The Hawthornden Prize
(est. 1919)
Hawthornden Castle International Retreat for Writers, Hawthornden Castle, Lasswade, Midlothian EH18 1EG, UK
The oldest British literary prize is awarded for the best work of fiction (including biography, history, essays, travel literature and verse) by a British author under 41 years of age.
1st prize £750
1989 **Alan Bennett** *Talking Heads* (BBC)

David Higham Prize for Fiction
(est. 1975)
Book Trust, Book House, 45 East Hill, London SW18 2QZ, UK
Awarded for the best first novel or book of short stories by a member of the British Commonwealth.
1st prize £1,000
1989 **Timothy O'Grady** *Motherland* (Chatto)

Georgette Heyer Historical Novel Prize
(est. 1977)
Mrs Jill Black, The Bodley Head, Random Century House, 20 Vauxhall Bridge Road, London SW1V 2SA, UK
Awarded for the best unpublished historical novel.
1st prize £5000
1989 **Janet Broomfield** *A Fallen Land*

The Calvin and Rose G. Hoffman Memorial Prize for Distinguished Publication on Christopher Marlowe
The Headmaster, The King's School, Canterbury CT1 2ES, UK
1st prize £7100
1989 **Professor Kurt Tetzeli von Rosador** (Univ. of Munster)

Winifred Holtby Memorial Prize
(est. 1966)
The Royal Society of Literature, 1 Hyde Park Gardens, London W2 2LT, UK
Awarded for the best regional novel of the year.
1st prize £500
1989 **Hilary Mantel** *Fludd*

The *Independent*/Fodor's Travel Writing Awards
(est. 1990)
The *Independent*/Fodor's Travel Writing Awards, The *Independent*, 40 City Road, London EC1Y 2DB, UK
Awarded for a piece of travel writing on a prescribed theme. Submissions by students judged in a separate category.
1st prize: Adventure holiday for two in northern Thailand
1st prize (students): Trailfinders round-the-world ticket

Institute of Journalists Gold Medal
(est. 1963)
Institute of Journalists, 1 Whitehall Place, London SW1A 2HE, UK
Awarded for outstanding service to journalism and promotion of the freedom of the press.
1989 No award

International Book Award
(est. 1973)
UNESCO, International Book Committee, Place de Fontenoy, 75700 Paris, France
Awarded to a group or individual for outstanding service to the cause of books.
1989 **Asian Cultural Centre for UNESCO** (Tokyo)

International Grand Prize for Poetry
(est. 1956)
Maison Internationale de la Poesie, 147 Chaussée de Maecht, 1030 Brussels, Belgium
Awarded for the published works of an internationally renowned poet.
1988 André du Buchet

Mary Vaughan Jones Award
Welsh National Centre for Children's Literature, Castell Brychan, Aberystwyth, Dyfed SY23 2JB, UK
Triennial award for outstanding contribution to Welsh children's literature.
1st prize £600 plus silver trophy
1988 **Emily Huws**

Sir Peter Kent Conservation Book Prize
(est. 1987)
The Book Trust, Book House, 45 East Hill, London SW18 2QZ, UK
Awarded for the best book on environment issues.
1st prize £2000
1989 **Philip Waire** *Operation Otter* (Chatto)

Lamberts Book of the Year Award
Editor, Journal of Alternative Medicine, Mariner House, 53A High Street, Bagshot, Surrey GU19 5AH
Awarded for outstanding contribution to the cause of alternative medicine
Prize of £500 plus trophy

Martin Luther King Memorial Prize
John Brunner, The Martin Luther King Memorial Prize, c/o NatWest Bank, 7 Fore Street, Chard, Somerset TA20 1PJ, UK
Awarded for a work reflecting the ideals of Martin Luther King.
1st prize £100
1989 **Taylor Branch** *Parting the Waters* (Macmillan)

Kraszna–Kransz Award: Best Book on Photography
John Chittock, Kraszna–Kransz Foundation, 37 Gower Street, London WC1E 6HH, UK
Biennial award of £5000
1988 **Paul Barkshire** *Unexplored London* (Lennard Publishing)

The Library Association Besterman Medal
The Library Association, Ridgmount Street, London WC1E 7AE, UK
Awarded for the best bibliography or guide to literature.
1989 **Philip O'Brien** *T.E. Lawrence: A Bibliography* (St Paul's Bibliography)

The Library Association Carnegie Medal
(SEE ABOVE)
Awarded for the best children's book.
1989 **Geraldine McCaughrean** *A Pack of Lies* (OUP)

The Library Association Kate Greenaway Medal
(SEE ABOVE)
Awarded to the best children's book illustrator.
1989 **Michael Foreman** *War Boy* (Pavilion)

The Library Association McColvin Medal
(SEE ABOVE)
Awarded for the most outstanding reference book.
1989 **Christopher Hibbert** (ed.) *Encyclopedia of Oxford* (Macmillan)

The Library Association Wheatley Medal
(SEE ABOVE)
Awarded for the best index.
1989 **Bobby Burke** for the index to *Halsbury's Laws of England* (4th edn, Butterworth)

Roger Machell Prize
(est. 1986)
Society of Authors, 84 Drayton Gardens, London SW10 9SB, UK
Awarded for the best book on the performing arts.
1st prize £2000
1989 **H.C. Robbins Landon** *1791: Mozart's Last Year* (Thames & Hudson)

The Macmillan Prize for a Children's Picture Book
Publicity Manager, Macmillan Children's Books, 18–21 Cavaye Place, London SW10 9PG, UK
Awarded for the best children's book illustrations by students in higher education.
1st prize £500
1989 **Amanda Harvey** (Chelsea School of Art)

Macmillan Silver Pen Awards for Fiction
(est. 1969)
PEN, 7 Dilke Street, Chelsea, London SW3 4JE, UK
Awarded for an outstanding collection of short stories.
1st prize £500
1990 **V.S. Pritchett** *A Careless Widow* (Chatto)

Kurt Maschler Emil Award
(est. 1982)
The Book Trust, Book House, 45 East Hill, London SW18 2QZ, UK
Awarded for a children's book of excellence in text and illustration.
1st prize £1000
1989 **Martin Waddell** – text and **Barbara Firth** – illustration *The Park in the Dark* (Walker)

Somerset Maugham Trust Awards
(est. 1947)
The Society of Authors, 84 Drayton Gardens, London SW10 9SB, UK
Awarded to British writers (under 35 years of age) of any promising literary work except dramatic pieces.
Prize – approx. £12,000 to be used for a period or periods of foreign travel.
1989 **Rupert Christiansen** *Romantic Affinities* (Bodley Head)
Alan Hollinghurst *The Swimming Pool Library* (Chattoo)
Deidre Madden *The Birds of the Innocent Wood* (Faber)

The McKitterick Prize
Society of Authors, 84 Drayton Gardens, London SW10 9SB, UK
Awarded to first novels by people over the age of 40.
1st prize £5000
1990 **Simon Mawer** *Chimera* (Hamish Hamilton)

The Enid McLeod Literary Prize
The Secretary of the Franco-British Society, Room 636, Linen Hall, 162–168 Regent Street, London W1R 5TB, UK
Awarded to the work of literature that contributes most to Franco-British understanding.
1st prize £100
1989 **Allan Massie** *A Question of Loyalties* (Century Hutchinson)

McVities Scottish Writer of the Year Award
Alan Clark, Michael Kelly Associates, 95 Bothwell Street, Glasgow G2 2BX, UK
1st prize £5000
1989 **Alan Bold** *MacDiarmid* (John Murray)

MIND Book of the Year – Allen Lane Award
(est.1981)
MIND, 22 Harley Street, London W1N 2ED, UK
Awarded to a book which advances public understanding of mental illness and handicap.
1st prize £1000
1989 No award as no book was found to meet the criterion

The Mother Goose Award
(est. 1979)
Sally Grindley, Books for Children, Park House, Dollar Street, Cirencester, Gloucestershire GL7 2AN, UK
£1000 plus bronze egg for an author's first major publication of a children's book
1990 **David Hughes** *Strat and Chatto* (Walker)

Shiva Naipaul Memorial Prize
(est. 1985)
The Spectator, 56 Doughty Street, London WC1N 2LL, UK
Awarded to the writer (under 35) of the best travel essay.
1st prize £1000
1989 **William Vollmann** *Amortortak* (Deutsch)

National Poetry Competition
National Poetry Competition, National Poetry Centre, 21 Earls Court Square, London SW5 9DE, UK
1989 1st prize £2000: **William Scammell** (Cumbria)

NCR Book Award for Non-Fiction
(est. 1987)
The Administrator, NCR Book Award, 206 Marylebone Road, London NW1 6LY, UK
Awarded for 'originality of thought, elegance of expression, and the ability of the author to express his or her knowledge of the subject to the widest possible readership'.
1st prize £25,000
1990 **Simon Schama** *Citizens: A Chronicle of the French Revolution* (Viking)

Nobel Prize for Literature
(est. 1901)
Swedish Academy, Kallargrand 4, S-111 29 Stockholm, Sweden
The income from the trust fund, established by the Swedish scientist Alfred Nobel, is distributed annually amongst six prizes: a) Physics; b) Chemistry; c) Physiology or Medicine; d) Economics; e) Peace; f) Literature.
1st prize £280,000
1989 **Camilo Jose Cela** Spain

The Noma Award for Publishing in Africa
(est. 1979)
H.M. Zell, The African Book Publishing Record, PO Box 56, Oxford, Oxfordshire OX1 3EL, UK
Awarded to an outstanding new book published on the continent of Africa.
1st prize $5000
1989 **Chenjerai Hove** (Zimbabwe) *Bones: A Novel* (Harare: Baobab Books)

Northern Arts Writers Award
Northern Arts, 10 Osborne Terrace, Jesmond, Newcastle upon Tyne NE2 1NZ, UK
Offered to established authors resident in the Northern Arts region on the basis of literary merit and financial need.
1989 recipients of 1 month residency: **David Imand** ed. *Panurge* magazine
Peter Mortimore ed. *Won* magazine
Anne Spillard fiction writer
1989 recipients of cash award: **John Murray**
Meg Peacocke
Linda France
Fiona Hall

Young Observer National Children's Poetry Competition
Sue Matthias, Observer Magazine, Chelsea Bridge House, Queenstown Road, London SW8 4NN, UK
£500 1st prize awarded for poems written on specified subjects in each category.
1989 Under-10s: **Grace Trinnaman** *The Burst of Light*
11–14: **Avril Huston** *Milking*
15–18: **Kerry Carson** *Mourne*
Schools prize: **Halesworth Middle School**
Painter Ash C.P. School
Thames Water Trophy: **Eynesbury C. of E. Primary School**

Odd Fellows (Manchester Unity) Social Concern Annual Book Awards
(est. 1977)
Book Trust, Book House, 45 East Hill, London SW18 2QZ, UK
Awarded for a book or pamphlet (10,000 words min.) which covers an area of social concern.
1st prize £2000
1989 **Catherine Caufield** *Multiple Exposures* (Secker)

Oppenheim-John Downes Memorial Trust
The Oppenheim–John Downes Memorial Trust, c/o 36 Whitefriars Street, London EC4Y 8BH, UK
Awarded to impoverished artists over 30.
Award varies from £50-£1500, depending on need.

Outposts Poetry Competition
Howard Sergeant, 72 Burwood Road, Walton-on-Thames, Surrey KT12 4AL, UK
Award for the best unpublished poem of less than 40 lines.
1st prize £1000
1989 **Christina Corser** *Meeting Elizabeth Bishop*

Catherine Pakenham Memorial Award
(est. 1970)
The Literary Editor, The Evening Standard, Northcliff House, 2 Derry Street, London W8 5EE, UK
Awarded to young women journalists for a newspaper article, TV or radio script.
1st prize £500
1989 **Amanda Mitchison** *Seeing Justice Done*

Parents Magazine Best Book for Babies Award
(est. 1985)
Book Trust, Book House, 45 East Hill, London SW18 2QZ, UK
Awarded for the best book for under-4s, babies and toddlers.
1st prize £1000
1990 **Martin Waddell** and **Penny Dale (illust.)** *Rosie's Babies* (Walker)

Peterloo Poets Open Poetry Competition
(est. 1986)
Peterloo Poets, 2 Kelly Gardens, Calstock, Cornwall PL18 9SA, UK
Awards in two categories: for best poem and best poem submitted by a competitor of Afro-Caribbean or Asian origin
1st prize £1000 and poem published in The *Guardian*
Afro-Caribbean or Asian prize £500 and poem published in The *Guardian*
1990 1st prize: **Maureen Wilkinson** *The Amnesiac's Dream*
Afro-Caribbean/Asian Prize: **David Simon** *Have Pity*
Mimi Khalvati *Amanuensis*

The Portico Prize
(est. 1985)
Portico Library, 57 Mosley Street, Manchester M2 3HY, UK
Awarded for a work of general interest and literary merit set in North-West England.
1st prize £1500

1989 **Anthony Burgess** *Any Old Iron* (Century Hutchinson)

Pulitzer Prizes in Letters
(est. 1917) (USA)
Secretary, Pulitzer Prize, Pulitzer Board, Columbia University, 702 Journalism Building, New York NY 10027, USA
In addition to the 13 different journalistic awards and an award for music, awards are also made to American authors in the following six literary genres: a) fiction; b) drama; c) history; d) biography or autobiography; e) poetry (1918/1919 gifted by the Poetry Society); f) general non-fiction (1962–).

1989 a) **Anne Tyler** *Breathing Lessons*
b) **Wendy Wasserstein** *The Heidi Chronicles*
c) **Taylor Branch** *Parting the Waters: America in the King Years 1954–63*
James M. McPherson *Battle Cry of Freedom: The Civil War Era*
d) **Richard Ellman** *Oscar Wilde*
e) **Richard Wilbur** *New and Collected Poems*
f) **Neil Sheehan** *A Bright Shining Lie: John Paul Vann and America in Vietnam*

Queen's Gold Medal for Poetry
(est. 1933)
The Queen occasionally awards gold medals to deserving poets, the potential recipients of which are chosen by a group of writers, under the chairmanship of the Poet Laureate.
1988 **Derek Walcott**

Radio Times Drama Awards
(est. 1973)
Radio Times, 35 Marylebone High Street, London W1M 4AA, UK
Biennial award for an original work for radio and television, which has not been previously produced. Awards totalling £15,000
1988 Television: **Martyn Hesford** and **Philip Goulding** (joint first)
Radio: **Patricia Finney**

Radio Times Radio Comedy Awards
(est. 1985)
(SEE ABOVE)
Awarded for an original half-hour radio script. Awards totalling £5000
1989 Max Russell

Trevor Reese Memorial Prize
(est. 1979)
The Director, Institute of Commonwealth Studies, 27–28 Russell Square, London WC1B 5DS, UK
Biennial award for an historical monograph on Imperial or Commonwealth history.
1st prize £500
1988 **James Belich** *New Zealand Wars* (Auckland Univ. Press)

The Margaret Rhondda Award
(est. 1968)
The Society of Authors, 84 Drayton Gardens, London SW10 9SB, UK
Triennial trust award to a woman writer to aid a journalistic research project.
1st prize £500
1990 **Mary London**
Clare Jenkins

John Llewellyn Rhys Memorial Prize
(est. 1942)
John Llewellyn Rhys Memorial Prize, c/o Book Trust, Book House, 45 East Hill, London SW18 2QZ, UK
Awarded to the writer (under 35) of the most promising and memorable literary work of the year.
1989 **Claire Harman** *Sylvia Townsend Warner* (Chatto)

Romantic Novelists' Association Major Award
(est. 1960)
(a.k.a. Boots Romantic Novel of the Year)
Hon. Secretary, Mrs Dorothy Entwistle, 20 First Avenue, Amersham, Buckinghamshire HP7 9BJ, UK
Awarded for the best romantic novel published in the year.
1st prize £5000
1989 **Sarah Woodhouse** *The Peacock Feather* (Century Hutchinson)

The Rooney Prize for Irish Literature
(est. 1976)
J.A. Sherwin, Strathin Enterprises Ltd, Strathin, Templecarrig, Delgany, County Wicklow, Eire
Awarded to encourage young Irish writers, and given either as a form of sponsorship or as an award for a particular piece of work.
1st prize IR£3000
1989 **Robert McLiam Wilson** *Ripley Bogle*

Routledge Ancient History Prize
Richard Stoneman, Senior Editor, Routledge, 11 New Fetter Lane, London EC4P 4EE, UK
1st prize of £500 plus publication by Routledge awarded for the unpublished work that makes the best contribution to understanding the history of the Greek and Roman world.
1989 **Guy Rogers** (Wellesley College, Massachusetts) 'The Foundation Myths of the Roman City of Ephesus'

The Royal Society of Literature Award under the W.H. Heinemann bequest
(est. 1923)
The Royal Society of Literature, 1 Hyde Park Gardens, London W2 2LT, UK
Awarded for a work of outstanding literary merit in any genre, but especially poetry, criticism, history and biography.
1989 **Roy Fuller** *Available for Dreams* (Collins Harvill)
Kit Wright *Short Afternoon* (Century Hutchinson)

Runciman Award
(est. 1985)
Book Trust, Book House, 45 East Hill, London SW18 2QZ, UK
Awarded for a literary work concerning Greece.
1st prize £1000
1989 **Rowland J. Mainstone** *Hagia Sophia: Architecture, Structure, and Liturgy of Justinian's Great Church* (Thames & Hudson)

The Saltire Society & The Scotsman Scottish Literary Award
The Saltire Society, 9 Fountain Close, High Street, Edinburgh EH1 1TF, UK
Two awards made to Scottish writers of: a) Scottish Book of the Year; b) Scottish First Book of the Year.
1989 Scottish Book of the Year: **Alan Massey** *A Question of Loyalty* (Hutchinson)
Scottish First Book of the Year: **Sian Hayton** *Cells of Knowledge* (Polygon)

The Science Book Prizes
COPUS, The Royal Society, 6 Carlton House Terrace, London SW1Y 5AG, UK
Prizes are awarded in three categories for popular non-fiction science and technology books which contribute most to the public understanding of science.
The Rhone-Poulenc Prize (£10,000) for books intended for general readership.
The COPUS/Science Museum Prize (£10,000) covers books written for under-14s and under-8s.
1989 Rhone-Poulenc Prize **Roger Penrose** *The Emperor's New Mind* (OUP)
Under-14 **Susan Mayes** *The Starting Point Science Series* (Usborne Publishing Ltd)
Under-8 **Ian Ridpath** *The Giant Book of Space* (Hamlyn)

The Schlegel-Tieck Prize
(est. 1964)
K. Pool, The Translators Association, 84 Drayton Gardens, London SW10 9SB, UK
Awarded for English translations of twentieth-century German literature.
1st prize £2200
1989 **Peter Tegel** trans. *The Snake Tree* by Ywe Tim (Picador)
Quentin Hoare trans. *The Town Park and Other Stories* by Herman Grab (Verso)

The Scott Moncrieff Prize
(est. 1964)
(SEE ABOVE)
Awarded for English translations of twentieth-century French literature.
1st prize £1400
1989 **Derk Mahon** *The Selected Poems of Phillippe Jaccotet* (Viking)

Scottish Arts Council Awards
Literature Department, The Scottish Arts Council, 19 Charlotte Square, Edinburgh EH2 4DF, UK
Usually awarded to Scottish writers, in any genre.
Autumn and spring book awards of £750
Previous winners:
Spring
1989 **Alan Bold** *MacDiarmid* (John Murray)
William Donaldson *The Jacobite Song* (Aberdeen University Press)
David Gilmour *The Last Leopard: A Life of Guiseppe di Lampedusa* (Quartet)
David Groves *James Hogg: The Growth of a Writer* (Scottish Academic Press)
Frances Hendry *Quest for a Maid* (Canongate)
Simon Louvish *City of Blok* (Collins)
Autumn
1989 **John Glenday** *The Apple Ghost* (Peterloo Poets)
James Kelman *A Disaffection* (Secker)
Ludovic Kennedy *On My Way to the Club* (Collins)
Frank Kuppner *A Very Quiet Street* (Polygon)
Carl MacDougall *Stone over Water* (Secker)
Candia McWilliam *A Little Stranger* (Bloomsbury)
Deborah Randall *The Sin Eater* (Bloodaxe)

SCSE Book Prizes
Prof. G.R. Batho, University of Durham, Leazes Rd, Durham DH1 1TA, UK
Awarded for the best education book.
1st prize £500

The Signal Poetry for Children Award
The Thimble Press, Lockwood, Station Road, South Woodchester, Stroud, Gloucestershire GL5 5EQ, UK
Awarded for an outstanding book of children's poetry (including anthologies).
1st prize £100
1989 **James Berry** *When I Dance* (Hamish Hamilton)

The André Simon Memorial Fund Book Awards
(est. 1977)
Tessa Hayward, 61 Church Street, Isleworth, Middlesex TW7 6BE, UK
Awarded for the best books on food and on drink.
Two prizes of £1500 each
1989 Food: **Peter Graham** *Classic Cheese Cookery* (Penguin)
Drink: **Tom Stevenson** *Sotheby's World Wine Encyclopedia* (Dorling Kindersley)

Smarties Prize
(est. 1985)
Book Trust, Book House, 45 East Hill, London SW18 2QZ, UK
Awarded to the best book for primary school children.
1st prize £8000
1989 1st prize – under 5s: **Michael Rosen** and **Helen Oxenbury** *We're Going on a Bear Hunt* (Walker)

The W.H. Smith Annual Literary Award
(est. 1959)
Michael S. Mackenzie, W.H. Smith & Son Ltd, Strand House, 7 Holbein Place, London SW1W 8NR, UK
Awarded to any book which has made an outstanding contribution to English Literature.
1st prize £10,000
1990 **V.S. Pritchett** *A Careless Widow* (Chatto)

The W.H. Smith Illustration Awards
Book Trust, Book House, 45 East Hill, London SW18 2QZ, UK
Awarded to the best illustrated book and the best illustrated magazine cover.
Book 1st prize £1000 plus £500 commended winners
Magazine 1st prize £1000 plus £500 commended winners
1989 Book: **Jeff Fisher** *A Better Beast of Burden* (New Scientist)
Magazine: **Richard Parent** 'Breakdown', *Director* vol. 41

The W.H. Smith Young Writers' Competition
Public Relations, W.H. Smith, 7 Holbein Place, London SW1W 8NR, UK
Awards for poetry or prose by writers under 17 years.
Prizes totalling £4000 (63 individual prize winners are published in paperback)
1989 Special prizewinners £100: **Kate Romany Beckinsale** *Hungerfruit/Heartsearch Nine Left One Departed*
Toby Peter Nicholson *An Early Frost/The Boulder Wall At Dummerdale*
Arjune Sen *A Test of Faith*

Southern Arts Literature Prize
Keiran Phelan, Southern Arts, 19 Southgate Street, Winchester, Hampshire SO23 9DQ, UK
Awarded to the best literary work by a writer in the Southern Arts region. Awards given in a three-year cycle of fiction, poetry and non-fiction.
1st prize £1000
1989 **Lyndell Gordon** *Eliot's New Life* (OUP)

The Spectator Young Writer Awards
The Spectator, 56 Doughty Street, London WC1N 2LL, UK
Awarded to the most promising young writer of an essay on the subject of his/her choice.
1st prize £1000 plus books and publication of the essay and a writing contract
1989 **Ross Clark** *From Cold War to Cold Store*

Stand Magazine International Short Story
Jon Silkin/Lorna Tracy, 179 Wingrove Road, Newcastle-upon-Tyne NE4 9DA, UK
Biennial award for an unpublished, original English short story (max. 8000 words).
1989 £1250: **Alison Dye** *On the Development of a Free Spirit*

Winifred Mary Stanford Prize
(est. 1977)
Winifred Mary Stanford Prize, c/o Hodder & Stoughton, 47 Bedford Square, London WC1B 3DP, UK
Biennial award for a book inspired by the Christian faith.
1st prize £1000
1988 **Robert Van Der Weyer** *Wickwyn* (SPCK)

Sunday Express Book of the Year Award
Graham Lord, The Sunday Express, 245 Blackfriars Road, London SE1 9UX, UK
Awarded to the author of an outstanding work of new fiction.
1st prize £20,000
1989 **Rose Tremain** *Restoration* (Hamish Hamilton)

The Dylan Thomas Award
(est. 1983)
The Dylan Thomas Award, The Poetry Society, 21 Earls Court Square, London SW5 9DE, UK
Awarded for the encouragement of writers working in the genres of poetry and short stories and awarded in alternate years to these two categories.
1st prize £1000
1989 **Carol Ann Duffy**

Time-Life Silver PEN Award for Non-Fiction
(est.1969)
PEN, 7 Dilke Street, Chelsea, London SW3 4JE, UK
Awarded for an outstanding work of non-fiction.
1st prize £1000
1989 **Brenda Maddox** *Nora* (Hamish Hamilton)

The Times Educational Supplement Information Book Awards
Times Educational Supplement, Priory House, St John's Lane, London EC1M 4BX, UK
Awarded to the two best information books for children, one for children under the age of 9, the other for children aged 10–16.
1st prize £500
1989 Under-9s: **Pete Sanders** *Why Do People Smoke?* (Franklin Watts)
10–16: **David Macaulay** *The Way Things Work* (Dorling Kindersley)

The Times Educational Supplement Schoolbook Awards
Heather Weill (Books editor)
(SEE ABOVE)
Awarded for the best school textbook.
1st prize £500 plus £250 to the illustrator (where appropriate)
1989 **Ann Miller, Liz Roselman** and **Marie-Therese Bougard** *Arc-en-ciel 2* (Mary Glasgow)

The Tir Na n-og Award
Welsh National Centre for Children's Literature, Castell Brychan, Aberystwyth, Dyfed SY23 2JB, UK
£350 awarded for the best original Welsh and English children's books.
1989 Fiction: **Irma Chilton** *Liw* (Gomer)
Jac Jones (ill.) *Ben y Garddwr a Storiau Eraill* (Cymedethas Lyfrau Ceredigion)
Best Book of the Year: **Gwyn** and **Margaret Thomas** *Culwch ac Olwen* (Gwasg Prifysgol Cymru)

The Tom-Gallon Trust
(est. 1943)
Society of Authors, 84 Drayton Gardens, London SW10 9SB, UK
Biennial award of £500 for writers of limited means who have had at least one short story published.
1988 **Alan Beard** *Taking Doreen out of the Sky*

The Betty Trask Awards
(est.1984)
The Society of Authors, 84 Drayton Gardens, London SW10 9SB, UK
Awarded for a first novel of traditional or romantic nature by a young author (under 35 years of age).
Total prize money of at least £20,000
1989 1st prize £10,000: **Nigel Watts** *The Life Game* (Hodder)
2nd prize £5000: **William Riviere** *Watercolour Sky* (Hodder)
3rd prize £2000: **Paul Houghton** *Harry's Last Wedding* (unpublished)
Alisdair McKee *Uncle Harry's Last Stand* (Chatto)

The Travelling Scholarship Fund
(est. 1946)
The Society of Authors, 84 Drayton Gardens, London SW10 9SB, UK
Awarded not for a particular work, but for the writer's work in general.
1990 **Roy Heath**
Adrian Mitchell
Elizabeth North

The TSB Peninsula Prize
(est. 1987)
The Administrator, TSB Peninsula Prize, Hennock Road, Exeter, Devon EX2 8RP, UK
Awarded for the best unpublished novel from a writer of the South and West of England.
1st prize £1500 plus hardback publication by Devon Books with £1000 royalty advance, trophy and leather-bound copy of the book
1989 **Philip Moyse** *If Greedy Wait...*

The Dorothy Tutin Award
(est. 1980)
Johnathon Clifford, National Poetry Foundation, 27 Mill Road, Fareham, Hampshire PO16 0TH, UK
Awarded to the person who has done most to encourage the writing and love of poetry.
1st prize of a carriage clock
1990 **Anne Lewis-Smith** (Envoi Magazine)

Ver Poets Open Competition
May Badman, Haycroft, 61/63 Chiswell Green Lane, St Albans, Hertfordshire AL2 3AG, UK
Awarded to unpublished poems of no more than 30 lines in length.
1st prize £500
1989 1st prize: **Billy Watt** *Porpoises on the Moray Firth*

Wandsworth London Writers' Competition
Assistant Director of Leisure and Amenity Services (Libraries, Museum and Arts), Wandsworth Town Hall, High Street, London SW18 2PU, UK
Awarded to previously unpublished work by Greater London Area writers (over 16 years of age) of poetry, short story and play.
1st prize £450 in each category
1989 Poetry **Sue Lenire** (Westminster) *A Little Bit on the Side*
Short Story **Patrick Cunningham** (Wandsworth) *Sticks and Stones*
Play **Stewart Harcourt** (Hounslow) *Small Talk*

The Welsh Arts Council's Awards to Writers
Literature Department, Welsh Arts Council, Museum Place, Cardiff CF1 3NX, UK
Awarded to writers of books of exceptional literary merit.
Bursaries and enabling grants totalling £40,000

1989 Fiction: **Christopher Meredith** *Shifts* (Seren)
Leslie Norris *The Girl from Cardigan* (Seren)
Poetry: **Tony Conran** *Blodeuwedd* (Seren)
Nigel Wells *Wilderness/Just Bounce* (Bloodaxe)
Young writer: **Catherine Fisher** *Immrama* (Seren)
Welsh Language
Fiction: **Rhydwen Williams** *Liwsi Regina* (Christopher Davies)
Non-Fiction: **Prys Morgan** *Beibl i Gymru* (Cambria)
D. Tecawyn Lloyd *John Saunders Lewis* (Gee)
Poetry: **Alan Llwyd** *Yn y Dirfawr Wag* (Barddas)
Donald Evans *Iasau* (Barddas)
Bursaries
English language: **Christine Evans, Catherine Fisher, Mike Jenkins**
Welsh language: **William Owen Roberts, Angharad Tomos, Llion Williams**

Whitbread Literary Awards
(est. 1971)
The Booksellers Association, 154 Buckingham Palace Road, London SW1 W9TZ, UK
Awarded in one stage until 1984. Since 1985 it has been judged in two stages: a) winners of five separate generic categories are awarded £1750 each; b) an overall winner is chosen from this shortlist of five and is awarded £20,250 on top of the first stage nomination award.
1989 Biography: **Richard Holmes** *Coleridge: Early Visions* (Hodder)
Novel: **Lindsay Clarke** *The Chymical Wedding* (Cape)
Children's Book: **Hugh Scott** *Why Weeps the Brogan?* (Walker)
First Novel: **James Hamilton-Paterson** *Gerontius* (Macmillan)
Poetry: **Michael Donaghy** *Shibboleth* (OUP)

Whitfield Prize
Executive Secretary, Royal Historical Society, University College London, Gower Street, London WC1E 6BT, UK
Awarded for the best work on English or Welsh history by an author under 40.
1st prize £1000
1989 **Gervase Rosser** *Mediaeval Westminster 1200–1540* (Clarendon Press)

John Whiting Award
(est. 1965)
Drama Director, Arts Council of Great Britain, 14 Gt Peter Street, London SW1 3NQ, UK
An award of £4000 given to a writer who in the preceding two years has been in receipt of an award through the Arts Council new theatre writing schemes.
1st prize £4000
1987 **Ian Heggey** *American Bagpipes*

The Mary and Alfred Wilkins Memorial Poetry Competition
Birmingham & Midland Institute, 9 Margaret Street, Birmingham B3 3BS, UK
Awarded to the writer of the best unpublished poem of not more than 40 lines in length.
First prize £200
1989 **Alison Chisholm**

Griffith John Williams Memorial Prize
Sian Ithel, Yr Academi Gymreig, Mount Stuart House, Mount Stuart Square, Cardiff CF1 6DQ, UK
Award for the best original Welsh volume. From 1990 awarded biennially and only to a first volume.
1st prize £200
1989 **Donald Evans**

H.H. Wingate Prizes
(est. 1977)
Norman Morris, Balfour Diamond Jubilee Trust, Balfour House, 741 High Road, London N12 0BQ, UK
£2500 awarded for fiction and non-fiction books which most stimulate an interest in and awareness of Jewish concerns.
1989 Non-Fiction: **Anthony Read** and **David Fisher** *Krystalnacht*
Fiction: **Aharon Applefeld** *Every Sin*

Wolfson Literary Awards for History
(est. 1972)
M. Paisner, Messrs Paisner & Co., Bouverie House, 154 Fleet Street, London EC4A 2DQ, UK
Awarded to a book on a historical subject or period which is judged to be readable and readily accessible to the general public.
1989 **Richard Fletcher** *The Quest for El Cid* (Hutchinson)
Prof. Donald Watt *How War Came* (Heinemann)

Young Observer National Children's Poetry Competition
(SEE OBSERVER)

Yorkshire Post Literary Awards
Secretary of the Book Awards, Yorkshire Post Newspapers Ltd., PO Box 168, Wellington Street, Leeds LS1 1RF, UK
Awarded to: a) Book of the Year; b) Best First Work of the Year; c) Works which have contributed most to the understanding and appreciation of Music and Art.
1989 a) 1st prize £1000: **Simon Schama** *Citizens*
b) £800: **William Dalrymple** *In Xanadu*
c) £800: **David Cairns** *Berlioz: The Making of an Artist* (vol. 1)

FILM AWARDS

American Academy of Motion Picture Arts and Sciences Awards (OSCARS)
8949 Wilshire Boulevard, Beverley Hills 90211, California, USA
Awarded March 1990 for 1989 films

Best film: **Driving Miss Daisy** (USA) Dir. Bruce Beresford
Best foreign language film: **Nuovo Cinema Paradiso (Cinema Paradiso)** (Italy) Dir. Giuseppe Tornatore
Best director: **Oliver Stone** for *Born on the Fourth of July*
Best actor: **Daniel Day Lewis** for *My Left Foot* (GB) Dir. Jim Sheridan
Best actress: **Jessica Tandy** for *Driving Miss Daisy*
Best supporting actor: **Denzel Washington** for *Glory* (USA) Dir. Edward Zwick
Best supporting actress: **Brenda Fricker** for *My Left Foot*
Best original screenplay: **Tom Schulman** for *Dead Poets Society* (USA) Dir. Peter Weir
Best screenplay adaptation: **Alfred Uhry** for *Driving Miss Daisy*
Best cinematography: **Freddie Francis** for *Glory*
Best editing: **David Brenner** and **Joe Hutching** for *Born on the Fourth of July*
Best original song: **Under the Sea** (Music Alan Menken, Lyrics Howard Ashman) from the *Little Mermaid* (USA-Walt Disney) Dir. John Musker
Best original music score: **Alan Menken** for the *Little Mermaid*
Best art direction: **Anton Furst** for *Batman* (USA) Dir. Tim Burton
Best set direction: **Peter Young** for *Batman*
Best costume design: **Phyllis Dalton** for *Henry V* (GB) Dir. Kenneth Brannagh
Best make-up: **Manlio Rocchetti**, **Lyn Barber** and **Kevin Haney** for *Driving Miss Daisy*
Best visual effects: **John Bruno, Dennis Muren, Hoyt Yeatman** and **Dennis Skotak** for the *Abyss* (USA) Dir. James Cameron
Best sound: **Donald O. Mitchell, Greg C. Rudloff, Elliot Tyson** and **Russell Williams II** for *Glory*
Best sound effects editing: **Ben Burtt** and **Richard Hymns** for *Indiana Jones and the Last Crusade* (USA) Dir. Steven Spielberg
Best short film (animated): **Balance** (USA) Prod. Christopher Lauenstein and Wolfgang Lauenstein
Best short film (live action): **Work Experience** (GB) Dir. James Hendrie
Best documentary feature: **Common Threads: Stories from the Quilt** (USA) Dir. Robert Epstein, Prod. Bill Couturie
Best documentary short: **Johnstown Flood** (USA) Prod. Charles Guggenheim
Academy honorary award: **Akira Kurosawa**
Ian Hersholt humanitarian award: **Howard W. Koch**
Gordon E. Sayer award: **Pierre Angenieux**

Berlin Film Festival Award For Best Film

The Berlin Film Festival was established in 1951. There was no award for best film in that year. Between 1952–55 the films were awarded marks by the audience. The Golden Bear award for best picture was first presented in 1956.

Awarded February 1990
GOLDEN BEARS
Grand prix: *Music Box* (USA) Dir. Costa Gavras
40th Anniversary special prize: Oliver Stone for *Born on the Fourth of July* (USA)
Short film: *Misteratao* (Italy) Dir. Bruno Bozetto

SILVER BEARS
Special jury prize: *Asteniceskij Sindrom* (*The Asthenic Syndrome*) (USSR) Dir. Kira Muratova
Best director: Michael Verhoeven for das *Schreckliche Madchen* (*Nasty Girl*) (W. Germany)
Best actor: Iain Glen for *Silent Scream* (GB) Dir David Hayman
Best joint performance: Jessica Tandy and Morgan Freeman for *Driving Miss Daisy* (USA) Dir. Bruce Beresford
Short film: *Ilha Das Flores* (*Island of Flowers*((Brazil) Dir. Jorge Furtado
Best film for sensitive handling of minorities: *Coming Out* (W. Germany) Dir. Heiner Carow
Outstanding single achievement: Xie Fie for *Ben Min Niam* (*Black Snow*) (China)

FIPRESCI prize: *Karaul* (*The Guard*) (USSR) dir. Aleksandr Rogoschkin
Alfred Bauer prize (to a film which opens new perspectives in cinematographic art): *Karaul*
OCIC (Catholic) prize: *Silent Scream*
Interfilm (Protestant) prize: *Schrekliche Madchen*
GDF (German Art Film Theatre Association) prize: *Driving Miss Daisy*
Berliner Morgenpost (audience) prize: *Schrekliche Madchen*
CIAE (International Confederation of Arts Cinemas) prize: *Rikyu* (Japan) Dir. Hiroshi Teshigahara
UNICEF prize: *Mahi* (*The Fish*) (Iran) Dir. Kambuzia Partovi
Best short film: *In and Out* (Canada) Dirs David Fine and Alison Snowden
CIFEJ (International Centre of Films for Children and Young People): *Kunst und Vliegwerk* (*At Stalling Speed*) (Netherlands) Dir. Karst van der Meulen

British Academy of Film and Television Arts (BAFTA)
195 Piccadilly, London W1V 9LG
Awarded March 1990 in London.
BAFTA special award 1990: **Dame Peggy Ashcroft**
Academy fellowship: **Paul Fox CBE**
Michael Balcon award for outstanding British contribution to cinema: **Lewis Gilbert**
Academy award: **Leslie Halliwell**
Desmond Davis award for outstanding creative contribuion to television: **John Lloyd** (BBC)
Writer's award: **Andrew Davis** for *Mother Love* (BBC)
Richard Dimbleby award: **Kate Adie** (BBC)

FILM
Best film: **Dead Poets Society** (USA) Dir. Peter Weir
Best achievement in direction: **Kenneth Brannagh** for *Henry V* (GB)
Best actress: **Pauline Collins** for *Shirley Valentine* (USA) Dir. Lewis Gilbert
Best actor: **Daniel Day Lewis** for *My Left Foot* (GB) Dir. Jim Sheridan
Best supporting actress: **Michelle Pfeiffer** for *Dangerous Liaisons* (USA) Dir. Stephen Frears
Best supporting actor: **Ray McAnally** for *My Left Foot*
Best original screenplay: **Nora Ephron** for *When Harry Met Sally* (USA) Dir. Rob Reiner
Best adapted screenplay: **Christopher Hampton** for *Dangerous Liaisons*
Best film score: **Maurice Jarre** for *Dead Poets Society*
Best foreign-language film: **Vie et Rien d'Autre (Life and Nothing But)** (France) Dir. Bertrand Tavernier, Prod. Rene Cleitman
Best short film: **Candy Show** (National Film and Television School) (Peter Hewits, David Freeman & Damian Jones)
Best short animated film: **Grand Day Out** (National Film and Television School) (Nicholas Park)

TELEVISION
Best single drama: **Accountant** (BBC) Prod. Paul Knight, Dir. Les Blair, Scr Geoffrey Case
Best drama series/serial: **Traffik** (Channel 4) Dir. Alastair Reid, Prod. Brian Eastman, Scr Simon Moore
Best factual series: **Forty Minutes** (BBC) Prod. Edward Mirzoeff
Best light entertainment programme: **Clive James on the '80s** (BBC) Prod. Elaine Bedell, Ed. Richard Drewett
Best comedy series: **Blackadder Goes Forth** (BBC)
Best news/OB coverage: **Tiananmen Square Massacre** (BBC News) Steve Selman
Best actress: **Diana Rigg** for *Mother Love* (BBC)
Best actor: **John Thaw** for *Inspector Morse* (Thames TV)
Best light entertainment performance: **Rowan Atkinson** for *Blackadder Goes Forth* (BBC)
Best original music: **Christopher Gunning** for *Agatha Christie's Poirot* (LWT)
Best children's programme (entertainment/drama): **Maid Marion and her Merry Men** (BBC)
Best children's programme (documentary/educational): **Really Wild Show** (BBC) Prod. Paul Appleby
Flaherty documentary award: **First Tuesday: Four Hours in My Lai** (YTV) Prod/Dir. Kevin Sim
Huw Wheldon award (best arts programme): **Art in the Third Reich** (BBC/Omnibus) Prod/Scr Peter Adam
Best foreign television programme: **Hotel Terminus: The Life and Times of Klaus Barbie** (France) Dir. Marcel Ophuls

BAFTA Craft Awards 1989
Awarded in Glasgow, 11 March 1990

FILM
Cinematography: **Peter Bizou** for *Mississippi Burning* (USA) Dir. Alan Parker
Production design: **Dante Ferretti** for the *Adventures of Baron Munchhausen* (GB/W. Germany) Dir. Terry Gilliam
Editing: **Gerry Hambling** for *Mississippi Burning*
Sound: **Bill Phillips, Danny Michael, Robert Litt, Elliot Tyson** and **Richard C. Kline** for *Mississippi Burning*
Achievement in special visual effects: **Ken Ralston, Michael Lantieri, John Bell** and **Steve Gawley** for *Back to the Future II* (USA) Dir. Robert Zemeckis
Make-up: **Maggie Weston, Fabrizio Szforza** and **Pam Meager** for the *Adventures of Baron Munchhausen*
Costume design: **Gabriella Pescucci** for the *Adventures of Baron Munchhausen*

TELEVISION
Video lighting: **Clive Thomas** for the *Ginger Tree* (BBC)
Design: **Hans Zillman** and **Martin Herbert** for *Traffik* (Channel 4)
Film cameraman: **Clive Tickner** for *Traffik*
Sound Supervisor: **Graham Haines** for *Love for Three Oranges* (BBC)
Film sound: **David Hildyard, David Old** and **Kim Weston** for *Traffik*
Film editor: **Howard Billingham** for *Around the World in 80 Days* (BBC)
Graphics: **Pat Gavin** for *Agatha Christie's Poirot* (LWT)
VTR editor: **John Baldwin** for *Spitting Image* (Central)
Make-up: **Hilary Martin, Christine Cant** and **Roseann Samuel** for *Agatha Christie's Poirot*
Costume design: **Linda Mattock** for *Agatha Christie's Poirot*
Video cameraman: **Ron Green** for the *Ginger Tree*

British Critics' Circle
Best English Language Film: **Distant Voices, Still Lives** (Terence Davies, GB)
Best Performance: **Daniel Day Lewis** in *My Left Foot* (Jim Sheridan, GB)
Best Director: **Terence Davies** for *Distant Voices, Still Lives* (GB)
Best Foreign Language Film: **Au Revoir Les Enfants** (Louis Malle, France)
Special Awards: **Sir Alec Guinness, Charles Crichton, Artifical Eye**

British Film Institute
1989 Technical Achievement Award: **The Adventures of Baron Munchausen** (Terry Gilliam)
Independent Achievement Award: **Amber Side Workshop** (Murry Martin)
Television Award: **Peter Kominsky** for *First Tuesday* programmes, *Afghansti* and *Murder in Ostankino Precinct*
Film Award: **British Screen Finance** (Simon Relph)
Archival Achievement: **Out of the Dolls' House** (Christine Whitaker)
Book Award: *The Hollywood Story* by **Joel Finler** (Octopus)
British Book Award: *Hidden Cinema* by **James Robertson** (Routledge)
A Career in the Industry: **Anette Caulkin**
Sutherland Trophy: **Pathfinder** (Nils Gaup)
Mari Kuuttna Award: **A Feet of Song** (Director Erica Russell, Producer Lee Stork)
The Grierson Award: **Concerning Cancer** (Adam Alexander)
Kodak Newcomers Award: **And I Was Such a Lovely Baby** (Bob Hartley, National Film & TV School)
The Anthony Asquith Award: **High Hopes** (Mike Leigh)
Young Composers Award: **Philip Appleby**
1989 BFI Fellowships: **Gerard Depardieu, Dame Peggy Ashcroft**

Cannes Film Festival
Palme d'Or for Best Picture
Awarded in 1990.
Palme D'Or: David Lynch's **Wild At Heart** (USA)
Grand Jury Prize: Idrissa Ouedraogo's **Tilai** (Burkina Faso) and Kohei Oguri's **The Sting Of Death** (Japan)
Best Director: **Pavel Lounguine** for *Taxi Blues* (USSR/France)
Best Actor: **Gerard Depardieu** for *Cyrano de Bergerac* (France)
Best Actress: **Christine Janda** for *The Interrogation* (Poland)
Best Artistic Contribution: **Gleb Panfilov for** *Mother* (USSR)
Jury Prize: **Ken Loach's** *Hidden Agenda* (UK)
Camera D'Or: Vitali Kanevski's **Lie Still And Rise Again** (USSR)
Palme D'Or, Short Film: Adam Davidson's **The Lunch Date** (US)
International Critics Prize: Oguri's **Sting Of Death** (Japan)

Edinburgh Film Festival
1989 Charles Chaplin Award: **Shaji** for *Piravi* [The Birth] (India)
Special Jury Prize: **My Twentieth Century** (Ildiko Enyedi, Hungary)
Young British Film-Maker Competition: **The Oil Gobblers** (Czechoslovakia)

Jerusalem Festival Prize for Comedy: **The Hill Farm** (Mark Baker, GB)

European Film Awards
(Paris)
1989 European Film of the Year: **Landscape in the Mist** (Theo Angelopoulos, Greece)
Special Jury Prizes: **Life and Nothing But** (Bertrand Tavernier, France)
Cinema Paradiso (Giuseppe Tornatore, Italy)
A Tale of the Wind (Joris Ivans & Marceline Loridan) [documentary]
European Actress of the Year: **Ruth Sheen** in *High Hopes* (Mike Leigh, UK)
European Actor of the Year: **Phillippe Noiret** in *Life and Nothing But* (France)
Best Supporting Player: **Edna Dore** in *High Hopes* (UK)
European Director of the Year: **Geza Beremenyi** for *The Midas Touch* (Hungary)
Young European Film of the Year: **300 Miles to Heaven** (Maciej Dejzer, Poland)
Career Award: **Federico Fellini** (Italy)

Evening Standard British Film Awards
1989 Best Film: **Henry V** (Kenneth Branagh)
Best Actor: **Daniel Day Lewis** in *My Left Foot*
Best Actress: **Pauline Collins** in *Shirley Valentine*
Peter Sellers Award for Comedy: **Mike Leigh** for *High Hopes*
Best Screenplay: **Willy Russell** for *Shirley Valentine*
Best Technical Achievement: **Anton Furst** for *Batman*
Most Promising Newcomer: **Andi Engel** for *Melancholia*
Special Award: **Peter Greenaway**

Locarno Film Festival
1989 Golden Leopard: **Why Did Bodhi-Dharma Leave for the Orient?** (Bae Yong-Kyan, S. Korea)
Silver Leopard: **Piravi** [The Birth] (Shaji, India)
Best Actor: **Adam Kamien** in *Kornblumenblau* (Poland)

Montreal Film Festival
1989 Best Actor: **Daniel Day Lewis** in *My Left Foot* (UK)

Venice Film Festival
Best Foreign Film 1934–42
Best Film Award 1946–68
Golden Lion Award inaugurated 1980
Awarded in 1989.
Golden Lion: **City of Sadness** (Hou Hsiao-hsien, Taiwan)
Special Grand Prize:
Silver Lion (and best direction): **Ken Kumai** for *Death of a Tea Master* (Japan)
Jose Cesar Monteiro for *Memories of the Yellow House* (Portugal)
Best Actor: **Marcello Mastroianni** and **Masimo Troisi** in *What Time Is It?* (Ettore Scola)
Best Actress: **Dame Peggy Ashcroft** and **Geraldine James** in *She's Been Away* (Peter Hall, GB)
International Critics Prize **Krzysztof Kieslowski** for *The Ten Commandments* (Poland)

MUSIC AWARDS: OPERA & CLASSICAL MUSIC

Joseph Bloch LRAM Prize
(est. 1987–8)
Sir James Caird's Travelling Scholarships Trust, 136 Nethergate, Dundee DD1 4PA, UK
1st prize £100 for the best string instrumentalist.
1989 **Malcom J. Johnston** (Aberdeen)

BP Peter Pears Award
The Administrator, 48 Canfield Gardens, London NW6 3EV, UK
Open international singing competition for women aged 21–28, and men aged 21–30.
1989 **Neal Davies** (baritone, Wales)

Robert William & Florence Amy Brant Pianoforte Competition
83 Windsor Road, Oldbury, Warley, West Midlands B68 8PB, UK
International competition for pianists aged 20–30.
1989 1st prize & £600: **Timothy Lissimore**

Brighton Philharmonic Piano Competition
Brighton Philharmonic Society Ltd, 50 Grand Parade, Brighton BN2 2QA, UK
Closed competition.
1989 **Steven Osborn**

British Violin Recital Prize
1 Parkfield Road, Cheadle Hulme, Cheshire SK8 6EX, UK
Junior prize (18 and under) and senior prize (19–26)

Britten Award for Composition
(est. 1989)
Britten-Pears Foundation, The Red House, Golf Lane, Aldeburgh, Suffolk IP15 5PZ, UK
1st prize £10,000 plus commercial recording of the work.
1990 **John Casker** for *Golem*

Benjamin Britten Composers' Competition
Britten-Pears School for Advanced Musical Studies, High Street, Aldeburgh, Suffolk IP15 5AX, UK
Biennial award.
1989 **Benedict Mason** *Double Concerto for Horn, Trombone & Chamber Ensemble*
Pawel Szymanski *A Study of Shade*

Ida Carroll Fellowship
Royal Northern College of Music, 124 Oxford Road, Manchester M13 9RD, UK
Biennial award of £2500 for post-graduate study.
1988 **John McLeod**

Clements Memorial Chamber Music Competition
Raymond Cassidy, Fernside, Copthall Green, Upshire, Waltham Abbey, Essex EN9 3SZ, UK
Biennial award for a chamber composition (3–6 players) with a minimum length of 15 minutes.
1988 **Benedict Mason**

John Clementi Collard Fellowship of Music
Royal Academy of Music, Marylebone Road, London NW1, UK
1989 1st prize £3000: **Benedict Mason** (composer)

Henry & Lily Davis Trust Fund
The Music Department, Arts Council of Great Britain, 14 Gt Peter Street, London SW1 3NQ, UK
1989 **Regina Nathan** (singer)
Helen Astrid (singer)
Virginia Shaw (oboist)

Carl Ebert Award
Glyndebourne Opera, Lewes, East Sussex BN8 5UU, UK
Nominated award to assist younger members of the Glyndebourne production staff to pursue their studies.
1989 **Kate Brown**

Decca-Kathleen Ferrier Prize
Royal Philharmonic Society, 10 Stratford Place, London W1N 9AE, UK
For British singers aged 21–26.
1989 1st Prize £5000: **Paul Clarke**

Vivian Ellis Prize for Young Writers for the Musical Stage
Administrator, Performing Rights Society, 29 Berners Street, London W1P 4AA, UK
Maximum age 30 years. 1st prize £3000.
1989 *House of Dreams* **Alison Gray**

English Song Award
44 New Road, Brynaston, Blandford Forum, Dorset DT12 0DR, UK
Open to singers aged 20–40.

Carl Flesch International Violin Competition
City Arts Trust Ltd., Bishopsgate Hall, 230 Bishopsgate, London EC2M 4QH, UK
Six main biennial prizes and special prizes plus concert engagements.
1st prize £5000
1990 1st prize: **Maxim Vengerov** (USSR)

Esso/Glyndebourne Touring Opera Singers Award
c/o Glyndebourne Opera, Lewes, East Sussex BN8 5UU, UK
Annual nominated award for young singers appearing with the Glyndebourne Touring Opera.
1989 **Sarah Pring**

Glasgow (City of) International Junior Violinists Competition
Iain Turpie, 12 Washington Street, Glasgow G3 8AZ, UK
For junior violinists aged 12–18.

Gramophone Record of the Year
177–179 Kenton Road, Harrow, Middlesex HA3 0HA, UK
1989 **The Emerson Quartet** *Bartok's Six Quartets* (Deutsche Grammophon)

Great Grimsby International Competition for Singers
(The Alice Redshaw Memorial Awards)
The Secretary, 23 Enfield Avenue, New Waltham, Grimsby, S. Humberside DN36 5RD, UK
Triennial award for singers aged 20–30.
1989 1st prize: **Jayne Carpenter** (soprano)
Teresa Shaw (mezzo)
Huw Rhys-Evans (tenor)
Stephen Gadd (bass-Baritone)

Walther Gruner International Lieder Competition
The Administrator, City Arts Trust Ltd., Bishopsgate Hall, 230 Bishopsgate, London EC2M 4QH, UK
Biennial award for singers and accompanists aged 28 and under.
1989 **Roman Trekel** (E. Germany): singer
Marina D'Ambroso (Italy): accompanist

Harvey Leeds International Pianoforte Competition
The University of Leeds, Leeds LS2 9JT, UK
Triennial awards. 1st prize of £5,000 & Gold Medal. Total prizes of £17,500 & Orchestral concerts and recitals worldwide.
1987 **Vladimir Ovchinikov** (USSR)

Anna Instone Memorial Grant
Susan Johnson, Capital Radio, PO Box 958, London NW1 3DR, UK
Annual award of £3000. Nominations only from the five London music colleges.
1989 **Rachael Tovey**

Interpretation Competition
International Organ Festival Society, PO Box 80, St Albans AL1 1BY, UK
Biennial award for organ music. 1st prize £1000 and recital at Chartres Cathedral plus BBC broadcast.
1989 **Mikhail Wahlin** (Sweden)

Julius Isserlis Scholarship
c/o Royal Philharmonic Society, 10 Stratford Place, London W1N 9AE, UK
Biennial competitive award worth £15,000 for two years' study abroad for anyone below the age of 21.
1989 **Sam Hayward**

Rowland Jones Award
Janet Kelly, 57 Borras Road, Rhosnesni, Wrexham, Clwydd WL12 7EN, UK
Awarded to young Welsh singers aged 18–30.
1st prize £1500 for extended training.
1990 **Neil Davies**

Kent Young Composers of the Year
Music Department, South-East Arts, 10 Mount Ephraim, Tunbridge Wells, Kent TN4 8AS, UK
1990 Celebration of three years of the scheme by all 18 previous winners.

Sascha Lasserson Memorial Prize
Brian Underwood, Flat Two, 81 Shepherds Hill, London N6 5RG, UK
Biennial award to violinists aged 16–35.
1988 **Aaron Stolow**

Miriam Licette Scholarship
Music Department, Arts Council of Great Britain, 14 Gt Peter Street, London SW1 3NQ, UK
Competition for women singers under 30 years of age to study in Paris. Arts Council musical awards system currently under review.

Llangollen International Musical Eisteddfod
International Eisteddfod Office, Llangollen, Clwydd, North Wales L20 8NG, UK
Annual musical festival, billed as a cultural olympics, attended in 1990 by 34 countries of the world. Considered the world's leading festival of choral music, folksong and dance, with over 12,000 competitors. Pavarotti competed here in 1955; Domingo in 1963, as a young Mexican tenor. 1990 was the 44th Eisteddfod, run by 12,000 volunteers. There is prize money for each competition but it is the International Trophy that is most important.

1990 results
Soprano Solo (£75): **Gail Regan**
Mezzo Soprano/Contralto (£75): **Clare Gray**
Tenor (£75): **Timothy Evans**
Baritone/Bass (£75): **Martin Boeg**
Princeps Cantorum (£75): **Gail Regan**
Vocal under 16 yrs (£20): **Lyndsey Vaughan Parry**
International Young Singer of the Year (£200): **Tatjana Davidova** (Bulgaria)
International Young Instrumentalist of the Year (£200): **Catrin Morris Jones** – Harp
Folk Song Groups (£300): **Brasov Philharmonic Choir** (Romania)
Folk Dance Groups (£300): **NEFAP Porto** (Portugal)
Folk Instrumental Solo/Group (£100): **Andre Gabriel** (France)
Folk Song over 16 yrs (£30): **Emine Akmese**
Folk Song under 16 yrs (£20): **Lindsey Vaughan Parry**
Choir of the World at Llangollen (£3000): **Ohio State University Men's Glee Club** (USA)
Mixed Choirs (£500): **Gruppo Polifonico F. Coradani, Arezzo** (Italy)
Female Choirs (£500): **Tallinn Teachers Female Choir** (Estonia)
Male Voice (£500): **Ohio State University Men's Glee Club** (USA)
Chamber Choirs (£500): **Joyful Company of Singers** (London)
Children's Choirs (£250): **Permonik, Karvina** (Czechoslovakia)
Youth Choirs (£250): **Kammarkoren Svenska Roster** (Sweden)

London International Piano Competition
28 Wallace Road, London N1 2PG, UK
Triennial award for pianists aged 30 and under.

London (formerly City of Portsmouth) International String Competition
Dennis Sayer, 62 High Street, Fareham, Hampshire PO16 7BG, UK
Triennial award to the best string quartet whose combined age is less than 120 years
1988 City of Portsmouth prize £6500: **Vanbrugh String Quartet** (UK)
IBM prize £3750: **Ysaye String Quartet** (France)
Schroder Life prize £2500: **Lafayette String Quartet** (USA)
Marks & Spencer Prize £2000: **Shanghai String Quartet** (China)
Duisberg prize £1250: **Sierra String Quartet** (USA)
Menuhin prize £500: **Martinu String Quartet** (Czechoslovakia)
British Reserve Insurance Audience prize £500: **Ysaye String Quartet** (France)

London Philharmonic/Pioneer Young Soloists of the Year Competition
London Philharmonic, 35 Doughty Street, London WC1N 2AA, UK
Biennial award of £2500 & concerto with orchestra, for instrumentalists aged 26 and under
1990 **Leon McCauley** (piano)

Menuhin Competition for Young Composers
City of Westmister Arts Council, Marylebone Library, Marylebone Road, London NW1 5PS, UK
Triennial award of £1250 and public performance of the work in London plus possibility of publication, broadcasting and recording of composition. Next held in 1991.
1987 **Evan Bennett** (USA)

Folkestone Menuhin International Violin Competition
Kallaway Ltd, 2 Portland Road, London W11 4LA, UK
Biennal award.
1989 Senior (under 20) 1st prize £3500: **Joji Hattorl** (Japan)
Junior (under 16) 1st prize £2500: **Livia Sohn** (USA)

National Early Music Competition
The Secretary, 7 Cinnamon Lane, Fearnhead, Warrington, Cheshire WA2 0AE, UK
For individuals and groups specializing in Early Music.
1989 **Tobias Schade**: harpsichord (Berlin)

Newport International Competition for Young Pianists
Leisure Services Department, Civic Centre, Newport, Gwent NP9 4UR, UK
Triennial award to pianists 25 and under.
1988 1st prize £2000 **Mark Anderson**

NFMS/Esso Young Concert Artists Award
Helen Ranger, 5 Summerfield Road, London W5 1ND, UK
Awarded to instrumentalists (aged 28 and under) and singers (aged 30 and under) in a four-year cycle.
1989 Female voices: **Maria Palazas** (soprano)

NFMS Special Award
(SEE ABOVE)
1989 **John Burgess Trio** (jazz trio)
Early Music Duo (Jane Booth – classic clarinet, Neal Perez da Costa – fortepiano)

North-West Arts Young Chamber Musicians' Platform
The Music/Dance Officer, North-West Arts, 12 Harter Street, Manchester M1 6HY, UK
Open to North-West musicians aged 20–30.
1989 **Apollo Saxophone Quartet**

Performing Rights Society Award for Composition
(SEE ROYAL OVER-SEAS LEAGUE)

Prudential Arts Awards
Kallaway Ltd, 2 Portland Road, London W11 4LA
Awards are made in five categories: Music, Theatre, Dance, Opera and Visual Arts. A £25,000 prize is awarded to the winner in each category, in order to encourage innovation. An overall winner is to be determined from the five categories in Nov. 1990.
1990 Music: **Royal Liverpool Philharmonic Society**
Opera: **City of Birmingham Touring Opera**

Pulitzer Prize in Music
Pulitzer Prize Board, 702 Journalism, Columbia University, New York NY 10027, USA
Awarded for distinguished composition by an American in any of the larger forms including Chamber, Orchestral, Choral, Opera, Song, Dance or other forms of musical theatre.
1st prize – $3000
1989 **Roger Reynolds** *Whispers out of Time* premiered on 11 December 1988

Dr William Baird Ross Prize for Church Music Composition

Alan Buchan, 4 Coillesdene Terrace, Edinburgh EH15 2JN, UK
Triennial award to Scottish composers

Royal Amateur Orchestral Society Silver Medal Awards
Royal Orchestral Society for Amateur Musicians, 100 Shakespeare Crescent, Manor Park, London E12 6LP, UK
Annual awards of the Royal Amateur Orchestral Society Silver Medal to the best young solo instrumentalist or singer under 28 years of age.
1989 Silver medal: **Julian Sperry** (flute)
Bronze medal: **Nicholas Unwin** (piano)

Royal National Eisteddfod of Wales
10 Park Grove, Cardiff CF1 3BN, UK
W. Towyn Roberts Scholarship worth £2500 awarded to the most promising vocalist.
1989 **Sharon Evans** (Bryn Teg, Anglesey)
The British Council Scholarship: The Blue Riband Instrumental Prize of travel to any European country for further training.
1989 **Gareth Small** (Swansea, West Glamorgan) [brass section]

Royal Over-Seas League Awards
(est. 1952)
Music Department, Park Place, St James's Street, London SW1A 1LR, UK
Competition open to Commonwealth citizens: Instrumental age limit 28; Singer age limit 30; Composer age limit 35.
Before 1952 the competition was non-competitive and was known as 'The Festival of Commonwealth Youth'. From 1960–1979 two equal first prizes were awarded to the best competitor from overseas and the best competitor from the UK. From 1980 one first prize has been awarded to the best musician from any country, chosen from the winners of the four main solo categories.
1989 Woodwind/Brass: **Jane Evans** (UK)
Singers: **Cheryl Baker** (UK)
Strings: **Nicola Hall** (UK)
Keyboard: **Alvin Moisey** (UK)
Miller Trophy & RTZ Ensemble Prize of £1000: **Apollo Saxophone Quartet** (UK)
Champagne Pommery Award 1st prize plus Festival Gold Medal £3000
Nicola Hall (Royal Northern College of Music) (Guitar)
Bernard Shore Memorial Scholarship for a viola player £2500
James Boyd
Heather Wallington
Performing Rights Society biennial award for composers £2500
Simon Holt *Capriccio Spettrale*
Overseas Trophy & Overseas Prize £500
Cheryl Baker (UK)
RVW Trust Contemporary Music Project II. Up to five prizes of £1000 each
Mark Richey *Piano Quartet* (UK)
John Kefala Kerr *Meltimi* (for String Quartet) (UK)
Andrew Lovett *String Quartet* (UK)
Andrew Toovey *Nobody'll Know* (cello and piano) (UK)
Philip Crawshaw Memorial Prize for a musician of promise from overseas £350
Charles Uzor (oboe) (Nigeria)
Australian Musical Association Prize £300
James Brawn (piano) (Australia)
Bank of New Zealand Award for a singer from overseas £300
Barry Patterson (baritone) (Australia)
New Zealand Society Prize for an instrumentalist of promise from New Zealand £400
James Eady (clarinet) (New Zealand)
New Zealand Society Prize for a singer of promise from New Zealand £400
Rhona Fraser (soprano) (New Zealand)
Foundation for Canadian Studies in the UK Award £500
Donna Bennett (soprano) (UK)
Marisa Robles Harp Prize £300
Catherine Beynon (UK)
Joan Davies Memorial Prize £150
Michael White (piano) (UK)
Sir Ernest Cassel Prize for a brass player £100
Richard Kennedy (horn) (UK)
Eric Rice Memorial Prize for an accompanist £100
Rebecca Holt (UK)
Ivor Walsworth Memorial Prize for a young string player of promise £100
Robert Max (cello) (UK)
J.G. John Award for a singer of promise £100
Julie Gossage (mezzo-soprano) (UK)

Royal Philharmonic Composition Prize
c/o Royal Philharmonic Society, 10 Stratford Place, London W1N 9AE, UK
1989 £2000: **Edward Newell, Robert Godman**

Sainsbury's Choir of the Year
Kallaway Ltd, 2 Portland Road, London W11 4LA, UK
Biennial award
Two awards, one for Youth Choir of the Year (under 18 years) and the other for Choir of the Year (over 18 years).
1988 **Chamber Choir of the Arts Educational Schools, Tring Park** (under 18 years)
Vasari Singers (over 18 years)

St Paul's School's Chamber Orchestra Composition Award
Jonathan Varcoe, St Paul's School, Lonsdale Road, London SW13 9JT, UK
Awarded irregularly (1991) to the composer of a piece for chamber orchestra.

Humphrey Searle Memorial Prize
The Secretary, 38 Agamemnon Road, London NW6 1EN, UK
Biennially awarded to a composer, aged 35 and under, for a chamber work.

Lewis Silkin National Young Composers Competition
R. Young, Lenwood Cottage, Lenham Heath, Maidstone, Kent ME17 2BS, UK
Biennial award to the composer, aged 35 and under, of a chamber choir piece.
1990 **Martin Craft** for *Eye of the Sea*

South-East Arts Fina Young Musicians Platform
Music Administrator, South-East Arts, 10 Mount Ephraim, Tunbridge Wells, Kent TN4 8AS, UK
Open to young musicians from Kent, East Sussex and Surrey.
Maximum age: 27 for instrumentalists, 30 for singers.

1989 **Tapestry** (clarinet, voice, piano)
Fiona Cross (clarinet)

Elsie Sykes Fellowship
Royal Northern College of Music, 124 Oxford Road, Manchester M13 9RD, UK
Annual award of £2500 for vocal studies.
1989 **Alison Duguid**

Richard Tauber Prize
Anglo-Austrian Society, 46 Queen Anne's Gate, London SW1H 9AU, UK
Biennial award including travel bursary, study grant and London recital. Prize for British or Austrian singers (21–30 years women, 21–32 years men).

Maggie Teyte Prize Competition
Felicity Guinness, 2 Keats Grove, London NW3 2RT, UK
Award of £1000 to a woman singer, maximum age 30 years.
1989 **Anita Morrison** (soprano)

Tournemire Prize
International Organ Festival Society, PO Box 80, St Albans, Hertfordshire AL1 1BY, UK
£750 biennial prize for improvisation on the organ.
1989 No award

Trianon Music Group Competition
Mrs J. Dann, Bath Road, Felixstowe, Suffolk IP11 7JW, UK
Biennial award.
1989 **Martin Storey**

Wiseman Prize
(est. 1967)
Sir James Caird's Travelling Scholarships Trust, 136 Nethergate, Dundee DD1 4PA, UK
1st prize £200 for best performance.
1989 **James Crabb** (Dundee)

Yorkshire Arts Association Young Composers Competition
The Music Officer, Yorkshire Arts Association, Glyde House, Bradford BD5 0BQ, UK
For British composers aged 30 and under.
1989 **Sohrab Uduman** *Movements* for piano trio
Nicholas Virgo *Sweet Luna* for piano trio

Young Concert Artists Trust Awards
(est. 1983)
General Administrator, 14 Ogle Street, London W1P 7LJ, UK
1989 **Laura Dimitrova** (piano)
Graham Scott (piano)
Laurence Scott (violin)

Young Musician of the Year (BBC TV) Competition
BBC, Kensington House, Richmond Way, London W14 0AX, UK
Biennial award.
1988 **David Pyatt** (French horn)

Young Pianist of the Year Award
The ABC Music Company, 85 High Street, Esher, Surrey KT10 9QA, UK
Biennial awards for pianists aged 18 and under.
1989 Under-10s: **Ricky Cheung** (Ealing)
Under-14s: **Min Jung Kim** (Northolt)
Under-18s: **Leon McCawley**

Young Welsh Singers Competition
Music Director, Welsh Arts Council, 9 Musuem Place, Cardiff CF1 3NX, UK
Triennial award to Welsh musicians aged 30 and under.
1988 **Bryn Terfel Jones** (bass-baritone)

ROCK, POP AND JAZZ AWARDS

Brit Awards
1989 Best British Newcomer: **Lisa Stansfield**
Best British Producer: **David A. Stewart**
Best Classical Music Recording: **Simon Rattle**
Best Movie Soundtrack: **Batman**
Best British Group: **Fine Young Cannibals**
Best Video Award: **The Cure**
Best International Group: **U2**
Best International Newcomer: **Neneh Cherry**
Best International Artist: **Neneh Cherry**
Best Album by a British Artist: **Fine Young Cannibals**
Best Single 1989: *Another Day in Paradise* by **Phil Collins**
Best Female Artist: **Annie Lennox**
Best Male Artist: **Phil Collins**
Special Award for Outstanding Contribution to British Music: **Queen**

1988 **Ivor Novello Awards**
Britain's Songwriter of the Year: **George Michael**, **Stock Aitkin & Waterman**
Outstanding Contribution to British Music: **Paul McCartney**, **Dire Straits**
Best Film Song: *Two Hearts* by **Phil Collins**
Best Seller of Last Year: *Mistletoe and Wine* by **Cliff Richard**
Best Song, Musically and Lyrically: *They Dance Alone* by **Sting**
Best Contemporary Song: *Love Changes Everything* by **Climie Fisher**

Top 10 Best-Selling Singles 1989
1 *Ride on Time* **Black Box**
2 *Swing the Mood* **Jive Bunny and the Master Mixers**
3 *Eternal Flame* **The Bangles**
4 *Too Many Broken Hearts* **Jason Donovan**
5 *Back to Life* **Soul II Soul** featuring **Caron Wheeler**
6 *Something's Gotten Hold of My Heart* **Marc Almond**, **Gene Pitney**
7 *That's What I Like* **Jive Bunny and the Master Mixers**
8 *Pump up the Jam* **Technotronic** featuring **Felly**
9 *Do They Know It's Christmas?* **Band Aid 2**
10 *Hand on Your Heart* **Kylie Minogue**

Top 10 Best-Selling Albums 1989
1 *Ten Good Reasons* **Jason Donovan**
2 *A New Flame* **Simply Red**
3 *But Seriously . . .* **Phil Collins**
4 *Anything for You* **Gloria Estefan and Miami Sound Machine**
5 *Cuts Both Ways* **Gloria Estefan and Miami Sound Machine**
6 *Enjoy Yourself* **Kylie Minogue**
7 *The Raw and the Cooked* **Fine Young Cannibals**
8 *Foreign Affair* **Tina Turner**
9 *Like A Prayer* **Madonna**
10 *Club Classics Vol 1* **Soul II Soul**
Charts courtesy of BPI, compiled by Gallup.

Grammy Awards. Jazz
1989 **The Guardian/The Wire Jazz Awards**

Best Instrumentalist: **Andy Sheppard**
Best Vocalist: **Cleveland Watkiss**
Best Composer: **Stan Tracey**
Best Band: **Loose Tubes**
Best New Band: **Road Side Picnic**
Best Newcomer: **Orphy Robinson**
Best Album: *Introductions in the Dark* by **Andy Sheppard**
The Milestone Award for Special Achievement: **George Russell**
Wire/Elephant Award: **John Surman**

VISUAL ARTS AWARDS

Athena Art Awards
Jill Copping, Pentos plc, New Bond Street House, No 1 New Bond Street, London W1Y 0SB, UK
1st prize £25,000
1988 **Jenefer Buwant** for *Thee and Back*

Barclays Bank Young Painters Prize
Application trhough any one of five London art coleges – Royal Academy of Art, Chelsea School of Art, Slade School of Art, Royal College of Art and Goldsmiths College.
Open to final year postgraduate students in Fine Arts at any of the five above-mentioned colleges of art.
Total prize of £20,000: £10,000 1st prize; £10,000 runners-up.
1989 **Helen Pavel** (Royal College of Art)

Birmingham Fine Art Award
Birmingham Arts Trust, Foyle House, Cannon Park, Birmingham
1989 **Mark Renn**

David Canter Memorial Fund Awards for Pottery
K. Canter, David Canter Memorial Fund, Devon Guild of Craftsmen, Riverside Mill, Bovey Tracey, Devon TQ13 9AE, UK
£500 each.
1989 **Carolyn Genders**
Mark Griffiths
Susan Nemeth
Jacqueline Norris

Graduate Artist of the Year Award
1st prize around-the-world trip plus £1000.
1989 **David Tebbs** (Humberside College of Higher Education)

Hunting Group Award
5th Floor, Bowater House East, 68 Knightsbridge, London SW1X 7LT, UK
Total prize money £13,000 awarded for the best painting.
1990 **Guss Cummins**

Inex Awards for Ceramics
Awards of £3000 each.
1989 **Henry Pim**
Steve Buck
Joanna Veevers
Jenny Bevan

International Exhibition of Miniature Arts Awards
Del Bello Gallery, Toronto, Canada
1989 1st prize: **Wendy Brown** for *Welsh Landscape*

International Print Exhibition Awards
Art for Offices (£200): **Joop Vegter** (Holland)
R.K. Burt Prizes (3 first prizes £100 + £50 paper vouchers): **Peter Rhoades** (UK), **Ferdynand Szypula** (Poland), **Christopher Cunliffe** (UK), **Kafumi Yamazaki** (Japan)
Printmakers Council Computer Prize (£50): **Michael King** (UK)
Intaglio Printmakers Etching Prize (£35 material vouchers): **Stuart Duffin** (UK)

John Moore's Exhibition of Contemporary Art Award
Walker Art Gallery, William Brown Street, Liverpool L3 8EL, UK
Biennial award of £14,000.
1989 1st prize £14,000: **Lisa Milroy** (Canada)

National Trust Award
36 Queen Anne's Gate, London SW1H 9AS, UK
£1000 1st prize.
1989 **Noreen Colwell** (textiles)

John Player Portrait Awards
National Portrait Gallery, St Martin's Place, London W1A 1AA, UK
1990 **Annabel Cullen**

Prudential Arts Awards
(SEE MUSIC)
1990 Visual Arts: **The Grizedale Society – Grizedale Forest Sculpture**

Readers Digest Young Illustrators' Competition
25 Berkeley Square, London W1X 6AB, UK
Awards are for the best narrative and the best non-fiction illustrations
1989 Narrative: **Janet Ponting**
Non-fiction: **Andrew Hutchinson**

Royal Academy Summer Exhibition Awards
Royal Academy of Arts, Piccadilly, London
1990 was the 22nd Summer Exhibition. The value of prizes offered to artists totalled over £40,000.
1990 awards:
The Charles Wollaston Award
£5,500 for the most distinguished work in the exhibition
Patrick Symons for *Mary Iliff's Viola, Played by Electric Light and Drawn by Gaslight*

Korn/Ferry International Award
£15,000 in total, donated by Korn/Ferry International Ltd for works of exceptional merit in any category: £1000 for each of the five artists chosen by a specially appointed panel and further prizes of £5000 each for the artist(s) chosen by ballot from the shortlist by the public and by the Members of the Royal Academy.
£1000 each to: **Gillian Ayres** for *Ding Dong Merrily on High*; **John Bellany** for *Death and the Maiden*, *Two Wives*, *Salome*, and *Conversation Piece*; **R.B. Kitaj** for *The First Time (Havana 1949)*; **Ben Panting** for *Untitled*; **Richard Rogers** for *European Court of Human Rights*

Bovis/AJ Awards for Architecture
£7250 donated by Bovis Construction Ltd in association with the *Architects' Journal*; £3500 and a bronze trophy (to be held for one year) for an exhibit displaying architectural merit and success in communicating the architect's intention to the public, open to non-members and Members of the Royal Academy; £1500 for an exhibit submitted by a non-member of the Royal Academy; £750 for a model, drawing or other graphic representation executed by the exhibitor or in his office. In addition, the judges may, at their discretion,

award £1500 worth of Architectural Press books for works of outstanding merit by younger architects and students.

£3500: **Richard Rogers** for *European Court of Human Rights*; £1500: **Goldstein Ween** for *Eurotunnel Information Ride Tourist Information Display*; £750: **Ben Johnson** for *Central Spine – Inmos*; £1500 of books: **Rosie Andrews** for *Fire Station*; **Paul Allen** for *Greensted Church*; **Neil Darby** for *Ecumenical Chapel: Detail*

Daler-Rowney Awards for Paintings
£6000 donated by Daler-Rowney Ltd for a prize for a painting in any media by a non-member of the Royal Academy under the age of 30 years.

£3000: **Anna Jefferson** for *In St James's Park*; £1000: **Liz Hough** for *The Farm Vilieux*; £1000: **Catherine Brerton** for *Crosby Row*; £1000: **Paul Layzell** for *Looks Like Rain*

CCA Galleries Award
£1000 donated by CCA Galleries plc for a print in any medium by a non-member of the Royal Academy.

£350 each: **Paul Hawden** for *Ponte Rotto, Rome*; **Chris Orr** for *A Short History of Motoring*; **Sasa Marinkov** for *Rebuilding Liverpool Street Station*

House & Garden Award
£1000 donated by House & Garden Magazine for a work in any medium depicting an interior.

Patrick Symons for *Mary Iliff's Viola, Played by Electric Light and Drawn by Gaslight*

The Goldhill Award for Sculpture
£2000 donated by Jack Goldhill for a sculpture.

F.E. McWilliam for *Waiting Figure*

The Blackstone Prize
£500 donated anonymously for a work chosen by an art critic, who is to remain anonymous also.

Gillian Ayres for *Ding Dong Merrily on High*

The Watercolour Foundation Prize
£3000 for a work, or works, in watercolour.

The late **Edward Bawden** for *Cat Among the Pigeons*

The Arts Club Prize
A purchase prize donated by The Arts Club, Dover Street, W1, whereby the artist is given the full purchase price, including the amount of the commission due to the Royal Academy.
Mary Fedden for *Lamplight*

Smith Biennial Award
Art Department, Scottish Arts Council, 19 Charlotte Square, Edinburgh EH2 4DF, UK
£1000 each for Scottish artists.
1989 **Steve Dilworth**
Moyne Flannigan
Douglas Gordon
Julie Roberts
Jane and **Louise Wilson**

Turner Prize
Tate Gallery, Millbank, London SW1P 4RG, UK
First awarded in 1984, the prize has been suspended from 1990 until a new sponsor is found. The 1989 winner won £10,000.
1989 **Richard Long** (sculptor)

Whitworth Young Contemporaries
Whitworth Art Gallery, Manchester
Biennial awards of £300 each.
1989 **Peter Bennett** (Canterbury College of Art)
Richard Clegg (Canterbury College of Art)
Dan Gardiner (Liverpool Polytechnic)
Derek Haworth (Manchester Polytechnic)
Thomas Neill (Humberside College of Higher Education)
Chris Ofili (Chelsea College of Art)

Wildlife Photographer of the Year Competition
BBC Wildlife Magazine/Natural History Museum in association with Fauna & Flora Preservation Society, c/o Broadcasting House, Whiteladies Rd, Bristol BS8 2LR, UK
Prize wildlife holiday for two and bronze sculpture.
1989 Jouni Ruuskanen (Finland) for 'Red-Throated Diver'

Young Wildlife Photographer of the Year Competition
BBC Wildlife Magazine/Natural History Museum, Broadcasting House, Whiteladies Rd, Bristol BS8 2LR, UK
Open to young photographers 17 years and under.
Prize £350 plus bronze sculpture.
1989 Teemu Helo (Finland) for 'Long-Tailed Skua'

THEATRE AWARDS

Barclays New Stages
Kallaway Ltd, 2 Portland Rd, London W11 4LA
Fringe theatre sponsorship award open to theatre companies based in the United Kingdom. Sponsorship of £500,000 over three years provides for at least eight new theatre productions a year and will enable a number of these to be performed at a three-to-four week season at the Royal Court Theatre, London.
Stage One: Jan. 1990
Stage Two: Jan. 1991

Edinburgh Festival Perrier Award Winner
Perrier UK Ltd, 6 Lygon Place, London SW1W OJR
1989 **Simon Fanshawe**

Evening Standard Drama Awards
Northcliffe House, 2 Derry Street, London W8 5EE, UK
1989 Best Play: *Ghetto* by **Joshua Sobol**
Best Actor: **Ian McKellen** in *Othello*
Best Actress: **Felicity Kendall** in *Much Ado about Nothing* and *Ivanov*
Best Comedy: *Henceforward* by **Alan Ayckbourn**
Best Musical: *Miss Saigon*
Best Director: (Sidney Edwards award): **Nicholas Hytner** for *Ghetto* and *Miss Saigon*
Most Promising Playwright: **Stephen Jeffreys** for *Valued Friends*
Special award: **Stephen Sondheim**

Linbury Prize for Stage Design
(est. 1988)
Open to all final-year students of theatre design at seven selected UK colleges. 1st prize £2000 from a total of £15,000 in prize money including commissioning fees; a guaranteed London production for three winners' designs; an exhibition at the National Theatre for three weeks of up to 15 designers.
1989 1st prize: **Kenny MacLellan**

Liverpool Playhouse Young Writers Award
(est. 1986)
Liverpool Playhouse, Williamson Square, Liverpool L1 1EL, UK
Depends on sponsorship, so an irregular award. Last prizewinner was **Andrew Cullen** in 1989 for *North* which won him £1000 plus Liverpool Playhouse production.

LWT Plays on Stage Competition:
LWT Plays on Stage, London Weekend Television, South Bank Television Centre, London SE1 9LT. UK
Three prizes totalling £48,000 for best production proposals.
1989 1st prize: £18,000: **Black Theatre Co-Operative** prod. of *The Pan-Beaters* by Stephen Landrigan
2nd prize: £16,000: **West Yorkshire Playhouse** prod. of *Safe in Our Hands* by Andy De La Tour
3rd Prize: £14,000: **Cumbernauld Theatre Co.** prod. of *The Tokyo Trip* by Stephen Greenhorn

Laurence Olivier Awards
Society of West End Theatre, Bedford Chambers, The Plaza, Covent Garden, London WC2E 8HQ, UK
1989 Best play: **Our Country's Good** (Timberlake Wertenbaker)
Best Comedy: **Shirley Valentine** (Willy Russell)
Best Musical: **Candide** (Hugh Wheeler)
Best Actor in a New Play: **David Haig** in *Our Country's Good*
Best Actress in a New Play: **Pauline Collins** in *Shirley Valentine*
Best Actor in a Revival: **Brian Cox** in *Titus Andronicus*
Best Actress in a Revival: **Harriet Walter** in *Twelfth Night*, *Three Sisters* and *A Question of Geography*
Best Comedy Performance: **Alex Jennings** in *Too Clever by Half*
Outstanding Actor Performance (Musical): **Con O'Neill** in *Blood Brothers*
Outstanding Actress Performance (Musical): **Patricia Routledge** in *Candide*
Outstanding Performance in a Supporting Role: **Eileen Atkins** in *Cymbeline, The Winter's Tale* and *Mountain Language*
Outstanding Newcomer: **Richard Jones** in *Too Clever by Half*
Best Director: **Deborah Warner** for *Titus Andronicus*
Best Designer: **Richard Hudson** for *Andromache*, *Bussy d'Ambois*, *Candide*, *One Way Pendulum*, *The Tempest* and *Too Clever by Half*
The Observer Award (in memory of Kenneth Tynan): **Maly Theatre of Leningrad** for *Stars in the Morning Sky*
Most Outstanding Achievement in Opera: **Leontina Vaduea** in *Manon*
Most Outstanding Achievement in Dance: **The Dancers of the Kirov Ballet**

Lloyds Bank Young Theatre Challenge
Kallaway Ltd, 2 Portland Rd, London W11 4LA
£250,000 sponsorship from Lloyds Bank for schools and youth drama, offering young people aged 11–18 an opportunity to perform on the stage of the Royal National Theatre. Entries by end Oct. 1990 for LBYTC three-day event at the National in July 1991.

Prudential Arts Awards
(SEE MUSIC)
1990 Theatre: **Theatre Royal Stratford East**

DESIGN AWARDS

The British Design Awards 1990
The Design Council, 28 Haymarket, London SW1 4SU, UK

Engineering Products

Planet Safe: fabricated in Ellox polymer, the safe offers improved protection against fire and theft.
Designed by **John Skelton** and **Leslie Stokes** of Racal-Chubb Ltd

Emma 220 Photoplotter: a compact photoplotter offering large-area photoplotting at low cost.
Designed by **in-house design team** of Marconi Instruments Ltd

Components

Turbine Gears: bulb water-turbine gears, the largest epicyclics made for water-power generation.
Designed by the **in-house design team** of Nei-Allen Ltd

Supreme Espagnolette Handle: with a unique latching device, the handle provides automatic and variable locking on a variety of windows.
Designed by **Leonard Fielding** and **Tracy Fletcher** of Worcester Parsons

Medical Equipment

Endolite: a prosthesis system for lower limbs based on new materials of carbon fibre and thermoplastics.
Designed by **Brian Blatchford, John Shorter** and **Victor Woolnough** of Chas A. Blatchford & Sons Ltd

Motor Equipment

Moveable Bulkhead: virtually 100% efficient in preventing thermal transfer, the bulkhead can be adapted for use in trailers carrying varying loads.
Designed by **Claude Endelin** of York Thermostar (UK) Ltd

Model 950 Pump: a heavy-duty plastic lever pump that costs half as much as its metal predecessor.
Designed by **Roy Lowbridge** and **Michael Chandler** of Ernest H. Hill Ltd

ST400 Intelligent Tachometer: the ST400, incorporating a stepper motor, is said to be a great improvement in accuracy, speed and data logging from a traditional tachometer.
Designed by the in-house team of **Trevor Tapping**, **Alan Rock** and **Angus Rock** of Stack Ltd

Computer Software

NewSPAper: an integrated full-colour desktop publishing package designed to enable school students to produce their own newspapers.
Designed by the **in-house design tream** of Software Production Associates Ltd

Autoroute Plus: a desktop mapping system which enables up to 20% of the costs of road journeys in Britain to be saved through route planning.
Designed by **John McCarthy** and the **in-house design team** of Nextbase Ltd

System 8000: an accurate and easy to use programme that enables medical staff to diagnose abnormalities that might otherwise be missed.
Designed by **Christopher Bunn**, **Professor G.S. Dawes**, **Dr C.W.G. Redman**, **Gary Murphy** and **Mary Moulden.** Oxford Sonicaid Ltd

Consumer Goods

Autohelm 4000: the first leisure sailing autopilot to

advance beyond an exposed-belt driven system.
Designed by **John Wickham** and the **in-house design team** of Nantech Ltd

Autohelm Seatalk System: an integrated navigation system in which the separate instruments share in formation without the need for a central computer.
Designed by **John Wickham** and the **in-house design team** of Nantech Ltd

Agenda: pocket electronic organizer containing a diary and personal data base and word processor.
Designed by **Sir Mark Weinberg**, **Cy Endfield** (user interface); **Chris Rainey** (electronics); **John Southgate** (software); **Stephen Steliou** (production design); **BIB Design Consultants Ltd** (industrial design) for Microwriter Systems plc

Nomix Super Pro: a chemical sprayer that reduces chemical drift and cuts operators' exposure to chemicals.
Designed by **David Ratto** (industrial design) and the **in-house design team** of Nomix Manufacturing Co. Ltd

Fox (Feedback Office Executive Terminal): a time and attendance recording device.
Designed by **Paul Durbin** and the **in-house design team** of Feedback Data Ltd

Dancall 5000 Cordless Telephone: pocket-sized cordless telephone.
Designed by **John Stoddard**, **Charles Ash** and **Nick Dorman** of Moggridge Associates for Dancall Radio A/S

Prince Philip Prize for the Designer of the Year

1990 **Barrie Weaver** (Robert Weaver) 7 Westbourne Grove Mews, London W11 2SA
Design research and new product development in the technological, commercial and consumer fields.

RSA Awards

Royal Society of Arts, 8 John Adams St, London WC2N 6EZ, UK
The **RSA Student Design Awards** offer 100 prizes every year in 30 design projects ranging from graphics and interiors to transport and technologies. Prizes include travel, medals and attachment to companies.

SPORTS FACTFILE

ABBREVIATIONS

General

A against
aet after extra time
aot after overtime
bt beat
C champions
CP Crystal Palace
D drawn
dec declared
f furlong(s)
F for
fav favourite
G–W Greenwich to Westminster
hr hour(s)
km kilometre(s)
L lost
m metre(s)
M mile(s)
MD men's doubles
min minute(s)
mph miles per hour
MS men's singles
MT men's team
no not out
NSD no score draw(s)
P played
pen penalties
Pts points
Q qualifying(ied)
qf quarter-final
r achieved during a relay
R relegated
rec record
SD score draw(s)
sec second(s)
sf semi-final
SP starting price
T team
u unratified for technical reasons
W won
WC wild card winner
WD women's doubles
WS women's singles
WT women's team
XD mixed doubles
y yard(s)

Countries

ANT Antigua
ARG Argentina
AUS Australia
AUT Austria
BAH Bahamas
BAN Bangladesh
BAR Barbados
BEL Belgium
BER Bermuda
BOL Bolivia
BRA Brazil
BUL Bulgaria
BVI British Virgin Islands
CAM Cameroon
CAN Canada
CHI Chile
CHN China
COL Colombia
CRC Costa Rica
CSR Czechoslovakia
CUB Cuba
CYP Cyprus
DEN Denmark
DOM Dominican Republic
ECU Ecuador
EGY Egypt
ENG England
ETH Ethiopia
FIJ Fiji
FIN Finland
FRA France
FRG Federal Republic of Germany (West Germany)
GBI Great Britain & Ireland
GBR Great Britain (United Kingdom)
GDR German Democratic Republic (East Germany)
GHA Ghana
GRE Greece
GUE Guernsey
GUY Guyana
HKG Kong Kong
HOL Holland (Netherlands)
HUN Hungary
ICE Iceland
INA Indonesia
IND India
IRE Ireland
ISR Israel
ITA Italy
JAM Jamaica
JAP Japan
JER Jersey
KEN Kenya
LUX Luxembourg
MAL Malaysia
MEX Mexico
MLT Malta
MNG Mongolia
MON Monaco
MOR Morocco
NAU Nauru
NGR Nigeria
NIR Northern Ireland
NKO North Korea
NOR Norway
NZL New Zealand
PAK Pakistan
PAN Panama
PHI Philippines
PNG Papua New Guinea
POL Poland
POR Portugal
PUE Puerto Rico
ROM Romania
SAF South Africa
SCO Scotland
SKO South Korea
SNM San Marino
SPA Spain
SRI Sri Lanka
SWE Sweden
SWI Switzerland
TAN Tanzania
THA Thailand
TRI Trinidad & Tobago
TUN Tunisia
TUR Turkey
UGA Uganada
URS USSR
URU Uruguay
USA United States of America
VEN Venezuela
VIS US Virgin Islands
WAL Wales
WSA Western Samoa
YUG Yugoslavia
ZAM Zambia
ZIM Zimbabwe

AMERICAN FOOTBALL

US 1989–90 SEASON

FINAL TABLES

	W	L	T*	F	A	
AFC – Eastern Division						
Buffalo Bills	9	7	0	409	317	C
Miami Dolphins	8	8	0	331	379	
Indianapolis Colts	8	8	0	298	301	
New England Patriots	5	11	0	297	391	
New York Jets	4	12	0	253	411	
AFC – Central Division						
Cleveland Browns	9	6	1	334	254	C
Houston Oilers	9	7	0	365	412	WC
Pittsburgh Steelers	9	7	0	265	326	WC
Cincinnati Bengals	8	8	0	405	285	
AFC – Western Division						
Denver Broncos	11	5	0	362	226	C
Los Angeles Raiders	8	8	0	315	297	
Kansas City Chiefs	8	7	1	318	286	
Seattle Seahawks	7	9	0	241	327	
San Diego Chargers	6	10	0	266	290	
NFC – Eastern Division						
New York Giants	12	4	0	368	252	C
Philadelphia Eagles	11	5	0	342	274	WC
Washington Redskins	10	6	0	386	308	
Phoenix Cardinals	5	11	0	258	377	
Dallas Cowboys	1	15	0	204	393	
NFC – Central Division						
Minnesota Vikings	10	6	0	351	276	C
Green Bay Packers	10	6	0	362	356	
Detroit Lions	7	9	0	312	364	
Chicago Bears	6	10	0	358	377	
Tampa Bay Buccaneers	5	11	0	320	419	
NFC – Western Division						
San Francisco 49ers	14	2	0	442	253	C
Los Angeles Rams	11	5	0	426	344	WC
New Orleans Saints	9	7	0	386	301	
Atlanta Falcons	3	13	0	279	437	

* Tied

WILD CARD PLAY-OFFS (31 Dec 89)

AFC	Houston Oilers	23	Pittsburgh Steelers*	26
NFC	Philadelphia Eagles	7	Los Angeles Rams	21

* aot

CHAMPIONSHIP SEMI-FINALS (6–7 Jan 90)

AFC	Buffalo Bills	30	Cleveland Browns	34
AFC	Pittsburgh Steelers	23	Denver Broncos	24
NFC	Minnesota Vikings	13	San Francisco 49ers	41
NFC	Los Angeles Rams*	19	New York Giants	13

* aot

CHAMPIONSHIP FINALS (14 Jan 90)

AFC	Cleveland Browns	21	Denver Broncos	37
NFC	Los Angeles Rams	3	San Francisco 49ers	30

SUPERBOWL XXIV (New Orleans 28 Jan 90)

San Francisco 49ers 55 Denver Broncos 10

San Francisco 49ers, who also won Superbowl XXIII, achieved two Superbowl records in 1990 – the highest ever score of 55, and the highest winning margin of 45 points. They equalled two more records – the most Superbowl wins (four by Pittsburgh Steelers: 1975, 1976, 1979 and 1980), and the fifth to retain the title (Green Bay Packers 1967–68, Miami Dolphins 1973–74, Pittsburgh Steelers 1975–76 and 1979–80).

PRO BOWL (Honolulu 4 Feb 90)

National Football Conf. 27 American Football Conf. 21

AMERICAN BOWL (Wembley 6 Aug 89)

Phildelpha Eagles 17 Cleveland Browns 13

ARCHERY

WORLD CHAMPIONSHIPS (7 & 9 Jul 89)

			pts
Men's Individual			
1	S. Zabrodsky	URS	332
2	S. Hallard	GBR	331
3	T. Poikolainen	FIN	331
Men's Team			
1	USSR		985
2	USA		976
3	South Korea		972
Women's Individual			
1	Kim Soo-nyung	SKO	338
2	Kim Kyung-wong	SKO	331
3	D. Parker	USA	331
Women's Team			
1	South Korea		995
2	Sweden		954
3	USSR		953

UK MASTERS (10 Jun 90)

Men		
1	S. Hallard	1254
2	R. Priestman	1239
3	A. Franks	1225
Women		
1	P. Edwards	1247
2	J. Edens	1237
3	S. Wilson	1229

ASSOCIATION FOOTBALL

14TH WORLD CUP FINALS (Italy 1990)

The Draw

The group draw was made in Rome on 9 December 1989. Two days earlier, FIFA announced that six teams would be seeded: Italy, Argentina, Brazil, West Germany, Belgium and England.

The Format

From the first round, played on a round-robin basis, the top two teams in each group qualified, plus four of the third place teams, decided firstly on points, then on goals scored and goal difference.

The sixteen qualifying teams entered a pre-determined draw and played on a knockout basis with the winners going forward to the next round.

First Round

Group A

9 Jun	Rome	Italy	1	Austria	0
10 Jun	Florence	Czechoslovakia	5	USA	1
14 Jun	Rome	Italy	1	USA	0
15 Jun	Florence	Czechoslovakia	1	Austria	0
19 Jun	Rome	Italy	2	Czechoslovakia	0
19 Jun	Florence	Austria	2	USA	1

	P	W	D	L	F	A	Pts
Italy	3	3	0	0	4	0	6Q
Czecho-slovakia	3	2	0	1	6	3	4Q
Austria	3	1	0	2	2	3	2
USA	3	0	0	3	2	8	0

Group B

8 Jun	Milan	Cameroon	1	Argentina	0
9 Jun	Bari	Romania	2	USSR	0
13 Jun	Naples	Argentina	2	USSR	0
14 Jun	Bari	Cameroon	2	Romania	1
18 Jun	Naples	Argentina	1	Romania	1
18 Jun	Bari	USSR	4	Cameroon	0

	P	W	D	L	F	A	Pts
Cameroon	3	2	0	1	3	5	4Q
Romania	3	1	1	1	4	3	3Q
Argentina	3	1	1	1	3	2	3Q
USSR	3	1	0	2	4	4	2

Group C

10 Jun	Turin	Brazil	2	Sweden	1
11 Jun	Genoa	Costa Rica	1	Scotland	0
16 Jun	Turin	Brazil	1	Costa Rica	0
16 Jun	Genoa	Scotland	2	Sweden	1
20 Jun	Turin	Brazil	1	Scotland	0
20 Jun	Genoa	Costa Rica	2	Sweden	1

	P	W	D	L	F	A	Pts
Brazil	3	3	0	0	4	1	6 Q
Costa Rica	3	2	0	1	3	2	4 Q
Scotland	3	1	0	2	2	3	2
Sweden	3	0	0	3	3	6	0

Group D

9 Jun	Bologna	Colombia	2	United Arab Emirates	0
10 Jun	Milan	West Germany	4	Yugoslavia	1
14 Jun	Bologna	Yugoslavia	1	Colombia	0
15 Jun	Milan	West Germany	5	United Arab Emirates	1
19 Jun	Milan	West Germany	1	Colombia	1
19 Jun	Bologna	Yugoslavia	4	United Arab Emirates	1

	P	W	D	L	F	A	Pts
West Germany	3	2	1	0	10	3	5 Q
Yugoslavia	3	2	0	1	6	5	4 Q
Colombia	3	1	1	1	3	2	3 Q
United Arab Emirates	3	0	0	3	2	11	0

Group E

12 Jun	Verona	Belgium	2	South Korea	0
13 Jun	Udine	Spain	0	Uruguay	0
17 Jun	Verona	Belgium	3	Uruguay	1
17 Jun	Udine	Spain	3	South Korea	1
21 Jun	Verona	Spain	2	Belgium	1
21 Jun	Udine	Uruguay	1	South Korea	0

	P	W	D	L	F	A	Pts
Spain	3	2	1	0	5	2	5 Q
Belgium	3	2	0	1	6	3	4 Q
Uruguay	3	1	1	1	2	3	3 Q
South Korea	3	0	0	3	1	6	0

Group F

11 Jun	Cagliari	England	1	Rep of Ireland	1
12 Jun	Palermo	Egypt	1	Holland	1
16 Jun	Cagliari	England	0	Holland	0
17 Jun	Palermo	Egypt	0	Rep of Ireland	0
21 Jun	Cagliari	England	1	Egypt	0
21 Jun	Palermo	Holland	1	Rep of Ireland	1

	P	W	D	L	F	A	Pts
England	3	1	2	0	2	1	4 Q
Rep of Ireland	3	0	3	0	2	2	3 Q
Holland	3	0	3	0	2	2	3 Q
Egypt	3	0	2	1	1	2	2

Second Round

23 Jun	Naples	Cameroon	2	Colombia	1	aet
23 Jun	Bari	Czechoslovakia	4	Costa Rica	1	
24 Jun	Turin	Argentina	1	Brazil	0	
24 Jun	Milan	West Germany	2	Holland	1	
25 Jun	Genoa	Rep of Ireland	0	Romania	0	aet
		Rep of Ireland won 5–4 on pen				
25 Jun	Rome	Italy	2	Uruguay	0	
26 Jun	Verona	Yugoslavia	2	Spain	1	aet
26 Jun	Bologna	England	1	Belgium	0	aet

Quarter-final Round

30 Jun	Florence	Argentina	0	Yugoslavia	0	aet
		Argentina won 3–2 on pen				
30 Jun	Rome	Italy	1	Rep of Ireland	0	
1 Jul	Milan	West Germany	1	Czecho-slovakia	0	
1 Jul	Naples	England	3	Cameroon	2	aet

Semi-final Round

3 Jul	Naples	Argentina	1	Italy	1	aet
		Argentina won 4–3 on pen				
4 Jul	Turin	West Germany	1	England	1	aet
		West Germany won 4–3 on pen				

3rd Place play-off

7 Jul	Bari	Italy	2	England	1

Final

8 Jul	Rome	West Germany	1	Argentina	0

Leading goalscorers:

S. Schillaci (ITA)	6
T. Skuhravy (CSR)	5
G. Lineker (ENG)	4
L. Matthäus (FRG)	4
M. Michel (SPA)	4
R. Milla (CAM)	4

HOME COUNTRIES' INTERNATIONAL MATCH RESULTS

England

6 Sep 89	World Cup Q	Sweden	0	England	0
11 Oct 89	World Cup Q	Poland	0	England	0
15 Nov 89	Friendly	England	0	Italy	0
13 Dec 89	Friendly	England	2	Yugoslavia	1
28 Mar 90	Friendly	England	1	Brazil	0
25 Apr 90	Friendly	England	4	Czechoslovakia	2
15 May 90	Friendly	England	1	Denmark	0
22 May 90	Friendly	England	1	Uruguay	2
2 Jun 90	Friendly	Tunisia	1	England	1
11 Jun 90	World Cup Grp	England	1	Rep of Ireland	1
16 Jun 90	World Cup Grp	England	0	Holland	0
21 Jun 90	World Cup Grp	England	1	Egypt	0
26 Jun 90	World Cup 2nd Rd	England	1	Belgium	0*
1 Jul 90	World Cup qf	England	3	Cameroon	2*
4 Jul 90	World Cup sf	West Germany	1	England	1
		West Germany won 4–3 on pen			
7 Jul 90	World Cup 3–4	Italy	2	England	1

* aet

Northern Ireland

6 Sep 89	World Cup Q	N. Ireland	1	Hungary	2
11 Oct 89	World Cup Q	Rep of Ireland	3	N. Ireland	0
18 May 90	Friendly	N. Ireland	1	Uruguay	0

Republic of Ireland

6 Sep 89	Friendly	Rep of Ireland	1	West Germany	1
11 Oct 89	World Cup Q	Rep of Ireland	3	N. Ireland	0
15 Nov 89	World Cup Q	Malta	0	Rep of Ireland	2
28 Mar 90	Friendly	Rep of Ireland	1	Wales	0
25 Apr 90	Friendly	Rep of Ireland	1	USSR	0
16 May 90	Friendly	Rep of Ireland	1	Finland	1
27 May 90	Friendly	Turkey	0	Rep of Ireland	0
2 Jun 90	Friendly	Malta	0	Rep of Ireland	3
11 Jun 90	World Cup Grp	England	1	Rep of Ireland	1
17 Jun 90	World Cup Grp	Rep of Ireland	0	Egypt	0
21 Jun 90	World Cup Grp	Rep of Ireland	1	Holland	1
25 Jun 90	World Cup 2nd Rd	Rep of Ireland	0	Romania	0
		Rep of Ireland won 5–4 on pen			
30 Jun 90	World Cup qf	Italy	1	Rep of Ireland	0

Scotland

6 Sep 89	World Cup Q	Yugoslavia	3	Scotland	1
11 Oct 89	World Cup Q	France	3	Scotland	0
15 Nov 89	World Cup Q	Scotland	1	Norway	1
28 Mar 90	Friendly	Scotland	1	Argentina	0
25 Apr 90	Friendly	Scotland	0	East Germany	1
16 May 90	Friendly	Scotland	1	Egypt	3
19 May 90	Friendly	Scotland	1	Poland	1
28 May 90	Friendly	Malta	1	Scotland	2
11 Jun 90	World Cup Grp	Scotland	0	Costa Rica	1
16 Jun 90	World Cup Grp	Scotland	2	Sweden	1
20 Jun 90	World Cup Grp	Scotland	0	Brazil	1

Wales

6 Sep 89	World Cup Q	Finland	1	Wales	0
11 Oct 89	World Cup Q	Wales	1	Holland	2
15 Nov 89	World Cup Q	West Germany	2	Wales	1
28 Mar 90	Friendly	Rep of Ireland	1	Wales	0
25 Apr 90	Friendly	Sweden	4	Wales	2
20 May 90	Friendly	Wales	1	Costa Rica	0

BARCLAYS ENGLISH FOOTBALL LEAGUE 1989–90

Division I

	P	W	D	L	F	A	Pts
1 Liverpool	38	23	10	5	78	37	79 C
2 Aston Villa	38	21	7	10	57	38	70
3 Tottenham Hotspur	38	19	6	13	59	47	63
4 Arsenal	38	18	8	12	54	38	62
5 Chelsea	38	16	12	10	58	50	60
6 Everton	38	17	8	13	57	46	59
7 Southampton	38	15	10	13	71	63	55
8 Wimbledon	38	13	16	9	47	40	55
9 Nottingham Forest	38	15	9	14	55	47	54
10 Norwich City	38	13	14	11	44	42	53
11 Queens Park Rangers	38	13	11	14	45	44	50
12 Coventry City	38	14	7	17	39	59	49
13 Manchester United	38	13	9	16	46	47	48
14 Manchester City	38	12	12	14	43	52	48
15 Crystal Palace	38	13	9	16	42	66	48
16 Derby County	38	13	7	18	43	40	46
17 Luton Town	38	10	13	15	43	57	43
18 Sheffield Wednesday	38	11	10	17	35	51	43 R
19 Charlton Athletic	38	7	9	22	31	57	30 R
20 Milwall	38	5	11	22	39	65	26 R

Division II

	P	W	D	L	F	A	Pts
1 Leeds United	46	24	13	9	79	52	85 P
2 Sheffield United	46	24	13	9	78	58	85 P
3 Newcastle United	46	22	14	10	80	55	80
4 Swindon Town	46	20	14	12	79	59	74
5 Blackburn Rovers	46	19	17	10	74	59	74
6 Sunderland	46	20	14	12	70	64	74
7 West Ham United	46	20	12	14	80	57	72
8 Oldham Athletic	46	19	14	13	70	57	71
9 Ipswich Town	46	19	12	15	67	66	69
10 Wolverhampton Wanderers	46	18	13	15	67	60	67
11 Port Vale	46	15	16	15	62	57	61
12 Portsmouth	46	15	16	15	62	65	61
13 Leicester City	46	15	14	17	67	79	59
14 Hull City	46	14	16	16	58	65	58
15 Watford	46	14	15	17	58	60	57
16 Plymouth Argyle	46	14	13	19	58	63	55
17 Oxford United	46	15	9	22	57	66	54
18 Brighton & Hove Albion	46	15	9	22	56	72	54
19 Barnsley	46	13	15	18	49	71	54
20 West Bromwich Albion	46	12	15	19	67	71	51
21 Middlesbrough	46	13	11	22	52	63	50
22 Bournemouth	46	12	12	22	57	76	48 R
23 Bradford	46	9	14	23	44	68	41 R
24 Stoke City	46	6	19	21	35	63	37 R

Play-off Semi-finals (13 & 16 May 90)

Sunderland	0	Newcastle United	0
Newcastle United	0	Sunderland	2

Sunderland won 2–0 on aggregate

Blackburn Rovers	1	Swindon Town	2
Swindon Town	2	Blackburn Rovers	1

Swindon Town won 4–2 on aggregate

Play-off Final (28 May 90)

Swindon Town 1 Sunderland 0 Swindon Town P

On 7 Jun 90, Swindon Town were relegated to Division III by the Football League as a result of irregularities over payments to players. Sunderland were promoted to Division I and Tranmere Rovers to Division II. This decision was changed on 2 Jul 90 following an appeal. Swindon Town stay in Division II, Sunderland are promoted to Division I and Tranmere Rovers stay in Division III.

Division III

	P	W	D	L	F	A	Pts
1 Bristol Rovers	46	26	15	5	71	35	93 C
2 Bristol City	46	27	10	9	76	40	91 P
3 Notts County	46	25	12	9	73	53	87
4 Tranmere Rovers	46	23	11	12	86	49	87
5 Bury	46	21	11	14	70	49	74
6 Bolton Wanderers	46	18	15	13	59	48	69
7 Birmingham City	46	18	12	16	60	59	66
8 Huddersfield Town	46	17	14	15	61	62	65
9 Rotherham United	46	17	13	16	71	62	64
10 Reading	46	15	19	12	57	53	64
11 Shrewsbury Town	46	16	15	15	59	54	63
12 Crewe Alexandra	46	15	17	14	56	53	62
13 Brentford	46	18	7	21	66	66	61
14 Leyton Orient	46	16	10	20	52	56	58
15 Mansfield Town	46	16	7	23	50	65	55
16 Chester City	46	13	15	18	43	55	54
17 Swansea City	46	14	12	20	45	63	54
18 Wigan Athletic	46	13	14	19	48	64	53
19 Preston North End	46	14	10	22	65	79	52
20 Fulham	46	12	15	19	55	66	51
21 Cardiff City	46	12	14	20	51	70	50 R
22 Northampton Town	46	11	14	21	51	68	47 R
23 Blackpool	46	10	16	20	49	73	46 R
24 Walsall	46	9	14	23	40	72	41 R

Play-off Semi-finals (13 & 16 May 90)

Bolton Wanderers	1	Notts County	1
Notts County	2	Bolton Wanderers	0

Notts County won 3–1 on aggregate

Bury	0	Tranmere Rovers	0
Tranmere Rovers	2	Bury	0

Tranmere Rovers won 2–0 on aggregate

Play-off Final (27 May 90)

Notts County 2 Tranmere Rovers 0 Notts County P

Division IV

	P	W	D	L	F	A	Pts
1 Exeter City	46	28	5	13	83	48	89 C
2 Grimsby Town	46	22	13	11	70	47	79 P
3 Southend United	46	22	9	15	61	48	75 P
4 Stockport County	46	21	11	14	68	62	74
5 Maidstone United	46	22	7	17	77	61	73
6 Cambridge United	46	21	10	15	76	66	73
7 Chesterfield	46	19	14	13	63	50	71
8 Carlisle United	46	21	8	17	61	60	71
9 Peterborough United	46	17	17	12	39	46	68
10 Lincoln City	46	18	14	14	48	48	68
11 Scunthorpe United	46	17	15	14	69	54	66
12 Rochdale	46	20	6	20	52	55	66
13 York City	46	16	16	14	55	53	64
14 Gillingham	46	17	11	18	46	48	62
15 Torquay United	46	15	12	19	53	66	57
16 Burnley	46	14	14	18	45	55	56
17 Hereford United	46	15	10	21	56	62	55
18 Scarborough	46	15	10	21	60	73	55
19 Hartlepool	46	15	10	21	66	88	55
20 Doncaster Rovers	46	14	9	23	53	60	51
21 Wrexham	46	13	12	21	51	67	51
22 Aldershot	46	12	14	20	49	69	50
23 Halifax Town	46	12	13	21	57	65	49
24 Colchester United	46	11	10	25	48	75	43 R

Play-off Semi-finals (13 & 16 May 90)

Cambridge United	1	Maidstone United	1
Maidstone United	0	Cambridge United	2

Cambridge United won 3–1 on aggregate

Chesterfield	4	Stockport County	0
Stockport County	0	Chesterfield	2

Chesterfield won 6–0 on aggregate

Play-off Final (26 May 90)

Cambridge United	1	Chesterfield	0
Cambridge United	P		

GM VAUXHALL CONFERENCE

	P	W	D	L	F	A	Pts
1 Darlington	42	26	9	7	76	25	87 P
2 Barnet	42	26	7	9	81	41	85
3 Runcorn	42	19	13	10	79	62	70
4 Macclesfield	42	17	15	10	56	41	66
5 Kettering Town	42	18	12	12	66	53	66
6 Welling United	42	18	10	14	62	50	64
7 Yeovil Town	42	17	12	13	62	54	63
8 Sutton United	42	19	6	17	68	64	63
9 Merthyr Tydfil	42	16	14	12	67	63	62

GM VAUXHALL CONFERENCE

	P	W	D	L	F	A	Pts
10 Wycombe Wanderers	42	17	10	15	64	56	61
11 Cheltenham Town	42	16	11	15	58	60	59
12 Telford United	42	15	13	14	56	63	58
13 Kidderminster	42	15	9	18	64	67	54
14 Barrow	42	12	16	14	51	67	52
15 Northwich Victoria	42	15	5	22	51	67	50
16 Altrincham	42	12	13	17	49	48	49
17 Stafford Rangers	42	12	12	18	50	62	48
18 Boston United	42	13	8	21	48	67	47
19 Fisher Athletic	42	13	7	22	55	78	46
20 Chorley	42	13	6	23	42	67	45 R
21 Farnborough Town	42	10	12	20	60	73	42 R
22 Enfield	42	10	6	26	52	89	36 R

B & Q SCOTTISH FOOTBALL LEAGUE 1989–90

Premier Division

	P	W	D	L	F	A	Pts
1 Rangers	36	20	11	5	48	19	51 C
2 Aberdeen	36	17	10	9	56	33	44
3 Hearts	36	16	12	8	54	35	44
4 Dundee United	36	11	13	12	36	39	35
5 Celtic	36	10	14	12	37	37	34
6 Motherwell	36	11	12	13	43	47	34
7 Hibernian	36	12	10	14	34	41	34
8 Dunfermline	36	11	8	17	37	50	30
9 St Mirren	36	10	10	16	28	48	30
10 Dundee	36	5	14	17	41	65	24 R

Division I

	P	W	D	L	F	A	Pts
1 St Johnstone	39	25	8	6	81	39	58 P
2 Airdrie	39	23	8	8	77	45	54 P
3 Clydebank	39	17	10	12	74	64	44
4 Falkirk	39	14	15	10	59	46	43
5 Raith Rovers	39	15	12	12	57	50	42
6 Hamilton Academicals	39	14	13	12	52	53	41
7 Meadowbank	39	13	13	13	41	46	39
8 Partick Thistle	39	12	14	13	62	53	38
9 Clyde	39	10	15	14	39	46	35
10 Ayr United	39	11	13	15	41	62	35
11 Morton	39	9	16	14	38	46	34
12 Forfar Athletic	39	8	15	16	51	65	29 *
13 Albion Rovers	39	8	11	20	50	78	27R
14 Alloa Athletic	39	6	13	20	41	70	25R

* 2 points deducted by the League

Division II

	P	W	D	L	F	A	Pts
1 Brechin City	39	19	11	9	59	44	49 P
2 Kilmarnock	39	22	4	13	67	39	48 P
3 Stirling Albion	39	20	7	12	73	50	47
4 Stenhousemuir	39	18	8	13	60	53	44
5 Berwick Rangers	39	18	5	16	66	57	41
6 Dumbarton	39	15	10	14	70	73	40
7 Cowdenbeath	39	13	13	13	58	54	39
8 Stranraer	39	15	8	16	57	59	38
9 East Fife	39	12	12	15	60	64	36
10 Queen of the South	39	11	14	14	58	69	36
11 Queens Park	39	13	10	16	40	51	36
12 Arbroath	39	12	10	17	48	61	34
13 Montrose	39	10	12	17	53	63	32
14 East Stirling	39	8	10	21	34	66	26

CUP RESULTS

TOYOTA CUP – WORLD CLUB CHAMPIONSHIP (17 Dec 89)
AC Milan ITA 1 Atletico Nacional COL 0 aet

EUROPEAN CHAMPIONS' CUP FINAL (23 May 90)
AC Milan ITA 1 Benfica POR 0

EUROPEAN CUP WINNERS' CUP FINAL (9 May 90)
Sampdoria ITA 2 Anderlecht BEL 0 aet

UEFA CUP FINAL

Ist leg (2 May 90)
Juventus ITA 3 Fiorentina ITA 1

2nd leg (16 May 90)
Fiorentina ITA 0 Juventus ITA 0
Juventus ITA won 3–1 on aggregate

ZENITH DATA SYSTEMS CHALLENGE CUP – UNOFFICIAL BRITISH CHAMPIONSHIP (Ibrox Park, Glasgow 19 Dec 89)
Arsenal ENG 2 Rangers SCO 1

TENNENT'S FA CHARITY SHIELD (12 Aug 89)
Liverpool 1 Arsenal 0

FA CUP FINAL (12 May 90)
Crystal Palace 3 Manchester United 3 aet

FA CUP FINAL – Replay (17 May 90)
Manchester United 1 Crystal Palace 0

LITTLEWOODS CUP FINAL – FA LEAGUE CUP (29 Apr 90)
Nottingham Forest 1 Oldham Athletic 0

ZENITH DATA SYSTEMS CUP FINAL – FULL MEMBERS' CUP (25 Mar 90)
Chelsea 1 Middlesbrough 0

LEYLAND DAF CUP FINAL – ASSOCIATE MEMBERS' CUP (20 May 90)
Tranmere Rovers 2 Bristol Rovers 1

FA TROPHY FINAL (19 May 90)
Barrow 3 Leek Town 0

FA VASE FINAL (5 May 90)
Bridlington Town 0 Yeading 0 aet

FA VASE FINAL – Replay (14 May 90)
Yeading 1 Bridlington Town 0

SCOTTISH FA CUP FINAL (12 May 90)
Aberdeen 0 Rangers 0 aet
Aberdeen won 9–8 on pen

SKOL CUP FINAL – SCOTTISH LEAGUE CUP (22 Oct 89)
Aberdeen 2 Rangers 1 aet

WELSH CUP FINAL (12 May 90)
Hereford United 2 Wrexham 1

BASS IRISH CUP FINAL (5 May 90)
Glentoran 3 Portadown 0

ATHLETICS

WORLD AND BRITISH RECORDS AS AT 8 JUL 90

Men

100 m	World	9.97	C. Lewis	USA	Seoul	24 Sep 88
	British	9.97	L. Christie	ENG	Seoul	24 Sep 88
200 m	World	19.72	P. Mennea	ITA	Mexico City	12 Sep 79
	British	20.09	L. Christie	ENG	Seoul	28 Sep 88
300 m	World	31.69	R. Hernández	CUB	Bratislava	20 Jun 90
	British	32.08	R. Black	ENG	London CP	8 Aug 86
400 m	World	43.29	H. Reynolds	USA	Zürich	17 Aug 88
	British	44.50	D. Redmond	ENG	Rome	1 Sep 87
600 m	World	1:12.81	J. Gray	USA	Santa Monica	24 May 86
	British	1:15.00	S. Coe	ENG	Florence	10 Jun 81

Event		Record	Name	Country	Venue	Date
800 m	World	1:41.73	S. Coe	ENG	Florence	10 Jun 81
	British	1:41.73	S. Coe	ENG	Florence	10 Jun 81
1000 m	World	2:12.18	S. Coe	ENG	Oslo	11 Jul 81
	British	2:12.18	S. Coe	ENG	Oslo	11 Jul 81
1500 m	World	3:29.46	S. Aouita	MOR	W. Berlin	23 Aug 85
	British	3:29.67	S. Cram	ENG	Nice	16 Jul 85
1 M	World	3:46.32	S. Cram	ENG	Oslo	27 Jul 85
	British	3:46.32	S. Cram	ENG	Oslo	27 Jul 85
2000 m	World	4:50.81	S. Aouita	MOR	Paris	16 Jul 87
	British	4:51.39	S. Cram	ENG	Budapest	4 Aug 85
3000 m	World	7:29.45	S. Aouita	MOR	Cologne	20 Aug 89
	British	7:32.79	D. Moorcroft	ENG	London CP	17 Jul 82
2 M	World	8:13.45	S. Aouita	MOR	Turin	28 May 87
	British	8:13.51	S. Ovett	ENG	London CP	15 Sep 78
5000 m	World	12:58.39	S. Aouita	MOR	Rome	22 Jul 87
	British	13:00.41	D. Moorcroft	ENG	Oslo	7 Jul 82
10000 m	World	27:08.23	A. Barrios	MEX	W. Berlin	18 Aug 89
	British	27:23.06	E. Martin	ENG	Oslo	2 Jul 88
Marathon	World	2:06:50	B. Dinsamo	ETH	Rotterdam	17 Apr 88
	British	2:07:13	S. Jones	WAL	Chicago	20 Oct 85
110 m Hurdles	World	12.92	R. Kingdom	USA	Zürich	16 Aug 89
	British	13.08	C. Jackson	WAL	Auckland	28 Jan 90
400 m Hurdles	World	47.02	E. Moses	USA	Koblenz	31 Aug 83
	British	48.12	D. Hemery	ENG	Mexico City	15 Oct 68
2000 m Steeplechase	World	5:18.32	A. Lambruschini	ITA	Verona	27 Sep 89
	British	5:19.86	M. Rowland	ENG	London CP	28 Aug 88
3000 m Steeplechase	World	8:05.35	P. Koech	KEN	Stockholm	3 Jul 89
	British	8:07.96	M. Rowland	ENG	Seoul	30 Sep 88
4 × 100 m Relay	World	37.83	Olympic Team S. Graddy/R. Brown/C. Smith/C. Lewis	USA	Los Angeles	11 Aug 84
	British	38.28	Olympic Team E. Bunney/J. Regis/M. McFarlane/L. Christie	GBR	Seoul	1 Oct 88
4 × 400 m Relay	World	2:56.16	Olympic Team V. Matthews/R. Freeman/L. James/L. Evans	USA	Mexico City	20 Oct 68
		2:56.16	Olympic Team D. Everett/S. Lewis/K. Robinzine/H. Reynolds	USA	Seoul	1 Oct 88
	British	2:58.86	World Championship Team D. Redmond/K. Akabusi/R. Black/P. Brown	GBR	Rome	6 Sep 87
High Jump	World	2.44	J. Sotomayor	CUB	San Juan, PUE	29 Jul 89
	British	2.34	D. Grant	ENG	Gateshead	28 Aug 89
Long Jump	World	8.90	R. Beaman	USA	Mexico City	18 Oct 68
	British	8.23	L. Davies	WAL	Berne	30 Jun 68
Triple Jump	World	17.97	W. Banks	USA	Indianapolis	16 Jun 85
	British	17.57	K. Connor	ENG	Provo	5 Jun 82
Pole Vault	World	6.06	S. Bubka	URS	Nice	10 Jul 88
	British	5.65	K. Stock	ENG	Stockholm	7 Jul 81
Shot	World	23.12	R. Barnes	USA	Los Angeles	20 May 90
	British	21.68	G. Capes	ENG	Cwmbran	18 May 80
Discus	World	74.08	J. Schult	GDR	Neubrandenburg	6 Jun 86
	British	64.32	W. Tancred	ENG	Woodford	10 Aug 74
Hammer	World	86.74	Y. Sedykh	URS	Stuttgart	30 Aug 86
	British	77.54	M. Girvan	NIR	Wolverhampton	12 May 84
Javelin	World	89.58	S. Backley	ENG	Stockholm	2 Jul 90
	British	89.58	S. Backley	ENG	Stockholm	2 Jul 90
Decathlon (new Javelin)	World	8811 pts	D. Thompson	ENG	Stuttgart	28 Aug 86
	British	8811 pts	D. Thompson	ENG	Stuttgart	28 Aug 86
Decathlon (old Javelin)	World	8847 pts	D. Thompson	ENG	Los Angeles	9 Aug 84
	British	8847 pts	D. Thompson	ENG	Los Angeles	9 Aug 84

Women

Event		Record	Name	Country	Venue	Date
100 m	World	10.49	F. Joyner (nee Griffith)	USA	Indianapolis	16 Jul 88
	British	11.10	K. Smallwood (now Cook)	ENG	Rome	5 Sep 81
200 m	World	21.34	F. Joyner (nee Griffith)	USA	Seoul	29 Sep 88
	British	22.10	K. Smallwood (now Cook)	ENG	Los Angeles	9 Aug 84
300 m	World	34.8	M. Koch	GDR	Athens	8 Sep 82
	British	35.46	K. Cook (nee Smallwood)	ENG	London CP	18 Aug 84

400 m	World	47.60	M. Koch	GDR	Canberra	6 Oct 85
	British	49.43	K. Cook (nee Smallwood)	ENG	Los Angeles	6 Aug 84
600 m	World	1:23.5	D. Melinte	ROM	Poiana Brasov	27 Jul 86
	British	1:26.18	D. Edwards	ENG	London CP	22 Aug 87
800 m	World	1:53.28	J. Kratochvilova	CSR	Munich	26 Jul 83
	British	1:57.42	K. McDermott (now Wade)	WAL	Belfast	24 Jun 85
1000 m	World	2:30.6	T. Providokhina	URS	Podolsk	20 Aug 78
	British	2:33.70	K. McDermott (now Wade)	WAL	Gateshead	9 Aug 85
1500 m	World	3:52.47	T. Kazankina	URS	Zürich	13 Aug 80
	British	3:59.96	Z. Budd	ENG	Brussels	30 Aug 85
1 M	World	4:15.61	P. Ivan	ROM	Nice	10 Jul 89
	British	4:17.57	Z. Budd	ENG	Zürich	21 Aug 85
2000 m	World	5:28.69	M. Puica	ROM	London CP	11 Jul 86
	British	5:29.58	Y. Murray	SCO	London CP	11 Jul 86
3000 m	World	8:22.62	T. Kazankina	URS	Leningrad	26 Aug 84
	British	8:28.83	Z. Budd	ENG	Rome	7 Sep 85
5000 m	World	14:37.33	I. Kristiansen	NOR	Stockholm	5 Aug 86
	British	14:48.07	Z. Budd	ENG	London CP	26 Aug 85
10000 m	World	30:13.74	I. Kristiansen	NOR	Oslo	5 Jul 86
	British	31:06.99	L. McColgan (nee Lynch)	SCO	Oslo	2 Jul 88
Marathon	World	2:21:06	I. Kristiansen	NOR	London G–W	21 Apr 85
	British	2:25:56	V. Marot	ENG	London G–W	23 Apr 89
100 m Hurdles	World	12.21	Y. Donkova	BUL	Stara Zagora	20 Aug 88
	British	12.82	S. Gunnell	ENG	Zürich	17 Aug 88
400 m Hurdles	World	52.94	M. Stepanova	URS	Tashkent	17 Sep 86
	British	54.03	S. Gunnell	ENG	Seoul	28 Sep 88
4 × 100 m Relay	World	41.37	World Cup Team	GDR	Canberra	6 Oct 85
			S. Gladisch/S. Rieger/I. Auerswald/M. Göhr			
	British	42.43	Olympic Team	GBR	Moscow	1 Aug 80
			H. Oakes/K. Smallwood/B. Callender/S. Lannaman			
4 × 400 m Relay	World	3:15.17	Olympic Team	GDR	Seoul	1 Oct 88
			T. Ledovskaya/O. Nazarova/M. Pinigina/O. Bryzgina			
	British	3:25.51	Olympic Team	GBR	Los Angeles	11 Aug 84
			M. Scutt/H. Barnett/G. Taylor/J. Hoyte-Smith			
High Jump	World	2.09	S. Kostadinova	BUL	Rome	30 Aug 87
	British	1.95	D. Elliott (now Davies)	ENG	Oslo	26 Jun 82
Long Jump	World	7.52	G. Chistyakova	URS	Leningrad	11 Jun 88
	British	6.90	B. Kinch	ENG	Helsinki	14 Aug 83
Shot	World	22.63	N. Lisovskaya	URS	Moscow	6 Jun 87
	British	19.36	J. Oakes	ENG	Gateshead	14 Aug 88
Discus	World	76.80	G. Reinsch	GDR	Neubrandenburg	9 Jul 88
	British	67.48	M. Ritchie	SCO	Walnut	26 Apr 81
Javelin	World	80.00	P. Felke	GDR	Potsdam	8 Sep 88
	British	77.44	F. Whitbread	ENG	Stuttgart	28 Aug 86
Heptathlon	World	7291 pts	J. Kersee (nee Joyner)	USA	Seoul	24 Sep 88
	British	6623 pts	J. Simpson (nee Livermore)	ENG	Stuttgart	30 Aug 86

KODAK AMATEUR ATHLETIC ASSOCIATION/WOMEN'S AMATEUR ATHLETIC ASSOCIATION CHAMPIONSHIPS (Birmingham 11–13 Aug 89)

Men

100 m	1	L. Christie	ENG	10.16
	2	M. Adam	ENG	10.34
	3	J. Regis	ENG	10.39
200 m	1	M. Adam	ENG	20.78
	2	A. Mafe	ENG	20.95
	3	L. Christie	ENG	21.02
400 m	1	P. Brown	ENG	46.26
	2	T. Bennett	ENG	46.40
	3	P. Crampton	ENG	46.43
800 m	1	I. Billy	ENG	1:48.01
	2	M. Yates	ENG	1:48.54
	3	K. McKay	ENG	1:48.97
1500 m	1	S. Coe	ENG	3:41.38
	2	A. Morrell	ENG	3:41.93
	3	N. Horsfield	WAL	3:42.14
3000 m	1	M. Giusto	USA	8:00.38
	2	A. Leonard	ENG	8:04.92
	3	G. Turnbull	ENG	8:06.01
5000 m	1	M. Rowland	ENG	13:32.05
	2	E. Martin	ENG	13:32.59
	3	G. Staines	ENG	13:34.83
110 m Hurdles	1	C. Jackson	WAL	13.19
	2	D. Nelson	ENG	13.57
	3	N. Walker	WAL	13.80
400 m Hurdles	1	M. Robertson	ENG	50.30
	2	A. Cuypers	BEL	50.63
	3	M. Bishop	ENG	51.39
3000 m S'chase	1	C. Walker	ENG	8:35.73
	2	E. Wedderburn	ENG	8:35.86
	3	M. Hawkins	ENG	8:45.36
10000 m Walk	1	M. Easton	ENG	41:39.93
	2	D. Stone	ENG	42:08.44
	3	P. Blagg	ENG	42:53.18

High Jump	1	D. Grant	ENG	2.33
	2	J. Holman	ENG	2.20
	3	S. Chapman	ENG	2.15
Long Jump	1	S. Faulkner	ENG	8.13
	2	J. King	ENG	7.89
	3	B. Williams	ENG	7.81
Triple Jump	1	J. Edwards	ENG	16.53
	2	V. Samuels	ENG	16.24
	3	E. McCalla	ENG	16.14
Pole Vault	1	M. Edwards	ENG	5.20
	2=	S. Arkell	AUS	5.10
	2=	I. Tullett	ENG	5.10
Shot	1	S. Williams	ENG	18.73
	2	M. Simson	ENG	17.75
	3	P. Edwards	WAL	17.27
Discus	1	P. Mardle	ENG	57.90
	2	A. Ekoku	ENG	56.82
	3	S. Casey	ENG	56.66
Hammer	1	J. Logan	USA	72.34
	2	P. Head	ENG	70.32
	3	D. Smith	ENG	68.96
Javelin	1	S. Backley	ENG	83.16
	2	M. Hill	ENG	79.94
	3	M. Roberson	ENG	78.64

Women

100 m	1	P. Dunn	ENG	11.32
	2	S. Douglas	ENG	11.34
	3	P. Smith	ENG	11.61
200 m	1	P. Dunn	ENG	23.43
	2	J. Stoute	ENG	23.61
	3	L. Keough	ENG	23.69
400 m	1	L. Keough	ENG	51.09
	2	J. Stoute	ENG	51.53
	3	A. Piggford	ENG	53.18
800 m	1	D. Edwards	ENG	2:01.24
	2	A. Williams	ENG	2:01.84
	3	L. Baker	ENG	2:02.23
1500 m	1	B. Nicholson	ENG	4:09.34
	2	A. Wyeth	ENG	4:10.83
	3	S. Bailey	ENG	4:11.15
3000 m	1	A. Wyeth	ENG	9:11.12
	2	R. Partridge	ENG	9:11.27
	3	S. McGeorge	ENG	9:12.12
100 m Hurdles	1	S. Gunnell	ENG	13.26
	2	K. Morley	WAL	13.35
	3	L–A. Skeete	ENG	13.38
400 m Hurdles	1	W. Cearns	ENG	56.05
	2	L. Hanson	ENG	56.70
	3	G. Retchakan	ENG	57.17
5000 m Walk	1	B. Sworowski	ENG	22:30.59
	2	L. Langford	ENG	23:40.68
	3	S. Brown	ENG	24:05.38
High Jump	1	D. Davies	ENG	1.85
	2	M. Wheeler	ENG	1.85
	3=	J. Boyle	NIR	1.80
	3=	L. Gittens	ENG	1.80
	3=	S. Hutchings	NIR	1.80
Long Jump	1	N. Boegman	AUS	6.74
	2	F. May	ENG	6..62
	3	K. Hagger	ENG	6.54
Shot	1	M. Augee	ENG	17.51
	2	Y. Hanson-Nortey	ENG	16.38
	3	M. Lynes	ENG	16.06
Discus	1	J. Picton	ENG	53.22
	2	S. Andrews	ENG	52.84
	3	K. Pugh	ENG	51.58
Javelin	1	T. Sanderson	ENG	58.64
	2	C. White	ENG	52.88
	3	A. Liverton	ENG	52.80

WORLD CROSS COUNTRY CHAMPIONSHIPS (Aix-les-Bains, FRA 24 Mar 90)

Men	1	K. Skah	MOR	34:21
	2	M. Tanui	KEN	34:21
	3	J. Korir	KEN	34:22
	T1	Kenya		42 pts
	T2	Ethiopia		96 pts
	T3	Spain		176 pts
Women	1	L. Jennings	USA	19:21
	2	A. Dias	POR	19:33
	3	E. Romanova	URS	19:33
	T1	USSR		37 pts
	T2	Ethiopia		75 pts
	T3	Portugal		80 pts

ADT LONDON MARATHON (Greenwich to Westminster 22 Apr 90)

Men	1	A. Hutton	SCO	2:10:10
	2	S. Bettiol	ITA	2:10:40
	3	J. Romero	SPA	2:10:48
Women	1	W. Panfil	POL	2:26:31
	2	F. Larrieu-Smith	USA	2:28:01
	3	L. Weidenbach	USA	2:28:16
BSAD Wheelchair	1	H. Ericsson	SWE	1:57:12
	2	W. Petersen	GDR	1:57:13
	3	J–F. Poitevin	FRA	1:58:24

PEARL ASSURANCE UK CHAMPIONSHIPS (Cardiff 2–3 Jun 90)

Men

100 m	1	L. Christie	ENG	10.13
	2	J. Livingston	ENG	10.31
	3	D. Clark	SCO	10.39
200 m	1	A. Mafe	ENG	21.13
	2	D. Clark	SCO	21.14
	3	M. Rosswess	ENG	21.26
400 m	1	R. Black	ENG	45.63
	2	P. Sanders	ENG	46.75
	3	M. Richardson	ENG	46.88
800 m	1	D. Sharpe	ENG	1:51.46
	2	M. Steele	ENG	1:51.63
	3	K. McKay	ENG	1:51.63
1500 m	1	N. Horsfield	WAL	3:48.39
	2	R. Whalley	ENG	3:49.07
	3	A. Geddes	ENG	3:49.18
3000 m	1	G. Turnbull	ENG	8:11.35
	2	R. Denmark	ENG	8:11.90
	3	T. Hanlon	SCO	8:12.71
5000 m	1	S. Mugglestone	ENG	13:43.7
	2	J. Richards	ENG	13:46.3
	3	D. McNeilly	NIR	13:47.7
110 m Hurdles	1	C. Jackson	WAL	13.10
	2	D. Nelson	ENG	13.62
	3	N. Walker	WAL	13.77
400 m Hurdles	1	K. Akabusi	ENG	51.50
	2	P. Harries	WAL	52.49
	3	M. Briggs	ENG	53.03
3000 m S'chase	1	K. Penney	ENG	8:50.90
	2	T. Buckner	ENG	8:54.84
	3	S. Newport	ENG	8:56.55
10000 m Walk	1	I. McCombie	ENG	41:16.00
	2	M. Easton	ENG	41:35.39
	3	A. Penn	ENG	44:10.67
High Jump	1	D. Grant	ENG	2.25
	2	G. Parsons	SCO	2.20
	3	B. Reilly	ENG	2.20
Long Jump	1	K. Liddington	ENG	7.62
	2	W. Griffith	ENG	7.58
	3	J. Shepherd	ENG	7.50

Triple Jump	1	F. Agyepong	ENG	16.06
	2	J. Edwards	ENG	15.49
	3	J. Sweeney	ENG	15.22
Pole Vault	1	A. Ashurst	ENG	5.30
	2	M. Edwards	ENG	5.20
	3	D. Mellor	ENG	5.00
Shot	1	P. Edwards	WAL	18.57
	2	M. Simson	ENG	18.52
	3	S. Whyte	SCO	17.24
Discus	1	P. Mardle	ENG	57.02
	2	A. Ekoku	ENG	56.46
	3	S. Casey	ENG	54.46
Hammer	1	P. Head	ENG	71.64
	2	M. Jones	ENG	68.24
	3	J. Byrne	ENG	67.98
Javelin	1	S. Backley	ENG	88.46
	2	M. Cottrell	ENG	72.54
	3	G. Jenson	ENG	72.20

Women

100 m	1	S. Short	WAL	11.36
	2	P. Smith	ENG	11.40
	3	H. Miles	WAL	11.45
200 m	1	P. Smith	ENG	23.97
	2	L. Stuart	ENG	24.00
	3	S. Short	WAL	24.04
400 m	1	D. Edwards	ENG	54.32
	2	S. Douglas	ENG	55.02
	3	P. Beckford	ENG	55.49
800 m	1	H. Thorpe	ENG	2:05.52
	2	M. Kitson	ENG	2:06.10
	3	S. Wheeler	ENG	2:07.36
1500 m	1	A. Wyeth	ENG	4:20.40
	2	L. York	ENG	4:21.04
	3	D. Gunning	ENG	4:21.24
3000 m	1	A. Wallace	ENG	9:08.1
	2	S. McGeorge	ENG	9:08.7
	3	A. Wyeth	ENG	9:08.9
100 m Hurdles	1	K. Morley	WAL	13.16
	2	S. Farquharson	ENG	13.33
	3	W. Jeal	ENG	13.40
400 m Hurdles	1	C. Sugden	ENG	57.52
	2	G. Retchakan	ENG	58.23
	3	J. Vine	ENG	59.82
5000 m Walk	1	B. Sworowski	ENG	22:31.59
	2	L. Langford	ENG	22:42.47
	3	J. Drake	ENG	23:03.24
High Jump	1	J. Bennett	ENG	1.84
	2	D. Marti	ENG	1.81
	3	L. Gittens	ENG	1.78
Long Jump	1	M. Berkeley	ENG	6.17
	2	J. Wise	ENG	6.08
	3	M. Griffith	ENG	5.90
Triple Jump	1	M. Griffith	ENG	12.94
	2	E. Finikin	ENG	12.87
	3	K. Hambrook	ENG	11.82
Shot	1	M. Augee	ENG	19.03
	2	J. Oakes	ENG	18.77
	3	Y. Hanson-Nortey	ENG	16.09
Discus	1	J. McKernan	NIR	55.36
	2	J. Picton	ENG	52.64
	3	S. Andrews	ENG	52.60
Javelin	1	S. Gibson	ENG	58.32
	2	A. Liverton	ENG	57.84
	3	F. Whitbread	ENG	51.50

AUSTRALIAN RULES FOOTBALL

FOSTER'S CUP (The Oval 22 Oct 89)

Melbourne	(12–10)	82	Essendon	(6–10)	46

BADMINTON

THOMAS CUP – WORLD MEN'S TEAM CHAMPIONSHIP (3 Jun 90)

MT	China	bt	Malaysia	4–1

UBER CUP – WORLD WOMEN'S TEAM CHAMPIONSHIP (2 Jun 90)

WT	China	bt	South Korea	3–2

WORLD CHAMPIONSHIPS (Djakarta 4 Jun 89)

MS	Yang Yang	CHN	bt	A. Wiranta	INA	15–10	2–15	15–5
WS	Li Lingwei	CHN	bt	Huang Hua	CHN	11–6	12–9	
MD	Li Yongbo/Tian Bingyi	CHN	bt	C. Kang/C. Hongyong	CHN	15–3	15–12	
WD	Lin Ying/Guan Weizhen	CHN	bt	Chung Myeong-hee/Hwang Hye-young	SKO	15–1	15–7	
XD	Park Joo-bong/Chung Myeong-hee	SKO	bt	E. Hartono/V. Fajrin	INA	15–9	15–9	

EUROPEAN CHAMPIONSHIPS (Moscow 10–14 Apr 90)

MS	S. Baddeley	ENG	bt	D. Hall	ENG	11–15	15–3	15–7	
WS	P. Nedergaard	DEN	bt	F. Smith	ENG	5–11	12–11	4–0	retired hurt
MD	J. Paulsen/H. Svarrer	DEN	bt	M. Gandrup/T. Lund	DEN	17–16	15–5		
WD	D. Kjaer/N. Nielsen	DEN	bt	E. Coene/E. van Dijck	HOL	15–5	15–6		
XD	J. Holst-Christiansen/G. Mogensen	DEN	bt	J-E. Antonsson/M. Bengtsson	SWE	15–7	15–8		

T1–2 Denmark	bt	Sweden	5–0
T3–4 England	bt	USSR	3–2

YONEX ALL-ENGLAND OPEN CHAMPIONSHIPS (17 Mar 90)

MS	Zhao Jianhua	CHN	bt	J. Suprianto	INA	15–4	15–1	
WS	S. Susanti	INA	bt	Huang Hua	CHN	12–11	11–1	
MD	Kim Moon-soo/Park Joo-bong	SKO	bt	Li Yongbo/Tian Bingyi	CHN	17–14	15–9	
WD	Chung Myeong-hee/Hwang Hye-young	SKO	bt	G. Clark/G. Gowers	ENG	6–15	15–4	15–4
XD	Park Joo-bong/Chung Myeong-hee	SKO	bt	J. Holst-Christiansen/G. Mogensen	DEN	15–6	15–3	

ORACLE ENGLISH NATIONAL CHAMPIONSHIPS (19 Dec 89)

MS	D. Hall	bt	S. Baddeley	15–18	15–4	15–4
WS	F. Smith	bt	H. Troke	11–1	11–7	
MD	M. Brown/A. Goode	bt	A. Fairhurst/C. Hunt	15–10	12–15	15–11
WD	G. Clark/G. Gowers	bt	K. Chapman/S. Sankey	9–15	17–15	15–7
XD	A. Goode/G. Clark	bt	M. Brown/J. Wallwork	15–8	18–13	

BASEBALL

WORLD SERIES (14–28 Oct 89)
THE AMERICAN LEAGUE CHAMPIONS (OAKLAND ATHLETICS) VERSUS THE NATIONAL LEAGUE CHAMPIONS (SAN FRANCISCO GIANTS)

Oakland Athletics bt San Francisco Giants 5–0
Oakland Athletics bt San Francisco Giants 5–1
Series interrupted by the San Francisco earthquake
Oakland Athletics bt San Francisco Giants 13–7
Oakland Athletics bt San Francisco Giants 9–6

Oakland Athletics won the World Series 4–0

NATIONAL CLUB CHAMPIONSHIP FINAL (22 Oct 89)
Enfield bt Sutton 15–9

BASKETBALL

US NATIONAL BASKETBALL ASSOCIATION CHAMPIONSHIP FINAL (14 June 90)

Detroit Pistons bt Portland Trail Blazers 107–101
Portland Trail Blazers bt Detroit Pistons 106–105 aot
Detroit Pistons bt Portland Trail Blazers 121–106
Detroit Pistons bt Portland Trail Blazers 112–109
Detroit Pistons bt Portland Trail Blazers 92–90

Detroit Pistons won the series 4–1

EUROPEAN RESULTS

EUROPEAN CHAMPIONSHIP (24 Jun 89)
Yugoslavia bt Greece 98–77

EUROPEAN WOMEN'S CHAMPIONSHIP (17 Jun 89)
USSR bt Czechoslovakia 64–61

EUROPEAN CHAMPIONS' CUP FINAL (19 Apr 90)
Jugoplastika Split YUG bt Barcelona SPA 72–67

3rd Place play-off
Limoges FRA bt Airs Salonika GRE 103–91

EUROPEAN CUP WINNERS' CUP FINAL (13 Mar 90)
Virtus Bologna ITA bt Real Madrid SPA 79–74

EUROPEAN MEN'S KORAC CUP FINAL

1st leg (22 Mar 90)
Scavolini Pesaro ITA 98 Joventut Badalona SPA 99

2nd leg (29 Mar 90)
Joventut Badalona SPA 98 Scavolini Pesaro ITA 86

Joventut Badalona won 197–184 on aggregate

EUROPEAN WOMEN'S RONCHETTI CUP FINAL

1st leg (15 Mar 90)
Primizie Parma ITA 79 Jedinstvo Aida Tuzla YUG 54

2nd leg (22 Mar 90)
Jedinstvo Aida Tuzla YUG 77 Primizie Parma ITA 71

Primizie Parma won 150–131 on aggregate

NATIONAL RESULTS

CARLSBERG LEAGUE – PREMIER DIVISION CHAMPIONS 1989–90
Kingston

NATIONAL LEAGUE – DIVISION I CHAMPIONS 1989–90
Oldham

NATWEST TROPHY FINAL (3 Dec 89)
Kingston bt Manchester Giants 86–77

COCA COLA NATIONAL MEN'S CUP FINAL (25 Mar 90)
Kingston bt Sunderland 76ers 103–78

COCA COLA NATIONAL TROPHY (25 Mar 90)
Oldham bt Brixton 87–81

COCA COLA NATIONAL WOMEN'S CUP (25 Mar 90)
Sheffield bt Brixton 64–46

CARLSBERG CHAMPIONSHIP PLAY-OFF FINAL (14 Apr 90)
Kingston bt Sunderland 76ers 87–82

3rd Place play-off
Manchester Giants bt Bracknell 110–103

ENGLISH WOMEN'S LEAGUE FINAL (14 Apr 90)
Northampton bt Sheffield 70–68

INVITATION CLUB CHAMPIONSHIP (Crystal Palace 29 Dec 89)

Men's Final
Murray Livingston SCO bt Bayer Leverkusen FRG 71–62

Women's Final
BCN Sao Paulo BRA bt Levski Spartak Sophia BUL 100–66

BILLIARDS

WORLD PROFESSIONAL CHAMPIONSHIP (23 Jul 89)
M. Russell ENG bt P. Gilchrist ENG 2242–1347

ROTHMANS WORLD MATCHPLAY CHAMPIONSHIP (28 May 89)
M. Russell ENG bt I. Williamson ENG 6–1

BRITISH OPEN CHAMPIONSHIP (8 Dec 89)
P. Gilchrist ENG bt N. Dagley ENG 1166–1008

STRACHAN UK PROFESSIONAL CHAMPIONSHIP (8 Mar 90)
M. Russell bt J. Murphy 1478–1058

ENGLISH AMATEUR CHAMPIONSHIP (13 May 90)
M. Goodwill bt P. Shelley 2371–1337

BOWLS

OUTDOOR EVENTS
NatWest British Isles Men's Championships (3 Jul 90)

Singles	J. Ottaway	ENG	bt	J. Baker	IRE	25–22
Pairs	J. Male/M. Chard	WAL	bt	G. Rees/M. Graham	IRE	21–16
Triples	J. Whyte/C. Craig/E. Parkinson	IRE	bt	P. Butler/C.Knight/A. Jordan	ENG	17–16
Fours	England		bt	Wales		23–21
	J. Chandler/J. Cross/T. Heppell/M.Sekjer			G. Hill/J. Evans/J. Anstey/N. Anstey		

NatWest British Isles Men's Home International Championship (6 Jul 90)
ENG 123 WAL 108, SCO 119 IRE 99, WAL 109 IRE 108, ENG 111 SCO 111, ENG 124 IRE 96, SCO 108 WAL 107.

Final Standings	P	W	D	L	F	A	Pts	
1 England	3	2	1	0	358	315	5	won on superior games total
2 Scotland	3	2	1	0	358	317	5	
3 Wales	3	1	0	2	324	339	2	
4 Ireland	3	0	0	3	303	352	0	

British Isles Women's Championships (28 Jun 90)

Singles	E. Wren	SCO	bt	J. Baker	ENG	25–14
Pairs	B. Johnson/N. Shaw	ENG	bt	A. Elliott/J. Mulholland	IRE	19–16
Triples	J. Evans/B. Mills/B. Morgan	WAL	bt	C. Webb/J. Andrews/J. Roylance	ENG	15–13
Fours	Wales		bt	Ireland		19–18
	D. Wallace/D. Hall/A. John/J. Ackland			B. Dunne/C. O'Gorman/M. Barber/A. Prodohl		

British Isles Women's Home International Championship (27 Jun 90)
ENG 112 IRE 105, SCO 107 WAL 100, ENG 119 SCO 96, WAL 103 IRE 94, ENG 157 WAL 92, SCO 115 IRE 112.

Final Standings	P	W	L	F	A	Pts
1 England	3	3	0	388	293	6
2 Scotland	3	2	1	318	331	4
3 Wales	3	1	2	295	358	2
4 Ireland	3	0	3	311	330	0

Woolwich English Bowling Association Men's National Championship (19–23 Aug 89)

Singles	J. Ottaway	bt	B. Croad	25–13
Pairs	P. Maynard/D. McCathie	bt	C. Tattersall/M. Leach	25–16
Triples	Southbourne (Sussex)	bt	Swindon (Wiltshire)	20–18
	P. Butler/C. Knight/A. Jordan		K. Norman/A. Jackson/H. Bowen	
Fours	Blackheath & Greenwich (Kent)	bt	Brush (Leics)	17–16

Middleton Cup Final 1989

	Kent	bt	Lancashire	117–107

Liverpool Victoria English Women's Bowling Association National Championships (12 Aug 89)

Singles	J. Baker	bt	W. Line	21–13
Pairs	B. Johnson/N. Shaw			19–18
Triples	North Walsham	bt	Sherwood	27–7
Fours	Kingsway, Hove	bt	W. Cornwall	20–13
	H. Dobbs/M. Curtis/J. Hardy/D. Whittingham		N. May/J. Smith/S. Coak/V. Ireland	
County Championship (Johns Trophy)				
	Sussex	bt	Yorkshire	112–106

INDOOR EVENTS

World Men's Indoor Championships (3–4 Mar 90)

Singles	J. Price	WAL	bt	I. Schuback	AUS	4–7 7–4 7–2 3–7 7–0
Pairs	T. Allcock/D. Bryant	ENG	bt	I. Schuback/J. Yates	AUS	3–7 7–4 3–7 7–3 7–2

Volkswagen World Women's Indoor Championship (22 Apr 90)

Singles	F. Bougourd	GUE	bt	E.Wren	SCO	6–7 7–6 7–5 4–7 7–2

CIS Insurance British Isles Men's Indoor Championships (2–3 Apr 90)

Singles	G. Robertson	SCO	bt	J. McMullan	IRE	21–7
Pairs	M. Craig/J. Baker	IRE	bt	Martin & Mick Tomlin	ENG	17–12
Triples	A. Rigby/D. Mogford/R. Price	WAL	bt	T. Mair/K. Williamson/J. Weir	SCO	27–16
Fours	England		bt	N. Ireland		19–13
	M. Sekjer/T. Heppell/G. Smith/A. Thomson			R. Bell/D. Johnston/M. Craig/J. Baker		

CIS Insurance British Isles Men's Indoor Home International Championship (6 Apr 90)

Final Standings	P	W	L	F	A	Pts	
1 England	3	2	1	387	319	4	won on superior games total
2 Wales	3	2	1	355	329	4	
3 Scotland	3	2	1	340	376	4	
4 Ireland	3	0	3	302	360	0	

British Isles Women's Indoor Championships (19 Mar 90)

Singles	M. Johnston	IRE	bt	G. Smith	ENG	21–12
Pairs	A. McFarlane/M. Spence	SCO	bt	J. Rowntree/G. Thomas	ENG	22–19
Triples	D. Wilson/S. King/J. Cammack	ENG	bt	M. Ferguson/M. Mungall/J. Adamson	SCO	23–11
Fours	England		bt	Scotland		24–16
	E. McKenna/P. Spence/J. Berry/N. Shaw			M. Hosie/R. Neil Jnr/J. Fraser/R. Neil Snr		

British Isles Women's Indoor Home International Championship (22 Mar 90)

Final Standings	P	W	L	F	A	Pts
1 England	3	3	0	385	297	6
2 Wales	3	2	1	375	323	4
3 Scotland	3	1	2	349	330	2
4 Ireland	3	0	3	262	421	0

CIS Insurance UK Men's Indoor Championship (5 Nov 89)

Singles	D. Bryant	ENG	bt	D. Corkhill	NIR	1–7 5–7 7–6 7–5 7–3

UK Women's Indoor Championship (1 Dec 89)

Singles	S. Froud	WAL	bt	M. Steele	ENG	5–7 7–6 7–0 5–7 7–2

English Men's National Indoor Championships (12–17 Mar 90)

Singles	A. Thomson (Cyphers)	bt	T. Allcock (Bentham)	21–7
Pairs	T. Scott/D. Webb (Gateshead)	bt	D. Snell/M. Biggs (Thamesdown)	22–10
Triples	Sunderland	bt	Bentham	23–17
	R. McKie/J. Lambert/G. Smith		T. Allcock/M. Jordan/P. Nelms	
Fours	Cyphers, Beckenham	bt	Preston Park, Brighton	26–6
County Championship (Liberty Trophy)				
	Middlesex	bt	Norfolk	128–102

English Women's National Indoor Championships (6–14 Mar 90)

Singles	G. Smith (Bentham)	bt	S. Franklin (Wisbech)	21–18
Pairs	D. Wilson/J. Cammack (Boston)	bt	J. Rowntree/G. Thomas (W. Cornwall)	22–12
Triples	D. Wilson/S. King/J. Cammack (Boston)	bt	D. Wickenden/D. Carpenter/A. Moore (Egerton Park, Bexhill)	26–11
Fours	Teeside	bt	Stone Lodge, Dartford	26–10
Team (Yetton Trophy)	Essex County	bt	Torbay	79–70
Champion of Champions	G. Thomas (W. Cornwall)	bt	J. Deacon (Croydon)	21–5

BOXING

Professional Champions – as at 1 Jul 90

There are, at present, four different world professional boxing bodies, each recognising its own world champion. They are the World Boxing Association, World Boxing Council, International Boxing Federation and World Boxing Organisation. To add further confusion, each describes the weight categories with varying names. Here, category names have been amalgamated and all world champions are listed.

Minimum/Straw/Mini-Fly

World WBA	Kim Bong-jun	SKO
World WBC	H. Ohashi	JAP
World IBF	F. Lookmingkwan	THA

Junior-Fly/Light-Fly

World WBA	Yuh Myung-woo	SKO
World WBC	H. Gonzales	MEX
World IBF	M. Kittikasem	THA
World WBO	J. de Jesus	PUE

Fly

World WBA	Lee Yul-woo	SKO
World WBC	S. Chitalada	THA
World IBF	D. McAuley	NIR
World WBO	P. Gonzales	USA
European	E. Can	DEN
Commonwealth	Vacant	
British	P. Clinton	ENG

Super-Fly/Junior-Bantam

World WBA	Khaosai Galaxy	THA
World WBC	Moon Sung-kil	SKO
World IBF	R. Quiroga	USA
World WBO	J. Ruiz	PUE

Bantam

World WBA	L. Espinosa	PHI
World WBC	R. Perez	MEX
World IBF	O. Canizares	USA
World WBO	I. Contreras	VEN
European	V. Belcastro	ITA
Commonwealth	R. Minus Jnr	BAH
British	W. Hardy	ENG

Super-Bantam/Junior-Feather

World WBA	J. Salud	USA Now vacant
	L. Mendoza and R. Palacios (both COL) fought a draw for the vacant title on 26 May 90.	
World WBC	P. Banke	USA
World IBF	W. N'cita	SAF
World WBO	O. Fernandez	PUE

Feather

World WBA	A. Esparragoza	VEN
World WBC	M. Villasana	MEX
World IBF	J. Paez	MEX
World WBO	L. Espinoza	USA
European	P. Hodkinson	ENG
Commonwealth	M. Napunyi	KEN
British	S. Murphy	ENG

Super-Feather/Junior-Light

World WBA	B. Mitchell	SAF
World WBC	A. Nelson	GHA Now vacant
World IBF	T. Lopez	USA
World WBO	Kamel Bou Ali	TUN
European	D. Londas	FRA
Commonwealth	M. Reefer	ENG
British	J. Jacobs	ENG

Light

World WBA	J. Nazario	PUE
World WBC	P. Whitaker	USA
World IBF	P. Whitaker	USA
World WBO	A. Castro	COL
European	P. Diaz	SPA
Commonwealth	C. Crook	ENG
British	S. Boyle	ENG

Super-Light/Junior-Welter/Light-Welter

World WBA	J.M. Coggi	ARG
World WBC	J.C. Chavez	MEX
World IBF	J.C. Chavez	MEX
World WBO	H. Camacho	USA
European	E. Calamati	ITA
Commonwealth	T. Ekubia	ENG
British	P. Barrett	ENG

Welter

World WBA	M. Breland	USA
World WBC	M. Starling	USA
World IBF	S. Brown	JAM
World WBO	G. Leon	MEX
European	K. Laing	ENG
Commonwealth	D. Boucher	CAN
British	K. Laing	ENG

Super-Welter/Junior-Middle/Light-Middle

World WBA	J. Jackson	VIS
World WBC	T. Norris	USA
World IBF	G. Rosi	ITA
World WBO	J. Jackson	USA
European	G. Dole	FRA
Commonwealth	T. Waters	AUS
British	G. Stretch	ENG

Middle

World WBA	M. McCallum	JAM
World WBC	R. Duran	PAN Now vacant
World IBF	M. Nunn	USA
World WBO	N. Benn	ENG
European	S. Kalambay	ITA
Commonwealth	M. Watson	ENG
British	H. Graham	ENG

Super-Middle

World WBA	C. Tiozzo	FRA
World WBC	Sugar Ray Leonard	USA
World IBF	L. Holmes	USA
World WBO	T. Hearns	USA
European	M. Galvani	ITA
British	S. Storey	ENG

Light-Heavy

World WBA	V. Hill	USA
World WBC	J. Harding	AUS
World IBF	C. Williams	USA
World WBO	M. Moorer	USA
European	E. Nicoletta	FRA
Commonwealth	G. Waters	AUS
British	T. Collins	ENG

Cruiser

World WBA	R. Daniels	USA
World WBC	C. de Leon	PUE
World IBF	J. Lampkin	USA
World WBO	M. Havnaa	NOR
European	A. Wamba	FRA
Commonwealth	D. Angol	ENG
British	J. Nelson	ENG

Heavy

World WBA	J. Douglas	USA
World WBC	J. Douglas	USA
World IBF	J. Douglas	USA
World WBO	F. Damiani	ITA
European	J-M. Chanet	FRA
Commonwealth	D. Williams	ENG
British	G. Mason	ENG

AMATEUR BOXING ASSOCIATION CHAMPIONSHIPS
Finals (Royal Albert Hall 2 May 90)

Light-Fly	N. Tooley	bt	P. Weir	Pts
Fly	J. Armour	bt	P. Ingle	Pts
Bantam	P. Lloyd	bt	P. Mullings	RSC 2nd
Feather	B. Carr	bt	J. Williams	Pts
Light	P. Gallagher	bt	W. Schwer	Pts
Light-Welter	J. Pender	bt	A. Stone	Pts
Welter	A. Carew	bt	P. Waudby	RSC 2nd
Light-Middle	T. Taylor	bt	J. Culwick	Pts
Middle	S. Wilson	bt	D. Griffiths	Pts
Light-Heavy	J. McCluskey	bt	M. Baker	RSC 2nd
Heavy	K. Inglis	bt	P. Lawson	RSC 2nd
Super-Heavy	K. McCormack	bt	T. Cherubin	Pts

CANOEING

1989 WORLD CHAMPIONS

Men

Kayak Singles	500m	M. Hunter	AUS
	1000m	Z. Gyulay	HUN
	10000m	A. Szabo	CSR
Kayak Doubles	500m	K. Bluhm/T. Gutsche	GDR
	1000m	K. Bluhm/T. Gutsche	GDR
	10000m	A. Abraham/S. Hodosi	HUN
Kayak Fours	500m	USSR	
	1000m	Hungary	
	10000m	USSR	
Canadian Singles	500m	M. Slivinsky	URS
	1000m	I. Klementiyev	URS
	10000m	I. Klementiyev	URS
Canadian Doubles	500m	N. Yuravsky/V. Renevsky	URS
	1000m	C. Frederiksen/A. Nielsson	DEN
	10000m	C. Frederiksen/A. Nielsson	DEN
Canadian Fours	500m	USSR	
	1000m	USSR	

Women

Kayak Singles	500m	K. Borchert	GDR
	5000m	K. Borchert	GDR
Kayak Doubles	500m	A. Northangel/H. Singer	GDR
	5000m	M. Bunke/R. Portwich	GDR
Kayak Fours	500m	East Germany	

1990 BRITISH SPRINT CHAMPIONSHIP (10 Jun 90)

Men

Kayak Singles	500m	G. Bourne
	1000m	G. Bourne
	10000m	G. Burns
Kayak Doubles	500m	I. Lawler/G. Bourne
	1000m	I. Lawler/G. Bourne

Women

Kayak Singles	500m	A. Dallaway
	5000m	H. Dresser
Kayak Doubles	500m	A. Dallaway/H. Dresser

CRICKET

TEST MATCH SERIES (Qualification for individual details: 40 runs and 4 wickets)
AUSTRALIA TOUR OF ENGLAND 1989

1st Cornhill Test (Headingley 13 Jun 89)

Australia	601–7 dec	S. Waugh 177 no, M. Taylor 136, D. Jones 79, M. Hughes 71, A. Border 66
	and 230–3 dec	M. Taylor 60, A. Border 60 no, D. Boon 43, D. Jones 40
England	430	A. Lamb 125, K. Barnett 80, R. Smith 66, T. Alderman 5–107
	and 191	G.Gooch 68, T. Alderman 5–44

Australia won by 210 runs

2nd Cornhill Test (Lords 27 Jun 89)

England	286	J. Russell 64 no, G. Gooch 60, D. Gower 57, M. Hughes 4–71
	and 359	D. Gower 106, R. Smith 96, T. Alderman 6–128
Australia	528	S. Waugh 152 no, D. Boon 94, G. Lawson 74, M. Taylor 62, J. Emburey 4–88
	and 119–4	D. Boon 84 no

Australia won by 6 wickets

3rd Cornhill Test (Edgbaston 11 Jul 89)

Australia	424	D. Jones 157, M. Taylor 43, S. Waugh 43, T. Hohns 40, A. Fraser 4–63
	and 158–2	M. Taylor 51, G. Marsh 42
England	242	I. Botham 46, J. Russell 42, T. Curtis 41

Match drawn

4th Cornhill Test (Old Trafford 1 Aug 89)

England	260	R. Smith 143, G. Lawson 6–72
	and 264	J. Russell 128, J. Emburey 64, T. Alderman 5–66
Australia	447	S. Waugh 92, M. Taylor 85, A. Border 80, D. Jones 69, G. Marsh 47
	and 81–1	

Australia won by 9 wickets

5th Cornhill Test (Trent Bridge 15 Aug 89)

Australia	602–6 dec	M. Taylor 219, G. Marsh 138, D. Boon 73, A. Border 65 no, Extras 61
England	255	R. Smith 101, T. Alderman 5–69
	and 167	M. Atherton 47

Australia won by an innings and 180 runs

6th Cornhill Test (The Oval 29 Aug 89)

Australia	468	D. Jones 122, A. Border 76, M. Taylor 71, D. Boon 46, I. Healey 44, D. Pringle 4–70
	and 219–4 dec	A. Border 51 no, D. Jones 50, M. Taylor 48
England	285	D. Gower 79, G. Small 59, T. Alderman 5–66
	and 143–5	R. Smith 77 no.

Match drawn

Australia regained the Ashes, winning the series 4–0 with two drawn

ENGLAND TOUR OF WEST INDIES 1990

1st Cable & Wireless Test (Kingston, JAM 1 Mar 90)

West Indies	164	A. Fraser 5–28
	and 240	C. Best 64, G. Small 4–58, D. Malcolm 4–77
England	364	A. Lamb 132, R. Smith 57, Extras 48, W. Larkins 46, C. Walsh 5–68
	and 41–1	
	England won by 9 wickets	

2nd Cable & Wireless Test (Georgetown, GUY 15 Mar 90)

Abandoned without any play through rain

3rd Cable & Wireless Test (Port of Spain, TRI 28 Mar 90)

West Indies	199	G. Logie 98, D. Malcolm 4–60
	and 239	D. Haynes 45, G. Greenidge 42, D. Malcolm 6–77
England	288	G. Gooch 84, W. Larkins 54, D. Capel 40, C. Ambrose 4–59
	and 120–5	
	Match drawn	

4th Cable & Wireless Test (Bridgetown, BAR 10 Apr 90)

West Indies	446	C. Best 164, V. Richards 70, R. Richardson 45, G. Greenidge 41, G. Small 4–109
	and 267–8 dec	D. Haynes 109, G. Logie 48, G. Small 4–74
England	358	A. Lamb 119, R. Smith 62, Extras 51, A. Stewart 45, I. Bishop 4–70
	and 191	J. Russell 55, R. Smith 40 no, C. Ambrose 8–45
	West Indies won by 164 runs	

5th Cable & Wireless Test (St. John's, ANT 16 Apr 90)

England	260	R. Bailey 42, I. Bishop 5–84
	and 154	C. Ambrose 4–22
West Indies	446	D. Haynes 167, G. Greenidge 149, D. Malcolm 4–126
	West Indies won by an innings and 32 runs	

West Indies won the series 2–1 with one drawn and one abandoned

NEW ZEALAND TOUR OF ENGLAND 1990

1st Cornhill Test (Trent Bridge 12 Jun 90)

New Zealand	208	M. Crowe 59, P. DeFreitas 5–53
	and 36–2	
England	345–9 dec	M. Atherton 151, R. Smith 55, R. Hadlee 4–89
	Match drawn	

2nd Cornhill Test (Lords 26 Jun 90)

England	334	G. Gooch 85, R. Smith 64, A. Stewart 54, D. Morrison 4–64
	and 272–4 dec	A. Lamb 84 no, M. Atherton 54, A. Stewart 42
New Zealand	462–9 dec	T. Franklin 101, J. Wright 98, Sir R. Hadlee 86, A. Jones 49, M. Greatbatch 47, D. Malcolm 5–94
	Match drawn	

ONE DAY INTERNATIONALS (Qualification for individual details – 30 runs and 3 wickets)

AUSTRALIA TOUR OF ENGLAND 1989

1st Texaco Match (Old Trafford 25 May 89)

England	231–9	G. Gooch 52, D. Gower 36, A. Lamb 35, R. Smith 35, G. Lawson 3–48 beat
Australia	136	S. Waugh 35, N. Foster 3–29, J. Emburey 3–31 by 95 runs

2nd Texaco Match (Trent Bridge 27 May 89)

England	226–5	A. Lamb 100 no, M. Gatting 37 tied with
Australia	226–8	S. Waugh 43, A. Border 39, G. Marsh 34

3rd Texaco Match (Lords 29 May 89)

England	278–7	G. Gooch 136, D. Gower 61, T. Alderman 3–36 lost to
Australia	279–4	G. Marsh 111 no, A. Border 53, S. Waugh 35 by 6 wickets

England won series by losing fewer wickets in the tied match

ENGLAND TOUR OF WEST INDIES 1990

1st Cable & Wireless Match (Port of Spain, TRI 14 Feb 90)

West Indies	208–8	R. Richardson 51, V. Richards 32
England	26–1	
	Match abandoned without result (rain affected)	

2nd Cable & Wireless Match (Port of Spain, TRI 17 Feb 90)

West Indies	13–0	
	Match abandoned without result (rain affected)	

3rd Cable & Wireless Match (Kingston, JAM 3 Mar 90)

England	214–8	A. Lamb 66, R. Smith 43, Extras 37, W. Larkins 33, I. Bishop 4–28 lost to
West Indies	216–7	R. Richardson 108 no, E. Hemmings 3–31 by 3 wickets

4th Cable & Wireless Match (Georgetown, GUY 7 Mar 90)

England	188–8	W. Larkins 34, G. Gooch 33 lost to
West Indies	191–4	C. Best 100, D. Haynes 50 by 6 wickets

5th Cable & Wireless Match (Bridgetown, BAR 3 Apr 90)

England	214–3	R. Smith 69, A. Lamb 55 no, Extras 36, W. Larkins 34 lost to
West Indies	217–6	R. Richardson 80, C. Best 51, D. Haynes 45, G. Small 3–29 by 4 wickets

West Indies won the series 3–0 with two abandoned

SPECIAL CABLE & WIRELESS MATCH (Georgetown, GUY 15 Mar 90)

England	166–9	G. Gooch 42, R. Bailey 42, C. Ambrose 4–18 lost to
West Indies	167–3	G. Greenidge 77, C. Lambert 48 by 7 wickets

NEW ZEALAND TOUR OF ENGLAND 1990

1st Texaco Match (Headingley 23 May 90)

England	295–6	R. Smith 128, G. Gooch 55, A. Stewart 34, D. Pringle 30 no lost to
New Zealand	298–6	M. Greatbatch 102 no, J. Wright 52, A. Jones 51, M. Crowe 46, C. Lewis 3–54 by 4 wickets

2nd Texaco Match (The Oval 25 May 90)

New Zealand	212–6	M. Greatbatch 111 lost to
England	213–4	G. Gooch 112 no, J. Russell 47 no by 6 wickets

England won the 1–1 tied series on a faster scoring rate

BRITANNIA ASSURANCE COUNTY CHAMPIONSHIP (14 Sep 89)

		P	W	L	D	Bonus Pts Bat	Bonus Pts Bowl	Pts
1	Worcestershire	22	12	3	7	44	83	319
2	Essex	22	13	2	7	59	71	313
3	Middlesex	22	9	2	11	50	72	266
4	Lancashire	22	8	5	9	57	65	250
5	Northamptonshire	22	7	8	7	47	63	222
6	Derbyshire	22	6	6	10	45	75	216
7	Hampshire	22	6	8	8	55	65	216
8	Warwickshire	22	5	4	13	44	75	207
9	Gloucestershire	22	6	11	5	38	70	204
10	Sussex	22	4	4	14	60	68	192
11	Nottinghamshire	22	6	6	10	54	65	190
12	Surrey	22	4	7	11	50	69	183
13	Leicestershire	22	4	8	10	43	74	181
14	Somerset	22	4	6	12	50	54	168
15	Kent	22	3	8	11	53	53	154
16	Yorkshire	22	3	9	10	41	60	149
17	Glamorgan	22	3	6	13	38	59	145

The Warwickshire total includes 8 points for levelling the scores in a drawn match Essex (at Southend) and Nottinghamshire (at Trent Bridge) were both penalised 25 points for sub-standard pitches

REFUGE ASSURANCE SUNDAY LEAGUE FINAL TABLE (27 Aug 89)

		P	W	L	Tied	NR	Pts
1	Lancashire	16	12	2	0	2	52
2	Worcestershire	16	11	4	0	1	46
3	Essex	16	11	4	0	1	46
4	Nottinghamshire	16	9	6	0	1	38
5	Derbyshire	16	9	6	0	1	38
6	Surrey	16	9	7	0	0	36
7	Hampshire	16	8	6	1	1	36
8	Northamptonshire	16	8	6	0	2	36
9	Middlesex	16	8	7	1	0	34
10	Somerset	16	7	8	1	0	30
11	Kent	16	7	9	0	0	28
12	Yorkshire	16	7	9	0	0	28
13	Sussex	16	6	8	1	1	28
14	Warwickshire	16	5	10	0	1	22
15	Leicestershire	16	5	10	0	1	22
16	Gloucestershire	16	3	13	0	0	12
17	Glamorgan	16	2	12	0	2	12

CUP FINALS

Benson & Hedges Cup Final (15 Jul 89)

Essex	243–7	A. Lilley 95 no, G. Gooch 48, M. Waugh 41 lost to
Nottinghamshire	244–7	T. Robinson 86, P. Johnson 54, D. Randall 49 by 3 wickets

NatWest Trophy Final (2 Sep 89)

Middlesex	210–5	D. Haynes 50, P. Downton 43 no lost to
Warwickshire	211–6	D. Reeve 42, G. Humpage 36, A. Lloyd 34, Asif Din 34 no by 4 wickets

Refuge Assurance League Cup Final (17 Sep 89)

Essex	160–5	P. Prichard 56, N. Hussain 32, G. Gooch 31 beat
Nottinghamshire	155	C. Broad 39, D. Pringle 4–20 by 5 runs

CURLING

WORLD CHAMPIONSHIPS (7 Apr 90)

Men	Canada	bt	Scotland	3–1
Women	Norway	bt	Scotland	4–2

CYCLING

WORLD CHAMPIONSHIPS (Lyon 15–27 Aug 89)

Men

Professional 1 km Sprint

1	C. Golinelli	ITA	2
2	Y. Kamiyama	JAP	0
3	H. Matsui	JAP	

Professional 5 km Individual Pursuit

1	C. Sturgess	GBR	5:52.40
2	D. Woods	AUS	5:54.06
3	R. Clere	FRA	faster sf

Professional Keirin

1	C. Golinelli	ITA	last 200m 10.88
2	P. Da Rocha	FRA	
3	M. Sako	JAP	

Professional 50 km Points Race

1	U. Freuler	SWI	45
2	G. Sutton	AUS	39
3	M. Penc	CSR	33

Professional 1-hour Motor-paced

1	G. Renosto	ITA
2	W. Brugna	ITA
3	T. Rellensmann	FRG

262.5 km Professional Road Road (Chambery)

1	G. LeMond	USA	6:45:59
2	D. Konychev	URS	6:45:59
3	S. Kelly	IRE	6:45:59

Amateur 1 km Sprint

1	B. Huck	GDR	2
2	M. Hubner	GDR	0
3	N. Kovsch	URS	

Amateur 1 km Time Trial

1	J. Glücklich	GDR	1:04.032
2	M. Vinnicombe	AUS	1:04.950
3	A. Kiritchenko	URS	1:05.060

Amateur 1 km Tandem Sprint

1	F. Coles/F. Magne	FRA	2
2	J. Illek/L. Hargas	CSR	0
3	A. Faccini/F. Paris	ITA	

Amateur 4 km Individual Pursuit

1	V. Yekimov	URS	4:35.58
2	J. Lehmann	GDR	4:42.17
3	S. Blochwitz	GDR	faster sf

Amateur 50 km Points Race

1	M. Satybaldiyev	URS	52
2	F. Baldato	ITA	44
3	L. Peelen	HOL	32

Amateur 4 km Team Pursuit

1	East Germany	4:16.59
2	USSR	4:18.54
3	Italy	faster sf

187.5 km Amateur Road Race (Chambery)

1	J. Halupczok	POL	4:52:54
2	E. Pichon	FRA	4:55:39
3	C. Manin	FRA	4:55:52

Amateur 100 km Team Time Trial

1	East Germany	2:02:36.29
2	Poland	2:03:19.35
3	USSR	2:03:37.35

Women

1 km Sprint

1	E. Salumyae	URS	2
2	G. Enuhina	URS	0
3	I. Gautheron	FRA	

3 km Individual Pursuit

1	J. Longo	FRA	3:54.45
2	P. Rossner	GDR	3:55.31
3	B. Ganz	SWI	faster sf

30 km Points Race

1	J. Longo	FRA	35
2	B. Ganz	SWI	29
3	J. Eickhoff	USA	50 at 1 lap

75 km Road Race (Chambery)

1	J. Longo	FRA	1:56:41
2	C. Marsal	FRA	2:00:46
3	M. Canins	ITA	2:00:46

50 km Team Time Trial

1	USSR	1:08:05.02
2	Italy	1:08:05.89
3	France	1:08:35.72

INTERNATIONAL EVENTS

TOUR DE FRANCE (23 Jul 89)

Men

1	G. LeMond	USA	87:38:35
2	L. Fignon	FRA	87:38:43
3	P. Delgado	SPA	87:42:09

Individual Points

1	S. Kelly	IRE	277 pts

King of the Mountains

1	G. Theunisse	HOL	441 pts

Women

1	J. Longo	FRA	21:59:38
2	M. Canins	ITA	22:08:22
3	I. Thompson	USA	22:12:02

KELLOGG'S PROFESSIONAL TOUR OF BRITAIN (3 Sep 89)

1	R. Millar	GBR	Z-Peugeot	20:45:10
2	M. Gianetti	SWI	Helvetia La Suisse	20:45:18
3	R. Stumpf	FRG	Toshiba	20:49:32

T1 Helvetia La Suisse
T2 PDM
T3 Teka

MILK RACE (Lands End to Liverpool 9 Jun 90)

1	S. Sutton	AUS	Banana-Falcon	48:26:22
2	R. Holden	GBR	Banana-Falcon	48:29:02
3	M. Vasicek	CSR	CSR	48:29:03

T1 Banana-Falcon
T2 Tulip Computers
T3 Czechoslovakia

Individual Points

1	J. McLoughlin	GBR	Ever Ready-Halfords	125 pts

King of the Mountains

1	G. Baker	GBR	Ever Ready-Halfords	130 pts

NATIONAL EVENTS

BCF NATIONAL CHAMPIONSHIPS (Leicester 30 Jul–5 Aug 89)

Men

Professional 1 km Sprint

1	P. McHugh	Pirelli	2
2	G. Coltman	Ever Ready Gold Seal	0
3	R. Williams	Ever Ready Gold Seal	

Professional 5 km Individual Pursuit

1	C. Sturgess	ADR	5:56.181
2	P. Curran	Percy Bilton	caught in 5:25.610
3	J. Walshaw	Percy Bilton	

Professional Keirin

1	P. McHugh	Pirelli	last 200m 11.529
2	N. Barnes	PMS-Falcon	
3	R. Williams	Ever Ready Gold Seal	

Professional Omnium – 10 km Scratch, 10 km Pts, 2 km Sprint, 1 km Time Trial

1	G. Coltman	Ever Ready Gold Seal	13
2	J. Walshaw	Percy Bilton	16
3	N. Barnes	PMS-Falcon	16

Pirelli Professional 30 km Grand Prix

1	A. Doyle	GBR	Ever Ready Gold Seal
2	A. Hughes	AUS	
3	D. Webster	GBR	Teka

Amateur 1 km Sprint

1	S. Brydon	City of Edinburgh RC	2
2	E. Alexander	City of Edinburgh RC	0
3	S. Paulding	City of Edinburgh RC	

Amateur 1 km Time Trial

1	S. Paulding	City of Edinburgh RC	1:08.288
2	S. Brydon	City of Edinburgh RC	1:08.697
3	A. Hawkins	Festival RC	1:08.794

Amateur 1 km Tandem Sprint

1	P. Boyd	Clayton Velo	
	G. Hibbert	Team Sportif Tameside	2
2	M. Borman	VC Nottingham	
	C. Pyatt	Stoke AC	0
3	D. Marsh		
	D. Cross	34th Nomads	

Amateur 4 km Individual Pursuit

1	C. Boardman	Manchester Wh.-Trumanns	4:55.404
2	B. Steel	Team Haverhill	4:56.960
3	G. Sword	Manchester Wh.-Trumanns	

Amateur 20 km Race

1	G. Sword	Manchester Wh.-Trumanns	25:52.92
2	P. Wain	Dinnington RC	
3	I. Wright	VC Lincoln	

Amateur 50 km Points Race

1	S. Lillistone	Team Haverhill	57
2	S. O'Brien	Manchester Wheelers	41
3	S. Wingrave	Team Haverhill	40

Amateur 4 km Team Pursuit

1	Manchester Wheelers-Trumanns	4:31.00
2	Team Haverhill	4:32.22
3	Zenith CC	

Open 50 km Motor-paced Race

1	N. Lett	Old Kent CC	42:41.757
2	J. Dale	VC Nottingham	@ 2 laps
3	L. Pegg	Birmingham Mercury	@ 6 laps

Women

1 km Sprint

1	L. Jones	Charnwood CRC	2
2	C. Rushworth	Manchester Wheelers	1
3	J. Harris	Team Haverhill	

1 km Time Trial

1	L. Jones	Charnwood CRC	1:16.739
2	A. Pockett	Halesowen A & CC	1:18.403
3	M. Johnson	Dinnington RC	1:18.670

3 km Individual Pursuit

1	S. McKenzie-Hodge	VC Ajax	4:04.107
2	M. Johnson	Dinnington RC	4:13.373
3	S. Dawes	Leicester RC	

15 km Points Race

1	L. Jones	Charnwood CRC	25
2	M. Johnson	Dinnington RC	25
3	S. McKenzie-Hodge	VC Ajax	24

NATIONAL ROAD RACES

National Professional 135-mile Road Race Championship (24 Jun 90)

1	C. Sturgess	Tulip Computers	5:14:24
2	B. Luckwell	Ever Ready-Halfords	5:14:24
3	H. Lodge	La William-Saltos	5:14:25

BCF National Amateur 123-mile Road Race Championship (1 Jul 90)

1	S. Hempsall	Chesterfield Coureurs	5:06:33
2	J. Hughes	Liverpool Mercury RC	5:06:36
3	G. Butler	Norwood Paragon CC	5:06:41

BCF National Women's 62.5-mile Road Race Championship (24 Jun 90)

1	M. Purvis	Ellan Vannin CC	2:51:17
2	A. Butter	Norwood Paragon CC	2:51:17
3	M. Johnson	Dinnington RC	2:51:17

RTTC National 24-hour Time Trial Championship (24 Jun 90)

1	P. Oxborough	St. Ives CC, Cambs.	455.48 M
2	R. Dadswell	Antelope RT	443.02 M
3	J. Baines	Selby CC	434.18 M

RTTC National 100-mile Time Trial Championship (23 Jul 89)

Men

1	I. Cammish	Manchester Wheelers	3:48:39
2	G. Longland	Antelope RT	3:52:34
3	G. Dighton	Team Chiltern	3:57:23
T1	Manchester Wheelers		11:50:24

Women

1	M. Allen	Knaresborough CC	4:20:38
2	K. Crisp	Chippenham & D. Wheelers	4:29:56
3	L. Wilkinson	East Anglian CC	4:33:54
T1	Knaresborough CC		13:59:34

British Professional 100 km Criterium (Circuit) Championship (1 Jul 90)

1	R. Holden	Banana-Falcon	2:03:06
2	H. McMurdo	Airmarshall-Kirk	2:03:36
3	A. Timmis	PCA	2:03:39

RTTC National 100 km Team Time Trial (16 Jul 89)

1	Manchester Wheelers C. Boardman/M. Gornall/P. Longbottom/B. Luckwell	2:03:07
2	Scotland D. Smith/A. Ferry/A. Mathieson/A. Young	2:07:34
3	BCF N. Midlands Division C. Creaghan/W. Randle/D. Spencer/J. Tanner	2:07:57

RTTC National Men's 50-mile Time Trial Championship (1 Jul 90)

1	D. Smith	Horwich CC	1:48:16
2	G. Gighton	Manchester Wheelers	1:52:46
3	M. Purshouse	Royal Sutton CC	1:53:21
T1	Manchester Wheelers		5:41:24

RTTC National Women's 50-mile Time Trial Championship (24 Jun 90)

1	M. Allen	Knaresborough CC	2:03:58
2=	C. Roberts	Team Kronos	2:04:51
2=	E. Ward	Scarborough Paragon	2:04:51
T1	East Anglian CC		6:29:51

RTTC National Women's 25-mile Time Trial (10 Jun 90)

1	A. Jones	Liverpool Mercury RC	1:00:47
2	S. Wright	Chelmer CC	1:01:15
3	L. Gornall	Horwich CC	1:02:02
T1	Liverpool Mercury CC		3:11:02

RTTC National Women's 10-mile Time Trial (16 Jul 89)

1	L. Brambini	Ravensthorpe CC	23:18
2	M. Allen	Knaresborough CC	23:22
3	S. Wright	Chelmer CC	23:47

CYCLO-CROSS

WORLD AMATEUR CHAMPIONSHIP (Getxi, SWI 3 Feb 90)

1	A. Buesser	SWI	48:27
2	M. Kvasnicka	CSR	48:39
3	T. Frischknecht	SWI	48:42

WORLD PROFESSIONAL CHAMPIONSHIP (Getxi, SWI 4 Feb 90)

1	H. Baars	HOL	1:03:14
2	A. van der Poel	HOL	1:03:19
3	B. Le Bras	FRA	1:03:19

FALCON CYCLES BRITISH CHAMPIONSHIP (6 Jan 90)

1	D. Baker	Cycles Peugeot	1:09:45
2	S. Barnes	Ace RT	1:10:51
3	S. Douce	Raleigh-Banana	1:12:32

DARTS

EMBASSY WORLD PROFESSIONAL CHAMPIONSHIP FINAL (13 Jan 90)

P. Taylor	ENG	bt	E. Bristow	ENG	6–1

WINMAU WORLD MASTERS FINALS (2 Dec 89)

Men

P. Evison	ENG	bt	E. Bristow	ENG	3–2

Women

M. Solomons	ENG	bt	S. Colclough	ENG	3–1

WEBSTERS BRITISH OPEN CHAMPIONSHIP FINALS (30 Dec 89)

Men

A. Warriner	ENG	bt	W. Jones	ENG	2–1

Women

S. Colclough	ENG	bt	S. Muir	ENG	3–0

NEWS OF THE WORLD CHAMPIONSHIP FINALS (2 Jun 90)

Men

P. Cook	ENG	bt	S. Hudson	ENG	2–0

Women

L. Ormond	ENG	bt	J. Stubbs	ENG	2–0

EQUESTRIAN EVENTS

SHOW JUMPING

VOLVO WORLD CUP (16 Apr 90)

1	J. Whitaker	GBR	Henderson Milton	4.0 faults
2	P. Durand	FRA	Jappeloup	12.5 faults
3	F. Sloothaak	FRG	Optiebeurs Walzerkoenig	14.0 faults

EUROPEAN CHAMPIONSHIP (18–20 Aug 89)

Individual

1	J. Whitaker	GBR	Next Milton	8.50 faults
2	M. Whitaker	GBR	Next Monsanta	9.03 faults
3	J. Lansink	HOL	Optiebeurs Felix	13.06 faults

Team

1	Great Britain		20.35 faults
	M. Whitaker	Next Monsanto	
	N. Skelton	Burmah Apollo	
	J. Whitaker	Next Milton	
	J. Turi	Country Classics Kruger	
2	France		33.41 faults
3	Switzerland		35.86 faults

SILK CUT HICKSTEAD DERBY (6 Aug 89)

1 N. Skelton	GBR	Burmah Apollo	4 faults 1:29.56
2 J. Turi	GBR	Country Classics Kruger	7 faults 1:27.15
3 P. Heffer	GBR	Viewpoint	8 faults 1:28.86

PRINCE OF WALES NATIONS CUP (Hickstead May 90)

1 Great Britain 8 faults, 3 faults in jump-off
M. Whitaker/D. Broome/E-J. Mac/J. Whitaker
2 Ireland 8 faults, 8 faults in jump-off
3= Switzerland 16 faults
3= West Germany 16 faults

KING GEORGE V GOLD CUP (23 Jun 90)

1 J. Whitaker	GBR	Henderson Milton	Clear 37.93
2 L. Philippaerts	BEL	Optiebeurs Fidelgo	4 faults 35.96
3 D. Broome	GBR	Countryman	4 faults 37.98

QUEEN ELIZABETH II CUP (23 Jun 90)

1 E-J. Mac	GBR	Everest Oyster	Clear 33.92
2 E. Edgar	GBR	Everest Asher	Clear 36.85
3 R. Tillson	GBR	Farasi Kuni	Clear 37.68

THREE DAY EVENTING

Remy Martin European Championship (10 Sep 89)

1	V. Leng	GBR	Master Craftsman	46.25 pen
2	J. Thelwell	GBR	King's Jester	59.20 pen
3	L. Clarke	GBR	Fearliath Mor	62.40 pen
T1	Great Britain			187.65 pen
T2	Holland			333.30 pen
T3	Ireland			363.10 pen

Barbour British Open Championship (Gatcombe Park 13 Aug 89)

1	M. Todd	NZL	Bahlua	46 pen
2	R. Powell	GBR	The Irishman	46 pen
3	J.Johnson	GBR	Timber Rua	47 pen

Todd won with a faster cross-country time

Whitbread Badminton Horse Trials (6 May 90)

1	Miss N. McIrvine	GBR	Middle Road	50.3 pen
2	B. Tait	NZL	Messiah	55.2 pen
3	Miss M. Thomson	GBR	King Boris	55.6 pen

FENCING

WORLD CHAMPIONSHIPS (11–15 Jul 89)

Men's Individual Foil Final
A. Koch FRG bt P. Omines FRA

Men's Team Foil Final
USSR bt West Germany

Men's Individual Epee Final
M. Pereira SPA bt S. Cuomo ITA

Men's Team Epee Final
Italy bt West Germany 9–4

Men's Individual Sabre Final
G. Kiriyenko URS bt J. Koniusz POL

Men's Team Sabre Final
USSR bt West Germany

Women's Foil Final
O. Velitchko URS bt A. Fichtel FRG

Women's Team Foil Final
West Germany bt USSR

Women's Individual Epee Final
A. Straub SWI bt U. Schäper FRG

Women's Team Epee Final
Hungary bt Italy

COMMONWEALTH CHAMPIONSHIPS (2–8 Jul 90)

Men's Foil Final
B.Giasson CAN bt J. Pitman ENG 2–1

Men's Team Foil Final
England bt Canada

Men's Epee Final
J-M. Chouinard FRA bt Q. Berriman WAL 2–1

Men's Team Epee Final
Canada bt Wales 5–2

Men's Sabre Final
J-P. Banos CAN bt I. Williams ENG 2–1

Men's Team Sabre Final
Canada bt Australia 5–3

Women's Foil Final
F. McIntosh SCO bt T. Tremblay CAN

Women's Team Foil Final
Canada bt England

Women's Epee Final
P. Tomlinson ENG bt F. Waterhouse AUS 2–1

Women's Team Epee Final
Canada bt Scotland 5–3

Wilkinson Trophy – Overall Team

1	Canada	40 pts
2	England	30 pts
3	Australia	12 pts

British Men's Epee Championship Final (11 Feb 90)
R. Johnson bt N. Mallett 2–0

British Men's Sabre Championship Final (10 Mar 90)
G. Fletcher bt I. Williams 2–0

British Men's Foil Championship Final (20 May 90)
W. Gosbee bt A. Royle

British Men's Foil Team Championship Final (10 Dec 89)
Hemel Hempstead bt Salle Paul 9–2

British Women's Foil Championship Final (20 May 90)
L. Strachan bt F. McIntosh

British Women's Foil Team Championship Final (17 Dec 89)
Salle Paul bt Cardiff

National Women's Epee Championship Final (27 May 90)
N. Twigg bt P. Tomlinson

GOLF

MEN'S PROFESSIONAL EVENTS

THE MAJOR OPENS

THE OPEN CHAMPIONSHIP (Royal Troon 23 Jul 89)

1	M. Calcavecchia	USA	275 4-hole play-off: –2
2=	W. Grady	AUS	275 4-hole play-off: +1
2=	G. Norman	AUS	275 4-hole play-off: conceded

AUSTRALIAN OPEN CHAMPIONSHIP (3 Dec 89)

1	P. Senior	AUS	271
2	P. Fowler	AUS	278
3	B. Ogle	AUS	279

US OPEN CHAMPIONSHIP (Medinah, Chicago, Ill. 18 Jun 90)

1	H. Irwin	USA	280 18-hole play-off: 74 won at 1st extra hole
2	M. Donald	USA	280 18-hole play-off: 74
3=	B.R. Brown	USA	281
3=	N. Faldo	GBI	281

THE MAJOR MASTERS

AUSTRALIAN MASTERS (Melbourne 18 Feb 90)

1	G. Norman	AUS	273
2=	M. Clayton	AUS	275
2=	N. Faldo	GBI	275
2=	J. Moore	USA	275

US MASTERS (Augusta, Georgia 8 Apr 90)

1	N. Faldo	GBI	278 won at 1st extra hole
2	R. Floyd	USA	278

3= J. Huston USA 283
3= L. Wadkins USA 283

DUNLOP BRITISH MASTERS (Woburn 3 Jun 90)
1 M. James GBI 270
2 D. Feherty GBI 272
3 C. Mason GBI 274

THE MAJOR PGAs

US PGA CHAMPIONSHIP (Kemper Lakes, Chicago, Ill. 3 Aug 89)
1 P. Stewart USA 276
2= A. Bean USA 277
2= M. Reid USA 277
2= C. Strange USA 277

AUSTRALIAN PGA CHAMPIONSHIP (12 Nov 89)
1 P. Senior AUS 274
2 J. Benepe USA 275
3 M. Harwood AUS 277

VOLVO PGA CHAMPIONSHIP (Wentworth 28 May 90)
1 M. Harwood AUS 271
2= J. Bland SAF 272
2= N. Faldo GBI 272

US PGA TOUR 1990

TOURNAMENT OF CHAMPIONS (La Costa, Carlsbad, Cal. 7 Jan 90)
1 P. Azinger USA 272
2 I. Baker-Finch AUS 273

TUCSON OPEN (14 Jan 90)
1 R. Gamez USA 270
2= M. Calcavecchia USA 274
2= J. Haas USA 274

BOB HOPE CHRYSLER CLASSIC – 90 HOLES (Palm Springs. Cal. 21 Jan 90)
1 P. Jacobsen USA 339
2= S. Simpsom USA 340
2= B. Tennyson USA 340

PHOENIX OPEN (Scottsdale 28 Jan 90)
1 T. Armour III USA 267
2 J. Thorpe USA 272

AT & T NATIONAL PRO-AM (Pebble Beach 4 Feb 90)
1 M. O'Meara USA 281
2 K. Perry USA 283

HAWAIIAN OPEN (Honolulu 11 Feb 90)
1 D. Ishii USA 279
2 P. Azinger USA 280

LOS ANGELES OPEN (25 Feb 90)
1 F. Couples USA 266
2 G. Morgan USA 269

DORAL RYDER OPEN (Miami, Fl. 4 Mar 90)
1 G. Norman AUS 273 won at 1st extra hole
2= P. Azinger USA 273
2= M. Calcavecchia USA 273
2= T. Simpson USA 273

HONDA CLASSIC (Coral Springs, Fl. 11 Mar 90)
1 J. Huston USA 282
2 M. Calcavecchia USA 284

TOURNAMENT PLAYERS' CHAMPIONSHIP (Pontra Vedra, Fl. 18 Mar 90)
1 J. Mudd USA 278
2 M. Calcavecchia USA 279

NESTLES INVITATIONAL (Orlando, Florida 25 Mar 90)
1 R. Gamez USA 274
2 G. Norman AUS 275

HOUSTON OPEN (1 Apr 90)
rain-reduced to 54 holes
1 A. Sills USA 204 won at 1st extra hole
2 G. Morgan USA 204

GREAT GREENSBORO OPEN (22 Apr 90)
1 S. Elkington AUS 282
2= M. Reid USA 284
2= J. Sluman USA 284

USF & G CLASSIC (New Orleans 29 Apr 90)
1 D. Frost SAF 276
2 G. Norman AUS 277

BYRON NELSON CLASSIC (Irving, Texas 6 May 90)
rain-reduced to 54 holes
1 P. Stewart USA 202
2 L. Wadkins USA 204

COLONIAL NATIONAL (Fort Worth, Texas 20 May 90)
1 B. Crenshaw USA 272
2= J. Mahaffey USA 275
2= C. Pavin USA 275
2= N. Price ZIM 275

ATLANTA CLASSIC (27 May 90)
1 W. Levi USA 275
2= K. Clearwater USA 276
2= L. Mize USA 276
2= N. Price ZIM 276

KEMPER OPEN (Potomac, Maryland 3 Jun 90)
1 G. Morgan USA 274
2 I. Baker-Finch AUS 275

WESTERN OPEN (Chicago, Ill. 10 Jun 90)
1 W. Levi USA 275
2 P. Stewart USA 279

BUICK WESTCHESTER CLASSIC (New York 24 Jun 90)
1 H. Irwin USA 269
2 P. Azinger USA 271

GREAT HARTFORD OPEN (Cromwell, Conn. 1 Jul 90)
1 W. Levi USA 267
2= M. Calcavecchia USA 269
2= B. Fabel USA 269
2= R. Mediate USA 269
2= C. Perry USA 269

EUROPEAN PGA TOUR 1989-90

KLM DUTCH OPEN CHAMPIONSHIP (Kennemer 30 Jul 89)
1 J-M. Olazabal SPA 277 won at 9th extra hole
2= R. Rafferty GBI 277
2= R. Chapman GBI 277 elim. at 1st extra hole

BELL'S SCOTTISH OPEN CHAMPIONSHIP (Gleneagles 16 Aug 89)
1 M. Allen USA 272
2= J-M. Olazabal SPA 274
2= I. Woosnam GBI 274

SCANDINAVIAN ENTERPRISE OPEN CHAMPIONSHIP (Drottningholm 6 Aug 89)
1 R. Rafferty GBI 268
2 M. Allen USA 270

BENSON & HEDGES INTERNATIONAL (Fulford 13 Aug 89)
1 G. Brand Jnr GBI 272
2 D. Cooper GBI 273

PLM OPEN (Malmo 20 Aug 89)
1 M. Harwood AUS 271
2 P. Senior AUS 272

WEST GERMAN OPEN GHAMPIONSHIP (27 Aug 89)
1 C. Parry AUS 266 won at 2nd extra hole
2 M. James GBI 266

EBEL EUROPEAN MASTERS/SWISS OPEN CHAMPIONSHIPS (Crans-sur-Sierre 3 Sep 89)
1 S. Ballesteros SPA 266
2 C. Parry AUS 268

PANASONIC EUROPEAN OPEN (Walton Heath 10 Sep 89)
1 A. Murray GBI 277
2 F. Nobilo NZL 278

LANCOME TROPHY (St. Non-la-Breteche 17 Sep 89)
1 E. Romero ARG 266
2= B. Langer FRG 267
2= J-M. Olazabal SPA 267

WEST GERMAN MASTERS (Stuttgart 8 Oct 89)
1 B. Langer FRG 276
2= J-M. Olazabal SPA 277
2= P. Stewart USA 277

BMW TOURNAMENT (Munich 15 Oct 89)

1	D. Feherty	GBI	269
2	F. Couples	USA	274

PORTUGUESE OPEN (Quinta do Lagos 22 Oct 89)

1	C. Montgomerie	GBI	264
2=	R. Davis	AUS	275
2=	M. Moreno	SPA	275
2=	M. Smith	USA	275

VOLVO MASTERS (Valderrama, SPA 29 Oct 89)

1	R.Rafferty	GBI	282
2	N. Faldo	GBI	283

EUROPEAN ORDER OF MERIT 1989

1	R. Rafferty	GBI	£400,311
2	J-M. Olazabal	SPA	£336,239
3	C. Parry	AUS	£277,321

VINHO VERDE ATLANTIC OPEN (18 Feb 90)

1	S. McAllister	GBI	288 won sudden death play-off
2=	R. Boxall	GBI	288
2=	S. Hamill	GBI	288
2=	R. Rafferty	GBI	288
2=	A. Sorensen	DEN	288
2=	D. Williams	GBI	288

EMIRATES DESERT CLASSIC (Dubai 25 Feb 90)

1	E. Darcy	GBI	276
2	D. Feherty	GBI	280

AMERICAN EXPRESS MEDITERRANEAN OPEN (Las Brisas, SPA 4 Mar 90) rain reduced to 54 holes

1	I. Woosnam	GBI	210
2=	M. Martin	SPA	212
2=	E. Romero	ARG	212

BALEARIC OPEN (Palma, Majorca 1 Mar 90)

1	S. Ballesteros	SPA	269 won at 1st extra hole
2	M. Persson	SWE	269

TENERIFE OPEN (18 Mar 90)

1	V. Fernandez	ARG	282 won at 3rd extra hole
2	M. Mouland	GBI	282

VOLVO OPEN (Ugolino, Florence, ITA 25 Mar 90)

1	E. Romero	ARG	265
2=	R. Claydon	GBI	266
2=	C. Montgomerie	GBI	266

AGF OPEN (Montpelier, FRA 1 Apr 90)

1	B. Ogle	AUS	278
2=	P. Curry	GBI	281
2=	W. Longmuir	GBI	281

EL BOSQUE OPEN (Valencia, SPA 8 Apr 90)

1	V. Singh	FIJ	278
2=	R. Boxall	GBI	280
2=	C. Williams	GBI	280

CREDIT LYONNAIS CANNES OPEN (16 Apr 90)

1	M. McNulty	ZIM	280
2	R. Rafferty	GBI	281

CEPSA MADRID OPEN (Puerta de Hierro 22 Apr 90)

1	B. Langer	FRG	270
2	R. Davis	AUS	271

PEUGEOT SPANISH OPEN CHAMPIONSHIP (Club de Campo, Madrid 29 Apr 90)

1	R. Davis	AUS	277
2=	N. Faldo	GBI	278
2=	P. Fowler	AUS	278
2=	B. Langer	FRG	278

BENSON & HEDGES INTERNATIONAL (St. Mellion 7 May 90)

1	J-M. Olazabal	SPA	279
2	I. Woosnam	GBI	280

BELGIAN OPEN CHAMPIONSHIP (Royal Waterloo, Brussels 13 May 90)

1	O. Sellberg	SWE	272
2	I. Woosnam	GBI	276

ITALIAN OPEN CHAMPIONSHIP (Milan 20 May 90)

1	R. Boxall	GBI	267
2	J-M. Olazabal	SPA	272

SCANDINAVIAN ENTERPRISE OPEN (Drottningholm 10 Jul 90)

1	C. Stadler	USA	268
2	C. Parry	AUS	272

WANG FOUR STARS (Moor Park 17 Jun 90)

1	R. Davis	AUS	271 won at 7th extra hole
2=	M. Clayton	AUS	271
2=	M. McNulty	ZIM	271
2=	W. Malley	USA	271

CARROLL'S IRISH OPEN CHAMPIONSHIP (Portmarnock 24 Jul 90)

1	J-M. Olazabal	SPA	282
2=	M. Calcavecchia	USA	285
2=	F. Nobilo	NZL	285

PEUGEOT FRENCH OPEN CHAMPIONSHIP (Chantilly 1 Jul 90)

1	P. Walton	GBI	275 won at 2nd extra hole
2	B. Langer	FRG	275

OTHER INTERNATIONAL EVENTS

MURPHY'S CUP STABLEFORD TOURNAMENT (St. Pierre 19 Aug 89)

1	H. Baiocchi	SAF	156 pts
2=	J. Bland	SAF	154 pts
2=	J. Hawkes	SAF	154 pts

THE JOHNNIE WALKER RYDER CUP (The Belfry 22–24 Sep 89)

Foursomes	EUR	1	USA	3	
Fourball	EUR	4	USA	0	
Foursomes	EUR	2	USA	2	
Fourball	EUR	2	EUR	2	
Singles	EUR	5	USA	7	
Final result	*EUR*	*14*	*USA*	*14*	*Europe retained the Cup*

DUNHILL CUP (St. Andrews 1 Oct 89)

Final			
USA	3.5	Japan	2.5
3rd Place			
England	2	Ireland	1

SUNTORY WORLD MATCHPLAY CHAMPIONSHIP (Wentworth 12–15 Oct 89)

1st Round					
R. Rafferty	NIR	bt	M. Reid	USA	3 & 2
J-M. Olazaba	SPA	bt	S. Hoch	USA	4 & 2
C. Beck	USA	bt	A. Ohmachi	JAP	8 & 6
D. Frost	SAF	bt	I. Baker-Finch	AUS	4 & 3
Quarter-finals					
R. Rafferty	NIR	bt	A. Lyle	SCO	1 hole
I. Woosnam	WAL	bt	J-M. Olazabal	SPA	3 & 2
S. Ballesteros	SPA	bt	C. Beck	USA	9 & 8
N. Faldo	ENG	bt	D. Frost	SAF	at 38th
Semi-finals					
N. Faldo	ENG	bt	S. Ballesteros	SPA	6 & 5
I. Woosnam	WAL	bt	R. Rafferty	NIR	2 & 1
Final					
N. Faldo	ENG	bt	I. Woosnam	WAL	1 hole

FOUR TOURS CHAMPIONSHIP (Tokyo 5 Nov 89)

Final				
USA	6	Europe	6	USA won 404–416 on strokes
3rd Place				
Japan	9	Australia/ New Zealand	3	

PHILIP MORRIS WORLD CUP (Las Brisas, SPA 19 Nov 89)
rain-reduced to 36 holes

1	AUS	(P. Fowler 137/W. Grady 141)	278
2	SPA	(J-M. Canizares 138/ J-M. Olazabal 143	281
3=	SWE	(M. Lanner 142/D. Sellberg 145)	287
3=	USA	(P. Azinger 141/M. McCumber 146)	287

Individual

1	P. Fowler	AUS	137

2=	A. Sorensen	DEN	138
2=	J-M. Canizares	SPA	138

SUN CITY MILLION DOLLAR CHALLENGE (10 Dec 89)

1	D. Frost	SAF	276
2	S. Hoch	USA	279
3	T. Simpson	USA	280

AMATEUR EVENTS

EUROPEAN TEAM CHAMPIONSHIP (2 Jul 89)

1	England	5
2	Scotland	2
3	Ireland	5
4	Sweden	2

THE WALKER CUP (Peachtree, Atlanta, Georgia 17 Aug 89)
Great Britain & Ireland bt USA 9–8 with 7 halved

THE AMATEUR CHAMPIONSHIP (Muirfield 9 Jun 90)
R. Muntz HOL bt M. Macara WAL 7 & 6

ENGLISH AMATEUR CHAMPIONSHIP (5 Aug 89)
S. Richardson bt R. Eggo 2 & 1

SCOTTISH AMATEUR CHAMPIONSHIP (5 Aug 89)
A. Thomson bt A. Tait 1 hole

WELSH AMATEUR CHAMPIONSHIP (30 Jul 89)
S. Dodd bt K. Jones 2 & 1

ENGLISH AMATEUR OPEN STROKEPLAY CHAMPIONSHIP (Burnham & Berrow 20 May 90)

1=	Olivier Edmond	FRA	287
1=	G. Evans	ENG	287

WOMEN'S EVENTS

THE MAJOR OPENS

US OPEN CHAMPIONSHIP (Indianwood, Mich. 16 Jul 89)

1	B. King	USA	278
2	N. Lopez	USA	282
3=	P. Bradley	USA	283
3=	P. Hammel	USA	283

WEETABIX BRITISH OPEN CHAMPIONSHIP (Ferndown 6 Aug 89)

1	J. Geddes	USA	274
2	F. Descampe	BEL	276
3	M-F. de Lorenzi	FRA	278

US LPGA TOUR

BOSTON FIVE CLASSIC (Boston, Mass. 23 July 89)
1 A. Alcott USA 272

LPGA CLASSIC (Bethesda 6 Aug 89)
1 B. Daniel USA 205

LPGA TOURNAMENT (Kent, Washington 17 Sep 89)
1 B. Daniel USA 273

LPGA TOURNAMENT (Buena Park, Cal. 24 Sep 89)
1 N. Lopez USA 277

LPGA CLASSIC (Lake Worth, Florida 4 Feb 90)

1	P. Bradley	USA	281	after play-off
2	D. Eggeling	USA	281	

KEMPER OPEN (Maui, Hawaii 4 Mar 90)
1 B. Daniel USA 283

TURQUISE LPGA CLASSIC (25 Mar 90)
1 P. Bradley USA 280

DINAH SHORE CLASSIC (1 Apr 90)
1 B. King USA 283

LPGA TOURNAMENT (Poway, Cal. 8 Apr 90)
1 K. Monaghan USA 276

LPGA TOURNAMENT (7 May 90)
1 A. Okamoto JAP 210

ATLANTIC CITY CLASSIC (17 Jun 90)
1 C. Johnson USA 275

ROCHESTER INTERNATIONAL (New York 24 Jun 90)
1 P. Sheehan USA 271

DU MAURIER CLASSIC (Kitchener, Ont. 1 Jul 90)
1 C. Johnson USA 276

EUROPEAN EVENTS

WEST GERMAN OPEN CHAMPIONSHIP (30 Jul 89)
1 A. Nicholas GBI 269

EXPEDIER EUROPEAN OPEN (Kingswood 17 Sep 89)
1 J. Connachan GBI 279

ITALIAN OPEN (Milan 1 Oct 89)
1 X. Wunsch-Ruiz SPA 278

AGF BIARRITZ OPEN (29 Oct 89)
1 D. Hutton AUS 274

QUALITAIR CLASSIC (La Manga, SPA 5 Nov 89)
1 A. Nicholas GBI 213

VALEXTRA CLASSIC (Rome 22 Apr 90)
1 F. Descampe FRA 279

FORD CLASSIC (Woburn 28 Apr 90)
1 M-L. de Lorenzi FRA 284

WPG HENNESSY CUP (St. Germain, Paris 13 May 90)
1 T. Johnson GBI 285

BMW EUROPEAN MASTERS (Bercuit 24 Jun 90)
1 K. Lunn AUS 285

BMW GERMAN CLASSIC (Hubbelrath 1 Jul 90)
1 D. Barnard GBI 278

NATIONAL EVENTS

BRITISH OPEN STROKEPLAY CHAMPIONSHIP (Southerness 25 Aug 89)
1 H. Dobson GBI 298

BRITISH AMATEUR OPEN CHAMPIONSHIP (Dunbar 18 Jun 90)
J. Hall ENG bt H. Wadswoth WAL 3 & 2

ENGLISH STROKEPLAY CHAMPIONSHIP (Hollinwell 10 Aug 89)

1	S. Robinson	302	at 1st extra hole
2	A. Shapcott	302	

WELSH AMATEUR OPEN 54–HOLE STROKEPLAY CHAMPIONSHIP (Newport 24 Jun 90)
1 L. Hackney ENG 218

ENGLISH WOMEN'S AMATEUR CLOSED CHAMPIONSHIP (Rye 26 May 90)
A. Uzielli bt L. Fletcher 2 & 1

SCOTTISH WOMEN'S AMATEUR CLOSED CHAMPIONSHIP (18 May 90)
E. Farquharson bt S. Huggan 3 & 2

WELSH WOMEN'S AMATEUR CLOSED CHAMPIONSHIP (18 May 90)
S. Roberts bt H. Wadsworth 3 & 2

IRISH WOMEN'S AMATEUR CLOSED CHAMPIONSHIP (25 May 90)
E. McDald bt L. Callen 2 & 1

OTHER EVENTS

EUROPEAN AMATEUR TEAM CHAMPIONSHIP (9 Jul 89)

1	France	4
2	England	3
3	Italy	4
4	Scotland	3

INTERNATIONAL AMATEUR DOUBLES BETTERBALL TEAM CHAMPIONSHIP (Sao Fernando, BRA 8 Oct 89)

1	GBI (H. Dobson/E. Farquharson)	278
2	SPA	279
3	COL	282

MIXED EVENT

BENSON & HEDGES MIXED PAIRS TROPHY (Marbella, SPA 12 Nov 89)

1	M. Jimenez/X. Wunsch-Ruiz	SPA	281
2	C. Mason/G. Stewart	GBI	283

GREYHOUND RACING

DAILY MIRROR/SPORTING LIFE DERBY FINAL – 480 m (Wimbledon 23 Jun 90)

	Greyhound	Owner	Trainer	SP	Time
1	Slippy Blue	Mrs. E. Fenn	K. Linzell	8–1	27.80 sec
2	Druids Johno	HRH Prince Edward	P. Byrne	4–7 fav	

GYMNASTICS

WORLD MEN'S CHAMPIONSHIP (Stuttgart 17–22 Oct 89)

Team

1	USSR		587.250
2	East Germany		580.850
3	China		579.300

Individual Overall

1	I. Korobchinsky	URS	59.250
2	V. Mogilny	URS	
3	Li Jing	CHN	

Floor Exercises

1	I. Korobchinsky	URS	9.937

High Bar

1	Li Chunyang	CHN	9.950

Parallel Bars

1=	V. Artemov	URS	9.900
1=	Lin Jing	CHN	9.900

Pommel Horse

1	V. Mogilny	URS	10.000

Rings

1	A. Aguilar	FRG	9.875

WORLD WOMEN'S CHAMPIONSHIP (Stuttgart 18–22 Oct 89)

Team

1	USSR		397.093
2	Romania		394.931
3	China		392.116

Individual Overall

1	S. Boginskaya	URS	39.900
2	N.Laschenova	URS	39.862
3	O. Strageva	URS	38.699

Assymetric Bars

1=	F. Di	CHN	10.000
1=	D. Silivas	ROM	10.000

Beam

1	D. Silivas	ROM	9.950

Floor Exercises

1=	S. Boginskaya	URS	10.000
1=	D. Silivas	ROM	10.000

Vault

1	O. Dudnik	URS	9.987

EUROPEAN MEN'S CHAMPIONSHIP (Lausanne, SWI 26–27 May 90)

Overall

1	V. Mogilny	URS	58.450
2	S. Kharkov	URS	58.300
3	Y. Chechi	ITA	58.200

Floor Exercises

1	V. Scherbo	URS	9.825
2	S. Kharkov	URS	9.800
3	A. Gal	ROM	9.700

High Bar

1	V. Scherbo	URS	9.912
2	R. Pluess	SWI	9.825
3	A. Kolman	YUG	9.800

Parallel Bars

1=	V. Mogilny	URS	9.800
1=	D. Giubellini	SWI	9.800
3	K. Hristozov	BUL	9.750

Pommel Horse

1	V. Mogilny	URS	9.937
2	J. Milbradt	GDR	9.837
3	S. Kharkov	URS	9.800

Rings

1	Y. Chechi	ITA	9.837
2	J. Milbradt	GDR	9.712
3	S. Csollany	HUN	9.687

Vault

1	V. Scherbo	URS	9.943
2	R. Buchner	GDR	9.724
3	N. Thomas	GBR	9.625

EUROPEAN WOMEN'S CHAMPIONSHIP (Athens, GRE 5–6 May 90)

Overall

1	S. Boginskaya	URS	39.874

Assymetric Bars

1	S. Boginskaya	URS

Beam

1	S. Boginskaya	URS

Floor Exercises

1	S. Boginskaya	URS

Vault

1	S. Boginskaya	URS

BRITISH MEN'S CHAMPIONSHIP (17–18 Mar 90)

Overall

1	N. Thomas	113.00
2	J. May	112.15
3	T. Bartlett	111.15

Floor Exercises

1=	T. Bartlett	9.450
1=	J. May	9.450

High Bar

1	M. Campbell	9.800

Parallel Bars

1	D. Cox	9.500

Pommel Horse

1	N. Thomas	9.500

Rings

1	M. Bone	9.400

Vault

1	N. Thomas	9.650

BRITISH WOMEN'S CHAMPIONSHIP (10 Mar 90)

Overall

1	S. Mercer	75.975
2	L. Redding	75.425
3	L. Mainwaring	74.675

HANDBALL

NATIONAL CUP FINALS 1990

Men

Ruislip Eagles	bt	Manchester United SSS	25–22

Women

Wakefield Metros	bt	Manchester United SSS	18–14

HOCKEY

7TH MEN'S WORLD CUP (Lahore 1990)

First Round

12 Feb	Group A	HOL 2	FRA 1	IND 1	URS 1
	Group B	ENG 2	IRE 0	PAK 6	SPA 3
13 Feb	Group A	AUS 4	ARG 1	HOL 5	URS 2
	Group B	FRG 4	CAN 1	PAK 2	IRE 1
14 Feb	Group A	ARG 5	IND 3	AUS 3	FRA 1
	Group B	ENG 2	CAN 0	FRG 2	SPA 0
15 Feb	Group A	FRA 2	IND 1		
	Group B	SPA 4	ENG 1		

16 Feb	Group A	AUS 3	URS 0	HOL 3	ARG 3
	Group B	FRG 4	IRE 0	PAK 1	CAN 0
17 Feb	Group A	FRA 0	URS 0	HOL 5	IND 3
	Group B	PAK 1	ENG 1	SPA 2	IRE 1
18 Feb	Group A	AUS 3	IND 2	FRA 1	ARG 0
	Group B	FRG 2	ENG 1	SPA 1	CAN 0
19 Feb	Group A	AUS 1	HOL 0	URS 3	ARG 1
	Group B	CAN 1	IRE 1	FRG 1	PAK 0

Group Tables

		P	W	D	L	F	A	Pts
Group A	AUS	5	5	0	0	14	4	10
	HOL	5	3	1	1	15	10	7
	FRA	5	2	1	2	5	6	5
	URS	5	1	2	2	6	10	4
	ARG	5	1	1	3	10	14	3
	IND	5	0	1	4	10	16	1
Group B	FRG	5	5	0	0	13	2	10
	PAK	5	3	1	1	10	6	7
	SPA	5	3	0	2	10	10	6
	ENG	5	2	1	2	7	7	5
	CAN	5	0	1	4	2	9	1
	IRE	5	0	1	4	3	11	1

21 Feb	5–8 Places	ENG 4	FRA 0	URS 2	SPA 1
	Semi-Finals	PAK 2	AUS 1	HOL 3	FRG 2
22 Feb	9–12 Places	ARG 4	IRE 1	IND 2	CAN 1
	7th Place	FRA 4	SPA 3		
	5th Place	ENG 1	URS 0		
23 Feb	11th Place	CAN 3	IRE 0		
	9th Place	ARG 1	IND 0		
	3rd Place	AUS 2	FRG 1		
	Final	HOL 3	PAK 1		

7TH WOMEN'S WORLD CUP (Sydney 1990)

First Round

2 May	Group A	AUS 3	CHN 0		
	Group B	CAN 1	NZL 0	SKO 7	SPA 0
		HOL 3	USA 0		
3 May	Group A	ENG 1	ARG 0	FRG 2	JAP 0
	Group B	NZL 1	SKO 0	CAN 1	USA 1
4 May	Group A	ENG 1	JAP 0	AUS 1	ARG 1
		FRG 3	CHN 1		
	Group B	HOL 3	SPA 0		
5 May	Group B	HOL 3	NZL 0	SKO 1	CAN 0
		SPA 3	USA1		
6 May	Group A	ENG 2	CHN 0	AUS 2	FRG 1
		ARG 0	JAP 0		
7 May	Group A	ENG 0	FRG 0	SPA 3	CAN 0
	Group B	HOL 0	SKO 0	NZL 6	USA 1
8 May	Group A	AUS 2	JAP 0	CHN 2	ARG 0
	Group B	NZL 1	SPA 1	SKO 9	USA 0
9 May	Group A	AUS 0	ENG 0	FRG 3	ARG 1
		CHN 1	JAP 1		
	Group B	HOL 2	CAN 0		

Group Tables

		P	W	D	L	F	A	Pts
Group A	AUS	5	3	2	0	8	2	8
	ENG	5	3	2	0	4	0	8
	FRG	5	3	1	1	9	4	7
	CHN	5	1	1	3	4	9	3
	ARG	5	0	2	3	2	7	2
	JAP	5	0	2	3	1	6	2
Group B	HOL	5	4	1	0	11	0	9
	SKO	5	3	1	1	17	1	7
	NZL	5	2	1	2	8	6	5
	SPA	5	2	1	2	7	12	5
	CAN	5	1	1	3	2	7	3
	USA	5	0	1	4	3	22	1

11 May	9–12 Places	ARG 4	USA 0	CAN 1	JAP 0
	5–8 Places	SPA 2	FRG 1	CHN 0	NZL 0 aet
				CHN won 5–4 on pen	
	Semi-Finals	AUS 2	SKO 1 aet	HOL 5	ENG 0
12 May	7th Place	NZL 4	FRG 1		
	5th Place	SPA 1	CHN 0		
13 May	11th Place	JAP 3	USA 1		
	9th Place	ARG 1	CAN 1 aet		
		ARG won 4–2 on pen			
	3rd Place	SKO 3	ENG2		
	Final	HOL 3	AUS 1		

LADA CLASSIC (Luton 1989)

Men

6 Oct	AUS 2	HOL 1	ENG 5	ARG 0
7 Oct	HOL 5	ENG 1	AUS 4	ARG 2
8 Oct	ARG 3	HOL 3	AUS 0	ENG 0

Final Standings

		P	W	D	L	F	A	Pts
1	AUS	3	2	1	0	6	3	5
2	HOL	3	1	1	1	9	6	3
3	ENG	3	1	1	1	6	5	3
4	ARG	3	0	1	2	5	12	1

Women (Friendly matches)

7 Oct	ENG 1	URS 0
8 Oct	URS 2	ENG 1

BMW TROPHY (Amsterdam 1990)

Seven-nation round-robin tournament

16 Jun	HOL 3	IND 1	PAK 4	SPA 1
17 Jun	AUS 3	HOL 2	FRG 3	SPA 3
	IND 2	GBR 1		
18 Jun	AUS 3	GBR 1	PAK 1	FRG 0
19 Jun	HOL 3	SPA 2	IND 4	PAK 2
20 Jun	AUS 2	SPA 1	FRG 2	GBR 1
21 Jun	AUS 4	PAK 4	HOL 1	GBR 0
	FRG 4	IND 3		
22 Jun	IND 1	SPA 1	PAK 2	HOL 1
23 Jun	FRG 3	AUS 2	GBR 3	SPA 1
24 Jun	AUS 6	IND 3	HOL 1	FRG 0
	PAK 5	GBR 2		

Final Standings

		P	W	D	L	F	A	Pts
1	AUS	6	4	1	1	20	14	9
2	PAK	6	4	1	1	18	12	9
3	HOL	6	4	0	2	11	8	8
4	FRG	6	3	1	2	12	11	7
5	IND	6	2	1	3	14	17	5
6	GBR	6	1	0	5	8	14	2
7	SPA	6	0	2	4	9	16	2

INAUGURAL EUROPEAN CUP WINNERS' CUP FINAL (3 Jun 90)

Hounslow GBR 3 Amsterdamsche HOL 2

EUROPEAN CLUBS' CHAMPIONSHIP (4 Jun 90)

Men

1	Uhlenhorst	FRG 2	
2	Atletico Terrassa	SPA 0	
3	Bloemendahl	HOL 4	
4	Frankfurt 1880	FRG 2	
5	Royal Leopold	BEL 1	3–1 on pen
6	Southgate	ENG 1	
7	Dynamo Alma Ata	URS	3
8	Lisnagarvey	NIR	2

Women

1	Amsterdamsche	HOL 4
2	Guytech Western	SCO 0
3	Kolos Borispol	URS 3
4	Campo de Madrid	SPA 2

5	Pegasus	NIR 0	4–3 on pen
6	Ealing	ENG 0	
7	Swansea	WAL 3	
8	Frankfurt 1880	FRG 1	

EUROPEAN INDOOR CUP FINAL (4 Mar 90)

Rot-Weiss Cologne FRG 8 Amsterdamsche HOL 4

WOMEN'S HOME COUNTRIES' CHAMPIONSHIP (31 Mar 90)

Scotland 0 Ireland 0, Wales 1 England 0, Ireland 1 England 0, Scotland 1 Wales 0, Ireland 4 Wales 0, England 2 Scotland 1.

Final Table		P	W	D	L	F	A	Pts
1	Ireland	3	2	1	0	5	0	5
2	Scotland	3	1	1	1	2	2	3
3	England	3	1	0	2	2	3	2
4	Wales	3	1	0	2	1	5	2

POUNDSTRETCHER NATIONAL LEAGUE – Final Tables 1989–90

1st Division

		P	W	D	L	F	A	Pts	
1	Hounslow	15	12	2	1	45	16	38	
2	East Grinstead	15	11	1	3	30	13	34	
3	Havant	15	10	3	2	36	15	33	
4	Slough	15	10	3	2	29	16	33	
5	Southgate	15	10	1	4	36	19	31	
6	Stourport	15	7	5	3	31	15	26	
7	Teddington	15	6	4	5	33	25	22	
8	Welton	15	6	4	5	24	24	22	
9	ISCA	15	6	2	7	28	26	20	
10	Bromley	15	5	2	8	24	25	17	
11	Indian Gymkhana	15	5	2	8	15	27	17	
12	Cannock	15	4	3	8	21	35	15	
13	Old Loughtonians	15	2	7	6	24	25	13	
14	Wakefield	15	3	2	10	17	39	11	
15	Harborne	15	1	2	12	15	58	5	R
16	Reading	15	0	1	14	10	40	1	R

2nd Division

		P	W	D	L	F	A	Pts	
1	St. Albans	15	13	2	0	50	17	41	P
2	Neston	15	9	4	2	41	24	31	P
3	Gore County	15	8	6	1	28	15	30	
4	Brean	15	8	4	3	29	13	28	
5	Bourneville	15	7	4	4	24	20	25	
6	Cambridge City	15	6	3	6	25	21	21	
7	Doncaster	15	5	5	5	28	26	20	
8	Lyons	15	6	2	7	26	31	20	
9	Guildford	15	5	3	7	25	26	18	
10	Warrington	15	4	5	6	22	26	17	
11	Canterbury	15	5	2	8	16	25	17	
12	Taunton Vale	15	4	4	7	15	21	16	
13	Richmond	15	4	3	8	28	30	15	
14	Broxborne	15	4	3	8	22	32	15	
15	Coventry	15	4	3	8	12	22	15	R
16	Peterborough	15	0	3	12	14	56	3	R

MEN'S COUNTY CHAMPIONSHIP FINAL (13 May 90)

Middlesex 2 Yorkshire 1 aet

NATIONWIDE ANGLIA MEN'S HOCKEY ASSOCIATION CUP FINAL (8 Apr 90)

Havant 3 Stourport 0

POUNDSTRETCHER HOCKEY LEAGUE CUP FINAL (6 May 90)

1st Division

Havant 3 Hounslow 2

2nd Division

Neston 3 St. Albans 2

TYPHOO NATIONAL WOMEN'S LEAGUE – Final Table 1989–90

		P	W	SD	NSD	L	F	A	Pts
1	Slough	9	8	1	0	0	30	5	34
2	Leicester	9	5	2	2	0	18	7	26
3	Sutton Coldfield	9	5	0	2	2	17	6	22
4	Hightown	9	4	2	1	2	19	12	21
5	Chelmsford	9	4	1	0	4	14	14	18
6	Clifton	9	3	1	1	4	7	9	15
7	Ealing	9	3	0	2	4	12	11	14
8	Orpington	9	1	2	0	6	6	23	8
9	Great Harwood	9	1	1	1	6	5	22	7
10	Exmouth	9	1	0	1	7	4	23	5

WOMEN'S COUNTY CHAMPIONSHIP FINAL (13 May 90)

Cheshire 4 Kent 2

ENGLISH WOMEN'S CLUB CHAMPIONSHIP FINAL (22 Apr 90)

Sutton Coldfield 1 Hightown 0

HORSE RACING

MAJOR FLAT RACING RESULTS 1989

	Horse	Age/ Weight	Owner	Trainer	Jockey	SP
CORAL ECLIPSE STAKES 1m 2f SANDOWN PARK 8 Jul 89						
1	Nashwan	3–8–8	Hamdan Al-Maktoum	W. Hern	W. Carson	2–5 fav
2	Opening Verse	3–8–8	Sheikh Mohammed	H. Cecil	N. Day	200–1
3	Indian Skimmer	5–9–4	Sheikh Mohammed	H. Cecil	S. Cauthen	11–2
KING GEORGE VI & QUEEN ELIZABETH DIAMOND STAKES 1m 4f ASCOT 22 Jul 89						
1	Nashwan	3–8–8	Hamdan Al-Maktoum	W. Hern	W. Carson	2–9 fav
2	Cacoethes	3–8–8	Lady Harrison	G. Harwood	G. Starkey	6–1
3	Top Class	4–9–7	Capt. M. Lemos	C. Brittain	M. Roberts	50–1
SCHWEPPES GOLDEN MILE (Handicap) 1m GOODWOOD 27 Jul 89						
1	Safawan	3–8–0	HH Aga Khan	M. Stoute	W. Carson	11–2
2	Serious Trouble	3–7–12	G. Moore	M. Prescott	J. Lowe	11–1
3	Mirror Black	3–8–5	Mrs C. Webster	P. Makin	P. Eddery	5–1
GOODWOOD CUP 2m 5f GOODWOOD 27 Jul 89						
1	Mazzacano	4–9–0	A. Ward	G. Harwood	P. Eddery	15–2
2	Sadeem	6–9–7	Sheikh Mohammed	G. Harwood	G. Starkey	3–10 fav
3	Princess Sobieska	3–7–7	Mrs D. Riley-Smith	J. Dunlop	W. Carson	7–1
JUDDMONTE INTERNATIONAL STAKES 1m 2f 110y YORK 22 Aug 89						
1	Ile de Chypre	4–9–6	A. Christodoulou	G. Harwood	A. Clark	16–1
2	Cacoethes	3–8–10	Lady Harrison	G. Harwood	G. Starkey	2–5 fav
3	Shady Heights	5–9–6	H. Furuoka	R. Armstrong	W. Carson	20–1
TOTE EBOR HANDICAP 1m 6f YORK 23 Aug 89						
1	Sapience	3–8–4	Marquesa de Moratalla	J. FitzGerald	P. Eddery	15–2
2	Bush Hill	4–8–0	Lord Matthews	I. Matthews	A. McGlone	50–1
3	Horn Dance	3–9–1	Sheikh Mohammed	G. Harwood	G. Starkey	5–2 fav

BEEFEATER GIN CELEBRATION MILE 1M GOODWOOD 26 Aug 87

1	Distance Relative	3–8–12	Wafic Said	B. Hills	M. Hills	2–1
2	Great Commotion	3–8–9	Maktoum Al Maktoum	A. Scott	P. Eddery	5–2
3	Reprimand	4–9–6	Sheikh Mohammed	H. Cecil	S. Cauthen	6–4 fav

LADBROKE SPRINT CUP 6f HAYDOCK PARK 2 Sep 89

1	Danehill	3–9–5	K. Abdulla	J. Tree	P. Eddery	3–1
2	Cricket Ball	6–9–10	R. Scully	J. Fellows (FRA)	W. Carson	7–2
3	A Prayer for Wings	5–9–10	S. Powell	J. Sutcliffe	M. Roberts	15–2

HOLSTEN PILS ST. LEGER STAKES 1M 6f 127y AYR 23 Sep 89
Transferred from Doncaster (16 Sep 89) due to course subsidence

1	Michelozzo	3–9–0	C. St. George	H. Cecil	S. Cauthen	6–4 fav
2	Sapience	3–9–0	Marquesa de Moratalla	J. FitzGerald	K. Fallon	15–1
3	Roseate Tern	3–8–11	Lord Carnarvon	W. Hern	W. Carson	5–2

QUEEN ELIZABETH II STAKES 1M ASCOT 30 Sep 89

1	Zilzal	3–8–11	Mana Al Maktoum	M. Stoute	W.R. Swinburn	Evens fav
2	Polish Precedent	3–8–11	Sheikh Mohammed	A. Fabre (FRA)	C. Asmussen	11–8
3	Distant Relative	3–8–11	Wafic Said	B. Hills	M. Hills	10–1

WILLIAM HILL CAMBRIDGESHIRE 1M 1f NEWMARKET 7 Oct 89

1	Rambo's Hall	4–8–6	B. Dixon	J. Glover	Dean McKeown	15–1
2	Dawn Success	3–7–10	Mrs C. Pateras	C. Brittain	S. Wood	33–1
3	Re-Release	4–7–9	J. Ennis	M. Pipe	J. Lowe	20–1

CIGA PRIX DE L'ARC DE TRIOMPHE 1m 4f LONGCHAMP 8 Oct 89

1	Carroll House	4–9–4	A. Balzarini	M. Jarvis (ENG)	M.J. Kinane
2	Behera	3–8–8	HH Aga Khan	A. de Royer-Dupre	A. Lequeux
3	Saint Andrews	5–9–4	F. Stronach	J-M. Beguigne	E. Legrix

DUBAI CHAMPION STAKES 1M 2f NEWMARKET 21 Oct 89

1	Legal Case	3–8–10	Sir G. White	L. Cumani	R. Cochrane	5–1
2	Dolpour	3–8–10	HH Aga Khan	M. Stoute	W.R. Swinburn	4–1 fav
3	Ile de Chypre	4–9–3	A. Christodoulou	G. Harwood	W. Carson	5–1

TOTE CESAREWITCH 2M 2f NEWMARKET 21 Oct 89

1	Double Dutch	5–9–10	L. Fuller	Miss B. Saunders	W. Newnes	15–2
2	Chelsea Girl	3–9–0	M. Hill	M. Jarvis	D. Biggs	12–1
3	Travelling Light	3–8–1	Mrs A. Sigsworth	Mrs J. Ramsden	A. Munro	9–4 fav

FINAL TABLE 1989

			1st	2nd	3rd	Unplaced
Jockeys	1	P. Eddery	171	126	91	450
	2	S. Cauthen	163	92	65	341
	3	W. Carson	137	126	122	482

			Winners	Win Prize Money
Owners	1	Sheikh Mohammed	130	£1,297,068
	2	Hamdan Al-Maktoum	98	£1,222,683
	3	K. Abdulla	61	£683,589

			1st	2nd	3rd	Unplaced
Trainers	1	M. Stoute	117	95	77	208
	2	H. Cecil	116	67	51	127
	3	G. Harwood	109	83	40	178

MAJOR FLAT RACING RESULTS 1990

WILLIAM HILL LINCOLN HANDICAP 1M DONCASTER 24 Mar 90

1	Evichstar	6–7–10	G. Meredith	J. FitzGerald	A. Munro	33–1
2	Vilanika	4–7–7	W. Gredley	C. Brittain	G. Bardwell	20–1
3	Inishpour	8–7–7	G. Russell	A. Robson	R. Fox	14–1

WESTMINSTER-MOTOR (TAXI) INSURANCE CITY & SUBURBAN STAKES (HANDICAP) 1M 2f EPSOM 24 Apr 90

1	Starlet	4–8–8	HM The Queen	W. Hastings-Bass	Dale Gibson	11–4 fav
2	Hateel	4–7–13	Hamdan Al-Maktoum	P. Walwyn	G. Carter	11–2
3	Dismiss	5–8–6	Mrs G. Smyth	R. Smyth	M. Hills	12–1

TRUSTHOUSE FORTE MILE 1M SANDOWN PARK 27 Apr 90

1	Markofdistinction	4–9–0	G. Leigh	L. Cumani	L. Dettori	9–2
2	Citidancer	4–9–0	I. Allan	H. Cecil	S. Cauthen	6–4 fav
3	Magic Gleam	4–9–1	Maktoum Al Maktoum	A. Scott	P. Eddery	4–1

GENERAL ACCIDENT 1000 GUINEAS 1M NEWMARKET 3 May 90

1	Salsabil	3–9–0	Hamdan Al-Maktoum	J. Dunlop	W. Carson	6–4 fav
2	Heart of Joy	3–9–0	J. Mabee	M. Stoute	W.R. Swinburn	4–1
3	Negligent	3–9–0	Mrs J. Corbett	B. Hills	P. Eddery	11–2

GENERAL ACCIDENT JOCKEY CLUB STAKES 1M 4f NEWMARKET 4 May 90

1	Roseate Tern	4–8–9	P. Brant	L. Cumani	L. Dettori	17–2
2	Ile de Nisky	4–8–7	Prince Yazid Saud	G. Huffer	G. Carter	12–1
3	Artic Envoy	4–8–7	G. Mazza	P. Kellaway	C. Asmussan	50–1

GENERAL ACCIDENT 2000 GUINEAS 1M NEWMARKET 5 May 90

1	Tirol	3–9–0	J. Horgan	R. Hannon	M.J. Kinane	9–1
2	Machiavellian	3–9–0	S. Niarchos	F. Boutin (FRA)	F. Head	6–4 fav
3	Anshan	3–9–0	Sheikh Mohammed	J. Gosden	W.R. Swinburn	6–1

INSULPAK VICTORIA CUP (HANDICAP) 7f ASCOT 2 May 90

1	Lomax	4–9–3	K. Abdulla	G. Harwood	P. Eddery	11–1

2	Profit a Prendre	6–7–2	P. Thorne	D. Wilson	N. Kennedy	33–1
3	Just Jennings	5–8–0	Mrs E. Haydn Jones	D. Haydn Jones	S. Dawson	33-1

LADBROKE CHESTER CUP (HANDICAP) 2M 2f 97y CHESTER 9 May 90

1	Travelling Light	4–9–1	Mrs A. Sigsworth	Mrs J. Ramsden	A. Munro	5–2 fav
2	Rambo Castle	4–8–9	P. Macari	N. Tinkler	D. Nicholls	25–1
3	Andorra	8–8–3	J. FitzGerald	J. FitzGerald	M. Roberts	11–1

WILLIAM HILL DANTE STAKES 1M 2f 110y YORK 16 May 90

1	Sanglamore	3–9–0	K. Abdulla	R. Charlton	P. Eddery	11–2
2	Karinga Bay	3–9–0	K. Higson	Denys Smith	B. Rouse	16–1
3	Anshan	3–9–0	Sheikh Mohammed	J. Gosden	W.R. Swinburn	Evens fav

PRIX DU JOCKEY CLUB LANCIA (FRENCH DERBY) 1M 4f CHANTILLY 3 Jun 90

1	Sanglamore	3–9–2	K. Abdulla	R. Charlton (ENG)	P. Eddery
2	Epervier Bleu	3–9–2	D. Wildenstein	E. Lellouche	D. Boeuf
3	Erdelistana	3–9–2	HH Aga Khan	A De Royer-Dupre	A. Cruz

EVER READY DERBY STAKES 1M 4f EPSOM 6 Jun 90

1	Quest For Fame	3–9–0	K. Abdulla	R. Charlton	P. Eddery	7–1
2	Blue Stag	3–9–0	R. Sangster	B. Hills	C. Asmussen	8–1
3	Elmaamul	3–9–0	Hamdam Al-Maktoum	W. Hern	W. Carson	10–1

HANSON CORONATION CUP 1M 4f EPSOM 7 Jun 90

1	In The Wings	4–9–0	Sheikh Mohammed	A. Fabre (FRA)	C. Asmussen	15–8 fav
2	Observation Post	4–9–0	R. Sangster	B. Hills	W. Carson	5–1
3	Ibn Bey	6–9–0	Fahd Salman	P. Cole	T. Quinn	5–1

GOLD SEAL OAKS STAKES 1M 4f EPSOM 9 Jun 90

1	Salsabil	3–9–0	Hamdan Al-Maktoum	J. Dunlop	W. Carson	2–1
2	Game Plan	3–9–0	Mrs H. Phillips	C. Brittain	B. Marcus	50–1
3	Knight's Baroness	3–9–0	Fahd Salman	P. Cole	T. Quinn	16–1

CORONATION STAKES 1M ROYAL ASCOT 20 Jun 90

1	Chimes of Freedom	3–9–0	S. Niarchos	H. Cecil	S. Cauthen	11–2
2	Hasbah	3–9–0	Hamdan Al-Maktoum	H. Thomson Jones	R. Hills	9–2
3	Heart of Joy	3–9–0	J. Mabee	M. Stoute	W.R. Swinburn	11–8 fav

ROYAL HUNT CUP (HANDICAP) 1M ROYAL ASCOT 20 Jun 90

1	Pontenuova	5–7–7	W. Mariti	D. Elsworth	G. Bardwell	50–1
2	Curtain Call	4–8–6	A. Hobbs	P. Makin	B. Raymond	10–1
3	Pride of Araby	4–9–5	K. Abdulla	R. Charlton	P. Eddery	6–1 fav

GOLD CUP 2M 4f ROYAL ASCOT 21 Jun 90

1	Ashal	4–9–0	Hamdam Al-Maktoum	H. Thomson Jones	R. Hills	14–1
2	Tyrone Bridge	4–9–0	P. Green	M. Pipe	P. Shanahan	7–1
3	Thethingaboutitis	5–9–2	Doublet Ltd	D. Elsworth	P. Eddery	20–1

HARDWICKE STAKES 1M 4f ROYAL ASCOT 22 Jun 90

1	Assatis	5–9–0	S. Harada	G. Harwood	R. Cochrane	50–1
2	Ile de Nisky	4–8–9	HH Prince Yazid Saud	G. Huffer	G. Carter	50–1
3	Old Vic	4–9–0	Sheikh Mohammed	H. Cecil	S. Cauthen	4–5 fav

WOKINGHAM STAKES 6f ROYAL ASCOT 22 Jun 90

1	Knight of Mercy	4–8–6	M. Grant	R. Hannon	P. Eddery	16–1
2	Amigo Menor	4–7–7	F. Glennon	K. Brassey	C. Rutter	33–1
3	Hana Marie	3–7–8	T. Nerses	G. Huffer	W. Carson	9–1 fav

BUDWEISER IRISH DERBY 1M 4f THE CURRAGH 1 Jul 90

1	Salsabil	3–9–0	Hamdan Al-Maktoum	J. Dunlop	W. Carson	11–4
2	Deploy	3–9–0	K. Abdulla	R. Charlton	W.R. Swinburn	16–1
3	Belmez	3–9–0	Sheikh Mohammed	H. Cecil	S. Cauthen	4–1

MAJOR NATIONAL HUNT RACING RESULTS 1989–90

HENNESSY COGNAC GOLD CUP HANDICAP CHASE 3M 2f 82y NEWBURY 25 Nov 89

1	Ghofar	6–10–0	Sir H. Dundas	D. Elsworth	H. Davies	5–1
2	Brown Windsor	7–11–3	W. Shand Kydd	N. Henderson	R. Dunwoody	7–4 fav
3	Mr. Frisk	10-11-8	Mrs H. Duffey	K. Bailey	Mr M. Armtage	16–1

KING GEORGE VI CHASE 3M KEMPTON PARK 26 Dec 89

1	Desert Orchid	10–11–10	R. Burridge	D. Elsworth	R. Dunwoody	4–6 fav
2	Barnbrook Again	8–11–10	M. Davies	D. Elsworth	B. Powell	13–2
3	Yahoo	8–11–10	A. Parker	J. Edwards	T. Morgan	11–2

TOTE GOLD TROPHY (HANDICAP HURDLE) 2M 200y NEWBURY 10 Feb 90

1	Deep Sensation	5–11–3	R. Eliot	J. Gifford	R. Rowe	7–1
2	Joyful Noise	7–11–5	S. Wood	A. Moore (IRE)	T. Taaffe	10–1
3	Imperial Brush	6–10–0	P. Pullen	D. Elsworth	P. Holley	33–1

WILLIAM HILL IMPERIAL CUP (HANDICAP HURDLE) 2M SANDOWN PARK 10 Mar 90

1	Moody Man	5–10–13	J. Burley	P. Hobbs	Peter Hobbs	20–1
2	Penny Forum	6–11–7	R. Surridge	J. Sutcliffe	D. McKeown	14–1
3	Joyful Noise	7–11–10	S. Wood	A. Moore (IRE)	T. Taaffe	5–1 fav

WATERFORD CRYSTAL CHAMPION HURDLE 2M CHELTENHAM 13 Mar 90

1	Kribensis	6–12–0	Sheikh Mohammed	M. Stoute	R. Dunwoody	95–40
2	Nomadic Way	5–12–0	R. Sangster	B. Hills	P. Scudamore	8–1
3	Past Glories	7–12–0	N. Hetherton	J. Hetherton	J.J. Quinn	150-1

TOTE GOLD CUP CHASE 3M 2f CHELTENHAM 15 Mar 90

1	Norton's Coin	9–12–0	S. Griffiths	S. Griffiths	G. McCourt	100–1
2	Toby Tobias	8–12–0	Mrs E. Hitchins	Mrs J. Pitman	M. Pitman	8–1
3	Desert Orchid	11–12–0	R. Burridge	D. Elsworth	R. Dunwoody	10–11 fav

SEAGRAM GRAND NATIONAL CHASE 4M 4f AINTREE 7 Apr 90

1	Mr. Frisk	11–10–6	Mrs H. Duffey	K. Bailey	Mr. M. Armytage	16–1
2	Durham Edition	12–10–9	R. Oxley	W. Stephenson	C. Grant	9–1
3	Rinus	9–10–4	A. Proos	G.W. Richards	N. Doughty	13–1

WHITBREAD GOLD CUP HANDICAP CHASE 3M 5f 18y SANDOWN PARK 28 Apr 90

1	Mr. Frisk	11–10–5	Mrs H. Duffey	K. Bailey	Mr. M. Armytage	9–2 fav
2	Durham Edition	12–10–9	R. Oxley	W. Stephenson	C. Grant	13–2
3	Four Trix	9–10–1	Mrs. S. Catherwood	G.W. Richards	D. Byrne	15–2

FINAL TABLES 1989–90

			1st	2nd	3rd	Unplaced
Jockeys	1	P. Scudamore	170	79	45	229
	2	R. Dunwoody	102	102	84	316
	3	G. McCourt	100	58	54	223

			1st	2nd	3rd	Unplaced
Trainers	1	M. Pipe	224	97	61	257
	2	W.A. Stephenson	116	88	62	253
	3	Mrs J. Pitman	93	62	33	147

			Winners	Win Prize Money
Owners	1	Mrs H. Duffey	3	£124,231
	2	P. Piller	38	£116,172
	3	Sheikh Mohammed	6	£106,533

HURLING

ALL-IRELAND FINAL – MCCARTHY CUP (3 Sep 89)

Tipperary	(4–24) 36	Antrim	(3–9) 18

JUDO

WORLD CHAMPIONSHIPS (Belgrade 10–15 Oct 89)

Men

Bantam	1	A. Totikashvili	URS
	2	K. Todanori	JAP
	3=	D. Battulga	MNG
	3=	H. Yoon	SKO
Feather	1	D. Becanovic	YUG
	2	U. Quellmatz	GDR
	3=	B. Carabetta	FRA
	3=	S. Kosmynin	URS
Light	1	T. Koga	JAP
	2	M. Swain	USA
	3=	L. Chang	NKO
	3=	G. Tenadze	URS
Light-Middle	1	B. Kim	SKO
	2	T. Mochida	JAP
	3=	W. Legien	POL
	3=	B. Varayev	URS
Middle	1	F. Canu	FRA
	2	B. Spykers	HOL
	3=	S. Freudenberg	FRG
	3=	A. Lobenstein	GDR
Light-Heavy	1	K. Kurtanidze	URS
	2	O. Baljuynnyan	MNG
	3=	M. Meiling	FRG
	3=	R. van der Walle	BEL
Heavy	1	N. Ogawa	JAP
	2	F. Moreno	CUB
	3=	R. Kubacki	POL
	3=	G. Veritchev	URS

Women

Bantam	1	K. Briggs	GBR
	2	F. Esaki	JAP
	3=	J. Gal	HOL
	3=	C. Nowak	FRA
Feather	1	S. Rendle	GBR
	2	A. Giungi	ITA
	3=	Cho Min-sun	SKO
	3=	C. Perez	CUB
Light	1	C. Arnaud	FRA
	2	A. Hughes	GBR
	3=	M. Blasco	SPA
	3=	Y. Sung	SKO
Light-Middle	1	C. Fleury	FRA
	2	E. Petrova	URS
	3=	T. Kobayashi	JAP
	3=	G. Ritschel	FRA
Middle	1	E. Pierantozzi	ITA
	2	H. Sasaki	JAP
	3=	C. Lecat	FRA
	3=	J. Reve	CUB
Light-Heavy	1	I. Berghmans	BEL
	2	Y. Tanabe	JAP
	3=	A. Batailler	FRA
	3=	W. Wu	CHN
Heavy	1	F. Gao	CHN
	2	R. Sigmund	FRG
	3=	N. Lupino	FRA
	3=	B. Maksymov	POL
Open	1	E. Rodriguez	CUB
	2	S. Lee	GBR
	3=	Y. Tanabe	JAP
	3=	Y. Zhang	CHN

EUROPEAN TEAM CHAMPIONSHIPS (Vienna 28–29 Oct 89)

Men

1 USSR
2 France
3= Great Britain
3= West Germany

Women

France	bt	Great Britain	4–1

EUROPEAN CHAMPIONSHIPS (Frankfurt 12 May 90)

Men

Bantam	1	P. Pradayrol	FRA
	2	N. Donohue	GBR
	3=	P. Botev	BUL
	3=	A. Totikashvili	URS
Feather	1	B. Carabetta	FRA
	2	U. Quellmatz	GDR
	3=	P. Laats	BEL
	3=	S. Patrascu	ROM
Light	1	G. Schumacher	FRG
	2	J. Korhonen	FIN
	3=	W. Blach	POL
	3=	B. Hajtos	HUN

Light-Middle	1	B. Varayev	URS
	2	Z. Zsoldos	HUN
	3=	B. Amoussou-Guenou	FRA
	3=	I. Rusu	ROM
Middle	1	W. Legien	POL
	2	A. Lobenstein	GDR
	3=	F. Canu	FRA
	3=	D. White	GBR
Light-Heavy	1	S. Traineau	FRA
	2	M. Meiling	FRG
	3=	F. Borkowski	GDR
	3=	K. Kurtanidze	URS
Heavy	1	S. Kossorotov	URS
	2	H. van Barneveld	BEL
	3=	M. Grozea	ROM
	3=	F. Möller	GDR
Open	1	L. Tolnai	HUN
	2	H. van Barneveld	BEL
	3=	D. Khakhalishvili	URS
	3=	A. von der Gröben	FRG
Women			
Bantam	1	C. Nowak	FRA
	2	K. Briggs	GBR
	3=	J. Perlberg	GDR
	3=	G. Tortora	ITA
Feather	1	S. Rendle	GBR
	2	K. Parrag	HUN
	3=	F. Boffin	FRA
	3=	C. Deliege	BEL
Light	1	C. Arnaud	FRA
	2	G. Hausch	FRG
	3=	N. Fairbrother	GBR
	3=	N. Flagothier	BEL
Light-Middle	1	B. Gomez	SPA
	2	D. Bell	GBR
	3=	G. Ritschel	FRG
	3=	S. Singer	GDR
Middle	1	A. Schreiber	FRG
	2	K. Howey	GBR
	3=	M. Alcibar	SPA
	3=	C. Lecat	FRA
Light-Heavy	1	K. Kruger	FRA
	2	E. Besova	URS
	3=	L. Meignan	FRA
	3=	U. Werbrouck	BEL
Heavy	1	C. Cicot	FRA
	2	R. Sigmund	FRG
	3=	M-T. Motta	ITA
	3=	M. van der Lee	HOL
Open	1	S. Lee	GBR
	2	N. Lupino	FRA
	3=	M. Aarts	HOL
	3=	T. Tomova	BUL

BRITISH OPEN CHAMPIONSHIPS (Crystal Palace 7 Apr 90)

Men			
Bantam	1	T. Dibert	FRA
Feather	1	M. Preston	ENG
Light	1	C. M'Bani	FRA
Light-Middle	1	R. Birch	ENG
Middle	1	M. Liebnitz	FRA
Light-Heavy	1	R. Stevens	ENG
Heavy	1	D. Douillet	FRA
Women			
Bantam	1	K. Briggs	ENG
Feather	1	S. Rendle	GBR
Light	1	N. Fairbrother	ENG
Light-Middle	1	D. Bell	GBR
Middle	1	K. Howey	GBR
Light-Heavy	1	E. Essombe	FRA
Heavy	1	S. Lee	ENG

MODERN PENTATHLON

WORLD CHAMPIONSHIPS (3 Sep 89)

Men's Individual			
1	L. Fabian	HUN	5654 pts
Men's Team			
1	Hungary		
Women's Individual			
1	L. Norwood	USA	5315 pts
Women's Team			
1	Poland		

BRITISH CHAMPIONSHIP (16 Jul 89)

Men's Individual			
1	G. Brookhouse	Spartan MPC	5813 pts
2	D. Mahony	Army	5707
3	R. Phelps	Spartan MPC	5675
Men's Team			
1	Spartan MPC		
Women's Individual			
1	T. Purton		5321 pts
Women's Team			
1	Pegasus MPC		

BRITISH OPEN CHAMPIONSHIP (10 Jun 90)

Men			
1	R. Phelps	Spartan MPC	5524 pts
2	G. Brookhouse	Spartan MPC	5435
3	D. Mahony	Army	5410

MOTOR SPORTS

Moto-Cross

1989 World 500 cc Champion

D. Thorpe GBR Honda

1989 British 500 cc Champion

K. Nicholl Kawasaki

British 500 cc Championship (24 Jul 809)

D. Thorpe GBR Honda

Motor Cycling

1989 WORLD CHAMPIONSHIPS – Final Standing

500 cc	1	E. Lawson	USA	Honda	228 pts
	2	W. Rainey	USA	Yamaha	210.5
	3	C.Sarron	FRA	Yamaha	165.5
250 cc	1	S. Pons	SPA	Honda	262 pts
	2	R. Roth	FRG	Honda	190
	3	J. Cornu	FRA	Honda	187
125 cc	1	A. Criville	SPA	JJ Cobas	166 pts
	2	H. Spaan	HOL	Honda	152
	3	E. Gianola	ITA	Honda	138
80 cc	1	M. Herreras	SPA	Derbi	90 pts
	2	S. Doerflinger	SWI	Krauser	88
	3	P. Getti	FRG	Krauser	75
Sidecar	1	S. Webster/A. Hewitt	GBR	LCR Krauser	145 pts
	2	E. Streuer/G. de Haas	HOL	LCR Krauser	134
	3	R. Biland/K. Waltisperg	SWI	LCR Krauser	127

1990 WORLD CHAMPIONSHIPS

JAPANESE GP (Suzuka 25 Mar 90)

500 cc	1	W. Rainey	USA	Yamaha	48:52.475

	2 W. Gardner	AUS	Honda	48:55.712
	3 K. Schwantz	USA	Suzuki	49:08.031
250 cc	1 L. Cadalora	ITA	Yamaha	45:55.994
	2 C. Cardus	SPA	Honda	45:59.694
	3 W. Zeelenberg	HOL	Honda	45:59.880
125 cc	1 H. Spaan	HOL	Honda	39:08.572
	2 S. Prein	FRG	Honda	39:12.884
	3 K. Takada	JAP	Honda	39:13.698

US GP (Laguna Seca 8 Apr 90)

500 cc	1 W. Rainey	USA	Yamaha	50:55.379
	2 M. Doohan	AUS	Honda	51:25.765
	3 P.Chili	ITA	Honda	51:54.612
250 cc	1 J. Kocinski	USA	Yamaha	44:59.738
	2 L. Cadalora	ITA	Yamaha	45:10.407
	3 W. Zeelenberg	HOL	Honda	45:17.742
Sidecar	1 A. Michel (FRA)/S. Birchall(GBR)		LCR Krauser	47:17.066
	2 S. Webster/G. Simons	GBR	LCR Krauser	47:37.682
	3 S. Abbott/S. Smith	GBR	Yamaha	47:48.166

SPANISH GP (Jerez 6 May 90)

500 cc	1 W. Gardner	AUS	Honda	52:58.021
	2 W. Rainey	USA	Yamaha	53:05.328
	3 K. Schwantz	USA	Suzuki	53:20.109
250 cc	1 J. Kocinski	USA	Yamaha	44:27.789
	2 L. Cadalora	ITA	Yamaha	44:27.998
	3 H. Bradl	FRG	Honda	44:34.945
125 cc	1 J. Martinez	SPA	JJ Cobas	43:06.406
	2 S. Prein	FRG	Honda	43:06.416
	3 F. Gresini	ITA	Honda	43:07.991
Sidecar	1 S. Webster/G. Simons	GBR	LCR Krauser	42:11.072
	2 A. Michel (FRA)/S. Birchall(GBR)		LCR Krauser	42:15.378
	3 R. Biland/K. Waltisperg	SWI	LCR Krauser	42:25.575

ITALIAN GP (Misano 20 May 90)

500 cc	1 W. Rainey	USA	Yamaha	46:21.150
	2 K. Schwantz	USA	Suzuki	46:23.271
	3 M. Doohan	AUS	Honda	46:29.020
250 cc	1 J. Kocinski	USA	Yamaha	39:33.533
	2 H. Bradl	FRG	Honda	39:47.943
	3 W. Zeelenberg	HOL	Honda	39:56.158
125 cc	1 J. Martinez	SPA	JJ Cobas	37:05.542
	2 D. Raudies	FRG	Honda	37:08.174
	3 L. Capirossi	ITA	Honda	37:10.071
Sidecar	1 R. Biland/K. Waltisperg	SWI	LCR Krauser	35:27.847
	2 S. Webster/G. Simons	GBR	LCR Krauser	35:33.299
	3 E. Streuer/G. de Haas	HOL	LCR Krauser	35:37.688

WEST GERMAN GP (Nurburgring 27 May 90)

500 cc	1 K. Schwantz	USA	Suzuki	50:18.517
	2 W. Rainey	USA	Yamaha	50:30.385
	3 N. Mackenzie	GBR	Suzuki	50:45.723
250 cc	1 W. Zeelenberg	HOL	Honda	46:53.199
	2 C. Cardus	SPA	Honda	46:53.265
	3 J. Kocinski	USA	Yamaha	46:53.305
125 cc	1 D. Rombini	ITA	Honda	43:11.803
	2 D. Raudies	FRG	Honda	43:15.077
	3 L. Capirossi	ITA	AGV Pileri	43:21.877
Sidecar	1 S. Webster/G. Simons	GBR	LCR Krauser	41:11.809
	2 P. Gudel/C. Gudel	SWI	Yamaha	41:28.612
	3 S. Abbott/S. Smith	GBR	Yamaha	41:33.403

AUSTRIAN GP (Salzburgring 10 Jun 90)

500 cc	1 K. Schwantz	USA	Suzuki	38:21.304
	2 W. Rainey	USA	Yamaha	36:21.865
	3 M. Doohan	AUS	Honda	36:46.608
250 cc	1 L. Cadalora	ITA	Yamaha	34:06.908
	2 M. Wimmer	FRG	Aprilia	34:07.397
	3 J. Kocinski	USA	Yamaha	34:07.607
125 cc	1 J. Martinez	SPA	JJ Cobas	36:05.777
	2 L. Capirossi	ITA	AGV Pileri	36:06.024
	3 S. Prein	FRG	Honda	36:11.110
Sidecar	1 E. Streuer/G. de Haas	HOL	LCR Krauser	36:09.948
	2 S. Webster/G. Simons	GBR	LCR Krauser	36:26.900
	3 A. Michel (FRA)/ S. Birchall (GBR)		LCR Krauser	36:51.648

YUGOSLAV GP (Rijeka 17 Jun 90)

500 cc	1 W. Rainey	USA	Yamaha	48:10.806
	2 K. Schwantz	USA	Suzuki	48:20.880
	3 N. Mackenzie	GBR	Suzuki	48:43.491
250 cc	1 C. Cardus	SPA	Honda	35:46.457
	2 J. Kocinski	USA	Yamaha	35:46.518
	3 M. Wimmer	FRG	Aprilia	35:46.688
125 cc	1 S. Prein	FRG	Honda	31:36.931
	2 L. Capirossi	ITA	AGV Pileri	31:36.961
	3 B. Casanova	ITA	Semprucci	31:37.049
Sidecar	1 A. Michel (FRA)/ S. Birchall (GER)		LCR Krauser	38:08.059
	2 E. Streuer/G. de Haas	HOL	LCR Krauser	38:08.116
	3 S. Webster/G. Simons	GBR	LCR Krauser	38:11.946

DUTCH GP (Assen 30 Jun 90)

500 cc	1 K. Schwantz	USA	Suzuki	45:39.074
	2 W. Rainey	USA	Yamaha	45:39.710
	3 E. Lawson	USA	Yamaha	46:04.524
250 cc	1 J. Kocinski	USA	Yamaha	43:35.983
	2 C. Cardus	SPA	Honda	43:36.959
	3 W. Zeelenberg	HOL	Honda	43:41.596
125 cc	1 D. Rombini	ITA	Honda	42:25.595
	2 B. Casanova	ITA	Semprucci	42:36.728
	3 A. Stadler	FRG	JJ Cobas	42:36.986
Sidecar	1 A. Michel (FRA)/ S. Birchall (GBR)		LCR Krauser	40:23.138
	2 R. Biland/K. Waltisperg	SWI	LCR Krauser	40:23.671
	3 E. Streuer/G. de Haas	HOL	LCR Krauser	40:29.165

ISLE OF MAN TOURIST TROPHY RACES (lap distance: 37.73 miles)

500 cc Senior TT (6 lapa: 226.38 miles)

1 C. Fogarty	750 Honda	2:02:25.2	110.95 mph
2 T. Nation	588 Norton	2:03:44.0	
3 D. Leach	750 Yahaha	2:03:54.8	

250 cc Junior TT (4 laps: 150.92 miles)

1 I. Lougher	250 Yamaha	1:18:37.6	115.16 mph
2 S. Hislop	250 Honda	1:18:39.4	
3 E. Laycock	250 Yamaha	1:20:24.0	

125 c Ultra Lightweight TT (3 laps: 113.19 miles)

1 R. Dunlop	125 Honda	1:05:40.2	103.41 mph
2 I. Newton	125 Honda	1:05:59.2	
3 M. Topping	125 Honda	1:07:30.2	

Sidecar TT – Race A (3 laps: 113.19 miles)

1 D. Saville/N. Roche	350 Yamaha	1:07:25.6	100.72 mph
2 M. Boddice/ D. Wells	600 Honda	1:09.07.4	
3 N. Smith/S. Mace	350 Yamaha	1:09:19.4	

Sidecar TT – Race B (rain reduced from 3 to 2 laps: 75.46 miles)

1 D. Saville/N. Roche	350 Yamaha	45:11.8	100.17 mph
2 G. Bell/J. Cochrane	350 Yamaha	47:29.6	
3 P. Krukowski/ C. McGahan	350 Yamaha	48:01.6	

FIM Formula One Coupe TT (6 laps: 226.38 miles)

1 C. Fogarty	750 Honda	1:54:45.6	118.35 mph
2 N. Jefferies	750 Yamaha	1:55:36.8	
3 R. Dunlop	588 Norton	1:55:58.2	

Supersport 400 TT (3 laps: 113.19 miles)

1 D. Leach	400 FZR Yamaha	1:03:02.2	107.73 mph
2 C. Fogarty	400 VFR Honda	1:03:10.4	
3 S. Ward	400 ZZR Kawasaki	1:03:14.2	

Supersport 600 TT (4 laps: 150.92 miles)

1 B. Reid	600 FZR Yamaha	1:20:51.6	111.98 mph
2 J. Rea	600 CBR Honda	1:21:57.6	
3 S. Cull	600 FZR Yamaha	1:22:05.4	

Motor Racing

1989 DRIVERS' CHAMPIONSHIP – FINAL TABLE (16 Grand Prix – best 11 points scores to count)

	BRA	SNM	MON	MEX	USA	CAN	FRA	GBR	FRG	HUN	BEL	ITA	POR	SPA	JAP	AUS	Best 11 Total
1 A. Prost (FRA)	6	6	6	2	9		9	9	6	3	6	9	6	4			76
2 A. Senna (BRA)		9	9	9					9	6	9			9			60
3 R. Patrese (ITA)				6	6	6	4		3			3		2	6	4	40
4 N. Mansell (GBR)	9						6	6	4	9	4						38
5 T. Boutsen (BEL)		3			1	9				4	3	4			4	9	37
6 A. Nannini (ITA)	1	4		3				4			2		3		9	6	32
7 G. Berger (AUT)												6	9	6			21
8 N. Piquet (BRA)						3		3	2	1					3		12
9 J. Alesi (FRA)							3					2		3			8
10 D. Warwick (GBR)	2	2							1		1				1		7
11=S. Johansson (SWE)							2						4				6
11=M. Alboreto (ITA)			2	4													6
11=E. Cheever (USA)					4					2							6
14=J. Herbert (GBR	3				2												5
14=P. Martini (ITA)								2					2			1	5
16=A. de Cesaris (ITA)						4											4
16=M. Gugelmin (BRA)	4																4
16=S. Modena (ITA)			4														4
16=A. Caffi (ITA)			3			1											4
16=M. Brundle (GBR)			1									1			2		4
21=C. Danner (FRG)					3												3
21=S. Nakajima (JAP)																3	3
23=R. Arnoux (FRA)						2											2
23=E. Pirro (ITA)																2	2
23=J. Palmer (GBR)		1											1				2
26=G. Tarquini (ITA)				1													1
26=O. Grouillard (FRA)							1										1
26=L. Perez Sala (SPA)								1									1
26=P. Alliot (FRA)														1			1

1989 WORLD FORMULA ONE GRAND PRIX CHAMPIONSHIP

FRENCH GP (Le Castellet 9 Jul 89)

1	A. Prost	FRA	MarlboroMcLaren-Honda
2	N. Mansell	GBR	Farrari
3	R. Patrese	ITA	Canon Williams-Renault

SHELL OILS BRITISH GP (Silverstone 16 Jul 89)

1	A. Prost	FRA	Marloboro McLaren-Honda
2	N. Mansell	GBR	Ferrari
3	A. Nannini	ITA	Benetton-Ford

WEST GERMAN GP (Hockenheim 30 Jul 89)

1	A. Senna	BRA	Marlboro McLaren-Honda
2	A. Prost	FRA	Marlboro McLaren-Honda
3	N. Mansell	GBR	Ferrari

HUNGARIAN GP (Hungaroring, Budapest 13 Aug 89)

1	N. Mansell	GBR	Ferrari
2	A. Senna	BRA	Marlboro McLaren-Honda
3	T. Boutsen	BEL	Canon Williams-Renault

BELGIAN GP (Spa-Francorchamps 27 Aug 89)

1	A. Senna	BRA	Marlboro McLaren-Honda
2	A. Prost	FRA	Marlboro McLaren-Honda
3	N. Mansell	GBR	Ferrari

ITALIAN GP (Monza 10 Sep 89)

1	A. Prost	FRA	Marlboro McLaren-Honda
2	G. Berger	AUT	Ferrari
3	T. Boutsen	BEL	Canon Williams-Renault

PORTUGUESE GP (Estoril 24 Sep 89)

1	G. Berger	AUT	Ferrari
2	A. Prost	FRA	Marlboro McLaren-Honda
3	S. Johansson	SWE	Onyx-Ford

SPANISH GP (Jerez de la Frontera 1 Oct 89)

1	A. Senna	BRA	Marlboro McLaren-Honda
2	G. Berger	AUT	Ferrari
3	A. Prost	FRA	Marlboro McLaren-Honda

JAPANESE GP (Suzuka 22 Oct 89)

1	A. Nannini	ITA	Benetton-Ford
2	R. Patrese	ITA	Canon Williams-Renault
3	T. Boutsen	BEL	Canon Williams-Renault

AUSTRALIAN GP (Adelaide 5 Nov 89)

1	T. Boutsen	BEL	Canon Williams-Renault
2	A. Nannini	ITA	Benetton-Ford
3	R. Patrese	ITA	Canon Williams-Renault

1989 CONSTRUCTORS' CHAMPIONSHIP – FINAL TABLE

	Constructor	Pts	Drivers and Pts
1	McLaren	141	A. Prost (FRA) 81/A. Senna (BRA) 60
2	Williams	77	R. Patrese (ITA) 40/T. Boutsen (BEL)37
3	Ferrari	59	N. Mansell (GBR) 38/G. Berger (AUT) 21
4	Benetton	39	A. Nannini (ITA) 32/J. Herbert (GBR) 5/E. Pirro (ITA) 2
5	Tyrrell	16	J. Alesi (FRA) 8/M. Alboreto (ITA) 6/ J. Palmer (GBR) 2/J. Herbert (GBR) 0
6	Lotus	15	N. Piquet (BRA) 12/S. Nakajima (JAP) 3
7	Arrows	13	D. Warwick (GBR) 7/E. Cheever (USA) 6
8=	Dallara	8	A. Caffi (ITA) 4/A. de Cesaris (ITA) 4
8=	Brabham	8	S. Modena (ITA) 4/M. Brundle (GBR) 4
10=	Onyx	6	S. Johansson (SWE) 6/B. Gachot (BEL) 0
10=	Minardi	6	P. Martini (ITA) 5/L. Perez Sala (SPA) 1
12	March	4	M. Gugelmin (BRA) 4/I. Capelli (ITA) 0
13=	Rial	3	C. Danner (FRG) 3/V. Weidler (FRG) O
13=	Ligier	3	R. Arnoux (FRA) 2/O. Grouillard (FRA) 1
15=	AGS	1	G. Tarquini (ITA) 1/P. Steiff (FRA) 0/ J. Winkehock (FRG) 0
15=	Lola	1	P. Alliott (FRA) 1/Y. Dalmas (FRA) 0

1990 WORLD FORMULA ONE GRAND PRIX CHAMPIONSHIP

US GP (Phoenix, Ariz. 11 Mar 90)

1	A. Senna	BRA	Marlboro McLaren-Honda
2	J. Alesi	FRA	Tyrrell-Ford
3	T. Boutsen	BEL	Canon Williams-Renault

BRAZILIAN GP (Interlagos, Sao Paulo 25 Mar 90)

1	A. Prost	FRA	Ferrari
2	G. Berger	AUT	Marlboro McLaren-Honda
3	A. Senna	BRA	Marlboro McLaren-Honda

SAN MARINO GP (Imola 13 May 90)

1	R. Patrese	ITA	Canon Williams-Renault
2	G. Berger	AUT	Marlboro McLaren-Honda
3	A. Nannini	ITA	Benetton-Ford

MONACO GP (Monte Carlo 27 May 90)

1	A. Senna	BRA	Marlboro McLaren-Honda
2	J. Alesi	FRA	Tyrrell-Ford
3	G. Berger	AUT	Marlboro McLaren-Honda

CANADIAN GP (Montreal 10 Jun 90)

1	A. Senna	BRA	Marlboro McLaren-Honda
2	N. Piquet	BRA	Benetton-Ford
3	N. Mansell	GBR	Ferrari

MEXICAN GP (Autodromo Hermanos Rodriguez 24 Jun 90)

1	A. Prost	FRA	Ferrari
2	N. Mansell	GBR	Ferrari
3	G. Berger	AUT	Marlboro McLaren-Honda

FRENCH GP (Le Castellet 8 Jul 90)

1	A. Prost	FRA	Ferrari
2	I. Capelli	ITA	Leyton House-Judd
3	A. Senna	BRA	Marlboro McLaren-Honda

OTHER EVENTS

1989 WORLD SPORTS PROTOTYPE CHAMPIONSHIP

Drivers'

1	J-L. Schlesser	FRA	Mercedes	115 pts
2	J. Mass	FRG	Mercedes	107
3	M. Baldi	ITA	Mercedes	102
4	K. Acheson	GBR	Mercedes	97
5	F. Jelinski	FRG	Porsche	84
6	R. Wollek	FRA	Porsche	72

Constructors'

1	Sauber Mercedes	155 pts
2	Joest Racing	84
3	Brun Motorsport	66

DAYTONA 24-HOUR RACE (4 Feb 90)

1 D. Jones (USA)/J. Lammers (HOL)/A. Wallace (GBR)
Jaguar XJR–12 761 laps/2709 M (rec)

1 M. Brundle (GBR)/P. Cobb (USA)/J. Nielsen (DEN)
Jaguar XJR–12 757 laps

1 D. Dobson (USA)/S. van der Merwe (SAF)/B. Wollek (FRA)
Porsche 962 755 laps

INDIANAPOLIS 500 (27 May 90)

1	A. Luyendyk	HOL	Lola-Chevrolet	185.984 mph
2	R. Rahal	USA	Lola-Chevrolet	
3	E. Fittipaldi	BRA	Penske-Chevrolet	

LE MANS 24-HOUR RACE (16–17 Jun 90)

1 M. Brundle (GBR)/P. Cobb (USA)/J. Nielsen (DEN)
Silk Cut Jaguar XJR12 358 laps/3034 M

2 F. Konrad (AUT)/J. Lammers (HOL)/A. Wallace (GBR)
Silk Cut Jaguar XJR12 354 laps

3 T. Needell (GBR)/A. Reid (GBR)/D. Sears (GBR)
Alpha Racing Team Porsche 962C 351 laps

Motor Rallying

1989 WORLD RALLY CHAMPIONSHIP (12 Oct 89)

Drivers'

1	M. Biasion	ITA	106 pts
2	A. Fiorio	ITA	65 pts
3=	D. Auriol	FRA	50 pts
4=	M. Eriksson	SWE	50 pts

Constructors'

1	Lancia	162 pts
2	Toyota	84 pts
3	Mazda	61 pts

LOMBARD RAC RALLY (23 Nov 89)

1 P. Airikkala	FIN		
R. McNamee	IRE	Mitsubishi Galant VR4	6:19:22
2 C. Sainz	SPA		
L. Moya	SPA	Toyotta Celica GR4	6:20:50
3 J. Kankkunen	FIN		
J. Piironen	FIN	Toyota Celica GR4	6:23:11

PARIS-DAKER RALLY (16 Jan 90)

1 A. Vatanen	FIN	Peugeot	39:08:59
2 B. Waldegard	SWE	Peugeot	40:18:50
3 A. Ambrosino	FRA	Peugeot	43:05:45

MONTE CARLO RALLY (25 Jan 90)

1 D. Auriol	FRA	Lancia Delta Integrale 16V	5:56:52
2 C. Sainz	SPA	Toyota	5:57:44
3 M. Biasion	ITA	Lancia	6:00:31

RACKETS

INAUGURAL LACOSTE WORLD DOUBLES CHAMPIONSHIP

Ist leg (16 Feb 90)

MD J. Male/ J. Prenn GBR bt S. Hazell/ N. Smith GBR 4 sets to 3
8–15 7–15 14–17 15–8 15–10 15–12 15–3

2nd leg (18 Feb 90)

MD J. Male/ J. Prenn GBR bt S. Hazell/ N. Smith GBR 4 sets to 2
5–15 15–5 11–15 15–11 15–7 15–13
Male and Prenn won the championship by 8 sets to 5

LACOSTE BRITISH OPEN CHAMPIONSHIP (25 Mar 90)

MS N. Smith GBR bt W. Boone GBR 15–5 15–7 15–9 15–11

LACOSTE BRITISH OPEN CHAMPIONSHIP (29 Apr 90)

MD J. Male/ J. Prenn GBR bt S. Hazell/ N. Smith GBR 15–9 15–9 5–15 15–10 15–9

BRITISH PROFESSIONAL CHAMPIONSHIP (11 Feb 90)

MS S. Hazell bt N. Smith 1–15 15–1 15–12 11–15 15–6

LACOSTE BRITISH AMATEUR CHAMPIONSHIP (10 Dec 89)

MS W. Boone bt J. Prenn 15–12 15–4 15–3

BRITISH AMATEUR CHAMPIONSHIP (11 Feb 90)

MD J. Male/J. Prenn bt C. Hue Williams/M. Hue Williams 7–15 15–1 15–6 15–0 15–9

REAL TENNIS

GEORGE WIMPEY BRITISH OPEN CHAMPIONSHIPS (13 Dec 89)

MS L. Deuchar AUS bt C. Ronaldson GBR 6–2 6–1 6–4
WS S. Jones ENG bt A. Warren-Piper GBR 6–4 6–1
MD L. Deuchar/ W. Davies AUS bt J. Howell/ K. Sheldon GBR 6–1 6–4 6–4

BRITISH PROFESSIONAL CHAMPIONSHIP (6 May 90)

MS L. Deuchar AUS bt D. Johnson GBR 6–1 6–0 6–3

BRITISH PROFESSIONAL DOUBLES CHAMPIONSHIPS (7 Jan 90)

MD C. Bray/ P. Brake GBR bt P. Meares (AUS)/ N. Wood (GBR) 6–3 6–3
WD M. Briggs/ A. Warren-Piper GBR bt M. Groszek/ J. Page GBR 6–1 6–4

BRITISH AMATEUR CHAMPIONSHIP (8 Apr 90)

MS J. Male bt J. Snow 6–4 6–4 6–4

LAURENT-PERRIER MASTERS (24 Sep 89)

MS L. Deuchar AUS bt C. Ronaldson GBR 6–3 6–5 6–4
WS P. Fellows GBR bt A. Warren-Piper GBR 6–2 6–3

ROWING

HENLEY ROYAL REGATTA (8 Jul 90)

Grand Challenge Cup	Hansa Dortmund	FRG bt	Leander Club/Univ of London	ENG	2 lengths	6:36
Ladies' Plate	Harvard Univ.	USA bt	Univ. of London	ENG	3 2/3 lengths	6:35
Thames Cup	Notts County	ENG bt	Harvard Univ. A	USA	2 lengths	6:50
Princess Elizebeth Cup	Eton College	ENG bt	Westminster School	ENG	2/3 length	6:58
Henley Prize	Imperial College London	ENG bt	Trinity College Dublin	IRE	1 3/4 lengths	7:00
Stewards' Cup	Star Club/Leander Club A	ENG bt	Star Club/Leander Club B	ENG	4 3/4 lengths	7:16
Prince Philip Cup	Hansa Dortmund	FRG bt	Levski Spartak	BUL	4 lengths	7:27
Queen Mother Cup	Danmarks Rocenter Roklub	DEN bt	ASR Nereus & Skadi	HOL	1/2 length	7:01
Visitors' Cup	Univ. of London A	ENG bt	Goldie	ENG	not rowed out	7:17
Wyfold Cup	London RC A	ENG bt	Notts County	ENG	1 1/3 lengths	7:26
Britannia Cup	Univ. College Galway	IRE bt	Cappoquin	IRE	2 lengths	7:47
Silver Goblets & Nickalls' Cup	K. Sinzinger/H. Bauer	AUT bt	M. Cross/T. Foster	ENG	1 foot	7:39
Double Sculls	A. Rudkin/P. Kittermaster	ENG bt	M. Alloway/C. Williams	ENG	1 3/4 lengths	8:28
Diamond Sculls	E. Verdonk	NZL bt	W. Van Belleghem	BEL	3/4 length	8:21

1990 HENLEY WOMEN'S REGATTA (24 Jun 90)

Eights	Tideway Scullers/Thames/Upper Thames	bt	Thames	4 lengths	4:33
Coxed Fours	Lea	bt	Kingston	4 lengths	5:18
Coxless Fours	Thames/Tideway Scullers A	bt	Thames/Tideway Scullers B	1.5 lengths	4:48
Coxless Pairs	Westminster School/Kingston	bt	Derby	3 lengths	ntt
Quadruple Sculls	Kingston	bt	LEH/Northwich/Queen's/Wallingford	easily	5:02
Double Sculls	Tideway Scullers/Kingston	bt	Hereford	3.5 lengths	5:34
Single Sculls A	F. Freckleton (Westminster School)	bt	J. Lloyd (Globe)	0.5 length	5:51
Single Sculls B	A. Gill (Upper Thames)	bt	R. Hurst (Notts County RA)	easily	5:39

WORLD CHAMPIONSHIPS (Bled, YUG 10 Sept 89)

Men			
Single Sculls	T. Lange	GDR	6:58.14
Double Sculls	Noway		6:23.40
Quadruple Sculls	Holland		6:03.99
Coxless Pairs	East Germany		6:39.95
Coxless Fours	East Germany		6:06.94
Coxed Pairs	Italy		6:54.81
Coxed Fours	Romania		6:14.90
Eights	West Germany		5:43.88
Men's Lightweight			
Single Sculls	F.Goebel	HOL	7:17.07
Double Sculls	Austria		7:03.33
Quadruple Sculls	West Germany		6:04.78
Coxless Fours	West Germany		6:28.70
Eights	Italy		5:47.95
Women			
Single Sculls	E. Lipa	ROM	7:27.96
Double Sculls	East Germany		7:01.71
Quadruple Sculls	East Germany		6:16.62
Coxless Pairs	East Germany		7:26.07
Coxless Fours	East Germany		6:45.81
Eights	Romania		6:07.92
Women's Lightweight			
Single Sculls	K. Karlson	USA	8:01.12
Double Sculls	USA		7:11.04
Coxless Fours	China		7:01.70

NATIONAL CHAMPIONSHIPS (16 July 89)

Men		
Single Sculls	S. Larkin (Notts County RA)	6:11.46
Double Sculls	Barclays Bank/Tideway Scullers	6:41.73
Quadruple Sculls	Notts County RA	6:11.46
Coxless Pairs	Notts County RA	7:01.36
Coxless Fours	Notts County RA	6:21.86
Coxed Pairs	Kingston BC	7:21.91
Coxed Fours	Thames Tradesmen	6:24.15
Eights	Castle Semple/Clydesdale/Stirling/ Glasgow Univ./Loch Lomond	5:59.27
Men's Lightweight		
Single Sculler	I. Hopkins (Thames Tradesmen)	7:09.21
Double Sculls	Leander Club	6:29.54
Quadruple Sculls	Boldie/Leander Club/Rob Roy	6:07.50
Coxless Fours	Notts County RA	6:19.55
Eights	Cambridge Univ.	6:03.58
Women		
Single Sculls	C. Baker (Tideway Scullers)	8:04.34
Double Sculls	G.B. National Squad A	7:16.57
Quadruple Sculls	Kingston BC	7:01.58
Coxless Pairs	Thames	7:40.37
Coxed Fours	G.B. National Squad A	7:04.40
Eights	Thames A	6:30.70
Women's Lightweight		
Single Sculls	E. Holmes (Tideway Scullers)	8:06.31
Double Sculls	G.B National Squad	7:22.02
Coxless Fours	G.B. National Squad	6:52.29

THAMES HEAD OF THE RIVER RACE (Mortlake to Putney 24 Mar 90)

1	GB National Squad	17:04.91
2	Notts County RA II	17:12.28
3	Univ. of London I	17:18.70

UNIVERSITY BOAT RACE (Putney to Mortlake 1 Apr 90)

Oxford 17:15 bt Cambridge 17:22 by 2.25 lengths

SCULLERS' HEAD OF THE RIVER RACE (Mortlake to Putney 7 Apr 90)

1	R. Henderson (Leander Club)	22:51
2	S. Larkin (Notts County RA)	23:05
3	C. Smith (Notts County RA)	23:08

WINGFIELD SCULLS (Putney to Mortlake 25 Apr 90)

R. Henderson 20:33 bt S. Redgrave 20:56

RUGBY LEAGUE

BRITISH COAL TEST SERIES

1st Test				
21 Oct 89	Great Britain	16	New Zealand	24
2nd Test				
28 Oct 89	Great Britain	26	New Zealand	6
3rd Test				
11 Nov 89	Great Britain	10	New Zealand	6

Great Britain won the series 2–1

BRITISH COAL TEST SERIES

Ist Test				
18 Mar 90	France	4	Great Britain	8
2nd Test				
7 Apr 90	Great Britain	18	France	25

GREAT BRITAIN TOUR OF PAPUA NEW GUINEA

1st Test				
27 May 90	Papua New Guinea	20	Great Britain	18
2nd Test				
2 June 90	Papua New Guinea	8	Great Britain	40

BRITISH COAL TEST SERIES

1st Test				
24 June 90	New Zealand	10	Great Britain	11

FOSTER'S WORLD CUP CHALLENGE (Old Trafford 4 Oct 89)

Widnes	GBR	30	Canberra Raiders	AUS 18

STONES BITTER PREMIERSHIP FINALS (13 May 90)

1st Division

Widnes	28	Bradford Northern	6

2nd Division

Oldham	30	Hull Kingston Rovers	29

SILK CUT CHALLENGE CUP FINAL (28 Apr 90)

Wigan	36	Warrington	14

REGAL TROPHY FINAL (13 Jun 90)

Wigan	24	Halifax	12

JOHN SMITHS YORKSHIRE CUP FINAL (4 Nov 89)

Bradford Northern	20	Featherstone Rovers	14

GREENALLS LANCASHIRE CUP FINAL (14 Oct 89)

Warrington	24	Oldham	16

RUGBY UNION

INTERNATIONAL EVENTS
1990 INTERNATIONAL CHAMPIONSHIP

20 Jan	England	23	Ireland	0
20 Jan	Wales	19	France	29
3 Feb	France	7	England	26
3 Feb	Ireland	10	Scotland	13
17 Feb	England	34	Wales	6
17 Feb	Scotland	21	France	0
3 Mar	Wales	9	Scotland	13
3 Mar	France	31	Ireland	12
17 Mar	Scotland	13	England	7
24 Mar	Ireland	14	Wales	8

Final Table	P	W	D	L	F	A	Pts
1 Scotland	4	4	0	0	60	26	8
2 England	4	3	0	1	90	26	6
3 France	4	2	0	2	67	78	4
4 Ireland	4	1	0	3	36	75	2
5 Wales	4	0	0	4	42	90	0

Scotland won the Grand Slam for the third time in history

BRITISH LIONS TOUR OF AUSTRALIA 1989

1st Test

1 Jul	Australia	30	British Isles	12

2nd Test

8 Jul	Australia	12	British Isles	19

3rd Test

15 Jul	Australia	18	British Isles	19

British Isles wond the series 2–1

OTHER HOME UNIONS' INTERNATIONAL MATCHES 1989–90

4 Oct 89	France	27	Home Unions XV	29
28 Oct 89	Scotland	38	Fiji	17
4 Nov 89	England	58	Fiji	23
4 Nov 89	Wales	9	New Zealand	34
18 Nov 89	Ireland	6	New Zealand	23
25 Nov 89	Barbarians	10	New Zealand	21
9 Dec 89	Scotland	32	Romania	0
2 Jun 90	Namibia	9	Wales	18
9 Jun 90	Namibia	30	Wales	34
16 Jun 90	New Zealand	31	Scotland	16
23 Jun 90	New Zealand	21	Scotland	18

NATIONAL EVENTS
COURAGE CLUBS' CHAMPIONSHIP 1989–90

Division I

		P	W	D	L	F	A	Pts
1	Wasps	11	9	0	2	250	106	18
2	Gloucester	11	8	1	2	214	139	17
3	Bath	11	8	0	3	258	104	16
4	Saracens	11	7	1	3	168	167	15
5	Leicester	11	6	0	5	248	184	12
6	Nottingham	11	6	0	5	187	148	12
7	Harlequins	11	6	0	5	218	180	12
8	Orrell	11	5	0	6	221	132	10
9	Bristol	11	4	0	7	136	144	8
10	Roselyn Park	11	4	0	7	164	243	8
11	Moseley	11	2	0	9	138	258	4
12	Bedford	11	0	0	11	70	467	0

Division II

1	Northampton	11	9	1	1	192	135	19
2	Liverpool St. Helens	11	8	2	1	154	106	18
3	Richmond	11	7	1	3	282	135	15
4	Coventry	11	6	1	4	206	185	13
5	London Irish	11	6	0	5	228	247	12
6	Rugby	11	5	0	6	238	172	10
7	Plymouth Albion	11	5	0	6	206	164	10
8	Headingley	11	5	0	6	161	226	10
9	Sale	11	4	0	7	153	182	8
10	Blackheath	11	3	2	6	141	205	8
11	Waterloo	11	3	0	8	147	193	6
12	Gosforth	11	1	1	9	108	266	3

Division III

1	London Scottish	11	11	0	0	258	92	22
2	Wakefield	11	7	1	3	210	126	15
3	West Hartlepool	11	5	2	4	175	110	12
4	Sheffield	11	6	0	5	176	174	12
5	Askeans	11	6	0	5	170	235	12
6	Exeter	11	5	1	5	149	153	11
7	Roundhay	11	5	0	6	156	166	10
8	Fylde	11	5	0	6	169	222	10
9	Vale of Lune	11	4	0	7	154	219	8
10	Nuneaton	11	4	0	7	127	196	8
11	Lydney	11	3	0	8	153	166	6
12	London Welsh	11	3	0	8	141	179	6

Area League North

1	Broughton Park	10	8	0	2	246	111	16
2	Morley	10	8	0	2	171	115	16
3	Stourbridge	10	7	0	3	146	133	14
4	Durham City	10	6	0	4	195	169	12
5	Kendal	10	6	0	4	130	136	12
6	Preston Grasshoppers	10	5	0	5	122	109	10
7	Lichfield	10	5	0	5	110	120	10
8	Northern	10	4	0	6	139	144	8
9	Winnington Park	10	4	0	6	142	152	8
10	Walsall	10	2	0	8	142	183	4
11	Stoke	10	0	0	10	88	259	0

Area League South

1	Metropolitan Police	10	9	0	1	255	74	18
2	Clifton	10	8	1	1	240	122	17
3	Redruth	10	7	0	3	151	84	14
4	Camborne	10	6	1	3	164	113	13
5	Havant	10	5	1	4	132	126	11
6	Sudbury	10	5	0	5	162	138	10
7	Southend	10	4	2	4	124	125	10
8	Basingstoke	10	3	1	6	138	144	7
9	Cheltenham	10	2	0	8	107	201	4
10	Maidstone	10	2	0	8	64	237	4
11	Salisbury	10	1	0	9	74	247	2

TOSHIBA ENGLISH COUNTY CHAMPIONSHIP FINAL (7 Apr 90)

Lancashire	32	Middlesex	9

PILKINGTON CUP FINAL (5 May 90)

Bath	48	Gloucester	6

SCHWEPPES WELSH CUP FINAL (5 May 90)

Neath	16	Bridgend	10

108th VARSITY MATCH (12 Dec 89)

Cambridge	22	Oxford	13

MIDDLESEX SEVENS FINAL (12 May 90)

Harlequins	26	Rosslyn Park	10

SHOOTING

QUEEN'S PRIZE (Bisley 22 Jul 89)

	Name	Association	Points	Shoot-off
1	J. Thompson	Central Bankers	288	25
2	J. Warburton	Huddersfield	288	23 4 5 5 5 4 5
3	L. Peden	OCRA	288	23 4 5 5 5 4 4

SNOOKER

PROFESSIONAL EVENTS

EMBASSY WORLD PROFESSIONAL CHAMPIONSHIP (29 Apr 90)
S. Hendry SCO bt J. White ENG 18–12

EVEREST WORLD MATCHPLAY CHAMPIONSHIP (16 Dec 89)
J. White ENG bt J. Parrott ENG 18–9

BRITISH CAR RENTAL WORLD TEAM CUP (24 Mar 90)
Canada bt Northern Ireland 9–5

STORMSEAL UK CHAMPIONSHIP (3 Dec 89)
S. Hendry SCO bt S. Davis ENG 16–12

PEARL ASSURANCE BRITISH OPEN (3 Mar 90)
R. Chaperon CAN bt A. Higgins NIR 10–8

HONG KONG OPEN (13 Aug 89)
M. Hallett ENG bt D. O'Kane NZL 9–8

ASIAN OPEN (26 Aug 89)
S. Hendry SCO bt J. Wattana THA 9–6

REGAL MASTERS (17 Sep 89)
S. Hendry SCO bt T. Griffiths WAL 10–1

BCE INTERNATIONAL (30 Sep 89)
S. Davis ENG bt S. Hendry SCO 9–4

ROTHMANS GRAND PRIX (22 Oct 89)
S. Davis ENG bt D. Reynolds ENG 10–0

DUBAI DUTY FREE CLASSIC (3 Nov 89)
S. Hendry SCO bt D. Mountjoy WAL 9–2

NORWICH UNION GRAND PRIX (12 Nov 89)
J. Johnson ENG bt S. Hendry SCO 5–3

MERCANTILE CREDIT CLASSIC (13 Jan 90)
S. James ENG bt W. King AUS 10–6

BENSON & HEDGES MASTERS (11 Feb 90)
S. Hendry SCO bt J. Parrott ENG 9–4

WELSH CHAMPIONSHIP (18 Feb 90)
D. Morgan WAL bt D. Mountjoy WAL 9–7

EUROPEAN OPEN (16 Mar 90)
J. Parrott ENG bt S. Hendry SCO 10–6

BENSON & HEDGES IRISH MASTERS (1 Apr 90)
S. Davis ENG bt Dn. Taylor NIR 9–4

CONTINENTAL AIRLINES LONDON MASTERS (15 May 90)
S. Hendry SCO bt J. Parrott ENG 4–2

AMATEUR EVENTS

IBSF WORLD AMATEUR CHAMPIONSHIP (19 Nov 89)
K. Doherty IRE bt J. Birch ENG 11–2

BCE ENGLISH AMATEUR CHAMPIONSHIP (26 May 90)
J. Swail NIR bt A. McManus SCO 13–11

WOMEN'S EVENTS

WORLD CHAMPIONSHIP (20 Oct 90)
A. Fisher ENG bt A–M. Farren ENG 6–5

UK OPEN CHAMPIONSHIP (25 Mar 90)
A. Fisher ENG bt S. Hillyard ENG 5–0

SPEEDWAY

WORLD INDIVIDUAL RIDERS' CHAMPIONSHIP FINAL (2 Sep 89)

1	H. Nielsen	DEN	15 pts	
2	S. Wigg	ENG	12 pts	after ride-off
3	J. Doncaster	ENG	12pts	

WORLD PAIRS CHAMPIONSHIP FINAL (5 Aug 89)

1	Denmark		48 pts
	H. Nielsen	28	
	E. Gundersen	20	
2	Sweden		44 pts
	J. Nilsen	23	
	P. Jonsson	21	
3	England		37 pts
	K. Tatum	21	
	P. Thorp	16	

SUNBRITE WORLD TEAM CHAMPIONSHIP FINAL (17 Sep 89)

1	England		48 pts
	J. Doncaster	13	
	K. Tatum	12	
	P. Thorp	12	
	S. Wigg	11	
2	Denmark		34 pts
	H. Nielsen	11	
	G. Handberg	9	
	J. Jorgensen	7	
	B. Karger	7	
3	Sweden		30 pts
	M. Blixt	10	
	P. Jonsson	8	
	T. Olsson	7	
	E. Stenlund	5	

WORLD LONG TRACK CHAMPIONSHIP (20 Aug 89)

1	S. Wigg	ENG	38 pts
2	A. Dryml	CSR	37 pts
3	M. Maier	FRG	33 pts

SUNBRITE BRITISH LEAGUE – 1989 FINAL STANDINGS

		P	W	D	L	Pts
1	Oxford	32	22	1	9	58
2	Wolverhampton	32	19	2	11	52
3	Cradley Heath	32	19	3	10	51

NATIONAL LEAGUE – 1989 FINAL STANDINGS

		P	W	D	L	Pts
1	Poole	34	26	1	7	53
2	Wimbledon	34	23	2	9	48
3	Berwick	34	23	0	11	46

GOLD CUP FINAL (23 Jun 90)
Oxford 47 Bradford 43
Bradford 63 Oxford 27
Bradford won 106–74 on aggregate

SQUASH

WORLD MEN'S OPEN CHAMPIONSHIP (17 Oct 89)
Jansher Khan PAK bt C. Dittmar AUS 10–15 6–15 15–4 15–11 15–10

WORLD WOMEN'S OPEN CHAMPIONSHIP (12 Mar 89)
M. le Moignan GBR bt S. Devoy NZL 4–9 9–4 10–8 10–8

WORLD MEN'S TEAM CHAMPIONSHIP (17 Oct 89)

1–2	Australia		bt Pakistan		3–0
	C. Robertson	AUS	bt Zarak Jahan Khan	PAK	3–9 7–9 9–2 9–2 9–0
	C. Dittmar	AUS	bt Jahangir Khan	PAK	6–9 9–5 9–3 9–0
	R. Martin	AUS	bt Jansher Khan	PAK	9–10 9–3 9–6 9–1
3–4	England		bt New Zealand		2–1
	S. Cunningham	NZL	bt J. Nicolle	ENG	9–2 9–7 9–4
	D. Harris	ENG	bt R. Norman	NZL	9–2 9–1 9–0
	B. Beeson	ENG	bt R. Watt	NZL	9–3 3–9 9–0 7–9 9–6

HI-TEC EUROPEAN MEN'S CHAMPIONSHIP (1 May 90)
C. Robertson AUS bt C. Dittmar AUS 15–10 10–15 15–6 15–6

EUROPEAN TEAM CHAMPIONSHIPS (5 May 90)
Men England bt West Germany 5–0
Women England bt Holland 3–0

HI-TEC BRITISH OPEN CHAMPIONSHIPS (23 Apr 90)
Men Jahangir Khan PAK bt R. Martin AUS 9–6 10–8 9–1
Women S. Devoy NZL bt S. Horner ENG 9–2 1–9 9–3 9–3

BRITISH CLOSED CHAMPIONSHIPS (12 Dec 90)

Men	D. Harris	bt B. Beeson	1–9 6–9 9–4 9–2 9–3
Women	L. Soutter	bt S. Horner	9–3 9–5 9–3

ECONOCOM BRITISH DOUBLES CHAMPIONSHIP (17 Dec 89)

Men	P. Gregory/ J. Lilley	bt S. Courtney/ J. Leslie	15–9 17–6
Women	D. Vardy/ S. Wright	bt F. Geaves/ R. Macree	16–18 15–10 18–17

HOME INTERNATIONAL CHAMPIONSHIP (7 Jan 90)

Men	1	England
	2	Scotland
	3	Wales
	4	Ireland
Women	1	England
	2	Scotland
	3	Ireland
	4	Wales

ENGLISH INTER-COUNTY CHAMPIONSHIP (28 Jan 90)

Men		Essex bt Surrey 3–2
Women	1	Yorkshire
	2	Essex
	3	Staffordshire

PIMMS PREMIER LEAGUE TROPHY – FINAL TABLE (22 Mar 90)

		P	W	L	F	A	Pts
1	Leekes Welsh Wizards	14	12	2	51	19	75
2	UTC Cannons	14	12	2	49	21	73
3	Village Leisure	14	11	3	49	21	71

SWIMMING

WORLD AND BRITISH RECORDS (in 50 m pools only) as at 8 Jul 90

Men

50 m Freestyle	World	21.81	T. Jager	USA	Nashville	24 Mar 90
	British	23.13	M. Foster	ENG	London CP	1 Aug 87
100 m Freestyle	World	48.42	M. Biondi	USA	Austin	10 Aug 89
	British	50.57	A. Jameson	ENG	Orlando	25 Mar 88
200 m Freestyle	World	1:46.69	G. Lamberti	ITA	Bonn	15 Aug 89
	British	1:50.68r	P. Howe	ENG	Auckland	26 Jan 90
400 m Freestyle	World	3:46.95	U. Dassler	GDR	Seoul	23 Sep 88
	British	3:50.01	K. Boyd	ENG	Seoul	23 Sep 88
800 m Freestyle	World	7:50.64	V. Salnikov	URS	Moscow	4 Jul 86
	British	8:01.87	K. Boyd	ENG	Orlando	26 Mar 88
1500 m Freestyle	World	14:54.76	V. Salnikov	URS	Moscow	22 Feb 83
		14:53.59u	G. Housman	AUS	Adelaide	12 Dec 89
	British	15:17.56	K. Boyd	ENG	Seoul	24 Sep 88
100 m Butterfly	World	52.84	P. Morales	USA	Orlando	23 Jun 86
	British	53.30	A. Jameson	ENG	Seoul	21 Sep 88
200 m Butterfly	World	1:56.24	M. Gross	FRG	Hanover	28 Jun 86
	British	2:00.21	P. Hubble	ENG	Split	11 Sep 81
100 m Backstroke	World	54.51	D. Berkoff	USA	Seoul	24 Sep 88
	British	57.60	M. Harris	ENG	Leeds	13 Apr 90
200 m Backstroke	World	1:58.14	I Polianskiy	URS	Erfurt	3 Mar 85
	British	2:03.20	G. Binfield	ENG	Auckland	27 Jan 90
100 m Breaststroke	World	1:01.49	A. Moorhouse	ENG	Bonn	15 Aug 89
		1:01.49	A. Moorhouse	ENG	Auckland	23 Jan 90
	British	1:01.49	A. Moorhouse	ENG	Bonn	15 Aug 89
		1:01.49	A. Moorhouse	ENG	Auckland	25 Jan 90
200 m Breaststroke	World	2:12.89	M. Barrowman	USA	Tokyo	19 Aug 89
	British	2:12.90	N. Gillingham	ENG	Bonn	18 Aug 89
200 m Individual Medley	World	2:00.11	D. Wharton	USA	Tokyo	19 Aug 89
	British	2:03.20	N. Cochran	ENG	Orlando	25 Mar 88
400 m Individual Medley	World	4:14.75	T. Darnyi	HUN	Seoul	21 Sep 88
	British	4:24.20	J. Davey	ENG	London CP	31 Jul 87
4 x 100 m Freestyle Relay	World	3:16.53	Olympic Team C. Jacobs/T. Dalbey/ T. Jager/M. Biondi	USA	Seoul	23 Sep 88
	British	3:21.71	Olympic Team A. Jameson/M. Foster/ M. Fibbens/R. Lee	GBR	Seoul	23 Sep 88
4 x 200 m Freestyle Relay	World	7:12.51	Olympic Team T. Dalbey/M. Cetlinski/ D. Gjertsen/M. Biondi	USA	Seoul	21 Sep 88
	British	7:24.78	Olympic Team N. Cochran/P. Easter/ P. Howe/A. Astbury	GBR	Los Angeles	30 Jul 84

4 x 100 m Medley Relay	World	3:36.93	Olympic Team D. Berkoff/R. Schroeder/ M. Biondi/C. Jacobs	USA	Seoul	25 Sep 88
	British	3:42.01	European Champ Team N. Cochran/A. Moorhouse/ A. Jameson/R. Lee	GBR	Strasbourg	23 Aug 87

Women

50 m Freestyle	World	24.98	Yang Wenyi	CHN	Guangzhou	10 Apr 88
	British	26.01	C. Woodcock	ENG	Bonn	20 Aug 89
100 m Freestyle	World	54.73r	K. Otto	GDR	Madrid	19 Aug 86
	British	56.60	J. Croft	ENG	Amersfoort	31 Jan 82
200 m Freestyle	World	1:57.55	H. Friedrich	GDR	E. Berlin	18 Jun 86
	British	1:59.74	J. Croft	ENG	Brisbane	4 Oct 82
400 m Freestyle	World	4: 03.85	J. Evans	USA	Seoul	22 Sep 88
	British	4:07.68	S. Hardcastle	ENG	Edinburgh	27 Jul 86
800 m Freestyle	World	8:16.22	J. Evans	USA	Tokyo	19 Aug 89
	British	8:24.77	S. Hardcastle	ENG	Edinburgh	29 Jul 86
1500 m Freestyle	World	15:52.10	J. Evans	USA	Orlando	26 Mar 88
	British	16:43.95	S. Hardcastle	ENG	Montreal	18 Apr 85
100 m Butterfly	World	57.93	M.T. Meagher	USA	Milwaukee	16 Aug 81
	British	1:01.33	M. Scarborough	ENG	Auckland	28 Jan 90
200 m Butterfly	World	2:05.96	M.T. Meagher	USA	Milwaukee	13 Aug 81
	British	2:11.97	S. Purvis	ENG	Los Angeles	4 Aug 84
100 m Backstroke	World	1:00.59	I. Kleber	GDR	Moscow	24 Aug 84
	British	1:03.61	B. Rose	ENG	Los Angeles	31 Jul 84
200 m Backstroke	World	2:08.60	B. Mitchell	USA	Orlando	27 Jun 86
	British	2:14.74	J. Deakin	ENG	Auckland	30 Jan 90
100m Breaststroke	World	1:07.91	S. Hörner	GDR	Strasbourg	21 Aug 87
	British	1:10.39	S. Brownsdon	ENG	Strasbourg	21 Aug 87
200 m Breaststroke	World	2:26.71	S. Hörner	GDR	Seoul	21 Sep 88
	British	2:31.57	J. Hill	SCO	Strasbourg	19 Aug 87
200 m Individual Medley	World	2:11.73	U. Geweniger	GDR	E.Berlin	4 Jul 81
	British	2:17.21	J. Hill	SCO	Edinburgh	21 Jul 86
400 m Individual Medley	World	4:36.10	P. Schneider	GDR	Guayaquil	1 Aug 82
	British	4:46.83	S. Davies	ENG	Moscow	26 Jul 80
4 x 100 m Freestyle Relay	World	3:40.57	World Champ. Team K. Otto/M. Stellmach/ S. Schulze/H. Friedrich	GDR	Madrid	19 Aug 86
	British	3:48.87	European Champ. Team K. Pickering/S. Davies/ C. Woodcock/J. Coull	GBR	Bonn	17 Aug 89
4 x 200 m Freestyle Relay	World	7:55.47	European Champ. Team M. Stellmach/A. Strauss/ A. Möhring/H. Friedrich	GDR	Strasbourg	18 Aug 87
	British	8:13.70	Commonwealth Games Team A. Cripps/S. Hardcastle/ K. Mellor/Z. Long	ENG	Edinburgh	25 Jul 86
4 x 100 m Medley Relay	World	4:03.69	European Champ. Team I. Kleber/S. Gerasch/ I. Giessler/B. Meineke	GDR	Moscow	24 Aug 84
	British	4:11.88	Commonwealth Games Team J. Deakins/S. Brownsdon/ M. Scarborough/K. Pickering	ENG	Auckland	29 Jan 90

EUROPEAN CHAMPIONSHIPS (14–20 Aug 89)

Men

50 m Freestyle

1	V. Tkachenko	URS	22.64
2	Y. Kotriaga	URS	22.67
3	N. Rudolph	GDR	22.76

100 m Freestyle

1	G. Lamberti	ITA	49.24
2	Y. Bashkatov	URS	50.13
3	R. Mazhoulis	URS	50.15

200 m Freestyle

1	G. Lamberti	ITA	1:46.69
2	A. Wojdat	POL	1:47.96
3	A. Holmertz	SWE	1:48.06

400 m Freestyle

1	A. Wojdat	POL	3:47.78
2	S. Pfeiffer	FRG	3:48.68
3	M. Podkoscielny	POL	3:49.29

1500 m Freestyle

1	J. Hoffman	GDR	15:01.52
2	S. Pfeiffer	FRG	15:01.93
3	M. Podkoscielny	POL	15:19.29

100 m Butterfly

1	R. Szukala	POL	54.47
2	B. Gutzeit	FRA	54.50
3	M. Herrmann	FRG	54.54

200 m Butterfly

1	T. Darnyi	HUN	1:58.87
2	R. Szukala	POL	2:00.62
3	M. Kozelj	YUG	2:00.73

100 m Backstroke

1	M. Lopez-Zubero	SPA	56.44
2	S. Zabolotnov	URS	56.45
3	D. Richter	GDR	56.52

200 m Backstroke

1	S. Battistelli	ITA	1:59.96
2	V. Selkov	URS	2:00.02
3	T. Weber	GDR	2:00.54

100 m Breaststroke

1	A. Moorhouse	GBR	1:01.71
2	D. Volkov	URS	1:01.94
3	N. Gillingham	GBR	1:02.12

200 m Breaststroke

1	N. Gillingham	GBR	2:12.90
2	G. O'Toole	IRE	2:15.73
3	J. Szabo	HUN	2:16.05

200 m Individual Medley

1	T. Darnyi	HUN	2:01.03
2	R. Hannemann	GDR	2:03.07
3	J. Hladky	FRG	2:03.21

400 m Individual Medley

1	T. Darnyi	HUN	4:15.25
2	P. Kuhl	GDR	4:16.08
3	S. Battistelli	ITA	4:19.13

4 x 100 m Freestyle Relay

1	West Germany	3:19.68
2	France	3:19.73
3	Sweden	3:19.76

4 x 200 m Freestyle Relay

1	Italy	7:15.39
2	West Germany	7:17.38
3	East Germany	7:17.79

4 x 100 m Medley Relay

1	USSR	3:41.44
2	France	3:43.09
3	Italy	3:43.14

10 m Highboard Diving

1	G. Chogovadze	URS	639.69 pts
2	J. Hempel	GDR	578.43
3	V. Timoshinin	URS	572.40

3 m Springboard Diving

1	A. Killat	FRG	672.75 pts
2	A. Gladchenko	URS	666.42
3	J. Hempel	GDR	663.84

1 m Springboard Diving

1	E. Jongejans	HOL	594.08 pts
2	V. Statsenko	URS	578.24
3	A. Gladchenko	URS	563.24

Women

50 m Freestyle

1	C. Plewinski	FRA	25.63
2	D. Hunger	GDR	25.64
3	K. Meissner	GDR	25.87

100 m Freestyle

1	K. Meissner	GDR	55.38
2	M. Stellmach	GDR	55.40
3	Marianne Muis	HOL	55.61

200 m Freestyle

1	M. Stellmach	GDR	1:58.93
2	Marianne Muis	HOL	1:59.96
3	M. Jacobsen	DEN	2:00.35

400 m Freestyle

1	A. Möhring	GDR	4:05.84
2	H. Friedrich	GDR	4:10.14
3	M. Melchiorri	ITA	4:10.89

800 m Freestyle

1	A. Möhring	GDR	8:23.99
2	A. Strauus	GDR	8:28.24
3	I. Dalby	NOR	8:28.59

100 m Butterfly

1	C. Plewinski	FRA	59.08
2	J. Jakob	GDR	1:00.42
3	K. Nord	GDR	1:00.81

200 m Butterfly

1	K. Nord	GDR	2:09.33
2	J. Jakob	GDR	2:10.94
3	M. Jacobsen	DEN	2:12.63

100 m Backstroke

1	K. Otto	GDR	1:01.86
2	K. Egerszegi	HUN	1:02.44
3	A. Eichhorst	GDR	1:03.10

200 m Backstroke

1	D. Hase	GDR	2:12.46
2	K. Egerszeki	HUN	2:12.61
3	K. Otto	GDR	2:14.29

100 m Breaststroke

1	S. Börnike	GDR	1:09.55
2	T. Dangalakova	BUL	1:09.65
3	M. Dalla Valla	ITA	1:10.39

200 m Breaststroke

1	S. Börnike	GDR	2:27.77
2	B. Becue	BEL	2:29.94
3	E. Volkova	URS	2:29.95

200 m Individual Medley

1	D. Hunger	GDR	2:13.26
2	Marianne Muis	HOL	2:15.85
3	Mildred Muis	HOL	2:17.23

400 m Individual Medley

1	D. Hunger	GDR	4:41.82
2	K. Egerszegi	HUN	4:44.75
3	G. Müller	GDR	4:46.06

4 x 100 m Freestyle Relay

1	East Germany	3:42.46
2	Holland	3:43.66
3	West Germany	3:46.15

4 x 200 m Freestyle Relay

1	East Germany	7:58.54
2	Holland	8:08.00
3	Italy	8:10.49

4 x 100 m Medley Relay

1	East Germany	4:07.40
2	Italy	4:10.78
3	Holland	4:11.53

10 m Highboard Diving

1	U. Wetzig	GDR	403.35 pts
2	I. Afonina	URS	400.83
3	J. Eichler	GDR	395.55

3 m Springboard Diving

1	M. Babkova	URS	514.23 pts
2	B. Baldus	GDR	510.72
3	S. Alexeyeva	URS	486.09

TSB AMATEUR SWIMMING ASSOCIATION CHAMPIONSHIPS (18 Jun 89)

Men

50 m Freestyle

1	M. Fibbens	Barnet Copthall	23.87
2	M. Foster	Southend	24.02
3	N. Metcalfe	City of Leeds	24.22

100 m Freestyle

1	M. Fibbens	Barnet Copthall	51.68
2	S. Dronsfield	City of Leeds	51.92
3	G. Bulpitt	City of Birmingham	51.98

200 m Freestyle

1	J. Broughton	City of Leeds	1:53.34

2	P. Brew	Kelly College	1.53.85
3	S. McQuaid	City of Manchester	1:54.15

400 m Freestyle

1	C. McNeil	Paisley	3:58.84
2	J. Broughton	City of Leeds	3:58.98
3	K. Boyd	South Tyneside	3:59.20

1500 m Freestyle

1	K. Boyd	South Tyneside	15:44.19
2	A. Day	City of Leeds	15:48.12
3	I. Wilson	Sunderland	15:57.47

100 m Butterfly

1	D. Parker	City of Coventry	55.33
2	M. Fibbens	Barnet Copthall	55.70
3	S. Dronsfield	City of Leeds	55.90

200 m Butterfly

1	A. Quinn	Sale	2:05.08
2	M. Watkins	Torfaen	2:05.88
3	C. Robinson	Killerwhales	2:06.06

100 m Backstroke

1	G. Binfield	Maxwell	58.52
2	G. Robins	Portsmouth Northsea	58.81
3	M. O'Connor	City of Manchester	59.00

200 m Backstroke

1	G. Binfield	Maxwell	2:05.26
2	P. Blake	Wigan Wasps	2:05.56
3	G. Robins	Portsmouth Northsea	2:06.45

100 m Breaststroke

1	A. Moorhouse	City of Leeds	1:03.31
2	N. Gillingham	City of Birmingham	1:03.61
3	J. Parrack	City of Leeds	1:04.24

200 m Breaststroke

1	N. Gillingham	City of Birmingham	2:18.45
2	N. Hudghton	Dundee	2:19.34
3	A. Moorhouse	City of Leeds	2:19.55

200 m Individual Medley

1	G. Robins	Portsmouth Northsea	2:06.05
2	P. O'Sullivan	Hounslow	2:06.14
3	J. Davey	City of Leeds	2:07.35

400 m Individual Medley

1	P. Brew	Kelly College	4:26.45
2	P. O'Sullivan	Hounslow	4:27.16
3	A. Day	City of Leeds	4:32.31

4 x 100 m Freestyle Relay

1	City of Leeds	3:30.14
2	City of Birmingham	3:34.40
3	Barnet Copthall	3:34.79

4 x 100 m Medley Relay

1	City of Leeds	3:49.27
2	City of Birmingham	3:51.33
3	Barnet Copthall	4:01.76

Women

50 m Freestyle

1	C. Woodcook	Haywards Heath	26.49
2	A. Sheppard	Milngavie & Bearsden	26.81
3	K. Pickering	Ipswich	26.92

100 m Freestyle

1	K. Pickering	Ipswich	58.21
2	L. Donnelly	Hamilton	58.57
3	J. Coull	City of Birmingham	58.33

200 m Freestyle

1	J. Coull	City of Birmingham	2:05.23
2	H. Mansfield	City of Chester	2:06.15
3	L. Donnelly	Hamilton	2:06.32

400 m Freestyle

1	K. Mellor	Sheffield	4:22.37
2	N. Atkinson	Stockport Metro	4:24.13
3	H. Walsh	Univ of Swansea	4:26.05

800 m Freestyle

1	K. Mellor	Sheffield	8:53.39
2	N. Atkinson	Stockport Metro	8:56.38
3	E. Arnold	Nottingham Northern	8:59.74

100 m Butterfly

1	M. Scarborough	Portsmouth Northsea	1:02.05
2	S. Purvis	Wigan Wasps	1:03.32
3	C. Foot	Millfield	1:03.33

200 m Butterfly

1=	S. Purvis	Wigan Wasps	2:15.24
1=	M. Scarborough	Portsmouth Northsea	2:15.24
3	H. Bewley	Univ. of Swansea	2:17.91

100 m Backstroke

1	K. Read	Barnet Copthall	1:04.70
2	H. Slatter	Kelly College	1:05.75
3	J. Deakins	Gloucester City	1:06.18

200 m Backstoke

1	K. Read	Barnet Copthall	2:16.11
2	H. Slatter	Kelly College	2:18.12
3	J. Deakins	Gloucester City	2:19.09

100 m Breaststroke

1	S. Brownsdon	Wigan Wasps	1:11.55
2	L. Coombes	Southampton	1:12.03
3	M. Hohmann	Wigan Wasps	1:12.16

200 m Breaststroke

1	S. Brownsdon	Wigan Wasps	2:35.01
2	M. Hohmann	Wigan Wasps	2:38.12
3	J. Hill	Cumbernauld	2:38.36

200 m Individual Medley

1	S. Davies	Bracknell	2:19.29
2	J. Hill	Cumbernauld	2:20.18
3	S. Brownsdon	Wigan Wasps	2:20.51

400 m Individual Medley

1	S. Brownsdon	Wigan Wasps	4:51.91
2	H. Walsh	Univ. of Swansea	5:02.00
3	S. Smart	City of Chester	5:05.35

4 x 100 m Freestyle Relay

1	City of Birmingham	3:58.54
2	Portsmouth Northsea	4:00.66
3	Bracknell	4:01.25

4 x 100 m Medley Relay

1	Wigan Wasps	4:27.29
2	City of Birmingham	4:29.86
3	Southampton	4:30.02

TSB BRITISH CLUBS' TEAM CHAMPIONSHIPS (15 Apr 90)
Final Standings

Men

1	City of Leeds	242	pts
2	Portsmouth Northsea	201	pts
3	Barnet Copthall	183	pts

Women

1	Wigan Wasps	212	pts
2	Portsmouth Northsea	195	pts
3	Warrington	175	pts

TABLE TENNIS

INAUGURAL TSP WORLD TEAM CUP (23 May 90)

MT	Sweden		bt	China		3–2
WT	China		bt	North Korea		3–0

EUROPEAN CHAMPIONSHIPS (16 Apr 90)

MS	M. Applegren	SWE	bt	A. Grubba	POL	21–15 15–21 21–14 21–19
WS	D. Guerguelcheva	BUL	bt	Yong Tu	SWI	17–21 21–15 21–18 21–16
MD	I. Lupulescu/Z. Primorac	YUG	bt	S. Fetzner/J. Rosskopf	FRG	22–20 22–20
WD	C. Batorfi/G. Wirth	HUN	bt	I. Palina/Y. Timina	URS	15–21 21–18 21–16
XD	J-P. Gatien/Wang Xiaoming	FRA	bt	J-M. Savie (BEL)/ G Wirth (HUN)		21–13 25–23
MT 1–2	Sweden		bt	West Germany		5–2
3–4	England		bt	Yugoslavia		5–1
WT 1–2	Hungary		bt	Czechoslovakia		3–0
3–4	Yugoslavia		bt	Holland		3–1

LEEDS ENGLISH OPEN CHAMPIONSHIP (7 Jan 90)

MS	Yu Shentong	CAN	bt	Chen Xinhua	ENG	Walkover
WS	M. Hoshina	JAP	bt	M. Hrachova	CSR	21–12 21–15 21–19
MD	Chen Longcan/ Wei Qingguang	CHN	bt	J. Rosskopf/S. Fetzner	FRG	19–21 21–15 21–17
WD	Lee Jung-ae/Kim Youn-sook	SKO	bt	M. Hrachova/R. Kasalova	CSR	21–16 18–21 21–19
XD	J-P. Gatien/Wang Xiaoming	FRA	bt	T. Janci/R. Kasalova	CSR	17–21 21–17 21–13
MT	China		bt	West Germany		3–2
WT	South Korea		bt	France		3–2

LEEDS ENGLISH NATIONAL CLOSED CHAMPIONSHIPS (7 May 90)

MS	D. Douglas	bt	C. Prean	8–21 21–17 21–17 17–21 21–12
WS	F. Elliot	bt	A. Holt	12–21 23–21 21–11 21–14
MD	A. Cooke/D. Douglas	bt	S. Andrew/N. Mason	21–15 21–18
WD	F. Elliot/L. Lomas	bt	A. Gordon/A. Holt	19–21 21–19 21–19
XD	S. Andrew/F. Elliot	bt	J. Holland/J. Billington	22–20 21–19

HOME INTERNATIONAL CHAMPIONSHIP (8 Oct 89)

Men		*Women*	
1	England	1	England
2	Ireland	2	Scotland
3	Wales	3	Wales
4	Scotland	4	Ireland

LEEDS MASTERS (16 Sep 89)

MS	J-P. Gatien	FRA	bt	D. Douglas	ENG	21–17 21–19

TENNIS

THE GRAND SLAM TOURNAMENTS

US OPEN CHAMPIONSHIPS (Flushing Meadow, New York 10 Sep 89)

MS	B. Becker	FRG	bt	I. Lendl	CSR	7–6 1–6 6–3 7–6
WS	S. Graf	FRG	bt	M. Navratilova	USA	3–6 7–5 6–1
MD	J. McEnroe (USA)/M. Woodforde (AUS)		bt	K. Flach/R. Seguso	USA	6–4 4–6 6–3 6–3
WD	H. Mandlikova (AUS)/ M. Navratilova (USA)		bt	M.J. Fernandez/P. Shriver	USA	5–7 6–4 6–4
XD	S. Cannon/R. White	USA	bt	R. Leach/M. McGrath	USA	3–6 6–2 7–5

AUSTRALIAN OPEN CHAMPIONSHIPS (Melbourne 28 Jan 90)

MS	I. Lendl	CSR	bt	S. Edberg	SWE	4–6 7–6 5–2 ret
WS	S. Graf	FRG	bt	M.J. Fernandez	USA	6–3 6–4
MD	P. Aldrich/D. Visser	SAF	bt	G. Connell/G. Michibata	CAN	6–4 4–6 6–1 6–4
WD	J. Novotna/H. Sukova	CSR	bt	P. Fendick/M.J. Fernandez	USA	7–6 7–6
XD	J. Pugh (USA)/N. Zvereva (URS)		bt	R. Leach/Z. Garrison	USA	4–6 6–2 6–3

FRENCH OPEN CHAMPIONSHIPS (Roland Garros, Paris 20 Jun 90)

MS	A. Gomez	ECU	bt	A. Agassi	USA	6–3 2–6 6–4 6–4
WS	M. Seles	YUG	bt	S. Graf	FRG	7–6 6–4
MD	S. Casal/E. Sanchez	SPA	bt	G. Ivanisevic (YUG)/ P. Korda (CSR)		7–5 6–3
WD	J. Novotna/H. Sukova	CSR	bt	L. Savchenko/N. Zvereva	URS	6–4 7–5
XD	J. Lozano (MEX)/A. Sanchez (SPA)		bt	D. Visser (SAF)/N. Provis (AUS)		7–6 7–6

THE ALL-ENGLAND OPEN CHAMPIONSHIPS (Wimbledon 8 Jul 90)

MS	S. Edberg	SWE	bt	B. Becker	FRG	6–2 6–2 3–6 3–6 6–4
WS	M. Navratilova	USA	bt	Z. Garrison	USA	6–4 6–1
MD	R. Leach/J. Pugh	USA	bt	P. Aldrich/D. Visser	SAF	7–6 7–6 7–6
WD	J. Novatna/H. Sukova	CSR	bt	K. Jordan (USA)/E. Smylie (AUS)		6–3 6–4
XD	R. Leach/Z. Garrison	USA	bt	J. Alexander/E. Smylie	AUS	7–5 6–2

OTHER OPEN CHAMPIONSHIPS

WEST GERMAN OPEN CHAMPIONSHIPS (13 & 20 May 90)

MS	J. Aguilera	SPA	bt	B. Becker	FRG	6–1 6–0 7–6
WS	M. Seles	YUG	bt	S. Graf	FRS	6–4 6–3

ITALIAN MEN'S OPEN CHAMPIONSHIP (20 May 90)

MS	T. Muster	AUT	bt	A. Chesnokov	URS	6–1 6–3 6–1
MD	S. Casal/E. Sanchez	SPA	bt	J. Courier/M. Davis	USA	7–6 7–5

ITALIAN WOMEN'S OPEN CHAMPIONSHIP (13 May 90)

WS	M. Seles	YUG	bt	M. Navratilova	USA	6–1 6–1
WD	H. Kelesi (CAN)/M. Seles (YUG)		bt	L. Garrone/L. Golarsa	ITA	6–3 6–4

INAUGURAL YUGOSLAV MEN'S OPEN CHAMPIONSHIP (20 May 90)

MS	G. Prpic	YUG	bt	G. Ivanisevic	YUG	6–3 4–6 6–4

OTHER INTERNATIONAL EVENTS

WIGHTMAN CUP (15–17 Sep 89)

	US		bt	Great Britain		7–0

NEC WOMEN'S FEDERATION CUP FINAL (9 Oct 90)

	USA		bt	Spain		3–0

EUROPEAN INDOOR CHAMPIONSHIP (22 Oct 89)

WS	S. Graf	FRG	bt	J. Novotna	CSR	6–1 7–6
WD	J. Novotna/H. Sukova	CSR	bt	N. Tauziat (FRA)/J. Wiesner (AUT)		6–3 3–6 6–4

EUROPEAN COMMUNITY INDOOR CHAMPIONSHIP (29 Oct 89)

MS	I. Lendl	CSR	bt	M. Mecir	CSR	6–2 6–2 1–6 6–4

MIDLAND BANK INDOOR CHAMPIONSHIP (29 Oct 89)

WS	S. Graf	FRG	bt	M. Seles	YUG	7–5 6–4

SILK CUT INDOOR CHAMPIONSHIP (12 Nov 89)

MS	M. Chang	USA	bt	G. Forget	FRA	6–2 6–1 6–1
MD	J. Hlasek (SWI)/J. McEnroe (USA)		bt	J. Bates (GBR)/K. Curren (USA)		6–1 7–6

VIRGINIA SLIMS CHAMPIONSHIPS (19 Nov 89)

WS	S. Graf	FRG	bt	M. Navratilova	USA	6–4 7–5 2–6 6–2
WD	M. Navratilova/P. Shriver	USA	bt	L. Savchenko/N. Zvereva	URS	6–3 6–2

EUROPEAN WOMEN'S TEAM TOURNAMENT (26 Nov 89)

	USSR		bt	Great Britain		2–1

NABISCO MASTERS INDOOR CHAMPIONSHIP (3 & 10 Dec 89)

MS	S. Edberg	SWE	bt	B. Becker	FRG	4–6 7–6 6–3 6–1
MD	J. Grabb/P. McEnroe	USA	bt	J. Fitzgerald (AUS)/ A. Jarryd (SWE)		7–5 7–6 5–7 6–3

DAVIS CUP FINAL (INDOOR – Stuttgart 15–17 Dec 89)

	West Germany		bt	Sweden		3–2
MS	M. Wilander	SWE	bt	C-U. Steeb	FRG	5–7 7–6 6–7 6–2 6–3
MS	B. Becker	FRG	bt	S. Edberg	SWE	6–2 6–2 6–4
MD	B. Becker/E. Jelen	FRG	bt	J. Gunnarsson/A. Jarryd	SWE	7–6 6–4 3–6 6–7 6–4
MS	B. Becker	FRG	bt	M. Wilander	SWE	6–2 6–0 6–2
MS	S. Edberg	SWE	bt	C-U. Steeb	FRG	6–2 6–4

HOPMAN CUP FINAL (Melbourne 1 Jan 90)

	Spain		bt	USA		2–1

WCT WORLD DOUBLES CHAMPIONSHIP (22 Apr 90)

MD	R. Leach/J. Pugh	USA	bt	K. Flach/R. Seguso	USA	7–6 4–6 7–6 6–4

APT MEN'S WORLD TEAM CUP (Dusseldorf 27 May 90)

MT	Yugoslavia		bt	USA		2–1

WOMEN'S NATIONS CUP (Marbella 27 May 90)

WT	Spain		bt	USA		3–2

TRIATHLON

1ST OFFICIAL WORLD SHORT COURSE CHAMPIONSHIPS (6 Aug 89)

Men

1	M. Allen	USA	1:58:46
2	G. Cook	GBR	2:00:04
3	R. Wells	NZL	2:00:56
T1	USA		6:05:04
T2	Australia		6:07:25
T3	Great Britain		6:12:29

Women

1	E. Baker	NZL	2:10;02
2	J. Ripple	USA	2:10:34
3	L.Samuelson	USA	2:12:50
T1	USA		6:36:36
T2	Canada		6:44:25
T3	West Germany		6:55:13

IRONMAN WORLD LONG COURSE CHAMPIONSHIPS (15 Oct 89)

Men

1	M. Allen	USA	8:09:14

Women

1	P. Newby-Fraser	ZIM	9:00;56

BRITISH SHORT COURSE CHAMPIONSHIPS (10 Sep 89)

Men

1	G. Cook	1:51:32

Women

1	S. Coope	2:08:04

VOLLEYBALL

WORLD CUP 1989

Men (26 Nov 89)

1	Cuba	14 pts
2	Italy	13 pts
3	USSR	12 pts

Women (12 Nov 89)

1	Cuba	14 pts
2	USSR	13 pts
3	China	12 pts

EUROPEAN CHAMPIONSHIP FINAL (1 Oct 89)

Italy bt Sweden 3–1

EUROPEAN CHAMPIONS' CUP FINAL 1990

Philip Modena ITA bt Frejus FRA 3–2

3rd Place play-off

CV Palma SPA bt CSKA Sophia BUL 3–2

EUROPEAN CUP-WINNERS' CUP FINAL 1990

Maxicono Parma ITA bt Sisley Treviso ITA 3–1

3rd Place play-off

Dinamo Moscow URS bt Hamburg FRG 3–0

BRITISH CHAMPIONSHIP FINAL 1990

Scotland bt England 3–1

3rd Place play-off

GB Students bt Wales 3–0

BRITISH WOMEN'S CHAMPIONSHIP (24 Jun 90)

FINAL STANDINGS	P	W	L	Pts
1 England	4	4	0	8
2 Scotland	4	3	1	6
3 Rep of Ireland	4	2	2	4
4 Wales	4	1	3	2
5 N. Ireland	4	0	4	0

ENGLISH CLUB CHAMPIONS 1990

Men Mizuno Malory

Women Brixton Knights

WATER POLO

EUROPEAN CHAMPIONSHIP FINAL (20 Aug 89)

West Germany bt Yugoslavia 10–9

3rd Place play-off

Italy bt USSR 12–11

HOME COUNTRIES' INTERNATIONAL CHAMPIONSHIP 1990

FINAL TABLE	P	W	L	F	A	Pts
1 England	3	3	0	46	20	6
2 Scotland	3	2	1	30	31	4
3 Wales	3	1	2	27	26	2
4 Ireland	3	0	3	15	41	0

BRITISH DEEPWATER CLUB CHAMPIONSHIP 1990

FINAL TABLE	P	W	L	F	A	Pts
1 Polytechnic	3	3	0	37	22	6
2 Sutton & Cheam	3	2	1	41	29	4
3 Penguin	3	1	2	29	33	2
4 Royton	3	0	3	27	50	0

WATER SKIING

1989 WORLD CHAMPIONS

Mens' Overall	P. Martin	FRA
Men's Slalom	A. Mapple	GBR
Men's Jump	G. Carrington	AUS
Men's Tricks	A. Bennet	FRA
Women's Overall	D. Mapple	USA
Women's Slalom	K. Laskoff	USA
Women's Jump	D. Mapple	USA
Women's Trick	T. Larsen	USA

1989 EUROPEAN CHAMPIONS

Men's Overall	A. Alessi	ITA
Women's Overall	N. Rumantseva	URS

1989 BRITISH CHAMPIONS

Men's Overall	P. Studd
Women's Overall	P. Roberts

WINTER SPORTS

Alpine Skiing

1989–90 WORLD CUP

FINAL STANDINGS – MEN

Downhill	1	H. Hoeflehner	SWI	166 pts
	2	A. Skaardal	NOR	120 pts
	3	P. Zurbriggen	SWI	105 pts
Super Giant Slalom	1	P. Zurbriggen	SWI	98 pts
	2	G. Mader	AUT	71 pts
	3	L-B. Eriksson	SWE	61 pts
Giant Slalom	1=	O.C Furuseth	NOR	96 pts
	1=	G. Mader	AUT	96 pts
	3	H. Strolz	AUT	71 pts
Slalom	1	A. Bittner	FRG	150 pts
	2=	O.C. Furuseth	NOR	95 pts
	2=	A. Tomba	ITA	95 pts
Overall	1	P. Zurbriggen	SWI	357 pts
	2	O.C. Furuseth	NOR	234 pts
	3	G. Mader	AUT	213 pts

FINAL STANDINGS – WOMEN

Downhill	1	K. Gutensohn-Knopf	FRG	110 pts
	2	P. Kronberger	AUT	106 pts
	3=	M. Figini	SWI	105 pts
	3=	M. Gerg	FRG	105 pts
Super Giant Slalom	1	C. Merle	FRA	99 pts
	2	M. Gerg	FRG	79 pts
	3	S. Wolf	AUT	73 pts
Giant Slalom	1	A. Wachter	AUT	133 pts
	2	M. Svet	YUG	89 pts
	3	P. Kronberger	AUT	85 pts
Slalom	1	V. Schneider	SWI	125 pts
	2	C. Strobl	AUT	108 pts
	3	I. Ladstaetter	AUT	98 pts
Overall	1	P. Kronberger	AUT	341 pts
	2	A. Wachter	AUT	300 pts
	3	M. Gerg	FRG	270 pts

NATIONS CUP (MEN & WOMEN COMBINED)

1	Austria	2816 pts
2	Switzerland	1968 pts
3	West Germany	1220 pts

Bobsleighing

WORLD TWO-MAN CHAMPIONSHIP (St. Moritz, SWI 4 Feb 90)

1	SWI I	G. Weder/B. Gerber	4:19.90
2	GDR II	H. Czudaj/A. Jang	4:20.30
3	GDR I	W. Hoppe/B Musiol	4:20.55

WORLD FOUR-MAN CHAMPIONSHIP (St. Moritz, SWI 11 Feb 90)

1	SWI I	G. Weder/B. Gerber/ L. Schindelholz/C. Morell	4:13.35
2	GDR II	H. Czudaj/T. Bonk/A. Szelig/A. Jang	4:13.84
3	AUT I	I. Appelt/G. Redl/J. Mandl/H. Winkler	4:13.94

EUROPEAN TWO-MAN CHAMPIONSHIP (Igls, AUT 21 Jan 90)

1	SWI I	G. Weder/C. Morell	3:33.33
2	URS I	S. Ekmanis/J. Tone	3:34.21
3	URS II	M. Poikans/A. Gorochov	3:34.52

EUROPEAN FOUR-MAN CHAMPIONSHIP (Igls, AUT 28 Jan 90)

1	AUT I	P. Kienast/T. Schroll/M. Riedl/H. Lindner	3:30.59
2	AUT II	I. Appelt/G. Redl/J. Mandl/H. Winkler	3:31.06
3	SWI I	G. Weder/B. Gerber/L. Schinderlholz/ C. Morell	3:31.07

BRITISH FOUR-MAN CHAMPIONSHIP (21 Oct 89)

1	T. De La Hunty/L. Paul/C. Rattigan/S. Redgrave	1:55.00
2	N. Phipps/V. Bramble/Murrain/Smith	1:56.11
3	M. Tout/Wilkinson/Newell/Rock	1:56.61

STELLA ARTOIS BRITISH TWO-MAN CHAMPIONSHIP (St. Moritz, SWI 22 Feb 90)

1	M. Lloyd/C. Davies	Team Canada
2	M. Tout/G. Farrell	Save & Prosper
3	N. Phipps/E. Haller	Team Stella Artois

Ice Hockey

1990 WORLD CHAMPIONSHIP – Final Standings

1	USSR
2	Czechoslovakia

EUROPEAN CHAMPIONSHIP (26 Apr 90)

Sweden	bt	Czechoslovakia	5–1

NORTH AMERICAN NHL PLAY-OFF CHAMPIONSHIP – Stanley Cup 1990

Edmonton Oilers	bt	Boston Bruins	3–2
Edmonton Oilers	bt	Boston Bruins	7–2
Boston Bruins	bt	Edmonton Oilers	2–1
Edmonton Oilers	bt	Boston Bruins	5–1
Edmonton Oilers	bt	Boston Bruins	4–1

Edmonton Oilers won the series 4–1

HEINEKEN LEAGUE PREMIER DIVISION – FINAL TABLE 1989–90

		P	W	D	L	F	A	Pts
1	Cardiff Devils	32	28	1	3	304	146	57
2	Murrayfield Racers	32	23	3	6	273	169	49
3	Durham Wasps	32	20	2	10	261	209	42
4	Solihull	32	16	1	15	218	209	33
5	Fife Flyers	32	14	3	15	226	264	31
6	Nottingham Panthers	32	12	2	18	184	188	26
7	Ayr	32	9	4	19	181	229	22
8	Peterborough	32	7	0	25	177	282	14
9	Whitley Bay	32	6	2	24	202	330	14

HEINEKEN CHAMPIONSHIP PLAY-OFF FINAL (22 Apr 90)

Cardiff Devils	bt	Murrayfield Racers	6–6 aot 6–5 pen

NORWICH UNION CUP FINAL (2 Dec 89)

Murrayfield Racers	bt	Durham Wasps	10–4

Ice Skating

WORLD CHAMPIONSHIPS (Halifax, Nova Scotia, CAN 7–10 Mar 90)

Men	1	K. Browning	CAN	3.0
	2	V. Petrenko	URS	3.8
	3	C. Bowman	USA	7.8
Women	1	J. Trenary	USA	5.4
	2	M. Ito	JAP	5.6
	3	H. Cook	USA	7.4
Pairs	1	S. Grinkov/Y. Gordeyeva	URS	1.5
	2	L. Eisler/I. Brasseur	CAN	4.0
	3	A. Dmitriev/N. Mishkutiunok	URS	4.0
Ice Dancing	1	S. Ponomarenko/M. Klimova	URS	3.0
	2	P. Duchesnay/I. Duchesnay	FRA	3.4
	3	A. Zhulin/M. Usova	URS	5.6

EUROPEAN CHAMPIONSHIPS (Leningrad 31 Jan–3 Feb 90)

Men	1	V. Petrenko	URS	3.6
	2	P. Barna	CSR	4.2
	3	V. Zagorodniuk	URS	6.6
Women	1	E. Grossmann	GDR	4.2
	2	N. Lebedyeva	URS	5.0
	3	M. Kielmann	FRG	8.2
Pairs	1	S. Grinkov/Y. Gordeyeva	URS	2.5
	2	O. Makarov/L. Selezneva	URS	3.0
	3	A. Dmitriev/N. Mishkutiunok	URS	3.5
Ice Dancing	1	S. Ponomarenko/M. Klimova	URS	2.0
	2	A. Zhulin/M. Usova	URS	4.0
	3	P. Duchesnay/I. Duchesnay	FRA	6.4

SKATE ELECTRIC BRITISH CHAMPIONSHIPS (Basingstoke 6–8 Nov 89)

Men	1	S. Cousins	4.4
	2	C. Newberry	5.0
	3	L. Yip	5.8
Women	1	E. Murdoch	4.0
	2	J. Conway	4.2
	3	G. Fulton	6.0
Pairs	1	a. Naylor/C. Peake	
	2	M. Aldred/C. Barker	
Ice Dancing	1	A. Place/L. Burton	2.4
	2	J. Blomfield/A. Hall	4.8
	3	A. Abretti/K. Quinn	5.8

WRESTLING

BRITISH SENIOR CHAMPIONSHIPS (17 Jun 90)

Light-Fly	A. Airlie
Fly	D. Connelly
Bantam	P. Morris
Feather	J. Melling
Light	P. Keech
Welter	F. Walker
Middle	S. Morley
Light-Heavy	G. English
Heavy	A. Singh
Super-Heavy	M. Clempner

YACHTING

1989–90 WHITBREAD 32,432-MILE ROUND THE WORLD RACE

1 Steinlage 2 (P. Blake)	NZL	128 days	9 hr 40 min
2 Fisher & Paykel (G. Dalton)	NZL	129 days	21 hr 18 min
3 Merit (P. Fehlmann)	SWI	130 days	10 hr 10 min
4 Rothmans (L. Smith)	GBR	131 days	4 hr 54 min
5 The Card (R. Nilson)	SWE	135 days	7 hr 15 min
6 Fortuna Extra Lights (J. Santana)	SPA	137 days	8 hr 14 min

Steinlager 2 won all six legs. The first-ever yacht to compete with an all-women crew, Maiden, skippered by T. Edwards, also finished.

CHAMPAGNE MUMM ADMIRAL'S (Cowes 10 Aug 89) Final Standings

1	Great Britain		748.0 pts
	Jamarella	321.5	
	Indulgence VII	217.0	
	Juno IV	209.5	
2	Denmark		730.5 pts
	Andelsbanken IV	263.5	
	Stockbroker's Container	281.5	
	4K	185.5	
3	New Zealand		667.5 pts
	Librah	285.5	
	Fair Share	203.0	
	Propaganda	179.0	

AMERICA'S CUP

The New Zealand challenge to the United States in the 27th staging of the America's Cup dissolved when they lost the series 2–0 on 9 September 1988. Considerable out-of-water arguments ensued between the two combatants over the American boat, 'Stars and Stripes,' a catamaran which the challengers claimed was ineligible to compete. The fight continued in the courts.

Judge Carmen Ciparick, sitting in the New York Supreme

Court on 28 March 1989, stated that the US entry, skippered by Dennis Conner, had "violated the spirit" of the America's Cup. In summary, she disqualified the San Diego Yacht Club and awarded the series to New Zealand.

On 19 September 1989, the Appellate Division of the New York Supreme Court gave back the Cup to the USA, reversing the original decision by a four to one majority. It declared that Judge Carmen Ciparick's ruling that the two boats should be "somewhat evenly matched" had no basis in the Deed of Gift, the 1887 trust document of the America's Cup.

THE XIV COMMONWEALTH GAMES (Auckland, New Zealand 24 Jan–3 Feb 1990)

ATHLETICS

Men

Event	Pos	Name	Country	Result
100 m	1	L. Christie	ENG	9.93
	2	D. Ezinwa	NGR	10.05
	3	B. Surin	CAN	10.12
200 m	1	M. Adam	ENG	20.10
	2	J. Regis	ENG	20.16
	3	A. Mafe	ENG	20.26
400 m	1	D. Clark	AUS	44.60
	2	S. Kitur	KEN	44.88
	3	S. Kipkemboi	KEN	44.93
800 m	1	S. Tirop	KEN	1:45.98
	2	N. Kiprotich	KEN	1:46.00
	3	M. Yates	ENG	1:46.62
1500 m	1	P. Elliott	ENG	3:33.39
	2	W. Kirochi	KEN	3:34.41
	3	P. O'Donoghue	NZL	3:35.14
5000 m	1	A. Lloyd	AUS	13:24.86
	2	J. Ngugi	KEN	13:24.94
	3	I. Hamer	WAL	13:25.63
10000 m	1	E. Martin	ENG	28:08.57
	2	M. Tanui	KEN	28:11.56
	3	P. Williams	CAN	28:12.71
Marathon	1	D. Wakiihuri	KEN	2:10.27
	2	S. Moneghetti	AUS	2:10:27
	3	S.R. Naali	TAN	2:10:38
30000 m Walk	1	G. Leblanc	CAN	2:08:28
	2	A. Jachno	AUS	2:09:09
	3	I. McCombie	ENG	2:09:20
110 m Hurdles	1	C. Jackson	WAL	13.08
	2	A. Jarrett	ENG	13:34
	3	D. Nelson	ENG	13:54
400 m Hurdles	1	K. Akabusi	ENG	48.89
	2	G. Yego	KEN	49.25
	3	J. Graham	CAN	50.24
3000 m Steeplechase	1	J. Kariuki	KEN	8:20.64
	2	J. Kipkemboi	KEN	8:24.26
	3	C. Walker	ENG	8:26.50
4 x 100 m Relay	1	England C. Callender/J. Regis/ M. Adam/L. Christie		38.67
	2	Nigeria V. Nwankwo/D. Ezinwa/ O. Ezinwa/A. Tetengi		38.85
	3	Jamaica W. Watson/J. Mair/ C. Wright/R. Stewart		39.11
4 x 400 m Relay	1	Kenya S. Kitur/S. Mwanzia/ D. Kitur/S. Kipkemboi		3:02.48
	2	Scotland M. Davidson/T. McKean/ D. Strang/B. Whittle		3:04.68
	3	Jamaica C. Wright/D. Morris/ T. Graham/H. Burnett		3:04.96
High Jump	1	N. Saunders	BER	2.36
	2	D. Grant	ENG	2.34
	3=	M. Ottey	CAN	2.33
	3=	G. Parsons	SCO	2.23
Long Jump	1	Y. Alli	NGR	8.39
	2	D. Culbert	AUS	8.20
	3	F. Igbinoghene	NGR	8.18
Triple Jump	1	M. Hadjiandreou	CYP	16.95
	2	J. Edwards	ENG	16.93
	3	E. Floreal	CAN	16.89
Pole Vault	1	S. Arkell	AUS	5.35
	2	I. Tullett	ENG	5.25
	3	S. Poelman	NZL	5.20
Shot	1	S. Williams	ENG	18.54
	2	A. Olukoju	NGR	18.48
	3	P. Edwards	WAL	18.17
Discus	1	A. Olukoju	NGR	62.62
	2	W. Reiterer	AUS	61.56
	3	P. Nandapi	AUS	59.94
Hammer	1	S. Carlin	AUS	75.66
	2	D. Smith	ENG	73.52
	3	A. Cooper	NZL	71.26
Javelin	1	S. Backley	ENG	86.02
	2	M. Hill	ENG	83.32
	3	G. Lovegrove	NZL	81.66
Decathlon	1	M. Smith	CAN	8525 pts
	2	S. Poelman	NZL	8207 pts
	3	E. Gilkes	ENG	7705 pts

Women

Event	Pos	Name	Country	Result
100 m	1	M. Otley	JAM	11.02
	2	K. Johnson	AUS	11.17
	3	P. Davis	BAH	11.20
200 m	1	M. Ottey	JAM	22.76
	2	K. Johnson	AUS	22.88
	3	P. Davis	BAH	23.15
400 m	1	F. Yusuf	NGR	51.08
	2	L. Keough	ENG	51.63
	3	C. Opara	NGR	52.01
800 m	1	D. Edwards	ENG	2:00:25
	2	A. Williams	ENG	2:0040
	3	S. Stewart	AUS	2:00.87
1500 m	1	A. Chalmers	CAN	4:08.41
	2	C. Cahill	ENG	4:08.75
	3	B. Nicholson	ENG	4:09.00
3000 m	1	A. Chalmers	CAN	8:38.38
	2	Y. Murray	SCO	8:39.46
	3	E. McColgan	SCO	8:47.66
10000 m	1	E. McColgan	SCO	32:23.56
	2	J. Hunter	ENG	32:33.21
	3	B. Moore	NZL	32:44.73
Marathon	1	L. Martin	AUS	2:25:28
	2	T. Ruckle	AUS	2:33:15
	3	A. Pain	ENG	2:36:35
10000 m Walk	1	K. Saxby	AUS	45:03
	2	A. Judkins	NZL	47:03
	3	L. Langford	ENG	47:23
100 m Hurdles	1	K. Morley	WAL	12.91
	2	S. Gunnell	ENG	13.12
	3	L-A. Skeete	ENG	13.31
400 m Hurdles	1	S. Gunnell	ENG	55.38
	2	D. Flintoff-King	AUS	56.00
	3	J. Laurendet	AUS	56.74
4 x 100 m Relay	1	Australia C. Freeman/K. Sambell/ M. Dunstan/K. Johnson		43.87
	2	England S. Douglas/J. Stoute/ S. Jacobs/P. Dunn		44.15
	3	Nigeria B. Utondu/F. Yusuf/ C. Opara/C. Ajunwa		44.67

4 x 400 m Relay	1	England A. Piggford/J. Stoute/ S. Gunnell/L. Keough		3:28.08
	2	Australia M. Holland/S. Stewart/ S. Andrews/D. Flintoff-King		
	3	Canada C. Allen/G. Harris/ R. Edeh/F. Garreau		3:33.26
High Jump	1	T. Murray	NZL	1.88 after jump-off
	2	J.Boyle	NIR	1.88
	3	T. Phillips	NZL	1.88
Long Jump	1	J. Flemming	AUS	6.78
	2	B. Utondu	NGR	6.65
	3	F. May	ENG	6.55
Shot	1	M. Augee	ENG	18.48
	2	J. Oakes	ENG	18.43
	3	Y. Hanson-Nortey	ENG	16.00
Discus	1	L-M. Vizaniari	AUS	56.38
	2	J. McKernan	NIR	54.86
	3	A. Vitols	AUS	53.84
Javelin	1	T. Sanderson	ENG	65.72
	2	S. Howland	AUS	61.18
	3	K. Farrow	AUS	58.98
Heptathlon	1	J. Flemming	AUS	6695 pts
	2	S. Jaklofsky-Smith	AUS	6115 pts
	3	J. Simpson	ENG	6085 pts

BADMINTON

Men's Singles	1	Rashid Sidek	MAL	15–8 15–10
	2	Foo Kok Keong	MAL	
	3	D. Hall	ENG	Walkover
Women's Singles	1	F. Smith	ENG	11–7 12–9
	2	D. Julien	CAN	
	3	H. Troke	ENG	11–0 11–0
Men's Doubles	1	Jaluni Sidek/ Razif Sidek	MAL	15–8 15–8
	2	Rashid Sidek/ Soon Chi	MAL	
	3	B. Blanshard/ M. Bitten	CAN	15–4 15–5
Women's Doubles	1	S. Sankey/F. Smith	ENG	18–14 2–15 15–9
	2	G. Clark/G. Gowers	ENG	
	3	J. Falardeau/D. Julien	CAN	18–13 15–2
Mixed Doubles	1	Chan Chi Choi/ Amy Chan	HKG	15–7 15–12
	2	M. Johnson/S. Sankey	ENG	
	3	A. Goode/G. Clark	ENG	Walkover
Team	1	England		5–0
	2	Canada		
	MS	D. Hall bt M. Butler		15–8 15–8
	WS	F. Smith bt D. Julien		7–11 11–1 11–0
	MD	S. Baddeley/A. Goode bt M. Bitten/B. Blanshard		15–5 15–8
	WD	G. Clarke/G. Gowers bt J. Falardeau/C. Sharpe		15–7 15–9
	XD	A. Goode/G. Gowers bt C. Sharpe/J. Falardeau		15–10 15–9
	3	Hong Kong		5–0
	4	New Zealand		
	MS	Yeung Yik Kei bt G. Stewart		15–6 3–15 15–12
	WS	Chan Man Wa bt L. Horne		11–5 11–8
	MD	Chan Chi Choi/Chan Siu Kwong bt K. Harrison/P. Horne		15–6 15–10
	WD	Amy Chan/Chan Man Wa bt J. Clarke/T. Whittaker		15–7 5–5
	XD	Chan Chi Choi/Amy Chan bt P. Horne/T. Whittaker		15–7 15–9

BOWLS

Men

Singles	1	R. Parrella	AUS	25–14
	2	M. McMahon	HKS	
	3	R. Corsie	SCO	25–17
Pairs	1	T. Morris/I. Schuback	AUS	23–15
	2	G. Boxwell/A. Wallace	CAN	
	3	R. Brassey/M. Symes	NZL	24–17
Fours	1	Scotland D. Love/G. Adrain/W. Wood/ I. Bruce		19–14
	2	N. Ireland S. Allen/J. Baker/J. McCloughlin/ R. McCutcheon		
	3	New Zealand K. Darling/S. McConnell/ P. Shaw/P. Skoglund		21–13

Women

Singles	1	G.V. Tau	PNG	25–18
	2	M. Khan	NZL	
	3	M. Johnston	NIR	25–15
Pairs	1	J. Howat/P. Watson	NZL	23–13
	2	E. Bonutto/M. Hobbs	AUS	
	3	M. Price/J. Roylance	ENG	22–14
Fours	1	Australia D. Roche/A. Rutherford/ D. Shaw/M. Stevens		20–18
	2	New Zealand M. Castle/A. Lambert/ L. McLean/R. Ryan		
	3	Hong Kong Sau Ling Chau/Yee Lai Lee/ N. Rozario/J. Wallis		21–20

BOXING

Light-Fly	1	J. Juko	USA	Pts
	2	A. Ramadhani	KEN	
	3=	D. Figliomeni	CAN	
	3=	D. Yadav	IND	
Fly	1	W. McCullough	NIR	Pts
	2	N. Tshabangu	ZIM	
	3=	M. Maina	KEN	
	3=	B. Siwakwi	ZAM	
Bantam	1	S. Mohammed	NGR	Pts
	2	G. Bie	CAN	
	3=	J. Chikwanda	ZAM	
	3=	W. Christmas	GUY	
Feather	1	J. Irwin	ENG	Pts
	2	H. Ally	TAN	
	3=	D. Gakuha	KEN	
	3=	J. Nicolson	AUS	
Light	1	G. Nyakana	UGA	Pts
	2	J. Rowsell	AUS	
	3=	D. Anderson	SCO	
	3=	B. Mambeya	TAN	
Light-Welter	1	C. Kane	SCO	Pts
	2	N. Odore	KEN	
	3=	D. Chinyadza	ZIM	
	3=	S. Scriggins	AUS	
Welter	1	D. Defiagbon	NGR	Pts
	2	G. Johnson	CAN	
	3=	G. Cheney	AUS	
	3=	A. Muramba	ZAM	
Light-Middle	1	R. Woodhall	ENG	Pts
	2	R. Downey	CAN	
	3=	A. Creery	NZL	
	3=	S. Figota	WSA	
Middle	1	C. Johnson	CAN	Pts
	2	A.J. Laryea	GHA	
	3=	M. Edwards	ENG	
	3=	C. Matata	UGA	

Light-Heavy	1	J. Akhasamba	KEN	Retired 3rd
	2	D. Brown	CAN	
	3=	N. Anderson	NZL	
	3=	A. Kaddu	UGA	
Heavy	1	G. Onyango	KEN	Pts
	2	P. Jordan	CAN	
	3=	E. Fainuulva	WSA	
	3=	K. Onwuka	NGR	
Super-Heavy	1	M. Kenny	NZL	Pts
	2	L. Alhassan	GHA	
	3=	P. Douglas	NIR	
	3=	V. Linklater	CAN	

CYCLING

Men

1000 m Sprint	1	G. Niewand	AUS	2–0
	2	C. Harnett	CAN	
	3	J. Andrews	NZL	2–1
1000 m Individual Time Trial	1	M. Vinnicombe	AUS	1:05.572
	2	G. Anderson	NZL	1:06.196
	3	J. Andrews	NZL	1:06.516
4000 m Individual Pursuit	1	G. Anderson	NZL	4:44.61
	2	M. Kingsland	AUS	4:52.75
	3	D. Winter	AUS	faster sf loser
4000 m Team Pursuit	1	New Zealand G. Anderson/N. Donnelly/G. McLeay/S. Williams		4:22.76
	2	Australia B. Aitken/S. McGlede/S. O'Brien/D. Winter		4:25.58
	3	England C. Boardman/S. Lillistone/B. Steel/G. Sword		faster sf loser
10 m Scratch race	1	G. Anderson	NZL	19:44.20
	2	S. O'Brien	AUS	19:44.22
	3	S. McGlede	AUS	19:44.26
50 km Points Race	1	R. Burns	AUS	81 Pts
	2	C. Connell	NZL	72 pts
	3	A. Irvine	NIR	39 pts
100 km Team Trial	1	New Zealand B. Fowler/G. Miller/I. Richards/G. Stevens		2:06:46.55
	2	Canada C. Koberstein/D. Spears/P. Verhesen/S. Way		2:09:19.59
	3	England C. Boardman/P. Longbottom/B. Luckwell/W. Randle		2:09:33.17
173 km Road Race	1	G. Miller	NZL	4:34:00.19
	2	B. Fowler	NZL	4:34:00.39
	3	S. Goguen	CAN	4:34:05.45

Women

1000 m Sprint	1	L. Jones	WAL	2–1
	2	J. Speight	AUS	
	3	S. Golder	NZL	2--1
3000 m Individual Pursuit	1	M.Harris	NZL	3:54.67
	2	K. Watt	AUS	3:54.78
	3	K-A. Way	CAN	fater sf loser
72 km Road Race	1	K. Watt	AUS	1:55:11.60
	2	L. Brambani	ENG	1:55:11.88
	3	K. Shannon	AUS	1:55:12.06

GYMNASTICS

Men

Artistic – All–round Team	1	Canada L. Bobkin/C. Hibbert/C. Latendresse/A. Nolet		171.800
	2	England T. Bartlett/D. Cox/J. May/N. Thomas		170.450
	3	Australia B. Dowrick/P. Hogan/T. Lees/K. Meredith		169.500
Artistic – All-round Individual	1	C. Hibbert	CAN	57.950
	2	A. Nolet	CAN	57.800
	3	J. May	ENG	57.400
Floor Exercises	1	N. Thomas	ENG	9.750
	2	A. Nolet	CAN	9.675
	3	C. Hibbert	CAN	9.600
Horizontal Bar	1=	C. Hibbert	CAN	9.850
	1=	A. Nolet	CAN	9.850
	3	B. Dowrick	AUS	9.800
Parallel Bars	1	C. Hibbert	CAN	9.800
	2	K. Meredith	AUS	9.675
	3	P. Hogan	AUS	9.600

Pommel Horse	1	B. Dowrick	AUS	9.825
	2	T. Lees	AUS	9.725
	3	J. May	ENG	9.700
Rings	1	C. Hibbert	CAN	9.775
	2	J. May	ENG	9.750
	3	K. Meredith	AUS	9.725
Vault	1	J. May	ENG	9.625
	2	C. Hibbert	CAN	9.575
	3	T. Lees	AUS	9.250
Women				
Artistic – All-round Team	1	Canada L. Lowing/J. Morin/L. Strong/S. Umeh		116.784
	2	Australia M. Allen/L. Read/K. Shadbolt/M. Telfer		115.272
	3	England L. Elliott/L. Grayson/L. Mainwaring/L. Redding		114.046
Artistic – All-round Individual	1	L. Strong	CAN	38.912
	2	M. Allen	AUS	38.687
	3	K. Shadbolt	AUS	38.499
Assymetrical Bars	1	M. Allen	AUS	9.875
	2	L. Strong	CAN	9.850
	3	M. Telfer	AUS	9.737
Beam	1	L. Strong	CAN	9.850
	2	L. Lowing	CAN	9.762
	3	K. Shadbolt	AUS	9.700
Floor Exercises	1	L. Strong	CAN	9.887
	2	L. Lowing	CAN	9.837
	3	K. Shadbolt	AUS	9.675
Vault	1	N. Jenkins	NZL	9.712
	2	L. Strong	CAN	9.643
	3	M. Allen	AUS	9.506
Rhythmic – All-round Individual	1	M. Fuzesi	CAN	37.65
	2	M. Gimotea	CAN	27.25
	3	A. Walker	NZL	36.90
Rhythmic Ball	1	M. Gimotea	CAN	9.450
	2	M. Fuzesi	CAN	9.400
	3	A. Walker	NZL	9.250
Rhythmic Hoop	1	M. Fuzesi	CAN	9.400
	2	M. Gimotea	CAN	9.200
	3=	R. Jack	NZL	9.100
	3=	A. Sands	ENG	9.100
	3	V. Seifert	ENG	9.100
Rhythmic Ribbon	1	M. Fuzesi	CAN	9.400
	2	M. Gimotea	CAN	9.300
	3=	R. Jack	NZL	9.200
	3=	V. Seifert	ENG	9.200
	3=	A. Walker	NZL	9.200
Rhythmic Rope	1	A. Walker	NZL	9.300
	2	M. Gimotea	CAN	9.275
	3	M. Fuzesi	CAN	9.250

JUDO

Men

Bantam – under 60 kg	1	C. Finney	ENG	Chui
	2	K. West	CAN	
	3=	J. Charles	WAL	
	3=	N. Singh	IND	
Feather – under 65 kg	1	B. Cooper	NZL	Ippon
	2	M. Preston	SCO	
	3=	M. Adshead	ENG	
	3=	J-P. Cantin	CAN	
Light – under 71 kg	1	R. Stone	ENG	Yuko
	2	M. Omagbaluwaje	NGR	
	3=	W. Cusack	SCO	
	3=	C. Savage	NIR	
Light-Middle – under 78 kg	1	D. Southby	ENG	Ippon
	2	G. Spinks	NZL	
	3=	R. Cote	CAN	
	3=	G. Kelly	AUS	
Middle – under 86 kg	1	D. White	ENG	Ippon
	2	W. Sweatman	SCO	
	3=	C. Bacon	AUS	
	3=	R. Dhanger	IND	
Light-Heavy – under 95 kg	1	R. Stevens	ENG	Shido
	2	D. Lampkin	AUS	
	3=	G. Campbell	SCO	
	3=	J. Kendrick	CAN	
Heavy – over 95 kg	1	E. Gordon	ENG	40 pts
	2	T. Greenaway	CAN	22 pts
	3	W. Watson	NZL	20 pts
Open – any weight	1	E. Gordon	ENG	Ippon
	2	M. Laroche	CAN	
	3=	G. Campbell	SCO	
	3=	M. Omagbaluwaje	NGR	

Women

Bantam – under 48 kg	1	K. Briggs	ENG	Ippon
	2	H. Duston	WAL	

	3=	J. Reardon	AUS	
	3=	D. Robertson	SCO	
Feather – under 52 kg	1	S. Rendle	ENG	Yuko
	2	C. Shiach	SCO	
	3=	C. Grainger	AUS	
	3=	L. Griffiths	WAL	
Light – under 56 kg	1	L. Cusack	SCO	Ippon
	2	S. Williams	AUS	
	3=	A. Hughes	ENG	
	3=	M. Sutton	WAL	
Light-Middle – under 61 kg	1	D. Bell	ENG	Yuko
	2	D. Guy-Halkyard	NZL	
	3=	M. Clayton	CAN	
	3=	L. Pace	MLT	
Middle – under 66 kg	1	S. Mills	ENG	Yuko
	2	K. Hayde	CAN	
	3=	N. Hill	AUS	
	3=	J. Malley	NIR	
Light-Heavy – under 72 kg	1	J. Morris	ENG	Yusei/Gachi
	2	A. Webb	CAN	
	3=	P. Knowles	WAL	
	3=	C. Obekpa	NGR	
Heavy – over 72 kg	1	S. lee	ENG	30 pts
	2	G. Dekker	AUS	17 pts
	3	Only four competed – no bronze medal awarded		
Open – any weight	1	S. Lee	ENG	Ippon
	2	J. Patterson	CAN	
	3=	G. Dekker	AUS	
	3=	N. Morris	NZL	

SHOOTING

Fullbore Rifle	**– Individual**	1	Colin Mallett	JER	394
		2	A. Tucker	ENG	390
		3	J. Corbett	AUS	390
	– Pairs	1	S. Belither/A. Tucker	ENG	580
		2	J. Corbett/B. Wood	AUS	565
		3	Cliff & Colin Mallett	JER	564
50 m Smallbore Rifle 3 Positions	**– Individual**	1	M. Klepp	CAN	1157
		2	M. Cooper	ENG	1154
		3	S. Dutta	IND	1143
	– Pairs	1	M. Klepp/J-F. Senecal	CAN	2272
		2	M. Cooper/R. Smith	ENG	2268
		3	R. Law/W. Murray	SCO	2258
50 m Smallbore Rifle Prone	**– Individual**	1	R. Harvey	NZL	591
		2	S. Petterson	NZL	590
		3	P. Scanlan	ENG	590
	– Pairs	1	R. Harvey/S. Petterson	NZL	1185
		2	M. Ashcroft/B. Sutherland	CAN	1184
		3	R. Jarvis/P. Scanlan	ENG	1180
10 m Air Rifle	**– Individual**	1	G. Lorion	CAN	583
		2	C. Hector	ENG	578
		3	M.Klepp	CAN	577
	– Pairs	1	M. Klepp/G. Lorion	CAN	1163
		2	C. Hector/R. Smith	ENG	1155
		3	S. Dutta/S. Bhagirath	IND	1148
50 m Free Pistol	**– Individual**	1	P. Adams	AUS	554
		2	B. Sandstrom	AUS	549
		3	G. U	HKG	549
	– Pairs	1	P. Adams/B. Sandstrom	AUS	1106
		2	B. Read/G. Yelavich	NZL	1084
		3	A. Rahman/A. Sattar	BAN	1078
25 m Centre Fire Pistol	**– Individual**	1	A. Pandit	IND	583
		2	S. Marwah	IND	577
		3	B. Quick	AUS	576
	– Pairs	1	P. Adams/B. Quick	AUS	1155
		2	B. O'Neale/G. Yelavich	NZL	1144
		3	A. Pandit/S. Marwah	IND	1142
25 m Rapid Fire Pistol	**– Individual**	1	A. Breton	GUE	583
		2	P. Murray	AUS	582
		3	M. Jay	WAL	579
	– Pairs	1	B. Favell/P. Murray	AUS	1153
		2	M. Howkins/S. Willis	CAN	1138
		3	B. Girling/J. Rolfe	ENG	1133
10 m Air Pistol	**– Individual**	1	B. Sandstrom	AUS	580
		2	P. Adams	AUS	574
		3	D. Lowe	ENG	574
	– Pairs	1	A. Rahman/A. Sattar	BAN	1138
		2	P. Adams/B. Sandstrom	AUS	1138
		3	J. Lawton/G. Yelavich	NZL	1137
10 m Running Target	**– Individual**	1	C. Robertson	AUS	539
		2	J. Maddison	ENG	539
		3	A. Clarke	NZL	535

	– Pairs	1	P. Carmine/A. Clarke	NZL	1091
		2	M. Bedlington/D. Lee	CAN	1070
			Only four competed – no bronze medal awarded		
Shotgun Trench	– individual	1	J. Maxwell	AUS	184
		2	K. Gill	ENG	183
		3	I. Peel	ENG	179
	– Pairs	1	K. Gill/I. Peel	ENG	181
		2	C. Evans/J. Birkett-Evans	WAL	178
		3	R. Mark/J. Maxwell	AUS	178
Shotgun Skeet	– Individual	1	K. Harman	ENG	187
		2	G. Sakellis	CYP	187
		3	A. Austin	ENG	184
	– Pairs	1	J. Dunlop/I. Marsden	SCO	189
		2	A. Austin/K. Harman	ENG	185
		3	T. Dodds/J. Woolley	NZL	183

SWIMMING AND DIVING

Men

50 m Freestyle	1 A. Baildon	AUS	22.76
	2 A. Waddell	AUS	23.03
	3 M. Foster	ENG	23.16
100 m Freestyle	1 A. Baildon	AUS	49.80
	2 C. Fydler	AUS	50.49
	3 M. Fibbens	ENG	50.76
200 m Freestyle	1 M. Roberts	AUS	1:49.58
	2 I. Brown	AUS	1:49.60
	3 T. Stachewicz	AUS	1:49.98
400 m Freestyle	1 I. Brown	AUS	3:49.91
	2 G. Housman	AUS	3:53.90
	3 C. Bowie	CAN	3:54.04
1500 m Freestyle	1 G. Housman	AUS	14:55.25
	2 K. Perkins	AUS	14:58.08
	3 M. McKenzie	AUS	15:09.95
100 m Butterfly	1 A. Baildon	AUS	53.98
	2 M. Gery	CAN	54.42
	3 J. Cooper	AUS	54.47
200 m Butterfly	1 A. Mosse	NZL	1:57.33
	2 M. Roberts	AUS	1:59.95
	3 J. Kelly	CAN	2:00.37
100 m Backstroke	1 M. Tewksbury	CAN	56.07
	2 G. Anderson	CAN	56.84
	3 P. Kingsman	NZL	57.07
200 m Backstroke	1 G. Anderson	CAN	2:01.69
	2 P. Kingsman	NZL	2:01.86
	3 K. Draxinger	CAN	2:02.02
100 m Breaststroke	1 A. Moorhouse	ENG	1:01.49
	2 J. Parrack	ENG	1:03.15
	3 N. Gillingham	ENG	1:03.16

200 m Breaststroke	1	J. Cleveland	CAN	2:14.96
	2	R. Lawson	AUS	2:15.68
	3	N. Gillingham	ENG	2:16.02
200 m Individual Medley	1	G. Anderson	CAN	2:02.94
	2	R. Bruce	AUS	2:03.78
	3	M. Roberts	AUS	2:04.03
400 m Individual Medley	1	R. Bruce	AUS	4:20.26
	2	R. Woodhouse	AUS	4:21.79
	3	J. Kelly	CAN	4:23.96
4 x 100 m Freestyle Relay	1	Australia T. Stachewicz/M. Renshaw/C. Fydler/ A. Baildon		3:20.05
	2	England M. Fibbens/N. Metcalfe/S. Dronsfield/ A. Shortman		3:22.61
	3	Canada S. Hebert/G. Van der Meulen/M. Gery/ D. Ward		3:22.79
4 x 200 m Freestyle Relay	1	Australia T. Stachewicz/G. Lord/I. Brown/ M. Roberts		7:21.17
	2	Canada E. Parenti/G. VanderMeulen/J. Kelly/ T. O'Hare		7:25.53
	3	New Zealand J. Steel/R. Tapper/A. Mosse/R. Anderson		7:30.10
4 x 100 m Medley Relay	1	Canada M. Tewksbury/J. Cleveland/T. Ponting/ M. Gery		3:42.45
	2	England G. Binfield/A. Moorhouse/M. Fibbens/ A. Shortman		3:43.88
	3	Australia T. Stachewicz/P. Rogers/A. Baildon/ C. Fydler		3:43.91

1 m Springboard	1	R. Butler	AUS	583.65 pts
	2	D. Bedard	CAN	547.35 pts
	3	S. McCormack	AUS	546.87 pts
3 m Springboard	1	C. Rogerson	AUS	594.84 pts
	2	M. Rourke	NZL	569.97 pts
	3	L. Flewwelling	CAN	569.79 pts
10 m Highboard	1	R. Morgan	WAL	639.84 pts
	2	D. Bedard	CAN	555.54 pts
	3	B. Fournier	CAN	544.50 pts
Women				
50 m Freestyle	1	L. Curry-Kenny	AUS	25.80
	2	K. Van Wirdum	AUS	26.00
	3	A. Nugent	CAN	26.26
100 m Freestyle	1	K. Van Wirdum	AUS	56.48
	2	L. Curry-Kenny	AUS	56.61
	3	P. Noall	CAN	56.67
200 m Freestyle	1	H.Lewis	AUS	2:00.79
	2	J. McMahon	AUS	2:02.43
	3	P. Noall	CAN	2:02.66
400 m Freestyle	1	H. Lewis	AUS	4:08.89
	2	J.McDonald	AUS	4:09.72
	3	J. Elford	AUS	4:10.74
800 m Freestyle	1	J. McDonald	AUS	8:30.27
	2	J. Elford	AUS	8:30.47
	3	S. Burge-Lopez	AUS	8:36.78
100 m Butterfly	1	L. Curry-Kenny	AUS	1:00.66
	2	S. O'Neill	AUS	1:01.03
	3	M. Scarborough	ENG	1:01.33
200 m Butterfly	1	H. Lewis	AUS	2:11.15
	2	H. Morris	AUS	2:11.76
	3	N. Redford	AUS	2:13.53
100 m Backstroke	1	N. Livingstone	AUS	1:02.46
	2	A. Simcic	NZL	1:02.55
	3	J. Griggs	AUS	1:03.69
200 m Backstroke	1	A. Simcic	NZL	2:12.32
	2	N. Livingstone	AUS	2:12.62
	3	K. Lord	AUS	2:14.53
100 m Breaststroke	1	K. Duggan	CAN	1:10.74
	2	G. Cloutier	CAN	1:11.22
	3	S. Brownsdon	ENG	1:11.54
200 m Breaststroke	1	N. Giguere	CAN	2:32.16
	2	G. Cloutier	CAN	2:32.91
	3	H. Morris	AUS	2:33.57
200 m Individual Medley	1	N. Sweetnam	CAN	2:15.61
	2	J. Clatworthy	AUS	2:17.10
	3	H. Lewis	AUS	2:17.13
400 m Individual Medley	1	H. Lewis	AUS	4:42.65
	2	J. Clatworthy	AUS	4:45.76
	3	D. Procter	AUS	4:47.38
4 x 100 m Freestyle Relay	1	Australia L. Curry-Kenny/S. O'Neill/A. Mullens/ K. Van Wirdum		3:46.85
	2	Canada A. Higson/E. Murphy/K. Paton/P. Noall		3:48.69
	3	England K. Pickering/S. Davies/Z. Long/J. Croft		3:51.26
4 x 200 m Freestyle Relay	1	Australia H. Lewis/J. McMahon/J. Elford/ J. McDonald		8:08.95
	2	England J. Coull/S. Davies/J. Lancaster/J. Croft		8:16.31
	3	New Zealand P. Langrell/M. Burke/L. Robinson/S. Hanley		8:22.60
4 x 100 m Medley Relay	1	Australia N. Livingstone/L. Hooiveld/L. Curry-Kenny/ K. Van Wirdum		4:10.87
	2	England J. Deakins/S. Brownsdon/M. Scarborough/ K. Pickering		4:11.88
	3	Canada L. Melien/K. Duggan/N. Sweetnam/ P. Noall		4:12.20

Event	Place	Name	Country	Result
Synchronised – Solo	1	S. Frechette	CAN	196.680 pts
	2	K. Shacklock	ENG	184.790 pts
		Only four competed – no bronze medal awarded		
Synchronised – Duet	1	K. Glen/C. Larsen	CAN	191.230 pts
	2	S. Northey/K. Shacklock	ENG	185.435 pts
		Only four competed – no bronze medal awarded		
1 m Springboard	1	M. De Piero	CAN	443.28 pts
	2	T. Cox	ZIM	423.93 pts
	3	P. Taylor	AUS	418.71 pts
3 m Springboard	1	J. Donnet	AUS	491.79 pts
	2	B. Bush	CAN	458.43 pts
	3	N. Cooney	NZL	457.29 pts
10 m Highboard	1	A. Dacyshyn	CAN	391.68 pts
	2	A. Adams	AUS	380.49 pts
	3	P. Gordon	CAN	380.43 pts

WEIGHTLIFTING

Class	Event	Place	Name	Country	Result
52 kg	**– Snatch**	1	C. Raghavan	IND	105.0
		2	V. Govindraj	IND	95.0
		3	G. Hayman	AUS	90.0
	– Clean & Jerk	1	C. Raghavan	IND	127.5
		2	G. Hayman	AUS	117.5
		3	V. Govindraj	IND	117.5
	– Total	1	C. Raghavan	IND	232.5
		2	V. Govindraj	IND	212.5
		3	G. Hayman	AUS	207.5
56 kg	**– Snatch**	1	R. Punnuswamy	IND	110.0
		2	A. Ogilvie	SCO	107.5
		3	D. Aumais	CAN	102.5
	– Clean & Jerk	1	R. Punnuswamy	IND	137.5
		2	G. Maruthachelam	IND	125.0
		3	A. Ogilvie	SCO	122.5
	– Total	1	R. Punnuswamy	IND	247.5
		2	A. Ogilvie	SCO	230.0
		3	G. Maruthachelam	IND	227.5
60 kg	**– Snatch**	1	M. Stephen	NAU	112.5
		2	P. Chandra Sharma	IND	112.5
		3	K. Sudalaimani	IND	110.0
	– Clean & Jerk	1	P. Chandra Sharma	IND	145.0
		2	M. Stephen	NAU	142.5
		3	K. Sudalaimani	IND	142.5
	–Total	1	P. Chandra Sharma	IND	257.5
		2	M. Stephen	NAU	255.0
		3	K. Sudalaimani	IND	252.5
67.5 kg	**– Snatch**	1	P. Sharma	IND	130.0
		2	L. Iquaibom	NGR	130.0
		3	M. Blair	AUS	127.5
	– Clean & Jerk	1	P. Sharma	IND	165.0
		2	L. Iquaibom	NGR	160.0
		3	M. Roach	WAL	155.0
	– Total	1	P. Sharma	IND	295.0
		2	L. Iquaibom	NGR	290.0
		3	M. Roach	WAL	280.0
75 kg	**– Snatch**	1	K. Mondal	IND	135.0
		2	K. Jones	WAL	135.0
		3	R. Laycock	AUS	132.5
	– Clean & Jerk	1	R. Laycock	AUS	177.5
		2	K. Mondal	IND	170.0
		3	D. Brown	AUS	167.5
	– Total	1	R. Laycock	AUS	310.0
		2	K. Mondal	IND	305.0
		3	B. Gagne	CAN	292.5
82.5 kg	**– Snatch**	1	D. Morgan	WAL	155.0
		2	M. Odusanya	NGR	152.5
		3	S. Leblanc	CAN	145.0
	– Clean & Jerk	1	D. Morgan	WAL	192.5
		2	S. Karupaswamy	IND	182.5
		3	M. Odusanya	NGR	180.0
	– Total	1	D. Morgan	WAL	347.5
		2	M. Odusanya	NGR	332.5
		3	A. Callard	ENG	317.5
90 kg	**– Snatch**	1	D. Dawkins	ENG	162.5
		2	K. Boxell	ENG	152.5
		3	H. Goodman	AUS	150.0
	– Clean & Jerk	1	D. Dawkins	ENG	195.0
		2	K. Boxell	ENG	192.5
		3	H. Goodman	AUS	190.0
	– Total	1	D. Dawkins	ENG	357.5
		2	K. Boxell	ENG	345.0
		3	H. Goodman	AUS	340.0
100 kg	**– Snatch**	1	A. Saxton	ENG	165.0
		2	P. May	ENG	145.0
		3	G. Greavette	CAN	140.0
	– Clean & Jerk	1	A. Saxton	ENG	197.5
		2	P. May	ENG	175.0
		3	G. Greavette	CAN	175.0
	– Total	1	A. Saxton	ENG	362.5
		2	P. May	ENG	320.0
		3	G. Greavette	CAN	315.0
110 kg	**– Snatch**	1	M. Thomas	ENG	160.0
		2	J. Roberts	AUS	152.5
		3	S. Wilson	WAL	152.5
	– Clean & Jerk	1	M. Thomas	ENG	197.5
		2	J. Roberts	AUS	192.5
		3	A. Arnold	WAL	187.5
	– Total	1	M. Thomas	ENG	357.5
		2	J. Roberts	AUS	345.0
		3	A. Arnold	WAL	335.0
over 110 kg	**– Snatch**	1	A. Davies	WAL	180.0
		2	A. Ojadi	NGR	177.5
		3	S. Kettner	AUS	172.5
	– Clean & Jerk	1	A. Davies	WAL	222.5
		2	A. Ojadi	NGR	222.5
		3	S. Kettner	AUS	205.0
	– Total	1	A. Davies	WAL	402.5
		2	A. Ojadi	NGR	400.0
		3	S. Kettner	AUS	377.5

TRIATHLON (Exhibition Sport)

Event	Place	Name	Country	Time
Men	1	R. Wells	NZL	1:52:01
	2	B. Beven	AUS	1:53:30
	3	G. Welch	AUS	1:53:30
Women	1	E. Baker	NZL	2:05:07
	2	C. Montgomery	CAN	2:05:45
	3	E. Christie	NZL	2:06:16

UK FACTFILE

BANKING AND INSURANCE

Historically located in the 'square mile' in the City of London, and now extending beyond it, is the United Kingdom's financial industry, one of the major financial centres of the world. The City (the various financial institutions located in and around the square mile) contains the greatest concentration of banks in the world (responsible for approximately one-quarter of total international bank lending); the world's biggest insurance market (accounting for approximately one-fifth of the international market); one of the world's largest stock exchanges and the principal centre for transactions in a large number of commodities. In 1987 the United Kingdom's financial industries accounted for 12.2% of UK total output, a sharp rise over the past decade, while in 1988 it accounted for 4% of total employment and had net identified overseas earnings amounting to £7,350 million.

Developments in the British financial industry since 1960

In the 1960s and 1970s the rate of international movements of capital increased and London, responding to this new market, became the international centre for activities such as bank lending and foreign-exchange trading, particularly in the Eurocurrency markets. In the 1980s, the increase in international competition, particularly in financial services, combined with developments in technology, encouraged rapid growth in the international securities market in which London now plays a leading role. The UK financial industry has also developed an important place in the Eurobond market in which it deals in a variety of currencies. These changes in the UK financial industry have, in part, been responsible for the reorganization of the International Stock Exchange, which has recently changed its membership rules and which, in turn, has had the effect of encouraging financial institutions in the City to form new alliances with one another. The government has also had to respond to these changes within the industry and, in the late 1980s, introduced three pieces of legislation – the Financial Services Act 1986, the Building Societies Act 1986, and the Banking Act 1987 – which, while encouraging growth and competition, provide safeguards for the new, investing public. Under the Financial Services Act, investment businesses (except wholesale money-market instruments) must be authorized – usually by becoming members of SROs (self-regulating organizations), recognized by the SIB (Securities and Investment Board) – and obey rules of conduct set down in legislation. All three Acts promote improvements in co-operation between the supervisory bodies of the various sectors of the financial industry (the Bank of England, the Building Societies Commission, the Department of Trade and Industry, the Securities and Investment Board and the SROs).

BANKING

The Bank of England

The Bank of England was first established in 1694, but was not nationalized until the implementation of the Bank of England Act 1946. The main responsibilities of the Bank are: to act as banker to the government and thereby arrange government borrowing; to execute monetary policy; to act as the note-issuing authority; and to exercise supervision over and provide banking facilities for the British banking system.

In England and Wales, the Bank of England has exclusive responsibility for issuing notes – with responsibility for the issuing of coins lying with the Royal Mint. These notes are no longer backed by gold, as once they were, but by government and other securities. In Scotland and Northern Ireland, however, the respective national banks have some limited ability to issue their own notes, although this occurs within strict limits and all notes issued must be fully covered by holdings of Bank of England notes.

The Bank of England also manages the Exchange Equalization Account (EEA), which holds Britain's official reserves of Gold, Foreign Exchange, Special Drawing Rights (SDRs) and European Currency Units (ECUs). These resources enable the Bank, when sometimes necessary, to check excessive fluctuations in the value of sterling by intervening in Foreign Exchange markets.

The Bank of England is also empowered under the Banking Act 1987 to act as the authorizing body for deposit-taking institutions; the Banking Act also increased the powers of the Bank of England to modify the rules governing the conduct of banking institutions and created a new supervisory board (the Board of Banking Supervision).

Deposit-taking institutions

These institutions can be broadly divided into two categories: those authorized and supervised by the Bank of England under the Banking Act 1987; and those authorized and supervised by the Building Societies Commission under the Building Societies Act 1986. In February 1990, there were 548 institutions authorized under the Banking Act 1987.

The Retail banks

Retail banks are primarily for personal customers and small businesses. In February 1990 there were 548 such authorized institutions in the United Kingdom. The major retail banks have large numbers of branches throughout the UK and provide services such as current accounts, loan facilities, cash withdrawal facilities and various systems for transferring funds which increasingly feature 'plastic-card technology'. Major retail banks in England and Wales include National Westminster, Midland, Lloyds, Barclays and the TSB Group; in Scotland, the Bank of Scotland and the Royal Bank of Scotland (see table on Branch Networks). These banks as well as the Standard Chartered Bank make up the Committee of London and Scottish Bankers, a liaison organization, representing members to the public, government and to each other.

In Northern Ireland, the total number of branches of retail banks is 334: Northern Bank, owned by the National Australian Bank (105), Ulster Bank, a subsidiary of National Westminster (85, plus 9 sub-branches), TSB Northern Ireland (54), the Bank of Ireland (43) and Allied Irish Bank (AIB) (38).

The Clearing System

The British inter-bank clearing systems are based in

Comparative Statistics Branch Networks in Great Britain

End-December	*1979*	*1981*	*1983*	*1985*	*1987*	*1989*
CLSB MEMBER BANKS						
Bank of Scotland	578	575	559	551	545	527
Barclays	3,012	2,986	2,912	2,874	2,767	2,645
Lloyds	2,317	2,292	2,276	2,229	2,162	2,184
Midland	2,464	2,454	2,345	2,311	2,127	2,042
National Westminster	3,239	3,216	3,226	3,172	3,101	2,997
The Royal Bank of Scotland[a]	915	903	894	864	835	842
Standard Chartered				23	25	14
TSB[b]	1,657	1,657	1,604	1,591	1,574	1,538
Abbey National[c]	553	635	676	674	677	678
Clydesdale	375	379	381	370	355	356
Co-operative Bank[d]	64	71	75	79	92	109
Girobank[e]	22,793	22,475	22,301	21,663	21,211	21,030
Yorkshire Bank	196	205	215	230	245	251
Building Societies[cf]	5,147	6,162	6,643	6,926	6,962	—

Notes
(a) Includes figures for Williams & Glyn's.
(b) Prior to 1982 the figures cover the 16 Regional TSB's. From 1982 onwards the figure covers TSB England & Wales, TSB Scotland and TSB Northern Ireland.
(c) Abbey National figures are also included in those shown for Building Societies up to and including 1988.
(d) Excludes some 4,000 in-store 'Handy Banks'.
(e) Number of Post Offices.
(f) Total number of offices (including one-office societies).

Source: *Abstract of Banking Statistics*, Committee of London and Scottish Bankers (CLSB).

London and administered by three separate companies (BACS Ltd, Cheque and Credit Clearing Co. Ltd, and CHAPS and Town Clearing Co Ltd), operating under the umbrella of the Association for Payment Clearing Services (APACS), established by the major banks in 1985 to manage the payment clearing systems and oversee money transmission in the UK. APACS also oversees the Currency Clearings in London and the Cheque Card and UK Uniform Eurocheque Schemes. Membership of APACS and the clearing companies is open to any bank or financial institution that meets a range of objective entry criteria.

Services
All the major retail banks have substantial networks of automatic teller machines and cash dispensers. In 1989, there were approximately 11,300 cash dispensers in Britain. Many banks also now offer home-banking services to their customers who can obtain account information and transfer funds by telephone; First Direct, a subsidiary of Midland now offers complete banking services over the telephone. Banks are also increasingly now open on Saturdays, enabling them to compete with building societies and allowing customers better access to banking facilities.

Cheque guarantee cards
Cheque guarantee cards entitle holders to reciprocal encashment facilities, and guarantee transactions with retailers (usually £50 per day). Another type of cheque card increasingly in use is the Eurocheque card. This card available from all major high-street banks allows the user to obtain cash or make payments anywhere in Britain and most of Europe.

Credit cards
Credit cards are an increasingly popular means of payment, the first of which, Barclaycard, began in 1966. The two main credit systems are Visa and Mastercard, which includes Access. Both organizations have approximately 320,000 retail outlets. In 1988 there were 15.3 million Visa card holders in the UK and 12.2 million Access holders; these figures represent an increase of 17% for Visa and 7% for Access since 1987. The increase in the use of credit cards is seen as a major contributor to the increase in the amount of consumer debt in recent years.

Debit cards
These cards allow payment to be deducted directly from the account of the card holder. The three most popular types of debit card are Switch (which is run jointly by Midland, National Westminster and the Royal Bank of Scotland) Barclay's Connect Card and Lloyd's Visa Payment Card.

Merchant and overseas banks
Although traditionally associated with accepting/guaranteeing commercial bills, merchant banks today have a diverse range of activities and important roles in international finance. These roles include managing investment holdings, and offering financial services to British industrial companies.

In April 1988 there were 370 overseas banks in Britain; in February 1989 this figure had dropped to 360. Of this figure, 46 were from the United States and 29 from Japan.

Discount houses
Discount houses are institutions peculiar to the City of London which developed there in the nineteenth century as bill brokers for industrialists, but which now act as intermediaries between the Bank of England and the rest of the banking sector. They do this by helping to promote an orderly flow of short-term funds between the government and the banks, enabling the Bank of England to keep short term interests within a certain band.

National Savings Bank

The National Savings Bank is run by the Department of Savings which is based in Glasgow. The bank provides its customers with services and provides facilities for depositing and withdrawing money at post-office counters throughout the country. At July 1990 the National Savings Bank reported that there were approximately 15,752,683 ordinary accounts with deposits amounting to £1,335,379,155 (where interest is earned at 5% per year, as long as the amount deposited is £500 or more, or 2.5% per year for accounts of less than £500 or on accounts opened and closed during the same year), and 4,734,695 investment accounts with deposits of £735,369,793. The 1990 Budget announced an increase of 1% on the interest rate on National Savings investment accounts from 11.75% to 12.75% on 3 April 1990 and on income bonds from 12.5% to 13.5% on 4 May 1990.

Building societies

At the beginning of 1990 there were 126 registered building societies, with assets totalling £168,000 million of which the three largest (Nationwide Anglia, Halifax and Woolwich) account for nearly 50%. Building societies are traditionally associated with the provision of long-term loans, in particular loans for house purchasing. In 1989, £45,000 million was advanced in new mortgages. However, the Building Societies Act 1986 has enabled building societies to diversify the number of services they can offer and allowed them to compete with other financial institutions. A variety of savings schemes and current-account facilities are now on offer including cheque books and automated-teller machines of which there are over 2500.

Since January 1990 building societies have been able to use a maximum of 17.5% of their total assets for purposes other than loans on mortgages, of which 7.5% can be used for the purposes of unsecured loans. These figures are expected to increase to 25% and 15% in 1993. The actual figures are much lower than these and around 98% of all building-society loans are still secured on housing.

The Building Societies Act 1986 established the Building Societies Commission as the supervisory body of the societies and enabled building societies, with the approval of their members, to become public limited companies (these companies thereby become an authorized institution under the Banking Act 1987). So far only Abbey National has become a public limited company.

In the 1990 Budget John Major announced the abolition of the composite rate of tax (1990/91 – 22%) on bank- and building-society interest from 1991/92. Non-taxpayers could not reclaim this tax. In future, non-taxpayers will be able to obtain their interest gross, while interest paid to taxpayers will be taxed at the full basic rate, currently 25%.

Savings Account Holding: by type of account

Percentage of Adults Holding:	*1981*	*1986*	*1987*
Building Society Account	36	51	53
Bank Account Earning Interest	23 (combined with Post Office)	23	22
Post Office Savings Account		10	10
Other Savings Account or Investments	5	9	15

INVESTING INSTITUTIONS

These are institutions which collect savings and invest them in securities and assets, in particular: insurance companies, pension funds, unit and investment trusts.

Insurance market

The London insurance market is responsible for 20% of international general insurance and is the world's leading insurance market. The services provided by the insurance market fall broadly into two categories: general and long-term life assurance. Insurance companies in the United Kingdom come under the Insurance Companies Act 1982 and, as a result of the Act, are supervised by the Department of Trade and Industry, with the Securities and Investments Board responsible for regulating the marketing of life and long-term insurance. At the end of 1989 there were 832 registered insurance businesses in the United Kingdom, with total invested funds of £334,657 million; the total UK premium income for long-term and general insurance in 1989 was £43,864 million. Some 440 of these companies belong to the Association of British Insurers and account for 90% of the British insurance business.

Investment of Funds

		Long-term Business		General Business	
		1988 £m	*1989 £m*	*1988 £m*	*1989 £m*
1.	Index-Linked British Government Securities	3,607	4,220	540	134
2.	British Government Authority Securities (excluding those in line 1)	30,002	29,086	5,642	5,665
3.	Other Government, Provincial and Municipal Stocks	6,494	6,706	7,384	7,043
4.	Debentures, Loan Stocks, Preference and Guaranteed Stocks and Shares	15,473	22,913	5,630	8,753
5.	Ordinary Stocks and Shares	102,456	145,226	11,921	16,184
6.	Mortgages	10,866	13,738	1,688	1,988
7.	Real Property and Ground Rents	35,983	42,585	3,533	4,324
8.	Other Invested Assets	11,207	13,824	6,391	7,219
9.	'Net Current Assets'	95	144	4,228	5,904
10.	Total Net Assets	216,093	277,442	46,957	57,214
11.	GROSS INCOME FOR YEAR ON INVESTMENT HOLDINGS (gross of tax and interest paid)	12,418	15,415	3,139	3,893
12.	INTEREST PAYABLE IN YEAR	312	447	221	358

Source: Association of British Insurers, 1990

Composition of credit in the United Kingdom

	1983	*1984*	*1985*	*1986*	*1987*	*1988*
Bank credit-card lending	13.7	14.9	15.8	17.1	16.5	15.6
Other lending from the monetary sector	64.6	63.2	62.2	61.4	62.3	64.7
Non-monetary sector credit companies	9.8	9.9	10.8	11.7	11.8	10.8
Insurance companies	1.9	3.1	2.9	2.7	2.3	2.2
Retailers	10.0	9.0	8.4	7.2	7.1	6.7
Amount of Credit outstanding at the end of year (= 100%) (£ billion)	18.9	22.3	26.1	30.5	36.6	42.8

Building Society Rates of Interest

Year	*Date of Recommendation/ Advice/Change*	*New Mortgages* 1 *Effective Date*	2 *Rate* %	*Ordinary Shares* 3 *Effective Date*	4 *Rate* %	5 *Gross Equivalent* %
1977	15th April	15.4.77	11.25	1.5.77	7.00	10.61
	10th June	10.6.77	10.50	1.7.77	6.70	10.15
	23rd September	23.9.77	9.50	1.11.77	6.00	9.09
1978	13th January	13.1.78	8.50	1.2.78	5.50	8.33
	9th June	9.6.78	9.75	1.7.78	6.70	10.00
	10th November	10.11.78	11.75	1.12.78	8.00	11.94
1979	13th July	1.1.80	12.50	1.8.79	8.75	12.50
	22nd November	22.11.79	15.00	1.12.79	10.50	15.00
1980	12th December	12.12.80	14.00	1.1.81	9.25	13.21
1981	13th March	13.3.81	13.00	1.4.81	8.50	12.14
	9th October	9.10.81	15.00	1.11.81	9.75	13.93
1982	12th March	12.3.82	13.50	1.4.82	8.75	12.50
	5th August	5.8.82	12.00	1.9.82	7.75	11.07
	12th November	12.11.82	10.00	1.12.82	6.25	8.93
1983	22nd June	22.6.83	11.25	1.7.83	7.25	10.36
1984	16th March	16.3.84	10.25	1.4.84	6.25	8.93
	13th July	13.7.84	12.50	1.8.84	7.75	11.07
	November		11.75–12.00		6.75	9.64
1985	January		12.75–13.00		7.50	10.70
	March		13.75–14.00		8.25	11.79
	August		12.75		7.00	10.00
1986	March		12.00		6.00	8.45
	May		11.00		5.25	7.39
	October		12.25–12.375		6.00	8.45
1987	March		11.25			
	June		10.50–11.25			
	August		11.25			
1988	December/January		10.00–10.30			
	April/May		9.50–9.80			
	July		11.50			
	September		12.75			
1989	January		13.50			
	November		14.50			
1990	February		15.40			

Notes:

1. The mortgage rates shown are gross and apply to annuity advances to owner-occupiers. The gross equivalent ordinary share rate shows the value of the (net) rate to a basic rate taxpayer.
2. From 1972 changes in recommended mortgage rates applied immediately for new loans. The rates on existing loans were normally changed on the first of the month following the month of the recommendation or as soon as practicable thereafter. In the case of an increase in rates, many mortgage deeds require between one and three months notice before a change can be implemented. The rate recommended on 13th July 1979 was unusual in that the date for implementation was deferred until 1st January 1980. In the event this recommendation was superseded by that made on 22nd November 1979 and thus the 12.50 per cent rate never became effective.
3. Between October 1983 and November 1984 the BSA's recommended rates were replaced by advised rates.
4. In November 1984 the previous advised rates were withdrawn. The rates charged and offered by the largest societies are shown from that date. Normally new share rates are applied from the first of the month following the month shown.
5. The ordinary share rate series has been discontinued from end-1986 as it no longer gives a useful guide to the rates paid by societies.

Source: *Housing Finance*, No. 6, May 1990.

Building Societies: Progress

Year	1 Number of Societies	2 Number of Branches	3 Number of Share-holders 000's	4 Number of Depositors 000's	5 Number of Borrowers 000's	Number of Staff 6 Full-time	7 Part-time	8 Share Balances £m	9 Deposit Loan Balances £m	10 Mortgage Balances £m	11 Total Assets £m	Advances during year 12 Number 000's	13 Amount £m
1900	2,286		585							46	60		9
1910	1,723		626							60	76		9
1920	1,271		748					64	19	69	87		25
1930	1,026		1,449	428	720			303	45	316	371	159	89
1940	952		2,088	771	1,503			552	142	678	756	43	21
1950	819		2,256	654	1,508			962	205	1,060	1,256	302	270
1960	726		3,910	571	2,349			2,721	222	2,647	3,166	387	560
1970	481	2,016	10,265	618	3,655	24,116	1,050	9,788	382	8,752	10,819	624	1,954
1980	273	5,684	30,636	915	5,383	46,418	6,309	48,915	1,762	42,437	53,793	936	9,503
1981	253	6,162	33,388	995	5,490	47,716	7,661	55,463	2,577	48,875	61,815	1,096	12,005
1982	227	6,480	36,607	1,094	5,645	49,102	9,047	64,968	3,532	56,696	73,033	1,322	15,036
1983	206	6,643	37,711	1,200	5,928	50,761	10,431	75,197	5,601	67,474	85,869	1,511	19,347
1984	190	6,816	39,380	1,550	6,314	51,660	11,454	88,087	8,426	81,882	102,689	1,658	23,771
1985	167	6,926	39,996	2,149	6,657	53,172	12,519	102,332	10,752	96,765	120,763	1,682	26,531
1986	151	6,954	40,559	2,850	7,023	55,830	13,436	115,538	16,862	115,669	140,603	2,062	35,913
1987	138	6,962	41,966	3,648	7,182	59,315	14,979	129,954	20,752	130,870	160,097	1,889	36,034
1988	131	6,915	43,813	4,306	7,369	63,917	16,231	149,791	26,529	153,015	188,844	2,002	46,929

Notes:

1. The figures are based on annual returns provided by all building societies in Great Britain. From 1986 figures include societies based in Northern Ireland.
2. The figures are the aggregation of figures for societies' financial years ending between 1st February in the year in question and 31st January of the following year. (Prior to 1930 the figures are the aggregation of figures for societies' financial years ending in the calendar year in question.) Because not all societies have financial years ending on 31st December the figures in Table 1 are not strictly compatible with figures in other tables which relate to calendar years.
3. Before 1930 borrowers who were not also shareholders were included in the number of shareholders.
4. The number of advances includes further advances and therefore does not indicate the number of home-buyers.

Source: Annual reports of the Chief Registrar of Friendly Societies, annual reports of the Building Societies Commission, BSA (for 1988, as reproduced in *Housing Finance*, No. 6, May 1990).

CHARITIES

The Charities Act 1960 is the most recent of the many laws that have regulated the activities of charities; its most important points are that charities must be registered, must state their aims (and apply their funds only to those aims) and publish annual accounts. The Charity Commission had 164,534 charities on its register at the end of 1988. The amount given to charity in 1989 has been estimated at £15,000 million, or £264 for every person in the country (this figure comes from the Charities Aid Foundation, which has also provided the data on individual charities given below).

Top 20 fund-raising charities, as ranked by voluntary income (donations and bequests)

	£ million	*Administration expenditure as % of total expenditure*
1. Oxfam	41.0	3.5
2. National Trust	40.6	3.4
3. RNLI	37.7	5.3
4. Imperial Cancer Research Fund	32.0	1.7
5. Cancer Research Campaign	31.0	2.1
6. Salvation Army	26.1	5.9
7. Barnardos	25.3	3.2
8. Save the Children Fund	24.1	2.5
9. Guide Dogs for the Blind Assn	19.9	5.2
10. Spastics Society	18.5	2.2
11. RSPCA	16.9	8.6
12. NSPCC	16.7	3.8
13. British Heart Foundation	16.5	3.1
14. Charity Projects	16.3	1.8
15. Christian Aid	16.0	3.1
16. Help the Aged	15.3	1.3
17. British Red Cross Society	13.7	3.6
18. Marie Curie Memorial Foundation	13.7	1.5
19. RNIB	13.6	1.4
20. Action Aid	12.9	5.7

Top 20 charities, by total income (including income from investments and trading)

	£ million	*Administration expenditure as % of total expenditure*
1. National Trust	85.3	3.4
2. Salvation Army	70.6	5.9
3. Nuffield Nursing Homes Trust	69.8	7.2
4. Barnardos	59.0	3.2
5. Imperial Cancer Research Fund	57.3	1.7
6. Oxfam	52.3	3.5
7. Spastics Society	46.6	2.2
8. RNLI	42.2	5.3
9. British Red Cross Society	38.5	3.6
10. Save the Children Fund	36.0	2.5
11. Cancer Research Campaign	35.5	2.1
12. Leonard Cheshire Foundation	31.8	1.9
13. Royal Opera House Covent Garden	30.9	14.3
14. RNIB	30.6	1.4
15. National Children's Home	30.5	4.4
16. Guide Dogs for the Blind Assn	28.7	5.2
17. Christian Aid	22.5	3.1
18. RSPCA	21.7	8.6
19. NSPCC	20.3	3.8
20. Unicef	19.9	2.0

Top 20 charities, by net assets

	£ million
1. National Trust	204.0
2. Salvation Army	172.1
3. Imperial Cancer Research Fund	108.6
4. Guide Dogs for the Blind Assn	97.0
5. Barnardos	88.3
6. RNLI	64.6
7. Nuffield Nursing Homes Trust	62.0
8. St Dunstan's	58.4
9. RSPCA	51.9
10. Leonard Cheshire Foundation	45.6
11. Masonic Trust for Boys and Girls	44.4
12. Cancer Research Campaign	39.2
13. Royal Masonic Hospital	37.9
14. Royal Masonic Benevolent Instn	37.2
15. National Children's Home	36.4
16. Church of England Children's Society	31.7
17. Church Army	31.5
18. RAF Benevolent Fund	31.3
19. British Heart Foundation	31.1
20. British Red Cross Society	29.7

AGE CONCERN ENGLAND

Age Concern England's aim is to make life better for elderly people, mainly by providing services through a network of 1000 independent local groups manned by 180,000 volunteers, many of whom are pensioners themselves. Services vary from district to district, but they include home and hospital visits, help with maintaining homes and gardens and filling in complicated forms, blankets and food in cold spells, and transport for shopping, day trips and visits to the doctor or to Age Concern's own day centres and luncheon clubs. National headquarters distributes £7 million a year in grants, campaigns for the elderly, publishes highly successful information for the elderly, publishes highly successful information books and leaflets, and responds direct to the 100,000 people who get in touch every year, mainly about personal finance and benefits entitlements. There are separate Age Concerns for Scotland, Wales and Northern Ireland.

Income 1988 £10.6 million (28% voluntary, 63% central and local government grants)
Expenditure 1988 £9.6 million (91% charitable, 6% fund-raising, 3% administration)
Chairman John Bettinson
Bernard Sunley House, 60 Pitcairn Rd, Mitcham, Surrey CR4 3LL, tel. 081-640 5431

BARNARDOS

Founded as an orphanage for destitute children by Dr Thomas Barnardo in 1867, Barnardos today is a Christian-based welfare charity helping children – and their parents – cope with a wide range of problems, including mental and physical handicaps, neglect and sexual abuse, loneliness and homelessness, drugs, drink and crime, and emotional and domestic traumas. Working in partnership with parents, local authorities and 17,000 active volunteers, its 3600 staff provide day centres and residential homes, a fostering and adoption service, support for teenagers living on their own, and help for families caring for handicapped or disturbed children at home. Barnardos operates in Ireland, Australia and New Zealand as well as the UK. About 18,000 children and families in the UK benefit from its services each year.

Income 1988 £59 million (43% voluntary, 36% local and central government fees)
Expenditure 1988 £45 million (83% charitable, 14% fund-raising, 3% administration)
Chairman Tessa Baring
Tanners Lane, Barkingside, Essex IG6 1QG, tel. 081-550 8822

BRITISH HEART FOUNDATION

The British Heart Foundation was formed in 1961 by a group of doctors convinced that only systematic research could provide the clue to the origin of heart disease (still the biggest single cause of death in Britain). The Foundation's main role is to fund heart research in hospitals and universities: 11 research groups and 21 professors currently depend on it for financial support. Many more doctors and scientists – working on about 400 different projects – receive grants. The Foundation also buys life-saving and other cardiac equipment for hospitals, ambulances and isolated GPs' surgeries. In fulfilling its educational role, the Foundation regularly disseminates the latest information on heart disease to all GPs, and provides films, leaflets and information packs to help ordinary people care for their own hearts.

Income 1988 £19.7 million (84% voluntary)
Expenditure 1988 £15.7 million (83% charitable, 13% fund-raising, 3% administration)
Chairman Professor Sir Raymond Hoffenberg KBE, MD, PHD, FRCP.
102 Gloucester Place, London W1H 4DH, tel. 071-935 0185

CHRISTIAN AID

Christian Aid was set up as the aid and development arm of the British Council of Churches after World War II. It is supported by nearly all the Christian denominations in the UK and Ireland, but not the Roman Catholic Church. Originally it was concerned with the plight of refugees in Europe, but it has now expanded its work to include natural disasters and human-rights abuses. Its main underlying aim, however, is to 'strengthen the poor' by tackling the long-term causes of poverty in the poorer countries, mainly by funding local projects originated and run by local people. Current projects include fish-farming in Tanzania, primary health care in Bangladesh and rubber-tapping in the Amazon. Christian Aid's work is based on the teaching of the Bible, though recipients do not have to be Christians to qualify for help. Christian Aid employs 207 people, all in the UK.

Income 1988 £22.5 million (71% voluntary, including 33% raised during Christian Aid Week in May)
Expenditure £20.9 million (87% charitable, 10% fund-raising, 3% administration)
Chairman Sir Brian Young
PO Box 100, London SE1 7RT, tel. 071-620 4444

CRISIS

Formerly known as Crisis at Christmas, Crisis was set up in 1967 to help single homeless people (currently estimated to be about 200,000 in the UK). It operates throughout the year raising money, mainly by a series of major fund-raising events in London and the south east. About £20,000 is spent on its Open Christmas when, with the help of 800 volunteers working in shifts, it converts a 'borrowed' building into a temporary home for 1000 homeless people over the Christmas period, and provides hot meals, accommodation, 'new' clothes and medical care free of charge. The rest of Crisis's income is distributed each May in grants to projects for hostels, advice centres and rehabilitation homes throughout the UK. Grants range in size from £100 to £20,000. To date, about 300 projects have been supported. Crisis is run almost entirely by volunteers and has only 2½ full-time staff.

Income 1988 £800,000 (95% voluntary)
Expenditure 1988 £700,000 (89% charitable, 4% fund-raising, 7% administration)
Chairman Freda Evans
212 Whitechapel Rd, London E1 1BJ, tel. 071-377 0489

THE DOGS' HOME BATTERSEA

The Dogs' Home Battersea is a refuge for stray and unwanted dogs (and several hundred cats) within a London catchment area bounded by the M25. Each year it takes in about 23,000 dogs, 2000 of them around Christmas. Two-thirds of the dogs are collected from London's police stations by the Home's five animal ambulances, in a daily round beginning at 6 a.m. In 1988 over 9000 dogs were rehomed or sold (for an average price of £21.65), 3000 were reclaimed by their rightful owners, and 9500 were put down. As well as its main centre in Battersea, South London, the Home also has four kennels in a quieter location at Old Windsor. Two of these are run commercially and earn enough to support the other two as a convalescent and maternity home, and a home for dogs belonging to prisoners on remand and to long-stay hospital patients. Since its foundation in 1860, the Home has cared for over 2½ million dogs.

Income 1988 £2.9 million (48% legacies, 35% sales, claim fees and police contracts)
Expenditure 1988 £1.2 million (80% charitable, 0.5% fund-raising, 19.5% administration)
Chairman Thomas Field-Fisher
4 Battersea Park Rd, London SW8 4AA, tel. 071-622 3626

GUIDE DOGS FOR THE BLIND ASSOCIATION

Training dogs as guides for blind people started in Germany after World War I. The British Guide Dogs Association, launched in 1934, is now the world's leading authority in the field, with a staff of 650. About 4000 blind people use dogs supplied by the Association (for the nominal sum of 50p). Over half the dogs are labrador/golden retriever crosses. The rest are mainly labradors, with a few pure golden retrievers and German shepherds. It takes about two years to train a guide dog properly and about a month to train a guide dog owner (on a residential course at one of the Association's seven training centres). 80% of puppies, all specially bred by the Association, go on to qualify as guide dogs. Just feeding the 6000-plus dogs maintained by the Association costs over £1 million a year (guide dog users receive a feeding allowance from the Association).

Income 1988 £28.7 million (69% voluntary, including 45% from legacies)
Expenditure 1988 £11.9 million (76% charitable, 19% fund-raising, 5% administration)
Chairman Dennis Armstrong
Alexandra House, Park St, Windsor, Berks SL4 1JR, tel. 0753 855711

HELP THE AGED

Founded in 1961, Help the Aged's object is to improve the quality of life for elderly people in need in the UK and overseas (where it is called HelpAge). Its main role is as a fund-raising and grant-making charity, supporting a wide range of local community projects. In the UK it gives money to day centres and luncheon clubs, day hospitals and hospices, rehabilitation units and residential homes. It also provides directly individual emergency alarms (6000 to date) and minibuses (650 to date) and manages 500 dwellings for the elderly, including sheltered homes. Overseas, HelpAge spends about a quarter of the charity's money in over 50 developing countries on health promotion, ophthalmic work, urban relief, income generation, refugee and disaster relief, and training schemes for age-care workers. The charity has over 700 paid staff.

Income 1988 £18.7 million (82% voluntary)
Expenditure 1988 £18.6 million (75% charitable, 23% fund-raising, 1% administration)
Chairman of Trustees William Menzies-Wilson CBE
St James's Walk, London EC1R 0BE, tel. 071-253 0253

IMPERIAL CANCER RESEARCH FUND

Founded in 1902 under the auspices of the Royal Colleges of Physicians and Surgeons, the Imperial Cancer Research Fund carries out research into the causes, prevention, treatment and cure of cancer. Responsible for about one-third of all cancer research in the UK, 70% of its money goes on prevention and cure, and 30% on looking for preventable causes of cancer. It employs a staff of over 1000, 900 of whom are doctors, scientists and technicians, many from overseas. Over 60 research teams work in the Fund's own laboratories in its London headquarters and at Clare Hall in Hertfordshire. Other researchers are based in laboratories and units in major teaching hospitals and universities around the country, bringing the benefits of research to cancer patients with minimum delay. The Fund also aims to educate the public about the dangers of cancer, and how to avoid it.

Income 1988 £57.3 million (56% voluntary, including 41% from legacies)
Expenditure 1988 £44.6 million (92% charitable, 6% fund-raising, 2% administration)
Chairman Sir David Innes Williams, MD, MCHIR, FRCS
PO Box 123, Lincoln's Inn Fields, London WC2A 3PX, tel. 071-242 0200

LEONARD CHESHIRE FOUNDATION

Founded in 1948 by Group Captain Leonard Cheshire VC, the Leonard Cheshire Foundation is best known for its famous Cheshire Homes. Altogether there are 79 in the UK, eight of them being for mentally handicapped adults and children, and four halfway houses for ex-psychiatric patients moving from institutional care to life in the community. The rest are for the disabled and sick. All homes make a point of encouraging residents to live as independently as possible and to participate as much as they can in the running of their home in conjunction with the local voluntary committee ultimately responsible for it. The Foundation also runs a growing network of Family Support Services (currently 27 in England) which look after disabled people in their own homes. Those who can, contribute financially towards the care they receive from the Foundation, with the balance coming from the DSS and fund-raising. Outside the UK, the Foundation is affiliated to a further 177 homes in 48 countries, including China.

Income 1988 £31.8 million (22% voluntary, 74% local and central government fees)
Expenditure 1988 £27.5 million (97.8% charitable, 0.3% fund-raising, 1.9% administration)
Chairman Peter Rowley
Leonard Cheshire House, 26–9 Maunsel St, London SW1P 2QN, tel. 071-828 1822

MENCAP (ROYAL SOCIETY FOR MENTALLY HANDICAPPED CHILDREN AND ADULTS)

Mencap provides special care and protection for Britain's mentally handicapped community (about 1–1½ million people), plus support and help for parents and families. It also tries to educate the public about mental problems and to secure fair provision from the public sector for the mentally handicapped. The society runs three residential homes for children and young people, a growing number of family-sized houses (currently over 200) for small groups of handicapped adults, three training centres preparing young people for life and work in the outside world, a special employment service and, through its network of 550 independent local societies, welfare visitors and numerous other personnel services. Over 700 Gateway clubs arrange leisure activities. Founded in 1946, Mencap has nearly 800 staff and 55,000 active members.

Income 1987 £9.6 million (21% voluntary, 53% local and central government grants)
Expenditure 1987 £9 million (89% charitable, 3% fund-raising, 8% administration)
Chairman Sir Brian Rix CBE, DL
123 Golden Lane, London EC1Y 0RT, tel. 071-253 9433

NATIONAL CHILDBIRTH TRUST

The NCT is the UK's foremost charity in the field of education for pregnancy, birth and early parenthood. In 1988 300,000 parents (men as well as women) attended the informal eight-session courses held by its 500 antenatal teachers. After birth, many women received friendly help and encouragement, particularly with breastfeeding. Through its 500 breastfeeding counsellors, the Trust promotes breastfeeding as the natural way to feed babies, but helps women who prefer bottle feeding just the same. The NCT also provides birth as opposed to sex education in schools, right down to primary level, and passes on its specialist knowledge and experience to nurses and doctors. All NCT's volunteer counsellors are thoroughly trained, although they are not normally medically qualified. Formed over 30 years ago, the Trust now has 348 local organizations and nearly 36,000 members.

Income 1988 £900,000 (28% voluntary)
Expenditure 1988 £500,000 (47% charitable, 3% fund-raising, 47% administration)
Chairman Janet Stephen
Alexandra House, Oldham Terrace, London W3 6NH, tel. 081-992 8637

NATIONAL SOCIETY FOR THE PREVENTION OF CRUELTY TO CHILDREN

The NSPCC was set up in 1884 by Congregational minister Benjamin Waugh and achieved its first success five years later with the passage of the Prevention of Cruelty to Children Act. Today the Society has over 60 highly trained Child Protection Teams spread across England, Wales and Northern Ireland, on call round the clock, seven days a week, to protect children from physical, sexual and emotional abuse and neglect. In 1987–8 it helped over 48,000 children, two-thirds of them aged under 10. Every call it gets (55% come from the public; 1% from children in danger) is immediately investigated and then dealt with either by the Society itself or by referral to social services or the police. The Society also tries to prevent abuse by extensive public information and education campaigns. The NSPCC Young League encourages fund-raising among young people and has 45,000-plus members.

Income 1988 £20.3 million (82% voluntary, including 64% from legacies)
Expenditure 1988 £22.7 million (86% charitable, 10% fund-raising, 4% administration)
Chairman Michael Moore
67 Saffron Hill, London EC1N 8RS, tel. 071-242 1626 (Child Protection Line in London: 071-404 4447)

THE NATIONAL TRUST FOR PLACES OF HISTORIC INTEREST AND NATURAL BEAUTY

Following a successful flight to maintain public access in the Lake District, the National Trust was set up in 1895 by Canon Rawnsley and others to preserve beautiful countryside and historically important places in England, Wales and Northern Ireland (a separate National Trust for Scotland was formed in 1931). After a century of gifts and purchases, the Trust now protects numerous sites, including 88 great country houses, large areas of Snowdonia, the Lake and Peak Districts, and one in six miles of coastline. In all, it owns over half a million acres of land, making it the largest private land-owner in the country. Most of its property is inalienable, meaning it can never be sold. Trust policy is decided by a 52-member council, while day-to-day work is carried out by 2400 staff. Over 9 million people buy tickets to visit the properties each year, and nearly 1.7 million people are members of the Trust.

Income 1988 £85.3 million (48% voluntary, including subscriptions, 24% rent and investments)
Expenditure 1988 £82.5 million (88% charitable, 9% fund-raising, 3% administration)
Chairman Dame Jennifer Jenkins
36 Queen Anne's Gate, London SW1H 9AS, tel. 071-222 9251

OXFAM

Famine in Greece in 1942 prompted the foundation of the Oxford Committee on Famine Relief – since 1965 Oxfam. Although Oxfam still devotes about one-third of its funds to disaster relief, its main priority is long-term overseas development. Oxfam is currently channelling funds, equipment and expertise to 2300 projects in 71 countries, mainly in the fields of health (16% of aid), agriculture (15%) and social development (including education and income generation – 33%). The philosophy behind its work is training local people to help themselves. In the UK, Oxfam concentrates on education and fund-raising. Its textile and aluminium recycling plant makes a profit for the charity, but its network of over 800 volunteer-run shops, with a turnover of £30 million, is its biggest donor. Oxfam employs about 1500 people, one-third overseas.

Income 1988 £52.3 million (78% voluntary, including 34% from fund-raising)
Expenditure 1988 £48.5 million (83% charitable, 13% fund-raising, 3.5% administration)
Chairman Mary Cherry
274 Banbury Rd, Oxford OX2 7DZ, tel. 0865 56777

ROYAL BRITISH LEGION

Formed in 1921 by the amalgamation of the four national ex-servicemen's organizations set up after World War I, the Royal British Legion offers practical help to ex-service men and women, their widows and dependants. About one-third of the entire UK population is entitled to call upon it for assistance. In practice 80,000 do so annually. Most get help through the national network of 3300 local welfare committees (staffed by 20,000-plus volunteers). Others receive care and treatment in five residential homes, three rest and convalescent homes and the Churchill Rehabilitation Centre. The Legion also provides work for 1500 people (including car-parking/security work and poppy-making) and is the country's largest employer of disabled people. Other services include a training school for London taxi drivers, War Graves Pilgrimages and help with war pension claims.

Income 1988 £15 million (68% voluntary, including 63% [9.3 million] from the poppy appeal)
Expenditure 1988 £13.4 million (84% charitable, 6% fund-raising, 10% administration)
Chairman David Knowles
48 Pall Mall, London SW1Y 5JY, tel. 071-930 8131

ROYAL NATIONAL INSTITUTE FOR THE BLIND

With nearly 2000 staff and 10,000 active volunteers, the RNIB is the world's largest organization for the visually handicapped. Its overall aim is to improve the quality of life for Britain's 300,000 blind and partially sighted people. Founded in 1868 by Dr Rhodes Armitage, a wealthy surgeon who became blind, the Institute runs special schools, colleges, employment rehabilitation centres, residential homes, seaside hotels and a London hostel. It transfers books, magazines, music, exam papers and even bank statements to tape, braille or Moon, and makes equipment like white sticks, talking thermometers and specially adapted games like Scrabble. The RNIB also provides advice and information for the visually handicapped, their parents, teachers and employers, funds research into the prevention of blindness, and campaigns on benefits, welfare and health issues.

Income 1988 £30.6 million (44% voluntary, 22% local and central government fees)
Expenditure 1988 £33.8 million (91% charitable, 8% fund-raising, 1% administration)
Chairman Duncan Watson CBE
224 Great Portland St, London W1N 6AA, tel. 071-388 1266

ROYAL NATIONAL LIFEBOAT INSTITUTION

The RNLI's sole purpose is to save lives at sea. Since its foundation in 1824 it has rescued over 118,000 people (at a human cost of 400 lifeboatmen). The Institution has 263 lifeboats (with a further 101 in reserve) berthed at 203 lifeboat stations round the coasts of Great Britain and Ireland. Boats are on call round the clock 365 days a year and operate up to 30 miles out to sea. 30% of launches take place in darkness. August is the busiest month of the year; December the quietest. All the lifeboat crews (some of which include women) are part-time volunteers. Station mechanics are usually full time and paid. There are 14 different types of lifeboat, ranging from the basic inflatable, costing £9000, to the most sophisticated self-righter, costing over £500,000. Current membership of the RNLI stands at over 135,000.

Lives saved in 1988 1343 (73% from pleasure craft)
Income 1988 £42.2 million (89% voluntary including 55% legacies)
Expenditure 1988 £29.1 million (81% charitable, 14% fund-raising, 5% administration)
Chairman Michael Vernon
West Quay Rd, Poole, Dorset BH15 1HZ, tel. 0202 671133

ROYAL SOCIETY FOR THE PREVENTION OF CRUELTY TO ANIMALS

Founded in 1824, the RSPCA is the world's largest animal welfare organization, with 209 volunteer-run local branches in England and Wales and nearly 800 staff. About 300 of these are uniformed inspectors – graduates of a special seven-month training course – whose job it is to monitor animal welfare and respond to complaints from the public about animal cruelty. In 1988, 80,000 complaints were investigated, resulting in over 1700 convictions, well over half involving cruelty to dogs (illegal dog-fighting is one of the Society's main worries). In addition, the Society treated 200,000 animals. New homes were found for 120,000 animals, but a similar number had to be put down (15,000 of them unwanted puppies and kittens). The Society also campaigns on behalf of animals and has special departments dealing with cruel farming methods, the use of animals in research and the ill-treatment of wild animals in, for example, circuses.

Income 1988 £21.7 million (78% voluntary, including 58% legacies)
Expenditure 1988 £14.4 million (86% charitable, 5% fund-raising, 9% administration)
Chairman Anelay Hart
Causeway, Horsham, W. Sussex RH12 1HG, tel. 0403 64181

ROYAL SOCIETY FOR THE PROTECTION OF BIRDS

The RSPB was founded in 1889 by a group of women opposed to the slaughter of birds to provide feathers for the fashion trade. They scored their first campaign success 32 years later when the importing of bird plumes was banned in 1921. Today the Society aims generally to protect (and where desirable add to) our natural heritage of wild birds. It does this mainly by conserving habitats, owning or managing 116 nature reserves covering 180,500 acres. The Society continues to campaign on behalf of birdlife (it played a leading part in getting a ban on DDT and other harmful pesticides) and through its local members' groups organizes events to raise public awareness of bird and wildlife (e.g. the RSPB Birdwatch and the Gardening for Wildlife Weekend in 1989). The Society has 600 staff and 570,000 members, including 110,000 in its junior section, the Young Ornithologists' Club.

Income 1988 £13.2 million (77% voluntary)
Expenditure 1988 £13.5 million (73% charitable, 16% fund-raising, 11% administration)
Chairman Adrian Darby
The Lodge, Sandy, Beds. SG19 2DL, tel. 0767 80551

THE SALVATION ARMY

Reflecting the intentions of its founder, London clergyman William Booth, who started the Army in 1865, the Salvation Army is both an evangelical church and a major welfare organization, today serving the poor and needy in 90 countries. In Britain it operates community service centres, inner city Goodwill centres, Eventide homes for 1000 elderly people, hostels for 5000 homeless people, alcohol detoxification and rehabilitation centres, bail units to keep accused people with no permanent address out of prison, and a prison chaplaincy service at over 100 penal centres. Tracking down missing persons is another of its tasks. Believing itself to be engaged in spiritual warfare, the Army uses quasi-military features such as ranks, uniforms, flags and bands. All Army officers are also ministers of religion and all Salvationists are teetotallers and non-smokers.

Income 1988 £70.6 million (37% voluntary, 28% local and central government grants)
Expenditure 1988 £46.6 million (87% charitable, 4% fund-raising, 6% administration)
General Gen. Eva Burrows
101 Queen Victoria St, London EC4P 4EP, tel. 071-236 5222

SAMARITANS

Founded in 1953 by City of London clergyman Chad Varah, the Samaritans provide a lifeline for the despairing and the suicidal. Anyone can ring them day or night throughout the year and be sure of a confidential talk with a sympathetic and caring listener. Special teams are mobilized at short notice to cope with major disasters such as Lockerbie and Hillsborough. About 2½ million calls are made on the Samaritans each year, 90% by phone, the rest in person or by letter. The organization has 22,000 trained volunteer befrienders who staff the phones at 183 local branches scattered across the UK and the Republic of Ireland. Each befriender donates on average 12 hours a month to Samaritans' work. The Samaritans' annual phone bill is about £500,000, amounting to 30% of its expenditure.

Income 1988 £1.1 million (75% voluntary)
Expenditure 1988 £1.2 million (55% charitable, 35% fund-raising, 8% administration)
Chairman Norman Keir
17 Uxbridge Rd, Slough SL1 1SN, tel. 0753 32713

SAVE THE CHILDREN FUND

The needs of children throughout the world are the prime concern of the Save the Children Fund. Founded as a disaster relief organization by Eglantyne Jebb in 1919, the Fund has a long tradition of emergency relief, but the main emphasis of its overseas work (on which it spends twice as much as it spends in the UK) is on long-term programmes concerned with mother and child health, nutrition, welfare and economic self-sufficiency. Instead of running its own projects, it provides technical support, funds, equipment and above all training so that local people learn to run their own services themselves. In the UK the Fund concentrates its efforts on minority and severely disadvantaged children – coloured, gypsies and travellers, the unemployed, young offenders and refugees. The Fund employs over 1800 people overseas (mostly local) and a further 800 in the UK.

Income 1988 £36 million (67% voluntary, 27% local and central government grants)
Expenditure 1988 £41.6 million (87% charitable, 11% fund-raising, 2% administration)
Chairman Viscount Boyd of Merton
Mary Datchelor House, 17 Grove Lane, London SE5 8RD, tel. 071-703 5400

SHELTER

Shelter was set up in 1966 as the national campaign for homeless people. Its main objective is decent, affordable homes for all. To achieve this, it runs campaigns to highlight the situation of people with housing problems, or with no home at all; researches the current housing situation; lobbies Parliament; raises funds for the campaign through its 70 local volunteer groups; funds eight independent housing advice centres and gives direct advice and practical help through its own national network of 11 housing advice centres. In 1988 these centres took on nearly 11,000 detailed cases and helped over 30,000 people, about 10% of the official (probably conservative) estimate of the number of homeless people. Shelter's casework ranges from defending tenants against harassment to contributing towards essential home repairs. The organization employs over 130 people.

Income 1988 £2.8 million (66% voluntary, 15% central and local government grants)
Expenditure 1988 £2.9 million (77% charitable, 13% fund-raising, 9% administration)
Chairman Lord Pitt
88 Old St, London EC1V 9HU, tel. 071-253 0202

SOCIETY FOR PROMOTING CHRISTIAN KNOWLEDGE

Founded in 1698, the SPCK is the oldest Anglican missionary organization. Communicating its message mainly through the printed word, it has its own publishing division turning over £1.5 million a year from prayer books, hymn books and also general books, the latter increasingly focusing on contemporary issues. Since 1835 it has also been in the retail book trade, a multi-million pound business with sales of over £5 million a year from mail order and 31 bookshops throughout Great Britain. Outside the UK the Society is active in over 100 countries. Through its project-funding arm, SPCK Worldwide, it distributes about £300,000 a year in grant aid to a variety of small projects, from photocopiers in Nepal to a Bible correspondence course in Burma. The SPCK has four offshoot organizations – in India, Australia, New Zealand and the US. The UK SPCK employs about 250 people.

Income 1988 £2.1 million (18% voluntary, 43% trading)
Expenditure 1988 £700,000 (80% charitable, nothing on fund-raising, 20% administration)
Chairman Lionel Scott
Holy Trinity Church, Marylebone Rd, London NW1 4DU, tel. 071-387 5282

THE SPASTICS SOCIETY

The Spastics Society was formed in 1952 by a group of parents with children with cerebral palsy, or cp (a physical disability of which spastic cp is the most common type). With nearly 3000 staff and 186 local groups, the Society is now a major provider of education, accommodation, information and social services in England and Wales for the cerebral palsied and their families. It has a network of 40 specialist social workers and runs schools and colleges for children aged 2 to 19, residential units, and various centres for skills development, sheltered work and day care. The Society also campaigns on behalf of those with cp and funds research into its causes and effects. Current priorities include providing computers and other microtech aids and enabling the residents of Society homes to move out into the community.

Income 1988 £46.6 million (40% voluntary and 41% local and central government fees)
Expenditure 1988 £45.7 million (78% charitable, 8% fund-raising, 2% administration)
Chairman Douglas Shapland
12 Park Crescent, London W1N 4EQ, tel. 071-636 5020

THE SUE RYDER FOUNDATION

The Sue Ryder Foundation is an international charity caring for sick and disabled people of all ages in Britain and many other countries, including Poland. It was set up in 1953 by Lady Ryder of Warsaw as a living memorial to all those who died during the two world wars and who still suffer today because of tyranny and persecution. The Foundation runs 80 homes providing nursing care for both long-term and some temporary residents. It als provides out-patient facilities for cancer sufferers and an informal social services network through its charity shops, of which there are over 360 in Britain alone. In addition, domiciliary care teams at some homes make thousands of home visits to the sick and bereaved. In Britain, the Foundation has 24 homes open or in the course of being established. They are mainly listed buildings and have a turnover of over 2000 patients a year. In total, Lady Ryder reckons to have helped about 350,000 people from over 50 countries through her Foundation.

Income 1988 £12 million (58% voluntary, 35% local and central government fees)
Expenditure 1988 £7.5 million (91% charitable, 0.2% fund-raising, 2.4% administration)
Chairman John Priest
Sue Ryder Home, Cavendish, Suffolk CO10 8AY, tel. 0787 280252

WAR ON WANT

Founded in 1952 by publisher Victor Gollancz, WOW fights worldwide against poverty, much of which it believes to be man-made rather than natural. Help takes the form of money or materials or technical know-how and covers the fields of health education, income generation, rural development, food production and human rights. Currently the charity is working in 35 countries on a range of locally initiated, predominantly long-term, self-help projects, including a 'people's school' in Bangladesh, tool-making machines for Vietnam, and bore-hole drilling to provide fresh water in Eritrea. In recent years nearly two-thirds of its money has gone to projects in North Africa and the Middle East. At home WOW lobbies for more effective use of overseas aid and campaigns on issues such as debt crises, women's rights in the Third World and conflict in South Africa. It has 65 local groups, 5000 members and 40 staff.

Income 1988 £7.4 million (99% voluntary)
Expenditure 1988 £6.7 million (84% charitable, 4% fund-raising, 11% administration)
Chairman Jenny Young
Fenner Brockway House, 37–9 Great Guildford St, London SE1 0ES, tel. 071-620 1111

WORLDWIDE FUND FOR NATURE

Formerly known as the World Wildlife Fund, WWF was founded in 1961 mainly to protect endangered animals like the giant panda. Nowadays it also tackles the kind of environmental problems that threaten all forms of life in the natural world, such as forest destruction, global warming and acid rain. Primarily a money-raising organization, the Fund is currently supporting some 240 projects worldwide, projects which increasingly involve sustainable development for local people (e.g. forestry for firewood in Nepal) rather than straight conservation. WWF UK is one of the largest members of the Fund's 23 national organizations, with over 120,000 members and 400,000 active supporters. Two-thirds of the money it raises goes overseas while one-third is spent helping other organizations like the Wildfowl Trust or the National Trust to establish bird reserves or buy threatened land. Of the £80 million plus spent by the Fund since it was set up, over £4 million has been spent in the UK.

Income 1987 £8.9 million (87% voluntary)
Expenditure 1987 £9.6 million (65% charitable, 29% fund-raising including membership servicing, 4% administration)
Chairman Sir Arthur Norman
Panda House, Weyside Park, Catteshall Lane, Godalming, Surrey GU7 1XR, tel. 0483 426444

CONSTITUTION

There is no written constitution for the United Kingdom. The constitutional arrangements have come about partly by Acts of Parliament, partly by common law, and partly by custom and convention; and the constitution can still be altered by any of these processes.

The Head of State is the sovereign, and the country is ruled in his or her name by a triangle of elements with Parliament at the top.

PARLIAMENT

House of Lords/House of Commons

↙ ↘

Judiciary	**Executive**
i.e. judges and magistrates	a. Cabinet and ministers b. Government departments c. Local authorities d. Public corporations

It is a key feature of the British style of constitution that the judiciary is independent both of the legislature and of the executive.

THE MONARCHY

The Queen combines several roles: apart from being the symbolic head of the country and the emblem of national unity, she is head of all three branches of government – legislature, executive and judiciary. She is also head of the Church of England and commander-in-chief of the armed forces. Her official title is 'Elizabeth II, by the Grace of God, of the United Kingdom of Great Britain and Northern Ireland and of her other Realms and Territories, Queen, Head of the Commonwealth, Defender of the Faith'.

The crown of the United Kingdom is directly inherited; kings and queens must be Protestant descendants of Princess Sophia Electress of Hanover (granddaughter of King James I of England and VI of Scotland), under a law passed in the reign of King William III. Sons and grandsons have precedence in the line of succession over daughters, but throughout British history it has always been legal for a woman to inherit the crown.

The new sovereign succeeds to the throne immediately on the death of his or her predecessor, taking on all the powers; this is proclaimed at an Accession Council, a special meeting of the Privy Council. The Coronation, a purely ceremonial event which confers no extra powers, is held at any convenient time after the accession. For the past 900 years it has been held at Westminster Abbey, where every sovereign from William the Conqueror (except Edward V and Edward VIII) has been crowned.

The Queen's powers have to a large extent been transmitted to her ministers but she still has several important functions. She appoints the Prime Minister although she does not choose who this should be, as it is automatically the leader of the party that has the majority in the House of Commons. She summons each Parliament and dissolves it, or (occasionally) prorogues it. Each year in October or November she opens the new session of Parliament with 'The Queen's Speech', not in fact written by her but a statement of the Government's plans for new legislation to be put before Parliament. Every Act of Parliament requires the Queen's signature – the Royal Assent – for it to become law. Many public appointments and honours are awarded by the Queen; she names judges, bishops and lords (hereditary and life), although almost all of these are in fact nominated by the Prime Minister, rather than chosen by the Queen personally. Technically the Queen as Head of State has the power to declare war and peace, though in modern times it would be impossible for a sovereign to do this other than on the advice of the Government.

Although her powers are so limited, the sovereign has been said to keep four rights in relation to the country's government: the right to be consulted, the right to advise, the right to encourage, and the right to warn. She is expected to keep herself fully informed of affairs of state and to give audiences to her ministers and others (e.g. heads of Commonwealth countries). However, she must be completely impartial politically.

If the Queen travels abroad her duties at home (with some limitations) are delegated to the Counsellors of State, normally close members of the Royal Family.

Members of the Royal Family have no statutory duties or responsibilities, although they do of course carry out a great many public engagements.

Royal Expenditure

The Queen's expenses in carrying out her duties come from three sources. About 85% comes from various government departments; for example, the Ministry of Defence pays for the royal yacht *Britannia* and the Queen's Flight, and the Department of the Environment takes responsibility for the royal palaces and parks. Every year Parliament votes to her and members of her family grants from the Civil List. In 1990 these were:

The Queen	£5,090,000
The Queen Mother	439,500
The Duke of Edinburgh	245,000
Duke of York	169,000
Prince Edward	20,000
Princess Royal	154,400
Princess Margaret	148,500
Princess Alice	60,500
Duke of Gloucester	119,500
Duke of Kent	161,500
Princess Alexandra	154,000
	6,762,000
Refunded by the Queen	435,000
Total	6,327,000

Note that the Prince of Wales has no income from the Civil List; his public funding is from the revenues of the Duchy of Cornwall. The Queen's private expenditure as sovereign comes from the Privy Purse, whose funds come mostly from the revenues of the Duchy of Lancaster; the annual total is now £2,250,000. It should be noted that the Queen is an extremely wealthy woman in her own right. She pays no income tax, but she pays into the Exchequer each year the amount of money that certain remoter members of the Royal Family are awarded in the Civil List.

THE PRIVY COUNCIL

The Privy Council (up to the 18th century a decision-making body, the equivalent of the Cabinet of today) is the sovereign's advisory body on the exercising of statutory and prerogative powers; it is now a purely formal body. There are about 400 Privy Councillors, appointed for life by the sovereign on the recommendation of the Prime Minister; they must be citizens of the UK or of a monarchical country within the Commonwealth. Cabinet Ministers automatically become members of the Privy Council. The full Council meets only to sign the proclamation of a new sovereign or on the sovereign announcing an intention to marry.

The committees of the Privy Council are important constitutionally. One of them, the Judicial Committee, is the final court of appeal for the UK's dependencies and for many of the Commonwealth countries. Another committee is responsible for the Channel Islands and the Isle of Man.

The post of Lord President of the Council, in charge of the Privy Council's office, is a cabinet post, but as the duties are not heavy, since 1964 the holder has combined it with being the Leader of the House of Commons.

THE ROYAL FAMILY

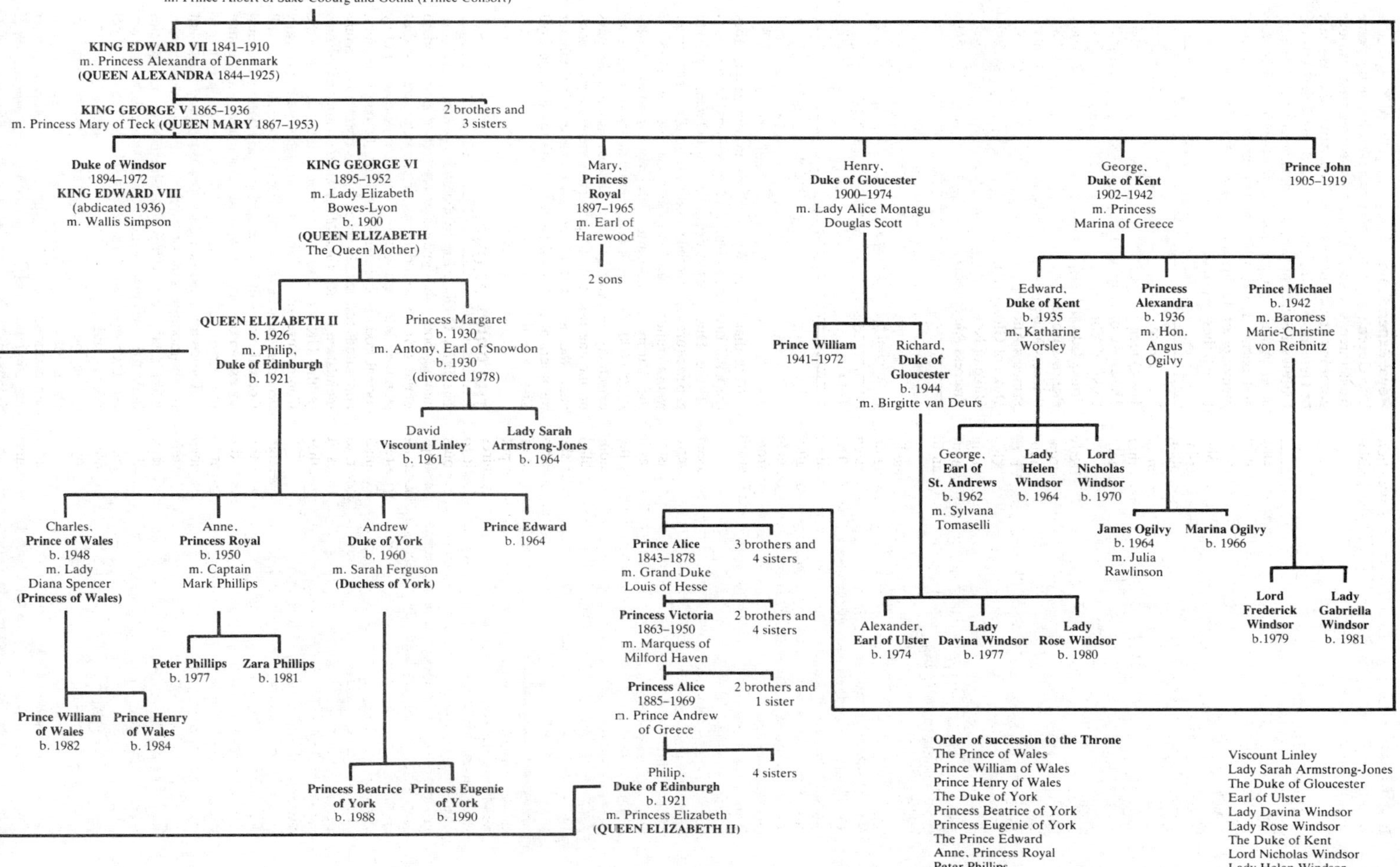

Order of succession to the Throne

The Prince of Wales
Prince William of Wales
Prince Henry of Wales
The Duke of York
Princess Beatrice of York
Princess Eugenie of York
The Prince Edward
Anne, Princess Royal
Peter Phillips
Zara Phillips
The Princess Margaret, Countess of Snowdon
Viscount Linley
Lady Sarah Armstrong-Jones
The Duke of Gloucester
Earl of Ulster
Lady Davina Windsor
Lady Rose Windsor
The Duke of Kent
Lord Nicholas Windsor
Lady Helen Windsor
Lord Frederick Windsor
Lady Gabriella Windsor

PARLIAMENT

The legislative authority of the United Kingdom is Parliament, which consists of the sovereign and the two Houses, the House of Commons and the House of Lords. Parliament's main function is to pass new laws or amend existing ones, but it also has to give its approval for the Government's expenditure plans, and scrutinizes government policy and administration. Matters of public importance are also debated by Parliament usually in an emergency debate.

A Parliament has a maximum duration of five years, after which it is dissolved by the sovereign. It may be dissolved earlier than this, if the Prime Minister chooses; the dissolution is again ordered by the sovereign. Each Parliament is divided into sessions, usually lasting one year from October or November. There are 'adjournments' every night and over weekends and Bank Holidays. The session ends when Parliament is prorogued (again by the sovereign), and the two Houses go into 'recess' until the beginning of the next session. Any legislation not completed before the prorogation is abandoned and must be started afresh in the new session. Recess lasts about three months (usually from late July to late October); the House of Commons sits for an average of 175 days per session, the Lords for an average of 155.

The House of Lords

The House of Lords consists of 1184 peers.

	Men	*Women*
Hereditary peers and peeresses	21	–
Archbishops and bishops	26	–
Peers by succession	763	20
Life peers under the Act of 1876	21	
Life peers under the Act of 1958	353	45
Total	1184	65
of whom		
Peers without writs of summons		95
Peers on leave of absence from the House		152

Irish peers do not sit in the House of Lords unless they hold a United Kingdom title. A peer who has not formally succeeded to his or her title does not receive a 'writ of summons' and therefore cannot sit (95 peers out of 1184); a peer may apply for leave of absence for all or part of a Parliament (152 out of the whole House). Average attendance at the sittings is about 320. A peer receives an expense allowance of up to £21 per day and £57 for an overnight stay plus travel expenses.

The president of the House of Lords is the Lord Chancellor, always a lawyer as he is also the head of the judiciary. He sits on the Woolsack, a seat in the shape of a large cushion.

The House of Lords can elect its members to sit on its own Select Committees to investigate particular matters, or to join members of the House of Commons on Joint Committees.

The House of Commons

The House of Commons consists of 650 elected members. To be eligible for election a person must be a citizen of Britain, a Commonwealth country or the Irish Republic and over 21 years old. All the following are disqualified: peers (not Irish ones), clergymen (of the Church of England and Scottish Episcopal Church, the Church of Scotland and the Roman Catholic Church), patients detained under current mental health legislation, undischarged bankrupts, civil servants, members of the regular armed forces, police officers and judges.

The United Kingdom is divided (for the purpose of parliamentary elections only) into constituencies, which is theory contain roughly equal members of electors (currently 69,500); to maintain this equal distribution, the four Boundary Commissions (for England, Wales, Scotland and Northern Ireland) are required to report every 10–15 years and to recommend changes in constituency boundaries. All British citizens, and citizens of the Commonwealth countries and the Irish Republic aged 18 and over are eligible to vote provided they are registered as resident in the annual electoral register in the given constituency; no one may vote in more than one constituency, even though they may be registered on more than one electoral register. 'Service Voters', i.e. members of the armed forces and civil servants and their families living abroad, can be registered in their home constituency and vote by post or by proxy. British citizens living abroad but who were registered electors within the previous five years are also eligible to vote by proxy. Voting is not compulsory.

Each candidate is required to lodge a deposit of £500 which is forfeit if he or she gains less than 5% of the vote. Election expenses are subject to a statutory limit of £3,648, plus a per-voter sum of 3.1 pence in a borough constituency and 4.1 for a county one.

In a general election voting in all the constituencies must take place on the same day; polling stations are open from 7 a.m. until 10 p.m.

Election is by a simple majority of votes. If the result if close, a candidate may ask for a recount, which the Returning Officer can allow or refuse at his or her own discretion; a second or subsequent recount may also be requested. If there were to be exactly equal numbers of votes cast for two candidates, the winner would be decided by lot.

After a general election the party with the majority of seats forms the next Government, and its leader becomes Prime Minister. (If no party has a majority, the leader of the party which can organize a working arrangement with one or more other parties must convince the Queen that he or she can form a viable government.) The new Prime Minister appoints a cabinet (and junior ministers) from among both MPs and Lords. In circumstances when the main party does not have an outright or substantial majority of seats in the Commons, the new Prime Minister may choose to bring in members of another party into the Government in a coalition. The largest minority party becomes the official Opposition party, and its leader appoints members of a shadow cabinet in the same way. Ministers and their opposite numbers in Opposition sit on the front benches, facing each other across the floor of the chamber; other MPs sit in the rows behind, hence the term 'back-benchers' to describe them. MPs receive a salary of £26,701 per year plus an Office Costs Allowance of £24,903 and expenses of £8,674 for the cost of staying away from home.

Parliamentary Procedure

The main part of the business of the Parliament is discussing Bills put forward by the Government. The process of the Bill becoming law is (a) **First Reading** –

no discussion; (b) **Second Reading** – discussion of general principles only; (c) **Committee Stage** – detailed consideration, amendments may be proposed; (d) **Report Stage** – the whole of the Commons discusses details and any amendments; (e) **Third Reading** – normally no discussion, vote taken on whether to accept or reject the Bill; (f) **Referral to the House of Lords** – the Lords may propose amendments but they cannot reject a Bill; (g) **Consideration of the Lords amendments** (if there are any); (h) **Royal Assent**.

Apart from the Government's own Bills, planned before the beginning of the parliamentary session and outlined in the Queen's Speech, there are four other main types of debate: **Emergency Debates**, called by any member at short notice and limited to three hours' discussion, **Private Members' Bills**, allocated by lottery to give individual members the chance to introduce their own legislation (these are often used where private conscience crosses party loyalties, e.g. the Abortion Act 1967), **Question Time**, in which ministers (including the Prime Minister on Tuesday and Thursday from 3.15 to 3.30) must answer questions previously submitted in writing by members, and the **Adjournment of the House**, a technicality permitting half-an-hour's debate each day on matters concerning MPs' constituents or of general immediate interest.

The Speaker

The House of Commons is presided over by the Speaker, elected by all MPs. The Speaker must act with absolute impartiality and therefore has to lay aside all political activity on behalf of his (or her) own party. The Speaker chooses who shall speak in debates, and makes rulings on whether MPs' words or behaviour are out of order or a breach of privilege; a Member can be suspended (barred from attending the Commons) for refusing to apologize for unacceptable conduct.

Voting

Voting in both Houses is by simple majority. The quorum in the Commons is 40, and in the Lords it is only 3, although 30 Lords are needed for a vote to take place. In the Commons the vote may be conducted verbally, with members shouting 'Aye' or 'No' and the Speaker ruling, e.g. 'The Ayes have it', but if the House is not happy with the decision a 'Division' is called, and each member must walk into the Aye lobby or the No lobby and be counted.

Whips

The Government and the Opposition each have a Chief Whip and a team of junior whips whose duties are to keep the MPs informed about forthcoming business in Parliament and to make sure that they attend the most important debates (this is indicated by underlining the item a certain number of times; a 'three-line whip' is the most important and constitutes an order from the party that the member must attend the vote). Whips also arrange 'pairing', an arrangement that enables MPs who want to be absent to agree with another from the opposite side to do the same so that the votes are neutralized.

Select Committees

Both Houses from time to time appoint a Select Committee to investigate a particular issue. The party composition of a Select Committee reflects that of its House. A Select Committee is authorised to 'send for persons, papers and records' from outside. At the end of its investigations the Select Committee agrees a report which is submitted to the House and either accepted or referred back to the Committee for revision.

Reporting

Sessions of Parliament are almost always open (the exception being when the country is at war) and may be attended by the public in the Strangers' gallery. The House of Lords has been televised since 1985, and the House of Commons began to be televised on 21 November 1989 for an experimental six months' period. *Hansard* is a verbatim record of the debates and is published daily.

GOVERNMENT

The Prime Minister

The Prime Minister is leader of his or her political party and therefore represents the interests of all members and supporters of that party, but is also formally responsible to the sovereign for the proper government of the state. Since the beginning of the 20th century, it has been felt that only a member of the House of Commons can effectively carry out this role.

The Prime Minister is also traditionally minister for the Civil Service and the First Lord of The Treasury. His or her most important function is to appoint ministers and to chair the cabinet. He or she also makes recommendations to the Queen for the appointment of many key figures in British public life, ranging from bishops and judges to BBC governors.

The Prime Minister's salary is £46,109 per year (Mrs Thatcher has chosen to drawn only the salary payable to an ordinary minister), plus the use of 10 Downing Street and Chequers.

The Cabinet

Members of the cabinet are each responsible for their own departments, but they are also responsible for coming to collective decisions on government policy. Every cabinet minister is held to be responsible for each cabinet decision. Thus if a minister cannot come to an unanimous agreement with his or her colleagues he or she must resign. The cabinet always meets in secret. There are specialized cabinet committees to handle some areas of government, but details of their existence and composition are by convention kept secret.

The title of a cabinet minister is generally Secretary of State for X, though some have individual titles, e.g. Chancellor of the Exchequer. Cabinet ministers are considered to be fully accountable to Parliament for everything done within their area of responsibility, whether it be work carried out by junior ministers or permanent civil servants.

A few posts in the cabinet – e.g. the Lord Privy Seal, the Chancellor of the Duchy of Lancaster – have light or only ceremonial duties; holders of these are available to take up any particular responsibility that the Prime Minister wishes to delegate.

Cabinet ministers receive £34,479 per year.

Other Ministers

Below the Secretaries of State comes Ministers of State (who may occasionally be of cabinet rank), and below them 'junior ministers', Parliamentary Under-Secretaries of State or Parliamentary Secretaries. Ministers of State who are members of the House of Lords receive £37,047 per year, and if they are MPs £24,209. Junior members receive £18,219 per year.

For a full list of H.M. Government as at 1 March 1990, see POLITICAL PARTIES.

Parliamentary Commissioner for Administration

The 'Ombudsman', as the Parliamentary Commissioner is generally known, is an independent officer who investigates cases in which a member of the public has suffered because of bad administration by the Government. Cases must be brought to the Ombudsman via the complainer's MP, and the report on the case is made to the MP not the individual. The Ombudsman has access to government papers and can question ministers and civil servants.

A similar system operates for complaints against National Health Service authorities. Here the complaint can be brought directly to the National Health Service Commissioner by the individual; no cases can be considered re clinical judgement by medical staff. There are three Health Service Commissioners, one each for England, Scotland and Wales, but all three are presently held by Sir Anthony Barrowclough, QC, who is also Parliamentary Commissioner for Administration.

In 1988 the Parliamentary Commissioner for Administration received 701 new complaints and carried over from the previous year another 216, amounting to a total of 917 complaints. Of these 917 complaints 120 full investigates were completed.

Departments

Ministry of Agriculture, Fisheries and Food
Minister: **Rt Hon. John Gummer MP**
Minister of State: **Baroness Trumpington**
Parliamentary secretaries: **David MacLean MP, David Curry MP**

As its title indicates the Ministry of Agriculture, Fisheries and Food is responsible for administering government policy relating to agriculture, horticulture, fisheries and food in England and the United Kingdom. However, it is not only British government policy for which the ministry is responsible. In association with other agricultural departments the ministry also administers the EC Common Agricultural Policy. Primarily the ministry is concerned with the supply and quality of food. It is also the Ministry of Agriculture, in association with the Department of Health and Social Security, which is responsible for alerting the public to possible food contamination, conducting research into various aspects of food production, e.g. irradiated food and compensation of farmers when cattle or crops are found to be unfit for human consumption, e.g. Mad Cow disease.

Estimated public expenditure of the department for the financial year 1990–91 is £1,833 million, the current workforce totalling 10,400.

Whitehall Place, London SW1A 2HH

H M Customs and Excise Department
H M Customs and Excise Department was first established on 1 April 1909 when the Excise Department, which had formerly been the responsibility of the Board of Inland Revenue, and the Customs Department, which was first established in 1671, were amalgamated. The responsibilities of the Customs and Excise department are: the collection and administration of customs duties and Valued Added Tax set by the Government, the prevention and prosecution of those evading the revenue laws, and the enforcement of restrictions on certain types of goods. The department also undertakes some work on behalf of other departments and advises the Chancellor of the Exchequer on matters relating to its particular field of expertise. For the financial year 1990–91 the department's budget was £641 million and its workforce totals 27,700.

New King's Beam House, 22 Upper Ground, London SE1 9PJ

Ministry of Defence
Secretary of State: **Rt Hon. Tom King MP**
Minister of State for Defence Procurement: **Hon. Alan Clarke MP**
Minister of State for the Armed Forces; **Hon. Archibald Hamilton MP**
Parliamentary Under Secretary for Defence Procurement: **Michael Neubert MP**
Parliamentary Under Secretary of State for the Armed Forces: **Earl of Arran**
See DEFENCE SECTION.

Department of Education and Science
Secretary of State: **Rt Hon. John MacGregor OBE MP**
Minister of State: **Mrs Angela Rumbold CBE MP**
Parliamentary Under Secretaries of State: **Robert Jackson MP, Alan Howarth MP**

It was not until the passing of the Education Act of 1944 that the Ministry of Education was founded although a number of other bodies which supervised education in the United Kingdom did exist prior to the passing of the Act. In 1839 a committee of the Privy Council was established to supervise the administration of grants such as the Maynooth Grant set up in 1834 and in 1899 the Board of Education, with a parliamentary secretary and chairman, was founded. In April 1964 the office of Minister of Science, previously without portfolio, was combined with the Ministry of Education to form the Department of Education and Science. The department is responsible for administering government policy on universities and education and also for carrying out scientific research. One of the subsidiary departments of the Ministry is H M Inspectorate of Schools which is responsible for supervising educational establishments in the United Kingdom and ensuring that standards set by the Government are adhered to. The Ministry's budget for the financial year 1990–91 is estimated at £6,590 million. The workforce totals 2,600.

Elizabeth House, York Road, London SE1 7PH

Department of Employment
Secretary of State: **Rt Hon. Michael Howard MP**
Minister of State: **Tim Eggar MP**
Parliamentary Under Secretaries of State: **Patrick Nicholls MP, Earl of Strathclyde**

The primary role of the Department of Employment is to implement Government policy to reduce the number of unemployed and increase the number of people engaged in full-time employment. The department is responsible for running schemes such as 'Job Club' and YTS which help people acquire and improve their skills and thereby improve their chances of gaining employment. In order to help it perform its tasks efficiently the department has at its disposal a number of other agencies which work within specific fields such as the Health and Safety Commission. The Department of Employment currently employs approximately 53,700 people and has an estimated public expenditure of £3,770 million.

Caxton House, Tothill Street, London SW1H 9NF

Department of Energy
Secretary of State: **Rt Hon. John Wakeham MP**
Minister of State: **Rt Hon. Peter Morrison MP**
Parliamentary Under Secretary of State: **Tony Baldry MP**

The Department of Energy is responsible for ensuring the implementation of Government policies relating to energy including nuclear-power, coal and electricity. The department also acts as the sponsoring department for the nuclear-power industry and the oil industry. The department is also responsible for conducting research into ways of harnessing other sources of energy such as water and wind, and also for maintaining relations with the larger oil-producing countries of the Middle East. The department's budget for the financial year 1990–91 is approximately £160 million whilst its workforce is currently 1,300.

1 Palace Street, London SW1E 5HE

Department of the Environment
Secretary of State: **Rt Hon. Christopher Patten MP**
Ministers of State:
Minister of the Environment and Countryside: **David Trippier MP**
Minister for Local Government and Inner Cities: **David Hunt MBE MP**
Minister for Housing and Planning: **Michael Spicer MP**
Parliamentary Under Secretaries of State: **Christopher Chope MP, Lord Hesketh, David Heathcote-Amory MP**
Minister for Sport: **Hon. Colin Moynihan MP**

In the light of its responsibilities the name of this department is perhaps misleading: in addition to being responsible for environmental protection, conservation and countryside affairs the Department of the Environment is also responsible for housing, construction and local government. This department is currently responsible for the implementation of the Community Charge (Poll Tax). The Department of the Environment currently employs a total of 19,400 people and has a budget of £20,485 million for local government, £6,268 million for housing and £1,406 million for other sectors covered by the department.

2 Marsham Street, London SW1P 3EB

Foreign and Commonwealth Office
Secretary of State: **Rt Hon. Douglas Hurd CBE MP**
Minister for Overseas Development: **Rt Hon. Lynda Chalker MP**
Ministers of State: **Rt Hon. William Waldegrave MP, Lord Brabazon of Tara, Hon Francis Maude MP**
Parliamentary Under Secretary: **Hon. Tim Sainsbury MP**

The Foreign and Commonwealth Office is responsible for maintaining communications between the British Government and the governments and international organizations of other countries. In order to facilitate this task the department maintains diplomatic missions throughout the world. Where relations with a particular country have broken down, as in the case of Iran, the Foreign and Commonwealth Office will arrange for British interests to be represented by another country. The department is also responsible for notifying the British Government of overseas developments, and the protection of British citizens. One of the major concerns of the department at the moment is the return of Hong Kong to the Chinese Government, due to take place in 1997. The Foreign and Commonwealth Office has an annual budget for the financial year 1990–91 of £2,600 million and it employs 8,300 people.

Downing Street, London SW1A 2AL

The Department of Health
Secretary of State for Health: **Rt Hon. Kenneth Clarke QC MP**
Minister of State: **Mrs Virginia Bottomley MP**
Parliamentary Under Secretaries of State: **Roger Freeman MP, Baroness Hooper**

The Department of Health was formed in July 1988 when the Department of Health and Social Security was divided and made into two separate departments. The department is responsible for running the NHS, social services provided by local government and for providing an efficient accident and emergency service. The department is currently responsible for attempting to promote the Government's opting-out policy whereby hospitals currently within the National Health Service are given the option to become self-governing. The estimated expenditure for the department amounts to £22,202 million and its workforce currently totals 11,400; this figure excludes those working in the National Health Service.

Richmond House, 79 Whitehall, London SW1A 2NS

The Home Office
Secretary of State: **Rt Hon. David Waddington MP**
Ministers of State: **Rt Hon. John Patten MP, David Mellor MP, Rt Hon. Earl Ferrers DL**
Parliamentary Under Secretary of State: **Peter Lloyd MP**

The Home Office is responsible for dealing with all those internal affairs that are not the responsibility of other departments; in particular, the department is responsible for the administration of justice, the penal system (including the prison and probation service), the police, immigration and nationality, licensing, e.g. marriage, liquor, theatre and cinema licensing, fire and civil-defence services and national broadcasting policies. The department budget for the financial year is £4,480 million and its current workforce totals 45,000.

50 Queen Anne's Gate, London SW1H 9AT

The Board of Inland Revenue
Chairman: **Sir Anthony Battishill**

The Board of Inland Revenue was established by the unification of the Board of Excise and the Board of Stamps and Taxes under the Inland Revenue Board Act of 1849. In 1909 a further reform of the Board occurred when the responsibility for the collection of excise duties was transferred to the Customs Board. The Board of Inland Revenue is responsible for the administration and collection of direct taxes (including income tax, capital gains tax and stamp duties). The Board has Inspectors of Taxes Boards throughout the United Kingdom. The Board has a staff of 67,200 and a budget for the financial year 1990–91 of £1,794 million.

Somerset House, London WC2R 1LB

Lord Chancellor's Department
Lord Chancellor: **The Lord Mackay of Clashfern**

The Lord Chancellor's Department is responsible for the administration of civil law including the procedure of civil courts, the administration of the Court of Appeal, the High Court, the Crown Court and the County Courts in England and Wales. The Lord Chancellor is responsible for appointing masters and registrars of the High Court and the magistrates and registrars of the District and County Courts. He also advises the Crown on the appointment of judges. One of the subsidiary departments of the Lord Chancellor's Department is the Office of the Clerk of the Crown in Chancery which is responsible for ensuring that formal documents and letters patent are passed in the proper manner under the Great Seal of the Realm of which the Lord Chancellor is custodian. The department's budget for the financial year 1990–91 is £1,267 million and it employs 30,200 people.

House of Lords, London SW1A 0PW

Overseas Development Administration

The Overseas Development Administration is responsible for the administration of British development assistance to overseas countries in the form of both capital and technical assistance. In 1989 the Overseas Development Administration employed 1,700 people and its budget for the financial year 1990–91 is £892 million.

Eland House, Stag Place, London SW1E 5DH
Abercrombie House, Eaglesham Road, East Kilbride, Glasgow G75 8EA

The Department of Social Security

Secretary of State for Social Security: **Rt Hon. Anthony Newton MP**
Minister of State for Social Security and the Disabled: **Rt Hon. Nicholas Scott MBE MP**
Parliamentary Under Secretaries of State: **Lord Henley, Mrs Gillian Shephard MP**

The Department of Social Security was formed in July 1988 when the Department of Health and Social Security was divided and made into two separate departments. The department is responsible for the administration of social services in England, Wales and Scotland.

(See HEALTH AND SOCIAL WELFARE.)

Richmond House, 79 Whitehall, London SW1A 2NS

Department of Trade and Industry

Secretary of State for Trade and Industry and President of the Board of Trade: **Rt Hon. Nicholas Ridley MP**
Ministers of State:
Minister for Trade: **Rt Hon. Lord Trefgarne**
Minister for Industry and Enterprise: **Hon. Douglas Hurd MP**
Parliamentary Under Secretaries of State:
Industry and Consumer Affairs: **Eric Fosworth MP**
Corporate Affairs: **John Redwood MP**

The Department of Trade and Industry is responsible for the administration of policies relating to international trade, industry, competition, consumerism, science technology and research; it is also responsible for the promotion of United Kingdom exports and assistance to exporters and the administration of company and corporate legislation. The department's budget for the financial year 1990–91 was £1,511 million and it employs 12,500 people.

2 Marsham Street, London SW1P 3EB

Department of Transport

Secretary of State for Transport: **Rt Hon. Cecil Parkinson MP**
Minister of State for Public Transport: **Michael Portillo MP**
Parliamentary Under Secretaries of State:
Minister for Roads and Traffic: **Robert Atkins MP**
Minister for Aviation and Shipping: **Patrick McLoughlin MP**

The Department of Transport which has staff of 16,000 is responsible for land, sea and air transport including general sponsorship of the transport industries, e.g. the subsidization of British Rail. It is also responsible for the administration of shipping, aviation and road-transport policy including the construction and maintenance of motorways and trunk roads, and for ensuring transport safety. The 1990–91 budget for the Department of Transport is £4,230 million. The department has recently announced a £12 billion road-building programme.

1–19 Victoria Street, London SW1H 0ET

The Treasury

Prime Minister, First Lord of the Treasury and Minister for the Civil Service: **Rt Hon. Margaret Thatcher FRS MP**
Chancellor of the Exchequer: **Rt Hon. John Major MP**
Chief Secretary: **Rt Hon. Norman Lamont MP**
Paymaster General: **Earl of Caithness**
Financial Secretary: **Peter Lilley MP**
Economic Secretary: **Richard Ryder MP**
Parliamentary Secretary to the Treasury: **Rt Hon. Tim Renton MP**
Lords Commissioners: **David Lightbrown MP, Kenneth Carlisle MP, Stephen Dorrell MP, John M. Taylor MP, Hon. Tom Sackville MP**
Assistant Whips: **Michael Fallon MP, Sydney Chapman MP, Greg Knight MP, Irvine Patnick MP, Nicholas Baker MP**

The Treasury is responsible for the control of public expenditure, public services, industry groups, overseas aid and export credit, efficiency in the public sector, procurement policy, monetary policy, the financial system, international financial business, European community business, the Royal Mint and Civil Service pay. At the pinnacle of the Treasury hierarchy are the Lord High Commissioners of HM Treasury of whom the First Lord of the Treasury and the Minister for the Civil Service is the Prime Minister Mrs Thatcher. The Treasury's budget for the financial year 1990–91 is £421 million and in order to perform all its responsibilities it employs 3,219 people.

Parliament Street, London SW1P 3AG

The Welsh Office

Secretary of State for Wales: **David Hunt MP** (announced intention to retire from politics at next election)
Minister of State: **Wyn Roberts MP**
Parliamentary Under Secretary of State: **Ian Grist MP**

The Welsh Office is responsible for administering a variety of functions which in England are carried out by separate departments. These include: health and personal social services, education, local government including housing, land use, town and country planning and conservation, water and sewage, sport, agriculture and tourism. The office is also responsible for promoting the Welsh language and culture and overseas economic affairs and regional planning in Wales. The Welsh Office employs 2,300 people and its budget for 1990 is £4,457 million.

Gwydyr House, Whitehall, London SW1A 2ER

Scottish Office

Secretary of State for Scotland: **Rt Hon. Malcolm Rifkind QC MP**
Ministers of State: **Ian Lang MP, Lord Sanderson of Bowden**
Parliamentary Under Secretaries of State:
Home Affairs and the Environment: **Lord James Douglas-Hamilton MP**
Health: **Michael Forsyth MP**

As with the Welsh Office, The Scottish Office is responsible for administering a variety of functions that in England are the responsibility of different departments. The statutory functions of the Scottish Office are administered by five departments which are: the Department of Agriculture and Fisheries for Scotland, the Scottish Development Department, the Scottish Education Department, the Industry Department for Scotland and the Scottish Home and Health Department. The Scottish Office's budget for the year 1990–91 is £9,576 million and it employs a total of 13,100 people

Dover House, Whitehall, London SW1A 2AU

The Northern Ireland Office
Secretary of State for Northern Ireland: **Rt Hon. Peter Brooke MP**
Minister of State: **Rt Hon. John Cope MP**
Parliamentary Under Secretaries of State: **Richard Needham MP, Peter Bottomley MP, Dr Brian Mawhinney MP, Lord Skelmersdale**

The Northern Ireland Office is the department through which the UK government governs Northern Ireland. The department is responsible for constitutional developments, security, law and order and electoral matters. In order to carry out these functions the Northern Ireland Office has a number of subsidiary departments responsible for specific areas of policy. These include: the Department of Agriculture for Northern Ireland, the Department of Education for Northern Ireland, the Department of Health and Social Services for Northern Ireland, the Department of the Environment for Northern Ireland, and the Department of Finance and Personnel. The budget for the Northern Ireland Office for the financial year 1990–91 is £5,968 million and its workforce totals 29,500.

Whitehall, London SW1A 2AZ

DEFENCE

The Sovereign as Head of State is technically the person in charge of the defence of the country, and is the only person who can made a declaration of war. The Sovereign is also head of all the armed forces, but Parliament is the ultimate source of decisions on defence, and the person responsible to Parliament for these matters is the Secretary of State for Defence. Policy decisions on defence are taken either by the Cabinet in full or, more usually, by its Defence and Overseas Policy Committee, which is chaired by the Prime Minister and includes the Secretary of State for Defence, the Foreign Secretary and the Home Secretary.

DEFENCE COUNCIL

The Defence Council, chaired by the Secretary of State for Defence, is responsible for running the armed forces, in peace-time as well as in war-time. Membership of the Defence Council consists of: politicians (two Ministers of State and two Parliamentary Under-Secretaries, as well as the Secretary of State); professional members of the armed forces; the Chief Scientific Adviser and the Chief of Defence Procurement, appointed by the Secretary of State.

Secretary of State for Defence Rt Hon. Tom King MP
Minister of State for the Armed Forces Hon. Archibald Hamilton MP
Parliamentary Under Secretary of State for the Armed Forces The Earl of Arran
Minister of State for Defence Procurement Hon. Alan Clark MP
Parliamentary Under Secretary of State for Defence Procurement Michael Neubert MP
Chief of the Defence Staff Marshal of the Royal Air Force Sir David Craig GCB, OBE, ADC
Permanent Under Secretary of State for Defence Sir Michael Quinlan KCB
Chief of the Naval Staff and First Sea Lord Admiral Sir William Staveley GCB, ADC
Chief of the General Staff Gen. Sir John Chapple GCB, CBE, ADC GEN
Chief of the Air Staff Air Chief Marshal Sir David Craig GCB, OBE, ADC
Chief Scientific Adviser Prof. Ronald Oxburgh
Chief of Defence Procurement Sir Peter Levene KBE
Second Permanent Under Secretary of State K. Macdonald CB

Ministry of Defence Main building, Whitehall, London SW1A 2HB. Tel. 071–218 9000

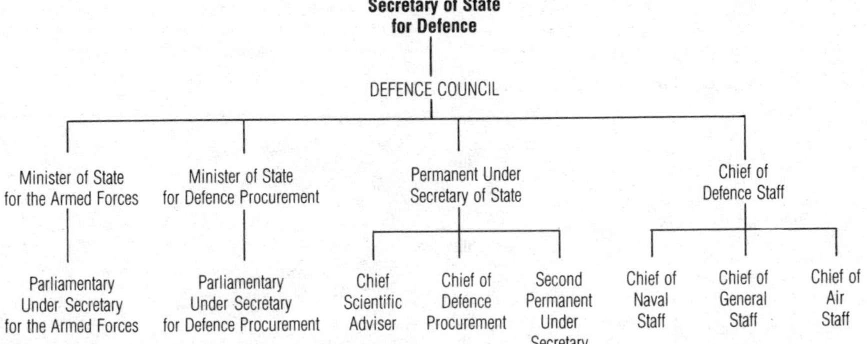

Defence Budget Analysis

£ million	*1985/6*	*1986/7*	*1987/8*	*1988/9*	*1989/90*	*1990/1*
Air Force general purpose forces	3,702	3,687	3,416	3,416	3,508	
Other support functions[1]	2,998	3,184	3,373	3,526	3,769	
European theatre ground forces	2,764	2,814	3,035	3,259	3,414	
Navy general purpose combat forces	2,505	2,625	2,491	2,425	2,398	
Research and development	2,304	2,327	2,337	2,257	2,350	
Training	1,294	1,257	1,277	1,249	1,357	
Equipment support and facilities (UK)	917	983	881	955	1,043	
War and contingency stocks	535	405	588	520	488	
Nuclear strategic force	509	658	882	1,072	1,158	
Reserves and auxiliaries	360	358	385	420	439	
Other Army combat forces	205	204	177	166	191	
Miscellaneous expenditure & receipts	–34	–23	–60	–50	28	
Total	18,059	18,479	18,782	19,215	20,143	

[1] Includes expenditure on local administration, meteorological services, family and personnel services, service pensions and organizations within Whitehall.

BUDGET

The Defence budget is the third biggest item in the national Budget, at £21,200 million (1990/1). (For a comparison with other countries' defence expenditure, see INTERNATIONAL STATISTICS.) The overall figure has shown a fall in real terms over the past five years, with expenditure down, after allowing for inflation, in all areas except nuclear strategic forces, up 100% after allowing for inflation.

ARMY

The Army is controlled by the Defence Council in the first place, but detailed management is in the hands of the Army Board. This is chaired by the Secretary of State for Defence, and the four subordinate Ministers are also members. The military side of the board is headed by the Chief of the General Staff and the other members are: the Adjutant General, responsible for manpower matters; the Quartermaster General, logistics, stores, buildings; the Master General of Ordnance, military equipment. Other members of the board are the Second Permanent Under-Secretary of State and the Controller of Establishments, Research and Nuclear Programmes.

HEADQUARTERS

All Army units in the UK are commanded from HQ United Kingdom Land Forces, Wilton, Wilts.; with the exception of units in Northern Ireland, which are controlled by the Ministry of Defence direct. There are three major commands overseas: Cyprus, Hong Kong, Germany (BAOR, British Army of the Rhine). There are permanent garrisons in: Belize, Berlin, Brunei, the Falkland Islands, Gibraltar.

NAMES AND SIZES OF UNITS

The regiments and corps of the Army maintain their traditions in many ways, including the terminology used for the names of their various sections. Thus the Infantry use platoon, company and battalion; the Royal Armoured Corps use troop, squadron and regiment: the Royal Artillery uses troop, battery and regiment. All have variations on these themes which can be confusing. Likewise each section will vary in size depending on its role at any particular time.

Cavalry

The group of regiments once known collectively as the Cavalry have now been separated into three groups: the Household Cavalry (H Cav) with two regiments; the Royal Armoured Corps (RAC) with 17 regiments; the Yeomanry with five regiments formed from the

Personnel
Strength of Army regular forces (including personnel training)

	1985	*1986*	*1987*	*1988*	*1989*
Male	155,600	154,900	153,300	151,800	149,700
Officers	16,300	16,300	16,400	16,300	16,300
Servicemen	139,300	138,600	136,900	135,500	133,400
Female	6,800	6,600	6,500	6,300	6,400
Officers	1,000	1,000	1,000	1,000	1,000
Servicewomen	5,800	5,600	5,500	5,300	5,400
Total male and female	162,400	161,500	159,800	158,100	156,000

Changes in numbers of Army regular forces

Recruitment	*1983/4*	*1984/5*	*1985/6*	*1986/7*	*1987/8*
Male	20,811	20,914	19,153	18,718	19,895
Officers	1,295	1,435	1,374	1,362	1,254
Servicemen	19,516	19,479	17,779	17,356	18,641
Female	1,537	1,364	1,095	1,200	1,146
Officers	173	160	151	154	148
Servicewomen	1,364	1,204	944	1,046	998
Total male and female	22,348	22,278	20,248	19,918	21,041
Outflow					
Male	18,854	20,286	19,999	20,473	21,393
Officers	1,701	1,703	1,790	1,654	1,651
Servicemen	17,153	18,583	18,209	18,819	19,742
Female	1,105	1,162	1,302	1,288	1,356
Officers	130	151	195	167	161
Servicewomen	975	1,011	1,107	1,121	1,195
Total male and female	19,959	21,448	21,301	21,761	22,749
Net gain or loss	+2,389	+830	−1033	−1843	−1708

The Army is studying ways of widening the range of jobs available to women in an attempt to keep numbers up in the face of the general trend of falling recruitment figures.

Territorial Army. The roles played by the Cavalry are: armoured regiments using main battle tanks such as the Chieftain; armoured reconnaissance regiments having some of the most complicated internal reporting structures in the Army and using light armoured vehicles such as the Scorpion; light reconnaissance regiments or Yeomanry reconnaissance regiments equipped with the Fox in BAOR and Land Rover in the UK. In addition, the Household Cavalry carries out ceremonial duties.

Infantry

In order to promote cross-battalion posting and flexibility between the formations it has been thought necessary for ease of administration to form the battalions into several divisions. These are: the Guards Division, containing eight battalions; the Scottish Division containing seven battalions; the Queen's Division containing nine battalions; the King's Division containing eight battalions; the Prince of Wales' Division containing nine battalions: the Light Division with six battalions; the Brigade of Gurkhas with five battalions; and the Parachute Regiment with three battalions. In addition, the 43 Territorial Army (TA) battalions are usually attached to regular battalions (though not the Guards).

Artillery

The two sections of the Artillery, the Royal Regiment of Artillery (RA) and the Royal Horse Artillery (RHA), have three major functions: air defence; indirect fire providing attack of enemy forces and support of friendly battle groups; nuclear warfare. The hierarchy of corps, brigades and commands is complicated with specialist artillery advisers in each armoured division and equipment such as the M110A2 self-propelled howitzer and Lance tactical ballistic missiles available for use as necessary. The Air Defence Group use towed or tracked Rapier surface-to-air missile systems and each armoured division has its artillery using shoulder-launched Javelin missiles. Control and planning are aided by modern computer and communications systems such as the BATES (Battlefield Target Engagement System) networking system. The Artillery gathers its own weather information and provides its own surveys for plotting gun positions.

Royal Engineers

The basis of the Royal Engineers is the individual soldier, the sapper, whose training gives him a triple role: as a soldier; as an engineer ready and able to handle a wide variety of equipment; as a specialized craftsman.

Among the tasks they carry out are: combat engineering, which can include road and airfield construction, demolition of obstacles, water supply and fortification of strategic points; airfield damage repair; bomb disposal (explosive ordnance disposal (EOD)) is the job of 33 Engineer Regiment (EOD) who are kept on almost permanent alert to respond to discoveries of suspect materials; postal and courier services; surveying, which means constantly updating old information and surveying by modern methods areas that may not have been covered before, complementing the hydrographic survey of the Royal Navy and providing information for all three branches of the forces; the Military Works Force (MWF), which is a specialist advisory body, defining problems and solutions, but not carrying out the construction work (sometimes done by private contractors as was the case with the Mount Pleasant airfield project in the Falklands).

Special Air Service (SAS)

Best known to the public in its counter-insurgency role, as demonstrated by its actions during the Iranian embassy siege in London in 1980, the SAS is a regiment trained to cause disruption behind enemy lines and gather information useful to friendly forces. Members of the SAS are volunteers from regular regiments who undergo strict selection and training (including parachute and free-fall training), becoming specialists in a particular skill, e.g. demolition or communications systems.

Royal Corps of Signals (R Signals)

The Royal Corps of Signals provides communications systems for the army. R Signals personnel are found throughout the structure of the Army, and account for almost 9% of the total Army manpower. Each armoured division has its own R Signals regiments providing communications to and from the headquarters. At brigade level, the Ptarmigan secure switching network works as a normal telephone system but with automatic rerouting if exchanges are put out of action. It carries computer-based information systems and the BATES artillery command system. Clansman portable radio equipment allows communication at unit level. Within NATO, R Signals are involved with Ace High and the satellite-based SATCOM programme, and to communicate with units further afield the FITS (Falkland Islands Trunk System) has been set up. R Signals are also responsible for electronic warfare (EW), a necessarily secretive branch of technology, which involves listening to and disrupting enemy signals, and avoiding the same treatment from the enemy.

Royal Corps of Transport (RCT)

Air, sea, rail and motor transport are covered by the RCT, whose job it is to transport the Army at all times. A transport regiment will have about 300 vehicles in which to carry supplies of all kinds to replenish men and machines. The RCT is also responsible for the ambulance squadrons and car squadrons providing staff cars. There is also a small fleet of vessels based near Southampton which carry supplies around the coast of Great Britain and to the Continent. In Germany the RCT has its own diesel railway upon which it trains technicians responsible for assisting on the German rail network in time of war. In addition to the regular army, this facility is supported by 275 Railway Squadron whose members are largely drawn from British Rail staff. Air transport is covered by 47 Air Despatch Squadron using RAF transport aircraft and helicopters to target and drop supplies by parachute.

Other sections

Among the other specialized sections of the Army are the *Army Air Corps*, operating almost entirely with helicopters (Lynx helicopters for anti-tank combat, and Gazelles for observation, patrol, casualty evacuation and movement of troops); *Royal Electrical and Mechanical Engineers* (*REME*), maintaining and repairing a very wide range of vehicles and equipment both in depots and in the field; *Royal Pioneer Corps*; *Gibraltar Regiment*.

Women's Royal Army Corps

The position of women in the army has improved over the past years, but they may still not take part in direct combat and may carry arms only for self-protection. On the career ladder the rule that they may not hold a post that would have to be filled by a man in time of war does not significantly reduce their prospects, although their pay is still below that of a man in the equivalent rank.

EQUIPMENT

Tanks

During 1988/9 a sixth regiment of Challenger 1 tanks was placed with BAOR with a further regiment on order. Replacement of the now ageing Chieftain tank will be either with Vickers' Challenger 2 Mk2 or with the American Abrams main battle tank.

Tanks

Name	*Crew*	*Max. speed*	*Armament*
FV4030/4 Challenger	4	56 km/h	1 × 120 mm L11A5 gun 1 × 7.62 mm L8A2 machine gun 1 × 7.62 mm L37A2 machine gun smoke dischargers
FV4201 Chieftain	4	48 km/h	1 × 120 mm L11A5 gun 1 × 7.62 mm L8A1 machine gun 1 × 7.62 mm L37A1 machine gun smoke dischargers
Scorpion series includes Striker, Spartan, Samaritan, Sultan, Samson, Scimitar, Stormer	3	80.5 km/h	1 × 76 mm L23A1 gun 1 × 7.62 mm L43A1 machine gun smoke dischargers (weapons vary)
FV721 Fox	3	104 km/h	1 × 30 mm Rarden L21 gun 1 × 7.62 mm L8A1 machine gun smoke dischargers
Ferret series	2	93 km/h	1 × 7.62 mm machine gun
FV510 Warrior	3	75 km/h	1 × 30 mm Rarden L21 gun 1 × 7.62 mm L94A1 chain gun
FV432 series	2+8–10	52 km/h	1 × 7.62 mm L7A2 machine gun smoke dischargers
Saxon	2+8	96 km/h	1 × 7.62 mm L7A2 machine gun
FV1611 Pig	2+6–8	64 km/h	Smoke or CS Gas discharger
Centurion	5	34.6 km/h	1 × 165 mm demolition gun 1 × 0.30 L3A3 machine gun 1 × 0.30 L3A4 machine gun smoke dischargers
FV180 Combat Engineer Tractor	2	56 km/h	1 × 7.62 mm L4A4 machine gun smoke dischargers

Infantry Weapons

Name	*Calibre*	*Rate of fire/magazine capacity*
L9A1 automatic pistol	9 mm	13 rounds
L2A3 sub-machine gun	9 mm	550 rpm/34 rounds

L1A1 rifle	7.62 mm	40 rpm/20–30 rounds
L42A1 rifle	7.62 mm	Single shot/10 rounds
M16 rifle	5.56 mm	700–950 rpm/20–30 rounds
L85A1 (Endeavour) individual weapon (SA 80)	5.56 mm	650–800 rpm/30 rounds
L86A1 (Engager) light support weapon	5.56 mm	700–850 rpm/30 rounds
L4A4 machine gun	7.62 mm	500–75 rpm/30 rounds
L7A2 general purpose machine gun	7.62 mm	625–750 rpm/100-round belt
L94A1 chain gun	7.62 mm	570 rpm/metal link belt
L3A3 & L3A4 machine gun	0.30 in	400–550 rpm/250-round belt
L1A1 machine gun	12.7 mm	450–600 rpm/metal-link belt
L10A1 mortar	51 mm	3 bombs per minute
LAW 80 (projectile launcher)	94 mm	500 m range
L16A2 Ordnance muzzle-loading	81 mm	15 bombs per min/5800 m range
L14A1 infantry gun	84 mm	6 rpm/1000 m range
Milan anti-tank missile	90 mm	2000 m range

Artillery weapons – Guns and howitzers

Name	*Calibre*	*Rate of fire*
L118 field gun	105 mm	6 rpm
L121 (FH-70) howitzer	155 mm	6 rpm
L13A1 gun		7–10 rpm
M185 howitzer		1–3 rpm
M113 gun		1 round every 2 mins; 2 rpm possible
M201 howitzer		1 round every 2 mins; 2 rpm possible

Self-propelled guns and howitzers

Name	*Crew*	*Speed*	*Armament*
FV433 field artillery self-propelled howitzer (Abbot)	4	48 km/h	1 × 105 mm L13A1 gun 1 × 7.62 mm L4A4 machine gun smoke dischargers
M109A2 self-propelled howitzer	6+2	56 km/h	1 × 155 mm M185 howitzer 1 × 7.62 mm L4A4 machine gun
M107 self-propelled gun	5+3	56 km/h	1 × 175 mm M113 gun
M110A2 self-propelled howitzer	5+8	56 km/h	1 × 8 in/203 mm M201 howitzer
MLRS (Multiple Launch Rocket System)	3/4	64 km/h	227 mm rocket/30,000 m range

Missiles

Name	*Length*	*Max. velocity*	*Range*
Lance (tactical nuclear)	6.146 m	Mach 3	4.8–121 km
Rapier (air defence)	2.235 m	Mach 2+	6800 m
Javelin	1.4 m	Mach 1+	4000+ m
Blowpipe	1.349 m	—	3000+ m
Starstreak (in development)		Mach 4	

Army Air Corps

Aircraft name	*Crew*	*Range*	*Armament*
Lynx AH1	2+ up to 8	630 km	8 × ITOW missiles 2 × 7.62 mm L20A1 machine guns reconnaissance flares
Lynx AH9	2+8	630 km	2 × 7.62 mm machine guns
Gazelle AH1	2+3	650 km	2 × 7.62 mm L20A1 machine guns reconnaissance flares
Scout AH1	2+4	488 km	None – used for reconnaissance
Turbine Islander AL1	2+7	1,000 km	None – used for support duties

Missiles

Name	*Length*	*Maximum range*
TOW (tube-launched, optically-guided, wire-guided)	1.168 m	3,750 m

ROYAL NAVY

The Navy is controlled by the Defence Council in the first place, but detailed management is in the hands of the Admiralty Board. This is chaired by the Secretary of State for Defence, and the four subordinate Ministers are also members. The naval side of the board is headed by the Chief of the Naval Staff and First Sea Lord (the same person), and the other members are the Chief of Naval Personnel and Second Sea Lord, the Controller of the Navy (responsible for ships, weapons and research and development) and the Chief of Fleet Support (logistics, stores, dockyards). Remaining members of the board are the Second Permanent Under-Secretary of State and the Controller of Establishments, Research and Nuclear Programmes.

Command Structure

The Royal Navy's Fleet is commanded by the Commander-in-Chief Fleet based at Northwood, Middx. The shore-based establishments are controlled by Area Flag Officers under the Commander-in-Chief Naval Home Command at Portsmouth. The Naval Air Stations and other aero units are commanded by the Flag Officer Naval Air Command, and the Royal Marines have their own Commandant General.

Since 1988 the nine destroyer and frigate squadrons of the Royal Navy, along with the five squadrons of mines counter-measures vessels (MCMVs), four squadrons of patrol vessels and four squadrons of submarines have been under the command of the Flag Officer First Flotilla. A senior captain is assigned a type of warship to oversee and is given a small staff with which to do this; categorizing the fleet by type of ship simplifies administration and sometimes leads to improvements of operation. On board ship the commanding officer is always called the captain, irrespective of his actual rank (he could be a lieutenant RN, lieutenant commander, or a commander) and the operating of the ship is divided into departments such

Personnel

Strength of Navy regular forces (including personnel in training)

	1985	*1986*	*1987*	*1988*	*1989*
Male	59,100	56,800	55,300	54,300	53,600
Officers	8,900	9,000	9,100	9,100	9,000
Servicemen	50,100	47,800	46,200	45,300	44,600
Female	3,700	3,500	3,400	3,300	3,400
Officers	400	400	400	400	400
Servicewomen	3,300	3,100	3,000	2,900	3,000
Total	62,800	60,300	58,700	57,600	57,000

Changes in numbers of Navy regular forces

Recruitment	*1983/4*	*1984/5*	*1985/6*	*1986/7*	*1987/8*
Male	4,223	4,231	3,987	4,791	4,601
Officers	445	537	568	592	455
Servicemen	3,778	3,694	3,419	4,199	4,146
Female	562	351	289	545	580
Officers	8	14	32	36	26
Servicewomen	554	337	257	509	554
Total	4,785	4,582	4,276	5,336	5,181
Outflow					
Male	4,514	5,011	6,356	6,295	5,603
Officers	796	567	648	620	671
Servicemen	3,718	4,444	5,708	5,675	4,932
Female	581	561	559	624	621
Officers	73	49	55	46	49
Servicewomen	508	512	504	578	572
Total	5,095	5,572	6,915	6,919	6,224
Net gain or loss	–310	–990	–2,639	–1,583	–1,043

as weapons, aviation, supply, etc. The structure of the ranks has evolved through centuries of tradition and the classes of officer, non-commissioned officer and rating are usually segregated, e.g. for accommodation, both ashore and afloat.

Royal Marines

Although they are part of the Royal Navy, the Royal Marines resemble a part of the Army in that the men are trained in combat techniques not seafaring. There are about 7700 Marines, including special units trained in commando techniques and equipped for action in the arctic regions. The bands throughout the Navy are staffed by the Marines.

Women's Royal Naval Service (WRENS)

Although still not given permanent postings on board ship, today's Wrens may spend short periods at sea, depending on their specialization. The new post of Wren Weapon Analyst, for example, demands their presence to assess the results of the projects they work on. Wrens are trained in the same way as their male colleagues, but specializations tend to fall into the areas of aviation and the more stereotyped (though still vital to the operations of the Fleet) such as medicine and clerical. Ranking and pay structures are independent of the male members of the Royal Navy.

Equipment

Of the total procurement budget for the armed forces in 1989/90, sea equipment accounted for 29.6%, and 4.1% of this will be used for the development of new projects. Since 1979 the Navy has ordered and brought into service (or is expecting a small balance to come into service soon) 11 submarines, 15 frigates, 25 mines counter-measures vessels, 10 patrol craft (three of these for use in the Falklands), six auxiliary vessels, and 82 aircraft. During 1989 seven new ships and submarines of various classes were brought into service. In the US development of the Trident D-5 missile programme continues with test firings on land and at sea. The warhead development is being carried out at various Atomic Weapons Establishments in the UK and support facilities at the Clyde Submarine base were completed in 1988.

The increasing importance of helicopters is indicated by an invitation to tender for an aviation support ship to provide dedicated helicopter-lifting facilities during amphibious operations, development of the Anglo-Italian Merlin (EH101) ASW helicopter, and the coming into service of RFA Argus (replacing RFA Engadine) as an aviation training ship with much improved helicopter training facilities.

In addition, the Navy is involved in development projects for T23 frigates, a single-role minehunter, an oiler replenishment vessel, and the Type 2400 Upholder submarine, all of which should become operational in the mid-1990s.

Strength of the Fleet

Strength shown at 1 Apr. 1989 and includes ships approved for disposal during 1989/90. All submarines, ASW carriers, assault ships, guided missile destroyers, frigates, offshore patrol ships, and MCMVs are assigned to NATO, and other ships could be made available to support NATO if national requirements permitted.

Strength of the Fleet
* = undergoing refit or on standby
\+ = engaged in trials or training

Name	*Pennant No.*	*Crew (officers & ratings)*	*Date commissioned*	*Home port*
SUBMARINES				
Polaris (SSBNs) nuclear-powered, ballistic missile carriers				
*Renown**	S26	(13+130)	Nov. 1968	Faslane
Repulse	S23	13+130	Sept. 1968	Faslane
Resolution	S22	13+130	Oct. 1967	Faslane
Revenge	S27	13+130	Dec. 1969	Faslane
Fleet submarines (SSNs) nuclear-powered, attack roles				
*Churchill**	S46	(13+90)	July 1970	Faslane
Conqueror	S48	13+100	Nov. 1971	Faslane
Courageous+	S50	13+96	Oct. 1971	Faslane
Sceptre	S104	12+85	Feb. 1978	Plymouth/Faslane
Sovereign	S108	12+85	July 1974	Plymouth/Faslane
Spartan+	S105	12+85	Sept. 1979	Plymouth/Faslane
*Splendid**	S106	(12+85)	Mar. 1981	Plymouth/Faslane
Superb	S109	12+85	Nov. 1976	Plymouth/Faslane
Swiftsure	S126	12+85	Apr. 1973	Plymouth/Faslane
Tireless	S117	12+85	Oct. 1985	Plymouth/Faslane
Torbay	S118	12+85	Feb. 1987	Plymouth/Faslane
Trafalgar	S107	12+85	May 1983	Plymouth/Faslane
Trenchant+	S91	(12+85)	Jan. 1989	Plymouth/Faslane
Turbulent	S110	12+85	Apr. 1984	Plymouth/Faslane
Valiant+	S102	14+96	July 1966	Faslane
*Warspite**	S103	(14+96)	Apr. 1967	Faslane
Type 2400 (SS/SSK) conventional power, patrol submarines				
Upholder	S40	7+37	Dec. 1989	not confirmed
Oberon Class (SS/SSK) diesel–electric power, patrol submarines				
Ocelot	S17	7+62	Jan. 1964	Portsmouth/Plymouth

Name	*Pennant No.*	*Crew (officers & ratings)*	*Date commissioned*	*Home port*
Odin	S10	6+62	May 1962	Portsmouth/Plymouth
Olympus	S12	6+64	July 1962	Portsmouth/Plymouth
Onslaught	S14	6+62	Aug. 1962	Portsmouth/Plymouth
Onyx	S21	6+62	Nov. 1967	Portsmouth/Plymouth
Opossum	S19	6+62	June 1964	Portsmouth/Plymouth
*Opportune**	S20	(6+62)	Dec. 1964	Portsmouth/Plymouth
Oracle	S16	7+58	Feb. 1963	Portsmouth/Plymouth
Osiris	S13	6+64	Jan. 1964	Portsmouth/Plymouth
Otter	S15	7+62	Aug. 1962	Portsmouth/Plymouth
Otus	S18	7+61	Oct. 1963	Portsmouth/Plymouth
ASW CARRIERS (CVSAs)				
Ark Royal	R07	131+869	Nov. 1985	Portsmouth
Illustrious	R06	131+869	June 1982	Portsmouth
Invincible+	R05	131+869	July 1980	Portsmouth
ASSAULT SHIPS (LPDs)				
*Fearless**	L10	(37+500)	Nov. 1965	Portsmouth
Intrepid	L11	37+500	Mar. 1967	Portsmouth
GUIDED-MISSILE DESTROYERS (DLG or DGH)				
Type 82 command, control, communications, and intelligence roles				
Bristol	D23	27+378	Mar. 1973	Portsmouth
Type 42 area air defence ships				
Batch 1				
Birmingham	D86	26+273	Dec. 1976	Portsmouth
Glasgow+	D88	21+249	May 1977	Portsmouth
Newcastle	D87	21+278	Mar. 1978	Portsmouth
Batch 2				
Cardiff+	D108	(20+260)	Sep. 1979	Portsmouth
*Exeter**	D89	(26+273)	Sep. 1980	Portsmouth
Liverpool	D92	26+273	July 1982	Portsmouth
Nottingham	D91	26+273	Apr. 1983	Portsmouth
*Southampton**	D90	(26+273)	Oct. 1981	long refit
Batch 3				
Edinburgh	D97	26+275	Dec. 1985	Portsmouth
Gloucester	D96	26+275	Sep. 1985	Portsmouth
Manchester	D95	26+275	Dec. 1982	Portsmouth
York	D98	26+275	Aug. 1985	Portsmouth
FRIGATES – general purpose/anti-submarine warfare				
Type 23				
Norfolk	F230		1989	
Type 22 – anti-submarine warfare				
Batch 1				
*Battleaxe**	F89	(20+203)	Mar. 1980	
*Brazen**	F91	(18+206)	July 1982	
Brilliant	F90	18+205	May 1981	
Broadsword	F88	25+225	May 1979	
Batch 2				
Beaver	F93	30+260	Dec. 1984	
Boxer	F92	30+260	Dec. 1983	
Brave	F94	30+260	Aug. 1986	
Coventry+	F98	30+260	June 1988	
London	F95	30+260	June 1987	
Sheffield	F96	30+260	Apr. 1988	
Batch 3				
Campbeltown+	F86	31+259	Feb. 1989	
Chatham	F87	31+259	Oct. 1989	
Cornwall+	F99	31+259	Apr. 1988	
Cumberland+	F85	31+259	July 1988	

Name	*Pennant No.*	*Crew (officers & ratings)*	*Date commissioned*	*Home port*
Type 21				
Active	F171	11+160	June 1977	
Alacrity	F174	11+160	July 1977	
Amazon	F169	11+159	May 1974	
Ambuscade	F172	12+168	Sep. 1975	
*Arrow**	F173	(13+167)	July 1976	
Avenger	F185	13+160	May 1978	
Leander:				
Batch 2A				
*Argonaut**	F56	(18+206)	Aug. 1966 Exocet mod 78–80	
Cleopatra	F28	20+230	Mar. 1966 Exocet mod 72–5	
Phoebe	F42	20+230	Apr. 1966 Exocet mod 74–7	
Sirius	F40	20+203	June 1966 Exocet mod 75–7	
Batch 2B				
Danae	F47	18+205	Sep. 1967 Exocet mod 77–8	
*Minerva**	F45	(18+210)	Sep. 1967 Exocet mod 76–9	
Penelope	F127	19+200	Oct. 1963 Exocet mod 80–2	
Batch 3				
Andromeda	F57	35+226	Dec. 1968 Exocet mod 77–81	
Charybdis	F75	18+196	June 1969 Exocet mod 79–82	
Hermione	F58	18+196	July 1969 Exocet mod 80–2	
Jupiter	F60	18+196	Aug. 1969 Exocet mod 80–3	
Scylla	F71	18+196	Feb. 1970 Exocet mod 80–3	
Batch 3B				
Achilles	F12	17+243	July 1970	
Ariadne+	F72	20+240	Feb. 1973 Sea-Wolf refit 71–3	
NAVIGATION TRAINING SHIP				
Offshore Patrol				
*Juno**	F52	(18 + 210)	Mar. 1967	Portsmouth
Castle Class (Falklands Patrol vessels)				
*Dumbarton Castle**	P265	(6+34)	Mar. 1982	Rosyth
Leeds Castle	P258	6+34	Aug. 1981	Rosyth
Island Class (Fisheries Protection)				
Alderney	P278	5+30	Oct. 1979	Rosyth
Anglesey	P277	4+29	June 1977	Rosyth
Guernsey	P297	5+30	Oct. 1977	Rosyth
Jersey	P295	5+30	Oct. 1976	Rosyth
Lindisfarne	P300	5+30	Mar. 1978	Rosyth
Orkney	P299	4+31	Feb. 1977	Rosyth
Shetland	P298	5+29	July 1977	Rosyth
MCMVs Mines Counter-Measures Vessels				
Minesweepers River Class (All except HMS *Blackwater* operated by Royal Naval Reserve)				
Arun	M2014		Aug. 1986	Littlehampton
Blackwater	M2008		June 1985	Rosyth
Carron	M2004		Sep. 1984	Bristol
Dovey	M2005		Dec. 1984	Glasgow
Helford	M2006		May 1985	Belfast
Helmsdale	M2010		Mar. 1986	Dundee
Humber	M2007		May 1985	London
Itchen	M2009		Sep. 1985	Southampton
Orwell	M2011		Nov. 1985	Newcastle
Ribble	M2012		Feb. 1986	Liverpool
Spey	M2013		Apr. 1986	Rosyth
Waveney	M2003		July 1984	Cardiff
Minesweepers Ton Class				
Cuxton	M1125	5+27	Oct. 1954	Portsmouth/Rosyth

Name	*Pennant No.*	*Crew (officers & ratings)*	*Date commissioned*	*Home port*
Soberton	M1200	5+27	Sep. 1957	Portsmouth/Rosyth
Upton	M1187	5+27	July 1956	Portsmouth/Rosyth
Minehunters Ton Class				
Brereton	M1113	5+33	July 1954	Rosyth
Brinton	M1114	5+33	Mar. 1954	
*Gavington**	M1140	(5+33)	July 1954	Reserve
Hubberston	M1147	5+33	Oct. 1955	Portsmouth
Iveston	M1151	5+33	June 1955	Portsmouth
Kedleston	M1153	5+33	July 1955	Rosyth
Kellington	M1154	5+33	Nov. 1955	Rosyth
*Kirkliston**	M1157	(5+33)	Aug. 1954	Reserve
*Nurton**	M1166	5+33	Aug. 1957	Portsmouth
Sheraton	M1181	5+33	Aug. 1956	Rosyth
Wilton	M1116	5+33	July 1973	Portsmouth
Minehunters Hunt Class				
Atherstone	M38	6+39	Jan. 1987	Portsmouth/Rosyth
Berkeley	M40	6+39	Nov. 1987	Portsmouth/Rosyth
Bicester	M36	6+39	Feb. 1986	Portsmouth/Rosyth
Brecon	M29	6+39	Mar. 1980	Portsmouth/Rosyth
*Brocklesbury**	M33	(6+39)	Feb. 1983	Portsmouth/Rosyth
Cattistock	M31	6+39	July 1982	Portsmouth/Rosyth
Chiddingfold	M37	6+39	Aug. 1986	Portsmouth/Rosyth
Cottesmore	M32	6+39	June 1983	Portsmouth/Rosyth
Dulverton	M35	6+39	Nov. 1983	Portsmouth/Rosyth
Hurworth	M39	6+39	June 1985	Portsmouth/Rosyth
Ledbury	M30	6+39	June 1981	Portsmouth/Rosyth
Middleton+	M34	6+39	Aug. 1984	Portsmouth/Rosyth
Quorn+	M41	6+39	Jan. 1988	Portsmouth/Rosyth
Single Role Minehunter				
Sandown	M101	7+27	May 1989	Portsmouth
PATROL CRAFT				
Bird Class (Northern Ireland)				
Cygnet	P261	3+25	July 1976	Belfast
Kingfisher+	P260	3+25	Oct. 1975	Belfast
(Training Craft)				
Petrel	P262	4+20	Feb. 1977	Dartmouth
Sandpiper	P263	4+20	Sep. 1977	Dartmouth
Redpole	P259	3+25	Mar. 1985	Belfast
Coastal Training Craft+ (Operated by Royal Naval Reserve and University Royal Navy Units)				
Archer	P264	2+8	Aug. 1985	Dundee
Biter	P270	2+8	Feb. 1986	Liverpool
Blazer	P279	2+8	Mar. 1988	Liverpool
Charger	P292	2+8	June 1988	Liverpool
Dasher	P280	2+8	Mar. 1988	Aberdeen
Puncher	P291	2+8	July 1988	London
Pursuer	P273	2+8	Feb. 1988	London
Ranger	P293	2+8	Sep. 1988	London
Smiter	P272	2+8	Feb. 1986	London
Trumpeter	P294	2+8	Sep. 1988	Liverpool
Attacker Class				
Attacker	P281	2+12	Mar. 1983	Glasgow
Chaser	P282	2+12	Mar. 1983	Aberdeen
Fencer	P283	2+12	Mar. 1983	Southampton
Hunter	P284	2+12	Mar. 1983	London
Striker	P285	2+12	Mar. 1983	Liverpool
Peacock Class – Hong Kong offshore patrol vessels				
Peacock	P239	6+38	July 1984	Hong Kong
Plover	P240	6+38	July 1984	Hong Kong
Starling	P241	6+38	Aug. 1984	Hong Kong

Name	*Pennant No.*	*Crew (officers & ratings)*	*Date commissioned*	*Home port*
Gibraltar Search & Rescue Craft				
Cormorant	P256	1+8	1976	Gibraltar
Hart	P257	1+8	1972	Gibraltar
SUPPORT SHIPS				
Submarine Tender/Target Ship				
Sentinel	P246	3+29	Jan. 1984	Faslane
Seabed Operations Vessel				
Challenger	K07	186	Aug. 1984	Portsmouth
Fleet Tankers				
*Black Rover**	A273	(16+31)	Aug. 1974	
Blue Rover	A270	16+31	July 1970	Portland
Gold Rover	A271	16+31	Mar. 1974	Portsmouth
*Green Rover**	A268	(16+31)	Aug. 1969	
Grey Rover	A269	16+31	Apr. 1970	Portsmouth
*Olmeda**	A124	27+62	Oct. 1965	Portsmouth
Olna	A123	27+62	Jan. 1966	Portsmouth
Olwen	A122	25+62	June 1965	Portsmouth
Tidespring+	A75	30+80	Jan. 1963	Portsmouth
Support Tankers				
Appleleaf	A79	20+40	Dec. 1979	Portsmouth
Bayleaf	A109	20+40	Mar. 1982	Portsmouth
Brambleleaf	A81	20+40	Jan. 1976	Portsmouth
Oakleaf	A111	36	1981	Portsmouth
Orangeleaf	A110	20+40	1979	Portsmouth
Fleet Replenishment Ships				
Fort Austin	A386	127 RFA 36 RNSTS	May 1979	Portsmouth
Fort Grange	A385	127 RFA 45 RN 3 36 RNSTS	Apr. 1978	Portsmouth
Regent	A486	134 RFA 37 RNSTS	June 1967	Portsmouth
*Resource**	A480	79 RFA 38 RN 137 aircrew	May 1967	Portsmouth
Helicopter Support Ship				
Argus	A135	79 RFA 38 RN 137 aircrew	June 1988	Portsmouth
LANDING SHIPS				
*Sir Bedivere**	L3004	(21+44)	May 1967	
Sir Galahad	L3005	17+32	Nov. 1987	
Sir Geraint	L3027	21+44	July 1967	
Sir Percivale	L3036	21+44	Mar. 1968	
Sir Tristram	L3505	21+44	Sep. 1967	
FORWARD REPAIR SHIPS				
Diligence	A132	31 RFA 90 RN	1981	Falkland Islands
Stena Seaspeed (on temporary charter)	–	31 RFA 90 RN	–	Falkland Islands
ROYAL YACHT/HOSPITAL SHIP				
Britannia	A00	21+256	Jan. 1954	Portsmouth
ICE PATROL SHIP				
Endurance		13+106	1968	Portsmouth

Name	*Pennant No.*	*Crew (officers & ratings)*	*Date commissioned*	*Home port*
SURVEY SHIPS				
Beagle	A319	6+40	May 1968	Plymouth
*Bulldog**	A317	(4+34)	Mar. 1968	Plymouth
Fawn	A325	5+37	Oct. 1968	Plymouth
Gleaner	A86	1+4	Dec. 1983	Plymouth
Hecate	A137	12+105	Dec. 1965	Portsmouth
Hecla	A133	12+105	Sep. 1965	Portsmouth
Herald	A138	12+106	Nov. 1974	Portsmouth
Roebuck	A130	7 +40	Oct. 1986	Plymouth

Naval Aircraft

Aircraft	*Crew*	*Date went into service*	*Squadrons*
Air Defence/Reconnaissance/Attack			
Sea Harrier FRS1	1	Aug. 1978	3
Harrier T4	1/2	Oct. 1969	1
Anti-Submarine			
Sea King HAS5	4+22	Oct. 1980	7
Anti-Submarine/Anti-Ship			
Lynx HAS 2/3	3+10	Feb. 1976	3
Airborne Early Warning			
Sea King AEW2		1982	1
Commando Assault			
Sea King HC4		1982	3
Aircrew Training			
Gazelle HT2	1/3+4	1967	1 (basic training)
Jetstream T2/3	1/2	1979	1 (observer training)
Chipmunk	1/2		(air experience)
Fleet Support Search and Rescue			
Sea King Mk5	4	Oct. 1980	1
Sea King Mk4		1982	1
Fleet Training and Support			
Hunter T8/GA11	1/2		Radar training, bomb practice
Canberra TT18			Target towing
Support			
Sea Devon	1/3+8	1955	
Sea Heron	1/3+14	1961	

Weaponry

Name	*Range*	*Type/calibre*	*Class of ship*
Weaponry			
Seacat	4.75 km	SAM/SSM	Hermes, County Leander, Amazon, Rothesay
Sea Dart	30 km	SAM/SSM	Invincible, Types 82, 42
Sea Wolf	10 km	SAM/SSM	Leander, Type 22
Sea Eagle	100km	ASM	Sea Harriers
Sea Skua	Medium	ASM	Lynxes HAS5
Exocet to be replaced			
by Harpoon in 1990s	38 km	SSM	County, Leander, Types 21, 22
Sub-Harpoon	–	Submarine SSM	Submarines
Mark 8	18 m depth	Torpedo	Patrol subs
Mk24 Tigerfish	300 m depth	Torpedo	SSKs, SSNs, SSBNs
Spearfish			
Stingray	–	AS Torpedo	Helicopters

Name	*Range*	*Type/calibre*	*Class of ship*
Ikara	24 km	ASW Torpedo launcher	Leanders
Vickers Mk8 Gun	22 km	114 mm	Types 21, 22
Oto Melara	16 km	76 mm	Peacock
Oerlikon	4 km	20 mm	most classes
Bofors	4 km	40 mm	most classes
Phalanx	1.85 km	20 mm	ASW, Type 42
Goalkeeper system			Type 22, ASW

Defensive countermeasures include chaff (metal strips to confuse radar), metal smoke (to confuse electro-optical tracking systems), and flares (to act as decoys for heat-seeking missiles).

Merchant Fleet

The Royal Navy is able to call upon ships of the Merchant fleet for defence use in its exercises and for military operations. Recently the number of ships suitable for this work has been dropping, but financial incentives such as the Merchant Shipping Act 1988, which enables the Government to provide assistance for training and the establishment of the Merchant Navy Reserve, along with provisions in the Finance Act 1988, which altered the rules on seamen's earnings from work overseas, seem to have slowed the drop. In addition, Britain is negotiating with flag-of-convenience states such as the Bahamas to enable use of British-owned vessels on their registers in time of need.

The types of vessel suitable for military use would be: large stern trawlers and other fishing vessels for off-shore support; tankers for transport of fuel; general cargo vessels for movement of provisions; cruise ships for use as troop carriers and hospital ships; roll-on-roll-off (ro-ro) ferries for passengers and transport; tugs for manoeuvring of ships. The figures for manpower are based upon those registered with the General Council of British Shipping and available for employment under National Maritime Board agreements and include about 1000 foreign sailors.

ROYAL AIR FORCE

Since 1964 the Royal Air Force has been under the control of the Ministry of Defence. Its administration is carried out under the Air Force Board whose chairman is the Secretary of State for Defence (though the vice-chairman, the Minister of State for the Armed Forces, usually officiates). The professional RAF members of the board are the Chief of the Air Staff, the Air Member for Personnel, Air Member for Supply and Organization, and Controller of Aircraft; other members are as for the Army and Admiralty Boards.

Command Structure

The RAF is divided into commands, according to the functions carried out.

Strike Command

This is the 'active' side of the RAF with detachments at various permanent or temporary bases around the world. It cooperates closely with NATO. Strike Command is divided into three Groups: no. 1, responsible for attack, reconnaissance, tanker, battlefield support and transport operations; no. 11, defence; no. 18, maritime operations. The RAFs air traffic control system also has the status of a Group within Strike Command.

Type and Numbers of Vessels in the Merchant Fleet

	1984	*1985*	*1986*	*1987*	*1988*
Vessels registered in UK:					
Large stern trawlers, etc.	404	377	335	318	343
Tankers	94	87	42	27	44
General cargo vessels	177	177	152	140	126
Cruise ships	3	3	2	2	4
Ro-Ro ferries	70	70	63	63	60
Tugs	102	106	96	93	86
Vessels registered in Crown Dependencies and Dependent territories:					
Large stern trawlers, etc.	—	—	2	8	5
Tankers	—	—	61	73	76
General cargo vessels	—	—	85	41	36
Cruise ships	—	—	—	—	1
Ro-ro ferries	—	—	10	11	9
Tugs	—	—	2	5	5
Manpower					
Officers	17,646	15,523	13,036	10,978	9,568
Ratings	20,251	19,095	17,612	15,835	13,638
Cadets	1,625	1,016	727	554	428

Support Command

This command provides support of all kinds, including all the training and communications facilities of the RAF. Maintenance of all types of aircraft is carried out at the Aircraft Engineering Units at RAF St Athan and RAF Abingdon, and storage of aircraft, when aeroplanes not in current use are kept ready for service should the need arise, is done at RAF Shawbury in Shropshire. The Field Repair Squadron based at Abingdon has the task not only of salvaging wrecked service aircraft from all over the world, but also of devising ways in which they can be repaired, and returning them to second-or third-line duties.

Signals fall into three main areas: telecommunications; signals engineering and ground radio repair; electronic warfare. The three major supply bases, at Stafford, Carlisle, and Quedgeley, have an annual turnover of more than 1 million items. To ensure the smooth running of the multitude of stations and specializations within Support Command, a dedicated computer network based at RAF Hendon works 24 hours a day recording and locating equipment.

To give military ground support to the airborne forces, the *RAF Regiment* with its Headquarters in Whitehall operates a range of equipment, including Scorpion light tanks and Rapier missiles, designed to defend airbases from ground and air attack.

Women's Royal Air Force

Women in the WRAF spend the first part of their training with the men, but not all specializations are open to them for further training. However, aircraft and electronic engineering now have growing numbers of women specialists and better-known areas of photographic interpretation, secretarial and management, and air traffic control are well staffed by members of the WRAF.

Equipment

The Lightning, which had been in service with the RAF for 28 years, was finally replaced by the Tornado F3 during 1988. The first Harrier GR5 Squadron became operational in late 1989 and 26 more Tornado GR1 and 15 more F3s are on order to replace predicted peacetime losses over the next few years. The Tucano basic training aircraft is coming into service, and development of the European Fighter Aircraft (EFA) to replace Phantoms and Jaguars and improvements to the Tornado GR1 are going ahead. The ALARM (Air-Launched Anti-Radar Missile) for the GR1 continues its development and test firings, and half of the 12 mobile radars supporting the UK Air Defence Ground environment system are now operative.

Deployment

All front-line aircraft are assigned or could be made available to NATO. In addition to normal deployment in the NATO area in 1989, RAF squadrons were posted in:

Falkland Islands Phantoms, Hercules, Chinooks, Sea

Strength of RAF regular forces (including personnel in training)

	1985	*1986*	*1987*	*1988*	*1989*
Male	87,500	87,200	87,300	87,000	85,800
Officers	14,500	14,500	14,700	14,700	14,400
Servicemen	73,000	72,700	72,600	72,300	71,400
Female	5,900	6,100	6,300	6,400	6,300
Officers	800	900	900	1,000	1,000
Servicewomen	5,100	5,200	5,400	5,400	5,300
Total	93,400	93,300	93,600	93,400	92,100

Changes in numbers of RAF regular forces

Recruitment	*1983/4*	*1984/5*	*1985/6*	*1986/7*	*1987/8*
Male	8,279	5,977	6,154	6,405	5,728
Officers	771	701	792	904	786
Servicemen	7,508	5,276	5,362	5,501	4,942
Female	1,132	930	860	1,157	885
Officers	124	126	144	170	188
Servicewomen	1,008	804	716	987	697
Total	9,411	6,907	7,014	7,562	6,613
Outflow					
Male	5,399	5,885	6,438	6,358	6,051
Officers	811	869	882	938	1,008
Servicemen	4,588	5,016	5,556	5,420	5,043
Female	772	736	779	855	907
Officers	101	98	101	121	118
Servicewomen	671	638	678	734	789
Total	6,171	6,621	7,217	7,213	6,958
Net gain or loss	+3,240	+286	–203	+349	–345

Front-Line Units

Aircraft/equipment	*Crew*	*Date of first production*	*No. and location of squadrons*
STRIKE/ATTACK			
Tornado	2	July 1980	2 × UK 7 × Germany
Buccaneer	2	July 1970	2 × UK
OFFENSIVE SUPPORT			
Harrier	1/2	Dec. 1967	1 × UK 2 × Germany (also reconnaissance role)
Jaguar	1/2	Oct. 1969	2 × UK
MARITIME PATROL			
Nimrod MR	3+9	June 1968	4 × UK
RECONNAISSANCE			
Canberra PR9	2/3		1 × UK (photo reconnaissance)
Jaguar	1/2	Oct. 1969	1 × UK
Tornado GR1a		July 1979	1 × Germany
AIR DEFENCE			
Tornado F3	2	Nov. 1985	3 × UK
Phantom FG1	2	1968	2 × UK
Phantom FGR2	2	1968	1 × UK 2 × Germany
AIRBORNE EARLY WARNING			
Shackleton	4+6–8	1951	1 × UK
AIR TRANSPORT			
VC10	4+150		1 × UK
Hercules	4	1966	4 × UK
HS125	2+8	1962	
Andover	2/3+58	1960	1 × UK
Gazelle helicopters	2+3	1972	
Andover	2/3+58	1968	1 × Germany
Chinook helicopters	3+44	Dec. 1980	1 × UK 1 × Germany
Wessex helicopters	2+16	1963	1 × UK
Pumä helicopters	2/3+16	1971	1 × UK 1 × Germany
TANKERS			
Victor K2	5	1977	1 × UK
VC10K2/3	4+18	July 1983	1 × UK
Tristar K1/KC1	3/4	July 1985	1 × UK
SEARCH AND RESCUE			
Sea King helicopters	4 + 19	1977	1 × UK
Wessex helicopters	2+16	1963	1 × UK
GROUND DEFENCE			
Light armour/ infantry weapons			5 × UK 6 × UK (RAuxAF) 1 × Germany

Weaponry: guided missiles

Name	*Range/calibre*	*Type*	*Aircraft*
Bloodhound	80 km	Radar guided	
Harpoon	110 km	Radar guided	Nimrod
Martel	60 km	Radar guided	Buccaneer
Sea Eagle	100 km	Radar guided	Buccaneer/Tornado
Sky Flash	40 km	Radar guided	Phantom/Tornado
Sparrow	40 km	Radar guided	Phantom

Name	Range/calibre	Type	Aircraft
ASRAAM (Advanced Short-range Air-to-Air Missile)			Tornado
Sidewinder	3.5 km	Infra-red seeking	Phantom/Buccaneer/Jaguar/Harrier/Nimrod
Red Top	12 km	Infra-red seeking	Lightning (training)
ALARM (Air-Launched Anti-Radar Missile)	10 km	Radar seeking	Tornado/Buccaneer
Shrike	12–16 km	Radar seeking	
JP233 Low Altitude Airfield Attack System			Tornado
BL755 Cluster Bomb			Harrier/Jaguar/Phantom/Buccaneer
SNEB rockets	68 mm	Various types	Harrier/Buccaneer/Hawk
M61A1 Vulcan gun	20 mm		Phantom
Mauser cannon	27 mm		Tornado
Aden gun (Mk 5)	30 mm		Jaguar/Hawk/Harrier
Aden 25	25 mm		Harrier

Kings, Rapier missiles (plus Hercules on Ascension Island for use in transporting personnel and equipment from the UK to the Falklands).
Cyprus Wessex helicopters plus one RAF Regiment Squadron.
Hong Kong One squadron Wessex helicopters.
Belize One flight Harriers, one flight Puma helicopters, half a squadron of an RAF Regiment.

RESERVES

The Reservist Forces accounted for 2.2% of the defence budget in 1989/90, at £439 million. They are not merely a back-up for the regular forces but are an integral part of defence planning: Reservists would form 45% of the front line in Germany in an emergency. Reservists have evening and weekend training sessions and must attend an annual two-week intensive training course (sometimes overseas); pay is £600 per year for those who have served at least three years.

ARMY RESERVES

Regular Reserves

Men and women who have completed their period of active service continue for a time to be liable to be called up as reserves. This is much the largest part of the Army's reserve force. The other reserves are all voluntary.

Territorial Army

This provides a trained and equipped force ready to form part of the BAOR and fill home defence roles (along with the HSF) such as guarding installations, reconnaissance, and maintenance of communications at times of national emergency. In the BAOR role, the TA would make up 45% of the infantry, logistic, and medical support.

Home Service Force (HSF)

This recent addition to the Volunteer Reserve Force intended to take a local guardian role at a low cost, thus allowing more highly-trained personnel to be used more effectively.

Ulster Defence Regiment (UDR)

Unique in several ways, this is the largest single regiment of the British Army (6500 serving members); the only regiment to accept women recruits; the newest regiment, having been founded in 1970; and the only regiment permanently on the front line and totally

All services

	1985	1986	1987	1988	1989
Regular Reserves					
Male	204,000	209,900	218,200	228,200	233,100
Female	1,600	1,700	1,800	1,900	2,000
Total	205,600	211,600	220,000	230,100	235,100
Volunteer Reserves and Auxiliary Forces					
Male	80,100	85,900	86,800	82,800	80,100
Female	8,500	9,400	9,900	10,000	10,500
Total	88,600	95,300	96,700	92,800	90,600
Cadets					
Male	135,400	132,500	132,100	128,700	126,800
Female	9,200	10,900	13,600	15,900	16,700
Total	144,600	143,400	145,700	144,600	143,500

dedicated to Northern Ireland. It provides military support for the Royal Ulster Constabulary (RUC), covering 85% of Northern Ireland, and over half the personnel are part-timers. Regular UDR members are full-time Army officers and NCOs; PCs (Permanent Cadre) are full-time members who only serve in Northern Ireland; PTs and Greenfinches (female personnel) are part-timers who spend evenings and weekends on duties such as routine patrols and other security tasks.

NAVY RESERVES

Royal Naval Reserve (RNR)

This consists of men and women who have completed their active service but continue for a time to be liable for reserve duties. In wartime the RNR would provide much of the Navy's mine counter-measures force, manning 41 ships in that capacity. Other essential support roles would be with medical and dental teams and naval control of shipping for resupply and co-ordination of reinforcements.

Royal Naval Auxiliary Service (RNXS)

This is formed of civilian volunteers, trained and administered by the Royal Navy. Defence of UK ports and maritime areas would be its role in wartime, along with assistance in naval control of shipping. Shore service can include communications work and general administration, whilst sea service is open to women as well as men, with several women commanding RNXS launches and patrol craft.

Royal Marine Reserve (RMR)

This was formed in 1963 from units of the Royal Marine Forces Volunteer Reserve, and provides specialist sub-units and individual reinforcements to the Royal Marines in times of tension. After four years' training the Reservist joins a Commando Company and begins further specialist training in the section which best suits his talents, for example the Special Boat Section or Mountain and Arctic Warfare.

Royal Fleet Auxiliary (RFA)

This originates from the times of Elizabeth I, and its role is to maintain the Navy at sea by transferring fuel, water, food, ammunition and other stores while both vessels are under way. Membership of the RFA is open to all UK merchant seamen or to cadets from school or college.

Royal Maritime Auxiliary Service (RMAS)

This is civilian-manned and provides local maritime support and naval bases. RMAS vessels can be distinguished by their colour scheme of black hull and buff-coloured upperworks and are often seen around the UK coastline.

ROYAL AIR FORCE RESERVES

Royal Auxiliary Air Force

This consists of former members of the RAF, and would in times of emergency be responsible for defence of front-line airfields and support of intelligence and communications sections. In addition they would have a guardianship role and responsibility for air movements and evacuation by air of wounded personnel.

RAF Volunteer Reserve

This consists of civilian volunteers, and takes its place with regular units to operate at home and abroad in public relations, intelligence and information gathering.

Army reserves

	1985	*1986*	*1987*	*1988*	*1989*
Regular Reserves					
Male	149,300	152,900	159,300	166,600	172,000
Female	900	1,000	1,100	1,100	1,100
Total	150,200	153,900	160,400	167,700	173,100
Territorial Army					
Male	67,200	70,600	71,000	67,000	64,700
Female	6,500	7,100	7,500	7,700	8,100
Total	73,700	77,700	78,500	74,700	72,800
Ulster Defence Regiment					
Male	5,700	5,800	5,800	5,600	5,600
Female	700	700	800	700	700
Total	6,400	6,500	6,600	6,300	6,300
Home Service Force					
Male only	900	3,000	3,300	3,100	3,000
Cadet Force					
Male	69,800	68,200	67,600	65,500	65,500
Female	2,300	2,700	3,600	3,800	3,800
Total	72,100	70,900	71,200	69,300	69,300

Navy reserves

	1985	1986	1987	1988	1989
Regular Reserves					
Male	23,100	23,900	24,200	24,400	25,100
Female	300	300	300	300	400
Total	23,400	24,200	24,500	24,700	25,500
Volunteer Reserves and Auxiliary Forces					
Male	4,000	4,200	4,300	4,300	4,200
Female	1,200	1,300	1,300	1,300	1,300
Total	5,200	5,500	5,600	5,600	5,500
Royal Marines					
Regular Reserves					
Male only	2,200	2,300	2,300	2,400	2,500
Volunteer Reserves and Auxiliary Forces					
Male only	1,000	1,200	1,200	1,300	1,200
Cadets					
Male	24,700	24,000	23,200	22,500	22,400
Female	3,700	4,000	4,300	4,500	4,600
Total	28,400	28,000	27,500	27,000	27,000

RAF reserves

	1985	1986	1987	1988	1989
Regular Reserves					
Male	29,400	30,700	32,300	34,900	33,600
Female	500	500	500	500	500
Total	29,900	31,200	32,800	35,400	34,100
Volunteer Reserves and Auxiliary Forces					
Male	1,100	1,100	1,300	1,400	1,300
Female	200	200	300	300	300
Total	1,300	1,300	1,600	1,700	1,600
Cadets					
Male	40,900	40,300	41,300	40,700	38,900
Female	3,200	4,200	5,700	7,600	8,200
Total	44,100	44,500	47,000	48,300	47,100

ROYAL OBSERVER CORPS

The ROC used to be part of the RAF but is now the operating arm of the United Kingdom Warning and Monitoring Organization (UKWMO) run by the Home Office as the nuclear observers for the UK. From their 870 monitoring stations dotted throughout the country these volunteers keep a constant look-out for nuclear explosions and maintain the systems that have been set up for warning and monitoring should an attack occur. The posts themselves are underground chambers spread at 16–20 km intervals with communications equipment enabling warning to be given direct to the BBC for transmission on radio and TV and to Carrier Control Points, which can be anything from local police stations to pubs. Observation and analysis of the nuclear incident is carried out by a network of instruments measuring such things as range, intensity and fall-out, and communicated to the ROC Headquarters near Stanmore, Middlesex for further action.

DEFENCE ESTATE

The total extent of the Defence Estate is now nearly 600,000 acres, of which 80% is used for training areas, ranges, and operational airfields.

Army training areas

	Acres
Salisbury Plain, Wiltshire	91,000
Otterburn, Northumberland	56,000
Sennybridge, Wales	30,000
Wassop, Cumbria	24,000
Catterick, North Yorkshire	21,000
Stanford, Norfolk	18,000
Dartmoor, Devon	15,000
Aldershot, Hampshire	11,000
Cinque Ports, south-seat coast	10,200
Castlemartin, Wales	5,900
Cultybraggan, Scotland	5,100

There are also other smaller training areas throughout the country.

The RAF have bombing ranges in the Wash area of East Anglia and Scotland. Low-flying areas are in North Wales and the Lake district, as well as using the above facilities. There are also arrangements with the US Air Force whereby RAF pilots and crew can gain experience in the clear skies and perfect weather conditions of Colorado, Nevada and Arizona.

Disposal of land and buildings raised over £77 million in 1987/8 and £155 million in 1988/9, but land is also purchased to provide more training areas and larger and safer ranges for weapons testing and experience. With more service personnel buying their own houses, married quarters are being disposed of (the stock declined from 85,900 rented units in 1984 to 78,500 in 1989) and whenever possible surplus housing stock is offered to local authorities or housing associations on short-term lease arrangements.

DEPLOYMENT OF UK SERVICE PERSONNEL OVERSEAS

The figures below include personnel on loan to countries in the areas shown. Royal Navy and Royal Marines personnel are counted in the area in which they served during the period shown; personnel on emergency tours of duty, e.g. earthquake relief, are counted in that area. Defence attachés and advisers are included in 'Other locations'.

UNITED STATES ARMED FORCES IN BRITAIN

US AIR FORCE

From June 1942 to Dec. 1945, 165 military installations in the UK were being used by US combat forces. After the end of World War II most of these were dismantled, but in 1948 the US Air Force returned to British soil to operate long-range B-29 strategic bombers from four East Anglian bases during the Berlin airlift. The Third Air Force is today headquartered at RAF Mildenhall in Suffolk from where it operates tactical air operations in support of NATO.

US NAVY

Grosvenor Square, London, is the US Naval Headquarters Europe and US Eastern Atlantic (UNCOMEASTLANT), home of the US Sixth Fleet

Deployment of UK Service Personnel Overseas

	1984	*1985*	*1986*	*1987*	*1988*
Army					
Europe					
West Germany	55,163	55,997	56,222	55,702	55,723
Other	3,909	3,853	3,877	3,830	4,133
Mediterranean, Near East, Gulf					
Gibraltar	815	771	744	781	723
Cyprus	3,307	3,177	3,317	3,346	2,981
Other	233	238	232	186	198
Far East					
Hong Kong	1,962	1,964	1,842	1,825	1,746
Other	235	235	222	224	204
Other locations	4,516	4,406	2,756	4,398	4,412
Total	70,140	70,641	69,212	70,292	70,120
Royal Navy and Royal Marines					
Europe					
West Germany	256	18	6	253	10
Other	838	867	514	824	620
Mediterranean, Near East, Gulf					
Gibraltar	816	733	766	529	677
Cyprus	20	19	16	20	14
Other	2,185	552	546	524	986
Far East					
Hong Kong	275	272	275	319	305
Other	58	114	334	61	60
Other locations	3,250	2,746	2,931	5,191	2,572
Total	7,698	5,321	5,388	7,721	5,244

Deployment of UK Service Personnel Overseas (contd)

	1984	*1985*	*1986*	*1987*	*1988*
Royal Air Force					
Europe					
West Germany	10,186	10,571	10,690	10,881	11,017
Other	1,803	1,623	1,591	1,674	1,697
Mediterranean, Near East, Gulf					
Gibraltar	465	455	405	387	398
Cyprus	1,626	1,539	1,610	1,584	1,643
Other	114	104	126	130	126
Far East					
Hong Kong	268	268	269	265	262
Other	13	9	7	9	6
Other locations	2,891	2,633	2,280	1,902	1,897
Total	17,366	17,202	16,978	16,832	17,046
Total all services	95,204	93,164	91,578	94,845	92,410

	1949	*1953*	*1969*	*1979*	*1985*	*1989*
US Air Force bases	5	43	9	8	9	8
Military personnel	5,818	46,634	23,473	24,254	26,873	25,000
Civilian personnel	1,420	3,478	6,897	4,621	4,532	21,000
Total	7,238[2]	78,548[1]	64,061[1]	59,763[1]	59,251[1]	77,606[1]
Mission aircraft	TDY only	312	330	288	346[3]	

[1] includes dependants
[2] does not include dependants
[3] estimate

command centre, and SUSLO (Special US Liaison Office) dealing with intelligence and communications. About 800 Naval personnel work there alongside other members of the American Embassy. It is also the centre of the WMCCS (Worldwide Military Command and Control System), which covers nuclear weapons plans and accounting systems and the Fleet Ocean Surveillance Information Centre (FOSIC).

Submarine Squadron 14 of the US Navy, with about 1800 personnel, ten SSBN submarines, one submarine tender, and a dry dock, operates refit site 1 at Holy Loch. Glen Douglas close by is a NATO nuclear and conventional weapons store supplying Holy Loch, which in addition to being a refit site for submarines also provides material, operational, and logistical support for the nuclear-powered ballistic missile submarines. Other US Navy bases include: Edzell, near Aberdeen (600 personnel), communications; Thurso (135), microwave communications; Brawdy, South Wales (280), US Navy Sonar Surveillance Centre, providing oceanographic data and probably plotting submarine and other vessel movements in the Atlantic.

US ARMY

There are few US Army personnel based in the UK and they are at: Burtonwood, near Liverpool, where there is a depot for Army Material Command 47th Area Support Group; RSA Caerwent, South Wales, and RSA Hythe, Kent, which is a subsidiary munitions store for Burtonwood and part of the 60th Ordnance Group; Felixstowe, Suffolk, which is a US Army Terminal; and Chessington, Surrey, which is an Army Medical Storage Facility.

NUCLEAR CAPABILITY

Figures for the UK's own nuclear capacity are usually combined with the other members of NATO to provide an overall figure compared with the Warsaw Pact forces. The total number of British nuclear warheads is unknown, but the following figures have been released at various times: 4 × Polaris submarines each with 16 missiles each carrying three MIRV Chevaline nuclear warheads (200kT each); 4 × Trident submarines each capable of carrying 16 Trident 2 D-5 SLBMs with 14 MIRVs each on order (Warheads are being manufactured at the Atomic Weapons Establishment, Aldermaston and support facilities at Clyde Submarine Base were completed in 1988. Latest estimated cost of this programme (Jan. 1989) is £9,089 million); 230 × Tornado aircraft with nuclear weapon carrying capability; 50 × Buccaneer with nuclear weapon carrying capability; 36 × Nimrod with nuclear weapon carrying capability; 40 × Sea Harriers with nuclear weapon carrying capability; 12 × Lance short-range missiles being upgraded to nuclear capability; 12 × M110 howitzers with 1 (BR) Corps and 100 × howitzers being upgraded to nuclear capability based in West Germany.

RESEARCH

11.7% of the defence budget in 1989/90 was spent on research and development, in which 0.3% of service manpower and 14% of the civilian manpower employed by the services is engaged.

US Air Force in Britain, 1988*

Base	*USAF personnel*	*US civilians*	*Dependants*	*Unit/equipment/purpose*
RAF Alconbury, Cambs.	3,220	207	5,243	10th Tactical Fighter Wing, 2 squadrons A-10 Thunderbolt II 17th Reconnaissance Wing, TR-1s for round-the-clock high-altitude surveillance
RAF Bentwaters/RAF Woodbridge Suffolk	4,264	235	5,437	81st Tactical Fighter Wing, 4 squadrons A-10 Thunderbolt II, 1 squadron F-16C Fighting Falcons, for training 67th Special Operations Squadron, HC-130N/P Hercules for refuelling 21st Special Operating Squadron, MC-53J Super Stallion helicopters
RAF Chicksands, Beds.	1,380	178	1,224	7274th Air Base Group, secure communications for US and NATO forces
RAF Fairford, Glos.**	1,173	134	1,421	7020th Air Base Group, supporting 11th Strategic Group, KC-10A Extenders and KC-135A stratotankers for refuelling
RAF Greenham Common, Berks.***	1,645	124	2,122	501st Tactical Missile Wing, cruise missiles (being returned to the US from Aug. 1989); base includes RAF Welford, with Europe's largest inventory of non-nuclear munitions
RAF Lakenheath, Suffolk	4,610	462	5,852	48th Tactical Fighter Wing (Statue of Liberty Wing), 4 squadrons F-111F fighters; base includes two USAF Contingency Hospitals
RAF Mildenhall, Suffolk	3,182	195	3,396	513th Airborne Command and Control Wing, operational control of more than half the USAF's tactical airlift capacity in Europe; over 30 subsidiary units including 306th strategic Wing, KC-135A Stratotankers for refuelling, 313th Tactical Airlift Group, C-130 Hercules, C-141 Starlifters and C-5A Galaxies for cargo and troop movements, Detachment 4, 9th Strategic Reconnaissance Wing, SR-71 Blackbird for high-altitude surveillance
RAF Upper Heyford, Oxon	4,662	341	5,620	20th Tactical Fighter Wing, 3 squadrons F-111E variable sweep wing and 1 squadron EF-111A Raven, long-range fighters
Other	857	237	1,291	

* Eight major bases. There are several other minor installations throughout England.

** Stand-by base only by 1 Oct. 1990

*** Stand-by base only by 31 May 1991

Defence Budget expenditure on research and development

(£ million)	*1986/7*	*1987/8*	*1988/9*
Ship construction and underwater warfare	377	348	378
Ordnance and other army	142	188	188
Military aircraft	667	628	631
Guided weapons	341	350	369
Other electronics	325	337	349
Other R&D	485	406	435
Total	2,337	2,257	2,350

MINISTRY OF DEFENCE RESEARCH ESTABLISHMENTS

Nuclear

Aldermaston, Berks.

Non-nuclear

Admiralty Research Establishment, Portsmouth (surface and underwater weaponry, marine technology); Aeroplane and Armament Experimental Establishment, Boscombe Down, near Salisbury; Chemical Defence Establishment, Porton Down, near Salisbury (chemical and biological techniques); Royal Aerospace Establishment, Farnborough (all aspects of aerospace except rocket motors and radar) with seven subsidiary units; Royal Armament Research and Development Establishment, Sevenoaks (weapons and integrated weapon systems), with Vehicles Department at Chessington, Surrey (research and testing of vehicles and bridges); Royal Signals and Radar Establishment, Malvern (radar, electronics, optical and infrared systems for military or civilian applications).

DEFENCE CONTRACTS

Approximately one-third of military research and development is carried out in the Ministry of Defence's own establishments.

Recipients of the largest contracts (1987/8, latest figures available) were: *over £250 million* – British Aerospace plc (Aircraft Group), British Aerospace plc (Dynamics Group), General Electric Co plc, Plessey Co plc, Rolls Royce plc, Vickers Shipbuilding & Engineering Ltd; *£100–250 million* – Boeing Aerospace Company, Devonport Management Ltd, Ferranti plc, FKI Babcock plc, Hunting Associated Industries plc, Racal Electronics plc, Royal Ordnance plc, Thorn EMI plc, Vickers plc, Westland plc; *£50–100 million* – British Petroleum Co plc, British Telecommunications plc, Dowty Group plc, Esso UK plc, GKN plc, Lucas Industries plc, Pilkington Brothers plc, Philips UK Ltd, The Rover group plc, The 'Shell' Transport and Trading Co plc, Short Bros plc, STC plc, Swan Hunter Shipbuilders Ltd.

SPECIALIST SERVICES

FISHERIES AND OFFSHORE OIL AND GAS PROTECTION

This service is run jointly by the Navy and the RAF. Since 1977 when the UK in common with the other EC nations extended her fishing limits to a 200-mile (370-km) radius, the RAF Fisheries Protection Squadron based at Rosyth, near Edinburgh, has had 270,000 sq. miles (9,699,300 km^2) to patrol. Aerial patrol is carried out by civilian aircraft on charter with Nimrods from RAF Kinloss in Scotland and RAF St Mawgan in Cornwall. Security patrols are provided for the many offshore oil and gas platforms in UK waters and on a smaller scale in inshore waters during the salmon season to deter poaching. In 1988, 2202 vessels were boarded, and there were 19 convictions for poaching; the entire service cost £16 million to run.

HYDROGRAPHIC SURVEY

This service is run by the Royal Navy. The survey ship *Vidal* launched in 1951 was the first ship of her type to be equipped with a flight deck and helicopter, enabling her survey parties to cover much wider areas on their missions, and she was the first warship designed for cafeteria messing. In 1964 the Cook class of specialist hydro-oceanographic ships began the task of surveying the Antarctic – a task continued today by the Ice Patrol Ship *Endurance* among others.

Constant survey and resurvey of the world's oceans is necessary because of developments such as: the increase of size and draught of merchant ships; the deeper diving capabilities of submarines; the development of new harbours; natural changes in the sea bed. The Department of Transport contributes towards the cost of survey in home waters, which has risen from £12.4 million in 1985/6 to an estimated £16.9 million in 1989/90.

MEDICAL SERVICES

All three forces run their own medical, dental and nursing services. The Army has 556 qualified doctors, 197 qualified dentists and 4552 support staff; Royal Navy 283, 82, 1446; Royal Air Force 363, 120, 2533.

In 1988, there were nine service hospitals in the UK and nine overseas, with total number of beds numbering 1766 and 981 respectively. The average percentage of beds occupied has dropped from 63.8% (54.5% overseas) in 1982 to 57.4% (48.2% overseas) in 1988 with a corresponding fall in the average number of days in hospital from 6.4 (5.6) to 5.1 (4.5). Sickness episodes (i.e. confined to bed for two days or more) have also dropped under most headings, partly as a result of reduced manpower, but have increased for infective and parasitic diseases (2963 in 1982, 3039 in 1987) and diseases of the musculoskeletal system (6974 in 1982, 7829 in 1987). Training and exercise injuries too have increased (934 in 1982, 1124 in 1987), as have medical discharges from all causes (800 in 1982 to 1109 in 1987).

METEOROLOGICAL OFFICE

The Meteorological Office, which is the source of most weather forecasts in the UK, is at present part of the Air Force. This situation originated during the early days of flying, when knowledge of weather all over the country and weather forecasting was much more vital to flight than it is now. The Met Office collects, publishes and distributes weather information worldwide and also undertakes research in the areas of meteorology and geophysics, using the Meteorological Research Flight based at Farnborough and the Meteorological Office College at Shinfield Park, Reading. In the late 1980s, the Meteorological Office was identified as one sector of operations to be designated an executive agency, thus removing it from direct military control. In 1989/90 the Office spent £74.3 million but received £27.2 million from selling forecasts and advice, so that its net expenditure was £47.1 million. There are 2200 civilian staff.

Meteorological Office, Bracknell, Berks RG12 2SZ. Tel. 0344 420242. London Weather Centre, Penderel House, 284–6 High Holborn, London WC1V 7HX. Tel. 071–430 5709.

SEARCH AND RESCUE (SAR)

The SAR service operated by the Royal Navy and the Royal Air Force primarily exists to rescue aircrew who have had to abandon their aircraft over land or sea, but it is better known as the service for civilians in distress around the British coastline. Call-outs are now occurring much more frequently, particularly from service personnel (up over 40% in five years). In response to this demand, call-out times of the RN Sea King helicopters have been shortened and the number of dedicated RN/RAF units equipped with Sea Kings has been doubled to eight. Co-operation with the Royal National Lifeboat Institution is enhanced by frequent combined exercises, and the RAF Mountain Rescue Teams contribute their special skills. During disasters both at home (the Lockerbie air crash, the Piper Alpha explosion) and abroad (Jamaican hurricane, Nepalese earthquake) SAR services are always needed and ready to respond.

The figures below show incidents which were handled by the two Rescue Co-ordinating Centres (Pitreavie and Mount Wise) and in which more than one Service may have been involved. It also includes medical incidents in which SAR facilities gave assistance, such as emergency airlifts between hospitals. Persons rescued means people who were removed alive from an incident or who were transported for medical treatment.

SAR call-outs

	1984	*1985*	*1986*	*1987*	*1988*
Call-outs:					
Royal Navy aircraft	265	272	259	346	438
Ships and auxiliary vessels	–	3	–	–	1
Army helicopters	1	–	–	–	–
RAF aircraft	1,001	1,005	1,066	1,220	1,377
RAF marine craft	8	1	–	–	–
RAF Mountain Rescue	56	33	73	79	80
Persons rescued:					
Civilians	1,004	826	747	863	1,129
Military	57	57	64	87	105
by Royal Navy	190	195	159	167	236
by Army	–	–	–	–	–
by RAF	840	674	638	726	958
by RAF Mountain Rescue	31	14	14	21	40

ECONOMY

THE BUDGET

The Budget is the annual financial review which takes place every March. Budgets are now normally delivered on Tuesdays. In election years, after a change of government, a Budget will usually be introduced by the incoming Chancellor, whether or not one has already been delivered by the outgoing Chancellor. In some years, an extra *mini* budget is necessary to adjust taxation levels.

Between 1641 and 1967 proposals for the raising of taxation originated in the Ways and Means Committee, but this was abolished in 1967. For the two annual taxes, income tax and corporation tax, Ways and Means resolutions followed by Finance Act clauses are still statutory requirements. The Chairman of Ways and Means (currently Harold Walker) usually occupies the chair during the Budget speech.

The tax proposals in the Chancellor's speech are immediately effected by virtue of the Provisional Collection of Taxes Act 1968. Under this act, tax changes and tax continuations, but no new taxes, can be validated by a single motion after the Budget speech. All the individual resolutions involving taxes and duties must be approved by the House within ten working days.

The Financial Bill is a Bill 'of aids and supplies' (Erskine May), which gives permanent legal effect to the Budget Resolutions and is usually presented the same day as the Budget proper. Committee stages for the Bill are often split between the House and a Standing Committee composed of about 30–40 members.

There is generally a large number of amendments proposed to the Bill, but it usually becomes law by July. Budget speeches generally last about an hour now and fall into two general parts – a resumé of the economic situation and then a detailed account of the budgetary measures necessary to raise the money required.

The Conservative Government's stated principal economic aims are to reduce inflation and taxation and to reduce public expenditure as a proportion of national output. The principal economic strategy used is referred to as the Medium Term Financial Strategy

(MTFS), the central objective of which is the defeat of inflation. The MTFS is summarized in the Financial Statement and Budget Report, which supplements the Chancellor's Budget Statement. This also charts developments in the UK economy over the previous financial year and provides economic forecasts for the current financial year, describes the Budget tax proposals and outlines the Government's plans. The November Autumn Statement reviews these plans, and details amendments and additions to the Budget Statement.

MARCH 1990 BUDGET

Chancellor of the Exchequer John Major in his debut Budget, stressed the primary economic objective of the Government was to bring down inflation and then to enter the EMS. He described the 1990 budget primarily as a 'Budget for savers. It will provide a range of incentives to save and a novel incentive to give. It will bring the introduction of independent taxation for married women. It will introduce important measures for business and keep up the pace of supply side reform. It will remove an old grievance from the tax system and make the social security system fairer and it will abolish two taxes.'

Savings. Savings measures were introduced to encourage 'high-street savers . . . essential to a capital-owning democracy'.

The composite rate of tax (1990/1 – 22%) on banks and building society deposits was abolished so that non-taxpayers did not have to pay. However, for taxpayers the composite rate was increased to 25%. Yield of Change: 1991/2, £550 million.

The 1990 Budget's Effect on Pay

Amounts in £ and pence	Annual Income	Monthly Income	NIC Change	89/90 Tax	90/91 Tax	Monthly Change
Single persons	3,000	250	0.65	1.35	0.00	2.00
	5,000	417	0.65	40.94	36.35	5.23
	10,000	833	0.65	139.90	135.31	5.23
	15,000	1,250	0.65	238.85	234.27	5.23
	20,000	1,667	[1](6.93)	337.81	333.23	(2.35)[1]
	25,000	2,083	[1](6.93)	440.08	432.75	0.40
	30,000	2,500	[1](6.93)	598.42	591.08	0.40
	40,000	3,333	[1](6.93)	915.08	907.75	0.40
	50,000	4,167	[1](6.93)	1,231.75	1,224.42	0.40
	80,000	6,667	[1](6.93)	2,181.75	2,174.42	0.40
	100,000	8,333	[1](6.93)	2,815.08	2,807.75	0.40
Married couple	5,000	417	0.65	0.00	0.00	0.65
(both earning, with	10,000	833	1.30	48.75	36.87	13.18
one partner earning 60%	15,000	1,250	1.30	147.71	135.83	13.17
of joint income, the	20,000	1,667	1.30	246.67	234.79	13.18
other earning 40%)	25,000	2,083	1.30	345.63	333.75	13.18
	30,000	2,500	[1](5.12)	452.58	432.71	14.76
	40,000	3,333	[1](6.28)	675.63	630.63	38.72
	50,000	4,167	[1](13.87)	936.23	866.98	55.38
	80,000	6,667	[1](13.87)	1,830.17	1,758.17	58.13
	100,000	8,333	[1](13.87)	2,463.50	2,391.50	58.13
Married couple,	3,000	250	0.65	0.00	0.00	0.65
(wife not working) or	5,000	417	0.65	7.81	0.52	7.94
single parent	10,000	833	0.65	106.77	99.48	7.94
	15,000	1,250	0.65	205.73	198.44	7.94
	20,000	1,667	[1](6.93)	304.69	297.40	0.36
	25,000	2,083	[1](6.93)	403.65	396.35	0.36
	30,000	2,500	[1](6.93)	545.42	533.75	4.73
	40,000	3,333	[1](6.93)	862.08	850.42	4.73
	50,000	4,167	[1](6.93)	1,178.75	1,167.08	4.73
	80,000	6,667	[1](6.93)	2,128.75	2,117.08	4.73
	100,000	8,333	[1](6.93)	2,762.08	2,750.42	4.73
Non-married couple	5,000	417	0.65	0.00	0.00	0.65
(both working, one	10,000	833	1.30	48.75	36.87	13.18
earning 60% of joint	15,000	1,250	1.30	147.71	135.83	13.17
income, the other 40%)	20,000	1,667	1.30	246.67	234.79	13.18
	25,000	2,083	1.30	345.63	333.75	13.18
	30,000	2,500	[1](5.12)	444.58	432.71	6.76
	40,000	3,333	[1](6.28)	642.50	630.63	5.59
	50,000	4,167	[1](13.87)	883.23	866.98	2.38
	80,000	6,667	[1](13.87)	1,777.17	1,758.17	5.13
	100,000	8,333	[1](13.87)	2,410.50	2,391.50	5.13

[1]( )Brackets indicate a loss. All figures assume 5% of gross income goes to a contributory pension scheme and individuals are contracted out of National Insurance (Serps).

Savings up to a limit of £1800 pa (or an initial one-off investment of £3000) became tax-free, as long as the principal sum is left untouched.

Mr Major announced the creation of a new tax-free savings account. Tax-Exempt Special Savings Accounts (TESSA) offer tax-free savings up to £9000 for five years from 1 Jan. 1991.

The amount of savings people can have without losing entitlement to means-tested benefits was increased from £6000 to £8000 for income support and family credit, doubling to £16,000 for housing or Community Charge/poll tax benefit.

An increase of 1% in the interest rate on National Savings Investment Accounts and income bonds.

Income Tax. From 6 Apr. 1990 married women to be taxed independently. Income Tax basic rate unchanged at 25%. Top rate also unchanged at 40%. Main allowances to increase by 7.7%, in line with inflation.

Mr Major maintained the Government's commitment to a 20% basic Income Tax rate, 'when the time was right'.

Personal allowance: £3005. Married couple's, additional personal allowance and widow's bereavement allowance: £1720. Aged 65–74, personal allowance: £3670. Aged 65–74, married couple's allowance: £2185. Aged 75 and over, personal allowance: £3820. Aged 75 and over, married couple's allowance: £2185. Blind person's allowance doubled: £1080. Income limit for age-related allowances: £12,300.

Excise duties. Increase of 10% in alcohol, tobacco and petrol excise duties, effecting an estimated 0.55% increase in the Retail Price Index (see also INFLATION).

Leaded petrol up 11p per gallon. Unleaded petrol up 9p per gallon, increasing the differential between unleaded and leaded petrol to 15.5p. Derv/diesel up 9p.

Vehicle excise duty (tax disc) unchanged at £100.

Tobacco: cigarettes up 10p for a packet of 20; cigars up 5p for a packet of five; hand-rolling tobacco up 30p for a 30 gramme packet; pipe tobacco unchanged.

Alcohol: spirits up 54p a bottle; wine up 7p a bottle; beer up 2p a pint.

Shares and employee shares. Estimated 11 million UK investors hold shares. Stamp duty and stamp duty reserve tax (0.5%) on shares and securities dealing to be abolished in 1991/2. Cost of Change: 1991/2, £800 million.

Employee Share Ownership Plans (ESOPs) made more attractive.

Business taxes. Mr Major announced increases in the qualifying levels of annual profits for corporation tax, from £150,000 to £200,000. The upper limit for full 35% corporation tax was increased by a third to £1 million.

Business Expansion Scheme tax limit raised to £750,000.

Tax relief introduced on company contributions to the Training and Enterprise Councils in an attempt to encourage private sector involvement.

Tax on private use of company cars increased by 20%. Yield of Change: 1990/1, £160 million.

Value added tax (VAT). VAT threshold raised from £23,000 to £25,400 (the maximum permissible under EC rules). VAT relief on bad debts.

Public sector finance. The debt repayment prediction for 1990/1 decreased from £10 billion to £7 billion. The budget surplus halved from 1988/9 from £14 billion to £7 billion in 1989/90. Mr Major budgeted for a £3 billion surplus in 1990/1 and no surplus in 1991/2 and 1992/3 when the election is due.

Inflation. Mr Major predicted that inflation would remain over 7% by the end of 1990, compared to his earlier, Autumn Statement forecast of 5.75%. He said he expected inflation to fall below 5% during 1991. Mr Major predicted high interest rates for some time to come and rejected the use of credit controls.

Mr Major predicted that the Community Charge/poll tax would add 1% to the Retail Price Index.

Monetary policy. Money Supply growth increased from 0%–4% to 1%–5%. However, it was currently estimated to be running at 6.4%.

No date was set for entry into the exchange-rate mechanism of the European Monetary System (EMS). The reducing of inflation is a pre-condition of entry into the EMS.

Equity investment. For the third consecutive year the limit on Personal Equity Plans was increased, from £4800 to £6000. The required rate of PEP portfolios in ordinary UK equities is reduced from 75% to 50%.

Unit trust and investment trusts limits are also increased to £3000.

Gifts and charity. Gift aid relief for single donations was set at between £600 and £5 million.

Limit on relief for charitable donations under payroll-giving, or Give-As-You-Earn (GAYE) schemes raised to £600. Estimated benefit to charity: £5 million.

Workplace nurseries. Workplace nurseries were exempted from taxation as a benefit in kind. However, there are only 3000 places at workplace nurseries, out of a total of 5.5 million under-5s. Furthermore, in Britain, less than 2% of under-two-year olds attend publicly-funded day-care nurseries, compared with 25% in France and Belgium and 44% in Denmark. Some 44% of 3–5-year old children in Britain attend nursery, compared with 95% in France.

Betting tax duty. Reduction to 40% in the pools betting tax duty. Yield to football: £100 million for safety improvements at football grounds.

Community Charge/poll tax. Doubling of the limit to £16,000, below which people will be eligible for Community Charge/poll tax rebates. This controversial move, whilst assisting 0.25 million voters in England and Wales, did not provide retrospective relief for poll tax payees in Scotland.

Inheritance tax. Inheritance tax threshold was increased from £118,000 to £128,000 from 6 Apr. 1990. Cost of change: 1990/1, £35 million.

Housing. Mortgage tax relief ceiling remained at £30,000.

Stamp duty unchanged on houses costing more than £30,000.

Economic forecasts. Mr Major predicted the economy would only grow by 1% in 1990, rising to 2.75% in 1991.

Balance of payments deficit forecast to decrease, from £21 billion in 1989/90 to £15 billion in 1990/1.

Public Expenditure planning total expected to be overshot by £2.25 billion.

Civil List 1990. The total expenditure on the civil list will increase from £6,195,000 in 1989 to £6,762,000 in 1990, a rise of 9% (see CONSTITUTION).

Reactions to the 1990 Budget

Parliamentary Labour Party. The Labour Leader, Mr Neil Kinnock, in reply to the Chancellor's speech, whilst welcoming some of the measures announced, such as VAT relief on bad debt and the increased tax differential between leaded and unleaded petrol, described the Budget as a 'bits and pieces', stop-gap Budget.

'He (Mr Major) truly showed himself to have the approach of a new broom. The problem is that won't be terribly convincing as long as the broomstick is ridden by the Prime Minister,' said Neil Kinnock.

Labour Party estimates that Conservative budgets

have given more to the top 5% of households than to the entire bottom 70%.

Trade unions. The trade unions attacked the Government's failure to cut interest rates and boost industrial investment and portrayed Mr Major's first budget as the product of a government ignoring real economic problems and paralysed by the prospect of electoral defeat.

Health organizations. The British Medical Association criticized the decision to add only 10p to a packet of 20 cigarettes, saying that children would only be discouraged to smoke if cigarettes cost £2.00.

ASH wanted to see a 17p increase in duty to put the price of cigarettes back to their January 1987 level, in line with inflation.

Alcohol Concern gave a guarded welcome.

Child Poverty Action Group. This was not the most satisfactory method of helping working mothers.

The City. The City was disappointed that the Chancellor had not been tough enough in his first Budget.

The pound closed down 2 pfennigs at DM2.7319, and down 1.5 cents against the dollar at $1.6110.

Sterling closed at 86% of its 1985 value, and against a basket of international currencies it closed 0.1% up.

FTSE closed at 2,259.7 points, up 21.7 points on the 100 Share Index.

Workplace Nurseries Campaign. Delighted by the Chancellor's announcement.

Equal Opportunities Campaign. Joanna Foster, chairwoman of EOC said, 'much more assistance is needed to enable working parents to combine their childcare and employment responsibilities'. The EOC estimated that providing comprehensive childcare facilities would cost £2 billion.

Save the Children. The tax relief would only help a small minority of parents.

Engineering Employers' Federation. Criticized the Government for not aiding industrial investment.

Association of British Chambers of Commerce. 'A triumphant Budget', which would boost savings and control inflation.

International Distillers and Vintners. Complained of the increasing differential between excise duty on spirits and other alcoholic drinks.

Confederation of British Industry (CBI). Welcomed 'a cautious budget' in the face of the challenge of inflation.

Environmental groups. Environmental groups complained that the Chancellor had 'wasted a green opportunity' in only increasing company car tax by 20% and not providing incentives for the fitting of catalytic converters.

Friends of the Earth voiced their concern that the Chancellor had not sought to encourage public transport.

Age Concern. Age Concern was delighted at the Chancellor's decision to increase the amount people can have in savings accounts and still be eligible for means-tested benefits. However, they were also worried that there would be no increase in pension income.

PUBLIC FINANCE

Public finance incorporates taxation, expenditure, borrowing by central and local government and the financing of public corporations. Her Majesty's Treasury is responsible for broad control of public finance and expenditure. The Bank of England is the Government's banker, financial adviser and enacts its monetary policy. General government expenditure is primarily met out of the Consolidated Fund (Exchequer) account at the Bank of England. Any excess of spending over income is financed via the National Loans Fund account, which receives money borrowed by the Government and in financing nationalized industries and other public corporations. The majority of public corporation borrowing is met by central government via the National Loans Fund, although temporary borrowing is met externally (usually the Treasury acts as guarantor). Local authority borrowing is met by central government, with Parliamentary approval, via the Public Works Loans Board. The Board is an independent body, but is merged administratively with the National Investment and Loans Office. The National Insurance Fund is primarily used for payment of social security benefits.

Central government raises and receives money from: individuals and companies via direct and indirect taxation, e.g. income tax and corporation tax; excise duties on alcohol and tobacco; interest and dividends on savings; National Insurance contributions.

Central government spends money on goods and services, e.g. health, and in payments to the public, e.g. pensions and social security.

Local government receives central government grants and raises revenue chiefly via rates (local property taxes) and, from 1 Apr. 1990, the Community Charge/poll tax (see LOCAL GOVERNMENT). From this revenue it provides services such as education, police and fire services, and refuse collection.

TAX REVENUE

There are three main sources of tax revenue for general government: income taxes; capital taxes; expenditure taxes.

Other revenue sources are: National Insurance contributions (which gives entitlement to a range of benefits); Community Charge or poll tax, which is set and collected by local authorities.

Tax thresholds and rate bands for income, inheritance and capital gains tax are automatically raised in line with inflation (Rooker-Wise Amendment), unless Parliament decides otherwise.

The Inland Revenue assesses and collects income and capital gains tax and stamp duty. HM Customs and Excise collects expenditure tax (VAT, most duties and car tax).

Vehicle Excise Duty is the Department of Transport's responsibility. National Insurance contributions are the responsibility of the Department of Social Security (DSS).

The Community Charge/poll tax is the responsibility of the Department of the Environment and the Scottish Office.

Income Taxes

Income tax. Generally, income tax is payable on all income which originates in Britain, though there are exemptions, e.g. social security benefits, interest on some government securities. It is also payable on all income earned broad by British residents, unless they have worked for a full year abroad, in which case they are entitled to 100% tax relief. Tax agreements exist with many countries and, if not, unilateral relief is provided to prevent double payment of tax.

For 1989/90 and 1990/1 the 25% basic rate of income tax applies to the first £20,700 of taxable income. Above this amount the rate increases to 40%. There are a number of allowances and reliefs, which reduce the amount of a person's taxable income, compared with gross income. The main allowances for 1990/1 have been statutorily indexed in line with 7.7% RPI inflation.

The system of independent taxation entitles all

taxpayers to a personal tax allowance against their income. From 6 Apr. 1990 married women will pay their own tax on the basis of their own income. Furthermore, there is a married couple's allowance, equal to the difference between the previous single and married allowances. Initially, this will go to the husband to ensure parity with his previous tax allowances. However, if he does not earn enough to use the allowance to the full extent, the unused portion of the allowance transfers to the wife.

The majority of salary and wage earners pay income tax under the Pay-As-You-Earn (PAYE) system, where tax is deducted by the employer and accounted for by the Inland Revenue.

Mortgage interest relief on repayment of borrowing for house purchase is given at source at the base rate, i.e. repayments are reduced to take account of the basic rate of income tax, the tax refund passing directly from the tax authorities to the bank or building society which provided the loan.

The Business Expansion Scheme provides relief for investors in trading companies without a stock market quotation on investment up to £40,000 in any one year. From 1 May 1990 the general limit for company investment in any tax year will be £750,000.

Corporation tax. Companies pay corporation tax on profits after allowances for deduction. Any company which distributes profits to shareholders has to make an advance payment of corporation tax to the Inland Revenue.

In 1990/1 the basic rate of corporation tax is 35%, though small companies with profits below £200,000 pa are liable for a reduced rate of 25%.

Marginal relief is also available between the main rate and the small companies rate for companies with profits of between £200,000 and £1 million.

The 1990 Budget allowed for corporation tax relief on bad debts. Relief for disposable losses will be phased.

Income tax relief and corporation tax relief will be available from 1 Oct. 1990 for charitable donations, between £600 and £5 million, by individuals and companies respectively.

From April 1991 unit trusts will be subject to corporation tax on income at the basic rate of 25%.

Plant and machinery investment qualifies for an annual allowance of 25%. The allowance is on a reducing balance, i.e. 25% of the total cost may be offset against tax in the first year, 25% of the remaining 75% in the second year, and so on. There are special arrangements for short-life plant and machinery assets. Scientific research qualifies for a 100% allowance.

Industrial and some other sorts of building and construction work qualify for annual tax allowances based on a 25-year life (4% pa for 25 years).

If available tax allowances are greater than taxable profits, then the excess can be carried forward and set against profits.

Petroleum revenue tax. Petroleum revenue tax (deductible in assessing profits for corporation tax) is charged on profits from the production (rather than refining or alternative methods of processing) of oil and gas under a British licence and on its continental shelf.

The rate of tax is 75%, which the oil field licensee is liable to pay after allowances and reliefs are deducted for exploration, appraisal and future development.

It is collected monthly and computed bi-annually.

Capital Taxes

Inheritance tax. Inheritance tax is applicable to transfers of wealth made on, or up to seven years before, the donor's death.

The first £128,000 of the capital transfer is not liable to tax, subject to certain allowances and reliefs.

Higher amounts are taxed at a rate of 40%. A sliding-scale of relief reduces the tax on wealth transfers made between three and seven years before the donor's death. Tax relief is scaled from 20% between three and four years prior to death, to 80% on transfers six and seven years prior to death.

Capital gains tax. Individual capital gains realised on asset disposal are liable to capital gains tax, capital gains of companies being liable to corporation tax.

Exemptions for individuals exist up to £5000 pa total net gain and £2500 in the case of most trusts.

Gains are taxed according to the appropriate income tax rate.

Only gains made since March 1982 are subject to tax and are indexed in line with inflation.

The tax on certain types of gifts and deemed disposals of assets can be deferred until sale of assets.

Some assets, including the principal private residence, possessions worth less than £6000 (and any possession with a predictable life of less than 50 years, except those which qualify for a capital allowance), private motor cars and National Savings Certificates and Bonds are all normally exempt; as are government securities, certain corporate bonds and PEP shares.

Expenditure taxes

Value added tax (VAT). VAT is set at 15% and charged to the consumer. It is collected at each stage in the production and distribution of goods and services by taxable persons (usually businesses with a turnover of more than £25,400 pa). The 1990 Budget announced the simplification of VAT registration requirements to a single limit based on the previous year's turnover.

On purchasing taxable goods and services, the supplier charges the taxable person VAT (input tax). When the taxable person supplies taxable goods or services to customers, then they are in turn charged VAT (output tax). The differences between the input and output taxes is paid to, or repaid by, HM Customs and Excise.

Relief on goods and services is provided in two broad ways: when a person or company is zero rated, or when exempt.

With zero-rate VAT a taxable person does not charge VAT to a customer, but reclaims any input tax paid to suppliers. It applies to: exports; foodstuffs; books; periodicals and newspapers; public transport fares; prescribed drugs and medicines; aids to handicapped persons; certain international services; houseboats and caravans; young children's clothing and footwear; charitable supplies; fuel (non-road use only); domestic power and residential construction.

A taxable person exempt from VAT does not charge a customer output tax and also cannot reclaim or deduct input tax. This system applies to: land and rents; education and health; supplies from trade unions and other professional bodies to their members; finance and insurance; postal services; betting and gaming (not lotteries or gaming machines).

Customs and Excise duties. Customs duties are charged in line with the EC Common Customs Tariff. No customs duties are charged on Community goods. Levies are charged on non-community agricultural products, but special procedures are in operation under the Common Agricultural Policy (CAP).

Excise duties are higher on hydrocarbon oils used for road fuel than those used for other purposes. (see also ENVIRONMENT)

For instance, kerosene and most lubricating oils used for industrial processes are duty-free.

There is an excise duty differential between leaded and unleaded petrol to encourage the use of the latter.

Duties are charged on the basis of alcoholic strength and volume for wine, beer, spirits, made-wine, pear wine and cider.

Spirits used for scientific, medicinal, industrial and research processes are usually free from duty.

The duty on tobacco is calculated on a percentage of retail price and on a charge for 100 cigarettes.

Duties are also charged on casino gaming, bingo and gaming machines, off-course betting and on pool betting. The 1990 Budget announced a reduction to 40% in the pools betting tax duty.

Vehicle excise duty (tax disc) is charged at the rate of £100 pa for a private motorcar or light van; for motorcycles the rate is £10, £20 or £40 pa, depending on the engine capacity.

Goods vehicle licence duty is charged on the basis of gross weight and, if over 12 tonnes, according to the number of axles. The duty is designed to ensure that the vehicles cover at least their road cost through tax (including both licence and fuel duties).

Taxis, buses and coaches are taxed according to their seating capacity.

Car Tax. Cars, motorcycles, scooters, mopeds and some motor caravans (whether imported or not) are taxed at the rate of 10% of wholesale value. Some motor caravans are charged at the rate of 10% of 60% of their wholesale value. VAT is charged on the price, including road tax.

Stamp Duty. Stamp duty is charged on certain kinds of transfer. These include: house sales (1% of total price above £30,000); declarations of trust (50p generally). Stamp duty and stamp duty reserve tax (0.5%) on shares and securities dealing is to be abolished in 1991/2.

National Insurance

There are four classes of National Insurance contributions:

Class 1 – paid by employers and their employees; employees with earnings up to £43 per week do not pay Class 1 contributions. Above this threshold contributions are set at 2% of the first £43 of total weekly earnings and 9% of the balance, up to the upper earnings limit of £325 per week.

Employers contributions are set at the same threshold. Above this threshold, contributions are on a sliding scale from 5% of total earning up to a maximum of 10.45% on earnings of £165 and above per week. There is no upper earnings limit.

Class 2 – a flat rate of £4.25 paid by the self-employed, who can claim exemption if profits are below £2350 pa.

Class 3 – a flat rate of £4.15 voluntary payment for pensions.

Class 4 – in addition to Class 2 contributions the self-employed pay National Insurance on taxable profits over a lower limit, currently £5050 and up to a set upper limit of £16,090. The rate is 6.3%.

Community Charge/poll tax and National Non-Domestic Rate

From April 1989 in Scotland and April 1990 in England and Wales the rates system of local government finance was replaced by the Community Charge/poll tax. It also reformed central government grants to local authorities and, in England and Wales, established a national non-domestic rate based on a re-evaluation of non-domestic properties. The proceeds of this are paid into a national pool and re-distributed to local authorities in proportion to the number of adults living in each authority.

PUBLIC SECTOR DEBT REPAYMENT AND BORROWING REQUIREMENT

In 1988/9 the Public Sector Debt Repayment stood at £14.5 billion, or 3% of GDP; excluding privatization proceeds it stood at £7.4 billion, or 1.5% of GDP. The 1989 Budget forecast a PSDR of £13.8 billion for 1989/90. However, the latest estimate of PSDR for 1989/90 is £7.1 billion (£2.9 billion, excluding the negative expenditure of privatization proceeds).

Perhaps the best measure of government debt is the net public sector debt, which calculates the public sector's net financial liabilities to the private sector and abroad, and is directly related to the PSDR; though there are slight differences due to the exchange rate and the inclusion of accrued index-linked government stocks in the net public sector debt calculation.

At the beginning of the 1988/9 financial year, net public sector debt stood at £158 billion, or 32% of money GDP. It is forecast to fall to £152 billion, or 28% of GDP at the end of 1989/90.

Another measure of debt is the National Debt.

The primary governmental debt instrument is gilt-edged stock, which is marketable and traded on the Stock Market.

Individuals can also make stock transactions through the Department for National Savings Stock Register at Post Offices. Pension funds and life insurance companies have majority holdings.

The Bank of England issues conventional and index-linked stock for the Government and, with high PSDRs, also buys gilt-edged stock by, for instance, reverse auctions.

National Savings are an important additional source of government revenue. 1988/9 (net additions): Income Bonds, £784 million; National Savings Certificates, £410 million; Investment Account, £344 million; Accrued interest, £166 million.

PUBLIC EXPENDITURE

The estimated sum of public expenditure for 1989/90 is £161,900 million. For 1990/1 expenditure is planned at £178,965 million, with £2,670 million planned reserve. The reserve is unallocated for planning years to cover all additional departmental costs. Central government spending is largely voted by Parliament through the annual Supply Estimates, which in 1989/90 provided for expenditure of £116,500 million. The estimates are submitted by each government department to the Treasury. These give details of the department's respective cash requirements for the financial year beginning the following April. Once Treasury approval is given the estimates are presented to Parliament usually at the same time as the Budget and are also approved in July as part of the Annual Appropriation Act.

The Supply Estimates may be supplemented, but if any supply estimate is overspent it must be scrutinized by the Public Accounts Committee before receiving parliamentary approval. Three 'estimate days' are set aside in each parliamentary session for debate on the Supply Estimates. Detailed examination of public expenditure is carried out in Commons select committees. These have the power to study individual departmental expenditure, and require ministerial and civil servant attendance for cross-examination.

Auditing of government expenditure is performed by the Public Accounts Committee and the Comptroller and Auditor General (John Bourn CB). The Comptroller and Auditor General has two distinct duties: (1) as Comptroller General, he ensures that all Exchequer

Public sector borrowing requirements

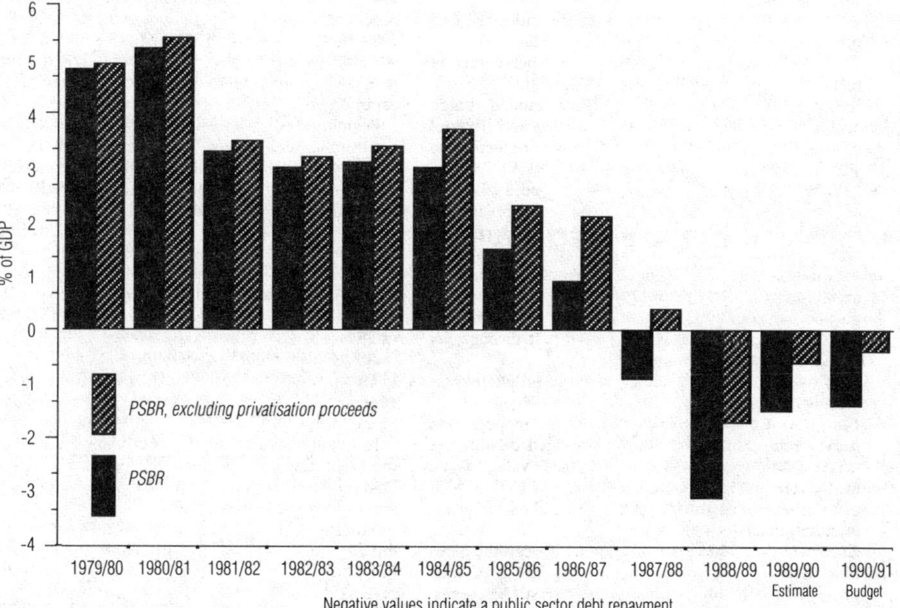

Net public sector debt

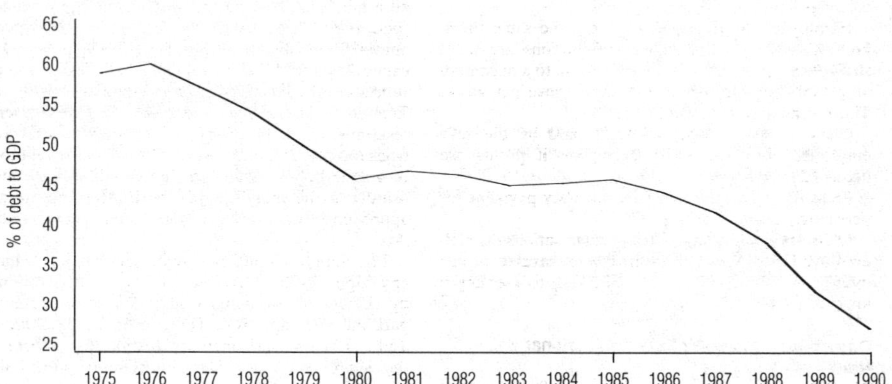

revenue and other public money payable to the National Loans Fund is paid and all payments out of these funds are statutorily authorized; (2) as Auditor General, he is responsible for endorsing government departmental and other public bodies' accounts. He is also responsible for examining revenue accounts and inventories and informing Parliament of his deliberations.

The Public Accounts Committee (15 members – *Chairman* Robert Sheldon) scrutinizes the departmental accounts and the reports of these accounts by the Comptroller and Auditor General. The committee receives evidence from departmental heads and public sector bodies and, in turn, submits its reports to Parliament.

NATIONAL INCOME AND EXPENDITURE

Gross Domestic Product (GDP) is the measure of the total value of all goods and services produced domestically by a nation during a year. It is equivalent to Gross National Product (GNP), minus net investment income from other countries.

GDP can be expressed either in terms of market prices (the prices people pay for the goods and services they buy), or at factor cost (the cost of the goods and services before adding taxes and subtracting subsidies). It can also be expressed at constant prices (that is, after removing the effects of inflation in order to measure the underlying growth in the economy). In 1989, GDP at current factor cost totalled £434,174 million, whilst GDP at constant factor cost (1985 prices) stood at £352,833 million.

In 1989 the GDP index (1985 = 100) was 115.4; an increase of 2.6% on the previous year.

The estimated GDP per capita for 1989 is £7,641 at current prices, or £6,166 at 1985 prices.

INFLATION

There is no exact measure of inflation, but the general index of retail prices (RPI) measures the change month by month in the level of prices of commodities and services purchased by almost all types of household in the United Kingdom.

The index monitors the change from month to month of the cost of a representative 'basket' of goods and services and can also be regarded as a measure of changes in the purchasing power of net income. The composition of the 'basket' (the weight attached to each of the goods and services) is annually revised on the basis of the data in the Family Expenditure Survey. It is affected by changes in indirect taxes, such as VAT and petrol duty, but not by changes in national insurance contributions or income tax, except tax relief on mortgages.

UK inflation remains high in relation to the average consumer prices of the seven major economic powers. Indeed, it is 50% above the average of the major industrialized powers.

Between 1979 and 1988 prices in Britain rose by 90%.

The greatest increases in inflation occurred in 1973 and 1979, with the increases in oil prices.

The present Conservative government has reiterated the primary importance of defeating inflation since its 1979 election pledge to reach a 0% rate of inflation.

In March 1990 the RPI stood at 8.1%. It is expected that inflation will rise sharply in the second quarter of 1990, mainly due to the implementation of the community charge/poll tax. In April 1990 inflation rose to 9.4% and in May to 9.7%, the highest for eight years and approaching the rate of inflation in 1979, when Mrs Thatcher took office. However, the Chancellor, John Major, has predicted that inflation will fall back to 7.25% by the fourth quarter of 1990. The government has made the lowering of the level of inflation a prerequisite for joining the Exchange Rate Mechanism (ERM) of the European Monetary System.

	Sterling Index (1985 = 100)	Relative Manufacturing Unit Labour Costs
(final quarter)		
1985	101.4	103.6
1986	85.1	82.6
1987	92.7	93.0
1988	96.7	98.1
1989	88.0	96.2

There is a close relationship between current market price GDP (or 'money GDP') and inflation. Large fluctuations in the growth of 'money GDP' are generally reflected in inflation, rather than real domestic growth.

The major instrument of the government's monetary policy to curb inflation has been the level of interest rates, which were raised quite dramatically in 1988/9 in an effort to resist the resurgence of inflationary pressures. Interest rates are now the highest of all major countries, and nearly double the German level. In March 1990 interest rates stood at 15.3%.

Thus, inflation has continued to rise and there has been criticism of the government's reliance on only one mechanism to curb inflation.

Another important concern in dealing with inflation is the rate of unit labour costs and pay settlements which, if high, may only serve to increase inflation and thus an inflationary spiral. Between 1981 and 1988 Britain's unit labour costs in manufacturing rose by an average of 3% per annum.

Factor Cost GDP at Current Market Prices 1978–89
Factor Cost GDP at Constant (1985) Prices 1978–90

	1978	1979	1980	1981	1982	1983	1984
Current	149,142	172,804	200,517	218,198	237,752	260,401	279,386
Constant	275,734	283,384	277,408	274,297	279,161	289,240	294,348
Index							

	1985	1986	1987	1988	1989	1990*
Current	305,872	324,256	355,788	396,181	434,174	
Constant	305,872	315,983	329,964	345,028	352,833	356,400
Index	100.0	103.3	107.9	112.8	115.4	116.5

* estimate

Factor Cost GDP Index Average Estimate (1985 = 100)

Workforce in Employment: By Sector (£ millions)

(mid-year estimates)	1961	1971	1976	1979	1981	1983	1984	1985	1986	1987	1988	1989	Feb. 1990
PUBLIC SECTOR	5.9	6.6	7.3	7.4	7.2	7.0	6.9	6.6	6.5	6.4	6.3		
General government	3.7	4.6	5.3	5.4	5.3	5.3	5.3	5.3	5.3	5.4	5.4		
Public corporations	2.2	2.0	2.0	2.1	1.9	1.7	1.6	1.3	1.2	1.0	0.9		
PRIVATE SECTOR	18.6	17.9	17.5	18.0	17.1	16.6	17.1	17.7	17.9	18.4	19.3		
Government training Programmes	–	–	–	–	–	–	0.2	0.2	0.2	0.3	0.3		
TOTAL WORKFORCE IN EMPLOYMENT	24.5	24.5	24.8	25.4	24.3	23.6	24.2	24.5	24.6	25.1	25.9	26.75	26.96

In 1989 unit labour costs rose faster in the United Kingdom than in other major industrial countries. However, with the decline in the value of sterling during 1989 actual costs were lower than in 1988.

INDUSTRIAL PRODUCTION

During the 1960s and early 1970s manufacturing output grew faster than the rest of the economy as a whole. The oil price rises in 1973–4 and 1979, together with increasing overseas competition, led to a sharp reduction in manufacturing output.

In 1989 manufacturing output and productivity rose by 4.75% on the previous year. However, the Budget forecast a freeze in growth in manufacturing output for 1990.

Production industry as a whole (water, energy and manufacturing) rose by 11% between 1979 and 1988. By 1986 energy output had more than doubled in a decade.

UK oil production has been falling since 1985, when it peaked at 127.6 million tonnes (£8,100 million oil surplus). By 1988 production was 5% lower and the oil surplus was down to about £2,300 million. This was due in part to the suspension of production from Piper, Fulmar and connected oil fields. Since 1979 North Sea oil has brought in £76 billion in revenue for the government.

In 1988 Britain was the seventh largest oil producer. It exports approximately 50% of production, mainly to other EC countries, yet is also imports crude oil.

It is estimated that there are only 570–1,800 million tonnes of recoverable oil reserves at existing fields (see ENERGY AND NATURAL RESOURCES and ECONOMY).

INVESTMENT

In the 1960s fixed investment increased by about 5% per annum, but from 1970 to 1983 remained fairly static. Since 1983 it has increased by almost 7% per annum (on average), due to rising company profits and overseas borrowing. The private sector accounts for an increasing majority of investment (88% in 1988), the service sector share of investment has also risen, but there has been a decline in manufacturing investment, which is still below 1979 levels.

The CBI industrial trends surveys suggest a decline in business and total investment for 1990.

UNEMPLOYMENT, EMPLOYMENT AND PRODUCTIVITY

In February 1990 Britain's workforce in employment totalled 26.96 million, an increase of 2.43 million since 1985.

Vacancies rose generally from 1981 to November 1987, since when they began to decrease, standing at 220,000 in July 1989.

According to government figures (the calculation of which have been subject to numerous revisions, thus rendering the series discontinuous) unemployment has fallen steadily since the end of 1986. In February 1990 the total adult unemployed (seasonally adjusted) stood at 1.61 million.

The severity of the recessions of 1974–6 and 1979–81 saw unemployment double to 1.5 million. The percentage of unemployment is 8.3%, still significantly higher than 1979 and high in comparison with other Western nations' rates of unemployment.

OVERSEAS SECTOR AND BALANCE OF PAYMENTS

Historically, trade has played a vital part in Britain's economy. Britain is still the fifth largest trading nation in the world. The European Community, of which Britain is a member, is the world's largest trading area and accounts for about 33% of all world trade. Membership of the European Community has had a profound effect on Britain's distribution of trade, increasing the proportion of trade with other member countries and reducing the share of trade with fellow Commonwealth nations. This trend is expected to become even more pronounced with the completion of the single European market in 1992.

The balance of payments is a measure of Britain's trading position *vis-à-vis* the rest of the world. As well as exports and imports, which make up the 'visible trade balance', account is taken of the earnings through 'invisibles' (such as tourism, banking and insurance). The balance indicates whether Britain has a surplus of income over expenditure. At present it is spending more than it earns. The current balance of payments account deficit is £20,851 million.

This compares with a US current account deficit of about $100 billion and a current account surplus of about $50 billion in Germany and $75 billion in Japan.

VISIBLE TRADE

In 1988 exports of goods and services accounted for over 25% of GDP.

In 1989 Britain's exports of goods (on a balance of payments basis) were valued at about £92,526 million and its imports valued at £115,638 million. The visible trade balance was thus in deficit by some £23,112 million.

Britain runs a visible trade deficit with every region of the globe, except North Africa and the Middle East.

UK balance of payments

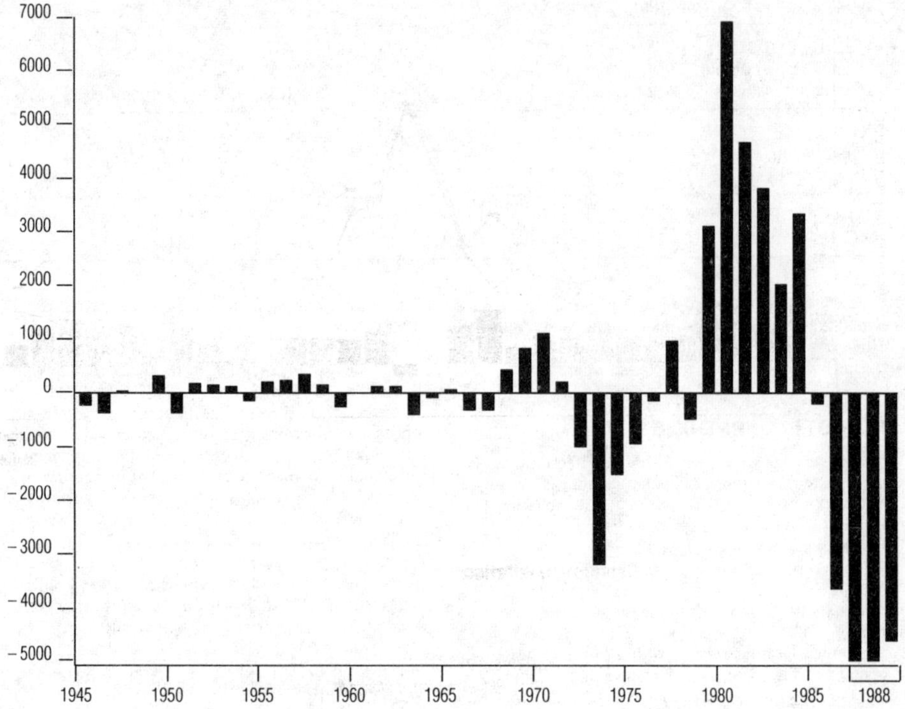

7000
6000
5000
4000
3000
2000
1000
0
−1000
−2000
−3000
−4000
−5000
1945
1950
1955
1960
1965
1970
1975
1980
1985
1988

Volume index of GDP at constant 1985 market prices (1985 = 100)

120
100
80
60
40
1967
1970
1973
1976
1979
1982
1985
1988

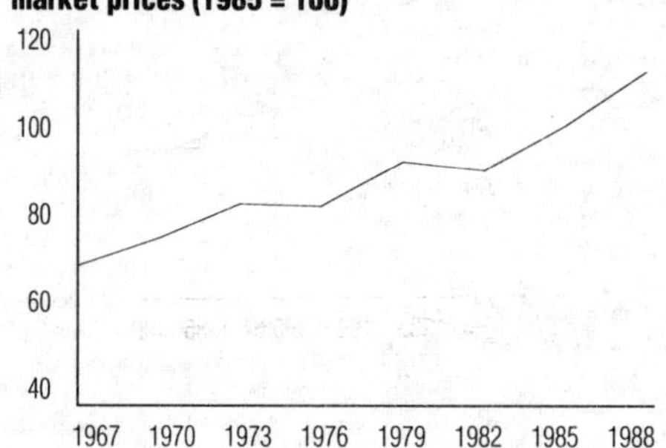

Government expenditure as a % of GDP

%
70
60
50
40
30
20
10
0
1945
1950
1960
1970
1980
1990

Invisible balance

£ billion
10
9
8
7
6
5
4
3
2
1
0
1980
1982
1984
1986
1988
1990
Forecast

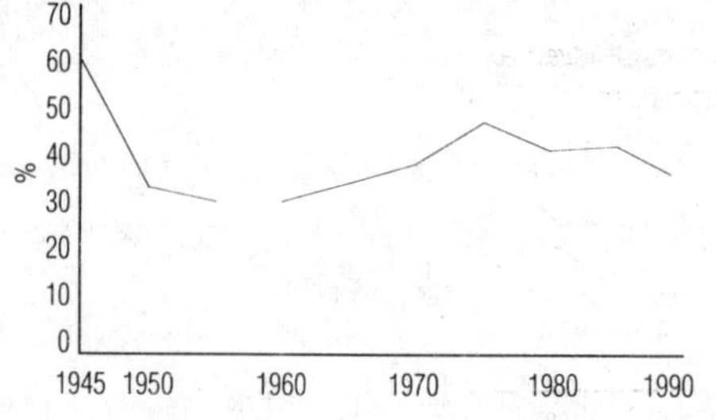

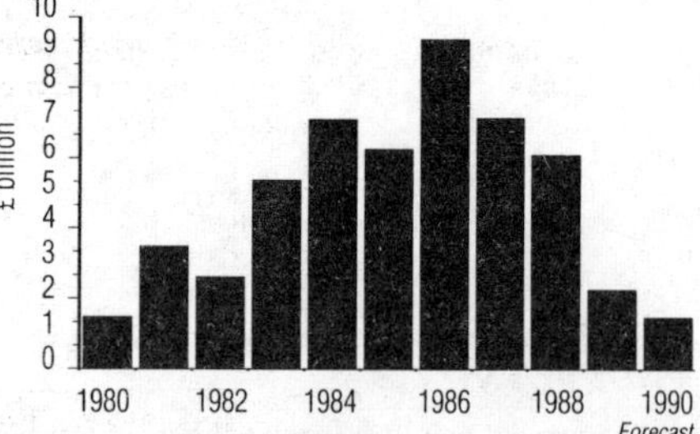

Money GDP, output and inflation

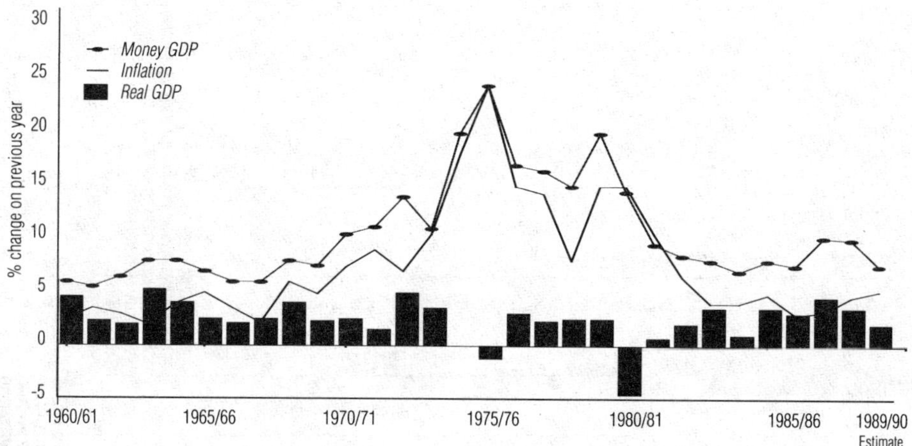

Retail price inflation

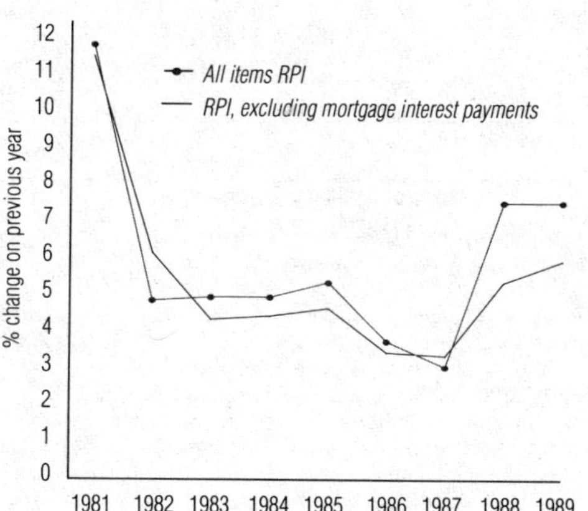

Major seven countries' consumer price inflation

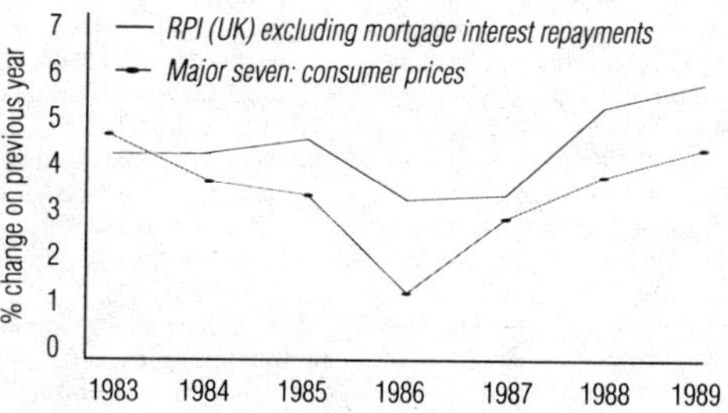

UK Balance of Payments, 1982–89 Current Account

£ millions	*1982*	*1983*	*1984*	*1985*	*1986*	*1987*	*1988*	*1989*	*Forecast 1990*	*1st Qtr. 1990*
Visible Trade:										
Exports (f.o.b)[a]	55,330	60,698	70,263	77,988	72,656	79,421	80,602	92,526		25,303
Imports (f.o.b.)[a]	53,422	62,207	75,432	81,120	82,020	90,350	101,428	115,638		30,893
Visible balance	1,908	-1,509	-5,169	-3,132	-9,364	-10,929	-20,826	-23,112	-16,500	-5,590
Invisible Trade:										
Credits	65,412	65,887	77,665	80,583	77,473	80,072	87,473	108,530		
Debits	62,714	60,584	70,542	74,290	68,148	72,965	81,319	106,268		
Invisible balance	2,698	5,303	7,123	6,293	9,327	7,106	6,154	2,261	1,500	
Current Account Balance of Payments	4,606	3,794	1,954	3,161	-39	-3,822	-14,762	-20,851	-15,000	-5,600

a = f.o.b. = free on board, i.e. all costs accruing up to the time of placing the goods on board, the exporting vessel having been paid by the seller.

UK Distribution of Visible Trade,1989

(Value of merchandise: '000 £)

Market:	*Exports*	*Imports*	*Balance*
European Community	47,140,164	63,494,966	–16,354,802
Rest of Western Europe	8,120,230	15,348,537	–7,228,307
North America	14,346,151	15,184,809	–838,658
Other developed countries	5,408,600	9,294,785	–3,886,185
Latin America	1,155,840	1,779,471	–623,631
Middle East and North Africa	6,280,125	2,717,505	+3,562,620
Other developing countries	8,118,074	9,955,649	–1,837,575
Centrally planned economies	1,786,256	2,280,638	–494,382
Low value trade	893,684	731,369	+162,315
Total	93,249,123	120,787,729	–27,538,606

Between 1972 and 1988 British exports within the Community rose from 34% to 50%, whilst exports to Commonwealth nations fell from 19% to 11%. Import distribution levels show a similar pattern. Trade with Japan and with the newly industrialized countries (NICs), such as Taiwan, Singapore, Korea and Malaysia, has increased substantially. Britain's principal export markets are, in order of importance, the United States, the Federal Republic of Germany, France and the Netherlands. Its main suppliers are, again in order of importance, the Federal Republic of Germany, the United States, France, the Netherlands and Japan.

Since World War II Britain has rarely been in surplus on the visible trading account (exceptions were 1956, 1958, 1971, 1980, 1981 and 1982). Therefore it has relied on invisible earnings, and in particular the reputation of the City of London as a major capital and financial centre, to keep the current account in surplus.

Since 1986 the decline in the visible trade balance (due to increased imports) and a corresponding decline in the surplus on invisible trade has fuelled the current balance of payments crisis. However, the Chancellor has forecast that the peak in the current account deficit has been reached and that the balance of payments deficit should fall back to some £15 billion in 1990, mainly due to an expected fall in domestic demand which will slow down the rate of increase in imports and an expected fall in the manufacturing trade deficit, which in the first three months of 1990 amounted to £3,644 million.

Britain exports 6% of the world's total visible exports. These include machinery, vehicles, aerospace products, electrical and electronic equipment, chemicals and oil.

The largest single component of Britain's balance of payments deficit is the £11,941 million deficit on finished manufactures (57% of the total deficit). At the peak of North Sea Oil production in the mid-1980s, oil exports accounted for over 20% of total national exports. By 1988 fuel accounted for approximately 7.1% of total exports and 4.8% of total imports. Britain imports over one-third of its foodstuffs. The deficit on trade in food, beverages and tobacco is £4,227 million.

IMPORT AND EXPORT CONTROLS

Britain has few international trade restrictions and is committed to further international market liberalization. Since joining the EC in 1973, Britain has conducted its commercial policy through the Community's common customs tariff at a trade-weighted average of 2.5% lower than most non-Community industrialized countries. The Single European Market, due for completion in 1992, is designed to remove the few existing barriers within the EC.

Almost all economic restrictions on the amounts of imports have been removed (some import restrictions are preserved against non-GATT countries). The remaining restrictions/protections apply mainly to the textile industry under the Multi-Fibre Agreement, due to expire in 1991.

Under European Community directives Britain has an import ban on certain iron and steel products from North Korea and South Africa. Despite national and

Commodity Analysis of Visible Trade, 1989

(Balance of payments: £ millions)

	Exports	*Imports*	*Balance*
Non-manufactures:			
Food, beverages and tobacco	6,494	10,721	–4,227
Basic materials	2,354	5,900	–3,546
Fuels	6,163	5,901	262
Total non-manufactures	15,011	22,522	–7,511
Manufactures:			
Semi-manufactures	26,817	31,011	–4,194
Finished manufactures	48,415	60,356	–11,941
Total manufactures	75,232	91,367	–16,135
Miscellaneous goods	2,283	1,749	534
TOTAL	92,526	115,638	–23,112

Current Account

£ billions (rounded)	*1988*	*1989*	*Forecast 1990*
Manufactures	–15	–16	–11
Oil	3	1½	2
Other	8½	–8½	–7½
Total visibles	–21	–23	–16½
Total invisibles	6	2½	1½
Current balance	–15	–21	–15
Balancing item	10	16½	

international pressure further sanctions against South Africa have been limited to the import of Kruger rands.

Other import controls exist on meat and poultry, animals, birds, bees, fish and plants, controlled drugs, offensive weapons, explosives, fireworks, certain citizens' band radios, 'indecent or obscene' articles, and products derived from endangered species.

Britain applies non-economic restrictions on imports and exports of firearms, ammunition, military equipment, nuclear materials and industrial goods of strategic importance.

However, the vast majority of British exports merely have to be presented and declared to HM Customs and Excise.

Export controls are placed on cocoa and cocoa products and, for health certification reasons, on horses, cattle, swine, sheep, goats, certain meat exports to other Community members, salmon and trout and endangered plants and species. There are also controls on certain cultural, historical and artistic works, such as photographic material over 50 years old and valued at £500 or more per item and most other articles over 50 years old valued at over £20,000 or more (£5,000 in the case of textiles and British historical portraits), and documents, manuscripts and archaeological items, controlled drugs, British spirits (beverages) and CAP products.

In 1979 Britain abolished exchange controls under EC directives and the OECD Code on Capital Movements.

TRADE AGREEMENTS

General Agreement on Tariffs and Trade (GATT)

Since 1947 there have been eight rounds of GATT multilateral trade negotiations aimed at reducing barriers to trading.

The eighth round of GATT negotiations (the Urugary Round) was launched in September 1986 and is expected to finish at the end of 1990. Fifteen trading issues are under discussion.

European Community Agreements

Britain applies the common customs tariff to all non-Community countries which do not have special arrangements with the Community.

EC members who joined before 1986 enjoy duty-free trade. Portugal and Spain, who joined after 1986, are subject to transitional arrangements, whereby industrial tariffs will be phased out at the beginning of 1993, but tariffs on agricultural produce will be dissolved at a later date.

Reciprocal agreements exist with the European Free Trade Association (EFTA) countries – Austria, Switzerland, Finland, Iceland, Norway and Sweden – providing for duty-free industrial tariffs. The 1984 Luxembourg Declaration committed the EC and EFTA to close economic co-operation.

Reciprocal, preferential terms of trading exist with Israel, Cyprus, Turkey and Malta.

Non-reciprocal agreements exist with Algeria, Morocco, Tunisia, Jordan, Egypt, the Occupied Territories, Lebanon, Syria and Yugoslavia.

Under the Third Lome Convention, 66 African, Caribbean and Pacific developing countries have free access (with certain safeguards) to the Community for industrial and agricultural products. The Fourth Lome Convention began at the end of 1988.

The Generalized Scheme of Preferences provides tariff preferences to developing countries, the Faroe Islands and overseas dependencies of EC member states.

Agreements for economic co-operation also exist with some Latin American countries, the People's

Republic of China and the six members of the Association of South-East Asian Nations.

Government Services for Exports

The British Overseas Trade Board
1 Victoria Street
London SW1H 0ET
President The Secretary of State for Trade and Industry, Rt Hon Peter Lilley MP
Chairman Sir James Cleminson MC; *Vice-Chairman* HRH The Duke of Kent KG GCMG GCVO.

This is the export arm of the Department of Trade and Industry (DTI) operating under the general authority of the Secretary of State for Trade and Industry. The board comprises members of trade and commerce (with personal involvement in exporting) and representatives of the DTI, Export Credits Guarantee Department (EGCD), and the Foreign and Commonwealth Office.

It disseminates export information and assistance to British exporters in appointing agents and researching potential export markets. Advice and assistance on exporting can be obtained on a regional basis from the regional offices of the DTI in England, the Welsh Office, the Scottish Export Office, the Industrial Development Board for Northern Ireland and from British Diplomatic Service posts outside the United Kingdom.

Export Credits Guarantee Department (ECGD)
England
P.O. Box 272
Export House
50 Ludgate Hill EC4M 7AJ

Wales
Crown Building
Cathays Park
Cardiff CF1 3NH

Established under the 1978 Export Guarantees and Overseas Investment Act, the ECGD is Britain's official export credit insurer. It is a separate government department responsible to the Secretary of State for Trade and Industry providing credit insurance for about 20% of Britain's export trade against non-payment by overseas purchasers. It also guarantees repayment to British banks providing finance for export credit on goods sold on credit for two or more years. Guarantees under Section 1 of the Act are given after consulting with the Export Guarantees Advisory Council. Investment insurance cover is provided against political risks, insolvency, expropriation and restrictions on remittances.

Queen's Awards for Export and Technology
The Secretary
The Queen's Awards Office
Dean Bradley House
52 Horseferry Road
London SW1P 2AG

The Queen's Award to Industry (est. 1965) was superseded by two separate awards in 1976: the Queen's Award for Export Achievement and the Queen's Award for Technological Achievement. The annual awards announced every 21 April (and held for five years) are made to encourage and recognize outstanding achievements in exporting goods or services from the United Kingdom. The Queen's Awards are granted on the recommendations of the Prime Minister's Advisory Committee, which includes senior representatives from industry, commerce, the trade unions and government departments.

Other awards include the Export Awards for Smaller Manufactures and the MacRobert Award for engineering.

INVISIBLE TRADE

In 1989 invisible trade credits stood at £108,530 million, whilst the debits stood at some £106,268 million, making an invisible balance of £2,261 million, the lowest for a decade, and partly reflecting the increasing internationalization of capital and finance and the competition from other financial centres.

Invisible trade transactions fall into three broad categories: services, interest, profits and dividends; and transfers.

Services are provided by general government, public corporations and the private sector. They include sea transport, civil aviation, travel and financial services.

In 1988 overseas earnings from services were equivalent to over 33% of total exports, yet the service sector alone is unlikely to bridge the balance of payments gap. The House of Lords Select Committee on Overseas Trade has estimated that each 1% fall in manufacturing exports requires a 3% increase in service exports to maintain the *same* level of economic activity. But Britain's share of world invisible trade (in percentage terms) over the last two decades has actually fallen by *more* than British manufactured exports' share of world trade.

Interest, profits and dividends and transfers are also provided by the three sectors. General government transactions are relatively unimportant in both the interest, profits and dividends and services accounts, but they form the majority of the transfer account. This is primarily as a result of EC subscriptions, other international organizations and bilateral aid. The deficit on general government transfers is expected to increase, partly as a result of new aid packages being announced for Eastern European countries.

As has already been noted, invisible trade plays a vital role in Britain's economy. In 1989 overseas earnings from invisible trade amounted to £108,530 million, second only to the United States. Britain has about a 15% share of world invisible trade.

However, the invisible surplus has fallen steadily since its 1986 peak at £9,327 million. The surplus is estimated to have declined from £6,154 million in 1988 to £2,261 million in 1989. The invisible surplus for 1990 is estimated to be £1,500 million. There is expected to be a slow rise in the services sector, but net earnings from interest, profits and dividends are expected to continue to fall. Transfers have almost always been in deficit.

In the second half of 1989 there was an increase in the United Kingdom's net payments to the EC and there was a sharp fall in net earnings from interest, profits and dividends.

The Conservative government argues that the expanding financial sector in general and the City in particular generates considerable wealth and invisible export earnings. However, these sectors are based primarily in the South-East and whether their 15% share of the world market can be further increased with the internationalization of money markets and *then* this wealth distributed throughout the rest of the United Kingdom is a matter of debate. However, it seems that since 1979 political, social and economic inequalities have increased.

There has long been an implicit 'subsidy' for the 'centre' (London and the South-East). However, further tax cuts and allowances (company and personal), transport subsidies, capital spending schemes, small business plans and the deregulation of the financial markets have all tended to accelerate the primacy of economic activity in the South, despite regional and industrial aid for the North of Britain. Even in the South of Britain this 'economic miracle' has been uneven and has also led to the problem of 'inflationary' overheating.

Between 1983 and 1987 the rise in the number of those in employment has been concentrated in the South, rising by 662,000 (6.2%) compared with an increase of 237,000 (2.3%) in the North.

The 'enterprise culture' (business creation) and the boom in 'popular capitalism' (share ownership) in the 1980s have also flourished predominantly in the South. In the South, and especially the South-East, earnings and personal incomes have risen by about 25% more than in the North and house price inflation (until 1988) had more than trebled property prices (see HOUSING). Furthermore, it is from the South that the 'booms' in mortgage debt and consumer credit have been most pronounced.

EXTERNAL ASSETS AND LIABILITIES

Transaction flows of external assets and liabilities indicate the flow of capital to and from Britain.

External assets include: British direct and portfolio investment overseas; deposits and lending overseas; official reserves and external assets of central government. The provisional total flow of external assets increased by £85,288 million in 1989. At the end of 1988 direct investment abroad by British residents totalled £102,000 million (approximately 35% of which went to the United States) and, by sector, oil companies accounted for about 32%, and manufacturing industry 28%, of overseas investment.

External liabilities include overseas investment in Britain (both direct and portfolio), borrowing from overseas and external liabilities of general government. In 1989 the provisional total flow of external liabilities increased by £89,629 million. At the end of 1988 direct investment in Britain from overseas was £66,000 million (51% from the United States, 41% in manufacturing and 34% for oil companies) and portfolio investment was £58,000 million.

Thus, for the second successive year, Britain imported more capital than it exported.

A further type of overseas transaction is company acquisitions and mergers. In 1988 British companies' acquisitions and mergers were valued at £13,200 (80% of which was from the United States) and overseas companies' acquisitions and mergers in Britain were valued at £5,000 million (22% of which were from the EC).

SECTORS OF THE ECONOMY

The manufacturing, service and construction industries account for about 93% of GDP, the rest coming from the energy production and agricultural sectors of the economy. The following sections outline the legislation, financial controls, industrial and commercial practice, governing these sectors.

General introduction

GOVERNMENT INDUSTRIAL AND COMMERCIAL LEGISLATION, CONTROLS AND POLICY

The most significant element of Mrs Thatcher's government's industrial policy has been the privatization programme, which has meant the selling of many nationalized industries (q.v.) and public companies, and government policy focusing mainly on the service sector of the economy and away from regional industrial aid to urban and general enterprise initiatives. The privatization of state-owned industry began in 1983. Those singled out for transference to the private sector have usually been the most profitable and possess a virtual market monopoly (British Telecom), those whose financial debts have been cancelled (Rolls Royce in 1988 and Shorts in 1989) and even those which include inducements or financial 'sweeteners' (Rover Group in 1989).

All in all, since 1979, the government has mounted 19 major public offers, the proceeds amounting to over £23,000 million. Other privatizations include British Aerospace, British Airways, the British Airports Authority, British Gas, British Steel, Cable and Wireless, National Freight Consortium, Amersham International, Jaguar, Enterprise Oil, Britoil, Associated British Ports, Royal Ordnance, most National Bus Company subsidiaries and British Shipbuilders. About 750,000 jobs have been transferred to the private sector. On 6 July 1989 Royal assent was given to the Water Act (1989), allowing for the privatization of the water and sewage industry in England and Wales, and companies were sold at the end of 1989. The electricity supply industry is to be transferred to the private sector in 1991, the date having been extended due to complications.

The Department of Trade and Industry (DTI) has the main responsibility for the government's relations with industry and commerce.

The DTI's specific responsibilities include technology and research, overseas trade and export promotion (q.v.), competition policy, consumer affairs, company legislation and the Patent Office. Through the Invest in Britain Bureau, it provides help and information for foreign companies investing and locating in Britain.

In 1988 a review of the organization and policies of the Department of Trade and Industry was published as a White Paper, *DTI – The Department for Enterprise*. This outlined the Conservative government's 'laissez-faire' belief in the free-market and in governmental responsibility being not to interfere but rather to create the right climate for markets to function properly. Thus, according to government policy, regional economic inequalities are to be resolved primarily by the market, without increased state intervention. In real terms regional industrial aid has declined by 25%, or £160 million, under Mrs Thatcher's administrations. In 1988/9 about £1,560 million was spent on regional and other forms of industrial support. The review seeks to shift industrial support further towards consultancy services, collaborative research and technological transfers.

The Treasury's macro-economic policies also have an influence on industrial and commercial policy. The Department of Employment is responsible for employment and training, small-firms counselling services and the promotion of tourism. The Scottish, Welsh and Northern Ireland Offices are responsible for the range of industrial policies in their respective areas.

Enterprise Initiative

This was launched in 1988, combining the DTI services for industry and commerce. The DTI emphasizes the promotion of open markets through competition, privatization, deregulation and international trade negotiations.

The emphasis is firmly on 'enterprise' (especially for small firms) and regional regeneration. The DTI industry divisions have been reorganized into market divisions, with the prioritizing of market goods and services.

'Enterprise initiatives' include six consultancy initiatives to advocate the use of external consultancy services for small and medium-sized businesses. Financial assistance is available to businesses with fewer than 500 employees at the rate of 50% of the project, except in the assisted and urban programme areas where assistance is given at 66% of the cost of the project. In 1989/90 £80 million was given to support 1,250 consultancies per month.

Regional industrial aid

Regional industrial policy in England and Wales is the responsibility of the DTI, in Scotland of the Scottish Office and in Wales of the Welsh Office. Government aid is focused on the 'assisted areas', both 'development areas' (e.g. Glasgow and its environs, Liverpool, Newcastle, Anglesey and Cornwall) and 'intermediate areas' (e.g. Plymouth and its environs, Cardiff, Birmingham and Manchester). Assistance comes in four main forms: (1) regional selective assistance, for firms in assisted areas which meet certain criteria; (2) regional enterprise grants, for small firms with fewer than 25 employees in development areas; (3) English Industrial Estates Corporation, providing premises in assisted areas of England with deficient private-sector provision; and (4) European Community aid. In 1975 the European Regional Development Fund was established to correct regional imbalances within the Community. In 1988 the fund was increased and concentrated on those areas most in need. Between 1975 and 1988 approximately £395 million was allocated to the UK, mainly for assisted areas and Northern Ireland. In 1989 the European Commission extended eligibility to certain non-assisted areas. Furthermore, the fund has provided £170 million for environmental and employment programmes.

The European Investment Bank (EIB) is a self-governing institution set up by the Treaty of Rome with member states giving subscription payments. Since 1973 the bank has lent almost £4,000 million to projects in Britain. The bank aims to encourage development in depressed areas, and conversion or modernization of industry. The EIB assists common projects undertaken by member countries. The European Coal and Steel Community (ECSC) distributes loans and grants to encourage rational distribution of production and a high level of productivity in the coal and steel industries while protecting employment and avoiding unfair competition.

Northern Ireland Northern Ireland also has a range of incentives provided under separate legislation. In 1982 the Industrial Development Board was formed under the aegis of the Northern Ireland Department of Economic Development. It offers incentives similar to those for assisted areas (sometimes at higher rates). Incentives for manufacturing include training grants and exemption from business rates. Industries which create jobs may be eligible for interest relief grants, favourable rent and assistance grants.

The board also provides capital for new businesses, assists high-technology industry and encourages links with overseas industry.

Other incentives available are relief of up to 80% on corporation tax and grants for energy conservation. The Local Enterprise Development Unit provides similar incentives for small businesses.

Scotland and Wales The Scottish and Welsh Development Agencies (SDA) promote industrial development in their respective countries. They encourage inward investment from overseas and mainly private loan capital for industrial projects. They also undertake land reclamation and urban renewal.

In 1988 the government published proposals to create a Scottish Enterprise Agency, incorporating some of the functions of the Scottish Development Agency and administering training programmes.

Rural development The Rural Development Commission advises the government on rural issues in England and promotes economic and social development with resources concentrated in rural 'development areas'. It also provides factories and workshops (built and managed by English Estates) and gives grants for conversion and renovation of disused buildings. Other functions include regional small business services and finance for rural housing.

The development agencies provide similar services for Scotland and Wales, except for two specific areas which have separate bodies. The Highlands and Islands Development Board (due to become Highland and Islands Enterprise) in Scotland provides capital for viable economic projects, builds factories and gives training grants. The Development Board for Rural Wales has all these functions and also general responsibility to promote mid-Wales and specific responsibility for Newtown, Powys.

Deregulation

Regulations which restrict competition, innovation or consumer choice in business by the public sector are scrutinized by the DTI's Enterprise and Deregulation Unit (*Director* M. Baker) for their impact on business. The last package of deregulation measures was announced in November 1988. The Bridge Programme seeks to increase links between business and the civil service.

Competition and Regulation

The DTI and the Office of Fair Trading (a government agency) is also responsible for controlling restrictive and anti-competitive policies. They scrutinize and regulate monopolies and mergers, anti-competitive and restrictive trade practices.

The Office of Fair Trading, headed by the Director General (Sir Gordon Borrie QC), administers the Fair Trading Act 1973 (monopolies and mergers); the Consumer Credit Act 1974; the Restrictive Trade Practices Act 1976; the Resale Prices Act 1976; the Estate Agents Act 1979; the Competition Act 1980; the provisions of the Financial Services Act 1986 which apply competition policy considerations to the financial sector, and the Control of Misleading Advertisements Regulations 1988. Various restrictive practices have also been removed: building societies are now able to offer more financial services; opticians' monopoly on spectacle dispensing and solicitors' monopoly on conveyancing and restrictions on advertising by some professional groups have also been lifted; and in 1989 the Director of Fair Trading sought assurances that doctors, consulting engineers and osteopaths do likewise.

Monopolies and mergers The Monopolies and Mergers Commission investigates these matters. They are an independent body whose members include lawyers, economists, industrialists and trade unionists. The Fair Trading Act 1973 defines a monopoly as a local or national situation where at least 25% of particular goods or services are supplied by a single person or company or group of connected companies which prevents, restricts or distorts competition. If the commission finds that a monopoly operates against the 'public interest', the Secretary of State for Trade and Industry can take action to solve or prevent the problem. The 1980 Competition Act empowers the Secretary of State to refer to the Monopolies and Mergers Commission any questions of abuse of monopoly, efficiency, costs and services in public sector industry.

A merger is where two or more companies are brought under common ownership or control. The Conservative government (as reaffirmed in the 1988 review of mergers policy) believes that the market is the best decision-maker as to whether mergers will adversely affect competition. However, if the merger threatens competition or results in a monopoly, or if the total value of gross assets to be taken over exceeds £30 million, then it may be referred to the Commission. If the Commission finds that the merger is against the public interest then the Secretary of State can prevent or impose conditions on it or ask the Director General of Fair Trading to gain undertakings.

The 1988 policy paper proposed three changes to existing legislation to improve controls: (1) voluntary pre-notification of proposed mergers to allow a speedy referral process; (2) charging for costs of merger control; (3) statutory undertakings by merger parties to prevent a full inquiry.

The 1973 Fair Trading Act contains special provisions for newspaper mergers.

Currently the commission is investigating 17 separate cases, two current examples of which are Tate & Lyle and Beresford, as well as an investigation into new motor cars and new motor car parts.

Restrictive trade practices The Restrictive Trade Practices Act 1976 ensures that restrictive trade agreements have to be notified for registration to the Director General of Fair Trading. When the parties supply the same goods or services and accept some limitation on their own decision-making on prices or conditions then the agreement must be registered. Failure to do so voids the restrictions and makes the party liable to legal proceedings.

Once an agreement is registered it then must be referred to the restrictive practices court, and the court must declare the restrictions contrary to the public interest unless it is satisfied that the parties have not acted unlawfully. The restrictions are voided and the court can place an order for the parties not to effect the agreement or make any similar new agreement. In practice agreements rarely reach the stage of court action.

In 1989 the government produced a White Paper detailing its proposed amendments to the existing legislation. These include the prohibition of restrictive trade agreements unless the economic benefits outweigh the adverse affect on competition; abolition of the registration procedure; strengthening of competition authorities' power; introduction of financial penalties for violation of the prohibition; authorities' decisions to be subject to appeal to the restrictive practices court; existing exemptions from the Act (e.g. professional services) may not be carried over into the new legislation.

European Community legislation The Treaty of Rome established competition rules and policy for the EC. Its central objective is to ensure that there is free and fair trading between member states and that dismantled international trade barriers are not supplanted by private barriers. It prohibits restrictive agreements and practices which impinge on trade between member states. However, exemptions exist for certain agreements, such as exclusive distribution and franchising, specialization, research and development, motor vehicle distribution and servicing and certain air services.

The treaty also forbids abuse of a dominant market position which adversely effects EC trade.

Consumer Protection

Again the government believes that the competitive market is the best ensurer of consumer protection.

However, this is reinforced by numerous Acts of Parliament in the last two decades (e.g. the Consumer Protection Act 1987).

The 1973 Fair Trading Act ensures the continuous review of consumer affairs in matters of unfair trading practices and the negotiation of self-regulatory trading standards.

British consumer organizations are represented in the EC by the Consumers in the European Community Group (UK). The EC's consumer legislation covers health and safety concerns, consumers' economic interests and consumer education.

In the UK, Citizens Advice Bureaux can provide general consumer assistance, as can local authority trading standards and consumer practice departments. There are also specialist consumer advice centres.

The National Consumer Council and similar councils in Scotland and Wales are independent non-statutory bodies with government funding. They exist to represent consumer interests and provide a lobbying service.

In Northern Ireland the General Consumer Council has similar responsibilities.

There are also consumer councils for nationalized industries.

The Consumer Association has over a million subscription-paying members. It publishes information, conducts test programmes and investigates concern with consumer goods and services.

Furthermore, there are local consumer groups, many of which are members of a national federation.

Research and Innovation

Research policy is determined by the Cabinet under the leadership of the Prime Minister. Assistance is provided for by the establishment of the Advisory Council on Science and Technology (ACOST), which functions as a secretariat in the Cabinet Office.

It is again government policy to encourage private sector investment and finance, rather than commit public funds to research and development. However, funding for basic scientific, strategic research is provided by government.

Expenditure 1987 industrial expenditure totalled £6,337 million, 69% from the private sector, 19% from government and 12% from overseas.

Research establishments A 1988 review announced that public sector research establishments should concentrate on government requirements, rather than industrial or commercial concerns.

The National Physical Laboratory provides common, internationally compatible measuring standards and calibration facilities and scientific and technological research. Its National Measuring Accreditation Service (NAMAS) is the centre for British voluntary accreditation of calibration testing facilities. Analytical measurement is the responsibility of the Laboratory of the Government Chemist (LGC). Both of these are DTI research establishments which are being considered for executive agency status. There are two other DTI research establishments: the National Engineering Laboratory, earmarked for privatization and dealing with research and development in mechanical engineering, and the Warren Spring Laboratory, an executive agency engaged in environmental process engineering.

The National Weights and Measures Laboratory

is responsible for administering the Weights and Measures Act 1985.

British Technology Group (BTG) BTG promotes the development of new technology (particularly in the public sector) into commercial products or processes. It possesses a portfolio of 6,788 British patents and patent applications, 537 licensees (providing 86% of total income) and 170 projects.

In its technology transfer role BTG provides up to 50% of development costs for British industrial innovation. BTG is commercially oriented, expecting to recover investment expenditure by a percentage levy on sales of the resulting product or process. Examples of technological achievement, for which BTG has been at least partly responsible, include pyrethin analogues and magnetic resonance imaging.

Company Law

The 1985 Companies Act regulates the establishment and conduct of companies. The Act is also concerned with capital structure, directors' and members' rights and duties, and company accounting.

Companies are 'incorporated' by registering with the Registrar of Companies in London, Cardiff, Edinburgh and Belfast. Most corporate businesses are 'limited liability' companies. Members of incorporated companies are not liable for its debts, whilst incorporated businesses are (unless the member is also a 'limited liability' company). The liability of members of a limited company is limited to contributing an amount in relation to their shareholding.

Companies may be public or private. A public limited company (plc) must fulfil three criteria: (1) it is limited by shares and possesses a share capital; (2) its memorandum of association explicitly states that it is a plc; (3) it has a minimum capital requirement. All other registered companies are, *de facto*, private and cannot engage in public share issues.

In 1985 a wealth of new company legislation passed onto the statute books: the Companies Act, which consolidates previous company law; the Business Name Act, which regulates the names under which people conduct business in the UK; the Company Securities (Insider Dealing) Act, which restates insider dealing laws; and the Insolvency Act, which introduced a licensing procedure, to ensure the status, standards and reputation of trustees, liquidators, receivers and administrators of insolvent and bankrupt companies and individuals. It also amended the Companies Act of the same year in legislation on winding-down limited companies and appointing receivers in Britain.

The 1986 Insolvency Act reinforced this legislation and, in April of the same year, the Company Directors Disqualifications Act came into effect. This provided a structure for the disqualification of directors unfit for office. In some cases, they are also made liable for company debts.

It is also now possible for debtors to reach agreement with creditors without resorting to formal bankruptcy or insolvency proceedings.

Scottish law is now separate with regard to individual insolvency proceedings.

Northern Ireland has analogous legislation to Britain.

Further legislation is planned to update company law to reflect the changing business environment. The major planned changes are the rules for disclosure of interest in shares (updating the Financial Services Act, which established powers of penalization and investigation of insider dealing).

Specialist legal services are provided by company lawyers.

A Serious Fraud Squad has been established to collaborate with police.

INDUSTRIAL AND COMMERCIAL ORGANIZATION AND OWNERSHIP

There are various forms and patterns of industrial and commercial ownership. These include: unincorporated business, e.g. sole traders and partnerships (1 million); public sector, government-owned industries; incorporated companies, i.e. on the Register of Companies; co-operatives (1,500); staff or management buyout (1982–8: 1,900, with a value of over £10,000 million).

Private companies generate 75% of total domestic income.

British Petroleum (BP) is Britain's largest and Europe's second largest company.

Nationalized industry now only accounts for about 5% of GDP and employs 3.1% of employees.

The major nationalized industries are:

(1) the electricity supply industry, including the Central Electricity Generating Board [CEGB], 12 area electricity boards in England and Wales, the South of Scotland Electricity Board and the North of Scotland Hydro-Electricity Board. The plans for privatization of the electricity industry in 1991 are still proceeding, despite resignations, various setbacks and anxieties and the retention of the nuclear-power industry in the public sector. Powergen and National Power have been established in advance for the privatization.
(2) British Coal (some pits are destined for privatization).
(3) British Rail (BR).
(4) The Post Office.
(5) London Regional Transport (LRT).

The managing boards are responsible to government ministers, who appoint the chairman and members of each board. Management strategies are worked out between ministers and managing boards. Performance, profit targets and external financing limits are set by government. There is also a 'required rate of return' of 8% in real terms on nationalized industrial investment.

Nationalized industries' affairs are annually scrutinized by the Monopolies and Mergers Commission and also, where appropriate, by management consultants. Parliamentary committees (such as the Public Accounts Committee) also examine public sector industrial concerns.

INDUSTRIAL FINANCE

In 1988 venture capital totalled £1,400 million.

Industrial finance is by and large internally generated wtihout government assistance. Banks are the principal source of external finance. Forms of short-term finance include overdrafts, credit and factoring (cash being exchanged for debts owed to a company, on a profit basis). Medium- and long-term finance services include bank loans, mortgages, securities and public share issues via the International Stock Exchange. Other financial sources include the government, the EC and industrial institutions.

VOLUNTARY INDUSTRIAL ASSOCIATIONS

The primary body representing British industry is the Confederation of British Industry (CBI), with 250,000 parent and subsidiary company members, 200 trade associations and 330 employers' organizations and the majority of public-sector industry. It provides a parliamentary lobby, a business forum and service.

The Association of British Chambers of Commerce is a regionalized body representing 70,000 businesses in 98 local chambers.

The 330 employers associations negotiate wage settlements and working conditions with trade unions in specific industrial sectors. Sometimes they combine this function with those of a trade association.

A trade association comprises companies who produce or retail the same products. They lobby the relevant government departments, regulate trading practices and provide services for member companies.

In addition to these there exist regional industrial development organizations and the Scottish Council for Development and Industry.

INDUSTRIAL MANAGEMENT, TRAINING AND EDUCATION

In 1987 the Council for Management Education and Development launched the Management Charter Initiative. In 1988 codes of management practice were introduced with 200 members.

'Industry Year 1986', launched by the Royal Society of Arts, was aimed at making industry more attractive to potential workers. It established greater links between companies and schools. This campaign continues under the title 'Industry Matters'. The DTI has sought to encourage links between industry and higher education, mainly through collaborative research projects, higher education equipment and new courses and city technology colleges (CTCs), established in 1986 to involve employers in the management of the colleges.

Other government programmes include the Enterprise Initiative (q.v.) and 'Managing into the '90s', which is designed to make business strategies more competitive in the use of design and quality, purchasing and supply and manufacturing management.

TECHNICAL AND VOCATIONAL TRAINING

The main responsibility for training in the United Kingdom rests with employers.

The Business and Technician Education Council (BTEC) is a private body which designs syllabuses and courses mainly at further education colleges for technicians and others. In Scotland the equivalent body is the Scottish Vocational Education Council.

Employment Training (ET) was started in September 1988 and is administered by the Department of Employment's Training Agency.

The Youth Training Scheme (YTS) is a controversial, compulsory training course for 16- or 17-year-old school-leavers offering work experience and training.

In 1983 the Open University Business School was opened and has since been used by over 3,000 companies; it is supported by the British Institute of Management. It offers part-time courses (for work and study) leading to a management diploma.

Economic Sectors

The following sections outline the characteristics of the main sectors in the British economy.

1989 Gross Domestic Product by Economic Sector, Changes from 1985 Index Base

Standard Industrial Classification		*Index (1985 = 100)*
0	Agriculture, forestry and fishing	98.0
1	Energy and water supply	89.8*
2–4	Manufacturing	119.6*
5	Construction	123.5*
6–9	Services	119.0

* = provisional figures

MANUFACTURING

In 1988 the manufacturing sector accounted for 24% of GDP and 33% of the total workforce in employment. In 1989 5.19 million people were employed in the manufacturing sector.

In 1989 total manufactures (semi-finished and finished) accounted for 81.3% of total visible exports and 79% of total visible imports. In 1989 manufactures accounted for £16,000 million of Britain's £21,000 million balance of payments deficit. Although Britain runs a loss on both semi-finished and finished manufactures, finished manufactures (52%) were the largest single component of Britain's balance of payments deficit in 1989. The trend remains poor in the first quarter of 1990 (53.5% of the quarterly total). The Chancellor, John Major, estimated that the deficit on total manufactures would fall by £5,000 million in 1990 to £11,000 million.

Since 1979 the United Kingdom's share of world manufacturing trade has fallen by 2%, both in value and volume.

The workforce in manufacturing has fallen from 7,253,000 in 1979 to 5,191,000 in 1989. Within the last two decades 'deindustrialization' has led to the loss of over 4 million production jobs in total (75% of which were in manufacturing). There are now fewer people employed in manufacturing than at the beginning of the twentieth century.

Between 1979 and 1987 some 2.4 million production jobs were lost from the production sector as a whole and trade union membership declined by 2.75 million (see TRADE UNIONS); some 70,000 industrial companies went into liquidation.

Thus, whilst Thatcherite deflationary monetary policy has meant increased productivity and profitability in the manufacturing sector of the United Kingdom economy, the actual size of the sector has contracted in terms of its ability to meet the growth in domestic demand and consumer credit and its contribution to the balance of payments. Furthermore, since the 1979 abolition of exchange controls much industrial investment and production has shifted outside the United Kingdom.

Output and Productivity Between 1979 and 1981 manufacturing output fell by 17%, employment by 1.2 million (16%) and capital investment by 33%. Since this recession manufacturing output and productivity have risen by about 5% per annum. Yet it was not until 1985/6 that manufacturing output climbed back to its 1979 level, by which time the level of manufacturing imports had risen by more than 33% and the visible trade deficit was too great to be offset by oil exports and invisible trade. In 1989 there was a sharp slowdown and the forecast growth rate for 1990 is 0%.

Productivity and output per head have improved partly through the shedding of labour. Manufacturing employment has fallen from 7.25 million in 1979 to 5.19 million in 1989.

To increase manufacturing profitability by reorganization and rationalization has led to the loss of more than 500,000 jobs in steel, coal, shipbuilding, British Aerospace, the motor industry and the railways.

High and advanced technology

At one level there has been a shift away from regional industrial aid towards research and development and 'white-heat' technology. Funding for innovation and technological development in micro-electronics, fibre optics, information technology and related fields has more than doubled, but at approximately £250 million per annum at current market prices it still remains lower than Britain's major competitors. Thus, both

Employees in Industry, 1971–1989[1]

thousands	*1971*	*1979*	*1981*	*1983*	*1986*	*1988*	*1989*
ALL INDUSTRIES AND SERVICES	22,139	23,173	21,892	21,067	21,387	22,226	22,452
Men	13,726	13,487	12,562	11,940	11,744	11,970	11,965
Women	8,413	9,686	9,331	9,127	9,644	10,257	10,488
Manufacturing	8,065	7,253	6,222	5,525	5,227	5,215	5,191
Services	11,627	13,580	13,468	13,501	14,297	15,168	15,427
Other	2,447	2,340	2,042	2,042	1,863	1,843	1,835
BY STANDARD INDUSTRIAL CLASS:							
Agriculture, forestry and fishing	450	380	363	350	329	313	299
Energy and water supply	798	722	710	648	545	487	468
Other minerals and ore extraction	1,282	1,147	939	817	729	687	673
Metal goods, engineering and vehicles	3,709	3,374	2,923	2,548	2,372	2,364	2,366
Other manufacturing industries	3,074	2,732	2,360	2,159	2,126	2,164	2,152
Construction	1,198	1,239	1,130	1,044	989	1,043	1,067
Distribution, catering and repairs	3,686	4,257	4,172	4,118	4,298	4,427	4,517
Transport and communication	1,556	1,479	1,425	1,345	1,298	1,324	1,347
Banking, finance, insurance, etc.	1,336	1,647	1,739	1,875	2,166	2,467	2,621
Other services	5,049	6,197	6,132	6,163	6,536	6,949	6,941

[1] = mid-year estimates.
Source: Department of Employment.

Self-employed in Industry, 1971–89[1]

thousands	*1971*	*1979*	*1981*	*1983*	*1986*	*1988*	*1989*
ALL INDUSTRIES AND SERVICES	2,026	1,906	2,119	2,221	2,627	2,986	3,770
Men	1,619	1,550	1,694	1,705	1,989	2,257	2,338
Women	407	357	425	516	637	729	772
Manufacturing	131	142	148	152	211	260	276
Services	1,231	1,126	1,298	1,379	1,646	1,856	1,935
Other	664	638	673	690	770	870	899
BY STANDARD INDUSTRIAL CLASS:							
Agriculture, forestry and fishing	314	286	276	272	274	268	267
Energy and water supply	–	1	1	1	1	1	1
Other minerals and ore extraction	4	6	8	9	11	12	13
Metal goods, engineering and vehicles	36	42	46	47	63	77	82
Other manufacturing industries	91	93	94	97	137	170	181
Construction	351	352	396	417	495	601	631
Distribution, catering and repairs	747	652	714	716	798	844	863
Transport and communication	66	88	101	94	113	138	143
Banking, finance, insurance, etc.	152	148	191	217	278	317	335
Other services	266	238	292	352	458	557	595

[1] = mid-year estimates.

regional aid and high technology, advance technology and innovative industry have been subordinated to the promotion of small firms and new businesses.

High-technology manufacturing industries are those with the highest levels of research and development expenditure, and include electrical, electronic and instrument engineering, chemicals and aerospace.

Advanced technology such as micro-electronics are increasingly used by British manufacturers. About 60% of all engineering plants use computer-aided design facilities.

Chemicals and man-made fibres

Britain's chemicals industry is the third largest in Western Europe and the fifth largest in the 'Western bloc'. Almost 50% of its production is exported and in 1988 it ran a trade surplus of £2,054 million. Much of the industry's production is accounted for by Imperial Chemicals Industries (ICI) which is the largest British manufacturing industry in terms of turnover, third largest company overall and the fourth largest chemicals producer in the world. Basic industrial chemicals still comprise about 40% of the industry's output, but the fastest growing is the production of chemicals such as pharmaceuticals, pesticides and cosmetics.

In 1988 pharmaceutical products were valued at over £1,800 million and ran a trade surplus of £867 million. British firms produce about 10 of the world's 50 best-selling drugs, including Glaxo's ulcer treatment and ICI's beta-blocker Tenormin which reduces high blood pressure; these are the world's first and third biggest selling drugs in the world. Other recent developments by British manufacturers or subsidiaries include Retrovir (treatment of AIDS and HIV); and the British

Celltech biotechnology company was the first to be licensed for the production of monoclonal antibodies (for identifying diseases and blood types and treating certain cancers) by the United States Food and Drug Administration.

A large percentage of the world's agrochemical research and development is conducted in Britain. British developments in this field include pyrethroid insecticides, which have similar chemical properties to Eurasian chrysanthemums. ICI has produced the world's first biodegradable thermoplastic, Biopol, which is used as a slow-release agent for drugs and herbicides and for films and bottles which are biodegradable. ICI is also the world's largest paint manufacturer.

The main types of man-made fibres are cellulosic fibres like viscose and synthetic fibres such as nylon polyamide, polyester and acrylics. In 1988, nearly 300,000 kilogrammes of unprocessed continuous filament yarn were produced.

From 1985 to 1989 Britain's chemical and man-made fibre output increased by 18.6%.

Mineral and metal products

Since 1985 metal manufacturing output has increased by 25%.

Iron and steel. Britain is the world's ninth largest steel-producing nation (by volume).

In 1988 British steel producers delivered 16.7 million tonnes of finished steel (65% to the domestic market).

British Steel is the fourth largest steel producer in the Western world, its major areas of production being in Scotland, Wales and northern England. In 1988/9 the company had a turnover of £4,900 million. Britain runs a trading surplus of £25 million in iron and steel products.

Non-ferrous metals. In 1988 non-ferrous metals (including aluminium, lead, copper, brass and tin) had sales of £2,270 million. Almost 50% of production is found in the Midlands and Wales. In 1988 exports of all precious non-ferrous metals totalled £296 million. Specialist developments include specialized alloys and 'superplastic' alloys, such as aluminium lithium produced by British Alcan Aluminium. Britain runs a trading deficit of £1,079 million in this category (1988).

Ceramics and heat-resistant goods. In 1988 total sales of ceramics totalled £1,120 million. The domestic pottery industry accounts for over half of this. Britain is the world's leading manufacturer of fine bone china, production of which is concentrated in Stoke-on-Trent. Britain runs a trading surplus in this category of £135 million.

Other mineral products. In 1988 glass and glassware accounted for £1,302 million sales, but imports were worth £594 million, £277 million more than Britain exported. Pilkington Brothers developed the float glass process for the production of flat glass.

Britain is the world's largest exporter of china clay (kaolin): 2.9 million tonnes (£197 million), primarily from English china clays.

Electrical, electronic and instrument engineering

In 1988 nearly 90% of this sector's products were exported, and since 1985 this sector's output has grown by 27%.

Britain is one of the top three markets in Western Europe for data processing, sales of which more than tripled between 1983 and 1988, and expenditure on data processing as a proportion of GDP is the highest in Western Europe.

British innovations include the transputer (which is a computer on a single chip), and British Telecom has led the way in the development of optical fibre communications systems. Over 50% of the world's undersea communications cables have been made and laid by STC Submarine Systems, and there is also radar and advanced electronic medical equipment, such as magnetic resonance imaging (MRI).

In 1988/9 British Telecommunications (BT) had a turnover of £11,071 million, and the General Electric Company (GEC) had a turnover of £5,878 million.

The Royal Charter 1981 established an Engineering Council with functions to further the science of engineering through educational courses, training and experience. The council has a register of 300,000 chartered engineers, incorporated engineers and engineering technicians and is advised by approximately 235 industrial engineering employers.

Mechanical engineering

In 1989 output grew by 5.4% in this sector.

In 1988 exports of mechanical engineering products amounted to 14% of all visible exports (£9,479 million) and sales totalled £23,425 million.

Britain is the Western world's largest producer of tractors, which comprise 75% of Britain's total output of agricultural equipment. Agricultural machinery and tractor sales in 1988 totalled £1,523 million (69% of which came from exports). Innovations in agricultural machinery include computer-controlled tractors.

Other goods in this sector include machine tools, textile machinery (i.e. weaving looms), mining and construction equipment and castings tools.

Motor vehicles and parts and other transport equipment

From 1985 to 1989 output of motor vehicles and parts increased by 25.3%.

Five car companies produce 95% of Britain's total output. These are Rover (owned by British Aerospace), Ford, Vauxhall, Peugeot-Talbot and Nissan. The remaining 5% is accounted for by specialist producers such as Jaguar (now owned by Ford) and Rolls Royce (owned by Vickers). Most of this production (66%) is concentrated in the West Midlands and the South-East. Sales of motor vehicles in 1988 totalled £12,137 million, yet the trade deficit on cars amounts to £5,598 million. In 1988 Rover Group exports alone amounted to £908 million (30% of total exports).

Motor vehicle parts are also in deficit to the tune of £527 million. British component manufacturers include GKN and Lucas.

Ford Motor Company is the largest car manufacturer in Britain, with a turnover of £5,936,000 in 1988.

Shipbuilding and marine engineering

This industry has also suffered during the 1980s, with many yards forced to close.

In 1987 British merchant shipbuilders had 65 orders in hand for the construction of ships of more than 100 gross tonnes, worth £622 million.

The largest sector is the building of warships, submarines, patrol craft, frigates etc. for the Royal Navy and other foreign powers.

Shipbuilders are also involved in the construction and conversion of offshore structures (mainly for oil purposes).

In 1987 the government leased the Royal Dockyards (ship repairers) to commercial management.

Aerospace

Britain's aerospace industry is the third largest in the world, behind the United States and the Soviet Union.

In 1989 aerospace and other transport equipment output grew by 8.4% on the previous year.

In 1988 the industry as a whole had a turnover of

£10,000 million and total sales of almost £8,500 million, and with exports totalling £5,241 million (over 50% of this total from British Aerospace) it contributed £1,690 million to the balance of payments. Over the past decade it has nearly doubled its productivity, turnover and the value of its exports.

In 1988 British Aerospace (Britain's main airframe manufacturer) had a turnover of £5,639 million, with an order book for 1989 of £11,000 million. BAe is the largest aerospace and communication satellite company in Europe. It is the world's third largest producer of communication satellites, and has been the prime contractor for all satellites launched by the European Space Agency, including the Olympus 1 launched in June 1989 – the world's most powerful communications satellite – as well as for scientific probes, such as the Giotto satellite. It produces military and civil aircraft, space equipment, electronic devices and missile systems.

BAe owns 20% of the European consortium Airbus Industrie (with sales of over 1,000 aircraft) and produces wings for all its aircraft, as well as 33% of the production of European Fighter Aircraft.

In 1988, amid controversy over £20 million of government 'sweeteners', BAe diversified into the production of motor vehicles, with its acquisition of the Rover Group from the public sector for a £150 million 'consideration' and a £547 million cash injection.

In June 1989 another major British aerospace manufacturer, Short Brothers of Belfast, was privatized by its sale to Bombardier. It produces the Turcano military trainer, guided missiles and airframe components.

Westland, whilst also producing aerospace equipment, is chiefly recognized for its manufacture of civil and military helicopters (e.g. Lynx and W30). It is also developing the EH101 three-engine helicopter for the Royal and Italian navies, in conjunction with Agusta of Italy. (In 1986 a Westland Lynx helicopter set a new helicopter world-speed record at over 249 mph/400kmh).

Rolls Royce (privatized in 1988) is one of the three largest manufacturers of civil and military aero-engines in the world, with a turnover of some £2,000 million in 1988 and a forward order book for 1989 of over £4,000 million. 75% of airlines using Boeing 757 airliners select Rolls Royce RB211-535 engines. It also provides gas turbine engines for 25 of the world's navies.

Rolls Royce is a partner in Eurojet, a business consortium from four countries involved in developing the EJ200 for European Fighter Aircraft.

Marconi Space systems (a subsidiary of GEC) is the principal contractor on many telecommunications satellite payloads.

The Aerospace Trade Association is the society of British Aerospace companies which organizes the bi-annual Farnborough Air Show in September each year.

Food, beverages and tobacco

(see also AGRICULTURE, FORESTY AND FISHERIES)

The 1989 deficit on trade in food, beverages and tobacco is £4,227 million and £1,285 million for the first quarter of 1990.

In 1988 food manufacturing had sales of £33,853, with a trade deficit of £4,164 million (the largest component of which was the £1,117 million deficit on meat products). In 1988 trading deficits were recorded on all food manufacturing, except flour-based products.

In 1989 sales of frozen food exceeded £2,000 million.

Scotch whisky is of major importance specifically to the British alcohol industry, but also generally to food, beverages and tobacco.

There are 114 distilleries in Scotland, and Guinness plc (having acquired Distillers Company and Arthur Bell & Sons) now accounts for 40% of Scotch whisky output and a 25% market share.

In 1988 whisky exports valued £1,300 million, with the major market being the United States.

Annual sales of beer in Britain exceed £9,000 million (2% of GDP) almost 50% of which is lager. There are six major brewery groups, the largest of which is Grand Metropolitan. In 1988/9 Grand Metropolitan announced a turnover of £9,298 million. Grand Metropolitan's interests include hotels, milk production and brewing, and the group employs over 152,000 people.

The British tobacco industry manufactures 91% of cigarettes and other tobacco goods sold in Britain. Three manufacturers (Imperial Tobacco, Gallaher and Carreras Rothmans) have virtually all the domestic market share.

Britain's most important sources of raw tobacco are Brazil, the United States, Zimbabwe, India and Canada.

In 1988 British American Tobacco (BAT) Industries had a turnover of £11,358 million and employed over 172,000 people.

In 1988 Unilever, who produces food products and detergents, had a turnover of £6,384 million and employed 155,000 people.

Sales of drinks (excluding duty-paid) totalled £6,081 million in 1988 and sales of tobacco amounted to £1,962 million.

In 1989 the manufacturing output index for beverages and tobacco (1985 = 100) was 107.3.

Textiles, footwear, clothing and leather

This sector employs 480,000 people, almost 10% of total manufacturing employment.

The textile industry is regionally concentrated in the North-West (cotton), West Yorkshire (wool), East Midlands (lace and knitwear) and Scotland (jute in Dundee, canvas and wool) and Northern Ireland (linen).

The industry has about 5,000 firms, including two leading multi-process companies, Coats Viyella and Courtaulds. In 1988/9 the latter was the 48th largest industrial company in the United Kingdom, with a turnover of over £2,600 million.

1988 textile sales amounted to £6,545 million, with a trade deficit (despite the Fourth 1986 Multi-Fibre Arrangement [MFA]) of £1,976 million. Much of this deficit (about 68%) is due to the declining British markets for cotton and silk, with increasing low-cost competition from Asia and the rest of Europe.

Britain has one of the largest wool industries in the world and the world's largest wool textile company, Illingworth Morris.

In 1989 textile output declined by 4.7% over the previous year.

The clothing industry is more diversified with about 9,000 companies, yet concentrations exist in urban conurbations such as Manchester, Leeds and London. It accounts for 4% of total manufacturing employment and supplies two-thirds of domestic demand. The British fashion design industry has also become more prominent.

The hosiery and knitwear industry (£1,860 million sales in 1988) consists of about 1,500 companies, located mainly in the East Midlands and Scotland.

British footwear manufacturers account for 36% of domestic demand, the rest being accounted for mainly by other European countries, such as Italy and Portugal.

Over 38% of leather and leather goods are exported,

yet Britain is in deficit here to the tune of £180 million.

Clothing, footwear and leather manufacturing output has increased by only 0.2% in the last four years.

Other manufacturing

This includes (i) the timber and furniture industry; (ii) paper and paper products; (iii) printing and publishing; (iv) rubber and plastics processing; and (v) toys and sports goods.

Timber and furniture. Sales of timber and wooden furniture exceeded £7.5 billion in 1988, with a trading deficit of £2,702 million.

There are 2,500 furniture companies, and in 1988 production of softwood timber totalled 911,000 metres^3/ 3.2 million feet^3.

Paper and paper products. Sales of paper and paper products totalled £8,850 million in 1988, with a trading deficit of £3,192 million, and there are about 33,000 people employed in 90 paper and board mills owned by 65 companies. 36% of British demand for newsprint is met by domestic producers, and waste paper provides about half of industry's needs.

Printing and publishing. Printing and publishing sales totalled £11,947 million in 1988.

There has been a large series of mergers and acquisitions in this sector in the 1980s, with many smaller independent publishers being bought out or having to close. The largest group in newspaper, magazine and book publishing is Maxwell Communications Corporation. Fragmentation of the industry has also occurred due to the introduction of new technologies.

The book publishing industry exports 33% of their production. In 1988 total employment in paper, printing and publishing was 491,000.

Rubber and plastic processing. Sales in this sector exceeded £10,000 million in 1988. The principal rubber manufactures are tyres and tubes (46%), other vehicle components, cables, latex foam, footwear and condoms.

Toys and sports goods. Sales of toys and sports goods totalled £573 million in 1988, by approximately 500 manufacturers.

CONSTRUCTION

In 1989 over a million people were employed in this sector and there were 631,000 self-employed.

In 1989 GDP in the construction sector of the economy had increased 23.5% from its 1985 index of 100, accounting for 6.5% of GDP. 1988 output was valued at £40,500 million, 58% of which was new work. Computer-based innovations have improved productivity and efficiency.

The Department of the Environment is responsible for the domestic construction market. The Secretary of State for the Environment is responsible for building regulations on both new and repair and maintenance construction. The regulations are usually administered and policed by the local authorities, although the Housing and Building Control Act 1985 provided for private certification in compliance with existing regulations.

Construction is carried out in both the public and private sectors, although over 90% of the work is carried out by private contractors. Out of 100,000 firms employing two or more people, 95% employ fewer than 25.

The Property Services Agency (PSA) (*Chief Executive* Sir Gordon Manzie), an arm of the Department of the Environment, is responsible for government construction programmes, although from April 1988 government departments have been able to use other agents on projects of over £150,000. The Building Research Establishment (part of the Department of the Environment) is the government's national research and advisory body on construction issues.

Housing

(see also HOUSING section)

In 1988 the construction of 245,000 houses was started in Britain (29,000 in the public sector and 216,000 in the private sector). New construction was valued at £8,550 million and repairs and maintenance at £9,300 million. 216,000 dwellings were completed (31,000 in the public sector and 185,000 in the private sector).

Civil Engineering

In 1988 construction companies had overseas contracts worth about £2,300 million. The most important external markets are the United States and the European Community.

Important civil engineering works completed (or in the process of being so) include the new British Library, the Queen Elizabeth II Conference Centre and the Channel Tunnel.

British companies provide consultancy engineering services for many of the world's largest projects (e.g. the Baghdad Metro in Iraq, worth £4,000 million).

SERVICE SECTOR

In 1988 services accounted for 63% of gross domestic product. In 1989 the service industries' GDP increased by 19% from an 1985 index base of 100. In 1988 service export earnings were nearly half the value of manufactures.

In 1989 in the service sector there were 15,427,000 employees and 1,935,00 self-employed in total, an increase of almost 1.85 million in the last decade. However, the shift from manufacturing or production to service sector industrial employment has been regionally disparate. Thus, while in Great Britain as a whole 3,413,000 manufacturing jobs were lost between 1966 and 1987, and 3,575,000 service industry jobs were gained, growth in service industry employment outstripped manufacturing industry job losses only in the South-East, the South-West, the East Midlands and East Anglia. This shift in the industrial base is accompanied by a 'consumer society'.

Distribution, wholesale, catering and repairs

In 1989 there were 5,380,000 employed and self-employed working in distribution, wholesale, catering and repairs (2.3 million retail employees, 1.1 million hotel and catering employees, 974,000 wholesale employees and 267,000 vehicle and other goods repairers). This sector accounts for approximately 14% of national income.

Wholesale trades. There are over 130,000 businesses engaged in wholesale and dealing. Sales of goods totalled £8,500 million in 1987. The main wholesale markets are New Covent Garden (fruit and vegetables), Smithfield (meat) and Billingsgate (fish).

The Co-operative Wholesale Society (CWS) serves the retail trade. In 1988/9 its turnover was £2,559 million.

Retail trades. In the 1980s consumer demand increased by 8% within six years. However, due to high interest rates, consumer spending slowed sharply during 1989. This was most evident in retail sales and the lower than usual demand for new cars in August 1990.

In 1989 the volume of retail sales for all of the retail industry at constant (1985) prices was 121.8 (an increase of 2.6% on the previous year), and their value (at current market prices) was 139.6. From April 1989 to April 1990 the value of retail goods increased by 9.1% (food retailing alone increased by 9.9%).

The fastest growing market in retail trade is in household goods, which increased their share of the retail market (in terms of turnover) by 3% and more than doubled their total turnover.

By 1990 there were about 240,000 retail trade businesses with about 345,000 outlets in Great Britain and a total turnover of approximately £110,000 million. The retail trade employs about 2.3 million people. As large multiple retailers (10 or more outlets) have grown in size and diversified the total number of retail businesses and outlets has diminished, especially independent businesses and co-operative societies.

In 1980 there were 186 co-operative retail societies; now there are only 90.

Large multiple retailers, whilst amounting to only 0.36% of total retail businesses, employ 53% of retail employees and have 60% of total retail turnover.

The largest multiple food retailers are the retail co-operatives Sainsbury, Tesco, the Gateway Corporation, the Argyll Group and the Asda Group. Retail co-operative societies are voluntary organizations run by their members, and they are also members (along with the Co-operative Wholesale Society) of the Co-operative Union, as are a number of other co-operative societies including the Co-operative Bank.

Sainsbury's are the largest food retailers in Britain and the 14th largest company overall, with a turnover in 1988/9 of £5,659 billion and employing 88,283 staff in their 284 stores.

Tesco had a turnover of over £4,700 million, employing 75,658 staff in their 380 outlets.

The Gateway Corporation had a turnover of over £4,500 million, employing some 83,318 staff.

Food retailing as a whole accounts for almost 31% of retail businesses, 28% of outlets, 35% of employees and about 36% of total retail turnover.

The leading mixed retail business is Marks & Spencer with a turnover of over £5,160 million in 1988/9 (almost 20% of total mixed retailing turnover) and employing over 55,000 staff.

Almost 20 million people shop by mail order each year.

Trends in retailing include large shopping centres and hypermarkets, market diversification, increasing use of electronic and computer technology (such as laser-scanning electronic checkouts), and 30,000 'electronic funds transfer at point of sale' (EFTPOS), such as Switch cards which instantly transfer funds from cardholders' accounts to the retailers' accounts, and 'in-store' credit cards.

Vehicle and petrol retailing. By the end of 1988 241,000 were employed in this sector of the economy.

Great Britain has about 20,000 petrol stations, one-third of which are owned by oil companies and about half of which are self-service.

Unleaded petrol is sold in half of all petrol stations and accounts for 25% of all petrol sales.

236,000 people were employed in garages for the repair of motor vehicles.

Hotels and catering. In June 1988 an estimated 1.1 million people were employed in the hotel and catering sector, of which 282,000 were in public houses and bars, 261,000 in hotels and residential establishments, 238,000 in restaurants, cafes and snack bars, 147,000 in clubs and 136,000 in canteens.

In 1987 there were about 12,800 hotel businesses (many with fewer than 20 rooms) with a combined turnover of £4,260 million.

Britain's largest hotel group is Trusthouse Forte plc, which owns over 240 hotels in Britain.

In the 1980s there has been significant growth in fast-food catering which, along with other industries owning the rights to a particular form of trading, has often resulted in licences to franchisees of individual branches.

There are about 75,000 public houses licensed to sell drinks (mainly alcohol) for consumption on the premises.

Business services

This sector includes advertising, auction houses, conference and exhibition centres, computing services, management consultancy and market research services.

Advertising. In 1988, according to the Advertising Authority, advertising expenditure rose 12% to £6,780 million, with the proportion of advertising revenue going to television increasing by 8%. Advertising in the press accounts for 63% of the total, television for 31%, posters 4%, and 2% commercial radio and cinema.

Government expenditure on advertising has also increased dramatically.

Most advertising is conducted along agency lines.

In 1988/9 Saatchi & Saatchi, Britain's largest advertising agency, had a turnover of over £4,364 million.

The fastest growing sector of the market is in the free distribution press and directories.

Auction houses. Britain's two largest auction houses for art, Sotheby's and Christie's, had turnovers of £1,356 million and £1,041 million respectively.

Conference and exhibition centres. Britain, along with the United States and France, is one of the world's three leading countries for international conferences. Major centres include the National Exhibition Centre (Birmingham), Wembley Conference Centre, the Queen Elizabeth II Conference Centre, the Barbican Centre for Arts and Conferences (London) and the Brighton Centre (Sussex).

Computing services. This industry is one of the fastest growing sectors of the economy (20% per annum).

This industrial sector includes systems houses (providing complete hardware and software computer services), software houses (writing of bespoke software), general software producers, computing consultancy services, facilities management and computer bureaux services (data processing).

In 1988 the turnover of the independent systems and software houses was approximately £2,500 million and they employed about 55,000 people.

There are about 440,000 'in-house' employees.

Management consultancy services. There are over 10,000 managment consultants in Britain, 3,400 of which are practising members of the Institute of Management Consultants. 29 companies are members of the Management Consultancy Association, which accounts for about 65% of the market. In 1988 the association's turnover totalled £385 million, 91% from the domestic market.

Market research services. 31 companies are members of the Association of Market Survey Organizations (AMSO), which accounts for about 75% of the market. In 1988 members of AMSO had a turnover of £179 million. 40% of revenue is spent on researching consumer goods (16% of which is spent on researching food and drinks) and the remainder is spent on business services and industrial goods.

Tourism and travel

In 1988 expenditure on tourism in Britain (including travel fares), both by residents and visitors, totalled about £19,000 million. Approximately 1.5 million people are employed in this sector of the economy and the British Tourist Authority forecast 200,000 new jobs will be created before 1993.

In 1988 overseas residents made 15.7 million visits to Britain, spending some £6,200 million. 60% of visitors came from Western Europe, 21% from North America and 18% from elsewhere in the world.

British residents made 29 million trips abroad and spent £8,190 million, giving a deficit on the travel account of about £2,000 million.

There are about 3,000 travel agencies with over 7,500 offices, 90% of which are members of the Association of British Travel Agents (ABTA). The largest agency is Lunn Poly with 507 branches nationwide.

683 tour operators are also members of ABTA. ABTA's functions for members include financial protection schemes, codes of conduct (in agreement with the Office of Fair Trading) and an independent conciliation and arbitration service for members' customers.

The British Tourist Authority (Thames Tower, Black's Road W6 9EL) is responsible for promoting tourism to Britain from overseas and the development of tourist facilities within Britain. The tourist boards for England, Scotland, Wales and Northern Ireland are responsible for developing, marketing and improving tourist amenities in their respective countries.

In 1987 the boards introduced a 1–5 crown classification scheme for hotel and service accommodation and a grading scheme for caravan and camping parks. This was later extended to self-catering accommodation. Registration is voluntary, and establishments which are registered are listed in the board's accommodation guides.

There are numerous regional tourist information centres.

Small firms

Small firms make a vital and increasing contribution to the British economy. They account for a quarter of those in employment and one-fifth of total turnover. The Conservative governments of the 1980s have sought to encourage small businesses. By 1989 new businesses were being started at a net rate of about 1,400 per week. However, many of these will close after a year or two of trading. The government runs a number of schemes providing direct assistance on business problems affecting small firms. These include the Small Firms Service (information and advice to prospective and established businesses), the Loan Guarantee Scheme (the government underwrites 70% – 85% in inner-city task force areas – of medium-term loans made by financial institutions), and the Business Expansion Schemes, designed to improve small firms equity finance by offering tax incentives to investors in qualifying unquoted companies. The Business Expansion Scheme provides relief for investors in trading companies without a stock market quotation, on investment up to £40,000 in any one year. From 1 May 1990 the general limit for company investment in any tax year is £750,000. Another scheme is the Enterprise Allowance Scheme (EAS), which allows people unemployed for six weeks or more to claim a £40 weekly allowance for the first year of their new business.

Other services

Approximately 500,000 people work in the arts in Britain (107,000 in research and development). There are about 12,600 film, theatre, literary, broadcasting and other businesses servicing the arts.

Other services include: over 13,000 sport, recreation, gaming and betting businesses; about 10,000 hairdressing and beauty parlours; dry cleaners; religious organizations; funeral services; tourist offices; employers and trade union organizations and photographic studios.

Film and television. The BBC and the commercial television companies have agreed to meet government targets of 25% of new material commissioned being made by independent producers by 1993.

Production of cinema films in the United Kingdom declined in the mid-1980s. In June 1990 the government announced an extra £5 million investment in British filmmaking.

In 1987 receipts from films and television companies totalled £382 million (£264 million from film, £118 million from television); expenditure was £268 million. The United States accounts for over 50% of the revenue in both cases.

International Unemployment Rates (adjusted to OECD concepts)

Percentages	1976	1977	1978	1979	1980	1981	1982	1983	1984	1985	1986	1987	1988
United Kingdom	5.6	6.0	5.9	5.0	6.4	9.8	11.3	12.4	11.7	11.2	11.2	10.2	8.3
Belgium	6.4	7.4	7.9	8.2	8.8	10.8	12.6	12.1	12.1	11.3	11.2	11.0	9.9
France	4.4	4.9	5.2	5.9	6.3	7.4	8.1	8.3	9.7	10.2	10.4	10.5	10.1
Germany (Federal Republic)	3.7	3.6	3.5	3.2	3.0	4.4	6.1	8.0	7.1	7.2	6.4	6.2	6.1
Italy	6.6	7.0	7.1	7.6	7.5	7.8	8.4	8.8	9.3	9.6	10.5	11.2	11.3
Netherlands	5.5	5.3	5.3	5.4	6.0	8.5	11.4	12.0	11.8	10.6	9.9	9.6	9.5
Portugal	–	–	–	–	–	–	–	7.9	8.4	8.5	8.5	7.0	5.7
Spain	4.6	5.2	6.9	8.5	11.2	13.9	15.8	17.2	20.1	21.4	21.0	20.1	19.1
Australia	4.7	5.6	6.2	6.2	6.0	5.7	7.1	9.9	8.9	8.2	8.0	8.1	7.2
Canada	7.1	8.0	8.3	7.4	7.4	7.5	10.9	11.8	11.2	10.4	9.5	8.8	7.7
Finland	3.8	5.8	7.2	5.9	4.6	4.8	5.3	5.4	5.2	5.0	5.3	5.0	4.5
Japan	2.0	2.0	2.2	2.1	2.0	2.2	2.4	2.6	2.7	2.6	2.8	2.8	2.5
Sweden	1.6	1.8	2.2	2.1	2.0	2.5	3.2	3.5	3.1	2.8	2.7	1.5	1.6
United States	7.6	6.9	6.0	5.8	7.0	7.5	9.5	9.5	7.4	7.1	6.9	6.1	5.4

AGRICULTURE, FORESTRY AND FISHERIES

Britain produces about 57% of its own food and feed. In 1989 there were 299,000 people employed in agriculture, forestry and fishery. This figure indicates a fall of 100,000 during the last decade and an even greater fall since 1946, when there were nearly a million farm workers alone. The 1989 index of changes in GDP (1985 = 100) showed a reduction to 98 in this sector of the economy.

Agriculture

Land use and countryside change. In 1988 agriculture contributed £5,436 million to GDP (1.4% of the total). Over 18 million hectares (ha) are used for agriculture, 77% of the total area of the United Kingdom. Since 1981 almost 200,000 ha of agricultural land have been lost. There are some 5.3 million ha of tillage land; 7 million ha, arable; 12.1 million ha, crops and grass; almost 6,000 ha, rough grazing in hill country (of which sole right land is the largest single contributor to the loss of agricultural land); 322,000 ha of woodland and 225,000 ha other agricultural land.

The third Agricultural Revolution occurred after World War II. The U-Boat campaign had revealed the vulnerability of Britain importing 70% of its food needs from its colonies and dependencies. Thus, with massive public funding, British agriculture was intensified with the aim to make Britain as self-sufficient in food as possible. The framework for this change was provided in the 1947 Town and County Planning and Agriculture Acts. The latter introduced the 'deficiency payment' scheme for farmers, providing a guaranteed minimum price for their products regardless of world-market fluctuations. In the 1970s this was superseded by the European Communities (EC) Common Agricultural Policy (CAP). Since 1929 all agricultural land and buildings have been exempt from paying rates. In 1986 the Government passed a new Agriculture Act, which was designed to achieve a balance between the interests of agriculture and the environment. However, many feel that the Act does not go far enough in addressing environmental concerns.

Areas of the countryside which have suffered the worst include semi-natural landscape and grassland. Nearly 25% of our semi-natural landscape and 20% of grassland has been lost since 1947. The Institute of Terrestrial Ecology 1978–84 survey revealed that losses of rough grazing included: 115,261 ha of rough grassland; 14,590, moorland; 8,754, scrub woodland; 5,836, degraded pasture; and 1,459, mountain grass. Losses of broadleaved woodland included: 24,700 ha of broadleaved woodland grubbed up and 11,200 ha planted with conifers. 177,000 ha were blanketed with conifer plantations, usually in upland grassland and moorland areas, mostly in Scotland and North Wales. It also reported the continuing loss of hedgerows (eight times as much as was planted). In 1947 there were 796,000 km of hedgerows, by 1980 this has declined to 653,000 km and by 1985 had fallen further to 621,000 km.

The Nature Conservancy Council's *Nature Conservation in Great Britain* (1984) reported on the changes to the British countryside since 1949. It found that: 95% of lowland neutral grasslands now lack significant wildlife interest and only 3% are left undamaged by intensive agriculture; 80% of chalk and Jurassic limestone, lowland grassland has been lost or damaged; 40% of lowland heaths on acidic soils have been eliminated; 30% of upland grasslands, heaths and blanket bogs have been lost or damaged; 45% of the limestone pavements in Northern England have been damaged or destroyed; 30–50% of ancient lowland, broadleaved woods have been lost; 50% of lowland fens, valley and basin mires have been lost or damaged and 60% of lowland raised mires have suffered a similar fate.

All these have had a 'knock-on' effect on animal and botanical species and the soil. The Soil Survey of England and Wales reported that 27,000 km^2 of soil (44% of all arable land) is now unstable and could be unproductive within 30 years. This problem has accelerated rapidly since the war, due to modern intensive farming and its reliance on (mainly chemical) fertilizers and pesticides. Of 55 resident breeding species of butterfly one, the large blue, became extinct in 1979; ten more species are vulnerable or seriously endangered; another 13 have declined substantially since 1960. There have been ten botanical extinctions since 1930 (qv *Environment*).

Farming. The pattern of farm management and organization has shifted towards large institutions and holdings; it is estimated that 12% of holdings in the largest size group accounted for 55.8% of activity, while small farmers (44%) account for 2.6% of activity. The 500,000 tractors and 54,500 combine harvesters and other machinery have all contributed to the decline in agricultural employment.

About 60% of full-time farms are livestock (mainly sheep and cattle) orientated, with the majority of sheep and cattle reared in the hill and moorland of Wales, Scotland, northern and south-western England and Northern Ireland.

Factory farming has increased dramatically. Every year some 33 million cattle, sheep and pigs are slaughtered in the United Kingdom (60 per minute) in 1,200 licensed slaughterhouses. The total number of animal and bird deaths is about 3,000 per minute, every working day. Intensive rearing and feeding practices can also have side effects on humans (e.g., the salmonella scare).

Cattle and sheep. The average yield of milk per dairy cow was 4,927 litres (1,084 gallons) and average consumption in the UK, 1988–89, was 2.29 litres per head a week: England and Wales, 2.27; Scotland, 2.32; and Northern Ireland, 2.52. In 1988 milk production stood at 14,400 million litres, just under 50% of which was sold as liquid milk. Milk and milk products sales exceeded £3.8 billion in 1988. The major products were (in tonnes): cheese (300,000 – 28,000, exported); butter (140,000 – 119,000, exported); condensed whole milk (85,000); condensed skimmed milk (42,000) and dried whole and skimmed milk (241,000 – 156,000 exported).

Dairy herds are not intensively farmed in the UK, though the average size of herds has steadily increased. In 1988 the average herd was about 61, with herds of 100 to 200 cows relatively common. The use of growth hormones was finally banned in the UK in 1989. Modern technology has meant that at least 60% of dairy cattle are bred by artificial insemination.

First identified in 1986, with some 14 cases by late 1986 and 1,000 in 1988, reported cases of Bovine Spongiform Encephalopathy (BSE) in Britain rose to a total of 15,467 by July 1990. Despite the government providing £12 million for research into BSE, the situation has deteriorated in June 1990 to the extent that France and other EC countries defied EC regulations and imposed a ban on British beef, which was lifted, with a settlement reached, after a few days. The suspected cause of BSE is infected mass-produced feed; since 1988 the feeding of ruminant protein to ruminants has been banned.

Pigs and poultry. Once more biotechnology and genetic scientific developments have signalled major changes in the production of poultry. Since 1977 poultry meat production has increased by almost 50%; in 1988, production was over 1 million tonnes (over 50% 'broilers'). By 1981 382 million chickens were kept in broiler units housing over 8,000 birds. It takes 7–8 weeks to produce a broiler chicken.

In 1988, despite the salmonella crisis, egg production was over 12,000 million. 35 million eggs are consumed in the UK per day. Over 66% of laying birds are in flocks of 20,000 or more. In 1961 19% of the UK's total egg production came from battery cages; by 1984 this had risen to 96%. Male chickens are destroyed; the national egg-laying flock is a little over 40 million females. Sales of 'free-range' eggs have increased in recent years. Policed by the Ministry of Agriculture, Egg Inspectorate, records have to be kept of all free-range egg production and sales and all free-range eggs have to be sold in pre-packs or cartons. The maximum stocking density for free-range egg production is 400 birds to the acre on the range; and 25 birds per m^2 in the house, if a perchery system is used – deep litter maximum density is 12 birds per m^2.

In 1988 about 8 million pigs were slaughtered. In 1960, more than 50% of our pig farmers had breeding stocks of less than 20 sows; by 1980, more than 50% of pig herds had over 100 sows. About 50%–70% are kept in close confinement.

Despite the various regulations, codes of conduct and recommendations for the welfare of farm animals some unnecessary pain and distress is still experienced by them. The State Veterinary Service monitor the conditions of farm animals and recommend necessary changes, the Farm Animal Welfare Council (an independent body set up by the government) reviews farm-animal welfare. The government are currently implementing some of its recommendations, including tighter controls on the marketing of calves.

Crops. Arable crops are found primarily in eastern and central-southern England and eastern Scotland. In 1988 in Britain 20.5 million tonnes of cereal were produced on 3.9 million ha, the lowest harvest since 1981. There was also a decline in 1988 in the area grown and yield of oilseed rape. Large-scale potato and vegetable production is to be found in the Fens (Cambridgeshire and South Lincolnshire) around the alluvial deposits of the Thames and Humber. Domestic production of sugar beet accounts for about half of requirements.

Horticulture. Over 200,000 ha are used for horticulture of which: vegetables grown in open fields account for 67.7% (37% of output value); orchards, 17.7%; small fruit, 7.4%; nursery stocks, 3.5%; flowers, 2.2%; glass-house crops, 0.2%.

Organic farming. Organic farms are becoming more widespread and attractive for farmers as the topsoil is gradually made barren by intensive use of agricultural chemicals and products. In 1987 Britain established the United Kingdom Register of Organic Food Standards.

Food irradiation. One of the most controversial pieces of legislation is the irradiation of food. Despite Government assurances of strict controls and clear labelling many consumer groups and large retail outlets are refusing to stock irradiated food. Food irradiation kills or reduces micro-organisms present in food and acts as a preservative, providing food with a longer 'shelf life'.

Exports in 1988. Agricultural exports totalled £6,506 million, of which exports of food and drink accounted for £5,280 million. In the same year Britain also exported £776 million of farm machinery.

Food From Britain is a national organization with the function of promoting food and agricultural produce marketing in domestic and overseas markets and has recently introduced a foodmark symbol which guarantees fresh and lightly processed foods. Support for the export sides comes from the British Food Export Council, while the British Agricultural Export Committee of the London Chamber of Commerce represents exporters of agricultural machinery.

The Royal International Agricultural Show (Stoneleigh, Warwickshire) is the major showcase for British agriculture. In 1988 it had over 227,000 visitors. Products are marketed by private traders, producers' co-operatives and marketing boards for milk, wool and potatoes. The marketing boards are producers' organizations (with an independent minority appointed by agricultural ministers); they have statutory powers of regulation and price stabilization.

The Role of the Government

The EC Common Agricultural Policy (CAP). CAP accounts for over 60% of the EC's budget. Its aims are: to ensure stable agricultural markets; a fair standard of living for farmers; and to guarantee food supplies at reasonable prices. Support prices and levies are calculated in European Currency Units (ECU) and are then converted to member state currencies at fixed 'green' rates of exchange. Monetary compensation amounts (import subsidies and export levies) are based on the percentage difference between the green and the market rate. The EC is committed to phasing out differentials by 1992. Minimum prices exist on many commodities and levies exist on imports to maintain support prices. Intervention stocks are disposed of within the community, as long as this does not disrupt internal markets. Export refunds are provided to meet any differential between EC and world prices. Direct payments are made to producers, especially in the beef and sheep sectors.

CAP agricultural production has increased considerably in the 1980s, while consumption has remained relatively stable. This has created surpluses and mountains of EC produce, while other regions of the globe face starvation. Although, since 1986 the butter mountain has fallen by 90% and the cereal mountain by almost 60%.

Britain has consistently sought reform of the CAP. In 1988/89 the European Council of Ministers introduced: a legal limit on CAP market support (restricting support for beef for instance); maximum support, to be given only in specified amounts and price-fixing settlement guidelines.

Market support. In 1988/89 expenditure in Britain was about £253 million for price guarantees, capital and production grants and subsidies and £1,240 million on CAP market regulation. £1,127 million was reimbursed through the community budget.

Smallholdings. There are about 5,900 statutory smallholdings in England and 950 in Wales, which are provided by local authorities. Tenants receive loans of up to 75% of working capital. Scottish land settlement has traditionally been the preserve of Government. Despite sales to sitting tenants it still administers about 116,000 ha of land-settlement statutes, 1,525 ha of which are crofts and holdings. The crofting areas of Scotland (Strathclyde, Highlands, Western Isles, Orkney and Shetland) are mainly owned by crofters and are administered by the Crofters Commission.

Agriculture and the protection of the countryside. The 1986 Agriculture Act gives agriculture ministers the duty of attaining a balance between environmental needs and those of the agricultural industry. It also requires the minister to encourage countryside conservation in the administration of farm-capital grant schemes, in both national parks and countryside areas of Special Scientific Interest (SSI), designated by the Nature Conservancy Council.

There are 19 Environmentally Sensitive Areas (ESAs) in the UK – 10 in England, 5 in Scotland, 2 in Wales and 2 in Northern Ireland. They are important for their natural, geographical and historical features and are particularly threatened by agricultural change. It is a voluntary scheme which provides farms with financial incentives for environmentally conscious farming. ESAs include: in England, the Norfolk and Suffolk Broads, Pennine Dales and Shropshire Borders; in Scotland, Breadalbane; in Wales, Lleyn Peninsula; and in Northern Ireland, Slieve Croob.

In 1988–89 a number of grant schemes were introduced to encourage farmers to seek other sources of revenue rather than produce surpluses. These included: Farm Diversification Scheme, which encourage farm business enterprises; Farm Woodland Scheme, (see FORESTRY); Farm and Conservation Grant Scheme, which aims to encourage the control of farm pollution and encourage conservation; EC 'Set Aside' Scheme, which offers compensation to farmers who set aside more than 20% of their arable land to lay fallow for more than five years.

Agricultural services. The government's Agricultural Development and Advisory Service (ADAS) is responsible for providing a range of scientific, technical, veterinary, and professional advice services for agricultural and associated industries. The majority of advice services are fee-paying, although in some areas, such as advice on conservation services, it is free. In Scotland these services are provided by the Department of Agriculture and Fisheries, the Scottish Agricultural Colleges and sectors of the state veterinary service, while in Northern Ireland, the Department of Agriculture has its own advisory and scientific service. These bodies are also responsible for advising the government on agricultural policy.

Agricultural and food research. Responsibility for conducting research into agriculture and food lies with the various agricultural departments of England, Northern Ireland, Scotland and Wales, the Agriculture Food and Research Council (AFRC), and private industry with government-funded research now amounting to £200 million a year. The AFRC is funded by the Department of Education and Science, the Ministry of Agriculture Fisheries and Food and other private bodies. Research is conducted at the AFRC's eight institutes in Britain, which specialize in conducting research into areas such as animal health, genetics, horticulture and animal production, and also by various university and polytechnic departments who are funded by the AFRC's research grants scheme. In Scotland, the Department of Agriculture Fisheries and Food funds five Scottish Agricultural Research Institutes which fulfil similar roles to those of the AFRC. In Northern Ireland, the Department of Agriculture in association with Queen's University of Belfast and the Agricultural Research Institute of Northern Ireland are responsible for conducting, promoting, and initiating research. However, the current Conservative government is planning to cut government expenditure on research and development services such as those provided by the AFRC and other bodies. A decision which has come at a time when public fears about food and Agricultural Safety are high (it is estimated that £30 million will be cut from the budget by 1991–92). The government is hoping that private industry will now take greater responsibility for conducting and initiating research programmes into food and agriculture.

Forestry

In 1987–88 total employment in the forestry industry was just over 22,000, with over 9,500 people working in the timber-processing industries. British woodlands meet only 12% of British consumption of wood and wood products.

There are 2.36 million ha of woodland in Britain (14.6% in Scotland, 11.9% in Wales, 7.3% in England and 5.2% in Northern Ireland). The area of productive woodland in 1988 was 2.1 million ha, nearly half of which is owned by the Forestry Commission (the biggest single landowner in Britain). In 1987–88 the Commission planted nearly 5,000 ha of new woodland and private woodland owners planted nearly 24,000 ha. However, 94% of the Forestry Commission's forests are predominantly conifer as opposed to broadleaved trees, which are rapidly dwindling. In 1985 an amendment to the Wild Life and Countryside Act gave the Forestry Commission the duty of achieving a balance between aforestation and environmental conservation. The Forestry Commission thus revised its grant policy to make broadleaved planting more financially attractive. In 1987–88 the commission grant-aided approximately 2,500 ha of new broadleaved planting (an 85% increase over the previous year). In 1988 the Commission introduced the Farm Woodlands Grant scheme, which consists in planting 36,000 extra ha in three years with incentives for broadleaved trees, and published its annual survey of UK tree health. It found that a quarter of trees had lost more than a quarter of their foliage and almost two-fifths had 11–25% loss of crown density. The Forestry Commission (established 1919) is financed partly by government and partly from sales and rents. It is responsible to the Ministry of Agriculture Fisheries and Food in England and the Secretaries of State for Scotland and Wales. Since 1981 the Crown has sold 72,000 ha and, by the year 2000, government expects to dispose of a further 100,000 hectares. The Forestry Commission also maintains two major research stations. The great storm of 1987 destroyed 15 million trees in southern England, 16,000 ha of woodland were badly damaged and 3.7 million m^3 of woodland timber were felled.

Fishing

The domestic fishing industry accounts for some two-thirds of Britain's fish supplies. There are about 20,000 fishermen in regular and occasional employment. In 1983 the EC's Common Fisheries Policy (CFP) was introduced. This policy establishes: territorial coastal fishing limits, (with British vessels able to fish within 6 miles of the mainland and EC member states between 6 and 12 miles); fish quotas, with world fish production in 1985 at 84 million tonnes – the Food and Agriculture Organization (FAO) estimates that the world's catch must not exceed 100 million tonnes per annum to avoid serious depletion of fish stocks and the CFP, in order to conserve stocks, annually sets a total allowable catch; conservation and management of fishing stocks and grants for improvements in the EC's fishing fleets.

Almost half of all fish caught in Britain are demersal. In 1988 733,000 tonnes of fish were landed by British vessels, of which cod and haddock accounted for 22% and 24% respectively. Britain imports about 403,000 tonnes of shellfish and fish, 206,000 tonnes of fishmeal and 164,000 tonnes of fish oil. In 1988 there were approximately 8,000 onshore fishing vessels under 80 feet in length and 273 deep-sea vessels. Major ports for fishing include; Aberdeen, Grimsby, Newlyn and Kilkeel in Northern Ireland. Developments in the

1980s include the ten-fold increase in fish farming. This sector has an estimated annual turnover of £120 million. The two fish most commonly farmed are salmon (18,000 tonnes) and trout (16,000 tonnes). The Government has provided the industry in Scotland with about £25 million in aid, through the Highlands and Islands Development Board.

The Sea Fish Industry Authority deals with all aspects of the industry including research and development, marketing and grant management. In England and Wales, the Ministry of Agriculture, Fisheries and Food is responsible for the administration of the fishing industry and also has a research directorate. In Scotland, this task falls to the Department of Agriculture and Fisheries for Scotland and in Northern Ireland to the Department of Agriculture.

UK INDUSTRIAL COMPANIES

The top companies in the United Kingdom are mostly multinationals. Only two wholly UK-owned companies appear in the list of the top 30 industrial companies which follows.

A table overleaf on pp. 838–9 lists the Top 20 Largest British Industrial Companies in the UK (i.e., excluding banks, etc.) in order of total turnover.

BRITISH PETROLEUM

Chairman **Robert Horton**

BP is a worldwide energy group mainly involved in oil and gas. Daily production of crude amounts to 1½ million barrels, equivalent to nearly 90% of Britain's daily consumption. Nearly half comes from Alaska and one-third from the North Sea, where BP's holding was boosted by the takeover of Britoil in 1988. The North Sea is also the source of nearly half BP's increasingly important natural gas production. Refining, trading and marketing BP's own and other producers' oil and gas generates nearly two-thirds of turnover and requires a huge infrastructure of refineries, tankers and petrol stations all over the world (though 40% of fixed assets are in the US). BP is also involved in petrochemicals (regarded as a core business alongside oil and gas), related products like plastics and detergents, food for humans, farm animals and pets, seed and breeding stock for farmers, coalmining and solar power. Founded in 1909 to develop the first commercial oil field in the Middle East, BP is Britain's largest company and the world's third largest oil producer. It employs 126,000 people, 29,000 in the UK.

	1987		*1988*	
	£ million		*£ million*	
Turnover	28,328		25,922	
UK turnover	11,454	(40%)	10,551	(40%)
Pre-tax profit	2,387		2,077	

Britannic House, Moor Lane, London EC2Y 9BU, tel. 071-920 8000

IMPERIAL CHEMICAL INDUSTRIES

Chairman **Sir Denys Henderson**

ICI is one of the world's leading chemical companies with a 15,000 strong product range covering agrochemicals, paints, dyes, explosives, films and fibres. Its main money-spinners, however, are petrochemicals, plastics and drugs, which together generated over half its 1988 pre-tax profits of £1,500 million. R&D is the company's lifeblood and currently absorbs about £550 million a year, half of this going into the big growth area of biological research. Since the company's formation out of a merger of Britain's four leading chemical companies in 1926, ICI has made 33,000 inventions, Perspex, Terylene and solid emulsion paint among them. Although UK-based, with 86% of its equity in British hands, ICI thinks and operates globally. It manufactures in 40 countries worldwide and sells in over 150. Foreign nationals comprise well over half its 130,000 workforce and fill one-third of the Group's top 500 jobs. In the UK ICI has over 50 plants and employs 55,000 people, mostly in Scotland and the north of England.

	1987		*1988*	
	£ million		*£ million*	
Turnover	11,123		11,699	
UK turnover	5,630	(51%)	5,694	(49%)
Pre-tax profit	1,312		1,470	

9 Millbank, London W1P 3JF, tel. 071-834 4444

BAT INDUSTRIES

Chairman **Patrick Sheehy**

Founded in 1902, British American Tobacco began to diversify out of tobacco in the 1960s and changed its name to BAT Industries in 1976. It is now one of the world's largest commercial enterprises and by turnover the UK's biggest company outside the oil sector. Generating one-third of its turnover in Europe, BAT is active in four main business sectors: tobacco, paper and pulp, financial services and retailing. Prompted by a takeover bid in 1989, BAT announced plans to sell its paper and retailing interests (which include Wiggins Teape, makers of Conqueror business stationery, and the Argos catalogue stores) and concentrate on tobacco and financial services, already responsible for 81% of turnover. Tobacco brands include Benson and Hedges and John Player Special. BAT's main financial companies are Eagle Star and Allied Dunbar in the UK and Farmer's Group in the US. BAT employs 310,000 people, one-tenth in the UK.

	1987		*1988*	
	£ million		*£ million*	
Turnover	11,402		11,522	
UK turnover	1,503	(13%)	1,624	(14%)
Pre-tax profit	1,394		1,641	

Windsor House, 50 Victoria St, London SW1H 0NL, tel. 071-222 7979

SAINSBURY

Chairman **Lord Sainsbury**

Sainsbury's is a supermarket group with over 400 stores in Britain and the US. About 300 of these are Sainsbury's supermarkets selling high-quality food and 'frequently purchased' household goods. They serve about 7 million customers a week, have an 11% share of the food and drink market making Sainsbury's Britain's largest food retailer, and are currently

Top 20 Largest Industrial Companies in the UK

Rank	Company name	Main activity	Chairman and Managing Director	Period end date	Turnover Latest £'000	Turnover Previous £'000
1 (1)	British Petroleum	Oil industry	Sir Peter Walthers (JMD)[1]	31–12–88	33,101,000	35,682,000
2 (2)	'Shell' Transport & Trading	Oil industry	Sir Peter Holmes (JMD), *J.S. Jennings*	31–12–88	22,329,000	23,924,000
3 (3)	Imperical Chemical Industries	Petrochemicals, pharmaceuticals, etc.	D.H. Henderson	31–12–89	13,171,000	11,699,000
4 (4)	Electricity Council	Electricity suppliers	Sir Philip Jones	31–03–89	12,373,800	11,358,100
5 (5)	BAT Industries	Tobacco, retailg, paper, finl services	P. Sheehy	31–12–88	11,358,000	11,252,000
6 (6)	British Telecommunications	Telecommunication services	I.D.T. Vallance, *G.D.W. Odgers*	31–03–89	11,071,000	10,185,000
7 (11)	Grand Metropolitan	Hotel props, milk prds, brewers, etc.	A.J.G. Sheppard (CE)	30–09–89	9,298,000	6,029,000
8 (8)	British Gas	Gas suppliers, etc.	R. Evans (CE)	31–03–89	7,526,000	7,364,000
9 (7)	Hanson	Consumer products, etc.	Lord Hanson	30–09–89	6,998,000	7,396,000
10 (9)	Shell UK	Oil industry	R.P. Reid (CE)	31–12–88	6,580,000	6,922,000
11 (10)	Unilever	Food products, detergents, etc.	M.R. Angus	31–12–88	6,384,000	5,428,000
12 (12)	Ford Motor Company	Motor vehicle manufacturers	D.D. Barron (CE), *R.F. Humm*	31–12–88	5,936,000	5,211,000
13 (16)	General Electric Company	Electrical engineers	Rt Hon Lord Prior, *Lord Weinstock*	31–03–89	5,878,100	5,552,500
14 (14)	J. Sainsbury	Retail distribution of food	Lord Sainsbury of Preston Candover	18–03–89	5,659,000	4,791,500
15 (15)	British Aerospace	Manufacture of aircraft, etc.	R. Smith, *Sir Raymond Lygo (CE)*	31–12–88	5,639,000	4,075,000
16 (17)	BTR	Construction, energy & electrical, etc.	Sir Owen Green, *J.C. Cahill*	31–12–88	5,472,700	4,149,200
17 (13)	Esso UK	Oil industry	Sir Archibald Forster, *D. Clayman, K.H. Taylor*	31–12–88	5,274,900	5,765,500
18 (19)	Marks and Spencer	General store proprietors	Lord Raynor, *C.V. Silver, R. Greenbury (CE)*	31–03–89	5,121,500	4,577,600
19 (20)	British Steel	Mfr & sale of steel	Sir Robert Scholey, *M.E. Llowarch (CE)*	01–04–89	4,906,000	0
20 (23)	Dalgety	International merchants	Sir Peter Carey, *M.E. Warren*	30–06–89	4,757,000	4,503,000

Note: 1 Managing directors – D.A.G. Simon, P.J. Gillam, H. Norton, B.R.R. Butter, R.B. Horton.
Source: Extel Financial Ltd, 1990.

Capital employed £'000	Rank Latest	Rank Previous	Net profit before interest and tax Latest £'000	Rank	Previous £'000	% Turnover Latest	% Capital Latest	Employed Previous	No. of employees	Equity market capital £M at 26.3.90
20,436,000	1	1	3,290,000	1	3,909,000	9.9	17.7	18.8	125,950	17,996.7
15,110,000	3	3	2,404,000	3	2,595,000	10.8	16.7	16.2	N/A	0.0
8,337,000	7	7	1,804,000	4	1,751,000	13.7	27.4	28.5	133,800	7,824.4
18,851,800	2	2	Loss 726,600	1000	1,284,400	0.0	0.0	8.4	131,179	NAT
7,064,000	8	6	1,745,000	5	1,542,000	15.4	27.3	22.0	172,715	12,096.7
13,375,000	4	4	2,832,000	2	2,661,000	25.6	23.5	23.4	242,723	17,309.2
4,454,000	9	11	1,042,000	8	667,000	11.2	26.5	19.9	152,175	5,884.0
8,364,000	6	5	1,577,000	6	1,462,000	21.0	19.5	19.5	81,832	9,117.3
8,682,000	5	8	1,394,000	7	1,167,000	19.9	22.7	24.0	89,000	10,937.1
3,705,000	15	14	687,000	16	1,096,000	10.4	18.6	31.3	18,233	HOL
2,580,000	30	23	632,000	17	527,000	9.9	24.7	18.4	155,000	5,296.4
2,410,000	33	26	704,000	15	366,000	11.9	29.6	16.1	47,900	USA
3,727,400	14	17	816,900	13	727,900	13.9	23.1	19.2	145,029	5,500.8
1,990,000	42	36	406,100	29	324,400	7.2	28.1	31.9	88,283	3,888.0
3,628,000	16	16	367,000	32	Loss 30,000	6.5	10.1	0.0	133,600	1,285.5
3,290,500	19	18	941,800	10	652,400	17.2	41.7	28.8	98,620	7,778.7
3,569,600	18	15	842,400	12	1,117,700	16.0	23.0	30.6	4,530	USA
2,361,000	35	29	570,600	20	507,600	11.1	24.1	30.3	76,313	5,280.8
4,329,000	11	10	738,000	14	0	15.0	17.0	0.0	55,200	2,920.0
826,000	107	108	168,000	98	143,000	3.5	23.8	20.7	22,503	843.0

expanding out of their South-East base at the rate of 20 new stores a year. Sainsbury's also owns the 50-store Homebase home improvement and garden-centre chain which it launched in 1979, the 7-store Savacentre hypermarket chain providing a complete shopping service for household goods, and, in New England in the US, 69 Shaw's supermarkets, bought in 1987 and similar in style to the British Sainsbury's (i.e. strong on quality, customer service and environmental responsibility). Founded as a dairy in Drury Lane in London by John and Mary Sainsbury in 1869, the company went public in 1973. 30% of its 88,000 staff are shareholders, representing one-quarter of the register.

	1988	*1989*
	£ million	*£ million*
Turnover	5,009	5,915
UK turnover	4,558 (91%)	5,084 (86%)
Pre-tax profit	332	401

Stamford House, Stamford St, London SE1 9LL, tel. 071-921 6000

BRITISH TELECOM

Chairman **Iain Vallance**

With 24 million customers and over 85,000 pay phones, BT is both much the larger of Britain's two national phone companies and the fifth largest telephone company in the western world. Thanks to a £3000 million a year investment programme, its increasingly modern network enables it to provide an ever-growing range of telephone and other telecommunications services, including mobile phones on the Cellnet network jointly owned with Securicor, the new high street telepoint system, information services like Prestel, fax, telex, share dealing via Sharelink, and television. BT owns and runs its own cable television systems in five new town locations, markets satellite television channels to companies like Sky Television, and provides broadcasting facilities to the four national television stations, plus national and local radio. Overseas, BT has always exported its equipment and expertise and is now investing heavily in foreign businesses similar to those at home. Separated from the Post Office in 1981 and privatized in 1984, BT is regulated by Oftel (the Office of Telecommunications) and employs nearly 250,000 people.

Telephone poles: 4,250,000, some 100 years old
Calls daily: 80 million
999 calls: 19 million a year, the cost borne by BT
Directory enquiries: over 500 million a year
Payphones: 96.5% working at any one time
Repairs: 95% of faults cleared within two working days

	1988	*1989*
	£ million	*£ million*
Turnover	10,185	11,071
Inland phone calls	3,960 (39%)	4,397 (40%)
International phone calls	1,400 (14%)	1,548 (14%)
Pre-tax profit	2,292	2,437

British Telecom Centre, 81 Newgate St, London EC1A 7AJ, tel. 071-356 5000

HANSON

Chairman **Lord Hanson**

Hanson PLC (Hanson Industries in the US) is an industrial management company which specializes in buying up poorly performing companies in Britain and America and bringing them back into profit. It uses a mixture of tried and tested methods and always aims to recoup its investment within three to four years. The Hanson philosophy is currently being applied to 175 companies producing an extraordinarily wide range of goods from batteries, car windscreen washers, bricks, gas meters and gas fires to chocolates, vacuum cleaners, toys, pool tables, shoes and hot dogs. Famous names in the Hanson stable include Imperial Tobacco, Ever Ready, Smith Corona and Jacuzzi. Started in 1964 by Lord Hanson and Sir Gordon White, Hanson moved into America in 1973 and now employs 105,000 people on both sides of the Atlantic, though less than 40% in the UK where it nevertheless makes over half its profit.

	1988	*1989*
	£ million	*£ million*
Turnover	6,682	7,396
UK turnover	4,003 (60%)	4,196 (57%)
Pre-tax profit	741	880

1 Grosvenor Place, London SW1X 7JH, tel. 071-245 1245

BRITISH GAS

Chairman and Chief Executive **Robert Evans**

The main business of British Gas is supplying gas in Great Britain. Although it operates its own rigs in Morecambe Bay and the North Sea, it has to buy over 90% of its gas from other North Sea suppliers. A little over half the gas goes to 16.8 million domestic customers, 96% of the company's total customer base and 80% of all households in Britain. The rest goes to commercial customers, such as offices and schools (16%), and to industry (29%). All in all, British Gas supplies about half the nation's total energy requirements. The company foresees its market maturing in the mid 1990s and has already begun to expand into oil and gas exploration overseas to sustain future growth. British Gas is also involved in selling, installing and servicing gas appliances, a business which occupies nearly a quarter of the 81,000 workforce but which generates only 9% of turnover. Created in 1948 when the 150-year-old gas industry was nationalized, the company was privatized in 1986.

	1988	*1989*
	£ million	*£ million*
Turnover	7,364	7,526
Pre-tax profit	1,008	1,054

Rivermill House, 152 Grosvenor Rd, London SW1V 3JL, tel. 071-821 1444

GEC

Chairman **Lord Prior**

GEC, standing for General Electric Company, is a worldwide electrical and engineering manufacturer with 70% of turnover being generated in the UK. The company specializes in power generation, transport, defence and communications and makes both individual pieces of equipment, ranging from tiny threads of optical fibre to locomotives and warships, and whole systems, including national telecommunications and rail networks and complete power stations. GEC also produces printing and office equipment, medical diagnostic imaging systems, factory robots, and washing machines, cookers and other white goods under such well-known UK brands as Hotpoint, Creda, Cannon and Osram. In all areas, GEC is at the forefront of technological progress, spending £700 million a year on R&D and employing 18,000 scientists and engineers among its 145,000 workforce (70% UK-based). Founded in 1886, the company merged with English Electric (including Marconi) and other companies in the 1960s, and in 1989 acquired Plessey, in partnership with Siemens of West Germany.

	1988		*1989*	
	£ million		*£ million*	
Turnover	5,915		6,806	
UK turnover	3,271	(55%)	3,532	(52%)
Pre-tax profit	708		797	

1 Stanhope Gate, London SW1A 1EH, tel. 071-493 8484

GRAND METROPOLITAN

Chairman and Group Chief Executive **Allen Sheppard**

Founded as a hotel company in 1962, Grand Met has grown by acquisition into one of the world's leading food, drinks and retailing companies, ranked no. 1 in wines and spirits (90 million cases sold a year), no. 2 in number of retail outlets (over 15,000) and no. 8 in food sales. Nearly half group turnover comes from the drinks business, embracing such famous brands as Croft sherry, Gilbey's gin, J and B Rare Scotch, Smirnoff vodka and Bailey's Irish Cream (all no. 1 or 2 in the world), and beers like Ruddles and Webster's. Food manufacturing is especially strong in dairy products, with brands such as Express Dairies, Eden Vale and Ski. Grand Met also owns several fast-food chains, including Burger King, Wimpy and Pizzaland, and a chain of optical stores in the US which is the largest in the world. Historically based in the UK and Ireland, the group moved into the US in the 1980s and is currently expanding fast in Europe and the Far East. It employs 140,000 people, 65,000 in the UK.

	1987		*1988*	
	£ million		*£ million*	
Turnover	5,705		6,028	
UK and Ireland turnover	3,558	(62%)	3,835	(64%)
Pre-tax profit	456		575	

11–12 Hanover Square, London W1A 1DP, tel. 071-629 7488

BRITISH AEROSPACE

Chairman **Prof. Roland Smith**

Formed out of BAC, Hawker Siddeley and Scottish Aviation in 1977, British Aerospace was a nationalized industry until privatized in two share issues in 1981 and 1985. Its main products are military and civil aircraft, defence systems, satellites and space craft and space equipment. Following the acquisition of Royal Ordnance and Ballast Nedam, a Dutch construction company, in 1987, Rover Group in 1988 and a UK property developer in 1989, it has expanded into ordnance and ammunition, car manufacture, property development and international construction – enabling it to supply, among other things, complete aerospace and defence systems to its customers. Now Britain's biggest car producer and manufacturing company generally, over 60% of its sales are made abroad, making it also Britain's biggest exporter of manufactured goods. The company operates on about 75 sites in the UK and employs 133,000 people.

	1987		*1988*	
	£ million		*£ million*	
Turnover	4,075		5,639	
UK turnover	1,994	(50%)	2,158	(38%)
Pre-tax profit	161		236	

11 Strand, London WC2N 5JT, tel. 071-930 1020

BTR

Chairman **Sir Owen Green**

Founded in 1924 as the UK subsidiary of a US tyre company, BTR went independent in 1934 and moved out of tyres in 1956 to become the broad-based international manufacturing and trading group it is today. The group comprises about 70 companies operating in five main sectors; industrial, transport, construction, energy and electrical, and consumer. It makes a wide variety of products, from conveyor belts and rubber hoses, cement and concrete, car axles and transmission systems to artificial limbs, Pretty Polly tights and Puma, Slazenger and Dunlop sports equipment (the latter company acquired in 1985). On the trading side, BTR sells Wellco DIY products, cash registers and runs chains of builders' merchants, electrical wholesalers and scaffolding and plant-hire companies. A worldwide company, its main centres of activity are the US, Australia and Europe including the UK, where it generates about half its turnover. BTR employs over 98,000 people, 43,000 in the UK.

	1987		*1988*	
	£ million		*£ million*	
Turnover	4,149		5,472	
Europe turnover	2,537	(61%)	2,796	(51%)
UK turnover	N/A		N/A	
Pre-tax profit	590		819	

Silvertown House, Vincent Square, London SW1P 2PL, tel. 071-834 3848

MARKS AND SPENCER

Chairman **Lord Rayner**

Marks and Spencer is an increasingly international retailer specializing in household goods, foods and clothes, the latter accounting for about half its turnover. Worldwide it owns 665 stores, 281 in the UK where it is the leading retailer with 14 million customers a week, and has market shares in food and clothes of 5% and 16% respectively. Overseas the company has 384 stores – in Canada (where it opened its first foreign outlet, in 1973), America, Ireland, France, Belgium, Hong Kong and Japan. 76 are Marks and Spencer stores; the rest belong to subsidiaries like Brooks Brothers, America's oldest clothing company, which was bought in 1988. There are also some franchise stores, including one in Hungary. All goods sold in Marks and Spencer stores carry a single brand – St Michael – launched in 1928. Founded in Leeds in 1894 by Russian refugee Michael Marks and his partner Tom Spencer, the company employs 76,000 people, 62,000 in the UK.

	1988		*1989*	
	£ million		*£ million*	
Turnover	4,577		5,121	
UK turnover	4,218	(92%)	4,488	(88%)
Pre-tax profit	501		529	

Michael House, 37–67 Baker St, London W1A 1DN, tel. 071-935 4422

TESCO

Chairman **Sir Ian MacLaurin**

Tesco is one of Britain's largest food retailers, with 374 stores all over Great Britain. 146 of them are superstores with over 25,000 sq ft of selling space. The company serves 10 million customers a week and has over 8% of the UK food and drinks market. In terms of superstore food retailing it is the biggest in the UK. With over 90 filling stations it is also the largest independent petrol retailer in the UK and was the first to sell unleaded petrol at all its outlets. Other signs of Tesco's pioneering commitment to the environment include the 200-odd paper and bottle banks in its car parks – more than any other similar retailer. Distribution is by a fleet of 365 lorries linking stores with computerized warehouses stocked with products from 2000 suppliers and manufacturers. Each year Tesco sells enough Liebfraumilch to fill 350 swimming pools and enough bananas to go round the M25 125 times. Launched in 1931 by ex-market-stall holder Jack Cohen, the company employs 75,000 people, over one-third of whom are shareholders.

	1988	*1989*
	£ million	*£ million*
Turnover	4,365	5,003
Pre-tax profit	225	276

Tesco House, Delamare Road, Cheshunt, Herts EN8 9SL, tel. 0992 32222

RTZ

Chairman **Sir Alistair Frame**

RTZ, standing for Rio Tinto Zinc, is predominantly a mining, smelting and refining company producing base and precious metals like gold, silver, aluminium, copper, zinc and tin, industrial minerals like borates, diamonds, silica sand and talc, and energy consumables such as coal and uranium. Outside the natural resources sector, which accounts for little more than half group turnover but over 80% of profits, it has diversified into related industries, mainly chemicals and products and services for the construction, aviation and automotive industries. RTZ is active in 40 countries, including the UK and Portugal, the US and Chile, Zimbabwe and Namibia, and Australia, Indonesia and Papua New Guinea, and employs 82,000 people, 18,000 in the UK. In 1989 it bought BP's minerals business for over US$ 4000 million, the most significant event in the history of the company since its foundation in 1962 following a merger between two old-established mining companies, the British Rio Tinto and the Australian Consolidated Zinc.

	1987		*1988*	
	£ million		*£ million*	
Turnover	4,209		4,922	
UK turnover	990	(23%)	1,378	(27%)
Pre-tax profit	594		879	

6 St James's Square, London SW1Y 4LD, tel. 071-930 2399

BRITISH STEEL

Chairman **Sir Robert Scholey**

British Steel was formed in 1967 by the nationalization of about 90% of Britain's steelmaking capacity. It has five major integrated plants in South Wales, South Humberside, Teeside and Scotland and produces about 15 million tonnes of steel a year. This makes it the western world's fourth largest steel producer. Following painful restructuring and privatization in the 1980s it is also one of the few major steelmakers to show a profit, even though it operates mainly at the high-volume, low-profitability end of the market. About 70% of British Steel's steel is used in the UK, where the company supplies about two-thirds of the market. The rest goes abroad, earning £1600 million in sales (62% in Europe) and making British Steel the UK's sixth largest exporter outside the oil sector. The company employs 55,000 people, the vast majority in the UK.

	1988		*1989*	
	£ million		*£ million*	
Turnover	4,116		4,906	
UK turnover	2,729	(66%)	3,248	(66%)
Pre-tax profit	419		593	

9 Albert Embankment, London SE1 7SN, tel. 071-735 7654

ALLIED LYONS

Chairman **Sir Derrick Holden-Brown**

Allied Lyons is an increasingly international food, drinks and leisure group, two-thirds of turnover being generated in Britain but about half its profits being earned overseas. It began life as Allied Breweries following the 1961 amalgamation of the Tetley, Ansells and Ind Coope breweries, and now produces about 14% of Britain's beer and lager with brands such as Double Diamond, Skol and Tetley's (Britain's biggest selling bitter). Entry into wines and spirits and food came in 1968 with the acquisition of Babycham and the J. Lyons food company. Now the group has hundreds of brands, amongst the best known being Courvoisier brandy, Harvey's Bristol Cream (the world's best-selling sherry), Tetley's Tea and Lyons Maid ice cream. Besides its seven breweries in the UK and the Netherlands, the group also owns vineyards in Spain and Portugal, about 7,000 pubs, bars and restaurants, over 1,000 off licences (mainly in the Victoria Wine chain), 42 Embassy hotels with 3,000 rooms, and Britain's biggest Mercedes car dealer. It employs 81,000 people, 65,000 in the UK.

	1988	*1989*
	£ million	*£ million*
Turnover	4,236	4,504
UK turnover	2,573 (61%)	2,797 (62%)
Pre-tax profit	436	502

24 Portland Place, London W1N 4BB, tel. 071-323 9000 9000

DALGETY

Chairman **Sir Peter Carey**

Dalgety is the world's leading food and agribusiness group. Through its subsidiary companies it is involved at all stages of food production and manufacture, from the supply of seeds, stock, fertilizer, machinery and expertise to farmers, to the manufacture of literally thousands of ingredients and a wide range of food products for human and animal consumption. As a food distributor and commodities trader, the group also supplies the bulk of the world's asparagus, keeps over half the Macdonald's in the US stocked up and handles 20% of the world's cocoa. In the UK, where it controls brands such as Golden Wonder, Homepride, Goldenlay and Winalot, it makes nearly half of Britain's flour and a quarter of its pet food. In Australia, where Dalgety was founded in 1846, the company is mainly a livestock auctioneer and wool broker, selling over 12 million beasts a year and handling 20% of wool production. Food technology breakthroughs have included a garlic-peeling laser and the world's biggest-selling breeding pig. Dalgety employs 23,000 people, 15,000 in the UK.

	1987	*1988*
	£ million	*£ million*
Turnover	5,003	4,503
Europe turnover	2,600 (52%)	2,231 (50%)
UK turnover	N/A	N/A
Pre-tax profit	93	100

19 Hanover Square, London SW1R 9DA, tel. 071-499 7712

BRITISH COAL

Chairman **Sir Robert Haslam**

British Coal was formed in 1947 when the coal industry was nationalized. It has 74 deep mines and 53 open-cast mines plus some small licensed mines which together produce over 100 million tonnes of coal a year, over 80% coming from the deep mines. About 80% of the coal is sold to power stations to generate electricity. The rest (apart from 1.8 million tonnes which is exported) goes to industry and for domestic use at home. British Coal supplies 90% of all coal used in Britain. Coal is mined all over England, Scotland and Wales, but over half (55%) comes from mines in the Nottinghamshire and Yorkshire coalfields. South Wales accounts for only 6% of total output. 88,000 people are employed by the company, about 85% underground. Owing to the most radical restructuring ever seen in British industry, British Coal has lost half its pits and workforce in recent years, yet doubled productivity has ensured virtually constant output.

	1988	*1989*
	£ million	*£ million*
Turnover	4,388	4,295
Pre-tax profit/loss	(495)	(203)

Hobart House, Grosvenor Place, London SW1X 7AE, tel. 071-235 2020

BRITISH AIRWAYS

Chairman **Lord King**

BA is the largest carrier of international airline traffic in the world (for details of its operations see under TRANSPORT). Created as a state-owned industry out of the old BEA and BOAC in 1974, BA was privatized in 1987 and took over British Caledonian in 1988. It now employs over 50,000 people, nearly 44,000 in the UK.

	1988	*1989*
	£ million	*£ million*
Turnover	3,756	4,257
UK turnover	378 (10%)	453 (11%)
Pre-tax profit	228	268

Speedbird House, Heathrow Airport, Hounslow TW6 2JA, tel. 081-759 5511

THE POST OFFICE

Chairman and Chief Executive **Sir Bryan Nicholson**

A government department from the 17th century, the Post Office was made a nationalized industry in 1969, separated from British Telecom in 1981 and reorganized into Letters, Parcels, Counters and Girobank in 1986. The biggest division is Royal Mail Letters which generates two-thirds of turnover. It collects 53 million items a day from 100,000 pick-up points and delivers them to 24 million addresses. Special aids include 37 mobile sorting offices on BR trains, address-reading sorting machines and a 6½-mile underground railway in London. Counters has 21,000 post offices, 1500 of them 'Crown' offices, and nearly 20,000 sub post offices. Most Post Office business is agency work (pensions, licences, cash handling, etc.) carried out for the government and other organizations like the Post Office's own Girobank (currently in the process of being sold off), which uses post offices as its branch network. The Post Office also administers the National Postal Museum and employs 205,000 people, 80% of them in Royal Mail Letters.

	1988	1989
	£ million	£ million
Turnover	3,790	3,914
Pre-tax profit	212	169

33 Grosvenor Place, London SW1 1PX, tel. 071-235 8000

The following ten wholly British-owned companies are among the next highest in terms of turnover per year (again banks and other service industries are excluded).

SAATCHI AND SAATCHI

Chairman **Maurice Saatchi**

Incorporating well over 100 companies and active in over 50 countries, Saatchi and Saatchi is the biggest communications and business services agency group in the world. Its business covers 16 different 'service lines' divided into two sectors: communications (advertising, PR, design, etc.), and consulting (human resources, market research, etc.). Communications is the biggest sector, generating about 80% of profits (though consulting is growing faster). Advertising, with over US$ 11,000 million worth of billings, equal to nearly 8% of the world market, is the biggest single business, reflecting the group's origins in the ad agency founded by brothers Maurice and Charles Saatchi in 1970. Over half Saatchi's profits come from the US. The UK, where Saatchi's is still regularly voted the no. 1 creative agency, produces under a fifth. At the last count, Saatchi's employed nearly 17,000 people.

	1987	1988
	£ million	£ million
Turnover	3,954	3,796
UK turnover	N/A	N/A
Pre-tax profit	124	138

Berkeley Square, London SW1X 5DH, tel. 071-495 5000

P&0

Chairman **Sir Jeffrey Sterling**

Originally a steamer service linking Britain first with the Iberian peninsula (Spain and Portugal) and then with the empire in the east, the Peninsular and Oriental Steam Navigation Company is one of the biggest shipping companies in the world, as well as a major international construction and service industry group. Shipping accounts for 40% of turnover and includes ferries between Britain, Ireland and the continent, bulk carriers, and a fleet of luxury cruise liners. The property business, carried on mainly through Bovis (bought by P&O in 1974), encompasses housebuilding (3000 up-market houses a year in Britain), property development, big construction projects like Euro-Disneyland, project management and investment. The group's service industries (mainly shipping-related) range from freight handling and port ownership (Felixstowe and Larne) to hiring out boiler suits and staging exhibitions (P&O owns Earl's Court and Olympia in London). The group employs 55,000 people, 35,000 in the UK and 9000 at sea.

	1987	1988
	£ million	£ million
Turnover	2,920	3,376
UK turnover	1,807 (62%)	2,093 (62%)
Pre-tax profit	274	316

79 Pall Mall, London SW1Y 5EJ, tel. 071-930 4343

LONRHO

Chairman **Rt Hon. Sir Edward du Cann KBE**

Lonrho is a diversified manufacturing and trading group comprising over 800 companies in 80 countries. Led by its ebullient chief executive, Tiny Rowlands, it has a strong presence in the UK where it generates nearly two-thirds of its turnover, and in Africa where it employs 70% of its 100,000 workforce. In both places it is the largest distributor of motor vehicles (motor and equipment distribution accounts for half group turnover). In Africa, where it owns the bulk of its 2 million acres of farmland, it is the largest commercial food producer, specializing in tea and sugar. Lonrho is also involved in gold and platinum mining in Africa, oil and gas production in the US, hotels and casinos in Mexico and the Bahamas, shipping and warehousing all over the world, currency and stamp printing and newspaper publishing in the UK (where it owns the *Observer* and 26 provincial papers), and many other businesses ranging from textiles to financial services. Lonrho was founded in 1909 as the London and Rhodesian Mining and Land Company and employs 15,000 people in the UK.

	1987	1988
£ million	£ million	
Turnover	3,013	3,266
UK turnover	1,837 (61%)	2,015 (61%)
Pre-tax profit	200	225

Cheapside House, 138 Cheapside, London EC2V 6BL, tel. 071-606 9898

ASDA

Chairman **John Hardman**

Asda is a retailing group with nearly 400 stores all over Great Britain. About half belong to Asda's subsidiary, Allied Carpets, which in 1989 acquired the brand names and most of the stores of the London-based Maples and Waring and Gillow furnishing companies. The other half are Asda superstores, selling increasingly up-market food, household and leisure goods, footwear and clothing (designed by George Davies of Next fame from 1990) to nearly 4 million customers a week. In spite of the near-equality in store numbers, the Asda stores generated over 90% of turnover in 1989, a proportion likely to increase in 1990 following the 1989 acquisition of 61 Gateway superstores from Isosceles. The group also has its own property company, Gazeley. Founded in the north of England in 1965 as Associated Dairies, Asda pioneered edge-of-town superstore family retailing, and is now the biggest such retailer in the UK, as well as the third-largest food retailer. It employs about 62,000 people.

	1988	*1989*
	£ million	*£ million*
Turnover	2,462	2,708
Pre-tax profit	215	246

Asda House, Southbank, Great Wilson St, Leeds LS11 5AD, tel. 0532 435435

GUINNESS

Chairman **Anthony Tennant**

Founded by the Guinness family in Dublin in 1759, Guinness is an international spirits and beer group. It is best known for its famous white-headed black stout, launched 200 years ago and now one of the few beers in the world with a truly international reputation. Newer 'blond' beers include Harp lager and two alcohol-free brands, Kaliber lager and Smithwick's bitter. The spirits business, which generates the greater part of group turnover following the controversial takeover of Distillers in 1986, has a stable of 200 leading brands, including Pimms, Cossack vodka, and two world leaders, Gordon's gin and Johnnie Walker Red Label whisky. Outside the drinks business, Guinness runs the Gleneagles Hotel and publishes the *Guinness Book of Records*, now in its 36th edition and the biggest-selling copyright book in the world. The company employs over 18,000 people, 10,000 in the UK and 3000 in Ireland, and earns 80% of its profits abroad.

	1987	*1988*
	£ million	*£ million*
Turnover	2,278	2,707
UK turnover	827 (36%)	920 (34%)
Pre-tax profit	408	521

39 Portman Square, London W1H 9HB, tel. 071-486 0288

BOOTS

Chairman **Robert Gunn**

Still based in Nottingham where it was founded over 100 years ago by herbalist Jesse Boot, Boots is Britain's biggest high street retailer of drugs, toiletries and cosmetics and a major manufacturer and supplier of similar products both in the UK and overseas. The retail side of the business is by far the biggest, generating over 80% of the company's £2700 million turnover. Most of this comes from Boots the Chemist's 1000-plus stores which serve half the women and a quarter of the men in Britain each week. Besides selling the more traditional products, many stores also develop photos and dispense spectacles (Boots has the second-largest retail optical chain in the UK). Overseas, Boots has a small retail presence in France and New Zealand and manufactures and/or markets in 18 countries. Following its £800 million takeover of the Ward White Group in 1989, the number of Boots' employees rose from 70,000 to 90,000, 80,000 in the UK.

	1988	*1989*
	£ million	*£ million*
Turnover	2,697	2,704
UK turnover	2,079 (77%)	2,254 (83%)
Pre-tax profit	267	306

The Boots Company Plc, Nottingham NG2 3AA, tel. 0602 506111

CADBURY SCHWEPPES

Chairman **Sir Graham Day**

Born out of a merger in 1969 between two famous old companies, Cadbury Schweppes is a major manufacturer of chocolate and soft drinks with a host of famous brands, many of them known all over the world. Drinks, made by both Cadbury and Schweppes, include Lilt, Five Alive, Kia Ora and of course Schweppes Ginger Ale and Tonic Water, both launched over a century ago. The best-known confectionery brands are sweets like Murray Mints and Fry's Turkish Delight and Cadbury's various chocolate products, such as Fruit and Nut, Flake, Crunchie, Bournville (named after Cadbury's old-established factory near Birmingham) and, biggest seller of them all, Diary Milk, launched in 1905. Although the UK is the company's single biggest market (it has around a quarter of the soft drinks market and over one-third of the confectionery market), Cadbury Schweppes earns over two-thirds of its revenue overseas, manufacturing in 60 countries and trading in over 120. More than half its 29,000 workforce are employed outside the UK.

	1987	*1988*
	£ million	*£ million*
Turnover	2,031	2,381
UK turnover	955 (47%)	1,049 (44%)
Pre-tax profit	176	215

1–4 Connaught Place, London W2 2EX, tel. 071-262 1212

TATE AND LYLE

Chairman and Chief Executive **Neil Shaw**

Founded in 1921 by a merger between the syrup and sugar refining firms of Henry Tate and Abram Lyle, Tate and Lyle is now a world leader in the production of sugar, 'sweeteners' and starch from beet, corn and cane. It also makes animal feed and malt and trades in sugar and molasses on a worldwide basis. Together, sweetener production, processing and trading accounted for over 90% of turnover and 75% of profits in 1988. Highly lucrative service businesses related to its main activities include insurance, bulk liquid storage and one of the developing world's largest farm management and consultancy services. Outside the commodity world, Tate and Lyle also builds ships and makes plastic and precision metal parts for cars, houses and the aerospace and defence industries. Active in over 40 countries from the Americas to Malaysia, around 60% of its assets and half its 17,000 workforce are now in North America following significant acquisitions in 1988. In the UK the company employs about 5,000 people.

	1987		*1988*	
	£ million		*£ million*	
Turnover	1,700		2,088	
UK turnover	517	(30%)	582	(28%)
Pre-tax profit	92		120	

Sugar Quay, Lower Thames St, London EC3R 6DQ, tel. 071-626 6525

TRUSTHOUSE FORTE

Chairman **Lord Forte**

Trusthouse Forte is an international hotel and catering group, the largest in the UK and the most profitable in the world. It has 75,000 rooms in its 800 hotels (all linked by computer to each other and to sales offices in 30 countries) and serves hundreds of millions of meals a year in its own hotels and restaurants, on the flights of 150 international airlines (including British Airways Concorde) and at contract outlets ranging from Wall Street banks and prestigious outdoor events like the Chelsea Flower Show, to factories, schools, oil rigs, and even Inter-City trains. THF earns 80% of its £2,000 million plus turnover in Britain where it owns 250 hotels and 1,000 eating outlets, including Little Chefs, the Cafe Royal and its flagship, the Grosvenor Hotel in London. Formed by the merger of Trusthouse Group and the company founded by Lord Forte in 1935, THF employs nearly 80,000 people from North America to the Middle East, 64,000 in the UK.

	1987		*1988*	
	£ million		*£ million*	
Turnover	1,778		2,044	
UK turnover	1,426	(80%)	1,638	(80%)
Pre-tax profit	180		232	

166 High Holborn, London WC1V 6TT, tel. 071-836 7744

Ten-year Record Table (*Net capital employed at beginning of year)

Rank by turnover	Company	Item		Accounting period ended
1	BRITISH PETROLEUM CO.	Net capital employed	£000	31 Dec.
		Ratio of turnover to *net capital employed		
		Net profit before interest and tax	£000	
		% to *net capital employed		
2	'SHELL' TRANSPORT & TRADING	Net capital employed	£000	31 Dec.
		Ratio of turnover to *net capital employed		
		Net profit before interest and tax	£000	
		% to *net capital employed		
3	IMPERIAL CHEMICAL INDUSTRIES	Net capital employed	£000	31 Dec.
		Ratio of turnover to *net capital employed		
		Net profit before interest and tax	£000	
		% to *net capital employed		
4	ELECTRICITY COUNCIL	Net capital employed	£000	31 Mar.
		Ratio of turnover to *net capital employed		
		Net profit before interest and tax	£000	
		% to *net capital employed		
5	BAT INDUSTRIES	Net capital employed	£000	30 Sept. 1978
		Ratio of turnover to *net capital employed		
		Net profit before interest and tax	£000	31 Dec. 1979–88
		% to *net capital employed		
6	BRITISH TELECOMMUNICATIONS	Net capital employed	£000	31 Mar.
		Ratio of turnover to *net capital employed		1982–89
		Net profit before interest and tax	£000	
		% to *net capital employed		
7	HANSON	Net capital employed	£000	30 Sept.
		Ratio of turnover to *net capital employed		
		Net profit before interest and tax	£000	
		% to *net capital employed		
8	BRITISH GAS	Net capital employed	£000	31 Mar.
		Ratio of turnover to *net capital employed		
		Net profit before interest and tax	£000	
		% to *net capital employed		
9	SHELL UK	Net capital employed	£000	31 Dec.
		Ratio of turnover to *net capital employed		
		Net profit before interest and tax	£000	
		% to *net capital employed		
10	UNILEVER	Net capital employed	£000	31 Dec.
		Ratio of turnover to *net capital employed		
		Net profit before interest and tax	£000	
		% to *net capital employed		

ROLLS-ROYCE

Chairman **Sir Francis Tombs**

Rolls-Royce today is the aero engine part of the original Rolls-Royce started by Charles Rolls and Frederick Royce in 1906. One of only three manufacturers in the western world capable of making the most powerful jet engines, it currently has about 20 engines in its product range and about 26,000 separate units in service around the world, some having been in continuous use since the 1950s. While Rolls-Royce engines are developed primarily as aero engines and are used to power a wide range of civil and military aircraft, some models have been successfully modified for industrial and marine use and now generate electricity, pump oil and gas through pipelines and drive the propellors of medium-sized ships like frigates and destroyers. Subsidiary Rolls-Royce companies provide the nuclear steam-raising plant for Britain's nuclear submarines and make rocket motors and components for the aerospace industry. Rolls-Royce employs 40,000 people, 38,000 in the UK, mainly at Derby and Bristol. The Ministry of Defence is its single biggest customer.

	1987	*1988*
	£ million	*£ million*
Turnover	2,059	1,973
UK turnover	543 (26%)	489 (25%)
Pre-tax profit	156	168

65 Buckingham Gate, London SW1E 6AT, tel. 071-222 9020

Ten-year Record Table ***continued***

1979	*1980*	*1981*	*1982*	*1983*	*1984*	*1985*	*1986*	*1987*	*1988*
10,230,200	11,447,000	16,010,000	17,370,000	19,171,000	23,188,000	21,096,000	20,817,000	18,624,000	20,436,000
2.5	2.5	2.7	2.2	2.2	2.3	2.0	1.6	1.7	1.8
4,823,200	5,448,000	6,616,000	5,589,000	5,606,000	7,021,000	7,053,000	2,199,000	3,909,000	3,290,000
53.6	51.7	57.8	34.7	32.3	36.6	30.4	10.4	18.8	17.7
6,754,000	7,828,000	9,198,000	11,838,000	15,213,000	18,153,000	15,835,000	16,050,000	14,355,000	15,110,000
2.5	2.3	2.4	2.4	2.1	1.9	1.6	1.4	1.5	1.6
2,622,400	2,690,800	2,915,000	3,246,000	3,837,000	4,529,000	4,088,000	2,505,000	2,595,000	2,404,000
46.5	39.8	37.2	35.6	32.4	29.8	22.5	15.8	16.2	16.7
4,549,000	4,753,000	5,294,000	5,370,000	5,541,000	6,333,000	5,910,000	6,425,000	6,154,000	6,585,000
1.3	1.3	1.4	1.4	1.5	1.8	1.7	1.7	1.7	1.9
747,000	538,000	736,000	724,000	1,107,000	1,426,000	1,310,000	1,295,000	1,574,000	1,751,000
18.2	11.8	15.5	14.2	18.9	25.7	20.5	21.9	24.5	28.5
7,299,700	7,779,000	31,343,200	32,950,000	34,396,500	36,350,200	36,882,300	38,113,600	15,342,300	16,271,500
0.8	0.8	0.2[2]	0.3	0.3	0.3	0.3	0.3	0.3	0.7
890,700	738,700	33,700	639,100	1,138,900	989,300	†1,230,300	957,200	2,001,800	1,586,600
12.9	10.1	1.1[2]	2.0	3.5	2.8	–	2.6	5.3	10.3
2,857,000	2,857,000	3,485,000	4,496,000	4,893,000	7,663,000	6,545,000	6,996,000	6,400,000	7,064,000
2.7	2.9	4.0	3.2	2.6	1.9	1.6	2.1	1.6	1.8
528,000pa	577,000	808,000	1,108,000	1,113,000	1,556,000	1,340,000	1,462,000	1,542,000	1,745,000
20.8pa	20.2	28.3	31.6	24.8	20.5	17.4	22.3	22.0	27.3
N/A	N/A	8,216,700	9,022,000	9,017,000	10,448,000	11,265,000	11,370,000	12,064,000	13,375,000
		0.7	0.8	0.8	0.7	0.8	0.8	0.9	0.9
		1,551,800	1,557,000	1,553,000	1,915,000	2,219,000	2,457,000	2,661,000	2,832,000
		18.9	18.9	17.2	18.3	21.2	21.9	23.4	23.5
179,900	203,200	433,900	563,200	981,300	1,615,800	2,409,700	5,141,000	4,871,000	6,128,000
4.4	3.8	2.0	2.0	1.5	1.5	1.6	0.8	1.3	1.5
40,800	49,900	76,000	110,900	145,100	266,100	374,600	714,000	1,041,000	1,167,000
27.3	27.7	17.5	19.7	14.8	16.5	23.0	13.9	20.2	24.0
1,775,400	2,271,500	9,912,500	10,992,600	12,069,400	13,232,900	16,889,600	18,438,000	7,496,000	8,092,000
1.6	1.5	0.4	0.5	0.5	0.5	0.5	0.5	1.0	1.0
618,300	721,100	433,300	394,900	765,600	775,900	744,200	808,000	1,395,000	1,462,000
32.6	40.6	4.4	4.0	7.0	6.4	5.6	4.8	18.6	19.5
2,800,400	3,081,000	3,519,800	3,741,000	3,656,000	3,827,000	3,886,000	3,504,000	3,698,000	3,705,000
1.3	1.3	1.7	1.9	2.1	2.6	2.3	1.7	2.0	1.8
621,416	629,200	843,000	1,213,700	1,924,000	2,344,000	2,236,000	1,112,000	1,096,000	687,000
27.6	22.5	27.4	36.9	51.4	64.1	57.6	28.6	31.3	18.6
1,750,000	1,899,800	2,156,200	2,394,000	2,519,000	2,997,000	2,739,000	2,863,000	2,558,000	2,580,000
2.5	2.5	2.6	2.5	2.2	2.3	2.1	2.2	1.9	2.5
335,200	338,700	412,100	412,00	400,000	465,000	514,000	531,000	527,000	632,000
20.9	19.4	21.7	20.8	16.7	18.5	16.9	19.4	18.4	24.7

Largest Takeovers of UK Public Companies
July 1988–June 1989

Rank	Date	Name	Target Company	Bid Value £m
1	06/07/88	Nestlé	Rowntree	2,550.00
2	01/12/88	Daily Mail & General Trust	Associated News Holdings	1,023.00
3	08/11/88	Mecca Leisure Group	Pleasurama	745.00
4	06/10/88	British Coal Staff Superannuation/ Mineworkers Pension	TR Industrial and General Trust	560.50
5	15/08/88	Lowndes Ventures	Harris Queensway	450.00
6	12/01/89	News International	William Collins	403.00
7	07/07/88	British Gas	Acre Oil	370.00
8	15/12/88	Blue Circle Industries	Birmid Qualcast	330.00
9	15/11/88	Williams Holdings	Pilgrim House Group	322.00
10	08/12/88	Cable & Wireless	Telephone Rentals	319.80
11	16/05/89	Rolls Royce	Northern Engineering Industries	310.00
12	13/01/89	Peel Holdings	London Shop	308.00
13	06/09/88	Wereldhave	Peachey Property Corporation	282.00
14	19/09/88	Wickes	Hunter	261.00
15	25/11/88	Pernod Ricard Group	Irish Distillers Group	248.90
16	04/01/89	Iceland Frozen Foods Holdings	Bejam Group	240.00
17	29/12/88	Kelt Energy	Carless	212.20
18	15/02/89	Ladbroke Group	Thomson T-Line	185.70
19	14/12/88	Leisure Investments	Land Leisure	164.10
20	08/09/88	Plessey Company	Hoskyns Group	164.00
21	24/04/89	Hambros	Hambros Investment Trust	163.00
22	09/11/88	Tarmac	Ruberoid	141.30
23	17/10/88	Travis Perkins	Travis & Arnold	139.00
24	09/12/88	Austrialian National Industrial	Aurora	138.10
25	15/11/88	Amec	Matthew Hall	131.00
26	26/10/88	Pergamon Professional & Financial Services	AGB Research	130.00
27	01/02/89	Textron Atlantic	Avdel	125.20
28	22/06/89	Omnicom (UK)	Boase Massimi Pollitt	125.00
29	04/04/89	Priest Marians Holding	Local London Group	110.90
30	01/12/88	Campbell Soup	Freshbake Foods Group	109.00
31	11/07/88	Glynwed International	Amari	105.30
32	01/04/89	Bank in Liechtenstein	G.T. Management	97.50
33	30/11/88	DMWS 99	Invergordon Distillers (Holdings)	93.10
34	20/04/89	Mid Kent Holdings	Mid Kent Water	93.00
35	06/03/89	Cadbury Schweppes	Bassett Foods	92.00
36	01/04/89	Yeoman International Group	CLF Holdings	89.00
37	23/05/89	Evode Group	Chamberlain Phipps	88.50
38	07/09/88	Davis (Godfrey) Holdings	Falcon Industries	87.19
39	08/09/88	Dowty Group	Case Group	81.20
40	15/06/89	Conrad Holdings	Marler Estates	80.90
41	01/02/89	Camacq Corporation	Cambrian & General Securities	77.30
42	01/06/89	Charles Church Holdings	Charles Church Developments	74.00
43	26/10/88	TI Group	Thermal Scientific	72.50
44	14/02/89	Digger	Ryan International	69.70
45	22/08/88	Pleasurama	Hard Rock International	63.00
46	01/12/88	LIT Holdings	Jersey General Investment Group	61.50
47	01/06/89	Lynrose	Smaller Companies International Trust	59.00
48	10/03/89	Saur Water Services	Mid-Southern Water	58.60
49	16/12/88	PLM	Redfearn	54.60
50	31/05/89	Fitzwilton	The Keep Trust	53.80

The UK's Top 10 Employers

Rank	Company	Employees
1	British Telecommunications	242,723
2	Post Office*	198,217
3	BAT Industries	172,715
4	General Electric Co.	157,262
5	Unilever	155,000
6	British Railways Board*	154,748
7	British Coal Corporation*	135,900
8	British Aerospace	133,600
9	Electricity Council*	131,398
10	Imperial Chemical Industries	130,400

* A nationalized industry.
Source: *The Times 1000.*

The UK's Top 10 in Capital Employed, 1964 and 1989

1964 Rank	Company	Capital employed £000s
1	Electricity Council	2,871,798
2	'Shell' Transport & Trading	1,265,975
3	British Rail	1,277,300
4	Post Office	1,203,927
5	Imperial Chemical Industries	943,300
6	British Petroleum	913,500
7	National Coal Board	904,300
8	Gas Board	689,382
9	Unilever	454,876
10	BAT Industries*	407,627

* Then British American Tobacco.
Source: The Times 1000.

1989 Rank	Company	Capital employed £000s	Ranking in 1964
1	British Petroleum Company	20,436,000	1
2	Electricity Council	16,271,500	4
3	'Shell' Transport & Trading	15,110,000	2
4	British Telecommunications	13,375,000	6
5	British Gas	8,092,000	8
6	BAT Industries*	7,064,000	5
7	Imperial Chemical Industries	6,585,000	3
8	Hanson	6,128,000	7
9	Allied Lyons	4,393,000	22
10	British Steel	4,329,000	20

* Then British American Tobacco.
Source: The Times 1000.

The UK's Top 10 Profit Makers 1964 and 1989

1964 Rank	Company	Profits* £000s
1	British Petroleum	217,200
2	Electricity Council	184,333
3	'Shell' Transport & Trading	179,228
4	Imperial Chemical Industries	117,200
5	BAT Industries†	76,892
6	The Post Office	72,558
7	Unilever Plc	59,607
8	National Coal Board	58,041
9	Distillers	39,838
10	Imperial Tobacco	39,107

* Before interest and tax. † Then British-American Tobacco. 1. Part of the Post Office in 1964.
Source: The Times 1000.

1989 Rank	Company	Profits* £000s	Ranking in 1964
1	British Petroleum	3,290,000	1
2	British Telecommunications[1]	2,832,000	6
3	'Shell' Transport & Trading	2,404,000	2
4	Imperial Chemical Industries	1,751,000	3
5	BAT Industries†	1,745,000	5
6	Electricity Council	1,586,600	4
7	British Gas	1,462,000	8
8	Hanson	1,167,000	7
9	Esso UK	1,117,700	13
10	BTRI	941,800	17

* Before interest and tax. † Then British-American Tobacco. 1. Part of the Post Office in 1964.
Source: The Times 1000.

EDUCATION

In general, policy for education is the responsibility of the Secretary of State for Education. However, in Wales, schools and all non-university education come under the Welsh Office, and in Scotland under the Scottish Education Department. All education in Northern Ireland comes under the Department of Education for Northern Ireland.

Although policy and overall targets for expenditure are set by Ministers, actual administration of the education service is decentralized: schools are run and funded by the relevant council (the county and metropolitan councils in England and Wales, the region and island councils in Scotland) which sets up a local education authority (LEA). In Northen Ireland, educational administration at all levels is carried out by five education and library boards.

EXPENDITURE

UK government expenditure on education reached £21,964 million in 1988/9. The level of expenditure is determined by central government, but the money for schools is actually raised by the local authorities as part of their income from the community charge and business rates, or by grant support from central government (all education expenditure in Northern Ireland is allocated from central funds). The largest item in schools expenditure is teachers' salaries, which are paid by the LEAs, although the teachers' terms and conditions are determined by the relevant Minister. Under the Education Reform Act 1988, control of schools' budgets (for all secondary and primary schools with more than 200 pupils) has been delegated to the governing body of the school.

The Department of Education and Science (DES) is directly responsible for financing the universities and (since 1989) polytechnics and colleges of higher education.

THE STATE-RUN SYSTEM OF EDUCATION

Under the Education Act 1944, full-time education is provided free of charge for all children of compulsory education age; in the UK this is from five years to 16 years. Children born from 1 Sept. to 31 Jan. remain at school until the end of the Easter term following their 16th birthday. Those born from 1 Feb. to 31 Aug. cease to be of compulsory school age on the Friday before the last Monday in May, and thus some of them leave school before they are 16. There is also state provision of education for pupils outside the compulsory age range, most notably for the over-16s in schools, colleges and universities.

EDUCATION AT HOME

Parents may educate a child at home, but must be able to satisfy their LEA that the child is receiving a full-time education suitable to its age and ability.

CORPORAL PUNISHMENT

Corporal punishment has been illegal in the UK since 1986 following a ruling in the European Court of Human Rights 1982.

NURSERY EDUCATION

Education at nursery level is not compulsory and there is uneven provision between different areas. The situation is complicated by the fact that children under five are offered quite different services: nursery education proper in nursery schools or nursery classes at primary schools; day care provided by LEAs in day nurseries, playgroups or with child-minders. There is a very extensive private sector, ranging from fee-paying nursery schools to parent-run playgroups and private child-minders.

Private Sector Nursery Schools in the UK

England	558
Wales	58
Scotland	596
N. Ireland	86
Total	1,298

In the UK as a whole, 49% of children aged three and four (866,000) receive some sort of nursery education. A further 38,000 have local authority day-care places, and 174,000 are cared for by registered child-minders (including local authority minders).

SCHOOLING

England and Wales

There are two patterns for state, i.e. publicly-maintained schools, in England and Wales. The first, and by far the most common, has *primary* schools for children aged 5–11, and *secondary* schools from 11 onwards. The primary school stage may be divided into infants (5–7) and junior (7–11); the secondary school may take children through to 18, or it may stop at 16, sending pupils on to sixth-form college or other tertiary college.

The second system consists of *first* schools for children aged 5–8, 9 or 10, followed by *middle* schools for pupils up to 14 (usually), then an *upper* school for 14–18 year olds.

Secondary schools. The majority of secondary schools are *comprehensive*, i.e. pupils are accepted without selection for ability, or *middle deemed secondary*, also unselective. Some LEAs have retained a system of selection, and offer *grammar schools* for academically able children, *technical schools* (England only) or *secondary modern schools* (11–16 only with an emphasis on vocational work). Two new types of secondary school were created by the Education Reform Act 1988: the *city technology colleges* and *city colleges for the technology of the arts*.

Funding arrangements. Within the public sector, schools can be either *county schools*, which are usually owned by the local authority, or *voluntary schools* whose buildings belong to some voluntary body (usually a church), but which are financed by the LEA. Voluntary schools are further divided into those that are *controlled*, with all costs paid by the LEA; those that are *aided*, with costs relating to the buildings paid by the voluntary body and everything else by the LEA; and schools that have a *special agreement* under which a voluntary body receives 50%–75% of the cost of providing buildings for a new school.

Since 1988, secondary schools and larger primary schools have had the right to opt out of LEA control and to have their public money paid to them direct

Number of public-sector educational establishments

	1978/79	1979/80	1980/81	1981/82	1982/83	1983/84	1984/85	1985/86	1986/87	1987/88
UNITED KINGDOM										
Nursery	1,213	1,236	1,251	1,254,	1,259	1,260	1,257	1,262	1,271	1,298
Primary	26,850	26,764	26,504	26,072	25,155	25,326	24,993	24,756	24,609	24,482
Secondary	5,585	5,571	5,542	5,506	5,437	5,328	5,262	5,161	5,091	5,020
Non-maintained	2,761	2,654	2,640	2,635	2,637	2,619	2.599	2,538	2,544	2,546
Special	2,018	2,016	2,011	1,994	1,989	1,972	1,949	1,923	1.915	1,900
Universities (including Open University)	46	46	46	46	46	46	46	46	46	46
Polytechnics, vocational, further education colleges and colleges of education:										
Public Sector	751	746	744	729	729	728	693	697	677	673
Assisted	67	63	62	58	57	57	56	56	52	51
Adult education centres (England and Wales)	5,303	4,926	4,628	4,318	4,542	4,513	4,227	2,874	2,523	2,632
ENGLAND										
Nursery	593	596	588	582	575	565	561	560	558	558
Primary	21,309	21,242	21,018	20,650	20,384	20,020	19,734	19,549	19,432	19,319
Secondary	4,694	4,680	4,654	4,622	4,553	4,444	4,382	4,286	4,221	4,153
Non-maintained	2,459	2,351	2,342	2,340	2,344	2,333	2,313	2,274	2,276	2,273
Special	1,599	1,597	1,593	1,571	1,562	1,548	1,529	1,493	1,470	1,443
Universities (including Open University)	35	35	35	35	35	35	35	35	35	35
Polytechnics	29	29	29	29	29	29	29	29	29	29
Other major establishments:										
Maintained and assisted	488	481	468	459	450	439	437	436	422	417
Grant-aided	40	36	35	34	33	33	32	31	29	29
Adult education centres	4,527	4,309	4,067	3,747	3,958	3,938	3,684	2,616	2,718	2,412
WALES										
Nursery	70	69	69	64	64	65	61	59	59	58
Primary	1,930	1,925	1,908	1,873	1,844	1,821	1,796	1,774	1,762	1,753
Secondary	244	241	239	241	238	236	237	237	234	233
Non-maintained	71	71	72	71	73	70	67	69	69	67
Special	74	75	73	73	71	69	68	67	65	65
Universities	1	1	1	1	1	1	1	1	1	1
Polytechnics	1	1	1	1	1	1	1	1	1	1
Other major establishments:										
Maintained and assisted	45	46	44	43	43	43	43	39	39	39
Grant-aided	1	1	1	1	1	1	1	1	1	1
Adult education centres	776	617	561	571	584	575	543	258	205	220
SCOTLAND										
Nursery	489	503	515	527	537	546	551	559	568	596
Primary	2,532	2,530	2,522	2.499	2,489	2,461	2.443	2,425	2.417	2,418
Secondary	443	445	444	439	442	444	440	440	440	438
Non-maintained	144	144	138	136	132	127	131	106	111	118
Special	319	320	319	324	336	330	328	339	356	346
Universities	8	8	8	8	8	8	8	8	8	8
Vocational further education colleges:										
Day	69	69	65	64	67	64	52	50	49	49
Evening	90	91	109	105	111	124	104	115	109	111
Central Institutions	14	14	14	14	14	14	14	16	16	15
Colleges of education	10	10	10	7	7	7	7	7	5	5
NORTHERN IRELAND										
Nursery	61	68	79	81	83	84	84	84	86	86
Primary	1,079	1,067	1,056	1,050	1,038	1,024	1,020	1,008	998	992
Secondary	204	205	205	204	204	204	203	198	196	196
Non-maintained	87	88	88	88	88	89	88	89	87	88
Special	26	24	26	26	26	25	24	24	24	46
Universities	2	2	2	2	2	2	2	2	2	2
Colleges of education	3	3	3	3	3	3	3	2	2	2
Polytechnics	1	1	1	1	1	1	—	—	—	—
Further education colleges	27	27	26	26	26	26	26	26	26	26

School Pupils in the UK – summary by type of school

	Actual	Projected			
(1,000s)	1988	1989	1991	1994	1998
Public Sector					
Nursery (part-time counted as 1)	100				
Primary					
Under 5	766				
Other	3,956				
Total	4,822	4,868	4,988	5,163	5,500
Secondary					
Under 16	3,305				
16 and over	381				
Total	3,686	3,573	3,423	3,540	3,681
Total all public sector	8,508	8,441	8,411	8,703	9,181
Independent	635	637	647	670	701
Special	117				
Total all schools	9,260	9,078	9,058	9,373	9,882

from the DES. The decision is made on the majority vote of the parents at the school (one vote per parent). Of the schools which have opted out of LEA control, by May 1990 there were 29 up and running, 10 about to start, 12 about to publish their proposals, and 6 about to ballot parents; 11 schools have had their proposals rejected by the Secretary of State.

City technology colleges and city colleges for the technology of the arts. These two new types of schools represent a new departure in the funding of public education, in that capital is provided jointly by the DES and by business sponsors. Running costs will be financed entirely by the Department. Pupils are selected according to their ability to benefit from the technological and business emphasis of the courses. By Sept. 1989, there were three city technology colleges in operation (Kingshurst, Solihull; Middlesbrough; Bradford), and the first city college for the technology of arts (Croydon) opened in 1990.

Scotland

Primary schools in Scotland are for children aged 5–12. The secondary schools are nearly all comprehensives, with courses lasting six years; but in some areas, e.g. remote places in the Highlands, it is not practicable to offer a wide enough range of teaching beyond the age of 16, so four-year comprehensives are provided, with the option for children to transfer to a six-year school for further study.

The great majority of Scottish schools (3733) belong to an education authority and are fully financed and managed by that authority. However, there are also a few grant-aided schools (19) run by voluntary bodies with funding from the Scottish Education Department. Under proposals contained in the Self-Governing Schools, etc. (Scotland) Bill, parents will be able to vote to remove their secondary school from LEA control and receive funding direct from the Educational Department. The same Bill includes the framework for setting up *technology academies* in urban areas, to be capitalized jointly by the Scottish Education Department and business sponsors; running costs will be provided by grants from the Department.

Northern Ireland

The age range for primary schools is 5–11 years. Secondary education is organized selectively as regards ability, and to a large extent is also divided along religious lines. *Controlled schools* are fully publicly funded by the five education and library boards. *Voluntary schools* are owned by a voluntary body, the majority of them by the Roman Catholic Church, but receive running costs from public funds. The *voluntary grammar schools*, some Roman Catholic and some non-denominational, with selective entry, receive direct grants from the Department of Education for Northern Ireland. These schools charge fees, but many pupils have the fees paid by their local education and library board. Legislation is to be introduced to encourage the setting up of schools having *grant-maintained integrated status*, which will provide integrated education for Protestant and Roman Catholic children.

Special Schools

Children may be in need of special education for a variety of reasons; data on individual handicaps are no longer kept, but in the last year recorded (1983) 68% of special-needs children were mentally handicapped, 12% physically handicapped, 11% maladjusted, 3.5% with total or partial loss of hearing, 2.4% with total or partial visual handicap. In England, Wales and Northern Ireland the education authorities have a duty to ensure that wherever possible a child with special needs is educated in a normal school; in 1989 there were 53,127 children such children aged 5–16 (0.7% of all pupils). In Scotland, the placing of a special-needs child is arranged between the LEA and the parents. The majority of special-needs children throughout the UK are taught in special schools; there are about 1500 day schools, 350 boarding schools, and 85 hospital special schools, which are educating about 120,000 children. These figures include schools run privately, generally by a charity, but assisted with local authority funds.

Independent schools
There are private schools for children of all ages from nursery to 18 years, attended by 584,306 children in 1988 (7% of all boys and 6.5% of all girls). There are about 2456 private schools in England, Wales and Scotland; the situation is rather different in Northern Ireland because fee-paying voluntary grammar schools are part of the arrangement for state education. Fees charged by independent schools range from about £400 per year for the youngest day pupils to £9000 per year for secondary-age boarding schools. There is a government-funded *assisted places scheme* which provides help for parents who could not otherwise afford to send children to independent schools; tuition fees are paid (in whole or in part, according to means) but not boarding charges. In 1988 there were 28,000 assisted places schemes run by nearly 280 schools.

The so-called *public schools* are the top 200 boys' boarding schools, many of them ancient foundations (more than 33% were founded prior to 1600, and four of them are over 1000 years old); there are also a few public schools for girls, and about 25% of the boys' public schools admit girls in the sixth form. The age range for public schools is 13–18. Pupils preparing for entrance to the public schools attend a *preparatory school* ('prep'), usually for 7–12 year olds, and these are traditionally single-sex. (In Scotland, the term 'public school' means a state-run school, and the term 'independent' is used to describe privately-run schools.)

CORE CURRICULUM
The Education Reform Act 1988 brought in the national curriculum, introduced in Sept. 1989 to the state primary and secondary schools of England and Wales. There will be a similar arrangement in Northern Ireland, but not Scotland. Independent schools are exempt.

There are three *core* subjects: English, mathematics and science. The *foundation subjects* are: art geography, history, music, physical education, technology (including design) and a foreign language (secondary only), plus the core subjects. All state schools are obliged to offer the *basic curriculum*, which consists of the foundation subjects plus religious education. Within this, schools must follow the *set programmes of study* for each of the four stages of pupils' school life: ages 5–7, 7–11, 11–14, and 14–16.

At the end of each stage pupils are measured against the *attainment target* for each foundation subject by means of a series of *standard assessment tasks* set by external examiners. These will be marked by the teacher and supplemented with the teacher's personal assessments. There are 10 levels of attainment (1 is the lowest, 10 the highest), and schools must publish the results of each age group from 11 upwards. Individual results are not published.

Owing to the shortage of specialist teachers, the national curriculum could not be introduced for all children simultaneously. Five-year olds began in Sept. 1989 on a reduced version of the national curriculum, and it will be brought in for core subjects only for 15-year olds in 1990, and 16-year olds in 1991. The complete system is expected to be in place by 1997.

HM INSPECTORATE OF SCHOOLS
The various ministers of education monitor the standards of education throughout the country by means of Her Majesty's Inspectorate. The inspectors visit schools (state-run and private) and colleges and further education establishments (not universities). They also give advice to the Ministers, to LEAs and to individual schools on good educational practice. There 469 inspectors in England, 49 in Wales, 111 in Scotland, and 55 in Northern Ireland. HMI Annual Report 1988/9 reported that 20% of higher and further education work was judged poor or very poor, and in schools 38% was judged poor or very poor. Less able pupils and students were more likely to experience poor provision.

EXAMINATION SYSTEM
England and Wales, Northern Ireland
The General Certificate of Secondary Education (GCSE). This was first awarded in Summer 1988. It replaces the earlier two-tier system of General Certificate of Education (GCE) and Certificate of Secondary Education (CSE). The GCSE is awarded partly by examination and partly by continuous assessment; pupils can enter for different papers within a subject according to their ability (pupils only attempting simpler papers cannot be awarded the higher grades). There are seven grades: at the top end, grades A to C equal the former GCE grades A to C or CSE grade 1; grades D to G (the lowest) are equivalent to the former CSE grades 2 to 5.

A level. For students staying on at school after 16, A level is the main examination and has remained more or less unchanged for 50 years. Two passes at A level are the minimum requirement for entry to university and to many of the professions. About 15% of school-leavers of both sexes reach this standard each year; this percentage has been more or less constant over the last 10 years for boys, but for girls it has risen gradually from 12% 10 years ago. The pass grades are from A (the highest) to E, with additional grades of N (narrow failure) and U (unclassified).

AS level. Introduced in 1987, the AS level covers similar ground to the A level in the same subjects, but takes only half the teaching and study time. Two passes at AS level are counted as one pass at A level for university entrance. It is hoped that students will use AS levels as a way of avoiding too narrow specialization from the age of 16.

S level. In 1989, the first year of AS level examination, S level candidates for A level could choose to take an extra paper at a higher standard. Successful students are awarded a special level or a scholarship level grade. There are only three grades: A (or 1), B (or 2) and U (unclassified).

The Certificate of Pre-vocational Training (CPVE). For non-academic pupils who want to continue in education after 16, the CPVE is awarded after one year's study at school or college, or two years part-time. There is no formal examination, the certificate being awarded entirely on credits for course work and achievements in work experience.

Scotland
The Scottish Certificate of Education Ordinary Grade. This is taken by pupils at the end of their fourth year of secondary school at the age of 16. This examination is fairly formal, corresponding to the old GCE, and is gradually being replaced with Standard Grade, which corresponds to GCSE in being adaptable to a wider range of abilities. Standard Grade is awarded on the basis of results of examination papers set at three different levels: candidates at Credit level can gain grade 1 or 2, at General level grade 3 or 4, and at Foundation level grade 5 or 6. Candidates generally sit Credit and General together, or General and Founda-

tion together, according to their expected results. Grade 7 is awarded without examination to pupils who have completed the course.

The Scottish Certificate of Education Higher Grade. This is taken one year after Ordinary/Standard Grade. The standard reached in each subject is therefore not as advanced as in A level, but pupils can study more subjects; commonly four or five for those who intend to go on to university or a profession. Pupils also often take more subjects at Ordinary/Standard Grade at this age, with the result that the average post-16 school-leavers in Scotland have a far greater breadth of knowledge than their counterparts in England, Wales and Northern Ireland.

The Certificate of Sixth-Year Studies (CSYS) . This was devised to give academic pupils, who have completed their Higher Grades, the opportunity to study in greater depth before going on to tertiary education. Taken at age 18 in not more than three subjects, CSYS requires a standard of work comparable to that of A level.

The National Certificate. Non-academic pupils of 16 plus, are awarded this certificate for a wide variety of vocational courses. The courses are standardized nationally and are based on study modules with continuous assessment, and work experience. Candidates may study at school or college, or at work with day-release.

TEACHERS

Training

Until 1989, the teaching profession was almost entirely restricted to graduate entrants. Teachers either take a BEd. degree or study any subject to degree level and take a year's Post-Graduate Certificate of Education (PGCE). About 7000 students per year qualify with a BEd. and about 8000 with a PGCE; of newly qualified teachers, 25% choose not to enter the teaching profession. Severe shortages of staff, particularly in city schools, led to the introduction in England and Wales of licensed teachers, who must have had the equivalent of two years' post-A level education, and who are trained on the job by LEAs. Licensed teachers can be declared fully qualified after two years, subject to approval from the DES. By May 1990, 48 licensed teachers had been appointed. In Scotland, all teachers must be graduates and must serve a two-year probation before being permanently appointed. (see PUBLIC SECTOR for pupil/teacher ratios)

SCHOOL COMPACTS

Compacts are locally-based agreements between schools and businesses guaranteeing pupils jobs and training when they leave school, if they attain certain measurable targets in areas like attendance, achievement, and educational standard. Compacts were launched by the Employment Department in 1988 and so far there are 29 up and running, with a further 21 in the pipeline. There are 3800 employers and training providers already involved, and the Government has promised £21 million over a four-year period (1990–4) to finance the scheme. The idea sprung from a similar initiative in Boston, USA, where children were leaving school without the necessary skills to gain employment in local industry.

UNIVERSITIES

There are 45 state-run universities in the UK: 34 in England, one in Wales, eight in Scotland, two in Northern Ireland. This is an increase of more than 100% from the 22 that existed 30 years ago. Student numbers have gone up even more steeply, from 104,000 (24% women) in 1959 to 260,000 (46% women) in 1987. There is also a privately-run university at Buckingham, offering a two-year degree course; it admits about 300 students per year.

Number of Pupils and Teachers in the UK, plus the Pupil/Teacher Ratio

(1,000s)	1988
Public Sector	
Nursery	
Pupils	57.6
Teachers	2.7
Ratio	21.3
Primary	
Pupils	4,598.9
Teachers	210.1
Ratio	21.9
Secondary	
Pupils	3,701.5
Teachers	244.9
Ratio	15.1
Special Schools	
Pupils	120.9
Teachers	19.3
Ratio	6.3
Totals	
Pupils	9,100.7
Teachers	531.1
Ratio	17.1
Of which	
England	17.2
Wales	18.0
Scotland	15.8
Northern Ireland	18.4

Full-time Students and Staff at UK Universities

	Students	Staff	Students per staff member	% annual change
1976/77	228,269	32,735	7.0	
1977/78	238,161	32,984	7.2	+2.9
1978/79	245,933	33,695	7.3	+1.4
1979/80	251,990	34,250	7.4	+1.4
1980/81	258,175	34,297	7.5	+1.3
1981/82	260,720	33,735	7.7	+2.7
1982/83	257,733	31,642	8.1	+5.2
1983/84	252,238	31,096	8.1	0.0
1984/85	254,819	31,043	8.2	+1.2
1985/86	256,340	31,412	8.2	0.0
1986/87	260,091	31,432	8.3	+1.2
Cumulative % change over 10 years				+18.6

Open University (OU)
The Open University celebrated its 21st anniversary in Jan. 1990 by awarding its 100,000th degree certificate. The university's degree courses are open to anyone resident in the UK and aged 18 or over. Study is part-time, and makes use of radio and television broadcasts, an extensive range of books, cassette tapes and other material published by the OU, plus correspondence and meetings with tutors. Degree courses are built up from a number of modules: six credits make an ordinary BA, eight credits earn an honours degree. There are about 72,000 students following degree courses, taught by about 2600 full-time staff and 5000 freelance tutors and counsellors.

The OU began its Open Business School in 1983, and has had 40,000 enrolments so far; students can take either the Certificate in Management, or (since 1989) the Master of Business Administration. The academic year runs from February to October for degree courses, but at other times for the Business School. Open University, Central Enquiry Service, PO Box 625, Walton Hall, Milton Keynes, MK1 1TY. Tel. 0908 274066.

Oxford and Cambridge Universities
The oldest universities in the UK, they have come to be regarded as particularly prestigious. They are however part of the general system of university education in the UK, and their degrees are at the same level as those of any other university. They have a different entrance system in that students are selected by the individual colleges, not the university itself; the university sets an approximate quota for each subject. Tuition is also slightly different, with tutorials (teaching sessions for one to three students, at which essays are presented) organized by colleges, but lectures, seminars and practicals provided by the university. Up until the late 1960s, the colleges were single-sex, with far more exclusively male: 19 men's and four women's at Cambridge, 22 men's and five women's at Oxford in 1965, not counting graduate colleges. Now all the former men-only colleges admit women, while four colleges are for women only: two at Cambridge and two at Oxford.

POLYTECHNICS AND COLLEGES

Under the Education Reform Act 1988, the 29 polytechnics in England and 55 other major institutions for higher education were removed from LEA control and placed under the general direction of the Polytechnics and Colleges Funding Council (PCFC). Each institution is now required to be run by an independent Higher Education Corporation, with a board of governors appointed by the Secretary of State for Education, consisting of further education teachers and at least half the board numbering people from business and industry.

Students at these colleges follow: vocational qualifications, e.g. Business and Technician Education Council (BTEC); first degrees in a wide range of subjects; teacher training courses; research degrees in mainly technical subjects. In Scotland the 15 Central Institutions carry out a similar role. As well as colleges funded by the PCFC, there are about 450 other colleges throughout the UK offering higher education, many of them at degree level. The number of students taking degrees in polytechnics and colleges is about double the number taking degrees in universities.

Council for National Academic Awards (CNAA)
Only universities are empowered to set their own degree courses; other colleges, including polytechnics, have to have their degrees validated by the CNAA, in order to ensure an even standard across all the hundreds of institutions involved. However, since 1987 it has been possible for colleges, whose degrees were CNAA approved, to apply to validate their own degrees as universities do; by 1989, a total of 29 colleges (mostly polytechnics) had done so.

GRANTS AND LOANS

Most UK students intending to take a higher education course are eligible for a grant from their LEA. The grant is mandatory for all degree courses (university or CNAA), for teacher training, and for the Higher National Diploma of BTEC; that is every student who gains a place on the course has a right to the grant. For other courses the grants are discretionary, i.e. LEAs decide their own policy for each course. Grants are means-tested against parental income, or spouse's income if the student is married. Students over 25 years old, who have been independent of their parents for three years, receive the grant in full. The annual grant for 1990/1 will be £1795 for a student living at home, and £2265 for all other except those in London who will get £2845.

From the academic year 1990/1 student grants will be frozen at the above levels. Students will, however, be able to obtain government-sponsored loans to top up their finances. In 1990/1, the amount that may be lent to a student is £420 per year (£460 in London). The loan becomes repayable from the April following graduation, but only if the graduate is earning over 85% of national average earnings. The permitted loan will be increased each year in line with inflation, until it equals the amount of the grant.

VOCATIONAL EDUCATION

Work-related qualifications at all levels are now co-ordinated by the National Council for Vocational Qualifications (NCVQ) founded in 1986 and covering England, Wales and Northern Ireland. The Scottish equivalent is the Scottish Vocational Education Council (SCOTVEC).

Principal examining bodies
Business and Technician Education Council. Address: Central House, Upper Woburn Place, London, WC1H OHH. TEL. 071-388 3288. The numbers of successful students in 1988 were: First Certificate 13,892; First Diploma 12,426; Ordinary National Certificate 28,948; Ordinary National Diploma 26,153; Higher National Certificate 18,164; Higher National Diploma 13,772.

City and Guilds of London Institute. Address: 76 Portland Place, London, W1N 4AA. TEL. 071-278 2468. The institute offers 380 subjects, and about 600,000 certificates are awarded each year.

Royal Society of Arts Examination Board. Address: Westwood Business Park, Westwood Way, Coventry, CV4 8HS. TEL. 0203 470033. Entries for 1988/9 totalled 892,041 for a variety of courses including modern languages, finance, numeracy, computer literacy.

The Technical and Vocational Education Initiative (TVEI)
This is a scheme run by the Employment Department that will eventually extend to all schools, providing children with experience and knowledge of the world of work. The Government has committed £900 million to TVEI over ten years (1990–9).

Youth Training (YT)
Youth Training (formerly Youth Training Scheme – YTS) is available for all 16–17 year olds who are not at school and not engaged in employment. YT aims to provide broad-based vocational education and training to raise the quality of young entrants into the labour market. Young people are guaranteed a place on the scheme, but failure to take up YT means they will not be eligible for Social Security payments if unemployed. Basically, YT provides on-the-job training with the Government paying participants a weekly allowance. As the new Training and Education Councils (TECs) come on stream, they will be responsible for local administration of the schemes. The annual budget for YT is currently £1000 million.

Employment Training (ET)
Also administered by the TECs, this scheme provides high-level training for longer-termed unemployed people. People who have been without a job for some time are retrained in skills that will enable them to join the workforce again.

YOUTH SERVICE
The youth service is a part of the education system in the UK, aiming to provide opportunities for young people to develop their personalities and social skills by participating in a wide range of voluntary activities. Although policy direction comes from the Ministers, the necessary money is put up, partly by LEAs, but to a far greater extent by the numerous voluntary organizations. The most important of these are: the Young Men's Christian Association (YMCA) with one million members; Youth Clubs UK 700,000 members; Girl Guides 700,000 members; Boy Scouts 550,000 members; National Association of Boys' Clubs 170,000 members. Information and advice for the youth service in England and Wales is co-ordinated by the National Youth Bureau.

ADULT EDUCATION
The National Centre for Adult continuing Education. Address: 19b De Montfort Street, Leicester, LE1 7GE. TEL. 0533551451. This organization acts as co-ordinator of information on all aspects of adult education.

Local Education Authorities
LEAs provide classes, almost all part-time or evening, in schools and colleges or at adult education centres. Some 1,663,000 people attended classes at 2632 centres in 1986/7.

University extra-mural departments
There are more than 30 of these departments providing courses for nearly 300,000 people.

Voluntary bodies
The Workers' Educational Association is the largest voluntary body; it has 900 branches throughout the UK, and has about 780,000 enrolments per year.

ENERGY AND NATURAL RESOURCES

In 1987 the approximate value of minerals produced was £18,193 million, about 4.4% of the Gross Domestic Product (GDP). Of this crude oil made up 53%, coal 24% and natural gas 14%. Of the mineral resources in Britain coal, oil, natural gas, silver and gold are all owned by the crown. All other mineral deposits are privately owned. On the United Kingdom Continental Shelf (UKCS), all rights to minerals and their extraction are owned by the crown. The right to extract coal rests exclusively with the British Coal Corporation, BCC (formally the National Coal Board, NCB).

ENERGY

Britain has the largest deposits of unexploited minerals in Europe. The main minerals extracted are coal, oil and natural gas, and these, along with nuclear energy are the main providers of electrical energy within the UK. There are also some small power contributions from wind and water power, though these sources have not yet been fully researched. Since the beginning of the 1980s Britain has been self-sufficient in energy as a result of offshore extraction in the UKCS.

Coal remains the largest single contributor to power generation and is expected, due to large unexploited reserves, to remain so into the twentieth century. Nuclear power provided about 20% of the UK's power requirements, in terms of its contribution to the national grid in 1988.

Offshore oil and gas production is the responsibility of privately owned companies, while, at present, the coal board is publicly owned. The electricity supply and creation industry is to be 'restructured' and sold to the private sector. The restructuring will involve the removal of the economically unattractive nuclear sector from the privatization.

Energy consumption

Energy consumption by final users in 1988 amounted to 59,471 million therms (1 therm = 105,506 kilojoules). Of this, transport consumed 30%, industry 28%, commerce, agriculture and public services 13% and domestic users about 28% (see table on Inland Energy Consumption).

Inland Energy Consumption (in terms of primary sources)

	1978	*1983*	*1986*	*1987*	*1988*
Oil	139.3	106.1	112.6	109.3	116.1
Coal	119.9	111.5	113.5	116.2	112.0
Natural Gas	65.1	74.8	83.6	85.9	81.5
Nuclear Energy	13.4	18.1	21.3	19.8	22.9
Hydro-Electric	2.1	2.4	2.4	2.1	2.4
Net imports of electricity	–	–	1.7	4.7	5.2
Total	339.8	312.9	335.1	338.0	340.1

Energy efficiency

The Government established the Energy Efficiency Office (EEO) in 1983. Its role is to promote more efficient use of natural resources. The EEO is predominantly an advisory body which emphasizes the importance of conservation within the realms of domestic, industrial and commercial applications.

The Community Insulation Programme has insulated 600,000 homes of those on low incomes and pensioners (1990).

However, the Association for the Conservation of Energy looked, in 1988, at three energy sectors; lighting, domestic fridges and industrial electric motors. It found that just in these three spheres, if the most energy efficient models were used and choosing from those readily available on the market, the national electricity saving could be as much as 11%.

Energy efficiency has increased in the United States by 20% in the last 5 years and by 50% in Japan; in Britain, however, energy conservation is still considered a novelty and as yet little action has been taken.

The Government also states its support for combined heat and power (CHP) technologies. Combined Heat and Power is a technique for improving the efficiency of electricity generation whilst using (recycling) its by-products. CHP power stations both generate electricity and use the heat generated by this process. Consequently the overall efficiency can be as high as 80%, or simply twice as efficient as a standard electricity-generating station. CHP is common outside the UK. There are stations in Germany, Denmark, Hungary, Sweden, Austria, Russia and the USA. In the UK, CHP provides 15% of the electricity for industry, but only 1% of heating supplies for the domestic market. The Department of Energy concluded in 1979 that CHP could eventually provide 30% of Britain's space and hot water needs and save up to an equivalent of 30 million tonnes of coal a year.

COAL

Coal mining in the eighteenth and nineteenth century fuelled the industrial revolution. The peak year for production was 1913, when the mines produced 292 million tonnes of coal and employed over one million workers. The National Coal Board (NCB) was established in 1947 and changed its name in 1987 to the British Coal Corporation (BCC). The present Government has announced its intention to privatize the industry if it is re-elected.

The BCC has almost totally exclusive rights over the extraction of coal in the UK and it also has the right to engage in certain petrochemical processes if they are deemed beneficial to the industry. In 1988–89 output of coal totalled 103.8 million tonnes. This included 83.5 million tonnes of deep-mined coal, 16.8 million tonnes from open-cast mines and 2.4 million tonnes from other sources. British Coal's capital investment in the industry amounted to £547 million in 1988–89.

Since the 1984 miners strike many pits have been closed down as the government has increased the output from the larger more efficient and modernized pits. As a consequence the workforce has declined significantly. Production at new pit complexes, such as the one at Selby in North Yorkshire, are designed to bring in yields of up to 10 million tonnes each year. Other new mines include those at Hawkhurst Moor in Warwickshire and Ashfordby in Leicestershire.

Consumption

In 1988–89 inland consumption of coal was 111.5 million tonnes. Of this power stations took 74%, coke ovens 10% and 6% was used by domestic consumers. For the generation of electricity 81 million tonnes of coal were mined. Exports were outbalanced by imports of coal at 1.8 million tonnes, compared to 12 million tonnes imported.

Research

The British Coal Corporation spent £33 million on research projects in 1988–89. This research was concentrated on techniques for the extraction of coal by remote control systems. The Department of Energy is spending £2.6 million on research into cleaner coal technologies. Furthermore they have stressed that continued research and new research by those wishing to exploit these technologies must be funded by the private sector.

OIL AND GAS

Britain's energy position has been greatly boosted by the discovery of oil and gas offshore, on the United Kingdom Continental Shelf (UKCS). These reserves have bolstered the British economy during the 1980s and have been one of the government's main sources of taxation revenue. The total area covered by production licences is 96,512 km^2, over which the UK has virtually exclusive rights to explore and exploit the seabed. Expenditure on exploration, both offshore and onshore, totalled £3,066 million in 1988. By the beginning of 1989, 3,331 sites had been or were being drilled in the UKCS. Britain's offshore supplies industry is one of the largest in the world. The Offshore Supplies Office has been established to provide British Industry with an equal opportunity to supply the UKCS with the goods and services that it requires. In 1988, some 84% of the entire orders from the UKCS were issued to British industries, these goods and services were valued at £2,131 million.

OIL

Britain is the world's seventh largest producer of crude oil. Output from the UKCS in 1988 averaged 2.3 million barrels a day.

North Sea Fields

During 1988 there were 36 offshore fields in operation. The Secretary of State for Energy has also issued a further 21 licenses for new developments. The two largest fields in operation at present are the Brent and Forties fields. UK oil production has been in steady decline since its peak in 1985, when output rose to 127.2 million tonnes for the year. Further, in 1985, there was an oil revenue surplus of £8,100 million. By 1988 production had dropped to 113.6 million tonnes and the oil surplus was down to £2,300 million. This lower total was, in part, due to the suspension of production, during 1988, from the Piper and Fulmer fields, due to accidents. The output of oil from the UKCS is expected to decline steadily with Britain just remaining self-sufficient in oil until the end of the 1990s. Since 1979 oil has brought in a government revenue of £76 billion from taxation. In the mid-1980s oil exports accounted for over 20% of total national exports. Various estimates predict that the UKCS has between 570 and 1,800 million tonnes of extractable oil left.

Structure

There are about 250 oil companies that operate or engage in work on the UKCS. The two largest being the British Petroleum Company, with a turnover of £33,101,000 million, and Shell, with a turnover of £22,329,000 million (1988). There are also some land-based fields, though output there is far less significant than at offshore equivalents. In 1988 total land-based oil output amounted to 761,000 tonnes, 60% of which came from Wytch farm in Dorset. At the start of 1989 there were 286 licenses for onshore exploration and extraction.

Britain has 13 refineries with a distillation capacity of 91 million tonnes per year.

Exports

Exports of crude oil in 1988 amounted to 63.8 million tonnes, predominantly to the other EEC countries, notably the Netherlands, France and West Germany. While Britain is almost self-sufficient in oil, it still relies upon the import of other grades of crude oil to enable a full range of products to be produced. Norway supplies 53% of Britain's crude oil imports.

Pipelines

There are 1,733 km (1,077 miles) of submarine pipelines in operation from the UKCS. Approximately 70% of all oil is now transported to the refineries through these pipes. Major pipelines include those from the Forties field to Grangemouth, Ekofisk to Teeside and Crudden Bay to Grangemouth. There are also some onshore lines including a 423 km (263 mile) line from Milford Haven to the Midlands and continuing to Manchester.

Research

Most research is conducted by the large, private oil companies or sponsored by them at other research establishment. Most government research is carried out by the Department of Energy. A Petroleum Science and Technology Institute is being established in Edinburgh, in conjunction with the Herriot Watt and Edinburgh universities. The Institute is to be funded by the Department of Energy in conjunction with the private oil industry.

GAS

Gas has been available to the public since the start of the ninteenth century, originally a by-product of coal. In the 1960s, with the discovery of town gas, a by-product of oil, supplies were changed to this alternative. With the discovery of gas offshore in the UKCS in 1965, town gas was replaced by natural gas. By 1977 natural gas had replaced town gas in the public supply system in Britain.

Structure

From 1946 until 1986 gas was a nationalized company. All assets and revenues were state owned. Under the Gas Act 1986, these assets passed to a privatized company renamed British Gas Plc. British Gas Plc has approximately 2.5 million shareholders and employs 79,000 people. In 1988–89 the turnover of British Gas and its subsidiary companies amounted to £7,526 million. Gas supply accounted for the vast majority of this, some £6,636 million. At current costs, operating profits for 1989 were £1,120 million. In 1989, it purchased a number of oil and gas production and exploration companies with activities in fifteen different nations. Revenue from these overseas concerns came to £357 million in 1988–89.

Consumption

British Gas has 17.4 million clients. About 55% of its total gas sales are for the domestic market, the other 45% for industrial and commercial use. Some 18,046 million therms of gas were supplied in 1988–89: 9,924 therms were sold for domestic use, 5,252 million therms, to industry and a further 2,870 million therms, for commercial or non-household use.

Production

In 1988 the total gross production of natural gas was 45,755 million m^3, of which 92% is available for sale after production company usage. A further 20% of British Gas's supplies came from Norway. There are at present 24 offshore gas fields in operation, of which the eight largest producers are: Leman, Frigg (UK), Indefatigable, North Alwyn, Viking, Hewett, West Sole and Victor. In 1988 the Department of Environment approved the further development of six new sites. Gas supplies in the UKCS are estimated to last for a further one or two decades. It is estimated that of recoverable gas reserves, including potential future discoveries there are between 850,000 million and 3 million m^3 of oil left.

Distribution and Storage

Throughout Britain there is a national high-pressure pipeline network 5,330 km (3,330 miles) long. This system is supplied from four North Sea terminals. Many different methods of storage can be used to enable the industry to cope with peak-time demands, particularly in winter. These include salt cavities and the storage of liquefied gas. More recently Rough Fields, a disused gas reservoir is being refilled and used for storage; this involves the pumping of gas back into the mine, from whence it may be accessed in times of peak demand.

Research

British Gas has 5 research centres throughout the country at which it spends £80 million a year. Research is carried out at both a national and international level within the private sector. Research is funded at universities and other educational establishments. British Gas also has an international consultancy service which sells its skills and expertise abroad.

Ofgas

The Office of Gas Supply is a regulatory body established by the Gas Act 1986. Its main role is to monitor British Gas's activities as the public gas supplier. It must also ensure that its customers and potential competitors are dealt with fairly.

WATER

Within England and Wales, authority and policy decisions concerning water and water supplies rest with the Secretary of State for the Environemnt. The Secretaries are responsible for the conservation and distribution of water supplies and the provision of sewerage and sewerage disposal services. They are also responsible for the quality of rivers and other inland waters.

Supply

Britain's water supplies come from two main sources: surface sources, such as lakes and rivers; and underground sources, such as wells and boreholes. Total water supply for England and Wales in 1987–88 amounted to 16,879 megalitres a day, this approximates to 336 litres per head of population per day. Within England and Wales around 26,847 megalitres of water are abstracted each day. Of this 16,879 megalitres are allocated for public supply. The Central Electricity Board takes around 4,578 megalitres a day, mainly for use in cooling electricity generators. Other industry uses around 3,712 megalitres a day and the remainder is used predominantly for fish farming and agriculture. Water supplies have previously been charged for on a level corresponding to the rateable value of the property supplied. With the introduction of the Community Charge, 'Poll Tax', this system is due to change. No plans are, as yet, established for the new method of payment. Industrial water supplies are paid for on an actual metered consumption system.

Water and sewerage companies

There are nine regional water authorities in England and the Welsh Water Authority in Wales. Under the Water Act 1989, which received Royal Assent in July 1989, the ten authorities (nine in England and the Welsh authority) have been privatized. The ten companies are responsible for water supplies, the development of water resources (storage and distribution), sewerage and sewerage disposal and pollution control. The Water Act 1989 also allows for the establishment of a National Rivers Authority. This body will take over the responsibilities from the regional authorities for their regulatory and river management functions. The regional companies supply 75% of all water supplies. The other 25% is supplied by 29 statutory water authorities which act as independent agents of supply. These 29 companies are all private companies and have previously been restricted to abstracting, purifying and supply. Should they now convert to a Plc status they are, since July 1989, able to become sewerage contractors within their regions.

Research and development

The Water Research Centre is the leading, official body for water research. It has three main laboratories for research into water supply and waste treatment. There are also some small-scale development programmes being undertaken.

Recently, there has been controversy over the quality of water supplies, and the national rivers and lakes. Many rivers and reservoirs have failed to meet European Community health standards. Legal action by the European courts has, as yet, only been delayed. The European Community has demanded that all rivers and water supplies must reach prescribed standards by 1992.

It is also predicted that over the next twenty years massive investment will be required to maintain water standards at their present levels, as the majority of Britain's sewerage system, built by the Victorians, is now in need of major overhaul.

ELECTRICITY

Since the Electricity Act 1947 electrical generation and supply in the UK has been under public ownership. Electricity from the National Grid is available to almost all premises throughout Britain. Investment in 1987–88 stood at £1,589 million and its income at £11,367 million. The total workforce stands at about 135,000 people.

Structure

The Electricity Act 1989 has provided for the sale of the industry within England, Scotland and Wales. The stock-market flotation is due to take place at the beginning of 1991.

In England, the present authority (the Central Electricity Generating Board) was split into four separate bodies, vested on 31 March 1990: Power Gen Plc, which will own 30% of current generating capacity, all non-nuclear; National Power Plc, which will own the remainder of the Boards' generating capacity, excluding nuclear generation; the National Grid Company Plc, which will control the national grid, ownership of which will be transferred to the 12 area electricity boards, to be privatized as regional supply companies; and Nuclear Electric who will control the nuclear-generating industry.

The Electricity Council is to be abolished as the central organizational body. A Director General of Electricity Supply will be assigned to ensure the protection of consumer interests, given that the organization will be operating within a market economy. Criticism of the nuclear industry, by both environmental and industrial groups have led to the Government's withdrawal of this sector from the privatization offer. The nuclear industry is no longer considered a viable economic option.

Consumption

Total electricity generated in 1988 amounted to 288,543 Gwh. Conventional steam power generated 77% of this total, nuclear stations 20.4% and gas turbine, hydro-electric power and diesel plants for 2.1%. There are 15 power stations in the UK with a capacity of 2,000 MW or above. The largest coal-fired power station in Western Europe is the Drax power station in North Yorkshire with a 4,000 MW output. The Central Electricity Generating Board, with Electricité de France, has constructed a cross-Channel submarine cable capable of handling 2,000 MW. (Nuclear Power: *see* Environment.)

ENVIRONMENT

BRITAIN'S ECOLOGY

Habitats

The basic habitat of the British Isles before human intervention through agriculture was broad-leaved woodland; this covered about two-thirds of the land area 5000 years ago. Now forests occupy only a small fraction of the country (and are mostly conifer plantations); only about 1% of the land area is native woodland, and the amount is still declining. Intensive agriculture is a far bigger threat to habitats than building development, and among the types of habitats that have been damaged or lost over the last 50 years are: lowland hay meadows (only 3% left undamaged), lowland sheep-walks (80% lost), lowland heaths on acidic soils (40% lost), limestone pavements in northern England (45% damaged or destroyed, largely by removal of stones to sell as rockery stones; only 3% completely undamaged), lowland fens (50% lost), upland grasslands, heaths and blanket bogs (30% lost or damaged, mostly by conifer afforestation). Higher mountains (ski developments) and sand-dunes are being damaged by recreational pressure, and shingle beaches are being seriously depleted by pebbles being taken for the construction industry.

Species

Mammals. There are 41 native species of land mammals in Britain, plus another 14 introduced by man. The otter has become rare or has disappeared in many parts of England and Wales. The common seal suffered from an epidemic caused by a virus related to canine distemper, and about 12,000 seals died during 1988. Of the 15 species of bat, two (the greater horseshoe and the mouse-eared) are at risk of extinction and three are rare (barbastelle, Bechstein's and Leisler's). Both the pine marten and the wild cat have increased slightly in numbers. There has been concern over the number of badgers, because they were gassed in large numbers in the 1970s as suspects for tuberculosis infection in cattle; no data on their numbers was available until the National Badger Survey (carried out by the Nature Conservancy Council) reported its findings in 1989. It seems that there are about 43,000 'social groups' of badgers in Britain, with very low densities in East Anglia and North-West Scotland. The coypu, originally introduced from South America, had caused immense ecological disruption especially in the Norfolk Broads, but is believed to have been exterminated, the last sighting having been in early 1988.

Reptiles and Amphibians. Of the 12 species, three (natterjack toad, sand lizard, smoothsnake) are endangered.

Birds. There are 229 species of bird that breed in Britain. Over the last 35 years there has been serious decline in the numbers of at least 36 species, owing to the loss or deterioration of habitat through agricultural intensification. This is more frequent in the lowlands (30 species) than the uplands (6 species).

Insects. There are 55 resident breeding species of butterflies in Britain. The large blue butterfly became extinct in 1979, and the chequered skipper became extinct in England in 1975 and is now found only in North-West Scotland. Another 13 species of butterfly have contracted substantially in range over the past 30 years. Of 43 species of dragonfly existing in 1953, three have since become extinct; the emerald damselfly, thought to be extinct in the early 1980s, has recolonized a very few sites in the Thames Estuary.

Plants. There have been 10 extinctions of species since 1930. Of the 1423 native flowering plants and ferns, 149 species have declined by at least 20% over the same time. Most of these (69) are wetland plants; others are from permanent grassland (32), woodland (18), sands and heaths (14).

Protected Species. Under the *Wildlife and Countryside Act 1981*, it is an offence to kill, injure, take, possess or sell any of the animals listed. The Nature Conservancy Council makes recommendations to Parliament from time to time to add species to the list; 22 were added in 1989. The 55 listed species are:

*Adder (*Vipera berus*)
Apus (*Triops canciformus*)
**Atlantic Stream Crayfish (*Austropotamobius paliper*)
Barberry Carpet Moth (*Parenlype berberata*)
Black-veined Moth (*Siona lineata* [or *Idgea lineata*])
Burbot (*Lota lota*)
*Common Frog (*Rena temporaria*)
Common Otter (*Lutra rutra*)
*Common Toad (*Bufo bufo*)
Dolphin (*Cetacea*)
Dormouse (*Muscardines avellanarius*)
Essex Emerald Moth (*Thetidia smaragderia*)
Fairy Shrimp (*Chirocephalus diaphanus*)
Fen Raft Spider (*Dolomedes plantarius*)
Field Cricket (*Gryllus campestris*)
Glutinous Snail (*Myxas glutinasa*)
†Grass Snake (*Natrix natrix* [*Natrix helvetica*])
Great Crested Newt [or Warty] (*Triturus cristatus*)
Horsehoe Bat (*Rhinophidae*, all species)
Ivell's Sea Anenome (*Edwardsia ivelli*)
Ladybird Spider (*Eresus niger*)
Lagoon Sand Shrimp (*Gammarus insensibilis*)
Lagoon Sandworm (*Armandia cirrhosa*)
Large Blue Butterfly (*Maculinea arion*)
Marine Turtle (*Dermochelyidae* [*Cheloniidae*, all species])
Medicinal Leech (*Hirado medicinalis*)
Mole Cricket (*Gryllotalpa gryllotalpa*)
Natterjack Toad (*Bufo calamita*)
New Forest Burnet Moth (*Zygaena viciae*)
New Forest Cicada (*Cicadetta montana*)
Norfolk Aeshna Dragonfly (*Aeshna isosceles*)
*Palmate Newt (*Triturus helveticus*)
Pine Marten (*Martes martes*)
Porpoise (*Cetacea*)
Rainbow Leaf Beetle (*Chrysolina cerealis*)
Reddish Buff Moth (*Acosmetia caliginosa*)
Red Squirrel (*Sciurus vulgaris*)
Sandbowl Snail (*Catinella arenaria*)
Sand Lizard (*Lacerta agilis*)
†Slow-worm (*Anguis hagilis*)
*Smooth Newt (*Triturus vulgaris*)
Smooth Snake (*Lovonella austriaca*)
Starlet Sea Anenome (*Nematosella vectensis*)
Swallowtail Butterfly (*Papilio machaon*)
Trembling Sea-Mat (*Victorella pavida*)
Typical Bat (*Vespertilionidae*, all species)
Vendace (*Coregonus albula*)
Violet Aick Beetle (*Limoniscus violaceus*)
Viper's Bugloss Moth (*Hadena irregularis*)
†Viviparous Lizard (*Lacerta vivipara*)
Walrus (*Odobenus vosmarus*)
Wart-biter Grasshopper (*Decticus verrucivorus*)
Whale (*Cetacea*)
Whitefish (*Coregonus lavaretus*)
Wild Cat (*Fetis silvestris*)
(* 'sale' only; ** 'taking' and 'sale' only; † 'killing, injuring' and 'sale')

There are also 90 species of plants which it is an offence to pick, uproot, sell or destroy. It is an offence to uproot any wild plant. The 90 listed species are:

Adder's-tongue Spearwort (*Ranunculus ophioglossifolius*)
Alpine Catchfly (*Lychnis alpina*)
Alpine Fleabane (*Erigeron borealis*)
Alpine Gentian (*Gentiana nivalis*)
Alpine Rock-cress (*Arabis alpina*)
Alpine Sow-thistle (*Cicerbita alpina*)
Alpine Woodsia (*Woodsia alpina*)
Bedstraw Broomrape (*Orobanche caryophllacea*)
Blue Heath (*Phyllodoce caerulea*)
Branched Horsetail (*Equisetum ramasissimum*)
Bristol Rock-cress (*Arabis stricta*)
Brown Galingale (*Gyperus fuscus*)
Cambridge Milk-parsley (*Selinum carvifolia*)
Cheddar Pink (*Dianthus gratianopolitanus*)
Childing Pink (*Petroraghia nanteuilli*)
Creeping Marshwort (*Apium veperis*)
Cut-leaved Germander (*Tencrium scordium*)
Diapensia (*Diapensia lapponica*)
Dickie's Bladder Fern (*Cystopteris dickieana*)
Downy Woundwort (*Stachys germanica*)
Drooping Saxifrage (*Saxifrage cerna*)
Early Spider Orchid (*Ophrys sphegodes*)
Early Star-of-Bethlehem (*Gagea bohemica*)
Fen Orchid (*Liparis loeselii*)
Fen Ragwort (*Senecio paludosus*)
Fen Violet (*Viola persicifolia*)
Field Cow-wheat (*Melampyrum arvense*)
Field Eryngo (*Eryngium campestre*)
Field Wormwood (*Artemisia campestris*)
Fingered Speedwell (*Veronica triphyllos*)
Foxtail Stonewort (*Lamprothamnium papulosum*)
Fringed Gentian (*Gentianella ciliata*)
Ghost Orchid (*Epipogium aphyllum*)

Grass-poly (*Lythrum hyssopifolia*)
Greater Yellow-rattle (*Rhinanthus serotinus*)
Green Hound's-tongue (*Cynoglossum germanicum*)
Holly-Leaved Naiad (*Najas marina*)
Jersey Cudweed (*Gnaphalium luteoalbum*)
Killarney Fern (*Trichomenes speciasum*)
Lady's-slipper (*Cypripedium calcealus*)
Late Spider Orchid (*Ophrys fuciflora*)
Least Adder's Tongue (*Ophioglossum lusitanicum*)
Least Lettuce (*Latuca saligna*)
Limestone Woundwort (*Stachys alpina*)
Lizard Orchid (*Himantoglossum hircinum*)
Lundy Cabbage (*Rhynchosinapis wrightii*)
Martin's Ramping-fumintory (*Fumaria martinii*)
Military Orchid (*Orchis militaris*)
Monkey Orchid (*Orchis simia*)
Norwegian Sandwort (*Arenaria norvegica*)
Oblong Woodsia (*Woodsia ilvensis*)
Oxtongue Broomrape (*Orobanche loricata*)
Pennyroyal (*Mentha pulegium*)
Perennial Knawel (*Sclerantus perennis*)
Pigmyweed (*Crassula aquatica*)
Plymouth Pear (*Pyrus cordata*)
Purple Colt's foot (*Homogyne alpina*)
Purple Spurge (*Euphorbia peplis*)
Red Helleborine (*Cephalanthera rubra*)
Red-tipped Cudweed (*Filago lutescens*)
Ribbon-leaved Water-plantain (*Alisma gramineum*)
Rock Cinquefoil (*Potentilla rupestris*)
Rough Marsh-mallow (*Althaea hirsuta*)
Round-headed Leek (*Allium sphaerocephalan*)
Sand Crocus (*Romulea columnae*)
Sea Knotgrass (*Polygonum maritimum*)
Sea Lavender (*Limonium paradoxam* [*Limonium recurrum*])
Sickle-leaved Hare's-ear (*Bupleurum falcatum*)
Slender Cottongrass (*Eriophorum gracile*)
Small Alison (*Alyssum alyssoides*)
Small Fleabane (*Pulicaria vulgaris*)
Small Hare's-ear (*Bupleurum baldense*)
Small Restharrow (*Ononis reclinata*)
Snowdon Lily (*Lloydia serotina*)
Spiked Speedwell (*Veronica spicata*)
Spring Gentian (*Gentiana verna*)
Starfruit (*Damasoniumalisma*)
Starved Wood-sedge (*Carex depauperata*)
Stinking Goosefoot (*Chenopodium hyssopifolia*)
Stinking Hawk's-Beard (*Crepis foetida*)
Strapwort (*Corrigiola litoralis*)
Teesdale Sandwort (*Minuartia stricta*)
Thistle Broomrape (*Orobanche reticulata*)
Triangular Club-rush (*Scirpus triquetrus*)
Tufted Saxifrage (*Saxifraga cespitosa*)
Viper's-grass (*Scorzonera humilis*)
Water Germander (*Teucrium scordium*)
Whorled Solomon's-seal (*Polygonatum verticillatum*)
Wild Cotoneaster (*Cotoneaster intergerrimus*)
Wild Gladiolus (*Gladiolus illyricas*)
Wood Calamint (*Calamintha sylvatica*)
Young's Helleborine (*Epipactis youngiana*)

POLLUTION

Automobiles

In 1950 there were 50 million cars in the world; by 1989 this figure had risen to about 400 million.

The increase in the number of cars on the roads far exceeds any previous estimates. The British Department of Transport estimated in 1985, a 25% increase in the number of cars and vans on the roads by the year 2000; this estimate was exceeded in 1988.

There are approximately 22 million vehicles in Britain, using about 30 million tonnes of fuel (petrol and diesel) per year.

There are four main automobile originating pollutants: lead, carbon monoxide, nitrogen oxides and hydrocarbons.

Lead. Continued exposure to lead in the atmosphere can impair children's development and their powers to perform intellectual ability tests. The dangers of lead in petrol are now widely accepted and the European Community countries now have a policy of advocating unleaded petrol.

In Britain there is a price differential of 10 pence per gallon between leaded and unleaded petrol to encourage the use of unleaded. Since 1986, the amount of lead in the air in Britain has been halved according to governmental figures. Britain agreed to an EEC directive requiring unleaded petrol to be available throughout the Community by October 1989, and from October 1990 all new cars are required to be able to run on unleaded petrol. By August 1989 unleaded petrol accounted for 23 % of all petrol sales in England.

Carbon monoxide. Excessive amounts of carbon monoxide reduce the oxygen-carrying capability of blood. Levels may build up gradually and ill health can occur without warning. Those who are most at risk are people who suffer from cardiovascular diseases and coronary artery problems.

Nitrogen oxides. The effects of exposure to nitrogen oxides have been linked to an increased susceptibility to respiratory infections, such as asthma. Nitrogen oxide emissions in London have breached EEC guidelines for the last three years.

Hydrocarbons. Hydrocarbons contain carcinogenic agents similar to those found in cigarettes. An American study shows that as much as 12% of lung cancers in the USA could be attributable to automobiles. If these figures were applied to a British scenario this would mean between 3000 and 4000 deaths per annum as a result of car pollution.

The World Health Organization estimates that London exceeds its upper 'safety' guidelines in three pollutants: carbon monoxide, nitrogen oxide and ozone, which becomes harmful in lower atmospheres.

Pollution problems are most apparent in London; however similar problems will be occurring, though of a smaller density, throughout the UK's other cities and rural areas.

The environmental effects of these emissions are hard to calculate. It is known that two of the key components of acid rain are nitrogen dioxides and hydrocarbons. 30% of the acidity of rain is made up of nitrogen pollution. This has a devastating effect on lakes, rivers and streams (see ACID RAIN).

The UK's vehicle emissions account for: 40% of all British nitrogen oxide pollution (700,000 tonnes), 86% of carbon monoxide pollution (4.45 million tonnes), and 33% of hydrocarbons pollution (538,000 tonnes). Since 1979, carbon monoxide emissions have risen by 13%, hydrocarbons by 14% and nitrous oxide by 18%.

Various solutions, both societal and technological have been suggested to solve the dilemma.

Societal solutions suggest reducing the total number of vehicles on the roads and limiting the misuse/overuse of these vehicles. Methods of application of these ideas vary from increasing road taxes, thus pricing people out of the market; to a complete redevelopment of the British public transport system, requiring vast capital expenditure to bring about a complete solution.

Present Government policy is to extend and widen our existing road networks and to develop new networks to cope with the predicted traffic increases. Environmental groups argue that this is a short-sighted approach as it fails to deal with the root issues and can only aggravate present pollution problems. Environmental groups recommend taking the strain off the roads by developing more efficient and better-serviced public transport systems.

A further suggestion is to ban cars from cities. This more radical approach has already been implemented in some European cities, i.e. Athens, Rome and West Berlin. This approach forces commuters to use public transport systems, thus limiting noxious exhaust emissions.

Technological solutions take a more short-term approach, arguing that as long as personal vehicular transport remains the main method of transport then vehicle emissions must be reduced.

The main pollution-limiting technologies available are: unleaded petrol, catalytic convertors and lean-burn engines.

Unleaded petrol has proved successful at limiting lead emissions in the UK, reducing lead emissions by up to 50% since January 1986.

The catalytic convertor was first introduced in 1975 in the USA. It is a filter in the car exhaust system, which use catalysts to change or reduce pollutants as they pass through. A three-way convertor can reduce emission of hydrocarbons, carbon monoxides and nitrogen oxides. It can only function with unleaded petrol. Since 1988, in Europe, catalytic convertors have been mandatory in Sweden, Norway, Austria and Switzerland. They are also mandatory in Canada, Japan, Australia, Denmark, Mexico, Taiwan, South Korea and Brazil. Also widely available in Germany and the Netherlands, all cars in America have been fitted with convertors since 1988.

In the UK there are no laws which require the fitting of convertors, nor are there any financial incentives to do so. However, some companies are now offering them as optional extras.

Lean-burn engines, by increasing the amount of air in the air-fuel mix in the combustion chamber, would reduce the amount of emissions coming from the exhaust. This would also extend the number of miles per gallon in a car fitted with such an engine. As of yet, little money has been invested in the development of such engines and catalytic convertors are accepted as being the most successful reducer of vehicle pollution.

Pesticides

'Pesticides' is a broad definition used to cover chemical substances used to kill insects, vegetation, fungus, rodents and other species.

Predominantly used in agriculture they are also sold for garden and household application. 800 pesticides have been approved for use in the UK, and these are used in about 4000 different formulations.

The argument in favour of pesticide usage is that they protect essential crops from unwanted pests and thus help maintain high crop yields.

Against this are presented many allegations of misuse: firstly by overuse, in the over-spraying of applications; and secondly because they decline in effectiveness as the pests become more resistant, leading in turn to more spraying and a vicious circle which becomes environmentally unacceptable. It is also argued that the safety checks and requirements supplied are inadequate or out-of-line with current thinking. This argument is often used against Britain and the Third World, where there are less stringent rules and regulations than in the rest of the developed world.

Approximately 1,000,000 million gallons of pesticide-containing liquids are sprayed on fields, parks and gardens in Britain each year. Most of the pesticides used in Britain are herbicides (65%), used for certain, or all, types of plants; fungicides (20%), used to control fungus growth, requiring pre-spraying to prevent possible build-ups; and insecticides (5%), used to kill all, or specific, species of insects.

The Government has withdrawn 20 pesticides after widespread use. There are a further 38 pesticides still in use in Britain which have been banned in other countries. Of the 140 pesticides banned in the USA, 24 are still in common use in Britain.

A report in February 1989, in the USA, argued that pre-school children faced unacceptably high risks of cancer because precautionary levels were based on adults and not on children. The tests ignored children's unusually high reliance on fresh fruit and vegetables. The most potent of these chemical carcinogens was identified as the Unsymmetrical Dimethylhydrazine, a by-product of Alar, the apple growth regulator.

Subsequently Alar was banned in New Zealand and the USA. In May 1989, after UK testing, it was passed for use on British-grown apples.

In June 1985, Oxfam, Friends of the Earth and the Soil Association published a list of the 'Dirty Dozen' particularly hazardous pesticides: 2, 4, 5–T, endrin, aldrin, paraquat, chlordane, lindane, DDT, camphechlor, chlordimeform, ethylene, dibromide, DDCP, dieldrin, ethylparathion and pentachlorophenol. (There are actually 14 here, but three – adrin, endrin and dieldrin are collectively known as the 'drins').

One of the main problems with pesticides is their misuse through overuse. Much machinery used for application is now old and inefficient; up to 70% of herbicides are 'lost', simply adding to soil pollution.

A new spraying technique called Controlled Droplet Application (CDA) has reduced the quantities of pesticides required by up to 80%, in tests in the UK.

Many species of pests are now becoming immune to existing pesticides. Respraying is often required for effective pest control several times in the course of a crop's growth.

A commonly occuring problem is 'spray-drift' where the pesticides miss their targets and drift onto adjacent fields and gardens. This can cause damage to humans and crops in other areas. Some crops, such as Brassicas, are particularly vulnerable to the pesticides being used. In Evesham in 1981, over £250,000 worth of crops were lost due to spray-drift.

Recently, as an environmental alternative, organic farms have started producing crops without the use of chemical aids. Here crop results may at first be poor, but it is hoped that as the soil loses its artificiality it will regain its fertility.

Organic produce is becoming widely available in supermarkets, as consumers have become wary over the use and misuse of pesticides.

Acid Rain

Acid rain is an international problem, in that all countries create it and suffer from it.

Acid rain is caused by the burning of coal and oil and the resulting polluting gases.

The results of this pollution can be disastrous, causing an imbalance in nature which can kill human beings, animals, trees, vegetation and lakes.

The process of burning coal and gas in power stations causes the release of sulphur dioxide gases. Similarly, nitrogen oxide gases are released. The process of burning also converts some of the nitrogen in the air to be converted to nitrogen oxide.

These gases float up the chimneys and are released into the atmosphere; 50% of the pollutants remain in the vicinity of the chimneys. These drift to earth within a 30 kilometre radius.

Some 30% of the pollutants mix with water in the clouds and fall as localised rain, snow, sleet and mist. The remainder, 20%, becomes mixed in with the prevailing wind currents and will travel with these, eventually falling to earth as dust, rain, snow and mist. Sulphur dioxide can travel for up to 100 hours and therefore cover great distances.

'Natural' rainfall is usually assumed to have an acidity pH of 5–6. The rain that falls on Britain and Southern Scandinavia has a pH range of 4 to 4.7. The great London fog of 1952, which killed 4000 people, had a pH of 1.7.

The pollutants can occur in their original states, as sulphur dioxide and nitrogen oxides; or in their acidic states as sulphuric or nitric acid; or, when the acids break into their component elements, as hydrogen, sulphates and nitrates. All of these states will destabilize the earth's natural processes.

Given the right weather conditions, nitrogen oxides can form ozone, this is a pollutant when industrially-created nearer the earth's surface.

The World Health Organization recommends that hourly ozone levels should not exceed 76–100 ppb, to protect human health. This hourly mean is regularly exceeded in South-East England, the highest ever recording being 258 ppb, registered in Britain in the summer of 1976.

The effects of acid rain are complex as they occur on a world-wide scale and are consequently hard to pinpoint.

Acid rain degrades lakes and streams causing the death of fish. In Norway 35,000 km^2 of lakelands have been affected. In Sweden 18,000 out of 85,000 lakes are acidified; 4000 of which are no longer able to support fish life. In Scotland at least 22 lakes have been acidified, likewise in Wales, Cumbria and parts of the Lake District.

Acid air pollution (acid rain being an element of this) destroys forests.

In Britain, though research has only recently been carried out (December 1987, UK Forestry Commission), it appears that damage levels are similar to those in West Germany, where 52% of all forests are damaged. In Switzerland there is 33% damage, in the Netherlands 50%, Poland 7–40% and Austria 16%.

Though little testing has been done on crops in the UK, testing in the USA shows 'severe' damage caused by exceptionally high ozone levels.

Acid pollution also has wide-spread effects on materials and upon many of Europe's major historical monuments, such as the Acropolis. Acid rain corrodes; sandstone, limestone, leather, certain metals and stained glass.

Certain birds can also be affected by acid changes, particularly if their food supply is disrupted. Some have suffered damage to their health due to aluminium contamination.

Solutions come in two main forms: those that aim to stop the pollution totally, by not allowing it to be emitted; and others that argue for more short-term solutions, which will clean up existing plants and thus alleviate the effects of acid rain.

Acid rain involves the interaction of the key pollutants: sulphur, nitrogens and hydrocarbons.

Sulphur emissions can be limited by preventing large scale burning of coal and oil deposits. This can be done by limiting demand, by conserving energy and investing in renewable sources which are less polluting.

Nitrogen emissions, which are also produced by power stations, can be reduced by using the same techniques as for sulphur emissions. These emissions could be further reduced by limiting car pollution (see AUTOMOBILES).

Hydrocarbons are produced by cars; by limiting the number of vehicles on the road and by pollution controls on these vehicles these pollutants can be reduced.

Hydrocarbons are also produced by solvent-based substances for which alternative substances, which are less environmentally damaging, are available.

By using these measures in combination, it is argued that acid rain pollution can be greatly reduced.

Short-term solutions can achieve significant reductions in pollution but will not solve the root issues.

Flue Gas Desulphurization (FGD) filters sulphur emissions out of power stations. This method is used in Japan, the USA and some European countries, though not in Britain.

Fluidized Bed Combustion, a method for burning coal efficiently, is favoured by the electricity industry, but has not yet been commercially developed.

There are also low-sulphur fuels, but the British industry has chosen not to use this alternative as the more polluting coal presently used is cheaper.

To reduce nitrogen emissions, special burners in power stations can cheaply achieve reductions of about 35%.

Flue Gas Denitrification is more efficient and can achieve pollution reductions of 90%. It is used in Japan, the USA and West Germany, but as yet nowhere else.

Catalytic convertors for automobiles can also help substantially reduce nitrogen emissions, as well as hydrocarbons.

Action within Europe against pollution, has been centred around the 30 Per Cent Club.

All members of the 30 Per Cent Club have pledged to reduce emissions, or exports, of sulphur by 1993; many countries have committed themselves further. Austria has pledged a 70% reduction by 1995, Belgium a 50% reduction by 1995, Canada 50% by 1994, Denmark 50% by 1995, Finland 50% by 1993, France 50% by 1990, Luxembourg 58% by 1990, Sweden 58% by 1995 and the FRG 65% by 1993.

There are only five Western European countries who are not members, they are: Britain, Eire, Spain, Portugal and Greece.

Greece argues that it cannot afford to make such pledges. All the other countries border Europe and as such do not suffer from its pollution.

Britain is the largest single pollutor of Western Europe, though it does not suffer from its emission. Britains' power stations and vehicles produce one-fifth of the region's sulphur pollution, most of which falls over North-East Europe.

Nitrates

The artifical fertilizers used in intensive agriculture consist to a large extent of compounds of nitrogen called nitrates. These get washed off land into rivers, lakes, reservoirs, etc., where they are accumulating. Under the EEC Drinking Water Directive, the 'Maximum Admissable Concentration' (MAC) is 50 mg nitrate to one litre of water. Two million people are supplied with water exceeding this maximum amount and 11 million people in Britain drink sub-standard water. Three Regional Water Authorities (Anglian, Severn-Trent and Thames) have supplied water which breached the directive. Three Water companies (Lee Valley, East Worcestershire and South Staffordshire) have also supplied water which has breached the directive. By the year 2000 it is estimated that peak levels will exceed 100 mg per litre due to the nitrates present in groundwater supplies. Whether the privatization of water will put profits before quality of water supply is still of great concern. The long-term effects on wildlife are being investigated by the Nature Conservancy Council.

The Greenhouse Effect

The greenhouse effect is the build-up in the atmosphere of polluting gases. These block heat coming away from the earth, so that it is no longer able to escape into space.

The sun emits heat in the form of radiation to the earth. Carbon dioxide allows visible light to pass through it. These light waves are absorbed by the earth, which in turn emits radiation. The carbon dioxide in the air absorbs this heat or reflects it back to earth.

Carbon dioxide in the atmosphere thus acts in the same manner as a greenhouse, allowing solar radiation to pass through (the 'glass'), but then holding back the radiation (heat) as it attempts to return.

This is a natural process, essential for maintaining the temperature on earth within its 'normal' levels.

The problem arises when carbon dioxide levels in the atmosphere rise above these 'natural' levels.

At present, it appears that carbon dioxide levels are escalating and consequently causing a greenhouse effect. The situation is exacerbated by the presence of other gases in the atmosphere which also act in the same way as carbon dioxide.

Carbon dioxide forms only a small percentage of the earth's atmosphere, about 0.03% or 2600,000 million tonnes. The oceans and forests of the world absorb much of the manufactured carbon dioxide; however approximately 8000,000 million tonnes each year are not assimilated.

Carbon dioxide concentrations have increased from 312 parts per million (ppm) in 1957 to 350 ppm in 1988, a 12% increase in three decades. Analysis of ice cores show earlier deposits, from pre-industrial times, with levels of 280 ppm. If this is the case then carbon dioxide levels have increased by 25% over the last 100 years.

If we assume that the greenhouse theory is correct, and there is now little doubt, then we should also be able to see a corresponding rise in the earth's temperature. Over the last 100 years global mean temperatures have risen by between 0.3°C to 0.7°C.

Estimates, notoriously hard to gather due to problems with earth models, suggest that if carbon dioxide levels continue rising at their present rates, this would mean that by the year 2030 temperatures will have risen globally by between 1.5 and 4.5°C. An increase of between 3–5° does not appear excessive; however this would be a greater increase than has so far occurred over the entire history of the human race.

Increases of this degree would have vast climatic effects, with problems arising in water supply, food, agriculture, forestry, soil moisture, flooding and consequently public health. Rainfall patterns throughout the world would change and many countries would be faced with environmental and subsequent economic disaster.

Some argue that the effects of the greenhouse phenomenon are already being felt.

In 1989 in the USA, half the country was listed as suffering from drought. Half the grain crop was lost. 2000 barges on the Mississippi were left stranded as water levels fell on the world's third largest drainage basin.

The previous year, 1988, was the hottest since records were first compiled by the British Meteorological Office 130 years earlier. The previous record holder was 1987 and then 1983, 1981 and 1980. Three-quarters of Bangladesh was flooded, 3000 died in flooding and 5000 in a tropical cyclone. In China 70,000 wells ran dry, whilst in other parts of the country 1400 people died in floods. Jamaica suffered its worst ever hurricane, with one in four losing their homes.

In England, the hottest summer on record was recorded in 1989, and in 1990 March and February were the hottest since records began.

None of these facts prove that the greenhouse effect exists, but if it were to, these kinds of climatic extremes would occur.

There are also other gases which contribute to the greenhouse effect: methane accounts for 18%, chlorofluorocarbons for 14%, tropospheric ozone 12% and nitrous oxide 6%.

Carbon dioxide is released in the burning of coal, oil and gas; coal being the main contributor. Equipment exists to remove these pollutants from the atmosphere by cutting down emissions at source, i.e. power stations. This would be an extremely expensive method of limiting emissions due to the cost of capping, and the disposal of the pollutants. A cheaper, more practical approach which has, as yet, not been used is to increase the efficiency of all fossil-fuel-burning technologies. By making better, more efficient use of energy, fossil fuel demand could be greatly reduced.

Chlorofluorocarbons are the second-largest contributor to the greenhouse effect; they deplete the ozone layer which allows further radiation from the sun to reach the earth and therefore increase the temperature.

Chlorofluorocarbons are not biodegradable; therefore recommendations are to reduce their creation, and to recycle those that are available, as in refrigerators.

Tropospheric ozone is the result of emissions of nitrous oxide and hydrocarbons primarily produced by power stations, vehicles and the use of solvents.

The technology for minimizing nitrous oxide and hydrocarbon emissions from automobiles already exists (see AUTOMOBILES).

Nitrous oxide emissions have increased over the last few decades due to the extensive use of nitrogen fertilizers and the burning of wood and fossil fuels.

Methane is released in the production of coal and natural gas, and by burning vegetation to make room for extensive cattle farming.

Nuclear power is sometimes quoted as the solution to the greenhouse effect. Unlike coal power stations, which contribute some 10% to the greenhouse gases, nuclear power stations produce less pollutants which can directly effect the global warming patterns. However, if all fossil-fuelled power stations were replaced with nuclear power stations this would only lead to a reduction of 10%. Furthermore one or two nuclear power stations would have to be built every day for the next 38 years to meet current energy demands.

The cost of such an investment would be unsupportable and environmentally disastrous; disposing of radioactive wastes created would be impractical and potentially highly hazardous.

Nuclear Power

Nuclear energy was born of research in the 1930s and '40s. The development of nuclear energy came as a by-product of the nuclear weapons programme.

In 1990, nuclear power generated some 15% of all the world's electricity.

Britain, though not the first country to develop nuclear power, was the first country to embark

Large-Scale Producers of Nuclear Electricity

Country	Existing reactors	Reactors under construction	Percentage of national electricity produced by nuclear power	Percentage of world nuclear electricity output
USSR	50	32	10.0	9.7
Canada	18	5	14.7	4.4
USA	99	21	16.6	27.0
UK	38	4	18.4	3.4
Japan	35	10	24.7	11.0
FRG	21	4	29.4	7.4
Sweden	12	–	50.3	4.4
France	49	14	69.8	15.2

on a civil nuclear power programme. The UK Atomic Energy Authority (UKAEA) was formed in 1954. At this time nine-tenths of atomic work in the UK was for military purposes.

In 1955 a White Paper announced plans to build nine nuclear power stations, producing a 2000 megawatt total output. After the Suez crisis a year later, this target was tripled. The first of these came on line in 1962.

The chairman of the UKAEA made a speech for-seeing a time that 'our children will enjoy electricity in their homes too cheap to meter'.

In 1990, of more than 150 countries in the world, 26 have nuclear power. Of these, 18 countries have less than 10 nuclear generators. The large bulk of nuclear power, four-fifths, is generated in only eight countries.

Some environmentalists argue that even these eight countries continue not solely for economic gain but for alternative reasons. The USA, USSR, UK and France all have large nuclear weapons programmes which require plutonium, which can be created as a by-product of nuclear energy. Hence, the research budgets and the weapons programmes cross-subsidize nuclear power's development.

Canada has developed its own nuclear reactors, which it is marketing. It also has large uranium reserves, essential in nuclear fission.

The FRG and Japan are still bound under Second World War obligations not to develop nuclear weapons capability and are indebted to the USA for financial and technical assistance in the development of their power programmes.

Finally, Sweden is to close its entire nuclear capacity in 2010, after a national referendum voted against its continuance.

At the end of 1986 there were 394 operational nuclear reactors in service and a further 137 under construction.

Since 1974, the International Atomic Energy Authority (IEAE) projections for nuclear power capacity by the year 2000, have been scaled down by 90%.

Austria and the Philippines each have a nuclear plant, which, after Chernobyl, they have decided not to operate.

Development of nuclear power plants has slowed down since the Chernobyl disaster. In the USSR, two planned and partially-constructed power plants have been left unfinished.

Greece, Yugoslavia, Finland, Italy, Brazil, Mexico, China, Egypt, Kuwait and Saudi Arabia have also postponed, cancelled or suspended work on their nuclear power programmes.

Nuclear energy was hailed as the cheapest form of energy yet discovered. In scientific theory this can be true, the potential for nuclear power appears limitless. Yet nuclear power has never fulfilled its promise of providing cheap and safe electricity and its history has been dogged by setbacks, price rises and fears over safety.

The first power station to be commissioned, Berkley in Somerset in 1962, cost three times that of the most modern fossil-fuelled power stations.

Construction over-runs for the Magnox power stations averaged two-and-a-half years.

The second generation of reactors, Advanced Gas Cooled Reactors (AGRs), achieved an average 10 year over-run. They now operate on only 60% capacity and cost twice their predicted prices.

The chairman of the British Central Electricity Generating Board (CEGB), Lord Marshall, has admitted that the economic benefit of nuclear power, has always been 'jam tomorrow'.

Nuclear power is not uneconomic in all countries. The OECD has stated that 'depending on applicable safety standards . . . nuclear power . . . (is) . . . either the cheapest or most expensive option relative to fossil fuels'.

The price per kilowatt installed may vary dependent on: safety levels, the cost of disposing of radio-active waste products and the predicted cost of decommissioning.

In France, the country most dependent on nuclear energy, the cost of installing a 1000 megawatt power station would be around $1000 million, in the USA this would be $3000 million and in Argentina $6000 million.

France's nuclear power programme has been cited as one of the most successful in the world, with 69.8% of all electricity generated from nuclear sources, but this has left Electricité de France in debt by £20,000 million, making it one of the largest debtors in the world.

The CEGB has predicted operational costs of 2.9 pence per kilowatt hour produced, at the Sizewell enquiry. Even if this figure proves accurate, and nuclear cost estimates are notoriously low, wind-power in the USA currently delivers energy at a rate of 2 pence per kilowatt hour.

Safety in nuclear power is perhaps the most controversial of issues. After the Chernobyl disaster the US Regulatory Commission predicted that Western Europe might expect a major accident every seven years.

Nuclear waste exists in various forms and strengths. It can be gas, liquid or solid; low, intermediate-short, intermediate-long and high level.

Low-level waste can be discharged directly into the environment, usually buried in trenches.

Intermediate-level and short-lived waste can be solid and semi-solid items such as sludges, resins and contaminated equipment. Previously, this has been dumped at sea, but is now stored at power stations, or the Sellafield reprocessing plant. Between 1949 and

1979, the UK dumped 67,337 tonnes of radioactive material in the sea, and between 1979 and 1983 the UK was responsible for 90% of all sea dumping.

The London Dumping Convention recommended a suspension of all nuclear dumping at sea in 1983. The UK Government announced its intentions to ignore this ban but was forced into compliance when the National Union of Seamen refused to take part in any more sea dumps. By 1989 the Irish sea was the most radioactive in the world, after one-third of a tonne of highly radioactive material was pumped into the sea from Sellafield.

Since 1985/6, funds for research into radioactive pollution have fallen by 42%.

Intermediate long-lived waste must be disposed of far from any human contact, suggestions are for deep depositories such as old mines.

High-level waste is intensely radioactive, it results from spent nuclear fuels. This generates large quantities of heat and needs to be cooled for a very long time.

Containment has now become the main method of waste disposal in the UK. Waste can remain radioactive for between 200 and 10,000 years, longer than recorded history. To store such high-risk waste for such long lengths of time causes many problems and risks.

On 1 January 1989, the UK Government stated that there were 42,000 cubic metres of intermediate waste; by February 1989 this had risen to 59,400 cubic metres. Total imports of hazardous wastes have risen from 4000 tonnes in 1981 to 80,000 tonnes in 1988.

A further problem is beginning to appear, the disposal of the nuclear reactors themselves. Once nuclear reactors have finished their useful working life they are intensely radioactive, they too need to be stored and safeguarded in the same manner as other nuclear wastes.

Estimated costs of decommissioning vary. The more modern and powerful power stations will prove harder to dispose of, as they are more radioactive, in proportion to the amount of power they create.

In the USA decommissioning cost estimates have ranged between $50 million and $3000 million per reactor. Most British estimates range between £200 million and £700 million. These can only be estimates, as yet no large scale (250 megawatts or above) nuclear power plant has been decommissioned.

In January 1989, the US Government released an estimate of $46,000 million over 20 years to 'clean-up' its radioactive and chemical pollutants created by its nuclear weapons, research and industrial plants.

ORGANIZATIONS CONCERNED WITH CONSERVATION

Nature Conservancy Council

The Nature Conservancy Council is the Government's official adviser on matters relating to conservation in Great Britain. The Secretary of State for the Environment appoints the members of the Council, and awards the annual grant, sometimes earmarking part of the grant for a particular purpose. The grant for 1989/90 was £40,150,000, with £500,000 earmarked for moors in Caithness and Sutherland; this was 5% below the 1988/9 grant after allowing for inflation. The NCC employs 770 permanent staff plus many scientists on short-term research contracts. It is organized regionally, and has its Welsh headquarters in Bangor, and Scottish in Edinburgh, but in 1990 the present NCC will be disbanded and re-formed into separate organizations for each country. The NCC works closely with voluntary bodies such as the Royal Society for the Protection of Birds, making funds available for the societies to buy land (a total of £911,945 was given to societies and trusts in 1988/9) and using their members as observers in collecting data. It also works closely with local authorities, in setting up nature reserves and advising on planning matters if conservation issues are affected; and with farmers, advising on environmentally friendly techniques.

The *Environmental Protection Bill* (Jan. 1990) announced the reorganization of the Nature Conservancy Council into three separate bodies for England, Scotland and Wales. If this is passed, it will become law from April 1991. Lord Cranbrook is chairman-designate of the English Conservancy Council.

Chairman Sir William Wilkinson
Director General T.R. Hornsby MA FRSA
Nature Conservancy Council, Northminster House, Peterborough PE1 1UA. Tel. 0733 40345

Countryside Commissions

The two Countryside Commissions (one for England and Wales, one for Scotland) are also official bodies appointed by and funded by the Government. Their concern is with the countryside as an amenity and as a place for recreation, not with wildlife conservation (on which they take advice from the Nature Conservancy Council). In England and Wales the Countryside Commission has given its official recognition to 222 country parks and 265 picnic sites; the Scottish Commission has recognized 35 country parks and awarded grants to many smaller sites. The Commission for England and Wales has powers to designate 'areas of outstanding natural beauty' and national parks, and to make money available to the landowners (private or public) in these areas to conserve or improve the landscape and give the public access to it. It also plans and administers national trails (long-distance footpaths).

National Parks. (total area 5258 sq miles, 9% of the area of England and Wales). The 10 National Parks are: Dartmoor, Exmoor, the Lake District, Northumberland, the North York Moors, the Peak District, the Yorkshire Dales, the Brecon Beacons, the Pembrokeshire coast, Snowdonia.

Areas of outstanding natural beauty. (total area 7450 sq miles, 12% of England and Wales). The 38 areas are: Arnside and Silverdale, Cannock Chase, Chichester Harbour, the Chiltern Hills, Cornwall, the Cotswold Hills, Cranborne Chase and the West Wiltshire Downs, Dedham Vale, Devon (East), Devon (North), Devon (South), Dorset, Forest of Bowland, Hampshire (East), Hampshire (South Coast), High Weald, the Howardian Hills, the Kent Downs, the Lincolnshire Wolds, the Malvern Hills, the Mendip Hills, the Norfolk Coast, the North Pennines, the Northumberland Coast, the North Wessex Downs, the Quantock Hills, the Scilly Isles, the Shropshire Hills, the Solway Coast, the Suffolk Coast and Heaths, the Surrey Hills, the Sussex Downs, the Isle of Wight, the Wye Valley; Anglesey, the Clwydian Range, the Gower Peninsula, the Lleyn Peninsula.

In Northern Ireland, Areas of Outstanding Natural Beauty are designated by the Department of the Environment for Northern Ireland (total area 695,166 acres, 20% of the country's area). The nine areas are: Antrim Coast and Glens, the Causeway Coast, the Lagan Valley, the Lecale Coast, the Mountains of Mourne, North Derry, South Armagh, Sperrin, Strangford Lough.

National Trails. (total length 1684 miles). The 10 trails are: Cleveland Way, North Downs Way, Offa's Dyke

Path, Peddars Way, Pembrokeshire Coast Path, Pennine Way, Ridgeway, South Downs Way, South West Coast Path (in four sections), Wolds Way.

Countryside Commission for England and Wales
Chairman Sir Derek Barber
Director General A.A.C. Phillips
John Dower House, Crescent Place, Cheltenham, Glos GL50 3RA. Tel. 0242 52138

Countryside Commission for Scotland
Chairman (part-time) J.R. Carr
Director D. Campbell
Battleby, Redgorton, Perth PH1 3EW. Tel. 0738 27921

Forestry Commission

This is primarily concerned with timber production as an industry (and is more fully described under AGRICULTURE), but is aware of the impact of forestry techniques on wildlife conservation. In particular it encourages landowners to plant broad-leaved trees, offering grants at rates three or four times higher than for conifers (depending on the area planted). However broad-leaved plantings are still a small proportion of new plantings, being only 3300 acres against 43,900 acres of conifers in 1986/7. The Commission has on its estates 340 SSSIs (see SITES OF SPECIAL SCIENTIFIC INTEREST), from which it has chosen 46 to be developed as Forest Nature Reserves. The Forestry Commission conducts an annual survey of forest health, monitoring the effects of environmental pollution on trees.

Natural Environment Research Council

Funded by the Department of Education and Science, the Natural Environment Research Council supports research into the environmental sciences; its scope is worldwide, not just confined to Britain. It has 11 research institutes (including the British Antarctic Survey, the British Geological Survey and the Sea Mammal Research Unit), supports research in other institutes and universities and gives grants to postgraduate students and research fellows. The Council's budget for 1989/90 is £160 million. All its work is research-orientated.

Chairman Prof. J. Knill PHD DSC
Polaris House, North Star Avenyue, Swindon, Wilts SN2 1EU. Tel. 0793 411500.

Rare Breeds Survival Trust

This charity is dedicated to preserving British farm animals threatened with extinction; partly because they are historically interesting in themselves, but partly because their unique genetic heritage may be needed again in the future as agriculture develops. Between 1900 and 1973 at least 20 breeds became extinct, but since the formation of the Trust in 1973 no more breeds have been lost. Some animals are owned by the Trust itself, such as its flock of seaweed-eating North Ronaldsay sheep on the Trust's own island of Linga Holm; but most are kept on private farms, some of which are open to the public as farm parks (14 of them RBST-approved). The Trust's annual income is about £400,000. Breeds are classified according to the number of breeding females: the numerical guidelines are 500 for goats and pigs, 750 for cattle, 1000 for horses/ponies, and 1500 for sheep.
Critical. Cattle: Gloucester, Irish Moiled, Kerry, Shetland. Sheep: Castle-milk Moorit, Leicester Longwool, Norfolk Longhorn, Portland. Pigs: Berkshire, British Lop, British Saddleback, Large Black, Middle White, Tamworth. Goats: Bagot. Horses/ponies: none.
Rare. Cattle: none. Sheep: Cotswold, Manx Loghtan, North Ronaldsay, Wensleydale. Pigs: Gloucester Old Spot. Goats: Golden Guernsey. Horses/ponies: Exmoor, Suffolk.
Vulnerable. Cattle: Beef Shorthorn, British White, Longhorn, Red Poll. Sheep: Grey-face Dartmoor, Lincoln Longwool, Whitefaced Woodland. Pigs: none. Goats: none. Horses/ponies: Dales.
Below numerical guidelines. Cattle: Dexter. Sheep: Shropshire, Southdown, Wiltshire Horn. Pigs: none. Goats: none. Horses/ponies: Cleveland Bay, Clydesdale.

Chairman Denis Vernon
4th Street, National Agricultural Centre, Stoneleigh, Kenilworth, War. CV8 2LG. Tel. 0203 696551.

Industry and Conservation Associations

The first Industry and Conservation Association (INCA) was established in February 1989. INCAs are self-help organizations in which local businesses, the local authority, conservation societies and individuals join together to raise the standards of conservation within the area. The first INCA covers the county of Cleveland, and was set up by the county council, ICI and local firms, plus a start-up grant from the Nature Conservancy Council.

Other Bodies

Numerous organizations are involved with conservation in Britain. International environmentalist groups such as Friends of the Earth are active in Britain (see PRESSURE GROUPS). Many of the voluntary bodies that own land used as nature reserves are charities; the two most important conservationist landowners are the National Trust and the Royal Society for the Protection of Birds (see CHARITIES).

NATURE RESERVES

National Nature Reserves

The *National Parks and Access to the Countryside Act 1949* gave the Nature Conservancy (now the Nature Conservancy Council) the power to establish National Nature Reserves (NNRs). Some of these are on land owned or leased by the NCC, but the majority are managed by the landowners under agreements with the NCC that guarantee best conservation practice. The public may visit most NNRs, but for some where plants and animals are highly sensitive to disturbance, a permit from the NCC is needed. There are 234 NNRs: 121 in England (totalling 102,040 acres), 68 in Scotland (277,235 acres) and 45 in Wales (30,332 acres). In Northern Ireland NNRs are established and managed by the Department of the Environment for Northern Ireland; there are 45 (10,736 acres).

Local Nature Reserves

The initiative in establishing Local Nature Reserves (LNRs) lies with the local authorities (England and Wales) and district councils (Scotland). Acting in consultation with the Nature Conservancy Council, they may acquire and manage land suitable for LNRs; many of these reserves have been established in or near urban areas. There are 154 LNRs: 133 in England (totalling 22,891 acres), 6 in Scotland (6642 acres) and 15 in Wales (8362 acres). Other reserves are non-statutory, i.e. they belong to a conservation trust or a charity (e.g. the Royal Society for the Protection of Birds, which owns over 100 reserves).

Marine Nature Reserves

Under the *Wildlife and Countryside Act 1981* the appropriate Secretary of State may designate sea areas as Marine Nature Reserves, on the recommendation of the Nature Conservancy Council (which then manages the reserve). Only one Marine Nature Reserve has so far been established: Lundy Island. Others proposed include: Bardsey Island, Loch Sween, the Menai Strait, St Abb's Head, the Scilly Isles, and Skomer Island.

Sites of Special Scientific Interest (SSSI)

If the Nature Conservancy Council considers a site to be of special interest because of its plants, animals or geological features, it can declare it to be a Site of Special Scientific Interest. To do this it must notify the local planning authority, the water and drainage companies, the relevant Secretary of State, and of course the owner(s) and occupier(s) of the site. The owner may object to the land being designated an SSSI, and in the last resort the NCC has to purchase the site to ensure that it can be designated. The NCC sends the owner(s) and occupier(s) of designated SSSIs a list of operations that they must not carry out on the site. Local authorities have a duty to consult the NCC before granting planning permission on any SSSI, but they do not have to accept the NCC's recommendation (at the end of 1989 there were major development proposals in hand re 23 SSSIs which would mean total or partial loss of the scientific interest). There are 5184 SSSIs: 3272 in England (totalling 1,688,566 acres), 1183 in Scotland (1,892,746 acres) and 729 in Wales (471,580 acres). In the year 1988/9 no SSSIs were totally lost, but 11 were partly lost, 31 suffered long-term damage (causing a permanent reduction in the scientific interest) and 160 suffered short-term damage (from which the object of scientific interest could recover). In Northern Ireland, Areas of Special Scientific Interest (ASSIs) are designated by the Department of the Environment for Northern Ireland; there are 24, totalling 16,348 acres.

GEOGRAPHY

GEOGRAPHY

The term *Great Britain* describes England, Scotland and Wales; the term *United Kingdom* also includes Northern Ireland (as is implied in its full version 'The United Kingdom of Great Britain and Northern Ireland'). Neither the Channel Islands nor the Isle of Man are part of the United Kingdom; they are direct dependencies of the Crown with their own independent systems of government (this is why they have no MPs in the British Parliament).

Dimensions

The maximum overall length of the mainland of Great Britain north to south is 605 miles (974 km) from Dunnet Head, Caithness (58°39′N) to the Lizard peninsula, Cornwall (49°57′30″N). The maximum overall width of the mainland from west to east is 330 miles (531 km) from Ardnamurchan Point, Argyll (6°12′W) to Lowestoft, Suffolk (1°46′)E). The maximum dimensions of the United Kingdom, including islands are: north to south 787 miles (1264 km) from Out Stack, off Unst, Shetland Islands, (60°51′N) to St Agnes, Scilly Isles, Cornwall (49°53′N); west to east 417 miles (670 km) from the western end of the former Co. Fermanagh, near Lough Melvin (8°11′W) to Lowestoft.

The land area of the United Kingdom is 94,247 sq miles (244,100 km^2), including inland water:

	Land, sq mls	Inland water, sq mls	Total area
England	50,070	293	50,363
Scotland	29,761	653	30,414
Wales	7,968	50	8,018
Northern Ireland	5,206	246	5,452
TOTAL	93,005	1,242	94,247

Physical geography

The British Isles can be thought of as being approximately divided into a Highland zone and a Lowland zone, the dividing line running NE to SW from the River Tees (around Newcastle) to the River Exe (Exeter). The most mountainous area is the Highlands of Scotland, consisting of great blocks of ancient granite rocks; two main ranges, the North West Highlands and the Grampians, are divided by the

County map of the United Kingdom

Town map of the United Kingdom

Meteorological areas in home waters

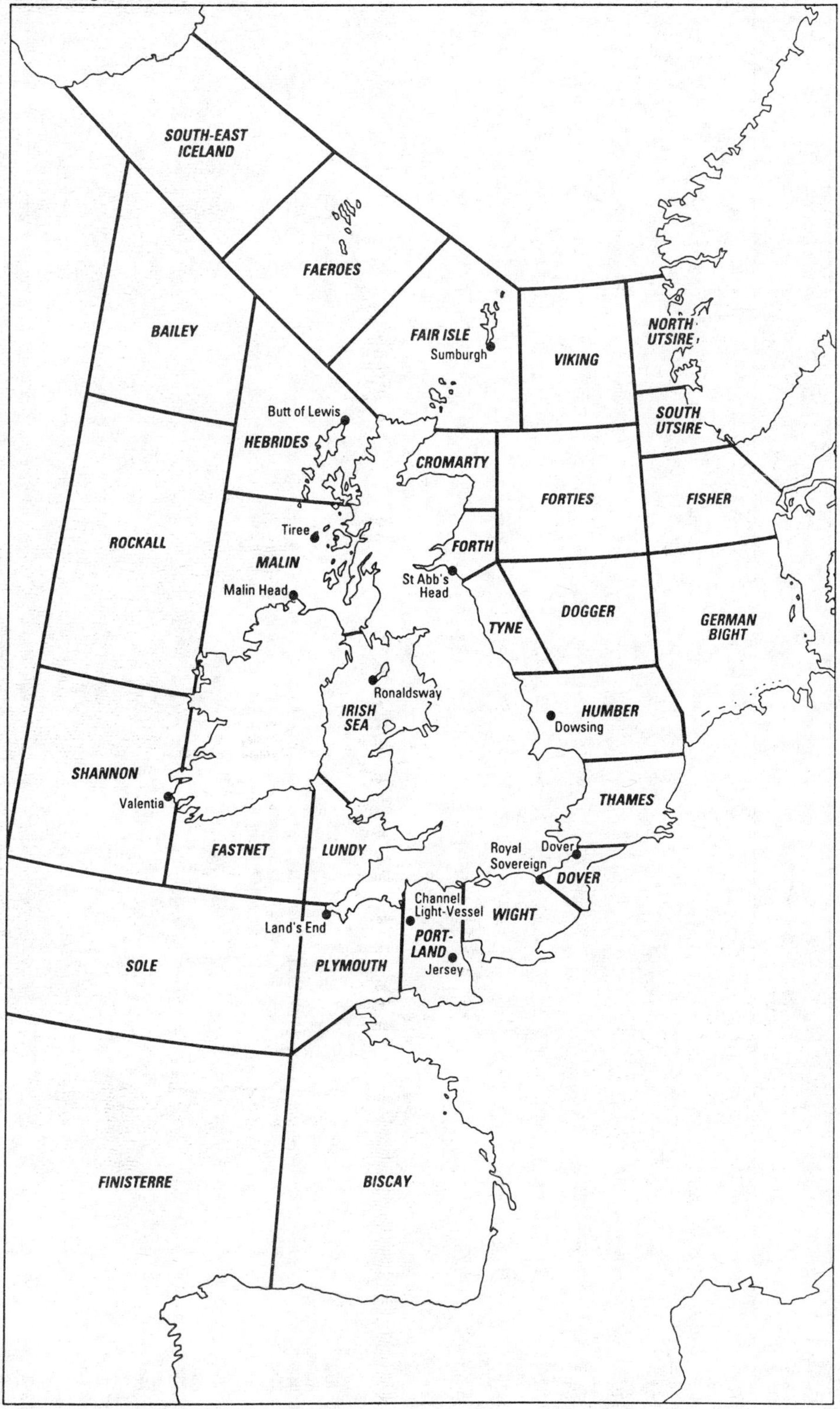

Cities and Towns

Town (County town = *)	Population	Cathedral	University	Cricket (County class)	Football league/rugby union/rugby league	Racecourse	Theatre	Orchestra/Opera	Airport	Main industry	Other
ABERDEEN,* Grampian	203,612	● + RC	●	●	Aberdeen FC	—	His Majesty's	—	Dyce	Oil; fishing; shipbuilding	
ABERYSTWYTH, Dyfed	8,666	—	Univ. Coll. of Wales	●	—	—	Aberystwyth Arts Centre	Orchestra of Wales & the Borders	—		National Library of Wales
ARMAGH	12,700	● + RC	—	—	—	—	—	—		Agriculture; linen	Former county town
AYLESBURY,* Bucks	48,159	—	—	●	—	—	—	—	Thame	Light engineering; printing	
AYR, Strathclyde	48,493	RC	—	—	Ayr United FC	●	Civic, Gaiety	—	Prestwick	Resort; agricultural engineering	
BANGOR, Gwynedd	12,174	●	Univ. Coll. of N Wales	—	—	●	Gwynedd	—	—	Engineering; tourism	
BARNSLEY, S Yorks	73,646	—		—	Barnsley FC	—	Civic	—	—	Coal; plastics; machinery	
BATH, Avon	79,965	—	●	●	Bristol Rovers FC; Bath (RU)	●	Theatre Royal	—	—	Tourism; electrical engineering	
BEDFORD,* Beds	74,245	—	—	●	Bedford (RU)	—	—	—	—	Engineering; brickmaking	
BELFAST	303,600	—	Queen's	●	—	—	Grand Opera Ho., Lyric Players	Opera Northern Ireland; Ulster Orchestra; Northern Ireland Symphony Orch.	Aldergrove & Harbour	Shipbuilding; engineering; aircraft	
BEVERLEY,* Humberside	16,433	—	—	—	—	●	—	—	—	Agricultural processing	Minster
BIRMINGHAM, W Midlands	924,000	● + RC	Birmingham; Aston	Warwicks CC at Egbaston	Aston Villa FC; B'ham City FC; W Bromwich Albion FC; Moseley (RU)	—	Alexandra, B'ham Repertory, Hippodrome, Cannon Hill Park	City of Birmingham Symphony Orch., Orchestra de Camera	Elmdon	Engineering; communications; chocolate	National Exhibition Centre
BLACKBURN, Lancs	139,000	●	—	—	Blackburn Rovers FC	—	Empire	—	—	Textiles; carpets; engineering	
BLACKPOOL, Lancs	146,297	—	—	—	Blackpool FC	—	Grand, North Pier, Opera Ho., South Pier	—	●	Resort; conferences; confectionery	
BOLTON, Gtr M'chester	143,960	—	—	—	Bolton Wanderers FC	—	Octagon	—	—	Aero engineering; textiles	
BOURNEMOUTH, Dorset	142,829	—	—	—	AFC, Bournemouth	—	Pavilion, Pier	Bournemouth Symphony Orch.	Hurn	Resort; light industry	
BRADFORD, W Yorks	280,691	●	●	—	Bradford City FC; Bradford Northern (RL)	—	Alhambra	—	Yeadon	Wool; engineering; printing	
BRIGHTON E Sussex	146,134	—	Sussex	—	Brighton and Hove Albion FC	●	Theatre Royal, Gardner Centre	Brighton Philharmonic	Shoreham	Conference centre	

BRISTOL,* Avon	387,977	● + RC	●	Gloucester-shire CC	Bristol City FC; Bristol (RU)	—	Hippodrome, New Vic, Theatre Royal	Philharmonia of Bristol; Bristol Sinfonia	Lulsgate	Aircraft; tobacco	
BUCKINGHAM, Bucks	6,627	—	● (private)	—	—	—	—	—	—	Light engineering; agriculture	
BURNLEY, Lancs	76,365	—	—	—	Burnley FC	—	Mechanics	—	—	Coalmining; textiles	
BURY ST EDMUNDS,* Suffolk	32,130	●	—	—	—	—	Theatre Royal	—	—	Market town; agriculture	
CAERNARFON, Gwynedd	9,506	—	—	—	—	—	—	—	—	Port; plastics	Castle
CAMBRIDGE,* Cambs	90,440	—	●	Fenner's	Cambridge United FC; Cambridge Univ. (RU)	—	Arts	Cambridge Symphony Orch.	●	Electronics; agriculture	
CANTERBURY, Kent	34,404	●	Kent	Kent CC	—	—	Marlowe	—	—	Tourism; light industry	
CARDIFF,* S. Glamorgan	273,856	● + RC	Univ. of Wales Coll. of Cardiff; Univ. of Wales Coll. of Medicine	Glamorgan CC	Cardiff City FC	—	New, Sherman	Welsh National Opera; BBC Welsh Symphony Orchestra	●	Port; engineering; iron and steel	
CARLISLE,* Cumbria	71,503	●	—	●	Carlisle United FC; Carlisle (RL)	●	Stanwix Arts Theatre	—	●	Textiles; food processing	
CARMARTHEN,* Dyfed	12,302	—	—	—	—	—	—	Thames Chamber Orch.	—	Dairy; agricultural engineering	
CHELMSFORD,* Essex	58,159	●	—	Essex CC	—	—	Civic	—	—	Electrics; radio engineering; agriculture	
CHELTENHAM, Glos.	87,188	—	—	—	—	●	Everyman	Cheltenham Chamber Orch.	Staverton	Aircraft components; service industries; GCHQ	
CHESTER,* Cheshire	58,436	●	—	—	Chester City FC	●	Gateway	—	Hawarden	Light engineering; electrical	
CHESTERFIELD, Derbys.	70,546	—	—	—	Chesterfield FC	—	Pomegranate	South Yorkshire Symphony Orch.	—	Engineering; ceramics; glass	
CHICHESTER,* W Sussex	24,189	●	—	—	—	Goodwood	Festival	Southern Chamber Orch.	Goodwood	Harbour; brewing; tanning	
COLCHESTER, Essex	81,945	—	Essex	●	Colchester United FC	—	Mercury	—	—	Oyster fisheries; engineering	
COVENTRY, W Midlands	317,124	●	Warwick	—	Coventry City FC	—	Belgrade	—	Baginton	Cars; engineering; chemicals	
CREWE, Cheshire	47,759	—	—	—	Crewe Alexandra	—	Lyceum	—	—	Railway engineering	
CWMBRAN,* Gwent	44,876	—	—	—	—	—	Congress	—	—	Coal; iron and steel; engineering	
DARLINGTON, Co Durham	85,396	—	—	—	Darlington FC	—	Civic	—	—	Heavy engineering	

Cities and Towns

Town (County town = *)	Population	Cathedral	University	Cricket (County class)	Football league/rugby union/rugby league	Racecourse	Theatre	Orchestra/Opera	Airport	Main industry	Other
DERBY, Derbys	215,736	●	—	Derby CC	Derby County FC	—	Playhouse	—	—	Rolls Royce; railway engineering; pottery	
DONCASTER, S Yorks	74,727	—	—	—	Doncaster Rovers FC; Doncaster (RL)	●	—	—	●	Railway engineering; confectionery	
DORCHESTER,* Dorset	14,049	—	—	●	—	—	—	—	—	Brewing; agriculture	
DOUGLAS, Isle of Man	19,944	—	—	—	—	—	Gaiety	—	Jurby Ronaldsway	Tourism; brewing; knitwear	
DOWNPATRICK	8,245	● + RC	—	—	—	●	—	—	—	Linen; brewing	Former county town of Co. Down
DUMFRIES,* Dumfries & Galloway	32,084	—	—	●	Queen of the South FC	—	—	—	—	Agricultural implements; clothing; chemicals	
DUNDEE,* Tayside	180,064	● + RC	●	—	Dundee FC; Dundee United FC	—	Dundee Repertory	—	●	Jute manufacture; engineering; marmalade	
DURHAM,* Durham	26,422	●	●	●	—	—	—	—	—	Agriculture; coal; carpets	
EDINBURGH,* Lothian	436,271	● + RC	Edinburgh; Heriot–Watt	●	Heart of Midlothian FC; Hibernian FC; Meadowbank Thistle FC	●	King's; Leith; Playhouse; Royal Lyceum, Traverse	Scottish Chamber Orchestra	Turnhouse	Printing; publishing; brewing	Arts Festival
ELY, Cambs	10,268	●	—	—	—	—	—	—	—	Market town; agriculture	
ENNISKILLEN	10,429	—	—	—	—	—	Ardhowen	—	—	Market town	Former county town of Co. Fermanagh
EXETER,* Devon	95,621	●	●	●	Exeter City FC	Devon & Exeter	Northcott	—	●	Market town, aircraft components	
GLASGOW,* Strathclyde	763,162	● + RC	Glasgow; Strathclyde	●	Celtic; Rangers; Queens Park; Clyde; Partick Thistle FCs	—	Citizen's, King's, Mitchell; Pavilion, Theatre Royal, Tron Theatre Club	BBC Scottish Symphony Orchestra; Scottish National Orchestra; Scottish Opera	●	Shipbuilding; iron and steel; engineering	
GLENROTHES* Fife	32,700	—	—	—	—	—	—	—	●	Coal; electronics; machinery	
GLOUCESTER,* Glos.	92,133	●	—	●	Gloucester (RU)	—	—	—	Staverton	Engineering; plastics; nylon	
GREAT YARMOUTH, Suffolk	54,777	—	—	—	—	●	Britannia, Gorleston Pavilion, Hippodrome, Royalty, Wellington Pier Pavilion	—	—	Fishing; resort; food processing	

GUILDFORD,* Surrey	56,652	•	Surrey	•	—	—	Civic Hall, Yvonne Arnaud	Guilford Philharmonic	—	Agricultural implements; light industry	
HALIFAX, W Yorks	76,675	—	—	—	Halifax Town FC Halifax (RL)	—	Civic	New London Sinfonia	—	Textiles; confectionery	
HEREFORD, Hereford & Worcs	47,652	•	—	•	Hereford United FC	•	New Hereford	—	—	Cider; engineering; timber	
HERTFORD,* Herts	21,412	—	—	•	—	—	—	—	—	Pharmaceuticals; flourmilling; brewing	
HULL (Kingston upon Hull) Humberside	268,302	—	•	•	Hull city FC; Hull (RL); Hull Kingston Rovers (RL)	—	Hull New, Spring Street	—	—	Port; fishing	Own telephone system
INVERNESS,* Highland	39,736	•	—	—	—	—	Eden Court	—	Dalcross	Distilling; iron; tourism	
IPSWICH,* Suffolk	120,447	—	—	•	Ipswich Town FC	—	Wolsey	—	•	Port; light industry	
KIRKWALL,* Orkney	5,947	•	—	—	—	—	—	—	•	Whisky; seaweed	
LANCASTER, Lancs	46,321	RC	•	—	—	—	Duke's Playhouse	—	—	Textiles	
LEEDS, W Yorks	448,528	RC	•	Yorkshire CC at Headingley	Leeds United FC; Leeds (RL); Hunslet (RL)	—	City Palace of Varieties, Civic, Grand Theatre and Opera Ho., Playhouse, W Yorks Playhouse	English Northern Philharmonia; Opera North	Yeadon	Clothing; engineering; paper; printing	
LEICESTER,* Leics	282,300	•	•	Leicester-shire CC	Leicester City FC; Leicester (RU)	•	Haymarket, Phoenix Arts Centre	—	•	Textiles; engineering; footwear	
LERWICK,* Shetland	7,223	—	—	—	—	—	—	—	•	Fishing	
LEWES,* E Sussex	14,971	—	—	—	—	—	—	Glyndebourne Festival Opera	—	Printing; light industry	
LICHFIELD, Staffs	26,310	•	—	—	—	—	Civic Hall	—	—	Agriculture; light industry	
LINCOLN,* Lincs	76,660	•	—	•	Lincoln City FC	—	Theatre Royal	Pavilion Opera	—	Agricultural and other machinery; brickmaking	
LIVERPOOL, Merseyside	544,861	• + RC	•	•	Liverpool FC; Everton FC; Liverpool St Helens (RU)	Aintree	Empire, Everyman, Playhouse, Neptune, Royal Court	Royal Liverpool Philharmonic; Liverpool Sinfonietta	Speke	Port; engineering; chemicals	
LLANDRINDOD WELLS, Powys	4,186	—	—	—	—	—	Albert Hall	—	—	Tourism	
LONDONDERRY	86,148	• + RC	—	—	—	—	—	—	—	Port; linen	Former county town
LOUGHBOR-OUGH, Leics	47,647	—	•	—	—	—	Charnwood	—	—	Engineering; electrical goods, chemicals	
LUTON, Beds	163,209	—	—	—	Luton Town FC	—	St George's	—	•	Cars; precision instruments	

Cities and Towns

*Town (County town = *)*	*Population*	*Cathedral*	*University*	*Cricket (County class)*	*Football league/rugby union/rugby league*	*Racecourse*	*Theatre*	*Orchestra/Opera*	*Airport*	*Main industry*	*Other*
MAIDSTONE,* Kent	72,311	—	—	●	Maidstone FC	—	Corn Exchange, Hazlitt	—	—	Brewing; paper manufacture	
MANCHESTER, Gtr Manchester	449,168	●	Manchester; Univ. of Manchester Inst. of Science and Technology (UMIST)	Lancashire CC at Old Trafford	Manchester City FC; Manchester United FC	—	Apollo, Contact, Forum, Library, Opera Ho., Palace, Royal Exchange	BBC Philharmonic; Hallé Orchestra	●	Engineering; chemicals; port	
MANSFIELD, Notts	71,325	—	—	—	Mansfield Town FC; Mansfield Marksman (RL)	—	Civic	—	—	Coalmining; hosiery	
MATLOCK,* Derbyshire	20,610	—	—	—	—	—	—	—	—	Spa; limestone quarries	
MIDDLES-BROUGH,* Cleveland	149,770	RC	—	●	Middlesbrough FC	—	Little	—	—	Iron and steel/port; chemicals	
MILTON KEYNES, Bucks	123,782	—	Open Univ. HQ	—	—	—	Jennie Lee, Stantonbury	Milton Keynes Chamber Orchestra	—	Light industry	
MOLD,* Clwyd	8,589	—	—	—	—	—	Clwyd	—	—	Agriculture; chemicals	
MORPETH,* Northumberland	14,545	—	—	—	—	—	—	—		Agricultural engineering; coal; iron	
MOTHERWELL,	149,914	RC	—	—	Motherwell FC	—	Civic	—	—	Iron and steel; engineering	
NEWCASTLE upon TYNE, Tyne and Wear	277,674	● + RC	●	●	Newcastle United FC	Gosforth	New Tyne Theatre and Opera Ho., People's, Playhouse, Theatre Royal	Northern Sinfonia of England	Woolsington	Shipbuilding; coal; chemicals	
NEWPORT,* Isle of Wight	23,570	—	—	—	—	—	Medina	—	—	Brewing; boat-building	
NORTH-ALLERTON,* N Yorks	9,622	—	—	—	—	—	—	—	—	Agriculture; engineering; plastics	
NORTHAMPTON,* *Northants	156,848	RC	—	Northants	Northampton Town FC; Northampton (RU)	— —	Derngate, Royal Theatre and Opera Ho.	Midland Philharmonic; Corelli Strings	—	Footwear; engineering; leather	
NORWICH,* Norfolk	122,270	● + RC	East Anglia	●	Norwich City FC	—	Theatre Royal	—	●	Footwear; mustard; engineering	
NOTTINGHAM,* Notts.	271,080	RC	●	Notts CC at Trent Bridge	Notts County FC; Nottm. Forest FC; Nottingham (RU)	●	Playhouse, Theatre Royal	East Midlands Music Theatre, East of England Orchestra	Tollerton	Textiles; lace; tobacco;	
OBAN, Strathclyde	8,134	● + RC	—	—	—	—	Highland	—	—	Port; tweed; whisky	

OLDHAM, Gtr Manchester	107,095	—	—	—	Oldham Athletic FC; Oldham (RL)	—	Coliseum, Grange Arts Centre	—	—	Textiles; engineering; paper	
OMAGH	14,627	—	—	—	—	—	—	—	—	Agriculture	Former county town of Co. Tyrone
OXFORD,* Oxon	98,521	●	●	The Parks	Oxford United FC; Oxford Univ. (RU)	—	Apollo, Playhouse	Oxford Pro Musica	Kidlington	Cars; tourism; publishing; printing	
PAISLEY, Strathclyde	84,789	RC	—	—	St Mirren FC	—	—	—	Renfrew (= Glasgow airport)	Textiles; engineering	
PERTH, Tayside	41,916	●	—	—	St Johnstone FC	●	Perth	—	—	Textiles; dyeing; cattle markets	Capital of Scotland 11th–15th centuries
PETERBOROUGH, Cambs	132,464	●	—	●	Peterborough United FC	—	The Cresset, Key	Peterborough String Orchestra	—	Engineering; bricks; agriculture	
PLYMOUTH, Devon	243,895	● + RC	—	—	Plymouth Argyle FC	—	Theatre Royal, Athenaeum	—	Roborough	Port; Naval base; fishing	
PORTSMOUTH, Hants	179,419	● + RC	—	●	Portsmouth FC	—	New Theatre Royal	—	●	Port; Naval base; shipbuilding	
PRESTON,* Lancs	86,913	—	—	—	Preston North End FC	—	Charter	—	Samlesbury	Textiles; engineering; aircraft	
READING,* Berks	132,037	—	●	●	Reading FC	—	Hexagon	—	—	Biscuits; printing; electronics	
RIPON, N Yorks	11,952	●	—	—	—	●	—	—	—	Tourism	
ROCHDALE, Gtr Manchester	97,292	—	—	—	Rochdale FC Rochdale Hornets (RL)	—	Gracie Fields	—	—	Textiles	
ROCHESTER, Kent	52,505	●	—	—	—	—	—	—	●	Heavy machinery; board and paper	
ST ALBANS, Herts	50,888	●	—	●	—	—	Abbey	—	—	Electronics; light industry	
ST ANDREWS, Fife	11,302	—	●	—	—	—	Byre	—	—	Tourism	Royal & Ancient Golf club
ST ASAPH, Clwyd	3,156	●	—	—	—	—	—	—	—	Agriculture	
ST DAVIDS, Dyfed	1,759	●	—	—	—	—	—	—	—	Agriculture	
ST HELIER, Jersey CI	25,698	—	—	—	—	—	Gloucester Hall, Opera Ho.	—	Jersey	Tourism; horticulture	
ST PETER PORT Guernsey CI	15,587	—	—	—	—	—	Beau Sejour	—	Guernsey	Tourism; horticulture	
SALFORD, Gtr Manchester	24,736	● + RC	●	—	Salford (RL)	—	—	—	—	Engineering; textiles; pharmaceuticals	
SALISBURY, Wilts	35,355	●	—	●	—	●	Playhouse	—	—	Engineering; food processing	
SHEFFIELD, S Yorks	536,770	● + RC	●	●	Sheffield United FC; Sheffield Wednesday FC; Sheffield Eagles (RL)	—	Crucible	—	—	Cutlery; steel; coal	
SHREWSBURY,* Shrops	87,300	RC	—	●	Shrewsbury Town FC	—	Music Hall	—	—	Engineering; agricultural equipment	

Cities and Towns

*Town (County town = *)*	*Population*	*Cathedral*	*University*	*Cricket (County class)*	*Football league/rugby union/rugby league*	*Racecourse*	*Theatre*	*Orchestra/Opera*	*Airport*	*Main industry*	*Other*
SOUTHAMPTON, Hants	204,406	—	•	Hampshire CC	Southampton FC	—	Mayflower, Nuffield	—	Eastleigh	Container port; ship repair, oil	
SOUTHWELL, Notts	6,370	•	—	—	—	•	—	—	—	Agriculture	
STAFFORD,* Staffs	55,497	—	—	•	—	—	Gatehouse	—	—	Electrical engineering; pottery; coal	
STIRLING,* Central	38,638	—	•	—	Stirling Albion FC	—	—	—	—	Agricultural engineering; carpets	
STOKE ON TRENT, Staffs	250,400	—	Keele (nearby)	•	Stoke City FC; Port Vale FC	—	Queen's	—	—	Pottery; coal; iron and steel	
STORNOWAY,* Outer Hebrides	8,660	—	—	—	—	—	—	—	•	Tweed	
SUNDERLAND, Tyne & Wear	195,064	—	—	—	Sunderland FC	—	Empire	—	Usworth	Shipbuilding; glass; paper	
SWANSEA,* W Glamorgan	167,796	RC	Univ. Coll. (Univ. of Wales)	•	Swansea City FC	—	Cwmtawe, Grand, Penyrheol	Welsh Philharmonic	Fairwood Common	Port; iron and steel; coal; oil refining	
SWINDON, Wilts	91,136	—	—	•	Swindon Town FC	—	Wyvern	—	—	Railway engineering; electronics; tobacco	
TAUNTON,* Somerset	35,326	—	—	Somerset CC	—	•	Brewhouse	Taunton Sinfonietta	—	Agriculture; cider; agricultural machinery	
TROWBRIDGE,* Wilts	22,984	—	—	•	—	—	—	—	—	Textiles; brewing; pork and dairy products	
TRURO,* Cornwall	16,277	•	—	•	—	—	—	—	—	Agriculture, tourism	
WAKEFIELD, W Yorks	311,787	•	—	—	Wakefield Trinity (RL); Featherstone Rovers (RL)	Pontefract	Theatre Royal and Opera Ho.	Yorkshire Philharmonic Orchestras	—	Coal; textiles; brewing	
WARWICK.* Warks	21,936	—	(Warwick Univ. is at Coventry)	—	—	•	—	—	—	Agricultural machinery; brewing	
WINCHESTER,* Hants	88,385	•	—	—	—	—	Theatre Royal	—	—	Agriculture	
WOLVERHAMP-TON, W Midlands	263,501	—	—	—	Wolverhampton Wanderers FC	• •	Grand	English Philharmonic Orch.	—	Engineeering, esp. locks	
WORCESTER,* Hereford & Worcs	74,790	•	—	Worcester-shire CC	—	•	Swan	—	—	Porcelain; sauce; gloves	
YORK, N Yorks	99.787	•	•	—	York City FC; York (RL)	•	Theatre Royal	—	—	Chocolate; railway workshops	

Great Glen (containing Loch Ness), which was created by a geological fault. The west coastline of the Highlands is deeply indented with sea-lochs, and there are many islands, large and small. The Outer Hebrides are the remains of a further ridge of mountains west of the North West Highlands, and the archipelagos of the Orkney and Shetland Islands (off the NE corner of Scotland) are also the remains of ancient mountains. The central area of Scotland, consisting of the valleys of the rivers Clyde, Forth and Tay, is relatively low-lying (and is also due to a geological fault). Southern Scotland and the northern part of England contain another block of mountains, the Southern Uplands, rather less high, with various ranges such as the Cheviots along the border. Extending southwards right down the centre of England as far as Derbyshire are the Pennine Mountains, a huge limestone ridge with scenery ranging from mountains to moors. To east and west lie the North York Moors and the Lake District (which includes the highest land in England). Northern Ireland has a ring of mountain ranges – Sperrin, Antrim and Mourne – surrounding the wide basin with Lough Neagh in the centre. In Wales most of the land is more or less mountainous, with various ranges from Snowdonia in the north to the Brecon Beacons in the south; islands are not a notable feature of the coast, apart from the large low-lying Anglesey in the north. Between the Welsh mountains and the southern end of the Pennines is the Mersey basin, a wide plain with southern Lancashire on one side and Cheshire on the other. The last section of the Highland zone lies in the extreme West of England, where Exmoor and Dartmoor rise as two ranges of granite hills.

The Lowland zone of England begins with the valleys of the Trent and Avon, which are more or less aligned and form a wide fertile plain across the middle of the country. The lowest-lying part of the country is the fenland of Cambridgeshire and Lincolnshire, where some of the land is below sea-level. The rest of England is low with periodical ranges of hills: first the Mendips and Cotswolds, which are limestone hills, and then the various chalk ranges, the Wiltshire, Berkshire, Kent and Sussex Downs, and the Chiltern Hills. The coastline of eastern and southern England is low-lying and mostly marshy or sandy; cliffs such as those at Dover occur only where a range of hills comes to the sea.

Land use

Overall, over three-quarters of the land area of the United Kingdom is used for agriculture, and 9% is forest. Urban and industrial use accounts for only about 11%, though this is increasing at about 0.1% of the land area per year.

The greater part of the Scottish Highlands and Islands consists of heather or other rough grazing and is used for raising sheep or for softwood forestry. This region is famous for its whisky, though the distilleries occupy tiny amounts of space and import all their grain from elsewhere. The North East of Scotland is the base for the North Sea oil industry, with Aberdeen and the Shetland Islands as its centres. There is also fishing and fish-farming round the coasts of Scotland. The Central Lowlands contain Scotland's centres of population and industry, with coalmining, shipbuilding and steelmaking still carried on, though on a reduced scale. Rural lowland areas are used for dairying and beef production. The Southern Uplands and the Pennines are more rough grazing and are used for sheep; the wool is utilized in local textile industries. In Northern Ireland the mountain areas are used for raising sheep and cattle, while the lowland was traditionally used for flax for the linen industry centred on Belfast; this and the shipbuilding have declined steeply since World War II. In Wales, the mountains are sheep areas but without the associated textile industries as in Scotland or N England; there is dairying in milder districts, particularly on the English border, and fishing in the West. Welsh industry and urban development is centred in the south, in the coalmining valleys and around the ports of Cardiff and Swansea. The traditional steelmaking is now in decline but replacement industries, e.g. car-making and electronics, have moved in. England's oldest industrial centres are those of the great conurbations of Tyneside, Merseyside, Greater Manchester, West Yorkshire, West Midlands, and London, all of which were originally based on manufacturing; even though manufacturing industry (especially heavy industry) is in decline, these conurbations have survived by diversifying into lighter industries and particularly into service industries. The conurbations still hold about 30% of the population. Agricultural lowland England is very roughly divided into dairying and beef production in the western half (with its wetter climate) and grain-growing in the drier eastern half. Market gardening is concentrated in fertile areas near the conurbations, e.g. the Vale of Evesham for West Midlands, Essex for London. Throughout lowland England are towns that have based their prosperity on one or other economic specialism, e.g. York (confectionary, railways) or Northampton (footwear); electronics is booming in a number of towns (e.g. Cambridge, Swindon). Ports of all sizes are still of great importance, though the planned Channel Tunnel (due to open in June 1993) will probably have an adverse effect on Dover and Folkstone and the other Channel ports.

Mountains

The highest mountain in the United Kingdom is Ben Nevis, at 4406 ft (1343 m); Scotland has all the peaks over 4000 ft, the others being Ben Macdui 4296 ft (1309 m), Braeriach 4248 ft (1295 m) and Cairn Gorm 4084 ft (1245 m). The highest mountain in Wales is Snowdon, in Gwynedd, at 3560 ft (1085 m); in England, Scafell Pike, in the Lake District, at 3210 ft (976 m); in Northern Ireland, Slieve Donard, in the former Co. Down, at 2786 ft (847 m).

Rivers

The longest river in the United Kingdom is the Severn, which rises in West Wales and flows through England to the Bristol Channel, with a total length of 220 miles (354 km). England's longest river is the Thames at 215 miles (346 km), Scotland's the Tay at 117 miles (188 km), Wales's the Towy, 68 miles (109 km), and Northern Ireland's the Mourne, 51 miles (82 km).

Man-made features

The longest bridge in the United Kingdom is the second Tay Bridge (railway) at 11,653 ft (3552 m); the Humber Bridge, near Hull, is a suspension bridge whose central span is 4626 ft (1406 m) – the longest in the world. The longest tunnel is London Underground's Northern Line from East Finchley to Morden via Bank, 17½ miles long (28 km); the longest railway tunnel is the Severn Tunnel at 4⅓ miles (6 km) and the longest road tunnel the Mersey Tunnel at just over 2 miles (3.4 km).

The tallest structure is the Independent Broadcasting Authority's mast near Horncastle, Lincs, which is 1272 ft (387 m) high and is supported by guy-lines; the tallest unsupported structure is another IBA mast, at Emley Moor, N Yorks, which is 1080 ft (329 m) high. The tallest building is one of the cooling towers at Drax Power Station, N Yorks, at 850 ft (259 m), and the tallest building for human occupation is the National Westminster Bank's headquarters in the City of London: it is 600 ft (183 m) tall and is the highest cantilevered building in the world. It will be superseded by an office block in the Canary Wharf development, in London's Dockland, which is planned to be over 850 ft (259 m) high.

Climate

The climate of the British Isles is temperate; by world standards, these islands do not experience anything extreme in either high or low temperatures. The warm Gulf Stream current flowing across the Atlantic Ocean from the Caribbean keeps the temperatures mild, particularly along the western coasts. This south-westerly airstream is the predominant factor in determining the weather, bringing depressions which cause wet weather; east or north winds bring dryer, colder weather. The climate is on average wetter and slightly warmer on the western side of the country, and there is also a gradient of temperature from the colder north to the warmer south. The lowest winter and summer averages come from Lerwick, Shetland Islands: 3°C (37°F) Dec.–Feb. and 11°C (52°F) June–Aug., and the highest are from the Isle of Wight: 5°C (41°F) and 16°C (61°F). Cities create 'heat islands' where temperatures are 2–4°F (1–2°C) higher than surrounding areas. Rainfall is only slightly seasonal, with most precipitation (i.e. rain, snow or sleet) occuring between September and January. Average annual rainfall is about 60 in (1600 mm) in western Britain and about 30 in (800 mm) in central and eastern Britain.

Records

The highest recorded temperature was 100.5°F (38.1°C) at Tonbridge, Kent, on 22 July 1868; the lowest, –17°F (–27.2°C) has been recorded twice at Braemar, Grampian, on 11 Feb. 1895 and 10 Jan. 1982. The wettest single day was 18 July 1955, when 11 in (279 mm) of rain fell at Martinstown, Dorset. The highest wind speed was 150 knots (172 mph) at Cairngorm, Highlands, on 20 Mar. 1986.

Population

The population of the United Kingdom grew steadily from the end of World War II to 1971 but since then its growth has slowed down, and the total is not expected to reach 60 million from the present 56.9 million until 2025. The factors that influence population growth are birth rate, death rate, and migration (immigration and emigration).

Birth rate

In 1987 there were 776,000 live births, which is 13.6 per 1000 population. The trend for births is slightly upwards again, after a fall from the 1964 peak.

Death rate

In 1987 there were 644,300 deaths, at rates per 1000 population of 11.2 for women and 11.5 for men. Life expectancy at birth was 77.5 years for women, 71.7 years for men.

Migration

Since 1983 there has been a net gain in population by excess of immigration over emigration, after nearly a decade of net losses.

The number of persons arriving from the EC countries has doubled over the past decade, and there

Growth of UK population, 1801–2025

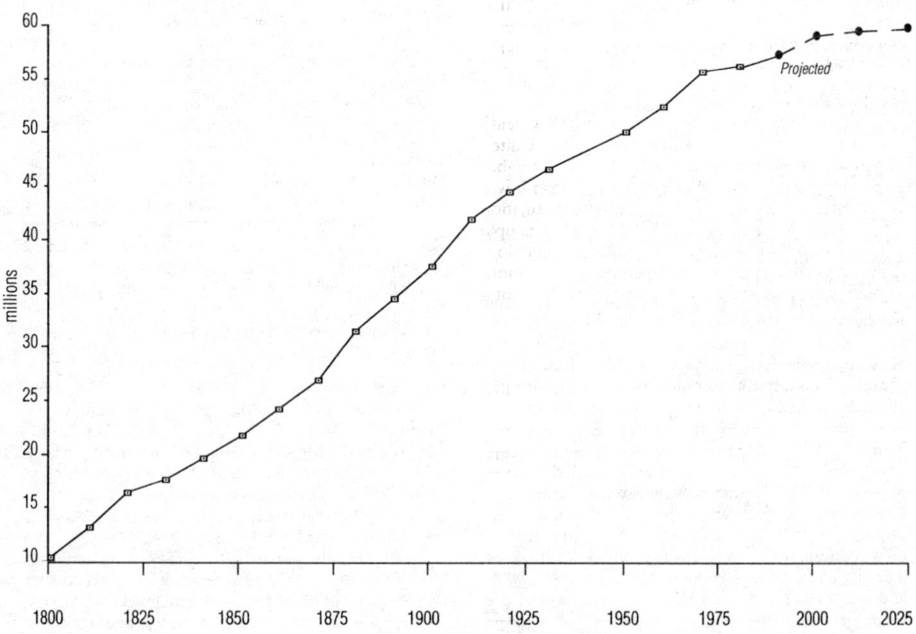

Birth rate per 1000 population, 1951–2006

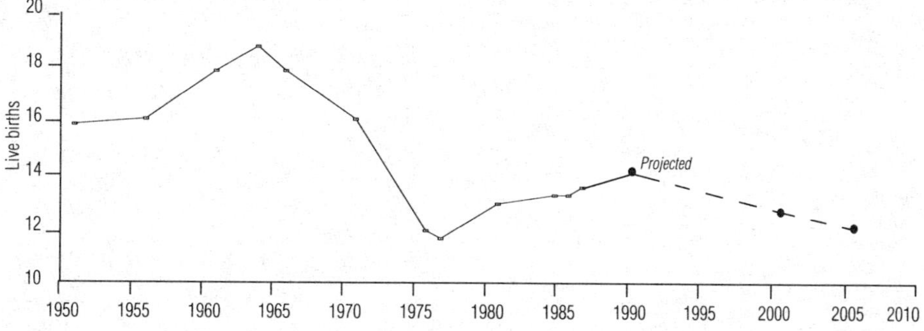

Death rate, per 1000 in each age group, 1986

	Age group								
	0–4	*5–14*	*15–24*	*25–34*	*35–44*	*45–54*	*55–64*	*65–74*	*75 and over*
Males	2.6	0.2	0.8	0.9	1.7	5.5	17.0	43.6	117.6
Females	2.0	0.2	0.3	0.5	1.1	3.3	9.5	24.0	87.4

has also been a 50% increase in the number coming from the United States over the same period: these two groups together account for very nearly the same as the total of all the Commonwealth countries put together.

Country of next or last residence	Inflow	1988 Outlfow	Net
Commonwealth countries	15,700	14,160	+1540
European Community	10,380	8,920	+1460
US	5,060	6,060	-1000
Others	12,780	8,700	+4080
TOTAL	43,920	37,840	+6080

Age distribution

The fall in the birth rate combined with a low death rate has meant that the population of the United Kingdom has become relatively older. The number of people aged 65 or over is 50% greater than it was in 1951; it is now just over 15% of the population (8.8 million in 1987). A further 10.8 million people are aged 15 and under, i.e. 19% of the population. These two combined give a dependency ratio (non-working-age persons as a pecentage of the total population) of 34%.

Location and density

Of the present 56.9 million population, over 80% live in urban areas.

	Population	Persons per km^2
England	47,407,000	363
Wales	2,836,000	137
Scotland	5,112,000	65
Northern Ireland	1,575,000	112
TOTAL	56,930,000	233

The population density in England, at 363 per km^2, is the highest of any country in the EC (next highest is Netherlands at 349 per km^2).

Ethnic groups

The great majority of the population is white (figures include white people of non-UK origin). (See also *Religions*, below).

Ethnic minorities in England, Wales and Scotland, 1986

Origin	*Number*	*Percent born in UK*	*Percent living in English metropolitan areas*
Indian	760,000	36%	66%
West Indian or Guyanese	534,000	53%	81%
Pakistani	397,000	42%	66%
Mixed	235,000	74%	58%
Chinese	115,000	24%	52%
African	103,000	35%	75%
Bangladeshi	103,000	31%	79%
Arab	66,000	11%	62%
Other	119,000	28%	63%
Total	2,432,000	42%	68%

Languages

English is the official language throughout the United Kingdom. In Wales, where 19% of the population can speak or read it, Welsh has some legal status: it has equal validity in law courts, and for some civil service posts applicants can be required to be Welsh-speakers. Gaelic has no official status, but some 100,000 people in Scotland are estimated to speak it; Manx, a closely-related language, is spoken by about 100 people on the Isle of Man.

No official statistics are kept of the languages spoken by immigrants, but estimates suggest that languages with substantial numbers of speakers include Chinese, Gujarati, Bengali, Panjabi, Urdu, Hindi, Jamaican Creole, Arabic, Turkish, Greek, Spanish and Japanese.

Households

There are 21.2 million households in the United Kingdom, and the numbers is projected to grow by 10% between now and 2001, because of the continuing rise in the number of one-person households.

Type of household	1961	1971	1981	1987
	Percentages			
Living alone	3.9	6.3	8.0	9.9
Married couple, childless	17.8	19.3	19.5	21.5
Married couple, with children (incl. non-dependent)	53.8	61.7	57.7	55.9
Single parents	2.5	3.5	5.8	4.7
Other	12.0	9.2	9.0	8.0

Marriages

Although the population has been growing, the number of marriages has shown a slight decline over the past two decades. However, remarriage has increased greatly over the same period, now accounting for over one-third of all marriages.

	1961	1971	1976	1981	1986	1987
	Thousands					
First marriage for both	340	369	282	263	254	260
First marriage for 1 ptr only	36	54	70	74	76	77
Second (or later) for both	21	36	54	61	63	61
Total marriages	397	459	406	398	393	398
Marriages per 1,000 pop.	7.5	8.2	7.2	7.1	6.9	7.0
Remarriages (of one or both ptrs) as % of all marriages	14	20	31	34	35	35

Divorce

The divorce rate increased very steeply after the passing of the Divorce Reform Act 1969 (England and Wales only), and again after the Matrimonial and Family Proceedings Act 1984 (also England and Wales only), which allowed a divorce petition to be filed after only one year from the date of marriage.

Divorce, 1961–1988

	1961	*1971*	*1976*	*1981*	*1984*	*1985*	*1986*	*1987*	*1988*
Decrees absolute granted (thousands)									
England & Wales	25	74	127	146	145	160	154	151	153
Scotland	2	5	9	10	12	13	13	12	11
N. Ireland	0.1	0.3	0.6	1.2	1.6	1.6	1.5	1.5	2
TOTAL UK	27	80	136	157	158	175	168	165	166
Persons divorcing per 1000 married people – England and Wales	2.1	6.0	10.1	11.9	12.0	13.4	12.9	12.6	12.8
Children under 16 whose parents divorced (thousands)	(n.a.)	77	153	160	149	155	152	149	150

HEALTH AND SOCIAL WELFARE

The British health and social welfare system comprises: the National Health Service (NHS); the personal social services; the social security system.

A co-ordinated welfare system, capable of providing a comprehensive service to the UK population, began to be put into place at the end of World War II. The Beveridge Report of 1942 provided the groundwork in the creation of the welfare state. In 1946 the National Insurance Act and the National Health Service Act were passed (despite Conservative opposition). In 1948 the National Assistance Act complemented these and, on 15 July 1948, the NHS came into being.

THE NATIONAL HEALTH SERVICE

The NHS is based on the principle that there should be a comprehensive range of publicly funded medical services, which are equally available to all, irrespective of means. The NHS is composed of: the Hospital and Community Health Services; the Family Practitioner Services, providing general medical, dental, dispensing, and some ophthalmic services, also covering the cost of medicines prescribed by general practitioners (GPs); the Central Health and Miscellaneous Services, providing a limited number of services which, it is thought, are best administered centrally, e.g. the Health Education Authority.

FINANCE AND EXPENDITURE

Approximately 78% of the cost of the NHS in Great Britain in 1989/90 was paid for out of general taxation. The Government re-affirmed its commitment to this method of finance in its white paper *Working for*

Patients. The remainder of the cost is met from National Insurance Contributions to the NHS, dental treatment, prescription charges and other receipts, e.g. land sales.

The total NHS current and capital expenditure out turn in 1988/9, for the UK as a whole, was £22,876 million. The total UK NHS estimated current and capital expenditure for 1989/90 is £24,826 million (80 % of which is allocated to England).

Whilst most governments have increased NHS resources in real and cash terms, all governments have also been faced with rising demands and costs in an ageing population. Over 45% of health authority expenditure on hospital, community and other related services is spent on care of the elderly.

A BBC Health Survey of 210 Regional Health Authorities (RHAs) revealed that since 1987: 123 were worse off; 91 had overspent; 51 had to make direct cuts to patient services.

The UK public health expenditure for 1989 was 5.7% of Gross Domestic Product (one of the lowest in OECD countries). Public expenditure as a percentage of total health spending (despite consistently reducing since 1980) still remains relatively high in relation to other OECD countries. This is perhaps one sign of a restriction of public expenditure and a corresponding reliance on private financing.

In 1980 the Health Services Act encouraged *pay beds* in National Health Service hospitals. In 1982 a Central Policy Review Staff leaked document suggested introducing charges for visits to GPs and hospital stays and, in the longer term, replacing the NHS with an insurance-based finance system. This leak prompted Mrs Thatcher to pledge that the NHS was 'safe in their hands', whilst the opposition claimed that the Government had a 'secret agenda' to privatise the NHS.

In 1983, after securing a second term, the Conservative Government introduced a 1% across-the-board reduction in the budgets of local health authorities, as well as revising the long-term revenue growth assumptions, which led to real reductions in resource-allocation to Thames Regional Health Authority. It also marked the beginning of competitive tendering for ancillary services, such as hospital cleaning, catering and laundry services. In 1987, £105 million was saved through this measure.

The emphasis on efficiency and value-for-money is central to government NHS strategy. Legislation has sought to impress upon health authorities the need for self-help and increasing commercialization in selling facilities and services for private use. Until 1988, NHS pay awards were consistently under-funded to ensure that District Health Authorities (DHAs) agreed to cost improvement programmes.

In 1988 the Health and Medicines Bill empowered health authorities to engage in income-generating activities to supplement their NHS allocations, by acting in a more commercial manner in selling facilities and services for non-NHS use to the public and organizations. Charitable finance has also been encouraged as part of the attempt to find alternative, non-Treasury sources of revenue for the NHS.

SECTORS OF THE NATIONAL HEALTH SERVICE

Hospitals, Community Health and Related Services

Community Child Health Service. This provides pre-school health services, usually at child health clinics, which monitor children's physical, mental and emotional well-being and development. The School Health Service provides mental and dental examination of school children and advises the Local Education Authority (LEA), school, parent and pupils of any special needs the pupils may require at school.

Hospital and specialist services. The Hospital and Community Health Services (HCHSs) provide a range of hospital services in district, general, specialist and children's hospitals. They also provide community services such as district nursing, ambulance services and public health services. Special Health Authorities (SHAs) are responsible for a variety of specialist services, such as those provided by the eight London special postgraduate hospitals, which combine treatment facilities with medical training and research.

In 1987/8 there were approximately 1737 hospitals in England alone. Hospitals provide facilities for the care of expectant and nursing mothers and young children, facilities for the prevention of illness and the care and after-care of persons suffering from illness, and other services which are needed for the diagnosis and treatment of illness. Private in-patients can be treated in NHS hospitals where they undertake to pay the full costs of hospital accommodation and services, and medical fees to a specialist. The total fee is agreed between doctor and patient. Hospital charges for private patients are determined by DHAs either on a local basis, or in line with a central recommended amount.

More patients than ever are being treated in fewer NHS hospital beds. Day-care attendances have increased by nearly 40% in the years 1981/7. There has been a continuing decline in the average number of private patients occupying beds in NHS hospitals. At the same time, the numbers of available beds in nursing homes and private hospitals has increased as well as the number of people with private medical insurance (see PRIVATE MEDICAL TREATMENT).

According to a report published on 8 Mar. 1990, there

are 1 million waiting to enter hospitals as in-patients. This is despite a government initiative, launched at the end of 1986, to improve the length of time people wait for hospital treatment, and the setting-up of a waiting list fund. This provided £31 million in 1988/90, and in 1990/1 will allocate £33 million. There are hugh regional variations in the numbers awaiting treatment (the highest is 85,000 in the North-East Thames RHA), as well as departmental variations in the numbers awaiting specialist treatment.

UK In-Patient Waiting List

1,000s	1976	1981	1986	1988	1989
General Surgery[1]	200.5	169.1	180.3	170.6	172.5
Orthopaedics	109.8	145.1	160.5	152.0	153.3
Ear, nose or throat	121.7	115.4	132.2	134.5	129.1
Gynaecology	91.8	105.6	106.6	98.3	98.5
Oral Surgery	26.5	35.5	56.3	51.4	51.3
Plastic Surgery	44.7	49.2	46.1	48.3	48.3
Ophthalmology	41.2	43.4	64.6	78.0	84.7
Urology[2]	22.0	29.1	42.7	46.6	48.4
Other	42.5	44.2	41.3	48.0	48.7
Total	700.8	736.6	830.6	827.7	834.8

[1] Included N. Ireland urology figures
[2] Great Britain only

At the end of March 1989, 53% of those on the in-patient waiting list and 68% of those on the day care list had been waiting for less than six months. However, 26% on the in-patient list had been waiting for over a year.

Many of the hospitals in the NHS are 19th century buildings. However, since 1979 over 270 health building schemes of over £1 million have been completed.

In 1990/91 over £300 million will be made available to

the NHS as a whole for the implementation of the NHS review and the white paper *Working for Patients*. The HCHS share of this will be around £180 million for current, and £70 million for capital expenditure. The white paper has been rejected by the Royal College of General Practitioners and the British Medical Association (BMA), the latter launching a campaign against the plans in 1989 and promising to block the implementation of the White Paper.

One of the most controversial proposals is the Government's intention to allow hospitals to apply for self-governing status as NHS Hospital Trusts. NHS Hospital Trusts would be able to earn revenue from the services they provided and be able to set rates of pay for their own staff and be able to borrow money. Finance would come directly from the Department of Health. In 1990 shadow boards of the first group of NHS Hospital Trusts will develop their future plans and by 1991 the first NHS Hospital Trusts will be established. The Labour Party has urged health workers to slow down the implementation of the reforms, since they would abandon the reforms once in office.

In September 1988 English HCHS staff in post totalled 793,400 whole time equivalents.

Primary health care services are offered by doctors, dentists, opticians, chiropodists and pharmacists within the health service, and by health visitors, district nurses and midwives employed by the health authorities; the latter working in close conjunction with the former. Health visitors are responsible for the preventative care and health education of all families, especially those with young children. About 15,000 district nurses give skilled nursing care in the home or elsewhere outside hospital; they also play an important role in preventative care and health education. Some ante-natal and most post-natal care is given in the community by midwives and GPs. The district nursing and health visiting services also include community psychiatric nursing for the mentally ill in the community and school nursing for children of all ages. A wide range of other services are offered. Remedial and therapeutic professions such as physiotherapy, occupational therapy and speech therapy are playing an increasingly important role in primary health care. Primary health care is also offered by community services run by DHAs, health centres and clinics, family planning clinics outside hospitals, and with preventative health services such as vaccination, immunisation, fluoridation and screening. The cervical screening programme aims to reduce deaths from cancer of the cervix by regularly screening women to identify and treat conditions that may develop into cancer. By 1988 all health authorities had computerised call and recall systems for women aged between 20 and 64 for cervical cancer screening. In 1987/8 almost 4.1 million smear tests were examined; 10.1% of these were positive. By 1988 all 14 regions in England had established their first breast screening centres and by 1990 all regions should have extended their services to provide a computerised call and recall system to screen all women aged between 50 and 64 every three years. It is planned to extend the service to cover all eligible women in the UK by 1991.

Family Practitioner Services

Family Practitioner Services (FPSs) comprise: the general medical services; the pharmaceutical services; the dental service; the general ophthalmic services. These services are provided by independent prac-

National Health Service Hospital Summary: All Specialities

	1971	1976	1981	1984	1985	1986	1987[1]
All In-Patients:							
Discharges and deaths (thousands)	6,437	6,525	7,179	7,666	7,884	7,959	8,088
Average number of staffed beds available daily (thousands)	526	484	450	429	421	409	392
Total average number of beds occupied daily (thousands)	436	394	366	347	341	330	317
Of which:-							
Maternities (thousands)	19	16	15	14	13	13	13
Other patients (thousands)	417	378	350	333	327	316	304
Patients treated per available bed	12.3	13.6	16.0	17.8	18.7	19.4	20.6
Average length of stay (days):							
Medical patients	14.7[2]	12.1	10.2[2]	9.1	8.7	8.5	—
Surgical patients	9.1[2]	8.6	7.6[2]	6.9	6.7	6.5	—
Maternities	7.0[2]	6.7	5.6[2]	4.9	4.7	4.5	—
% of live births in hospital[2]	89.8	97.6	98.9	99.0	99.1	99.1	99.2[4]
Private In-Patients:[3]							
Discharges and deaths (thousands)	115	95	98	79	71	—	—
Average number of beds occupied daily	2	2	1	1	1	—	—
Day case attendances (thousands)		565[2]	863	1,081	1,166	1,288	1,207
New out-patients (thousands)							
Accidents and emergency	9,358	10,463	11,342	12,279	12,492	12,682	12,797
Other out-patients	9,572	9,170	9,816	10,376	10,604	10,758	10,350
Average attendances per new patient:-							
Accidents and emergency	1.6	1.6	1.4	1.4	1.3	1.3	1.3
Other out-patients	4.2	4.0	4.4	4.3	4.3	4.3	4.2

1 Financial year ending 31 March 1988
2 Great Britain only
3 England and Wales only
4 United Kingdom

Health and Personal Social Services Staff in the UK

1,000s	1981	1983	1984	1985	1986	1987
Regional and District Health Authorities						
Medical and dental (excluding locums)	49.7	51.2	51.4	52.1	52.4	52.0
Nursing and Midwifery (excluding agency staff)	492.8	502.0	500.8	505.1	505.4	507.3
Professional and technical	80.2	84.7	89.2	91.2	93.4	96.8
Administration and clerical	133.3	135.2	135.5	136.7	137.2	141.2
Ancillary	220.1	213.6	198.1	184.1	167.4	156.6
Other non-medical	56.2	56.2	55.4	55.1	55.3	54.4
Total	1,032.3	1,042.9	1,030.4	1,024.3	1,011.1	1,008.3
Family Practitioner Services	54.3	56.8	58.2	59.3	57.3	58.4
Personal Social Services						
Social work staff	28.4	29.4	30.1	30.8	32.2	33.4
Managerial, administritive and ancillary	27.7	28.6	29.1	29.5	30.4	32.0
Other	194.8	204.9	207.1	211.8	217.7	222.7
Total	250.9	262.9	266.3	272.1	280.3	288.1
Total Health Service, Personal Social Services and Family Practitioner Services Staff	1,337.5	1,362.6	1,354.9	1.355.7	1.348.1	1.354.8

Department of Health and Office of Population Census and Surveys Expenditure Breakdown and Planned Expenditure 1984–1993 (£ million)

(England Only)	Out Turn				Estimated Out Turn	Planned Totals			
	1984/5	1985/6	1986/6	1987/8	1988/9	1989/90	1990/1	1991/2	1992/3
National Health Service Total Expenditure Current & Capital	13,396	14,159	15,165	16,649	18,391	19,962	21,982	23,260	24,430
Of which:- (Voted & Non-Voted)									
Hospitals, Community Health and Related Services	9,887	10,410	11,133	12,210	13,448	14,579	15,895	16,650	17,300
Family Practioner Services	3,090	3,274	3,513	3,899	4,401	4,738	5,386	5,880	6,370
Departmental Administration	117	136	150	150	164	204	229	240	240
Central Health and Miscellaneous Services	302	339	370	389	398	442	471	490	510
General Practice Finance Corporation					–20[1]				
Personal Social Services (Voted & Non-Voted)	15	15	16	18	17	23	27	20	30
Total Central Government Support to Local Authorities	86	93	88	92	106	116	144	130	140
Public Corporations	23	23	27	12	–49				
Total Department of Health	13,520	14,250	15,296	16,771	18,465	20,102	22,153	23,410	24,600
Total Office of Population, Census and Surveys	24	26	27	28	24	32	49	90	30
Total Department of Health/Office of Population Censuses and Surveys	13,544	14,315	15,323,	16,800	18,489	20,133	22,202	23,510	24,630

[1] Sale of share capital to Norwich Union Life Insurance Society for £145 million

titioners who may also treat fee-paying patients. Extensive use is made of the FPS not only by those who are ill, but also by those apparently in good health who seek advice and screening.

The FPS is administered by three bodies: Family Practitioner Committees (FPCs), in England and in Wales. FPCs, are, in turn, to be brought under the control of RHAs. They directly employ about 4000 staff; the Prescription Pricing Authority (PPA), who employ about 1720 staff; the Dental Practice Board (DPB), which employs about 1328 staff.

Cash expenditure on the FPS totalled £4401 million in 1988/9.

Family Doctor Service (General Medical Services). In 1988/9 there were 25,322 unrestricted principal general medical practitioners in England alone. Unrestricted principals provide a full range of general medical services and their lists are not limited to any particular type of person. There are about 200 million consultations a year with family doctors. The gross current expenditure on general medical services per medical practitioner (cash terms) is £55,229.

Family doctors usually provide the first diagnosis in the case of illness and either prescribe a course of treatment, or refer a patient to the more specialized services and hospital consultants.

Family doctors are remunerated for their NHS work in a variety of ways, including: a basic practice allowance; payment for out of hours work; capitation fees and reimbursement of certain practice expenses. They can also have fee-paying private patients. About 80% of family doctors in Britain work in partnership or group practices.

Anyone over 16 can choose their own doctor, and the doctor is also free to accept a person or not if they so choose. A person may change their doctor if they wish. Either at once, if they have changed address or obtained permission from the doctor on whose list they are, or by informing the FPC, in which case a fortnight must elapse before they can be accepted on the new doctor's list. The average list size for a family doctor service is 1999.

When people are away from home they can still use the general medical service as *temporary residents* and, in an emergency, any doctor in the service should give treatment and advice.

Patients are treated at the doctor's surgery or, when necessary, at home. Doctors may prescribe all drugs and medicines necessary for their treatment. They may also prescribe a certain number of surgical appliances (the rest being available from hospitals).

The *Working for Patients* White Paper includes new and controversial changes in funding for general practices. It is proposed to bring in: a performance-related contract for GPs, rewarding those who attract most patients and provide a greater range of services; FPC cash limited funds for GP staff; indicative drug budgets; GP funds; an enhanced managerial role for FPCs.

Pharmaceutical Services. Patients may obtain medicines, appliances and oral prescriptions prescribed under the NHS from any pharmacy registered with the FPC. Almost all pharmacies are registered in this manner. In England and Wales in 1988 there were about 10,400 registered pharmacies. In 1988/9 there were 9768 in England alone. There are also specialist appliance contractors and doctors' surgeries mainly in country areas may also dispense.

Charges for medical prescriptions were first introduced in 1951 to meet rising costs and demand in the newly-established NHS. The prescription charge of one shilling (5p), which was introduced, created a split in the then Labour Government.

Between the years 1976–89 charges rose from 20p per item to the present £3.05 per item. Contraceptives are provided free of charge. In fact, around 76% of prescriptions are still provided free of charge due to exemptions.

Exemptions cover: children under 16; students under 19 in full time education; men aged 65 and over; women aged 60 and over; pregnant women and mothers who have had a baby within the last year; people who suffer from certain medical disabilities; people who receive Income Support or Family Credit; people on low income; war pensioners (for their accepted disablements). People who are not exempt, but require frequent prescriptions can limit the amount they have to pay by purchasing a prepayment certificate, which covers all charges for a fixed term. These cost £14.50 for four months, or £40 for 12 months. Prepayment application is made on form FP 95 (EC95 in Scotland). The claim form for prescription exemption is AG1. Further information about prescription exemptions and prepayment arrangements is given in leaflet P11. All these can be obtained from local Social Security offices, surgeries, dentists, opticians, hospitals and post offices.

In 1988/9, about 376 million prescriptions were dispensed or administered. The gross cost of the pharmaceutical service per prescription (in cash terms) was £5.94. The total cost per person, including dispensing fees and cost was £44.10. This is the largest single element of total expenditure by the FPS.

There are wide regional variations in drug costs and the number of prescriptions, reflecting varying attitudes towards prescriptions and methods of treatment. In an attempt to contain the rise of medicinal costs the Government introduced a *Selected List* of drugs, which doctors may prescribe and an information system was formed to collect prescribing pattern data. With the NHS and Community Care Bill, which includes the *Working for Patients* White Paper recommendation and had by June 1990 received two Commons' readings, the Government intends to introduce indicative drug budgets for general practitioners. RHAs will have to set an annual drug budget for each FPC. The FPCs, after discussions with GPs will then set indicative drug budgets for each practice and then monitor the spending of practices. The performance of the FPCs is in turn monitored by the RHAs. The Government will only allow practices to exceed their budget in exceptional circumstances.

Under the Medicines Act 1968 the Health and Agriculture Ministers are responsible for licensing the manufacture, marketing and importation of medicines for human and veterinary use. The Medicines Commission advises the relevant Ministers on policy regarding medicinal products. The Committee on Safety of Medicines, on Dental and Surgical Materials and on the Review of Medicines, advise on the safety, quality and efficacy of medicinal products.

General practice pharmacists and hospital pharmacists have to be registered with the Pharmaceutical Society of Great Britain or the Pharmaceutical Society of Northern Ireland. Pharmacists take a three-year degree course before registration.

The Dental Service. Dentists, like doctors, can both take part in the service and have private patients. In 1988, there were 15,070 dentists in general practice in England alone. They are responsible to the FPC.

Patients are free to visit any dentist who takes part in the service and is willing to take them. Dentists are, at present, paid not per capita like doctors, instead they receive payment for items of treatment for individual patients. However, this method of payment is currently being reviewed.

Dental patients pay 75% of NHS dental treatment costs. The maxium charge for a course of treatment is £150. There is no charge for the arrest of bleeding, repairs to dentures, dental home visits or re-opening a surgery in an emergency. The same exemption rules apply for dental treatment as for the prescription service. The Health Departments have reached agreement in principle with the General Dental Services Committee (GDSC) of the British Dental Association on a proposed new contract for dentists, a final response from the GDSC is expected in July 1990. The main proposals are: all adult patients will be offered a treatment plan; emergency cover; guaranteed replacement at no cost to the patient. There is agreement to move to a national capitation system, rather than on an item of service basis, i.e. for each filling etc.

General Ophthalmic Services. General Ophthalmic Services form part of the NHS ophthalmic services and are administered by FPCs. The free NHS sight test from April 1989 is now restricted to certain priority groups: children under 16; full-time students under the age of 19; people and dependents in receipt of Family Credit or Income Support; others exempt on low income grounds; those entitled to complex lenses under the NHS voucher scheme; the registered blind and partially sighted; diagnosed diabetic and glaucoma patients; close relatives aged 40 or over of diagnosed glaucoma patients.

Certain groups are automatically entitled to help with the purchase of glasses under an NHS voucher scheme. These are: children under 16; full-time students under 19; people in receipt of Income Support or Family Credit and their dependents; people wearing certain complex lenses. The value of the voucher depends on the lenses required. Vouchers are used to offset the payment for glasses or contact lenses of the patient's choice. The same exemption forms apply.

Diagnosis and specialist treatments of sight defects and eye diseases are available through the Hospital Eye Service, as well as special types of glasses. Sight testing may only be carried out by ophthalmic medical practitioners or ophthalmic opticians and can cost up to £10.

The optician must hand the prescription, and a voucher if eligible, to the patient who can take this to registered ophthalmic and dispensing opticians. Only registered opticians can supply glasses to children, and those who are registered blind or partially sighted. Unregistered opticians can supply glasses to other adults only under prescribed conditions.

In 1988/9 there were 6210 opticians in England and nearly 12.5 million sight tests were performed.

The General Optical Council regulates the ophthalmic and dispensing optician profession. Training of ophthalmic opticians lasts four years, including one year in practice. Dispensing opticians, on the other hand, take a two-year course with a year's practical experience or a part-time day release course while employed with an optician.

Chiropody. In 1987/88, there were 2644 chiropodists and almost 1,950,000 people were treated.

NHS Administration

This is an increasingly complex area of health care in the UK. The Department of Health (which became a separate department with its own Secretary of State in July 1988) is responsible for NHS strategic planning, policy and service in England. In Scotland this task is performed by the Scottish Home and Health Departments; in Wales, by the Welsh Office and in Northern Ireland by the Department of Health and Social Services. The Department of Health, as well as its general functions as a central health department, includes the NHS Management Executive. Some 64% of its estimated £204 million expenditure is spent on general public health functions and the administration, management and policy development of the HPSS programmes. The dominant priority for 1989/90 is the implementation of the White Paper *Working for Patients*.

The Health Ministers (the Secretary of State for Health in England and the Secretaries of State for Scotland, Wales and Northern Ireland) are ultimately responsible for all aspects of the health services in their respective countries. It is their duty to promote a comprehensive Health Service designed to improve the mental and physical health of the people and the prevention, diagnosis and treatment of illness.

In 1973, the NHS Re-organisation Act changed the structure of NHS administration into a two tier system. The 1980 Health Services Act led to further structural changes in the administration. From April 1982, Area Health Authorities were removed and DHAs, 190 in England and nine in Wales, were made responsible for planning and operational management of all health services. In Scotland this task is performed by Health Boards. England has, in addition, a tier of 14 RHAs, which are responsible for: regional planning DHA resources allocation; major capital building work; the promotion of national policies and priorities and some hospital services. The Chairman and members of RHAs are appointed by the Secretary of State.

FPCs in England and Wales and Health Boards in Scotland arrange for the provision of services by doctors, dentists, pharmacists and opticians, as well as contributing to the planning of health services. All members of FPCs are appointed by and accountable to the Secretary of State.

Local and public opinion is represented on Community Health Councils in England and Wales, Health Councils in Scotland, and District Committees in Northern Ireland. Like Scotland, Northern Ireland has Health Boards which are responsible for the health services in their areas. Public opinion is represented on district committees.

Complaints from the public, which have not been resolved to their satisfaction by the RHA complaints procedure, are referred to the three separate health commissioners for England, Scotland and Wales. In Northern Ireland this role is provided by the Commissioner for Complaints.

The Parliamentary Commissioner and Health Service Commissioner is Sir Anthony Barrowclough QC Address: Church House, Great Smith Street, London SW1P 3BW. Tel: 071 276 3000.

The Griffiths Report of 1983 was responsible for the installation of general managers, from both inside and outside the NHS. General managers have responsibility for particular units and to monitor performance and encourage financial control.

On 31 January 1989 (following the NHS review commissioned by Mrs Thatcher), the Government's proposal for improving the hospital service and the organization of the NHS generally, were presented to parliament by Kenneth Clarke (Secretary of State for Health), Peter Walker (Wales), Malcolm Rifkind (Scotland) and Tom King (Northern Ireland). The resulting Bill is at present receiving its third reading in the Commons and has yet to receive the approval of the Lords. The Labour shadow health secretary, Mr Robin Cook, called the White Paper a prescription for a National Health Service run by accountants, written by people who will always put a healthy balance before healthy patients.

As part of these reforms new arrangements for the central management of the NHS have been introduced, including the establishment of the NHS Policy Board, with the Secretary of State as Chairman. This will determine the strategy, objectives and finances of the NHS in the light of Government policy. The former NHS Management Board has been restructured and relocated in Leeds as the NHS Management Executive, headed by D. Nichols CBE. This has responsibility for the operation and management of the NHS. It will set objectives for health authorities in line with Conservative Government policies and within given resources, and will monitor their performance. The executive will be accountable to the Policy Board for its operational management of the health service.

Central Health and Miscellaneous Services (CHMSs)

The objective of the CHMSs is to perform those functions which, it it said, are most effectively undertaken centrally, and to assist in the funding of health and personal social services provided through external public bodies and those in the voluntary sector. The three largest services it provides are the Welfare Food programme, the Disablement Services Authority and the Special Hospitals Service Authority. Expenditure on health information and education services is expected to be £42 million in 1989/90. It is planned to increase to £46 million in 1990/91. In England, health education is promoted by the Health Education Authority, whose functions are to: advise the Government on health education; plan and carry out national, regional, or local programmes in co-operation with health authorities and other bodies; sponsor research and evaluation; assist the provision of training; publish and distribute material; provide a national centre of information and advice on health education. In Wales, these functions are delegated to the Welsh Health Promotion Authority. Health education support services in Northern Ireland are provided by a Health Promotion Unit and legislation is being prepared to give this body statutory powers. In Scotland, health education is promoted by the Scottish Health Education Group.

General Practice Finance Corporation

On 22 March 1989, the Secretary of State announced that the Government had accepted an offer of £145 million from Norwich Union Life Insurance Society for the acquistion of all the share capital of the General Practice Finance Corporation.

Other NHS Services

Ambulance Services. For those in medical need, free transport by ambulance is provided by the health authorities. The ambulance service performs emergency work (dealing with sudden illness, urgent maternity cases, and accidents) and non-emergency services (providing transport for people needing out-patient treatment at hospitals, clinics and day hospitals). In some areas the non-emergency service is augmented by voluntary organizations using their own vehicles, competitive tendering to private firms, or by volunteers using their own cars. This is the sector which the Government wished to see increase. Indeed, a leaked management document not only disclosed plans to privatize non-emergency ambulance services in London, but also to run the accident and emergency service on commercial lines, and in the longer term to run the London Ambulance Service (LAS) as a self-governing trust, similar to the plans for hospitals (see HOSPITALS AND SPECIALIST SERVICES).

The London Ambulance Service is the largest in the world and its vehicles make a total of 1.6 million non-emergency journeys each year. It receives 2000 emergency calls a day.

There are 22,500 ambulance officers and ambulancemen/women. Ambulancemen/women constitute 81% of this total.

After a six-month pay dispute a settlement was reached on the 23 February 1990; it offered minimum increases of 17.6% on the basic wage by next April, but was unsupported by a long-term pay formula. The deal allowed both sides to claim victory. The cost to the health authorities of providing police and military ambulance cover during the six-month dispute is likely to be £30 million: three times the unions' original pay claim. The Department of Health has refused to make extra funds available to cover the cost for the substitute services.

There are now several air ambulance services in the UK.

Blood Transfusion Services. In 1987/8 in England and Wales this service collected 1981 million blood donations, 70% of which were packed red cells. Some 90,000 voluntary, unpaid donors give plasma each year; in Scotland the figures are 285,000 and 8000 respectively. The regional transfusion centres organise donor sessions and recruit donors, as well as: testing and grouping donated blood; maintaining blood banks; providing a hospital consultancy service; teaching in medical schools; providing instruction for doctors, nurses and technicians. Blood is manufactured and research undertaken at central laboratories. Blood is increasingly separated out into components, such as plasma, for specific uses. In 1987, a blood products laboratory was established in Elstree, Hertfordshire for the purpose of fulfilling the need for all blood products in England and Wales.

Organ transplants. The United Kingdom Transplant Service provides a centralised organ matching and distribution service for kidney, cornea, liver, heart, lung and pancreas organs. By the end of 1987 about 7600 people were living with functioning kidney transplants, and during 1988 over 1500 transplants were performed. In 1983, cornea transplant services were provided for the first time, about 1500 are transplanted each year.

There are four heart transplantation operational units at Papworth Hospital, Cambridgeshire (est. 1979), Harefield Hospital, West London (est. 1980), Freeman Hospital, Newcastle-upon-Tyne (est. 1986) and Wythenshawe Hospital, Manchester (est. 1988). Two further centres in London and Sheffield are expected to be opened in April 1990. A programme of combined heart and lung transplants is also operative. In 1988, 375 heart and heart-lung transplants were performed. In 1987, the world's first combined heart, lung and liver transplant was performed at Papworth Hospital. In 1988, over 200 liver transplants were completed. Pancreas transplants are also carried out.

Donor cards, available from surgeries and hospitals, enable people to indicate their consent to become organ donors when they die. A publicity campaign in 1988 was responsible for the distribution of 14 million donor cards. Several recent scandals concerning the sale of organs and donor consent (which led to the resignation of Dr R. Crockett as medical director of the National Kidney Centre) have been partly rectified by the Human Organ Transplants Act 1989, which placed a statutory ban on commercial dealings in organ transplantation and placed restrictions on the transplanting of human organs between people who are not genetically related.

Abortion. The Abortion Act 1967 allowed for the termination of pregnancy by a registered doctor before the 28th week of gestation, if two registered doctors considered that its continuance would involve a greater risk to the life of the pregnant woman (or injury to her physical or mental health or that of any existing children in the family) than if the pregnancy were terminated.

Termination may also be allowed if two doctors consider there is a substantial risk that the child would be born with a serious physical or mental handicap. Abortions are carried out in NHS hospitals, or in private premises approved by the Secretary of State. In 1988 the total number of terminations in England increased by 5.5% over 1987 to 179,612 – 65,077 in NHS hospitals; 114,535 in the private sector. 151,197 (84%) of abortions were performed in the first 12 gestation weeks.

On 24 April 1990 MPs voted by 382 to 141 to reduce the upper weekly limit for abortion to 24 weeks. However, a motion calling for a greater reduction to 18 weeks was rejected by 375 votes to 165.

Hospices. The hospice movement was founded in the UK and is now worldwide. A number of hospices provide care for the terminally ill, either in residential homes or through nursing and other assistance in the patient's own home. The major responsibility of the modern hospice service is the control of symptoms and therapeutic, psychological support for the patient and the patient's family. Only some of the hospices in the UK are NHS run; the remainder, some of which still receive public funding, are run by independent charities. As part of the Government's general health policy, greater co-operation is encouraged between the voluntary, private sector and public health authorities.

Rehabilitation. Rehabilitation services are vital for elderly, young disabled, mentally ill and mentally handicapped people, who need such help to resume life in the community. Co-ordinated services are available in hospitals, community centres and patients' own homes by a gamut of professional health workers, including doctors, nurses, physiotherapists, dietitians and social workers. These staff often work in close conjunction with other local authority and government departments. Medical services, appliances, and nursing aids are also available.

Research. Approximately £15.7 million was spent on health research in 1989/9, not including expenditure on the Medical Research Council. The Medical Research Council is the primary agency for biomedical and clinical research. Priority is accorded to AIDS research, primary health care, community care and child abuse.

International health care arrangements. European Community (EC) residents are entitled to receive free or reduced-cost medical treatment anywhere in the Community. There are also reciprocal arrangements to cover people who go to work or live in other countries. Available from Post Offices, form E111 covers travellers for health expenses in the EC. In addition, there are reciprocal arrangements with some other countries under which urgent medical treatment is available to visitors.

NHS Staff (see table HEALTH AND PERSONAL SOCIAL SERVICES STAFF IN THE UK)

The NHS is one of the largest employers in the world. Total UK NHS staff totalled over one million in 1988. When including personal social service and Family Practitioner Service staff the figure increases to 1,354,900 (1987).

Practising doctors and dentists in the NHS must be registered. They are taught in university medical and dental schools. Full registration for a doctor usually takes five or six years' training, with an additional year's practical training. Full registration for a dentist normally requires four or more years' training.

The medical profession is regulated by the General Medical Council (see QUANGOS); the regulatory body for dentists is the General Dental Council (see QUANGOS). The main professional associations for doctors and dentists are the British Medical Association and the British Dental Association respectively. For the nursing profession usually a minimum three years' training is required, before registration as a first-level nurse. Including senior nurses 1–8 and tutorial nursing staff, there were 118,299 qualified, registered nurses in England in 1987; as well as 66,074 enrolled nurses. Enrolled nurses require second-level registration and two years' (18 months training in Scotland).

Midwifery training for registered general nurses takes 18 months, and for other student midwives in England three years. There were a total of 19,000 hospital midwives in 1987. Health visitors (10,333) are registered general nurses, with midwifery or obstetric experience, who have successfully completed a year's health visiting training.

District nurses (8691) are registered general nurses who have successfully completed a six-month course followed by a period of supervised district nursing.

The UK examing bodies for all these professions respectively are the National Boards for Nursing, Midwifery and Health Visiting.

The regulatory and registry body is the United Kingdom Central Council for Nursing, Midwifery and Health Visiting.

State registration is also compulsory for NHS employment of chiropodists, dietitians, occupational therapists and physiotherapists, orthoptists, medical laboratory scientific officers and radiographers. There are seven governing boards for each of these professions, all of which are under the general supervision of the Council for Professions Supplementary to Medicine.

GOVERNMENT PUBLIC HEALTH AIMS

The Secretary of State has outlined some specific public health aims: to safeguard public health through effective policies on drug abuse (including smoking and drinking); food and water safety; environmental hazards, diet and the prevention of communicable disease; to carry forward the Government's decisions on community care (see PERSONAL SOCIAL SERVICES); to maintain momentum on containing HIV infection and AIDS; to ensure adequate services for the victims of child abuse.

Drug Abuse

Alcohol. The far-reaching effects of alcohol misuse in terms of illness, family disruption, inefficiency at work, loss of earnings, accidents and crime are widely acknowledged. The Government considers that the reduction of such misuse requires a range of action by central and local government, voluntary and community bodies, the health professions, business and trade unions.

The Conservative Government believes that emphasis should be placed on policies to prevent alcohol misuse, and continues to seek better information about the causes of problem drinking, to encourage a healthier living style, and to provide earlier identification and help for the problem drinker.

According to the Office of Population Censuses and Surveys, average weekly consumption of alcohol by adult females increased by 14% between 1978 and 1987, though it still remains significantly lower than the units of alcohol males consume per week (15.5 units, overall average). The most marked increase is the 50% rise in the consumption patterns for divorced or separated males. There is also the worrying relationship between road accidents and drinking. During the late evening and early morning, more than half of all those killed in road accidents are found to have blood alcohol levels in excess of the legal limit and 80% of pedestrians killed between 10pm and 4am have high levels.

Treatment and rehabilitation for alcoholics include in-patient and out-patient services in general and psychiatric hospitals and specialized alcoholism treatment units. An integral role is also played by primary health care teams and voluntary organizations providing hostels, day centres and counselling services. Close co-operation exists between statutory and voluntary bodies; the national voluntary agency, Alcohol Concern, received a government grant of £680,000 in 1988/9. Alcohol Concern plays a prominent role in prevention of misuse, training for professional and voluntary workers and improving the network of local voluntary agencies and their co-operation with statutory authorities. In 1988, Al-Anon Family Groups (including Alateen), which provide support for families and friends of problem drinkers in the UK and the Republic of Ireland, had 12,200 clients. Alcoholics Anonymous in Britain received 45,000 clients.

Smoking. Cigarette smoking is the greatest preventable cause of disease and death. It accounts for no fewer than 100,000 premature deaths and 30 million lost working days each year, and costs £500 million a year for the treatment of diseases attributable to smoking. A quarter of all deaths in 1988 were from cancer. In particular, death from lung cancer amongst women in 1988 was 50% higher than in 1974. (Yet, the largest cancer killer of woment is cancer of the breast). Smoking by pregnant women can cause prematurity and low birth weight in infants. National publicity and media campaigns are the main thrust of government policy to discourage and reduce the level of smoking. In 1988, tobacco accounted for £7,945 million (2.8%) of household expenditure. The Government aims to reduce adult smoking from a current level of 33% and to halve smoking by young people.

A multi-media campaign directed at teenage smoking was launched on 11 Dec. 1989 and is expected to continue until 1994. The Government considers it particularly imperative to get the message across to teenage girls, who are twice as likely to smoke as boys. A sample of over 1,500 children showed that in 1988 just under 60% of 11–15 year olds in England had never smoked. However, 12% of boys and 14% of girls were regular or occasional smokers. Since 1984 smoking amongst schoolchildren has been declining.

In recent years voluntary restrictions on smoking in public places, such as trains, buses and theatres, have been introduced. Commercial premises have also restricted smoking to smoking rooms or banned it altogether. Ford, TSB, British Gas, British Telecom and the Prudential are among them. Marks and Spencers staff have been liable for dismissal since 1959 for smoking in cigarette-free zones. The voluntary body, Action on Smoking and Health (ASH), has done much to promote changes in this and other fields. The Government estimates that passive smoking causes several hundred lung cancer deaths each year.

Voluntary agreements between the Government and the tobacco industry regulate the advertising and promotion of tobacco products, changes in these products, and sports sponsorship by tobacco companies. On Mar. 14 1990 (National No Smoking Day), the European Parliament voted for a total ban on all forms of tobacco advertising. In the UK an agreement on tobacco advertising was introduced in 1986. This provides for the use of six different health warnings about the dangers of smoking. Many health workers were concerned that the link between smoking and heart disease, lung cancer and bronchitis was still not explicitly stated on the packet. The agreement also provided measures to protect particularly vulnerable groups, such as children, young people, and young women in early chilbearing years. The Protection of Children (Tobacco) Act 1986 makes the sale of any type of tobacco product to children illegal. Cigarette advertising is banned on television and radio by law. In 1987 a new voluntary agreement on sports sponsorship came into force. This covers levels of overall expenditure, restrictions on sponsorship for sports events whose spectators are mainly under 18 years, and controls over the siting of display advertising at televised events. Proposals to ban certain oral tobacco products which are causally linked to cancer have also been announced.

Illicit drugs. In 1988, some 30,315 persons were found guilty, cautioned or dealt with by compounding, for drug offences. 86% of these were for unlawful possession offences. The increase in the misuse of hard drugs such as heroin, cocaine and now crack, has become a serious social and health problem. The Government has made the fight against illicit drug misuse one of its major priorities. Its strategy is multifold: to halt the supply from source; to provide more effective law enforcement by police and the customs service; to tighten controls on drugs produced and supplied in Britain; to provide stricter sentences for offenders; to discourage youths from expermenting with drugs; to develop effective treatment and rehabilitation for drug misusers. In 1988, an interdepartmental, ministerial group was formed to review implementation of these measures and develop further strategies.

A significant part of prevention is public education. In 1985, a campaign was launched aimed primarily at dissuading young people from taking drugs and informing parents, teachers and others on the ways to recognise the problems of drug dependency. In 1987, the campaign was broadened to include warning of the dangers of sharing needles and syringes in the transmission of the AIDS virus. Another phase of the campaign, begun in 1988, was directed at those in the 16–25 age group who were occasional injectors of amphetamines or users of pharmaceutical drugs. The problem of legally prescribed drugs is, numerically at least, a greater one. Despite significant reductions, in 1987 there were over 25 million benzodiazepine prescriptions and over 1 million barbiturate prescriptions. This compares to 4630 notified heroin addicts, 576 notified methadone addicts and 462 notified cocaine addicts.

In 1988, some £9.5 million was made available by English health authorities for treatment and rehabilitation services for drug addicts. This includes £1 million for services to deal with the spread of HIV infection. In 1989/90, the total is estimated to increase to £15 million. Similar services are available in Scotland, Wales and Northern Ireland.

The Government has set up a drugs advisory service to advise DHAs on the availability of services in their areas. The Government is, in turn, advising on drug misuse matters and associated social concerns by the Advisory Council on the Misuse of Drugs.

Drug dependency treatment is usually provided on an out-patient basis. Many NHS hospitals provide specialist treatment, or special drug treatment units for drug misusers. Family practitioners also treat drug misusers, but only some specialist doctors are licensed to prescribe heroin, methadone, cocaine and dipipanone (Diconal). All doctors are duty-bound to notify authorities of any patient who is addicted to controlled drugs; other medical practice guidelines have been issued to all Britain's doctors. The Home Secretary has statutory powers for dealing with doctors who have prescribed irresponsibly.

A number of mainly voluntary agencies combine and co-operate with the health authorities. These include advice and rehabilitation services in residential facilities. Community support is provided by the probation services and local social services departments.

Also of concern is the incidence of solvent abuse, e.g. glue sniffing, by young people. In 1983, Scottish legislation added solvent abuse to the reason why a child might be considered for community care. From 1985 it became an offence in England and Wales to supply solvents to children under 18 in the knowledge or suspicion that they are to be used for intoxication. Public information and guidance leaflets have also been issued.

Food and Water Safety

Food Safety. The average annual figure of formally notified cases of food poisoning in the 1980s is 90% greater than the same figure for the 1970s. This can be attributable only in part to increased public awareness with the recent eggs and salmonella bacteria scare, dangerous amounts of benzine in Perrier bottled spring water, and listeria in soft cheeses and paté. In February 1989, the Government established the Committee on Microbiological Food Safety. Its function is to examine the increasing incidence of food-borne illnesses (particularly from salmonella, botulism, listeria and campylobacter) and to recommend action where necessary. Proposals to strengthen food safety laws were published in white paper form in July 1989. They include tighter controls and new enforcement measures on food unfit for consumption, extended powers to cover new technical developments (one controversial recent development is the proposal to sell food which has been irradiated to give it a longer shelf-life) and the introduction of compulsory registration of premises (where food and drink is prepared, handled, stored or sold) in order to enforce tighter hygiene standards. Special regulations govern safety levels of foods such as milk, eggs, meat, ice-cream and shellfish. Local Authority Environmental health officers are responsible for taking and analysing samples of food, both at retail and distribution levels.

Water Safety. (see NITRATES)

Environmental Hazards, Diet and the Prevention of Communicable Disease

Environmental Hazards. Environmental health officers are also responsible for the control of air and noise pollution; occupational health and safety aspects in both civic, commercial and private buildings; investigating unfit, dangerous housing; in some cases for refuse collection and home safety. At ports and airports they are responsible in addition for the inspection of imported foods and disease control. In Northern Ireland these duties are performed by district councils. An example of the work that environmental health officers perform is their inspection of Irish meat products, which they discovered had bovine spongiform encephalopathy (BSE) or mad cow disease. The beef had supposedly been allowed into the food chain through a loophole in government regulations concerning BSE in imported meat, although the Agriculture Minister (John MacGregor) stated on 21 December 1989 that it had not entered the food chain. Reported cases of BSE in Britain totalled 10,736 in March 1990. The Government have provided £12 million for research into BSE.

Diet. In 1988, heart diseases, including heart attacks and strokes accounted for nearly a half of all deaths.

There has been an increasing public awareness of the importance of a healthy, balanced diet. The nutritional content of a person's diet relies on the balance of foods that are consumed. The 1984 report on diet and cardiovascular disease produced by the Government recommended a reduction of fat (especially saturated fatty acids) in the diet to reduce or delay the incidence of cardiovascular disease. The British Dietary Foundation and the Scottish Health Education Group produce practical dietary information.

Fatty acids increase the cholesterol level in susceptible individuals, which in turn is associated with an increased risk of coronary heart disease. It is also planned to make the labelling of fat content in foods a statutory requirement, in addition to the present voluntary nutritional labelling of foodstuffs. Total fat intake has fallen by approximately 15% between 1959 and 1988, yet total energy intake has fallen by a similar proportion thus the percentage of energy derived from fat has remained at about 42%. Still, there is a shift in the types of fat consumed: consumption of saturated fatty acids has fallen by nearly a third since 1969, whilst the intake of polyunsaturated fatty acids has risen by 29%. The Department of Health has recommended that people should reduce their fat intake to 35%, or below, of their energy intake. Similarly, it recommends limiting consumption of saturated and trans fatty acids to a maximun of 15% of energy intake.

High intakes of some kinds of dietary fibre are associated with a reduced incidence of coronary heart disease. However, despite an increase in the consumption of wholemeal bread and bran breakfast cereals, it appears that the total fibre content of the average diet in the UK has not changed significantly in the century. The importance of healthy eating as a means of preventing illness and disease is emphasised in programmes such as the Look After Your Heart campaign. The Chief Medical Officer's Committee on Medical Aspects of Food Policy (COMA) has been reviewing the latest scientific evidence in two important dietary areas: the consumption of sugars, on which a report was published on 13 December 1989, and daily requirements for nutrients.

Infectious Diseases. Since 1981 there has been a dramatic decline in the number of deaths from infectious diseases. Measles remains the most prevalent notifiable infectious disease (39,825 in 1987); like the majority of infectious diseases there is an epidemic cycle about every three years, the last being in 1988. However, the peaks of successive epidemics decrease as the uptake of measles vaccination increases. In October 1988, a new combined, single-injection vaccine against measles, mumps and rubella was introduced. In 1989, some £7.8 million was allocated for the purchase of this new vaccine. The programme has a 90% take-up target in line with the World Health Organisation recommendations. A batch of this vaccine was withdrawn for analysis following the death of an 11-year old boy from inflammation of the brain shortly after he had been vaccinated.

Food poisoning is the next largest notifiable infectious disease (19,048 in 1987), more than doubling in the last decade. Notifications of whooping cough dropped rapidly between 1951 and 1961, since then there have been occasional epidemics as whooping cough has a three to four year cycle. The last peak was in 1986 with 34,361 notifications, almost half of the previous cycle peak (62,470 in 1982), again because of increased immunisation through vaccines. Immunisation uptake rates more than doubled in the last decade; immunisation is voluntary.

Acute poliomyelitis is, thanks to immunisation, now virtually eliminated and great progress has also been made in reducing the risk of the various tubercular diseases.

The Public Health Laboratory Service provides a national network of bacteriological and virological laboratories throughout England and Wales, which conduct research and assist in the diagnosis, prevention and control of communicable disease. The primary site is the Central Public Health Laboratory, Colindale, North-West London. This includes the National Collection of Type Cultures, the Food Hygiene Laboratory and reference laboratories specialising in identification of infective micro-organisms. Two surveillance centres, one in England and one in Scotland, investigate and monitor human communicable diseases. Microbiological work in Scotland and Northern Ireland is usually undertaken by hospital laboratories.

Community Care (see PERSONAL SOCIAL SERVICES)

Human Immunodeficiency Virus (HIV) and **Acquired Immune Deficiency Syndrome (AIDS)**

HIV, which is the cause of AIDS, is transmitted through: vaginal, oral, or anal intercourse; injection into the bloodstream of blood from an infected person (usually in the process of injecting drugs); receiving infected blood products and from an infected mother to her baby. Breakthroughs in the treatment of the disease have been limited to the development and use of drugs. At the beginning of 1987 the launch of a new £14.8 million research programme was announced; this aims to provide a vaccine against HIV infection and new anti-viral drugs for those already infected. There is, as yet, no known cure for AIDS. However a new drug called Retrovir (zidovudine-AZT) which can prolong the life and improve the health of some AIDS sufferers, has been developed. It is likely that almost all those infected with HIV will die within 15 years. The total UK AIDS figures for 1989 are 2830 of which 1612 (57%) have died so far. Eighty per cent of the total were homosexual or bisexual males. About 2% are believed to have contracted AIDS through heterosexual intercourse. The UK has an average of 41.7 cases of AIDS per million of the population, below the European average. The World Health Organisation (WHO) reports a worldwide total of just under 178,000 cases of AIDS, 100,000 of which are in the USA. By the end of June 1989, some 10,794 HIV antibody-positive cases had been reported in the UK. Nearly half of these cases were homosexual or bisexual males, with male injecting drug users and male haemophiliacs being the next largest groups with 10% of the total.

Some 1200 haemophiliacs were infected with HIV in the early 1980s from being given contaminated manufactured Factor VIII (a blood-clotting agent) imported from the USA. Since 1985 all blood has been screened for the HIV antibody, and blood products for haemophiliacs have been heat treated where possible. A government grant of £10 million to the Haemophilia Society in Britain established a trust fund for those who have become infected with the AIDS virus via contaminated blood products.

In the present situation health education and other preventive strategies to engender change in sexual and drug misusing behaviour seem to offer the most effective way of combating the spread of AIDS. In England the Health Education Authority has executive and budgetary responsibility for public education about AIDS. For those already infected or at risk, the Government provides diagnostic and treatment facilities, counselling and support services. Much of this work is done by voluntary agencies such as the Terence Higgins Trust, London Lighthouse and Scottish AIDS Monitor. Both London Lighthouse and the Mildmay Mission Hospital provide hospice care (SEE HOSPICES) and community support. These agencies received about £1.8 million in 1989.

Funding is also made available to health authorities for treatment and counselling services, experimental schemes, e.g. Maryland Centre, counselling of drug misusers and the exchange of clean needles and syringes for used, since the sharing of equipment is one of the main ways by which the AIDS virus spreads among drug users. Under the AIDS (Control) Act 1987, each health authority is required to publish annual reports on provided and planned services.

1986 saw the launch of a major public education campaign involving most areas of media, broadcasting and entertainment, leafleting to all British households, as well as the establishment of a free national telephone advisory service. In 1988, more campaigns were launched aimed at the general population, business people travelling within the UK and abroad and drug-misusers. By March 1989 some £32.5 million had been spent on public health education. The planned total for the AIDS publicity campaign is £10 million in 1990/1. In 1989/90 health authorities were allocated £122 million as a contribution to the costs of providing HIV related services.

Another important measure in controlling the spread of AIDS is international co-operation, not only through the European Community, but also by the work of the WHO. Britain has committed £12.25 million to WHO's Global Programme on AIDS, which is helping developing countries establish national AIDS control programmes. It has also agreed to give £6.34 million in support of African and Caribbean programmes, and is to give about £1.6 million to the International Planned Federation for AIDS-related activities.

In January 1988, Britain hosted the World Summit of Ministers of Health on Programmes for AIDS Prevention. The resulting London Declaration stressed the need for governments to take urgent action in the face of the global threat from AIDS and stated the primary role of education in this process and the need to protect human rights.

Services for the Victims of Child Abuse

In 1988, a survey conducted of 40,900 children and young persons on the Child Protection Registers in England and Wales showed that younger children were more likely to be on the register than older children and of those the highest rates were in the 1–4 and 5–9 age ranges. Overall girls were more likely to be on the list, especially in the age range 16 and over, where girls were nearly three times as likely to be on the register. Twenty-eight per cent of the total had suffered physical abuse, 15% sexual abuse and 37% were of grave concern. Later that year the Cleveland Enquiry report into the high incidence of children being removed to a place of safety because of suspected child abuse in Cleveland was published.

The Department of Health's response was to issue, in turn, *Working Together*, an inter-agency guide to co-operation in the protection of children from abuse. The Criminal Justice Act 1988, and in Northern Ireland the Police and Criminal Evidence (Northern Ireland) Act 1989, made it possible for children under the age of 14 to give live television evidence to courts. (see PERSONAL SOCIAL SERVICES)

Private Medicine

The Conservative Government has sought to encourage private-sector medical treatment in a number of ways, including tax concessions. From 6 April 1990, income tax relief is provided on private medical insurance premiums for those aged 60 and over at a cost of £40 million to the Exchequer in 1990/1.

The scale of private practice is small in relation to the NHS. There are 10,000 beds available in the private-health sector. By 1986, some 65,100 beds were available in registered nursing homes and private hospitals, nearly doubling in five years. One thousand NHS beds are occupied daily by private patients. Approximately 3000 beds in English health service hospitals are authorised for the treatment of private patients. Some health authorities share facilities with private hospitals, and NHS patients are occasionally treated in private hospitals.

It is estimated that about 75% of those receiving acute treatment in private hospitals or NHS hospital pay-beds are covered by provident schemes providing for private health care in return for annual payments. In 1985, it was estimated that British United Provident Association, Private Patients Plan and Western Provident Association accounted for 92% of all private medical insurance subscription income. Over 2.5 million people subscribe to private medical insurance schemes, and in 1987 over 5.3 million people were insured privately for private treatment. Some 45% of policy holders had part or all of their subscriptions paid by an employer in 1987.

Private practice may also be undertaken by family doctors and dentists. Alternative medical treatment such as homeopathy, osteopathy and acupuncture are usually practised outside the NHS.

Perhaps the most internationally recognized centre for private treatment in the UK is Harley Street.

Personal Social Services

In England and Wales, responsibility for personal social services rests with local authority social services departments; in Scotland, with the social work departments; in Northern Ireland, with the social services board.

Personal social services are required for the aged, children and young people, families, people with mental illness, people with physical or mental handicaps, juvenile offenders, and other socially disadvantaged, vulnerable members of the public.

The primary services offered include residential care, day care, domiciliary services and other social work. Local authorities also have responsibilities to provide services for children who cannot be cared for by their own parents. In Scotland, local authorities have the additional responsibility of probation and prison after-care services.

However, public expenditure economies have meant increasing voluntary and private-sector involvement in personal social services. Government policy has shifted away from the statutory sector hospitals and homes, to community care for those in need.

Government proposals for the future management and organisation of community care services are encapsulated in the White Paper *Caring for People: Community Care in the Next Decade and Beyond*, which was published in November 1989. This will establish a new financial and managerial framework for the personal social services, following the 1988 review. The NHS and Community Care Bill 1989 to bring into effect the Government's care proposals, which place more emphasis and responsibility on the voluntary sector to meet the extra demand. The voluntary sector includes self-help groups and families. (see VOLUNTARY SERVICES)

Elderly Persons

In 1988, there were 8.9 million people aged 65 and over (15.6% of the total UK population), an increase of 3.4 million within the last four decades. By 2006, it is projected that 16.2% of the resident population will be over 65. An increasingly ageing population means greater demand for health and social services. In 1987, nearly 243,000 people (2.7%) aged 65 and over were resident in local authority, registered voluntary or private homes in the UK. Homes for the elderly are registered under the Registered Homes Act 1984. Recently, there has been some controversy about facilities for the elderly in some privately-run homes. This is particularly worrying considering the shift in the burden for elderly care from the public sector to the voluntary and private sectors. In 1980, a third of elderly residents were in registered voluntary and private homes; by 1987 this had risen to a half.

Social service authorities provide residential homes for the elderly and infirm, and are in charge of registering and inspecting homes run by voluntary and private organizations. Provision for the elderly includes social work, advice and help, meals-on-wheels, sitters, night attendants and laundry services, as well as day centres (588 in England), luncheon clubs and recreation facilities. Local authorities also usually provide free or subsidised travel for elderly people.

As part of their responsibility for public housing, local authories also provide specially-designed accommodation (some of which is sheltered). Housing associations and private contractors also build this type of housing.

Disabled

Britain has approximately 6 million adults with one or more disabilities, 400,000 (7%) of which live in a communal environment. There are also 1,227,600 people registered as substantially and permanently handicapped.

Local social services help with social rehabilitation, counselling, adjustment and care for those with disabilities. They are also responsible for: registering disabled persons in their areas; occupational, educational, social and recreation facilities; adaptations to private dwellings (76,400 in England) and local authority dwellings (17,400 in England), such as wheelchair ramps and disabled toilets; installation of living aids, such as communications equipment (in 1987, 14,800 telephones were installed): installing some televisions and radios; meals-on-wheels (33,100 in England in 1988); care attendant help; orange vehicle badges for the disabled (778,400 on issue to individuals in England in 1988).

In June 1988, a £5 million Independent Living Fund was established by the Government to provide financial support for the 761,000 very severely handicapped in England. The scheme will run for five years.

Mental Handicaps

Social service authorities are responsible for services to people with mental handicaps and their families. Such services can include day and short-term care, domestic support for families, accommodation provisions and adult training centres. In 1988, there were 585 such local authority day centres and adult training centres for the mentally-handicapped. The principal aims of the service are to help ensure that all people with mental handicaps can lead full lives in their own communities and that no person should be admitted to hospital, unless on strictly medical grounds. Specialized residential health provision is available for those with special needs.

In 1987, there were a total of 647 local authority homes and hostels in England with some 3512 places.

Mentally ill

Local authority social services departments are responsible for providing preventative and after-care services for the mentally ill. These include day centres (171 in England), social centres and residential care.

Social workers work with patients and families to deal with social and family problems, which may arise from mental illness.

In 1983 (1984 in Scotland, 1986 in Northern Ireland) the rights of compulsorily-detained patients were extended by statute law, and the Mental Health Act Commission was established to ensure stringent safeguards.

Families

The Conservative Government has stressed the centrality of the family to social well-being, despite the fact that one in three marriages is now likely to end in divorce and the UK having the second largest divorce rate in the EC.

Social services authorities, via social and other workers, give various sorts of help to families with special problems. This includes services for: children at risk of injury, abuse or neglect who require care away from the family unit; support for family carers looking after elderly and other family members. There are also services for single parents (4.7% of the population), including unmarried mothers, and women's refuges run by local authorities or voluntary organisations. Refuge is provided for women who face intolerable home conditions. These refuges provide vital support and short term accommodation, and attempt to alleviate the women's problems.

Many authorities also contribute to voluntary family social work (such as the Marriage Guidance Council, now known as Relate).

In September 1989, the Government provided funds worth £2 million for encouraging voluntary-sector provision of research and day-care services for families in temporary accommodation.

Children (see also CHILD ABUSE)

Local authorities, voluntary bodies and private institutions provide day-care facilities for children under 5. Local authorities in England provide some 688 day nurseries for 34,398 children; they also run 109 playgroups for 3,205 children.

Priority for places is given to children with special social or health needs for day care. They also register, give support and advice to childminders and private day nurseries. In England in 1988, there were 73,686 registered childminders, 17,026 registered playgroups and 1355 registered day nurseries.

Authorities are obliged to receive into their care any child under 17 who has no parent or guardian, or who has been abandoned, or whose parents are unable to look after them, only if they are satisfied that intervention is in the child's interest or well-being. In 1987, there were approximately 66,000 in local authority care (.06% of all under 18s in the UK). The child may remain in care until 18, unless discharged to the care of parents, other relatives or friends. In some cases the local authority might assume the rights and duties of one or both parents. The parents must be told, and if they object, the matter is referred to a law court.

In England and Wales, children who are neglected, maltreated, exposed to moral danger, out of the control of their parents, not attending school (10 or over), or have committed an offence (other than homicide), can be brought before a juvenile court. However, it must be proven that the children need care and control, which cannot be provided without a court order.

Local authorities are responsible for implementing inquiries via social workers and parental consultation, schools and the police. Children may either be committed to local authority control, or placed under probation officer or social worker supervision.

Greater use is being made of intermediate treatment, which provides a community-based service with supervised activities, group work and individual counselling. A requirement to attend such a programme can be made by the court.

In Northern Ireland, there is as yet no intermediate provision, but the court may send children in need or trouble to a training school, commit them to the care of a fit person, or make a supervision order.

In Scotland, children in trouble or in need can be brought before a children's hearing, which can impose a supervision requirement on a child if it thinks that compulsory measures of care are appropriate. These are reviewed at less than annual intervals, until the requirement is taken away by a children's hearing or by the Secretary of State.

The Children Act 1989, which the Government intends to implement by October 1991, will reform the legislative framework for child services, care and protection. A specific grant was introduced in 1989/90 to provide support of £7 million towards expenditure of £10 million on training for social services staff working in the child-care field, with particular emphasis on training for those dealing with child protection and child abuse. In 1990/1 £7.3 million will be provided to support expenditure of £10.4 million.

Adoption

Local authorities are required by law to provide an adoption service, either directly, or in conjunction with a voluntary organization. Agencies may offer prospective adoptive families an allowance if this helps to find a family for a child. Adoption procedures are strictly regulated by statute, and adoption societies must be approved by the respective social services Minister. The Registrars-General keep confidential registers of adopted children. Adopted people may be given details of their original birth record on reaching the age of 18, and counselling is provided to help them understand the circumstances of their adoption. Adoption orders cannot be revoked.

Custodianship

In Britain, a person, e.g. foster parent or step-parent, who has cared for a child for some time may apply to a court for a custodianship order giving him or her legal custody of the child. The custodian assumes parental rights and duties. The order may, however, be revoked.

Personal Social Services Staff

Social Workers

Social work training courses, e.g. CQSW, are offered in universities, polytechnics, Scottish Central Institutions and colleges of further education. The length of the course can be one to four years, depending on educational qualifications and previous work experience. The Central Council for Education and Training in Social Work is the regulatory, statutory body responsible for social work training and also acts as an advisory body for those considering a career in the profession. The council has also proposed a range of improvements in the present training systems. Address: Derbyshire House, St. Chad's Street, London WC1H 8AD. Director: A. Hall.

The effective operation of the personal social services in the UK depends to a large extent on professionally qualified social workers trained in social work methods.

Voluntary Social Services. The Conservative government is placing increasing emphasis and financial encouragement on this sector of social services. Co-operation between the public and voluntary sectors is vital to the shift towards local community care. Government interests are represented in the voluntary sector by the Home Office Voluntary Services Unit.

Voluntary organizations derive their incomes in various ways: voluntary public contributions; central and local government grants; commercial activities and investments; from contractual charges for services provided for local and central government. Over 500 voluntary bodies are given direct grant aid from government health and social services departments. In 1987/8, this amounted to in excess of £37 million out of total central government funding of £293 million. Futhermore, tax inducements in recent budgets have helped the voluntary movement secure more donations from individuals and institutions. The Charities Aid Foundation is an independent body responsible for ensuring the flow of funds from individuals, grant-making trusts and institutions.

Over 65,000 voluntary organizations are registered as charities with the Charity Commission, which also provides advice to charitable organizations and holds charitable investments. Charitable status is afforded to voluntary organizations if they are founded for: poverty relief; educational and religious advancement; promotion of other social benefits such as the prevention of racial discrimination; the promotion of equal opportunities.

The most rapidly expanding area of the voluntary sector are self-help groups, e.g. voluntary playgroups and women's groups. Many voluntary organizations belong to larger associations, or are represented on local or national co-ordinating councils or committees. Some are concerned with providing personal services, whilst others deal with the formation of public opinion and exchange of information. An expanding part of the sector are voluntary cultural and environmental groups (the largest being the National Trust with 1,634,000 members in 1988).

The main co-ordinating bodies (England – National Council for Voluntary Organizations; Scotland – Scottish Council for Community and Voluntary Organizations; Northern Ireland – Council for Voluntary Action) seek to establish co-operation between the public, private and voluntary sectors.

Voluntary organizations which specialize in personal social services include the National Association for the Prevention of Cruelty to Children (NSPCC), marriage guidance councils who are affiliated to Relate; Child Poverty Action Group; the Samaritans.

Young people's voluntary groups include the Scouts and Girl Guides and the Community Service Volunteers.

Voluntary groups which contribute to the care of sick and disabled people include the British Red Cross Society (57,000 members); St John Ambulance (78,600 members in the UK in 1988 excluding Scotland), who were drafted into public-sector ambulance work during the ambulance dispute; the Women's Royal Voluntary Service (160,000 members in 1988); the League of Hospital Friends. Societies which help with specific disabilities and difficulties include: the Royal National Institute for the Blind (in 1988 there were 133,700 registered blind persons in England alone); the Royal National Institute for the Deaf (in 1988 there were 34,100 registered deaf persons and 63,400 registered hard-of-hearing persons); the Royal Association for Disability and Rehabilitation; the Disabled Living Foundation; the Disablement Income Group; National Association for Mental Health (MIND); the Royal Society for Mentally Handicapped Children and Adults (MENCAP); the Spastics Society; Alcoholics Anonymous; Age Concern; Help the Aged; other equivalent organizations in Wales, Scotland and Northern Ireland.

The Women's Royal Voluntary Service provides: meals-on-wheels services to the elderly and the disabled; flats and residential clubs for the aged; family problem counselling; assists in hospital and clinics during emergencies.

Enquiries, explanation and advice on rights and the social services available in each area is available from the Citizen's Advice Bureaux (CAB), law centres and housing advice centres.

HISTORY

Until c.18,000 BC, ice made all but a narrow strip of southern England uninhabitable. The area was not yet cut off from the mainland of Europe, and early humans crossed the land bridge as seasonal visitors during this ice age: Lower Palaeolithic hunters (c.250,000–100,000 BC), Neanderthalers (c.130,000–40,000 BC), and modern homo sapiens from c.38,000 BC onwards. As the ice retreated and tundra yielded to forest, human occupation spread northwards into Scotland. By c.7500 BC Mesolithic hunters with domesticated dogs and bows and arrows prevailed. By 6000 BC Britain was an island.

The first Neolithic farmers arrived from the Continent in the 4th millenium BC and began forest clearance, making permanent settlements and building megalithic tombs and the earliest stone circles. Occupation spread to poorer, lighter soils during the 3rd millenium, and social elites emerged with widespread trading contacts. Late Neolithic immigrants (c.2500–1800 BC) introduced copper, the horse, the wheel, and perhaps an Indo-European language. Between 1800 and 1000 BC the climate warmed and settlement spread to the high uplands. Wealthy warrior elites emerged, with marked regional differences. Bronze working was established, trade goods from the Mycenean world appeared, and the final monumental phase of Stonehenge was completed.

Around 1000 BC the climate deteriorated, causing retreat from high land. A proliferation of defended settlements and of weapons (soon of iron) suggests stressful times during which the tribal structure of Iron-Age Britain was laid down. The ancestors of the Picts arrived from Northern Europe during the 7th and 6th centuries; around 400 BC Celts from the Paris Basin settled in Yorkshire, and by the end of the 2nd century Belgae from Picardy were settling in Kent.

Julius Caesar made brief forays in 55 and 54 BC, but Britain's multitude of quarrelsome petty kings did not invite formal conquest. The ensuing century of trading contact with Roman Gaul produced two exceptionally strong kingdoms in southern Britain which reached their height under Cunobelin and Verica in the AD 30s. Inland, beyond a ring of less centralized tribal kingdoms, life continued much as before in northern Britain and Scotland.

Dynastic disputes after Cunobelin and Verica died in 40 prompted Claudius' invasion in 43. Roman armies quickly engulfed the large southern kingdoms and moved on to Cornwall and Wales. Roman exactions were resented, but suppression of Boudicca's revolt in 60 only brought tighter control. By 78 Wales had been conquered, and in 84 Agricola annihilated the last great Celtic army in Scotland at Mons Graupius.

Roman armies always fared badly against tribal enemies, and northward expansion faltered at the end of the 1st century AD. In 105 there was a planned withdrawal from the furthest outposts, and in c.122 Hadrian had a formidable stone wall built from the Tyne to the Solway to separate the warlike provincial Brigantes from their associates in Scotland, and to make a permanent frontier. An attempt under Antoninus Pius (138–61) to establish a more northerly frontier from Clyde to Forth was soon abandoned.

Within the province, towns flourished and Roman civilization took root. In 212 all free subjects of the empire received Roman citizenship. Beyond Hadrian's Wall, the tribes of Scotland formed two large and potentially threatening confederate groups during the 2nd century: Maeatae in the south, uneasily allied with Rome, and Caledonians further north (known as Picts by 297).

Turmoil at the heart of the Roman empire (55 emperors between 244 and 284) had repercussions in Britain, which shared in the extreme monetary inflation of the period and produced its own imperial usurpers in Carausius and Allectus (286–96), who strengthened the south-eastern sea defences against the growing threat of Saxon piracy. In the 4th century, civilian life in Britain flourished. Villas abounded, London was a great city, and Britain was as populous as it would be in 1500. Christianity also arrived, and by 314 there was an urban episcopate.

In 342 Picts together with Scots from Ireland attacked protected lands north of the Wall and in 360 launched the first of many devastating raids into the province: town defences were modernized to take artillery. By the end of the 4th century the Scots had formed permanent settlements in Wales and founded the kingdom of Dál Riada in Argyll. In the south, Saxon raids were renewed at the end of the century, attracted by Britain's great wealth and by the permanent garrisons of their kinsmen which the Romans had already settled in the south-east. The 4th-century crisis in Roman Gaul caused repeated troop withdrawals from Britain in 383–407. In 410 Honorius withdrew the remainder and told Britain to see to its own defence.

At first the framework of Roman civilization was maintained, with the Picts seen as chief enemy. The British leader Vortigern actually summoned Saxon help against them in c.425. Then in 442 the Saxons rebelled, causing widespread havoc. Many Britons emigrated to Brittany in c.460, squeezed out by the Irish and Scots in the west and north and Germanic invaders in the east.

Roman administrative structures had been replaced by a network of essentially tribal groupings which coalesced against the Saxons. It was probably the King Arthur of subsequent Camelot legend who led the Britons to victory at Mount Badon in c.500, a victory followed by two generations of peace. Saxon conquests resumed after 550, and by 600 most of Britain had fallen to Germanic kingdoms except in the far west and north. All the British kings were Christians, but the Germanic kings were pagans until Aethelbert of Kent (560–616) accepted Christianity and hosted Augustine's mission from Rome. By the 8th century organized paganism had gone.

Anglo-Saxon politics were governed by the sword, and in the 7th to early 8th centuries consisted of struggles among rival petty kings, although a high king or Bretwalda might be recognized from among the larger kingdoms of Mercia, Wessex, Northumbria, East Anglia, and Kent. The reigns of Offa of Mercia (757–96) and his contemporary Aethelred of Northumberland marked the end of the heroic age of Anglo-Saxon England. Offa abolished sub-kings, and put himself on a level with Charlemagne. His earthen dyke along the entire length of the Welsh border is a monument to his ambitions.

The subsequent history of Anglo-Saxon England was shaped by resistance to Vikings from Scandinavia. Opportunist Viking raids began in 786, attacking towns and monasteries. The threat intensified when in 865 a 'great army' under Danish royal leadership invaded to conquer Northumberland (867), East Anglia (869), and most of Mercia (874–77). Viking savagery coupled with rooted paganism was profoundly disruptive to Christian kingdoms. Under Alfred (871–99), Wessex alone managed to beat off the Danes and actually expanded, taking London in 886. Alfred negotiated with the Danes and established separate spheres of influence for the English and the Danes, divided along the line of Watling Street. The key to Alfred's success was the network of burhs or garrisoned towns he created; he also further centralized the monarchy, instituted legal reforms, and presided over a revival of Latin learning centred on the monasteries.

The Danes were gradually pushed further back by a series of English successes. The last Danish outposts fell in 924 under Alfred's son, Edward the Elder, who also converted the kingdom of Wessex into the kingdom of England. His son Aethelstan consolidated it, receiving homage from kings and lords of Scotland and expanding into Wales. In 939 Norse Vikings returned to take Northumbria; when Eadred expelled them in 954 he extorted recognition as king of England from Northumbria.

Edgar's reign (959–75 crowned formally in 973) was prosperous and peaceful. From his death until 1066, however, England was racked by dynastic disputes, aggravated by a renewed Danish onslaught in Aethelred II's reign (978–1016). A series of English defeats resulted in payment to the Danes of colossal tributes in silver between 991 and 1040. In

1013 the last phase of Viking conquest opened. King Sweyn of Denmark ousted Aethelred and seized the English throne, succeeded by his son Cnut in 1014. The English fought back; after Aethelred's death (April 1016), his son Edmund Ironside held Wessex but was compelled to reach a settlement defining spheres of influence, with London and Mercia falling to Cnut's larger sphere. When Edmund died in November 1016, all England accepted Cnut, whose rule gave the country 20 years of peace, following Aethelred's policies with some success. Cnut's administration depended heavily upon deputies. In 1017 he divided England into four earldoms, Northumbria, East Anglia, Mercia, and Wessex, and unified Wessex (previously divided in three) under a single quasi-royal earl, Godwine.

Cnut died in 1035, and a protracted dynastic crisis ensued. In 1042 Edward the Confessor became king, but depended heavily upon alliance with the Duchy of Normandy both for security against further Viking raids and for an heir (William). This choice was contested by Godwine, who promoted the claim of his own son Harold, who succeeded him as earl of Wessex when he died. By 1062 Harold and his relatives held all the English earldoms. Edward the Confessor died in Jan. 1066. Harold claimed the throne but was promptly challenged both in Northumbria by Harold Hardrada, king of Norway (whose army he defeated at Stamford Bridge, Yorkshire), and in the south by William of Normandy, to whom he fell at Hastings on his return from Stamford Bridge. The Norman conquest opened a new chapter in English history.

The crowning of William the Conqueror as king of England on Christmas Day, 1066, heralded about 150 years of dramatic change within English government and society. William developed the existing feudal system, created a king's Curia Regis (the precursor of the modern cabinet), extended the system of national taxation, reorganized the administration of central and local government, ensured a stronger administration of justice with the use of the jury becoming commonplace, and protected his territories with extremely secure castles. The compilation of his detailed and unique 'Domesday' survey of the country's land in 1086, used as a major resource for the collection and operation of taxation, emphasised the reputation of the king as an efficient administrator and practitioner of strong government.

The strength of the crown was maintained under his two sons, William II (1087–1100) and Henry I (1100–35). William II was killed before he achieved his principal ambition of rejoining Normandy with England, while Henry I gained control of Normandy in 1106 after a prolonged battle with his brother Robert.

Henry was succeeded by his nephew, Stephen of Blois, whose reign (1135–54) was marked by civil war and anarchy. Henry I's daughter Matilda had expected to become queen, and attempted to capture the succession in a number of battles during the period 1139–48. Stephen was succeeded in 1154 by Matilda's son, Henry Plantagenet of Anjou.

The reign of Henry II (1154–89) was notable for his determination to advance the administration of justice, and also for his struggle with Thomas Becket, whom he appointed Archbishop of Canterbury in 1162, over the issue of whether the monarchy or the Church should be supreme in matters of Church discipline. Becket was murdered by Henry's knights in Canterbury Cathedral (1170).

Richard the Lionheart became king when his father Henry died in 1189. He reigned for a decade (1189–99) and spent much of his time at the Crusades, attempting to recover Jerusalem. Richard was killed in battle in France and was succeeded by his brother John (1199–1216). John had by 1204 lost Normandy to France, and then faced a rebellion of his barons and widespread civil war. The king was compelled to accept limits on his authority, embodied in the Magna Carta (signed in 1215), a general declaration of liberty and justice, including the principle that every alleged criminal should have a fair trial.

Henry III (1216–72) and Edward I (1272–1307) reigned during a period which saw the emergence of something approaching parliamentary government. In 1258 Henry III agreed to the appointment of a joint committee of 12 of his own supporters and 12 dissident barons, the latter group being led by his brother-in-law, Simon de Montfort. The committee produced the Provisions of Oxford which determined the organization of the king's government. These arrangements began to come apart in 1260 when, firstly, Henry suspected collusion between his son Edward and his opponents, and secondly, the King dismissed his government after the Pope relieved him of his oath to support the Provisions. From Apr. 1264 Simon de Montfort and the king fought for supremacy. Henry, Edward and their associates were captured, following which Simon called two parliaments and effectively governed in place of the King. In May 1265 Edward escaped; Simon was defeated in battle, and killed in Aug. 1265. The last seven years of Henry's reign saw the re-emergence of a parliament in which representatives of the poorer classes in the towns, as well as the barons, were allowed to assemble, a practice first adopted by Simon de Montfort. Edward became king in 1272 on the death of his father, and it was during his reign that statute law began to accompany the established common law of the land. Edward I summoned regular and more representative parliamentary assemblies.

In Scotland, the growing strength of the monarchy south of the border posed a serious threat to Scottish independence. (The hereditary monarchy in Scotland itself had begun to develop only after the defeat of Macbeth and the reign of his successor Malcolm, 1057–1093.) The death of Alexander III of Scotland in 1286 and of his only heir, Margaret, in 1290, enabled Edward I to begin an attempt to control Scotland. Under Edward's arbitration, John Balliol, a descendant of William the Lion (king of Scotland 1165–1214), became the new Scottish king. However, he was forced to surrender in 1296 by the English army. The ensuing struggle against English rule over Scotland was dominated firstly by William Wallace, executed in London in 1305, and then by Robert Bruce, who as Robert I, king of Scotland (1306–1329), secured the independence of his country at the Battle of Bannockburn (1314).

Meanwhile, the period following the Norman Conquest of England saw the steady progress of the Normans into Wales. Although William II failed three times in his efforts to invade Wales, by 1093 the Normans had made enough of an advance to exercise major powers over many Welsh communities. Welsh princes held out against them in the kingdoms of Gwynedd (whose most famous ruler, 1194–1240, was Llywelyn the Great), Powys and Deheubarth. Edward I completed the English conquest of Wales; the military defeat (1282) of the prince of Snowdonia, Llewelyn ap Gruffydd, and his brother David, enabled the English king to give his heir Edward, born at Caernarvon in 1284, the title Prince of Wales

– a title formally conferred upon him at the Lincoln parliament in 1301 and subsequently conferred by successive English monarchs upon their eldest sons. Edward I also embarked upon a programme of castle building in Wales and reorganized its arrangements for government as a principality under the English crown. Henry VIII's reign saw the full annexation of Wales under the acts of 1536 and 1543 which extended English parliamentary taxation to Wales and created 13 counties, applied English common law there, and provided for the representation of each Welsh shire in the English Parliament.

In England, during the reign of Edward II (1307–27), the political relationship between the King and his parliament made further progress towards a fully developed constitutional monarchy. Conflict surfaced intermittently between the King and his barons, however, and Edward was eventually overthrown, forced to abdicate, murdered, and succeeded by his son, Edward III (r.1327–77). The Black Death, or plague, engulfed Europe in the years 1348–50, killing 33–50% of the population of England, and recurring occasionally up to the late 17th century. The economic and social consequences were severe at a time when the growth of the cloth trade was forcing the development of new forms of economic organization: there was a major shortage of labour to work on the land, and a fall in the value of farms, and wages rose very quickly. The Statute of Labourers (1351), an attempt to impose maximum wages, was bitterly opposed throughout the country and eventually led, indirectly, to a national Peasants' Revolt led by Wat Tyler (1381). It was during the reign of Edward III that the Hundred Years' War (1338–1453) began with France, a conflict both dynastic and economic, as England sought to retain access to markets for its wool and cloth trades.

The grandson of Edward III, Richard II, became king in 1377 and although his monarchy survived the 1381 revolt it did not survive complaints of extravagance, inefficiency and the abuse of personal patronage. His rule ended in 1399, when he was deposed by his cousin Henry of Lancaster, and murdered in prison.

The period 1399–1485 was dominated by fierce rivalry between the rival houses of Lancaster (whose emblem was a red rose) and York (a white rose), both descended from sons of Edward III. Lancastrian kings were Henry IV (r.1399–1413), Henry V (r.1413–22) and Henry VI (r.1422–61 and 1470–71), while the Yorkists held control of the monarchy under Edward IV (r.1461–70 and 1471–83) and Richard III (r.1483–85). The strong Lancastrian upper hand in the first part of this period was based on the successes of Henry IV as a practical statesman who consolidated the role of parliament in the affairs of the realm, and of Henry V as a popular king who conquered northern France, achieving his most notable victory at Agincourt in 1415. The death of Henry V in 1422, however, left as his heir his son, Henry VI, who was less than one year old. Henry VI's long reign saw the reversal of English fortunes in the war against France, and the emergence of a powerful Yorkist claim for the throne. Richard Duke of York gained power as protector, or regent, in 1453 when Henry VI was declared insane, but in 1454 the King had a son, who stood in the way of Richard's claim as heir apparent. Following a number of battles between the two sides as the Wars of the Roses gathered pace, Richard was killed (1460) but his son Edward eventually became king the following year, forcing the Lancastrians to retreat northwards. During Edward's reign, Henry VI made a brief recovery of the throne 1470–71, but Edward returned as king and ruled over a period of unusual calm both at home and abroad.

When Edward IV died in 1483, his two sons, Edward (nominally Edward V) and Richard, were left in the protection of their uncle Richard, Duke of Gloucester. The two boy princes apparently disappeared, and subsequently entered popular history as the Princes in the Tower, supposedly murdered in the Tower of London on their uncle's orders. Richard of Gloucester did indeed have himself proclaimed king as Richard III in 1483, reigning for two years before suffering defeat at Bosworth (1485) by Henry Tudor, whose landing from France was the last successful invasion of Britain. The charge of killing the princes, and other murders, appears to have been laid at Richard III's door by Tudor apologist historians and the Tudor dramatist William Shakespeare.

England under the Tudors (1485–1603) saw a number of gradual but remarkable changes in its economic, social and cultural life which transformed the country from a medieval to a modern nation. These changes included the widespread adoption of the English language in all walks of life and in all forms of written communication, including parliamentary and political documents and in literature. Geoffrey Chaucer (1340–1400), author of *The Canterbury Tales*, had written in English, while William Caxton (1422–91), who as the first English printer set up his press in 1476, successfully laid the foundations of the English literary tongue. The transformation from a solely agricultural society was shown by the fact that, by the beginning of the 16th century, woollen cloth rather than production of raw wool had become the leading economic activity. Henry VII (r.1485–1509) gained a reputation as an extremely efficient monarch in matters of finance, justice and government. His son Henry VIII experienced a much more eventful and spectacular reign (1509–47); he married six times, sought to divorce his first wife (Catherine of Aragon) in order to meet the need for a male heir, rejected the supremacy of the Catholic Church (executing his recalcitrant former archbishop, Thomas More, in 1535), authorized the dissolution of the monasteries, and established Protestantism during the period of the European Reformation.

The government of Edward VI (r.1547–53) – who was nine years old on becoming king – was conducted first by the Duke of Somerset up to 1549 and then by the Duke of Northumberland. Edward was induced to name Lady Jane Grey – the granddaughter of Mary, sister of Henry VIII – as his successor. When he died in 1553, however, the daughter of Catherine of Aragon, Mary I (a Catholic) became queen (r.1553–58). Mary tried unsucessfully but bloodily to return England to the Catholic Church; some 300 Protestants were burned to death, as bishops Latimer and Ridley (Oct. 1555) and Cranmer (Mar. 1556) set inspiring examples of bravery at the stake.

Mary was succeeded by her Protestant sister, Elizabeth I (r.1558–1603). Confirming a Protestant identity for England despite pressure from Catholic France and Spain (by the Acts of Supremacy and Uniformity, 1559), she sent her armies into Scotland to support Protestant nobles there against French influence (1560), later making a prisoner (in 1568) of the Catholic claimant to her throne, Mary Queen of Scots, and ultimately having her executed in Feb. 1587 after the third in a series of plots aimed at making Mary queen in her place.

England's conflict with Spain, fuelled by the piratical raids of great navigators such as Drake against Spanish silver fleets crossing the Atlantic, reached a peak with the planned Spanish invasion in 1588, frustrated by the destruction of the great Armada by the English fleet and the bad weather (July–Aug. 1588). Despite continuous warfare with Spain thereafter, in the Netherlands, France, the Spanish empire and Ireland, Elizabeth's reign was actually a remarkably stable period of English history, the so-called First Elizabethan Age, characterized by the flowering of literature and the arts, and the worldwide explorations of Elizabethan seamen.

In Scotland, the 14th and 15th centuries saw a continuing period of unrest reflected in the war with England, a parliament which was not so well developed as its English counterpart, and a fairly primitive economy based upon the export of raw materials and imported luxury goods. The Scottish king James VI, the son of Mary Stuart, became also king of England (as James I, r.1603–25) on the death of Elizabeth. In 1605, in the Gunpowder Plot, a group of English Catholics attempted to blow up the Houses of Parliament; Guy Fawkes was caught in the act and executed.

James I's son Charles I (r.1625–49) decided in 1629 to attempt to rule without parliament, whose leading members (notably John Pym and John Hampden) continued to resist arbitrary royal taxation without parliamentary approval. They impeached the King's ministers Stafford and Laud (1641) and published a Grand Remonstrance passed by parliament against the King (Nov. 1641). Charles's attempt to have them arrested in the Houses of Parliament (4 Jan. 1642) set the two sides on a course which led to civil war (1642–46). Parliament, with its armies led by Pym, Thomas Fairfax and Oliver Cromwell, gained the upper hand with decisive victories at Marston Moor (July 1644) and Naseby (1645). The King's forces surrendered the following year, and Charles himself was taken prisoner (June 1647) by an army faction increasingly at odds with the more moderate majority in parliament. Cromwell, asserting military command structures and discipline against the radicalism of the Levellers, marched north to defeat an invading Scottish army at Preston, while the army dispersed all but 60 radical members of parliament and ruled through the rest, the Rump Parliament (1649–53), after Charles had been arrested and beheaded (30 Jan. 1649). A Commonwealth of England was declared (19 May 1649); Cromwell, after brutally reconquering Ireland (massacre of Drogheda 11 Sept. 1649), put down a Scottish rising (1650–51) led by the future Charles II, who famously hid in an oak tree while escaping back to France. By now army commander-in-chief, Cromwell became Lord Protector (Dec. 1653), his rule becoming effectively a conservative one as the contending factions of idealists showed themselves unsympathetic to his emphasis on effective government. The republic survived his death (3 Sept. 1658) by less than two years, as Charles arrived at Dover (25 May 1660) under a negotiated settlement to restore the monarchy.

The Restoration under Charles II (r.1660–85) and his brother James II (r.1685–88) has become chiefly remembered for loose morals in high society, artistic achievement, and the Great Plague (Sept. 1665) and Fire of London (Sept. 1666). James, a Catholic, attempted unsuccessfully to restore a Catholic domination in England; his opponents invited in the Dutch Protestant William of Orange, to whose standard the nobility and gentry defected as he marched on London (the Glorious Revolution of 1688) and James escaped to France and exile. Parliament passed legislation to debar Catholics from the throne (1689). William and his wife Mary, daughter of James II, ruled as joint monarchs, their army defeating James's Catholic rising in Ireland (1690, the Battle of the Boyne). After Mary's death in 1694 William's military and diplomatic successes against Louis XIV of France were prematurely ended by his death after a riding accident in 1702.

In 1707, under Queen Anne (r.1702–14), the English and Scottish parliaments both passed an Act of Union, giving England military peace of mind and Scotland economic security. Under the Act Scotland kept its legal system and Presbyterian Church, but the country's parliament was replaced by seats in both the House of Commons and the House of Lords in London.

Meanwhile John Churchill, 1st Duke of Marlborough, led the war effort with a string of major victories (Blenheim, Ramillies, Oudenarde and Malplaquet, 1704–09).

The period of rule by the first Hanoverian kings, George I (1714–27) and George II (1727–60), was one of unique constitutional and political development. Sir Robert Walpole (1676–1745) emerged in 1721 as the first (or prime) minister to lead an executive of a single political party in control of the legislature; the institution of the British Cabinet began to emerge at this time as an effective and important part of parliamentary government. George II survived in 1745 the last Jacobite rebellion, when Charles Edward Stuart (Bonnie Prince Charlie) landed in Scotland, raised support for an attempt to restore him to the throne, and marched south into England as far as Derby, hoping to spark off a rising and a French invasion. Neither materialized, he turned back to Scotland, and was defeated at Culloden (16 Apr. 1746) by an English army under the Duke of Cumberland who then hunted down and killed the highlanders who had backed the rising.

It was under George II that the development of Britain as a maritime and colonial power was given primacy in the vision of William Pitt the Elder. A powerful critic of European wars if they obscured this purpose (such as the 1740–48 War of the Austrian Succession), Pitt nevertheless brought the Seven Years' War (1756–63) into perspective as an opportunity to gain a global ascendancy over France, and to 'win Canada on the banks of the Elbe'. George III (r.1760–1820), grandson of George II, faced problems of the national debt burden, the loss of the American colonies (1776) and the questioning of English power in both India and Ireland. The repression of Wolf Tone's United Irishmen movement from 1793, and its eventual military defeat in 1798, was followed by legislative union with Great Britain under the Act of Union which established the United Kingdom of Great Britain and Ireland (1 Jan. 1801).

1789–1815, the period of the French Revolution and of the ministries of William Pitt the Younger (1784–1801 and 1804–06), saw Europe engulfed by war and France declaring war on England in 1793. Adml Horatio Nelson (1758–1805) defeated Napoleon at Trafalgar in 1805; on land, the British contribution to the eventual defeat of the French came principally under the Duke of Wellington's command in the Peninsular War (1809–14) and at Waterloo (1815).

It was during this period, and in particular in the years 1730–1850, that the Industrial Revolution in

England transformed a largely agricultural economy into a largely industrial one, beginning with mechanization of the textile industry, and with startling progress in mining, the organization of industry, and transport (improved roads and the birth of the canal age in 1759). Industrial change was driven forward by the development of coal and iron industries, and by the use of the steam-engine as a source of power. Although the industrial revolution made Britain one of the wealthiest countries in the world, the long period of technological and economic development also emphasised such social characteristics of British society as child labour, long working days, slums, and the poverty and misery experienced by the urban poor. Whereas Britain abolished the slave trade (1807) and then outlawed slavery itself throughout the Empire (1833), domestically there was widespread fear and loathing of the workhouses set up under the new Poor Law Amendment Act of 1834, the year which also saw the conviction and transportation of the 'Tolpuddle Martyrs', poor Dorset labourers who had illegally sworn a secret oath to uphold their union.

Scotland continued to retain and indeed expand its own distinctive elements of the law, its Church and its education system, where the Presbyterian Church was perhaps more authoritarian in its influence upon the community. Intellectually, Scotland began to secure worldwide acclaim for the quality of its universities and contributions such as those of Adam Smith (1723–90) in economics and David Hume (1711–76) in philosophy. Economic growth in Scotland depended heavily on fishing, linen, woollens and then the manufacture of cotton; in Wales, meanwhile, it was principally coal and iron which were added to the traditional livestock and wool industries.

George III was succeeded by his son, George IV (r.1820–30), who had already been Prince Regent because of his father's madness since 1811. William IV (r.1830–37), younger brother to George IV and notably more favourable to political reform, was in turn succeeded by his niece Victoria (r.1837–1901).

Queen Victoria's record 64-year reign saw the advent and expansion of the British railway network in the 1840s and beyond, owing much to the engineering genius of men like Isambard Brunel; a long period of peace in Europe save for the Crimean War (1853–56), and of imperial expansion, particularly in Africa, in the latter part of the Victorian era; and an increasing prosperity across nearly all parts of the country's growing population. The electoral Reform Bills of 1832, 1867 and 1884 implemented a major redistribution of constituencies and extended the right to vote, in effect granting many of the democratic political rights for which the radical Chartist movement had campaigned in 1838–48. In 1846, Sir Robert Peel (1788–1850) as home secretary repealed the Corn Laws, which for 500 years had protected British agriculture with duties on imported grain which kept up the price of corn. The Public Health Act of 1848 was the first piece of national legislation which recognized the role of Parliament in the improvement and monitoring of public sanitation. William Gladstone (1809–98), prime minister 1868–74, 1880–85, 1886 and 1892–94, was responsible for much notable reforming legislation in similar vein, but failed to implement Home Rule for Ireland and deeply divided his Liberal Party in the process. His great political rival Benjamin Disraeli, the Tory leader and prime minister 1868 and 1874–80, combined a commitment to social reform (as the original 'one nation Conservative') with devotion to the furtherance of Empire.

The death of Queen Victoria (22 Jan. 1901) and the accession of her son as Edward VII (r.1901–1910) ended the reign of one of the most successful and popular monarchs in the history of the country, and ended an era in which 'Victorian Britain' had come to represent self-confidence both at home and abroad. Britain began the 20th century with a massive empire, one of the most advanced economies and equitable democracies in the world, and a powerful navy which stamped its presence on international politics. In the 90 years since, Britain has undergone profound changes; its colonies have become independent states, and the 'mother country' has faced sometimes painful choices over participating in the integration of Europe. On the home front, greater national cohesion, stemming partly from the effort of fighting two World Wars, exposed anachronisms in Britain's rigid class system, and pointed a way forward to a welfare state and consensus politics in post-war Britain.

The foundation of the Labour Movement (27 Feb. 1900) signalled a warning to the Conservatives, in government under Lord Salisbury, and to the Liberal opposition, that a new force, the urban proletariat, demanded a voice in parliament. The economy was emerging from two decades of depressed prices, but while this hit the rural aristocracy and peasantry, it released more money for spending in the growing cities, boosted by the railways. Urbanization, however, brought its own problems, including sanitation and the control of disease: in 1900, 50 people a day died from influenza in London alone. The budget was strained, meanwhile, by foreign wars. In British-ruled South Africa, the Boer War (1899–1902), fought in response to an independence revolt by White Afrikaners ('Boers'), was controversial for the British use of mass internment in concentration camps to cut Boer fighters off from their support among the White population. In China, the British joined with other European powers in military action to put down the bloody anti-European Boxer rebellion (July 1900–Sept. 1901).

Lord Salisbury and his Conservatives were re-elected (Oct. 1900), adamantly opposing the growing Irish demand for independence, an issue which split the opposition Liberals into Radical and Imperialist camps. Arthur Balfour succeeded Salisbury as prime minister (July 1902), Lord Rosebery formed a breakaway Liberal League (Feb. 1902), and in 1903 the Tory Joseph Chamberlain formed the Tariff League, demanding preferential trading with the Empire; fears of resulting food price rises were eventually to force Balfour's Tory Government to resign in 1905. Campbell-Bannerman's Liberals enjoyed a landslide electoral victory (Feb. 1906), while Keir Hardie's Labour Party won 29 seats.

As Labour's strength grew at the polls, the Liberal Government moved to enact far-reaching legislation on social issues, introducing the first old-age pensions in 1908, labour exchanges in 1909, compulsory medical insurance and a limited unemployment insurance for workers in the great National Insurance Act of 1911, and a limited working week for shop workers in the same year, and a minimum wage for coal miners in 1912. Unions could now also levy political funds. Newly formed unions, however, worried by mounting unemployment and stagnant wages, and drawing a sense of solidarity from the Trades Union Congress (TUC), often opted for strike action; coal miners in 1907, 1910, 1911 and 1915, Lancashire cotton-workers in 1908, dockers and railwaymen in 1910. Violent protest also came from an unexpected quarter, the Women's Social and Political Union (the 'Suffragettes'), formalized as a movement under Emily Pankhurst (10 Oct. 1903). In 1905 a bill to allow women to vote was defeated in Parliament, and later that year Suffragettes were imprisoned for assaulting police. A further bill introduced by Hardie was defeated in 1907. Suffragette direct action continued, and the cause gained a martyr in Emily Davison, who threw herself in front of the King's horse at the Derby (4 June 1913). Throughout 1914 Suffragettes attacked churches, museums, Parliament and even leading politicians – but it was not until the Representation of People Act in 1917 that wives over 30 could vote, as well as all men over 21 (a proposal dropped as 'too radical' before the war). In 1918 Parliament allowed for women MPs.

The Liberal Herbert Asquith, who succeeded Campbell-Bannerman as prime minister in 1908, attacked the power of the House of Lords, backed by rising star David Lloyd George, who believed the nation's problems stemmed from such outdated structures with vested interests. In 1909 Asquith presented the radical 'People's Budget', seen as paying for social welfare by supertaxing the rich. The Lords rejected it (30 Nov.); Asquith called an election (Jan.–Feb. 1910) and emerged with a Liberal government dependent on Labour and Irish Nationalist support. Asquith tried to force through a law to curb the Lords' veto rights, and threatened to create enough sympathetic peers to swamp the largely pro-Tory House of Lords. The new King, George V (r.1910–1936), had secretly agreed (after his predecessor died in May) to create new peers if a further election backed Asquith's course. The year's second election (Nov.–Dec. 1910) produced almost identical results, and the Lords ultimately accepted (by passing the Parliament Act in Aug. 1911) strict limitations on the power of the upper house to hold up the passage of legislation.

British governments began to accept the idea of Irish Home Rule, but faced a dilemma over Ulster, a largely Protestant province. In May 1907 the Government proposed an Irish Council, though this was soon abandoned in the face of opposition from Nationalist MPs who felt it did not go far enough. Violence rose in succeeding years, and in 1912 there were huge Loyalist (Protestant) rallies in Ulster. The House of Commons passed a Home Rule Bill (mid-1912), amended to exclude Ulster; delayed by defeat in the Lords (Jan. 1913), it nevertheless became law (Sept. 1913). An Ulster Volunteer Force mobilized under Sir Edward Carson to threaten civil war if Home Rule was implemented in Ulster. In July 1914 King George V, already King for four years but crowned only the previous month, came out on the side of the Unionists, and the government thereupon shelved the Irish issue, preoccupied with impending world war.

When Germany invaded Belgium, and Britain declared war in response (4 Aug. 1914), the popular belief was that it would be 'over by Christmas'. Facing the reality of a long war, an all-party coalition government was formed under Asquith (May 1915), succeeded in Dec. 1916 by Lloyd George. Despite the huge numbers who volunteered to serve, Parliament voted for conscription in Jan. 1916. Thousands were dying in the attritional trench warfare in Flanders; the 1915 spring offensive at Ypres succumbed to German gas attacks, and the July 1916 Somme offensive cost 60,000 British casualties in a week. In the Near East, the Turks held off Britain and her allies, inflicting 25,000 casualties at Gallipoli (1915), before the Arab revolt of June 1916 gave the British, urged on by T.E. Lawrence, the chance to harness this nationalism against the Ottoman empire. Meanwhile at Jutland (May 1916) Adml. Jellicoe won a naval victory sufficient to drive the German fleet back to port. The collapse of the Russian front was counterbalanced by the United States entering the war on the side of Britain and its allies (6 Apr. 1917); together they withstood the 1918 German offensive launched at Ypres, and (11 Nov. 1918) Germany finally surrendered. In four years of war some 750,000 British troops had died, as had 200,000 Empire troops, a third of them Indian. The war cost Britain US$35,000 million – more than any nation except Germany.

Euphoria greeted the returning 'Tommies', and Lloyd George's coalition swept back to power in a general election (Dec. 1918), but rising unemployment reached 2.2 million by June 1921. Unemployment benefit was increased to cope with hardship. Food and coal rationing were re-introduced during a national rail strike and Glasgow general strike in 1919. Coal miners and even police went on strike in 1920, but a planned general strike (Apr. 1921) was called off in the face of government willingness to take emergency powers. Killer epidemics of influenza swept across Europe, still capable of causing deaths of 1,000 in a week in Britain as late as 1927. But despite economic stringencies, the sense of relief after the war was irrepressible, and showed itself during the 1920s in a welter of new fashions, avant-garde art, theatre and literature. Women, having proven themselves capable in war work, won not only the vote but the right, after 1921, to use birth control clinics.

Millions in Britain's colonies were inspired by ideas of freedom expressed in the post-war creation of the League of Nations, and during the 1920s British forces were repeatedly called out, facing the gravest challenge in India (where Gandhi launched the massive campaigns of passive resistance). Particularly volatile, too, was the Middle East, where Britain and France divided most of the old Turkish Empire between them in mandated territories. The Imperial Conference of 1926 agreed that Canada, Australia, New Zealand, South Africa and Newfoundland would be self-governing dominions, equal in status to Britain.

In Ireland, meanwhile, the Free State compromise offered to the South (Dec. 1921) had extricated Britain from the attempt to sustain its rule by martial law, using 'black and tan' demobbed soldiers as special constables through months of bitter fighting (1920–July 1921).

Britain itself faced a period of political volatility, with parties seldom winning outright majorities at elections. The wartime coalition ended in 1922 with the acrimonious unseating of Lloyd George. The Tories did win the ensuing election outright (Nov. 1922), and Labour under Ramsay MacDonald became the official opposition. As prime minister, Andrew Bonar Law was succeeded in May 1923 by Stanley Baldwin, who called and lost an election in Nov. 1923 over his pro-tariff policy. The first Labour government, with Liberal support, lasted just one year, its fall encouraged by the faked Zinoviev Letter suggesting Labour links with the Bolsheviks. Baldwin returned to office, with the former Liberal Winston Churchill joining his Conservative cabinet as chancellor of the Exchequer and returning Britain to the gold standard (Apr. 1925) as a sign, he said, of postwar economic recovery. Britain's first general strike (3–12 May 1926), backed by the TUC in support of action by coal miners, rekindled class animosities; the miners' strike ended in defeat (Nov. 1926), wage cuts and an eight-hour day, and new legislation curbed union powers.

After the inconclusive May 1929 elections, Ramsay MacDonald formed his second minority Labour government (June 1929–Aug. 1931), committed to a fiscal conservatism which it sustained despite the international depression and unemployment which followed the Oct. 1929 stock market crash on Wall Street. Impatient with the Government's failure to halt unemployment (over 2,000,000 by Aug. 1930), Sir Oswald Mosley left the cabinet and founded the fascistic New Party (28 Feb. 1931), which over succeeding years became notorious for aggressive demonstrations, until London East Enders organized to stop the fascists marching at Cable Street (11 Oct. 1936; 80 injured, over 80 arrested). Far from sharing Mosley's belief in state intervention, Ramsay Macdonald backed draconian spending cuts, losing the support of his own Labour Party but surviving as prime minister of an all-party National Government (from Aug. 1931), and winning a landslide at the Oct. 1931 election with 554 (mostly Tory) seats. The austerity measures precipitated nationwide strikes and even a navy mutiny at Invergordon (Sept. 1931), and Britain left the gold standard and devalued the pound. Hunger marches, and protests over the means test applied to the recipients of relief, became a feature of the depressed 1930s, with violent protests in London hitting headlines in Oct. 1932, and jobless workers from Jarrow marching on London four years later (Oct.–Nov. 1936).

Faced with belligerent Nazism in Germany and Fascism in Italy, the Government reversed its policy of cutting arms spending (Nov. 1933), but Labour gained support for a pacifist stance. (The Spanish Civil War, from 1936, was to provide a counter to pacifism on the left, with 3,000 from Britain joining the International Brigades to fight the fascists, and 500 of them dying in Spain.) In Sept. 1934 the nation was temporarily united over the Wrexham pit disaster, when 262 miners died. Stanley Baldwin, succeeding MacDonald as prime minister under the National Coalition in June 1935, led the Conservatives to a huge general election victory (Nov. 1935), but his new government faced public outrage at appeasement of Italy over Abyssinia, and foreign minister Samuel Hoare was sacked (Dec. 1935).

1936 began with the death of King George V, and ended with the shock abdication (11 Dec. 1936) of his successor, Edward VIII, compelled to step down because he intended to marry the American divorcee Wallis Simpson. Successive budgets increased taxation to pay for unemployment benefits and defence spending. In May 1937 George VI (r.1936–1952) was crowned king, and Neville Chamberlain succeeded Baldwin as prime minister. The House of Commons voted to erect air raid shelters in anticipation of war, and in Apr. 1938 approved a deal with France to defend Czechoslovakia against a threatened German invasion. Chamberlain, however, clung to the belief that appeasement would avert war, and described as 'peace in our time' his Munich agreement with Hitler (30 Sept. 1938), allowing Germany to take over the Sudetenland from Czechoslovakia on the understanding that Hitler had no further territorial ambitions. When Hitler broke his promise by invading Czechoslovakia six months later, Britain formed a military pact with Poland and France (Apr. 1939) and introduced conscription. The US remained neutral, so when Germany and USSR signed a surprise non-aggression pact in August, Britain began evacuating children from the cities. Germany later invaded Poland and Britain declared war on 3 Sept. 1939.

As in 1914, all other issues – unrest in Palestine and in India, the threat of IRA attacks and economic and social legislation at home – were shelved as Britain went to war. Backed by its loyal colonies, Britain introduced food rationing, censorship and an Emergency Powers Act, banning strikes and commandeering goods. Blackouts were commonplace, a Home Guard was formed, and there were new taxes on purchases, profits and luxuries. But Britain and its allies failed to halt Germany's invasion of Norway; MPs lambasted Chamberlain over this debacle (May 1940) and he resigned, Winston Churchill replacing him as prime minister at the head of an all-party Coalition Government and offering 'nothing but blood, toil, tears and sweat'.

Hitler's rapid blitzkrieg invasion of France and Holland in 1940 forced the expeditionary forces to retreat from Dunkirk (27 May–4 June; 338,000 evacuated). Germany conquered the British Channel Islands and attacked shipping. The Royal Air Force (RAF) bombed Berlin and Hamburg in retaliation, while the Navy blockaded German ports. By August Britain stood alone against German aerial bombing of London, Coventry and other major cities. The RAF beat off many Luftwaffe aircraft in what was known as the Battle of Britain (July–Sept. 1940), but the raids continued. By mid-1941 bombs were falling at a rate of up to 100,000 a night, and 10,000 Londoners a month were killed at the height of the Blitz (daylight bombing raids in Sept. and early Oct. 1940, and night raids over the succeeding seven months). Women joined war work (compulsory for all in 1943), and by December were being conscripted into the forces. In 1944 German V-1 bombs fell on England, but by now the tide had turned. In North Africa, the victory of Gen. Montgomery's Eighth Army at El Alamein (24 Oct.–4 Nov. 1942) had ended Rommel's German advance; in the USSR, German armies faced stalemate and then counter-offensive. The US had entered the war on the Allied side (Dec. 1941), having already leased bases and lent arms to Britain, and cemented their 'special relationship' by stating their common aspirations in the Atlantic Charter in Aug. 1941; and with US help Britain was regaining Far Eastern territories lost to Japan. Britain became a virtual armed camp for Allied troops, preparing for the invasion of German-ruled Europe on D-Day (6 June 1944). By October the Allies entered Germany itself. In Feb. 1945 the RAF and US Air Force bombed Dresden, killing 130,000. The surrender of Germany was celebrated as VE Day (7 May); three months later came the end of the war in the East (14 Aug.) after US atomic bombs had broken Japan's determination to fight on.

The war cost some 55 million lives in all, including half a million from Britain and the Empire/Commonwealth. In Britain the economic cost was devastating - city centres destroyed, an immense debt owed to the US, the task of demobilizing a million soldiers and a million munitions workers. A rash of strikes broke out in late 1944. Churchill called the first election since the Coalition took power in 1935. Surprising many, Clement Atlee's Labour won a landslide victory (5 July 1945), and for the first time enjoyed an absolute majority. They launched plans for a welfare state, national health service (NHS) and widespread nationalization. Much of the groundwork had been laid in the Beveridge Plan of 1943 and the 1944 White

Paper which called for free state schooling for children up to 16. Between 1946 and 1948 the new Parliament voted to nationalize the 'commanding heights of the economy', including the Bank of England, railways, ports and civil aviation, coal, electricity, gas and atomic energy. The legislation on nationalising steel took longer, going through finally in Nov. 1949. Aneurin Bevan presented proposals for the NHS (free medical treatment for all) in March 1946. After much protest from doctors it opened, along with National Insurance offices, in July 1948.

In opposition Churchill warned that an 'iron curtain has descended' across Europe (speech in Fulton, Missouri, March 1946) and spoke of a 'cold war' between Western powers, now led by the US, and their erstwhile ally, the USSR, which now occupied Eastern Europe. Britain held a permanent seat as one of five major powers on the newly formed United Nations Security Council (founded in London in Jan. 1946) but was clearly now a junior partner to the US. In 1949 the North Atlantic Treaty Organization (NATO) was set up under US patronage. The 1940s also saw Britain begin to divest itself of its colonies. Between 1948 and 1956 British forces crushed a Communist guerrilla campaign in Malaya, but in Palestine (where British forces left in 1947) and India/ Pakistan and Burma (independent in Aug. 1947 and in Feb. 1948) there was no controlling the contending parties.

In 1946 Britain accepted a £936 million loan from the USA, and had to re-introduce wartime rationing, some of which continued until 1949. Britain also obtained almost a quarter of the total funding made available by the US Marshall Aid plan. Coal shortages further hampered economic recovery, as did a severe winter in early 1947. Troops were called in under a new Supplies and Services Act when hauliers went on strike; Attlee launched a string of new austerity measures. After hosting the 'austerity Olympics' in Aug. 1948, Britain began lifting manufacturing restrictions, but had to devalue the pound by 30% in Sept. 1949. The official Labour Party line, as espoused by Herbert Morrison, now played down socialism, while a left wing led by Bevan demanded accelerated nationalization. In Feb. 1950 Labour returned to power, but with a tiny majority; the turnout of almost 84 per cent was a record. This administration proved short-lived. Bevan and Harold Wilson resigned in Apr. 1951 over Chancellor Gaitskell's policy of high defence spending (14 per-cent of GNP) and having the NHS charge for false teeth and spectacles. Attlee argued that military costs were unavoidable as Britain had committed itself to the Korean War. Even the lavish Festival of Britain in May 1951, which gave London its South Bank Arts Centre, provoked criticism for costliness.

In Oct. 1951 Churchill and the Tories returned to power, thanks largely to the collapse of the Liberal vote. In Feb. 1952 King George VI died, and his elder daughter became Queen Elizabeth II. That same month Churchill revealed that Britain had the atom bomb. There were other signs of Britain's renascent technological progress – the first jet airliner, the Comet, and Britain's own Vulcan jet bomber. Maintaining an imperial role, British troops captured Ismailia in Egypt to enforce a defence pact and Suez Canal agreement, and flew into Kenya (Oct. 1952) in response to the Mau Mau unrest, declaring a state of emergency which lasted almost uninterrupted till 1959.

Important issues in 1953–54 were economic reflation, the death penalty, equal pay for women, nuclear defence, commercial television (ITV began in 1955) and the impact of new Caribbean immigrants. An ill Churchill handed over the leadership in Apr. 1955 to Sir Anthony Eden, who won a snap election but inherited other problems – the Burgess and Maclean spy scandal, riots against British rule in Cyprus, a dock strike and Royal embarrassment over Princess Margaret's cancelled engagement. Attlee resigned as Labour leader and was replaced by Hugh Gaitskell, a victory for the right-wing. In 1956 Chancellor Harold Macmillan launched the tightest credit squeeze since 1931 to stifle inflation. Young people, less willing to accept austerity, sought a new identity in Teddy Boy fashions, rock 'n roll or the plays of the Angry Young Men.

Eden's biggest challenge came when Nasser nationalized the Suez Canal (July 1956). Britain froze its Egyptian assets and arranged for a joint Anglo-French force to bombard Suez while Israel attacked from the north (end Oct.). Britain then seized the canal zone and declared acceptance of a UN-backed cease-fire, but had to withdraw (23 Nov.) under US pressure and the threat of a run on sterling. Eden resigned because of illness and handed the premiership to Harold Macmillan in Jan. 1957. Macmillan did not join the new European Economic Community (EEC) set up that year but emphasised the UK-US 'special relationship', accepting US nuclear missiles in Britain. A Campaign for Nuclear Disarmament (CND) grew stronger in 1958, aided by worries over leaks at the Windscale nuclear plant. In 1960 the Labour Party voted for unilateral nuclear disarmament, against the wishes of its leader Hugh Gaitskell. Macmillan, meanwhile, introduced cheaper home loans and luxury taxes and opened the first motorway (1958). Overseas, he could welcome peaceful independence for Malaya, but sent troops to quell unrest in Cyprus and Jordan.

In Oct. 1959 Macmillan won an election after a popular reflationary budget. The new Government promised independence to Nigeria and Cyprus, and in Feb. 1960 he delivered his 'wind of change' speech to South Africa's Whites-only Parliament, heralding a decade of decolonization on the African continent.

Regarding Europe, Macmillan favoured membership of a European Free Trade Association (EFTA, founded 1959) and continued preferential trade with the British Commonwealth. In Aug. 1961, however, Britain formally applied to join the EEC, but France's Pres. de Gaulle vetoed the idea of British membership on special terms.

In 1961 birth control pills became available on the NHS, and in 1962 *Private Eye* magazine and satirical radio programmes openly mocked the Government. The Government passed a stricter Commonwealth Immigrants Act in July 1962 to stem immigration from the Caribbean and Indian sub-continent. A new budget cut purchase taxes and bolstered hire purchase, but this fuelled a consumer boom. When Macmillan urged pay restraint, voters turned against him at by-elections. He axed a third of his cabinet, but little changed, and 1963 brought a spate of sex and spy scandals involving ministers, most damaging being the case of John Profumo, who resigned as war secretary (5 June 1963) after allegations of an affair with Christine Keeler, a call girl also consorting with Soviet officials. Macmillan faced a backbench rebellion over the issue, but was temporarily spared embarrassment when public opinion turned to the Great Train Robbery and the UK-US-USSR nuclear test ban treaty. The Denning report then condemned his handling of the Profumo affair, and he resigned (Oct.

1963) in favour of Sir Alec Douglas-Home.

Home inherited an altered Britain. Harold Wilson as Labour leader touted a new socialism based on scientific revolution; reports called for new universities and new towns; Beatlemania swept the country; and youth cult Mods and Rockers clashed on the beaches. Labour won the first Greater London Council (GLC) elections in Apr. 1964, and narrowly won the general election (Oct. 1964). Committed to a national economic plan under a young team, Wilson faced immediate crises. To stop the fall in sterling he raised income tax, set an import tax and borrowed more than £1,000 million. In Jan. 1965 Winston Churchill died, aged 91, and received a huge and affectionate state funeral, marking his passing as the end of an era. In a new liberal Britain, the death penalty was abolished (1965), protests grew over support for the US in Vietnam (100 MPs later joining condemnations of US bombing in 1967, and violence erupting outside the US Embassy in 1968), and a woman became a High Court judge, while Tory MPs for the first time elected a new leader, Edward Heath. In 1968 'permissive' bills legalized abortion and adult homosexuality, and abolished stage censorship. Huge open-air rock concerts took place in the summer of 1969. From Jan. 1970, the age of majority was cut from 21 to 18.

Labour had greatly increased its majority in the March 1966 election, and in May of that year. Wilson declared a state of emergency to quell a 'communist-inspired' dock strike, and with TUC support the Government passed a law to freeze wages and prices for six months. National gloom lifted when England won the football World Cup for the first time, but returned after the Aberfan disaster in Wales, when a coal slag heap slid down on the village school, killing 144, mainly children (27 Oct. 1966).

A huge majority of MPs had supported Wilson's new application for EEC membership, but de Gaulle dismissed it (16 May 1967). After an influx of East African Asians with British passports in 1968, the Labour government rushed through a new Commonwealth Immigrants Act to impose stricter controls on entry, but also legislated, through the Race Relations Act of 1968, to strengthen anti-discrimination powers first enacted in 1965. The right-wing conservative Enoch Powell's notorious 'rivers of blood' speech (21 Apr. 1968) condemned immigration. As inflation climbed in 1968, Michael Foot led 41 Labour MPs in a revolt against spending cuts, while others launched an 'I'm Backing Britain' campaign. In March George Brown resigned as foreign secretary and Labour lost three by-election seats to the Tories.

Ulster's Catholics and Protestants rioted in Londonderry and Armagh respectively, and in early 1969 Protestant leader Ian Paisley was jailed for unlawful assembly. Ulster's Prime Minister O'Neill resigned (Apr. 1969), and British troops were sent in (Aug. 1969); Catholic protests continued, so troops and police erected a 'peace wall' to keep the communities apart. Bernadette Devlin, the Ulster civil rights MP, was jailed (Dec. 1969) for 'incitement to riot'.

The 1970s began with some 4,000 dying from Hong Kong influenza. Employment Secretary Barbara Castle steered through a bill giving women equal pay with men, but had been unsuccessful in 1969 in promoting the 'In Place Of Strife' proposals to curb union strikes, and despite a budget exempting two million from paying tax, Labour lost the June 1970 elections to Heath. Immediately the new Government faced a dockers' strike. Troops were on standby, but dockers accepted the pay deal. In Belfast, troops used rubber bullets and CS gas for the first time. After a year of Heath's leadership, strikes were at their highest level since 1926, with 8.8 million working days lost. Heath set up an Industrial Relations Court to fine unions who endorsed wildcat strikes. In 1971 postmen went on strike for the first time, and the first British soldier died in Ulster. A new 'provisional' wing of the Catholic IRA started a terror campaign against British troops. The troubles claimed their 100th victim in September. IRA members were interned and all marches banned. Then the IRA detonated a bomb in London's Post Office Tower – the first of many attacks in Britain itself.

Conversion to decimal currency (15 Feb. 1971) came amid rising inflation, and unemployment climbed inexorably. The Government pushed for EEC membership and were supported by 100 rebel Labour MPs. Meanwhile they decided not to bail out 'lame duck' industries, like the Clydeside ship-builders. Britain finally joined the EEC (22 Jan. 1972) after getting special terms for certain Commonwealth products.

A miners' strike over pay led to blackouts in early 1972, as electricity failed. The IRA bombed a British Army parachute headquarters at Aldershot, killing seven, and Heath imposed direct rule on Ulster (March-April), supported by the Irish Government; the following year a fresh IRA bombing campaign hit London, the Government proposed trials without juries in Ulster, a new Ulster Assembly met in June, and in December leaders from Dublin, Belfast and London set up a Council of Ireland to discuss issues of mutual concern, but the initiative had collapsed by May 1974 and direct rule was resumed.

Meanwhile, after two years of boom the economy was in difficulties again. In an effort to quell inflation and sustain sterling, the Government floated the pound on the money markets, and asked the TUC and CBI (Sept. 1972) to keep a voluntary prices and pay policy. When this failed, Heath imposed a mandatory 90-day wage and price freeze, echoing previous Labour policy. In Nov. 1973 new Arab oil price increases threatened petrol rationing. A crisis pre-Christmas budget ordered businesses to go on to a three-day week to save electricity, after strikes by miners and power workers; £1,200 million was cut from public spending, and credit was squeezed.

During 1973 there was an influx of Asians expelled from Uganda, The Distillers' Company finally agreed to pay compensation to those who, in the 1950s, had suffered birth defects when pregnant women used the Thalidomide sedative drug. In May two ministers, Earl Jellicoe and Lord Lambton, resigned after a sex scandal.

An election was called for Mar. 1974. Miners shunned Heath's appeals to end their strike. Neither Labour nor the Tories won an outright majority. Heath could not get the support of the 14 Liberal MPs (backed by 23.6% of the vote) and Harold Wilson returned to office. He conceded almost all the miners' demands. In May Unionist strikers brought down the Ulster power-sharing Executive, and Dublin suffered a spate of car bombs. One Labour success was Foreign Secretary Callaghan's signing of a peace deal and new constitution in war-torn Cyprus. A second election in October returned Labour with a majority of three. In the worst IRA outrage yet in Britain, 17 died in pub blasts in Birmingham, and a new Prevention of Terrorism Act was brought in. As 1974 ended, inflation stood at 26%; a budget raised VAT and initiated defence spending cuts to save £4,700 million over ten years.

In Feb. 1975 Margaret Thatcher ousted Heath as Tory leader, becoming the first woman to head a British political party. With a referendum on EEC membership pending, the Labour cabinet split; the electorate voted two to one in favour (June 1975). Controversial legislation froze wage increases on salaries above £8,500; the Sex Discrimination Act and Equal Pay Act were passed. A North Sea oil pipeline came into operation, the value of the reserves being estimated at £200 billion. British trawlermen suffered badly from the dispute over fishing around Iceland, when Britain backed down after the Cod War (to June 1976).

When Wilson resigned unexpectedly in Mar. 1976, James Callaghan narrowly beat left-winger Michael Foot to become Labour leader and prime minister. Then Jeremy Thorpe resigned as Liberal leader after claims that he had had a homosexual affair. The worst drought for 240 years dried up reservoirs, worsening economic problems. Britain borrowed £2,300 million from the International Monetary Fund to support sterling.

By Mar. 1977 Labour needed Liberal support to stave off a no-confidence vote; under the Lib-Lab pact Liberals had a say in policy. The violent Grunwick dispute over the closed shop (compulsory union membership) raised fears of 'hard left' influence; the 'social contract' between unions and Government collapsed as unions condemned the incomes policy (Oct. 1978) and sought higher wage deals. Fresh strikes hit Britain in the 'winter of discontent' of early 1979, with rubbish piling up and patients turned away from hospitals. The TUC and Government made a new contract but strikes continued and sapped support for Labour. When Callaghan stalled on home rule legislation for Scotland, he lost the votes of Scottish Nationalists, and the Liberals and Ulster Unionists deserted Labour, allowing the Tories to win a no-confidence vote (28 Mar. 1979). A general election followed in May which the Tories won with a majority of 43 seats.

New Prime Minister Thatcher vowed to take a tougher line with the IRA after the assassination of Lord Mountbatten (27 Aug. 1979). Her cabinet had both hardliners and moderate conservatives, dubbed the 'wets'. Abrasively she demanded and secured rebates to cut Britain's EEC budget contribution from £1,100 million to £250 million. Rhodesia's 14 years of UDI ended in the Lancaster House peace deal signed in London (21 Dec. 1979). In May 1980 the SAS stormed the Iranian Embassy to free hostages held by gunmen. The advent of American cruise missiles in Britain prompted the biggest CND protests for 20 years. Oil price rises fuelled inflation, and by squeezing the money supply, Thatcher caused industrial retrenchment – by Aug. 1980 two million were out of work, and inner-city riots broke out in the Black area of St Pauls in Bristol. Striking steelworkers had their benefits cut, and inefficient plants were closed.

In 1981 a 'Gang of Four' broke from Labour (now led by Michael Foot) and founded the centrist Social Democratic Party, which allied itself with Liberals in June. Thatcher outlined her privatization policy: selling off nationalized industries, starting with half the shares in British Aerospace and proceeding over the next decade with British Gas, Electricity, British Telecommunications, British Steel and most recently, the water boards. A new 'share-owning democracy' would at one stroke break class barriers and boost government revenue. In April Black and White youths rioted in Brixton (South London). In July there was renewed rioting in Toxteth (Liverpool), London, Birmingham and Preston; Michael Heseltine visited Merseyside and promised aid to inner city areas. The Scarman report admitted 'racial disadvantage' and police attitudes fuelled the riots. Meanwhile in Ulster in May there were riots in Belfast in protest at the death by hunger strike of IRA MP Bobby Sands. But most eyes were fixed on the wedding of Prince Charles to Lady Diana Spencer (29 July 1981).

By Jan. 1982 unemployment topped three million, upsetting Tory 'wets'. The government recovered its popularity, however, over the Falklands War; Argentina invaded the islands, a British dependency, in April, and Mrs Thatcher responded with a show of strength, sending a task force which sank the *Belgrano* (May 2) and retook the islands (29 May–14 June), with losses of 255 British dead and 652 Argentinians. CND women encircled the Greenham Common and in 1983 the Upper Heyford cruise missile sites and clashed with police. In the 1983 pre-election budget taxes were cut, and Tories promised to abolish the Greater London Council (GLC), while Labour endorsed unilateral disarmament and EEC withdrawal. On June 10 the electorate returned Thatcher with a 144-seat majority. Labour was almost wiped out in the south; the SDP-Liberal Alliance got 25% of the votes but only 23 seats. Michael Foot and Roy Jenkins resigned as leaders of Labour and SDP respectively, and were replaced by Neil Kinnock and the one-time Labour foreign secretary David Owen.

A bitter one-year miners' strike (Mar. 1984–Mar. 1985) saw half the pits shut down, police clashing with pickets, and union funds sequestrated by the courts. Kinnock distanced his party from condoning miners' violence. Britain broke off relations with Libya, sending home diplomats who were held responsible for shooting WPC Yvonne Fletcher in the square outside the Libyan Embassy (17 Apr. 1984). In Oct. 1984 an IRA bomb intended to kill the whole cabinet exploded in a Brighton hotel; four died and Employment Secretary Norman Tebbit was among the injured. In 1985 Clive Ponting, accused of breaking the Official Secrets Act by passing information on the Falklands War to an MP, was acquitted (a similar situation occurred with the *Spycatcher* book in 1986). In May 1985 two football disasters, the Bradford fire (over 40 dead) and the Heysel stadium rampage (38 dead), shocked the nation. A different spirit prevailed at the Live Aid rock concert for Ethiopia famine victims (7 July). The November 1985 Anglo-Irish accord gave Eire a role to play in Ulster but many Unionists were appalled. Later, Thatcher fumed about Irish refusal to extradite IRA suspects, and the accord was strained. In May John Stalker was removed as head of an inquiry into an alleged 'shoot to kill' policy by Ulster police.

The Anglo-French Channel Tunnel got the go-ahead in 1986; the Westland crisis, ostensibly over the future of a helicopter manufacturer, damaged the government with rows about leaks and the resignations of Michael Heseltine and Leon Brittan (Jan. 86). In March the GLC was abolished; the City, epitome of the new enterprise spirit, was streamlined in the October Big Bang, but then came scandals involving abuses by Guinness and Barlow Clowes.

In Mar. 1987 Thatcher visited Pres. Gorbachev in the USSR. At home overspending Labour councils were rate-capped. In June the Tories were elected for a third time, but with a reduced majority; the first four Black MPs entered Parliament, all for Labour, and the SDP-Liberal Alliance broke down in failure.

Unemployment fell below three million, but in October a surprise Stock Market collapse wiped out £50,000 million and forced the Government to halt the BP shares flotation. The King's Cross underground fire and Clapham Junction rail crash moved transport up the political agenda, as did the railway strikes which ended in July 1989.

In 1988 the trade deficit deepened while house prices soared. Nurses went on strike for better pay, saying that underfunding of the NHS was harming the service, and complaining that the new cost-budgeting health bill dismantled the NHS, rather than rationalized it. Food minister Edwina Currie resigned, denounced by farmers when she said that eggs contained salmonella (Dec. 1988). A Pan Am airliner crashed over Lockerbie in Scotland (21 Dec.), the victim of anti-US terrorism.

In Mar. 1989 Muslims held mass protests against Salman Rushdie's allegedly blasphemous book *The Satanic Verses*. The Tiananmen Square massacre in China made Hong Kong citizens apply in droves to come to Britain, but only some categories of skilled professionals got passports, and Norman Tebbit led a campaign to keep them all out. The EEC criticised British food and water standards, undermining Tory claims to be a party of environmentalist action. Britain promoted the integrated EEC of 1992, yet in a speech at Bruges Mrs Thatcher stated that 1992 could threaten parliamentary sovereignty. She rejected the Social Charter and the European Monetary System (EMS); Nigel Lawson at the Exchequer evidently favoured EMS: he later resigned and was replaced by John Major (Oct. 1989). In June the Tories lost the European Parliament elections to Labour by 32 to 45 seats, and the Greens made a good showing. In the Commonwealth Britain alone opposed full sanctions against South Africa. The year ended with Thatcher claiming that East European revolution vindicated her belief that freedom, not socialism, was what people wanted. The Christmas ambulance strike won general public support, and ended with a compromise, while the government moved towards a further storm over plans for a Community Charge ('Poll Tax') to replace the rates on property in financing local government.

HOUSING

During the 1980s there have been major changes in Government housing policy which have led to a reversal of the housing trends prevalent since World War II. One of these changes has been the introduction, in 1980, of council tenants' 'right to buy'; correspondingly the Government has dramatically cut council-house building, by 64% from the previous Government, whilst encouraging a move towards home ownership.

There has also been a decline in privately rented dwellings with an increase in housing associations offering homes. Government policy has stated that 'they [the Government] wanted to encourage owner-occupation and give very substantial incentives to do that' (M. Heseltine, Secretary of State for the Environment, 1980). In 1951 there were about 4 million owner-occupied dwellings; by 1989 this had risen to 13,076,000. 26% of all homes were owner-occupied in 1945 in England and Wales; by 1966 the proportion had risen to 47%, and in 1983 to 63%. Owner-occupation also has regional variations. From Scotland only 45% of all dwellings are owner-occupied in comparison to England where 73% are owner-occupied.

There are 22.5 million dwellings in Britain, 50% of which are in post-1945 homes. 95% of households in 1987 had exclusive use of a bath or shower. 73% had central heating and 64% of all households had use of at least one car. The responsibility for the planning and supervision of housing policy rests with the Secretary of State for the Environment.

Construction and modernizations are governed by building regulations under the law. House building in the private sector has been regulated by an independent organization, the National House Building Council. Through this council a 10-year guarantee against structural defects and a 2-year guarantee against faulty workmanship are issued. Further, in 1989, the new Housing Standard Company Ltd, a private company, began operating and providing certification and 15-year guarantees.

PUBLIC-SECTOR HOUSING

The 460 local housing authorities and New Town authorities provide most public-sector housing. Public-housing authorities own approximately 6 million houses and flats. The number of houses owned by each authority varies greatly. The Northern Ireland Housing Executive owns about 125,000 homes, whilst the average is between 2,500 and 15,000. Local authorities build new houses and can recoup the costs of such works by raising loans on the open market and by borrowing from the independent statutory body, the Public Works Loans Board. Since 1980 local authorities can also raise money from the receipts raised by the sale of council houses and council lands.

The Housing Act 1980 has established a charter for public-sector tenants in England and Wales. Public-sector tenants of at least two years' standing can purchase their houses or flats at a discount which is dependent on the duration of their occupation. Over 1.4 million council houses have been sold (1989). The absolute number of council houses and the proportion of the total stock has fallen sharply since 1979, whilst owner-occupation has increased. The previous Government cut housing expenditure by 18% and the present Government has increased this cut by a further 64% between 1979–80 and 1988–9. Since the 1982 peak of 207,000 sales of council houses/flats sales have fallen. The average discount given in 1983 was 41%; this has since risen whilst the length of tenure required for eligibility (for purchasing application) has dropped.

Between 1971 and 1980 average local-authority new-house construction stood at 111,000 new homes per annum. By 1981 Government cut-backs had reduced this to 58,000. This figure has continually declined since 1980 and in 1988 only 21,000 new council homes were constructed (see Fig. 1).

In 1980, the Government announced large-scale council-rent increases. These were non-mandatory but

Housing Supply Average Annual Change in Dwelling Stock (1000s)

UNITED KINGDOM	*1961 –70*	*1971 –80*	*1981*	*1982*	*1983*	*1984*	*1985*	*1986*	*1987*	*1988*
NEW CONSTRUCTION										
Private enterprise	198	161	118	128	152	165	162	174	182	192
Housing associations	4	16	19	13	17	17	14	13	12	12
Local authorities	152	111	58	36	37	35	29	24	20	21
New town corporations	9	12	10	4	2	2	1	1	1	–
Government departments	5	2	1	–	–	–	–	–	1	1
Total new construction	368	302	206	182	208	220	206	212	215	226
OTHER CHANGES										
Slum clearance	−65	−55	−30	−26	−18	−15	−14	−11	−10	−11
Other[1]	−44	−19	−9	3	−1	−6	5	4	1	1
Total other changes	−109	−74	−39	−23	−19	−21	−8	−7	−9	−10
TOTAL NET GAIN	258	228	167	158	189	199	198	205	206	216

[1] Comprises net gains from conversions and other causes, and losses other than by slum clearance.

Any discrepancies within the table are as reported by government statistics and due to limitations of categorization.

Source: Dept. of Environment

were 'assumed' to have been implemented for the sake of calculating the levels of Government subsidy towards each local authority. Irrespective of whether or not the local authorities had actually implemented these rent increases, their levels of central Government subsidy was reduced as though they had.

Increasing emphasis has been placed by the Government on enabling the elderly to remain in their existing homes by providing more local home-based services and the modernization of their homes. Similarly, the Government has encouraged a new programme of 'care in the community', enabling the mentally handicapped to return to the community and into special needs housing (see HOMELESSNESS). Local authorities have a legal duty to provide accommodation to the homeless with dependent children or those who are vulnerable on the grounds of age or disability.

PRIVATE RENTED SECTOR

There has been a long-term and steady decline in the number of rented houses from private landlords and landladies since World War II – from over 50% of the housing stock in 1951 to just 7% in England in 1988. This has occurred due to the increase in the demand for owner-occupied dwellings. Many landlords and landladies operate on a small scale, whilst there are also large property owners and some property companies. The Government's policy has been to encourage the growth of the privately rented sector. To enable this the Government has relaxed and deregulated many previous restrictions, such as the 'fair rents' scheme.

The Housing Act of 1988 has provided for the deregulation of private-sector accommodation, for the creation of Housing Action Trusts, the reform of housing associations' finances, and, for council tenants, the right to choose new landlords/ladies if dissatisfied with their services. Prior to the Housing Act of 1988 most private lettings were protected under the Rent Act 1977.

Along with a wide degree of security of tenure where property was a fully protected 'regulated tenancy', the tenant or landlord/lady were able to apply for a 'fair rent' to be fixed by independent rent officers. This scheme was designed to limit the effect of an unregulated market economy, which would be able to set any rent desired. The fair-rent scheme meant that tenants could apply for independent officers to assess the true value of their property and apply rents accordingly, with recourse to the law if deemed necessary.

Under the new Housing Acts 1980 and 1988 two forms of tenancy have been created: the assured tenancy, which is designed to give long-term security in return for market rent levels, to be negotiated between landlord/ladies and tenant, and the assured shorthold tenancy. This is for a fixed term, at a rent negotiated between landlord/lady and tenant. The holder of a shorthold tenancy is eligible to apply to a rent assessment committee for rent to be determined. The committee may reduce rent demands if they are deemed excessive by comparison to other equivalent market rates for the area. The emphasis has thus been changed from fair rents to market rates. The previous fair-rents scheme is still continuing for those with existing lettings.

The Acts have also been designed to strengthen the laws concerning the harassment of tenants. Tenants and most other residential occupiers may not be evicted without a court order. The relaxation of controls is designed to lead to a rise in free-market rent setting. This in turn will lead to a growth in the number of properties available, as landlords/ladies are able to charge higher market rents.

Depending on personal circumstances householders may be eligible for housing benefit to assist in the payment of rent; in 1988 there were 5.18 million households claiming benefit.

Some confusion has arisen over the community charge, or poll tax, which has replaced rates previously paid by landlords/ladies out of rents with taxes for which tenants are now directly responsible. Rents will theoretically drop, allowing the 'saved' money to be used in part-payment of the new tax.

In Northern Ireland both tenants and landlords/ladies may apply to rent-assessment committees if the current rent is considered inappropriate. Rent increases are only permitted for properties which meet prescribed standards. There are no assured tenancies in Northern Ireland, but lets under the shorthold concept are available.

HOUSING ASSOCIATIONS

Housing associations provide a full range of accommodation for rent and sometimes sale. They normally cater for those who would otherwise have been provided for by their local authorities. With the sale of council housing there has been a corresponding increase in the stock of housing-association dwellings, from 281,000 in 1976 to 522,000 in 1988 in Britain. Housing-association stock as a percentage of total housing stock has risen from 1.6% in 1976 to 2.7% in 1988. As well as 522,000 homes they also provide 37,000 beds in hostels. Housing associations also provide for those with special needs, such as the elderly, disabled and single people. The associations are non-profit-making and are making an increasing contribution to low-cost housing. In Britain housing schemes qualify for Government grants if they are among the 2600 registered with housing corporations, Scottish Homes or Homes for Wales. These are statutory bodies which pay grants to, supervise and monitor associations in England, Scotland and Wales.

Housing associations provide accommodation on a shared-ownership basis. The occupiers are able to part-rent, part-own a home and are able to buy outright older homes which are in need of modernization. In England the Tenants' Guarantee initiated under the Housing Act 1988, assures rights covering tenancy terms; rent levels and the allocation of tenancies are protected. Associations aim, and are required, to set levels of rent which can be affordable to those on lower incomes.

MODERNIZATION AND GOVERNMENT HOUSING PROJECTS

The trend during the 1980s has been towards retaining existing buildings. Rather than demolishing old buildings the Government has placed emphasis on modernization and conversion. The emphasis has been switched from slum clearance and rebuilding to 'area renewal' or renovation.

In the late 1980s the Government has focused on inner-city problems, especially upon high-density local-authority estates, from where the urban unrest which led to riots began. Authorities aim to tackle these problems through refurbishment or sale to the private sector. The Government has also created a range of options and special private-investment schemes designed to alleviate these problems.

Estates Action Programme

This programme was started in 1985 and aims to provide a solution to run-down council-housing estates. The aim is to remove autonomy from the local authorities and to allow the tenants control in the management of their estates. This will be through tenant management co-operatives. Between 1986 and 1989 approval was given for 440 such schemes involving £260 million. Available total resources for 1989/90 are £190 million.

Priority Estates Projects

PEPs were set up in England in 1976, and in Wales in 1983. They aim to promote local housing management. Landlord/lady services are devolved to a local management team with emphasis placed on consultation with residents.

Housing Action Trusts

These were established under the Housing Act of 1988 for areas where social problems and housing disrepair are at their worst. The Government's solution has been to transfer council estates to the private rented sector for renovation. The trusts may take over responsibility from the local authority in specifically designated areas, where they renovate and improve the estates and then the control is handed to management/owner groupings, similar to co-ops and housing associations. New landlords may be chosen and must abide by the Tenants' Guarantee. Trusts are designed to stimulate community facilities such as shops, advice centres and local enterprise. This move towards the private rented sector has been designed to remove responsibility from those local councils deemed by the Government to be inefficient.

Home Improvement Grants

Between 1980 and 1988 about 1.6 million HIGs were paid to private sector dwellings in Britain. There are many categories of eligibility for grants: for renovation of older homes, provision of standard amenities, structural repairs and insulation. Under the Local Government and Housing Bill new means-tested grants will be allocated under new more 'objective fitness' standards.

Housing Action Areas and General Improvement Areas

In HAAs there is poor-condition and poor-quality housing and the areas are categorized by bad environmental and social conditions. There are about 200 HAAs in England and Wales. There are 1800 GIAs with fundamentally sound housing and stable populations. Government grants are available to improve these areas, particularly the externalities of the buildings and landscapes. Home improvement grants are also available for up to 75% of the costs. In Scotland HAAs can be established in areas where half the dwellings fail to meet statutory tolerable standards. In Northern Ireland 50 HAAs have been established since 1977.

MORTGAGE LOANS

Most homes are purchased with a loan, for which the property acts as security. Building societies are the main source of such loans, though in recent years banks and other financial institutions have raised their stake in the market. First-time buyers can usually receive up to 90% of the value of their property from the lenders. Loans are repayable over a fixed period of time at monthly intervals. Mortgages are available to those with average or above-average incomes. Those on lower incomes are not usually able to obtain a mortgage but may be able to share one with a housing association or similar institution. Owner-occupiers are entitled to tax relief on interest payments for their mortgage loans of up to £30,000 per individual. The number of mortgages has grown substantially over the last two decades, from 3,896,000 in 1971 to 7,674,000 in 1989, corresponding to the general trend to owner-occupation (see Fig. 2). UK mortgage interest has also risen substantially over the last two years, from 9.6% in 1988 to 15.2% in May 1990 (see Fig. 3).

Regional Trends

House prices and the rates of house-price inflation vary regionally, and this disparity has increased over the last decade (see Fig. 4). In 1971/2 and 1979/80 the price of the average London house was double that of the equivalent house in the North and Yorkshire and Humberside. By 1987 this price differential had increased to 2.7 times. The price of terraced housing

Mortgages, Mortgage Arrears and Repossessions

	ALL MORTGAGES			LOANS IN ARREARS AT END-PERIOD (Thousands)		
	Number of mortgages ('000s)	Balance due on mortgages (£m)	Average mortgage balance (£)	By 6–12 months	By over 12 months	Properties taken into possession in period ('000s)
1971	3,896	10,332	2,652	...	...	...
1976	4,609	22,565	4,896	...	...	...
1981	5,490	48,875	8,903	18.7	...	4.2
1982	5,645	56,696	10,044	23.8	4.8	6.0
1983	5,928	67,474	11,382	25.6	6.5	7.3
1984	6,314	81,882	12,968	41.9	8.3	10.9
1985	6,657	96,775	14,498	49.6	11.4	16.8
1986	7,023	115,699	16,474	45.3	11.3	21.0
1987	7,182	130,870	18,222	48.2	13.0	22.9
1988	7,369	153,167	20,785	37.4	8.9	16.2
1989	7,674	164,146	21,390	45.1	9.3	6.4

may vary by up to a factor of four. From an average of £20,000 in Yorkshire and Humberside to £79,300 in London in 1987. These differentials have decreased as London house prices have remained relatively static since late 1988, whilst prices in the North of England, Yorkshire, Lancashire and Humberside have continued to rise.

HOMELESSNESS

Since 1978 the number of registered homeless households, in England, has doubled, from 53,100 in 1978 to 112,550 in 1988. By 1989 this figure had risen further, reaching 126,240. Councils now turn away more homeless people than they are able to agree to help: since 1981, 1.5 million applicants for housing assistance have been refused. Of these, a large proportion are now categorized as 'intentionally homeless'.

Between 1988 and 1989 the number of households housed in temporary accommodation – bed & breakfast and squats – rose by 26% from 30,100 to 37,900. The number of households in bed & breakfast accommodation in London has risen from 1000 in 1981 to 4000 by 1985. The length of stay varies, since Government legislation after 1987 reduced the ability of many to claim for supplementary benefit whilst in this type of housing. The cost of such accommodation is relatively high: top-up payments in London in 1987 were estimated at £92 per week per household, a total of £15 million per year. In the long run, it is estimated that the cost of building new council houses would be cheaper than paying out top-up loans. However, councils have been unable to build such housing due to the financial limits placed upon them.

Homelessness has traditionally been defined as an urban problem only affecting the larger cities. Nonetheless, in 1988 42% of all homeless households were not in big cities. Salisbury saw a 52% rise in homelessness, Colchester 48% and Gateshead 27%. The most common reason stated for homelessness (44%) was that 'parents, relatives or friends were no longer willing or able to accommodate these individuals'. The breakdown of a relationship with a partner was the reason for 19% of homelessness. Mortgage arrears accounted for 7%, loss of private rented dwelling 11% and rent arrears (to private and local authorities) 4%.

The Pat Niner report estimated that there are 180,000 single homeless people in Britain. Of these, the Salvation Army estimates that 75,000 are in London. Estimates of homelessness and in particular sleeping rough are inevitably hard to gather, but most estimates state that between 1000 and 4000 sleep rough in the capital each night. A further 25,000 people sleep in temporary bed & breakfast accommodation each night and 30,000 sleep in squats. Centrepoint, a housing charity specifically aimed to alleviate youth homelessness, estimates that there are at least 50,000 young homeless in central London between the ages of 16 and 19.

Growing concern has highlighted the problems surrounding previous patients of psychiatric hospitals. Since the Government's 'Care in the Community' programme started 25,000 beds in psychiatric hospitals have been shut down. Correspondingly only 4000 new residential places have been established within the community. This has led to questions as to the whereabouts of these people, some of whom must have become homeless.

One of the key reasons for the growing number of homeless has been the national trend away from rented accommodation towards home ownership. The number of rented dwellings, both public and private, has decreased from 7,404,000 in 1976 to 6,269,000 in 1988. The Department of the Environment estimates that between 1979 and 1987 574,000 dwellings were removed from the private rented sector. In London this amounts to a loss of 17,000 dwellings a year. The private rented sector now stands at two-thirds of its 1981 figure. This decrease can partly be explained by the decline in local-authority, Government-funded house constructions, from 140,000 new public housing completions in 1977 to 24,800 in 1988.

Local-authority housing investment has fallen from £3700 million in 1980–1 to £1127 million in 1988–9. Government subsidies to local authorities for housing has decreased by 77% during the last nine years (1981–90), from £2060 million in 1978–9 to £473 million in 1987/8.

Home ownership has risen correspondingly from 7,197,000 dwellings in 1966 to 10,451,000 dwellings in 1980 and 13,076,000 in 1989. As house prices have more than doubled since 1980 and earnings have risen at a lower ratio (see Fig. 4) home ownership has become increasingly difficult for those on a lower income. Higher interest rates during 1989 and 1990 have led to a rise in mortgage defaulting and repossessions. Building-society repossessions have risen from 2530 in 1979 to 16,150 in 1988.

LAW

THE LEGAL SYSTEM

The legal systems of all four countries of the United Kingdom make a distinction between criminal law (wrongful acts harmful to the community) and civil law (disputes between individuals or organizations). However, Scottish law and the legal structure are very different from those of England and Wales. Northern Ireland's legal structure is very similar to England and Wales but many of the laws themselves are different.

ENGLAND AND WALES

CRIMINAL LAW

The initial decision as to whether a person should be charged with a crime lies with the police; if they do bring a charge the papers go to the Crown Prosecution Service (headed by the Director of Public Prosecutions) which decides whether or not the case should go to court.

The most serious offences – murder, manslaughter, rape, etc. – can only be tried on *indictment* by a judge and a jury in the Crown Court. Less serious crimes are known as *summary* offences and can be tried by voluntary magistrates without a jury: these are the vast majority of cases tried. In between come the 'either way' offences (e.g. burglary and malicious wounding) which can go either to the magistrates or the Crown Court at the decision of the Crown Prosecution Service or the defendant (who may prefer to be heard by a jury). The accused person is presumed innocent; the trial consists of a contest in which the prosecution attempts to prove the person guilty while the defence tries to show that the case has not been proved (the defence does not have positively to show the accused to be innocent). Prosecution and defence lawyers share access to the same documents so that neither side is at a disadvantage re information. The way in which statements are taken from the accused person and witnesses are controlled by 'judges' rules' and if these are disregarded the statements cannot be used as evidence in court.

Magistrates' Courts

The first level of criminal court is the magistrates' court, normally consisting of three voluntary justices (JPs) advised by a professional clerk; in London and other large cities the court has a professional ('stipendiary', i.e. paid) magistrate sitting alone. There are 24,521 lay magistrates (including 12,577 women) and 64 stipendiaries. The magistrates' courts try over 97% of all criminal cases. For summary offences they have the power to pass a sentence of up to 6 months' imprisonment or a fine of up to £2000. They also hold preliminary hearings of indictable offences that must be tried in the Crown Court, unless a point of law is involved in which case it goes to the High Court.

Crown Court

The second level of courts was set up in 1971 to replace the quarter sessions and assizes; it is part of the Supreme Court of the Judicature (see table). The advantage of the Crown Court is that it can meet in any place and as frequently as needed so as to respond to the workload. There are now 92 places in England and Wales where Crown Court sessions are held. They are presided over by a High Court judge, or a circuit judge, or a recorder (a part-time judge), always sitting with a jury of 12. The Crown Court hears cases of serious crimes (indictable offences) and appeals from the magistrates' court, and can also pass sentence on persons convicted at the magistrates' court but not sentenced because the magistrates felt their range of sentence insufficient for the case. Any appeal from the Crown Court goes to the Court of Appeal (Criminal Division).

Court of Appeal

The Court of Appeal with its two divisions, Criminal and Civil, is the highest part of the Supreme Court of the Judicature. The Criminal Division consists of the Lord Chief Justice (or another Lord Justice) with a number of High Court judges (usually two or four, to make a 'bench' of three or five judges); there is no jury. It hears appeals from decisions in the Crown Court on indictable cases. Appeals involving a point of law are brought by right, but other appeals need the permission of the Crown Court. Appeals from the Court of Appeal can be made to the House of Lords.

House of Lords

Sitting as a law court, the House of Lords consists of the Lord Chancellor, the Lords of Appeal in Ordinary (ten of them) and any other Lords who have been senior judges. It hears appeals from the Court of Appeal in criminal cases, but only if a point of law of general public importance is involved.

At the very last resort, in cases for which sentence of death has been passed (abolished for murder in 1965 but still in force for certain categories of treason and piracy) an appeal can be made for a reprieve by royal prerogative. The decision whether or not to grant this is made on the advice of the Home Secretary.

CIVIL LAW

All civil cases are initiated by the party which considers that it has ben harmed (this can be an individual, a company, or a public body); this party is termed the *plaintiff*. The other party (or parties) are termed the *defendant(s)*. As all civil cases are private matters between parties concerned, they can be dropped at any time if a mutually satisfactory compromise can be reached out of court. For actions in the county court, the plaintiff notifies the court of the complaint, and the court issues a summons to the defendant. In High Court cases, the plaintiff sends a writ direct to the defendant, who either concedes the matter (and pays the damages demanded or whatever) or else notifies the court that the matter will be contested. Either party may request that their case be heard before a jury, who can rule on matters of fact and/or the size of damages. The judge can order the costs to be charged either to the winner or loser; sometimes they are borne as a public expense.

Magistrates' Courts

The lowest courts for civil cases are the magistrates' courts (see above), which can hear cases on certain family matters (adoption, guardianship, custody and

COURT SYSTEMS OF THE UNITED KINGDOM

ENGLAND & WALES

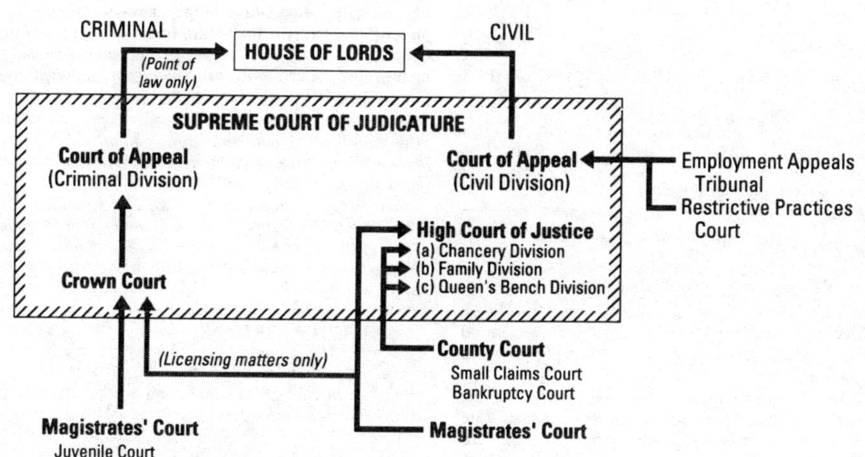

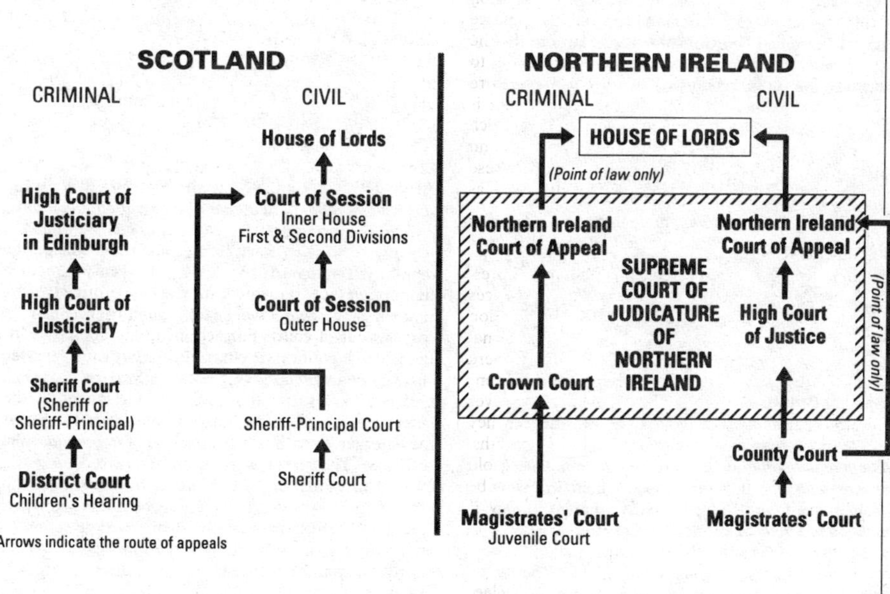

maintenance, but not divorce), and on public health. They also grant licences for public houses and betting shops (appeals for relicensing decisions go to the Crown Court, as for criminal cases). Appeals against their decisions on civil cases go to the High Court.

County Courts

The great majority of civil cases are dealt with by the county courts (of which there are 274, each presided over by a circuit judge). Cases heard here include divorce (except contested cases which go to the High Court), bankruptcy (except in London), landlord-and-tenant, probate (i.e. wills) contract, tort (i.e. harming another party's interests in situations not covered by a contract), and cases involving sexual or racial discrimination. If the sums involved are above a certain limit (£5000 in contract and tort cases) the matter goes to the High Court, as do appeals from county court decisions.

Related to the county courts are certain specialist courts. The *small claims courts* deal with complaints if the sum involved is under £500 with fixed costs of 10% of the sum up to £300, £37 above that. The *Bankruptcy Court* only deals with cases in the Greater London area.

High Court

The High Court of Justice forms part of the Supreme Court of the Judicature (see table). It consists of three divisions: (i) Chancery, which deals with probate, bankruptcy, patents and copyright (11 judges, no women); (ii) Queen's Bench, which deals with the law of the sea, cases involving money or property over the value that county courts can deal with, and appeals from the county or magistrates' courts (54 judges, no women); (iii) Family Court (16 judges, one woman). Cases being heard for the first time come before a judge sitting alone, but appeals are usually heard by two or three judges (occasionally the Lord Chancellor authorizes a judge to hear an appeal alone). Any appeal from the High Court Divisions goes to the Civil Division of the Court of Appeal (or very occasionally direct to the House of Lords).

Court of Appeal

The Civil Division of the Court of Appeal consists of its President – the Master of the Rolls – and 27 Lord Justices of Appeal (one woman) who sit in either twos or threes. The Court hears appeals not only from the Higher Court but also from some specialized courts, such as the restrictive practices court, and the Employment Appeal Tribunal (see below). Any appeal from the Civil Division of the Court of Appeal goes to the House of Lords (see above), the final authority for civil matters.

Special Courts

Several special-purpose courts lie outside the main civil/criminal system.

Coroners' courts. A coroner is either a lawyer or a doctor who presides over a court held to investigate violent deaths or sudden deaths where the cause is unknown. Such deaths may be reported by members of the public, public authorities, doctors, the police or the registrar of births, marriages and deaths. The coroner may, if the cause of death is unknown, order a post-mortem examination; if the result of this satisfies the coroner that the death is natural no inquest need be held. In other circumstances, including all violent deaths and all deaths in prison or police custody, the coroner must establish time, place and cause of death; usually the coroner sits alone but occasionally there is a jury. The verdicts that the coroner can bring are: death from natural causes, accidental death, misadventure, unlawful killing, open, suicide, and death due to drug dependency. In many cases a rider is added, e.g. due to lack of care. Coroners also have jurisdiction over cases of treasure trove.

Restrictive practices court. This hears complaints about restrictive trade agreements, which are legal only if they operate to the benefit of the general public. It is presided over by a High Court judge with four other judges, but lay persons with appropriate expertise (up to ten of them) may also sit. Appeals from this court go to the Court of Appeal (Civil Division).

Employment Tribunal. This hears appeals against the decisions of the industrial tribunals and of the certification officer. A High Court judge hears the appeal, assisted by two lay persons with industrial-relations experience, one from the employers' and one from the trade unions' side (sometimes there are two from each side). Appeals from the Tribunal are heard by the Court of Appeal (Civil Division).

NORTHERN IRELAND

The legal system in Northern Ireland is very similar to that in England and Wales (see table above). The administration of the Northern Ireland Court Service is directed by the Lord Chancellor, and there is a separate Director of Public Prosecutions for Northern Ireland responsible to the Attorney General.

Under the Northern Ireland (Emergency Provisions) Act 1978 certain serious crimes can be tried by a judge with no jury (the so-called 'Diplock' courts). It is also possible for a court in Northern Ireland to try a person for a terrorism-connected offence committed in the Irish Republic.

SCOTLAND

Scotland's judicature is very different from that of the rest of the United Kingdom in terms of the system of courts, the procedures used, and the laws themselves.

CRIMINAL LAW

The chief legal officer is the Lord Advocate. He is ultimately responsible for all criminal prosecutions, both in deciding whether a person should go for trial and in preparing the case. At higher levels this is done by officers of the Crown Office, and the prosecution is conducted in court by the Lord Advocate, or his deputy, or (more usually) one of a number of advocates known as Crown Council. In the lower courts the case is prepared and the prosecution conducted by a procurator fiscal, a local law officer. (Procurator fiscals also investigate violent or unexplained death.)

Since 1987 it has been possible for the procurator fiscal to offer a suspected person a fixed penalty as an alternative to being prosecuted, for certain minor offences. The person is not obliged to accept.

Offences are classified according to how serious they are, and the minor ones are tried under summary procedure (with judge only) while serious ones are tried on indictment (with judge and jury). The accused is presumed to be innocent, but there are three possible verdicts: 'guilty', 'innocent' or 'not proven'. Unlike in England and Wales, an accused person cannot be found guilty on their confession alone without corroborating evidence. The jury consists of 15 people who reach their verdict by a simple majority.

Court Structure

The administration of all courts in Scotland is managed by the Scottish Courts Administration, which is part of the Scottish Office and therefore completely separate from the Lord Advocate's Department which runs the judiciary.

District Courts

The lowest courts are the district courts, established in each local-authority district and presided over by lay justices. They have limited power in terms of what offences they can deal with and what penalties they can impose; they always use summary procedure (i.e. they sit without a jury). In Glasgow there are four stipendiary magistrates in the district courts, with powers equivalent to a sheriff (see below) but still only using summary procedure. Appeals from decisions of the district court go before the sheriff.

Sheriffs' Courts

The courts of the sheriffs and sheriffs-principal are the core of the Scottish system. The country is divided into six sheriffdoms, each with a sheriff-principal, and below these are a total of 45 sheriff-court districts, each with a full time sheriff (or sheriffs).

In criminal cases, the powers of the sheriffs-principal and the sheriffs are the same. Under summary procedure they try less serious offences; sitting with a jury they can try all serious criminal offences committed within the sheriffdom (unless it is one of the gravest crimes which can only be tried by the High court of Justiciary) and hear appeals from the lower courts. In civil cases, the sheriff's is the first court available for a complaint, and the great majority of cases are settled there. Appeals from decisions in criminal cases go to the High Court, in civil cases either to the sheriff-principal or to the Court of Session.

High Court of Justiciary

For criminal cases, the High Court of Justiciary is the senior court. It tries all the most serious cases (murder, rape, treason etc.). It also acts as the final appeal court for any cases tried on indictment, either in the High Court itself or in the Sheriffs' courts; as an appeal court the High Court of Justiciary can sit only in Edinburgh. There are 24 judges, all men.

There is no appeal in criminal cases to the Houses of Lords.

Court of Session

This sits only in Edinburgh, and consists of two parts, the Outer House and the Inner House. The Outer House is the senior court hearing civil cases in their first instance (dealing with cases where the value claimed is over the limit for the sheriffs' courts). The Inner House consists of two equal divisions, and hears appeals on civil cases both from the sheriffs' courts and from the Outer House. An appeal may be made from the Inner House to the House of Lords. The judges of the Court of Session are the same people as in the High Court of Justiciary.

JURY SYSTEM

Throughout the United Kingdom the qualifications for serving as a juror are the same: everyone who is on the electoral register, is aged 18–70 and has lived for five years in the United Kingdom, the Channel Islands or the Isle of Man since reaching the age of 13 is eligible. Certain classes of people are ineligible; they are: (i) the judiciary (judges of all ranks, including JPs); (ii) others concerned with the administration of justice (all solicitors and barristers or advocates, police officers, prison officers, probation officers etc.); (iii) the clergy (including monks and nuns); (iv) mentally ill persons. Some people are disqualified on account of their criminal record, e.g. if they have ever received a life sentence, or have been in prison or youth custody within the last ten years, or have been placed on probation within the last five years. Many people can claim to be excused from jury service on account of their profession; these include MPs, members of the House of Lords and of the European Parliament, members of the armed forces, and practising medical professionals (including doctors, dentists, midwives, veterinary surgeons and pharmaceutical chemists). Anyone can ask to be exempted if they have served as a juror within the previous two years, or can ask for their attendance to be deferred if it is at a time that causes them severe inconvenience.

All the people summoned to serve as jurors at a particular time have their names put on long lists, known as 'panels'. The jury for a particular case is chosen by ballot from one of the panels, and generally that jury will try the one case only, unless it is so short that the next case starts within 24 hours of the first. However, each juror will have been required to serve a certain number of days, and when the first case they have tried is over their name will go onto a panel for possible selection for another case, until they have fulfilled their service. In a case being tried on indictment, the accused can challenge any juror, but only for a specified reason; it is up to the judge to decide whether the reason is sufficient for the juror to be taken off the case. There is no limit to the number of jurors that can be challenged.

The jury has to decide whether the accused is guilty or not guilty. In England and Wales, the jury normally consists of 12 people (but it is sometimes reduced if jurors fall ill during the trial), and if they cannot agree unanimously the judge may rule after the jury has deliberated for two hours that a majority verdict will be acceptable; 10 jurors must agree, or 9 if the total jury is only 10. If the jury cannot agree, the judge must order a new trial with a different jury but this is extremely unusual. In Scotland, the jury is normally 15 people, and verdicts are always reached by simple majority; there is however a third verdict in Scotland – 'not proven' – which results in the acquittal of the accused (they cannot be tried again for the same offence). Jury arrangements in Northern Ireland are very similar to those in England and Wales (one difference being that teachers and university lecturers can claim exemption from service).

THE LEGAL PROFESSION

The legal profession is divided into two branches. (i) *Solicitors* provide legal services to the public, including general advice, drafting documents, e.g. wills, trusteeship, conducting negotiations, e.g. house conveyancing, conducting family matters, e.g. divorce or adoption, and engaging and briefing barristers for court cases. Solicitors can also appear in court. Most solicitors work in partnerships, and most are assisted by legal executives on less specialised areas of law. The profession is governed by the Law Society of England and

Wales, the Law Society of Northern Ireland, and the Law Society of Scotland. (ii) *Barristers* (in Scotland known as advocates) represent people in higher courts, and also give advice on legal matters. They are not allowed to deal direct with the public, so a solicitor is always involved in giving the brief or submitting questions for advice. Senior barristers are awarded the title of Queen's Council (QC). The governing bodies for the profession are the General Council for the Bar, the General Council for the Bar in Northern Ireland, the Executive Council of the Inn of Court of Northern Ireland and the Faculty of Advocates.

Both barristers and solicitors may be appointed by judges. All judges are appointed by the Queen (on the advice of the Prime Minister) and hold office for life. A junior judge can be dismissed for misconduct or proven incapacity. A senior judge in England, Wales and Northern Ireland can be dismissed only if both Houses of Parliament present an address to the Queen; in Scotland dismissal is not possible.

Table of income per week and the proportion of the cost that must be paid by someone in receipt of legal advice and assistance

More than	*But not exceeding*	*Contribution*
£61	£69	£5
£69	£75	£12
£75	£81	£19
£81	£87	£25
£87	£93	£32
£93	£98	£37
£98	£103	£42
£103	£108	£48
£108	£113	£53
£113	£118	£59
£118	£123	£64
£123	£128	£70

LEGAL ASSISTANCE

Duty Solicitor Scheme

Under the Legal Aid Acts of 1974, 1982 and 1988 solicitors are available either in attendance or on call at magistrates' courts; they may give advice to people accused of a criminal offence, make an application for bail, and give limited other kinds of help. The service is free. From 1 January 1986 the service was extended to cover police stations, where solicitors are now available 24 hours a day (in attendance or on call) to give advice to suspects before or after they are charged. This service is also free. The police-stations scheme cost £12.5 million to run in its first year, rising by 72% to £21.5 in 1987 and again by 30% to £28 million in 1988; there is no record of how many people were helped.

Legal Advice and Assistance Scheme

This scheme (known as the Green Form Scheme in England and Wales and the Pink Form Scheme in Scotland) gives the poorest people a limited amount of legal advice. The work a solicitor can do for a client is limited to two hours (or, in England and Wales only, three hours for an undefended divorce or legal separation); exceptionally the solicitor can apply for an extension to complete work over the fixed time. The help given does not usually include representing the client in any court (for which legal aid is available; see below), and normally only covers advice on points of law, negotiating, writing letters, getting a barrister's or advocate's advice, or preparing documents for a tribunal hearing.

To qualify for the scheme an applicant must have (a) savings of less than £890, (b) a weekly income of less than £128 after deducting the following: income tax, National Insurance, £32.75 for spouse, and an allowance for each dependent or child (£34.25 if over 18, £26.00 if aged 16–17, £21.70 if 11–15 and £14.70 if under 11). All persons on family credit or income support automatically qualify, subject to the savings limit. If the 'disposable weekly income' (as calculated above) is under £61 the person will get a completely free service, but above that may have to pay a proportion of the cost.

Sometimes if as a result of advice given under the scheme a person wins a case involving money or property, part of their 'winnings' will be deducted to pay the solicitor.

About 994,606 people were helped under the scheme in 1988/9.

Legal Aid – Civil Courts

Legal aid is also available to people who need to bring a civil case to court or to defend a case brought against them. This help will cover preparation of the case and representation in court. The applicant has to go first to a solicitor who will fill in the form and send it to the Legal Aid Board (or the Scottish Legal Aid Board or the Law Society of Northern Ireland). The board will approve the application if they believe the person has reasonable grounds for going to court or making a defence; then the papers go to the Department of Social Security, who assess the applicant's capital and income and issue a legal aid certificate. (As there is usually a long delay at this stage, it is possible to get 'emergency legal aid' for urgent cases.) The financial criteria are (a) savings under £6000, (b) a weekly disposable income under £116.06 (allowances are made for spouse and dependent relatives, at the same rates as for the legal advice and assistance scheme, and all essential costs such as mortgage payments, fares to and from work, child care expenses are also allowable. If the weekly disposable income is over £48.37, or if the person has savings of between £3000 and £6000, a contribution towards legal costs will have to be made. As with the legal advice and assistance scheme, if a person wins a case involving money or property the cost of their legal aid may be deducted from their 'winnings' and only the remainder paid to them (this does not happen if the case was about maintenance payments or state benefits).

In 1987/8 a total of 237,000 people received legal aid for civil cases; over half of the cases (108,000) involved divorce proceedings, for which 29,000 men and 79,000 women got legal aid.

Legal Aid and Criminal Courts

The largest part of the state-supported legal assistance scheme is legal aid for persons accused of a criminal offence. Legal aid pays for a solicitor to prepare the defence and a barrister or advocate to appear in court, and also covers applications for bail.

The position in England and Wales is that, subject to a means test, legal aid will be granted to an applicant 'if it appears to be in the interests of justice' to do so. In practice this covers the vast majority of cases, and legal aid is always granted (subject to a means test) for cases of murder, and is generally granted where defendants are likely to go to prison or to lose their jobs if convicted, or if they are unable (through physical or mental disability or because of poor English) to understand court proceedings. Legal aid is very rarely given for motoring or other minor charges. Legal aid can be given to children facing criminal charges, subject to their parents' means. The court itself assesses what contribution, if any, a person must make towards the cost of their legal aid.

In Scotland and Northern Ireland the position is similar, except that no contribution is required; persons qualifying for criminal legal aid get the entire costs of their defence paid.

SENTENCES

Prison sentences are imposed in the minority of cases, fines being by far the most usual form of punishment for criminal offences.

PRISONERS

The prison population consists not only of people sentenced to imprisonment but also the following categories: (a) people awaiting trial who have been refused bail (19% of prison population); (b) people convicted in a lower court awaiting sentence in a higher

Breakdown of persons sentenced for indictable offences 1987/88

	Men (%)	*Women (%)*
Absolute discharge	0.6	0.8
Conditional discharge	11.1	28.1
Probation order	8.3	18.1
Supervision order	1.8	1.2
Fine	39.4	34.4
Community Service order	8.5	3.8
Attendance centre order	2.2	6.4
Care order	0.1	0.1
Young offender institution	6.7	1.3
Imprisonment		
Fully suspended	7.3	5.7
Partly suspended	0.7	0.6
Unsuspended	11.7	4.2
Other sentence or order	1.5	1.4
Total number of offenders	337,500	46,100

Length of prison sentences

	Men (over 21)			*Women (over 21)*		
	1971	*1984*	*1987*	*1971*	*1984*	*1987*
England & Wales						
Life	770	1760	2170	20	50	60
Over 4 years (exl. life)	3320	4220	6590	20	60	150
18 months to 4 years	9580	7550	9890	170	200	390
6 to 18 months	8230	6500	6110	210	300	310
Less than 6 months	2970	3730	2920	130	270	180
Total	24,870	23,770	27,680	540	880	1090
Scotland						
Life	134	313	349	2	7	6
Over 3 years (excl. life)	500	752	1221	5	7	26
18 months to 3 years	481	280	404	6	7	10
6 to 18 months	503	448	472	12	13	10
Less than 6 months	1275	896	909	33	29	65
Total	2893	2689	3356	58	63	117
Northern Ireland						
Life	N/A	292	335	N/A	2	6
Over 4 years (excl. life)	N/A	587	369	N/A	11	7
18 months to 4 years	N/A	205	243	N/A	1	2
6 to 18 months	N/A	124	154	N/A	3	4
Less than 6 months	N/A	62	100	N/A	2	4
Total	N/A	1270	1201	N/A	19	23

Average daily population of prisons

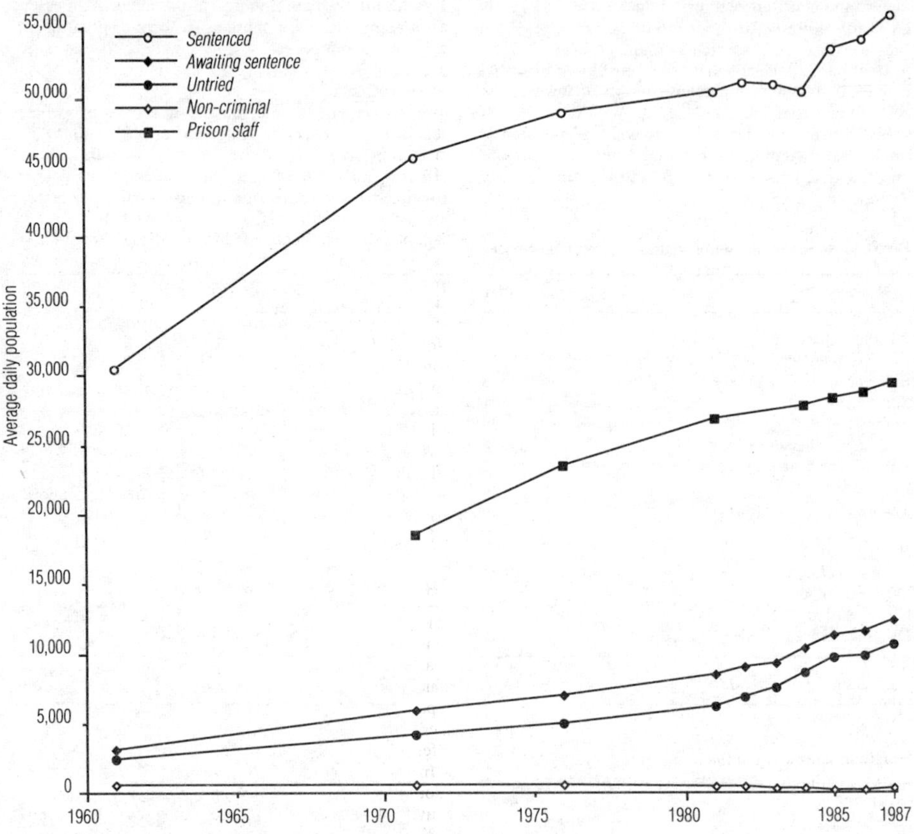

court (3%); (c) non-criminal people, including immigrants and people in default of court orders (0.5%).

The prison population is increasing much faster than the rate of increase in the population as a whole, mainly because of the increase in the number of people awaiting trial, but also because of the longer average sentences.

Prisoners' Classification

Immediately after they are sentenced, prisoners are classified according to the security risk they present (not according to the crime committed).

Category A. 'Those whose escape would be highly dangerous to the public, the police or the security of the State.' These prisoners are kept in dispersal prisons, where their numbers must not exceed 15% of the total prison population.

Category B. 'Those for whom the highest conditions of security are not required but for whom escape must be made very difficult.' These prisoners are kept either in dispersal prisons with category A prisoners or in local prisons; some are in closed training prisons.

Category C. 'Those who cannot be trusted in open conditions but who do not have the ability or resources to make a determined escape attempt.' The great majority of prisoners come under this classification. These prisoners are generally kept in closed training prisons although some are in local prisons.

Category D. 'Those who can reasonably be trusted to serve their sentence in open conditions.'

Young offenders. Young offenders' prisons can be either open or closed depending on the nature of the crime committed.

EXPENDITURE

The annual cost of the Prison Department (England and Wales only) rose in the ten years 1977–87 from £219.9 million to £786.4 million, an increase of 63% after allowing for inflation. This includes capital costs for building new prisons.

PAROLE BOARD

The Parole Board constituted under Section 59 of the Criminal Justice Act is an independent body which can make recommendations to the Home Secretary for the early release of prisoners. To qualify for consideration for parole a prisoner must have served at least one-third of the sentence or six months minimum. Members of the Parole Board are: Viscount Colville of Culross QC, Hon. Mr Justice Garland, T.J. Wilkie, and the three of them sit together. In 1988 the board heard 23,136 applications and recommended parole in 12,796 cases (55%). A prisoner on parole is freed under the terms of the parole licence and is liable to be recalled to prison if the conditions set are not complied with (about one in 20 paroled prisoners were recalled in 1987).

The Parole Board of Scotland works in a similar way, making its recommendation to the Secretary of State for Scotland. It generally recommends fewer cases for parole (370 out of 1167 – 32% – in 1987). There is no parole in Northern Ireland.

LIFE PRISONERS

Prisoners serving life sentences can be released on licence on the recommendation of the appropriate Parole Board; the Home Secretary or the Secretary of State for Scotland then consults the judiciary but the final decision is theirs alone. In Northern Ireland there is an independent review body to make recommendations to the Secretary of State for Northern Ireland, who takes into account not only the prisoner's own circumstances but also the political situation in the country.

YOUNG OFFENDERS

In all parts of the United Kingdom there is a lower age limit below which a child is not responsible for its actions and cannot be charged with any crime (even in circumstances when it is obvious that the child did commit the crime); in Scotland the age is 8, and in England, Wales, and Northern Ireland it is 10.

Courts

In England, Wales and Northern Ireland children aged between 10 and 16 can be brought before a juvenile court, either because the local authority believes the child needs to be taken into care for its own good, or because the child is accused of an offence. The juvenile court is a special magistrates' court with three justices (at least one man and one woman). It is held on separate premises from the magistrates' court and is not open to the public; the press is not permitted to report any details about a person appearing before a juvenile court.

In Scotland it is very unusual for a child aged between 8 and 15 to be prosecuted at all, and this can only be done on the personal authority of the Lord Advocate (normally only for serious crimes or in cases where the child is jointly accused with someone older). Children of this age who are considered to need to be taken into care, or who are accused of an offence, appear before a children's hearing. This consists of a group of three lay people from a panel of residents of the region or islands concerned.

After reaching the age of 17 (16 in Scotland) a young person can be tried in the same courts as adults.

Sentences

The great majority of young offenders do not come before a court or a hearing at all but are dealt with by being cautioned by (or on the authoirty of) a senior policeman.

Every effort is made to deal with young offenders by other means than custodial sentences. Many are required to pay fines and/or compensation; the parents can be made to pay if the young person cannot. Under a care order, the local authority decides where the child should live, which may be at home, with foster parents or in a community home. A supervision order usually means that the child lives at home but has to comply with directions from a superior or probation officer, which may include training courses. For older children who have committed the type of offence for which an adult would be sent to prison there are two further possibilities; compulsory attendance on Saturdays at an attendance centre, or community service (to which the sentenced person has to give their consent).

A child or young person accused of murder or manslaughter or any other serious crime will be taken into care as soon as the charge is made, and if they are particularly unruly will be looked after in a remand centre (provided that they are 15 or over if a boy, 17 or over if a girl). Young persons under the age of 20 cannot be sentenced to go to an adult prison. If they must be kept in custody they are sentenced to a young offenders' institution (England, Wales and Scotland) or young offenders' centre (Northern Ireland). A person under 18 years old who has been convicted of murder cannot be sentenced to life imprisonment but is detained during Her Majesty's pleasure (England and Wales and Northern Ireland) or without limit as directed by the Secretary of State (Scotland). For other offences a person aged 17–20 (England, Wales and Northern Ireland) or 16–20 (Scotland) who has committed a crime for which an adult would be imprisoned is kept in custody for an appropriate length of time, including a life sentence for the most serious crimes.

A young person can also be committed to a young offenders' institution for being in default of a fine (and in fact the majority of inmates at a young offenders' institution in Scotland are defaulters – nearly 60% in 1987).

THE PROBATION SERVICE

One of the characteristics of the British legal system is its use of both custodial and non-custodial sentencing to deal with those who break the law. The decision as to which sentence would be most suitable with regard to a particular offence committed is at the discretion of the court and is based on the nature and gravity of the offence and information about the offender.

In the postwar era the tendency of the courts to adopt non-custodial sentencing as a penalty for criminal activity has increased considerably. In 1948 only 41% of adults convicted of offences were given non-custodial sentences but by 1979 this had increased to 66%. In 1988 136,000 people commenced supervision by the probation service, and by 31 December 1988 this figure has increased to 146,000.

The upward trend in the use of non-custodial sentencing has in part been influenced by reservations about the efficacy of imprisonment for certain types of offender. As a consequence a wide range of non-custodial sentences are now available including probation, community service, suspended sentencing and fines. In 1988 the Government issued a consultative document on punishment in the community suggesting that the courts in England and Wales should be able to impose a new supervision and restriction order on an offender which would include compensation to the victim, community service, residence at a hostel or other appointed place, prescribed activities at a day centre or elsewhere, curfew or house arrest, or tracking an offender's whereabouts. In 1989 the government introduced electronic tagging on an experimental basis for the first time.

THE PROBATION AND AFTER CARE SERVICE

The Probation and After Care Service is responsible for organizing and administering the bulk of non-custodial sentences. In the United Kingdom there are 56 probation areas. In England and Wales the service is run locally through committees, comprising local magistrates and co-opted members of the legal profession. In Northern Ireland the service is adminis-

Young offenders in the UK

	Age 8	9	10	11	12	13	14	15	16	17	18	19	20
Age of criminal responsibility													
E & W	–	–	●										
N Ireland	–	–	●										
Scotland	●												
Trial in juvenile court													
E & W	–	–	●	●	●	●	●	●	●				
N Ireland	–	–	●	●	●	●	●	●	●				
Scotland: children's hearings	●	●	●	●	●	●	●	●					
Sentences:													
Care order													
E & W	–	–	●	●	●	●	●	●	●	●	●	[●]	
N Ireland	–	–	●	●	●	●	●	●	●	●			
Scotland	●	●	●	●	●	●	●	●	●				
Supervision													
E & W	–	–	●	●	●	●	●	●	●				
N Ireland	–	–	–	–	–	–	–	–	–				
Scotland	●	●	●	●	●	●	●	●	●	●	●		
Probation													
E & W	–	–	–	–	–	–	–	–	–	●	●	●	●
N Ireland	–	–	●	●	●	●	●	●	●	●	●	●	●
Scotland	–	–	–	–	–	–	–	–	●	●	●	●	●
Attendance centre													
E & W	–	–	–	–	–	–	← max 24 hrs →			← max 36 hrs →			
N Ireland (Belfast only)	–	–	–	–	–	–	●	●	●	●	●	●	●
Scotland	–	–	–	–	–	–	–	–	–	–	–	–	–
Community service													
E & W	–	–	–	–	–	–	–	–	40–120 hrs	← 40–240 hrs →			
N Ireland	–	–	–	–	–	–	–	–	–	●	●	●	●
Scotland	–	–	–	–	–	–	–	–	–	●	●	●	●
Detention													
E & W: Young Offenders' Institutions	–	–	–	–	–	–	Boys 3 wks to 4 mths	Boys max 12 mths Girls min 4 mths max 12 mths		●	●	●	●
N Ireland:													
Training schools	–	–	–	–	–	–	●	●	●	–	–	–	–
Young Offenders' Centres	–	–	–	–	–	–	–	–	–	●	●	●	●
Scotland: Young Offenders' Institutions	–	–	–	–	–	–	–	–	●	●	●	●	●

tered by the Northern Ireland Office and in Scotland the functions of the service are run by the social work departments of local authorities, but there is no separate service as in England and Wales.

The main functions of the probation service are to rehabilitate offenders, to provide prison and welfare services and to provide social inquiry reports on offenders for the courts. Between 1987 and 1988 the probation service prepared about 215 social inquiry reports and 35,000 criminal reports, the average caseload per main-grade officer amounting to 29.

Probation

Probation is designed to secure the rehabilitation of an offender while he continues his or her normal life under the supervision and guidance of a probation officer. Before placing an offender on probation which may last from six months to three years, the court must explain the order in ordinary language ensuring that the offender consents to the requirements of the order and understands that failure to comply with them will make him or her liable to a penalty or to being dealt with for the original offence. In order to be eligible for probation the offender must be aged 17 or more in England and Wales, over 16 in Scotland, and over 10 in Northern Ireland. The order can require the offender to attend a particular place at a particular time and/or to take part in activities or it may require the offender to attend one of a number of day centres set up by the Probation and After Care Service which provide training programmes including such items as group counselling, remedial education, instruction in home budgeting and simple training in woodwork, decorating and car maintenance, for a maximum of 60 days.

Types of crimes committed by young persons sentenced to custody

England and Wales 1987	*Males*				*Females*			
	14–16yrs		17–20yrs		14–16yrs		17–20yrs	
Burglary	359	(46%)	2934	(37%)	3	(30%)	31	(15%)
Theft, handling stolen goods, fraud, forgery	160	(20%)	1406	(18%)	0		71	(36%)
Violence against the person	97	(12%)	1499	(19%)	0		32	(16%)
Robbery	74	(9%)	891	(11%)	6	(60%)	20	(10%)
Sexual offences	6	(1%)	176	(2%)	0		0	
Other offences	74	(9%)	1023	(13%)	1	(10%)	43	(22%)
Offence not known	18	(2%)	39	n.s.	0		2	(1%)
Total offenders	788		7968		10		199	

Northern Ireland 1986	*Juveniles (both sexes) 17–20 yrs*	
Theft, handling stolen goods, taking motor vehicles, fraud and forgery	497	(27%)
Burglary and robbery	385	(21%)
Motoring offences	370	(20%)
Assaults and offences against the person	141	(8%)
Disorderly behaviour	123	(7%)
Malicious damage	28	(2%)
Sexual offences	22	(1%)
Other offences	257	(14%)
Total offenders	1823	

Increasingly the probation service is finding itself supervising more serious offenders on probation – the proportion of those on probation who are known to have had a previous custodial sentence has risen from 20% in 1979 to 36% in 1988; 66% of those placed on probation with a condition to attend a day centre had a previous custodial sentence.

Community Service

The Probation and After Care Service is also responsible for administering community service orders. Under this system an offender aged 16 or over (17 in Northern Ireland) convicted of an imprisonable offence may, with his or her consent, be given a community service order. A community service order may require an offender to work anything from 40 to 240 unpaid hours in and for the community (up to 160 hours in England for those aged 16). Types of work done under a community service order can include doing repairs for the elderly, helping to run or build adventure play rounds for children or helping out in hospitals. Since 1979 the number of offenders receiving community service orders has risen by 122%.

Suspended Sentences

Suspended sentences are another aspect of the British system of non-custodial sentencing for which the Probation and After Care Service sometimes has responsibility. In England, Wales and Northern Ireland a court is free to pass a suspended sentence of not more than two years. This sentence is not served unless the offender is convicted of a further offence which is punishable with imprisonment. If an offender is sentenced to a suspended sentence of longer than six months then he may also be placed under the supervision of a probation officer.

Towards the end of 1989 there was speculation that the Government was planning to reform the Probation Service and its policy on sentencing. In December, in a letter to Graham Smith who had asked what the Government's intentions were with regard to the Probation Office, John Patten replied that he saw the Probation Service moving centre stage and dealing with even greater numbers of more serious offenders in the community. In February 1990 the Government produced its Green Paper entitled *Supervision and Punishment in the Community: A Framework for Action* in which it proposed a number of reforms of the present probation and prison system, including the privatization of bail hostels, the imposition of national controls on local probation services, the merging of some small probation areas, and reforms in probation training creating stronger links with the judiciary, the intention being to create a 'new model probation officer'.

In reply to the Government's Green Paper the National Association of Probation Officers said that the Home Office was proposing to take control of the service by abolishing 20% of funding that comes from local authorities and taking over the entire responsibility for financing the Probation Service and imposing an 'unworkable framework' of punishment in the country.

THE POLICE SERVICE

In the United Kingdom there are 52 police forces (43 in England and Wales, eight in Scotland, and one in Northern Ireland). Each force is responsible for law enforcement in its own area, their main functions being crime prevention, crime investigation, the preservation of the peace and the bringing to trial of offenders. Outside London most counties (regions or islands in the case of Scotland) have their own police forces although there are some combined forces, e.g. Avon and Somerset. The policing of London is performed by the Metropolitan Police Force which is responsible for an area within a radius of approximately 24 kilometres from the centre but excluding the City of London which has its own force.

POLICE AUTHORITIES

Most of the 52 regular police forces are maintained by police authorities. In England and Wales the authorities comprise local councillors and magistrates with the exception of the Metropolitan Force where the Home Secretary acts as the authority and the City of London Force which is responsible to the Court of Common Council. In Scotland the police authority is the regional or island council and in Northern Ireland the Secretary of State appoints an authority which is 'representative of the community'. The primary role of the police authority is to provide an adequate and efficient police force for its particular area. In performing this role the authorities have the power to appoint and dismiss the Chief Constable, Deputy Chief Constable and assistant chief constables. They must also provide and maintain buildings and decide upon the numbers of policemen necessary to police their regions effectively.

Funding of the police authorities and as a consequence the various police forces in the country comes from both central and local government. The central government contribution amounts to approximately half of the approved expenditure (one-third in the City of London) but is conditional upon the Home Secretary and the Secretaries of State for Scotland and Northern Ireland, who have ultimate responsibility for the preservation of law and order, being satisfied that the respective authorities under their jurisdiction are being efficiently administered and maintained. The Home Secretary and the Secretaries of State for Northern Ireland and Scotland also have a number of other powers available to ensure effective policing in the country. They approve the appointments of and may require the retirement of Chief Constables, order reports from Chief Constables on any matters relating to the policing of the various authorities, and/or order local inquiries to be held on specific aspects of policing in any of the 52 areas. The Secretaries of State are also empowered to make regulations to which all police authorities must comply covering such matters as police ranks, qualifications for appointment, promotions and retirement, hours of duty, discipline, uniform and equipment, leave and pay.

British police officers are agents of the law of the land not of the police authorities or of the Government. Consequently they may be sued or prosecuted for breaking the law in the course of carrying out their duties. Members of the public can make complaints about police officers and their conduct by appealing to the Police Complaints Authority or by contacting their local station. Investigations into the conduct of particular police officers are initially carried out by a senior police officer sometimes from a different force who, having made inquiries, must send a report to the Director of Public Prosecutions if he is satisfied that an offence has been committed. The Police Complaints Authority is 'an independent body' appointed by the Home Secretary. The Authority reviews the decisions of deputy chief constables with regard to disciplinary action taken against particular officers, investigates complaints from members of the public and can also call for disciplinary hearings and inflict penalties on an officer found guilty of misconduct.

THE CRIMINAL INJURIES COMPENSATION BOARD

The Criminal Injuries Compensation Board was established in 1964 to administer the Criminal Injuries Compensation Scheme which provides *ex gratia* payments of compensation to victims of crimes of violence. Appointments to the Board are made by the Secretary of State after consultation with the Lord Chancellor, and occasionally the Lord Advocate. Those appointed to the Board must hold or have held a judicial office in England, Wales or Scotland and initially serve up to five years, although their positions are renewable where the Secretary of State deems it appropriate. The Board is provided with money through a grant-in-aid from the Home Office and the Scottish Home and Health Office out of which compensation payments are awarded. The Board is entirely responsible for deciding the amount of compensation to be paid in individual cases and once made these decisions are not subject to appeal or to ministerial review, although the general working of the scheme is kept under review by the Government.

THE CRIMINAL INJURIES COMPENSATION SCHEME

Since its implementation in 1964 the Criminal Injuries Compensation Scheme has been modified in a number of respects. Under the 1990 revision which came into effect on 1 February 1990 you can apply for compensation if you sustained personal injury directly attributable to: (a) a crime of violence (including arson or poisoning); (b) either an incident when you were trying to stop someone from committing a crime, or when trying to apprehend a suspect after a crime, or when assisting the police to apprehend someone; (c) an offence of trespass on a railway (the Board will consider applications from people who suffer mental injury after witnessing suicides on railway tracks).

Applications for compensation are only accepted if they are made within three years of the incident which gave rise to the injury. In assessing compensation payments the Board bases its awards on common-law damages, which means that, subject to the other provisions of the scheme, the Board will award what a civil court would award in 'damages' for the same injury. The awards given by the Criminal Injuries Compensation Scheme do however differ in two respects from the awards given in a civil court. Firstly, in assessing the amount to be paid to a person making a claim, the Board will deduct all benefits received as a result of his/her injury, and secondly there is a lower limit which prevents the Board from making an award if the damages a civil court would award are less than £750.

Furthermore even if the total sum payable is equal to or more than the lower limit of £750 if the balance of compensation payable after the deduction of social benefits is less than £750 no compensation can be paid at all.

In the first full year of its existence the Board received 2452 applications for compensation and disposed of 1375. In 1988/9 the Criminal Injuries Compensation Board received 43,385 new applications for compensation bringing the overall total of claims for compensation since the Board was established to

498,000. Of the total number of complaints received in 1988/9 the Board made 27,752 awards, 32% more than in 1987/8. With the current caseload and a predicted intake of 50,000 new applications for 1989/90 the time taken by the Board to resolve cases has become a matter of concern; in 1988 25,581 cases took 12 months or more to resolve. The Board is still awaiting approval to proceed with a computer system.

Crimes reported in England and Wales during 1989

Type of offence	*No. of offences*	*% increase on 1988*
Violence against the person	176,900	11.8
Sexual offences	29,700	12.0
Robbery	33,200	5.5
Burglary in dwelling	437,700	–0.8
Other burglary	388,100	3.0
Theft from the person	25,400	–4.4
Theft from a shop	222,900	3.1
Theft from a vehicle	628,800	1.3
Theft/taking a vehicle	393,300	7.2
Other theft/handling	737,900	5.9
Fraud and forgery	134,500	0.5
Criminal damage	630,000	6.1
Other offences	27,700	21.9
Total	3,866,100	4.2

LOCAL GOVERNMENT

Local government in England comes under the direction of the Department of the Environment; in Wales the Welsh Office has control, in Scotland the Scottish Office, and in Northern Ireland the Department of the Environment for Northern Ireland. The extent of the powers and duties of each layer of local government is laid down by Parliament, and can only be changed by an Act of Parliament (or by the appropriate Minister acting with Parliament's authority). Within this remit, each local authority is free to act in its own way. The expenditure of local authorities in England and Wales is subject to scrutiny by the Audit Commission; the equivalent Scottish body is the Commission for Local Authority Accounts, and in Northern Ireland there is a local authority audit section within the Department of the Environment for Northern Ireland.

LOCAL GOVERNMENT STRUCTURE

England and Wales

In England and Wales there are three levels of elected councils: county, district and parish.

County. There are 39 counties in England and eight in Wales. Each has an elected council of 60–100 members. The responsibilities of the county councils are: formulating county structure plans; roads, traffic and transport; education, public libraries and museums; police; fire service; consumer protection; refuse disposal; social services. The councils employ executives to manage these functions, and are also the employers of all the staff in these areas.

There are also six metropolitan counties (Greater Manchester, Merseyside, South Yorkshire, Tyne & Wear, West Midlands, West Yorkshire) which do not have county councils. The county functions are carried out by the district councils within them, as is also the case in Greater London.

The members of the county council are generally organized along party political lines, and the policies of the council will therefore reflect the political priorities of the party having the majority. Council officers, however, are required to be politically neutral in carrying out their duties; senior staff are not allowed to be elected members of other councils. The councillors elect from among themselves a chairman to serve for one year.

Of the 47 counties in England and Wales, 17 are controlled by the Conservatives, 13 by Labour, one by the SLD (Isle of Wight), and two are Independent-controlled. Fourteen counties have no overall party control.

District. There are 332 districts in England (264 non-metropolitan, 36 within the metropolitan counties and 32 boroughs in London) and 37 in Wales. The councils of non-metropolitan districts consist of 30–60 members, metropolitan ones have 50–80 members. The councillors elect one of themselves annually to act as chairman, and in districts that are also boroughs or cities, this person takes the title of Mayor (in very large cities, Lord Mayor). The responsibilities of non-metropolitan districts are: housing; markets; refuse collection; planning and building regulations; environmental health; licensing for pubs and restaurants; registration of electors and of births, marriages and deaths; off-street parking and some road maintenance; aerodromes; cemetries and crematoria.

The metropolitan districts carry out all of the above, and also the functions of the county councils, except that in some cases there are joint authorities covering the entire metropolitan area (police, fire services, civil defence and public transport). London is exceptional in that the Metropolitan Police (responsible to the Home Secretary) and London Regional Transport (responsible to the Minister of Transport) are controlled by the

Government and not by any form of locally elected authority.

In 1986 district councils were given the right to choose one of two ways in which to organize their electoral system. They could either run elections every four years and councillors would serve for the next four years, whereupon they would all be eligible for re-election or retirement (as in a general election); or they could run the 'thirds' system, whereby a third of the councillors retire or stand for election every year except in the fourth year, when there are county council elections (thus some councillors would serve four years). The majority of districts opted for the first choice, and Greater London was obliged by the Government to do so; consequently the local government elections held in these areas in 1990 were the first to be held for four years.

As for county councils, councillors are organized along party political ines, while paid staff carry out their duties with political neutrality.

Parish and Community. There are about 10,000 parishes in England, though these do not cover the entire area of the country; about 8000 of them have elected councils. Parishes with populations under about 200 do not have a council but hold meetings of all parishioners at least twice a year. In Wales, boundaries have been drawn up to divide the entire county into about 1000 communities, of which about 770 have elected councils. Elections for both parish and community councils are held every four years, at the same time as the district council elections. The functions of parish and community councils are similar, and include: burial and cremation facilities; public halls; allotments; recreation facilities; public lavatories; street lighting; footpaths; encouragement of arts and crafts. Parish and community councils have the right to be consulted on any planning applications affecting their own area. They do not employ any full-time staff.

Scotland

There are two tiers of council in mainland Scotland: region and district. The island regions – Orkney, Shetland and the Western Isles – each have a single all-purpose island council.

Region. There are nine regions in Scotland, each with an elected council with membership varying according to the population (from 19 to 103). Elections are held every four years, the most recent being May 1990. The responsibilities of the regional councils are: strategic planning; roads and transport; water, sewerage and flood protection; police, fire service and civil defence; education; social services; registration of electors and of births, marriages and deaths. The councillors are organized along party lines, but there are relatively more independent or non-party members than in the English and Welsh county councils; Labour controls four of the regions, but the other five have no overall control.

District. The Scottish regions are subdivided into 53 districts, each of which has a council elected for four years (next elections due in 1992). The membership of the councils varies, according to the population, from 10 to 60. The districts generally deal with more local matters than the regions, and their functions include: housing; planning and building regulations; environmental health (including inspection of premises, collection and disposal of refuse, etc.); burial and cremation; licensed premises and places of entertainment; allotments; administration of district courts.

Island. The councils for the three main groups of islands in Scotland (Orkney, Shetland and the Western Isles) combine the functions of the region and district councils on the mainland. Councillors are elected for a four-year term. The majority of councillors are Independent, with a few Island Movement and Labour councillors.

Community Councils. The community councils in Scotland, organized in a similar way to the parish and community councils of England and Wales, are not formally part of the local government system and do not have power to spend any public money. They exist to provide a forum for consultation on planning or other proposals affecting the local community.

Northern Ireland

The 'Six Counties' that form Northern Ireland have been abolished as units of local government. The country is divided into 26 districts, each of which has a council elected for a four-year term by proportional representation. The position is unlike that in Great Britain, in that many of the services are provided by central government departments rather than local government. The district councils act in three different ways. First, they are responsible for providing local services in: environmental health; refuse collection and disposal; recreation and cultural facilities; consumer protection; enforcement of building regulations; development of tourism. Secondly, they send representatives to the boards responsible for the various services such as education, health and social services, which are run by departments of central government. Thirdly, they act as a means of consultation for the local community on matters affecting the area, e.g. planning and highways.

OMBUDSMAN FOR LOCAL GOVERNMENT

Any member of the public who feels that he or she has suffered through maladministration by the local authority, or through the authority's failure to provide a statutory service, can take the complaint to the Local Commissioner, applying either personally or through a councillor. The Commissioner, appointed by the Crown on the recommendation of a Secretary of State, is impartial. Unfortunately the Commissioner's decision is not binding upon the council, which can refuse to change its practice or to pay any compensation if it is found to be in the wrong.

England. Commission for Local Administration in England, 21 Queen Anne's Gate, London SW1H 9BU. Tel. 071 222 5622.

Wales. Commission for Local Administration in Wales, Derwen House, Court Road, Bridgend CF31 1BN. Tel. 0656 61325.

Scotland. Commission for Local Administration in Scotland, 5 Shadwick Place, Edinburgh EH2 4RG. Tel. 031 229 4472.

In Northern Ireland most local services are administered by departments of central government, so complaints about them have to be directed to the Parliamentary Commissioner for Administration (the Ombudsman), who can only be approached via an MP.

In 1988/9 (the first year in which complaints could be presented direct rather than via a councillor), the Local Ombudsman received a total of 8366 complaints, an increase of 40% over the previous year.

LOCAL GOVERNMENT FINANCE

Up until April 1989 in Scotland and April 1990 in England and Wales, money for local authorities was raised as follows: 33% from receipts for services, including council house/flat rents, fees for adult educa-

Complaints to the Local Ombudsman, 1988/9

	England	Wales	Scotland	Total
Total complaints received	7055	511	800	8366
Complaints not proceeded with (settled locally, outside jurisdiction etc.)	6394	463	744	7601
Investigations resulting in findings of:				
Maladministration causing injustice	212	27	20	259
Maladministration, no injustice	30	1	1	32
No maladministration	60	20	29	109
TOTAL	302	48	50	400
Most frequent subject of complaints (and as % of all complaints received)				
– Housing	2889 (41%)	143 (28%)	380 (47%)	
– Planning	2075 (29%)	152 (30%)	87 (11%)	
– Highways	423 (6%)	38 (7%)	23 (3%)	
– Environmental Health	248 (3.5%)	15 (3%)	16 (2%)	
– Education	248 (3.5%)	14 (3%)	16 (2%)	

Note: The figures on the table for complaints not investigated and the results of investigations do not add up to the total complaints received. This is because of the delay in processing the complaints: many of the investigations are the results of complaints made in 1987/8, while some 20% of complaints made in 1988/9 were carried forward into the next year.

tion, library charges, etc; 16% from domestic rates; 18% from business rates; 33% Rate Support Grant from central government.

(These figures were the national average for England; individual councils varied greatly.)

Under the new system, money for local authorities is to be raised in three ways: Community Charge; national non-domestic rates; government grants.

Community Charge

This replaces the domestic rates, and is a flat rate set annually by each district or borough and payable by all persons over 18 years old. There are some exemptions including: long-term hospital patients and residents of nursing homes, people with a severe mental handicap, prisoners (except people in prison for refusing to pay the Community Charge), monks and nuns, some charity volunteers, 18 year olds at school, foreign diplomats or service personnel serving in Britain. Students (apart from student nurses who pay the full rate) pay 20% of the Community Charge. People with low incomes may apply for a rebate, but in no case will this be greater than 80% of the set charge.

Payment of the Personal Community Charge (widely known as the 'poll tax') is the responsibility of each individual named on the Register, but in some circumstances wives and husbands can be compelled to pay the bill if the other has defaulted. In lodging houses or other places where the turnover of residents is so fast that it is not feasible for everyone to be on the Register, a daily rate of Community Charge is paid by each resident to the landlord, who passes it on to the council (this is the Collective Community Charge).

Unoccupied houses, including second homes occupied only occasionally, are subject to the Standard Community Charge, which is set by the council at any level up to twice the level of the Personal Charge.

National Non-domestic Rates

The rate on business premises is now set at the same rate – 34.8p per £ of valuation – throughout the country, and any increase must be no greater than the rate of inflation. The valuations on which the business rates are based are being completely revised. The money raised through the business rates is pooled nationally and distributed to each council according to the number of resident adults. The system therefore acts to redistribute money from areas with many businesses but few residents (e.g. the City of London), to other areas where there are more residents and consequently more demand for council services; it also acts to discourage businesses from decentralizing, as there is no longer an advantage in doing so in the shape of lower rates.

In the first few years of operation of the new system, a safety net will operate to ensure that the amount that any person is required to pay does not rise too sharply in any year (particularly in the year of transition from rates to poll tax). This works by a system of allocating to certain councils more cash from the pool of business rate receipts than the number of residents would strictly justify.

Government Grants

Local authorities will be given financial help from central government in the form of Revenue Support Grant. An authority will qualify for one of these grants if it needs one in order to make its provision of a certain service match the theoretical national standard for that service. The grant is earmarked for spending on one particular service and cannot be simply added to the council's budget.

FIRE SERVICES

Throughout Great Britain the fire services are organized at local level: by county or metropolitan district councils in England and Wales and by region or island councils in Scotland. These authorities are supervised by the Home Secretary or by the Secretary of State for Scotland, and funding is partly through locally raised finance (the community charge and business rate) and partly through grants from central government. In Northern Ireland the service is entirely supported by central funds and is the direct responsibility of the Secretary of State.

Fire Brigades' Duties

The brigades in the UK answer over 800,000 calls per year. The majority – over one-third – are fires, but there are also many calls to provide 'special services',

Local authority current expenditure 1988/9

	England			Wales			Scotland			Northern Ireland	
	£ million	£ per head		£ million	£ per head		£ million	£ per head		£ million	£ per head
Education	14,590	308		862	304		1846	361	(incl. arts and libraries)	837	531
Police, fire services, etc	4531	96	(see Home Office, below)	–	–		447	87		609	387
Social Security	3370	71		–	–		–	–		1528	970
Health & personal social services	3035	64		150	53		407	80		845	536
Environmental services	3015	64		223	77		461	90		251	159
Roads & transport	1950	41		126	44		331	65		122	77
Housing	629	13		10	4		24	5		338	215
Arts & libraries	480	10		22	8		62	12	(see Education, above)	–	–
Industry, trade & employment	195	4		5	2		13	3		390	247
Agriculture, fisheries & food	162	3		–	–		–	–		172	109
	31,957	674	Home Office services	231	81						
						Tourism	4	1		–	–
			Housing benefit	210	74	Housing benefit	428	84		–	–
			Higher & further education	46	16		–	–		–	–
			Other services	10	4	Other services	20	4	Other services	54	34
				1895	667		4043	792		5146	3625

Fire services, 1988

	England	Metropolitan counties (inc. London)	Wales	Scotland	N. Ireland
Divisions	100	34	18	18	5
Stations	1135	322	153	392	7 full-time 52 retained
Staff					
Uniformed					
Wholetime	16,551	16,727	1701	4351	733
Part-time	11,207	525	1547	3468	1023
Control room	885	534	138	188	181
Non-uniformed	2687	2744	297	605	
Total	31,330	20,530	3683	8612	1937
Equipment					
Water tenders	2002	267	234	453	N/A
Pumps	82	514	15	28	N/A
Light pumps	461	2	49	156	N/A
Turntable ladders, hydraulic platforms, Simonitors	144	97	20	36	N/A
Fire boats	14	3	–	–	
Emergency tenders	53	35	14	11	N/A
Rescue tenders, apparatus tenders	114	15	12	14	N/A
Other special appliances	249	121	52	106	N/A
Cars and vans	2139	881	277	335	N/A

Fire brigade calls answered, 1987/8

	England	Metropolitan counties (inc. London)	Wales	Scotland	N. Ireland
Fires	149,131	127,825	19,816	45,431	342,203
Special services	68,275	93,679	6935	5441	174,330
False alarms:					
Good intent	52,908	38,943	4816	12,436	109,103
Electrical/ mechanical	35,598	26,148	2690	7075	71,511
Malicious	40,064	60,797	6731	12,691	120,283
Total false alarms	128,570	125,888	14,237	32,202	300,897
Total calls	345,976	347,392	40,988	83,074	817,430

which can mean anything from air or rail crashes to rescuing cats. False alarms are a serious problem, with malicious false alarms amounting to nearly 20% of calls in some areas.

Fire Casualties

Fatalities caused by fires do not show any particular trend, but non-fatal casualties have increased by nearly 10% per year (up to the most recently available figures, for 1986).

	1982	1983	1984	1985	1986
Fatal	728	710	692	700	753
Non-fatal	6659	7137	7757	8501	9403

The causes of accidental fires in occupied buildings (1986) were: cooking appliances 40%, smokers' materials 12%, electrical equipment 11%, space-heating appliances 9%, matches 8%, faulty electrical wiring 6%.

AMBULANCE SERVICES

See Health and Social Welfare

POLICE SERVICES

See Law

MEDIA AND COMMUNICATIONS

CINEMA

Within the United Kingdom at the end of 1989, there were 1,316 cinema screens operating at 661 sites. Of these Great Britain accounted for 642 sites with 1,284 screens (England, 518 sites with 1,088 screens, Scotland, 58 sites with 106 screens, Wales, 50 sites with 71 screens) and Northern Ireland with 16 sites operating 19 screens. In 1990 independent cinemas account for 449 sites, the first increase in the number of sites for over 15 years. The leading cinema chains, members of the Cinema Exhibitors panel, operated 268 sites in 1990.

The total number of admissions for 1988 was 61.8 million, a drop from the 1987 total of 64.6 million. It is estimated that this figure will have risen again in 1989–90. Results for attendance and admissions are only current up to the third quarter of 1989. They show, however, that with seasonal adjustment there has been an increase in overall takings and admissions: in the third quarter of 1989 admissions totalled 18.5 million, a 34% increase on the third quarter of 1988; average revenue per admission equalled £2.03.

Cinema attendance has declined greatly over the previous 30 years since its peak in the mid-1950s. The main reason for this appears to be the growth of television, and, more recently, home videos. In 1955 the annual rate of visits to the cinema stood at 23 per person per year. By 1984 this had become only one visit per person per year, but this situation has since improved, however, and the most recent figures show an average rate of visits of 1.4 in 1988. The rise, since 1985, was partly the result of British Film Year, which helped to promote British films and cinemas. Gross box-office takings for 1988 were £113.8 million, an increase of £15.7 million on the previous year. The total for the first three-quarters of 1989 was £102.9 million, showing an almost inevitable increase when the full figures become available.

The 1980s has seen the arrival of the *multiplex*, the fastest expanding aspect of the cinema industry. The multiplex is a North American concept whereby a completely new complex, housing around 10 screens with appropriate facilities, is created. Multiplexes tend to represent fresh investment in areas of large catchment populations, relying heavily on a mobile audience. The concept is similar to the Superstore innovation in retailing. They provide on site restaurants, parking and have pricing policies encouraging off-peak visits. The multiple auditoria are designed with variable capacities, flexible enough to cater for more or less popular films.

Major Cinema Chains

Cannon Established in 1982, Cannon cinemas control 140 sites with 382 screens. Cannon became the largest UK exhibitor, following its acquisition of Thorn EMI Screen Entertainment, Star and Classic circuits in 1986. In 1989 they also acquired the remaining Granada cinema sites. The company, which was established by the Golum brothers, particularly Menachem, is no longer owned by them, but by the Pathé Communications Corporation headed by Giancarlo Parretti. Recent developments include a buy-out bid for MGM-UA in America and the development of cinema sites in Europe. Cannon has established multiplex operations within the UK, Salford Keyes, Manchester was the second multiplex to open in the UK on the 7 Dec. 1986. This was followed by The Forge, Parkhead, Glasgow in Apr. 1989 and Ocean Village, Southampton in July 1989. A fourth is planned for Shawridge, Swindon, due to open in 1991.

United Cinema International (UCI) UCI, formerly American Multi-Cinema, established the first multiplex in Britain on the 29 Nov. 1985 at The Point, Milton Keynes. The Point, with 10 screens, was the start of a new concept in British cinema, designed to bring large audiences away from television and back into cinemas. With a choice of 10 films to see, new comfort levels, competitive pricing, food and drink (fast and seated) and free parking for all cars, UCI has had a great deal of success.

UCI now owns 16 locations with a total of 151 screens, its growth and expansion has been rapid, opening three new sites in the last five weeks of 1989 alone. The company also plans to open seven more sites in the next 18 months. Average annual attendance for the sites open for a year or more stands at 1,176,000 (Oct. 1988–9). The first multiplex, The Point, Milton Keynes had 1,300,000 visitors in the same year.

Odeon, Rank Film Distribution Rank Films were incorporated on 27 May 1935 and they now control 75 sites operating 253 screens. This makes them the second largest cinema circuit within Britain, following the Cannon Group. They have approximately 23–25% of the market share for admissions, totalling some 15 million visitors for 1989.

Odeon cinemas have also started to develop multiplex sites. Their first site was the Stoke Festival Park complex with 8 screens, which opened at the end of 1989. In January 1990, a further site was opened at Kingston-upon-Hull also with 8 screens. Future sites are already planned for Romford, Cardiff and Uxbridge.

Cinema attendance

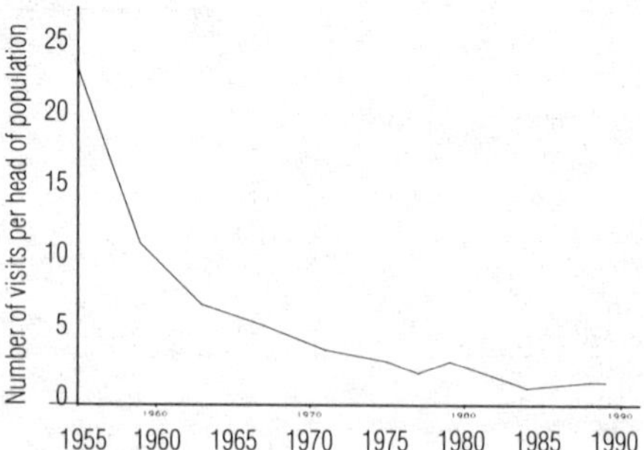

OPERA

In 1989, the seven major companies produced 742 performances in theatres with a seating capacity of 800 or above. 1,171,782 tickets were sold, averaging out at 1579 people per performance. Theatres performed to an average of 85% capacity. Total box office receipts reached £17.9 million, the highest total since figures were first compiled in 1971–2.

The seven major companies are: English National Opera (ENO), Glyndebourne Touring Opera, Kent

Opera, Opera North (Leeds), Royal Opera, Scottish Opera, Welsh National Opera. Of these the ENO is the largest and accounts for 36% of all ticket sales.

The most performed artists were Puccini, Verdi and Mozart.

The majority of works performed (54%) were 19th century works, 17% of works performed were 18th century, 19% were pre-war 20th century and 10% post-war.

DANCE

The six major companies produced 753 performances in theatres with a seating capacity of 800 or above. 851,000 tickets were sold, averaging out at 1130 people per performance. Theatres performed to an average of 74% capacity. Total box office receipts amounted to £8.9 million.

The figures on dance are particularly hard to compile due to problems with categorization. The figures here involve only Contemporary dance and Ballet. Therefore, Modern, Jazz, Tap, Ballroom and other dancing styles are left out of these statistics.

The six major companies within England are: London Contemporary Dance Theatre, Rambert Dance Company (the oldest dance company in Britain), English National Ballet, Northern Ballet Theatre, Royal Ballet, Sadler's Wells.

BOOKS AND PUBLISHING

In 1988 British publishers sold some 505 million books in the UK; there were, in addition, some 525 million loans from public libraries: both figures each averaged around nine books per person. In the past decade the average price of a book has more than tripled, as book prices have risen exactly in line with inflation; the current average price of a book is £3.88.

In 1989, British publishers issued 66,619 separate titles. Of these, 50,225 were new titles, of which 1,750 were translations; 16,394 were reprints and new editions. In 1989 book exports totalled £537 million, confirming a rising trend due to the work of several promotional agencies, notably the Book Development Council. The British Council publicizes British books overseas through their 116 libraries in over 60 countries. Other promotional bodies include the Publishers Association (with some 200 members), the Booksellers Association and Book Trust.

Book Production and Exports

Year	Total value of books produced in UK (£ million)	Total value of books exported from UK (£ million)
1986	1068.3	315.4
1987	1191.2	342.2
1988	1296.3	358.8
1989	1044.0	340.9

Consumer Trends

One of the general trends of book consumerism in the 1980s was parochialism. This is reflected in the fact that of the top sellers in the last decade only 5 were foreign language writers: Gabriel Garcia Marquez, Patrick Suskind, Umberto Eco, Dominique Lapierre, Edward Topol. Generally the spoils are divided amoung British and American writers. However, the American performance has steadily declined from a half-share in the early eighties, down to almost a third today.

The evidence of the last 10 years shows little change in popular taste. Over 70% of the listings are 'entertainment' fiction (including romance, sagas, thrillers, fantasy and spy genres). A tenth of the market consists of 'serious' fiction, or novels which editors might recommend for literary review. Yet the increase in media coverage of literary awards (see ARTS FACTFILE 1989–90), particularly the Whitbread and the Booker Prizes, have helped to boost this market. Furthermore, the recent notoriety of Salman Rushdie's *The Satanic Verses* and the renewal of the *fatwah* (death sentence) passed upon him, has perhaps brought this market sharply back into public focus. The final 20% share of the market is taken up by a combination of miscellaneous genres, astrology, humour and diet.

The overall largest seller of the 1980s was Sue Townsend's *The Secret Diary of Adrian Mole*, which sold over 3 million copies and beat Jeffrey Archer into second place. It is also interesting to note that every author in the top 20 for 1989 has been placed before.

Public Lending Right

The Public Lending Right (PLR) was created by the

Books Published in GB, 1988

Classification (15 largest)	Total	Reprints and New Editions	Translations	Limited Editions
Art	1,703	292	58	4
Biography	2,131	594	79	8
Children's	5,063	1,203	151	7
Commerce	2,033	514	15	2
Education	1,429	204	5	–
Fiction	6,496	3,074	270	3
History	2,153	412	76	4
Law & Public Administration	1,932	441	13	–
Literature	1,574	216	44	3
Medical Science	3,423	729	29	–
Political Science & Economics	4,307	778	68	1
Religion & Theology	2,047	331	117	2
School Texts	2,007	332	16	–
Sociology	1,284	168	27	–
Travel & Guide Books	1,333	426	17	–
Totals	38,915	9,714	985	34

Who Borrows Whom
Public Lending Right's Most Borrowed Authors

Top 10 adult-fiction authors
(21.3m loans = 3.4 per cent)

- Agatha Christie
- Catherine Cookson
- Dick Francis
- Jack Higgins
- Victoria Holt
- Ed McBain
- Alistair Maclean
- Ruth Rendell
- Wilbur Smith
- Danielle Steel

Top 100 adult-fiction authors
(93m loans = 14.9 per cent)

- Ted Allbeury
- Charlotte Vale Allen
- Margery Allingham
- Lucilla Andrews
- Virginia Andrews
- Evelyn Anthony
- Jeffrey Archer
- Desmond Bagley
- Barbara Taylor Bradford
- Iris Bromige
- Elizabeth Cadell
- Victor Canning
- Phillippa Carr
- John le Carré
- Barbara Cartland
- James Hadley Chase
- Agatha Christie
- Jon Cleary
- Virginia Coffman
- Jackie Collins
- Catherine Cookson
- Jilly Cooper
- Sara Craven
- Janet Dailey
- Len Deighton
- R F Delderfield
- Dorothy Eden
- J T Edson
- Elizabeth Ferrars
- Colin Forbes
- Helen Forrester
- Frederick Forsyth
- Dick Francis
- Alexander Fullerton
- John Gardner
- Catherine Gaskin
- Michael Gilbert
- Winston Graham
- Graham Greene
- John Harris
- James Herbert
- Georgette Heyer
- Jack Higgins
- Patricia Highsmith
- Jane Aitken Hodge
- Victoria Holt
- Hammond Innes
- Michael Innes
- Brenda Jagger
- P D James
- Penny Jordan
- Marie Joseph
- M M Kaye
- Lena Kennedy
- Alexander Kent
- Stephen King
- Louis L'amour
- Charlotte Lamb
- Norah Lofts
- Robert Ludlum
- Helen MacInnes
- Alistair Maclean

Top 100 adult authors continued

- Ngaio Marsh
- Graham Masterton
- Anne Mather
- Daphne Du Maurier
- Ed McBain
- Philip McCutchan
- Carole Mortimer
- Maisie Mosco
- Betty Neels
- Christopher Nicole
- Pamela Oldfield
- Ellis Peters
- Jean Plaidy
- Dudley Pope
- Anthony Price
- Claire Rayner
- Miss Read
- Douglas Reeman
- Ruth Rendell
- Harold Robbins
- Denis Robins
- Tom Sharpe
- Sarah Shears
- Sidney Sheldon
- Nevil Shute
- Helen Van Slyke
- Wilbur Smith
- Danielle Steel
- Jessica Steel
- Mary Stewart
- Jessica Stirling
- Leslie Thomas
- E V Thompson
- John Wainwright
- Phyllis A Whitney
- Kate Williams
- Sara Woods
- Margaret Yorke

Top 10 adult non-fiction authors
(1.6m loans = 0.2 per cent)

- Hunter Davies
- Gerald Durrell
- Bill Gunston
- James Herriot
- Spike Milligan
- Chapman Pincher
- Doris Stokes
- Miriam Stoppard
- Derek Tangye
- Colin Wilson

Top 20 children's authors
(13m loans = 2.1 per cent)

- Jean & Gareth Adamson
- Joan Alken
- Rev W Awdry
- Val Biro
- Judy Blume
- Enid Blyton
- Michael Bond
- Dick Bruna
- John Burningham
- John Cunliffe
- Roald Dahl
- Terrance Dicks
- René Goscinny
- Hergé
- Eric Hill
- Shirley Hughes
- Pat Hutchins
- Carolyn Keene
- Penelope Lively
- Beatrix Potter

Source: Public Lending Right, as reproduced in *The Bookseller*, 13 July 1990

Public Lending Right Act 1979. Under the system, authors (writers, translators and illustrators) whose books are lent out from public libraries are given a payment from public funds. The amount is proportionate to the number of times that his or her books are lent out in the course of the year, based upon a sample of 30 libraries. The rules for administering the PLR are set out in the Public Lending Right Scheme 1982. For 1990–91, parliament allocated £3,500,000 for this system. The government has announced that £4.25 million will be available in 1991–2. Minimum payment limits are set at £1.00 per annum and the top limit (for 1989–90) was £6000. In 1988 16,034 authors were registered under the PLR.

Net Book Agreement

The Net Book Agreement (NBA) is an arrangement, approved by the Restrictive Practices Court, designed to act in the public's interest. It is designed to improve availability to booksellers of wide-ranging stocks, secure in the knowledge that the prices of their books and the value of their stocks will not be undermined by other retailers offering lesser services and stock levels.

The Agreement, operated by the Publishers Association, enables (but does not legally require) any publishers who are signatories to enforce a minimum retail price (the net price) for individual books. Thus, booksellers can be secure in the knowledge that they will not be undercut and can keep less popular titles in stock, particularly those of literary and academic value.

THEATRE

Within the *British Performing Arts Yearbook* are listed over 700 companies. This includes all theatres in Britain; professional and amateur.

There are about 300 theatres intended for professional use, which can seat between 200 and 2,300 people. Some are privately owned, whilst others are owned municipally or by non-profit-making organizations.

London has the largest number of privately owned, and Arts Council funded, theatres. There are approximately 100 West End and suburban theatres, including 30 Arts Council funded theatres. London is also the home of the Royal National Theatre (established in 1963).

Top 20 Paperback Sales, 1989

No.	Title	Genre	Author	Imprint	Price £	Month	Home	Export	Gross	Product £
1	A Twist in the Tale	Stories	J. Archer (GB)	Coronet	3.50	July	572,841	437,748	1,010,589	3,537,061
2	To be the Best	Saga	B. Taylor Bradford (GB)	Grafton	4.50	June	586,521	251,375	837,896	3,770,532
3	Complete Hip and Thigh Diet	Health	R. Conley (GB)	Arrow	3.50	Jan.	669,085	147,055	816,140	2,856,490
4	Rock Star	Saga	J. Collins (GB)	Pan	3.99	May	481,217	320,832	802,049	3,200,175
5	Rivals	Novel	J. Copper (GB)	Corgi	4.99	Apr.	601,823	151,864	753,687	3,760,898
6	Cultured Handmaiden	Novel	C. Cookson (GB)	Corgi	3.50	Mar.	437,201	143,856	581,057	2,033,699
7	The Edge	Thriller	D. Francis (GB)	Pab	3.99	Dec.	350,293	212,303	562,596	2,244,758
8	Spyhook	Thriller	L. Deighton (GB)	Grafton	3.50	Oct.	322,296	239,253	561,549	1,965,421
9	Fallen Hearts	Saga	V. Andrews (US)	Fontana	3.99	Sept.	326,809	219,898	546,707	2,181,360
10	The Icarus Agenda	Thriller	R. Ludlum (US)	Grafton	4.50	Mar.	265,156	258,943	524,099	2,358,445
11	The Long Dark Teatime of the Soul	Humour	D. Adams (GB)	Pan	3.99	Oct.	284,955	237,641	522,596	2,085,158
12	Haunted	Horror	J. Herbert (GB)	NEL	3.50	Aug.	397,526	106,083	503,609	1,762,631
13	Tommyknockers	Horror	S. King (US)	NEL	4.99	Nov.	309,945	189,678	499,623	2,493,118
14	Till We Meet Again	Novel	J. Krantz (US)	Bantam	3.99	Sept.	283,592	190,246	473,838	1,890,613
15	Prime Time	Novel	J. Collins (GB)	Arrow	3.50	June	301,135	166,754	467,889	1,637,611
16	1990 Horoscopes	Astrology	R. Grant (GB)	Star	1.99	June	374,748	90,363	465,111	925,570
17	Matilda	Childrens	R. Dahl (GB)	Puffin	3.50	Oct.	380,874	77,598	458,472	1,604,652
18	Easy People × 12	Childrens	Hargreaves & Jolliffe (GB)	Pan	1.50	July	272,788	184,508	457,296	685,944
19	Zoya	Romance	D. Steel (US)	Sphere	3.99	July	351,672	80,118	431,790	1,722,842
20	Stark	Novel	Ben Elton (GB)	Sphere	3.50	Mar.	349,394	74,159	423,553	1,482,435

Outside London the Arts Council funds a further 21 theatres (1988), though this figure excludes touring companies and companies funded for one-off productions or on a temporary basis.

Most regional repertory theatres perform between 8 and 10 productions a year; several have studio theatres, as well as a main house, where new and experimental productions can be performed. Often, if they are successful, they may transfer to London's West End. In return the national companies, the Royal National Theatre (RNT) and the Royal Shakespeare (RSC), tour many of the larger regional theatres.

Recently (February 1990) there has been much controversy over the RSC's decision to shut their London theatres, the Barbican and the Pit, for four months due to lack of government funding. This will be the first time for 28 years that these theatres will have to go 'dark'. Despite the Government's own report recommending an increase in their grant from its 1984–5 levels of £5.44 million, no action has yet, or seems likely, to be taken.

British Arts Council Subsidized Theatres

Figures for 1987–8 financial year show 41 repertory theatres, 23 studio theatres (subsidiaries of the former), eight small venues and two national companies funded by the Arts Council. This excludes the RSC's touring performances, totalling 128 with 62,400 ticket sales and box office receipts totalling £337,700. There were 85 platform performances at the RNT with 8,500 ticket sales and box-office receipts totalling £14,800.

British repertory theatres gave 11,024 performances, which 172,200 people attended. Box office receipts totalled £5,891,000.

Small venue theatres performed 2,309 times, with 257,100 people attending. Box office receipts totalled £15,758,000.

Major Companies Performing In-house Productions

Some companies are unable, or choose not, to give box office totals. It must be noted that these figures are not an accurate indicator of success as they exclude grants and funding. Figures refer to 1989 unless otherwise stated.

Royal Shakespeare Company. Barbican Theatre, London, EC2Y 8BQ. Tel. 071-628 3351
Number of productions: 13 Stratford; 22 London, including the Almeida
Number of performances: 1,612
Touring productions: 7 Newcastle, 75 performances
RSC–British Telecom 2 productions, 136 performances
RSC–Royal Insurance 1 production, 91 performances
Box office total (net including VAT) £10,640
Artistic director: Terry Hands
Royal National Theatre. National Theatre, South Bank, London, SE1 9PX. Tel. 071–928 2033
Number of productions: 32 main house, no studio figures available
Number of performances: 1,146
Total attendance: 628,019
Box office total not available
Artistic director: Richard Ayer
Old Vic Theatre. Waterloo Road, London, SE1 8NB. Tel. 071–240 7200.
Number of productions: 5 (J. Miller season); 7 (English Stage Company at Royal Court).
Box office total not available.
Artistic Director: Dr Jonathan Miller.
Theatre Royal, Norwich. Theatre Street, Norwich, NR2 1RL. Tel. 0603–623562
Number of productions: 90
Number of performances: 480
Box office total (including VAT): £1,767,952
Managing director: Mr Condon
Birmingham Repertory Theatre. Broad Street, Birmingham, B1 2EP. Tel. 0203 56431
Number of productions: 10 main house; 35 studio
Number of performances: 440
Box office total (financial year 1988–9): £888,801
Artistic director: John Adams
Nottingham Playhouse. Wellington Circus, Notts., NG1 5AF. Tel. 0602–474361
Number of productions: 13 independent; 11 amateur
Number of performances: 283 independent; 38 amateur
Box office total: £684,524
Artistic director: Kenneth Alan Taylor
Scarborough Theatre Trust Ltd. Stephen Joseph Theatre in the Round, Scarborough. Valley Bridge, North Yorkshire, YO11 2PL. Tel. 0273–370540
Number of productions: 7 main house; 6 studio
Number of performances: 217 main house; 69 studio
No box office total available.
Artistic director: Alan Ayckbourn
Royal Exchange Theatre, Manchester. St Annes Square, Manchester, M2 7DH. Tel. 061–833 9333
Number of productions: (Financial year 1989–90) 8
Number of performances: 345
Box office total: £1,020,000 main house, £20,000 approx. special events
Artistic director: Michael Fox
Royal Lyceum Theatre Company, Edinburgh. Grindlay Street, Edinburgh, EH3 9AX. Tel. 031–229 7404
Number of productions: 6 main house
Number of performances: 278 main house; 112 studio; 24 (RLT Touring); 27 (Edinburgh Festival performances at RLT; 116 (Communicado experimental touring company)
Total performances: 557
Box office total (gross): 1988–9 £708, 635
Artistic director: Ian Wooldridge
Glasgow Citizens' Theatre. 119 Gorbals Street, Gorbals, Glasgow, G5 9DS. Tel. 041–429 5561
Number of productions: 11
Number of performances: 182 in-house, 54 summer season
Total box office: £297,145
Artistic directors: Giles Havergel, Philip Prowse, Robert David McDonald
Lyric Players Theatre, Ireland. 55 Ridgeway Street, Stanmils, Belfast, B29 5FP. Tel. 0232–669660
Number of productions: 7 in-house; 1 week touring
Number of performances: 204
No box office figures available.
Artistic director: Roland Jaquarello

NEWSPAPERS

National Newspapers: Circulation, Ownership and Politics

Circulation data for August 1989 to January 1990 unless otherwise stated.
Daily Express (established 1900)
Ludgate House, 245 Blackfriars Rd, London, SE1 9UX.
Controlled by: United Newspapers.
Circulation: 1,574,466
Politics: populist right.
Daily Mail (established 1896)
Northcliffe House, 2 Derry St, London, EC4Y 0JA.
Controlled by: Associated Newspapers Group.
Circulation: 1,709,494
Politics: Tory, middle class/popular.
Daily Mirror (established 1903)

Magazine Readership in Great Britain

	Percentage of adults reading each magazine in 1988			Readership (millions)		Readers per copy (numbers)
	Men	Women	All Adults	1971	1988	1988
General magazines						
TV Times	19	21	20	9.1	9.1	3.0
Radio Times	19	21	20	9.5	9.0	2.9
Reader's Digest	14	14	14	9.2	6.4	4.0
Smash Hits	3	4	4	–	1.7	2.6
Exchange and Mart	5	2	3	–	1.6	7.4
What Car	6	1	3	–	1.6	11.3
Women's magazines						
Woman's Own	3	17	10	7.2	4.6	4.1
Woman	2	13	7	8.0	3.3	3.2
Woman's Weekly	2	12	7	4.7	3.1	2.5
Best	2	9	6	–	2.6	2.2
Prima	1	9	5	–	2.5	2.3
Family Circle	2	9	5	4.4	2.4	3.4

Source: Regional Trends 1990.

Holborn Circus, London, EC1P 1DQ.
Controlled by: Mirror Group Newspapers, R. Maxwell.
Circulation: 3,084,090
Politics: left of centre.
Daily Star (established 1978)
Ludgate House, 245 Blackfriars Rd, London, SE1 9UX
Controlled by: United Newspapers.
Circulation: 894,116
Politics: Tory, right
The People (established 1881)
Holborn Circus, London, EC1P 1DQ.
Controlled by: Mirror Group Newspapers, R. Maxwell.
Circulation: 2,654,491
Politics: right of centre.
The Sunday Correspondent (established 1989)
21 Clerkenwell Close, London, EC1R 0AA.
Controlled by: Sunday Newspaper Publishing plc.
Circulation: 246,000 (Oct. 1989–Mar. 1990)
Politics: left of centre.
The Sunday Express (established 1918)
Ludgate House, 245 Blackfriars Rd, London, SE1 9UX.
Controlled by: United Newspapers.
Circulation: 1,842,526
Politics: popular conservative, Thatcherite.
Sunday Mirror (established 1963)
Holborn Circus, London, EC1P 1DQ.
Controlled by: Mirror Group Newspapers, R. Maxwell.
Circulation: 2,907,872
Politics: left of centre.
Sunday Telegraph (established 1961)
181 Marsh Wall, Peterborough Court, London, E14 9SR.
Controlled by: Hollinger, Conrad Black.
Circulation: 633,000
Politics: right of centre.
Today (established 1986)
70 Vauxhall Bridge Road, Pimlico, London, SW1V 2RP.
Controlled by: News International, R. Murdoch.
Circulation: 587,228
Politics: right.
The Mail on Sunday (established 1982)
Northcliffe House, London, EC4Y 0JA.
Controlled by: Associated Newspapers Group.
Circulation: 1,896,820
Politics: Tory, populist right.
News of the World (established 1843)
1 Virginia Street, London, E1 9XR.
Controlled by: News International, R. Murdoch.
Circulation: 5,163,650
Politics: right.
The Observer (established 1791)
Chelsea Bright House, Queenstown Road, London, SW8 4NN.
Controlled by: Lonhro International.
Circulation: 635,439
Politics: centre.
Morning Star (established 1966)
74 Luke St, London, EC2A 4PY.
Controlled by: Morning Star Co-operative Society.
Circulation: 29,000
Politics: Marxist communist.
Racing Post (established 1986)
120 Coombe Lane, Raynes Park, London, SW20 0AB.
Controlled by: Sheikh Mohamed of Dubai.
Circulation: 48,000 (March 1990)
Politics: None.
Sporting Life (established 1859)
Orbit House, New Fetter Lane, London, EC4A 1AR.
Controlled by: R. Maxwell.
Circulation: 100,000 (approx.)
Politics: none.
The Sun (established 1964, from the retitled *Daily Herald*)
1 Virginia St, London, E19 XP.
Controlled by: News International, R. Murdoch.
Circulation: 4,002,021
Politics: extreme right.
The Times (established 1785)
1 Pennington St, London, E1 9XN.
Controlled by: News International, R. Murdoch.
Circulation: 428,784
Politics: right of centre.
The Sport (established 1987)
19 Great Ancoats St, Manchester M60 4BT.
Controlled by: Sport Newspapers, David Sullivan.
Circulation: Wed. edn: 300,000; Fri. edn: 285,000; Thurs. edn: publication from 23 Aug. 1990
Politics: right wing.
Daily Telegraph (established 1855)
Peterborough Court, South Quay Plaza, 181 Marsh

Wall, London, E14 9SR.
Controlled by: Hollinger, Conrad Black.
Circulation: 1,103,000
Politics: right of centre.
Financial Times (established 1888)
1 Southwark Bridge Rd, London, SE1 9LH.
Controlled by: Pearson.
Circulation: 288,009
Politics: centre.
The Guardian (established 1821)
119 Farringdon Rd, London, EC1R 3ER.
Controlled by: the Guardian and Manchester Evening News.
Circulation: 434,000
Politics: left of centre.
The Independent (established 1986)
40 City Rd, London, EC1Y 2DB.
Controlled by: Newspaper Publishing plc.
Circulation: 412,516
Politics: centre left/independent
Sunday Sport (established 1988)
Marten House, 39–47 East Road, London, N1 6AH.
Controlled by: Sport Newspapers, David Sullivan.
Circulation: 482,370
Politics: none
Sunday Times (established 1822)
1 Pennington Street, London, E1 9XW.
Controlled by: News International, R. Murdoch.
Circulation: 1,244,890
Politics: right of centre.
Independent on Sunday (established 1990)
Controlled by: Newspaper Publishing plc.
Circulation: 332,284
Politics: centre left/independent.

Regional Newspapers in the UK

There are 89 regional newspapers, including morning and evening dailies and Sunday papers. There are a further 750 newspapers appearing once or twice a week. As well as these there are another 950 free-distribution papers which are predominantly financed by advertising. Over the last five years these papers have grown in numbers, and it is now estimated that they have an average weekly circulation figure of 40 million. The daily papers provide regional and national news but also tend to cover international news. Evening papers tend to be more apolitical, whilst the dailies tend to have a more political approach, generally adopting a more conservative opinion.

Weekly regional papers tend to have smaller circulation figures, within the 5,000 to 60,000 range.

Circulation, Major Regional Evening and Daily Papers

		Circulation (approximate)
Daily		
England	Yorkshire Post (Leeds)	92,000
	Eastern Daily Press (Norwich)	92,000
Wales	Western Mail (Cardiff)	74,000
Scotland	The Scotsman (Edinburgh)	88,261 (July–Dec. 1989)
	Glasgow Herald	121,595 (July–Dec. 1989)
Evening		
England	Manchester Evening News	291,000
	Birmingham Evening Mail	233,000
	Wolverhampton Express and Star	239,000
	Liverpool Echo	207,000
	Evening Standard (London)	493,000
Wales	South Wales Echo (Cardiff)	28,000–95,000
	South Wales Argus (Newport)	
	South Wales Evening Post (Swansea)	
Scotland	Evening News (Edinburgh)	12,000–167,082
	Evening Times (Glasgow)	
	Evening Telegraph (Dundee)	

TELEVISION

Television and Radio: average viewing and listening per week

In general, people watch far more television than listen to the radio. In 1988 average television viewing time per week was 25 hours 21 minutes for all age groups. People over the age of 65 watched up to 50% more than this per week, averaging out at 37 hours 25 minutes.

In most age groups television viewing has declined since 1985. This does not, however, take into account the rise in home video usage and may therefore well imply that more, rather than less, hours are now spent in front of the television.

Unlike television viewing hours, which increase with age, radio listening constantly peaks between the ages of 16 and 34.

In 1988 an average of half-an-hour less time was spent watching television by those under the age of 16 than in 1984.

Radio listening has increased for all age groups since 1984 and now stands at 9 hours 12 minutes per week, on average.

Audiences for television and radio vary widely throughout the day. Radio is still far more popular in the morning with 15.5% of all age groups listening between 8.00 and 8.30am: 40.3% of the population watch television between 9.00 and 9.30pm.

Television audiences overtake radio audiences from about 1.00pm onwards. The television lunch-time peak has viewing audiences of approximately 26 million, roughly half of the UK population.

British Broadcasting Corporation

The British Broadcasting Company was established by Royal Charter on the 18 October 1922. Broadcasting began on the 14 November 1922 with the news. The Company's first *Director General* was John C.W. Reith. When in 1927 the organization changed its name to the British Broadcasting Corporation (BBC), there were two million licence holders each paying 10 shillings a year. High-definition television broadcasts first began in 1936 and in 1964 BBC2 switched to 625 lines.

The Constitution of the BBC is two-pronged: firstly, the Royal Charter which gives the Corporation legal existence, fixed objectives and established advisory bodies; and secondly, the licence and agreement which sets the terms and conditions for broadcasting and finance.

The Government has ultimate control over the broadcasting of materials. This veto has only been used once in October 1988 when the government chose to use the powers against the BBC, ITV and ILR to restrict broadcast coverage of statements supporting terrorism in Northern Ireland.

The BBC is regulated by a Board of Governors whose members are appointed by the Queen in council

Television and Radio: Average Viewing and Listening in the UK

TV Viewing Age Groups	1984	1985	1986	1987	1988
			Hours:minutes per week		
4–15 years	16:10	19:59	20:35	19:14	18:34
16–34 years	18:16	21:36	21:10	20:03	20:36
35–64 years	23:24	28:04	27:49	27:25	27:17
65 & over	29:50	36:35	36:55	37:41	37:25
Reach (percentages)					
Daily	74	79	78	76	77
Weekly	90	94	94	93	94
All aged 4 years & over	23:03	26:33	25:54	25:25	25:21

on the advice of the government. There are 12 Governors including national Governors for Scotland, Wales and Northern Ireland.

The BBC's services include two national television services which are complementary to each other. The four national radio networks were joined by a fifth on 27 August 1990, devoted predominantly to sport and education with an emphasis on youth appeal. It also carries some of the World Service.

The World Service broadcasts in English and 36 other languages. The running costs are not included in the licence fee and are paid for by a Parliamentary grant-in-aid, although editorial control still rests with the BBC.

The BBC still has a strong regional structure and is divided into four English regions: North, Midlands, South and East, South and West; along with Scotland, Wales and Northern Ireland. The regions make programmes for their local audience as well as contributing to the networks. Between them, they are responsible for 35 local radio stations, with a further four new stations opening in 1991.

The BBC's finances are far smaller than those of Independent Television. Its income is fixed to the Retail Price Index (RPI), which the BBC argues is not an accurate costing and means it no longer has enough money to invest in and develop the modern technologies which have become crucial to broadcasting in the 1990s. The BBC's income for 1988–9 stands at £788 million, as opposed to ITV's £1,425 million per annum. There are 19.5 million licence payers paying £62.50 per annum for this service. The commercial side of the BBC is handled by BBC Enterprises Ltd. It is responsible for the raising of income through the sale of programmes, books, videos, records, tapes and the *Radio Times*. Breaking down expenditure, the costs of BBC1 are £426 million per annum, BBC2 £209 million, and regional broadcasting (including television, radio, and programmes made for network) £250 million. Re-equipment costs £119 million per annum, licence fee collection £71 million, and transmission and distribution £40 million.

Recent Developments The Government's White Paper *Broadcasting in the '90s; Competition Choice and Quality* has stated that the BBC should maintain its role as the 'cornerstone of British broadcasting'; it continues that the BBC should 'provide high-quality programming across the full range of public tastes and interests, including programmes of minority interests, and offer education, information and cultural material as well as entertainment'.

In 1988 the government established the Broadcasting Standards Authority to develop a code on the portrayal of sex and violence and to be 'fair, accurate and impartial'. The chairman is Lord Rees Mogg. New Producers Guidelines have brought together all the policies and practices that will ensure consistent high standards and these have been welcomed by the BBC.

Contentiously the Paper suggests a move towards subscription as the primary source of future television funding. On this the BBC recommends a more cautious approach, suggesting waiting to see what happens with the recently established subscription satellite and cable channels, BSB and SKY. They also can see no practical manner in which radio can be incorporated into such a system.

Generally the BBC agrees with the White Paper. However it has three central queries which it has put forward in its response. Firstly it is concerned that major national sporting events should not be exclusive to subscription channels, thus denying national audiences; and secondly, that cable operators should carry public-service channels. The BBC feels that unless they are incorporated within any cable system they may be 'displaced' and the public will lose their services. Finally, it says that there should be no transfer or removal of existing frequencies which may impede future technological developments.

Michael Checkland states that, 'We look forward to the expansion of broadcasting in Britain. Of course, it will challenge us. But we are confident it will also give opportunities – and benefits – for our audience.'

The organization is already developing new technologies for the nineties such as the 'down-loading' of encoded programmes, a new service started in 1989 providing subscription information for specialist fields specifically, at the moment, the medical profession.

Radio Listening Age Groups	1984	1985	1986	1987	1988
			Hours:minutes per week		
4–15 years	2:46	2:24	2:12	2:07	2:13
16–34 years	11:42	11:42	11:24	11:18	11:40
35–64 years	9:59	9:43	9:56	10:16	10:33
65 & over	8:01	8:04	8:27	8:44	8:49
All aged 4 years and over	8:44	8:40	8:40	8:52	9:12
Reach (percentages)					
Daily	46	43	43	43	43
Weekly	81	78	75	74	73

The BBC also plans to start stereo broadcasts in the Autumn of 1991 and is co-operating with BSB in the development of satellite technologies.

The Independent Broadcasting Authority

The Independent Television Authority was founded by an Act of Parliament in 1954 to provide an alternative/additional television broadcasting service to that offered by the British Broadcasting Company (BBC). In 1972 it was renamed the Independent Broadcasting Authority (IBA) and its functions were extended to cover independent local radio.

The IBA provides television and radio services of information, education and entertainment. Basing its policy on the Broadcasting Act 1981, the IBA is both a 'regulator' and a 'publisher'.

The IBA has four main functions: the selection and appointment of programme companies, the supervision of programme planning, the control of advertising and the transmission of programmes.

There are 15 ITV companies with contracts for 14 different regions (there are two companies in London: Thames and London Weekend Television). Each company must produce programmes of interest to the viewers of its area with distinct regional character. TV-AM, the 16th company, provides breakfast-time viewing.

Independent Television News (ITN) supplies news information to Channel 4 and ITV, and is a non-profit-making organization owned by the ITV companies.

Channel 4 is a wholly-owned subsidiary of the IBA, designed to complement the ITV service. It is financed by subscription from the ITV companies which sell advertising time on the channel in their own regions.

Supervision of programme planning is carried out by the IBA who is ultimately responsible to Parliament and the public for all it transmits. The IBA must ensure the maintenance of a balance between entertainment, information, education and also maintain impartiality, accuracy, 'good taste' and decency. The IBA has a censoring role, though this is rarely used – the responsibility generally resting within the independent companies' authority.

The IBA also controls advertising on ITV, Channel 4 and Independent Local Radio (ILR). The Broadcasting Act again lays strict rules and codes of practice governing taste, accuracy and duration. All advertisements are checked against the code of Advertising Standards in consultation with the IBA's Advertising Advisory Committee.

The IBA builds, owns, maintains and operates all transmitters which cover around 99% of the UK. Engineering accounts for two-thirds of IBA's staff and capital commitment. There are approximately 1,500 transmitters.

Independent Local Radio, ILR Similar principles apply to ILR services. The 46 stations are appointed by and under contract to the IBA. They provide radio broadcasts to 85% of the population, again aiming to suit local needs and regional interests.

They operate under the IBA's control and are financed by advertising revenue. News coverage is supplied by a common service, Independent Radio News. On Monday 4 March 1990 Jazz FM, London's newest independent radio station, started broadcasting after receiving the Government's go-ahead and its contract from the IBA.

Channel Four Television Company

Channel 4 is a national television channel, broadcasting for more than 112 hours per week, with a national service available to nearly 99% of the British population (excluding Wales where there is a separate service). It is operated by the Channel Four Television Company Ltd, a wholly owned subsidiary of the Independent Broadcasting Authority (IBA).

The channel is non-profit-making but is funded indirectly from advertising, through a subscription which the regional television companies are required to pay in return for the right to sell and insert advertisements in Channel 4's national service in their own areas. The subscription is based on an agreed proportion of the previous year's advertising revenues for both channels.

Channel 4 commenced broadcasting on 2 November 1982, the first new television company to be launched for 18 years.

Under the 1981 Broadcasting Act, the channel is required to plan its programming in a manner wholly different to that of the other IBA companies; to cater for tastes, interests and audiences not previously served by ITV, or any other broadcast channel and to provide a substantial proportion of educational programming.

Unlike Britain's other three channels, Channel 4 is charged not to produce its own programmes but to obtain them from other sources, that is, independent producers. The number of such producers has grown enormously since the start of Channel 4. Independent producers provide 28% of total programming hours transmitted in 1988–9. ITV and ITN produce some 29% of programming hours, whilst the other 43% is made up from purchased programmes, acquired material and feature films.

The channel must also schedule its programmes to complement ITV at all times, and must obey the same rules on fairness, balance and control of content, as govern the ITV companies under the IBA.

S4C, Sianel Pedwar Cymru Channel 4 is national, except for Wales. The Welsh fourth channel is separate, created to serve a distinct purpose; its main aim is to 'provide a service of programmes in the Welsh language for Welsh speakers'. S4C was brought into being partly because of the perceived need for a Welsh channel emphasised by the threatened hunger strike of Gwynfor Evans, leader of Plaid Cymru.

It schedules over 25 hours a week in Welsh. Work is commissioned by S4C in the same manner as that of Channel 4 in London. The Welsh channel is run by a separate authority, the Welsh Fourth Channel Authority. The service is relayed to viewers, like Channel 4, via the IBA's transmitters.

Recent developments Now in the review stage, the Government's White Paper, *Broadcasting in the 90s: Competition, Choice and Quality*, was first presented to Parliament in November 1988. It delineates a complete re-shaping of the commercial sector and redefines Channel 4's placement within this new framework. The Government's propositions are based on two clear prerequisites: that Channel 4's airtime should be separately and competitively sold; and that its programming remit, which is described as 'a striking success', should be maintained. The paper is still in the review stage and Channel 4 is recommending following the second option. This advocates the channel selling its own airtime underpinned to a guaranteed minimum level by income from other sources. As an incentive to efficiency, they suggested that this safety net should be set at 14% of all terrestrial net advertising revenue.

At the moment it appears that the Government will accept these recommendations. Channel 4 believes that this funding formula will afford advertisers the competitive sale of airtime that they seek, and may also eradicate the potential damage which might occur with a policy which only aims to increase ratings.

Channel 4: analysis of programming

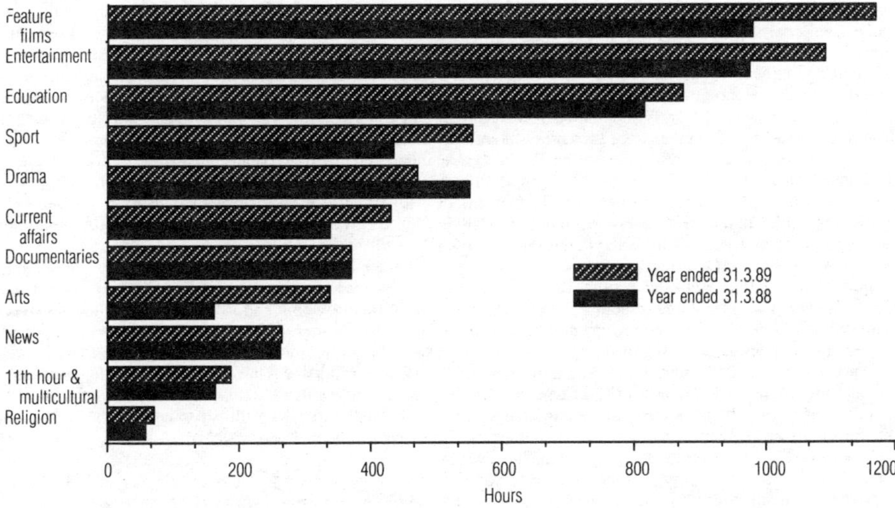

Source: Report and Accounts, Channel 4.

Total hours broadcast

Sky Television

On 8 June 1988 Rupert Murdoch announced his plans to set up a satellite broadcasting service, to be called Sky Television.

Transmission started on 5 February 1989. These were broadcasted via the Astra satellite, with four initial channels: Sky One, Sky News, Sky Movies and Eurosport. Also available from the Astra satellite are Sky Radio, MTV (Music Television) and W.H. Smith's two channels: Screensports and Lifestyle.

The estimated total viewing audience, as at May 1990, was 4,000,000 people in 1,363,297 homes. There were 135,000 standing orders for systems and in March 1990 there were 78,000 new systems installed. The total number of Sky satellite dishes now installed in the UK and Irish Republic is 718,297; added to this are the 570,000 cable subscribers able to receive Sky and the 75,000 SMATV receivers (shared rental schemes).

These services have been put together with the aid of 15 European Broadcasting Union members.

Sky Movies Sky's movie channel appears to be the most popular of all satellite channels yet available. On 6 April 1990 there were 449,134 subscribers paying £2.29 per month to receive 400 films a year, including 40 different titles per month. None of these films are interrupted by advertising.

The Movie channel, which started as a free service to those with receiving capability, moved over to subscription-based funding in February 1990.

Agreements have been reached with three of the major studios: Warner Brothers, Twentieth Century Fox and Touchstone Pictures.

15 of 1989's top twenty video releases will be shown on Sky's movie channel as compared to five on BSB's equivalent. This involves showing 16 hours of films per day, seven days a week.

Sky One Sky One aims to provide 20 hours of family entertainment every day. The service starts with children's programmes in the morning, moving to daytime drama and game-shows. The evenings have comedy shows, mini-series, drama and special events.

The special events category is for the broadcasting of major events, the first of these to be shown was the Bruno/Tyson World Heavyweight fight. Since then, live concerts by Elton John and Bros have been shown. In February 1990 live coverage of the cricket test in the West Indies was shown.

Sky News Sky News is the first 24-hour television news station.

The service includes extensive Parliamentary coverage, national, international and business news as well as special features including interview programmes, documentaries and current-affairs shows.

It aims to be the fastest service for live news coverage, and aided this by being the first to show live footage of the dismantling of the Berlin Wall. Each afternoon Sky News shows the largest percentage of coverage, of any station, of the House of Commons.

Eurosport Operated by a European consortium on behalf of members of the European Broadcasting Union, this channel has an 18 million viewing audience in 22 European countries.

The programme features European and international sporting events and is broadcast with a three language soundtrack option: English, German or Dutch.

Sports shown are: athletics, basketball, cycling, figure skating, football, golf, motor racing, show jumping, skiing and tennis.

Satellite Shop The Satellite Shop home shopping service was launched in May 1989. It has been backed by the Next and Grattan retail chains. The service will act like existing mail-order services, with the Grattan chain's delivery service promising a 48-hour delivery time.

Regulatory bodies At present Sky, like the other satellite services, is monitored by the Cable Authority. This will change when the new Independent Television Commission comes into being (once the Government's paper *Broadcasting in the '90s* is passed).

Transmission standards Sky operates on the PAL system which is the existing system used by current earth television. It has chosen not to use the High Definition System opted for by BSB, but states that it will 'consider . . . HD Television when it becomes available towards the end of this century'.

Broadcasting Bill The Government's White Paper *Broadcasting in the '90s* has been welcomed by Sky for its deregulatory tendencies, which it argues will allow for choice without sacrificing standards.

The new Astra 1B satellite will enable 32 new satellite channels to be broadcast; this is due to start at the beginning of 1991.

David Mellor, the Broadcasting Minister, has said that 'there is potentially open-ended scope for Astra-type developments under diverse ownership'.

British Satellite Broadcasting

On 27 August 1989, British Satellite Broadcasting (BSB) launched its satellite, the Marcopolo I. This was the start of the first British-based satellite service.

BSB started full satellite broadcasting on 29 April 1990; cable broadcasting commenced at the end of March 1990.

BSB stated that this expansion in broadcasting, 'will double the number of UK-regulated mainstream channels'.

The satellite revolution in Britain is rapidly progressing. In 1990 the British public is able to receive two new satellite services offering twenty-one new channels between them.

Anthony Simonds-Gooding, BSB's Chief Executive, has promised that 'BSB will be a regulated extension of choice for the British public'.

The service is regulated by the Independent Broadcasting Authority (IBA). Under the new White Paper *Broadcasting in the '90s*, the newly established Broadcasting Standards Council and the Broadcasting Complaints Commission will be its watchdogs.

BSB, which was selected by the IBA after tendering, will offer five new channels and a news service.

The Movie channel will offer six films a day on subscription, a new idea within television pioneered by the satellite companies. During the afternoons free 'classic', old films will be shown. BSB has signed major deals with some of the large Hollywood companies and offers 24 films a month to British television.

The Now channel is an information service covering leisure, hobbies, environmental issues, education, health, the arts, fashion, news and parliamentary coverage.

Galaxy is an entertainment channel for the family, offering children's programming during the day and drama, soaps and comedy in the evenings.

Sports will show top events at peak times live. BSB has secured the rights to the International, Scottish and English FA cup finals.

The Power station provides a music channel with bias towards rock and pop and issues of interest to teenagers.

The news service is available on all channels and has been contracted out, primarily to Crown Communications/IRN.

BSB had to delay its opening date by six months due to technical difficulties, firstly with its 'Squarials' and then with its decoders. Using new D-Mac transmission standards, offering better pictures, stereo sound and parental control has not been without its difficulties.

The original budget of £625 million has been exceeded and now stands at £1.3 billion. Whilst BSB predicts that there will be 3 million satellite owners by 1991, independent surveys suggest a figure between 1.6 and 2.2 million as being more realistic for 1991.

Of those able to receive BSB's services at present, 55% receive the transmissions through cable and only 45% through satellite.

On 30 April, the launch date, there were only 5,000 satellite receivers installed. This was due to further technical problems and, argue BSB, should be overcome by autumn 1990 when receivers will be easily available in the shops.

BSB accepts that it has had some 'teething' problems, but it believes the situation will improve and that it is entering the market with a product that it feels is far superior to any yet on offer.

COMMUNICATIONS

Telecommunications

One of the most rapidly expanding service sectors today is telecommunications. Under the British Telecom Act 1981, the functions of the Post Office were split between two organizations. The Post Office remained in the public sector providing postal services and British Telecom was privatized to provide telecom services.

The Telecom Act 1984 removed British Telecom's monopoly and opened the industry to competition. The Act required that the running of telecom systems be licensed by the Secretary of State for Trade and Industry.

British Telecom is empowered to continue to provide telecom services throughout the country; they must meet all reasonable demands and continue to provide essential services, such as the public emergency services.

The Telecom Act 1984 also created the Office of Telecommunications (Oftel) as the independent regulatory body. Oftel is a non-ministerial government department. Its role is to ensure that the holders of telecom licences comply with their conditions. Oftel also aims to promote and create effective competition. The *Director General*, Prof. Sir Brian Carsberg, has some powers to control anti-competitive practices and monopolistic actions.

There are, at present, three licensed fixed-link Public Telecom Operators (PTOs) in the UK; British Telecom, Mercury Communications Ltd and the Kingston-upon-Hull City Council Exchange.

In August 1989 further liberalization measures occurred with the new version of the branch system general licence. This covers most public and business uses. It sets up new guidelines within which private users may connect their own wiring and extensions and take advantage of private lines which can now be leased from private operators. The licence now covers value-added and data services which had previously been covered under a separate class of licence.

The new version has further liberalized the industry and has simplified the regulatory procedures.

In 1988 the government announced plans for six new operator agreements to provide one-way satellite communications systems for a third party by 1990.

In December 1989 the Trade and Industry Minister, Eric Forth, granted three Personal Communication Network (PCN) licences. These are a digital wireless communications system designed to foresee the advances and limitations of the present cellular phone networks. The licences went to: Mercury in a consortium with Motorola and Telefonica; British Aerospace and a consortium (called Unitel) of STC, US West, Thorn EMI; and finally the West German Bundespost.

British Telecom When British Telecom became a public limited company in 1984 it was the largest ever stock-market flotation in Britain. It now has 1.2 million shareholders, including 98% of its 244,000 employees.

British Telecom operates 18.7 million residential lines and 5.2 million business lines. There are 109,000 telex connections, 85,500 public payphones and a wide range of specialist services.

International Direct Dialing (IDD) is now available from any phone in the UK to 190 countries; this represents over 90% of the world's telephones.

Pre-tax profits for 1988–9 were £2,437 million on a turnover of £11,071 million.

British Telecom is constantly reinvesting in modernizing equipment and in research. £2,500 million is reinvested each year on modernization and expansion of the network. Of this £711 million went on modernizing exchanges with digital equipment. There are now over 2,000 digital exchanges in service. These involve digital-exchange switching, digital-transmission techniques, new optical-fibre cable and microwave radio links. Approximately £214 million was spent last year on research and development.

British Telecom runs many general services. Several of these are free, including calls to the emergency services; fire, police, ambulance, coastguard, lifeboat, air-sea rescue, and non-emergency services such as the directory of inquiries. Chargeable calls include; transfer calls, alarm calls and Timeline (formerly the speaking clock).

In 1988 a new optical-fibre flexible-access system was installed in the City (of London), at a cost of £70 million, to aid the ever-growing demand placed by business for voice and data traffic.

£160 million has been spent on modernizing the payphone network; as well as 85,500 payphones there are also now 17,000 public phonecard installations.

Prestel, British Telecom videotext service, is now installed in 95,000 terminals.

British Telecom also operates and is investing in the modernization of international services. These are mainly operated from British Telecom's three earth satellite stations.

The world's first undersea international fibre-optical cable began operating in 1986, between Britain and Belgium. TAT 8, the first underwater transatlantic optical-fibre cable, entered service in December 1988 and a further cable, TAT 9, is planned for 1991. This will cost £250 million and be able to handle 75,000 calls simultaneously.

Mercury Mercury Communications Ltd is a wholly-owned subsidiary of Cable and Wireless plc. It operates under licence as the competing telecom company. It is licensed to provide national and international telephone services for residential and business needs, utilizing Mercury's new 6,200-mile wholly-digital trunk network, costing £1 billion, and centred in Birmingham.

Mercury's services began in 1986 and they now provide: public payphones (1988), national and international telexes, international packet data services, electronic messaging to telex via computer, data network services and nationwide radiopaging.

International services are handled by satellite networks, based in London's Docklands.

Cable and Wireless, the owner of Mercury, has now extended its operations and is active in over 40 countries throughout the world. It has provided and maintained telecommunications networks in 36 countries under franchise with the governments concerned.

Cable and Wireless, like British Telecom, has also started to lay an underwater network of digital optical-fibre lines. This global digital Highway (GDH) is due to be completed in 1991.

Other services Recently, there are a growing number of new private services. Most of these are information services, including; weather reports, stock market updates, horoscopes and Chatlines.

These services must adhere to the codes of practice of the Independent Committee for the Supervision of

Phones per 100 people

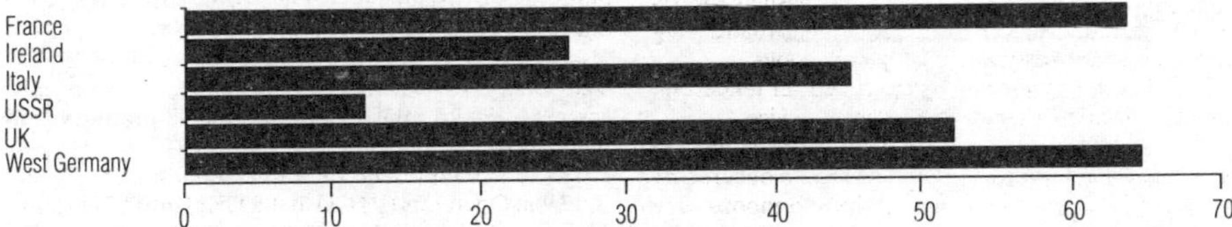

Percentage of households with telephones in GB

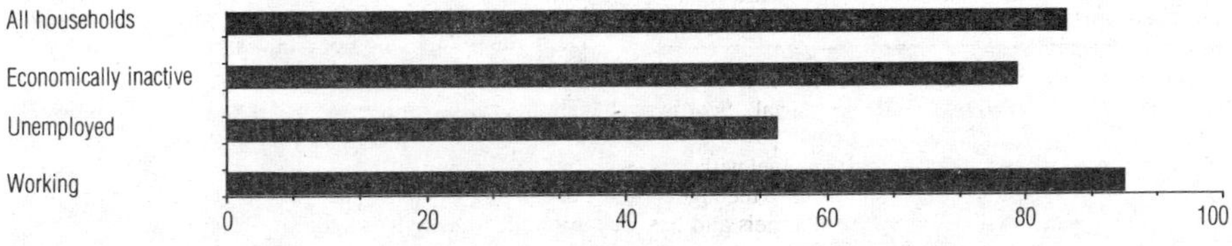

Standards of Telephone Information Practice.

On 6 May 1990 London prefix codes were extended to provide for the ever-growing number of lines required, particularly due to the increase in the number of facsimile (fax) machines and modem computer links. The new codes replace 01 with 071 for Inner London and 081 for Outer London.

Mobile telephone systems (cellular) have been in operation since 1985. Two companies were licensed by the Department of Trade and Industry to provide this service: Cellnet, jointly owned by British Telecom and Securicor; and Vodaphone Ltd, owned by the Racal electronics group.

In June 1989 it was estimated that there were 600,000 cellular phones in operation. In January 1989 a further three companies were licensed to enter this market; Ferranti, Phonepoint and Mercury's Callpoint.

Postal Services

The first Royal service for the delivery of Government dispatches was set up in 1516. Conveyance of public correspondence began in 1635, and the Post Office (PO) was the first to issue adhesive stamps as proof of advance payment for mail.

The Post Office became a Parliamentary responsibility in 1657. Telegraphs came under the Post Office responsibility in 1870 and the Telephone Service began in 1880. The National Girobank began in 1968.

In 1969 the Post Office ceased being a Government department and responsibility for postal, telecom, Girobank and remittance services were transferred to a public authority called the Post Office.

In 1981 the British Telecommunications Act split the functions of the Post Office and it became solely responsible for postal services and Girobank. This was further split in 1990 when Girobank was privatized.

The Chairman and members of the Post Office Board are appointed by the Secretary of State, but responsibility for the Post Office rests wholly with the Board.

The Royal Mail delivers to nearly 24 million addresses and handles over 50 million letters and parcels each day, totalling approximately 13,000 million items a year.

Mail is collected from 100,000 posting boxes, as well as post offices and larger users.

Girobank provides a wide range of corporate and personal banking facilities. In 1988 the government announced its plans for privatization. This was due to occur at the end of June 1990 with a buy-out by the Alliance and Leicester Building Society.

Financial Results: Post Office Group, 1988–9

£ million	
Turnover	3,914.8
Trading profit, pre-tax	169.7
Letters and parcels:	
Turnover	3,125.2
Pre-tax profits	107.9
Counters:	
Turnover	798.4
Pre-tax profits	45.5
Girobank:	
Turnover	234.2
Pre-tax profits	21.6

The Post Office now has 80 sorting offices with mechanical handling equipment. These are taking over from the 100 or so independent sorting offices handling letters manually. There are 27 large parcel centres, each serving a group of counties, which have taken over from the 1200 offices which previously manually handled parcels.

There are nearly 21,000 post offices, of which some 1,500 are operated directly by the Post Office and the remainder on an agency basis controlled by sub-postmasters.

£80 million pounds has been invested in a premium parcel service for business, called Royal Mail Parcelforce. This service was launched on the 27 February 1990 and is a competitor to the growing private sector courier service. Parcelforce has 150 depots which are independent of the general post offices. Some 95% of its users are businesses and it is now the market leader with a 33% share. Parcelforce has taken over the role of Datapost, which now operates within the wider organization.

The British Telecommunications Act 1981 gave the Secretary of State for Trade and Industry powers to suspend the Post Office monopoly in certain areas. This enables licences to be given to other bodies to provide alternative services. Non-post-office bodies are now allowed to transfer mail between document exchanges and deliver letters, provided a minimum fee of £1 is charged. Charitable organizations are allowed to carry and deliver Christmas and New Year cards.

At present there is a two-tiered postal delivery system, with first-class letters normally arriving the next day and second-class post within two days.

Sales of postage stamps have been extended to include outlets other than the post offices, including newsagents and stationers.

Postal Orders are issued and paid out at nearly all Post Offices in the UK. Other services include: Cash on Delivery, certificate of posting, compensation, newspaper post, recorded delivery, re-direction and registration (first class only). There are also restrictions on prohibited articles, and undelivered mail is returned to sender, where possible.

The Royal Mail facsimile service is the first international 'fax' service for public use in sending letters and documents electronically between 100 post offices in Britain and to over 40 other countries.

The Philatelic Bureau, in Edinburgh, handles a third of all philatelic business.

The British Postal Consultancy Service offers advice and assistance on all aspects of the postal business, and nearly 40 countries have used its services since 1965.

The Royal Mail also operates a special delivery service, with special message treatment for first class letters and packages. Swiftair is an express delivery service for air-mail letters and packets to anywhere in the world.

Private courier services are now allowed to handle time-sensitive and valuable mail; again this is subject to a minimum fee of £1.

The courier industry has grown rapidly, by about 20% per year, and the estimated value of items now handled is £200 million per annum.

Attendances at National Museums and Galleries in UK, 1979 to 1988

	1979	1984	1985	1986	1987	1988
			millions			
England:						
National Art Museums & Galleries:						
British Museums (a)	4.1	3.5	4.1	3.9	4.0	4.2
National Gallery (a)	2.6	2.9	3.2	3.2	3.6	3.3
National Portrait Gallery (a)	0.4	0.6	0.5	0.6	0.6	0.6
Tate Gallery (a)	1.1	1.3	1.0	1.2	1.7	2.1
Victoria and Albert (b)	2.1	2.1	2.1	1.4	1.4	1.4
Wallace Collection (a)	0.1	0.2	0.2	0.2	0.2	0.2
Total	10.3	10.6	11.1	10.5	11.5	11.8
Science and Other Museums:						
Imperial War Museum (c)	1.4	1.4	1.3	1.2	1.2	1.1
National Army Museum (a, d)	0.1	0.1	0.1	0.1	0.1	0.1
National Maritime Museum (h)	1.1	0.6	0.6	0.4	0.4	0.7
National Museum of Photography Film and Television (a, e)	N/A	0.4	0.5	0.7	0.7	0.8
National Railway Museum (f)	1.2	0.9	1.1	0.9	0.6	0.6
National History Museum (g)	2.9	3.0	3.4	3.2	2.0	1.7
Royal Airforce Museum (h)	0.6	0.4	0.4	0.3	0.3	0.3
Royal Armouries (i)	2.4	2.0	2.1	1.8	2.0	2.2
Science Museum (j)	3.9	3.2	3.0	3.2	3.4	2.5
Total	13.6	12.0	12.5	11.8	10.7	10.0
Scotland:						
National Museums (a)	0.7	0.7	0.8	0.7	0.8	0.7
National Galleries (a)	0.4	0.5	0.5	0.5	0.5	0.5
Total	1.1	1.2	1.3	1.2	1.3	1.2
Wales:						
National Museums (k)	0.7	0.8	0.8	0.8	1.0	0.8
Northern Ireland:						
Ulster Museum (a)	0.2	0.3	0.3	0.3	0.3	0.4
Ulster Folk & Transport Museum	0.2	0.2	0.1	0.2	0.2	0.2
Total	0.4	0.5	0.4	0.5	0.5	0.6

(a) No entry admission charged.
(b) Voluntary donations introduced Nov. 1985.
(c) Imperial War Museum, attendance: Main M 282,000, HMS *Belfast* 209,000, Duxford Airfield 377,000, Cabinet War Rooms 219,000.
(d) Funded by MOD.
(e) Opened in 1984.
(f) Charges introduced April 1987.
(g) Includes Geological Museum, charges introduced April 1987.
(h) Funded by MOD, charges introduced April 1988.
(i) Funded DOE.
(j) Charges introduced Oct. 1988.
(k) Charges introduced Dec. 1988.
Source: Museums and Galleries Commission.

English National Museums and Galleries: Effect of Admission Charges on Attendance

	1979	1984	1985	1986	1987	1988
			millions			
Free Museums (a)	8.4	9.0	9.6	9.9	10.9	11.3
Museums and Galleries Charging Admission (b):						
Imperial War Museum (1989)	1.4	1.4	1.3	1.2	1.2	1.1
National Maritime Museum (1984)	1.1	0.6	0.6	0.4	0.4	0.7
National Railway Museum (1987)	1.2	0.9	1.1	0.9	0.6	0.6
Natural History Museum (1987)	2.9	3.0	3.4	3.2	2.0	1.7
RAF Museum (1988)	0.6	0.4	0.4	0.3	0.3	0.3
Science Museum (1988)	3.9	3.2	3.0	3.2	3.4	2.5
Victoria and Albert (c) (1985)	2.0	2.1	2.1	1.4	1.4	1.4

(a) British M, National G, National Portrait G, Tate G, Wallace Collection, National Army M, National Museum of Photography, Film and Television (since 1984).
(b) Date of introduction of charge or voluntary contribution.
(c) Voluntary donation.
Source: Museums and Galleries Commission.

MEMBERS OF PARLIAMENT

Abbreviations

ACTT	Association of Cinematograph, Television and Allied Technicians
AEU	Amalgamated Engineering Union
All.	Alliance
All. (NI)	Alliance Party Northern Ireland
APEX	Association of Professional, Executive, Clerical, and Computer Staff (part of GMB)
Apr.	April
ASH	Action on Smoking and Health
assn	Association
asst	assistant
ASTMS	now MSF
Aug.	August
AUT	Association of University Teachers
b.	born
BACM	British Association of Colliery Management
BALPA	British Air Line Pilots Association
Beds.	Bedfordshire
BEM	British Empire Medal
Berks.	Berkshire
Bt	Baronet
Bucks.	Buckinghamshire
C of E	Church of England
Cambs.	Cambridgeshire
Capt.	Captain
Chmn	Chairman
Cllr	Councillor
CMG	Companion, Order of St Michael and St George
CND	Campaign for Nuclear Disarmament
Co.	County
COHSE	Confederation of Health Service Employees
Col	Colonel
Coll.	*College*
Con.	Conservative
CPWSML	Capital Punishment Will Save More Lives
cttee	committee
DCP	Democratic Commonwealth Party
Dec.	December
dept	department
Derbys.	Derbyshire
dir.	director
DUP	Democratic Unionist Party
E. Sussex	East Sussex
ed.	educated and editor
EC	European Economic Community
EETPU	Electrical, Electronic, Telecommunication and Plumbing Union
EMS	European Monetary System
ERD	Emergency Reserve Decoration
FBU	Fire Brigades Union
Feb.	February
FRAME	Fund for the Replacement of Animals in Medical Experiments
FRCP	Fellow, Royal College of Physicians
FRS	Fellow, Royal Society
GLC	Greater London Council
Glos.	Gloucestershire
GMB	General, Municipal, Boilermakers
govt	government
h	hour
Hants.	Hampshire
Herts.	Hertfordshire
HGV	Heavy Goods Vehicle

HM Her Majesty
Hon. Honorary/Honorable
Hosp. Hospital

Inst. Institute
IRA Irish Republican Army
ISTC Iron and Steel Trades Confederation

Jan. January
JP Justice of the Peace
jtly jointly

KBE Knight Commander, Order of the British Empire
KCMG Knight Commander, Order of St Michael and St George

Lab. Labour
Lancs. Lancashire
l.d. lost deposit
Leics. Leicestershire
Lib. Liberal
Lib. Dem. Social and Liberal Democrat
Lincs. Lincolnshire
LOMRP Loony Official Monster Raving Party
Lt Lieutenant
Lt-Col Lieutenant-Colonel

m metre
MA Master of Arts
Mar. March
Marq. Marquess
MATSA Managerial and Technical Staff Association
MBE Member, Order of the British Empire
MC Military Cross
MEP Member of European Parliament
min. minute
MP Member of Parliament
MSF Manufacturing, Science and Finance

NALGO National and Local Government Officers' Association
NATFHE National Association of Teachers in Further and Higher Education
NCB National Coal Board
NCU National Communications Union
NFFG National Front Flag Group
NFU National Farmers' Union
NGA National Graphical Association
NHS National Health Service
Northants. Northamptonshire
Notts. Nottinghamshire
Nov. November
NSPCC National Society for the Prevention of Cruelty to Children
NUJ National Union of Journalists
NUM National Union of Mineworkers
NUPE National Union of Public Employees
NUR National Union of Railwaymen
NUS National Union of Seamen
NUT National Union of Teachers

OBE Officer, Order of the British Empire
Oct. October
OFB Official Fidgeyitous Party
OOBPC Only Official Best Party Candidate
OUP Official Unionist Party
Oxon. Oxfordshire

PC Privy Councillor (see also Rt Hon.)
PGA Professional Golfers' Association
Pl.C. Plaid Cymru
Poly. Polytechnic
PPS Parliamentary Private Secretary
Pres. President
Prof. Professor
PRP Protestant Reformation Party
PSA Property Services Agency

QC Queen's Counsel
QSO Queen's Service Order

RAF Royal Air Force
RC Roman Catholic
RCP Return Capital Punishment
RD Naval Reserve Decoration
Rev. Reverend
RNLI Royal National Lifeboat Institution
RSPCA Royal Society for the Prevention of Cruelty to Animals
Rt Hon. Right Honourable (see also PC)

s. succeeded
S. Glamorgan South Glamorgan
S. Yorks. South Yorkshire
Sch. School
SDLP Social Democratic and Labour Party
SDP Social Democrat Party
Sept. September
SNP Scottish National Party
SOGAT '82 Society of Graphical and Allied Trades
St Saint
Staffs. Staffordshire

TGWU Transport and General Workers' Union
TSSA Transport Salaried Staffs' Association
TUC Trade Union Congress

UAE United Arab Emirates
UCATT Union of Construction, Allied Trades and Technicians
UCW Union of Communications Workers
UK United Kingdom
UN United Nations
Univ. University
UPUP Ulster Popular Unionist Party
USDAW Union of Shop, Distributive and Allied Workers
UU Ulster Unionist

Vice-Pres. Vice-President
Visc. Viscount
VSO Voluntary Service Overseas

W. Glamorgan West Glamorgan
W. Midlands West Midlands
W. Sussex West Sussex
W. Yorks. West Yorkshire
Warks. Warwickshire
Wilts. Wiltshire
WP Workers' Party (Northern Ireland)
WRP Workers' Revolutionary Party

ABBOTT, Diane Lab., Hackney North and Stoke Newington (1987) **b.** 27 Sept. 1953 **ed.** Harrow Co. Girls' Grammar Sch.; Newnham Coll., Cambridge **Profession** civil servant, broadcaster **Political interests** race relations, housing, social services, nuclear disarmament **Political career** Westminster City Cllr 1982–6 **Member** Anti-Apartheid; CND **Unions** ACTT; NUJ **Other** The first Black woman MP

ADAMS, Allen Lab., Paisley North (1983) **b.** 16 Feb. 1946 **ed.** Camphill High Sch., Paisley; Reid-Kerr Technical Coll., Paisley **Profession** computer analyst **Political interests** child care, health, disabled, motor industry, local issues; pro-devolution **Political career** Strathclyde Regional Cllr 1972–80; MP for Paisley 1979–83 **Parliamentary career** Opposition Scottish Whip 1987– **Unions** GMB (APEX partnership) **Other** JP, former Chief Magistrate of Paisley Borough

ADAMS, Gerry Sinn Fein, Belfast West (1983) **b.** 6 Oct. 1948 **ed.** St Mary's Coll., Belfast **Political career** founder, Northern Ireland Civil Rights Association; Northern Ireland Assembly 1982–6; Pres. Provisional Sinn Fein 1983– (Vice-Pres. 1978–83) **Publications include** *Falls Memories* **Other** Absentee MP. The leading political voice of the Provisional IRA (in spite of ban on Sinn Fein broadcasting since 19 Oct. 1988) and a former internee. Ousted Gerry Fitt from his long-held Belfast West seat in 1983

ADLEY, Robert Con., Christchurch (1983) **b.** 2 Mar. 1935 **ed.** Uppingham Sch. **Profession** hotel group marketing dir., author **Political interests** railways, transport, tourism, Asia, Middle East, marketing, publishing **Political career** Slough Borough Cllr 1965–8; contested Birkenhead 1966; MP for Bristol North East 1970–4, for Christchurch and Lymington 1974–83 **Member** Founder and first chmn of the Brunel Society **Publications include** *In Praise of Steam*; *Covering My Tracks*; *Tunnel Vision* **Other** Railway enthusiast

AITKEN, Jonathan Con., Thanet South (1983) **b.** 30 Aug. 1942 **ed.** Eton; Christ Church, Oxford **Profession** journalist, broadcaster, company dir. (TV-am 1981–8) **Political interests** foreign affairs, Middle East, EC, health, employment, police, media **Political career** Private Secretary to Selwyn Lloyd 1964–6; contested Meriden 1966; MP for Thanet East 1974–83 **Publications include** *Land of Fortune: A Study of Australia*; *Officially Secret*; articles in *Spectator*, *Washington Post*, *Sunday Telegraph*, *Guardian* **Other** Great-nephew of Lord Beaverbrook

ALEXANDER, Richard Con., Newark (1979) **b.** 29 June 1934 **ed.** Dewsbury Grammar Sch.; Univ. Coll., London; Inst. of Advanced Legal Studies, London Univ. **Profession** solicitor **Political interests** environment, health and social security, home affairs, foreign affairs, arts, heritage, Commonwealth, inter-parliamentary relations **Political career** Retford Borough Cllr 1965–74; Bassetlaw District Cllr 1975–9; Mayor of Retford 1977–8; Notts. Co. Cllr 1967–74; contested Lincoln 1966, 1970

ALISON, Rt Hon. Michael Con., Selby (1983) **b.** 27 June 1926 **ed.** Eton; Wadham Coll., Oxford **Profession** Coldstream Guards 1944–8, Conservative Research Dept 1958–63, company dir. **Political interests** Northern Ireland, home affairs, church affairs, transport, energy, agriculture, economy; anti-pornography **Political career** Kensington Borough Cllr 1956–9; MP for Barkston Ash 1964–83 **Parliamentary career** Under-Secretary of State for Health 1970–4; Minister of State for Northern Ireland 1979–81; PC 1981; Minister of State for Employment 1981–3; PPS to the Prime Minister, Margaret Thatcher, 1983–7 **Other** Second Church Estate Commissioner 1987–

ALLASON, Rupert Con., Torbay (1987) **b.** 8 Nov. 1951 **ed.** Downside Sch.; Grenoble Univ., France; Univ. Hall, Buckland **Profession** journalist, author **Political interests** police, intelligence, security, defence, new technology, home affairs, media, housing, transport **Political career** contested Kettering 1979 and Battersea 1983 **Publications include** (as Nigel West) *MI5*; *MI6*; *The Branch*; *The Unreliable Witness*; editor of *Intelligence Quarterly* 1985–

ALLEN, Graham Lab., Nottingham North (1987) **b.** 11 Jan. 1953 **ed.** Forest Fields Grammar Sch., Nottingham; City of London Poly.; Leeds Univ. **Profession** Labour Party and union research officer **Political interests** trade unions, socialism, reform of Parliament, economy, employment **Unions** TGWU

ALTON, David Lib. Dem. (Lib. 1979–88), Liverpool Mossley Hill (1983) **b.** 15 Mar. 1951 **ed.** Edmund Campion Sch., Hornchurch; Christ's Coll. of Education, Liverpool **Profession** teacher of handicapped children **Political interests** foreign affairs, economy, environment, housing, inner cities, human rights, Northern Ireland; anti-abortion and racism **Political career** Liverpool City Cllr 1972–80; Merseyside Co. Cllr 1973–8 (Deputy Leader 1978); MP for Liverpool Edge Hill 1979–83 **Parliamentary career** Lib. Spokesman on Housing and Local Govt 1979–81, on Home Affairs 1981–2; Parliamentary Aide to David Steel 1982–3; Lib. Chief Whip 1985–7; sponsored Private Member's Bill to reduce time limit for abortions 1987; All. Spokesman on Northern Ireland 1987–8 **Member** National Vice-Pres. of LIFE **Unions** NUT **Publications include** *What Kind of Country*; *Whose Choice Anyway: The Right to Life* **Other** Britain's youngest-ever city councillor when elected at 21 and the youngest MP when he entered Parliament in 1979

AMERY, Rt Hon. Julian Con., Brighton Pavilion (1969) **b.** 27 Mar. 1919 **ed.** Eton; Balliol Coll., Oxford **Profession** RAF and Army 1940–4, company dir., author **Political interests** foreign affairs, defence, economy, housing, energy, aviation; pro-South Africa, anti-hanging **Political career** contested Preston 1945; MP for Preston North 1950–66 **Parliamentary career** Under-Secretary of State for War 1957–8, for the Colonies 1958–60; PC 1960; Secretary of State for Air 1960–2; Minister of Aviation 1962–4, of Public Buildings and Works 1970, for Housing and Construction 1970–2, for Foreign and Commonwealth Affairs 1972–4 **Publications include** *The Life of Joseph Chamberlain*; *Sons of the Eagle* **Other** Son-in-law of Harold Macmillan

AMESS, David Con., Basildon (1983) **b.** 26 Mar. 1952 **ed.** St Bonaventure's Grammar Sch.; Bournemouth Coll. of Technology **Profession** chmn of specialist employment agency **Political interests** employment, local govt, housing, health, education, transport, environment; anti-abortion, pro-hanging **Political career** Redbridge Cllr 1982–6; contested Newham North West 1979

AMOS, Alan Con., Hexham (1987) **b.** 10 Nov. 1952 **ed.** St Albans Sch.; St John's Coll., Oxford **Profession**

teacher, Conservative Research Dept 1984–6 **Political interests** transport, local govt, education, agriculture, economy; anti-abortion and smoking **Political career** Enfield Borough Cllr 1978– (Deputy Leader 1983–); contested Walthamstow 1983

ANDERSON, Donald Lab., Swansea East (1974) **b.** 17 June 1939 **ed.** Swansea Grammar Sch.; Univ. Coll., Swansea **Profession** diplomat, lecturer, barrister **Political interests** foreign affairs, housing, law, transport, environment, Welsh affairs; pro-EC and anti-devolution **Political career** MP for Monmouth 1966–70; Royal Borough of Kensington and Chelsea Cllr 1971–5 **Parliamentary career** Opposition Spokesman on Foreign and Commonwealth Affairs 1983– **Unions** sponsored by NUR **Other** Methodist lay preacher

ARBUTHNOT, James Con., Wanstead and Woodford (1987) **b.** 4 Aug. 1952 **ed.** Eton; Trinity Coll., Cambridge **Profession** barrister **Political interests** foreign affairs, legal affairs, taxation **Political career** Royal Borough of Kensington and Chelsea Cllr 1978– (Deputy Mayor 1983–4); contested Cynon Valley 1983, 1984 **Other** Son of Sir John Arbuthnot, MP for Dover 1950–64

ARCHER, Rt Hon. Peter Lab., Warley West (1974) **b.** 20 Nov. 1926 **ed.** Wednesbury Boys' High Sch.; London Sch. of Economics; Univ. Coll., London **Profession** barrister (QC 1971) **Political interests** human rights, law, Northern Ireland, conservation, Third World, world govt, mining **Political career** contested Hendon South 1959 and Brierley Hill 1964; MP for Rowley Regis and Tipton 1966–74 **Parliamentary career** Solicitor General 1974–9; PC 1977; Opposition Spokesman on Legal Affairs 1979–82; Opposition Spokesman on Trade, Prices and Consumer Protection 1982–3, on Northern Ireland 1983–7 **Member** founder member of Amnesty International (Chmn British section 1971–4) **Unions** sponsored by GMB (APEX partnership) **Publications include** *The International Protection of Human Rights*; (jtly) *Freedom at Stake*; *Purpose in Socialism* **Other** He refused a knighthood in 1974

ARMSTRONG, Hilary Lab., Durham North West (1987) **b.** 30 Nov. 1945 **ed.** Monkwearmouth Comprehensive Sch., Sunderland; West Ham Coll. of Technology; Birmingham Univ. **Profession** VSO in Kenya 1967–9, lecturer in community and youth work **Political interests** education, employment, environment, regional and overseas development **Political career** Durham Co. Cllr 1985–8 **Parliamentary career** Opposition Spokesman on Education 1988– **Member** Anti-Apartheid **Unions** MSF **Other** Daughter of Ernest Armstrong, the previous MP for Durham North West

ARNOLD, Jacques Con., Gravesham (1987) **b.** 27 Aug. 1947 **ed.** in Brazil; London Sch. of Economics **Profession** banker, company dir. **Political interests** finance, economy, foreign affairs, Latin America, education **Political career** Northants. Co. Cllr 1981–5; contested Coventry South East 1983

ARNOLD, Sir Thomas Con., Hazel Grove (1974) **b.** 25 Jan. 1947 **ed.** Le Rosey, Geneva; Pembroke Coll., Oxford **Profession** impresario, publisher **Political interests** theatre, Europe, Third World **Political career** contested Manchester Cheetham 1970 and Hazel Grove 1974 **Parliamentary career** Vice-Chmn Conservative Party (Research Dept and Candidates) 1983– **Member** Society of West End Theatre **Unions** MSF **Other** Knighted 1990

ASHBY, David Con., Leicestershire North West (1983) **b.** 14 May 1940 **ed.** Royal Grammar Sch., High Wycombe; Bristol Univ. **Profession** barrister, company dir. **Political interests** law, music, arts, sport and recreation, Africa, Italy, Central America, coal, allergies; anti-hanging **Political career** Hammersmith Borough Cllr 1968–71; Greater London Cllr 1977–81

ASHDOWN, Rt Hon. Paddy Leader of the Liberal Democrats Lib. Dem. (Lib. 1983–8), Yeovil (1983) **b.** 27 Feb. 1941 **ed.** Bedford Sch.; Hong Kong Univ. **Profession** Marine commando 1960–72, diplomat, youth officer **Political interests** foreign affairs, Northern Ireland, defence, industry, new technology, education, unemployment, youth **Political career** contested Yeovil 1979 **Parliamentary career** Lib. Spokesman on Trade and Industry 1985–7; All. Spokesman on Education and Science 1987–8; Leader of the Liberal Democrats and Spokesman on Northern Ireland 1988– ; PC 1989 **Unions** AEU

ASHLEY, Rt Hon. Jack Lab., Stoke-on-Trent South (1966) **b.** 6 Dec. 1922 **ed.** St Patrick's Elementary Sch., Widnes; Ruskin Coll., Oxford; Gonville and Caius Coll., Cambridge **Profession** labourer, BBC producer **Political interests** disabled, health, drugs, social services, women's rights, industrial relations, broadcasting, poverty, Hong Kong and China; fighter for the rights of Thalidomide victims **Political career** Widnes Borough Cllr 1946–7; contested Finchley 1951 **Parliamentary career** Chmn All-Party Lords and Commons Disablement Group 1969– ; PC 1979 **Member** Founder and Pres., Hearing and Speech Trust 1985– **Unions** sponsored by GMB **Publications include** *Journey into Silence* **Other** He is deaf. Companion of Honour 1975

ASHTON, Joe Lab., Bassetlaw (1968) **b.** 9 Oct. 1933 **ed.** High Storrs Grammar Sch.; Rotherham Technical Coll. **Profession** design engineer, journalist (*Labour Weekly*, *Daily Star*, *Sunday People*) **Political interests** employment, trade unions, industry, energy, media, economy **Political career** Sheffield City Cllr 1962–8 **Parliamentary career** PPS to Tony Benn 1974–6; Asst Whip 1976–7; Opposition Spokesman on Energy 1979–80 **Unions** sponsored by AEU **Publications include** *Grassroots*; *A Majority of One*

ASPINWALL, Jack Con., Wansdyke (1983) **b.** Feb. 1933 **ed.** Prescot Grammar Sch., Bootle; Marconi Coll., Chelmsford **Profession** RAF 1949–56, company dir., publican **Political interests** trade and industry, aviation, health and social services **Political career** former Avon Co. and Kingswood District Cllr; contested Kingswood 1974 as Lib. candidate; joined Conservative Party 1975; MP for Kingswood 1979–83 **Publications include** *Kindly Sit Down!* (a compilation of the best after-dinner stories from the Houses of Parliament)

ATKINS, Robert Con., South Ribble (1983) **b.** 5 Feb. 1946 **ed.** Highgate Sch. **Profession** Lloyd's marine insurance broker **Political interests** defence, aviation, industry, transport, Northern Ireland, sport **Political career** Haringey Borough Cllr 1968–77; contested Luton West 1974; MP for Preston North 1979–83 **Parliamentary career** Under-Secretary of State for Trade and Industry 1987–9, for Transport 1989–90,for the Environment (Minister for Sport) 1990-

ATKINSON, David Con., Bournemouth East (1977) **b.** 24 Mar. 1940 **ed.** St George's Coll., Weybridge; Southend Coll. of Technology; Coll. of Automobile and Aeronautical Engineering, Chelsea **Profession** motor retailer, company dir. **Political interests** foreign affairs, human rights, health, privatization, small business, arts, heritage, space technology; pro-hanging **Political career** Southend Co. Borough Cllr 1969–72; National Chmn Young Conservatives 1970–1; Essex Co. Cllr 1973–8; contested Newham North West Feb. 1974 and Basildon Oct. 1974

BAKER, Rt Hon. Kenneth Chancellor of the Duchy of Lancaster and Chmn of the Conservative Party Con., Mole Valley (1983) **b.** 3 Nov. 1934 **ed.** St Paul's Sch.; Magdalen Coll., Oxford **Profession** company dir., author **Political interests** education, training, environment, local govt, technology, industry **Political career** Twickenham Borough Cllr 1960–2; contested Poplar 1964 and Acton 1966; MP for Acton 1968–70, for St Marylebone 1970–83 **Parliamentary career** Secretary for the Civil Service Dept 1972–4; PPS to the Leader of the Opposition, Edward Heath, 1974–5; Executive of 1922 Cttee 1975–81; Minister of State for Industry and Information Technology 1981–4, for Local Govt 1984–5; PC 1984; Secretary of State for the Environment 1985–6, for Education and Science 1986–9; Chancellor of the Duchy of Lancaster and Chmn of the Conservative Party 1989– **Publications include** *I Have No Gun But I Can Spit* (comic verse); *London Lines* (poetry anthology)

BAKER, Nicholas Con., Dorset North (1979) **b.** 23 Nov. 1938 **ed.** Clifton Coll.; Exeter Coll., Oxford **Profession** solicitor, company dir., Lloyd's underwriter **Political interests** business, defence, children with learning disabilities, countryside **Political career** contested Southwark Peckham Feb. and Oct. 1974 **Parliamentary career** Asst Whip 1989– **Member** Bow Group **Publications include** *Better Company* (a Bow Group publication concerning company law reform); *This Pleasant Land* (a planning strategy)

BALDRY, Tony Con., Banbury (1983) **b.** 10 July 1950 **ed.** Leighton Park Sch.; Sussex Univ.; Lincoln's Inn **Profession** barrister, publishing company dir. **Political interests** employment, youth training, publishing, industrial law, legal affairs, agriculture, overseas aid, EC, children; pro-hanging and EC **Political career** Personal aide to Margaret Thatcher 1974–5; contested Thurrock 1979 **Parliamentary career** Under-Secretary of State for Energy 1990– **Member** Bow Group

BANKS, Robert Con., Harrogate (1974) **b.** 18 Jan. 1937 **ed.** Haileybury **Profession** furniture manufacturer, Lloyd's underwriter **Political interests** tourism, defence, arts, architecture, environment, alcohol problems **Political career** Paddington Borough Cllr 1959–65 **Member** Alcohol Education and Research Council 1982– **Publications include** (jtly) *Britain's Home Defence Gamble*; *New Jobs from Pleasure*

BANKS, Tony Lab., Newham North West (1983) **b.** 8 Apr. 1943 **ed.** Archbishop Tenison's Grammar Sch., London; York Univ.; London Sch. of Economics **Profession** AEU research dept 1969–75, union official **Political interests** trade unions, industrial relations, Northern Ireland, media, arts, economy **Political career** Lambeth Borough Cllr 1971–4; Greater London Cllr 1970–7, 1981–6 (Chmn 1985–6); contested East Grinstead 1970, Newcastle North 1974, and Watford 1979 **Parliamentary career** Opposition Whip 1987–8 **Member** Co-operative Party **Unions** sponsored by TGWU

BARNES, Harry Lab., Derbyshire North East (1987) **b.** 22 July 1936 **ed.** Ryhope Grammar Sch.; Ruskin Coll., Oxford; Hull Univ. **Profession** lecturer **Political interests** mining, energy, environment, industrial relations, education, local govt, nuclear disarmament **Member** Amnesty International; CND

BARNES, Rosie SDP, Greenwich (1987) **b.** 16 May 1946 **ed.** Bilborough Grammar Sch.; Birmingham Univ. **Profession** market researcher **Political interests** education, housing, health **Parliamentary career** SDP Spokesman on Education and Health 1987–

BARRON, Kevin Lab., Rother Valley (1983) **b.** 26 Oct. 1946 **ed.** Maltby Hall Secondary Modern Sch.; Ruskin Coll., Oxford **Profession** miner **Political interests** coal, energy, environment, home affairs, human rights, nuclear disarmament **Parliamentary career** PPS to the Leader of the Opposition, Neil Kinnock, 1985–7; Opposition Spokesman on Energy 1988– **Unions** sponsored by NUM

BATISTE, Spencer Con., Elmet (1983) **b.** 5 June 1945 **ed.** Carmel Coll.; Sorbonne, Paris; Queens' Coll., Cambridge; Coll. of Law **Profession** solicitor, company dir. **Political interests** trade and industry, coal, energy, education, information technology, space

BATTLE, John Lab., Leeds West (1987) **b.** 26 Apr. 1951 **ed.** St Michael's Coll.; Upholland Coll.; Leeds Univ. **Profession** trained for RC priesthood; research officer; National Co-ordinator of Church Action on Poverty 1983–7 **Political interests** poverty, Third World, urban development, industry, housing, economy **Political career** Leeds City Cllr 1980– ; contested Leeds North West 1983 **Member** World Development Movement; Child Poverty Action Group; Catholic Institute for International Relations

BEAUMONT-DARK, Anthony Con., Birmingham Selly Oak (1979) **b.** 11 Oct. 1932 **ed.** Cedarhurst Sch., Solihull; Birmingham Coll. of Art; Birmingham Univ. **Profession** stockbroker, company dir. **Political interests** treasury affairs, economy, trade and industry, transport **Political career** Birmingham City Cllr 1956–67 (Alderman 1967–); contested Birmingham Aston 1959 and 1964

BECKETT, Margaret Shadow Chief Secretary to the Treasury Lab., Derby South (1983) **b.** 15 Jan. 1943 **ed.** Notre Dame High Sch., Norwich; John Dalton Poly., Manchester; Manchester Coll. of Science and Technology **Profession** metallurgist, Labour Party researcher, Granada TV researcher **Political interests** education, social services, industry, nuclear disarmament, economy **Political career** contested Lincoln 1974; MP for Lincoln 1974–9 **Parliamentary career** Asst Whip 1975–6; Under-Secretary of State for Education and Science 1976–9; Opposition Spokesman on Social Security 1984–9; Labour National Executive Cttee 1988– ; Shadow Chief Secretary to the Treasury 1989– **Member** Amnesty International; Anti-Apartheid; Campaign Group; CND; Fabian Society; Tribune Group **Unions** ACTT; NUJ; sponsored by TGWU

BEGGS, Roy OUP, Antrim East (1983) **b.** 20 Feb. 1936 **ed.** Ballyclare High Sch.; Stranmillis Training Coll., Belfast **Profession** teacher **Political interests** education, trade and industry **Political career** Larne Borough Cllr

1973– (Mayor 1978–83); Northern Ireland Assembly 1982–6; resigned House of Commons seat Dec. 1985 to protest against Anglo-Irish agreement and was re-elected Jan. 1986

BEITH, Alan Lib. Dem. (Lib. 1973–88), Berwick-upon-Tweed (1973) **b.** 20 Apr. 1943 **ed.** King's Sch., Macclesfield; Balliol Coll. and Nuffield Coll., Oxford **Profession** lecturer **Political interests** foreign affairs, treasury affairs, parliamentary and constitutional affairs, art and architecture; anti-pornography and abortion **Political career** Hexham Rural District Cllr 1969–74; contested Berwick 1970 **Parliamentary career** Lib. Spokesman on Home Affairs 1973–6, on Northern Ireland 1974–6; Lib. Chief Whip 1976–85; Lib. Spokesman on Education and Fisheries 1976–83, on Northern Ireland 1982, on Foreign Affairs 1985–7; Deputy Leader of the Liberal Party 1985–8; All. Spokesman on Foreign Affairs 1987; Lib. Spokesman on the Treasury 1987; Lib. Dem. Spokesman on the Treasury 1988– **Other** Methodist lay preacher

BELL, Stuart Lab., Middlesbrough (1983) **b.** 16 May 1938 **ed.** Hookergate Grammar Sch., Durham; Gray's Inn **Profession** barrister, writer, Lloyd's underwriter **Political interests** economy, law, education, police, Ireland, EC, Middle East **Political career** contested Hexham 1979; Newcastle City Cllr 1980–3 **Parliamentary career** PPS to the Deputy Leader of the Opposition, Roy Hattersley, 1983–4; Opposition Spokesman on Northern Ireland 1984–7 **Member** Co-operative Society; Fabian Society **Unions** GMB **Publications include** *Paris 69*; *Days That Used to Be*; *How to Abolish the Lords*

BELLINGHAM, Henry Con., Norfolk North West (1983) **b.** 29 Mar. 1955 **ed.** Eton; Magdalene Coll., Cambridge; Council for Legal Education **Profession** barrister, Lloyd's underwriter, farmer, company dir. **Political interests** small business, farming, Northern Ireland, defence; pro-hanging **Member** NFU; National Executive of Small Business Bureau 1981– **Other** former amateur jockey

BENDALL, Vivian Con., Ilford North (1983) **b.** 14 Dec. 1938 **ed.** Coombe Hill House; Broad Green Coll., Croydon **Profession** estate agent **Political interests** law and order, transport, employment, trade unions, foreign affairs; pro-hanging; anti-abortion, immigration **Political career** Croydon Borough Cllr 1964–78; Greater London Cllr 1970–3; contested Hertford and Stevenage 1974; MP for Redbridge Ilford North 1978–83

BENN, Rt Hon. Anthony Wedgwood (Tony) Lab., Chesterfield (1984) **b.** 3 Apr. 1925 **ed.** Westminster; New Coll., Oxford **Profession** RAF pilot, BBC producer, writer **Political interests** foreign affairs, industry, technology, energy, media, socialism and Labour history, democracy, constitutional affairs, political theory **Political career** MP for Bristol South East 1950–60, when he was debarred from the Commons by the death of his father, Visc. Stansgate; re-elected 1961, unseated by election court, and renounced his peerage; MP for Bristol South East 1963–83 **Parliamentary career** Lab. National Executive Cttee 1959– ; PC 1964; Postmaster General 1964–6; Minister of Technology 1966–70, of Power 1969–70; Opposition Spokesman on Trade and Industry 1970–4; Chmn Labour Party 1971–2; Secretary of State for Industry and Minister of Posts and Telecommunications 1974–5; Secretary of State for Energy 1975–9 (Pres. EEC Energy Council of Ministers 1977) **Unions** GMB; NUJ; NUM; SOGAT '82; TGWU **Publications include** *Regeneration of Britain*; *Arguments for Socialism*; *Arguments for Democracy*; *Parliament, People and Power*; *Out of the Wilderness: Diaries 1963–7*; *Office without Power: Diaries 1968–72*; *Fighting Back* **Other** son of William Wedgwood Benn (Visc. Stansgate), former Lab. MP for Aberdeen North and Gorton

BENNETT, Andrew Lab., Denton and Reddish (1983) **b.** 9 Mar. 1939 **ed.** Hulme Grammar Sch., Manchester; Birmingham Univ. **Profession** teacher **Political interests** education, housing, poverty, civil liberties, Northern Ireland **Political career** Oldham Borough Cllr 1964–74; contested Knutsford 1970; MP for Stockport North 1974–83 **Parliamentary career** Opposition Spokesman on Education 1985–8 **Unions** NUT

BENNETT, Nicholas Con., Pembroke (1987) **b.** 7 May 1949 **ed.** Sedgehill Sch.; North London Poly.; London Univ.; Sussex Univ. **Profession** teacher **Political interests** foreign affairs, Northern Ireland, law and order, defence, health, transport, education, local govt, housing, agriculture; pro-EC, anti-abortion **Political career** Lewisham Borough Cllr 1974–82; contested Hackney Central 1979

BENYON, William Con., Milton Keynes (1983) **b.** 17 Jan. 1930 **ed.** Royal Naval Coll., Dartmouth **Profession** Royal Navy 1947–56, farmer **Political interests** constitutional affairs, local govt, heritage, conservation, Africa, Northern Ireland **Political career** Berkshire Co. Cllr 1964–74; MP for Buckingham 1970–83 **Parliamentary career** Opposition Whip 1974–6; Executive of 1922 Cttee 1982– **Member** Royal Agricultural Society of England; Country Landowners' Association **Other** JP 1960–77; Deputy Lieutenant Berks. 1970; grandson of 3rd Marquis of Salisbury, three times Prime Minister

BERMINGHAM, Gerald Lab., St Helens South (1983) **b.** 20 Aug. 1940 **ed.** Wellingborough Grammar Sch.; Sheffield Univ. **Profession** solicitor, teacher **Political interests** law, home affairs, penal reform, energy, race relations and immigration **Political career** Sheffield City Cllr 1975–9, 1980–2; contested Derbyshire South East 1979 **Member** Campaign for Criminal Justice; Co-operative Party; Liberty; Tribune Group **Unions** GMB (APEX partnership); TGWU

BEVAN, David Gilroy Con., Birmingham Yardley (1979) **b.** 10 Apr. 1928 **ed.** King Edward's Sch., Birmingham **Profession** estate agent, company dir. **Political interests** transport, home affairs, urban affairs, employment, small business, tourism, recreation; pro-hanging **Political career** contested Birmingham Aston 1957; Birmingham City Cllr 1959–73; W. Midlands Co. Cllr 1973–81 **Other** Chmn House of Commons Yacht Club 1988

BIDWELL, Sydney Lab., Ealing Southall (1974) **b.** 14 Jan. 1917 **ed.** elementary sch. and evening classes **Profession** teacher and organizer, National Council of Labour Colleges **Political interests** race relations and immigration, transport **Political career** Southall Borough Cllr 1951–5; contested Hertfordshire East 1959 and Hertfordshire South West 1964; MP for Southall 1966–74 **Parliamentary career** introduced bill to exempt Sikhs wearing motorcycle helmets 1975 and introduced bill to ban incitement to racial hatred 1981 (both became acts) **Member** Co-operative Party;

Tribune Group (Chmn 1975) **Unions** Writers' Guild; NUR; sponsored by TGWU **Publications include** *Red, White and Black*; *Turban Victory*

BIFFIN, Rt Hon. John Con., Shropshire North (1983) **b.** 3 Nov. 1930 **ed.** Dr Morgan's Grammar Sch., Bridgwater; Jesus Coll., Cambridge **Profession** economist, management consultant, company dir. **Political interests** economy, trade and industry, small business, energy, technology **Political career** contested Coventry East 1959; MP for Oswestry 1961–83 **Parliamentary career** Executive of 1922 Cttee 1967–76; Opposition Spokesman on Energy 1976, on Industry 1976–7, on Small Business and Self-Employed 1978–9; PC 1979; Chief Secretary to the Treasury 1979–81; Secretary of State for Trade 1981–2; Lord President of the Council 1982–3; Leader of the House of Commons and Lord Privy Seal 1982–7

BLACKBURN, John Con., Dudley West (1979) **b.** 2 Sep. 1933 **ed.** Liverpool Collegiate Sch.; Liverpool Univ.; Berlin Univ. **Profession** Liverpool City Police 1954–63, sales manager, company dir. **Political interests** foreign and home affairs, church affairs, arts, heritage, Jewish affairs, Israel; pro-capital and corporal punishment; anti-EC **Political career** Wolverhampton District Cllr 1970–81

BLAIR, Tony Shadow Employment Secretary Lab., Sedgefield (1983) **b.** 6 May 1953 **ed.** Fettes Coll.; St John's Coll., Oxford **Profession** barrister **Political interests** legal affairs, trade unions, taxes, economy, trade and industry, employment **Political career** contested Beaconsfield 1982 **Parliamentary career** Opposition Spokesman on Treasury and Economic Affairs 1984–7, on Trade and Industry 1987–9; Shadow Employment Secretary 1989– **Unions** sponsored by TGWU **Other** He produced reviews with Mel Smith at Oxford

BLAKER, Rt Hon. Sir Peter Con., Blackpool South (1964) **b.** 4 Oct. 1922 **ed.** Shrewsbury Sch.; Toronto Univ.; New Coll., Oxford **Profession** Canadian Infantry 1942–6, barrister, diplomat, farmer, Lloyd's underwriter, company dir. **Political interests** defence, foreign and Commonwealth affairs, tourism **Parliamentary career** Opposition Whip 1966–7; Executive of 1922 Cttee 1967–70; Under-Secretary of State for Defence (Army) 1972–4, at the Foreign and Commonwealth Office 1974; Minister of State at the Foreign and Commonwealth Office 1979–81, for Defence (Armed Forces) 1981–3 (announced closure of Chatham and sale of 19 Navy vessels 1982); PC 1983 **Other** KCMG 1983

BLUNKETT, David Lab., Sheffield Brightside (1987) **b.** 6 June 1947 **ed.** Royal Normal Coll. for the Blind; Sheffield Univ.; Huddersfield Coll. of Education **Profession** tutor **Political interests** local govt, education, economy, environment, health and social services, disabled **Political career** Sheffield City Cllr 1970–88 (Leader 1980–7); S. Yorks. Co. Cllr 1973–7; contested Sheffield Hallam 1974 **Parliamentary career** Labour National Executive Cttee 1983– ; Opposition Spokesman on Environment 1988– **Unions** NATFHE; NUPE **Other** He is blind

BOATENG, Paul Lab., Brent South (1987) **b.** 14 June 1951 **ed.** Accra Academy; Apsley Grammar Sch.; Bristol Univ.; Coll. of Law **Profession** solicitor **Political interests** home affairs, housing, inner city, race relations, police, civil liberties, legal affairs, education, environment, South Africa, Third World **Political career** Greater London Cllr 1981–6; contested Hertfordshire West 1983 **Parliamentary career** Opposition Spokesman on Treasury and Economic Affairs 1989– **Member** legal adviser to Scrap Sus Campaign 1977–81; Vice-Moderator of World Council of Churches Commission to combat racism 1984– ; Police Training Council 1981–5; Executive of National Council for Civil Liberties (now Liberty) 1980–6

BODY, Sir Richard Con., Holland with Boston (1966) **b.** 18 May 1927 **ed.** Reading Sch. **Profession** barrister, farmer, writer, Lloyd's underwriter **Political interests** agriculture, animal rights, environment, home affairs, Third World; anti-EC and farm subsidies **Political career** contested Rotherham 1950, Abertillery 1950 and Leek 1951; MP for Billericay 1955–9 **Member** Chmn of Council of Get Britain Out Referendum Campaign 1974; Chmn of Consumer Watch 1988 **Publications include** *Agriculture: the Triumph and the Shame*; *Farming in the Clouds*; *Red or Green for Farmers (and the Rest of Us)* **Other** KBE 1986

BONSOR, Sir Nicholas Con., Upminster (1983) **b.** 9 Dec. 1942 **ed.** Eton; Keble Coll., Oxford **Profession** barrister, farmer, company dir., Lloyd's underwriter **Political interests** defence, foreign affairs, criminal law, agriculture, heritage, tourism; anti-EC **Political career** contested Newcastle-under-Lyme 1974; MP for Nantwich 1979–83 **Member** Chmn of British Field Sports Society 1988– **Other** He is a baronet and was an Oxford heavyweight boxing blue

BOOTHROYD, Betty Deputy Speaker of the House of Commons Lab., West Bromwich West (1974) **b.** 8 Oct. 1929 **ed.** Dewsbury Coll. of Commerce and Art **Profession** dancer, political asst, company dir. **Political interests** foreign affairs, public finance, health service; pro-EC, abortion **Political career** Hammersmith Borough Cllr 1965–8; contested Leicester South East 1957, Peterborough 1959, Nelson and Colne 1968 and Rossendale 1970; MP for West Bromwich 1973–4; MEP 1975–7 **Parliamentary career** Asst Whip 1974–5; Speaker's Panel of Chairmen 1979– ; Labour National Executive Cttee 1981–7; Second Deputy Chmn Ways and Means and Deputy Speaker of the House of Commons 1987– **Unions** sponsored by GMB

BOSCAWEN, Hon. Robert Con., Somerton and Frome (1983) **b.** 17 Mar. 1923 **ed.** Eton; Trinity Coll., Cambridge **Profession** Coldstream Guards 1942–5 (won MC in 1944 battle to relieve Arnhem); Lloyd's underwriter, company dir. **Political interests** social services, disabled, agriculture; pro-hanging **Political career** contested Falmouth and Camborne 1964 and 1966; MP for Wells 1970–83 **Parliamentary career** Asst Whip 1979–81; Lord Commissioner of the Treasury (Govt Whip) 1981–3; Vice-Chamberlain of the Household 1983–6; Comptroller of the Household (No. 3 Whip) 1986–8

BOSWELL, Timothy Con., Daventry (1987) **b.** 2 Dec. 1942 **ed.** Marlborough Coll.; New Coll., Oxford **Profession** Conservative Research Dept 1966–73, farmer **Political interests** agriculture, finance, taxation; pro-EC **Political career** contested Rugby 1974 **Parliamentary career** Govt Whip 1990– **Member** NFU

BOTTOMLEY, Peter Con., Eltham (1983) **b.** 30 July 1944 **ed.** Westminster; Trinity Coll., Cambridge

Profession industrial relations officer, marketing consultant, company dir. **Political interests** social and economic policy, child welfare, the family, employment, health and social services, transport **Political career** contested Greenwich, Woolwich West 1974; MP for Greenwich, Woolwich West 1975–83 **Parliamentary career** Under-Secretary of State for Employment 1984, for Transport (Minister for Roads and Traffic) 1986–9, for Northern Ireland 1989–90 **Member** Bow Group **Other** Husband of Virginia Bottomley, MP for Surrey South West; former captain of the House of Commons Football Club

BOTTOMLEY, Virginia Con., Surrey South West (1984) **b.** 12 Mar. 1948 **ed.** Putney High Sch.; Essex Univ.; London Sch. of Economics **Profession** psychiatric social worker **Political interests** child welfare, elderly, education, health service, prisons, defence, overseas aid **Political career** contested Isle of Wight 1983 **Parliamentary career** Under-Secretary of State for the Environment 1988–9; Minister of State for Health 1989– **Other** Wife of Peter Bottomley, MP for Eltham; magistrate in Inner London Juvenile Courts 1975–84

BOWDEN, Andrew Con., Brighton Kemptown (1970) **b.** 8 Apr. 1930 **ed.** Park Town Sch., Johannesburg; Ardingly Coll., Sussex **Profession** personnel consultant, company dir. **Political interests** pensioners, ex-servicemen, animal rights; anti-abortion and fluoride **Political career** Wandsworth Borough Cllr 1956–62; National Chmn Young Conservatives 1960–1; contested Hammersmith North 1955, Kensington North 1964 and Brighton Kemptown 1966 **Other** MBE 1961

BOWDEN, Gerald Con., Dulwich (1983) **b.** 26 Aug. 1935 **ed.** Battersea Grammar Sch.; Magdalen Coll., Oxford; Coll. of Estate Management; Gray's Inn **Profession** barrister, lecturer, chartered surveyor, Lloyd's underwriter **Political interests** education, housing, inner cities, law reform, police, local govt, heritage, conservation, arts, trade unions, defence; pro-hanging **Political career** Greater London Cllr 1977–81 **Unions** NATFHE **Publications include** *An Introduction to the Law of Contract and Tort* **Other** Lt-Col. in the Territorial Army; Territorial Decoration 1971

BOWIS, John Con., Battersea (1987) **b.** 2 Aug. 1945 **ed.** Tonbridge Sch.; Brasenose Coll., Oxford **Profession** Conservative Central Office 1979; Public Affairs Dir., British Insurance Brokers Association 1983–8 **Political interests** education, inner cities, insurance industry, industrial relations, arts **Political career** Kingston upon Thames Cllr 1982–6 **Other** OBE 1981

BOYES, Roland Lab., Houghton and Washington (1983) **b.** 12 Feb. 1937 **Profession** teacher, asst dir. of Durham Co. Social Services Dept 1975–9 **Political interests** environment, defence, nuclear disarmament, social services, poverty, education, local issues, water; anti-EC **Political career** Peterlee Parish Cllr 1969–73; Peterlee Town Cllr 1976–9; Easington District Cllr 1973–6; MEP for Durham 1979–84 **Parliamentary career** Opposition Spokesman on the Environment 1985–8, on Defence and Disarmament and Arms Control 1988– **Member** Tribune Group (Chmn 1985–6) **Unions** GMB

BOYSON, Rt Hon. Sir Rhodes Con., Brent North (1974) **b.** 11 May 1925 **ed.** Haslingden Grammar Sch.; Manchester Univ.; London Sch. of Economics; Corpus Christi Coll., Cambridge **Profession** teacher, writer, publisher (Chmn Churchill Press and Constitutional Book Club 1969–79) **Political interests** religion and morality, education, social issues; pro-hanging **Political career** Haslingden Cllr 1957; left Labour Party and joined Conservative Party 1964; Waltham Forest Borough Cllr 1968–74; contested Eccles 1970 **Parliamentary career** Under-Secretary of State for Education and Science 1979–83; Minister of State for Social Security 1983–4, for Northern Ireland 1984–6, for Local Govt 1986–7; PC 1987 **Member** National Council for Educational Standards (Chmn 1974–9) **Publications include** *Education: Threatened Standards*; *Centre Forward: A Radical Conservative Programme* **Other** Knighted 1987

BRADLEY, Keith Lab., Manchester Withington (1987) **b.** 17 May 1950 **ed.** Bishop Vesey's Grammar Sch.; Manchester Poly.; York Univ. **Profession** health service administrator **Political interests** local govt, housing, health, social security, poverty, environment, transport, aviation **Political career** Manchester City Cllr 1983–8 **Member** Co-operative Party **Unions** NALGO

BRAINE, Rt Hon. Sir Bernard Father of the House of Commons Con., Castle Point (1983) **b.** 24 June 1914 **ed.** Hendon Co. Grammar Sch. **Profession** served in Africa, Europe and Asia in World War II; company dir., consultant **Political interests** foreign affairs, the Commonwealth, overseas aid, refugees, human rights, alcoholism and drug addiction; anti-racism, abortion, video nasties **Political career** contested Leyton East 1945; MP for Billericay 1950–5, for Essex South East 1955–83 **Parliamentary career** Executive of 1922 Cttee 1958–60; Parliamentary Secretary at the Ministry of Pensions 1960; Under-Secretary of State for Commonwealth Relations 1961; Parliamentary Secretary at the Ministry of Health 1962–4; Opposition Spokesman on Commonwealth Affairs and Overseas Aid 1967–70; PC 1985; Father of the House of Commons 1987 **Member** National Council on Alcoholism (Chmn 1975–82); Greater London Alcohol Advisory Services (Pres. 1983–); Society for Defence of the Unjustly Prosecuted; trustee of the Commonwealth Institute **Other** Knighted 1972; Deputy Lieutenant Essex 1978

BRANDON-BRAVO, Martin Con., Nottingham South (1983) **b.** 25 Mar. 1932 **ed.** Latymer Upper Sch. **Profession** textiles company dir. **Political interests** industry, local govt, housing, race relations, transport, sport and recreation **Political career** Nottingham City Cllr 1968–70, 1976–87; contested Nottingham East 1979 **Other** Former executive member of National Rowing Council and an international rowing umpire

BRAY, Dr Jeremy Lab., Motherwell South (1983) **b.** 29 June 1930 **ed.** Kingswood Sch.; Jesus Coll., Cambridge **Profession** mathematician, lecturer, journalist, consultant, company dir. **Political interests** science and technology, industry, energy, steel, economy, overseas development, Hong Kong **Political career** contested Thirsk and Malton 1959; MP for Middlesbrough West 1962–70, for Motherwell and Wishaw 1974–83 **Parliamentary career** Parliamentary Secretary at the Ministry of Power 1966–7, at the Ministry of Technology 1967–9; Opposition Spokesman on Science and Technology 1983– **Member** Christian Aid (Deputy Chmn 1972–83); Fabian Society (Chmn 1971); Tribune Group **Unions** TGWU **Publications include** *Decision in Government*

BRAZIER, Julian Con., Canterbury (1987) **b.** 24 July 1953 **ed.** Wellington Coll.; Brasenose Coll., Oxford **Profession** management consultant **Political interests** defence, law and order, education, unemployment, conservation **Political career** contested Berwick-upon-Tweed 1983 **Member** Bow Group

BRIGHT, Graham Con., Luton South (1983) **b.** 2 Apr. 1942 **ed.** Hassenbrook Comprehensive Sch.; Thurrock Technical Coll. **Profession** food company dir. **Political interests** trade and industry, food industry, motor industry, aviation and airports, small business, privatization, economy, Europe; anti-pornography **Political career** Thurrock Borough Cllr 1966–79; Essex Co. Cllr 1967–70; National Vice-Chmn Young Conservatives 1970–2; contested Thurrock 1970 and Feb. 1974, Dartford Oct. 1974; MP for Luton East 1979–83 **Parliamentary career** introduced Private Member's Bill to regulate video nasties which became Video Recordings Act 1984 **Publications include** (jtly) *Moving Forward: Small Business and the Economy*

BROOKE, Rt Hon. Peter Secretary of State for Northern Ireland Con., City of London and Westminster South (1977) **b.** 3 Mar. 1934 **ed.** Marlborough Coll.; Balliol Coll., Oxford; Harvard Business Sch. **Profession** management consultant, Lloyd's underwriter, company dir., journalist **Political interests** finance, education, Northern Ireland; anti-pornography **Political career** Camden Borough Cllr 1968–9; contested Bedwellty 1974 **Parliamentary career** Asst Whip 1979–81; Lord Commissioner of the Treasury (Govt Whip) 1981–3; Under-Secretary of State for Education and Science 1983–5; Minister of State for the Treasury 1985–7; Paymaster General 1987; Chmn Conservative Party 1987–9; PC 1988; Secretary of State for Northern Ireland 1989– **Other** Son of Baron (Henry) Brooke of Cumnor, former Con. MP for Hampstead and Home Secretary, and of Baroness (Barbara) Brooke of Ystradfellte, former Vice-Chmn Conservative Party

BROWN, Dr Gordon Shadow Trade and Industry Secretary Lab., Dunfermline East (1983) **b.** 20 Feb. 1951 **ed.** Kirkcaldy High Sch.; Edinburgh Univ. (Rector 1972–5) **Profession** lecturer, TV journalist **Political interests** economy, employment, trade and industry, health and social security, Scottish affairs, shipbuilding, education, media **Political career** contested Edinburgh South 1979; Chmn Scottish Labour Party 1983– **Parliamentary career** Opposition Spokesman on Trade and Industry 1985–7; Shadow Chief Secretary to the Treasury 1987–9; Shadow Trade and Industry Secretary 1989– **Unions** NUJ; sponsored by TGWU **Publications include** *Scotland: The Real Divide*; (jtly) *The Politics of Devolution and Nationalism*

BROWN, Michael Con., Brigg and Cleethorpes (1983) **b.** 3 July 1951 **ed.** Andrew Cairns Secondary Modern Sch., Littlehampton; York Univ. **Profession** lecturer, company dir. **Political interests** Northern Ireland, steel, agriculture; anti-EC **Political career** MP for Brigg and Scunthorpe 1979–83

BROWN, Nicholas Lab., Newcastle-upon-Tyne East (1983) **b.** 13 June 1950 **ed.** Tunbridge Wells Technical High Sch.; Manchester Univ. **Profession** GMB legal adviser **Political interests** law, economy, housing **Political career** Newcastle-upon-Tyne City Cllr 1980–3 **Parliamentary career** Opposition Spokesman on Legal Affairs 1985– , on Treasury and Economic Affairs 1988– **Unions** GMB

BROWN, Ron Lab., Edinburgh Leith (1979) **b.** June 1940 **ed.** Ainslie Park High Sch., Edinburgh; Bristo Technical Institute, Edinburgh **Profession** fitter, convenor of shop stewards **Political interests** Middle East, shipbuilding **Political career** Lothian Regional Cllr 1974–9 **Parliamentary career** twice expelled from the House **Unions** sponsored by AEU **Other** found guilty of causing criminal damage 1990

BROWNE, John Con., Winchester (1979) **b.** 17 Oct. 1938 **ed.** Malvern Coll.; Sandhurst; Cranfield Inst. of Technology; Harvard Business Sch. **Profession** Grenadier Guards 1957–67; merchant banker, company dir. **Political interests** finance, defence, foreign affairs, small businesses, conservation; pro-hanging **Political career** Westminster City Cllr 1974–8 **Parliamentary career** suspended from the House for one month for failing to declare UK and Middle East business interests Mar. 1990 **Member** NFU

BRUCE, Ian Con., Dorset South (1987) **b.** 14 Mar. 1947 **ed.** Chelmsford Technical High Sch.; Bradford Univ.; Mid-Essex Technical Coll. **Profession** employment agency and consultancy group dir. **Political interests** employment, trade and industry, tourism, energy, defence **Political career** contested Burnley 1983

BRUCE, Malcolm Lib. Dem. (Lib. 1983–8), Gordon (1983) **b.** 17 Nov. 1944 **ed.** Wrekin Coll., Shropshire; St Andrews Univ.; Strathclyde Univ. **Profession** journalist, publisher **Political interests** energy, oil and gas, trade and industry, the deaf; pro-devolution **Political career** contested Angus North and Mearns 1974, Aberdeenshire West 1979 **Parliamentary career** Lib. Spokesman on Energy 1986–7, on Education 1986, on Trade and Industry 1987–8; All. Spokesman on Employment 1987; Lib. Dem. Spokesman on Natural Resources (Energy and Conservation) 1988– ; Leader of Scottish Liberal Democrats 1988– **Unions** NUJ **Other** Rector of Dundee Univ. 1986–

BUCHAN, Norman Lab., Paisley South (1983) **b.** 27 Oct. 1922 **ed.** Kirkwall Grammar Sch.; Glasgow Univ. **Profession** teacher, journalist, poet **Political interests** arts, education, agriculture, media, Scottish affairs, nuclear disarmament; anti-EC **Political career** left Communist Party after invasion of Hungary and joined Labour Party 1957; MP for Renfrew West 1964–83 **Parliamentary career** Under-Secretary of State for Scotland 1967–70; Opposition Spokesman on Scottish Affairs 1970–3, on Agriculture and Food 1973–4; Minister of State for Agriculture 1974 (resigned over Common Market); Opposition Spokesman on Social Security 1980–1, on Food, Agriculture and Fisheries 1981–3, on the Arts 1983–7 **Member** CND; Council of Poetry Societies; Tribune Group (Chmn 1981–2) **Unions** sponsored by TGWU **Publications include** (ed.) *101 Scottish Songs*; *The Scottish Folksinger*; *The Macdunciad* **Other** Husband of Janey Buchan MEP

BUCHANAN-SMITH, Rt Hon. Alick Con., Kincardine and Deeside (1983) **b.** 8 Apr. 1932 **ed.** Edinburgh Academy; Glenalmond Coll.; Pembroke Coll., Cambridge; Edinburgh Univ. **Profession** farmer **Political interests** Scottish affairs, energy, agriculture; pro-devolution **Political career** contested Fife West 1959; MP for Angus North and Mearns 1964–83 **Parliamentary career** Opposition Spokesman on Scotland and Agriculture 1969–70; Under-Secretary of State at the Scottish Office 1970–4; Opposition

Spokesman on Scotland 1974–6 (resigned over devolution); Minister of State for Agriculture, Fisheries and Food 1979–83; PC 1981; Minister of State for Energy 1983–7

BUCK, Sir Antony Con., Colchester North (1983) **b.** 19 Dec. 1928 **ed.** King's Sch., Ely; Trinity Hall, Cambridge; Inner Temple **Profession** barrister (QC 1974), company dir. **Political interests** defence, legal affairs; pro-NATO **Political career** MP for Colchester 1961–83 **Parliamentary career** Executive of 1922 Cttee 1972, 1974; Under-Secretary of State for Defence (Royal Navy) 1972–4; Opposition Spokesman on Defence 1974–5; Chmn Conservative Defence Cttee 1979– **Other** Knighted 1983

BUCKLEY, George Lab., Hemsworth (1987) **b.** 6 Apr. 1935 **ed.** South Kirkby Sch.; Doncaster Technical Coll.; Leeds Univ. **Profession** miner **Political interests** employment, education, environment, housing, mining, trade unions, economy **Political career** South Kirkby Town Cllr 1973–83; Wakefield District Cllr 1973–87 **Unions** NUM **Other** JP 1972–86

BUDGEN, Nicholas Con., Wolverhampton South West (1974) **b.** 3 Nov. 1937 **ed.** St Edward's Sch., Oxford; Corpus Christi, Cambridge **Profession** barrister, farmer **Political interests** Northern Ireland, legal affairs; anti-immigration, EC, hanging **Political career** contested Birmingham Small Heath 1970 **Parliamentary career** Asst Whip 1981–2 (resigned over Northern Ireland Bill)

BURNS, Simon Con., Chelmsford (1987) **b.** 6 Sept. 1952 **ed.** Christ the King Sch., Accra; Stamford Sch.; Worcester Coll., Oxford **Profession** company dir. **Political interests** employment, trade and industry, foreign affairs **Political career** worked for George McGovern's presidential campaign against Richard Nixon 1972; asst to Sally Oppenheim, former MP for Gloucester, 1975–81; contested Alyn and Deeside 1983 **Member** Amnesty International

BURT, Alistair Con., Bury North (1983) **b.** 25 May 1955 **ed.** Bury Grammar Sch.; St John's Coll., Oxford **Profession** solicitor **Political interests** housing, education, local govt, trade and industry, paper industry, energy, race relations, Third World, human rights, South Africa, church affairs; anti-hanging **Political career** Haringey Borough Cllr 1982–4 **Member** Bow Group

BUTCHER, John Con., Coventry South West (1979) **b.** 13 Feb. 1946 **ed.** Huntingdon Grammar Sch.; Birmingham Univ.; Inst. of Strategic Studies, London **Profession** computer industry executive **Political interests** employment, education, defence, foreign affairs; anti-EC **Political career** Birmingham City Cllr 1972–8; contested Birmingham Northfield 1974 **Parliamentary career** Under-Secretary of State for Trade and Industry 1982–8, for Education and Science 1988–9 **Member** Bow Group **Publications include** *The Big Steal*; *A Glimpse of Nirvana* (Bow Group pamphlets)

BUTLER, Christopher Con., Warrington South (1987) **b.** 12 Aug. 1950 **ed.** Cardiff High Sch. for Boys; Emmanuel Coll., Cambridge **Profession** market researcher; Conservative Research Dept 1977–80; Political office 10 Downing St 1980–3 **Political interests** health service, AIDS, prisons, foreign affairs, Wales **Political career** contested Brecon and Radnor 1985

BUTTERFILL, John Con., Bournemouth West (1983) **b.** 14 Feb. 1941 **ed.** Caterham Sch.; Coll. of Estate Management, London **Profession** chartered surveyor, company dir. **Political interests** trade and industry, housing, health, environment, tourism, foreign affairs; pro-EC, anti-hanging **Political career** contested Croydon North West 1981

CABORN, Richard Lab., Sheffield Central (1983) **b.** 6 Oct. 1943 **ed.** Hurfield Comprehensive Sch.; Granville Coll.; Sheffield Poly. **Profession** engineer, convenor of shop stewards **Political interests** unions, steel, EC; pro-nuclear disarmament, anti-apartheid **Political career** MEP for Sheffield 1979–84 **Parliamentary career** Opposition Spokesman on Trade and Industry 1988– **Member** Anti-Apartheid (National Executive); CND **Unions** AEU

CALLAGHAN, James Lab., Heywood and Middleton (1983) **b.** 28 Jan. 1927 **ed.** Manchester Univ.; London Univ. **Profession** art lecturer **Political interests** education, health, arts, transport; anti-EC, pro-nuclear disarmament **Political career** Middleton Borough Cllr 1971–4; MP for Middleton and Prestwich 1974–83 **Other** Football Association referee and coach

CAMPBELL, Menzies Lib. Dem. (Lib. 1987–8), Fife North East (1987) **b.** 22 May 1941 **ed.** Hillhead High Sch., Glasgow; Glasgow Univ.; Stanford Univ., US **Profession** advocate (QC 1982) **Political interests** law, defence, sport, arts **Political career** contested Greenock and Port Glasgow Feb. and Oct. 1974, Fife East 1979, Fife North East 1983; Chmn Scottish Liberal Party 1975–7 **Parliamentary career** Lib. Spokesman on Arts, Broadcasting and Sport 1987–8; Lib. Dem. Spokesman on Defence and Sport 1988– **Member** UK Sports Council 1965–8; Scottish Sports Council 1971–81 **Other** A sprinter who competed in the Tokyo Olympics and held the UK 100 m record 1967–74; CBE 1987

CAMPBELL, Ronald Lab., Blyth Valley (1987) **b.** 14 Aug. 1943 **ed.** Ridley High Sch., Blyth **Profession** miner **Political interests** mining, health, housing, employment **Political career** Blyth Borough Cllr 1969–74; Blyth Valley Cllr 1974– **Unions** sponsored by NUM

CAMPBELL-SAVOURS, Dale Lab., Workington (1979) **b.** 23 Aug. 1943 **ed.** Keswick Sch.; Sorbonne **Profession** clock manufacturing company dir., export agent **Political interests** foreign affairs, Italy, education, health service, public ownership, industry; pro-nuclear disarmament, EC; anti-abortion **Political career** Ramsbottom Urban District Cllr 1972–4; contested Darwen Feb. and Oct. 1974, Workington 1976 **Unions** TGWU; sponsored by COHSE

CANAVAN, Dennis Lab., Falkirk West (1983) **b.** 8 Aug. 1942 **ed.** St Columba's High Sch., Cowdenbeath; Edinburgh Univ. **Profession** mathematics teacher **Political interests** foreign affairs, social services, health service, poverty, education, Northern Ireland, sport; pro-nuclear disarmament and devolution, anti-apartheid and royalty **Political career** Stirling District Cllr 1973–4; MP for Stirlingshire West 1974–83 **Parliamentary career** Chmn Scottish Parliamentary Labour Group 1980–1 (Vice-Chmn 1979–80) **Member** Co-operative Party; Fabian Society **Unions** sponsored by COHSE

CARLILE, Alex Lib. Dem. (Lib. 1983–8), Montgomery (1983) **b.** 12 Feb. 1948 **ed.** Epsom Coll.; King's Coll., London; Council of Legal Education **Profession** barrister (QC 1984) **Political interests** home and foreign affairs, United Nations, law, consumer rights, human rights, agriculture, arts **Political career** contested Flintshire East 1974, 1979; Chmn Welsh Liberal Party 1980–2 **Parliamentary career** Lib. Spokesman on Home Affairs and Law 1985–8; All. Spokesman on Legal Affairs 1987; Lib. Dem. Spokesman on Foreign Affairs 1988–

CARLISLE, John Con., Luton North (1983) **b.** 28 Aug. 1942 **ed.** Bedford Sch.; St Lawrence Coll., Ramsgate; Coll. of Estate Management, London **Profession** grain trader, company dir. **Political interests** sport and politics, immigration, trade and industry, commodity trading, airports; pro-South Africa, hanging and corporal punishment; anti-unions **Political career** MP for Luton West 1979–83 **Member** British South Africa Group (Chmn 1987–)

CARLISLE, Kenneth Con., Lincoln (1979) **b.** 21 Mar. 1941 **ed.** Harrow Sch.; Harvard Coll., California; Magdalen Coll., Oxford; Inner Temple **Profession** barrister, farmer **Political interests** trade and industry, employment, conservation, agriculture; pro-EC **Parliamentary career** Asst Whip 1987–8; Lord Commissioner of the Treasury (Govt Whip) 1988– **Member** Bow Group; NFU

CARRINGTON, Matthew Con., Fulham (1987) **b.** 19 Oct. 1947 **ed.** The Lycée, London; Imperial Coll., London Univ.; London Graduate Sch. of Business Studies **Profession** banker **Political interests** finance, education, Middle East **Political career** contested Tottenham 1979, Fulham 1986

CARTTISS, Michael Con., Great Yarmouth (1983) **b.** 11 Mar. 1938 **ed.** Great Yarmouth Technical High Sch.; Goldsmiths Coll., London Univ.; London Sch. of Economics **Profession** teacher **Political interests** education, health, local govt **Political career** Norfolk Co. Cllr 1966–85; Great Yarmouth Borough Cllr 1973–82 (Leader 1980–2)

CARTWRIGHT, John SDP (Lab. 1974–81), Woolwich (1983) **b.** 29 Nov. 1933 **ed.** Woking Co. Grammar Sch. **Profession** civil servant, Labour Party agent **Political interests** foreign affairs, housing, environment, local govt, transport, defence **Political career** joined Labour Party 1951; Greenwich Borough Cllr 1967–75 (Leader 1971–5); contested Bexley 1970, Bexleyheath 1974; Labour National Executive Cttee 1971–8; MP for Woolwich East 1974–83; joined the SDP 1981 **Parliamentary career** PPS to Shirley Williams 1976–8; SDP Spokesman on Foreign Affairs, Defence, Housing, Local Govt and Transport 1981–7, on Defence and Urban Affairs 1987– ; SDP Whip 1983– ; Vice-Pres. SDP 1987–8, Pres. 1988–90 **Other** JP 1970–

CASH, Bill Con., Stafford (1984) **b.** 10 May 1940 **ed.** Stonyhurst Coll.; Lincoln Coll., Oxford **Profession** solicitor **Political interests** trade and industry, small businesses, employment, tourism, heritage, complementary medicine, law, EC, media; anti-pornography and abortion **Member** Bow Group **Other** Dir. of Ironbridge Gorge Museum Trust 1980–

CHALKER, Rt Hon. Lynda Con., Wallasey (1974) **b.** 29 Apr. 1942 **ed.** Roedean Sch.; Heidelberg Univ.; Westfield Coll., London Univ.; Central London Poly. **Profession** statistician **Political interests** health and social services, disabled, women's issues, foreign affairs, overseas aid, trade, transport; pro-EC **Political career** National Vice-Chmn Young Conservatives 1970–1 **Parliamentary career** Opposition Spokesman on Social Services 1976–9; Under-Secretary of State for Health and Social Security 1979–82, for Transport 1982–3; Minister of State for Transport 1983–6, at the Foreign and Commonwealth Office 1986– ; PC 1987

CHANNON, Rt Hon. Paul Con., Southend West (1959) **b.** 9 Oct. 1935 **ed.** Eton; Christ Church, Oxford **Profession** company dir., shareholder **Political interests** arts, housing, environment, civil service, trade and industry, transport, Northern Ireland **Political career** selected at age 23 to succeed his father as MP (the Guinness family has held the seat for over 65 years) **Parliamentary career** Executive of 1922 Cttee 1965–6; Opposition Spokesman on Arts and Amenities 1967–70; Joint Secretary to the Ministry of Housing and Local Govt 1970; Joint Under-Secretary of State for the Environment 1970–2; Minister of State for Northern Ireland 1972, for Housing and Construction 1972–4; Opposition Spokesman on Price and Consumer Affairs 1974, on the Environment 1974–5; Minister of State in the Civil Service Dept 1979–81, for the Arts 1981–3, for Trade 1983–6; PC 1980; Secretary of State for Trade and Industry 1986–7, for Transport 1987–9 **Other** A multi-millionaire and member of the Guinness family. His daughter Olivia died from a drugs and alcohol overdose at Oxford Univ.

CHAPMAN, Sydney Con., Chipping Barnet (1979) **b.** 17 Oct. 1935 **ed.** Rugby Sch.; Manchester Univ. **Profession** architect, town planner, company dir. **Political interests** environment, trees, Green Belt, conservation, architecture, heritage, building, inner city; pro-EC and hanging **Political career** contested Stalybridge and Hyde 1964; National Chmn Young Conservatives 1964–6; MP for Birmingham Handsworth 1970–4 **Parliamentary career** Asst Whip 1988– **Member** Arboricultural Association (Pres. 1983–); London Green Belt Council (Pres. 1985–); Patron of Tree Council **Publications include** *Town and Countryside: Future Planning Policies for Britain*

CHOPE, Christopher Con., Southampton Itchen (1983) **b.** 19 May 1947 **ed.** Marlborough Coll.; Dundee Univ.; St Andrews Univ.; Inner Temple **Profession** barrister **Political interests** environment, local govt, defence, health, shipbuilding, home affairs, education; pro-hanging and privatization **Political career** Wandsworth Borough Cllr 1974–83 (Leader 1979–83) **Parliamentary career** Under-Secretary of State for the Environment (Local Govt and PSA) 1986– **Other** OBE 1982

CHURCHILL, Winston Con., Davyhulme (1983) **b.** 10 Oct. 1940 **ed.** Eton; Christ Church, Oxford **Profession** journalist, Lloyd's underwriter, company dir. **Political interests** defence, foreign affairs, human rights, refugees, elderly, kidney patients; pro-hanging **Political career** contested Manchester Gorton 1967; MP for Stretford 1970–83 **Parliamentary career** Opposition Spokesman on Defence 1976–8; Executive of 1922 Cttee 1979–85 (Treasurer 1987–8) **Member** English Speaking Union (Governor 1975–80); trustee of Winston Churchill Memorial Trust **Publications include** *First Journey*; *Six Day War*; *Defending the West* **Other** Grandson of Sir Winston Churchill. He is a volunteer pilot for St John's Air Wing, transporting kidneys and medical transplant teams

CLARK, Hon. Alan Con., Plymouth Sutton (1974) **b.** 13 Apr. 1928 **ed.** Eton; Christ Church, Oxford; Inner Temple **Profession** barrister, military historian **Political interests** defence, foreign affairs, trade and industry, employment; anti-EC **Parliamentary career** Under-Secretary of State for Employment 1983–6; Minister of State for Trade and Industry 1986–9, for Defence 1989– **Publications include** *The Fall of Crete*; *Barbarossa: The Russo-German Conflict 1941–45*; *Aces High: The War in the Air over the Western Front 1914–1918* **Other** Son of Lord (Kenneth) Clark

CLARK, Dr David Shadow Agriculture Minister Lab., South Shields (1979) **b.** 19 Oct. 1939 **ed.** Windermere Grammar Sch.; Morecambe Coll. of Further Education; Manchester Univ.; Sheffield Univ. **Profession** teacher **Political interests** agriculture, food, health, environment, conservation, industry, defence; pro-nuclear disarmament **Political career** contested Manchester Withington 1966; MP for Colne Valley 1970–Feb. 1974; contested Colne Valley Oct. 1974 **Parliamentary career** Opposition Spokesman on Agriculture, Fisheries and Food 1972–4, on Defence 1980–1, on the Environment 1981–7; Shadow Agriculture Minister 1987– **Member** CND **Unions** sponsored by NUPE **Publications include** *Industrial Manager*; *Colne Valley: Radicalism to Socialism*; *Victor Grayson: Labour's Lost Leader*

CLARK, Dr Michael Con., Rochford (1983) **b.** 8 Aug. 1935 **ed.** King Edward VI Grammar Sch., East Retford; King's Coll., London; Minnesota Univ.; St John's Coll., Cambridge **Profession** industrial chemist, management consultant **Political interests** energy, industry, unions, science and technology, education, environment, animal welfare; pro-hanging **Political career** contested Ilkeston 1979

CLARK, Rt Hon. Sir William Con., Croydon South (1974) **b.** 18 Oct. 1917 **Profession** accountant, company dir. (Caribbean sugar) **Political interests** finance, trade and industry, sugar cane, insurance, housing; pro-hanging **Political career** Wandsworth Borough Cllr 1949–52; contested Northampton 1955; MP for Nottingham South 1959–66, for Surrey East 1970–4 **Parliamentary career** Opposition Spokesman on Treasury Affairs 1964–6; Deputy Chmn Conservative Party 1975–7; PC 1990 **Other** Knighted 1980

CLARKE, Rt Hon. Kenneth Secretary of State for Health Con., Rushcliffe (1970) **b.** 2 July 1940 **ed.** Nottingham High Sch.; Gonville and Caius Coll., Cambridge **Profession** barrister (QC 1980) **Political interests** social services, education, health, employment, industry, transport; pro-EC **Political career** contested Mansfield 1964, 1966 **Parliamentary career** PPS to the Solicitor General, Geoffrey Howe (working on Industrial Relations Bill and the European Community enabling legislation) 1971–2; Asst Whip 1972–4; Lord Commissioner of the Treasury (Govt Whip) 1974; Opposition Spokesman on Social Services 1974–6, on Industry 1976–9; Parliamentary Secretary in the Ministry of Transport 1979–80; Under-Secretary of State for Transport 1980–2; Minister of State for Health 1982–5; PC 1983; Paymaster General and Minister of State for Employment 1985–7; Chancellor of the Duchy of Lancaster and Minister of State for Trade and Industry 1987–8; Secretary of State for Health 1988– **Publications include** *New Hope for the Regions*

CLARKE, Tom Lab., Monklands West (1983) **b.** 10 Jan. 1941 **ed.** Columba High Sch., Coatbridge **Profession** asst dir. of Scottish Film Council 1966–82 **Political interests** foreign affairs, Central America, Philippines, civil service, health and social services, housing, Scottish affairs, local govt, film industry; pro-devolution **Political career** Coatbridge Town Cllr 1964–74; Monklands District Cllr 1974–82 (Provost 1974–82); MP for Coatbridge and Airdrie 1982–3 **Parliamentary career** Opposition Spokesman on Scottish Affairs 1986–7, on Health 1987– **Member** British Amateur Cinematographers' Central Council **Unions** GMB **Other** JP 1972; CBE 1980

CLAY, Robert Lab., Sunderland North (1983) **b.** 2 Oct. 1946 **ed.** Bedford Sch.; Gonville and Caius Coll., Cambridge **Profession** bus driver, union official **Political interests** transport, shipbuilding, coal, industry, unions, Northern Ireland; pro-nuclear disarmament **Member** CND; Co-operative Party **Unions** GMB; NUM

CLELLAND, David Lab., Tyne Bridge (1985) **b.** 27 June 1943 **ed.** Kelvin Grove Boys' Sch.; Gateshead Technical Coll.; Hebburn Technical Coll. **Profession** electrical fitter **Political interests** local govt, transport, social services, health, unions, home affairs **Political career** Gateshead Borough Cllr 1972–86 (Leader 1984–6); National Secretary of Association of Cllrs 1981–5 **Unions** sponsored by AEU

CLWYD, Ann Lab., Cynon Valley (1984) **b.** 21 Mar. 1937 **ed.** Queen's Sch., Chester; Univ. Coll., Bangor **Profession** teacher, journalist (*Guardian*, *Observer* 1964–79) **Political interests** defence, foreign affairs, health, the arts, education **Political career** contested Denbigh 1970, Gloucester 1974; MEP for Mid and West Wales 1979–84; Labour National Executive Cttee 1983–4 **Parliamentary career** Opposition Spokesman on Education 1987–8; Shadow Minister for Overseas Development and Co-operation 1989– **Member** Co-operative Party; CND; Tribune Group (Chmn 1986–7) **Unions** NUJ; sponsored by TGWU **Other** Welsh speaker

COHEN, Harry Lab., Leyton (1983) **b.** 10 Dec. 1949 **Profession** accountant **Political interests** defence, Middle East, Northern Ireland, immigration, women's rights, ecology, conservation, animal welfare **Political career** Waltham Forest Borough Cllr 1972–83 **Unions** NALGO

COLEMAN, Donald Lab., Neath (1964) **b.** 19 Sep. 1925 **ed.** Cadoxton Boys' Sch., Barry; Cardiff Technical Coll. **Profession** metallurgist **Political interests** Welsh affairs, industry, steel, unions; pro-nuclear disarmament, anti-devolution **Parliamentary career** Opposition Whip 1970–4; Lord Commissioner of the Treasury (Govt Whip) 1974–9; Vice-Chamberlain of the Royal Household 1978–9; Opposition Whip 1979–81; Opposition Spokesman for Wales 1981–3; Speaker's Panel of Chairmen 1983– **Member** CND; Co-operative Party **Unions** sponsored by ISTC **Other** A former tenor with the Welsh National Opera Company. JP 1962; CBE 1979; Deputy Lieutenant West Glamorgan 1985

COLVIN, Michael Con., Romsey and Waterside (1983) **b.** 27 Sep. 1932 **ed.** Eton; Sandhurst; Royal Agricultural Coll., Cirencester **Profession** Grenadier Guards 1950–7, Conservative Research Dept 1974–9; farmer, publican, company dir., Lloyd's underwriter **Political interests** aviation and aerospace, training, employment, small businesses, pubs, environment, countryside **Political career** Tangley Parish Cllr 1964–76; Andover Rural District Cllr 1965–73; Hants. Co. Cllr 1970–75; Test Valley District Cllr 1972–4; MP for Bristol North West 1979–83 **Member** Bow Group; Council for Country Sports (Chmn 1987–); British Field Sports Society (Vice-Chmn 1986–) **Unions** NFU, MSF **Other** parliamentary consultant to National Union of Licensed Victuallers

CONWAY, Derek Con., Shrewsbury and Atcham (1983) **b.** 15 Feb. 1953 **ed.** Beacon Hill Boys' Sch.; Gateshead Technical Coll.; Newcastle-upon-Tyne Poly.; London Academy of Music and Dramatic Art **Profession** charity organizer (National Fund for Research into Crippling Diseases), company dir. **Political interests** Territorial Army, defence, law and order, medicine, health and social services, local govt, transport, agriculture, countryside **Political career** National Vice-Chmn Young Conservatives 1973–5; Gateshead Metropolitan Borough Cllr 1974–81; Tyne and Wear Metropolitan Co. Cllr 1977–83 (Leader 1979–82); contested Durham 1974, Newcastle-upon-Tyne East 1979 **Member** Council for the Protection of Rural England **Unions** NFU

COOK, Frank Lab., Stockton North (1983) **b.** 3 Nov. 1935 **ed.** Corby Sch., Sunderland; De La Salle Coll., Manchester; Inst. of Education, Leeds **Profession** construction manager, teacher **Political interests** engineering industry, expatriate workers, alternative energy, ecology, social services, pensioners, education, race relations; pro-nuclear disarmament **Parliamentary career** Opposition Whip 1987– **Unions** sponsored by AEU

COOK, Robin Shadow Health Secretary Lab., Livingston (1983) **b.** 28 Feb. 1946 **ed.** Aberdeen Grammar Sch.; Edinburgh Univ. **Profession** adult education tutor, journalist **Political interests** health, social services, education, prisons, trade and industry, railways, defence, environment; pro-nuclear disarmament **Political career** Edinburgh Town Cllr 1971–4; contested Edinburgh North 1970; MP for Edinburgh Central 1974–83 **Parliamentary career** assisted Neil Kinnock in his campaign for leadership 1983; Labour National Executive Cttee 1988– ; Opposition Spokesman on Treasury and Economic Affairs 1980–3, on European and Community Affairs 1983–4, on the City 1986–7; Campaign Co-ordinator 1984–6; Shadow Health Secretary 1987– **Member** Tribune Group **Unions** sponsored by NUR

COOMBS, Anthony Con., Wyre Forest (1987) **b.** 18 Nov. 1952 **ed.** Charterhouse; Worcester Coll., Oxford **Profession** founder and dir. of building company **Political interests** education, housing, inner cities, sports, arts, economy **Political career** Birmingham City Cllr 1978–88; contested Coventry North West 1983 **Member** Bow Group

COOMBS, Simon Con., Swindon (1983) **b.** 21 Feb. 1947 **ed.** Wycliffe Coll., Stroud; Reading Univ. **Profession** British Telecom marketing executive, company dir. **Political interests** transport, tourism, health, disabled, nuclear energy, information technology, cable TV, record industry, music, arts, local govt, environment; pro-hanging **Political career** Reading Borough Cllr 1969–83 **Parliamentary career** Chmn All-Party Cable Cttee 1987–

COPE, Rt Hon. John Con., Northavon (1983) **b.** 13 May 1937 **ed.** Oakham Sch. **Profession** accountant, company dir., Conservative Research Dept 1965–7 **Political interests** small businesses, aerospace, agriculture, employment, Northern Ireland **Political career** contested Woolwich East 1970; MP for Gloucestershire South 1974–83 **Parliamentary career** Asst Whip 1979–81; Lord Commissioner of the Treasury (Govt Whip) 1981–3; Treasurer of the Household and Deputy Chief Whip 1983–7; Minister of State for Employment (Small Firms) 1987–9, for Northern Ireland 1989– ; PC 1988 **Publications include** (with Bernard Weatherill) *Acorns to Oaks (Policy for Small Business)*

CORBETT, Robin Lab., Birmingham Erdington (1983) **b.** 22 Dec. 1933 **ed.** Holly Lodge Grammar Sch., Smethwick **Profession** journalist **Political interests** home affairs, police, civil rights, children's rights, animal welfare, motor industry, agriculture, environment, the press, disabled; pro-alternative energy, abortion, single parents; anti-nuclear **Political career** contested Hemel Hempstead 1966, Derbyshire West 1967, Hemel Hempstead Feb. 1974; MP for Hemel Hempstead 1974–9 **Parliamentary career** Opposition Spokesman on Home Affairs 1984– **Member** Committee for Reform of Animal Experiments; Farm Animal Welfare Co-ordinating Executive (Chmn); Save the Children Fund **Unions** NUJ

CORBYN, Jeremy Lab., Islington North (1983) **b.** 26 May 1949 **ed.** Adams Grammar Sch., Shropshire **Profession** NUPE official **Political interests** socialism, health and social services, Ireland, Latin America, refugees, foreign affairs, defence, environment, transport; anti-imperialism and racism **Political career** Haringey Borough Cllr 1974–83 **Parliamentary career** organized Gerry Adams's visit to the House of Commons 1983 **Unions** sponsored by NUPE

CORMACK, Patrick Con., Staffordshire South (1983) **b.** 18 May 1939 **ed.** Havelock Sch., Grimsby; Hull Univ. **Profession** history teacher, hotel company dir., writer **Political interests** arts and heritage, defence, NATO, education, electoral reform, industrial relations, human rights; anti-pornography; defender of old churches and historic buildings **Political career** contested Bolsover 1964, Grimsby 1966; MP for Staffordshire Cannock 1970–4, for Staffordshire South West 1974–83 **Parliamentary career** Chmn All Party-Cttee for Heritage 1979– ; Speaker's Panel of Chairmen 1983– **Member** Staffordshire Historic Buildings Trust (Pres. 1983–); Historic Churches Preservation Trust (trustee); Heritage in Danger (founder and Vice-Chmn) **Publications include** *Heritage in Danger*; *Westminster: Palace and Parliament*; *English Cathedrals*

COUCHMAN, James Con., Gillingham (1983) **b.** 11 Feb. 1942 **ed.** Cranleigh Sch.; King's Coll., Newcastle **Profession** company dir., publican **Political interests** defence, Northern Ireland, China and Hong Kong, health and social services, small business, licensing legislation, aviation **Political career** Bexley Borough Cllr 1974–82; contested Chester-le-Street 1979 **Member** National Union of Licensed Victuallers

COUSINS, James Lab., Newcastle-upon-Tyne Central (1987) **b.** 23 Feb. 1944 **ed.** New Coll., Oxford; London Sch. of Economics **Profession** lecturer, research worker **Political interests** health, local govt, income policies, industrial relations, employment, steel, shipbuilding, regional affairs, transport, environment, science, world trade, Third World; pro-nuclear disarmament **Political**

career Wallsend Borough Cllr 1969–73; Tyne and Wear Co. Cllr 1973–86 **Member** CND **Unions** MSF

COX, Tom Lab., Tooting (1974) **b.** 1930 **ed.** London Sch. of Economics **Profession** electrician at Battersea Power Station **Political interests** education, industrial relations, elderly; pro-nuclear disarmament, anti-racism **Political career** Fulham Borough Cllr; contested Stroud 1966; MP for Wandsworth Central 1970–4 **Parliamentary career** Asst Whip 1974–7; Lord Commissioner of the Treasury (Govt Whip) 1977–9 **Member** CND; Co-operative Party **Unions** sponsored by EETPU

CRAN, James Con., Beverley (1987) **b.** 28 Jan. 1944 **ed.** Ruthrieston Sch.; King's Coll., Aberdeen Univ. **Profession** Conservative Research Dept 1970–1; National Association of Pension Funds 1971–9; Confederation of British Industry 1979–87 **Political interests** trade and industry, regional policy, pensions **Political career** Sutton Borough Cllr 1974–9; contested Glasgow Shettleston 1974, Gordon 1983

CRITCHLEY, Julian Con., Aldershot (1970) **b.** 8 Dec. 1930 **ed.** Shrewsbury Sch.; Sorbonne; Pembroke Coll., Oxford **Profession** author **Political interests** defence, security, media, churches **Political career** MP for Rochester and Chatham 1959–64; contested Rochester and Chatham 1966 **Member** Bow Group (Chmn 1966–7) **Publications include** *NATO in the 80s*; *Westminster Blues*; *Cruise, Pershing and S.S.20s*; *Heseltine: The Unauthorised Biography* **Other** Steward, British Boxing Board of Control 1987–

CROWTHER, Stan Lab., Rotherham (1976) **b.** 30 May 1925 **ed.** Rotherham Grammar Sch.; Rotherham Coll. of Technology **Profession** served in Royal Signal Corps, World War II; journalist, folk singer **Political interests** urban problems, employment, transport, steel, vehicle industry, animal welfare, conservation, regional affairs, public services; anti-EC, pro-nuclear disarmament **Political career** Rotherham Borough Cllr 1958–9, 1961–76; Mayor of Rotherham 1971–2, 1975–6 **Parliamentary career** Speaker's Panel of Chairmen 1983– **Member** CND **Unions** sponsored by TGWU

CRYER, Bob Lab., Bradford South (1987) **b.** 3 Dec. 1934 **ed.** Salt Sch., Shipley; Hull Univ. **Profession** teacher **Political interests** trade and industry, health and safety at work, transport, law, education; anti-EC, pro-nuclear disarmament **Political career** contested Lancashire Darwen 1964; Keighley Borough Cllr 1971–4; MP for Keighley 1974–83; MEP for Sheffield 1984–9 **Parliamentary career** Under-Secretary of State for Industry 1976–8 **Unions** NATFHE; TGWU **Publications include** *Steam in the Worth Valley* **Other** Founder of Keighley and Worth Valley Railway

CUMMINGS, John Lab., Easington (1987) **b.** 6 July 1943 **ed.** Murton Senior Sch.; Easington Technical Coll. **Profession** colliery electrician **Political interests** mining, water, tourism, energy, environment **Political career** Easington District Cllr 1970–87 (Chmn 1975–6, Leader 1979–87) **Unions** NUM

CUNLIFFE, Lawrence Lab., Leigh (1979) **b.** 25 Mar. 1929 **ed.** St Edmund's Sch., Manchester; Ruskin Coll., Oxford **Profession** mining engineer **Political interests** mining, energy, trade and industry, aerospace **Political career** Farnworth Borough Cllr 1960–74; Bolton Metropolitan District Cllr 1974–9; contested Rochdale 1972, 1974 **Parliamentary career** Opposition Whip 1985–7 **Unions** sponsored by NUM **Other** JP 1967–79

CUNNINGHAM, Dr Jack Shadow Leader of the House of Commons Lab., Copeland (1983) **b.** 4 Aug. 1939 **ed.** Jarrow Grammar Sch.; Bede Coll., Durham Univ. **Profession** chemist, lecturer **Political interests** energy, nuclear industry, chemical industry, environment, regional policy, housing, foreign affairs, world development **Political career** Chester-le-Street Urban District Cllr 1969–74; MP for Whitehaven 1970–83 **Parliamentary career** PPS to James Callaghan 1974–6 (leading his campaigns to become Leader and Prime Minister); Under-Secretary of State for Energy 1976–9; Opposition Spokesman on Industry 1979–83; Shadow Environment Secretary 1983–9; Shadow Leader of the House of Commons 1989– **Unions** sponsored by GMB

CURRIE, Edwina Con., Derbyshire South (1983) **b.** 13 Oct. 1946 **ed.** Liverpool Inst. for Girls; St Anne's Coll., Oxford; London Sch. of Economics **Profession** economics teacher **Political interests** health and social services, housing, education, local govt, energy; pro-hanging **Political career** Birmingham City Cllr 1975–86 **Parliamentary career** Under-Secretary of State for Health 1986–88 (resigned over salmonella in eggs issue) **Unions** NATFHE

CURRY, David Con., Skipton and Ripon (1987) **b.** 13 June 1944 **ed.** Ripon Grammar Sch.; Corpus Christi Coll., Oxford; Kennedy Sch. of Govt, Harvard Univ. **Profession** journalist (*Financial Times* 1970–9) **Political interests** agriculture, finance, trade, foreign affairs, EC **Political career** contested Morpeth 1974; MEP for Essex North East 1979–89 **Parliamentary career** Secretary for Agriculture, Fisheries and Food 1989– **Publications include** *The Food War: The EEC, the US and the Battle for World Food Markets*

DALYELL, Tam Lab., Linlithgow (1983) **b.** 9 Aug. 1932 **ed.** Eton; King's Coll., Cambridge; Moray House, Edinburgh **Profession** teacher, author **Political interests** science, defence, education, conservation, economy, kidney transplants; anti-devolution, Falklands War; pro-nuclear power, EC **Political career** contested Roxburgh, Selkirk and Peebles 1959; MEP 1975–9; MP for West Lothian 1962–83 **Parliamentary career** PPS to Richard Crossman 1964–70; Opposition Spokesman on Science 1980–2 (sacked because of opposition to Falklands War); frequent questioner about the sinking of the *Belgrano* 1982–4; Labour National Executive Cttee 1986–7 **Unions** sponsored by NUR **Publications include** *Devolution: End of Britain*; *One Man's Falklands*; *A Science Policy for Britain*; *Thatcher's Torpedo*; *Misrule*

DARLING, Alistair Lab., Edinburgh Central (1987) **b.** 28 Nov. 1953 **ed.** Loretto Sch.; Aberdeen Univ. **Profession** advocate **Political interests** transport, education, health and social services, housing, economy **Political career** Lothian Regional Cllr 1982–7 **Parliamentary career** Opposition Spokesman on Home Affairs 1988– **Unions** GMB (APEX partnership)

DAVIES, Rt Hon. Denzil Lab., Llanelli (1970) **b.** 9 Oct. 1938 **ed.** Queen Elizabeth Grammar Sch., Carmarthen; Pembroke Coll., Oxford; Gray's Inn **Profession** barrister **Political interests** foreign affairs, economy, Welsh affairs, defence and disarmament, law, EC **Parliamentary career** Minister of State at the Treasury 1975–9; PC 1978; Opposition Spokesman on the

Treasury and Economic Affairs 1979–80, on Foreign and Commonwealth Affairs 1980–1, on Defence and Disarmament 1981–8; Shadow Welsh Secretary 1983

DAVIES, Quentin Con., Stamford and Spalding (1987) **b.** 29 May 1944 **ed.** Leighton Park Sch.; Gonville and Caius Coll., Cambridge; Harvard Univ. **Profession** diplomat 1967–74; merchant banker, company dir. **Political interests** trade and industry, banking, finance, economy, agriculture, health **Political career** contested Birmingham Ladywood 1977

DAVIES, Ron Lab., Caerphilly (1983) **b.** 6 Aug. 1946 **ed.** Bassaleg Grammar Sch.; Portsmouth Poly.; Univ. of Wales Coll., Cardiff; London Univ. **Profession** further education teacher and officer **Political interests** agriculture, regional affairs, environment, poverty, employment, adult education, EC **Political career** Bedwas and Machen Urban District Cllr and Rhymney Valley District Cllr 1969–84 **Parliamentary career** Opposition Whip 1985–7; Opposition Spokesman for Agriculture and Rural Affairs 1987– **Unions** sponsored by NUPE

DAVIS, David Con., Boothferry (1987) **b.** 23 Dec. 1948 **ed.** Bec Grammar Sch.; Warwick Univ.; London Business Sch.; Harvard Business Sch. **Profession** company dir. **Political interests** trade and industry, agriculture, health, law and order

DAVIS, Terry Lab., Birmingham Hodge Hill (1983) **b.** 5 Jan 1938 **ed.** King Edward VI Grammar Sch., Stourbridge; Univ. Coll., London; Univ. of Michigan **Profession** motor industry manager **Political interests** health and social services, economy, motor industry, US politics **Political career** Yeovil Rural District Cllr 1967–8; contested Bromsgrove 1970; MP for Bromsgrove 1971–4; contested Bromsgrove and Redditch 1974, Birmingham Stechford 1977; MP for Birmingham Stechford 1979–83 **Parliamentary career** Opposition Whip 1979–80; Opposition Spokesman on the Health Service 1980–3, on Treasury and Economic Affairs 1983–6, on Trade and Industry 1986–7 **Member** Co-operative Party; Fabian Society **Unions** sponsored by MSF

DAY, Stephen Con., Cheadle (1987) **b.** 30 Oct. 1948 **ed.** Otley Secondary Modern Sch.; Park Lane Coll. of Further Education; Leeds Poly. **Profession** sales and marketing executive **Political interests** education, law and order, environment, local govt, defence **Political career** Otley Town Cllr 1975–6, 1979–83; Leeds City Cllr 1975–80; contested Bradford West 1983

DEAN, Sir Paul Deputy Speaker of the House of Commons Con., Woodspring (1983) **b.** 14 Sep. 1924 **ed.** Ellesmere Coll., Shropshire; Exeter Coll., Oxford **Profession** served with Welsh Guards during World War II; Conservative Research Dept 1958–64; company dir., consultant, farmer **Political interests** health and social services, pensions, small businesses **Political career** contested Pontefract 1962; MP for Somerset North 1964–83 **Parliamentary career** Opposition Spokesman on Social Services 1969–70; Under-Secretary of State for Health and Social Security 1970–4; co-authored the Social Security Act 1973; Speaker's Panel of Chairmen 1979–82; Second Deputy Chmn of Ways and Means and Asst Deputy Speaker 1982–7; First Deputy Chmn of Ways and Means and Deputy Speaker of the House of Commons 1987– **Other** Knighted 1985

DEVLIN, Timothy Con., Stockton South (1987) **b.** 13 June 1959 **ed.** Dulwich Coll.; London Sch. of Economics; City Univ.; Lincoln's Inn **Profession** barrister **Political interests** regional development, EC, foreign affairs, defence, housing, health and social security, transport, law and order, charity law

DEWAR, Donald Shadow Scottish Secretary Lab., Glasgow Garscadden (1978) **b.** 21 Aug. 1937 **ed.** Glasgow Academy; Glasgow Univ. **Profession** solicitor **Political interests** Scottish affairs, law, housing; pro-devolution **Political career** contested Aberdeen South 1964; MP for Aberdeen South 1966–70 **Parliamentary career** Opposition Spokesman on Scottish Affairs 1981–4; Shadow Scottish Secretary 1984– **Unions** sponsored by NUR

DICKENS, Geoffrey Con., Littleborough and Saddleworth (1983) **b.** 26 Aug. 1931 **ed.** East Lane Sch., Wembley; Harrow Technical Coll.; Acton Technical Coll. **Profession** company dir. (aids for the elderly) **Political interests** energy, steel, petro-chemical industry, transport, data protection, human rights, child protection; campaigner against child molesters and child pornography **Political career** Sandridge Parish Cllr 1961–73 (Chmn 1969–70); St Albans District Cllr 1967–73 (Chmn 1970–1); Herts. Co. Cllr 1970–5; contested Middlesbrough Feb. 1974, Ealing North Oct. 1974; MP for Huddersfield West 1979–83 **Other** JP 1968; he saved two children from drowning in heavy seas 1972

DICKS, Terry Con., Hayes and Harlington (1983) **b.** 17 Mar. 1937 **ed.** Oxford; London Sch. of Economics **Profession** local govt officer **Political interests** local govt, housing, police, law and order, foreign affairs; pro-hanging, anti-immigration **Political career** Hillingdon Borough Cllr 1974–87; contested Bristol South 1979

DIXON, Don Lab., Jarrow (1979) **b.** 6 Mar. 1929 **ed.** Ellison Elementary Sch., Jarrow **Profession** shipyard worker, trade union official **Political interests** unions, employment, shipbuilding, maritime affairs, housing, transport, social services, local govt, industry, solvent abuse; pro-nuclear disarmament **Political career** Jarrow Borough Cllr 1963–74 (Leader 1966–74); South Tyneside District Cllr 1974–81 **Parliamentary career** Opposition Whip 1984–7; Deputy Chief Opposition Whip 1987– **Unions** sponsored by GMB

DOBSON, Frank Shadow Energy Secretary Lab., Holborn and St Pancras (1983) **b.** 15 Mar. 1940 **ed.** Archbishop Holgate's Grammar Sch., York; London Sch. of Economics **Profession** administrator with Central Electricity Generating Board and Electricity Council **Political interests** energy, transport, education, environment, local affairs, foreign affairs, socialism, govt reform; anti-EC, nuclear, apartheid **Political career** Camden Borough Cllr 1971–6 (Leader 1973–5); MP for Holborn and St Pancras South 1979–83 **Parliamentary career** Opposition Spokesman on Environment 1979–81, on Education 1982–3; Shadow Health Minister 1983–7; Shadow Leader of the House of Commons and Campaigns Co-ordinator 1987–9; Shadow Energy Secretary 1989– **Member** Anti-Apartheid (National Cttee 1980–) **Unions** sponsored by NUR

DORAN, Frank Lab., Aberdeen South (1987) **b.** 13 Apr. 1949 **ed.** Leith Academy; Dundee Univ.; Aberdeen Univ. **Profession** solicitor **Political interests**

energy, mental health, child care and the family, social welfare, law **Parliamentary career** Opposition Spokesman on Energy 1988– **Unions** GMB

DORRELL, Stephen Con., Loughborough (1979) **b.** 25 Mar. 1952 **ed.** Uppingham Sch.; Brasenose Coll., Oxford **Profession** company dir. (industrial clothing) **Political interests** economy, trade and industry, consumer affairs, Third World, EC, foreign affairs; anti-racism, monetarism, hanging **Political career** contested Kingston upon Hull East 1974 **Parliamentary career** Asst Whip 1987–8; Lord Commissioner of the Treasury (Govt Whip) 1988–90; Under-Secretary of State for Health 1990– **Member** Tory Reform Group

DOUGLAS, Dick Lab., Dunfermline West (1983) **b.** 4 Jan. 1932 **ed.** Govan Secondary Sch.; Scottish Coll. of Commerce, Glasgow; Loughborough Co-operative Coll.; Strathclyde Univ. **Profession** engineer, lecturer, company dir., consultant **Political interests** energy, maritime affairs, defence, foreign affairs, Scottish affairs; pro-EC **Political career** contested Angus South 1964, Edinburgh West 1966, Glasgow Pollok 1967; MP for Stirlingshire East and Clackmannan 1970–4, for Dunfermline East 1979–83 **Member** sponsored by Co-operative Party **Unions** AEU **Other** He ran the 1983 London Marathon in 4 h 40 min

DOUGLAS-HAMILTON, Lord James Con., Edinburgh West (1974) **b.** 31 July 1942 **ed.** Eton; Balliol Coll., Oxford; Edinburgh Univ. **Profession** advocate, author, Lloyd's underwriter **Political interests** foreign affairs, defence, Scottish affairs, law, conservation, arts; pro-devolution **Political career** Murrayfield District Cllr 1972–4; contested Hamilton Feb. 1974 **Parliamentary career** Opposition Whip 1976–9; Lord Commissioner of the Treasury (Govt Whip) 1979–81; Under-Secretary of State at the Scottish Office 1987– **Publications include** *Motive for a Mission: The Story behind Hess's Flight to Britain*; *The Air Battle for Malta: The Diaries of a Fighter Pilot*; *Roof of the World: Man's First Flight over Everest* **Other** Son of 14th Duke of Hamilton; an Oxford boxing blue and Hon. Pres. of Scottish Boxing Association 1975–

DOVER, Den Con., Chorley (1979) **b.** 4 Apr. 1938 **ed.** Manchester Grammar Sch.; Manchester Univ. **Profession** civil engineer, company dir. **Political interests** transport, health, housing, education, construction industry, new towns, inner cities, sport; pro-hanging; anti-EC, immigration **Political career** Barnet Borough Cllr 1968–71; contested Caerphilly 1974

DUFFY, Patrick Lab., Sheffield Attercliffe (1970) **b.** 17 June 1920 **ed.** London Sch. of Economics; Columbia Univ., New York **Profession:** Royal Navy 1940–6, economist, lecturer **Political interests** economy, defence, education **Political career** contested Tiverton 1950, 1951, 1955; MP for Colne Valley 1963–6 **Parliamentary career** Under-Secretary of State for Defence (Royal Navy) 1976–9; Opposition Spokesman on Defence 1979–80, 1983–4 **Unions** sponsored by GMB **Other** Pres. North Atlantic Assembly 1989–90

DUNN, Robert Con., Dartford (1979) **b.** 14 July 1946 **ed.** Manchester Poly.; Brighton Poly.; Salford Univ. **Profession** senior buyer, J. Sainsbury Ltd **Political interests** environment, education; pro-privatization; anti-unions **Political career** contested Eccles 1974; Southwark Borough Cllr 1974–8 **Parliamentary career** Under-Secretary of State for Education and Science 1983–8

DUNNACHIE, James Lab., Glasgow Pollok (1987) **b.** 17 Nov. 1930 **Profession** engineer, shop steward **Political interests** health and social services, housing, industry, employment **Political career** Glasgow Corporation Cllr 1972–4; Glasgow District Cllr 1974–77; Strathclyde Regional Cllr 1978–87 **Parliamentary career** Opposition Whip 1988– **Member** Tribune Group **Other** JP

DUNWOODY, Hon. Gwyneth Lab., Crewe and Nantwich (1983) **b.** 12 Dec. 1930 **ed.** Fulham Co. Secondary Sch.; Convent of Notre Dame **Profession** company dir., actress, scriptwriter **Political interests** transport, health and social services, arts, Middle East, foreign affairs; anti-EC, devolution; pro-abortion **Political career** Totnes Borough Cllr 1963–6; contested Exeter 1964; MP for Exeter 1966–70, for Crewe 1974–83; MEP 1975–9 **Parliamentary career** Opposition Spokesman on Foreign and Commonwealth Affairs 1979–80, on the Health Service 1980–3, on Parliamentary Campaigning and Information 1983–4, on Transport 1984–5; Labour National Executive Cttee 1981– **Unions** TGWU; sponsored by NUR **Other** Daughter of Morgan Phillips, former General Secretary of the Labour Party, and of Baroness (Norah) Phillips, Labour whip

DURANT, Tony Con., Reading West (1983) **b.** 9 Jan. 1928 **ed.** Bryanston Sch. **Profession** Conservative Party Agent 1952–62; National Organizer of Young Conservatives 1962–7; company dir., consultant **Political interests** housing, environment, town planning, transport, local govt, employment, inland waterways, film industry, single-parent families, EC, foreign affairs **Political career** Woking Urban District Cllr 1968–74; contested Rother Valley 1970; MP for Reading North 1974–83 **Parliamentary career** Asst Whip 1984–6; Lord Commissioner of the Treasury (Govt Whip) 1986–8; Crown Estates Paving Commissioner 1987– ; Vice-Chamberlain of the Royal Household 1988–90

DYKES, Hugh Con., Harrow East (1970) **b.** 17 May 1939 **ed.** Weston-super-Mare Grammar Sch.; Collège de Normandie, France; Pembroke Coll., Cambridge **Profession** stockbroker, consultant **Political interests** defence, taxation, human rights, Europe, Middle East; pro-EC, Israel; anti-hanging, monetarism **Political career** contested Tottenham 1966; MEP 1974–6 **Parliamentary career** chief sponsor of the Heavy Commercial Vehicles Act (the Dykes Act) 1973; Chmn All-Party Euro Group for Commons and Lords 1988– **Member** Bow Group **Publications include** (ed.) *Westropp's Invest £100*; *Westropp's Start Your Own Business*

EADIE, Alexander Lab., Midlothian (1966) **b.** 23 June 1920 **ed.** Buckhaven Secondary Sch.; Buckhaven Technical Coll., Fife **Profession** miner **Political interests** energy, coal, electricity, nuclear power, industry, Scottish affairs, law, local govt, education, devolution, industry, mentally handicapped people **Political career** Fife Co. Cllr 1953–73; contested Ayr 1959, 1964 **Parliamentary career** Opposition Spokesman on Energy 1970–4; Under-Secretary of State for Energy 1974–9; Opposition Spokesman on Energy 1979–87 **Unions** sponsored by NUM **Other** JP 1951; BEM 1960

EASTHAM, Kenneth Lab., Manchester Blackley (1979) **b.** 11 Aug. 1927 **ed.** Openshaw Technical Coll. **Profession** planning engineer **Political interests** economy, trade and industry **Political career** Manchester City Cllr 1962–80 **Parliamentary career** Opposition Whip 1987– **Unions** sponsored by AEU

EGGAR, Tim Con., Enfield North (1979) **b.** 19 Dec. 1951 **ed.** Winchester Coll.; Magdalene Coll., Cambridge; Coll. of Law, London **Profession** barrister, merchant banker, company dir. **Political interests** economy, energy, privatization, overseas aid, foreign affairs **Parliamentary career** Under-Secretary of State at the Foreign and Commonwealth Office 1985–9; Minister of State for Employment 1989–90, for Education 1990–

EMERY, Sir Peter Con., Honiton (1967) **b.** 27 Feb. 1926 **ed.** Scotch Plains, New Jersey; Oriel Coll., Oxford **Profession** RAF 1943–7; company dir. **Political interests** trade and industry, purchasing and supply, consumer affairs, energy, parliamentary procedure, Africa, Commonwealth, US, Third World **Political career** Hornsey Borough Cllr 1951–9; contested Poplar 1951, Lincoln 1955; MP for Reading 1959–66 **Parliamentary career** Secretary 1922 Cttee 1964–6; Opposition Spokesman on Trade, Treasury and Economic Affairs 1965–6; Under-Secretary of State for Industry 1972, for Industry and Consumer Affairs 1973–4, for Energy 1974; Procedure Cttee 1976– (Chmn 1983–) **Member** Bow Group (joint founder and first secretary 1951) **Other** Knighted 1982; captain of House of Commons Bridge Team 1984–

EVANS, David Con., Welwyn Hatfield (1987) **b.** 23 Apr. 1935 **ed.** Raglan Sch., Enfield; Tottenham Technical Coll. **Profession** footballer (Aston Villa) and cricketer (Wark. and Glos.); company dir. (office cleaning) **Political interests** environment, law and order, defence, local govt, sport **Political career** Wheathampstead Parish Cllr 1979–87; St Albans City and District Cllr 1980–4 **Other** Chmn The Lord's Taverners 1982–4; Chmn Luton Town Football Club 1984–

EVANS, John Lab., St Helens North (1983) **b.** 19 Oct. 1930 **ed.** Jarrow Central Sch. **Profession** shipyard worker, union official **Political interests** employment, energy, transport, industry, shipbuilding, health and safety, industrial relations, EC; pro-nuclear power, anti-nuclear weapons **Political career** Hebburn Urban District Cllr 1962–74 (Leader 1969–74, Chmn 1972–3); South Tyneside Metropolitan District Cllr 1973–4; MEP 1975–8; MP for Newton 1974–83 **Parliamentary career** Asst Whip 1978–9; Opposition Whip 1979–80; PPS to Michael Foot, Leader of the Opposition, 1980–3; Labour National Executive Cttee 1982– ; Shadow Employment Minister 1983–7 **Unions** sponsored by AEU

EVENNETT, David Con., Erith and Crayford (1983) **b.** 3 June 1949 **ed.** Buckhurst Hill Co. High Sch. for Boys; London Sch. of Economics **Profession** marine insurance broker, Lloyd's underwriter, company dir. **Political interests** education, transport, employment, insurance, health and social services, economy **Political career** Redbridge Borough Cllr 1974–8; contested Hackney South and Shoreditch 1979 **Member** Bow Group **Other** He is the first Conservative to win this seat since 1935

EWING, Harry Lab., Falkirk East (1983) **b.** 20 Jan. 1931 **ed.** Beath High Sch., Cowdenbeath **Profession** foundry man, postman, union official **Political interests** health and social services, trade and industry, aircraft industry, home affairs, education, economy, sport; pro-devolution, anti-EC **Political career** contested Fife East 1970, MP for Stirling and Falkirk 1971–4, for Stirling, Falkirk and Grangemouth 1974–83 **Parliamentary career** Under-Secretary of State at the Scottish Office (Devolution) 1974–9; Opposition Spokesman on Scotland 1979– **Unions** sponsored by UCW

EWING, Margaret SNP, Moray (1987) **b.** 1 Sept. 1945 **ed.** Biggar High Sch.; Glasgow Univ.; Strathclyde Univ.; Jordan Hill Coll. of Education **Profession** teacher, journalist **Political interests** agriculture, education, social services **Political career** contested Dunbartonshire East Feb. 1974; MP for Dunbartonshire East Oct. 1974–9 (as Margaret Bain); contested Dunbartonshire East 1979, Strathkelvin and Bearsden 1983 **Parliamentary career** SNP Whip 1976–9; sponsored Divorce Law Reform Act (Scotland) 1976; SNP Parliamentary Leader and Spokesman on Education, Health, Social Services, Agriculture, Defence, Foreign Affairs 1988– **Other** Daughter-in-law of Winifred Ewing, former MP and MEP

FAIRBAIRN OF FORDELL, Sir Nicholas Con., Perth and Kinross (1983) **b.** 24 Dec. 1933 **ed.** Loretto Sch.; Edinburgh Univ. **Profession** advocate (QC 1972), company dir., writer, farmer **Political interests** foreign affairs, defence, Africa, Scottish affairs, home affairs, law, agriculture, arts **Political career** contested Edinburgh Central 1964, 1966; MP for Kinross and West Perthshire 1974–83 **Parliamentary career** Solicitor General for Scotland 1979–82 **Member** Historic Buildings Council for Scotland (Chmn 1988–); Edinburgh Festival Council 1971– **Other** Knighted 1988

FALLON, Michael Con., Darlington (1983) **b.** 14 May 1952 **ed.** Epsom Coll.; St Andrews Univ. **Profession** asst to Lord Carrington 1974–7; Conservative Research Dept 1975–9; lecturer, writer, company dir. **Political interests** trade and industry, EC, constitutional affairs, local affairs, public sector; pro-hanging **Political career** contested Darlington by-election Mar. 1983 **Parliamentary career** Asst Whip 1988–90; Under-Secretary of State for Education 1990– **Publications include** (jtly) *The Quango Explosion*; *Sovereign Members?*; *The Rise of the Euroquango*

FARR, Sir John Con., Harborough (1959) **b.** 25 Sept. 1922 **ed.** Harrow Sch. **Profession** Royal Navy 1940–6; land-owner (12,000 acres in England, Ireland, Zimbabwe), company dir., Lloyd's underwriter **Political interests** foreign affairs, Northern Ireland, agriculture, conservation **Political career** contested Ilkeston 1955 **Parliamentary career** Chmn British-Zimbabwe Parliamentary Group 1980– ; Chmn British-Korea Parliamentary Group 1984– **Member** British Shooting Sports Council (Chmn 1977–86); The Shooting Sports Trust (Vice-Pres. 1972–86) **Other** Knighted 1984

FATCHETT, Derek Lab., Leeds Central (1983) **b.** 8 Aug. 1945 **ed.** Lincoln Sch.; Birmingham Univ.; London Sch. of Economics **Profession** lecturer in industrial relations **Political interests** industrial relations, employment, education, housing, health and social services, local govt, economy, Northern Ireland **Political career** Wakefield Metropolitan Borough Cllr 1980–4; contested Bosworth 1979 **Parliamentary career**

Opposition Whip 1986–7; Deputy Campaign Co-ordinator 1987– ; Opposition Spokesman on Education 1987– , on Employment 1988– **Unions** sponsored by MSF **Publications include** *Trade Unions and Politics in the 1980s*; (jtly) *Workers' Participation in Management*; (jtly) *Worker Participation: Industrial Control and Performance*

FAULDS, Andrew Lab., Warley East (1974) **b.** 1 Mar. 1923 **ed.** Stirling High Sch.; Glasgow Univ. **Profession** actor **Political interests** foreign affairs, Middle East, arts, heritage, media; anti-racism, Zionism; pro-EC **Political career** contested Stratford-upon-Avon 1963, 1964; MP for Smethwick 1966–74 **Parliamentary career** Opposition Spokesman for the Arts 1970–3, 1979–82 **Other** He played Jet Morgan in *Journey into Space*

FAVELL, Anthony Con., Stockport (1983) **b.** 29 May 1939 **ed.** St Bees Sch., Cumbria; Sheffield Univ. **Profession** solicitor, company dir. **Political interests** health and social security, law and order, aviation, mentally handicapped people; pro-hanging **Political career** contested Bolsover 1979

FEARN, Ronnie Lib. Dem. (Lib. 1987–8), Southport (1987) **b.** 6 Feb. 1931 **ed.** King George V Grammar Sch., Southport **Profession** banker **Political interests** banking and finance, local govt, environment, education, health and social services, arts **Political career** Southport Borough Cllr 1963–74; Sefton Borough Cllr 1974–87; Merseyside Co. Cllr 1974–86; contested Southport 1970, 1974, 1979 **Parliamentary career** Lib. Spokesman on Health and Social Services 1987–8; Lib. Deputy Whip 1987–8; Lib. Dem. Spokesman on Health, Personal Social Services and Tourism 1988– **Other** OBE 1985

FENNER, Dame Peggy Con., Medway (1983) **b.** 12 Nov. 1922 **ed.** Ide Hill Sch., Kent **Profession** lecturer, drawing office employee **Political interests** agriculture, local govt, Europe **Political career** Sevenoaks Urban District Cllr 1957–71 (Chmn 1962–3); contested Newcastle-under-Lyme 1966; MP for Rochester and Chatham 1970–4, 1979–83; MEP 1974–5 **Parliamentary career** Under-Secretary of State for Agriculture 1972–4, 1981–6; voted against Royal Navy cuts which closed Chatham dockyard 1981 **Other** DBE 1986

FIELD, Barry Con., Isle of Wight (1987) **b.** 4 July 1946 **ed.** Bembridge Sch.; Victoria Street Coll. **Profession** undertaker, company dir., Lloyd's underwriter **Political interests** tourism, maritime affairs, local govt, privatization; pro-hanging **Political career** Horsham District Cllr 1983–6; Isle of Wight Co. Cllr 1986– **Other** Territorial Decoration 1984

FIELD, Frank Lab., Birkenhead (1979) **b.** 16 July 1942 **ed.** St Clement Danes; Hull Univ. **Profession** teacher, Dir. Child Poverty Action Group 1969–79 and Low Pay Unit 1974–80, writer **Political interests** poverty, welfare state, health and social security, taxation, education, industry, church affairs **Political career** Hounslow Borough Cllr 1964–8; contested Buckinghamshire South 1966 **Parliamentary career** Opposition Spokesman on Education 1980–1 **Member** Tribune Group **Publications include** *Freedom and Wealth in a Socialist Future*; (jtly) *To Him Who Hath: A Study of Poverty and Taxation*; *The Politics of Paradise*

FIELDS, Terry Lab., Liverpool Broadgreen (1983) **b.** 8 Mar. 1937 **ed.** De la Salle Grammar Sch. **Profession** fireman **Political interests** socialism, employment, drug abuse, fire service

FINSBERG, Sir Geoffrey Con., Hampstead and Highgate (1983) **b.** 13 June 1926 **ed.** City of London Sch. **Profession** company dir. **Political interests** foreign affairs, defence, housing, local govt, health and social services, environment, industrial relations; pro-hanging **Political career** Hampstead Borough Cllr 1949–65; Camden Borough Cllr 1964–74 (Leader 1968–70); National Chmn Young Conservatives 1954–7; contested Islington East 1955; MP for Hampstead 1970–83 **Parliamentary career** Executive 1922 Cttee 1974–6; Opposition Spokesman on Greater London 1974–9; Vice-Chmn Conservative Party 1975–9, 1984–7; Under-Secretary of State for the Environment 1979–81, for Health and Social Security 1981–3; co-sponsored bill against video nasties 1983; Leader of UK delegation to Council of Europe and Western European Union 1987– **Other** MBE 1959; JP 1962; knighted 1983

FISHBURN, Dudley Con., Kensington (1988) **b.** 8 June 1946 **ed.** Eton; Harvard Univ. **Profession** journalist (executive ed. *Economist* 1979–88), company dir. **Political interests** foreign affairs, economy, privatization, inner cities **Political career** won this seat in the by-election of 14 July 1988 **Member** Pres. Harvard Club of London

FISHER, Mark Lab., Stoke-on-Trent Central (1983) **b.** 29 Oct. 1944 **ed.** Eton; Trinity Coll., Cambridge **Profession** film producer, teacher, writer **Political interests** education, health and social services, arts, foreign affairs; pro-nuclear disarmament **Political career** Staffs. Co. Cllr 1981–5; contested Leek 1979 **Parliamentary career** Opposition Whip 1985–6; Opposition Spokesman on Arts and Media 1987– **Member** CND; Socialist Educational Association **Unions** NUT **Publications include** *City Centres, City Cultures* **Other** Son of Sir Nigel Fisher, Con. MP for Hitchin 1950–5, Surbiton 1955–74 and Kingston upon Thames 1974–83

FLANNERY, Martin Lab., Sheffield Hillsborough (1974) **b.** 2 Mar. 1918 **ed.** De la Salle Grammar Sch., Sheffield; Coll. of Education, Sheffield **Profession** Royal Scots 1940–6; teacher **Political interests** education, housing, union affairs, countryside, British Rail, Northern Ireland, foreign affairs, Latin America, South Africa, human rights; pro-nuclear disarmament, anti-Falklands War **Political career** left Communist Party 1956 and joined Labour Party 1957 **Member** Tribune Group (Chmn 1980–1) **Unions** NUT (Chmn National Advisory Cttee on Primary Education 1972–4; Parliamentary Consultant 1974–); sponsored by MSF

FLYNN, Paul Lab., Newport West (1987) **b.** 9 Feb. 1935 **ed.** St Illtyd's Coll., Cardiff; Univ. of Wales Coll., Cardiff **Profession** industrial chemist **Political interests** environment, housing, education, poverty, broadcasting, maritime affairs, Welsh affairs, industry, EC, civil liberties; anti-apartheid **Political career** Gwent Co. Cllr and Newport Borough Cllr 1972–83; contested Denbigh 1974 **Parliamentary career** Opposition Spokesman on Social Security 1988– **Other** He speaks Welsh

FOOKES, Dame Janet Con., Plymouth Drake (1974) **b.** 21 Feb. 1936 **ed.** Hastings High Sch. for Girls; Royal Holloway Coll., London Univ. **Profession** teacher

Political interests education, penal reform, mental health, animal rights, women's issues, housing, defence **Political career** Hastings Borough Cllr 1960–1, 1963–70; MP for Merton and Morden 1970–4 **Parliamentary career** Speaker's Panel of Chairmen 1976– ; Chmn Parliamentary Group for Animal Welfare 1985– **Member** RSPCA Council (Chmn 1979–81, Vice-Chmn 1981–3) **Other** consultant to English Tourist Board 1983– ; DBE 1989

FOOT, Rt Hon. Michael Former Leader of the Labour Party Lab., Blaenau Gwent (1983) **b.** 23 July 1913 **ed.** Leighton Park Sch., Reading; Wadham Coll., Oxford **Profession** journalist (ed. *Evening Standard* 1942–3; political columnist *Daily Herald* 1944–64; managing dir. *Tribune* 1960–74) **Political interests** employment, coal, steel, energy, nuclear disarmament **Political career** left Liberal Party and joined Labour Party 1934; contested Monmouth 1935; MP for Plymouth Devonport 1945–55; contested Plymouth Devonport 1959; MP for Ebbw Vale 1960–83 **Parliamentary career** Labour National Executive Cttee 1947–50, 1972–83; Opposition Spokesman on Trade and Industry (Power and Steel) 1970–2, on the Common Market 1972–4; Shadow Leader of the House of Commons 1971–2; Secretary of State for Employment 1974–6; PC 1974; Leader of the House of Commons and Lord Pres. of the Council 1976–9; Deputy Leader of the Labour Party 1976–80; Leader of the Labour Party 1980–3 **Member** CND (one of the first sponsors of the Aldermaston March 1958) **Publications include** *Parliament in Danger*; *Another Heart and Other Pulses*; *Debts of Honour*; *Aneurin Bevan*; *Isaac Foot* **Other** Son of Isaac Foot, Lib. MP for Bodmin 1922–4, 1929–35; husband of Jill Craigie, film maker and feminist writer

FORMAN, Nigel Con., Carshalton and Wallington (1983) **b.** 25 Mar. 1943 **ed.** Shrewsbury Sch.; New Coll., Oxford; Coll. of Europe, Bruges; Harvard Univ.; Sussex Univ. **Profession** Conservative Research Dept 1974–6, lecturer, author, consultant **Political interests** economy, unemployment, energy, environment, education, science and technology, North-South divide **Political career** contested Coventry North East 1974; MP for Sutton Carshalton 1976–83 **Publications include** *Towards a More Conservative Energy Policy*; *Another Britain*; *Mastering British Politics*

FORSYTH, Michael Con., Stirling (1983) **b.** 16 Oct. 1954 **ed.** Arbroath High Sch.; St Andrews Univ. **Profession** public relations consultant **Political interests** privatization, health service, mentally handicapped people, local govt, environment, Scottish affairs; pro-hanging **Political career** Westminster City Cllr 1978–83 **Parliamentary career** Under-Secretary of State at the Scottish Office 1987– **Publications include** *The Case for a Poll Tax*; *Reservicing Health*; *The Myths of Privatisation*

FORSYTHE, Clifford OUP, Antrim South (1983) **b.** 24 Aug. 1929 **ed.** Glengormley Public Elementary Sch. **Profession** footballer (Linfield and Derry City), plumbing and heating contractor **Political interests** transport, communications, environment **Political career** Newtownabbey Borough Cllr 1981–5 (Mayor 1982–3); Northern Ireland Assembly 1982–6; resigned House of Commons seat Dec. 1985 to protest against Anglo-Irish agreement and was re-elected Jan. 1986 **Parliamentary career** OUP Spokesman on Transport and Communications 1983–

FORTH, Eric Con., Worcestershire Mid (1983) **b.** 9 Sep. 1944 **ed.** Jordanhill Coll. Sch., Glasgow; Glasgow Univ. **Profession** management consultant, company dir. **Political interests** economy, EC, trade and industry, computer industry, local govt; pro-hanging, anti-immigration **Political career** Brentwood Urban District Cllr 1968–72; contested Barking 1974; MEP for Birmingham North 1979–84 **Parliamentary career** Under-Secretary of State for Trade and Industry 1988– **Publications include** *Regional Policy – A Fringe Benefit?*

FOSTER, Derek Lab., Bishop Auckland (1979) **b.** 25 June 1937 **ed.** Bede Grammar Sch., Sunderland; St Catherine's Coll., Oxford **Profession** youth and community worker, further education organizer **Political interests** youth affairs, community development, education and training, transport, economy, regional policy, Third World **Political career** Sunderland Co. Borough Cllr 1972–4; Tyne and Wear Co. Cllr 1973–7 **Parliamentary career** Opposition Whip 1981–2; Opposition Spokesman on Social Security 1982–3; PPS to Neil Kinnock, Leader of the Opposition, 1983–5; Opposition Chief Whip 1985– **Member** Capt in Salvation Army **Unions** NUT

FOULKES, George Lab., Carrick, Cumnock and Doon Valley (1983) **b.** 21 Jan. 1942 **ed.** Haberdashers' Aske's Sch., Hampstead; Edinburgh Univ. **Profession** public relations consultant, dir. of Age Concern Scotland 1973–9 **Political interests** foreign affairs, human rights, social services, pensioners, taxation, education, aviation, coal, energy; pro-EC and devolution; anti-Fortress Falklands **Political career** Edinburgh Corporation Cllr 1970–5; Lothian Regional Cllr 1974–9; contested Edinburgh West 1970, Edinburgh Pentlands 1974; MP for Ayrshire South 1979–83 **Parliamentary career** Opposition Spokesman on Europe 1983–5, on Foreign and Commonwealth Affairs 1985– **Member** sponsored by Co-operative Party; Fabian Society **Unions** GMB (APEX partnership) **Other** JP 1975

FOWLER, Rt Hon. Sir Norman Con., Sutton Coldfield (1974) **b.** 2 Feb. 1938 **ed.** King Edward VI Sch., Chelmsford; Trinity Coll., Cambridge **Profession** journalist (*The Times* 1961–70) **Political interests** home affairs, transport, social services, employment, race relations **Political career** MP for Nottingham South 1970–4 **Parliamentary career** Opposition Spokesman on Home Affairs 1974–5, on Social Services 1975–6, on Transport 1976–9; PC 1979; Minister for Transport 1979–81; Secretary of State for Transport 1981, for Social Services 1981–7, for Employment 1987–90 **Member** Bow Group **Unions** NUJ **Publications include** *After the Riots: The Police in Europe*; (jtly) *Crisis in Crime* **Other** Knighted 1990

FOX, Sir Marcus Con., Shipley (1970) **b.** 11 June 1927 **ed.** Wheelwright Grammar Sch., Dewsbury **Profession** Duke of Wellington's Regiment and Green Howards 1945–8; company dir., consultant **Political interests** transport, housing, environment, race relations; pro-hanging, sport with South Africa; anti-abortion, immigration, EC **Political career** Dewsbury Co. Cllr 1956–63; National Vice-Chmn Young Conservatives 1962; contested Dewsbury 1959, Huddersfield West 1966 **Parliamentary career** Asst Whip 1972; Lord Commissioner of the Treasury (Govt Whip) 1973–4; Opposition Spokesman on Environment 1974, on Housing 1974–5, on Transport 1975–6; Vice-Chmn Conservative Party (Candidates) 1976–9; Under-Secretary of State for the Environment 1979–81; Executive of 1922 Cttee 1981– (Vice-Chmn 1983–);

Chmn of Cttee of Selection 1984– ; Chmn Association of Conservative Clubs 1988– **Other** MBE 1963; knighted 1986

FRANKS, Cecil Con., Barrow and Furness (1983) **b.** 1 July 1935 **ed.** Manchester Grammar Sch.; Manchester Univ. **Profession** solicitor, company dir. **Political interests** economy, local govt, housing, law, defence, privatization; pro-hanging **Political career** left Labour Party and joined Conservative Party 1965; Salford City Cllr 1960–74 (Alderman 1967–74, Leader 1968–72); Manchester City Cllr 1975–84

FRASER, John Lab., Norwood (1966) **b.** 30 June 1934 **ed.** Sloane Grammar Sch., Chelsea; Co-operative Coll., Loughborough; Law Society Sch. of Law **Profession** solicitor **Political interests** housing, inner city, employment, law, consumer affairs, environment; anti-racism, pro-Esperanto **Political career** Lambeth Borough Cllr 1962–8; contested Norwood 1964 **Parliamentary career** Opposition Spokesman on Home Affairs 1972–4; Under-Secretary of State for Employment 1974–6; Minister of State for Prices and Consumer Protection 1976–9; Opposition Spokesman on Trade, Prices and Consumer Protection 1979–83, on Housing 1983–4, on the Environment 1984–7, on Legal Affairs 1987– **Member** Co-operative Society; Fabian Society **Unions** GMB

FREEMAN, Roger Con., Kettering (1983) **b.** 27 May 1942 **ed.** Whitgift Sch., Croydon; Balliol Coll., Oxford **Profession** accountant, investment banker, company dir. **Political interests** trade and industry, shoe industry, finance, pensions, health, defence **Political career** contested Don Valley 1979 **Parliamentary career** Under-Secretary of State for the Armed Forces 1986–8, for Health 1988–90; Minister of State for Transport 1990– **Member** Bow Group **Publications include** *Professional Practice*; *Fair Deal for Water*

FRENCH, Douglas Con., Gloucester (1987) **b.** 20 Mar. 1944 **ed.** Glyn Grammar Sch., Epsom; St Catharine's Coll., Cambridge; Inns of Court Sch. of Law **Profession** barrister, company dir. **Political interests** taxation, finance, pensions, law, insurance, small business, housing **Political career** research asst to Sir Geoffrey Howe 1976–9, 1982–3; contested Sheffield Attercliffe 1979 **Member** Bow Group (Chmn 1978–9)

FRY, Peter Con., Wellingborough (1969) **b.** 26 May 1931 **ed.** Royal Grammar Sch., High Wycombe; Worcester Coll., Oxford **Profession** teacher, insurance broker, company dir. **Political interests** transport, local govt, health and social services, insurance, shoe industry; anti-EC, unions **Political career** Bucks Co. Cllr 1961–7; contested Nottingham North 1964, Willesden East 1966 **Parliamentary career** Opposition Spokesman on Transport 1978–9; Joint Chmn All-Party Roads Study Group

FYFE, Maria Lab., Glasgow Maryhill (1987) **b.** 25 Nov. 1938 **ed.** Notre Dame High Sch., Glasgow; Strathclyde Univ. **Profession** lecturer in trade union studies **Political interests** unions, employment law, industrial health and safety, women's rights, local govt, elderly, disabled, nursery schools **Political career** Glasgow District Cllr 1980–7; Labour Party Scottish Executive 1982–8 **Parliamentary career** Opposition Spokesman on Women 1988– **Unions** TGWU

GALBRAITH, Dr Sam Lab., Strathkelvin and Bearsden (1987) **b.** 18 Oct. 1945 **ed.** Greenock High Sch.; Glasgow Univ. **Profession** neurosurgeon **Political interests** health, science, foreign affairs, defence **Parliamentary career** Opposition Spokesman on Health 1988– , on Scotland 1988– **Publications include** *Introduction to Neurosurgery* **Other** The first brain surgeon to sit in the House of Commons

GALE, Roger Con., Thanet North (1983) **b.** 20 Aug. 1943 **ed.** Hardye's Sch., Dorchester; Guildhall Sch. of Music and Drama **Profession** radio and TV broadcaster, dir. and producer (Radio Caroline, Radio Scotland, Radio 1's *Newsbeat*, Radio 4's *Today*, *Blue Peter*, Thames TV) **Political interests** union reform, education, media, broadcasting, cable TV, communications, tourism, leisure industries, animal welfare, transport, pubs **Political career** contested Birmingham Northfield 1982 **Member** Chmn of FRAME 1984– **Unions** ACTT; Equity; NUJ

GALLOWAY, George Lab., Glasgow Hillhead (1987) **b.** 16 Aug. 1954 **ed.** Harris Academy, Dundee **Profession** General Secretary War on Want 1983–7 **Political interests** foreign affairs, defence, Third World, charities, Scottish affairs **Political career** Chairman Scottish Labour Party 1981–2 **Member** Tribune Group **Unions** TGWU **Other** defeated Roy Jenkins to take seat

GARDINER, George Con., Reigate (1983) **b.** 3 Mar. 1935 **ed.** Harvey Grammar Sch., Folkestone; Balliol Coll., Oxford **Profession** journalist (Thomson Newspapers 1964–74, ed. *Conservative News 1972–9*), company dir. **Political interests** industrial relations, economy, privatization, EC, home affairs; anti-smoking, devolution, unions; pro-hanging, sport with South Africa **Political career** contested Coventry South 1970; MP for Reigate and Banstead 1974–83 **Parliamentary career** Executive of 1922 Cttee 1982, 1987– **Unions** NUJ **Publications include** *The Changing Life of London*; *Margaret Thatcher: From Childhood to Leadership*

GAREL-JONES, Tristan Con., Watford (1979) **b.** 28 Feb. 1941 **ed.** King's Sch., Canterbury; La Casa Inglesa, Madrid **Profession** merchant banker, Lloyd's underwriter, principal of language school in Spain **Political interests** alcohol abuse, Spain; anti-hanging, abortion **Political career** contested Caernarvon Feb. 1974, Watford Oct. 1974; asst to Lord Thorneycroft, Conservative Party Chmn, 1978–9 **Parliamentary career** Asst Whip 1982–3; Lord Commissioner of the Treasury (Govt Whip) 1983–6; Vice-Chamberlain of the Household (Govt Whip) 1986–8; Comptroller of the Household (No. 3 Whip) 1988–9; Treasurer of the Household (Deputy Chief Whip) 1989–90; Minister of State at the Foreign Office 1990– **Unions** MSF **Other** He speaks Welsh and Spanish

GARRETT, John Lab., Norwich South (1987) **b.** 8 Sep. 1931 **ed.** Sir George Monoux Sch., Walthamstow; Univ. Coll., Oxford; Graduate Business Sch., Univ. of California **Profession** management consultant **Political interests** trade and industry, economy, health and social services, education, civil service, parliamentary reform, environment **Political career** Greenwich Borough Cllr 1971–4; MP for Norwich South 1974–83 **Parliamentary career** Opposition Spokesman on Treasury and Economic Affairs 1979–80, on Industry 1980–3, on Energy 1987–8, on Trade and Industry 1988– **Member** CND; Friends of the Earth **Publications include** *The Management of Government*; *Managing Human Resources*; *Managing the Civil Service*

GARRETT, Ted Lab., Wallsend (1964) **b.** 21 Mar. 1920 **ed.** Prudhoe Elementary Sch.; London Sch. of Economics **Profession** engineer **Political interests** economics, local govt, agriculture, industry (engineering, machine tool, chemical), Commonwealth and foreign affairs **Political career** left Communist Party and joined Labour Party 1939; Prudhoe Urban District Cllr 1948–64; Northumberland Co. Cllr 1954–64; contested Hexham 1955, Doncaster 1959 **Unions** sponsored by AEU

GEORGE, Bruce Lab., Walsall South (1974) **b.** 1 June 1942 **ed.** Mountain Ash Grammar Sch.; Univ. Coll. of Swansea; Warwick Univ. **Profession** lecturer in politics, defence and security **Political interests** defence, international relations, education, health and social services, housing; pro-NATO **Political career** contested Southport 1970 **Member** consultant to Confederation of Long Distance Pigeon Racing Associations **Unions** GMB (APEX partnership); NATFHE **Publications include** *The Politics of Parliamentary Reform* **Other** Founder and former capt. of the House of Commons Football Club

GILBERT, Rt Hon. Dr John Lab., Dudley East (1974) **b.** 5 Apr. 1927 **ed.** Merchant Taylors' Sch., Northwood; St John's Coll., Oxford; New York Univ. **Profession** economist, accountant **Political interests** defence, foreign affairs, human rights, economy, finance, transport, conservation **Political career** contested Ludlow 1966, Dudley 1968; MP for Dudley 1970–4 **Parliamentary career** Opposition Spokesman on Treasury Matters 1972–4; Financial Secretary to the Treasury 1974–5; Minister of State for Transport 1975–6, for Defence 1976–9; PC 1978 **Member** Amnesty International; Co-operative Party; Fabian Society **Unions** GMB

GILL, Christopher Con., Ludlow (1987) **b.** 28 Oct. 1936 **ed.** Shrewsbury Sch. **Profession** butcher, farmer, chmn of family meat business **Political interests** agriculture **Political career** Wolverhampton Borough Cllr 1965–72 **Member** Bacon and Meat Manufacturers' Association; Rare Breeds Survival Trust; NFU **Other** RD 1971

GILMOUR, Rt Hon. Sir Ian Con., Chesham and Amersham (1974) **b.** 8 July 1926 **ed.** Eton; Balliol Coll., Oxford; Inner Temple **Profession** Grenadier Guards 1944–7; barrister, journalist (owner of *Spectator* 1954–67), company dir. **Political interests** defence, home affairs, Northern Ireland, agriculture; pro-EC, proportional representation; anti-monetarism, Zionism **Political career** contested Hounslow West 1962; MP for Norfolk Central 1962–74 **Parliamentary career** Under-Secretary of State for Defence (Army) 1970–1; Minister of State for Defence 1971–4; PC 1973; Secretary of State for Defence 1974; Chmn Conservative Research Dept 1974–5; Opposition Spokesman on Defence 1974, on Northern Ireland 1974–5, on Home Affairs 1975–6, on Defence 1976–9; Lord Privy Seal 1979–81; voted against the abolition of the GLC 1984 **Publications include** *The Body Politic*; *Inside Right: A Study of Conservatism*; *Britain Can Work* **Other** Inherited the title of Baronet 1977

GLYN, Dr Sir Alan Con., Windsor and Maidenhead (1974) **b.** 26 Sept. 1918 **ed.** Westminster; Gonville and Caius Coll., Cambridge; St Bartholomew's Hosp.; St George's Hosp.; Middle Temple **Profession** served World War II, doctor, barrister **Political interests** defence, foreign affairs, health **Political career** Chelsea Borough Cllr 1959–62; MP for Wandsworth Clapham 1959–64, for Berkshire Windsor 1970–4 **Publications include** *Let's Think Again*; *Witness to Vietnam* **Other** One of Earl Marshal's Green Staff Officers at the Investiture of HRH The Prince of Wales 1969; knighted 1990

GODMAN, Dr Norman Lab., Greenock and Port Glasgow (1983) **b.** 19 Apr. 1937 **ed.** Westbourne Street Boys' Sch., Hull; Hull Univ.; Heriot-Watt Univ. **Profession** shipwright, lecturer **Political interests** housing, social services, education, law, human rights, shipbuilding, fishing, agriculture **Political career** contested Aberdeen South 1979 **Parliamentary career** Opposition Spokesman on Agriculture and Rural Affairs 1988– **Member** CND **Unions** AUT; sponsored by TGWU

GOLDING, Llin Lab., Newcastle-under-Lyme (1986) **b.** 21 Mar. 1933 **ed.** Caerphilly Girls' Grammar Sch.; Cardiff Radiography Sch. **Profession** radiographer **Political interests** health and social services, unions, children's rights, home affairs **Political career** asst to John Golding MP 1972–86 **Parliamentary career** Opposition Whip 1987– **Unions** NUPE **Other** Daughter of Ness Edwards, former MP for Caerphilly, and wife of John Golding, MP for Newcastle-under-Lyme 1969–86

GOODHART, Sir Philip Con., Beckenham (1957) **b.** 3 Nov. 1925 **ed.** Hotchkiss Sch., US; Trinity Coll., Cambridge **Profession** served World War II; journalist (*Daily Telegraph* 1950–5, *Sunday Times* 1955–7), land-owner **Political interests** defence, foreign affairs, Northern Ireland, consumer issues **Political career** contested Consett 1950 **Parliamentary career** Secretary of 1922 Cttee 1960–79; Opposition Spokesman on the Army 1964–5, on Home Affairs 1965–6; Under-Secretary of State for Northern Ireland 1979–81, for Defence 1981, for the Armed Forces 1981 **Member** Bow Group (dir. of publications 1960–); Consumers Association (Vice-Pres. 1983–) **Publications include** *The 1922: The History of the 1922 Committee*; *War without Weapons*; *Stand on Your Own Four Feet*; *Jobs Ahead* **Other** Knighted 1981

GOODLAD, Alastair Con., Eddisbury (1983) **b.** 4 July 1943 **ed.** Marlborough; King's Coll., Cambridge **Profession** company dir., Lloyd's underwriter **Political interests** agriculture, trade and industry, energy, Northern Ireland, South-East Asia **Political career** contested Crewe 1970; MP for Northwich 1974–83 **Parliamentary career** Asst Whip 1981–2; Lord Commissioner of the Treasury (Govt Whip) 1982–4; Under-Secretary of State for Energy 1984–7; Comptroller of the Household (No. 3 Whip) 1989–90; Treasurer of the Household (Deputy Chief Whip) 1990–

GOODSON-WICKES, Dr Charles Con., Wimbledon (1987) **b.** 7 Nov. 1945 **ed.** Charterhouse; St Bartholomew's Hosp.; Inner Temple **Profession** Life Guards (Surgeon Capt.) 1973–7; doctor, barrister **Political interests** foreign affairs, defence, education, health, heritage, law **Political career** contested Islington Central 1979 **Publications include** *The New Corruption*

GORDON, Mildred Lab., Bow and Poplar (1987) **b.** 24 Oct. 1923 **ed.** Raines Foundation Sch., Stepney; Forest Training Coll., Walthamstow; Emergency Teacher Training Coll. **Profession** teacher of history and English **Political interests** education, race relations, immigration, prisons, women's issues, children's rights, health

GORMAN, Teresa Con., Billericay (1987) **b.** 30 Sep. 1931 **ed.** Fulham Co. Sch.; Brighton Coll. of Education; Univ. Coll., London **Profession** teacher, company dir. (teaching equipment) **Political interests** education, housing, local govt, women's health, small businesses, elderly, foreign affairs **Political career** Westminster City Cllr 1982–6; contested Lambeth Streatham (as Theresa Moore, Independent) 1974 **Member** Alliance of Small Firms and Self-Employed People (Founder and Chmn 1974–)

GORST, John Con., Hendon North (1970) **b.** 28 June 1928 **ed.** Ardingly Coll.; Corpus Christi Coll., Cambridge **Profession** company dir.; industrial and public relations consultant **Political interests** media, broadcasting, local radio, consumer protection, advertising and public relations, employment, unions, Jewish affairs **Political career** contested Chester-le-Street 1964, Bodmin 1966 **Member** Telephone Users' Association (Founder and Secretary 1964–70); Local Radio Association (Founder and Secretary 1964–70)

GOULD, Bryan Shadow Environment Secretary Lab., Dagenham (1983) **b.** 11 Feb. 1939 **ed.** Dannevirke High Sch., New Zealand; Univ. of New Zealand (Victoria and Auckland Univ. Colls.); Balliol Coll., Oxford **Profession** diplomat, law tutor, broadcaster (presenter and reporter *TV Eye* 1979–83) **Political interests** economy, international relations, trade and industry, countryside, environment **Political career** contested Southampton Test Feb. 1974; MP for Southampton Test Oct. 1974–9 **Parliamentary career** Opposition Spokesman on Trade and Industry 1983–6, on the Treasury 1986–7; Labour National Executive Cttee 1987– ; Shadow Trade and Industry Secretary 1988–9; Shadow Environment Secretary 1989– **Unions** NUJ **Publications include** *Monetarism or Prosperity?*; *Socialism and Freedom*

GRAHAM, Tommy Lab., Renfrew West and Inverclyde (1987) **b.** 5 Dec. 1943 **ed.** Crookston Castle Secondary Sch.; Stow Coll. of Engineering, Glasgow **Profession** engineer, office manager **Political interests** health and social security, elderly, disabled, unemployment, shipbuilding, agriculture, foreign affairs **Political career** Strathclyde Regional Cllr 1978–

GRANT, Sir Anthony Con., Cambridgeshire South West (1983) **b.** 29 May 1925 **ed.** St Paul's Sch.; Brasenose Coll., Oxford **Profession** served with 3rd Dragoon Guards in World War II; solicitor, company dir. **Political interests** defence, civil defence, foreign affairs, Europe, finance, trade and industry, civil aviation; pro-hanging **Political career** contested Hayes and Harlington 1959; MP for Harrow Central 1964–83 **Parliamentary career** Opposition Whip 1966–70; Parliamentary Secretary to the Board of Trade 1970; Under-Secretary of State for Industry 1970–2, for Industrial Development 1972–4; Vice-Chmn Conservative Party 1974–6; Executive of 1922 Cttee 1979– **Member** Guild of Experienced Motorists (Pres.) **Other** Knighted 1983

GRANT, Bernie Lab., Tottenham (1987) **b.** 17 Feb. 1944 **ed.** St Stanislaus Coll., Georgetown, Guyana; Tottenham Technical Coll., London; Heriot-Watt Univ. **Profession** local govt officer **Political interests** local govt, housing, unemployment, education, equal opportunities, race relations, Third World, peace, mining **Political career** Haringey Borough Cllr 1978–87 (Leader 1983–7) **Parliamentary career** Founder and Chmn Parliamentary Black Caucus 1988– **Member** executive of Anti-Apartheid 1988– **Unions** NUPE

GREENWAY, Harry Con., Ealing North (1979) **b.** 4 Oct. 1934 **ed.** Warwick Sch.; Coll. of St Mark and St John, London; Univ. of Caen, Normandy **Profession** teacher **Political interests** education, arts, animal welfare, racing and bloodstock, housing, pensioners, NATO, defence; pro-caning, anti-sex education in schools **Political career** contested Stepney 1970, Stepney and Poplar 1974 **Member** Council of British Horse Society 1973– ; Council of Open University 1980– **Publications include** *Adventure in the Saddle* **Other** Founder of the Lords and Commons Hockey Club

GREENWAY, John Con., Ryedale (1987) **b.** 15 Feb. 1946 **ed.** Sir John Deane's Grammar Sch., Northwich; Hendon Police Coll.; London Coll. of Law **Profession** policeman, insurance broker, financial consultant (advising dentists), journalist (*British Dental Journal*, *The Dentist*) **Political interests** insurance, personal finance, taxation, small businesses, education, law and order, tourism, agriculture, media, health service, arts **Political career** N. Yorks. Co. Cllr 1985–7 **Publications include** *Finance and the Dental Practitioner*

GREGORY, Conal Con., York (1983) **b.** 11 Mar. 1947 **ed.** King's Coll. Sch., Wimbledon; Sheffield Univ.; Worshipful Company of Vintners (Master of Wine 1979) **Profession** wine consultant and journalist, company dir. **Political interests** transport, tourism, heritage, EC, food industry, housing, environment, consumer affairs, arts **Political career** Norfolk Co. Cllr 1977–81 **Member** Bow Group; British Atlantic Group of Young Politicians (Chmn 1988–9) **Publications include** *A Caterer's Guide to Drinks*; (jtly) *Beers of Britain*; (with Robert Adley MP) *A Policy for Tourism*

GRIFFITHS, Sir Eldon Con., Bury St Edmunds (1964) **b.** 25 May 1925 **ed.** Ashton Grammar Sch.; Emmanuel Coll., Cambridge **Profession** journalist (*Time*, *Life*, *Newsweek*, *Washington Post*), Conservative Research Dept 1963–4, company dir., pig farmer **Political interests** police, foreign affairs (US, India, Gulf States), defence, pollution, environment, countryside, transport; pro-hanging, sport with South Africa **Parliamentary career** Executive of 1922 Cttee 1969– ; Parliamentary Secretary to Ministry of Housing and Local Govt 1970; Under-Secretary of State for the Environment (Minister for Sport) 1970–4; Opposition Spokesman on Trade and Industry 1974–5, on Europe 1975–6 **Other** Adviser to the Police Federation 1966–70, 1974– , to the National Caravan Council 1982– ; knighted 1985

GRIFFITHS, Nigel Lab., Edinburgh South (1987) **b.** 20 May 1955 **ed.** Hawick High Sch.; Edinburgh Univ.; Moray House Coll. of Education **Profession** Mencap official **Political interests** health and social services, disabled, mentally handicapped, housing, education, Scottish affairs, arts, economy, trade and industry **Political career** Edinburgh District Cllr 1980–7 **Parliamentary career** Opposition Whip 1987–9; Opposition Spokesman on Trade and Indsutry 1989– **Member** Anti-Apartheid; Amnesty International; Friends of the Earth; War on Want; National Trust **Publications include** *Rights Guide for the Mentally Handicapped*; *A Guide to DHSS Claims and Appeals*; *Council Housing on the Point of Collapse* **Other** JP

GRIFFITHS, Peter Con., Portsmouth North (1979) **b.** 24 May 1928 **ed.** West Bromwich Grammar Sch.; City of Leeds Training Coll.; London Sch. of Economics; Birmingham Univ. **Profession** teacher

Political interests education, foreign affairs, defence, race relations, unions, deaf, elderly, heritage, tourism; anti-EC, immigration; pro-sport with South Africa **Political career** Smethwick Borough Cllr 1955–64 (Alderman 1964–6); contested Smethwick 1959; MP for Smethwick 1964–6; contested Portsmouth North 1974 **Parliamentary career** one of five Con. MPS to rebel against Royal Navy cuts 1981 **Publications include** *A Question of Colour?*

GRIFFITHS, Win Lab., Bridgend (1987) **b.** 11 Feb. 1943 **ed.** Brecon Boys' Grammar Sch.; Univ. of Wales Coll., Cardiff **Profession** teacher **Political interests** education, EC, charities, disabled, regional policy, energy, animal welfare, overseas development **Political career** Vale of Glamorgan Borough Cllr 1973–6; MEP for South Wales 1979–89 (Vice-Pres. European Parliament 1984–7) **Member** Amnesty International; Anti-Apartheid; CND; Christian Socialist Movement; Fabian Society **Other** Methodist lay preacher

GRIST, Ian Con., Cardiff Central (1983) **b.** 5 Dec. 1938 **ed.** Repton; Jesus Coll., Oxford **Profession** Conservative Party official, Conservative Research Dept 1970–4 **Political interests** Welsh affairs, West Africa, human rights, victims of violence; anti-devolution **Political career** contested Aberavon 1970; MP for Cardiff North 1974–83 **Parliamentary career** Under-Secretary of State at the Welsh Office 1987–

GROCOTT, Bruce Lab., The Wrekin (1987) **b.** 1 Nov. 1940 **ed.** Hemel Hempstead Grammar Sch.; Leicester Univ.; Manchester Univ. **Profession** lecturer, broadcaster (presenter and producer, Central Television 1979–87) **Political interests** foreign affairs, overseas aid, media, health and social services, prisons, local govt **Political career** Bromsgrove Urban District Cllr 1971–4; contested Hertfordshire South West 1970, Lichfield and Tamworth Feb. 1974; MP for Lichfield and Tamworth Oct. 1974–9; contested The Wrekin 1983 **Parliamentary career** Deputy Shadow Leader of the House and Deputy Campaigns Co-ordinator 1987–

GROUND, Patrick Con., Feltham and Heston (1983) **b.** 9 Aug. 1932 **ed.** Beckenham and Penge Co. Grammar Sch.; Lycée Guy Lussac, Limoges; Selwyn Coll., Cambridge; Magdalen Coll., Oxford; Inner Temple **Profession** barrister (QC 1981) **Political interests** health and social services, environment, aviation, law, local govt, housing, foreign affairs **Political career** Hammersmith Borough Cllr 1968–71; contested Hounslow, Feltham and Heston 1974, 1979

GRYLLS, Michael Con., Surrey North West (1974) **b.** 21 Feb. 1934 **ed.** Royal Navy Coll., Dartmouth; Paris Univ.; Madrid Univ. **Profession** Marine Commando, company dir., consultant **Political interests** trade and industry, small businesses; pro-monetarism, privatization, hanging; anti-smoking **Political career** St Pancras Borough Cllr 1959–62; Greater London Cllr 1967–8; contested Fulham 1964, 1966; MP for Chertsey 1970–4 **Other** Spokesman for the Institute of Directors 1979–

GUMMER, Rt Hon. John Selwyn Minister of Agriculture Con., Suffolk Coastal (1983) **b.** 26 Nov. 1939 **ed.** King's Sch., Rochester; Selwyn Coll., Cambridge **Profession** publisher, journalist, company dir. **Political interests** employment, agriculture, church affairs; anti-abortion, pro-EC **Political career** contested Greenwich 1964, 1966; MP for Lewisham West 1970–4, for Eye 1979–83 **Parliamentary career** Vice-Chmn of Conservative Party 1972–4; Asst Whip 1981; Lord Commissioner of the Treasury (Govt Whip) 1981–3; Under-Secretary of State for Employment 1983; Minister of State for Employment 1983–4; Chmn of Conservative Party 1983–5; Paymaster-General 1984–5; PC 1985; Minister of State for Agriculture, Fisheries and Food 1985–8, for Local Govt 1988–9; Minister of Agriculture 1989– **Member** General Synod of the Church of England **Publications include** *The Permissive Society*; *The Christian Calendar*; (jtly) *Faith in Politics*

HAGUE, William Con., Richmond (1989) **b.** 26 Mar. 1961 **ed.** Wath-on-Dearne Comprehensive Sch.; Magdalen Coll., Oxford; INSEAD Business Sch., France **Profession** management consultant **Political interests** agriculture, health and social services, economy, defence **Political career** contested Wentworth 1987; won seat in Feb. 1989 by-election

HAMILTON, Hon. Archie Con., Epsom and Ewell (1978) **b.** 30 Dec. 1941 **ed.** Eton **Profession** Coldstream Guards 1960–2, farmer, company dir. **Political interests** defence, finance, taxation, economy, trade and industry **Political career** Kensington and Chelsea Borough Cllr 1968–71; contested Dagenham 1974 **Parliamentary career** Asst Whip 1982–4; Lord Commissioner of the Treasury (Govt Whip) 1984–6; Under-Secretary of State for Defence Procurement 1986–7; PPS to the Prime Minister, Margaret Thatcher, 1987–8; Minister of State for Defence (Armed Forces) 1988– **Member** Bow Group

HAMILTON, Neil Con., Tatton (1983) **b.** 9 Mar. 1949 **ed.** Amman Valley Grammar Sch.; Univ. Coll. of Wales, Aberystwyth; Corpus Christi Coll., Cambridge; Middle Temple **Profession** barrister, economist **Political interests** small businesses, economy, finance, taxation, trade and industry, privatization, law, agriculture, energy, arts, Europe, foreign affairs; pro-hanging **Political career** contested Abertillery 1974, Bradford North 1979 **Parliamentary career** Govt Whip 1990– **Publications include** *The Facts on State Industry*; *UK – US Double Taxation Treaty*; *The European Community: A Policy for Reform* **Other** He won a £20,000 libel action in 1986 against the BBC for a Panorama programme alleging links with right-wing extremists

HAMPSON, Dr Keith Con., Leeds North West (1983) **b.** 14 Aug. 1943 **ed.** King James I Grammar Sch., Bishop Auckland; Bristol Univ.; Harvard Univ. **Profession** lecturer in American history **Political interests** education, youth employment and training, local govt, defence, environment **Political career** asst to Edward Heath in 1966 and 1970 elections; contested Ripon 1973; MP for Ripon 1974–83 **Other** adviser to AUT 1983–

HANLEY, Jeremy Con., Richmond and Barnes (1983) **b.** 17 Nov. 1945 **ed.** Rugby Sch. **Profession** accountant, company dir., lecturer **Political interests** race relations, immigration, home affairs, transport, trade and industry, animal welfare, pensioners; anti-racism, pro-hanging **Political career** contested Lambeth Central 1978, 1979 **Member** Bow Group; European Movement; Mensa; FRAME; RSPCA **Other** adviser to Institute of Chartered Accountants in England and Wales 1987–

HANNAM, John Con., Exeter (1970) **b.** 2 Aug. 1929 **ed.** Yeovil Grammar Sch. **Profession** Army 1947–51, company dir. (hotels, travel, oil) **Political interests** disabled, energy, education, small businesses, housing, environment, arts and leisure **Political career** Somerset Co. Cllr 1967–9 **Parliamentary career** Joint Secretary 1922 Cttee 1987– **Member** Bow Group; Disabled Drivers' Assn (Vice-Pres. 1977–) **Other** Capt. Lords and Commons Tennis Club 1975– ; adviser to Pharmaceutical Society of Great Britain 1979–

HARDY, Peter Lab., Wentworth (1983) **b.** 17 July 1931 **ed.** Wath-upon-Dearne Grammar Sch.; Westminster Coll., London; Sheffield Univ. **Profession** teacher **Political interests** conservation, wildlife, agriculture, education, environment, energy, employment, regional development, defence, foreign affairs; anti-EC **Political career** Wath-upon-Dearne Urban District Cllr 1960–70 (Chmn 1968–9); contested Scarborough and Whitby 1964, Sheffield Hallam 1966; MP for Rother Valley 1970–83 **Parliamentary career** Leader of Labour delegation to Council of Europe and Western European Union 1983– **Member** NSPCC; RSPB **Unions** NUPE; sponsored by NACODS **Publications include** *A Lifetime of Badgers*

HARGREAVES, Andrew Con., Birmingham Hall Green (1987) **b.** 15 May 1955 **ed.** Eton; St Edmund Hall, Oxford **Profession** merchant banker **Political interests** economy, urban affairs, sport, defence **Political career** contested Blyth Valley 1983 **Member** Bow Group

HARGREAVES, Kenneth Con., Hyndburn (1983) **b.** 1 Mar. 1939 **ed.** St Mary's Coll., Blackburn; Burnley Municipal Coll.; Manchester Coll. of Commerce **Profession** office manager **Political interests** local govt, housing; anti-abortion, Sunday trading; pro-hanging **Political career** Oswaldtwistle Urban District Cllr 1965–74; Hyndburn Borough Cllr 1974–83 (Mayor 1979–80); won seat in 1983 by 21 votes

HARMAN, Harriet Lab., Peckham (1982) **b.** 30 July 1950 **ed.** St Paul's Sch.; York Univ. **Profession** solicitor, NCCL (Liberty) legal officer **Political interests** civil liberties, law, child care, health and social services, women's issues **Parliamentary career** Opposition Spokesman on Health 1984– **Unions** sponsored by TGWU **Publications include** *Sex Discrimination in Schools*; *Justice Deserted: The Subversion of the Jury*

HARRIS, David Con., St Ives (1983) **b.** 1 Nov. 1937 **ed.** Mount Radford Sch., Exeter **Profession** journalist (*Daily Telegraph* 1961–79) **Political interests** fishing industry, agriculture, tourism, regional policy **Political career** Greater London Cllr 1968–77; contested Mitcham and Morden 1974; MEP for Cornwall and Plymouth 1979–84 **Unions** NUJ

HASELHURST, Alan Con., Saffron Walden (1977) **b.** 23 June 1937 **ed.** King Edward VI Sch., Birmingham; Cheltenham Coll.; Oriel Coll., Oxford **Profession** company dir., consultant **Political interests** education, aviation, youth affairs, agriculture; pro-EC; anti-apartheid, racism, hanging **Political career** National Chmn Young Conservatives 1966–8; MP for Middleton and Prestwich 1970–4

HATTERSLEY, Rt Hon. Roy Deputy Leader of the Labour Party and Shadow Home Secretary Lab., Birmingham Sparkbrook (1964) **b.** 28 Dec. 1932 **ed.** Sheffield City Grammar Sch.; Hull Univ. **Profession** journalist (*Guardian*; *Listener*; *Punch*; *Observer*) **Political interests** foreign affairs, defence, housing, education, consumer affairs, the press, unemployment, economy; pro-EC, NATO **Political career** Sheffield City Cllr 1957–65; contested Sutton Coldfield 1959 **Parliamentary career** Under-Secretary of State for Employment and Productivity 1967–9, for Labour 1967–8; Minister of State for Defence (Administration) 1969–70; Opposition Spokesman on Foreign and Commonwealth Affairs 1970–2, on Defence 1972, on Education and Science 1972–4; Minister of State for Foreign and Commonwealth Affairs 1974–6; PC 1975; Secretary of State for Prices and Consumer Protection 1976–9; Shadow Environment Secretary 1979–80; Shadow Home Secretary 1980–3; Shadow Chancellor 1983–7; Deputy Leader of the Labour Party 1983– ; Shadow Home Secretary 1987– **Unions** MSF; NUJ; sponsored by USDAW **Publications include** *A Yorkshire Boyhood*; *Choose Freedom: The Future for Democratic Socialism*; *Politics Apart*

HAWKINS, Christopher Con., High Peak (1983) **b.** 26 Nov. 1937 **ed.** Bristol Grammar Sch.; Bristol Univ. **Profession** economist, lecturer **Political interests** economy, industry, unemployment, education, health; anti-hanging, pro-council house sales **Political career** Coventry City Cllr 1964–6 **Publications include** *Theory of the Firm*; *The British Economy: What Will Our Children Think?*; *Britain's Economic Future: An Immediate Programme for Revival*

HAYES, Jeremy Con., Harlow (1983) **b.** 20 Apr. 1953 **ed.** Oratory Sch.; London Univ.; Middle Temple **Profession** barrister **Political interests** health and social services, home affairs, race relations, Northern Ireland, human rights, disabled, law and order, defence, economy, unemployment; anti video nasties, hanging **Member** Amnesty International; Bow Group; FRAME

HAYHOE, Rt Hon. Sir Barney Con., Brentford and Isleworth (1974) **b.** 8 Aug. 1925 **ed.** Stanley Technical Sch., Croydon; Croydon Borough Poly. **Profession** Conservative Research Dept 1965–70, mechanical engineer, company dir., Lloyd's underwriter **Political interests** defence, employment, health and social services, civil service; pro-EC, NATO **Political career** contested Lewisham South 1964; MP for Heston and Isleworth 1970–4 **Parliamentary career** Opposition Spokesman on Employment 1974–9; Under-Secretary of State for Defence (Army) 1979–81; Minister of State for the Civil Service 1981, at the Treasury 1981–5, for Health 1985–6; PC 1985 **Other** Knighted 1987

HAYNES, Frank Lab., Ashfield (1979) **b.** 8 Mar. 1926 **ed.** London secondary sch. **Profession** miner **Political interests** health and social services, coal, railways **Political career** Notts. Co. Cllr 1965–81 **Parliamentary career** Opposition Whip 1981– **Unions** sponsored by NUM **Other** JP

HAYWARD, Robert Con., Kingswood (1983) **b.** 11 Mar. 1949 **ed.** Maidenhead Grammar Sch.; Univ. of Rhodesia **Profession** personnel manager **Political interests** transport, aviation, energy, trade and industry, communication, information technology **Political career** contested Carmarthen 1974; National Vice-Chmn Young Conservatives 1976–7; Coventry City Cllr 1976–8

HEAL, Sylvia Lab., Mid Staffordshire (1990) **b.** 20 July 1942 **ed.** Coleg Harlech; Swansea Univ. **Profession** social worker **Political interests** health and social services, employment, the disabled, women's issues, education **Political career** Won this seat in the by-election of 22 Mar. 1990 **Other** JP 1973

HEALEY, Rt Hon. Denis Lab., Leeds East (1955) **b.** 30 Aug. 1917 **ed.** Bradford Grammar Sch.; Balliol Coll., Oxford **Profession** served in World War II (received MBE in 1945 for role as beachmaster at Anzio); journalist, broadcaster, lecturer **Political interests** foreign affairs, defence, trade and industry, economy, arts **Political career** member of Communist Party 1936–9; contested Pudsey and Otley 1945; MP for Leeds South East 1952–5 **Parliamentary career** Opposition Spokesman on Foreign Affairs 1959–63, on the Colonies 1961, on Defence 1963; PC 1964; Secretary of State for Defence 1964–70; Opposition Spokesman on Foreign Affairs 1970–2, on Economics 1972–4; Chancellor of the Exchequer 1974–9; Opposition Spokesman on the Treasury and Economic Affairs 1979–80; Deputy Leader of the Labour Party 1980–3; Opposition Spokesman on Foreign and Commonwealth Affairs 1980–7; Labour National Executive Cttee 1970–5, 1980–3 **Unions** sponsored by GMB (APEX partnership) **Publications include** *Labour Britain and the World*; *Labour and a World Society*; *Beyond Nuclear Deterrence*; *Socialism with a Human Face*; *The Time of My Life* **Other** MBE 1945, Companion of Honour 1979

HEATH, Rt Hon. Edward (Ted) Former Prime Minister and Leader of the Conservative Party Con., Old Bexley and Sidcup (1983) **b.** 9 July 1916 **ed.** Chatham House Sch.; Balliol Coll., Oxford **Profession** served in World War II (MBE 1946), author, company dir. **Political interests** trade and industry, employment, EC, economy, defence, foreign affairs **Political career** MP for Bexley 1950–74, for Bexley Sidcup 1974–83 **Parliamentary career** Opposition Whip 1951; Lord Commissioner of the Treasury (Govt Whip) 1951–2; Deputy Chief Whip 1952–5; PC 1955; Secretary to the Treasury and Chief Whip 1955–9; Minister of Labour 1959–60; Lord Privy Seal 1960–3; Secretary of State for Industry, Trade and Regional Development and Pres. of the Board of Trade 1963–4; Opposition Spokesman on Economics and Treasury Affairs 1964–5; Leader of the Conservative Party 1965–75; appointed Margaret Thatcher Opposition Spokesman on Education 1969; Prime Minister, First Lord of the Treasury and Minister for the Civil Service 1970–4; resigned as Leader of the Conservative Party 1975 **Member** Bach Choir (Vice-Pres. 1970–); European Community Youth Orchestra (1977–80); London Symphony Orchestra (Hon. member 1974–) **Publications include** (jtly) *One Nation: A Tory Approach to Social Problems*; *Sailing: A Course of My Life*; *Music: A Joy for Life* **Other** Winner of Sydney to Hobart Ocean Race 1969; Capt., Britain's Admiral's Cup Team 1971, 1979, and of Britain's Sardinia Cup Team 1980

HEATHCOAT-AMORY, David Con., Wells (1983) **b.** 21 Mar. 1949 **ed.** Eton; Oxford **Profession** accountant, Lloyd's underwriter, company dir., farmer **Political interests** trade and industry, agriculture, forestry, defence, arms control, energy; pro-hanging for terrorists **Political career** contested Brent South 1979 **Parliamentary career** Asst Whip 1988–9; Lord Commissioner of the Treasury (Govt Whip) 1989; Under-Secretary of State for the Environment 1989– **Other** A member of the famous thread family and nephew of Derick Heathcoat-Amory, Chancellor of the Exchequer 1958–60

HEFFER, Eric Lab., Liverpool Walton (1964) **b.** 12 Jan. 1922 **ed.** Longmore Senior Sch., Hertford **Profession** RAF 1941–5, carpenter, journalist **Political interests** foreign affairs, Europe, housing and construction, local govt, health and social services, trade and industry, unemployment, church affairs; pro-animal rights, nuclear disarmament **Political career** member of Communist Party 1940–8; Liverpool City Cllr 1960–6 **Parliamentary career** Opposition Spokesman on Industrial Relations 1970–2; Minister of State for Industry 1974–5; Labour National Executive Cttee 1975–86; Opposition Spokesman on European and Community Affairs 1981–3, on Housing and Construction 1983–5; Vice-Chmn Labour Party 1982–3, Chmn 1983–4; contested Labour Party Leadership 1983 **Member** League against Cruel Sports (Vice-Chmn 1977–) **Unions** sponsored by UCATT **Publications include** *The Dilemma of Eurocommunism*; *The Class Struggle in Parliament*; (jtly) *Faith in Politics*

HENDERSON, Douglas Lab., Newcastle-upon-Tyne North (1987) **b.** 9 June 1949 **ed.** Waid Academy, Fife; Central Coll., Glasgow; Strathclyde Univ. **Profession** trade union official **Political interests** economy, trade and industry, employment, regional policy, science, sport **Parliamentary career** Opposition Spokesman on Trade and Industry 1988– **Member** Anti-Apartheid **Unions** sponsored by GMB

HESELTINE, Rt Hon. Michael Con., Henley (1974) **b.** 21 Mar. 1933 **ed.** Shrewsbury Sch.; Pembroke Coll., Oxford **Profession** publisher, company dir. (Haymarket Group) **Political interests** defence, environment, transport, trade and industry, aviation; anti-hanging, racism **Political career** contested Gower 1959, Coventry North 1964; MP for Tavistock 1966–74 **Parliamentary career** Opposition Spokesman on Transport 1969–70; Under-Secretary of State for Transport 1970, for the Environment (Local Govt and Development) 1970–2; Minister of State for Trade and Industry (Aerospace and Shipping) 1972–4; Opposition Spokesman on Industry 1974–6, for the Environment 1976–9; PC 1979; Secretary of State for the Environment 1979–83, for Defence 1983–6; resigned over Westland Helicopters controversy 1986 **Publications include** *Reviving the Inner Cities*; *Where There's a Will*

HICKS, Maureen Con., Wolverhampton North East (1987) **b.** 23 Feb. 1948 **ed.** Brokenhurst Grammar; Furzedown Coll. of Education, London **Profession** dir. of Stratford Motor Museum 1976–82, lecturer on tourism and retail management **Political interests** education, tourism, retail trade, local govt, inner cities, law and order **Political career** Stratford District Cllr 1978–83 **Member** Heart of England Tourist Board Executive

HICKS, Robert Con., Cornwall South East (1983) **b.** 18 Jan. 1938 **ed.** Queen Elizabeth Grammar Sch., Crediton; Univ. Coll., London; Exeter Univ. **Profession** lecturer **Political interests** agriculture, fishing industry, regional policy, Europe, Middle East, sport; pro-EC, Arabs **Political career** National Vice-Chmn Young Conservatives 1964–6; contested Aberavon 1966; MP for Bodmin 1970–Feb. 1974 (when he lost his seat by nine votes), Oct. 1974–83 **Parliamentary career** Asst Whip 1973–4 **Other** adviser to British Hotels, Restaurants and Caterers Assn 1974– , and to the Milk Marketing Board 1985–

HIGGINS, Rt Hon. Terence Con., Worthing (1964) **b.** 18 Jan. 1928 **ed.** Alleyn's Sch., Dulwich; Gonville and Caius Coll., Cambridge; Yale Univ. **Profession** economist, company dir. **Political interests** finance, trade and industry, economy, transport, foreign affairs, sport **Parliamentary career** Opposition Spokesman on Treasury and Economic Affairs 1967–70; Minister of State at the Treasury 1970–2; Financial Secretary to the Treasury 1972–4; Opposition Spokesman on Treasury and Economic Affairs 1974, on Trade 1974–6; PC 1979; Executive of 1922 Cttee 1980–5; Chmn House of Commons Liaison Cttee 1984– ; Chmn Select Cttee on the Treasury and Civil Service 1984– **Other** A sprinter on the British Olympic Team 1948 and 1952, and on the Commonwealth Games Team 1950

HILL, James Con., Southampton Test (1979) **b.** 21 Dec. 1926 **ed.** Regents Park Sch.; Univ. Coll., Southampton **Profession** served in World War II, BOAC pilot, company dir. **Political interests** Europe, Third World, foreign affairs, aviation, transport, agriculture **Political career** Southampton City Cllr 1966–70, 1976–8; contested Southampton Test 1968; MP for Southampton Test 1970–Oct. 1974; MEP 1973–5 **Other** Chmn House of Commons Flying Club

HINCHLIFFE, David Lab., Wakefield (1987) **b.** 14 Oct. 1948 **ed.** Cathedral Secondary Sch.; Wakefield Technical Coll.; Leeds Poly.; Bradford Univ. **Profession** social worker **Political interests** health and social services, employment **Political career** Wakefield City Cllr 1971–4; Wakefield Metropolitan District Cllr 1979– **Unions** NUPE

HIND, Kenneth Con., Lancashire West (1983) **b.** 15 Sept. 1949 **ed.** Woodhouse Grove Sch., Bradford; Leeds Univ.; Inns of Court **Profession** barrister **Political interests** law and order, defence, home affairs, health and social services, agriculture, horticulture, energy, regional policy; pro small businesses, cyclists

HOEY, Kate Lab., Vauxhall (1989) **b.** 21 June 1946 **ed.** Belfast Royal Academy; Ulster Coll. of Physical Education; City of London Coll. **Profession** lecturer, sports writer **Political interests** civil rights, health and social services, education, transport, sport **Political career** Hackney Borough Cllr 1978–82; contested Dulwich 1983, 1987; Southwark Borough Cllr 1988– ; won Vauxhall in by-election 15 June 1989 **Other** Former Northern Ireland high jump champion

HOGG, Hon. Douglas Con., Grantham (1979) **b.** 5 Feb. 1945 **ed.** Eton; Christ Church, Oxford; Lincoln's Inn **Profession** barrister, journalist **Political interests** agriculture, home affairs, trade and industry; pro reform of Lords **Parliamentary career** Asst Whip 1983–4; Under-Secretary of State at the Home Office 1986–9; Minister of State for Trade and Industry 1989– **Publications include** (jtly) *Contempt of Court*; (jtly) *Bill of Rights*; (jtly) *Law of Privacy* **Other** Son of Lord Hailsham of St Marylebone, former Lord Chancellor

HOGG, Norman Lab., Cumbernauld and Kilsyth (1983) **b.** 12 Mar. 1938 **ed.** Ruthrieston Secondary Sch., Aberdeen; Aberdeen Coll. of Commerce **Profession** local govt officer, union official **Political interests** Scottish affairs, trade and industry, transport, local govt **Political career** MP for Dunbartonshire East 1979–83 **Parliamentary career** Opposition Whip 1982–3; Opposition Deputy Chief Whip 1983–7; Opposition Spokesman on Scottish Affairs 1987– **Unions** NALGO (consultant 1980–)

HOLT, Richard Con., Langbaugh (1983) **b.** 2 Aug. 1931 **ed.** Wembley Co. Grammar Sch.; Hendon and Harrow Technical Colls. **Profession** Royal Navy 1949–54; personnel consultant, betting-shop owner **Political interests** trade and industry, racing industry, furniture industry, licensing laws, water, Alzheimer's Disease; pro-capital and corporal punishment **Political career** Brent Borough Cllr 1963–74; Wycombe District Cllr 1976– (Leader 1978–83); Bucks. Co. Cllr 1981– ; contested Brent South 1974 **Other** consultant to the National Association of Bookmakers 1985–

HOME ROBERTSON, John Lab., East Lothian (1983) **b.** 5 Dec. 1948 **ed.** Ampleforth Coll.; Perugia Univ., Italy; West of Scotland Agricultural Coll. **Profession** farmer **Political interests** Scottish affairs, agriculture, disabled, Palestine; pro-devolution, EC **Political career** Berwickshire District Cllr 1974–8; MP for Berwick and East Lothian 1978–83 **Parliamentary career** Opposition Whip 1983–4; Opposition Spokesman on Agriculture 1984–7, on Scottish Affairs 1987–9, on Agriculture 1989– **Unions** NUPE; sponsored by TSSA

HOOD, Jimmy Lab., Clydesdale (1987) **b.** 11 May 1949 **ed.** Lesmahagow Higher Grade Sch.; Motherwell Technical Coll.; Nottingham Univ. **Profession** miner, NUM official **Political interests** trade and industry, unions, coal, energy, industrial safety, health and social services, environment, local govt, education, home affairs **Political career** Newark and Sherwood District Cllr 1973– ; Notts. Co. Cllr 1973–87 **Unions** NUM

HORDERN, Sir Peter Con., Horsham (1983) **b.** 18 Apr. 1929 **ed.** Geelong Grammar Sch., Australia; Christ Church, Oxford **Profession** stockbroker, company dir., Lloyd's underwriter, journalist **Political interests** finance **Political career** MP for Horsham 1964–74, for Horsham and Crawley 1974–83 **Parliamentary career** Executive of 1922 Cttee 1967– (Joint Secretary 1988–); Chmn Public Accounts Commission 1987– **Other** Knighted 1985

HOWARD, Michael Secretary of State for Employment Con., Folkestone and Hythe (1983) **b.** 7 July 1941 **ed.** Llanelli Grammar Sch.; Peterhouse, Cambridge; Inner Temple **Profession** barrister (QC 1982), Lloyd's underwriter **Political interests** employment, trade union law reform, town and country planning, trade and industry **Political career** contested Liverpool Edge Hill 1966, 1970 **Parliamentary career** Under-Secretary of State for Trade and Industry 1985–7; Minister of State for the Environment (Local Govt 1987–8) (Water and Planning 1988–) 1987–90; Secretary of State for Employment 1990– **Member** Bow Group (Chmn 1970–1)

HOWARTH, Alan Con., Stratford-upon-Avon (1983) **b.** 11 June 1944 **ed.** Rugby Sch.; King's Coll., Cambridge **Profession** research asst to Field-Marshal Montgomery 1965–7, teacher, dir. Conservative Research Dept 1979–81, merchant banker **Political interests** economy, employment, education, arts, heritage, charities, finance **Political career** asst to William Whitelaw and Lord Thorneycroft, Chmn of the Conservative Party, 1974–9; Vice-Chmn Conservative Party 1980–1 **Parliamentary career** Asst Whip 1987–8; Lord Commissioner of the Treasury (Govt Whip) 1988–9; Under-Secretary of State for Education and Science 1989– **Publications include** *Montgomery at Close Quarters*; *The Arts: The Next Move Forward*; *Save Our Schools* **Other** CBE 1982

HOWARTH, George Lab., Knowsley North (1986) **b.** 29 June 1949 **ed.** Huyton; Liverpool Poly.; Salford

Univ. **Profession** engineer, teacher **Political interests** trade and industry, unions, education **Political career** Huyton Borough Cllr 1971– ; Knowsley Borough Cllr 1975–86 (Deputy Leader 1982–3) **Unions** sponsored by AEU

HOWARTH, Gerald Con., Cannock and Burntwood (1983) **b.** 12 Sep. 1947 **ed.** Bloxham Sch., Banbury; Southampton Univ. **Profession** banker, company dir. **Political interests** law and order, economy, defence, aviation, media, education, privatization, industrial relations **Political career** Hounslow Borough Cllr 1982–3

HOWE, Rt Hon. Sir Geoffrey Leader of the House of Commons and Deputy Prime Minister Con., Surrey East (1974) **b.** 20 Dec. 1926 **ed.** Winchester Coll.; Trinity Hall, Cambridge; Middle Temple **Profession** barrister (QC 1965), company dir. **Political interests** trade and industry, economy, law, health and social services, foreign affairs **Political career** contested Aberavon 1955, 1959; MP for Bebington 1964–6, for Reigate 1970–4 **Parliamentary career** Opposition Spokesman on Labour and Social Services 1965–6; Solicitor General 1970–2; PC 1972; Minister for Trade and Consumer Affairs 1972–4; Opposition Spokesman on Social Services 1974–5; contested the Leadership of Conservative Party 1975; Opposition Spokesman on Treasury and Economic Affairs 1975–9; Chancellor of the Exchequer 1979–83; Secretary of State for Foreign and Commonwealth Affairs 1983–9; Lord Pres. of the Council, Leader of the House of Commons and Deputy Prime Minister 1989– **Member** Bow Group (a founding member 1951, Chmn 1955) **Other** Knighted 1970

HOWELL, Rt Hon. David Con., Guildford (1966) **b.** 18 Jan. 1936 **ed.** Eton; King's Coll., Cambridge **Profession** economist, journalist (*Daily Telegraph*), company dir. **Political interests** economy, finance, energy, oil, Ireland, employment, transport, science and technology **Political career** contested Dudley 1964 **Parliamentary career** Lord Commissioner of the Treasury (Govt Whip) 1970–1; Parliamentary Secretary in the Civil Service Dept 1970–2; Under-Secretary of State for Employment 1971–2, for Northern Ireland 1972; Minister of State for Northern Ireland 1972–4, for Energy 1974; Opposition Spokesman on Energy 1974, on Treasury and Economic Affairs 1974–7, on Home Affairs 1977–9; PC 1979; Secretary of State for Energy 1979–81, for Transport 1981–3; Chmn Select Cttee on Foreign Affairs 1987– **Member** Bow Group (Chmn 1962) **Publications include** *The Conservative Opportunity*; *Freedom and Capital*; *Blind Victory: A Study in Income, Wealth and Power*

HOWELL, Rt Hon. Denis Lab., Birmingham Small Heath (1961) **b.** 4 Sept. 1923 **ed.** Handsworth Grammar Sch., Birmingham **Profession** clerk, Football League referee 1956–70, company dir., consultant **Political interests** trade and industry, health and social services, environment, arts, local govt, immigration, sport, EC; anti-Militant, racism **Political career** Birmingham City Cllr 1946–56; contested Kings Norton 1951; MP for Birmingham All Saints 1955–9 **Parliamentary career** Under-Secretary of State for Education and Science (Sport) 1964–9; set up the Sports Council 1965; Minister of State for Housing and Local Govt (Sport) 1969–70; Opposition Spokesman for Local Govt and Sport 1970–4; Minister of State for Environment (Sport, Recreation, Water, PSA) 1974–9; named Minister for Drought 1976; PC 1976; Opposition Spokesman on the Environment 1979–83, on Home Affairs (Sport, Immigration, Broadcasting) 1983–4, on the Environment (Sport) 1984– ; Labour National Executive Cttee 1982–3 **Member** Chmn Lab. Movement for Europe **Unions** sponsored by GMB (APEX partnership) (Pres. 1971–83) **Publications include** *Soccer Referee*; *The Howell Report on Sports Sponsorship*

HOWELL, Ralph Con., Norfolk North (1970) **b.** 25 May 1923 **ed.** Diss Grammar Sch. **Profession** RAF 1941–6; farmer, company dir., Lloyd's underwriter **Political interests** agriculture, defence, foreign affairs, taxation, employment, local govt, health and social services; pro-hanging, South Africa; anti-unions, welfare scroungers **Political career** Mitford and Launditch District Cllr 1961; MEP 1974–9 **Parliamentary career** Executive of 1922 Cttee 1984– **Publications include** *Why Work?*

HOWELLS, Geraint Lib. Dem. (Lib. 1974–88), Ceredigion and Pembroke North (1983) **b.** 15 Apr. 1925 **ed.** Ardwyn Grammar Sch., Aberystwyth **Profession** hill farmer, company dir. **Political interests** agriculture, Welsh language and culture, wool, Third World; pro-devolution, small businesses **Political career** Cardiganshire Co. Cllr 1952–73; contested Brecon and Radnor 1970; MP for Cardigan 1974–83 **Parliamentary career** Leader Welsh Liberal Party 1979–88; Lib. Spokesman on Wales 1974–88, on Agriculture 1976–88, on Small Businesses 1979–88; Lib. Dem. Spokesman on Welsh Affairs 1988– **Member** Wool Producers of Wales Ltd (Chmn 1977–); British Wool Marketing Board (Vice-Chmn 1971–83) **Other** A champion sheep-shearer

HOWELLS, Kim Lab., Pontypridd (1989) **b.** 27 Nov. 1947 **ed.** Mountain Ash Grammar Sch.; Hornsey Coll. of Art; Cambridge Coll. of Advanced Technology; Warwick Univ. **Profession** lecturer, NUM research officer, journalist, broadcaster **Political interests** environment, energy, transport, art, EC **Political career** won seat in by-election 23 Feb. 1989 **Unions** NUM

HOYLE, Doug Lab., Warrington North (1983) **b.** 17 Feb. 1930 **ed.** Adlington Sch.; Horwich Technical Coll.; Bolton Technical Coll. **Profession** sales engineer **Political interests** trade and industry, unions, employment, health and social services, immigration, youth, arts, foreign affairs; anti-EC **Political career** contested Clitheroe 1964, Nelson and Colne 1970 and Feb. 1974; MP for Nelson and Colne Oct. 1974–9, for Warrington 1981–3 **Parliamentary career** Labour National Executive Cttee 1978–82, 1983–5 **Unions** sponsored by MSF (Pres. 1977–81, 1985–) **Other** JP 1958

HUGHES, John Lab., Coventry North East (1987) **b.** 29 May 1925 **ed.** Durham secondary sch. **Profession** served with Fleet Air Arm in Pacific 1943–6, miner, warehouseman **Political interests** trade and industry, mining **Political career** Coventry City Cllr 1974–82 **Unions** sponsored by TGWU

HUGHES, Robert Lab., Aberdeen North (1970) **b.** 3 Jan. 1932 **ed.** Benoni High Sch., Transvaal; Pietermaritzburg Technical Coll., Natal **Profession** engineering draughtsman **Political interests** African affairs, overseas development, agriculture, fishing industry, transport, health and social services; anti-apartheid **Political career** contested Angus North and

Mearns 1959; Aberdeen Town Cllr 1962–70 **Parliamentary career** Opposition Spokesman on Scottish Affairs 1973–4; Under-Secretary of State at the Scottish Office 1974–5; Opposition Spokesman on Transport 1981–3, on Agriculture, Fisheries and Food 1983–4, on Transport 1984–8 **Member** Anti-Apartheid (Chmn 1977); CND (a founding member 1958, Chmn 1976–); Tribune Group (Vice-Chmn 1984–5) **Unions** sponsored by AEU

HUGHES, Robert Con., Harrow West (1987) **b.** 14 July 1951 **ed.** Spring Grove Grammar Sch., Hounslow; Harrow Coll. of Technology and Art **Profession** BBC TV news picture editor **Political interests** Middle East, housing, inner cities, London **Political career** Hounslow Borough Cllr 1974–8; National Chmn Young Conservatives 1979–80; Greater London Cllr 1980–6; contested Stepney and Poplar 1979, Bermondsey 1983 **Unions** NUJ

HUGHES, Roy Lab., Newport East (1983) **b.** 9 June 1925 **ed.** Pontllanfraith Grammar Sch.; Ruskin Coll., Oxford **Profession** miner, motor company executive **Political interests** steel, coal, motor industry, transport, sport, foreign affairs; anti-EC, Zionism; pro-nuclear disarmament **Political career** Coventry City Cllr 1962–6; MP for Newport 1966–83 **Parliamentary career** Speaker's Panel of Chairmen 1982–4; Opposition Spokesman on Welsh Affairs 1984–8 **Member** CND **Unions** sponsored by TGWU

HUGHES, Simon Lib. Dem. (Lib. 1983–8), Southwark and Bermondsey (1983) **b.** 17 May 1951 **ed.** Llandaff Cathedral Sch., Cardiff; Christ Coll., Brecon; Selwyn Coll., Cambridge; Inns of Court; Coll. of Europe, Bruges **Profession** barrister **Political interests** human rights, civil liberties, youth, law, housing, environment, health and social services, inner cities, EC, devolution, Ireland, South Africa **Political career** MP for Bermondsey Southwark Feb.– June 1983, winning the previously safe Labour seat with a record swing of 44% **Parliamentary career** Lib. Spokesman on the Environment 1983–8; All. Spokesman on Health 1987; Lib. Dem. Spokesman on the Environment 1988– **Member** Amnesty International; Liberty **Publications include** (jtly) *Human Rights in Western Europe – The Next Thirty Years*; *Across the Divide – Liberal Values for Defence and Disarmament*; *The Prosecutorial Process in England and Wales*

HUME, John SDLP, Foyle (1983) **b.** 18 Jan. 1937 **ed.** St Columb's Coll., Derry; St Patrick's Coll., Maynooth **Profession** lecturer **Political interests** EC, Northern Ireland, Third World, nuclear disarmament, poverty, credit management; pro-Anglo-Irish agreement **Political career** Northern Ireland Parliament 1969–73; Northern Ireland Assembly 1973–5; Northern Ireland Constitutional Convention 1975–6; MEP for Northern Ireland 1979– ; contested Londonderry 1974; founder member and Deputy Leader of the SDLP 1970–9, Leader 1979–

HUNT, David Secretary of State for Wales Con., Wirral West (1983) **b.** 21 May 1942 **ed.** Liverpool Coll.; Montpellier Univ., France; Bristol Univ.; Coll. of Law, Guildford **Profession** solicitor, company dir., Lloyd's underwriter **Political interests** law, finance, energy, youth, EC **Political career** National Chmn Young Conservatives 1972–3; contested Bristol South 1970, Kingswood 1974; MP for Wirral 1976–83 **Parliamentary career** Asst Whip 1981–3; Lord Commissioner of the Treasury (Govt Whip) 1983–4; Vice-Chmn Conservative Party 1983–4; Under-Secretary of State for Energy 1984–7; Treasurer of the Household (Deputy Chief Whip) 1987–9; Minister of State for the Environment 1989–90; Secretary of State for Wales 1990– **Publications include** *Europe Right Ahead*; *A Time for Youth* **Other** MBE 1973

HUNT, John Con., Ravensbourne (1974) **b.** 27 Oct. 1929 **ed.** Dulwich Coll. **Profession** stockbroker, public-relations consultant **Political interests** environment, race relations, education, foreign affairs; pro-EC, hanging; anti-racism **Political career** Bromley Borough Cllr 1953–65 (Alderman 1961–5, Mayor 1963–4); contested Lewisham South 1959; MP for Bromley 1964–74 **Parliamentary career** Speaker's Panel of Chairmen 1980–

HUNTER, Andrew Con., Basingstoke (1983) **b.** 8 Jan. 1943 **ed.** St George's Sch., Harpenden; Durham Univ.; Jesus Coll., Cambridge **Profession** classics teacher **Political interests** education, agriculture, conservation, environment, health and social services, defence, foreign affairs; anti-racism; pro small farmers, Green Belt, sport with South Africa, hanging **Political career** contested Southampton Itchen 1979 **Member** National Prayer Book Society (Vice-Pres. 1987–); British Field Sports Society (Chmn Falconry Cttee 1988–); NFU

HURD, Rt Hon. Douglas Foreign Secretary Con., Witney (1983) **b.** 8 Mar. 1930 **ed.** Eton; Trinity Coll., Cambridge **Profession** HM Foreign Service 1952–66, Conservative Research Dept 1966–8, author **Political interests** foreign affairs, EC, home affairs, police, broadcasting policy **Political career** secretary to Edward Heath 1968–74; MP for Oxfordshire Mid 1974–83 **Parliamentary career** Opposition Spokesman on Europe 1976–9; Minister of State at the Foreign and Commonwealth Office 1979–83, at the Home Office 1983–4; PC 1982; Secretary of State for Northern Ireland 1984–5; Home Secretary 1985–9; Foreign Secretary 1989– **Publications include** *End to Promises*; *Vote to Kill*; *Truth Game*; *Scotch on the Rocks* **Other** Son of Lord (Anthony) Hurd, MP for Newbury 1945–64, and grandson of Sir Percy Hurd, MP for Devizes 1924–45; CBE 1974

ILLSLEY, Eric Lab., Barnsley Central (1987) **b.** 9 Apr. 1955 **ed.** Barnsley Holgate Grammar Sch.; Barnsley Coll. of Technology; Leeds Univ. **Profession** NUM official **Political interests** unions, mining, energy, health and social services, law **Unions** sponsored by NUM

INGRAM, Adam Lab., East Kilbride (1987) **b.** 1 Feb. 1947 **ed.** Cranhill Senior Secondary Sch.; Open Univ. **Profession** computer programmer, NALGO official **Political interests** local govt, unions, industrial relations, energy, prisons, arts **Political career** East Kilbride District Cllr 1980–7 (Leader 1984–7); contested Strathkelvin and Bearsden 1983 **Parliamentary career** PPS to Neil Kinnock, Leader of the Labour Party, 1988– ; Opposition Whip 1988– **Member** Tribune Group **Unions** sponsored by TGWU **Other** JP 1980

IRVINE, Michael Con., Ipswich (1987) **b.** 21 Oct. 1939 **ed.** Rugby; Oriel Coll., Oxford **Profession** barrister **Political interests** law **Political career** contested Bishop Auckland 1979 **Other** Son of Rt Hon. Sir Arthur Irvine QC, Lab. MP for Liverpool Edge Hill 1947–78

IRVING, Sir Charles Con., Cheltenham (1974) **b.** 4 May 1923 **ed.** Cheltenham Grammar Sch.; Lucton

Sch., Herefordshire **Profession** company dir. (hotels, public relations) **Political interests** mental health, prisons, drug abuse, the homeless, health and social services, housing, environment, animal welfare; anti-hanging, EC; a defender of victims of violence and non-violent criminals **Political career** Cheltenham Borough and District Cllr 1947–74 (Alderman 1959–67; Deputy Mayor 1959–63, 1972–3; Mayor 1958–60, 1971–2); Glos. Co. Cllr 1948–74 (Alderman 1965–74); contested Staffordshire Bilston 1970, Kingswood 1974 **Parliamentary career** Chmn All-Party Mental Health Cttee 1979– ; Chmn House of Commons Catering Cttee 1979– **Member** National Council for the Care and Resettlement of Offenders (Vice-Chmn); National Victims Assn (founder and Chmn); National Victim Support Scheme (Pres.) **Unions** NUJ **Other** Knighted 1990

JACK, Michael Con., Fylde (1987) **b.** 17 Sep. 1946 **ed.** Bradford Grammar Sch.; Bradford Technical Coll.; Leicester Univ. **Profession** sales dir. **Political interests** health and social services, transport, nuclear industry, horticulture, North of England **Political career** National Vice-Chmn Young Conservatives 1975–6, Chmn 1976–7; contested Newcastle-upon-Tyne Central 1974

JACKSON, Robert Con., Wantage (1983) **b.** 24 Sep. 1946 **ed.** Falcon Coll., Rhodesia; St Edmund Hall, Oxford **Profession** consultant, writer, editor (*International Affairs*; *The Round Table: The Commonwealth Journal of International Affairs*), Fellow of All Soul's Coll., Oxford 1968–86 **Political interests** EC, foreign affairs, agriculture, science **Political career** Oxford City Cllr 1969–71; contested Manchester Central 1974; adviser to Sir Christopher (Lord) Soames 1974–6 and to Lord Soames, Governor of Rhodesia, 1980; MEP for Upper Thames 1979–84 **Parliamentary career** Under-Secretary of State for Education and Science 1987–90, for Employment 1990– **Publications include** *The Powers of the European Parliament*; *Reforming the European Budget*; *Tradition and Reality: Conservative Philosophy and European Integration* **Other** Husband of Caroline Jackson, MEP for Wiltshire

JANMAN, Timothy Con., Thurrock (1987) **b.** 9 Sept. 1956 **ed.** Sir William Borlase Grammar Sch., Marlow; Nottingham Univ. **Profession** marketing representative **Political interests** economy, education, law and order, union reform, immigration, privatization, foreign affairs; anti-abortion **Political career** Southampton City Cllr 1987

JANNER, Hon. Greville Lab., Leicester West (1974) **b.** 11 July 1928 **ed.** St Paul's Sch.; Trinity Hall, Cambridge; Harvard Law Sch. **Profession** barrister (QC 1971), writer **Political interests** foreign affairs, Jewish affairs, human rights, Commonwealth, India, Middle East, law, employment law, industrial relations, consumer rights, media, education **Political career** contested Wimbledon 1955; MP for Leicester North West 1970–4 **Parliamentary career** Vice-Chmn All-Party Cttee for Release of Soviet Jewry 1971– ; Chmn All-Party Industrial Safety Group 1975– **Member** Executive of World Jewish Congress 1986– ; Commonwealth Jewish Council (Pres. 1983–); Magic Circle **Unions** NUJ; NUM **Publications include** *Race and Equality and Equal Pay*; *Compendium of Health and Safety Law*; *Complete Speechmaker* (over 60 books on industrial relations, law, employment, public speaking) **Other** Son of Sir Barnett (Lord) Janner, MP for Leicester North West 1950–70, and father of Daniel Janner, who contested Bosworth 1983

JESSEL, Toby Con., Twickenham (1970) **b.** 11 July 1934 **ed.** Royal Naval Coll., Dartmouth; Balliol Coll., Oxford **Profession** company dir. **Political interests** environment, arts, immigration; anti-EC, Heathrow expansion **Political career** Southwark Borough Cllr 1964–5; Greater London Cllr 1967–73; contested Peckham 1964, Hull North 1966

JOHNSON SMITH, Sir Geoffrey Con., Wealden (1983) **b.** 16 Apr. 1924 **ed.** Charterhouse; Lincoln Coll., Oxford **Profession** Royal Artillery 1942–7, broadcaster, company dir. **Political interests** defence, media, agriculture, environment, energy, education **Political career** member of the Labour Party 1942–50; London Co. Cllr 1955–8; MP for Holborn and St Pancras South 1959–64, for East Grinstead 1965–83 **Parliamentary career** Opposition Whip 1965; Vice-Chmn Conservative Party 1965–71; Under-Secretary of State for Defence (Army) 1971–2; Parliamentary Secretary to the Civil Service Dept 1972–4; Executive of 1922 Cttee 1979– ; Chmn House of Commons Select Cttee on Members' Interests 1980– ; Leader of UK Delegation to North Atlantic Assembly 1987– **Other** Knighted 1982; DL East Sussex 1986

JOHNSTON, Sir Russell Lib. Dem. (Lib. 1964–88), Inverness, Nairn and Lochaber (1983) **b.** 28 July 1932 **ed.** Portree Secondary Sch., Skye; Edinburgh Univ.; Moray House Coll. of Education **Profession** history teacher **Political interests** foreign affairs, Commonwealth, Scottish affairs, energy, transport, the blind, human rights; pro-devolution, EC, SDP-Lib. merger **Political career** research asst with Liberal Party 1963; MEP 1973–5, 1976–9; MP for Inverness 1964–83 **Parliamentary career** Lib. Spokesman on Scotland 1964–87, on Foreign and Commonwealth Affairs 1970–5, 1979–85, 1987–8, on EC 1986–8; All. Spokesman on Scotland and EC 1987; Lib. Dem. Spokesman on Foreign and Commonwealth Affairs 1988– ; Leader of Scottish Liberal Party 1974–88; Pres. Scottish Liberal Democrats and Deputy Leader of Liberal Democrats 1988– **Other** Knighted 1985

JONES, Barry Shadow Welsh Secretary Lab., Alyn and Deeside (1983) **b.** 26 June 1938 **ed.** Hawarden Grammar Sch.; Bangor Coll. of Education **Profession** English teacher, NUT official **Political interests** Welsh affairs, education, unemployment, regional policy **Political career** contested Northwich 1966; MP for Flint East 1970–83 **Parliamentary career** Under-Secretary of State for Wales 1974–9; Opposition Spokesman on Employment 1980–3; Shadow Welsh Secretary 1983– **Unions** sponsored by TGWU; adviser to NUT 1970–

JONES, Gwilym Con., Cardiff North (1983) **b.** 1947 **ed.** Caerphilly Grammar-Technical Sch.; Cardiff Coll. of Commerce **Profession** insurance broker **Political interests** Welsh affairs, local govt, transport **Political career** Cardiff City Cllr 1969–72, 1973–83 **Member** FRAME

JONES, Ieuan Pl.C., Ynys Mon/Anglesey (1987) **b.** 22 May 1949 **ed.** Bala Comprehensive Sch., Meirionnydd; Liverpool Poly.; London Univ. **Profession** solicitor **Political interests** Welsh affairs, home affairs, law, employment, agriculture, transport, education, industry, the elderly **Political career** contested Denbigh West 1974 and 1979, Ynys Mon 1983; Vice-Chmn Plaid Cymru 1975–9, Chmn 1980–2 **Other** He speaks Welsh

JONES, Martyn Lab., Clwyd South West (1987) **b.** 1 Mar. 1947 **ed.** Grove Park Grammar Sch.,

Wrexham; Liverpool Coll. of Commerce; Liverpool Poly.; Trent Poly. **Profession** microbiologist **Political interests** science, agriculture, ecology, brewing industry, local govt **Political career** Clwyd Co. Cllr 1981– **Parliamentary career** Opposition Whip 1988– **Unions** TGWU

JONES, Robert Con., Hertfordshire West (1983) **b.** 26 Sept. 1950 **ed.** Merchant Taylors' Sch.; St Andrews Univ. **Profession** consultant, writer **Political interests** trade and industry, small businesses, new technology, housing, construction, planning, transport, environment; pro-monetarism, privatization, hanging; anti-racism **Political career** St Andrews Burgh Cllr 1972–5; Fife Co. Cllr 1973–5; Chiltern District Cllr 1979–83; contested Kirkaldy 1974, Stockton-upon-Tees 1979 **Publications include** *Economy and Local Government*; *Roads and the Private Sector*; *Town and Country Chaos: Critique of the Planning System*

JOPLING, Rt Hon. Michael Con., Westmorland and Lonsdale (1983) **b.** 10 Dec. 1930 **ed.** Cheltenham Coll.; King's Coll., Newcastle-upon-Tyne; Durham Univ. **Profession** farmer, Lloyd's underwriter, company dir. **Political interests** agriculture, fishing, food, trade and industry, science, technology **Political career** Thirsk Rural District Cllr 1958–64; contested Wakefield 1959; MP for Westmorland 1964–83 **Parliamentary career** Asst Whip 1971–3; Lord Commissioner of the Treasury (Govt Whip) 1973–4; Oppposition Whip 1974; Opposition Spokesman on Agriculture 1974–9; PC 1979; Parliamentary Secretary to the Treasury and Chief Whip 1979–83; Minister of Agriculture, Fisheries and Food 1983–7 **Member** NFU

KAUFMAN, Rt Hon. Gerald Shadow Foreign Secretary Lab., Manchester Gorton (1983) **b.** 21 June 1930 **ed.** Leeds Grammar Sch.; Queen's Coll., Oxford **Profession** journalist (*Daily Mirror* 1955–64, *New Statesman* 1964–5) **Political interests** foreign affairs, home affairs, environment, trade and industry, media, immigration and race relations **Political career** contested Bromley 1955, Gillingham 1959; MP for Manchester Ardwick 1970–83 **Parliamentary career** Under-Secretary of State for the Environment 1974–5, for Industry 1975; Minister of State for Industry 1975–9; PC 1978; Opposition Spokesman on the Environment 1979–83; Shadow Home Secretary 1983–7; Shadow Foreign Secretary 1987– **Member** Fabian Society **Unions** sponsored by GMB **Publications include** *How to be a Minister*; *Renewal: Labour's Britain in the 1980s*; *Inside the Promised Land*

KELLETT-BOWMAN, Dame Elaine Con., Lancaster (1970) **b.** 8 July 1924 **ed.** The Mount Sch., York; St Anne's Coll., Oxford; Barnet House, Oxford **Profession** social worker, barrister, farmer **Political interests** health and social security, disabled, elderly, local govt, agriculture, taxation; anti-abortion, pro-hanging **Political career** Denbigh Borough Cllr 1951; Camden Borough Alderman 1968–74; contested Nelson and Colne 1955, Norfolk South West 1959, Buckingham 1964, 1966; MEP 1975–9, MEP for Cumbria 1979–84 **Other** Wife of Edward Bowman, MEP for Lancashire East 1979–84; DBE 1988

KENNEDY, Charles Lib. Dem. (SDP 1983–8), Ross, Cromarty and Skye (1983) **b.** 25 Nov. 1959 **ed.** Lochaber High Sch., Fort William; Glasgow Univ.; Indiana Univ., US **Profession** teacher, broadcaster (BBC Highlands 1982–) **Political interests** Scottish affairs, health and social security, broadcasting, foreign affairs; anti-hanging **Parliamentary career** All. Spokesman on Social Security 1987; SDP Spokesman on Scotland and Social Security 1987–8; Lib. Dem. Spokesman on Trade and Industry 1988– ; Lib. Dem. Pres. 1990–

KEY, Robert Con., Salisbury (1983) **b.** 22 Apr. 1945 **ed.** Sherborne Sch.; Clare Coll., Cambridge **Profession** teacher, consultant **Political interests** foreign affairs, defence, environment, agriculture, education, arts, broadcasting, AIDS; pro-EC **Political career** contested Holborn and St Pancras South 1979 **Member** ALICE Trust for Autistic Children (founder and Chmn 1977–) **Unions** MSF **Other** A tenor with the chorus of the Academy of St Martin-in-the-Fields 1975–

KILFEDDER, James UPUP (UU 1970–9), Down North (1970) **b.** 16 July 1928 **ed.** Portora Royal Sch., Enniskillen; Trinity Coll., Dublin; King's Inn, Dublin **Profession** barrister **Political interests** foreign affairs, nuclear disarmament, human rights, housing, employment, law; pro-devolution **Political career** Northern Ireland Assembly 1973–4, 1982–6; Northern Ireland Convention 1975–6; MP for Belfast West 1964–6 **Parliamentary career** UU Chief Whip 1970–4; Founder and Leader of Ulster Popular Unionist Party 1980– ; resigned seat Dec. 1985 in protest against Anglo-Irish agreement and was re-elected Jan. 1986

KING, Roger Con., Birmingham Northfield (1983) **b.** 26 Oct. 1943 **ed.** Solihull Sch. **Profession** automobile engineer, motor accessory dealer **Political interests** transport, motor industry, trade and industry, defence; pro-hanging **Political career** contested Cannock 1974 **Member** Institute of the Motor Industry **Other** Winner of the Lords and Commons Brands Hatch Charity Motor Race 1985, 1986

KING, Rt Hon. Tom Secretary of State for Defence Con., Bridgwater (1970) **b.** 13 June 1933 **ed.** Rugby Sch.; Emmanuel Coll., Cambridge **Profession** farmer, company dir. **Political interests** employment, transport, environment, local govt, energy, Northern Ireland, defence **Parliamentary career** Opposition Spokesman on Industry 1975–6, on Energy 1976–9; PC 1979; Minister of State for Environment (Local Govt and Environmental Services) 1979–83; Secretary of State for Environment 1983, for Transport 1983, for Employment 1983–5, for Northern Ireland 1985–9, for Defence 1989–

KINNOCK, Rt Hon. Neil Leader of the Labour Party and Leader of the Opposition Lab., Islwyn (1983) **b.** 28 Mar. 1942 **ed.** Lewis Sch., Pengam; Univ. of Wales Coll., Cardiff **Profession** adult education teacher, Labour Research Dept 1974–9, journalist (*Tribune*, *Guardian*, *New Statesman*) **Political interests** education, employment, health and social services, race relations, nuclear disarmament **Political career** MP for Bedwellty 1970–83 **Parliamentary career** PPS to Michael Foot 1974–5; Labour National Executive Cttee 1978– ; Shadow Cabinet 1979– ; Opposition Spokesman on Education 1979–83; Leader of the Labour Party and Leader of the Opposition 1983– ; PC 1983 **Member** Socialist Education Association; Anti-Apartheid; CND **Unions** sponsored by TGWU **Publications include** *Why Vote Labour?*; *Wales and the Common Market*; *Making Our Way*

KIRKHOPE, Timothy Con., Leeds North East (1987) **b.** 29 Apr. 1945 **ed.** Newcastle Royal Grammar Sch.; Coll. of Law, Guildford **Profession** solicitor, company dir. **Political interests** defence, foreign affairs, eastern Europe, housing, health and social services, law, broadcasting, aviation **Political career** Northumberland Co. Cllr 1981–5; contested Durham 1974, Darlington 1979; successor to Sir Keith Joseph as MP for Leeds North East **Parliamentary career** Govt Whip 1990–

KIRKWOOD, Archy Lib. Dem. (Lib. 1983–8), Roxburgh and Berwickshire (1983) **b.** 22 Apr. 1946 **ed.** Cranhill Sch.; Heriot-Watt Univ. **Profession** solicitor **Political interests** health and social services, human rights, law, freedom of information, Scottish affairs **Political career** asst to David Steel 1971–5, 1977–8 **Parliamentary career** Lib. Spokesman on Health and Social Services 1985–7, on Scotland 1987–8; All. Spokesman on Overseas Development 1987; Lib. Dem. Convenor on Welfare, Health and Education 1988–

KNAPMAN, Roger Con., Stroud (1987) **b.** 20 Feb. 1944 **ed.** All Hallows Sch., Lyme Regis; Royal Agricultural Coll., Cirencester **Profession** surveyor, farmer, Lloyd's underwriter **Political interests** agriculture, small businesses, insurance, environment, foreign affairs

KNIGHT, Gregory Con., Derby North (1983) **b.** 4 Apr. 1949 **ed.** Alderman Newton's Grammar Sch., Leicester; Coll. of Law, Guildford **Profession** solicitor, music studio proprietor, company dir. **Political interests** consumer law, licensing laws, animal welfare, music, arts, home affairs **Political career** Leicester City Cllr 1976–9; Leics. Co. Cllr 1977–83 **Parliamentary career** Asst Whip 1989– **Publications include** (jtly) *Westminster Words*

KNIGHT, Dame Jill Con., Birmingham Edgbaston (1966) **b.** 9 July 1923 **ed.** King Edward Grammar Sch., Birmingham **Profession** lecturer, journalist **Political interests** health and social services, child care, trade and industry; anti-abortion, immigration, welfare scroungers; pro-hanging **Political career** Northampton Co. Borough Cllr 1956–66; contested Northampton 1959, 1964 **Parliamentary career** Chmn Lords and Commons All-Party Family and Child Protection Group 1975– ; Executive of 1922 Cttee 1979– (Secretary 1983–7, Vice-Chmn 1987–) **Member** Lifeline (pregnancy counselling) (Chmn 1974–84) **Other** MBE 1964, DBE 1985

KNOWLES, Michael Con., Nottingham East (1983) **b.** 21 May 1942 **ed.** Clapham Coll. **Profession** sales manager, export executive **Political interests** EC, Third World, housing, trade and industry, inner cities, local govt; pro-hanging **Political career** Kingston upon Thames Borough Cllr 1971–83 (Leader 1974–83); contested Merthyr Tydfil Feb. 1974, Brent East Oct. 1974

KNOX, David Con., Staffordshire Moorlands (1983) **b.** 30 May 1933 **ed.** Lockerbie Academy; Dumfries Academy; London Univ. **Profession** economist, management consultant **Political interests** economy, human rights, world govt; pro-EC, proportional representation, devolution **Political career** contested Birmingham Stechford 1964 and 1966, Nuneaton 1967; MP for Leek 1970–83 **Parliamentary career** Vice-Chmn Conservative Party 1974–5; Speaker's Panel of Chairmen 1983–

LAMBIE, David Lab., Cunninghame South (1983) **b.** 13 July 1925 **ed.** Ardrossan Academy; Glasgow Univ.; Geneva Univ.; Jordanhill Coll. of Education **Profession** geography teacher **Political interests** Scottish affairs, trade and industry, chemicals, aircraft, shipbuilding, steel, energy, health and social services, pensions, housing, education, local govt; anti-EC, pro-devolution **Political career** contested Ayrshire North and Bute 1958, 1959, 1964, 1966; Chmn Scottish Labour Party 1964; MP for Ayrshire Central 1970–83 **Parliamentary career** Chmn Scottish Affairs Select Committee 1981–7 **Member** CND **Unions** sponsored by USDAW

LAMOND, James Lab., Oldham Central and Royton (1983) **b.** 29 Nov. 1928 **ed.** Coupar Angus Sch., Perthshire **Profession** engineering draughtsman **Political interests** nuclear disarmament, foreign affairs, United Nations, unions; anti-devolution **Political career** Aberdeen Town Cllr 1959–71 (Lord Provost and Lord Lieutenant 1970–1); MP for Oldham East 1970–83 **Parliamentary career** Speaker's Panel of Chairmen 1979– **Member** Campaign Group; World Peace Council (Vice-Pres. 1975–) **Unions** sponsored by AEU **Other** JP

LAMONT, Rt Hon. Norman Chief Secretary to the Treasury Con., Kingston-upon-Thames (1972) **b.** 8 May 1942 **ed.** Loretto Sch.; Fitzwilliam House, Cambridge **Profession** Conservative Research Dept 1966–8, merchant banker, journalist **Political interests** economy, finance, consumer affairs, trade and industry, energy, health and social services, foreign affairs **Political career** contested Hull East 1970 **Parliamentary career** Opposition Spokesman on Prices and Consumer Affairs 1975–6, on Industry 1976–9; Under-Secretary of State for Energy 1979–81; Minister of State for Trade and Industry 1981–5, for Defence (Procurement) 1985–6; PC 1986; Financial Secretary to the Treasury 1986–9; Chief Secretary to the Treasury 1989– **Member** Bow Group (Chmn 1971–2)

LANG, Ian Con., Galloway and Upper Nithsdale (1983) **b.** 27 June 1940 **ed.** Rugby Sch.; Sidney Sussex Coll., Cambridge **Profession** company dir., Lloyd's underwriter **Political interests** Scottish affairs, employment **Political career** contested Ayrshire Central 1970, Glasgow Pollok 1974; MP for Galloway 1979–83 **Parliamentary career** Asst Whip 1981–3; Lord Commissioner of the Treasury (Govt Whip) 1983–6; Vice-Chmn Scottish Conservative Party 1983–7; Under-Secretary of State for Employment 1986, at the Scottish Office 1986–7; Minister of State at the Scottish Office 1987– **Publications include** (jtly) *The Scottish Conservatives: A Past and Future*

LATHAM, Michael Con., Rutland and Melton (1983) **b.** 20 Nov. 1942 **ed.** Marlborough Coll; King's Coll., Cambridge; New Coll., Oxford **Profession** Conservative Research Dept 1965–7, builder, company dir. **Political interests** building and housing, environment, energy, local govt, agriculture, foreign affairs, Israel, Middle East, Gibraltar; anti-EC **Political career** Westminster City Cllr 1968–71; contested Liverpool West Derby 1970; MP for Melton 1974–83 **Member** House Builders' Federation (dir. 1971–3); Building Societies Assn (Vice-Pres. 1981–)

LAWRENCE, Ivan Con., Burton (1974) **b.** 24 Dec. 1936 **ed.** Brighton, Hove and Sussex Grammar Sch.; Christ Church, Oxford; Inner Temple **Profession** barrister (QC 1981) **Political interests** foreign affairs, human rights, civil liberties, law, police, prison, race relations, brewing industry; pro-hanging, Israel; anti-fluoride **Political career** contested Peckham 1966, 1970 **Member** Bow Group **Publications include** *The Conviction of the Guilty*; *Towards a New Nationality*; *Financing Strikes*

LAWSON, Rt Hon. Nigel Con., Blaby (1974) **b.** 11 Mar. 1932 **ed.** Westminster; Christ Church, Oxford **Profession** journalist (*Financial Times* 1956–60, *Sunday Telegraph* 1961–3, *Spectator* 1966–70), company dir. **Political interests** economy, finance, energy **Political career** asst and speech writer to the Prime Minister, Sir Alec Douglas-Home, 1963–4; contested Eton and Slough 1970; adviser Conservative Party Headquarters 1973–4 (wrote the 1974 Manifesto) **Parliamentary career** Opposition Whip 1976–7; Opposition Spokesman on Treasury and Economic Affairs 1977–9; Financial Secretary to the Treasury 1979–81; PC 1981; Secretary of State for Energy 1981–3; Chancellor of the Exchequer 1983–9; resigned from the Cabinet 26 Oct. 1989 because he felt that he did not have the Prime Minister's support for his pro-EMS stance **Publications include** *The Power Game*; (jtly) *Britain and Canada*; (jtly) *The Coming Confrontation*

LEADBITTER, Ted Lab., Hartlepool (1964) **b.** 18 June 1919 **ed.** Easington Colliery Sch.; Cheltenham Teacher Training Coll. **Profession** gunnery instructor with Royal Artillery in World War II; teacher **Political interests** energy, transport, ports, regional policy, housing, town planning, education, health and social services, women's rights, finance **Political career** West Hartlepool Borough Cllr 1954–67 **Parliamentary career** Speaker's Panel of Chairmen 1979– **Unions** sponsored by NUPE **Other** Pres. Hartlepool Football Club 1983–

LEE, John Con., Pendle (1983) **b.** 21 June 1942 **ed.** William Hulme's Grammar Sch., Manchester **Profession** accountant, stockbroker, company dir. **Political interests** small businesses, employment, defence **Political career** contested Manchester Moss Side 1974; MP for Nelson and Colne 1979–83 **Parliamentary career** Under-Secretary of State for Defence (Procurement) 1983–6, for Employment 1986–9

LEIGH, Edward Con., Gainsborough and Horncastle (1983) **b.** 20 July 1950 **ed.** Oratory Sch., Berks.; The Lycée, London; Durham Univ.; Inner Temple **Profession** Conservative Research Dept 1973–5, barrister **Political interests** defence, civil defence, foreign affairs, agriculture, energy; pro-hanging, anti-CND **Political career** contested Middlesbrough 1974; Richmond Borough Cllr 1974–8, Greater London Cllr 1977–81; correspondence secretary to Margaret Thatcher, Leader of the Opposition, 1976–7 **Member** National Council for Civil Defence (Chairman 1980–2); Coalition for Peace through Security (dir. 1981–3) **Publications include** *Right Thinking*

LEIGHTON, Ron Lab., Newham North East (1979) **b.** 24 Jan. 1930 **ed.** Bifrons Sch., Barking; Ruskin Coll., Oxford **Profession** printer, shop steward **Political interests** employment, industrial relations, trade and industry, printing industry, economy, nuclear disarmament, countryside; pro-nuclear disarmament, anti-EC **Political career** contested Middleton and Prestwich 1964, Horsham and Crawley 1974 **Parliamentary career** Dir. All-Party Common Market Safeguards Campaign 1970–3; organizer of National Referendum Campaign which opposed entry into Common Market 1975; Opposition Whip 1981–4; Chmn Select Cttee on Employment 1984– **Member** CND; Tribune Group **Unions** sponsored by SOGAT '82 **Publications include** *The Labour Case against Entry to the Common Market*; *What Labour Should Do about the Common Market*

LENNOX-BOYD, Hon. Mark Con., Morecambe and Lunesdale (1983) **b.** 4 May 1943 **ed.** Eton; Christ Church, Oxford; Middle East Centre for Arabic Studies, Lebanon; Inner Temple **Profession** barrister, company dir. **Political interests** energy, finance, Middle East **Political career** contested Brent South 1974; MP for Morecambe and Lonsdale 1979–83 **Parliamentary career** Asst Whip 1984–6; Lord Commissioner to the Treasury (Govt Whip) 1986–8; PPS to the Prime Minister, Margaret Thatcher, 1988–90; Under-Secretary of State at the Foreign Office 1990– **Other** Son of Rt Hon. Viscount Boyd of Merton (Alan Lennox-Boyd), MP for Mid Bedfordshire 1931–60, and Lady Patricia Guinness

LESTER, Jim Con., Broxtowe (1983) **b.** 23 May 1932 **ed.** Nottingham High Sch. **Profession** company dir., consultant **Political interests** employment, local govt, overseas development, Third World; pro-EC **Political career** Notts. Co. Cllr 1967–74; contested Bassetlaw 1968, 1970; MP for Beeston 1974–83 **Parliamentary career** Opposition Whip 1975–9; Under-Secretary of State for Employment 1979–81 **Member** CARE (Conservative Action to Revive Employment) (founder and Chmn 1985–); British Refugee Council (Chmn Africa Committee); Save the Children Fund (Overseas Advisory Cttee)

LESTOR, Joan Lab., Eccles (1987) **b.** 13 Nov. 1931 **ed.** William Morris Secondary Sch., Walthamstow; London Univ. **Profession** nursery school teacher **Political interests** education, employment, race relations, women's and children's rights, homosexual rights, foreign affairs, Third World, nuclear disarmament **Political career** Wandsworth Borough Cllr 1958–68; London Co. Cllr 1962–4; contested Lewisham West 1964; MP for Eton and Slough 1966–83 **Parliamentary career** Labour National Executive Cttee 1967–82, 1987– ; Under-Secretary of State for Education and Science 1969–70, at the Foreign and Commonwealth Office 1974–5, for Education and Science 1975–6; Vice-Chmn Labour Party 1976–7, Chmn 1977–8; Opposition Spokesman on Women's Rights 1981–3, on Overseas Development 1987–9, on Children 1989– **Member** CND (National Council 1983–); Defence for Children International (Chmn UK Branch) **Unions** sponsored by GMB

LEWIS, Terry Lab., Worsley (1983) **b.** 29 Dec. 1935 **ed.** Our Lady of Mount Carmel Sch., Salford **Profession** personnel officer **Political interests** local govt, health and social services, education **Political career** Kearsley Urban District Cllr 1971–4; Bolton Borough Cllr 1976–84 **Unions** MSF; sponsored by TGWU

LIGHTBOWN, David Con., Staffordshire South East (1983) **b.** 30 Nov. 1932 **ed.** Derby Sch. of Art; Derby Technical Coll. **Profession** engineer, company dir. **Political interests** law and order, employment, trade and industry, engineering, education, local govt, regional policy, finance **Political career** Lichfield District Cllr 1975–87 (Leader 1977–83); Staffs. Co. Cllr 1977–85 (Deputy Leader 1979–81) **Parliamentary career** Asst Whip 1986–7; Lord Commissioner of the Treasury (Govt Whip) 1987–

LILLEY, Peter Secretary of State for Trade and Industry Con., St Albans (1983) **b.** 23 Aug. 1943 **ed.** Dulwich Coll.; Clare Coll., Cambridge **Profession** Dir. Conservative Research Dept 1980–3, investment adviser, company dir. **Political interests** economy, finance, energy, EC, education, race relations **Political career** contested Haringey Tottenham 1974 **Parliamentary career** Economic Secretary to the Treasury 1987–9; Financial Secretary to the Treasury 1989–90; Secretary of State for Trade and Industry 1990– **Member** Bow Group (Chmn 1973–5) **Publications include** *Do You Sincerely Want to Win?*; *Lessons for Power*; (jtly) *The Delusion of Incomes Policy*

LITHERLAND, Bob Lab., Manchester Central (1979) **b.** 23 June 1930 **ed.** North Manchester High Sch. **Profession** sales representative for a printing firm **Political interests** defence, foreign affairs, housing and construction, unions, health and social services, employment, environment, local govt; anti-Falklands War **Political career** contested Manchester Withington 1967, Manchester Old Moat 1968; Manchester City Cllr 1971–9 **Member** Campaign Group; CND **Unions** sponsored by SOGAT '82

LIVINGSTONE, Ken Lab., Brent East (1987) **b.** 17 June 1945 **ed.** Tulse Hill Comprehensive Sch.; Fawcett Coll. of Education **Profession** laboratory technician, teacher **Political interests** local govt, education, minority rights, Northern Ireland **Political career** Lambeth Cllr 1971–8; Camden Cllr 1978–82; Greater London Cllr 1973–86 (Leader 1981–6); contested Hampstead 1979 **Parliamentary career** Labour National Executive Cttee 1987–9 **Publications include** *If Voting Changed Anything They'd Abolish It*

LIVSEY, Richard Lib. Dem. (Lib. 1985–8), Brecon and Radnor (1985) **b.** 2 May 1935 **ed.** Bedales Sch.; Seale-Hayne Agricultural Coll.; Reading Univ. **Profession** farmer, farm management lecturer **Political interests** agriculture, Welsh affairs, local govt, education, environment, regional policy **Political career** contested Perth and East Perthshire 1970, Pembroke 1979, Brecon and Radnor 1983 **Parliamentary career** Lib. Spokesman on Agriculture 1985–7, on Welsh Affairs 1987–8; All. Spokesman on the Countryside 1987; Leader of the Welsh Liberal Democrats and Spokesman on Wales and Water 1988–

LLOYD, Sir Ian Con., Havant (1983) **b.** 30 May 1921 **ed.** Michaelhouse, Natal; Witwatersrand Univ.; King's Coll., Cambridge; Staff Coll., Henley **Profession** South African Air Force 1941–5, economic adviser, company dir. **Political interests** energy, information technology, science, computer literacy, education, shipping, South Africa, Japan; pro-EC, nuclear power **Political career** MP for Portsmouth Langstone 1964–74, for Havant and Waterloo 1974–83 **Parliamentary career** Chmn Select Cttee on Energy 1979– **Publications include** *Rolls-Royce* **Other** Knighted 1986

LLOYD, Peter Con., Fareham (1979) **b.** 12 Nov. 1937 **ed.** Tonbridge Sch.; Pembroke Coll., Cambridge **Profession** marketing manager, Lloyd's underwriter **Political interests** employment, education, science, Northern Ireland, health and social services; anti-abortion, pornography, EC; pro-Sunday trading **Political career** contested Nottingham West 1974 **Parliamentary career** Asst Whip 1984–6; Lord Commissioner of the Treasury (Govt Whip) 1986–8; Under-Secretary of State for Social Security 1988– **Member** Bow Group (Chmn 1972–3)

LLOYD, Tony Lab., Stretford (1983) **b.** 25 Feb. 1950 **ed.** Stretford Grammar Sch.; Nottingham Univ.; Manchester Business Sch. **Profession** lecturer **Political interests** civil liberties, human rights, foreign affairs, defence, disarmament, overseas development, immigration, race relations, trade and industry, education, health and social services, employment, housing, environment **Political career** Trafford District Cllr 1979–84 **Parliamentary career** Opposition Spokesman on Employment 1988– **Unions** GMB (APEX partnership); AUT; sponsored by NGA

LOFTHOUSE, Geoffrey Lab., Pontefract and Castleford (1978) **b.** 18 Dec. 1925 **ed.** Featherstone Secondary Sch.; Leeds Univ. **Profession** miner, British Coal personnel manager **Political interests** mining, industrial relations, energy, local govt, housing, education, human rights **Political career** Pontefract Borough Cllr 1962–74 (Mayor 1967–8); Wakefield Metropolitan District Cllr 1973–9 **Parliamentary career** Speaker's Panel of Chairmen 1987– **Unions** GMB (APEX partnership); BACM; NUM **Publications include** *A Very Miner MP* **Other** JP 1970

LORD, Michael Con., Suffolk Central (1983) **b.** 17 Oct. 1938 **ed.** William Hulme's Grammar Sch., Manchester; Christ's Coll., Cambridge **Profession** arboricultural consultant, lecturer **Political interests** agriculture, forestry, environment, countryside, sport, education; pro-South Africa, anti-unions **Political career** North Beds. Borough Cllr 1974–7; Beds. Co. Cllr 1981–3; contested Manchester Gorton 1979 **Member** Arboricultural Assn (Vice-Pres.) **Other** Cambridge rugby blue

LOYDEN, Edward Lab., Liverpool Garston (1983) **b.** 3 May 1923 **ed.** Friary Sch., Liverpool **Profession** seaman, port worker **Political interests** ports and shipping, transport, employment, health and social services, economy, housing, local govt, defence, foreign affairs **Political career** Liverpool City Cllr 1960–74, 1980–3; Merseyside Co. Cllr 1973– ; Liverpool District Cllr 1973– ; MP for Liverpool Garston 1974–9 **Unions** sponsored by TGWU

LUCE, Rt Hon. Richard Con., Shoreham (1974) **b.** 14 Oct. 1936 **ed.** Wellington Coll.; Christ's Coll., Cambridge; Wadham Coll., Oxford **Profession** company dir. **Political interests** foreign affairs, defence, transport, arts; pro-EC **Political career** contested Hitchin 1970; MP for Arundel and Shoreham 1971–4 **Parliamentary career** Opposition Whip 1974–5; Opposition Spokesman for Foreign and Commonwealth Affairs 1977–9; Under-Secretary of State for Foreign and Commonwealth Affairs 1979–81; Minister of State at the Foreign and Commonwealth Office 1981–2 (resigned due to Foreign Office failure to warn of Falklands invasion), 1983–5; Minister of State at the Privy Council Office (Minister for the Arts) 1985–90; PC 1986

LYELL, Rt Hon. Sir Nicholas Con., Bedfordshire Mid (1983) **b.** 6 Dec. 1938 **ed.** Stowe Sch.; Christ Church, Oxford; Coll. of Law, Guildford **Profession** barrister (QC 1980), Lloyd's underwriter **Political interests** home affairs, employment, prison, law, environment, defence **Political career** contested Lambeth Central 1974; MP for Hemel Hempstead 1979–83 **Parliamentary career** Under-Secretary of State for Health and Social Security 1986–7; Solicitor General 1986– ; PC 1990 **Member** Bow Group **Other** Knighted 1987

McALLION, John Lab., Dundee East (1987) **b.** 13 Feb. 1948 **ed.** St Augustine's Secondary Sch.,

Glasgow; St Andrews Univ.; Dundee Coll. of Education **Profession** teacher **Political interests** trade and industry, employment, education, housing; pro-devolution **Political career** Tayside Regional Cllr 1984–7 (Convenor 1986–7) **Member** CND; Child Poverty Action Group; Tribune Group

McAVOY, Tom Lab., Glasgow Rutherglen (1987) **b.** 14 Dec. 1943 **ed.** St Columbkille's Secondary Sch. **Profession** storeman, shop steward **Political interests** health and social services, housing, employment, co-operatives **Political career** Rutherglen Community Cllr (Chmn 1980); Strathclyde Regional Cllr 1982–7 **Member** Co-operative Party **Unions** AEU

McCARTNEY, Ian Lab., Makerfield (1987) **b.** 25 Apr. 1951 **ed.** Lenzie Academy; Langside Coll. **Profession** seaman, local govt official, party organizer **Political interests** local govt, fire service, civil defence, health and social services, disabled, tourism, environment **Political career** Wigan Cllr 1982–7 **Member** MENCAP; Tribune Group **Unions** TGWU **Other** Son of Hugh McCartney, MP for Dunbartonshire East 1970–4, Dunbartonshire Central 1974–83 and Clydebank and Milngavie 1983–7

McCREA, Rev. William DUP, Ulster Mid (1983) **b.** 6 Aug. 1948 **ed.** Cookstown Grammar Sch.; Theological Hall, Free Presbyterian Church **Profession** Free Presbyterian minister, gospel singer, company dir. **Political interests** law and order, education, health and social services, elderly, disabled, foreign affairs **Political career** Magherafelt District Cllr 1973– (Chmn 1977–81); Northern Ireland Assembly 1982–6 **Parliamentary career** resigned seat Dec. 1985 in protest at the Anglo-Irish agreement; re-elected Jan. 1986; DUP Whip 1987– ; DUP Spokesman on Education 1987–8, on Health and Social Services 1988– **Publications include** *In His Pathway – The Story of the Reverend William McCrea*

McCRINDLE, Sir Robert Con., Brentwood and Ongar (1974) **b.** 19 Sep. 1929 **ed.** Allen Glen's Coll., Glasgow **Profession** insurance broker, company dir. (travel trade), journalist (*Travel Trade Gazette*, *Insurance Week*, *Financial Adviser*) **Political interests** trade and industry, aviation, travel and tourism, banking, insurance, health and social services **Political career** contested Dundee East 1959, Thurrock 1964; MP for Billericay 1970–4 **Parliamentary career** Chmn All-Party Aviation Group **Member** Bow Group **Other** consultant to British Insurance and Investment Brokers Assn and British Transport Police Federation; knighted 1990

MacDONALD, Calum Lab., Western Isles (1987) **b.** 7 May 1956 **ed.** Bayble Sch.; Nicolson Institute; Edinburgh Univ. **Profession** teacher, crofter **Political interests** agriculture, education; anti-abortion **Unions** TGWU

McFALL, John Lab., Dumbarton (1987) **b.** 4 Oct. 1944 **ed.** St Patrick's Secondary Sch., Dumbarton; Paisley Coll. of Technology; Strathclyde Univ.; Open Univ. **Profession** teacher **Political interests** defence, trade and industry, health and social services, education; anti-abortion **Unions** GMB

MACFARLANE, Sir Neil Con., Sutton and Cheam (1974) **b.** 7 May 1936 **ed.** Bancroft Sch., Woodford Wells **Profession** oil executive, company dir. **Political interests** oil and gas, environment, science, law and order, employment, sport, recreation; anti-football hooligans **Political career** contested East Ham North 1970, Sutton and Cheam 1972 **Parliamentary career** Under-Secretary of State for Education and Science and for the Arts 1979–81, for the Environment (Minister for Sport) 1981–5 **Member** PGA (Vice-Pres. 1985–); Sports Aid Foundation (Chmn 1986) **Publications include** *Politics and Sport – A World Divided* **Other** Knighted 1988

McGRADY, Eddie SDLP, Down South (1987) **b.** 3 June 1935 **ed.** St Patrick's High Sch., Downpatrick; Belfast Technical Coll. **Profession** accountant **Political interests** housing, environment, local govt **Political career** Downpatrick Urban District Cllr 1961–73 (Chmn 1964–73); Down District Cllr 1973– (Chmn 1974, 1976, 1978); Northern Ireland Assembly 1973–5, 1982–6; Northern Ireland Constitutional Convention 1975–6; contested Down South 1979, 1983, 1986; defeated Enoch Powell to win his seat 1987; a founder member and first Chairman of SDLP 1970–2 **Parliamentary career** SDLP Spokesman on Housing, Local Govt and Environment 1987–

MacGREGOR, Rt Hon. John Secretary of State for Education and Science Con., Norfolk South (1974) **b.** 14 Feb. 1937 **ed.** Merchiston Castle Sch., Edinburgh; St Andrews Univ.; King's Coll., London Univ. **Profession** merchant banker, company dir., Conservative Research Dept 1965 **Political interests** economy, finance, agriculture, trade and industry, housing, countryside, education; pro-EC, anti-devolution **Political career** asst to Sir Alec Douglas Home 1963–4; head of private office of Edward Heath 1965–8 **Parliamentary career** Opposition Whip 1977–9; Lord Commissioner of the Treasury (Govt Whip) 1979–81; Under-Secretary of State for Industry (Small Businesses) 1981–3; Minister of State for Agriculture, Fisheries and Food 1983–5; PC 1985; Chief Secretary to the Treasury 1985–7; Minister of Agriculture, Fisheries and Food 1987–9; Secretary of State for Education and Science 1989– **Member** Bow Group (Chmn 1963–4) **Other** OBE 1971

McKAY, Allen Lab., Barnsley West and Penistone (1983) **b.** 5 Feb. 1927 **ed.** Hoyland Kirk Balk Secondary Sch.; Sheffield Univ. **Profession** mining electrical engineer, British Coal industrial relations officer **Political interests** coal, health and social services, disabled, local govt, environment, regional development, defence **Political career** Hoyland District Cllr 1965–74 (Chmn 1973–4); Barnsley Borough Cllr 1974–8; MP for Penistone 1978–83 **Parliamentary career** Opposition Whip 1981 **Unions** BACM; NUM **Other** JP 1970

MacKAY, Andrew Con., Berkshire East (1983) **b.** 27 Aug. 1949 **ed.** Solihull Sch. **Profession** estate agent, company dir. (house building) **Political interests** foreign affairs, trade and industry, construction industry, environment, law and order; anti-immigration, pro-hanging **Political career** MP for Birmingham Stechford 1977–9

McKELVEY, Willie Lab., Kilmarnock and Loudoun (1983) **b.** 1 July 1934 **ed.** Morgan Academy; Dundee Coll. of Technology **Profession** engineer, union official **Political interests** Scottish affairs, housing, prisons, industrial relations, nuclear disarmament, Central America, Middle East; pro-devolution, PLO; anti-Falklands War **Political career** MP for Kilmarnock 1979–83 **Member** Campaign Group (a founder member); CND **Unions** sponsored by AEU

MACLEAN, David Con., Penrith and the Border (1983) **b.** 16 May 1953 **ed.** Fortrose Academy; Aberdeen Univ. **Profession** security consultant, company dir. **Political interests** defence, agriculture, law and order, transport **Political career** contested Inverness, Nairn and Lochaber 1983; won seat in July 1983 by-election **Parliamentary career** Asst Whip 1987–8; Lord Commissioner of the Treasury (Govt Whip) 1988–9; Parliamentary Secretary for Agriculture, Fisheries and Food 1989–

McLEISH, Henry Lab., Fife Central (1987) **b.** 15 June 1948 **ed.** Buckhaven High Sch., Fife; Heriot-Watt Univ., Edinburgh **Profession** local govt officer, lecturer **Political interests** Scottish affairs, employment, training, education, trade and industry, energy, local govt, health and social services, economy **Political career** Kirkcaldy District Cllr 1974–7; Fife Regional Cllr 1978–87 (Leader 1982–7); contested Fife North East 1979 **Parliamentary career** Opposition Spokesman on Scotland 1988–9, on Employment 1989– **Unions** sponsored by NUPE

MACLENNAN, Robert Lib. Dem. (Lab. 1966–81, SDP 1981–8), Caithness and Sutherland (1966) **b.** 26 June 1936 **ed.** Glasgow Academy; Balliol Coll., Oxford; Trinity Coll., Cambridge; Columbia Univ., US **Profession** barrister **Political interests** nuclear energy, agriculture, constitutional affairs; pro-EC, devolution **Parliamentary career** Opposition Spokesman on Scottish Affairs 1970–1, on Defence 1971–2; Under-Secretary of State for Prices and Consumer Protection 1974–9; Opposition Spokesman on Foreign and Commonwealth Affairs 1980–1; left Labour Party and joined SDP 1981; SDP Spokesman on Agriculture 1981–7, on Scotland 1982–7, on Home and Legal Affairs 1983–7, on Northern Ireland 1983–7, on Economic Affairs 1987–8; Leader of the SDP 1987–8; All. Spokesman on Agriculture 1987; Lib. Dem. Spokesman on Home Affairs 1988–

McLOUGHLIN, Patrick Con., Derbyshire West (1986) **b.** 30 Nov. 1957 **ed.** Cardinal Griffin Comprehensive Sch., Cannock **Profession** miner, British Coal marketing executive **Political interests** coal, agriculture, education, transport; anti-abortion **Political career** Cannock Chase District Cllr 1980–6; Staffs. Co. Cllr 1981–6; National Vice-Chmn Young Conservatives 1982–4; contested Wolverhampton South East 1983 **Parliamentary career** Under-Secretary of State for Transport 1989–

McNAIR-WILSON, Sir Michael Con., Newbury (1974) **b.** 12 Oct. 1930 **ed.** Eton **Profession** company dir., public relations consultant **Political interests** health and social services, kidney patients, home affairs, education, Northern Ireland, defence; anti-pollution, pornography **Political career** contested Lincoln 1964; MP for Walthamstow East 1969–74 **Member** Bow Group **Publications include** (jtly) *Blackshirt: A Biography of Mussolini*; (jtly) *No Tame or Minor Role* **Other** Brother of Patrick McNair-Wilson MP; knighted 1988; the first MP on kidney dialysis treatment

McNAIR-WILSON, Patrick Con., New Forest (1968) **b.** 28 May 1929 **ed.** Eton **Profession** Coldstream Guards 1946–52; company dir., public relations consultant **Political interests** energy, steel, information technology, economics, transport, Middle East **Political career** MP for Lewisham West 1964–6 **Parliamentary career** Opposition Spokesman on Fuel and Power 1965–6, on Energy 1974–6; Chmn Joint Lords and Commons Select Cttee on Private Bill Procedure 1987– **Other** Brother of Sir Michael McNair-Wilson MP

McNAMARA, Kevin **Principal Opposition Spokesman on Northern Ireland** Lab., Kingston upon Hull North (1983) **b.** 5 Sep. 1934 **ed.** St Mary's Coll., Crosby; Hull Univ. **Profession** lecturer in law **Political interests** Northern Ireland, defence, nuclear disarmament, unions, education; anti-abortion, blood sports **Political career** contested Bridlington 1964; MP for Kingston upon Hull North 1966–74, for Kingston upon Hull Central 1974–83 **Parliamentary career** Opposition Spokesman on Defence (Armed Forces) 1983–7; Principal Opposition Spokesman on Northern Ireland 1987– **Member** CND; Tribune Group **Unions** sponsored by TGWU

McWILLIAM, John Lab., Blaydon (1979) **b.** 16 May 1941 **ed.** Leith Academy; Heriot-Watt Univ., Edinburgh; Napier Coll. of Science and Technology **Profession** telephone engineer **Political interests** telecommunications, science, technology, education, arts, defence, parliamentary affairs, local govt, unions **Political career** Edinburgh Co. Cllr 1970–5; contested Edinburgh Pentlands 1974 **Parliamentary career** Deputy Shadow Leader of the House of Commons 1983–4; Opposition Whip 1984–7 **Member** CND **Unions** sponsored by NCU

MADDEN, Max Lab., Bradford West (1983) **b.** 29 Oct. 1941 **ed.** Pinner Grammar Sch. **Profession** journalist, press and information officer, publicity dir. of Labour Party 1979–82 **Political interests** employment, trade and industry, industrial safety, textile industry, health and social services, media; anti-EC, asbestos **Political career** contested Sudbury and Woodbridge 1966; Wandsworth Borough Cllr 1971–4; MP for Sowerby 1974–9 **Parliamentary career** Opposition Spokesman on Health and Social Services 1983–4 **Member** Campaign Group; CND **Unions** sponsored by TGWU

MADEL, David Con., Bedfordshire South West (1983) **b.** 6 Aug. 1938 **ed.** Uppingham Sch.; Keble Coll., Oxford **Profession** advertising executive, consultant, company dir. **Political interests** education, employment, banking, finance **Political career** contested Erith and Crayford 1965, 1966; MP for Bedfordshire South 1970–83 **Member** Bow Group

MAGINNIS, Ken OUP, Fermanagh and South Tyrone (1983) **b.** 21 Jan. 1938 **ed.** Royal Sch., Dungannon; Stranmillis Teacher Training Coll., Belfast **Profession** teacher **Political interests** security, terrorism, defence, Northern Ireland, education, Brazil; anti-hanging **Political career** contested Fermanagh and South Tyrone 1981; Dungannon District Cllr 1981– ; Northern Ireland Assembly 1982–6 **Parliamentary career** OUP Spokesman on Security 1983– ; resigned seat Dec. 1985 in protest at the Anglo-Irish agreement; re-elected Jan. 1986 **Member** Ulster Special Constabulary 1958–65; Ulster Defence Regiment 1970–81

MAHON, Alice Lab., Halifax (1987) **b.** 28 Sept. 1937 **ed.** Bradford Univ. **Profession** lecturer in trade union studies **Political interests** unions, employment, equal opportunities, local govt, education, health and social services **Political career** Calderdale District Cllr 1981–

MAJOR, Rt Hon. John **Chancellor of the Exchequer** Con., Huntingdon (1983) **b.** 29 Mar. 1943 **ed.** Rutlish Grammar Sch. **Profession** banker **Political interests** economy, finance, health and social services, housing, local govt, agriculture, environment; anti-racism, hanging **Political career** Lambeth Borough Cllr 1968–71; contested St Pancras North 1974; MP for Huntingdonshire 1979–83 **Parliamentary career** Asst Whip 1983–4; Lord Commissioner of the Treasury (Govt Whip) 1984–5; Under-Secretary of State for Health and Social Services 1985–6; Minister of State for Health and Social Services (Social Security and the Disabled) 1986–7; PC 1987; Chief Secretary to the Treasury 1987–9; Foreign Secretary July – Oct. 1989; Chancellor of the Exchequer Oct. 1989– **Other** His father was a trapeze artist

MALINS, Humfrey Con., Croydon North West (1983) **b.** 31 July 1945 **ed.** St John's Sch., Leatherhead; Brasenose Coll., Oxford; Coll. of Law, Guildford **Profession** solicitor, company dir. **Political interests** law, housing, charities, sport, EC; pro-proportional representation **Political career** Mole Valley District Cllr 1973–83; contested Liverpool Toxteth 1974, Lewisham East 1979

MALLON, Seamus SDLP, Newry and Armagh (1986) **b.** 17 Aug. 1936 **ed.** Abbey Grammar Sch., Newry; St Joseph's Coll. of Education, Belfast **Profession** teacher **Political interests** law, education, health and social services **Political career** Armagh District Cllr 1973–; Northern Ireland Assembly 1973–4, 1982; Northern Ireland Convention 1975–6; Irish Senate 1981–2; contested Newry and Armagh 1983; Deputy Leader of SDLP 1978– **Parliamentary career** SDLP Spokesman on Justice 1986– **Publications include** *Adam's Children*

MANS, Keith Con., Wyre (1987) **b.** 10 Feb. 1946 **ed.** Berkhamsted Sch.; RAF Coll., Cranwell; Open Univ. **Profession** RAF pilot 1967–77; retail manager **Political interests** defence, aviation; pro-EC, anti-CND **Political career** New Forest District Cllr 1983–7; contested Stoke-on-Trent Central 1983 **Member** Bow Group

MAPLES, John Con., Lewisham West (1983) **b.** 22 Apr. 1943 **ed.** Marlborough Coll.; Downing Coll., Cambridge; Harvard Business Sch. **Profession** barrister, consultant, Lloyd's underwriter **Political interests** inner city, housing, taxation, rates, economy, small businesses; anti-GLC **Parliamentary career** Economic Secretary to the Treasury 1990–

MAREK, Dr John Lab., Wrexham (1983) **b.** 24 Dec. 1940 **ed.** Chatham House Grammar Sch.; King's Coll., London Univ. **Profession** mathematics lecturer **Political interests** transport, health, economy, conservation **Political career** Ceredigion District Cllr 1979–83; contested Ludlow 1974 **Parliamentary career** Opposition Spokesman on Health 1985–7, on Treasury Matters 1987– **Unions** sponsored by NUR

MARLAND, Paul Con., Gloucestershire West (1979) **b.** 19 Mar. 1940 **ed.** Gordonstoun Sch.; Trinity Coll., Dublin; Grenoble Univ., France **Profession** farmer, company dir., Lloyd's underwriter **Political interests** agriculture, energy **Political career** North Cotswold Rural District Cllr; contested Bedwellty 1970, Gloucestershire West 1974

MARLOW, Tony Con., Northampton North (1979) **b.** 17 June 1940 **ed.** Wellington Coll.; Royal Military Academy, Sandhurst; St Catharine's Coll., Cambridge **Profession** Royal Engineers 1960–9; farmer, management consultant **Political interests** foreign affairs, defence, Middle East; anti-EC, immigration, unions, abortion, welfare scroungers; pro-South Africa, hanging, dog control **Political career** contested Normanton Feb. 1974, Rugby Oct. 1974

MARSHALL, David Lab., Glasgow Shettleston (1979) **b.** 7 May 1941 **ed.** Woodside Senior Secondary Sch., Glasgow **Profession** bus conductor, party official **Political interests** transport, drug and solvent abuse, industrial relations, Scottish affairs, Third World, conservation; pro-devolution **Political career** Glasgow Corporation Cllr 1972–5; Strathclyde Regional Cllr 1974–9 **Parliamentary career** Chmn Select Cttee on Transport 1987– ; Joint Chmn All-Party Road Passenger Transport Group 1986– **Member** CND; Co-operative Party **Unions** sponsored by TGWU

MARSHALL, James Lab., Leicester South (1987) **b.** 13 Mar. 1941 **ed.** Sheffield City Grammar Sch.; Leeds Univ. **Profession** lecturer, research scientist **Political interests** housing, education, local govt, energy, economy, EC, Northern Ireland **Political career** Leeds City Cllr 1965–8; Leicester City Cllr 1971–6 (Leader 1974); contested Leicestershire Harborough 1970, Leicester South Feb. 1974; MP for Leicester South Oct. 1974–83, losing his seat by seven votes **Parliamentary career** Asst Whip 1977–9; Opposition Spokesman on Home Affairs 1982–3, on Northern Ireland 1988–

MARSHALL, John Con., Hendon South (1987) **b.** 19 Aug. 1940 **ed.** Harris Academy, Dundee; Glasgow Academy; St Andrews Univ. **Profession** economics lecturer, stockbroker **Political interests** economics, trade and industry, EC, education, local govt, Middle East; pro-monetarism **Political career** Aberdeen Town Cllr 1968–70; Ealing Borough Cllr 1971–86; contested Dundee East 1964 and 1966, Lewisham East 1974; MEP for London North 1979–89

MARSHALL, Sir Robert (Michael) Con., Arundel (1974) **b.** 21 June 1930 **ed.** Bradfield Coll.; Harvard Univ., US; Stanford Univ., US **Profession** company dir. (steel industry), writer, broadcaster (BBC cricket commentator 1964–9) **Political interests** trade and industry, steel, information technology, defence, media **Political career** contested Hartlepool 1970 **Parliamentary career** Under-Secretary of State for Industry 1979–81; Chmn Information Technology Cttee 1986– **Unions** Equity **Publications include** *The Book of Comic and Dramatic Monologues*; (ed.) *The Stanley Holloway Monologues*; *The Timetable of Technology* **Other** Knighted 1990

MARTIN, David Con., Portsmouth South (1987) **b.** 5 Feb. 1945 **ed.** Kelly Coll., Tavistock; Governor Dummer Academy, US; Fitzwilliam Coll., Cambridge; Inner Temple **Profession** barrister, company dir. **Political interests** defence, housing, local govt, law **Political career** Teignbridge District Cllr 1979–83; contested Yeovil 1983

MARTIN, Michael Lab., Glasgow Springburn (1979) **b.** 3 July 1945 **ed.** St Patrick's Boys' Sch., Glasgow **Profession** sheet-metal worker, union official **Political interests** trade and industry, industrial relations, employment, health and social services, housing, local govt, drug abuse, women's rights, human rights, Canada and US, finance **Political career** Glasgow Corporation Cllr 1973–4; Glasgow District Cllr 1974–9 **Parliamentary career** Speaker's Panel of Chairmen 1987– **Unions** sponsored by AEU

MARTLEW, Eric Lab., Carlisle (1987) **b.** 3 Jan. 1949 **ed.** Harraby Secondary Sch.; Carlisle Technical Coll.

Profession personnel manager **Political interests** transport, health and social services, agriculture, industrial relations, local govt **Political career** Carlisle Borough Cllr 1972–4; Cumbria Co. Cllr 1973–87 (Chmn 1983–5)

MATES, Michael Con., Hampshire East (1983) **b.** 9 June 1934 **ed.** Blundell's Sch.; King's Coll., Cambridge **Profession** Queen's Dragoon Guards 1954–74; company dir., consultant **Political interests** defence, home affairs, Northern Ireland **Political career** MP for Petersfield 1974–83 **Parliamentary career** Chmn All-Party Anglo-Irish Group 1979– ; Secretary 1922 Cttee 1987–8; Chmn House of Commons Defence Cttee 1987–

MAUDE, Hon. Francis Con., Warwickshire North (1983) **b.** 4 July 1953 **ed.** Abingdon Sch.; Corpus Christi Coll., Cambridge; Inner Temple **Profession** barrister **Political interests** foreign affairs, economics, trade and industry, energy, coal, privatization, employment, law, health and social services, education; pro-hanging **Political career** Westminster City Cllr 1978–84 **Parliamentary career** Asst Whip 1985–7; Under-Secretary of State for Trade and Industry (Corporate Affairs) 1987–9; Minister of State at the Foreign Office 1989–90; Financial Secretary to the Treasury 1990– **Other** Son of Lord (Angus) Maude, MP for Ealing South 1950–8 and Stratford-on-Avon 1963–83

MAWHINNEY, Dr Brian Con., Peterborough (1979) **b.** 26 July 1940 **ed.** Royal Belfast Academical Institution; Queen's Univ., Belfast; Michigan Univ., US; London Univ. **Profession** radiation biologist, lecturer, company dir. **Political interests** Northern Ireland, health and social services, race relations, trade and industry, economy, railways, foreign affairs, Middle East, US; anti-pornography, NHS waste **Political career** contested Stockton-on-Tees 1974 **Parliamentary career** Under-Secretary of State for Northern Ireland 1986– **Member** General Synod of the Church of England 1985– **Publications include** (jtly) *Conflict and Christianity in Northern Ireland* **Other** He is a lay preacher

MAXTON, John Lab., Glasgow Cathcart (1979) **b.** 5 May 1936 **ed.** Lord Williams' Grammar Sch., Thame; Univ. Coll., Oxford **Profession** lecturer in social studies **Political interests** Scottish affairs, education, environment, housing, trade and industry; pro-devolution, anti-Falklands War **Parliamentary career** Opposition Whip 1984–5; Opposition Spokesman on Scotland 1985– **Member** Tribune Group **Unions** MSF

MAXWELL-HYSLOP, Robin Con., Tiverton (1960) **b.** 6 June 1931 **ed.** Stowe Sch.; Christ Church, Oxford **Profession** Rolls-Royce executive **Political interests** economy, trade and industry, motor and aerospace industries, self-employment, agriculture, Brazil and South America, parliamentary procedure **Political career** contested Derby North 1959

MAYHEW, Rt Hon. Sir Patrick Attorney General Con., Tunbridge Wells (1974) **b.** 11 Sep. 1929 **ed.** Tonbridge Sch.; Balliol Coll., Oxford; Middle Temple **Profession** barrister (QC 1972), farmer **Political interests** law, home affairs, employment, immigration; anti-capital and corporal punishment **Political career** contested Camberwell Dulwich 1970 **Parliamentary career** Executive of 1922 Cttee 1976–9; Under-Secretary of State for Employment 1979–81; Minister of State at the Home Office 1981–3; Solicitor General 1983–7; PC 1986; Attorney General 1987– **Other** Knighted 1983

MEACHER, Michael Shadow Secretary for Social Security Lab., Oldham West (1970) **b.** 4 Nov. 1939 **ed.** Berkhamsted Sch.; New Coll., Oxford; London Sch. of Economics **Profession** lecturer in social administration, journalist **Political interests** health and social services, education, employment, housing, civil liberties, media, arts, govt reform, trade and industry, economics, wealth, defence; anti-Falklands War **Political career** contested Colchester 1966, Oldham West 1968 **Parliamentary career** Under-Secretary of State for Industry 1974–5, for Health and Social Security 1975–6, for Trade 1976–9; Labour National Executive Cttee 1983– ; contested Deputy Leadership of Labour Party 1983; Shadow Cabinet 1983– ; Shadow Secretary for Health and Social Security 1983–7; Shadow Employment Secretary 1987–9; Shadow Secretary for Social Security 1989– **Member** Campaign Group; Fabian Society; Child Poverty Action Group **Unions** sponsored by COHSE **Publications include** *The Care of Old People*; *Socialism with a Human Face: The Political Economy in the 1980s*

MEALE, Alan Lab., Mansfield (1987) **b.** 31 July 1949 **ed.** St Joseph Roman Catholic Sch., Bishop Auckland; Durham Univ.; Ruskin Coll., Oxford **Profession** researcher, union official **Political interests** home affairs, poverty, drug abuse, unemployment, health and social services, transport, media **Political career** adviser to Michael Meacher MP 1983– **Member** Anti-Apartheid; Child Poverty Action Group; Campaign Group; CND; Tribune Group **Unions** sponsored by TGWU

MELLOR, Rt Hon. David Con., Putney (1979) **b.** 12 Mar. 1949 **ed.** Swanage Grammar Sch.; Christ's Coll., Cambridge; Inner Temple **Profession** barrister (QC 1987), consultant **Political interests** law, home affairs, foreign affairs, health, energy **Political career** contested West Bromwich East 1974 **Parliamentary career** Under-Secretary of State for Energy 1981–3, at the Home Office 1983–6; Minister of State at the Home Office 1986–7, at the Foreign and Commonwealth Office 1987–8, for Health 1988–9, at the Home Office 1989–90; PC 1990; Minister of State for the Arts 1990–

MEYER, Sir Anthony Con., Clwyd North West (1983) **b.** 27 Oct. 1920 **ed.** Eton; New Coll., Oxford **Profession** Scots Guards 1941–5; diplomat, company dir., Lloyd's underwriter **Political interests** foreign affairs, trade and industry, Welsh affairs; pro-EC, UN; anti-hanging, Falklands War **Political career** MP for Eton and Slough 1964–6, for West Flintshire 1970–83 **Parliamentary career** Chmn Franco-British Group 1979– ; Speaker's Panel of Chairmen 1985– ; contested leadership of Conservative Party 1989 **Publications include** *A European Technological Community*; *Europe – Should We Join?* **Other** Son of Sir Frank Meyer Bt, MP for Great Yarmouth 1924–9; succeeded 1935

MICHAEL, Alun Lab., Cardiff South and Penarth (1987) **b.** 22 Aug. 1943 **ed.** Colwyn Bay Grammar Sch.; Keele Univ. **Profession** journalist, youth and community worker **Political interests** local govt, housing, youth affairs, juvenile courts, employment, education, environment, Welsh affairs, media, economy, co-operative movement **Political career** Cardiff City Cllr 1973– ; succeeded Jim Callaghan as MP for Cardiff South and Penarth **Parliamentary career**

Opposition Whip 1987–8; Opposition Spokesman on Welsh Affairs 1988– **Member** sponsored by Co-operative Party **Other** He speaks Welsh; JP 1972

MICHIE, Bill Lab., Sheffield Heeley (1983) **b.** 24 Nov. 1935 **ed.** Abbeydale Secondary Sch., Sheffield **Profession** electrician, laboratory technician, shop steward **Political interests** trade and industry, local govt, employment, health and social services; anti-EC **Political career** Sheffield City Cllr 1970–84; S. Yorks. Co. Cllr 1974–86 **Member** Co-operative Party; Campaign Group **Unions** sponsored by AEU

MICHIE, Ray Lib. Dem. (Lib. 1987–8), Argyll and Bute (1987) **b.** 4 Feb. 1934 **ed.** Aberdeen High Sch. for Girls; Lansdowne House, Edinburgh; Edinburgh Coll. of Speech Therapy **Profession** speech therapist **Political interests** Scottish affairs, crofting and farming, Gaelic, women's issues, health, education, constitutional reform; pro-devolution **Political career** contested Argyll 1979, Argyll and Bute 1983 **Parliamentary career** Lib. Spokesman on Transport and Rural Development 1987–8; Lib. Dem. Spokesman on Scotland and Women's Issues 1988–

MILLER, Sir Hal Con., Bromsgrove (1983) **b.** 6 Mar. 1929 **ed.** Eton; Merton Coll., Oxford; London Univ. **Profession** colonial civil servant, company dir. **Political interests** West Midlands motor industry, Third World, Hong Kong and China, sport **Political career** contested Barrow-in-Furness 1970, Bromsgrove 1971; MP for Bromsgrove and Redditch 1974–83 **Parliamentary career** Joint Chmn All-Party Motor Industry Group 1978; Vice-Chmn Conservative Party 1984–7 **Other** Knighted 1988

MILLS, Iain Con., Meriden (1979) **b.** 21 Apr. 1940 **ed.** Prince Edward Sch., Zimbabwe; Cape Town Univ. **Profession** chemical engineer, designer and manager of Dunlop racing tyres, company dir. **Political interests** trade and industry, car industry, transport, road safety, unions, employment, the disabled, conservation, animal welfare **Political career** Lichfield District Cllr 1974–6

MISCAMPBELL, Norman Con., Blackpool North (1962) **b.** 20 Feb. 1925 **ed.** St Edward's Sch., Oxford; Trinity Coll., Oxford; Inner Temple **Profession** barrister (QC 1974) **Political interests** Northern Ireland, law, environment **Political career** Hoylake Urban District Cllr 1955–61; contested Newton-le-Willows 1955, 1959

MITCHELL, Andrew Con., Gedling (1987) **b.** 23 Mar. 1956 **ed.** Rugby Sch.; Sandhurst; Jesus Coll., Cambridge **Profession** banker, wine merchant **Political interests** foreign affairs, defence, economy, inner cities, job creation, trade and industry, health and social services **Political career** contested Sunderland South 1983 **Other** Son of Sir David Mitchell MP

MITCHELL, Austin Lab., Great Grimsby (1983) **b.** 19 Sep. 1934 **ed.** Bingley Grammar Sch.; Manchester Univ.; Nuffield Coll., Oxford **Profession** lecturer, TV journalist and broadcaster, writer **Political interests** trade and industry, fishing industry, employment, poverty, economy, media, education; pro-proportional representation, anti-EC **Political career** Sheffield City Cllr; S. Yorks. Co. Cllr; MP for Grimsby 1977–83, succeeding Anthony Crosland **Parliamentary career** Opposition Whip 1979–82; Opposition Spokesman on Trade and Industry 1988–9 **Member** Fabian Society **Unions** NUJ **Publications include** *Yes Maggie There is an Alternative*; *Westminster Man*; *Four Years in the Death of the Labour Party*; *Yorkshire Jokes*

MITCHELL, Sir David Con., Hampshire North West (1983) **b.** 20 June 1928 **ed.** Aldenham **Profession** farmer, wine merchant **Political interests** transport, Northern Ireland, small businesses, agriculture; anti-closed shop **Political career** St Pancras Borough Cllr 1956–9; contested St Pancras North 1959; MP for Basingstoke 1964–83 **Parliamentary career** Opposition Whip 1965–7; Executive of 1922 Cttee 1976–7; Under-Secretary of State for Industry 1979–81, for Northern Ireland 1981–3, for Transport 1983–6; Minister of State for Transport 1986–8 **Other** Knighted 1988; father of Andrew Mitchell MP; his family owns El Vino's in Fleet Street

MOATE, Roger Con., Faversham (1970) **b.** 12 May 1938 **ed.** Latymer Upper Sch., Hammersmith **Profession** insurance broker, company dir. **Political interests** transport, Norway; anti-EC, immigration, Public Lending Right; pro-hanging **Political career** contested Faversham 1966 **Parliamentary career** Chmn British-Norwegian Group 1987–

MOLYNEAUX, Rt Hon. James OUP, Lagan Valley (1983) **b.** 27 Aug. 1920 **ed.** Aldergrove Sch., Co. Antrim **Profession** RAF 1941–6; printer **Political interests** Northern Ireland, local govt, constitutional affairs, mental health **Political career** Antrim Co. Cllr 1964–73; MP for Antrim South 1970–83; Northern Ireland Assembly 1982–6 **Parliamentary career** Leader Ulster Unionist Coalition 1974–7; Leader OUP 1979–; PC 1983 **Member** Orange Order (Deputy Grand Master 1964–) **Other** He survived an assassination attempt 1982; JP 1957–86

MONRO, Sir Hector Con., Dumfries (1964) **b.** 4 Oct. 1922 **ed.** Canford Sch.; King's Coll., Cambridge **Profession** RAF 1941–6; farmer, company dir. **Political interests** Scottish affairs, agriculture, sport, heritage, aviation, defence; pro-devolution, hanging **Political career** Dumfries Co. Cllr 1952–67 **Parliamentary career** Asst Whip 1967–70; Lord Commissioner of the Treasury (Govt Whip) 1970–1; Under-Secretary of State for Scotland 1971–4; Opposition Spokesman on Scottish Affairs 1974–5, on Sport 1974–9; Under-Secretary of State for the Environment (Minister for Sport) 1979–81 **Member** Scottish Rugby Union 1957–77 (Pres. 1976–7); Nature Conservancy Council 1982– ; National Small-bore Rifle Association (Pres. 1987–); NFU **Other** DL Dumfries 1973; knighted 1981

MONTGOMERY, Sir Fergus Con., Altrincham and Sale (1974) **b.** 25 Nov. 1927 **ed.** Jarrow Grammar Sch.; Bede Coll., Durham **Profession** Royal Navy 1946–8; teacher, finance company dir. **Political interests** home affairs, aviation, education, police, law and order; anti-abortion **Political career** Hebburn Urban District Cllr 1950–8; National Chmn Young Conservatives 1957–8; contested Consett 1955; MP for Newcastle-upon-Tyne East 1959–64 (the first Con. to represent this seat), for Brierley Hill 1967–Feb. 1974; contested Dudley West 1974 **Parliamentary career** PPS to Margaret Thatcher, Secretary of State for Education and Science and Leader of the Opposition, 1973–6 **Other** Knighted 1985

MOONIE, Dr Lewis Lab., Kirkcaldy (1987) **b.** 25 Feb. 1947 **ed.** Grove Academy, Dundee; St Andrews Univ.; Edinburgh Univ. **Profession** community health specialist **Political interests** health and social services, education, local govt, peace **Political career** Fife Regional Cllr 1982–6 **Member** sponsored by Co-operative Party **Unions** MSF; TGWU

MOORE, Rt Hon. John Con., Croydon Central (1974) **b.** 26 Nov. 1937 **ed.** Licensed Victuallers' Sch., Slough; London Sch. of Economics **Profession** investment banker, company dir., Lloyd's underwriter **Political interests** health and social services, energy, finance, transport; pro-hanging, privatization; anti-racism **Political career** Merton Borough Cllr 1971–4 **Parliamentary career** Vice-Chmn Conservative Party 1975–9; Under-Secretary of State for Energy 1979–83; Economic Secretary to the Treasury 1983; Financial Secretary to the Treasury 1983–6; PC 1986; Secretary of State for Transport 1986–7, for Social Services 1987–8, for Social Security 1988–9

MORGAN, Rhodri Lab., Cardiff West (1987) **b.** 29 Sep. 1939 **ed.** Whitchurch Grammar Sch., Cardiff; St John's Coll., Oxford; Harvard Univ., US **Profession** economist, local govt officer **Political interests** Welsh affairs, coal, steel, energy, conservation, regional policy, economy, EC, health and social services **Parliamentary career** Opposition Spokesman on Energy 1988– **Member** Anti-Apartheid; Tribune Group **Unions** TGWU **Other** He speaks Welsh

MORLEY, Elliot Lab., Glanford and Scunthorpe (1987) **b.** 6 July 1952 **ed.** St Margaret's High Sch., Liverpool; Hull Coll. of Education **Profession** teacher **Political interests** education, public transport, local govt, agriculture, conservation, nuclear disarmament, the disabled; anti-nuclear dumping **Political career** Hull City Cllr 1979–86; contested Beverley 1983 **Parliamentary career** Opposition Spokesman on Agriculture 1989– **Member** CND; Friends of the Earth; Greenpeace **Unions** NUT; sponsored by GMB

MORRIS, Rt Hon. Alfred Lab., Manchester Wythenshawe (1964) **b.** 23 Mar. 1928 **ed.** Manchester Elementary Sch.; Ruskin Coll., Oxford; St Catherine's Coll., Oxford; Manchester Univ. **Profession** Army 1946–8; industrial relations officer **Political interests** disabled, science, education, technology, health and social services, co-operative movement, regional development, airports, Commonwealth; anti-EC, abortion **Political career** contested Liverpool Garston 1951, Manchester Wythenshawe 1959 **Parliamentary career** Opposition Spokesman on Social Services 1970–4; Under-Secretary of State for Health and Social Security (Minister for the Disabled) 1974–9 (the first Minister for the Disabled); PC 1979; Opposition Spokesman for the Disabled 1979– ; Chmn Parliamentary and Scientific Cttee 1988– **Member** CND; sponsored by the Co-operative Party; Chmn of World Planning Group appointed to draft *Charter for the 80s* for disabled people worldwide, published in the International Year of Disabled People 1981 **Publications include** *The Growth of Parliamentary Scrutiny by Committee*; (jtly) *No Feet to Drag* **Other** Brother of Charles Morris, MP for Openshaw 1963–83; QSO 1989

MORRIS, Rt Hon. John Shadow Attorney General Lab., Aberavon (1959) **b.** 5 Nov. 1931 **ed.** Ardwyn Grammar Sch., Aberystwyth; Univ. Coll. of Wales, Aberystwyth; Gonville and Caius Coll., Cambridge; Academy of International Law, The Hague; Gray's Inn **Profession** barrister (QC 1973) **Political interests** law, Welsh affairs, agriculture, steel, coal, transport, defence; pro-devolution, NATO **Parliamentary career** Parliamentary Secretary Ministry for Power 1964–6, for Transport 1966–8; Minister of Defence (Equipment) 1968–70; PC 1970; Opposition Spokesman on Defence 1970–4; Secretary of State for Wales 1974–9; Shadow Attorney General 1979–81, 1983– **Unions** sponsored by GMB (APEX partnership)

MORRIS, Michael Con., Northampton South (1974) **b.** 25 Nov. 1936 **ed.** Bedford Sch.; St Catharine's Coll., Cambridge **Profession** advertising executive, company dir., communications consultant **Political interests** food and nutrition, health and social services, trade and industry, energy, exports, environment, EC, Sri Lanka, South-East Asia **Political career** Islington Borough Cllr 1968–74 (Leader 1969–71, Alderman 1971–4); contested Islington North 1966 **Parliamentary career** Speaker's Panel of Chairmen 1985– ; Joint Founder of Food and Health Cttee **Member** Bow Group **Publications include** (jtly) *Helping the Exporter*; *The Disaster of Direct Labour*

MORRISON, Hon. Sir Charles Con., Devizes (1964) **b.** 25 June 1932 **ed.** Eton; Royal Agricultural Coll., Cirencester **Profession** Life Guards 1950–2, farmer, company dir., Lloyd's underwriter **Political interests** constitutional affairs, education, agriculture, local govt, economy, foreign affairs; pro-proportional representation, GLC; anti-hanging **Political career** Wilts. Co. Cllr 1958–65 **Parliamentary career** Opposition Spokesman on Sport 1967–70; Vice-Chmn 1922 Cttee 1974–83 **Member** National Cttee for Electoral Reform (Chmn 1985–); Game Conservancy (Chmn 1987–) **Other** Son of Baron Margadale (John Morrison), MP for Salisbury 1942–64, and brother of Peter Morrison MP; knighted 1988

MORRISON, Rt Hon. Peter Con., City of Chester (1974) **b.** 2 June 1944 **ed.** Eton; Keble Coll., Oxford **Profession** farmer, company dir. **Political interests** energy, trade and industry, small businesses, youth training, employment, agriculture; anti-proportional representation, welfare scroungers; pro-hanging **Parliamentary career** Opposition Whip 1976–9; Lord Commissioner of the Treasury (Govt Whip) 1979–81; Under-Secretary of State for Employment 1981–2; Minister of State for Employment 1983–5, for Industry 1985–6; Deputy Chmn Conservative Party 1986– ; Minister of State for Energy 1987–90; PC 1988; PPS to the Prime Minister, Margaret Thatcher, 1990– **Other** Son of Baron Margadale (John Morrison), MP for Salisbury 1942–64, and brother of Charles Morrison MP

MOSS, Malcolm Con., Cambridgeshire North East (1987) **b.** 6 Mar. 1943 **ed.** Audenshaw Grammar Sch.; St John's Coll., Cambridge **Profession** teacher, insurance broker, company dir. **Political interests** finance, insurance, small business, energy, education, housing, trade and industry, rural development **Political career** Wisbech Town Cllr 1979–87; Fenland District Cllr 1983–7; Cambs. Co. Cllr 1985–7; defeated Clement Freud to gain seat

MOWLAM, Dr Marjorie Lab., Redcar (1987) **b.** 18 Sep. 1949 **ed.** Coundon Court Comprehensive Sch., Coventry; Durham Univ.; Iowa Univ., US **Profession** lecturer **Political interests** Northern Ireland, energy, education, trade and industry, media, nuclear disarmament **Parliamentary career** Opposition Spokesman on Northern Ireland 1988–9, on Trade and Industry 1989– **Member** CND **Unions** TGWU;

sponsored by COHSE **Publications include** (ed.) *Debate on Disarmament*; (jtly) *Over Our Dead Bodies*

MOYNIHAN, Hon. Colin Con., Lewisham East (1983) **b.** 13 Sep. 1955 **ed.** Monmouth Sch.; Univ. Coll., Oxford **Profession** company dir. **Political interests** sport, inner city, foreign affairs, overseas aid, refugees, environment, probation service, trade and industry **Parliamentary career** Under-Secretary of State for the Environment (Minister for Sport) 1987–90, for Energy 1990– **Member** Bow Group; British Boxing Board of Control (Steward 1979–87); Sports Aid Trust (Trustee 1984–7) **Other** Double Oxford blue for coxing and boxing; he won an Olympic silver medal for rowing, Moscow 1980

MUDD, David Con., Falmouth and Camborne (1970) **b.** 2 June 1933 **ed.** Truro Cathedral Sch. **Profession** journalist **Political interests** transport, energy, minerals, fishing industry, industrial safety; pro-devolution, hanging; anti-EEC, immigration, fluoride **Political career** Tavistock Urban District Cllr 1963–5; Cornwall Co. Cllr 1967–9 **Publications include** *The Cruel Cornish Sea*; *The Cornish Edwardians*; *Cornwall in Uproar*

MULLIN, Chris Lab., Sunderland South (1987) **b.** 12 Dec. 1947 **ed.** St Joseph's Coll., Ipswich; Hull Univ. **Profession** journalist **Political interests** Vietnam, foreign affairs, Northern Ireland, media, regional policy, shipbuilding **Political career** contested Devon North 1970, Kingston upon Thames 1974 **Unions** MSF; NUJ **Publications include** *Error of Judgement – The Truth about the Birmingham Pub Bombings*; *The Last Man out of Saigon*; *A Very British Coup*

MURPHY, Paul Lab., Torfaen (1987) **b.** 25 Nov. 1948 **ed.** West Monmouth Sch., Pontypool; Oriel Coll., Oxford **Profession** lecturer in history and politics **Political interests** Welsh affairs, local govt, education, housing, youth employment, economy, foreign affairs; anti-devolution **Political career** Torfaen Borough Cllr 1973–87; contested Wells 1979; succeeded Leo Abse in this seat **Parliamentary career** Opposition Spokesman on Welsh Affairs 1988– **Unions** sponsored by TGWU

NEALE, Gerry Con., Cornwall North (1979) **b.** 25 June 1941 **ed.** Bedford Sch. **Profession** solicitor, company dir. **Political interests** defence, telecommunications, employment, education, environment; pro-hanging, anti-welfare scroungers **Political career** Milton Keynes Borough Cllr 1973–9 (Mayor 1976–7); contested Cornwall North 1974; defeated John Pardoe to win this seat

NEEDHAM, Richard Con., Wiltshire North (1983) **b.** 29 Jan. 1942 **ed.** Eton **Profession** company dir., Lloyd's underwriter **Political interests** Northern Ireland, trade and industry, foreign affairs, employment **Political career** Somerset Co. Cllr 1967–74; contested Pontefract and Castleford Feb. 1974, Gravesend Oct. 1974; MP for Chippenham 1979–83 **Parliamentary career** Under-Secretary of State for Northern Ireland 1985– **Publications include** *Honourable Member* **Other** He is the 6th Earl of Kilmorey, but does not use the title. Four of his ancestors were MPs for Down South

NELLIST, David Lab., Coventry South East (1983) **b.** 16 July 1952 **ed.** Guisborough Grammar Sch. **Profession** council storeman **Political interests** employment, industrial relations, privatization, poverty, youth, immigration, human rights, South Africa, Middle East **Political career** W. Midlands Co. Cllr 1982–6 **Member** Campaign Group **Unions** sponsored by AEU

NELSON, Anthony Con., Chichester (1974) **b.** 11 June 1948 **ed.** Harrow; Christ's Coll., Cambridge **Profession** merchant banker, company dir. **Political interests** economy, finance, defence, foreign affairs, EC, Middle East, Canada, technology, housing; pro-EMS, anti-City fraud **Political career** contested Leeds East 1974 **Parliamentary career** Chmn British-Canadian, British-Oman, British-UAE, British-Bahrain Groups **Member** Bow Group

NEUBERT, Michael Con., Romford (1974) **b.** 3 Sept. 1933 **ed.** Bromley Grammar Sch.; Royal Coll. of Music, London; Downing Coll., Cambridge **Profession** tour operator, hospital administrator, travel and industrial consultant **Political interests** local govt, travel and tourism, arts, heritage, economy, defence **Political career** Bromley Borough Cllr 1960–74 (Leader 1967–70, Alderman 1968–74, Mayor 1972–3); contested Hammersmith North 1966, Havering Romford 1970 **Parliamentary career** Asst Whip 1983–6; Lord Commissioner of the Treasury (Govt Whip) 1986–8; Vice-Chamberlain of the Household (Govt Whip) 1988; Under-Secretary of State for Defence (Armed Forces) 1988–90 **Publications include** *Running Your Own Society*

NEWTON, Rt Hon. Antony Secretary of State for Social Security Con., Braintree (1974) **b.** 29 Aug. 1937 **ed.** Friends' Sch., Saffron Walden; Trinity Coll., Oxford **Profession** Conservative Research Dept 1961–74; economist, lecturer, company dir. **Political interests** social security, health and social services, disabled, child care, taxation, building industry, trade and industry **Political career** contested Sheffield Brightside 1970 **Parliamentary career** Asst Whip 1979–81; Lord Commissioner of the Treasury (Govt Whip) 1981–2; Under-Secretary of State for Social Security 1982–4 (Minister for the Disabled 1983–4); Minister of State for Social Security and the Disabled 1984–6, for Health 1986–8; PC 1988; Chancellor of the Duchy of Lancaster (Minister for Trade and Industry) 1988–9; Secretary of State for Social Security 1989– **Member** Bow Group **Other** OBE 1972

NICHOLLS, Patrick Con., Teignbridge (1983) **b.** 14 Nov. 1948 **ed.** Redrice Coll., Andover; Coll. of Law, Guildford **Profession** solicitor **Political interests** home affairs, law, employment, defence; pro-hanging, US **Political career** East Devon District Cllr 1980–4 **Parliamentary career** Under-Secretary of State for Employment 1987– **Member** British Boxing Board of Control (Steward 1985–7)

NICHOLSON, David Con., Taunton (1987) **b.** 17 Aug. 1944 **ed.** Queen Elizabeth's Grammar Sch., Blackburn; Christ Church, Oxford; London Sch. of Economics **Profession** Conservative Research Dept 1972–82; Association of British Chambers of Commerce 1982–7 (Deputy Dir.-General 1986–7) **Political interests** economy, employment, local govt, environment, planning, education, foreign affairs **Political career** contested Walsall South 1983 **Publications include** (joint ed.) *The Diaries of L. S. Amery*

NICHOLSON, Emma Con., Devon West and Torridge (1987) **b.** 16 Oct. 1941 **ed.** St Mary's Sch., Wantage; Royal Academy of Music **Profession** computer programmer and consultant, fund-raising dir. of Save the Children Fund 1977–85 **Political interests** charities, information technology, agriculture, health and social services **Political career** contested Blyth 1976, 1979; Vice-Chmn Conservative Party 1983–7 **Member** Friends of the Duke of Edinburgh Award Scheme (Chmn 1988–); Suzy Lamplugh Educational Project (Chmn 1988–) **Other** Daughter of Sir Godfrey Nicholson Bt, MP for Morpeth 1931–5 and Farnham 1937–66

NORRIS, Steven Con., Epping Forest (1988) **b.** 24 May 1945 **ed.** Liverpool Inst.; Worcester Coll., Oxford **Profession** car dealer, company dir. **Political interests** motor industry, health and social services, local govt, civil liberties, animal welfare; anti-hunting **Political career** Berks. Co. Cllr 1977–85; MP for Oxford East 1983–7; won Epping Forest in by-election 15 Dec. 1988 **Other** He went to school with Paul McCartney and George Harrison

OAKES, Rt Hon. Gordon Lab., Halton (1983) **b.** 22 June 1931 **ed.** Wade Deacon Grammar Sch., Widnes; Liverpool Univ. **Profession** solicitor, consultant **Political interests** trade and industry, law, environment, pollution, energy, transport, local govt, tourism; pro-consumer rights, NATO; anti-abortion **Political career** Widnes Borough Cllr 1952–66 (Mayor 1964–5); contested Bebington 1959, Manchester Moss Side 1961; MP for Bolton West 1964–70, for Widnes 1971–83 **Parliamentary career** Opposition Spokesman on Local Govt 1972–4; Under-Secretary of State for the Environment 1974–6, for Energy 1976; Minister of State for Education 1976–9; PC 1979; Opposition Spokesman on the Environment 1979–83 **Unions** sponsored by TGWU **Publications include** *The Management of Higher Education in the Maintained Sector*

O'BRIEN, Bill Lab., Normanton (1983) **b.** 25 Jan. 1929 **ed.** Leeds Univ. **Profession** miner **Political interests** environment, local govt, mining, water industry, housing **Political career** Knottingley Urban District Cllr 1951– ; Wakefield Cllr 1973–83 (Deputy Leader 1974–83); W. Riding Co. Cllr 1969–78 **Parliamentary career** Opposition Spokesman on the Environment 1987– **Unions** NUM **Other** JP 1979

O'NEILL, Martin Principal Opposition Spokesman on Defence Lab., Clackmannan (1983) **b.** 6 Jan. 1945 **ed.** Trinity Academy, Edinburgh; Heriot-Watt Univ., Edinburgh; Moray House Coll. of Education, Edinburgh **Profession** teacher **Political interests** education, defence, Scottish affairs **Political career** contested Edinburgh North 1974; MP for Clackmannan and East Stirlingshire 1979–83 **Parliamentary career** Opposition Spokesman on Scotland 1980–4, on Defence and Disarmament and Arms Control 1984–8; Principal Spokesman on Defence 1988– **Member** Tribune Group **Unions** GMB; MATSA; sponsored by NGA

ONSLOW, Rt Hon. Cranley Con., Woking (1964) **b.** 8 June 1926 **ed.** Harrow; Royal Military Academy, Sandhurst; Oriel Coll., Oxford; Geneva Univ. **Profession** Royal Armoured Corps 1944–8, diplomat, MI6, company dir. **Political interests** defence, foreign affairs, aviation, conservation, trade and industry; pro-field sports **Political career** Dartford Rural District Cllr 1960–2; Kent Co. Cllr 1961–4 **Parliamentary career** Executive of 1922 Cttee 1968–72, 1981–2, 1983– (Chmn 1984–); Under-Secretary of State for Trade and Industry (Aerospace) 1972–4; Opposition Spokesman on Health and Social Security 1974–5, on Defence 1975–6; Chmn Select Cttee on Defence 1981–2; Minister of State at the Foreign and Commonwealth Office 1982–3; PC 1988 **Other** A descendant of three Speakers of the House of Commons (the first in 1566)

OPPENHEIM, Phillip Con., Amber Valley (1983) **b.** 20 Mar. 1956 **ed.** Harrow; Oriel Coll., Oxford **Profession** journalist, publisher, company dir., farmer **Political interests** information technology, computers, motor industry, aerospace, trade and industry, publishing, agriculture, health and social services, animal welfare, EC **Publications include** *A Handbook of New Office Technology*; *Telecommunications: A User's Handbook*; *A Word Processing Handbook*; co-founder and co-editor of *What to Buy for Business* 1980–5 **Other** Son of Baroness Oppenheim-Barnes (Sally Oppenheim), MP for Gloucester 1970–87

ORME, Rt Hon. Stanley Lab., Salford East (1983) **b.** 5 Apr. 1923 **ed.** Springfield Road Elementary Sch.; National Council of Lab. Colleges; Workers' Education Association **Profession** RAF 1942–7; engineer **Political interests** trade and industry, industrial relations, public ownership, energy, health and social services, Northern Ireland, foreign affairs; anti-EC, pro-Irish reunification **Political career** Sale Borough Cllr 1958–65; contested Stockport South 1959; MP for Salford West 1964–83 **Parliamentary career** Opposition Spokesman on Northern Ireland 1973–4; PC 1974; Minister of State for Northern Ireland 1974–6, for Health and Social Security 1976–9; Shadow Secretary for Health and Social Security 1979–80, for Industry 1980–3, for Energy 1983–7; Chmn Parliamentary Labour Party 1987– **Member** CND; Tribune Group **Unions** sponsored by AEU

OWEN, Rt Hon. Dr David Leader of the SDP SDP (Lab. 1966–81), Plymouth Devonport (1974) **b.** 2 July 1938 **ed.** Bradfield Coll.; Sidney Sussex Coll., Cambridge; St Thomas's Hospital, London **Profession** doctor **Political interests** health and social services, child care, drug abuse, energy, constitutional reform, human rights, defence, foreign affairs **Political career** contested Torrington 1964; MP for Plymouth Sutton 1966–74 **Parliamentary career** Under-Secretary of State for Defence (Royal Navy) 1968–70; Opposition Spokesman on Defence 1970–2; Under-Secretary of State for Health 1974; Minister of State for Health and Social Services 1974–6; PC 1976; Minister of State at the Foreign and Commonwealth Office 1976–7; Secretary of State for Foreign and Commonwealth Affairs 1977–9; Shadow Energy Secretary 1979–80; a founder of the SDP, launched by the Limehouse Declaration 26 Mar. 1981; Deputy Leader of the SDP 1982–3, Leader 1983–7; resigned over merger with Liberal Party; re-elected Leader of SDP 1988– **Member** Independent Commission on International Humanitarian Issues 1983– **Unions** MSF **Publications include** *Face the Future*; *A Future That Will Work*; *A United Kingdom*; *Speaking Personally*; *Our NHS*

PAGE, Richard Con., Hertfordshire South West (1979) **b.** 22 Feb. 1941 **ed.** Hurstpierpoint Coll.; Luton Technical Coll. **Profession** mechanical engineer, company dir. **Political interests** small businesses, trade and industry, science and technology **Political career** Banstead Urban District Cllr 1968–71; contested Workington 1974; MP for Workington 1976–9

PAICE, James Con., Cambridgeshire South East (1987) **b.** 24 Apr. 1949 **ed.** Framlingham Coll.; Writtle Agricultural Coll., Essex **Profession** farmer, company dir. **Political interests** small businesses, employment, agriculture **Political career** Suffolk Coastal District Cllr 1976–87 (Chmn 1982–3); contested Caernarfon 1979

PAISLEY, Rev. Ian DUP, Antrim North (1970) **b.** 6 Apr. 1926 **ed.** Ballymena Model Sch.; Ballymena Technical High Sch.; South Wales Bible Coll.; Reformed Presbyterian Theological Coll., Belfast; Bob Jones Univ., US **Profession** minister, publisher, writer **Political interests** foreign affairs, Northern Ireland, religion, constitutional affairs **Political career** Stormont MP 1970–2; Northern Ireland Assembly 1973–4, 1982–6; Constitutional Convention 1975–6; MEP for Northern Ireland 1979– **Parliamentary career** Leader and co-founder of DUP 1971– ; resigned seat Dec. 1985 in protest at Anglo-Irish agreement; re-elected Jan. 1986 **Member** Moderator of Free Presbyterian Church of Ulster 1951– ; World Congress of Fundamentalists (Co-Chmn 1978–); Pres. of Whitefield Coll. of the Bible 1980– **Publications include** *No Pope Here*; (jtly) *Ulster – The Facts*; *Paisley's Pocket Preacher*; *Jonathan Edwards: The Theologian of Revival*

PARKINSON, Rt Hon. Cecil Secretary of State for Transport Con., Hertsmere (1983) **b.** 1 Sep. 1931 **ed.** Royal Grammar Sch., Lancaster; Emmanuel Coll., Cambridge **Profession** accountant, company dir. **Political interests** trade and industry, energy, transport; pro-hanging **Political career** contested Northampton 1970; MP for Enfield West 1970–4, for Hertfordshire South 1974–83 **Parliamentary career** Asst Whip 1974; Opposition Whip 1974–6; Opposition Spokesman on Trade 1976–9; Minister of State for Trade 1979–81; PC 1981; Paymaster General 1981–2; Chmn of Conservative Party 1981–3; Chancellor of the Duchy of Lancaster 1982–3; Secretary of State for Trade and Industry 1983; resigned over Sara Keays affair; Secretary of State for Energy 1987–9, for Transport 1989– **Other** Cambridge running blue

PARRY, Robert Lab., Liverpool Riverside (1983) **b.** 8 Jan. 1933 **ed.** Bishop Goss Roman Catholic Sch., Liverpool **Profession** construction worker, union official **Political interests** human rights, overseas development, foreign affairs, Korea, Hong Kong, Northern Ireland, housing; anti-EC, Falklands War; pro-united Ireland **Political career** Liverpool City Cllr 1963–74; MP for Liverpool Exchange 1970–4, for Liverpool Scotland Exchange 1974–83 **Member** Campaign Group (co-founder 1982); Co-operative Party **Unions** sponsored by TGWU

PATCHETT, Terry Lab., Barnsley East (1983) **b.** 11 July 1940 **ed.** Wombwell Technical Coll.; Sheffield Univ. **Profession** miner **Political interests** coal, energy, local govt, health and social services, Third Word, peace, nuclear disarmament **Political career** Wombwell Urban District Cllr 1969–73 **Member** Tribune Group **Unions** sponsored by NUM

PATNICK, Irvine Con., Sheffield Hallam (1987) **b.** Oct 1929 **ed.** Central Technical Sch.; Sheffield Poly. **Profession** building contractor, company dir. **Political interests** local govt, building industry **Political career** Sheffield City Cllr 1967–70; Sheffield Metropolitan District Cllr 1971–88; S. Yorks. Co. Cllr 1973–86; contested Sheffield Hillsborough 1970, 1979 **Parliamentary career** Asst Whip 1989– **Other** OBE 1980

PATTEN, Chris Secretary of State for the Environment Con., Bath (1979) **b.** 12 May 1944 **ed.** St Benedict's Sch., Ealing; Balliol Coll., Oxford **Profession** Conservative Research Dept 1966–70 (Dir. 1974–9), company dir., journalist, consultant **Political interests** foreign affairs, overseas development, defence, Northern Ireland, economy, education, environment; anti-hanging, pro-proportional representation **Political career** asst to Lord Carrington, Chmn of Conservative Party 1972–4; contested Lambeth Central 1974 **Parliamentary career** Under-Secretary of State at the Northern Ireland Office 1983–5; Minister of State for Education and Science 1985–6, at the Foreign Office (Overseas Development) 1986–9; Secretary of State for the Environment 1989– **Publications include** *The Tory Case*

PATTEN, Rt Hon. Dr John Con., Oxford West and Abingdon (1983) **b.** 17 July 1945 **ed.** Wimbledon Coll.; Sidney Sussex Coll., Cambridge **Profession** lecturer in geography **Political interests** home affairs, health and social services, housing, Northern Ireland; anti-hanging **Political career** Oxford City Cllr 1973–6; MP for Oxford 1979–83 **Parliamentary career** Under-Secretary of State for Northern Ireland 1981–3, for Health 1983–5; Minister of State for the Environment (Housing, Urban Affairs and Construction) 1985–7, at the Home Office 1987– ; PC 1990 **Publications include** (jtly) *The Conservative Opportunity*; *Pre-Industrial England*; (jtly) *The Penguin Guide to the Landscape of England and Wales*

PATTIE, Rt Hon. Sir Geoffrey Con., Chertsey and Walton (1974) **b.** 17 Jan. 1936 **ed.** Durham Sch.; St Catharine's Coll., Cambridge; Gray's Inn **Profession** barrister, company dir. **Political interests** defence, trade and industry, technology, aviation, mental health **Political career** Greater London Cllr 1967–70; contested Barking 1966, 1970 **Parliamentary career** Under-Secretary of State for Defence (RAF) 1979–81, for Defence (Procurement) 1981–3; Minister of State for Defence (Procurement) 1983–4, for Trade and Industry (Information Technology) 1984–7; PC 1987 **Member** Bow Group; General Synod of the Church of England 1970–5 **Publications include** *Towards a New Defence Policy*; *A New World Role for the Medium Power: The British Opportunity* **Other** Knighted 1987

PAWSEY, James Con., Rugby and Kenilworth (1983) **b.** 21 Aug. 1933 **ed.** Coventry Technical Sch.; Coventry Technical Coll. **Profession** company dir., Lloyd's underwriter **Political interests** education, trade and industry, health and social security, environment, law and order, foreign affairs; pro-capital and corporal punishment; anti-EC, abortion **Political career** Rugby Rural District Cllr 1965–73; Rugby Borough Cllr 1973–5; Warks. Co. Cllr 1974–9; MP for Rugby 1979–83 **Member** European Reform Group **Other** He is the father of six sons, including two sets of twins

PEACOCK, Elizabeth Con., Batley and Spen (1983) **b.** 4 Sep. 1937 **ed.** St Monica's Convent, Skipton **Profession** administrator, consultant **Political interests** health and social services, education, drug abuse, employment, textile industry, trade and industry, regional policy, law and order; anti-video nasties, pro-hanging **Political career** N. Yorks. Co. Cllr 1981–4 **Parliamentary career** Executive of 1922 Cttee 1987– **Member** National Assn of Approved Driving Instructors (Honorary Pres. 1984–) **Other** JP 1982

PENDRY, Tom Lab., Stalybridge and Hyde (1970) **b.** 10 June 1934 **ed.** St Augustine's Sch., Ramsgate;

Plater Hall, Oxford **Profession** union official **Political interests** industrial relations, industrial law, housing, health and social services, environment, sport and recreation, Northern Ireland, finance; anti-EC **Political career** Paddington Borough Cllr 1962–5 **Parliamentary career** Opposition Whip 1971–4; Lord Commissioner of the Treasury (Govt Whip) 1974–7; Under-Secretary of State for Northern Ireland 1978–9; Opposition Spokesman on Northern Ireland 1979–82, on Overseas Development 1981–2, on Regional Affairs and Devolution 1982– ; Chmn All-Party Football Cttee 1980– **Member** Co-operative Party; Fabian Society; British Boxing Board of Control (Steward 1987–) **Unions** sponsored by NUPE **Other** Middleweight Colonial champion Hong Kong 1957

PIKE, Peter Lab., Burnley (1983) **b.** 26 June 1937 **ed.** Hinchley Wood Co. Secondary Sch. **Profession** factory inspector, party official **Political interests** local govt, housing, transport, race relations, environment, energy, employment, trade and industry, health and social services **Political career** Merton and Morden Urban District Cllr 1962–3; Burnley Borough Cllr 1976–84 (Leader 1980–3) **Member** Anti-Apartheid; CND **Unions** sponsored by GMB

PORTER, Barry Con., Wirral South (1983) **b.** 11 June 1939 **ed.** Birkenhead Sch.; Univ. Coll., Oxford **Profession** solicitor, company dir. **Political interests** trade and industry, transport, tourism and leisure, Northern Ireland **Political career** Birkenhead Borough Cllr 1967–74; Wirral Borough Cllr 1975–9; contested Liverpool Scotland Exchange 1971, Newton le Willows Feb. 1974, Chorley Oct. 1974; MP for Bebington and Ellesmere Port 1979–83

PORTER, David Con., Waveney (1987) **b.** 16 Apr. 1948 **ed.** Lowestoft Grammar Sch.; New Coll. of Speech and Drama, London **Profession** drama teacher **Political interests** local govt, transport, education, regional policy, fishing industry, arts **Political career** Waveney District Cllr 1979–84, 1985–7

PORTILLO, Michael Con., Enfield Southgate (1984) **b.** 26 May 1953 **ed.** Harrow Co. Sch. for Boys; Peterhouse, Cambridge **Profession** Conservative Research Dept 1976–9, consultant **Political interests** health and social services, transport, energy, privatization, taxation **Political career** contested Birmingham Perry Barr 1983 **Parliamentary career** Asst Whip 1986–7; Under-Secretary of State for Health and Social Security 1987–8; Minister of State for Transport (Public Transport) 1988–90, for the Environment (Local Govt) 1990–

POWELL, Ray Lab., Ogmore (1979) **b.** 19 June 1928 **ed.** Pentre Grammar Sch., Rhondda; National Council of Labour Colleges; London Sch. of Economics **Profession** water authority administrator **Political interests** trade and industry, coal, steel, water, railways, retail trade, small business, employment, Welsh affairs, nuclear disarmament; anti-Sunday trading, Falklands War; pro-devolution **Political career** Ogwr Borough Cllr 1973–6; Chmn of Welsh Labour Party 1977–8 **Parliamentary career** Opposition Whip 1984– **Member** CND; Campaign Group **Unions** sponsored by USDAW

POWELL, William Con., Corby (1983) **b.** 3 Aug. 1948 **ed.** Lancing Coll.; Emmanuel Coll., Cambridge; Lincoln's Inn **Profession** barrister **Political interests** foreign affairs, EC, US, defence, overseas aid, election law, copyright, trade and industry; anti-hanging

PRESCOTT, John Shadow Transport Secretary Lab., Kingston upon Hull East (1970) **b.** 31 May 1938 **ed.** Grange Secondary Modern Sch., Ellesmere Port; Ruskin Coll., Oxford; Hull Univ. **Profession** seaman, union official **Political interests** transport, energy, shipping, regional policy, unions, economy, nuclear disarmament; anti-Falklands War, EC **Political career** contested Southport 1966; MEP 1976–9 **Parliamentary career** Opposition Spokesman on Merchant Shipping 1972–4, on Transport 1979–81, on Regional Affairs and Devolution 1981–3; Shadow Transport Secretary 1983–4; Shadow Employment Secretary 1984–7; Shadow Energy Secretary 1987–8; Shadow Transport Secretary 1988– ; Labour National Executive Cttee 1989– **Member** CND; Tribune Group **Unions** sponsored by NUS **Publications include** *Not Wanted on Voyage*

PRICE, Sir David Con., Eastleigh (1955) **b.** 20 Nov. 1924 **ed.** Eton; Trinity Coll., Cambridge; Yale Univ. **Profession** Scots Guards 1942–6; industrial consultant, company dir. **Political interests** science and technology, trade and industry, shipping, food industry, economy, health and social services, arts, heritage; anti-monetarism; pro-EC, US **Parliamentary career** Parliamentary Secretary to the Board of Trade 1962–4; Opposition Spokesman on Science and Technology 1965–70; Parliamentary Secretary at the Ministry of Technology 1970, for Aviation Supply 1970–1; Under-Secretary of State for Trade and Industry (Aerospace) 1971–2; Chmn Scientific Cttee 1973–5, 1979–82 **Member** Institute of Industrial Managers (Vice-Pres. 1980–) **Other** Knighted 1980; DL Hampshire 1982

PRIMAROLO, Dawn Lab., Bristol South (1987) **b.** 2 May 1954 **ed.** Thomas Bennett Comprehensive Sch.; Bristol Poly.; Bristol Univ. **Profession** secretary, research asst **Political interests** education, housing, employment, women's issues, energy, Nicaragua, Chile **Political career** Avon Co. Cllr 1985–7

QUIN, Joyce Lab., Gateshead East (1987) **b.** 26 Nov. 1944 **ed.** Whitley Bay Grammar Sch.; Newcastle Univ.; London Sch. of Economics **Profession** lecturer in French and politics **Political interests** EC, trade and industry, regional policy, shipbuilding, fishing industry, women's issues; pro-EC **Political career** MEP for Tyne and Wear 1979–89 **Parliamentary career** Opposition Spokesman on Trade and Industry 1989– **Member** Fabian Society **Unions** sponsored by TGWU

RADICE, Giles Lab., Durham North (1983) **b.** 4 Oct. 1936 **ed.** Winchester; Magdalen Coll., Oxford; London Sch. of Economics **Profession** union researcher, writer **Political interests** trade and industry, unions, education, employment, foreign affairs **Political career** contested Chippenham 1964, 1966; MP for Chester-le-Street 1973–83 **Parliamentary career** Opposition Spokesman on Foreign Affairs 1981, on Employment 1982–3, on Education 1983–7 **Member** Fabian Society (Chmn 1976–7) **Unions** sponsored by GMB **Publications include** (jtly) *Socialists in Recession*; *The Industrial Democrats*; *More Power to People*

RAFFAN, Keith Con., Delyn (1983) **b.** 21 June 1949 **ed.** Trinity Coll., Glenalmond; Corpus Christi Coll., Cambridge **Profession** journalist **Political interests** Welsh affairs, regional policy, tourism, employment, drug abuse **Political career** contested Dulwich Feb. 1974, Aberdeenshire East Oct. 1974 **Unions** NUJ

RAISON, Rt Hon. Timothy Con., Aylesbury (1970) **b.** 3 Nov. 1929 **ed.** Eton; Christ Church, Oxford

Profession journalist, company dir. **Political interests** education, environment, home affairs, foreign and Commonwealth affairs **Political career** Richmond Borough Cllr 1967–71 **Parliamentary career** Under-Secretary of State for Education 1973–4; Opposition Spokesman on Social Services and Education 1974, on Prices and Consumer Affairs 1974–5; Shadow Environment Secretary 1975–6; Minister of State at the Home Office 1979–83, at the Foreign and Commonwealth Office (Overseas Development) 1983–6; PC 1982; Chmn of Select Cttee on Education 1987–9 **Member** Bow Group **Publications include** *Power and Parliament*; *Why Conservative?*; (ed.) *Youth in New Society*; founder and editor of *New Society*

RANDALL, Stuart Lab., Kingston upon Hull West (1983) **b.** 22 June 1938 **ed.** Plymouth Technical Secondary Sch.; Univ. of Wales Coll., Cardiff **Profession** systems engineer, consultant **Political interests** information technology, fishing industry, agriculture, home affairs **Political career** contested Worcestershire South 1974 **Parliamentary career** Opposition Spokesman on Agriculture 1985–7, on Home Affairs 1987– **Unions** sponsored by EETPU

RATHBONE, John (Tim) Con., Lewes (1974) **b.** 17 Mar. 1933 **ed.** Eton; Christ Church, Oxford; Harvard Business Sch. **Profession** advertising executive, company dir. **Political interests** foreign affairs, education, arts, media, consumer affairs, drug abuse; pro-proportional representation, Lords reform, EC, local radio; anti-hanging **Parliamentary career** Founder and Chmn All-Party Cttee on Drug Misuse 1984– **Member** Conservatives for Fundamental Change in South Africa (founder 1985); National Committee for Electoral Reform **Other** Son of John Rathbone, MP for Bodmin 1935–40

REDMOND, Martin Lab., Don Valley (1983) **b.** 15 Aug. 1937 **ed.** Woodlands Roman Catholic Sch.; Sheffield Univ. **Profession** HGV driver **Political interests** mining, disabled, health and social services, nuclear disarmament; anti-EC **Political career** Doncaster Borough Cllr 1975–83 (Leader 1982–3) **Member** CND **Unions** sponsored by NUM

REDWOOD, John Con., Wokingham (1987) **b.** 15 June 1951 **ed.** Kent Coll., Canterbury; Magdalen Coll., Oxford; St Antony's Coll., Oxford **Profession** Fellow All Souls Coll., Oxford 1972–87, head of Prime Minister's policy unit 1983–5, investment analyst, company dir. **Political interests** finance, economy, privatization, popular capitalism, inner cities, education **Political career** Oxon. Co. Cllr 1973–7; contested Southwark Peckham 1982 **Parliamentary career** Under-Secretary of State for Trade and Industry 1989– **Publications include** *Popular Capitalism*; *Equity for Everyman*; (jtly) *Controlling Public Industries*

REES, Rt Hon. Merlyn Lab., Leeds South and Morley (1983) **b.** 18 Dec. 1920 **ed.** Harrow Weald Grammar Sch.; Goldsmiths' Coll., London; London Sch. of Economics; London Univ. Inst. of Education; Nottingham Univ. **Profession** RAF 1941–6; teacher and lecturer in economics and history **Political interests** Northern Ireland, home affairs, employment, housing, education, prisons, defence, economy, energy **Political career** contested Harrow East 1955, 1959; selected for Leeds South on the death of Hugh Gaitskell; MP for Leeds South 1963–83 **Parliamentary career** Under-Secretary of State for Defence (Army) 1965–6, for Defence (RAF) 1966–8, at the Home Office 1968–70; Opposition Spokesman on Home Affairs 1970–2, on Northern Ireland 1972–4; PC 1974; Secretary of State for Northern Ireland 1974–6, at the Home Office 1976–9; Opposition Spokesman on Home Affairs 1979–80, on Energy 1980–2, on Industry and Employment Co-ordination 1982–3 **Member** Fabian Society **Unions** GMB; NUT **Publications include** *Northern Ireland: A Personal Perspective*

REID, Dr John Lab., Motherwell North (1987) **b.** 8 May 1947 **ed.** St Patrick's Senior Secondary Sch., Coatbridge; Stirling Univ. **Profession** researcher, union official **Political interests** trade and industry, steel, employment, unions, education, housing, health and social services, Central America, foreign affairs, nuclear disarmament **Unions** sponsored by TGWU

RENTON, Timothy Commons Chief Whip Con., Sussex Mid (1974) **b.** 28 May 1932 **ed.** Eton; Magdalen Coll., Oxford **Profession** company dir., Lloyd's underwriter **Political interests** trade and industry, unions, privatization, employment, finance, home affairs, conservation; pro-EMS, EC, proportional representation **Political career** contested Sheffield Park 1970 **Parliamentary career** Under-Secretary of State at the Foreign and Commonwealth Office 1984–5; Minister of State at the Foreign and Commonwealth Office 1985–7, at the Home Office 1987–9; Parliamentary Secretary to the Treasury (Commons Chief Whip) 1989– **Unions** GMB (APEX partnership)

RHODES JAMES, Robert Con., Cambridge (1976) **b.** 10 Apr. 1933 **ed.** Sedbergh Sch.; Worcester Coll., Oxford **Profession** Commons clerk 1955–64, Fellow All Souls Coll., Oxford 1964–8, company dir., publisher, historian **Political interests** foreign affairs, defence, education **Parliamentary career** Speaker's Panel of Chairmen 1988– **Member** History of Parliament Trust (Chmn 1983–); Stop Polio Campaign of the Save the Children Fund (Chmn 1983–) **Publications include** *Albert: Prince Consort*; (ed.) *The Complete Speeches of Sir Winston Churchill*; *Ambition and Realities: British Politics 1964–70*

RICHARDSON, Jo Lab., Barking (1974) **b.** 28 Aug. 1923 **ed.** Southend-on-Sea High Sch. for Girls **Profession** secretary to Ian Mikardo MP 1945–60, company dir. **Political interests** women's issues, civil liberties, public ownership, defence, nuclear disarmament, foreign affairs; pro-abortion, anti-Falklands War **Political career** Hornsey Borough Cllr 1951–5; Hammersmith Borough Cllr 1962–5; contested Monmouth 1951 and 1955, Hornchurch 1959, Harrow East 1964 **Parliamentary career** Labour National Executive Cttee 1979– ; Opposition Spokesman on Women 1983– ; Chmn of Labour Party 1988– **Member** Co-operative Party; CND (Vice-Pres.); Tribune Group (Chmn 1978–9); Campaign Group **Unions** GMB (APEX partnership); MSF

RIDDICK, Graham Con., Colne Valley (1987) **b.** 26 Aug. 1955 **ed.** Stowe Sch.; Warwick Univ. **Profession** sales manager, Lloyd's underwriter **Political interests** trade and industry, small businesses, local govt, education; pro-NATO, anti-unions

RIDLEY, Rt Hon. Nicholas Con., Cirencester and Tewkesbury (1959) **b.** 17 Feb. 1929 **ed.** Eton; Balliol Coll., Oxford **Profession** civil engineer, company dir. **Political interests** trade and industry, technology, transport, environment, arts, foreign affairs; pro-monetarism **Political career** contested Blyth 1955

Parliamentary career Opposition Spokesman on Power 1964–5, and 1967–8, on Defence 1965–6, on Labour Relations 1966–7, on Trade and Technology 1969–70; Under-Secretary of State for Technology 1970, for Trade and Industry 1970–2; Minister of State at the Foreign and Commonwealth Office 1979–81; Financial Secretary to the Treasury 1981–3; PC 1983; Secretary of State for Transport 1983–6, for the Environment 1986–9, for Trade and Industry 1989–90; resigned from Cabinet 14 July 1990 after *Spectator* interview attacking the EC

RIDSDALE, Sir Julian Con., Harwich (1954) **b.** 8 June 1915 **ed.** Tonbridge Sch.; Royal Military Academy, Sandhurst; Oriental Sch. of Languages, London Univ. **Profession** Army 1935–46; fruit farmer, company dir. **Political interests** defence, NATO, foreign affairs, Japan, finance; pro-hanging **Political career** contested Paddington North 1951 **Parliamentary career** Under-Secretary of State for Defence (Air Ministry) 1962–4, for Defence (RAF) 1964; Chmn British Japanese Group 1964– ; Chmn All-Party Group for Engineering Development 1985– **Other** Nephew of Stanley Baldwin and of Sir Aurelian Ridsdale, Lib. MP for Brighton 1906–10; CBE 1977; knighted 1981

RIFKIND, Rt Hon. Malcolm Secretary of State for Scotland Con., Edinburgh Pentlands (1974) **b.** 21 June 1946 **ed.** George Watson's Coll., Edinburgh; Edinburgh Univ. **Profession** advocate (QC 1985) **Political interests** Scottish affairs, foreign affairs, overseas development; pro-devolution, anti-hanging **Political career** Edinburgh Town Cllr 1970–4; contested Edinburgh Central 1970 **Parliamentary career** Opposition Spokesman on Scottish Affairs 1975–6 (resigned over devolution); Minister of State at the Scottish Office (Home Affairs and the Environment) 1979–82; Under-Secretary of State at the Foreign and Commonwealth Office 1982–3; Minister of State at the Foreign and Commonwealth Office 1983–6; PC 1986; Secretary of State for Scotland 1986–

ROBERTS, Sir Ieuan (Wyn) Con., Conwy (1970) **b.** 10 July 1930 **ed.** Harrow; Univ. Coll., Oxford **Profession** journalist, TV executive and producer of Welsh language programmes **Political interests** Welsh affairs, media, education, tourism, small businesses, transport, conservation, economy; pro-Welsh language, anti-Plaid Cymru **Parliamentary career** Opposition Spokesman on Welsh Affairs 1974–9; Under-Secretary of State at the Welsh Office 1979–87; Minister of State at the Welsh Office 1987– **Member** Gorsedd of Bards of the Royal National Eisteddfod 1966– **Other** He is a Welsh-language poet; knighted 1990

ROBERTSON, George Lab., Hamilton (1978) **b.** 12 Apr. 1946 **ed.** Dunoon Grammar Sch., Argyll; St Andrews Univ.; Dundee Univ. **Profession** union official **Political interests** foreign affairs, Scottish affairs, defence, industrial relations, car safety; pro-devolution, EC **Political career** Chmn Scottish Labour Party 1977–8 **Parliamentary career** Opposition Spokesman on Scotland 1979–80, on Defence 1980–1, on Foreign and Commonwealth Affairs 1981– **Member** Manifesto Group; Operation Raleigh Council 1982– ; Seatbelt Survivors' Club (Chmn 1981–) **Unions** sponsored by GMB

ROBINSON, Geoffrey Lab., Coventry North West (1976) **b.** 25 May 1938 **ed.** Emmanuel Sch., London; Clare Coll., Cambridge; Yale Univ. **Profession** motor industry executive **Political interests** science and technology, trade and industry, motor industry, aerospace, new technology, economy, regional policy **Parliamentary career** Opposition Whip 1980–2; Opposition Spokesman on Science 1982–3, on Trade and Industry and Regional Affairs 1983–7 **Unions** TGWU

ROBINSON, Peter DUP, Belfast East (1979) **b.** 29 Dec. 1948 **ed.** Annadale Grammar Sch., Belfast; Castlereagh Coll. of Further Education **Profession** publishing company dir. **Political interests** Northern Ireland, terrorism, housing, community services, shipbuilding, aerospace; pro-hanging **Political career** Castlereagh Borough Cllr 1977– (Mayor 1986); Northern Ireland Assembly 1982–6 **Parliamentary career** Deputy Leader of the DUP 1980–7, 1988– ; resigned Dec. 1985 in protest at Anglo-Irish agreement; re-elected Jan. 1986 **Publications include** *The North Answers Back*; (jtly) *Ulster – The Facts*; *Capital Punishment for Capital Crime*

ROE, Marion Con., Broxbourne (1983) **b.** 15 July 1936 **ed.** Croydon High Sch.; English Sch. of Languages, Switzerland **Political interests** transport, agriculture and horticulture, environment, health and social services, local govt, home affairs; pro-hanging **Political career** Bromley Borough Cllr 1975–8; Greater London Cllr 1977–86; contested Barking 1979 **Parliamentary career** Under-Secretary of State for the Environment 1987–8 **Member** Women's National Cancer Control Campaign (Vice-Pres. 1985–)

ROGERS, Allan Lab., Rhondda (1983) **b.** 24 Oct. 1932 **ed.** Bargoed Secondary Sch.; Univ. Coll., Swansea **Profession** geologist, teacher **Political interests** health and social security, education, environment, energy, defence; anti-EC **Political career** Rhondda District Cllr 1965–71; Glamorgan Co. Cllr 1970–9; MEP for South East Wales 1979–84 (Vice-Pres. of the European Parliament 1979–82) **Parliamentary career** Opposition Spokesman on Defence 1988– **Unions** sponsored by COHSE

ROOKER, Jeffrey Lab., Birmingham Perry Barr (1974) **b.** 5 June 1941 **ed.** Handsworth Technical Coll.; Aston Univ.; Warwick Univ. **Profession** production engineer, lecturer **Political interests** local govt, housing, environment, trade and industry, construction industry, regional development, economy, women's issues, education, devolution, Northern Ireland; anti-British troops in Ulster, sexism; pro-animal welfare **Parliamentary career** Opposition Spokesman on Social Security 1979–83, on Treasury and Economic Affairs 1983–4, on the Environment 1984–8 **Unions** sponsored by MSF

ROSS, Ernest Lab., Dundee West (1979) **b.** 27 July 1942 **ed.** St John's Junior Secondary Sch. **Profession** quality control engineer **Political interests** foreign affairs, Middle East, Africa, Latin America, defence, trade and industry, employment, education, health and social services, defence; anti-Falklands War, Israel **Member** Campaign Group **Unions** sponsored by AEU

ROSS, William OUP, Londonderry East (1983) **b.** 4 Feb. 1936 **ed.** Dungiven Primary Sch. **Profession** farmer **Political interests** agriculture, local govt, housing, disabled, firearms legislation, defence; pro-hanging, anti-power sharing in Ulster **Political career** Limavady District Cllr; MP for Londonderry 1974–83 **Parliamentary career** OUP Spokesman on Agriculture

1974– ; OUP Whip and Spokesman on Local Govt 1977– ; resigned seat Dec. 1985 in protest at the Anglo-Irish agreement; re-elected Jan. 1986 **Member** Apprentice Boys of Derry; Orange Order; Ulster Farmers' Union

ROSSI, Sir Hugh Con., Hornsey and Wood Green (1983) **b.** 21 June 1927 **ed.** Finchley Catholic Grammar Sch.; King's Coll., London **Profession** solicitor, company dir. **Political interests** environment, housing, planning, construction industry, pensions, Northern Ireland, human rights, Cyprus, Italy; anti-abortion, pro-EC **Political career** Hornsey Borough Cllr 1956–65 (Leader 1965); Middx Co. Cllr 1961–5; Haringey Borough Cllr 1964–8; MP for Hornsey 1966–83 **Parliamentary career** Asst Whip 1970–2; Lord Commissioner of the Treasury (Govt Whip) 1972–4; Under-Secretary of State for the Environment 1974; Opposition Spokesman on the Environment (Housing, Planning and Land) 1974–9; Minister of State for Northern Ireland 1979–81, for Social Security and the Disabled 1981–3; Chmn British-Italian Group 1983– ; Chmn Select Cttee on the Environment 1983– **Publications include** *Guide to Community Land Act*; *Guide to Landlord and Tenant Act*; *Guide to Rent (Agriculture) Act* **Other** Knighted 1983

ROST, Peter Con., Erewash (1983) **b.** 19 Sep. 1930 **ed.** Aylesbury Grammar Sch.; Birmingham Univ. **Profession** stockbroker, company dir., financial journalist, energy consultant **Political interests** energy, trade and industry, small businesses, privatization, aviation, science and technology, conservation; anti-pornography, pro-Channel tunnel **Political career** contested Sunderland North 1966; MP for Derbyshire South East 1970–83

ROWE, Andrew Con., Kent Mid (1983) **b.** 11 Sep. 1935 **ed.** Eton; Merton Coll., Oxford **Profession** lecturer, company dir., journalist **Political interests** small businesses, employment, franchising, conservation, voluntary organizations; anti-hanging **Member** Conservative Small Business Bureau (founder and dir.) **Publications include** *Somewhere to Start*; *Democracy Renewed: The Community Council in Practice*; editor of the newspaper *Small Business*

ROWLANDS, Ted Lab., Merthyr Tydfil and Rhymney (1983) **b.** 23 Jan. 1940 **ed.** Wirral Grammar Sch.; King's Coll., London **Profession** lecturer in modern history and govt **Political interests** foreign affairs, overseas aid, energy, education, disabled, publishing, arts; pro-devolution **Political career** MP for Cardiff North 1966–70, for Merthyr Tydfil 1972–83 **Parliamentary career** Under-Secretary of State at the Welsh Office 1969–70 and 1974–5, at the Foreign and Commonwealth Office 1975–6; Minister of State at the Foreign and Commonwealth Office 1976–9; Opposition Spokesman on Foreign and Commonwealth Affairs 1979–80, on Energy 1980–7 **Unions** MSF; sponsored by USDAW

RUDDOCK, Joan Lab., Lewisham Deptford (1987) **b.** 28 Dec. 1943 **ed.** Pontypool Grammar Sch. for Girls; Imperial Coll., London **Profession** charity dir. **Political interests** foreign affairs, defence, nuclear disarmament, environment, housing, employment, race relations, women's issues **Political career** contested Newbury 1979 **Parliamentary career** Opposition Spokesman on Transport 1989– **Member** CND (Chmn 1981–5, Vice-Chmn 1985–) **Unions** sponsored by TGWU **Publications include** *CND Scrapbook*; *Voices for One World*

RUMBOLD, Angela Con., Mitcham and Morden (1982) **b.** 11 Aug. 1932 **ed.** Ealing High Sch.; King's Coll., London **Profession** public relations company dir. **Political interests** home affairs, law and order, transport, education, environment, health and social services, small businesses, trade and industry, defence; pro-capital and corporal punishment, monetarism **Political career** Kingston Borough Cllr 1976–82 **Parliamentary career** Under-Secretary of State for the Environment 1985–6; Minister of State for Education and Science 1986–90, at the Home Office 1990– **Other** CBE 1981

RYDER, Richard Con., Norfolk Mid (1983) **b.** 4 Feb. 1949 **ed.** Radley; Magdalene Coll., Cambridge **Profession** journalist, farmer, company dir. **Political interests** economy, foreign affairs, education, agriculture **Political career** contested Gateshead East 1974; political secretary to Margaret Thatcher 1975–81 **Parliamentary career** Asst Whip 1986–8; Parliamentary Secretary at the Ministry of Agriculture, Fisheries and Food 1988–9; Economic Secretary to the Treasury 1989–90; Paymaster General 1990– **Other** OBE 1981

SACKVILLE, Hon. Tom Con., Bolton West (1983) **b.** 26 Oct. 1950 **ed.** Eton; Lincoln Coll., Oxford **Profession** banker, company dir. **Political interests** defence, disarmament, health and social services, drug abuse, aerospace, finance; anti-hanging **Political career** contested Pontypool 1979 **Parliamentary career** Asst Whip 1988– **Publications include** *Heroin, Threat to a Generation*

SAINSBURY, Hon. Timothy Con., Hove (1973) **b.** 11 June 1932 **ed.** Eton; Worcester Coll., Oxford **Profession** company dir. **Political interests** foreign affairs, Israel, defence, environment, retail trade; anti-Sunday trading, pornography **Parliamentary career** Asst Whip 1983–5; Lord Commissioner of the Treasury (Govt Whip) 1985–7; Under-Secretary of State for Defence (Procurement) 1987–9, at the Foreign Office 1989–90; Minister of State for Trade and Industry 1990– **Member** Bow Group **Other** Member of the Sainsbury supermarket family

SALMOND, Alexander SNP, Banff and Buchan (1987) **b.** 31 Dec. 1954 **ed.** Linlithgow Academy; St Andrews Univ. **Profession** economist **Political interests** fishing industry, agriculture, energy, oil, Scottish affairs, economy, Third World **Parliamentary career** SNP Spokesman on Energy, Treasury and Fishing 1987–

SAYEED, Jonathan Con., Bristol East (1983) **b.** 20 Mar. 1948 **ed.** Woolverstone Hall, Suffolk; Royal Naval Coll., Dartmouth; Royal Naval Engineering Coll., Manadon **Profession** Royal Navy 1966–72; marine insurance consultant, Lloyd's underwriter, company dir. **Political interests** shipping, defence, foreign affairs, home affairs; anti-apartheid, video nasties **Political career** defeated Tony Benn to win seat in 1983

SCOTT, Nicholas Con., Chelsea (1974) **b.** 5 Aug. 1933 **ed.** Clapham Coll.; City of London Coll.; City Lit. **Profession** company dir. **Political interests** environment, housing, education, employment, Northern Ireland, law and order, health and social services, disabled, defence, printing and publishing; pro-EC; anti-racism, hanging **Political career** Holborn Borough Cllr 1956–9, 1962–5; National Chmn Young Conservatives 1963; contested Islington South West

1959, 1964; MP for Paddington South 1966–74 **Parliamentary career** Under-Secretary of State for Employment 1974; Opposition Spokesman on Housing 1974–5; Executive of 1922 Cttee 1978–81; Under-Secretary of State for Northern Ireland 1981–6; Minister of State for Northern Ireland 1986–7, for Social Services and the Disabled 1987–8, for Social Security 1988– **Member** Tory Reform Group (Pres. 1975–) **Other** JP 1961; MBE 1964

SEDGEMORE, Brian Lab., Hackney South and Shoreditch (1983) **b.** 17 Mar. 1937 **ed.** Heles Sch., Exeter; Corpus Christi, Oxford **Profession** barrister, TV researcher, writer **Political interests** economy, law, housing **Political career** Wandsworth Borough Cllr 1971–4; MP for Luton West 1974–9 **Member** Campaign Group; Fabian Society **Unions** ACTT; NUJ **Publications include** *The Secret Constitution*; *Power Failure*; *Big Bang 2000*

SHAW, David Con., Dover (1987) **b.** 14 Nov. 1950 **ed.** King's Coll. Sch., Wimbledon; City of London Poly. **Profession** accountant, company dir. **Political interests** trade and industry, small businesses, economy, defence, foreign affairs, local govt, housing, education, privatization; anti-Channel tunnel **Political career** Kingston upon Thames Borough Cllr 1974–8; contested Leigh 1979 **Member** Bow Group (Chmn 1983–4)

SHAW, Sir Giles Con., Pudsey (1974) **b.** 16 Nov. 1931 **ed.** Sedbergh Sch.; St John's Coll., Cambridge **Profession** company dir. **Political interests** trade and industry, textiles, food marketing, environment, water industry, Northern Ireland, home affairs; pro-EC, EMS **Political career** Flaxon Rural District Cllr 1957–64; contested Hull West 1966 **Parliamentary career** Under-Secretary of State for Northern Ireland 1979–81, for the Environment 1981–3, for Energy 1983–4; Minister of State at the Home Office 1984–6, for Trade and Industry 1986–7; Treasurer of 1922 Cttee 1988– **Other** Knighted 1987

SHAW, Sir Michael Con., Scarborough (1974) **b.** 9 Oct. 1920 **ed.** Sedbergh Sch. **Profession** accountant **Political interests** fishing industry, prisons, EC; pro-hanging **Political career** contested Dewsbury 1955, Brighouse and Spenborough 1959; MP for Brighouse and Spenborough 1960–4, for Scarborough and Whitby 1966–74; MEP 1974–9 **Parliamentary career** Speaker's Panel of Chairmen 1979– **Other** JP 1953; DL W. Yorks. 1977; knighted 1982

SHEERMAN, Barry Lab., Huddersfield (1983) **b.** 17 Aug. 1940 **ed.** Hampton Grammar Sch.; Kingston Technical Coll.; London Sch. of Economics; London Univ. **Profession** lecturer **Political interests** trade and industry, education, youth, small businesses, employment, home affairs, aviation, transport, media, energy, finance; pro-seatbelts, anti-alcohol **Political career** Loughor Urban District Cllr 1972–4; Lliw Valley Borough Cllr 1973–8; contested Taunton 1974; MP for Huddersfield East 1979–83 **Parliamentary career** Opposition Spokesman on Employment 1983–8, on Education 1983–7, on Home Affairs 1988– **Member** sponsored by Co-operative Party; Fabian Society **Unions** MSF; AUT

SHELDON, Rt Hon. Robert Lab., Ashton-under-Lyne (1964) **b.** 13 Sep. 1923 **ed.** Burnley Grammar Sch.; Salford Technical Coll.; Burnley Technical Coll.; Stockport Technical Coll.; London Univ. **Profession** engineer, company dir. **Political interests** civil service, economy, textiles **Political career** contested Manchester Withington 1959 **Parliamentary career** Opposition Spokesman on Civil Service, Treasury Matters and Machinery of Govt 1970–4; Minister of State for the Civil Service 1974, at the Treasury 1974–5; Financial Secretary to the Treasury 1975–9; PC 1977; Shadow Deputy Leader of the House of Commons and Opposition Spokesman on Treasury and Economic Affairs 1980–3; Chmn Public Accounts Cttee 1983– **Unions** TGWU **Publications include** (jtly) *Administrative Reform: The Next Step*

SHELTON, Sir William Con., Streatham (1974) **b.** 30 Oct. 1929 **ed.** Radley Coll.; Tabor Academy, US; Worcester Coll., Oxford; Texas Univ. **Profession** advertising executive, company dir., Lloyd's underwriter **Political interests** foreign affairs, education, pensioners; pro-monetarism **Political career** Greater London Cllr 1967–70; MP for Wandsworth Clapham 1970–4 **Parliamentary career** PPS to Margaret Thatcher, Leader of the Opposition, 1975; Under-Secretary of State for Education and Science 1981–3 **Other** Knighted 1989

SHEPHARD, Gillian Con., Norfolk South West (1987) **b.** 22 Jan. 1940 **ed.** North Walsham Girls' High Sch.; St Hilda's Coll., Oxford **Profession** school inspector **Political interests** health and social services, education, prisons, agriculture, economy, EC **Political career** Norfolk Co. Cllr 1977–87 **Parliamentary career** Under-Secretary of State for Social Security 1989– **Other** JP

SHEPHERD, Colin Con., Hereford (1974) **b.** 13 Jan. 1938 **ed.** Oundle Sch.; Gonville and Caius Coll., Cambridge; McGill Univ., Canada **Profession** marketing dir. **Political interests** Welsh affairs, agriculture, conservation, tourism, animal welfare, Commonwealth affairs

SHEPHERD, Richard Con., Aldridge-Brownhills (1979) **b.** 6 Dec. 1942 **ed.** Isleworth Grammar Sch.; London Sch. of Economics; Sch. of Advanced International Studies, Johns Hopkins Univ., US **Profession** company dir. (retail food), Lloyd's underwriter **Political interests** trade and industry, retail trade, unions, civil service, freedom of information; anti-EC **Political career** contested Nottingham East 1974

SHERSBY, Michael Con., Uxbridge (1972) **b.** 17 Feb. 1933 **ed.** John Lyon Sch., Harrow **Profession** company dir., Dir. General of the Sugar Bureau 1977–88 **Political interests** sugar industry, film industry, public accounts, environment, conservation, human rights, Falkland Islands, foreign affairs **Political career** Paddington Borough Cllr 1959–64; Westminster City Cllr 1964–71 **Parliamentary career** Speaker's Panel of Chairmen 1983– **Member** UK Sugar Industry Association (Secretary 1978–88)

SHORE, Rt Hon. Peter Lab., Bethnal Green and Stepney (1983) **b.** 20 May 1924 **ed.** Quarry Bank Grammar Sch., Liverpool; King's Coll., Cambridge **Profession** political economist, broadcaster, writer **Political interests** foreign affairs, Middle East, Northern Ireland, economy, employment, race relations, home affairs; pro-NATO, Commonwealth; anti-EC **Political career** contested St Ives 1950, Halifax 1959; MP for Stepney 1964–74, for Stepney and Poplar 1974–83 **Parliamentary career** PPS to the Prime Minister, Harold Wilson, 1965–6; Parliamentary

Secretary at the Ministry of Technology 1966–7; Under-Secretary of State for Economic Affairs 1967; PC 1967; Secretary of State for Economic Affairs 1967–9; Minister without Portfolio and Deputy Leader of the House of Commons 1969–70; Opposition Spokesman on Europe 1971–4; Secretary of State for Trade 1974–6, for the Environment 1976–9; Opposition Spokesman on Foreign Affairs 1979–80, on Treasury and Economic Affairs 1980–3; contested leadership of the Labour Party 1983; Opposition Spokesman on Trade and Industry 1983–4; Shadow Leader of the House of Commons 1983–7 **Member** Fabian Society **Unions** sponsored by TGWU **Publications include** *Entitled to Know*; *Europe: The Way Back*; *Industry and Society*

SHORT, Clare Lab., Birmingham Ladywood (1983) **b.** 15 Feb. 1946 **ed.** St Paul's Grammar Sch., Birmingham; Keele Univ.; Leeds Univ. **Profession** charity dir. **Political interests** race relations and immigration, employment, low pay, home affairs, women's issues, health and social services, Middle East; pro-united Ireland **Parliamentary career** attended meeting with Gerry Adams 1983; launched All-Party Group on Race Relations 1985; Opposition Spokesman on Employment 1985–8, on Social Security 1989– ; Labour National Executive Cttee 1988– **Member** Campaign Group **Unions** sponsored by NUPE **Publications include** *Talking Blues: A Study of Young West Indians' Views of Policing*; *Handbook of Immigration Law* **Other** Wife of Alex Lyon, MP for York 1966–83

SILLARS, James SNP (Lab. 1970–6, Scottish Lab. 1976–9), Glasgow Govan (1988) **b.** 4 Oct. 1937 **ed.** Ayr Academy **Profession** railwayman, fireman, union official, management consultant, political journalist **Political interests** Scottish affairs, education, health and social services, industrial relations; pro-devolution **Political career** MP for Ayrshire South 1970–9; left Labour Party to found Scottish Labour Party 1976; leader of Scottish Labour Party 1976–9; joined SNP 1980; contested Linlithgow 1987 **Unions** TGWU **Publications include** *Scotland – The Case for Optimism* **Other** Husband of Margo MacDonald, MP for Glasgow Govan 1973–4

SIMS, Roger Con., Chislehurst (1974) **b.** 27 Jan. 1930 **ed.** St Olave's Grammar Sch., London **Profession** export manager, company dir. **Political interests** Hong Kong, Japan, Sri Lanka, home affairs, law and order, juvenile crime, alcoholism, health and social services, children, education, trade and industry, whisky industry; anti-tobacco; pro-Greenbelt, hanging **Political career** Chislehurst and Sidcup Urban District Cllr 1956–62; contested Shoreditch and Finsbury 1966, 1970 **Parliamentary career** Chmn All-Party ASH (Action on Smoking and Health) Group 1983– **Member** NSPCC (Central Executive Cttee 1980–) **Other** JP 1960; adviser to the Scotch Whisky Association 1980–

SKEET, Sir Trevor Con., Bedfordshire North (1983) **b.** 28 Jan. 1918 **ed.** King's Coll., Auckland; Univ. of New Zealand **Profession** served in World War II with New Zealand forces; barrister, industrial consultant **Political interests** energy, oil, science and technology, race relations **Political career** contested Stoke Newington and Hackney North 1951, Llanelly 1955; MP for Willesden East 1959–64, for Bedford 1970–83 **Parliamentary career** Chmn All-Party Minerals Group 1979– ; Chmn Parliamentary and Scientific Cttee 1985–8, Vice-Pres. 1988– **Other** Knighted 1986

SKINNER, Dennis Lab., Bolsover (1970) **b.** 11 Feb. 1932 **ed.** Tupton Hall Grammar Sch.; Sheffield Univ.; Ruskin Coll., Oxford **Profession** miner **Political interests** energy, coal, industrial relations, economy, education, environment, pensions, inland waterways, Third World; anti-EC, Lords **Political career** Clay Cross Urban District Cllr 1960–70; Derbys. Co. Cllr 1964–70 **Parliamentary career** Labour National Executive Cttee 1978– (Chmn 1988–9); Vice-Chairman Labour Party 1987– **Member** Tribune Group (Chmn 1973–4); Campaign Group **Unions** sponsored by NUM

SMITH, Andrew Lab., Oxford East (1987) **b.** 1 Feb. 1951 **ed.** Reading Grammar Sch.; St John's Coll., Oxford **Profession** officer of Oxford and Swindon Co-operative Society **Political interests** trade and industry, car industry, retail industry, education, housing, employment, youth affairs, economy, Third World **Political career** Oxford City Cllr 1976–87; contested Oxford East 1983 **Parliamentary career** Opposition Spokesman on Education 1988– **Unions** sponsored by USDAW

SMITH, Dr Chris Lab., Islington South and Finsbury (1983) **b.** 24 July 1951 **ed.** George Watson's Coll., Edinburgh; Pembroke Coll., Cambridge; Harvard Univ. **Profession** housing officer **Political interests** housing, local govt, environment, police, home affairs, human rights, gay rights, civil liberties, justice, economy, Northern Ireland, nuclear disarmament, foreign affairs **Political career** Islington Borough Cllr 1978–83; contested Epsom and Ewell 1979 **Parliamentary career** Opposition Whip 1986–7; Opposition Spokesman on Treasury and Economic Affairs 1987– **Member** Tribune Group (Secretary 1984–); Labour Campaign for Criminal Justice (Chmn 1985–); Liberty (Executive 1986–); Co-operative Party; Fabian Society; CND **Unions** sponsored by ACTT and MSF **Publications include** (jtly) *The Economics of Prosperity*; *National Parks*

SMITH, Sir Cyril Lib. Dem. (Lib. 1972–88), Rochdale (1972) **b.** 28 June 1928 **ed.** Rochdale Grammar Sch. **Profession** company dir. **Political interests** housing, health and social services, employment, education, immigration; anti-abortion, closed shop; pro-local govt, hanging **Political career** joined Labour Party 1950; Rochdale Borough Cllr 1952–74 (Alderman 1966–74, Mayor 1966–7); joined Liberal Party 1967; contested Rochdale 1970 **Parliamentary career** Lib. Chief Whip 1975–6; Lib. Spokesman on Employment 1976–7, 1979–83, 1987–8 **Publications include** *Big Cyril*; *Industrial Participation* **Other** MBE 1966; knighted 1988

SMITH, Sir Dudley Con., Warwick and Leamington (1968) **b.** 14 Nov. 1926 **ed.** Chichester High Sch. **Profession** management consultant, journalist, company dir. **Political interests** foreign affairs, China, Turkey, defence, travel and tourism, immigration and race relations, employment, trade and industry, pharmaceutical industry, conservation, parliamentary reform; anti-EC, pro-hanging **Political career** Middx Co. Cllr 1958–65; contested Peckham 1955; MP for Brentford and Chiswick 1959–66 **Parliamentary career** Opposition Whip 1964–6; Opposition Spokesman on Employment and Productivity 1969–70; Under-Secretary of State for Employment 1970–4, for Defence (Army) 1974 **Publications include** *Harold Wilson: A Critical Biography* **Other** Knighted 1983

SMITH, Rt Hon. John Shadow Chancellor of the Exchequer Lab., Monklands East (1983) **b.** 13 Sep. 1938 **ed.** Dunoon Grammar Sch.; Glasgow Univ. **Profession** advocate (QC 1983) **Political interests** economy, trade and industry, employment, energy, law, Scottish affairs, arts; pro-devolution **Political career** contested Fife East 1961, 1964; MP for Lanarkshire North 1970–83 **Parliamentary career** Under-Secretary of State for Energy 1974–5; Minister of State for Energy 1975–6, at the Privy Council Office (with responsibility for devolution) 1976–8; PC 1978; Secretary of State for Trade 1978–9; Opposition Spokesman on Trade, Prices and Consumer Protection 1979–82, on Energy 1982–3, on Employment 1983–4, on Trade and Industry 1984–7; Shadow Chancellor of the Exchequer 1987– **Member** Fabian Society **Unions** sponsored by GMB

SMITH, John Lab., Vale of Glamorgan (1989) **b.** 17 Mar. 1951 **ed.** Penarth Grammar Sch.; Univ. of Wales Coll., Cardiff **Profession** carpenter, lecturer in business studies **Political interests** home affairs, industrial relations **Political career** Vale of Glamorgan Borough Cllr 1979–88; contested Vale of Glamorgan 1987; Chmn Wales Labour Party 1988– ; won seat at by-election 4 May 1989 **Member** Chmn Wales Anti-Apartheid **Unions** sponsored by MSF

SMITH, Tim Con., Beaconsfield (1982) **b.** 5 Oct. 1947 **ed.** Harrow; St Peter's Coll., Oxford **Profession** accountant **Political interests** economy, trade and industry, company law, taxation, privatization, home affairs **Political career** MP for Ashfield 1977–9 **Other** Consultant to the Institute of Chartered Accountants 1982–

SMYTH, Rev. Martin OUP, Belfast South (1982) **b.** 15 June 1931 **ed.** Methodist Coll., Belfast; Magee Univ. Coll., Londonderry; Trinity Coll., Dublin; Presbyterian Coll., Belfast; San Francisco Theological Seminary, US **Profession** Presbyterian minister **Political interests** health and social services, education, transport, human rights, religious affairs, foreign affairs; pro-hanging **Political career** Northern Ireland Constitutional Convention 1975; Northern Ireland Assembly 1982–6; succeeded the murdered Rev. Robert Bradford in this seat **Parliamentary career** OUP Spokesman on Health and Social Services 1983– ; resigned seat Dec. 1985 in protest against Anglo-Irish agreement; re-elected Jan. 1986 **Member** Grand Orange Lodge of Ireland (Grand Master 1972–); Grand Orange Council of the World (Grand Master 1973–82, Pres. 1985–8) **Publications include** *The Battle for Northern Ireland; Why Presbyterian?*; (ed.) *Faith for Today*

SNAPE, Peter Lab., West Bromwich East (1974) **b.** 12 Feb. 1942 **ed.** Dial Stone Secondary Modern Sch., Stockport **Profession** railwayman **Political interests** transport, motorways, environment, housing, home affairs, defence, nuclear disarmament **Political career** Bredbury and Romiley Urban District Cllr 1971–4 **Parliamentary career** Asst Whip 1975–7; Lord Commissioner of the Treasury (Govt Whip) 1977–9; Opposition Spokesman on Defence 1979–82, on Home Affairs 1982–3, on Transport 1983– **Unions** sponsored by NUR **Other** Adviser to the Musicians' Union 1976–

SOAMES, Hon. Nicholas Con., Crawley (1983) **b.** 12 Feb. 1948 **ed.** Eton **Profession** 11th Hussars 1967–70; Equerry HRH Prince of Wales 1970–2; stockbroker, company dir. **Political interests** defence, foreign affairs, environment, trade and industry **Political career** contested Dumbartonshire Central 1979 **Other** Grandson of Winston Churchill and son of Lord (Christopher) Soames, MP for Bedford 1950–76

SOLEY, Clive Lab., Hammersmith (1983) **b.** 7 May 1939 **ed.** Downshall Secondary Modern Sch., Ilford; Newbattle Abbey Adult Education Coll.; Strathclyde Univ.; Southampton Univ. **Profession** probation officer **Political interests** defence, foreign affairs, China, Middle East, civil liberties, prisons, Northern Ireland, inner cities, law and order, environment, housing; pro-united Ireland **Political career** Hammersmith Borough Cllr 1974–8; MP for Hammersmith North 1979–83 **Parliamentary career** Opposition Spokesman on Northern Ireland 1982–4, on Home Affairs 1984–7, on Environment 1987– **Member** Labour Campaign for Criminal Justice (Chmn 1983–); Tribune Group; Co-operative Party **Unions** GMB **Other** Consultant to the Society of Civil and Public Servants 1984–

SPEARING, Nigel Lab., Newham South (1974) **b.** 8 Oct. 1930 **ed.** Latymer Upper Sch., Hammersmith; St Catharine's Coll., Cambridge **Profession** geography teacher **Political interests** foreign and Commonwealth affairs, environment, education, transport, inland waterways, civil liberties; anti-EC, alcohol, tobacco; pro-Thames barrier, Commonwealth **Political career** contested Warwick and Leamington 1964; MP for Acton 1970–4 **Parliamentary career** Select Cttee on European Legislation 1979– (Chmn 1983–) **Member** British Anti-Common Market Campaign (Chmn 1977–83); River Thames Society (Vice-Pres.) **Unions** NUT **Publications include** *The Thames Barrier – Barrage Controversy* **Other** Congregational preacher

SPEED, Keith Con., Ashford (1974) **b.** 11 Mar. 1934 **ed.** Bedford Modern Sch.; Royal Naval Coll., Dartmouth and Greenwich **Profession** Royal Navy 1947–56; marketing manager, company dir. **Political interests** defence, Navy, transport, trade and industry, tourism, local govt, foreign affairs **Political career** contested St Helens 1964; MP for Meriden 1968–74 **Parliamentary career** Asst Whip 1970–1; Lord Commissioner of the Treasury (Govt Whip) 1971–2; Under-Secretary of State for the Environment 1972–4; Opposition Spokesman on Local Govt 1976–7, on Home Affairs 1977–9; Under-Secretary of State for Defence (Navy) 1979–81; sacked for resisting Navy cuts 1981 **Publications include** *Sea Change*; *Blue Print for Britain* **Other** RD 1967; adviser to Professional Association of Teachers 1982–

SPELLER, Tony Con., Devon North (1979) **b.** 12 June 1929 **ed.** Exeter Sch.; London Univ.; Exeter Univ. **Profession** dir. of chain of photocopying and graphic art shops **Political interests** energy, alternative energy sources, small businesses, information technology, tourism, catering, alternative medicine, foreign affairs, Africa, US; anti-immigration, pro-hanging **Political career** Exeter City Cllr 1964–74; contested Devon North 1974; defeated Jeremy Thorpe to win this seat **Parliamentary career** Chmn All-Party Alternative Energy Cttee 1983–

SPICER, Sir James Con., Dorset West (1974) **b.** 4 Oct. 1925 **ed.** Latymer Sch. **Profession** Army 1943–57; farmer, company dir. **Political interests** Turkey, South Africa, foreign affairs, defence, NATO, agriculture, health and social services, hospices, environment; pro-EC **Political career** contested Southampton Itchen 1971; MEP 1975–8 and MEP for Wessex 1979–84

Parliamentary career Chmn British-Turkish Group 1978– ; Vice-Chmn Conservative Party 1984– **Other** Knighted 1988

SPICER, Michael Con., Worcestershire South (1974) **b.** 22 Jan. 1943 **ed.** Wellington Coll.; Emmanuel Coll., Cambridge **Profession** economist, Conservative Research Dept 1966–8; company dir., novelist **Political interests** transport, aviation, energy; pro-EC **Political career** contested Easington 1966, 1970 **Parliamentary career** Vice-Chmn Conservative Party 1981–3, Deputy Chmn 1983–4; Under-Secretary of State for Transport (Minister for Aviation) 1984–7, for Energy 1987–90; Minister of State for the Environment (Housing and Planning) 1990– **Publications include** *Final Act*; *Prime Minister Spy*; *Cotswold Manners*

SQUIRE, Robin Con., Hornchurch (1979) **b.** 12 July 1944 **ed.** Tiffin Sch., Kingston upon Thames **Profession** accountant **Political interests** local govt, housing, environment, health and social services, children, freedom of information, trade and industry, finance; anti-racism, hanging; pro-EC, proportional representation **Political career** Sutton Borough Cllr 1968–82 (Leader 1976–9); National Vice-Chmn Young Conservatives 1974–5; contested Hornchurch 1974 **Member** Tory Reform Group; Conservative Action for Electoral Reform (Chmn 1983–6); Shelter (board member 1982–) **Publications include** (jtly) *Set the Party Free*

STANBROOK, Ivor Con., Orpington (1970) **b.** 13 Jan. 1924 **ed.** Willesden Central Sch.; Birkbeck Coll., London; Univ. Coll., London; Pembroke Coll., Oxford **Profession** RAF 1943–6; colonial civil servant, barrister **Political interests** home affairs, Northern Ireland, law, extradition law, EC, foreign affairs, Africa, constitutional affairs, animal welfare; anti-immigration, pornography; pro-hanging **Political career** contested East Ham South 1966 **Parliamentary career** Chmn British-Nigerian, British-Zambian, British-Southern Africa Groups **Publications include** *A Year in Politics*; *Extradition – The Law and Practice*; *British Nationality – The New Law*

STANLEY, Rt Hon. Sir John Con., Tonbridge and Malling (1974) **b.** 19 Jan. 1942 **ed.** Repton Sch.; Lincoln Coll., Oxford; Syracuse Univ., US **Profession** Conservative Research Dept 1967–8; financial executive, company dir. **Political interests** defence, environment, housing, Northern Ireland **Political career** contested Newton le Willows 1970 **Parliamentary career** PPS to Margaret Thatcher, Leader of the Opposition, 1976–9; Minister for Housing and Construction 1979–83, for Defence (Armed Forces) 1983–7, for Northern Ireland 1987–8; PC 1984 **Publications include** (jtly) *The International Trade in Arms* **Other** Knighted 1988

STEEL, Rt Hon. Sir David Lib. Dem. (Lib. 1965–88), Tweeddale, Ettrick and Lauderdale (1983) **b.** 31 Mar. 1938 **ed.** Prince of Wales Sch., Nairobi; George Watson's Coll., Edinburgh; Edinburgh Univ. **Profession** journalist, broadcaster **Political interests** foreign affairs, Scottish affairs, home affairs, housing, environment, abortion; anti-apartheid; pro-EC, NATO, proportional representation **Political career** contested Roxburgh, Selkirk and Peebles 1964; MP for Roxburgh, Selkirk and Peebles 1965–83 **Parliamentary career** sponsored 1966 Abortion Bill which became the Abortion Act 1967; Lib. Whip 1967–75; Lib. Spokesman on Foreign Affairs 1975–6; Leader of the Liberal Party 1976–88; PC 1977; joint founder of the Liberal Democrats 1988; Lib. Dem. Convenor on Foreign Affairs 1988– **Member** Anti-Apartheid (Pres. 1966–9) **Publications include** *David Steel's Border Country*; *A House Divided*; *Partners in One Nation*; (jtly) *Mary Stuart's Scotland* **Other** Rector of Edinburgh Univ. 1982–5; knighted 1990

STEEN, Anthony Con., South Hams (1983) **b.** 22 July 1939 **ed.** Westminster Sch.; Gray's Inn **Profession** barrister, Lloyd's underwriter, youth and community worker, company dir. **Political interests** inner cities, community and youth work, planning, environment, conservation, footpaths, cycling, law, health and social services, charities, aviation **Political career** MP for Liverpool Wavertree 1974–83 **Parliamentary career** Chmn Urban and New Town Affairs Cttee 1979–80, 1987– ; Chmn Urban and Inner City Cttee 1987– **Publications include** *Public Land Utilisation Management Schemes (PLUMS)*; *Tested Ideas for Political Success*; *New Life for Old Cities*

STEINBERG, Gerald Lab., Durham, City of (1987) **b.** 20 Apr. 1945 **ed.** Johnston Grammar Sch.; Sheffield Coll. of Education; Newcastle Poly. **Profession** teacher **Political interests** local govt, education, finance, housing, sport **Political career** Pittington and Sherburn Parish Cllr 1970–6; Durham City Cllr 1976–87 **Member** Anti-Apartheid **Unions** NUT

STERN, Michael Con., Bristol North West (1983) **b.** 3 Aug. 1942 **ed.** Christ's Coll. Grammar Sch., Finchley **Profession** accountant **Political interests** taxation, pensions, economy, education, ports, mentally handicapped; pro-EC **Political career** Ealing Borough Cllr 1980–3; contested Derby South 1979 **Member** Bow Group (Chmn 1977–8) **Publications include** *The Needle's Eye of a Socialist Heaven: A Critique of Labour's Taxes on Capital*

STEVENS, Lewis Con., Nuneaton (1983) **b.** 13 Apr. 1936 **ed.** Oldbury Grammar Sch., Worcs.; Liverpool Univ.; Lanchester Technical Coll., Coventry **Profession** industrial engineer **Political interests** trade and industry, manufacturing industry, industrial training, industrial relations, new technology, employment, education; pro-hanging **Political career** Nuneaton Borough Cllr 1966–72; contested Nuneaton 1979 **Other** MBE 1982

STEWART, Allan Con., Eastwood (1983) **b.** 1 June 1942 **ed.** Bell Baxter High Sch., Cupar; St Andrews Univ.; Harvard Univ. **Profession** Scottish dir. Confederation of British Industry 1971–9; company dir. **Political interests** Scottish affairs, trade and industry, sport; anti-devolution, pro-hanging **Political career** Bromley Borough Cllr 1974–6; contested Dundee East 1970; MP for Renfrewshire East 1979–83 **Parliamentary career** Under-Secretary of State at the Scottish Office (Minister for Health and Social Work) 1981–2; Minister of State at the Scottish Office (Home Affairs and the Environment) 1982–3, (Industry and Education) 1983–6

STEWART, Andrew Con., Sherwood (1983) **b.** 27 May 1937 **ed.** Strathaven Academy, Lanark; West of Scotland Agriculture Coll. **Profession** farmer **Political interests** coal, agriculture, conservation, environment **Political career** Caunton Parish Cllr 1973–83; Notts. Co. Cllr 1974–83 **Member** NFU

STEWART, Rt Hon. Ian Con., Hertfordshire North (1983) **b.** 10 Aug. 1935 **ed.** Haileybury; Jesus Coll.,

Cambridge **Profession** merchant banker, company dir. **Political interests** finance, taxation, economy, Northern Ireland, defence, foreign affairs, disabled, charities; pro-Sunday trading **Political career** contested Hammersmith North 1970; MP for Hitchin 1974–83 **Parliamentary career** Opposition Spokesman on the Development Land Tax Bill 1976, on the Banking Bill 1978–9; Under-Secretary of State for Defence (Procurement) 1983; Economic Secretary to the Treasury 1983–7; Minister of State for Defence (Armed Forces) 1987–8, for Northern Ireland 1988–9; PC 1989 **Member** Bow Group **Publications include** *The Scottish Coinage*; *Scottish Mints*; (jtly) *Studies in Numismatic Method* **Other** An expert on Scottish medieval coinage; RD 1972

STOKES, Sir John Con., Halesowen and Stourbridge (1974) **b.** 23 July 1917 **ed.** Temple Grove; Haileybury; Queen's Coll., Oxford **Profession** Royal Fusiliers 1939–46; personnel consultant, company dir. **Political interests** the monarchy, church affairs, law and order, home affairs, foreign affairs, defence, trade and industry; pro-sport with South Africa, police, hanging; anti-immigration, strikers **Political career** contested Gloucester 1964, Hitchin 1966; MP for Oldbury and Halesowen 1970–4 **Member** General Synod of the Church of England 1985– **Other** Knighted 1988

STOTT, Roger Lab., Wigan (1983) **b.** 7 Aug. 1943 **ed.** Greenbank Secondary Modern Sch.; Rochdale Technical Coll.; Ruskin Coll., Oxford **Profession** telephone engineer **Political interests** information technology, aerospace, trade and industry, industrial relations, transport, agriculture, economy, Middle East **Political career** Rochdale Cllr 1970–4; contested Cheadle 1970; MP for Westhoughton 1973–83 **Parliamentary career** PPS to James Callaghan 1976–80; Opposition Spokesman on Transport 1980–3, on Trade and Industry (Information Technology) 1983–9, on Northern Ireland 1989– **Unions** sponsored by NCU **Other** CBE 1979

STRADLING THOMAS, Sir John Con., Monmouth (1970) **b.** 10 June 1925 **ed.** Rugby Sch.; Royal Veterinary Coll., London **Profession** farmer, company dir. **Political interests** Welsh affairs, agriculture **Political career** Carmarthen Borough Cllr 1961–4; contested Aberavon 1964, Cardiganshire 1966 **Parliamentary career** Asst Whip 1971–2; Lord Commissioner of the Treasury (Govt Whip) 1973–4; Opposition Whip 1974–9; Deputy Chief Whip and Treasurer of the Household 1979–83; Minister of State for Wales 1983–5 **Member** Bow Group; NFU **Other** Knighted 1985

STRANG, Dr Gavin Lab., Edinburgh East (1970) **b.** 10 July 1943 **ed.** Morrison's Academy, Crieff; Edinburgh Univ.; Churchill Coll., Cambridge **Profession** agrarian research scientist **Political interests** agriculture, energy, employment, Middle East, nuclear disarmament; anti-Falklands War **Parliamentary career** Opposition Spokesman on Trade and Industry 1973–4; Under-Secretary of State for Energy 1974; Parliamentary Secretary to the Ministry of Agriculture 1974–9; Opposition Spokesman on Agriculture 1979–82, on Employment 1987– **Member** CND; Co-operative Party; Fabian Society **Unions** sponsored by TGWU

STRAW, Jack Shadow Secretary for Education Lab., Blackburn (1979) **b.** 3 Aug. 1946 **ed.** Brentwood Sch.; Leeds Univ.; Inns of Court Sch. of Law **Profession** barrister, broadcaster **Political interests** education, health and social services, local govt, housing, police, law, taxation, economy, EC **Political career** Islington Borough Cllr 1971–8; adviser to Barbara Castle, Secretary of State for Social Services, 1974–6; contested Tonbridge and Malling 1974; succeeded Barbara Castle in this seat **Parliamentary career** Opposition Spokesman on Treasury and Economic Affairs 1980–3, on Environment 1983–7; Shadow Education Secretary 1987– **Member** Fabian Society; Tribune Group **Unions** ACCT; sponsored by GMB **Other** Adviser to AUT 1984–

SUMBERG, David Con., Bury South (1983) **b.** 2 June 1941 **ed.** Tettenhall Coll., Wolverhampton; Coll. of Law, London **Profession** solicitor **Political interests** trade and industry, paper industry, food and drink industry, local govt, law, foreign affairs, human rights, Soviet Jewry **Political career** Manchester City Cllr 1982–4; contested Manchester Wythenshawe 1979

SUMMERSON, Hugo Con., Walthamstow (1987) **b.** 21 July 1950 **ed.** Harrow Sch.; Royal Agricultural Coll., Cirencester **Profession** chartered surveyor, company dir. **Political interests** agriculture, environment, inner cities, defence **Political career** contested Barking 1983

TAPSELL, Sir Peter Con., Lindsey East (1983) **b.** 1 Feb. 1930 **ed.** Tonbridge Sch.; Merton Coll., Oxford **Profession** Conservative Research Dept 1954–7; stockbroker, company dir. **Political interests** economy, finance, banking, foreign and Commonwealth affairs; anti-monetarism **Political career** asst to the Prime Minister, Sir Anthony Eden, in 1955 election campaign; contested Wednesbury 1957; MP for Nottingham West 1959–64, Horncastle 1966–83 **Parliamentary career** Opposition Spokesman on Foreign and Commonwealth Affairs 1976–7, on Treasury and Economic Affairs 1977–8 **Other** Knighted 1985

TAYLOR, Ann Lab., Dewsbury (1987) **b.** 2 July 1947 **ed.** Bolton Sch.; Bradford Univ.; Sheffield Univ. **Profession** teacher **Political interests** education, housing, home affairs, regional policy, health and social services, economy **Political career** Holmfirth Urban District Cllr 1972–4; contested Bolton West Feb. 1974; MP for Bolton West Oct. 1974–83; contested Bolton North East 1983 **Parliamentary career** Asst Whip 1977–9; Opposition Spokesman on Education 1979–81, on Housing 1981–3, on Home Affairs 1987–8, on the Environment 1988– **Unions** GMB (APEX partnership) **Publications include** (jtly) *Political Action*

TAYLOR, Ian Con., Esher (1987) **b.** 18 Apr. 1945 **ed.** Whitley Abbey Sch., Coventry; Keele Univ.; London Sch. of Economics **Profession** merchant banker, corporate financial consultant, company dir. **Political interests** economy, small businesses, trade and industry, environment, defence, foreign affairs; pro-EC **Political career** contested Coventry South East 1974 **Other** MBE 1974

TAYLOR, John Con., Solihull (1983) **b.** 19 Aug. 1941 **ed.** Bromsgrove Sch.; Coll. of Law, Guildford **Profession** solicitor, company dir. **Political interests** law, trade and industry, environment, heritage, EC, foreign affairs **Political career** Solihull Co. Borough Cllr 1971–4; W. Midlands Co. Cllr 1973–86 (Leader 1977–9); MEP Midlands East 1979–84; contested Dudley East 1974 **Parliamentary career** Asst Whip

1988–9; Lord Commissioner of the Treasury (Govt Whip) 1989–

TAYLOR, Rt Hon. John OUP, Strangford (1983) **b.** 24 Dec. 1937 **ed.** Royal Sch., Armagh; Queen's Univ., Belfast **Profession** civil engineer, publisher, company dir. **Political interests** Northern Ireland, EC, Turkey, Cyprus, Asia, Gibraltar, regional policy, agriculture, engineering; anti-EMS **Political career** Stormont MP 1965–73; PC 1970; Northern Ireland Assembly 1973–5, 1982–6; Northern Ireland Constitutional Convention 1976–7; MEP for Northern Ireland 1979–89 **Parliamentary career** resigned seat Dec. 1985 in protest against Anglo-Irish agreement; re-elected Jan. 1986 **Publications include** (jtly) *Ulster – The Facts* **Other** He survived an assassination attempt 1972

TAYLOR, Matthew Lib. Dem. (Lib. 1987–8), Truro (1987) **b.** 3 Jan. 1963 **ed.** Treliske Sch., Truro; Univ. Coll., London; Lady Margaret Hall, Oxford **Profession** economic researcher for David Penhaligon MP **Political interests** education, employment, trade and industry, energy, local govt, youth, environment, transport, economy **Political career** succeeded David Penhaligon in this seat **Parliamentary career** Lib. Spokesman on Energy 1987–8; Lib. Dem. Spokesman on England (Local Govt, Housing, Transport) 1988–

TAYLOR, Teddy Con., Southend East (1980) **b.** 18 Apr. 1937 **ed.** High Sch. of Glasgow; Glasgow Univ. **Profession** journalist, industrial relations officer, company dir. **Political interests** home affairs, environment, law and order, Scottish affairs; anti-EC, alcohol, abortion, devolution; pro-capital and corporal punishment **Political career** Glasgow City Cllr 1960–4; contested Glasgow Springburn 1959; MP for Glasgow Cathcart 1964–79 **Parliamentary career** Under-Secretary of State for Scotland 1970–1, 1974; Opposition Spokesman on Trade 1976, on Scotland 1976–9 **Member** European Reform Group **Unions** NUJ **Publications include** *Hearts of Stone*

TEBBIT, Rt Hon. Norman Con., Chingford (1974) **b.** 29 Mar. 1931 **ed.** Edmonton Co. Grammar Sch. **Profession** BOAC pilot 1953–70; company dir. **Political interests** aviation, science and technology, housing, trade and industry **Political career** MP for Epping 1970–4 **Parliamentary career** Under-Secretary of State for Trade 1979–81; Minister of State for Industry 1981; PC 1981; Secretary of State for Employment 1981–3, for Trade and Industry and Pres. of the Board of Trade 1983–5; Chancellor of the Duchy of Lancaster and Chmn Conservative Party 1985–7 **Unions** BALPA **Publications include** *Upwardly Mobile* **Other** He was seriously injured and his wife was paralyzed in the Brighton bombing 1984; CH 1987

TEMPLE-MORRIS, Peter Con., Leominster (1974) **b.** 12 Feb. 1938 **ed.** Hillstone Sch., Malvern; St Catharine's Coll., Cambridge; Inner Temple **Profession** barrister, company dir. **Political interests** foreign affairs, Middle East and Iran, human rights, refugees, agriculture, transport, local govt, taxation **Political career** contested Newport 1964 and 1966, Norwood Lambeth 1970 **Parliamentary career** Executive of British Branch of Inter-Parliamentary Union 1977– (Chmn 1982–5) **Member** Iran Society (Council 1968–80); Bow Group **Other** Son of Sir Owen Temple-Morris, MP for Cardiff East 1931–42

THATCHER, Rt Hon. Margaret Prime Minister and Leader of the Conservative Party Con., Finchley (1959) **b.** 13 Oct. 1925 **ed.** Kesteven and Grantham Girls' High Sch.; Somerville Coll., Oxford; Lincoln's Inn **Profession** research chemist, barrister **Political interests** foreign and Commonwealth affairs, EC, education, trade and industry, chemical industry, transport, home affairs, law and order, economy; pro-hanging, NATO **Political career** contested Dartford (as Margaret Roberts) 1950, 1951 **Parliamentary career** Parliamentary Secretary at the Ministry of Pensions and National Insurance 1961–4; Opposition Spokesman on Pensions and National Insurance 1964–5, on Housing and Land 1965–6, on Treasury Affairs 1966–7, on Power 1967–8; Shadow Minister of Transport 1968–9; Shadow Education Minister 1969–70; PC 1970; Secretary of State for Education and Science 1970–4; Shadow Environment Secretary 1974; Opposition Treasury Spokesman 1974–5; Leader of the Conservative Party 1975– ; Leader of the Opposition 1975–9; Prime Minister, First Lord of the Treasury and Minister for the Civil Service 4 May 1979– **Publications include** *In Defence of Freedom* **Other** The first woman Prime Minister

THOMAS, Dafydd Pl.C., Meirionnydd Nant Conwy (1983) **b.** 18 Oct. 1946 **ed.** Ysgol Dyffryn Conwy; Univ. Coll. of North Wales, Bangor **Profession** lecturer, broadcaster, writer **Political interests** Welsh affairs, Welsh language, media; pro-devolution **Political career** contested Conway 1970; MP for Merioneth 1974–83 **Parliamentary career** Pl.C. Chief Whip 1974–80; Pl.C. Spokesman on Agriculture 1974–5, on Social, Educational and Cultural Policy 1975–9; Vice-Pres. Plaid Cymru 1980–2, Pres. 1984– **Unions** TGWU **Other** Welsh speaker and author

THOMPSON, Donald Con., Calder Valley (1983) **b.** 13 Nov. 1931 **ed.** Hipperholme Grammar Sch. **Profession** farmer, butcher, company dir. **Political interests** agriculture, small business, engineering, textile industry, energy, health and social services, sport **Political career** West Riding Co. Cllr 1967–74; W. Yorks. Co. Cllr 1973–7; Calderdale District Cllr 1975–9; contested Batley and Morley 1970; contested Sowerby 1974; MP for Sowerby 1979–83 **Parliamentary career** Asst Whip 1981–3; Lord Commissioner of the Treasury (Govt Whip) 1983–6; Parliamentary Secretary at the Ministry of Agriculture 1986–9

THOMPSON, John Lab., Wansbeck (1983) **b.** 27 Aug. 1928 **ed.** Bothal Sch.; Ashington Mining Coll.; Ashington Technical Coll. **Profession** miner, electrical engineer **Political interests** mining, science and education, mental health, energy, trade and industry, chemical industry, environment, local govt **Political career** Newbiggin by the Sea Urban District Cllr 1970–4; Wansbeck Distict Cllr 1974–9; Northumberland Co. Cllr 1974–85 (Leader 1981–3) **Unions** sponsored by NUM

THOMPSON, Patrick Con., Norwich North (1983) **b.** 21 Oct. 1935 **ed.** Felsted Sch.; Emmanuel Coll., Cambridge **Profession** physicist, electrical engineer, teacher **Political interests** education, science, engineering, transport, employment, defence; pro-EC **Political career** contested Bradford North 1974, Barrow-in-Furness 1979 **Publications include** *Elementary Calculations in Physics*

THORNE, Neil Con., Ilford South (1979) **b.** 8 Aug. 1932 **ed.** City of London Sch.; London Univ. **Profession** chartered surveyor, Lloyd's underwriter, company dir. **Political interests** defence, civil defence, foreign affairs,

Israel, Nepal, housing, environment, transport; anti-abortion **Political career** Redbridge Borough Cllr 1965–8 (Alderman 1975–8); Greater London Cllr 1967–73; contested Ilford South 1974 **Member** House of Commons Motor Club (Chmn 1985–); Royal British Legion (Vice-Pres.); National Council for Civil Defence (Chmn 1982–6) **Publications include** *Pedestrianised Streets: A Study of Europe and America* **Other** Territorial Decoration 1969; OBE 1980

THORNTON, Malcolm Con., Crosby (1983) **b.** 3 Apr. 1939 **ed.** Wallasey Grammar Sch.; Liverpool Nautical Coll. **Profession** River Mersey pilot **Political interests** shipping, housing, local govt, education, law and order, police, Southern Africa; pro-capital and corporal punishment **Political career** Wallasey Co. Borough Cllr 1965–74; Wirral Metropolitan Cllr 1973–9 (Leader 1974–7); MP for Liverpool Garston 1979–83; defeated Shirley Williams to win this seat **Other** consultant to NALGO 1981–

THURNHAM, Peter Con., Bolton North East (1983) **b.** 21 Aug. 1938 **ed.** Oundle Sch.; Peterhouse Coll., Cambridge; Cranfield Inst. of Technology; Harvard Business Sch. **Profession** engineer, farmer, company dir. **Political interests** trade and industry, chemical industry, employment, economy, medicine, handicapped children; pro-hanging **Political career** South Lakeland District Cllr 1982–4 **Publications include** *When Nature Fails – Why Handicap?*; *Operation Long Stop: Putting a Time Limit on Unemployment*

TOWNEND, John Con., Bridlington (1979) **b.** 12 June 1934 **ed.** Froebel House; Hymer's Coll., Hull **Profession** wine merchant, accountant, company dir., Lloyd's underwriter **Political interests** small businesses, taxation, finance, employment, law and order, Southern Africa; pro-hanging; anti-immigration, pornography **Political career** Hull City Cllr 1966–74; Humberside Co. Cllr 1973–9 (Leader 1977–9); contested Hull North 1970

TOWNSEND, Cyril Con., Bexleyheath (1974) **b.** 21 Dec. 1937 **ed.** Bradfield Coll.; Royal Military Academy, Sandhurst **Profession** Durham Light Infantry 1958–68; Conservative Research Dept 1970–4 **Political interests** foreign affairs, South Atlantic, Middle East, Cyprus, defence, home affairs, children's welfare; anti-Fortress Falklands, hanging, racism **Political career** asst to Rt Hon. Edward Heath 1968–70 **Member** Bow Group **Publications include** *Helping Others to Help Themselves: Voluntary Action in the Eighties*

TRACEY, Dick Con., Surbiton (1983) **b.** 8 Feb. 1943 **ed.** King Edward VI Sch., Stratford-upon-Avon; Birmingham Univ. **Profession** journalist, broadcaster, sports writer **Political interests** local govt, transport, environment, education, law and order, home affairs, sport, economy; pro-hanging **Political career** contested Northampton North 1974 **Parliamentary career** Under-Secretary of State for the Environment (Minister for Sport) 1985–7 **Member** Bow Group; Special Olympics UK (Vice-Chmn 1988–) **Publications include** (jtly) *The World of Motor Sport*; (jtly) *Hickstead: The First Twelve Years* **Other** JP 1977

TREDINNICK, David Con., Bosworth (1987) **b.** 19 Jan. 1950 **ed.** Eton; Mons Officer Cadet Sch.; Graduate Sch. of Business, Cape Town; St John's Coll., Oxford **Profession** Grenadier Guards 1968–71; computer marketing manager, company dir. **Political interests** defence, foreign affairs, EC, home affairs, law and order, housing, trade and industry, employment, high technology, agriculture **Political career** contested Cardiff South and Penarth 1983 **Member** Bow Group

TRIMBLE, David OUP, Upper Bann (1990) **b.** 15 Oct. 1944 **ed.** Bangor Grammar Sch.; Queen's Univ., Belfast **Profession** barrister, lecturer in law **Political interests** constitutional affairs, foreign affairs, legal affairs, housing and planning **Political career** Northern Ireland Constitutional Convention 1975–6; won this seat in the by-election of 17 May 1990

TRIPPIER, David Con., Rossendale and Darwen (1983) **b.** 15 May 1946 **ed.** Bury Grammar Sch. **Profession** stockbroker, company dir. **Political interests** trade and industry, employment, small business, footwear industry, textile industry, defence, local govt, disabled, environment, finance **Political career** Rochdale Cllr 1969–78; contested Rochdale 1972, Oldham West 1974; MP for Rossendale 1979–83 **Parliamentary career** Under-Secretary of State for Trade and Industry 1983–5, for Employment 1985–7, for the Environment 1987–9; Minister of State for the Environment 1989– **Publications include** *Defending the Peace* **Other** JP 1975; RD 1983

TROTTER, Neville Con., Tynemouth (1974) **b.** 27 Jan. 1932 **ed.** Shrewsbury Sch.; King's Coll., Durham Univ. **Profession** accountant, company dir. **Political interests** transport, trade and industry, shipping, aviation, employment, regional policy, health and social services, the elderly, solvent abuse, defence, foreign affairs **Political career** Newcastle City Cllr 1963–74 (Alderman 1970–4); Tyne and Wear Metropolitan Cllr 1973–4; contested Consett 1970 **Other** JP 1973

TURNER, Dennis Lab., Wolverhampton South East (1987) **b.** 26 Aug. 1942 **ed.** Stonehead Secondary Sch.; Bilston Coll. of Further Education **Profession** dir. of a social, sports and leisure co-operative **Political interests** health and social services, education, housing, steel **Political career** Wolverhampton Borough Cllr 1966–86; W. Midlands Co. Cllr 1973–86; contested Halesowen and Stourbridge 1974 **Member** sponsored by Co-operative Party

TWINN, Dr Ian Con., Edmonton (1983) **b.** 26 Apr. 1950 **ed.** Cambridge Grammar Sch.; Univ. Coll. of Wales, Aberystwyth; Reading Univ. **Profession** lecturer in town planning **Political interests** environment, planning, transport, conservation, heritage, education, constitutional reform, energy, food and drink industries; pro-hanging **Unions** NATFHE **Publications include** *Public Involvement or Public Protest*; (ed.) *Use of Computers in Town Planning*

VAUGHAN, Dr Sir Gerard Con., Reading East (1983) **b.** 11 June 1923 **ed.** London Univ.; Guy's Hospital Medical Sch.; Maudsley's **Profession** psychiatrist, Lloyd's underwriter, company dir. **Political interests** health and social services, pharmaceutical industry, science and technology, publishing, trade and industry, education, inland waterways **Political career** London Co. Cllr 1955–64; Greater London Cllr 1966–70 (Alderman 1970–2); contested Poplar 1955; MP for Reading 1970–4, for Reading South 1974–83 **Parliamentary career** Opposition Whip 1974–5; Opposition Spokesman on Health 1975–9; Minister of State for Health 1979–82, for Trade (Consumer Affairs) 1982–3 **Other** Knighted 1984

VAZ, Keith Lab., Leicester East (1987) **b.** 26 Nov. 1956 **ed.** St Joseph's Convent, Aden; Latymer Upper Sch., Hammersmith; Gonville and Caius Coll., Cambridge; Coll. of Law, London **Profession** solicitor **Political interests** local govt, law, home affairs, race relations, education, peace **Political career** contested Richmond and Barnes 1983 **Unions** NUPE

VIGGERS, Peter Con., Gosport (1974) **b.** 13 Mar. 1938 **ed.** Portsmouth Grammar Sch.; Trinity Hall, Cambridge; Gray's Inn **Profession** solicitor, company dir. (oil), Lloyd's underwriter **Political interests** defence, Northern Ireland, trade and industry, energy, finance; pro-NATO **Parliamentary career** Under-Secretary of State for Northern Ireland (Industry) 1986–9 **Member** Bow Group; National Cttee RNLI 1979–

WADDINGTON, Rt Hon. David Home Secretary Con., Ribble Valley (1983) **b.** 2 Aug. 1929 **ed.** Sedbergh; Hertford Coll., Oxford; Gray's Inn **Profession** barrister (QC 1971), company dir. (textiles) **Political interests** home affairs, employment, textile industry, law; anti-pornography, racism, welfare scroungers **Political career** contested Farnworth 1955, Nelson and Colne 1964, Heywood and Royton 1966; MP for Nelson and Colne 1968–74, for Clitheroe 1979–83 **Parliamentary career** Lord Commissioner of the Treasury (Govt Whip) 1979–81; Under-Secretary of State for Employment 1981–3; Minister of State at the Home Office (Immigration) 1983–7; PC 1987; Parliamentary Secretary to the Treasury and Govt Chief Whip 1987–9; Secretary of State at the Home Office Oct. 1989–

WAKEHAM, Rt Hon. John Secretary of State for Energy Con., Colchester South and Maldon (1983) **b.** 22 June 1932 **ed.** Charterhouse **Profession** accountant, company dir., farmer, Lloyd's underwriter **Political interests** small businesses, trade and industry, economy, energy **Political career** contested Coventry East 1966, Putney 1970; MP for Maldon 1974–83 **Parliamentary career** Asst Whip 1979–81; Lord Commissioner of the Treasury (Govt Whip) 1981; Under-Secretary of State for Trade and Industry 1981–2; Minister of State at the Treasury 1982–3; PC 1983; Parliamentary Secretary to the Treasury and Govt Chief Whip 1983–7; Lord Privy Seal 1987–8; Leader of the House of Commons 1987–9; Lord Pres. of the Council 1988–9; Secretary of State for Energy 1989– **Publications include** *The Case against Wealth Tax*; *A Personal View* **Other** JP 1972; his wife was killed, and he was seriously injured, in the Brighton bombing 1984

WALDEGRAVE, Rt Hon. William Con., Bristol West (1979) **b.** 15 Aug. 1946 **ed.** Eton; Corpus Christi, Oxford; Harvard Univ. **Profession** Fellow All Souls Coll., Oxford 1971–86; member of political staff at 10 Downing Street and in the Leader of the Opposition's Office 1973–5; company dir. **Political interests** foreign affairs, home affairs, housing, arts, education, environment, energy **Parliamentary career** Under-Secretary of State for Education and Science 1981–3, for the Environment 1983–5; Minister of State for the Environment 1985–8, at the Foreign and Commonwealth Office 1988– ; PC 1990 **Publications include** *The Binding of Leviathan – Conservatism and the Future* **Other** JP 1974

WALDEN, George Con., Buckingham (1983) **b.** 15 Sept. 1939 **ed.** Latymer Upper Sch., Hammersmith; Jesus Coll., Cambridge; Moscow Univ.; Hong Kong Univ.; Harvard Univ.; Ecole Nationale d'Administration, Paris **Profession** diplomat, journalist **Political interests** foreign affairs, education, arts, economy **Parliamentary career** Under-Secretary of State for Education and Science 1985–7 **Publications include** *The Shoeblack and the Sovereign* **Other** CMG (Companion of St Michael and St George) 1981

WALKER, William Con., Tayside North (1983) **b.** 20 Feb. 1929 **ed.** Logie Sch., Dundee; Trades Coll., Dundee; Coll. of Art, Dundee; Coll. for Distributive Trades, London **Profession** pilot and flying instructor, company dir. (airline), management consultant **Political interests** aviation, defence, trade and industry, youth; anti-EC; pro-capital and corporal punishment **Political career** contested Dundee East 1974; MP for Perth and East Perthshire 1979–83 **Member** European Reform Group

WALKER, Cecil OUP, Belfast North (1983) **b.** 17 Dec. 1924 **ed.** Methodist Coll., Belfast **Profession** timber merchant **Political interests** Northern Ireland, housing, local govt, fishing industry, timber, conservation, elderly; pro-devolution, anti-EC **Political career** Belfast City Cllr 1977– ; contested Belfast North 1979 **Parliamentary career** resigned seat Dec. 1985 in protest against Anglo-Irish agreement; re-elected Jan. 1986 **Other** JP 1966

WALKER, Rt Hon. Harold Chairman of Ways and Means and Deputy Speaker of the House of Commons Lab., Doncaster Central (1983) **b.** 12 July 1927 **ed.** Manchester Coll. of Technology **Profession** Fleet Air Arm 1946–8; engineer **Political interests** industrial relations, industrial safety, employment, trade and industry, mentally handicapped, cancer, nuclear disarmament **Political career** MP for Doncaster 1964–83 **Parliamentary career** Asst Whip 1967–8; Under-Secretary of State for Employment 1968–70; Opposition Spokesman on Employment 1970–4; Under-Secretary of State for Employment 1974–6; Minister of State for Employment 1976–9; PC 1979; Opposition Spokesman on Employment 1979–83; Chmn of Ways and Means and Deputy Speaker of the House of Commons 1983– **Member** Co-operative Party **Unions** sponsored by AEU

WALKER, Rt Hon. Peter Con., Worcester (1961) **b.** 25 Mar. 1932 **ed.** Latymer Sch. **Profession** company dir. (Slater Walker), Lloyd's underwriter, farmer **Political interests** transport, environment, agriculture, energy, defence, Welsh affairs, trade and industry; pro-proportional representation, anti-monetarism **Political career** National Chmn Young Conservatives 1958–60; contested Dartford 1955, 1959 **Parliamentary career** Opposition Spokesman on Financial Affairs 1965–6, on Transport 1966–9, for Housing and Local Govt 1969–70; Minister for Housing and Local Govt 1970; PC 1970; Secretary of State for the Environment 1970–2, for Trade and Industry 1972–4; Opposition Spokesman on Trade and Industry 1974, on Defence 1974–5; Minister of Agriculture, Fisheries and Food 1979–83; Secretary of State for Energy 1983–7, for Wales 1987–90 **Member** Tory Reform Group **Publications include** *The Ascent of Britain*; *Trust the People* **Other** MBE 1960

WALL, Pat Lab., Bradford North (1987) **b.** 6 May 1933 **ed.** Liverpool Inst. Grammar Sch. **Profession** hardware buyer **Political interests** economy, health and social services, disabled, Asia **Political career** Liverpool City Cllr 1961–4; Bingley Urban District Cllr 1964–73;

contested Bradford North 1983 **Member** Child Poverty Action Group

WALLACE, James Lib. Dem. (Lib. 1983–8), Orkney and Shetland (1983) **b.** 25 Aug. 1954 **ed.** Annan Academy, Dumfriesshire; Downing Coll., Cambridge; Edinburgh Univ. **Profession** advocate **Political interests** Scottish affairs, law, conservation, agriculture, fishing, transport, employment, energy, defence, civil liberties; pro-devolution **Political career** contested Dumfriesshire 1979; succeeded Jo Grimond in this seat **Parliamentary career** Lib. Spokesman on Energy 1983–5, on Fishing 1985–7, on Defence 1985–8; Lib. Deputy Whip 1985–7, Chief Whip 1987–8; All. Spokesman on Transport 1987–8; Lib. Dem. Chief Whip and Spokesman on Employment 1988– **Member** Amnesty International

WALLER, Gary Con., Keighley (1983) **b.** 24 June 1945 **ed.** Rugby Sch.; Lancaster Univ. **Profession** journalist **Political interests** trade and industry, textile industry, information technology, transport, health and social services, home affairs **Political career** contested Rother Valley 1974; MP for Brighouse and Spenborough 1979–83 **Parliamentary career** Chmn All-Party Wool Textile Group 1984– **Member** Friends of the Settle-Carlisle Line Association (Vice-Pres. 1987–)

WALLEY, Joan Lab., Stoke-on-Trent North (1987) **b.** 23 Jan. 1949 **ed.** Biddulph Grammar Sch.; Hull Univ.; Univ. Coll., Swansea **Profession** environmental health officer **Political interests** environment, health and social services **Political career** Lambeth Borough Cllr 1982–6 **Parliamentary career** Opposition Spokesman on the Environment 1988– **Member** CND; Institute of Environmental Health Officers (Vice-Pres.) **Unions** sponsored by COHSE

WALTERS, Sir Dennis Con., Westbury (1964) **b.** 28 Nov. 1928 **ed.** Downside Sch.; St Catharine's Coll., Cambridge **Profession** served with Italian Resistance 1943–4; company dir. (investment, oil), investment adviser, journalist **Political interests** foreign and Commonwealth affairs, Middle East, energy, oil, medicine; pro-Arab, anti-Zionist **Political career** asst to Viscount (now Lord) Hailsham, Chmn of Conservative Party, 1957–9; contested Blyth 1959, 1960 **Parliamentary career** Chmn British-Kuwaiti Group 1970– **Member** Bow Group (founder member); Asthma Research Council (Chmn 1969–); Council for the Advancement of Arab-British Understanding (Chmn 1970–82) **Other** MBE 1960; knighted 1988

WARD, John Con., Poole (1979) **b.** 8 Mar. 1925 **ed.** Romford Co. Technical Sch.; St Andrews Univ. **Profession** RAF 1943–7; civil engineer, company dir. (Taylor Woodrow) **Political interests** trade and industry, exports, industrial relations, employment, health and social services, defence, EC, foreign affairs, animal welfare **Political career** contested Portsmouth North 1974 **Member** FRAME **Other** CBE 1973

WARDELL, Gareth Lab., Gower (1982) **b.** 29 Nov. 1944 **ed.** Gwendraeth Grammar Sch.; London Sch. of Economics **Profession** lecturer in geography **Political interests** Welsh affairs, health and social services, education, housing, energy, transport, drugs, pornography, Sri Lanka **Parliamentary career** Chmn Select Cttee on Welsh Affairs 1984– **Unions** GMB (APEX partnership); NATFHE **Other** Welsh speaker

WARDLE, Charles Con., Bexhill and Battle (1983) **b.** 23 Aug. 1939 **ed.** Tonbridge Sch.; Lincoln Coll., Oxford; Harvard Business Sch. **Profession** merchant banker, engineering company dir. **Political interests** trade and industry, engineering, employment, economy **Member** CBI Council 1980–4

WAREING, Robert Lab., Liverpool West Derby (1983) **b.** 20 Aug. 1930 **ed.** Alsop High Sch., Liverpool; Bolton Coll. of Education; London Univ. **Profession** lecturer **Political interests** health and social services, disabled, trade and industry, motor car industry, aviation, regional policy, environment, economy, foreign affairs, Latin America, Eastern Europe, Middle East **Political career** Merseyside Co. Cllr 1981–3; contested Berwick-upon-Tweed 1970, Liverpool Edge Hill 1979 **Parliamentary career** Opposition Whip 1987– **Member** Campaign Group **Unions** MSF; NATFHE

WARREN, Kenneth Con., Hastings and Rye (1983) **b.** 15 Aug. 1926 **ed.** Aldenham Sch.; De Havilland Aeronautical Technical Sch.; King's Coll., London; London Sch. of Economics **Profession** aeronautical engineer, company dir. **Political interests** science and technology, trade and industry, aviation, defence, foreign affairs, Soviet Union, conservation, mentally handicapped **Political career** Paddington Borough Cllr 1953–65; contested St Pancras North 1964; MP for Hastings 1970–83 **Parliamentary career** Chmn Select Cttee on Trade and Industry 1983– ; Chmn British-Soviet Group 1986–

WATSON, Mike Lab., Glasgow Central (1989) **b.** 1 May 1949 **ed.** Dundee High Sch.; Heriot-Watt Univ., Edinburgh **Profession** union official **Political interests** Scottish affairs, foreign affairs, employment, education and training; pro-devolution **Political career** won seat in by-election 15 June 1989 **Member** Tribune Group **Unions** sponsored by MSF

WATTS, John Con., Slough (1983) **b.** 19 Apr. 1947 **ed.** Bishopshalt Grammar Sch., Hillingdon; Gonville and Caius Coll., Cambridge **Profession** accountant **Political interests** finance, taxation, accountancy, vocational training, local govt, animal welfare; pro-hanging **Political career** Hillingdon Borough Cllr 1973–86 (Leader 1978–84); defeated Joan Lestor to gain seat

WEATHERILL, Rt Hon. Bernard Speaker of the House of Commons Con. (until he was elected Speaker 1983), Croydon North East (1964) **b.** 25 Nov. 1920 **ed.** Malvern Coll. **Profession** Bengal Lancers 1941–5; master tailor, company dir., Lloyd's underwriter **Parliamentary career** Opposition Whip 1967–70; Lord Commissioner of the Treasury (Govt Whip) 1970–1; Vice-Chamberlain of the Household (Govt Whip) 1971–2; Comptroller of the Household (No. 3 Whip) 1972–3; Treasurer of the Household (Deputy Chief Whip) 1973–4; Opposition Deputy Chief Whip 1974–9; Chmn of Ways and Means and Deputy Speaker 1979–83; PC 1980; Speaker of the House of Commons 1983– ; Chmn Commonwealth Speakers and Presiding Officers 1986–8 **Publications include** *Acorns to Oaks*

WELLS, Bowen Con., Hertford and Stortford (1983) **b.** 4 Aug. 1935 **ed.** St Paul's Sch., London; Exeter Univ.; Poly. of Central London **Profession** Commonwealth Development Corporation executive, company dir. **Political interests** foreign affairs, West Indies, Commonwealth, Third World, overseas development,

UN, trade and industry, charities, employment, finance; pro-abortion **Political career** MP for Hertford and Stevenage 1979–83; defeated Shirley Williams to gain seat in 1979 **Parliamentary career** Chmn British-Caribbean Group 1983– ; Chmn UN All-Party Group 1983–

WELSH, Andrew SNP, Angus East (1987) **b.** 19 Apr. 1944 **ed.** Govan High Sch.; Glasgow Univ. **Profession** lecturer **Political interests** education, local govt, Scottish affairs **Political career** Stirling District Cllr 1974; contested Dunbarton Central Feb. 1974; MP for Angus South Oct. 1974–9; contested Angus East 1983; Angus District Cllr 1984–7 (Provost 1984–7) **Parliamentary career** SNP Spokesman on Housing 1974–9, on Agriculture 1974–9, on Self-Employed and Small Businesses 1975–9; SNP Whip 1978–9, 1987–

WELSH, Michael Lab., Doncaster North (1983) **b.** 23 Nov. 1926 **ed.** Woodlands Elementary Sch.; Sheffield Univ.; Ruskin Coll., Oxford **Profession** miner **Political interests** mining, trade and industry, local govt, foreign affairs, nuclear disarmament **Political career** Doncaster Local Authority Cllr 1962–9; MP for Don Valley 1979–83 **Member** Co-operative Party; CND **Unions** sponsored by NUM

WHEELER, Sir John Con., Westminster North (1983) **b.** 1 May 1940 **ed.** County Sch., Suffolk; Inst. of Criminology, Cambridge Univ.; Prison Services Staff Coll., Wakefield **Profession** prison governor, Lloyd's underwriter **Political interests** home affairs, law and order, police, prisons, crime prevention, race relations, immigration, inner cities, housing, environment, Jewish affairs; anti-hanging **Political career** MP for City of Westminster Paddington 1979–83 **Parliamentary career** Chmn All-Party Penal Affairs Group 1986– (Vice-Chmn 1979–86); Chmn Select Cttee on Home Affairs 1987– **Member** British Security Industry Association (Dir.-General 1976–); National Inspectorate of Security Guard Patrol and Transport Services (Chmn 1982–); Security Systems Inspectorate (Chmn 1987–); Tory Reform Group **Publications include** *Who Prevents Crime?* **Other** JP 1978; knighted 1990

WHITNEY, Ray Con., Wycombe (1978) **b.** 28 Nov. 1930 **ed.** Wellingborough Sch.; Royal Military Academy, Sandhurst; Sch. of Oriental and African Studies, London Univ.; Hong Kong Univ.; Australian National Univ. **Profession** Army 1951–63; diplomat, company dir., export consultant **Political interests** foreign and Commonwealth affairs, defence, disarmament, economy, health and social services, employment, education **Parliamentary career** Under-Secretary of State at the Foreign and Commonwealth Office 1983–4, for Social Security 1984–5, for Health 1985–6; Chmn All-Party British-Latin American Group 1987– **Other** OBE 1968

WIDDECOMBE, Ann Con., Maidstone (1987) **b.** 4 Oct. 1947 **ed.** La Sainte Union Convent, Bath; Birmingham Univ.; Lady Margaret Hall, Oxford **Profession** university administrator **Political interests** defence, education; pro-nuclear, anti-abortion **Political career** Runnymede District Cllr 1976–8; contested Burnley 1979, Plymouth Devonport 1983 **Member** Women and Families for Defence (Vice-Chmn 1982–); Society for the Protection of Unborn Children **Unions** AUT **Publications include** *A Healthier Future*; *Choosing Our Rulers – A Study of Candidate Selection in the Conservative Party*; *A Layman's Guide to Defence*

WIGGIN, Jerry Con., Weston-super-Mare (1969) **b.** 24 Feb. 1937 **ed.** Eton; Trinity Coll., Cambridge **Profession** farmer, company dir., Lloyd's underwriter **Political interests** agriculture, defence, NATO; anti-Sunday trading; pro-hanging, compulsory seatbelts **Political career** contested Montgomeryshire 1964, 1966 **Parliamentary career** Parliamentary Secretary at the Ministry of Agriculture 1979–81; Under-Secretary of State for Defence (Armed Forces) 1981–3; Chmn Select Cttee on Agriculture 1987– (Vice-Chmn 1974–9) **Other** Territorial Decoration 1970

WIGLEY, Dafydd Pl.C., Caernarfon (1974) **b.** 1 Apr. 1943 **ed.** Rydal Sch., Colwyn Bay; Manchester Univ. **Profession** industrial economist **Political interests** Welsh affairs, Welsh language, disabled, mentally handicapped, health and social services, trade and industry, employment; pro-EC, proportional representation **Political career** Merthyr Tydfil Co. Borough Cllr 1972–4; contested Merioneth 1970 **Parliamentary career** Pres. Plaid Cymru 1981–4; Chmn All-Party Social Service Group 1985– ; Pl.C. Whip 1987– **Member** CND; Wales Council for the Disabled (Vice-Pres.) **Unions** MSF **Publications include** *An Economic Plan for Wales*; *Tourism in Wales* **Other** Welsh speaker

WILKINSON, John Con., Ruislip-Northwood (1979) **b.** 23 Sept. 1940 **ed.** Eton; RAF Coll., Cranwell; Churchill Coll., Cambridge **Profession** RAF pilot and instructor; Conservative Research Dept 1969; company dir., business consultant **Political interests** defence, arms control, aviation, trade and industry, technology, EC, foreign affairs, race relations **Political career** MP for Bradford West 1970–Feb. 1974; contested Bradford West Oct. 1974 **Parliamentary career** Chmn Aerospace Cttee 1986– **Member** Bow Group **Publications include** (jtly) *The Uncertain Ally*; *British Defence: A Blueprint for Reform*

WILLIAMS, Rt Hon. Alan Lab., Swansea West (1964) **b.** 14 Oct. 1930 **ed.** Cardiff High Sch.; Cardiff Coll. of Technology; Univ. Coll., Oxford **Profession** lecturer in economics, journalist, company dir. **Political interests** economics, trade and industry, regional policy, employment, science and technology, education, Welsh affairs, consumer affairs, civil service; anti-devolution **Political career** contested Poole 1959 **Parliamentary career** Under-Secretary of State for Economic Affairs 1967–9; Parliamentary Secretary at the Ministry of Technology 1969–70; Opposition Spokesman on Industry 1970–1, on Higher Education 1971–2, on Consumer Affairs 1973–4; Minister of State for Prices and Consumer Protection 1974–6, for Industry 1976–9; PC 1977; Chmn All-Party Minerals Cttee 1979– ; Opposition Spokesman on Wales 1979–80, 1987–8, on the Civil Service 1980–3, on Industry 1983–7; Shadow Deputy Leader of the House 1983– ; Campaigns Co-ordinator 1988– **Member** Co-operative Party; Fabian Society **Unions** NATFHE; sponsored by TSSA

WILLIAMS, Alan Lab., Carmarthen (1987) **b.** 21 Dec. 1945 **ed.** Carmarthen Grammar Sch.; Jesus Coll., Oxford **Profession** lecturer in environmental science **Political interests** environment, ecology, energy, education

WILSHIRE, David Con., Spelthorne (1987) **b.** 16 Sep. 1943 **ed.** Kingswood Sch., Bath; Fitzwilliam House, Cambridge **Profession** political consultant, company dir. **Political interests** local govt **Political career** Wansdyke District Cllr 1976–87 (Leader 1981–7); Avon Co. Cllr 1977–81

WILSON, Brian Lab., Cunninghame North (1987) **b.** 13 Dec. 1948 **ed.** Dunoon Grammar Sch.; Dundee Univ.; Univ. of Wales Coll., Cardiff **Profession** founder, editor and publisher of *West Highland Free Press* 1972– **Political interests** Scottish affairs, media; anti-devolution **Political career** contested Ross and Cromarty 1974, Inverness 1979, Western Isles 1983 **Parliamentary career** Opposition Spokesman on Scotland 1988– **Publications include** *Celtic: A Century with Honour*

WINNICK, David Lab., Walsall North (1979) **b.** 26 June 1933 **ed.** London Sch. of Economics **Profession** administrator **Political interests** race relations, immigration, housing, home affairs, environment, foreign policy; anti-racism **Political career** Willesden Borough Cllr 1959–64; Brent Borough Cllr 1964–6; contested Harwich 1964; MP for Croydon South 1966–70; contested Croydon Central 1974, Walsall North 1976 **Member** Co-operative Party; Tribune Group (Chmn 1984–5); United Kingdom Immigrants' Advisory Service (Chmn 1984–) **Unions** sponsored by GMB (APEX partnership)

WINTERTON, Ann Con., Congleton (1983) **b.** 6 Mar. 1941 **ed.** Erdington Grammar Sch. for Girls **Profession** plant-hire company executive **Political interests** trade and industry, textiles, pharmaceuticals and chemicals, agriculture, transport; anti-abortion, CND; pro-hanging, South Africa **Member** South Staffs. Hunt (Master 1959–64) **Other** Wife of Nicholas Winterton MP

WINTERTON, Nicholas Con., Macclesfield (1971) **b.** 31 Mar. 1938 **ed.** Rugby Sch. **Profession** plant-hire company sales manager **Political interests** trade and industry, textiles, paper, local govt, health and social services, sport, foreign affairs; pro-capital and corporal punishment, South Africa; anti-EC **Political career** Warks. Co. Cllr 1967–72; contested Newcastle under Lyme 1969, 1970 **Parliamentary career** Chmn All-Party Group for the Paper and Board Industries 1983– ; Chmn All-Party Group for Cotton and Allied Textiles; Chmn British-Namibia All-Party Group **Other** Husband of Ann Winterton MP

WISE, Audrey Lab., Preston (1987) **b.** 4 Jan. 1935 **ed.** Rutherford High Sch. **Profession** typist, market researcher **Political interests** women's issues, health and social services, environment, local govt, shopworkers, poverty, nuclear disarmament, Nicaragua; anti-EC, NATO **Political career** Tottenham Borough Cllr 1956–60; MP for Coventry South West 1974–9; contested Woolwich 1983; Labour National Executive Cttee 1982–7 **Member** War on Want; CND; Labour Action for Peace; Nicaragua Solidarity **Unions** sponsored by USDAW **Publications include** *Eyewitness in Revolutionary Portugal*; *Women and the Struggle for Workers' Control*

WOLFSON, Mark Con., Sevenoaks (1979) **b.** 7 Apr. 1934 **ed.** Eton; Pembroke Coll., Cambridge **Profession** personnel dir. (Hambros Bank), business consultant **Political interests** defence, human rights, trade and industry, industrial relations, industrial training, employment, inner cities; pro-hanging **Political career** Wandsworth Borough Cllr 1968–70; contested Islington North Feb. 1974, City of Westminster Paddington Oct. 1974

WOOD, Timothy Con., Stevenage (1983) **b.** 13 Aug. 1940 **ed.** King James's Grammar Sch., Knaresborough; Manchester Univ. **Profession** computer programer, computer executive **Political interests** high technology industries, new towns, aerospace, education, health and social security, local govt, defence, Northern Ireland **Political career** Bracknell District Cllr 1975–83 (Leader 1976–8) **Parliamentary career** Asst Whip 1990– **Member** Bow Group

WOODCOCK, Michael Con., Ellesmere Port and Neston (1983) **b.** 10 Apr. 1943 **ed.** Queen Elizabeth's Grammar Sch., Mansfield **Profession** accountant, company dir., management consultant, writer, Lloyd's underwriter **Political interests** small businesses, management, trade and industry, energy, oil, conservation; pro-hanging **Publications include** *Unblocking Your Organisation*; *Management Development Manual*; *50 Activities for Teambuilding* **Other** JP 1971

WORTHINGTON, Tony Lab., Clydebank and Milngavie (1987) **b.** 11 Oct. 1941 **ed.** City Sch., Lincoln; London Sch. of Economics; York Univ.; Durham Univ.; Glasgow Univ. **Profession** sociology lecturer **Political interests** home affairs, race relations, prisons, youth work, education, regional policy, inner cities, media, Third World, nuclear disarmament **Political career** Strathclyde Regional Cllr 1974–87 **Parliamentary career** Opposition Spokesman on Scotland 1989– **Member** CND; Tribune Group

WRAY, Jimmy Lab., Glasgow Provan (1987) **b.** 28 Apr. 1938 **ed.** St Bonaventure's, Gorbals **Profession** HGV driver **Political interests** health and social services, housing, inner cities, drug abuse, education, foreign affairs **Political career** Glasgow Corporation Cllr 1972–5; Strathclyde Regional Cllr 1976–88 **Unions** TGWU

YEO, Timothy Con., Suffolk South (1983) **b.** 20 Mar. 1945 **ed.** Charterhouse; Emmanuel Coll., Cambridge **Profession** company dir., charity administrator **Political interests** charities, health and social services, home affairs, employment, economy, agriculture, Third World **Political career** contested Bedwellty 1974 **Member** Charities VAT Reform Group (Chmn 1981–8) **Publications include** *Public Accountability and Regulation of Charities*

YOUNG, David Lab., Bolton South East (1983) **b.** 12 Oct. 1930 **ed.** Greenock Academy; Glasgow Univ.; St Paul's Coll., Cheltenham **Profession** history teacher **Political interests** education, economy, employment, pensions, health and social services, defence, nuclear disarmament, foreign affairs **Political career** Nuneaton District Cllr; contested Worcestershire South 1959, Banbury 1966, Bath 1970; MP for Bolton East 1974–83 **Member** Fabian Society; CND; Co-operative Party **Unions** NUPE; TGWU

YOUNG, Sir George Con., Ealing Acton (1974) **b.** 16 July 1941 **ed.** Eton; Christ Church, Oxford; Surrey Univ. **Profession** economist **Political interests** race relations, environment, housing, health and social services, disabled; anti-smoking, racism **Political career** Lambeth Borough Cllr 1968–71; Greater London Cllr 1970–3 **Parliamentary career** Opposition Whip 1976–9; Under-Secretary of State for Health and Social Services 1979–81, for the Environment 1981–6; Comptroller of the Household (No. 3 Whip) 1990– **Member** Tory Reform Group **Publications include** *Tourism – Blessing or Blight?*; *Accommodation Services in the UK 1970–80* **Other** He succeeded his father as 6th Baronet 1960

YOUNGER, Rt Hon. George Con., Ayr (1964) **b.** 22 Sep. 1931 **ed.** Winchester; New Coll., Oxford **Profession** Argyll and Sutherland Highlanders 1950–65; brewer and company dir. (George Younger and Son Ltd), farmer **Political interests** Scottish affairs, arts, aviation, trade and industry, small business, brewing, finance, defence; pro-EC **Political career** contested Lanarkshire North 1959 **Parliamentary career** Opposition Whip 1965–7; Deputy Chmn Conservative Party in Scotland 1967–70, Chmn 1974–75; Under-Secretary of State at the Scottish Office (Development) 1970–4; Minister of State for Defence 1974; Opposition Spokesman on Defence 1974–6, on Scotland 1976–9; PC 1979; Secretary of State for Scotland 1979–86, for Defence 1986–9 **Other** Son and heir of Viscount Younger of Leckie; Territorial Decoration 1964; DL Stirlingshire 1968

POLITICAL PARTIES

General Elections and By-elections in the United Kingdom, 1979–89

	General Election 03/05/79	*May 1979 to June 1983*	*General Election 09/06/83*	*June 1983 to June 1987*	*General Election 11/06/87*	*June 1987 to June 1989*	*June 1989 to June 1990*
Number of By-elections		20		31		8	11
Percentage Turnout	76.0	61.2	72.7	62.4	75.3	56.8	57.9
Party Percentages:							
Conservative	43.9	23.8	42.4	16.0	42.3	26.6	23.8
Labour	36.9	25.7	27.6	14.9	30.8	36.4	38.4
Liberal Democrat[1]	13.8	9.0	13.7	15.0	12.8	11.7	10.4
Social Democratic Party (SDP)[1]		14.2	11.6	5.6	9.7	8.8	6.5
Plaid Cymru	0.4	0.5	0.4	0.3	0.4	4.1	2.8
Scottish National Party	1.6	1.7	1.1		1.3	8.1	5.6
Northern Ireland Parties	2.2	23.3	2.5	47.4	2.2		7.7
Green Party[2]	0.1	0.3	0.2		0.3	2.4	2.4
Others	1.1	1.6	0.5	0.8	0.2	1.9	2.4
Total voting electorate[3]	31,221	715	30,671	1,235	32,530	281	409

1 In 1983 and 1987 the Liberals and SDP contested the general elections as the Liberal-SDP Alliance. Combine percentages for the Liberals and SDP to find total Alliance percentage of vote in these general elections. In 1988 the Social and Liberal Democrats were formed, after which the Democrats and the SDP contested elections separately.

2 Known as the Ecology Party before 1977.

3 In thousands.

Members Elected in the 1987 General Election

Conservative Party	375
Labour Party	229
Liberal Party	17
Ulster Unionist Party	9
Social Democratic Party	5
Scottish National Party	3
Plaid Cymru	3
Ulster Democratic Unionist Party	3
Social Democratic and Labour Party	3
Ulster Popular Unionist Party	1
Sinn Fein	1
Speaker	1
Total	650

HOUSE OF COMMONS

The State of Parties 1990 (as of 11 July 1990)

Conservative Party	372
Labour Party	226
Liberal Democrat Party	19
Ulster Unionist Party	9
Scottish National Party	4
Social Democrat Party	3
Ulster Democratic Unionist Party	3
Plaid Cymru	3
Social Democratic and Labour Party	3
Sinn Fein	1
Ulster Popular Unionist Party	1
Independent – Labour	1
Vacant seat (Knowsley South)	1
Speaker and 3 deputies	4
Total	650

POLITICAL PARTIES

The highest intake of female MPs at a general election was in 1987, when 41 women were elected to Parliament – 6.3% of the House – when Kate Hoey was elected Labour MP for Vauxhall in 1989, the number rose to 42 (6.5%); rising to 43 (6.6%) with Sylvia Heal's election as Labour MP for Mid-Staffordshire. This puts the United Kingdom third from the bottom in percentages of women elected to parliament in a Western European country.

CONSERVATIVE AND UNIONIST PARTY

Central Office, 32 Smith Square, Westminster, London SW1P 3HH Tel: (071) 222 9000
Chairman: Rt Hon. K. Baker MP
Deputy Chairman: Rt Hon. the Lord of Graffham
Vice Chairmen: T. Arnold MP, Dame J. Seccombe OBE, Sir J. Spicer MP
Hon. Treasurers: Lord McAlpine of West Green, Sir O. Wade, Sir H. Laing

The Scottish Conservative Party

Central Office, 3 Chester Street, Edinburgh EH3 7RF Tel: (031) 226 4426
Chairman: M.B. Forsyth MP
Deputy Chairman: W. Hughes
Hon. Treasurer: Sir M. Goodwin CBE
Chief Executive: J.J. MacKay

The Tory Party became generally known as the Conservative Party after Sir Robert Peel's declaration in his election address to the constituents of Tamworth in 1834. The repeal of the Corn Laws in 1846 split the Conservative Party, one group led by Disraeli (the Protectionists) opposing the repeal, and another group, in which Gladstone was prominent (the Peelites), supporting Peel's free trade policy. The Peelites gradually merged with the Whigs and the Radicals during the 1850s and 1860s to produce a new Liberal Party. In 1886, however, the issue of Home Rule split the Liberals, with Joseph Chamberlain leading a group who favoured the maintenance of Irish union with Britain into a 'Unionist' alliance. This was eventually acknowledged by the changing of the party's name in 1912 to the Conservative and Unionist Party. The first Conservative Prime Minister proper was the Earl of Derby who took office on 25 February 1858.

Party Structure

The Conservative Party leader chooses either the cabinet, or shadow cabinet, depending on whether the party is in government or opposition. The leader also makes policies, approves the party manifesto and indirectly controls central headquarters by the power of appointment of the Party Chairman. The leader is elected by the parliamentary party. Both individual members and constituency associations provide the party with finance and select election candidates. The National Conservative Association (formed in 1867) represents the mass membership of about 1.5 million in the various constituency associations in England and Wales. The Scottish Conservative Association is a separate, but parallel body.

Central Office (established in 1870) is the central,

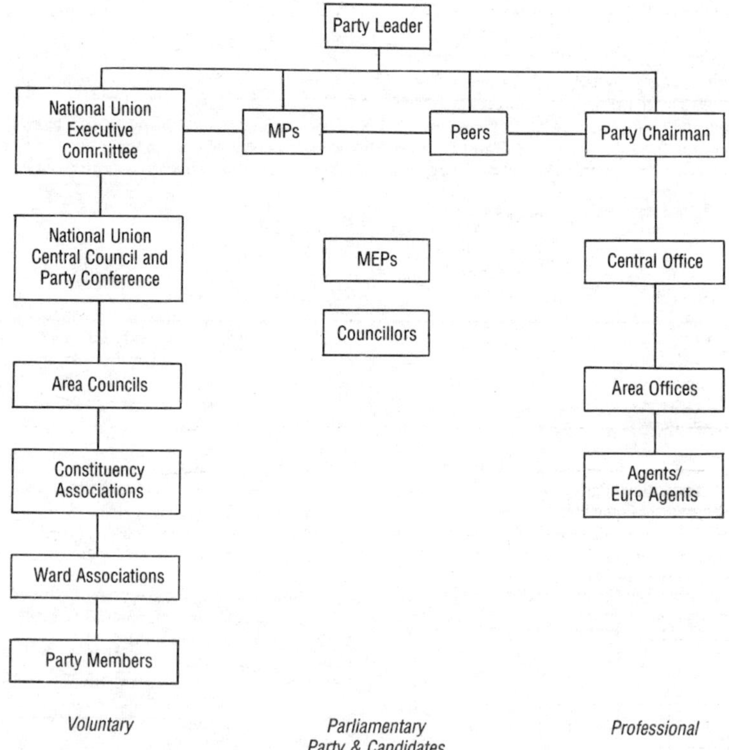

professional administrative structure which supervises the running of the local organizations. Attached to Central Office are the Conservative Research Department, the Centre for Policy Studies and the Conservative Political Centre.

The basis of Conservative Party organization in Parliament is the 1922 Committee, which is composed of all Conservative backbenchers.

The Conservative Party is the richest of the political parties. In 1989 it received some £8.1 million and its total expenditure stood at £7.8 million. Corporations and companies donate over a third of all party finance.

Mrs Thatcher is the longest consecutive serving Prime Minister in British Parliamentary history. The Conservative Party's overall majority of 101 seats is the second largest since the 1945 general election.

LABOUR PARTY

150 Walworth Road, London SE17 1JT Tel: (071) 703 0833

Scottish Labour Party

Keir Hardie House, 1 Lyne Doch Place, Glasgow, G3 6AB

Chairman: Rt Hon. N. Kinnock MP
Vice-Chairman: D. Skinner MP
General Secretary: L. Whitty
Treasurer: S. McCluskie
Director of Organization: Mrs J. Gould
Director of Campaigns and Co-ordination: P. Mandelson
Director of Policy Development: G. Bish
Director of Personnel, Resources and Training: M. Watts
Parliamentary Party Leader: Rt Hon. Neil Kinnock MP
Deputy Leader: Rt Hon. R. Hattersley MP
Leader of the Labour Peers: Lord Cledwyn of Penrhos CH

Members of Shadow Cabinet:

Leader of the Opposition: Rt Hon. N. Kinnock MP
Deputy Leader and Shadow Home Secretary: Rt Hon. R. Hattersley MP
Chief Whip: D. Foster MP
Chairman of Parliamentary Party: Rt Hon. S. Orme MP
Chief Secretary to the Treasury: M. Beckett MP
Shadow Chancellor: Rt Hon. J. Smith MP
Shadow Foreign Secretary: Rt Hon. G. Kaufman MP
Agriculture, Food and Rural Affairs: Dr D. Clark MP
Health: R. Cook MP
Social Security: M. Meacher MP
Leader of the House and Campaign Co-ordinator: Dr J. Cunningham MP
Trade and Industry: G. Brown MP
Energy: F. Dobson MP
Employment: A. Blair MP
Education: J. Straw MP
Children's Rights: J. Lestor MP
Overseas Development and Co-operation: A. Clwyd MP
Women's Rights: J. Richardson MP
Transport: J. Prescott MP
Scotland: D. Dewar MP
Wales: B. Jones MP
Environment: B. Gould MP
Leader of the Labour Peers: Rt Hon. Lord Cledwyn of Penrhos CH
Chief Whip, Lords: Lord Ponsonby of Shulbrede
Labour Peers Representative: The Lord Dean of Beswick

Labour candidates stood for the first time in the 1892 general election. In 1900 the Labour Representation Committee was formed in an attempt to get working class representation in Parliament via a distinct party grouping. In 1906 the name was changed to the Labour Party, and between 1906 and 1922 the Labour Party grew to replace the Liberals as one of the two major parties.

The first Labour Party Prime Minister was J. Ramsay MacDonald, who took office on 22 January 1924.

Party Structure

The Labour Party leader has the power to elect the cabinet only when in government. The parliamentary Labour Party, when in opposition, elects a Parliamentary Committee which forms the basis of the opposition frontbench spokesmen and thus shadow cabinet. The leader and deputy leader of the Labour Party are chosen at the party conference by an electoral

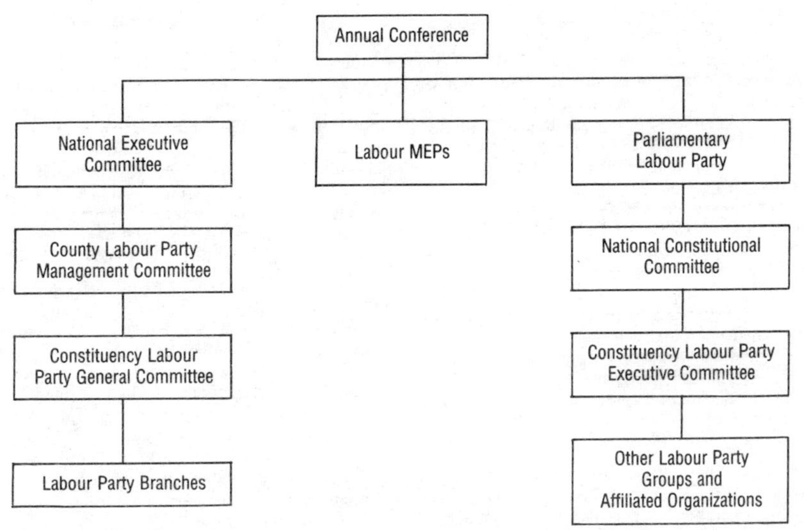

college. The annual conference is also the policy-making body.

The National Executive Committee (NEC) of the Labour Party (elected by party conference) usually meets monthly. The NEC is composed of 29 members, including the leader and deputy leader. The Central Secretary, and other senior members of the party bureaucracy, are appointed by and responsible to the NEC. The NEC supervises the whole party organization outside Parliament, approves the manifesto and can also make policy (which must be ratified by a two-thirds majority at the party conference). The constituency parties choose both the election candidates and, as part of the conference, elect the leadership.

Constituency parties and individual members provide party finance, as do the unions which contribute about 75% of the Labour Party funds. The Trade Unions Act 1984 required unions to ballot their members to determine whether the unions should continue to give financial support to the Labour Party. All the major unions secured majorities in favour of the political fund. The Labour Party receives about £5,586,000 p.a. (1988) and its total expenditure is approximately £5,579,000 p.a. (1988). In 1988 its total membership stood at 265,927, a 7.7% reduction on the previous year.

LIBERAL DEMOCRAT PARTY

4 Cowley Street, London SW1P 3NP Tel: (071) 222 7999

The Scottish Liberal Democrats

4 Clifton Terrace, Edinburgh, EH12 5DR Tel: (031) 337 2314

Leader of the Party: Rt Hon. P. Ashdown MP
Deputy Leader: Sir Russell Johnston MP
Chief Whip: Jim Wallace MP
Deputy Whip: Simon Hughes MP
Deputy Whip and Campaign Co-ordinator: Archie Kirkwood
President: Charles Kennedy MP
Deputy Chair: Trevor Jones
Hon. Treasurer: T. Razzell
General Secretary: Graham Elson
Leader of the L D Peers: Rt Hon. Lord Jenkins
Deputy Leader in the Lords: Rt Hon. the Baroness Seear
L D Whip in the Lords: The Lord Tordoff
Deputy L D Whip in the Lords: The Viscount Falkland

With the splitting of the Conservative Party in 1846, after the repeal of the Corn Laws, the Peelites gradually merged with the Whigs and Radicals to produce a new Liberal Party. The Liberal Registration was founded in 1861 and, in 1877, Joseph Chamberlain created the National Liberal Federation, with its headquarters in London. Between 1906 and 1922 the Labour Party grew to replace the Liberals as one of the two major parties. The last Liberal government was that of H.H. Asquith who took office on 8 April 1908. In 1981 the then newly formed and now disbanded (1990) Social Democratic Party (SDP) and the Liberals agreed to work jointly as an alliance, although a merger of the two parties was then rejected. In 1988 a majority of the SDP agreed on a merger with the Liberals, which took place in March 1988 as the Social and Liberal Democrats. In a ballot of members in October 1989 the party decided to shorten its title to Liberal Democrats.

Party Structure

The party has a federal structure with parties in Scotland, Wales and England. Each 'state' party is responsible for the operation of local parties' parliamentary candidate selection. In England there is an English Conference, a Co-ordinating Committee and a Council of the Regions of England. In Scotland there is a Conference, Executive and a Policy Committee. In Wales there is a Council, a National Executive and a Policy Sub-committee. The Federal Policy Committee is elected annually by the Federal Conference and is responsible for initiating and developing policy. It has 27 members, including the leader and the President of the party.

The Federal Executive is responsible for directing, co-ordinating and implementing policy. It has 24 members, including the leader and the president. The Federal Conference meets at least twice annually and is composed of local party representatives. The Conference is the sovereign decision-making body in the party.

GREEN PARTY

10 Station Parade, Balham High Road, SW12 9AZ Tel: (081) 673 0045

Office Manager: John Bishop
Press Officer: Caroline Lucas

The British Green Party is the oldest in Western Europe. It was founded in February 1973 as the People Party, which contested its first national elections in February 1974, standing in five constituencies. In 1975 the party's name was changed to the Ecology Party. It was not until September 1985 that the party acquired its present name. In 1978 the Ecology Party Conference decided to contest 50 seats in the 1979 general election and thus, for the first time, were able to broadcast party policies.

Number of candidates and percentage of vote in general elections

Years	*1974*	*1974*	*1979*	*1983*	*1987*
No. of candidates	3	4	53	109	133
Percentage of votes	1.8	0.7	1.5	1.0	1.4

In the June 1989 European elections the Green Party achieved their largest percentage of the vote on a national basis (15 per cent; 2.25 million votes). This was the highest percentage of any Green Party in the world contesting nationwide elections, yet no MEPs were returned. At local level, the Green Party has over 100 parish councillors, 13 district councillors and one county councillor. Present membership of the Green Party stands at 17,122, twice the previous year. Its income is approximately £106,584 p.a. (1988/9) and its expenditure stands at £89,590 p.a. (1988/9).

Party Structure

The 250 local parties decide on candidates and elections and undertake the majority of the campaigning. They are semi-autonomous and banded into geographical regions. They follow the principles of the Green Party's latest *Manifesto for a Sustainable Society*. The policy-making body is the twice-annually convened National Conference, which is open to all party members. The Conference elects the Party Council which administers the national party. The Party Council elects three co-chairs and the speakers as Green Party representatives, since the Green Party does not have a hierarchical leadership structure.

The cornerstone of Green Party politics is a commitment to policies which preserve the planet, the environment and its peoples.

PLAID CYMRU (WELSH NATIONALIST)

51 Cathedral Road, Cardiff, CF1 94D Tel: (0222) 231944

Chairman: D. Huws
Deputy Chairman: I.W. Jones
Hon. Treasurer: D. Watkins
Secretary: D. Williams
Party President: D.E. Thomas MP
Vice President: D. Iwan

Plaid Cymru was founded in 1925. Its aims are self-government for Wales within the European Community (regional autonomy within a federal Europe). They also seek to preserve the Welsh language which by 1960 was spoken by only a quarter of the population from half the population in 1900. Their power base is in North-West Wales. Their first success was the July 1966 by-election at Carmarthen, the first indication of an upsurge of nationalism in the 1960s and 1970s.

A Royal Commission, on examining devolution proposals, rejected the principle of Welsh separatism in 1973, but proposed the creation of a Welsh Assembly. With the renewed success of Plaid Cymru in 1974 the Labour Party set up a 'devolution unit'. A joint Scotland and Wales Bill was introduced in 1976 but successfully blocked. A separate Bill for Wales was presented in the next parliamentary session and an agreement was reached that the Act should only be put into force after devolution received the support of 40% of the electorate as a whole (not just voters in Wales). The Scottish and Welsh referendums were held in March 1979. The Wales Act was rejected with only 20% of those voting (12% of the total Welsh electorate) supporting it.

Plaid Cymru has three MPs in the present United Kingdom Parliament: D.W. Wigley – Caernarvon (Gwynedd); D.E. Thomas – Meirionnydd Nant Conwy (Gwynedd); I.W. Jones – Ynys Mon/Anglesey (Gwynedd). In the 1989 European Parliament election Plaid Cymru received 12.9% of the vote in Wales.

Its current membership total stands at 10,000 and its annual budget is £120,000.

Party Structure

The annual Conference is the sovereign policy-making body and is also responsible for electing the leadership. The National Council which meets four times yearly is responsible for policy matters when the Conference is not in session. The National Council also ratifies the manifesto which is drawn up by the Vice-Chair of Research and Policy. The National Executive Committee is the main administrative body and meets on a monthly basis. Selection of candidates is the responsibility of the 36 Rhanberths (District Committees).

SCOTTISH NATIONAL PARTY

6 North Charlotte Street, Edinburgh, EH2 4JH Tel: (031) 226 3661

National Governor: G. Wilson
Deputy Vice Governor: A. Salmond MP
National Treasurer: A. Morgan
National Secretary: J. Swinney
Parliamentary Party Leader: Mrs M.W. Ewing MP
Chief Whip: A. Welsh MP

The SNP was founded in 1934 and scored its first parliamentary success when Dr R. McIntyre won the Motherwell by-election in 1945. Its major aim is the establishment of a democratic Scottish Parliament. The SNP has had continuous Parliamentary representation since November 1967 when Winnie Ewing overturned a 10,000 Labour majority to win the Hamilton by-election. (Mrs E. Ewing is now the sole SNP MEP). This upsurge in nationalist support in Scotland was most clearly reflected in the October 1974 general election when 11 SNP MPs were elected and the party polled over 30% of the total vote. After the proposal of the Scottish Constitutional Committee in 1970 to create a separate Scottish Assembly without executive powers, the tension in the devolution debate eased slightly after the 1970 election saw the return of only one SNP MP. However, their support increased again in the February 1974 election and the October 1974 result persuaded the Labour government to create a 'devolution' unit. A joint Scotland and Wales Bill was introduced in 1976 but successfully blocked by devolution opponents. A separate Bill for Scotland was presented in the next parliamentary session and an agreement was reached that the Act should only be put

Percentage share of the vote in selected general elections in Wales

Years	*1945*	*1959*	*1970*	*Oct. 1974*	*1979*	*1983*	*1987*
Parties							
Plaid Cymru	1.1	4.8	19.7	10.8	8.1	7.8	7.3
Conservative	23.9	32.6	27.7	23.9	32.2	31.1	29.5
Liberal/Alliance	15.0	5.5	6.8	15.5	10.6	23.2	17.9
Labour	58.4	56.4	51.6	49.5	48.5	37.5	45.1

Percentage share of the vote in selected general elections in Scotland

Years	*1945*	*1959*	*1970*	*Oct. 1974*	*1979*	*1983*	*1987*
Parties:							
SNP (Nationalist)	1.3	0.8	11.1	30.4	17.3	11.7	14.0
Conservative Party	41.0	47.2	38.0	24.7	31.4	28.4	24.0
Liberal Party/Alliance	5.6	4.1	5.5	8.3	9.0	24.5	19.2
Labour Party	47.5	46.7	44.5	36.3	41.4	35.1	47.4
Other						0.3	0.3

into force after devolution received the support of 40% of the electorate as a whole (not just voters in Scotland). The Scottish and Welsh referendums were held in March 1979. The Scottish Act was supported by 52% of those voting but as they amounted to only a third of the Scottish electorate the Act failed to meet the 40% requirement. 32.5% voted 'Yes', while 30.4% voted 'No'. However, the Scottish National Party faced more serious problems than 'unfriendly' amendments, in that less than half the SNPs own supporters were in favour of the party's ultimate aim of an independent Scotland. Two months after the referenda the Conservative Party, which remains opposed on its Unionist principles to devolved assemblies, won the British general election and the SNP lost nine of its eleven seats. In the 1987 election the SNP returned three MPs. On 10th November 1988 the SNP achieved a result as spectacular as the 1967 by-election, when Jim Sillars overturned a Labour majority of 19,509 to win the Glasgow, Govan by-election with 48.75% of the vote and a majority of 3,554.

The other SNP MPs returned in 1987 were: Margaret Ewing – Moray (Grampian); Alex Salmond – Banff and Buchan (Grampian); Andrew Welsh – Angus East (Tayside).

THE ULSTER UNIONIST COUNCIL (Northern Ireland) [Official Unionist Party]

3 Glengall Street, Belfast BT12 5AE Tel: (0232) 324601

Parliamentary Party Leader: Rt Hon. J.H. Molyneaux MP
Chairman: J. Allen
Vice-Chairman: A.J. Wilson
Hon. Treasurer: J. Cunningham
Party Secretary and Chief Executive: J.H. Wilson

9 MPs elected at the 1987 general election:

Education, Trade & Industry: R. Beggs MP
Transport, Communications, Local Government: C. Forsythe MP
Defence, Security: K. McGuinnis MP
Constitutional Affairs: Rt Hon. J.H. Molyneaux MP
Foreign Affairs, Employment: R. McCusker MP
Treasury: W. Ross MP
Health and Social Services, Regional Affairs: Rev. M. Smyth BA BD MP
EC, Agriculture: Rt Hon. J. Taylor BSC MP
Housing, Environment: C. Walker MP

1 MEP at the 1989 European Elections: J. Nicholson MEP

The Unionist Parties severed links with the Conservative Party and split into two factions: the Ulster Democratic Unionist Party (q.v.) and the Ulster Unionist Council. The Ulster Unionist Council (Official Unionist Party) traces its foundation to the Ulster Unionist Party, established in 1892 and the sole voice of Northern Ireland's Protestant population until the late 1960s. The Ulster Unionist Council remains the largest Unionist Party in the province. It is split between integrationists (J.H. Molyneaux) and devolutionists. The latter is the official party stance. The Ulster Unionist Council MPs resigned their seats on 17 December 1985, as a protest vote against the Anglo-Irish Agreement, seeking re-election on 23 January 1986.

ULSTER DEMOCRATIC UNIONIST PARTY (DUP)

296 Albert Bridge Road, Belfast BT5 4GX Tel. (0232) 458597

Parliamentary Party Leader: Rev. I.R.K. Paisley MP MEP
Deputy Leader: P. Robinson MP
Chairman: J. McClure
Deputy Chairman: S. Gibson
Hon. Treasurer: D. Herron
Secretary: A. Kane

The Democratic Unionist Party (DUP) was founded in 1971. Its predominant voice is that of 'Paisleyism'. The DUP regards itself as 'right-wing in terms of being strong on the constitution, but to the left on social policies'. It has been engaged in a battle with the Ulster Unionist Council to establish itself as the dominant Unionist party in the province. The DUP MPs also resigned their seats on 17 December 1985, in protest against the Anglo-Irish Agreement. The resulting by-elections were also held on 23 January 1986.

3 MPs were returned at the 1987 general election: Rev. I.R.K. Paisley – Antrim North; P.D. Robinson – Belfast East; Rev. R.T.U. McCrea – Mid Ulster.

ULSTER POPULAR UNIONIST PARTY

Eastonville Millisle, Co. Down, N. Ireland Tel: (0247) 883222

Leader of the Party: J. Kilfedder MP
1987 election, 1 MP: J. Kilfedder MP – North Down

The Ulster Popular Unionist Party (UPUP) is in favour of Northern Ireland devolution and proportional representational elections to the House of Commons. It also supports the desegregation of Northern Ireland's schools. J. Kilfedder, along with the other Ulster Unionist MPs, resigned his seat on 17 December 1985 in protest against the Anglo-Irish Agreement. He was returned in the by-election on 23 January 1986.

SOCIAL DEMOCRATIC AND LABOUR PARTY (SDLP)

38 University Street, Belfast BT7 1FZ Tel: (0232) 323428

Parliamentary Party Leader: J. Hume MP MEP
Deputy Leader: S. Mallon MP
Chief Whip: E.K. McGrady MP
Chair: A. Maginness
Deputy Chair: M. Durkan, G. Murphy
Hon. Treasurer: P. Brannigan
General Secretary: P. McGlone

The SDLP was founded in 1970 by ex-civil rights activists. It united members of the old Nationalist Party, the National Democratic Party and the Republican Labour Party. Its present membership is about 4,000. Its aims are a socialist state in the mould of European social democracy and Irish unity based on majority consent in Northern Ireland. It demands the right to share power, a new constitution and thus an institutional tie with the Republic of Ireland. In the 1987 general election they returned 3 MPs to Westminster: E.K. McGrady MP – South Down; S. Mallon MP – Newry and Armagh; J. Hume MP – Foyle.

SINN FEIN (OURSELVES ALONE)

44 Parnell Square, Dublin, Irish Republic Tel: (0001) 726932

In 1969 the Irish Republican Army Council voted to give token recognition to the parliaments in Westminster, Dublin, Stormont; this change in policy created a fissure in the movement. The faction opposing the change formed the 'Provisional' Irish Republican Army (PIRA) and its political counterpart, 'Provisional' Sinn Fein, while those supporting recognition became the 'Official' IRA and 'Official' Sinn Fein (now the Workers Party). Sinn Fein contested the last all-Ireland election in 1918, winning 75% of the 105 Irish seats (69.5% of the vote). 36 of those elected were in prison. Sinn Fein set up their own judicial procedures and formed the Dail Eireann which, as the elected body, unilaterally declared a state of independence. Negotiations with the Westminster Parliament began in 1921, after the British government prepared to save the North of Ireland and Ulster in particular. From the 1921 Anglo-Irish Treaty a split developed in the organization of Sinn Fein in the South (Eire). Fine Gael originated in the pro-treaty wing; Fianna Fail (the largest political party in the republic) opposed the Anglo-Irish Treaty and is thus regarded as the more staunchly 'republican' party. As an independent state, Eire has its own Parliament in Dublin, votes for its own MEPs, and does not have representatives in the British Parliament.

In 1981 the Maze hunger-striker and member of Provisional Sinn Fein, Bobby Sands, was elected to the Westminster Parliament as MP for Fermanagh-South Tyrone, with the SDLP deciding not to contest the election in a head-to-head confrontation with Provisional Sinn Fein which would split the Catholic vote. This infuriated the Unionists who accused the SDLP of electoral complicity with the IRA. Recently, Sinn Fein has twice (1983 and 1987) won a parliamentary seat in West Belfast. However, the MP for West Belfast, Gerry Adams, chooses not to sit at the Westminster Parliament. Mr Adams is also the President of Sinn Fein. Sinn Fein's aims are national self-determination for 'the island of Ireland', thus demanding an end to partition; British troop withdrawal; a constitutional conference to establish a new constitution. It seeks to establish a socialist, thirty-two county republic, with collective ownership. It also seeks a restoration of Irish language and culture. At the beginning of 1988 Sinn Fein and the SDLP had a series of discussions on the Irish constitution. Sinn Fein does not support the Anglo-Irish Agreement.

FULL LIST OF HM GOVERNMENT AS AT 16 JANUARY 1990

Members of the Cabinet

Prime Minister, First Lord of the Treasury and Minister for the Civil Service – Rt Hon Margaret Thatcher FRS MP
Lord President of the Council and Leader of the House of Commons – Rt Hon Sir Geoffrey Howe QC MP
Lord Chancellor – Rt Hon Lord Mackay of Clashfern
Secretary of State for Foreign and Commonwealth Affairs – Rt Hon Douglas Hurd CBE MP
Chancellor of the Exchequer – Rt Hon John Major MP
Secretary of State for the Home Department – Rt Hon David Waddington QC MP
Secretary of State for Wales – Rt Hon Peter Walker MBE MP
Secretary of State for Defence – Rt Hon Tom King MP
Secretary of State for Trade and Industry and President of the Board of Trade – Rt Hon Nicholas Ridley MP
Chancellor of the Duchy of Lancaster – Rt Hon Kenneth Baker MP
Secretary of State for Health – Rt Hon Kenneth Clarke QC MP
Secretary of State for Education and Science – Rt Hon John MacGregor OBE MP
Secretary of State for Scotland – Rt Hon Malcolm Rifkind QC MP
Secretary of State for Transport – Rt Hon Cecil Parkinson MP
Secretary of State for Energy – Rt Hon John Wakeham MP
Lord Privy Seal and Leader of the House of Lords – Rt Hon Lord Belstead
Secretary of State for Social Security – Rt Hon Antony Newton OBE MP
Secretary of State for the Environment – Rt Hon Christopher Patten MP
Secretary of State for Northern Ireland – Rt Hon Peter Brooke MP
Minister of Agriculture, Fisheries and Food – Rt Hon John Gummer MP
Chief Secretary to the Treasury – Rt Hon Norman Lamont MP
Secretary of State for Employment – Rt Hon Michael Howard QC MP

Law Officers

Attorney-General – Rt Hon Sir Patrick Mayhew QC MP
Lord Advocate – Rt Hon Lord Fraser of Carmyllie QC
Solicitor-General – Rt Hon Sir Nicholas Lyell QC MP
Solicitor-General for Scotland – Alan Rodger Esq QC*

Ministers not in the Cabinet

Parliamentary Secretary to the Treasury – Rt Hon Tim Renton Esq MP
Minister of State, Privy Council Office, (Minister for the Arts) – Rt Hon Richard Luce MP
Minister for Overseas Development – Rt Hon Lynda Chalker MP
Ministers of State, Foreign and Commonwealth Office
 Rt Hon William Waldegrave MP
 Lord Brabazon of Tara
 Hon Francis Maude MP
Paymaster General – Earl of Caithness
Financial Secretary to the Treasury – Peter Lilley Esq MP
Ministers of State, Home Office –
 Rt Hon John Patten Esq MP
 David Mellor Esq QC MP
 Rt Hon Earl Ferrers DL
Minister of State for Welsh Office – Wyn Roberts Esq MP
Ministers of State, Ministry of Defence
 Minister of State for Defence Procurement – Hon Alan Clark MP
 Minister of State for the Armed Forces – Hon Archibald Hamilton MP
Ministers of State, Department of Trade and Industry –
 Minister for Industry and Enterprise – Hon Douglas Hogg MP
 Minister for Trade – Rt Hon Lord Trefgarne
Minister of State, Department of Health – Mrs Virginia Bottomley MP
Minister of State, Department of Education and Science – Mrs Angela Rumbold CBE MP
Ministers of State, Scottish Office –
 Ian Lang Esq MP
 Lord Sanderson of Bowden
Minister of State, Department of Transport –
 Minister for Public Transport – Michael Portillo Esq MP
Minister of State, Department of Energy – Rt Hon Peter Morrison MP
Minister of State, Department of Social Security – Rt

Hon Nicholas Scott MBE MP
Ministers of State, Department of the Environment
Minister for Environment and Countryside – David Trippier Esq JP MP
Minister for Local Government and Inner Cities – David Hunt Esq MBE MP
Minister for Housing and Planning – Michael Spicer Esq MP
Minister of State, Northern Ireland Office – Rt Hon John Cope MP
Minister of State, Ministry of Agriculture, Fisheries and Food – Baroness Trumpington
Minister of State, Department of Employment – Tim Eggar Esq MP

Departments of State and Ministers

Agriculture, Fisheries and Food –
Minister – Rt Hon John Gummer MP
Minister of State – Baroness Trumpington
Parliamentary Secretaries – David Maclean Esq Mp, David Curry Esq MP

Arts and Libraries, Office of –
Minister for the Arts – Rt Hon Richard Luce MP

Chancellor of the Duchy of Lancaster – Rt Hon Kenneth Baker MP

Civil Service, Office of the Minister for
Prime Minister and Minister for the Civil Service – Rt Hon Margaret Thatcher FRS MP
Minister of State, Privy Council Office (Minister for the Arts) – Rt Hon Richard Luce MP

Defence –
Secretary of State – Rt Hon Tom King MP
Minister of State for Defence Procurement – Hon Alan Clarke MP
Minister of State for the Armed Forces – Hon Archibald Hamilton MP
Parliamentary Under-Secretary of State for Defence Procurement – Michael Neubert Esq MP
Parliamentary Under-Secretary of State for the Armed Forces – Earl of Arran

Education and Science –
Secretary of State – Rt Hon John MacGregor OBE MP
Minister of State – Mrs Angela Rumbold CBE MP
Parliamentary Under-Secretaries of State – Robert Jackson Esq MP, Alan Howarth Esq CBE MP

Employment –
Secretary of State – Rt Hon Michael Howard QC MP
Minister of State – Tim Eggar Esq MP
Parliamentary Under-Secretary of State – Patrick Nicholls Esq MP, Earl of Strathclyde

Energy –
Secretary of State – Rt Hon John Wakeham MP
Minister of State – Rt Hon Peter Morrison MP
Parliamentary Under-Secretary of State – Tony Baldry Esq MP

Environment –
Secretary of State – Rt Hon Christopher Patten MP
Ministers of State
Minister for the Environment and Countryside – David Trippier Esq MP
Minister for Local Government and Inner Cities – David Hunt Esq MBE MP
Minister for Housing and Planning – Michael Spicer Esq MP
Parliamentary Under-Secretaries of State – Christopher Chope Esq OBE MP, Lord Hesketh, David Heathcoat-Amory Esq MP
Minister for Sport – Hon Colin Moynihan MP

Foreign and Commonwealth Affairs –
Secretary of State – Rt Hon Douglas Hurd CBE MP
Minister for Overseas Development – Rt Hon Lynda Chalker MP
Ministers of State – Rt Hon William Waldegrave MP, Lord Brabazon of Tara, Hon Francis Maude MP
Parliamentary Under-Secretary of State – Hon Tim Sainsbury MP

Health –
Secretary of State for Health – Rt Hon Kenneth Clarke QC MP
Minister of State – Mrs Virginia Bottomley MP
Parliamentary Under-Secretaries of State – Roger Freeman Esq MP, Baroness Hooper

Home Office –
Secretary of State for the Home Department – Rt Hon David Waddington QC MP
Ministers of State – Rt Hon John Patten Esq MP, David Mellor Esq QC MP, Rt Hon Earl Ferrers DL
Parliamentary Under-Secretary of State – Peter Lloyd Esq MP

Law Officers' Department –
Attorney-General – Rt Hon Sir Patrick Mayhew QC MP
Solicitor-General – Rt Hon Sir Nicholas Lyell QC MP

Lord Advocate's Department –
Lord-Advocate – Rt Hon Lord Fraser of Carmyllie QC
Solicitor-General for Scotland – Alan Rodger Esq QC*

Lord Chancellor – Rt Hon Lord Mackay of Clashfern

Northern Ireland Office –
Secretary of State for Northern Ireland – Rt Hon Peter Brooke MP
Minister of State – Rt Hon John Cope MP
Parliamentary Under-Secretaries of State – Richard Needham Esq MP, Peter Bottomley Esq MP, Dr Brian Mawhinney MP, Lord Skelmersdale

Paymaster General – Earl of Caithness

Privy Council Office –
Lord President of the Council and Leader of the House of Commons – Rt Hon Sir Geoffrey Howe QC MP
Lord Privy Seal and Leader of the House of Lords – Rt Hon Lord Belstead DL
Minister of State – Rt Hon Richard Luce MP

Scottish Office –
Secretary of State for Scotland – Rt Hon Malcolm Rifkind QC MP
Ministers of State – Ian Lang Esq MP, Lord Sanderson of Bowden
Parliamentary Under-Secretaries of State –
Minister for Home Affairs and the Environment – Lord James Douglas-Hamilton MP
Minister for Health – Michael Forsyth Esq MP

Social Security –
Secretary of State for Social Security – Rt Hon Antony Newton OBE MP
Minister of State for Social Security and the Disabled – Rt Hon Nicholas Scott MBE MP
Parliamentary Under-Secretaries of State – Lord Henley, Mrs Gillian Shephard MP

Trade and Industry –
Secretary of State for Trade and Industry and President of the Board of Trade – Peter Lilley MP

Government departments and related bodies

DEPARTMENT	*Responsibilities*	*England*	*Wales*	*N.I.*	*Scot.*	*SUBSIDIARY DEPARTMENTS, etc.*	*England*	*Wales*	*N.I.*	*Scot.*	*'QUANGOS' and other related bodies*
AGRICULTURE, FISHERIES AND FOOD, MINISTRY OF	Policy for farming, horticulture and fishing	•	•	–	–	Agricultural Development and Advisory Service (ADAS)	•	•	–	–	Agricultural and Food Research Council
	Administration of EC agricultural policies	•	•	–	–						
	Animal health and welfare	•	•	–	•						
	Food and drink processing and distribution	•	•	–	–						
ARTS AND LIBRARIES, OFFICE OF	Promotion of the Arts	•	•	–	•						Arts Council (and its subsidiaries the Scottish and Welsh Arts Councils), British Film Institute, Crafts Council
	Library and information services	•	(•)	(•)	–						British Library
	Museums	•	–	–	–						National Heritage Memorial Fund
DEFENCE, MINISTRY OF	Defence policy; administration of the armed forces and related services	•	•	•	•	Meteorological Office	•	•	•	•	Ordnance Survey
EDUCATION AND SCIENCE, DEPARTMENT OF	Education policy	•	–	–	–	HM Inspectorate of Schools	•	–	–	–	
	Universities' policy	•	•	–	•						University Funding Council
	Scientific research	•	•	•	•						Advisory Board for the Research Councils (and the five councils: Agricultural and Food, Economic and Social, Medical, Natural Environment, Science and Engineering)
EMPLOYMENT, DEPARTMENT OF	Policy on all aspects of employment: labour utilization, unemployment, health and safety at work, industrial relations, equal opportunities	•	•	–	•						Advisory Conciliation and Arbitration Service (ACAS), Health and Safety Commission, Training Commission
	Tourism	•	•	–	•						British Tourist Authority, English Tourist Board, Scottish Tourist Board, Welsh Tourist Board
ENERGY, DEPARTMENT OF	Policy for energy supply and use	•	•	•	•						British Coal, Electricity Council, Central Electricity Generating Board, Office of Gas Supply, United Kingdom Atomic Energy Authority
ENVIRONMENT, DEPARTMENT OF THE	Planning, development, new towns, housing, construction	•	–	–	–						Ordnance Survey, Housing Corporation

Government departments and related bodies ***continued***

DEPARTMENT	*Responsibilities*	*England*	*Wales*	*N.I.*	*Scot.*	*SUBSIDIARY DEPARTMENTS, etc.*	*England*	*Wales*	*N.I.*	*Scot.*	*'QUANGOS' and other related bodies*
	Conservation, countryside, water, environmental protection	•	–	–	–	HM Inspectorate of Pollution	•				Countryside Commission, Royal Commission on Environmental Pollution, Natural Environment Research Council, Nature Conservancy
	Local government	•	–	–	–						Audit Commission, Commission for Local Administration in England
	Sport and recreation	•	–	–	–						Sports Council
	Ancient monuments, historic buildings, royal palaces and parks	•	–	–	–						English Heritage
	Government property and estates	•	•	–	•						
FOREIGN AND COMMONWEALTH OFFICE	Britain's relations with other countries	•	•	•	•	Overseas Development Administration	•	•	•	•	BBC (World Service), British Council
HEALTH, DEPARTMENT OF	The National Health Service, social and health services provided by local authorities, public hygiene	•	–	–	–	Office of Population Censuses and Surveys					Health Education Authority, Medical Research Council, Public Health Laboratory Service
HOME OFFICE	Justice and law enforcement	•	•	–	–	Police Department	•	•	–	–	Criminal Injuries Compensation Board, Parole Board, Police Complaints Authority, Probation Service
						Prisons Department	•	•	–	–	
	Fire and civil defence services	•	•	–	–						
	Licensing laws	•	•	–	–						
	Gaming and lotteries	•	•	–	•						Gaming Board
	Electoral regulations	•	•	–	–						Boundary Commissions for England and Wales
	Broadcasting	•	•	•	•						BBC, Broadcasting Standards Council, Cable Authority, Independent Broadcasting Authority
	Immigration, passports, race relations	•	•	•	•						Commission for Racial Equality
	Sex discrimination	•	•	•	•						Equal Opportunities Commission
											Office of the Data Protection Registrar, Charity Commission

Government departments and related bodies ***continued***

DEPARTMENT	*Responsibilities*	*England*	*Wales*	*N.I.*	*Scot.*	*SUBSIDIARY DEPARTMENTS, etc.*	*England*	*Wales*	*N.I.*	*Scot.*	*'QUANGOS' and other related bodies*
LANCASTER, DUCHY OF	There are only ceremonial duties, but the Chancellor of the Duchy of Lancaster has a seat in the cabinet.										
LAW OFFICERS' DEPARTMENT	Legal advice to the Government and representation of the Crown in court										
	Attorney General	•	•	•	–	Director of Public Prosecutions	•	•	–	–	
						Director of Public Prosecution for N.I.land	–	–	•	–	
						Serious Fraud Office	•	•	•	–	
	Solicitor General	•	•	–	–						
LORD CHANCELLOR'S DEPARTMENT	Administration of Courts of Appeal, High Courts, Crown Courts, County Courts	•	•	•	–	Legal Aid and Advice Scheme					
	Appointment of judges and magistrates										
	Promotion of legal reforms										Law Commission
						HM Land Registry	•	•	–	–	
						Public Record Office	•	•	–	–	
PRIVY COUNCIL OFFICE	Duties are mainly formalities, but the Lord President of the Council has a seat in the Cabinet and is also Leader of the House of Commons										
SOCIAL SECURITY, DEPARTMENT OF	Administration of social security	•	•	–	•		•	•	–	–	
TRADE AND INDUSTRY, DEPARTMENT OF	Industrial and commercial policy	•	•	•	•	Export Credits Guarantee Department	•	•	•	•	British Standards Institution, British Technology Group, Design Council, Monopolies and Mergers Commission, Office of Fair Trading
						Patent Office	•	•	•	•	
	Communications	•	•	•	•						OFTEL (Office of Telecommunications), Post Office
	Radio regulation	•	•	–	•						
	Consumer protection	•	•	•	•						National Consumer Council, Securities and Investments Board

Government departments and related bodies ***continued***

DEPARTMENT	*Responsibilities*	*England*	*Wales*	*N.I.*	*Scot.*	*SUBSIDIARY DEPARTMENTS, etc.*	*England*	*Wales*	*N.I.*	*Scot.*	*'QUANGOS' and other related bodies*
TRANSPORT, DEPARTMENT OF	Transport policy	•	•	•	•	HM Coastguard Service	•	•	•	•	British Rail, Civil Aviation Authority, London Regional Transport, Trinity House and the Commissioners of Northern Lighthouses
HM TREASURY	The Prime Minister is First Lord of the Treasury but does not manage any aspects of its day-to-day work. The Chancellor of the Exchequer is therefore directly in charge of the Treasury and is responsible for Britain's economic strategy. There are four other ministers:					Crown Estate Office, Central Statistical Office					National Economic Development Council
	Chief Secretary: control of public expenditure	•	•	•	•						
	Financial Secretary					Board of Inland Revenue	•	•	•	•	
	Economic Secretary: monetary policy and international financial affairs	•	•	•	•	Department of National Savings	•	•	•	•	
	Paymaster General					HM Customs & Excise	•	•	•	•	
						Royal Mint	•	•	•	•	
						HM Stationery Office	•	•	•	•	
						Central Office of Information	•	•	•	•	
											National Audit Office (*not* part of the Treasury; reports direct to Parliament's Public Accounts Cttee)
WELSH OFFICE	Agriculture and fisheries	–	•	–	–						
	Education (except teachers' pay and conditions; universities)	–	•	–	–	HM Inspectorate of Schools (Wales)	–	•	–	–	
	Environment: local government, planning, housing, water and sewerage, conservation and land use, ancient monuments and historic buildings, sport	–	•	–	–						Commission for Local Administration in Wales
	European Regional Development Fund and other EC matters	–	•	–	–						
	Health and personal social services	–	•	–	–						
	Roads	–	•	–	–						
	Tourism	–	•	–	–						Wales Tourist Board
	Training	–	•	–	–						
	Welsh language and culture	–	•	–	–						National Library of Wales

UK FACTFILE : POLITICAL PARTIES 28

Table 8 of POLITICAL PARTIES (pp. 24-27)

Government departments and related bodies *continued*

DEPARTMENT	*Responsibilities*	*England*	*Wales*	*N.I.*	*Scot.*	*SUBSIDIARY DEPARTMENTS, etc.*	*England*	*Wales*	*N.I.*	*Scot.*	*'QUANGOS' and other related bodies*
TRANSPORT, DEPARTMENT OF	Transport policy	•	•	•	•	HM Coastguard Service	•	•	•	•	British Rail, Civil Aviation Authority, London Regional Transport, Trinity House and the Commissioners of Northern Lighthouses
HM TREASURY	The Prime Minister is First Lord of the Treasury but does not manage any aspects of its day-to-day work. The Chancellor of the Exchequer is therefore directly in charge of the Treasury and is responsible for Britain's economic strategy. There are four other ministers:					Crown Estate Office, Central Statistical Office					National Economic Development Council
	Chief Secretary: control of public expenditure	•	•	•	•						
	Financial Secretary					Board of Inland Revenue	•	•	•	•	
	Economic Secretary: monetary policy and international financial affairs	•	•	•	•	Department of National Savings	•	•	•	•	
	Paymaster General					HM Customs & Excise	•	•	•	•	
						Royal Mint	•	•	•	•	
						HM Stationery Office	•	•	•	•	
						Central Office of Information	•	•	•	•	
											National Audit Office (*not* part of the Treasury; reports direct to Parliament's Public Accounts Cttee)
WELSH OFFICE	Agriculture and fisheries	–	•	–	–						
	Education (except teachers' pay and conditions; universities)	–	•	–	–	HM Inspectorate of Schools (Wales)	–	•	–	–	
	Environment: local government, planning, housing, water and sewerage, conservation and land use, ancient monuments and historic buildings, sport	–	•	–	–						Commission for Local Administration in Wales
	European Regional Development Fund and other EC matters	–	•	–	–						
	Health and personal social services	–	•	–	–						
	Roads	–	•	–	–						
	Tourism	–	•	–	–						Wales Tourist Board
	Training	–	•	–	–						
	Welsh language and culture	–	•	–	–						National Library of Wales

Ministers of State –
Minister for Trade – Rt Hon Lord Trefgarne
Minister for Industry and Enterprise – Hon Douglas Hogg MP
Parliamentary Under-Secretaries of State –
Parliamentary Under-Secretary of State for Industry and Consumer Affairs – Eric Forth Esq MP
Parliamentary Under-Secretary of State for Corporate Affairs – John Redwood Esq MP

Transport –
Secretary of State for Transport – Rt Hon Cecil Parkinson MP
Minister of State –
Minister for Public Transport – Michael Portillo Esq MP
Parliamentary Under-Secretaries of State –
Minister for Roads and Traffic – Robert Atkins Esq MP
Minister for Aviation and Shipping – Patrick McLoughlin Esq MP

Treasury –
Prime Minister, First Lord of the Treasury and Minister for the Civil Service – Rt Hon Margaret Thatcher FRS MP
Chancellor of the Exchequer – Rt Hon John Major MP
Chief Secretary – Rt Hon Norman Lamont MP
Paymaster General – Earl of Caithness
Economic Secretary – Richard Ryder Esq OBE MP
Parliamentary Secretary to the Treasury – Rt Hon Tim Renton Esq MP
Lords Commissioners – David Lightbown Esq MP, Kenneth Carlisle Esq MP, Stephen Dorrell Esq MP, John M Taylor Esq MP, Hon Tom Sackville MP
Assistant Whips – Michael Fallon Esq MP, Sydney Chapman Esq MP, Greg Knight Esq MP, Irvine Patrick Esq OBE MP, Nicholas Baker Esq MP

Welsh Office –
Secretary of State for Wales – Rt Hon Peter Walker MBE MP
Minister of State – Wyn Roberts Esq MP
Parliamentary Under-Secretary of State – Ian Grist Esq MP

Her Majesty's Household –
Lord Chamberlain – Rt Hon The Earl of Airlie GCVO
Lord Steward – Viscount Ridley
Master of the Horse – Rt Hon The Earl of Westmorland KCVO
Treasurer – Tristan Garel-Jones Esq MP
Comptroller – Alastair Goodlad Esq MP
Vice-Chamberlain – Tony Durant Esq MP
Captain of the Honourable Corps of Gentlemen-at-Arms – Rt Hon Lord Denham
Captain of The Queen's Bodyguard of the Yeomen of the Guard – Viscount Davidson
Lords in Waiting – Viscount Long, Viscount Ullswater, Lord Reay, Earl of Strathmore and Kinghorne
Baroness in Waiting – Baroness Blatch

Second Church Estates Commissioner, Representing Church Commissioners – Rt Hon Michael Alison MP

*Alan Rodger is not a Member of the House of Commons.

QUANGOS

Quasi-autonomous non-governmental organizations

There are approximately 1,600 quangos. Some are purely advisory while others execute government policy and distribute public funds (e.g. the University Grants Committee). Quangos are organizations through which government ministers can distance themselves while still retaining ultimate control over some social, cultural or economic services.

They operate within broad policy guidelines set by ministers but are not staffed by civil servants and are not subject to day-to-day ministerial control.

There are three types of quango: executive bodies (for instance the Arts Council of Great Britain), advisory bodies (such as the Boundary Commissions) and tribunal bodies (e.g. Social Security Tribunals).

Among the most important quangos are:

ADVERTISING STANDARDS AUTHORITY

Established in 1962, the Advertising Standards Authority aims to maintain the quality of advertisements so that they are 'legal, decent, honest and truthful'. The Authority's main activities are monitoring advertisements for their compliance with the British Code of Advertising. It has no binding legal powers, but can apply to the Director General of Fair Trading to seek court injunctions against 'damaging and misleading advertisements'.

Brook House, 2–16 Torrington Place, London, WC1E 7HN

(ACAS) ADVISORY, CONCILIATION AND ARBITRATION SERVICE

(q.v. Trade Unions)

ARTS COUNCIL OF GREAT BRITAIN

Chairman **Sir Peter Palumbo**

The Arts Council is Britain's principal channel for public financial support of the arts and was established by Royal Charter in 1946.

The Council is responsible for funding major organizations within England as well as the regional arts associations and the Scottish and Welsh Arts Councils. The Council is funded by a government grant which for the year 1989–90 totalled £155 million.

105 Piccadilly, London, W1V 0AU

BOUNDARY COMMISSIONS

The Boundary Commissions were constituted under the 1986 Parliamentary Constituencies Act. In the United Kingdom there are four Commissions which are required to keep the particular constituencies they are responsible for under review. The three Boundary

Commissions within Great Britain are also expected to review the European Parliamentary constituencies.

England: St Catherine's House, 10 Kingsway, London, WC2B 6JP
Wales: see England
Scotland: St Andrew's House, Edinburgh, EH1 3DE

BRITISH COUNCIL

Chairman **Sir David Orr** MC
The British Council is an independent, non-political organization established in 1934 and incorporated by Royal Charter in 1940. The aim of the British Council is to promote British culture in the fields of language, the arts, the sciences and technology. The Council is represented in more than 80 countries and for the financial year 1989–90 had a turnover of £312 million including grants.

10 Spring Gardens, London, SW1A 2BN

BRITISH FILM INSTITUTE

Director **Wilf Stevenson**
The British Film Institute was founded in 1933 to 'encourage the use and development of cinema as a means of entertainment and instruction'. Partly funded by government, the Institute includes the National Film Archive (founded in 1935), the National Film Theatre (founded in 1951) and a library, a stills collection and educational information.

21 Stephen Street, London W1P 1PL

BRITISH STANDARDS INSTITUTE

Director General **Dr I. Dunstan**
The British Standards Institute is most commonly known for its certification trade marks (the 'Kite Mark' and the 'Safety Mark'). The Institute prepares standards relating to nearly every sector of industry and trade including consumer goods. The British Standards are usually issued for voluntary adoption although for some products the standards are required by legislation. There are over 20,000 subscribing members of the British Standards Institute.

2 Park Street, London, W1A 2BS

BRITISH TECHNOLOGY GROUP

Chairman **C. Barker**
The British Technology Group is a self-financing group appointed by the government to license new scientific and engineering products to industry. It aims to promote the commercial use of new developments in technology research from United Kingdom institutions: universities, polytechnics and research councils. The British Technology Group can also provide financial backing where necessary.

101 Newington Causeway, London, SE1 6BU

CENTRAL OFFICE OF INFORMATION

Director General **G.M. Devereau**
The Central Office of Information provides consultancy, design and production facilities for all publicity activities within all fields while specializing in government organizations. In the United Kingdom it conducts government display advertising, television, film production, exhibitions, marketing, publications, radio, photography and market research. The costs of the Office are recovered from its customers. It is estimated that the total costs of the Central Office of Information for the financial year 1989–90 will be £144 million.

Hercules Road, London, SE1 7DU

CHARITY COMMISSION

Chief Commissioner **R.I.L. Guthrie**
The Charity Commissioners are appointed under the Charities Act of 1960. The principal roles of the Charity Commission are: to work for charities in England and Wales as an advisory and information body and to investigate alleged abuses of charitable status. The Commission also gives advice on the administrative machinery of charities and maintains a full register of such organizations.

St Albans House, 57–60 Haymarket, London, SW1Y 4QX

CHURCH COMMISSIONERS

Chief Commissioner **Sir D. Lovelock**
The Church Commissioners were established on 1 April 1948. The main task of the Commissioners is to improve stipends and housing for Church of England clergy and their widows and to provide adequate housing and pensions for those in retirement. In 1988 the income of the Church Commissioners was £183.5 million.

1 Millbank, London, SW1P 3JZ

CIVIC TRUST

Director **M.C. Bradshaw**
The Civic Trust was founded in 1957 and is supported by voluntary contributions. Its aim is to stimulate interest in, and action for, the improvement of the environment. It acts as the spokesman on issues of national environmental control. The Trust is often consulted by the government and is the founder member of the United Kingdom 2,000 initiative. Its total membership is 249,000.

17 Carlton House Terrace, London, SW1Y 5AW

COMMISSION FOR RACIAL EQUALITY

Chairman **M. Day** OBE
The Commission for Racial Equality was established on 13 July 1977. The Commission aims to work towards the elimination of discrimination and to promote equality of opportunity and good relations between different racial groups, in compliance with the Race Relations Act of 1976 which provided for its formation.

Elliot House, 10–12 Allington Street, London, SW1E 5EH

COMMONWEALTH INSTITUTE

Director General **J.F. Porter**
The Commonwealth Institute is the centre for information on the Commonwealth: a voluntary association of 50 independent sovereign states which were all at some point formerly associated with Britain. The Institute is funded by the British government and contributions from other Commonwealth countries. The Institute, based in London, houses permanent exhibitions from all the Commonwealth nations as well as educational resources.

Kensington High Street, London, W8 6NQ

CONFEDERATION OF BRITISH INDUSTRY

President **Sir T. Holdsworth**
The Confederation was founded in 1965 and is a non-party political body financed by industry and commerce. It exists so that governments can understand the needs and problems of industry. It is recognized as the spokesman on the needs of business and represents, both directly and indirectly, some 250,000 companies.

Centre Point, 103 New Oxford Street, London, WC1A 1DU

COUNTRYSIDE COMMISSION

The Countryside Commission was founded in 1968 to promote the conservation and enhancement of the landscapes of England and Wales and to provide access to open-air recreation areas. Since 1982 the Commission has been funded by annual grants from the Department of the Environment which is also responsible for appointing members of the Commission.

John Dower House, Crescent Place, Cheltenham, Gloucestershire, GL50 3RA

CROWN ESTATE COMMISSIONERS

First Commissioner **The Earl of Mansfield**

The Crown Estate Commissioners are responsible for collecting revenues from the Crown Estates that were surrendered by King George III in 1760. In the year ending 31 March 1989 the gross income from the Crown Estates totalled £81.5 million; the sum of £41 million was paid as surplus to the Exchequer. Land revenues in Ireland were transferred to the funds in 1923. In Eire, the Republic of Ireland government collects the revenues itself while revenues in Scotland were transferred to the Commissioners in 1833.

13–16 Carlton House Terrace, London, SW1Y 5AH

DATA PROTECTION REGISTRAR

Registrar **E.J. Howe**

With the creation of the Data Protection Act in 1984 the office of Registrar was formed. It is the Registrar's job to maintain the Data Users and Computer Bureau and enable the public to examine the Register. The Registrar also aims to promote the use of codes of practice by the trade associations. The Registrar must report annually to parliament on his functions under the Act.

Springfield House, Water Lane, Wilmslow, Cheshire, SK9 5AX

DESIGN COUNCIL

Chairman **Sir S. Hornby**

The main aim of the Design Council is to improve the design of British products. It does this by advising companies on modern practice in engineering and industrial designs. The annual Design Awards are aimed to promote these functions. There is a Design Centre in London and Council offices all around the country.

28 Haymarket, London, SW1Y 4SV

ENGLISH HERITAGE

Chairman **Lord Montague**

Previously part of the Department of the Environment, English Heritage was founded in 1984. Its main aim is to preserve the ancient monuments and buildings within England. It also endeavours to preserve the character of conservation areas and to promote general public awareness and enjoyment of historic sites. It employs 2,000 people throughout England.

Fortress House, 23 Savile Row, London, W1X 1AB

EQUAL OPPORTUNITIES COMMISSION

Chairman **Mrs J. Foster**

The Equal Opportunities Commission was set up by Parliament as a result of the Sex Discrimination Act of 1975. The Commission works towards the elimination of discrimination by sex or marital status and to promote equality of opportunity between men and women in all spheres of life.

Overseas House, Quay Street, Manchester, M3 3HN

FORESTRY COMMISSION

Chairman **J.R. Johnstone CBE**

The Forestry Commission has the legal status of, and functions as, a government department. It is responsible for the formation and implementation of forestry policy, forestry research and the administration of grants to private woodlands. One of its main purposes is to achieve a balance between the needs of industry and conservation.

231 Corstorphine Road, Edinburgh, EH12 7AT

GENERAL DENTAL COUNCIL

President **Prof D. Mason CBE FDSRCS**

The Council is a statutory body founded by the Dental Act of 1984. The role of the Council is to promote dental education and awareness and also to set the standards for professional conduct. The Council also prepares and maintains a complete Dental Register. It has a disciplinary function and is able to 'strike-off' dentists for serious misconduct.

37 Wimpole Street, London, W1M 8DQ

GENERAL MEDICAL COUNCIL

President **Sir Peter Kilpatrick**

Like the General Dental Council, the General Medical Council is a statutory body which was founded by the Medical Act of 1983. The aim of the Medical Council is to promote general medical education and to set and maintain standards for professional conduct. The Council also prepares and maintains a full register of United Kingdom and European Community doctors. The Council has authority to try cases of professional misconduct and in 1988 brought about 71 convictions.

44 Hallam Street, London, W1N 6AE

HEALTH EDUCATION AUTHORITY

Chairman **Sir Donald Maitland**

The main aim of the Health Education Authority is the promotion of health education. The Authority has major executive responsibilities and an appropriate budget. It plans and executes national awareness programmes such as the Aids Awareness Campaign. It has a national centre for information based in London which publishes and distributes material.

Hamilton House, Mabledon Place, London, WC1H 9OX

HEALTH AND SAFETY COMMISSION

(q.v. Law Section UK Factfile)

HER MAJESTY'S COASTGUARDS

Chief Coastguard **Commander D.T. Ancona**

Her Majesty's Coastguard was established in 1822 as a predominantly anti-smuggling organization. Initially the Coastguards were the responsibility of the Board of Trade. In 1972 the Coastguards were reorganized into six major regions. Today the main role of the Coastguards is as lifesavers and they are responsible for conducting all maritime search and rescue operations around the British coastline and up to 1,000 miles into the Atlantic. In the mid-1980s the Coastguards became the responsibility of the Department of Transport.

Sunley House, 90–93 High Holborn, London, WC1V 6LP

HER MAJESTY'S LAND REGISTRY

First introduced in 1862, the Land Registry now operates under the Land Registration Acts of 1925 and 1986. The object of Her Majesty's Land Registry is to create and maintain a register of landowners whose title is guaranteed by the state and to simplify the transfer mortgage and other dealings with real property. Registration of title throughout England and Wales is not yet universal.

Lincoln's Inn Fields, London, WC2A 3PH

HER MAJESTY'S STATIONERY OFFICE

Chief Executive **P.I. Freeman**
HMSO was established in 1786 and is the British government's agency for printing, binding and office supplies. The Office is the government's publisher and it must compete for its business with other commercial suppliers. *Hansard* and Bills and Acts of Parliament account for approximately 20% of the Office's output.

Head Office, St Crispin's, Duke Street, Norwich, NR3 1PD
London branch, 51 Nine Elms Lane, London, SW8 5DR

THE METEOROLOGICAL OFFICE

Director General **Dr J.T. Houghton CBE DPhil FRS**
The Meteorological Office is a state-run and funded service. It forms part of the Ministry of Defence and its costs are borne by the Ministry. The expenditure of the Office totals £69 million per annum with approximately £25 million recovered from outside bodies for special services rendered and sales of meteorological equipment.

London Road, Bracknell, Berkshire

THE MONOPOLIES AND MERGERS COMMISSION

Chairman **M.S. Lipworth**
The Monopolies and Mergers Commission was established in 1948 but did not become known as the Monopolies and Mergers Commission until 1973. The role of the Commission is to investigate and report on:
a) the existence or possible existence of monopolies not registered under the Restrictive Trade Practices Act of 1976 relating to the supply of goods or services in the United Kingdom or the supply of goods for export;
b) the transfer of a newspaper or a newspaper's assets;
c) the creation or possible creation of a merger qualifying for investigation within the meaning of the Fair Trading Act of 1973.

The Competition Act of 1980 also provides reference to the Commission on possible abuse of monopolies in the public sector. Recent work embarked on by the Commission includes the investigation into the Allied Lyons takeover bid for the Distiller Group.

New Court, Carey Street, London, WC2A 2JT

NATIONAL AUDIT OFFICE

Controller and Auditor General **J.B. Bourn CBE**
The National Audit Office came into existence under the National Audit Act of 1983. The Office is totally independent both financially and operationally from the government, though it maintains a close relationship with Parliament.

The Office provides independent advice, information and assurance to Parliament about all aspects of the government's financial operations. It does this by examining the accounts of government organizations and regularly reporting and publishing these results to Parliament and the public sector.

157–197 Buckingham Palace Road, London, SW1W 9SP

NATIONAL CONSUMER COUNCIL

Chairman **Baroness Oppenheim-Barnes PC**
The National Consumer Council, which was established in 1975, is funded by the Department of Trade and Industry. The Council's role is to safeguard and further the interests of consumers. It also acts as spokesman to the public utilities, business, industry, the professions and government.

20 Grosvenor Gardens, London, SW1W 0DH

NATIONAL ECONOMIC DEVELOPMENT COUNCIL

Chairman **The Chancellor of the Exchequer, Rt Hon. John Major MP**
The National Economic Development Council unites government, management and trade unions to tackle issues vital to employment and economic growth by identifying problems to economic development and promoting change.

NEDO, Millbank Tower, Millbank, London, SW1P 4QX

NATURE CONSERVANCY COUNCIL

Chairman **Lord Cranbrook** (Chairman designate of English Conservancy Council)
The Nature Conservancy Council is in charge of the establishment, maintenance and management of the National Nature Reserves and is responsible for advising the government on nature conservation policies. The Environmental Protection Bill of 15 January 1990 proposes to restructure the Council and divide it into three separate bodies for England, Scotland and Wales. If passed this will take effect from April 1990.

NUCLEAR INDUSTRY RADIOACTIVE WASTE EXECUTIVE (UK NIREX LTD)

Managing Director **Mr P.T. McInerney**
Nirex is the government body responsible for the disposal of most low- and intermediate-level radioactive waste. It disposes of material for the United Kingdom nuclear industry and of radioactive waste from hospitals, industry, research and the Ministry of Defence. The Executive was set up by the government in 1982 and was reconstituted as UK Nirex Ltd in 1985. Shares in Nirex are held by British Nuclear Fuels Ltd, Nuclear Electrics (formerly CEGB), Scottish Nuclear Ltd and the United Kingdom Atomic Energy Authority.

Curie Avenue, Harwell, Didcot, Oxfordshire, OX11 0RA

OFFICE OF FAIR TRADING

Director General **Sir Gordon Borrie QC**
The Office of Fair Trading monitors commercial activities within the UK. It aims to protect consumers within five main sectors: consumer affairs, consumer credit, monopolies and mergers, restrictive trade practices and anti-competitive practices.

The Office administers the Fair Trading Act of 1973, the Consumer Credit Act of 1974, the Restrictive Trade Practices Act of 1976, the Estate Agents Act of 1979, the Competition Act of 1980 and Misleading Advertisement Regulations established in 1988.

Field House, Bream's Buildings, London, EC4A 1PR

OFFICE OF POPULATION CENSUSES AND SURVEYS

Director General **Mrs G.T. Banks**

The Office of Population Censuses and Surveys, created in 1970, holds records and controls registration of marriages, births and deaths within England and Wales. Central indexes are compiled annually and are generally available. Since 1841 the Registrar has also been responsible for population censuses. The Office also makes available a wide range of statistics including: population, fertility, births, marriages, deaths and their causes, and sickness, etc.

St Catherine's House, 10 Kingsway, London, WC2B 6JD

ORDNANCE SURVEY

Director General **P. McMaster**

The Ordnance Survey is the national mapping organization for Britain. It produces some 220,000 large-scale maps per annum on three scales: 1:1,250 for urban areas, 1:2,500 for rural areas and 1:10,000 for mountains and moorlands. Ordnance Survey also produce a range of small-scale maps for general use.

Romsey Road, Maybush, Southampton, SO9 4DH

PATENT OFFICE

(including the Industrial Property and Copyright Department)

Controller General **P.J. Cooper**

The main function of the Patent Office is the administration of the Copyright, Designs and Patents Act 1988. It also deals with questions arising from the Copyrights Acts. The Office provides an information service concerning patent specifications. The number of patents issued by the Office in 1988 totalled 11,456.

D T I, State House, 67–71 High Holborn, London, WC1R 4TP

PRESS COUNCIL

Chairman **L. Blom-Cooper QC**

The Press Council was established in its present form of 36 members, half of which are members of the press, the others being laymen, in 1978. Its aims are to preserve the character and freedom of the British press, to deal with complaints in an appropriate manner and to review developments and report on them with a view to the best interests of the public.

1 Salisbury Square, London, EC4Y 8AE

PUBLIC RECORD OFFICE

Since the Public Records Act of 1958, the Public Record Office has come under the direction of the Lord Chancellor. The role of the Office is to co-ordinate and supervise a collection of the records of government departments and the English law courts for permanent preservation. Under the Public Records Act of 1967, these records are usually available for public scrutiny after 30 years.

Chancery Lane, London, WC2

THE RESEARCH COUNCILS

AGRICULTURAL AND FOOD RESEARCH COUNCIL

Chairman **Earl of Selborne KBE**

The Agricultural and Food Research Council is an independent body established by Royal Charter. Funding for the Council comes from the Department of Education and Science. The Council is responsible for commissioning research carried out at its institutes and United Kingdom university departments, the latter being funded from a research grants scheme.

Central Office, Wiltshire Court, Farnsby Street, Swindon, SN1 5AT

ECONOMIC AND SOCIAL RESEARCH COUNCIL

Chairman **Prof. H. Newby**

The Economic and Social Research Council was set up by Royal Charter in 1965 to promote research in the field of social sciences. The Council carries out this role by awarding grants and bursaries, initiating research, funding research centres and by awarding postgraduate grant awards. In addition the Council works in an advisory and information capacity.

Cherry Orchard East, Kembry Park, Swindon, SN2 6VQ

MEDICAL RESEARCH COUNCIL

Chairman **Earl Jellicoe KBE DSO MC PC**

The Medical Research Council is the government's main body for the promotion of medical and related research. The Council has its own research staff and also provides grants for institutions and individuals. These facilities complement the resources at universities and hospitals.

20 Park Crescent, London, W1N 4AL

SCIENCE AND ENGINEERING RESEARCH COUNCIL

Chairman **Prof E.W.J. Mitchell**

The Science and Engineering Research Council is funded by the Department of Education and Science. Its aim is to 'develop the natural and social sciences, including engineering, to maintain a fundamental capacity of research and scholarship and support for relevant postgraduate education'.

Polaris House, North Star Avenue, Swindon, SN2 1ET

ROYAL GREENWICH OBSERVATORY

Director **Prof A. Bokenberg FRS**

The Royal Greenwich Observatory was founded by Charles II in 1675. After World War II, due to excessive smog and pollution, the Observatory moved to Herstmonceux in East Sussex. Traditional work in positional astronomy still remains one of its key functions, although it now makes use of European satellite information. The Observatory also prepares scientific data which is published through a subsidiary arm. In 1990 the Observatory will again be moving, its new base being in Cambridge.

Herstmonceux, East Sussex, BN27 1RP

ROYAL MINT

Deputy Master and Comptroller **A.D. Garret**

The Royal Mint is the centre for the printing and pressing of British currency. Ultimate control for the Mint lies with the Chancellor of the Exchequer.

Llantrisant, North Pontyclun, Mid Glamorgan, CF7 8YT

SCOTTISH ARTS COUNCIL

Chairman **Sir Alan Peacock**

The Scottish Arts Council is a subsidiary of the Arts Council of Great Britain (qv) and as such receives its financing from the main parent body while having a large degree of autonomy.

19 Charlotte Square, Edinburgh, EH2 4DF

SCOTTISH CIVIC TRUST

Director **Mrs C. Douglas**
The Scottish Civic Trust is an associate trust to the English parent body (q.v.). Its main aims are educational and informational, specializing in environmental and conservational areas.

24 George Square, Glasgow, G2 1EF

THE TRAINING AGENCY

(Formerly: Manpower Services Commission)

Director General **R. Dawe CBE OBE**
The Training Agency was established in 1988 when the Manpower Services Commission was dissolved. The Training Agency is now the national training authority of the UK. Funded by its parent body, the Department of Employment, the Agency aims to create a more skilled workforce, improve job education, and raise the standards and quality of training within Britain.

Moorfoot, Sheffield, S1 4PQ

CORPORATION OF TRINITY HOUSE

Deputy Master **Capt. P.M. Edge**
Master **H.R.H. the Duke of Edinburgh**
The Corporation of Trinity House was established by Henry VIII in 1614 as the first general lighthouse and pilotage authority. The Corporation is the body concerned with lighthouses and navigational information throughout England, Wales and the Channel Islands. It is also responsible for wrecks dangerous to navigation. In October 1988 responsibility for pilotage was handed over to the harbour authorities.

Trinity House, Tower Hill, London, EC3N 4DH

RELIGION

CHRISTIAN CHURCHES

Church of England

The Church in England was established by St Augustine in AD 597. The Church of England was founded by Henry VIII in the 16th Century as a product of the Reformation. Its form of worship is embodied in the Book of Common Prayer first compiled in 1549 and followed in 1612 by the James I Bible.

The Church of England, established by the State, incorporates mutual obligations. The Sovereign must always be a member of the Church, and promise to uphold it. The archbishops, bishops and deans are appointed by the Sovereign on the advice of the Prime Minister. Recently this power has been challenged by the Bishop of Durham, who wished to break the link between State and Church by ending government appointments.

All clergy must take an oath of allegiance to the Crown. The two Archbishops of Canterbury and York, the Bishops of London, Durham and Winchester and 21 other bishops sit in the House of Lords. Clergy of the Church are not allowed to sit in the House of Commons.

The Church has two provinces: Canterbury comprising 30 diocese and York, with 14 diocese. These diocese are divided into 13,250 parishes.

In 1987 some 230,000 people were baptised into the Church (29% of all live births). In the same year there were 65,850 confirmations. Attendance at services for a normal Sunday is around 1.2 million.

The central governing body, the General Synod, has both spiritual authority and legislative powers. Bishops, clergy and lay members are all involved with decisions. The General Synod deals with such matters as educaion, inter-church relations, social questions, church buildings and works. More recently the question of women's ordination has arisen. At present there are 1000 female deacons though no priests, bishops or higher clergy. However the issue has been much debated and will be raised again in 1992.

Head of the Church of England is the *Archbishop of Canterbury* Most Rev. and Rt Hon. Robert Runcie.

Church of Scotland

The Church of Scotland has a Presbyterian constitution. Its status as a national church derives from the Scottish Reformation, consolidated in the Treaty of Union in 1707 and the Church of Scotland Act 1921; this confirmed its complete freedom in spiritual matters.

It is governed by the Kirk Session, consisting of the ministers and the elected elders of the church. Above the Kirk Session is the Court of Presbytery, the Court of Synods and ultimately the General Assembly. This is presided over by a moderator chosen annually by the Assembly.

The Sovereign is represented at the General Assembly by the Lord High Commissioner, who is also appointed by the Crown.

The country, for church purposes, is divided into 12 Synods and 46 Presbyteries. There are approximately 1400 ministers of both sexes presiding over 1716 churches. The adult communicant membership of the Church of Scotland is nearly 823,000.

Roman Catholic Church

The Roman Catholic Church has a long history in the UK and yet it was not until 1850 in England and Wales and 1875 in Scotland that the hierarchies were restored.

There are seven Roman Catholic provinces in Britain, each under an archbishop. There are 30 episcopal diocese, 22 in England and Wales and eight in Scotland with 3000 parishes. In Northern Ireland there six diocese.

Only men are accepted into the priesthood.

The present Pope is His Holiness Pope John Paul II, who paid a visit to Britain in 1982, the first visit by a reigning pontiff.

The Roman Catholic Church in England and Wales is governed by two bodies: the Bishops' Conference, headed by the president, Cardinal Basil Hume and the vice-president, Archbishop Worlock; and the Bishops' Standing Committee.

The Bishops' Standing Conference has departments which are responsible for: Christian Life and Worship, Mission and Unity, Christian Doctrine and Formation, Social Responsibility, Christian Citizenship, and International Affairs.

The *Apostolic Pro-Nuncio to the United Kingdom of Great Britain and Northern Ireland* The Most Rev.

Luigi Barbarito is the Pope's representive in the UK.

The Most Rev. Archbishop of Westminster, HE Cardinal Basil Hume leads the Roman Catholic Church in the UK.

Methodist Church

This is the largest of the "Free" churches, that is Protestant churches which unlike the Church of England and the Church of Scotland are not established as Churches of the State. All Free churches accept both men and women into the ministry.

The Methodist Church was founded by the Wesley brothers in 1739 and now has some 450,406 adult full members and a community of 1.3 million.

The Methodist Church of Great Britain was founded in 1932 with the union of most of the separate Methodist churches. The Methodist Church in Britain is governed by Conference, District Synod and the Circuit Meeting of ministers and lay officers of each Circuit. *President of the Conference* Rev Dr Donald English heads the Methodist Church.

Baptist Union

There are 35,000,000 members of Baptist churches throughout the world. Within England these are for the most part grouped in the Association of Churches; the majority of these belong to the Baptist Union which was formed in 1812.

Total membership of the 2111 churches stands at 167,466 in England. There are separate churches for Scotland, (166 churches with 14,600 members), Wales (586 churches with 29,593), and Ireland (92 churches with 8550 members). *President of the Baptist Union of Britain* Rev. Dr John Biggs leads the majority of Baptist churches in England.

Orthodox Church

The Orthodox Church in the UK is comprised largely of the Greek Orthodox Church, the Serbian Orthodox Church and the Russian Orthodox Church (Patriarchate of Moscow), as well as the Russian Orthodox Church Outside Russia.

Religious Society of Friends, Quakers

Founded in the 17th century by George Fox, the Quakers have no separate ministry. Silent worship is central to their observations, as is working for peace and the relief of suffering throughout the world.

In Britain there are 462 places of worship with 18,010 adult members.

United Reform

The United Reform Church was formed by the union of the Congregational Church in England and Wales and the Presbyterian Church of England in 1972.

In 1981 there was a further union with the Reformed Association of Churches of Christ. The Church is divided into 12 provinces and 70 districts; there are some 128,000 members served by 1000 ministers.

General Secretary Rev. B.G. Thorogood is head of the United Reform Church.

Salvation Army

The Salvation Army, first known as the Christian Mission, was founded in 1865 by William Booth in London's East End.

It has a quasi-military governing structure, headed by the General with Territorial Commanders and Colonels.

In 1988 there were 929 corps (churches), and 135 social services centres involving 1575 officers within Britain.

The social services activities involve hostels for the sick, homeless, elderly, abused children and teenagers on probation. They also provide chaplaincy to over 1000 prisons. Leader of the Salvation Army is *General* Eva Burrows.

Charismatic Renewal

From the early 1970s, the UK has seen the emergence of the charismatic renewal movement which has affected both Anglican and Roman Catholic churches, as well as generating the new House Church movement and many other new independent churches.

Charismatic renewal places emphasis on the 'born again' experience and the gifts of the Holy Spirit, praying in tongues, healing, etc., with a return to traditional Christian teaching and values.

It is difficult to estimate membership, as charismatic churches cross the denominational boundaries, but House Churches and the new independent churches now number more than 1300 with attendance figures of 170,000. One of the unique characteristics of charismatic churches is the major growth in attendance, while the traditional denominations have experienced a marked decline in congregations.

Watch Tower Bible and Tract Society (Jehovah's Witnesses)

A Christian church of American origin, the followers believe that the end of the world is nigh, that all other churches are false or evil, that all war is unlawful, and that civil law should be resisted whenever it conflicts with their own Church's religious principles. An emphasis is put on conversion and missionary work.

NON CHRISTIAN FAITHS

Islam

Britain's Muslim population now stands at 1.5 million. This community, which originates mainly from Pakistan, Bangladesh, India and the Arab world, established its first mosque in England in 1890 in Woking, Surrey. There is now a large British-born Muslim community.

There are 385 mosques with numerous other prayer centres throughout the country. Mosques within Britain act not only as religious centres but also as cultural and social centres giving instruction in the Muslim way of life, whilst also maintaining welfare traditions.

The Central Mosque in London with its associated Islamic Cultural Centre is the largest in Britain. The congregation, for major festivals, can number as many as 30,000. Other important centres include Liverpool, Manchester, Leicester, Bradford and Glasgow.

Muslim beliefs centre around the religion of Islam, having the Koran as its sacred scripture and teaching that there is only one God and that Mohammed is his prophet.

Sikhism

The British Sikh community now stands at approximately 500,000. This community, originating predominantly from India, has long been established in Britain. The first Gurdwara (temple), was established in London in 1908, and the largest is now is Southall, Middlesex where congregations for festivals number up to 5000.

The Gurdwaras cater for cultural, social and welfare activities with an emphasis placed on the maintenance of traditional values and principles.

The Sikh religion is a reformed schism of the Hindu faith, founded in the 16th century, that teaches monotheism. The Granth is its main religious document which rejects the authority of the Hindu Vedas.

Hinduism

There are at present some 300,000 Hindus living within Britain today, worshipping at Mandirs. The largest communities are located in Leicester, North and North West London, Birmingham and Bradford. Emphasis is

Religious Ministers and Buildings in the UK

1,000s	Ministers 1970	1980	1987	Buildings 1970	1980	1987
Trinitarian Churches						
Anglican	17.4	14.7	13.8	20.3	19.4	18.7
Presbyterian	4.2	3.7	3.4	6.6	6.1	5.7
Methodist	4.5	3.9	3.7	10.0	8.6	7.8
Baptist	2.5	2.4	2.4	3.7	3.3	3.4
Other Protestant	6.6	8.5	9.8	7.8	8.5	9.5
Roman Catholic	8.1	7.6	6.2	5.1	4.1	4.4
	43.3	40.8	39.3	53.5	50.0	49.5
Non-Trinitarian Churches						
Mormon	3.5	7.3	9.8	0.1	0.2	0.4
Jehovah's Witness	7.0	8.1	10.4	0.6	1.2	1.2
Spiritualist	0.2	0.3	0.4	0.6	0.6	0.6
Other Non-Trinitarian	0.7	1.2	1.2	1.1	1.1	1.1
	11.4	16.9	21.8	2.4	3.1	3.3
Other religions						
Muslim	0.4	1.5	2.1	0.1	0.2	0.4
Sikh	0.1	0.1	0.2	–	0.1	0.2
Hindu	0.1	0.1	0.2	0.1	0.1	0.2
Jew	0.4	0.4	0.4	0.3	0.3	0.3
Other	0.1	0.6	0.9	0.1	0.2	0.3
	1.1	2.7	3.8	0.6	0.9	1.4

Marriages in Great Britain: religious and civil ceremonies, 1971 and 1988

1,000s	1971 All marriages	1988 First marriages	Second marriages	All marriages
Manner of solemnisation				
Religious Ceremony				
Church of England/Church in Wales	160	111	8	119
Church of Scotland	20	11	3	14
Roman Catholic	48	27	2	29
Other Christian	37	17	19	36
Jewish and other religions	2	2	–	2
Civil marriages	180	76	107	183
Total	447	244	139	383
Civil marriages as a percentage of all marriages				
England and Wales	41	31	78	48
Scotland	31	29	70	42
Great Britain	40	31	77	48

placed on cultural and social welfare activities as well as religion within the community.

Hinduism involves a complex set of beliefs, values and customs, centering around the worship of many gods, including Brahma the supreme being. Hinduism also involves a belief in reincarnation and the ability for self improvement within this life to improve future incarnations.

Judaism

The present Jewish community dates from 1656 when Cromwell's Commonwealth allowed religious freedom within England. Most of these earlier settlers were of Spanish, Portuguese and Middle-Eastern origins. More recently, during the 20th century, settlers have come from Germany and the Eastern European countries.

The present community, numbering 330,000, is the second largest in Europe. The community is divided into two groups; the Ashkenazim, coming from Europe, and the Sephardim originating in Spain and Portugal.

The Ashkenazim, the majority group, have the Chief Rabbi as their spiritual head whilst the Sephardim have a Haham. Despite being split, the two groups still have close ties and there are few religious differences.

Within the Ashkenzi community there are the Liberal and Progressive Movement, established in 1840, and the Reform Movement, established in 1901.

There are 300 synagogues (churches/temples) and many denominational schools. The officially recognized representative body is the Board of Deputies of the British Jews.

Judaism was the first monotheistic religion. Beliefs are based upon the Old Testament and the Talmud.

Buddhism

Within Britain today there are 134 Buddhist groups with 55 centres. There are 13 monasteries and several temples, including the Peace Pagoda in Battersea Park, London.

All Buddhist schools of thought have some representation within Britain. The Buddhist Society, whose headquarters are in London, represents all of the schools. They also publicize the teachings and beliefs of the movement and encourage study and practice.

Buddhism is a religious teaching as taught by the Buddha, a man not a God, which declares that by eliminating greed, hatred, and self illusion one can eliminate suffering and thus attain enlightenment.

Active members of religious faiths in the UK

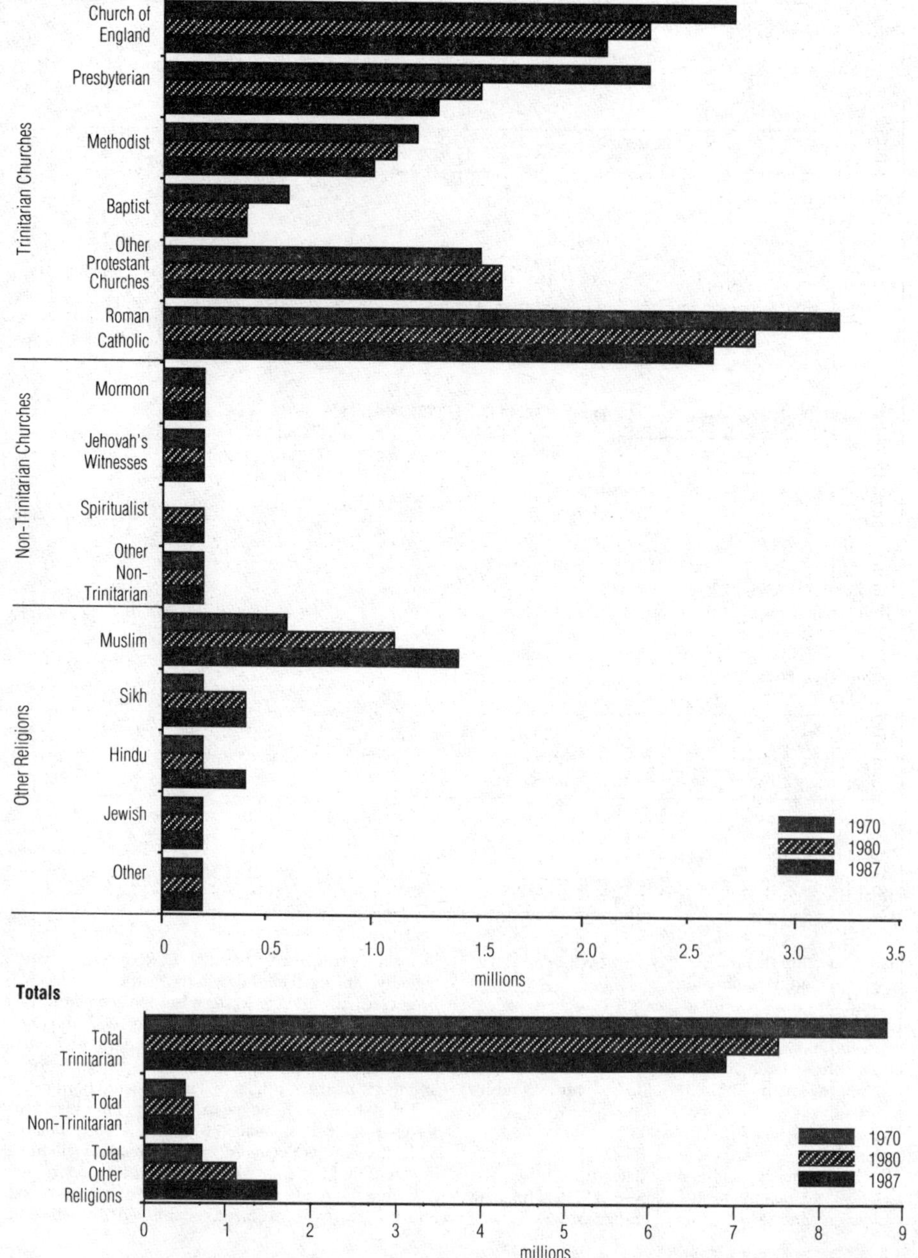

Religious adherents in the United Kingdom of Great Britain and Northern Ireland

Year	1900		mid-1970		Annual change, 1970–1980				mid-1975		mid–1980		2000	
Name	*Adherents*	%	*Adherents*	%	*Natural*	*Conversion*	*Total*	*Rate*	*Adherents*	%	*Adherents*	%	*Adherents*	%
Christians	37,125,000	97.4	49,298,000	88.8	168,118	−101,518	66,600	0.13	49,604,000	87.9	49,964,000	86.9	51,182,000	81.5
professing	37,125,000	97.4	49,298,000	88.8	168,118	−101,518	66,600	0.13	49,604,000	87.9	49,964,000	86.9	51,182,000	81.5
Anglicans	25,100,000	65.9	31,624,000	57.0	109,007	−4,307	104,700	0.32	32,163,000	57.0	32,671,000	56.8	33,909,000	54.0
Protestants	9,475,000	24.9	9,432,000	17.0	30,597	−110,997	−80,400	−0.89	9,028,000	16.0	8,628,000	15.0	7,535,000	12.0
Roman Catholics	2,530,000	6.6	7,212,000	13.0	24,860	7,440	32,300	0.44	7,335,000	13.0	7,535,000	13.1	8,352,000	13.3
Marginal Protestants	12,000	0.0	550,000	1.0	2,000	6,300	8,300	1.41	590,000	1.0	633,000	1.1	816,000	1.3
Orthodox	2,000	0.0	360,000	0.6	1,244	256	1,500	0.41	367,000	0.6	375,000	0.6	420,000	0.7
Third-World indigenous	0	0.0	80,000	0.1	285	515	800	0.95	84,000	0.1	88,000	0.2	120,000	0.2
Catholics (non-Roman)	6,000	0.0	40,000	0.1	125	−725	−600	−1.62	37,000	0.1	34,000	0.1	30,000	0.0
nominal	998,600	2.6	5,406,777	9.7	22,165	208,037	230,202	3.52	6,539,800	11.6	7,708,800	13.4	9,587,000	15.3
affiliated	36,126,400	94.8	43,891,223	79.1	145,953	−309,555	−163,602	−0.38	43,064,200	76.3	42,255,200	73.5	41,595,000	66.2
total practising	30,707,440	*85*	28,369,700	*65*	91,950	−351,353	−259,403	−0.96	27,130,450	*63*	25,775,670	*61*	23,293,200	*56*
non-practising	5,418,960	*15*	15,521,520	*35*	54,003	41,798	95,801	0.60	15,933,750	*37*	16,479,530	*39*	18,301,800	*44*
Anglicans	24,536,400	64.4	29,063,241	52.4	97,725	−139,649	−41,924	−0.15	28,834,000	51.1	28,644,000	49.8	28,257,000	45.0
Evangelicals	12,954,000	34.0	7,556,000	13.6	27,365	76,335	103,700	1.28	8,074,000	14.3	8,593,000	14.9	10,675,000	17.0
Anglican pentecostals	0	0.0	60,000	0.1	1,017	52,983	54,000	18.00	300,000	0.5	600,000	1.0	1,200,000	1.9
Protestants	9,144,000	24.0	8,357,343	15.1	26,582	−131,816	−105,234	−1.34	7,843,000	13.9	7,305,000	12.7	6,405,000	10.2
Evangelicals	5,715,000	15.0	2,164,000	3.9	7,650	11,750	19,400	0.86	2,257,000	4.0	2,358,000	4.1	2,826,000	4.5
Neo-pentecostals	0	0.0	20,000	0.0	305	17,695	18,000	20.00	90,000	0.2	200,000	0.3	400,000	0.6
Roman Catholics	2,429,000	6.4	5,543,431	10.0	18,359	−43,502	−25,143	−0.46	5,417,000	9.6	5,292,000	9.2	5,651,000	9.0
Catholic pentecostals	0	0.0	2,000	0.0	41	2,259	2,300	19.17	12,000	0.0	25,000	0.0	100,000	0.2
Marginal Protestants	10,000	0.0	480,888	0.9	1,745	5,166	6,911	1.34	515,000	0.9	550,000	1.0	754,000	1.2
Orthodox	2,000	0.0	351,100	0.6	1,213	177	1,390	0.39	358,000	0.6	365,000	0.6	400,000	0.6
Third-World indigenous	0	0.0	74,470	0.1	262	311	573	0.74	77,300	0.1	80,200	0.1	110,000	0.2
Catholics (non-Roman)	5,000	0.0	20,750	0.0	67	−242	−175	−0.88	19,900	0.0	19,000	0.0	18,000	0.0
Non-religious	720,000	1.9	4,248,400	7.7	6,500	73,100	79,600	1.73	4,610,900	8.2	5,044,400	8.8	7,819,000	12.5
Jews	235,000	0.6	450,000	0.8	1,620	−20	1,600	0.35	458,000	0.8	466,000	0.8	505,000	0.8
Muslims	0	0.0	635,000	1.1	14,400	5,100	19,500	2.67	730,000	1.3	830,000	1.4	1,130,000	1.8
Ahmadis	0	0.0	8,000	0.0	140	60	200	2.22	9,000	0.0	10,000	0.0	15,000	0.0
Atheists	10,000	0.0	300,000	0.5	1,149	9,151	10,300	3.04	339,000	0.6	403,000	0.7	942,000	1.5
Hindus	0	0.0	220,000	0.4	10,423	5,577	16,000	5.33	300,000	0.5	380,000	0.7	560,000	0.9
Sikhs	0	0.0	200,000	0.4	1,050	−50	1,000	0.49	205,000	0.4	210,000	0.4	310,000	0.5
Buddhists	0	0.0	30,000	0.1	303	8,797	9,100	11.30	80,500	0.1	121,000	0.2	230,000	0.4
Spiritists	10,000	0.0	20,000	0.0	64	−264	−200	−1.05	19,000	0.0	18,000	0.0	16,000	0.0
Chinese folk-religionists	0	0.0	15,000	0.0	47	−247	−200	−1.43	14,000	0.0	13,000	0.0	10,000	0.0
Baha'is	0	0.0	13,600	0.0	50	150	200	1.37	14,600	0.0	15,600	0.0	25,000	0.0
Other religionists	0	0.0	50,000	0.1	176	244	400	0.77	52,000	0.1	54,000	0.1	65,000	0.1
Country's population	**38,100,000**	**100.0**	**55,480,000**	**100.0**	**203,900**	**0**	**203,900**	**0.36**	**56,427,000**	**100.0**	**57,519,000**	**100.0**	**62,794,000**	**100.0**

Source: *World Christian Encyclopedia*, ed. D.B. Barrett, OUP, 1982.

TRADE UNIONS

TRADE UNIONISM AND THE TRADES UNION CONGRESS (TUC)

Chairman **Miss A. Maddocks OBE (NALGO)**
General Secretary **Norman Willis**

The forerunners of trade unions were the journeyman guilds that existed in the Middle Ages, and later the combinations of wage-earners formed in the 18th century and outlawed in Britain in 1800. The modern trade union, which is an organization for improving workers' pay and conditions by collective bargaining with employers, had its origin in the Industrial Revolution. Even after the repeal of the Combination laws in 1824–5 however, trade unionists continued to be persecuted and trade unions did not achieve proper legitimacy until the Trade Union Acts 1871–6.

Established in 1868, the Trades Union Congress (TUC) is a voluntary association of 78 independent trade unions representing some 8.8 million workers of whom nearly one-third are women. (In law, an independent trade union is one that is not subject to domination, control or interference by employers or employer groups.) Trade union members are found in every industry and service and include top managers and professional staff as well as scientists and technicians, clerical staff, skilled workers and labourers. Total trade union membership at the end of 1988 (the latest year for which figures are available) was 10,387,238. The major unions with a membership of over 100,000 accounted for 8,342,064 members or 80% of the total. The returns show that in 1988 total trade union membership fell for the ninth consecutive year since 1979 when it reached a peak of 13.2 million. However, the relatively small fall of 92,912 during the year to a total of 10.4 million is a further reflection of the levelling off in the downward trend noted for 1987.

Gross income from members' subscriptions to all trade unions totalled £429.7 million, of which £8.1 million was paid to the TUC in affiliation fees. During 1988 the TUC's total funds increased from £604 million to £620 million.

Although the TUC is a non-political organization, some 40 affiliated unions maintain a voluntary political fund to support the Labour Party. At the end of 1988 the fund stood at £11.9 million, made up of contributions by almost 6 million trade union members.

TUC policy is decided at its annual congress, which meets during the first week of September. Congress consists of more than 1000 delegates from all the constituent unions, the larger unions having proportionally greater representation. However, each union, irrespective of size, is entitled to table two motions for debate. Voting is normally by a show of hands or, exceptionally, by a 'card vote', when unions vote according to their numbers of members.

To run the TUC between congresses, a General Council of 48 members, presided over by the General Secretary, meets once a month. The largest unions are each entitled to four seats on the Council, and any union with more than 100,000 members has automatic representational rights. A further 11 seats are contested by smaller unions in secret ballots, and another six are reserved for women trade unionists. Nine standing committees each dealing with a specific area of policy (such as education and training, employment legislation, equal rights and European strategy) report to the General Council.

In 1989 the TUC was particularly concerned with promoting the European Social Charter to guarantee workers' basic rights in the run-up to the Single European Market of 1992. Unions were encouraged to draw up checklists of demands based on the Charter and to forge closer links with unions in Europe. Lobbying took place in the European Parliament through the European Trade Confederation, to which the TUC is closely allied, and a mass rally and march were held in Brussels in October.

Congress House, 23–8 Great Russell St, London WC1B 3LS. Tel. 071–636 4030

MAJOR TRADE UNIONS

Given here are details on the most significant of the trade unions. A complete list of TUC-affiliated unions is given at the end.

AMALGAMATED ENGINEERING UNION (AEU)

General Secretary **Gavin Laird**
President **Bill Jordan**

One of the biggest British trade unions, the AEU represents members in every sphere of manufacturing in the public and private sectors, including the aircraft and shipbuilding industries, railway workshops, foundries, scientific instruments and heavy, medium and light engineering. The union, which is affiliated to the TUC, has about 794,000 members of whom 13% are women. All of the AEU's 167 full-time officials are elected by the members. In addition to operating a political fund, the union sponsors 12 Labour MPs: Richard Caborn (Sheffield Central), David Clelland (Tyne Bridge), Jimmy Dunnachie (Glasgow Pollok), Ken Eastham (Manchester Blackley), John Evans (St Helens North), Ted Garrett (Wallsend), George Howarth (Knowsley North), Robert Hughes (Aberdeen North), William McKelvey (Kilmarnock and Louden), Bill Michie (Sheffield Heeley), Stan Orme (Salford East) and Harold Walker (Doncaster Central).

The AEU has pressed for improvements in safety standards on oil rigs, following the Piper Alpha disaster of 1988, and, as the largest member of the Confederation of Shipbuilding and Engineering Unions, has led the campaign to reduce the working week from 39 to 35 hours.

110 Peckham Rd, London SE15 5EL. Tel. 071–703 4231

ASSOCIATED SOCIETY OF LOCOMOTIVE ENGINEERS AND FIREMEN (ASLEF)

General Secretary **Neil Milligan**

The union consists mainly of train drivers and driver trainees working for British Rail (BR), train operators and guards on the London Underground and train operators on the Tyne and Wear Metro. There are currently 19,117 members, of whom 52 are women. ASLEF has nine salaried officials including the General Secretary and Deputy General Secretary. It is affiliated to the TUC and has a voluntary political fund, but does not sponsor any MPs.

In the summer of 1989 ASLEF, together with the NUR (National Union of Railwaymen), went into dispute with BR over a claim for a 'substantial' pay increase, and management proposals to dismantle the national negotiating machinery. Having earlier rejected an offer of 7%, members imposed an indefinite ban on overtime and restday working, resulting in the cancellation of one quarter of the services. After a week of this action, which coincided with the fifth week of one-day strikes by the NUR, ASLEF accepted an improved pay offer of 8.8% and agreed to resolve the question of bargaining structure through ACAS. In a second dispute, with London Underground, ASLEF and NUR train operators achieved an 8.75% pay rise, after seeking a 'substantial increase', and a further two-stage pay award by ACAS of £7.64 a week for working one-person-operated trains. The dispute lasted from April to August and involved ASLEF members in five official weekly one-day strikes, from early July, as well as earlier unofficial strike action.

9 Arkwright Rd, London NW3 6AB. Tel. 071–431 0275

ASSOCIATION OF CINEMATOGRAPH, TELEVISION AND ALLIED TECHNICIANS (ACTT)

General Secretary **Alan Sapper**

The union is open to all those working on the technical side of the television, film, video- and audio-recording industries, including transmission and distribution. It has 29,390 members of whom 7774 are women, and is serviced by 19 full-time paid officials. It is a TUC affiliate and operates a political fund. Since 1984 ACTT has had a parliamentary committee, with representatives in both Houses and in Europe. Committee members in mid-1989 (all Labour) were Lord Dormand of Easington, Lord Graham of Edmonton, Lord Jenkins of Putney, Margaret Beckett MP (Derby South), Norman Buchan MP (Peckham), Bob Cryer MP (Bradford South), Mark Fisher MP (Stoke-on-Trent Central), Bruce Grocott MP (Wrekin), Tom Pendry MP (Stalybridge and Hyde), Chris Smith MP (Islington South and Finsbury), Ken Collins MEP (Strathclyde East) and Henry McCubbin MEP (Scotland North East). In 1989 ACTT had a three-month dispute with the BBC over a pay claim for 16.6%, but finally agreed to accept 8.8%. The dispute was conducted jointly with the Broadcasting and Entertainment Trades Alliance (BETA) and the National Union of Journalists (NUJ) and involved 12 days of action, including overtime bans as well as half-day and full-day strikes. The union has also been in dispute with TV-AM since 1987 over the sacking of 229 technicians.

111 Wardour St, London W1V 4AY. Tel. 071-437 8506

ASSOCIATION OF UNIVERSITY TEACHERS (AUT)

General Secretary **Diana Warwick**

The AUT represents university lecturers as well as senior administrative staff and senior research, library and computer staff working in universities. It has about 32,000 members of whom some 20% are women, and is administered by 11 full-time officials with 25 support staff. Since 1976 the union has been affiliated to the TUC. The AUT has no political fund and does not sponsor any MPs, but it does use the services of two MPs, Keith Hampson (Con., Leeds North West) and Jack Straw (Lab., Blackburn) as advisers. From October 1988 until April 1989 the union was in dispute with the Committee of Vice-Chancellors and Principals (the university authorities) over a pay claim for a minimum of 9% for its members. After industrial action involving withdrawal from student appraisal and the examination process, members accepted an offer of 7%.

United House, 1 Pembridge Rd, London W11 3HJ. Tel. 071-221 4370

BANKING, INSURANCE AND FINANCE UNION (BIFU)

General Secretary **Leif Mills**

The union represents staff in all the major banks in Great Britain, British banks overseas, foreign and Commonwealth banks, clearing banks, finance houses and credit card companies, building societies, insurance companies and other financial institutions. The largest banking union in Europe, it has 168,400 members, including 54% women and 6% part-time employees, and is serviced by some 40 full-time officials. BIFU is affiliated to the TUC, but does not sponsor MPs or operate a political fund. It does, however, have two parliamentary consultants, Jeremy Bray (Lab., Motherwell South) and David Madel (Con., South Bedfordshire). A dispute in 1989 with Barclay's Bank over parity payments for data-processing workers lasted several months and led to an overtime ban before the parties agreed to resume talks. There were also local disputes over pay, mainly within the banking sector, that involved overtime bans in some cases.

Sheffield House, 1b Amity Grove, London SW20 0LG. Tel. 081-946 9151

BRITISH ACTORS' EQUITY ASSOCIATION (incorporating the Variety Artistes' Federation) (EQUITY)

General Secretary **Peter Plouviez**

The trade union accepts as members all professional actors and other professionals involved in entertainment on stage, in films, in radio or in television, including producers and others. It has 40,388 members, of whom 19,531 are women, and 30 full-time bargaining officials. Equity is a TUC affiliate, but does not operate a political fund or sponsor an MP.

8 Harley St, London W1N 2AB. Tel. 071–637 9311

CIVIL AND PUBLIC SERVICES ASSOCIATION (CPSA)

General Secretary **John Ellis**

The membership of this TUC-affiliated trade union includes all administrative, secretarial and clerical grades of employee in the civil service and related bodies. It is the largest of the civil service unions, with around 126,000 members of whom two-thirds or more are women. The CPSA has 17 full-time officials involved in industrial relations, including the General Secretary and Deputy General Secretary. Frank Field MP (Lab., Birkenhead) is sponsored by the union which up to 1989 did not have a political fund. Since 1984 the union has been in dispute with the Government over the trade union ban at Government Communications Headquarters (GCHQ) Cheltenham. However, despite protest industrial action taken over the period, including a series of one-day strikes, the last of the 150 employees who refused to renounce their union membership were forced to quit GCHQ at the beginning of 1989.

160 Falcon Rd, London SW11 2LN. Tel. 071-924 2727

CONFEDERATION OF HEALTH SERVICE EMPLOYEES (COHSE)

General Secretary **Hector McKenzie**

The largest of the health unions, COHSE recruits all grades of health-care workers, principally nurses and ancillary staff, and has members in the NHS, in local authorities and in the voluntary and private sectors. A total of some 80 paid officials serve the membership numbering about 220,000 and including 79% women. The union is TUC-affiliated, has a political fund and sponsors six Labour MPs: Dale Campbell-Savours (Workington), Dennis Canavan (Falkirk West), Michael Meacher (Oldham West), Marjorie Mowlam (Redcar) and Joan Walley (Stoke-on-Trent North). During 1989 COHSE opposed the hospital managements' imposition of a new clinical structure as being discriminatory against ancillary nursing staff and the lower-paid. It also campaigned vigorously against the proposals for the health service set out in the Government's White Paper, in the belief that health-care provision would suffer as a result of their implementation.

Glen House, High St, Banstead, Surrey SM7 2LH. Tel. 0737 353322

ELECTRICAL, ELECTRONIC, TELECOMMUNICATION AND PLUMBING UNION (EETPU)

General Secretary **Eric Hammond**

The union organizes skilled and non-skilled workers over a wide range of industries, principally electrical engineerng, construction, electronics, telecommunications and plumbing. It also has a clerical, technical and administrative section, the Electrical and Engineering Staff Association (EESA). Out of a total membership of around 360,000, of whom some 40,000 are women, EESA accounts for nearly 10%. The union employs 135 paid officials, including the General Secretary. EETPU is not affiliated to the TUC, having been expelled in 1988 after a disagreement over the signing of single-union no-strike deals with employers. The union operates a political fund and sponsors the Labour MPs Tom Cox (Tooting) and Stuart Randall (Hull West).

Hayes Court, West Common Rd, Hayes, Bromley, Kent BR2 7AU. Tel. 081-462 7755

EQUITY: see British Actors' Equity Association

GMB/APEX PARTNERSHIP (GMB)

General Secretary **John Edmonds**

In March 1989 the General, Municipal, Boilermakers and Allied Trade Union (GMBATU) merged with the Association of Professional, Executive, Clerical and Computer Staff (APEX) to form the second-largest of Britain's trade unions. GMB/APEX is a general union, organizing, among others, staff in local government, public utilities such as gas, water and electricity, the health service, hotels, the food drink and tobacco industries, retail, the security industry, merchant banking, the shipyards and engineering. The TUC-affiliated union has about 864,000 members, of whom some 275,000 are women, with 231 full-time serving officials (including the General Secretary). Besides maintaining a political fund, the union also sponsors 15 Labour MPs: Denis Howell (Birmingham Small Heath) and David Winnick (Walsall North), both sponsored by APEX, and Jack Ashley (Stoke-on-Trent South), Betty Boothroyd (West Bromwich West), Tom Clarke (Monklands West), John Cunningham (Copeland), Don Dixon (Jarrow), Patick Duffy (Sheffield Attercliffe), Doug Henderson (Newcastle upon Tyne North), Gerald Kaufman (Manchester Gorton), Joan Lestor (Eccles), Giles Radice (Durham North), George Robertson (Hamilton), Clive Soley (Hammersmith) and John Smith (Monklands East), who are all GMB-sponsored.

In 1989, at the end of a month-long dispute, members in the electricity supply industry won a 9.2% pay rise. The initial claim for a 'substantial increase' had been met by offers of 7–7.5%, but a settlement was reached after members endorsed a ballot for strike action. As a member of the Confederation of Shipbuilding Unions, in 1989 the union pressed for a 35-hour week within the industries concerned, and was also involved in campaigns directed against Government plans for the NHS and the privatization of water and electricity. GMB/APEX was active in the TUC's 1989 'Inspect and Protect' health and safety campaign and in the health field generally. The union campaigned on the dangers of repetitive strain injury (RSI) in new-technology industries, and sought compensation for its members in a number of court actions against employers. It also launched in 1989 a campaign to focus attention on women's health at the workplace.

Thorne House, Ruxley Ridge, Claygate, Esher, Surrey KT10 0TL. Tel. 0732 62081

IRON AND STEEL TRADES CONFEDERATION (ISTC)

General Secretary **Roy Evans**

Membership of the ISTC is open to anyone in the metal-working industries. The union has 41,920 members, including 2500 women, whose interests are looked after by 22 paid officials. The TUC-affiliated union maintains a political fund and sponsors the Labour MP Donald Coleman (Neath).

Swinton House, 324 Gray's Inn Rd, London WC1X 8DD. Tel. 071-837 6691

MANUFACTURING SCIENCE FINANCE (MSF)

General Secretary **Ken Gill**

MSF is a white-collar union formed by an amalgamation in January 1988 of TASS (Technical Administrative and Supervisory Section of the Amalgamated Engineering Union) and ASTMS (Association of Scientific, Technical and Managerial Staffs). It organizes over a wide range of industries, particularly those involved with new technology, but also has members in commerce, health and education and many other professions and industries. A hundred or so paid officials look after the interests of some 653,000 members, of whom 126,000 are women. The union operates a political fund and sponsors 16 Labour MPs: Hilary Armstrong (Durham North West), Joe Ashton (Bassetlaw), Frank Cook (Stockton North), Jim Cousins (Newcastle upon Tyne Central), Terry Davis (Birmingham Hodge Hill), Derek Fatchett (Leeds Central), Martin Flannery (Sheffield Hillsborough), Doug Hoyle (Warrington North), James Lamond (Oldham Central and Royton), Michael Martin (Glasgow Springburn), Alan Meale (Mansfield), Dawn Primarolo (Bristol South), Jo Richardson (Barking), Jeff Rooker (Birmingham Perry Bar), Ernie Ross (Dundee West) and Chris Smith (Islington South and Finsbury). In 1989 MSF campaigned through Parliament, and on the basis of health and safety legislation, for improvements in the working conditions on offshore rigs, while the union's Medical Practitioners' Union section called for a reduction in the number of hours worked by junior hospital doctors. MSF was also active as a member of the Confederation of Shipbuilding Unions in the campaign for a 35-hour working week.

79 Camden Rd, London NW1 9ES. Tel. 071-267 4422

NATIONAL AND LOCAL GOVERNMENT OFFICERS' ASSOCIATION (NALGO)

General Secretary **John Daly**

The union is for clerical, administrative, professional and technical employees in local government; the health service; public utilities such as water, gas and electricity; transport and universities. It has a membership of about 754,000 of whom about half are women. NALGO officials include 40 or more at the union's headquarters and around 150 in district offices across the country. The union is TUC-affiliated and has a political fund. It does not sponsor any MPs but has a number of parliamentary advisers who offer their services free of charge. During 1989, members in local government embarked on six days of one-day strike action, involving half a million workers, following a dispute over pay and proposals to dismantle the national bargaining structure. At the end of six weeks, and after further all-out strikes in selected target areas, the union settled for 8.8% (between 8.6% and 9.5% weighted toward the lower-paid), having at first sought a 12% increase. It also succeeded in preventing the devolution of negotiations to local level.

1 Mabledon Place, London WC1H 9AJ.
Tel. 071-388 2366

NATIONAL ASSOCIATION OF SCHOOLMASTERS/UNION OF WOMEN TEACHERS (NAS/UWT)

General Secretary **Fred Smithies**

The second largest teaching union, the NAS/UWT represents qualified teachers and instructors employed on Baker scales (from 1987) in schools throughout Britain. The union is about 120,000 strong, with 40% women. There are 25 senior officials of whom about half are deployed in the regions. A TUC affiliate, the union sponsors no MPs, but its 1989 Conference voted for the first time to have a political fund.

Hillscourt Education Centre, Rose Hill, Rednal, Birmingham B45 8RS. Tel. 021-453 6150

NATIONAL ASSOCIATION OF TEACHERS IN FURTHER AND HIGHER EDUCATION (NATFHE)

General Secretary **Geoff Wolf**

The union organizes academic staff in all areas of post-school, further, higher and adult education. It has about 82,000 members, one-third of whom are women, and 17 full-time bargaining officials (excluding the General Secretary and Deputy General Secretary). NATFHE is an affiliate to the TUC and operates a political fund. In common with other education unions it does not sponsor any MPs, but employs the services of parliamentary consultants. In 1989 these were Malcolm Thornton (Con., Crosby) and Paul Murphy (Lab., Torfaen).

A two-year dispute with Hereford and Worcester County Council over the breaking of national agreements resulted in a return in 1989 to previous conditions, following a series of one-day strikes and the blacklisting of the authority as an employer by the union. In colleges of further education the refusal of employers to accept a £3400 flat-rate claim, and the union's rejection of an offer of 5.3% plus proposals to change working practices, led to a one-day strike on 17 October and a second on 14 December accompanied by an indefinite examination boycott. An improved offer of 8% payable from September together with a two-stage payment of £700, but with flexible working included as part of the package, was made at the end of December. In higher education, members sought a 9.25% increase, but the Polytechnic and College Employers' Forum (PCEF) offered only 5.4%, which was later increased to 6%, with changes to condition of employment. When no agreement had been reached by November, the union imposed an examination boycott amid threats by the PCEF to dock pay and withdraw from national bargaining.

27 Britannia St, London WC1X 9JP. Tel. 071-837 3636

NATIONAL GRAPHICAL ASSOCIATION (NGA)

General Secretary **Tony Dubbins**
General President **Bryn Griffiths**

The union accepts as members qualified workers in printing and allied trades, including camera workers, artists and designers; as well as apprentices and office staff, electricians and technicians. A TUC affiliate, the NGA organizes across the whole of Britain and in the Irish Republic. It has around 125,000 members, 6% of whom are women, supported by a team of more than 70 full-time paid officials. The union maintains a political fund and sponsors three Labour MPs: Martin O'Neill (Clackmannan), Tony Lloyd (Stretford) and Jim Marshall (Leicester South).

Graphic House, 63–7 Bromham Rd, Bedford, Beds MK40 2AG. Tel. 0234 51521

NATIONAL UNION OF JOURNALISTS (NUJ)

General Secretary **Harry Conroy**

The union is open to journalists, including photographers and creative artists, working editorially in newspapers, magazines, books, broadcasting, public relations and teletext and viewdata services. It has about 32,000 members, of whom one-third are women, with 17 full-time officials (all NUJ members). The union is a TUC affiliate, but does not have a political fund or sponsor any MPs.

In 1989, a five-month dispute over pay with the BBC, conducted jointly with the Association of Cinematograph, Television and Allied Technicians (ACCT) and the Broadcasting and Entertainment Trades Alliance (BETA), resulted in 12 days of action, including one-day and half-day strikes. At the end of August the 3000 NUJ members involved voted 3:1 by ballot to accept an 8.8% increase, having at first claimed 16.6% and been offered 4.5%. A dispute with Robert Maxwell's Pergamon Press, a publisher of journals and books, remained unresolved after 23 journalists who struck in support of recognition of the union's right to represent a sacked member were themselves dismissed in May. As the Pergamon dispute continues into 1990, the NUJ is also negotiating in a number of other disputes within the publishing industry.

In London in November 1989 VNU Business Publications entered into a dispute with the NUJ over an individual case that escalated into a dispute over union derecognition. The strike was called off by the union in May 1990 and journalists at this company are now working under personal (individual) contracts.

Recognition disputes were especially prominent in the newspaper sector, where managements sought to scrap collective agreements and impose personal contracts. In the provincial press, some 3000 journalists up and down the country were affected. At the *Essex Chronicle*, owned by Northcliffe Newspapers, a subsidiary of Associated Newspapers, 14 were sacked in June 1989 for striking in defence of the union and the issue had still not been settled by June 1990. In Aberdeen, 115 journalists on the *Evening Express* and other publications belonging to Thomson Regional

Newspapers struck twice over derecognition and allegations of victimization; the second action, begun in October 1989, failed to produce a result by June 1990.

Among national newspapers, journalists working for the Mirror Group and Express Newspapers agreed to accept personal contracts after lengthy negotiations. However, similar moves were rejected at the *Daily* and *Sunday Telegraph*, where members imposed a 36-hour strike in October and awaited a resolution of the dispute through ACAS in December. By January 1990 the bulk of union members had accepted personal contracts. Likewise journalists on the *Daily Mail*, *Mail on Sunday* and *Evening Standard* – all published by Associated Newspapers – rejected the imposition of individual contracts and voted in December for oppositional action such as work-to-rule or 36-hour strikes. Once again, the bulk of union members accepted personal contracts during 1990. The concerted attempt by employers to phase out collective bargaining in the industry prompted the NUJ to call for a conference of all the media unions in the new year.

The union is affiliated to the Campaign for Press and Broadcasting Freedom and campaigns in its own right for the lifting of broadcasting restrictions imposed by the Government and for the repeal of the Official Secrets Act and other censorship laws.

Acorn House, 314–20 Gray's Inn Rd, London WC1X 8DP. Tel. 071-278 7916

NATIONAL UNION OF MINEWORKERS (NUM)

General Secretary **Peter Heathfield**
President **Arthur Scargill**

A staunch TUC-affiliate, the NUM organizes manual and clerical workers employed in Britain's coalmining industry and in all related industries and ancillary undertakings. At the beginning of 1989 it had a membership of around 77,300, including 3500 women, and there were altogether more than 100 paid officials and other staff. However, the volatile nature of the industry – eight pit closures and the loss of some 6000 jobs in less than a year – made any figures subject to rapid change. By August 1990, membership had decreased to 60,000. The union has a political fund and sponsors 13 Labour MPs: Kevin Barron (Rother Valley), George Buckley (Hemsworth), Ronnie Campbell (Blyth Valley), John Cummings (Easington), Lawrence Cunliffe (Leigh), Alex Eadie (Midlothian), Jimmy Hood (Clydesdale), Eric Illsley (Barnsley Central), Terry Patchett (Barnsley East), Martin Redmond (Don Valley), Dennis Skinner (Bolsover), Jack Thompson (Wansbeck) and Mick Welsh (Doncaster North).

Holly St, Sheffield, S. Yorks S1 2GT. Tel. 0742 766900

NATIONAL UNION OF PUBLIC EMPLOYEES (NUPE)

General Secretary **Rodney Bickerstaffe**

Members of the union include manual and clerical workers in municipal authorities, nurses, midwives, ambulance and ancillary staffs in the NHS, water authority workers and non-teaching staffs at universities. A TUC-affiliate, NUPE employs 181 full-time officials to look after the interests of its 640,500 members, 74% of whom are women. The union maintains a political fund and sponsors 10 Labour MPs: David Blunkett (Sheffield Brightside), David Clark (South Shields), Jeremy Corbyn (Islington North), Ron Davies (Caerphilly), David Hinchliffe (Wakefield), Henry McLeish (Fife Central), Alice Mahon (Halifax), Tom Pendry (Stalybridge and Hyde), Clare Short (Birmingham Ladywood) and Keith Vaz (Leicester East).

NUPE has consistently campaigned with other unions against Government plans to privatize the water industry and to introduce compulsory competitive tendering by local authorities. It has also jointly opposed Government proposals for reforming the NHS, which, it believes, will worsen the quality of the service. Instead, NUPE has argued for better pay and equal opportunities for its predominantly female membership, including a clinical grading review for 90,000 NUPE nurses. The union is a staunch opponent of privatization proposals of NHS support services, such as cleaning, catering and laundering.

The rejection of a 6.5% pay offer by ambulance crews, officers and control assistants seeking the restoration of parity with firefighters (which had lapsed after 1986) led to a lengthy dispute, beginning in the autumn of 1989. NUPE's ambulance workers, who accounted for more than half of the 22,500 affected, imposed a national overtime ban and work-to-rule following management's refusal to take the dispute to arbitration. First in London, and later in other parts of the country, the dispute escalated when the army and police were deployed after ambulance staffs had been suspended with cuts in pay for withdrawing some non-emergency cover provision. A new offer of 9% over 18 months failed to resolve the dipsute, and by Christmas 95% of ambulance staffs from NUPE, TGWU, COHSE, GMB and NALGO were operating a restricted service on reduced pay (some were being paid nothing at all), with the army, police and volunteers acting largely as non-emergency back-up. The dispute was finally resolved on 13 March 1990 and a two-year agreement reached which offered an increase of 17.6% on salary levels. In return for improvements in efficiency in the ambulance service, pay will be increased by a further 2% from 1 October 1990. As part of the settlement ambulance staff also received lump-sum payments ranging from £615 to £915. Furthermore, to facilitate future pay negotiations both sides agreed to take account of relevant pay movements in the National Health Service, internal pay differentials, affordability, recruitment and retention problems as well as the need to identify and solve career and pay structure problems. Relevant pay movements in the NHS will be those of the pay review bodies such as the Nursing Staff, Midwives and Health Visitors Pay Review Body.

Civic House, 20 Grand Depot Rd, Woolwich, London SE18 6SF. Tel. 081-854 2244

NATIONAL UNION OF RAILWAYMEN (NUR)

General Secretary **Jimmy Knapp**
President **Alan Foster**

The union represents workers in the transport industry, mainly railways, but including some ancillary services such as hotels, as well as London Transport staff on the underground and the buses. A membership of 110,256, 5530 of whom are women, is served by 40 paid officials, made up of a full-time executive (21), elected every three years, and 19 Divisional Officers. The union is a TUC affiliate and operates a political fund. It also sponsors eight Labour MPs: Donald Anderson (Swansea East), Robin Cook (Livingston), Tam Dalyell (Linlithgow), Frank Dobson (Holborn and St Pancras), Gwyneth Dunwoody (Crewe and Nantwich), John Marek (Wrexham) and Peter Snape (West Bromwich East).

A six-week dispute with British Rail (BR) during the summer of 1989 yielded an 8.8% pay rise. BR's first offer of 7% in response to the NUR's claim, and that of ASLEF (Associated Society of Locomotive Engineers and Firemen), for a 'substantial increase' provoked a series of one-day weekly strikes before a settlement was reached. A further grievance over BR's proposal to break up the national bargaining machinery was shelved pending further talks. Members on the London Underground, together with ASLEF, also sought a 'substantial increase' but eventually settled for 8.75% after a four-month dispute that included 14 one-day stoppages (half of them unofficial). A parallel conditions-of-service dispute over one-person-operated trains was resolved when ACAS recommended a two-stage award of £7.64 per week, backdated and payable in April 1989 and January 1990.

Unity House, Euston Rd, London NW1 2BL.
Tel. 071-387 4771

NATIONAL UNION OF SEAMEN (NUS)

General Secretary **Sam McCluskie**

Membership of the NUS is open to anyone working afloat including ratings (not officers), deck or engine-room workers, catering staff, divers and offshore oil- or gas-rig workers. A TUC affiliate, the union has around 22,000 members, of whom some 2000 are women, and 20 full-time officials. The union operates a political fund and is represented in Parliament by the Labour MP John Prescott (Hull East). A 16-month dispute with P & O over safety and conditions of service on cross-channel ferries ended in May 1989, when strike action by ferry workers, who had been sacked by the company, was finally called off. The union had opposed increases in working hours and reductions in staffing levels in the interests of safety, but faced fines and court costs of over £2 million and the sequestration of its funds when it tried to spread the strike. Beginning in 1990, the union will hold talks with the NUR with a view to forming a single transport union.

Maritime House, Old Town, London SW4 0JP.
Tel. 071-236 8998

NATIONAL UNION OF TEACHERS (NUT)

General Secretary **Doug McAvoy**

The union is open to qualified teachers in England and Wales but also includes student members. A TUC affiliate, it is the biggest of the teaching unions, with a membership of around 180,000, of whom 70% are women. The NUT employs 50–60 full-time officials at head office and across the country. In common with other teaching unions, there is no political fund or MP sponsorship but instead the NUT uses the services of parliamentary consultants on a paid-retainer basis. Currently they are the Labour MPs Hilary Armstrong (Durham North West), Mark Fisher (Stoke-on-Trent Central), Martin Flannery (Sheffield Hillsborough) and Barry Jones (Alyn and Deeside). Although not involved in any disputes in 1989, the union consistently campaigned for improvements in educational standards and opposed Government legislation on education reform and teachers' pay and conditions.

Hamilton House, Mabledon Place, London WC1H 9BD.
Tel. 071388 6191

PRISON OFFICERS ASSOCIATION (POA)

General Secretary **David Evans**

The union is open to prison officers including principal officers, senior officers and below, storemen, night patrol staff, and nurses in prisons or special hospitals such as Broadmoor. Its total membership is about 24,000, including 10% women, and it has 16 paid officials. POA is affiliated to the TUC but has no political fund. It is represented in Parliament by the Labour peer Lord Graham of Edmonton. A year-long dispute over the interpretation of national agreements and conditions of service in Wandsworth prison erupted at the end of January 1989, when prison officers were locked out for 10 days while policemen and prison governors did their work. Since then, the prison authorities have agreed to talks to help resolve union grievances, in particular over new rota systems, staffing levels and numbers of prisoners.

Cronin House, 245 Church Street, London N9 9HW.
Tel. 081-803 1761

ROYAL COLLEGE OF NURSING OF THE UNITED KINGDOM (RCN)

General Secretary **Christine Hancock**

The RCN, which is not affiliated to the TUC, admits as members registered nurses employed in hospitals or as health visitors or midwives, and offers a category of student membership. Nine-tenths of its estimated 290,000 members are women and it claims to be the fastest-growing union in the country. The RCN employs a total of around 400 full-time, paid officials and operates a no-strike policy. The union is also non-party-political, but has a panel of 10 unpaid parliamentary advisers from both Houses and representing all the major political parties. Like other health unions, the RCN in 1989 campaigned against proposals in the Government White Paper on reform of the NHS. It argued that the creation of self-governing hospitals would be divisive and that both standards of care and nurses' pay and conditions would suffer as a consequence.

20 Cavendish Square, London W1M 0AB.
Tel: 071-409 3333

SOCIETY OF GRAPHIC AND ALLIED TRADES '82 (SOGAT '82)

General Secretary **Brenda Dean**
General President **Danny Sergeant**

The union's members are primarily manual and clerical workers in the printing, publishing, packaging and paper-making industries, and include bookbinders. A TUC affiliate, SOGAT '82 employs 150 full-time officials to look after a membership of around 193,000, some two-thirds of whom are women. The union maintains a political fund and sponsors the Labour MPs Ron Leighton (Newham North East) and Bob Litherland (Manchester Central).

Sogat House, 274–88 London Rd, Hadleigh, Benfleet, Essex SS7 2DE. Tel. 0702 554111

TRANSPORT AND GENERAL WORKERS UNION (TGWU)

General Secretary **Ron Todd**

With 1.29 million members, the TGWU is by far the biggest of Britain's trade unions. Its membership, which includes 208,000 women, spans every industry and covers both manual and non-manual workers as well as unemployed youth. A team of around 500 paid officials acts on behalf of the membership. An affiliate of the TUC, and as the largest union the most powerful voice within it, the TGWU also operates a political fund and sponsors 33 Labour MPs. They are Graham Allen (Nottingham North), Tony Banks (Newham North West), Margaret Beckett (Derby South), Sid Bidwell (Ealing Southall), Tony Blair (Sedgefield), Gordon Brown (Dunfermline East), Norman Buchan

(Paisley South), Ann Clywd (Cynon Valley), Stan Crowther (Rotherham), Maria Fyfe (Glasgow Maryhill), George Galloway (Glasgow Hillhead), Norman Goodman (Greenock and Port Glasgow), Harriet Harman (Peckham), Roy Hughes (Newport East), Adam Ingham (East Kilbride), Barry Jones (Alyn and Deeside), Neil Kinnock (Islwyn), Terry Lewis (Worsley), Eddie Loyden (Liverpool Garston), Ian McCartney (Makerfield), Kevin McNamara (Hull North), Max Madden (Bradford West), David Marshall (Glasgow Shettleston), Eric Martlew (Carlisle), Paul Murphy (Torfaen), Gordon Oakes (Halton), Bob Parry (Liverpool Riverside), Joyce Quin (Gateshead East), John Reid (Motherwell North), Allan Roberts (Bootle), Joan Ruddock (Lewisham Deptford), Peter Shore (Bethnal Green) and Gavin Strang (Edinburgh East).

In the summer of 1989 the union was involved in a dispute lasting several months over conditions of service for dock-workers, following Government moves to scrap the Dock Labour Scheme. Court action by employers failed to prevent a strike ballot from going ahead, resulting in the withdrawal of labour by some 9000 dockers at ports all round the country. However, the action quickly succumbed to employers' threats to sack the strikers, and after two weeks was officially called off. In a second dispute, between the TGWU and London Transport, bus drivers imposed a series of weekly one-day strikes in June and July, in pursuit of a claim for a pay increase to cover inflation and changes to conditions of service. At the end of eight weeks, a settlement was reached on both issues giving drivers an extra 9%-plus on pay.

Transport House, Smith Square, London SW1 3JB. Tel. 071-828 7788

UNION OF COMMUNICATION WORKERS (UCW)

General Secretary **Alan Tuffin**

Union membership consists primarily of manual and lower-grade clerical workers in the Post Office and in British Telecom. The union has 13 paid officials looking after the interests of its 197,500 members, of whom just under a quarter are women. A TUC affiliate, the UCW maintains a political fund and sponsors the Labour MPs Harry Ewing (Falkirk East) and Kate Hoey (Lambeth).

UCW House, Crescent Lane, London SW4 9RN. Tel. 071-720 6853

UNION OF CONSTRUCTION, ALLIED TRADES AND TECHNICIANS (UCATT)

General Secretary **Albert Williams**

The union organizes primarily building and construction workers in the private sector, but also has members in engineering, local authorities, the health service, furniture-making and shipbuilding, and includes some clerical and administrative staff. The TUC-affiliated union is about 260,000 strong, with women representing less than one-tenth of the membership, and has a team of 126 paid officials, including a full-time executive council. The union maintains a political fund and sponosrs Eric Heffer (Lab., Liverpool Walton).

Since 1986 the union has campaigned for a national register of construction workers in order to improve standards within the building industry, and launched a campaign *Action for homes and jobs* in 1989 to build houses for the homeless.

UCATT House, 177 Abbeville Rd, London SW4 9RL. Tel. 071-622 2442

UNION OF DEMOCRATIC MINEWORKERS (UDM)

President/Secretary **Roy Link**

The UDM, which formed as a breakaway union from the National Union of Mineworkers after the strike of 1984, is open to workers in the coalmining and quarrying industries and ancillary services such as transport. It also has a clerical and supervisory staffs section. Eight full-time officials are responsible to a membership totalling 21,568, of which a tiny percentage are women. Since 1989 the union has had a political fund, but does not sponsor any MPs and is not a TUC affiliate.

The Sycamores, Moor Rd, Bestwood, Nottingham NG6 8UE. Tel. 0602 763468

UNION OF SHOP, DISTRIBUTIVE AND ALLIED WORKERS (USDAW)

General Secretary **D. Garfield Davies**

The union organizes in co-operative wholesale and retail, and wholesale and retail generally, warehousing and mail order trade, service industries such as catering, the footwear trade, butchers, food manufacturing, chemicals and insurance among others. It also has a white-collar section, SATA (Supervisory, Administrative and Technical Association). A TUC affiliate, USDAW has about 390,000 members, of whom 268,000 are women, and employs 122 full-time officials to look after the membership. The union maintains a political fund and sponsors nine Labour MPs: Robin Corbett (Birmingham Erdington), Derek Foster (Bishop Auckland), Thomas Graham (Renfrew West and Inverclyde), Roy Hattersley (Birmingham Sparkbrook), David Lambie (Cunninghame North), Ray Powell (Ogmore), Ted Rowlands (Merthyr Tydfil and Romney), Andrew Smith (Oxford East) and Audrey Wise (Preston).

Oakley, 188 Wilmslow Rd, Fallowfield, Manchester M14 6LJ. Tel. 061-224 2804

TUC-AFFILIATED UNIONS

A complete listing of all unions affiliated to the TUC (with 1989 membership figures):

Amalgamated Association of Beamers, Twisters and Drainers	470
Amalgamated Engineering Union	813,072
Amalgamated Society of Textile Workers and Kindred Trades	2,838
Associated Society of Locomotive Engineers and Firemen	20,034
Association of Cinematograph, Television & Allied Technicians	28,680
Association of First Division Civil Servants	9,063
Association of Professional Executive, Clerical & Computer Staff (merged with the General Municipal Boilermakers and Allied Trades Union March 1989 to form GMB)	79,691
Association of University Teachers	32,339
Bakers, Food and Allied Workers' Union	34,461
Banking, Insurance and Finance Union	163,839
British Actors' Equity Association	36,421
British Air Line Pilots Association	3,900
British Association of Colliery Management	10,757
Broadcasting and Entertainment Trades Alliance	30,195
Card Setting Machine Tenters' Association	100
Ceramic and Allied Trades Union	29,957
Civil and Public Services Association	149,484
Communication Managers Association	19,200

Confederation of Health Service Employees	207,841
Educational Institute of Scotland	40,037
Engineering and Fastener Trade Union (formerly the Screw, Nut, Bolt and Rivet Trade Union)	400
Engineers' and Managers' Association	40,389
Film Artistes' Association	2,190
Fire Brigades Union	45,503
Furniture, Timber and Allied Trades Union	47,008
General Union of Associations of Loom Overlookers	1,173
GMB/APEX	803,319
Greater London Staff Association	12,122
Health Visitors' Association	16,701
Hospital Consultants and Specialists Association	2,370
Inland Revenue Staff Federation	52,970
Institute of Professionals, Managers and Specialists (formerly IPCS)	90,820
Iron and Steel Trades Confederation	67,000
Manufacturing Science and Finance	653,000
Military and Orchestral Musical Instrument Makers Trade Society	21
Musicians' Union	39,738
National and Local Government Officers' Association	758,780
National Association of Colliery Overmen, Deputies and Shotfirers	8,835
National Association of Co-operative Officials	4,423
National Association of Licensed House Managers	12,800
National Association of Probation Officers	6,310
National Association of Schoolmasters and Union of Women Teachers	120,544
National Association of Teachers in Further and Higher Education	79,918
National Communications Union	151,407
National Graphical Association (1982)	124,638
National League of the Blind and Disabled	2,883
National Union of Civil and Public Servants	118,740
National Union of Domestic Appliances and General Operatives	3,100
National Union of Footwear, Leather and Allied Trades	35,065
National Union of Hosiery and Knitwear Workers	47,238
National Union of Insurance Workers	17,697
National Union of Journalists	30,178
National Union of Dock and Metal Workers	5,240
National Union of Marine, Aviation, and Shipping Transport Officers	21,201
National Union of Mineworkers	77,300
National Union of Public Employees	650,930
National Union of Railwaymen	117,594
National Union of Scalemakers	935
National Union of Seamen	20,963
National Union of Tailors and Garment Workers	76,868
National Union of Teachers	178,294
Northern Carpet Trades' Union	842
Power Loom Carpet Weavers' and Textile Workers' Union	3,200
Prison Officers' Association	24,358
Rossendale Union of Boot, Shoe, and Slipper Operatives	4,457
Scottish Prison Officers' Association	3,255
Scottish Union of Power-Loom Overlookers	60
Sheffield Wool Shear Workers Union	17
Society of Graphical and Allied Trades '82	193,838
Society of Shuttlemakers	41
Society of Telecom Executives	28,834
Transport and General Workers' Union	1,348,712
Transport Salaried Staffs' Association	40,980
Union of Communication Workers	197,758
Union of Construction, Allied Trades and Technicians	255,883
Union of Shop, Distributive & Allied Workers	387,207
United Road Transport Union	20,545
Wire Workers' Union	5,103
Writers Guild of Great Britain	1,551
Yorkshire Association of Power-Loom Overlookers	561

EMPLOYMENT LEGISLATION

Recent Legislation

Since the Conservative Government came in it has brought in a great deal of legislation affecting the way that the trade unions carry out their work. The Acts listed below apply to England, Wales and Scotland.

Employment Act 1980. This limited picketing to the employee's own place of work and placed restrictions on secondary action (i.e. sympathetic strikes at workplaces other than the one(s) involved in a dispute). It made funds available for unions to run secret ballots (a move to reduce the ability of unions' executive committees to make decisions).

Employment Act 1982. This increased compensation for workers dismissed for membership or non-membership of a union. It made unlawful any discrimination against non-union labour in the awarding of contracts; and action by workers to persuade an employer not to use non-union suppliers was also made unlawful. Trade unions lost their immunity from civil actions except in respect of what they did 'in furtherance or contemplation of a trade dispute', and the definition of what is a trade dispute was narrowed.

Trade Union Act 1984. This required that all voting members of the executive committee should be subject to re-election every five years (people principally affected were long-serving general secretaries). It made it necessary for a union to hold a secret ballot before taking strike or other industrial action; if the membership votes for the action, it must be carried out within a month or the 'permission' lapses. If any strike or other action is taken without a ballot the union loses its immunity from civil action. The Act also required all unions that have political funds to ballot their members regularly on whether to continue the fund.

Employment Act 1988. This removed the power of a union to discipline a member for refusing to support official industrial action. It outlawed the closed shop and any actions in support of closed shops. It provided for a Commissioner to assist members wanting to sue their unions.

Advisory Conciliation and Arbitration Service (ACAS)

Although the members of the Council of ACAS are appointed by the Secretary of the State for Employment (who also provides the grant for running the service – an estimated £16 million in 1988–89), the service is completely independent of government control. There is a full-time chairman and nine part-time council members, all of whom are experienced in industrial relations: three are from the employers' side (nominated by the CBI), three from the unions (nominated by the TUC) and three are independent. The Service has 618 permanent staff, and has offices in Aldershot, Birmingham, Bristol, Cardiff, Glasgow, Leeds, Liverpool, London, Manchester, Newcastle upon Tyne and Nottingham. (It does not cover Northern Ireland, where a similar service is provided by the Labour Relations Agency.) ACAS's work falls into three parts:

Advice. The service gives general advice on employment and industrial relations policy to employers, unions and individuals. This is by far the largest part of its work, and it receives some 400,000 enquiries each year (320,000 in 1988).

Conciliation. In the case of a dispute, either side may call on ACAS for assistance. One or more members of ACAS's staff visit the participants in the dispute, making suggestions for negotiating points and acting as go-between; but the dispute is settled by the parties themselves. ACAS provided this sort of assistance in 1163 disputes in 1988. Another aspect of conciliation is intervention in an individual's disputes with an employer, such as complaints of unfair dismissal or claims under the Equal Pay Act 1970, the Sex Discrimination Acts 1975 and 1986 or the Race Relations Act 1976. ACAS conciliated in 44,443 such cases in 1988.

Arbitration. If no agreement can be reached, ACAS can provide arbitration. This can only happen if both sides agree, and commit themselves to accept the outcome. ACAS sometimes uses a single arbitrator, sometimes a board; it may occasionally refer a case to the Central Arbitration Committee. The process of arbitration can take several weeks, as ACAS's arbitrator(s) need to become familiar with the detailed position of each side. There were 145 arbitrations in 1987.

Chairman **D.B. Smith CB**

27 Wilton St, London SW1X 7AX. Tel. 071-210 3000

Health and Safety at Work

The Health and Safety at Work Act 1974. The principle act governing health and safety at work in Great Britain is the *Health and Safety at Work Act 1974.* The purpose of the Act is to secure the health, safety and welfare of people at work and to protect the general public from work activities within the community that might be hazardous to their health. The act established the current system whereby employers in association with their employees have the responsibility for working out health and safety arrangements, within the confines of the Act, for their own workplaces. The passing of the Act was seen as the first step towards replacing the mass of earlier legislation with a new set of regulations codes and practices incorporated within one act rather than having a system of specific acts governing specific types of work.

The Health and Safety Commission. Established under the provisions of the *Health and Safety at Work Act 1974*, the Health and Safety Commission is responsible for developing policies and codes of practice governing health and safety at work, and advises the Secretary of State for Employment in these areas. The Commission is comprised of: an independent chairman, Dr J. McCullen; three representatives of employers organizations; three representatives of Trade Unions and two other members chosen by local authority associations.

The Health and Safety Executive. Like the Health and Safety Commission, the Health and Safety Executive was established under the 1974 Health and Safety Act. The Executive is responsible for ensuring that the law with regard to health and safety at work is enforced. The Executive is comprised of government inspectorates covering a range of working activities including the Factory Inspectorate, the Inspectorate for Mines and Quarries, etc. These inspectors have powers of entry and enforcement and seek compliance with Health and Safety legislation.

1992. The run-up to the single-market in 1992 and the *1989 European Framework Directive* will introduce further reforms in legislation governing health and safety at work. To coincide with the changes, 1992 will be the European Year of Health and Safety.

Wages Councils

Wages Councils are responsible for setting statutory minimum pay for 2.5 million workers aged 21 and over. In Great Britain there are 26 of these councils which are comprised of equal numbers of representatives from employers and employees organizations. Under the *1986 Wages Act* the councils are responsible for setting minimum hourly rates, overtime rates, and limits on the amount employers can charge employees for accommodation. The functions of Wages Councils are rapidly being eroded as the current Conservative government does not see a statutory system for pay determination as necessary in the 1990s and has already introduced procedures to abolish the Councils.

TRANSPORT

Comparative Use of Different Transport within Great Britain 1961–87 (1,000 million passenger miles)

	1961	1971	1976	1981	1983	1984	1985	1986	1987	1988
Air	0.6	1.2	1.2	1.9	1.9	1.9	2.5	2.5	2.5	3.1
Rail	24.2	22.4	20.5	21.1	21.1	21.7	22.4	23.0	24.2	25.5
Road										
1	41.6	31.7	32.9	26.1	26.1	26.1	26.1	25.5	25.5	25.5
2	88.2	176.5	195.1	254.8	261.6	274.0	277.8	292.7	313.8	324.9
3	6.2	2.5	2.5	2.5	3.7	3.7	3.7	3.1	3.7	3.1

1 = buses and coaches
2 = cars, taxis and motorcycles
3 = bicycles

Road and rail passenger transport use, Great Britain

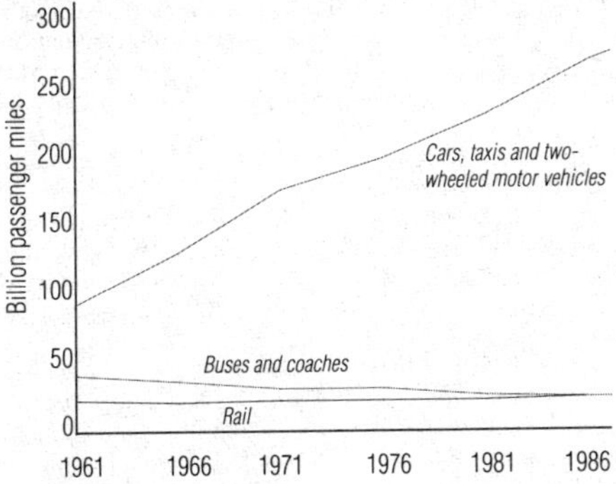

Source: Social Trends, 1989

ROAD TRANSPORT

Over the past decade the total length of surfaced roads in Great Britain increased by 5%, to 219,675 miles, with England accounting for more than 75% of the road network. The greatest growth was in motorways, which expanded by 25% between 1978 and 1988.

Length of Highways in Great Britain

miles	1987	1988
Motorways	1,849	1,859
Trunk roads	7,717	7,755
Principal roads	21,740	21,710
Others	187,849	188,837
Total	219,155	220,161

In December 1989, the Government announced plans to spend £12 billion on a road-building programme for inter-urban motorways and trunk roads; £6 billion of this is to be allocated to four roads programmes under assessment in London. This is still in the consultation stage, generating many objections from local and community groups.

Motorway Traffic

The volume of motorway traffic increased by 1.5% during 1988, representing a 14.3% share of all traffic on all roads (0.3% down on 1987).

Volume of Passenger and Goods Vehicles on Motorways

(billion vehicle miles)	1987	1988
Passenger vehicles	23.86	24.81
Goods vehicles	7.22	7.39
All vehicles on all roads	217.29	225.14
As a % of all vehicles on all roads		
Passenger vehicles	10.98	11.02
Goods vehicles	3.32	3.28

The density of traffic on motorways is now 20 times greater than on other roads.

Number of Vehicles

Between 1978 and 1988, the number of licensed vehicles on Great Britain's roads rose by nearly 30%, to 23 million; more than 18 million of these were private cars. By the end of 1988, there were 1 million more cars on the roads than at the beginning of the year; an increase of 6% over 1987, the biggest for 15 years. However, the number of motorcycles, which in 1987 fell below a million for the first time in 14 years, declined by a further 7% to 910,000 in 1988. There was a 3% increase in buses and coaches in 1988, to around 72,000 vehicles, but their share of all passenger road journeys remained the same as the previous year, at around 7%. Heavy lorries in 1988 numbered over 460,000, a 4% rise over the previous year.

In 1988, road transport accounted for 93% of passenger transport (excluding sea travel) in Great Britain.

Freight

Road transport continues to gain share from the railways, including the carriage of national newspapers from London to the provinces, traditionally a task for the railways until recent times. In 1987, 81% of all goods lifted (except fuel products) were done so on the roads; this was 1,542 billion tonnes in all. By 1988, the figure had increased to 82%, some 1,758 billion tonnes. The number of heavy goods vehicles on the roads in 1987 was 444,000; this increased by 4% in 1988 to 462,000.

Accidents

Since 1972, road accident deaths have shown a consistent decline, with the 1988 total of 5011 fatalities the lowest since 1954. Deaths peaked in the mid 1960s, but then fell due to the introduction of new speed limits in 1966, before rising again during the early 1970s. The reduced fatality rate has taken place despite the marked growth in traffic on Britain's roads in recent years.

The number of fatal accidents per vehicle has shown an even more dramatic decline since pre-war days, when each vehicle was 14 times as likely to be involved in a fatal accident as it would be now.

In 1988, 432,000 vehicles were involved in accidents and 80% of these were cars or motorcycles; almost 7800 vehicles were involved in fatal accidents, 5000 of these being cars. Teenagers and young adults are most likely to be injured in an accident; in 1988, nearly 20% of all casualties were aged 15–19.

Some 75% of accidents occur on built-up roads and 70% of these occur at or near junctions. The probability of accidents occurring varies with time of day, and day of the week; accidents peak on Fridays, and during morning and evening rush hour periods from Monday to Friday.

RAILWAYS

British Rail (BR)

With the 1947 Transport Act, Great Britain's four major private railway companies came under public ownership to form British Rails (from 1965 called British Rail). In the early 1960s, faced with mounting losses as a result of growing competition from road transport and reduced government subsidies, BR drastically cut its rail network; under Dr Robert Beeching (chairman 1963–5), BR aimed to concentrate on the more profitable routes. Between 1959 and 1969 the routes open to passenger traffic were reduced by 33%, a cut of some 6200 miles, and annual investment

Number of cars and motorcyles in Great Britain, 1903–88 (000s)

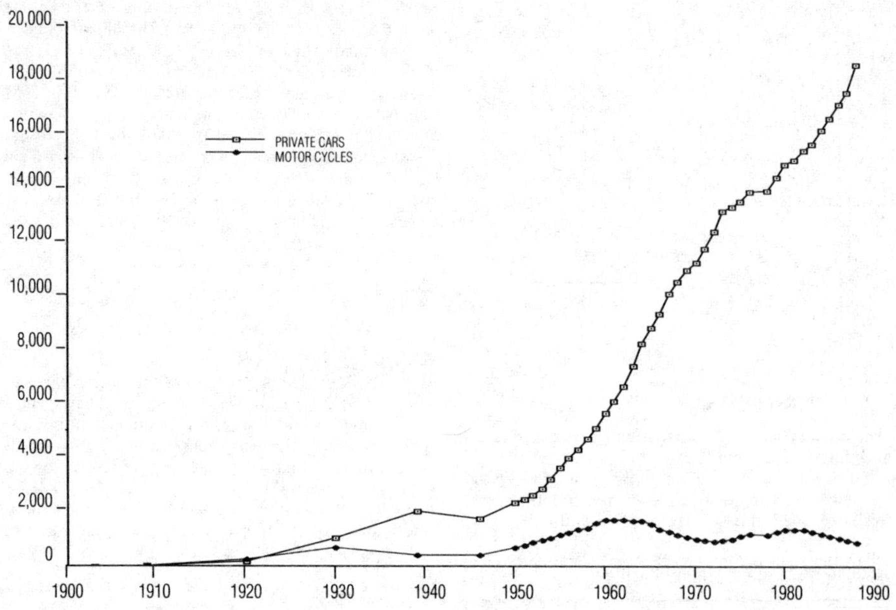

Road-accident deaths, Great Britain, 1927–88

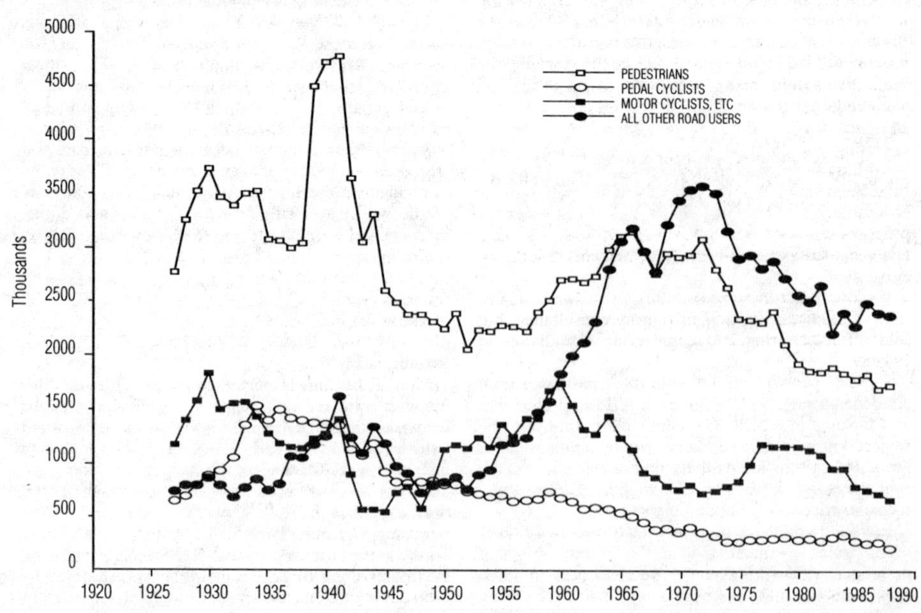

Fatal accidents per thousand vehicles on the road, 1930–88

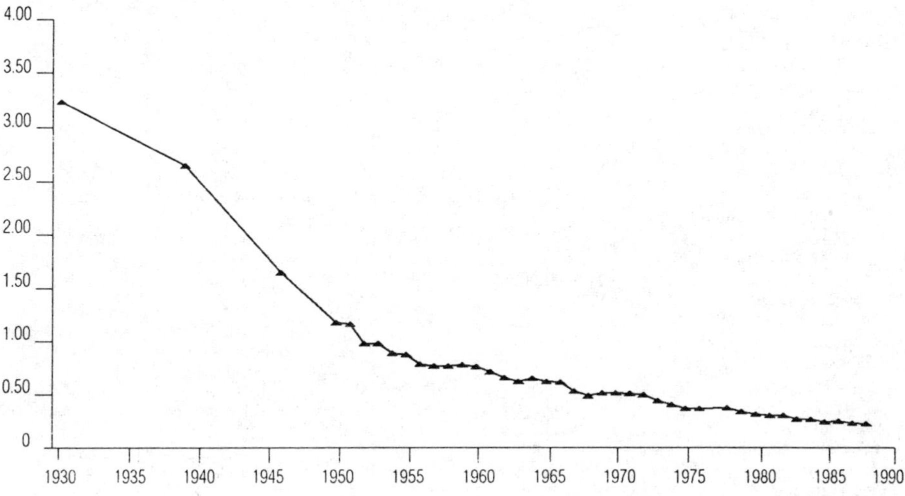

fell by the equivalent of nearly £1000 million, at today's prices. Since then, rail routes have declined by a further 25%, though from 1983 passenger revenue has increased in real terms by 22%, and investment by 69%.

BR Route and Track Open for Traffic 1984–9

	1984/5	1987/8	1988/9
Route open for traffic (miles)	10,416	10,311	10,292
Track open for traffic (miles)	24,769	23,498	23,473

As head of a nationalized company, BR's chairman is a government appointee who is responsible to the Secretary of State for Transport for the railway's profitability. Since 1983, public subsidy to BR has been more than halved, and in 1988/9 the InterCity services were required to run unsupported for the first time. Even so, at the end of the year InterCity showed an operating profit of £54.7 million. Together, Network SouthEast and provincial services utilized public service subsidies of some £550 million (£50 million less than the government-set target) in 1988/9, but the Government proposes to halve the present grant over the next few years, phasing out subsidy to Network SouthEast altogether.

BR owns subsidiary companies in railway freight, railway maintenance, and in railway consultancy, but sold off its catering and engineering subsidiaries in 1988/89.

Some 42 people were killed in three passenger train accidents during 1988/9. The most serious of them was at Clapham in which 35 people died; this was the subject of a public enquiry whose findings have prompted BR to increase its investment programme over the next few years by £500 million, to pay for the recommended safety improvements.

BR has permission to invest £356 million in high-speed trains to meet the needs of cross-Channel passengers when the Channel Tunnel opens in 1993. New international passenger terminals are being planned as well as a new rail link from London to the Kent coast; these moves have aroused considerable controversy and specific locations of terminals and routes have yet to be decided.

Chairman Sir Robert Reid CBE. Address: British Rail, Euston Square, 24 Eversholt Street, PO Box 100, London, NW1 1DZ. Tel. 071–928 5151.

CHANNEL TUNNEL

The idea of a tunnel under the Channel (a fixed link between Britain and the European mainland) was advanced by the French at the beginning of the 19th century, and has since been revived no fewer than 27 times. In 1883, a tunnel that had begun two years earlier on both sides of the Channel was abandoned because Britain feared infiltration by subversives. In 1975, an Anglo–French project, launched in the previous decade, was scrapped on economic grounds. Finally, on 12 Feb. 1986, Britain and France signed the Channel Tunnel Treaty, committing both countries to the development.

Responsibility for the present scheme rests with Eurotunnel, a private-sector Anglo–French consortium, which was awarded a 55-year concession (until 2042) to build the tunnel and operate a cross-Channel rail link. The possibility of a drive-through tunnel for road vehicles was also considered; this was ruled out because of problems of expelling exhaust fumes, and the unknown effects of long tunnels on drivers' concentration.

The Eurotunnel system will incorporate three tunnels: two rail tunnels; a service tunnel running between them to provide ventilation and routine maintenance. Terminals near Folkestone in England and at Coquelles near Calais in France will connect the tunnels with motorway and rail networks. The terminals will also serve as frontier controls and offer travellers shopping and other facilities. Eurotunnel will run its own shuttle trains between the terminals, carrying private cars and coaches (up to 200 vehicles at a time) with their drivers and passengers, and transporting

British Rail 1979–88

	1979	1983	1987	1988
British Rail Staff				
salaried	52,600	44,300	38,800	37,800
wage-earning	129,400	111,100	94,600	89,600
Rolling stock				
diesel locomotives	3,261	2,603	2,040	1,920
electric locomotives	310	247	230	260
coaches	21,511	16,963	14,648	14,258
freight wagons	157,000	70,400	44,200	40,200
Passenger traffic (million miles)				
InterCity	7,800,000	7,600,000	8,000,000	8,400,000
Network SouthEast	8,000,000	7,800,000	8,800,000	9,400,000
provincial	3,300,000	2,900,000	3,200,000	3,500,000
Passenger stations	2,365	2,363	2,426	2,435
Passenger revenue (£ millions, 1988 prices)	1,521	1,447	1,630	1,786
Freight traffic (1,000 tonnes)				
coal and coke	93,500	87,900	77,700	78,800
all freight	169,300	145,100	141,000	149,500
Freight revenue (£1,000s, 1988 prices)	853,400	676,600	585,800	642,400
Parcels (tonnes)	1,200,000	900,000	700,000	700,000
Parcels revenue (£1,000s, 1988 prices)	253,900	147,300	129,200	126,600
Freight depots	442	253	114	125
Government grant (£1,000, 1988 prices)	1,028,900	1,217,400	862,500	606,500
Surplus grant on rail operations (£1,000, 1988 prices)	67,300	81,100	112,200	161,400

freight vehicles. At peak times the passenger shuttles will run every 12 minutes, and freight shuttles every 15 minutes; the crossing between terminals will take about 35 minutes.

There will be direct high-speed passenger trains connecting European cities provided by the British, French and Belgian railways. BR plans to operate hourly passenger services (more frequent at peak times) from Waterloo Station in London to Gare du Nord in Paris, and to Brussels; journey times will be cut by half, to three hours and two hours 40 minutes respectively. BR will take delivery of 14 high-speed trains, capable of 186 mph, from the TransManche Super Train Group, a mainly Anglo–French concern in which GEC is a dominant partner. There will also be through freight trains serving the European markets. A new, dedicated line between London and the tunnel entrance has been proposed, reducing the journey time by a further 25–30 minutes.

The building of the tunnel has been subcontracted to TransManche Link (TML), a consortium of 10 British and French construction firms, who are responsible to Eurotunnel for completing the work by 15 June 1993. Around £5000 million was raised for the project in 1987, 83% of which has been promised as loans by an international syndicate of banks, while the remainder will come from investments. The total cost of the project is now estimated to be £7500 million.

By autumn 1989, the landward sections of the service tunnel had broken through on both sides of the Channel, and a total of 25 miles of tunnelling had been bored and lined. Altogether, 11 tunnel-boring machines, each weighing more than 1000 tonnes with precision positioning controlled by lasers, are required to cut through the undersea chalk marl to build the system. The linings, of concrete or iron, are brought to the faces by special railwagons and erected mechanically. Each tunnel will be 30.6 miles long, with the running tunnels 25 feet in diameter, and the service tunnels 16 feet in diameter. The tunnels will generally be between 81 and 132 feet below the sea bed, with a maximum 328 feet below sea level. The service tunnel, which will act as a pilot for the running tunnels, is scheduled for completion by the beginning of 1991. On the British side, the construction work and terminal site at Folkestone have provided about 5000 jobs, about half of which have gone to local people.

Eurotunnel's Revenue and Traffic Forecasts

	1993	2003
Passengers (millions)		
shuttle	15.8	22.9
rail	13.6	21.0
Freight (million gross tonnes)		
shuttle	9.0	14.2
rail	6.4	10.6
Revenue (£ millions, 1989 values)		
shuttle	352.2	519.0
rail	207.3	272.6
ancillary	19.2	27.9
total	578.7	819.5

LONDON REGIONAL TRANSPORT (LRT)

Set up in 1984 under the London Regional Transport Act, LRT is a public-sector company responsible to the Secretary of State for Transport. It replaced the Transport Executive, which earlier had been answerable to the Greater London Council (abolished in 1986) for the operation of the London parent company with three main subsidiaries: London Underground Ltd, London Buses Ltd, Docklands Light Railway Ltd (since 1987). Its services include some 470 underground trains carrying passengers between 263 stations to all parts of London, as well as over 5000 buses operating over 487 routes. A total of 815 million journeys were made on the Underground in 1988/9 (a 2% increase over the previous year) and 1244 million on the buses (marginally less than in 1987/8).

In 1988/9, London Buses Ltd set up 12 subsidiaries, including 11 bus companies, to cover its present area of operation, and London Coaches for sightseeing and tourism. These changes took effect from April 1989. London Buses Ltd also subcontracts services covering about a quarter of its network to private bus firms. In addition to its three main subsidiaries, LRT owns a number of other transport-related businesses, including most recently Victoria Coach Station Ltd (acquired in October 1988), and the London Transport Museum in Covent Garden, which attracted 187,000 visitors in 1988/9, with a turnover of £700,000.

In 1988/9, LRT received £190 million in pubic subsidies to cover its operating losses, representing a cut in real terms of 25% since 1987/8. Thre was a 3% increase in staff on the London Underground, with the addition of nearly a 1000 more engineers; partly a reflection of the need for improved safety measures following the Fennel Report into the fire at King's Cross in November 1987, when 32 people lost their lives, and partly because of the need for more automated systems. The sharpest increase, however, (62%) was in business administration staff, whose numbers rose to nearly 1000; correspondingly, the number of train-operating staff fell by 940, over the same 1988/9 period. *Chairman* Wilfred Newton CBE. Address: London Regional Transport, 55 Broadway, London, SW1H 0BD. Tel. 071–227 3178/071–222 5600.

AIR TRANSPORT

Air travel within the UK increased by over 50% in the 10 years between 1977 and 1987, from 151,000 scheduled flights to 266,266; the number of passengers uplifted increased only a little less, from 5.5 million to 10.1 million. At the same time cargo, including mail, showed some decline from its 1977 figure of 41,413 tonnes, but finished with 23% growth at 50,783 tonnes.

Domestic Air Services in the UK

	Aircraft flights	Miles flown (1,000s)	Passengers uplifted (1,000s)	Cargo (incl. mail) (tonnes)
1977	151,900	27,000	5,500	41,413
1978	176,628	31,000	6,400	44,608
1979	199,101	34,400	7,200	39,339
1980	201,227	35,800	7,200	31,005
1981	188,534	32,900	6,600	35,212
1982	201,887	34,800	7,100	37,993
1983	221,560	37,600	7,200	39,739
1984	254,064	41,700	8,300	45,529
1985	258,502	43,000	9,000	46,337
1986	255,764	44,100	9,100	47,550
1987	266,226	45,600	10,100	50,783

Source: *Annual Abstract of Statistics*

London Regional Transport 1980–9

	1980	1983	1987/8	1988/9
London Underground				
stations	248	247	248	248
railway cars	4,400	3,900	3,900	4,000
staff	23,600	23,900	18,900	19,600
passenger miles (1,000s)	2,700,000	2,700,000	3,900,000	3,900,000
London Buses				
vehicle stock	6,200	5,600	5,300	5,300
staff	34,500	32,400	19,800	19,800
vehicle miles (1,000s)	173,000	163,000	155,000	151,000
Docklands Light Railway				
stations			15	15
railway cars			11	11
staff			187	146
LRT income (£1,000s, 1989 values)				
traffic income			711,000	770,000
other income			48,000	56,000
total income			758,000	826,000
Operating loss before grant			222,000	212,000
Grants and benefits			217,000	213,000
Underground investment expenditure (£1,000s)			218,000	206,000
Other investment expenditure			93,000	106,000
Average bus fare per passenger mile (pence)			11.4	11.8
Average underground fare per passenger mile (pence)			10.9	10.9
Bus operating costs per passenger mile (pence)			15.5	15.9
Underground operating costs per passenger mile (pence)			12.7	13.5

UK Airlines: aircraft miles flown (monthly averages)

(1,000s)	All services	Domestic Services	International Services
1982	17,137	2,912	14,225
1983	16,810	3,143	13,667
1984	18,118	3,488	14,630
1985	19,235	3,587	15,648
1986	19,926	3,686	16,240
1987	21,003	3,807	17,196
1988	22,719	4,005	18,714

Civil Aviation Authority (CAA)

The Civil Aviation Authority was established in 1971 to co-ordinate civil aviation functions that had earlier been undertaken by the Department of Trade and Industry, the Air Transport Licensing Board, and the Air Registration Board. It acts as both a public-service enterprise and regulatory body whose wide-ranging duties include the provision of air-traffic control and telecommunications services: NATS (Nation Air Traffic Services). NATS operations are conducted jointly with the Ministry of Defence, with whom the costs are shared.

The CAA is also responsible for: economic regulation (including approval of airline takeovers, such as that of British Caledonian Airways by British Airways in 1988); ensuring airworthiness and operational safety in the air and on the ground; licensing civil air transport and air-travel organizers; approving air fares; sometimes airport charges. It advises the government on all matters of civil aviation and carries out research and development in close contact with government research establishments. The CAA offers overseas consultancy and training services, and has a subsidiary company, Highlands and Islands Airports Ltd, which owns and operates eight airports in Scotland.

In 1988/9, there was an 11% increase in the volume of air traffic handled by civil controllers, on top of the 9% increase of the previous year; this was reflected in severe flight delays and passenger congestion at airports during the holiday season.

The increase in operating costs over the previous year of £35 million was in part due to launching the £600 million investment programme for new air-traffic control facilities. The CAA's average return on capital employed for the past four years was 7.7%, exceeding a government-set target of 7% and only marginally short of the new government target of 8% for the following three years.

Chairman Christopher Tugendhat. Address: CAA House, 45/49 Kingsway, London, WC2B 6TE. Tel. 071–379 7311.

British Airports Authority plc (BAA)

Established in 1965, BAA began trading as a public-sector company in the following year. Initially, it owned and controlled Heathrow, Gatwick and Stansted airports in South East England, and Prestwick in Scotland. But by the mid 1970s it had acquired Glasgow, Edinburgh and Aberdeen airports. The BAA also manages airports at Southampton, Southend, Exeter and Biggin Hill on behalf of their owners.

Since it was privatized in July 1987, BAA has diversified into areas complementary to the core airport business. These include hotels; property development; cargo-handling; airport management and consultancy abroad. BAA is the only international airport company to be quoted on the stock exchange.

Airport operational activities, including charges for landing and departure of aircraft, duty and tax free sales, and rents for airline offices, and so on, account for 80% of BAA's annual revenue. BAA and its subsidiaries employ about 8500 staff, of whom nearly 7000 work at the airports. Since 1983, the average number of airport staff has risen by 6%.

Measured by the number of international passengers, Heathrow and Gatwick airports, BAA's two main subsidiaries, are the busiest international airports in the world. Heathrow also ranks fifth largest by the number of terminal passengers using it, that is those boarding or leaving an aircraft there for domestic or international destinations.

Chairman Sir Norman Payne. Address: 130 Wilton Road, London SW1V 1LQ. Tel. 071–834 9449.

UK Airports 1979–88

	1979	1986	1987	1988
Aircraft movements: take-offs or landings (1,000s)	2,198	2,439	2,614	2,868
Commercial air transport aircraft movements (1,000s)	924	1,125	1,193	1,280
Terminal passengers (1,000s)	56,992	75,161	86,041	93,162
Air cargo (1,000 tonnes)	797	881	976	1,088
Commercial air transport reported air misses	90	75	70	95
Commercial air transport estimated hours flown (1,000s)	475	573	606	655

Civil Aviation Authority 1987–89

	1987/88	1988/89
Number of staff		
air traffic services	4,882	4,895
all (incl. Highlands and Islands Airports Ltd)	6,485	6,477
Staff wages and salaries (£ millions)	115.0	129.3
Turnover (£ millions)	284.2	301.1
Net operating costs (£ millions)	259.4	294.4
Net profit (£ millions)	9.0	6.3

British Airways plc (BA)

Formed from a merger of Britain's two nationalized airlines, BOAC (British Overseas Airways Corporation) and BEA (British European Airways), BA began operations in 1974. Following the Civil Aviation Act of 1980, it was re-established as British Airways plc, and subsequently privatized in 1987. In the following year, the company acquired British Caledonian Airways (BCal), Britain's largest independent airline, and absorbed its scheduled services. British Airways' charter airline subsidiary, British Airtours, was renamed British Caledonian Airways and expanded to include some of BCal's former charter-flight services. The merger resulted in the loss of some 2500 jobs.

British Airways operates a network of routes across

British Airports Authority 1979–89

	1979/80	1983/4	1987/8	1988/9
Revenue (£ millions)	191	316	523	641
Pre-tax profit (£ millions)	45	84	166	198
Terminal Passengers (1,000s)				
Heathrow	28,543	26,976	35,638	38,058
Gatwick	8,836	12,745	20,091	21,057
all BAA airports	43,149	45,867	63,654	68,004
Cargo (tonnes)				
Heathrow	490,700	487,400	594,100	656,100
Gatwick	119,700	115,600	199,600	193,600
all BAA airports	666,500	652,100	845,200	918,100
Mail (tonnes)				
Heathrow	59,800	65,300	68,200	66,900
Gatwick	5,300	11,900	16,300	11,700
all BAA airports	71,400	93,700	106,400	102,700
Aircraft movements (take-offs and landings)				
Heathrow	303,445	286,909	336,893	355,120
Gatwick	143,483	152,842	195,151	200,199
Aberdeen	105,303	107,512	94,660	100,457
Edinburgh	79,754	73,078	95,821	100,413
all BAA airports	800,723	781,683	913,957	1,007,243

British Airways 1984–9

	1984/5	1987/8	1989/90
Scheduled services			
revenue passenger miles (millions),	23,852	30,524	35,912
no. of passengers carried (1,000s)	15,951	20,169	22,578
revenue per passenger mile (pence)	9.45	9.37	9.50
cargo tonne miles (million)	803	1,114	1,398
tonnes of cargo carried	259,000	361,000	459,000
revenue per cargo tonnes mile (pence)	83.85	79.82	79.82
Total airline operations (includes BCal)			
average fleet size	153	171	203
average no. of airline staff employed	36,861	42,709	48,760
Group turnover (£ millions)	2,943	3,756	4,257
turnover from airline operations (£ millions)	2,797	3,523	4,132
operating surplus from airline operations (£ millions)	303	241	340
pre-tax profit (£ millions)	191	228	268
retained profit for the year (£ millions)	174	101	119

the globe, covering 44,000 miles, from Anchorage in Alaska to Auckland in New Zealand. Its 209-strong airline fleet includes seven Concordes (BA's supersonic flagship), 40 Boeing 747s, eight McDonnell Douglas DC10s, 49 Boeing 737s, 35 Boeing 757s, 17 Lockheed TriStars, four Airbus A320s, 34 BAC One-Elevens, four British Aerospace ATPs, and 11 HS748s. Another 73 aircraft are on order, or awaiting delivery. The company also owns, or part owns, 25 subsidiary companies involved in airline operations, package holidays, retail, computer and management services, and airline marketing.

Worldwide, in 1988–9, BA employed around 50,200 staff (compared with 44,000 in 1987–8), of whom more than 95% were involved with airline operations, at a cost of £1040 million. In 1988–9, the chairman, Lord King, received a total salary of £385,791, representing a 117% increase of the figure he received in the previous 12 months.

With 22.5 million passengers on international or domestic scheduled flights in 1988/9, BA ranks sixth largest airline in the world, and fifth in terms of passenger miles (around 36,000 million). However, measured solely by the number of international passengers carried (16.9 million in 1988) BA is the largest airline, well ahead of Air France, in second place with 11.6 million. BA is also the world's fifth-largest carrier of air freight.

Chairman Lord King of Wartnaby. *Chief Executive* Sir Colin Marshall. Address: Speedbird House, Heathrow Airport, London, TW6 2JA. Tel. 081–759 5511.

Accidents

A total of 18 people were killed in UK aviation accidents in 1988; 13 fewer than in 1987. But in January 1989, a British Midland Boeing 737, with 126 people on board, crashed near Kegworth, killing 47 people and seriously injuring 74.

WATERBORNE TRANSPORT

In 1988, the tonnage of freight handled by British ports (imports and exports) increased for the seventh successive year, to reach 4.8 million tonnes. Export freight tonnage, having risen in the decade up to 1987, largely due to North Sea oil (which peaked at 103 million tonnes in 1985), fell for the first time as a result of the continuing decline in bulk fuel exports. Between 1983 and 1988 imported freight through British ports rose by 40%, of which bulk fuel accounted for some 38% (13% less than in 1978). Bulk fuel also made up 64% of Great Britain's waterborne exports in 1988, and in total a half of foreign traffic tonnage.

All Foreign and Domestic Freight Handled by Great Britain's Ports

(million tonnes)	1979	1983	1987	1988
London	52.08	46.95	48.88	53.71
Sullom Voe, Shetlands (mostly oil)	19.97	54.33	50.03	50.56
Tees and Hartlepool	40.24	33.84	50.03	50.56
Grimsby and Immingham	26.25	29.00	32.24	34.96
Milford Haven	41.48	30.74	32.67	33.26
Southampton	25.21	25.29	27.21	31.42
All ports	426.78	426.01	456.28	476.46

Domestic Freight

Throughout the UK as a whole, movement of freight by water (sea, river or canal) accounted for about 7% of all freight lifted (tonnage), but 28% of all goods moved (weight × distance, measured in tonne-km). Goods lifted on rivers and inland waterways have increased by more than 10% in the last decade, to around 70 million tonnes. Since 1978 crude oil and petroleum have represented nearly a half of all domestic goods moved by water, and 80%–90% of Great Britain's waterborne goods.

Unitized Traffic

In 1988, the growth of unitized traffic (container and roll-on/roll-off traffic) continued as a result of increasing non-oil trade with the EC. Consequently, the east coast ports carried on expanding, particularly at the expense of those on the west coast with traditional deep-sea markets. The number of roads goods vehicles using roll-on/roll-off (ro-ro) services nearly doubled from 1979, to reach 1.2 million in 1988. Over the same period there was a 30% increase in private cars using ro-ros, to 4.2 million; the number of coaches increased by nearly 100,000 (130%).

Merchant Fleet

Britain's merchant fleet, after reaching a peak of tonnage of 52 million deadweight tons (dwt) in 1975 (mainly due to expansion in tankers, dry bulk carriers and container ships) contracted rapidly in the following decade to around 4.8 million dwt, or 9.3 gross tons (Gt) by the end of 1988 (1 dwt = 1 tonne, and is a measure of the load a ship can carry; 1 Gt = 1000 ft^3). A large tonnage of tankers and other ships was scrapped or sold off. Between 1978 and 1988, the number of UK-registered vessels of 500 Gt or more fell by 66% to less than 500; there was also a 60% reduction in the seafarers employed. The age distribution of the merchant fleet also changed. About 40% of the present vessels are less than 10 years old, whereas in 1978 the equivalent figure was 80%. Some 75% of the ships in Britain's merchant fleet were built 5–15 years ago, and 6% built 20 years ago (compared with only 1% in 1978). About 30% of the fleet is in the 20–50,000-tonne band (double the equivalent proportion of 10 years ago). Large bulk carriers and tankers of over 100,000 dwt made up only 4% of total dwt tonnage and only 3% of the ships in the fleet, in 1988. (see also ROYAL NAVY)

UK-Registered Merchant Vessels of 500 gross tons or Above

	1978	1983	1987	1988
Number				
passenger and cargo vessels	1,023	562	381	326
tankers	398	304	165	156
all	1,421	866	546	482
Weight (millions)				
Gt	28.1	15.9	8.0	6.6
dwt	47.1	24.9	12.1	9.3

Employment of Registered Seafarers in UK Shipping Industry

(1,000s)	1979	1983	1987	1988
Officers	33.3	20.6	9.9	9.3
Ratings	31.6	22.5	14.3	12.9
All	67.7	46.1	24.7	22.6

Overseas Trade

Some 94% of the UK's overseas trade (imports and exports) by weight, and 77% by value, is carried by sea.

Freight Traffic to and from Great Britain's Ports

(1,000 tonnes)	1979	1985	1987	1988
Exports				
bulk fuel	71,958	103,114	100,179	91,129
all	107,537	147,814	150,650	141,693
Imports				
bulk fuel	76,877	57,249	57,284	62,890
all	157,073	139,869	151,776	166,448
All foreign traffic	264,610	287,683	302,426	308,141
All foreign and domestic freight	426,783	449,330	456,281	476,459

Waterborne Domestic Freight, and as a % of all such Domestic Freight Lifted

(million tonnes/%)	1979		1983		1987		1988	
Petroleum products	74	(28%)	73	(31%)	67	(30%)	72	(29%)
Coal and coke	10	(6%)	11	(7%)	8	(5%)	7	(5%)
Other commodities	56	(5%)	61	(4%)	68	(4%)	73	(4%)
Total share of all domestic freight lifted		(8%)		(7%)		(7%)		(7%)

Foreign and Domestic Unitized Traffic Handled by Great Britain's Ports (units/million tonnes)

	1979		1983		1987		1988	
London	382	(3.62)	346	(3.37)	453	(4.75)	458	(5.34)
Felixstowe	366	(4.44)	635	(7.35)	977	(11.50)	1,144	(13.61)
Dover	577	(5.70)	610	(8.00)	842	(10.15)	810	(9.85)
All ports	3,519	(41.70)	4,208	(49.93)	5,175	(65.14)	5,267	(72.11)

UK International Seaborne Trade

	1979	1983	1987	1988
Tanker cargo (million tonnes)	124.2	122.3	148.0	131.3
value (£100 millions)	93.9	183.3	131.7	92.2
% carried by UK-registered vessels	27%	20%	18%	18%
All cargo (million tonnes)	251.3	247.1	297.9	289.6
value (£100 millions)	695.4	996.0	1,332.6	1,416.2
% carried by UK-registered vessels	41%	35%	37%	32%

Manufactured goods and foodstuffs account for 80% of the £ Sterling value of this cargo, of which, in 1988, about 20% by weight and 32% by value was carried by UK-registered ships (a fall of 2% and 5% respectively from 1987). Some 70% of UK exports sent by sea were to destinations in Europe and 66% of Britain's seaborne imports also come from there.

Passengers

There was a decline in the number of passengers travelling to or from the UK by sea from 1978–83. This was due mostly to an appreciable reduction in the number of journeys by sea, to and from Europe.

UK Passenger Movements by Sea

(1,000s)	1979	1983	1987	1988
Europe	21,074	26,617	25,938	24,833
Other	40	35	40	33
All	21,289	26,776	26,103	24,994

Accidents

The incidents of search and rescue reported by HM Coastguard rose by 68% between 1979 and 1988, and the figure of 379 lives lost at sea in 1988 was also 68% higher than for 1979 (but 84% higher than the 1987 figure). On average, from 1978 to 1988, an accidental death at sea occurred every 5530 million passenger miles.

INTERNATIONAL STATISTICS

Food production
Import and export of food and animals, 1986

Country	*Value in US$ million* *Imports*	*Exports*
Algeria	1,768.60	8.10
Argentina	303.10	3,002.55
Australia	769.64	5,330.75
Austria	1,143.07	795.85
Bahamas	120.13	0.50[1]
Bahrain	204.51	0.12[1]
Bangladesh	257.21	64.11
Belgium/Luxembourg	5,965.93	6,082.16
Brazil	1,997.33	6,615.53
Brunei	88.77	7.60
Burma	5.80	131.33
Canada	3,939.42	4,902.94
Congo	54.30	13.81
Cuba	785.97	5,151.56
Cyprus	128.82	128.27
Czechoslovakia	1,064.66	459.85
Denmark	16,539.40	4,462.16
Dominican Republic	132.33	421.55
Egypt	2,841.11	200.64
Ethiopia	266.65	375.58
Finland	745.16	373.72
France	11,430.50	13,750.40
Germany, West	18,712.10	9,732.40
Ghana	56.90	500.66
Greece	1,560.64	1,199.29
Greenland	40.40	0.16
Hong Kong	2,134.67	631.51
Hungary	515.02	1,480.38
Iceland	83.09	15.20
India	549.21	1,794.09
Indonesia	586.17	1,439.25
Ireland	1,270.06	2,812.77
Israel	622.48	641.95
Italy	11,663.60	4,947.90
Jamaica	140.56	126.47
Japan	11,880.10	521.70
Kenya	94.62	827.88
Korea Republic	1,307.37	343.79
Kuwait	891.49	58.55
Liberia	67.76	25.55
Malawi	10.14	85.14
Malaysia	1,010.94	625.26
Malta	91.32	11.12
Mauritius	77.64	285.64
Mexico	861.13	2,141.12
Morocco	432.91	413.03
Netherlands	8,933.40	13,960.10
New Zealand	266.24	2,246.57
Nigeria	684.90	329.29
Norway	943.05	166.05
Panama	114.76	146.82
Pakistan	610.75	461.49
Peru	503.92	342.11
Philippines	434.10	678.89
Poland	825.61	823.44
Portugal	742.93	188.59
Samoa	9.98	3.86
Saudi Arabia	3,165.10	83.10
Singapore	1,522.77	1,004.82
South Africa	393.17	903.11
Spain	2,692.90	3,231.45
Sri Lanka	303.93	425.44
Sweden	1,692.21	609.21
Switzerland	2,265.75	970.31
Syria	424.73	87.55
Tanzania	71.50	269.53
Turkey	256.41	1,735.19
UK	11,628.10	4.935.30
United Arab Emirates	797.21	90.05
Uruguay	50.37	338.91
USA	15,947.80	16,417.50
USSR	12,005.90	680.50
Venezuela	519.46	140.50
Yugoslavia	651.20	780.44
Zambia	28.90	18.90

Note:
1. FAO estimate.

Source: UN/FAO, *Trade Year Book 1987*

Crude oil production, 1986

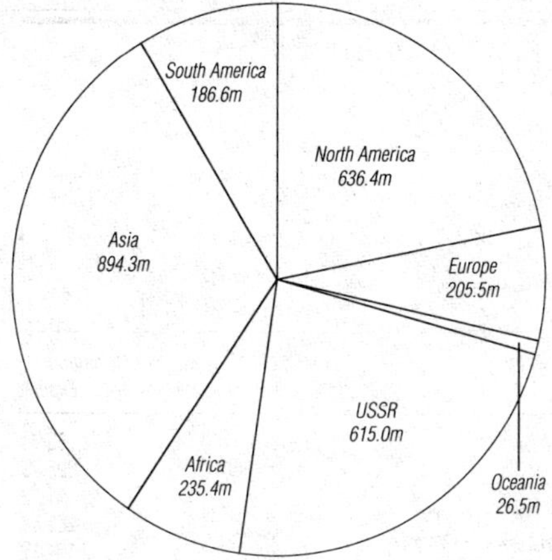

World oil production: 2800.2 million metric tonnes

Source: Euromonitor, *International and European Marketing Data and Statistics 1988/89*

Oil production

Country	Quantity (million metric tonnes)
Albania	3.0
Algeria	27.8
Angola	13.9
Argentina	22.2
Australia	25.2
Austria	1.1
Bahrain	2.1
Bangladesh	0.023
Barbados	0.07
Bolivia	1.0
Brazil	28.7
Bulgaria	0.3
Burma	1.4[1]
Canada	72.0
Chile	1.4
China	130.6
Colombia	15.6
Cuba	0.9
Czechoslovakia	0.1
Denmark	3.6
Ecuador	14.5
Egypt	40.2
France including Monaco	2.9
Germany, East	0.039
Germany, West	5.6
Greece	1.2
Guatemala	0.2
Hungary	2.0
India	31.1
Indonesia	71.0
Iran	93.3
Iraq	82.6
Israel	0.012
Italy and San Marino	2.5
Japan	0.6
Jordan	0.015
Kuwait	71.5
Malaysia	24.4
Mexico	126.2
Netherlands	4.6
New Zealand	1.2
Nigeria	72.8
Norway	40.5
Oman	27.6
Pakistan	1.9
Peru	8.7
Philippines	0.3
Poland	0.1
Qatar	16.0[1]
Romania	10.5
Saudi Arabia	251.6
Spain	1.8
Sweden	0.004
Syrian Arab Republic	9.2
Thailand	1.0
Trinidad and Tobago	8.7
Turkey	2.3
UK	121.1
United Arab Emirates	66.2[1]
USA	428.1
USSR	615.0
Venezuela	93.9
Yemen	0.3
Yugoslavia	4.1

Note:
1. UN Statistical Office estimate

Source:
UN Energy Statistics Yearbook 1986

World oil consumption, 1938–1987

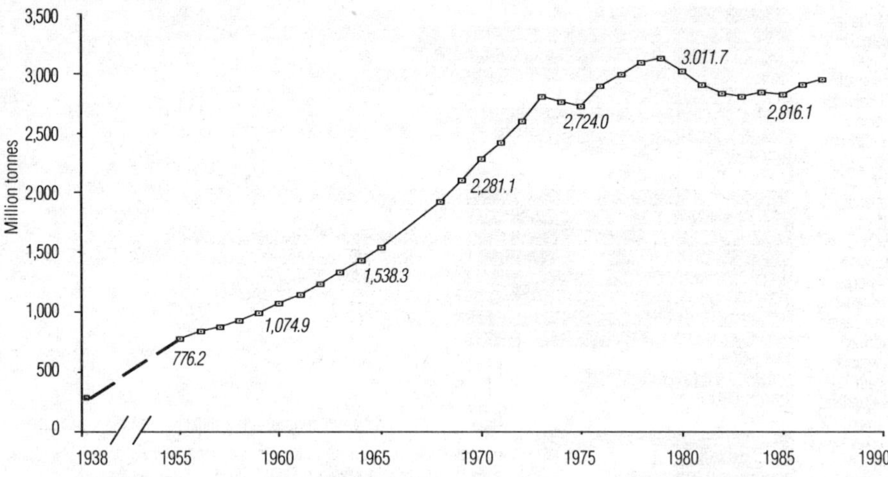

Sources: BP, *Statistical Review of the World Oil Industry 1965*; BP, *Statistical Review of World Energy 1988*

Forest land as percentage of total land area (latest available figures)

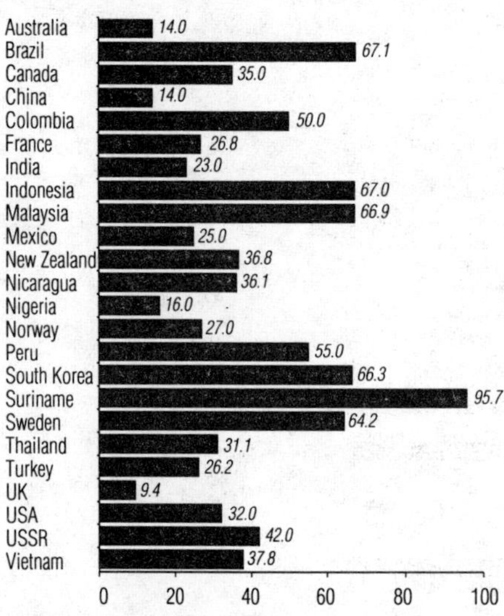

Sources: Euromonitor, *International Marketing Data and Statistics 1988/9; European Marketing Data and Statistics 1988/9*

Reforestation ('000 hectares)

Brazil	448.6
Canada	720.0
India	126.0
Indonesia	131.4
USA	1,775.0
USSR	4,540.0
Others	<100.0

Deforestation and reforestation, 1981–1985

Country	*Annual deforestation ('000 hectares)*	*Annual reforestation ('000 hectares)*
Bolivia	117	1.4
Brazil	2,530	448.6
Burma	105	0.2
Colombia	890	8.4
Ecuador	340	4.4
India	147	126.0
Indonesia	620	131.4
Ivory Coast	510	6.0
Laos	130	1.4
Madagascar	156	12.0
Malawi	150	4.0
Malaysia	235	20.0
Mexico	615	22.2
Mozambique	120	3.6
Nicaragua	121	1.0
Nigeria	400	25.8
Paraguay	212	0.6
Peru	270	6.4
Sudan	504	13.4
Thailand	379	24.4
Venezuela	245	18.8
Zaire	370	0.4
Others	<100	

Note:
1. Data not avaliable for Australia, Canada, China, Middle East, Korea, New Zealand, South Africa, USA, USSR. See below for Europe.

Education expenditure, 1986

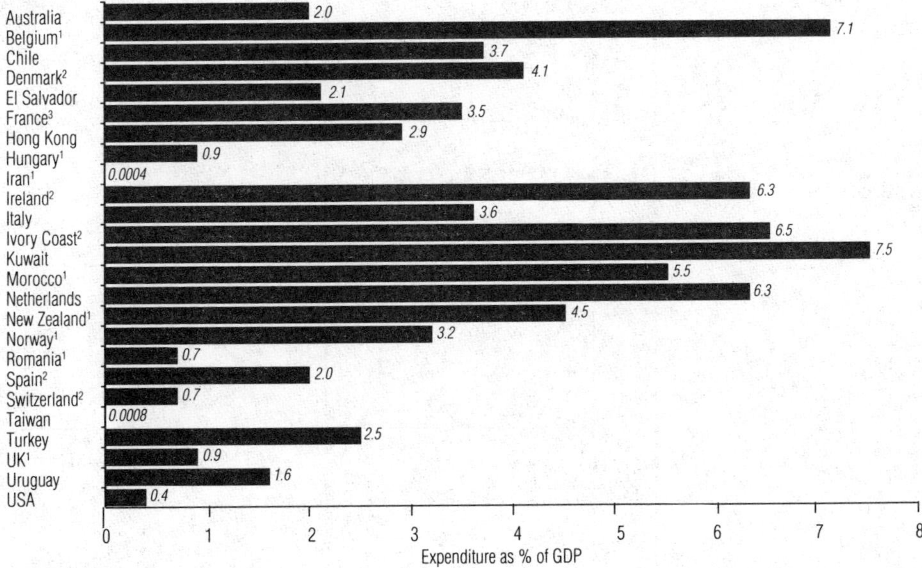

Notes:

1. 1985. 2. 1984. 3. 1983.

No figures available for USSR.

Source: Euromonitor, *International Marketing Data and Statistics*; *European Marketing Data and Statistics*

Defence expenditure, 1985

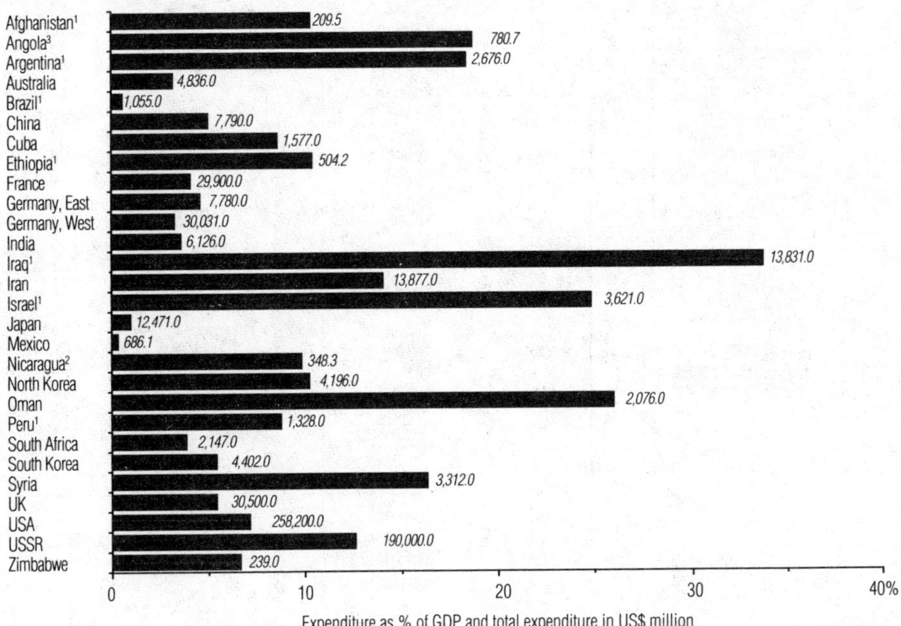

Notes:

1. 1984 figures. 2. 1983 figures. 3. 1982 figures.

The expenditure reflects those parts of the world where active unrest is taking place or where countries exert world influence by defence expenditure.

Sources: Euromonitor, *International Marketing Data and Statistics 1988/9*, 13th Edition; *European Marketing Data and Statistics 1987/8*; *Defence & Foreign Affairs Handbook 1989*

Unemployment, 1969–1988

Country	Unemployment as % of workforce																			
	1969	*1970*	*1971*	*1972*	*1973*	*1974*	*1975*	*1976*	*1977*	*1978*	*1979*	*1980*	*1981*	*1982*	*1983*	*1984*	*1985*	*1986*	*1987*	*1988*
Argentina	4.3	4.8	6.0	6.6	5.6	3.4	2.3	4.5	2.8	2.8	2.0	2.3	4.5	4.8	4.2	3.8	5.3	4.4	5.2	NA
Austria	2.8	2.4	2.1	1.9	1.6	1.5	2.0	2.0	1.8	2.1	2.0	1.9	2.4	3.7	4.5	4.5	4.8	5.2	5.6	5.3
Canada	4.7	5.9	6.4	6.3	5.6	5.4	6.9	7.1	8.1	8.3	7.4	7.5	7.5	11.0	11.9	11.3	10.5	9.6	8.9	7.8
China[1]	1.9	1.7	1.7	1.5	1.3	1.5	2.4	1.8	1.72	5.3	NA	4.9	3.8	3.2	2.3	1.9	1.8	2.0	2.0	NA
Denmark	3.9	2.9	3.1	NA	1.1	2.5	6.0	6.1	6.4	7.3	6.1	7.0	9.2	10.0	10.5	10.1	9.1	8.1	8.0	8.8
Germany, West	0.9	0.7	0.8	1.1	1.2	2.6	4.7	4.6	4.5	4.3	3.8	3.8	5.5	7.5	9.1	9.1	9.3	9.0	8.9	8.7
Italy	3.4	3.2	3.2	3.7	3.5	2.9	3.3	3.7	7.2	7.2	7.7	7.6	8.4	9.1	9.9	10.0	10.3	11.1	11.9	12.0
Japan	1.1	1.2	1.2	1.4	1.3	1.4	1.9	2.0	2.0	2.2	2.1	2.0	2.2	2.4	2.6	2.7	2.6	2.8	2.8	2.5
Puerto Rico	10.0	10.8	11.6	11.9	11.6	13.2	18.1	19.5	19.9	18.1	17.0	17.1	19.9	22.8	23.4	20.7	21.8	18.9	16.8	NA
South Korea	4.8	4.5	4.5	4.5	4.0	4.1	4.1	3.9	3.8	3.2	3.8	5.2	4.5	4.4	4.1	3.8	4.0	3.8	3.1	2.5
UK	2.5	2.7	3.7	4.1	2.8	3.5	4.4	5.8	6.3	5.7	5.3	6.8	10.4	10.9	11.6	11.7	11.9	11.9	10.7	8.4
USA	3.5	4.9	5.9	5.6	4.9	5.6	8.5	7.7	7.0	6.0	5.8	7.0	7.5	9.5	9.5	7.4	7.1	6.9	6.1	5.4

Notes:
1. The early year figures, produced by China, are much lower than the later 'international' figures.

Method of counting changes from time to time, e.g. exclusion of certain age-groups previously in total or vice versa.
No figures available for USSR.

Sources: International Labour Office *Year Book of Labour Statistics 1988* China, 1969–77 – *Statistical Year Book Rep China 1988*

Inflation, 1974–1989

Country	*Annual inflation rates, % increase*															
	1974	*1975*	*1976*	*1977*	*1978*	*1979*	*1980*	*1981*	*1982*	*1983*	*1984*	*1985*	*1986*	*1987*	*1988*	*1989*
Australia	15.1	15.1	13.5	12.3	7.9	9.1	10.1	9.7	11.1	10.1	4.0	6.7	9.1	8.5	7.2	NA
Brazil	27.6	28.9	41.9	43.7	38.7	52.7	82.8	105.6	97.8	142.1	197.0	226.9	145.2	229.7	682.3	1,118.1
China	47.5	5.2	2.5	6.8	0.7	1.9	7.5	2.5	2.0	2.0	2.7	11.5	6.0	7.3	20.7	NA
Germany, West	7.0	5.9	4.5	3.6	2.8	4.1	5.4	6.3	5.3	3.3	2.4	2.2	– 0.2	0.3	1.2	3.0
Hong Kong	—	NA	—	5.6	5.8	11.7	14.8	13.8	10.6	9.9	8.5	3.4	3.2	5.3	7.4	10.4
India	27.8	5.6	– 7.8	8.4	2.5	6.4	11.4	13.0	7.9	11.9	8.3	5.6	8.7	8.8	9.4[2]	NA
Italy	19.1	17.0	16.8	17.0	12.1	14.8	21.3	19.5	16.5	14.6	10.8	9.2	5.9	4.7	5.0	5.7
Japan	24.3	11.9	9.3	8.2	4.2	3.7	7.7	4.9	2.7	1.9	2.2	2.0	0.6	0.1	0.7	1.0
Korea	23.8	26.3	15.4	10.1	14.4	18.3	28.7	21.3	7.3	3.4	2.3	2.5	2.8	3.0	7.1	5.3
South Africa	11.7	13.5	11.1	11.1	10.2	13.1	13.8	15.2	14.7	12.3	11.7	16.2	18.6	16.1	12.8	13.5
UK	16.0	24.2	16.6	15.9	8.3	13.4	18.0	11.9	8.6	4.6	5.0	6.1	3.4	4.2	4.9	7.9
USA	10.9	9.2	5.8	6.5	7.6	11.3	13.5	10.4	6.2	3.2	4.3	3.6	1.9	3.7	4.0	5.1
USSR[1]	—	—	NA	—	—	1.0	1.1	1.3	3.3	0.6	– 1.0	– 2.0	2.0	—	NA	—

Notes:
1. USSR 1987/8 and 1988/9. Official estimate 2%, but probably higher.
2. Estimated.

Sources:
Euromonitor, *International Marketing Data and Statistics 1988/9*; Euromonitor, *European Marketing Data and Statistics 1988/9*; IMF, *International Financial Statistics*

Health-care provision

Region	Year of WHO data	Doctors per 10,000 pop.	Dentists per 10,000 pop.	Nurses/midwives per 10,000 pop.
EUROPE & USSR				
Austria	1985	26.1	4.1	55.1
Bulgaria	1984	27.6	6.3	64.2
Denmark	1984	25.1	8.8	164.4
Germany, East	1985	22.5	7.0	69.1
France	1986	31.9	7.2	—
Hungary	1985	31.9	—	56.5
Ireland	1984	14.7	3.2	71.5
Italy		42.4	0.6	—
Norway	1984	22.2	8.9	175.0
Switzerland	1985	14.6	4.9	—
UK	1987	18.8	7.1	71.0
USSR	1985	42.1[1]	—	—
Germany, West	1984	25.6	—	53.8
E. MEDITERRANEAN				
Iran	1987	3.3	0.5	8.4
Iraq	1987	5.5	0.9	5.8
Israel	1983	29.0	7.1	93.7
Jordan	1984	11.4	2.4	9.9
Kuwait	1986	15.1	1.8	47.3
Libya	1983	13.8	1.1	15.3
AMERICAS				
Argentina	1984	27.0	2.2	12.3
Bahamas	1984	9.8	1.4	48.3
Bolivia	1984	7.2	0.6	1.9
Brazil	1984	9.3	1.3	8.4
Canada	1984	19.6	4.9	34.3[2]
Cayman Islands	1984	21.5	3.0	41.0
Jamaica	1984	4.9	0.5	20.6
Peru	1984	9.5	2.2	7.8
USA	1984	21.4	5.9	137.2
Venezuela	1984	14.3	2.6	9.0
ASIA				
Afghanistan	1987	2.0	0.2	1.5
Bangladesh	1985	0.7	—	1.0
Dem. People's Rep. Korea	1982	23.8	—	—
India	1984	3.9	0.1	5.8
Indonesia	1983	1.0	0.1	7.8
Nepal	1984	0.3	—	1.4
Sri Lanka	1985	1.2	0.2	7.1
Thailand	1984	1.6	0.3	14.1
WESTERN PACIFIC				
Australia	1986	22.9	—	93.4
China	1986	9.1	—	7.2
Hong Kong	1986	9.3	—	41.5
Japan	1984	15.1	—	54.1
New Zealand	1986	17.4	—	123.8
Philippines	1984	1.5	—	3.7
Vietnam	1986	3.1	—	15.8
AFRICA				
Algeria	1984	4.3	1.5	30.4
Angola	1984	0.6	—	7.6
Burkina Faso	1983	0.2	—	19.2
Egypt	1985	2.0	—	2.7
Ethiopia	1984	0.1	—	1.8
Kenya	1982	1.2	0.1	10.4
Niger	1984	0.3	—	23.3
Rwanda	1983	0.3	—	2.7
Senegal	1984	0.5	0.1	4.4
Somalia	1984	0.6	0.0	6.3
Sudan	1984	1.0	0.1	8.1
Zambia	1983	1.4	—	10.7

Notes:
1. Includes dentists.
2. Nursing auxiliaries only.

Source: WHO Statistics Annual 1988; UK – Department of Health Figures

Mortality
Cause of death

Country	*Malnutrition*	*Infectious diseases*	*Respiratory diseases*	*Heart & circulatory diseases*	*Cancers*	*Road accidents*	*Murder*	*Suicide*
EUROPE								
Austria	—	5.8	60.4	634.2	280.7	20.1	1.4	27.7
Belgium	0.2	7.8	57.4	479.8	247.3	19.9	1.7	23.8
France	2.8	13.4	28.2	356.8	242.7	20.0	1.3	22.0
Germany, West	—	8.4	64.9	588.3	298.3	13.1	1.2	20.7
Greece	—	7.5	26.8	413.2	197.3	21.1	0.9	3.9
Ireland	0.3	7.6	91.5	472.2	215.6	15.3	0.8	8.0
Italy	0.1	5.7	49.2	444.4	247.4	17.5	2.1	7.4
Netherlands	0.5	4.8	44.1	375.5	234.8	9.8	0.9	11.3
Norway	0.7	8.1	97.6	486.4	235.5	10.5	(no data)	14.1
Portugal	0.9	9.2	47.3	424.6	178.9	25.6	1.4	9.7
Spain	0.1	11.0	46.5	353.1	144.7	16.4	1.0	4.4
Sweden	0.6	8.3	86.1	550.7	239.9	10.0	(no data)	18.2
Switzerland	0.4	6.4	45.2	387.9	253.0	14.3	(no data)	25.0
UNITED KINGDOM								
England & Wales	0.1	5.1	82.0	560.2	320.3	10.1	0.7	8.7
Scotland	0.3	5.7	98.3	629.2	320.5	11.9	1.3	11.1
N. Ireland	0.1	3.3	122.8	515.5	241.6	12.5	3.7	7.5
REST OF WORLD								
Australia	—	3.7	24.7	349.0	150.5	17.4	1.9	11.0
Brazil	1.2	46.6	32.0	154.9	61.8	15.5	13.4	3.5
Canada	0.6	4.2	30.8	311.3	204.7	15.8	2.3	13.7
Cape Verde	15.9	163.4	52.3	123.4	49.7	2.7	1.7	2.4
Cuba	0.2	11.4	44.9	260.1	131.0	12.9	4.7	4.7
Egypt	—	170.6	106.3	185.3	21.8	1.7	0.5	0.5
Hong Kong	—	14.5	56.5	135.2	150.7	5.3	1.5	13.1
Israel	0.4	13.3	21.7	283.2	170.7	9.9	1.4	5.4
Japan	0.2	10.0	49.6	245.6	163.7	10.3	0.8	19.4
Mexico	5.7	70.0	53.1	94.7	34.4	21.5	17.9	1.6
New Zealand	—	5.3	55.5	371.7	212.1	21.1	1.2	12.0
Poland	—	12.4	52.8	522.7	204.8	13.9	1.6	13.3
USA	1.0	9.8	32.5	420.4	215.4	18.5	8.5	12.1

Note:
No Third World countries available apart from Cape Verde; WHO considers that the Third World data are too inaccurate so they do not publish it at all.
Rates are the number of deaths from each cause per 100,000 population.

Source: United Nations Demographic Yearbook, 1986

Public expenditure, 1986

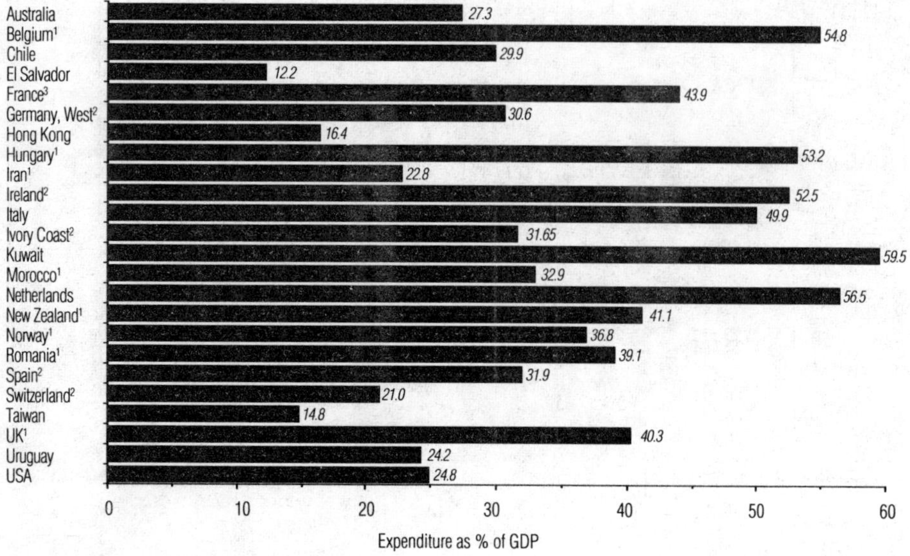

Notes:
1. 1985 figures.
2. 1984 figures.
3. 1983 figures.

No figures available for USSR.
Public expenditure includes: public services, defence, education, health, social security and welfare, housing and community amenities, other social services, economic services and other purposes.

Sources: Euromonitor, *International Marketing Data and Statistics*; Euromonitor, *European Marketing Data and Statistics*

Interest rates, 1980–1989

Country	*Base lending rate p.a.*									
	1980	*1981*	*1982*	*1983*	*1984*	*1985*	*1986*	*1987*	*1988*	*1989*
Australia	10.58	12.92	14.55	14.04	14.46	15.96	19.85	19.83	18.52	20.25
Canada	18.25	17.25	12.50	11.17	12.06	10.58	10.52	9.52	10.83	13.50
Finland	9.77	8.84	9.32	9.56	10.49	10.41	9.08	8.91	9.72	9.90
Germany, West	12.04	14.69	13.50	10.05	9.82	9.53	8.75	8.36	8.33	9.26
Greece	21.30	21.30	20.50	20.50	20.50	20.50	20.50	21.82	22.89	22.02
Italy	19.03	18.36	17.37	22.27	22.23	18.15	14.64	13.50	13.57	13.37
Japan	8.32	7.79	7.23	7.05	6.66	6.52	5.91	5.09	4.93	4.94
Kuwait	6.80	6.80	6.80	6.80	6.80	6.80	6.80	6.80	6.80	6.80
South Africa	9.50	17.00	18.00	16.67	22.33	21.50	14.33	12.50	15.33	19.00
South Korea	18.00	17.38	11.79	10.00	10.00	10.00	10.00	10.00	10.00	11.50
UK	16.17	13.25	11.79	9.79	9.65	12.29	10.83	9.63	10.29	13.00
USA	15.27	18.87	14.86	10.79	12.04	9.93	8.35	8.21	9.32	11.50

Sources: IMF, *International Financial Statistics* Euromonitor *European Marketing Data and Statistics 1988/9*